Teachers

iCheck Series

Microsoft Office 2007 Real World Applications

Log on to the Online Learning Center through

glencoe.com!

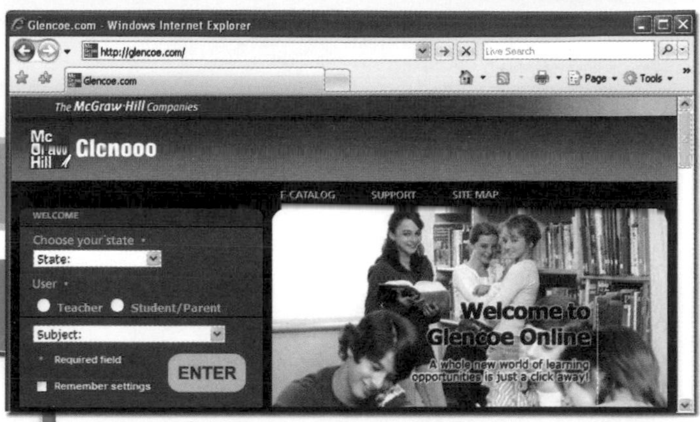

Integrated Academics

- Academic Skills: English Language Arts and Math
- Writing Matters
- Math Matters
- Academic Vocabulary
- Academic Connections

New Student Edition Features

- Quick Write Activities
- Study Skills
- 21st Century Workplace Skills
- Ethics in Action
- Careers and Technology
- Go Online: Real World Connections
- What's New in Office 2007

Technology

- Teacher Resource DVD with Data Files and Solution Files
- *ExamView® Assessment Suite* CD
- Lesson Planner Plus DVD
- *Presentation Plus!*™ PowerPoint Presentations DVD
- Online Student Edition

Online Learning Center

- Self-Check Quizzes and Reviews
- Rubrics
- Data Files and Solution Files
- Technology Handbook
- Math Skills Handbook
- Advanced Microsoft Word, Excel, Access, and PowerPoint Exercises
- Microsoft Outlook and Windows Vista Exercises
- *Presentation Plus!*™ PowerPoint Presentations
- Additional Projects
- Study-to-Go

Teacher Annotated Edition

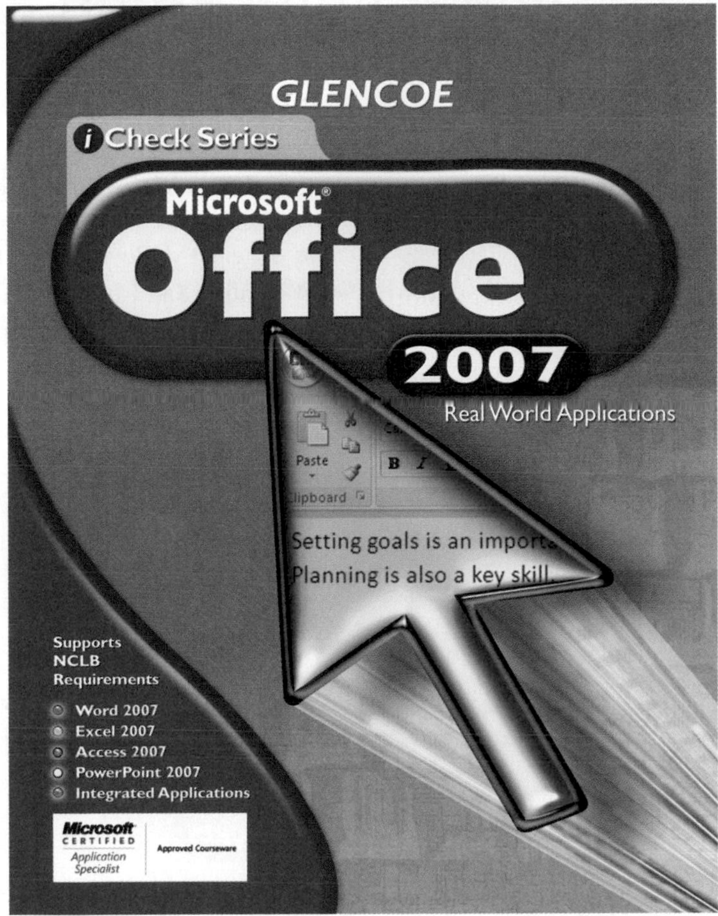

Lead Consultants

C. Jacqueline Schultz, Ph.D.
Career and Business Education Instructor
Warrensville Heights High School
Warrensville Heights, Ohio

Linda Wooldridge, M.B.A.
School of Information Technology Instructor
Santa Susana High School
Simi Valley, California

Lesson Planning Guide

Focus

Consider showing a slide show that includes a hyperlink and an action button. Ask students how they think they might use these features.

At this time you may want students to view PowerPoint Lesson 4 of the *Presentation Plus!* DVD.

Teach

- **Step-By-Steps**
  Throughout the lesson, have students perform the Step-By-Steps to complete each exercise.
- **Troubleshooting Tips**
  Students are taught how to publish presentations as Web pages. Check that you do not need parental permission to post student work.
- **Differentiated Instruction**
  For advanced students, ask them to cover the Quick Reference Guide on pages 696–706 except for the button icons and identify their functions.
- **Classroom Management Tips**
  Consider using a phrase each time you need students to stop what they are doing at the computer and direct their attention to you.
- **Reading and Writing Support**
  Remind students to enclose direct quotations in quotation marks. Barbara told me, *"Your class will not be canceled for any reason."*

Assess

Have students complete the following:

- After You Read, p. 666
- Practice It Activities, on pp. 667–669

Reteach

- **Independent Practice**
  Assign You Try It Activities, pp. 670–671.
- **Differentiated Instruction**
  Assign Challenge Yourself Projects, p. 673.

Assess

There are multiple formats for assessment provided for this lesson. These include:

- Interactive Review—Online Learning Center
- Online Self Check—Online Learning Center
- Critical Thinking Activities, p. 672
- Rubrics for Challenge Yourself Projects—Online Learning Center. Refer to page TM38 for an explanation of how rubrics can help students enhance self-evaluation techniques.
- *ExamView* for PowerPoint Lesson 4

Close

Ask students why it would be helpful to have a printout of the outline and notes pages for a presentation they are viewing.

Answers

- **21st Century Skills (p. 638)** Answers will vary. Students should describe a situation in which they took initiative by making informed decisions.
- See Lesson Resources on the previous page for a list of Solution Files provided in this lesson.
- See answers to After You Read on p. 666 and Critical Thinking Activities on p. 672.
- **21st Century Workplace: Communicate Effectively (p. 665)**
  1. Students should recognize that knowing their audience will help them explain the new information in a way the audience will understand.
  2. Students' guidelines should include at least four suggestions for communicating effectively, such as thinking through the purpose of your communication, knowing your audience, using appropriate media, and considering ahead of time possible questions from the audience.
  3. Maia means that people are more likely to tell others about a bad job than about a good one. This emphasizes how important good communication is to the success of a business.

Glencoe

The McGraw·Hill Companies

Printed in the United States of America

Send all inquiries to:

Glencoe/McGraw-Hill
21600 Oxnard Street, Suite 500
Woodland Hills, CA 91367

MHID 0-07-878605-3 (Student Edition)
ISBN 978-0-07-878605-1 (Student Edition)
MHID 0-07-880260-1 (Teacher Annotated Edition)
ISBN 978-0-07-880260-7 (Teacher Annotated Edition)

1 2 3 4 5 6 7 8 9 043/027 11 10 09 08 07

Lesson Planning Guide

LESSON 4 Manage Presentations

Key Concepts

After completing this lesson, students will be able to:

- Add, delete, and rearrange slides
- Add hyperlinks and action buttons
- Use grids and guides
- Create custom shows
- Rehearse timings
- Mark up presentations electronically with a pen or highlighter
- Prepare your presentations by saving them in various formats
- Preview slides and modify printing options

iCheck Lesson Resources

The following components and resources have been provided to help you teach this lesson.

- Glencoe's Lesson Planner Plus DVD
  - Create your lesson plans with a few, simple clicks
  - Access blackline masters and resources
- Teacher Resource DVD
  - Data Files for PowerPoint Lesson 4
  - Solution Files for PowerPoint Lesson 4
- *Presentation Plus!* DVD
- Online Learning Center at **glencoe.com**
  - Data Files for PowerPoint Lesson 4
  - Solution Files for PowerPoint Lesson 4
  - Interactive Review for PowerPoint Lesson 4
  - Online Self Check for PowerPoint Lesson 4
  - Challenge Yourself Project Rubrics for PowerPoint Lesson 4
- *ExamView* CD, PowerPoint Lesson 4 Test

Standards

See page 638 for a list of Microsoft Certified Application Specialist objectives and ISTE/NETS standards that students will meet by completing this activity. See page TM33 for a correlation of 21st Century Skills and Workplace Competencies.

Lesson 4	Pg #	Data File
EX 4-1	640	Literacy.pptx
EX 4-3	642	Publicity.pptx
EX 4-5	645	Publicity.pptx
EX 4-7	647	Worksheet.docx
EX 4-9	649	Reading.wmv
EX 4-9	650	Volunteer.wav
EX 4-19	661	Literacy.wav
EX 4-19	661	Worksheet.docx
PIA 1	667	Activities.pptx
YTI 4	670	Habits.pptx
BCA 6	672	Mow.pptx
SAW 7	672	Publicity.pptx
Ch. Yrslf. 9	673	Activities.pptx
Ch. Yrslf. 10	673	Activities.pptx
Ch. Yrslf. 11	673	Activities.pptx

Lesson 4	Pg #	Solution File
EX 4-11	652	p4-7a-SF.docx and p4-7b-SF.docx
EX 4-19	662	Found in LiteracyCD-SF folder
EX 4-19	662	Found in LiteracyCD-SF folder
EX 4-1 to 4-21	664	Literacy-SF.pptx
PIA 1	667	Activities1-SF.pptx
PIA 2	668	Activities2-SF.pptx
PIA 3	669	Activities3-SF.pptx
YTI 4	670	Habits4.pptx
YTI 5	671	Habits5.pptx

Table of Contents

Lesson Planning Guide

Teach

- **Step-By-Steps**
  Throughout the lesson, have students perform the Step-By-Steps to complete each exercise.
- **Troubleshooting Tips**
  It is common for PowerPoint users to change the type of bullet for one bulleted item in a list, when they meant to change all the bullets. Encourage students to click in the bulleted list and press **CTRL** + **A** to select all bulleted items.
- **Differentiated Instruction**
  Occasionally begin class by showing students the solution file for the current lesson. Seeing the final result will help visual learners picture the goal of the exercises.
- **Classroom Management Tips**
  If you do not have a printer in your classroom, have students use **Print Preview**. From **Print Preview**, students can choose slides, notes pages, outlines view, or any type of handout from the **Print What** drop-down list.
- **Reading and Writing Support**
  Remind students to capitalize the days of the week, months, and holidays. *She will decide on Wednesday whether her party will be in September or October.*

Assess

After the students finish the lesson, have them complete the following assessment activities:

- After You Read, p. 630
- Practice It Activities, on pp. 631–633

Reteach

- **Independent Practice**
  Assign the You Try It Activities on pp. 634–635.
- **Differentiated Instruction**
  Assign Challenge Yourself Projects on p. 637.

Assess

There are multiple formats for assessment provided for this lesson. These include:

- Interactive Review—Online Learning Center
- Online Self Check—Online Learning Center
- Critical Thinking Activities, p. 636
- Rubrics for Challenge Yourself Projects—Online Learning Center. Refer to page TM38 for an explanation of how rubrics can help students enhance performance and self-evaluation techniques.
- *ExamView* for PowerPoint Lesson 3

Close

Ask students to identify when they think it is appropriate to add Clip Art such as cartoon characters to a presentation. When might they use fancy backgrounds and colors? When is it appropriate to use a more conservative design?

Answers

- **21st Century Skills (p. 601)** Answers will vary. Students should consider ethical behaviors related to schoolwork.
- See Lesson Resources on the previous page for a list of Solution Files provided in this lesson.
- See answers to After You Read on p. 630 and Critical Thinking Activities on p. 636.
- **Writing Matters: Copyrights (p. 629)**
  1. Students should recognize that copyrights exist to keep people from taking original work and using it as their own.
  2. Answers may vary, but students will probably suggest that photographs, video clips, and audio clips could all be used in a presentation about famous movie soundtracks. Students should know that they would have to check the copyright guidelines for each such item before using it in a presentation.
  3. Answers may vary, but students should understand that copyrights exist to protect individuals who create original works.

Table of Contents

Planning Guides and Answer Keys

Lesson Planning Guide

LESSON 3 Format Content

Key Concepts

After completing this lesson, students will be able to:

- Customize slide backgrounds
- Modify slide layouts, fonts, and text
- Modify and add effects to pictures, shapes, and graphics
- Apply animation and transition effects
- Work with slide masters
- Modify page setup
- Use headers and footers

iCheck Lesson Resources

The following components and resources have been provided to help you teach this lesson.

- Glencoe's Lesson Planner Plus DVD
  - Create your lesson plans with a few, simple clicks
  - Access blackline masters and resources
- Teacher Resource DVD
  - Data Files for PowerPoint Lesson 3
  - Solution Files for PowerPoint Lesson 3
- *Presentation Plus!* DVD
- Online Learning Center at **glencoe.com**
  - Data Files for PowerPoint Lesson 3
  - Solution Files for PowerPoint Lesson 3
  - Interactive Review for PowerPoint Lesson 3
  - Online Self Check for PowerPoint Lesson 3
  - Challenge Yourself Project Rubrics for PowerPoint Lesson 3
- *ExamView* CD, PowerPoint Lesson 3 Test

Standards

See page 601 for a list of Microsoft Certified Application Specialist objectives and ISTE/NETS standards that students will meet by completing this activity. See page TM33 for a correlation of 21st Century Skills and Workplace Competencies.

Lesson 3	Pg #	Data File	Lesson 3	Pg #	Solution File
EX 3-1	603	Music.pptx	Ex 3-1 to 3-18	622	Music-SF.pptx
EX 3-19	623	Staff.pptx	Ex 3-19 to 3-22	628	Staff-SF.pptx
PIA 1	631	Copyrights.pptx	PIA 1	631	Copyrights1-SF.pptx
			PIA 2	632	Copyrights2-SF.pptx
			PIA 3	633	Copyrights3-SF.pptx
YTI 4	634	Questions.pptx	YTI 4	634	Questions4-SF.pptx
			YTI 5	635	Questions5-SF.pptx
SAW 7	636	p3rev7.pptx			

Focus

Ask students what they might need to keep in mind when formatting a PowerPoint presentation. Text in a presentation needs to be large enough so it is easy to read. To make key points stand out, students can change the color, italicize them, or use other formatting. Students should understand that too much formatting can ruin a presentation and make it difficult to read. Share examples of printed or on-screen presentations that contain too much or inconsistent formatting. Point out that presentations that are formatted inconsistently can be hard to follow.

At this time you may want students to view PowerPoint Lesson 3 of the *Presentation Plus!* DVD. This presentation program uses an engaging format to introduce students to the key concepts of this lesson.

Connect Students *to* Careers *and* Community

This student edition has been designed with a number of features that can help students increase comprehension and remember information. Use the following pages to familiarize yourself with the student edition features. Then have students complete the Cyberhunt activity on pages xix–xx of their textbooks.

Teaching with the Unit Opener

The student textbook is divided into four units. There is one unit for each of the Microsoft Office applications: Word 2007, Excel® 2007, Access™ 2007, and PowerPoint® 2007.

Unit Objectives give students an overview of the lessons covered in the unit.

Why It Matters feature helps students understand the real-world use of the application taught in the unit. It explains why learning the application is important to students now and in the future.

Real World Connections feature allows students to visit **glencoe.com** to learn more about a key topic covered in the unit.

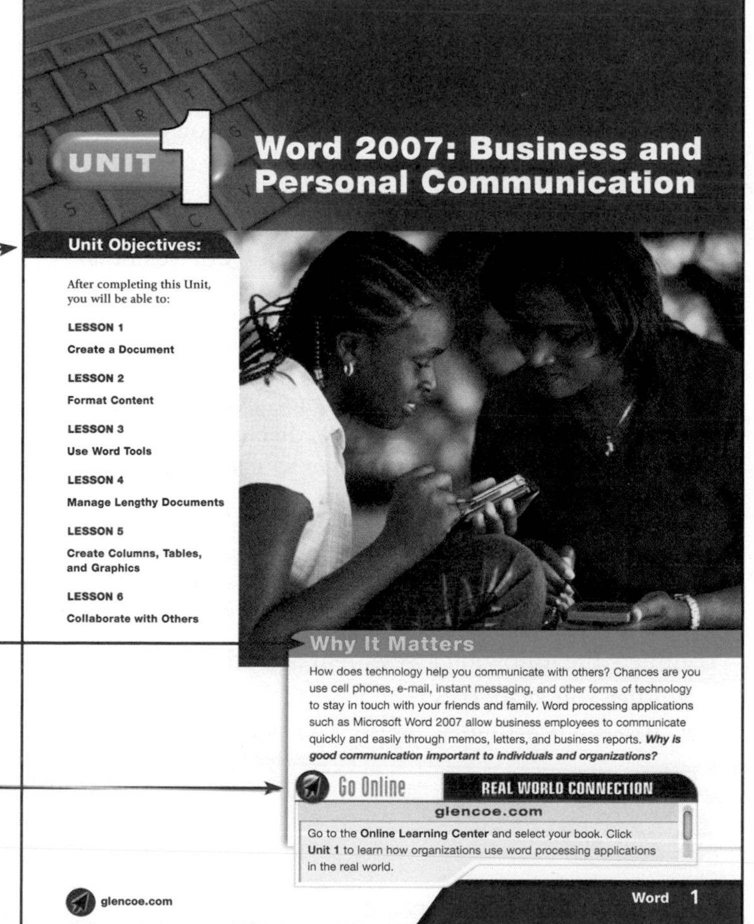

UNIT 1 Word 2007: Business and Personal Communication

Unit Objectives:

After completing this Unit, you will be able to:

LESSON 1
Create a Document

LESSON 2
Format Content

LESSON 3
Use Word Tools

LESSON 4
Manage Lengthy Documents

LESSON 5
Create Columns, Tables, and Graphics

LESSON 6
Collaborate with Others

Why It Matters

How does technology help you communicate with others? Chances are you use cell phones, e-mail, instant messaging, and other forms of technology to stay in touch with your friends and family. Word processing applications such as Microsoft Word 2007 allow business employees to communicate quickly and easily through memos, letters, and business reports. ***Why is good communication important to individuals and organizations?***

Go Online — REAL WORLD CONNECTION

glencoe.com

Go to the **Online Learning Center** and select your book. Click **Unit 1** to learn how organizations use word processing applications in the real world.

glencoe.com

Word 1

Careers and Technology The second page of the Unit Opener contains current career information for high-interest jobs and illustrates how technology is used in those careers.

Lesson Planning Guide

Teach

- **Step-By-Steps**
  Throughout the lesson, have students perform the Step-By-Steps to complete each exercise.
- **Troubleshooting Tips**
  If the datasheet disappears when students are modifying a chart, have them double-click the chart.
- **Differentiated Instruction**
  When students learn a new skill, have them write down the name of the topic and a one-sentence reminder of how the topic works. By the end of a lesson, they will have a one-page summary of the topics in a lesson.
- **Classroom Management Tips**
  Students can easily lose focus when they learn about topics such as Clip Art, organization charts, pie charts, shapes, and WordArt. To help students focus while learning about topics like these, keep the examples that you use business based. The topic is still enjoyable to learn about, but business-based scenarios will help the student remain focused.
- **Reading and Writing Support**
  Tell students not to spell out numbers if they are measurements of time, money, distance, or weight: *I will start on my 400-mile trip tomorrow at 5 a.m.*

Assess

After the students finish the lesson, have them complete the following assessment activities:

- After You Read, p. 593
- Practice It Activities, on pp. 594–596

Reteach

- **Independent Practice**
  Assign You Try It Activities on pp. 597–598.
- **Differentiated Instruction**
  Assign students the Challenge Yourself Projects on p. 600.

Assess

There are multiple formats for assessment provided for this lesson. These include:

- Interactive Review—Online Learning Center
- Online Self Check—Online Learning Center
- Critical Thinking Activities, p. 599
- Rubrics for Challenge Yourself Projects—Online Learning Center. Refer to page TM38 for an explanation of how rubrics can help students enhance performance and self-evaluation techniques.
- *ExamView* for PowerPoint Lesson 2

Close

Write the following list on the board: organization chart, table, pie chart. Invite volunteers to come to the board and, next to one of the objects, write down how it might be used. See if students can come up with several uses for each type of object.

Answers

- **21st Century Skills (p. 569)** Answers will vary. Students should identify local charities, groups, or organizations, for which they could volunteer.
- See Lesson Resources on the previous page for a list of Solution Files provided in this lesson.
- See answers to After You Read on p. 593 and Critical Thinking Activities on p. 599.
- **21st Century Workplace: Develop Media Literacy (p. 592)**
  1. Answers will vary, but students should explain that to be "media literate" means to be able to recognize, analyze, and question the messages we get from the media.
  2. Students' journals should note a variety of media—radio, newspaper, television, Internet, CDs, etc.—encountered at different times during the day. Students should identify which type of media they encountered most.
  3. Students should evaluate whether or not the local and national newspapers present different perspectives.

Teaching with the Unit Closer

Unit closing material offers additional features and practice for skills students have learned.

Academic Connections cross-curriculum feature connects computer applications to language arts, science, math, and social studies.

Ethics in Action case study gives students a chance to decide how to handle various ethical issues.

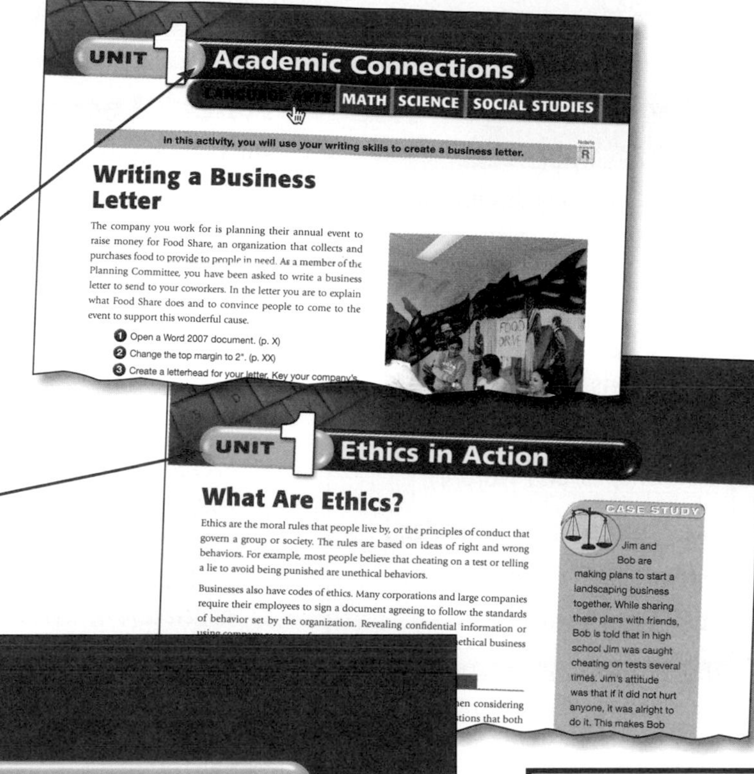

UNIT 1 Academic Connections

LANGUAGE ARTS | MATH | SCIENCE | SOCIAL STUDIES

In this activity, you will use your writing skills to create a business letter.

Writing a Business Letter

The company you work for is planning their annual event to raise money for Food Share, an organization that collects and purchases food to provide to people in need. As a member of the Planning Committee, you have been asked to write a business letter to send to your coworkers. In the letter you are to explain what Food Share does and to convince people to come to the event to support this wonderful cause.

1. Open a Word 2007 document. (p. X)
2. Change the top margin to 2". (p. XX)
3. Create a letterhead for your letter. Key your company's

UNIT 1 Ethics in Action

What Are Ethics?

Ethics are the moral rules that people live by, or the principles of conduct that govern a group or society. The rules are based on ideas of right and wrong behaviors. For example, most people believe that cheating on a test or telling a lie to avoid being punished are unethical behaviors.

Businesses also have codes of ethics. Many corporations and large companies require their employees to sign a document agreeing to follow the standards of behavior set by the organization. Revealing confidential information or

CASE STUDY

Jim and Bob are making plans to start a landscaping business together. While sharing these plans with friends, Bob is told that in high school Jim was caught cheating on tests several times. Jim's attitude was that if it did not hurt anyone, it was alright to do it. This makes Bob

Portfolio Project provides a four-page, four-part project that wraps up student learning for the unit.

Rubrics for students and teachers are included for each project on the Online Learning Center.

Math and language arts connections are included in many projects.

Have You...? Project Checklists allow students to check their own work.

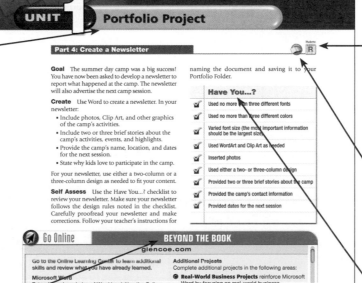

Beyond the Book feature directs students to the Online Learning Center to complete additional projects and exercises.

UNIT 1 Portfolio Project

Part 4: Create a Newsletter

Goal The summer day camp was a big success! You have now been asked to develop a newsletter to report what happened at the camp. The newsletter will also advertise the next camp session.

Create Use Word to create a newsletter. In your newsletter:

- Include photos, Clip Art, and other graphics of the camp's activities.
- Include two or three brief stories about the camp's activities, events, and highlights.
- Provide the camp's name, location, and dates for the next session.
- State why kids love to participate in the camp.

For your newsletter, use either a two-column or a three-column design as needed to fit your content.

Self Assess Use the Have You...? checklist to review your newsletter. Make sure your newsletter follows the design rules noted in the checklist. Carefully proofread your newsletter and make corrections. Follow your teacher's instructions for naming the document and saving it to your Portfolio Folder.

Have You...?

- Used no more than three different fonts
- Used no more than three different colors
- Varied font size (the most important information should be the largest size)
- Used WordArt and Clip Art as needed
- Inserted photos
- Used either a two- or three-column design
- Provided two or three brief stories about the camp
- Provided the camp's contact information
- Provided dates for the next session

Go Online BEYOND THE BOOK

glencoe.com

Go to the Online Learning Center to learn additional skills and review what you have already learned.

Microsoft Word
Extend your knowledge of Word by visiting the Online Learning Center for more MCAS-based exercises. Select **Advanced Word Exercises>Lessons**.

Windows Vista
Select **Windows Vista Exercises>Lessons** to explore Microsoft's operating system fully.

Microsoft Outlook
Want to learn all about Outlook and how to use e-mail communication and scheduling? Select **Microsoft Outlook Exercises>Lessons** for all you need to know.

Additional Projects
Complete additional projects in the following areas:

- **Real-World Business Projects** reinforce Microsoft Word by focusing on real-world business applications.
- **Presentation and Publishing Projects** Use your Word skills to create exciting PowerPoint presentations and desktop publishing activities.
- **Academic Projects** Integrate academic skills while enriching your understanding of Microsoft Word.

More Online Resources
Access additional Web sites and online information relating to key topics covered in Glencoe's *iCheck Series*. Select **Additional Resources>Links**.

Unit 1: Portfolio Project — Word 199

Lesson Planning Guide

LESSON 2 Create Content and Collaborate

Key Concepts

After completing this lesson, students will be able to:

- Promote and demote text
- Create diagrams, tables, and charts
- Insert Clip Art, pictures, shapes, and WordArt
- Use Spelling Checker and Thesaurus
- Track changes

iCheck Lesson Resources

The following components and resources have been provided to help you teach this lesson.

- Glencoe's Lesson Planner Plus DVD
  - Create your lesson plans with a few, simple clicks
  - Access blackline masters and resources
- Teacher Resource DVD
  - Data Files for PowerPoint Lesson 2
  - Solution Files for PowerPoint Lesson 2
- *Presentation Plus!* DVD
- Online Learning Center at **glencoe.com**
  - Data Files for PowerPoint Lesson 2
  - Solution Files for PowerPoint Lesson 2
  - Interactive Review for PowerPoint Lesson 2
  - Online Self Check for PowerPoint Lesson 2
  - Challenge Yourself Project Rubrics for PowerPoint Lesson 2
- *ExamView* CD, PowerPoint Lesson 2 Test

Standards

See page 569 for a list of Microsoft Certified Application Specialist objectives and ISTE/NETS standards that students will meet by completing this activity. See page TM33 for a correlation of 21st Century Skills and Workplace Competencies.

Lesson 2	Pg #	Data File	Lesson 2	Pg #	Solution File
Ex 2-3	573	Outline.docx	Ex 2-1 to 2-18	591	Garden-SF.pptx
Ex 2-13	586	Flowers.jpg			
PIA 1	594	Fundraiser .pptx	PIA 1	594	Fundraiser1-SF.pptx
PIA 1	594	PI_Outline .docx			
			PIA 2	595	Fundraiser2-SF.pptx
			PIA 3	596	Fundraiser3-SF.pptx
YT1 4	597	Theater.pptx	YTI 4	597	Theater4-SF.pptx
YT1 4	597	Theater.wmf			
			YTI 5	598	Theater5-SF.pptx
BCA 6	599	Sales.pptx			

Focus

Ask the class to brainstorm about possible uses for PowerPoint. Guide students by giving them a few examples. Students should understand that PowerPoint presentations communicate information. PowerPoint could be used for sales presentations, employee orientation, training presentations, or announcements to a company. You might tell students that on-screen presentations are often used at trade shows to give an overview of services or products. The presentation loops continually, and passersby can stop and watch any part of the presentation.

At this time you may want students to view PowerPoint Lesson 2 of the *Presentation Plus!* DVD. This presentation program uses an engaging format to introduce students to the key concepts of this lesson.

Inside the Student Edition

Teaching with the Lesson Opener

Each unit is divided into multiple lessons. The lesson opener helps direct students' attention to the material presented.

Key Concepts present lesson objectives.

21st Century Skills highlight essential workplace competencies.

Standards list ISTE NETS and Microsoft Certified Application Specialist standards covered in the lesson.

LESSON 1 Create a Document

In this lesson, you will learn how to key and edit text. You will also learn how to name, save, print, open, and close a document. Knowing these basic skills is an essential part of becoming a word processing expert.

Key Concepts

- Identify parts of the Word screen
- Name and save a document
- Key text into a document
- Edit text
- Print a document
- Close a document

Standards

The following standards are covered in this lesson. Refer to pages xxv and 715 for a description of the standards listed here.

ISTE Standards Correlation

NETS•S

3b, 3c, 5b, 6a, 6b, 6d

Microsoft Certified Application Specialist

Word

1.4, 5.1

21st CENTURY SKILLS

Set Realistic Goals Recall the first time you tried to ride a skateboard or play basketball. How long did it take before you felt confident with your performance? Like skateboarding and basketball, it takes time to learn word processing skills. Along the way, you will make mistakes. Allowing yourself to make mistakes, and knowing how to learn from those mistakes, is an important part of setting realistic goals. *What is your goal for this class?*

Word 3

Before You Read, Read to Learn and **Main Idea** reading strategies help prepare students to learn lesson material.

Vocabulary list contains both key terms and academic vocabulary.

Academic Standards box notes national language arts and math standards met in the lesson.

LESSON 1 Reading Guide

Before You Read

Survey Before starting the lesson, survey the content by reading exercise titles, bolded terms, and figures. Do they help you predict the information in the lesson?

Read To Learn

- Consider how the Word screen allows you to enter commands easily into the application.
- Explore file management as a vital skill.
- Discover how creating and editing documents is part of good business communication.

Main Idea

Microsoft Word is a word processing application that you can use to create and organize documents.

Vocabulary

Key Terms

button	insertion point	status bar
command	pointer	tab
cursor	Quick Access Toolbar (QAT)	title bar
dialog box	Ribbon	
document	ScreenTip	
edit	scroll bar	
folder		
group		

Academic Vocabulary

These words appear in your reading and on your tests. Make sure you know their meanings.

consider
determine

Quick Write Activity

Describe On a separate sheet of paper, describe why it is important to edit and proofread a document before you consider it to be final. What steps do you take when you proofread a document?

Study Skills

Stay On Task If you are easily distracted in class, try sitting at the front of the room or near the teacher's desk. This will make it easier to focus on what the teacher is saying.

Academic Standards

English Language Arts

NCTE 1 Read texts to acquire new information.
NCTE 4 Use written language to communicate effectively.
NCTE 5 Use different writing process elements to communicate effectively.
NCTE 6 Apply knowledge of language structure and conventions to discuss texts.
NCTE 7 Conduct research and gather, evaluate, and synthesize data to communicate discoveries.
NCTE 8 Use information resources to gather information and create and communicate knowledge.

Lesson 1: Reading Guide Word 4

Quick Write Activity allows students to practice their writing skills.

Study Skills provide strategies for student academic success.

Lesson Planning Guide

Teach

Step-By-Steps
Throughout the lesson, have students perform the Step-By-Steps to complete each exercise.

Troubleshooting Tips
Encourage students to press **CTRL** + **S** often to avoid losing any of their work.

Differentiated Instruction
Consider beginning this lesson by having students explore the PowerPoint screen on their own. Have them read the ScreenTips of the buttons on the screen. Then, have them explore the different tabs.

Classroom Management Tips
Students will want to share what they learn about PowerPoint with their friends during class. In order to minimize disruption in class, consider making this "sharing" time official, but set a time limit. Invite students to talk about what they have learned with their friends. Then, have students return to their seats and continue class.

Reading and Writing Support
Point out to students that there should be one space before a zip code. *Please send the information to 72 Mount Washington Lane, Malden Hills, OH 45101.*

Assess

After the students finish the lesson, have them complete the following assessment activities:

- After You Read, p. 561
- Practice It Activities, on pp. 562–564

Reteach

Independent Practice
Assign You Try It Activities on pp. 565–566.

Differentiated Instruction
Assign Challenge Yourself Projects on p. 568.

Assess

There are multiple formats for assessment provided for this lesson. These include:

- Interactive Review—Online Learning Center
- Online Self Check—Online Learning Center
- Critical Thinking Activities, p. 567
- Rubrics for Challenge Yourself Projects—Online Learning Center. Refer to page TM40 for an explanation of how rubrics can help students enhance performance and self-evaluation techniques.
- *ExamView* for PowerPoint Lesson 1

Close

Have students brainstorm as many ways as possible to move around in a presentation. Possible answers include using the scroll bar, pressing Page Down and other keys on the keyboard, using Slide Sorter view, using the Slides pane, and using the Outlines pane.

Answers

- **21st Century Skills (p. 542)** Answers will vary. Students may say that if you catch your audience's interest, they are more likely to pay attention.
- See Lesson Resources on the previous page for a list of Solution Files provided in this lesson.
- See answers to After You Read on p. 561 and Critical Thinking Activities on p. 567.
- **Writing Matters: Know your Audience (p. 560)**
  1. Answers will vary. Students might ask the following questions: What are their ages? What do they already know about the subject? What do I want them to know?
  2. Answers may vary, but students should recognize that understanding their audience will help them decide what information to provide, get the audience's attention, and explain the subject in a way the audience will understand.
  3. Students should key a paragraph that introduces the comic book collection, and is aimed at fifth and sixth graders.

How to Use the iCheck Step-By-Steps

Each step-by-step exercise page is specially designed to help maximize students' learning. Text is kept to a minimum, key terms are highlighted, steps are brief, and select screen captures provide a visual for students' reference.

Step-By-Steps are easy-to-follow steps that guide students through the skills presented.

iCheck Icon iCHECK reminds students to compare their work against the correct examples shown in the figures.

Academic Skills help students connect computer application skills to core academic concepts. Other mini-features provide students with helpful point-of-use information.

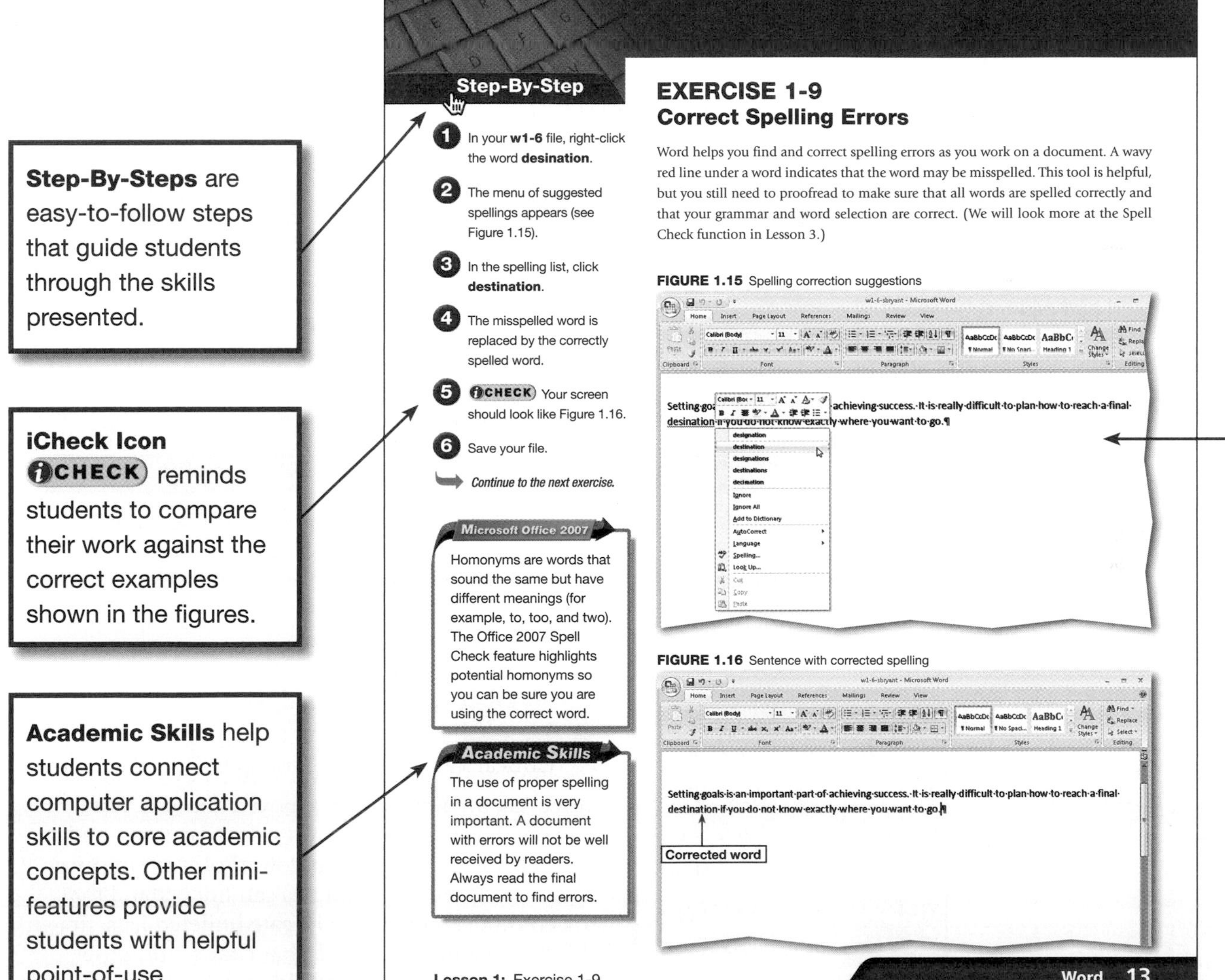

Step-By-Step
1 In your w1-6 file, right-click the word desination.
2 The menu of suggested spellings appears (see Figure 1.15).
3 In the spelling list, click destination.
4 The misspelled word is replaced by the correctly spelled word.
5 iCHECK Your screen should look like Figure 1.16.
6 Save your file.
Continue to the next exercise.
Microsoft Office 2007
Homonyms are words that sound the same but have different meanings (for example, to, too, and two). The Office 2007 Spell Check feature highlights potential homonyms so you can be sure you are using the correct word.
Academic Skills
The use of proper spelling in a document is very important. A document with errors will not be well received by readers. Always read the final document to find errors.
EXERCISE 1-9
Correct Spelling Errors
Word helps you find and correct spelling errors as you work on a document. A wavy red line under a word indicates that the word may be misspelled. This tool is helpful, but you still need to proofread to make sure that all words are spelled correctly and that your grammar and word selection are correct. (We will look more at the Spell Check function in Lesson 3.)
FIGURE 1.15 Spelling correction suggestions
FIGURE 1.16 Sentence with corrected spelling
Setting·goals·is·an·important·part·of·achieving·success.·It·is·really·difficult·to·plan·how·to·reach·a·final·destination·if·you·do·not·know·exactly·where·you·want·to·go.¶
Corrected word
Lesson 1: Exercise 1-9
Word 13

Figures are color images with callouts that give students a model for checking their work.

Lesson Planning Guide

LESSON 1 PowerPoint Basics

Key Concepts

After completing this lesson, students will be able to:

- Identify parts of the PowerPoint screen
- Work with the Ribbon, Office button, and dialog boxes
- Open an existing presentation
- Insert and edit text on slides
- Start and run slide shows
- Preview and print a presentation

iCheck Lesson Resources

The following components and resources have been provided to help you teach this lesson.

- Glencoe's Lesson Planner Plus DVD
  - Create your lesson plans with a few, simple clicks
  - Access blackline masters and resources
- Teacher Resource DVD
  - Data Files for PowerPoint Lesson 1
  - Solution Files for PowerPoint Lesson 1
- *Presentation Plus!* DVD
- Online Learning Center at **glencoe.com**
  - Data Files for PowerPoint Lesson 1
  - Solution Files for PowerPoint Lesson 1
  - Interactive Review for PowerPoint Lesson 1
  - Online Self Check for PowerPoint Lesson 1
  - Challenge Yourself Project Rubrics for PowerPoint Lesson 1
- *ExamView* CD, PowerPoint Lesson 1 Test

Standards

See page 542 for a list of Microsoft Certified Application Specialist objectives and ISTE/NETS standards that students will meet by completing this activity. See page TM33 for a correlation of 21st Century Skills and Workplace Competencies.

Lesson 1	Pg #	Data File	Lesson 1	Pg #	Solution File
EX 1-3	546	Tips.pptx	Ex 1-3 to 1-16	559	Tips-SF.pptx
PIA1	562	Pizza.pptx	PIA 1	562	Pizza1-SF.pptx
			PIA 2	563	Pizza2-SF.pptx
			PIA 3	564	Pizza3-SF.pptx
			YTI 4	565	Tips4-SF.pptx
			YTI 5	566	Tips5-SF.pptx
			SAW 7	567	Tips7-SF.pptx

Focus

Ask students if they have ever seen a PowerPoint slide show. Ask them what they enjoyed about it. Students may say that a slide show has colors, pictures, and fancy effects. Point out that PowerPoint is not only used for slide shows. Students can understand that PowerPoint can be used to create bulleted lists, drawn objects, organization charts, bar charts, and other graphics. Share a variety of slide printouts. Ask students what features they see that they would like to learn more about.

At this time you may want students to view PowerPoint Lesson 1 of the *Presentation Plus!* DVD. This presentation program uses an engaging format to introduce students to the key concepts of this lesson.

Teaching with the Features

There are three different full-page features scattered throughout the text—Writing Matters, Math Matters, and 21st Century Workplace. Each feature provides students with pertinent and practical real-world information.

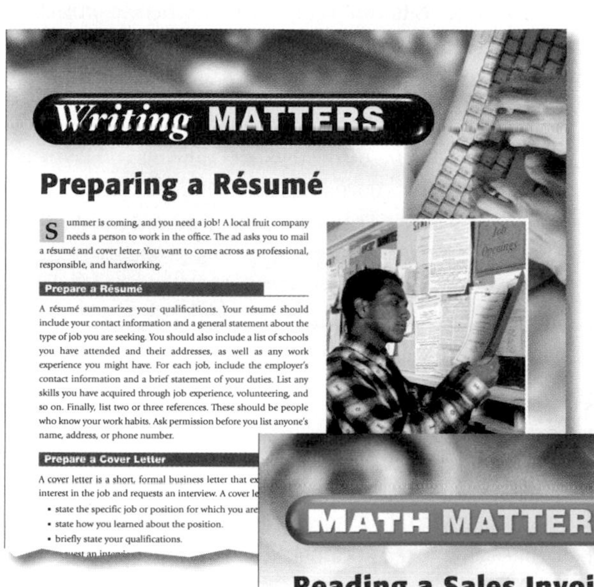

Writing MATTERS

Preparing a Résumé

Summer is coming, and you need a job! A local fruit company needs a person to work in the office. The ad asks you to mail a résumé and cover letter. You want to come across as professional, responsible, and hardworking.

Prepare a Résumé

A résumé summarizes your qualifications. Your résumé should include your contact information and a general statement about the type of job you are seeking. You should also include a list of schools you have attended and their addresses, as well as any work experience you might have. For each job, include the employer's contact information and a brief statement of your duties. List any skills you have acquired through job experience, volunteering, and so on. Finally, list two or three references. These should be people who know your work habits. Ask permission before you list anyone's name, address, or phone number.

Prepare a Cover Letter

A cover letter is a short, formal business letter that ex... interest in the job and requests an interview. A cover le...

- state the specific job or position for which you are...
- state how you learned about the position.
- briefly state your qualifications.

Writing Matters These features provide students with information and activities related to business and academic writing. Business and personal letters, business and academic reports, and essays are just a few of the topics covered in these features. Each feature gives students a chance to develop their reading and writing skills.

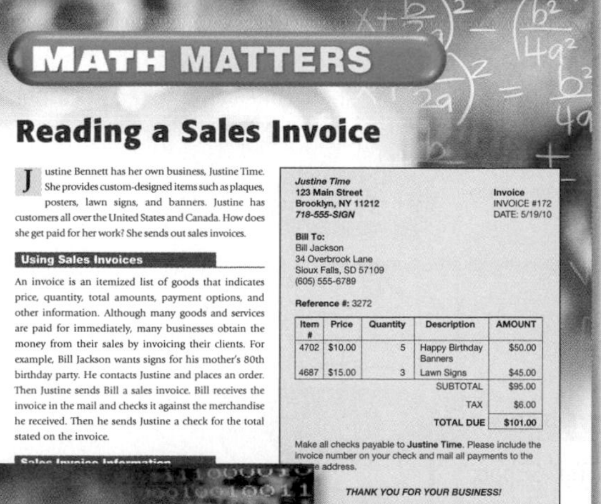

MATH MATTERS

Reading a Sales Invoice

Justine Bennett has her own business, Justine Time. She provides custom-designed items such as plaques, posters, lawn signs, and banners. Justine has customers all over the United States and Canada. How does she get paid for her work? She sends out sales invoices.

Using Sales Invoices

An invoice is an itemized list of goods that indicates price, quantity, total amounts, payment options, and other information. Although many goods and services are paid for immediately, many businesses obtain the money from their sales by invoicing their clients. For example, Bill Jackson wants signs for his mother's 80th birthday party. He contacts Justine and places an order. Then Justine sends Bill a sales invoice. Bill receives the invoice in the mail and checks it against the merchandise he received. Then he sends Justine a check for the total stated on the invoice.

Justine Time
123 Main Street
Brooklyn, NY 11212
718-555-SIGN

Invoice
INVOICE #172
DATE: 5/19/10

Bill To:
Bill Jackson
34 Overbrook Lane
Sioux Falls, SD 57109
(605) 555-6789

Reference #: 3272

Item #	Price	Quantity	Description	AMOUNT
4702	$10.00	5	Happy Birthday Banners	$50.00
4687	$15.00	3	Lawn Signs	$45.00
			SUBTOTAL	$95.00
			TAX	$6.00
			TOTAL DUE	**$101.00**

Make all checks payable to **Justine Time**. Please include the invoice number on your check and mail all payments to the ...e address.

THANK YOU FOR YOUR BUSINESS!

...s use invoices to let customers know how much ... for items or services they have purchased.

Math Matters Students use math every day—even if it is just counting out money to buy a juice drink at the campus store. The Math Matters features show students many different ways math is used in business and personal life. These features provide students with basic background information on several topics. Some of the topics students will learn about include balance sheets, reading charts and diagrams, and reading sales invoices.

21st Century WORKPLACE

Learn to Collaborate

Collaboration means working with other people. It means sharing ideas and tasks to make a project run well. Since most jobs involve the efforts of many people, knowing how to collaborate is a critical skill in today's workplace.

People bring different backgrounds and skills to each project. For projects to run smoothly, it is important that team members treat each other with respect. Being a good team member can thus involve looking at ideas and tasks from someone else's point of view. Ultimately, all team members benefit by being open to each other's ideas and suggestions.

MEET THE MANAGER

Sweet Potato Kids in Baltimore, Maryland, is a hands-on museum for children ages 1–10. Working collaboratively allows Michelle Hall-Davis, the museum's manager and owner, and her staff to provide the best possible activities and programs to their community. "Sweet Potato Kids is in a diverse neighborhood," notes Michelle. "Our employees need to be sensitive to the cultural, religious, economic, and racial backgrounds of our customers. They are also sensitive to these differences among themselves. Because we all work together, Sweet Potato Kids has

Working well with others is a critical skill to learn in today's workplace.

21st Century Workplace Topics of the 21st Century Workplace features include the "soft" skills that students need to be successful in getting and keeping a job. Information and communication skills, thinking and problem-solving skills, and interpersonal and self-direction skills are covered. Each feature includes a short quote from a real-life manager that highlights how the topic skill is valued in the workplace.

Unit 4 PowerPoint Overview

Focus

Motivation

- **Why It Matters** Review the Why It Matters feature on page 540. Discuss with students how being able to use PowerPoint 2007 will help them at both school and work.
- **Go Online: Real World Connection Activity** Have students complete the Go Online: Real World Connection Activity on page 540 to learn more about how different organization use database applications.
- **Careers and Technology** The ability to use PowerPoint can help one present information to a group, from demonstrating a product concept to training a group of employees. The effective use of PowerPoint can impress one's co-workers and one's superiors.
- **Answers to Reading Check (p. 541)**
  1. Answers will vary. Students should be able to identify three ways that presentation skills might be useful in an occupation.
  2. Postsecondary teachers.

Teach

Guided Practice

- ***Presentation Plus! PowerPoint Presentations*** A special PowerPoint presentation has been provided to help you introduce PowerPoint, including how people use PowerPoint at both school and work.

Independent Practice

Additional exercises and projects are available at the book's Online Learning Center at glencoe.com.

- **Additional Exercises**
  - Microsoft Word
  - Microsoft Excel
  - Microsoft Access
  - Microsoft PowerPoint
  - Microsoft Outlook
  - Windows Vista
- **Additional Projects**
  - Real-World Business Applications
  - Present and Publish Projects
  - Academic Projects

Assess

- **Portfolio Project** The Portfolio Project on pages 676–679 allows students to complete a business-oriented project. Students can complete all four parts, or focus on only one part of the project. Students can print copies of their projects, or create an electronic copy for their portfolios.
- **Rubrics** Rubrics are provided to help students and teachers assess the Portfolio Projects. Rubrics can be accessed on the Online Learning Center at glencoe.com.

Unit 4 Closer	Pg #	Data File
Portfolio Proj. pt. 2	677	Certificate-SF.pptx

Reteach

- **Academic Connections** Review the feature on page 674 with students to show how the technical skills developed in this unit can be used to complete an academic project.

Assess

- ***ExamView® Assessment Suite*** **PowerPoint Unit 4 Test**

Close

- **Ethics in Action** The feature on page 675 focuses on an important ethical issue that students may encounter. Have students read the feature and complete the questions to develop their decision-making skills.

  Answers to You Decide and **Application Activity (p. 675)**
  1. Answers may vary, but students should recognize that an involved citizen puts privileges into action, tries to bring about change, and participates in debates.
  2. Answers will vary. Students should list the advantages and disadvantages of each candidate and identify who they would vote for and why.
  3. Students should save their work as a PowerPoint presentation. In their slide shows, students should explain why they are the best candidate for class president.

Teaching with the Lesson Review

The lesson review offers students many different ways to review and reinforce the material presented.

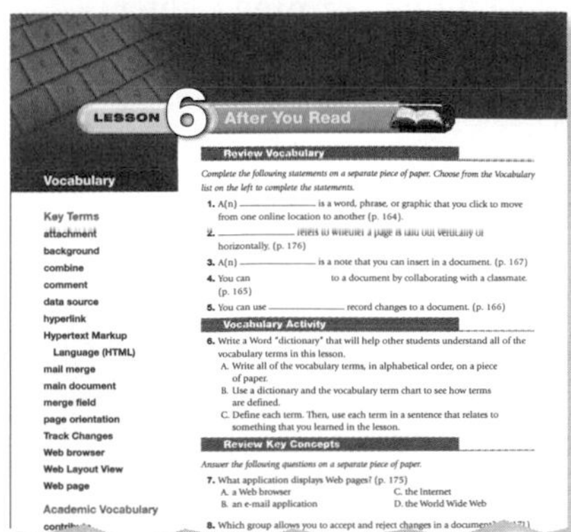

After You Read At the end of each lesson, the After You Read page compiles all of the Vocabulary and Key Concepts covered in the lesson into three review activities.

Practice It Activities These basic review activities contain step-by-step directions that walk students through one of the skills learned in the lesson. There are three Practice It Activities for each lesson.

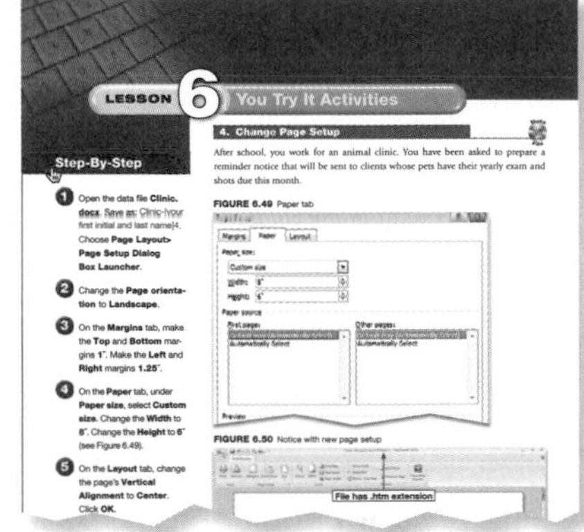

You Try It Activities Students are provided with guided practice for skills covered in the lesson in the You Try It Activities. There are two You Try It Activities in each lesson.

Critical Thinking Activities Students complete three exercises that integrate standards-based and real-world skills.

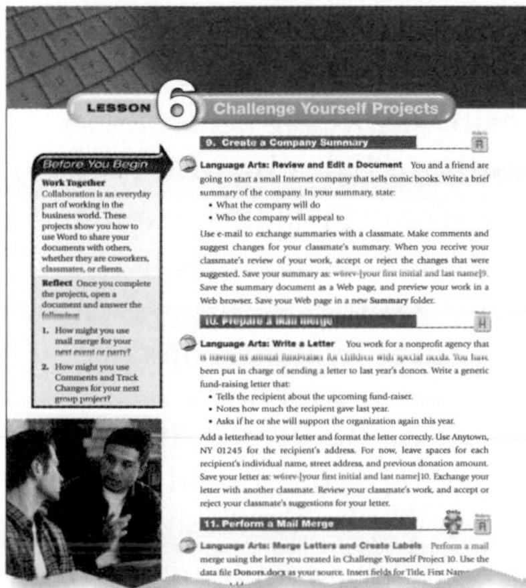

Challenge Yourself Projects These projects provide students with additional independent practice of the skill presented in the lesson. There are three different projects for each lesson and each project is leveled—beginning, intermediate, or advanced.

- Before You Begin appears in every Challenge Yourself Project, and gives students real-world context for the projects they will be creating.
- A rubric **R** is provided online at **glencoe.com** for each Challenge Yourself Project.
- Academic and technical standards are reinforced in these exercises.
- Data files  are provided when needed.

Lesson Planning Guide

Focus

Explain to students that as you develop a database, you create relationships between objects. If you delete a field or table you no longer need, you may cause problems with other objects.

At this time you may want students to view Access Lesson 5 of the *Presentation Plus!* DVD.

Teach

- **Step-By-Steps**
  Throughout the lesson, have students perform the Step-By-Steps to complete each exercise.
- **Troubleshooting Tips**
  This book was designed for Office 2007. Students may not be able to do the exercises in other versions.
- **Differentiated Instruction**
  Have advanced students create a simple database on a topic of their choice.
- **Classroom Management Tips**
  Hands on computer classes are engaging but can be rowdy. Consider using a sound to focus students' attention, like a bicycle horn.
- **Reading and Writing Support**
  Tell students to hyphenate two-word adjectives that come before the noun (unless the first word ends in *–ly*). *Julio bought a five-day pass.*

Assess

After the students finish the lesson, have them complete the following assessment activities:

- After You Read, p. 526
- Practice It Activities, on pp. 527–529

Reteach

- **Independent Practice**
  Assign You Try It Activities, pp. 530–531.
- **Differentiated Instruction**
  Assign Challenge Yourself Projects, p. 533.

Assess

There are multiple formats for assessment provided for this lesson. These include:

- Interactive Review—Online Learning Center
- Online Self Check—Online Learning Center
- Critical Thinking Activities, p. 532
- Rubrics for Challenge Yourself Projects—Online Learning Center. Refer to page TM40 for an explanation of how rubrics can help students enhance self-evaluation techniques.
- *ExamView* for Access Lesson 5

Close

Ask students to explain the difference between Print Preview and Layout Preview of a report. Students should explain that Print Preview shows a preview of the entire report. Layout Preview shows a preview of a few pages of the report, using a sample of the records.

Answers

- **21st Century Skills (p. 508)** Answers will vary. Students should describe things they could have done more of or differently in a task they recently completed.
- See Lesson Resources on the previous page for a list of Solution Files provided in this lesson.
- See answers to After You Read on p. 526 and Critical Thinking Activities on p. 532.
- **Math Matters: Reading a Sales Invoice (p. 525)**
  1. To detail the transaction, including naming the purchaser, the seller, the date, the items purchased, and their costs.
  2. Answers will vary. Students should describe invoices they or someone they know received and the information on the invoice. If no invoice was received, students should describe a situation in which they might receive one.
  3. Answers will vary. Students should understand the advantages and disadvantages of having an invoicing system.

Choose Proven Teaching Solutions *for* Effective Results

The *Teacher Annotated Edition* of *iCheck Microsoft Office 2007* is a comprehensive resource designed to help you motivate and involve your students throughout the learning process. The *Teacher Annotated Edition* provides teaching suggestions both at the beginning of the text and at point of use within each lesson. These suggestions guide you in introducing and reviewing the lesson in ways suited to your students' needs.

Teaching with the Annotations

Annotations within the lessons and in features provide suggestions for teaching the class and also provide ideas for student involvement within the text.

- **NCLB** indicate at point-of-use when a National Language Arts or National Math standard is being addressed.
- **EL** offer ideas for helping English Language Learners understand the content.
- **Differentiated Instruction** provide ideas for including the visually and physically impaired student in your class.
- **Inclusion Strategies** provide tips on how to include all levels of learners in daily class instruction.
- **Teaching Tips** offer many point-of-use tips to help you and your students get the most out of the textbook.
- **Step-By-Step Tips** offer additional information for a step within an exercise.
- **Troubleshooting** offer ideas for helping students avoid and solve computer-related difficulties they might encounter while working through an activity.
- **Different Strokes** give alternative methods for completing a step or skill.
- **Level** indicate the difficulty level of many of the projects provided in the text.
- **Answers** are provided for all of the activities. Many answers are provided at point of use.

Annotations Point-of-use annotations provide information when you need it.

LESSON 4 Critical Thinking Activities

Beyond the Classroom Activity Students' worksheets should look similar to solution file **e4rev6-SF.xlsx.**

Standards at Work Activity Students' final files should look like the solution file **e4rev7-SF.xlsx.**

21st Century Skills Activity Students' worksheets should look similar to solution file **e4rev8-SF.xlsx.**

NCLB/Math (Number and Operations) To reinforce students' understanding of meanings and operations and how they relate to one another, ask students to calculate and include the grand total for all four weeks.

6. Beyond the Classroom Activity

Math: Create an Income Sheet Each week you earn money doing the following chores for your neighbors:

- For sweeping one neighbor's sidewalk and porch, you earn $5.00.
- For mowing another neighbor's lawn, you earn $20.00.
- For cleaning another neighbor's windows, you earn $15.00.

Create a worksheet that has columns for three chores and rows for four weeks. For each week, show the amount you earn for each chore and use the **SUM** function to show how much you earned that week.

Save your worksheet as: e4rev-[your first initial and last name]6.

7. Standards at Work Activity

Microsoft Certified Application Specialist Correlation
Excel 4.1 *Create and Format Charts*

Create a Column Chart Your supervisor has asked you to create a clustered column chart comparing January and February sales in your **Books** file.

Open the latest version of your **Books** file. Save it as: e4rev-[your first initial and last name]7. Select cells **A1:C10**. Use the **Chart Tools** to create a **Clustered Column** chart. Enlarge the chart and position it so that it does not cover the data in your worksheet.

8. 21st Century Skills Activity

Design an Academic Calendar One way to manage your time well is to create a calendar to schedule your schoolwork. Imagine that you have a five-page English paper due in two weeks. Use Excel to create a schedule for working on your English paper. Your schedule should include the following steps:

A. Research
B. Write a draft
C. Edit the draft
D. Write a final draft

Remember that you have five pages to write. Make sure you schedule all ten weekdays in the two weeks you have to finish the paper. Give yourself at least three days to research and at least one day to complete each of the remaining stages of the writing process.

Save your worksheet as: e4rev-[your first initial and last name]8.

Go Online **e-REVIEW**
glencoe.com

Go to the **Online Learning Center** to complete the following review activities.

Online Self Check
To test your knowledge of the material, click **Unit 2> Lesson 4** and choose **Self Checks**.

Interactive Review
To review the main points of the lesson, click **Unit 2> Lesson 4** and choose **Interactive Review.**

Lesson 4: Critical Thinking Activities Excel 311

LESSON 5 Manage Databases

Key Concepts

After completing this lesson, students will be able to:

- Identify object dependencies
- Preview reports
- Print documentation on database objects
- Repair databases

iCheck Lesson Resources

The following components and resources have been provided to help you teach this lesson.

- Glencoe's Lesson Planner Plus DVD
  - Create your lesson plans with a few, simple clicks
  - Access blackline masters and resources
- Teacher Resource DVD
  - Data Files for Access Lesson 5
  - Solution Files for Access Lesson 5
- *Presentation Plus!* DVD
- Online Learning Center at **glencoe.com**
  - Data Files for Access Lesson 5
  - Solution Files for Access Lesson 5
  - Interactive Review for Access Lesson 5
  - Online Self Check for Access Lesson 5
  - Challenge Yourself Project Rubrics for Access Lesson 5
- *ExamView* CD, Access Lesson 5 Test

Standards

See page 508 for a list of Microsoft Certified Application Specialist objectives and ISTE/NETS standards that students will meet by completing this activity. See page TM33 for a correlation of 21st Century Skills and Workplace Competencies.

Lesson 5	Pg #	Data File	Lesson 5	Pg #	Solution File
			Ex 5-1 to 5-10	522	Sports5-SF.accdb
EX 5-11	523	Sports5b.mdb	EX 5-11	523	Sports5b-SF.mdb
			EX 5-12	524	a5-12-SF.accdb
			PIA 1	527	Sports5-SF.accdb
			PIA 2	528	Sports5b2003-SF.accdb
			PIA 3	529	a5-p3-SF.accdb
			YTI 5	531	CustomerOrders form (located in Sports5-SF.accdb)
			Ch. Yslf. 10	533	Query Order_PivotChart10-SF (located in Sports5-SF.accdb)
			Ch. Yslf. 11	533	Query Order_PivotChart11-SF (located in Sports5-SF.accdb)

The Six-Step Teaching Plan

The Teacher Manual in the *Teacher Annotated Edition* of *iCheck Microsoft Office 2007* is designed to make full and effective use of a proven pedagogical approach: Focus, Teach, Assess, Reteach, Assess, and Close.

Step 1—Focus As a teacher, you know that the first step in presenting new material is to capture students' interest. Special features, such as Why It Matters and Quick Write Activity in the *Student Edition* are designed to engage students in the material presented in the coming unit or lesson.

Step 2—Teach The second step in the instruction process involves the presentation and exploration of new material. The teaching plan is designed to give you maximum flexibility in meeting the needs of your class.

Step 3—Assess This third step involves an assessment of students' learning. Because students have different learning styles and learn at different rates, the Assess section provides a selection of evaluation activities designed to accommodate a wide range of learning abilities.

Step 4—Reteach The fourth step is a reinforcement of the concepts and ideas learned in the material. The Reteach section provides activities designed to reteach students the concepts they need to know as they complete the material.

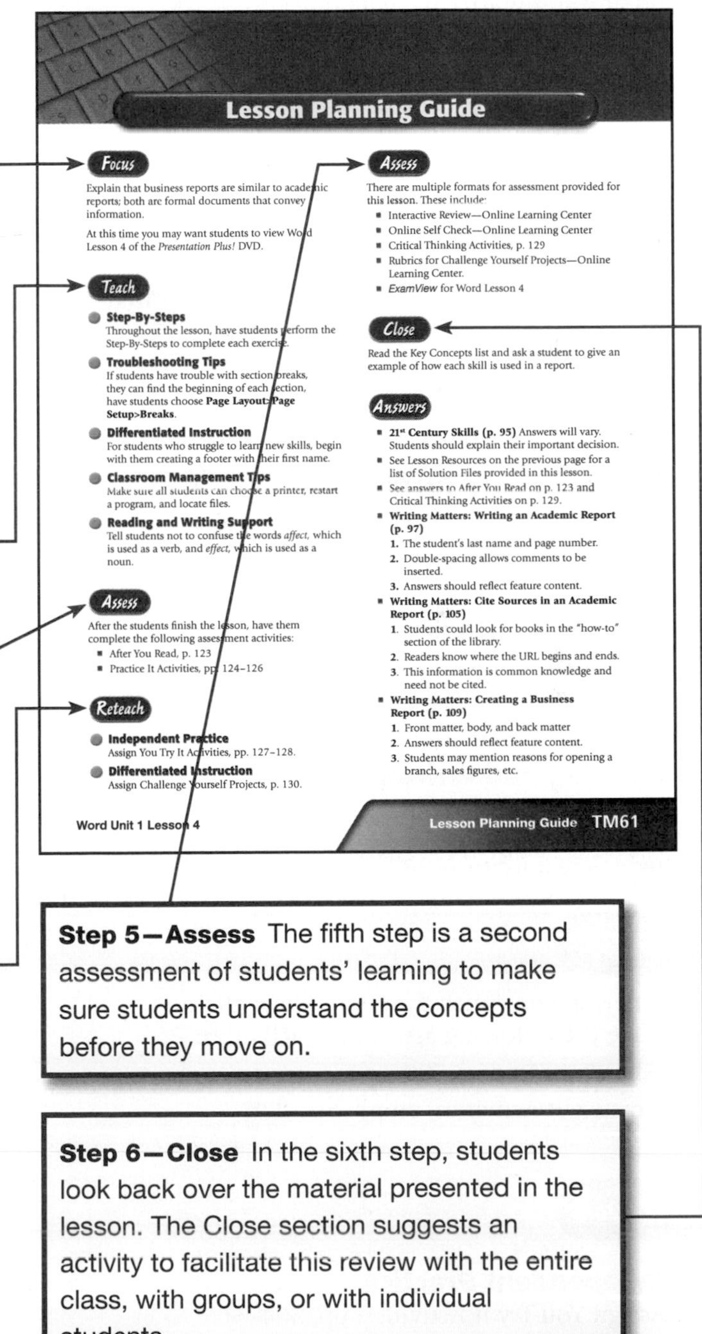

Lesson Planning Guide

Focus

Explain that business reports are similar to academic reports; both are formal documents that convey information.

At this time you may want students to view Word Lesson 4 of the *Presentation Plus!* DVD.

Teach

- **Step-By-Steps**
  Throughout the lesson, have students perform the Step-By-Steps to complete each exercise.
- **Troubleshooting Tips**
  If students have trouble with section breaks, they can find the beginning of each section, have students choose **Page Layout>Page Setup>Breaks**.
- **Differentiated Instruction**
  For students who struggle to learn new skills, begin with them creating a footer with their first name.
- **Classroom Management Tips**
  Make sure all students can choose a printer, restart a program, and locate files.
- **Reading and Writing Support**
  Tell students not to confuse the words *affect,* which is used as a verb, and *effect,* which is used as a noun.

Assess

After the students finish the lesson, have them complete the following assessment activities:

- After You Read, p. 123
- Practice It Activities, pp. 124–126

Reteach

- **Independent Practice**
  Assign You Try It Activities, pp. 127–128.
- **Differentiated Instruction**
  Assign Challenge Yourself Projects, p. 130.

Assess

There are multiple formats for assessment provided for this lesson. These include:

- Interactive Review—Online Learning Center
- Online Self Check—Online Learning Center
- Critical Thinking Activities, p. 129
- Rubrics for Challenge Yourself Projects—Online Learning Center.
- *ExamView* for Word Lesson 4

Close

Read the Key Concepts list and ask a student to give an example of how each skill is used in a report.

Answers

- **21st Century Skills (p. 95)** Answers will vary. Students should explain their important decision.
- See Lesson Resources on the previous page for a list of Solution Files provided in this lesson.
- See answers to After You Read on p. 123 and Critical Thinking Activities on p. 129.
- **Writing Matters: Writing an Academic Report (p. 97)**
  1. The student's last name and page number.
  2. Double-spacing allows comments to be inserted.
  3. Answers should reflect feature content.
- **Writing Matters: Cite Sources in an Academic Report (p. 105)**
  1. Students could look for books in the "how-to" section of the library.
  2. Readers know where the URL begins and ends.
  3. This information is common knowledge and need not be cited.
- **Writing Matters: Creating a Business Report (p. 109)**
  1. Front matter, body, and back matter
  2. Answers should reflect feature content.
  3. Students may mention reasons for opening a branch, sales figures, etc.

Word Unit 1 Lesson 4

Lesson Planning Guide TM61

Step 5—Assess The fifth step is a second assessment of students' learning to make sure students understand the concepts before they move on.

Step 6—Close In the sixth step, students look back over the material presented in the lesson. The Close section suggests an activity to facilitate this review with the entire class, with groups, or with individual students.

Lesson Planning Guide

Focus

Explain to students that Access offers the ability to import thousands of records from outside sources, including Excel spreadsheets. Queries can then be built to sort and summarize the data quickly.

At this time you may want students to view Access Lesson 4 of the *Presentation Plus!* DVD.

Teach

- **Step-By-Steps**
  Throughout the lesson, have students perform the Step-By-Steps to complete each exercise.
- **Troubleshooting Tips**
  Encourage students to use Design View to troubleshoot problems in Access.
- **Differentiated Instruction**
  Have students ask parents who use Access at work for a sample report. Seeing completed reports will help visual learners.
- **Classroom Management Tips**
  If you notice students have the same troubles on the same exercises, do the exercises out loud as a class. Have students help each other.
- **Reading and Writing Support**
  Remind students to put a comma between adjacent adjectives. *He is a successful, talented actor.*

Assess

After the students finish the lesson, have them complete the following assessment activities:

- After You Read, p. 500
- Practice It Activities, on pp. 501–503

Reteach

- **Independent Practice**
  Assign You Try It Activities, pp. 504–505.
- **Differentiated Instruction**
  Assign Challenge Yourself Projects, p. 507.

Assess

There are multiple formats for assessment provided for this lesson. These include:

- Interactive Review—Online Learning Center
- Online Self Check—Online Learning Center
- Critical Thinking Activities, p. 506
- Rubrics for Challenge Yourself Projects—Online Learning Center. Refer to page TM40 for an explanation of how rubrics can help students enhance performance and self-evaluation techniques.
- *ExamView* for Access Lesson 4

Close

Explain to students that there are various circumstances in which you will need to link to an external source rather than importing it. Ask them what these circumstances might include. The goal in making this decision is to accommodate the needs of the user.

Answers

- **21st Century Skills (p. 470)** Answers will vary. Students should identify and describe a recently completed task.
- See Lesson Resources on the previous page for a list of Solution Files provided in this lesson.
- See answers to After You Read on p. 500 and Critical Thinking Activities on p. 506.
- **21st Century Workplace: Problem Solving (p. 499)**
  1. Maria identifies the problem's source, which allows her to come up with a possible solution.
  2. Students might offer the alternate solution of trying to bargain with Douglas. Students might list issues such as the difficulty of finding new clients and whether it is possible to bargain.
  3. Students should describe an impending problem and how they will apply the "go slow to go fast" strategy to solve it.

Explore Technology Solutions *for* Instructional Support

Glencoe's *iCheck Series* includes a number of resources developed to support you in meeting your course objectives and in maximizing student learning.

Technology Resources

Glencoe's *iCheck Series* contains technology that allows teachers to customize classroom resources. The program includes customizable tests and lesson plans, as well as Data Files, Solution Files and PowerPoint presentations that preview important topics.

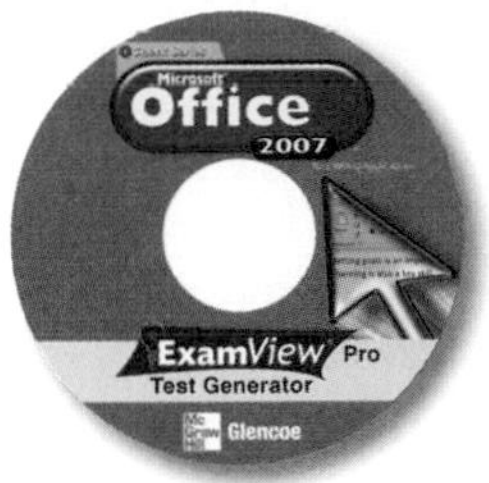

ExamView® Assessment Suite CD

A fully enabled copy of the *ExamView®* software is provided on this CD. This software can be used to print out ready-made tests, complete with answer keys for each lesson in the textbook. You can also modify the testbanks provided on the CD or create your own tests. The software can be run on either Macintosh or Windows platforms.

Lesson Planner Plus DVD

Custom design your lesson plan with this easy-to-use DVD. The electronic format allows teachers to select a preset plan or to create their own planning guide. Either way, it offers access to electronic files of all reproducible resources at the click of a button.

Presentation Plus! PowerPoint Presentations

Presentation Plus! contains highly visual presentations that summarize each lesson in the text. The overviews highlight the skills students will learn and show how these skills can be used in real world situations. The presentations allow students to preview and review material covered in the text.

This is an exciting and easy-to-use teaching tool that is PowerPoint based. With the full version of PowerPoint, you can customize presentations to meet your needs, add and rearrange slides, or update information.

Teacher Resource DVD

The Teacher Resource DVD contains Data Files and Solution Files used in the Student Edition.

Lesson Planning Guide

LESSON 4 Maximizing Database Functions

Key Concepts

After completing this lesson, students will be able to:

- Link to external data sources
- Import and export data
- Sort and filter data within different database objects
- Save and run import and export specifications

iCheck Lesson Resources

The following components and resources have been provided to help you teach this lesson.

- Glencoe's Lesson Planner Plus DVD
  - Create your lesson plans with a few, simple clicks
  - Access blackline masters and resources
- Teacher Resource DVD
  - Data Files for Access Lesson 4
  - Solution Files for Access Lesson 4
- *Presentation Plus!* DVD
- Online Learning Center at **glencoe.com**
  - Data Files for Access Lesson 4
  - Solution Files for Access Lesson 4
  - Interactive Review for Access Lesson 4
  - Online Self Check for Access Lesson 4
  - Challenge Yourself Project Rubrics for Access Lesson 4
- *ExamView* CD, Access Lesson 4 Test

Standards

See page 470 for a list of Microsoft Certified Application Specialist objectives and ISTE/NETS standards that students will meet by completing this activity. See page TM33 for a correlation of 21st Century Skills and Workplace Competencies.

Lesson 4	Pg #	Data File	Lesson 4	Pg #	Solution File
EX 4-1	472	Sports4.accdb	Ex 4-1 to 4-19	498	Sports4-SF.accdb
			PIA 1	501	DetailedOrders query (located in Sports4-SF.accdb)
			PIA 2	502	CustOrdAmt By Order Date query (located in Sports4-SF.accdb)
			PIA 3	503	CustomerOrders form (located in Sports4-SF.accdb)
			YTI 4	504	Sport Record Holders3 table (located in Sports4-SF.accdb)
			YTI 5	505	Sports Record Holders3.rtf
			Ch. Yrslf. 9	507	DetailedOrders-9SF query (located in Sports4-SF.accdb)
			Ch. Yrslf. 10	507	DetailedOrders-10SF.xlsx
			Ch. Yrslf. 11	507	From Sales file (located in Sports4-SF.accdb)

Online Learning Center

The Online Learning Center at **glencoe.com** contains numerous resources for students and teachers to support instruction in the computer education classroom.

Online Student Center

The Online Student Learning Center at **glencoe.com** provides students with a variety of materials to enhance their learning experience.

Online Self Checks provide students with multiple choice questions they can use to review the main ideas of the lesson.

Online Review offers students an exciting game format to review and assess their understanding of the topics covered in the lesson.

Data Files used in the lessons and activities are provided for students to download.

Student Resource Links give students access to additional information that relates to the information covered in the text.

Real World Connection Activities teach students how Microsoft Office applications are used in their future careers.

Business Application Projects include twenty reproducible projects that focus on real-world business applications.

Present and Publish contains in-depth activities in which students create exciting PowerPoint presentations and desktop publishing projects.

Integrated Curriculum Projects contain projects to help integrate academic skills into the computer applications classroom.

Advanced Exercises Also Available:

- Microsoft Word 2007
- Microsoft Excel 2007
- Microsoft Access 2007
- Microsoft PowerPoint 2007
- Microsoft Outlook 2007
- Windows Vista

Online Teacher Center

The Online Teacher Resource Center at **glencoe.com** provides you with additional resources to use as you teach your computer applications course, including

Resource Links provide you with a wealth of information relating to such topics as professional development, funding, teaching strategies, and rubrics.

Solution Files for each activity in the text as well as for Business Application projects, Integrated Curriculum projects, and Present and Publish projects are provided at the resource center.

Inclusion in the Computer Technology Classroom Practical information on how to help special-needs students succeed in the computer applications classroom is presented in this booklet for teachers.

(ID = iCheck, Password = the last word on page TM5.)

Lesson Planning Guide

Focus

Ask students what would be important to them if they needed to retrieve information from a database. Explain that in this lesson they will learn how to make data easy to find.

At this time you may want students to view Access Lesson 3 of the *Presentation Plus!* DVD.

Teach

Step-By-Steps
Throughout the lesson, have students perform the Step-By-Steps to complete each exercise.

Troubleshooting Tips
Students can press **CTRL** + the plus key (+) before they can enter data to create a new, blank record.

Differentiated Instruction
Ask volunteers to read the introductory text of each exercise. This will help auditory learners.

Classroom Management Tips
To help less skilled students, ask advanced students to prepare a 5-minute lesson on a new topic.

Reading and Writing Support
Tell students that to make the possessive of a plural noun that ends with *s,* they should add an apostrophe. *The turkeys' home was a small farm.*

Assess

After the students finish the lesson, have them complete the following assessment activities:

- After You Read, p. 462
- Practice It Activities, on pp. 463–465

Reteach

Independent Practice
Assign You Try It Activities, pp. 466–467.

Differentiated Instruction
Assign Challenge Yourself Projects, p. 469.

Assess

There are multiple formats for assessment provided for this lesson. These include:

- Interactive Review—Online Learning Center
- Online Self Check—Online Learning Center
- Critical Thinking Activities, p. 468
- Rubrics for Challenge Yourself Projects—Online Learning Center. Refer to page TM40 for an explanation of how rubrics can help students enhance performance and self-evaluation techniques.
- *ExamView* for Access Lesson 3

Close

Discuss why it is important to set up forms and reports so that the controls are aligned and evenly spaced.

Answers

- **21st Century Skills (p. 425)** Answers will vary. Students should think about the main activities in their lives and then identify the most important.
- See Lesson Resources on the previous page for a list of Solution Files provided in this lesson.
- See answers to After You Read on p. 462 and Critical Thinking Activities on p. 468.
- **Math Matters: Showing a Profit or Loss (p. 461)**
  1. Revenue − Expenses = Net Profit or Net Loss.
  2. Answers will vary, but students should recognize that if you know the status of your business' finances, you can make sound decisions about whether to expand your business or adjust how you run it.
  3. Students' profit and loss statements should include the three basic elements and should show accurate calculations.
  4. Students' paragraphs should include a description of the software and why they think it is appropriate for a small business.

Make Your Teaching Adaptable *to* Any Schedule

Unit Organizers

The charts on pages TM15 through TM17 provide an overview of the units and lessons in Glencoe's *iCheck Series*. Use Glencoe's *Lesson Planner Plus* DVD to develop personalized electronic teaching plans for individual lessons.

	FOCUS	FEATURES	PROJECTS	ASSESSMENT
UNIT 1	Word 2007: Business and Personal Communication	Academic Connections: Social Studies—Writing a Business Letter (p. 194) Ethics in Action: What Are Ethics? (p. 195)	Portfolio Project (p. 196) Beyond the Book Online Projects (p. 199)	*ExamView* Portfolio Project (p. 196)
Lesson 1	Create a Document	Writing Matters: Proofread to Avoid Mistakes (p. 22)	Challenge Yourself Projects (p. 30)	*ExamView* Challenge Yourself Projects (p. 30)
Lesson 2	Format Content	Writing Matters: Writing a Memo (p. 33) Writing Matters: Formatting a Memo (p. 34)	Challenge Yourself Projects (p. 63)	*ExamView* Challenge Yourself Projects (p. 63)
Lesson 3	Use Word Tools	Writing Matters: Business Letters (p. 66) Writing Matters: Business and Personal Business Letters (p.67)	Challenge Yourself Projects (p. 94)	*ExamView* Challenge Yourself Projects (p. 94)
Lesson 4	Manage Lengthy Documents	Writing Matters: Writing an Academic Report (p. 97) Writing Matters: Citing Sources in an Academic Report (p. 105) Writing Matters: Creating a Business Report (p. 109)	Challenge Yourself Projects (p. 130)	*ExamView* Challenge Yourself Projects (p. 130)
Lesson 5	Columns, Tables, and Graphics	Math Matters: Reading Charts, Graphs, and Diagrams (p. 153)	Challenge Yourself Projects (p. 161)	*ExamView* Challenge Yourself Projects (p. 161)
Lesson 6	Collaborate with Others	21st Century Workplace: Learn to Collaborate (p. 185)	Challenge Yourself Projects (p. 193)	*ExamView* Challenge Yourself Projects (p. 193)

Lesson Planning Guide

LESSON 3 Enter and Organize Data

Key Concepts

After completing this lesson, students will be able to:

- Enter, edit, and delete records from a datasheet
- Create, change, and format forms and reports
- Define and format controls
- Create multiple item, split, and subforms, and PivotTables
- Create and print labels

iCheck Lesson Resources

The following components and resources have been provided to help you teach this lesson.

- Glencoe's Lesson Planner Plus DVD
  - Create your lesson plans with a few, simple clicks
  - Access blackline masters and resources
- Teacher Resource DVD
  - Data Files for Access Lesson 3
  - Solution Files for Access Lesson 3
- *Presentation Plus!* DVD
- Online Learning Center at **glencoe.com**
  - Data Files for Access Lesson 3
  - Solution Files for Access Lesson 3
  - Interactive Review for Access Lesson 3
  - Online Self Check for Access Lesson 3
  - Challenge Yourself Project Rubrics for Access Lesson 3
- *ExamView* CD, Access Lesson 3 Test

Standards

See page 425 for a list of Microsoft Certified Application Specialist objectives and ISTE/NETS standards that students will meet by completing this activity. See page TM33 for a correlation of 21st Century Skills and Workplace Competencies.

Lesson 3	Pg #	Data File
Ex 3-1	427	Sports.accdb

Lesson 3	Pg #	Solution File
Ex 3-1 to 3-21	460	Sports-SF.accdb
PIA 1	463	Product Form (located in Sports-SF.accdb)
PIA 2	464	Order Detail report (located in Sports-SF.accdb)
PIA 3	465	Inventory Labels report (located in Sports-SF.accdb)
YTI 4	466	Customer Split View form (located in Sports-SF.accdb)
YTI 5	467	Orders With Groups report (located in Sports-SF.accdb)
Ch. Yslf 9	469	Product9-SF form (located in Sports-SF.accdb)
Ch. Yslf 10	469	ProdReport10-SF report (located in Sports-SF.accdb)
Ch. Yslf 11	469	ProdLabels11-SF table (located in Sports-SF.accdb)

Course Planning

	FOCUS	FEATURES	PROJECTS	ASSESSMENT
UNIT 2	Unit 2 Excel 2007: Business and Personal Finances	Academic Connections: Math—Calculate Percentages (p. 342) Ethics in Action: Using Online Resources Responsibly (p. 343)	Portfolio Project (p. 344) Beyond the Book Online Activities (p. 347)	*ExamView* Portfolio Project (p. 344)
Lesson 1	Excel Basics	Math Matters: Introduction to Excel (p. 204)	Challenge Yourself Projects (p. 225)	*ExamView* Challenge Yourself Projects (p. 225)
Lesson 2	Create Data and Content	Math Matters: Using Math Formulas (p. 240)	Challenge Yourself Projects (p. 248)	*ExamView* Challenge Yourself Projects (p. 248)
Lesson 3	Format Data and Content	21st Century Workplace: Develop Interview Skills (p. 273)	Challenge Yourself Projects (p. 281)	*ExamView* Challenge Yourself Projects (p. 281)
Lesson 4	Analyze Data	Math Matters: Presenting Information Graphically (p. 304)	Challenge Yourself Projects (p. 312)	*ExamView* Challenge Yourself Projects (p. 312)
Lesson 5	Manage Workbooks	Math Matters: Balancing an Account (p. 333)	Challenge Yourself Projects (p. 341)	*ExamView* Challenge Yourself Projects (p. 341)

Lesson Planning Guide

Focus

Tell students that their role has changed from database user to designer. Students should understand that creating an Access database requires careful planning and an understanding of relational databases.

At this time you may want students to view Access Lesson 2 of the *Presentation Plus!* DVD.

Teach

- **Step-By-Steps**
  Throughout the lesson, have students perform the Step-By-Steps to complete each exercise.
- **Troubleshooting Tips**
  Remind students to think about all data when creating an input mask, such as an input mask for the field First Name that capitalizes the first letter.
- **Differentiated Instruction**
  Write the names of 20 database fields on index cards. As a class, group the fields by topic.
- **Classroom Management Tips**
  When new students join your class, have them try some of the You Try It Activities from previous lessons to assess their skills.
- **Reading and Writing Support**
  Tell students to spell out a number if it is the first word in a sentence. *Five new stores opened this week.*

Assess

After the students finish the lesson, have them complete the following assessment activities:

- After You Read, p. 417
- Practice It Activities, on pp. 418–420

Reteach

- **Independent Practice**
  Assign You Try It Activities, pp. 421–422.
- **Differentiated Instruction**
  Assign Challenge Yourself Projects, p. 424.

Assess

There are multiple formats for assessment provided for this lesson. These include:

- Interactive Review—Online Learning Center
- Online Self Check—Online Learning Center
- Critical Thinking Activities, p. 423
- Rubrics for Challenge Yourself Projects—Online Learning Center. Refer to page TM40 for an explanation of how rubrics can help students enhance performance and self-evaluation techniques.
- *ExamView* for Access Lesson 2

Close

Have students review this lesson's vocabulary. Ask students to choose three terms that they do not understand. Find these terms and review them.

Answers

- **21st Century Skills (p. 380)** Answers will vary. Students may say that being patient would allow them to spend sufficient time interpreting information and doing assignments.
- See Lesson Resources on the previous page for a list of Solution Files provided in this lesson.
- See answers to After You Read on p. 417 and Critical Thinking Activities on p. 423.
- **Writing Matters: Prepare a Resume (p. 416)**
  1. Students should list personal contact information, general statement about the job being sought, schools attended, work experience, honors/activities, and references.
  2. Students should prepare a draft of their résumé and cover letter. These pieces should follow the guidelines described in the feature.
  3. Students may say that an Access database of information about prospective employers can be useful in keeping track of a job search. Students can store the names of employers and contact persons, company addresses, phone numbers, and directions to the office.

Course Planning

	FOCUS	FEATURES	PROJECTS	ASSESSMENT
UNIT 3	Access 2007: Use Databases	Connections: Science—Keep Track of the Temperature (p. 534) Ethics in Action: Corporate Responsibility (p. 535)	Portfolio Project (p. 536) Beyond the Book Online Activities (p. 539)	*ExamView* Portfolio Project (p. 536)
Lesson 1	Access Basics	21st Century Learner: Can You Be Counted On? (p. 371)	Challenge Yourself Projects (p. 379)	*ExamView* Challenge Yourself Projects (p. 379)
Lesson 2	Structure a Database	Writing Matters: Preparing a Résumé and Cover Letter (p. 416)	Challenge Yourself Projects (p. 424)	*ExamView* Challenge Yourself Projects (p. 424)
Lesson 3	Enter and Organize Data	Math Matters: Showing a Profit or Loss (p. 461)	Challenge Yourself Projects (p. 469)	*ExamView* Challenge Yourself Projects (p. 469)
Lesson 4	Maximize Database Functions	21st Century Workplace: Problem Solving (p. 499)	Challenge Yourself Projects (p. 507)	*ExamView* Challenge Yourself Projects (p. 507)
Lesson 5	Manage Databases	Math Matters: Reading a Sales Invoice (p. 525)	Challenge Yourself Projects (p. 533)	*ExamView* Challenge Yourself Projects (p. 533)

UNIT 4	PowerPoint 2007: The Power of Presentations	Academic Connections: Social Studies—Create a Town Hall Presentation (p. 674) Ethics in Action: Citizenship (p. 675)	Portfolio Project (p. 676) Beyond the Book Online Activities (p. 679)	*ExamView* Portfolio Project (p. 676)
Lesson 1	PowerPoint Basics	Writing Matters: Know Your Audience (p. 560)	Challenge Yourself Projects (p. 568)	*ExamView* Challenge Yourself Projects (p. 568)
Lesson 2	Create Content and Collaborate	21st Century Workplace: Develop Media Literacy (p. 592)	Challenge Yourself Projects (p. 600)	*ExamView* Challenge Yourself Projects (p. 600)
Lesson 3	Formatting Content	Writing Matters: Copyrights (p. 629)	Challenge Yourself Projects (p. 637)	*ExamView* Challenge Yourself Projects (p. 637)
Lesson 4	Manage Presentations	21st Century Workplace: Communicate Effectively (p. 665)	Challenge Yourself Projects (p. 673)	*ExamView* Challenge Yourself Projects (p. 673)

LESSON 2 Structure a Database

Key Concepts

After completing this lesson, students will be able to:

- Use database templates and create blank databases
- Create tables and change their structure
- Create relationships between tables
- Create different types of queries

iCheck Lesson Resources

The following components and resources have been provided to help you teach this lesson.

- Glencoe's Lesson Planner Plus DVD
  - Create your lesson plans with a few, simple clicks
  - Access blackline masters and resources
- Teacher Resource DVD
  - Data Files for Access Lesson 2
  - Solution Files for Access Lesson 2
- *Presentation Plus!* DVD
- Online Learning Center at **glencoe.com**
  - Data Files for Access Lesson 2
  - Solution Files for Access Lesson 2
  - Interactive Review for Access Lesson 2
  - Online Self Check for Access Lesson 2
  - Challenge Yourself Project Rubrics for Access Lesson 2
- *ExamView* CD, Access Lesson 2 Test

Standards

See page 380 for a list of Microsoft Certified Application Specialist objectives and ISTE/NETS standards that students will meet by completing this activity. See page TM33 for a correlation of 21st Century Skills and Workplace Competencies.

Lesson 2	Pg #	Data File	Lesson 2	Pg #	Solution File
			Ex 2–3	385	Contacts table (located in Database-SF.accdb)
			Ex 2–4	386	Companies table (located in Database-SF.accdb)
Ex 2–5	387	Depot.accdb	Ex 2–5 to 2–16	403	Depot-SF.accdb
Ex 2–10	396	Baseball.gif			
Ex 2–17	404	Warehouse.accdb	Ex 2–17 to 2–22	415	Warehouse-SF.accdb
			PIA 1	418	Find duplicates for Detailed Orders query (located in Warehouse-SF.accdb)
			PIA 2	419	Contacts table (located in Warehouse-SF.accdb)
			PIA 3	420	Quantities query (located in Warehouse-SF.accdb)
			YTI 4 to YTI 5	421 to 422	Quantities More Than 2 query (located in Warehouse-SF.accdb)

Course Planning

Suggested Pacing Schedules

The following chart suggests how Glencoe's *iCheck Series, Microsoft Office 2007* may be used to teach both a semester-long course (18 weeks) and a year-long course (36 weeks). Glencoe's *Lesson Planner Plus* DVD offers teachers a convenient and efficient method to incorporate all of the program resources into their daily lesson planning.

	18-WEEK COURSE	36-WEEK COURSE
Week 1	Unit 1, Lessons 1, 2	Unit 1, Lesson 1
Week 2	Unit 1, Lesson 3	Unit 1, Lesson 2
Week 3	Unit 1, Lesson 4	Unit 1, Lesson 3
Week 4	Unit 1, Lesson 5	Unit 1, Lesson 4
Week 5	Unit 1, Lesson 6, Portfolio Project	Unit 1, Lesson 4
Week 6	Unit 2, Lessons 1, 2	Unit 1, Lesson 5
Week 7	Unit 2, Lesson 3	Unit 1, Lesson 5
Week 8	Unit 2, Lesson 4	Unit 1, Lesson 6
Week 9	Unit 2, Lesson 5, Portfolio Project	Unit 1, Lesson 6
Week 10	Unit 3, Lesson 1	Unit 1, Portfolio Project
Week 11	Unit 3, Lesson 2	Unit 2, Lesson 1
Week 12	Unit 3, Lesson 3	Unit 2, Lesson 2
Week 13	Unit 3, Lesson 4	Unit 2, Lesson 3
Week 14	Unit 3, Lesson 5, Portfolio Project	Unit 2, Lesson 4
Week 15	Unit 4, Lesson 1	Unit 2, Lesson 4
Week 16	Unit 4, Lesson 2	Unit 2, Lesson 5
Week 17	Unit 4, Lesson 3	Unit 2, Lesson 5
Week 18	Unit 4, Lesson 4, Portfolio Project	Unit 2, Portfolio Project
Week 19		Unit 3, Lesson 1
Week 20		Unit 3, Lesson 2
Week 21		Unit 3, Lesson 2
Week 22		Unit 3, Lesson 3
Week 23		Unit 3, Lesson 3
Week 24		Unit 3, Lesson 3
Week 25		Unit 3, Lesson 4
Week 26		Unit 3, Lesson 4
Week 27		Unit 3, Lesson 4
Week 28		Unit 3, Lesson 5
Week 29		Unit 3, Lesson 5
Week 30		Unit 3, Portfolio Project
Week 31		Unit 4, Lesson 1
Week 32		Unit 4, Lesson 2
Week 33		Unit 4, Lesson 3
Week 34		Unit 4, Lesson 4
Week 35		Unit 4, Lesson 4
Week 36		Unit 4, Portfolio Project

Lesson Planning Guide

Teach

- **Step-By-Steps**
  Throughout the lesson, have students perform the Step-By-Steps to complete each exercise.
- **Troubleshooting Tips**
  When students open a database, they may receive the following message: "This file may not be safe. Do you want to open this file or cancel the operation?" A malicious program can be disguised as an Access database, but if you know the source of the file, you can click **Open.**
- **Differentiated Instruction**
  After students complete this lesson, they will describe the sports equipment company portrayed in the exercises. Asking students to think about the data in the exercises will help them understand how a database organizes information.
- **Classroom Management Tips**
  Since Access does not include a Save As feature, students will need to copy each supplied database to their own folder before working in the database. Show students how and where to copy and save their databases before starting the exercises.
- **Reading and Writing Support**
  Warn students not to confuse the words *than* and *then. I watch more movies than he does. I need to feed my cat, and then I will be ready to go.*

Assess

After the students finish the lesson, have them complete the following assessment activities:

- After You Read, p. 372
- Practice It Activities, on pp. 373–375

Reteach

- **Independent Practice**
  Assign You Try It Activities, pp. 376–377.
- **Differentiated Instruction**
  Assign Challenge Yourself Projects, p. 379.

Assess

There are multiple formats for assessment provided for this lesson. These include:

- Interactive Review—Online Learning Center
- Online Self Check—Online Learning Center
- Critical Thinking Activities, p. 378
- Rubrics for Challenge Yourself Projects—Online Learning Center. Refer to page TM40 for an explanation of how rubrics can help students enhance performance and self-evaluation techniques.
- *ExamView* for Access Lesson 1

Close

Ask students what they learned about databases that they did not know at the beginning of this lesson. Then ask what they would like to learn about Access in the next four lessons.

Answers

- **21st Century Skills (p. 350)** Answers will vary. Students should describe the methods they use to organize test assignments, due dates, etc.
- See Lesson Resources on the previous page for a list of Solution Files provided in this lesson.
- See answers to After You Read on p. 372 and Critical Thinking Activities on p. 378.
- **21st Century Workplace: Can You be Counted On? (p. 371)**
  1. Students might say that it would be frustrating to walk or drive to the shop expecting it to be open and find it closed—especially in an emergency.
  2. Students should recognize that customers are more likely to be loyal to businesses whose owners and employees are reliable. It is important that owners be able to rely on employees to do work and that employees be able to rely on owners to compensate them.
  3. Students' stories should reflect the information they collected by interviewing a classmate, neighbor, or relative about reliability.

Course Planning

Data and Solution Files

The following data and solution files are provided on the Teacher Resource DVD and at the Online Teacher Resource Center at **glencoe.com**.

UNIT 1					
Lesson/Exercise	**Pg #**	**Data File**	**Lesson/Exercise**	**Pg #**	**Solution File**
Lesson 1					
			EX 1-6 to 1-12	16	w1-6-SF.docx
EX 1-13	17	Goals.docx	EX 1-14 to 1-17	21	Goals-SF.docx
			PIA 1	24	w1rev1-SF.docx
			PIA 2	25	w1rev2-SF.docx
			PIA 3	26	w1rev3-SF.docx
YTI 4	27	Letter.docx	YTI 4	27	w1rev4-SF.docx
CYP 9	30	Jobs.docx			
Lesson 2					
EX 2-1	35	Schedule_Memo.docx	EX 2-1 to 2-2	37	Schedule_Memo-SF.docx
EX 2-3	38	Memo.docx	EX 2-3 to 2-7	42	Memo-SF.docx
EX 2-8	43	Meeting_Notes.docx	EX 2-8 to 2-13	49	Meeting_Notes-SF.docx
EX 2-14	50	Meeting_Outline.docx	EX 2-14	50	Meeting_Outline-SF.docx
EX 2-15	51	Flyer.docx	EX 2-15 to 2 -19	55	Flyer-SF.docx
PIA 1	57	Fonts.docx	PIA 1	57	Fonts1-SF.docx
PIA 2	58	Paragraphs.docx	PIA 2	58	Paragraphs2-SF.docx
PIA 3	59	PI_Memo.docx	PIA 3	59	PI_Memo3-SF.docx
YTI 4	60	Volunteers.docx	YTI 4	60	Volunteers4-SF.docx
YTI 5	61	Yearbook.docx	YTI 5	61	Yearbook5-SF.docx
			BCA 6	62	w2rev6-SF.docx
			SAW 6	62	w2rev7-SF.docx
			21stC 8	62	w2rev8-SF.docx
			Ch. Yslf. 9	63	w2rev9-SF.docx
			Ch. Yslf. 10	63	w2rev10-SF.docx
			Ch. Yslf. 11	63	w2rev11-SF.docx
Lesson 3					
EX 3-1	68	Business_Letter.docx	EX 3-1 to 3-10	77	Business_Letter-SF.docx
EX 3-11	78	Fay_Memo.docx	EX 3-11 to 3-13	80	Fay_Memo-SF.docx
EX 3-14	81	Profiles.docx	EX 3-14	82	Profiles_SF. docx
			EX 3-15	84	Leadership-SF.docx
EX 3-16	85	Leadership.docx	EX 3-16	85	Leadership2-SF.docx
			EX 3-17	86	Letterhead-SF.docx
PIA 1	88	Park_Letter.docx	PIA 1	88	Park_Letter1-SF.docx
			PIA 2	89	Park_Letter2-SF.docx
			PIA 3	90	Park_Letter3-SF.docx
YTI 4	91	Hillside_Letter.docx	YTI 4	91	Hillside_Letter4-SF.docx
YTI 5	92	Wkshop_Memo.docx	YTI 5	92	Wkshop_Memo5-SF.docx
			SAW 7	93	w3rev7-SF.docx
			Ch. Yrslf. 9	94	w3rev9-SF.docx
			Ch. Yrslf. 10	94	w3rev10-SF.docx
			Ch. Yrslf. 11	94	w3rev11-SF.docx
Lesson 4					
EX 4-2	99	Earthquakes.docx	EX 4-1 to 4-8	106	Academic-SF.docx
EX 4-9	107	Endnotes.docx	EX 4-9	107	Endnote-SF.docx
EX 4-10	108	Footnotes.docx	EX 4-10	108	Footnote-SF.docx
EX 4-11	110	Business.docx	EX 4-11 to 4-18	118	Business-SF.docx
EX 4-20	120	Report_Outline.docx	EX 4-20	121	Report_Outline-SF.docx
PIA 1	124	Washington.docx	PIA 1	124	Washington1-SF.docx
			PIA 2	125	Washington2-SF.docx
			PIA 3	126	Washington3-SF.docx
YTI 4	127	New Zealand.docx	YTI 4	127	NewZealand4-SF.docx
			YTI 5	128	NewZealand5-SF.docx
			BCA 6	129	w4rev6-SF.docx
SAW 7	129	Conflict.docx	SAW 7	129	Conflict7-SF.docx
Ch. Yrslf. 9	130	Marketing_Report.docx	Ch. Yrslf. 9	130	Marketing_Report9-SF.docx
			Ch. Yrslf. 10	130	Marketing_Report10-SF.docx
			Ch. Yrslf. 11	130	Marketing_Report11-SF.docx

LESSON 1 Access Basics

Key Concepts

After completing this lesson, students will be able to:

- Identify parts of the Access screen
- Open a database
- Insert and format data
- View and print data from a database
- Copy a database
- Compact and close a database

iCheck Lesson Resources

The following components and resources have been provided to help you teach this lesson.

- Glencoe's Lesson Planner Plus DVD
  - Create your lesson plans with a few, simple clicks
  - Access blackline masters and resources
- Teacher Resource DVD
  - Data Files for Access Lesson 1
  - Solution Files for Access Lesson 1
- *Presentation Plus!* DVD
  - Online Learning Center at **glencoe.com**
  - Data Files for Access Lesson 1
  - Solution Files for Access Lesson 1
  - Interactive Review for Access Lesson 1
- Online Self Check for Access Lesson 1
  - Challenge Yourself Project Rubrics for Access Lesson 1
- *ExamView* CD, Access Lesson 1 Test

Standards

See page 350 for a list of Microsoft Certified Application Specialist objectives and ISTE/NETS standards that students will meet by completing this activity. See page TM33 for a correlation of 21st Century Skills and Workplace Competencies.

Lesson 1	Pg #	Data File	Lesson 1	Pg #	Solution File
EX 1-4	355	Sports Equipment.accdb	Ex 1-4 to 1–19	370	Sports Equipment-SF .accdb; Sports Equipment Split-SF .accdb
PIA 1	373	Camp.accdb	PIA 1 and PIA2	373 and 374	Activity Info table (located in Camp-SF .accdb)
			PIA 3	375	Hart Lodge Activities query (located in Camp-SF.accdb)
			YTI 5	377	Order Info and Product Info tables (located in Sports Equipment-SF.accdb)
Ch. Yrslf. 10	379	My Collections .accdb			
Ch. Yrslf. 11	379	Registration .accdb			

Focus

Invite students to share what they already know about databases. Students should understand that a database stores information and allows you to retrieve the information in various ways. You might give the students a few examples of data that could be stored in a database. A database might contain information about DVD rentals, student grades, charitable donations, or sales data for a flower shop. If students are familiar with Excel, point out that Excel has some database capabilities, but Access is more powerful and complex and has more capabilities than Excel.

At this time you may want students to view Access Lesson 1 of the *Presentation Plus!* DVD. This presentation program uses an engaging format to introduce students to the key concepts of this lesson.

Data and Solution Files (Continued)

Lesson/Exercise	Pg #	Data File	Lesson/Exercise	Pg #	Solution File
Lesson 5					
EX 5-1	133	Newsletter.docx	EX 5-1 to 5-16	150	Newsletter-SF.docx
EX 5-17	151	Sales.docx	EX 5-17 to 5-18	152	Sales-SF.docx
PIA 1	155	Hillside.docx	PIA 1	155	Hillside1-SF.docx
			PIA 2	156	Hillside2-SF.docx
			PIA 3	157	Hillside3-SF.docx
			YTI 4	158	w5rev4-SF.docx
			YTI 5	159	Hillside5-SF.docx
Ch. Yrslf. 10	161	Theater_Newletter.docx	Ch. Yrslf. 10	161	Theater_Newsletter10-SF.docx
Ch. Yrslf. 11	161	Grades.docx	Ch. Yrslf. 11	161	Grades-SF.docx
Lesson 6					
EX 6-1	164	Flyer_Memo.docx	EX 6-1 to 6-2	165	Flyer_Memo-SF.docx
EX 6-3	166	Flyer.docx	EX 6-3 - 6-9	173	Combined-SF.doc
EX 6-12	176	Notice.docx			
			EX 6-13 to 6-14	179	Notice-Landscape-SF.docx
			EX 6-16	181	Labels-SF.docx
			EX 6-17	182	Notice-SF.doc, Notice-SF.rtf
			EX 6-18	184	Letterhead-SF.docx
PIA 1	187	Book Sale.docx	PIA 1	187	Book Sale1-SF.docx
			PIA 2	188	Book Sale2-SF.docx
			PIA 3	189	Book Sale3-SF.docx
YTI 4	190	Clinic.docx	YTI 4	190	Clinic4-SF.docx
YTI 5	191	Clients.docx	YTI 5	191	Clinic5-SF.docx
Ch. Yrslf. 11	193	Donors.docx			
Closer	**Pg #**	**Data File**	**Closer**	**Pg #**	**Solution File**
Portfolio Proj. pt. 2	197	Schedule.docx			

UNIT 2

Lesson/Exercise	Pg #	Data File	Lesson/Exercise	Pg #	Solution File
Lesson 1					
			EX 1-6 to 1-13	217	e1-6-SF.xlsx
There are no data files for this lesson			PIA 1	219	e1rev1-SF.xlsx
			PIA 2	220	e1rev2-SF.xlsx
			PIA 3	221	e1rev3-SF.xlsx
			YTI 4	222	e1rev4-SF.xlsx
			YTI 5	223	e1rev5-SF.xlsx
			Crit. Think. 7	224	e1rev7-SF.xlsx
			Crit. Think. 8	224	e1rev8-SF.xlsx
			Ch. Yslf. 9	225	e1rev9-SF.xlsx
			Ch. Yslf. 10	225	e1rev10-SF.xlsx
			Ch. Yslf. 11	225	e1rev11-SF.xlsx
Lesson 2					
EX 2-1	228	Budget.xlsx	EX 2-1 to 2-12	239	Budget-SF.xlsx
PIA 1	242	clients.xlsx	PIA 1	242	Clients1-SF.xlsx
			PIA 2	243	Clients2-SF.xlsx
			PIA 3	244	Clients3-SF.xlsx
YTI 4		Teams.xlsx	YTI 4	245	Teams4-SF.xlsx
			YTI 5	246	Sporting5-SF.xlsx
Ch. Yrslf. 9	248	Sandwich.docx	Ch. Yrslf. 9	248	e2rev9-SF.xlsx
Ch. Yrslf. 10	248	Sandwich.docx	Ch. Yrslf. 10	248	e2rev10-SF.xlsx
Ch. Yrslf. 11	248	Sandwich.docx	Ch. Yrslf. 11	248	e2rev11-SF.xlsx
Lesson 3					
EX 3-1	251	Goals.xlsx	EX 3-1 to 3-6	259	Goals-SF.xlsx
EX 3-7	260	Supplies.xlsx	EX 3-7 to 3-11	264	Supplies-SF.xlsx
EX 3-12	265	Computers.xlsx	EX 3-12 to 3-18	272	Computers-SF.xlsx
EX 3-16	269	CompuBold.JPG			
PIA 1	275	Office.xlsx	PIA 1	275	Office1-SF.xlsx
			PIA 2	276	Office2-SF.xlsx
PIA 3	277	OfficeInc.JPG	PIA 3	277	Office3-SF.xlsx
YTI 4	278	Planner.xlsx	YTI 4	278	Planner-SF.xlsx
YTI 5	279	Backpacking.xlsx	YTI 5	279	Backpacking-SF.xlsx
YTI 5	279	Pack.JPG			
SAW 7	280	Pottery.xlsx			

Unit 3 Access Overview

Focus

- **Why It Matters** Review the Why It Matters feature on page 348. Discuss with students how being able to use Access 2007 will help them at both school and work.
- **Go Online: Real World Connection Activity** Have students complete the Go Online: Real World Connection Activity on page 348 to learn more about how different organization use database applications.
- **Careers and Technology** The organization, manipulation, and protection of large amounts of data are an important part of business. Because of this, the demand for people who know how to work with databases is projected to increase.
- **Answers to Reading Check (p. 349)**
  1. The amount of information that must be organized and protected continues to increase.
  2. It is expected to double.

Teach

Guided Practice

- ***Presentation Plus! PowerPoint Presentations*** A special PowerPoint presentation has been provided to help you introduce Access, including how people use Access at both school and work.

Independent Practice

Additional exercises and projects are available at the book's Online Learning Center at **glencoe.com**.

- **Additional Exercises**
  - Microsoft Word
  - Microsoft Excel
  - Microsoft Access
  - Microsoft PowerPoint
  - Microsoft Outlook
  - Windows Vista
- **Additional Projects**
  - Real-World Business Applications
  - Present and Publish Projects
  - Academic Projects

Assess

- **Portfolio Project** The Portfolio Project on pages 536–539 allows students to complete a business-oriented project.
- **Rubrics** Rubrics can be accessed on the Online Learning Center at **glencoe.com**.

Closer	Pg #	Data File
PP pt. 1	536	Fundraiser.docx
	Pg #	**Solution File**
PP pt. 1	536	Totals table (located in BakeSale-SF.mdb)
PP pt. 2	537	Fundraiser Totals query (located in BakeSale-SF.mdb)
PP pt. 3	538	Fundraiser Totals query (located in BakeSale-SF.mdb)
PP pt. 4	539	Fundraiser PerStudent report (located in BakeSale-SF.mdb)

Reteach

- **Academic Connections** Review the feature on page 534 with students to show how the technical skills developed in this unit can be used to complete an academic project.

Assess

- ***ExamView® Assessment Suite* Access Unit 3 Test**

Close

- **Ethics in Action** The feature on page 535 focuses on an important ethical issue that students may encounter. Have students read the feature and complete the questions to develop their decision-making skills.

Answers to You Decide and **Application Activity (p. 535)**

1. The company has a replanting program.
2. Answers will vary. Students should discuss each argument and decide which they agree with.
3. Students should create an Access database that includes a table of expenses and a query.

Data and Solution Files (Continued)

Lesson/Exercise	Pg #	Data File	Lesson/Exercise	Pg #	Solution File
Lesson 4					
EX 4-1	284	February Sales.xlsx	EX 4-1 to 4-2	285	February Sales-SF.xlsx
EX 4-3	286	Bonus.xlsx	EX 4-3 to 4-6	289	Bonus-SF.xlsx
EX 4-7	290	Books.xlsx	EX 4-7 to 4-10	293	Books.SF.xlsx
EX 4-11	294	Shoes.xlsx	EX 4-11 to 4-14	297	Shoes-SF.xlsx
EX 4-15	298	Expenses.xlsx	EX 4-15	299	Expenses-SF.xlsx
EX 4-16	300	Car.xlsx	EX 4-16 to 4-17	303	Car-SF.xlsx
PIA 1	306	Commission.xlsx	PIA 1	306	Commission1-SF.xlsx
			PIA 2	307	Commission2-SF.xlsx
			PIA 3	308	Commission3-SF.xlsx
YTI 4	309	Homework.xlsx	YTI 4	309	Homework4-SF.xlsx
			YTI 5	310	Homework5-SF.xlsx
			BCA 6	311	e4rev6-SF.xlsx
			SAW 7	311	e4rev7-SF.xlsx
			21stC 8	311	e4rev8-SF.xlsx
			Ch. Yrslf. 9	312	e4rev9-SF.xlsx
			Ch. Yrslf. 10	312	e4rev10-SF.xlsx
			Ch. Yrslf. 11	312	e4rev11-SF.xlsx
Lesson 5					
			EX 5-1 to 5-4	318	Timecard-SF.xlsx
EX 5-5	319	Insurance.xlsx	EX 5-5 to 5-17	332	Insurance-SF.xlsx
Ex 5-6	320	Guidelines.xlsx			
EX 5-6	320	Pricing.xlsx	EX 5-7	321	Sales Numbers-SF.htm
PIA 1	335	Costs.xlsx	PIA 1	335	Costs1-SF.xlsx
			PIA 2	336	Costs2-SF.xlsx
			PIA 3	337	Costs3-SF.xlsx
			YTI 4	338	Expenses4-SF.xlsx
YTI 5	339	Subjects.xlsx	YTI 5	339	Subjects5-SF.xlsx
BCA 6	340	Hours.docx	BCA 6	340	e5rev6-SF.xlsx
SAW 7	340	Web.xlsx			
Closer	**Pg #**	**Data File**	**Closer**	**Pg #**	**Solution File**
Port. Proj. pt. 1	344	Hours.docx			
Port. Proj. pt. 3	346	Lawns.docx			

UNIT 3

Lesson/Exercise	Pg #	Data File	Lesson/Exercise	Pg #	Solution File
Lesson 1					
EX 1-4	355	Sports Equipment.accdb	EX 1-4 to 1-19	370	Sports Equipment-SF.accdb and Sports Equipment Split-SF.accdb
PIA 1	373	Camp.accdb	PIA 1 and PIA 2	373, 374	Activity Info table (located in Camp-SF.accdb)
			PIA 3	375	Hart Lodge Activities query (located in Camp-SF.accdb)
			YTI 5	377	Order Info and Product Info tables (located in Sports Equipment-SF.mdb)
Ch. Yrslf. 10	379	My Collections.accdb			
Ch. Yrslf. 11	379	Registration.accdb			
Lesson 2					
			EX 2-3	385	Contacts table (located in Database-SF.accdb)
			EX 2-4	386	Warehouse-SF.accdb
EX 2-5	387	Depot.accdb	EX 2-5 to 2-16	403	Depot-SF.accdb
EX 2-10	396	Baseball.gif			
EX 2-17	404	Warehouse.accdb	EX 2-17 to 2-22	415	Warehouse-SF.accdb
			PIA 1	418	Find duplicates for Detailed Orders query (located in Warehouse-SF.accdb)
			PIA 2	419	Contacts table (located in Warehouse-SF.accdb)
			PIA 3	420	Quantities query (located in Warehouse-SF.accdb)
			YTI 4 to YTI 5	421 to 422	Quantities more than 2 query (located in Warehouse-SF.accdb)

Lesson Planning Guide

Teach

- **Step-By-Steps**
  Throughout the lesson, have students perform the Step-By-Steps to complete each exercise.
- **Troubleshooting Tips**
  If the entire worksheet does not print, a print area may be set. To remove the print area, choose **Page Layout>Page Setup>Print Area>Clear Print Area.**
- **Differentiated Instruction**
  As students are stepping through the exercises, have them take note of and write on a sheet of paper a tip that they like. Have them note a tip that they do *not* understand and want to discuss. Making these notes will help students focus on what they are reading.
- **Classroom Management Tips**
  In computer classes, students often ask to cover topics that are not part of the curriculum. Often the topics relate to graphics, photos, colors, charts, drawing, etc. Keep track of these requests and create a supply of "bonus" topics. When students are restless, help them focus by offering to teach a bonus topic if time allows at the end of class.
- **Reading and Writing Support**
  Tell students to use pronouns *me, him, her, us,* and *them* when they are objects in a sentence. *Please give your form to Brenda or me.*

Assess

After students finish the lesson, have them complete the following assessment activities:

- After You Read, p. 334
- Practice It Activities, pp. 335–337

Reteach

- **Independent Practice**
  You Try It Activities on pp. 338–339.
- **Differentiated Instruction**
  Assign Challenge Yourself Projects on p. 341.

Assess

There are multiple formats for assessment provided for this lesson. These include:

- Interactive Review—Online Learning Center
- Online Self Check—Online Learning Center
- Critical Thinking Activities, p. 340
- Rubrics for Challenge Yourself Projects—Online Learning Center. Refer to page TM40 for an explanation of how rubrics can help students enhance performance and self-evaluation techniques.
- *ExamView* for Excel Lesson 5

Close

Ask students how they might use a multiple-sheet workbook to organize information. Write the ideas on the board. If necessary, give them an example.

Answers

- **21st Century Skills (p. 313)** Answers will vary. Students should describe a recent incident in which honesty, or lack of honesty, played a role.
- See Lesson Resources on the previous page for a list of Solution Files provided in this lesson.
- See answers to After You Read on p. 334 and Critical Thinking Activities on p. 340.
- **Math Matters: Balancing an Account (p. 333)**
  1. Answers will vary. Students should recognize that balancing an account tells them how much money is available—and, therefore, whether or not they can afford to make certain withdrawals or payments. Businesses must balance their accounts to make sure money is available to pay employees, rent, and other expenses.
  2. Students should recognize that failure to balance an account may result in a financial crisis, such as being overdrawn.
  3. Students should know that one should pay a credit card bill after receiving and depositing a paycheck and before the bill's due date. The balance in the account after paying the bill will be $77.02.

Data and Solution Files (Continued)

Lesson/Exercise	Pg #	Data File	Lesson/Exercise	Pg #	Solution File
Lesson 3					
EX 3-1	427	Sports.accdb	EX 3-1 to 3-21	460	Sports-SF.accdb
			PIA 1	463	Product Form (located in Sports-SF.accdb)
			PIA 2	464	Order Detail report (located in Sports-SF.accdb)
			PIA 3	465	Inventory Labels report (located in Sports-SF.accdb)
			YTI 4	466	Customer Split View form (located in Sports-SF.accdb)
			YTI 5	467	Orders With Groups report (located in Sports-SF.accdb)
			Ch. Yrslf. 9	469	Product9-SF form (located in Sports-SF.accdb)
			Ch. Yrslf. 10	469	ProdReport10-SF report (located in Sports-SF.accdb)
			Ch. Yrslf. 11	469	ProdLabels11-SF table (located in Sports-SF.accdb)
Lesson 4					
EX 4-1	472	Sports4.acccdb	EX 4-1 to 4-19	498	Sports4-SF.accdb
			PIA 1	501	DetailedOrders query (located in Sports4-SF.accdb)
			PIA 2	502	CustOrdAmt by Order Date query (located in Sports4-SF.accdb)
			PIA 3	503	CustomerOrders form (located in Sports4-SF.accdb)
			YTI 4	504	Sport Record Holders3 table (located in Sports4-SF.mdb)
			YTI 5	505	Sport Record Holders3 .rtf
			Ch. Yrslf. 9	507	DetailedOrders-9SF query (located in Sports4-SF.accdb)
			Ch. Yrslf. 10	507	DetailedOrders-10SF.xlsx
			Ch. Yrslf. 11	507	From Sales file (located in Sports4-SF.accdb)
Lesson 5					
			EX 5-1 to 5-10	522	Sports5-SF.accdb
EX 5-11	523	Sports5b.mdb	EX 5-11	523	Sports5b-SF.mdb
			EX 5-12	524	a5-12-SF.accdb
			PIA 1	527	Sports5-SF.accdb
			PIA 2	528	Sports5b2003-SF.accdb
			PIA 3	529	a5-p3-SF.accdb
			YTI 5	531	CustomerOrders form (located in Sports5-SF.accdb)
			Ch. Yrslf. 10	533	Query Order_PivotChart10-SF (located in Sports5-SF.accdb)
			Ch. Yrslf. 11	533	Query Order_PivotChart11-SF (located in Sports5-SF.accdb)
Closer	**Pg #**	**Data File**	**Closer**	**Pg #**	**Solution File**
Portfolio Proj. pt. 1	536	Fundraiser.docx			

UNIT 4

Lesson/Exercise	Pg #	Data File	Lesson/Exercise	Pg #	Solution File
Lesson 1					
EX 1-3	546	Tips.pptx	EX 1-3 to 1-16	559	Tips-SF.pptx
			PIA 1	562	Pizza1-SF.pptx
			PIA 2	563	Pizza2-SF.pptx
			PIA 3	564	Pizza3-SF.pptx
			YTI 4	565	Tips4-SF.pptx
			YTI 5	566	Tips5-SF.pptx
			SAW 7	567	Tips7-SF.pptx
Lesson 2					
EX 2-3	573	Outline.docx			
EX 2-13	586	Flowers.jpg	EX 2-1 to 2-18	591	Garden-SF.pptx
PIA 1	594	Fundraiser.pptx			
PIA 1	594	PI_Outline.docx	PIA 1	594	Fundraiser1-SF.pptx
			PIA 2	595	Fundraiser2-SF.pptx
			PIA 3	596	Fundraiser3-SF.pptx
YTI 4	597	Theater.pptx			
YTI 4	597	Theater.wmf	YTI 4	597	Theater4-SF.pptx
			YTI 5	598	Theater5-SF.pptx
BCA 6	599	Sales.pptx			
Lesson 3					
EX 3-1	603	Music.pptx	EX 3-1 to 3-18	622	Music-SF.pptx
EX 3-19	623	Staff.pptx	EX 3-19 to 3-22	628	Staff-SF.pptx
PIA 1	631	Copyrights.pptx	PIA 1	631	Copyrights1-SF.pptx
			PIA 2	632	Copyrights2-SF.pptx
			PIA 3	633	Copyrights3-SF.pptx
YTI 4	634	Questions.pptx	YTI 4	634	Questions4-SF.pptx
			YTI 5	635	Questions5-SF.pptx
SAW 7	636	p3rev7.pptx			

Lesson Planning Guide

LESSON 5 Managing Workbooks

Key Concepts

After completing this lesson, students will be able to:

- Use a template
- Organize worksheets
- Split, freeze, hide, and arrange workbooks
- Save and preview worksheets as Web pages
- Set up pages for printing
- Rename folders and covert files to different formats

iCheck Lesson Resources

The following components and resources have been provided to help you teach this lesson.

- Glencoe's Lesson Planner Plus DVD
  - Create your lesson plans with a few, simple clicks
  - Access blackline masters and resources
- Teacher Resource DVD
  - Data Files for Excel Lesson 5
  - Solution Files for Excel Lesson 5
- *Presentation Plus!* DVD
- Online Learning Center at **glencoe.com**
  - Data Files for Excel Lesson 5
  - Solution Files for Excel Lesson 5
  - Interactive Review for Excel Lesson 5
  - Online Self Check for Excel Lesson 5
  - Challenge Yourself Project Rubrics for Excel Lesson 5
- *ExamView* CD, Excel Lesson 5 Test

Standards

See page 313 for a list of Microsoft Certified Application Specialist objectives and ISTE/NETS standards that students will meet by completing this activity. See page TM33 for a correlation of 21st Century Skills and Workplace Competencies.

Lesson 5	Pg #	Data File	Lesson 5	Pg #	Solution File
			EX 5-1 to 5-4	318	Timecard-SF.xlsx
EX 5-5	319	Insurance.xlsx	EX 5-5 to 5-17	332	Insurance-SF.xlsx
EX 5-6	320	Guidelines.xlsx			
EX 5-6	320	Pricing.xlsx	Ex 5-7	321	Sales Numbers-SF.htm
PIA 1	335	Costs.xlsx	PIA 1	335	Costs1-SF.xlsx
			PIA 2	336	Costs2-SF.xlsx
			PIA 3	337	Costs3-SF.xlsx
			YTI 4	338	Expenses4-SF.xlsx
YTI 5	339	Subjects.xlsx	YTI 5	339	Subjects5-SF.xlsx
BCA 6	340	Hours.docx	BCA 6	340	e5rev6-SF.xlsx
SAW 7	340	Web.xlsx			

Focus

Consider bringing a variety of forms to class, such as an employment application and an order form from an office supply store. Explain that a template is similar to these forms. Students should understand that when they use an Excel template, a copy of the template opens, which they then fill in with specific data. Ask students when they might use a template in Excel. What type of file would they use again and again, filling in different information each time? Students might say that they would create a template for a monthly budget or a weekly time card.

At this time you may want students to view Excel Lesson 5 of the *Presentation Plus!* DVD. This presentation program uses an engaging format to introduce students to the key concepts of this lesson.

Data and Solution Files (Continued)

Lesson/Exercise	Pg #	Data File	Lesson/Exercise	Pg #	Solution File
Lesson 4					
EX 4-1	640	Literacy.pptx			
EX 4-3	642	Publicity.pptx			
EX 4-5	645	Publicity.pptx			
EX 4-7	647	Worksheet.pptx			
EX 4-9	649	Reading.pptx			
EX 4-9	650	Volunteer.pptx			
			EX 4-11	652	p4-7a-SF.docx and p4-7b-SF.docx
EX 4-19	661	Literacy.wav	EX 4-19	662	Found in LiteracyCD-SF folder
EX 4-19	661	Worksheet.docx	EX 4-19	662	Found in LiteracyCD-SF folder
			EX 4-21	664	Literacy-SF.pptx
PIA 1	667	Activities.pptx	PIA 1	667	Activities1-SF.pptx
			PIA 2	668	Activities2-SF.pptx
			PIA 3	669	Activities3-SF.pptx
YTI 4	670	Habits.pptx	YTI 4	670	Habits4-SF.pptx
			YTI 5	671	Habits5-SF.pptx
BCA 6	672	Mow.pptx			
SAW 7	672	Publicity.pptx			
Ch. Yrslf. 9	673	Activities.pptx			
Ch. Yrslf. 10	673	Activities.pptx			
Ch. Yrslf. 11	673	Activities.pptx			
YTI 4	190	Clinic.docx	YTI 4	190	Clinic4-SF.docx
YTI 5	191	Clients.docx	YTI 5	191	Clinic5-SF.docx
Ch. Yrslf. 11	193	Donors.docx			
Closer	**Pg #**	**Data File**	**Closer**	**Pg #**	**Solution File**
Portfolio Proj. pt. 2	677	Certificate-SF.pptx			

APPENDIX A

Lesson/Exercise	Pg #	Data File	Lesson/Exercise	Pg #	Solution File
App. A Ex 1	682	Rental.docx	App. A EX 1	683	Rental-SF.docx
App. A EX 1	682	Properties.xlsx			
App. A EX 1	683	Cleaning.xlsx			
App. A EX 2	684	Budget.xlsx	App. A EX 5	687	Budget-SF.xlsx
App. A EX 2	684	Memo.docx	App. A EX 5	687	Memo-SF.docx
App. A EX 6	688	Estate.accdb	App. A EX 7	690	Estate-SF.accdb
App. A EX 6	688	Recent.xlsx			
App. A EX 7	690	Repairs.xlsx			
			App. A EX 8	691	Current-SF.xlsx
			App. A EX 9	692	Realty-SF.rtf
App. A EX 10	693	Added.txt			
			App. A EX 10	693	Listings table (located in Estate-SF.accdb)
App. A EX 11	694	Historic.pptx	App. A EX 12	695	Historic-SF.pptx

Lesson Planning Guide

Focus

Ask for a volunteer to explain what it means to *analyze* data. Students might say something like, "To look at it closely."

At this time you may want students to view Excel Lesson 4 of the *Presentation Plus!* DVD.

Teach

- **Step-By-Steps**
  Throughout the lesson, have students perform the Step-By-Steps to complete each exercise.
- **Troubleshooting Tips**
  If a formula results in an error value, encourage students to study the formula to make sure that it is logical.
- **Differentiated Instruction**
  After learning a challenging topic, such as the PMT of the IF function, consider having students explain the topic to a partner.
- **Classroom Management Tips**
  When new students join your class, consider having them step through previous lessons.
- **Reading and Writing Support**
  Explain to students that a verb should be plural if it refers to an impossible condition. *If I were an eagle, I would perch at the top of the tallest tree.*

Assess

After students finish the lesson, have them complete the following assessment activities:

- After You Read, p. 305
- Practice It Activities, pp. 306–308

Reteach

- **Independent Practice**
  You Try It Activities on pp. 309–310.
- **Differentiated Instruction**
  Assign Challenge Yourself Projects on p. 312.

Assess

There are multiple formats for assessment provided for this lesson. These include:

- Interactive Review—Online Learning Center
- Online Self Check—Online Learning Center
- Critical Thinking Activities, p. 311
- Rubrics for Challenge Yourself Projects—Online Learning Center. Refer to page TM40 for an explanation of how rubrics can help students enhance performance and self-evaluation techniques.
- *ExamView* for Excel Lesson 4

Close

Explain to students that different types of charts are best for certain kinds of information. Show students a sample line chart, pie chart, and column chart. Ask the students when they think they might use each type of chart.

Answers

- **21st Century Skills (p. 282)** Answers will vary. Students should think about their current goals that require successful self-management.
- See Lesson Resources on the previous page for a list of Solution Files provided in this lesson.
- See answers to After You Read on p. 305 and Critical Thinking Activities on p. 311.
- **Math Matters: Presenting Information Graphically (p. 304)**
  1. A business report might analyze sales, present a proposal, or examine the overall performance of a business.
  2. A graphic such as a chart or diagram can show a person immediately whether, for example, sales are increasing or decreasing.
  3. People need math skills to analyze numbers and read or create graphs and charts. People need good writing skills to communicate ideas and findings effectively. With basic knowledge of Excel, one can create effective charts and graphs that would enhance a business report.

Microsoft Certified Application Specialist Standards

Glencoe's *iCheck Series* covers the Microsoft Certified Application Specialist (MCAS) standards for Word 2007, Excel 2007, Access 2007, PowerPoint 2007, Outlook 2007, and Windows Vista. Advanced MCAS exercises are available at the Online Learning Center at **glencoe.com**. Because this program is designed specifically for secondary school students, standards are introduced, developed, and mastered.

WORD 2007 MCAS STANDARDS				
Microsoft Certified Application Specialist Standard		Textbook Correlation		
	Skill Sets and Skills	Introduced	Developed	Mastered
1	CREATING AND CUSTOMIZING DOCUMENTS			
1.1	Create and format documents	42, 54	83, 99	173, 189, 192, 193
1.2	Lay out documents	35, 69	99, 100, 101, 133, 135, 176,	190
1.3	Make documents and content easier to find	111, 117, 118	164, Adv. Word L1, L2	172, 192
1.4	Personalize Office Word 2007	8, 29	76, 80, Adv. Word L3	98, 165
2	FORMATTING CONTENT			
2.1	Format text and paragraphs	38, 41, 42, 48, 98	39, 40, 44, 47, 51, 53, 113, Adv. Word L1, L2	114, 124
2.2	Manipulate text	70, 79	71, 72, 81	88, 89, 92, 94
2.3	Control pagination	103, 110	112	125, 127
3	WORKING WITH VISUAL CONTENT			
3.1	Insert illustrations	143	147, 148	157, 159, 161
3.2	Format illustrations	144, 147	148, Adv. Word L1	157
3.3	Format text graphically	150	155	Adv. Word L1
3.4	Insert and modify text boxes	145	146	161
4	ORGANIZING CONTENT			
4.1	Structure content by using Quick Parts	85, 86	92, Adv. Word L2	94
4.2	Use tables and lists to organize content	45	46, 50, 152	156, 158, 160, 161
4.3	Modify tables	138, 139, 140	141, 142	152, 156, 158
4.4	Insert and format references and captions	106, 107, 108	114, 115, 116	126, 130
4.5	Merge documents and data sources	77, 177	178, 180, 181	191, 193
5	REVIEWING DOCUMENTS			
5.1	Navigate documents	19, 78, 79	90, 92	119, 125
5.2	Compare and merge document versions	169	Adv. Word L3	Adv. Word L3
5.3	Manage Track Changes	166, 167	171, Adv. Word L3	187, 188
5.4	Insert, modify, and delete comments	167	187, 188	193
6	SHARING AND SECURING CONTENT			
6.1	Prepare documents for sharing	182	Adv. Word L3	Adv. Word L3
6.2	Control document access	Adv. Word L3	Adv. Word L3	Adv. Word L3
6.3	Attach digital signatures	Adv. Word L3	Adv. Word L3	Adv. Word L3

Adv. = Advanced lessons are available at the Online Learning Center at **glencoe.com**.

Lesson Planning Guide

LESSON 4 Analyze Data

Key Concepts

After completing this lesson, students will be able to:

- Filter and sort data
- Write, edit, and use formulas
- Use absolute, relative, and mixed references
- Create, modify, and position diagrams
- Create, modify, and position charts

iCheck Lesson Resources

The following components and resources have been provided to help you teach this lesson.

- Glencoe's Lesson Planner Plus DVD
  - Create your lesson plans with a few, simple clicks
  - Access blackline masters and resources
- Teacher Resource DVD
  - Data Files for Excel Lesson 4
  - Solution Files for Excel Lesson 4
- *Presentation Plus!* DVD
- Online Learning Center at **glencoe.com**
  - Data Files for Excel Lesson 4
  - Solution Files for Excel Lesson 4
  - Interactive Review for Excel Lesson 4
  - Online Self Check for Excel Lesson 4
  - Challenge Yourself Project Rubrics for Excel Lesson 4
- *ExamView* CD, Excel Lesson 4 Test

Standards

See page 282 for a list of Microsoft Certified Application Specialist objectives and ISTE/NETS standards that students will meet by completing this activity. See page TM33 for a correlation of 21st Century Skills and Workplace Competencies.

Lesson 4	Pg #	Data File	Lesson 4	Pg #	Solution File
EX 4-1	284	February Sales.xlsx	Ex 4-1 to 4-2	285	February Sales-SF.xlsx
EX 4-3	286	Bonus.xlsx	Ex 4-3 to 4-6	289	Bonus-SF.xlsx
EX 4-7	290	Books.xlsx	Ex 4-7 to 4-10	293	Books-SF.xlsx
EX 4-11	294	Shoes.xlsx	Ex 4-11 to 4-14	297	Shoes-SF.xlsx
EX 4-15	298	Expenses.xlsx	EX 4-15	299	Expenses-SF.xlsx
EX 4-16	300	Car.xlsx	EX 4-16 to 4-17	303	Car-SF.xlsx
PIA 1	306	Commission.xlsx	PIA 1	306	Commission1-SF.xlsx
			PIA 2	307	Commission2-SF.xlsx
			PIA 3	308	Commission3-SF.xlsx
YTI 4	309	Homework.xlsx	YTI 4	309	Homework4-SF.xlsx
			YTI 5	310	Homework5-SF.xlsx
			BCA 6	311	e4rev6-SF.xlsx
			SAW 7	311	e4rev7-SF.xlsx
			21stC 8	311	e4rev8-SF.xlsx
			Ch. Yrslf. 9	312	e4rev9-SF.xlsx
			Ch. Yrslf. 10	312	e4rev10-SF.xlsx
			Ch. Yrslf. 11	312	e4rev11-SF.xlsx

EXCEL 2007 MCAS STANDARDS				
Microsoft Certified Application Specialist Standards		Textbook Correlation		
	Skill Sets and Skills	Introduced	Developed	Mastered
1	CREATING AND MANIPULATING DATA			
1.1	Insert data using AutoFill	234, 238	259	
1.2	Ensure data integrity	Adv. Excel L1	Adv. Excel L1	Adv. Excel L1
1.3	Modify cell contents and formats	251, 252	Adv. Excel L1	Adv. Excel L1
1.4	Change worksheet views	212, 219, 221, 222	319, 320, 326	335
1.5	Manage worksheets	268, 270	317, 318	Adv. Excel L4
2	FORMATTING DATA AND CONTENT			
2.1	Format worksheets	267, 268, 269	275, Adv. Excel L3	277, 346
2.2	Insert and modify rows and columns	234, 235, 236, 237, 243, 248	254, 261, 262, 263, 264, 265	342, 344
2.3	Format cells and cell content	239, 247, 251, 252, 254, 300	259, 264, 265, 266, 278, 279	281, 344, 346
2.4	Format data as a table	254, 255, 257	260, 276	280, 342
3	CREATING AND MODIFYING FORMULAS			
3.1	Reference data in formulas	291, 292, 293	307, 309, 311, 312	345
3.2	Summarize data using a formula	215, 221, 223, 225	229, 244, 246, 248, 281, 298	306, 307, 309, 311, 312, 340, 341, 342
3.3	Summarize data using subtotals	Adv. Excel L1	Adv. Excel L1	Adv. Excel L1
3.4	Conditionally summarize data using a formula	Adv. Excel L2	Adv. Excel L2	Adv. Excel L2
3.5	Look up data using a formula	Adv. Excel L2	Adv. Excel L2	Adv. Excel L2
3.6	Use conditional logic in a formula	302, Adv. Excel L2	312, Adv. Excel L2	Adv. Excel L2
3.7	Format or modify text using formulas	Adv. Excel L2	Adv. Excel L2	Adv. Excel L2
3.8	Display and print formulas	Adv. Excel L2	Adv. Excel L2	Adv. Excel L2
4	PRESENTING DATA VISUALLY			
4.1	Create and format charts	294	308, 310, 311	347
4.2	Modify charts	295, 296	297, 308, Adv. Excel L3	310
4.3	Apply conditional formatting	Adv. Excel L3	Adv. Excel L3	Adv. Excel L3
4.4	Insert and modify illustrations	271	281, Adv. Excel L3	Adv. Excel L3
4.5	Outline data	Adv. Excel L1	Adv. Excel L1	Adv. Excel L1
4.6	Sort and filter data	284	285	347
5	COLLABORATING AND SECURING DATA			
5.1	Manage changes to workbooks	Adv. Excel L1, L4	Adv. Excel L4	Adv. Excel L4
5.2	Protect and share workbooks	Adv. Excel L4	Adv. Excel L4	Adv. Excel L4
5.3	Prepare workbooks for distribution	Adv. Excel L4	Adv. Excel L4	Adv. Excel L4
5.4	Save workbooks	321, 332	335, Adv. Excel L4	340
5.5	Set print options for printing data, worksheets, and workbooks	323–327	329, 330, 336, 337	339

Adv. = Advanced lessons are available at the Online Learning Center at **glencoe.com**.

Lesson Planning Guide

Teach

Step-By-Steps
Throughout the lesson, have students perform the Step-By-Steps to complete each exercise.

Troubleshooting Tips
When changing column width by dragging, students may inadvertently hide a column. To unhide the column, select the columns on either side of the hidden column and choose **Home>Cells>Format>Hide & Unhide**.

Differentiated Instruction
Students who are struggling may have trouble completing the activities at the end of each lesson. Consider having students complete activities that cover the essential topics in the lesson.

Classroom Management Tips
It can be tempting for students to save files on the desktop. This can create a file management headache for the teacher. Consider establishing a class rule that at the end of every day, all files on the desktop will be deleted. Be sure to enforce this rule.

Reading and Writing Support
Remind students to place a comma after each item except for the last when you have a series of three or more items. *There will be hamburgers, salad, and drinks at the picnic.*

Assess

After students finish the lesson, have them complete the following assessment activities:

- After You Read, p. 274
- Practice It Activities, pp. 275–277

Reteach

Independent Practice
Assign students the You Try It Activities on pages 278–279.

Differentiated Instruction
Assign students the Challenge Yourself Projects on page 281.

Assess

There are multiple formats for assessment provided for this lesson. These include:

- Interactive Review—Online Learning Center
- Online Self Check—Online Learning Center
- Critical Thinking Activities, p. 280
- Rubrics for Challenge Yourself Projects—Online Learning Center. Refer to page TM40 for an explanation of how rubrics can help students enhance performance and self-evaluation techniques.
- *ExamView* for Excel Lesson 3

Close

End this lesson with a class discussion about formatting in Excel. Ask students why someone would use each type of formatting. Possible answers: Borders make it easier to read lists of data; Changing font color makes important information stand out, etc.

Answers

- **21st Century Skills (p. 249)** Answers will vary. Students should describe when they had to be flexible to meet a goal.
- See Lesson Resources on the previous page for a list of Solution Files provided in this lesson.
- See answers to After You Read on p. 274 and Critical Thinking Activities on p. 280.
- **21st Century Workplace: Develop Interview Skills (p. 273)**
  1. Students should list at least five pointers, possibly including those mentioned in the feature.
  2. Answers will vary. Students could ask about what tasks the job entails, hours, pay, benefits, training on the job, possibilities for promotion, number of women working for the company, number of people of color, etc.
  3. Answers will vary. Students should write a sentence about their choice for the most important behavior and then rank the other four in importance.

Technical and Academic Standards

ACCESS 2007 MCAS STANDARDS				
Microsoft Certified Application Specialist Standards		Textbook Correlation		
	Skill Sets and Skills	Introduced	Developed	Mastered
1	**STRUCTURING DATABASES**			
1.1	Define data needs and types	393	394, Adv. Access L1	Adv. Access L1
1.2	Define and print table relationships	399, 401, 403	400, 402	424
1.3	Add, set, change, or remove primary keys	386	Adv. Access L1	Adv. Access L1
1.4	Split databases	367		
2	**CREATING AND FORMATTING DATABASE ELEMENTS**			
2.1	Create databases	382	384	534, 536
2.2	Create tables	385, 386	419, 424	534, 536, 538
2.3	Modify tables	385	387, 389, 391	393
2.4	Create fields and modify field properties	386, 389, 393, 394	396, 398	419, 424, 534, 536, 538
2.5	Create forms	430, 432, 433, 435, 436, 438	440, 463	466, 468, 469
2.6	Create reports	449, 451, 453, 455	459, 464, 465, 467, 469	513, 516, 539
2.7	Modify the design of reports and forms	442–445, 447	457	539
3	**ENTERING AND MODIFYING DATA**			
3.1	Enter, edit, and delete records	361, 379, 427	428	534, 536
3.2	Navigate among records	357	360	374
3.3	Find and replace data	429		
3.4	Attach documents to and detach documents from records	Adv. Access L1	Adv. Access L1	Adv. Access L1
3.5	Import data	472	474	475
4	**CREATING AND MODIFYING QUERIES**			
4.1	Create queries	404, 406, 408, 410, 412, 414	418, 420, 421, 422, 423	537
4.2	Modify queries	477, 478, 480, 482, 483	484, 501, 506	537, 538

Adv. = Advanced lessons are available at the Online Learning Center at **glencoe.com**.

Lesson Planning Guide

LESSON 3 Format Data and Content

Key Concepts

After completing this lesson, students will be able to:

- Change font, font size, font style, and font color
- Convert text to columns
- Apply cell and table styles
- Modify the size of rows and columns
- Hide and unhide rows, columns, and worksheets
- Change horizontal and vertical alignment
- Insert, move, and modify SmartArt graphics

iCheck Lesson Resources

The following components and resources have been provided to help you teach this lesson.

- Glencoe's Lesson Planner Plus DVD
  - Create your lesson plans with a few, simple clicks
  - Access blackline masters and resources
- Teacher Resource DVD
  - Data Files for Excel Lesson 3
  - Solution Files for Excel Lesson 3
- *Presentation Plus!* DVD
- Online Learning Center at **glencoe.com**
  - Data Files for Excel Lesson 3
  - Solution Files for Excel Lesson 3
  - Interactive Review for Excel Lesson 3
  - Online Self Check for Excel Lesson 3
  - Challenge Yourself Project Rubrics for Excel Lesson 3
- *ExamView* CD, Excel Lesson 3 Test

Standards

See page 249 for a list of Microsoft Certified Application Specialist objectives and ISTE/NETS standards that students will meet by completing this activity. See page TM33 for a correlation of 21st Century Skills and Workplace Competencies.

Lesson 3	Pg #	Data File	Lesson 3	Pg #	Solution File
EX 3-1	251	Goals.xlsx	Ex 3-1 to 3-6	259	Goals-SF.xlsx
EX 3-7	260	Supplies.xlsx	Ex 3-7 to 3-11	264	Supplies-SF.xlsx
EX 3-12	265	Computers.xlsx	Ex 3-12 to 3-18	272	Computers-SF.xlsx
EX 3-16	269	CompuBold.JPG			
PIA 1	275	Office.xlsx	PIA 1	275	Office1-SF.xlsx
			PIA 2	276	Office2-SF.xlsx
PIA 3	277	OfficeInc.JPG	PIA 3	277	Office3-SF.xlsx
YTI 4	278	Planner.xlsx	YTI 4	278	Planner-SF.xlsx
YTI 5	279	Backpacking.xlsx	YTI 5	279	Backpacking-SF.xlsx
YTI 5	279	Pack.JPG			
SAW 7	280	Pottery.xlsx			

Focus

Students should know that Excel has extensive formatting capabilities. Excel can be used to present information in an attractive, professional way. Brainstorm with students about types of businesspeople who might use Excel. Accountants will probably be one of the first professions that students mention. Encourage students to expand the list to include occupations such as salespeople and high school teachers.

At this time you may want students to view Excel Lesson 3 of the *Presentation Plus!* DVD. This presentation program uses an engaging format to introduce students to the key concepts of this lesson.

Technical and Academic Standards

ACCESS 2007 MCAS STANDARDS				
Microsoft Certified Application Specialist Standards		Textbook Correlation		
	Skill Sets and Skills	Introduced	Developed	Mastered
5	PRESENTING AND SHARING DATA			
5.1	Sort data	485, 486	502, 503	537–539
5.2	Filter data	488, 490, 492,	493, 495	504, 507
5.3	Create and modify charts	511	512	533
5.4	Export data	496, 497, 498	505	507
5.5	Save database objects as other file types	523	Adv. Access L1	Adv. Access L1
5.6	Print database objects	365, 375, 378	513, 515, 516, 517	531, 534, 538, 539
6	MANAGING AND MAINTAINING DATABASES			
6.1	Perform routine database operations	355, 368, 370, 373	523, 524	528, 529
6.2	Manage databases	366	514, 518, 519, 521	522, 527, 528, 530, 532, 533

Adv. = Advanced lessons are available at the Online Learning Center at **glencoe.com**.

Lesson Planning Guide

Teach

Step-By-Steps
Throughout the lesson, have students perform the Step-By-Steps to complete each exercise.

Troubleshooting Tips
Make sure students know the correct syntax for functions. For example, the word *Minimum* is abbreviated *Min* in a formula, but the word *Average* is not abbreviated.

Differentiated Instruction
Help students see the connection between Excel formulas and math problems. For example, in a simple worksheet, create a function such as *=average (B3:B6)*. Then have a student write the equivalent math problem on the board, such as *=(245+871+89+199)/4*.

Classroom Management Tips
When students learn about certain features, such as the Fill handle, it may be difficult to rein them back in. Consider covering topics like that in the last 15 minutes or so to allow students to experiment, while limiting the time spent on the topic.

Reading and Writing Support
Tell students to use one space after a colon. *The following classes are now being offered in the evening: Jewelry Making, Pottery, and Cooking.*

Assess

After the students finish the lesson, have them complete the following assessment activities:

- After You Read, p. 241
- Practice It Activities, pp. 242–244

Reteach

Independent Practice
Assign students the You Try It Activities on pages 245–246.

Differentiated Instruction
Assign students the Challenge Yourself Projects on page 248.

Assess

There are multiple formats for assessment provided for this lesson. These include:

- Interactive Review—Online Learning Center
- Online Self Check—Online Learning Center
- Critical Thinking Activities, p. 247
- Rubrics for Challenge Yourself Projects—Online Learning Center. Refer to page TM40 for an explanation of how rubrics can help students enhance performance and self-evaluation techniques.
- *ExamView* for Excel Lesson 2

Close

Ask for volunteers to name the four functions covered in this lesson. Write these on the board. Then, invite students to come to the board and write a description next to each function. Students should name and describe the four functions as follows: **AutoSum** is a function used to add values in rows or columns. **AVERAGE** is the average value of a range of cells. **MIN** is the smallest value in a range of cells. **MAX** is the largest value in a range of cells.

Answers

- **21st Century Skills (p. 226)** Answers will vary, but most students should agree that a budget would help them better manage their money.
- See Lesson Resources on the previous page for a list of Solution Files provided in this lesson.
- See answers to After You Read on p. 241 and Critical Thinking Activities on p. 247.
- **Math Matters: Using Math Formulas (p. 240)**
  1. Excel will do the calculations in the following order: multiplication, division, addition, subtraction.
  2. The order of precedence is important because if one does a calculation two different ways, one can get two different answers.
  3. The answer is 14.

Technical and Academic Standards

POWERPOINT 2007 MCAS STANDARDS				
Microsoft Certified Application Specialist Standards		Textbook Correlation		
	Skill Sets and Skills	Introduced	Developed	Mastered
1	CREATING AND FORMATTING PRESENTATIONS			
1.1	Create new presentations	571, 636, 637	655, 672, 674	676, 677, 678, 694
1.2	Customize slide masters	623	625-626	632, 637
1.3	Add elements to slide masters	627, 628	632, Adv. PowerPoint L2	637
1.4	Create and change presentation elements	622,633	634, 636, 637	674, 676
1.5	Arrange slides	549, 550	563, 565	567, 640
2	CREATING AND FORMATTING SLIDE CONTENT			
2.1	Insert and format text boxes	643-644	663	Adv. PowerPoint L1
2.2	Manipulate text	574, 575, 588, 594, 596, 600	605–610	635, 637, 678, 679
2.3	Add and link existing content to presentations	641, 642, 645, 646	649, 667	672, 673, 677, 678, 679
2.4	Apply, customize, modify, and remove animations	618, 620	600, 622	635, 679
3	WORKING WITH VISUAL CONTENT			
3.1	Create SmartArt diagrams	580	595, Adv. PowerPoint L2	599
3.2	Modify SmartArt diagrams	580, 582	595, Adv. PowerPoint L1	599
3.3	Insert illustrations and shapes	578, 586, 587	594, 597, 598, 599	637, 673, 674, 678
3.4	Modify illustrations	611, 612	615, 633, 635, 637	673, 677
3.5	Arrange illustrations and other content	611, 614, 615, 616	619, 635, 648	667, 670, 672, 673
3.6	Insert and modify charts	583, 585	597, 600	673, 674
3.7	Insert and modify tables	576, 577	598	600
4	COLLABORATING ON AND DELIVERING PRESENTATIONS			
4.1	Review presentations	591	596, 600	673, 674
4.2	Protect presentations	Adv. PowerPoint L2	Adv. PowerPoint L2	Adv. PowerPoint L2
4.3	Secure and share presentations	660, 663	664	669, 671, 672
4.4	Prepare printed materials	558, 559, 564	568, 628, 652	669, 670, 672, 676, 678, 679
4.5	Prepare for and rehearse presentation delivery	554, 555, 564, 567, 568	654, 655, 657, 658, 659, 661	668, 670–673, 679

Adv. = Advanced lessons are available at the Online Learning Center at **glencoe.com**.

Lesson Planning Guide

LESSON 2 Create Data and Content

Key Concepts

After completing this lesson, students will be able to:

- Enter, edit, clear, find, and replace cell contents
- Use AutoSum, AVERAGE, MIN, and MAX functions
- Use Cut, Copy, and Paste
- Use the Fill handle tool
- Insert, modify, and remove hyperlinks

iCheck Lesson Resources

The following components and resources have been provided to help you teach this lesson.

- Glencoe's Lesson Planner Plus DVD
  - Create your lesson plans with a few simple clicks
  - Access blackline masters and resources
- Teacher Resource DVD
  - Data Files for Excel Lesson 2
  - Solution Files for Excel Lesson 2
- *Presentation Plus!* DVD
- Online Learning Center at **glencoe.com**
  - Data Files for Excel Lesson 2
  - Solution Files for Excel Lesson 2
  - Interactive Review for Excel Lesson 2
  - Online Self Check for Excel Lesson 2
  - Challenge Yourself Project Rubrics for Excel Lesson 2
- *ExamView* CD, Excel Lesson 2 Test

Standards

See page 226 for a list of Microsoft Certified Application Specialist objectives and ISTE/NETS standards that students will meet by completing this activity. See page TM33 for a correlation of 21st Century Skills and Workplace Competencies.

Lesson 2	Pg #	Data File	Lesson 2	Pg #	Solution File
EX 2-1	228	Budget.xlsx	Ex 2-1 to 2-12	239	Budget-SF.xlsx
PIA 1	242	Clients.xlsx	PIA 1	242	Clients1-SF.xlsx
			PIA 2	243	Clients2-SF.xlsx
			PIA 3	244	Clients3-SF.xlsx
YTI 4	245	Teams.xlsx	YTI 4	245	Teams4-SF.xlsx
			YTI 5	246	Sporting5-SF.xlsx
Ch. Yrslf. 9	248	Sandwich.docx	Ch. Yrslf. 9	248	e2rev9-SF.xlsx
Ch. Yrslf. 10	248	Sandwich.docx	Ch. Yrslf. 10	248	e2rev10-SF.xlsx
Ch. Yrslf. 11	248	Sandwich.docx	Ch. Yrslf. 11	248	e2rev11-SF.xlsx

Focus

Invite students to share what they already know about monthly budgets. Students should understand that a budget helps a person, family, company, or organization manage its money. A designated amount of money is set aside for categories such as school supplies, food, rent, or entertainment. Consider creating a simple budget for a high school student on the board. Encourage students to help you come up with categories and realistic amounts for each category.

At this time you may want students to view Excel Lesson 2 of the *Presentation Plus!* DVD. This presentation program uses an engaging format to introduce students to the key concepts of this lesson.

Technical and Academic Standards

OUTLOOK 2007 MCAS STANDARDS				
Microsoft Certified Application Specialist Standards		Textbook Correlation		
	Skill Sets and Skills	Introduced	Developed	Mastered
1	MANAGING MESSAGING			
1.1	Create and send an e-mail message	Adv. Outlook L1	Adv. Outlook L4	Adv. Outlook L4
1.2	Create and manage your signature and automated messages	Adv. Outlook L1	Adv. Outlook L1	Adv. Outlook L1
1.3	Manage e-mail message attachments	Adv. Outlook L1	Adv. Outlook L1	Adv. Outlook L1
1.4	Configure e-mail message sensitivity and importance settings	Adv. Outlook L1	Adv. Outlook L1	Adv. Outlook L1
1.5	Configure e-mail message security settings	Adv. Outlook L1	Adv. Outlook L1	Adv. Outlook L1
1.6	Configure e-mail message delivery options	Adv. Outlook L1	Adv. Outlook L1	Adv. Outlook L1
1.7	View e-mail messages	Adv. Outlook L1	Adv. Outlook L1	Adv. Outlook L1
2	MANAGING SCHEDULING			
2.1	Create appointments, meetings, and events	Adv. Outlook L3	Adv. Outlook L3	Adv. Outlook L3
2.2	Send meeting requests	Adv. Outlook L3	Adv. Outlook L3	Adv. Outlook L3
2.3	Update, cancel, and respond to meeting requests	Adv. Outlook L3	Adv. Outlook L3	Adv. Outlook L3
2.4	Customize Calendar settings	Adv. Outlook L3	Adv. Outlook L3	Adv. Outlook L3
2.5	Share your Calendar with others	Adv. Outlook L3	Adv. Outlook L3	Adv. Outlook L3
2.6	View other Calendars	Adv. Outlook L3	Adv. Outlook L3	Adv. Outlook L3
3	MANAGING TASKS			
3.1	Create, modify, and mark tasks as complete	Adv. Outlook L3	Adv. Outlook L3	Adv. Outlook L3
3.2	Accept, decline, assign, update, and respond to tasks	Adv. Outlook L3	Adv. Outlook L3	Adv. Outlook L3
4	MANAGING CONTACTS AND PERSONAL CONTACT INFORMATION			
4.1	Create and modify contacts	Adv. Outlook L2	Adv. Outlook L2	Adv. Outlook L2
4.2	Edit and use an electronic business card	Adv. Outlook L2	Adv. Outlook L2	Adv. Outlook L2
4.3	Create and modify distribution lists	Adv. Outlook L2	Adv. Outlook L2	Adv. Outlook L2
4.4	Create a secondary address book	Adv. Outlook L2	Adv. Outlook L2	Adv. Outlook L2
5	ORGANIZING INFORMATION			
5.1	Categorize Outlook items by color	Adv. Outlook L4	Adv. Outlook L4	Adv. Outlook L4
5.2	Create and manage Outlook data files	Adv. Outlook L4	Adv. Outlook L4	Adv. Outlook L4
5.3	Organize mail folders	Adv. Outlook L4	Adv. Outlook L4	Adv. Outlook L4
5.4	Locate Outlook items by the search feature	Adv. Outlook L4	Adv. Outlook L4	Adv. Outlook L4
5.5	Create, modify, and remove rules to manage e-mail messages	Adv. Outlook L4	Adv. Outlook L4	Adv. Outlook L4
5.6	Customize your Outlook experience	Adv. Outlook L4	Adv. Outlook L4	Adv. Outlook L4

Adv. = Advanced lessons are available at the Online Learning Center at **glencoe.com**.

Lesson Planning Guide

Teach

- **Step-By-Steps**
  Throughout the lesson, have students perform the Step-By-Steps to complete each exercise.
- **Troubleshooting Tips**
  Double-clicking a cell switches to Edit mode and places a cursor in the cell. If students double-click a cell inadvertently, have them press the Esc key. Pressing Esc cancels Edit mode and saves a lot of frustration.
- **Differentiated Instruction**
  Occasionally read the Step-By-Step instructions aloud to the class. Students will enjoy the variety, and this exercise will help auditory learners.
- **Classroom Management Tips**
  When new students join your class, have them try some of the Critical Thinking Activities or You Try It Activities from previous lessons. Use these review activities to assess the skills of incoming students.
- **Reading and Writing Support**
  Tell students not to confuse the words *farther* and *further*. Suggest that they use the word *far* in the word *farther* to remind them that *farther* refers to distance. *I can hit the baseball farther than I could last year. We will talk about benefits further if you are offered the job.*

Assess

After students finish the lesson, have them complete the following assessment activities:

- After You Read, p. 218
- Practice It Activities, pp. 219–221

Reteach

- **Independent Practice**
  Assign students the You Try It Activities on pages 222–223.
- **Differentiated Instruction**
  Assign students the Challenge Yourself Projects on page 225.

Assess

There are multiple formats for assessment provided for this lesson. These include:

- Interactive Review—Online Learning Center
- Online Self Check—Online Learning Center
- Critical Thinking Activities, p. 224
- Rubrics for ChallengeYourself Projects—Online Learning Center. Refer to page TM40 for an explanation of how rubrics can help students enhance performance and self-evaluation techniques.
- *ExamView* for Excel Lesson 1

Close

End this lesson with a quick vocabulary game. Quiz the students aloud on the vocabulary's definitions. Call on a student to define a term—or read a definition and call on a student to identify the term. Keep track of the correct answers and declare a winner.

Answers

- **21st Century Skills (p. 202)** Answers will vary. Students should attempt to describe the methods they usually use to organize their work.
- See Lesson Resources on the previous page for a list of Solution Files provided in this lesson.
- See answers to After You Read on p. 218 and Critical Thinking Activities on p. 224.
- **Math Matters: Introduction to Excel (p. 204)**
  1. Possible answers include: to organize product data, to track customer information, etc.
  2. Students should recognize that using Excel's built-in formulas may be more efficient and accurate than using a calculator since Excel's calculations are automated and not keyed in.
  3. Students should identify the main differences between a word processing and a spreadsheet application.
  4. Answers will vary, but students should describe a new use for Excel that they found on the Internet.

Technical and Academic Standards

WINDOWS VISTA MCAS STANDARDS				
Microsoft Certified Application Specialist Standards		Textbook Correlation		
	Skill Sets and Skills	Introduced	Developed	Mastered
1	PROTECTING YOUR COMPUTER			
1.1	Manage Windows Firewall	Adv. Vista L1	Adv. Vista L1	Adv. Vista L1
1.2	Manage malicious software (also called malware) protection	Adv. Vista L1	Adv. Vista L1	Adv. Vista L1
1.3	Configure Windows Update settings	Adv. Vista L1	Adv. Vista L1	Adv. Vista L1
1.4	Lock a computer	Adv. Vista L1	Adv. Vista L1	Adv. Vista L1
1.5	Manage Windows Internet Explorer security	Adv. Vista L1	Adv. Vista L1	Adv. Vista L1
1.6	Configure local user accounts	Adv. Vista L1	Adv. Vista L1	Adv. Vista L1
2	MANAGING MOBILE AND REMOTE COMPUTING			
2.1	Manage the computer power state	Adv. Vista L2	Adv. Vista L2	Adv. Vista L2
2.2	Manage network connections	Adv. Vista L2	Adv. Vista L2	Adv. Vista L2
2.3	Manage remote access to your computer	Adv. Vista L2	Adv. Vista L2	Adv. Vista L2
2.4	Connect to another computer	Adv. Vista L2	Adv. Vista L2	Adv. Vista L2
2.5	Access files stored in shared network folders when your computer is offline	Adv. Vista L2	Adv. Vista L2	Adv. Vista L2
3	MANAGING SOFTWARE, DISKS, AND DEVICES			
3.1	Manage software	Adv. Vista L3	Adv. Vista L3	Adv. Vista L3
3.2	Manage disks	Adv. Vista L3	Adv. Vista L3	Adv. Vista L3
3.3	Manage devices and drivers	Adv. Vista L3	Adv. Vista L3	Adv. Vista L3
3.4	Manage display settings	Adv. Vista L3	Adv. Vista L3	Adv. Vista L3
3.5	Configure multiple monitors	Adv. Vista L3	Adv. Vista L3	Adv. Vista L3
3.6	Install and configure a printer	Adv. Vista L3	Adv. Vista L3	Adv. Vista L3
4	MANAGING FILES AND FOLDERS			
4.1	Manage Windows Explorer settings	Adv. Vista L4	Adv. Vista L4	Adv. Vista L4
4.2	Manage and secure folders	Adv. Vista L4	Adv. Vista L4	Adv. Vista L4
4.3	Share folders	Adv. Vista L4	Adv. Vista L4	Adv. Vista L4
4.4	Search for files and folders	Adv. Vista L4	Adv. Vista L4	Adv. Vista L4
4.5	Organize files within folders	Adv. Vista L4	Adv. Vista L4	Adv. Vista L4
4.6	Manage files	Adv. Vista L4	Adv. Vista L4	Adv. Vista L4
4.7	Back up and restore files and folders	Adv. Vista L4	Adv. Vista L4	Adv. Vista L4

Adv. = Advanced lessons are available at the Online Learning Center at **glencoe.com**.

Lesson Planning Guide

LESSON 1 Excel Basics

Key Concepts

After completing this lesson, students will be able to:

- ✓ Identify parts of the Excel screen
- ✓ Open and close workbooks
- ✓ Insert and edit cell contents
- ✓ Name and save a workbook
- ✓ Calculate a sum
- ✓ Print a worksheet

iCheck Lesson Resources

The following components and resources have been provided to help you teach this lesson.

- Glencoe's Lesson Planner Plus DVD
  - Create your lesson plans with a few, simple clicks
  - Access blackline masters and resources
- Teacher Resource DVD
  - Data Files for Excel Lesson 1
  - Solution Files for Excel Lesson 1
- *Presentation Plus!* DVD
  - Online Learning Center at **glencoe.com**
  - Data Files for Excel Lesson 1
  - Solution Files for Excel Lesson 1
  - Interactive Review for Excel Lesson 1
  - Online Self Check for Excel Lesson 1
  - Challenge Yourself Project Rubrics for Excel Lesson 1
- *ExamView* CD, Excel Lesson 1 Test

Standards

See page 202 for a list of Microsoft Certified Application Specialist objectives and ISTE/NETS standards that students will meet by completing this activity. See page TM33 for a correlation of 21st Century Skills and Workplace Competencies.

Lesson 1	Pg #	Data File
There are no data files for this lesson.		

Lesson 1	Pg #	Solution File
Ex 1-6 to 1-13	217	e1-6-SF.xlsx
PIA 1	219	e1rev1-SF.xlsx
PIA 2	220	e1rev2-SF.xlsx
PIA 3	221	e1rev3-SF.xlsx
YTI 4	222	e1rev4-SF.xlsx
YTI 5	223	e1rev5-SF.xlsx
Crit. Think. 7	224	e1rev7-SF.xlsx
Crit. Think. 8	224	e1rev8-SF.xlsx
Ch. Yrslf. 9	225	e1rev9-SF.xlsx
Ch. Yrslf. 10	225	e1rev10-SF.xlsx
Ch. Yrslf. 11	225	e1rev11-SF.xlsx

Focus

Ask students if they know the purpose of a spreadsheet. Students might already know that people use spreadsheets to perform calculations. Consider passing a variety of Excel files around the class. The printouts might include formulas, lists of data, shaded cells, a pie chart, etc. Ask students to discuss some of the features that they see in the Excel files.

At this time you may want students to view Excel Lesson 1 of the *Presentation Plus!* DVD. This presentation program uses an engaging format to introduce students to the key concepts of this lesson.

Technical and Academic Standards

WINDOWS VISTA MCAS STANDARDS				
Microsoft Certified Application Specialist Standards		Textbook Correlation		
	Skill Sets and Skills	Introduced	Developed	Mastered
5	COLLABORATING WITH OTHER PEOPLE			
5.1	Collaborate in real time	Adv. Vista L2	Adv. Vista L2	Adv. Vista L2
5.2	Present information to an audience	Adv. Vista L2	Adv. Vista L2	Adv. Vista L2
6	CUSTOMIZING YOUR WINDOWS VISTA EXPERIENCE			
6.1	Customize and modify the Start menu	Adv. Vista L5	Adv. Vista L5	Adv. Vista L5
6.2	Customize the taskbar	Adv. Vista L5	Adv. Vista L5	Adv. Vista L5
6.3	Personalize the appearance and sound of a computer	Adv. Vista L5	Adv. Vista L5	Adv. Vista L5
6.4	Manage the Windows Sidebar	Adv. Vista L5	Adv. Vista L5	Adv. Vista L5
7	OPTIMIZING AND TROUBLESHOOTING YOUR COMPUTER			
7.1	Increase processing speed	Adv. Vista L6	Adv. Vista L6	Adv. Vista L6
7.2	Locate troubleshooting information	Adv. Vista L6	Adv. Vista L6	Adv. Vista L6
7.3	Locate system information	Adv. Vista L6	Adv. Vista L6	Adv. Vista L6
7.4	Repair a network connection	Adv. Vista L6	Adv. Vista L6	Adv. Vista L6
7.5	Recover from software errors	Adv. Vista L6	Adv. Vista L6	Adv. Vista L6
7.6	Troubleshoot printing errors	Adv. Vista L6	Adv. Vista L6	Adv. Vista L6
7.7	Recover the operating system from a problem	Adv. Vista L6	Adv. Vista L6	Adv. Vista L6
7.8	Request and Manage Remote Assistance	Adv. Vista L6	Adv. Vista L6	Adv. Vista L6

Adv. = Advanced lessons are available at the Online Learning Center at **glencoe.com**.

Unit 2 Excel Overview

Focus

Motivation

- **Why It Matters** Review the Why It Matters feature on page 200. Discuss with students how being able to use Excel 2007 will help them at both school and work.
- **Go Online: Real World Connection Activity** Have students complete the Go Online: Real World Connection Activity on page 200 to learn more about how different organizations use spreadsheet applications.
- **Careers and Technology** The Careers and Technology feature on page 201 illustrates the high demand for computer jobs. Discuss with students how learning computer applications will affect their career paths.
- **Answers to Reading Check (p. 201)**
  1. Spreadsheet software knowledge is used in the management of money or other assets in order to complete projects. Managers make more money than those they manage.
  2. Computer software engineer.

Teach

Guided Practice

- ***Presentation Plus! PowerPoint Presentations*** A special PowerPoint presentation has been provided to help you introduce Excel, including how people use Excel at both school and work.

Independent Practice

Additional exercises and projects are available at the book's Online Learning Center at **glencoe.com**.

- **Additional Exercises**
  - Microsoft Word
  - Microsoft Excel
  - Microsoft Access
  - Microsoft PowerPoint
  - Microsoft Outlook
  - Windows Vista
- **Additional Projects**
  - Real-World Business Applications
  - Present and Publish Projects
  - Academic Projects

Assess

- **Portfolio Project** The Portfolio Project on pages 344–347 allows students to complete a business-oriented project. Students can complete all four parts, or focus on only one part of the project. Students can print copies of their projects, or create an electronic copy for their portfolios.
- **Rubrics** Rubrics are provided to help students and teachers assess the Portfolio Projects. Rubrics can be accessed on the Online Learning Center at **glencoe.com**.

Unit 2 Closer	Pg #	Data File
Portfolio Proj. pt. 1	344	Hours.docx
Portfolio Proj. pt. 3	346	Lawns.docx

Reteach

- **Academic Connections** Review the feature on page 342 with students to show how the technical skills developed in this unit can be used to complete an academic project.

Assess

- ***ExamView® Assessment Suite* Excel Unit 2 Test**

Close

- **Ethics in Action** Have students read the feature on page 343 and complete the questions.

  Answers to You Decide and **Application Activity (p. 343)**
  1. Use a government or university source.
  2. Answers will vary but students should indicate that Samantha should tell Jay his solution is unethical, they need to cite their source, and they need to find a reputable source with reliable information.
  3. Students' worksheets should list ethical guidelines for using books, periodicals, and online resources.

ISTE NETS Standards

The International Society for Technology in Education (ISTE) has developed NETS (National Educational Technology Standards) to effectively define educational technology standards for students.

NETS STANDARDS	PERFORMANCE INDICATORS	TEXTBOOK CORRELATION
1. **Creativity and Innovation** Students demonstrate creative thinking, construct knowledge, and develop innovative products and processes using technology.	a. apply existing knowledge to generate new ideas, products, or processes. b. create original works as a means of personal or group expression. c. use models and simulations to explore complex systems and issues. d. identify trends and forecast possibilities.	29, 56, 62, 63, 65, 87, 94, 123, 129, 132, 154, 160, 161, 185, 186, 192–194, 196–199, 218, 227, 239, 241, 247, 250, 273, 280, 305, 334, 351, 372, 378, 381, 417, 423, 426, 469, 561, 570, 593, 599, 630, 637, 666, 674
2. **Communication and Collaboration** Students use digital media and environments to communicate and work collaboratively, including at a distance, to support individual learning and contribute to the learning of others.	a. interact, collaborate, and publish with peers, experts or others employing a variety of digital environments and media. b. communicate information and ideas effectively to multiple audiences using a variety of media and formats. c. develop cultural understanding and global awareness by engaging with learners of other cultures. d. contribute to project teams to produce original works or solve problems.	22, 31, 33, 34, 62–64, 67, 75, 94, 97, 129, 134, 162, 163, 165–171, 185, 192, 193, 214, 224, 273, 283, 508, 541, 542, 560, 614, 636, 637, 665, 672
3. **Research and Information Fluency** Students apply digital tools to gather, evaluate, and use information.	a. plan strategies to guide inquiry. b. locate, organize, analyze, evaluate, synthesize, and ethically use information from a variety of sources and media. c. evaluate and select information sources and digital tools based on the appropriateness to specific tasks. d. process data and report results.	30, 74, 76, 93, 95, 153, 199, 204, 315, 343, 369, 462, 513, 525, 533, 556, 568, 592, 629, 679
4. **Critical Thinking, Problem-Solving, and Decision-Making** Students use critical thinking skills to plan and conduct research, manage projects, solve problems and make informed decisions using appropriate digital tools and resources.	a. identify and define authentic problems and significant questions for investigation. b. plan and manage activities to develop a solution or complete a project. c. collect and analyze data to identify solutions and/or make informed decisions. d. use multiple processes and diverse perspectives to explore alternative solutions.	32, 63, 94, 95, 109, 153, 161, 203, 224, 225, 240, 247–249, 280–282, 294, 296, 304, 311, 312, 333, 340–342, 344–347, 350, 423, 424, 461, 468, 471, 499, 506, 507, 532, 538, 543, 602, 673
5. **Digital Citizenship** Students understand human, cultural, and societal issues related to technology and practice legal and ethical behavior.	a. advocate and practice safe, legal, and responsible use of information and technology. b. exhibit a positive attitude toward using technology that supports collaboration, learning, and productivity. c. demonstrate personal responsibility for lifelong learning. d. exhibit leadership for digital citizenship.	2, 3, 29, 30, 66, 93, 105, 129–132, 160, 195, 201, 202, 224, 226, 230, 313, 340, 343, 349, 371, 380, 416, 423, 425, 470, 509, 535, 567, 569, 586, 599, 601, 629, 636, 638, 650, 672, 673, 675
6. **Technology Operations and Concepts** Students demonstrate a sound understanding of technology concepts, systems and operations.	a. understand and use technology systems. b. select and use applications effectively and productively. c. troubleshoot systems and applications. d. transfer current knowledge to learning of new technologies.	5–21, 27, 35–55, 68–86, 93, 95, 96, 98–122, 134–152, 165–184, 205–217, 228–240, 251–273, 284–303, 315–332, 352–370, 382–415, 427–460, 472–498, 510–524, 536–539, 544–559, 571–591, 603–628, 640–664

Lesson Planning Guide

Teach

Step-By-Steps
Throughout the lesson, have students perform the Step-By-Steps to complete each exercise.

Troubleshooting Tips
Let students know that if you key the name of a Web site or e-mail address, Word automatically creates a hyperlink. One can right-click the hyperlink and choose **Remove Hyperlink** if desired.

Differentiated Instruction
To help visual learners understand a Mail Merge, hold up a business letter in one hand and a list of names and addresses in the other. Explain that documents are merged to create a stack of personalized letters.

Classroom Management Tips
If some students move through exercises more quickly than other students, ask advanced students to help other students. The advanced students will learn by teaching.

Reading and Writing Support
Remind students that when two subjects are joined by or, the verb must agree with the subject that is closer to the verb. *My cousins or uncle is helping me.*

Assess

After the students finish the lesson, have them complete the following assessment activities:

- After You Read, p. 186
- Practice It Activities, pp. 187–189

Reteach

Independent Practice
Assign students the You Try It Activities on pages 190–191.

Differentiated Instruction
Assign students the Challenge Yourself Projects on page 193.

Assess

There are multiple formats for assessment provided for this lesson. These include:

- Interactive Review—Online Learning Center
- Online Self Check—Online Learning Center
- Critical Thinking Activities, p. 192.
- Rubrics for Challenge Yourself Projects—Online Learning Center. Refer to page TM40 for an explanation of how rubrics can help students enhance performance and self-evaluation techniques.
- *ExamView* for Word Lesson 6

Close

Ask students to think of a scenario in which a high school student might use a mail merge. Invite students to share their ideas with the class.

Answers

- **21st Century Skills (p. 162)** Answers will vary. Students should attempt to reconstruct the way they handled a recent conflict.
- See Lesson Resources on the previous page for a list of Solution Files provided in this lesson.
- See answers to After You Read on p. 186 and Critical Thinking Activities on p. 192.
- **21st Century Workplace: Learn to Collaborate (p. 185)**
  1. Students may describe difficulties in understanding others or coming to agreements. Benefits may be success of the project; learning how to compromise, or to get along with, other people.
  2. Students may say that collaboration is important, and employees can improve technical skills; or they may say the reverse. Students should give concrete examples.
  3. Students should save their work as a Word document. Students' flyers should give collaboration tips and examples and be illustrated by Clip Art or other graphics.

21st Century Skills and Workplace Competencies

Today's workplace is highly competitive and demands skilled employees. Successful employees deal with the varied demands of the fast-paced workplace, which requires decision making, creative problem solving, and the ability to interact with diverse groups—employees, managers, investors, customers, or clients. The business and workplace skills covered in Glencoe's *iCheck Series* have been identified by the Secretary's Commission on Achieving Necessary Skills (SCANS) and by 21st Century Skills as skills needed by successful employees. Glencoe's *iCheck Series* provides students with opportunities to learn and acquire the following skills.

SKILL	TEXTBOOK CORRELATION	SKILL	TEXTBOOK CORRELATION
Interpersonal Skills		**Personal Qualities**	
Resolving conflict	162, 192	Responsibility	131, 160
Demonstrating leadership	64, 93	Managing money	226, 247, 333
Communicating with others	67, 540, 665, 673	Understanding the role of the media	592
Working as a team	31, 62, 185	Setting realistic goals	3, 29
Developing interviewing skills	273	Patience	380, 423
Understanding audience	542, 560, 567	Prioritizing tasks	425, 468
Being active in the community	569, 599, 675	Demonstrating ethical behavior	601, 636
		Self-initiative	638, 672
		Making decisions	95, 129
		Perseverance	470
		Productivity	202,224
		Flexibility	249, 280
		Honesty	313, 341
		Organization	282, 311, 350, 378

LESSON 6 Collaborating with Others

Key Concepts

After completing this lesson, students will be able to:

- Insert and edit hyperlinks
- Send documents for review
- Use Track Changes
- Compare and merge documents
- Create and preview a Web page
- Perform a mail merge
- Select printing options
- Create and print labels
- Convert documents into different formats
- Create a letterhead

iCheck Lesson Resources

The following components and resources have been provided to help you teach this lesson.

- Glencoe's Lesson Planner Plus DVD
  - Create your lesson plans with a few, simple clicks
  - Access blackline masters and resources
- Teacher Resource DVD
  - Data Files for Word Lesson 6
  - Solution Files for Word Lesson 6
- *Presentation Plus!* DVD
- Online Learning Center at **glencoe.com**
  - Data Files for Word Lesson 6
  - Solution Files for Word Lesson 6
  - Interactive Review for Word Lesson 6
  - Online Self Check for Word Lesson 6
  - Challenge Yourself Project Rubrics for Word Lesson 6
- *ExamView* CD, Word Lesson 6 Test

Standards

See page 162 for a list of Microsoft Certified Application Specialist objectives and ISTE/NETS standards that students will meet by completing this activity. See page TM33 for a correlation of 21st Century Skills and Workplace Competencies.

Lesson 6	Pg #	Data File	Lesson 6	Pg #	Solution File
EX 6-1	164	Flyer_Memo.docx	EX 6-1 to 6-2	165	Flyer_Memo-SF.docx
EX 6-3	166	Flyer.docx	EX 6-3 to 6-9	173	Combined-SF.docx
EX 6-12	176	Notice.docx			
			EX 6-13 to 6-14	179	Notice-Landscape-SF.docx
			EX 6-16	181	Labels-SF.docx
			EX 6-17	182	Notice-SF.doc; Notice-SF.rtf
			EX 6-18	184	Letterhead-SF.docx
PIA 1	187	Book Sale.docx	PIA 1	187	Book Sale1-SF.docx
			PIA 2	188	Book Sale2-SF.docx
			PIA 3	189	Book Sale3-SF.docx
YTI 4	190	Clinic.docx	YTI 4	190	Clinic4-SF.docx
YTI 5	191	Clients.docx	YTI 5	191	Clinic5-SF.docx
Ch. Yrslf. 11	193	Donors.docx			

Focus

Begin this lesson by asking students what it means to collaborate with others. Ask students to discuss school projects they did with other students.

At this time you may want students to view Word Lesson 6 of the *Presentation Plus!* DVD. This presentation program uses an engaging format to introduce students to the key concepts of this lesson.

National Language Arts Standards

Use these language arts standards to incorporate literacy skills (reading, writing, listening, speaking, and viewing) into your computer applications classroom.

STANDARD	TEXTBOOK CORRELATION
1. Students read a wide range of print and non-print texts to build an understanding of texts, of themselves, and of the cultures of the United States and the world; to acquire new information; to respond to the needs and demands of society and the workplace; and for personal fulfillment. Among these texts are fiction and nonfiction, classic and contemporary works.	5–9, 11, 14, 28, 273, 371, 548, 592
2. Students read a wide range of literature from many periods in many genres to build an understanding of the many dimensions (e.g., philosophical, ethical, aesthetic) of human experience	4, 22, 27, 30, 32, 33, 34, 66, 67, 96, 97, 105, 109, 132, 163, 227, 250, 283, 314, 342, 351, 381, 416, 426, 471, 509, 535, 543, 560, 570, 602, 629, 639, 675
3. Students apply a wide range of strategies to comprehend, interpret, evaluate, and appreciate texts. They draw on their prior experience, their interactions with other readers and writers, their knowledge of word meaning and of other texts, their word identification strategies, and their understanding of textual features (e.g., sound-letter correspondence, sentence structure, context, graphics).	30, 47, 105, 139, 163, 166, 195, 203, 204, 283
4. Students adjust their use of spoken, written, and visual language (e.g., conventions, style, vocabulary) to communicate effectively with a variety of audiences and for different purposes.	14, 22, 34, 66, 74, 78, 94, 97, 101, 109, 134, 179, 185, 193, 214, 224, 515, 551, 553, 560, 605, 609, 636–637, 665, 674, 678, 679
5. Students employ a wide range of strategies as they write and use different writing process elements appropriately to communicate with different audiences for a variety of purposes.	22, 33, 39, 42, 67, 75, 94, 99, 104, 149, 166, 273, 552, 562, 567, 573, 575, 589, 603, 614, 665, 672, 677
6. Students apply knowledge of language structure, language conventions (e.g., spelling and punctuation), media techniques, figurative language, and genre to create, critique, and discuss print and non-print texts.	13, 22, 72, 161, 192, 194, 196, 198, 199, 414, 556, 590
7. Students conduct research on issues and interests by generating ideas and questions, and by posing problems. They gather, evaluate, and synthesize data from a variety of sources (e.g., print and non-print texts, artifacts, people) to communicate their discoveries in ways that suit their purpose and audience.	6, 76, 90, 93, 97, 105, 109, 115, 116, 130, 185, 194, 568, 629, 654
8. Students use a variety of technological and information resources (e.g., libraries, databases, computer networks, video) to gather and synthesize information and to create and communicate knowledge.	20, 30, 105, 116, 194, 217, 361, 387, 441, 484, 586, 651
9. Students develop an understanding of and respect for diversity in language use, patterns, and dialects across cultures, ethnic groups, geographic regions, and social roles.	73, 165
10. Students whose first language is not English make use of their first language to develop competency in the English language arts and to develop understanding of content across the curriculum.	73, 80, 144, 165, 166, 264, 291, 517, 521, 572, 589, 659
11. Students participate as knowledgeable, reflective, creative, and critical members of a variety of literacy communities.	166, 592, 599, 600
12. Students use spoken, written, and visual language to accomplish their own purposes (e.g., for learning, enjoyment, persuasion, and the exchange of information).	33, 91, 114, 119, 175, 331, 371, 416, 468, 487, 499, 599, 629, 652, 676

*These standards have been developed by the *National Council of Teachers of English* and the *International Reading Association.*

Lesson Planning Guide

Teach

- **Step-By-Steps**
  Throughout the lesson, have students perform the Step-By-Steps to complete each exercise.
- **Troubleshooting Tips**
  If students have trouble working with columns, have them click the **Show/Hide** button. Clicking this button displays both column breaks and section breaks, which often reveals the source of the problem.
- **Differentiated Instruction**
  For visual learners, provide real-world examples of the features that students are learning. Seeing the outcome of a skill or process in a sample can help students visualize the goal of an exercise so that the skill is more easily learned.
- **Classroom Management Tips**
  Keep a stockpile of brainteasers for times when students become restless. Take a short break and have students solve one of these puzzles as a class. You can buy books of brainteasers or search for them on the Internet.
- **Reading and Writing Support**
  Point out to students that they can use a semicolon instead of a period to join two closely related independent clauses. *They celebrated; we did not.*

Assess

After the students finish the lesson, have them complete the following assessment activities:

- After You Read, p. 154
- Practice It Activities, pp. 155–157

Reteach

- **Independent Practice**
  Assign students the You Try It Activities on pages 158–159.
- **Differentiated Instruction**
  Assign students the Challenge Yourself Projects on page 161.

Assess

There are multiple formats for assessment provided for this lesson. These include:

- Interactive Review—Online Learning Center
- Online Self Check—Online Learning Center
- Critical Thinking Activities, p. 160
- Rubrics for Challenge Yourself Projects—Online Learning Center. Refer to page TM40 for an explanation of how rubrics can help students enhance performance and self-evaluation techniques.
- *ExamView* for Word Lesson 5

Close

Have students think of a scenario when they might use columns, an organizational chart, and WordArt in the same document. Possible answers include a company newsletter introducing new employees. The organization chart would show where the new employees fit in the organization. The title of the newsletter could be created using WordArt.

Answers

- **21st Century Skills (p. 131)** Answers will vary. Students should identify behavior that would make them more responsible.
- See Lesson Resources on the previous page for a list of Solution Files provided in this lesson.
- See answers to After You Read on p. 154 and Critical Thinking Activities on p. 160.
- **Math Matters: Reading Charts, Graphs, and Diagrams (p. 153)**
  1. To represent statistical information visually. Data is often easier to understand in this format.
  2. Answers will vary. Students may respond that important business information, such as sales and product data, is often expressed in the form of charts and graphs. An employee who can read charts and graphs is valuable.
  3. One would be more likely to market Lar's Quest to 16–19-year-olds. Based on the data, more teens in this age group preferred it.

National Math Standards

Glencoe's *iCheck Series* provides students with opportunities to practice the math skills indicated in the national math standards developed by the *National Council of Teachers of Mathematics.*

National Council of Teachers of Mathematics Standards for Grades 9–12	
STANDARD	**TEXTBOOK CORRELATIONS**
Number and Operation	
Understand numbers, ways of representing numbers, relationships among numbers, and number systems	104, 153, 204, 224, 247, 260, 281, 298, 301, 311, 333, 344, 387–388, 424, 478, 506, 518, 558, 584, 615
Understand meanings of operations and how they relate to one another	215, 257, 258, 286, 291, 292, 311, 333, 456, 538
Compute fluently and make reasonable estimates	100, 160, 221, 223, 225, 229, 230, 239, 244, 246, 248, 301, 302, 316, 340, 341, 345, 346, 619
Algebra	
Understand patterns, relations, and functions	285, 312
Represent and analyze mathematical situations and structures using algebraic symbols	240, 281, 283, 288, 290–293, 306–307, 309, 342, 482, 484
Use mathematical models to represent and understand quantitative relationships	286, 287, 312, 333, 342, 461, 533
Geometry	
Analyze characteristics and properties of two- and three-dimensional geometric shapes and develop mathematical arguments about geometric relationships	147, 349, 541, 582, 635, 648
Measurement	
Understand measurable attributes of objects and the units, systems, and processes of measurement	38, 51, 59, 60, 69, 88, 91, 114, 212, 219, 327, 363, 534, 611, 644, 651
Apply appropriate techniques, tools, and formulas to determine measurements	35, 51, 53, 59, 60, 69, 88, 91, 114, 613
Data Analysis and Probability	
Select and use appropriate statistical methods to analyze data	294, 296, 298, 300, 301, 302, 304, 306, 349
Problem Solving	
Solve problems that arise in mathematics and in other contexts	248, 333, 344
Apply and adapt a variety of appropriate strategies to solve problems	225, 226, 239, 247, 300, 341, 424, 461, 468, 507
Monitor and reflect on the process of mathematical problem solving	499, 506
Communication	
Organize and consolidate mathematical thinking through communication	151, 152
Communicate mathematical thinking coherently and clearly to peers, teachers, and others	160, 225, 424, 461, 506
Analyze and evaluate the mathematical thinking and strategies of others	153, 201, 304, 525
Connections	
Understand how mathematical ideas interconnect and build on one another to produce a coherent whole	153, 521
Recognize and apply mathematics in contexts outside of mathematics	201, 304, 468, 532
Representation	
Create and use representations to organize, record, and communicate mathematical ideas	151, 152, 160, 295, 308, 310, 347, 349, 511–512, 525, 533, 583–584, 597, 673
Select, apply, and translate among mathematical representations to solve problems	152, 294, 296, 327
Use representations to model and interpret physical, social, and mathematical phenomena	153, 304, 310, 342, 541, 585, 673

LESSON 5 Columns, Tables and Graphs

Key Concepts

After completing this lesson, students will be able to:

- Create and format columns
- Insert and modify a table and a chart
- Insert and manipulate Clip Art, SmartArt, and WordArt
- Work with a text box
- Insert, position, and modify a shape

iCheck Lesson Resources

The following components and resources have been provided to help you teach this lesson.

- Glencoe's Lesson Planner Plus DVD
  - Create your lesson plans with a few, simple clicks
  - Access blackline masters and resources
- Teacher Resource DVD
  - Data Files for Word Lesson 5
  - Solution Files for Word Lesson 5
- *Presentation Plus!* DVD
- Online Learning Center at **glencoe.com**
  - Data Files for Word Lesson 5
  - Solution Files for Word Lesson 5
  - Interactive Review for Word Lesson 5
  - Online Self Check for Word Lesson 5
  - Challenge Yourself Project Rubrics for Word Lesson 5
- *ExamView* CD, Word Lesson 5 Test

Standards

See page 131 for a list of Microsoft Certified Application Specialist objectives and ISTE/NETS standards that students will meet by completing this activity. See page TM33 for a correlation of 21st Century Skills and Workplace Competencies.

Lesson 5	Pg #	Data File	Lesson 5	Pg #	Solution File
Ex 5-1	133	Newsletter.docx	EX 5-1 to 5-16	150	Newsletter-SF.docx
Ex 5-17	151	Sales.docx	EX 5-17 to 5-18	152	Sales-SF.docx
PIA 1	155	Hillside.docx	PIA 1	155	Hillside1-SF.docx
			PIA 2	156	Hillside2-SF.docx
			PIA 3	157	Hillside3-SF.docx
			YTI 4	158	w5rev4-SF.docx
			YTI 5	159	Hillside5-SF.docx
Ch. Yrslf. 10	161	Theater_ Newsletter.docx	Ch. Yrslf. 10	161	Theater_ Newsletter 10-SF.docx
Ch. Yrslf. 11	161	Grades.docx	Ch. Yrslf. 11	161	Grades-11 SF.docx

Focus

Consider bringing to class a variety of newsletters and newspaper articles. Point out how columns of text in newsletters and newspapers wrap from the bottom of one column to the top of the next. You might also show the class a sample pie chart and organization chart. Ask students why someone might use charts like these. Students should understand that charts sometimes convey information more clearly than paragraphs of text can.

At this time you may want students to view Word Lesson 5 of the *Presentation Plus!* DVD. This presentation program uses an engaging format to introduce students to the key concepts of this lesson.

Improve Student Performance

Assessment Strategies

In response to the growing demand for accountability in the classroom, educators must use multiple assessment measures to accurately gauge student performance. In addition to quizzes, tests, essay exams, and standardized tests, assessment today incorporates a variety of performance-based measurements and portfolio opportunities.

Performance assessment activities provide hands-on approaches to learning concepts. Through activities students are able to actually experience these concepts rather than just reading and hearing about them. These types of activities also help students become aware of diverse audiences for their work.

Performance-Based Assessments

One good way to present a performance assessment is in the form of an open-ended question.

- Journals—Students write from the perspective of a businessperson or a consumer of a particular historical era.
- Letters—Students write a letter from one businessperson to another or to another audience.
- Position Paper or Editorial—Students explain a controversial issue and present their own opinions and recommendations, supported with strong evidence and convincing reasons.
- Newspaper—Students write stories from the perspective of a business reporter.
- Biographies and Autobiographies—Students write about business leaders either from the third person point of view (biography) or from the first person (autobiography).
- Creative Stories—Students integrate business events into a piece of fiction.
- Poems and Songs—Students follow the conventions of a particular type of song or poem as they tell about a business event or person.
- Research Reports—Students synthesize information from a variety of sources into a well-developed research report.

Oral Presentations

Oral presentations allow students to demonstrate their business literacy in front of an audience. Oral presentations are often group efforts, although this need not be the case.

- Simulations—Students hold simulations of actual events, such as a role play in a business scenario.
- Debates—Students debate two or more sides of a business policy or issue.
- Interview—Students conduct a mock interview of a business leader or worker.
- Oral Reports—Students present the results of research efforts in a lively oral report. This report may be accompanied by visuals.
- Skits and Plays—Students use business events as the basis for a play or skit.

Lesson Planning Guide

Focus

Explain that business reports are similar to academic reports; both are formal documents that convey information.

At this time you may want students to view Word Lesson 4 of the *Presentation Plus!* DVD.

Teach

- **Step-By-Steps**
  Throughout the lesson, have students perform the Step-By-Steps to complete each exercise.
- **Troubleshooting Tips**
  If students have trouble with section breaks, they can find the beginning of each section, have students choose **Page Layout>Page Setup>Breaks**.
- **Differentiated Instruction**
  For students who struggle to learn new skills, begin with them creating a footer with their first name.
- **Classroom Management Tips**
  Make sure all students can choose a printer, restart a program, and locate files.
- **Reading and Writing Support**
  Tell students not to confuse the words *affect,* which is used as a verb, and *effect,* which is used as a noun.

Assess

After the students finish the lesson, have them complete the following assessment activities:

- After You Read, p. 123
- Practice It Activities, pp. 124–126

Reteach

- **Independent Practice**
  Assign You Try It Activities, pp. 127–128.
- **Differentiated Instruction**
  Assign Challenge Yourself Projects, p. 130.

Assess

There are multiple formats for assessment provided for this lesson. These include:

- Interactive Review—Online Learning Center
- Online Self Check—Online Learning Center
- Critical Thinking Activities, p. 129
- Rubrics for Challenge Yourself Projects—Online Learning Center.
- *ExamView* for Word Lesson 4

Close

Read the Key Concepts list and ask a student to give an example of how each skill is used in a report.

Answers

- **21st Century Skills (p. 95)** Answers will vary. Students should explain their important decision.
- See Lesson Resources on the previous page for a list of Solution Files provided in this lesson.
- See answers to After You Read on p. 123 and Critical Thinking Activities on p. 129.
- **Writing Matters: Writing an Academic Report (p. 97)**
  1. The student's last name and page number.
  2. Double-spacing allows comments to be inserted.
  3. Answers should reflect feature content.
- **Writing Matters: Cite Sources in an Academic Report (p. 105)**
  1. Students could look for books in the "how-to" section of the library.
  2. Readers know where the URL begins and ends.
  3. This information is common knowledge and need not be cited.
- **Writing Matters: Creating a Business Report (p. 109)**
  1. Front matter, body, and back matter
  2. Answers should reflect feature content.
  3. Students may mention reasons for opening a branch, sales figures, etc.

Visual Presentations

Visual presentations allow students to demonstrate their understanding in a variety of visual formats. Visual presentations can be either group or individual projects.

- Model—Students make a model to demonstrate or represent a business process.
- Museum Exhibit—Students create a rich display of materials around a topic. Typical displays might include models, illustrations, photographs, videos, writings, and presentation software.
- Graph or Chart—Students analyze and represent data in a line graph, bar graph, table, or other chart format.
- Drawing—Students represent a business event or historical period through illustration, including cartoons.
- Posters and Murals—Posters and murals may include maps, time lines, diagrams, illustrations, photographs, and written explanations that reflect students' understanding of business information.
- Quilt—Students sew or draw a design for a patch-work quilt that shows a variety of perspectives, events, or issues related to a key business topic.
- Videotapes—Students film a video to show a simulation of a business event.
- Multimedia Presentation—Students create a computer-generated presentation or slide show containing business information and an analysis of the information presented.

How Are Performance Assessments Scored?

There are a variety of means used to evaluate performance tasks.

- Scoring Rubrics—A scoring rubric is a set of guidelines for assessing the quality of a process and/or product. It sets out criteria used to distinguish acceptable responses from unacceptable ones. Rubrics may be used as guidelines as the students prepare their products. They are also commonly used for peer-to-peer assessment and self-assessment.
- Models of Excellent Work—Teacher-selected models of excellent work help students set goals for their own projects.
- Student Self-Assessment—Common methods of self-assessment include ranking work in relation to the model, or using a scoring rubric. Students can write their own goals and then evaluate how well they have met the goals they set for themselves.
- Peer or Audience Assessment—Many of the performance tasks target an audience other than the teacher. If possible, peers should give feedback. Have the class create rubrics for specific projects together.
- Observation—As students carry out their performance tasks, you may want to formally observe them at work. Develop a checklist that identifies all the specific behaviors you expect students to demonstrate.
- Interviews—As a form of ongoing assessment, you may want to conduct interviews with students, asking them to analyze, explain, and assess their participation in performance tasks.

LESSON 4 Manage Lengthy Documents

Key Concepts

After completing this lesson, students will be able to:

- Format an academic report
- Create headers and footers
- Insert page numbers
- Insert and delete page and section breaks
- Insert footnotes and endnotes
- Create a table of contents
- Use Word Count and modify Document Properties
- Use different views

iCheck Lesson Resources

The following components and resources have been provided to help you teach this lesson.

- Glencoe's Lesson Planner Plus DVD
  - Create your lesson plans with a few, simple clicks
  - Access blackline masters and resources
- Teacher Resource DVD
  - Data Files for Word Lesson 4
  - Solution Files for Word Lesson 4
- *Presentation Plus!* DVD
- Online Learning Center at **glencoe.com**
  - Data Files for Word Lesson 4
  - Solution Files for Word Lesson 4
  - Interactive Review for Word Lesson 4
  - Online Self Check for Word Lesson 4
  - Challenge Yourself Project Rubrics for Word Lesson 4
- *ExamView* CD, Word Lesson 4 Test

Standards

See page 95 for a list of Microsoft Certified Application Specialist objectives and ISTE/NETS standards that students will meet by completing this activity. See page TM33 for a correlation of 21st Century Skills and Workplace Competencies.

Lesson 4	Pg #	Data File	Lesson 4	Pg #	Solution File
			EX 4-1 to 4-8	106	Academic-SF.docx
EX 4-2	99	Earthquakes.docx			
EX 4-9	107	Endnotes.docx	EX 4-9	107	Endnote-SF.docx
EX 4-10	108	Footnotes.docx	EX 4-10	108	Footnote-SF.docx
EX 4-11	110	Business.docx	EX 4-11 to 4-18	118	Business-SF.docx
EX 4-20	120	Report_Outline.docx	EX 4-20	121	Report_Outline-SF.docx
PIA 1	124	Washington.docx	PIA 1	124	Washington1-SF.docx
YTI 4	127	New Zealand.docx	YTI 4	127	Washington2-SF.docx
			YTI 5	128	Washington3-SF.docx
			BCA 6	129	w4rev6-SF.docx
SAW 7	129	Conflict.docx	SAW 7	129	Conflict7-SF.docx
Ch. Yrslf. 9	130	Marketing_Report.docx	Ch. Yrslf. 9	130	Marketing_Report9-SF.docx
			Ch. Yrslf. 10	130	Marketing_Report10-SF.docx
			Ch. Yrslf. 11	130	Marketing_Report11-SF.docx

Test-Prep Strategies

Students can follow the steps below to prepare for the standardized assessments they are required to take.

- Read about the Test—Students can familiarize themselves with the format, the types of questions, and the amount of time they will have to complete the test. Emphasize that it is very important for students to budget their time during test-taking.
- Review the Content—Consistent study will help students build knowledge and understanding. Help students review facts or skills based on test objectives.
- Practice—Provide practice, ideally with real tests, to build students' familiarity with the content, format, and timing of the real exam. Students should practice all the types of questions they will encounter on the test.
- Pace—Students should pace themselves differently depending on how the test is administered. As students practice, they should try to increase the number of questions they can answer correctly.
- Analyze Practice Results—Help students improve test-taking performance by analyzing their test-taking strengths and weaknesses. Help students identify what kinds of questions they found most difficult.

Test-Taking Strategies

It's not enough for students to learn facts and concepts—they must be able to show what they know in a variety of test-taking situations.

Objective Tests

Apply the following strategies to help students do their best on objective tests.

Multiple-Choice Questions

- Students should read the directions carefully to learn what answer the test requires—the best answer or the right answer. This is important when answer choices include "all of the above" or "none of the above."
- Advise students to watch for negative words in the questions, such as *not, except, unless, never,* and so forth.
- Students should try to mentally answer the question before reading the answer choices.
- Students should read all the answer choices and eliminate those that are obviously wrong.

True/False Questions

- It is important that students read the entire question before answering. For an answer to be true, the entire statement must be true. If one part of a statement is false, the answer should be marked false.
- Remind students to watch for words such as *all, never, every,* and *always.* Statements containing these words are often false.

Matching Questions

- Students should read through both lists before they mark any answers.
- Students should cross out answers as they use them, unless the choice can be used again.
- Using what they know about grammar can help students find the right answer. For instance, when matching a word with its definition, the definition is often the same part of speech (noun, verb, adjective, and so forth) as the word.

Lesson Planning Guide

Focus

Have students create a list of reasons why someone in their position might want to write a business letter—to thank someone, to complain, to ask for information, etc. At this time you may want students to view Word Lesson 3 of the *Presentation Plus!* DVD.

Teach

- **Step-By-Steps**
  Throughout the lesson, have students perform the Step-By-Steps to complete each exercise.
- **Troubleshooting Tips**
  Remind students to use **Undo** when using drag-and-drop to move text.
- **Differentiated Instruction**
  For kinesthetic learners, ask students to rearrange text by literally cutting and pasting parts of a newspaper article.
- **Classroom Management Tips**
  If advanced students finish early, have them create a new business letter using skills from Word Lesson 3.
- **Reading and Writing Support**
  Tell students to use a singular verb with the following pronouns: anybody, each, either, everybody, everyone, much, neither, no one, nobody, and one. *Each of the students is willing to volunteer for two hours.*

Assess

After the students finish the lesson, have them complete the following assessment activities:

- After You Read, p. 87
- Practice It Activities, pp. 88–90

Reteach

- **Independent Practice**
  Assign You Try It Activities, pp. 91–92.
- **Differentiated Instruction**
  Assign Challenge Yourself Projects, p. 94.

Assess

There are multiple formats for assessment provided for this lesson. These include:

- Interactive Review—Online Learning Center
- Online Self Check—Online Learning Center
- Critical Thinking Activities, p. 93
- Rubrics for Challenge Yourself Projects—Online Learning Center. Refer to page TM40 for an explanation of how rubrics can help students enhance self-evaluation techniques.
- *ExamView* for Word Lesson 3

Close

As a class, create a simple business letter on the board. The letter should include letterhead, the date, the recipient's name and address, salutation, the body, the closing and the sender's name and job title.

Answers

- **21st Century Skills (p. 64)** Answers will vary. Students should identify one leadership skill and explain why it is important.
- See Lesson Resources on the previous page for a list of Solution Files provided in this lesson.
- See answers to After You Read on p. 87 and Critical Thinking Activities on p. 93.
- **Writing Matters: Business Letters (p. 66)**
  1. A business letter presents information, makes requests, or responds to a query.
  2. Business letters may pass along information, ask or answer questions, etc.
  3. One must consider a company's interests and policies rather than his or her own.
- **Writing Matters: Business and Personal Business Letters (p. 67)**
  1. Block format creates a neat, clear letter.
  2. Fonts and designs will vary, but letterhead will include the company's name and address.
  3. A business letter must reflect a professional image. In a personal business letter, the address precedes the date because it has no letterhead.

Essay Tests

Essay tests require students to provide thorough and well-organized written responses, in addition to telling what they know. Help students use these strategies on essay tests.

Read the Question

The key to writing successful essay responses lies in reading and interpreting questions correctly. Teach students to identify and underline key words to guide them in understanding the question.

Plan and Write the Essay

Students should follow the writing process to develop their answer. Encourage students to follow these steps to plan and write their essays.

1. Map out an answer. Make lists, webs, or an outline to plan the response.
2. Decide on an order in which to present the main points.
3. Write an opening statement that directly responds to the essay question.
4. Write the essay. Expand on the opening statement. Support key points with specific facts, details, and reasons.
5. Write a closing statement that brings the main points together.
6. Proofread to check for spelling, grammar, and punctuation.

The table below defines purposes for different writing strategies.

Writing Strategies	
Analyze	To analyze means to examine all parts of an issue or event systematically and critically.
Classify or Categorize	To classify or categorize means to put people, things, or ideas into groups based on a common set of characteristics.
Compare and Contrast	To compare is to show how things are similar, or alike. To contrast is to show how things are different.
Describe	To describe means to present a sketch or impression. Rich details, especially details that appeal to the senses, improve descriptions.
Discuss	To discuss means to write systematically about all sides of an issue or event.
Evaluate	To evaluate means to make a judgment and support it with evidence.
Explain	To explain means to clarify or make plain.
Illustrate	To illustrate means to provide examples or to show with a picture or other graphic.
Infer	To infer means to read between the lines or to use knowledge and experience to draw a conclusion, make a generalization, or form a prediction.
Justify	To justify means to prove or to support a position with specific facts and reasons.
Predict	To predict means to tell what is likely to happen in the future, based on an understanding of prior events and behaviors.
State	To state means to present information briefly and concisely.
Summarize	To summarize means to give a brief overview of the main points of an issue or event.
Trace	To trace means to present the steps or stages in a process or event in sequential or chronological order.

Lesson Planning Guide

LESSON 3 Use Word Tools

Key Concepts

After completing this lesson, students will be able to:

- Create a business letter
- Cut, paste, copy, and move text
- Use the Thesaurus and the Research tool
- Check spelling and grammar
- Print an envelope
- Find and replace text
- Customize AutoCorrect
- Create and use templates
- Create and use Building Blocks and Quick Parts

iCheck Lesson Resources

The following components and resources have been provided to help you teach this lesson.

- Glencoe's Lesson Planner Plus DVD
  - Create your lesson plans with a few, simple clicks
  - Access blackline masters and resources
- Teacher Resource DVD
  - Data Files for Word Lesson 3
  - Solution Files for Word Lesson 3
- *Presentation Plus!* DVD
- Online Learning Center at **glencoe.com**
  - Data Files for Word Lesson 3
  - Solution Files for Word Lesson 3
  - Interactive Review for Word Lesson 3
  - Online Self Check for Word Lesson 3
  - Challenge Yourself Project Rubrics for Word Lesson 3
- *ExamView* CD, Word Lesson 3 Test

Standards

See page 64 for a list of Microsoft Certified Application Specialist objectives and ISTE/NETS standards that students will meet by completing this activity. See page TM33 for a correlation of 21st Century Skills and Workplace Competencies.

Lesson 3	Pg #	Data File	Lesson 3	Pg #	Solution File
EX 3-1	68	Business_Letter.docx	EX 3-1 to 3-10	77	Business_Letter-SF.docx
EX 3-11	78	Fay_Memo.docx	EX 3-11 to 3-13	80	Fay_Memo-SF.docx
EX 3-14	81	Profiles.docx	EX 3-14	82	Profiles-SF.docx
			EX 3-15	84	Leadership-SF.docx
EX 3-16	85	Leadership.docx	EX 3-16	85	Leadership2-SF.docx
			EX 3-17	86	Letterhead-SF.docx
PIA 1	88	Park_Letter.docx	PIA 1	88	Park_Letter1-SF.docx
			PIA 2	89	Park_Letter2-SF.docx
			PIA 3	90	Park_Letter3-SF.docx
YTI 4	91	Hillside_Letter.docx	YTI 4	91	Hillside_Letter4-SF.docx
YTI 5	92	Wkshop_Memo.docx	YTI 5	92	Wkshop_Memo5-SF.docx
			SAW 7	93	w3rev7-SF.docx
			Ch. Yrslf. 9	94	w3rev9-SF.docx
			Ch. Yrslf. 10	94	w3rev10-SF.docx
			Ch. Yrslf. 11	94	w3rev11-SF.docx

Program Assessment

Evaluation of student performance is fundamental to the teaching and learning process. Glencoe's *iCheck Series* offers a variety of ways to help you assess what your students have learned.

After You Read

The **After You Read** at the end of each lesson provides students an opportunity to recall important concepts covered in the lesson. **Reviewing Vocabulary** and **Vocabulary Activity** give students two ways to review the important new vocabulary presented in the lesson.

iCheck Self-Assessment

Throughout Glencoe's *iCheck Series* students are provided with opportunities to evaluate their own progress.

Exercises contain one or more iCheck steps, reminding students to check that their computer screen looks like the text figure.

Rubrics are provided for the **Challenge Yourself Projects**, **Academic Connections** feature, and **Portfolio Projects**. The rubrics provide students with a checklist to use to evaluate how closely they followed directions to complete the project.

Critical Thinking Activities

Three different **Critical Thinking Activities** are provided for each lesson. **Beyond the Classroom Activity** allows students to use the skills they have learned in the lesson in a scenario that takes place in a real world environment outside the classroom. **Standards at Work Activity** gives students another look at the Microsoft Certified Application Specialist standards covered in the lesson. **21st Century Skills Activity** provides students with real world practice in a business and workplace skill.

ExamView

The multitude of practices, activities, and projects in Glencoe's *iCheck Series* allow teachers to observe and assess student performance. When you wish to use traditional testing methods, turn to the *ExamView* testbank on the CD-ROM. The *ExamView Assessment Suite* allows you to build customized tests to assess student understanding of the concepts presented in Glencoe's *iCheck Series*.

Project-Based Assessment Options

Project-based assessment allows students to apply their knowledge in context. It focuses on what students know rather than on what they don't know. It is also an excellent tool to meet the needs of students with diverse learning styles, cultural backgrounds, English proficiency levels, and ability levels.

Challenge Yourself Projects offer students three opportunities to apply the skills they have acquired in the lesson in real world scenarios. Students are given minimal direction, which allows them to use their acquired knowledge as well as their creativity to complete the projects. The **Before You Begin** feature provides context for the three projects and offers the opportunity for students to reflect on the work they have completed.

Portfolio Projects are provided at the end of each unit. One project is divided into four parts, which build on one another and allow students to exhibit their mastery of the skills learned in the unit. You might want to have students create a special folder for their Portfolio Projects. These projects will provide students (and you) with a history of their progress through the course.

Lesson Planning Guide

Teach

- **Step-By-Steps**
  Throughout the lesson, have students perform the Step-By-Steps to complete each exercise.
- **Troubleshooting Tips**
  Creating and modifying tab stops can be very tricky. Consider doing a class demonstration to show students how to clear tab stops. Select the text, choose **Home>Paragraph>Dialog Box Launcher>Tabs**. In the **Tabs** dialog box, choose **Clear All**.
- **Differentiated Instruction**
  For students who have trouble remembering a lot of information, encourage them to focus on using the ScreenTips.
- **Classroom Management Tips**
  When new students join your class, have them try activities from previous lessons.
- **Reading and Writing Support**
  Tell students that when a date is written within text, commas should be used after the day and after the year. For example: *We plan to arrive in Los Angeles on June 24, 20XX, to visit with friends.*

Assess

After the students finish the lesson, have them complete the following assessment activities:

- After You Read, p. 56
- Practice It Activities, pp. 57–59

Reteach

- **Independent Practice**
  Assign You Try It Activities, pp. 60–61.
- **Differentiated Instruction**
  Assign Challenge Yourself Projects, pp 63.

Assess

There are multiple formats for assessment provided for this lesson. These include:

- Interactive Review—Online Learning Center
- Online Self Check—Online Learning Center
- Critical Thinking Activities, p. 62
- Rubrics for Challenge Yourself Projects—Online Learning Center. Refer to page TM40.
- *ExamView* for Word Lesson 2

Close

Ask students to create a short memo proposing a new photography club at your school. The memo should be addressed to all teachers.

Answers

- **21st Century Skills (p. 31)** Answers will vary. Encourage students to think about how their individual contribution helped the team.
- See Lesson Resources on the previous page for a list of Solution Files provided in this lesson.
- See answers to After You Read on p. 56 and Critical Thinking Activities on p. 62.
- **Writing Matters: Writing a Memo (p. 33)**
  1. A memo is an informal communication used to pass information along quickly to others.
  2. Guide words include TO (to whom the memo is sent), FROM (who is sending it), CC (the other people receiving a copy of the memo), DATE (date it is sent), and SUBJECT (its subject or topic).
  3. Memos provide a quick, informal way to distribute necessary information.
- **Writing Matters: Formatting a Memo (p. 34)**
  1. The heading, body, and closing.
  2. Answers may vary, but students should recognize that in a formatted memo, the sender knows exactly what information to include.
  3. Student memos should reflect the formatting described in this feature.

Base Your Teaching on Best Practices

Reading Strategies for All Students

Today's classroom is composed of students with various backgrounds, skill levels, and characteristics that affect their ability to read and process information at grade level. These students include:

- Struggling and striving readers
- English Learners (EL)
- Students with physical disabilities
- Students with learning difficulties
- Gifted and talented students

Universal Design for Learning

Every student needs to develop reading skills in order to succeed in school and in the workplace. To help meet this goal, Glencoe has developed *Inclusion in the Computer Technology Classroom.* (See page TM14.) This booklet contains reading and learning strategies designed to reach students of all performance levels and abilities. The booklet follows the Universal Design for Learning, a classroom approach that emphasizes how making a classroom inclusive helps all students—challenged or not—to learn, grow, and reach their potential.

To help make your classroom more inclusive, you may wish to adapt some of the strategies summarized on pages TM42 through TM43.

Lesson Planning Guide

LESSON 2 Format Content

Key Concepts

After completing this lesson, students will be able to:

- Work with templates
- Set margins
- Set and change tab stops
- Modify font size, style, and color
- Apply and remove styles
- Align paragraphs
- Create numbered and bulleted lists
- Create outlines

iCheck Lesson Resources

The following components and resources have been provided to help you teach this lesson.

- Glencoe's Lesson Planner Plus DVD
  - Create your lesson plans with a few, simple clicks
  - Access blackline masters and resources
- Teacher Resource DVD
  - Data Files for Word Lesson 2
  - Solution Files for Word Lesson 2
- *Presentation Plus!* DVD
  - Online Learning Center at **glencoe.com**
  - Data Files for Word Lesson 2
  - Solution Files for Word Lesson 2
  - Interactive Review for Word Lesson 2
  - Online Self Check for Word Lesson 2
  - Challenge Yourself Project Rubrics for Word Lesson 2
- *ExamView* CD, Word Lesson 2 Test

Standards

See page 31 for a list of Microsoft Certified Application Specialist objectives and ISTE/NETS standards that students will meet by completing this activity. See page TM33 for a correlation of 21st Century Skills and Workplace Competencies.

Lesson 2	Pg #	Data File	Lesson 2	Pg #	Solution File
EX 2-1	35	Schedule_Memo.docx	EX 2-1 to 2-2	37	Schedule_Memo-SF.docx
EX 2-3	38	Memo.docx	EX 2-3 to 2-7	42	Memo-SF.docx
EX 2-8	43	Meeting_Notes.docx	EX 2-8 to 2-13	49	Meeting_Notes-SF.docx
EX 2-14	50	Meeting_Outline.docx	EX 2-14	50	Meeting_Outline-SF.docx
EX 2-15	51	Flyer.docx	EX 2-15 to 2 -19	55	Flyer-SF.docx
PIA 1	57	Fonts.docx	PIA 1	57	Fonts1-SF.docx
PIA 2	58	Paragraphs.docx	PIA 2	58	Paragraphs2-SF.docx
PIA 3	59	PI_Memo.docx	PIA 3	59	PI_Memo3-SF.docx
YTI 4	60	Volunteers.docx	YTI 4	60	Volunteers4-SF.docx
YTI 5	61	Yearbook.docx	YTI 5	61	Yearbook5-SF.docx
			BCA 6	62	w2rev6-SF.docx
			SAW 7	62	w2rev7-SF.docx
			21stC 8	62	w2rev8-SF.docx
			Ch. Yslf. 9	63	w2rev9-SF.docx
			Ch. Yslf. 10	63	w2rev10-SF.docx
			Ch. Yslf. 11	63	w2rev11-SF.docx

Focus

Ask students if they have ever written or received a memo. You might want to explain to students that memos are used for communication within an organization. Consider reviewing with students the parts of a memo: the heading, the body, and the closing.

At this time you may want students to view Word Lesson 2 of the *Presentation Plus!* DVD.

EL and LEP Strategies

Glencoe's *iCheck Series* has integrated many reading strategies and study skills to help both proficient and struggling readers process the text. A partial definition of Limited English Proficiency (as found in Title IX) includes students "whose difficulties in speaking, reading, writing, or understanding the English language may be sufficient to deny the individual the ability to meet the state's 'proficient' level of performance, to successfully achieve in the classroom where the language of instruction is English, or the opportunity to participate fully in society."

An English Learner may be defined as a student whose "native use is not English; . . . who comes from an environment where a language other than English has had a significant impact on the individual's level of English proficiency."

You may wish to adapt the following Before, During, and After reading strategies to help students master the key terms and the academic vocabulary associated with the step-by-step instructions and the activities in this text.

Before Reading Activities and Strategies

- Conduct verbal walkthroughs of the lessons, including picture walkthroughs, predicting the text, and verbal summaries. Teach text features: help students learn where to find important vocabulary and concepts by pointing out vocabulary lists and important key terms that are bolded and highlighted.
- Encourage students to verbalize what they know and can say about the topic as you preview the subject matter. Ask students to restate the task to confirm they understand the goal or assignment.
- Tap prior knowledge. Assign students a question about the new unit/topic to ask about at home (in student's native language).
- Have students play "Password." Student A gives a definition or describes a vocabulary word. Student B tries to guess what the word is.
- Create pronunciation exercises. Give students the opportunity to hear and practice the pronun ciation of vocabulary items. This will build their aural as well as their visual memory of the word.

During Reading Activities and Strategies

- Use a *paired-reading* strategy where a proficient and struggling reader take turns reading aloud from vocabulary lists or introductory text.
- Break reading into "chunks." Ask students to orally summarize key concepts at regular intervals.
- Revisit vocabulary words introduced at the beginning of the lesson.
- Create an interesting visual of important words (a "word splash") from the new lesson, as an overhead transparency and as a handout. Then discuss words students know and predict the meaning of new ones.
- Provide native language support. Allow students to discuss or clarify new vocabulary items in their native language with same-language peers.
- Label figures and graphs. Use figures and graphs from the text, delete significant text and have students label them.

Lesson Planning Guide

Teach

- **Step-By-Steps**
  Throughout the lesson, have students perform the Step-By-Steps to complete each exercise.
- **Troubleshooting Tips**
  If a document does not print, check to see where the print job was sent. Have the student choose **File>Print** and make sure that the correct printer is selected.
- **Differentiated Instruction**
  Occasionally read the Step-By-Step instructions aloud to the class. Students will enjoy the variety, and this exercise will help auditory learners.
- **Classroom Management Tips**
  If you have a wide range of abilities in your class, consider seating students who work quickly with students who are struggling. Ask the skilled students to help the less skilled students.
- **Reading and Writing Support**
  Remind students that when keying data they should always space once after a period, question mark, or exclamation point at the end of a sentence.

Assess

After the students finish the lesson, have them complete the following activities:

- After You Read, p. 23
- Practice It Activities, pp. 24–26

Reteach

- **Independent Practice**
  Assign students the You Try It Activities on pages 27–28.
- **Differentiated Instruction**
  Assign students the Challenge Yourself Projects on page 30.

Assess

There are multiple formats for assessment provided for this lesson. These include:

- Interactive Review—Online Learning Center
- Online Self Check—Online Learning Center
- Critical Thinking Activities, p. 29
- Rubrics for Challenge Yourself Projects—Online Learning Center. Refer to page TM40 for an explanation of how rubrics can help students enhance performance and self-evaluation techniques.
- *ExamView* for Word Lesson 1

Close

As a class, have students create a list of five skills in this lesson that allow the students to make changes to a document. Possible answers include keying text, correcting spelling, deleting text, and Undo.

Answers

- **21st Century Skills (p. 3)** Answers will vary. Encourage students to think about how the skills they will learn may help them to achieve goals.
- See Lesson Resources on the previous page for a list of Solution Files provided in this lesson.
- See answers to After You Read on p. 23 and Critical Thinking Activities on p. 29.
- **Writing Matters: Proofread to Avoid Mistakes (p. 22)**
  1. a. Sales increased from $100,000 to $150,000.
     b. Maria said they're getting new computers in their office.
     c. My supervisor, Julie Long, is in Boston on a business trip.
     d. Hard work has its rewards.
     e. Many jobs in the United States require computer skills.
  2. Answers will vary, but students should understand that errors make a document seem unprofessional and may affect accuracy.

- Use bilingual dictionaries. Spanish speaking students who come to high school from other countries are usually literate in their first language and can make efficient use of bilingual dictionaries. Students can also use the *Glosario* at the back of the text.
- Provide opportunity to have directions read aloud to assist with reading comprehension.
- Provide checkpoints for long-term assignments.
- Use Two Column Notes. (Possible headings include Main Idea/Details; Questions/Answers; Problem/Solution; Stated/Inferred; Fact/Opinion, etc.)

After Reading Activities and Strategies

- Orally summarize to review what was read.
- Ask and respond to written questions about the text, including brief constructed response and/or selected response items that have been adapted for the student's proficiency level.
- Graphic organizers provide visual reinforcement for new vocabulary items and help students organize and remember new material. Students can create a visual dictionary using *Alphaboxes* to collect terms, or students may draw buttons to mimic computer application functions.
- Allow additional time to complete research assignments.

Academic Vocabulary

Academic English and academic vocabulary are two examples of ways that students can learn more reading skills in the classroom. *Glencoe iCheck Series Microsoft Office 2007* features both academic English and academic vocabulary.

What Is Academic English?

by Robin Scarcella, Ph.D.

Academic English is the language commonly used in business and education. It is the language used in academics, and courts of law. It is the type of English used in professional books, including textbooks, and it contains specific linguistic features that are associated with all disciplines. Proficiency in reading and using academic English is strongly related to long-term success in all parts of life.

What Is Academic Vocabulary?

By the time children have completed elementary school, they must have acquired the knowledge needed to understand academic vocabulary. How many words should they acquire to be able to access their textbooks? A basic 2,000-word vocabulary of high-frequency words makes up 87% of the words. Three percent of the remaining words are technical words. The remaining 2% are low-frequency words. There may be as many as 123,000 low-frequency words in academic texts.

Why Should Students Learn Academic Vocabulary?

English Language Learners who have mastered a basic 2,000-word vocabulary are ready to acquire the majority of general words found in their texts and on standardized tests.

Knowledge of academic words, combined with continued acquisition of general words, can significantly boost an English Learner's comprehension level of academic texts. English Learners who learn and practice these words before they graduate from high school are likely to be able to master academic material with more confidence and speed. They waste less time and effort in guessing words than those students who know only the basic 2,000 words that characterize general conversation.

LESSON 1 Create a Document

Key Concepts

After completing this lesson, students will be able to:

- Identify parts of the Word screen
- Name and save a document
- Key text into a document
- Edit text
- Print a document
- Close a document

iCheck Lesson Resources

The following components and resources have been provided to help you teach this lesson.

- Glencoe's Lesson Planner Plus DVD
  - Create your lesson plans with a few, simple clicks
  - Access blackline masters and resources
- Teacher Resource DVD
  - Data Files for Word Lesson 1
  - Solution Files for Word Lesson 1
- *Presentation Plus!* DVD
- Online Learning Center at **glencoe.com**
  - Data Files for Word Lesson 1
  - Solution Files for Word Lesson 1
  - Interactive Review for Word Lesson 1
  - Online Self Check for Word Lesson 1
  - Challenge Yourself Project Rubrics for Word Lesson 1
- *ExamView* CD, Word Lesson 1 Test

Standards

See page 3 for a list of Microsoft Certified Application Specialist objectives and ISTE/NETS standards that students will meet by completing this lesson. See page TM33 for a correlation of 21st Century Skills and Workplace Competencies.

Lesson 1	Pg #	Data File	Lesson 1	Pg #	Solution File
			Ex 1-6 to 1-12	16	w1-6-SF.docx
EX 1-13	17	Goals.docx	EX 1-14 to 1-17	21	Goals-SF.docx
			PIA 1	24	w1rev1-SF.docx
			PIA 2	25	w1rev2-SF.docx
			PIA 3	26	w1rev3-SF.docx
YTI 4	27	Letter.docx	YTI 4	27	w1rev4-SF.docx
CYP9	30	jobs.docx			

Focus

Students should understand that simple documents are the foundation for more involved documents. Students will learn more about the different kinds of documents in upcoming lessons. You may want to bring in a variety of word processing documents, such as memos, formal business letters, annual reports, order forms, invoices, solicitation letters, and newsletters. Ask students to discuss the main features and purposes of each document.

At this time you may want students to view Word Lesson 1 on the *Presentation Plus!* DVD. This presentation program uses an engaging format to introduce students to the key concepts of this lesson.

Academic Vocabulary and Academic English in the Computer Education Classroom

Teachers can provide their students with rich samples of academic vocabulary and help students understand the academic English of their text. To develop academic English, students must have already acquired a large amount of basic proficiency in the grammar of everyday English.

Academic English should be taught within contexts that make sense. Academic English arises not only from a knowledge of linguistic code and cognition but also from social practices in which academic English is used to accomplish communicative goals. The acquisition of academic vocabulary and grammar is necessary to advance the development of academic English.

Tips for Teaching Academic Vocabulary:

- **Expose Students to Academic Vocabulary**—Students learn academic vocabulary through use and in reading content. You do not need to call attention to all academic words students are learning because they will acquire them subconsciously.
- **Do Not Correct Students' Mistakes When Using Academic Vocabulary**—All vocabulary understanding and spelling errors are developmental and will disappear once the student reads more.
- **Help Students Decode the Words Themselves**—Once students learn the alphabet, they should be able to decode words. Decoding each word they do not recognize will help them more than trying to focus on sentence structure. Once they can recognize words, they can read "authentic" texts.
- **Do Not Ignore the English Learner in This Process**—English Learners can learn academic vocabulary before they are completely fluent in spoken English.
- **Helping Students Build Academic Vocabulary Leads to Broader Learning**—Students who have mastered the basic academic vocabulary are ready to continue acquiring words from the rest of the vocabulary groups. Use the Internet to find lists of appropriate vocabulary word lists.

There are a number of guidelines that teachers can follow when teaching academic English and vocabulary:

Guidelines for Teaching Academic Vocabulary

1. Use direct and planned instruction.
2. Employ models that have increasingly difficult language.
3. Focus attention on form by pointing out linguistic features of words.
4. Provide practice opportunities.
5. Motivate student interest and self-confidence.
6. Provide instructional feedback.
7. Use assessment tools on a regular basis.

Unit 1 Word Overview

Focus

Motivation

- **Why It Matters** Review the Why It Matters feature on page 1. Discuss with students how being able to use Word 2007 will help them at both school and work.
- **Go Online: Real World Connection Activity** Have students complete the Go Online: Real World Connection Activity on page 1 to learn more about how different organizations use word processing applications.
- **Careers and Technology** The Careers and Technology feature on page 2 illustrates the high demand for computer jobs. Discuss with students how learning computer applications will affect their career paths.
- **Answers to Reading Check (p. 2)**
  1. Word processing skills are needed in the health care field for tasks varying from filling out forms and reports to submitting invoices and payments.
  2. Approximately 38%.

Teach

Guided Practice

- ***Presentation Plus! PowerPoint Presentations*** A special PowerPoint presentation has been provided to help you introduce Word, including how people use Word at both school and work.

Independent Practice

Additional exercises and projects are available at the book's Online Learning Center at **glencoe.com**.

- **Additional Exercises**
  - Microsoft Word
  - Microsoft Excel
  - Microsoft Access
  - Microsoft PowerPoint
  - Microsoft Outlook
  - Windows Vista
- **Additional Projects**
  - Real-World Business Applications
  - Present and Publish Projects
  - Academic Projects

Assess

- **Portfolio Project** The Portfolio Project on pages 196-199 allows students to complete a business-oriented project. Students can complete all four parts, or focus on only one part of the project. Students can print copies of their projects, or create an electronic copy for their portfolios.
- **Rubrics** Rubrics are provided to help students and teachers assess the Portfolio Projects. Rubrics can be accessed on the Online Learning Center at **glencoe.com**.

Unit 1 Closer	Pg #	Data File
Portfolio Proj. pt. 2	197	Schedule.docx

Reteach

- **Academic Connections** Review the feature on page 194 with students to show how the technical skills developed in this unit can be used to complete an academic project.

Assess

- ***ExamView® Assessment Suite*** **Word Unit 1 Test**

Close

- **Ethics in Action** Have students read the feature on page 195 and complete the questions:

  Answers to You Decide and **Application Activity (p. 195)**
  1. Answers may vary, but students should include the four questions listed under Making Ethical Decisions.
  2. Answers will vary. Students should be prepared to explain their decisions using the criteria discusses in the feature.
  3. Answers will vary. Students' codes should have a business aspect and students should be prepared to explain their code using the criteria discussed in the feature.

Teaching Strategies

The following strategies can be used to address the diverse needs of students in a computer education classroom.

Self-Directed Study

Self-directed study, sometimes called independent study, can be a useful addition to your computer applications class. If you have students who consistently finish early or are always ahead of the rest of the class, you might consider helping them plan a self-directed study project.

There are some guidelines you will need to discuss with your students before allowing them to work on their own. To effectively complete a self-directed study course or project, students must:

- be self-disciplined and motivated to work on their own.
- organize their time and materials to successfully complete the assignment.
- complete and turn in assignments when they are due.
- discuss their progress with you on a regular basis.

If students feel that they can comply with these requirements, they may be good candidates for a self-directed study course or project.

Peer Teaching

Peer teaching occurs when one child instructs another child of the same or similar age. In the classroom, peer teaching can take different forms. In some cases, students with a high need level are trained as peer teachers or tutors. Typically, though, students who are "experts" in certain skills or subject areas are trained to teach students who need additional or one-on-one help. Peer teaching can have a number of benefits—from the obvious learning of academic skills to the development of social relationships.

In the computer applications classroom, peer teaching can be utilized in a number of different ways. Advanced or gifted students can be challenged to share their knowledge and expertise with students who may need additional help. English Learners can also benefit from peer teaching. Even if the "teacher" doesn't speak the learner's language, the one-on-one help offered will benefit the English Learner.

New Student Strategies

Peer teaching can be an effective new student strategy. As new students enter your class, pair them with students who have a good understanding of the material being covered. Throughout this *Teacher Annotated Edition*, there are numerous annotations titled **New Student Strategy**. These strategies will give you point-of-use ideas to help you focus on the needs of students who are new to your computer applications class.

Integrating Ethics

As your students engage in business transactions and act as employees and managers, they will encounter ethical dilemmas requiring sound decision-making skills. Students should understand that unethical behavior is often perceived as unethical only after the action or decision has been taken or made.

The purpose of introducing ethics into your instruction is to help your students integrate ethical considerations and basic values into their decision-making process. Students are

What's New in Microsoft Office 2007

New Features of Access 2007

- **Create Databases with the Ribbon**
  The new Ribbon feature groups all tools together by feature and functionality and places all frequently used commands in an area where users can easily access them.
- **Use the Getting Started Page**
  The Getting Started page is a new addition to Access. It appears everytime Access 2007 is started. This page includes a section of professionally designed database templates for tracking contacts, events, and other types of data.
- **Preview Form Layouts**
  The new Layout View allows you to make design changes while you view data in a form or report. Layout View allows you to easily rearrange fields, columns, and rows.
- **Use the Field List Pane**
  The Field List Pane allows you to drag fields from multiple tables into your database so that you join tables and improve query results.
- **Export Data**
  You can export data to a PDF or XPS file format for printing, publishing, and distribution. You can also import and export data to Word or Excel.
- **Use Enhanced Filtering and Sorting Features**
  Filtering and sorting records has become easier with the new enhanced features. You can now focus on a specific set of values in the database when you sort and filter data.
- **Use the Split Form**
  The new Split Form enables you to view both Datasheet View and a Form View at the same time. You can set properties in Access to view forms on the top, bottom, left, or right.

New Features of PowerPoint 2007

- **Create Presentations with the Ribbon**
  Presentation tools are grouped together by task so that users can access frequently used commands.
- **Create Custom Slide Layouts**
  You can create your own custom layouts with unlimited numbers of placeholders and elements, as well as multiple slide masters.
- **Use New Text Options**
  New character styles provide several professional-looking options. New text styles include all caps, small caps, strikethrough options, and various 3-D effects.
- **View Slides in Presenter View**
  You can use the thumbnails in this to move slides out of sequence and create a customized presentation. Speaker's notes appear in large, clear type so that you can use them as a script.
- **Share and Reuse Slides with the Slide Library**
  The Slide Library keeps presentations up to date by linking all slides in a presentation with those in the Library. If a slide is updated, the Slide Library will prompt you to make updates.
- **Use the Live Preview Feature**
  The Live Preview feature enables the user to preview a style or theme before it is placed into a presentation. By rolling over available styles and colors, the user can see what the slides will look like if created in that format.
- **Presentation Clean Up**
  Use the presentation clean up feature to check for and remove comments, hidden text, and personal information before giving a final presentation.

directed to develop a process for considering both the business and the ethical ramifications of a decision before that decision is made. Even though basic values are set in childhood, people do make different decisions as they gain knowledge and insight.

Teaching Ethics

Educational instruction of ethics as a discipline is an aspect of teaching that is commonly ignored. Yet, you do know how to make decisions and most likely have had personal experiences with decisions involving ethical ramifications. You need not be an ethics theorist to incorporate discussions of ethical actions into your instruction.

The Ethical Decision-Making Model

The ethical decision-making model described below will help your students analyze a situation, evaluate alternatives, consider ramifications of each decision, and choose among the alternatives. This eight-step model is one possible approach to making an ethical decision. (The following model is based on the work of S. Lovey, 1998.) You might have students use this model when you assign the **Ethics in Action** features at the end of each unit in Glencoe's *iCheck Series*.

Step 1: Identify the problem. State it clearly and briefly.

Step 2: Identify the potential issues involved.

Step 3: Review relevant ethical guidelines. What is the school or work policy on this subject?

Step 4: Know relevant laws and regulations. Are there any legal issues involved?

Step 5: Obtain consultation. Discuss the dilemma or problem with others whose opinions you respect.

Step 6: Consider possible and probable courses of action.

Step 7: List the consequences of the probable courses of action. List all possible effects, not just the most likely.

Step 8: Decide on what appears to be the best course of action.

You may wish to share the **"SELF"** ethical decision-making mnemonic with students. Would your decision withstand **S**crutiny by friends, family, and coworkers? Does your decision **E**nsure that you comply with known laws and policies? Does your decision show **L**eadership through integrity and accountability? Finally, is your decision **F**air to yourself and to others?

Generate Results *with* New Technology

New Features of Word 2007

- **Format with the Ribbon**
  The new Ribbon feature groups style and format tools together and allows you to automatically preview formatting changes.
- **Work with Building Blocks**
  Building Blocks were created to place preformatted information into documents. A company can save its logo and address as a Building Block address and attach it to a document without having to key it in.
- **Use the Contextual Spelling Checker**
  The spelling checker can now find and flag contextual spelling errors. This option helps in finding mistakes involving similar words, such as "there" and "their."
- **Compare and Combine Documents**
  It is now easier to track and review changes in a document. The new layout allows you to compare and combine documents so that you can preview what has been deleted, moved, or inserted.
- **Add a Digital Signature**
  You can provide authenticity to your documents by adding a digital signature. The signature can either be invisible or on a signature line in the document.
- **Use SmartArt Graphics**
  The new diagramming tool helps create visually appealing graphics in a document. Some of its capabilities include 3-D shapes, transparencies, and drop shadows.

New Features of Excel 2007

- **Work with the Ribbon**
  The Ribbon feature groups all tools together by task and places all frequently used data functions and commands in one area.
- **Manage Large Amounts of Data**
  An Excel 2007 worksheet contains 1,048,576 rows and 16,384 columns. This is 1,500% more rows and 6,300% more columns than what was available in Excel 2003.
- **Recover Damaged Files**
  The Office software is designed to save files in a compressed, segmented format. This feature reduces file size and makes it easier to recover damaged or corrupted files.
- **Format with Themes and Styles**
  The data in your Excel 2007 worksheet can easily be formatted by applying a theme and style to the information.
- **Write Formulas**
  The Formula Bar now automatically resizes to fit long, complex formulas. This prevents formulas from overlapping other cell material.
- **Add Charts and Graphics**
  New enhanced graphics and charting capabilities give visual appeal to data.
- **Check Compatibility**
  You can check an Excel 2007 workbook and see if it contains features or elements that are not compatible with earlier versions of Excel. Now you can make any changes necessary for backward compatibility.

Research-Based Classroom Solutions

Classroom Inclusion Strategies

The current emphasis on accountability for student achievement affects you as a teacher of computer applications because reinforcement of basic literacy skills is a responsibility shared by all educators. Glencoe's *iCheck Series* provides teachers and students with a variety of activities that reinforce the literacy strategies listed below.

STRATEGIES	iCHECK OFFICE 2007 ACTIVITIES	LOCATION
Identify Essential Course Content		
• Provide a course outline. • Have students use lesson organizers. • Use guided notes and handouts in class.	• Unit Contents • Key Concepts • Reading Guide • Rubrics	• Unit opener • Lesson opener • Online Learning Center
Use a Variety of Instructional Methods and Groupings		
• Have peers teach peers. • Use cooperative learning. • Allow small group discussions.	Annotations throughout the *Teacher Annotated Edition* direct the teacher to pair students with a classmate for a variety of activities.	
Provide Information in Multiple Formats		
• Demonstrate ideas verbally, physically, and in writing. • Use pictures, posters, and other visuals to convey main ideas. • Use color to help students identify important ideas and organize information. • Use graphic organizers to help students visualize relationships among information.	• Careers and Technology • Reading circle • Step-By-Steps • Figures • Key Terms • PowerPoint presentation	• Unit opener • Unit opener • Exercises • *Presentation Plus!* PowerPoint Presentations
Use Multiple Methods of Assessment		
• Self-assessment • Multimedia presentations • Student portfolios	• iCheck • Challenge Yourself Projects • Portfolio Projects • Rubrics	• Exercises • Lesson review • Unit review • Online Learning Center
Use Technology		
• Put content online so students can use screen readers to access information. • Use text to speech software. • Use CDs and multimedia to provide multiple ways to access information.	• PowerPoint presentations • Various online activities for students • The very nature of this course—Computer Applications—requires students to use technology throughout the class period.	• *Presentation Plus!* PowerPoint Presentations • Online Learning Center

Guidelines for the Classroom

Publishing Web Sites

Some activities encourage students to publish Web sites. Please review the options available at your school for publishing Web sites. Because of the potential legal ramifications of students publishing Web sites under the school's name or auspices, it is critical that students understand their responsibility to avoid inappropriate content. You may want to review appropriate and inappropriate content guidelines with students before they publish any Web sites.

Suggested Classroom Resources

Students may want to use the following materials for reference when learning skills and completing activities and projects.

- Computer catalogs and magazines
- User guides for computers and software

Using the Data Files

To complete some activities and projects in this book, Data Files are required.

- When you see the Data File icon, locate needed files *before* beginning the activity.

- Data Files are available on the Teacher Resource DVD and on the book Web site at **glencoe.com**.

Teachers need to review how best to distribute these files to students. Some options may include:

1. Saving the files in a folder on the school network
2. Posting the files on the teacher's course Web site
3. Saving the files to the hard drive of each computer with read-only access (students can resave file to their location as a writeable file)

A chart outlining each data file and where it is used in the textbook is included on pages TM20 through TM23.

Using Equipment

Because of the wide variety of manufacturers, platforms, and configurations, this text does not discuss specific ways to use technology tools such as scanners and digital cameras. Review the operating procedures for any technology tools that you have available in the classroom, and make sure that students understand how to use this equipment responsibly. Also, consider posting operating instructions or user manuals for hardware and software in a convenient location for easy reference.

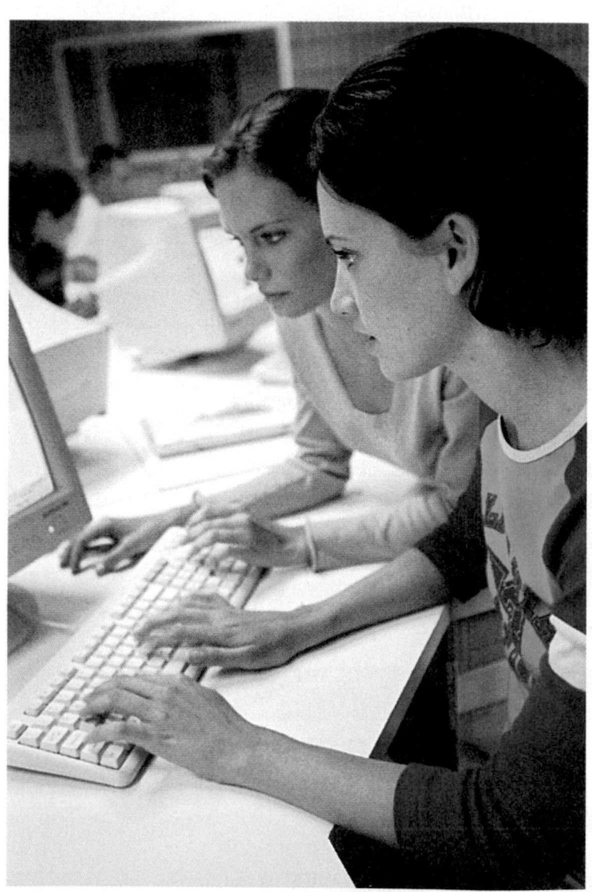

Deliver Effective Instruction *in the* Computer Application Classroom

Students will use computer technology throughout the course. Help students demonstrate responsible technology use by discussing the following guidelines with them. (These guidelines are also discussed in features throughout the student edition.)

Using the Internet

To enhance or enrich activities and projects, students may be instructed to access Web sites. Where possible, suggested Web sites are provided in the student edition and in this *Teacher Annotated Edition.* Although suggested live sites have been thoroughly reviewed, they are not under the control of Glencoe/McGraw-Hill. Site content and URLs may also change over time. We therefore strongly encourage teachers to preview these sites before assigning their students individual activities.

Acceptable Use Policies

Teachers should also check with their schools to learn about their district's acceptable use policy (AUP). Most AUPs provide a statement of responsibilities of educators, parents, and students for using the Internet, guidelines for appropriate online behavior, and a description of the consequences should the school district's AUP be violated. Teachers, parents, guardians, and students should all be familiar with their school's AUP before any Internet activities are assigned.

Downloading Files

Students are sometimes instructed to locate and download files to complete activities and projects. Review your school's policies on downloading files from the Internet. If students will not have that capability, supply appropriate files and let students know where to find them. Students should always review a Web site's Terms of Use before downloading and using any files.

Copyright Guidelines

When necessary, students should include copyright information and credit lines on their pages to acknowledge their sources. Some general points include:

1. It is illegal and unethical to use a person's or company's intellectual property without first obtaining their permission.
2. A person or company does not have to obtain a copyright notice to have rights over intellectual property. Therefore, even if a site does not have a copyright notice, the content included on that site is still protected.
3. Another person's or company's intellectual property can only be used if written permission is obtained to use this property, or if it is stated on the Web site that all content is royalty free and can be used without permission.
4. If an individual places a copyright notice on a work, then he or she must defend that work if he or she knows that the work is being used without permission. Failure to defend a copyright can result in the loss of that copyright.

Web Strategies

In today's world, computer applications teachers must teach students how to find and evaluate sources on their own. Many of the suggestions here will provide students with tips to use when they need to do research on the Internet.

What's Available on the Internet?

You can use the following online resources to support student learning.

Teacher-Focused Web Sites These Web sites provide teaching tips, detailed lesson plans, and links to other sites of interest to teachers.

Statistics Government Web sites are rich depositories for statistics of all kinds.

Reference Sources Students can access encyclopedias, dictionaries, atlases, and other reference books, as well as journal and newspaper articles.

News Traditional media sources, including television, radio, newspapers, and news magazines, sponsor Internet sites that provide news updates, in-depth news coverage, and analysis.

Topical Information Among the most numerous Web sites are those organized around a particular topic or issue, such as the stock market.

Organizations Many organizations post Web sites that contain a variety of information.

How Do I Teach Students to Evaluate Web Sites?

You can teach students to critically evaluate Web resources using the questions and criteria below.

1. **Purpose:** What is the purpose of the Web site or Web page? Is it an informational Web page, a news site, a business site, an advocacy site, or a personal Web page?
2. **URL:** What is the URL, or Web address? Where does the site originate? URLs with .edu and .gov domain names indicate that the site is connected to an educational institution or a government agency, respectively. A .com suffix usually means that a commercial or business interest hosts the Web site. A nonprofit organization's Web address may end with .org.
3. **Authority:** Who wrote the material or created the Web site? What qualifications does the person or group have? Who has ultimate responsibility for the site? If the site is sponsored by an organization, are the organization's goals clearly stated?
4. **Accuracy:** How reliable is the information? Are sources listed so that they can be verified? Is the Web page free from surface errors in spelling and grammar?
5. **Objectivity:** If the site presents itself as an informational site, is the material free from bias? If there is advertising, is it easy to tell the difference between the ads and other features? If the site mixes factual information with opinion, can you spot the difference between the two?
6. **Currency:** When was the information first placed on the Web? Is the site updated on a regular basis? When was the last revision?
7. **Coverage:** What topics are covered on the Web site? What is the depth of coverage? Are all sides of an issue presented? How does the coverage compare with other Web and print sources?

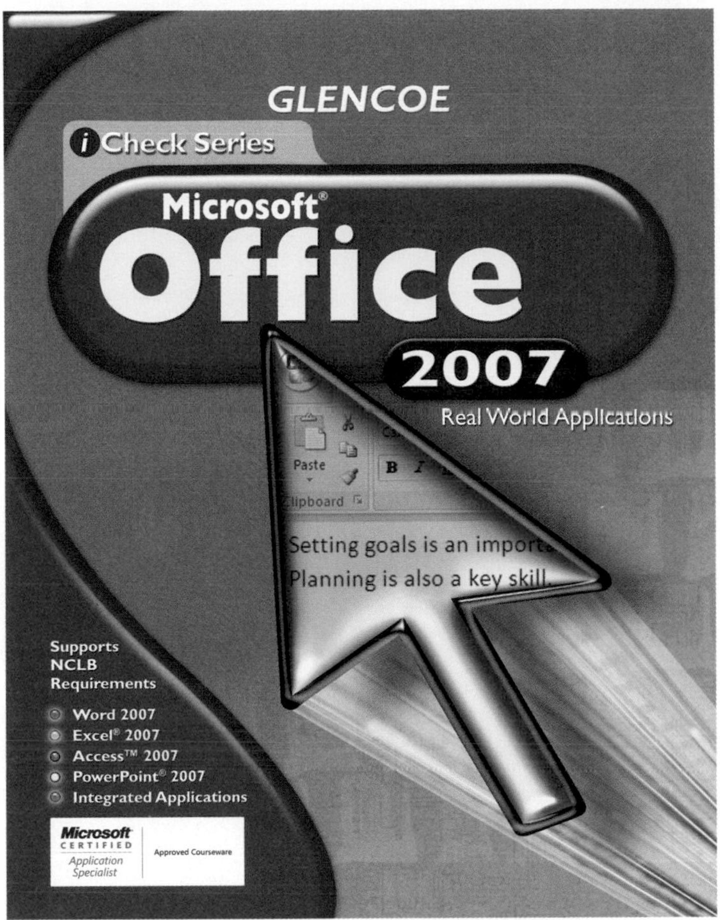

GLENCOE
iCheck Series
Microsoft®
Office
2007
Real World Applications
Setting goals is an import
Planning is also a key skill.
Supports
NCLB
Requirements
Word 2007
Excel® 2007
Access™ 2007
PowerPoint® 2007
Integrated Applications
Microsoft CERTIFIED
Application Specialist
Approved Courseware

Lead Consultants

C. Jacqueline Schultz, Ph.D.
Career and Business Education Instructor
Warrensville Heights High School
Warrensville Heights, Ohio

Linda Wooldridge, M.B.A.
School of Information Technology Instructor
Santa Susana High School
Simi Valley, California

The McGraw·Hill Companies

Printed in the United States of America

Send all inquiries to:

Glencoe/McGraw-Hill
21600 Oxnard Street, Suite 500
Woodland Hills, CA 91367

MHID 0-07-878605-3 (Student Edition)
ISBN 978-0-07-878605-1 (Student Edition)
MHID 0-07-880260-1 (Teacher Annotated Edition)
ISBN 978-0-07-880260-7 (Teacher Annotated Edition)

1 2 3 4 5 6 7 8 9 043/027 11 10 09 08 07

Advisory Review Board

Erik Amerikaner
Oak Park High School
Oak Park, California

Elisa Bunn
East Coweta High School
Sharpsburg, Georgia

Gordon S. DeFacis
Mifflinburg Area High School
Mifflinburg, Pennsylvania

Dawn Johnston
Northwestern High School
Kokomo, Indiana

Judie Reasons
Peabody High School
Trenton, Tennessee

David Salem
John Dewey High School
Brooklyn, New York

Marilyn L. Satterwhite
Professor, Business and Technology Division
Danville Area Community College
Danville, Illinois

Dan Shuster
Royal High School
Simi Valley, California

Kelley Todd
Van Buren High School
Van Buren, Arkansas

Reviewers

Marsha Bass
Art Institute of Pittsburg
Elkhart, Indiana

Juana Benson
Guthrie High School
Guthrie, Oklahoma

Doug Bergman
Porter-Gaud School
Charleston, South Carolina

Robert Bloom
Chaparral High School
Las Vegas, Nevada

Scott Ciarlone
Cohoes High School
Cohoes, New York

Earl W. Cobb
Hilldale High School
Muskogee, Oklahoma

Suzi Cotton
Pea Ridge High School
Pea Ridge, Arkansas

Daryl Daniels
New Milford High School
New Milford, Connecticut

Carol Evans
Adolfo Camarillo High School
Camarillo, California

Leah Franco
Comanche High School
Comanche, Texas

Lori C. Houck
Anderson County High
Clinton, Tennessee

Margaret Irby
Permian High School
Odessa, Texas

Regina W. Johnson
McBee High School
McBee, South Carolina

Robert Kane
Newton North High School
Newtonville, Massachusetts

Dorothy Lewis
Dougherty Comprehensive High School
Albany, Georgia

Angie Marquart
Clear Fork High School
Bellville, Ohio

Linda Robinson
Winter Haven High School
Winter Haven, Florida

Ann Rosborough
Decatur Middle School
Indianapolis, Indiana

Joan Staley
Grayslake High School
Grayslake, Illinois

Gwin D. Wyatt
Murrah High School
Jackson, Mississippi

PHOTO CREDITS

TM41 Jonathan Nourok/PhotoEdit; **TM46** Jose Luis Palaez, Inc./Corbis; **TM50** Richard G./StockImage/Age Fotostock; **vi** Esbin Anderson/Age Fotostock America, Inc.; **viii** Royalty-free/Masterfile; **x** Royalty-Free/Alamey; **xi** Charles Gupton/CORBIS; **xiv** Michael Newman/PhotoEdit; **xv** Michael Newman/PhotoEdit; **xvii** RyanStock/Getty Images; **xxiv** Royalty-free/Photodisc/Getty Images; **1** Royalty-free/Creatas/Jupiterimages; **3** Roy Morsch/CORBIS; **22** Royalty-free/Andrew Woodley/Alamy Images; **30** Rob Crandall/The Image Works; **31** Paul Barton/CORBIS; **33** Superstock; **63** Steve Skjold/PhotoEdit; **64** Jon Riley/Getty Images; **66** Royalty-free/Francisco Cruz/SuperStock; **94** Royalty-free/Adam Smith/Superstock; **95** Royalty-free/Digital Vision/Getty Images; **130** Jose Louis Pelaez, Inc./Corbis; **131** Jose Luis Pelaez, Inc/CORBIS; **161** Cleve Bryant/ PhotoEdit; **162** Royalty-free/Masterfile; **185** RNT Productions/Corbis; **193** Jose Luis Pelaez, Inc./Corbis; **194** Michael Newman/PhotoEdit; **196** Anna Lundgren/SuperStock; **197** James Marshall/CORBIS; **198** Yellow Dog Productions/Getty Images; **202** Walter Hodges/Getty Images; **225** Rob Glodmen/Getty Images; **226** Robert E. Daemmrich/Getty Images; **240** Doug Menuez/Getty Images; **248** Alexander Walter/Getty Images; **249** Klaus Lahnstein/Getty Images; **273** Royalty-free/Hemera/Images.com; **281** Ron Fehling/Masterfile; **282** Esbin-Anderson/Age Fotostock America, Inc.; **312** Bob Daemmrich/PhotoEdit; **313** Jeff Maloney/Getty Images; **341** Jose Luis Pelaez Inc./Corbis; **342** Mug Shots/Corbis; **344** David Young-Wolff/Getty Images; **345** David Young-Wolff/PhotoEdit; **346** Jeff Greenberg/Age Fotostock America, Inc.; **348** Mina Chapman/CORBIS; **350** Royalty-free/MedioImages/SuperStock; **371** Michael Newman/PhotoEdit; **379** Dana White/PhotoEdit; **380** Royalty Free/CORBIS; **416** Dana White/PhotoEdit; **424** Getty Images; **425** David Young-Wolff/PhotoEdit; **461** Royalty-free/Image Source Ltd./Age Fotostock; **469** Royalty-Free/CORBIS; **470** David Young-Wolff/PhotoEdit; **499** Rick Gomez/Masterfile; **507** Chuck Savage/Corbis; **508** Ariel Skelley/CORBIS; **533** Michelle D. Bridwell/PhotoEdit; **534** David Young-Wolff/PhotoEdit; **536** Bob Daemmrich/The Image Works; **537** Michael Newman/PhotoEdit; **538** Michael Newman/PhotoEdit; **540** Michael Newman/PhotoEdit; **542** Charles Gupton/CORBIS; **560** Royalty-free/Stockbyte/SuperStock; **568** Richard G./StockImage/Age Fotostock; **569** Royalty-free/SW Productions/Getty Images; **592** Dwayne Newton/PhotoEdit; **600** Jim Cummins/Getty Images; **601** Gabe Palmer/CORBIS; **637** Royalty-free/Stockbyte/Getty Images; **665** Tony Freeman/PhotoEdit, **673** Scott Barrow, **674** David Stoecklein/CORBIS; **676** Michael Newman/PhotoEdit; **677** Bob Daemmerich/PhotoEdit; **678** Lou Jones/Getty Images;

SCREEN CAPTURE CREDITS

Abbreviation Key: MS = Screen shots used by permission from Microsoft Corporation.
©2007 MS Word **5-21**, **24-26**, **35-36**, **38-55**, **57-58**, **69-83**, **85-86**, **98-104**, **106-108**, **110-122**, **124-128**, **133-152**, **155-159**, **164-184**, **187-191**; ©2007 MS Excel **204-217**, **219-223**, **228-239**, **242-246**, **251-272**, **275-279**, **284-303**, **306-310**, **315-333**, **335-340**; ©2007 MS Access **352-370**, **373-377**, **382-415**, **418-422**, **427-460**, **463-467**, **472-498**, **501-505**, **510-524**, **527-531**; ©2007 MS PowerPoint **544-559**, **562-566**, **571-591**, **594-598**, **603-628**, **631-635**, **640-656**, **659-664**, **667-671;** ©2007 Fender Musical Instruments Corp. **629**

Table of Contents

Z

Table of Contents

U

V

W

Table of Contents

T

Table of Contents

Table of Contents

S

Table of Contents

Q

R

Table of Contents

P

Table of Contents

N

O

Table of Contents

J

K

L

M

Table of Contents

G

H

I

Table of Contents

Table of Contents

E

F

Table of Contents

FEATURE CONTENTS

Writing MATTERS

MATH MATTERS

21st Century WORKPLACE

D

Why Study Computer Applications?

When you master the computer skills used in Microsoft Office 2007, you will benefit in both your business and academic careers. There is no business today that is untouched by computers. Whether you plan to become a mechanic, an architect, a photographer, or the CEO of a corporation, you will be expected to have some basic computer skills. In any business, time is money. People who can use the computer to save time give themselves a competitive advantage in the job market.

Book reports that are free of misspelled words and research papers that include accurate citations and footnotes will result in better grades. The student who knows how to import tables or graphics into a report will be able to make a stronger case for a particular point of view.

The architectural firm described below illustrates how Microsoft Office is used in every aspect of a typical business.

- **Microsoft Word** is used to generate detailed drawing notes that are inserted into computer-aided-drafting. Large projects require specification books that are thousands of pages long. These books make sure that builders meet critical safety codes. Careful documentation is required in memo form to communicate with every member of a design team.
- **Microsoft Excel** is used to calculate costs for code requirements. Excel files are inserted into computer-drafted drawings for door schedules, window schedules, and finish schedules. Area calculations for large buildings use Excel spreadsheets to make sure that the required space is provided to exit a building in the case of an emergency.

Why Study Computer Applications? (Continued)

- **Microsoft Access** databases are used to track the use of building materials on a project. Databases are also used to track documentation and to manage the contact information of the many members of design and construction teams.
- **Microsoft PowerPoint** is used by the initial architect to communicate his or her ideas to clients and to the community. PowerPoint is the tool used to create presentations in many industries and professions.
- **Microsoft Outlook** extends beyond sending and receiving e-mail. It is an organizational tool that allows team members to schedule meetings with design team members, check their schedules, and organize communication to groups within the team.
- **Windows Vista** is an operating system used on personal computers, including home and business desktops, notebooks, and tablet PCs. More than just an operating system, Vista contains graphical interfaces not seen in other operating systems. It also has a higher level of security not seen in its predecessors.

The managers in an architecture firm require all staff members, from architects to accountants to administrative personnel, to know these software applications well. In today's competitive job market, the person with the greatest computer abilities is often placed at the top of the hiring list.

Throughout the book, you will notice this logo. This logo indicates that the exercise or activity meets one of the **Microsoft Certified Application Specialist** standards. These standards cover topics from the Microsoft Certified Application Specialist certification exam.

The Microsoft Certified Application Specialist logo means that this book has been approved by the Microsoft Certified Application Specialist Program to help you master Microsoft Office desktop applications. This book can also help you prepare for the Microsoft Certified Application Specialist certification exam. For more information about Microsoft Certified Application Specialist certification, see page 714.

C

Take the iCheck Office 2007 Cyberhunt!

Did you know that your text contains many features that can **make learning easier for you**? Explore how to get the most out of your textbook by following the clues on pages xvii-xviii to discover useful features, activities, tips, and tools that are integrated into the lessons in this text. Then use these elements to help reach your computer applications learning goals.

Get Started

The scavenger hunt on these pages highlights features that will help you get the most out of your textbook. Collect points as you complete each step.

1. **It is easier to learn a new skill if you understand how this knowledge will help you get ahead and stay ahead. How could learning Excel help you reach personal goals?** *(8 points. Hint: see* **Why It Matters** *on page 200.)*

2. **You will move through projects more quickly if you know the basics before you begin. What will the projects on page 248 teach you about the hiring process?** *(4 points. Hint: See* **Before You Begin**.*)*

3. **Improving interpersonal ("soft") skills, such as communication and goal setting, will help you succeed in school, in work, and in daily life. What 21st Century Workplace skill is featured on page 499?** *(4 points. Hint: Working well with others is a very important skill in today's business world.)*

4. **Learning new skills is made easier by breaking them into small steps, so any one task or exercise does not seem too hard or time consuming. In the Use the Office Clipboard exercise, how many Step-By-Steps are included to complete the activity?** *(9 points. Hint: See page 81.)*

5. **All people learn and progress at different rates. How does the iCheck icon help you know if you are completing an exercise correctly or not?** *(4 points. Hint: See Exercise 3-1 on page 601.)*

6. **You need to repeat a skill or action many times to become proficient. Practicing the skills you have learned earlier will help you become proficient with Office. How many opportunities do you have to complete the Practice It Activities in a single lesson?** *(3 points. Hint: see pages 463-465.)*

7. **What additional program resources are highlighted in the Beyond the Book section, in the Unit Closers?** *(5 points. Hint: See page 347.)*

8. **Reading, writing, and arithmetic are fundamental skills for lifelong learning. In any career you choose, you will need to be able to read and to perform basic calculations. What expensive error did the sign painters make in the Writing Matters feature on page 14?** *(6 points. Hint: proofreading is critical!)*

Index

A

B

WD=Word, EX=Excel, AC=Access, PP=PowerPoint, AP=Appendixes

9 Before an assessment, it can be helpful to know whether you have really learned the lessons. What activities can be found on the Online Learning Center to help you reinforce the skills you have learned? *(6 points. Hint: the quizzes are not in the text. See page 280.)*

10 The real importance of learning new skills is to be able to apply this knowledge to create something of your own. What original Portfolio Projects do you create after completing Unit 4 on PowerPoint? *(10 points. Hint: See page 676.)*

11 When beginning a new lesson, it is very important to know what topics you will be reading about. It is also necessary to know what vocabulary words and ideas you will need to think about while reading. All this information can be found in the Reading Guide. What section of the Reading Guide can give you tips on reading before you start a lesson? *(4 points. Hint: See page 132.)*

12 What new feature is highlighted in the Microsoft Office 2007 minifeature on page 5? *(5 points)*

13 Summarizing reference material is a very useful tool for reviewing and reinforcing what you have learned. Which material does the Quick Reference Summary give to you in Appendix B? *(5 points. Hint: See page 696.)*

14 What section of the Reading Skills Handbook might you review to learn how to understand and remember text that you just read? *(4 points. Hint: See page xxxiv.)*

15 What activities on the After You Read page help you review the Key Terms and Academic Vocabulary taught in a lesson? *(4 points. Hint: See page 526.)*

16 In Appendix A, Integrated Applications, what Microsoft Office suites are included in the exercises? *(5 points. Hint: See page 681.)*

17 The Data File icon appears in the top right corner of some exercises. What is the purpose of the Data File icon? *(4 points. Hint: See page 228.)*

18 If you read and come across a key term and you are not certain of its meaning, what section of the book can you use to find the word and its definition? *(5 points. Hint: See page 740.)*

19 The Academic Skills minifeature shows you how learning computer skills can also help you learn academic skills. In Unit 2 Excel, Lesson 4, how many Academic Skills minifeatures are present? *(4 points. Hint: See page 318.)*

20 The Microsoft Certified Application Specialist (MCAS) standards were created to help you take the Microsoft Certified Application Specialist exams for each Office 2007 application. The exams can certify you as a Specialist for each application area. Where in the lesson opener can you find a listing of the MCAS standards hit in that particular lesson? *(5 points. Hint: See page 470.)*

Template/Plantilla Guía que contiene el formato de un documento, presentación o libro de trabajo específico. (pp. 83, 315)

Text/El Texto Las palabras en una página o en un doculento (pp. 14, 99-100, 252–253, 553, 574, 568)

Text box/Cuadro de texto Rectángulo movible, que se puede cambiar de tamaño y que contiene texto. (pp. 145, 442, 643)

Theme/Tema Colección de elementos de diseño, gráficas y colores que dan a los documentos, presentaciones y páginas Web una imagen consistente. (pp. 255, 571)

Thesaurus/Diccionario de sinónimos(Tesoro) Colección de palabras con sus sinónimos, semejante a un diccionario. (pp. 74, 659)

Timing/Tiempo de transición Característica de PowerPoint que determina el tiempo que dura visible una diapositiva durante una presentación antes de moverse automáticamente a la siguiente. (p. 659)

Title bar/Barra de título Barra de la parte superior de la pantalla que muestra el nombre de la ventana actual. (pp. 10, 205, 353, 544)

Totals row/Renglón de totales Función capaz de resumir las columnas de datos en una tabla para calcular totales, promedios, máximos, mínimos y otros cálculos de manera simple y rápida. (p. 387)

Track Changes/Revisar Cambios Característica que permite seguir la pista de los cambios que se hacen a un documento. (p. 166)

Transition/Transición Efecto que ocurre entre diapositivas en una presentación visual. (p. 622)

Typeface/Tipo de letra El diseño de un conjunto de caracteres. (También llamado fuente.) (pp. 38, 605)

U

Union Query/Consulta de Unión Consulta que combina los datos de consultas separadas en una sola. (p. 515)

Unmatched query/Consulta no comparativa Localiza registros sin comparar los datos relacionados. (p. 408)

Vary/Variar Crear diferencias entre elementos. (p. 177)

Version/Versión Forma o variante de un tipo u original. (pp. 300, 523)

Vertical alignment/Alineación vertical Colocación vertical de los contenidos de una celda. (p. 255)

Visual/Visual Capaz de ser visto; visible. (p. 148)

W

Web browser/Navegador (Explorador de Web) Aplicación que muestra la página Web. (p. 175)

Web Layout view/Vista de Diseño Web Vista que permite observar cómo se verá un documento como página Web. (p. 173)

Web page/Página Web Página de un sitio Web. (p. 193)

Wildcard/Comodines Caracteres similares al criterio de búsqueda de información. (p. 429)

Window/Ventana Área en la pantalla de la computadora donde puede verse y usarse una aplicación. (pp. 122, 320, 441)

WordArt/WordArt Gráfico de texto que puede ser alargado, sombreado y se le puede dar forma. (pp. 15, 588)

Word Count/Contar palabras Comando que cuenta el número de palabras, caracteres y párrafos de un documento o de parte de un texto. (p. 104)

Word processor/Procesador de palabras Aplicación de computadora que produce documentos de texto. (p. 2)

Workbook/Libro de trabajo Archivo de Excel que contiene una o más hojas de trabajo. (p. 207)

Worksheet/Hoja de trabajo Hoja de celdas organizada en filas y columnas. (p. 207)

Zoom/La Ampliación Un instrumento que aumenta o reduce el tamaño de los objetos dentro de la ventana. (pp. xliii, 19)

What Is Your Cyberhunt Skill Rating?

POINTS	CYBERHUNT RATING
90 to 100	You really know how to let your textbook work for you!
70 to 89	You know how to find your way around a textbook!
Less than 70	Consider working with your teacher or classmates to learn how to use your textbook more effectively—you will gain skills you can use your whole life.

1. If you are a skilled Excel user, you will be a good candidate for a variety of jobs. Excel can also help you now. You could use Excel to create a budget for yourself or to keep track of friends' addresses.
2. The projects on page 248 will teach you how to create a resume and how to prepare for an interview.
3. Collaborating with others.
4. Nine
5. When you you see the iCheck icon, compare your screen to the figure shown on the exercise page. If your screen looks like the figure, then you are completing the steps correctly. you can verify your screen with the figures located on the exercise page. Your screen should look like the called out figure.
6. Three
7. Beyond the Book highlights the additional exercises, projects, and resources available on the Online Learning Center.
8. They did not proofread their work so they spelled "DINING" incorrectly.
9. Self Check quizzes and Interactive Reviews.
10. Portfolio Project—Planning a Town Recreation Center: Part 1: Create a Slide, Part 2: Create a Certificate of Excellence, Part 3: Create a Presentation, Part 4: Create a Proposal
11. Before You Read
12. The Microsoft Office 2007 minifeature gives information about new features associated with the Office 2007 software such as the new Office Button, or the new Ribbon.
13. The Quick Reference Summary shows you how to use buttons, menus, and keyboard shortcuts to perform specific tasks.
14. Techniques to Understand and Remember What You Read
15. Review Vocabulary and Vocabulary Activity
16. Word, Excel, Access, and PowerPoint
17. The Data File icon lets you know that you will need to access a data file to complete an exercise.
18. Glossary
19. 6
20. In the Standards Box

Sheet tab/Pestaña de hoja Pequeña parte en la parte inferior de una hoja de trabajo que despliega el nombre de la hoja de trabajo y te permite moverte de una hoja de trabajo a otra en el mismo libro de trabajo. (p. 208)

Shortcut/Un Atajo Una manera simplificada de ejecutar una tarea. Algunos requieren que se haga clic en un icono que abre automáticamente un programa específico, un archivo, o una carpeta. Otros atajos piden que se oproma una combinación de teclas. (pp. 40, 354, 606, 657)

Shortcut menu/Menú atajo Menú que se abre cuando haces un clic derecho sobre un icono. (p. 657)

Sizing handle/Manija de tamaño Señala en un pequeño cuadro un objeto seleccionado que puede ser arrastrado para cambiar su tamaño. (p. 145)

Slide/Diapositiva Página de una presentación. (p. 546)

Slide Finder/Buscador de diapositivas Despliega una miniatura de cada diapositiva en una presentación que tú puedes seleccionar e insertar en la presentación en uso actual. (p. 623)

Slide icon/Icono de diapositiva En el panel de Esquema, es la pequeña imagen de diapositiva localizada a un lado del contenido de la diapositiva. Haz clic en la imagen para moverte de una diapositiva a otra. (p. 523)

Slide layout/Diseño de la diapositiva Arreglo del texto y gráficos en una diapositiva. (p. 604)

Slide Master/Master de diapositiva Diapositiva que sirve de modelo para las demás diapositivas en una presentación, excepto para la diapositiva del título. (p. 623)

SmartArt/SmartArt Galería que contiene seis tipos de diagramas adaptables. (pp. 147, 271)

Snap/Alinear Ajustar algo a una cuadrícula o guía cuando se arrastra cerca de ella. (p. 648)

Sort/Ordenar Hacer una lista de datos en orden ascendente o descendente. (pp. 285, 453)

Source/Fuente Lugar de donde se obtiene información. (p. 515)

Split/Dividir Dividir una ventana en dos paneles para poder desplazarte independientemente. (p. 319)

Split form/Forma Dividida Forma que contiene una hoja de datos en una mitad y una forma en la otra. (p. 433)

Spreadsheet/Hoja de cálculos Tabla de datos numéricos que están organizados en columnas y filas. (pp. 204, 207, 315)

Start Menu/Menú de inicio En Windows es un menú que proporciona herramientas para localizar documentos, encontrar ayuda, modificar parámetros del sistema y correr programas. (p. 5)

Status bar/Barra de estado Barra en la parte inferior de la pantalla que despliega información como el número de la página en uso o el número de diapositiva y el número total de páginas o diapositivas que hay en el documento. (pp. 5, 544)

Style/Estilo Conjunto de características definidas de formato. (pp. 40, 142)

Subform/Subforma Forma insertada en otra forma. (p. 435)

Survey/Encuesta Inspección crítica detallada. (p. 136)

Symbol/Símbolo Carácter así como un símbolo de moneda que no aparece en el teclado pero que puede insertarse por medio del cuadro de diálogo Símbolo. (p. 73)

Synonym/Sinónimo Palabra con el mismo significado que otra. (p. 74)

T

Tab/Pestaña Pequeña solapa en la barra que muestra un botón (o instrucción). (pp. 6, 206, 354, 545)

Tab stop/Parada de tabulador Configuración que determina dónde parará el punto de inserción al pulsar la tecla del tabulador. (pp. xxxix, 6, 206, 356, 576)

Table/Tabla Conjunto de filas y columnas en que se organiza la información. (pp. 136, 356, 576)

Table Analyzer Wizard/Asistente Analizador de Tablas Asistente que evalúa la información de una tabla específica y hace cambios para hacer más eficientes los datos. (p. 391)

Table of contents/Tabla de contenidos Lista de los temas de un documento que va con los números de sus páginas. (pp. 109, 111, 117)

Table Style/Estilo de Tabla Conjunto predefinido de formatos que pueden aplicarse a un rango de datos. (p. 255)

Task pane/El Cristal de Tarea Un crystal que se puede utilizar para simplificar last areas. Por ejemplo, el crystal de tarea ClipArt se utiliza para reducir los terminus de búsqueda cuando se busca en la Galería de ClipArt. (pp. 217, 369, 578–579, 620)

Online Learning Center

Follow these steps to access the textbook resources on the Student Online Learning Center.

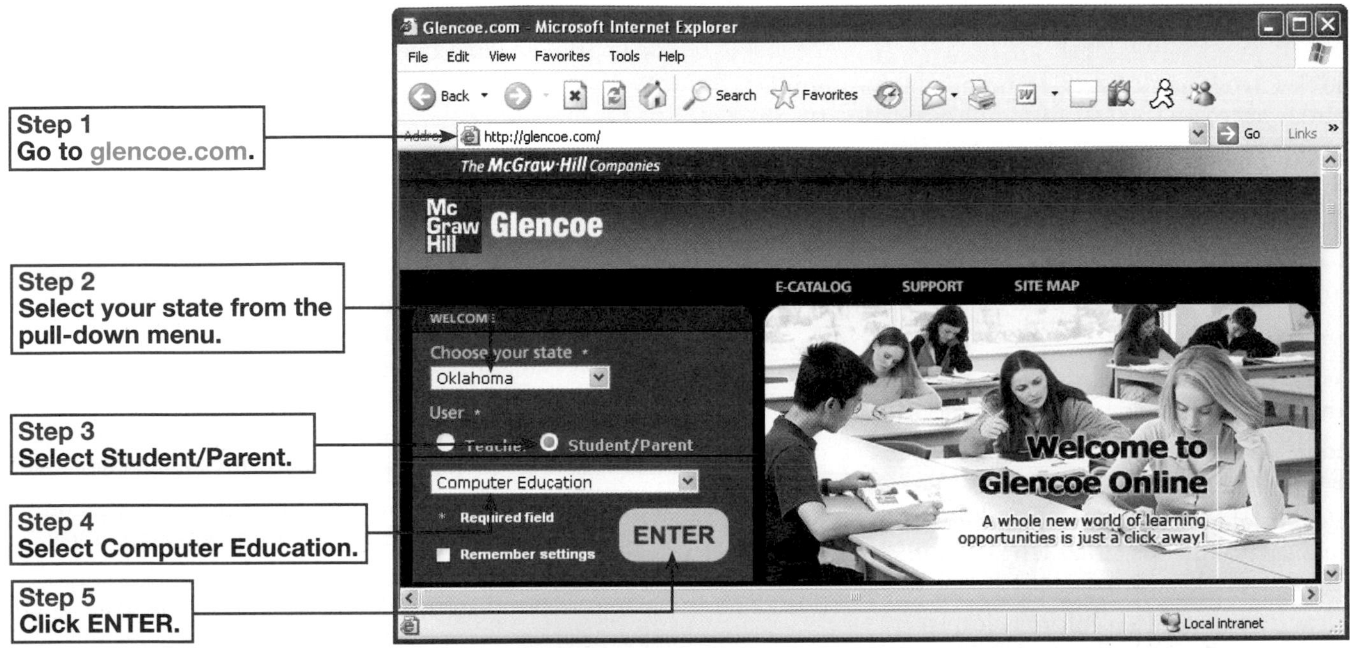

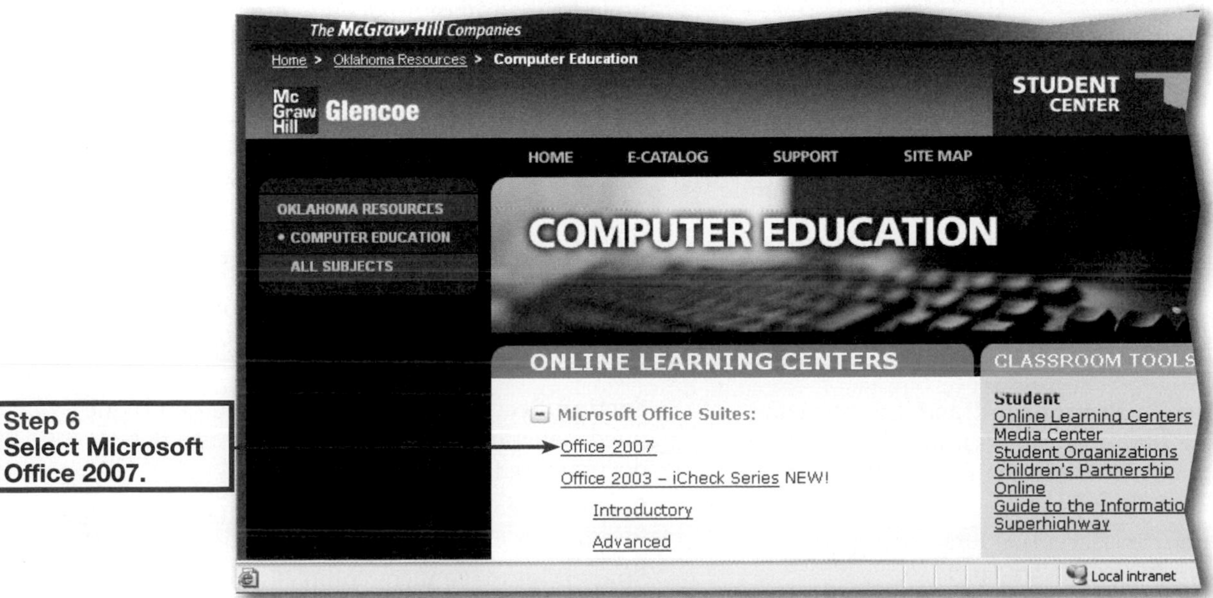

Q

Query/Consulta Instrucción que le dice a la base de datos que muestre sólo cierta información. (p. 357)

Quick Access Toolbar (QAT)/Barra de Herramientas de Acceso Rápido Barra de herramientas que permite a los usuarios localizar instrucciones rápidamente. (pp. xlii, 8, 205, 353, 544)

Quick Parts/Quick Parts Herramienta que permite guardar texto, imágenes y formatos especiales. (p. 85)

Quick Print/Impresión rápida Opción de impresión que imprime el reporte de inmediato sin abrir el cuadro de diálogo de Impresión. (p. 516)

Quick Styles/Estilos Rápidos Característica que permite aplicar fácilmente nuevos estilos al texto. (p. 54)

R

Range/Rango Un conjunto de celdas. (p. 284)

Record/Registro Conjunto de datos que describen un objeto y que se muestra en una fila de una tabla. (p. 284)

Referential integrity/Integridad referencial Evita que los datos de dos tablas tengan conflictos por medio de una relación. (p. 401)

Refine/Refinar Filtrar información (p. 478)

Relationship/Relación Vínculo entre dos tablas basado en un campo común. (p. 399)

Relative reference/Referencia relativa Una referencia de celda que cambia cuando se copia la fórmula en una nueva ubicación. (p. 291)

Replace/Reemplazar Herramienta que se usa para reemplazar datos localizados. (p. 429)

Report/Informe (Reporte) Documento formal que se usa para comunicar información. (p. 98)

Resize/Modificar tamaño Aumentar o reducir el tamaño de una ventana; Hacer los controles de un formulario o reporte más grandes o más pequeños. (p. 458)

Responsibility/La Responsabilidad La obligación. Cuando le dé a uno una responsabilidad, éste se encarga de ser alguien de confianza y de llevarla hasta el fin. (pp. 131, 226, 371)

Restore/Restaurar Hacer que una ventana ya reducida sea visible de nuevo. (p. 152)

Revise/Revisar Examinar nuevamente con el fin de corregir o mejorar. (p. 449)

Ribbon/Cinta Panel en Microsoft Office que organiza instrucciones en pestañas. La Cinta cambia dependiendo de los programas y herramientas que estén activos. (pp. 6, 206, 354, 545)

Right-outer join/Combinación externa derecha Combinación que le indica a una consulta regresar todas las filas de la segunda tabla y únicamente las filas de la primera tabla que coincidan con la segunda tabla. (p. 480)

Rotate/Rotar Dar vuelta a un objeto, generalmente 90 grados, a la derecha o a la izquierda. (p. 615)

S

Save As dialog box/Una Cajita de Diálogo Marcada Guardar Como Una cajita que se presenta cuando uno hace clic en el botón Guardar o en el botón Guardar Como. En la cajita Guardar Como, se cambia el nombre del archivo, el tipo de archivo, o la situación del archivo. (pp. lii, 9, 209, 407, 664)

Scale/Escala Cambia el tamaño de un carácter. (p. 53)

Scanner/Escáner (Digitalizador) Hardware que codifica digitalmente texto, gráficas y fotografías. (p. 586)

ScreenTip/ScreenTip Descripción de un botón que aparece cuando apuntas hacia ese botón. (pp. 7, 356, 551)

Scroll/Desplazar Moverse por arriba o por abajo o de un lado al otro por un documento usando la barra de desplazamiento u oprimiendo los botones del teclado. (p. 5)

Scroll bar/Barra de desplazamiento Barra que se encuentra a la derecha o en la parte inferior de la pantalla y que te permite moverte hacia arriba o hacia abajo o a la izquierda o derecha de un documento o hoja de trabajo. (pp. 7, 229, 382, 525)

Search box/La Cajita de Buscar Una característica que se utiliza para buscar información usando los teclados. La característica Ayuda en Office utiliza una cajita de Buscar. (p.20)

Section/Sección Porción de un documento que puede tener distinto formato que el resto del documento. (p. 109)

Section break/Salto de sección Espacio que se inserta para empezar una nueva sección. (p. 109)

Shape/Figura Gráficos como círculos, cuadros, estrellas y flechas. (p. 148)

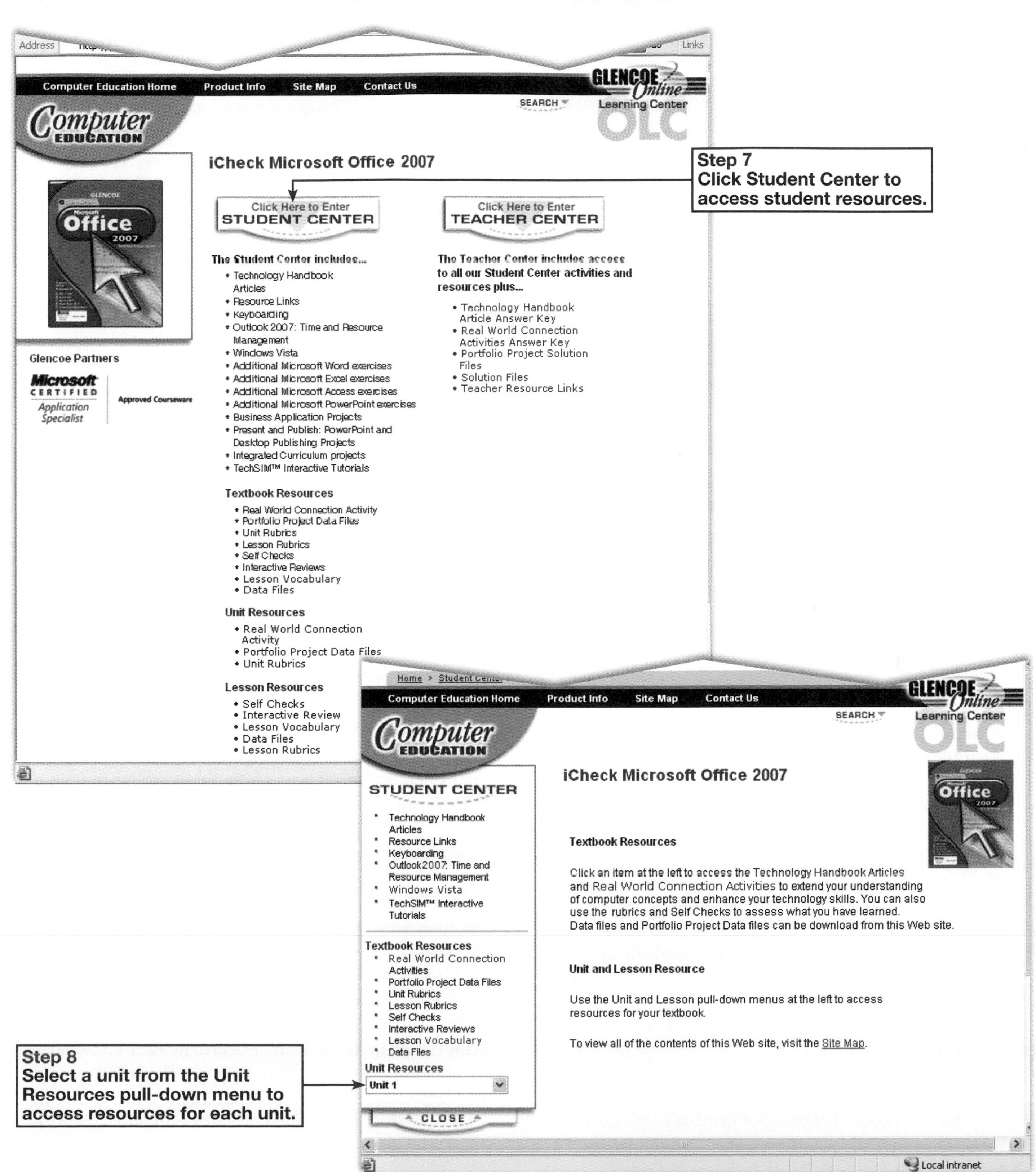
Address
Links
Computer Education Home
Product Info
Site Map
Contact Us
GLENCOE Online Learning Center
SEARCH
OLC
Computer EDUCATION
iCheck Microsoft Office 2007
Step 7
Click Student Center to access student resources.
Click Here to Enter STUDENT CENTER
Click Here to Enter TEACHER CENTER
The Student Center includes...
Technology Handbook Articles
Resource Links
Keyboarding
Outlook 2007: Time and Resource Management
Windows Vista
Additional Microsoft Word exercises
Additional Microsoft Excel exercises
Additional Microsoft Access exercises
Additional Microsoft PowerPoint exercises
Business Application Projects
Present and Publish: PowerPoint and Desktop Publishing Projects
Integrated Curriculum projects
TechSIM™ Interactive Tutorials
The Teacher Center includes access to all our Student Center activities and resources plus...
Technology Handbook Article Answer Key
Real World Connection Activities Answer Key
Portfolio Project Solution Files
Solution Files
Teacher Resource Links
Glencoe Partners
Microsoft CERTIFIED Application Specialist
Approved Courseware
Textbook Resources
Real World Connection Activity
Portfolio Project Data Files
Unit Rubrics
Lesson Rubrics
Self Checks
Interactive Reviews
Lesson Vocabulary
Data Files
Unit Resources
Real World Connection Activity
Portfolio Project Data Files
Unit Rubrics
Lesson Resources
Self Checks
Interactive Review
Lesson Vocabulary
Data Files
Lesson Rubrics
Home > Student Center
Computer Education Home
Product Info
Site Map
Contact Us
SEARCH
GLENCOE Online Learning Center
OLC
Computer EDUCATION
STUDENT CENTER
Technology Handbook Articles
Resource Links
Keyboarding
Outlook 2007: Time and Resource Management
Windows Vista
TechSIM™ Interactive Tutorials
Textbook Resources
Real World Connection Activities
Portfolio Project Data Files
Unit Rubrics
Lesson Rubrics
Self Checks
Interactive Reviews
Lesson Vocabulary
Data Files
Unit Resources
Unit 1
CLOSE
iCheck Microsoft Office 2007
Textbook Resources
Click an item at the left to access the Technology Handbook Articles and Real World Connection Activities to extend your understanding of computer concepts and enhance your technology skills. You can also use the rubrics and Self Checks to assess what you have learned. Data files and Portfolio Project Data files can be download from this Web site.
Unit and Lesson Resource
Use the Unit and Lesson pull-down menus at the left to access resources for your textbook.
To view all of the contents of this Web site, visit the Site Map.
Local intranet
Step 8
Select a unit from the Unit Resources pull-down menu to access resources for each unit.

P

Package for CD/Empaquetar para CD Modo rápido de agrupar una presentación de PowerPoint y todos los archivos relacionados (tales como archivos vinculados y el Visor de PowerPoint) dentro de una sola carpeta. (p. 661)

Page break/Salto de página Lugar donde termina una página impresa y empieza la otra. Un salto de página automático se produce cuando Word automáticamente mueve el texto a una nueva página. Un salto de página manual o forzado se produce cuando el usuario inserta manualmente el texto en una nueva página. (pp. 103, 326)

Page orientation/Orientación de la página Se refiere a la orientación vertical u horizontal de la página. (pp. 176, 323)

Parameter/Parámetro Límite. Se puede aplicar un parámetro a una consulta. (p. 478)

Password/Contraseña Serie de caracteres usados para encriptar una base de datos. (p. 518)

Paste/Pegar Insertar texto previamente cortado o copiado en otro documento. (pp. 70, 234, 547)

Picture/Una Imagen Un gráfico, una foto, u otra obra de arte que se inserta en un documento de Word, en una diapositiva de PowerPoint, en una hoja de Excel, en un formulario de Access. (p. 586)

Phrase/Frase Grupo de palabras que funciona como una sola unidad. (p. 78)

PivotTable/Tabla Pivote Tabla que puede mostrar información y presentarla de varias maneras diferentes. (p. 438)

Placeholder/Marcador de posición Texto que te dice qué tipo de contenido debe ir en las diferentes áreas de una diapositiva. (p. 552)

Plagiarism/El Plagio El acto de tomar las palabras y las ideas de otra persona como si fueran las suyas de usted. (pp. 105, 343)

PMT/PAGO Función que calcula los pagos de un préstamo basándose en la tasa de interés, número de abonos y cantidad total del préstamo. (p. 300)

Point/Punto Unidad de medida para el tamaño de fuente. (p. 38)

Pointer/Apuntador (Puntero) Flecha que se usa para seleccionar objetos en pantalla como menús y botones. En Excel, al apuntador cambia a una flecha doble para cambiar el tamaño de columnas. Cambia a un cuadro y signo de menos sobre las celdas de la hoja de trabajo y cambia a un signo de más negro sobre la manija de llenar de una celda. (pp. 5, 354)

Portion/Porción Parte o porción de algo. (p. 281)

Portrait/Orientación vertical Orientación de la página, la hoja de trabajo o la presentación que se muestra más alta que ancha. (pp. 323, 623)

PowerPoint Viewer/Visor de PowerPoint Aplicación de computadora que te permite ver una diapositiva sin usar PowerPoint. (p. 661)

Presentation/Presentación Archivo de PowerPoint. Una presentación puede incluir texto, imágenes, gráficas, vínculos a otras páginas y otros objetos. (p. 546)

Preview/Vista previa Muestra de una página en pantalla de un formulario o informe. (p. 510)

Primary Key/Llave Primaria Campo en una base de datos que identifica cada registro como único. (p. 386)

Print area/Área de impresión Parte de una hoja de trabajo que puede imprimirse. (p. 324)

Print Layout View/La Vista del Expuesto de los Impresos La indicación por defecto para examinar los documentos. La Vista del Expuesto de los Impresos expone cómo se verá el documento al imprimirlo. (pp. 7, 69, 704)

Print Preview/Preestreno Impreso Un preestreno de los documentos, las hojas de ejercicio, o de las diapositivas para imprimir. (pp. 21, 216, 365, 557, 704)

Printer/Impresora Dispositivo de salida que se usa para transferir información del monitor al papel. (p. 21)

Process Diagram/Diagrama de Proceso Diagrama que muestra cómo cambia la información en un proceso. (p. 271)

Productivity/La Productividad Una medida de la capacidad de un individuo o de un equipo a conseguir los resultados. (p. 202)

Promote/Aumentar nivel En esquemas, cambia el texto seleccionado al siguiente nivel superior de encabezado (subir un nivel, mover a la izquierda). (p. 575)

Proofread/La Corrección de Pruebas Leer para encontrar y corregir los errors. (pp. 22, 245, 677)

Property/Propiedad Detalle acerca de un objeto, por ejemplo tamaño o valor predeterminado. (p. 386)

Property sheet/Hoja de propiedades Ventana en que se muestran las propiedades de un objeto. (p. 389)

Prepare for 21st Century Success!

ISTE and NETS

The International Society for Technology in Education (ISTE) has developed National Educational Technology Standards to define educational technology standards for students (NETS•S). The activities in this book are designed to meet ISTE standards. The Standards box on each lesson opening page indicates which standards and performance indicators are covered in the lesson.

NETS•S Standards

To live, learn, and work successfully in an increasingly complex and information-rich society, students must be able to use technology effectively. Althought the ISTE standards identify skills that students can practice and master in school, the skills are also used outside of school, at home, and at work. For more information about ISTE and the NETS, please visit **www.iste.org**.

Media Information/La Información de Medios de Comunicación Unas Fuentes como tall as revistas, los periódicos, la radio, la television, y el Internet. (p 592)

Memo/Memorándum Nota informal que generalmente se envía entre las personas de un negocio u organización. (pp. 33-35)

Merge/Intercalar Combinar. Por ejemplo, se puede intercalary dos documentos o se puede intercalar dos celdas en una tabla. (pp. 141,169, 698)

Merge field/Campo de combinación Código en el documento principal de una combinación de correspondencia que muestra el lugar donde se insertará información. (p. 178)

MIN/Mínimo Función que se usa para identificar el valor más pequeño de un grupo de celdas. (p. 229)

Minimize/Reducir Quitar una ventana del escritorio (o fondo de la pantalla) sin cerrarla. (p. 221)

Mini Toolbar/Mini Barra de Herramientas Cuando se elige un texto, una barra de herramientas de formateo en miniatura desde la cual se puede cambiar el estilo de letras, el color del estilo de letras, y más. La mini Barra de Herramientas es semitransparente hasta que se mueva el cursor por encima. Cuando el cursor se quede en la barra de herramientas, se hace opaco. (pp. xliv, 12)

Mixed reference/Referencia mixta Referencia de celda que contiene una parte relativa y una parte absoluta. (p. 293)

MLA (Modern Language Association) /La Asociación de Lenguas Modernas Una organización que public alas directrices para formatear y citar las fuentes en un informe académica de investigación. (pp. 9, 105, 115)

Monitor/Controlar Vigilar y confirmar. Se refiere también a la parte de la computadora que expone la pantalla. (pp. liv, 552)

Multiple item form/Forma de elementos múltiples Forma que muestra múltiples elementos en una hoja de datos. (p. 432)

N

Navigate/Navegar Moverse en el documento a un lugar en particular. (p. 102)

Navigation Pane/El Cristal de Navegación Un cristal que aparece por el lado izquierdo de la pantalla en Access. El Cristal de Navegación hace un listado de las preguntas, las tablas, y otros objetos en su base de datos. Haga clic en un objeto en el Cristal de Navegación para abrirlo. (p. 353)

Network/Red Un grupo de computadoras que están conectadas la una con la otra. (p. 2)

Newsletter/Boletín de noticias Reporte impreso que usa una compañía para mantener informados a los empleados acerca de eventos importantes. (p. 133)

Normalize/Normalizar Asegurarse de que una tabla esté correctamente estructurada y que no se repitan grupos de información. (p. 472)

NOW/AHORA Función que despliega la fecha y la hora en que se abre o usa una hoja de trabajo. (p. 300)

Numbered list/Lista numerada Lista de objetos que deben aparecer en una secuencia en particular. Cada objeto es precedido por un número o letra. (p. 50)

O

Object/Un Objeto Cualquier artículo que uno puede elegir y manipular individualmente. Un gráfico es un objeto, tambi´n son porciones individuales de una base de datos, como tal una pregunta. (p. 514)

Object dependency/Dependencia de objeto Se refiere al hecho de que una base de datos que usa un objeto de una segunda base de datos depende de ese segundo objeto. (p. 521)

Office Button/Un Botón de Despacho Un botón situado en el rincón de arriba a la izquierda de Microsoft Word, Excel, Access, y PowerPoint. Haga clic en este botón para abrir , guardar, e imprimir los archivos. (pp. xli, 5)

Operating system/El Sistema de Operación El programa total que controla todos los otros programas de software en una máquina y que permite a funcionar correctamente los mecanismos de hardware. Windows XP y Windows Vista son los sistemas de operación en los cuales funciona Office 2007. (p. xlix)

Operator/Operario Un símbolo que representa una función matemática. (p. 286)

Organizational chart/Organigrama Tabla gráfica que muestra el arreglo jerárquico de una organización. (p. 271)

Outline View/Vista Esquema Vista de un documento que muestra el texto con sangría para poder ver el nivel del encabezado. (p. 120)

Outlook/Outlook Programa de Microsoft Office que envía, recibe y organiza los mensajes de correo electrónico. (pp. 730, 733)

National Educational Technology Standards and Performance Indicators for Students

The NETS are divided into the six broad categories that are listed below. Activities in the book meet the standards within each category.

❶ Creativity and Innovation

Students demonstrate creative thinking, construct knowledge, and develop innovative products and processes using technology. Students:

- **a.** apply existing knowledge to generate new ideas, products, or processes.
- **b.** create original works as a means of personal or group expression.
- **c.** use models and simulations to explore complex systems and issues.
- **d.** identify trends and forecast possibilities.

❷ Communication and Collaboration

Students use digital media and environments to communicate and work collaboratively, including at a distance, to support individual learning and contribute to the learning of others. Students:

- **a.** interact, collaborate, and publish with peers, experts or others employing a variety of digital environments and media.
- **b.** communicate information and ideas effectively to multiple audiences using avariety of media and formats.
- **c.** develop cultural understanding and global awareness by engaging with learners of other cultures.
- **d.** contribute to project teams to produce original works or solve problems.

❸ Research and Information Fluency

Students apply digital tools to gather, evaluate, and use information. Students:

- **a.** plan strategies to guide inquiry.
- **b.** locate, organize, analyze, evaluate, synthesize, and ethically use information from a variety of sources and media.
- **c.** evaluate and select information sources and digital tools based on the appropriateness to specific tasks.
- **d.** process data and report results.

Indent/Sangría Distancia a la izquierda o a la derecha de los márgenes del texto. (pp. 51, 117)

Inner join/Una Juntura Interior La juntura por omission que le dice a una pregunta que combine las filas de dos tables que comparten el mismo valor. (p. 480)

Input mask/Entrada Permite a los usuarios aplicar cierto tipo de formato a los datos ingresados en la base de datos. (p. 398)

Insert/Insertar Añadir un texto a un documento; añadir artículos como tall as filas o las columnas a un documento, a una diapositiva, a una hoja de cálculo o a un archivo de base de datos. (pp. 11, 236)

Insertion point/Punto de inserción Barra vertical parpadeante que indica el punto en que aparecerá el texto que se ha ingresado. También se llama cursor. (pp. 6, 11)

J

Join/Juntar Un campo que conecta dos tables en un base de datos Access. El campo juntura pertenece a las dos tables y la información de las tablas juntadas se combina, resultando en las respuestas más acertadas a una pregunta. (p. 480)

K

Key/Entrar Introducir el texto a un documento (p. 137)

Keyboard shortcut/El Atajo de Teclado Una manera alternativa de realizar una tarea oprimiendo las teclas en el teclado en vez de hacer clic en una opción o en un icono. Por ejemplo, oprim [CTRL] + [B] para hacer en negrita el texto. (pp. 40, 44, 78, 137, 354, 696))

L

Label/Etiquetar Describir o designar con una etiqueta o como si se usara una. (p. 459)

Landscape/Orientación horizontal Orientación en que la página, hoja de trabajo o diapositiva es más ancha que alta. (pp. 323, 392, 623)

Layout view/Vista de Diseño Vista que permite ver qué aspecto tendrán los datos cuando se impriman. (p. 440)

Learn/Aprender Familiarizarse con algo. (p. 205)

Left-outer join/Combinación externa izquierda Combinación que le indica a una consulta regresar todas las filas de la primera tabla y únicamente las filas de la segunda tabla que coincidan con la primera tabla. (p. 480)

Letterhead/El Membrete El papel de escribir que incluye el nombre y la información de contrato del remitente. Las empresas frecuentemente crean un membrete que incluye el logotipo del negocio. Los individuos pueden crear el membrete personal.(pp. 183–184)

Line color/Color de línea Color aplicado a una línea o al borde de una forma. (p. 611)

Link/Vinculado Acción de relacionar una fuente de datos con otra. (p. 472)

Literacy/La Alfabetización La capacidad de leer, escribir, analizar y evaluar. Por ejemplo, la alfabetización de los medios de comunicación es la capacidad de analizar y evaluar la información de muchas Fuentes. (p. 592)

Live Preview/El Preestreno En Vivo Un instrumento en Office 2007 que le deja prever los cambios de formateo antes de aplicarlos. Si se aplica Quick Styles a un documento, Live Preview preestrena los estilos. (p. 54)

Locate/Localizar Determinar o indicar el lugar, sitio o límites de algo. (p. 331)

Log/Bitácora Registro escrito. (p. 114)

Lookup field/Campo de búsqueda Muestra las opciones de entrada de otra tabla para que puedas ingresar los datos al escogerlos de una lista. (p. 394)

M

Mail merge/Combinación de correspondencia Proceso que crea múltiples copias de la misma carta, sobre o etiqueta e inserta datos personalizados. (p. 177)

Main document/Documento principal Carta, sobre o etiqueta que se usa en una combinación de correspondencia. (p. 178)

Margin/Margen Espacio en blanco que aparece entre el texto y la orilla de la página. (pp. 35, 327)

Mark as Final/Indicar como Final Una orden que hace su documento sólo-leer, impidiendo algún cambio.(p. xlviii)

Markup/Marca Cuadros de leyendas que contienen el nombre del revisor, la fecha y detalles de los comentarios y cambios que se hicieron. (p. 615)

MAX/Máximo Función que se usa para identificar el valor más grande de un grupo de celdas. (p. 229)

Maximize/Aumentar Aumentar una ventana para que llene la pantalla. (p. 320)

❹ Critical Thinking, Problem-Solving, and Decision-Making

Students use critical thinking skills to plan and conduct research, manage projects, solve problems and make informed decisions using appropriate digital tools and resources. Students:

- **a.** identify and define authentic problems and significant questions for investigation.
- **b.** plan and manage activities to develop a solution or complete a project.
- **c.** collect and analyze data to identify solutions and/or make informed decisions.
- **d.** use multiple processes and diverse perspectives to explore alternative solutions.

❺ Digital Citizenship

Students understand human, cultural, and societal issues related to technology and practice legal and ethical behavior. Students:

- **a.** advocate and practice safe, legal, and responsible use of information and technology.
- **b.** exhibit a positive attitude toward using technology that supports collaboration, learning, and productivity.
- **c.** demonstrate personal responsibility for lifelong learning.
- **d.** exhibit leadership for digital citizenship.

❻ Technology Operations and Concepts

Students demonstrate a sound understanding of technology concepts, systems and operations. Students:

- **a.** understand and use technology systems.
- **b.** select and use applications effectively and productively.
- **c.** troubleshoot systems and applications.
- **d.** transfer current knowledge to learning of new technologies.

Footnote/Nota al pie Nota en la parte inferior de la página, usada para citar referencias o proporcionar más información. (pp. 42, 108)

Form/Formulario Despliegue de la pantalla en donde los datos pueden agregarse o cambiarse. (p. 430)

Format/Formato Hacer que un documento o una presentación tenga la misma apariencia por medio de cambiar la manera de que las palabras y los párrafos se ven; proceso en que la computadora asegura que un disco funciona bien y después crea direcciones para la información en un disco. (pp. 67, 98, 109)

Format Painter/Copiar Formato Herramienta que copia el formato de un objeto a otro. (p. 41, 608)

Formatting/Modificación de formato Cualquier cambio hecho a la apariencia del texto o contenido de una diapositiva. (pp. 40, 98, 603)

Formula/Fórmula Ecuación que contiene valores, referencias de celda o ambas. (p. 215)

Formula Bar/Barra de Fórmulas Barra que despliega el contenido de una celda. (p. 211)

Freeze/Congelar Mantener los encabezados en su lugar mientras te desplazas por la hoja de trabajo. (p. 319)

Function/Función Lista de fórmulas previamente configuradas que se usan para resolver ecuaciones. (pp. 288, 354)

G

Gradient/Gradiente El sombreado gradual de un gráfico de un lado al otro. (p. 612)

Graphic/Gráfico Elemento visual creado usando herramienta como WordArt, Autoformas, escáneres y cámaras digitales. (p. 148)

Graphical list/Lista gráfica Gráficos que pueden usarse en una lista con viñetas o numerada. (p. 271)

Graphical User Interface (GUI)/Interfaz gráfica de usuario (IGU) Interfaz de computadora que facilita el uso de la computadora al permitirles a los usuarios hacer clic con un ratón sobre iconos gráficos para hacer los comandos. (p. xxxix)

Grid/Cuadrícula Serie de líneas verticales y horizontales puesta sobre una diapositiva para ayudarte a alinear objetos. (p. 648)

Group/Grupo Conjunto organizado de instrucciones que se relaciona con una actividad específica. (pp. 6, 206, 354, 545)

Group Header/Encabezado de grupo Herramienta que afina los reportes clasificando la información en grupos (p.453)

Guide/Guía Línea vertical u horizontal que se coloca en una diapositiva para alinear los objetos. (p. 648)

H

Header/Encabezado Texto que aparece en la parte superior de cada página o presentación. (pp. 101, 325, 628)

Help Menu/Menú de ayuda Menú que ofrece instrucciones y sugerencias sobre varios temas relacionados con las aplicaciones. (pp. 20, 217, 556, 701)

Horizontal/Horizontal De izquierda a derecha. (p. 36)

Horizontal alignment/Alineación horizontal Colocación paralela del contenido de una celda. (p. 264)

HTML Ve *Hyptertext Markup Language/Lenguaje de Marcado de Hipertexto.*

Hyperlink/Hiperenlace (Hipervínculo) Enlace en un documento que lleva a una página Web o a otro documento. (pp. 164, 239, 646)

Hypertext Markup Language (HTML)/Lenguaje de Marcado de Hipertexto (HTML) Lenguaje de programación usada por los navegadores de Internet para leer y mostrar las página Web. (p. 173)

I

Icon/Icono Pequeña imagen o gráfico que representa visualmente programas, archivos de documentos, enlaces Web u otros objetos en la computadora. (pp. 38, 548)

IF/SI Función que verifica que si se cumple una condición, se obtiene un resultado si es falsa y otro si es verdadera. (p. 301)

Illustrate/Ilustrar Mostrar claramente. (p. 216)

Import/Importar Traer datos de una aplicación a otra, con la opción de guardar el mismo formato. (pp. 472, 573, 688, 694)

Import specifications/Especificaciones de importación Requerimientos que pueden guardarse para indicar la manera en que se importarán los datos. (p. 475)

Incorporate/Incorporar Unir o trabajar en algo que ya existe con el fin de formar un todo indistinguible. (p. 642)

Microsoft Certified Application Specialist Standards

What is the Microsoft Business Certification Program?

The Microsoft Business Certification Program allows users to show that they have proven expertise in Microsoft Office programs. Users who prove this expertise achieve the Microsoft Certified Application Specialist certification. The Microsoft Business Certification Program is the only Microsoft-approved certification program of its kind, recognized by businesses and schools around the world.

How can I get Microsoft Certified Application Specialist (MCAS) certification?

In order to achieve MCAS certification, a user must pass an exam based on specific skill sets within a Microsoft® Office application. Users can take as many exams as they want and can achieve as many certifications as they want. The Application Specialist exams include:

- Using Microsoft® Office Word 2007
- Using Microsoft® Office Excel® 2007
- Using Microsoft® Office Access 2007
- Using Microsoft® Office PowerPoint® 2007
- Using Microsoft® Office Outlook® 2007
- Using Microsoft® Windows Vista™

How can Glencoe iCheck Microsoft Office 2007 help me achieve certification?

Glencoe iCheck Microsoft Office 2007 has been written to cover all standards necessary to complete and pass the Application Specialist exams listed above. A correlation to the Microsoft Certified Application Specialist standards is provided on page 714. This correlation indicates where specific standards are covered in the Student Edition or on the Online Learning Center. The beginning of every lesson also contains a Standards box that shows you which MCAS standards are taught in that lesson.

Display/Mostrar Poner o exhibir ante el espectador. (pp. 521, 544)

Distinct/Distinto Que se puede distinguir visual o mentalmente de manera discreta; separado. (p. 259)

Distribution list/El Listado de Distribución Una lista de direcciones a las cuales se envían cartas o correo electrónico. Por ejemplo, cuando se usa la característica Word Mail Merge, se envían las cartas al listado de distribución. (p. 177)

Document/Documento Archivo en el cual se teclea texto. Los documentos pueden contener texto, imágenes, gráficas y otros objetos. (pp. 5, 449, 493)

Documenter/Documentador Herramienta que reporta las características de objetos de base de datos y sus partes. (p. 514)

Drag/Arrastrar Mover texto seleccionándolo, dejando presionado el botón del ratón y moviendo el ratón. (pp. 72, 290)

Duplicate query/Consulta múltiple Localiza registros con los mismos datos de un campo. (p. 408)

E

Edit/Editar Hacer cambios en un documento, en el contenido de una celda o en una presentación. (pp. 14, 230)

Electronic mail (E-mail)/Correo electrónico (E-mail) Comunicación enviada de una persona a otra por medio de Internet. (pp. 165, 699)

Element/Elemento Parte integrante de algo. (p. 486, 641)

Emphasis/Énfasis Importancia o significado especial. (p. 606)

Enable/Permitir Hacer posible, práctico o fácil. (p. 164)

Encrypt/Encriptar Usar una contraseña para incrementar la seguridad de los datos. (pp. 518, 523)

Encryption/Encriptación Es una forma segura de guardar la información codificándola conforme se transmite por una red de comunicaciones o por Internet. (pp. 518, 523)

Endnote/Nota final Nota al final del documento o sección, que se usa para citar referencias o proporcionar más información. (p. 107)

Enhance/Realzar Mejorar un documento (p. 39)

Ensure/Asegurarse Tener certeza, seguridad, certidumbre. (p. 522)

Evaluate/Evaluar Determinar el significado, valor o condición de algo por medio de una valoración y estudio cuidadoso. (p. 570)

Export/Exportar Para guardar los datos que se ha creado en una aplicación para que se los pueda acceder usando una aplicación diferente. Se puede exportar una tabla desde una base de datos Access para que se la pueda abrir en Word. (p. 496)

Export specification/Especificaciones de exportación Requerimientos que permiten definir la composición de los registros que se exportarán hacia un destino. (p. 498)

F

Field/Campo Porción de información que describe algo. (p. 356)

File format/El Formato de Archivos El tipo de fichero, como tal .docx o .rtf. Se puede cambiar el formato de archivo de un documento para que los usuarios que no usen Microsoft Office pueden leer sus datos. (p. 332)

File management/Control de archivos Utilidad que organiza los archivos e información para que se puedan localizar fácilmente. (pp. 9, 10)

Fill color/Color de relleno Color que se aplica al interior de una forma. (p. 611)

Fill handle/Manija de llenado Herramienta que te permite llenar múltiples celdas con el mismo contenido usando una celda como ejemplo. (p. 238)

Filter/Filtrar Elemento que te permite ver sólo la información que necesitas. (pp. 284, 406)

Find/Buscar Herramienta que se usa para encontrar datos específicos en una tabla o documento. (pp. 79, 232, 429)

Folder/Carpeta Objeto que le ayuda al usuario a organizar archivos. (pp. 9, 209, 362, 547)

Font/Fuente Diseño general de un conjunto de caracteres. (También llamado tipo de letra.) (pp. 38, 251, 605)

Font style/Estilo de fuente Efecto que puede aplicarse a una fuente, tal como negritas, cursivas y subrayado. (pp. 39, 251, 605)

Footer/Nota El texto que se encuentra a pie de página en un documento, un formulario, o una presentación. (pp. 100, 452)

Prepare *for* Academic Success!

National Language Arts Standards

To help incorporate literacy skills (reading, writing, listening, and speaking) into *Glencoe iCheck Microsoft Office 2007*, each lesson contains a listing of the language arts skills covered. These skills have been developed into standards by the *National Council of Teachers of English and International Reading Association*.

- Read texts to acquire new information.
- Read literature to build an understanding of the human experience.
- Apply strategies to interpret texts.
- Use written language to communicate effectively.
- Use different writing process elements to communicate effectively.
- Apply knowledge of language structure and conventions to discuss texts.
- Conduct research and gather, evaluate, and synthesize data to communicate discoveries.
- Use information resources to gather information and create and communicate knowledge.
- Develop an understanding of diversity in language used across cultures.
- Use first language to develop competency in English language arts and develop an understanding of content across the curriculum.
- Participate as members of literacy communities.
- Use language to accomplish individual purposes.

National Math Standards

Glencoe's iCheck Series provides students with opportunities to practice the math skills indicated in the national math standards developed by the *National Council of Teachers of Mathematics*. The basic skills are:

- Number and Operations
- Algebra
- Geometry
- Measurement
- Data Analysis and Probability
- Problem Solving
- Communication
- Connections
- Representation

Corporate/Corporativo Relacionado con un negocio o una corporación. (p. 535)

COUNT/Contar Función que cuenta el número de celdas en el rango que contiene números. (p. 298)

COUNTA/CONTARA Función que se usa para encontrar el número de celdas en un rango que contiene datos (tanto números como texto). (p. 298)

Count Numbers/Contar Números Función que se usa para encontrar el número de celdas en un rango que contiene números. (p. 298)

Cover letter/Una Carta Por Separada Una corta carta correcta de negocio que expresa el interés del remitente en un empleo y que pide una entrevista. (p. 416)

Criteria/Criterios Condiciones que se establecen en una consulta. (p. 357)

Crosstab query/Consulta de referencia cruzada Calcular una suma, promedio, conteo u otro tipo de total de datos que están agrupados en dos campos, uno a lo ancho de la parte superior y el otro en cada fila de la hoja de trabajo. (p. 408)

Cursor/Cursor Barra vertical parpadeante que indica el lugar donde el texto ingresado aparecerá en la pantalla. También conocido como punto de inserción. (pp. 11, 553)

Cut/Cortar Seleccionar y borrar texto, normalmente con el propósito de pegarlo en alguna otra parte de un documento o aplicación. (pp. 80, 260)

D

Data/Datos Información factual usada como base para razonar, discutir o calcular. (pp. 204, 356)

Data source/Origen de datos Archivo que contiene la información para combinar correspondencia. (p. 177)

Data type/Tipo de datos Te dice qué tipo de datos pueden caber en un campo. Por ejemplo, un campo de números sólo puede almacenar números. (p. 386)

Database/Base de datos Manera organizada para almacenar información para que la computadora pueda buscar la información fácilmente. (pp. 348, 352)

Database object/Objeto de base de datos Cualquiera de las partes de la base de datos que se muestra en la Ventana de Base de Datos. Una tabla, consulta, formulario, reporte, página, módulo o macro. (p. 376)

Database template/Plantilla de Base de Datos Una muestra de base de datos usada por el asistente de base de datos para crear una nueva base de datos. (p. 302)

Datasheet/Una Hoja de Datos Una representación visual de los datos contenidos en una tabla Access o los resultados devueltos por una pregunta. (p. 432)

Decision/Una Decisión Una posición, una opinión o un juicio que se logra después de estar estudiado. (p. 95)

Default/Un Defecto Un fijo que un programa elige automáticamente si no se especifica un sustituto. Por ejemplo, Word 2007 contiene fijos de defectos de margen que se puede cambiar. (pp. 35, 43, 54)

Delete/Suprimir Tachar o borrar (pp. 14, 43, 54)

Delimiter/Delimitador Divisores que separan texto. (p. 254)

Demote/Disminuir nivel En esquemas, cambia el texto seleccionado al siguiente nivel inferior de encabezado (bajar un nivel, mover a la derecha). (pp. 120, 575)

Describe/Describir Resumir. (p. 98)

Design/Diseñar Idear para una función o fin específico. (pp. 161, 488)

Design View/Vista Diseño Vista que te permite cambiar la estructura de un objeto de base de datos. (pp. 386, 512)

Determine/Determinar Resolver o decidir, eligiendo de entre alternativas o posibilidades. (pp. 8, 229)

Diagram/Diagrama Gráfica que representa o ilustra algo o que se puede usar para organizar y presentar visualmente la información en una diapositiva. (pp. 147, 580)

Dialog box/Cuadro de diálogo Cuadro abierto por algunos comandos del menú que permite seleccionar opciones o especificar información para efectuar el comando. (pp. 9, 206, 362, 547)

Dialog Box Launcher/El Lanzamiento del Cuadro de Diálogo Un botón en donde se puede hacer clic que aparece en el rincón abajo a la derecha de un grupo en la Cinta (Ribbon). El lanzamiento del Cuadro de Diálogo indicado Párrafo en Word abre la ventana Párrafo Cuadro de Diálogo. (p. xli)

Digital signature/La Firma Digital Una característica de seguridad que autentifica la información digital que Ud. crea. Insertando una firma digital significa que no se ha cambiado el contenido desde que se ha firmado el documento. (p. xlviii)

Reading Skills Handbook

Reading: What's in It for You?

What role does reading play in your life? The possibilities are countless. Are you on a sports team? Perhaps you like to read about the latest news and statistics in your sport or find out about new training techniques. Are you looking for a part-time job? You might be looking for advice about résumé writing, interview techniques, or information about a company. Are you enrolled in an English class, an algebra class, or a business class? Then your assignments require a lot of reading.

Improving or Fine-tuning Your Reading Skills Will:

- Improve your grades
- Allow you to read faster and more efficiently
- Improve your study skills
- Help you remember more information accurately
- Improve your writing

The Reading Process

Good reading skills build on one another, overlap, and spiral around in much the same way that a winding staircase goes around and around while leading you to a higher place. This handbook is designed to help you find and use the tools you will need **before**, **during**, and **after** reading.

Strategies You Can Use

- Identify, understand, and learn new words
- Understand why you read
- Take a quick look at the whole text
- Try to predict what you are about to read
- Take breaks while you read and ask yourself questions about the text
- Take notes
- Keep thinking about what will come next
- Summarize

Vocabulary Development

Word identification and vocabulary skills are the building blocks of the reading and the writing process. By learning to use a variety of strategies to build your word skills and vocabulary, you will become a stronger reader.

Cell reference/Referencia de celda La letra de la columna y el número de la fila de una celda. (pp. 211, 291)

Cell style/Formato de celda Grupo de rasgos de formato al que se ha dado un nombre específico. (p. 260)

Character/Carácter Cada una de las letras, números, símbolos y signos de puntuación. (pp. 38, 53)

Chart/Gráfica (Gráfico) Presentación gráfica que organiza visualmente los datos. Las gráficas comunes incluyen las gráficas circulares, las de barras y las de líneas. (pp. 150, 294, 511, 583)

Chicago Style/Estilo Chicago Las directrices creadas por el *Chicago Manual of Style* para formatear y para citar las fuentes en un informe de investigación académica. (p. 116)

Clear/Borrar Quitar todos los contenidos de una celda. (pp. 40, 231)

Clip Art/Imágenes prediseñadas Imágenes o gráficos que se han hecho previamente y que pueden insertarse en un documento o una presentación. (pp. 143, 578)

Clipboard/Portapapeles Lugar donde se almacena el texto cortado o copiado para usarse después. (pp. 70, 234, 549)

Collaborate /Colaborar Trabajar juntos para completar un proyecto. (pp.185, 193)

Color scheme/Esquema de color Los ocho colores usados en el diseño de una diapositiva. Cada plantilla de diseño tiene un esquema de color que se usa para el fondo de la presentación, el texto y las líneas, el sombreado, texto del título, llenados, acentos e hipervínculos. (p. 625)

Column/Columna Celdas arregladas verticalmente bajo un encabezado de letras. (pp. 133, 139, 254, 363)

Column break/Salto de columna Separación de texto entre una columna y la parte superior de la siguiente columna. (p. 134)

Combine/Combinar Fusionar dos copias distintas del mismo documento en un solo documento. (p. 169)

Command/Comando Controles que señalan que la computadora realice una tarea específica. (pp. 6, 206, 354, 544)

Comment/Comentario Notas que pueden agregarse a un documento o una presentación sin que aparezcan como cambios reales. (pp. 167, 591)

Common/Común Compartido por dos o más partes. (pp. 315, 480)

Communicate/Comunicar Transmitir información, pensamiento, o sentimiento para que sea recibido o comprendido de modo satisfactorio. (p. 1)

Compare/Comparar Examinar y prestar atención a las semejanzas o diferencias. (p. 359)

Compatible/Compatible Capaz de funcionar en versiones anteriores. (p. 663)

Compatibility Checker/Control de Compatabilidad Un instrumento de Office 2007 que identifica características en un documento de Word, Excel, Access, or PowerPoint que no funcionará correctamente si se abre con una versión previa del software, como tal Office 2003 o Office 2000. (p. 663)

Computer/Computadora (Computador) Dispositivo electrónico que procesa los datos y los convierte en información que se puede usar. (pp. 2, 201, 349)

Condition/Condición Regla. (p. 302)

Conditional formatting /El Formateo Condicional Un formato que está fijado para aparecer de una cierta manera si ciertas condiciones o reglas están cumplidas. (pp. 447–448)

Consider/Considerar Meditar cuidadosamente. (p. 6)

Content/Los Contenidos El texto, los gráficos y los datos que se contienen en un archivo de Word, Excel, Access, o PowerPoint. (pp. 111, 117, 571)

Contextual tab/Cinta contextual Pestaña que aparece en la Cinta y que contiene instrucciones que pueden usarse solamente en un orden elegido. (pp. xlv, 101, 572)

Contribute/Contribuir Participar de manera significativa para llevar a cabo una meta o resultado. (p. 165)

Control/Control Objeto en un formulario o reporte que muestra información como por ejemplo un cuadro de texto o una casilla de verificación o un botón, que permite a los usuarios controlar un programa. (pp. 355, 389, 442)

Convert/Convertir Cambiar el formato de un documento o de un archivo. (pp. 152, 254, 321)

Convey/Transmitir Comunicar visualmente. (p. 275)

Copy/Copiar Seleccionar y reproducir texto en alguna otra parte del documento o aplicación. (pp. 81, 260)

Copyright/Los Derechos de Autor El derecho exclusivo de publicar y vender las obras literarias, musicales, o artísticas. (pp. 586, 629, 650)

Use Context to Determine Meaning

The best way to expand and extend your vocabulary is to read widely, listen carefully, and participate in a rich variety of discussions. When reading on your own, though, you can often figure out the meanings of new words by looking at their **context,** the other words and sentences that surround them.

Tips for Using Context

Look for clues such as:

A synonym or an explanation of the unknown word in the sentence:
Elise's shop specialized in ***millinery,*** *or* ***hats for women.***

A reference to what the word is or is not like:
An ***archaeologist,*** *like a* ***historian,*** *deals with the past.*

A general topic associated with the word:
The ***cooking*** *teacher discussed the best way to* ***braise*** *meat.*

A description or action associated with the word:
He used the ***shovel*** *to* ***dig up*** *the garden.*

Predict a Possible Meaning

Another way to determine the meaning of a word is to take the word apart. If you understand the meaning of the **base,** or **root,** part of a word, and also know the meanings of key syllables added either to the beginning or end of the base word, you can usually figure out what the word means.

Word Origins Since Latin, Greek, and Anglo-Saxon roots are the basis for much of our English vocabulary, having some background in languages can be a useful vocabulary tool. For example, *astronomy* comes from the Greek root *astro,* which means "relating to the stars." *Stellar* also has a meaning referring to stars, but its origin is Latin. Knowing root words in other languages can help you determine meanings, derivations, and spellings in English.

Prefixes and Suffixes A prefix is a word part that can be added to the beginning of a word. For example, the prefix *semi* means "half" or "partial," so *semicircle* means "half a circle." A suffix is a word part that can be added to the end of a word. Adding a suffix often changes a word from one part of speech to another.

Recognize Word Meanings Across Subjects
Have you learned a new word in one class and then noticed it in your reading for other subjects? The word might not mean exactly the same thing in each class, but you can use the meaning you already know to help you understand the word's meaning in another subject area.

A

Absolute reference/Referencia absoluta Referencia de celda que no cambia cuando se copia una fórmula en otro lugar. (pp. 292, 319)

Action Button/Botón de acción Botón que cuando se pulsa ejecuta una acción en una presentación de diapositivas, como avanzar a otra diapositiva. (p. 647)

Adjust/Ajustar Adaptar o conformar. (p. 289)

Affect/Afectar Producir un efecto sobre algo. (p. 381)

Aggregate function/Función agregada Se usa para calcular cuentas, sumas, promedios y otras estadísticas para grupos de registros. (p. 455)

Alias/Alias Nombre alternativo dado a una tabla o campo en una expresión. (p. 483)

Alignment/Alineación Manera en que el texto se alinea con respecto a los márgenes o tabuladores. (pp. 44, 264, 607)

Analyze/Analizar Estudiar o determinar la naturaleza y relación de las partes de un componente. (pp. 54, 408)

Animation scheme/Esquema de animación Efecto que cuando se aplica hace que el texto y los gráficos se muevan y se desplieguen de manera específica. (p. 620)

Annotation/Anotación Marca o nota que se hace con una herramienta de pluma cuando se ve una diapositiva. (p. 658)

Anticipate/Anticipar Acto de esperar ansiosamente. (p. 620)

Application/Aplicación Programa diseñado para un tipo específico de tarea, así como escribir una carta o calcular un presupuesto. (p. 1)

Arrange/Organizar Organizar al mismo tiempo más de una ventana en la pantalla. (p. 345)

Attachment/Anexo Archivo que se envía con un mensaje de correo electrónico. (pp. 165, 397)

Attachment field/Campo de anexo Campo que se usa para relacionar archivos y otros objetos a una base de datos. (p. 396)

AutoCorrect/Autocorrección Herramienta de Word que automáticamente corrige errores comunes de ortografía. (pp. 80, 519)

AutoFormat/Autoformato Formato disponible en Access que puede aplicarse a un objeto de base de datos existente. (p. 457)

AutoSum/Autosuma Función que se usa para agregar valores en filas o columnas. (p. 229)

AVERAGE/Promedio Función que se usa para determinar el promedio numérico de un grupo de celdas. (p. 229)

B

Background/Fondo (Segundo plano) Gráfico que aparece detrás de la información en una hoja de trabajo; Colores, estampados o figuras que llenan toda la diapositiva y aparecen detrás del contenido de la diapositiva. (pp. 173, 269, 625)

Backup/Respaldo (Copia de seguridad) Copia de una base de datos que se guarda para proteger el trabajo y la información. (p. 368)

Border/Borde Línea o cuadro que enmarca a un texto o una celda. (pp. 52, 252)

Browser/Navegador Programa de software que se usa para navegar en Internet e interactuar con sitios Web. (p. 321)

Budget/Presupuesto Cálculo aproximado de ingresos y egresos durante cierto período de tiempo. (p. 228)

Building Block/Bloque de Construcción Elemento que se guarda mediante la herramienta Quick Parts. (p. 85)

Bullet/Viñeta Símbolo, figura o imagen, como por ejemplo un punto, diamante o flecha. Las viñetas se usan comúnmente en listas no ordenadas. (p. 46)

Bulleted list/Lista con viñetas Serie de textos precedidos por un símbolo especial como un punto o una flecha. (p. 46)

Business letter/Carta de negocios Carta formal escrita por una empresa o un individuo acerca de un asunto relacionado con los negocios. (pp. 67, 68)

Button/Botón Icono gráfico en el que se hace clic para efectuar una tarea específica. (pp. xxxix, 6, 206, 354, 544, 609)

C

Caption/Título Nombre para desplegar. Encabezado de columna de un campo en la Vista Hoja de Datos. El texto en un control etiqueta. (p. 393)

CD-ROM/CD-ROM Disco óptico que puede almacenar hasta 1 gigabyte de información. (p. 661)

Cell/Celda Intersección de una fila y una columna en una tabla o hoja de trabajo. (pp. 137, 211)

Cell content/Contenido de celda Letras, números y símbolos que aparecen dentro de una celda. (p. 228)

Dictionary Entry

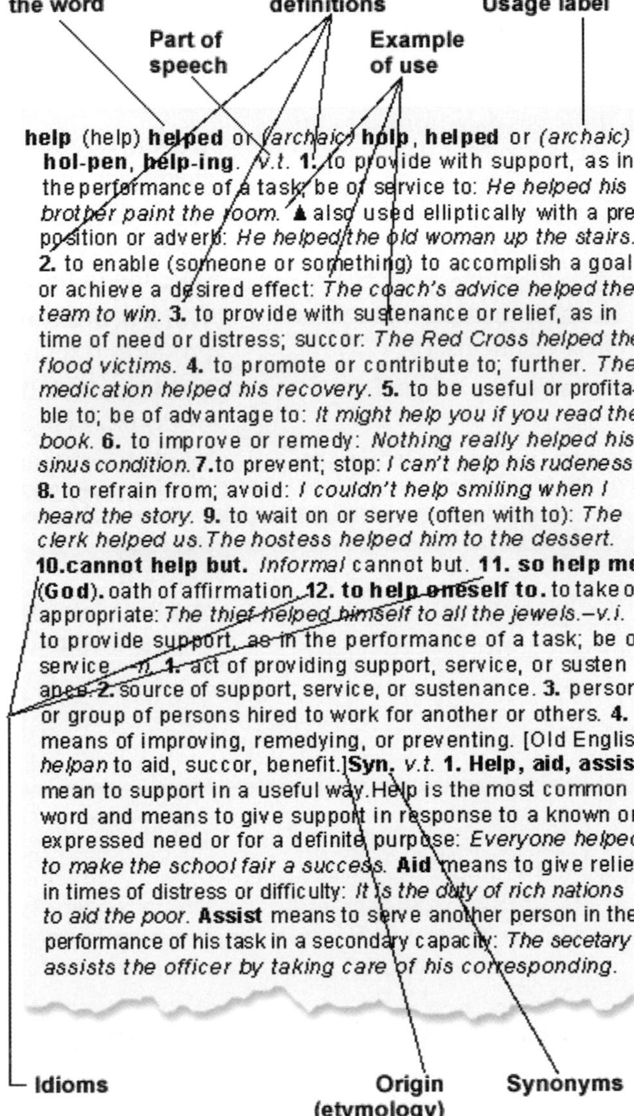

help (help) **helped** or *(archaic)* **holp**, **helped** or *(archaic)* **hol-pen, help-ing**. *v.t.* **1.** to provide with support, as in the performance of a task; be of service to: *He helped his brother paint the room.* ▲ also used elliptically with a preposition or adverb: *He helped the old woman up the stairs.* **2.** to enable (someone or something) to accomplish a goal or achieve a desired effect: *The coach's advice helped the team to win.* **3.** to provide with sustenance or relief, as in time of need or distress; succor: *The Red Cross helped the flood victims.* **4.** to promote or contribute to; further. *The medication helped his recovery.* **5.** to be useful or profitable to; be of advantage to: *It might help you if you read the book.* **6.** to improve or remedy: *Nothing really helped his sinus condition.* **7.** to prevent; stop: *I can't help his rudeness.* **8.** to refrain from; avoid: *I couldn't help smiling when I heard the story.* **9.** to wait on or serve (often with to): *The clerk helped us. The hostess helped him to the dessert.* **10. cannot help but.** *Informal* cannot but. **11. so help me (God).** oath of affirmation. **12. to help oneself to.** to take or appropriate: *The thief helped himself to all the jewels.*—*v.i.* to provide support, as in the performance of a task; be of service. —*n.* **1.** act of providing support, service, or susten ance. **2.** source of support, service, or sustenance. **3.** person or group of persons hired to work for another or others. **4.** means of improving, remedying, or preventing. [Old English *helpan* to aid, succor, benefit.] **Syn.** *v.t.* **1. Help, aid, assist** mean to support in a useful way. Help is the most common word and means to give support in response to a known or expressed need or for a definite purpose: *Everyone helped to make the school fair a success.* **Aid** means to give relief in times of distress or difficulty: *It is the duty of rich nations to aid the poor.* **Assist** means to serve another person in the performance of his task in a secondary capacity: *The secetary assists the officer by taking care of his corresponding.*

Using Dictionaries A dictionary provides the meaning or meanings of a word. Look at the sample dictionary entry above to see what other information it provides.

Thesauruses and Specialized Reference Books A thesaurus provides synonyms and often antonyms. Specialized dictionaries, such as *Barron's Dictionary of Business Terms* or *Black's Law Dictionary,* list terms and expressions that are not commonly included in a general dictionary. You can also use online dictionaries.

Glossaries Many textbooks and technical works contain condensed dictionaries that provide an alphabetical listing of words used in the text and their specific definitions.

Transition An effect that occurs between slides during a slide show. (p. 622)

Typeface The overall design of a full set of characters. Also known as font. (pp. 38, 605)

U

Union Query A query that merges data from separate queries into one query. (p. 515)

Unmatched query A query that finds records without matching related data. (p. 408)

V

Vary To make differences between items. (p. 177)

Version A form or variant of a type or original. (pp. 300, 523)

Vertical alignment The top-to-bottom placement of the contents of a cell. (p. 255)

Visual Capable of being seen; visible. (p. 148)

W

Web browser An application that displays Web pages. (p. 175)

Web Layout view A view that allows you to see how your document will look as a Web page. (p. 173)

Wildcard Using characters similar to your criteria to find information. (p. 429)

Window An area on the computer screen where an application can be viewed and accessed. (pp. 122, 320, 441)

WordArt A tool used to create text that is stretched, shadowed, or shaped. (p. 150, 588)

Word Count The command that counts the number of words, characters, and paragraphs in a document or selection of text. (p. 104)

Word processor A computer application that produces text documents. (p. 2)

Workbook An Excel file that contains one or more worksheets. (p. 207)

Worksheet A sheet of cells organized into rows and columns. (p. 207)

Z

Zoom A tool that increases or decreases the size of objects within the window (pp. xliii, 19)

Understanding What You Read

Reading comprehension means understanding—deriving meaning from—what you have read. Using a variety of strategies can help you improve your comprehension and make reading more interesting and more fun.

Read for a Reason

To get the greatest benefit from what you read, you should **establish a purpose for reading**. In school, you have many reasons for reading. Some of them are:

- To learn and understand new information
- To find specific information
- To review before a test
- To complete an assignment
- To prepare (research) before you write

As your reading skills improve, you will notice that you apply different strategies to fit the different purposes for reading. For example, if you are reading for entertainment, you might read quickly, but if you read to gather information or follow directions, you might read more slowly, take notes, construct a graphic organizer, or reread sections of text.

Draw on Personal Background

Drawing on personal background may also be called activating prior knowledge. Before you start reading a text, ask yourself questions like these:

- What have I heard or read about this topic?
- Do I have any personal experience relating to this topic?

Using a KWL Chart A KWL chart is a good device for organizing information you gather before, during, and after reading. In the first column, list what you already **know**, then list what you **want** to know in the middle column. Use the third column when you review and you assess what you **learned**. You can also add more columns to record places where you found information and places where you can look for more information.

K (What I already know)	W (What I want to know)	L (What I have learned)

Adjust Your Reading Speed Your reading speed is a key factor in how well you understand what you are reading. You will need to adjust your speed depending on your reading purpose.

Scanning means running your eyes quickly over the material to look for words or phrases. Scan when you need a specific piece of information.

Skimming means reading a passage quickly to find its main idea or to get an overview. Skim a text when you preview to determine what the material is about.

Sizing handle Points on a small square around a selected object that can be dragged to change the object's size. (p. 145)

Slide One page in a presentation. (p. 546)

Slide Finder A pane displaying a miniature of each slide in a presentation that you can select and insert into the current presentation. (p. 623)

Slide icon The small slide image that is located next to the slide content in the Outline pane. Click the image to move among slides. (p. 523)

Slide layout The arrangement of text and graphics on a slide. (p. 604)

Slide Master A slide that serves as a model for every slide in a presentation except the Title slide. (p. 623)

SmartArt A gallery that contains six types of customizable diagrams. (pp. 147, 271)

Snap To line up with a grid or guide when something is dragged close to it. (p. 648)

Sort To put a list of data in ascending or descending order. (pp. 285, 453)

Source One that provides information. (p. 515)

Split To divide a window into two panes that you can scroll independently. (p. 319)

Split form A form that is split into a datasheet in one half and a form in the other. (p. 433)

Spreadsheet A table of numerical data organized into columns and rows. (pp. 204, 207, 315)

Start Menu A Windows menu that provides tools to locate documents, find help, change system settings, and run programs. (p. 5)

Status bar The bar at the bottom of the screen that displays information such as the current page or slide number and the total number of pages or slides in the document. (pp. 5, 544)

Style A set of defined formatting characteristics. (pp. 40, 142)

Subform A form inserted into another form. (p. 435)

Survey A detailed critical inspection. (p. 136)

Symbol A character such as a monetary symbol that does not appear on the keyboard but can be inserted using the Symbol dialog box. (p. 73)

Synonym A word with the same meaning as another word. (p. 74)

T

Tab A clickable area of the Ribbon that displays menu options. (pp. 6, 206, 354, 545)

Tab stop A setting that determines where the insertion point will stop when you press the Tab key. (pp. xxxix, 6, 206, 356, 576,)

Table A set of rows and columns used to organize information. (pp. 136, 356, 576)

Table Analyzer Wizard A wizard that evaluates the information in a chosen table and then makes changes to streamline the data. (p. 391)

Table of contents A list of the topics presented in a document, along with their corresponding page numbers. (pp. 109, 111, 117)

Table Style A pre-defined set of formats that can be applied to a range of data. (p. 255)

Task pane A pane that can be used to simplify tasks. For example, the Clip Art task pane is used to narrow down search terms when the Clip Art Gallery is searched. (pp. 217, 578-579, 620, 369)

Template A guide that contains the formatting of a particular type of document, workbook, or presentation. (pp. 83, 315)

Text Words on a page or in a document. (pp. 14, 99-100, 252-253, 553, 568, 574)

Text box A moveable, resizable rectangle that contains text. (pp. 145, 442, 643)

Theme A collection of design elements, graphics, and colors that help items such as documents, presentations, and Web pages maintain a consistent image. (pp. 255, 571)

Thesaurus A collection of words and their synonyms, similar to a dictionary. (pp. 74, 659)

Timing A PowerPoint feature that determines how long a slide should remain visible during a slide show before automatically moving to the next slide. (p. 659)

Title bar The bar at the top of the screen that displays the name of the current window. (pp. 10, 205, 353, 544)

Totals row A function can summarize columns of data in a table to give you totals, averages, maximums, minimums, and other calculations simply and quickly. (p. 387)

Track Changes A feature that keeps track of the changes you make to a document. (p. 166)

Reading for detail involves careful reading while paying attention to text structure and monitoring your understanding. Read for detail when you are learning concepts, following complicated directions, or preparing to analyze a text.

Techniques to Understand and Remember What You Read

Preview

Before beginning a selection, it is helpful to **preview** what you are about to read.

Previewing Strategies

- Read the title, headings, and subheadings of the selection.
- Look at the illustrations and notice how the text is organized.
- Skim the selection: Take a glance at the whole thing.
- Decide what the main idea might be.
- Predict what the selection will be about.

Predict

Have you ever read a mystery, decided who committed the crime, and then changed your mind as more clues were revealed? You were adjusting your predictions. Did you smile when you found out you guessed the murderer? You were verifying your predictions.

As you read, take educated guesses about story events and outcomes; that is, **make predictions** before and during reading. This will help you focus your attention on the text and it will improve your understanding.

Determine the Main Idea

When you look for the **main idea**, you are looking for the most important statement in a text. Depending on what kind of text you are reading, the main idea can be located at the very beginning (as in news stories in a newspaper or a magazine) or at the end (as in a scientific research document). Ask yourself:

- What is each sentence about?
- Is there one sentence that is more important than all the others?
- What idea do details support or point out?

Q

Query An instruction that tells a database to show only certain information. (p. 357)

Quick Access Toolbar (QAT) A toolbar that allows users to quickly find commands. (pp. xlii, 8, 205, 353, 544)

Quick Parts A tool that allows you to save text, images, and special formats. (p. 85)

Quick Print A print option that prints the report right away without opening the Print dialog box. (p. 516)

Quick Styles A feature that lets you easily apply new styles to text. (p. 54)

R

Range A group of cells. (p. 284)

Record The set of data that describes one item, shown in one row of a table. (p. 356)

Referential integrity Prevents conflicting data between two tables by enforcing a relationship. (p. 401)

Refine To filter information. (p. 478)

Relationship A link between two tables based on a common field. (p. 399)

Relative reference A cell reference that changes when a formula is copied to a new location. (p. 291)

Replace A tool used to replace found data. (p. 429)

Report A formal document used to communicate information. (p. 98)

Resize To make a window larger or smaller; To make controls on a form or report larger or smaller. (p. 458)

Responsibility An obligation. When a person is given a responsibility, he or she has a duty to be reliable and to follow through. (pp. 131, 226, 371)

Restore To make a window that was minimized visible again. (p. 152)

Revise Look over again in order to correct or improve. (p. 449)

Ribbon A panel in Microsoft Office that organizes commands into tabs. The Ribbon changes depending on which applications and tools are activated. (pp. 6, 206, 354, 545)

Right-outer join A join that tells the query to return all the rows from the second table and only the rows from the first table that match the second table. (p. 480)

Rotate To turn an object, usually 90° to the left or right. (p. 615)

S

Save As dialog box A dialog box that appears when you click the Save or the Save As button. In the Save As dialog box, you change the filename, file type, or location of the file. (pp. lii, 9, 209, 407, 664)

Scale Changes the size of a character. (p. 53)

Scanner Hardware that digitally encodes text, graphics, and photographs. (p. 586)

ScreenTip A description that appears when you point to a button. (pp. 7, 356, 551)

Scroll To move up or down or side to side through a document by using the scroll bar or by pressing buttons on the keyboard. (p. 5)

Scroll bar A bar at the right side or bottom of the screen that allows you to move up and down or left and right in a document or a worksheet. (pp. 7, 229, 382, 525)

Search box A feature used to seek out information using keywords. The Help feature in Office uses a Search box. (p. 20)

Section A portion of a document that can have different formatting from the rest of the document. (p. 109)

Section break A break that you insert to start a new section. (p. 109)

Shape Graphics including circles, squares, stars, and arrows. (p. 148)

Sheet tab A small flap at the bottom of a worksheet that displays the name of the worksheet, and allows you to move from one worksheet to another within the same workbook. (p. 208)

Shortcut A simplified means of performing a task. Some require you to click an icon that automatically opens a particular program, folder, or file. Other shortcuts require you to press a combination of keys. (pp. 40, 354, 606, 657)

Shortcut menu A menu that opens when you right-click an icon. (p. 657)

Taking Notes

Cornell Note-Taking System There are many methods for note taking. The **Cornell Note-Taking System** is a well-known method that can help you organize what you read. To the right is a diagram that shows how the Cornell Note-Taking System organizes information.

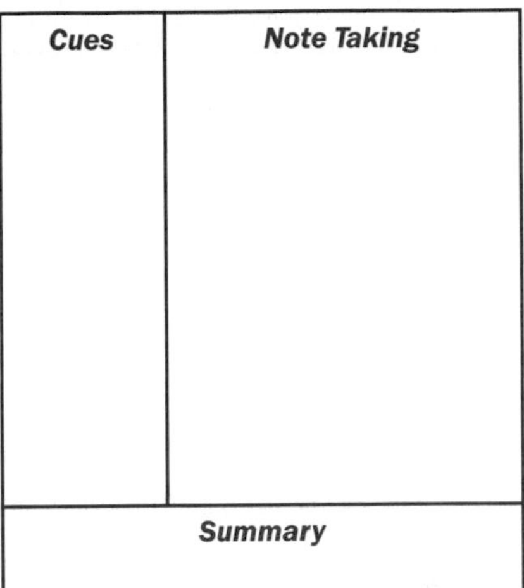

Graphic Organizers Using a graphic organizer to retell content in a visual representation will help you remember and retain content. You might make a **chart** or **diagram**, organizing what you have read. Here are some examples of graphic organizers:

Venn diagrams When mapping out a compare-and-contrast text structure, you can use a Venn diagram. The outer portions of the circles will show how two characters, ideas, or items contrast, or are different, and the overlapping part will compare two things, or show how they are similar.

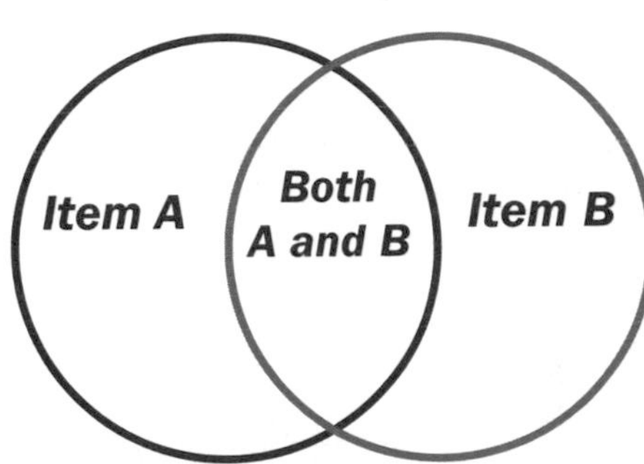

Flow charts To help you track the sequence of events, or cause and effect, use a flow chart. Arrange ideas or events in their logical, sequential order. Then draw arrows between your ideas to indicate how one idea or event flows into another.

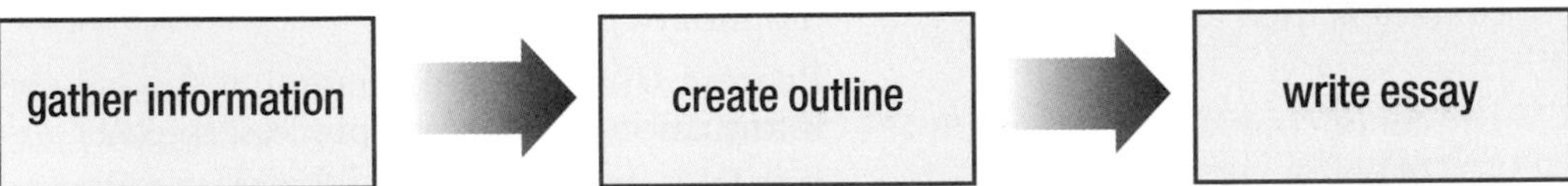

Visualize

Try to form a mental picture of scenes, characters, and events as you read. Use the details and descriptions the author gives you. If you can **visualize** what you read, it will be more interesting and you will remember it better.

Question

Ask yourself questions about the text as you read. Ask yourself about the importance of the sentences, how they relate to one another, if you understand what you just read, and what you think is going to come next.

Operating system The overall program that controls all the other software programs on a machine and allows hardware devices to work properly. Windows XP and Windows Vista are the operating systems on which Office 2007 runs. (p. xlix)

Operator A symbol that represents a mathematical function. (p. 286)

Organizational chart A chart that demonstrates an organizational arrangement. (p. 271)

Outline View The view of a document that displays the text, indented to show the heading level. (p. 120)

Outlook A Microsoft Office program that sends, receives, and organizes e-mail messages. (pp. 730, 733)

P

Package for CD A fast way to group a PowerPoint presentation and all related files (such as linked files and PowerPoint Viewer) into one folder. (p. 661)

Page break The place where one printed page ends and the next begins. A soft page break automatically moves text to a new page. A hard page break can be inserted to force text to a new page. (pp. 103, 326)

Page orientation Refers to whether a page is laid out vertically (Portrait) or horizontally (Landscape). (pp. 176, 323)

Parameter A limit. You can apply a parameter to a query. (p. 478)

Password A string of characters used to encrypt a database. (p. 518)

Paste To place previously cut or copied text into a document. (pp. 70, 234, 574)

Picture A graphic, photograph, or other piece of artwork that is inserted into a Word document, PowerPoint slide, Excel worksheet, or Access form. (p. 586)

Phrase A group of words that functions as a single unit. (p. 78)

PivotTable A table that can display information and present it in several different ways. (p. 438)

Placeholder Preset text boxes. (p. 552)

Plagiarism The act of taking another person's words and ideas as one's own. (pp. 105, 343)

PMT A function that calculates payments for a loan based on interest rate, number of payments and the amount of the loan. (p. 300)

Point Unit of measure for font size. (p. 38)

Pointer The arrow used to select on-screen items, such as menus and buttons. In Excel, the pointer changes to a two-headed arrow to resize columns. It changes to a block plus sign over the worksheet cells and it changes to a black plus sign over the fill handle of a cell. (pp. 5, 354)

Portion A part or share of something. (p. 281)

Portrait The orientation of a page, worksheet, or presentation that is taller than it is wide. (pp. 323, 623)

PowerPoint Viewer A computer application that allows people to view a slide show without using PowerPoint. (p. 661)

Presentation A PowerPoint file. A presentation can contain text, pictures, charts, links to other pages, and other objects. (p. 546)

Preview An on-screen sample of a page from a form or report. (p. 510)

Primary Key A column in a table whose values uniquely identify the rows in the table. (p. 386)

Print area The part of a worksheet that prints. (p. 324)

Print Layout View The default setting for viewing documents. Print Layout View displays how the document will look when printed. (pp. 7, 69, 704)

Print Preview A preview of documents, worksheets, or slides to be printed. (pp. 21, 216, 365, 557, 704)

Printer A device used to transfer information from a monitor to paper. (p. 21)

Process Diagram A diagram that shows how information changes in a process. (p. 271)

Productivity A measure of a person or team's ability to achieve results. (p. 202)

Promote In outlines, changes selected text to the next-higher heading level (up one level, to the left). (p. 575)

Proofread To read for the purpose of finding and correcting errors. (pp. 13, 22, 245, 677)

Property A detail about an object, such as the size or default value. (p. 386)

Property sheet A window listing the properties for an object. (p. 389)

Clarify

If you feel you do not understand meaning (through questioning), try these techniques:

What to Do When You Do Not Understand

- Reread confusing parts of the text.
- Diagram (chart) relationships between chunks of text, ideas, and sentences.
- Look up unfamiliar words.
- Talk out the text to yourself.
- Read the passage once more.

Review

Take time to stop and review what you have read. Use your note-taking tools (graphic organizers or Cornell notes charts). Also, review and consider your KWL chart.

Monitor Your Comprehension

Continue to check your understanding by using the following two strategies:

Summarize Pause and tell yourself the main ideas of the text and the key supporting details. Try to answer the following questions: Who? What? When? Where? Why? How?

Paraphrase Pause, close the book, and try to retell what you have just read in your own words. It might help to pretend you are explaining the text to someone who has not read it and does not know the material.

Understanding Text Structure

Good writers do not just put together sentences and paragraphs. They organize their writing with a specific purpose in mind. That organization is called text structure. When you understand and follow the structure of a text, it is easier to remember the information you are reading. There are many ways text may be structured. Watch for **signal words**. They will help you follow the text's organization. Also, remember to use these techniques when you write.

Compare and Contrast

The compare and contrast structure shows similarities and differences between people, things, and ideas. This is often used to demonstrate that things that seem alike are really different, or vice versa.

Signal words: similarly, more, less, on the one hand/on the other hand, in contrast, but, however

Live Preview previews the styles as the cursor moves over them. (p. 54)

Locate To determine or indicate the place, site, or limits of. (p. 331)

Log A written record. (p. 114)

Lookup field Displays input choices from another table so you can enter data by choosing from a list. (p. 394)

M

Mail Merge The tool in Word that creates multiple copies of the same letter, envelope, or label and inserts personalized data. (p. 177)

Main document The letter, envelope, or label document that is used in a mail merge. (p. 178)

Margin The amount of space between the text and the edge of the page. (pp. 35, 327)

Mark as Final A command that makes your document read-only, preventing any changes from being made to it. (p. xlviii)

Markups Any extra text added as comments to a document or slide. (p. 615)

MAX A function used to identify the largest value in a group of cells. (p. 229)

Maximize To make a window fill up the screen. (p. 320)

Media Information that comes from sources such as magazines, newspapers, radio, television, and the Internet. (p. 592)

Memo An informal note sent to one or more people, usually within a business or organization. (pp. 33-35)

Merge To combine. For example, you can merge two documents or you can merge two cells in a table. (pp. 141, 169, 698)

Merge field Code in a mail merge main document that shows where data will be inserted. (p. 178)

MIN A function used to identify the smallest value in a group of cells. (p. 229)

Minimize To take a window off the desktop without closing it. (p. 221)

Mini Toolbar When text is selected, a miniature formatting toolbar from which you can change font, font size, font color, and more. The Mini Toolbar is semitransparent until the mouse pointer is moved over it. When the pointer rests on the toolbar, it becomes opaque. (pp. xliv, 12)

Mixed reference A cell reference that is part relative and part absolute. (p. 293)

MLA (Modern Language Association) An organization that publishes guidelines on how to format and cite sources in an academic research report. (pp. 9, 105, 115)

Monitor To watch and confirm. Also refers to the part of a computer that displays the screen. (pp. liv, 552)

Multiple item form A form that shows multiple items in a datasheet. (p. 432)

N

Navigate To move through your document to a particular location. (p. 102)

Navigation Pane A pane that appears along the left side of the screen in Access. The Navigation Pane lists the queries, tables, and other objects in your database. Click an object in the Navigation Pane to open it. (p. 353)

Network A group of computers that are connected to each other. (p. 2)

Newsletter A printed report used by a company to keep employees informed about important events. (p. 133)

Normalize To make sure that a table is structured correctly and that there are no repeated groups of information. (p. 472)

NOW A function that displays the date and time that a worksheet is opened or used. (p. 300)

Numbered list A list of items that must appear in a particular sequence. Each item is preceded by a number or letter. (p. 50)

O

Object Any item that can be individually selected and manipulated. A graphic is an object, as are individual portions of a database, such as queries. (p. 514)

Object dependency Refers to the fact that a database object that uses a second database object is dependent on that second object. (p. 521)

Office Button A button located in the upper-left corner of Microsoft Word, Excel, Access, and PowerPoint. Click this button to open, save, and print files. (pp. xli, 5)

Cause and Effect

Writers use the cause and effect structure to explore the reasons for something happening and to examine the results, or consequences, of events.

Signal words: so, because, as a result, therefore, for the following reasons

Problem and Solution

When they organize text around the question "how?", writers state a problem and suggest solutions.

Signal words: how, help, problem, obstruction, overcome, difficulty, need, attempt, have to, must

Sequence

Sequencing tells you the order in which to consider thoughts or facts. Examples of sequencing are:

Chronological order refers to the order in which events take place.

Signal words: first, next, then, finally

Spatial order describes the organization of things in space (to describe a room, for example).

Signal words: above, below, behind, next to

Order of importance lists things or thoughts from the most important to the least important (or the other way around).

Signal words: principal, central, main, important, fundamental

Reading for Meaning

It is important to think about what you are reading to get the most information out of a text, to understand the consequences of what the text says, to remember the content, and to form your own opinion about what the content means.

Interpret

Interpreting is asking yourself, "What is the writer really saying?" and then using what you already know to answer that question.

Infer

Writers do not always directly state everything they want you to understand. By providing clues and details, they sometimes imply certain information. An **inference** involves using your reason and experience to develop the idea on your own, based on what an author implies or suggests. When drawing inferences, be sure that you have accurately based your guesses on supporting details from the text. If you cannot point to a place in the selection to help back up your inference, you may need to rethink your guess.

H

Header Text that appears at the top of every page or presentation. (pp. 101, 325, 628)

Help feature A feature that offers instructions and tips about many application-related topics. (pp. 20, 217, 556, 701)

Horizontal Left to right. (p. 36)

Horizontal alignment The side-to-side placement of the contents of a cell. (p. 264)

HTML See *Hypertext Markup Language.*

Hyperlink A link in a document to a Web page or to another document. (pp. 164, 239, 646)

Hypertext Markup Language (HTML) A programming language used by Internet browsers to read and display Web pages. (p. 173)

Icon A small picture or graphic that visually represents programs, document files, Web links, or other items on the computer. (pp. 38, 548)

IF A function that checks to see if a condition is met and then has one result if it is true and another if it is false. (p. 302)

Illustrate To show clearly. (p. 216)

Import To bring data from one application into another with the option of keeping the same formatting. (pp. 472, 573, 688, 694)

Import specifications Specifications that can be saved to indicate how data should be imported. (p. 475)

Incorporate Unite or work into something already existent so as to form an indistinguishable whole. (p. 642)

Indent The distance from the left or right margin to the text. (pp. 51, 117)

Inner join The default join that tells a query to combine rows from two tables that share a common value. (p. 480)

Input mask Allows users to apply a specific type of format to data entered into a database. (p. 398)

Insert To add text to a document; to add items such as rows or columns to a document, slide, spreadsheet, or database file. (pp. 11, 236)

Insertion point A blinking vertical bar that indicates where the text you key will appear on the screen. Also known as a cursor. (pp. 6, 11)

Join A field that connects two tables in an Access database. The join field belongs to both tables, and information from the joined tables is combined, resulting in more accurate query results. (p. 480)

K

Key To enter text into a document (p. 137)

Keyboard shortcut An alternate manner of performing a task by pressing keys on the keyboard instead of clicking an option or icon. For example, press **CTRL+B** to make text boldface. (pp. 40, 44, 78, 137, 354, 696)

L

Label To describe or designate with or as if with a label. (p. 459)

Landscape The orientation of a page, worksheet, or a slide that is wider than it is tall. (pp. 323, 392, 623)

Layout view A view that allows you to see how your data will look when printed. (p. 440)

Learn To become familiar with. (p. 205)

Left-outer join A join that tells the query to return all the rows from the first table and only the rows from the second table that match the first table. (p. 480)

Letterhead Stationary that includes the name and contact information of the sender. Companies often create letterhead that includes the business' logo. Individuals can create personal letterhead. (pp. 183-184)

Line color The color applied to a line or to the border of a shape. (p. 611)

Link The action of attaching one data source to another. (p. 472)

Literacy The ability to read, write, analyze, and evaluate. For example, media literacy is the ability to analyze and evaluate information from many sources. (p. 592)

Live Preview A tool in Office 2007 that allows users to preview formatting changes before you apply them. If Quick Styles are applied to a document, for example,

Draw Conclusions

A conclusion is a general statement you can make and explain with reasoning, or with supporting details from a text. If you read a story describing a sport in which five players bounce a ball and throw it through a high hoop, you may conclude that the sport is basketball.

Analyze

To understand persuasive nonfiction (a text that discusses facts and opinions to arrive at a conclusion), you need to analyze statements and examples to see if they support the main idea. To understand an informational text (such as a textbook, which gives you information, not opinions), you need to keep track of how the ideas are organized to find the main points.

Hint: Use your graphic organizers and notes charts.

Distinguish Facts and Opinions

Learning to determine the difference between facts and opinions is one of the most important reading skills you can learn. A fact is a statement that can be proven. An opinion is what the writer believes. A writer may support opinions with facts, but an opinion cannot be proven. For example:

Fact: California produces fruit and other agricultural products.

Opinion: California produces the best fruit and other agricultural products.

Evaluate

Would you seriously consider an article on nuclear fission if you knew it was written by a comedic actor? If you need to rely on accurate information, you need to find out who wrote what you are reading and why. Where did the writer get information? Is the information one-sided? Can you verify the information?

Reading for Research

You will need to **read actively** in order to research a topic. You might also need to generate an interesting, relevant, and researchable **question** on your own and locate appropriate print and nonprint information from a wide variety of sources. Then you will need to **categorize** that information, evaluate it, and **organize** it in a new way in order to produce a research project for a specific audience. Finally, **draw conclusions** about your original research question. These conclusions may lead you to other areas for further inquiry.

Encryption A way to keep information secure by scrambling it as it is being transmitted over a network or over the Internet. (pp. 518, 523)

Endnote A note at the end of the document or section that cites a reference or gives more information. (p. 107)

Enhance To make a document better. (p. 39)

Ensure To make sure, certain, or safe. (p. 522)

Evaluate To determine the significance, worth, or condition of, usually by careful appraisal and study. (p. 570)

Export To save data that was created in one application so that it can be accessed using a different application. You can export a table from an Access database so that it can be opened in Word. (p. 496)

Export specifications Terms that allow users to define how data will be exported from Access to another destination. (p. 498)

F

Field One piece of data that describes something. (p. 356)

File format The file type, such as .docx or .rtf. You can change the file format of a document so that users who do not use Microsoft Office can read your data. (p 332)

File management A utility that organizes files and information so that they are easy to locate. (pp. 9, 10)

Fill color The color applied to the interior of a shape. (p. 611)

Fill handle A tool that lets you fill multiple cells with the same content by using one cell as an example. (p. 238)

Filter A feature that allows you to look at only the data that you need. (pp. 284, 406)

Find A tool used to find specific data in a table or document. (pp. 79, 232, 429)

Folder An item that helps the user organize files. (pp. 9, 209, 362, 547)

Font The overall design of a full set of characters. Also known as typeface. (pp. 38, 251, 605)

Font style An effect that can be applied to a font, such as bold, italic, or underline. (pp. 39, 251, 605)

Footer Text that appears at the bottom (foot) of every page or presentation. (pp. 100, 452)

Footnote A note at the bottom of the page used to cite references or give more information. (pp. 42, 108)

Form An onscreen display where data can be added or changed (p. 430)

Format To make a document or presentation look a certain way by changing the appearance of words and paragraphs; a process in which the computer makes sure a disk works and then creates addresses for the information on a disk. (pp. 67, 98, 109)

Format Painter A tool that allows you to copy formatting from one object and paste it into another object. (pp. 41, 608)

Formatting Any change made to the appearance of the text or content on a slide. (pp. 40, 98, 603)

Formula An equation containing values, cell references, or both. (p. 215)

Formula Bar The bar that displays the contents of a cell. (p. 211)

Freeze To keep headings in place while you scroll through a worksheet. (p. 319)

Function A list of preset formulas that are used to solve equations. (pp. 288, 354)

G

Gradient The gradual shading of a graphic from one side or corner to the other. (p. 612)

Graphic A visual element created using tools such as WordArt, AutoShapes, scanners, and digital cameras. (p. 148)

Graphical list A graphic that may be used in a list, such as a bulleted or numbered list. (p. 271)

Graphical User Interface (GUI) A computer interface that makes computing easy by allowing users to click a mouse and graphical icons to perform commands. (p. xxxix)

Grid A series of horizontal and vertical lines laid over a slide to help align items on a slide. (p. 648)

Group An organized set of commands that relates to a specific activity. (pp. 6, 206, 354, 545)

Group Header A tool that refines reports by sorting information into groups. (p. 453)

Guide A horizontal or vertical line you place on a slide to help align objects. (p. 648)

Locate Appropriate Print and Nonprint Information

In your research, try to use a variety of sources. Because different sources present information in different ways, your research project will be more interesting and balanced when you read a variety of sources.

Literature and Textbooks These texts include any book used as a basis for instruction or a source of information.

Book Indexes A book index, or a bibliography, is an alphabetical listing of books. Some book indexes list books on specific subjects. Others are more general. Some list a variety of topics or resources.

Periodicals Magazines and journals are issued at regular intervals, such as weekly or monthly. One way to locate information in magazines is to use the *Readers' Guide to Periodical Literature.* This guide is available in print form in most libraries.

Technical Manuals A manual is a guide, or handbook, intended to give instruction on how to perform a task or operation. A vehicle owner's manual might give information on how to operate and service a car.

Reference Books Reference books include encyclopedias and almanacs, and are used to locate specific pieces of information.

Electronic Encyclopedias, Databases, and the Internet There are many ways to locate extensive information using your computer. Infotrac, for instance, acts as an online readers guide. CD-ROM encyclopedias can provide easy access to all subjects.

Organize and Convert Information

As you gather information from different sources, taking careful notes, you will need to think about how to **synthesize** the information, or convert it into a unified whole, as well as how to change it into a form your audience will easily understand and that will meet your assignment guidelines.

1. First, ask yourself what you want your audience to know.
2. Then, think about a pattern of organization, a structure that will best show your main ideas. You might ask yourself the following questions:
   - When comparing items or ideas, what graphic aids can I use?
   - When showing the reasons something happened and the effects of certain actions, what text structure would be best?
   - How can I briefly and clearly show important information to my audience?
   - Would an illustration or even a cartoon help to make a certain point?

Cursor A vertical bar that indicates where the text you key will appear on the screen. Also known as an insertion point. (pp. 11, 553)

Cut To select and remove text, usually for the purpose of pasting somewhere else in a document or application. (pp. 80, 260)

D

Data Factual information used as a basis for reasoning, discussion, or calculation. (pp. 204, 356)

Data source A file that contains the information for a mail merge. (p. 177)

Data type Tells what type of data a field can hold. For instance, a number field can store numbers only. (p. 386)

Database An organized way to store information so that it is easy for the computer to search for information. (pp. 348, 352)

Database object Any of the parts of the database shown in the Database window. A table, query, form, report, page, module, or macro. (p. 376)

Database template A sample database used by the Database Wizard to create a new database. (p. 302)

Datasheet A visual representation of the data contained in an Access table, or the results returned by a query. (p. 432)

Decision A position, opinion, or judgment reached after consideration. (p. 95)

Default A setting that a program automatically selects if you do not specify a substitute. For example, Word 2007 has default margin settings that you can change. (pp. 35, 43, 54)

Delete To remove or erase (pp. 14, 43, 54)

Delimiter A divider that separates text. (p. 254)

Demote In an outline, to change selected text to a lower heading level. (pp. 120, 575)

Describe To summarize. (p. 98)

Design To devise for a specific function or purpose. (pp. 161, 488)

Design View The view that allows you to change the structure of a database object. (pp. 386, 512)

Determine To identify or decide by weighing alternatives or possibilities. (pp. 8, 229)

Diagram A graphic that represents or illustrates a concept or process. Diagrams can be used to organize and present information visually. (pp. 147, 580)

Dialog box A box opened by a menu commands that allows you to select options or specify information to perform the command. (pp. 9, 206, 362, 547)

Dialog Box Launcher A clickable button that appears in the lower-right corner of a group on the Ribbon. For example, the Paragraph Dialog Box Launcher in Word opens the Paragraph dialog box. (p. xli)

Digital signature A security feature that authenticates the digital information you create. Inserting a digital signature signifies that that the content has not been changed since the document was signed. (p. xlviii)

Display To put or spread before the viewer. (pp. 521, 544)

Distinct Distinguishable to the eye or mind as discrete; separate. (p. 259)

Distribution list A list of addresses to which letters or e-mail messages are sent. For example, when Word's Mail Merge feature is used, letters are sent to a distribution list. (p. 177)

Document A file into which text is keyed. Documents can contain text, pictures, charts, and other objects. (pp. 5, 449, 493)

Documenter A tool that reports the characteristics of database objects and their parts. (p. 514)

Drag To move text by selecting it, holding down the mouse button, and moving the mouse. (pp. 72, 290)

Duplicate query A database query that finds records with the same data in a field. (p. 408)

E

Edit To make changes to a document, contents of a cell, or presentation. (pp. 14, 230)

Electronic mail (e-mail) A communication sent from one person to another over the Internet. (pp. 165, 699)

Element A constituent part. (pp. 486, 641)

Emphasis Special importance or significance. (p. 606)

Enable To make possible, practical, or easy. (p. 164)

Encrypt To use a password to add security to your data. (pp. 518, 523)

New Features in Microsoft Office 2007

Microsoft Office 2007 is a collection of software applications, including Word, Excel, Access, and PowerPoint. Like previous versions of Office, Microsoft Office 2007 allows you to create, communicate, and work in a productive manner. Office 2007 contains new features that allow users to create and format documents with greater ease and with a more professional look.

Interface Tools

The Office Ribbon

The Microsoft Office 2007 interface is based around a new tool called the **Ribbon**. The Ribbon groups tools by their functions. The Ribbon is broken into three different portions:

- The **tabs** are divided among the different tasks you can do in an application.
- The **groups** within each tab break the tasks into subtasks. The groups replace the menus used in previous versions of Office.
- The **buttons** within each group carry out commands or display menus of subcommands.

The **Word Ribbon** provides you with related tasks for formatting text. For example, on the Home tab, every task related to fonts is in the Font group. Next to the Font group is the Paragraph group, where you can format text. Other tabs, such as Page Layout and Review, contain tools for those areas.

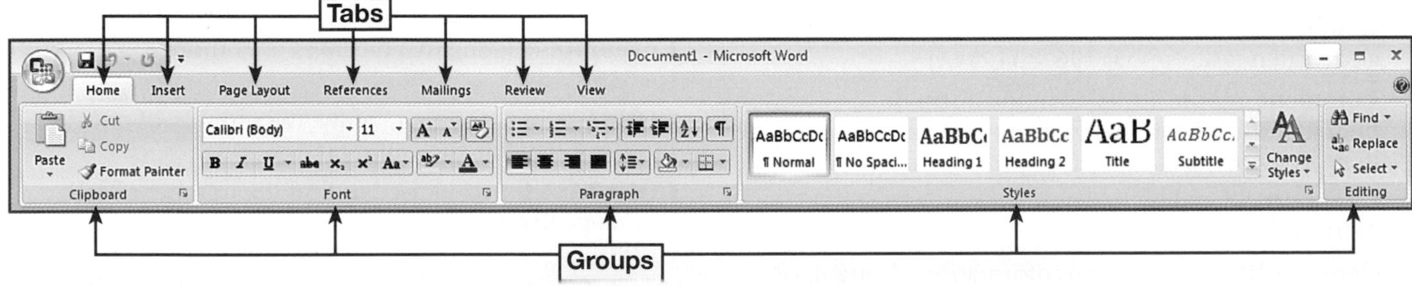

The **Excel Ribbon** allows you to find related tasks involving cell formatting. For example, on the Formulas tab, you can find all major commands involving functions in the Function Library group.

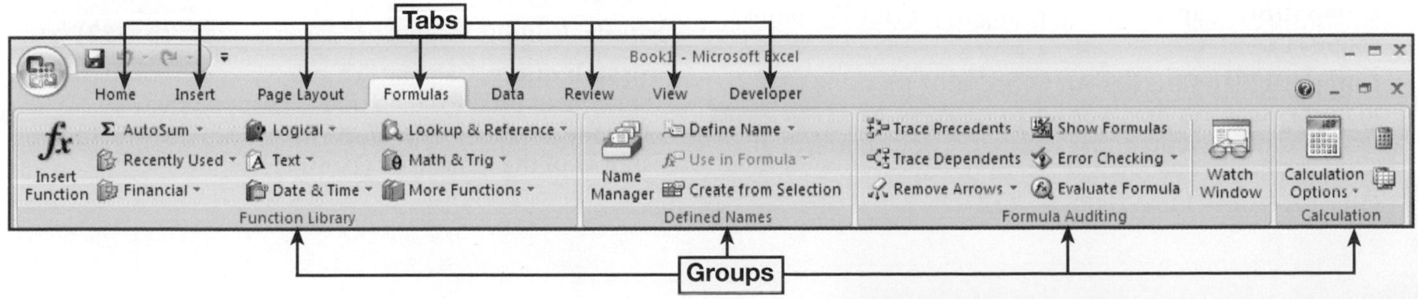

Chart A graphic that organizes data visually. Common charts are pie charts, bar charts, and line charts. (pp. 151, 294, 511, 583)

Chicago Style Guidelines established in the *Chicago Manual of Style* for formatting and citing sources in an academic research report. (p. 116)

Clear To remove all of the contents. You can clear the contents of a cell or of a text box. (pp. 40, 231)

Clip Art Images or pre-made graphics that can be inserted into a document or presentation. (pp. 143, 578)

Clipboard A place where cut or copied text is stored so that it can be copied into a document in the future. (pp. 70, 234, 549)

Collaborate To work together to complete a project. (pp. 185, 193)

Color scheme The eight colors used in a slide's design. Each design template has a specific color scheme that is used for the presentation's background, text, lines, shadows, title text, fills, accents, and hyperlinks. (p. 625)

Column All of the cells arranged vertically under a lettered column heading. (pp. 133, 139, 254, 363)

Column break Separation of text from one column to the top of the next column. (p. 134)

Combine To merge two different copies of the same document into one document. (p. 169)

Command Controls that tell the computer to perform a particular task. (pp. 6, 206, 354, 544)

Comment A note added to a document or presentation without making any changes to the text itself. (pp. 167, 591)

Common Shared by two or more parties. (pp. 315, 480)

Communicate To transmit information, thought, or feeling so that it is satisfactorily received or understood. (p. 1)

Compare To examine and note the similarities or differences of. (p. 359)

Compatible Capable of operating in previous versions (p. 663)

Compatibility Checker An Office 2007 tool that identifies features in a Word, Excel, Access, or PowerPoint document that will not operate correctly if opened with a previous version of the software, such as Office 2003 or Office 2000. (p. 663)

Computer An electronic device that processes data and converts it into information that people can use. (pp. 2, 201, 349)

Condition A rule. (p. 302)

Conditional formatting Formatting that is set to appear a certain way if certain conditions, or rules, are met. (pp. 447-448)

Consider To think about carefully. (p. 6)

Content The text, graphics, and data that are contained in a Word, Excel, Access, or PowerPoint file. (pp. 111, 117, 571)

Contextual tab A tab that appears on the Ribbon that contains commands that can only be used with a selected object. (pp. xlv, 101, 572)

Contribute To play a significant part in bringing about an end or result. (p. 165)

Control An object on a form or report that displays data, such as a text box or check box, or a button that lets users control a program. (pp. 355, 389, 442)

Convert To change the format of a document or file. (pp. 152, 254, 321)

Convey To visually communicate. (p. 275)

Copy To select and reproduce text somewhere else in a document or application. (pp. 81, 260)

Copyright The exclusive right to publish and sell literary, musical, or artistic work. (pp. 586, 629, 650)

Corporate Relating to a business or corporation. (p. 535)

COUNT A function that counts the number of cells in the range that contain numbers. (p. 298)

COUNTA A function used to find the number of cells in a range that contain data (both numbers and text). (p. 298)

Count Numbers A function used to find the number of cells in a range that contain numerals. (p. 298)

Cover letter A short, formal business letter that expresses the sender's interest in a job and requests an interview. (p. 416)

Criteria Conditions that are set in a query. (p. 357)

Crosstab query Calculates a sum, average, count, or other type of total for data that is grouped by two fields-one across the top of the datasheet, the other in each row of the datasheet. (p. 408)

The **Access Ribbon** makes it easy to create and use a database:

- You can insert records into a datasheet with the Records group on the Home tab.
- You can then use the Database Tools tab to examine the records more closely.
- The Show/Hide group, located in the Database Tools tab, allows you to see relationships between multiple records as well as multiple databases.

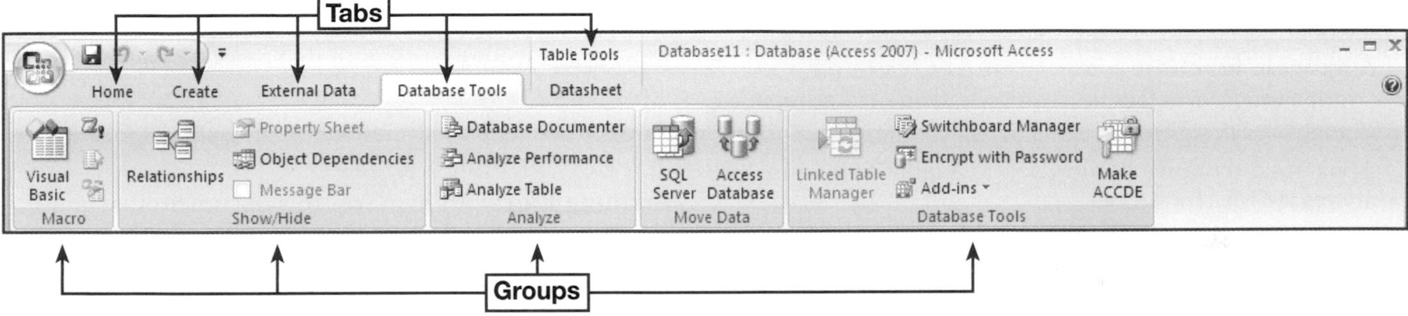

The **PowerPoint Ribbon** helps you to design and create presentations with ease:

- You can manage a presentation with the Slide Show tab, which includes the Set Up group and the Start Slide Show group.
- The other tabs separate the basic areas of presentations, such as design and animation, and enable you to create a visual and informative slide show.

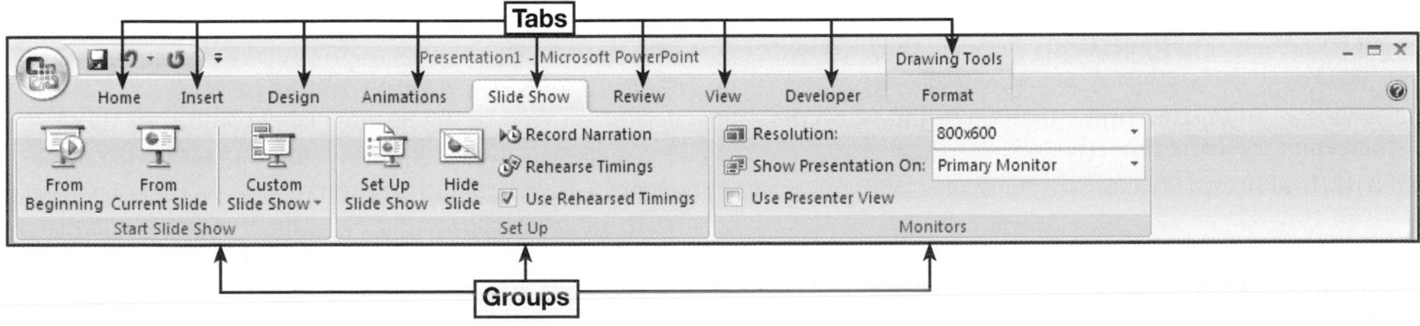

Glossary

A

Absolute reference A cell reference that does not change when a formula is copied to a new location. (pp. 292, 319)

Action Button A button that, when clicked, performs an action during a slide show, such as advancing to another slide. (p. 647)

Adjust To adapt or conform. (p. 289)

Affect To produce an effect upon. (p. 381)

Aggregate function A formula used to calculate counts, totals, averages, and other statistics for groups of records. (p. 455)

Alias An alternative name given to a table or field in an expression. (p. 483)

Alignment The way text lines up with respect to margins or tabs; the position of text and graphics in relation to a text box's margins and to other text and graphics on a slide. (pp. 44, 264, 607)

Analyze To study or determine the nature and relationship of component parts. (pp. 54, 408)

Animation scheme An effect that, when applied, causes text and graphics to move and display on-screen in specific ways. Animation schemes can be Subtle, Moderate, or Exciting. (p. 620)

Annotation A mark or note made with a pen tool by a presenter during a slide show. (p. 658)

Anticipate The act of looking forward. (p. 620)

Application A program designed for a particular type of task, such as writing a letter or calculating a budget. (p. 1)

Arrange To organize more than one window on the screen at the same time. (p. 345)

Attachment A file that is sent with an e-mail message. (pp. 165, 397)

Attachment field A field that is useful for linking files and other objects to a database. (p. 396)

AutoCorrect A tool that automatically corrects common errors. (pp. 80, 519)

AutoFormat A format available in Access to apply to your existing database object. (p. 457)

AutoSum A function used to add values in rows or columns. (p. 229)

Average A function used to find the numeric average of a group of cells. (p. 229)

B

Background A graphic that appears behind the information in a worksheet; solid colors, patterns, or pictures that fill the entire slide and appear behind the slide's content. (pp. 173, 269, 625)

Backup A copy of a file that is created to protect one's work and data. (p. 368)

Border A line or box that frames text or a cell. (pp. 52, 252)

Browser A software program that can surf the Web and interact with Web sites. (p. 321)

Budget A detailed estimate of income and expenses over a period of time. (p. 228)

Building Block An item within a document that you save using the Quick Parts tool to be reused in other documents. (p. 85)

Bullet A symbol, shape, or image such as a dot, diamond, or arrow. Bullets are often used in unordered lists. (p. 46)

Bulleted list A list of items preceded by a special symbol, such as a dot or an arrow. (p. 46)

Business letter A formal letter written by a company, or an individual, on a business-related subject. (pp. 67, 68)

Button A graphic icon that can be clicked to perform a specific task. (pp. xxxix, 6, 206, 354, 544, 609)

C

Caption A label that corresponds with a picture or diagram; in Access, a field's column heading in Datasheet View or the text in a label control. (p. 393)

CD-ROM An optical disk that can hold up to one gigabyte of information. (p. 661)

Cell The intersection of a row and a column in a table or worksheet. (pp. 137, 211)

Cell content The words, numbers, and symbols that appear inside a cell. (p. 228)

Cell reference The column letter and row number of a cell. (pp. 211, 291)

Cell style A set of formatting traits that has been given a name. (p. 260)

Character An individual letter, number, symbol, or punctuation mark. (pp. 38, 53)

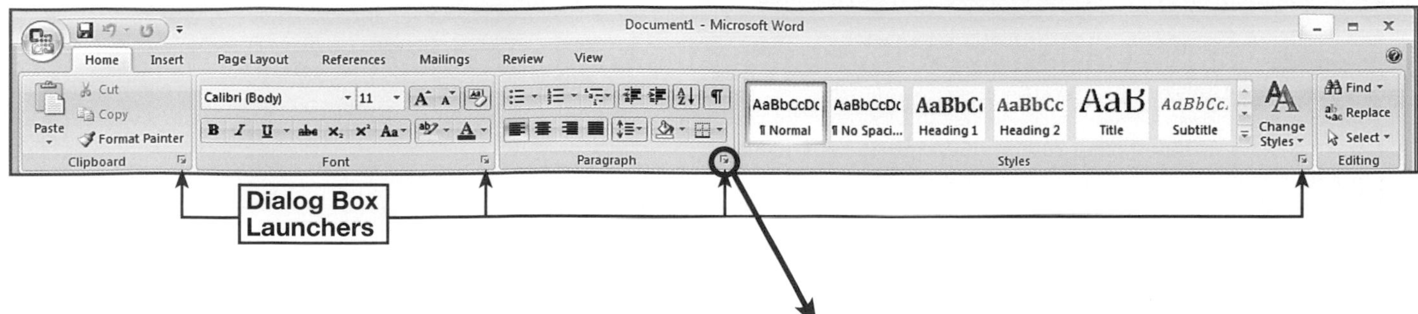

The Dialog Box Launcher

In Office 2007, the dialog boxes have been moved to the appropriate groups in the Ribbon. If a dialog box is available, the **Dialog Box Launcher** will be in the bottom right corner of the group and will open a dialog box with the same name as the group. For example, the Paragraph group's Dialog Box Launcher opens the Paragraph dialog box.

Paragraph Dialog Box

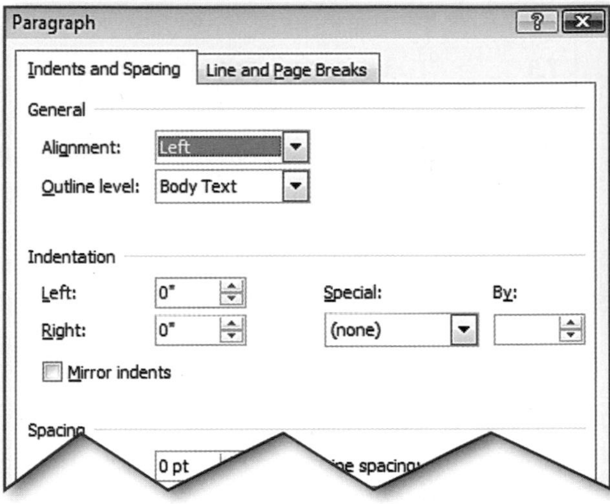

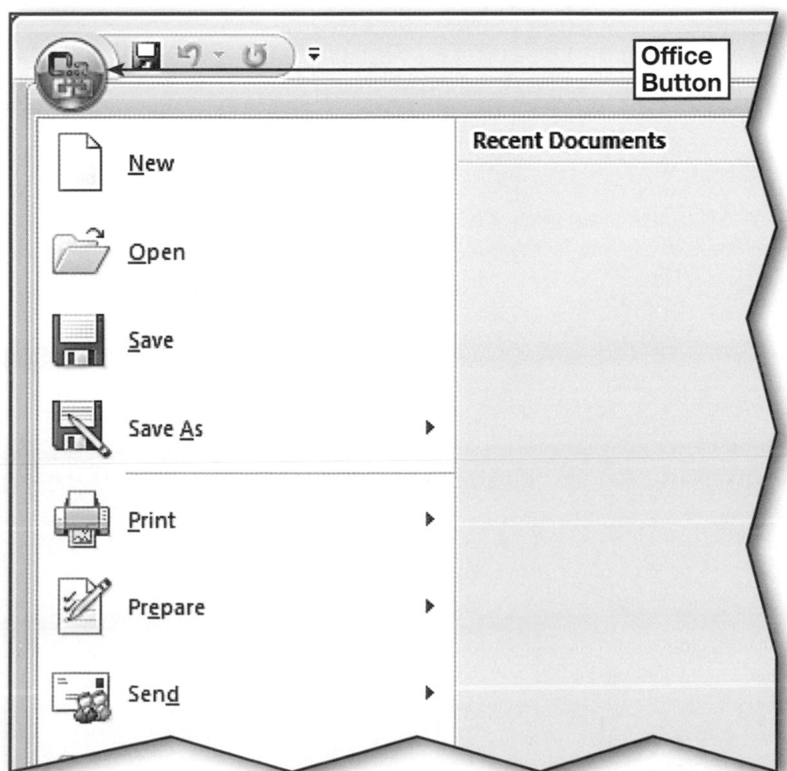

The Microsoft Office Button

The Microsoft Office Button, located in the upper-left corner of Microsoft Word, Excel, Access, and PowerPoint, replaces the File menu. You can use the Office Button to open, save, and print your files. The Publish command, new in Office 2007, also allows you to save your file to a server or to sign your document digitally.

Windows Vista 2007 Certified Application Specialist Standards (continued)		
Standard	**Skill Sets and Skills**	**Text Correlation**
6	**Customizing Your Windows Vista Experience**	
6.1	Customize and modify the Start menu	Adv. Vista L5
6.2	Customize the taskbar	Adv. Vista L5
7.1	Increase processing speed	Adv. Vista L6
7.2	Locate troubleshooting information	Adv. Vista L6
7.3	Locate system information	Adv. Vista L6
7.4	Repair a network connection	Adv. Vista L6
7.5	Recover from software errors	Adv. Vista L6
7.6	Troubleshoot printing errors	Adv. Vista L6
7.7	Recover the operating system from a problem.	Adv. Vista L6
7.8	Request and manage Remote Assistance	Adv. Vista L6

The Quick Access Toolbar

The Quick Access Toolbar (or QAT) contains frequently used commands. The default location of the QAT is in the upper-left corner of the screen, next to the Microsoft Office Button. To maximize the work area on your screen, keep the Quick Access Toolbar in its default location.

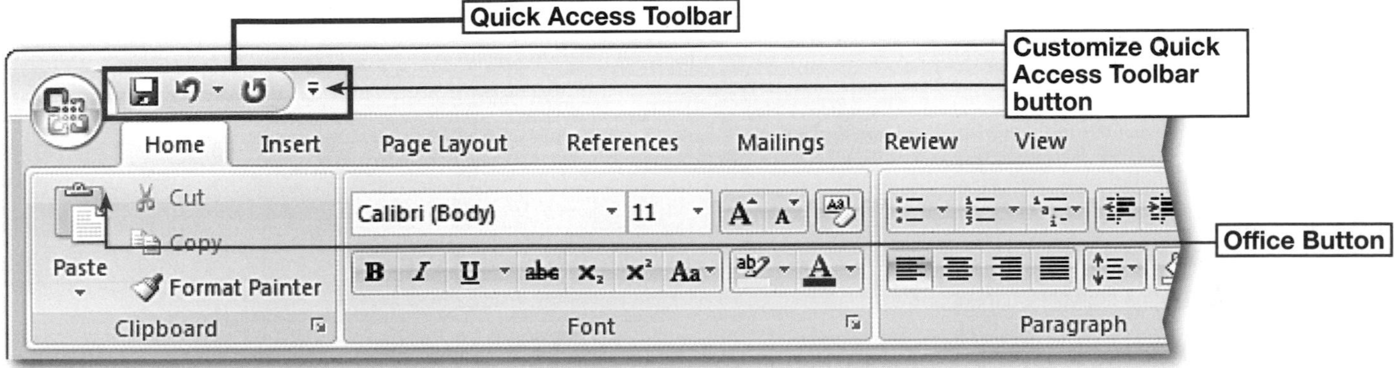

The **Quick Access Toolbar is customizable**, which means that you can add any command to it. To add a command to the Quick Access Toolbar:

- Click the appropriate tab
- Locate the command you want to add
- Right-click the command
- Select Add to Quick Access Toolbar from the shortcut menu

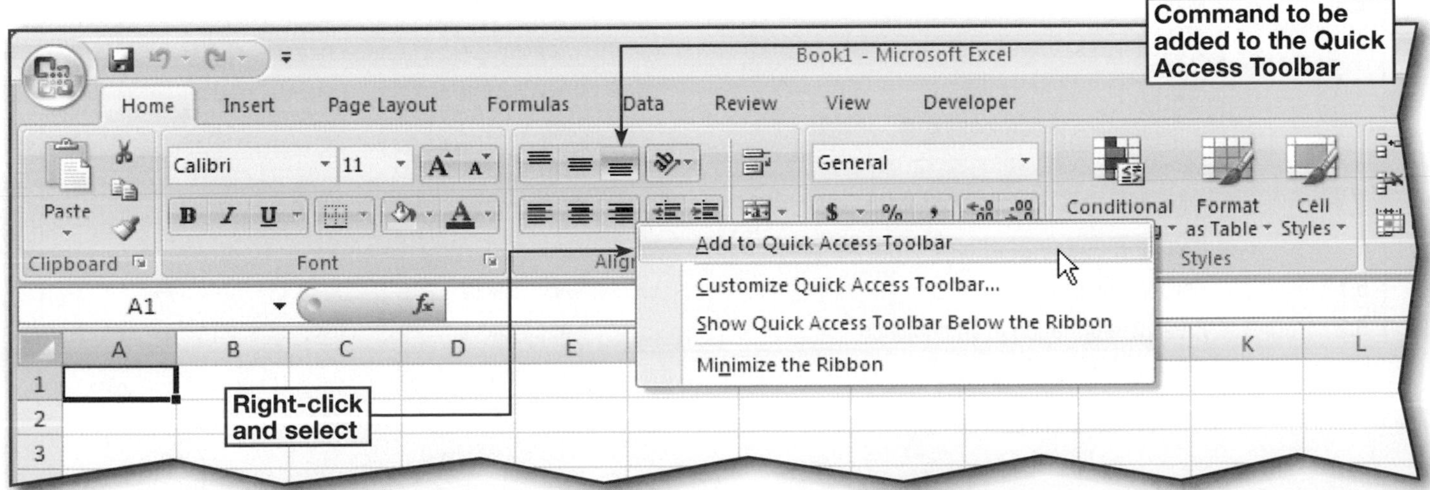

Windows Vista 2007 Certified Application Specialist Standards		
Standard	**Skill Sets and Skills**	**Text Correlation**
1	**Protecting Your Computer**	
1.1	Manage Windows firewall	Adv. Vista L1
1.2	Manage malicious software (also called malware) protection	Adv. Vista L1
1.3	Configure Windows Update settings	Adv. Vista L1
1.4	Lock a computer	Adv. Vista L1
1.5	Manage Windows Internet Explorer security	Adv. Vista L1
1.6	Configure local user accounts	Adv. Vista L1
2	**Managing Mobile and Remote Computing**	
2.1	Manage the computer power state	Adv. Vista L2
2.2	Manage network connections	Adv. Vista L2
2.3	Manage remote access to your computer	Adv. Vista L2
2.4	Connect to another computer	Adv. Vista L2
2.5	Access files stored in shared network folders when your computer is offline	Adv. Vista L2
3	**Managing Software, Disks, and Devices**	
3.1	Manage software	Adv. Vista L3
3.2	Manage disks	Adv. Vista L3
3.3	Manage devices and drivers	Adv. Vista L3
3.4	Manage display settings	Adv. Vista L3
3.5	Configure multiple monitors	Adv. Vista L3
3.6	Install and configure a printer	Adv. Vista L3
4	**Managing Files and Folders**	
4.1	Manage Windows Explorer settings	Adv. Vista L4
4.2	Manage and secure folders	Adv. Vista L4
4.3	Share folders	Adv. Vista L4
4.4	Search for files and folders	Adv. Vista L4
4.5	Organize files within folders.	Adv. Vista L4
4.6	Manage files	Adv. Vista L4
4.7	Back up and restore files and folders	Adv. Vista L4
5	**Collaborating with Other People**	
5.1	Collaborate in real time	Adv. Vista L2
5.2	Present information to an audience	Adv. Vista L2

Zoom Settings

The zoom level of the screen increases or reduces the size of objects within the window. When proofreading a Word document, you might want a higher zoom level in order to see the text more clearly. When working in a large Excel worksheet, you might want a lower zoom level to see all of the data at once.

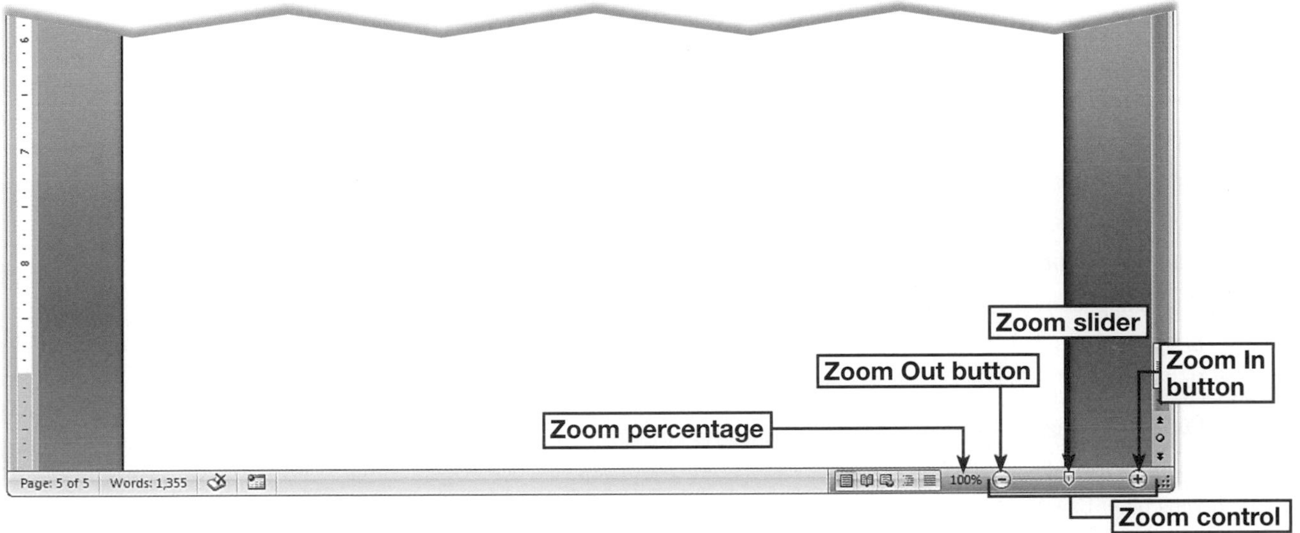

To adjust the zoom level of a program window, use the **Zoom control** at the lower-right corner of the window.

- Click the Zoom In or Zoom Out button to increase or decrease the size of the items on screen by 10 percent increments.
- You can also use the slider to select a specific zoom amount.

You can also adjust the zoom level in the **Zoom dialog box**. To access the Zoom dialog box:

- Click the View tab.
- In the Zoom group, select the Zoom button.

The Zoom dialog box allows you to select a preset zoom level or to enter a specific custom zoom level.

Zoom Dialog box

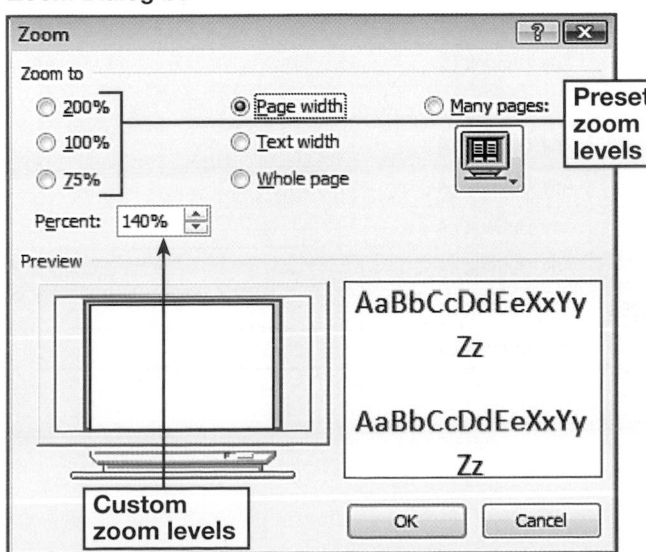

Microsoft Outlook 2007 Certified Application Specialist Standards		
Standard	**Skill Sets and Skills**	**Text Correlation**
1	**Managing Messaging**	
1.1	Create and send an e-mail message	Adv. Outlook L1, Adv. Outlook L4
1.2	Create and manage your signature and automated messages	Adv. Outlook L1
1.3	Manage e-mail message attachments	Adv. Outlook L1
1.4	Configure e-mail message sensitivity and importance settings	Adv. Outlook L1
1.5	Configure e-mail message security settings	Adv. Outlook L1
1.6	Configure e-mail message delivery options	Adv. Outlook L1
1.7	View e-mail messages	Adv. Outlook L1
2	**Managing Scheduling**	
2.1	Create appointments, meetings, and events	Adv. Outlook L3
2.2	Send meeting requests	Adv. Outlook L3
2.3	Update, cancel, and respond to meeting requests	Adv. Outlook L3
2.4	Customize Calendar settings	Adv. Outlook L3
2.5	Share your Calendar with others	Adv. Outlook L3
2.6	View other Calendars	Adv. Outlook L3
3	**Managing Tasks**	
3.1	Create, modify, and mark tasks as complete	Adv. Outlook L3
3.2	Accept, decline, assign, update, and respond to tasks	Adv. Outlook L3
4	**Managing Contacts and Personal Contact Information**	
4.1	Create and modify contacts	Adv. Outlook L2
4.2	Edit and use an electronic business card	Adv. Outlook L2
4.3	Create and modify distribution lists	Adv. Outlook L2
4.4	Create a secondary address book	Adv. Outlook L2
5	**Organizing Information**	
5.1	Categorize Outlook items by color	Adv. Outlook L4
5.2	Create and manage Outlook data files	Adv. Outlook L4
5.3	Organize mail folders	Adv. Outlook L4
5.4	Locate Outlook items by the search feature	Adv. Outlook L4
5.5	Create, modify, and remove rules to manage e-mail messages	Adv. Outlook L4
5.6	Customize your Outlook experience	Adv. Outlook L4

The Mini Toolbar

The Mini Toolbar appears when you select text and enables you to format the text at the point of use in the document instead of with the Ribbon. The Mini Toolbar includes fonts, font styles, font size, alignment, indentation, bullets, and text color.

When text is selected, the Mini Toolbar is semitransparent until you roll your pointer over it. When the pointer rests on the toolbar, it becomes opaque.

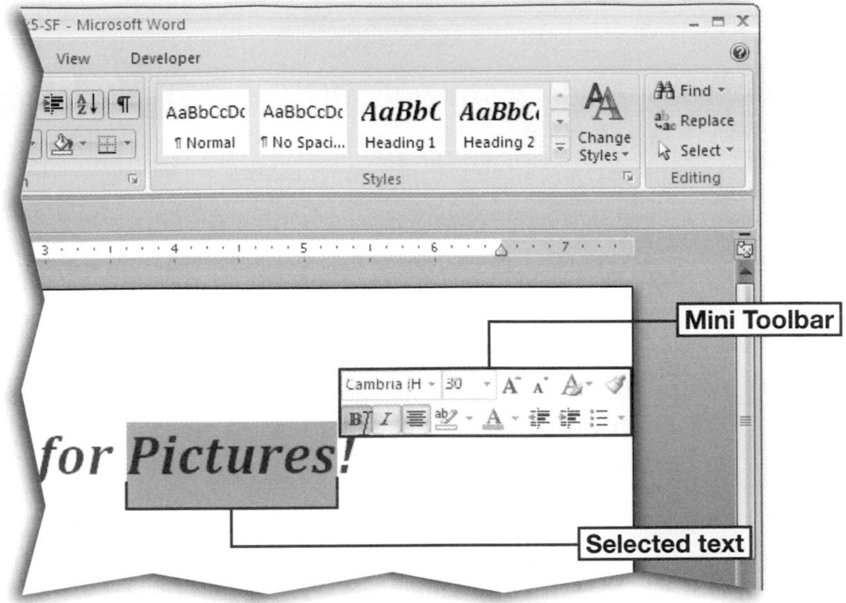

Options Dialog box

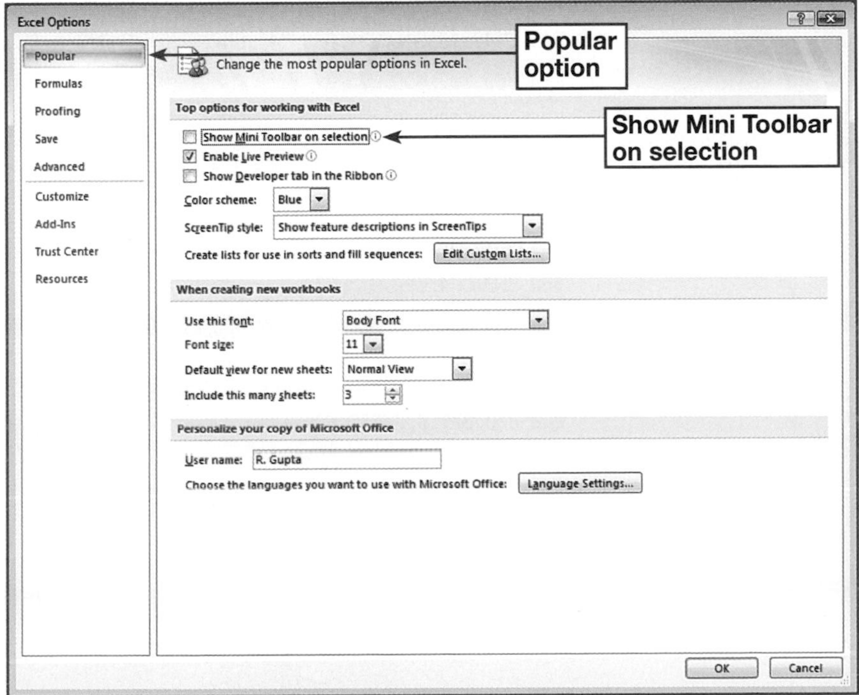

To turn off the Mini Toolbar:

- Click the Microsoft Office Button
- Select the application's Options button in the lower-right corner
- Select Popular from the listing of options
- Clear the Show Mini Toolbar on selection check box.

To turn the Mini Toolbar back on:

- Click the Microsoft Office Button
- Select the application's Options button in the lower-right corner
- Select Popular from the listing of options
- Select the Show Mini Toolbar on selection check box

Microsoft PowerPoint 2007 Certified Application Specialist Standards		
Standard	**Skill Sets and Skills**	**Text Correlation**
1	**Creating and Formatting Presentations**	
1.1	Create new presentations	571, 636, 637, 655, 672, 674, 676, 677, 678, 694
1.2	Customize slide masters	623, 625-626, 632, 637
1.3	Add elements to slide masters	627, 628, 632, 637
1.4	Create and change presentation elements	622,633, 634, 636, 637, 674, 676
1.5	Arrange slides	549, 550, 563, 565, 567, 640
2	**Creating and Formatting Slide Content**	
2.1	Insert and format text boxes	643-644, 663
2.2	Manipulate text	574, 575, 588, 594, 596, 600, 605, 606, 607, 608, 609, 610, 635, 637, 678, 679
2.3	Add and link existing content to presentations	641, 642, 645, 646, 649, 667, 672, 673, 677, 678, 679
2.4	Apply, customize, modify, and remove animations	600, 618, 620, 622, 635, 679
3	**Working with Visual Content**	
3.1	Create SmartArt diagrams	580, 595, 599
3.2	Modify SmartArt diagrams	580, 582, 595, 599
3.3	Insert illustrations and shapes	578, 586, 587, 594, 597, 598, 599, 637, 673, 674, 678
3.4	Modify illustrations	611, 612, 615, 633, 635, 637, 673, 677
3.5	Arrange illustrations and other content	611, 614, 615, 616, 619, 635, 648, 667, 670, 672, 673
3.6	Insert and modify charts	583, 585, 597, 600, 673, 674
3.7	Insert and modify tables	576, 577, 598, 600
4	**Collaborating on and Delivering Presentations**	
4.1	Review presentations	591, 596, 600, 673, 674
4.2	Protect presentations	Adv. PowerPoint L2
4.3	Secure and share presentations	660, 663, 664, 669, 671, 672
4.4	Prepare printed materials	558, 559, 564, 568, 628, 652, 669, 670, 672, 676, 678, 679
4.5	Prepare for and rehearse presentation delivery	554, 555, 564, 567, 568, 654, 655, 657, 658, 659, 661, 668, 670, 671, 672, 673, 679

Contextual Tabs

Contextual tabs appear only when you work with certain objects. Contextual tabs are available with objects such as charts, tables, and pictures.

In Microsoft Word 2007 and Microsoft PowerPoint 2007, the Picture Tools contextual tab appears when you insert a picture into a document or slide. Included in the Picture Tools tab is the Format tab, which contains groups to help you adjust, place, and style the picture.

When you have finished working with the picture, select an area outside of the picture's boundaries. The Picture Tools tab disappears.

In Microsoft Excel 2007, the Chart Tools contextual tab appears when you want to insert a chart into a worksheet. Included in the Chart Tools tab are the Design, Layout, and Format tabs, which all contain groups to help you insert a chart.

When you have finished working on the chart and select an area outside of the chart's boundaries, the Chart Tools tab disappears.

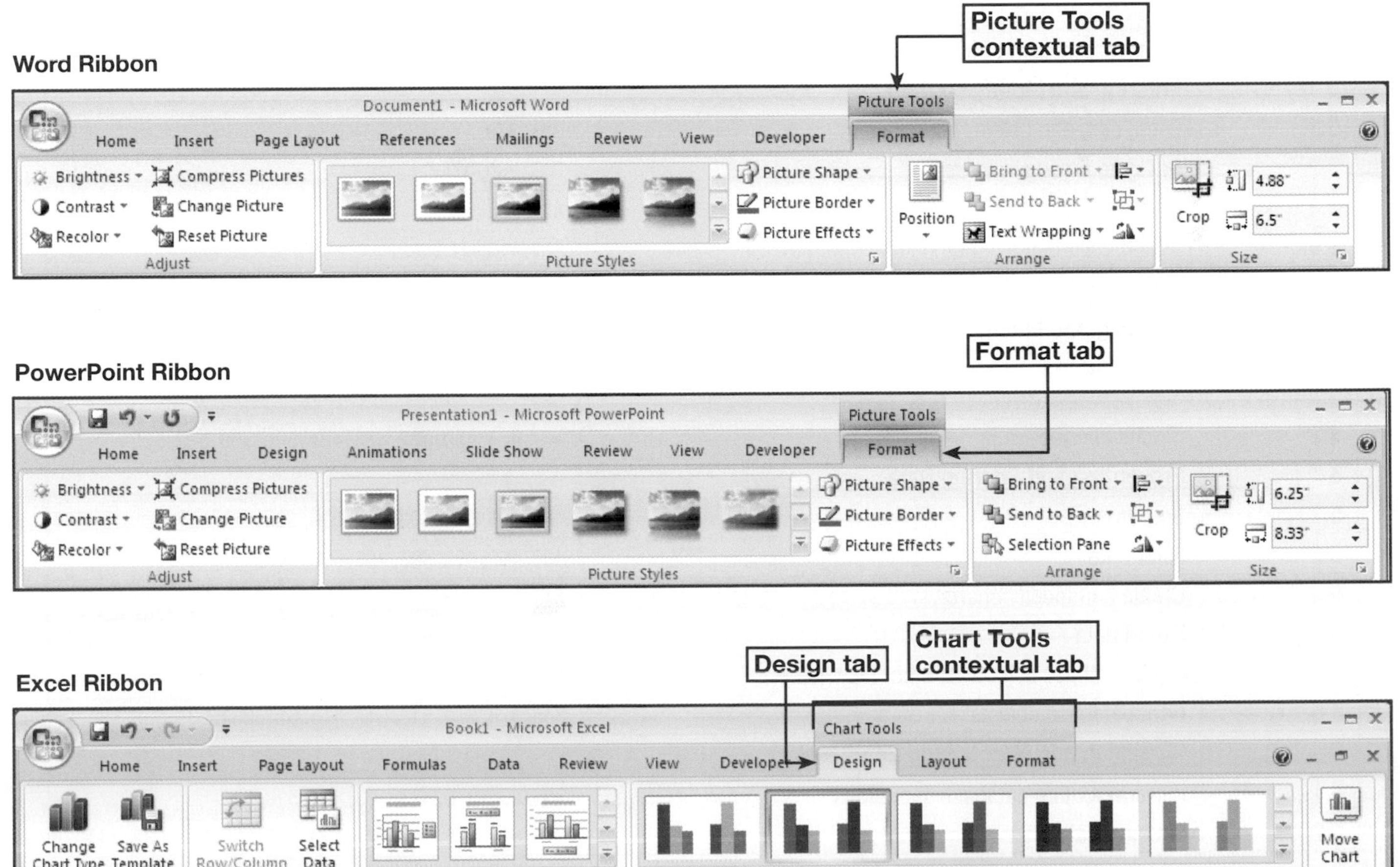

Microsoft Access 2007 Certified Application Specialist Standards		
Standard	Skill Sets and Skills	Text Correlation
1	**Structuring a Database**	
1.1	Define data needs and types	393, 394, Adv. Access L1
1.2	Define and print table relationships	399, 400, 401, 402, 403, 424
1.3	Add, set, change, or remove primary keys	Adv. Access L1
1.4	Split databases	367
2	**Creating and Formatting Database Elements**	
2.1	Create databases	382, 384, 534, 536
2.2	Create tables	385, 386, 419, 424, 534, 536, 538
2.3	Modify tables	385, 387, 389, 391, 393
2.4	Create fields and modify field properties	386, 389, 393, 394, 396, 398, 419, 424, 534, 536, 538
2.5	Create forms	430, 432, 433, 435, 436, 438, 440, 463, 466, 468, 469
2.6	Create reports	449, 451, 453, 455, 459, 464, 465, 467, 469, 513, 516, 539
2.7	Modify the design of reports and forms	442, 443, 444, 445, 447, 457, 539
3	**Entering and Modifying Data**	
3.1	Enter, edit, and delete records	361, 379, 427, 428, 534, 536
3.2	Navigate among records	357, 360, 374
3.3	Find and replace data	429
3.4	Attach documents to and detach from records	Adv. Access L1
3.5	Import data	472, 474, 475
4	**Creating and Modifying Queries**	
4.1	Create queries	404, 406, 408, 410, 412, 414, 418, 420, 421, 422, 423, 537
4.2	Modify queries	477, 478, 480, 482, 483, 484, 501, 506, 537, 538
5	**Presenting and Sharing Data**	
5.1	Sort data	485, 486, 502, 503, 537, 538, 539
5.2	Filter data	488, 490, 492, 493, 495, 504, 507
5.3	Create and modify charts	511, 512, 533
5.4	Export data	496, 497, 498, 505, 507
5.5	Save database objects as other file types	523, Adv. Access L1
5.6	Print database objects	365, 375, 378, 513, 515, 516, 517, 531, 534, 538, 539
6	**Managing and Maintaining Databases**	
6.1	Perform routine database operations	355, 368, 370, 373, 523, 524, 528, 529
6.2	Manage Databases	366, 514, 518, 519, 521, 522, 527, 528, 530, 532, 533

Design and Layout Tools

The enhanced design and layout functions in Microsoft Office 2007 allow you to produce professional-looking documents quickly and easily.

Themes

Themes can be applied with one click to provide consistent fonts, charts, shapes, tables, and so on throughout an entire document.

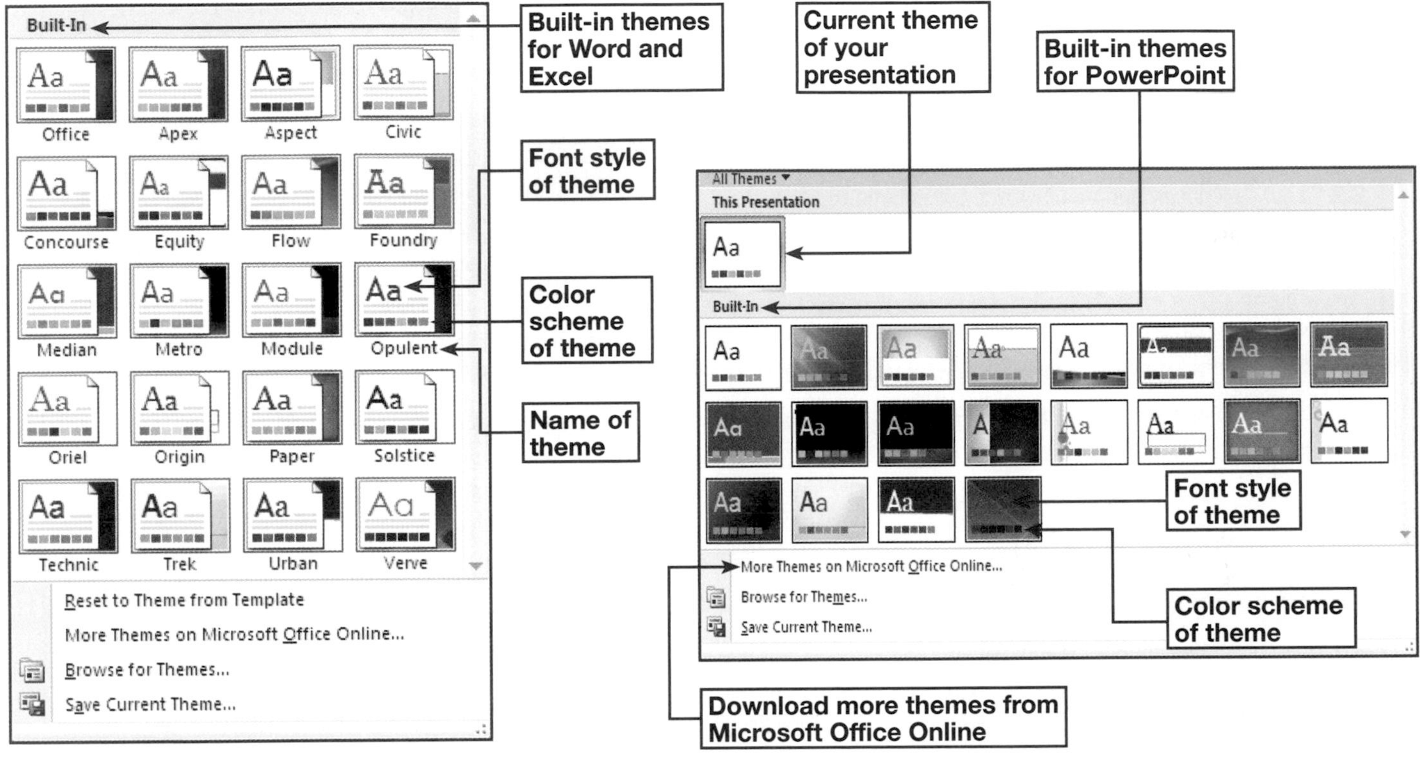

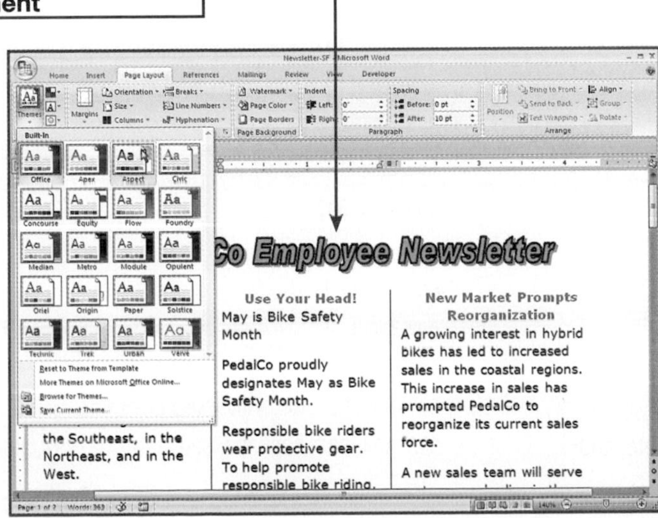

The entire document is linked to a theme. If the theme is changed, new colors, fonts, and effects are applied to the entire document.

Microsoft Office 2007 also allows you to see how a theme would look in a document without applying the theme. As the pointer is rolled over each theme, the document changes to show a Live Preview of what it would look like with each theme. Additional themes are available through Microsoft Office Online.

Microsoft Certified Application Specialist Certification

Microsoft Excel 2007 Certified Application Specialist Standards		
Standard	**Skill Sets and Skills**	**Text Correlation**
1	**Creating and Manipulating Data**	
1.1	Insert data using AutoFill	234, 238, 259
1.2	Ensure data integrity	Adv. Excel L1
1.3	Modify cell contents and formats	251, 252, Adv. Excel L1
1.4	Change worksheet views	212, 219, 221, 222, 319, 320, 326, 335
1.5	Manage worksheets	268, 270, 317, 318
2	**Formatting Data and Content**	
2.1	Format worksheets	267, 268, 269, 275, 277, 346
2.2	Insert and modify rows and columns	234, 235, 236, 237, 243, 248, 254, 261, 262, 263, 264, 265, 342, 344
2.3	Format cells and cell content	239, 247, 251, 252, 254, 259, 264, 265, 266, 278, 279, 281, 300, 344, 346
2.4	Format data as a table	254, 255, 257, 260, 276, 280, 342
3	**Creating and Modifying Formulas**	
3.1	Reference data in formulas	291, 292, 293, 307, 309, 311, 312, 345
3.2	Summarize data using a formula	215, 221, 223, 225, 229, 244, 246, 248, 281, 298, 306, 307, 309, 311, 312, 340, 341, 342
3.3	Summarize data using subtotals	Adv. Excel L1
3.4	Conditionally summarize data using a formula	Adv. Excel L2
3.5	Look up data using a formula	Adv. Excel L2
3.6	Use conditional logic in a formula	302, 312, Adv. Excel L2
3.7	Format or modify text using formulas	Adv. Excel L2
3.8	Display and print formulas	Adv. Excel L2
4	**Presenting Data Visually**	
4.1	Create and format charts	294, 308, 310, 311, 347
4.2	Modify charts	295, 296, 297, 308, 310
4.3	Apply conditional formatting	Adv. Excel L3
4.4	Insert and modify illustrations	271, 281, Adv. Excel L3
4.5	Outline data	Adv. Excel L1
4.6	Sort and filter data	284, 285, 347
5	**Collaborating and Securing Data**	
5.1	Manage changes to workbooks	Adv. Excel L4
5.2	Protect and share workbooks	Adv. Excel L4
5.3	Prepare workbooks for distribution	Adv. Excel L4
5.4	Save workbooks	321, 332, 335, 340, Adv. Excel L4
5.5	Set print options for printing data, worksheets, and workbooks	323, 324, 325, 326, 327, 329, 330, 336, 337, 339

Quick Styles

While themes change the overall colors, fonts, and effects of a document, Quick Styles determine how those elements are combined and which color, font, and effect will be the dominant style. Roll your pointer over each Quick Style to get a Live Preview.

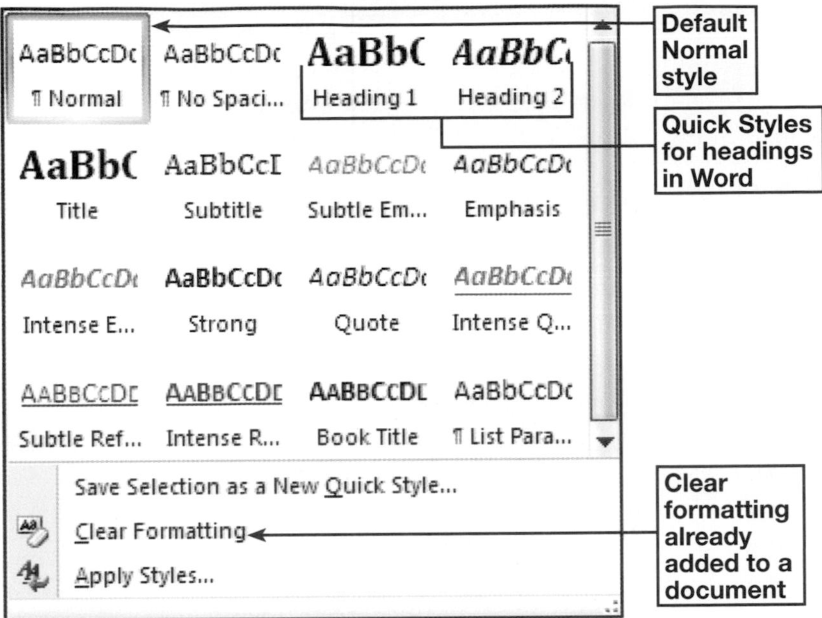

Word 2007 allows you to choose from specific styles for headings, quotations, and titles, or you can choose from a Style Set list to format your entire document. You can even choose a Style Set first and then apply Quick Styles to some elements.

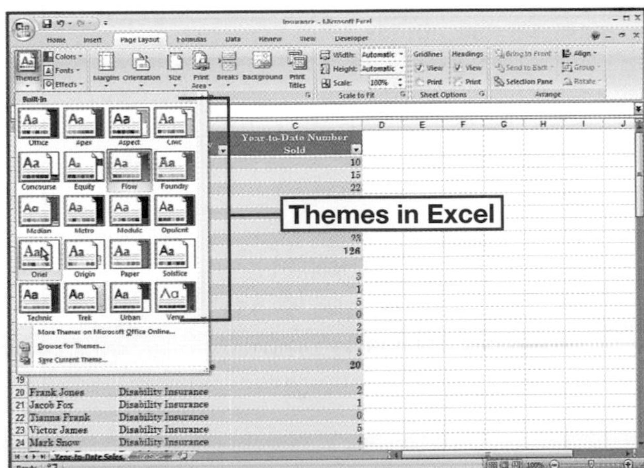

Excel 2007 offers cell styles that work like Quick Styles. In the Themes group, click the Themes drop-down arrow to choose a theme.

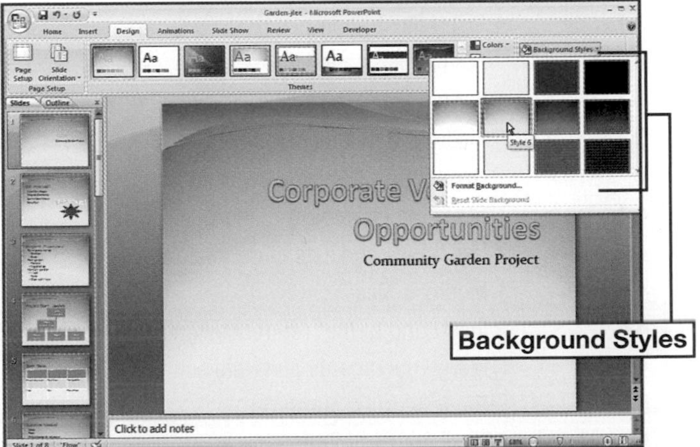

PowerPoint 2007 uses Quick Styles with the Background Styles function, located on the Design tab. The background styles can be used with any of the themes in PowerPoint.

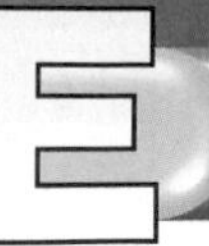

Microsoft CERTIFIED Application Specialist | Approved Courseware

Microsoft Certified Application Specialist Standards

iCheck Microsoft Office 2007 covers the Microsoft Certified Application Specialist (MCAS) standards for Word, Excel, Access, PowerPoint, Outlook, and Vista. This chart provides an overview of the coverage of the MCAS standards standards in *iCheck Microsoft Office 2007*.

Microsoft Word 2007 Certified Application Specialist Standards		
Standard	**Skill Sets and Skills**	**Text Correlation**
1	**Creating and Customizing Documents**	
1.1	Create and format documents	42, 54, 83, 99, 173, 189, 192, 193
1.2	Lay out documents	35, 69, 99, 100, 101, 133, 135, 176, 190
1.3	Make documents and content easier to find	111, 117, 118, 164, 172, 192
1.4	Personalize Office Word 2007	8, 29, 76, 80, 98, 165
2	**Formatting Content**	
2.1	Format text and paragraphs	38, 39, 40, 41, 42, 44, 47, 48, 51, 53, 98, 113, 114, 124
2.2	Manipulate text	70, 71, 72, 79, 81, 88, 89, 92, 94
2.3	Control pagination	103, 110, 112, 125, 127
3	**Working with Visual Content**	
3.1	Insert illustrations	143, 147, 148, 157, 159, 161
3.2	Format illustrations	144, 147, 148, 157
3.3	Format text graphically	150, 155, Adv. Word L1
3.4	Insert and modify text boxes	145, 146, 161
4	**Organizing Content**	
4.1	Structure content by using Quick Parts	85, 86, 92, 94
4.2	Use tables and lists to organize content	45, 46, 50, 152, 156, 158, 160, 161
4.3	Modify tables	138, 139, 140, 141, 142, 152, 156, 158
4.4	Insert and format references and captions	106, 107, 108, 114, 115, 116, 126, 130
4.5	Merge documents and data sources	77, 177, 178, 180, 181, 191, 193
5	**Reviewing Documents**	
5.1	Navigate documents	19, 78, 79, 90, 92, 119, 125
5.2	Compare and merge document versions	169, Adv. Word L3
5.3	Manage track changes	166, 167, 171, 187, 188
5.4	Insert, modify, and delete comments	167
6	**Sharing and Securing Content**	
6.1	Prepare documents for sharing	182, Adv. Word L3
6.2	Control document access	Adv. Word L3
6.3	Attach digital signatures	Adv. Word L3

Adv. Advanced lessons are available at the Online Learning Center at **glencoe.com**.

Security Tools

Microsoft Office 2007 includes new security features that protect your documents and computer from hacking and identity theft.

Mark as Final

After you have finished a document, you can use the Mark as Final command to make the document read-only, which prevents any changes from being made. This allows you to share the document with others without the fear of anything being lost or changed.

The Mark as Final command is located in the Microsoft Office Button menu, in the Prepare section.

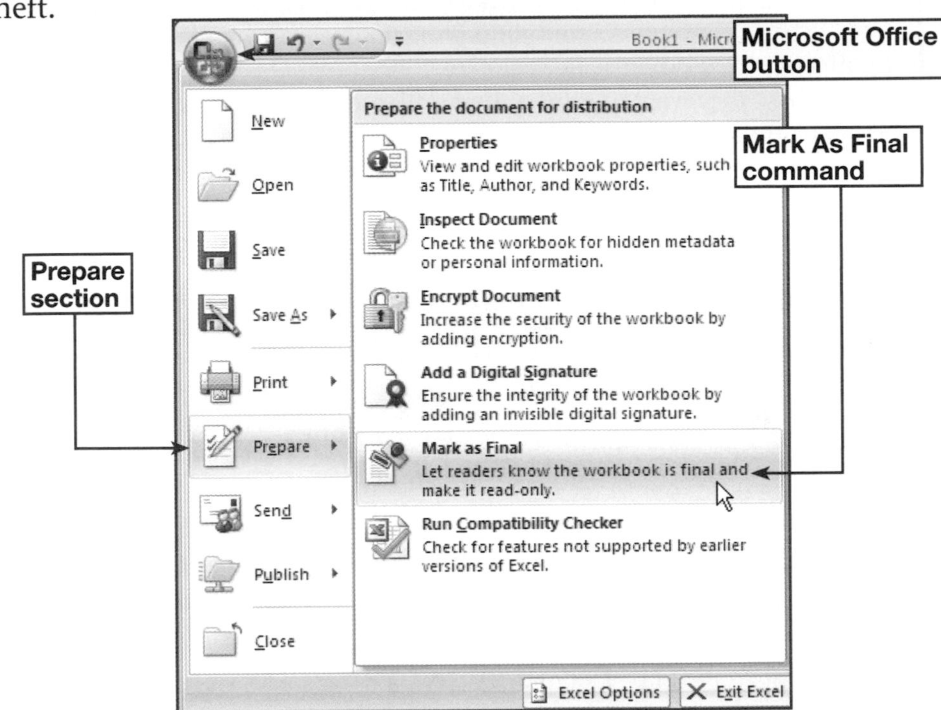

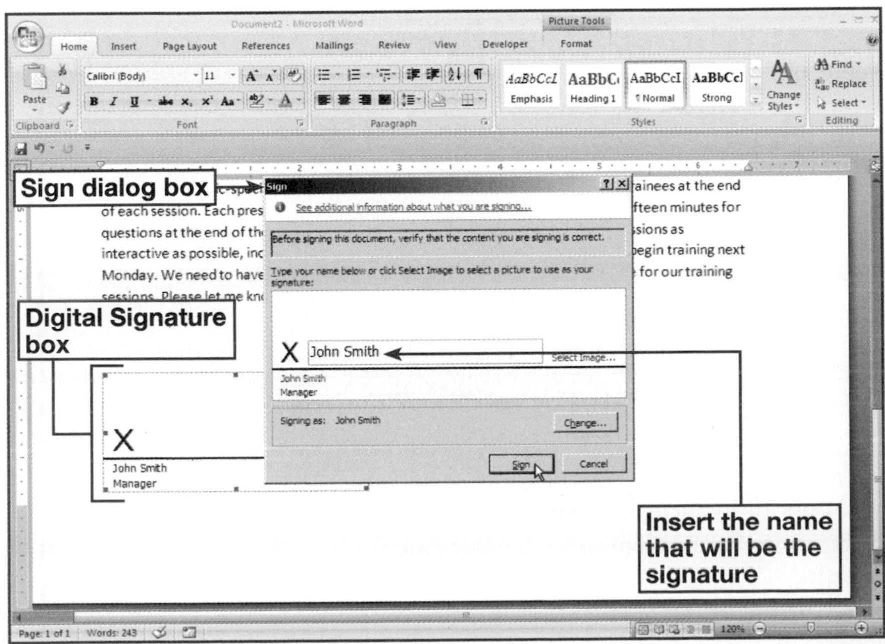

Digital Signatures

You can also digitally sign a document to authenticate any digital information that you create, such as documents, e-mails, macros, and databases. Cryptography assures that the content has not been changed since the document was signed.

What is the Microsoft Business Certification Program?

The Microsoft Business Certification Program enables candidates to show that they have something exceptional to offer—proven expertise in Microsoft Office programs. The two certification tracks allow candidates to choose how they want to exhibit their skills, either through validating skills within a specific Microsoft product or taking their knowledge to the next level and combining Microsoft programs to show that they can apply multiple skills sets to complete more complex office tasks. Recognized by businesses and schools around the world, over 3 million certifications have been obtained in over 100 different countries. The Microsoft Business Certification Program in the only Microsoft-approved certification program of its kind.

What is the Microsoft Certification Application Specialist Certification?

The Microsoft Certified Application Specialist Certification exams focus on validating specific skill sets within each of the Microsoft® Office system programs. The candidate can choose which exam(s) they want to take according to which skills they want to validate. The available Application Specialist exams include:

- Using Microsoft® Windows Vista™
- Using Microsoft® Office Word 2007
- Using Microsoft® Office Excel® 2007
- Using Microsoft® Office PowerPoint® 2007
- Using Microsoft® Office Access 2007
- Using Microsoft® Office Outlook® 2007

What does the Microsoft Business Certification Vendor of Approved Coursework logo represent?

The logo validates that the courseware has been approved by the Microsoft® Business Certification Vendor program that these courses cover objectives that will be included in the relevant exam. It also means that after utilizing this courseware, you may be prepared to pass the exams required to become a Microsoft Certified Application Specialist.

For more information:

To learn more about the Microsoft Certified Application Specialist exam, visit **microsoft.com/learning/msbc**. To learn about other Microsoft Certified Application Specialist approved courseware from Glencoe/McGraw-Hill, visit **www.glencoe.com**.

*The availability of Microsoft Certified Application exams varies by Microsoft Office program. program version and language. Visit **www.microsoft.com/learning** for exam availability.

Operate Microsoft Office 2007 Using Windows XP

Glencoe's *iCheck Series Microsoft Office 2007* has been created and written to show Microsoft Office 2007 on the new Windows Vista operating system. Microsoft Office 2007 can also be used with the Windows XP operating system.

Most tasks can be completed on either operating system with the instructions in this book. However, there are a few tasks that have slightly different instructions or may not look exactly the same as in the textbook. This section shows the steps needed to complete these tasks with Windows XP.

The following steps are shown using Microsoft Word 2007, but the steps apply to all Office 2007 applications. Depending on how hardware and software was installed on your computer, you may need to ask your teacher for further instruction.

Use Windows XP to Start a Program

1. In the Windows taskbar, click the Start button.
2. In the Start menu, select Programs.
3. In the Programs menu, select Microsoft Office.

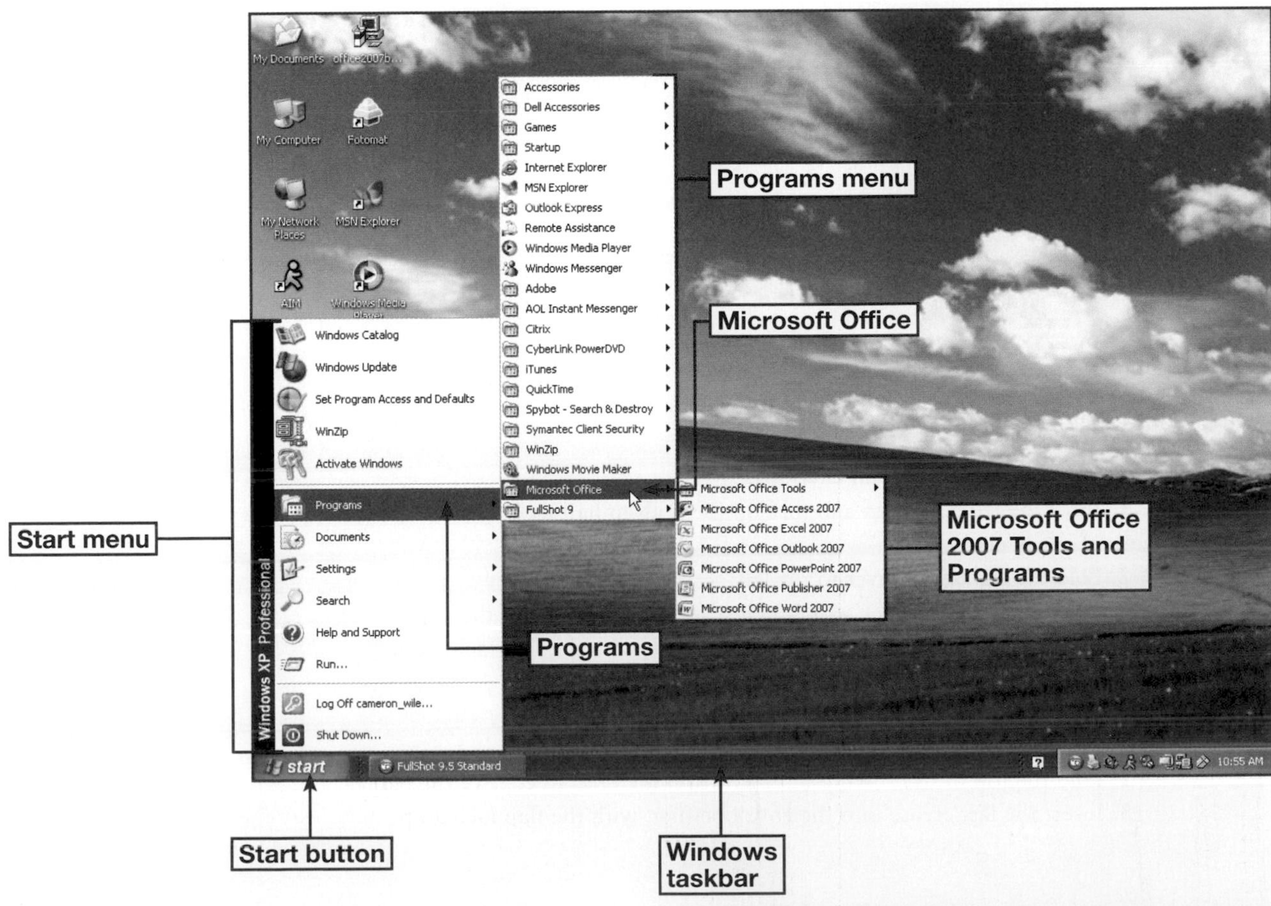

APPENDIX  Reference Guide for Formatting Documents

Format for Envelopes

A standard large (No. 10) envelope is 9½ by 4⅛ inches. A standard small (No. 6¾) envelope is 6½ by 3⅝ inches. The format shown is recommended by the U.S. Postal Service for mail that will be sorted by an electronic scanning device.

Your Name
4112 Bay View Drive
San Jose, CA 95192

Mrs. Maria Chavez
1021 West Palm Blvd.
San Jose, CA 95192

6021 Brobeck Street
Flint, MI 48532

Dr. John Harvey
Environmental Science Department
Central College
1900 W. Innes Blvd.
Salisbury, NC 28144

How to Fold Letters

To fold a letter for a small envelope:

1. Place the letter *face up* and fold up the bottom half to 0.5 inch from the top edge of the paper.
2. Fold the right third over to the left.
3. Fold the left third over to 0.5 inch from the right edge of the paper.
4. Insert the last crease into the envelope first, with the flap facing up.

To fold a letter for a large envelope:

1. Place the letter *face up* and fold up the bottom third.
2. Fold the top third down to 0.5 inch from the bottom edge of the paper.
3. Insert the last crease into the envelope first, with the flap facing up.

Operate Microsoft Office 2007 Using Windows XP (Continued)

Use Windows XP to Start a Program (Continued)

4. Select the program you would like to open.
5. Depending on your screen settings, your window may not be fully maximized. To maximize the window, select the Maximize button, located next to the Close button.

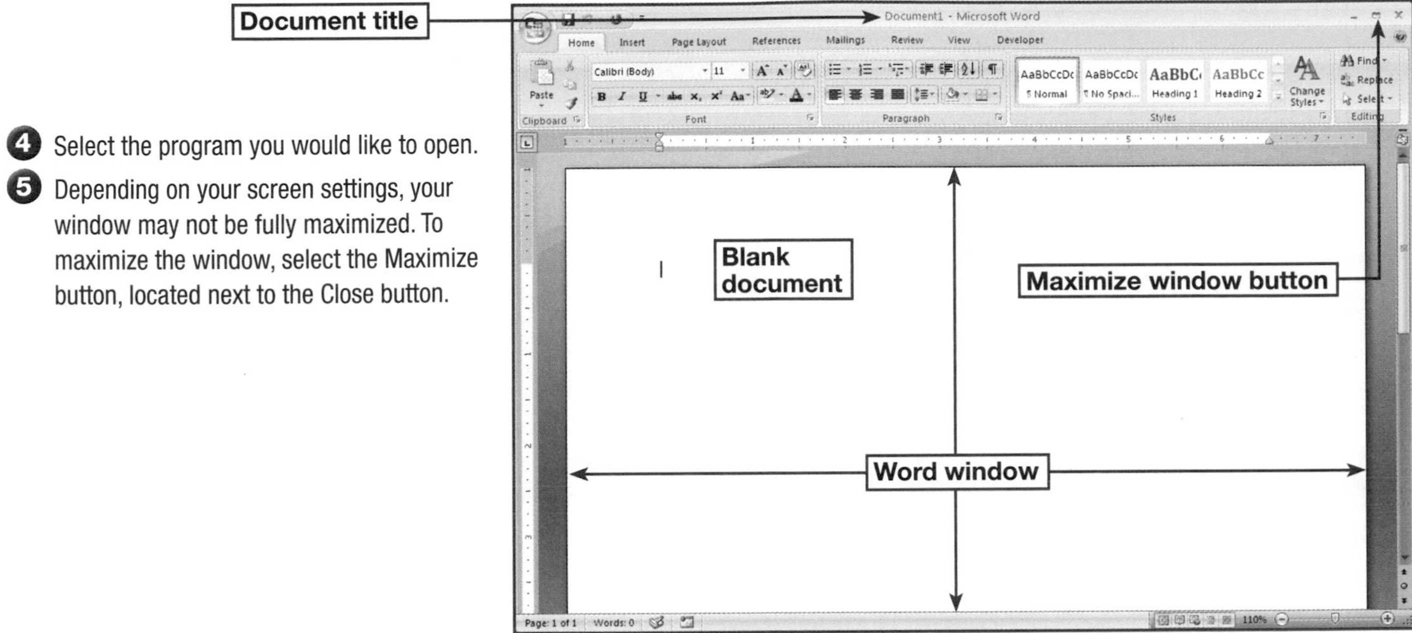

Use Windows XP to Open a Document

1. Start the desired Office program.
2. In the program window, select the Office Button to open the Office menu.
3. In the Office menu, select Open. The Open dialog box will appear.

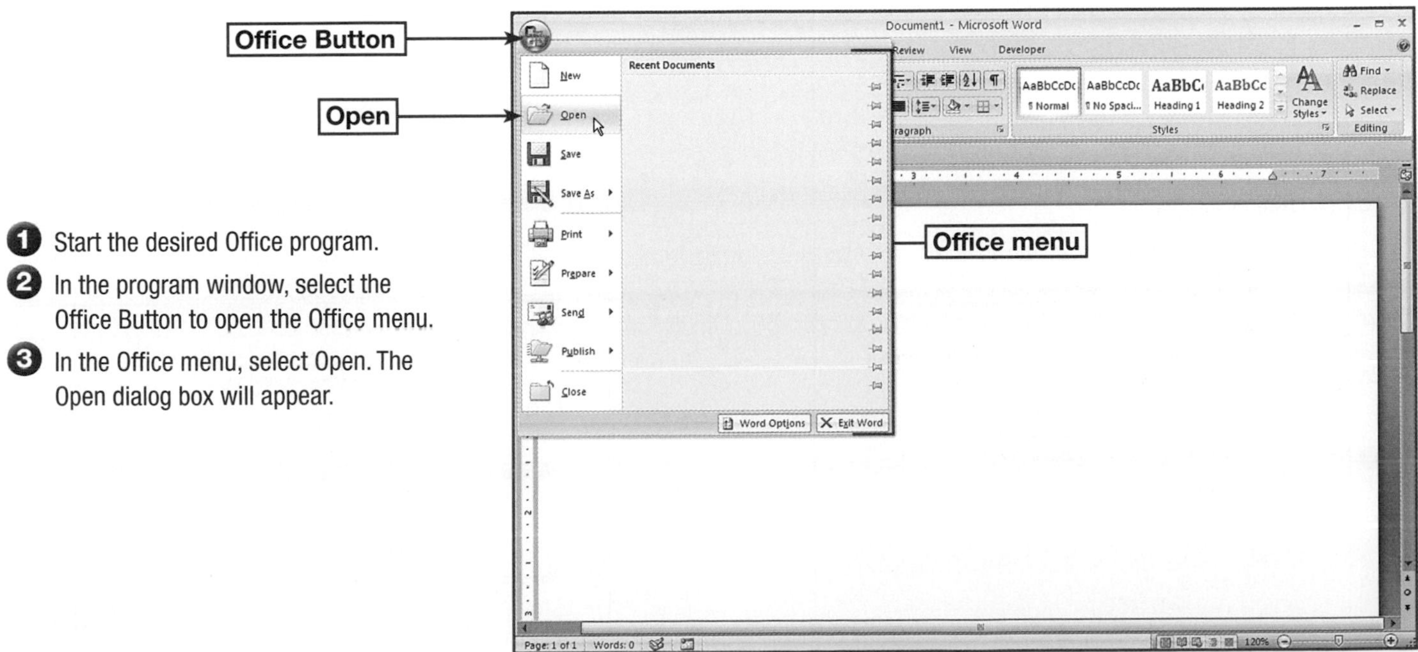

APPENDIX D Reference Guide for Formatting Documents

Boxed Table

Bills Passed for E-Waste or E-Cycling	
State	Bill
Arkansas	SB807, Enacted 6/20/10
California	SP1253, Introduced 2/20/09 SB1619, Introduced 6/13/09
Florida	SB1922, Introduced 7/23/10
Georgia	HB2, Passed the House, in the Senate, 7/9/09
Hawaii	HB1638, Carried over to the 2011 session
Idaho	S1416, Sent to Committee 9/22/09
Illinois	HB14464, Passed the House, in the Senate 4/24/09
Maryland	HB111, Unfavorable Environmental Committee Report

Contents

CONTENTS

Introduction 1
Problem 1
Hypothesis 1
Research 2
The Experiment 5
Materials 5
Procedures 5
Results 7
Conclusion 8
Bibliography 9

Cover Letter

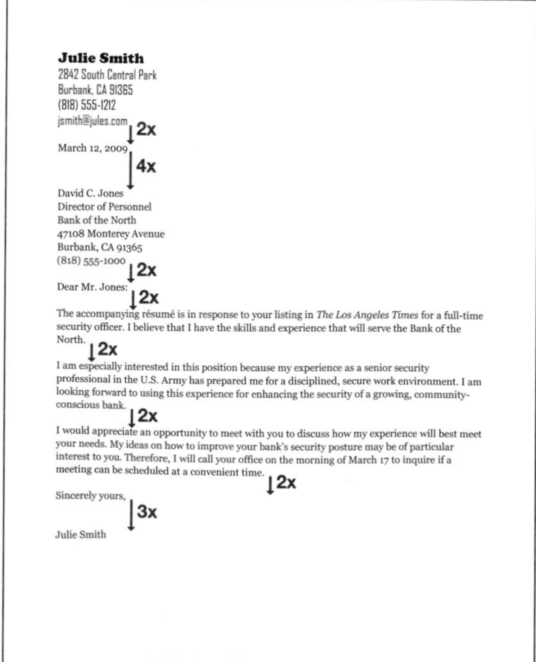

Julie Smith
2842 South Central Park
Burbank, CA 91365
(818) 555-1212
jsmith@jules.com

↓ 2x

March 12, 2009

↓ 4x

David C. Jones
Director of Personnel
Bank of the North
47108 Monterey Avenue
Burbank, CA 91365
(818) 555-1000

↓ 2x

Dear Mr. Jones:

↓ 2x

The accompanying résumé is in response to your listing in *The Los Angeles Times* for a full-time security officer. I believe that I have the skills and experience that will serve the Bank of the North.

↓ 2x

I am especially interested in this position because my experience as a senior security professional in the U.S. Army has prepared me for a disciplined, secure work environment. I am looking forward to using this experience for enhancing the security of a growing, community-conscious bank.

↓ 2x

I would appreciate an opportunity to meet with you to discuss how my experience will best meet your needs. My ideas on how to improve your bank's security posture may be of particular interest to you. Therefore, I will call your office on the morning of March 17 to inquire if a meeting can be scheduled at a convenient time.

↓ 2x

Sincerely yours,

↓ 3x

Julie Smith

Résumé

Julie Smith
2842 South Central Park Burbank, CA 91365
(818) 555-1212
jsmith@jules.com

OBJECTIVE
Experienced and dependable security guard dedicated to ensuring the safety of employees and visitors while minimizing potential losses. Proficient in operating security systems, including two-way radios, CCTVs, and two-way/convex wall mirrors. Committed to enhancing knowledge of security techniques. Completed intensive security training program through ABC Retail Company. Possess clean California driver's license; drug free; physically fit; and available to work various shifts.

TARGET JOB
Desired Job Type: Employee, Temporary/Contract
Desired Status: Full-Time
Career Level: Mid Career (2+ years of experience)

EXPERIENCE
Security Guard
10/2007 to Present ABC Retail Company Burbank, CA
Provide a high profile presence in the 10,000-square foot retail store, monitoring the facility to prevent loss and ensure the full protection of occupants. Operate surveillance systems and patrol the grounds to protect against possible hazards. Write informative reports to update management on all emergency situations. Exercise sound judgment and maintain confidentiality at all times. Highlights:

- Offered a full-time position after two months of temporary employment based on exemplary performance
- Awarded "Certificate of Achievement" (5/2009) for identifying and reporting internal theft, potentially saving the company tens of thousands of dollars annually.
- Apprehended numerous shoplifters by recognizing suspicious behavior, using available surveillance systems, and taking action at the appropriate time.
- Completed two-week security training program.

EDUCATION
10/2007 ABC Retail Company Burbank, CA
Certification
Professional Training: Crisis Intervention, Public Relations, Report Writing, Legal Authority and Limitations, Risk Analysis, First Aid, CPR, Fire Protection, Crime Prevention, Arrest Procedures, CCTV Surveillance
6/2005 ABC High School Burbank, CA
Academic diploma

REFERENCES
References are available on request.

Operate Microsoft Office 2007 Using Windows XP (Continued)

Use Windows XP to Open a Document (Continued)

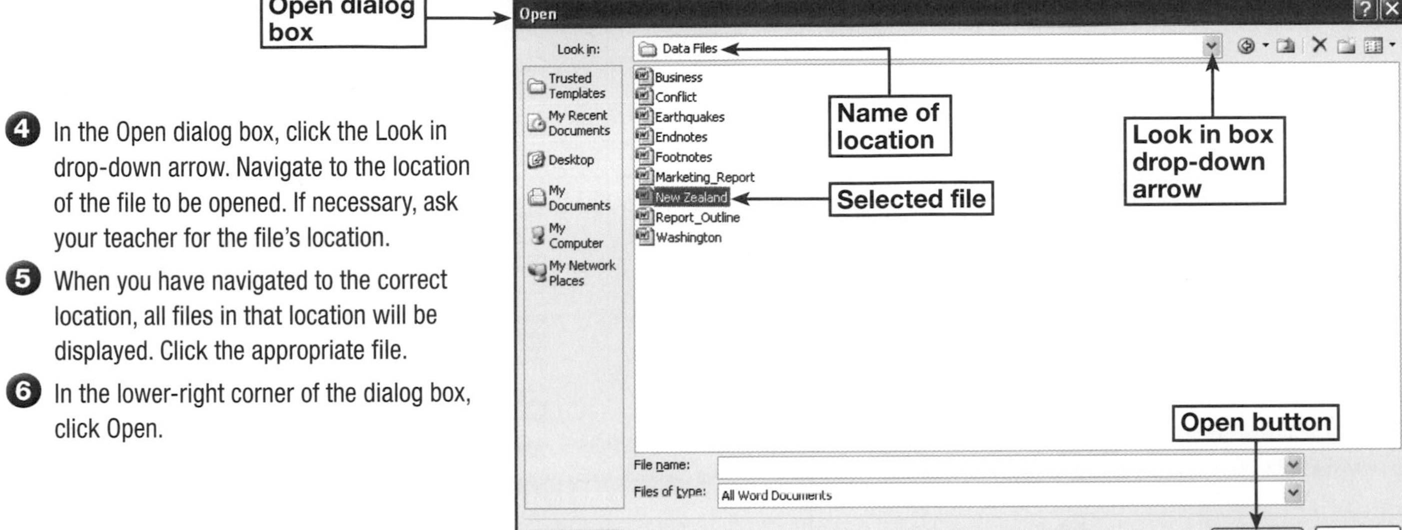

4. In the Open dialog box, click the Look in drop-down arrow. Navigate to the location of the file to be opened. If necessary, ask your teacher for the file's location.
5. When you have navigated to the correct location, all files in that location will be displayed. Click the appropriate file.
6. In the lower-right corner of the dialog box, click Open.

Use Windows XP to Save a Document

1. When you are ready to save a file, click the Office Button to display the Office menu.
2. In the Office menu, click Save. If the file has been saved before, it will be saved, with your changes, to the same location with the same file name. If the file has not been saved before, the Save As dialog box will open.
3. In the Save As dialog box, select the Save in box drop-down arrow. Ask your teacher where the file should be saved, and navigate to that location.
4. Double-click the name of the save location. The name should now be the only item located in the Save in box.
5. In the File name box, key the name under which you would like to save the file. Click the Save button in the lower-right corner.

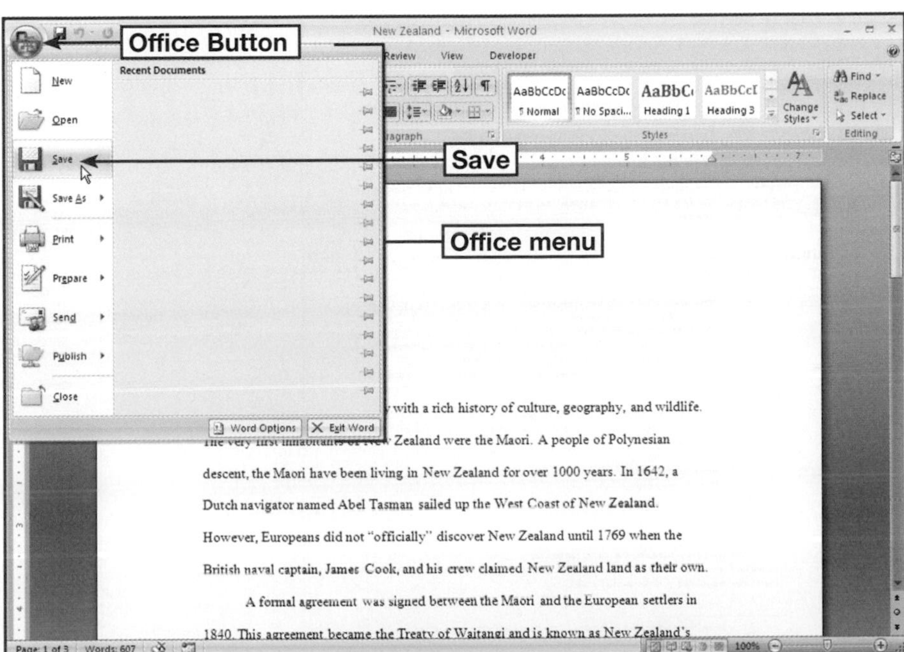

APPENDIX D Reference Guide for Formatting Documents

Title Page

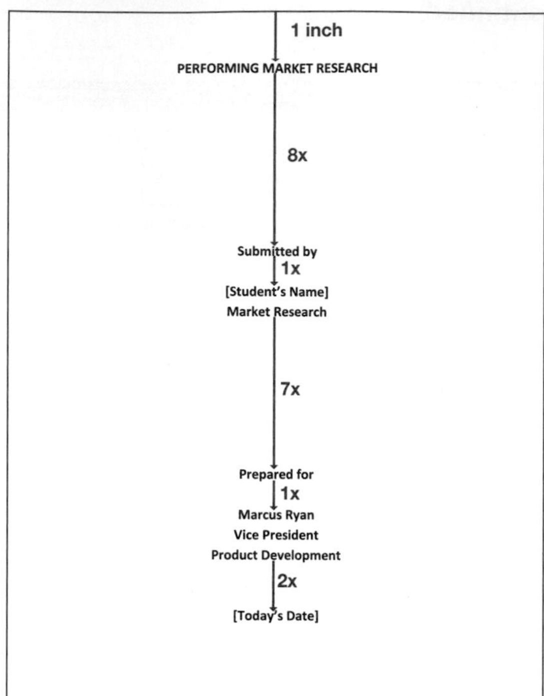
1 inch

PERFORMING MARKET RESEARCH

8x

Submitted by

1x

[Student's Name]

Market Research

7x

Prepared for

1x

Marcus Ryan

Vice President

Product Development

2x

[Today's Date]

Simple Business Report

1 inch

.5 inch

Marketing Research 1

Market Research—Why?

Your new product is terrific. Your planned service support for the new product is outstanding. However, even if you have the greatest product and the best service support, your new venture can still fail if you do not have effective marketing.

People cannot purchase a product if they do not know that that product exists. It is up to you to let your potential customers know what you have to offer. Effective marketing begins with careful, systematic research. It is dangerous to assume that you are already familiar with your intended market. You must perform market research to make sure you are on track. Use the business planning process as your opportunity to uncover data and to question your marketing efforts. Your time will be well spent.

Market Research—How?

There are two kinds of market research: primary and secondary. Both types of research are necessary for an effective marketing campaign.

Primary Research

Primary research means gathering your own data. For example, performing your own traffic count at a proposed location is a form of primary research. Using the yellow pages to identify competitors, and doing surveys or focus-group interviews to learn about consumer preferences are also forms of primary research. Hiring professional market researchers can be very costly. If money is tight, you can look for a book that illustrates how small business owners can perform effective research themselves. Such books are plentiful, and will help you perform your own primary research.

1 inch

1 inch

Secondary Research

Secondary research means using published information to research your market. Published information can include industry profiles, trade journals, newspapers, magazines, census data, and demographic profiles.[1] This type of information is available at many locations, including public libraries, industry associations, and Chambers of Commerce. You can also get important information from vendors who sell to your industry, and from government agencies.

When performing secondary research, try starting with your local library. Most librarians are pleased to guide you through their business data collection. You will be amazed at what is there. In particular, ask the librarian to help you navigate the many online sources that inevitably exist for your industry. You will probably find that there are more online sources than you could ever possibly use!

Beside the library, search for information at your local Chamber of Commerce. The Chamber of Commerce usually has comprehensive information about the local area. Trade associations and trade publications often have excellent industry-specific data.

[1] Keiko Kimura, "Sources for Secondary Market Research," *Marketing Research Essentials*, New York: All Biz Publishing, 2009, pp. 47-58.

Simple Business Report continued

Marketing Research 2

Market Research—Get the Facts

When performing marketing research, you need to focus on identifying some important facts about your industry. These facts will help you better understand your market. This, in turn, will help you decide what marketing efforts you need to implement to promote your product.

Developing the Marketing Plan

Use your primary and secondary research to develop a marketing plan for your product. Be as specific as possible in your marketing plan. Provide statistics, numbers, and sources. It is important that you be as exact as possible, for your marketing plan will become the basis, later on, for your all-important sales projections.[1]

Define Your Market

1 inch

1 inch

Market research will also help you narrow your focus. When researching your market, ask the following questions:

- What is the total size of your market?
- What percent share of the market will you have? (This is important only if you think you will be a major factor in the market.)
- What is the current demand in your target market?
- What are the current trends in your target market? Try to identify growth trends, trends in consumer preferences, and trends in product development.
- What is the growth potential and opportunity for a business of your size in this market?

Identify Barriers

When researching the market, you also need to try and identify potential barriers to success. What factors may prevent you from successfully entering the market with your new product? Some typical barriers to consider include:

- High capital costs
- High production costs
- High marketing costs
- Consumer acceptance and brand recognition

Conclusion

Introducing a new product to the market can be a scary experience. You and many others have invested time, money, and sweat into the new product, and you all want it to succeed. Careful market research can help you help your product to succeed.

[1] Trey Smith, "Developing Sales Projections," *Sales Review Monthly*, October 2010, p. 67-73.

Bibliography

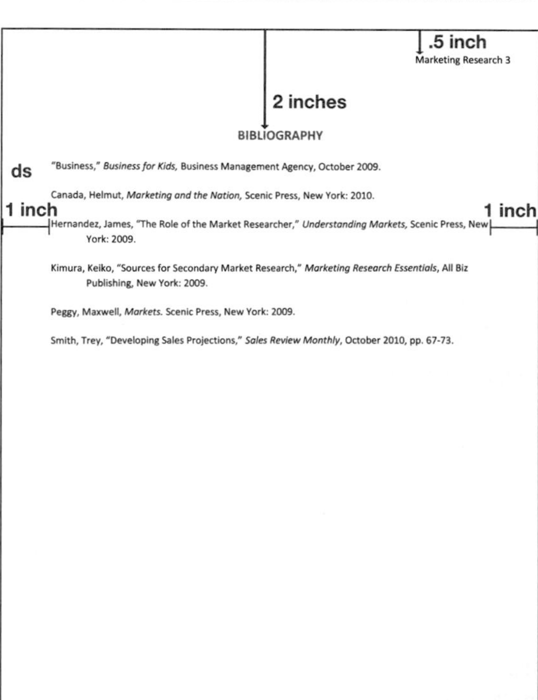
.5 inch

Marketing Research 3

2 inches

BIBLIOGRAPHY

ds

"Business," *Business for Kids*, Business Management Agency, October 2009.

Canada, Helmut, *Marketing and the Nation*, Scenic Press, New York: 2010.

1 inch

1 inch

Hernandez, James, "The Role of the Market Researcher," *Understanding Markets*, Scenic Press, New York: 2009.

Kimura, Keiko, "Sources for Secondary Market Research," *Marketing Research Essentials*, All Biz Publishing, New York: 2009.

Peggy, Maxwell, *Markets*. Scenic Press, New York: 2009.

Smith, Trey, "Developing Sales Projections," *Sales Review Monthly*, October 2010, pp. 67-73.

Operate Microsoft Office 2007 Using Windows XP (Continued)

Use Windows XP to Save a Document (Continued)

Sometimes you might want to use the Save As function instead of the Save function. The Save As and Save functions perform differently. The Save function will replace the original file with the new file. The Save As function will leave the original document as it was and will save the revised document as a separate file with a new name.

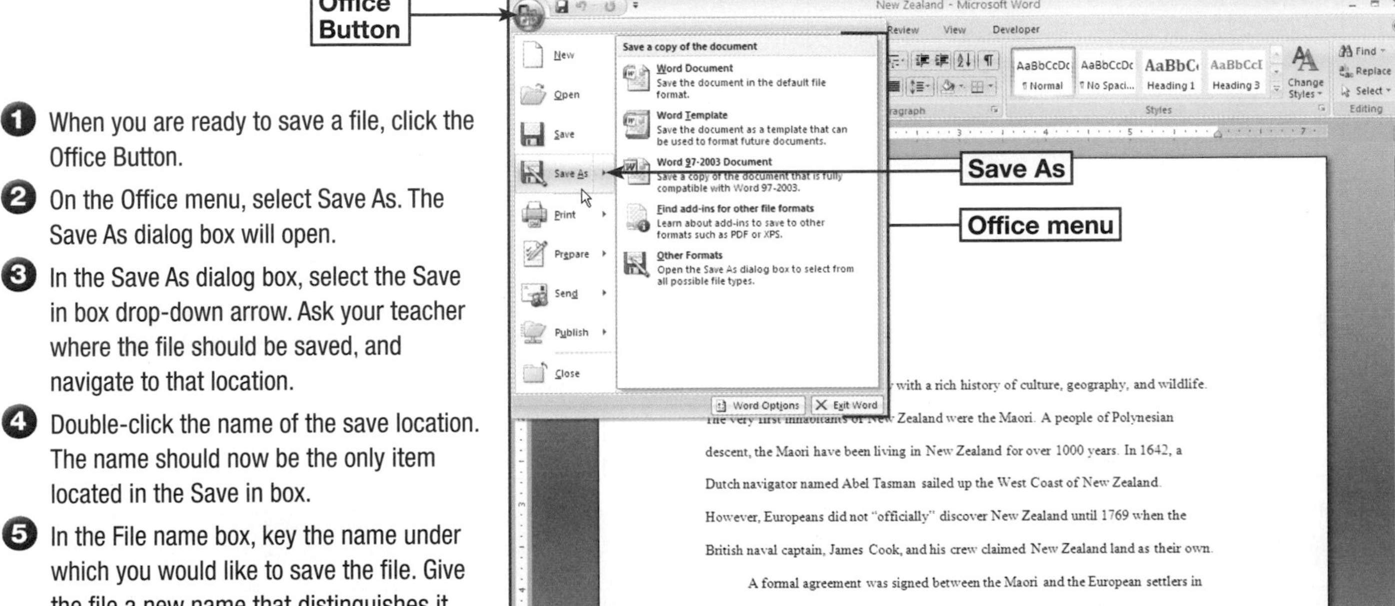

1. When you are ready to save a file, click the Office Button.
2. On the Office menu, select Save As. The Save As dialog box will open.
3. In the Save As dialog box, select the Save in box drop-down arrow. Ask your teacher where the file should be saved, and navigate to that location.
4. Double-click the name of the save location. The name should now be the only item located in the Save in box.
5. In the File name box, key the name under which you would like to save the file. Give the file a new name that distinguishes it from the original document. Click the Save button in the lower-right corner to save your file.

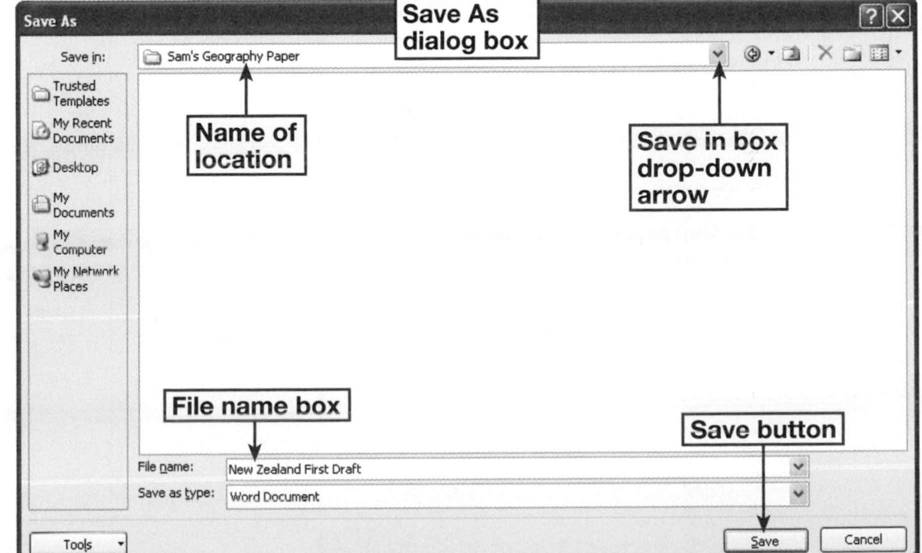

APPENDIX D Reference Guide for Formatting Documents

Newsletter

The Hillside High Gazette

Band Tryouts on Tuesday

Show off your school spirit and your musical talent by joining the band! Band tryouts will be this Tuesday, from 3:30-5:30 in the North field. Please bring your own instrument.

The Hillside High Band is in need of all musicians, especially trumpet and flute players. Band rehearsals will be held every Monday, Wednesday, and Friday after school during football season. Off-season, rehearsals will be held every Monday and Wednesday after school.

The tryouts will be judged by our band leader Mr. Schaefer, as well as by two senior band members in each instrumental group.

Recycling Challenge

Hillside High is proud to announce the first annual Recycling Challenge. Each homeroom class will compete to see who can bring in the most paper, plastic bottles, cans, and boxes. The winning homeroom class will receive a free pizza party.

Bike Week Continues

The Bicycle Club would like to acknowledge the efforts of Janet McSimmons, Steve Yuan, Maggie Estevez, Jill Pierce, James Mazur, Jason Trevor, and Yolanda Washington, who organized our first annual Bike Week. The event wraps up this Friday with the competition finals.

We had great turnout for all the rides, from spectators and participants alike. Leaders in each category will compete for the grand prize—a free PedalCo bike, helmet, and safety pads. Good luck to all the competitors! Here is a list of events and times to beat.

Event	Type of Bike	Time to Beat
Hills Ride	Mountain Bike	1:05:24
Distance Ride	Road Bike	1:42:07
Obstacle Course	Hybrid	15:32
Beach Ride	Beach Cruiser	37:59
Speed Ride	Racing Bike	25:30

MLA Style Academic Report

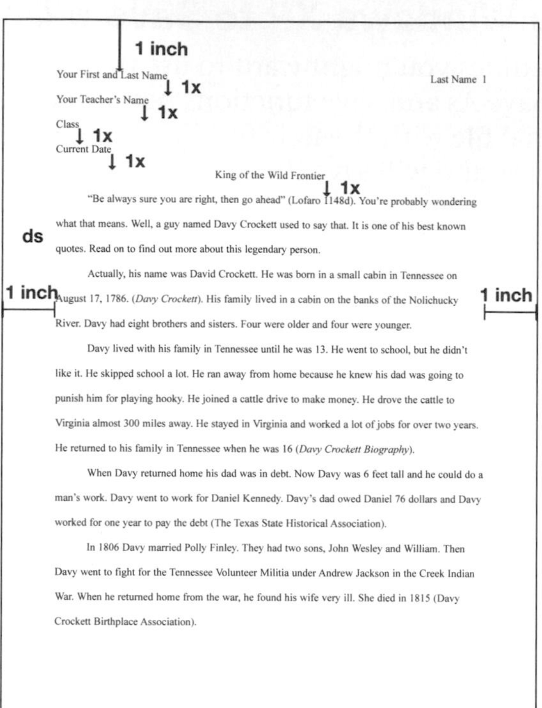

1 inch

Your First and Last Name ↓ 1x

Last Name 1

Your Teacher's Name ↓ 1x

Class ↓ 1x

Current Date ↓ 1x

King of the Wild Frontier ↓ 1x

ds

1 inch | 1 inch

"Be always sure you are right, then go ahead" (Lofaro 1148d). You're probably wondering what that means. Well, a guy named Davy Crockett used to say that. It is one of his best known quotes. Read on to find out more about this legendary person.

Actually, his name was David Crockett. He was born in a small cabin in Tennessee on August 17, 1786. (*Davy Crockett*). His family lived in a cabin on the banks of the Nolichucky River. Davy had eight brothers and sisters. Four were older and four were younger.

Davy lived with his family in Tennessee until he was 13. He went to school, but he didn't like it. He skipped school a lot. He ran away from home because he knew his dad was going to punish him for playing hooky. He joined a cattle drive to make money. He drove the cattle to Virginia almost 300 miles away. He stayed in Virginia and worked a lot of jobs for over two years. He returned to his family in Tennessee when he was 16 (*Davy Crockett Biography*).

When Davy returned home his dad was in debt. Now Davy was 6 feet tall and he could do a man's work. Davy went to work for Daniel Kennedy. Davy's dad owed Daniel 76 dollars and Davy worked for one year to pay the debt (The Texas State Historical Association).

In 1806 Davy married Polly Finley. They had two sons, John Wesley and William. Then Davy went to fight for the Tennessee Volunteer Militia under Andrew Jackson in the Creek Indian War. When he returned home from the war, he found his wife very ill. She died in 1815 (Davy Crockett Birthplace Association).

MLA Style Academic Report cont.

1 inch

.5 inch

Last Name 2

ds

1 inch | 1 inch

Davy then married Elizabeth Patton in 1817. She was a widow and she had two children of her own, George and Margaret Ann (The Texas State Historical Association).

Davy was well known in Tennessee as a frontiersman. He was a sharpshooter, a famous Indian fighter, and a bear hunter. In 1821, he started his career in politics as a Tennessee legislator. People liked Davy because he had a good humor and they thought he was one of their own. He was re-elected to the Legislature in 1823, but he lost the election in 1825.

In 1827 Davy was elected to Congress. He fought for the land bill. The land bill allowed those who settled the land to buy it at a very low cost. He was re-elected to Congress in 1829 and again in 1833, but he lost in 1836 (Lofaro, 1148d).

Many Americans had gone to Texas to settle. In 1835, Davy left his kids, his wife, his brothers, and his sisters to go to Texas. He loved Texas. When the Texans were fighting for their independence from Mexico, Davy joined the fight. He was fighting with a group of Tennessee volunteers defending the Alamo in San Antonio on March 6, 1836 (The Texas State Historical Association). He was 49 years old.

Works Cited

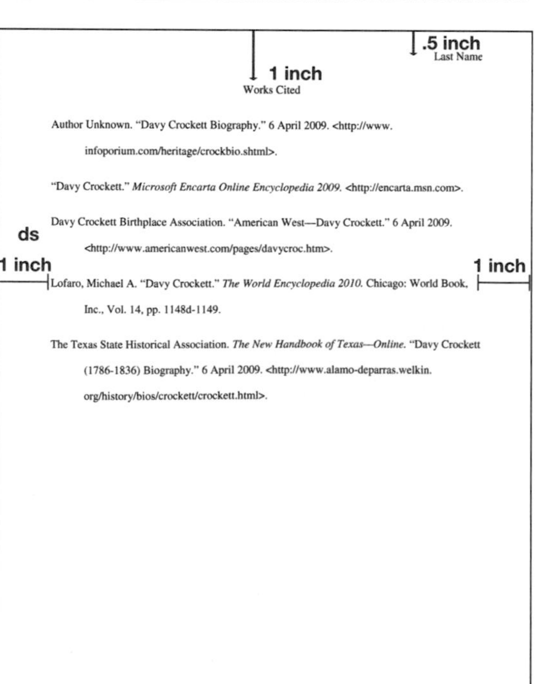

.5 inch

Last Name

1 inch

Works Cited

ds

1 inch | 1 inch

Author Unknown. "Davy Crockett Biography." 6 April 2009. <http://www.infoporium.com/heritage/crockbio.shtml>.

"Davy Crockett." *Microsoft Encarta Online Encyclopedia 2009.* <http://encarta.msn.com>.

Davy Crockett Birthplace Association. "American West—Davy Crockett." 6 April 2009. <http://www.americanwest.com/pages/davycroc.htm>.

Lofaro, Michael A. "Davy Crockett." *The World Encyclopedia 2010.* Chicago: World Book, Inc., Vol. 14, pp. 1148d-1149.

The Texas State Historical Association. *The New Handbook of Texas—Online.* "Davy Crockett (1786-1836) Biography." 6 April 2009. <http://www.alamo-deparras.welkin.org/history/bios/crockett/crockett.html>.

Operate Microsoft Office 2007 Using Windows XP (Continued)

Use Windows XP and Insert SmartArt

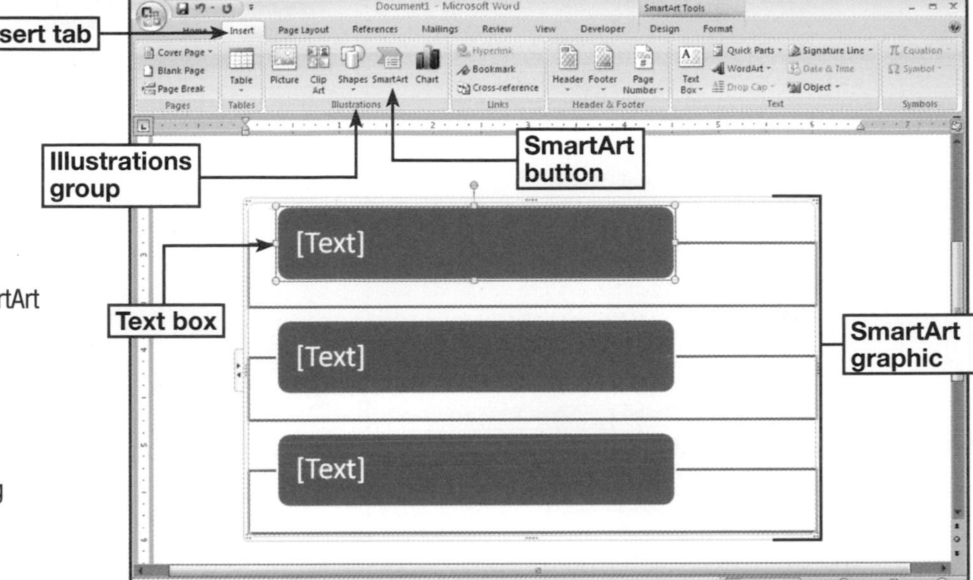

1. Click where you want to insert the SmartArt graphic.
2. On the Ribbon, on the Insert tab, in the Illustrations group, select the SmartArt button.
3. In the Choose a SmartArt Graphic dialog box, select the type and layout of the SmartArt graphic.
4. The graphic will appear in the area that you designated. On the left side of the SmartArt graphic is the Text Pane Launcher. Click the Launcher to enter text into the graphic.
5. The Text pane will open either on the left or right side of the graphic, depending on the space available. Key your text into the appropriate spots in the Text pane. The Live Preview function shows the text in the graphic as you key it in the Text pane.
6. To close the Text pane, select the Text pane close button in the top-right corner of the pane.

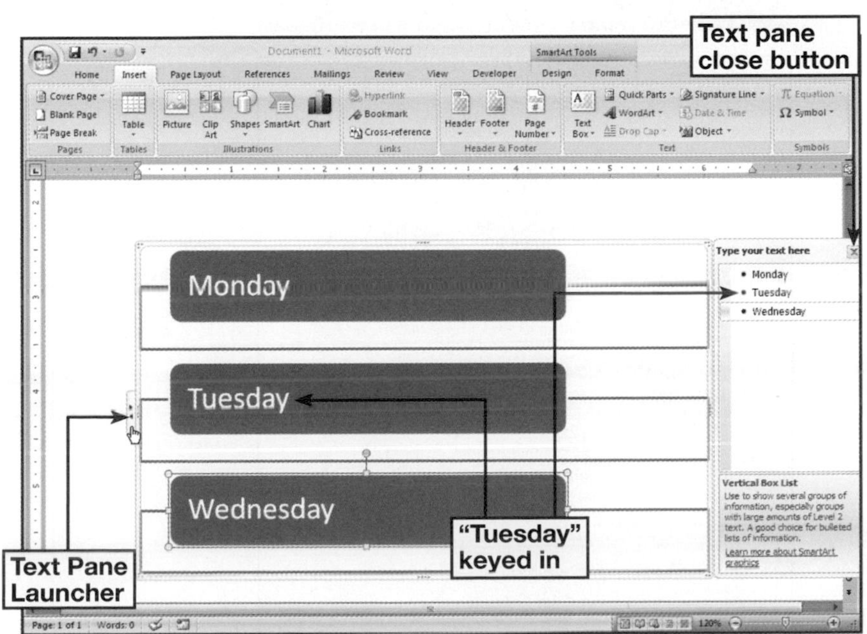

APPENDIX D Reference Guide for Formatting Documents

Memo

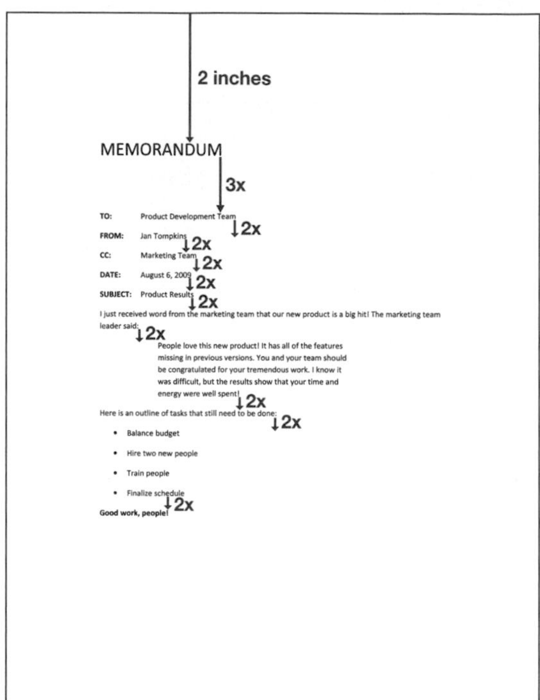

MEMORANDUM

TO: Product Development Team

FROM: Jan Tompkins

CC: Marketing Team

DATE: August 6, 2009

SUBJECT: Product Results

I just received word from the marketing team that our new product is a big hit! The marketing team leader said:

> People love this new product! It has all of the features missing in previous versions. You and your team should be congratulated for your tremendous work. I know it was difficult, but the results show that your time and energy were well spent!

Here is an outline of tasks that still need to be done:

- Balance budget
- Hire two new people
- Train people
- Finalize schedule

Good work, people!

Business Letter

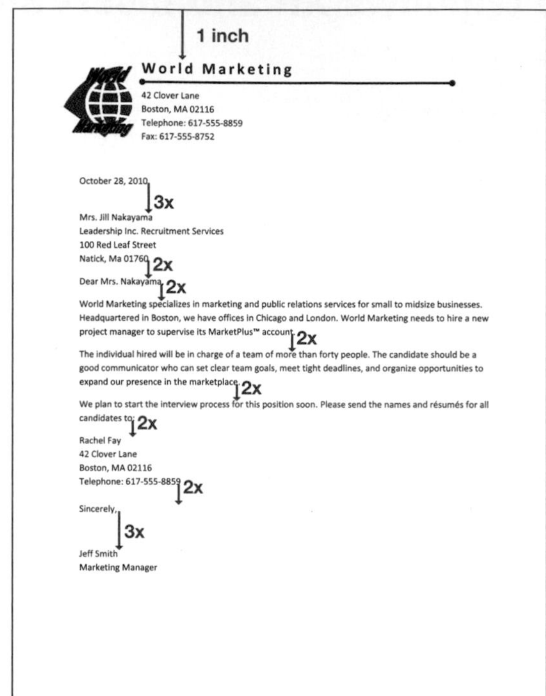

World Marketing

42 Clover Lane
Boston, MA 02116
Telephone: 617-555-8859
Fax: 617-555-8752

October 28, 2010

Mrs. Jill Nakayama
Leadership Inc. Recruitment Services
100 Red Leaf Street
Natick, Ma 01760

Dear Mrs. Nakayama:

World Marketing specializes in marketing and public relations services for small to midsize businesses. Headquartered in Boston, we have offices in Chicago and London. World Marketing needs to hire a new project manager to supervise its MarketPlus™ account.

The individual hired will be in charge of a team of more than forty people. The candidate should be a good communicator who can set clear team goals, meet tight deadlines, and organize opportunities to expand our presence in the marketplace.

We plan to start the interview process for this position soon. Please send the names and résumés for all candidates to:

Rachel Fay
42 Clover Lane
Boston, MA 02116
Telephone: 617-555-8859

Sincerely,

Jeff Smith
Marketing Manager

Personal Business Letter

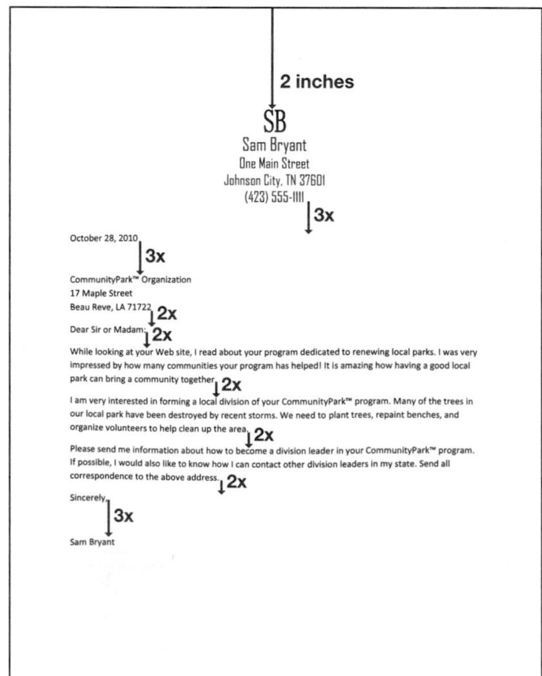

SB
Sam Bryant
One Main Street
Johnson City, TN 37601
(423) 555-1111

October 28, 2010

CommunityPark™ Organization
17 Maple Street
Beau Reve, LA 71722

Dear Sir or Madam:

While looking at your Web site, I read about your program dedicated to renewing local parks. I was very impressed by how many communities your program has helped! It is amazing how having a good local park can bring a community together.

I am very interested in forming a local division of your CommunityPark™ program. Many of the trees in our local park have been destroyed by recent storms. We need to plant trees, repaint benches, and organize volunteers to help clean up the area.

Please send me information about how to become a division leader in your CommunityPark™ program. If possible, I would also like to know how I can contact other division leaders in my state. Send all correspondence to the above address.

Sincerely,

Sam Bryant

Outline

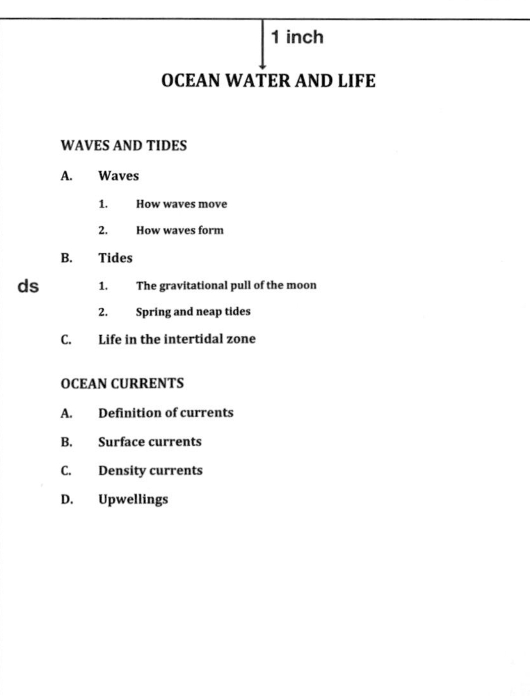

OCEAN WATER AND LIFE

WAVES AND TIDES

A. Waves
 1. How waves move
 2. How waves form
B. Tides
 1. The gravitational pull of the moon
 2. Spring and neap tides
C. Life in the intertidal zone

OCEAN CURRENTS

A. Definition of currents
B. Surface currents
C. Density currents
D. Upwellings

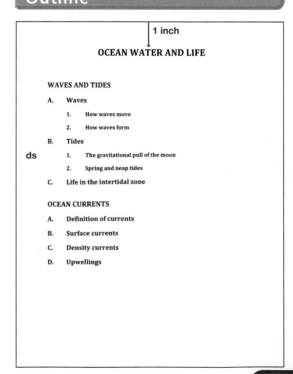

Operating Your Computer

The following tips should be used to operate your computer correctly. Your teacher may provide you with additional instructions.

Turning the computer on

- ✓ Make sure there are no disks in the computer's disk drives.
- ✓ Power on the computer and monitor.
- ✓ Wait for the start-up process to finish before starting any programs. You may be required to enter a network user ID and password at this time.
- ✓ Insert disks, DVDs, and CDs.

Turning the computer off

- ✓ Save data and files if necessary and close all windows.
- ✓ Remove any disks, DVDs, and CDs.
- ✓ Use the desktop shut-down procedure. Click Start on the taskbar, click Shut Down, choose the Shut down option, and click OK.
- ✓ Power off the computer and monitor (if necessary).

Disks and CD-ROMs

- ✓ Handle disks, DVDs, and CDs carefully, holding them by the edges.
- ✓ Protect disks, DVDs, and CDs from dirt, scratches, moisture, extremes in temperature, and magnetic fields.
- ✓ Insert and remove disks, DVDs, and CDs gently.
- ✓ Do not attempt to remove a disk, DVD, or CD when the drive indicator light is on.

Work area

- ✓ Keep the area around your computer neat and free from dust and dirt.
- ✓ Do not eat or drink near your computer, as spilled food and drinks can cause damage to the computer.

Using Student Data Files

To complete some Exercises in this book, Data Files are required.

- When you see the Data File icon, locate the needed files before beginning the exercise.
- Data Files are available at the Student Online Learning Center at **glencoe.com**. Your teacher will tell you where to find these files.
- Some exercises require you to continue working on a file you created in an earlier exercise. If you were absent and could not complete the previous exercise, your teacher may choose to provide you with the Solution File for the missed exercise.

How To Use the Reference Guide

The information on the following pages will help you format various kinds of documents. Use the Contents below to quickly locate the type of document you are creating. Then use the examples shown as a guide to help you format your document properly. The arrows and numbers shown in red on each sample tell you how many times to press Enter on your keyboard to separate items in your document. Double space is indicated by ds.

Remember that your work should reflect your own original research and content and that the information provided here is for reference purposes only. If you use other sources to create your documents, remember to cite your sources properly.

Contents

UNIT 1 Word 2007: Business and Personal Communication

Unit Objectives:

After completing this Unit, you will be able to:

LESSON 1

Create a Document

LESSON 2

Format Content

LESSON 3

Use Word Tools

LESSON 4

Manage Lengthy Documents

LESSON 5

Columns, Tables, and Graphics

LESSON 6

Collaborate with Others

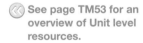

See page TM53 for an overview of Unit level resources.

Why It Matters Have students identify times when good communication was important in their lives. Help students understand why good communication is important to running a successful business.

Why It Matters

You probably use cell phones, e-mail, instant messaging, and other technology to stay in touch with friends and family. Word processing applications such as Microsoft Word 2007 allow business employees to communicate quickly and easily through memos, letters, and business reports. ***Why is good communication important to individuals and organizations?***

Go Online **REAL WORLD CONNECTION**

glencoe.com

Go to the **Online Learning Center** and select your book. Choose **Unit 1** to learn how organizations use word processing applications in the real world.

APPENDIX C Proofreader's Glossary

Proofreader's Marks		Draft	Final Copy
~~	Boldface	Chapter Title	**Chapter Title**
ital	Italics	ital Business Week	*Business Week*
u/l	Underline	u/l Business Week readers	Business Week readers
¶	New paragraph	¶ Once upon a time	Once upon a time
○	Spell out	There were (5).	There were five.
⁐	Close up; omit space	no thing	nothing
# ^	Insert space	allright	all right
∨ or ∧	Insert	Dont go there. (over)	Don't go over there.
⊙	Insert period	She went home⊙	She went home.
∧	Insert comma	Alex said "Let's go."	Alex said, "Let's go."
∂	Delete	the ~~very~~ last time	the last time
•••	Don't delete; stet	a ~~red~~ ball	a red ball
≡	Capitalize	Third avenue	Third Avenue
/	Make lowercase	the Teacher	the teacher
when ~~if~~	Change word	Wear the ~~blue~~ hat. (orange)	Wear the orange hat.
∽	Transpose	is it cold	it is cold
⊐	Move right	$93.87	$93.87
⊏	Move left	Shall we	Shall we dance
♂	Move as shown	Let's go (dance)	Let's go
SS	Single-space	SS I heard that you are leaving.	I heard that you are leaving.
ds	Double-space	ds When will it take place?	When will it take place?

UNIT 1 Careers and Technology

How Can Word Processing Advance Your Career?

Word processing is an important skill for most jobs today. Students and professionals use word processors to create and edit documents and to communicate effectively. But do you know how word processing skills can help you get a high-demand job?

Career Checklist

To use word processing as an effective communication tool in the workplace, remember to:

- ✓ Define your goals.
- ✓ Stay brief, focused, and to-the-point.
- ✓ Use proper formatting.
- ✓ Apply Spell-Check.
- ✓ Re-read your document.
- ✓ Revise your document.
- ✓ Get feedback.

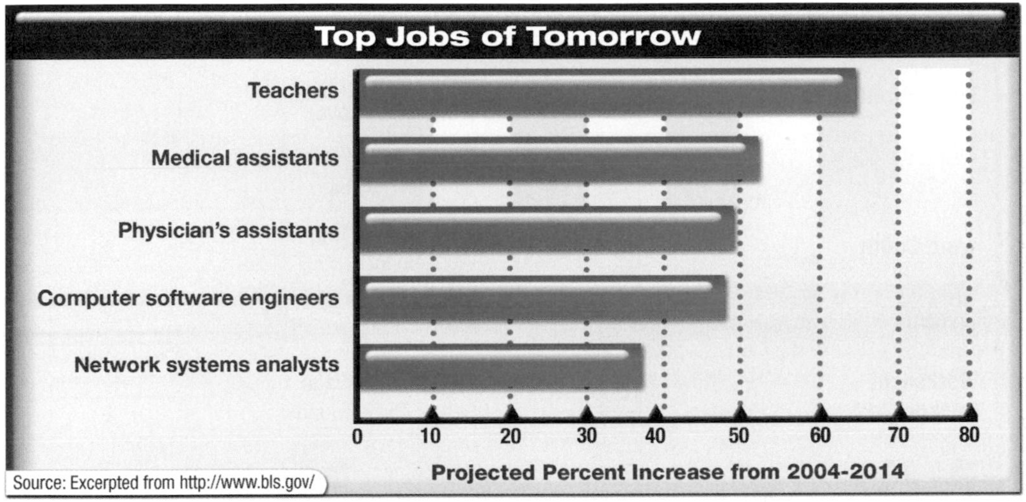

Differentiated Instruction/Advanced Students Have students write a paragraph describing how the career of their choice uses word processing.

NCLB/Math (Representation) Have students visit the Online Learning Center for this book at **glencoe.com** to learn more about math theory. Click the link to the Math Handbook.

Health Care

You can see in the chart above that health care workers are in high demand. Why do health care professionals need word processing skills? Good communication and record keeping is essential to good health care. Like most office jobs, health care requires some word processing, from filling out forms and reports to submitting invoices and payments.

Computers and Networks

A network systems analyst or computer software engineer needs to manage information using the word processing skills you will learn in this Unit. Being able to create and edit text and images is vital to professionals who build, analyze, edit, and maintain computer systems, explain technical information in writing, develop user documentation and manuals, and communicate with other employees and clients.

READING CHECK

1. **Evaluate** How can excellent word processing skills improve your ability to find and keep a job in the health field?
2. **Math** According to the chart, what is the approximate percent increase of network systems analysts from 2004–2014?

See page TM53 for answers to the Reading Check.

Function	Button	Ribbon	Keyboard Shortcuts	Application
Undo		Quick Access Toolbar>Undo	CTRL + Z	Word, Excel, Access, PowerPoint
Unfreeze panes		View>Window>Freeze Panes>Unfreeze Panes		Excel
Update Table of Contents		References>Table of Contents>Update Table		Word
View in Full Screen Mode		View>Workbook Views>Full Screen		Excel
Web Layout View		Page Layout>Document Views>Web Layout		Word
Windows Side by Side		View>Window> View Side by Side		Word
Word Count		Review>Proofing> Word Count		Word
WordArt		Insert>Text>WordArt		Word, Excel, PowerPoint
Worksheet Background		Page Layout>Page Setup>Background		Excel
Zoom In or Out		View>Zoom>Zoom		Word, Excel, PowerPoint

LESSON 1 Create a Document

In this lesson, you will learn how to key and edit text. You will also learn how to name, save, print, open, and close a document. Knowing these basic skills is an essential part of becoming a word processing expert.

Key Concepts

- Identify parts of the Word screen
- Name and save a document
- Key text into a document
- Edit text
- Print a document
- Close a document

Standards

The following standards are covered in this lesson. Refer to pages xxv and 715 for a description of the standards listed here.

ISTE Standards Correlation

NETS•S

3b, 3c, 5b, 6a, 6b, 6d

Microsoft Certified Application Specialist

Word

1.4, 5.1

21st CENTURY SKILLS

See page TM55 for answer to 21st Century Skills.

Set Realistic Goals Recall the first time you tried to ride a skateboard or play basketball. How long did it take before you felt confident with your performance? Like skateboarding and basketball, it takes time to learn word processing skills. Along the way, you will make mistakes. Allowing yourself to make mistakes, and knowing how to learn from those mistakes, is an important part of setting realistic goals. *What is your goal for this class?*

APPENDIX B Quick Reference Summary

Function	Button	Ribbon	Keyboard Shortcuts	Application
Start Word		Start>Programs>Microsoft Office>Microsoft Office Word 2007		Word
Styles		Home>Styles>Change Styles		Word
Switch Between Open Windows		View>Window>Switch Windows>[Name of Window]	SHIFT + F6	Word, Excel, Access, PowerPoint
Symbol		Insert>Symbols> Insert Symbol		Word, PowerPoint
Symbol		Insert>Text>Symbol		Excel
Table		Insert>Tables>Table		Word, Excel, PowerPoint
Table Borders		Table Tools>Design> Table Styles>Borders		Word, PowerPoint
Table in Database		Create>Tables>Table Design		Access
Table of Contents		References>Table of Contents		Word
Table Styles		Design>Table Styles>More		Word, PowerPoint
Text Box		Insert>Text>Text Box		Word, Excel, PowerPoint
Text Box to a Form		Design>Controls>Text Box		Access
Text to Table		Insert>Tables>Table>Convert Text to Table		Word
Thesaurus		Review>Proofing>Thesaurus	SHIFT + F7	Word, Excel, PowerPoint
Total Data		Home>Records>Totals		Access
Track Changes		Review>Tracking>Tracking Changes	CTRL + SHIFT + E	Word
Transition Effects		Animations>Transition to This Slide>[Transition]		PowerPoint
Turn Filter On and Off		Home>Sort & Filter>Toggle Filter		Access
Underline		Home>Font>Underline		Word, Excel, Access, PowerPoint

LESSON 1 Reading Guide

Before You Read

See page TM42 for English Learner activity suggestions.

Survey Before starting the lesson, survey the content by reading exercise titles, bolded terms, and figures. Do they help you predict the information in the lesson?

Read To Learn

- Consider how the Word screen allows you to enter commands easily into the application.
- Explore file management as a vital skill.
- Discover how creating and editing documents is part of good business communication.

Main Idea

Microsoft Word is a word processing application that you can use to create and organize documents.

Vocabulary

Key Terms

button
command
cursor
dialog box
document
edit
folder
group
insertion point
pointer
Quick Access Toolbar (QAT)
Ribbon
ScreenTip
scroll bar
status bar
tab
title bar

Academic Vocabulary

These words appear in your reading and on your tests. Make sure you know their meanings.

consider
determine

Quick Write Activity

Describe On a separate sheet of paper, describe why it is important to edit and proofread a document before you consider it to be final. What steps do you take when you proofread a document?

Study Skills

Stay on Task If you are easily distracted in class, try sitting at the front of the room or near the teacher's desk. This will make it easier to focus on what the teacher is saying.

Academic Standards

English Language Arts

NCTE 1 Read texts to acquire new information.
NCTE 4 Use written language to communicate effectively.
NCTE 5 Use different writing process elements to communicate effectively.
NCTE 6 Apply knowledge of language structure and conventions to discuss texts.
NCTE 7 Conduct research and gather, evaluate, and synthesize data to communicate discoveries.
NCTE 8 Use information resources to gather information and create and communicate knowledge.

Function	Button	Ribbon	Keyboard Shortcuts	Application
SmartArt		Insert>Illustrations>SmartArt		Word, Excel, PowerPoint
Sort		Home>Paragraph>Sort		Word
Sort Ascending Order		Data>Sort & Filter> Sort A to Z		Excel
Sort Ascending Order		Home>Sort & Filter> Ascending		Access
Sort Descending Order		Data>Sort & Filter> Sort Z to A		Excel
Sort Descending Order		Home>Sort & Filter> Descending		Access
Sound		Insert>Media Clips>Sound		PowerPoint
Spelling		Review>Proofing>Spelling	F7	Excel, PowerPoint
Spelling		Home>Records>Spelling	F7	Access
Spelling and Grammar		Review>Proofing> Spelling & Grammar	F7	Word
Split Database		Database Tools>Move Data>Access Database		Access
Split Form		Create>Forms>Split Forms		Access
Split Window		View>Window>Split		Word, Excel
Start Access		Start>Programs>Microsoft Office>Microsoft Office Access 2007		Access
Start Excel		Start>Programs>Microsoft Office>Microsoft Office Excel 2007		Excel
Start PowerPoint		Start>Programs>Microsoft Office>Microsoft Office PowerPoint 2007		PowerPoint
Start Slide Show from Beginning		Slide Show>Start Slide Show>From Beginning	F5	PowerPoint

Step-By-Step

1. To start Word, click the **Start** button (see Figure 1.1). Choose **Programs> Microsoft Office®> Microsoft Office Word 2007**. A new document opens.

2. **iCHECK** Your screen should look like Figure 1.1.

3. Locate the **title bar**. The name of your document should be **Document 1**.

4. Locate the **Office** button at the top of the screen.

5. Click **Office**. The first option in the drop-down menu is **New**.

6. Locate the **Quick Access Toolbar**. The first option on the toolbar is **Save**.

7. Locate the **scroll bar** on the right side of the screen (see Figure 1.1). Practice scrolling up and down in your document.

8. Locate the **status bar**. You should be on **Page 1 of 1**.

Continue to the next exercise.

Teaching Tip Review with students the purpose of the iCheck icon in **Step 2** on this page. The iCheck icon lets the student know that their screen should look like the figure at that step.

EXERCISE 1-1
Identify Parts of the Word Screen

Word 2007's Microsoft Office Button provides access to basic commands such as open, save, and print. The **title bar** displays the name of the current **document** or file. The **status bar** tells you the page you are on and the total page count. **Scroll bars** move a document up and down or left and right on the screen. The **pointer** arrow lets you select commands on screen.

FIGURE 1.1 The Word screen

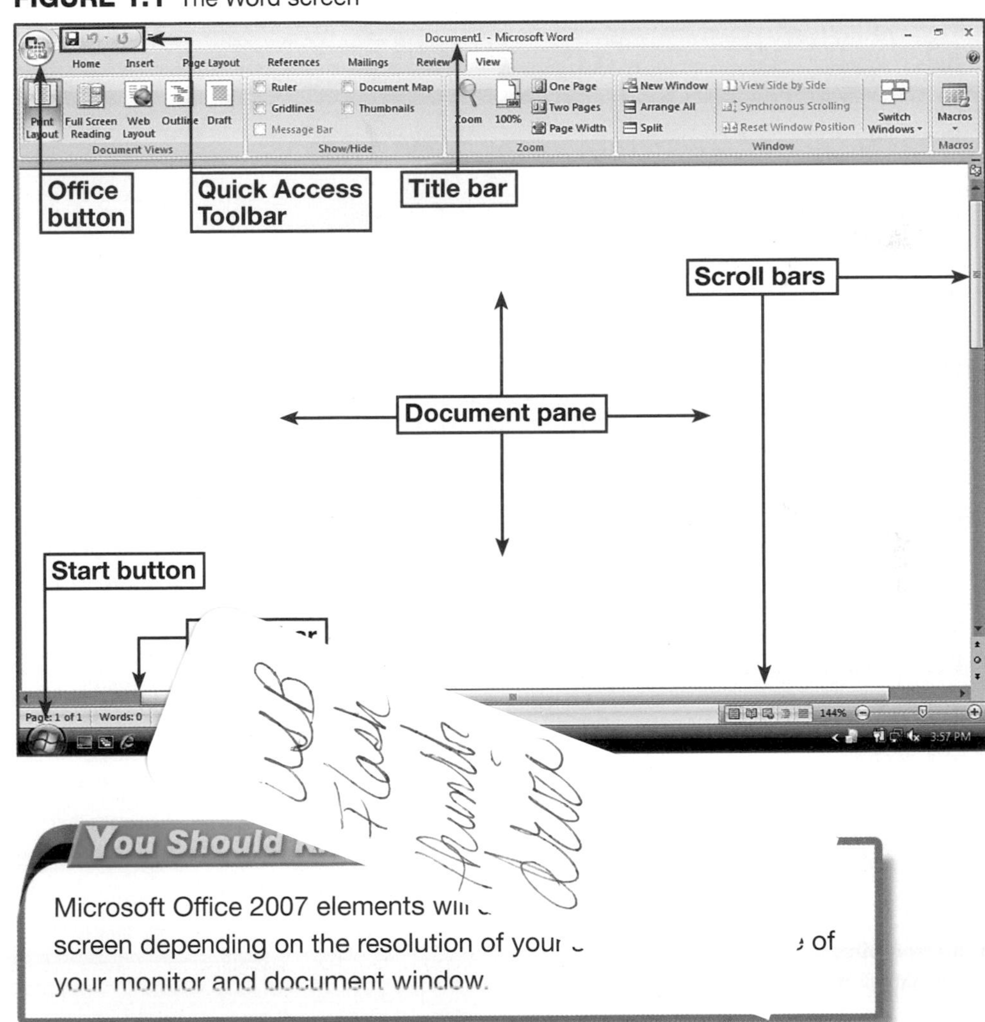

You Should K...

Microsoft Office 2007 elements will ... screen depending on the resolution of your ... of your monitor and document window.

Microsoft Office 2007

The Office button is a new Office 2007 feature. You can use this button to perform important tasks such as creating, saving, and printing a document.

APPENDIX  Quick Reference Summary

Function	Button	Ribbon	Keyboard Shortcuts	Application
Report		Create>Reports>Report		Access
Report in Design View		Create>Reports>Design		Access
Report Labels		Create>Reports>Labels		Access
Report Wizard		Create>Reports>Report Wizard		Access
Run Query		Design>Results>Run		Access
Save		Office>Save	CTRL + S	Word, Excel, Access, PowerPoint
Save As		Office>Save As	F12	Word, Excel, Access, PowerPoint
Select All		Home>Editing>Select> Select All		Word, PowerPoint
Set Up Slide Show		Slide Show>Set Up> Set Up Slide Show		PowerPoint
Shade Tables		Design>Table>Styles> Shading		Word, PowerPoint
Show Markup		Review>Comments> Show Markup		Excel
Show Markup		Review>Tracking> Show Markup		Word
Show Nonprinting Characters		Home>Paragraph> Show/Hide	CTRL + *	Word
Show or Hide Relationships		Database Tools>Show/ Hide>Relationships		Access
Show or Hide Worksheet Gridlines		View>Show/Hide>Gridlines		Excel
Show or Hide Worksheet Headings		View>Show/Hide>Headings		Excel
Slide Layout		Home>Slides>Layout		PowerPoint
Slide Master View		View>Presentation Views> Slide Master		PowerPoint
Slide Orientation		Design>Page Setup>Slide Orientation		PowerPoint
Slide Sorter View		View>Presentation Views>Slide Sorter		PowerPoint

Step-By-Step

1. In Word, on the **Ribbon**, click the **Home** tab (see Figure 1.2).
2. Roll your pointer arrow over the five different groups in the **Home** tab (see Figure 1.3).
3. Click the seven different tabs across the Ribbon. Identify the groups displayed in each tab.
4. Click the **Home** tab. In the **Styles** group, click **Change Styles** .
5. Move the pointer to **Style Set**. The submenu automatically opens.
6. **CHECK** Your screen should look like Figure 1.2.
7. Click in a blank area on the screen to close the **Change Styles** menu.

Continue to the next exercise.

EXERCISE 1-2
Use the Ribbon, Tabs, and Groups

The **Ribbon** is designed to help you quickly find a **button** (or **command**), which is a small image that can be clicked to perform various tasks. The buttons are organized under tabs and groups. Each **tab** contains several related groups, and each **group** contains closely related buttons. Consider, or think about, the common text commands grouped under the Home tab.

NCLB/Language Arts (NCTE 7) Have students review the Ribbon and evaluate why certain buttons are placed in certain groups.

FIGURE 1.2 Style and Set submenu

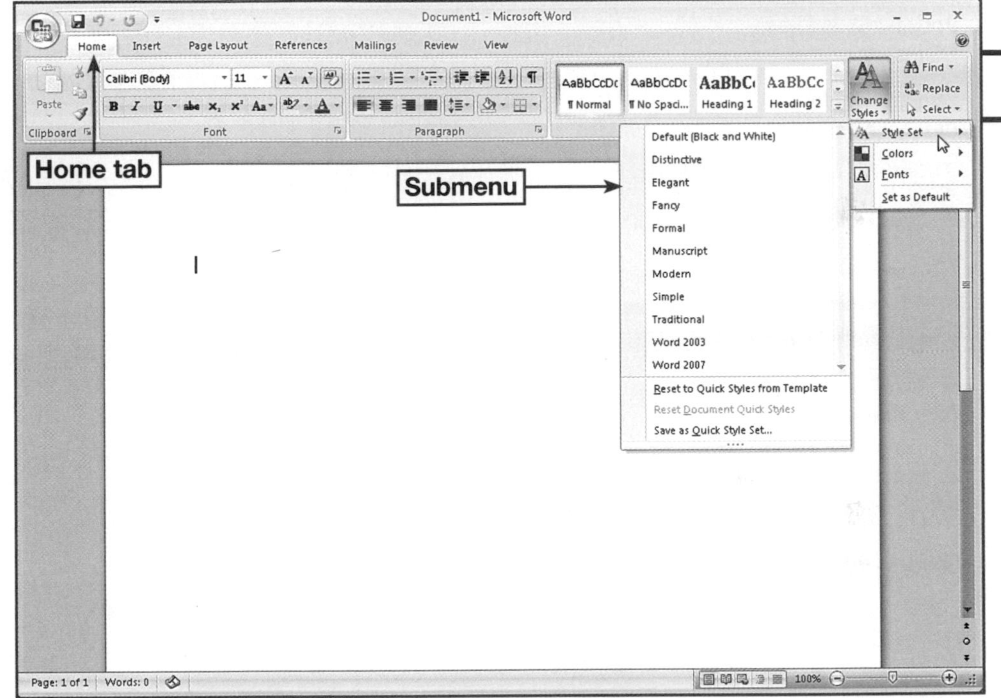

FIGURE 1.3 Ribbon and Home tab menu

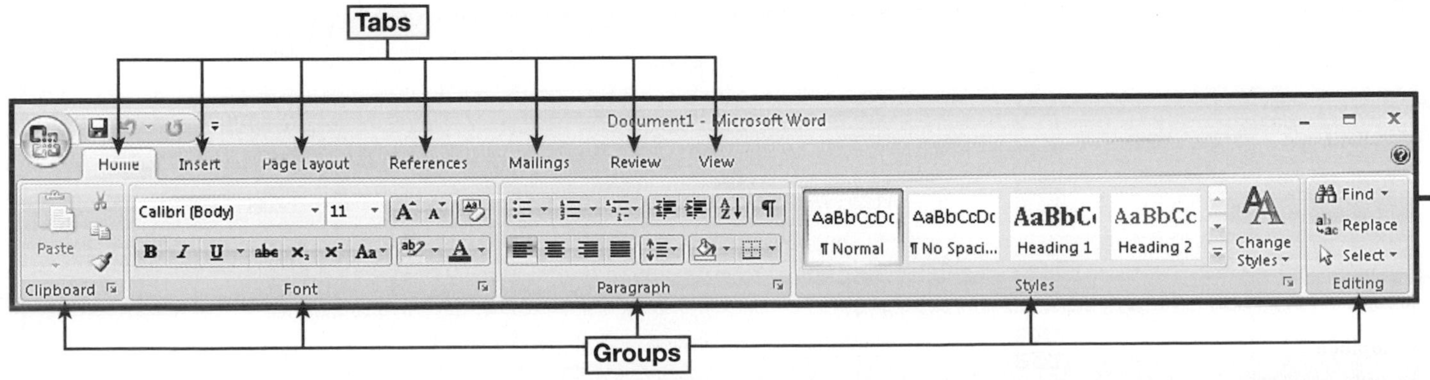

Differentiated Instruction/ Advanced Students Students who favor learning by touching and exploring may be tempted to click on all the buttons. You may wish to allow extra time for some "free exploration."

Function	Button	Ribbon	Keyboard Shortcuts	Application
Password for Database		Database Tools>Database Tools>Encrypt with Password		Access
Paste		Home>Clipboard>Paste	CTRL + V	Word, Excel, Access PowerPoint
Paste Special		Home>Clipboard>Paste> Paste Special		Word, Excel, Access, PowerPoint
Preview Slide Show Animations		Animations>Preview> Preview		PowerPoint
Primary Key for Database Table		Design>Tools>Primary Key		Access
Print		Office>Print	CTRL + P	Word, Excel, Access, PowerPoint
Print Area		Page Layout>Page Setup> Print Area		Excel
Print Layout View		View>Document Views>Print Layout	CTRL + ALT + P	Word
Print Preview		Office>Print>Print Preview		Word, Excel, Access, PowerPoint
Promote Text to Heading Level 1		Outlining>Outline Tools> Promote to Heading Level 1		Word
Query in Design View		Create>Other>Query Design		Access
Query Wizard		Create>Other>Query Wizard		Access
Reject Suggested Changes		Review>Changes> Reject and Move to Next		Word
Relationship Report		Design>Tools>Relationship Report		Access
Remove Filters		Home>Sort & Filter> Advanced>Clear All Filters		Access
Remove Split in Window		View>Window>Remove Split		Word
Remove Split in Window		View>Window>Split		Excel
Repeat		Quick Access Toolbar>Redo	CTRL + Y	Word, Excel, Access, PowerPoint
Replace		Home>Editing>Replace	CTRL + H	Word, PowerPoint
Replace	Replace	Home>Find>Replace		Access

Step-By-Step

1. On the **Home** tab, in the **Clipboard** group, move the pointer over the **Format Painter** button . A **ScreenTip** appears.
2. Read the **ScreenTip** for each button in the **Font** group.
3. In the **Font** group, click the arrow next to the **Font Color** button. The drop-down menu is displayed.
4. In the **Font** group, click the **Dialog Box Launcher** (see Figure 1.4).
5. **CHECK** Your screen should look like Figure 1.4. Click the **Close** button on the dialog box.
6. At the bottom-right of the screen, click **Full Screen Reading** .
7. Click the **Close** button at the top right corner to return to the default **Print Layout** view.

Continue to the next exercise.

Different Strokes You can also show students how to change the view by clicking the **Full Screen View** button at the bottom of their screens.

EXERCISE 1-3
Use ScreenTips and Different Views

When you point to a button, a **ScreenTip** appears to show you the name of the command. If the picture on a button is dimmed, the button is not available. For example, Undo would not be available if you have not performed any actions to undo.

At the bottom of the screen there are buttons which allow you to change the screen display. Print Layout View lets you see how the document will look when it is printed. Full Screen View displays the entire page on the screen. To see how your document will appear on the World Wide Web, choose Web View.

FIGURE 1.4 Print Layout View with Font dialog box

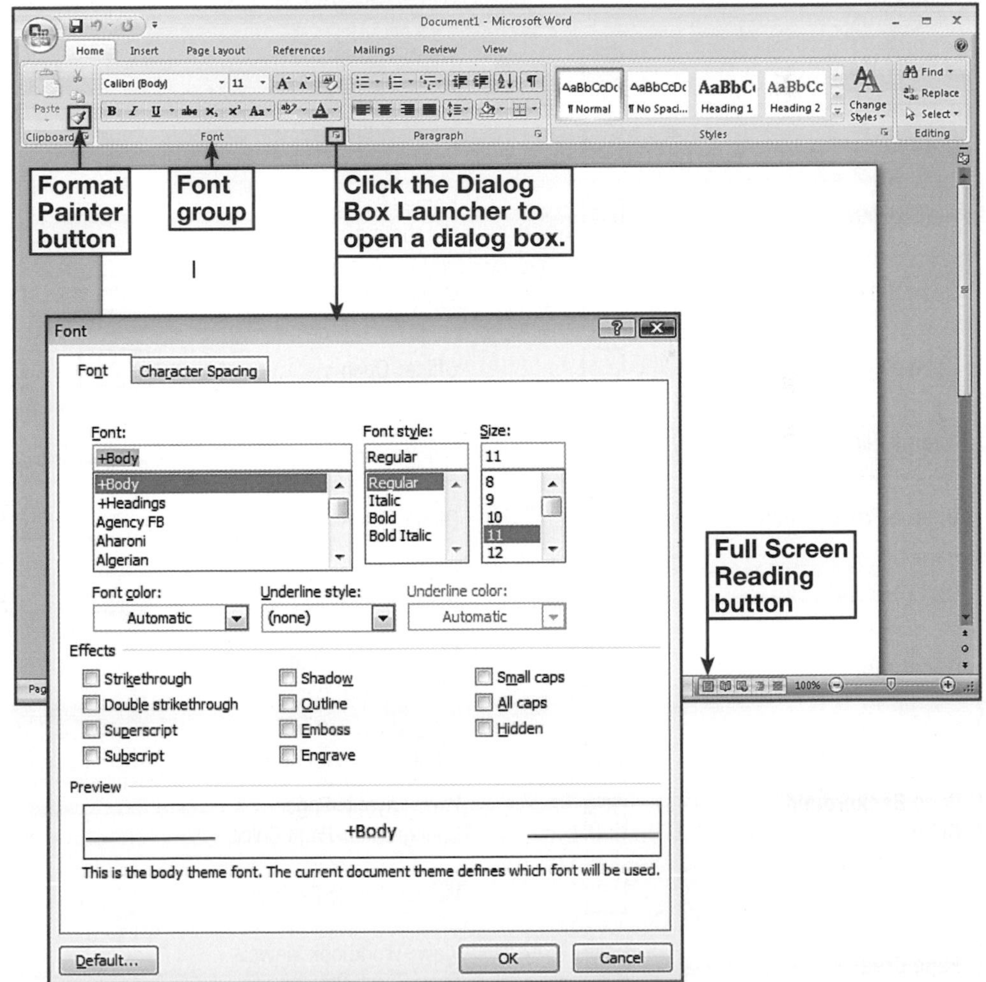

APPENDIX  Quick Reference Summary

Function	Button	Ribbon	Keyboard Shortcuts	Application
Multilevel List		Home>Paragraph> Multilevel List		Word
Multiple Item Form		Create>Forms>Multiple Items		Access
New Comment		Review>Comments> New Comment		Word, Excel, PowerPoint
New Page		Insert>Pages>Blank Page		Word
New Slide		Home>Slides>New Slide		PowerPoint
Normal View		View>Presentation Views>Normal View		PowerPoint
Normal View		View>Workbook Views>Normal View		Excel
Numbering		Home>Paragraph> Numbering		Word, PowerPoint
Open a Database		Office>Open	CTRL + O	Access
Open a Document		Office>Open	CTRL + O	Word
Open a File		Office>Open	CTRL + O	Word, Excel, Access, PowerPoint
Open a Presentation		Office>Open	CTRL + O	PowerPoint
Open a Workbook		Office>Open	CTRL + O	Excel
Orientation		Page Layout>Page Setup>Orientation		Word, Excel
Orientation		Slide Master>Page Setup>Slide Orientation		PowerPoint
Page Background Color		Page Layout>Page Background>Page Color		Word
Page Break		Insert>Pages>Page Break	CTRL + ENTER	Word
Page Break Preview		View>Workbook Views> Page Break Preview		Excel
Page Number		Insert>Header & Footer> Page Number		Word

Step-By-Step

1. At the top of your screen, locate the **Quick Access Toolbar (QAT)**.
2. To the right of the **QAT**, click **Customize Quick Access Toolbar** (see Figure 1.5).
3. In the drop-down **Customize** menu, click **Open**. Notice that **Open** is added to the toolbar.
4. In the **Customize** menu, click **Open** again. Notice that **Open** has been removed.
5. In the **Customize** menu, click **Show Below the Ribbon**. Notice that the **QAT** has moved below the Ribbon.
6. CHECK Your screen should look like Figure 1.6.
7. Click **Show Above the Ribbon**. The **QAT** returns to its default location.
8. In the **Customize** menu, click **Minimize the Ribbon**.
9. Click **Minimize the Ribbon** again to restore the Ribbon.

Continue to the next exercise.

EXERCISE 1-4
Customize the Quick Access Toolbar

The **Quick Access Toolbar** (QAT) is a customizable toolbar for easy access to your most commonly used command buttons (default buttons include Save, Undo, and Redo). **Determine**, or decide, which commands you want to have easy access to as you work. Other commands that can be added to the **QAT** include Spelling & Grammar, Open, and Print Preview.

FIGURE 1.5 Customize Quick Access Toolbar drop-down menu

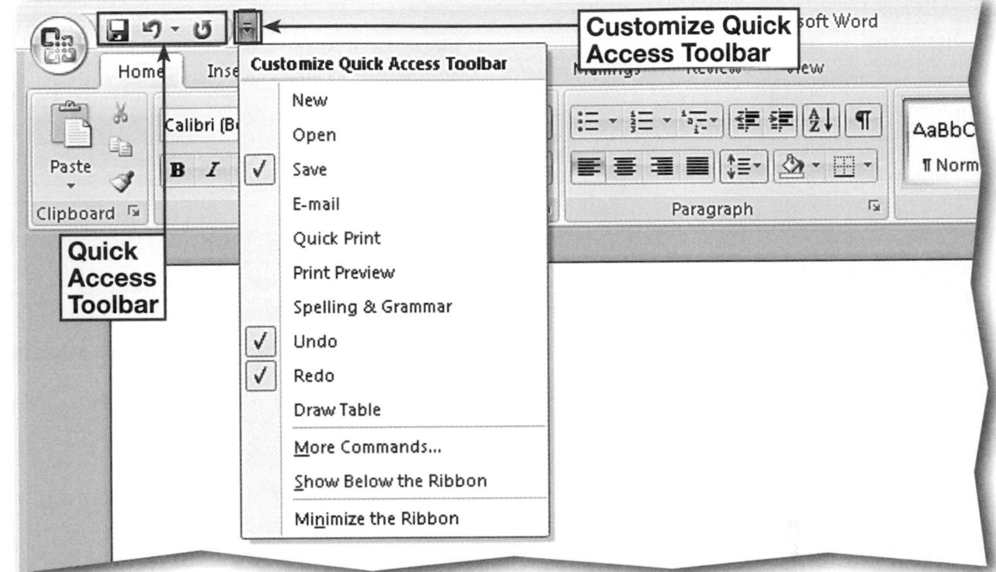

FIGURE 1.6 The QAT placed beneath the Ribbon

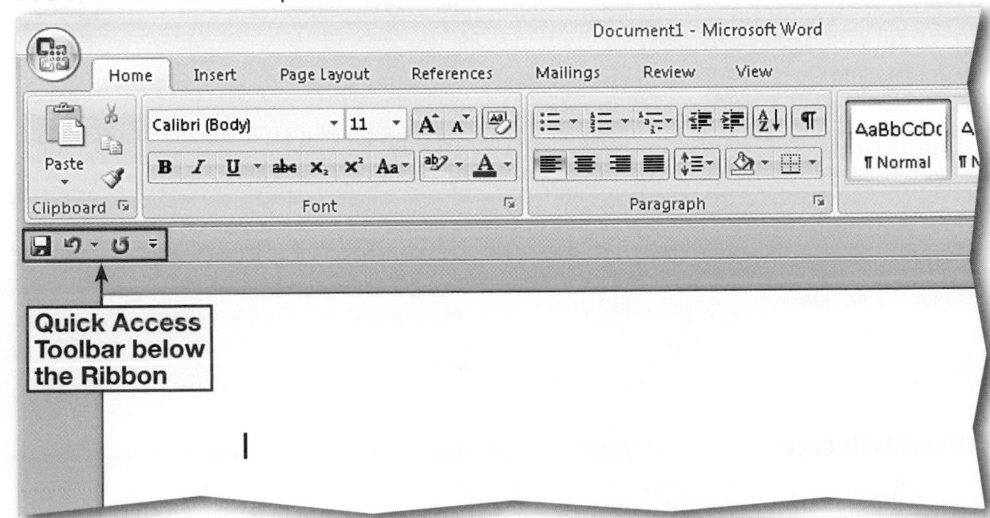

Teaching Tip The **More Commands** option in the **Customize** menu allows students to view all the commands that can be added to the **QAT**, but students can also change settings. If you allow students to explore this option, make sure they understand how to use it responsibly.

APPENDIX  Quick Reference Summary

Function	Button	Ribbon	Keyboard Shortcuts	Application
Hide Slide		Slide Show>Set Up> Hide Slide		PowerPoint
Hide Window		View>Window>Hide		Excel
Highlight Text		Home>Font>Text Highlight Color		Word
Hyperlink		Insert>Links>Hyperlink	CTRL + K	Word, Excel, PowerPoint
Import Excel File to Database		External Data>Import>Excel		Access
Import Text File to Database		External Data>Import> Text File		Access
Increase Indent Level		Home>Paragraph> Increase Indent	CTRL + M	Word, PowerPoint
Increase List Level		Home>Paragraph> Increase List Level	CTRL + M	Word, PowerPoint
Insert Table Row Above		Layout>Rows & Columns>Insert Above		Word, PowerPoint
Insert Worksheet		Insert>Cells>Insert> Insert Sheet		Excel
Insert Worksheet Cells		Home>Cells>Insert> Insert Cells		Excel
Italic		Home>Font>Italic	CTRL + I	Word, Excel, PowerPoint, Access
Line Spacing		Home>Paragraph> Line Spacing		Word, PowerPoint
Lookup Field		Datasheet>Fields & Columns>Lookup Column		Access
Mail Merge Wizard		Mailings>Start Mail Merge>Start Mail Merge		Word
Make-Table Query		Design>Query Type> Make Table		Access
Margins		Page Layout>Page Setup> Margins		Word, Excel
Merge Table Cells		Layout>Merge>Merge Cells		Word, PowerPoint
Move Chart to New Worksheet		Design>Location>Move Chart		Excel
Movie		Insert>Media Clips>Movie		PowerPoint

Step-By-Step

1. Click **Office**.
2. In the **Office** drop-down menu, click **Save As**. The **Save As** dialog box opens.
3. With your teacher's permission, click the **New Folder** button (see Figure 1.7).
4. In the **New Folder** text box that appears, key your first initial and last name (for example, *sbryant*).
5. Click outside the text box. The new folder opens automatically.
6. In the upper left, click the **Back to** button.
7. CHECK Your screen should look like Figure 1.8.
8. Click **Close** to close the dialog box.

Continue to the next exercise.

Troubleshooter

If you are using Windows XP, go to page li to learn how to complete the steps in this exercise and in Exercise 1-6.

Step-By-Step Tip In Step 5, tell students to watch the address bar as the new folder is added. Explain that the path shows them where on their computer the folder is located.

EXERCISE 1-5
Create a New Folder

Intervention Strategy Make sure students understand where their new folder is located on the computer or server. They will need this skill to save and locate folders and files throughout the course.

You can organize your documents in a **folder**. Using the Save As command, you can create a new folder for yourself. Use the Save As **dialog box** to enter specific information to perform a particular task, such as naming and saving a document.

FIGURE 1.7 Create and name a new folder

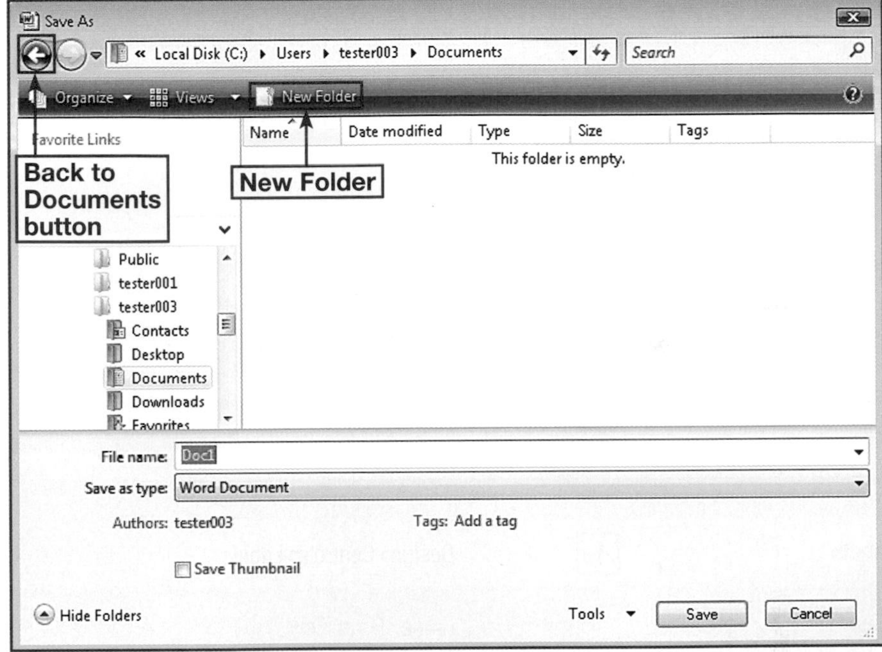

Teaching Tip You may refer students to the Technology Handbook (located on the Online Learning Center) to have them learn more about file management.

FIGURE 1.8 Verify the folder location

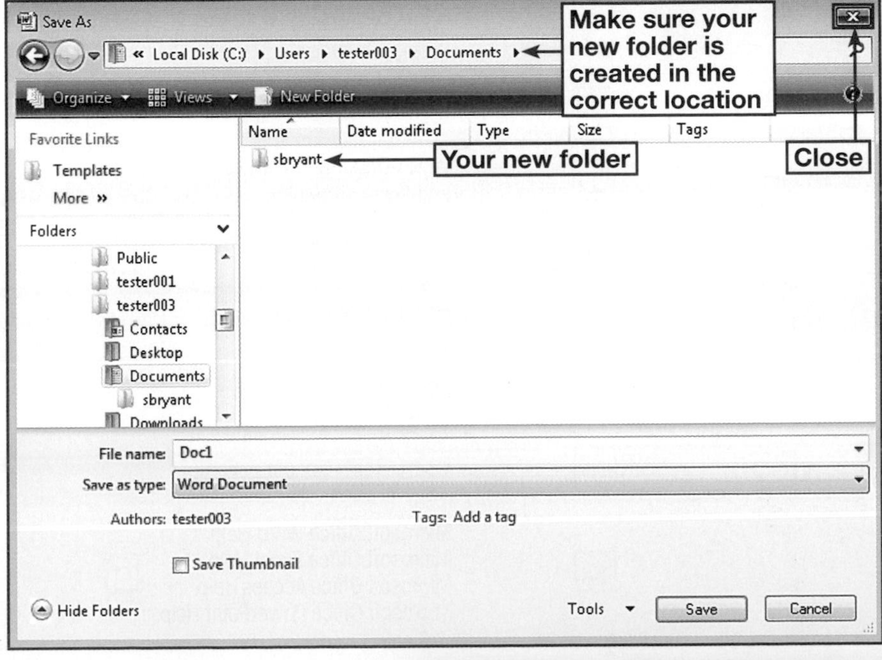

APPENDIX B Quick Reference Summary

Function	Button	Ribbon	Keyboard Shortcuts	Application
Find		Home>Editing>Find & Select	CTRL + F	Excel
Find		Home>Editing>Find	CTRL + F	Word, PowerPoint
Find		Home>Find>Find	CTRL + F	Access
Find a Synonym		Review>Proofing>Thesaurus	SHIFT + F7	Word, Excel, PowerPoint
Font		Home>Font>Font		Word, Excel, Access, PowerPoint
Font Color		Home>Font>Font Color		Word, Excel, Access, PowerPoint
Font Size		Home>Font>Font Size		Word, Excel, Access, PowerPoint
Footer		Insert>Header & Footer>Footer		Word
Form		Create>Forms>Form		Access
Form Labels		Design>Controls>Label		Access
Form View		Home>Form View		Access
Format Cells in Worksheet		Home>Cells>Format		Excel
Format Painter		Home>Clipboard> Format Painter		Word, Excel, Access, PowerPoint
Freeze Panes		View>Window>Freeze Panes		Excel
Full Screen Reading		View>Document Views> Full Screen Reading		Word
Function		Formulas>Function Library> Insert Function	SHIFT + F3	Excel
Group Report Data		Format>Grouping & Totals>Group & Sort		Access
Header		Insert>Header & Footer> Header		Word
Header		Insert>Text>Header & Footer		Excel, PowerPoint
Help		Microsoft Office Word Help Microsoft Office Excel Help Microsoft Office Access Help Microsoft Office PowerPoint Help	F1	Word, Excel, Access, PowerPoint

Step-By-Step

1. Click **Office** and choose **Save As**. The **Save As** dialog box opens.
2. In the **File name** box, key: w1-6-. Then key your first initial and your last name (for example, *w1-6-sbryant*).
3. In the **Save in** box, click the drop-down arrow. Locate the folder you created in Exercise 1-5 or ask your teacher for the location you should choose (see Figure 1.9).
4. Click **Save** in the **Save As** dialog box.
5. **CHECK** Your screen should look like Figure 1.10. The document's name appears on the title bar.

Continue to the next exercise.

Troubleshooting Emphasize the difference between **Save** and **Save As**. It is very important for beginning word processing students to understand the different reasons for using these functions. Explain to students that, if they use **Save As**, they will end up with two documents (one with the file's original name, and one with the file's new name).

Teaching Tip Point out to students that the first line of text in the document automatically becomes the default file name when the document is saved.

EXERCISE 1-6
Name and Save a Document

You can use the Save command to save a document with its current name. Use the Save As command if you want to rename a document, or create a second document that is based on the original. The Save As dialog box allows you to name and save a document so that you can find it and work on it again. You should save every 5 to 10 minutes to protect your work from being lost.

FIGURE 1.9 Save As dialog box

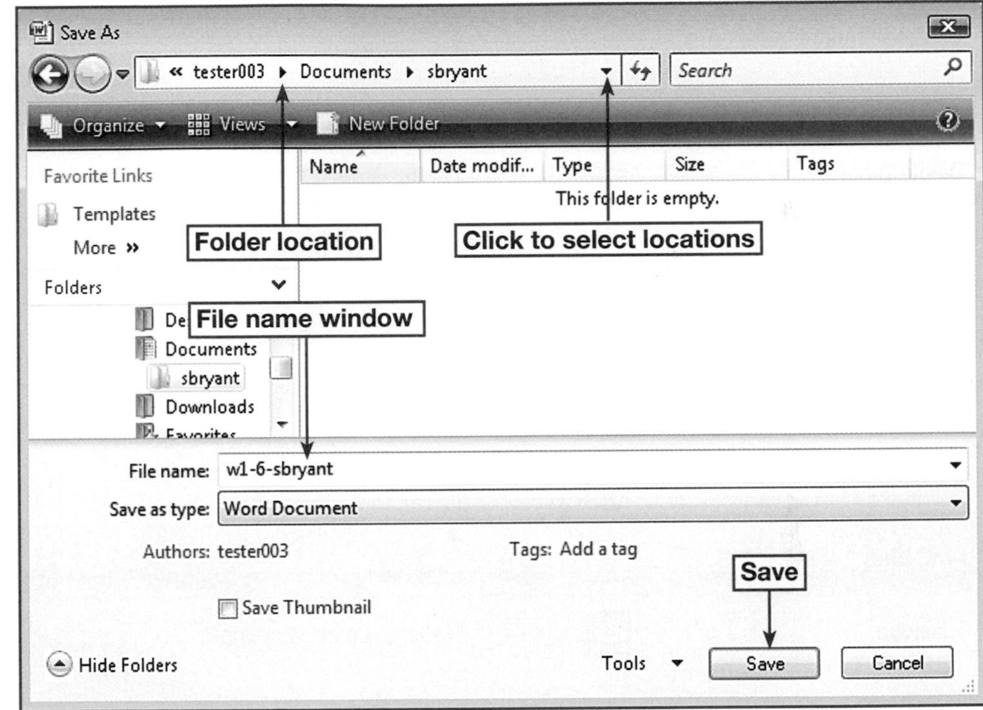

FIGURE 1.10 Saved document

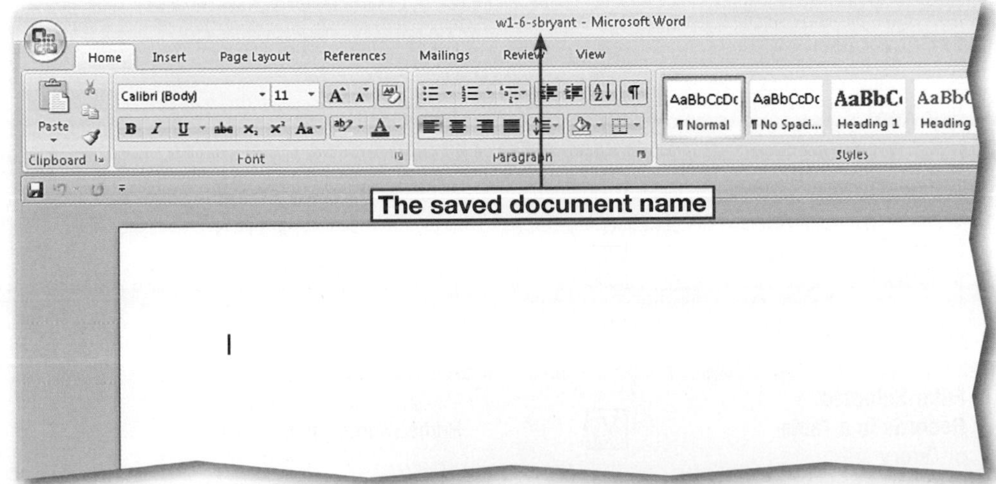

APPENDIX  Quick Reference Summary

Function	Button	Ribbon	Keyboard Shortcuts	Application
Database Table Templates		Create>Tables> Table Templates		Access
Datasheet View		Home>Views>View> Datasheet View		Access
Decrease Indent		Home>Paragraph> Decrease Indent	CTRL + SHIFT + M	Word
Decrease Indent		Home>Paragraph> Decrease List Level		PowerPoint
Delete Datasheet Records		Home>Records>Delete		Access
Delete Table Columns		Layout>Rows & Columns> Delete>Delete Columns		Word
Delete Table Rows		Layout>Rows & Columns> Delete>Delete Rows		Word
Delete Worksheet Cells		Home>Cells>Delete> Delete Cells		Excel
Demote Text to Lower Level		Outlining>Outline Tools> Demote		Word
Design View		Home>Views>View> Design View		Access
Draft View		View>Document Views> Draft View		Word
Envelope		Mailings>Create>Envelopes		Word
Exit Access		Office>Exit Access		Access
Exit Excel		Office>Exit Excel		Excel
Exit PowerPoint		Office>Exit PowerPoint		PowerPoint
Exit Word		Office>Exit Word		Word
Export Database Table to Word		External Data>Export>Word		Access
Filter a Table, Query, or Report		Home>Sort & Filter>Filter		Access
Filter Selected Cells		Data>Sort & Filter>Filter	CTRL + SHIFT + L	Excel
Filter Selected Records in a Table or Query		Home>Sort & Filter>Selection		Access

Step-By-Step

1. In your **w1-6** file, click in the document pane and key: Setting goals.
2. Choose the **Home tab> Paragraph group> Show/Hide ¶** ¶ button.
3. CHECK Your screen should look like Figure 1.11.
4. Click just before the word **goals**. The insertion point appears where you clicked.
5. Click at the end of the word **goals**.
6. Press the **spacebar** once. Key: is an important part of achieving success.
7. CHECK Your screen should look like Figure 1.12. The insertion point is at the end of the sentence.
8. Click **Save** on the **QAT** to save your work.

Continue to the next exercise

Microsoft Office 2007

When the **>** symbol appears in a step, it means that you need to follow a path to complete a task. For example, **Home>Font>Bold** means go to the **Home** tab, then go to the **Font** group, then click the **Bold** button.

EXERCISE 1-7
Insert Text into a Document

To insert, or add, text to a document, click in the document where you want the new text to begin. The blinking I-pointer (also called a **cursor**) shows where the **insertion point** is located. The insertion point shows where new text will begin. Then type, or key, text into the document pane. The Show/Hide ¶ button allows you to see hard returns (paragraph marks), spaces, and other characters that will not appear in the document when it is printed.

FIGURE 1.11 Keyed text and non-printing characters

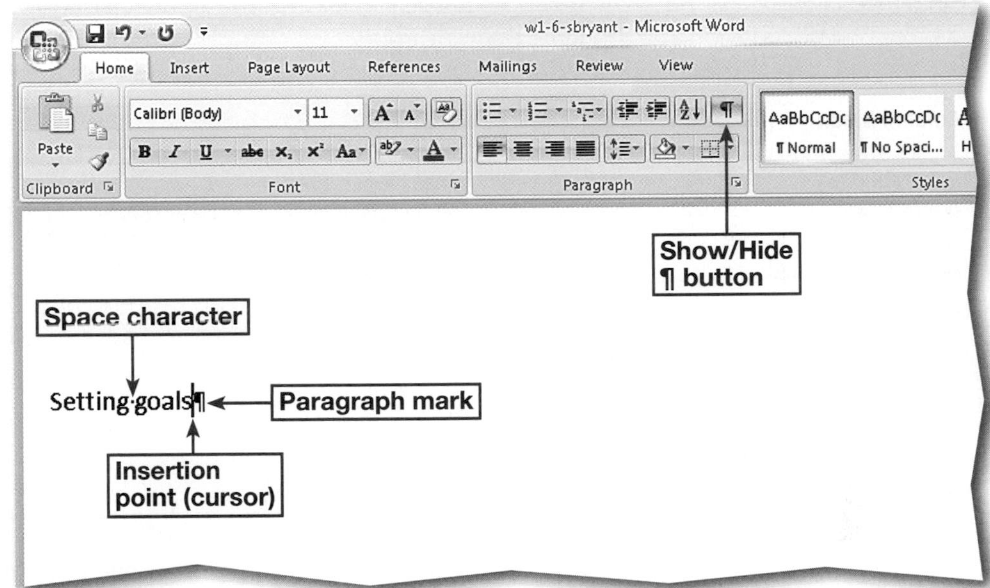

FIGURE 1.12 Insertion point at the end of the sentence

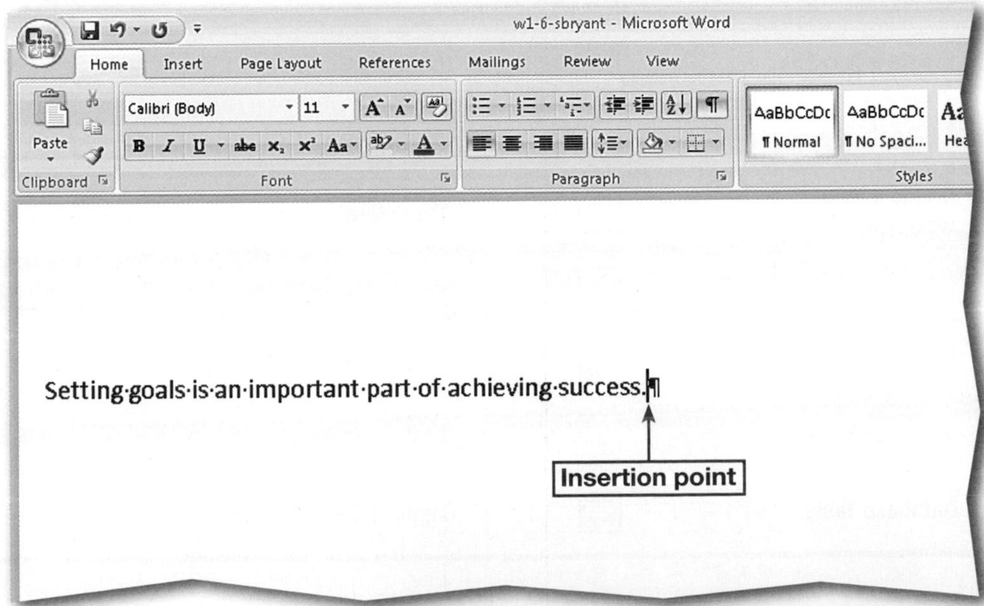

Function	Button	Ribbon	Keyboard Shortcuts	Application
Close a Presentation		Office>Close	CTRL + W *or* CTRL + F4	PowerPoint
Close a Window		Office>Close	CTRL + W *or* CTRL + F4	Word, Excel, PowerPoint
Close a Workbook		Office>Close	CTRL + W *or* CTRL + F4	Excel
Column Break		Page Layout>Page Setup>Breaks>Column		Word
Columns in a Document		Page Layout>Page Setup>Columns		Word
Columns on a Slide		Home>Paragraph>Columns		PowerPoint
Combine Documents		Review>Compare>Combine		Word
Compare Documents		Review>Compare>Compare		Word
Copy		Home>Clipboard>Copy	CTRL + C	Word, Excel, Access, PowerPoint
Create a New Database		Office>New	CTRL + N	Access
Create a New Document		Office>New	CTRL + N	Word
Create a New File		Office>New	CTRL + N	Word, Excel, Access, PowerPoint
Create a New Presentation		Office>New	CTRL + N	PowerPoint
Create a New Workbook		Office>New	CTRL + N	Excel
Cut		Home>Clipboard>Cut	CTRL + X	Word, Excel, Access, PowerPoint
Database Form		Create>Forms>Form		Access
Database Report		Create>Reports>Report		Access
Database Table		Create>Tables>Table Design		Access

Step-By-Step

1. In your **w1-6** file, double-click anywhere in the word **Setting**. The word is selected and the **Mini Toolbar** appears (see Figure 1.13).
2. Click anywhere in the document pane. The text is no longer selected.
3. Move the pointer to the left of the sentence until it changes to an arrow. Click. The entire line is selected.
4. Click anywhere in the document pane to deselect the text.
5. Click at the end of the sentence. Press the **spacebar** once.
6. Key: It is really difficult to plan how to reach a final desination if you do not know exactly where you want to go. (Note misspelling of *desination*.)
7. Hold down CTRL. Click anywhere in the first sentence. The entire sentence is selected.
8. CHECK Your screen should look like Figure 1.14.
9. Save your file.

Continue to the next exercise.

Step-By-Step Tip In **Step 6**, reassure students that they should ignore the misspelling in the sentence and key it as shown.

EXERCISE 1-8
Wrap and Select Text

When you get to the end of a line of text, Word will automatically wrap your text, or move it to the next line. You do not have to press Enter to move down to the next line. To edit specific text, you need to select it. Selected text has a colored background. When text is selected, a Mini Toolbar appears on screen with formatting commands.

Teaching Tip Let students know that pressing **Enter** puts in a *hard return*, which Word considers the end of a paragraph.

FIGURE 1.13 Select a line

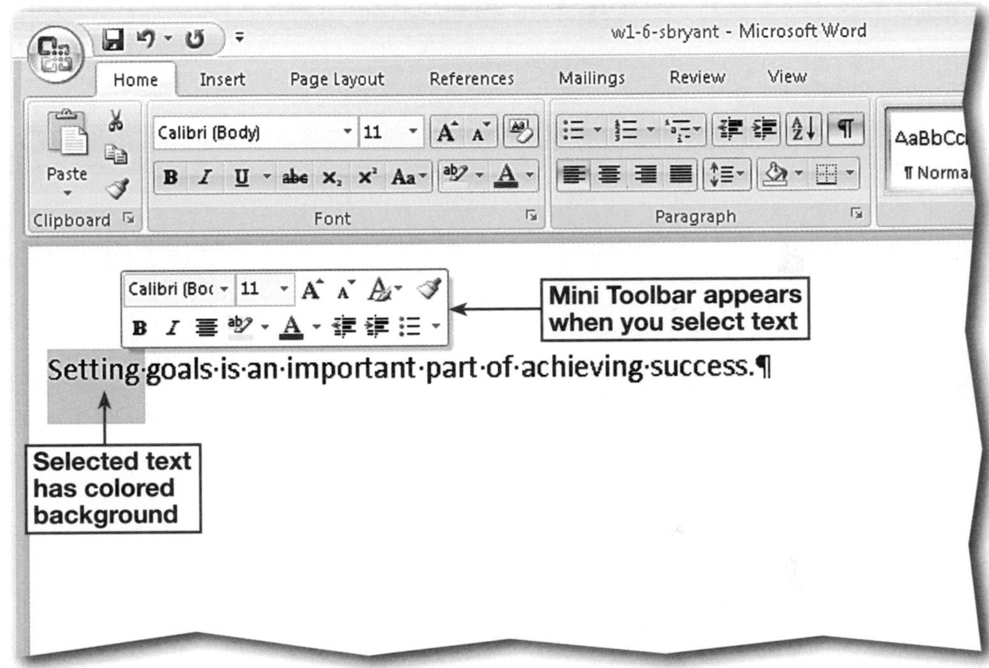

FIGURE 1.14 Select a sentence

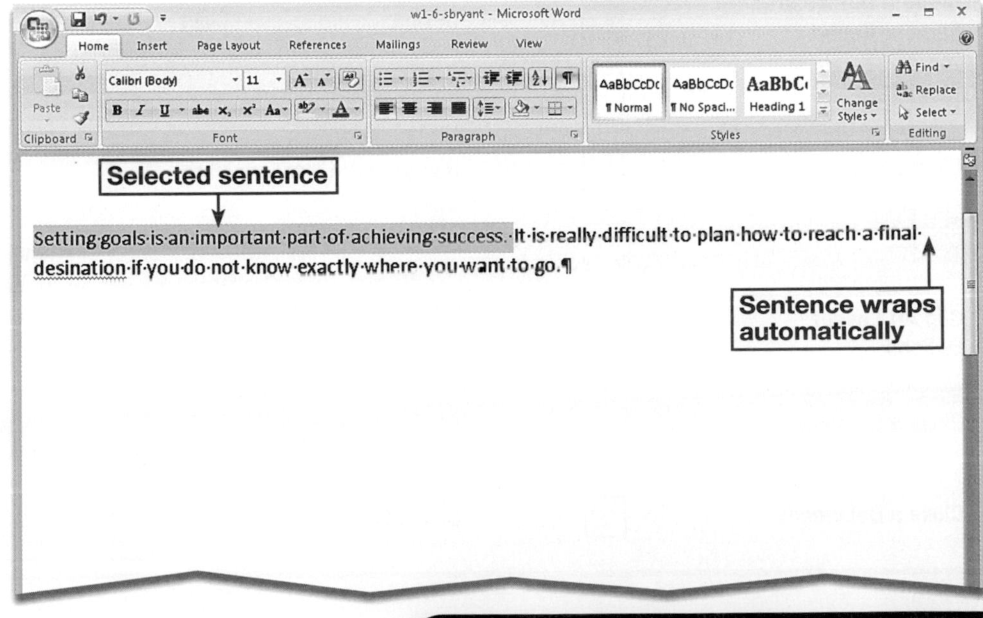

Function	Button	Ribbon	Keyboard Shortcuts	Application
Axis Titles of a Chart		Layout>Labels>Axis Titles		Excel
Bibliography Style		References>Citations & Bibliography>Style		Word
Bold		Home>Font>Bold	CTRL + B	Word, Excel, Access, PowerPoint
Borders		Home>Paragraph>Border		Word
Borders		Home>Font>Border		Excel
Bullets		Home>Paragraph>Bullets		Word, PowerPoint
Cell Styles		Home>Styles>Cell Styles		Excel
Change Case		Home>Font>Change Case		Word, PowerPoint
Change Chart Type		Design>Type>Change Chart Type		Excel
Change Order of Slides		View>Presentation Views>Slide Sorter		PowerPoint
Chart		Insert>Illustrations>Chart		Word, PowerPoint
Chart		Insert>Charts>[Chart Type]		Excel
Chart in Database Form or Report		Design>Controls>Insert Chart		Access
Chart Title		Layout>Labels>Chart Title		Excel
Clear Formatting		Home>Font>Clear Formatting		Word, PowerPoint
Clip Art		Insert>Illustrations>Clip Art		Word, Excel, PowerPoint
Clip Art Layout Options		Format>Arrange>Text WraPowerPointing>More Layout Options		Word
Close a Database		Office>Close Database		Access
Close a Document		Office>Close	CTRL + W *or* CTRL + F4	Word

Step-By-Step

1. In your **w1-6** file, right-click the word **desination**.
2. The menu of suggested spellings appears (see Figure 1.15).
3. In the spelling list, click **destination**.
4. The misspelled word is replaced by the correctly spelled word.
5. **CHECK** Your screen should look like Figure 1.16.
6. Save your file.

Continue to the next exercise.

Microsoft Office 2007

Homonyms are words that sound the same but have different meanings (for example, to, too, and two). The Office 2007 Spell Check feature highlights potential homonyms so you can be sure you are using the correct word.

Academic Skills

The use of proper spelling in a document is very important. A document with errors will not be well received by readers. Always read the final document to find errors.

NCLB/Language Arts (NCTE 6) Reinforce the importance of proper spelling in a document.

EXERCISE 1-9
Correct Spelling Errors

Teaching Tip In this exercise, we introduce the spelling drop-down menu. See Exercise 3-8 for information on the Spelling and Grammar commands.

Word helps you find and correct spelling errors as you work on a document. A wavy red line under a word indicates that the word may be misspelled. This tool is helpful, but you still need to proofread to make sure that all words are spelled correctly and that your grammar and word selection are correct. (We will look more at the Spell Check function in Lesson 3.)

EL Students should choose the correct word carefully, as choices may look similar.

FIGURE 1.15 Spelling correction suggestions

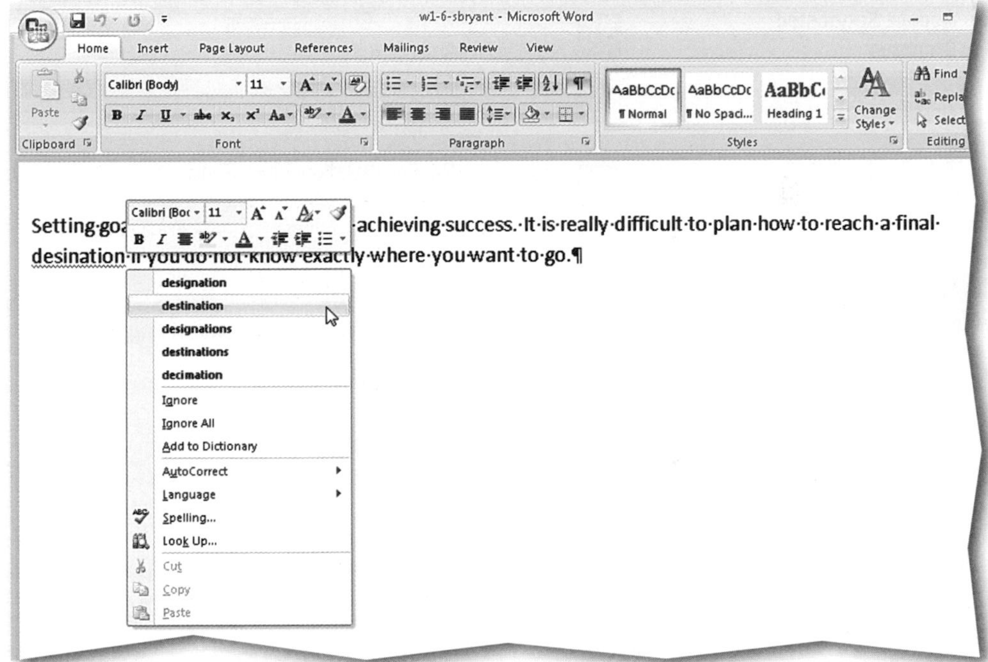

FIGURE 1.16 Sentence with corrected spelling

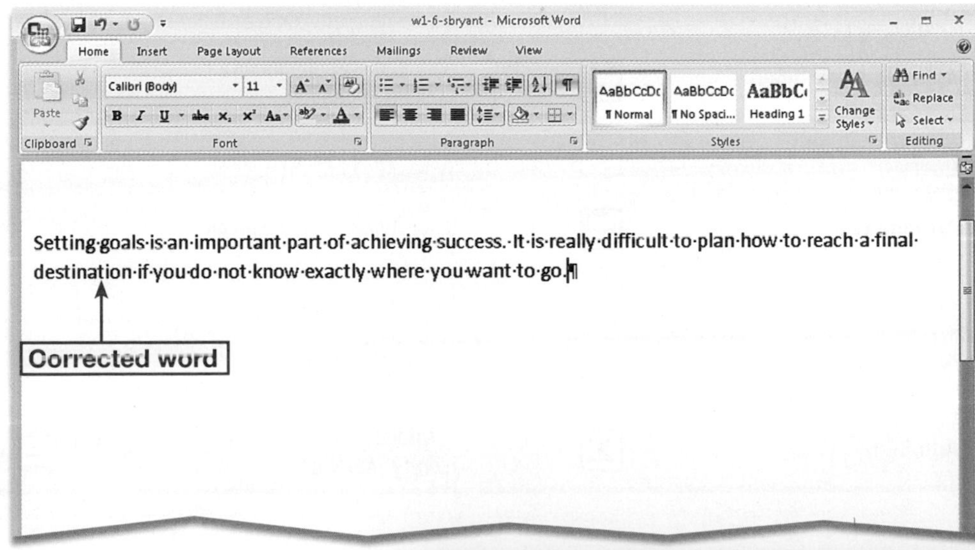

APPENDIX B Quick Reference Summary

The following commands were covered in this book.

All of the commands have speech function accessibility, with the proper Office setup. See **Help>Speech Functions> Accessibility** in any Microsoft Office application for instructions.

Function	Button	Ribbon	Keyboard Shortcuts	Application
Accept Suggested Changes		Review>Changes>Accept and Move to Next		Word
Add Fields to a Form		Design>Tools>Add Existing Fields		Access
Add Tables to Relationship Window		Design>Relationships>Show Table		Access
Advanced Filter		Home>Sort & Filter> Advanced>Advanced Filter/Sort		Access
Align Cell Contents in Worksheet		Home>Alignment> [Alignment Option]		Excel
Align Center		Home>Paragraph>Center	CTRL + E	Word, PowerPoint
Align Justified		Home>Paragraph>Justify	CTRL + J	Word, PowerPoint
Align Left		Home>Paragraph> Align Text Left	CTRL + L	Word, PowerPoint
Align Right		Home>Paragraph> Align Text Right	CTRL + R	Word, PowerPoint
Analyze Database Table		Database Tools>Analyze>Analyze Table		Access
Animate Slide Show		Animations>Animations> Custom Animation		PowerPoint
APowerPointend Query		Design>Query Type>APowerPointend		Access
Arrange Windows		View>Window>Arrange All		Word, Excel, PowerPoint
AutoFilter		Data>Sort & Filter>Filter	CTRL + SHIFT + L	Excel
AutoFit Table Contents		Layout>Cell Size> AutoFit>AutoFit Contents		Word
AutoSum		Formulas>Function Library>AutoSum	ALT + =	Excel

Step-By-Step

1. In your **w1-6** file, click immediately before the word **difficult** (see Figure 1.17).
2. Press DELETE nine times to delete each letter of **difficult**. Key: hard.
3. Click after the word **really**.
4. Press ←BACKSPACE seven times to delete the word and the extra space.
5. Click before the word **final**.
6. Hold down CTRL and press DELETE. The word **final** is deleted.
7. Click at the end of the word **exactly**.
8. Hold down CTRL and press ←BACKSPACE. The word **exactly** is deleted.
9. **CHECK** Your screen should look like Figure 1.18. Save your file.

Continue to the next exercise.

NCLB/Language Arts (NCTE 4) Reinforce to students that deleting redundant words in a document can help improve how the document is received by an audience.

Different Strokes The **Undo** command is introduced in Exercise 1-11. However, if students accidentally erase the wrong text, show them the **Undo** button on the **Quick Access Toolbar**, or the keyboard shortcut **CTRL + Z**.

EXERCISE 1-10
Delete Text

Sometimes you need to **edit**, or change, your document by deleting text. There are several ways to delete, or remove, unwanted text from a document. Some of these ways are outlined in Table 1.1.

Troubleshooting Warn students that pressing **Backspace** or **Delete** when a sentence is selected will delete the entire sentence.

TABLE 1.1 Ways to delete text

Keyboard Shortcut	Result
←BACKSPACE	Deletes the character to the left of the insertion point
CTRL + ←BACKSPACE	Deletes the word to the left of the insertion point
DELETE	Deletes the character to the right of the insertion point
CTRL + DELETE	Deletes the word to the right of the insertion point

FIGURE 1.17 Use the Delete key to delete characters to the right

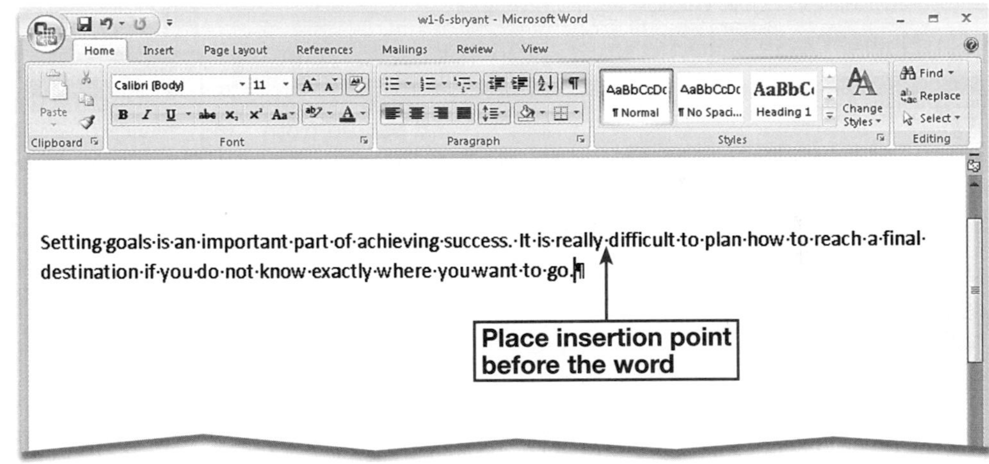
w1-6-sbryant - Microsoft Word
Setting goals is an important part of achieving success. It is really difficult to plan how to reach a final destination if you do not know exactly where you want to go.
Place insertion point before the word

FIGURE 1.18 Final text with words deleted

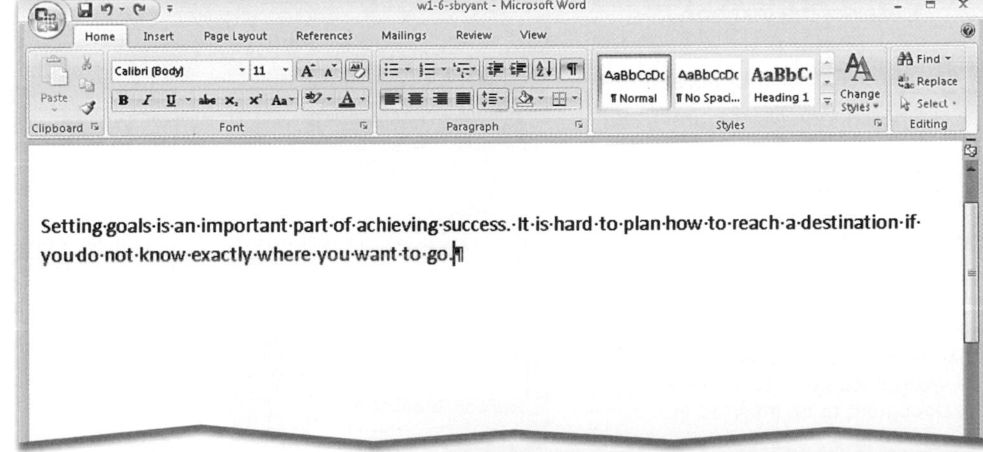
w1-6-sbryant - Microsoft Word
Setting goals is an important part of achieving success. It is hard to plan how to reach a destination if you do not know exactly where you want to go.

POWERPOINT INTEGRATION

Exercise 12: Copy and Paste Data between Applications

1. In your **Historic** presentation, move to **Slide 2**.
2. Start **Word**. Locate and open the data file **Founder.docx**.
3. Select the bulleted list. Click **Home>Copy**. Save and close the document.
4. Switch to your **Historic** presentation. Click in the **Slide 2** text box. Press ←BACKSPACE once. Click **Home>Paste**.
5. Click the **Paste Options** drop-down arrow. Confirm that **Use Destination Theme** is selected (see Figure 1.27).
6. Select the text **First mayor of Greenhaven** and **Founder of Greenhaven University**. Click **Paragraph> Increase List Level**. Deselect the text box.
7. CHECK Your screen should look like Figure 1.28.
8. Save and close your files.

Step By Step Tip In **Step 2**, make sure that students do not use the Open feature in PowerPoint to open the Word document. This will cause the document to be inserted into a new slide show.

You can use the Cut, Copy, and Paste functions to insert information created in a Word document into a PowerPoint slide. If the slide has a bulleted format, each paragraph of the pasted material will become a bulleted item. Use Paste Options to specify if the pasted information will retain its original formatting.

Use the file **Historic-SF.pptx** as a solution file for Exercises 11 and 12.

FIGURE 1.27 Paste Options drop-down menu

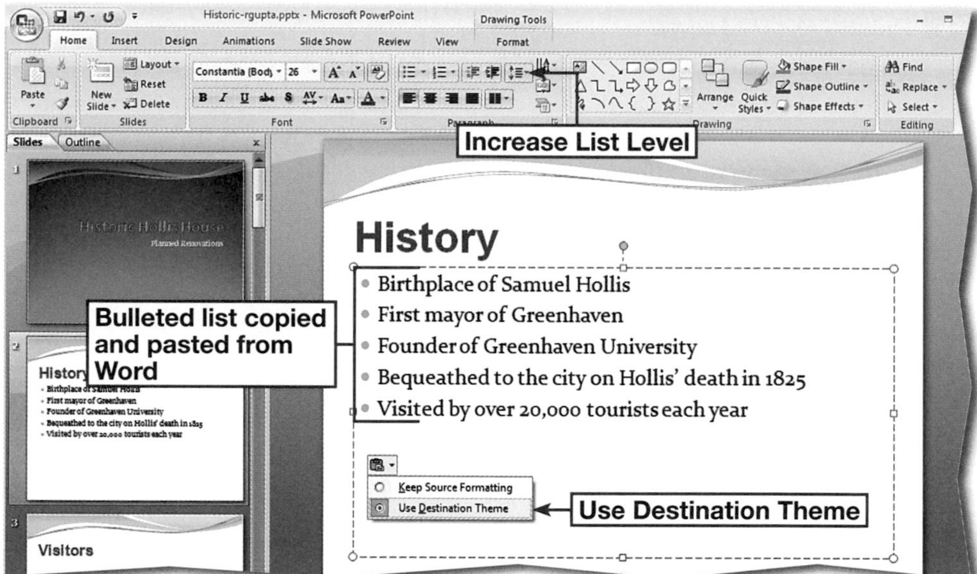

FIGURE 1.28 Text pasted in PowerPoint and formatted

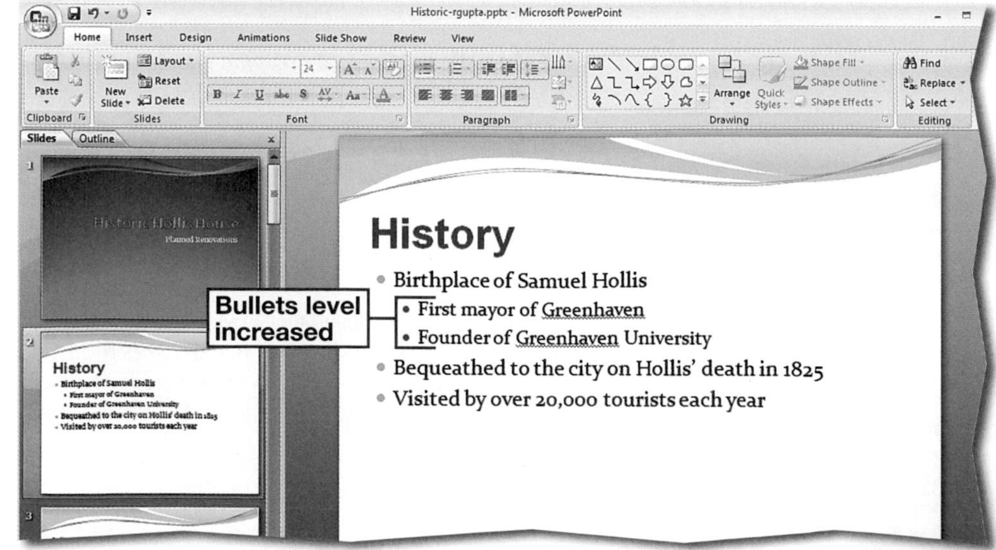

Step-By-Step

1. In your **w1-6** file, click at the end of the second sentence. Press the **spacebar** once. Key: However.

2. On the **Quick Access Toolbar**, click **Undo** [Undo icon]. The word **However** disappears.

3. On the **QAT**, click **Redo** [Redo icon]. The word reappears.

4. CHECK Your screen should look like Figure 1.19.

5. Click **Undo**. The word disappears again.

6. Select the first word **Setting**. Press DELETE.

7. Move your pointer over **Undo**. Notice the ScreenTip now reads **Undo Clear**.

8. Click **Undo** [Undo icon]. The word **Setting** is restored.

9. CHECK Your screen should look like Figure 1.20.

Continue to the next exercise.

Microsoft Office 2007

The **Repeat** button [Repeat icon] appears on the word QAT by default. The **Redo** button only appears when you can redo an action.

EXERCISE 1-11
Undo and Redo Actions

You may decide not to keep a change that you have just made to a document. You can click Undo to erase a step you have just performed. If you want to restore the change, click Redo to bring it back. Click the Undo drop-down arrow to see how many changes you can undo in your document.

FIGURE 1.19 Text has been reinserted using the Redo function

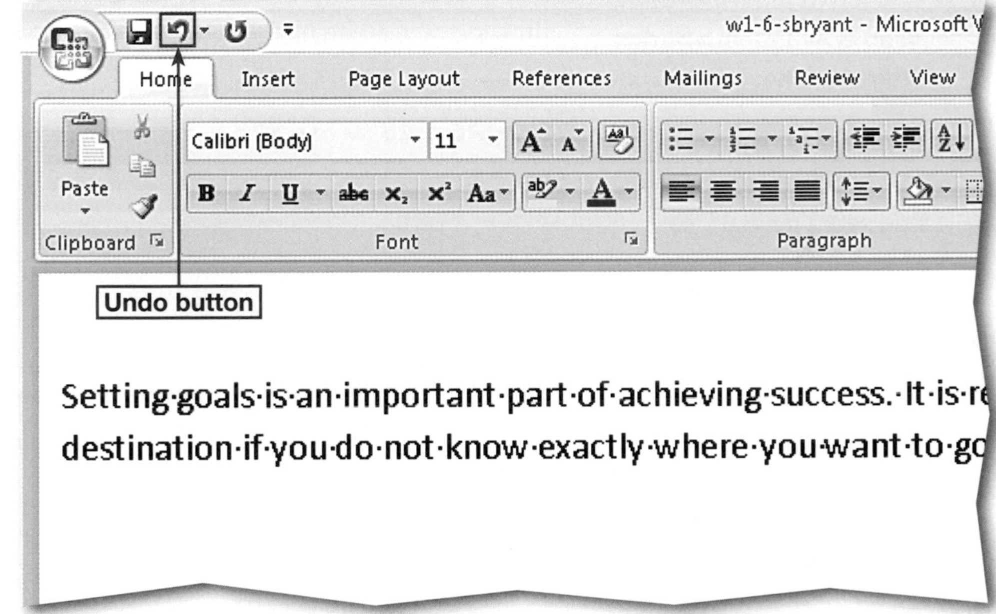

FIGURE 1.20 Deleted text is restored using the Undo function

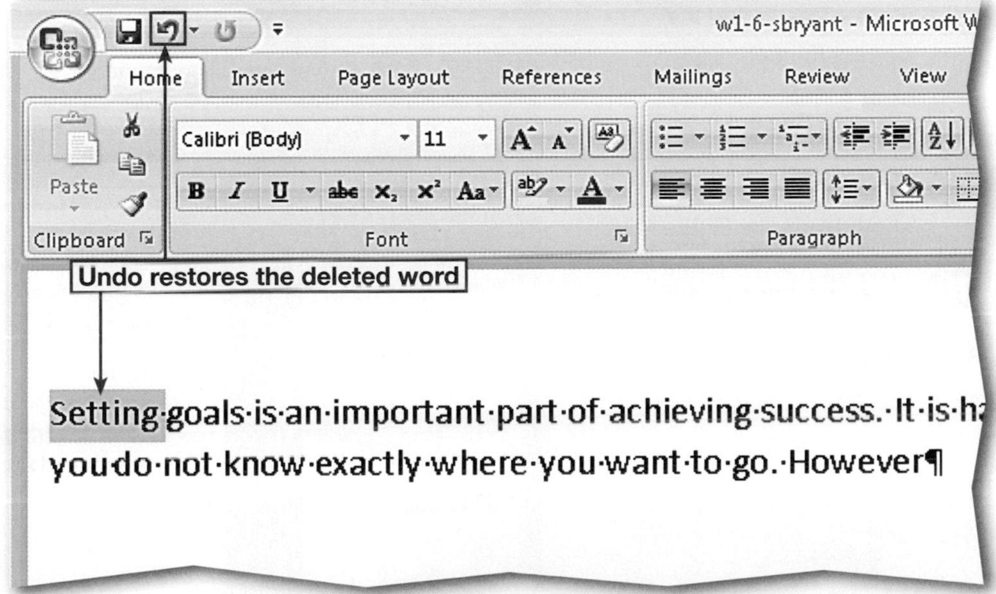

Step-By-Step

1. Start **PowerPoint**.
2. Locate and open the data file **Historic.pptx**. Save as: Historic-[your first initial and last name].
3. Choose **Home>New Slide drop down menu>Slides from Outline**.
4. In the **Insert Outline** dialog box, browse to and select the data file **Needs.docx**. Click **Insert**.
5. Choose **Home>Slides> Layout**. Change the layout of the second slide to **Title and Content**.
6. **CHECK** Your screen should look like Figure 1.25.
7. Choose **Design>Themes drop down arrow>More**. Select the **Flow** theme (use ScreenTips to find the correct theme).
8. Move to **Slide 4**.
9. **CHECK** Your screen should look like Figure 1.26.
10. Save and close your files.

Continue to the next exercise.

POWERPOINT INTEGRATION

Exercise 11: Insert Word Outlines into PowerPoint

You can use Word's Outline View to key the text of a presentation and then import the Word outline into PowerPoint. When you import an outline into PowerPoint, text that is formatted Level 1 becomes Title text, while Level 2 text is inserted into the body of the slides. Once you have imported your text, you can use the PowerPoint functions to design your presentation.

FIGURE 1.25 Word outline inserted into presentation

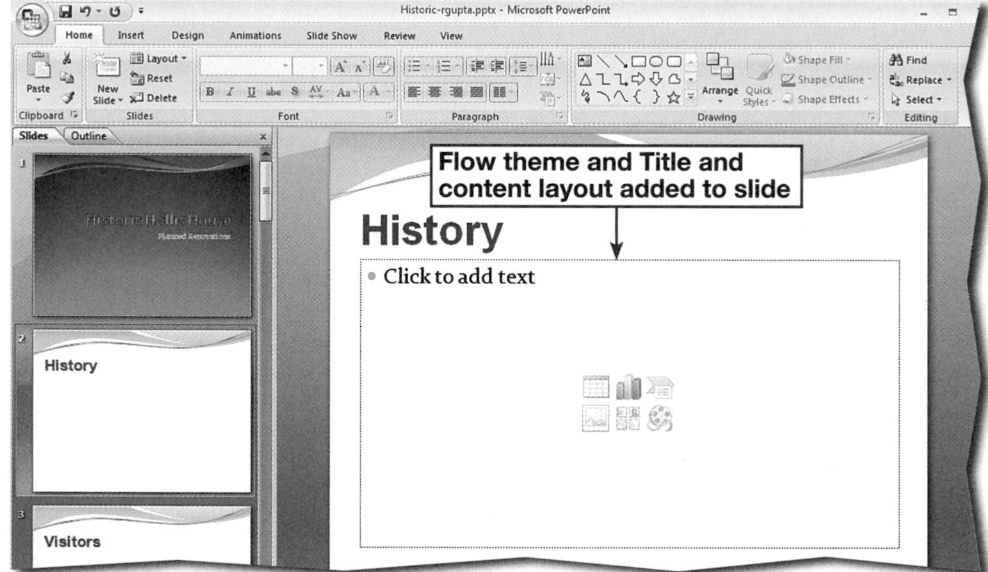

FIGURE 1.26 PowerPoint slide created from Word outline

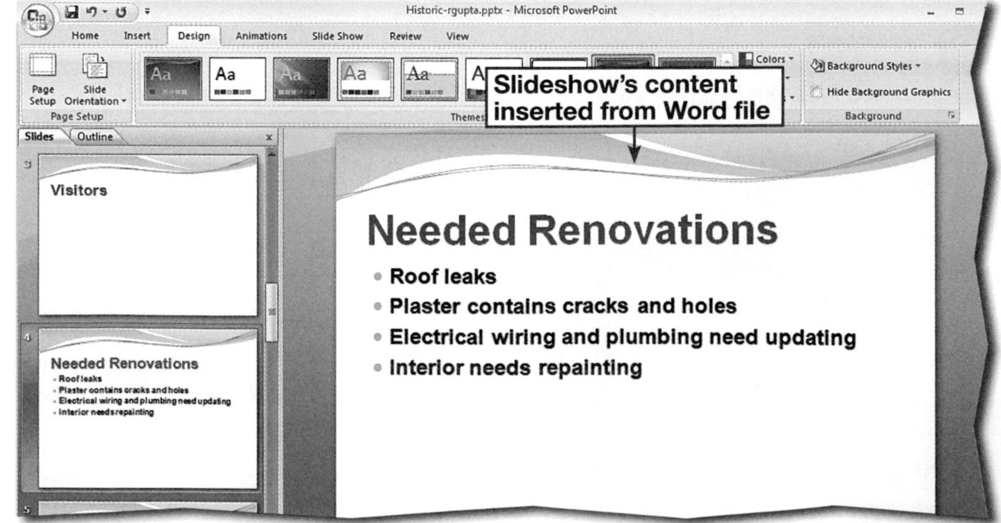

Step-By-Step

1. In your **w1-6** file, click **Office** .
2. Locate but do NOT click the **Exit Word** button in the **Office** menu (see Figure 1.21). Clicking **Exit Word** would close Word and all Word documents you have open.
3. In the **Office** menu, locate but do NOT click the **Close** button. Clicking **Close** would close the Word document you have open.
4. Click outside the menu to close the **Office** menu.
5. Click **Close** (see Figure 1.22). Your Word document closes.
6. **CHECK** Your screen should look like Figure 1.22.

Continue to the next exercise

You Should Know

Clicking the **Close** button on the title bar closes one open document at a time. If only one document is open, clicking the **Close** button will exit Word.

Solution Use the file **w1-6-SF** as a solution file for Exercises 1-6 to 1-12.

Troubleshooting Let students know they may be prompted to save their changes after they click **Close** or **Exit Word** in the **Office** menu.

EXERCISE 1-12
Close a Document

After you have finished and saved your work in a document, you can close it. Your document will still be available to you if you need to work on it at a later time.

FIGURE 1.21 Use the Office menu to close a document

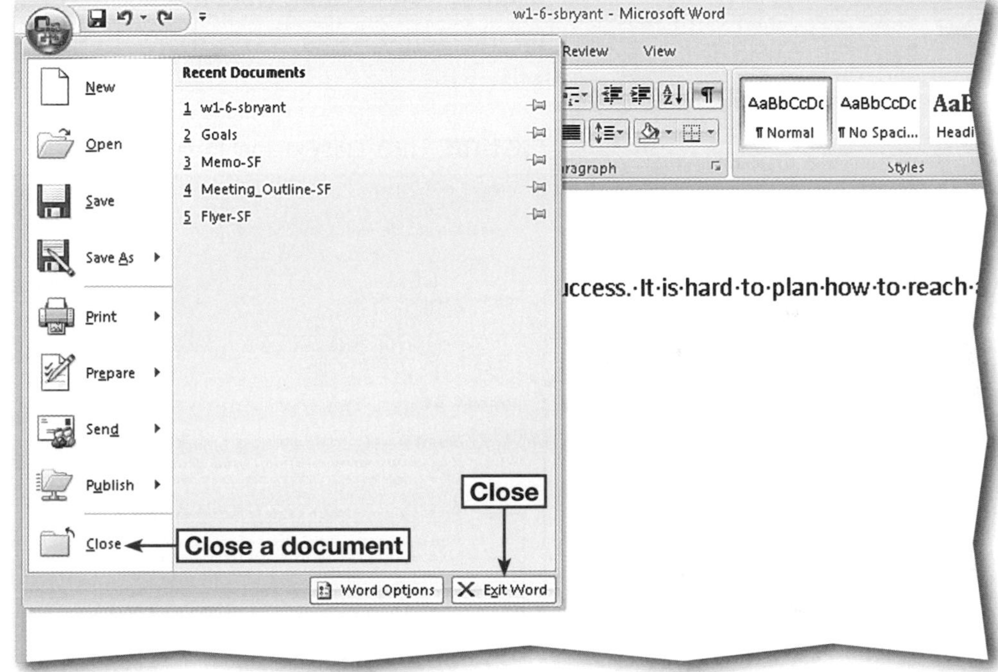

FIGURE 1.22 Word document closed

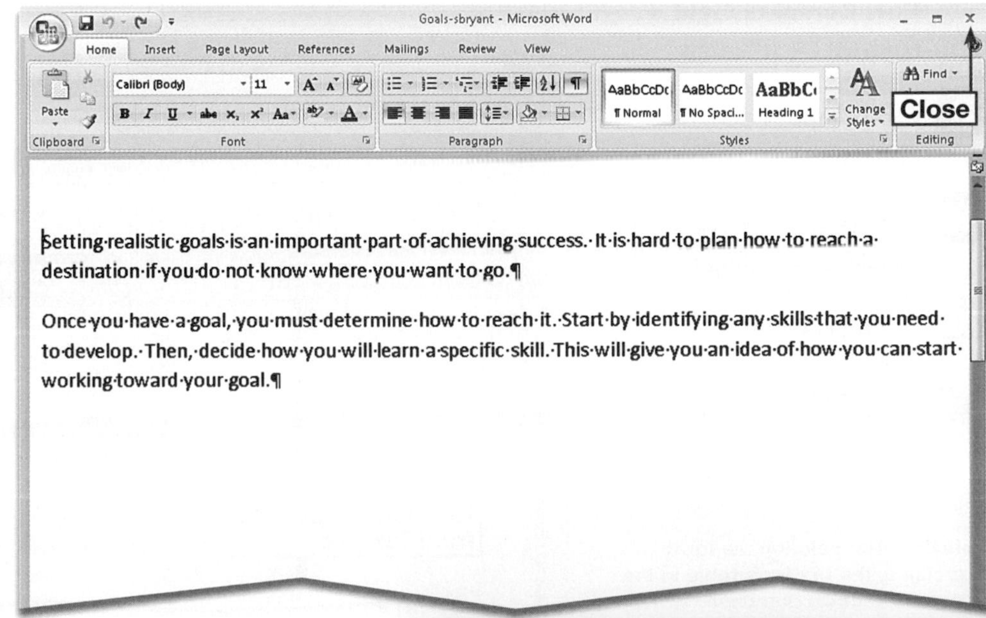

ACCESS INTEGRATION

Exercise 10: Import Word Data

You can transfer data from Word to Access. To do so, you must first save the Word document in a Plain Text Format. Saving a Word document as a plain text file (.txt) removes the formatting from that document. Importing Word data, such as customer information, into an Access database is very similar to importing Excel data into a database.

Step-By-Step

1. In your **Estate** database, close the **Listings** table.
2. Choose **External Data> Import>Text File**.
3. In the **Get External Data– Text File** dialog box, click the **Browse** button.
4. In the **File Open** dialog box, locate and select the data file **Added.txt**. Click **Open**.
5. Select **Append a copy of the records to the Table:**, then click the drop-down arrow and choose **Listings**.
6. **CHECK** Your dialog box should look like Figure 1.23.
7. Click **OK**. Click **Next**. Click the check box next to **First Row Contains Field Names**. Click **Finish**.
8. Click **Close**. Open the **Listings** table.
9. **CHECK** Your screen should look like Figure 1.24.
10. Close the table.

Continue to the next exercise.

Solution The solution file for this exercise is the **Listings** table in the **Estate-SF.accdb** database.

FIGURE 1.23 Get External Data dialog box

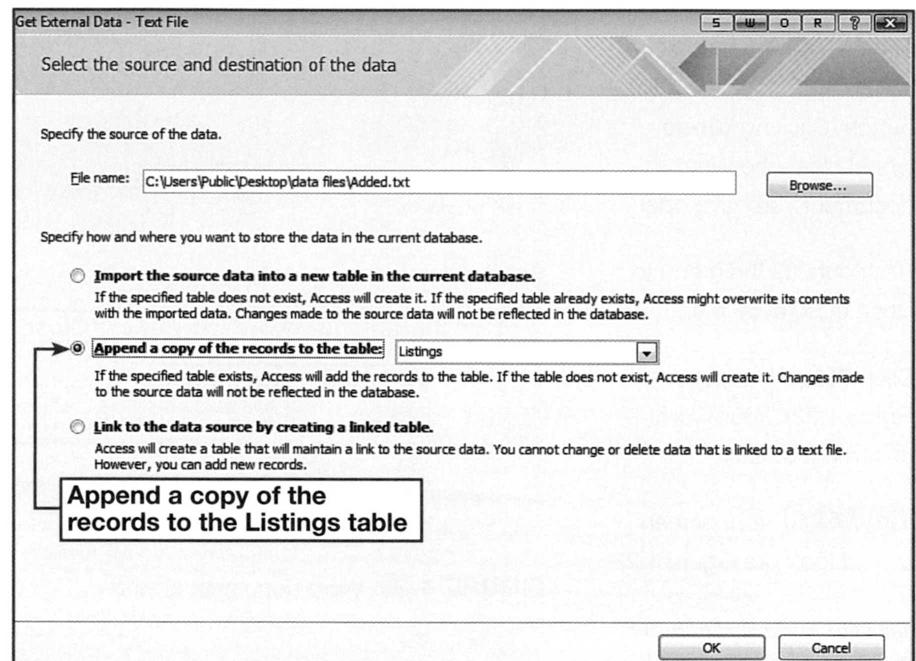

FIGURE 1.24 Text data imported into Access

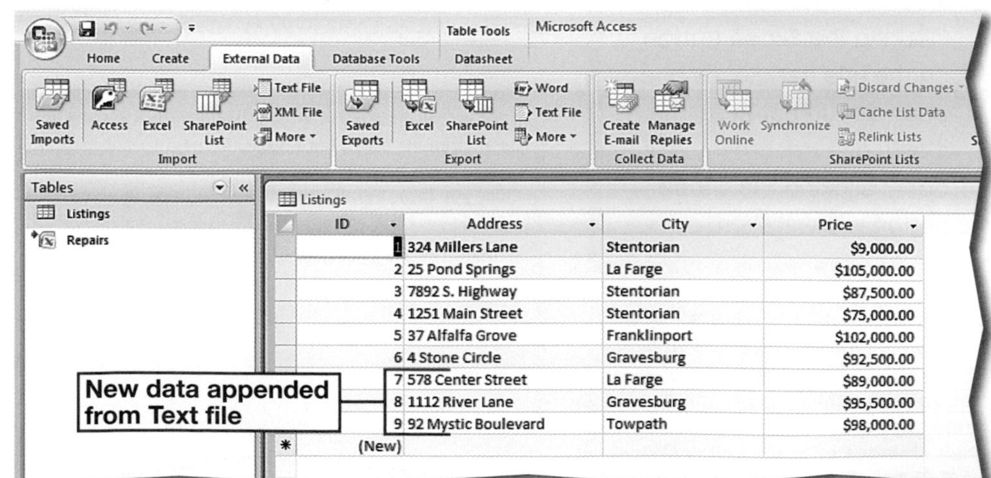

Step-By-Step

1. Choose **Office>Open**.
2. In the **Open** dialog box, click the **Previous Locations** box drop-down arrow. Select the location of your data files. Ask your teacher for the correct location.
3. **CHECK** Your screen should look like Figure 1.23.
4. Click the file **Goals.docx**. Click **Open**.
5. Choose **Office>Save As**. In the **File name** box, key: Goals-[your first initial and last name] (for example, *Goals-sbryant*).
6. In the **Save in** box, locate your folder.
7. In the **Save As** dialog box, click **Save**.
8. **CHECK** Your screen should look like Figure 1.24.

Continue to the next exercise.

Troubleshooting Make sure students know where to locate data files and where to save their own files. Explain to students that the first time they open a data file, they will save it as [file name]-[student's first initial and last name]. Students will work in this file throughout the rest of the lesson.

EXERCISE 1-13
Open an Existing Document

You can open and use an existing document that has been saved. This can be very useful if, for example, you are working on a team project and you need to work on a document created by you or one of your team members.

FIGURE 1.23 Open dialog box

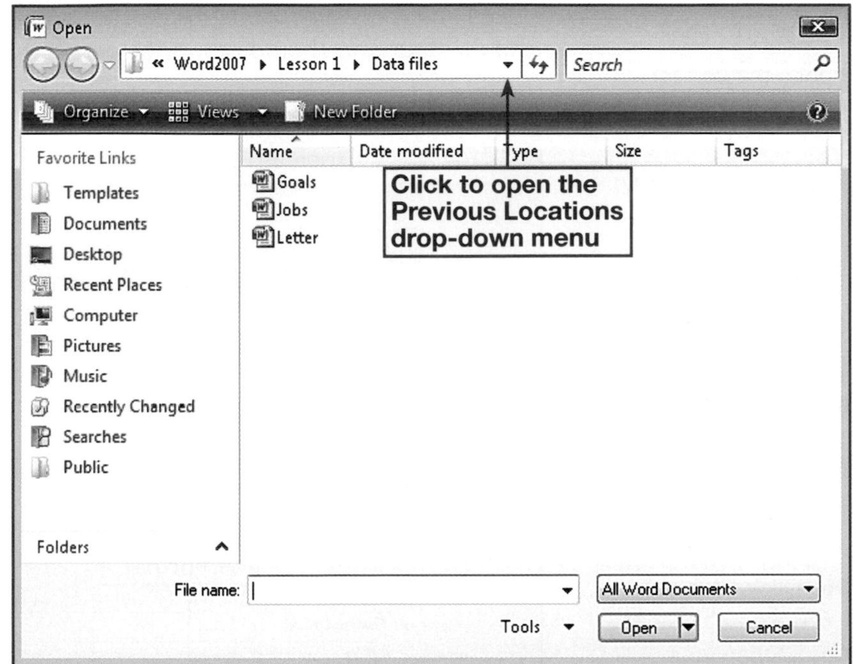

FIGURE 1.24 Document resaved with student name

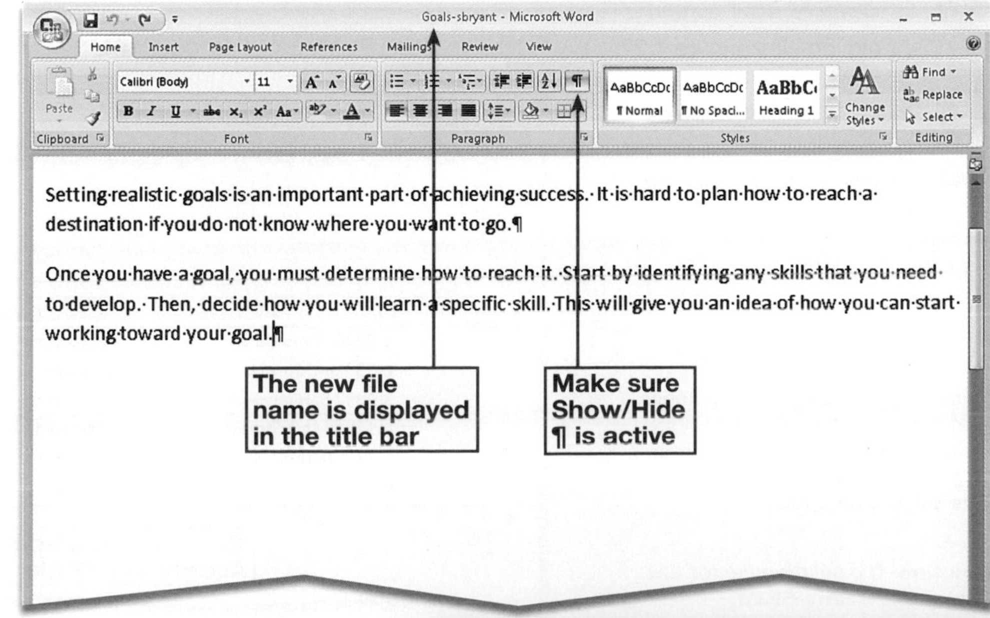

ACCESS INTEGRATION
Exercise 9: Export Access Data to Word

You might want to include data from an Access database in a Word document. For example, if you need the data for a business report, this is a quick and accurate option. You can export data from Access to Word while preserving the original formatting. If you are not sure what type of word processor you, or another person, will use later to read the data, you should export the data in Rich Text Format. Most word processors can read .rtf files.

FIGURE 1.21 Export as Rich Text Format

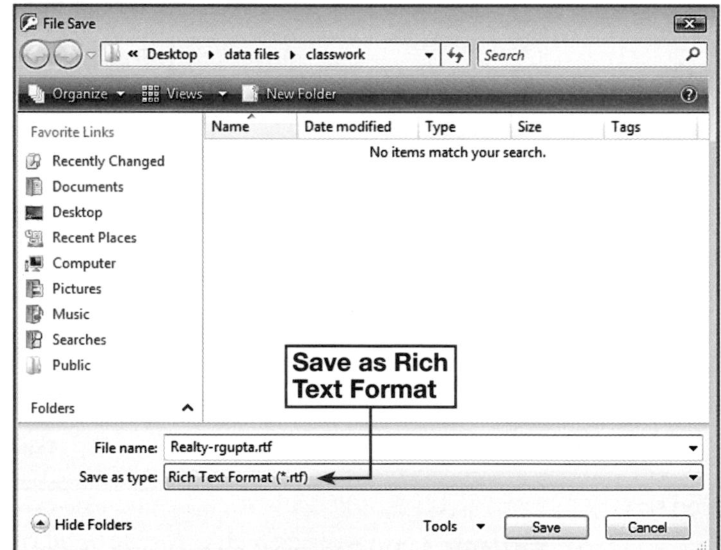

FIGURE 1.22 Access data exported to Word

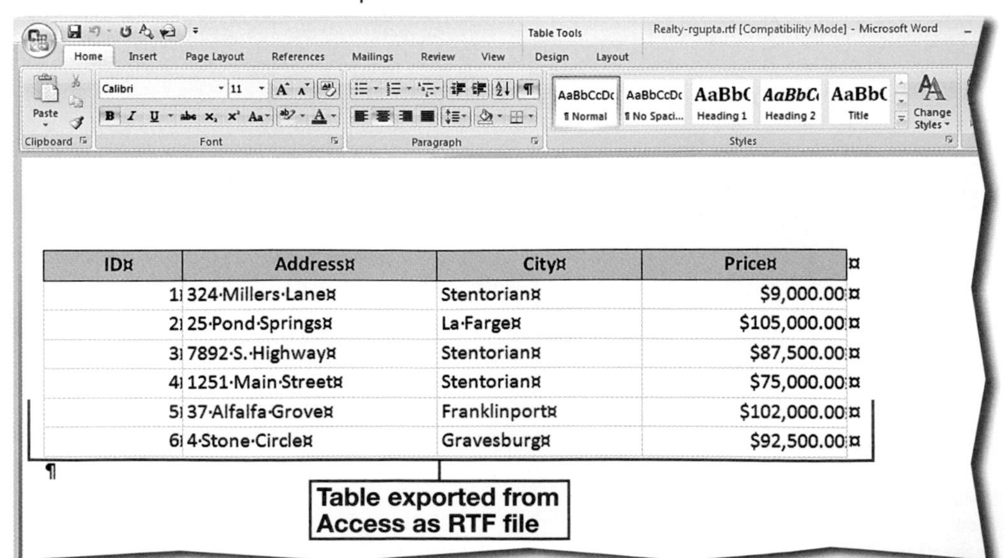

ID	Address	City	Price
1	324 Millers Lane	Stentorian	$9,000.00
2	25 Pond Springs	La Farge	$105,000.00
3	7892 S. Highway	Stentorian	$87,500.00
4	1251 Main Street	Stentorian	$75,000.00
5	37 Alfalfa Grove	Franklinport	$102,000.00
6	4 Stone Circle	Gravesburg	$92,500.00

1. In your **Estate** database, open the **Listings** table. Choose **External Data> Export>Word**.
2. In the **Export–RTF file** dialog box, click **Browse**. In the **File Save** dialog box, choose the correct location to save the file.
3. In the **File name** box, key: Realty-[your first initial and last name].
4. In the **Save as type** box, make sure **Rich Text Format** is selected.
5. **CHECK** Your dialog box should look like Figure 1.21. Click **Save**. Click **OK**. Click **Close**.
6. Start Word. Open your **Realty.rtf** file.
7. **CHECK** Your screen should look like Figure 1.22.
8. Save and close your files.

Continue to the next exercise.

Teaching Tip Let students know that they can also export Access data as plain text files, but formatting details such as font and font size will not be preserved.

Solution The solution file for this exercise is **Realty-SF.rtf**.

Step-By-Step

1. In your **Goals** file, make sure **Show/Hide ¶** is on. At the end of the first paragraph, click after the period following the word **go**.
2. Press DELETE once to delete the space between paragraphs.
3. Press the **spacebar** once to insert a space between the sentences.
4. CHECK Your screen should look like Figure 1.25.
5. Click after the period following the word **go**. Press DELETE once to delete the space between the sentences.
6. Press ENTER once to add a space between paragraphs.
7. CHECK Your screen should look like Figure 1.26. Save your file.

Continue to the next exercise.

Shortcuts

You can get help for tasks you are performing by pressing F1.

EXERCISE 1-14
Combine and Split Paragraphs

As you write, you might decide that one long paragraph should be made into two paragraphs. Or, you might decide that two paragraphs should be combined into one. Word makes it easy to perform these tasks.

FIGURE 1.25 Combine paragraphs

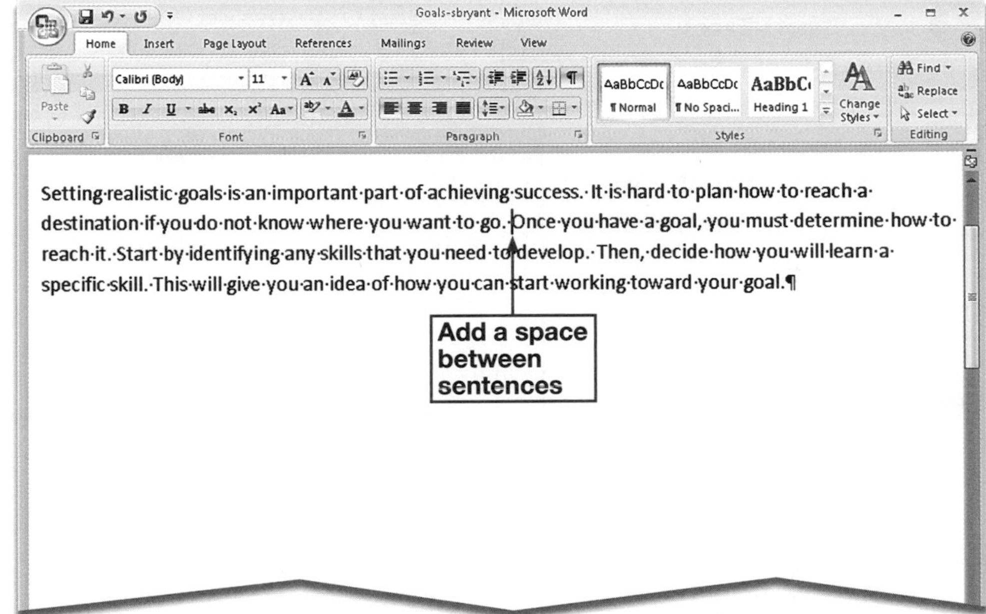

FIGURE 1.26 Split one paragraph into two paragraphs

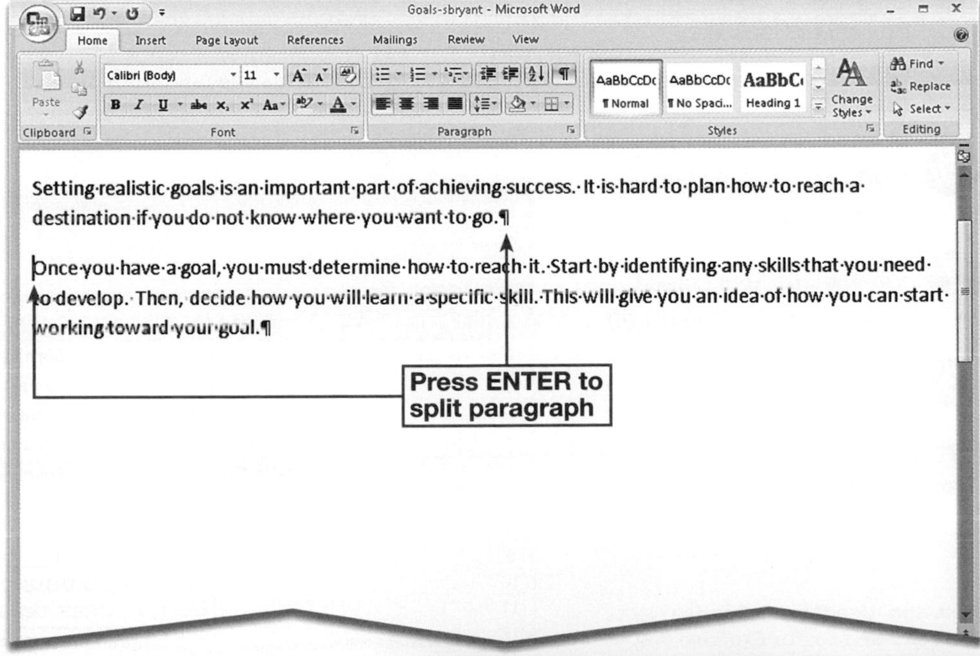

ACCESS INTEGRATION

Exercise 8: Export Access Data to Excel

Sometimes people need to use data in Excel instead of Access. Exporting data from Access to Excel is as easy as importing data from Excel. For example, you can export the data from a table in an Access database and save it as an Excel worksheet.

Step By Step Tip In **Step 4**, explain to students that if they check the **Save Formatted** check box, the resulting Excel worksheet will automatically adjust the column width to fit the data.

1. Open your copy of the **Estate** file. Open the **Listings** table in **Datasheet** view. Select **External Data>Export> Excel**.
2. In the **Export-Excel Spreadsheet** dialog box, click **Browse**. In the **File Save** dialog box, choose the correct location to save your file. In the **File name** box, key: Current-[your first initial and last name]. Click **Save**.
3. Click the **File Format** drop-down arrow. Choose **Excel Workbook (*.xlsx)**.
4. Check the **Export Data with formatting and layout** box.
5. CHECK Your dialog box should look like Figure 1.19. Click **OK**. Click **Close**.
6. Start Excel. Open your **Current.xlsx** file.
7. CHECK Your screen should look like Figure 1.20.
8. Save and close your **Current** file.

Continue to the next exercise.

Solution Use the solution file **Current-SF.xlsx** for Exercise 8 is.

FIGURE 1.19 Export dialog box

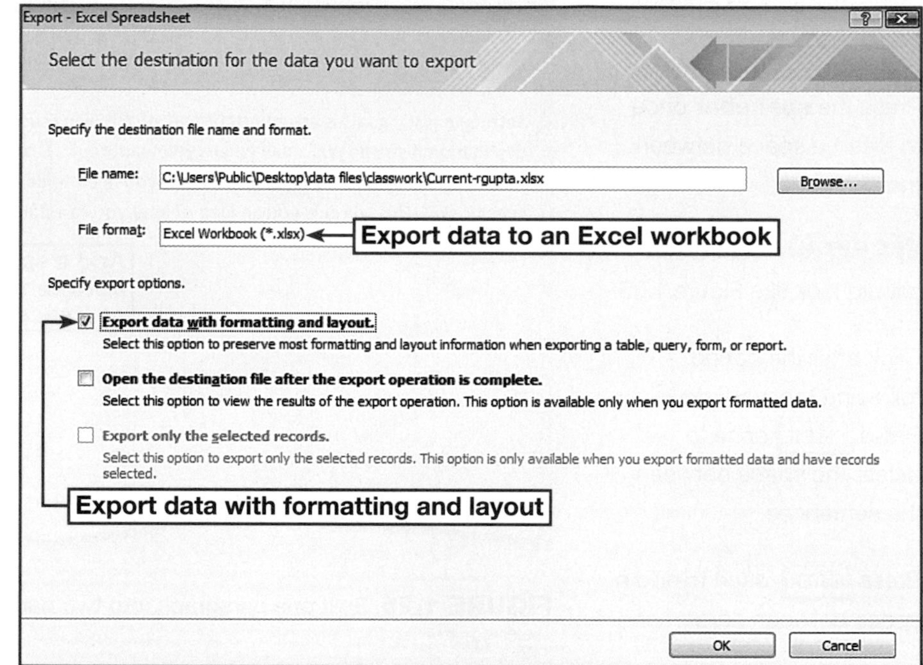

FIGURE 1.20 Excel file with exported Access data

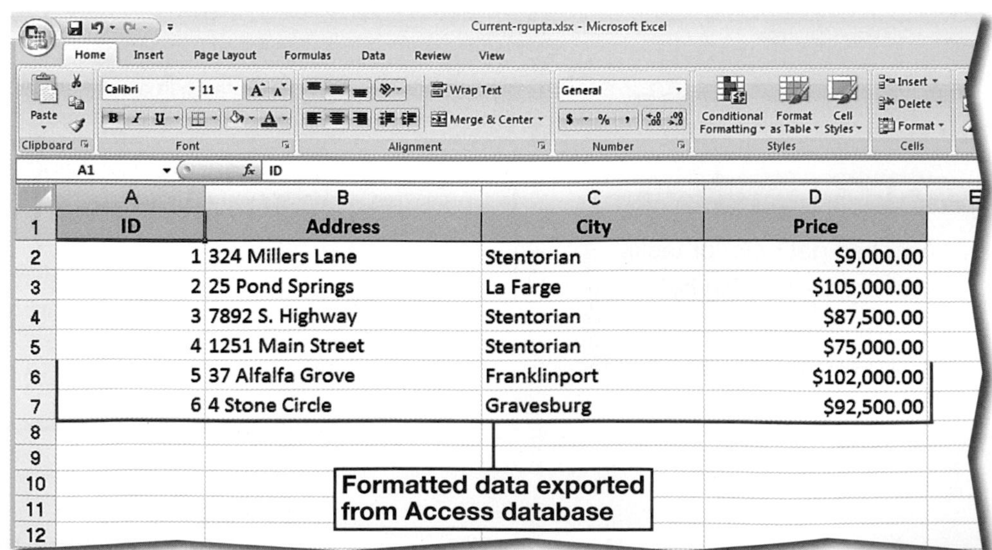

ID	Address	City	Price
1	324 Millers Lane	Stentorian	$9,000.00
2	25 Pond Springs	La Farge	$105,000.00
3	7892 S. Highway	Stentorian	$87,500.00
4	1251 Main Street	Stentorian	$75,000.00
5	37 Alfalfa Grove	Franklinport	$102,000.00
6	4 Stone Circle	Gravesburg	$92,500.00

Step-By-Step

1. In your **Goals** file, choose **View>Zoom>Zoom** .
2. In the **Zoom** dialog box, under **Zoom to**, click **200%**.
3. CHECK Your dialog box should look like Figure 1.27. Click **OK**. The text in your document appears larger.
4. Choose **View>Zoom> 75%**.
5. CHECK Your screen should look similar to Figure 1.28. Your text appears smaller.
6. Find the **Zoom** slider on the status bar. Slide the percentage zoom to the normal or default setting (see Figure 1.28).
7. Save your file.

Continue to the next exercise.

Microsoft Office 2007

The Zoom Slider allows you to see automatically how changing the zoom affects the look of your screen.

EXERCISE 1-15
Use the Zoom Options

Zoom options can make it easier to read items on the screen. Zoom changes the magnification. You can zoom in to make content easier to read, or zoom out to see more of a document on the screen.

FIGURE 1.27 Zoom at 200%

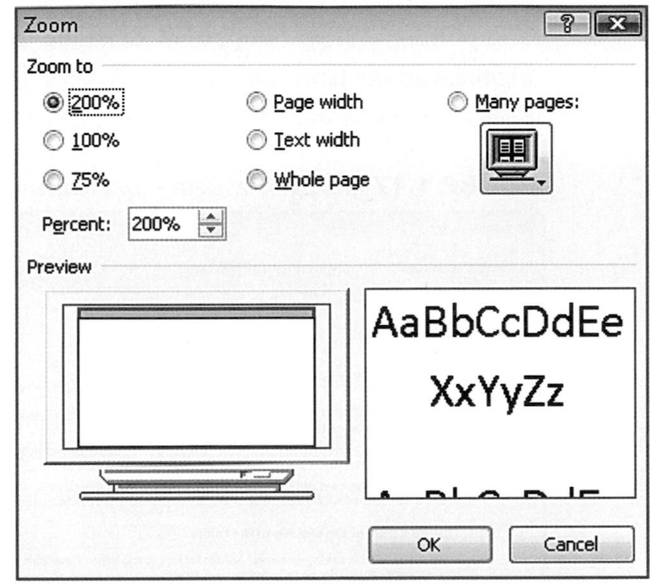

FIGURE 1.28 The Zoom slider located on the status bar

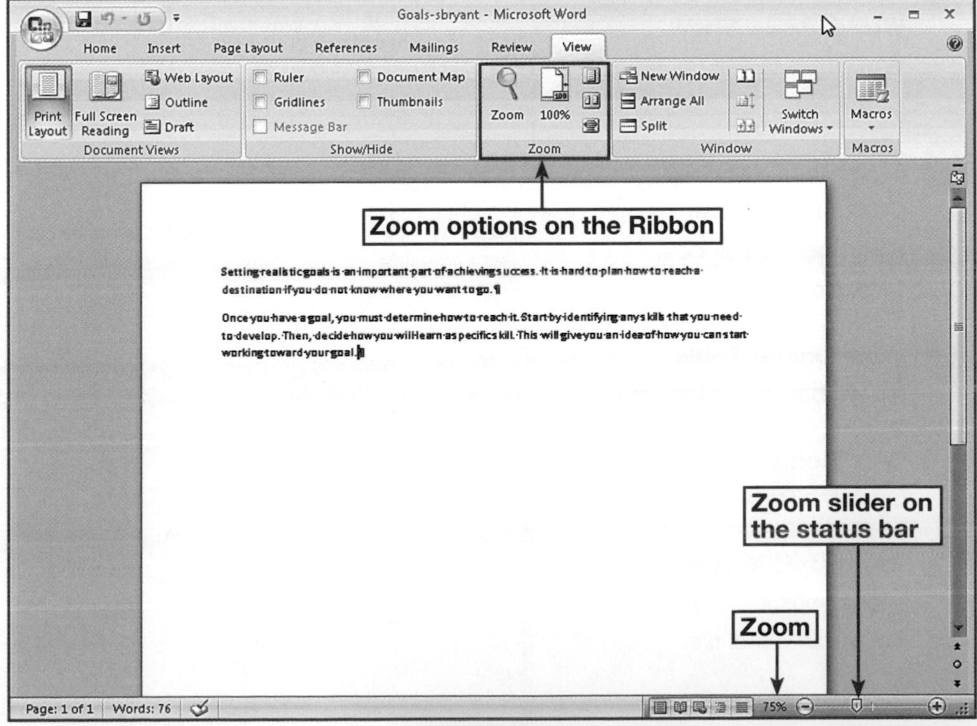

ACCESS INTEGRATION
Exercise 7: Link Excel Data to Access

You can link an Excel worksheet to a new Access table. When linking a table, you must create a new linked table in Access. You cannot link the Excel worksheet to an existing Access table. There are a few benefits to linking an Excel file to a database, as opposed to importing it. If you import an Excel file to a database and make changes to the original, you will have to reimport it. When a database is linked to an Excel file, the link is always to the most recent version of the Excel file. **Use the file Estate-SF.accdb as a solution file for Exercises 6 and 7.**

FIGURE 1.17 Get External Data—Excel Spreadsheet dialog box

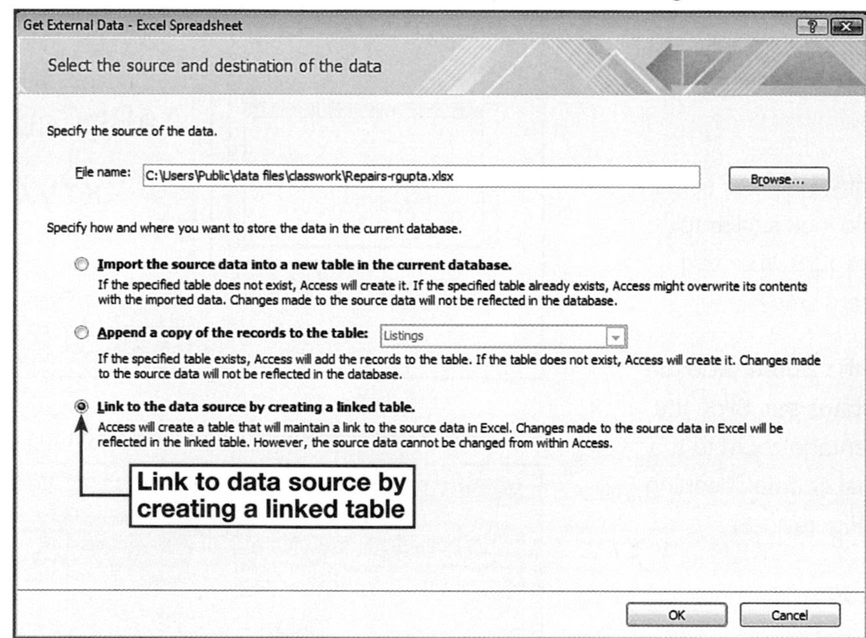

FIGURE 1.18 New Access table linked to Excel worksheet

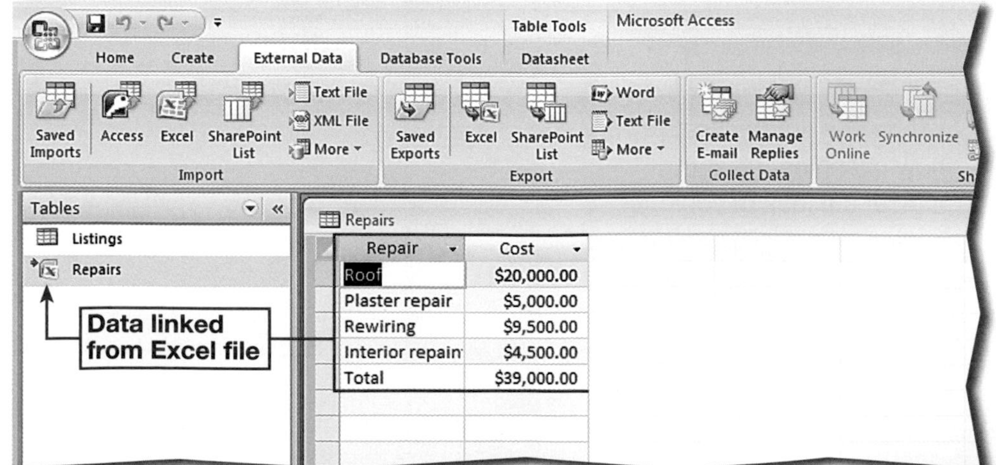

Step-By-Step

1. Open the data file **Repairs.xlsx**. Save as: Repairs-[your first initial and last name]. Exit Excel.
2. Open the data file **Estate.accdb**. Copy the file to your folder.
3. Choose **External Data>Import>Excel**. In the **Get External Data–Excel Spreadsheet** dialog box, in the **File name** box, navigate to your saved **Repairs.xlsx** file. Click **Open**.
4. Select **Link to the data source by creating a linked table** (see Figure 1.17). Click **OK**.
5. In the **Link Spreadsheet Wizard**, select **Show Worksheets** and click **Next**.
6. Check the **First Row Contains Column Headings** check box. Click **Next**.
7. In the **Linked Table Name** box, key: Repairs.
8. Click **Finish**. Click **OK**. Open the **Repairs** table.
9. **CHECK** Your screen should look like Figure 1.18. Save your Excel file.

Continue to the next exercise.

Step-By-Step

1. In your **Goals** file, click the **Help** on the top right corner of the screen. The **Word Help** window opens.

2. In the **Search** box, key: save a document.

3. CHECK Your screen should look like Figure 1.29.

4. Click **Search**. A list of topics appears in a new window.

5. Scroll down the list and click **Save a document** to open instructions on how to save documents.

6. In the toolbar at the top of the screen, click **Show Table of Contents**.

7. CHECK Your screen should look similar to Figure 1.30. Notice that the topic is listed under *Saving and printing*.

8. Click **Close** [x] in the **Word Help** window.

Continue to the next exercise.

NCLB/Language Arts (NCTE 8) Reinforce to students that the **Help** feature is laid out just like a book, with its own Table of Contents.

Step-By-Step Tip If classroom computers are connected to the Internet, be aware that **Step 2** may send students online.

Different Strokes Show students that they can also press **F1** to open the **Help** window.

EXERCISE 1-16
Use the Help Feature

As you write, you may have many questions about how certain Word features work. Word Help can answer these questions for you. Enter a topic into the Help window Search box and Word will produce a list of search results for you.

FIGURE 1.29 Word Help window

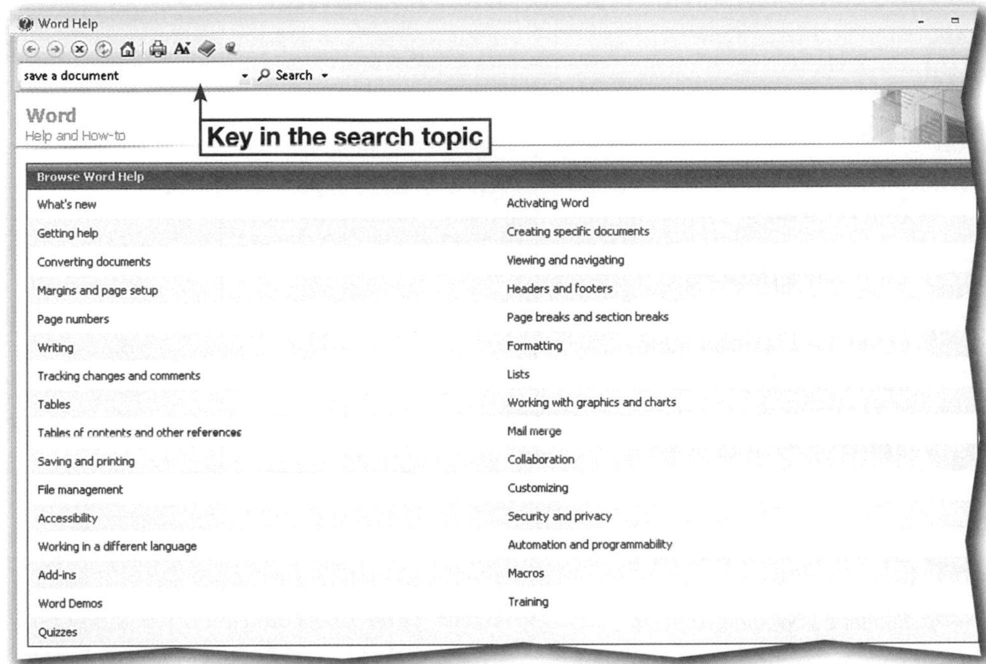

FIGURE 1.30 Search Result and Table of Contents

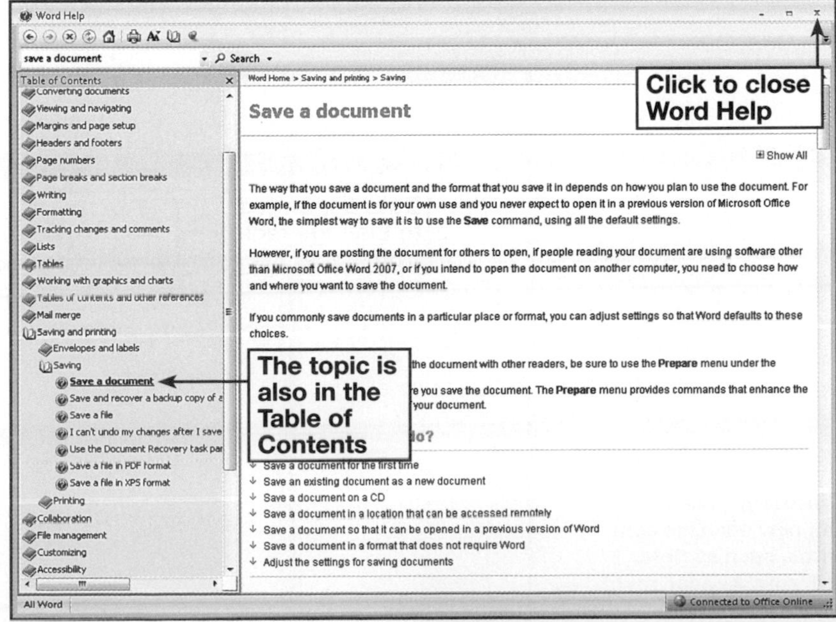

ACCESS INTEGRATION

Exercise 6: Import Excel Data (Continued)

8. Click **OK**.
9. Save and close the table. Click **Next**. The **Import Spreadsheet Wizard** dialog box appears (see Figure 1.15).
10. Click **Next**.
11. Click **Finish**. In the dialog box that opens, click **Save Import Steps**.
12. Click **Save Import**.
13. Open the **Listings** table from the **Tables** task pane.
14. **CHECK** Your screen should look like Figure 1.16.
15. Save and close your files.

Continue to the next exercise.

FIGURE 1.15 Import Spreadsheet Wizard dialog box

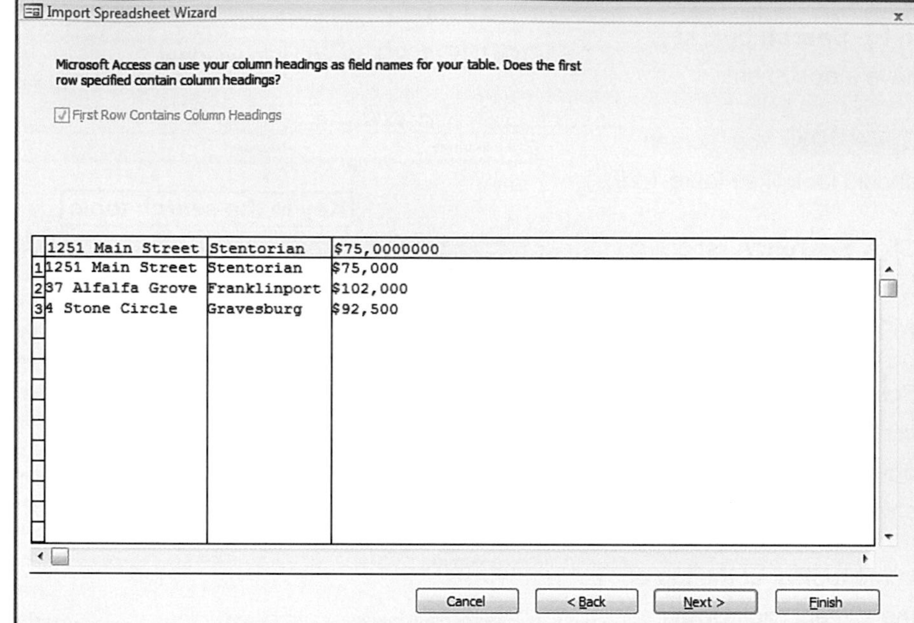

FIGURE 1.16 Excel data imported into Access

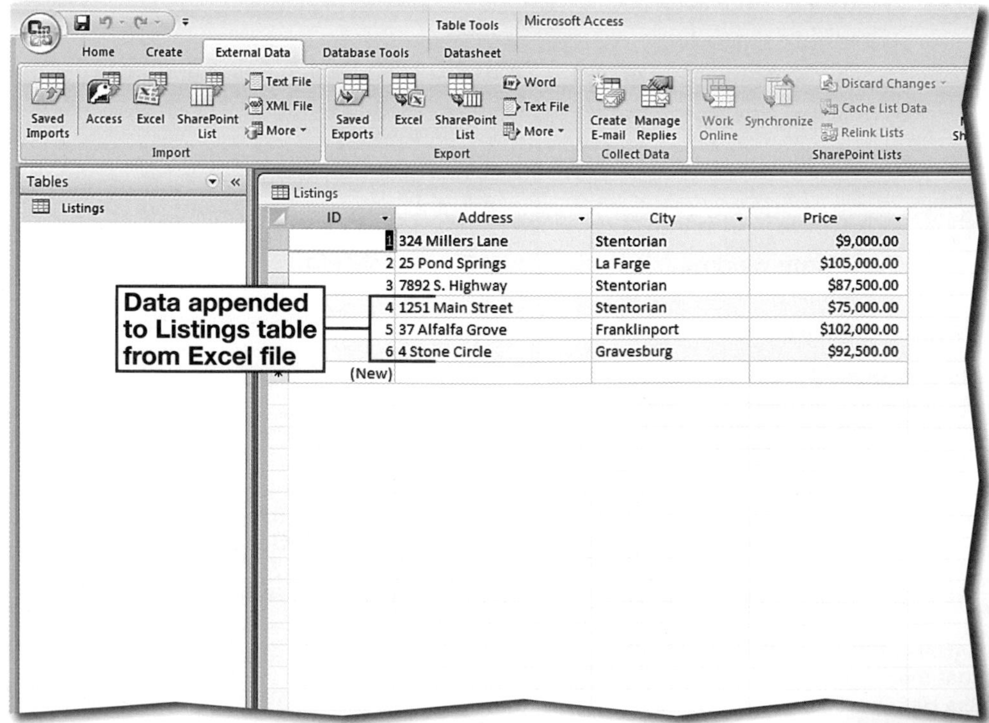

New Student Strategy If necessary, review with new students common Access terms, such as **field**, **column**, **record**, **row**, **header row**, and **column headings**.

Step-By-Step

1. In your **Goals** file, click **Office**. Move your pointer over **Print** to open the **Print Options** pane.
2. Click **Print Preview**.
3. CHECK Your screen should look like Figure 1.31.
4. In the **Preview** group, click **Close Print Preview**.
5. Choose **Office>Print**. The **Print** dialog box opens as shown in Figure 1.32.
6. Check with your teacher to make sure that the correct printer name is in the **Name** box.
7. Check that the number **1** is in the **Number of copies** box.
8. With your teacher's permission, click **OK** to print the document.
9. Save your file. Choose **Office>Close** to close your document.
10. Click **Close** to exit the Word program (see Figure 1.31).

Solution Use the file **Goals-SF.docx** as a solution file for Exercises 1-14 to 1-17.

EXERCISE 1-17
Preview and Print a Document

Print Preview allows you to see the page as it will appear when printed. Once you are satisfied with the document, the Print dialog box allows you to make choices such as the number of copies, or which printer you will use.

FIGURE 1.31 Document displayed in Print Preview view

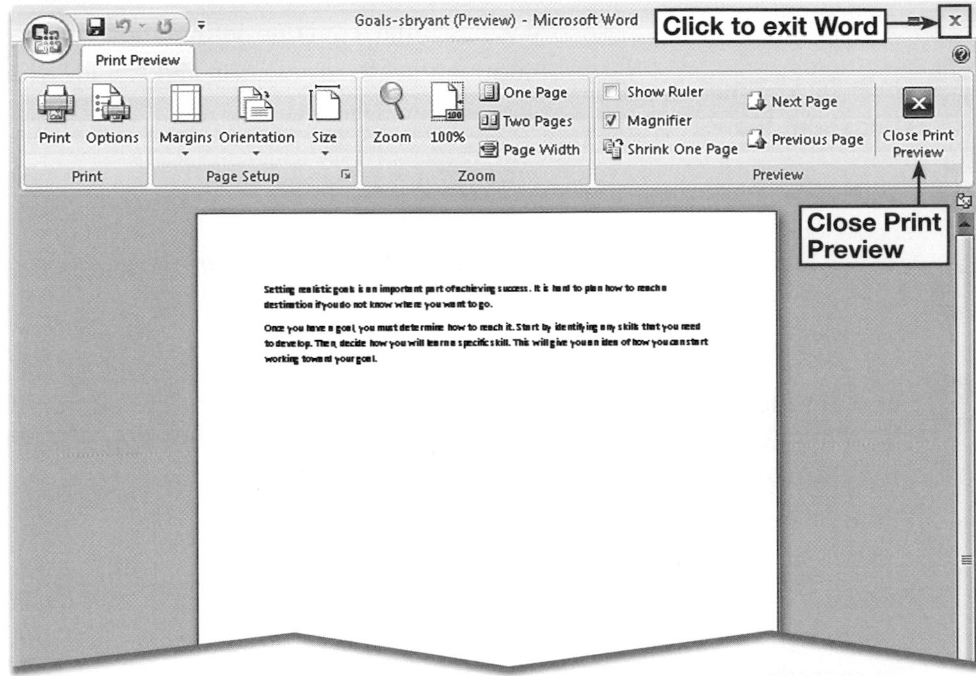

FIGURE 1.32 Print dialog box

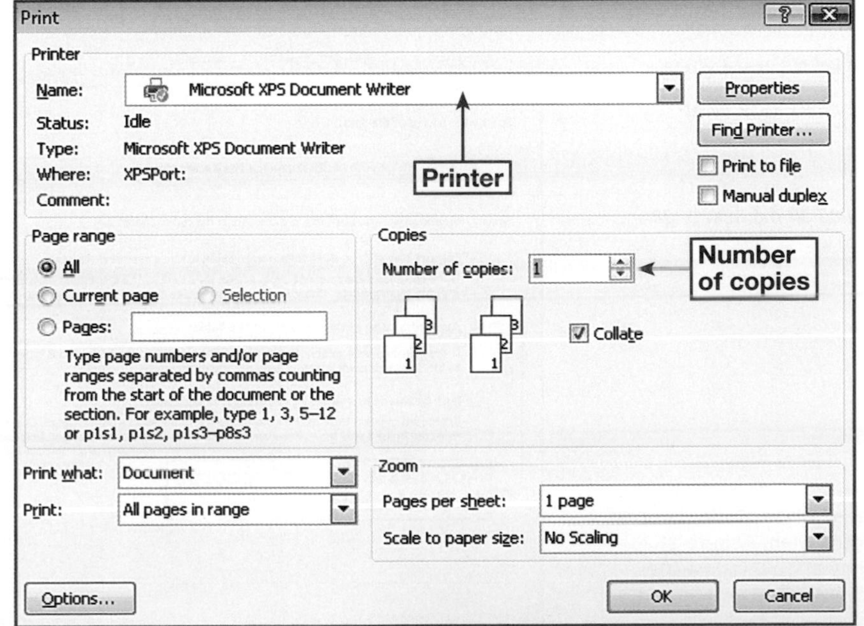

1. Start **Access**.
2. With your teacher's help, locate the data file **Estate.accdb**. Copy the database to your folder before working in it.
3. Open the **Listings** table in **Datasheet View**.
4. **CHECK** Your screen should look like Figure 1.13.
5. Choose **External Data> Import>Excel**.
6. The **Get External Data–Excel Spreadsheet** dialog box opens. In the **File name** box, browse to and select the data file **Recent.xlsx**. Click **Open**. Click **Append a copy of the records to the table:** and select **Listings** from the drop-down menu.
7. **CHECK** Your dialog box should look like Figure 1.14.

Continued on the next page.

Troubleshooting A security warning may appear when students open the Access data files. Assure students that they should follow the Access-recommended action and disable macros.

ACCESS INTEGRATION
Exercise 6: Import Excel Data

Both Excel and Access allow you to organize and analyze related information. For example, you might use Excel to perform calculations on data. However, you might want to put that data into an Access database. For example, if you are creating a database that contains information about your customers, and some of that information already exists in an Excel file, you can import data from Excel to Access without having to rekey the data.

FIGURE 1.13 Listings table

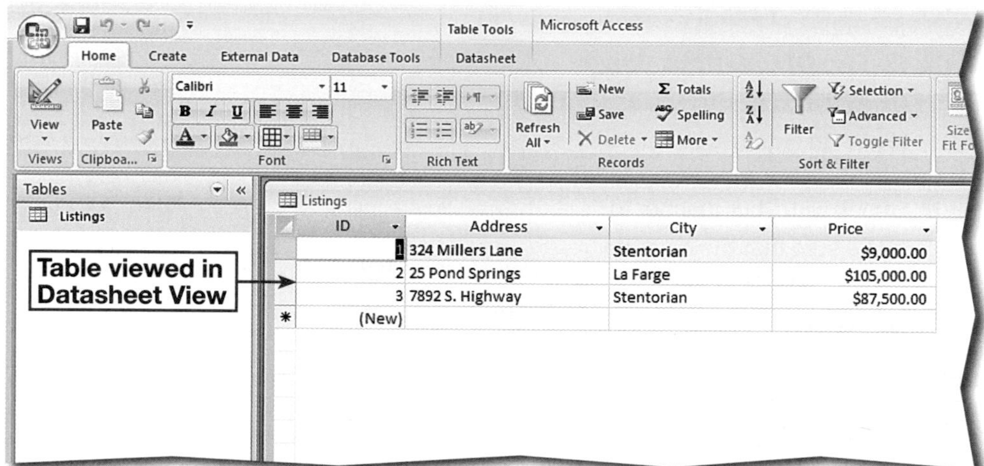

FIGURE 1.14 External Data—Excel dialog box

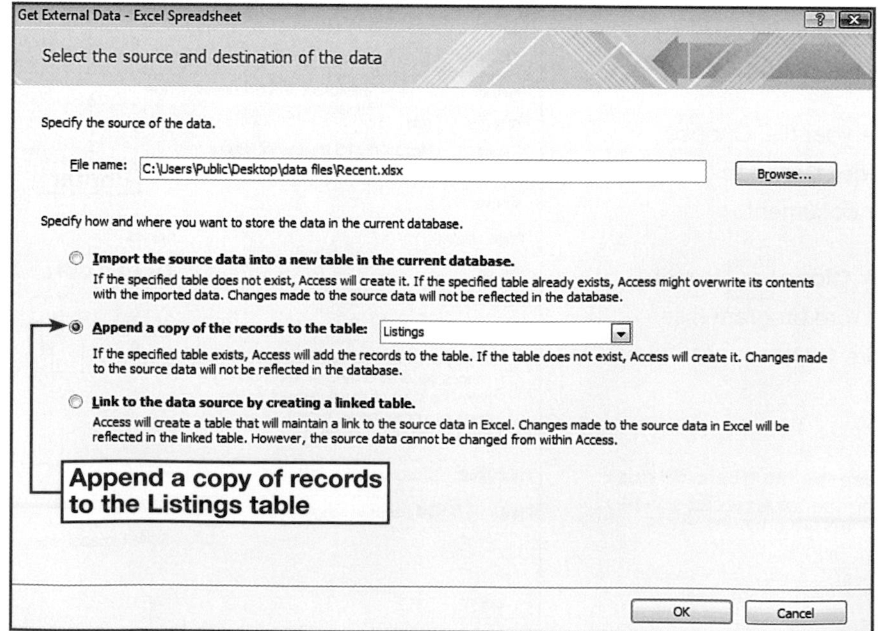

Writing MATTERS

Proofread to Avoid Mistakes

You may have read about the student who wrote his teacher that he needed "a bite of help." Or, maybe you saw the newspaper headline proudly announcing, "New York Yankees Take a Walk to Tie Store." These examples might make you smile, but mistakes in reports or business letters are more likely to cause confusion.

The time you spend proofreading your document—whether it is a research report or a business letter—is just as important as gathering data or summarizing your proposal.

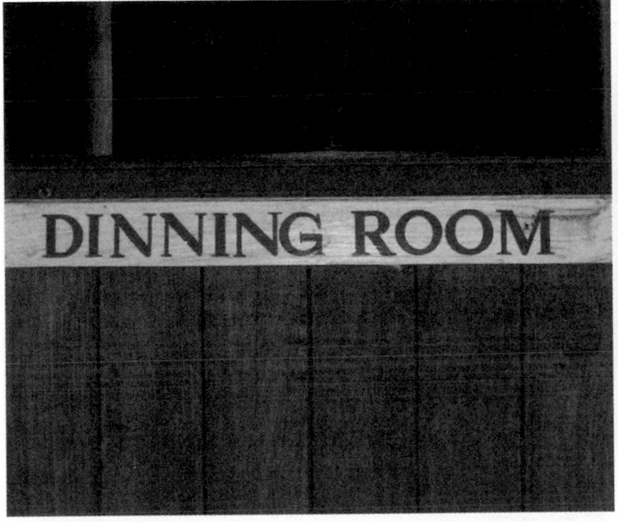

Proofreading can help you catch errors before it is too late!

NCLB/Language Arts (NCTE 4) Reinforce to students that correct spelling is vital to effective written communication.

(NCTE 5) Students should understand that proofreading is not an optional, but rather necessary, element of the writing process.

(NCTE 6) Reinforce that proofreading brings student knowledge of spelling and grammar into the creation of all documents.

Proofreading Steps

Follow these suggestions for checking your paper for mistakes.

1. **Print the copy** from the computer, if possible, and read the printed copy.
2. **Read the copy out loud.** It helps to read out loud, because
   - **a.** you are forced to slow down, and
   - **b.** you hear what you are reading.
3. **Let someone else read.** Choose a proofreading partner, and have one person read aloud as the other looks at the paper.

SKILLBUILDER

1. **Identify** Find the mistakes in the following sentences. Write the corrected sentences on a separate sheet of paper.
   - **a.** Sales increased form $100,000 to $150,000.
   - **b.** Maria said their getting new computers in their office.
   - **c.** My supervisor Julie Long is in Boston on a business trip.
   - **d.** Hard work has it's rewards.
   - **e.** Many jobs in the Untied States require computer skills.
2. **Evaluate** Why do you think managers might demand error-free documents?

SkillBuilder answers can be found on page TM55.

EXCEL INTEGRATION
Exercise 5: Create a Linked Object in Excel

A linked object is a file, table, worksheet, chart, or graphic that is inserted into an Excel workbook but is not located within the actual document. Instead, the content of a linked object is in a separate file known as the source file. In this exercise you will insert a Word document as a linked object in an Excel workbook.

1. In your **Memo.docx** file, under the heading **Board Members**, select the list **President—Sam Said** through **Technical—Neville Jones**.
2. Click **Copy**.
3. In your **Budget.xlsx** file, select the **Board Members** tab. Click cell **A3**.
4. On the **Home** tab, select the **Paste** drop-down arrow. Select **Paste Special**.
5. In the **Paste Special** dialog box, select the button next to **Paste link**. Click **Text**.
6. CHECK Your dialog box should look like Figure 1.11. Click **OK**.
7. In your **Memo** file, select the name **Neville**. Click **Cut**. Key: Faye. Press the **spacebar** once.
8. Click **Save**.
9. Go to your **Budget** workbook. Click in cell **A2**.
10. CHECK Your screen should look like Figure 1.12.
11. Save and close your files.

Continue to the next exercise.

Solution Use the files **Budget-SF.xlsx** and **Memo-SF.docx** as solution files for Exercises 2 through 5.

FIGURE 1.11 Paste Special dialog box

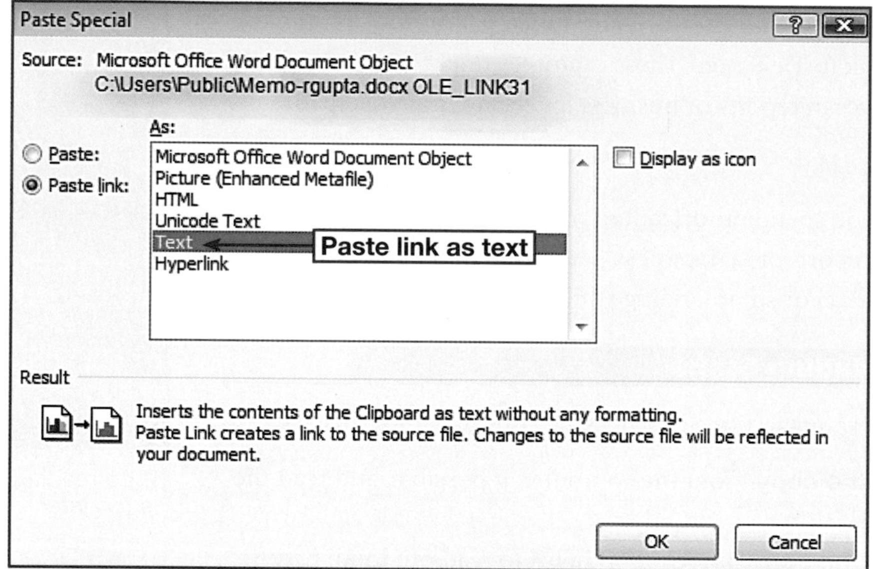

FIGURE 1.12 Linked object in Excel worksheet

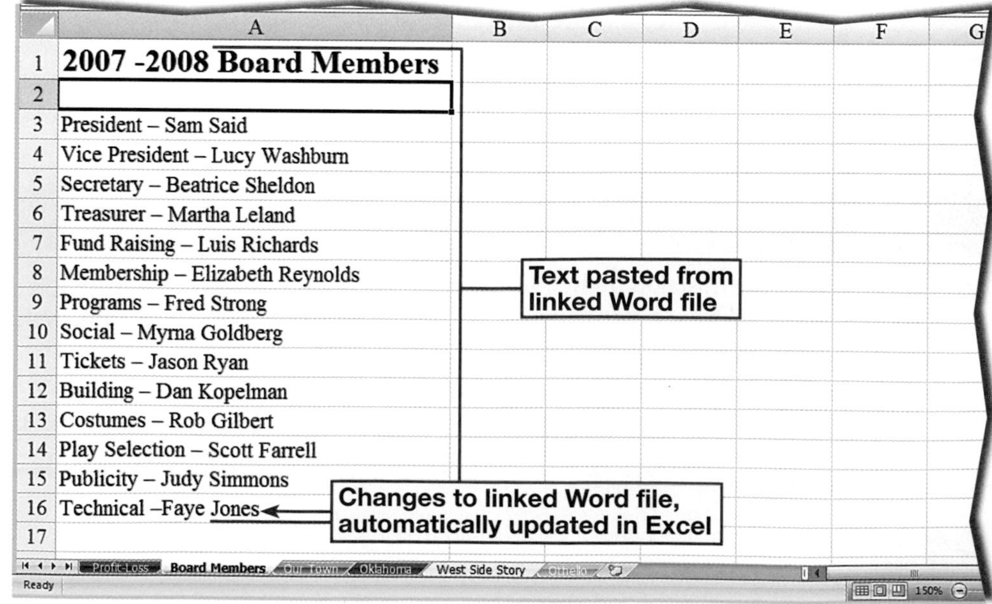

LESSON 1 After You Read

Review Vocabulary

Complete the following statements on a separate piece of paper. Choose from the Vocabulary list on the left to complete the statements.

1. A(n) ScreenTip is text that tells you what a button does. (p. 7)
2. The Ribbon contains groups of command buttons that you can click to perform tasks. (p. 6)
3. You can add frequently-used commands to the Quick Access Toolbar (QAT). (p. 8)
4. Related groups are collected under a(n) tab. (p. 6)
5. When customizing the Quick Access Toolbar you need to think about, or consider, what commands you would place on the QAT. (p. 6)

Vocabulary Activity

6. Create a five-question quiz based on this lesson's vocabulary and their definitions.
   A. Decide what the format of the questions will be (for example, fill-in-the-blank, multiple choice, matching).
   B. After you have created your quiz, team up with a classmate and exchange quizzes.
   C. Take each other's quizzes. Note any terms that you get wrong and identify the correct answer. Focus on any terms you did not understand as you read the lesson.

Review Key Concepts

Answer the following questions on a separate piece of paper.

7. Which of the following is located in the paragraph menu? (p. 11)
   A. Open
   B. Print
   C. Save
   (D.) Show/Hide
8. Which task can you do from the Save As dialog box? (p. 9)
   A. Format text
   (B.) Name a document
   C. Open a file
   D. Close a file
9. What tool lets you change a document's magnification? (p. 19)
   A. Office button
   B. Quick Access Toolbar
   (C.) Zoom
   D. Scroll bar
10. What is a quick way to select a sentence? (p. 12)
    A. Double-click the sentence.
    (B.) Hold down Ctrl and click in the sentence.
    C. Click the sentence.
    D. Click to the right of the sentence.

Vocabulary

Key Terms

button
command
cursor
dialog box
document
edit
folder
group
insertion point
pointer
Quick Access Toolbar (QAT)
Ribbon
ScreenTip
scroll bar
status bar
tab
title bar

Academic Vocabulary

consider
determine

Answer to Vocabulary Activity
Student answers will depend on the questions they ask. You may want to collect the quizzes and use the questions as an oral review or basis for a Jeopardy-type game for students.

Step-By-Step

1. In your **Budget.xlsx** file, choose **Office>Excel Options**.
2. In the **Excel Options** dialog box, click **Advanced**.
3. Under **Cut, Copy, and Paste**, make sure the **Show Paste Options buttons** check box is selected. Click **OK**.
4. In your **Memo.docx** file, select all the text in the table **Event Net** (through **$5,845.00**). Click **Copy**.
5. In your **Budget** file, select the **Othello** tab. Click cell **B27**. Click **Paste**.
6. Move your mouse over **Paste Options** so that the drop-down arrow appears.
7. Click the arrow. On the drop-down list, choose **Keep Source Formatting** (see Figure 1.9). Click cell **A31**.
8. **CHECK** Your screen should look like Figure 1.10.
9. Save your files.

Continue to the next exercise.

EXCEL INTEGRATION

Exercise 4: Use Paste Options

Use Paste Options to specify the format of the information you are pasting into Excel from another file or application. For example, you can use Paste Options to copy a long list of names from Word and paste them into a workbook. Paste Options allows you to choose whether pasted content should keep the formatting used in your source file, match the formatting used in your destination file, or apply no formatting at all.

FIGURE 1.9 Paste Options drop-down list

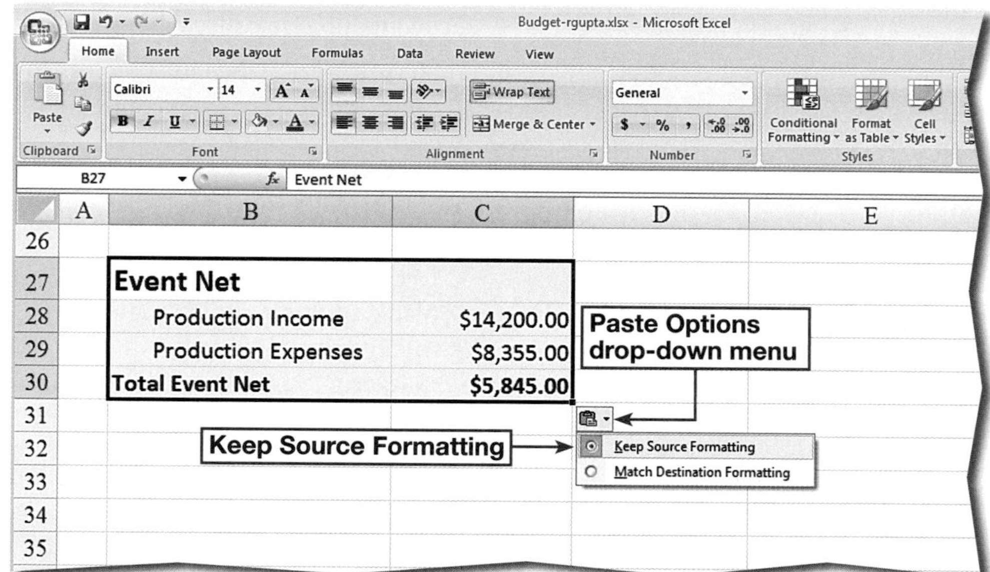

FIGURE 1.10 Document with pasted information

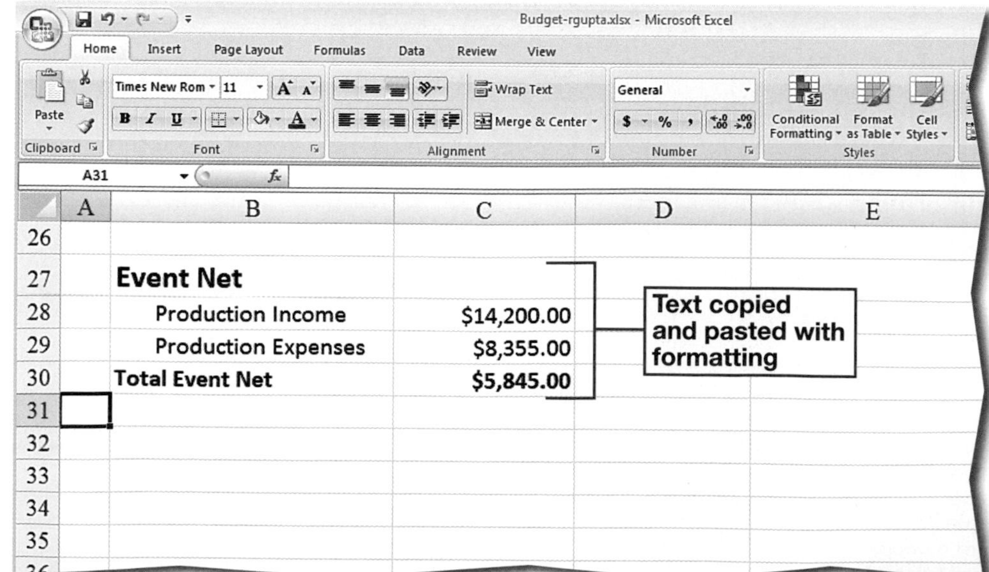

LESSON 1 Practice It Activities

1. Explore the Word Screen

Follow the steps to complete the activity.

Step-By-Step

1. Create a new Word document. Save your document as: w1rev-[your first initial and last name]1. Ask your teacher where to save the file.
2. Choose **Home>Paragraph> Show/Hide** ¶ [¶].
3. Key: The Word Screen.
4. CHECK Your screen should look like Figure 1.33.
5. On the **Ribbon,** on the **Home** tab**,** in the **Paragraph** group, roll your pointer over each button to read the **ScreenTip**.
6. Roll over and display the **ScreenTip** for the **Shading** command.
7. CHECK Your screen should look like Figure 1.34. Click Save [Save].
8. Click **Office>Close** to close the document.
9. Click **Close** [X] to exit Word.

FIGURE 1.33 The Word screen with text inserted

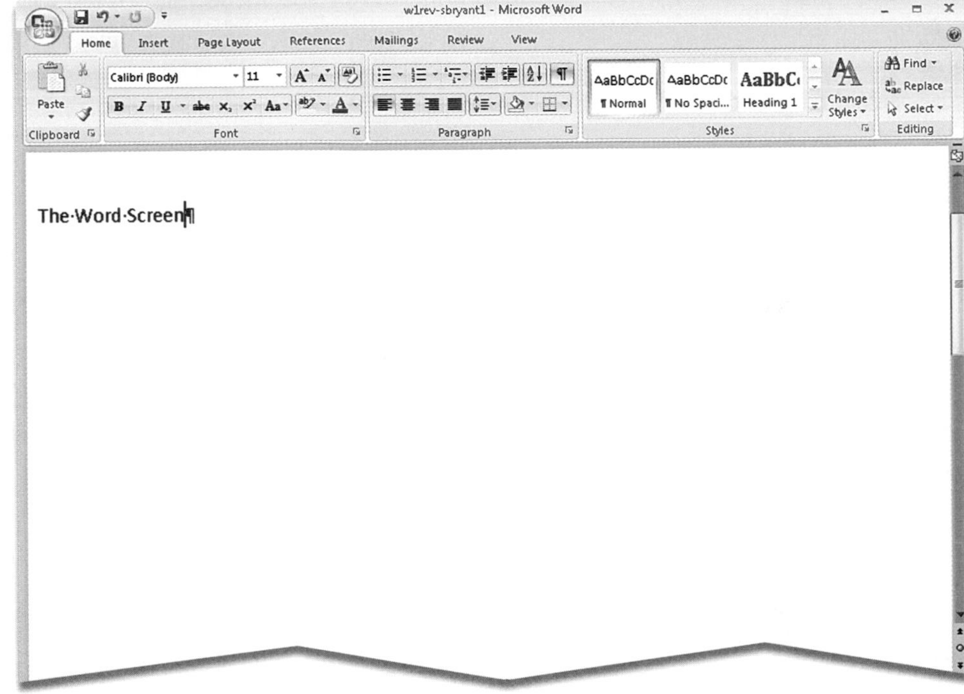

FIGURE 1.34 Shading ScreenTip displayed

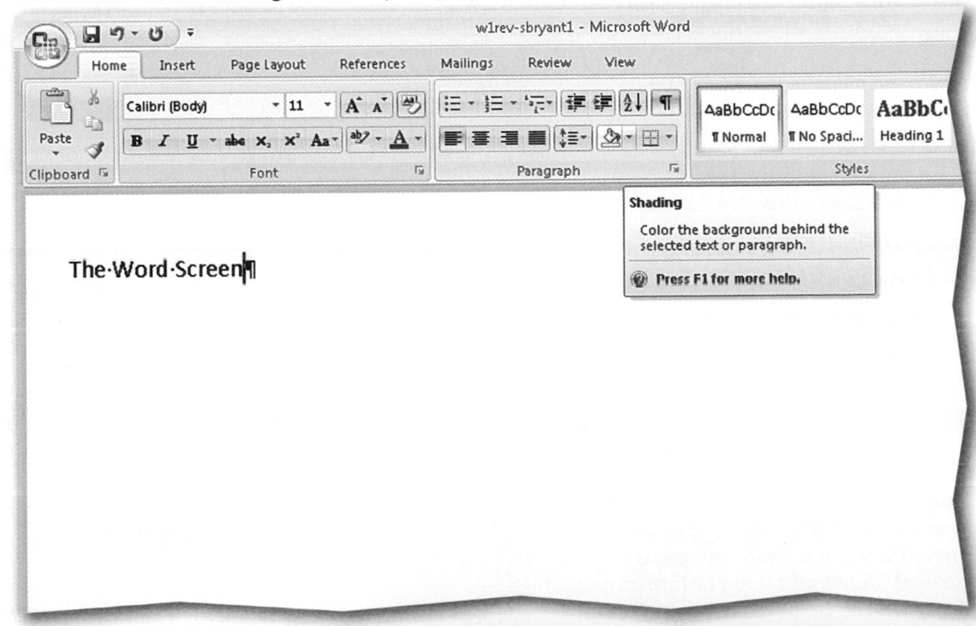

Step-By-Step

1. In your **Memo.docx** file, select all the text in the table **Production Income** (through **$14,200.00**). Click **Home>Clipboard> Copy**.
2. In your **Budget.xlsx** file, select the **Othello** tab. Click cell **B21**.
3. Choose **Home>Paste**. Click the **Paste Special** drop-down arrow.
4. In the **Paste Special** dialog box, under **As:**, choose **Text**.
5. **CHECK** Your dialog box should look like Figure 1.7. Click **OK**.
6. **CHECK** Your screen should look like Figure 1.8.
7. Insert dollar signs into the table. Save your files.

Continue to the next exercise.

You Should Know

Use **Paste Special** to choose the file format of pasted data. Use **Paste Options** to format pasted text.

Step-By-Step Tip In **Step 6**, students may notice that the dollar signs were erased when the table was pasted. Have students add them before saving the file.

EXCEL INTEGRATION

Exercise 3: Use Paste Special

Use Paste Special to specify the file format of the information you are pasting into Excel from another file or application. Using Paste Special, you can paste information in a variety of formats, including rich text format (RTF) and HTML. You can also paste content as a hyperlink or as a picture.

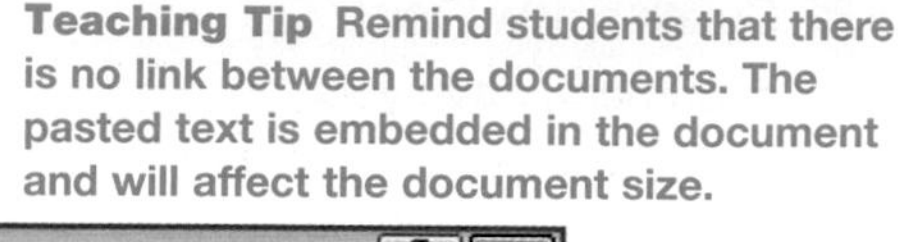

Teaching Tip Remind students that there is no link between the documents. The pasted text is embedded in the document and will affect the document size.

FIGURE 1.7 Paste Special dialog box

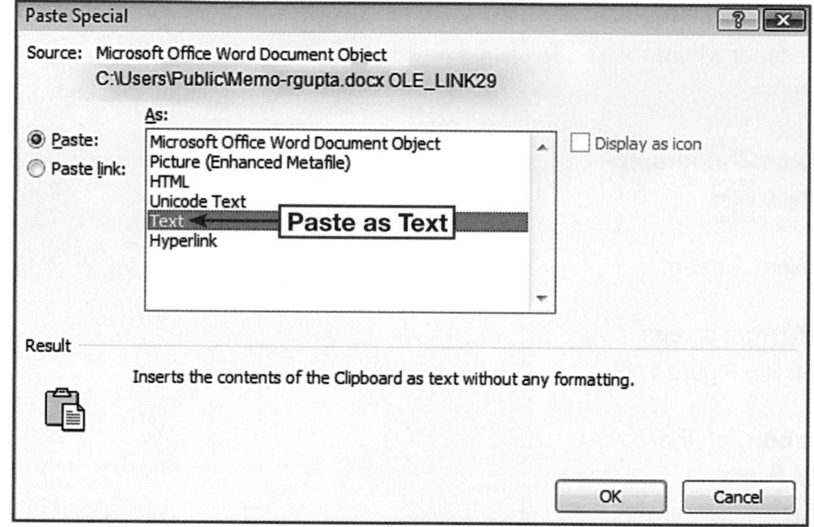

FIGURE 1.8 Document with pasted information

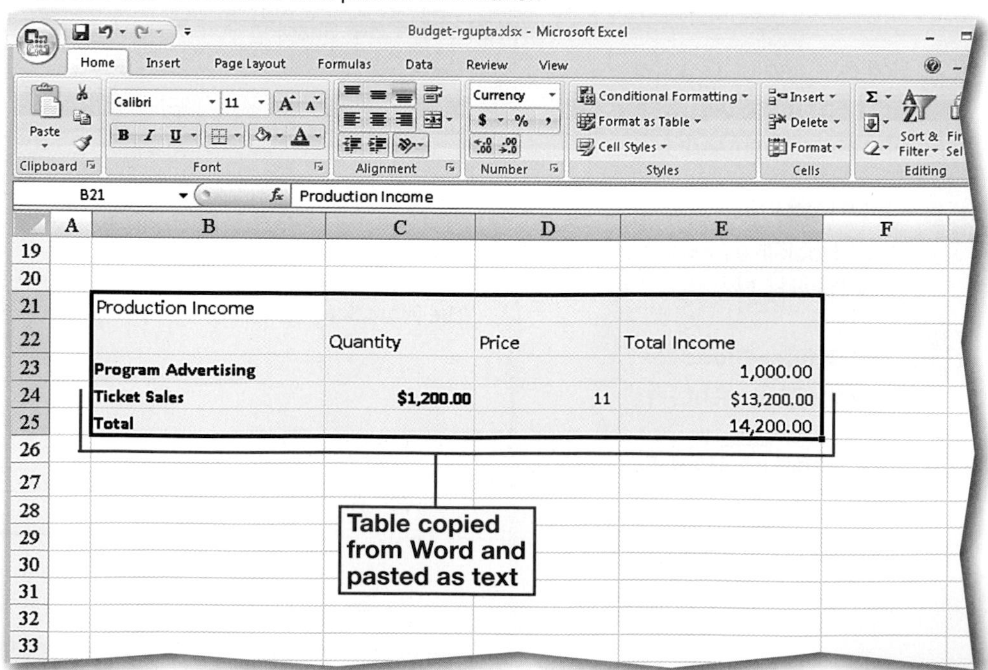

Step-By-Step

1. Create a new Word document. Save your document as: w1rev-[your first initial and last name]2.
2. Turn on **Show/Hide** ¶ [¶]. Key the text shown in Figure 1.35.
3. Click before the word **part**. Key: an important. Press the **Spacebar** once.
4. Click before the word **new**. Hold down [CTRL] and press [DELETE].
5. Hold down [CTRL] and press [←BACKSPACE] to delete the word **insert**.
6. Key: delete.
7. Your screen should look like Figure 1.36.
8. In the **QAT**, click **Save** [Save icon].
9. Click **Office>Close** to close the document.

Solution The solution for this activity is **Figure 1.36**.

2. Insert and Delete Text

Follow the steps to complete the activity.

FIGURE 1.35 Original text

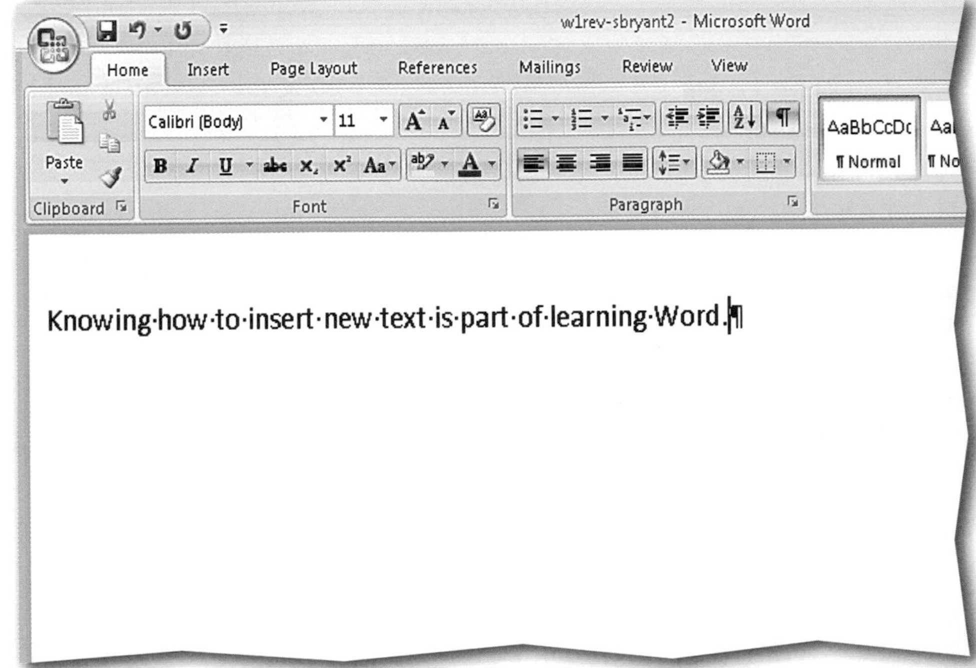

FIGURE 1.36 Edited text

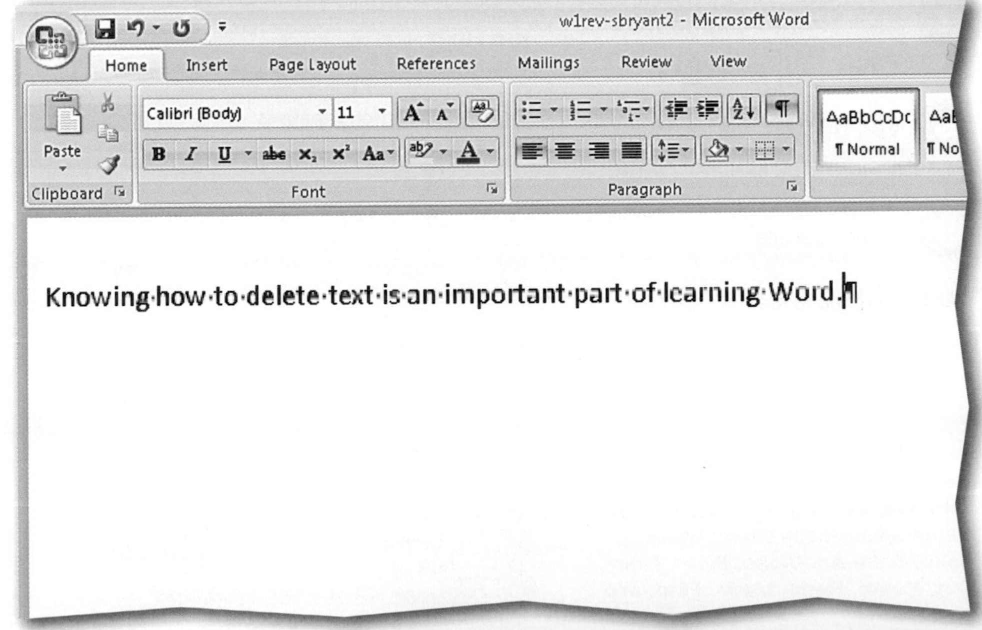

1. Start **Excel**.
2. Locate and open the data file **Budget.xlsx**. Save as: Budget-[your first initial and last name] (for example, *Budget-rgupta*).
3. Start **Word**. Locate and open the data file **Memo.docx**. Save as: Memo-[your first initial and last name].
4. In the memo, select all the text in the table **Production Expenses**. Click **Home>Clipboard>Copy**.
5. **CHECK** Your screen should look like Figure 1.5.
6. Switch to your **Budget** file. Select the **Othello** tab. Click cell **B1**.
7. Click **Home>Clipboard>Paste**. Click **A20**.
8. **CHECK** Your screen should look like Figure 1.6.
9. Save your files.

Continue to the next exercise.

New Student Strategy Review with new students the features that Office applications share: **Open, Save, Save As, Close, Print, Copy, Cut, Paste, Redo, Undo, Find,** and **Replace.**

EXCEL INTEGRATION

Exercise 2: Copy and Paste between Applications

If you have information in a Word document that you would like to import to an Excel spreadsheet, you can use the Copy and Paste functions on the Clipboard to copy text from Word and paste it into an Excel worksheet. When you copy and paste text instead of cutting and pasting, the text remains in both the original and the destination file.

Step-By-Step Tip In **Step 3**, remind students that they can select an entire table by using the **Move Handle.**

FIGURE 1.5 Text copied in Word document

Production Expenses			
	Quantity	Price	Total Expenses
Fees			
Rights and Rentals			$2,500.00
Theater Fees			$500.00
Posters	250	$3.00	$750.00
Programs	600	$1.50	$900.00
Copying			$40.00
Postal Fees			$50.00
Scene Shop Rental			$500.00
Daily Advertising			
Half Page Ad			$85.00
Full Page Ads	2	$165.00	$330.00
Technical Costs			
Costumes			$1,000.00
Props			$250.00
Set			$1,250.00
Lighting			$200.00
Total			$8,355.00

FIGURE 1.6 Text pasted into Excel worksheet

	A	B	C	D	E
1		Production Expenses			
2			Quantity	Price	Total Expense
3		Fees			
4		Rights and Rentals			$2,500.00
5		Theater Fees			$500.00
6		Posters	250	$3.00	$750.00
7		Programs	600	$1.50	$900.00
8		Copying			$40.00
9		Postal Fees			$50.00
10		Scene Shop Rental			$500.00
11		Daily Advertising			
12		Half Page Ad			$85.00
13		Full Page Ads	2	$165.00	$330.00
14		Technical Costs			
15		Costumes			$1,000.00
16		Props			$250.00
17		Set			$1,250.00
18		Lighting			$200.00
19		Total			$8,355.00

3. Create, Save, and Print a Document

Follow the steps to complete the activity.

Step-By-Step

1. Create a new Word document. Save your document as: w1rev-[your first initial and last name]3.
2. Turn on **Show/Hide** ¶ [¶]. Key: Microsoft Word is a word processing application. You can use Word to create memos, reports, and letters.
3. Press [ENTER]. Key: Knowing how to name and save a document is an important part of learning Word. You use the Save As dialog box to name a document.
4. CHECK Your screen should look like Figure 1.37.
5. Choose **Office>Print> Print Preview**.
6. Your screen should look like Figure 1.38. Click **Close Preview**.
7. Choose **Office>Print**. With your teacher's permission, click **OK** to print the document.
8. Click **Save** [Save]. Close the document.

Solution The solution file for this activity is **Figure 1.38**.

FIGURE 1.37 The document with keyed text

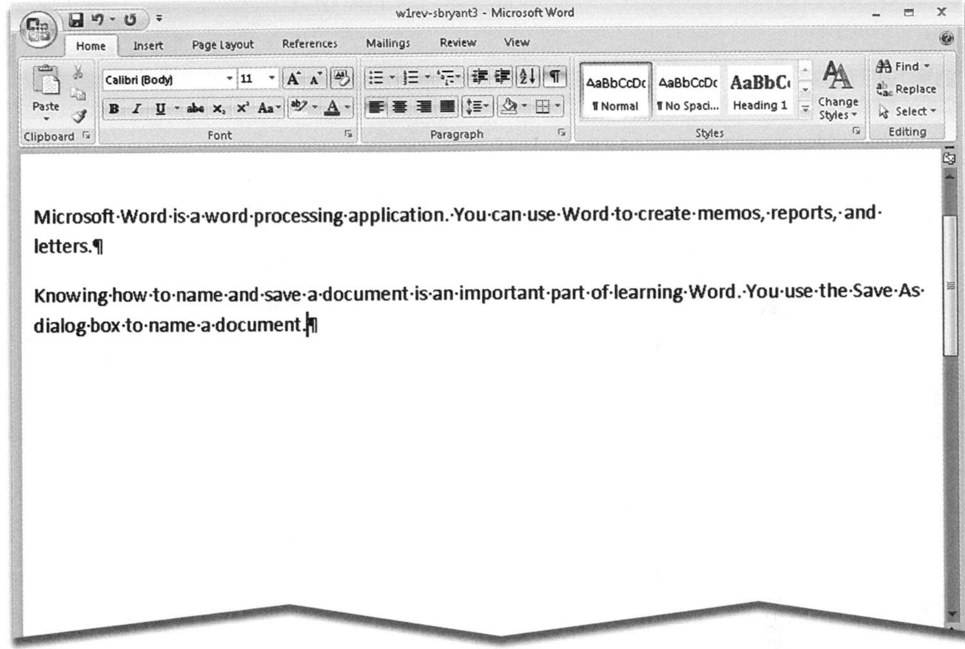

FIGURE 1.38 Print Preview

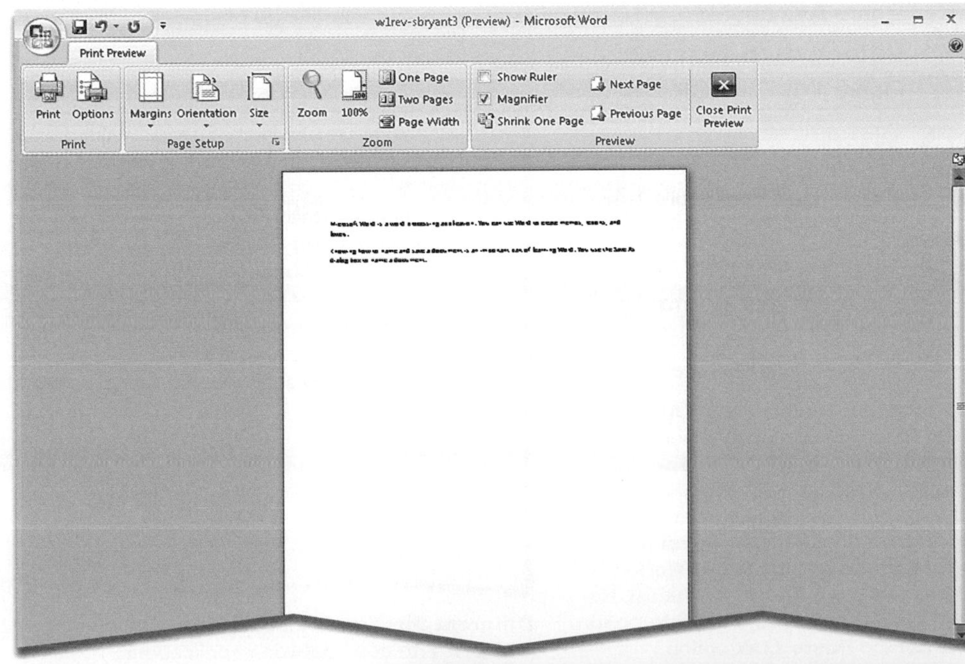

WORD INTEGRATION

Exercise 1: Copy and Paste between Applications (Continued)

Solution Use the file **Rental-SF.docx** as a solution file for Exercise 1.

8 If the table gridlines do not show, choose **Table Tools>Layout>Table> View Gridlines**. Select the table and click **Align Center**.

9 Switch to **Excel**. Close the **Properties.xlsx** data file. Click **No**. Open the **Cleaning.xlsx** data file. Save as: Cleaning-[your first initial and last name]. Select cells **A2** through **A6**. Click **Home>Clipboard>Copy**.

10 In your **Rental** file, click at the end of the sentence that ends **here are their names** and press ENTER twice.

11 On the **Home** tab, click the **Paste** drop-down arrow. Select **Paste Special**. Under **As:**, choose **Unformatted Text** (see Figure 1.3). Click **OK**.

12 CHECK Your screen should look like Figure 1.4.

13 Close the Excel file. Save and close your **Rental** file.

Continue to the next exercise.

Differentiated Instruction/Advanced Students Demonstrate embedding a worksheet using the **Paste Special** feature. (Copy worksheet cells to the clipboard. Switch to the Word document and choose **Paste Special**. Select the **Microsoft Excel Worksheet Object** option in the **As** list. Be sure students choose the **Paste** option and not the **Paste Link** option.)

FIGURE 1.3 Paste Special dialog box

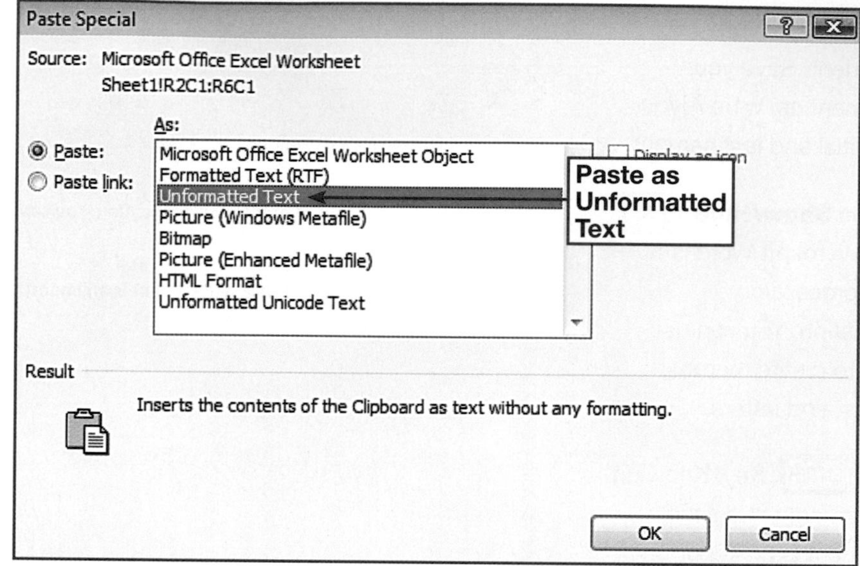

FIGURE 1.4 Document with pasted information

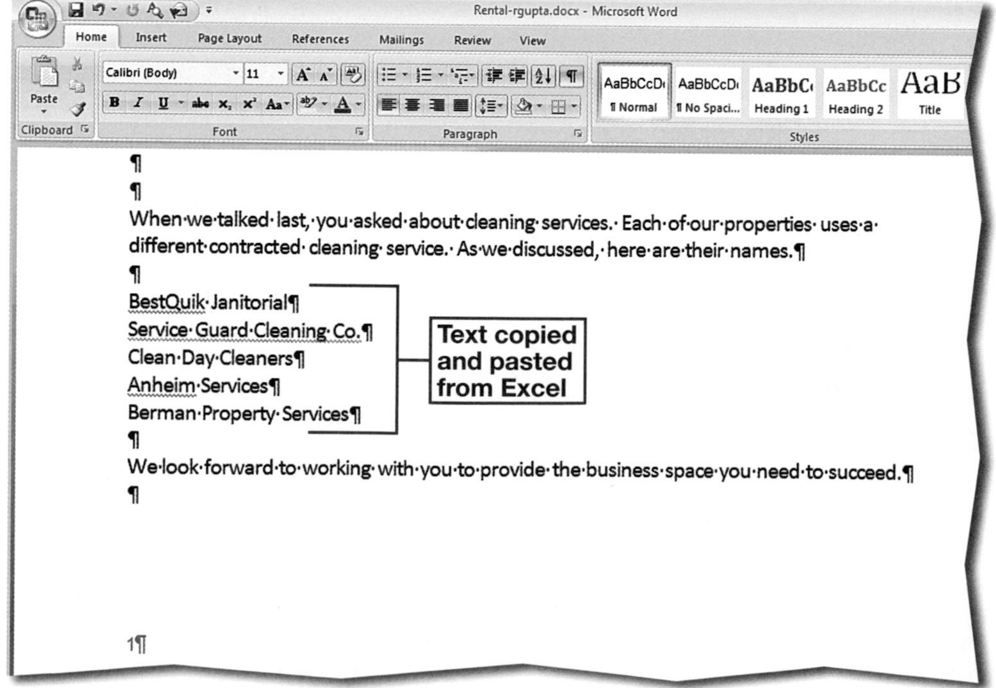

Different Strokes Point out to students that they can also use **CTRL** + **C** and **CTRL** + **V** to copy between applications.

4. Edit a Business Letter

Your boss has asked you to edit a business letter. Part of this letter is shown below. The letter contains some keying mistakes that you need to fix before it can be sent out.

Step-By-Step

1. Open the data file **Letter .docx**. You will see the text shown in Figure 1.39.
2. Save the file as: w1rev-[your first initial and last name]4.

In the text:

3. Change **Alic** to **Alice**.
4. Combine the first line with the line that begins with **working**.
5. Change the question mark at the end of the first sentence to a period.
6. Change **too** to **to**.
7. Change the colon to a comma after **said**.
8. Change the single quotation marks to double quotation marks (two times).
9. Add a space between the closing quotation mark and **We**.
10. Your letter should look like Figure 1.40. Save and close your document.

Solution The solution for this activity is **Figure 1.40** or the file **w1-rev-SF.docx**.

FIGURE 1.39 Unedited letter

Dear Alic:

I am happy that we are going to be
working together on the new project? I think we should get together as soon as possible to discuss how we plan too complete the project. As you know our supervisor, Mr. Jones, said: 'This is the most important new project our company has had in years.' We definitely need to decide how to finish the project on time and within budget.

FIGURE 1.40 Edited letter

Dear Alice:

I am happy that we are going to be working together on the new project. I think we should get together as soon as possible to discuss how we plan to complete the project. As you know, our supervisor, Mr. Jones, said, "This is the most important new project our company has had in years." We definitely need to decide how to finish the project on time and within budget.

1 Start **Word**. Open the data file **Rental.docx**. Save as: Rental-[your first initial and last name] (for example, *Rental-rgupta*).

2 Start **Excel**. Open the data file **Properties.xlsx**. Save as: Properties-[your first initial and last name].

3 Select cells **A1** through **E6**. Click **Home>Clipboard> Copy**.

4 **CHECK** Your screen should look like Figure 1.1.

5 Switch to your **Rental** file. Click at the end of the sentence that begins with **Below is**. Press ENTER twice.

6 Click **Home>Clipboard> Paste**. The Excel data is inserted in its original format.

7 **CHECK** Your screen should look like Figure 1.2.

Continued on the next page.

Step-By-Step Tip If the **Paste Options** button does not appear in **Step 6**, have students choose **Office>Word Options>Advanced**. Under **Cut, Copy,** and **Paste,** click the **Show Paste Options Buttons** option. Click **OK**.

WORD INTEGRATION

Exercise 1: Copy and Paste between Applications

By now you are familiar with using Copy and Paste as functions in various Microsoft Office programs. You can use the Clipboard to paste data from one file to another file in another application, just like you do within a single application. Use Paste Special to specify the file format of the information you are pasting from another file or application. Use Paste Options to specify the format of the pasted information.

FIGURE 1.1 Data copied in Excel source file

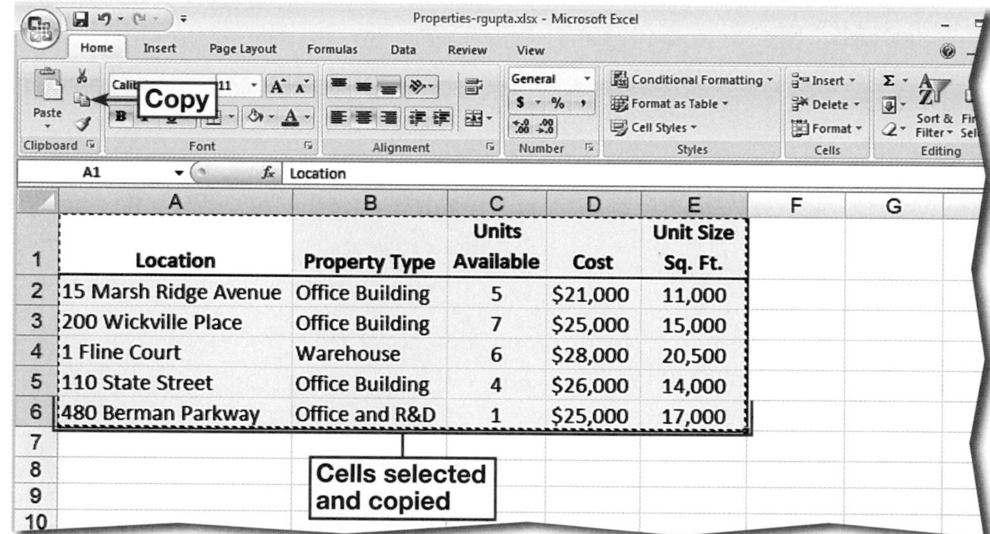

	A	B	C	D	E
1	Location	Property Type	Units Available	Cost	Unit Size Sq. Ft.
2	15 Marsh Ridge Avenue	Office Building	5	$21,000	11,000
3	200 Wickville Place	Office Building	7	$25,000	15,000
4	1 Fline Court	Warehouse	6	$28,000	20,500
5	110 State Street	Office Building	4	$26,000	14,000
6	480 Berman Parkway	Office and R&D	1	$25,000	17,000

FIGURE 1.2 Excel data pasted into Word destination file

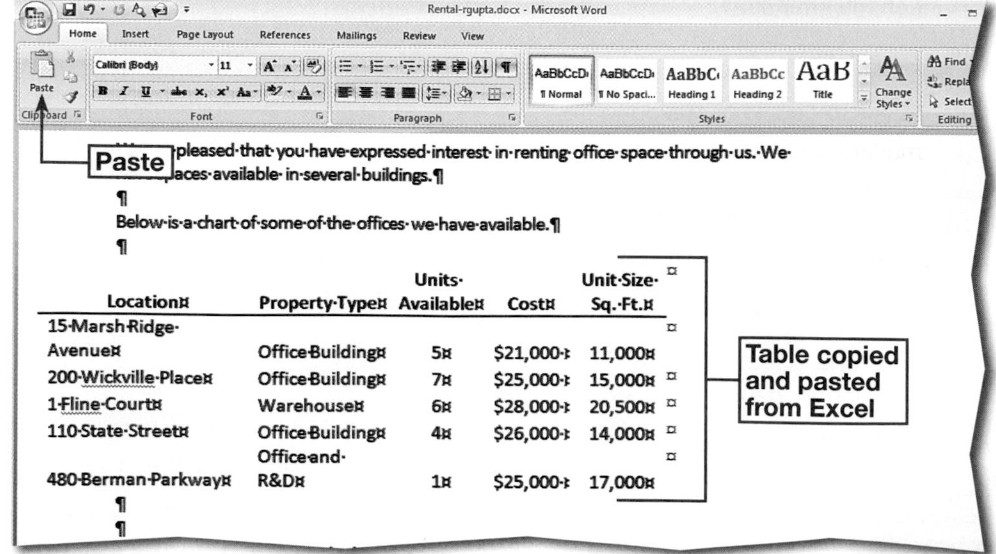

Location	Property Type	Units Available	Cost	Unit Size Sq. Ft.
15 Marsh Ridge Avenue	Office Building	5	$21,000	11,000
200 Wickville Place	Office Building	7	$25,000	15,000
1 Fline Court	Warehouse	6	$28,000	20,500
110 State Street	Office Building	4	$26,000	14,000
480 Berman Parkway	Office and R&D	1	$25,000	17,000

5. Create a "How to" Guide

You have a new coworker who does not know anything about Word. Your supervisor has asked you to teach your new coworker how to open a Word document, key text, print a document, and save a document.

Step-By-Step

1. Create a new document. Save it as: w1-rev[your first initial and last name]5.
2. Key the first four lines of information in Figure 1.41. Press ENTER after each line.
3. Key a paragraph that explains why your coworker needs to know Word and how he or she might use Word at work. Press ENTER.
4. Key a second paragraph that lists the steps needed to perform one of the following tasks:
   - open a document
   - print a document
   - save a document
   - insert text
   - delete text

   Press ENTER after each step.
5. Key a concluding paragraph that tells your coworker how to use the Help feature.
6. Save and print your document. Close the file and exit Word.

Solution Students' documents should be formatted like **Figure 1.41.** Text will vary.

FIGURE 1.41 Sample document

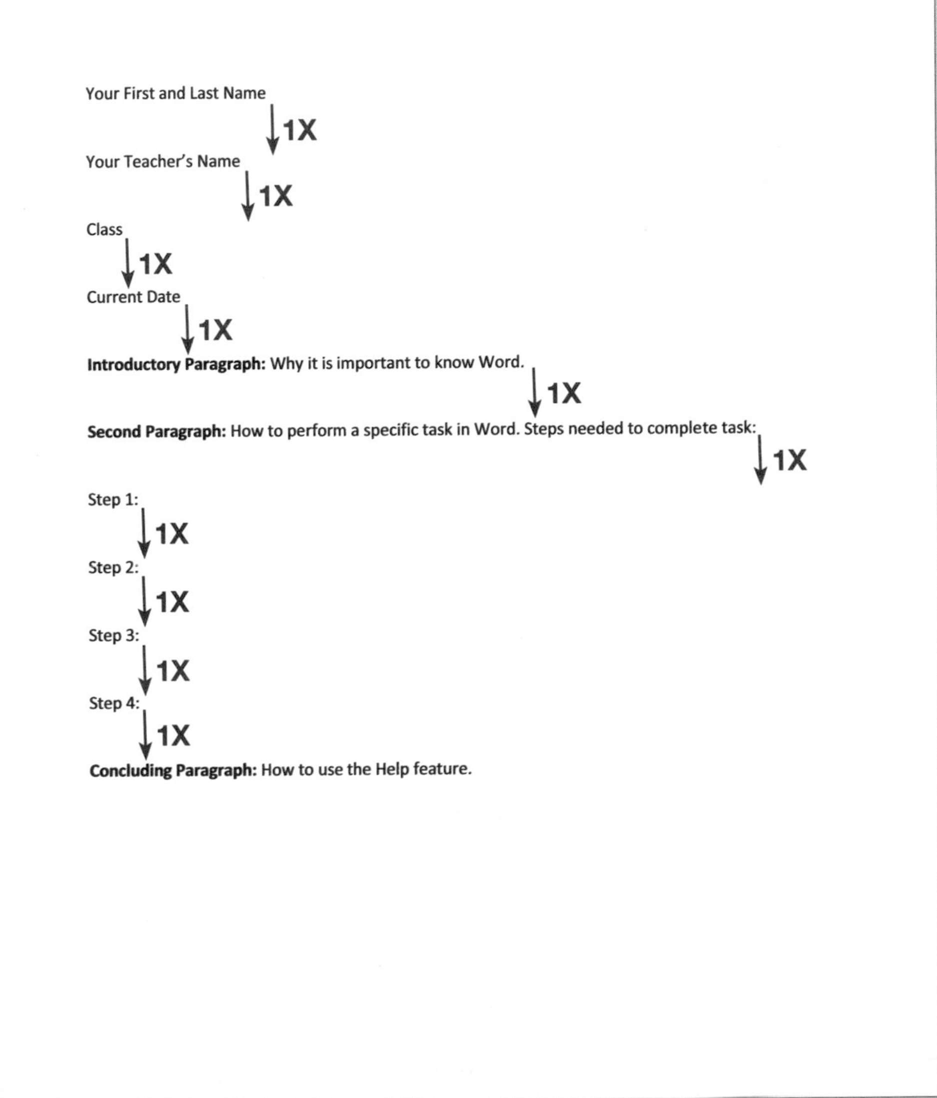

Your First and Last Name
1X
Your Teacher's Name
1X
Class
1X
Current Date
1X
Introductory Paragraph: Why it is important to know Word.
1X
Second Paragraph: How to perform a specific task in Word. Steps needed to complete task:
1X
Step 1:
1X
Step 2:
1X
Step 3:
1X
Step 4:
1X
Concluding Paragraph: How to use the Help feature.

NCLB/Language Arts (NCTE 1) Reinforce that the structure of a "How-to" document is very important. The steps need to be laid out logically so that the information is organized in a way that readers can understand.

Table of Contents

Beyond the Classroom Activity Students key three paragraphs about a place they want to visit. Students should identify the place they want to visit, explain why they want to visit, and the steps they must take to accomplish their visit.

Standards at Work Activity Students key instructions in three paragraphs. Students should explain a) the rationale behind customizing this feature, b) specific instructions for how to do so, and c) suggestions for ideal commands to include.

21st Century Skills Activity Students key a paragraph that identifies a personal goal they have for the course and list the steps they will take to achieve this goal.

Teaching Tip Reinforce that Activity 7 uses the "How-to" format learned in Activity 5.

Go Online e-REVIEW

glencoe.com

Go to the **Online Learning Center** to complete the following review activities.

Online Self Check
To test your knowledge of the material, click **Unit 1> Lesson 1** and choose **Self Checks**.

Interactive Review
To review the main points of this lesson, click **Unit 1> Lesson 1** and choose **Interactive Review.**

6. Beyond the Classroom Activity

Language Arts: Describe Your Dream Vacation Think about one place you really want to visit. This place can be anywhere—in the United States, in Africa, or even on the moon! Then, open a Word document and key three paragraphs:

- Identify the place you want to visit and state where it is located.
- Explain why you want to visit this place (to see an attraction, to meet different people, and so on).
- Describe what steps you would need to take to visit this place (for example, earn money, book a ticket, and so on).

Save your document as: w1rev-[your first initial and last name]6.

7. Standards at Work Activity

Microsoft Certified Application Specialist Correlation
Word 1.4 *Personalize Office Word 2007*

Write Instructions Your supervisor has asked you to write instructions for trainees on how to customize the Quick Access Toolbar in Microsoft Word 2007. Open a document and key three short paragraphs.

- In the first paragraph, state why an employee might want to customize their Quick Access Toolbar.
- In the second paragraph, instruct trainees how to customize the QAT. Include the pathways (specific instructions on which command buttons to click) to accomplish this.
- In the third paragraph, recommend the most commonly used command buttons they might want quick access to when using Word.

Save your document as: w1rev-[your first initial and last name]7.

8. 21st Century Skills Activity

Set Goals You have to set a goal before you can decide what steps you must take to reach that goal. Locate the key concepts list in the Lesson Opener. This list is designed to help you identify the tasks (steps) you need to master in order to complete the lesson (goal).

Key a paragraph that identifies a personal goal you have for this course. In your paragraph, list at least five steps you will take to achieve that goal.

Save your document as: w1rev-[your first initial and last name]8.

Contents of Appendixes

LESSON 1 Challenge Yourself Projects

Before You Begin

The Job Hunt An important challenge in life is finding the right job. These projects teach you how to use the Web to search for job opportunities, identify skills needed to perform a job, and plan to develop those skills.

Reflect Once you complete the projects, open a document and answer the following:

1. What did you like most about the Web site you used? What did you like the least?
2. What job skills do you already have?
3. What job skills are you currently learning?

Answers Teacher and student rubrics for each Challenge Yourself Project are available at **glencoe.com**. You may want to download the rubrics and make them available to students as they complete each project.

9. Search for Jobs

LEVEL This is an intermediate level project.

Language Arts: Summarize Research Go to a job search Web site. Use the site's search function to find a job you might like to have in the future. In your search, you will be asked to select a job category. Pick a category that really interests you, such as technology, health care, or marketing.

If you do not have access to the Internet, read about available jobs in the classified section of a local newspaper or in the data file **Jobs**.

Carefully read the job descriptions in your chosen category. Look up the meanings of any job-related terms you do not understand. When you are finished reading:

- Select three job descriptions.
- Briefly summarize each job in a Word document.
- For each job summary, key a short paragraph that explains why the job interests you.

Save your document as: w1rev-[your first initial and last name]9.

10. Identify Job Qualifications

Rubric R

LEVEL This is an intermediate level project.

Language Arts: Identify Important Content Open a Word document and save it as: w1rev-[your first initial and last name]10. Save the file to the location specified by your teacher.

Select one of the job descriptions you read in the previous exercise. Identify the qualifications needed to perform that job. Job qualifications can include:

- educational requirements
- prior experience
- skills you need to perform the job

Key a paragraph summarizing the qualifications needed to perform the job you selected.

11. Plan Career Goals

LEVEL This is an advanced level project.

Language Arts: Evaluate Information Review the job qualifications you identified in Project 10. After each job qualification, insert a sentence describing what you would do in order to meet the qualification. For example, if the job qualification is, "The candidate must have a Bachelor of Arts degree," insert the statement, "To meet this qualification, I will go to college and earn a Bachelor of Arts degree." Save the revised file as: w1rev-[your first initial and last name]11.

UNIT 4 Portfolio Project

Part 4: Create a Proposal

LEVEL This is an advanced level project.

Goal Based on the meeting's results, the town planner is going to propose the construction of a multi-use recreation center. She would like you to help create the presentation that promotes this proposal.

Create Create a new blank presentation.

- Choose a **Theme**. Key content for the proposal on the slides. Include a minimum of six slides in your presentation and a Title slide with a logo for the recreation center.
- Add graphics such as Clip Art, WordArt, SmartArt, charts, or diagrams as needed.
- Add an **Action Button**.
- Add transitions between the slides.
- Add animation to elements on at least two slides.
- Add notes to use during your presentation to the **Notes Pane** on each slide.

Self Assess Use the Have You...? checklist to review your presentation. Carefully preview your presentation and make corrections. With your teacher's permission, print your presentation in Notes Pages format. Follow your teacher's instructions for naming the presentation and saving it in your Portfolio Folder.

	Have You...?
✓	Included a minimum of six slides
✓	Created a logo for the Title Slide
✓	Added graphics as needed
✓	Added an Action Button
✓	Added slide transitions
✓	Made necessary corrections
✓	Rehearsed timings
✓	Added notes to the Notes Pane on each slide
✓	Printed the Notes Pages of the presentation

Go Online BEYOND THE BOOK

glencoe.com

Go to the Online Learning Center to learn additional skills and review what you have already learned.

Microsoft PowerPoint
Extend your knowledge of PowerPoint by visiting the Online Learning Center for more MCAS-based exercises. Select **Advanced PowerPoint Exercises>Lessons**.

Windows Vista
Select **Windows Vista Exercises>Lessons** to explore Microsoft's operating system fully.

Microsoft Outlook
Want to learn all about Outlook and how to use e-mail communication and scheduling? Select **Microsoft Outlook Exercises>Lessons** for all you need to know.

Additional Projects
Complete additional projects in the following areas:

- **Real-World Business Projects** reinforce Microsoft Word by focusing on real-world business applications.
- **Presentation and Publishing Projects** Use your Word skills to create exciting PowerPoint presentations and desktop publishing activities.
- **Academic Projects** Integrate academic skills while enriching your understanding of Microsoft Word.

More Online Resources
Access additional Web sites and online information relating to key topics covered in Glencoe's *iCheck Series*. Select **Additional Resources>Links**.

LESSON 2

Format Content

Key Concepts

- Work with templates
- Set margins
- Set and change tab stops
- Modify font size, style, and color
- Apply and remove styles
- Align paragraphs
- Create numbered and bulleted lists
- Create outlines

Standards

The following standards are covered in this lesson. Refer to pages xxv and 715 for a description of the standards listed here.

ISTE Standards Correlation

NETS•S

1a, 1b, 2a, 2b, 2d, 3c, 5a, 5b, 6a, 6b

Microsoft Certified Application Specialist

Word

1.1, 1.2, 2.1, 4.2. 

A written document's formatting, or overall appearance, will be the first thing that any reader will note. You can change a document's margins, add color and styles, or create lists to help make your document more interesting and easy to read. In this lesson, you will learn how to enhance, or make the most of, your document's appearance.

21st CENTURY SKILLS

See page TM57 for answer to 21st Century Skills.

Team Work Think about a time when you worked as part of a sports team to win a game or on a school team to accomplish a task. A good team member is committed to the team, is concerned for and supportive of the other team members, and works with others to make good decisions. An effective team member also listens, encourages other team members, and is committed to the team's goals. *What are some ways in which you have helped a team succeed?*

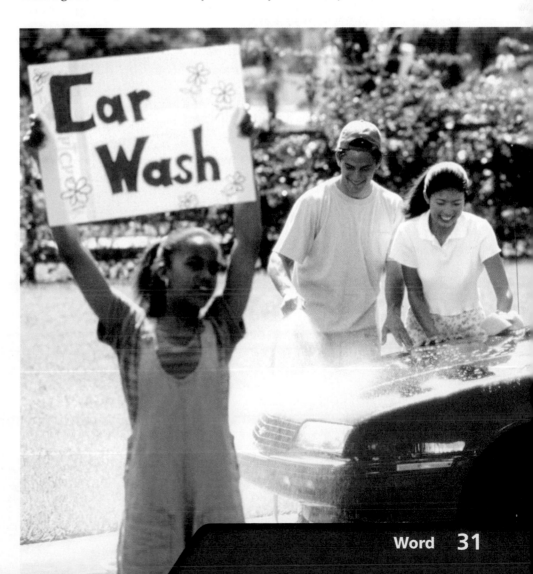

UNIT 4 Portfolio Project

Part 3: Create a Presentation

LEVEL This is an intermediate level project.

Goal You are a teenager who lives in the town. You read the flyer about the town meeting and have an idea you want to present. You decide to create a short presentation about your idea.

Create Think of businesses that might attract you to your town's business district. For example, you may think the town needs a movie theater, a skating rink, a recreation center, or an arcade.

Use a Theme to create a presentation proposing your idea. In your presentation, include the following items:

- A Title slide with a title.
- A slide that describes the business you would like to see in your town.
- A bulleted slide with information about your selected business.
- A piece of **WordArt**, a **Shape**, and another graphic such as a chart or diagram.
- Transitions between slides.

Self Assess Use the Have You...? checklist to review your presentation. View the slide show. With your teacher's permission, print a handout of your presentation. Follow your teacher's instructions for naming the presentation and saving it in your Portfolio Folder.

When finished, proceed to Part 4.

	Have You...?
✓	Included a Title slide
✓	Included a slide describing your business
✓	Included a slide with a bulleted list
✓	Included WordArt
✓	Included a Shape
✓	Included a chart of diagram
✓	Added slide transitions
✓	Printed a handout of your presentation

LESSON 2 Reading Guide

Before You Read

See page TM42 for English Learner activity suggestions.

Vocabulary To gain a better understanding of vocabulary, create a Vocabulary Journal. Divide a piece of paper into three columns. Label the first column *Vocabulary.* Then, label the other columns: *What is it? What else is it like?* Write down each word and answer the questions as you read the lesson.

Read To Learn

- Discover how to change the format, or appearance, of text to improve your message.
- Practice how to format paragraphs and pages to improve your written communication.
- Understand why formatting needs to be consistent in a document.

Main Idea

Formatting documents is essential to good written communication.

Vocabulary

Key Terms

alignment	Format Painter	point
bullet	formatting	Quick Styles
bulleted list	indent	scale
character	margin	style
font	memo	tab stop
font style	numbered list	typeface

Academic Vocabulary

These words appear in your reading and on your tests. Make sure you know their meanings.

analyze
enhance
horizontal

Quick Write Activity

Analyze On a separate sheet of paper, write a brief paragraph explaining how you would feel if you received a flyer or advertisement from a business that was difficult to read and contained spelling errors. Would you use that business? Why or why not?

Study Skills

Take Good Notes To help review for tests, take good notes. Write down key words and important information that you will need to review. Read through your notes after you finish a lesson and add any missing items.

Academic Standards

English Language Arts

NCTE 3 Apply strategies to interpret texts.

NCTE 4 Use written language to communicate effectively.

NCTE 5 Use different writing process elements to communicate effectively.

NCTE 12 Use language to accomplish individual purposes.

Math

NCTM (Measurement) Understand measurable attributes of objects and the units, systems, and processes of measurement.

NCTM (Measurement) Apply appropriate techniques, tools, and formulas to determine measurements.

UNIT 4 Portfolio Project

Part 2: Create a Certificate of Excellence

LEVEL This is an intermediate level project.

Goal At the start of the town meeting, the president of the Town Council will recognize students who volunteered their time in town.

Create Pretend three of your classmates will be given certificates of excellence. Use the data file **Certificate.pptx** to create the certificates:

- Use **Design>Colors** to change the color of the border.
- Select the image and use **Picture Tools>Format** to add Picture Effects.
- Use **Home>New Slide drop down arrow>Duplicate Select Slides** to duplicate the **Certificate** slide for each classmate.

Tailor a certificate for each of the three classmates you selected. Certificates should include each student's name and the current date. You should also include your town's name. Add the name of any specific projects for which your classmates have volunteered. Sign your name as the person presenting the certificate.

NCLB/Language Arts (NCTE 12) PowerPoint can be used for purposes other than presentations. Ask students to name other documents that could be made using PowerPoint. Answers may include Web pages, flyers, handouts, and worksheets.

Self Assess Use the Have You...? checklist to review the certificates. Proofread each slide and make any necessary edits. With your teacher's permission, print the certificates. Follow your teacher's instructions for naming the presentation and saving it in your Portfolio Folder.

When finished, proceed to Part 3.

	Have You...?
✓	Changed the color of the border
✓	Added **Picture Effects** to the image of the ribbon
✓	Duplicated the **Certificate** slide to create three slides
✓	Tailored a slide for each classmate
✓	Signed your name to each certificate
✓	Proofread and made necessary corrections
✓	Printed the slides

Writing MATTERS

Writing a Memo

As treasurer of your school's soccer club, you need to remind club members to pay their dues by a particular date. You decide to send a memo to all of the club's members.

How Memos Are Used

A memo (or memorandum) is an informal communication. Memos share information quickly within an organization. Memos usually provide information, make a request, or suggest a change.

Identify Memo Content

A memo's heading usually contains the following guide words:

- TO: (the main person or people receiving the memo)
- FROM: (the person sending the memo)
- CC: (the other people receiving a copy of the memo)
- DATE: (the date the memo was sent)
- SUBJECT: (the memo's subject or topic)

The body of the memo contains the information being distributed. Unlike a business letter, a memo does not have a salutation or a close. The writer's initials and an enclosure notation are sometimes included after the body of the memo.

Create Memo Content

Memos are usually short and to the point. In a memo, identify:

1. Who should receive the memo.
2. What the reader needs to know, and why.
3. Any important time or date requirements.

Key a memo when you need to provide information to others quickly.

NCLB/Language Arts (NCTE 5) Discuss with students how a memo compares to e-mail. Both are brief communications, but they may be used for different purposes. Ask students to consider a situation in which they might want to send a memo and a situation in which they might send an e-mail.

NCLB/Language Arts (NCTE 12) Reinforce to students that a memo is not always the best way to communicate. Sometimes a presentation or meeting may be more effective, as the audience must listen instead of read.

SKILLBUILDER

1. **Identify** What is a memo?
2. **Summarize** What five guide words do most memos contain, and what does each guide word indicate?
3. **Evaluate** Why are memos a useful communication tool for most businesses?

SkillBuilder answers can be found on page TM57.

UNIT 4 Portfolio Project

Planning a Town Recreation Center

You are a volunteer for your Town Council which recently hired a planner to help stimulate economic growth. Benefits of growth include higher-quality jobs and the construction of more schools, parks, homes, and roads. The planner has asked you to organize a town meeting to discuss how to increase business from teens.

Answers Rubrics for each part of the Portfolio Project are available at **glencoe.com**. You may want to download the rubrics and make them available to students as they complete each project.

Part 1: Create a Slide

LEVEL This is a beginning level project.

Goal Your first task is to generate interest in the upcoming town meeting. Teens will be invited to offer their ideas about businesses they would like to see in town. You decide to create a flyer to attract their interest.

Create Create a single-slide presentation which you will print and use as a flyer that informs teens of the town meeting. Change the orientation to **Portrait**. Apply a Theme and include a title to catch teens' interest. Make it clear that this is an opportunity to meet the planner and offer ideas directly to her. Also include a description of what the meeting is about, as well as the meeting's location, date, and time. Note that attendees will be limited to five minutes to present their ideas.

Self Assess Use the Have You...? checklist to review your slide. Then print and proofread your flyer and make necessary corrections. Follow your teacher's instructions for naming the flyer and saving it in your Portfolio Folder.

When finished, proceed to Part 2.

	Have You...?
✓	Changed the orientation to Portrait
✓	Selected an appropriate theme
✓	Selected a theme that is readable when printed
✓	Included a title to capture teens' attention
✓	Included a description
✓	Included location, date, and time information
✓	Included a note about a time limit

Writing MATTERS

Formatting a Memo

Although a memo is an informal communication, it still uses a specific format. You can format your own document or use a memo template, which is a pre-formatted document available in Word. Even when using a template, be sure to format the memo correctly.

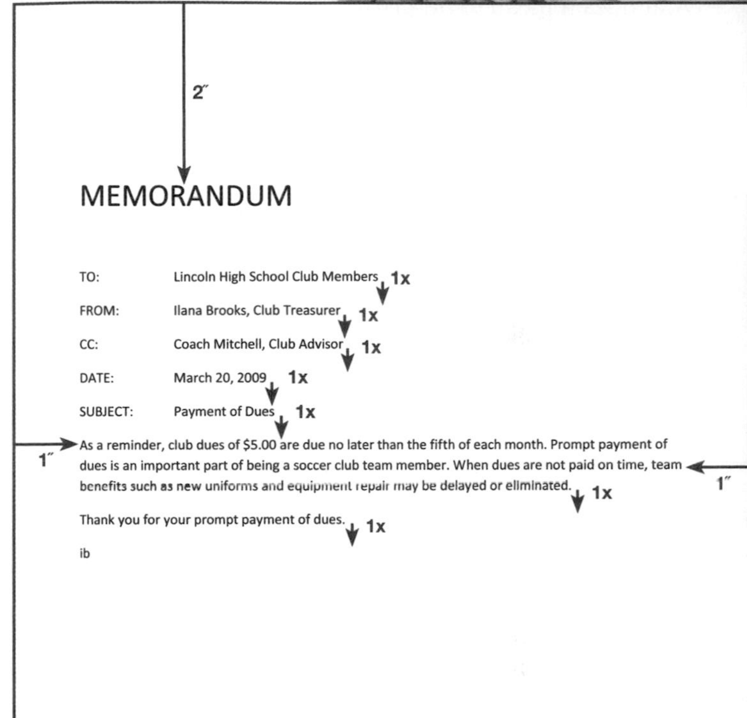

Be careful about spacing when formatting a memo.

NCLB/Language Arts (NCTE 4) Compare various types of business documents, including letters, memos, and formal reports. Explain to students that memos are used for efficient communication since they require less formatting than a formal letter. Business letters require more formatting, and reports are far more extensive.

Parts of a Memo

A memo has three main parts:

- A heading that contains the memo's guide words.
- A body that contains the information being shared.
- A closing that can contain the writer's initials and enclosure information.

The figure to the right indicates how many spaces should be included between each part.

Formatting Guidelines

Word 2007 makes it easy to format a memo:

1. Use a 2″ top margin and 1″ margins for left and right margins. If the memo is very short, you might reset the margins to 1.25″.
2. Press ENTER between each line in the heading.
3. Press ENTER after the last guide word to begin writing the content.
4. Press ENTER after every paragraph.
5. Insert the initials of the writer or person who keyed it.
6. Press ENTER after the initials if there are any other notations (such as an enclosure or distribution list).

SKILLBUILDER

1. **Summarize** What are the three main parts of a memo?
2. **Evaluate** Why is it important to follow a consistent format for a memo?
3. **Write** You are part of a group of students working on a report for your history class. Key a memo to the other members of your group informing them of the deadlines for completing their portion of the report.

SkillBuilder answers can be found on page TM57.

Citizenship

What does it mean to be a citizen? According to early U.S. President Theodore Roosevelt, "The first requisite of a good citizen in this Republic of ours is that he shall be able and willing to pull his own weight." For Roosevelt, good citizens are people willing to work hard to support themselves and to help their community.

You could also describe a citizen as a person in a nation who is entitled to its protection and its privileges. Citizenship involves putting those privileges into action. For example, in the United States, if you are 18 years or older, you have the privilege and right to vote.

Getting Involved

Instead of sitting back and letting things happen, involved citizens participate in the decision-making process. They take part in debate, exercise their rights, and try to bring about change. They speak out when they agree or disagree with something. Margaret Mead, a famous American anthropologist, author, and environmentalist, once wrote "Never doubt that a small group of thoughtful, committed citizens can change the world; indeed, it's the only thing that ever has."

Consider ways to get involved at your school or in your community. For example, you could support your sports teams, sing in a chorus, or help with a school play. You could volunteer to be an after-school tutor. You could run for class office, or simply make your voice heard by voting for class officers.

In your community, you could participate in town meetings, volunteer at the library or a soup kitchen, or write a letter to your congressional representative. You can do so much as a citizen. Take action and get involved!

CASE STUDY

Your class is about to elect a class president. One candidate is popular, but seems to be interested only in having the title of class president. Another candidate is bright and active, but you do not agree with what she wants to accomplish. A third candidate has expressed values that agree with yours, but he does not strike you as a person who can get things done. You want your vote to count but you do not know which candidate you should vote for.

See page TM88 for answers to You Decide and Application Activity.

YOU DECIDE

1. **Identify** What is one thing that an involved citizen does?
2. **Evaluate** Make a list of advantages and disadvantages of each candidate in the case study above. Which candidate would you vote for? Explain your reasons.

APPLICATION ACTIVITY

3. **Create a Presentation** You have decided to run for class president. Create a presentation explaining why you think you are the best candidate for the job. Use your proactive attitude toward citizenship to support your candidacy.

Step-By-Step

1. Start **Word**. Turn on **Show/Hide** ¶ [¶].
2. Locate and open the data file **Schedule_Memo**. Save as: Schedule_Memo-[your first initial and last name] (for example, *Schedule_Memo-sbryant*).
3. In the **View** tab, **Show/Hide** group, check **Ruler**. The ruler appears.
4. Choose **Page Layout>Page Setup>Dialog Box Launcher** [↘]. (see Figure 2.1).
5. In the **Page Setup** dialog box, under **Margins**, use the arrows to change the **Top** to **2″**.
6. Confirm the **Left** and **Right** margins are set to the default **1″**.
7. **CHECK** Your dialog box should look like Figure 2.2. Click **OK**. Save your file.

Continue to the next exercise.

Academic Skills

Take out a sheet of paper and a ruler. Measure and draw 1″ margins on all sides. This margin will match your computer screens.

EXERCISE 2-1
Set Margins

In this exercise, you will set the margins for a **memo** (an informal note sent to a group of people, usually within an office or organization). A **margin** measures the distance from the edge of the page to the text. Word contains automatic, or default, margin settings of 1″ at the top and bottom of the page, and 1″ for the left and right margins. You can change these margins if a document such as a memo must have different settings.

Differentiated Instruction/Visually Impaired Students with visual impairments can enlarge a document by using the Zoom tool.

FIGURE 2.1 Existing document

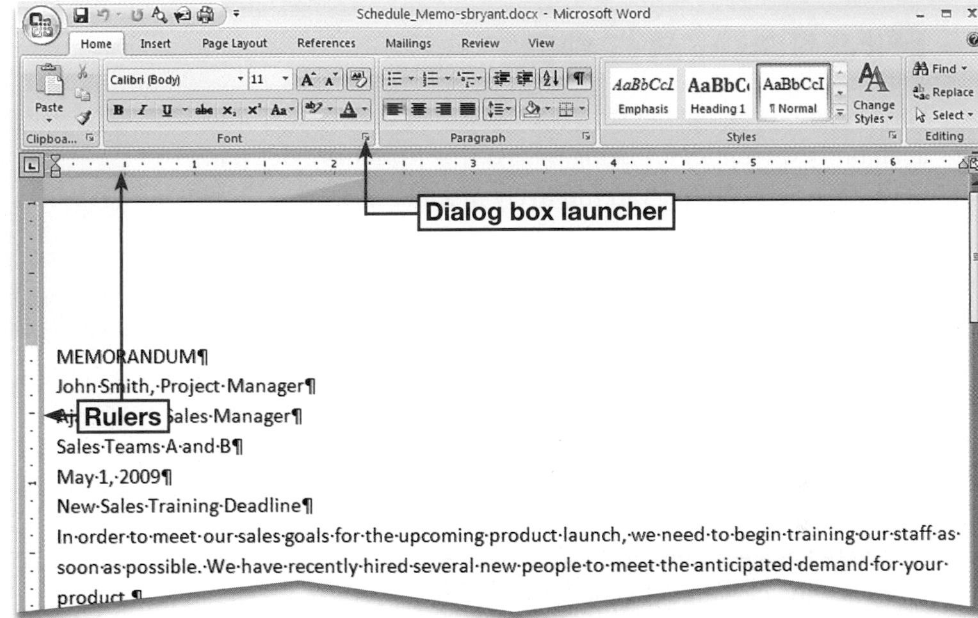

FIGURE 2.2 Page Setup dialog box

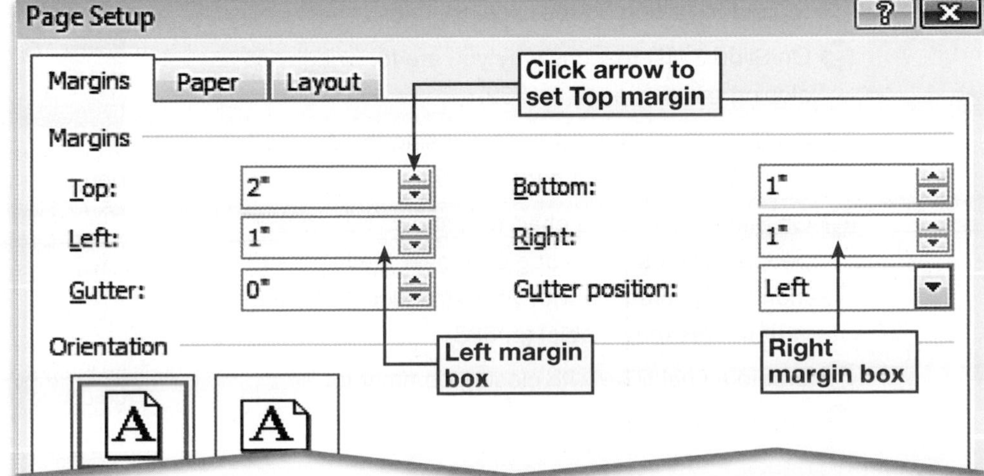

NCLB/Math (Measurement) Student drawings should have 1″ margins.

In this activity, you will create a presentation in which you support a specific point of view. Rubric

Create a Town Hall Presentation

You live in a town that has strict leash laws. Pets must be on leashes at all times when they are being walked. The town has a dog park, however, where your pet can run freely in a fenced area.

Recently, some townspeople have argued that the town should close the dog park and create a monument park in its place. Residents can voice their opinions about this proposal at a town meeting. This is your only chance to be heard. Create a PowerPoint presentation for or against the closing of the dog park.

1. Create a new presentation. (p. 571)
2. Apply a **Theme** to your presentation. (p. 571)
3. Create a **Title** slide that clearly supports or opposes the closing of the dog park. (p. 571)
4. On Slide 2, introduce yourself and your dog. If necessary, pretend you own a dog. Include a picture or photograph of a dog on the slide. (p. 586)
5. On Slide 3, list reasons why you are for or against closing the dog park. (p. 552)
6. On Slide 4, list alternatives to closing the dog park or building a monument park. (p. 552)
7. On Slide 5, include a chart that shows how many people have used the dog park over the last four months. Be creative with your statistics, but make your figures reasonable! (p. 583)
8. Create a final slide with closing comments.
9. Add transitions between slides. (p. 622)

NCLB/Language Arts (NCTE 5) Tell students to consider the possible opposing arguments that people may make. Students should anticipate the reactions and be prepared to respond.

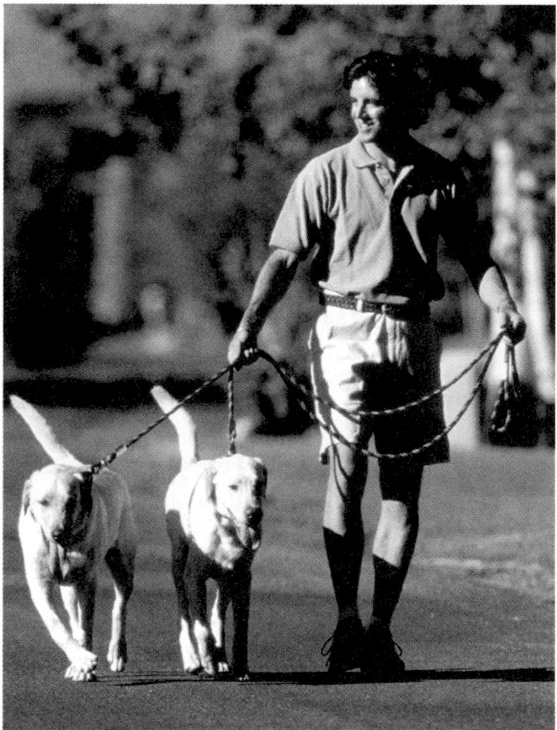

You can use a PowerPoint presentation to let people know your opinion about a topic, such as whether your town needs a dog park.

NCLB/Language Arts (NCTE 12) Set up a mock town hall meeting in your class. Divide students up into groups. One group should pretend to be dog owners who support the dog park. One group should be opposed to the dog park. The final group should be supporters of the monument park. Allow time for groups to brainstorm before they present their cases.

Answer to Academic Connections Go to the Online Learning Center at **glencoe.com** to access the rubric for this activity. If students need help remembering how to complete specific skills, have them turn to the page number listed after selected steps.

Step-By-Step

1. In your **Schedule_Memo** file, select the first five lines of text under **MEMORANDUM**.
2. In the **Home** tab, click the **Paragraph** group **Dialog Box Launcher**.
3. At the bottom of the **Paragraph** dialog box, click the **Tabs** button.
4. In the **Tabs** dialog box, under **Tab stop position**, key: 1″ (see Figure 2.3).
5. Under **Alignment**, make sure **Left** is selected. Under **Leader**, make sure **1 None** is selected. Click **Set**. Click **OK**.
6. Click anywhere in the document to deselect the text. Press CAPS LOCK.
7. Click before the text **John Smith**. Key: MEMO TO:. Press TAB.
8. Repeat Step 7 to key and position the guide words FROM:, CC:, DATE:, and SUBJECT:. Press CAPS LOCK to deselect it.
9. CHECK Your screen should look like Figure 2.4. Select **View>Show/Hide** and click **Ruler** to deactivate the ruler.

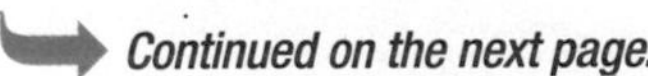
Continued on the next page.

EXERCISE 2-2
Set Tab Stops

A **tab stop** is a marker on the horizontal, or left-to-right, ruler that shows where the insertion point will jump to when you press the Tab key. Word has default tab stops every half inch along the ruler. Tab stops can help you to correctly format the heading of a memo.

FIGURE 2.3 Tabs dialog box

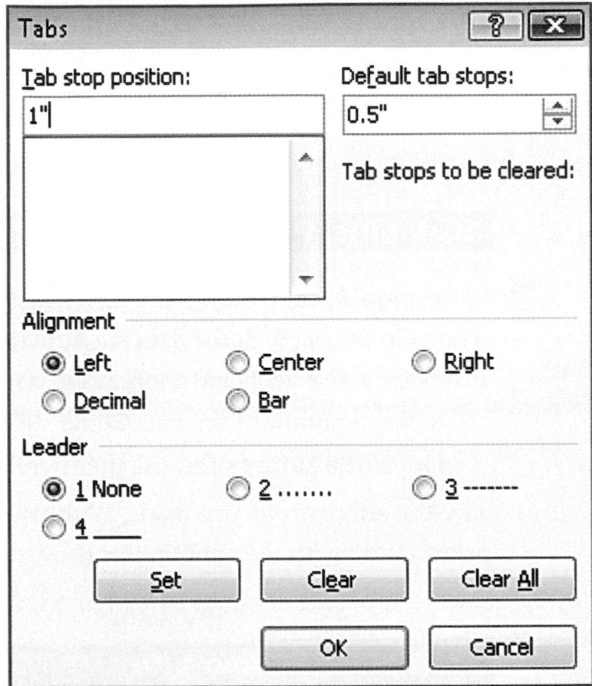

FIGURE 2.4 Memo heading with new tab stop

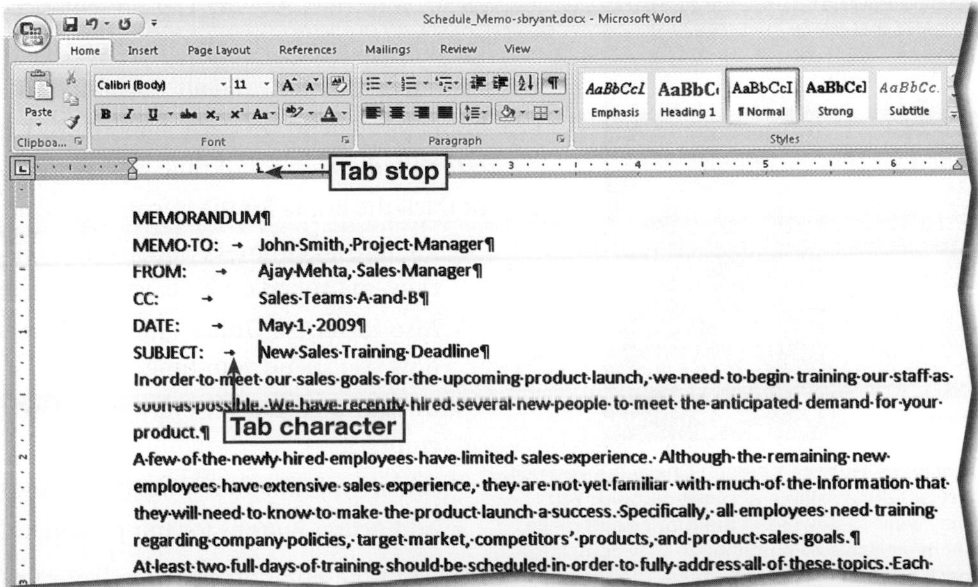

LESSON 4 Challenge Yourself Projects

Before You Begin

Manage Your Time
Learning how to manage your time is an essential skill. Look at how you currently spend your time and figure out how you can rearrange your schedule to accomplish your goals.

Reflect Once you complete the projects, open a Word document and answer the following:

1. Which activities take up the majority of your time?
2. Which activities do you wish you had more time to for? Which do you feel you could spend less time doing?
3. How can budgeting your time help you meet more of your goals?

Answers Rubrics for each Challenge Yourself Project are available at **glencoe.com**. You may want to download the rubrics and make them available to students as they complete each project.

9. Add Finishing Touches

Data File Rubric

LEVEL This is an intermediate level project.

Language Arts: Deliver a Custom Presentation Use the presentation you created in Project 9, or the data file **Activities.pptx**, to create a custom presentation. Only include the **Title**, **Summary**, and **Goals** slide. Create a new slide for your presentation that lists all the categories of activities you tracked. In your presentation, add a hyperlink to a new document or to a Web page. Show the slide show to a classmate. When you are finished, package the presentation for a CD.

Save your presentation as: p4rev-[your first initial and last name]9.

10. Lights, PowerPoint, Action!

Data File Rubric

LEVEL This is an intermediate level project.

Language Arts: Deliver a Presentation Using the presentation you created in Project 9, or the data file **Activities.pptx**, show the slide show to a classmate. Use keyboard shortcuts to navigate through the show.

- Make annotations on your **Goals** slide using the Felt Tip Pen.
- On the **Saturday** slide, use the Highlighter.

Save the annotations you made. With your teacher's permission, print the presentation with the annotations showing.

Save your presentation as: p4rev-[your first initial and last name]10.

11. A Week in Your Life

Data File Rubric

LEVEL This is an advanced level project.

Math: Create a Pie Chart Using the data file **Activities.pptx** as a model, create your own Activity Log presentation. Your activity categories should include homework, television, phone time, sports and after-school activities, volunteer activities, and after-school or weekend jobs. Track the number of hours you spend on each activity every day of the week. You can either estimate the amount of time you spent on each activity the previous week, or track the hours for the upcoming week. In your presentation:

- Include a **Summary** slide with a pie chart that illustrates how much time you spend on each activity during one week.
- Also include a **Goals** slide that lists three ways you intend to modify how you spend your time.
- Include a graphic in every slide. Use the grid feature to position your graphics.
- Add a hyperlink from one slide to another slide in the presentation.
- Add Action Buttons to your presentation.

Save your presentation as: p4rev-[your first initial and last name]11.

Step-By-Step

10 Click after the title **MEMORANDUM**. Press ENTER twice.

11 At the end of the first line, click after the words **John Smith, Project Manager**. Press ENTER.

12 Click at the end of the second line. Press ENTER. Repeat this step for the third and fourth lines.

13 Click at the end of the fifth line. Press ENTER once.

14 At the end of the first paragraph, click after the word **product**. Press ENTER.

15 At the end of the second paragraph, click after the word **goals**. Press ENTER.

16 At the end of the third paragraph, click after the word **appropriate**. Press ENTER. Click after the word **problem** in the last paragraph. Press ENTER.

17 CHECK Your memo should look similar to Figure 2.5. Save your file.

Continue to the next exercise.

Teaching Tip Ask students to compare FROM:, CC:, DATE:, and RE: to the header information contained in an e-mail or on the title page of a report. How is this information similar or different in various documents?

Solution Use the file **Schedule_ Memo-SF.docx** as a solution file for Exercises 2-1 through 2-2.

EXERCISE 2-2 (Continued)
Set Tab Stops

FIGURE 2.5 Memo with correct margins, spacing, and heading

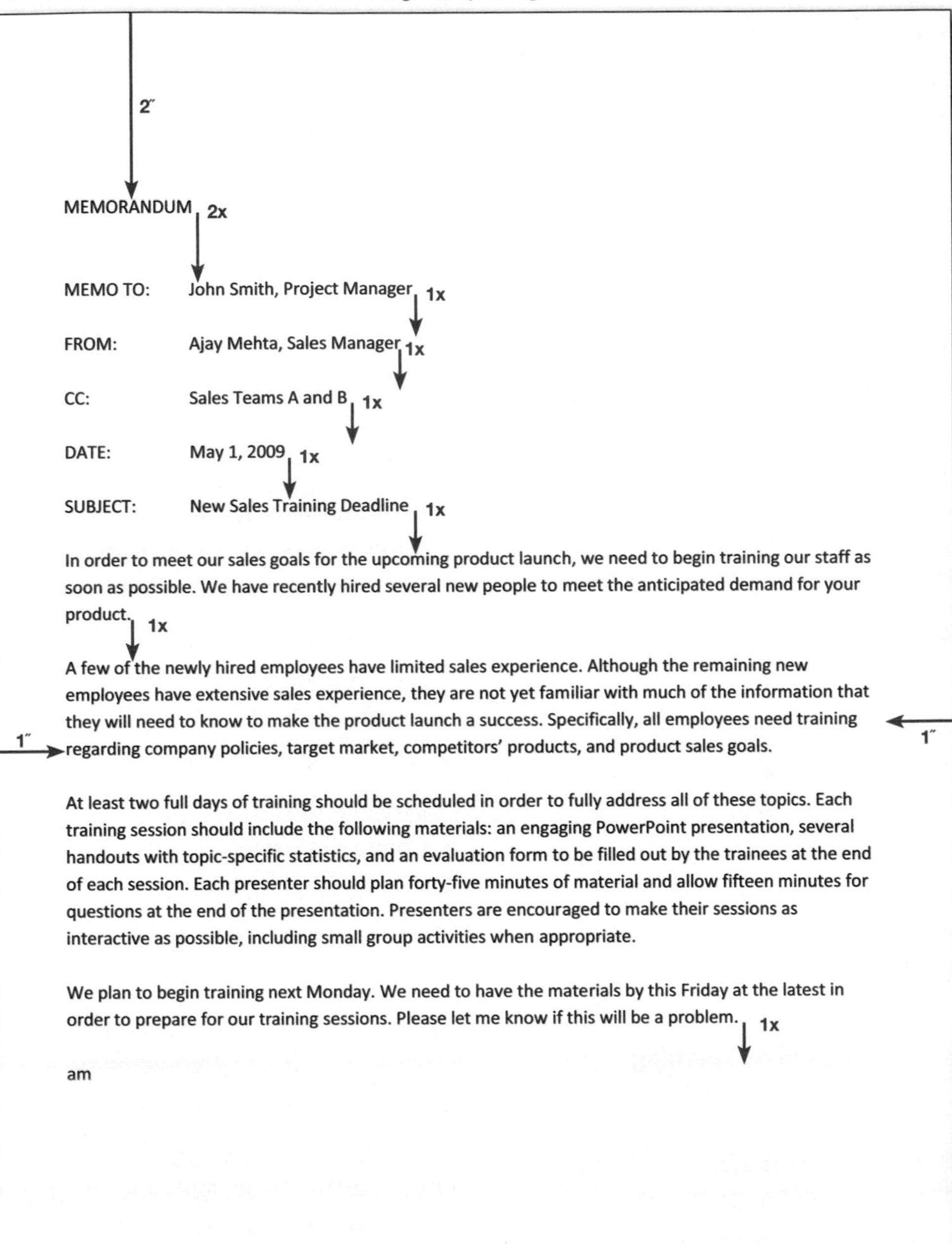

EL Make sure EL students understand what the ″ (inch) symbol represents.

LESSON 4 Critical Thinking Activities

NCLB/Language Arts (NCTE 5) Students should understand that they need to consider their audience as they create presentations. Make certain that the presentation and all of its elements are accessible to their audience.

Beyond the Classroom Activity Students should customize the data file so it is appropriate for an audience of potential clients. Students should use grids and guides to position the graphic on the title slide and add an Action button to the presentation.

Standards at Work Activity Students practice delivering the **Publicity** slide show. Students should add appropriate timings to the slide show. They should use the felt tip pen and highlighter to make annotations. Students should write notes for the presentation in the **Notes** pane.

21st Century Skills Activity Student presentations will vary, but should be consistent with the assignment.

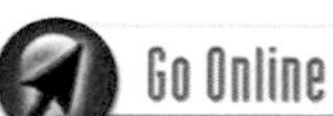

Go Online **e-REVIEW**

glencoe.com

Go to the **Online Learning Center** to complete the following review activities.

Online Self Check
To test your knowledge of the material click **Unit 4> Lesson 4** and choose **Self Checks**.

Interactive Review
To review the main points of this lesson, click **Unit 4> Lesson 4** and choose **Interactive Review**.

6. Beyond the Classroom Activity

Language Arts: Create a Custom Show for a Specific Audience You have started your own lawn-mowing business. When you started your business, you created a PowerPoint presentation to recruit employees. You now want to give the presentation to recruit new clients. Open the data file **Mow.pptx**.

Create a Custom Show directed to potential clients.

- Only display the slides that are relevant to customers.
- Use grids and guides to line up the graphic on the title slide.
- Add an Action Button to the presentation.

Save your presentation as: Mow-[your first initial and last name]6.

7. Standards at Work Activity

Microsoft Certified Application Specialist Correlation
PowerPoint 4.5 *Prepare and Rehearse Presentation Delivery*

Use Presentation Tools You are a spokesperson for the Reading Reach literacy organization. You need to practice delivering the presentation contained on the data file **Publicity.pptx**. Open the data file and:

- Practice using the felt tip pen and highlighter to emphasize points.
- Rehearse and set timings.
- Copy a slide from the **Literacy** presentation to the **Publicity** presentation.
- Add notes to the Notes pane.
- Print the notes page, as well as an an outline of the presentation.

Save your file as: Publicity-[your first initial and last name]7.

8. 21st Century Skills Activity

Show Initiative Create a 5- to 7-slide PowerPoint presentation about a person who took initiative and changed a situation for the better. You can choose a historical person, a public figure, someone from your family or community, or yourself. Give examples of how initiative was taken and explain what might have happened if nobody had taken the lead.

- Select an appropriate audience for your presentation.
- Run the Compatibility Checker.
- Address any issues that will not work in a previous version of PowerPoint.
- Save your file to run as a slide show (.pps).

Save your file as: p4rev-[your first initial and last name]8.pps.

Step-By-Step

1. Open the data file **Memo**. Save as: Memo-[your first initial and last name] (for example, *Memo-sbryant*).

2. Choose **Home>Editing> Select**. Click **Select All**.

3. In the **Home** tab, click the **Font** group **Dialog Box Launcher**. In the **Font** dialog box, click the **Font** tab.

4. In the **Font** box, scroll down and click **Calibri**. In the **Size** box, click **11**.

5. **CHECK** Your dialog box should look like Figure 2.6. Click **OK**. Deselect the text.

6. Select the text **Memorandum**. In the **Font** group, click the **Font Size** drop-down arrow. Click **24**. Deselect the text.

7. **CHECK** Your screen should look like Figure 2.7. Save your file.

Continue to the next exercise.

Tech Tip

In standard fonts, one point equals 1/72 of an inch.

NCLB/Math (Measurement) Ask students to compare point size with another unit of measurement, such as inches or centimeters.

EXERCISE 2-3
Modify Font and Size

A **character** is an individual letter, number, symbol, or punctuation mark. A **font** (also called a **typeface**) is the unique design of a set of characters. For example, the default font in Word 2007 is Calibri. Font size refers to how large or small characters are. Font size is measured in **points**. Many teachers require students to use specific fonts and font sizes in their work.

Teaching Tip Point out to students that as they run the pointer over the choices in the Font and Font Size menus, they can preview how their documents will look.

FIGURE 2.6 Font dialog box

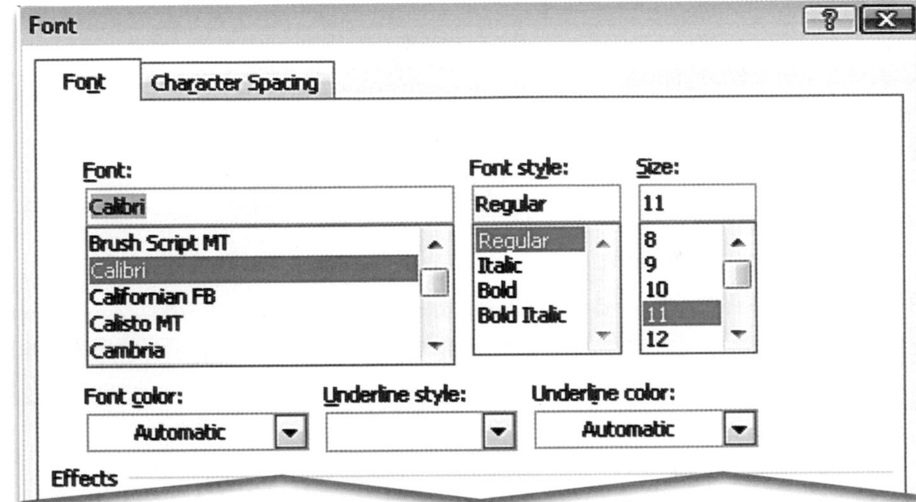

FIGURE 2.7 Memo with new font and font sizes

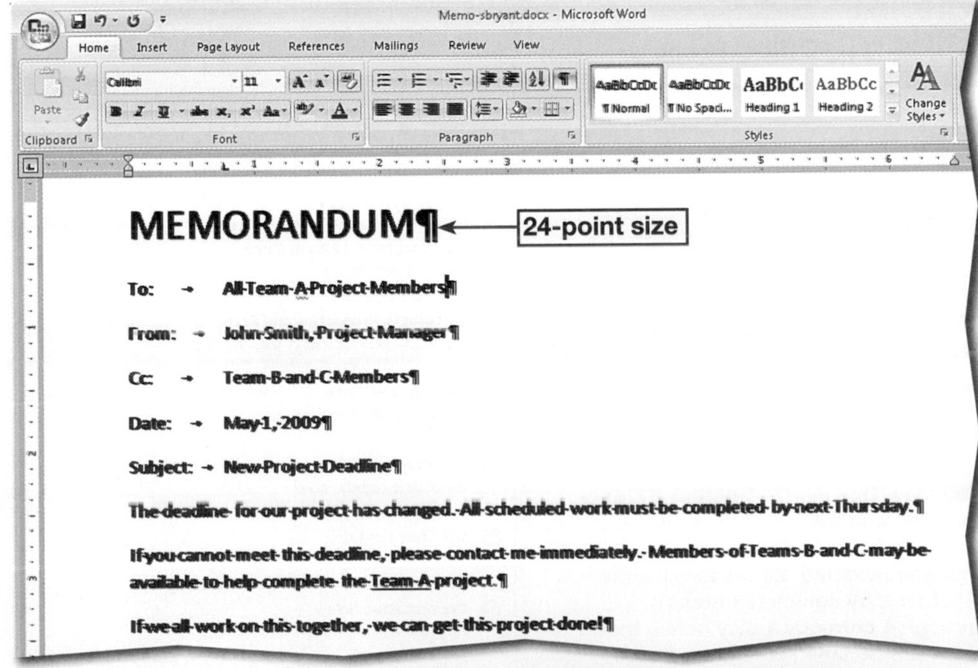

Different Strokes Students can **Select All** by using the keyboard shortcut **CTRL + A**.

LESSON 4 You Try It Activities

Step-By-Step

1. Open your **Habits-4** file. Save as: Habits-[your first initial and last name]5.
2. Create a new custom show named **Exercise**. Include **Slides 1-5**, **8**, **9**, and **11**.
3. In the **Set Up Show** dialog box, make sure the **Custom show** setting is selected.
4. Rehearse the timings for the **Exercise** slide show. Save your file.
5. **CHECK** Your screen should look similar to Figure 4.58.
6. Choose **Office>Prepare>Inspect Document**.
7. Click **Remove All** to erase the information from the file. **Reinspect** the file.
8. **CHECK** Your screen should look like Figure 4.59. Save and close your file.

Solution Use the file **Habits5-SF.pptx** as a solution file for this activity.

Troubleshooting Students will know whether they completed Steps 1 through 4 correctly if they notice that there are no time settings for Slides 6, 7, 10, and 12 (see Figure 4.58).

5. Customize a Presentation

Your teacher asked you to give your health presentation to a different audience that is interested only in the information about exercise. You must create a custom show for this audience and set the show's timings. Be sure to inspect the document to remove personal or other inappropriate information from the file.

FIGURE 4.58 Timings set for Custom Show

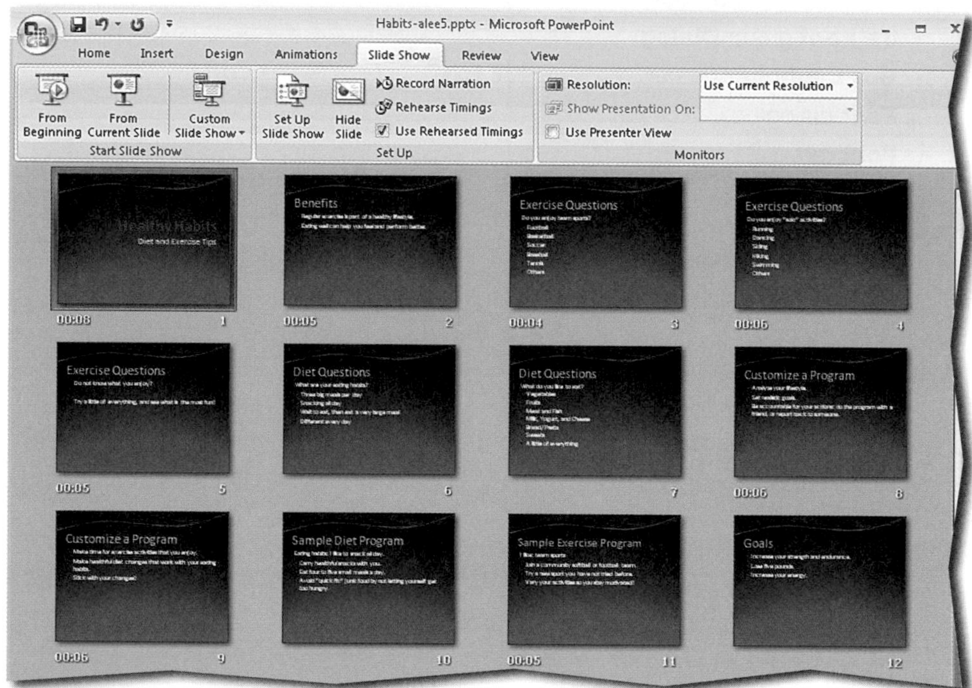

FIGURE 4.59 Document Inspector inspection results dialog box

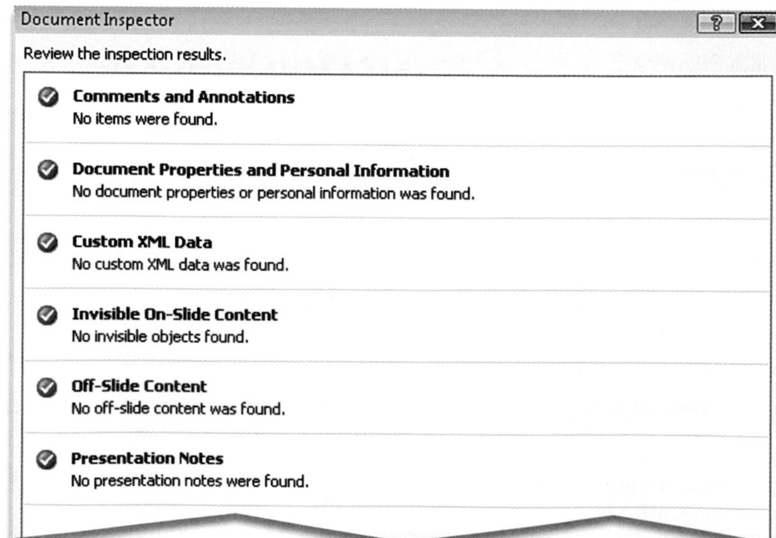
Document Inspector

Review the inspection results.

Comments and Annotations
No items were found.

Document Properties and Personal Information
No document properties or personal information was found.

Custom XML Data
No custom XML data was found.

Invisible On-Slide Content
No invisible objects found.

Off-Slide Content
No off-slide content was found.

Presentation Notes
No presentation notes were found.

Step-By-Step

1. In the first line of your **Memo** file, click before the word **To:**. Press ENTER. Double-click the word **must**.

2. In the **Mini toolbar** that appears, click **Italic** *I* (see Figure 2.8).

3. Choose **Home>Font> Underline** U. Select the word **Thursday**.

4. Click the **Font** group **Dialog Box Launcher**. In the **Font** dialog box, under **Font style**, click **Bold** **B**. Click the **Font Color** A drop-down arrow. Click **Red**. Click **OK**.

5. Select the word **completed**. In the **Font** group, click the **Font Color** drop-down arrow. Click **Red**. Deselect the text.

6. CHECK Your screen should look like Figure 2.9. Save your file.

Continue to the next exercise

Academic Skills

Do not format your document heavily. Having too much formatting can be a distraction to readers and take away from your intended goal.

EXERCISE 2-4
Modify Font Style and Color

The **font style** refers to effects such as **bold**, *italic*, and underline. You can apply these effects to words and phrases to add emphasis. A change of color can help make text stand out and can enhance a document, or make it better.

NCLB/Language Arts (NCTE 5) Show students a document that is over-formatted. Ask students to identify the problems caused by heavy formatting.

FIGURE 2.8 Use the Mini Toolbar to change font styles

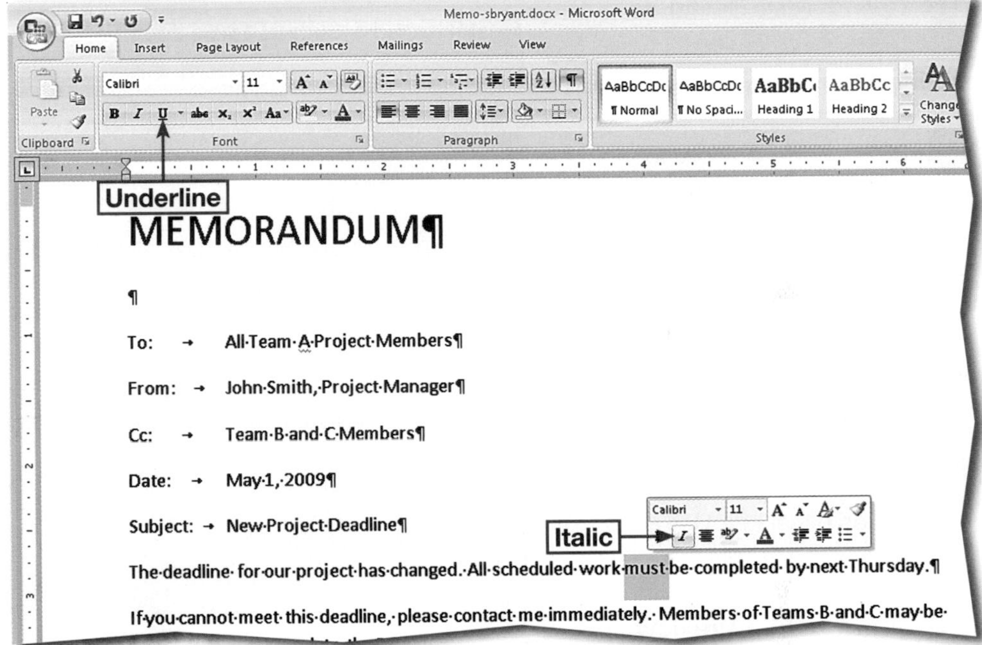

Differentiated Instruction/Visually Impaired In **Step 5**, students with colorblindness can use the mouse to see the ScreenTip that identifies each color's name.

FIGURE 2.9 Memo with styles applied to fonts

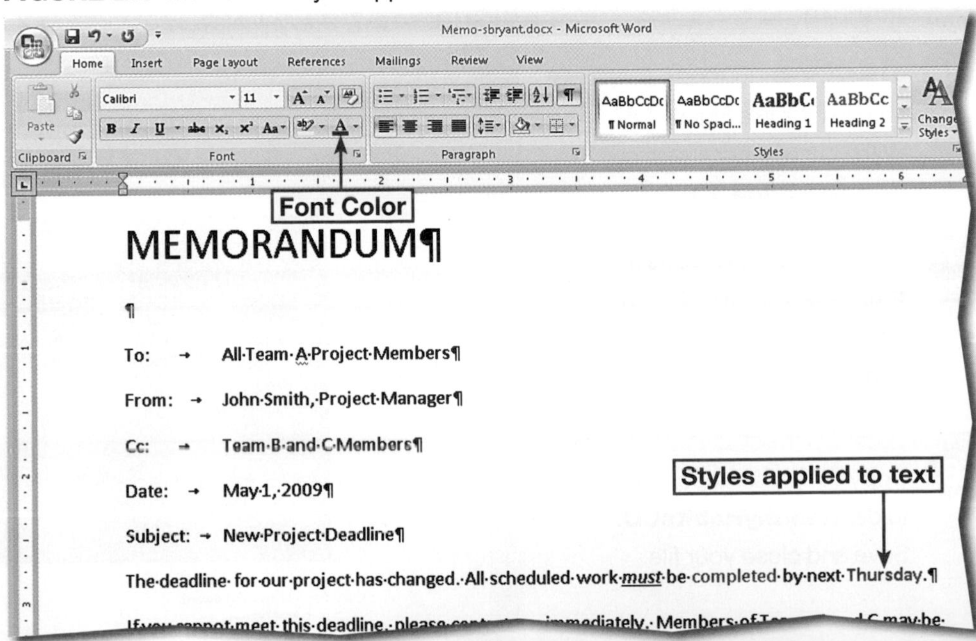

LESSON 4 You Try It Activities

Step-By-Step

1. Open the data file **Habits .pptx**. Save as: Habits-[your first initial and last name]4.
2. Delete **Slide 3**. Move to **Slide 12**. Click in the slide. Zoom in **150%**.
3. **CHECK** Your screen should look like Figure 4.56. In the **Zoom** group, click **Fit to Window**.
4. Move to **Slide 13**. In the **Notes** pane, key: Use a fun activity as a reward.
5. Switch to **Print Preview**. Under **Print What**, select **Notes Pages**. Scroll to **Slide 13**.
6. **CHECK** Your screen should look like Figure 4.57. With your teacher's permission, print **Slide 13**.
7. Choose **Office>Publish> Package for CD**. Name it **HealthyHabitsCD**. Click **Options**. Select **Embedded TrueType fonts**.
8. Copy the presentation to the folder **HealthyHabitsCD**. Save and close your file.

4. Promote Healthy Habits

Data File

For your health class, you must create a PowerPoint presentation about healthy exercise and diet habits. Your teacher has asked you to print any notes and to package your presentation as a CD.

Solution Use the file **Habits4-SF.pptx** as a solution file for this activity.

FIGURE 4.56 Slide at 150% zoom

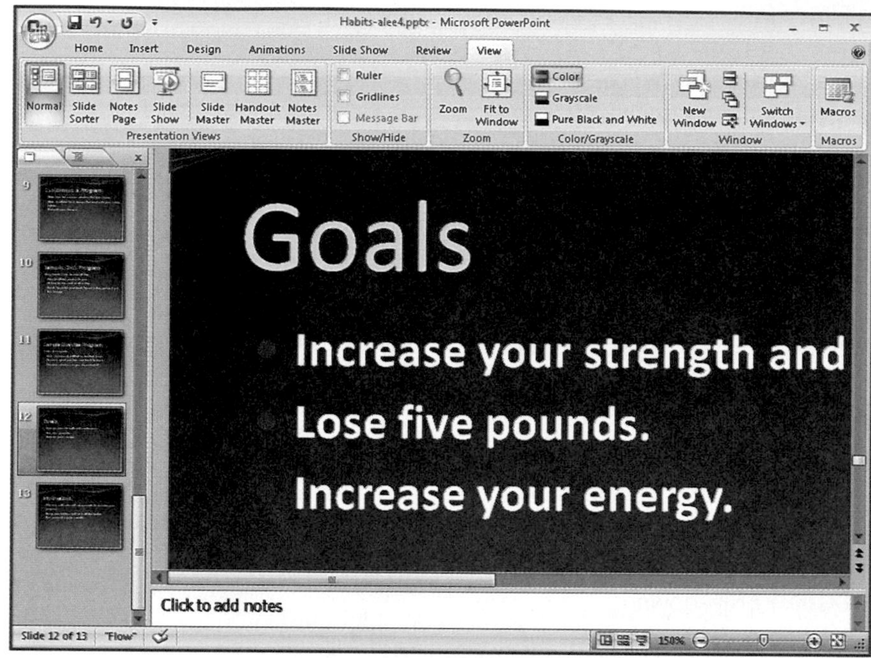

FIGURE 4.57 Preview of Notes page

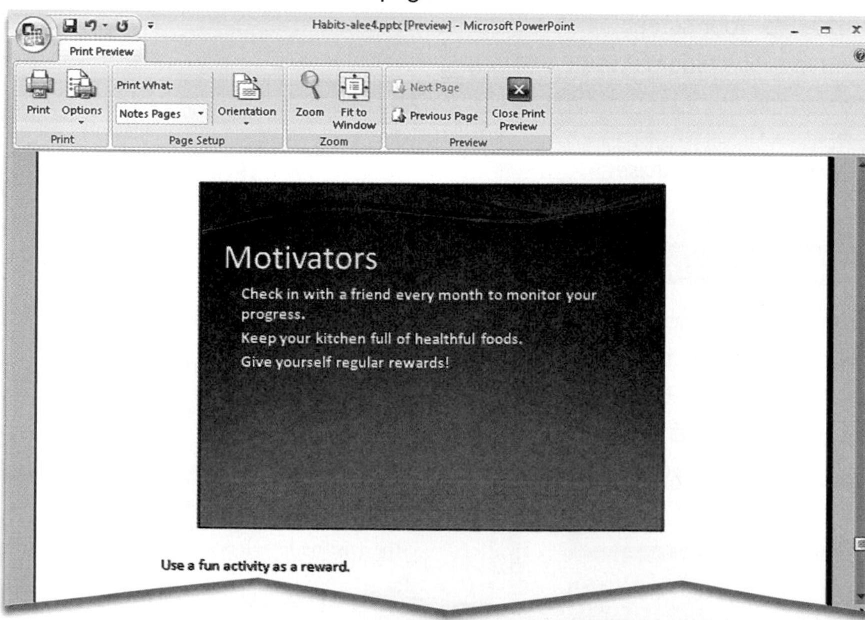

Step-By-Step

1. In your **Memo** file, in the first paragraph, select the word **completed**. Click **Bold** **B**.

2. In the second paragraph, select the word **immediately**.

3. Choose **Home>Styles>Dialog Box Launcher**.

4. In the **Styles** pane, click **Calibri, Bold, Red** (see Figure 2.10). Close the **Styles** pane. Deselect the text.

5. In the first paragraph, select the word **completed** again. Choose **Home>Styles>Dialog Box Launcher**.

6. In the **Styles** pane, click **Clear All**. Close the **Styles** pane. Deselect the text.

7. **CHECK** Your screen should look like Figure 2.11. Save your file.

Continue to the next exercise.

Shortcuts

To apply bold, italic, and underline, you can use the keyboard shortcuts CTRL + B, CTRL + I, and CTRL + U.

EXERCISE 2-5
Apply and Clear Styles from Text

Formatting is the overall look of a document, including the individual characters, paragraphs, and pages. You can use the Styles pane to apply, create, or delete a **style**, which is a defined formatting characteristic.

FIGURE 2.10 Apply the style listed in the Styles pane

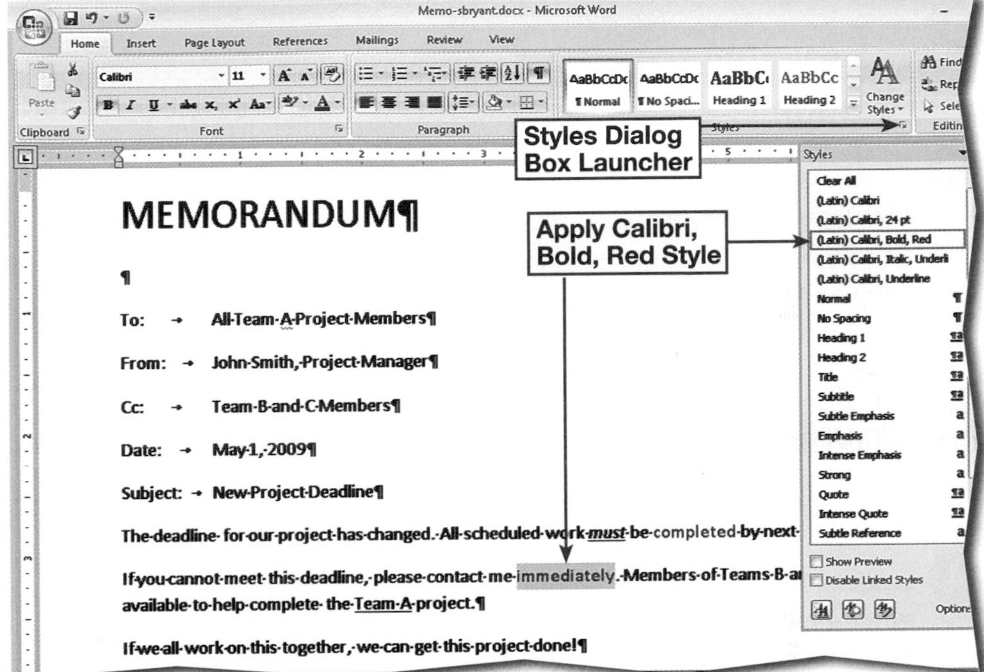

FIGURE 2.11 Styles applied to and cleared from text

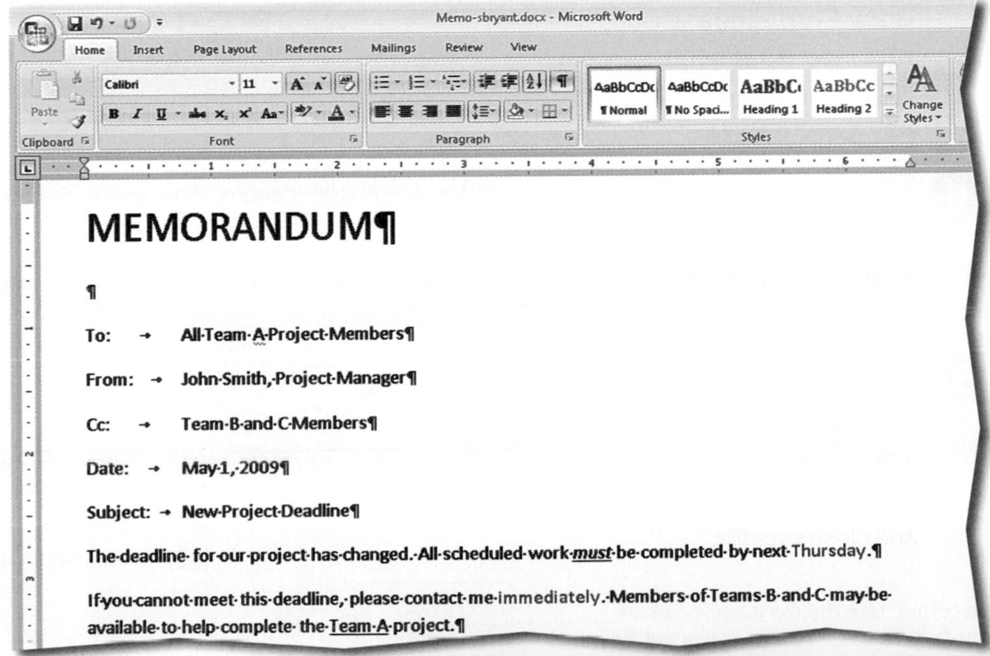

LESSON 4 Practice It Activities

3. Save Files in Different Formats and Print Presentation Items

Follow the steps to complete the activity. You must complete Practice It Activity 2 before doing this activity.

New Student Strategy Students just entering the class can use **Activities2-SF.pptx** as the data file for this activity.

Step-By-Step

1. Open your **Activities-2** file. Save as: Activities-[your first initial and last name]3.
2. Choose **Office>Save As.** Click **New Folder**. Key: Activities Presentation. Under **Save as type**, click **PowerPoint 97-2003 Show**.
3. **CHECK** Your dialog box should look like Figure 4.54. Click **Save**.
4. In the **Microsoft Office PowerPoint Compatibility Checker**, click **Continue**.
5. Choose **Office>Print.** Under **Print range**, select **All**. Under **Print what**, select **Handouts**. In **Slides per page**, select **6**.
6. Select **Scale to fit paper**, **Frame slides**, and **Print comments and ink markup**.
7. **CHECK** Your dialog box should look like Figure 4.55. With your teacher's permission, click **OK**. Save and close your file.

Solution Use the file **Activities3-SF.pptx** as a solution file for this activity.

FIGURE 4.54 Save As dialog box

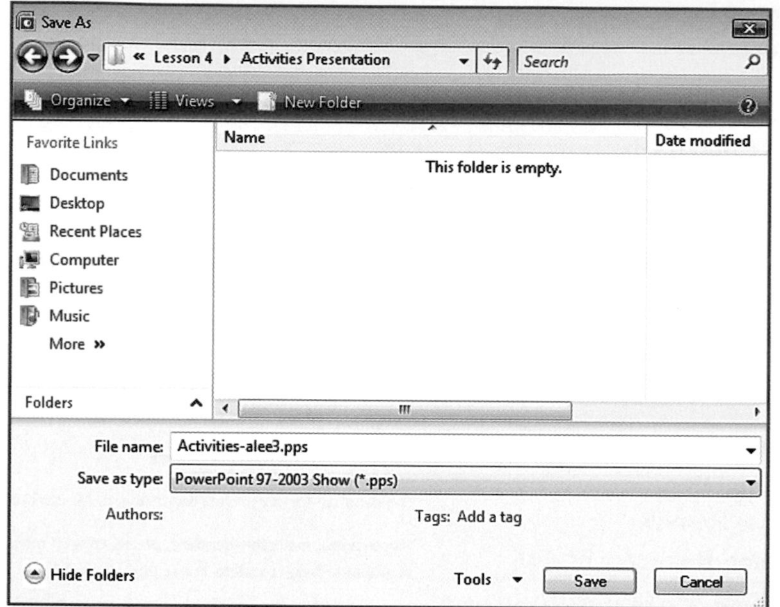

FIGURE 4.55 Print dialog box

Print range
All
Current slide
Selection
Custom Show:
Slides:
Enter slide numbers and/or slide ranges. For example, 1,3,5-12
Number of copies:
1
Collate
Print what:
Handouts
Color/grayscale:
Color
Handouts
Slides per page: 6
Order: Horizontal Vertical
Scale to fit paper
Frame slides
Print comments and ink markup
Print hidden slides
High quality
Preview
OK
Cancel

Step-By-Step

1. In your **Memo** file, select **To:** in the memo heading. Select **Home>Font> Change Case** [Aa].

2. In the **Change Case** drop-down menu, click **UPPERCASE**. With **TO:** still selected, click **Bold** [B]. Deselect the text.

3. **CHECK** Your screen should look like Figure 2.12. Select **TO**: again. On the **Home** tab, in the **Clipboard** group, click **Format Painter**.

4. In the memo heading, with **TO**: still selected, select **From:**. The formatting is applied.

5. With **FROM:** still selected, double-click **Format Painter**. Select the following: **Cc:**, **Date:**, and **Subject:**. Click **Format Painter** to turn it off. Deselect the text.

6. **CHECK** Your screen should look like Figure 2.13. Save your file.

Continue to the next exercise.

Step-By-Step Tip In **Step 5**, point out to students that they must first select the text with the style that they want to copy before clicking **Format Painter**.

Troubleshooting In **Step 5**, if the **Format Painter** does not change the letters to uppercase, instruct the students to highlight the word and use the Change Case button, choosing UPPERCASE.

EXERCISE 2-6
Change Font Case and Use Format Painter

The **Format Painter** is a tool that allows you to copy multiple formats from one part of a document to another. For example, you can copy a character that is bold, red, and italic and apply all three formats to another set of characters. Clicking Format Painter changes the pointer to a small paintbrush. Click Format Painter once to copy formatting once. Double-click Format Painter to copy formatting multiple times.

FIGURE 2.12 Text with font case changed

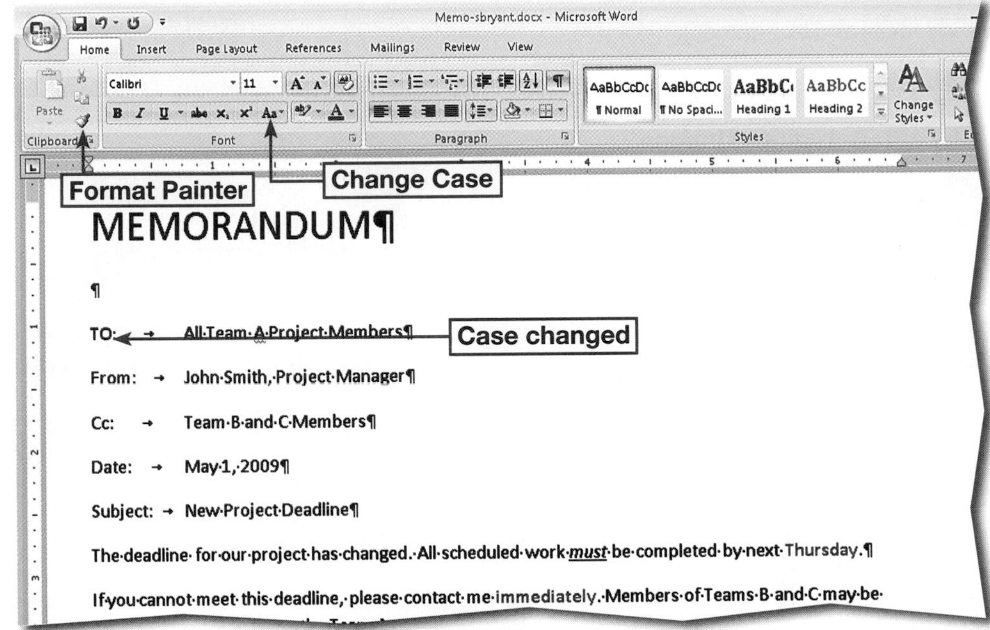

FIGURE 2.13 Format copied to more than one location

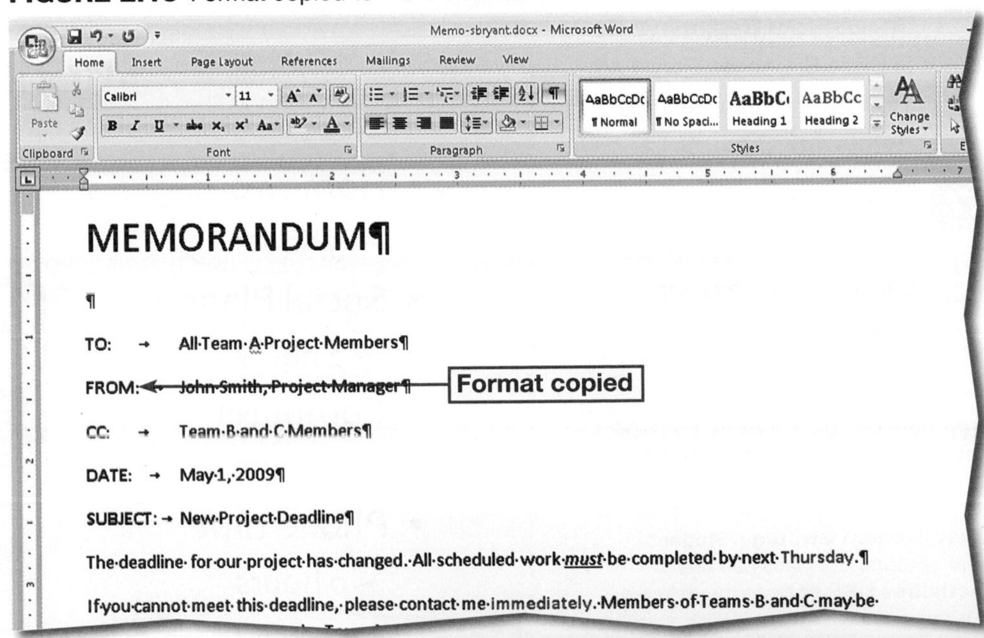

LESSON 4 Practice It Activities

Step-By-Step

1. Open your **Activities-1** file. Save as: Activities-[your first initial and last name]2.
2. Choose **Slide Show>Set Up>Rehearse Timings**.
3. Run through the slide show. Read each slide aloud before advancing to the next slide.
4. Click **Yes** to save the timings. Click **Slide 10**. Click **Hide Slide**.
5. **CHECK** Your screen should look like Figure 4.52. Click **Hide Slide** again.
6. Click **Normal View**. Choose **Slide Show>Start Slide Show>From Beginning**. Go to **Slide 8**. Choose **Pen>Felt Tip Pen**. Circle the text **Homework-5 hours**.
7. **CHECK** Your screen should look like Figure 4.53. End the show. Save and close your file.

Solution Use the file **Activities2-SF .pptx** as a solution file for this activity.

New Student Strategy Students just entering the class can use **Activities1-SF.pptx** as the data file for this activity.

2. Rehearse Timings, Hide Slides, and Use Pens

Follow the steps to complete the activity. You must complete Practice It Activity 1 before doing this activity.

FIGURE 4.52 Slide hidden in Slide Sorter View

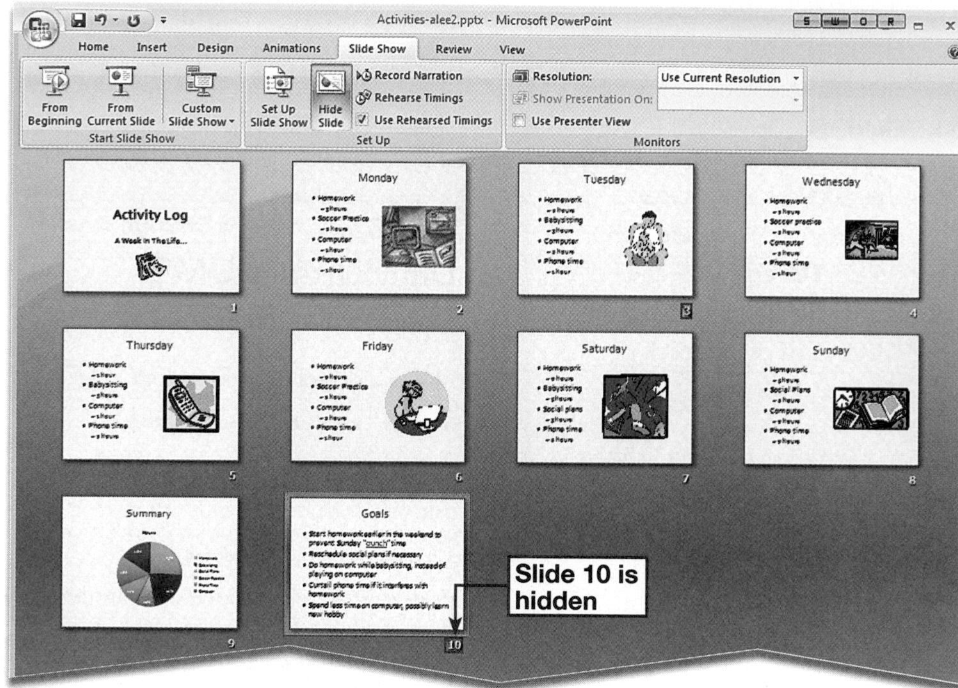

FIGURE 4.53 Slide with pen annotation

Step-By-Step

1. In your **Memo** file, in the first paragraph, delete the word **Next**. Click after **Thursday** and key: , May 28th. Select **th** in 28th.
2. Choose **Home>Font> Dialog Box Launcher**.
3. In the **Font** dialog box, under **Effects**, select **Superscript**. Click **OK**.
4. Select the text **Thursday, May 28th**.
5. In the **Font** group, click the **Text Highlight Color** drop-down arrow. Make sure **Yellow** is selected. Deselect the text.
6. CHECK Your screen should look like Figure 2.14.
7. With your teacher's permission, print the memo. Save and close your file.

Continue to the next exercise.

Academic Skills

When taking study notes, you only highlight important points. You should also be careful not to overuse Word's highlighting feature. If a whole memo is highlighted, recipients will not know where to focus.

NCLB/Language Arts (NCTE 5)

EXERCISE 2-7
Apply Character Effects and Highlighting

The Font dialog box has an Effects section that lets you apply special formatting to your characters. Some effects are also on the Ribbon. Available effects are shown in Table 2.1. Highlighting applies color behind the text to draw attention to it.

Solution Use the file **Memo-SF.docx** as a solution file for Exercises 2-3 through 2-7.

TABLE 2.1 Character Effects

Effect	Purpose
Strikethrough	Applies a ~~horizontal line~~ through text that indicates text to be deleted.
Double Strikethrough	Applies a ~~double horizontal line~~ through text that indicates text to be deleted.
Superscript	Raises text above other characters; often used to indicate footnotes and exponents.
Subscript	Places text below other characters; often used in scientific formulas.
Shadow	Applies a decorative **shadow** behind text.
Outline	Decorative element that shows the outline of selected text.
Emboss	Decorative element that makes selected text look like it is raised off the page.
Engrave	Decorative element that makes selected text look like it is **imprinted on** the page.
Small Caps	Makes all lowercase text small caps; often used for abbreviations such as B.C.
All Caps	Makes all text UPPERCASE; often used in report titles.
Hidden	Allows you to hide text that you do not want to appear on screen or in a printed document.

FIGURE 2.14 Character effect and highlighting applied to text

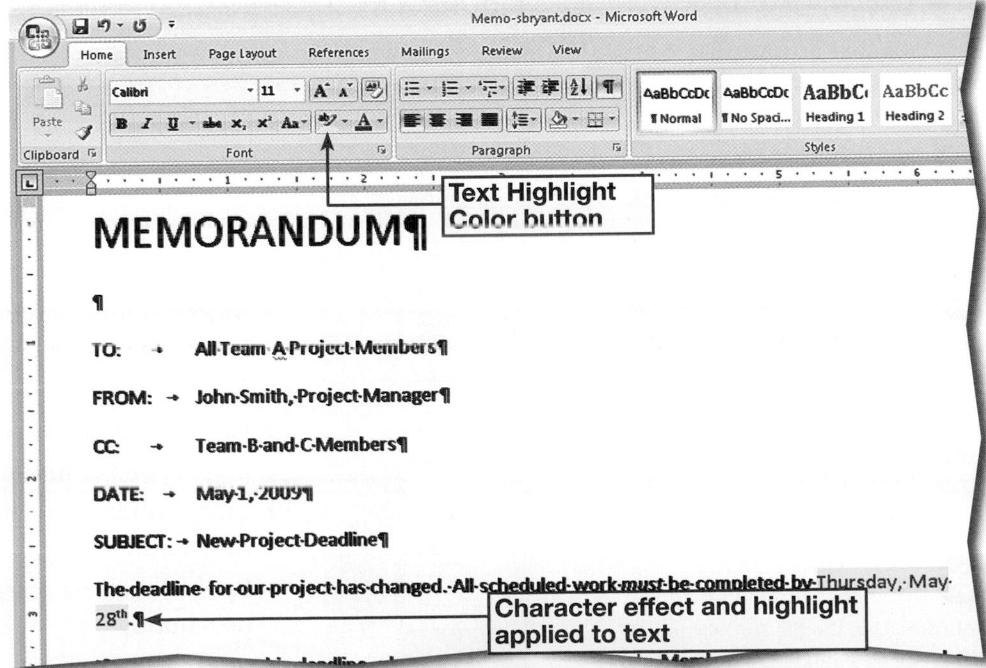

LESSON 4 Practice It Activities

Step-By-Step

1. Open the data file **Activities.pptx**. Save as: Activities-[your first initial and last name]1.
2. Choose **View>Slide Sorter**. Click **Slide 2** and drag it between **Slides 4** and **5**.
3. Choose **View>Normal**. Move to **Slide 9**. Click in the **Notes** pane and key: Take time to explain pie chart.
4. **CHECK** Your screen should look like Figure 4.50.
5. Move to **Slide 10**. Select the text **crunch**. Choose **Insert>Hyperlink**.
6. In the **Insert Hyperlink** dialog box, click **Place in This Document**.
7. Under **Select a place in this document**, click **8. Sunday**. Click **OK**. Deselect the text.
8. **CHECK** Your screen should look like Figure 4.51.
9. Save and close your file.

Solution Use the file **Activities1-SF.pptx** as a solution file for this activity.

1. Rearrange Slides, Use Notes Panes, and Create Hyperlinks

Data File

Follow the steps to complete the activity.

FIGURE 4.50 Note added to Notes pane

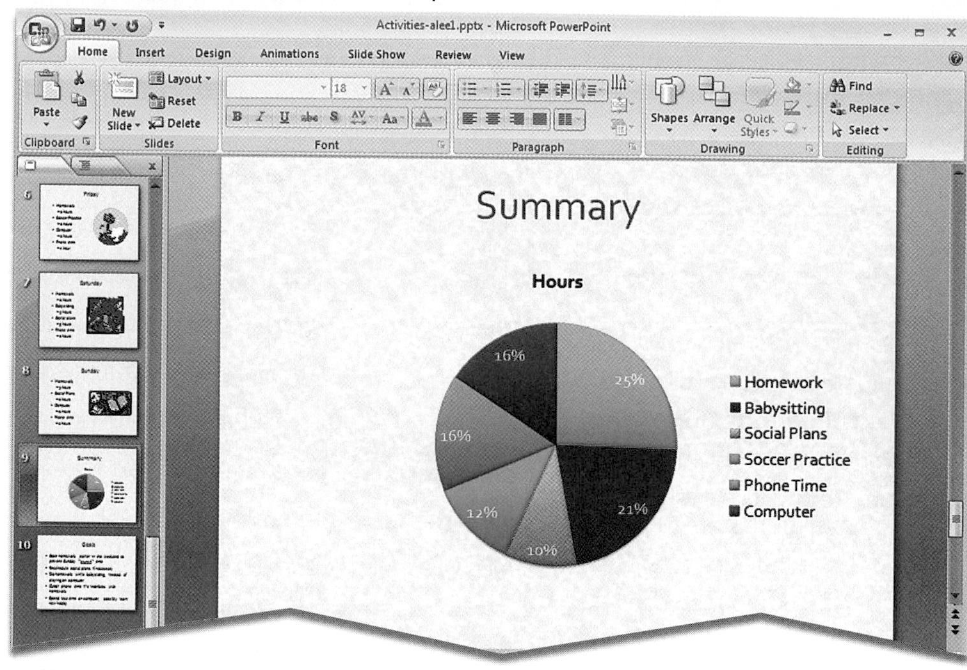

FIGURE 4.51 Hyperlink inserted into slide

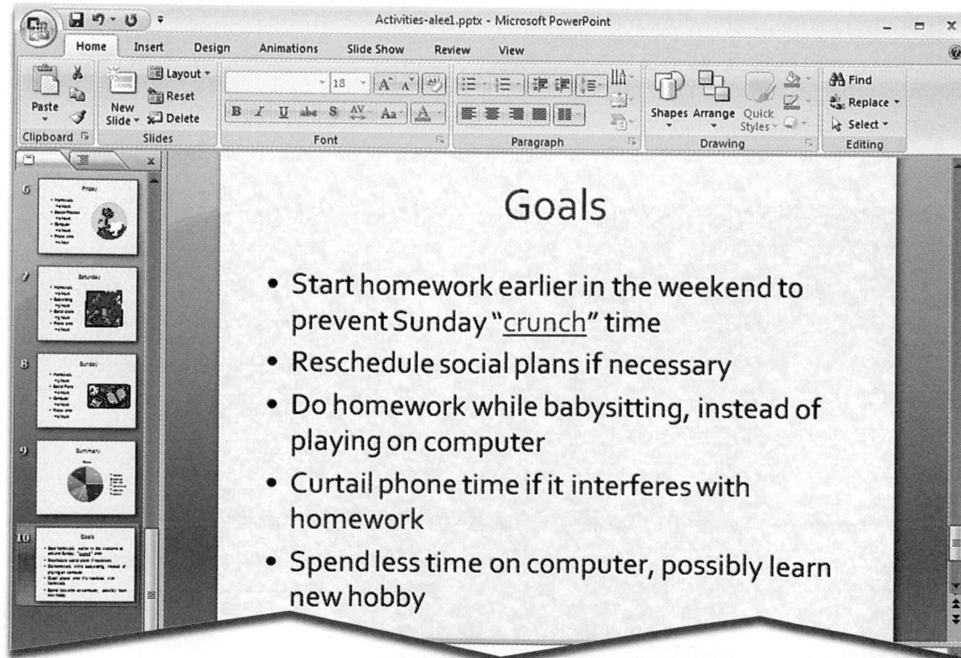

Step-By-Step

1. Open the data file **Meeting_Notes.docx**.
2. Save as: Meeting_Notes-[your first initial and last name].
3. In the document, select the text from **Project Meeting** through **Training of sales team**.
4. Choose **Home>Paragraph>Dialog Box Launcher** .
5. In the **Paragraph** dialog box, click the **Indents and Spacing** tab.
6. Under **Line spacing**, click the drop-down arrow and select **Single**. Click **OK**. Deselect the text.
7. **CHECK** Your screen should look like Figure 2.15. Click **OK**.
8. Select the remaining body text (from **Conclusions:** to the end of the page).
9. On the **Home** tab, in the **Paragraph** group, click the **Line spacing** drop-down arrow. Click **1.0**. Deselect the text.
10. **CHECK** Your screen should look like Figure 2.16. Save your file.

Continue to the next exercise.

EXERCISE 2-8
Change Line Spacing

Word lets you change the spacing between lines and paragraphs. The default for Word 2007 is 1.15 pt between lines and 10 pt between paragraphs. While these are generally very readable settings, you may need to change them for certain documents. For example, you may need to decrease the space between lines to help fit a document on one page.

FIGURE 2.15 First paragraph with new line spacing applied

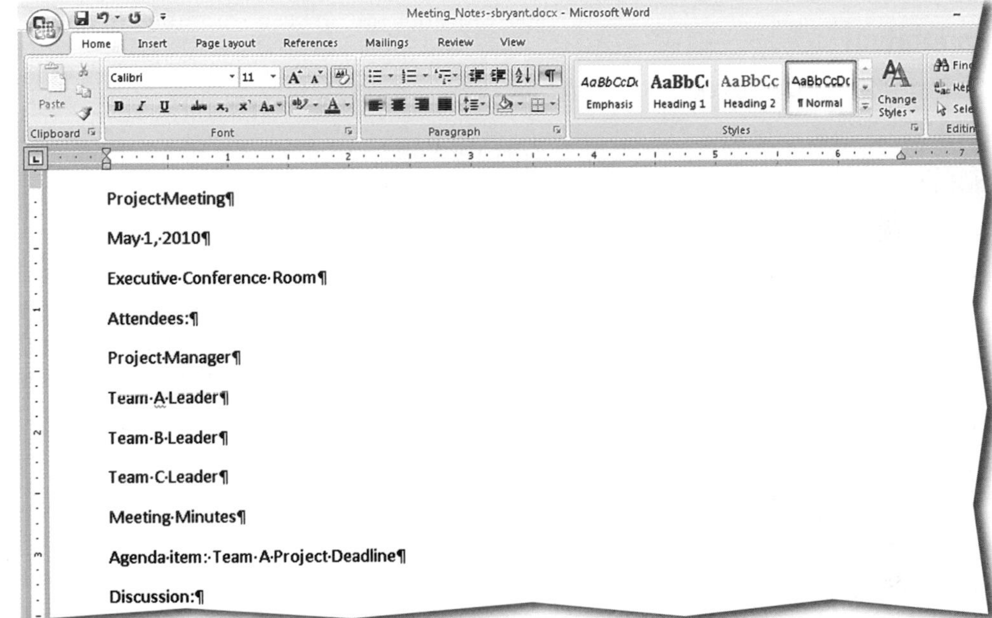

FIGURE 2.16 Body text with new line spacing applied

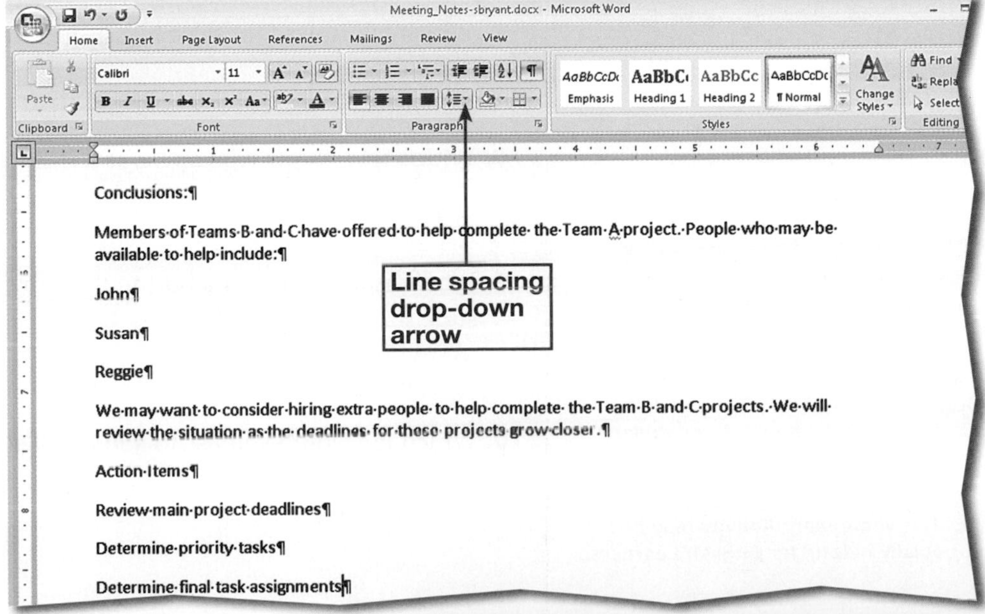

LESSON 4 After You Read

Vocabulary

Key Terms

Action button
annotation
Compatibility Checker
grid
guide
hyperlink
Package for CD
PowerPoint Viewer
Print Preview
snap
timing

Academic Vocabulary

compatible
element
incorporate

Answer to Vocabulary Activity Cryptograms will vary but should be logical and include seven vocabulary terms.

EL The Vocabulary Activity may be especially helpful for English Learners.

Reviewing Vocabulary

Complete the following statements on a separate piece of paper. Choose from the Vocabulary list on the left to complete the statements.

1. A(n) ___grid___ is a series of horizontal and vertical lines that helps align objects. (p. 648)

2. A(n) ___hyperlink___, when clicked, takes you to another slide, opens another file on your computer, or opens a Web page on the Internet. (p. 646)

3. If you do not have PowerPoint, you can view a presentation using ___PowerPoint Viewer___. (p. 661)

4. You can use the Felt Tip Pen or Highlighter to make a(n) ___annotation___ on a slide. (p. 658)

5. Some features of PowerPoint 2007 will not work, or are not ___compatible___, with earlier versions of PowerPoint. (p. 663)

Vocabulary Activity

6. Select seven vocabulary terms and create a cryptogram.
A. For each letter in the alphabet, assign a number. No two letters can have the same number.
B. For each vocabulary term, draw a box to represent each letter in the term.
C. Below each box, write the number that matches that letter.
D. See if your friends can decode each vocabulary term. Decode one of the terms to get them started, or give them a hint, such as 3=F.

Reviewing Key Concepts

Answer the following questions on a separate piece of paper.

7. Which tab is used to create a custom show? (p. 655)
A. Animations
B. Insert
C. Slide Show (circled)
D. View

8. Which Save As file type opens as a slide show automatically? (p. 664)
A. .pptx
B. .ppsx (circled)
C. .potx
D. .ppt

9. Which is the name for a button that connects you to another slide during a slide show? (p. 647)
A. Motion button
B. Advance button
C. Go To button
D. Action button (circled)

10. Which tab would you use to add a video clip to a slide? (p. 649)
A. Insert (circled)
B. Animation
C. Design
D. Home

EXERCISE 2-9
Change Paragraph Alignment

Paragraph **alignment** is when paragraphs are lined up along a document's left or right margins.

- Align Left lines up text along the left margin. This is the default setting.
- Align Right lines up text along the right margin. Page numbers are often right aligned.
- Center aligns text between the left and right margins. Titles are often centered.
- Justify lines up text so that it starts at the left margin and ends at the right margin. Newspapers, magazines, and other professional publications often use justified text.

Different Strokes Tell students that the keyboard shortcuts for **Left, Center, and Right** alignment are **Ctrl** + **L**, **Ctrl** + **E**, and **Ctrl** + **R**.

FIGURE 2.17 Document title centered and bold

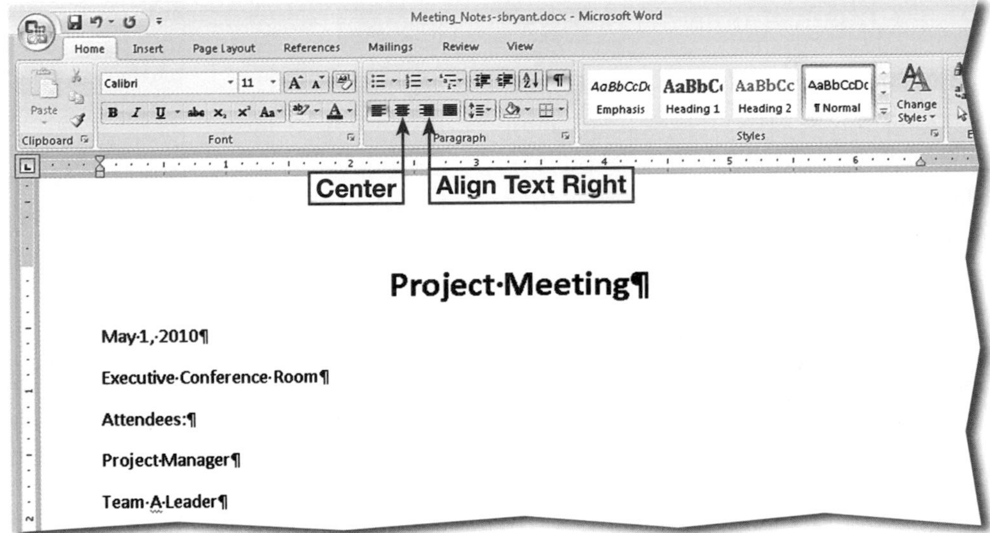

FIGURE 2.18 Text aligned right

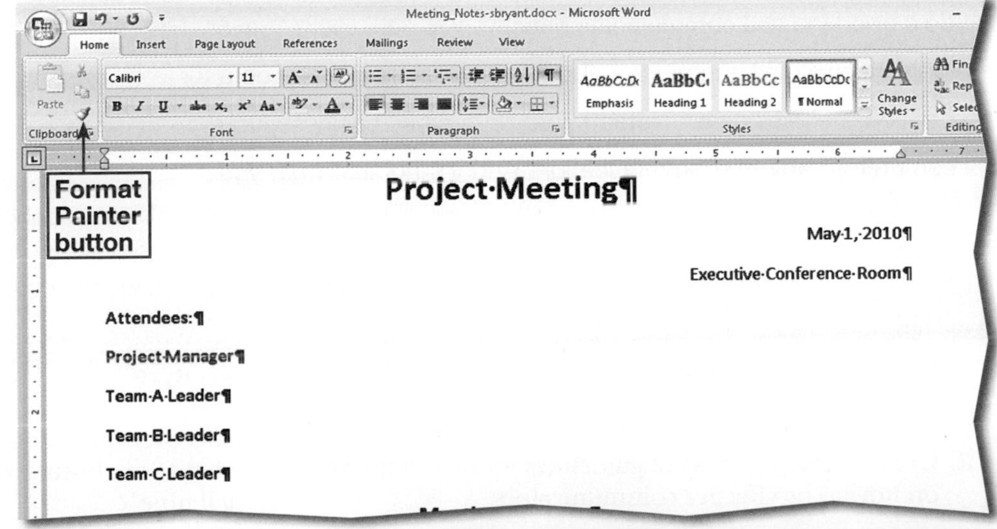

Step-By-Step

1. In your **Meeting Notes** file, select the text **Project Meeting**. Select **Home>Paragraph>Dialog Box Launcher**.
2. In the **Paragraph** dialog box, under **General**, click the **Alignment** drop-down arrow. Select **Centered**. Click **OK**. With the text still selected, click **Bold** **B**. In the **Font Size** box, select **20**. Deselect the text.
3. **CHECK** Your screen should look like Figure 2.17. Select the text **Meeting Minutes**. Choose **Home>Paragraph>Center**. Make the text **Bold, 14pt**.
4. Select the text **May 1, 2010** and **Executive Conference Room**. Click **Align Text Right**.
5. Select **Attendees:** Format the text **Bold**. With the text still selected, double-click **Format Painter**. Select the following text: **Agenda item:**, **Discussion:**, **Conclusions:**, and **Action Items**. Click **Format Painter**. Deselect the text.
6. **CHECK** Your screen should look like Figure 2.18. Save your file.

Continue to the next exercise.

21st Century WORKPLACE

Communicate Effectively

When you introduce a new idea, you need to determine the best way to communicate it to your audience. Thinking about your audience's needs will help you decide how best to deliver your new information. For example, when talking with younger people, it may be better to show them what you mean in addition to explaining your ideas in words.

Use Presentation Tools

Using presentation tools can also make you a more effective communicator. For example, if you are presenting complex ideas, you may want to provide handouts that explain your ideas in more detail. Pens, Highlighters, and other annotation tools can also help you emphasize important points when you are delivering a PowerPoint presentation.

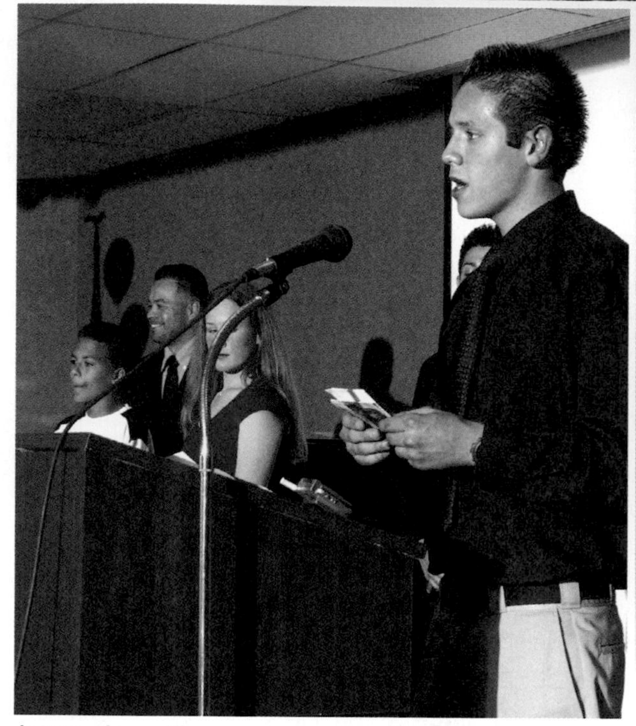

Interacting with your audience will make you a more effective presenter.

NCLB/Language Arts (NCTE 5) Students should understand how good presentation skills improve the quality of their message.

MEET THE MANAGER

Maia Rosenfeld is the manager and chief photographer of Maia Rosenfeld Photography in Los Angeles, California. Since she gets many new clients through word-of-mouth recommendations, she knows the importance of effective communication. "If you do a good job and communicate effectively to your client," says Maia, "he will tell one person about your business. If you do a bad job, he'll tell nine." Notes Maia, "In a small business, you can't afford any miscommunication. And it's not just *what* you say; it's *how* you say it."

SkillBuilder answers can be found on page TM96.

SKILLBUILDER

1. **Explain** Why is it important to know your audience when you communicate new information?
2. **Create** Develop a set of guidelines for new employees on how to be effective communicators.
3. **Analyze** What does Maia mean when she says, "If you do a good job and communicate effectively to your client, he will tell one person about your business. If you do a bad job, he'll tell nine"?

Step-By-Step

1 In your **Meeting Notes** file, select the tasks **Final review of product, Creation of training manual**, and **Training of sales team**.

2 Choose **Home> Paragraph> Numbering** drop-down arrow.

3 In the **Numbering Library** menu, click the option shown in Figure 2.19.

4 Keep the text selected. Right click. In the menu, select **Adjust List Indents**.

5 In the **Adjust List Indents** dialog box, under **Number position**, key: .5″. Under **Text indent**, key: .1″. Click the **Follow number with** drop-down arrow and select **Space**.

6 **CHECK** The **Adjust List Indents** dialog box should look like Figure 2.20. Click **OK**. Save your file.

Continue to the next exercise.

Microsoft Office 2007

Microsoft Office 2007 contains many new list styles to enhance your documents.

EXERCISE 2-10
Create and Customize a Numbered List

In a **numbered list**, a sequential number or letter comes before each new line of text. A numbered list can be used when you want to indicate that items in a list should be performed or viewed in a particular order. They are also helpful when you need to refer to a particular item in a list.

FIGURE 2.19 Numbering Library

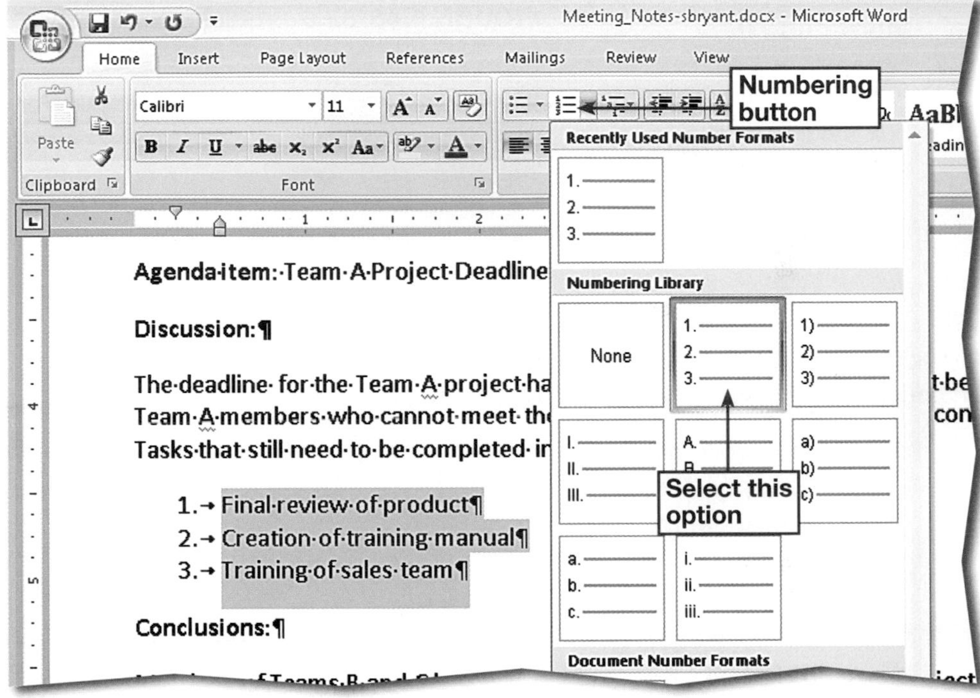

FIGURE 2.20 Customized numbered list format

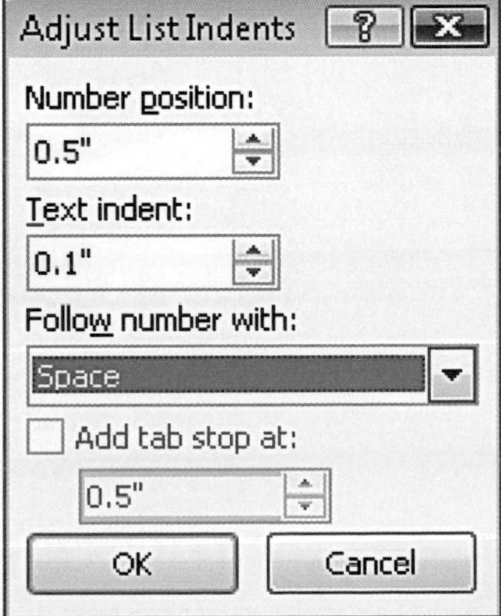

Step-By-Step Tip In **Step 3**, show students how they can move their pointer over each numbering option to preview how it looks in their document.

Step-By-Step

1. In your **Literacy.pptx** file, choose **Office>Save As> PowerPoint Show**.
2. In the **Save As** dialog box, be sure the **Save as type** box reads **PowerPoint Show (*.ppsx)**.
3. **CHECK** Your dialog box should look like Figure 4.48.
4. Click **Save**.
5. Choose **Office>Save As> Other Formats**.
6. In the **Save As** dialog box, click the drop-down arrow in the **Save as type:** box. Select **PowerPoint 97-2003 Show (*.pps)**.
7. Click **Save**. In the **Microsoft Office PowerPoint Compatibility Checker**, click **Continue**.
8. Click **Close** to exit PowerPoint.
9. Navigate to your saved **Literacy.pps** file. Double-click the file to open it.
10. **CHECK** Your screen should look like Figure 4.49.
11. Click through the presentation.

Solution The solution files for Exercise 4-21 are **Literacy-SF.pps and Literacy-SF.ppsx.**

EXERCISE 4-21
Save Presentations as a Slide Show

You can save a presentation to open directly in Slide Show View. Once you open a file in this format, the first slide of the presentation appears in full screen. You can then click through the slides as you normally would. Presentations can be saved as either ppsx or pps files, depending on whether they will be viewed on computers equipped with PowerPoint 2007 or an earlier version.

Troubleshooter If students are using Windows XP, have them go to page xlix to complete steps 4-7, and to learn how to save a file.

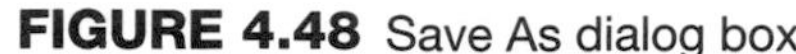

FIGURE 4.48 Save As dialog box

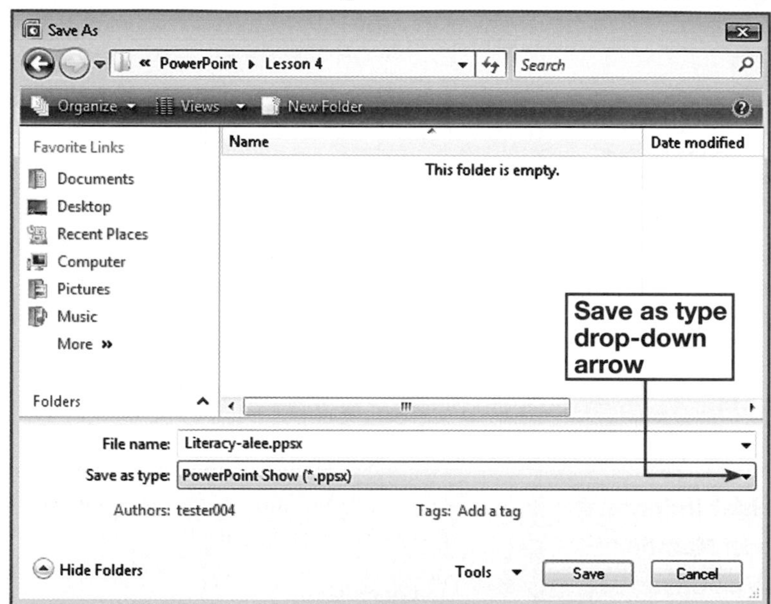

FIGURE 4.49 Opened PowerPoint Show .pps file.

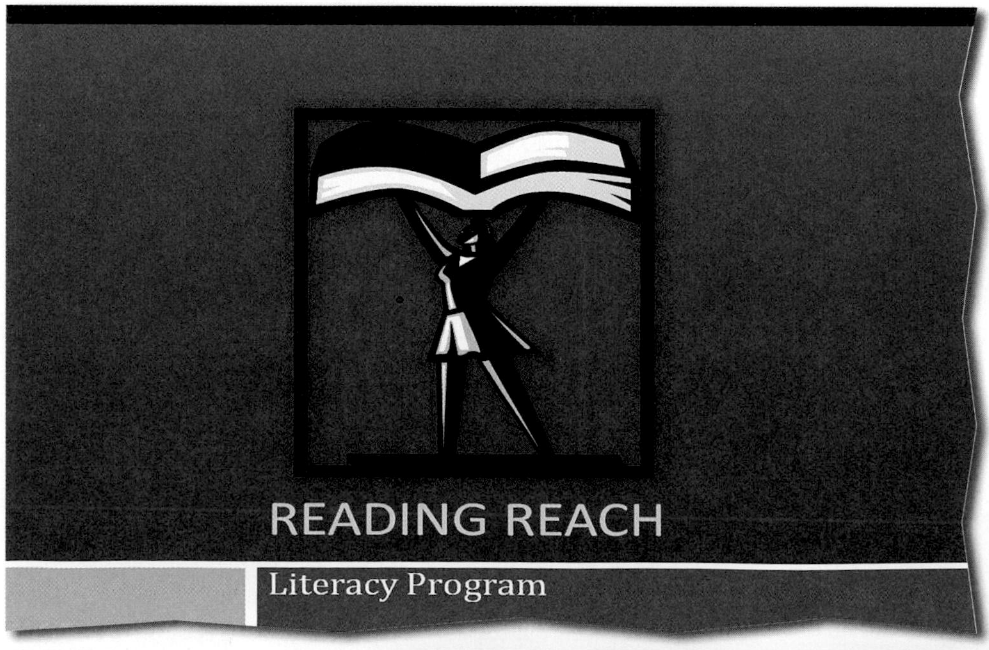

Step-By-Step

1. In your **Meeting Notes** file, select the three tasks at the bottom of the document (starts with **Review main project deadlines**).
2. Choose **Home> Paragraph>Bullets** drop-down arrow.
3. In the **Bullet Library** menu, click the option shown in Figure 2.21.
4. With the text still selected, right click. In the menu, select **Adjust List Indents**.
5. In the **Adjust List Indents** dialog box, under **Bullet position**, key: 0″. Under **Text indent**, key: .1″. Click the **Follow number with** drop-down arrow and select **Space**. Click **OK**.
6. **CHECK** Your screen should look like Figure 2.22. Save your file.

Continue to the next exercise.

Troubleshooting The Bullet Library and the Number Library may look different from the figure, but that should not affect students' results.

EXERCISE 2-11
Create and Customize a Bulleted List

In a **bulleted list**, each item begins with a **bullet**. Bullets are symbols, shapes, or images such as dots, diamonds, or arrows. A bullet is placed in front of each item in a list to call attention to that item. You might use a bulleted list if it does not matter in which order the items in the list are displayed. You might list the members of your team in a bulleted list.

FIGURE 2.21 Bullet Library

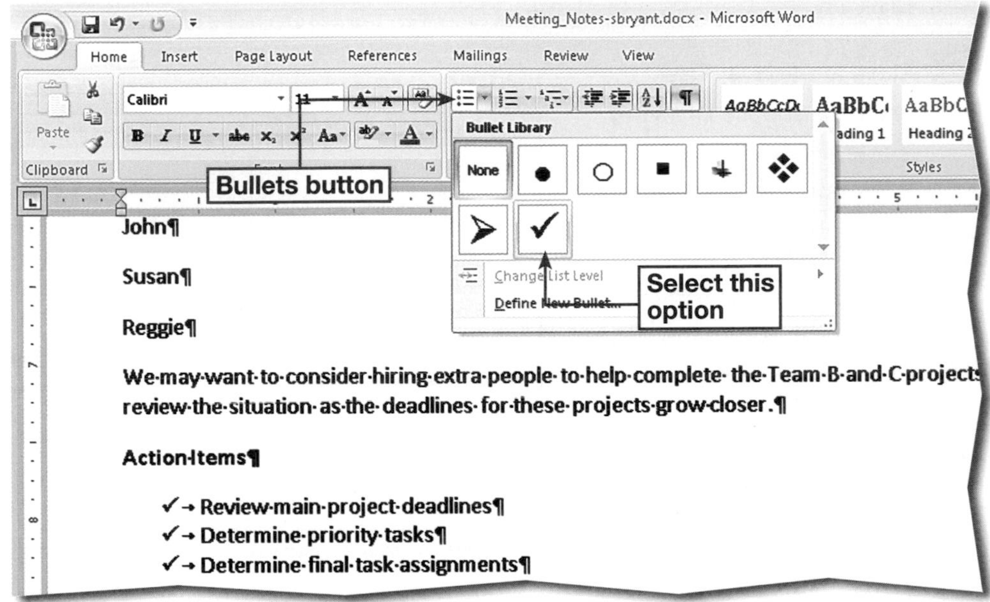

FIGURE 2.22 Customized bulleted list

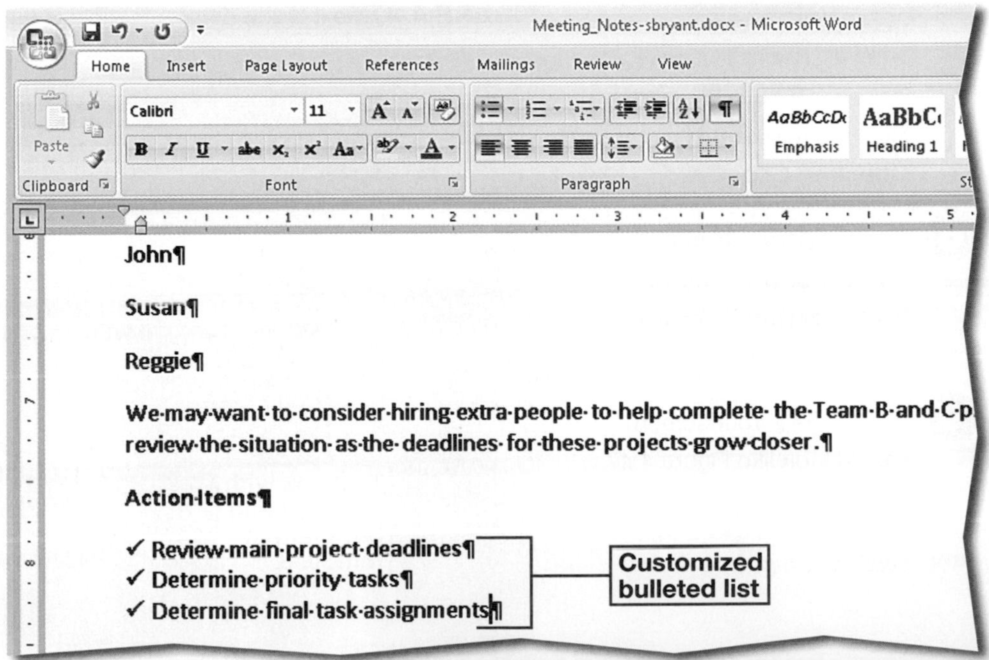

Step-By-Step

1. In your **Literacy** file, choose **Office>Prepare>Run Compatibility Checker**.
2. CHECK Your screen should look like Figure 4.46. Click **OK**.
3. Move to **Slide 8**. Select the text box. Choose **Drawing Tools>Format>Shape Effects>Bevel>No Bevel**.
4. Select the text in the text box. Choose **Home>Paragraph>Columns**. Click **One Column**.
5. Choose **Drawing Tools>Format>Size**. Change the width to **5.5″**.
6. In the **Arrange** group, click **Align**. Choose **Align Center**. Deselect the text.
7. Choose **Office>Prepare>Run Compatibility Checker**. Click **OK**.
8. Choose **Office>Save As>PowerPoint 97-2003 Presentation**. Click **Save**. Click **Continue**.
9. CHECK Your screen should look like Figure 4.47. Close your file

Continue to the next exercise.

EXERCISE 4-20
Identify Features Not Supported by Previous Versions

The **Compatibility Checker** will show you any features used in your PowerPoint presentation that are not compatible, or capable of operating in previous versions of PowerPoint. If you plan to run a presentation on a computer that has an earlier version of PowerPoint, you can check your file and fix any elements that are incompatible with PowerPoint 97–2003. You will not be able to edit incompatible elements.

Teaching Tip The second issue in Figure 4.46 refers to the ScreenTips in the slide show. In earlier versions of PowerPoint these elements may not work.

FIGURE 4.46 Microsoft Office PowerPoint Compatibility Checker dialog box

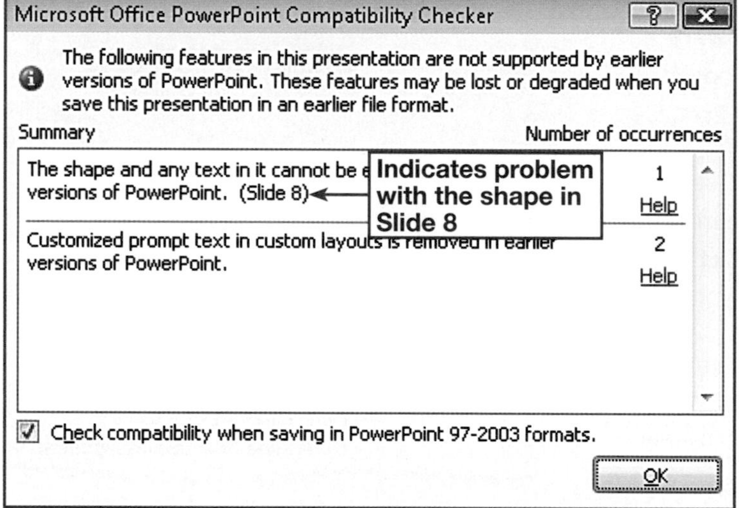

FIGURE 4.47 Text box with incompatible features removed

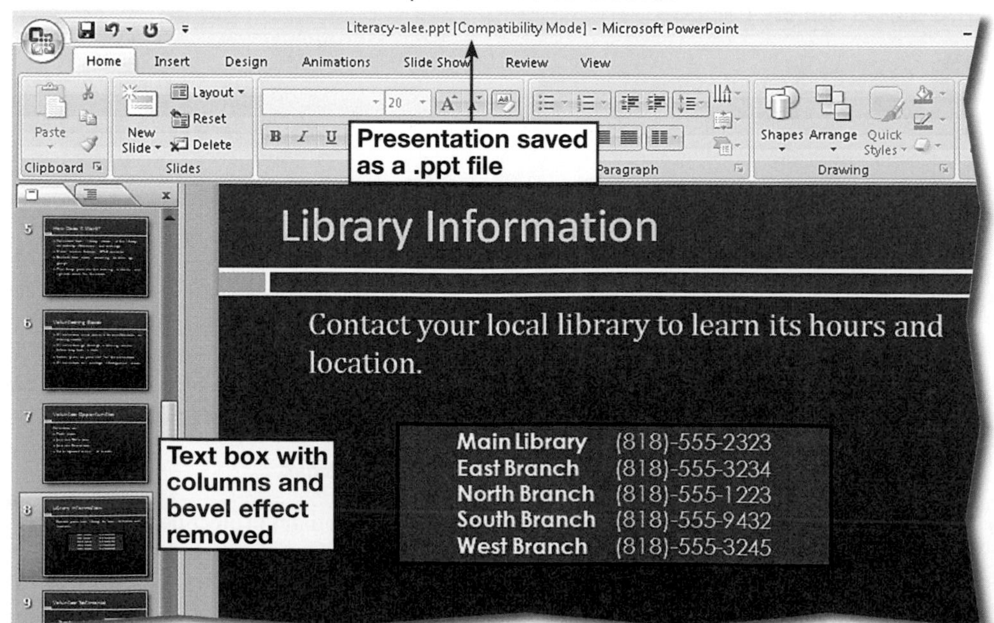

Step-By-Step

1. In your **Meeting Notes** file, select the four titles under **Attendees** (starts with **Project Manager**).

2. Choose **Home>Styles> Dialog Box Launcher**. In the **Styles** pane, click **List Paragraph**.

3. With the text still selected, in the **Styles** pane, click **Clear All**. With the text still selected, in the **Styles** pane, click **No Spacing**. Deselect the text.

4. CHECK Your screen should look like Figure 2.23.

5. Select the names **John, Susan, Reggie**. In the **Styles** pane, select **List Paragraph**. With the text still selected, click **Bullets**. Close the **Styles** pane.

6. CHECK Your screen should look like Figure 2.24. Save your file.

Continue to the next exercise.

Academic Skills

Different fonts can be used to convey different moods. Some fonts might be appropriate in a letter to friends but not in a letter to a boss. What fonts might be appropriate for business documents?

EXERCISE 2-12
Apply and Clear Styles from Lists

You might want to clear formatting from a list you have created. Use the Styles panel to apply and clear styles from lists quickly and easily.

FIGURE 2.23 Formatting cleared and applied using Styles pane

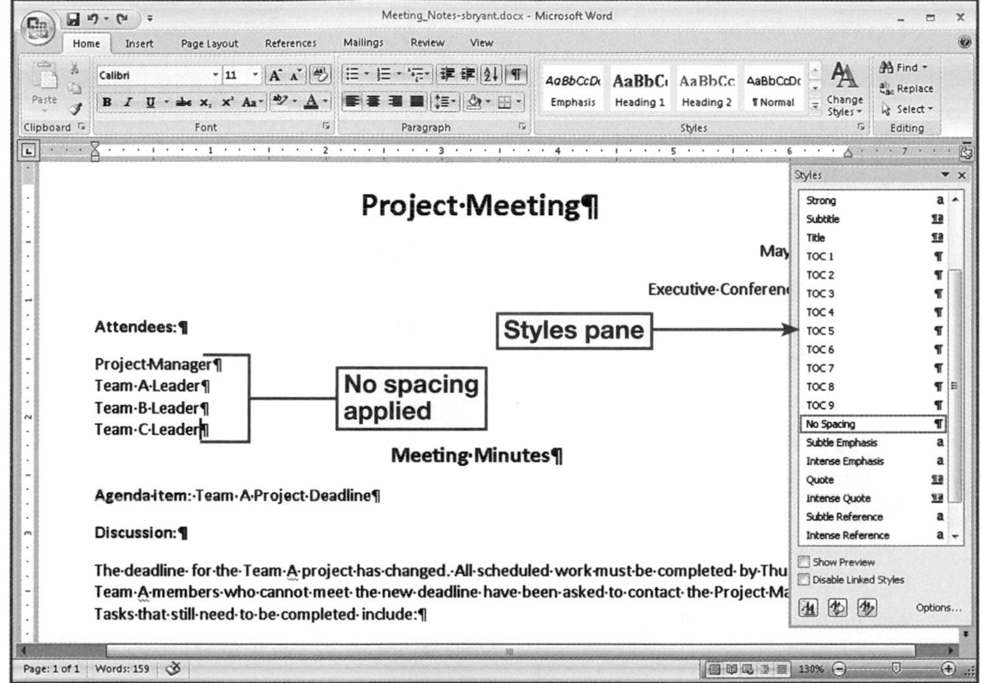

FIGURE 2.24 Formatting added to list

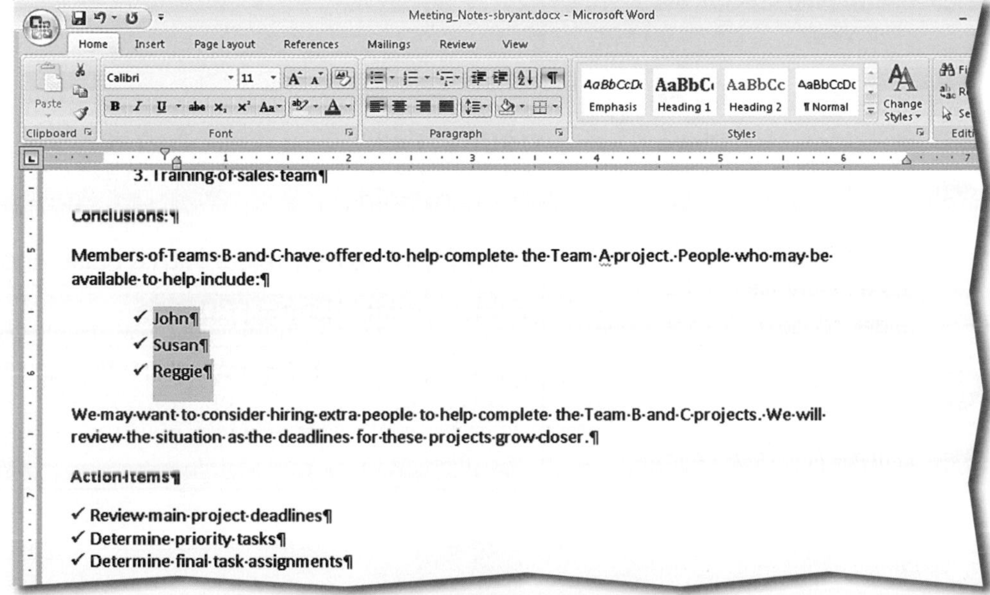

NCLB/Language Arts (NCTE 3) Tell students that Calibri and Times New Roman are examples of professional business fonts.

Step-By-Step

EXERCISE 4-19 (Continued)
Package Presentations for Storage on a CD

8. Click **Options**. Be sure the **Linked files** check box is checked.
9. Check the **Embedded TrueType fonts** check box.
10. CHECK Your **Options** dialog box should look like Figure 4.44. Click **OK**.
11. Click **Copy to Folder**. In the **Folder name** box, be sure **LiteracyCD-[your first initial and last name]** appears.
12. CHECK Your dialog box should look like Figure 4.45. Click **Browse**. Ask your teacher which location to select in the **Location** box. Click **OK**.
13. If a warning box opens, click **Yes**.
14. In the **Package for CD** dialog box, click **Close**.
15. Locate and open your **LiteracyCD** folder. Note the different files in the folder. Close the folder.
16. Save your file.

Continue to the next exercise.

FIGURE 4.44 Package for CD Options dialog box

Options

Package type

(●) Viewer Package (update file formats to run in PowerPoint Viewer)

Select how presentations will play in the viewer:

Play all presentations automatically in the specified order

( ) Archive Package (do not update file formats)

Include these files

(These files will not display in the Files to be copied list)

[✓] Linked files

[✓] Embedded TrueType fonts

Enhance security and privacy

Password to open each presentation:

Password to modify each presentation:

[ ] Inspect presentations for inappropriate or private information

OK | Cancel

FIGURE 4.45 Copy to Folder dialog box

Copy to Folder

Copy files to a new folder with a name and location you specify.

Folder name: LiteracyCD-alee

Location: C:\Users\tester004\Documents\ | Browse...

OK | Cancel

Solution The solution folder for Exercise 4-19 is **LiteracyCD-SF**.

Step-By-Step

1. If your horizontal ruler is not visible, choose **View> Show/Hide>Ruler**.

2. In your **Meeting Notes** file, select the text **Action Items** and the three checked items at the end of the document.

3. Choose **Home> Paragraph>Dialog Box Launcher** . At the bottom of the **Paragraph** dialog box, click **Tabs**.

4. In the **Tabs** dialog box, under **Tab stop position**, key: 3.5″. Under **Alignment**, select **Left**. Under **Leader**, click **1 None**. Click **Set**. Click **OK**.

5. On the far left side of the horizontal ruler, click the **Left Tab** button (see Figure 2.25). Click **5″** on the ruler. Deselect the text.

6. Click after **Action Items**. Press TAB. Key: Team Responsible. Press TAB. Key: Deadline.

7. CHECK Your screen should look like Figure 2.26. Select the line of text from **Action Items** to **Deadline**. Use **Home>Paragraph> Dialog Box Launcher** to open the **Tabs** dialog box.

Continued on the next page.

EXERCISE 2-13
Modify and Remove Tabs

You can modify tab stops to align text anywhere within a document. The Tab key automatically moves the insertion point to the next tab stop in the document. Word has default tab stops every half inch along the ruler. If you no longer need a particular tab stop, you can easily remove it.

Teaching Tip Show students the View Ruler command at the top of the right vertical scroll bar.

FIGURE 2.25 Tab button on ruler

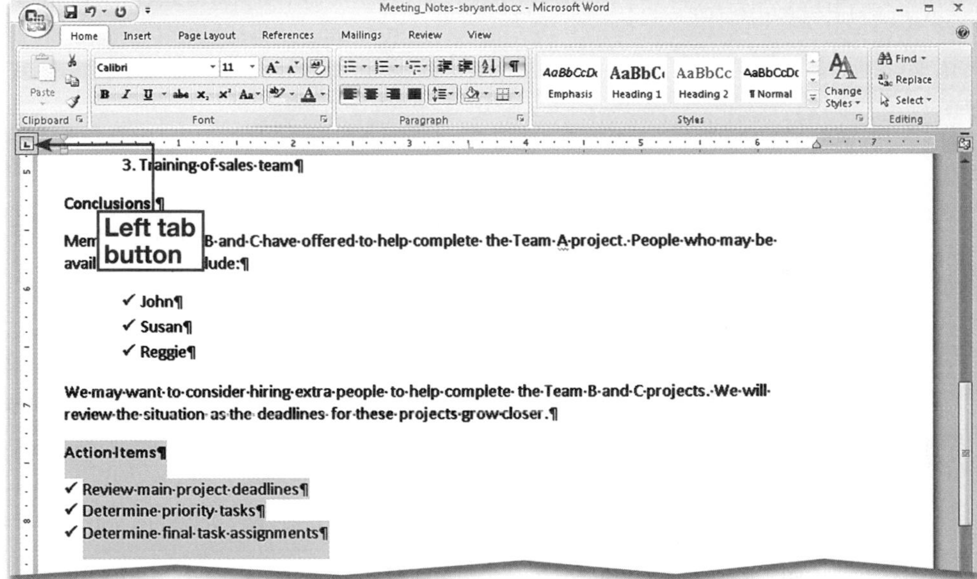

FIGURE 2.26 Left tab set

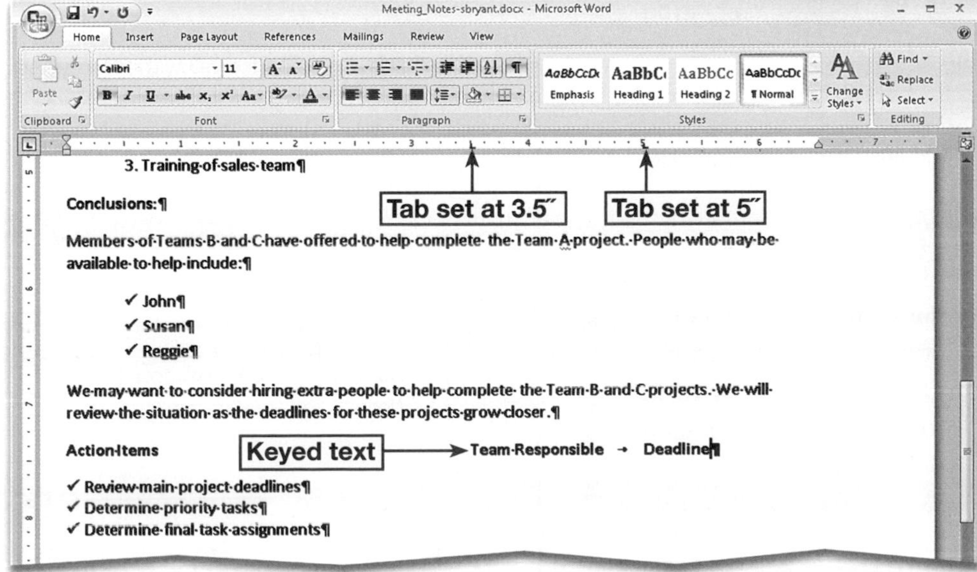

Step-By-Step Tip In **Step 5**, if the button does not match the button shown in Figure 2.25, have students click the button until the Left Tab button cycles around.

Step-By-Step

1. In your **Literacy** file, choose **Office>Publish> Package for CD**.
2. In the **Warning** box that appears, click **OK**.
3. In the **Package for CD** dialog box, in the **Name the CD** box, key: LiteracyCD-[your first initial and last name] (see Figure 4.42).
4. Click **Add Files**. On the **Presentations and Shows** drop-down arrow and select **All Files (*.*)**.
5. Locate and select the data files **Worksheet.docx** and **Literacy.wav**.
6. Click **Add**.
7. **CHECK** Your dialog box should look like Figure 4.43.

Continued on the next page.

Shortcuts

If you have a CD writer connected to your computer, choose **Copy to CD** to burn your presentation onto a CD.

Step-By-Step In **Step 5**, students can click CTRL to select both files at once

EL Consider pairing English Learners with native English speakers for this exercise.

EXERCISE 4-19
Package Presentations for Storage on a CD

Burning a presentation to a CD makes it easy to store and transport your work. Many different text and graphics files are used to create one presentation. When you use the **Package for CD** feature, PowerPoint automatically creates a folder that stores all these files. If you have hyperlinked to a file, you must add this file to the folder so PowerPoint can locate it. **PowerPoint Viewer** allows someone to view a slide show without using PowerPoint itself.

FIGURE 4.42 Package for CD dialog box

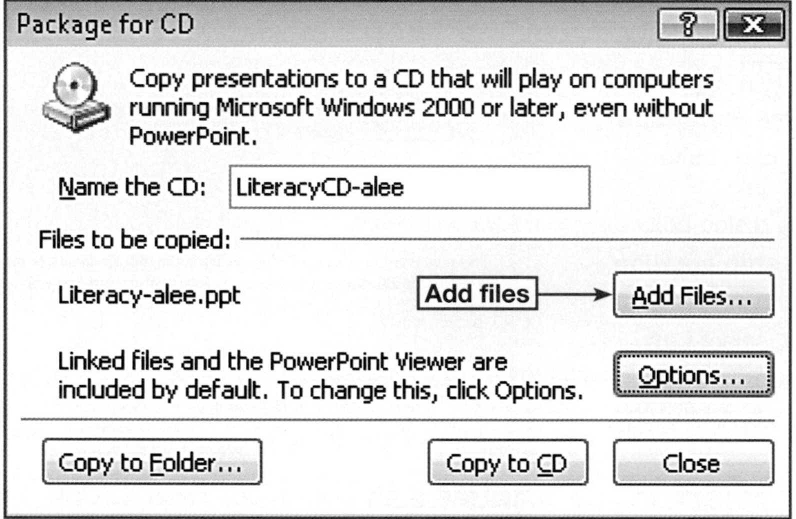

FIGURE 4.43 Package for CD with files added

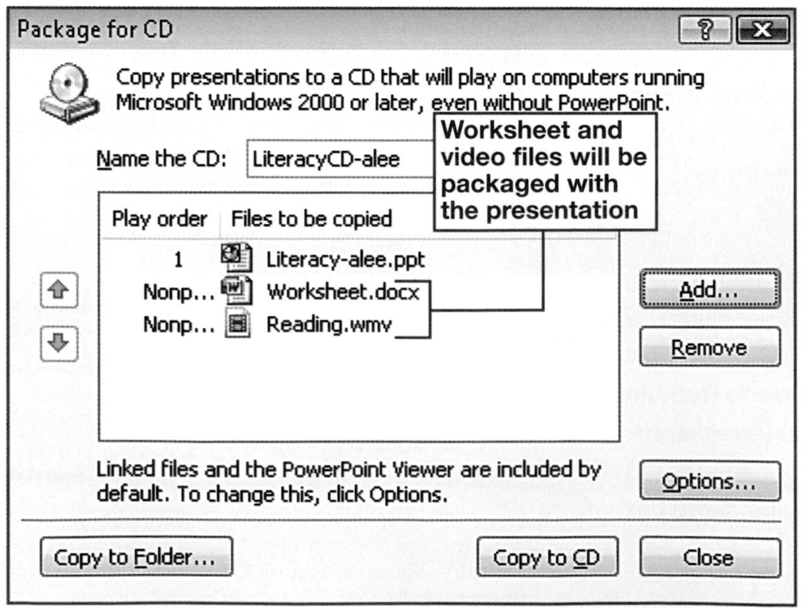

EXERCISE 2-13 (Continued)

Modify and Remove Tabs

Solution Use the file **Meeting_Notes-SF .docx** as a solution file for Exercises 2-8 through 2-13.

8 In the **Tabs** dialog box, under **Tab stop position**, select **3.5″**. Click **Clear** to clear the tab. Under **Tab stop position**, key: 2.5″. Click **Set**. Click **OK**. Click after the first checked item under **Action Items**. Press TAB. Key: Team A. Press TAB. Key: 5/5.

9 Click after the second checked item. Press TAB. Key: Team A. Press TAB. Key: 5/10. Click after the third checked item. Press TAB. Key: Teams A, B, C. Press TAB. Key: 5/15.

10 CHECK Your screen should look like Figure 2.27. Select all header text (from **Action Items** to **Deadline**) and all text under the headers. Choose **Home>Paragraph>Dialog Box Launcher>Tabs**.

11 In the **Tabs** dialog box, under **Tab stop position**, select **2.5″** and **5″**. Click **Clear All**. Under **Tab stop position**, key: 3″. Click **Set**. Under **Tab stop position**, click **5.5″**. Click **Set**. Click **OK**.

12 CHECK Your screen should look like Figure 2.28. Hide the ruler. Save and close your file.

Continue to the next exercise.

FIGURE 2.27 Right tab set to 5″

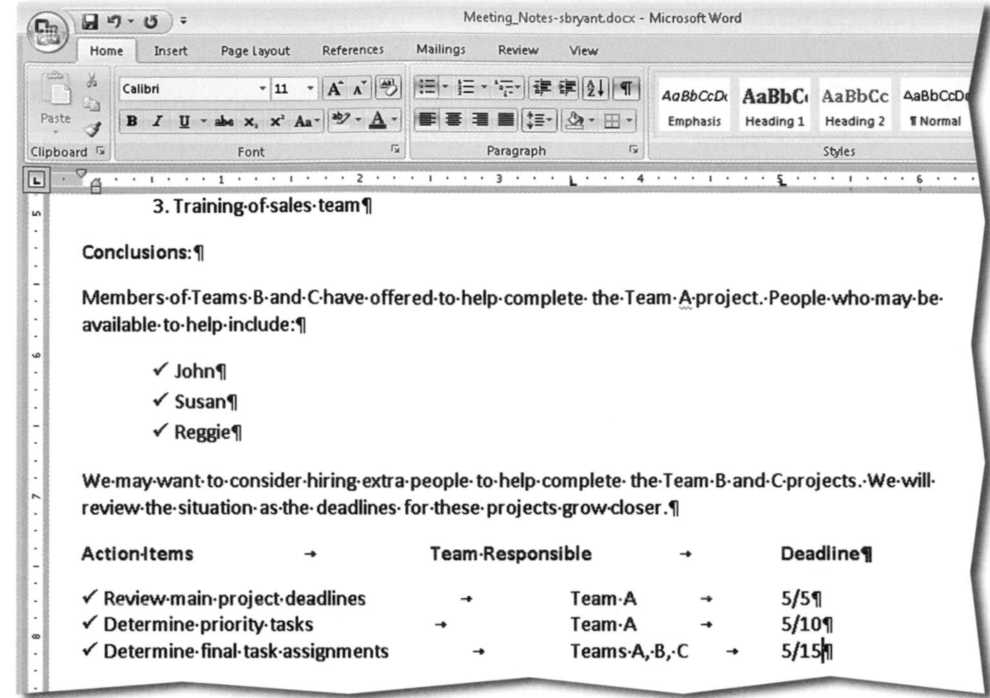

FIGURE 2.28 Left tabs set at 3″ and 5.5″

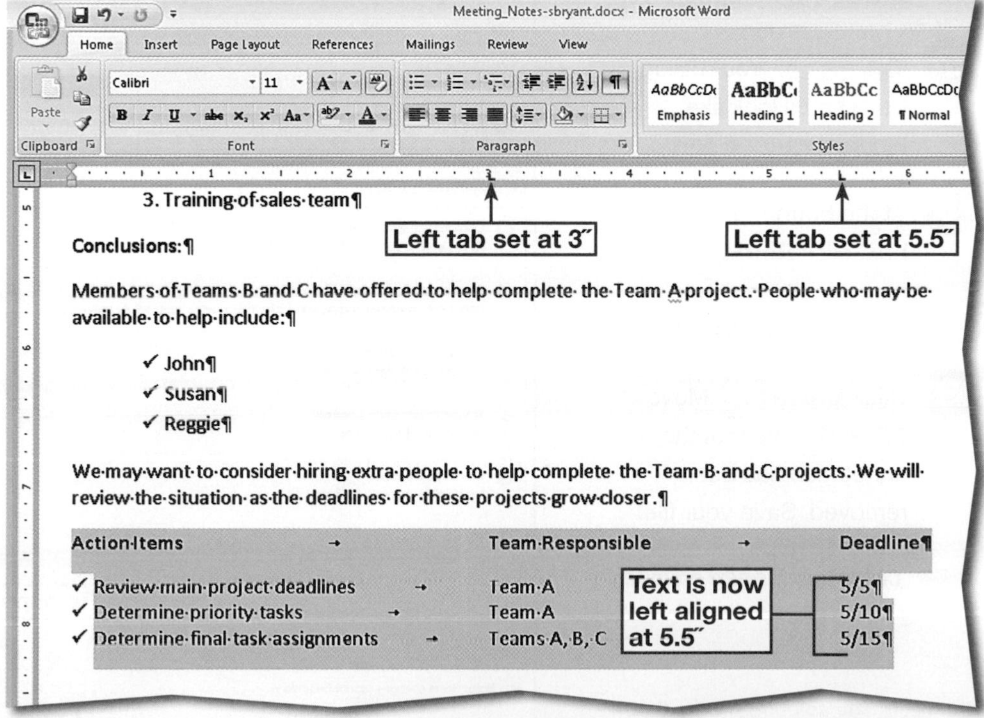

Step-By-Step

1. In your **Literacy** file, choose **Office>Prepare>Inspect Document**.
2. In the **Document Inspector** dialog box, be sure all content check boxes are selected.
3. CHECK Your dialog box should look like Figure 4.40. Click **Inspect**.
4. Next to **Comments and Annotations**, click **Remove All**.
5. Next to **Document Properties and Personal Information**, click **Remove All**.
6. Next to **Presentation Notes**, click **Remove All**.
7. CHECK Your dialog box should look like Figure 4.41.
8. At the bottom of the dialog box, click **Reinspect**. Be sure all content items are selected. Click **Inspect**.
9. Click **Close** [x]. Move to **Slide 5**. Note that the annotation has been removed. Save your file.

Continue to the next exercise.

Solution The solution file for Exercises 4 to 4-18 is **Literacy-SF.pptx**.

EXERCISE 4-18
Use the Document Inspector to Remove Information

If you plan to make your presentation available for other people to view and use, you can use the Document Inspector to remove sensitive information that you may not want to share. The Document Inspector allows you to review and remove hidden or personal information from the presentation itself and from the file's properties.

FIGURE 4.40 Document Inspector dialog box

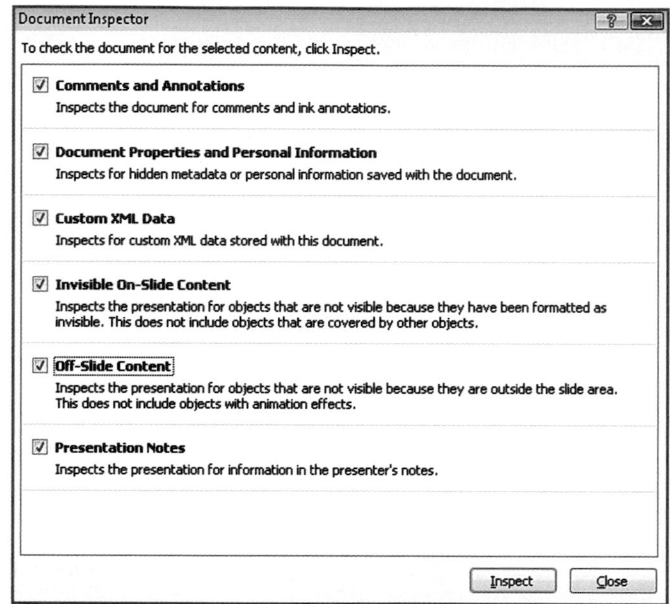

FIGURE 4.41 Document Inspector inspection results

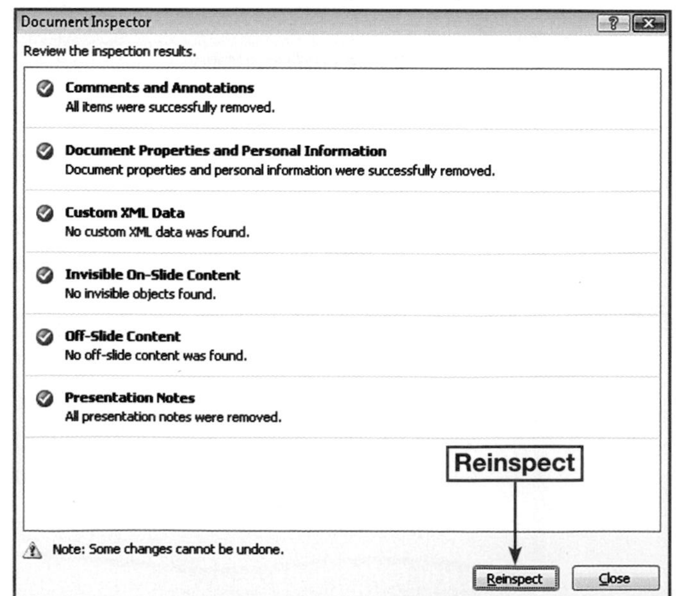

Step-By-Step

1. Open the data file **Meeting_Outline.docx**. Save as: Meeting_Outline-[your first initial and last name].

2. Select all three paragraphs. Choose **Home>Paragraph>Multilevel List**. Click the box to the right of the **None** box (see Figure 2.29). The document automatically formats.

3. Select the last three lines of the first paragraph. Choose **Home>Paragraph>Increase Indent**.

4. With the last three lines of the first paragraph still selected, choose **Home>Paragraph>Decrease Indent**. Reselect the three lines and click **Increase Indent**.

5. Select the last three lines of the second paragraph. Click **Increase Indent**. Select the last four lines of the third paragraph. Click **Increase Indent**.

6. **CHECK** Your screen should look like Figure 2.30. With your teacher's permission, print the document. Save and close the file.

Continue to the next exercise.

EXERCISE 2-14
Create an Outline Numbered List

An outline numbered list looks just like an outline that you might create on paper to take notes or to study from. You can subdivide the list into a maximum of nine levels.

Solution Use the file **Meeting_Outline-SF.docx** as a solution file for Exercise 2-14.

FIGURE 2.29 Multilevel List drop-down menu

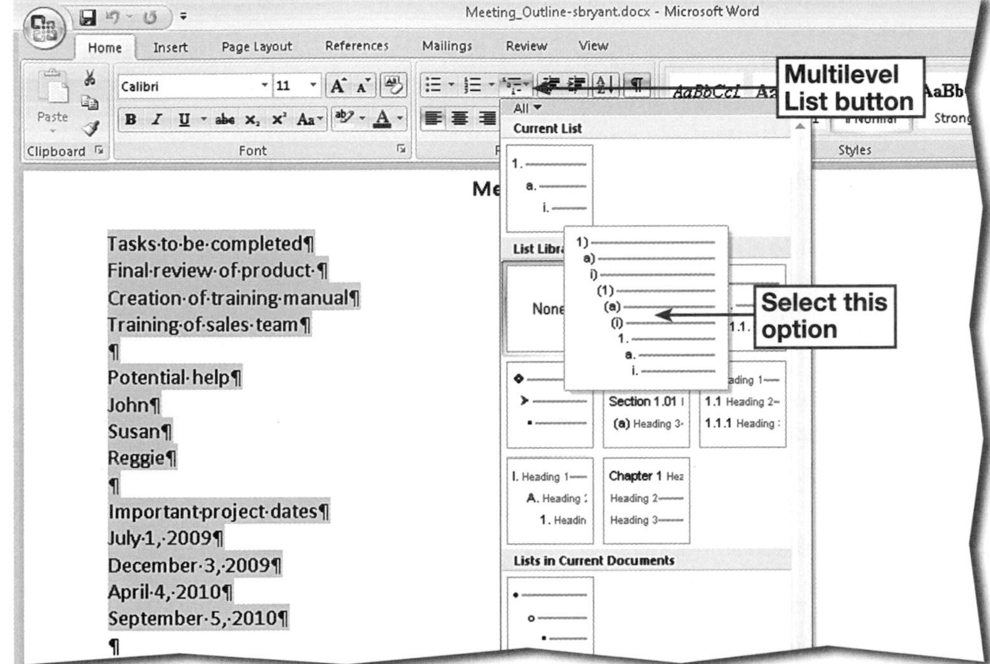

FIGURE 2.30 An outline numbered list

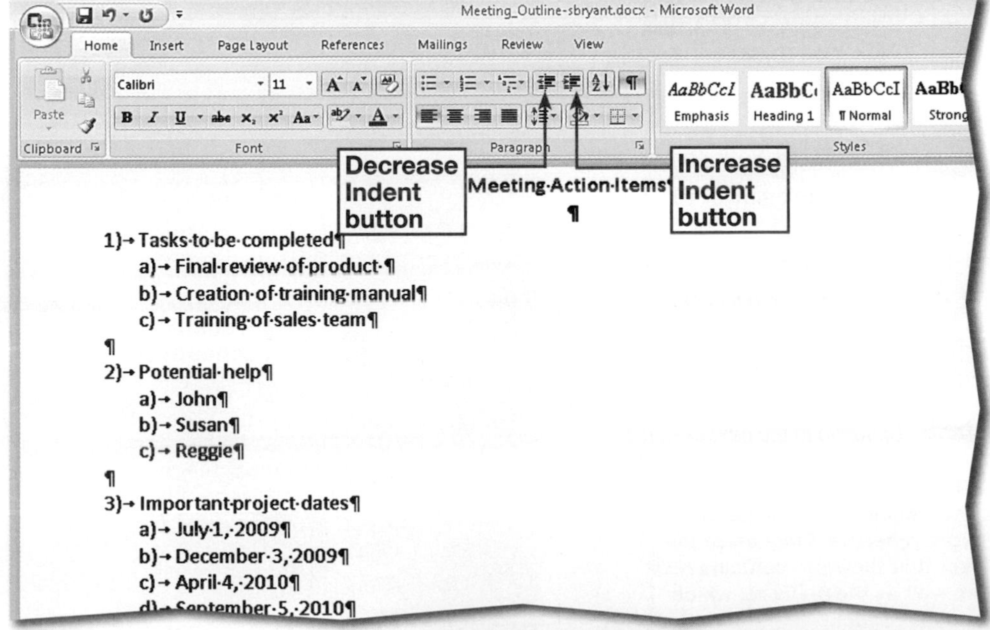

Step-By-Step

1. In your **Literacy** file, on the **Animations** tab, in the **Transition to this Slide** group, under **Advance Slide**, select **Automatically after**. Key: 00:15.

2. **CHECK** Your screen should look like Figure 4.38. Click **Apply to All**.

3. On the **Slide Show** tab, on the **Set Up** group, click **Rehearse Timings**.

4. Slowly read each slide aloud. Practice any comments you plan to make. Click **Next** on the **Rehearsal** toolbar (upper-left corner of the screen) to move to the next slide.

5. After you have read the last slide, in the **Rehearsal** toolbar, click **Close**. Click **Yes** to save the timing for each slide.

6. **CHECK** Your screen should look similar to Figure 4.39.

7. Switch to **Normal View**.

8. Save your file.

Continue to the next exercise.

EL Make sure English Learners understand the meaning of the word *rehearse*. Emphasize the fact that the word contains *hear*, as well as the prefix *re*, which means "again."

EXERCISE 4-17
Rehearse and Save Timings

To set a show's **timing**, or how long each slide appears, rehearse the presentation. Make sure you and your audience have enough time to read each slide. Use the Rehearsal toolbar to move from slide to slide, to track the presentation's total time, and to pause if necessary while setting timings. When finished, test your timings by viewing the slide show again.

Solution Use the file **Literacy-SF.pptx** as a solution file for Exercises 4-1 through 4-14.

FIGURE 4.38 Automatic timing set at 15 seconds

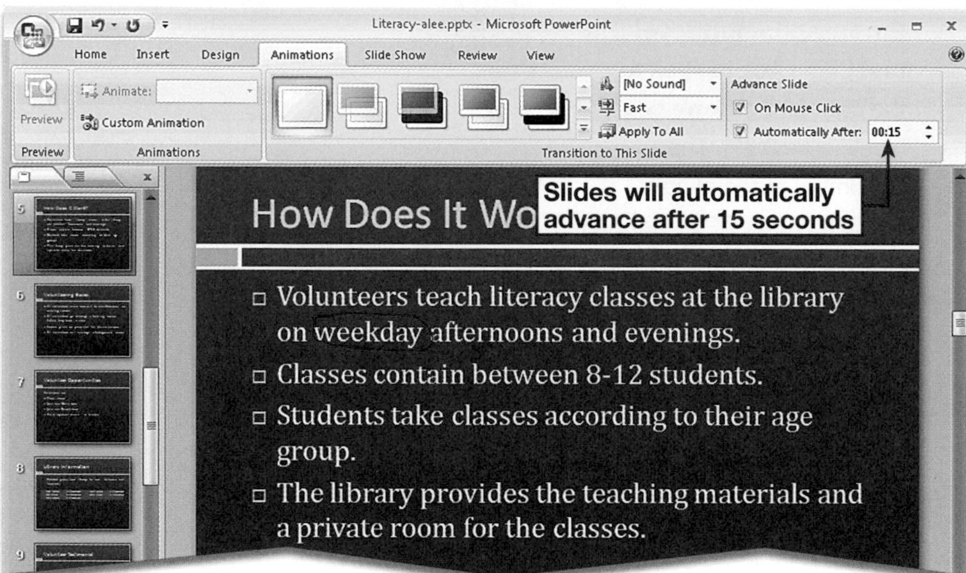

FIGURE 4.39 Saved timings

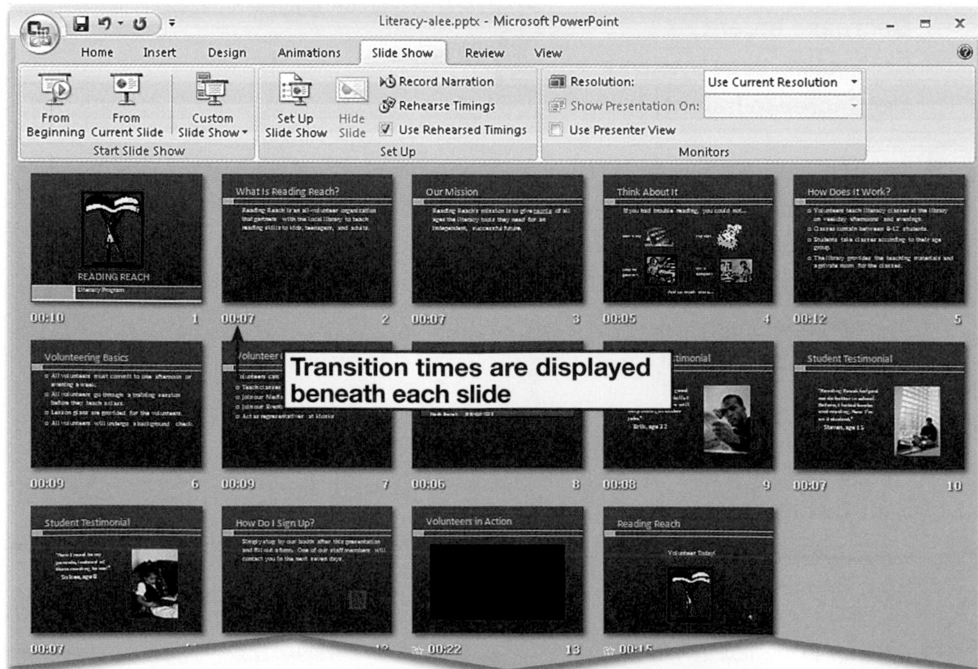

Step-By-Step

1. Open the data file **Flyer.docx**. Save as: Flyer-[your first initial and last name].

2. Choose **View>Show/Hide>Ruler** to display the ruler. Return to the **Home** tab.

3. Select the last line of text in the document. On the ruler, click and drag the **First Line Indent** marker to the **0.5″** mark. Deselect the text.

4. **CHECK** Your screen should look like Figure 2.31. Notice that the line of text is now indented. Reselect the line of text.

5. Click and drag the **First Line Indent, Left Indent**, and **Hanging Indent** markers to the **1″** mark.

6. Drag the **Right Indent** marker to the **5″** mark. Deselect the text.

7. **CHECK** Your screen should look like Figure 2.32.

8. Save your file.

Continue to the next exercise.

Differentiated Instruction/ Physically Impaired If students have problems indenting using the ruler, they can set indentations by selecting the text and using **Page Layout>Paragraph>Dialog box launcher>Indents and Spacing>Indentation.**

EXERCISE 2-15
Set Indents Using the Ruler

An **indent** is the space between the margin and the text. A first line indent moves the first line of a paragraph in and is often used to set off a new paragraph. A left indent moves the left edge of an entire paragraph in. A right indent moves the right edge of a paragraph. A hanging indent moves the second line in a paragraph and then aligns the next lines below it.

FIGURE 2.31 Indent markers on the ruler

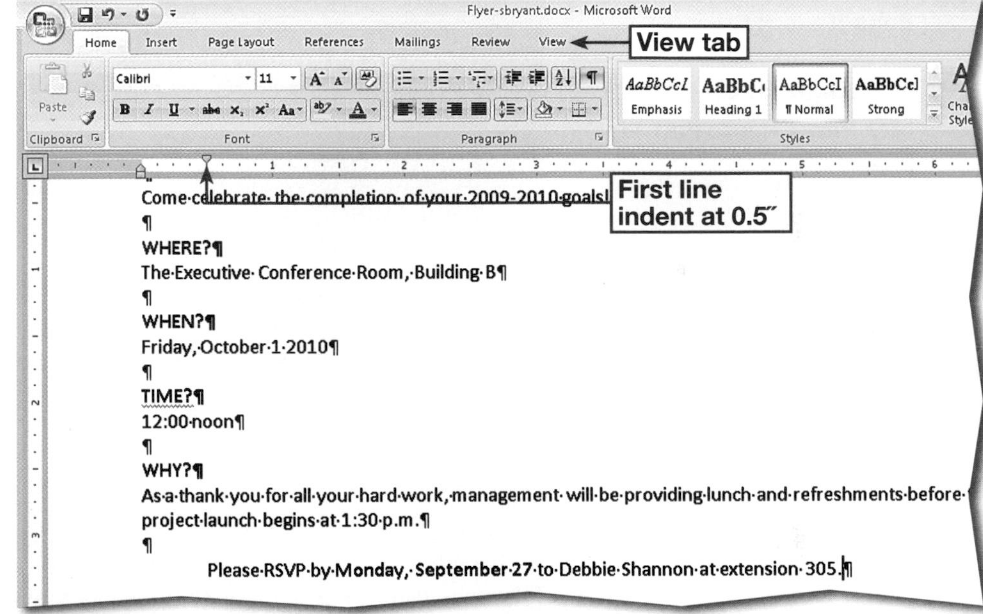

FIGURE 2.32 Set margins and indents using the ruler

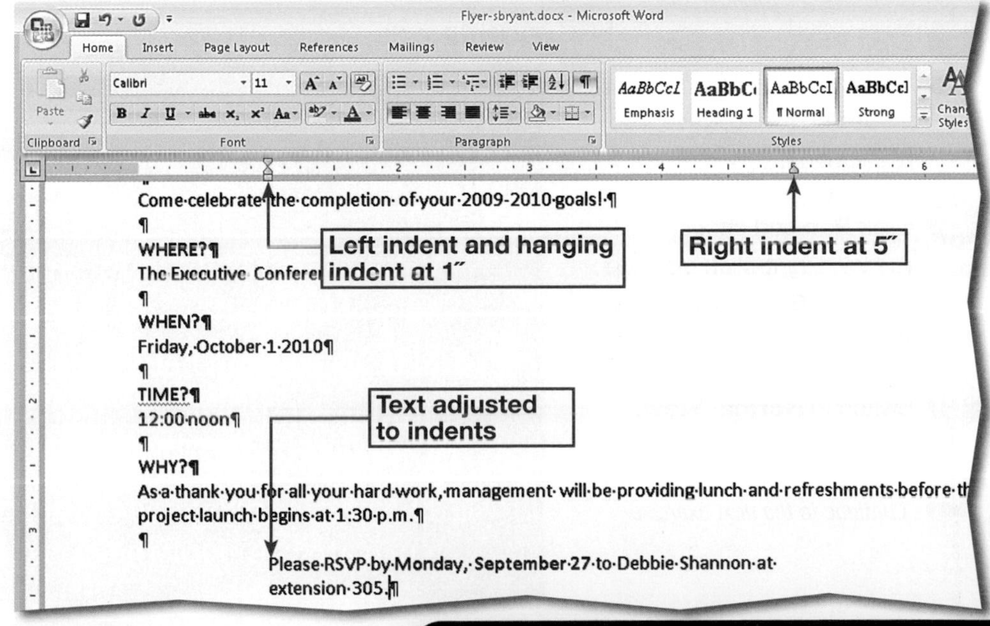

EXERCISE 4-16
Use Pens, Highlighters, and Arrows

Use a Pen to highlight or circle items, and use an arrow to point to parts of a slide. You can change the color of the pen and erase an **annotation**, or mark. You can choose whether to save or not save your annotations. Select Print Comments and Ink Markup from print options to print your annotations.

Step-By-Step

1. In your **Literacy** file, choose **Slide Show>Start Slide Show>From Beginning**. Move the mouse to display the **Slide Show** toolbar.
2. Move to **Slide 5. How does it work?**
3. In the **Slide Show** toolbar, click **Pen**. Choose **Felt Tip Pen**.
4. Hold down the mouse button to circle **weekday** (see Figure 4.36).
5. Click **Pen** and choose **Highlighter**. Choose **Ink Color>Light Green**. Hold down the mouse button to highlight **library** in the last bullet point.
6. CHECK Your screen should look like Figure 4.37.
7. Click **Pen** and choose **Eraser**. Hold down the mouse button to erase the highlighting.
8. Click **Pen** and choose **Arrow**. Right-click the slide and click **End Show**. In the dialog box, click **Keep**.
9. Switch to **Normal View**. Save your file.

Continue to the next exercise.

FIGURE 4.36 Text circled with Felt Tip Pen

How Does It Work?
Volunteers teach literacy classes at the library on weekday afternoons and evenings.
Classes contain between 8-12 students.
Students take classes according to their age group.
The library provides the teaching materials and a private room for the classes.
Pen tool

FIGURE 4.37 Highlighted text

How Does It Work?
Volunteers teach literacy classes at the library on weekday afternoons and evenings.
Classes contain between 8-12 students.
Students take classes according to their age group.
Highlighted text
The library provides the teaching materials and a private room for the classes.

Step-By-Step

1. In your **Flyer** file, select the last line of text.
2. Choose **Page Layout> Page Background>Page Borders**. The **Borders and Shading** dialog box opens.
3. Click the **Borders** tab. Under **Setting**, click **Box**. Under **Style**, click the solid line.
4. Under **Color**, select **Red**. Under **Width**, click **3 pt**.
5. In the **Preview** box, click **Bottom Border** (see Figure 2.33).
6. Click the **Shading** tab. Under **Fill**, select **Yellow**. Click **OK**.
7. Click the **Home> Paragraph>Border** drop-down arrow. Click **Outside Border**.
8. Choose **Home> Paragraph>Justify**. Deselect the text.
9. **CHECK** Your screen should look like Figure 2.34.
10. Save your file.

Continue to the next exercise.

Intervention Strategy If students have trouble adding borders, have them click **None** to clear the borders. Then have them add the borders.

EXERCISE 2-16
Add Borders and Shading to Text

To make text stand out, you can add a border or shading. A border can be a single line or a box that frames text. Shading adds color or a pattern to the background of text.

FIGURE 2.33 Borders and Shading dialog box

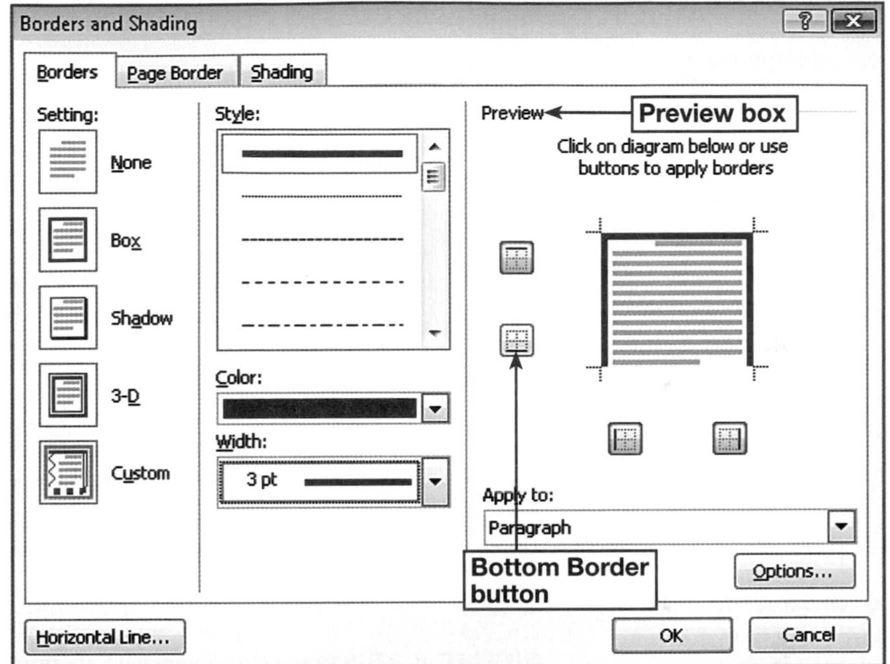

FIGURE 2.34 Text with border and shading applied

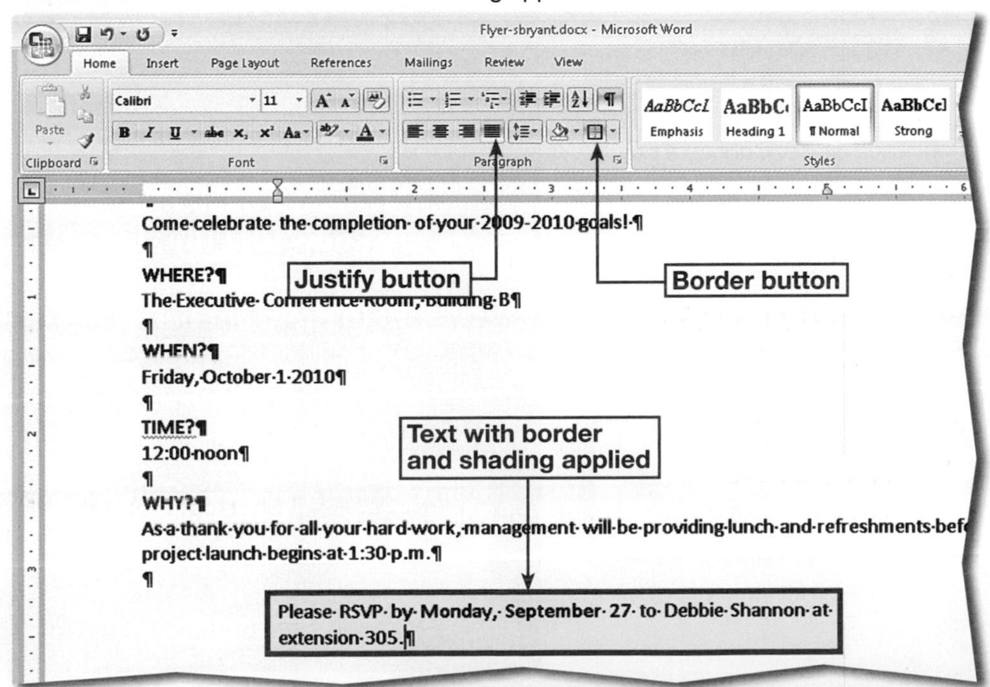

Step-By-Step

1. In your **Literacy** file, choose **Slide Show> Start Slide Show>From Beginning**. The slide show begins.
2. Move your mouse to display the **Slide Show** toolbar.
3. Click the **Next** arrow to move to **Slide 2**.
4. Click **Slide** to open the shortcut menu. Review the commands described in Table 4.1.
5. Click **Slide**. Choose **Next** to go to **Slide 3**.
6. Click **Slide**. Choose **Go to Slide**. Click **9. Volunteer Testimonial**. Click **Slide** to open the shortcut menu.
7. **CHECK** Your screen should look like Figure 4.35.
8. Click **Slide**. Choose **End Show**.
9. Save your file.

Continue to the next exercise.

Shortcuts

To exit a slide show quickly, press ESC.

EXERCISE 4-15
Navigate in Slide Show View

If you move the mouse during a slide show, the Slide Show toolbar appears. Use the Slide Show toolbar arrows and the Slide shortcut menu to navigate forward, backward, or to a specific slide. The Slide shortcut menu also allows you to access a custom show, help information, or screen options. Some shortcut functions are shown in Table 4.1.

TABLE 4.1 Slide shortcut menu navigation options

Shortcut	Command Function
Next	Moves to next slide
Previous	Moves to previous slide
Last Viewed	Moves to last slide viewed
Go to Slide	Moves to a specified slide
Custom Show	Starts a custom show
Screen	Changes screen appearance options
Pause	Pauses show
End Show	Ends show

FIGURE 4.35 Slide Show toolbar with shortcut menu open

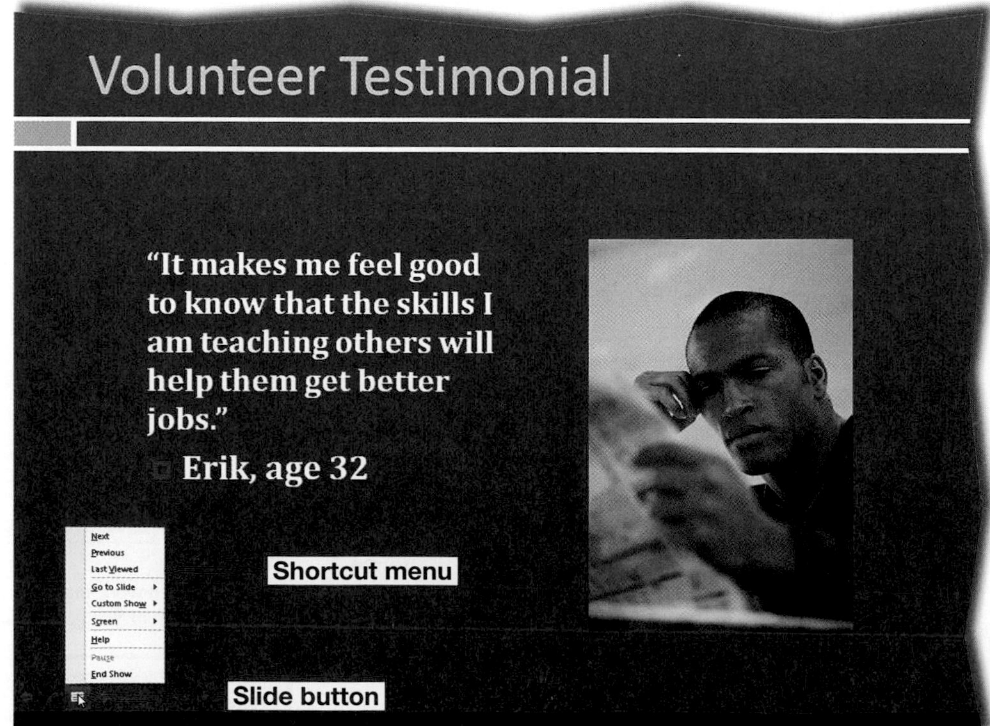

EXERCISE 2-17
Modify Character Spacing and Scale

Changing the spacing between characters in your document makes text more attractive and easier to read. **Scale** changes the size of a character. Scaling text more than 100 percent will stretch the text. Scaling text less than 100 percent will compress it.

FIGURE 2.35 Character Spacing in the Font dialog box

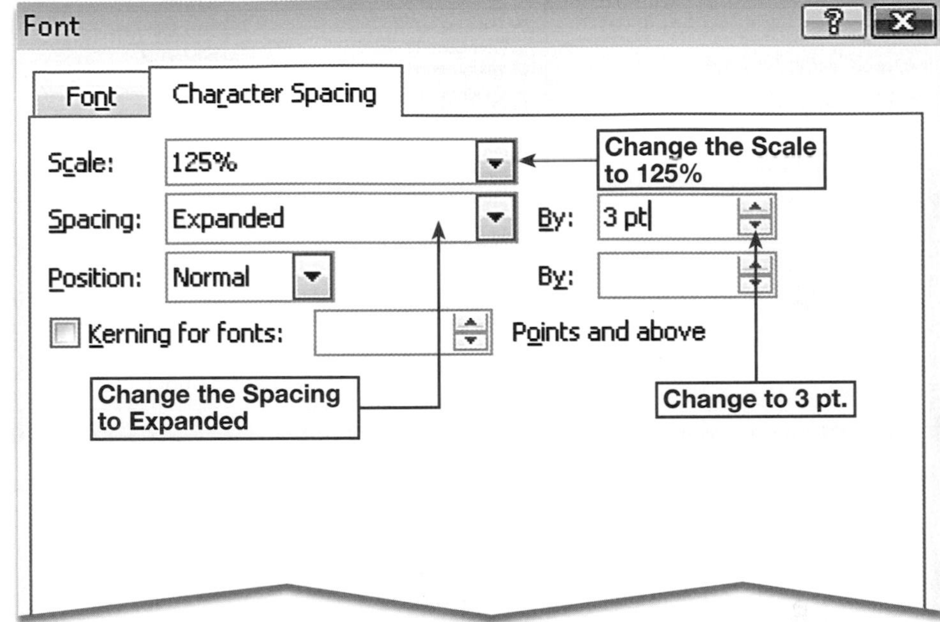

FIGURE 2.36 Modified character spacing and scale

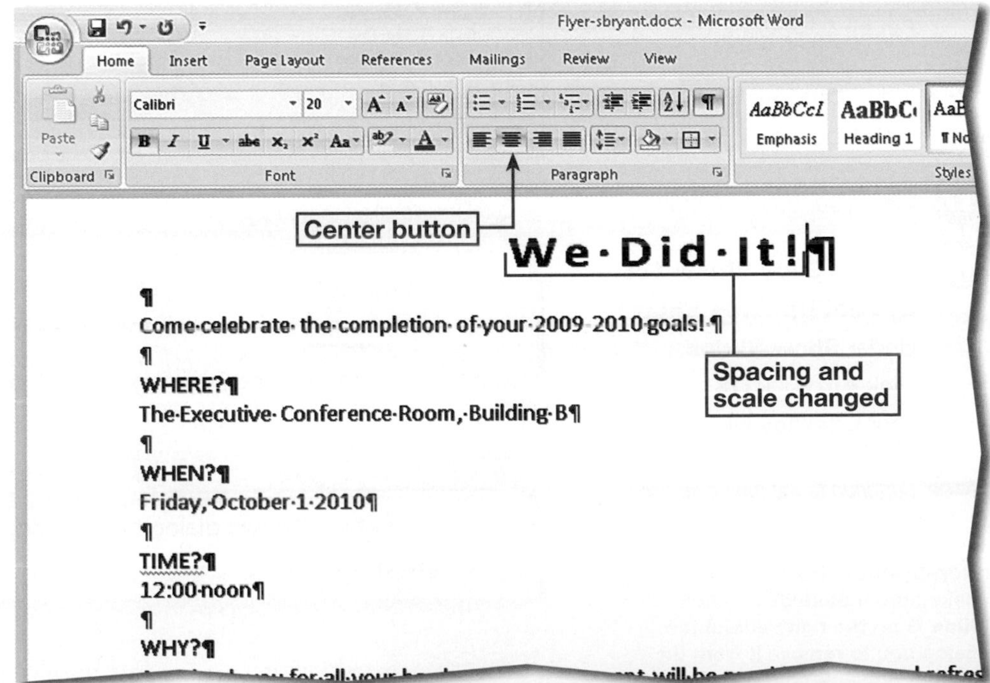

Step-By-Step

1. In your **Flyer** file, click the **View Ruler** button on the vertical scrollbar to close the rulers.
2. Select **We Did It!**. Change the **Font** to **Calibri**. Change the **Font Size** to **20 pt.**
3. Choose **Home>Font Dialog Box Launcher**. Select the **Character Spacing** tab.
4. In the **Scale** window, delete the setting that is displayed. Key: 125%.
5. In the **Spacing** window, select **Expanded**. In the **By** box, key: 3 pt.
6. **CHECK** Your dialog box should look like Figure 2.35. Click **OK**.
7. Select the text **We Did It!**. Choose **Home>Paragraph>Center**.
8. **CHECK** Your screen should look like Figure 2.36. Save your file.

Continue to the next exercise.

NCLB/Math (Measurement)
Reinforce to students the mathematical nature of spacing and scale. Inform students that the scale of an object is measured in point size just as the length of an object is measured in inches.

Step-By-Step

EXERCISE 4-14 (Continued)
Create and Edit a Custom Show

10 Click **Edit**. In the **Define Custom Show** dialog box, under **Slides in presentation**, click **14. Reading Reach**. Click **Add**.

11 Under **Slides in custom show**, click **3. Our Mission**. Click the **up arrow** button once.

12 CHECK Your dialog box should look like Figure 4.33. Notice that **Slide 3** has become the second slide in the list.

13 Under **Slides in custom show**, click **8. Library Information**.

14 Click **Remove**.

15 CHECK Your dialog box should look like Figure 4.34. Click **OK**.

16 In the **Custom Shows** dialog box, click **Show**.

17 View your custom show.

18 Choose **Slide Show>Set Up>Set Up Slide Show**. Under **Show Slides**, click **All**. Click **OK**.Save your **Literacy** file.

Continue to the next exercise.

Step-by-Step Tip In Step 13, make sure that students click **Slide 8** on the right side of the dialog box to remove it from the custom presentation.

FIGURE 4.33 Rearranging slides in the custom presentation

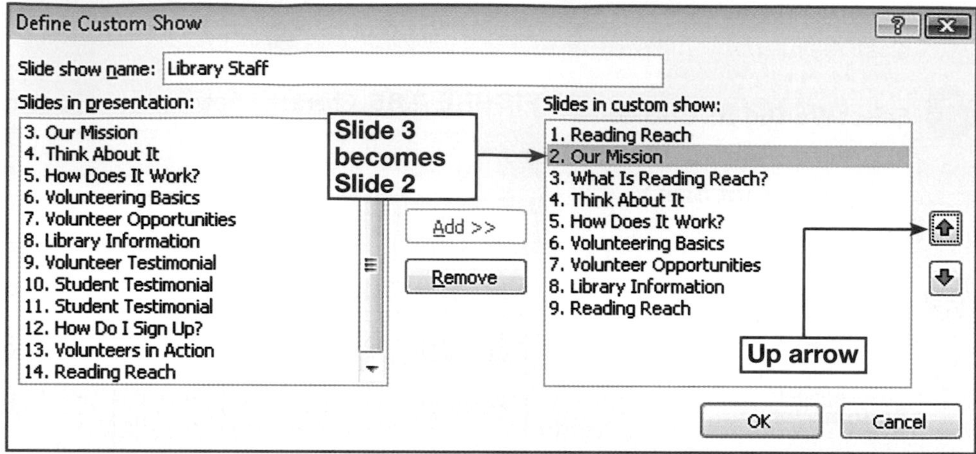

FIGURE 4.34 Edited custom show

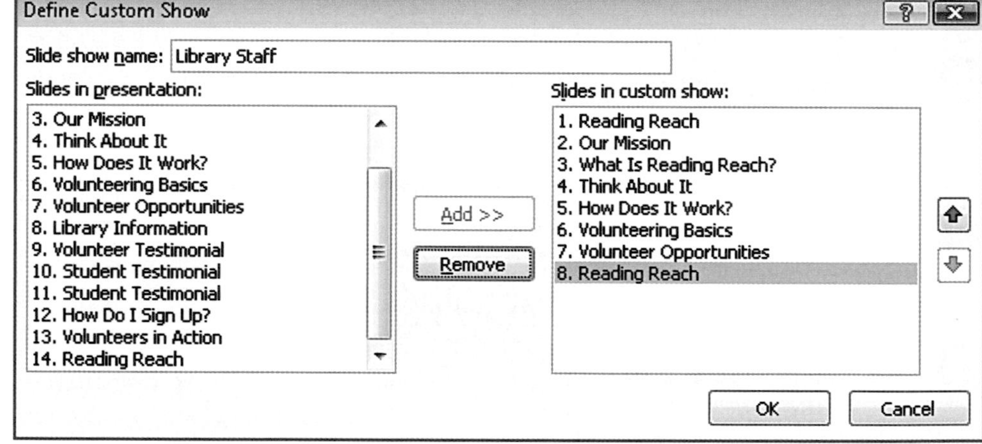

Shortcuts

To select multiple slides in the **Define Custom Show** dialog box, hold down CTRL as you click the slides.

You Should Know

Use the **Custom Shows** dialog box to add, modify, remove, or copy a custom show.

Step-By-Step

1. In your **Flyer** file, select the heading **WHERE?**.
2. In **Home>Styles**, click the **More** arrow [button] to open the **Quick Styles** gallery.
3. Move your pointer over the style options. **Live Preview** allows you to see how the title in your document would change (see Figure 2.37).
4. Click the **Emphasis** style to apply it to your heading.
5. Select the heading **WHEN?**. Repeat Step 4.
6. Repeat Step 4 for the remaining two headings, **TIME?** and **WHY?**.
7. Select the headings **WHERE?**, **WHEN?**, **TIME?**, and **WHY?** and format them **Bold**.
8. **CHECK** Your screen should look like Figure 2.38. Save your file.

Continue to the next exercise.

Troubleshooter

The Style Set shown here is the program default. The styles displayed on your screen may look different than the figure.

EXERCISE 2-18
Apply Quick Styles to a Document

Word 2007 has a feature called **Quick Styles**, which lets you easily apply new styles to text. The styles are grouped in sets so that colors and formats create a design with a unified look. Creating a uniform, professional appearance in your documents with Quick Styles can help make the document easier to analyze, or study.

FIGURE 2.37 Preview the style options in the Quick Styles gallery

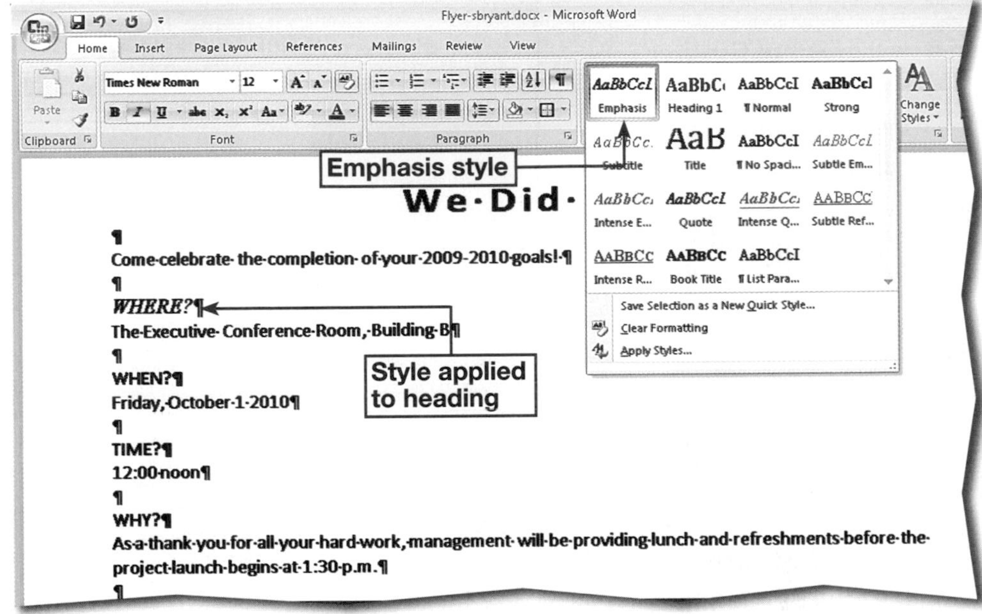

FIGURE 2.38 The Quick Styles applied to the text

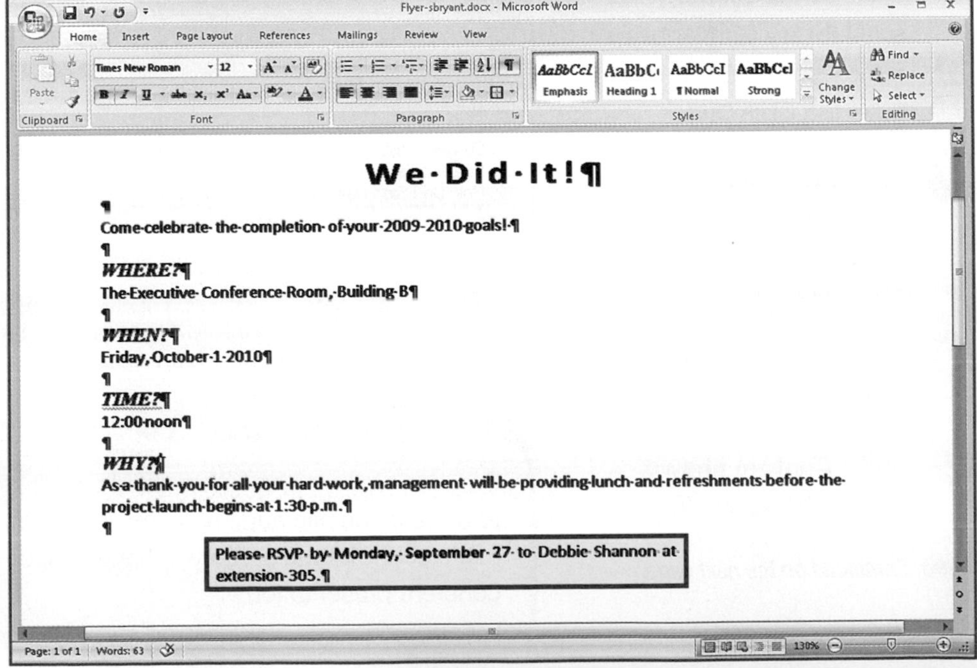

Step-By-Step

1. In your **Literacy** file, choose **Slide Show> Custom Slide Shows**.
2. In the **Custom Shows** dialog box, click **New** (see Figure 4.31).
3. In the **Define Custom Show** dialog box, click in the **Slide show name** box. Key: Library Staff.
4. Hold down CTRL. Select Slides **1-8**. Click **Add**.
5. **CHECK** Your dialog box should look like Figure 4.32. Click **OK**. Click **Close** in the **Custom Shows** dialog box.
6. Choose **Slide Show>Set Up**. Click **Set Up Show** and select **Custom Show** under **Show Slides**. Make sure **Library Staff** appears in the **Custom Show** drop-down list. Click **OK**.
7. In the **Start Slide Show** group, click **From Beginning**. View your custom show.
8. Choose **Custom Slide Show>Custom Shows**.
9. Under **Custom shows**, select **Library Staff**.

Continued on the next page.

EXERCISE 4-14
Create and Edit a Custom Show

Another way to tailor an existing presentation for different audiences is to create a custom show. A custom show includes slides from an existing slide show. You can edit a custom show by adding, removing, and rearranging slides.

New Student Strategy If students are just joining the class, show them how to run a slide show.

FIGURE 4.31 Custom Shows dialog box

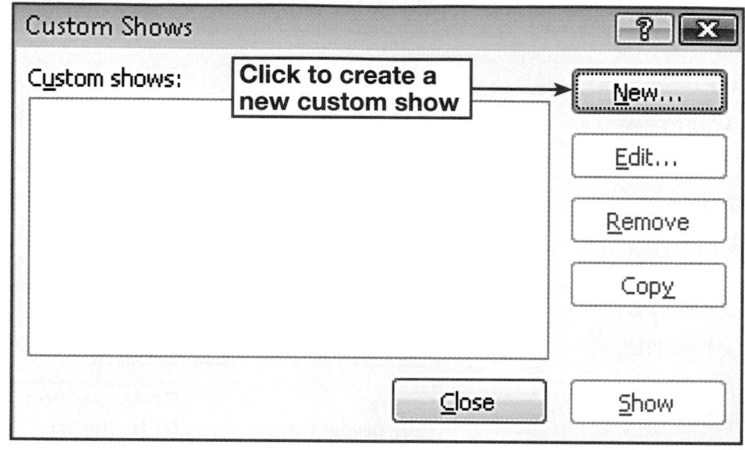

FIGURE 4.32 Define Custom Show dialog box

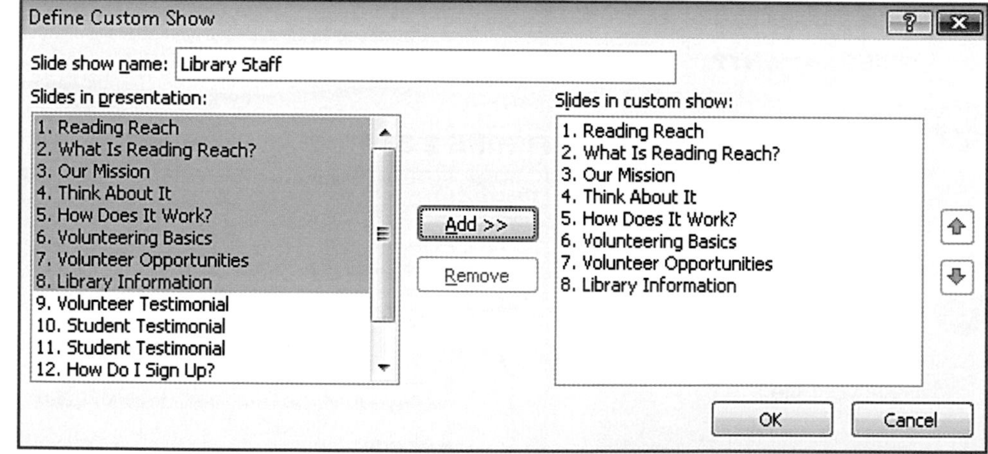

NCLB/Language Arts (NCTE 12) Tell students that taking slides out of a presentation can be like taking pages out of a book. Students need to be certain that their overall point is not weakened when they customize a presentation.

Academic Skills

Creating custom shows is a good way to gear a larger presentation to a more specific audience. Preview your customized show to make sure that the slides you have chosen create a complete and coherent presentation.

Step-By-Step

1. In your **Flyer** file, choose **Home>Styles>Change Styles>Style Set**. A drop-down menu appears.
2. Move your pointer over the different style set options to see how they look in your document. Choose **Modern** (see Figure 2.39).
3. Click **Change Styles**. Choose **Colors**.
4. Choose **Aspect**.
5. Select the document title. Click the **Font Color** drop-down arrow.
6. Use the **Color** menu ScreenTips to choose **dark green, accent 4**.
7. **CHECK** Your screen should look like Figure 2.40. Save and close your file.

You Should Know

Quick Styles can help format various assignments. For example, if you are writing a term paper, use Quick Styles to format the headings in the document and allow the reader to see each section clearly.

Troubleshooting Since you may not be able to print in color in the classroom, show students the gray-scale option in the Color menu.

EXERCISE 2-19
Change the Style Set and Color Themes

The Quick Styles options displayed on your ribbon and the Quick Styles gallery can change depending on the style set that you are using. Each style set offers a different combination of fonts, formats, and colors that are designed to be used together to give your document a distinct look. You can further modify the styles by changing the color theme.

Solution Use the file **Flyer-SF.docx** as a solution file for **Exercises 2-15** through **2-19**.

FIGURE 2.39 Preview the Style Set options

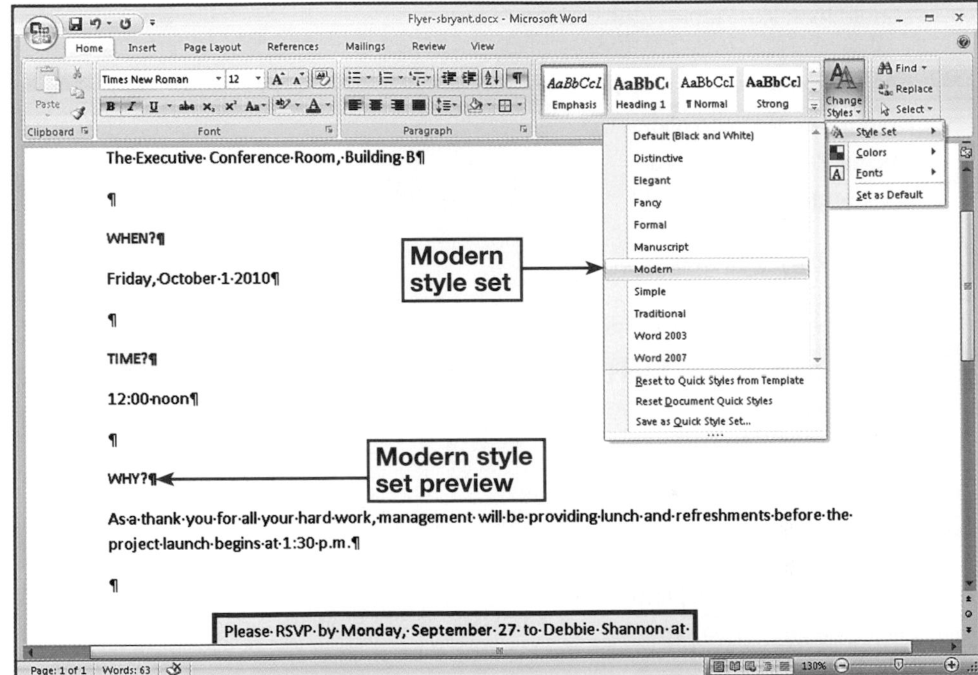

FIGURE 2.40 The Style Set applied to the text

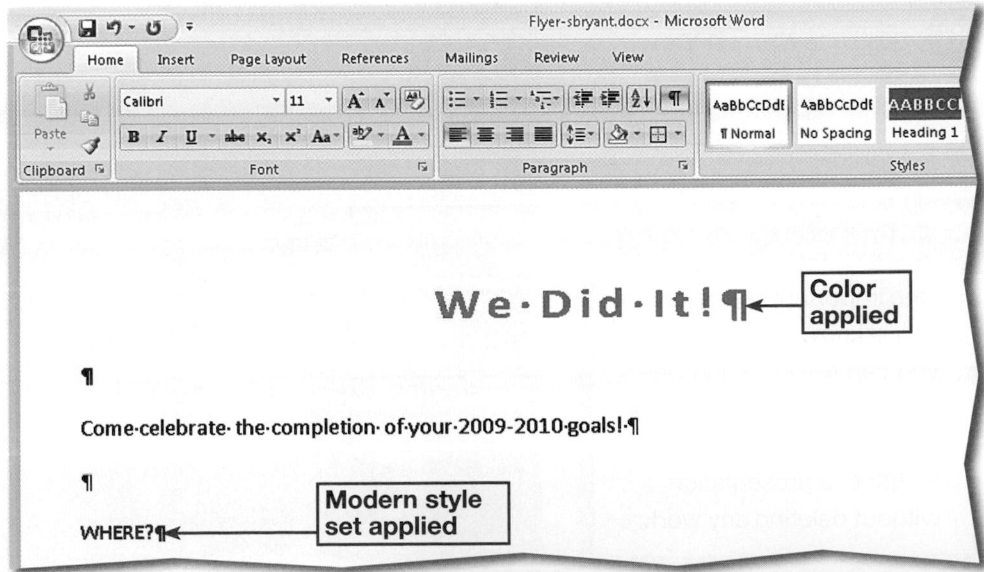

Step-By-Step

1. In your **Literacy** file, click **Slide Sorter View**.
2. Click **Slide 4**. Choose **Slide Show>Set Up> Hide Slide** .
3. CHECK Your screen should look like Figure 4.29.
4. Click **Slide 6**. Press CTRL. Hold the button and click **Slides 7**, **9**, **12**, and **13**. Click **Hide Slide** .
5. CHECK Your screen should look like Figure 4.30.
6. Choose **Slide Show>Start Slide Show>From Beginning** .
7. After viewing the show, in **Slide Sorter View**, click **Slide 4**. Press CTRL and click **Slides 6**, **7**, **9**, **12**, and **13**. Click **Hide Slide** again to unhide the slides.
8. Switch to **Normal View**. Save your file.

Continue to the next exercise.

Academic Skills

One important presentation skill is knowing how much you can say in a short period of time. Hiding slides is a quick way to reduce the length of a presentation without deleting any work.

EXERCISE 4-13
Hide Slides

Depending on your audience, you may want to customize your presentations. Instead of deleting slides that you do not want to use, simply hide them by using the Hide Slide button. The Hide Slide button is available only in Slide Sorter view. Select Print hidden slides in the Print dialog box to print slides you have hidden.

NCLB/Language Arts (NCTE 7) Remind students to evaluate if their presentations are too specific. They can include hidden slides as handouts to provide extra details to interested audience members.

FIGURE 4.29 Hidden slide in Slide Sorter View

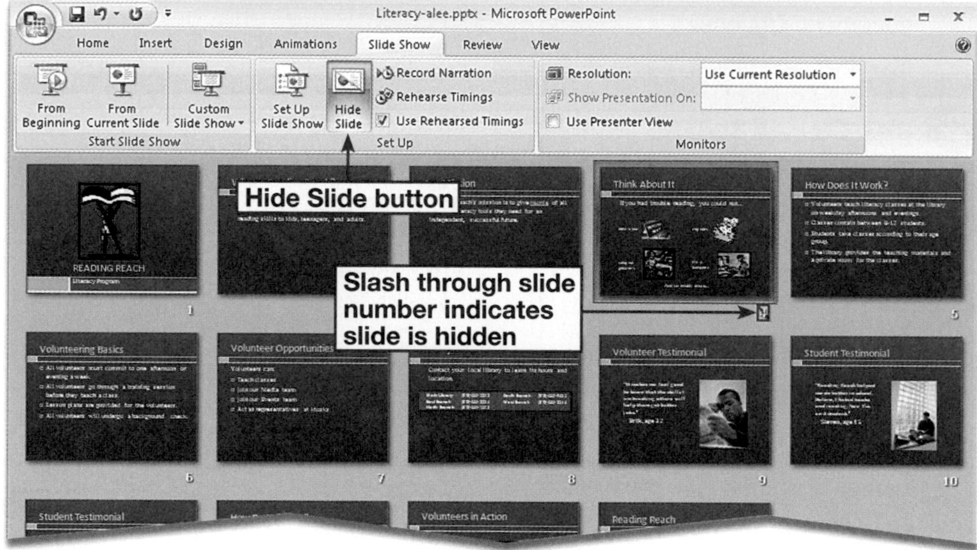

FIGURE 4.30 Multiple slides hidden

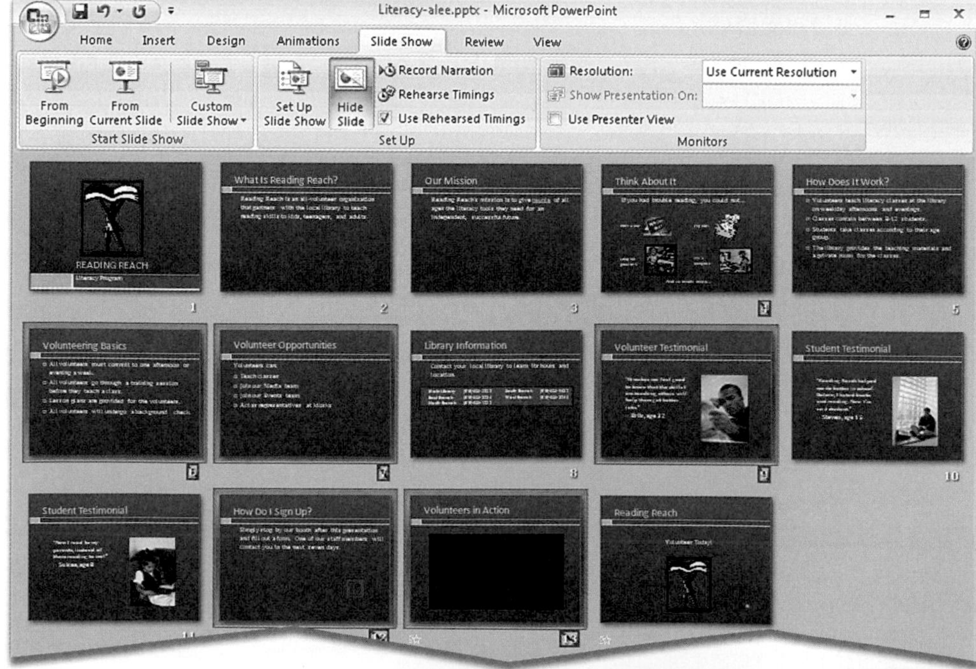

LESSON 2 After You Read

Vocabulary

Key Terms

alignment
bullet
bulleted list
character
font
font style
Format Painter
formatting
indent
margin
memo
numbered list
point
Quick Styles
scale
style
tab stop
typeface

Academic Vocabulary

analyze
enhance
horizontal

Answer to Vocabulary Activity
Students create a word search using ten vocabulary words from the lesson. Word searches will vary.

Review Vocabulary

Complete the following statements on a separate piece of paper. Choose from the Vocabulary list on the left to complete the statements.

1. A(n) ___point___ is used to measure font size. (p. 38)

2. The ___font___ is the unique design of a set of characters. (p. 38)

3. In Word, a default ___tab stop___ is set every .5 inches. (p. 36)

4. You can easily apply styles to a document using ___Quick Styles___. (p. 54)

5. Left and right page margins can be set on the ___horizontal___ ruler. (p. 36)

Vocabulary Activity

6. Create a word search using ten of the Vocabulary terms from this lesson.
A. Decide which ten terms to use in the word search.
B. Write the definitions for each Vocabulary term. These will be the "clues" for your word search.
C. Create a block of letters. Your ten terms should be hidden in this block, with letters spelling out the ten terms written horizontally, vertically, diagonally, or backwards.
D. Exchange your word search with a classmate. Try your classmate's word search. Use the definitions to find the terms in the block of letters.

Review Key Concepts

Answer the following questions on a separate piece of paper.

7. Which of the following is NOT an example of formatted text? (p. 40)
A. Red
B. Bold
C. 11 pt.
(D.) Tab

8. Which of the following is NOT a type of paragraph alignment? (p. 44)
A. Align right
(B.) Horizontal
C. Justify
D. Center

9. The Tabs command is found by clicking ______. (p. 36)
A. Home>Paragraph>Tabs
(B.) Home>Paragraph> Dialog Box Launcher
C. Page Layout>Page Set Up>Tabs
D. Page Layout>Paragraph>Indent

10. Which of the following lists should be performed or viewed in a particular order and, therefore, should be formatted as a numbered list? (p. 45)
A. A grocery list
B. A list of team members
(C.) Directions to a friend's house
D. A list of items in your desk

11. The three parts of a memo are: (p. 34)
A. heading, salutation, body
B. salutation, body, closing
C. date, body, closing
(D.) heading, body, closing

Step-By-Step

1. In your **Literacy** file, switch to **Normal View**.
2. Click **Office>Print>Print Preview**. Under **Print what**, select **Handouts (4 Slides Per Page)**.
3. Click the **Options** drop-down arrow. Select **Scale to Fit Paper** and **Frame Slides**.
4. Under **Options**, choose **Printing Order> Horizontal**. Click **Next Page** twice. Click **Orientation> Landscape**.
5. **CHECK** Your screen should look like Figure 4.27.
6. Click **Orientation> Portrait**. Click **Options>Header and Footer**. On the **Notes and Handouts** tab, select only **Header**. In the **Header** box, key: Reading Reach Presentation. Click **Apply to All**.
7. **CHECK** Your screen should look like Figure 4.28. Close **Print Preview**. Save your file.

Continue to the next exercise.

Differentiated Instruction/Visually Impaired Discuss with students the usefulness of distributing handouts to an audience. They can get a closer look at the content and take notes.

EXERCISE 4-12
Change Preview Options

Use **Print Preview** to see how slides, notes pages, outlines, and handouts will look when you print them. For example, if you want to hand out a paper copy of your presentation to your audience, conserve paper by printing more than one slide per page. Use the Print What drop-down arrow to preview different views. You can also add frames, headers, and footers.

FIGURE 4.27 Preview of slide with options applied

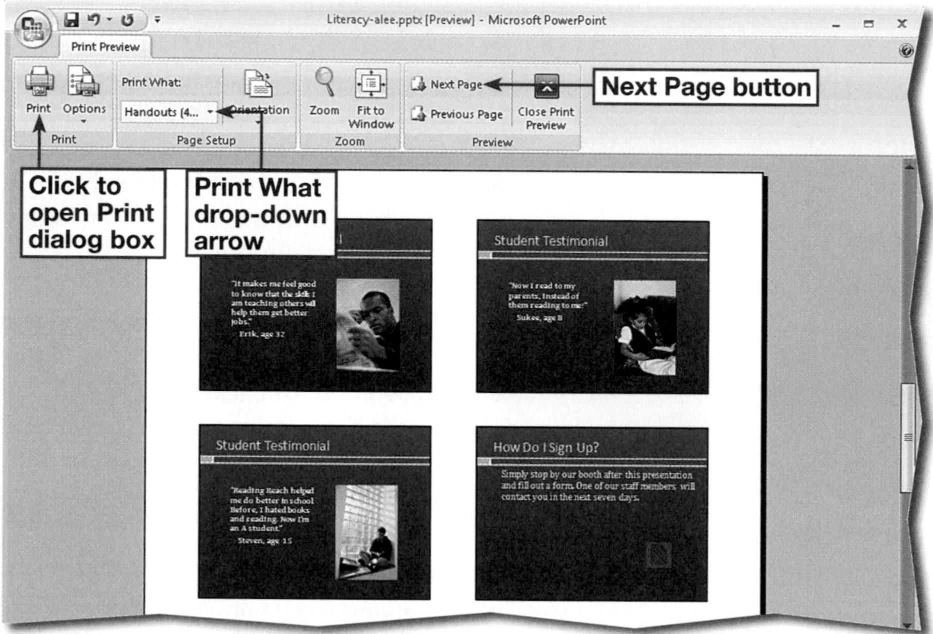

FIGURE 4.28 Preview of handout with options applied

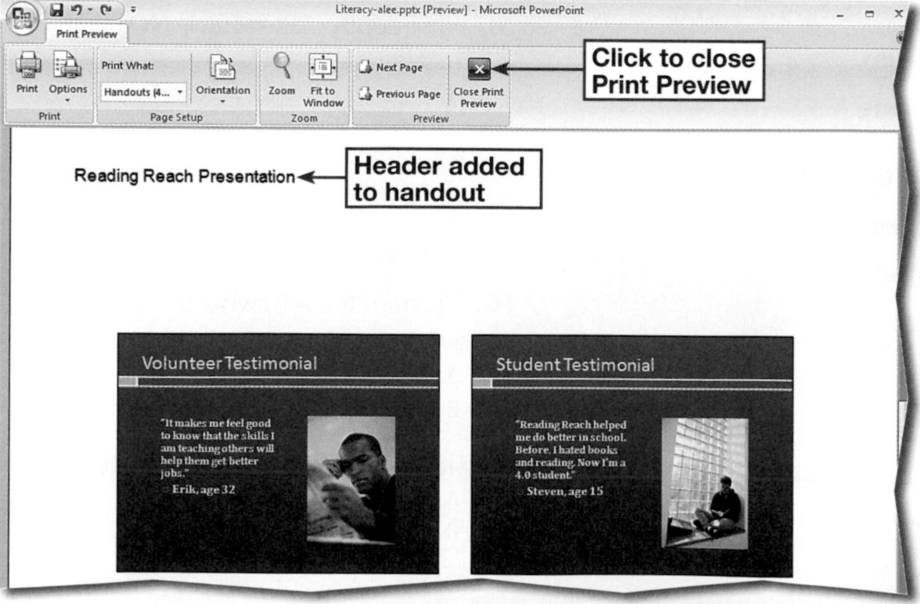

LESSON 2 Practice It Activities

1. Format Fonts

Follow the steps to complete the activity.

Step-By-Step

1. Open the data file **Fonts.docx**. Save as: Fonts-[your first initial and last name]1.
2. Select the word **Typeface**. Change the **Font** to **Times New Roman**.
3. Select the word **Style**. Click **Italic**.
4. Select the word **Size**. Change the **Font Size** to **20**.
5. Select the word **Color**. Change the **Font Color** to **Red**. Deselect the text.
6. **CHECK** Your screen should look like Figure 2.41.
7. Select the four words you just formatted. Click [bullets button].
8. Select the word **superscript**. On the **Home** tab, click [x² button].
9. Select the word **highlighter**. Click [highlight button].
10. **CHECK** Your screen should look like Figure 2.42. Save and close the file.

Solution The solution file for this activity is **Fonts1-SF.docx**.

FIGURE 2.41 Modify fonts

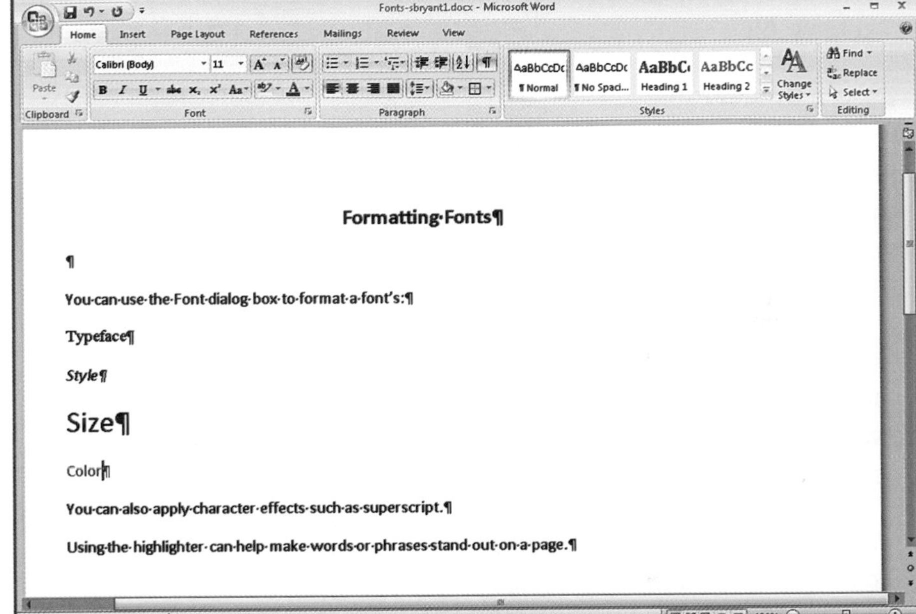

FIGURE 2.42 Format a bulleted list

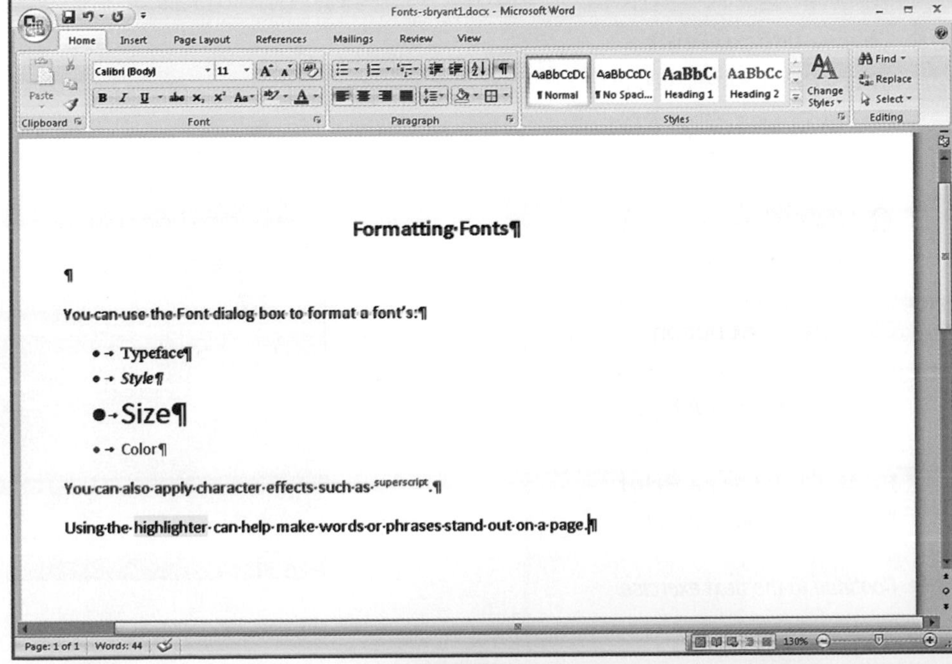

Step-By-Step

1. With your **Literacy** file open in **Normal View**, click the **Outline** pane.

2. Right-click in the **Outline** pane and select **Collapse> Collapse All**.

3. Choose **Office>Print**. In the **Print** dialog box, under **Print what**, choose **Outline View**. Click **Preview**. Zoom to **100%** and scroll up.

4. **CHECK** Your screen should look like Figure 4.25. With your teacher's permission, click **Print**.

5. Click **Close Print Preview**. Right-click in the **Outline** pane and select **Expand> Expand All**. Click the **Slides** pane.

6. Choose **Office>Print**. Under **Print what**, choose **Notes Pages**. Click **Preview**. Scroll to **Page 14**.

7. **CHECK** Your screen should look like Figure 4.26.

8. Click the **Print** button. Under **Print range**, select **Current slide**. With your teacher's permission, click **Print**. Click **Close Print Preview**. Save your file.

Continue to the next exercise.

EXERCISE 4-11
Print Outlines and Speaker Notes

To print only the text of a presentation, use Outline View. Before you print, use the Outlining toolbar in the Outline pane to choose the number of levels of text that you want to print. You can also print slides along with their notes pages.

NCLB/Language Arts (NCTE 12) Reinforce for students how useful **Outline View** is for organizing the overall presentation. Explain the similarities between creating an outline for an essay and an outline for a presentation.

FIGURE 4.25 Preview of Outline View at 100% zoom

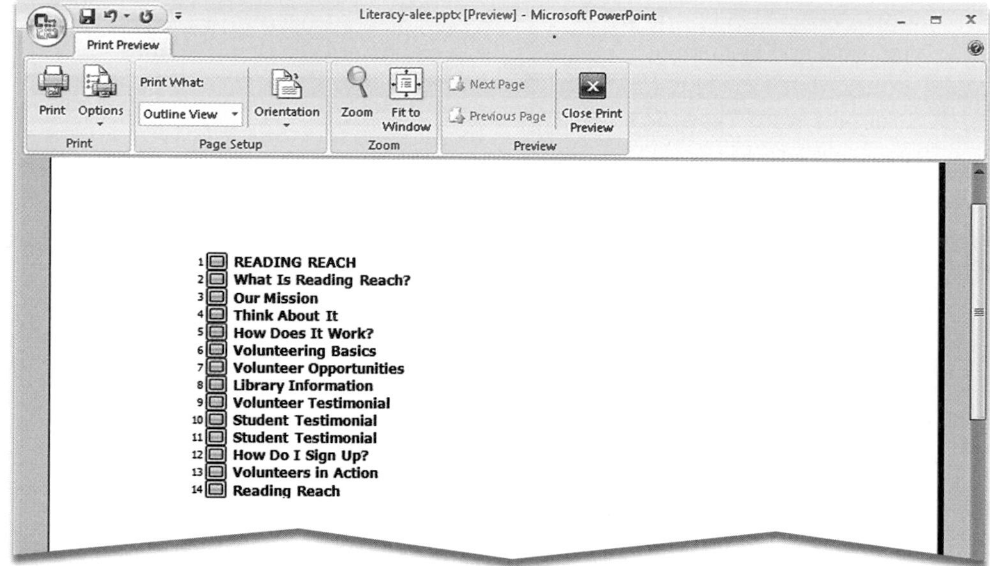

Solution The solution files for this exercise are **p4-7a-SF.docx** and **p4-7b-SF.docx**.

FIGURE 4.26 Preview of Notes Page

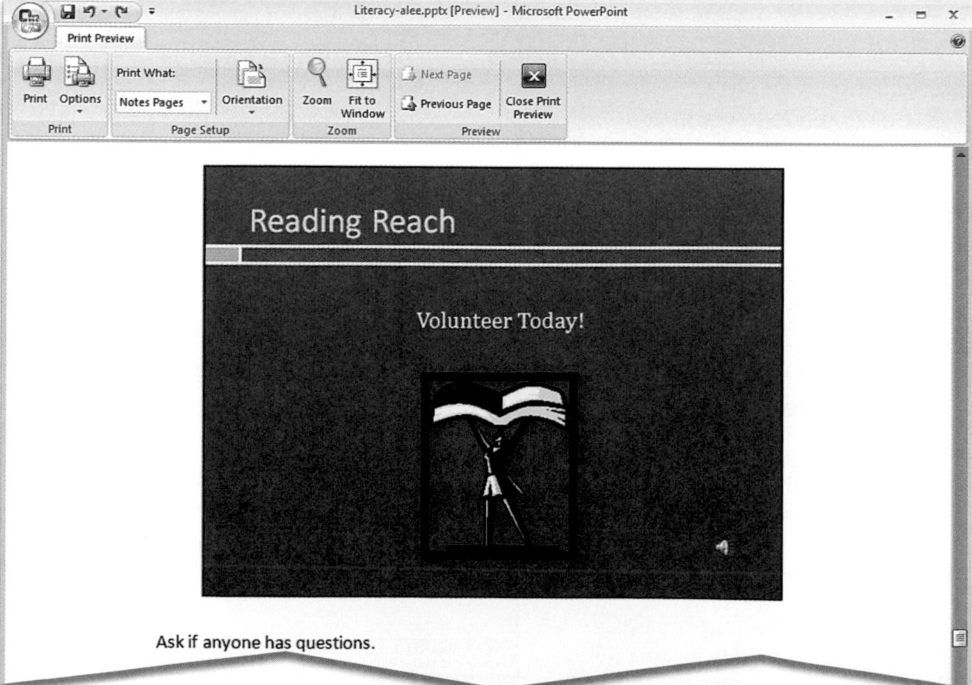

LESSON 2 Practice It Activities

2. Format Paragraphs

Follow the steps to complete the activity.

Solution The solution file for this activity is **Paragraphs2-SF.docx.**

Step-By-Step

1. Open the data file **Paragraphs.docx**. Save as: Paragraphs-[your first initial and last name]2.
2. **Center** align the second paragraph.
3. **Right** align the third paragraph.
4. **Justify** the fourth paragraph.
5. CHECK Your screen should look like Figure 2.43.
6. Select the title **Formatting Paragraphs**. Apply **Quick Styles Heading 2**. Change the color to a shade of **Red**.
7. Change the document's **Line Spacing** to **1.5**. Deselect the text.
8. Select the words **Align left** and click **Highlight**. Double-click [icon].
9. Select the words **Center**, **Align Right**, and **Justify**. Click **Format Painter**.
10. CHECK Your screen should look like Figure 2.44. Save and close the file.

FIGURE 2.43 Formatted paragraphs

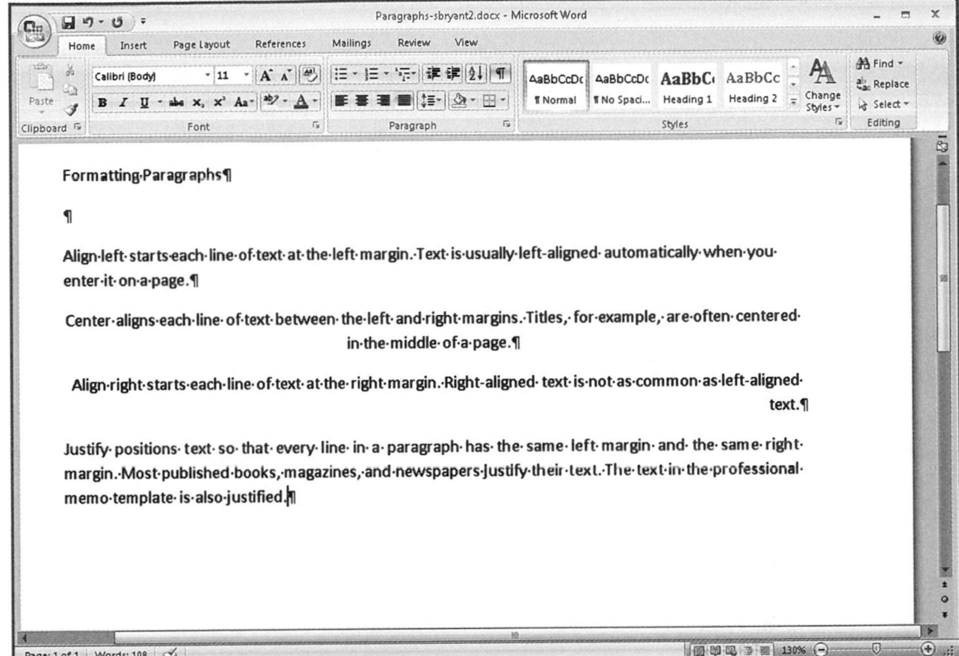

FIGURE 2.44 Paragraphs with copied formats

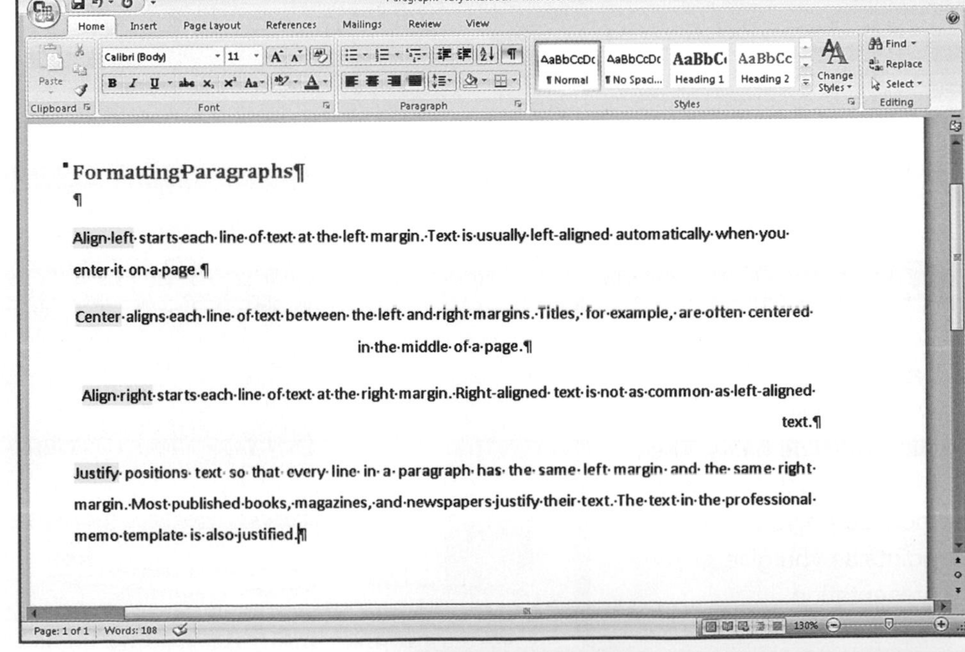

Step-By-Step

1. In your **Literacy** file, move to **Slide 14**. Make sure you are in **Normal View**.
2. Click in the **Notes** pane. Key: Ask if anyone has questions.
3. **CHECK** Your screen should look like Figure 4.23.
4. Choose **View> Presentation Views> Notes Page**.
5. Click **View>Zoom**. In the **Zoom** dialog box, click **100%**. Click **OK**.
6. **CHECK** Your screen should look like Figure 4.24.
7. Choose **View>Zoom> Fit to Window**. Click **Normal View**.
8. **CHECK** Your screen should again look like Figure 4.23.
9. Save your file.

Continue to the next exercise.

Academic Skills

You can use the **Notes** pane to write notes about what you will say on a slide-by-slide basis. These notes can help you stay focused on your main points as you give a presentation.

EXERCISE 4-10
Use Notes Pages and Zoom Views

In Normal View, use the Notes pane to add notes to your presentation. To see your notes, use Page View. The Zoom tool increases and decreases the display size.

FIGURE 4.23 Normal View with note added to Notes pane

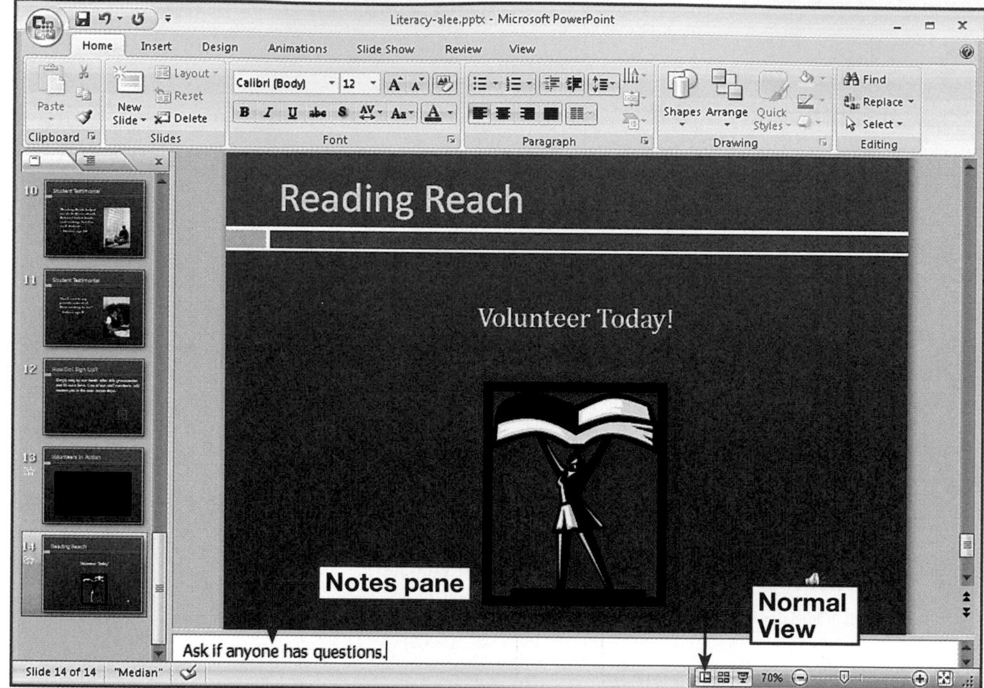

FIGURE 4.24 Notes Page view at 100% zoom

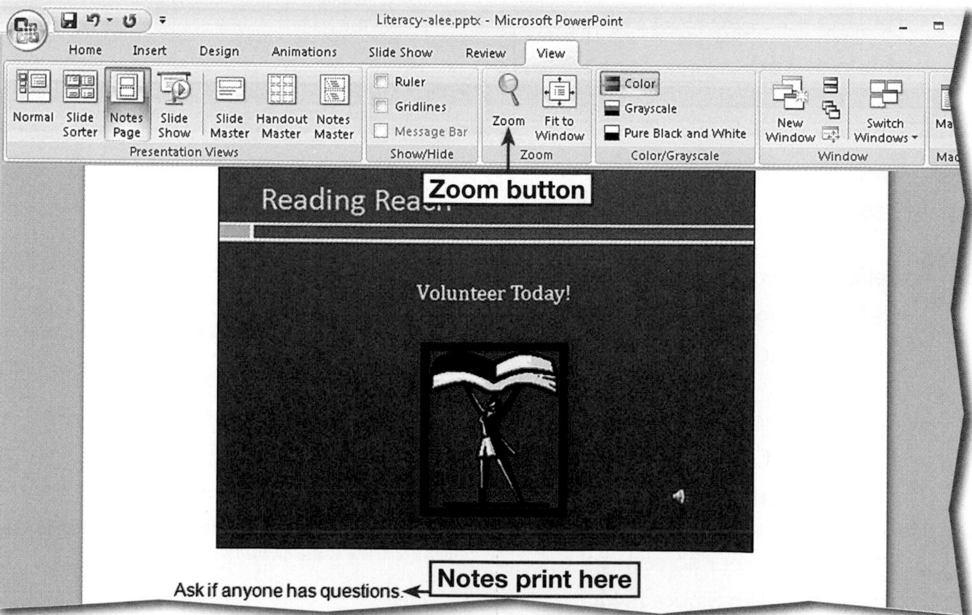

NCLB/Language Arts (NCTE 8) Remind students of the importance of outlining their ideas in short, organized lists when they prepare reports and presentations.

3. Format a Memo

Data File

Follow the steps to complete the activity.

Step-By-Step

1. Open the data file **PI_Memo.docx**. Save as: PI_Memo-[your first initial and last name]3. Choose **Page Layout>Page Setup>Dialog Box Launcher**. Set the **Top** margin to **2″**. Set the **Left** and **Right** margins at **1″**. Click **OK**.

2. Select the five lines under **MEMORANDUM**. Launch the **Paragraph** dialog box. Select **Tabs**. Under **Tab stop position**, key: .75. Click **Set**. Click **OK**.

3. Click before **Product Team Development**. Key: TO:. Press TAB. Repeat to create the guide words: **FROM:**, **CC:**, **DATE:**, **SUBJECT:** (see Figure 2.45). Bold all five words.

4. Select the second paragraph in the memo body. Set the **First Line Indent**, **Hanging Indent**, and **Left Indent** to **1″**. Set the **Right Indent** to **4.5″**.

5. CHECK Your screen should look like Figure 2.45. Save and close the file.

FIGURE 2.45 Formatted memo

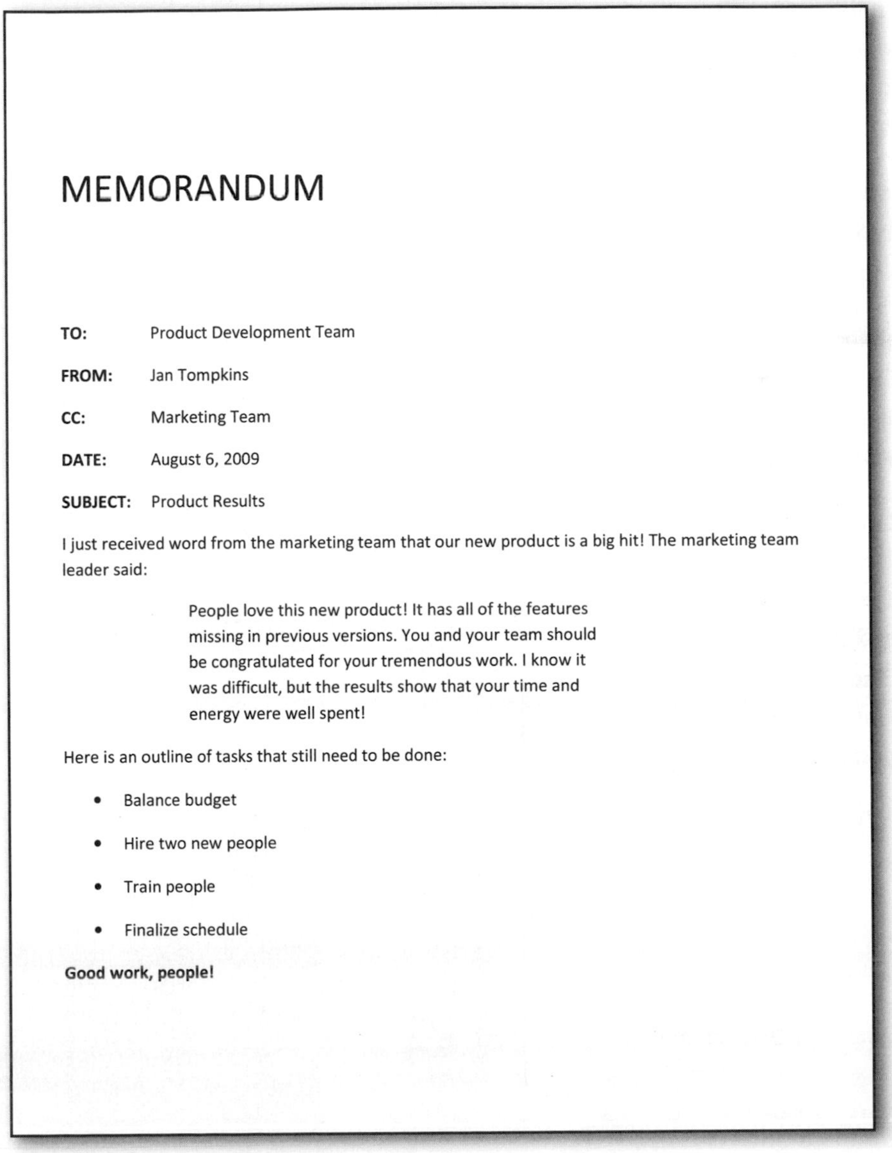

MEMORANDUM

TO: Product Development Team

FROM: Jan Tompkins

CC: Marketing Team

DATE: August 6, 2009

SUBJECT: Product Results

I just received word from the marketing team that our new product is a big hit! The marketing team leader said:

> People love this new product! It has all of the features missing in previous versions. You and your team should be congratulated for your tremendous work. I know it was difficult, but the results show that your time and energy were well spent!

Here is an outline of tasks that still need to be done:

- Balance budget
- Hire two new people
- Train people
- Finalize schedule

Good work, people!

Solution The solution file for this activity is **PI-Memo3-SF.docx.**

Step-By-Step

8. Move to **Slide 14**. Choose the **Insert>Media Clips> Sound** drop-down arrow. Select **Sound from File**.

9. In the **Insert Sound** dialog box, navigate to and select the data file **Volunteer.wav**.

10. **CHECK** Your dialog box should look like Figure 4.21. Click **OK**.

11. In the **Microsoft Office PowerPoint** dialog box that opens, click **Automatically**.

12. On the **Sound Tools Options** tab, in the **Sound Options** group, select the box next to **Hide During Show**. Move the speaker icon to the lower-right corner of the slide.

13. **CHECK** Your screen should look like Figure 4.22.

14. Click **Preview**. Click ESC. Save your file.

Continue to the next exercise.

You Should Know

Most media clips are copyright protected. It is not acceptable to use media clips without the owner's permission.

EXERCISE 4-9 (Continued)
Insert Media Clips into Slides

FIGURE 4.21 Insert Sound dialog box

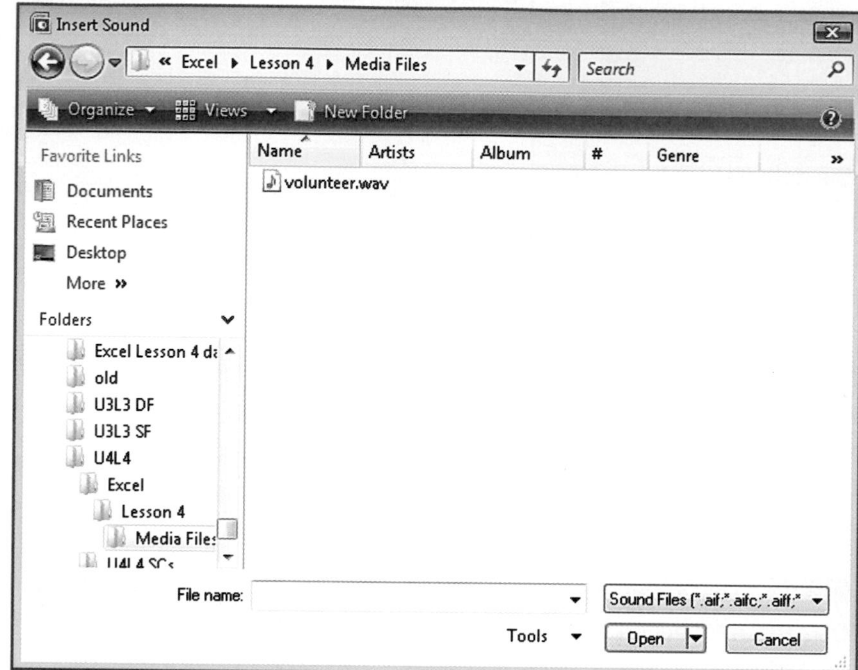

Differentiated Instruction/Advanced Students Encourage students to experiment with the other movie and sound options.

FIGURE 4.22 Final slide of presentation

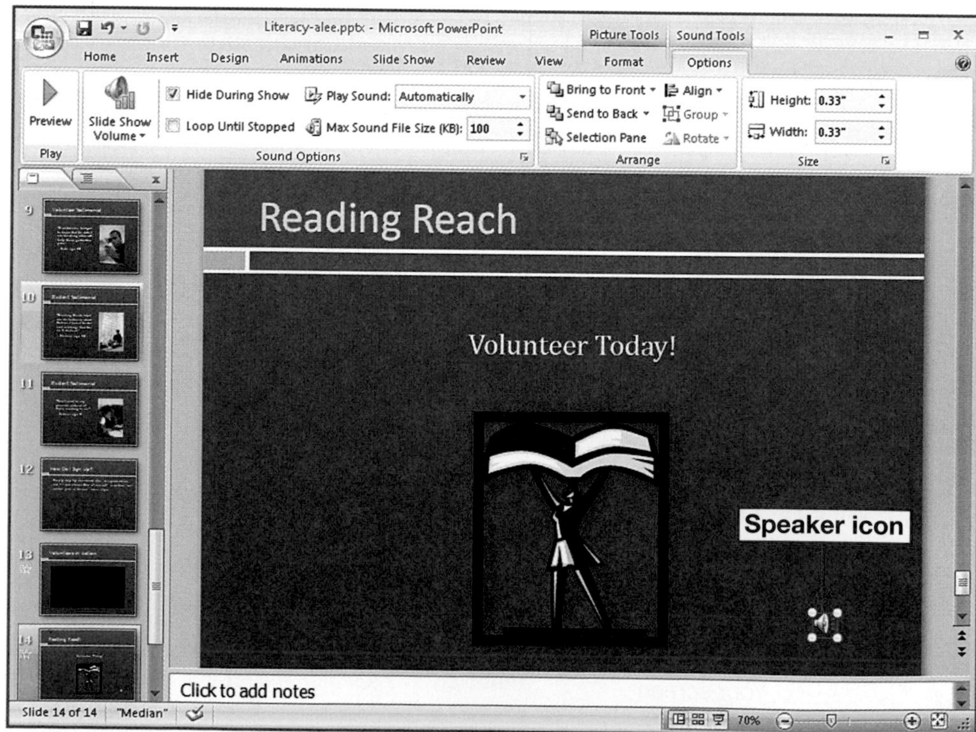

Teaching Tip Turn to page TM48 for more information about copyright guidelines.

LESSON 2 You Try It Activities

4. Create and Format a Memo

You are a member of your local Community Center's event planning committee. As fall approaches, you decide to create a memo to help coordinate the Center's many volunteers.

Solution The solution file for this activity is **Volunteers4-SF.docx**.

Step-By-Step

1. Open the data file **Volunteers.docx**. Save as: Volunteers-[your first initial and last name]4.
2. Set the memo's margins as shown in Figure 2.46.
3. Format the heading as shown. Use a 1″ tab stop. Add the guide words and format them bold.
4. Select the list of fall events. Create a numbered list as shown.
5. Format the first three lines in the memo's form as shown. (The form starts with **Name:** and ends with **Friday Saturday**.)
6. Use a **2″ Left** aligned tab stop to format the days of the week as shown.
7. Select the entire form. Set the **Right Indent** to **2.75″**. Add a border and shading as shown.
8. **CHECK** Your memo should look like Figure 2.46. Save and close your file.

Differentiated Instruction/ Advanced Students Encourage students to key the document instead of using the data file.

FIGURE 2.46 Community Center memo

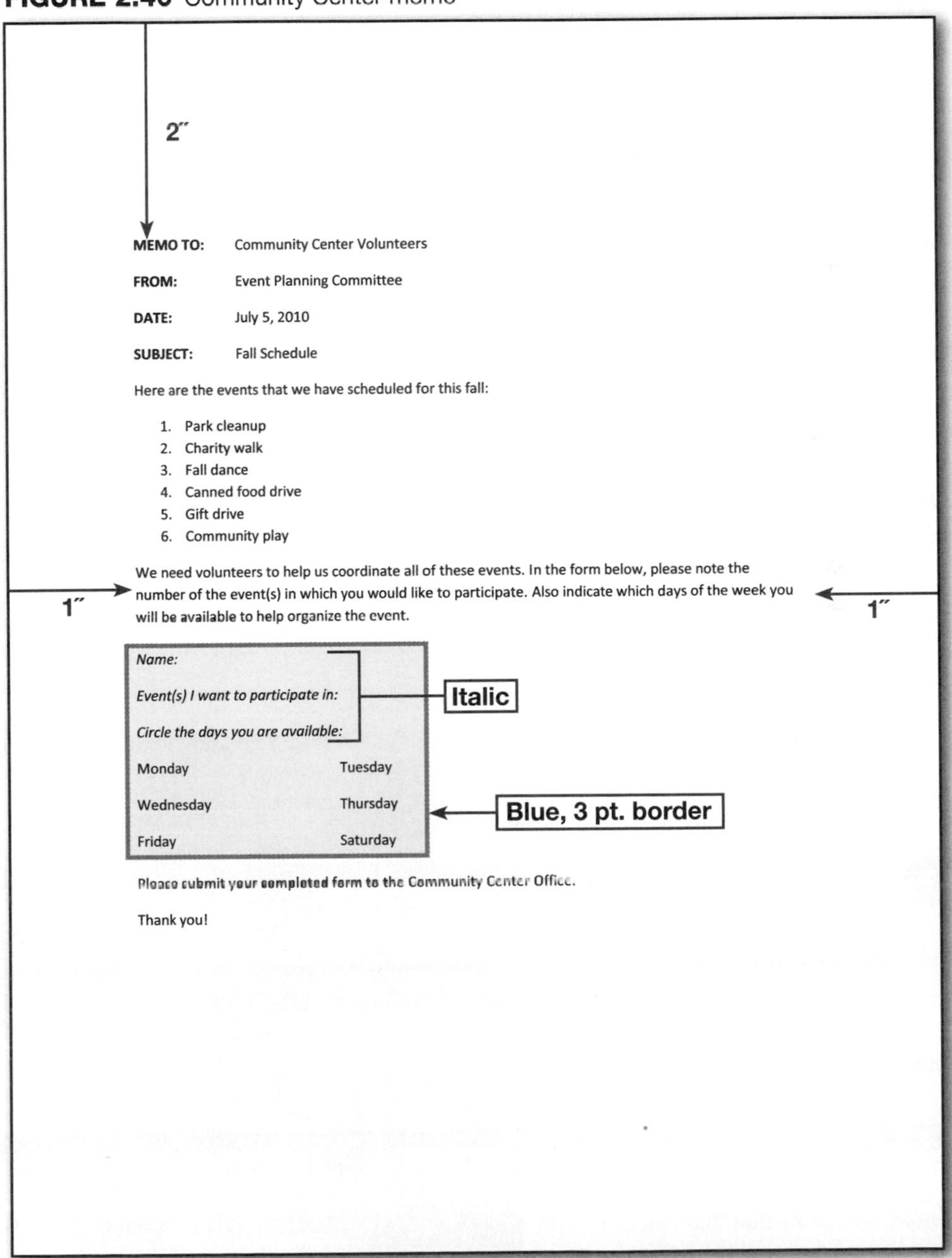

Step-By-Step

1. In your **Literacy** file, move to **Slide 12**. Choose **Home>Slides>New Slide>Title and Content Slide**. In the title, key: Volunteers in Action.

2. Choose **Insert>Media Clips>Movie>Movie from File**.

3. **CHECK** Your screen should look like Figure 4.19

4. In the **Insert Movie** dialog box, select the data file **Reading.wmv**. Click **OK**. In the **Microsoft Office PowerPoint** dialog box, click **Automatically**.

5. Click on the movie image. On the **Movie Tools Options** tab, change the **Width** to **7″**. Press ENTER.

6. Place the box as shown in Figure 4.20. Choose **Movie Tools Options>Arrange>Align>Align Center**.

7. **CHECK** Your screen should look like Figure 4.20. Click **Preview** to view the movie clip. Save your file.

Continued on the next page.

Step-by-Step Tip In **Step 5**, tell students to move the box so that it does not block the title of the slide **Volunteers in Action.** Students can drag the movie box down as they would drag a text box.

EXERCISE 4-9
Insert Media Clips into Slides

To insert sound and movie files into a presentation, use the Insert tab. Be sure to choose clips that add to your overall presentation. Clips that are too long or seem unconnected to the presentation's message will distract your audience.

FIGURE 4.19 Insert Movie dialog box

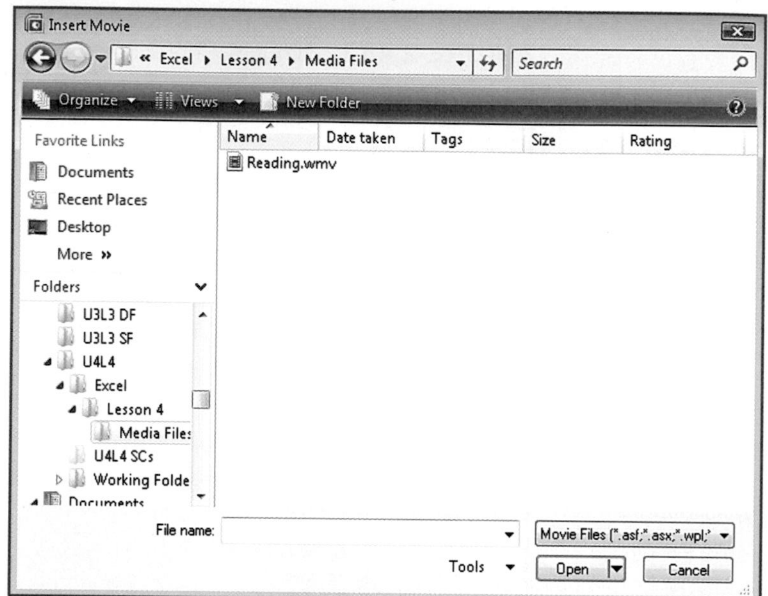

FIGURE 4.20 Movie clip inserted into slide

5. Apply Styles to a Flyer

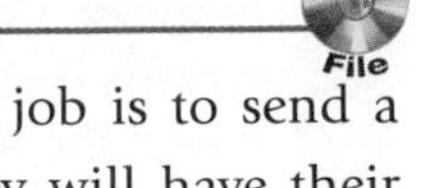

You are a member of your school's yearbook committee. Your job is to send a flyer to the sophomore class telling them when and where they will have their pictures taken.

Step-By-Step

1. Open the data file **Yearbook.docx**. Save as: Yearbook-[your first initial and last name]5.
2. Click **Change Styles**. Set the **Style Set** to **Manuscript**. Set the **Colors** to **Module**.
3. Format **Where?**, **When?**, and **What If I Miss the Date?** as shown.
4. Format the text under **Where?**, **When?**, **What If I Miss the Date?** as shown. Add bullets.
5. Format **It's Time for Pictures!** and **See you there!** in **Title** style.
6. Select **It's Time for Pictures!** Center align the text. Change the **Font Color** to **Red, Accent 6**.
7. Select **See you there!** Center align the text. Change the **Font Color** to **Red, Accent 6**. In the **Font** dialog box, select **Small caps**.
8. **CHECK** Your flyer should look like Figure 2.47. Save and close your file.

FIGURE 2.47 Yearbook flyer

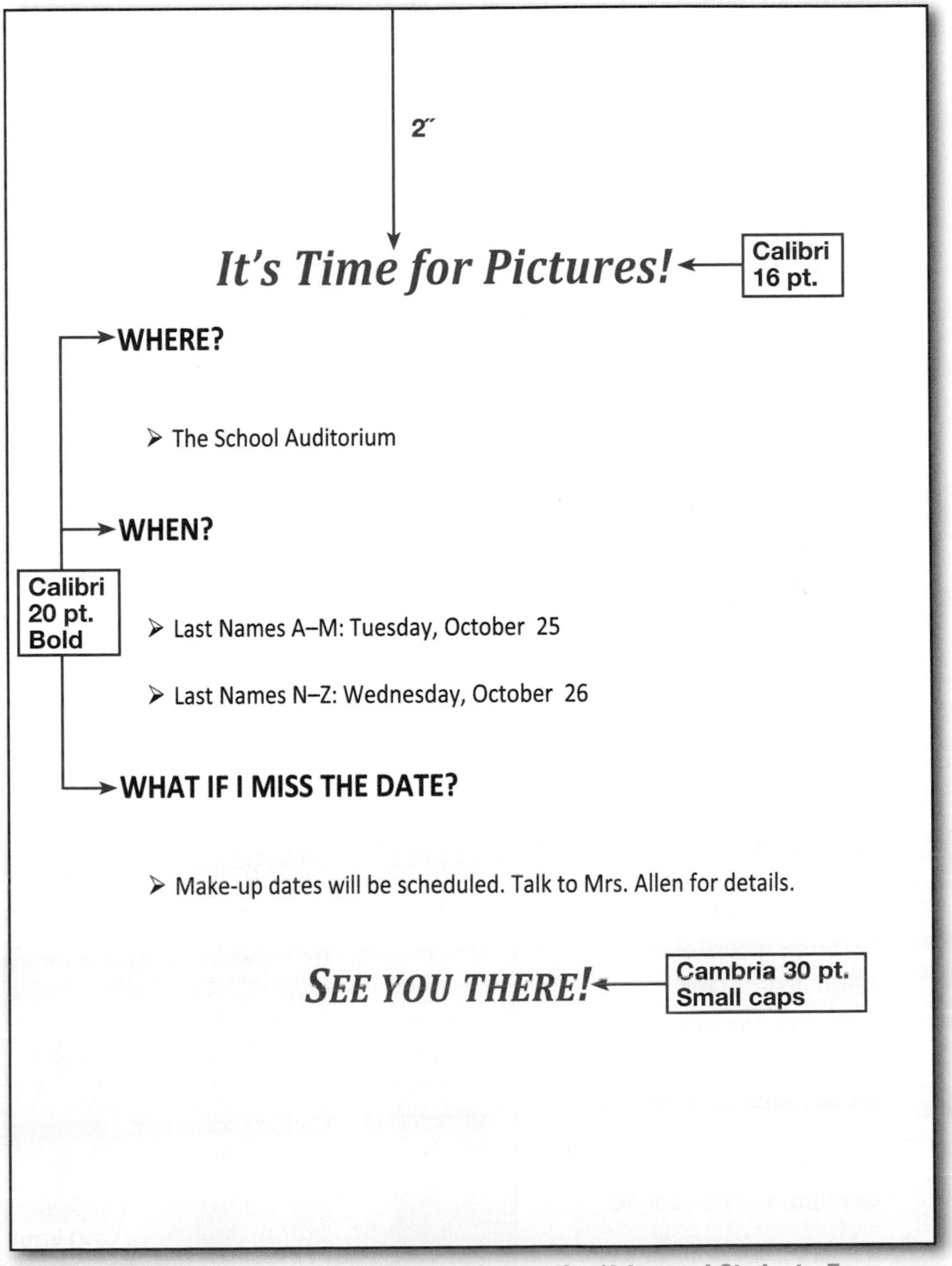

2″

It's Time for Pictures! ← Calibri 16 pt.

WHERE?

- The School Auditorium

WHEN?

Calibri 20 pt. Bold

- Last Names A–M: Tuesday, October 25
- Last Names N–Z: Wednesday, October 26

WHAT IF I MISS THE DATE?

- Make-up dates will be scheduled. Talk to Mrs. Allen for details.

SEE YOU THERE! ← Cambria 30 pt. Small caps

Solution The solution file for this activity is **Yearbook5-SF.docx.**

Differentiated Instruction/Advanced Students Encourage students to key the document instead of using the data file.

Step-By-Step

1. In your **Literacy** file, move to **Slide 12**.
2. Select the Action button. Select **Drawing Tools> Format>Arrange>Align**. Select **Grid Settings**. In the **Grid and Guides** dialog box, under **Snap to**, select **Snap objects to grid**.
3. Select **Display grid on screen**. Select **Display drawing guides on screen**.
4. **CHECK** Your dialog box should look like Figure 4.17. Click **OK**.
5. Drag the Action button up and position its bottom edge within the guide lines. Press CTRL and use ← and → to position the button more accurately.
6. **CHECK** Your screen should look similar to Figure 4.18.
7. On the **Format** tab in the **Arrange** group, click **Align**. Select **Grid Settings**. Deselect **Display drawing guides on screen**. Click **OK**.
8. Click **Align**. Deselect **View Gridlines**. Save your file.

Continue to the next exercise.

EXERCISE 4-8
Display Grids and Guides

Grids and guides make it easier to create, modify, and align text and graphics. A **grid** is a series of horizontal and vertical lines that look similar to graph paper. A **guide** is an adjustable horizontal or vertical line on a slide to help you align objects. When you drag an object close to a grid or guide, it will **snap** into place.

FIGURE 4.17 Grid and Guides dialog box

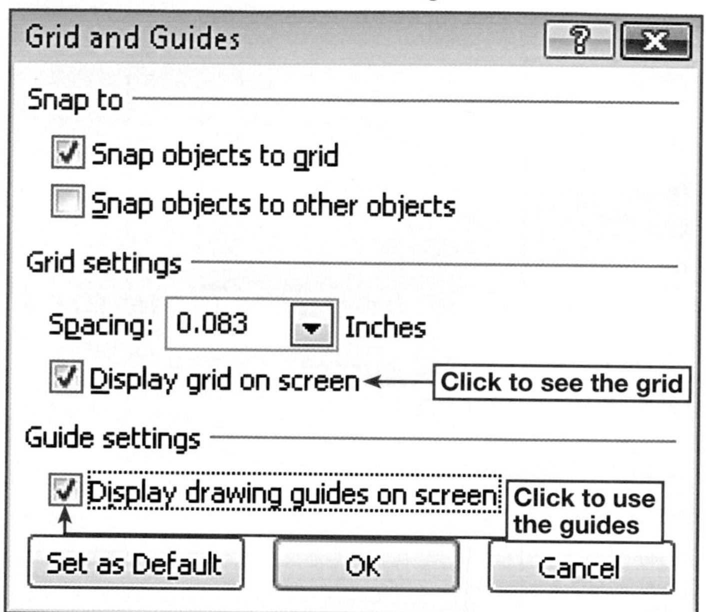

FIGURE 4.18 Action button positioned using grids and guides

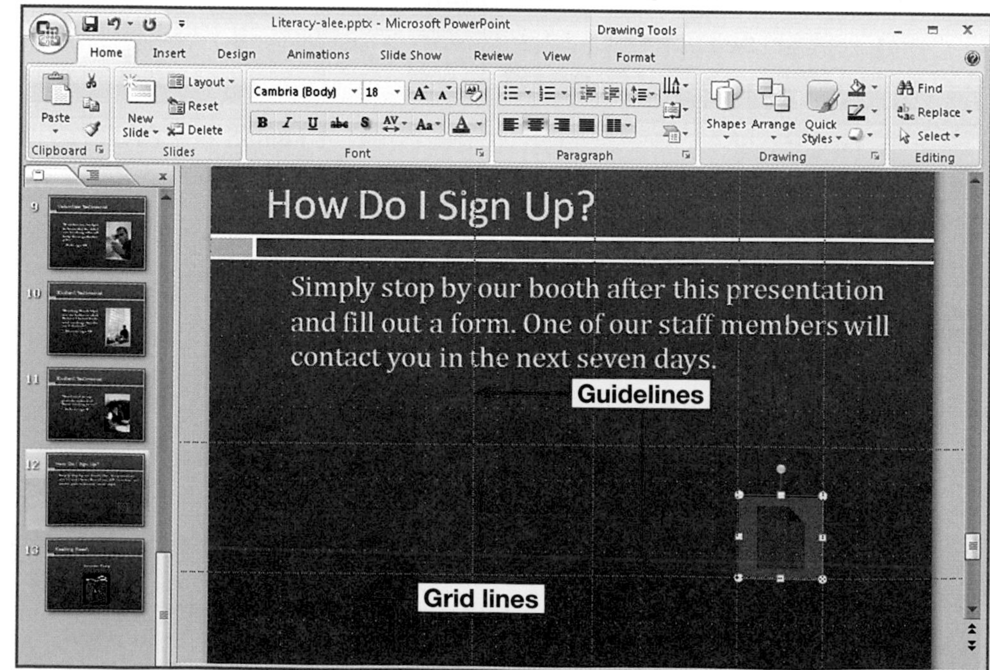

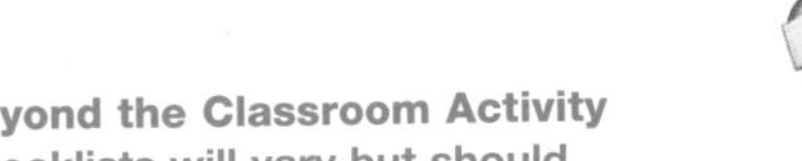

LESSON 2 Critical Thinking Activities

6. Beyond the Classroom Activity

Beyond the Classroom Activity Checklists will vary but should describe the Style Set used; title/head font size and style; body font type and size; default paragraph alignment and line spacing; and any special formatting. Students should explain their choices.

Standards at Work Activity Student lists should use a standard memo format and should include a bulleted list of three employees and a numbered list of three tasks.

21st Century Skills Activity Students should create two numbered lists of five items each, one list of qualities one wants in a team member and the other of undesirable team member qualities. Students can use Quick Styles or other techniques to format the document and text.

Language Arts: Create a Formatting Checklist You want documents in your company to have a consistent look, so you decide to create a formatting checklist that details the styles and formats you will apply to memos and agendas. Create a sample memo or agenda. Then, in your checklist, note the following:

- The Style Set you are using
- Title/heading font size and style
- Body font type and size
- Default paragraph alignment and line spacing
- Any special formatting (colors, styles, etc.)

Explain the reasoning behind your formatting choices.

Save your file as: w2rev-[your first initial and last name]6.

7. Standards at Work Activity

 **Microsoft Certified Application Specialist Correlation**

Word 2.1 *Format Text and Paragraphs*

Create and Format a Memo You are training three new employees in your company and will write a memo to your manager explaining your training agenda.

- Insert a memo heading and title.
- Create a bulleted list that identifies the three employees you are training.
- Create a numbered list that identifies three tasks you plan to teach them.

Save your file as: w2rev-[your first initial and last name]7.

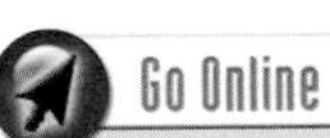

Go Online e-REVIEW

glencoe.com

Go to the **Online Learning Center** to complete the following review activities.

Online Self Check
To test your knowledge of the material, click **Unit 1> Lesson 2** and choose **Self Checks**.

Interactive Review
To review the main points of the lesson, click **Unit 1> Lesson 2** and choose **Interactive Review**.

8. 21st Century Skills Activity

Prioritize Team Member Qualities In order to help your team work well together, you must be a good team member.

- Create a numbered list that identifies the top five qualities a team member should have.
- Items in the list should go from most important (number 1) to least important (number 5).
- Create a second numbered list that identifies five qualities that prevent a team from working together.
- Add a title and headers. Format your text and document to create a unique look.

Save your file as: w2rev-[your first initial and last name]8.

Step-By-Step

1. In your **Literacy** file, click **Slide 12**. Choose **Insert>Shapes**.

2. In the **Shapes** drop-down menu, at the bottom of the menu, under **Action Buttons**, select **Action Button: Document** .

3. The pointer turns into a cross. Click once in the lower-right corner to place the Action button.

4. In the **Action Settings** dialog box, under **Action on click**, select **Hyperlink to:**. Scroll down and select **Other File** (see Figure 4.15).

5. Navigate to and select the data file **Worksheet.docx**. Click **OK**.

6. CHECK Your screen should look like Figure 4.16.

7. Save your file.

Continue to the next exercise.

Academic Skills

Test the file by clicking the **Slide Show** and clicking the Action button. The file that opens is for people interested in signing up for the program. What other types of documents might you want to incorporate into your presentations?

EXERCISE 4-7
Add Action Buttons to Slides

An **Action button** is a button displayed on a slide. Like a hyperlink, it allows you to link to another slide, presentation, document, or Web page. Some buttons can help you navigate among slides. Others take you to the first slide in your presentation, to more information, to the Help screen, or to a selected document.

FIGURE 4.15 Insert Action Settings dialog box

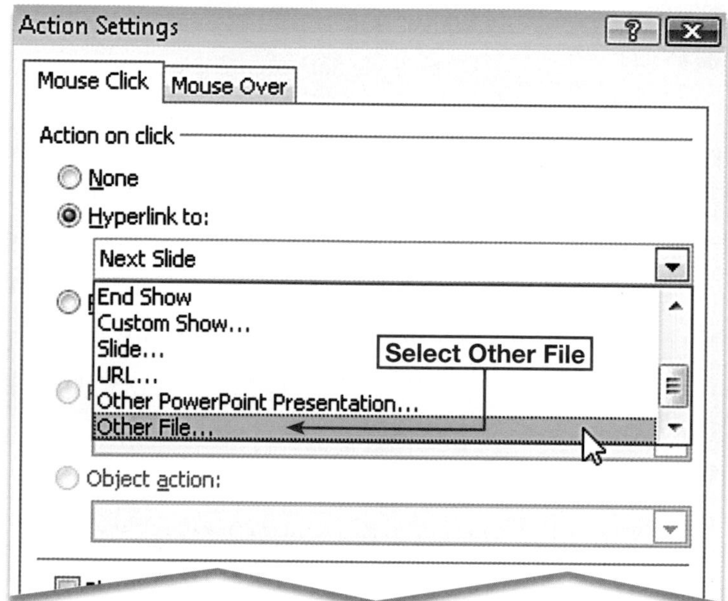

NCLB/Language Arts (NCTE 12) Explain to students that using Action buttons to add documents to their presentations is a great way to ecourage people to participate in and respond to a presentation.

FIGURE 4.16 Document Action button

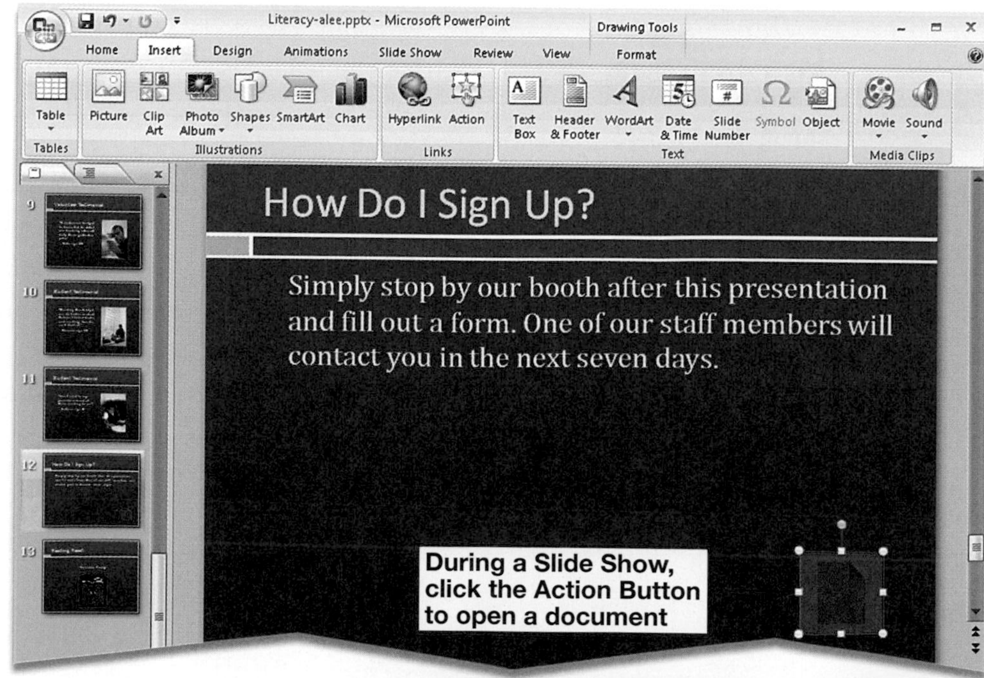

LESSON 2 Challenge Yourself Projects

Before You Begin

The Hiring Process Understanding the hiring process will give you an idea of what to expect when you look for a job. It will also prepare you for the time when you might have to hire others.

Reflect Once you complete the projects, open a new document and answer the following:

1. How can a good job description help to attract the right candidate for the job?
2. Why is it important to prepare interview questions in advance?
3. What questions might a job candidate ask an interviewer?

9. Create a Job Advertisement

Rubric

LEVEL This is an intermediate level project.

Language Arts: Write a Job Description You are a manager for a bicycle shop. You need to hire someone who can sell and repair bikes. To save money, you decide to post a job description in the local supermarket.

Write a one-paragraph job description for this position. You want somebody who:

- Has at least three years experience in sales.
- Can repair bicycles.
- Can work weekends.

Format your job description so that it catches people's attention. Use different fonts, colors, and shading as needed to emphasize important points.

Save your file as: w2rev-[your first initial and last name]9.

10. Create Lists

Rubric

LEVEL This is an advanced level project.

Language Arts: List Interview Questions You have scheduled interviews for the new position. Now you need to generate a list of five questions that you want to ask the candidates.

- Brainstorm a bulleted list of five questions.
- Organize your five questions into a numbered list.
- Put the most important question first and the least important question last.

Save your file as: w2rev-[your first initial and last name]10.

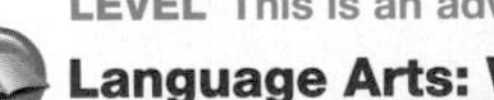

11. Create a Memo

Rubric

LEVEL This is an advanced level project.

Language Arts: Write a Summary You have found someone that you think is perfect for the bike shop job! The owner of the bike shop has asked you to write a brief memo that explains why you want to hire the candidate you have chosen. Remember that you need to express to your boss why you feel this applicant is the best candidate for the position. In order to professionally communicate, create a professional memo for your boss.

- In your memo, state the name of the person you want to hire.
- Give a brief description of the person's qualifications.
- Include a bulleted list that identifies three reasons why you want to hire this individual.

Save your file as: w2rev-[your first initial and last name]11.

Answers Rubrics for each Challenge Yourself Project are available at **glencoe.com**. You may want to download the student rubrics and make them available to students as they complete each project.

EXERCISE 4-6
Add Hyperlinks to Slides

A **hyperlink** is clickable text that takes users to a new location. Use hyperlinks in your presentations to quickly move to a different slide within the same presentation, to another file on your computer, or to a Web page.

Step-By-Step Tip In **Step 3**, be sure students select Slide 10, not Slide 11.

FIGURE 4.13 Insert Hyperlink dialog box

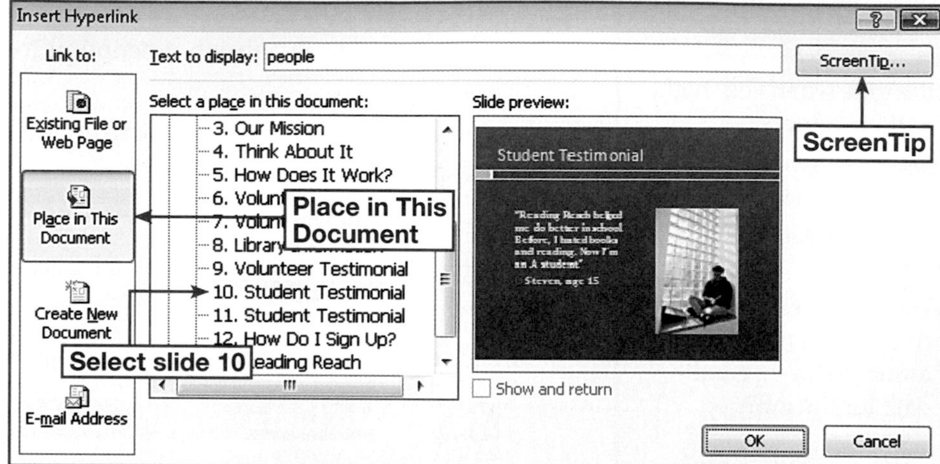

FIGURE 4.14 Hyperlink inserted into slide

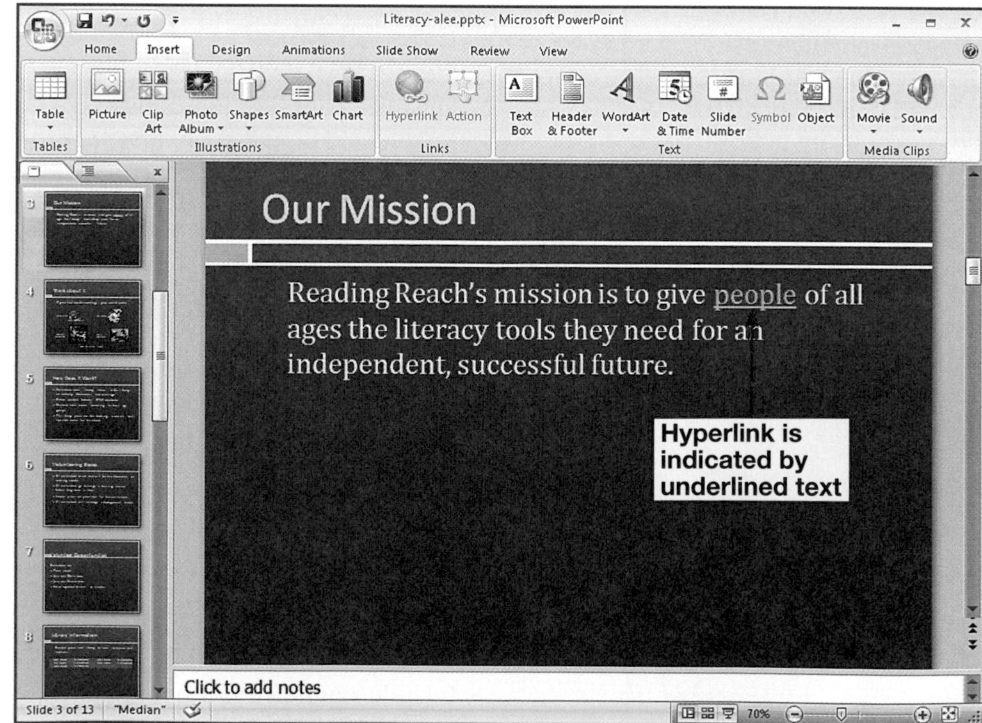

Step-By-Step

1. In your **Literacy** file, move to **Slide 3**. In the slide, select the text **people**.
2. Choose **Insert>Links>Hyperlink**. In the **Insert Hyperlink** dialog box, under **Link to**, click **Place in This Document**.
3. Under **Select a place in this document**, click **10. Student Testimonial**.
4. Click **ScreenTip**. In the **Set Hyperlink ScreenTip** dialog box, key: Click to go to Slide 10. Click **OK**.
5. **CHECK** Your dialog box should look like Figure 4.13.
6. Click **OK**. Deselect the text.
7. **CHECK** Your screen should look like Figure 4.14.
8. On the **status bar**, Click **Slide Show**. Click the hyperlink. Press ESC. Save your file.

Continue to the next exercise.

Tech Tip

You can change hyperlink colors by choosing **Design>Themes>Colors**. Click **Create New Theme Colors** and choose new colors for **Hyperlink** and **Followed Hyperlink**.

Teaching Tip Have students run the slide show at the end of this exercise. On Slide 3, have them hover the cursor over the hyperlink so they can see the **ScreenTip**.

LESSON 3 Use Word Tools

Just as you might use tools to fix a car or build a deck, you can use Word tools to help you work more efficiently. Becoming proficient in Word tools will allow you to do your job better, both as a student and in your career.

Key Concepts

- Create a business letter
- Cut, paste, copy, and move text
- Use the Thesaurus and the Research tool
- Check spelling and grammar
- Print an envelope
- Find and replace text
- Customize AutoCorrect
- Use templates
- Create and use Building Blocks and Quick Parts

Standards

The following standards are covered in this lesson. Refer to pages xxv and 715 for a description of the standards listed here.

ISTE Standards Correlation

NETS•S

1a, 1b, 1c, 2b, 3a, 3b, 3c, 6a

Microsoft Certified Application Specialist

Word

1.1, 1.2, 1.4, 2.2, 4.1, 4.5, 5.1

21st CENTURY SKILLS

See page TM59 for answer to 21st Century Skills.

Identify Leadership Qualities Think about a time when you were a member of a group that had a good leader. What made that leader effective? Perhaps he or she communicated well, respected different points of view, or acted with the interests of the larger community in mind. A good leader may possess one or all of these traits. Identifying leadership skills can be the first step in becoming a leader yourself. *Which leadership skill do you think is most important? Why?*

EXERCISE 4-5
Copy Slides Between Presentations

Instead of re-creating a slide every time you need to display the same information, you can reuse a slide from another presentation. If you select Keep source formatting, the slide keeps its original formatting. If you do not, the slide takes on the design of the new presentation. You may need to adjust the layout of the copied slide to ensure that the contents fit correctly.

Intervention Strategy Be sure students know to save their file if they close it at the end of an exercise.

FIGURE 4.11 Reuse Slides task pane

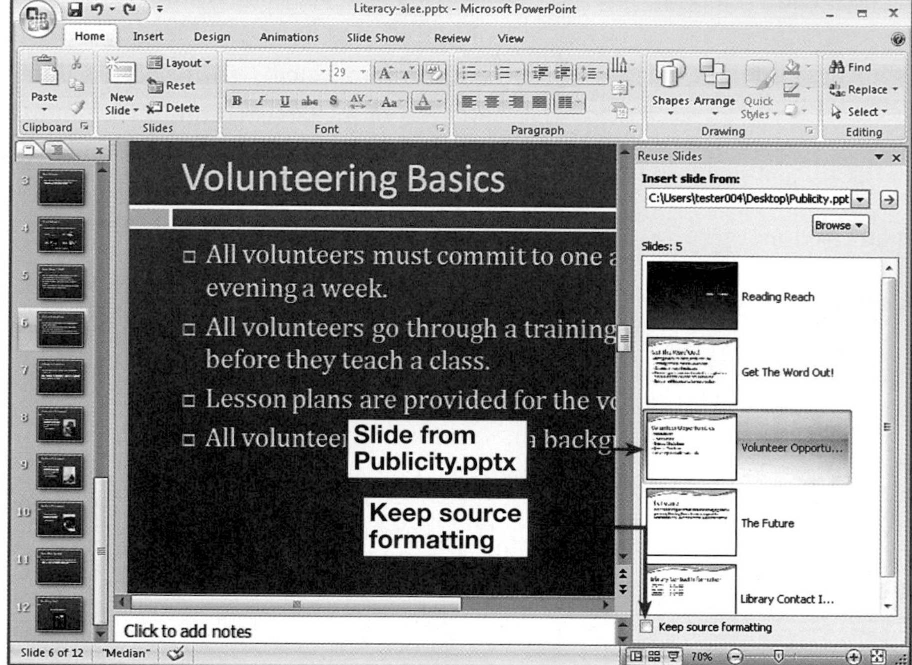

FIGURE 4.12 New slide inserted from different presentation

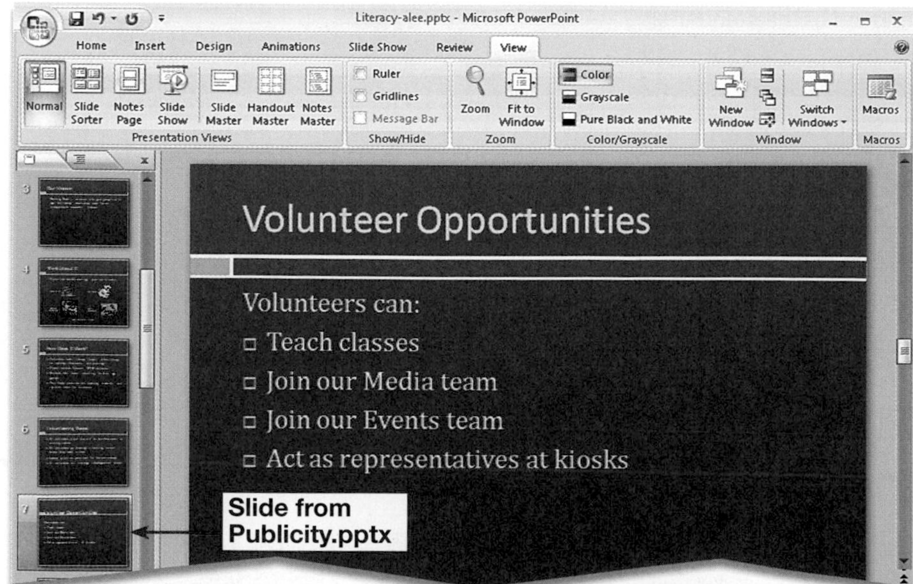

Step-By-Step

1. In your **Literacy** file, move to **Slide 6**.
2. On the **Home** tab, choose the **New Slides** drop-down arrow. Select **Reuse Slides**.
3. In the **Reuse slides** task pane, click **Browse> Browse File**.
4. Locate and click the data file **Publicity.pptx**.
5. Click **Open**.
6. In the **Reuse Slides** task pane, at the bottom of the pane, make sure **Keep source formatting** is not checked (see Figure 4.11).
7. Click **Slide 3**, **Volunteer Opportunities**.
8. Close the task pane.
9. Choose **Home>Slides> Layout**. Select **Title and Text**.
10. **CHECK** Your screen should look like Figure 4.12.
11. Save your file.

Continue to the next exercise.

Teaching Tip Let students know that if they have access to a Microsoft Office SharePoint server, they can also save individual slides in a Slide Library that is accessible to anyone on the server.

Before You Read

See page TM42 for English Learner activity suggestions.

Adjust Reading Speed Improve your comprehension by adjusting reading speed to match the difficulty of the text. Slow down and, if needed, reread each paragraph. Reading slower may take longer, but you will understand and remember more.

Read To Learn

- Consider the various uses of business letters.
- Learn the parts and format of a business letter.
- Understand how Word tools, such as the Spelling and Grammar check and the Thesaurus, can help you create professional documents.
- Explore using Building Blocks and templates to customize business letters and other documents.

Main Idea

Use Word's various features to master advanced editing skills and create formal business letters.

Vocabulary

Key Terms

AutoCorrect	content control	paste
building block	copy	Quick Part
business letter	cut	symbol
Clipboard	drag	thesaurus

Academic Vocabulary

These words appear in your reading and on your tests. Make sure you know their meanings.

phrase
synonym

Quick Write Activity

Identify Think about the type of information a business might want to communicate to its customers. In a Word document, identify three ways that a business letter might be different from a personal letter to a friend or family member.

Study Skills

Set Study Goals Make a list of everything you need to study, decide which assignments to do first, and break long assignments into manageable sections. Try to meet your goals before you stop your study session.

Academic Standards

English Language Arts

NCTE 4 Adjust use of language to communicate effectively with a variety of audiences.

NCTE 5 Employ a wide range of strategies while writing to communicate effectively with different audiences.

NCTE 6 Apply knowledge of language structure and conventions to discuss texts.

NCTE 7 Conduct research and gather, evaluate, and synthesize data to communicate their findings.

NCTE 9 Develop an understanding of diversity in language use across cultures.

NCTE 12 Use spoken, written, and visual language to accomplish their own purposes.

Math

NCTM (Measurement) Apply appropriate techniques, tools, and formulas to determine measurements.

Step-By-Step

EXERCISE 4-4 (Continued)
Size and Format Text Boxes

9. Click the center sizing handle on the left side of the text box and drag it to the **4.5**″ line on the left side of the ruler (see Figure 4.9).

10. Click the center sizing handle on the right side of the text box and drag it to the **4.5**″ line on the right side of the ruler. Choose **Home>Paragraph>Columns**. Select **Two Columns**.

11. Click the center sizing handle at the bottom of the text box and drag it up between the **North Branch** and **South Branch** lines. Deselect the text box.

12. CHECK Your screen should look like Figure 4.10.

13. Choose **View>Show/Hide>Ruler** to turn off the ruler. Save your file.

Continue to the next exercise.

FIGURE 4.9 Text box resized using ruler

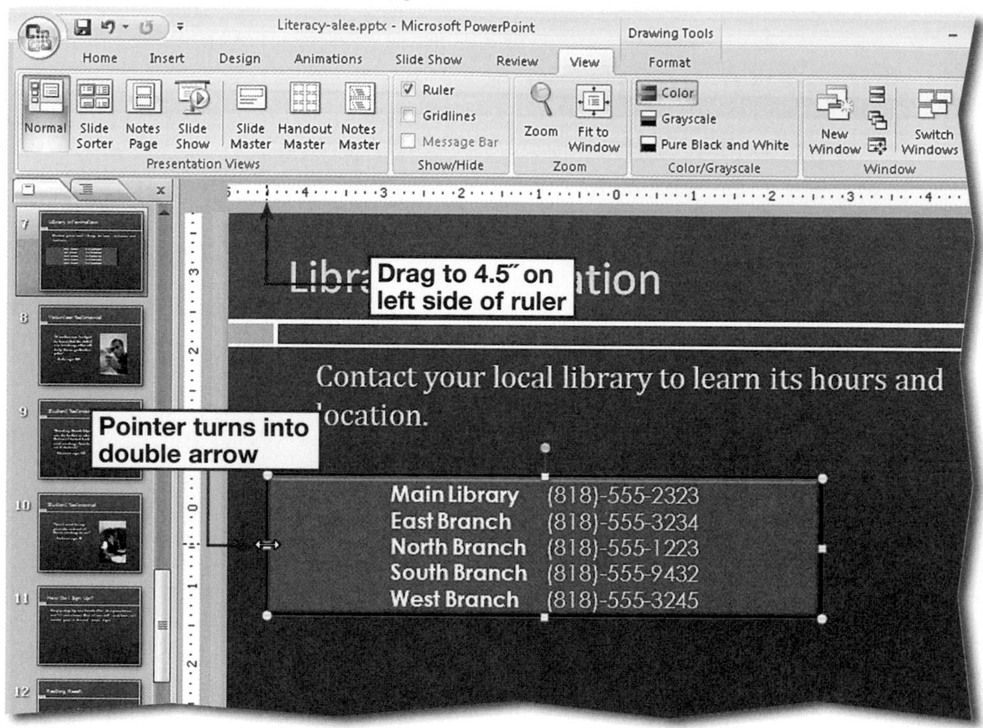

FIGURE 4.10 Text box with two columns

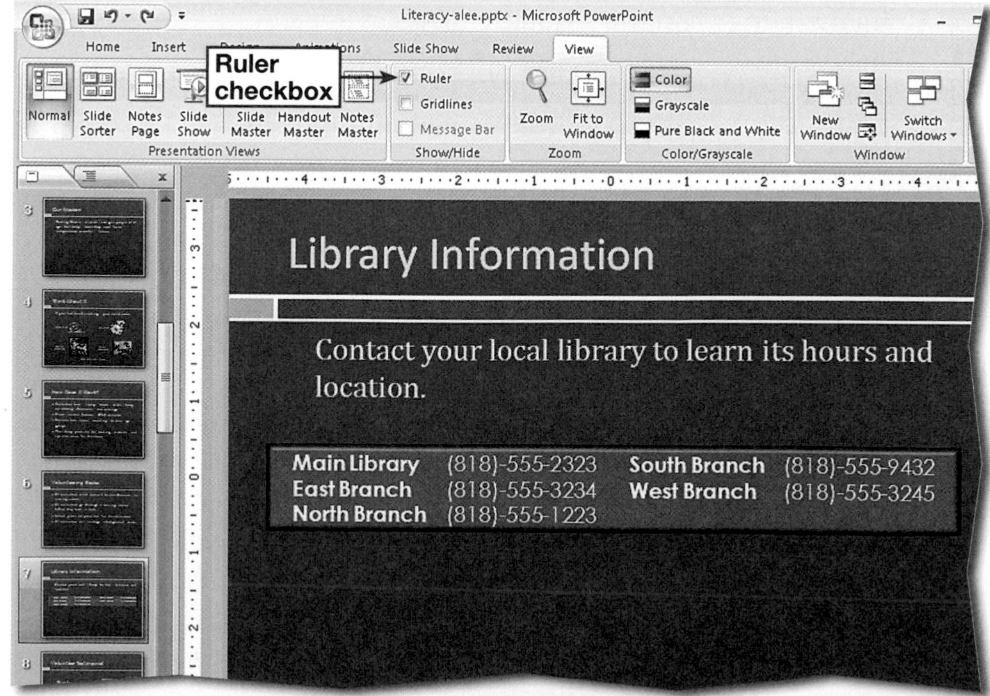

Academic Skills

The PowerPoint ruler measures from the center of each slide, instead of from the left margin.

NCLB/Math (Measurement) Demonstrate sliding the text box handle 1.5″ to the left so that students can see how the PowerPoint ruler can be used to center objects on a slide.

Writing MATTERS

Business Letters

At your after-school job at a mail-order tool company, your supervisor has asked you to write thank-you letters to customers who return tools, encouraging them to use the service again. You are supposed to use a standard business format for the letters and to key them on company letterhead. How should you start?

Businesses often use letters to thank customers or to ask or answer questions.

NCLB/Language Arts (NCTE 4) Explain to students that, unlike a personal letter, a business letter must contain seven specific elements. In order for a business letter to be effective, all of the seven elements must be present.

Business Letter Basics

A business letter is a formal document written by people who work for a business or organization. Businesses send letters for many reasons. Some letters pass along information, while others gather market data. Business letters generally represent a company or an organization, rather than an individual person.

Business Letter Content

An effective business letter should include the following elements:

- A letterhead that includes the company's name and address. Phone and fax numbers are also helpful. Sometimes Web addresses and e-mail addresses are included.
- Today's date.
- The recipient's name and address, also known as the inside address.
- A salutation, or greeting, such as Dear Mr. Smith:.
- The body, consisting of three or more paragraphs.
- A closing.
- The sender's name and job title.

By following the accepted business format, you will present customers with a professional document that provides all the information customers need if they want to contact the company.

SkillBuilder answers can be found on page TM59.

SKILLBUILDER

1. **Define** What is a business letter?
2. **Identify** What are some of the reasons businesses send letters?
3. **Analyze** Why is it important to remember that a business letter represents a company or organization, and not an individual person? How does that fact influence how a letter is composed?

Step-By-Step

1. In your **Literacy** file, on **Slide 7**, hold down SHIFT and select both the large text box and the smaller text box that contains the library phone numbers.
2. On the **Drawing Tools Format** tab, in the **Arrange** group, click **Align**. Select **Align Center**.
3. Click **Align**. Select **Align Middle**. Deselect both text boxes.
4. Select the smaller text box. On the **Drawing Tools Format** tab, in the **Shape Styles** group, select **Shape Fill**. Select **Red, Accent 1**.
5. Select **Shape Styles> Shape Effects**. Select **Bevel>Cool Slant**.
6. Click **Shape Outline**. On the drop-down menu, select **Red, Accent 1, Darker 50%**. Select **Weight**. On the drop-down-menu, select **3pt**. (see Figure 4.7.) Deselect the text box.
7. **CHECK** Your screen should look like Figure 4.8.
8. Select the text box. Choose **View>Show/Hide>Ruler** to show the Ruler.

Continued on the next page.

EXERCISE 4-4
Size and Format Text Boxes

Text boxes allow you to place text anywhere on a slide. They are especially useful when you know you want to include some text but you do not yet know what you want to say. Simply add a text box to reserve space for the text you want to include. You can resize text boxes, apply shape styles, and organize the text into columns.

FIGURE 4.7 Shape Outline drop-down menu

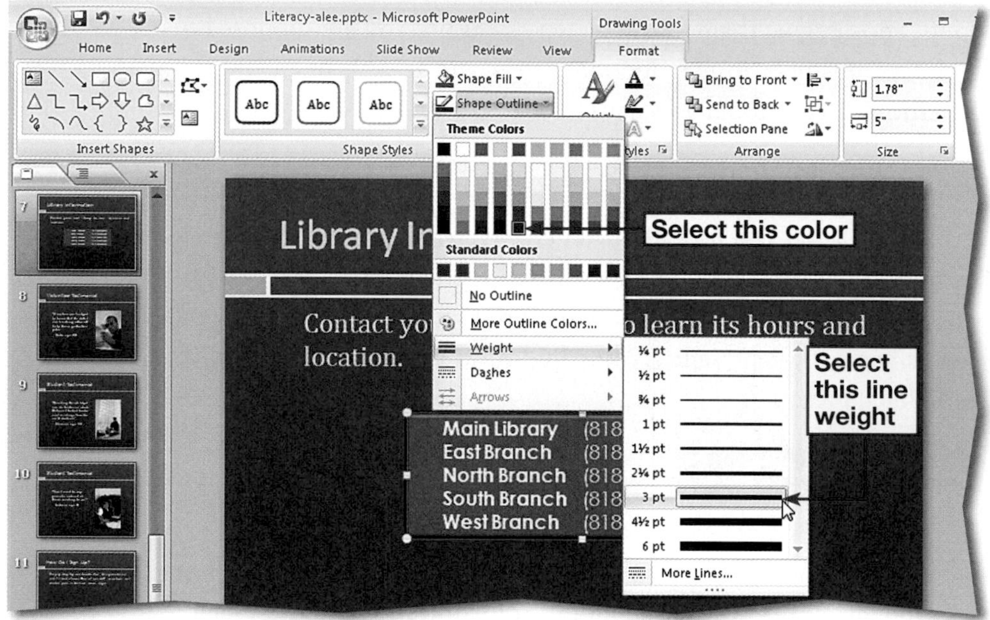

FIGURE 4.8 Formatted text box

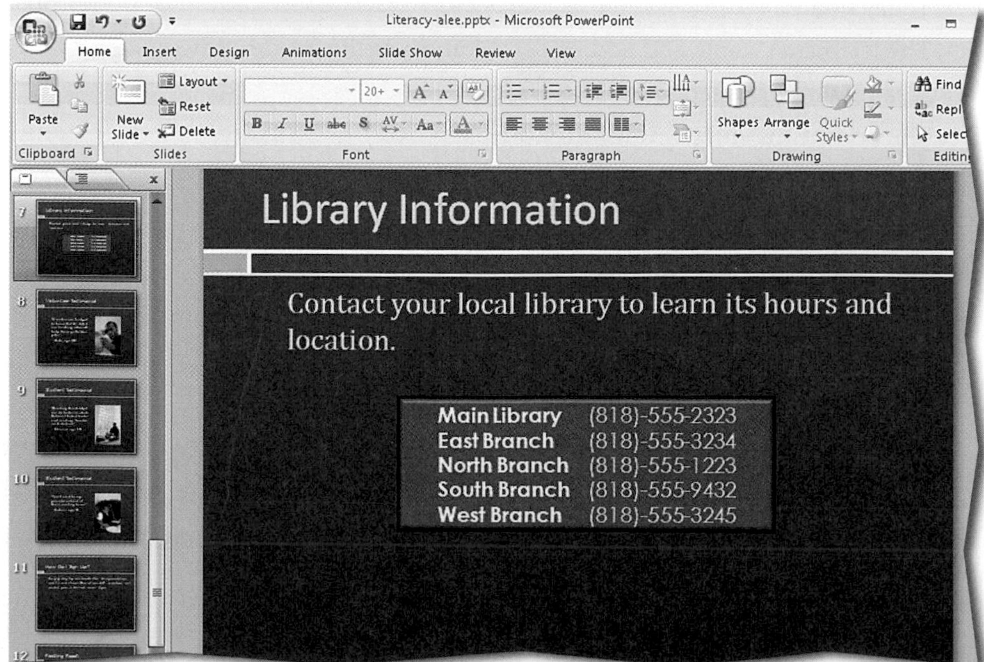

Writing MATTERS

Business and Personal Business Letters

NCLB/Language Arts (NCTE 5)
Explain to students that a personal business letter is appropriate when an individual is writing to a business.

Businesses or organizations send professional business letters that their customers can immediately identify. A personal business letter is a letter written by an individual to a business or organization.

Block Style Format

Both types of business letters usually use the block style format because they are easy to key and have a clean, organized look. In block style formatting, all lines of the letter align at the left margin. The body of the letter has 1.15 pt. line spacing, 10 pt. paragraph spacing (or spacing after each hard return), a 2″ top margin, and 1″ side and bottom margins.

Personal Business Letter Format

The main difference between personal business letters and business letters is that a personal business letter does not use letterhead. The individual's home address precedes the date line at the top of the letter. Use the personal business letter format when your letter represents only yourself and not a separate business or organization.

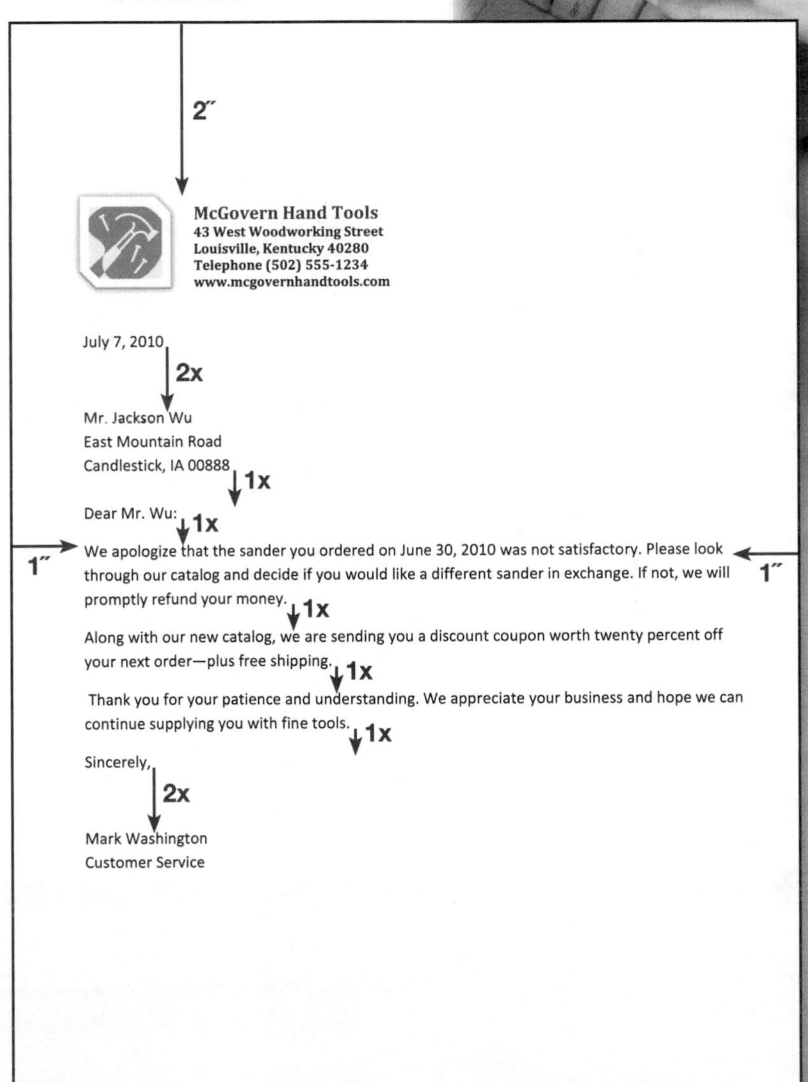

2″

McGovern Hand Tools
43 West Woodworking Street
Louisville, Kentucky 40280
Telephone (502) 555-1234
www.mcgovernhandtools.com

July 7, 2010 2x

Mr. Jackson Wu
East Mountain Road
Candlestick, IA 00888 1x

Dear Mr. Wu: 1x

1″ We apologize that the sander you ordered on June 30, 2010 was not satisfactory. Please look through our catalog and decide if you would like a different sander in exchange. If not, we will promptly refund your money. 1x 1″

Along with our new catalog, we are sending you a discount coupon worth twenty percent off your next order—plus free shipping. 1x

Thank you for your patience and understanding. We appreciate your business and hope we can continue supplying you with fine tools. 1x

Sincerely, 2x

Mark Washington
Customer Service

Pay attention to margins and spacing when formatting a business letter as shown.

SKILLBUILDER

1. **Explain** What is the block style format?
2. **Evaluate** Why is it important to format a business letter correctly?
3. **Compare** How does the formatting of a personal business letter differ from that of a business letter? Why are the two different?

SkillBuilder answers can be found on page TM59.

Step-By-Step

1. In your **Literacy** file, move to **Slide 7**. Choose **Office>Open**. Open the data file **Publicity.pptx**.

2. In the **Publicity** file, move to **Slide 5**. Select the text in the text box. Choose **Home>Clipboard>Copy**.

3. Choose **Office>Close**.

4. On **Slide 7** of your **Literacy** file, choose **Home>Clipboard>Paste**. Click **Home>Paragraph>Center**.

5. **CHECK** Your screen should look like Figure 4.5.

6. Select all of the text in the text box. On the **Home** tab, in the **Font** group, change the **Font** to **Century Gothic**. Change the **Font size** to **20**.

7. **CHECK** Your screen should look like Figure 4.6.

8. Save your file.

Continue to the next exercise.

Troubleshooter

If you have trouble selecting the text you have copied into your **Literacy** file, double-click next to the first word and drag the cursor to select all text.

EXERCISE 4-3
Copy Elements Between Presentations

You can also incorporate, or add in, an element from one presentation to another. You may need to adjust the formatting of the element to match the new presentation.

FIGURE 4.5 Text box pasted from one presentation to another

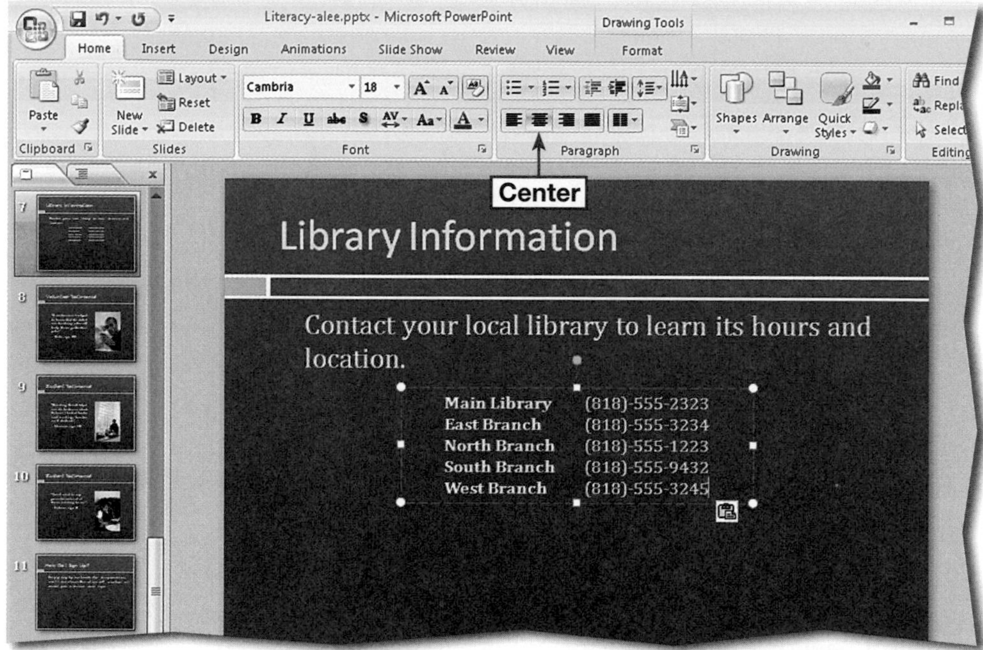

FIGURE 4.6 Text box with new font and font size

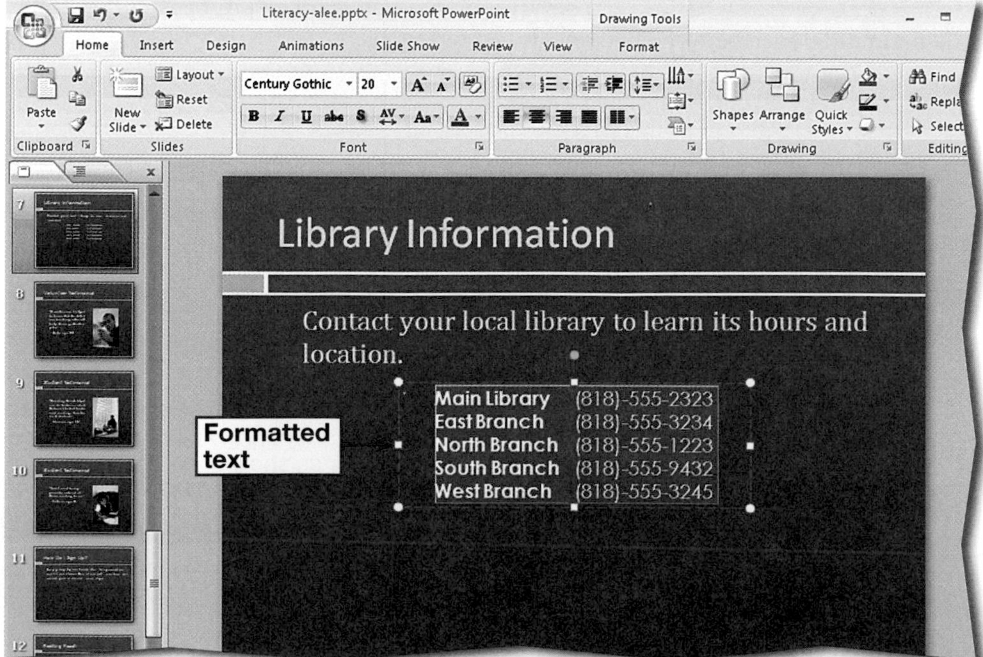

Step-By-Step

1. Start **Word**. Open the data file **Business_Letter.docx**. Save as: Business_Letter-[your first initial and last name] (for example, *Business_Letter-sbryant*).
2. Click after the Fax number. Press ENTER two times.
3. Key: October 28, 2010. Press ENTER twice.
4. Key the recipient's name and address as shown in Figure 3.1. Press ENTER.
5. Key the salutation as shown.
6. Click after **candidates to:** at the end of the letter's body. Press ENTER once.
7. Key the closing as shown. Press ENTER twice. Key the sender's name and job title.
8. Select the first three lines of the inside address. Choose **Page Layout>Paragraph Spacing**. Set **Before:** and **After:** to **0 pt**.
9. Select the sender's name and title. Repeat Step 9 to remove the **10 pt spacing**.
10. CHECK Your screen should look similar to Figure 3.1. Save your file.

Continue to the next exercise.

EXERCISE 3-1
Create a Business Letter

A **business letter** is a formal letter written on company letterhead regarding a business-related subject. Business letters use a specific format. In this exercise, you will use the block letter format.

FIGURE 3.1 Partially formatted business letter

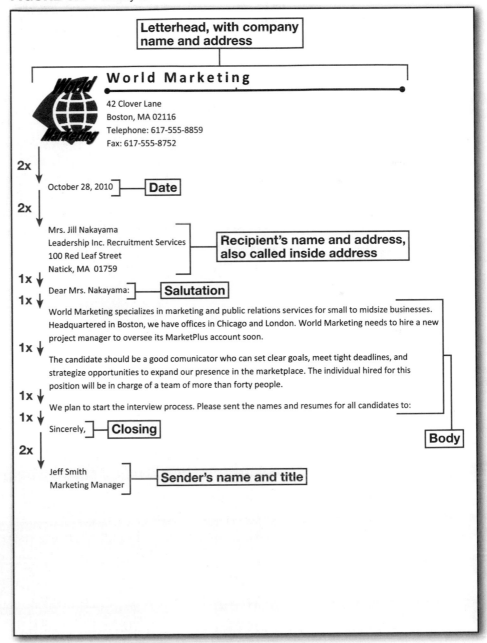

Teaching Tip The letter shown is incomplete and contains intentional errors that students will correct in the lesson.

Step-By-Step

1. In your **Literacy** file, move to **Slide 1**.
2. Select the image. Choose **Home>Clipboard>Copy** .
3. Move to **Slide 12**. Click **Paste** . Click the **Format** tab.
4. **CHECK** Your screen should look like Figure 4.3.
5. On the **Picture Tools Format** tab, in the **Size** group, change the **Height** to **3″**. Press ENTER.
6. With the image still selected, press SHIFT and select the text box that says **Volunteer Today!** Both elements are now selected.
7. On the **Drawing Tools Format** tab, in the **Arrange** group, click **Align** and click **Align Center**.
8. Click **Align** again and click **Align Bottom**. Deselect the text box and image.
9. **CHECK** Your screen should look like Figure 4.4.
10. Save your file.

Continue to the next exercise.

EXERCISE 4-2
Copy Elements from One Slide to Another

You can improve the overall consistency of a presentation by repeating an element, or essential part, on more than one slide. An image such as a company logo or slogan might appear on both the first and last slide.

FIGURE 4.3 Image copied on Slide 12

FIGURE 4.4 Image aligned and resized

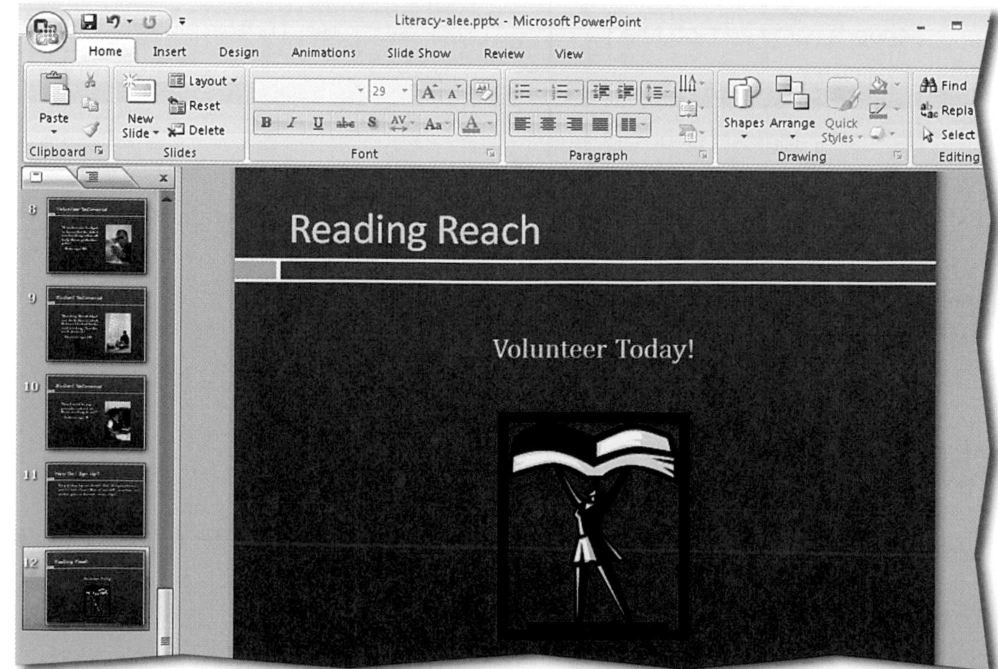

Step-By-Step

1. Open your **Business Letter** file. Choose **Page Layout>Page Setup>Dialog Box Launcher**.
2. In the **Page Setup** dialog box, click the **Layout** tab. Under **Page**, change the **Vertical alignment** to **Center**.
3. **CHECK** Your dialog box should look like Figure 3.2. Click **OK**.
4. If rulers are not visible, click **View Ruler** and scroll to the top of the document.
5. Along the left side of the screen, position the pointer on the vertical ruler between the blue and white areas. The pointer becomes a double-headed arrow (see Figure 3.2).
6. Press ALT and drag the double-headed arrow down until you see **2″** in the blue margin area.
7. **CHECK** Your screen should look like Figure 3.3.
8. Close the rulers. Save your file.

Continue to the next exercise.

NCLB/Math (Measurement) Show students how the ability to use a ruler aids in formatting documents.

EXERCISE 3-2
Set Margins in Print Layout View

In Print Layout View, you can change a document's top and bottom margins using the vertical ruler or the left and right margins using the horizontal ruler. On the rulers, margin areas are blue, and the text area is white. If a business letter is short, you can center the letter vertically rather than set a fixed top margin.

FIGURE 3.2 The Page Setup dialog box

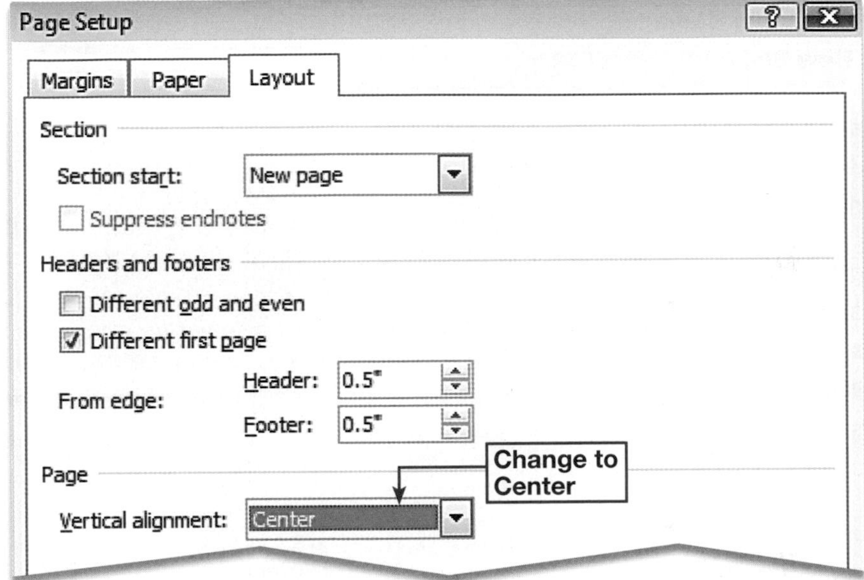

FIGURE 3.3 Use the vertical ruler to set the top margin to 2 inches

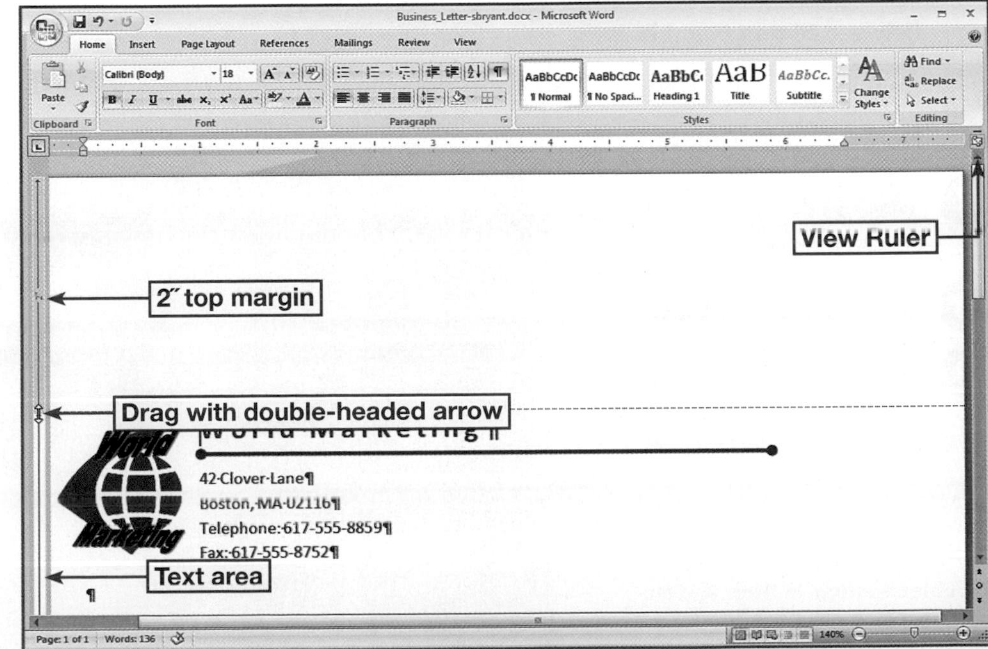

Step-By-Step

1. Open the data file **Literacy.pptx**. Save as: Literacy-[your first initial and last name]. (For example, *Literacy-alee.*)
2. In the **Slide** pane, click **Slide 7**. On the **Home** tab, click **New Slide**.
3. In the title box of the new slide, key: Library Information.
4. Click in the text box. Press ←BACKSPACE. Press TAB. Key: Contact your local library to learn its hours and location. (see Figure 4.1.)
5. Choose **View> Presentation Views> Slide Sorter View**. Click **Slide 2** and drag it between **Slides 6** and **7**.
6. Click **Slide 4**. Choose **Home>Slides>Delete**.
7. **CHECK** Your screen should look like Figure 4.2.
8. Switch to **Normal View**.
9. Save your file.

Continue to the next exercise.

Intervention Strategy Be sure students know where to find and save their data files.

Troubleshooting In **Step 2**, if students accidentally click the **New Slide** drop-down arrow, tell them to choose **Title and Text** from the **New Slide Layout** menu that pops up.

EXERCISE 4-1
Add, Delete, and Rearrange Slides

As you create a presentation, you can add, delete, and rearrange slides at any time so the presentation flows in a logical order and shows all the essential information.

FIGURE 4.1 New slide inserted into presentation

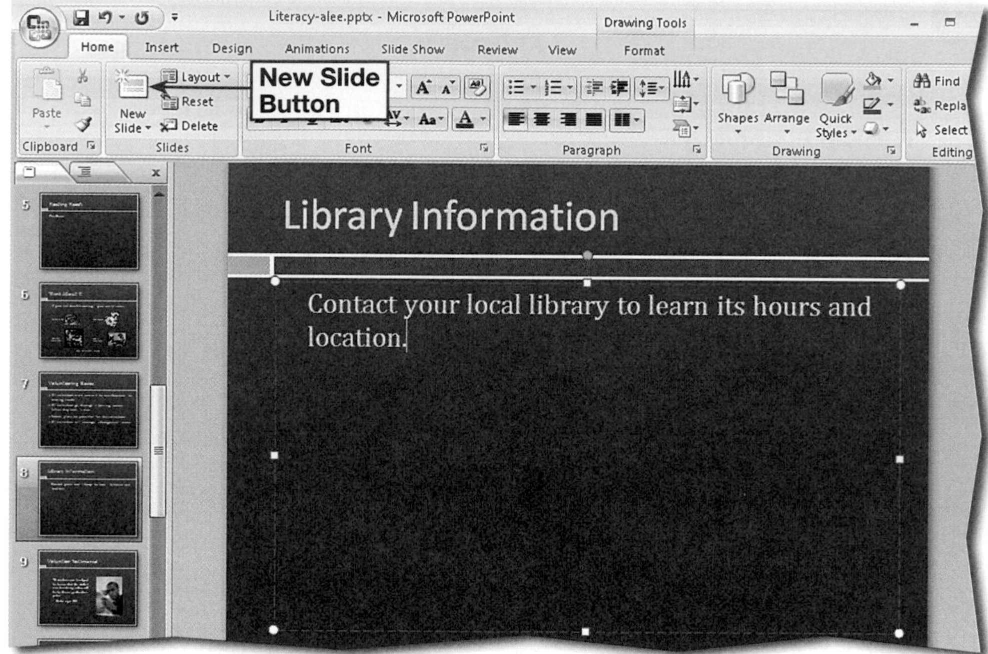

FIGURE 4.2 View with slides deleted and rearranged

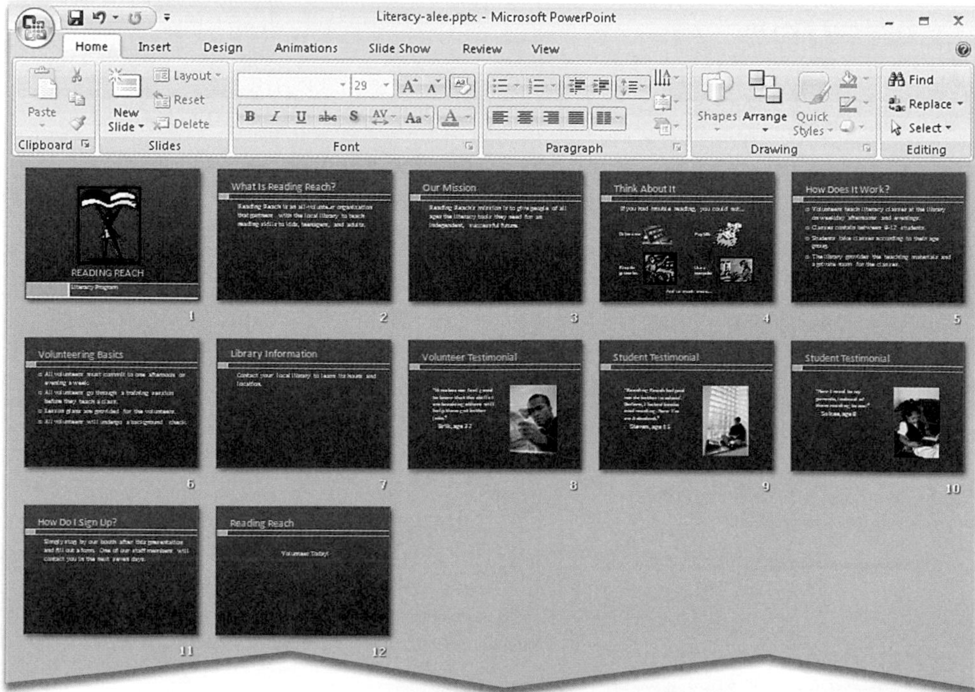

EXERCISE 3-3
Cut and Paste Text

When writing or editing a document, you may want to move text from one location to another. Word lets you do this quickly with **Cut** and **Paste**. When you cut text, it is removed from the document. The text that you most recently cut is stored on the **Clipboard**. You can then paste the cut content elsewhere in your document. You determine where the pasted text will go by moving the mouse and clicking to create an insertion point.

FIGURE 3.4 Pasted text

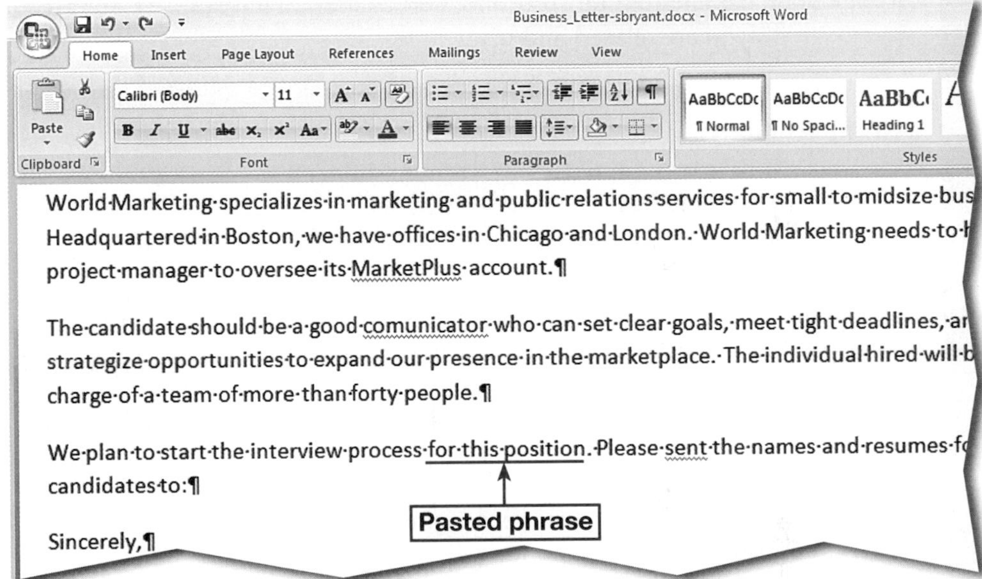

FIGURE 3.5 Text is pasted into a new location

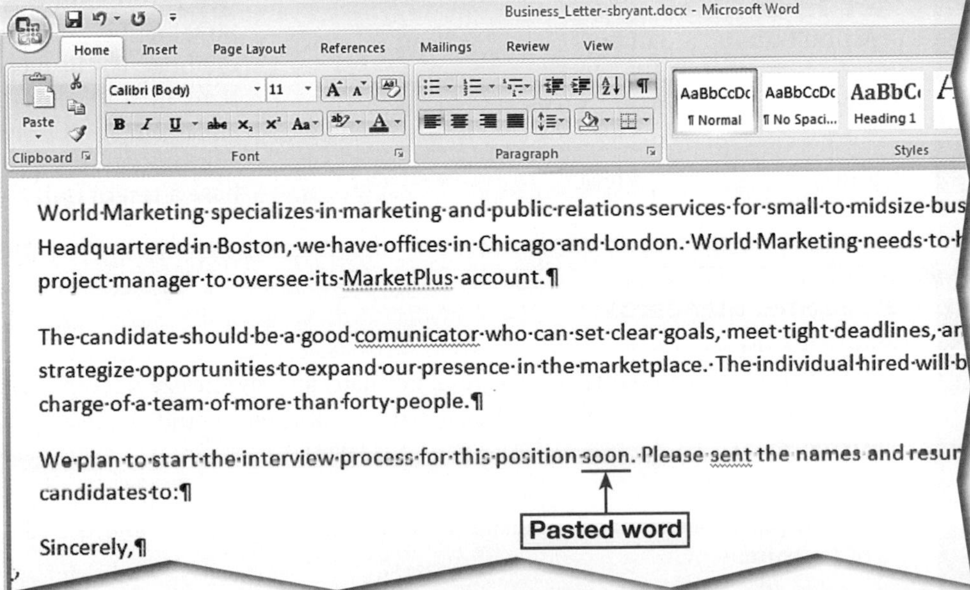

Step-By-Step Tip In **Step 3** and **Step 6**, have students check the spacing in their sentences to make sure they have not added or lost a space between words or punctuation.

Step-By-Step

1. In your **Business Letter** file, select **for this position** in the second paragraph. Choose **Home> Clipboard>Cut** .
2. Click after the word **process** in the last paragraph. Choose **Home>Clipboard> Paste** .
3. **CHECK** Your screen should look like Figure 3.4.
4. In the letter's first paragraph, select the word **soon**. Right-click the selected word. Click **Cut**.
5. In the last paragraph, right-click after the word **position**. Choose **Paste** from the menu.
6. **CHECK** Your screen should look like Figure 3.5. Save your file.

Continue to the next exercise.

Troubleshooter

By double-clicking a word, you can quickly select it without selecting any of the accompanying punctuation.

Differentiated Instruction/ Physically Impaired Ask other students to assist physically impaired students with their text selections.

LESSON 4 Reading Guide

Before You Read

See page TM42 for English Learner activity suggestions.

Take Guilt-Free Days of Rest The reason for resting is to refresh oneself. However, if you feel guilty about resting ("I really should be reading"), then your precious rest period will only create more stress. The brain has a hard time absorbing new data when it is stressed. Your reading skills will be much more effective if you are relaxed and ready to learn.

Read To Learn

- Consider how you can reuse one or more slides in a new presentation.
- Think about how you can enhance your presentation with audio and video clips.
- Prepare your presentation for your audience by rehearsing and making custom slide shows.
- Evaluate how your presentation can be viewed by audiences that do not have Office 2007.

Main Idea

PowerPoint contains many features designed to help you finish your presentation.

Vocabulary

Key Terms

Action button
annotation
Compatibility Checker
grid
guide
hyperlink
Package for CD
PowerPoint Viewer
Print Preview
snap
timing

Academic Vocabulary

These words appear in your reading and on your tests. Make sure you know their meanings.

compatible
element
incorporate

Quick Write Activity

Analyze On a separate sheet of paper, consider how you use your computer to manage your collections of music, homework, or other groups of files. How does having this information organized ensure that you can always find what you need?

Study Skills

Use a Mnemonic A mnemonic (pronounced nuh-MON-ick) is a sentence or phrase that jogs your memory. For instance, ROY G BIV is an easy way to remember the colors of the rainbow. Mnemonics are also helpful in remembering key terms or vocabulary. Try using mnemonics the next time you have a test or quiz.

Academic Standards

English Language Arts

NCTE 7 Conduct research and gather, evaluate, and synthesize data to communicate discoveries.

NCTE 8 Use information resources to gather information and create and communicate knowledge.

NCTE 12 Use language to accomplish individual purposes.

Math

NCTM (Measurement) Understand measurable attributes of objects and the units, systems, and processes of measurement.

Step-By-Step

1. In your **Business Letter** file, click after **candidates to:** at the end of the third paragraph. Press ENTER. Key: Rachel Fay.
2. Select the return address and telephone number in the letterhead. Choose **Home>Clipboard> Copy** (see Figure 3.6).
3. Position the insertion point after the text **Rachel Fay**. Choose **Page Layout> Paragraph>Spacing**. Set **After:** to **0**. Press ENTER.
4. Choose **Home> Clipboard>Paste**.
5. In the second sentence in the second paragraph, select the word **team**. Right-click the selected word and click **Copy**.
6. In the first sentence in the second paragraph, right-click before the word **goals**. Click **Paste**.
7. **CHECK** Your screen should look like Figure 3.7. Save your file.

Continue to the next exercise.

Troubleshooter

Be sure to check spacing between words when you cut, copy, or paste text.

EXERCISE 3-4
Copy and Paste Text

Sometimes you may want to have exactly the same text appear more than once in your document. To save time, you can **copy** text in one location and paste it in another. Like photocopying, in Word you can create an exact copy without destroying the original. You can avoid errors by copying and pasting addresses, names, and phone numbers within a document.

Teaching Tip Show students that if **Copy** is dimmed in the Ribbon or pop-up menu, they have not selected any text.

FIGURE 3.6 Text to be copied

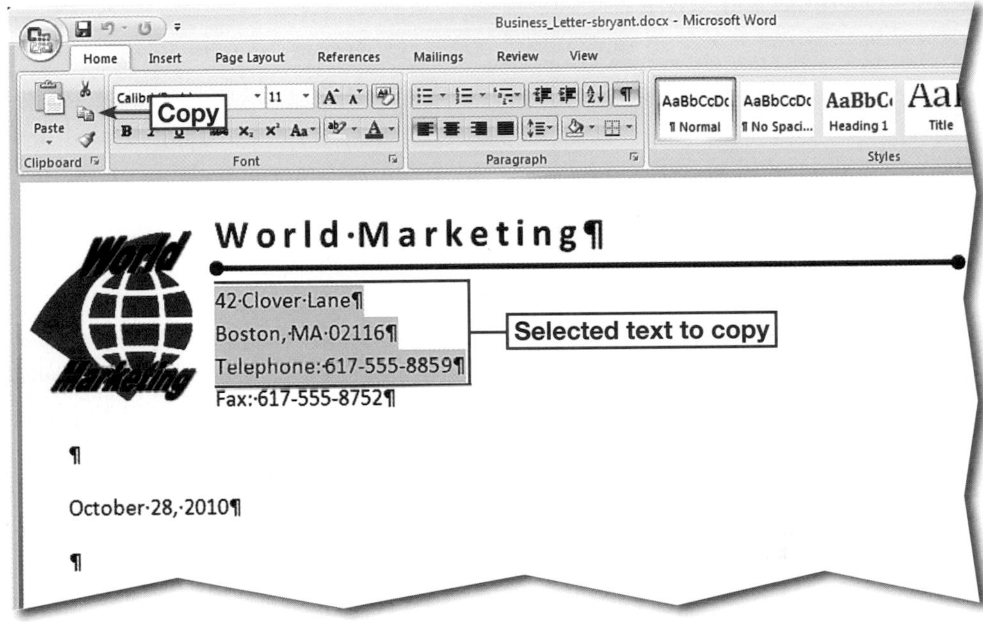

FIGURE 3.7 Pasted text

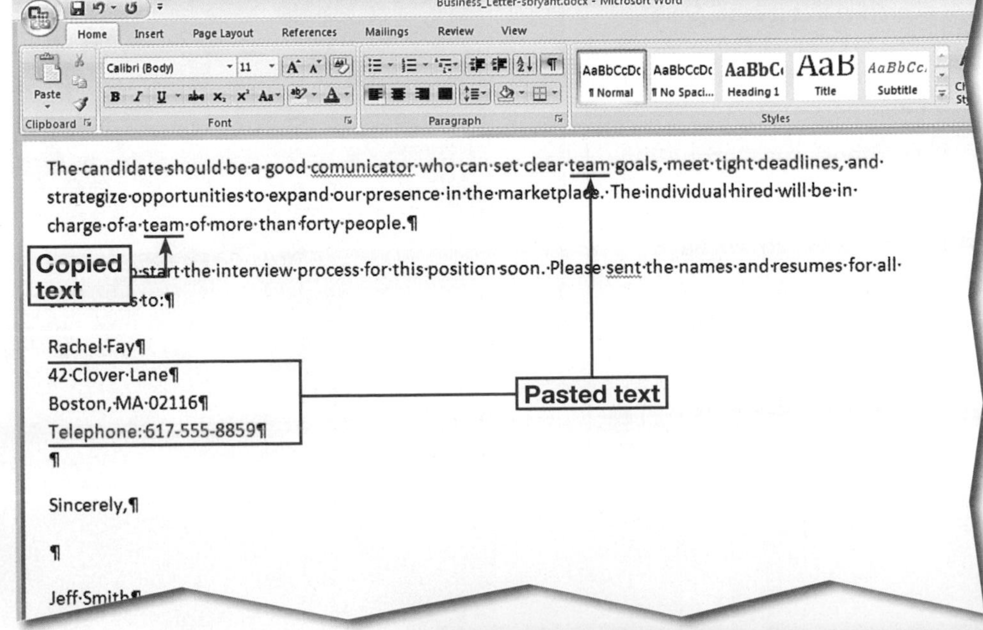

LESSON 4 Manage Presentations

Key Concepts

- Add, delete, and rearrange slides
- Add hyperlinks and Action buttons
- Use grids and guides
- Preview slides and modify printing options
- Create custom shows
- Rehearse timings
- Mark up presentations electronically with the Felt Tip Pen or Highlighter features
- Prepare your presentations by saving them in various formats

Standards

The following standards are covered in this lesson. Refer to pages xxv and 715 for a description of the standards listed here.

ISTE Standards Correlation

NETS•S

1b, 1c, 1d, 2a, 2b, 4b, 6a, 6b

Microsoft Certified Application Specialist

PowerPoint

1.1, 1.5, 2.1, 2.3, 3.5, 4.3, 4.4, 4.5

In this lesson, you will learn how to finalize many aspects of your presentation so that you can focus on delivering it flawlessly. You will save the presentation in different formats, copy elements between presentations, and add video files. Learning how to prepare your presentation for an audience will help you maximize its effectiveness.

See page TM96 for answer to 21st Century Skills.

Take Initiative Imagine a time when you were faced with a challenging problem, either at school, at work, or with friends. Did you avoid the problem, or did you take initiative and tackle it head-on? Taking initiative means making informed decisions and acting on them. You can take initiative by focusing on a challenge, writing down your goals, and taking steps to achieve them. *When was the last time you took initiative?*

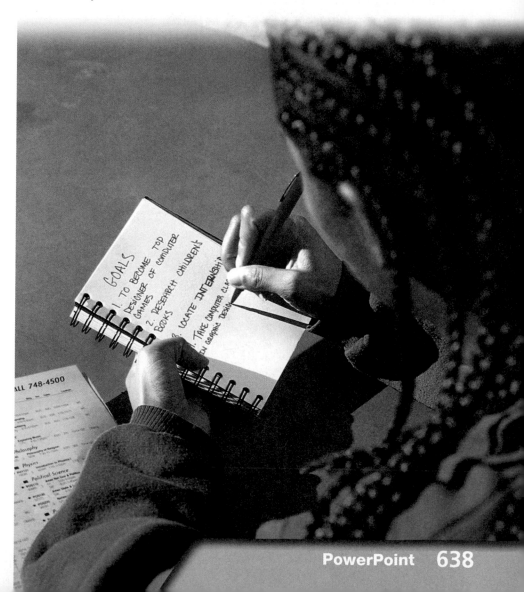

Step-By-Step

1. In your **Business Letter** file, select the second sentence in the second paragraph (starts with **The individual**).
2. Point in the selected sentence. The pointer takes the shape of an arrow.
3. Click and hold the mouse button while you move the pointer. A dotted line and dotted box appear when you drag the mouse.
4. Position the dotted line at the beginning of the second paragraph (see Figure 3.8).
5. Release the mouse button and press SPACE.
6. CHECK Your screen should look like Figure 3.9. Save your file.

Continue to the next exercise.

Academic Skills

Many computer terms such as *cut* and *paste* are metaphors. When you cut or paste text, you are not physically cutting or pasting the text. The terms are used because they are similar to the actions that they represent.

NCLB/Language Arts (NCTE 6) Ask students to name other computer terms that are metaphors.

EXERCISE 3-5
Use Drag-and-Drop to Move Text

Use drag-and-drop when you want to move text around as an alternative to copying and pasting text from one location in a document to another. When you **drag** text, you select the text, hold down the left mouse button, and drag the mouse where you want to move the text. Then you release the left mouse button. When you drag text, the pointer becomes a dotted box arrow.

Differentiated Instruction/Physically Impaired If students cannot drag and drop text, they can use **Cut** and **Paste** instead.

FIGURE 3.8 Drag-and-drop arrow

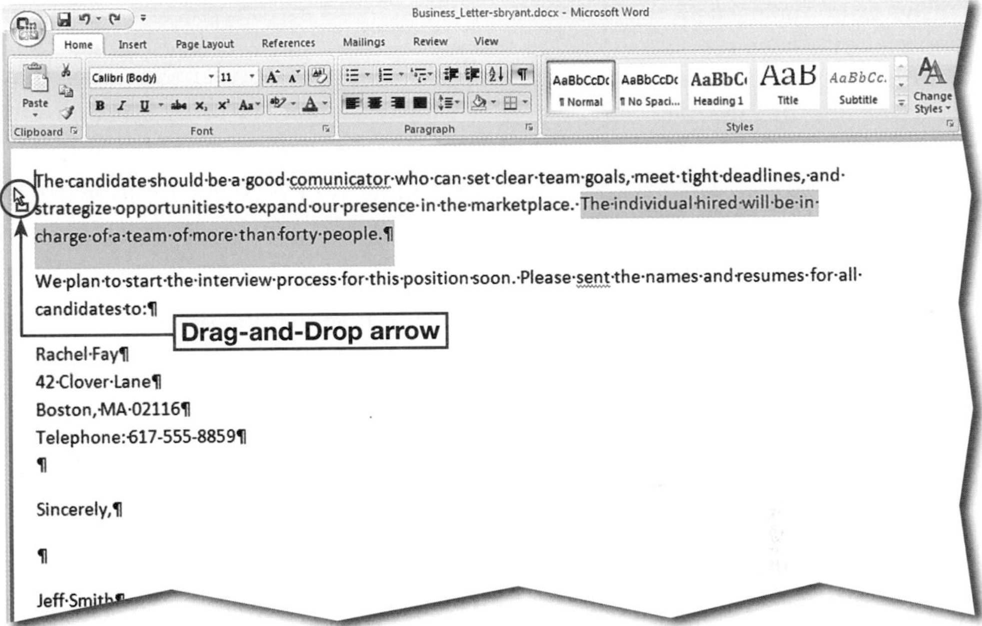

FIGURE 3.9 Text moved with drag-and-drop

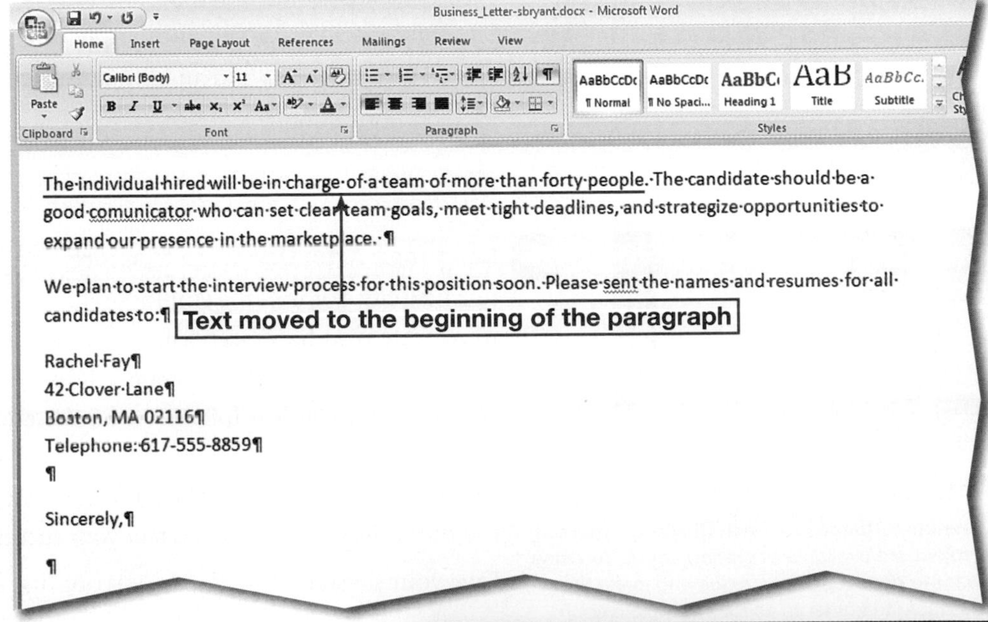

LESSON 3 Challenge Yourself Projects

Before You Begin

Understand and Respond to Your Audience To promote a business, you need to understand what the business offers and what the clients want. You need to show how the business meets the needs of the customer base. Identify the ways that businesses have marketed themselves to you. Consider the advertising you see daily.

Reflect Once you complete the projects, open a Word document and answer the following:

1. What types of advertising are most effective?
2. When you adapted the presentation for prospective employees, what were the main changes that you made?
3. How do employee needs differ from customer needs?

Answers Rubrics for each Challenge Yourself Project are available at **glencoe.com**. You may want to download the rubrics and make them available to students as they complete each project.

9. Promote a Restaurant

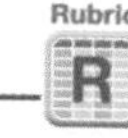

LEVEL This is an intermediate level project

Language Arts: Create Slides You work for a public relations firm that has been hired to promote a new Italian restaurant. Your job is to create a presentation that tells the owners how you plan to promote their restaurant.

- Identify the customers—will the restaurant target an older or a younger crowd? Is it a casual pizza parlor or a fancy gourmet restaurant?
- Create a 5- to 7-slide presentation that describes how you will promote the restaurant (by using flyers, advertisements, free offers, and so on). Make sure your promotion ideas match the customer base.
- Format your presentation to match the restaurant's image. Use fonts, colors, backgrounds, and graphics that reflect whether the restaurant is casual or more formal.

Save your presentation as: p3rev-[your first initial and last name]9.

10. Present a Business Proposal

LEVEL This is an intermediate level project

Apply Effects The restaurant was pleased with your presentation. Now they want you to adapt the presentation as an introduction for prospective employees. Consider the different jobs available at the restaurant. Think about how an employer can make a company attractive to potential employees. Then, adapt your **p3rev9** presentation into a 5- to 7-slide presentation to be used before employee interviews. In your presentation, include:

- At least three images that have effects applied to them (fill color, transparency, custom animation, and so on)
- Slide transitions and an animation scheme on at least one slide

Save your presentation as: p3rev-[your first initial and last name]10.

11. Create an Employee Orientation

LEVEL This is an advanced level project

Language Arts: Use Slide Masters The restaurant is opening a franchise in a new city. Some of the employees have been asked if they would be willing to relocate. You have been asked to create a presentation to help employees learn more about this city. Create a 5- to 10-slide presentation about a city of your choice. Include information for the employees about the city's climate, lifestyle, and history. Use the Slide Master to keep formatting consistent. Create the restaurant's logo and place it on every slide. Apply a design theme and customize its color scheme to suit your presentation.

Save your presentation as: p3rev-[your first initial and last name]11.

EXERCISE 3-6
Insert Symbols and Special Characters

Word allows you to insert **symbols** and special characters that do not appear on the keyboard. Using the Symbol dialog box makes it easy to insert accents, trademarks, and other characters into a document. **NCLB/Language Arts (NCTE 9)** **Direct students who speak or study foreign languages to other useful symbols included in the Symbol dialog box.**

FIGURE 3.10 Symbol dialog box

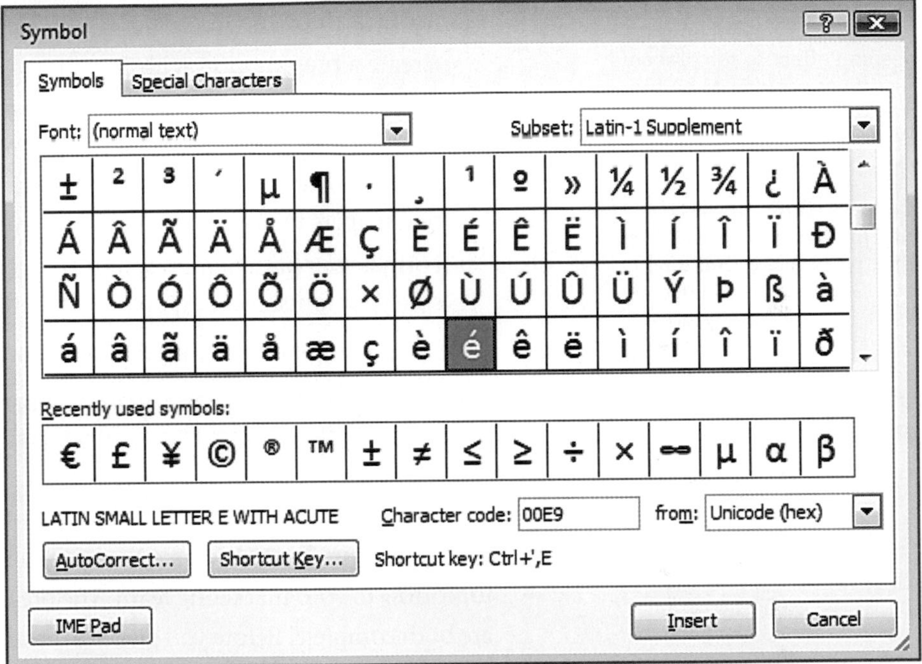

FIGURE 3.11 Document with symbol and special character added

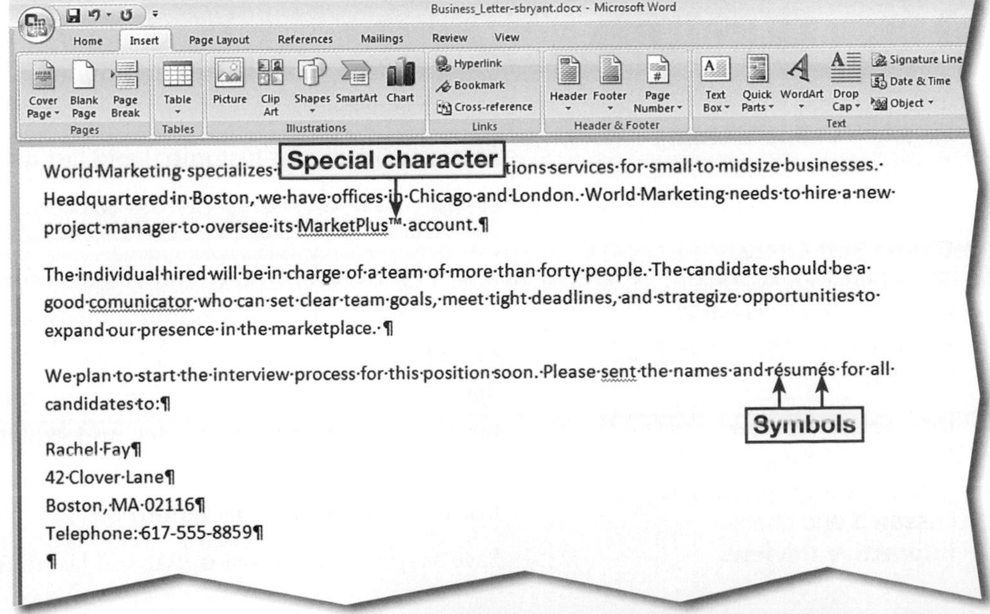

Step-By-Step

1. In your **Business Letter** file, select the first **e** in the word **resumes** near the end of the letter.
2. Choose **Insert>Symbols> Symbol** [Ω]. Choose **More Symbols**.
3. In the **Symbol** dialog box, scroll and select the symbol **é** (see Figure 3.10).
4. Click **Insert**. Click **Close** to close the dialog box.
5. Select the **é** you inserted. Click **Copy**. Select the second **e** in **résumes**. Click **Paste**. Click after **MarketPlus** in the first paragraph. Choose **Insert>Symbol** [Ω].
6. Click the **Special Characters** tab. Select Trademark **™**. Click **Insert**. Close the dialog box.
7. **CHECK** Your screen should look like Figure 3.11. Save your file.

Continue to the next exercise.

Academic Skills

The symbol that you add in Step 3 is called an *acute accent*. The accents help distinguish the noun *résumé* from the verb *resume*, which means to start again.

LESSON 3 Critical Thinking Activities

6. Beyond the Classroom Activity

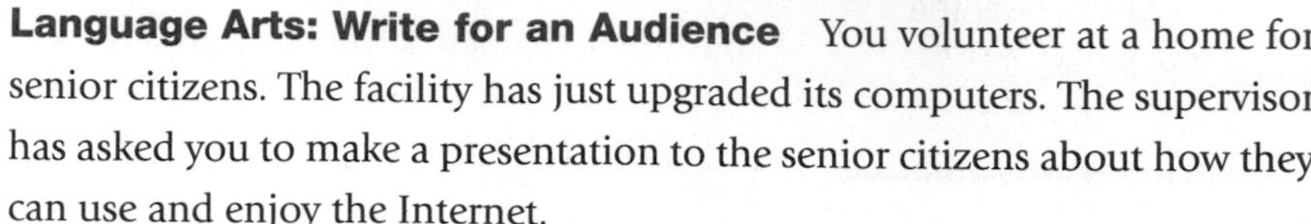

Language Arts: Write for an Audience You volunteer at a home for senior citizens. The facility has just upgraded its computers. The supervisor has asked you to make a presentation to the senior citizens about how they can use and enjoy the Internet.

- Create a presentation with five slides.
- Add content that highlights the different uses for the Internet. You may want to discuss using e-mail to communicate with loved ones, finding message boards to meet others with common interests, or reading online newspapers to keep up with current events around the world.
- Format your presentation so it is appropriate for an older audience. Make sure your fonts, colors, graphics, and other objects are large and readable.

Save as: p3rev-[your first initial and last name]6.

7. Standards at Work Activity

Data File

Microsoft Certified Application Specialist Correlation
PowerPoint 1.4 *Create and Change Presentation Elements*

Apply Slide Transitions You are scheduled to give a presentation tomorrow to your marketing team. The presentation's content and formatting are both complete. Before you give the presentation, however, you need to add transition effects to the slides.

- Open the data file **p3rev7.pptx**.
- Apply a transition effect to the entire presentation.
- Modify the speed of the effect and add a sound effect. Make sure that the effects you select are appropriate for your presentation's tone and audience.

Save as: p3rev-[your first initial and last name]7.

8. 21st Century Skills Activity

Identify Role Models Individuals often look to their role models for ethical guidance. Think about someone who you think is a good role model. This person may be a family member, a teacher, or even an historical figure. Create a brief presentation about this person. Identify why you think he or she is a good role model, and explain how your actions have been influenced by this person. Use at least three PowerPoint features learned in this lesson in your presentation.

Save as: p3rev-[your first initial and last name]8.

Beyond the Classroom Activity
Slides should include different uses for the Internet. The format should include large fonts and should be easy to read.

Standards at Work Activity
Students should apply an appropriate transition effect to the presentation. The effect should not be too fast, and the sound effect should not be distracting.

21st Century Skills Activity
Students' presentations should discribe their role models and their influence. Students should use at least three PowerPoint features.

glencoe.com

Go to the **Online Learning Center** to complete the following review activities.

Online Self Check
To test your knowledge of the material, click **Unit 4> Lesson 3** and choose **Self Checks**.

Interactive Review
To review the main points of the lesson, click **Unit 4> Lesson 3** and choose **Interactive Review**.

Step-By-Step

1. In your **Business Letter** file, select the word **strategize** in the second paragraph.
2. Choose **Review>Proofing>Thesaurus** .
3. In the **Research** task pane, under **Thesaurus**, place the pointer over **organize**. Click the drop-down arrow.
4. **CHECK** Your screen should look like Figure 3.12.
5. Click **Insert**. Close the task pane.
6. Right-click the word **oversee** in the first paragraph.
7. In the shortcut menu, choose **Synonyms**. Click **supervise**.
8. **CHECK** Your screen should look like Figure 3.13. Save your file.

Continue to the next exercise.

Academic Skills

Write a sentence using the word *save*. List three synonyms for the word save. If you replace the word *save* with each synonym, the sentence should still make sense.

EXERCISE 3-7
Use the Thesaurus

Word has a **thesaurus** to help you find a **synonym** (a word that has the same or similar meaning to another word). The thesaurus can help you find alternatives for words so that you can add a variety of word choices to your document. You can also use the thesaurus to find the word that best expresses what you are trying to say.

FIGURE 3.12 Choose a synonym using the Thesaurus

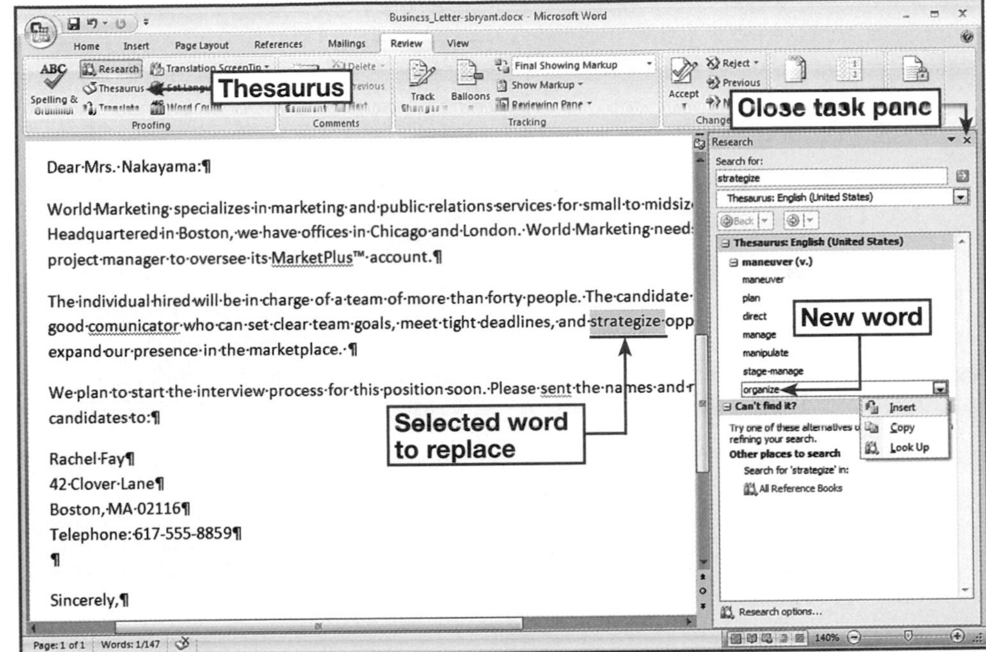

FIGURE 3.13 Replaced word with its synonym

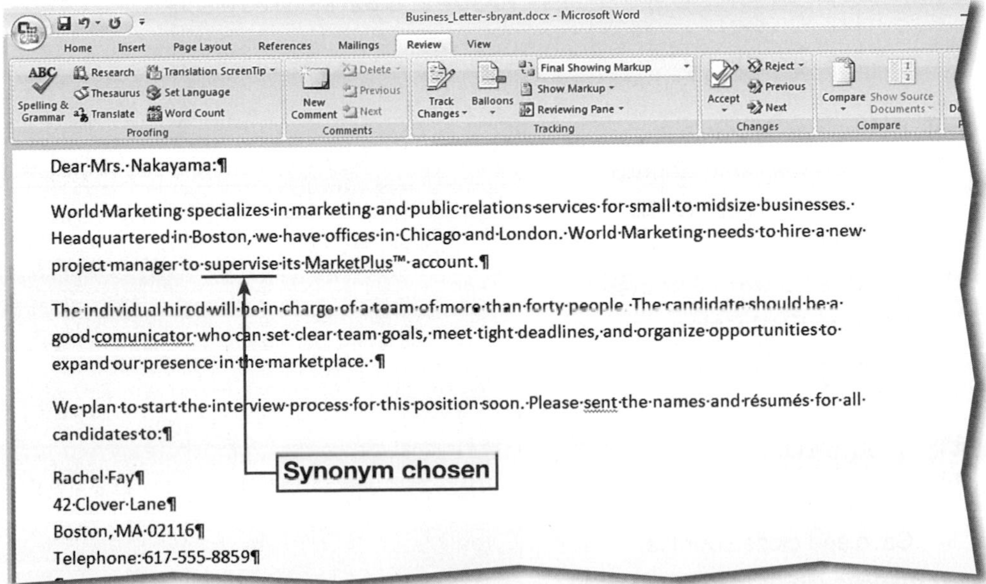

NCLB/Language Arts (NCTE 4) Ask students to share their synonyms. Emphasize that there is more than one correct answer depending on the context of the original sentence.

5. Rotate, Align, and Add Effects to Graphics

Your presentation is almost ready to show. All you have to do is finish the final slide. To do this, you must modify Clip Art, WordArt, and shapes to make your content presentable. You must complete You Try It Activity 4 before doing this activity.

Solution The solution file for this exercise is **Questions5-SF.pptx**.

Step-By-Step

1. Open your **Questions** file. Save as: Questions-[your first initial and last name]5.
2. Select **Slide 6**. Rotate the image of the man to the left **90°**. Use **Picture Effects** to place a glow effect on the central image.
3. **CHECK** Your screen should look like Figure 3.61. Select the URL address. Change its **Font** to **Cooper Black**. Use a **Straight arrow connector** to connect the information symbol to the URL.
4. Align the information symbol with the two images using **Align Middle**.
5. Select the URL. Select **Animations>Animations> Custom Animation**. Click **Add Effect**. Choose **Emphasis>More Effects> Change Font Color**. Under **Modify**, change **Font Color** to **Yellow**.
6. **CHECK** Your screen should look like Figure 3.62. Save and close your file.

New Student Strategy If a student did not complete You Try It Activity 4, then the solution file for that activity can be used as a data file for this activity.

FIGURE 3.61 Rotated and recolored images

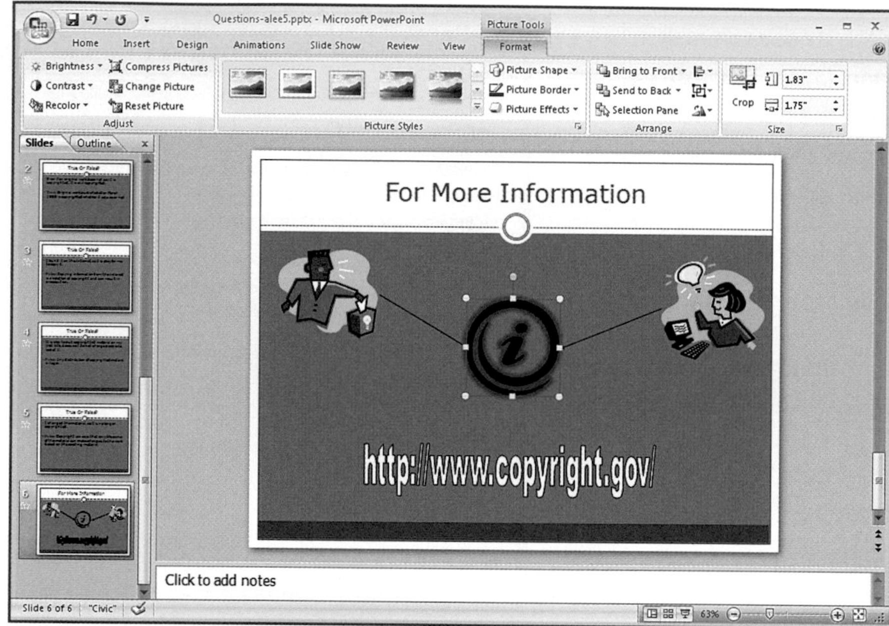

FIGURE 3.62 Modified graphics

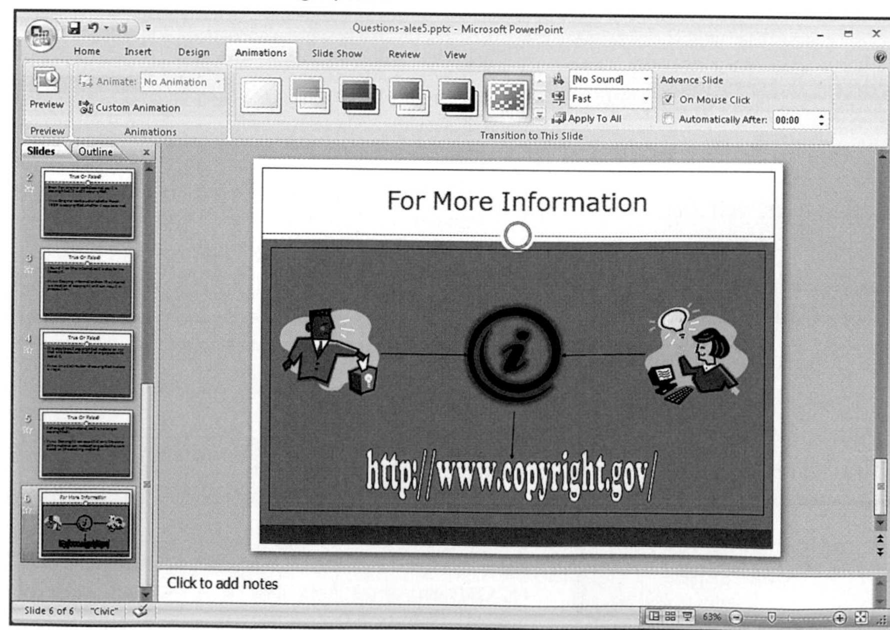

Step-By-Step

1. In your **Business Letter** file, click before the first line of the body.
2. Choose **Review>Proofing>Spelling & Grammar**. In the dialog box, under **Not in Dictionary**, the word **MarketPlus** is selected in red. Click **Ignore Once**.
3. Under **Not in Dictionary**, the misspelled word **comunicator** is shown in red (see Figure 3.14).
4. Under **Suggestions**, select **communicator**. Click **Change**. Under **Subject-Verb Agreement**, the word **sent** is selected in green.
5. Under **Suggestions**, select **send**. Click **Change**. Click **OK** in the **Readability Statistics** dialog box.
6. **CHECK** Your screen should look like Figure 3.15. Save the file.

Continue to the next exercise.

Academic Skills

Word's review and editing tools are helpful, but you should still proofread each document. Why is it important to proofread documents?

NCLB/Language Arts (NCTE 5)

EXERCISE 3-8
Spell and Grammar Check a Document

Your document might have red and green squiggles under words. Red indicates a spelling error and green signifies a grammar error. These marks, along with a spelling and grammar check, can help you edit a document's spelling and grammar.

Troubleshooting Have students' check settings by choosing **Office>Word Options>Proofing**. Under the **When checking spelling and grammar in Word** heading, check all options.

FIGURE 3.14 Spelling and Grammar dialog box

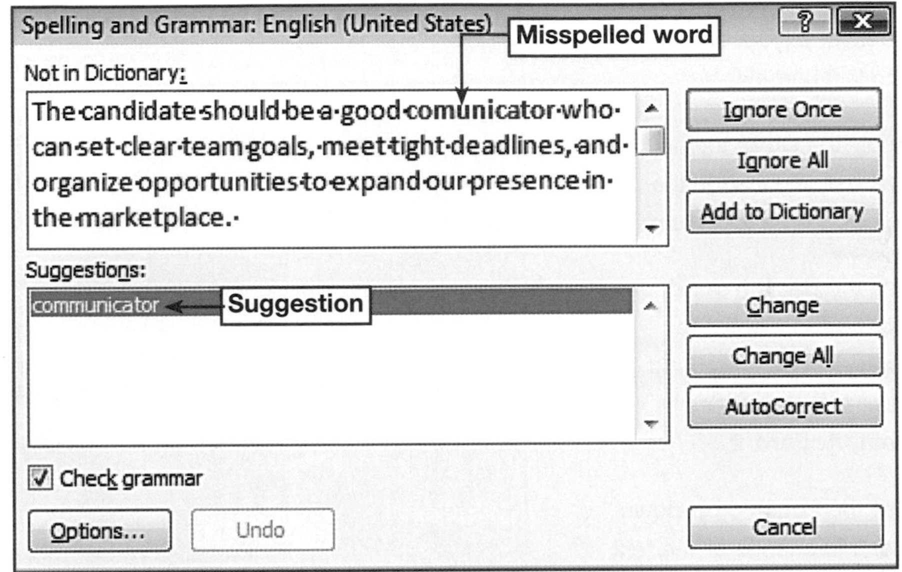

FIGURE 3.15 Letter with correct spelling and grammar

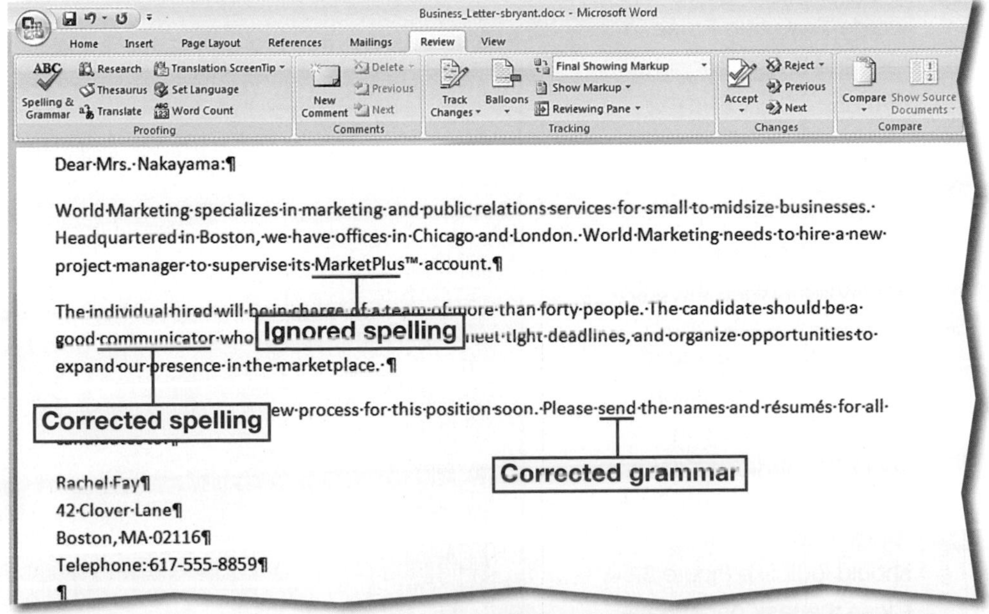

Step-by-Step Tip In **Step 5**, the Readability Statistics dialog box may not appear. If it does not, move on to **Step 6**.

LESSON 3 You Try It Activities

4. Format Slides and Add Transition Effects

You work on your school's Web site. Your supervisor has asked you to put together a brief presentation to help new students understand what materials they can and cannot include on the Web site. You have created the content for your presentation and are ready to format the slides and apply transition effects.

Solution The solution file for this activity is **Questions4-SF.pptx**.

Step-By-Step

1. Open the data file **Questions.pptx**. Save as: Questions-[your first initial and last name]4.
2. Apply the **Civic** theme to every slide. Change the color scheme to **Urban**.
3. Use the **Background Styles** drop-down to change the background color of all the slides to **Teal, Accent 2**.
4. Use the **Fonts** drop-down menu to change all the text to **Verdana**.
5. On **Slides 2** to **5**, make the words **True** and **False** in the slide body dark purple and bold. Click **Slide 2**.
6. **CHECK** Your screen should look like Figure 3.59. Add the **Dissolve** transition to all the slides in the show.
7. Add the **Camera** sound effect to each transition. Change the transition speed to medium.
8. **CHECK** Your screen should look like Figure 3.60. Close the task pane. Save your file.

FIGURE 3.59 Slide 2 with new formatting

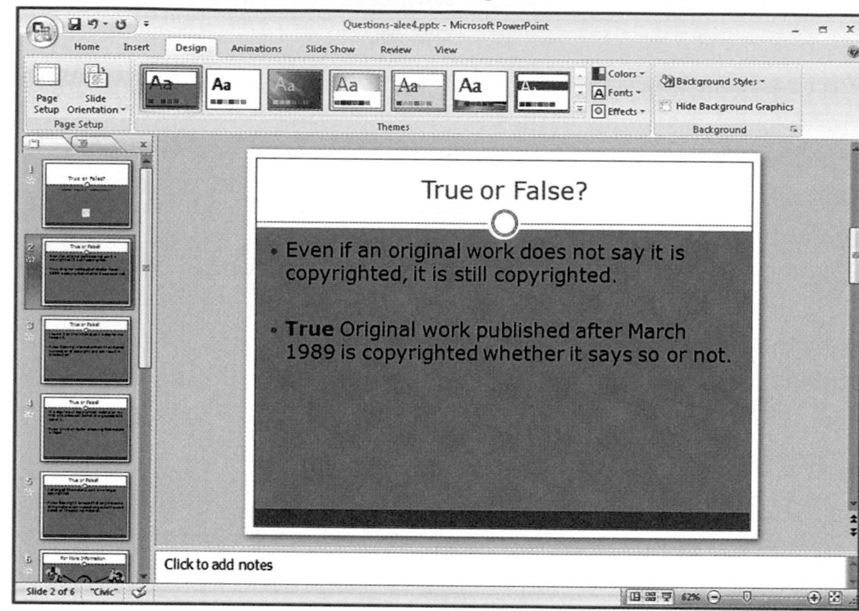

FIGURE 3.60 Transition effect applied to slides

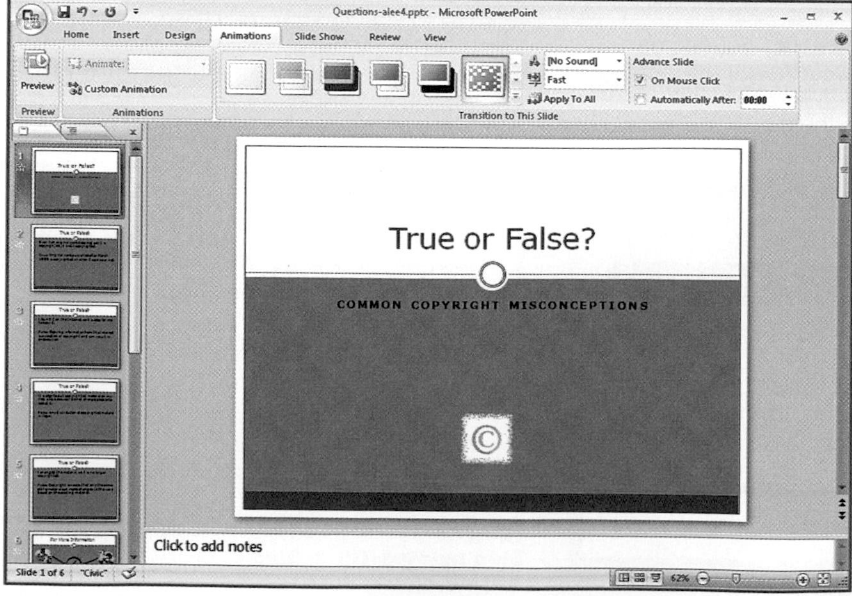

Step-By-Step

1. In your **Business Letter** choose **Review>Proofing> Research**.
2. In the **Research** task pane, under **Search for**, key: city zip codes.
3. In the **Search for** drop-down list, click **MSN Search**.
4. Click **Start searching** .
5. **CHECK** Your screen should look similar to Figure 3.16.
6. Scroll down and click the U.S. Postal Service (USPS) link. On the USPS site, enter **Natick, MA**. Click **Submit**.
7. In your Business Letter, change the zip code in the inside address from **01759** to **01760**. Close the task pane.
8. **CHECK** Your screen should look like Figure 3.17.
9. With your teacher's permission, print the letter. Save the file.

Continue to the next exercise.

Troubleshooter

If you do not see USPS in your search results at first, scroll down in the menu.

EXERCISE 3-9
Research Information

Word's Research task pane allows you to search online or offline for information. Offline, the Research options are limited to information on your own computer, such as the thesaurus. Online, however, you can use the Research tool to search the Web for information.

Teaching Tip If students cannot go online, review the features of the **Research** tool with them.

FIGURE 3.16 Task pane displays Research results

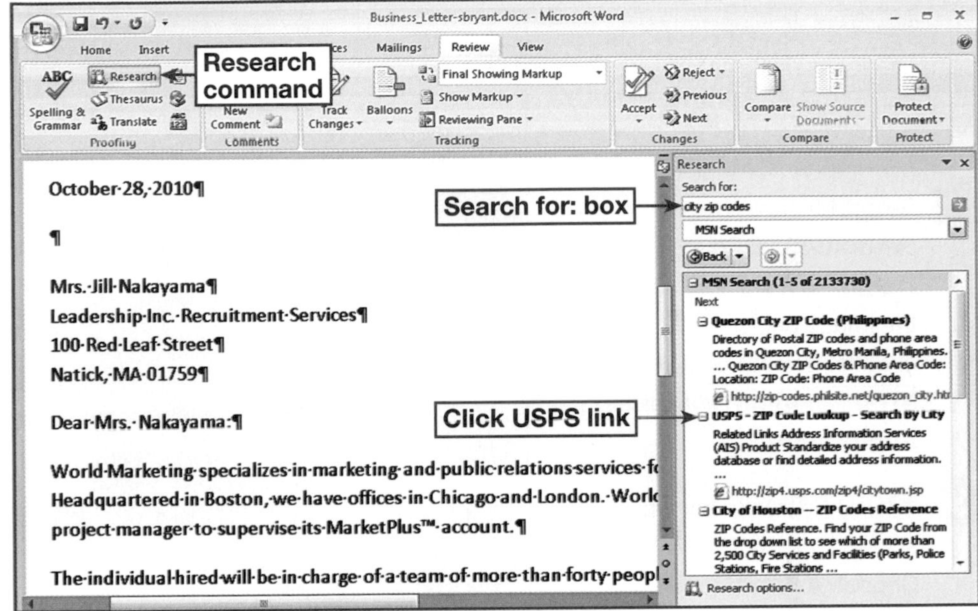

FIGURE 3.17 Information inserted using the Research tool

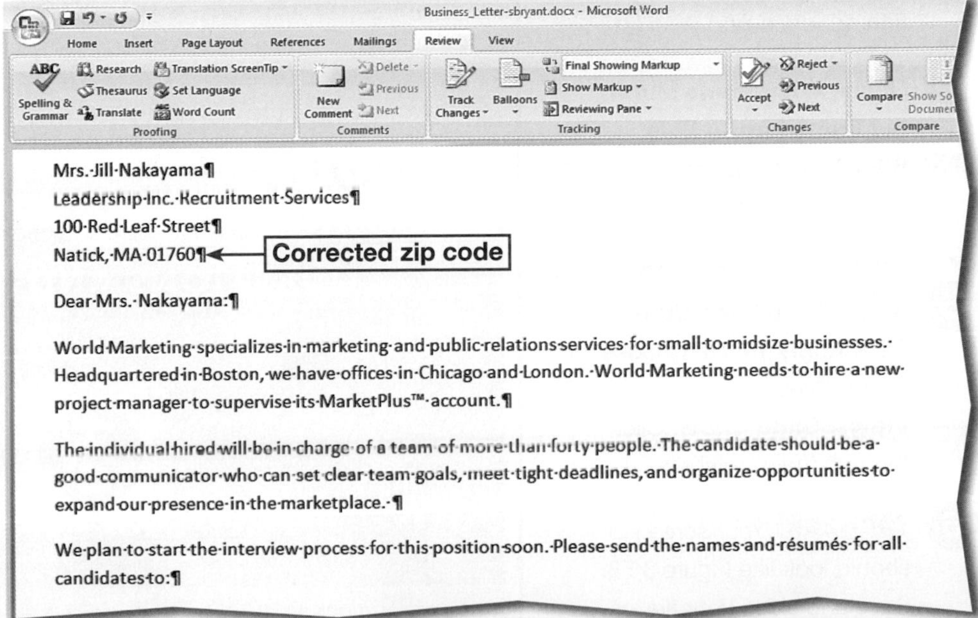

LESSON 3 Practice It Activities

Step-By-Step

1. Open your **Copyrights-2** file. Save as: Copyrights-[your first initial and last name]3. Click **Slide 1**. Select the graphic.

2. Select **Picture Tools> Format>Size**. Change **Height** to **2** inches. Move the image below the subtitle. Select **Format> Arrange>Align** . Click **Align Center**.

3. **CHECK** Your screen should look like Figure 3.57. Choose **Animations> Transition to This Slide> More** drop-down arrow. Under **Wipes**, choose the fifth option, called **Wedge**.

4. On the **Animations** tab, in the **Transition to This Slide** group, click the **Sound** drop-down arrow. Select **Click**.

5. Select **Speed>Medium**. Click **Apply to All**. Choose **View>Presentation Views>Slide Show**. Click through the slide show.

6. **CHECK** Your screen should look like Figure 3.58. Save and close your file.

3. Modify Graphics and Apply Transition Effects

Follow the steps to complete the activity. You must complete Practice It Activity 2 before doing this activity.

Solution The solution file for this exercise is **Copyrights3-SF.pptx.**
New Student Strategy If a student did not complete Practice It Activity 2, then the solution file for that activity can be used as a data file for this activity.

FIGURE 3.57 Graphic resized and aligned

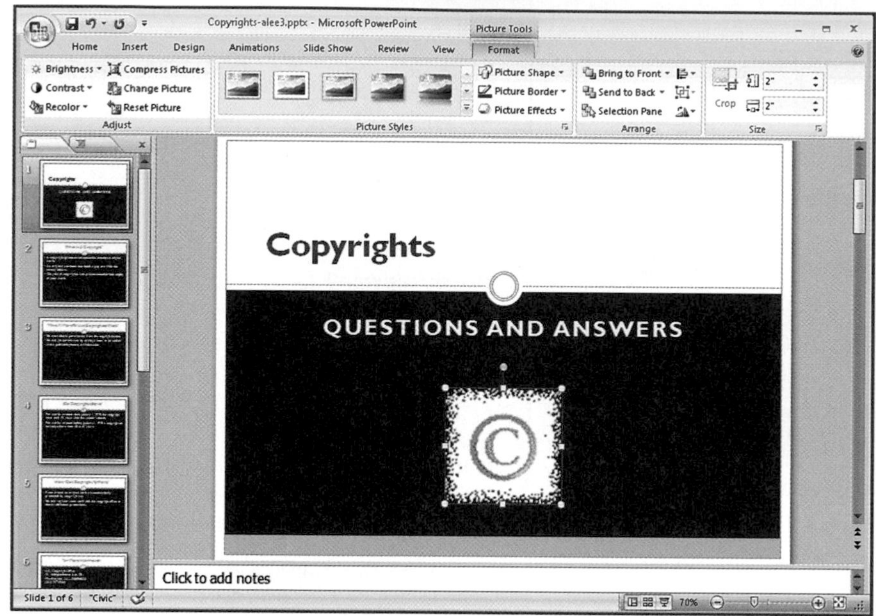

FIGURE 3.58 Slide 1 in Slide Show view

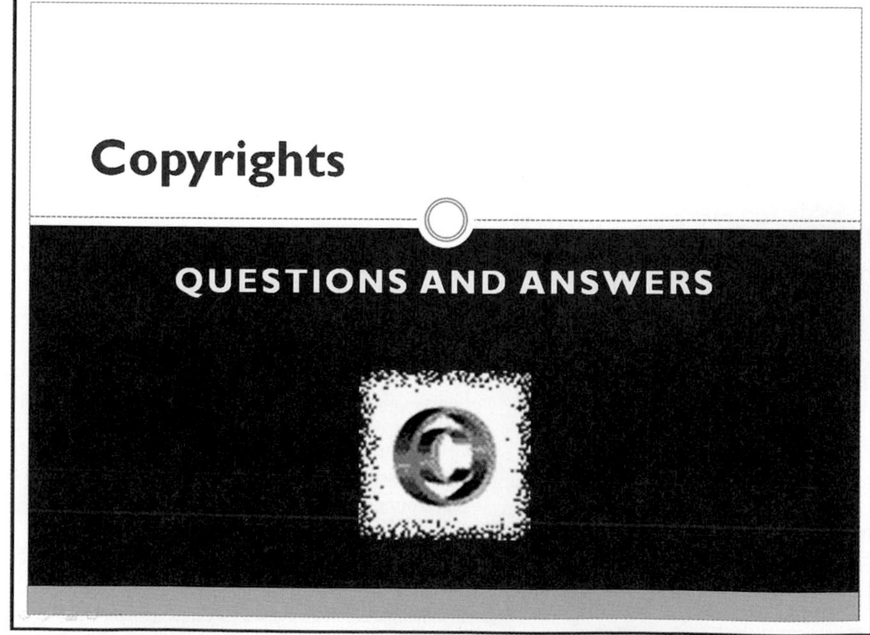

Step-By-Step

1. In your **Business Letter** file, select the entire inside address (see Figure 3.18).
2. Choose **Mailings> Create>Envelopes**.
3. In the **Envelopes and Labels** dialog box, click the **Envelopes** tab.
4. **CHECK** Your dialog box should look like Figure 3.18.
5. In the **Return address** box, key the World Marketing address shown on the **Business Letter**.
6. Make sure the **Add electronic postage** and **Omit** boxes are not checked in the dialog box.
7. **CHECK** Your dialog box should look like Figure 3.19.
8. With your teacher's permission, click **Print**. In the dialog box that appears, click **No**.
9. Save and close your **Business Letter** file.

Continue to the next exercise.

Differentiated Instruction/ Advanced Students In the **Envelopes and Labels** dialog box, have students click **Options** and explore envelope size, font, and other options.

EXERCISE 3-10
Print an Envelope

Use the Envelopes and Labels dialog box to create an envelope automatically using an address in a document. You can also key an address directly into the dialog box.

Solution Use the file **Business Letter-SF.docx** as a solution file for Exercises 3-1 through 3-10.

FIGURE 3.18 Select the address you want on the envelope

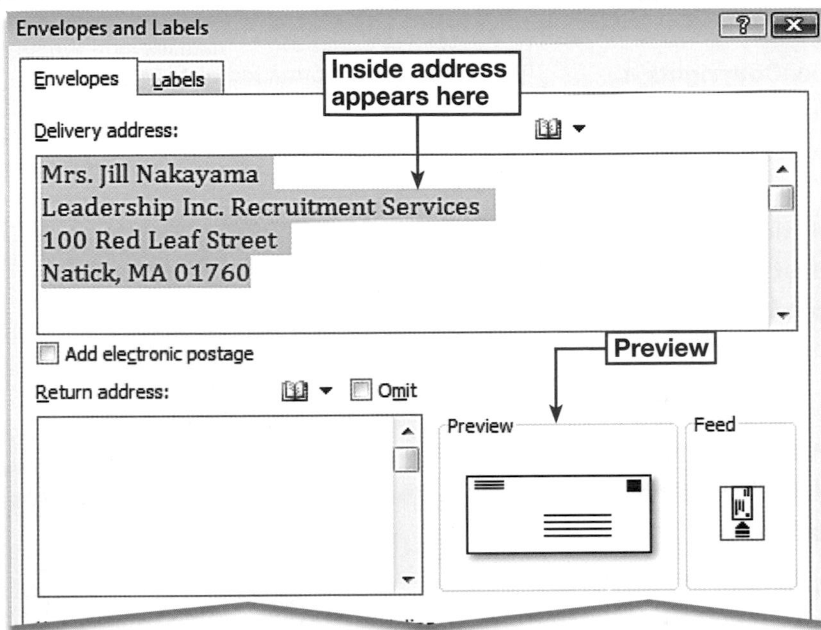

FIGURE 3.19 Delivery and return addresses added to dialog box

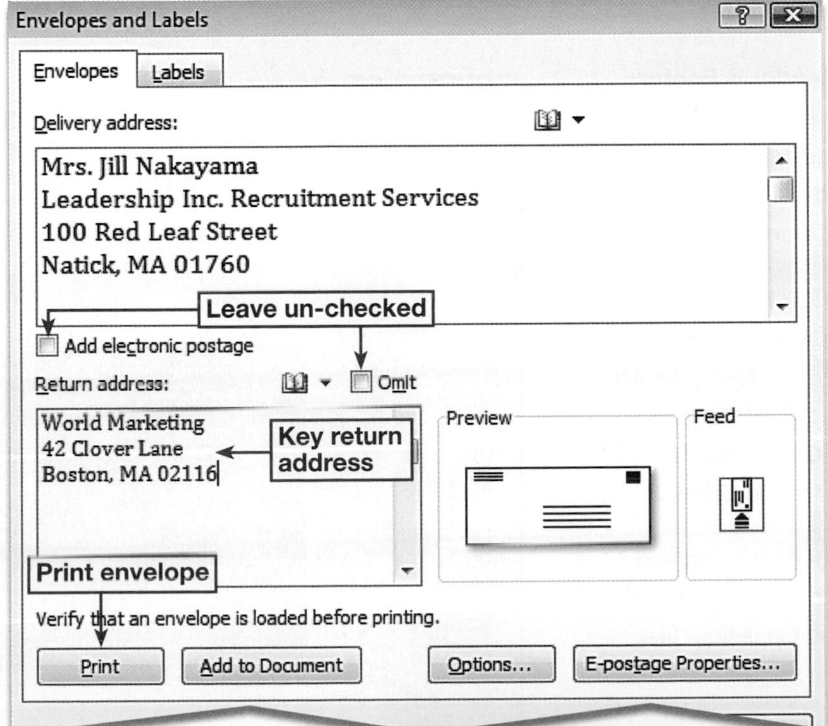

2. Modify Slide Masters, Headers, and Footers

Follow the steps to complete the activity. You must complete Practice It Activity 1 before doing this activity.

Solution The solution file for this exercise is **Copyright2-SF.pptx.**
New Student Strategy If a student did not complete Practice It Activity 1, then the solution file for that activity can be used as a data file for this activity.

Step-By-Step

1. Open your **Copyrights-1** file. Save as: Copyrights-[your first initial and last name]2. Choose **View>Presentation Views>Slide Master**. Click the **Title Slide Layout: used by slide(s) 1** thumbnail.
2. Select the **Click to Edit Master Subtitle Style** placeholder. Change the **Font Size** to **28 pt**.
3. **CHECK** Your screen should look like Figure 3.55. Choose **Insert>Text>Header & Footer**.
4. In the **Header & Footer** dialog box, on the **Slide** tab, click **Date and Time** and **Update automatically**. Leave the default date as is.
5. Click **Slide Number**. Click **Don't show on title slide**. Select **Apply to All**. Choose **Slide Master>Close>Close Master View**. Move to **Slide 2**.
6. **CHECK** Your screen should look like Figure 3.56. Save and close your file.

FIGURE 3.55 Formatted Slide Master

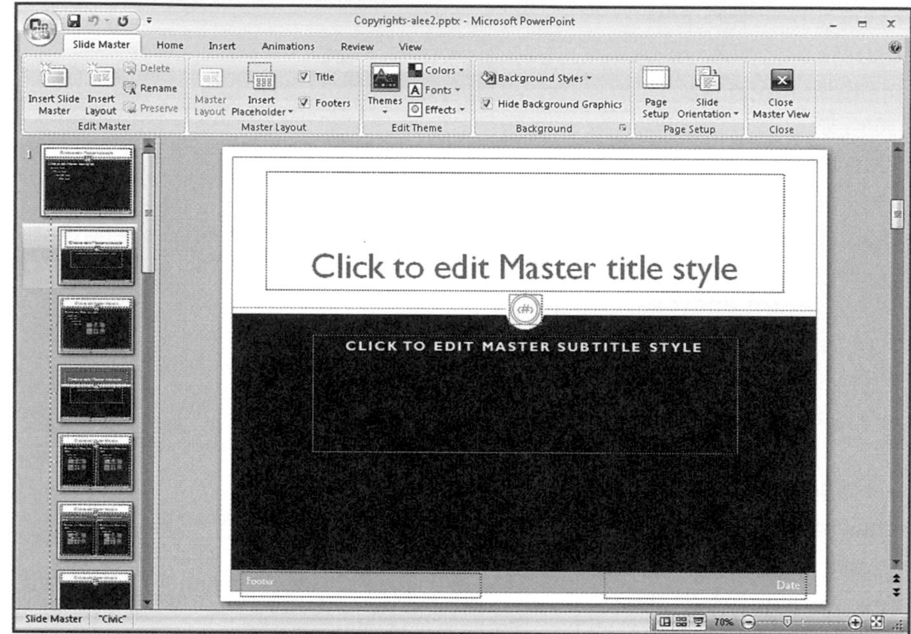

FIGURE 3.56 Formatted footer

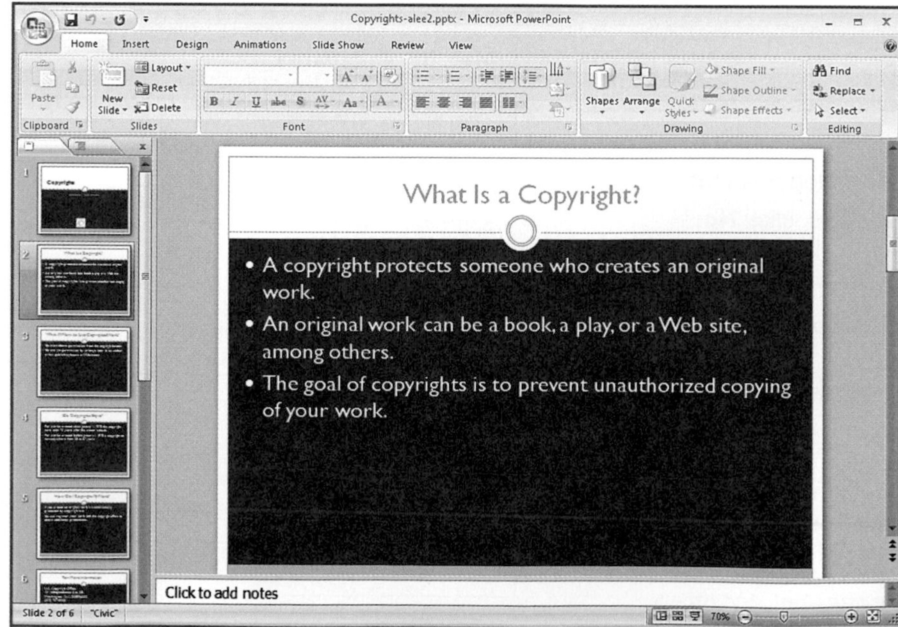

Step-By-Step

1 Open the data file **Fay_Memo.docx**. Save as: Fay_Memo-[your first initial and last name].

2 Choose **Home>Editing>Find** . In the **Find and Replace** dialog box, in the **Find what** box, key: LeaderShip.

3 CHECK Your dialog box should look like Figure 3.20.

4 Click **Find Next**. Click in the memo and change **LeaderShip** to **Leadership**.

5 In your dialog box, click the **Go To** tab. Under **Go to what:** choose **Line**.

6 In the **Enter line number:** box, key: 9. Click **Go To** (see Figure 3.21).

7 The insertion point moves to the beginning of the ninth line of your memo. Close the dialog box and save your document.

Continue to the next exercise.

NCLB/Language Arts (NCTE 4)
Explain to students that they can use **Find** to locate and correct words. If they discover that a name that they have used in a document is misspelled, they can find the misspelling and replace it in each spot where it occurs.

EXERCISE 3-11
Use the Find and Go To Commands

Word allows you to find text in your document. Key a word or group of words, also know as a phrase, in the Find dialog box. Word will find every place where that word or phrase appears in your document. The Go To command is used to find specific parts of your document. This feature is especially useful in long documents because you can tell Word to go to individual pages, tables, or sections.

FIGURE 3.20 Find tab

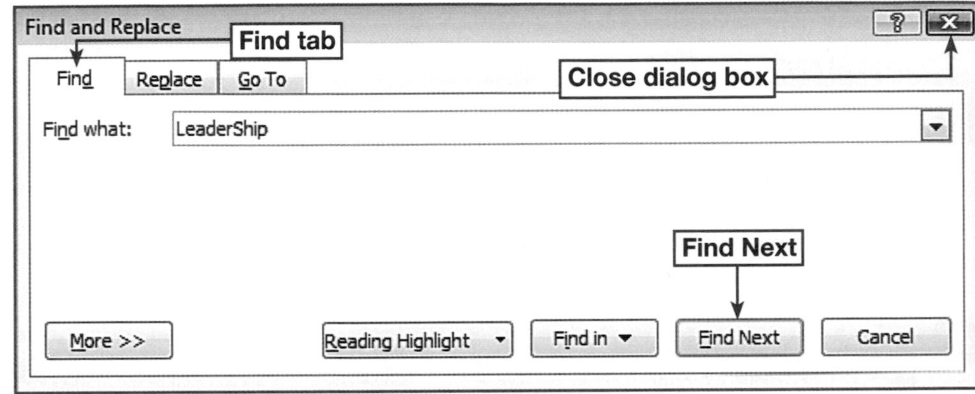

FIGURE 3.21 Go To tab

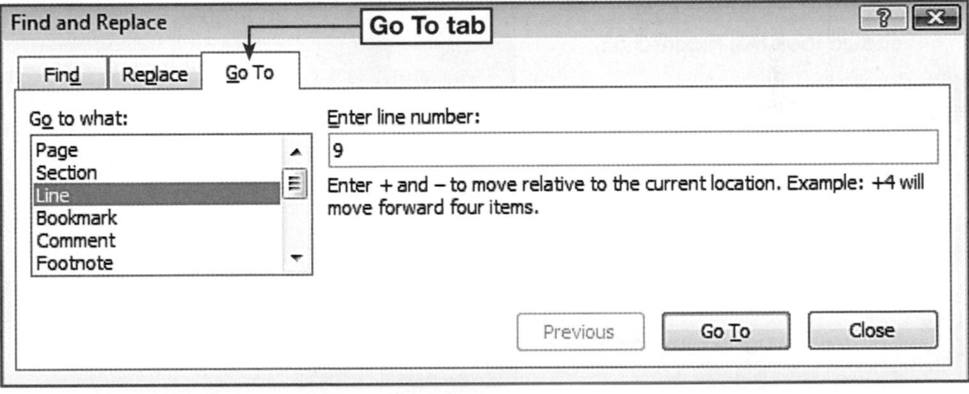

Shortcuts

To open the **Find** tab in the dialog box, press CTRL + F. To open the **Go To** tab, press CTRL + ALT + HOME or click **Select Browse Object** beneath the horizontal scroll bar.

Microsoft Office 2007

Word now indicates contextual errors with a wavy blue line. This feature is designed to catch incorrect uses of words such as to, two, and too.

LESSON 3 Practice It Activities

1. Apply and Modify Themes and Format Slides

Data File

Follow the steps to complete the activity.

Step-By-Step

1. Open the **Copyrights.pptx** data file. Save as: Copyrights [your first initial and last name]1.
2. Select **Slide 1**. Choose **Home>Slides>Layout** . In the **Slide Layout** drop-down menu, click **Title Slide**.
3. Choose **Design>Themes>More** drop-down arrow. Select **Civic**.
4. **CHECK** Your screen should look like Figure 3.53.
5. Choose **Design>Background>Background Styles**. Click **Style 3**.
6. Choose **Design>Themes>Colors**. Click **Office**.
7. Choose **Design>Themes>Fonts**. Scroll down to select **Solstice**.
8. **CHECK** Your screen should look like Figure 3.54.
9. Save and close your file.

Solution The solution file for this activity is **Copyright1-SF.pptx**.

FIGURE 3.53 Slide with modified layout and design

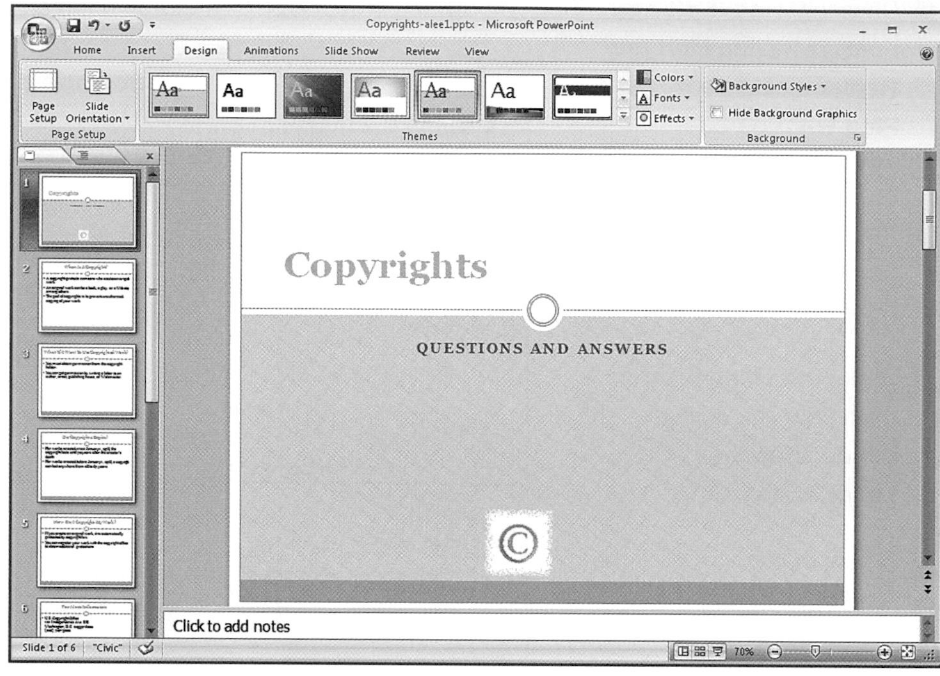

FIGURE 3.54 Slide with modified background and transition effect applied

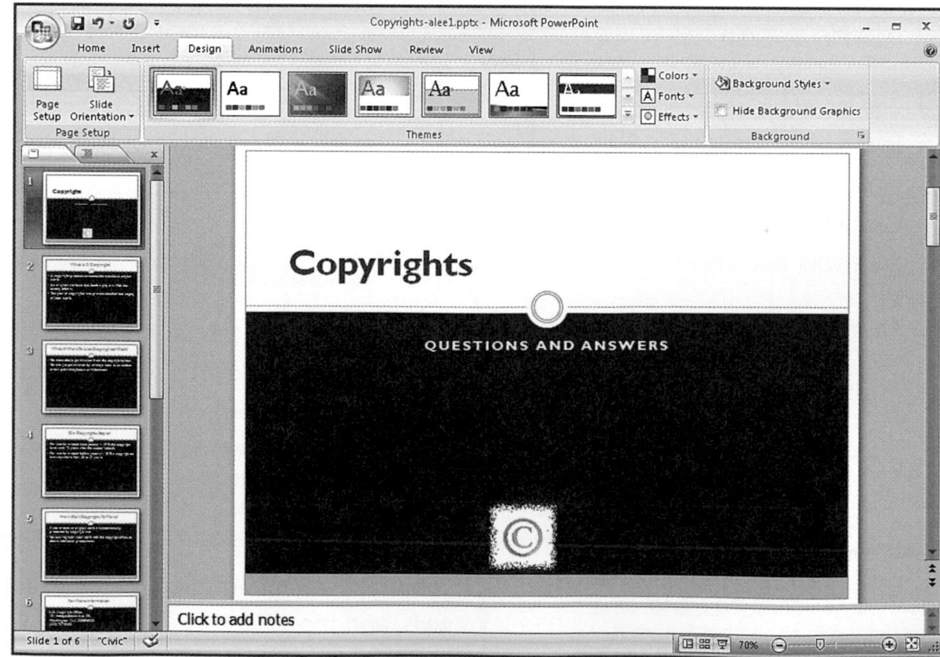

Step-By-Step

1. In Your **Fay Memo** file, choose **Home>Editing> Replace** .
2. In the **Find and Replace** dialog box, in the **Find what**: box, clear the box and key: applicant.
3. In the **Replace with**: box, key: candidate.
4. CHECK Your dialog box should look like Figure 3.22.
5. In the dialog box, click **Replace**. Click **Replace** again to replace **applicant** with **candidate**.
6. The word **applicant** is selected again in the memo. In the dialog box, click **Replace All**.
7. Click **OK** in the **Word** dialog box. Close the dialog box.
8. CHECK Your screen should look like Figure 3.23. Save your file.

Continue to the next exercise.

Shortcuts

To open the **Replace** tab in the **Find and Replace** dialog box using keyboard keys, press CTRL + H.

EXERCISE 3-12

Find and Replace Text

You can use the Find and Replace dialog box to replace text in your document by keying the word that you want to replace and the word that should replace it. Word will then automatically replace one word with the other.

Step-By-Step Tip Remind students to be careful in **Step 6** when they click the **Replace All** button.

FIGURE 3.22 Replace tab

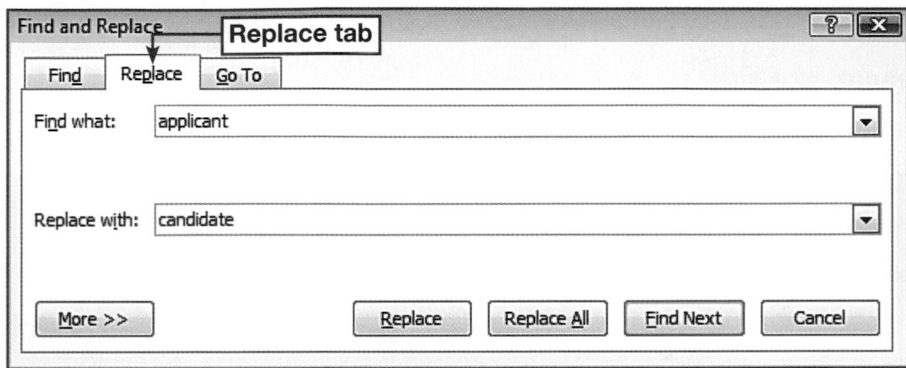

FIGURE 3.23 Text found and replaced

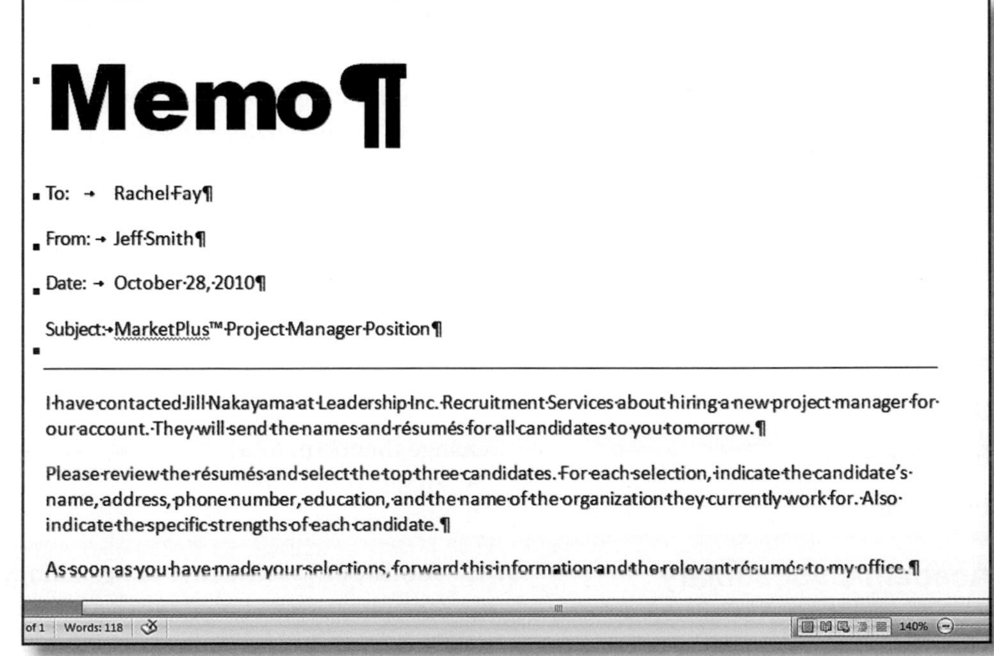

LESSON 3 After You Read

Vocabulary

Key Terms

alignment
animation scheme
background
color scheme
fill color
font
font style
footer
Format Painter
formatting
gradient
header
landscape
line color
portrait
rotate
slide layout
Slide Master
transition
typeface

Academic Vocabulary

anticipate
emphasis

Answer to Key Term Activity
Slide shows will vary, but each slide should include one term and its definition.

Review Key Terms

Complete the following statements on a separate piece of paper. Choose from the Vocabulary list on the left to complete the statements.

1. A text's __alignment__ refers to whether it is lined up along the left margin, along the right margin, along both margins, or in the center of the text box. (p. 607)

2. A(n) __color scheme__ is the colors used in a slide's design. (p. 625)

3. The color inside a graphic is called __fill color__. (p. 611)

4. Bold, underline, and shadow are all types of __font style__. (p. 605)

5. Increasing font size or adding color to text is a way to add __emphasis__ to the text. (p. 606)

Key Term Activity

6. Create a PowerPoint Key Term quiz.
A. Organize into groups of four or five students.
B. Have each group member select a different Key Term.
C. Have each member create one slide. Place the Key Term definition at the top of the slide. Use the **Fade in one by one** animation scheme to have the Key Term drop into the slide.
D. Run the slide show. Have each group member guess which Key Term is being defined before revealing the Key Term on the slide.

Reviewing Key Concepts

Answer the following questions on a separate piece of paper.

7. Which of the following can you use to join two graphics? (p. 616)
A. Rotate or Flip
B. Align or Distribute
(C.) Connectors
D. Join

8. If you want to change all of the bullets in a presentation, where should you change them? (p. 623)
A. Presentation Master
(B.) Slide Master
C. Slide Sorter View
D. Show Master

9. The footer of a presentation can contain which of the following information? (p. 628)
A. Date
B. Slide number
C. Presentation title
(D.) All of the above

10. What makes objects on a screen appear one by one? (p. 620)
A. Slide Transition
(B.) Animation Scheme
C. Color Scheme
D. Background Styles

Step-By-Step

1. In your **Fay Memo** file, position the insertion point at the end of the second paragraph. Press the **spacebar** once.
2. Key exactly as shown: We can thne schedule interveiws. Press the **spacebar** once.
3. CHECK Your screen should look like Figure 3.24.
4. Choose **Office>Word Options>Proofing> AutoCorrect Options**. Click **AutoCorrect Options**.
5. In the **AutoCorrect Options** dialog box, under **Replace**:, key: aech. Under **With:**, key: each.
6. Click **Add**. Click **Close**. Click **OK**.
7. Key: with aech candidate.
8. CHECK Your screen should look like Figure 3.25. Save and close the file.

Continue to the next exercise.

Step-By-Step Tip In **Step 2**, students should watch the screen closely when they key to see how AutoCorrect works.

EL Ask English Learner students which English words they find most difficult and guide them as they enter those words into the AutoCorrect Options dialog box.

EXERCISE 3-13
Customize and Use AutoCorrect

AutoCorrect is a Word feature that automatically corrects common spelling errors. You can also customize AutoCorrect to catch your frequent keying or spelling errors.

Solution Use the file **Fay_Memo-SF.docx** as the solution file for Exercises 3-10 through 3-14.

FIGURE 3.24 AutoCorrect changed misspelled words

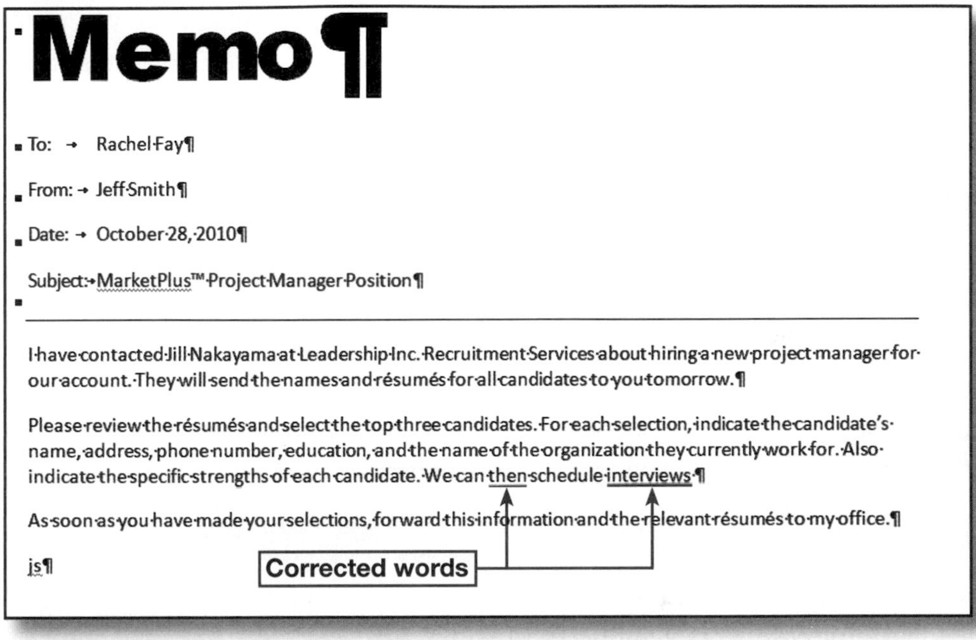

Memo¶

To: → Rachel Fay¶

From: → Jeff Smith¶

Date: → October 28, 2010¶

Subject: → MarketPlus™ Project Manager Position¶

I have contacted Jill Nakayama at Leadership Inc. Recruitment Services about hiring a new project manager for our account. They will send the names and résumés for all candidates to you tomorrow.¶

Please review the résumés and select the top three candidates. For each selection, indicate the candidate's name, address, phone number, education, and the name of the organization they currently work for. Also indicate the specific strengths of each candidate. We can then schedule interviews.¶

As soon as you have made your selections, forward this information and the relevant résumés to my office.¶

js¶

Corrected words

FIGURE 3.25 Errors corrected using customized AutoCorrect

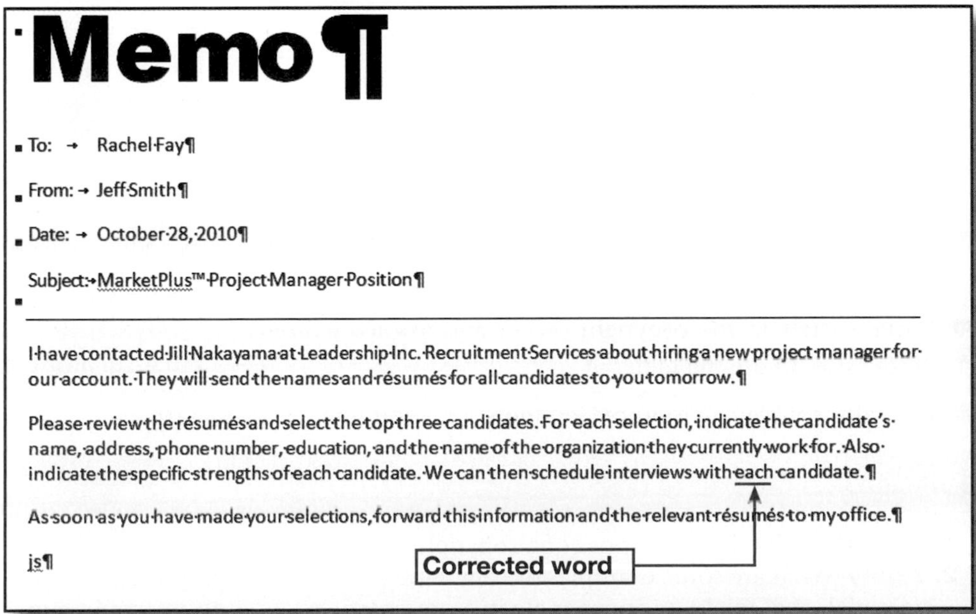

Memo¶

To: → Rachel Fay¶

From: → Jeff Smith¶

Date: → October 28, 2010¶

Subject: → MarketPlus™ Project Manager Position¶

I have contacted Jill Nakayama at Leadership Inc. Recruitment Services about hiring a new project manager for our account. They will send the names and résumés for all candidates to you tomorrow.¶

Please review the résumés and select the top three candidates. For each selection, indicate the candidate's name, address, phone number, education, and the name of the organization they currently work for. Also indicate the specific strengths of each candidate. We can then schedule interviews with each candidate.¶

As soon as you have made your selections, forward this information and the relevant résumés to my office.¶

js¶

Corrected word

Writing MATTERS

Copyrights

You have written a great short story for your creative writing class. When a friend asks to read it, you are flattered by his interest. Later, you learn that your friend has taken your ideas, changed the words slightly, and turned the story in to his teacher without giving you any credit. What would you say to this friend?

Respect Other People's Work

When a work is copyrighted, it is illegal for someone else to use it and pass it off as his or her own. When you create an original work, it is automatically copyrighted. That means even if you do not see the copyright symbol, ©, on an item, the artist or writer is protected by copyright law. Published authors usually apply for a copyright notice through the U.S. Copyright Office. Books, artistic works, and ideas are all copyrighted. Material found on the Internet is also protected by the same copyright laws.

How to Use Copyrighted Material

Sometimes when you are preparing a report or presentation, you find a piece of writing, music, or video clip that perfectly illustrates your point. While all of these items are copyrighted, this does not necessarily mean that you cannot use them. Rules for using copyrighted material are different depending upon whether the purpose is educational or commercial. To get permission to use copyrighted material:

- Find out who owns the material you want to use. Many Web sites have a Terms of Use page that lets you know who owns the material and what you can and cannot use from the site.
- Write a letter to the copyright owner and ask for written permission to use the material.
- Cite your source in a footnote, endnote, or credit line.

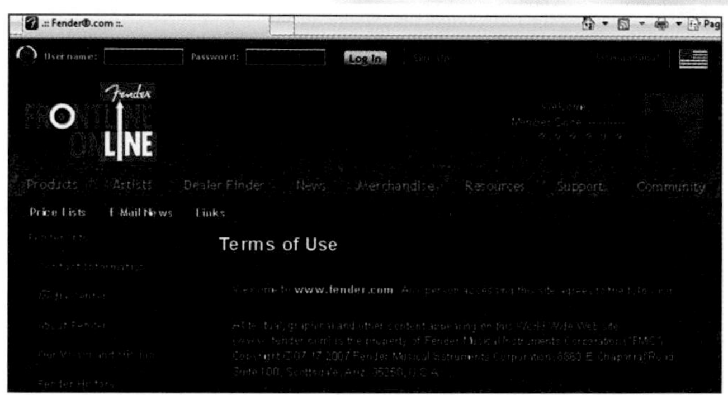

Read a Web site's Terms of Use page to find out who owns the material on the site.

NCLB/Language Arts (NCTE 7) Be sure students understand how to cite sources in their work.

NCLB/Language Arts (NCTE 12) Students should understand how to write a letter to ask permission to use copyrighted materials.

SKILLBUILDER

1. **Identify** What is the purpose of a copyright?
2. **Apply** What are some examples of copyrighted materials that might be appropriate in a presentation about famous movie soundtracks?
3. **Evaluate** Why do you think copyright laws are important? In your own words, describe what you think would happen if these laws did not exist. Give examples.

SkillBuilder answers can be found on page TM94.

Step-By-Step

1. Open the data file **Profiles .docx**. Save as: Profiles-[your first initial and last name].

2. Choose **Home> Clipboard>Dialog Box Launcher** .

3. Select the five lines of text under **Three Top Candidates**. Click **Copy** .

4. **CHECK** Your screen should look like Figure 3.26.

5. Click after **Current Organization:**. Press ENTER twice. Click the item in the **Clipboard**.

6. Press ENTER. Click the item in the **Clipboard** again.

7. **CHECK** Your screen should look like Figure 3.27.

8. Select the text **of résumés** near the top of the document. Click **Copy** .

9. Click before the word **reviewed** in the line below. Click **of résumés** in the **Clipboard**.

Continued on the next page.

You Should Know

The Clipboard appears on the left side of the screen. You can move it by clicking and dragging it.

EXERCISE 3-14
Use the Office Clipboard

Any time you cut or copy text, that text is stored on the Word Clipboard. The Word Clipboard stores only one item at a time. As soon as you cut or copy another item, the previous item is replaced. Unlike the Word Clipboard, the Office Clipboard can store up to 24 separate cut or copied items. Use the Office Clipboard when you want to store and reuse several words, phrases, or paragraphs.

Inclusion Strategy Show students a clipboard with items clipped to it to help them see how the Clipboard works.

FIGURE 3.26 Office Clipboard

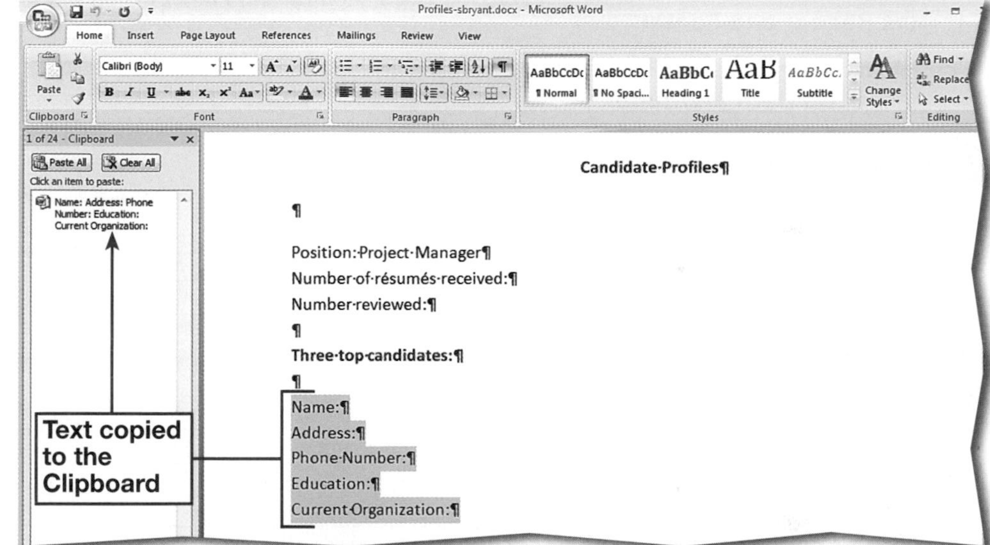

FIGURE 3.27 Clipboard items pasted

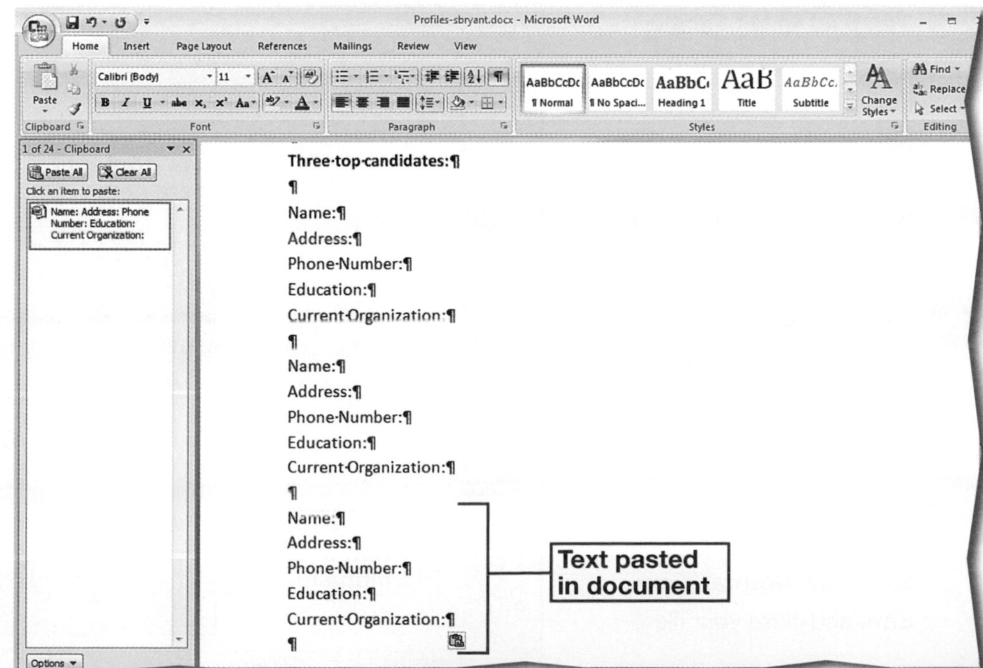

Step-By-Step

1. In your **Staff** file, select the **Title and Content Layout: used by Slides 3-4, 6-7** thumbnail, if necessary.

2. Choose **Insert>Text> Header and Footer**. In the **Header and Footer** dialog box, on the **Slide** tab, select **Date and time**.

3. Select **Update automatically**. Click the date drop-down arrow. Click the date and time style shown in Figure 3.51.

4. Select **Slide number**. Select **Footer**. In the **Footer** box, key: Satellite Sound Waves Staff. Select **Don't show on title slide**.

5. **CHECK** Your dialog box should look like Figure 3.51. On the **Notes and Handouts** tab, select **Header**. In the **Header** box, key: Staff Orientation. Click **Apply to All**.

6. Select **View>Notes Page**. On the status bar, click **Zoom In** until the **Zoom Level** is at **120%**.

7. **CHECK** Your screen should look similar to Figure 3.52. Click **Normal View**. Save and close your file.

EXERCISE 3-22
Use Footers and Headers with Slide Masters

A **footer** is text that appears at the bottom of every slide in a presentation. Footers often contain the date, presentation title, and slide number. You can choose not to include footers on specific slides, such as title slides. A **header** is information that appears at the top of every notes page or presentation handout.

FIGURE 3.51 Header and Footer dialog box

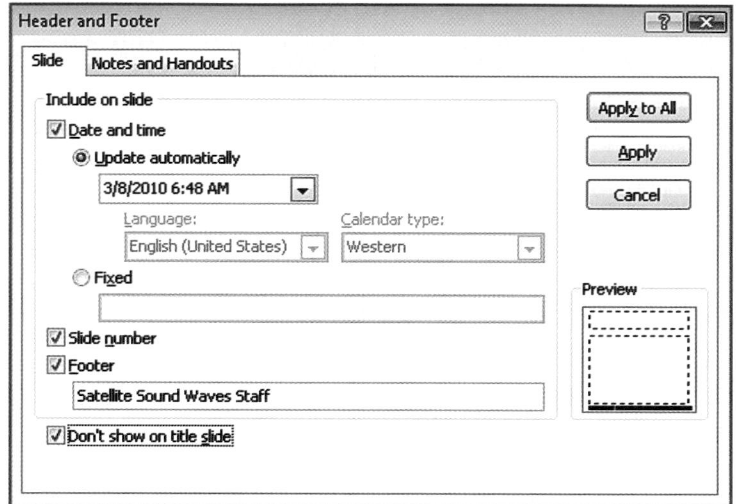

Solution Use the file **Staff-SF.pptx** as a solution file for Exercises 3-19 through 3-22.

FIGURE 3.52 Header and footer on notes page

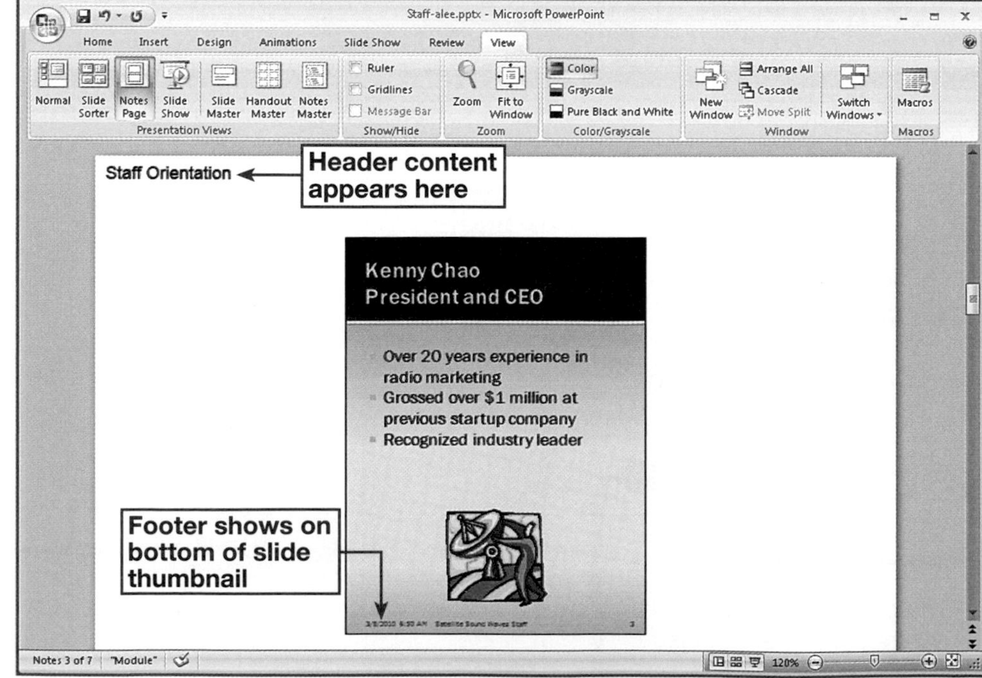

Step-By-Step

EXERCISE 3-14 (Continued)
Use the Office Clipboard

10 CHECK Your screen should look like Figure 3.28.

11 Click after **Current Organization:** in the first listing. Press ENTER. Key: Specific Strengths:

12 Select **Specific Strengths:**. Click **Copy**.

13 Click under **Current Organization:** in the second listing. Click **Specific Strengths:** in the Clipboard.

14 Click under **Current Organization:** in the third listing. Click **Specific Strengths:** in the Clipboard.

15 CHECK Your screen should look like Figure 3.29.

16 Close the **Clipboard** task pane. With your teacher's permission, print the document. Save and close your file.

Continue to the next exercise.

You Should Know

You can paste all Clipboard items at once by clicking **Paste All**. If you no longer need any of the items in the Clipboard, click **Clear All** to remove them.

FIGURE 3.28 More Clipboard items pasted

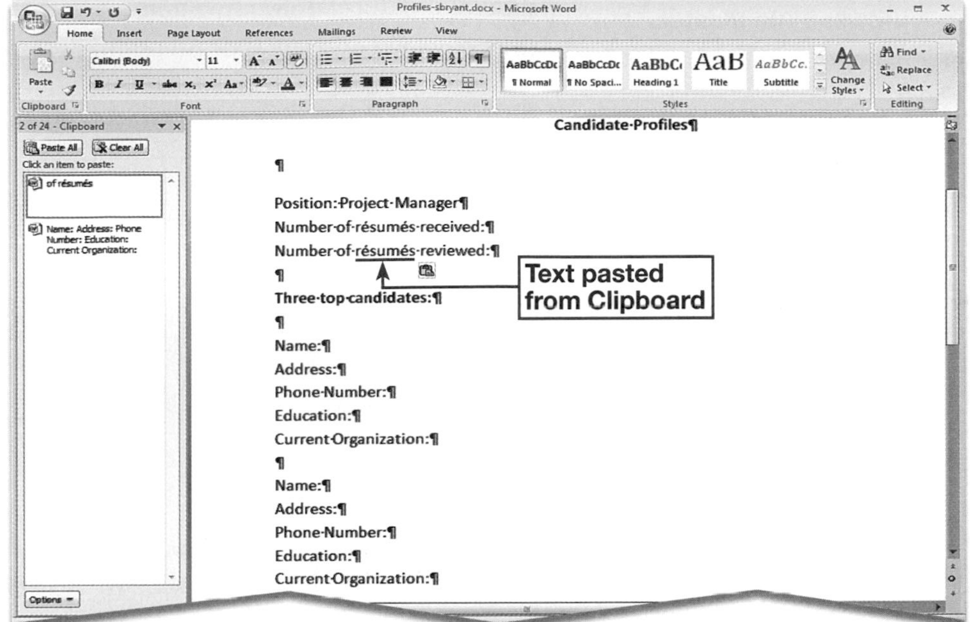

Solution The solution file for this exercise is **Profiles-SF.docx**.

FIGURE 3.29 All Clipboard items pasted

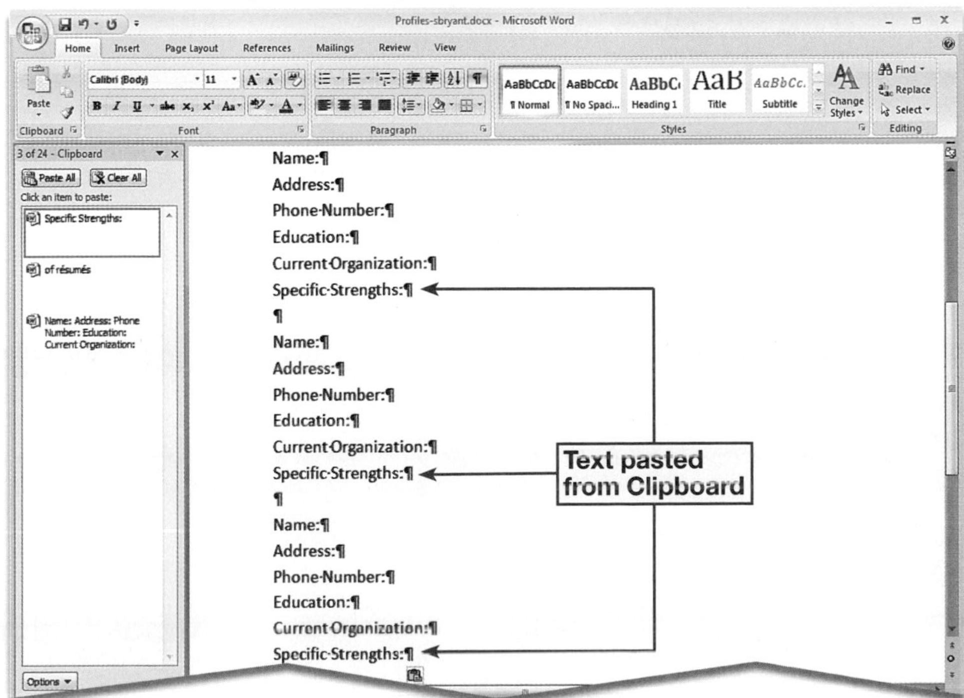

Step-By-Step

1. In your **Staff** file, choose **View>Presentation Views>Slide Master**.
2. In the **Slide Master** overview pane, scroll down and select **Title and Content Layout: used by Slides 3-4, 6-7**.
3. Choose **Insert> Illustrations>Clip Art**. In the **Clip Art** task pane, in the **Search for:** box, key: antennas. Click **Go**. Double click the Clip Art shown in Figure 3.49.
4. **CHECK** Your screen should look like Figure 3.49. With the Clip Art image selected, press SHIFT and click inside the content text box to select it.
5. On the **Picture Tools** contextual tab, on the **Format** tab, in the **Arrange** group, click **Align**. Click **Align Selected Objects**.
6. Click **Align** again. Select **Align Bottom**. Click outside the text box to deselect it.
7. **CHECK** Your screen should look like Figure 3.50. Close the **Clip Art** task pane. Save your file.

Continue to the next exercise.

EXERCISE 3-21
Add Graphical Elements to Slide Masters

Slide Masters allow you to add graphics to every slide in a presentation or to every slide of a particular layout within a presentation. With this tool, you can insert a company logo on every slide or just on slides with a particular layout.

Troubleshooting If students cannot find the Clip Art, direct them to the file provided for this lesson.

FIGURE 3.49 Graphic inserted into background

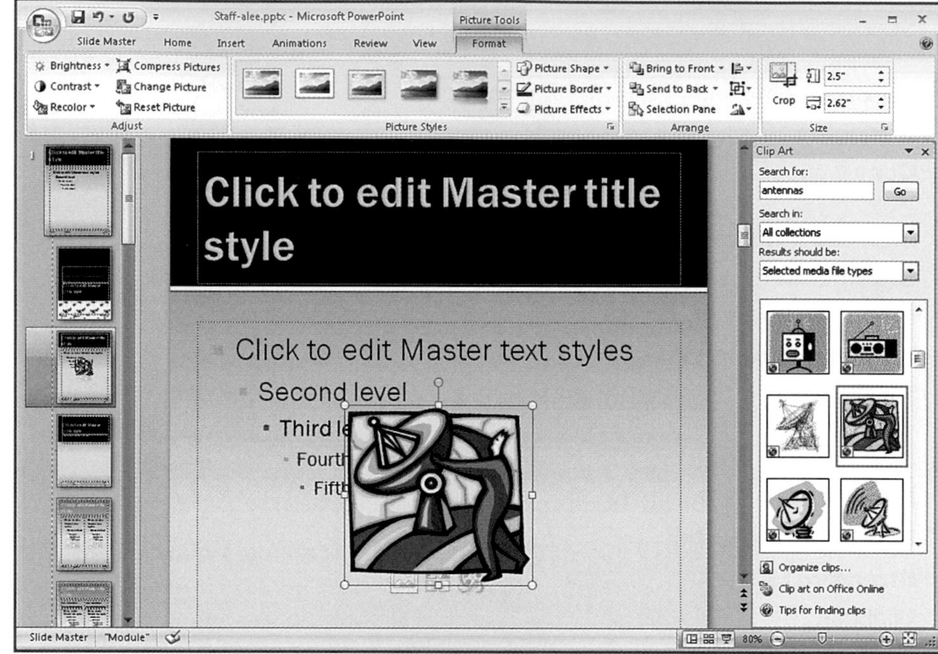

FIGURE 3.50 Background image aligned in slide

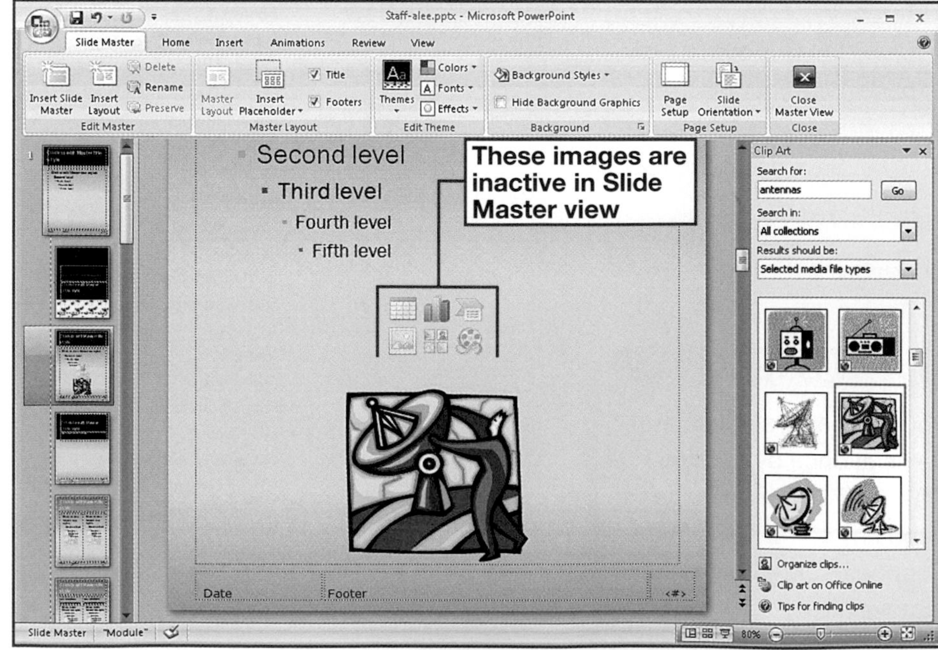

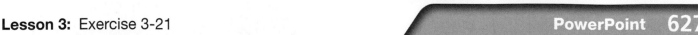

Step-By-Step

1. Choose **Office>New**. In the **New Document** task pane, click **Installed Templates**. Choose **Equity Letter** style.

2. In the **Preview** window, next to **Create new**, click **Document**. Click **Create**.

3. **CHECK** Your screen should look like Figure 3.30. Save as: w3-15-[your first initial and last name].

4. Right-click the content control below the date. Choose **Remove Content Control**. Select the word again and delete it.

5. In the **Type sender company name** content control, key: Leadership Inc. Recruitment Services. In the **Type company address** content control box, enter the address shown in Figure 3.31.

6. In the **Type recipient name** content control, key: Rachel Fay. In the **Type recipient address** content control, key the return address.

7. **CHECK** Your screen should look like Figure 3.31.

Continued on the next page.

EXERCISE 3-15
Use a Template to Create a Business Letter

A template is a formatted guide that can help you create documents. Placeholder text tells you what information you should key into each **content control**, or specific text field, in the document. You can use templates to create many types of common documents, including professional business letters.

FIGURE 3.30 Create a letter from an installed template

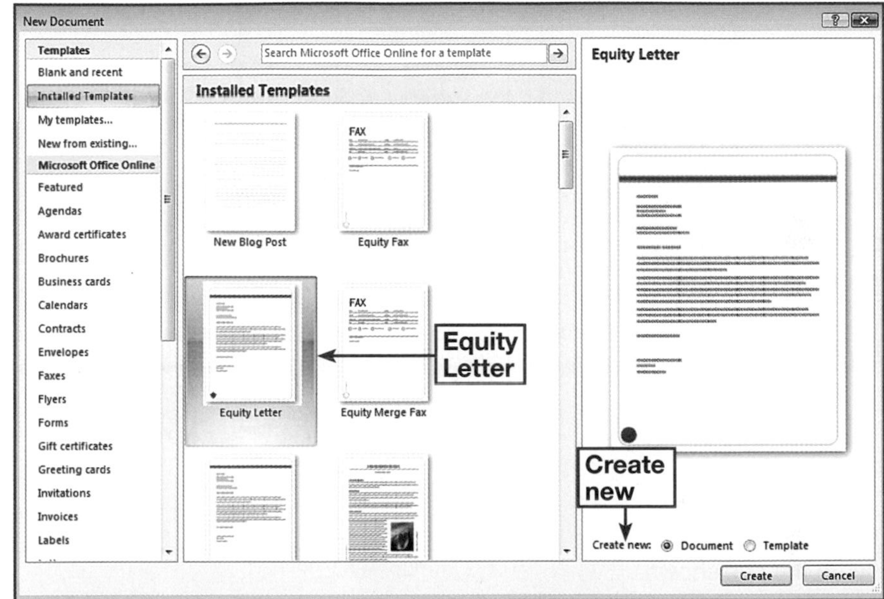

FIGURE 3.31 Enter the return and inside addresses

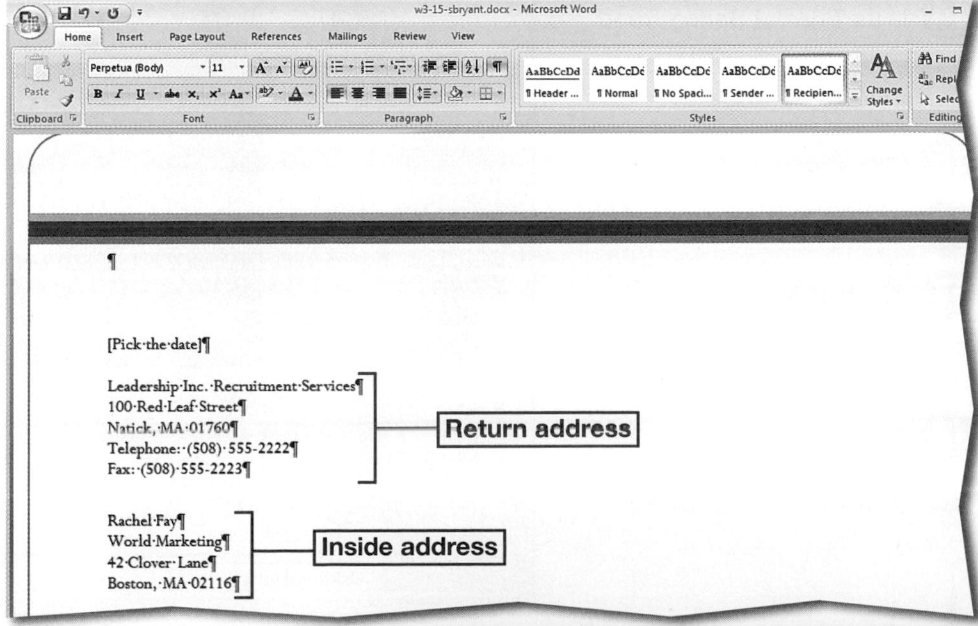

Step-By-Step

EXERCISE 3-20 (Continued)
Customize Slide Backgrounds Using Slide Masters

8. In the **Overview** pane, click **Title Slide Layout: used by slide(s) 1-2, 5** (it is second from the top).
9. On the **Slide Master** tab, click the **Background** dialog box launcher.
10. In the **Format Background** dialog box, under **Fill**, select **Picture or texture fill**.
11. Under **Insert from:** click **Clip Art**.
12. In the **Select Picture** dialog box, in the **Search text:** box, key: satellite. Click **Go**.
13. Select Clip Art of a satellite similar to the one shown in the dialog box in Figure 3.47. Click **OK**.
14. In the **Format Background** dialog box, click **Tile picture as texture**.
15. Click **Close**.
16. Click **Close Master View**.
17. **CHECK** Your screen should look similar to Figure 3.48.
18. Save your file.

Continue to the next exercise.

FIGURE 3.47 Select Picture dialog box

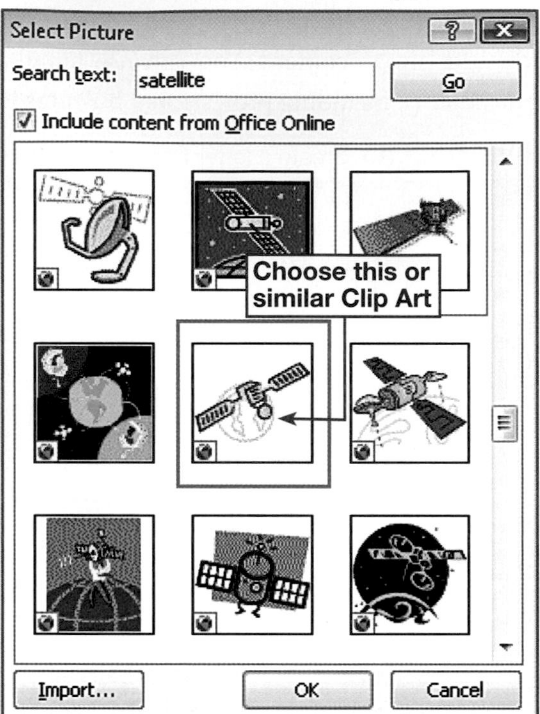

Troubleshooting If students do not have access to the Internet or cannot find the appropriate Clip Art, provide them with the Satellite data file provided with this lesson.

Troubleshooting In this exercise, if the top half of the screen (the black colored half) does not appear, have students make sure that Hide Background Graphics is not selected.

FIGURE 3.48 Title slide with customized background

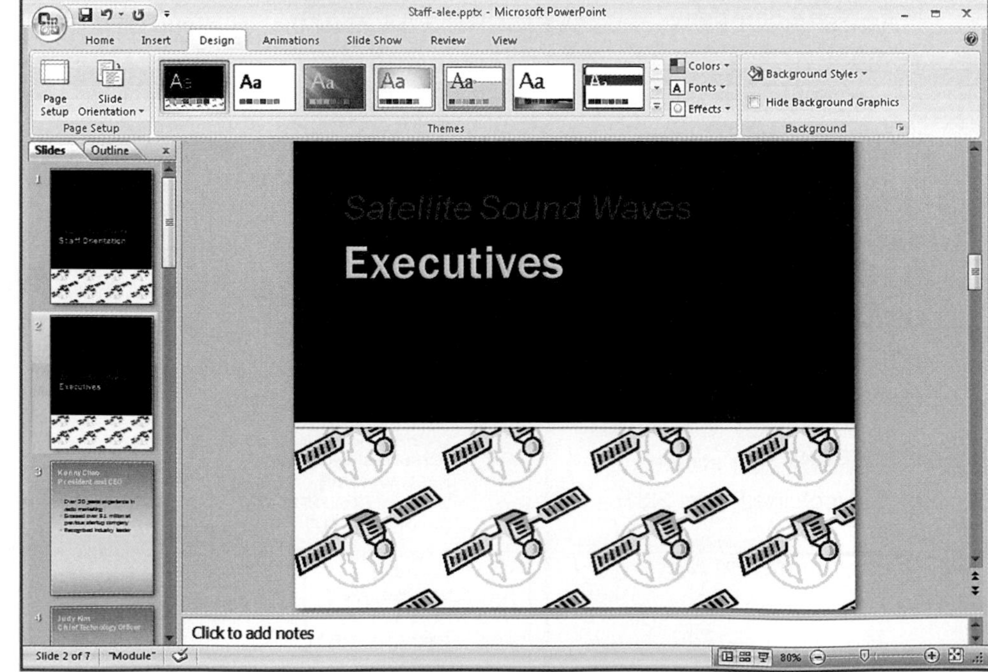

Step-By-Step

8 Choose **Page Layout> Paragraph Dialog Box Launcher** . Change the **Spacing Before** to **0**. Change the **Spacing After** to **0**. Click **OK**.

9 Click the arrow to the right of the **Choose today's date** content control. Click **Today**.

10 Select the **Date** content control and choose **Home> Cut** . Choose **Home> Paste** before Rachel Fay's name in the inside address. Press ENTER.

11 In the **Type salutation** content control, key: Dear Rachel:. Select the text you just keyed. Deselect **Bold**.

12 Select the **Type the body of the letter here** content control and key the letter's body as shown. Key the closing, sender's name, and sender's title also.

13 Format the top company name **Arial Black**, **14 pt**. and the remaining text **Arial**, **12 pt**.

14 CHECK Your finished letter should look like Figure 3.32. Save the file as: Leadership-[your first initial and last name].

Continue to the next exercise.

EXERCISE 3-15 (Continued)
Use a Template to Create a Business Letter

Solution File Use the file **Leadership-SF** as a solution file for Exercise 3-15.

FIGURE 3.32 Text in the Equity Letter template

Leadership Inc. Recruitment Services
100 Red Leaf Street
Natick, MA 01760
Telephone: (508) 555-2222
Fax: (508) 555-2223

10/29/2010

Rachel Fay
World Marketing
42 Clover Lane
Boston, MA 02116

Dear Rachel:

Enclosed please find the names and résumés of individuals interested in applying for your company's project manager position. All of the candidates have been carefully screened by my staff.

Our team has assembled a strong group of candidates. Each candidate has demonstrated an ability to successfully set goals and maintain schedules. The candidates also have the skills and vision needed to develop your MarketPlus™ account.

I will continue to forward names and résumés to you as they become available. Please let me know if you have any questions or need additional information.

Sincerely,

Sam Bryant
Recruitment Specialist
Leadership Inc. Recruitment Services

You Should Know

To properly format a business letter, place the date between the return address and the recipient's address.

Step-By-Step

1. In your **Staff** file, choose **View>Presentation Views>Slide Master**.
2. Select the **Module Slide Master**.
3. Choose **Slide Master> Background> Background Styles**. Select **Format Background**.
4. In the **Format Background** dialog box, under **Fill**, click the **Gradient fill** radio button.
5. Click the **Preset colors** drop down arrow. Select **Fog** (see Figure 3.45).
6. Click **Apply to All**. Click **Close**.
7. CHECK Your screen should look similar to Figure 3.46.

Continued on the next page.

Shortcuts

To open the **Background** dialog box, right-click a blank area of the slide and click **Format Background**.

Differentiated Instruction/ Advanced Students Have students try different background colors with their presentations. Ask them to explain why different background colors do or do not work with the rest of the presentation.

EXERCISE 3-20
Customize Backgrounds Using Slide Masters

A **background** is a solid color, pattern, or picture that appears behind content on a slide. You can add a background to a single slide or add the same background to an entire presentation. Using the Format Shape dialog box, you can apply a **gradient** effect to the background. This effect gives the background gradual shading that changes from one side or corner to the other. Every theme has a background color that is part of its **color scheme**.

FIGURE 3.45 Format Background dialog box

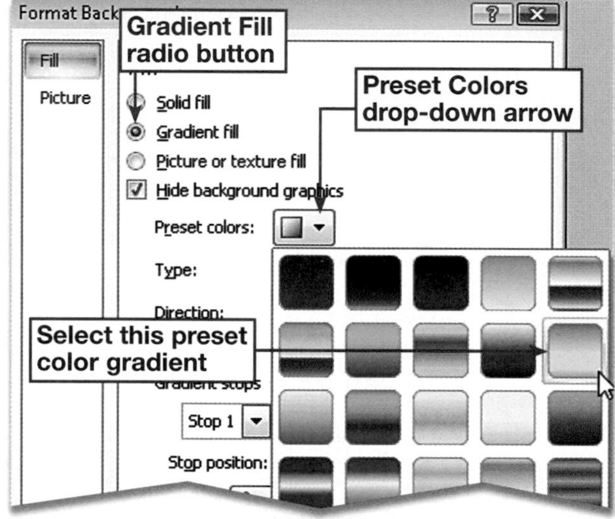

FIGURE 3.46 New background applied to slides

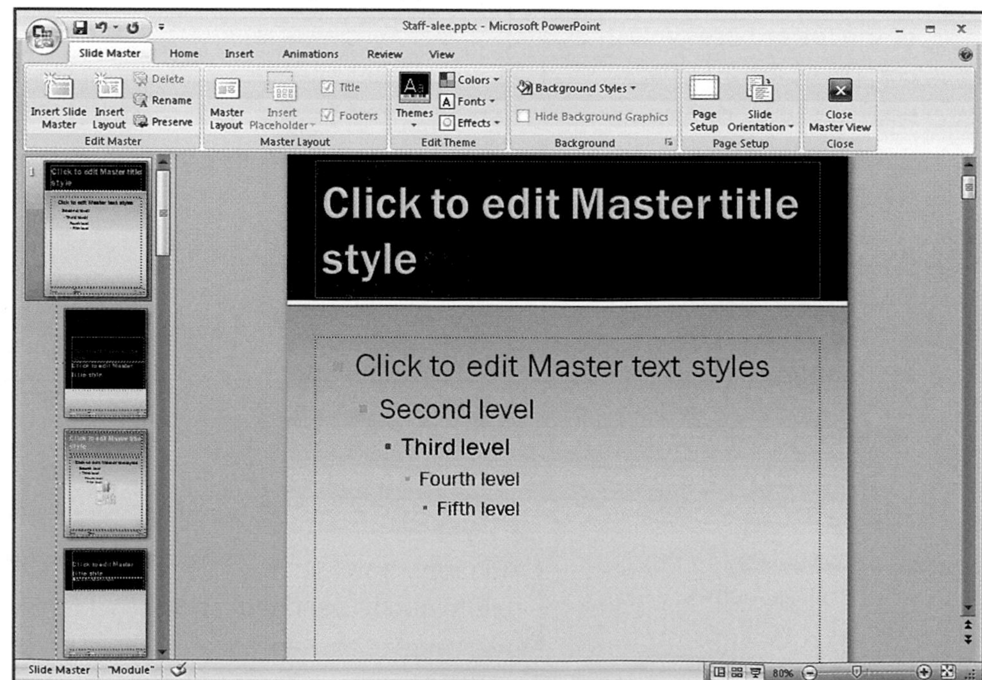

EXERCISE 3-16
Create and Insert Building Blocks

Word makes it easy to insert text, images, and special formats that you use frequently by creating a **building block**. Building blocks are the items that you save using the **Quick Part** tool so that you can reuse them in your document.

FIGURE 3.33 Create New Building Block dialog box

Create New Building Block

Name: Leadership Inc.

Gallery: Quick Parts

Category: General

Description:

Save in: Building Blocks.dotx

Options: Insert content only

OK Cancel

Solution File Use the file **Leadership-SF.docx** as a solution file for Exercise 3-15 for Exercise 3-16.

FIGURE 3.34 Building block inserted into document

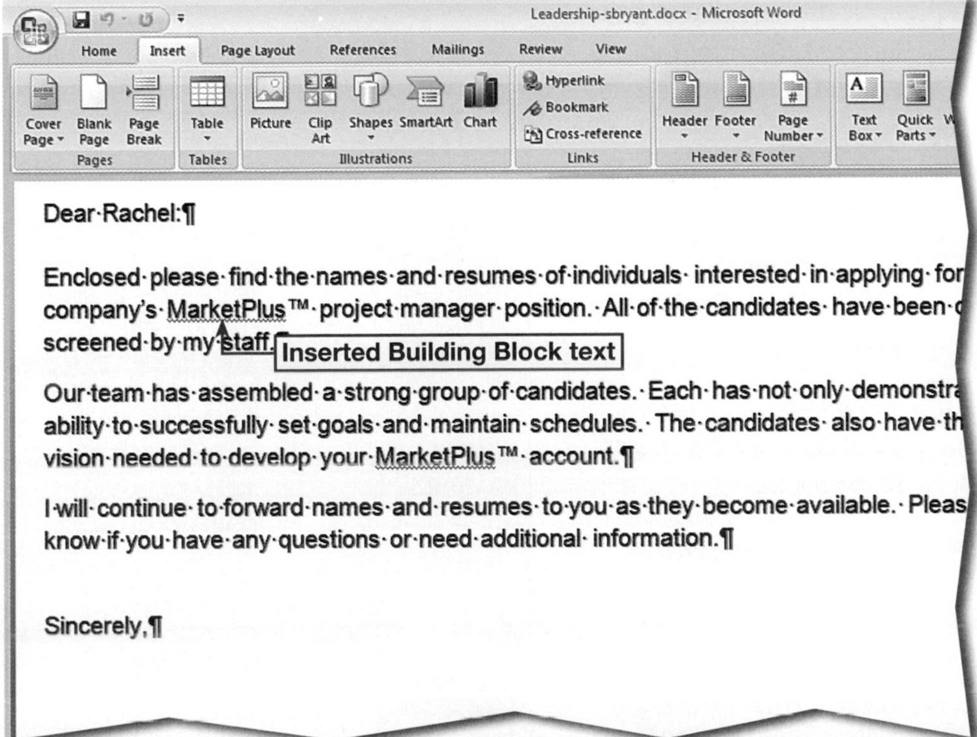

Dear·Rachel:¶

Enclosed·please·find·the·names·and·resumes·of·individuals·interested·in·applying·for company's·MarketPlus™·project·manager·position.·All·of·the·candidates·have·been·c screened·by·my·staff.¶

Our·team·has·assembled·a·strong·group·of·candidates.·Each·has·not·only·demonstr ability·to·successfully·set·goals·and·maintain·schedules.·The·candidates·also·have·th vision·needed·to·develop·your·MarketPlus™·account.¶

I·will·continue·to·forward·names·and·resumes·to·you·as·they·become·available.·Pleas know·if·you·have·any·questions·or·need·additional·information.¶

Sincerely,¶

Troubleshooting In **Step 2**, students may not be able to tell that they selected both the text and the image. Both the logo and the address will appear in the **Quick Parts** gallery.

Step-By-Step

1. Open your **Leadership** file. Save as: Leadership-[your first initial and last name]2.
2. Select the letterhead **logo**, **name**, and **contact information**.
3. Choose **Insert>Text>Quick Parts>Save Selection to Quick Part Gallery**. In the **Name** text box, key: Leadership Inc.
4. **CHECK** Your dialog box should look like Figure 3.33. Click **OK**.
5. Select **MarketPlus™** at the end of the second paragraph.
6. Choose **Insert>Text>Quick Parts>Save Selection to Quick Part Gallery**. In the **Name** text box, key: MarketPlus trademark. Click **OK**.
7. Click before **project** in the first paragraph. Choose **Insert>Text>Quick Parts**. In the **Quick Parts** menu, under **General**, select **MarketPlus™**. Press SPACE
8. **CHECK** Your screen should look like Figure 3.34. Save your file.

Continue to the next exercise.

Step-By-Step

EXERCISE 3-19 (Continued)
Use a Slide Master

7. Choose **Slide Master>Edit Theme>Fonts.** Select the **Trek** font theme.

8. In the **Overview** pane, click on the **Title Slide Layout: used by slide(s) 1-2, 5** thumbnail.

9. Click in the **Click Here to Edit Master Subtitle Style** box. Click three times on the text in this box to select it.

10. On the **Home** tab, in the **Font** group, click the **Font Size** drop-down arrow. Change the size to **36**.

11. Use the floating toolbar to apply **Italics** and change the **Font Color** to **Red, Accent 6**.

12. **CHECK** Your screen should look like Figure 3.43.

13. Choose **Slide Master>Close>Close Master View**.

14. **CHECK** Your screen should look like Figure 3.44. Save your file.

Continue to the next exercise.

Teaching Tip Point out to students that they did not change the content in this exercise. They only changed the formatting. The formatting they changed was applied to slides 1, 2, and 5, the slides that use this master slide.

FIGURE 3.43 New styles applied to the Master subtitle style

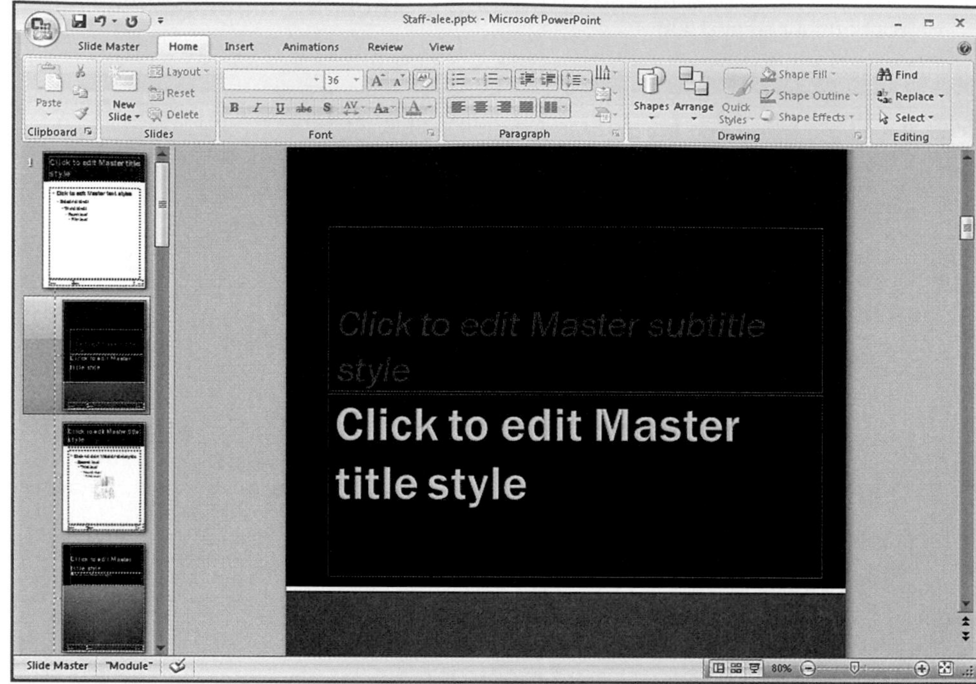

FIGURE 3.44 Changes shown in normal view

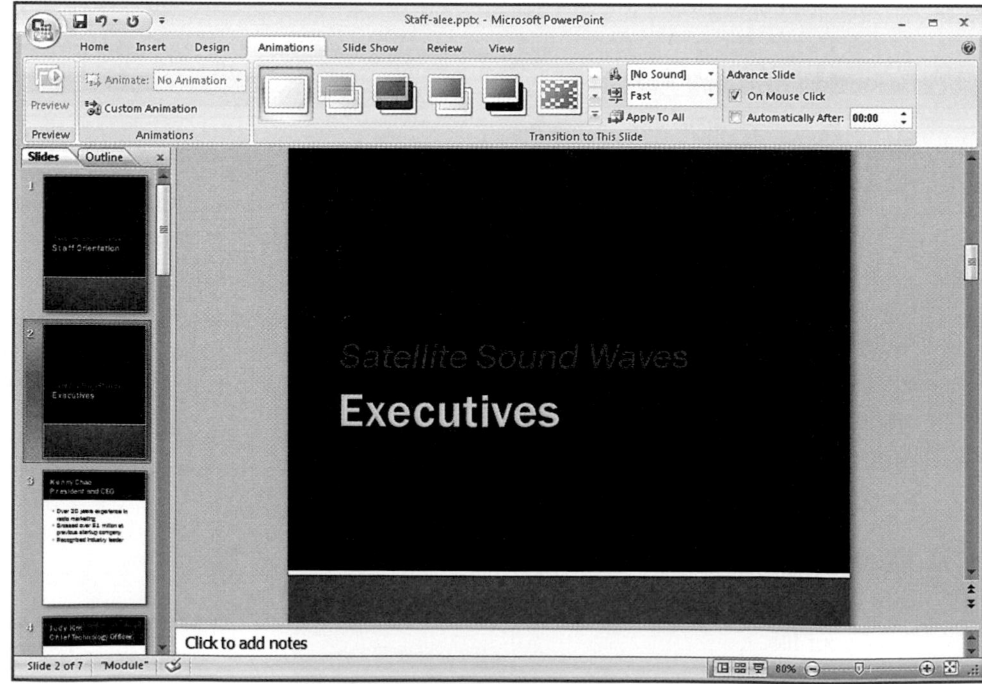

Step-By-Step

1. In your **Leadership2** document, choose **Insert>Text>Quick Parts>Building Blocks Organizer**.

2. In the **Building Blocks Organizer** dialog box, click the **Category** column head. In the **Name** column, scroll down and select **Leadership Inc.**

3. **CHECK** Your screen should look like Figure 3.35.

4. Click **Edit Properties**. In the **Modify Building Block** dialog box, under **Name:**, key: Leadership Inc. Return Address.

5. **CHECK** Your dialog box should look like Figure 3.36. Click **OK**. Click **Yes**. Close the dialog box, and then close the **Leadership2** file without saving it.

6. Choose **Office>New>Blank Document**. Click **Create**. In the new document, choose **Insert>Text**. Click the **Quick Parts** drop-down menu. Choose **Leadership Inc. Return Address**. Save your file as Leadership Letterhead-[your first initial and last name].

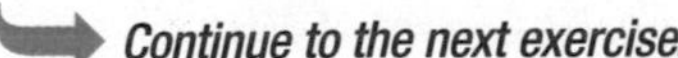

Continue to the next exercise.

EXERCISE 3-17
Sort and Edit Building Blocks

Word 2007 provides building blocks for works cited pages, graphics, page numbers, and more. Use the Building Blocks Organizer to sort them by name, category, or gallery. From here, you can also edit, preview, and insert building blocks into your document. Formatting of building blocks changes to match Word 2007 themes.

Solution File Use the file **Leadership_Letterhead-SF** as a solution file for Exercise 3-17.

FIGURE 3.35 Building blocks sorted by Name

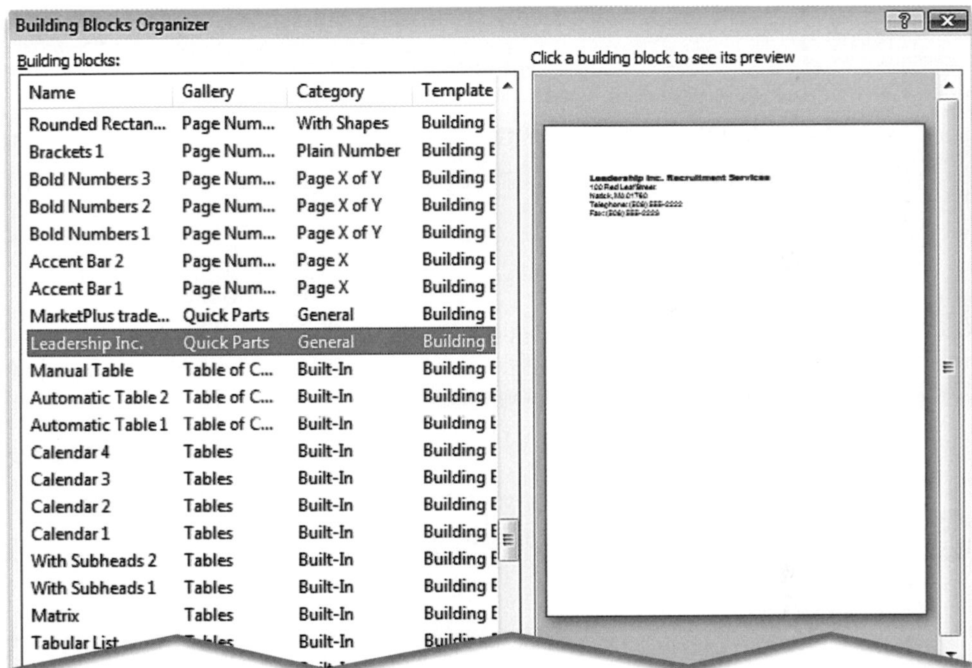

Name	Gallery	Category	Template
Rounded Rectan...	Page Num...	With Shapes	Building E
Brackets 1	Page Num...	Plain Number	Building E
Bold Numbers 3	Page Num...	Page X of Y	Building E
Bold Numbers 2	Page Num...	Page X of Y	Building E
Bold Numbers 1	Page Num...	Page X of Y	Building E
Accent Bar 2	Page Num...	Page X	Building E
Accent Bar 1	Page Num...	Page X	Building E
MarketPlus trade...	Quick Parts	General	Building E
Leadership Inc.	Quick Parts	General	Building E
Manual Table	Table of C...	Built-In	Building E
Automatic Table 2	Table of C...	Built-In	Building E
Automatic Table 1	Table of C...	Built-In	Building E
Calendar 4	Tables	Built-In	Building E
Calendar 3	Tables	Built-In	Building E
Calendar 2	Tables	Built-In	Building E
Calendar 1	Tables	Built-In	Building E
With Subheads 2	Tables	Built-In	Building E
With Subheads 1	Tables	Built-In	Building E
Matrix	Tables	Built-In	Building E
Tabular List	Tables	Built-In	Buildin...

FIGURE 3.36 Modified building block properties

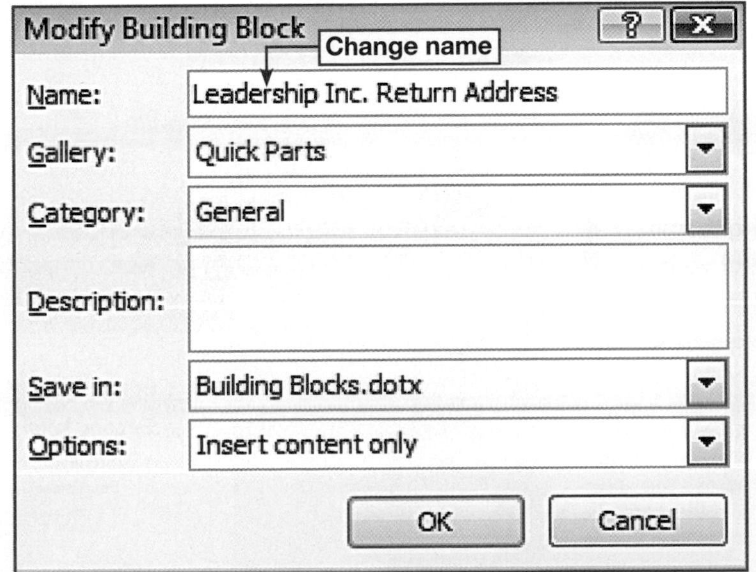

Troubleshooting If the Quick Styles menu does not display any gallery options, you must rebuild the gallery. Navigate to the hard drive and locate **Documents and Settings\Student name\Application Data\Microsoft\Document Building Blocks\1033**. You need to **Cut** the **1033** folder and **Paste** it onto the student's desktop. Restart Word. The galleries will appear.

Step-By-Step

1. Open the data file **Staff.pptx**. Save as: Staff-[your first initial and last name].
2. Choose **View> Presentation Views> Slide Master**.
3. On the **Overview** pane, select the **Default Design Slide Master: used by slide(s) 1-7** (see Figure 3.41).
4. On the **Slide Master** tab, in the **Page Setup** group, click **Slide Orientation**. Select **Portrait**.
5. Choose **Slide Master> Edit Theme>Themes**. Select **Module**.
6. **CHECK** Your screen should look like Figure 3.42.

Continued on the next page.

Microsoft Office 2007

The Slide Master enables you to change the theme and appearance of your entire presentation quickly.

Teaching Tip In **Step 3**, explain to students that they can use different kinds of master slides for particular types of information. For example, as they move the pointer across the slide masters on the left side of the screen, they might see master slides for title slides, pictures with captions, and various layouts for presenting content.

EXERCISE 3-19
Use a Slide Master

Presentations are based on a **Slide Master**, which contains one or more layouts that control the appearance of every slide in a presentation. The Slide Master is part of a template that stores information such as the fonts, font sizes and styles, bullet styles, background colors, and color schemes used in the presentation. Changes made to a Slide Master are repeated on every slide in the presentation. Use Page Setup to change a presentation's size and orientation. If you want your slides to be wider than they are tall, set the orientation to **landscape**. Set the orientation to **portrait** for slides to be taller than they are wide.

FIGURE 3.41 Default Design Master Slide in Slide Master view

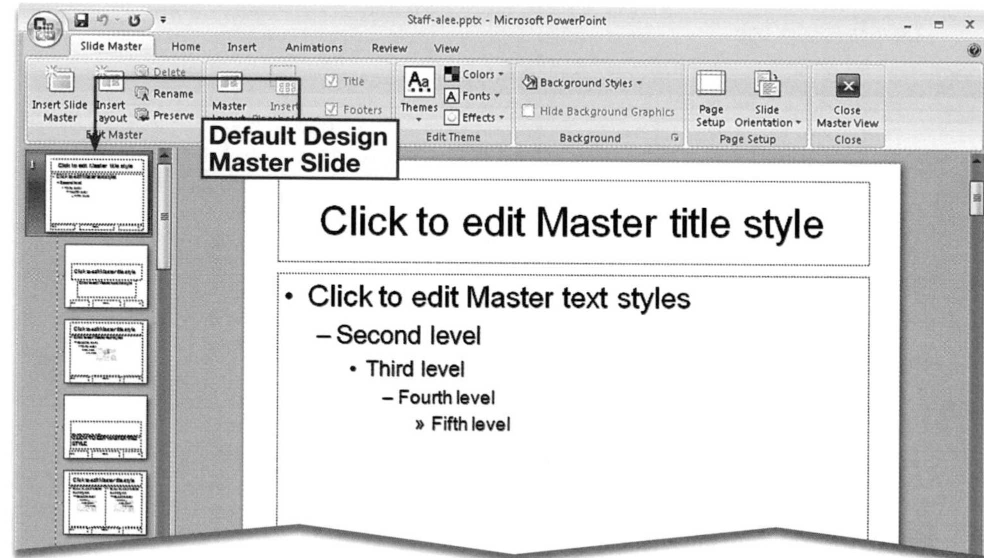

FIGURE 3.42 Module Master Slide in portrait view

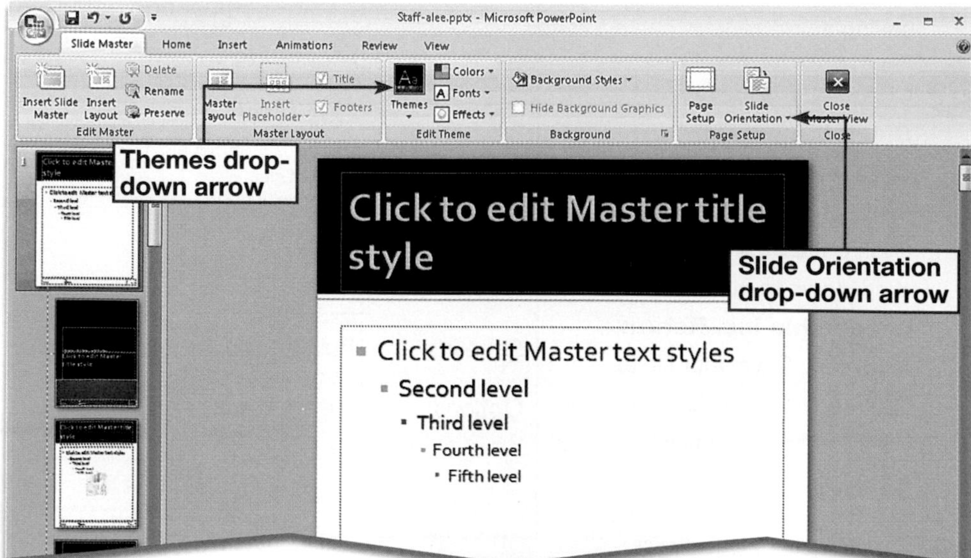

LESSON 3 After You Read

Review Vocabulary

Complete the following statements on a separate piece of paper. Choose from the Vocabulary list on the left to complete the statements.

1. A(n) ___business letter___ is a formal letter written by a company or an individual on a business-related subject. (p. 68)

2. The Office ___Clipboard___ can store up to 24 cut or copied entries. (p. 70)

3. You can use the ___cut___ button to remove a word from your document. (p. 70)

4. A(n) ___Quick Part___ is predefined text, a symbol, or formatting that you can quickly insert in your document. (p. 85)

5. The thesaurus can help you find a(n) ___synonym___ for a word. (p. 74)

Vocabulary Activity

6. Create a matching quiz to review the vocabulary used in this lesson.

A. Key seven vocabulary terms into a document. Format the terms as a numbered list.

B. Key the definitions for the seven vocabulary terms underneath the numbered list. Use your own words when creating the definitions. Be sure to mix up the order of the definitions so that they do not match the order of the numbered list.

C. Exchange quizzes with a classmate. Take each other's quiz by placing the number of the vocabulary terms next to the term's definition. Check each other's work and review any terms that you miss.

Review Key Concepts

Answer the following questions on a separate piece of paper.

7. What is the Paste button used for? (p. 70)

A. To insert a symbol
B. To format a business letter
(C.) To insert cut or copied text
D. To close the Research task pane

8. Which Word feature automatically corrects simple spelling and grammar errors? (p. 80)

(A.) AutoCorrect
B. AutoFix
C. Clipboard
D. Thesaurus

9. Which Word feature allows you to search for words with a similar meaning? (p. 74)

A. Research task pane
(B.) Thesaurus
C. Spelling
D. Dictionary

10. Which of the following is a template? (p. 83)

(A.) A pre-formatted letter
B. A blank document
C. A clipboard
D. Copied text

Vocabulary

Key Terms

AutoCorrect
building block
business letter
Clipboard
content control
copy
cut
drag
paste
Quick Part
symbol
thesaurus

Academic Vocabulary

phrase
synonym

Answer to Vocabulary Activity
Students' quizzes will vary, but should reflect a broad understanding of the vocabulary terms covered in the Lesson.

Step-By-Step

1. In your **Music** file, select **Slide 1**.
2. Choose the **Animations** tab. In the **Transition to This Slide** group, click the **More** drop-down arrow.
3. Under **Wipes**, select **Box Out** (see Figure 3.39).
4. Click the **Transition Speed** drop-down arrow. Select **Medium**.
5. Click the **Transition Sound** drop-down arrow. Select **Laser**. Click **Apply To All**.
6. **CHECK** Your screen should look like Figure 3.40.
7. At the bottom of the task pane, click **Slide Show**. Press ESC to move from slide to slide.
8. On **Slide 7**, press ENTER to display each image and its connector line. Click through the remainder of the slide show.
9. Close the task pane. Save and close your **Music** file.

Continue to the next exercise.

Solution Use the file **Music-SF.pptx** as a solution file for Exercises 3-1 through 3-18.

EXERCISE 3-18
Apply Transition Effects and Run the Slide Show

To choose the way one slide changes to the next during a slide show, apply a **transition** effect. You can apply a transition effect to one slide or to an entire presentation. You can also modify the speed of transition effects and add sound effects that play when you move from slide to slide. To remove transitions, select No Transition in the task pane.

FIGURE 3.39 Slide Transition drop-down menu

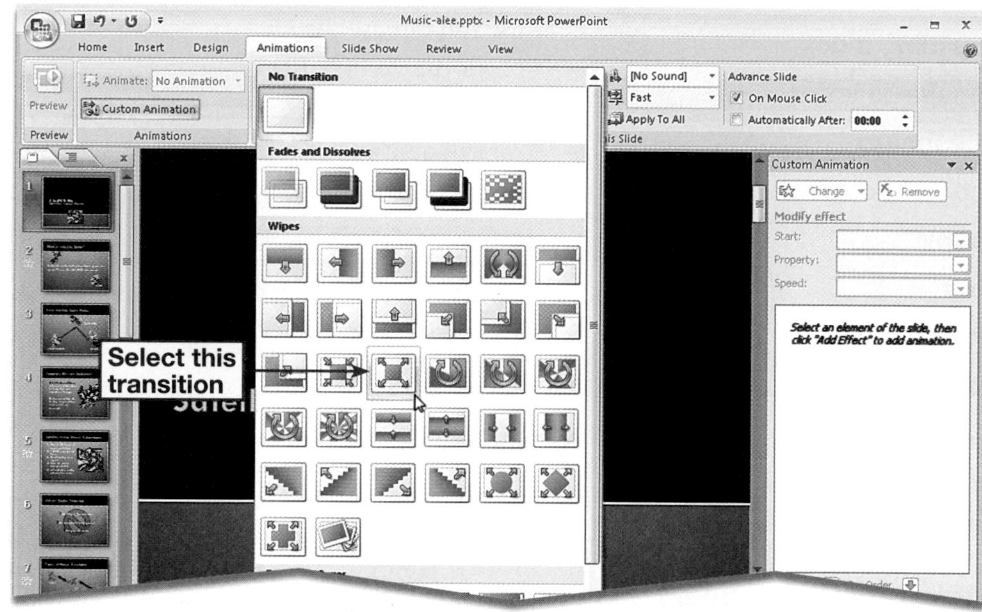

FIGURE 3.40 Slide Transition selections

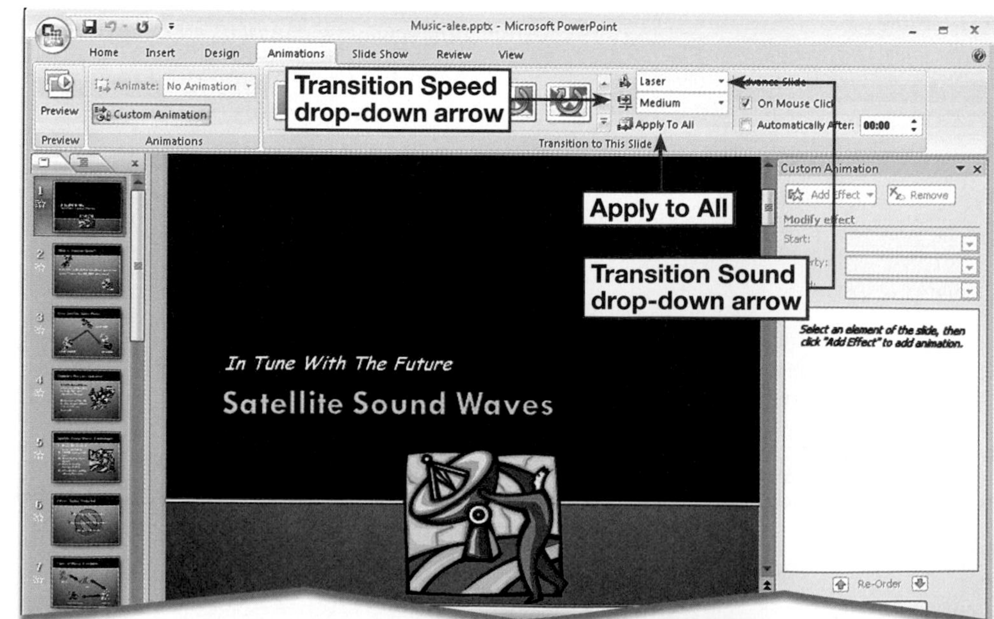

LESSON 3 Practice It Activities

Step-By-Step

1. Open the data file **Park_ Letter.docx**. Save as: Park_Letter-[your first initial and last name]1.
2. Choose **Page Layout> Page Setup>Dialog Box Launcher** .
3. In the **Page Setup** dialog box, click the **Margins** tab. Adjust the top margin to **2″**. Click **OK**.
4. Replace the letterhead with your personal information.
5. In the second paragraph, select the last sentence (starts with **I am very interested**).
6. Drag-and-drop the selected sentence to the beginning of the same paragraph (before **We need to plant**). Press the **spacebar** once.
7. Select the text **[Your Name]**. Key your own name.
8. **CHECK** Your screen should look similar to Figure 3.37. Save and close the file.

Solution The solution file for this activity is **Park_Letter1-SF.docx.**

1. Create a Personal Business Letter

Data File

Follow the steps to complete the activity.

FIGURE 3.37 Personal business letter

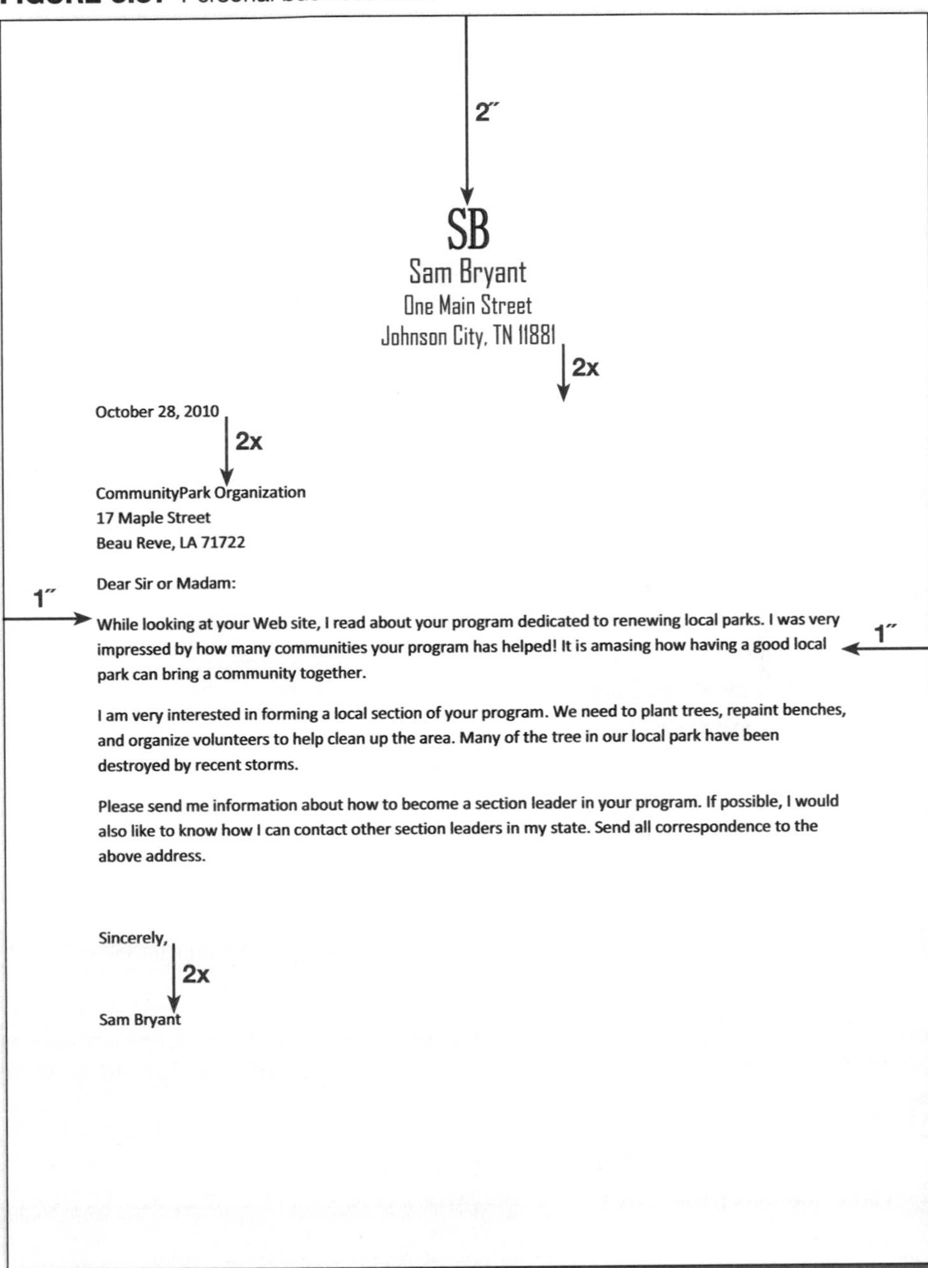

2″

SB
Sam Bryant
One Main Street
Johnson City, TN 11881

2x

October 28, 2010

2x

CommunityPark Organization
17 Maple Street
Beau Reve, LA 71722

Dear Sir or Madam:

1″ 1″

While looking at your Web site, I read about your program dedicated to renewing local parks. I was very impressed by how many communities your program has helped! It is amasing how having a good local park can bring a community together.

I am very interested in forming a local section of your program. We need to plant trees, repaint benches, and organize volunteers to help clean up the area. Many of the tree in our local park have been destroyed by recent storms.

Please send me information about how to become a section leader in your program. If possible, I would also like to know how I can contact other section leaders in my state. Send all correspondence to the above address.

Sincerely,

2x

Sam Bryant

Teaching Tip The letter shown is incomplete and contains intentional errors that students will correct in the lesson.

Step-By-Step

1. In your **Music** presentation, select **Slide 2**.
2. Choose **Animations>Animations>Custom Animation**.
3. In the **Custom Animation** task pane, click **Play** to view the animation.
4. In the task pane, click the first animation (see Figure 3.37). Click **Remove**.
5. Click the small box to the upper left of the image of the satellite.
6. Click **Change>Entrance>Fly In**.
7. In the **Custom Animation** task pane, under **Modify: Fly In**, click the **Direction** drop-down arrow. Click **From Right**.
8. Click the **Speed** drop-down arrow. Click **Medium**.
9. Click the **Start** drop-down arrow. Click **With Previous**. Click **Play** to view the slide animation.
10. **CHECK** Your slide should look like Figure 3.38. Close the task pane. Save your file.

Continue to the next exercise.

EXERCISE 3-17
Create and Modify Custom Animations

You can apply animation effects to individual elements on a slide, and you can customize animations to better fit the theme of the presentation. It is very important to keep your audience focused on your message instead of on any unnecessary movements in your slides. If you decide an animation is distracting, you can remove it from a slide.

FIGURE 3.37 Custom Animation task pane

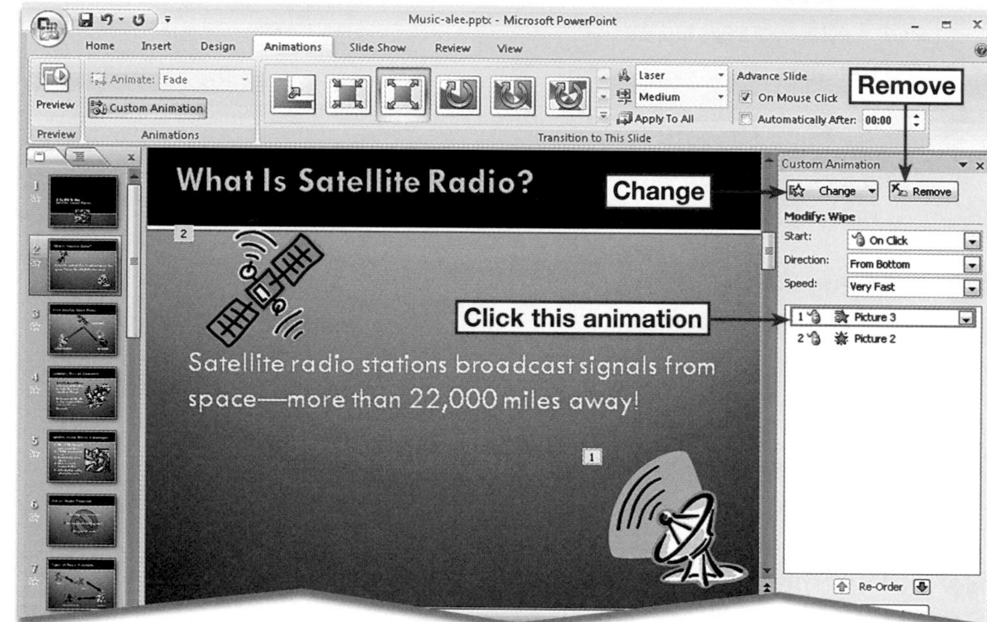

FIGURE 3.38 Slide with animation applied to image

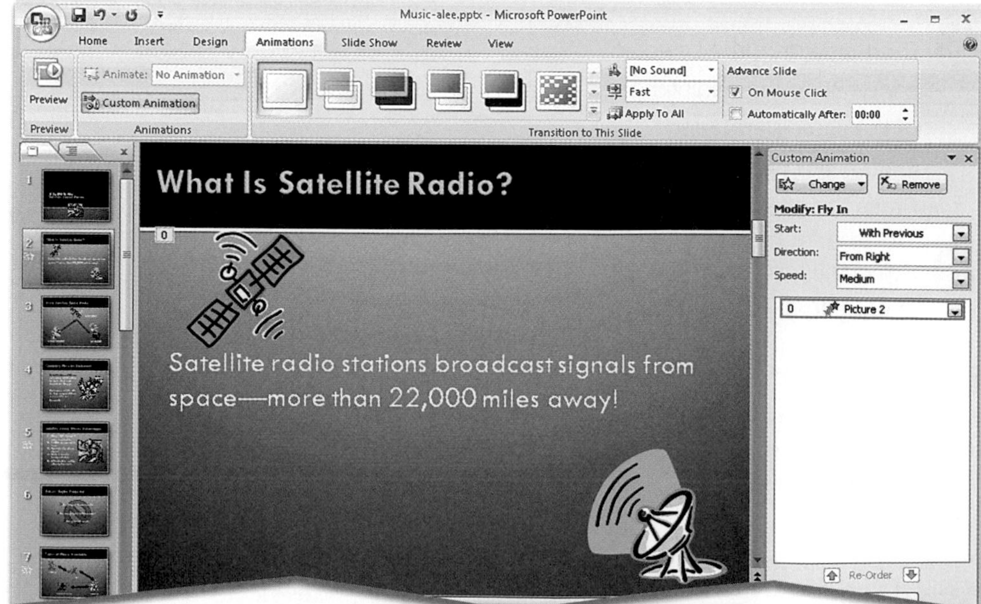

LESSON 3 Practice It Activities

Step-By-Step

1. Open your **Park_Letter-1** file. Save as: Park_Letter-[your first initial and last name]2.
2. Select the last sentence in the second paragraph. Click **Cut**.
3. Click after the first sentence in the second paragraph. Press the **spacebar** once. Choose **Edit>Paste**.
4. Select **CommunityPark™**. Click **Copy**. Click before **program** in the second paragraph. Click **Paste**. Press the **spacebar** once.
5. Choose **Home>Clipboard>Dialog Box Launcher**. Click before **program** in the first sentence in the last paragraph.
6. Click **CommunityPark™** in the clipboard. Press the **spacebar** once. Close the task pane.
7. **CHECK** Your letter should look similar to Figure 3.38. Save and close the file.

2. Cut, Copy, and Paste Text

Follow the steps to complete the activity. You must complete Practice It Activity 1 before doing this activity.

New Student Strategy If a student did not complete Practice It Activity 1, then the solution file for that activity can be used as a data file for this activity.

FIGURE 3.38 Cut and copied text

SB
Sam Bryant
One Main Street
Johnson City, TN 37601
(423) 555-1111

October 28, 2010

CommunityPark™ Organization
17 Maple Street
Beau Reve, LA 71722

Dear Sir or Madam:

While looking at your Web site, I read about your program dedicated to renewing local parks. I was very impressed by how many communities your program has helped! It is amasing how having a good local park can bring a community together.

I am very interested in forming a local section of your CommunityPark™ program. Many of the tree in our local park have been destroyed by recent storms. We need to plant trees, repaint benches, and organize volunteers to help clean up the area.

Please send me information about how to become a section leader in your CommunityPark™ program. If possible, I would also like to know how I can contact other section leaders in my state. Send all correspondence to the above address.

Sincerely,

Sam Bryant

Solution The solution file for this activity is **Park_Letter2-SF.docx**.

Step-By-Step

1. In your **Music** file, select **Slide 5**. Select the bulleted list.
2. On the **Animations** tab, in the **Animations** group, click the **Animate** drop-down arrow.
3. On the drop-down menu, under **Fly In**, click **By 1st Level Paragraphs** (see Figure 3.35).
4. On the **Status Bar**, click **Slide Show** to preview the animation. Click to show each bullet point. Click ESC to close the slide show.
5. Choose **Animations>Animations>Custom Animation**.
6. In the task pane, click the animation **Rectangle 3: Over**.
7. Under **Modify: Fly In**, click the **Start** drop-down arrow. Click **After Previous**.
8. Choose **Animations>Preview>Preview** to preview the animation. Click ESC to close the slide show.
9. **CHECK** Your screen should look like Figure 3.36. Save your file.

Continue to the next exercise.

EXERCISE 3-16
Apply an Animation Scheme

An **animation scheme** adds movement to individual slides or to an entire presentation. You can apply built-in animation schemes. For example, you can have each item in a slide's bulleted list fade, wipe, or fly in when you click the mouse. You can also customize these schemes to operate automatically. The preview function will allow you to **anticipate**, or know in advance, what to expect when you run the slide show.

Step-By-Step Tip In **Step 2**, tell students that the preview function will start to show animations immediately.

FIGURE 3.35 Animation schemes

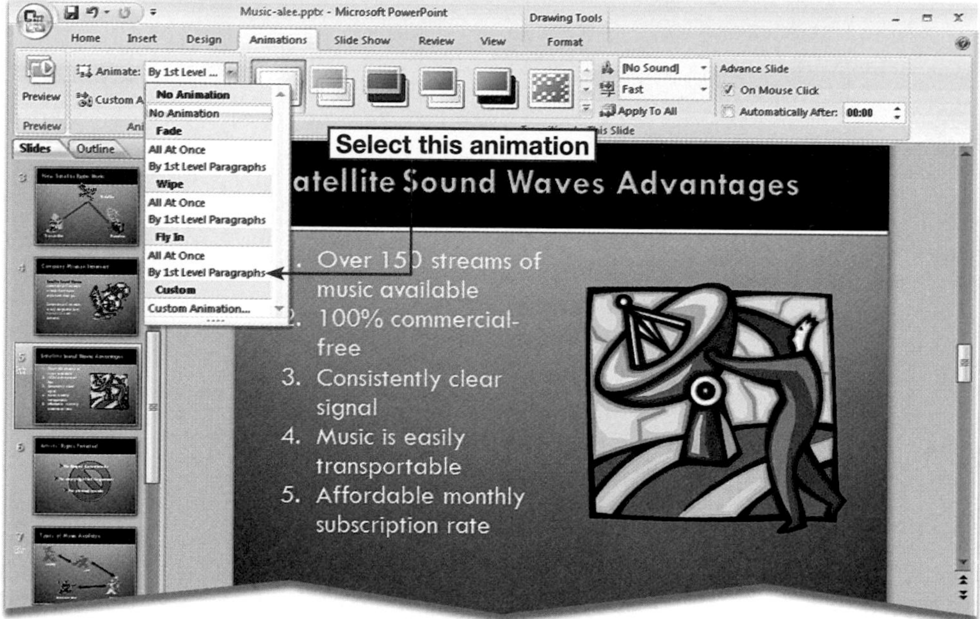

Troubleshooting The yellow boxes on the left side of Figure 3.36 indicate the order of animation.

FIGURE 3.36 Animation scheme applied to slide

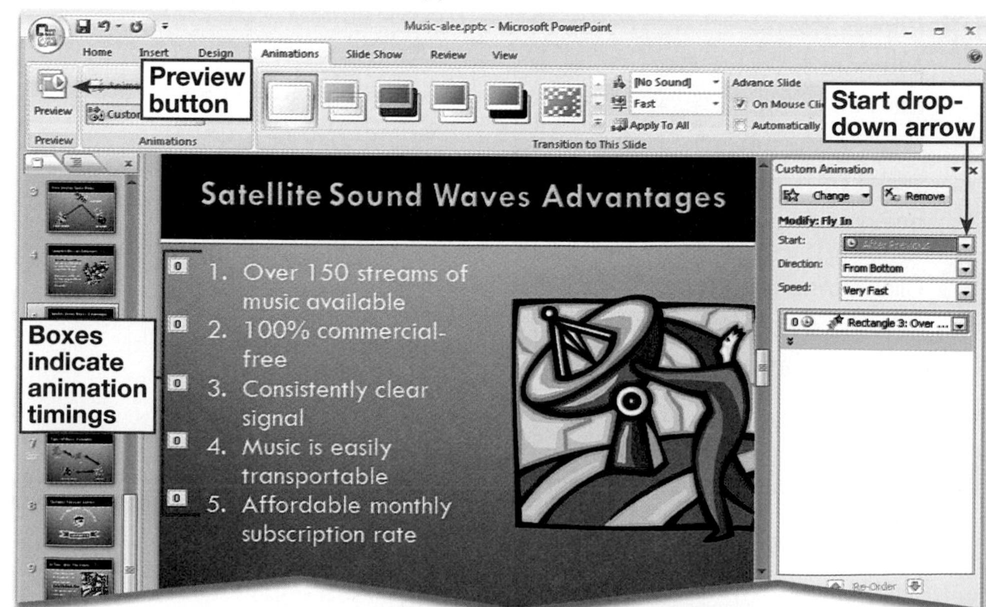

3. Edit a Personal Letter

Follow the steps to complete the activity. You must complete Practice It Activity 2 before doing this activity.

New Student Strategy If a student did not complete Practice It Activity 2, then the solution file for that activity can be used as a data file for this activity.

Step-By-Step

1. Open your **Park_Letter-2** file. Save as: Park_Letter-[your first initial and last name]3.
2. Select the word **section** in the second paragraph. Choose **Review>Proofing> Thesaurus**.
3. Click the drop-down arrow next to **division**. Click **Insert**. Close the task pane.
4. Choose **Editing> Replace**. Under **Find what:**, key: section. Under **Replace with:**, key: division.
5. Click **Replace All**. Click **Close**.
6. Click **Spelling & Grammar**.
7. Use the **Spelling and Grammar** dialog box to change *tree* to *trees*. Change *amasing* to *amazing*.
8. **CHECK** The finished letter should look similar to Figure 3.39. Save and close the file.

FIGURE 3.39 Edited text

SB
Sam Bryant
One Main Street
Johnson City, TN 37601
(423) 555-1111

October 28, 2010

CommunityPark™ Organization
17 Maple Street
Beau Reve, LA 71722

Dear Sir or Madam:

While looking at your Web site, I read about your program dedicated to renewing local parks. I was very impressed by how many communities your program has helped! It is amazing how having a good local park can bring a community together.

I am very interested in forming a local division of your CommunityPark™ program. Many of the trees in our local park have been destroyed by recent storms. We need to plant trees, repaint benches, and organize volunteers to help clean up the area.

Please send me information about how to become a division leader in your CommunityPark™ program. If possible, I would also like to know how I can contact other division leaders in my state. Send all correspondence to the above address.

Sincerely,

Sam Bryant

Solution The solution file for this activity is **Park_Letter3-SF.docx**.

Step-By-Step

1. In your **Music** file, select **Slide 8**.

2. Click **100% Customer Satisfaction**. On the **Format** tab, choose **WordArt Styles**. Click the **Text Fill** drop-down arrow. Select the color **White**.

3. Place the pointer over the **Rotation Handle** that appears.

4. Click the **Rotation Handle**. Hold the mouse button down and rotate to the left until the green dot is at the top of the slide (see Figure 3.33). Release the mouse.

5. With the text still selected, press SHIFT. Click the Clip Art and the **Guaranteed** banner so all three items are selected.

6. On the **Drawing Tools Format** tab, choose **Align>Align to Slide**. Click **Align Center** to center the objects. Deselect the three images.

7. CHECK Your screen should look like Figure 3.34.

8. Save your file.

Continue to the next exercise.

NCLB/Math (Geometry) Ask students to estimate how many degrees they must rotate the object to the left. Students' answers should be that they rotated the object about 32 degrees to the left.

EXERCISE 3-15
Rotate and Align Shapes and Other Graphics

As with pictures, you can rotate shapes and graphics to turn them 90 degrees to the right or left. You can also align shapes and graphics so they are correctly grouped together on a slide.

FIGURE 3.33 Rotated text

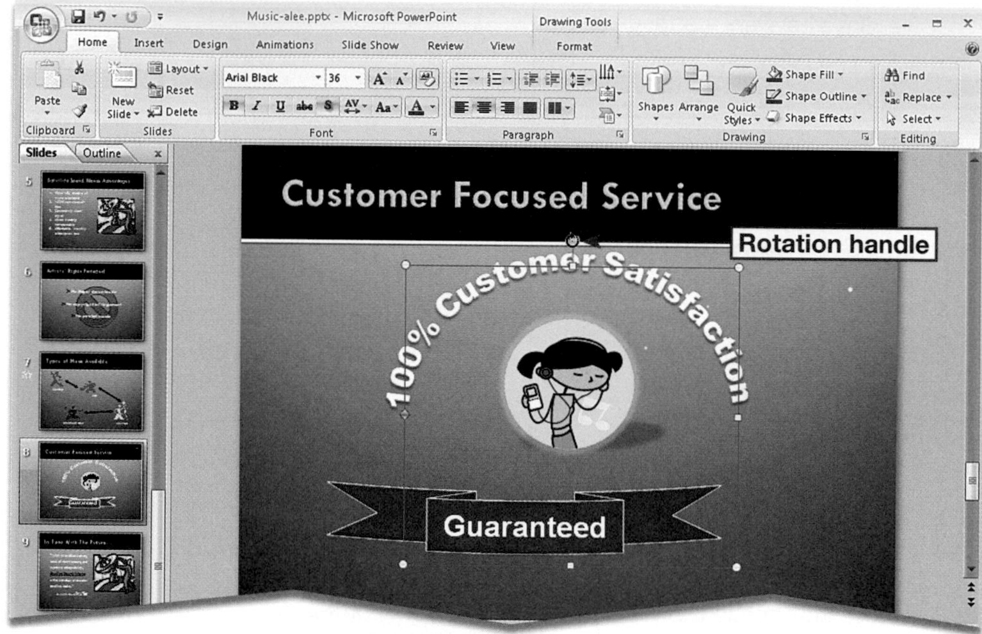

FIGURE 3.34 Images center aligned

LESSON 3 You Try It Activities

4. Create a Fund-Raising Letter

You need to raise money to support your school's art and sports programs. As student leader of the fund-raising committee, your first task is to write a letter to a local business owner asking whether he or she wants to contribute to the after-school program fund.

Step-By-Step

1. Open the data file **Hillside_ Letter.docx**. Save as: Hillside_Letter-[your first initial and last name]4.
2. Set the letter's top margin to **2″** and the left and right margins to **1″**.
3. Key the business's name and address as shown.
4. Key your name and title as shown.
5. Format the letter as shown. Be sure you have correctly spaced items in the letter (see Figure 3.40).
6. Check your document for spelling and grammar.
7. **CHECK** Your finished letter should look like Figure 3.40.
8. Save and close the file.

FIGURE 3.40 Fund-raising letter

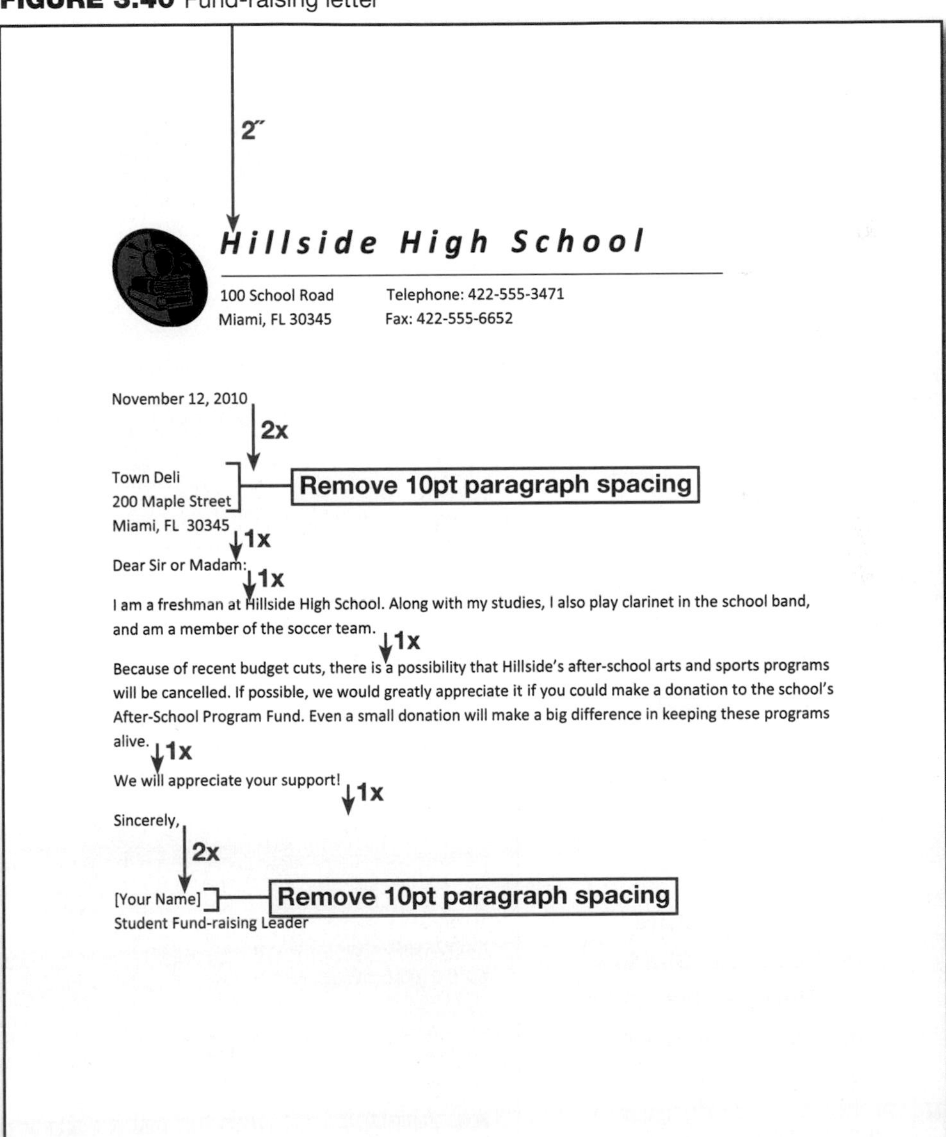

2″

Hillside High School

100 School Road
Miami, FL 30345

Telephone: 422-555-3471
Fax: 422-555-6652

November 12, 2010

2x

Town Deli
200 Maple Street
Miami, FL 30345

Remove 10pt paragraph spacing

1x

Dear Sir or Madam:

1x

I am a freshman at Hillside High School. Along with my studies, I also play clarinet in the school band, and am a member of the soccer team.

1x

Because of recent budget cuts, there is a possibility that Hillside's after-school arts and sports programs will be cancelled. If possible, we would greatly appreciate it if you could make a donation to the school's After-School Program Fund. Even a small donation will make a big difference in keeping these programs alive.

1x

We will appreciate your support!

1x

Sincerely,

2x

[Your Name]
Student Fund-raising Leader

Remove 10pt paragraph spacing

Solution The solution file for this activity is **Hillside_Letter4-SF.docx.**

Step-By-Step

1. In your **Music** file, select **Slide 7**. Click the connector between **Classical** and **Rock/ Alternative**. On the **Animations** tab, click **Custom Animation**.
2. Choose **Add Effect> More Effects>Wipe**. Under **Modify: Wipe**, click the **Direction** drop-down arrow. Click **From Right**. Select the **Rock/ Alternative** image. Choose **Add Effect> Entrance>Fly In**.
3. **CHECK** Your screen should look like Figure 3.31. Click **Play** to preview the slide. Close the task pane.
4. Move to **Slide 8**. Click the central image. On the **Format** tab, click **Picture Effects**. Select **Glow**. Under **Glow Variations**, select **Accent Color 1, 11 pt. Glow**.
5. With the image still selected, click **Picture Effects**. Choose **Shadow**. Under **Perspective**, select **Diagonal Upper Right**. Deselect the image.
6. **CHECK** Your screen should look like Figure 3.32. Save your file.

Continue to the next exercise.

EXERCISE 3-14
Add Animation and Effects to Connectors and Pictures

You can add effects to connectors and pictures. For example, you can add animation effects to make the connectors and pictures move on the slide. As with other graphics, you can also add effects to pictures to make them more visually interesting.

FIGURE 3.31 Animation added to connector and picture

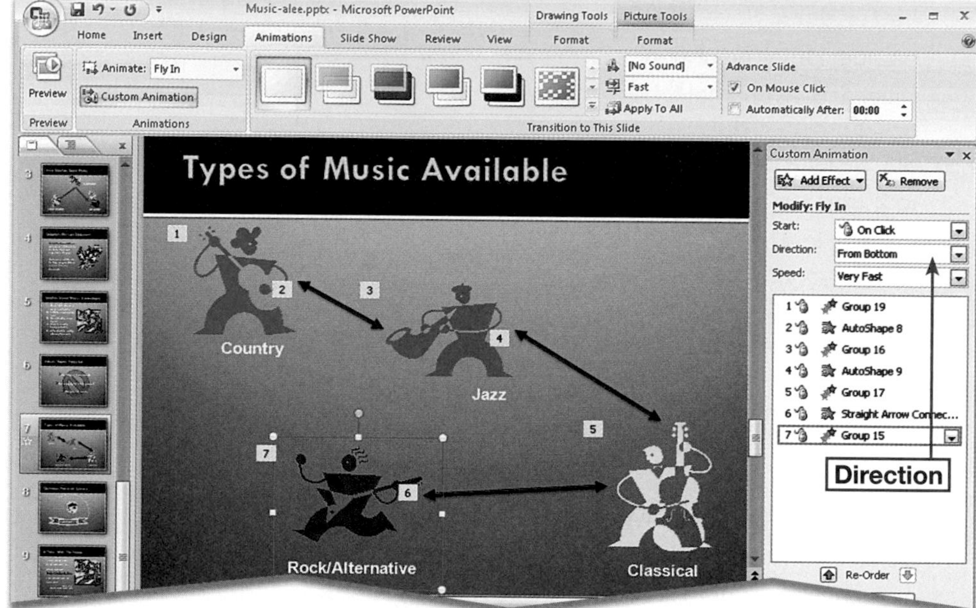

Troubleshooting In Step 2, if Wipe does not appear on the Entrance effects menu have students click More Effects and choose Wipe.

FIGURE 3.32 Picture with fill and shadow effect

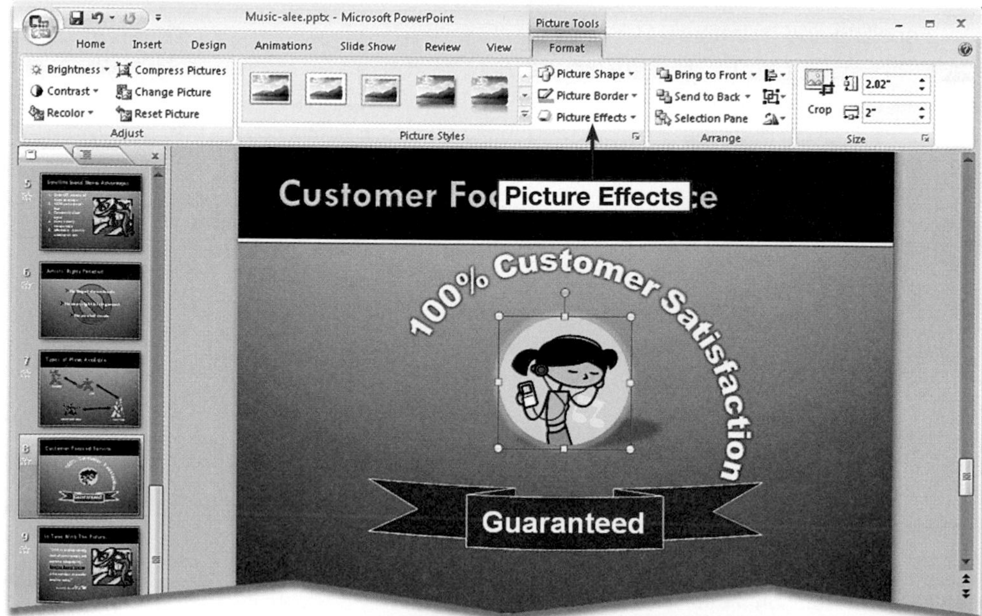

5. Edit a Memo with Word Tools

As the Director of Human Resources for a large advertising company, you are responsible for organizing professional development workshops for employees. You send a memo to all employees asking them to choose workshops they would be interested in attending.

Solution The solution file for this activity is **Wkshop_Memo5-SF.docx.**

Step-By-Step

1. Open the data file **Wkshop_Memo.docx**. Save as: Wkshop_Memo-[your first initial and last name]5.
2. Select the text **Title:**, **Name:**, **Seminars:**, **Time:**. Create a Building Block called **Workshop Information**.
3. Insert the Quick Part **Workshop Information** two times. Press ENTER once between each insertion.
4. Use **Find** to locate and delete each instance of the word **Time:** from the list.
5. Use **Replace** to change **Seminars** to **Workshops**.
6. Use drag-and-drop to reverse the order of **Title:** and **Name:** in each list.
7. Use the **Thesaurus** to change the word **sponsor** to **support**.
8. CHECK Your finished memo should look like Figure 3.41. Save and close the file.

FIGURE 3.41 Finished workshop memo

Advertising, Inc.

Memo

To: All Employees
From: Human Resources
Date: August 30, 2010
Subject: Workshop Topics

This year, our professional development workshops will revolve around the theme of leadership. Please take some time and note what topics you would be most interested in learning more about. We need your input to determine which workshops we will support!

Possible Topics:

Running Team Meetings
Giving Effective Presentations
Increasing Team Communication
Improving Time Management Skills
Developing a Vision
Taking Responsibility

Name:
Title:
Workshops:

Name:
Title:
Workshops:

Name:
Title:
Workshops:

Step-By-Step

8 Hold the left mouse button down and draw a connector line to the **Rock/Alternative** image.

9 Position your pointer over the red box to the right of the **Rock/Alternative** image. Release the mouse button.

10 CHECK Your screen should look like Figure 3.29.

11 Select the arrow connecting **Jazz** and **Classical**. Click the **Format Painter**.

12 Click the arrow connecting **Classical** and **Rock/Alternative**.

13 Select the **Classical** image. With the image still selected, press SHIFT. Click the **Rock/Alternative** image.

14 With the two objects selected, on the contextual **Drawing Tools** tab, on the **Format** tab, choose **Align>Align Bottom**. Deselect the images.

15 CHECK Your screen should look like Figure 3.30.

16 Save your file.

Continue to the next exercise.

Differentiated Instruction/Advanced Students Have students discuss and create examples of other uses for connectors.

EXERCISE 3-13 (Continued)
Align and Connect Pictures

FIGURE 3.29 Two images connected with a connector

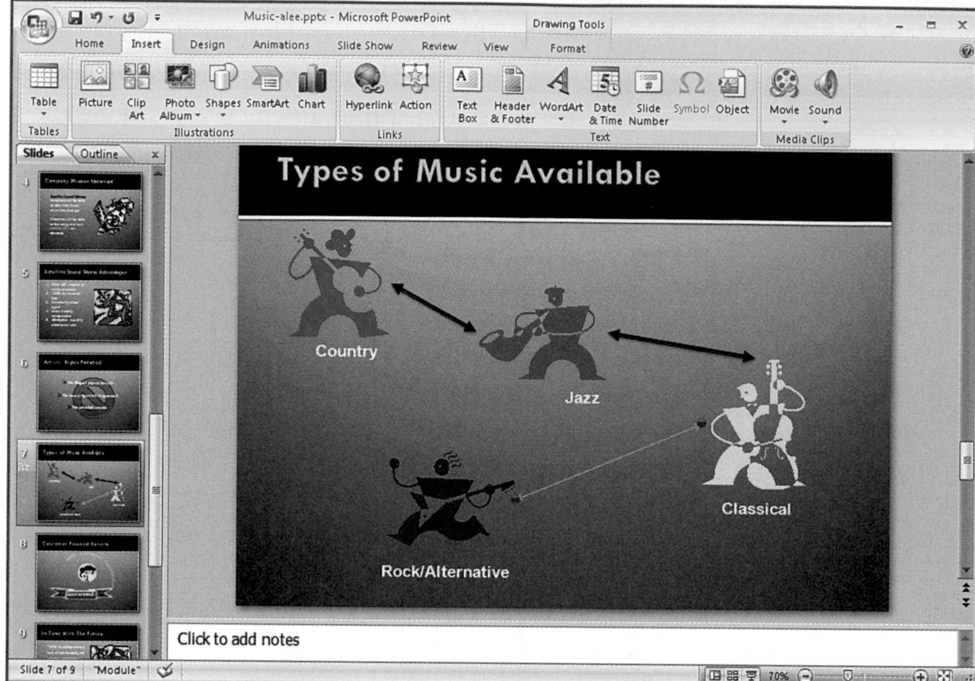

Differentiated Instruction/Advanced Students Have students discuss and create examples of other uses for connectors.

FIGURE 3.30 Connected images aligned

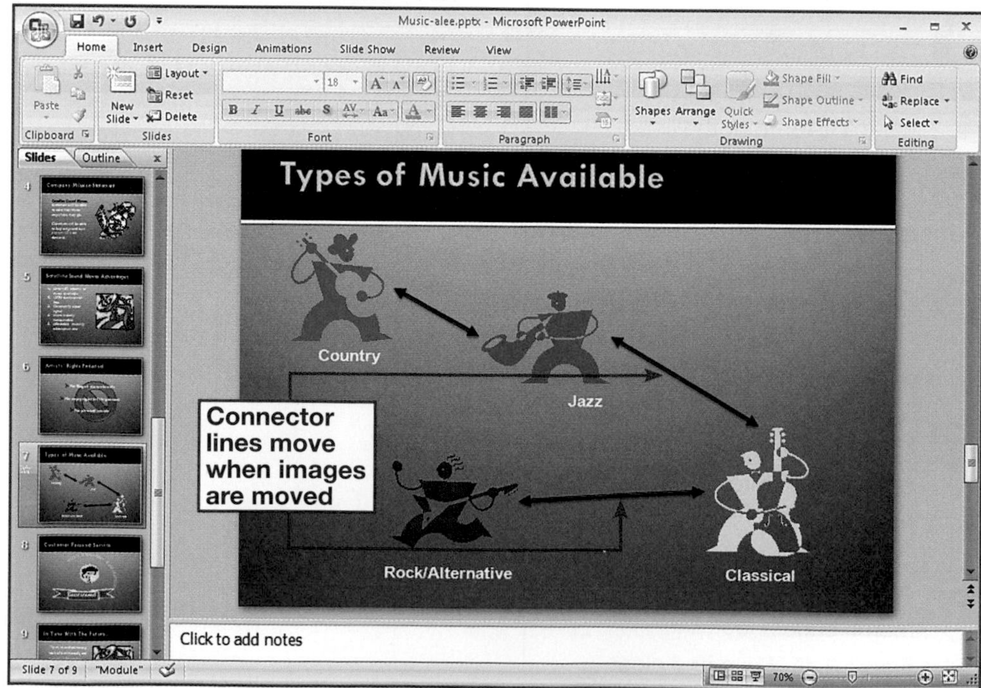

LESSON 3 Critical Thinking Activities

Beyond the Classroom Activity Students could use **Edit>Find** to locate the name and correct each time as needed. Or they could use **Find>Replace** to replace incorrect spelling with correct spelling. They could create a **Building Block/ Quick Part**, add the name to the spell check dictionary, or add the name to the **AutoCorrect** options so Word would automatically correct it. Paragraphs should reflect how each tool can be used to catch spelling errors that spell check would not normally be able to correct.

Standards at Work Activity Use the file **w3rev7-SF.docx** as a solution file for this activity.

21st Century Skills Activity Student paragraphs will vary but should include a description of one characteristic of a good leader and an explanation of why the characteristic is important to leadership.

6. Beyond the Classroom Activity

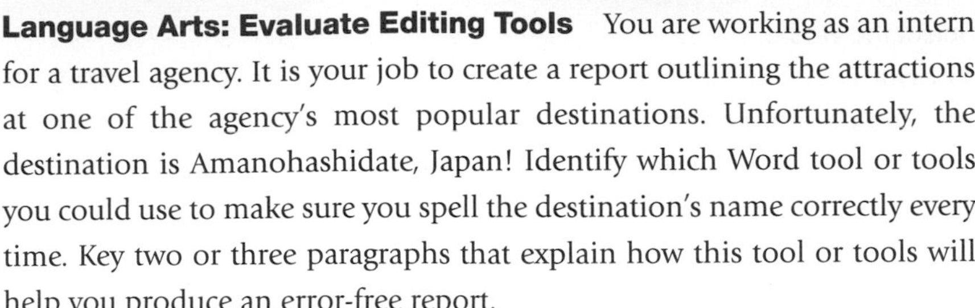

Language Arts: Evaluate Editing Tools You are working as an intern for a travel agency. It is your job to create a report outlining the attractions at one of the agency's most popular destinations. Unfortunately, the destination is Amanohashidate, Japan! Identify which Word tool or tools you could use to make sure you spell the destination's name correctly every time. Key two or three paragraphs that explain how this tool or tools will help you produce an error-free report.

Save your document as: w3rev-[your first initial and last name]6.

7. Standards at Work Activity

Microsoft Certified Application Specialist Correlation
Word 1.2 *Lay Out Documents*

Language Arts: Format a Business Letter Your supervisor has given you a letter to send to clients. Before you send the letter, you must make sure it is properly formatted.

Open your **w3rev6** file.

- Change the margins to 1″ on the left and right sides.
- Change the top margin to 2″.
- Add the correct spacing between items in the letter.
- Modify the correct paragraph spacing for the inside address and sender.

Save the file as: w3rev-[your first initial and last name]7.

8. 21st Century Skills Activity

Evaluate Leadership Skills Think of a person who you believe is a good leader. This person could be a family member, a teacher, a member of your community, or even a world leader. Next, evaluate why you think this person is a good leader. For example, he or she might be:

- A good communicator
- Honest
- Responsible

Key a paragraph that describes one characteristic that you think makes your chosen individual a good leader. Explain why you think this characteristic is an important part of that person's ability to lead.

Save your file as: w3rev-[your name and first initial]8.

Go Online e-REVIEW
glencoe.com

Go to the **Online Learning Center** to complete the following review activities.

Online Self Check
To test your knowledge of the material, click **Unit 1> Lesson 3** and choose **Self Checks**.

Interactive Review
To review the main points of this lesson, click **Unit 1> Lesson 3** and choose **Interactive Review**.

Step-By-Step

1. In your **Music** file, select **Slide 7**.
2. Select the **Rock/ Alternative** image and the text **Rock/Alternative** by holding SHIFT down while clicking both objects.
3. On the **Drawing Tools Format** tab, select **Arrange>Align**. Choose **Align Center**.
4. With the objects still selected, choose **Group>Group**.
5. CHECK Your screen should look like Figure 3.27.
6. On the **Insert** tab, click the **Shapes** drop-down arrow. Select **Double Arrow**. The pointer becomes a plus sign.
7. Move the pointer over the **Classical** image. Place the pointer over the left red circular connection site (see Figure 3.28).

Continued on the next page.

Intervention Strategy Aligning objects can be tricky. You may want to do a demo of this for the class.

Differentiated Instruction/ Physically Impaired Have physically impaired students partner with students with full mobility to complete this exercise.

EXERCISE 3-13
Align and Connect Pictures

As with text, you can align objects, such as pictures, on a slide. Once you have objects aligned correctly, you can group them so they will always stay together. You can also join objects by using connectors. When you group objects together, the connectors between the objects move with the objects when you rearrange them on the screen.

FIGURE 3.27 Objects aligned and grouped

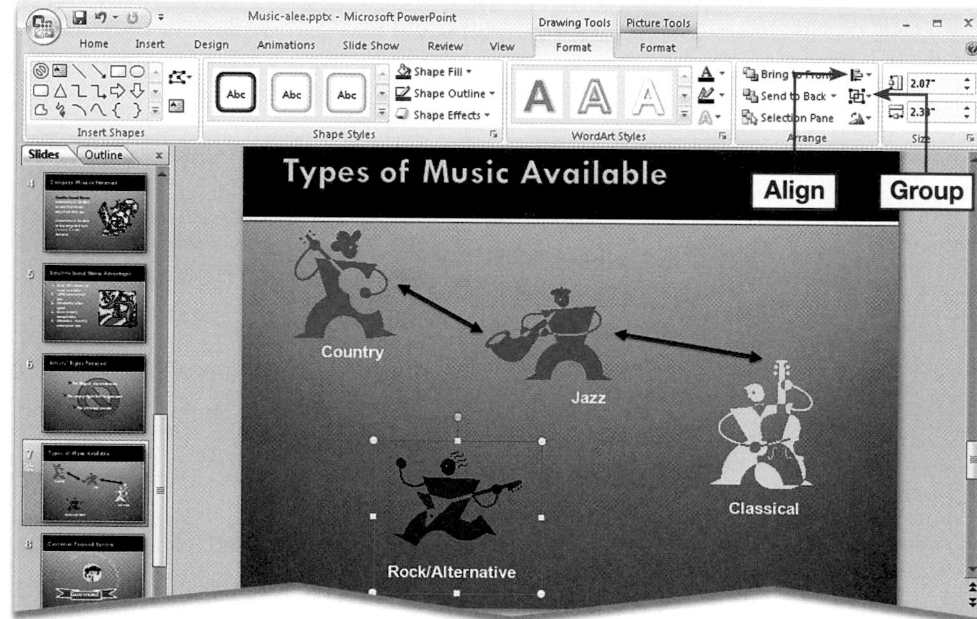

FIGURE 3.28 Classical image connection site

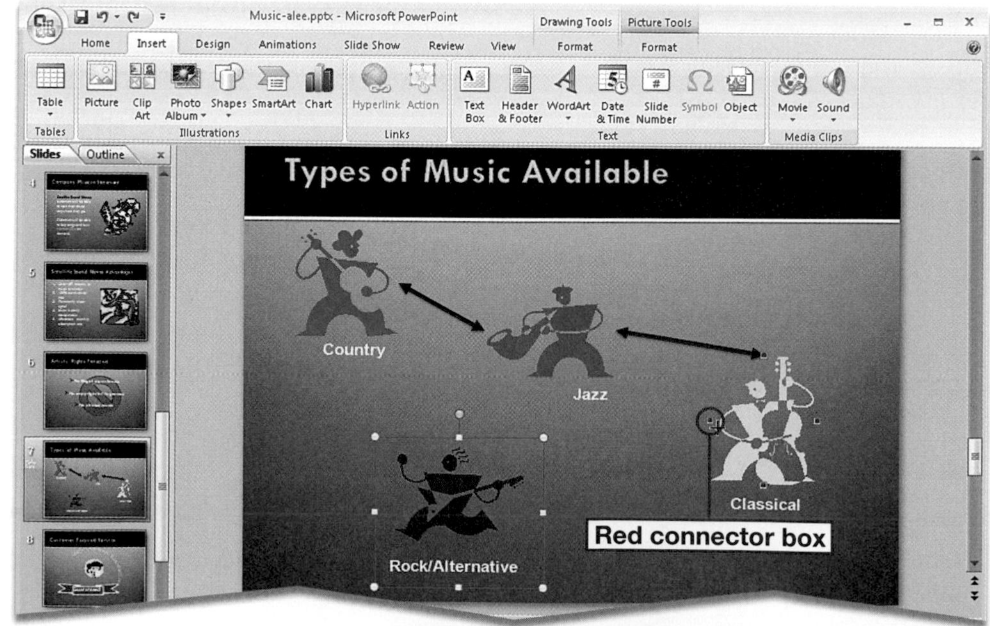

LESSON 3 Challenge Yourself Projects

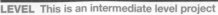

Before You Begin

How To Hire One challenge in business is hiring the right candidate for a job. These projects will take you through the process of identifying and evaluating applicants, much the same way you might in the real world.

Reflect Once you complete the projects, open a Word document and answer the following questions:

1. What are the most important qualities a job applicant should have?
2. If two applicants have similar skills, what other factors might you use to make your decision?

Answers Rubrics for each Challenge Yourself Project are available at **glencoe.com**. You may want to download the rubrics and make them available to students as they complete each project.

9. Identify Job Candidates

Rubric 

LEVEL This is an intermediate level project

Language Arts: Create a Letter You manage a successful construction company. The company's board of directors has asked you to identify five potential candidates for vice-president of your company. Create a document that includes the following information for each candidate: name, title, and years of work experience. Then, use one of Word's installed templates to key a letter that identifies your five candidates.

- Address your salutation to the Board of Directors.
- Give your company a name with a trademark. Key your return address. Insert the current date into the letter.
- Create a Building Block of the company name and trademark.
- Key a recipient address for your Board of Directors (assume that your address is different from the Board's address.)

Make sure your letter is formatted correctly. Save your file as: w3rev-[your first initial and last name]9.

Solution Use the file **w3rev9-SF.docx** as a sample solution file for this project.

10. Edit the Candidate List

Rubric

LEVEL This is an intermediate level project

Language Arts: Edit a Letter After looking at your letter, the board of directors has asked you to cut your list down to two candidates. Open your **w3rev-9** letter. Then, key a memo that says: Please note the final list of candidates.

- Use the Clipboard to copy the candidates listed in your letter. Paste your final two candidates into your memo.
- Use drag-and-drop to place the two names in alphabetical order, if necessary.

Solution Use the file **w3rev10-SF.docx** as a sample solution file for this project.

Save your memo file as: w3rev-[your first initial and last name]10.

11. Evaluate Candidates

Rubric

LEVEL This is an advanced level project

Language Arts: Analyze and Describe Along with your revised list of names, the board of directors wants you to provide a formal letter that explains your decision. Open a Word document to create a professional letter. Be sure to include all parts of a formal letter (salutation, etc.).

Key your candidate evaluations into the letter's body. Explain why you selected both candidates and why you rejected the other three. Format your document as standard business letter in Calibri, 11 pt. Save your file as: w3rev-[your first initial and last name]11.

Solution Use the file **w3rev11-SF.docx** as a sample solution file for this project.

Step-By-Step

1. In your **Music** file, select **Slide 7**. Click the **Rock/Alternative** image to select it.
2. On the **Format** tab, in the **Size** group, click the **Size Dialog Box Launcher**.
3. In the **Size and Position** dialog box, on the **Size** tab, under **Size and rotate**, change the **Rotation** to **0°**. Click **Close**.
4. CHECK Your screen should look like Figure 3.25.
5. On the **Format** tab, in the **Size** group, change the **Height** to **1.5″**. Press ENTER.
6. On the **Format** tab, in the **Adjust** group, click **Recolor**.
7. In the **Recolor** drop-down menu, under **Light Variations**, select **Accent Color 6 Light**.
8. Choose **Format>Adjust>Contrast**. Click **+30%**.
9. Choose **Format>Adjust>Brightness**. Click **−10%**.
10. CHECK Your screen should look like Figure 3.26. Deselect the image. Save your file.

Continue to the next exercise.

EXERCISE 3-12
Rotate, Resize, and Recolor a Picture

Using Clip Art is an easy way to add visual interest to a presentation. When you select a piece of Clip Art, you usually have to modify it in some way to fit your presentation. For example, you can **rotate** an object to turn it 90 degrees to the right or left. As with other graphics, you can resize Clip Art to better fit your slides. You can also recolor Clip Art and adjust its contrast and brightness so it better suits the design and needs of your presentation.

Teaching Tip Show students how to use **Rotate** or **Flip** to flip ClipArt images.

FIGURE 3.25 Rotated picture

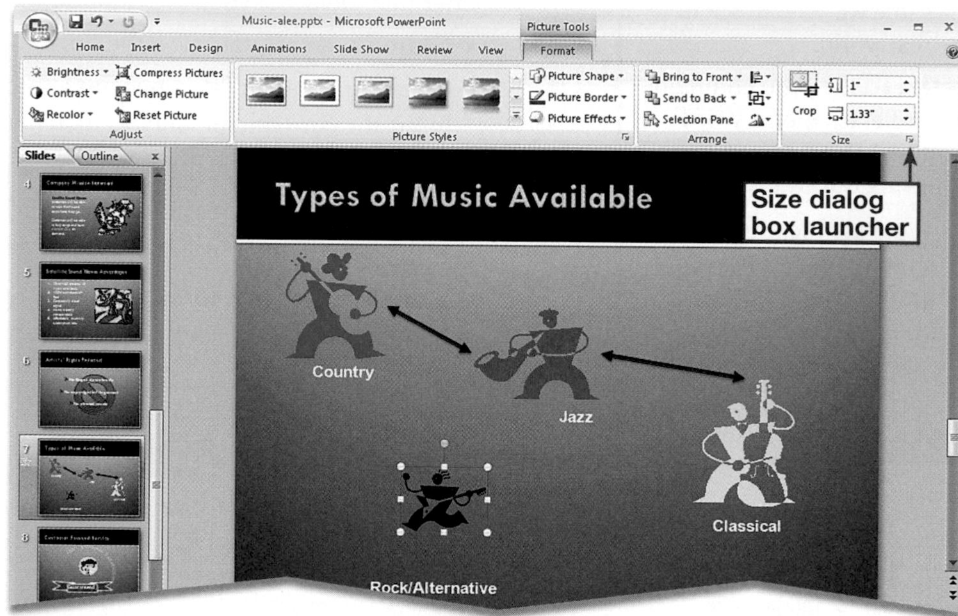

FIGURE 3.26 Picture resized and recolored

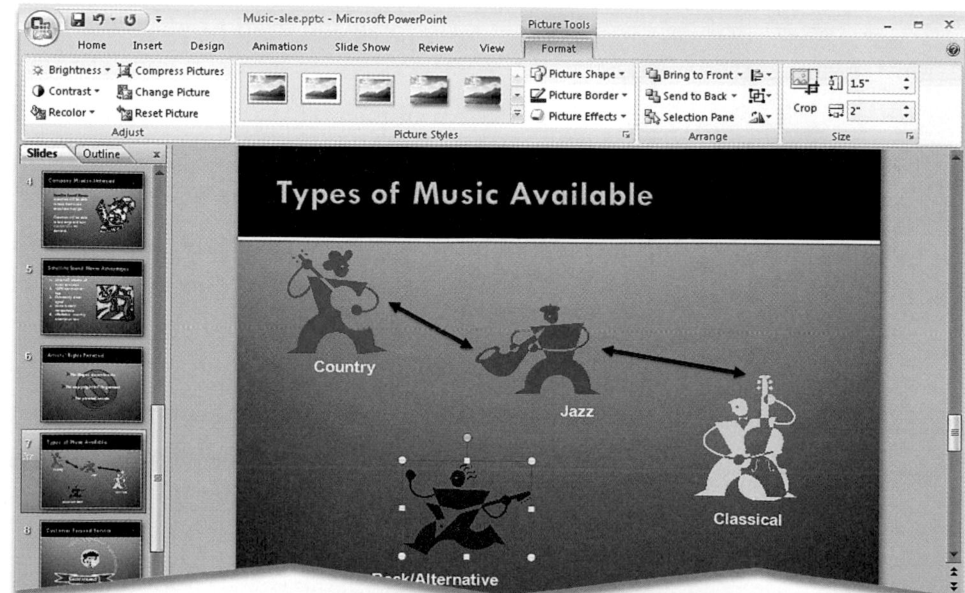

LESSON 4 Manage Lengthy Documents

Key Concepts

- Format an academic report
- Insert page numbers
- Create headers and footers
- Insert and delete page and section breaks
- Insert footnotes and endnotes
- Create a table of contents
- Use Word Count
- Modify Document Properties
- Use different views

Standards

The following standards are covered in this lesson. Refer to pages xxv and 715 for a description of the standards listed here.

ISTE Standards Correlation

NETS•S

1a, 1b, 2a, 2b, 2d, 3a, 3b, 3c, 3d, 4b, 4c, 4d, 5a, 5b, 5c, 5d, 6a, 6b, 6c, 6d

Microsoft Certified Application Specialist

Word

1.2, 1.3, 2.1, 2.3, 4.2, 4.4, 5.1

In school, you are often asked to take a point of view and support it with facts. In the business world, you will be asked to create reports that make recommendations and explain how you reached your conclusions. Organizing information and communicating with others are important lifelong skills. In this lesson, you will learn about Word tools that you can use to format and manage lengthy documents such as reports.

See page TM61 for answer to 21st Century Skills.

21st CENTURY SKILLS

Make Informed Decisions The first step in making informed decisions is to research, or gather information. Data used to make decisions should be as current as possible and should directly relate to your needs. Too many facts may confuse the situation. For example, if you are trying to decide what type of computer system to buy, you need to know about the newest products on the market and the costs. You can ignore information on computer systems that are more powerful than you need or that are out of your price range. *What strategy did you use to make an important decision recently?*

Step-By-Step

1. In your **Music** file, on **Slide 6**, select the **"No" Symbol**.
2. On the **Format** tab, in the **Arrange** group, click the **Send to Back** drop-down arrow (see Figure 3.23).
3. Click **Send to Back**.
4. Click **Bring to Front**.
5. **CHECK** Your screen should look like Figure 3.23.
6. Click **Send to Back** once more.
7. Deselect the image.
8. **CHECK** Your screen should look like Figure 3.24.
9. Save your file.

Continue to the next exercise.

Academic Skills

As you create a presentation, remember to choose topics and designs that are appropriate for your audience and are easy for them to read. Compare the difference in readability when an illustration is in front of the text and when it is behind the text.

NCLB/Language Arts (NCTE 5) Have students brainstorm different audiences and discuss how the language and design of a presentation might need to be different for each audience.

EXERCISE 3-11
Place Illustrations in Order

You can move illustrations behind text to improve the readability of the words. You can arrange illustrations using the Formatting tab on the Drawing Tools contextual tab. Using the Arrange group, you can send illustrations to the back or move them in front of other illustrations.

FIGURE 3.23 Send to Back drop-down menu

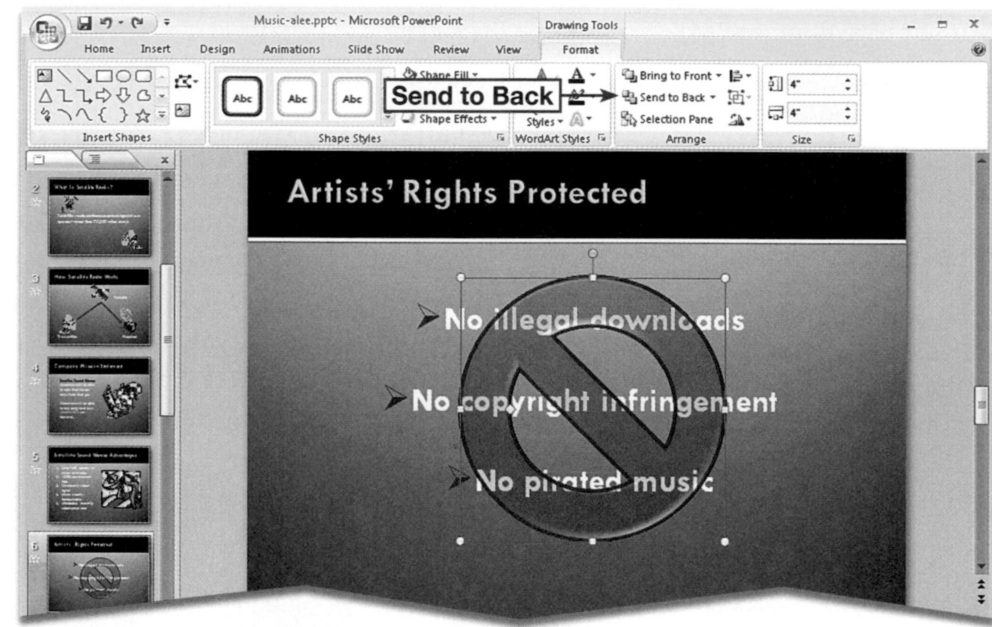

FIGURE 3.24 Image moved behind text

LESSON 4 Reading Guide

Before You Read

See page TM42 for English Learner activity suggestions.

Create an Outline Use the lesson's exercise titles to create an outline. Make the titles into Level 1 main ideas. Add supporting information to create Level 2 and 3 details. Use the outline to predict what you are about to learn.

Read To Learn

- Explore how you can use page numbers, headers, and footers to make your reports easier to read.
- Format citations correctly.
- Understand how you can use page breaks and section breaks to organize your message.
- Consider how navigational tools in long documents improve the quality of your work.

Main Idea

Organize information and communicate your knowledge by learning how to create and manage lengthy documents.

Vocabulary

Key Terms

bibliography
endnote
footer
footnote
header
Outline View
page break
report
section
section break
table of contents
Word Count

Academic Vocabulary

These words appear in your reading and on your tests. Make sure you know their meanings.

describe
log
navigate

Quick Write Activity

Describe On a separate sheet of paper, describe the essays and reports you have written for your English, history, and science classes. What elements are common among all papers? How are titles, page numbers, and citations used differently in a short essay as opposed to a longer report?

Study Skills

Improve Concentration Skills Increase your concentration by dividing your study time or task into short-term goals. Assign a deadline for each goal or task. Determine a few specific objectives and stick to your time schedule. Complete your goals one at a time.

Academic Standards

English Language Arts

NCTE 4 Use written language to communicate effectively.

NCTE 5 Use different writing process elements to communicate effectively.

NCTE 7 Conduct research and gather, evaluate, and synthesize data to communicate discoveries.

NCTE 8 Use information resources to gather information and create and communicate knowledge.

NCTE 12 Use language to accomplish individual purposes.

Math

NCTM Measurement Apply appropriate techniques, tools, and formulas to determine measurements.

Step-By-Step

7. In the **Format Shape** dialog box, under **Fill**, select **Solid fill**. Change the **Transparency** to **75%**. Click the **Color** drop-down arrow. Select **Dark Red**.

8. **CHECK** Your dialog box should look like Figure 3.21. Click **Close**.

9. Choose **Format>Shape Styles>Shape Outline**. Click **Dark Red**.

10. Choose **Format>Shape Styles>Shape Effects** .

11. On the drop-down menu, select **Bevel**. In the menu, under **Bevel**, in the second row, click **Soft Round**.

12. Select the shape and position it in the center of the bulleted list. Deselect the shape.

13. **CHECK** Your screen should look similar to Figure 3.22.

14. Save your file.

Continue to the next exercise.

NCLB/Math (Measurement) In **Step 7**, explain that transparency indicates that you can see through something. Ask students to tell you what they would expect to see if they changed the transparency to 25%. What might they see if they changed it to 100%? The higher the percentage, the greater the transparency.

EXERCISE 3-10 (Continued)
Format and Add an Effect to a Shape

FIGURE 3.21 Format Shape dialog box

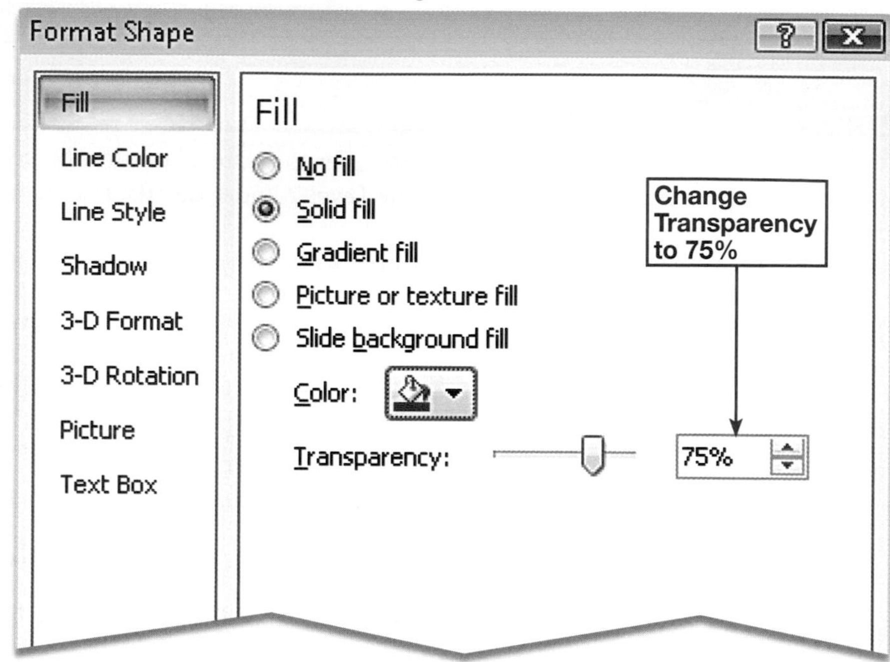

FIGURE 3.22 Modified shape with effects applied

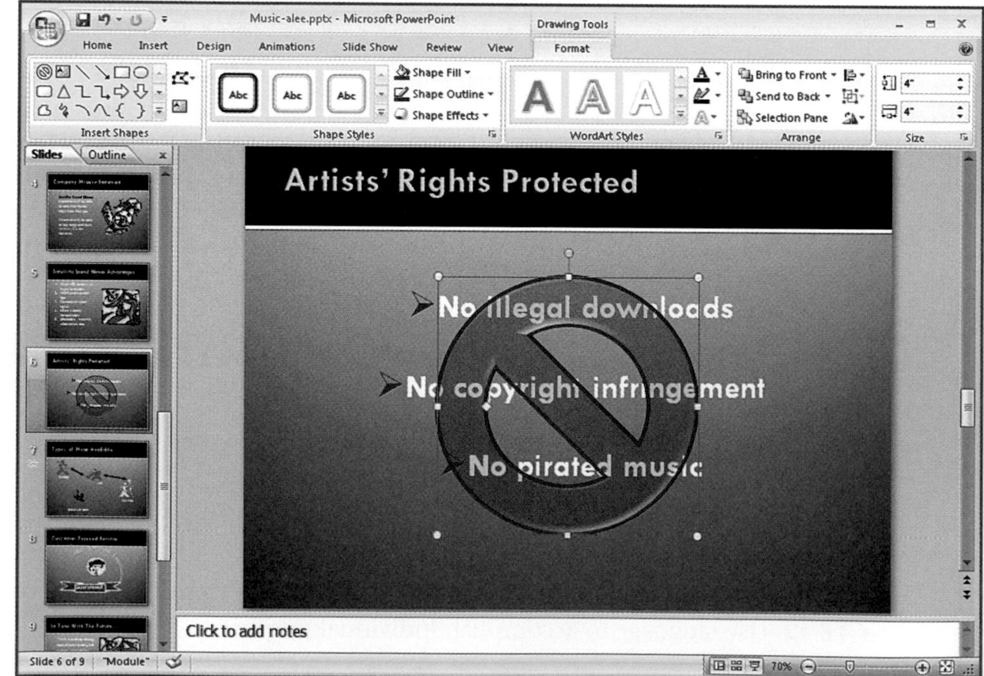

Writing MATTERS

Writing an Academic Report

What interests you? The history of the Underground Railroad? Recycling? You have probably written many interesting reports!

Information, Please

In a research report, you are asked to present information to your reader. The main components of an academic research report are the title and introduction, the body, and the conclusion.

An academic report should also include a Works Cited page, which lists the information for every source used to create the report (see **Citing Sources in an Academic Report** on page 105 for more information on this topic).

Formatting an Academic Report

The **Modern Language Association (MLA)** publishes guidelines on how to format a research report. Here are some important guidelines:

- Set all margins 1 inch from the edge of the page.
- Double-space your entire report, including the Works Cited page.
- Indent the first line of each paragraph 0.5 inch.
- Include only one space between end punctuation and a new sentence.
- Create a heading, including your name, the name of the class and teacher, and the date, at the top left of the page.
- Center the title, but do not make it bold.
- Right-align your last name and the page number in the report's header.

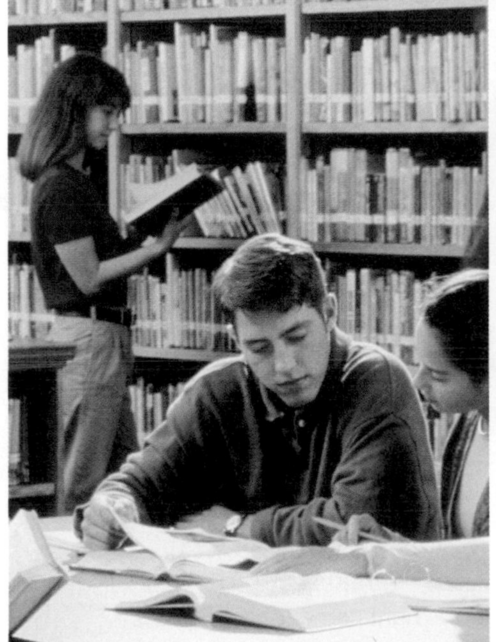

In a research report, you gather information from different sources and bring it together in one organized paper.

NCLB/Language Arts (NCTE 4) Remind students that correctly formatting an academic report is essential to communicating with other students and teachers about a topic.

NCLB/Language Arts (NCTE 7) Explain to students that by following the rules set forth here, they are conducting proper research and writing guidelines.

SKILLBUILDER

1. **Identify** What information should be displayed in an academic report's header?
2. **Evaluate** Why do you think the MLA recommends double-spacing an academic report?
3. **Connect** Think about a research report you have written recently. What were its main components? How might you have organized the report differently knowing what you now know about formatting reports?

SkillBuilder answers can be found on page TM61.

Step-By-Step

1. In your **Music** file, select **Slide 6**.
2. On the **Insert** tab, in the **Illustrations** group, click the **Shapes** drop-down arrow. Under **Basic Shapes**, select **"No" Symbol**.
3. Click in the middle of the bulleted list on the slide.
4. CHECK Your screen should look similar to Figure 3.19.
5. On the **Format** tab, change the **Shape Height** to **4″** and the **Shape Width** to **4″** (see Figure 3.20).
6. Click the **Dialog Box Launcher** in the bottom right corner of the **Shape Styles** group.

Continued on the next page.

Microsoft Office 2007

PowerPoint 2007 contains built-in basic shapes and shape styles. You can change the style of a shape to create a wide variety of graphic effects for a presentation.

EXERCISE 3-10
Format and Add an Effect to a Shape

You can resize and add color and effects to shapes. For example, you can change the size of shapes so that they fit your slide. You can also use the Fill Effects dialog box to add texture, patterns, or pictures to shapes and to change their color.

FIGURE 3.19 Shape inserted into slide

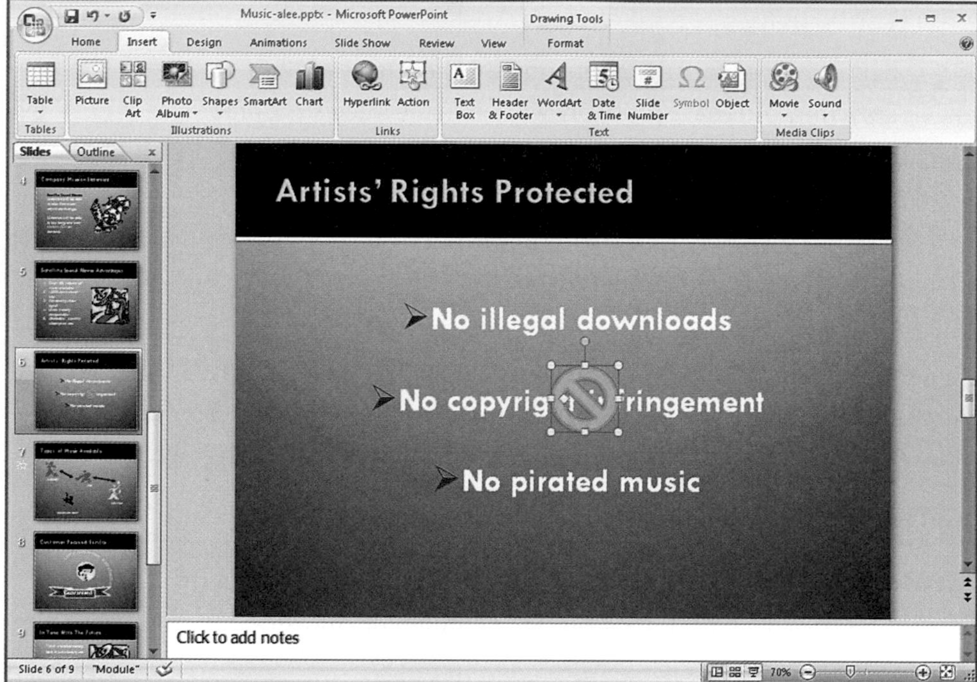

FIGURE 3.20 Size group

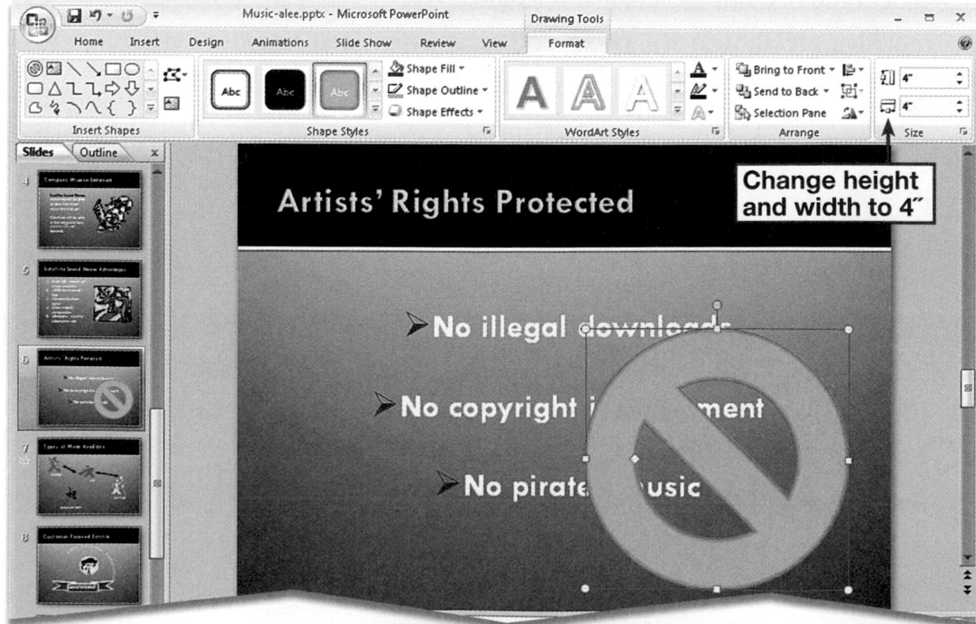

Step-By-Step

1. Start **Word**. Save a new document as: Academic-[your first initial and last name] (for example, *Academic-sbryant*).

2. Click **Customize Quick Access Toolbar** (see Figure 4.2). Choose **More Commands**.

3. In the **Word Options** dialog box, select **All Commands** (see Figure 4.1). Select **Reveal Formatting**. Click **Add**. Click **OK**.

4. In the **QAT**, click **Reveal Formatting**. In the **Reveal Formatting** task pane, click **Font**. Change to **Times New Roman**, **12 pt**. Click **Default**. Click **No**. In **Paragraph**, click **Alignment**. In **Indentation**, confirm that **Right** is set to **0″**.

5. Under **Spacing**, change **Line spacing** to **Double**. Click **Default**. Click **No**.

6. Click the **plus sign** next to **Section**. Confirm all four **Margins** are **1″**.

7. **CHECK** Your task pane should look like Figure 4.2. Close the pane. Save your file.

Continue to the next exercise.

EXERCISE 4-1
Use Reveal Formatting to Format an Academic Report

A **report** is a formal document that describes, or represents in words, facts and information. To help the reader understand the report, specific formatting guidelines are followed. For instance, MLA reports should have 1-inch margins and be double spaced. Use the Reveal Formatting task pane to make sure your document is formatted correctly. (**Note**: Reveal Formatting must be added to the QAT using the Customize Quick Access Toolbar command.)

Troubleshooting In **Steps 4 and 5**, when students click **Default**, they should be sure to click **No** when they are asked if they would like the change to affect all new documents.

FIGURE 4.1 Reveal Formatting added to the QAT

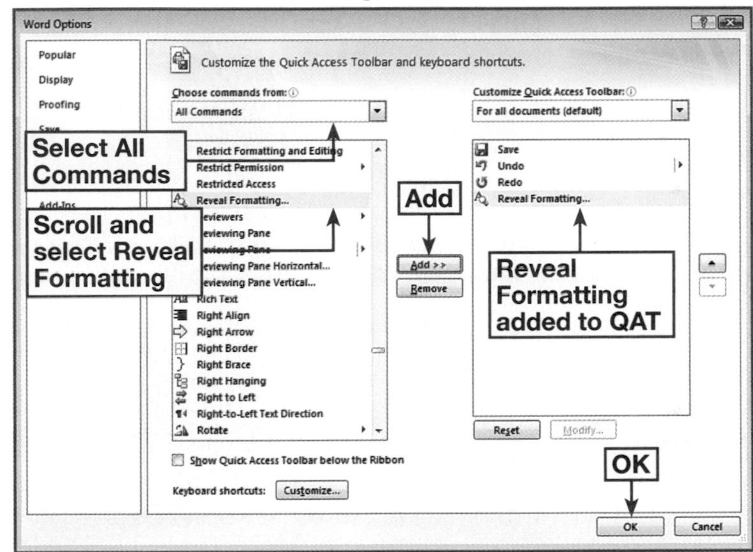

FIGURE 4.2 Reveal Formatting task pane

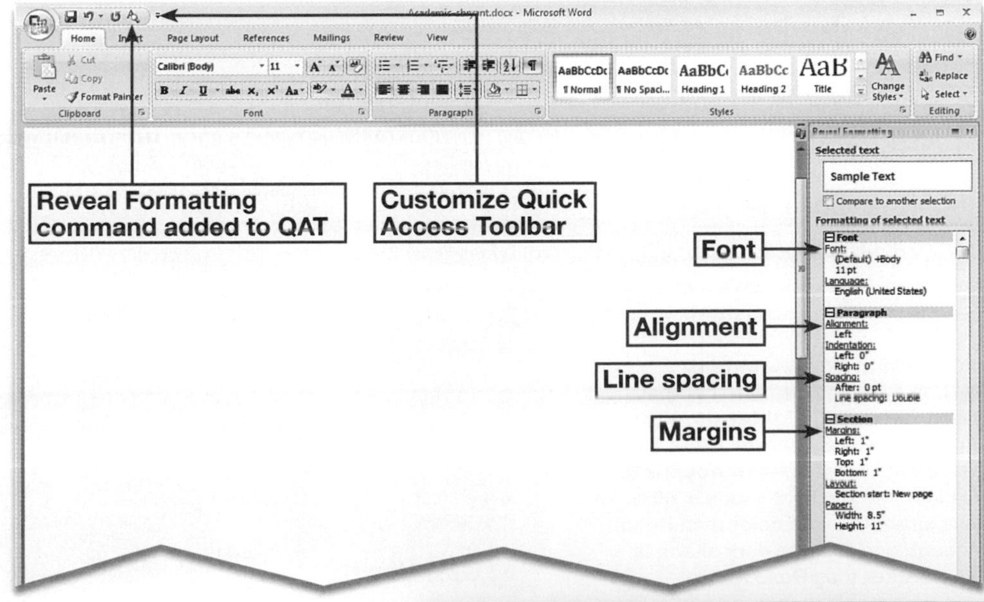

Step-By-Step

1. In your **Music** file, select **Slide 8**. Select the ribbon graphic. The **Drawing Tools Format** tab appears in the upper-right corner.
2. On the **Format** tab, in the **Shape Styles** group, click the **Shape Fill** drop-down arrow.
3. Click **Rose, Accent 3, Darker 25%**.
4. Click **Shape Effects**. Select **Shadow**.
5. In the **Inner** category, select **Inside Center** (see Figure 3.17).
6. On the **Format** tab, in the **Shape Width** box, key: 6. Press ENTER. Deselect the ribbon shape.
7. **CHECK** Your screen should look like Figure 3.18. Save your file.

Continue to the next exercise.

Step-By-Step Tip In **Step 4**, if students are having trouble finding the right shade, tell them to slowly move the pointer over each color until they see a ScreenTip naming them.

NCLB/Math (Measurement)
In Step 4, ask students to compare **Rose Accent 3, Lighter 60%** to **Rose Accent 3, Darker 60%**. Then ask them to locate **Rose Accent 3**. Explain that the light shade is 60% less saturated with color than Rose Accent, and that the dark shade is 60% darker than Rose Accent.

EXERCISE 3-9
Change the Size and Color of a Graphic

When you resize a graphic, you make it larger or smaller so it fits better on a slide. In Lesson 2, you learned how to use sizing handles to resize graphics. If you want a graphic to be a specific height or width, you can key the exact measurement you need into the formatting dialog box. You can also use the dialog box to change the **fill color** inside the graphic and the **line color** of the graphic's outside edge.

FIGURE 3.17 Shape Effects drop-down menu

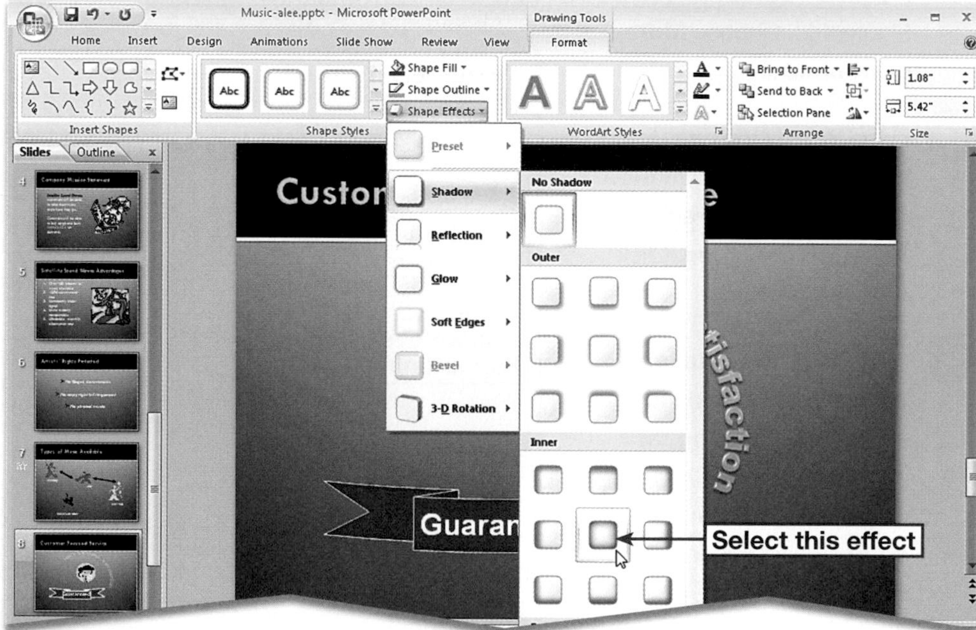

FIGURE 3.18 Graphic with modified size and color

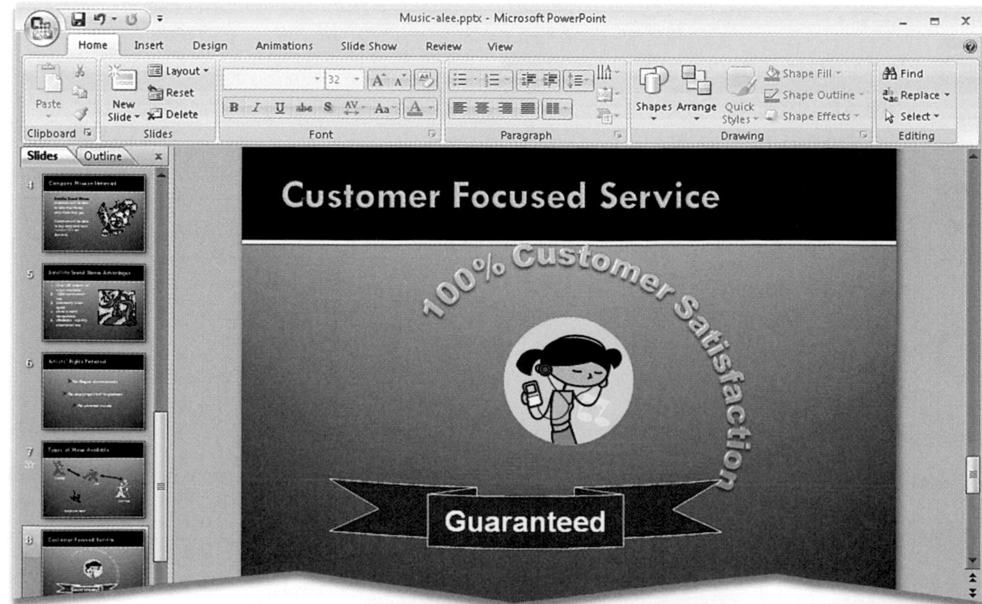

Step-By-Step

1. In your **Academic** file, make sure that **Show/Hide** ¶ [¶] is activated. Move the insertion point to the top left corner.
2. Key the heading shown in Figure 4.3. Press [ENTER] after each line. When you have keyed the final line, press [ENTER].
3. Key the title: Earthquakes. Press [ENTER] once. Select the text **Earthquakes**. Click **Center** [≡].
4. Click before the paragraph mark under the title. Press [TAB]. Key the report's first paragraph as shown in Figure 4.3. Press [ENTER].
5. Choose **Insert>Text>Object>Text from File**. In the **Insert File** dialog box, browse to and select **Earthquakes.docx**. Click **Insert**. Click **OK**. Scroll to the top of the first page.
6. **CHECK** Your screen should look like Figure 4.4. Save your file.

Continue to the next exercise.

Academic Skills

The report on earthquakes used in this lesson is a research report that includes academic citations.

EXERCISE 4-2
Create the First Page of a Report

When creating a report in MLA format, place a heading at the top of the report's first page. This heading includes your name, your teacher's name, the class name and period, and the date. You then key the report's title, followed by the first paragraph of your report.

FIGURE 4.3 Report with heading, title, and first paragraph

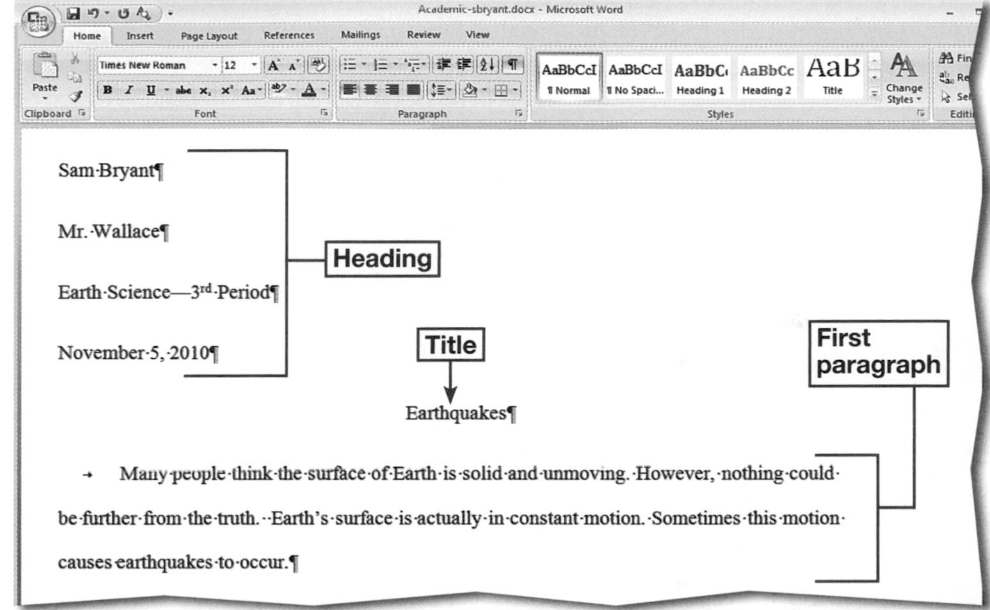

FIGURE 4.4 Report with file inserted

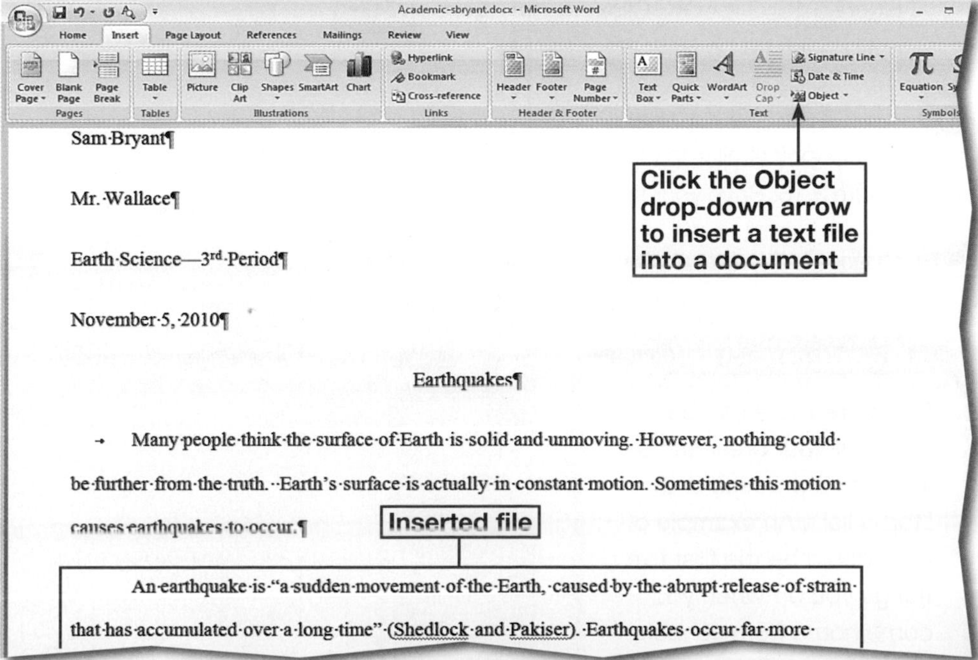

NCLB/Language Arts (NCTE 5) Discuss with students the difference between a personal essay and an academic report. In an academic report, observations should be based on research, and students should never use "I."

Step-By-Step

1. In your **Music** file, select **Slide 5**. Select the bulleted points.

2. Choose **Home>Paragraph**. click the **Numbering** drop-down arrow. Click **Bullets and Numbering**.

3. In the **Bullets and Numbering** dialog box, on the **Numbered** tab, in the first row, click the second box from the left.

4. In the **Size** box, increase the size to **100%** of text.

5. Click the **Color** drop-down arrow. Under **Theme Colors**, select **White**.

6. **CHECK** Your dialog box should look like Figure 3.15. Click **OK**. Click outside the text box.

7. **CHECK** Your screen should look similar to Figure 3.16. Save your file.

Continue to the next exercise.

Academic Skills

Numbered lists can be very helpful if your presentation includes a process or a "top 5 list". An example of a list could be the first five things you do when you come home from school.

NCLB/Language Arts (NCTE 5)

EXERCISE 3-8
Add and Modify Numbered Lists

Like bulleted lists, numbered lists are common in PowerPoint presentations. Numbered lists present text in a specific order. Use a numbered list if giving instructions that must be followed in the order in which they are presented. Numbered lists can also be used to show the relative importance of points. As with other text, you can modify the appearance of a numbered list. Use the Bullets and Numbering dialog box to change the type, size, and color of the numbers used on a slide.

FIGURE 3.15 Bullets and Numbering dialog box

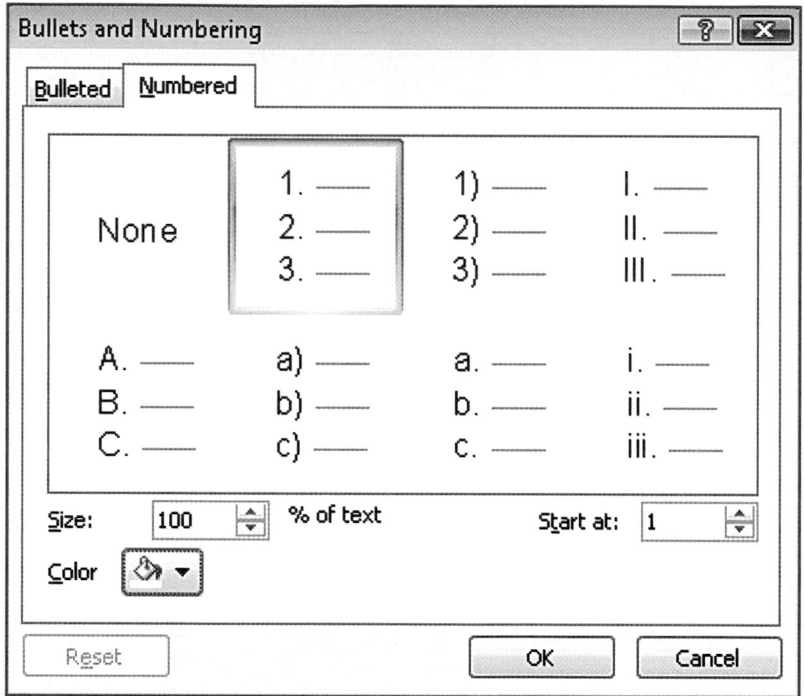

FIGURE 3.16 Modified numbered list

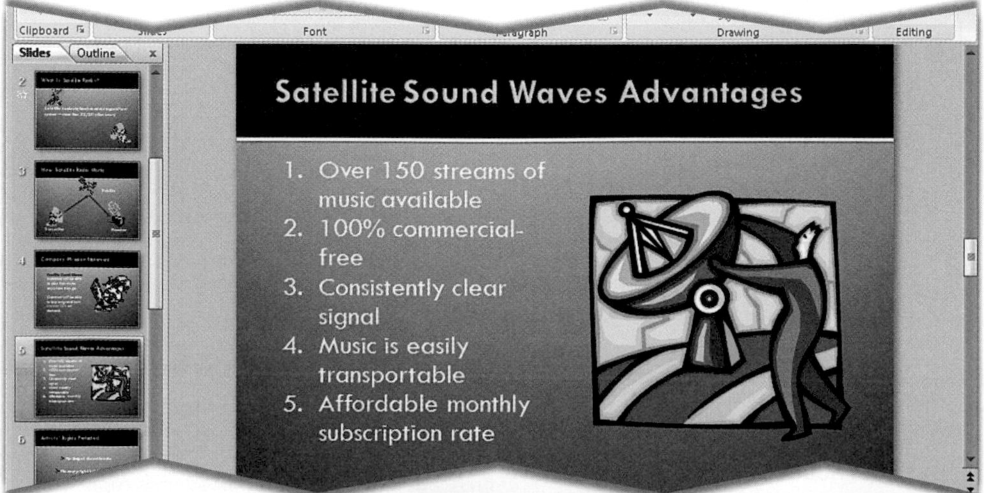

Step-By-Step

1. In your **Academic** file, choose **Insert>Header & Footer>Page Number**.
2. In the **Page Number** menu, select **Top of Page**.
3. Click **Plain Number 1** (see Figure 4.5).
4. In your document, at the top of the first page, select and right-click the page number **1**.
5. In the menu, click **Paragraph**. In the **Paragraph** dialog box, under **General**, change **Alignment** to **Right**. Click **OK**.
6. **CHECK** Your screen should look like Figure 4.6. In the **Header & Footer Tools** contextual tab, click **Close Header and Footer** . Save your file.

Continue to the next exercise.

You Should Know

Although an MLA report should have a page number on the first page, a business report should not. To remove it, select the first page number. In the **Header & Footer Tools** contextual tab, choose **Design>Options>Different First Page**.

EXERCISE 4-3
Insert and Modify Page Numbers

Page numbers help readers to locate information quickly in a document. When you insert a page number, a number prints on every page unless you specify otherwise. In an MLA report, the page number should be aligned with the right margin on every page and be positioned .5″ from the top margin (the default in Word). Use the Page Number menu to position numbers in the top right corner of every page.

NCLB/Math (Number and Operations) Ask students to determine the indent for the first line of each paragraph. The margin is 1" and the indent is .5".

FIGURE 4.5 Page Numbers options

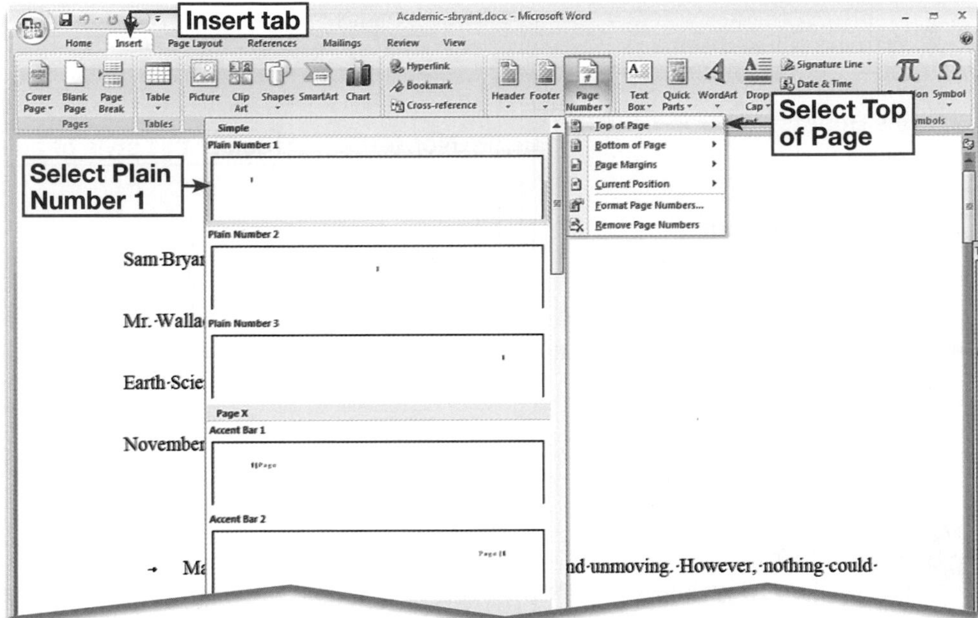

FIGURE 4.6 Document with modified page number

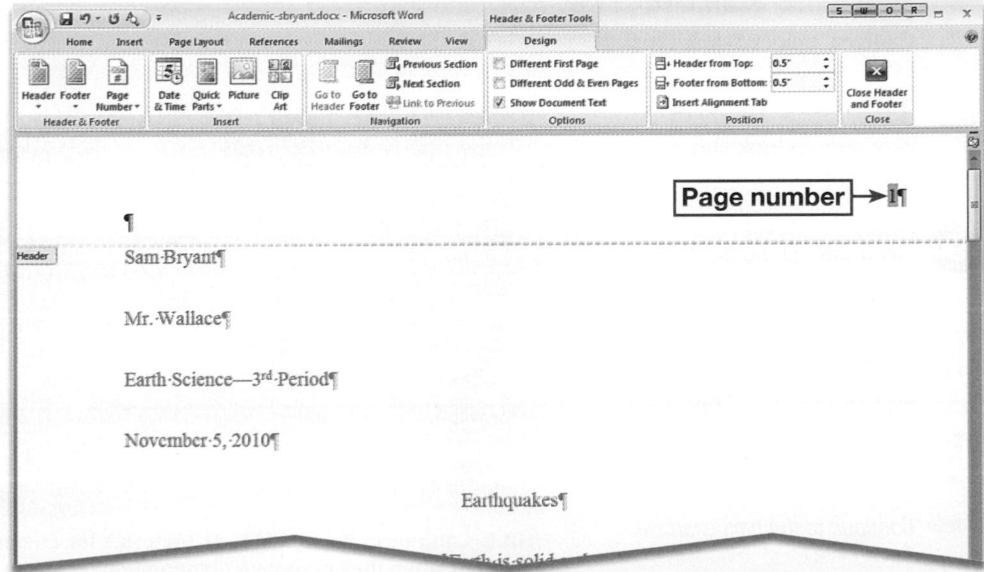

Teaching Tip Point out to students that the Header & Footer Tools contextual tab appears only when changes are being made to the header or footer

Step-By-Step

1. In your **Music** file, select **Slide 6**.
2. Select the three lines of text. On the **Home** tab, in the **Paragraph** group, click **Bullets**. Square bullets are added.
3. With the bulleted items in the slide still selected, click the **Bullets** drop-down arrow.
4. Click **Bullets and Numbering**.
5. In the **Bullets and Numbering** dialog box, on the **Bulleted** tab, in the second row, click the third box from the left.
6. In the **Size** box, increase the size to **110%** of text.
7. Click the **Color** drop-down arrow. Under **Standard Colors**, select **Dark Red**.
8. **CHECK** Your dialog box should look like Figure 3.13.
9. Click **OK**. Deselect the bulleted text.
10. **CHECK** Your screen should look like Figure 3.14.
11. Save your file.

Continue to the next exercise.

EXERCISE 3-7
Add and Modify Bulleted Lists

Bulleted lists are common in PowerPoint presentations because they allow you to present information in short, readable sections. As with other text, you can modify the appearance of a bulleted list. Use the Bullets and Numbering dialog box to change the type, size, and color of the bullets used on a slide.

FIGURE 3.13 Bullets and Numbering dialog box

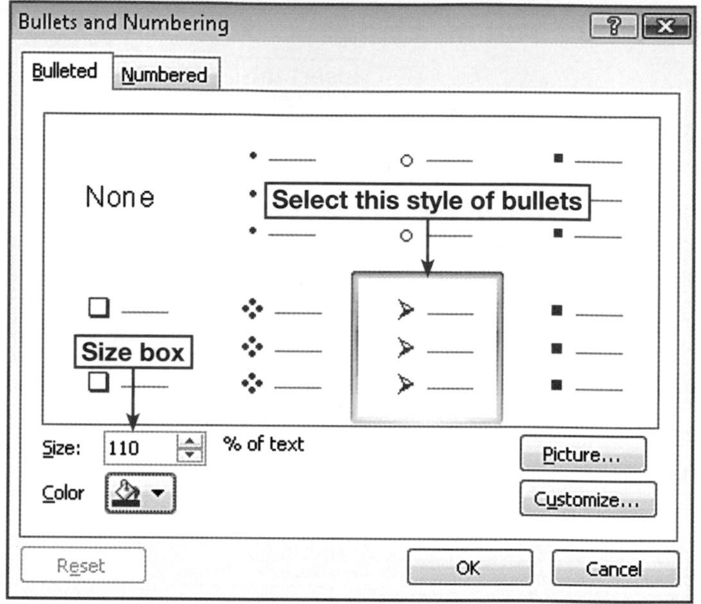

FIGURE 3.14 Modified bullets

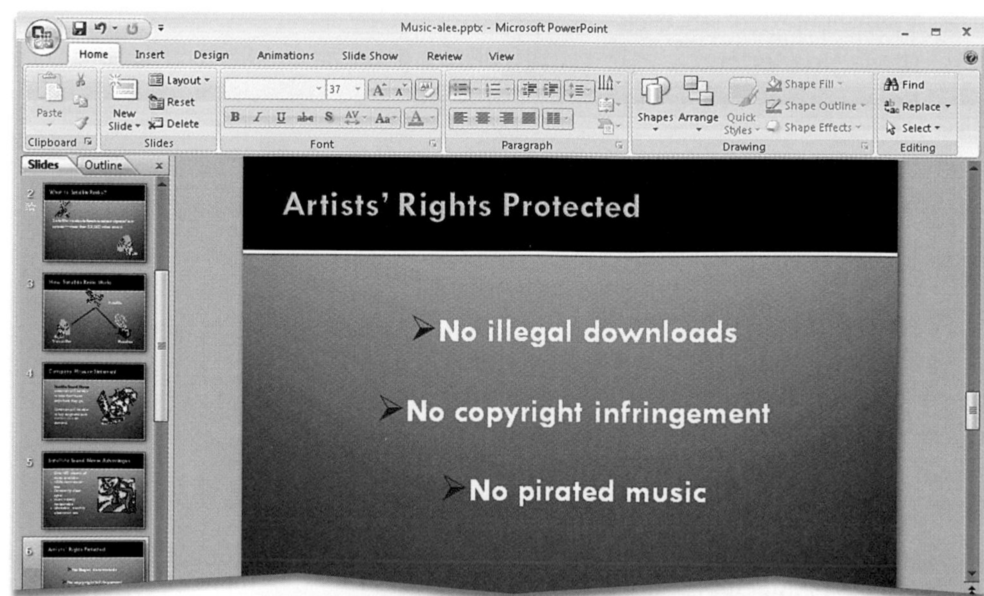

NCLB/Language Arts (NCTE 4) Reiterate for students the importance of organizing their thoughts when they prepare a presentation. Just like an essay, a presentation should be organized around a central thesis statement with fluid transitions between important points.

Step-By-Step

1. In your **Academic** file, choose **Insert>Header & Footer>Header>Edit Header**.
2. In the first page's header, click before the page number **1**. Key: Sam Bryant. Press the **spacebar**.
3. **CHECK** Your screen should look like Figure 4.7. Select the text **Sam**. Press DELETE.
4. **CHECK** Your screen should look like Figure 4.8.
5. In the **Header & Footer Tools** contextual tab, click **Close Header and Footer**. Save your file.

Continue to the next exercise.

Academic Skills

Although Word has many fonts, MLA requirements are very specific. Follow your teacher's guidelines. When in doubt, use the MLA-accepted **Times New Roman 12 pt.** font.

Microsoft Office 2007

The **Header & Footer Tools** contextual tab appears in the Ribbon only when you work in the **Header & Footer** group.

EXERCISE 4-4
Create and Modify a Header and Footer

A **header** contains text that appears at the top of every page. A header in an MLA report displays the student's last name followed by the page number. Both items should be right aligned. A **footer** contains text that appears at the bottom of every page. MLA reports generally do not display any information in footers, but footers are used in business reports and other documents. You can edit and format the text in a header or footer just as you would any other text in a document.

Teaching Tip Have students read the ScreenTip for each button on the **Header & Footer Tools** contextual tab.

FIGURE 4.7 Header added to report

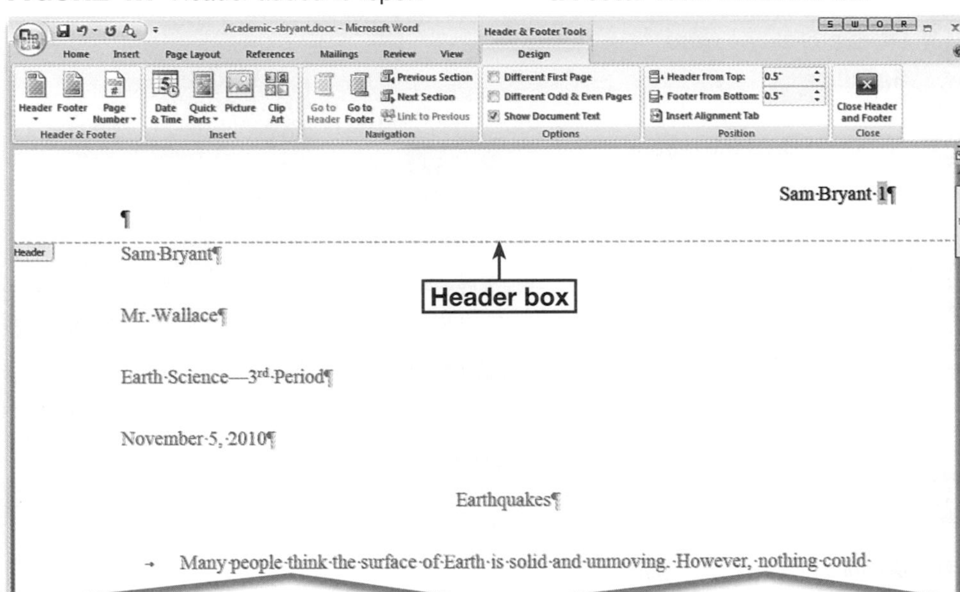

NCLB/Language Arts (NCTE 4) Have students go online to find and discuss MLA formatting requirements.

FIGURE 4.8 Report with modified header

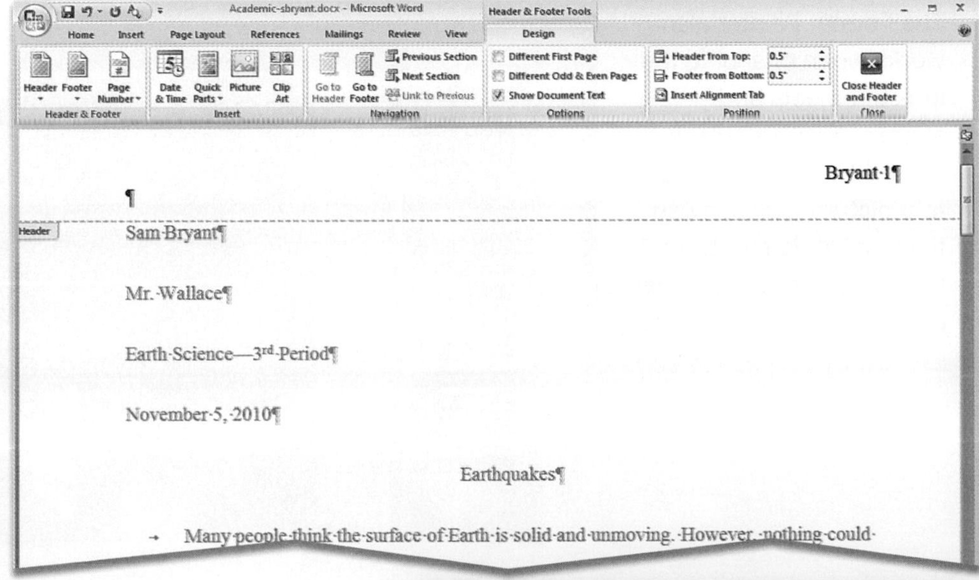

Step-By-Step

1. Select **Slide 2**. Select the title of the slide.
2. Double-click the **Format Painter** . The pointer will turn into a paintbrush (see Figure 3.11).
3. Move to **Slide 1**.
4. Double-click the word **Satellite**.
5. Click and drag the cursor across the phrase **Satellite Sound Waves**.
6. Deselect the text.
7. **CHECK** Your screen should look similar to Figure 3.12.
8. Save your file.

Continue to the next exercise.

Tech Tip

The Format Painter also works when changing the look of objects and shapes. For example, if you add a border or effect to a picture, you can use the Format Painter to add the same effect to another picture in your presentation.

EXERCISE 3-6
Use the Format Painter

The **Format Painter** allows you to apply all of the text styling from selected text to other text in the same presentation. By selecting text, clicking or double-clicking the Format Painter, and then selecting other text, you can transfer the same color, font, size, effects, and any other attributes to the text.

FIGURE 3.11 Format Painter

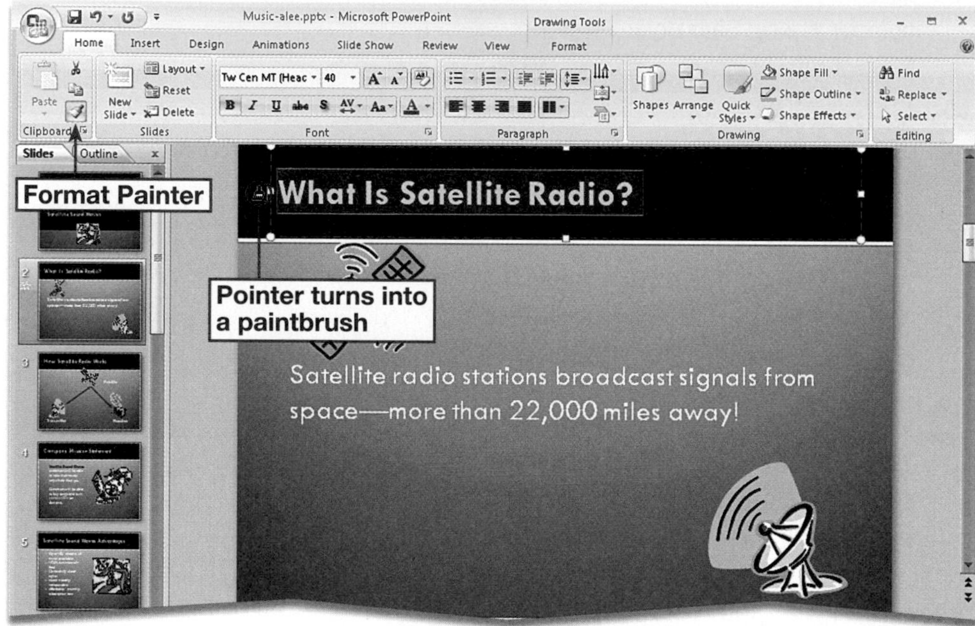

FIGURE 3.12 Formatting applied with Format Painter

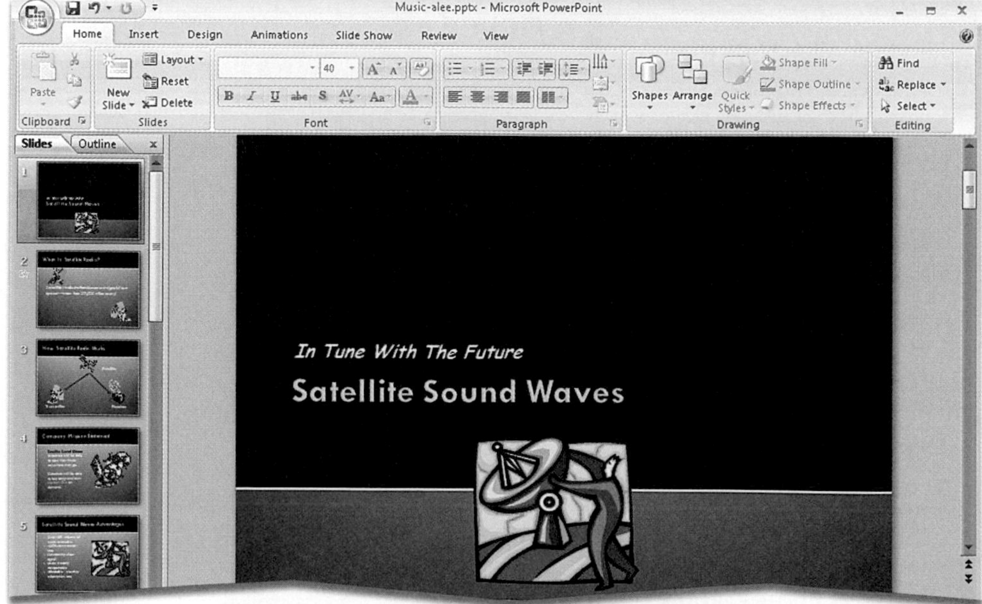

Step-By-Step

1. In your **Academic** file, scroll down to the end of the document. Select CTRL + HOME. You are at the beginning of the document.
2. On the scroll bar, click **Next Page** (see Figure 4.9). You are on Page 2.
3. Click **Next Page** again.
4. Click **Previous Page** (see Figure 4.9).
5. CHECK Your screen should look like Figure 4.9.
6. On the keyboard, press PAGE UP. You have moved up to the previous screen.
7. Press PAGE UP again.
8. Press PAGE DOWN.
9. CHECK Your screen should look like Figure 4.10.
10. Save your file.

Continue to the next exercise.

Differentiated Instruction/Physically Impaired Suggest that students who have trouble scrolling with the mouse use the keyboard shortcuts discussed here.

EXERCISE 4-5
Navigate a Document

Word provides different options to help you **navigate**, or move through, a multiple-page document such as a report. On the scroll bar, the Previous Page and Next Page buttons can help you move from page to page. Use the Page Up and Page Down keys to change your view of a document one full screen at a time.

FIGURE 4.9 Page 2 of the report

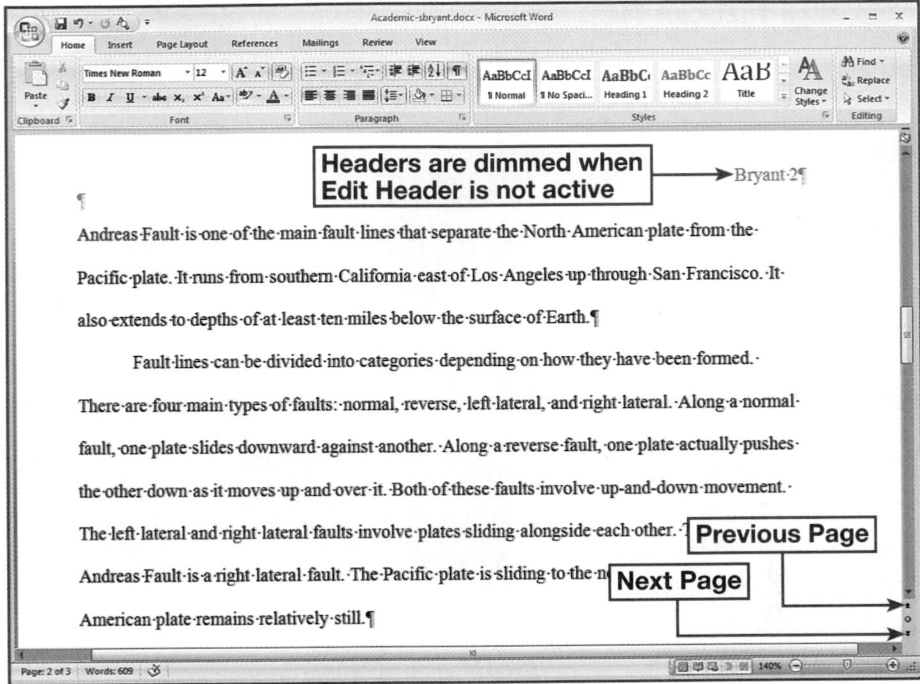

FIGURE 4.10 Bottom of Page 1

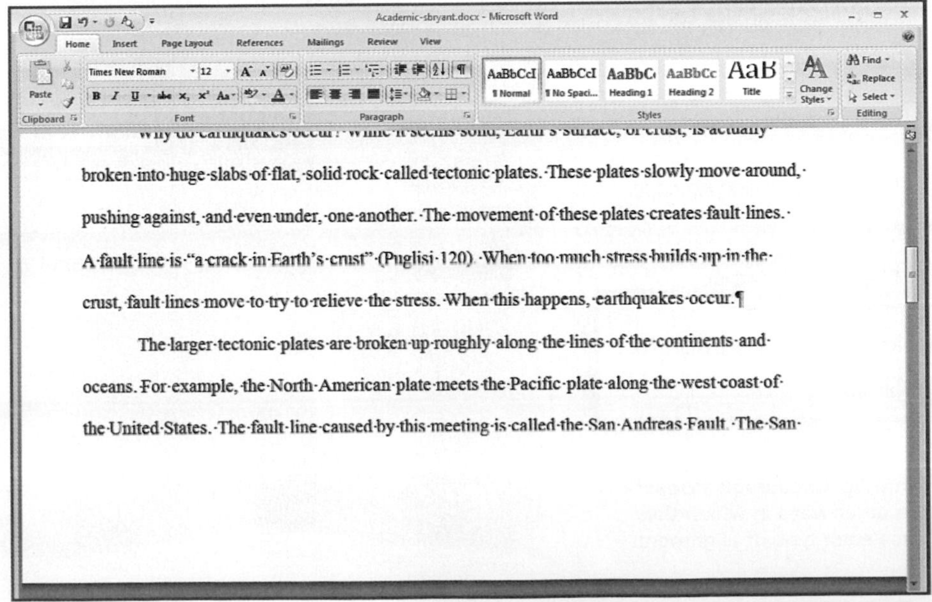

Step-By-Step

1. In your **Music** file, select **Slide 9**.
2. Select the paragraph under the title **In Tune with the Future**.
3. Click **Align Text Left** .
4. Deselect the text.
5. CHECK Your screen should look similar to Figure 3.9.
6. Select the name and title at the bottom of the slide.
7. Click **Align Text Right** .
8. Select the paragraph under the title **In Tune with the Future**. Click the **Line Spacing** drop-down arrow. Choose **1.5**. Deselect the text.
9. CHECK Your screen should look similar to Figure 3.10.
10. Save your file.

Continue to the next exercise.

Shortcuts

Triple-click a paragraph to select it.

Teaching Tip Encourage students to share other ways in which they might use each type of alignment.

EXERCISE 3-5
Align Text and Change Line Spacing

A text's **alignment** refers to where the text lines up in relation to a text box's margins. Left-aligned text lines up along a text box's left side. Right-aligned text lines up along a text box's right side. Centered text is positioned in the middle of a text box. You can also justify text so it lines up with both the left and right sides of the text box.

FIGURE 3.9 Left-aligned text

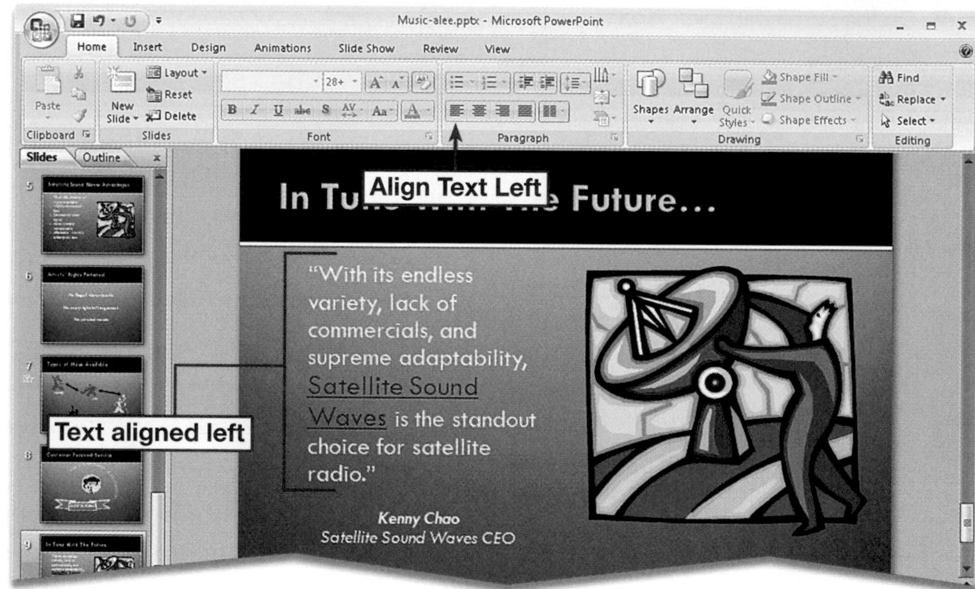

FIGURE 3.10 Right-aligned text

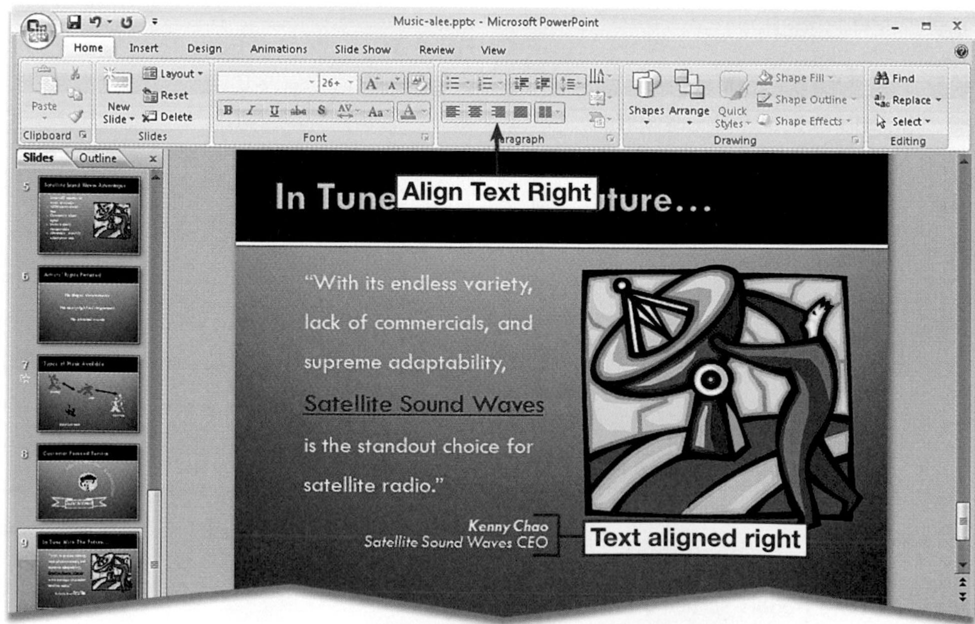

Step-By-Step

1. In your **Academic** file, click before the text **Works Cited** on Page 3.
2. Choose **Insert>Pages>Page Break**.
3. CHECK Your screen should look like Figure 4.11.
4. Click **Page Break** on Page 3 once. When the cursor appears to the left of the break, press DELETE twice.
5. CHECK Your screen should look like Figure 4.12.
6. Press CTRL + ENTER.
7. CHECK Your screen should again look like Figure 4.11. Save your file.

Continue to the next exercise.

Tech Tip

To see the hard page breaks in a document, choose **Home>Paragraph>Show/Hide ¶**.

Troubleshooting Students may try to insert page breaks by pressing **Enter** until they reach the bottom of the page. Explain that they should not do this because inserting any content into these pages will cause the page breaks to move around and appear in unplanned places. Tell students that if blank pages are printing in a document, they should click **Show/Hide ¶** to display and delete any extra page breaks in their document.

EXERCISE 4-6
Insert and Delete Page Breaks

A **page break** is the point at which one page ends and another begins. When you key text and reach the end of a page, Word automatically moves text to a new page. This is known as a soft page break. You can control where a new page begins by inserting a hard page break. In documents such as formal reports, you should make sure that certain parts, such as a Works Cited page, do not begin or end on the same page as others. A hard page break lets you control where parts of a report begin and end.

FIGURE 4.11 Page break inserted into a document

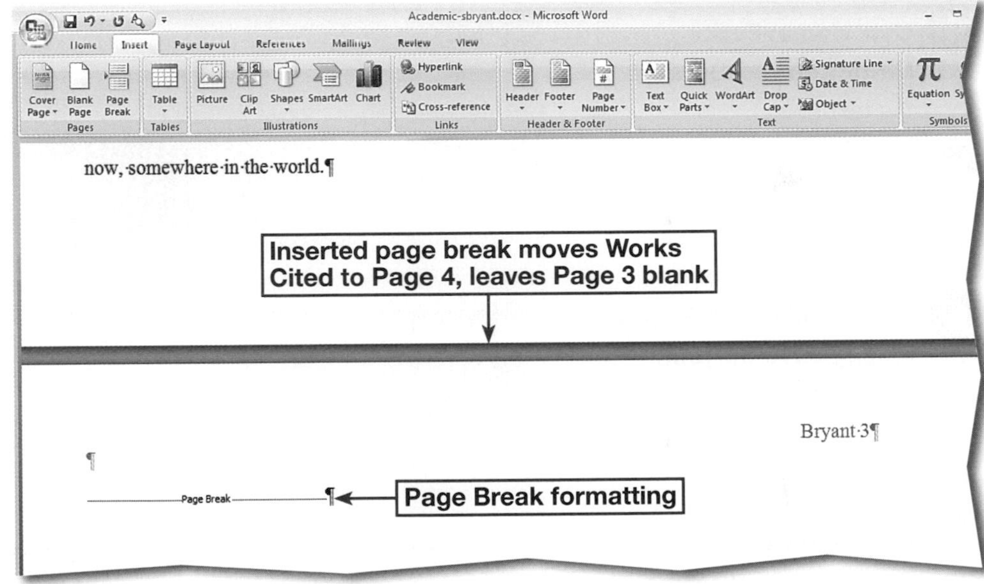

FIGURE 4.12 Page break deleted

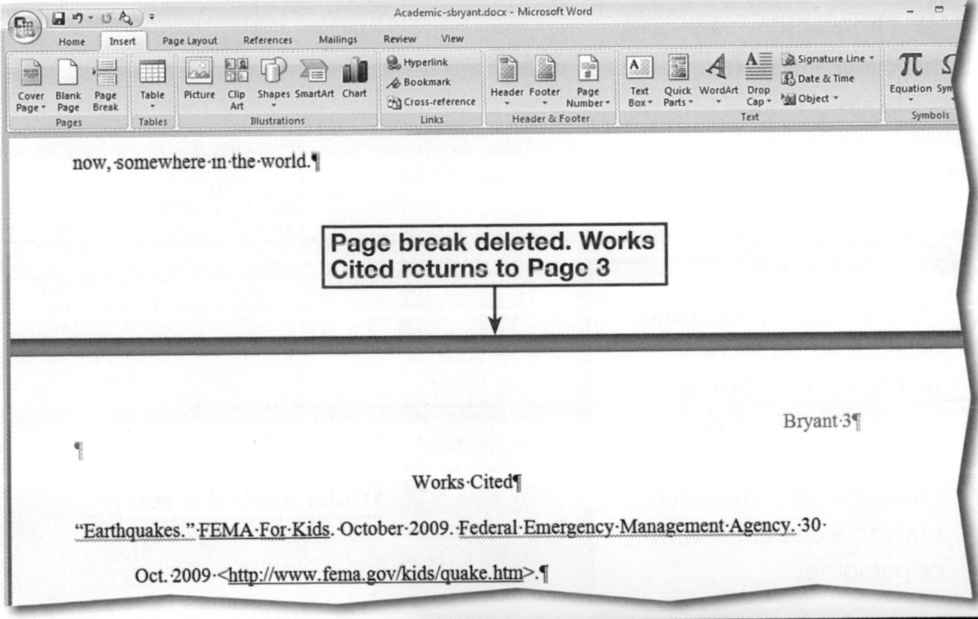

Step-By-Step

1. In your **Music** file, select **Slide 9**.
2. Select the text **Satellite Sound Waves**.
3. On the **Home** tab, click the **Font Size** drop-down arrow. Click **32**.
4. Click **Home>Font>Underline** U. Deselect the text.
5. CHECK Your screen should look similar to Figure 3.7.
6. Reselect **Satellite Sound Waves**. Click the **Font Color** A drop-down arrow.
7. In the menu, under **Standard Colors**, select **Dark Red**. Deselect the text.
8. CHECK Your screen should look similar to Figure 3.8. Save your file.

Continue to the next exercise.

Tech Tip

You can quickly add **bold**, *italic*, or an underline to text by clicking **Ctrl+B** (for bold), **Ctrl+I** (for italic), or **Ctrl+U** (for underline). You can apply all of these formats to a character, word, or paragraph.

EXERCISE 3-4
Modify Font Size and Color

Font size refers to how large or small characters are. Consider how much **emphasis**, or importance, you want to give the text when choosing its font size. For example, title text is generally large so that the title is highly visible. Adding color to a font can also bring attention to a key point. When using different colored fonts, make sure the colors you select contrast with the slide background. Light fonts work best on a dark background, while dark fonts are more readable against a light background.

Teaching Tip Point out to students that some colors may be difficult to read during an on-screen slide show.

FIGURE 3.7 Text with increased font size

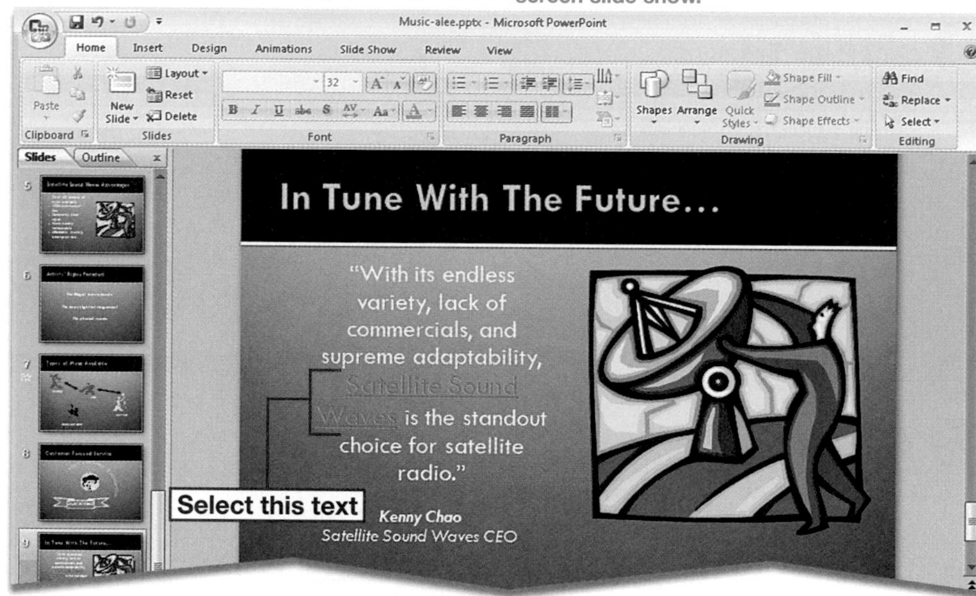

FIGURE 3.8 Text with modified color

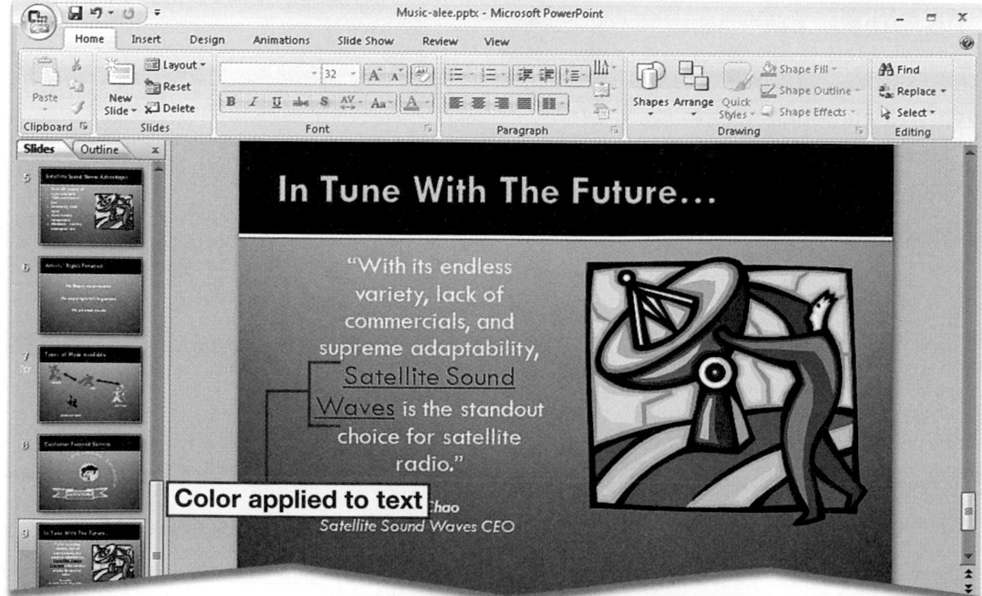

Step-By-Step

1. In your **Academic** file, choose **Review>Proofing> Word Count** .
2. In the **Word Count** dialog box, notice that the document contains 609 words (see Figure 4.13). Click **Close**.
3. On Page 1, click after the last sentence in the second paragraph (ends with **ocean floor**.).
4. Press the **spacebar** once. Key: Earthquakes can also occur well beneath Earth's surface.
5. On the **status bar**, click the text **Words: 617** to open the **Word Count** dialog box.
6. **CHECK** Your screen should look like Figure 4.14. Save your file.

Continue to the next exercise.

Academic Skills

The **Word Count** feature gives you a general sense of a document's length. Avoid cutting text to reach an exact target. Most teachers will not mind if your report is a little long if you support your ideas.

EXERCISE 4-7
Use Word Count

When creating documents such as reports, you may be asked to have a minimum or maximum number of words. **Word Count** tracks the number of words in a document or selection of text. You can also use this command to count the number of characters, paragraphs, and lines in a document. As you add or delete text, use this feature to recount the number of words in the document.

FIGURE 4.13 Word Count dialog box

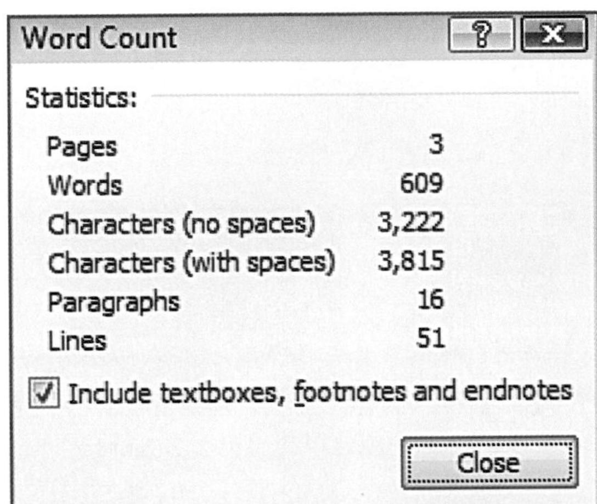

Step-By-Step Tip In **Step 3,** remind students that they can use **Find** to locate specific words or phrases in a document.

Differentiated Instruction/ Advanced Students You may want to give advanced students a general word limit for the report and have them decide which information they should remove to meet this limit.

NCLB/Language Arts (NCTE 5) Reinforce that students should not spend more time cutting or adding text to meet a target word count than they do communicating their original ideas.

FIGURE 4.14 Document with changed word count

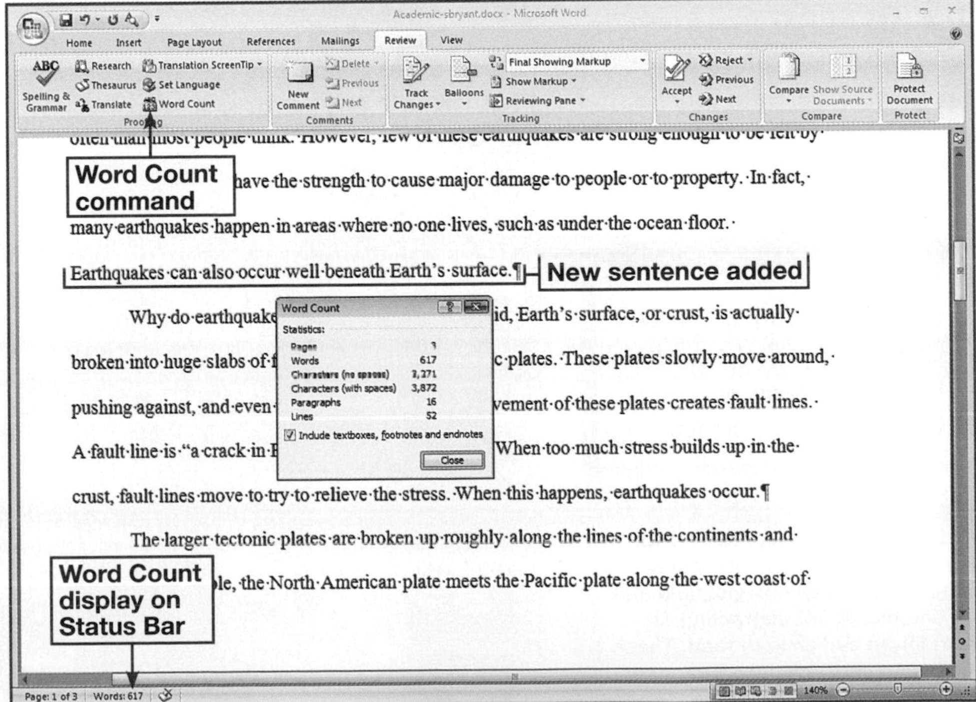

Step-By-Step

1. In your **Music** file, select **Slide 1**.
2. Select the text **In Tune with the Future**. Click the **Font Dialog Box Launcher**.
3. In the **Font** dialog box, under **Latin text font**, select **Comic Sans MS**.
4. Under **Font Style**, click **Bold**. Click **OK**.
5. Click anywhere in the slide to deselect the text.
6. **CHECK** Your screen should look similar to Figure 3.5.
7. Reselect the text **In Tune with the Future**. Click **Italic** *I*. Deselect the text.
8. **CHECK** Your screen should look similar to Figure 3.6. Save your file.

Continue to the next exercise.

You Should Know

Be aware of your audience. Choose fonts that are easy to read for those with vision-based difficulties.

NCLB/Language Arts (NCTE 4) Remind students that when they choose a font style they should look for one that is not distracting or hard for an audience to read. These kinds of styles can draw attention away from the presentation.

EXERCISE 3-3
Modify Fonts and Font Styles

Characters are individual letters, numbers, symbols, and punctuation marks. A **font** (also called a **typeface**) is the unique design of a set of characters. Some fonts are more serious (Times New Roman), while others are more fun (Comic Sans MS). Choose fonts that match the tone of your presentation. The **font style** refers to effects such as bold, italic, underline, and shadow. To preserve consistency, try not to use too many different fonts and styles when creating slides.

EL If you have English Learner students, point out fonts that have special characters such as é and ü. On the **Insert** tab, select **Symbol**.

FIGURE 3.5 Text with new font and style applied

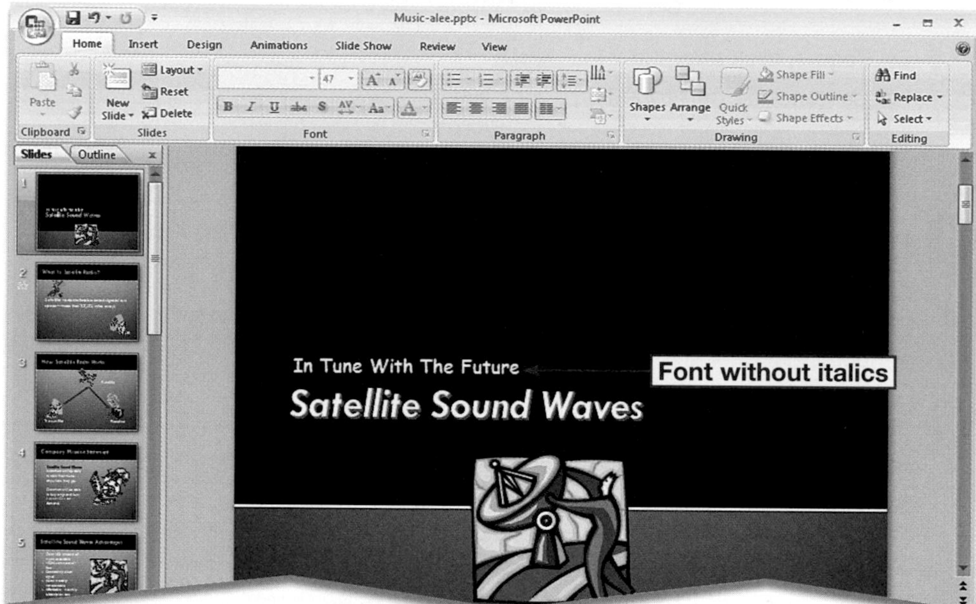

FIGURE 3.6 Text with Italic style applied

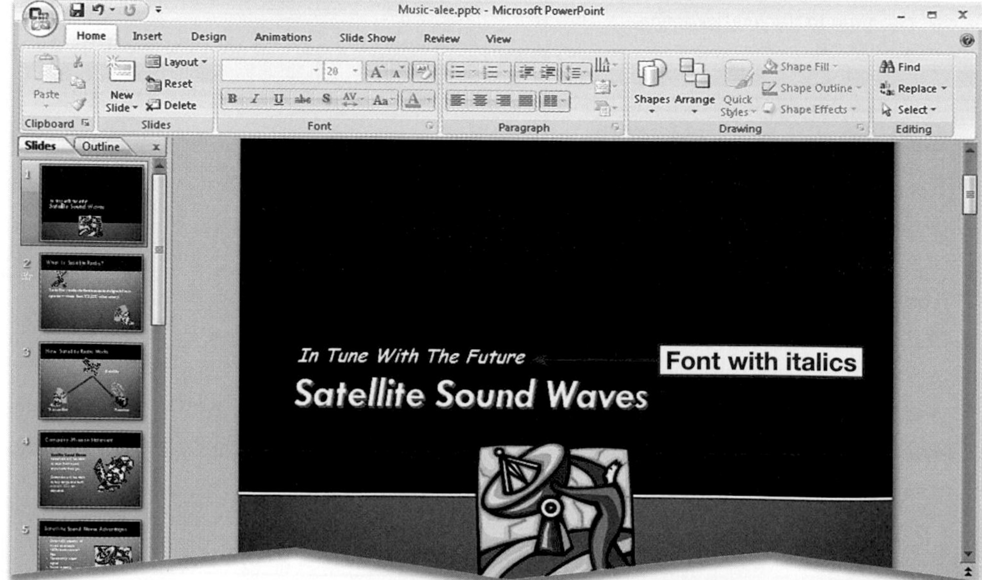

Writing MATTERS

Citing Sources in an Academic Report

When writing a research paper, give proper credit to the sources of your ideas. Presenting someone else's ideas or expressions as your own is plagiarism, which is a form of cheating.

Documenting Sources

The **Modern Language Association (MLA)** publishes guidelines on what information you should provide for all types of sources, including books, articles, and online sources. In general, you need to include the author's name, title of the work, and publication information, such as when and where the source was published. For Web sites, you also need to cite the date on which you accessed the page. Model citations are shown to the right.

Formatting Sources

Some general MLA formatting guidelines include:

- Entries in a Works Cited list should use hanging indention with the first line of each entry flush left and subsequent lines indented.
- Titles in a Works Cited list should be underlined and not italic.
- URLs (Internet addresses) should be surrounded by angle brackets <like this> in a Works Cited list.

Article Citation
Belanger, Ryan. "Hands-On Repairs."
Bicycling Magazine July 2009: 38–39.

Book Citation
Cole, Steve, and Sarah Rakitin.
Kids' Easy Bike Care: Tune-Ups, Tools, and Quick Fixes.
Charlotte, Vermont: Williamson, 2009.

Web Site Citation
Langley, Jim. "Fixing Flats Is Fun."
Bicycle Repair Page. Dec. 2009. Wrench Online.
9 Jan. 2010 <http://www.jimlangley.net/wrench/flattire.html>.

Different sources require different citations.

NCLB/Language Arts (NCTE 7) Emphasize to students how citing sources is an essential component to researching, evaluating, and synthesizing source material into an academic report.

NCLB/Language Arts (NCTE 8) It is important for students to choose a variety of sources, both electronic and print, that both support and refute the claims they raise in their academic research. Students should avoid picking only data with which they agree.

SKILLBUILDER

1. **Identify** What sources could you use to research a paper on how to repair a bicycle tire?
2. **Evaluate** Why do you think the MLA recommends using angle brackets to surround a URL in a Works Cited list?
3. **Analyze** Explain why you would or would not need to cite the source of the following information in a research paper: Driving over a sharp object will most likely cause a bicycle tire to puncture.

SkillBuilder answers can be found on page TM61.

Step-By-Step

1. In your **Music** file, select **Slide 5**.
2. Choose **Home>Slides>Layout** .
3. In the **Layout** drop-down menu, click the **Title, Text, and Content** layout (see Figure 3.3).
4. In the content placeholder, click the **Clip Art** icon.
5. In the **Search for** box, key: antennas.
6. Select an image similar to the one in Figure 3.4.
7. On the slide, use the sizing handles to enlarge the Clip Art.
8. **CHECK** Your screen should look similar to Figure 3.4. Save your file. Close the **Clip Art** task pane.

Continue to the next exercise.

You Should Know

Your presentation will be more interesting if you vary the layouts. For example, to add more text to the layout in this exercise, resize the picture and choose **Insert>Textbox**. PowerPoint lets you customize the layouts to meet your needs.

EXERCISE 3-2
Modify Slide Layout

Slide layout refers to how text, graphics, and other content are arranged on a slide. PowerPoint has two main slide layouts—Title and Title and Text. You can change a slide's layout to better fit the content you want to include. You can apply a new layout before you add content to a slide, or you can change the layout of a slide you have already created.

Step-By-Step Tip In **Step 5,** if students do not have access to appropriate Clip Art, they can use the Satellite data file supplied with the lesson.

FIGURE 3.3 Slide Layout drop-down menu

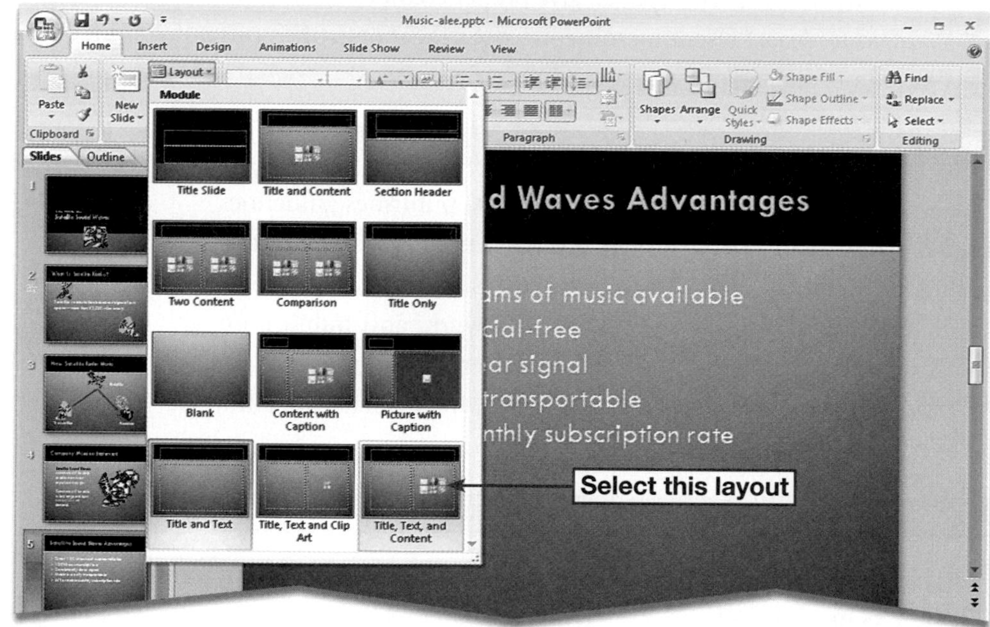

FIGURE 3.4 Slide with new layout and Clip Art

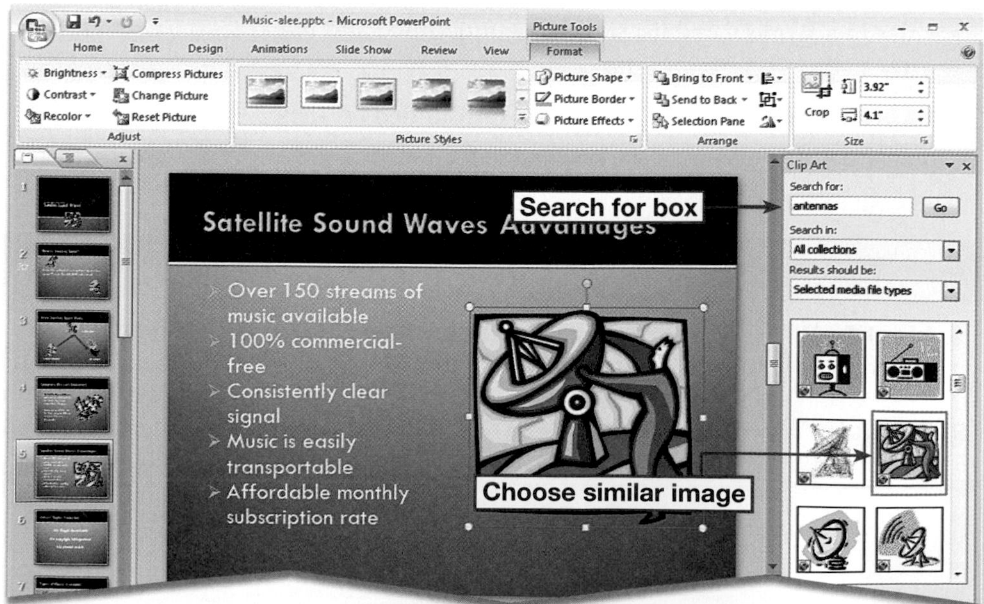

Step-By-Step

1. In your **Academic** file, on Page 2, in the second paragraph, click after the quotation mark that follows **factors** in the fourth line.

2. Press the **spacebar** once. Key: (Hernandez 33). Do not forget the period.

3. CHECK Your screen should look like Figure 4.15.

4. Move to the **Works Cited** list on Page 3. Click at the end of the first citation. Press ENTER once.

5. Key: Hernandez, Jaime. "The Role of the Seismologist." Understanding Earthquakes. Ed. Lynn Walters. Chicago: Earth Science Press, 2010. 32-40.

6. Select **Understanding Earthquakes**. Choose **Home>Font>Underline** U.

7. Select the citation. Choose **Paragraph>Dialog Box Launcher**. In the dialog box, under **Indentation**, in the **Special** box, make sure **Hanging** is selected. Click **OK**. Deselect the text.

8. CHECK Your screen should look like Figure 4.16. Save and close your file.

Continue to the next exercise.

EXERCISE 4-8
Insert and Format a Citation

MLA reports usually use parenthetical citations in the report body. These citations note the author's name and the page where the cited information is located. Every parenthetical citation has a corresponding citation in the Works Cited list. A complete citation includes such information as the author's name, the book or journal's title, and publication information. In MLA style, citations on the Works Cited page use a hanging indent.

Solution Use the file **Academic-SF.docx** as a solution file for **Exercises 4-1** through **4-8**.

FIGURE 4.15 Parenthetical citation added to academic report

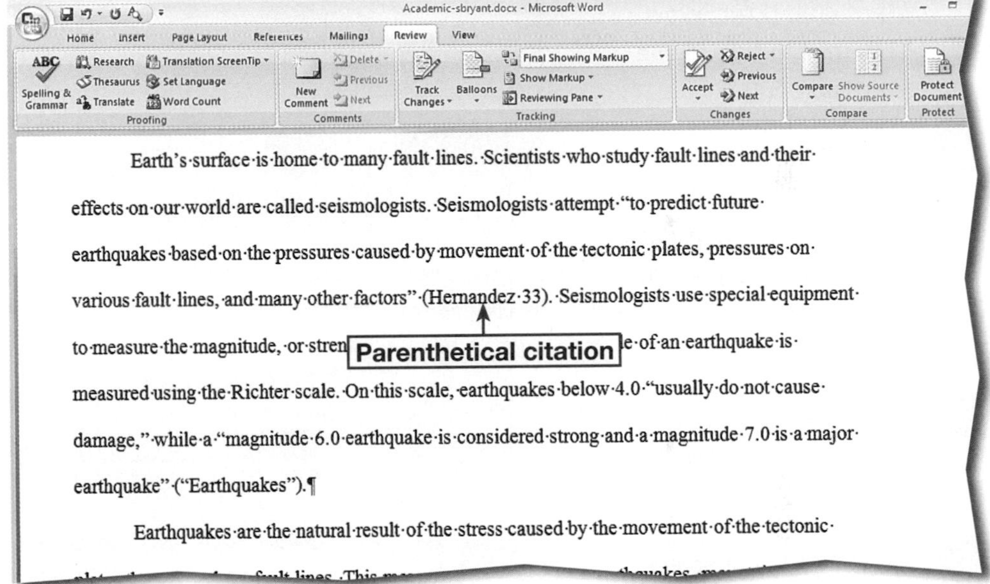

FIGURE 4.16 Citation added to Works Cited page

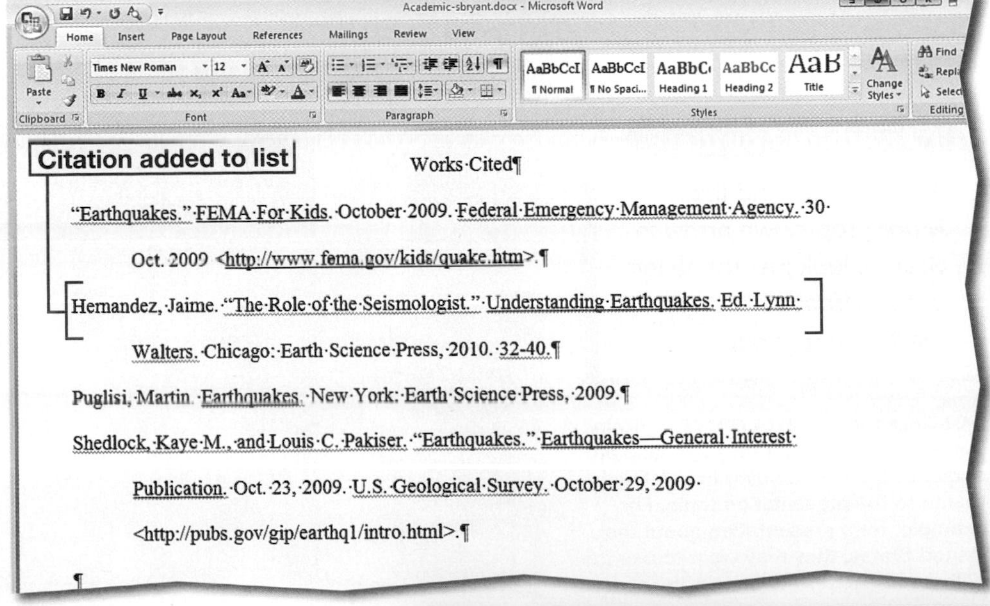

Step-By-Step

1. Locate and open the data file **Music.pptx**. Save as: Music-[your first initial and last name] (for example, *Music-alee*). In the **Slides** pane, select **Slide 1**.

2. On the **Design** tab, in the **Themes** group, click the **More** drop-down arrow. Click the **Module** theme (see Figure 3.1).

3. Select **Slide 2**. On the **Design** tab, in the **Background** group, click **Background Styles**. In the drop-down menu, click **Style 7**.

4. On the **Design** tab, in the **Themes** group, click **Fonts**. Select **Median**.

5. **CHECK** Your screen should look like Figure 3.2. Save your file.

Continue to the next exercise.

Troubleshooter

If you cannot find the **More** drop-down arrow in **Step 3**, look just to the left of the **Effects** button in the **Themes** group.

NCLB/Language Arts (NCTE 5) Reinforce to students that they can help an audience's understanding by relating a theme to the presentation topic. For example, for a presentation about the United States, they may want to use the colors red, white, and blue in the slides.

EXERCISE 3-1
Apply Design Themes

A theme is a type of template that adds visual interest to a presentation and helps to give it a consistent look, or **formatting**. When selecting a theme, think about what you want the tone of your presentation to be. Some combinations of colors and fonts set a serious tone, while other combinations create a fun look. Know your audience, and select a theme that supports or matches the purpose of your presentation.

Step-By-Step Tip In Step 1, be sure students know where to find and where to save their data files.

FIGURE 3.1 More Themes drop-down menu

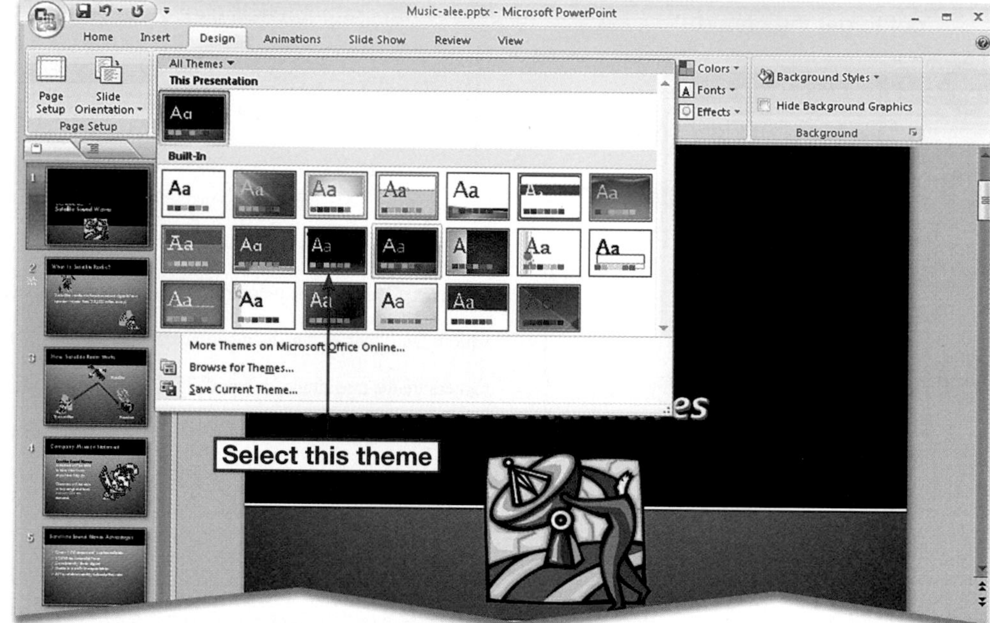

FIGURE 3.2 Design applied to slide

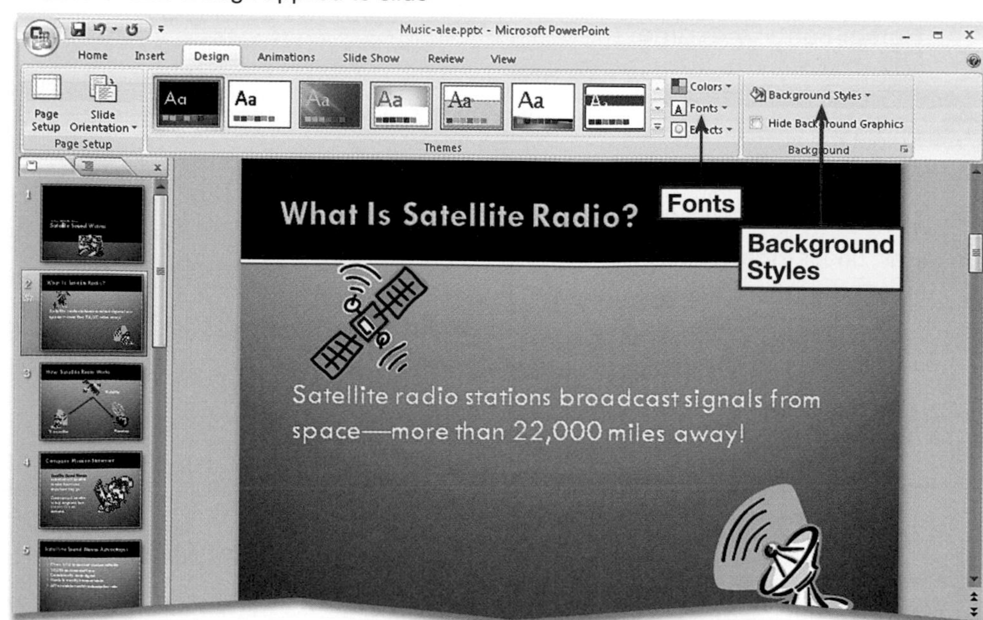

Step-By-Step

1 Locate and open the data file **Endnotes.docx**. Save as: Endnotes-[your first initial and last name].

2 On Page 2, click after the quotation mark after **factors** in the fourth line of the second paragraph.

3 Choose **References> Footnotes>Dialog Box Launcher**.

4 In the dialog box, under **Location**, click **Endnotes**. Make sure **End of document** is selected. In the **Number format** box, make sure **1, 2, 3** is selected (see Figure 4.17). Click **Insert**.

5 On the **Notes** page, select **3**. Format the font **Times New Roman, 12 pt**.

6 Click after the **3**. Key the endnote text shown in Figure 4.18. Press ENTER.

7 Select the citation. Choose **Home>Paragraph>Dialog Box Launcher**. In the **Special** box, select **First line**. In the **Line spacing** box, select **Double**. Click **OK**. Deselect the text.

8 **CHECK** Your screen should look like Figure 4.18. Save and close your file.

Continue to the next exercise.

EXERCISE 4-9
Insert and Format an Endnote

An **endnote** is used to cite references or to give more detail about something in the text. Endnotes appear at the end of the document or at the end of a section. Although endnotes are not generally used in MLA style, they can be used in place of parenthetical citations to provide source information. If you use endnotes, they should appear at the end of the document on a separate page titled Notes.

Step-By-Step Tip In **Step 5,** if students have difficulty seeing the **3,** have them increase the **Zoom.**

FIGURE 4.17 Footnote and Endnote dialog box

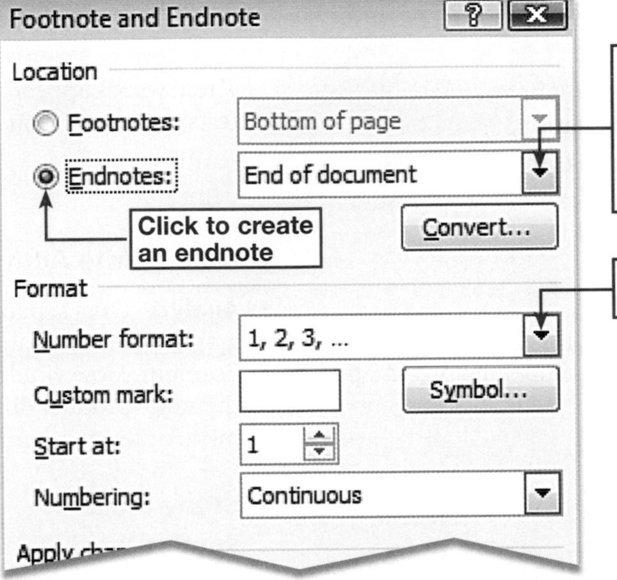

Teaching Tip Let students know they can choose **References> Insert Endnote** to quickly insert an endnote.

FIGURE 4.18 Endnote inserted at end of document

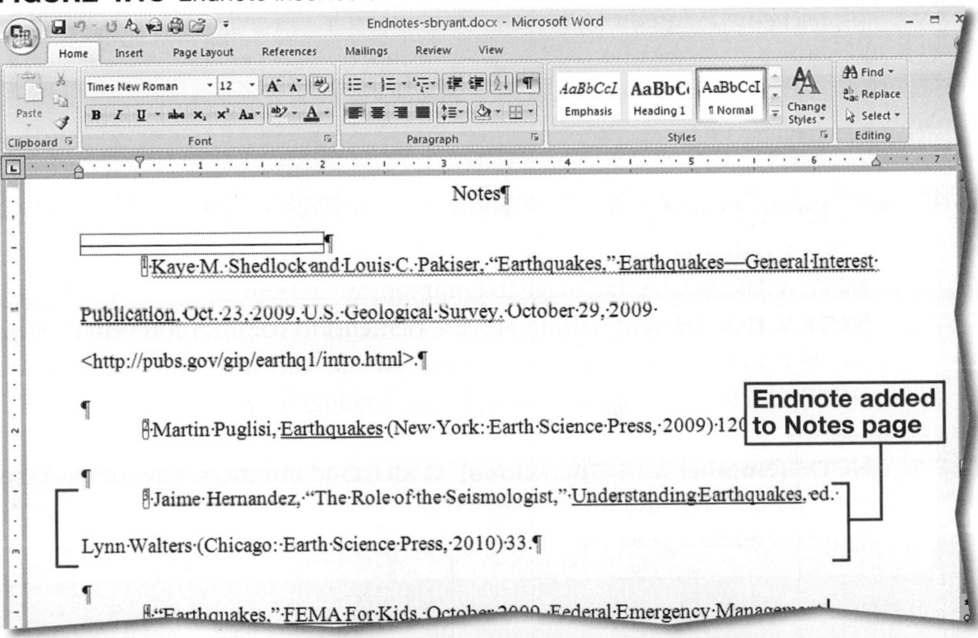

Solution Use the file **Endnote-SF.docx** as a solution file for this activity.

LESSON 3 Reading Guide

Before You Read

See page TM42 for English Learner activity suggestions.

Pace Yourself Short blocks of concentrated reading repeated frequently are more effective than one long session. Focus on reading for 10 minutes. Take a short break. Then read for another 10 minutes.

Read To Learn

- Choose fonts, colors, and effects that work with the goals of your presentation.
- Animate graphics to enhance your presentation.
- Explore how transitions can make your presentation more professional in appearance.

Main Idea

PowerPoint features many formatting options that allow you to create visually compelling presentations.

Vocabulary

Key Terms

alignment
animation scheme
background
color scheme
fill color
font
font style
footer
Format Painter
formatting
gradient
header
landscape
line color
portrait
rotate
slide layout
Slide Master
transition
typeface

Academic Vocabulary

These words appear in your reading and on your tests. Make sure you know their meanings.

anticipate
emphasis

Quick Write Activity

Analyze On a separate sheet of paper, analyze how graphics and formatting impact a magazine advertisement. How would a PowerPoint presentation for the same product differ from the ad? Would you use more or fewer graphics or text?

Study Skills

Routine Break Taking regular study breaks can actually help you to get your work done faster. When you feel your attention drifting, take a few minutes to change your environment, and then go back to your studies.

Academic Standards

English Language Arts

NCTE 4 Use written language to communicate effectively.

NCTE 5 Use different writing process elements to communicate effectively.

NCTE 7 Conduct research and gather, evaluate, and synthesize data to communicate discoveries.

NCTE 12 Use language to accomplish individual purposes.

Math

NCTM (Number and Operations) Understand numbers, ways of representing numbers, relationships among numbers, and number systems.

NCTM (Number and Operations) Compute fluently and make reasonable estimates.

Step-By-Step

1. Locate and open the data file **Footnotes.docx**. Save as: Footnotes-[your first initial and last name].

2. On Page 2, click after the quotation mark after **factors** in the fourth line of the third paragraph.

3. Choose **References>Footnotes>Dialog Box Launcher**.

4. In the dialog box, under **Location**, select **Footnotes** and **Bottom of page** (see Figure 4.19).

5. Under **Format**, for **Number format**, make sure **1, 2, 3** is selected. Click **Insert**.

6. At the bottom of the page, select the **3** that was just inserted. Format the font **Times New Roman, 12 pt.**

7. Click after the **3**. Key the footnote text in Figure 4.20.

8. Select the citation. Choose **Home>Paragraph>Dialog Box Launcher**. In the **Special** box, select **First line**. In the **Line spacing** box, select **Double**. Click **OK**. Deselect the text.

9. **CHECK** Your screen should look like Figure 4.20. Save and close your file.

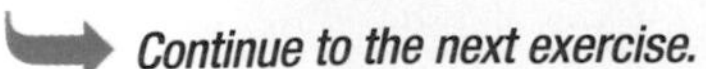
Continue to the next exercise.

EXERCISE 4-10
Insert and Format a Footnote

Like an endnote, a **footnote** is used to cite sources or to give more detail about something in the text. While endnotes appear at the end of a document, footnotes appear at the bottom, or the foot, of the page. Although footnotes, like endnotes, are not generally used in MLA style, they can be used in place of parenthetical citations to provide source information.

FIGURE 4.19 Footnote and Endnote dialog box

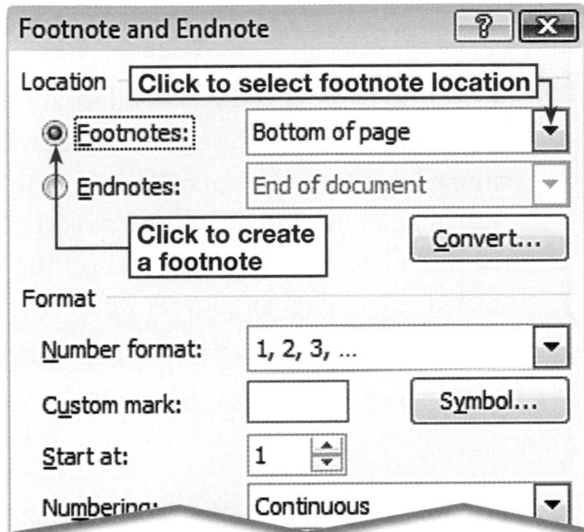

FIGURE 4.20 Report with footnote inserted

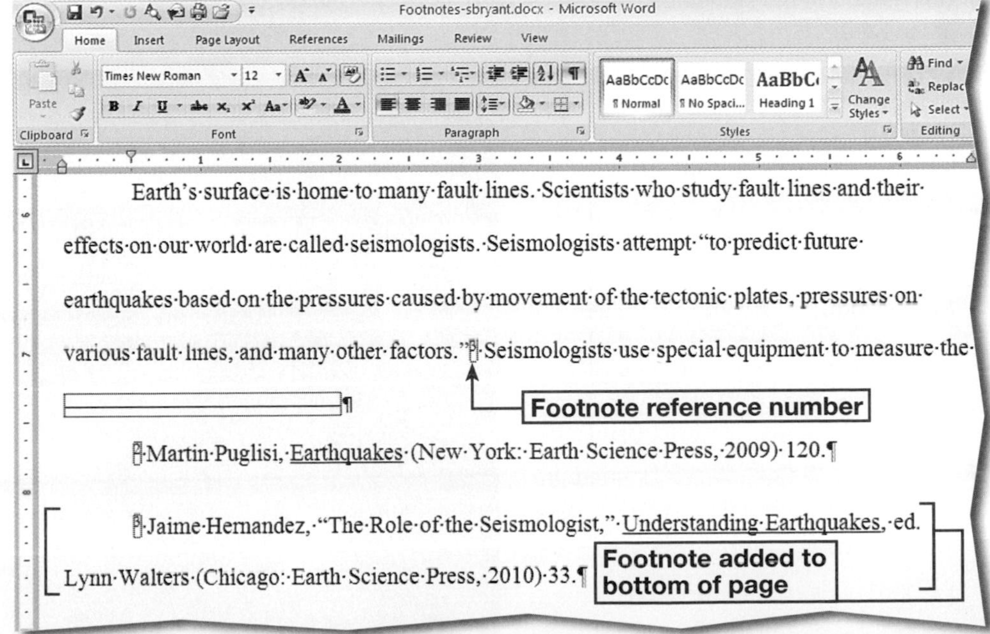

Solution Use the file **Footnotes-SF.docx** as a solution file for this exercise.

LESSON 3 Format Content

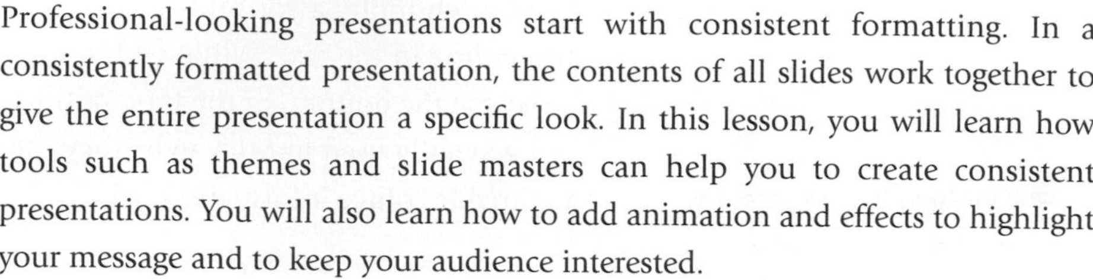

Professional-looking presentations start with consistent formatting. In a consistently formatted presentation, the contents of all slides work together to give the entire presentation a specific look. In this lesson, you will learn how tools such as themes and slide masters can help you to create consistent presentations. You will also learn how to add animation and effects to highlight your message and to keep your audience interested.

Key Concepts

- Customize slide backgrounds
- Modify slide layouts, fonts, and text
- Modify and add effects to pictures, shapes, and graphics
- Apply animation and transition effects
- Work with slide masters
- Modify page setup
- Use headers and footers

Standards

The following standards are covered in this lesson. Refer to pages xxv and 715 for a description of the standards listed here.

ISTE Standards Correlation

NETS•S

1a, 1b, 2a, 2b, 3b, 3c, 5a, 5b, 5c, 5d, 6a, 6b, 6d

Microsoft Certified Application Specialist

PowerPoint

1.2, 1.3, 1.4, 2.2, 2.4, 3.4, 3.5, 4.4

21st CENTURY SKILLS

See page TM94 for answer to 21st Century Skills.

Practice Ethical Behavior Ethics are the principles of conduct that govern a group or society. Practicing ethical behavior is an important part of a successful future. An ethical code of behavior is one where you behave in a way you feel is just and fair. For instance, if you took credit for a friend's hard work, that would be unethical. Your friend should get the credit if they worked hard and completed something. Employees who behave ethically do not lie, cheat, or steal. *What ethical behaviors should you practice at school?*

Writing MATTERS

Creating a Business Report

The main purpose of a business report is to present and analyze information. What information you present, and how, will depend on the purpose of the report.

Parts of a Business Report

Most business reports have three main parts: front matter, body, and back matter. The front matter includes pages such as the title page and the table of contents. The body contains the report's main information. Headings are often used to separate topics in the body if the report is long. The end matter contains pages such as the end notes page and the bibliography.

Format the Report

Here are some guidelines for formatting a simple business report:

- Use default side and bottom margins.
- Leave an approximate 2-inch top margin on select pages, including the first page of the report body and the Table of Contents, Endnote, and Bibliography pages.
- Use headers and footers to display page numbers, the name of the report, the date, and other information. The title page should not display any header or footer information.

Cite Sources in a Business Report

You can use either footnotes or endnotes to cite your sources in a business report. Models for both citations are shown on the right.

Footnote

[1] Hahn Jack, "Using Focus Groups," *Collected Business Essays,* New York, All Biz Publishing, 2009.

Endnote

1. Fine Cecilia, "Location is Everything," *Business Analysis Monthly,* August, 2010.

Footnotes and endnotes are formatted similarly.

NCLB/Language Arts (NCTE 4) Reinforce the differences between an academic audience and a business audience. A business report is likely to be very different than an academic report on the same topic.

NCLB/Language Arts (NCTE 7) Explain to students that the research skills they practice in school will be applied in the business world as well.

Skillbuilder answers can be found on page TM61.

SKILLBUILDER

1. **Identify** What are the three main parts of a business report?
2. **Summarize** What are three guidelines that you should remember when formatting a business report?
3. **Plan** You work for a CD store, and you want to propose opening a branch of the store in a new neighborhood. Key an informal paragraph explaining what you would include in your business report.

LESSON 2 Challenge Yourself Projects

Before You Begin

Present Yourself Giving a good presentation is an extension of making a good impression. These projects teach you how to use your skills to give a professional and error-free presentation.

Reflect Once you complete the projects, open a Word document and answer the following:

1. What types of visual elements did you add to the presentation and why?
2. What types of errors did you find when you reviewed your classmate's presentation?
3. Which project took you the longest time and why?

Answers Rubrics for each Challenge Yourself Project are available at **glencoe.com.** You may want to download the rubrics and make them available to students as they complete each project.

9. Create a Presentation

Rubric

LEVEL This is an intermediate level project

Language Arts: Identify Text for Slides You have a client who is coming to town for an important meeting. Your client has never been to your town. Use a theme to create a presentation that will prepare your client for her visit. In your presentation:

- Identify where your client is staying.
- Identify where the meeting is being held.
- Identify two sites that your client should know about (for example, places to eat, where the local movie theater is, and so on).
- Provide a brief schedule in a table for your client. Include when the client will arrive in town, when the meeting is being held, and when the client will leave town.

Your presentation should include at least five slides. Save your presentation as: p2rev-[your first initial and last name]9.

10. Add Content to Slides

Rubric

LEVEL This is an intermediate level project

Language Arts: Create Contact Information Using Visuals Open the presentation you created in Project 9. Add at least one piece of Clip Art or a photo and at least one piece of WordArt or an AutoShape.

Add a table to your presentation that provides important contact information for your client (e.g., the hotel's telephone number, your telephone number, etc.). Add a second slide that uses an organizational chart to give your client an overview of your company's structure.

Save your presentation as: p2rev-[your first initial and last name]10.

11. Review a Presentation

Rubric

LEVEL This is an advanced level project

Language Arts: Edit Content With your teacher's permission, team up with another member of your class. Exchange the presentations that you each created in Projects 9 and 10. Review your classmate's presentation. As you review:

- Correct any misspellings or other errors you might find.
- Use the Thesaurus to suggest a change of wording on one slide.
- Insert comments with constructive suggestions.
- When finished, go back over your classmate's suggestions.
- Make any edits that you think will improve your presentation.

Save your presentation as: p2rev-[your first initial and last name]11.

Step-By-Step

1 Locate and open the data file **Business.docx**. Save as: Business-[your first initial and last name].

2 Go to Page 2. Click before the head **Business Overview**.

3 Choose **Page Layout> Page Setup>Breaks**. Under **Section Breaks**, select **Next Page**.

4 CHECK Your page should look like Figure 4.21.

5 Click **Section Break**. When the cursor appears to the left of the break, press DELETE.

6 Repeat **Step 3** two more times.

7 Scroll up. Click before the second section break. Press ENTER.

8 CHECK Your screen should look like Figure 4.22. Save your file.

Continue to the next exercise.

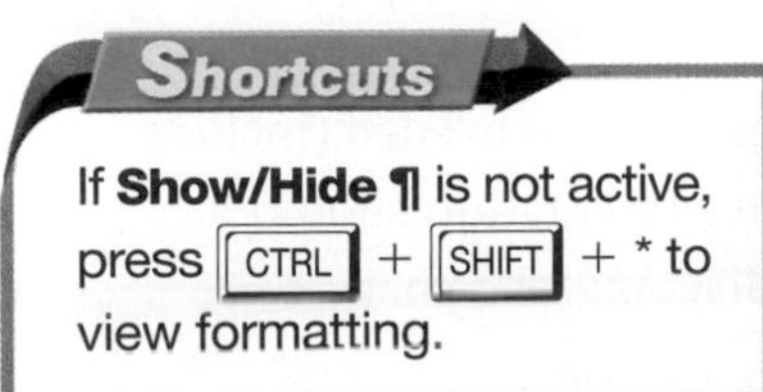

Shortcuts
If **Show/Hide ¶** is not active, press CTRL + SHIFT + * to view formatting.

Teaching Tip If the section indicator is not visible in the status bar as shown in Figure 4.21, have students right-click inside the status bar and select **Section**.

EXERCISE 4-11
Insert and Delete Section Breaks

A blank Word document consists of one **section**, or part. A simple report usually has three main sections: the front matter, the report body, and the end matter. Inserting a **section break** divides a document into different sections. Each section in a document can be formatted differently. Dividing a report into sections makes it easier to apply specific margins and other formatting to the report's individual parts.

FIGURE 4.21 Section break inserted into a document

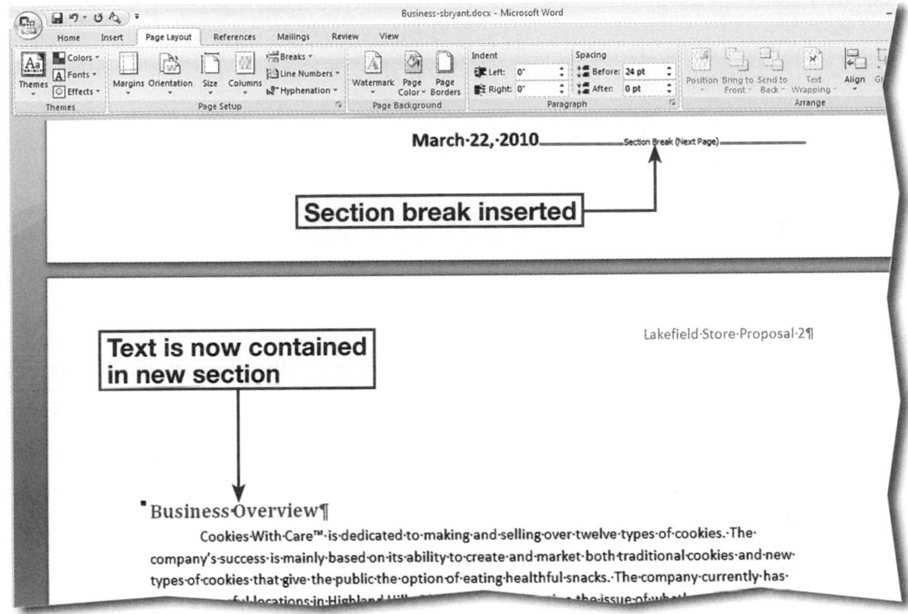

FIGURE 4.22 A new page created using section breaks

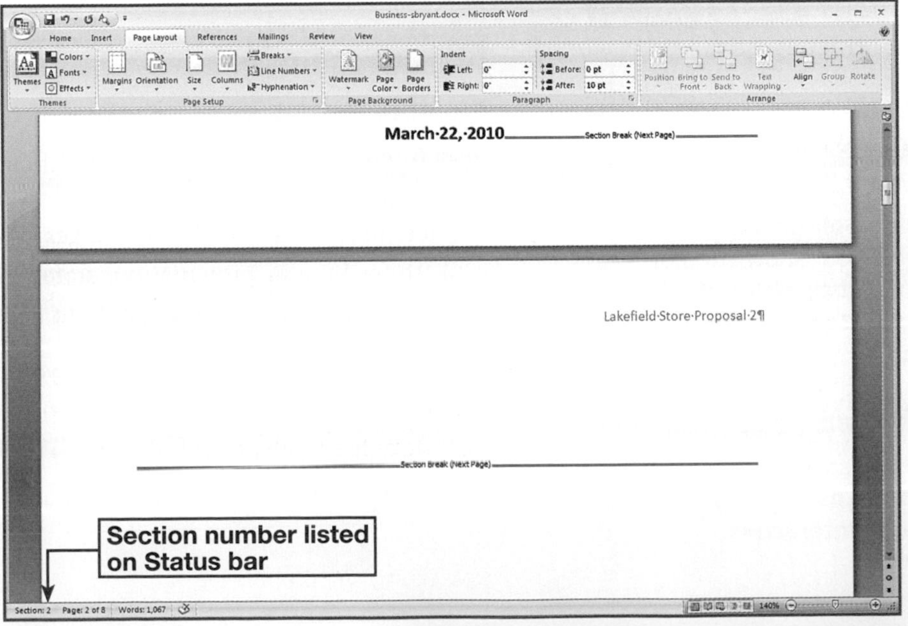

LESSON 2 Critical Thinking Activities

Beyond the Classroom Activity
The presentation should be free of spelling errors, contain several comments, and have at least one word that has been changed.

Standards at Work Activity
Students should add a new slide to their Sales-6 presentation. The slide should contain a hierarchical SmartArt diagram with all boxes filled in and recolored and restyled using Quick Styles.

21st Century Skills Activity
Students should create a presentation including at least two illustrations and a table, chart, or diagram. The presentation should encourage audience participation in a charity walkathon.

6. Beyond the Classroom Activity

Language Arts: Review a Presentation You are reviewing a coworker's presentation. Open the data file **Sales.pptx**. Save as: Sales-[your first initial and last name]6. Use what you learned in this lesson to edit the presentation and suggest changes. You should:

- Check spelling.
- Add comments.
- Use the Thesaurus to change at least one word.
- Include a comment evaluating the theme, color scheme, and graphics used in the presentation. Suggest some alternatives.

7. Standards at Work Activity

Microsoft Certified Application Specialist Correlation
PowerPoint 3.1 *Create SmartArt diagrams*

Create a Hierarchy Diagram You decide that your **Sales** presentation should include a SmartArt diagram showing the hierarchy of the sales department. Open your saved **Sales-6** file. On a new slide, create a hierarchical SmartArt diagram. Make the following changes to the diagram:

- Add the names and titles of the Sales Department employees
- Change the color of the diagram
- Add effects using Quick Styles

Save your work as: Sales-[your first initial and last name]7.

8. 21st Century Skills Activity

Promote Getting Involved A local charity is planning a walkathon to raise money for cancer research. As a member of the charity, you want to encourage people to participate in the event. Use a design theme to create a brief presentation that encourages people to get involved with the walkathon. In your presentation, state what the issue is, why the issue is important, and what people can do to get involved.

Add Clip Art, photos, and WordArt to your presentation as needed (include at least two graphics in your presentation). Your presentation should also include at least one of the following: a table, a diagram, or a chart.

Save your file as: p2rev-[your first initial and last name]8.

Go Online **e-REVIEW**
glencoe.com

Go to the **Online Learning Center** to complete the following review activities.

Online Self Check
To test your knowledge of the material, click **Unit 4> Lesson 2** and choose **Self Checks**.

Interactive Review
To review the main points of this lesson, choose **Unit 4>Lesson 2** and choose **Interactive Review.**

EXERCISE 4-12
Create and Format a Table of Contents

A **table of contents** lists the topics in a document along with their page numbers. You can create a table of contents automatically. By default, the table of contents will include all text that is formatted as the style Heading 1, Heading 2, or Heading 3.

FIGURE 4.23 Table of contents inserted into Section 2

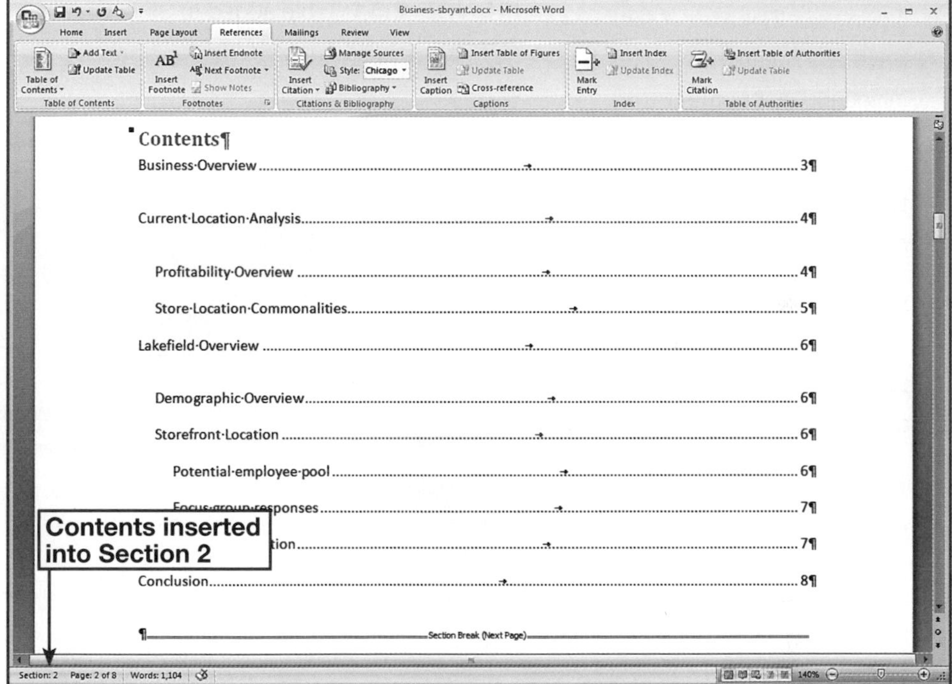

FIGURE 4.24 Modified table of contents

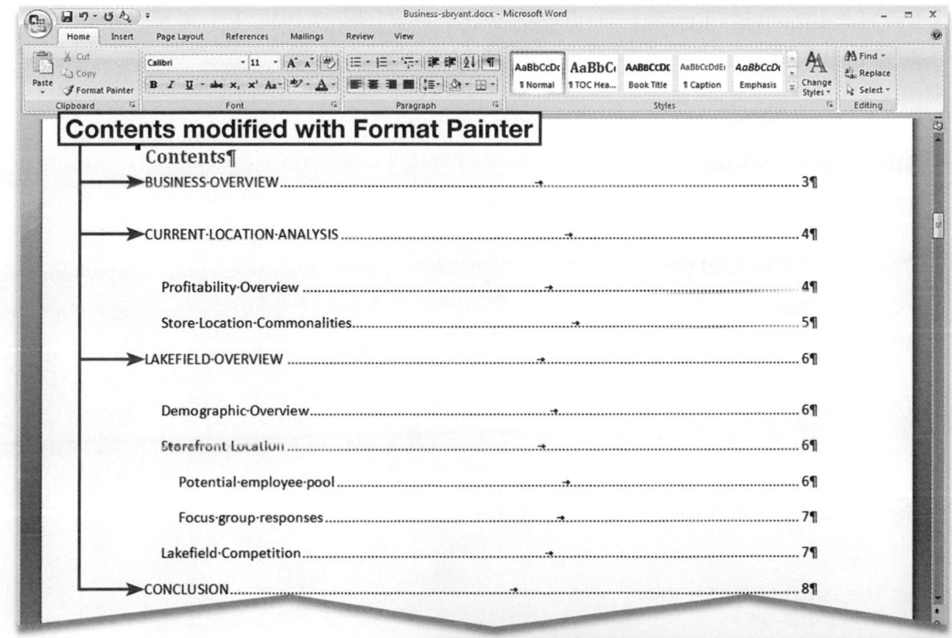

Step-By-Step

1. In your **Business** file, select the paragraph mark next to the second section break. Choose **Home>Font>Clear Formatting**.
2. Choose **References>Table of Contents>Automatic Table 1**.
3. **CHECK** Your screen should look like Figure 4.23. Select the text **Business Overview**. Choose **Home>Font>Dialog Box Launcher**. Check **All Caps**. Click **OK**.
4. With the text still selected, double-click **Format Painter**. Select **Current Location Analysis**, **Lakefield Overview**, and **Conclusion**.
5. Click **Format Painter** once. Deselect the table of contents.
6. **CHECK** Your screen should look like Figure 4.24. Save your file.

Continue to the next exercise.

Differentiated Instruction/ Advanced Students Have students explore the other formatting options in the Font dialog box.

LESSON 2 You Try It Activities

Step-By-Step

1. Open your **Theater-4** file. Save as: Theater-[your first initial and last name]5.
2. Select **Slide 5**. Insert a table with 3 columns and 4 rows.
3. Fill the table in using the information shown in Figure 2.51. Resize the table as necessary.
4. CHECK Your screen should look like Figure 2.51.
5. Check spelling. Make any needed corrections to **Slide 2**.
6. Add a new **Slide 8**. Add the text shown in Figure 2.52 to the slide.
7. Choose **AutoShapes> Stars and Banners** to add a star to **Slide 8**.
8. Use WordArt to add the word **Welcome!** to **Slide 8**.
9. CHECK Your screen should look like Figure 2.58.
10. Save and close the file.

Solution The solution file for this activity is **Theater5-SF**.

5. Create Tables and Check Spelling

You need to add a table including all of the managers' contact information for all employees. You must complete You Try It Activity 4 before doing this activity.

New Student Strategy If a student did not complete You Try It Activity 4, then the solution file for that activity can be used as a data file for this activity.

FIGURE 2.51 Table added to Slide 5

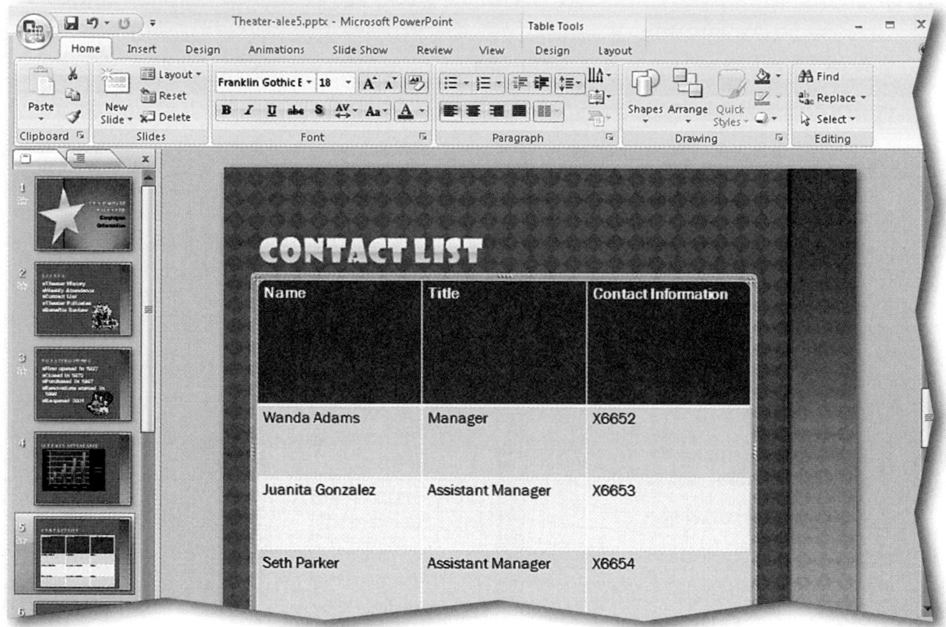

FIGURE 2.52 New Slide 8

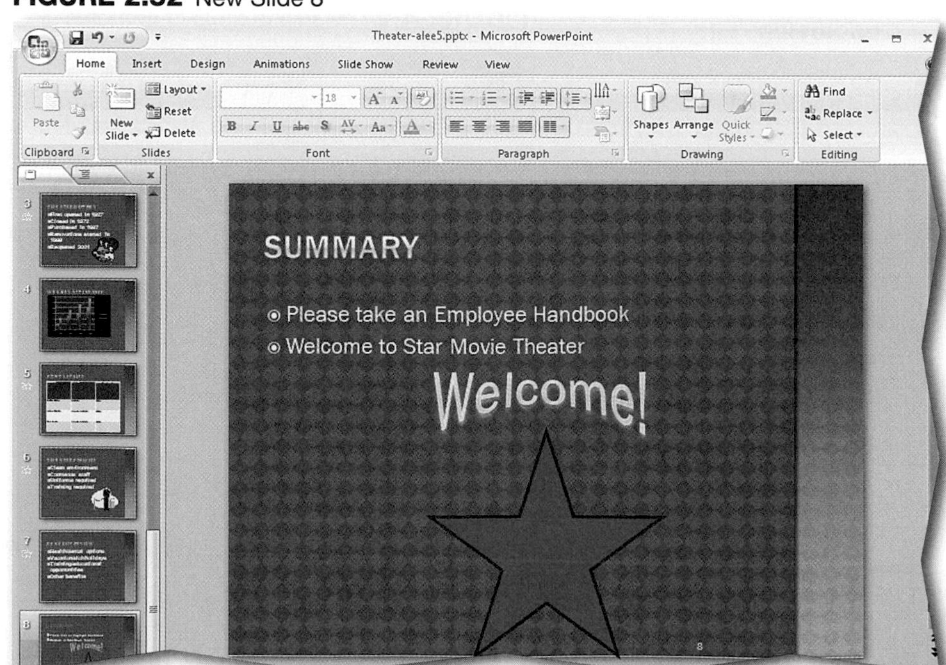

EXERCISE 4-13
Format Different Sections in a Document

Section breaks can help you to create an appropriate header and footer for each part of a formal report. The first page of a formal report should not display any header or footer information. Other introductory pages, such as the table of contents, should display a roman numeral in the page's footer. Unlinking headers and footers from other sections allows you to change headers and footers on individual pages in the document while leaving others unchanged.

Step-By-Step Tip In **Step 4**, let students know that the ScreenTip for **Next Section** reads *Show Next*.

FIGURE 4.25 Page number removed from Section 1 header

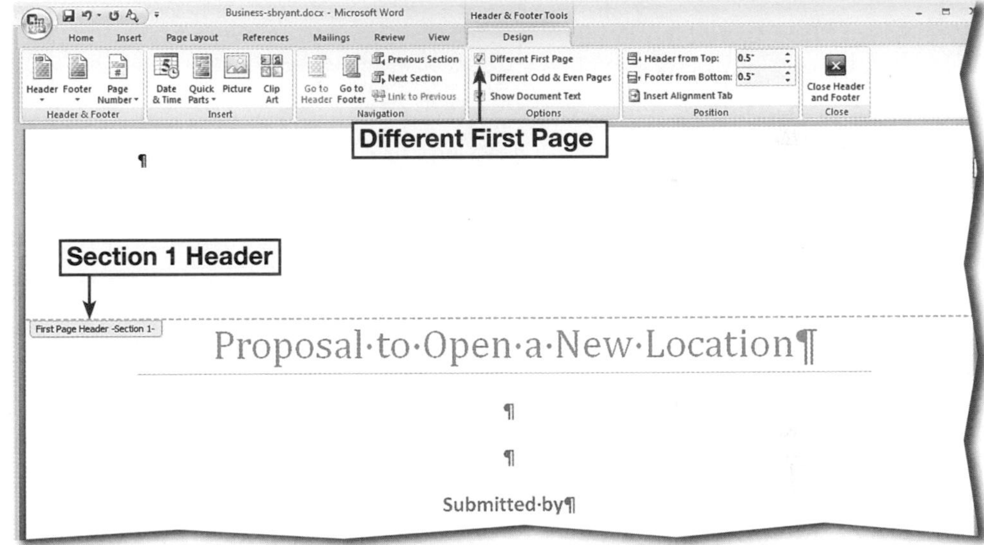

FIGURE 4.26 Section 2 header unlinked from Section 1 header

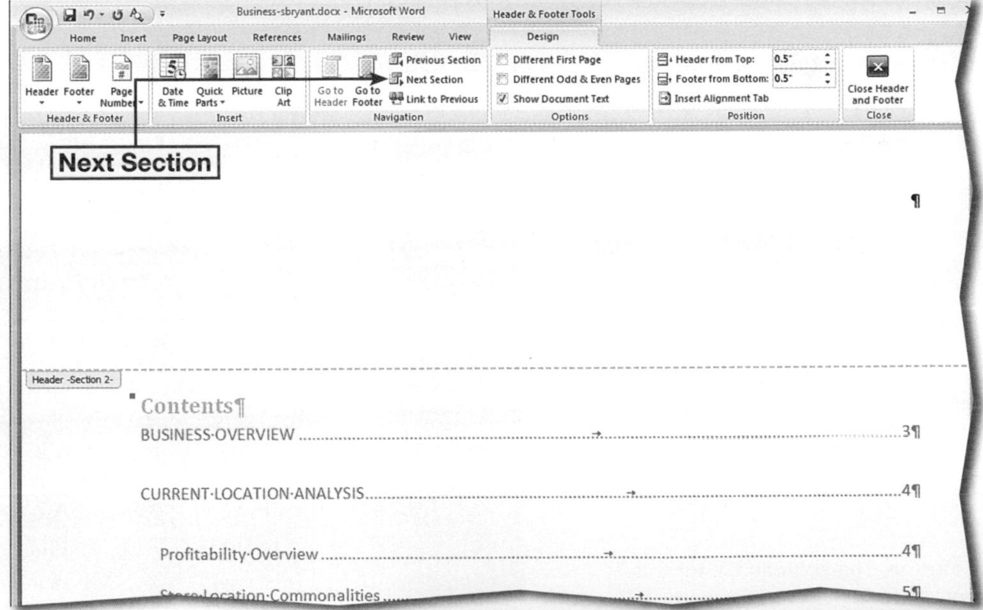

Step-By-Step

1. In your **Business** file, press CTRL + HOME. Choose **Insert>Header & Footer>Header>Edit Header**.
2. Under **Header & Footer Tools>Design>Options**, check **Different First Page**.
3. **CHECK** Your screen should look like Figure 4.25. Click **Header & Footer Tools>Design> Navigation>Next Section**. With the insertion point in the Section 2 header, in the **Navigation** group, click **Link to Previous** to deselect it. Delete the header text.
4. **CHECK** Your screen should look like Figure 4.26. In the **Navigation** group, click **Go to Footer**.
5. With the insertion point in the Section 2 footer, deselect **Link to Previous**.
6. In the **Header & Footer** group, choose **Page Number>Current Position>Plain Number**.
7. Choose **Insert>Header & Footer>Page Number> Format Page Numbers**.

Continued on the next page.

LESSON 2 You Try It Activities

4. Add Content to Slides

Data File

You are an assistant manager for the Star Movie Theater. Your manager asked you to develop a PowerPoint presentation to help orient new employees.

Step-By-Step

1. Open the data file **Theater.pptx**. Save as: Theater-[your first initial and last name]4.
2. Select **Slide 2**. Add the data file **Theater.wmf** to the slide. Resize the image as necessary.
3. Select **Slide 4**. Add a **clustered column** chart to the slide.
4. Fill in the chart worksheet using the information shown in Figure 2.49.
5. CHECK Your screen should look like Figure 2.49.
6. Close the Excel worksheet.
7. Apply **Style 42** from the **Chart Styles** drop-down menu.
8. CHECK Your screen should look like Figure 2.50.
9. Save and close the file.

Solution The solution file for this activity is **Theater4-SF**.

FIGURE 2.49 Chart added to Slide 4

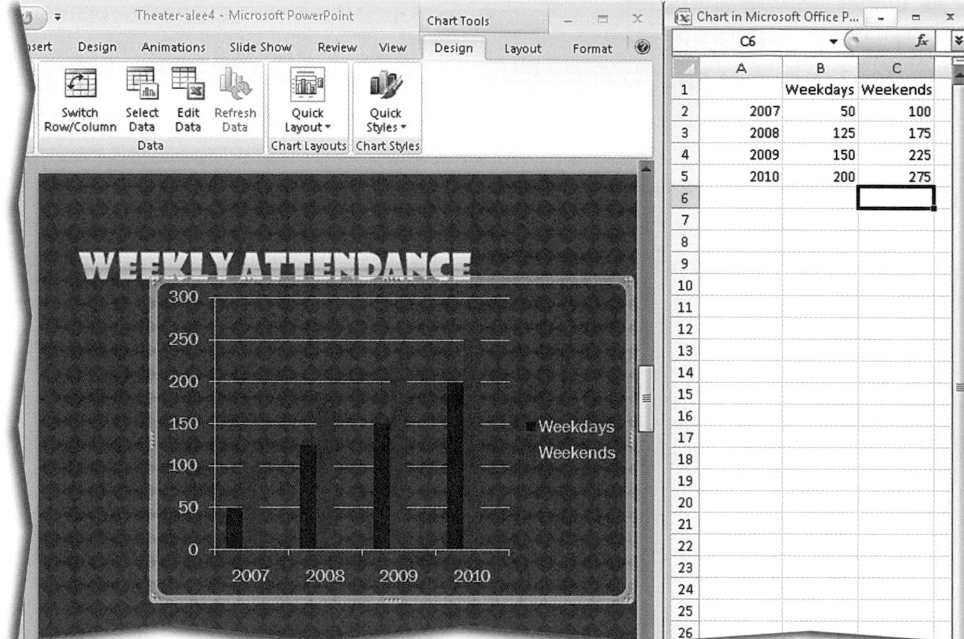

FIGURE 2.50 Chart with Chart Styles applied

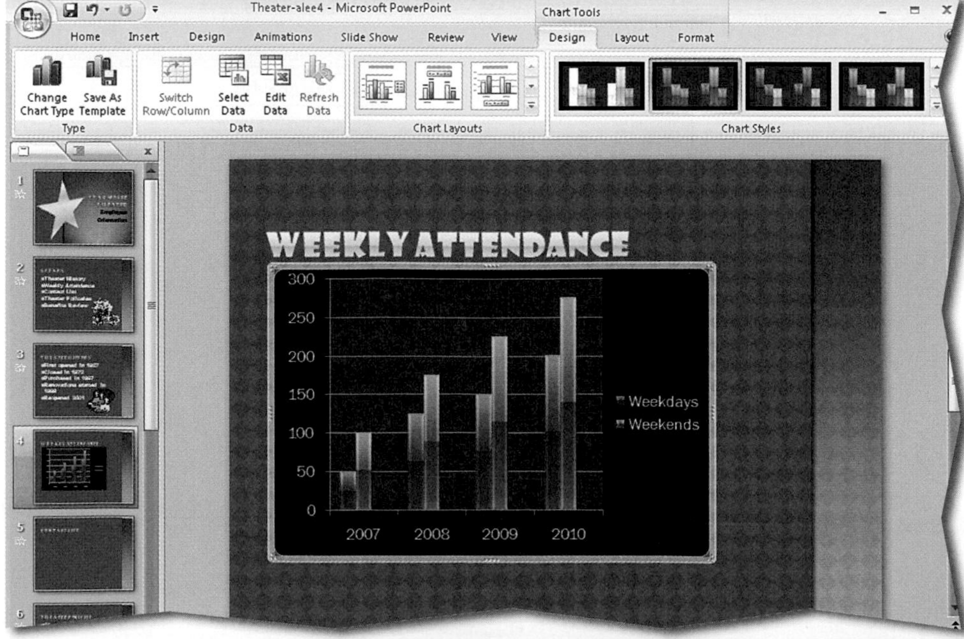

Step-By-Step

EXERCISE 4-13 (Continued)
Format Different Sections in a Document

EL When inserting page numbers, make sure EL students understand the correlation between **1, 2, 3** and **i, ii, iii.**

8. In the **Page Number Format** dialog box, under **Number format**, select **i, ii, iii**. In **Page numbering**, click the **Start at** box and key: ii. Click **OK**. In the footer, select **ii**. In the mini toolbar, click **Center**. Deselect the text.

9. CHECK Your screen should look like Figure 4.27. Click the Section 3 header. Deselect **Link to Previous**.

10. Key: Lakefield Store Proposal. Press the spacebar once. Choose **Insert>Header & Footer>Page Number> Current Position> Plain Number**.

11. Select the number. Choose **Insert>Header & Footer> Page Number>Format Page Numbers**. Under **Page numbering**, click the **Start at** box. Key: 1. Click **OK**. Deselect the text.

12. CHECK Your screen should look like Figure 4.28. Click the Section 3 footer. Deselect **Link to Previous**. Delete the page number. Click **Close Header and Footer**. Save your file.

Continue to the next exercise.

FIGURE 4.27 Roman numeral added to Section 2 footer

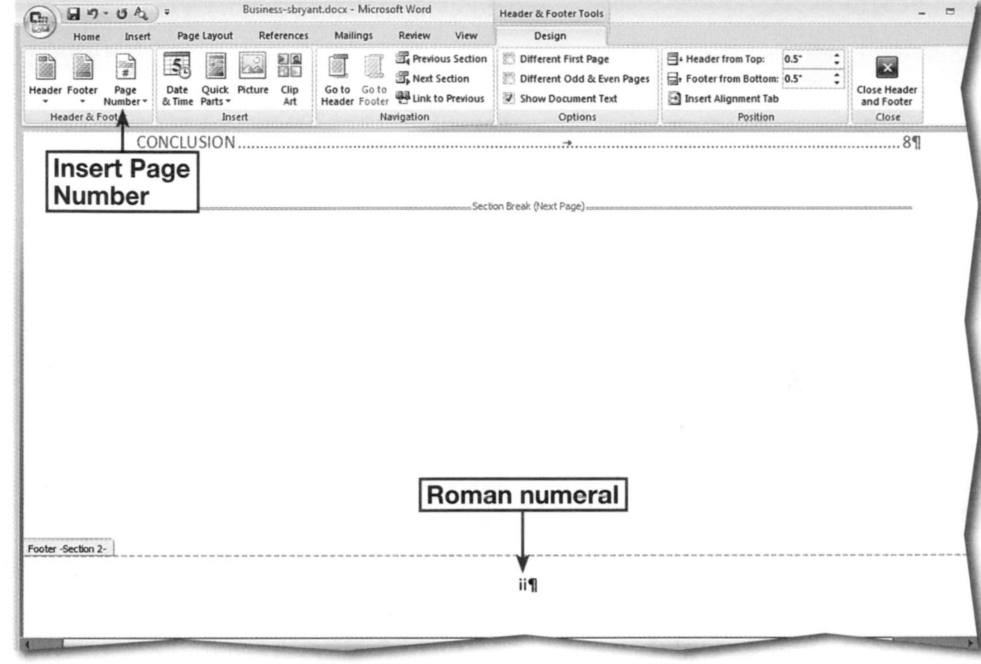

FIGURE 4.28 Section 3 header modified

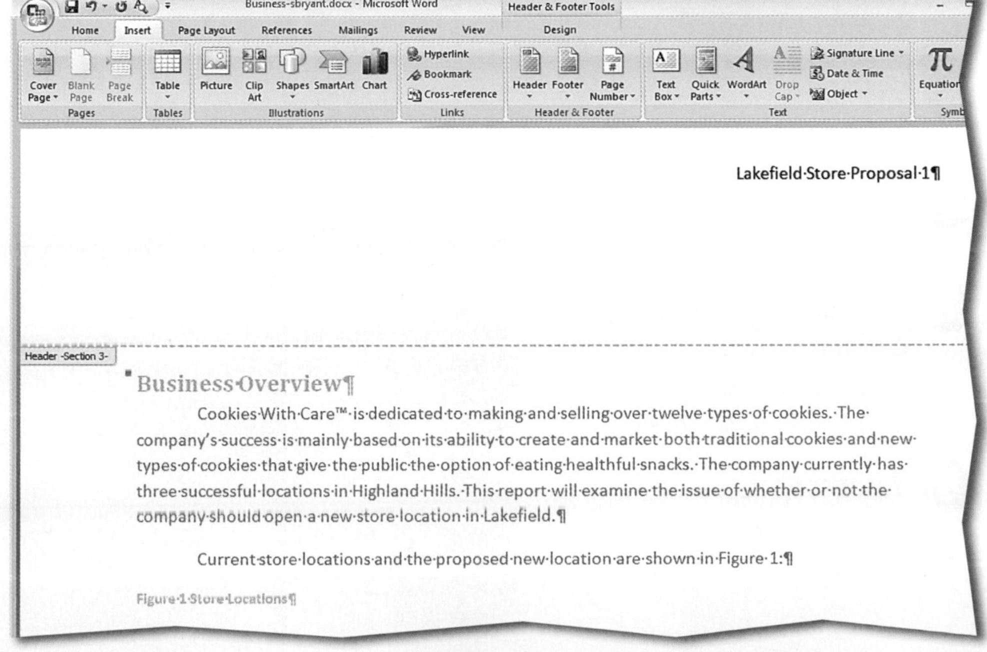

LESSON 2 Practice It Activities

3. Add WordArt and Correct a Presentation

Follow the steps to complete the activity. You must complete Practice It Activity 2 before doing this activity.

New Student Strategy If a student did not complete Practice It Activity 2, then the solution file for that activity can be used as a data file for this activity.

Step-By-Step

1. Open your **Fundraiser-2** file. Save as: Fundraiser-[your first initial and last name]3.
2. Select **Slide 5**. On the **Home** tab, click the **New Slide** drop-down arrow. Click **Title Only**. Key the title: Fundraiser Results.
3. Choose **Insert>Text> WordArt**.
4. Click the third box in the fifth row **(Fill-Accent 2, Warm Matte Bevel)**. Click **OK**. Key: Total Raised. Press ENTER. Key: $375.00. Click **OK**.
5. **CHECK** Your screen should look like Figure 2.47.
6. Click **Review>Proofing> Spelling**.
7. Under **Suggestions**, click **Community**. Click **Change**. Click **OK**. Click anywhere outside the text.
8. **CHECK** Your screen should look like Figure 2.48. Save and close your file.

Solution The solution file for this activity is **Fundraiser3-SF**.

FIGURE 2.47 Slide 5 with WordArt

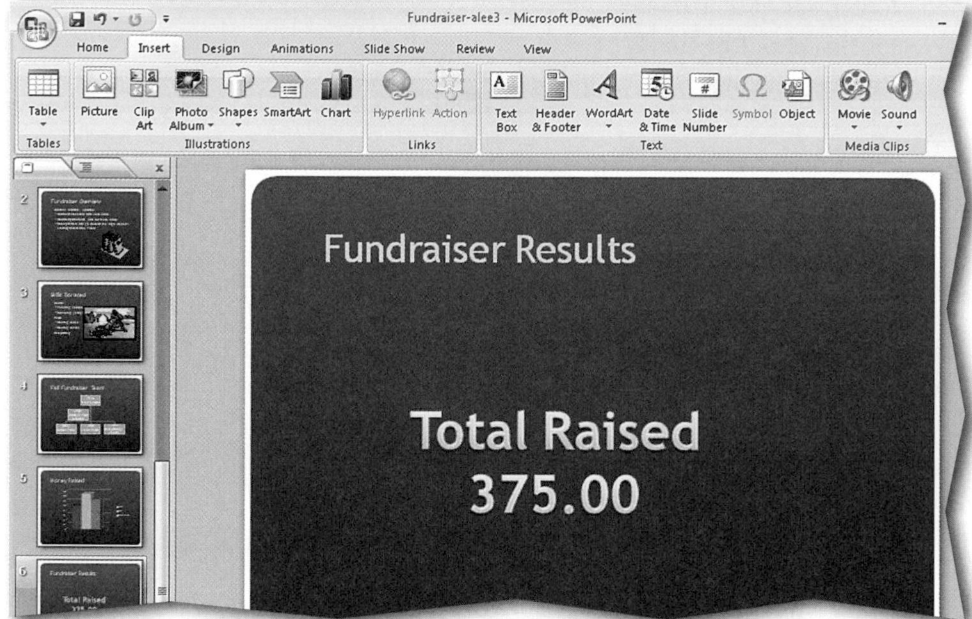

Step-by-Step Tip In **Step 4** depending on whether your students are using Windows XP or Windows Vista, a text box may appear asking to enter the text. For further information have them refer to pages l through liv for XP versus Vista differences.

FIGURE 2.48 Slide 2 with corrected spelling

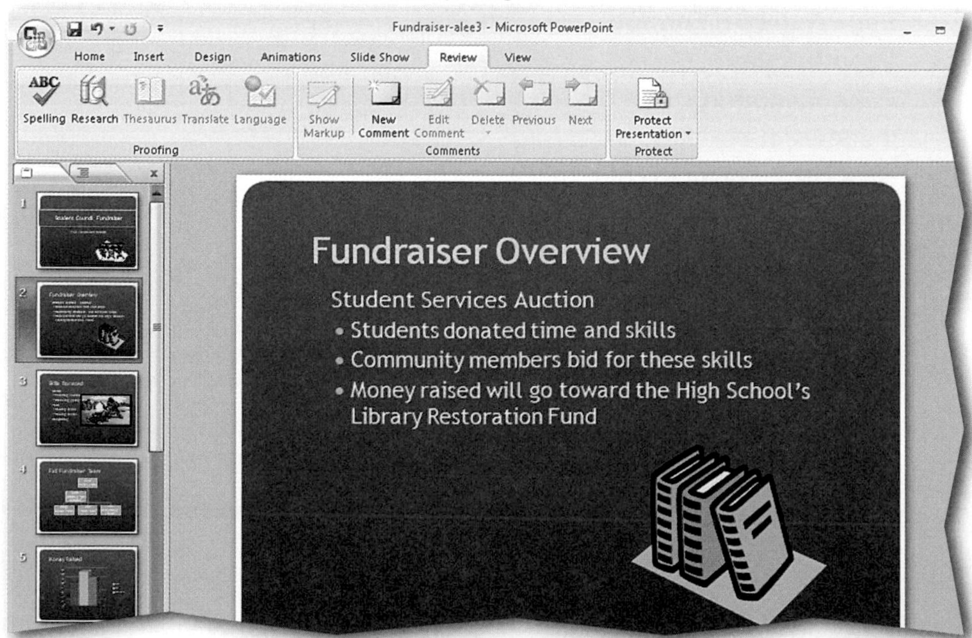

Step-By-Step

1. In your **Business** file, go to Page 5.
2. In the first paragraph, click after the text **commented:**. Press ENTER.
3. Select the entire quote (starts with **My family** and ends with **With Care™!**). Choose **Home>Paragraph>Dialog Box Launcher**.
4. In the **Paragraph** dialog box, set the **Left** and **Right Indentation** to **0.5″**. Set **Special** to **(none)** (see Figure 4.29). Click **OK**. Deselect the text.
5. CHECK Your screen should look like Figure 4.30. Save your file.

Continue to the next exercise.

Academic Skills

You should limit the number of long quotations in your academic or business reports and aim to keep most quotations about one sentence long. Block quotes should only be included if they represent an important idea that cannot be condensed or paraphrased.

EXERCISE 4-14
Format Long Quotations

A long quotation, or block quote, that runs four or more lines requires special formatting. Do not use quotation marks. Instead, indent the quote a half-inch from each side margin and leave a blank line above and below it. You should also remove the first line indentation from the long quote and remaining paragraph, since they are not new paragraphs.

NCLB/Language Arts (NCTE 12) One of the greatest challenges for students writing research papers is quoting too much. Remind students that quotes should be just long enough to highlight their own ideas.

FIGURE 4.29 Paragraph dialog box

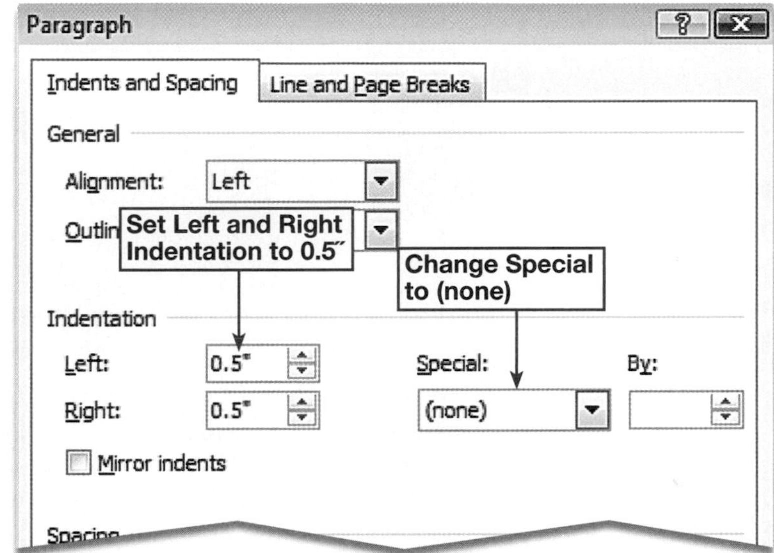

FIGURE 4.30 Properly formatted long quote

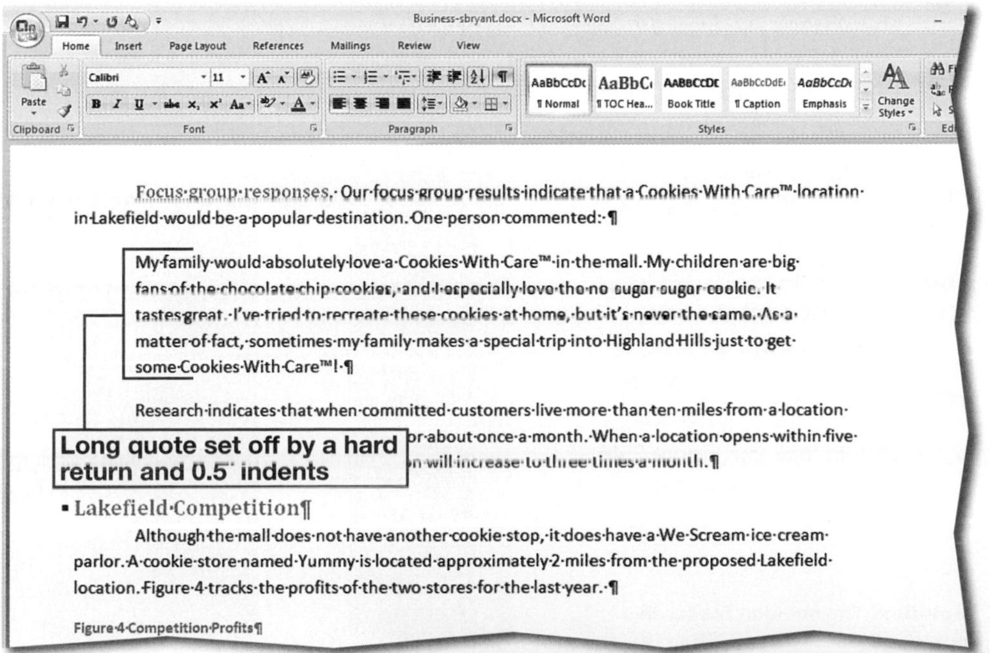

LESSON 2 Practice It Activities

Step-By-Step

1. Open your **Fundraiser-1** file. Save as: Fundraiser-[your first initial and last name]2. Close the task pane.
2. Click **Slide 4**. Choose **Insert>Illustrations> SmartArt**. Click **Hierarchy**. Click **Organization Chart**. Click **OK**.
3. In the top box, key: Paul. Press ENTER. Key: Team Leader. Fill in the remaining four boxes as shown in Figure 2.45.
4. CHECK Your screen should look like Figure 2.45.
5. Under the **SmartArt Tools** contextual tab, choose **Design>SmartArt Styles>Change Colors**.
6. In the drop-down menu, under **Accent 3**, click **Colored Fill - Accent 3**.
7. CHECK Your screen should look like Figure 2.46. Save and close your file.

Solution The solution file for this activity is **Fundraiser2-SF**.

2. Insert Diagrams

Follow the steps to complete the activity. You must complete Practice It Activity 1 before doing this activity. **New Student Strategy** If a student did not complete Practice It Activity 1, then the solution file for that activity can be used as a data file for this activity.

FIGURE 2.45 Organization chart added to slide

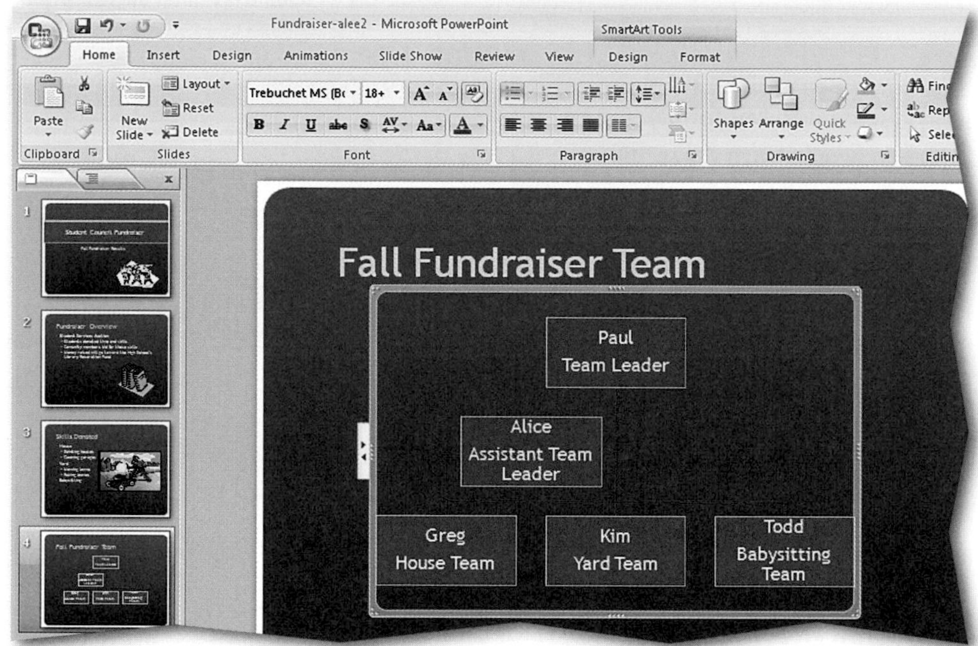

FIGURE 2.46 SmartArt styles applied to chart

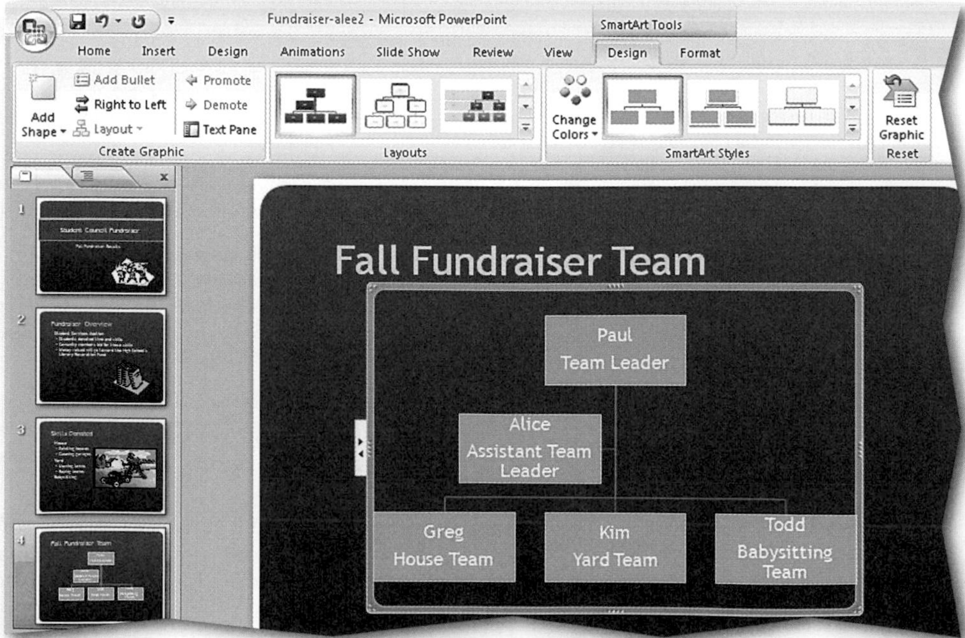

Step-By-Step

1. In your **Business** file, choose **References> Citations & Bibliography>Style** . Click the **Style** drop-down arrow and select **Chicago**.

2. Go to Page 5. Click after the sentence that ends with the text **three times a month**. Be sure to click before the period.

3. Choose **References> Citations & Bibliography>Insert Citation>Add New Source** .

4. In the **Create Source** dialog box, under **Type of Source**, select **Book Section**.

5. Fill out the remaining fields as shown in Figure 4.31. Press TAB to navigate among the fields. Click **OK**.

6. CHECK Your screen should look like Figure 4.32. Save your file.

Continue to the next exercise.

Microsoft Office 2007

The **Style** menu lets you apply different formatting to citations. Business reports often use the Chicago style. MLA style is used for academic reports.

EXERCISE 4-15

Select Reference Styles and Add a Citation Source

Word 2007's Citations & Bibliography tool allows you to log, or record, your citation sources as part of your file. You can insert and reuse multiple properly formatted citations. **NCLB/Language Arts (NCTE 8)** Tell students that the elements of a bibliographical reference are like those of an MLA reference in a Works Cited list. All citations, regardless of style, should give credit to the author, title, publisher, and date of publication.

FIGURE 4.31 Create Source dialog box

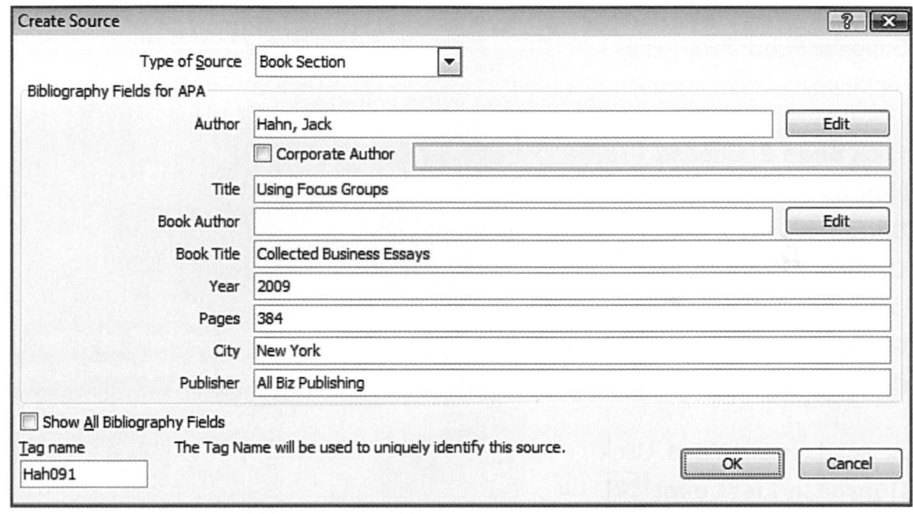

FIGURE 4.32 The source has been added as an inline citation.

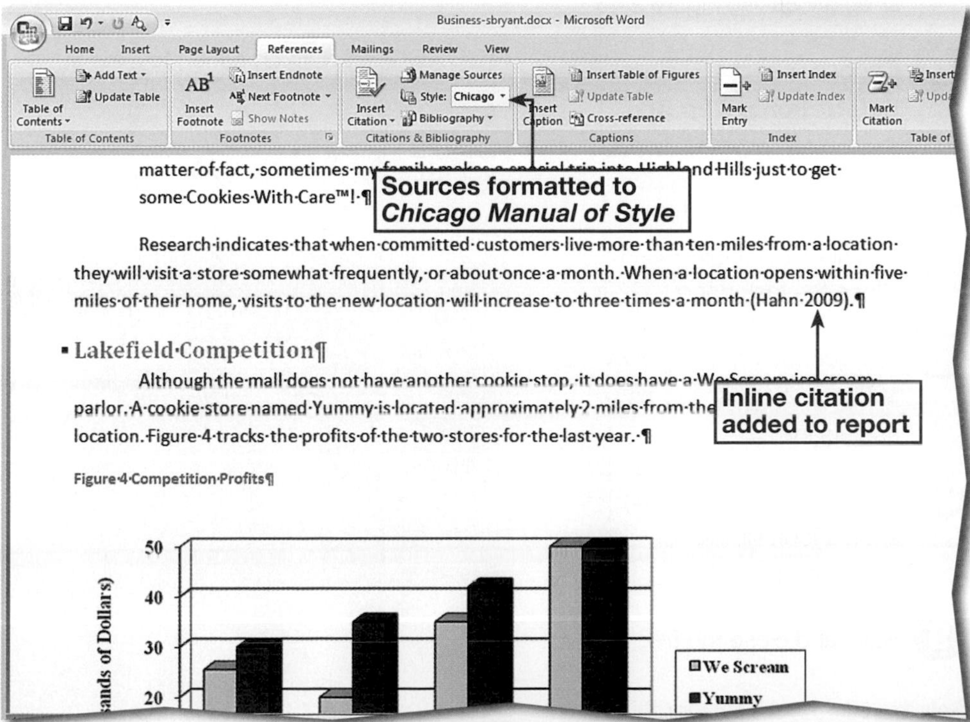

LESSON 2 Practice It Activities

1. Create a Slide

Follow the steps to complete the activity.

Step-By-Step

1. Start PowerPoint. Open the data file **Fundraiser.pptx**. Save as: Fundraiser-[your first initial and last name]1.
2. Click **Slide 2**. Choose **Home>Slides>New Slides>Slides from Outline**. Locate and select the data file **PI_Outline.docx**. Click **Insert**.
3. Select the word **Yard**. Click **Decrease List Level** .
4. CHECK Your screen should look like Figure 2.43.
5. Choose **Insert>Illustrations>Clip Art**. Search for: mowing lawns.
6. Select an image similar to that shown in Figure 2.44. Close the task pane.
7. Position the clip as shown in Figure 2.44. Resize as necessary.
8. CHECK Your screen should look similar to Figure 2.44.
9. Save and close the file.

Solution The solution file for this activity is **Fundraiser1-SF**.

FIGURE 2.43 Slide 3

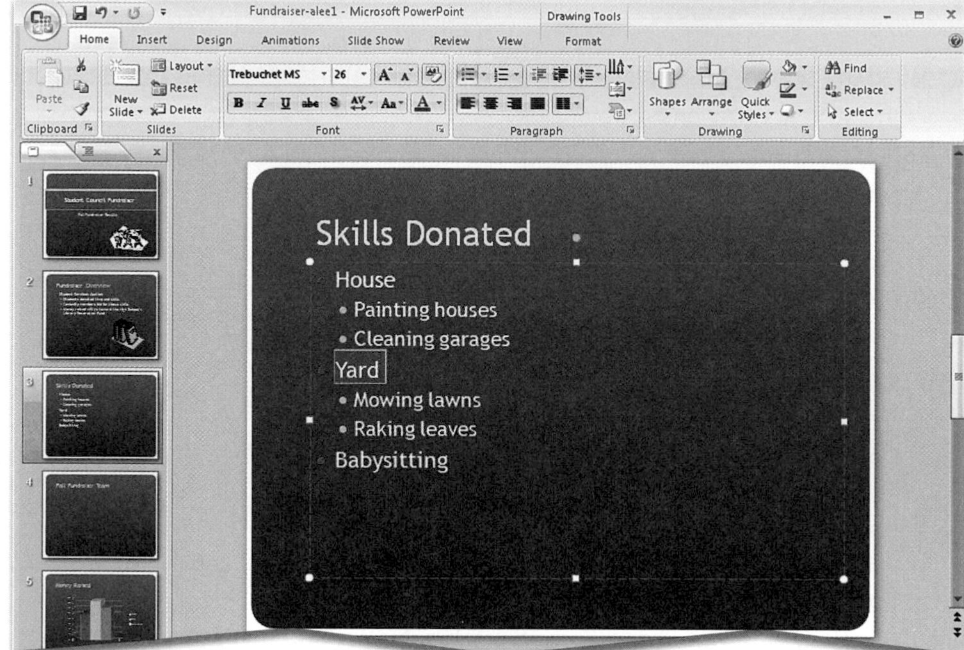

FIGURE 2.44 Clip art added to Slide 3

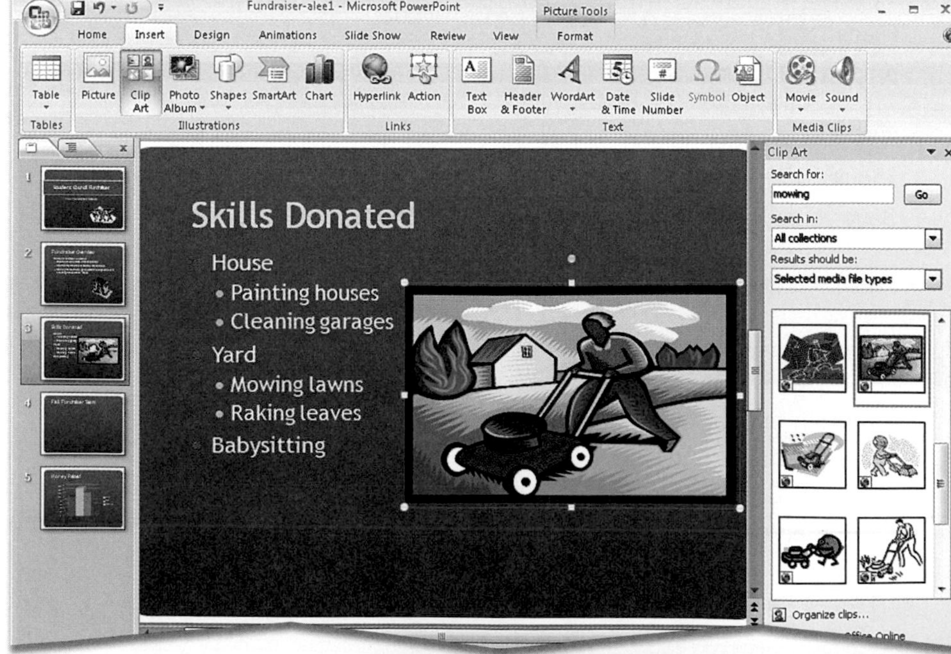

Step-By-Step

1. In your **Business** file, press CTRL + END.
2. Choose **Insert>Pages> Blank Page**.
3. Choose **References> Citations & Biblio-graphy>Bibliography> Bibliography** (see Figure 4.33).
4. Select the publication month, day, and year **August 12, 2010** in the first citation. Press DELETE. Key: July 2009.
5. CHECK Your screen should look like Figure 4.34.
6. Save your file.

Continue to the next exercise.

Academic Skills

Summarizing or paraphrasing ideas from a source without a citation is a form of plagiarism. You should cite sources even when you are not using a direct quotation in your documents. Think of a citation as a tool for giving credit to a source, not just for his or her words, but also for his or her ideas.

NCLB/Language Arts (NCTE 8) Even if a source is not being quoted, a citation is necessary. When in doubt, students should err on the side of citing a source rather than giving no credit.

EXERCISE 4-16
Insert a Bibliography

After you have added all of your sources and citations, you can create a **bibliography**. A bibliography is a list of works cited in a report. At the click of a button, Word 2007's Citations & Bibliography tool compiles all your source information and formats a bibliography or works cited list that matches the reference style you have chosen.

FIGURE 4.33 Bibliography options

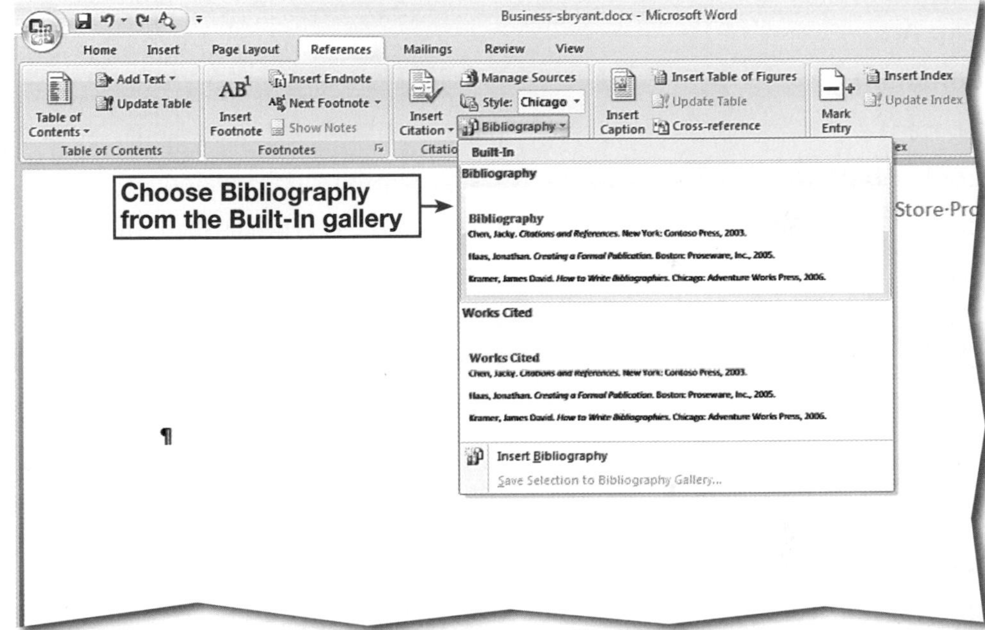

FIGURE 4.34 Inserted bibliography

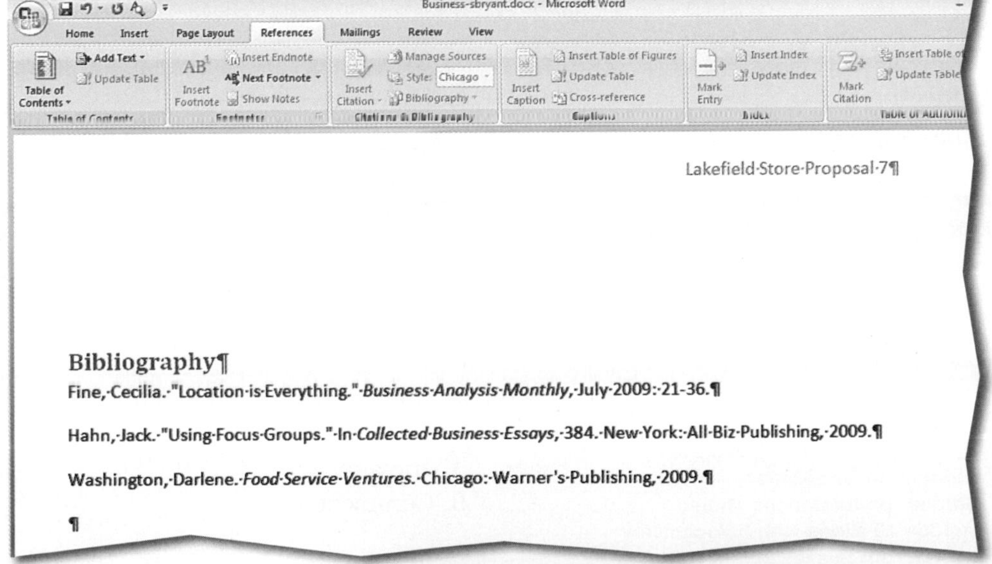

LESSON 2 After You Read

Vocabulary

Key Terms

chart
Clip Art
comment
content
contextual tab
copy
cut
demote
diagram
markup
paste
promote
table
theme
thesaurus
WordArt

Academic Vocabulary

import
subordinate

Answer to Vocabulary Activity
Student presentations should include 10 slides with 5 Vocabulary words from this lesson.

Review Vocabulary

Complete the following statements on a separate piece of paper. Choose from the Vocabulary list on the left to complete the statements.

1. Use the Increase List Level button to ___promote___, or change text to the next higher level. (p. 575)

2. A ___contextual tab___ appears on the Ribbon only when specific types of objects are selected. (p. 572)

3. When creating a PowerPoint presentation you may need to ___import___ information from other slides or documents. (p. 573)

4. The ___comment___ feature allows you to quickly and easily view and add suggestions to a presentation. (p. 591)

5. Decorative text such as shadowed, rotated, and stretched text is called ___WordArt___. (p. 588)

Vocabulary Activity

6. Create a five-question quiz in the form of a PowerPoint presentation based on this lesson's Vocabulary words and their definitions.

A. Choose five terms. Describe each term in your own words.
B. Create a 10-slide presentation. On the first slide, display one term. On the second slide, display the term's definition.
C. Create slides for the remaining four terms.
D. Present your quiz to a classmate or to the entire class.

Review Key Concepts

Answer the following questions on a separate piece of paper.

7. Where can you find a list of themes to use when creating a new presentation? (p. 571)

(A.) Design tab C. Review tab
B. Drawing toolbar D. Thesaurus

8. What appears as small yellow boxes on a slide? (p. 591)

A. Pictures C. Clip Art
B. WordArt (D.) Comments

9. Which button would you use to demote selected text? (p. 575)

A. Lower C. Demote
(B.) Decrease List Level D. Delete

10. You can use which tool to find a word, similar in meaning to another word? (p. 589)

(A.) Thesaurus C. Diagrams
B. Comments D. Demote

1. In your **Business** file, go to Page ii. Click anywhere inside the table of contents.
2. Choose **References> Table of Contents> Update Table**.
3. In the **Update Table of Contents** dialog box, choose **Update entire table**. Click **OK**.
4. CHECK Your screen should look like Figure 4.35. Notice that the **Bibliography** page has been added to the table of contents.
5. Select the text **Business Overview**. Choose **Home>Font>Dialog Box Launcher**. Check **All Caps**. Click **OK**.
6. With the text still selected, double-click **Format Painter**. Select **Current Location Analysis**, **Lakefield Overview**, **Conclusion**, and **Bibliography**.
7. Click **Format Painter** once. Deselect the table of contents.
8. CHECK Your screen should look like Figure 4.36. Save your file.

Continue to the next exercise.

EXERCISE 4-17
Update a Table of Contents

Headings, page numbers, and sections often change as you create and revise a document. Each time these changes occur, you should update the table of contents. Use Reveal Formatting to identify the different headings used in a document, and to apply heading styles as needed to selected text.

Different Strokes Tell students that they can also update the table of contents by pressing **F9**.

FIGURE 4.35 Updated table of contents

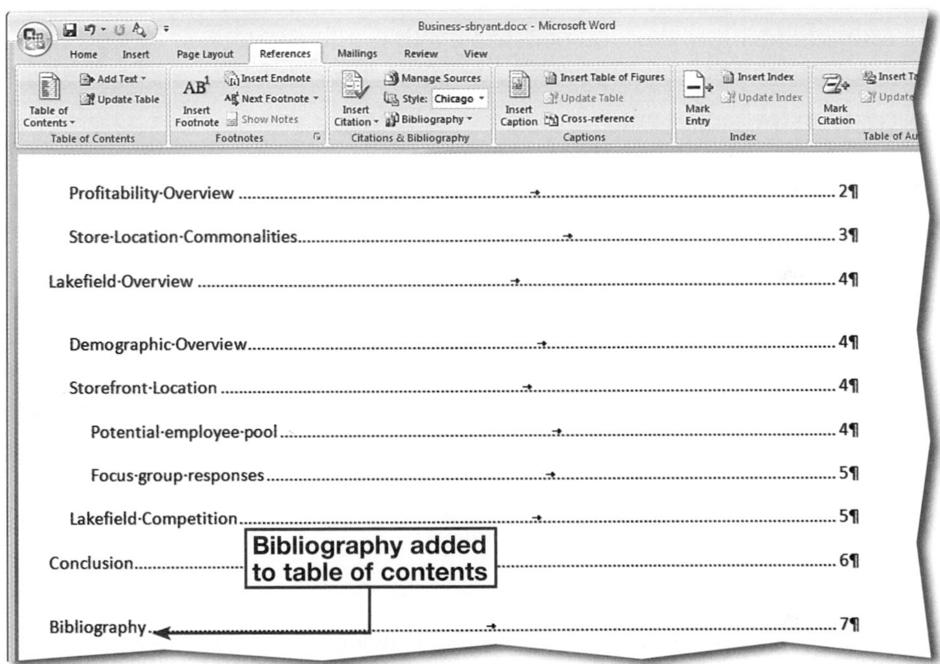

FIGURE 4.36 Updated table of contents with correct formatting

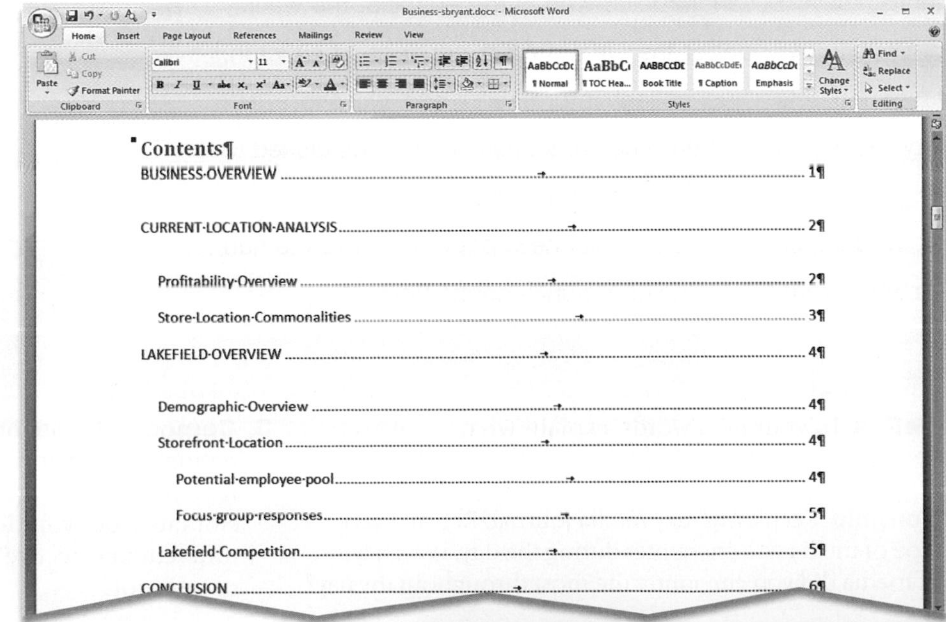

21st Century WORKPLACE

Develop Media Literacy

Two rival baseball teams play a major game. In the winning team's hometown, the local newspaper tells one story. In the losing team's hometown, the local newspaper tells a different story. You ask yourself, "Why do the two newspapers have different perspectives on the same game?"

When people use the term "literacy," they are usually referring to the ability to read and write. "Media literacy" means having the ability to analyze and evaluate the hundreds of messages you get every day from all types of media. These media can include print, video, radio, and the Internet. Anything from the media contains a message that is created for a purpose. Being "media literate" means learning to recognize and evaluate the purposes behind the messages that you are hearing, seeing, or reading.

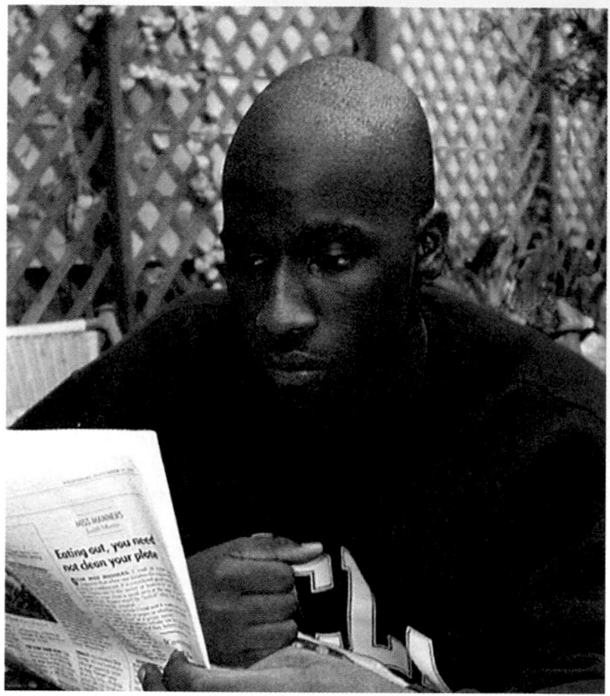

Being media literate means taking a critical look at everything you read, hear, or see.

MEET THE MANAGER

Media literacy is important because the media can have a tremendous influence on how you see your world and your community. "We are the eyes, ears, and voice of the community," says Susan Tordella, who is the editor of the weekly community newspaper the *Littleton Independent*, in Littleton, Massachusetts. "We collect information and we share it. I judge our success when I see our stories and photos tacked to refrigerators and bulletin boards at schools and businesses." Ms. Tordella believes community newspapers are like the hub of a wheel that keeps the community connected.

NCLB/Language Arts (NCTE 11) Reinforce to students that to be "media literate" one must read many sources to get different opinions. This means reading articles not only from a newspaper or web site, but from both. Sources of information may have different opinions and views and in order to be "media literate" you need to know all sides.

SkillBuilder answers can be found on page TM92.

SKILLBUILDER

1. **Define** In your own words, explain what it means to be "media literate."

2. **Compile** Keep a one-day media journal. Record every type of media you encounter during the day. Which type of media did you encounter the most throughout the day?

3. **Compare** Locate one local newspaper and one national newspaper. Compare the first pages of each newspaper. How are they different, and how are they similar? Does your local newspaper seem to have a different perspective than a national newspaper? Why or why not?

Step-By-Step

1. In your **Business** file, choose **Office>Prepare> Properties**.
2. The **Document Information Panel** opens above your document. Click **Document Properties** and select **Advanced Properties**.
3. In the **Document Properties** dialog box, click the **Summary** tab.
4. In the **Title** box, key: Proposal to Open a New Location.
5. In the **Subject** box, key: Lakefield Storefront Proposal.
6. In the **Author** box, key: Tina Yee.
7. In the **Company** box, key: Cookies with Care.
8. **CHECK** Your screen should look like Figure 4.37. Click **OK**.
9. In the upper-right corner of the **Document Information Panel**, click **Close** [X] to close the panel. Save your file.

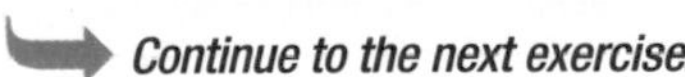
Continue to the next exercise.

EL Explain to English Learners that *property* has more than one meaning. Here, it is a trait that identifies a document, but *property* can also refer to a piece of land that is owned.

EXERCISE 4-18
Review and Modify Document Properties

Properties help to define and describe a document, such as title, subject, or author. Properties stay with a document from computer to computer and can be viewed by anybody. You might add properties to an official business document to identify it as a draft or to distinguish it from a similar document. Word allows you to save properties and document information through the Document Information Panel.

Solution Use the file **Business-SF.docx** as a solution file for Exercises 4-11 through 4-18.

FIGURE 4.37 Modified Document Summary

Business-sbryant.docx Properties

General | Summary | Statistics | Contents | Custom

Title: Proposal to Open a New Location
Subject: Lakefield Storefront Propodal
Author: Tina Yee
Manager:
Company: Cookies with Care
Category:
Keywords:
Comments:
Hyperlink base:
Template: Normal.dotm
Save Thumbnails for All Word Documents
OK | Cancel

You Should Know

Document properties can be used by individuals and by companies to summarize contents, identify authors, and to highlight important changes to document drafts.

Tech Tip

File properties are not actually associated with a file until that file is saved.

Step-By-Step

1. In your **Garden** file, select **Slide 2**.
2. On the **Review** tab, in the **Comments** group, click **New Comment**. In the comment box, key: Change color of WordArt.
3. CHECK Your screen should look like Figure 2.41.
4. Repeat **Step 2**. Key: Delete sunshine .
5. Click outside the comment box. Place your pointer over the first comment box. Right-click the comment box. Click **Edit Comment**.
6. Replace the text with: Add effect to WordArt. Click outside the box. Place your pointer over the comment.
7. Choose **Review>Comments>Show Markup**. Click the **Show Markup** button again.
8. Right-click the second comment box. Click **Delete Comment**.
9. CHECK Your screen should look like Figure 2.42.
10. With your teacher's permission, print the document. Save and close the file.

Continue to the next exercise.

EXERCISE 2-18
Add, Edit, and Delete Comments

Before you deliver a presentation, you might want to have classmates or coworkers review it and suggest improvements. Or, you might review a coworker's presentation. You can add **comments** to the presentation so he or she can see what your suggestions are. Comments are like sticky notes that appear as small boxes on the slide. If you want to look at a presentation without the comments showing, you can hide the extra text, called **markup**.

Solution Use the file **Garden-SF** as a solution file for Exercises 2-1 through 2-18.

FIGURE 2.41 Comment added to slide

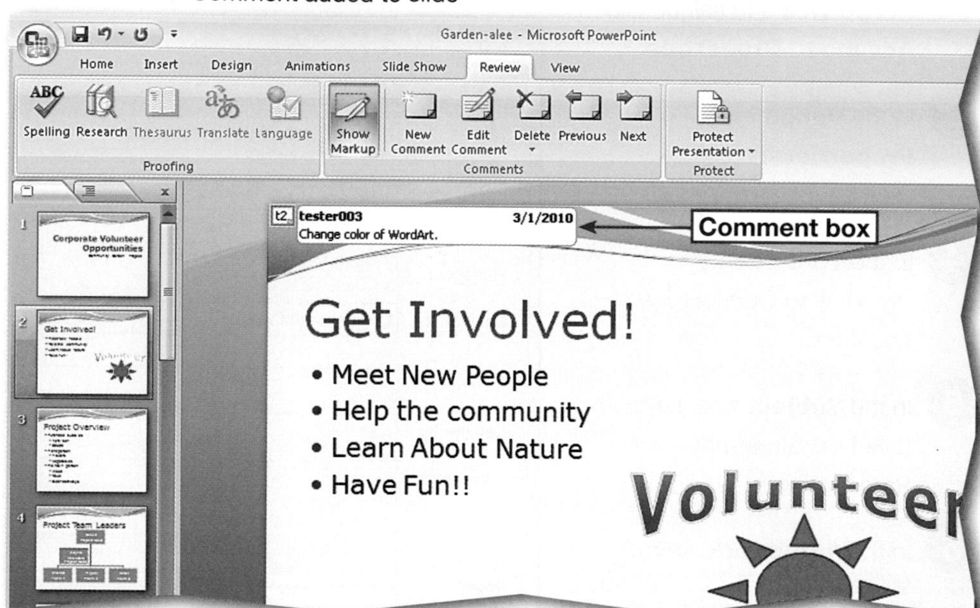

FIGURE 2.42 Slide with edited comment

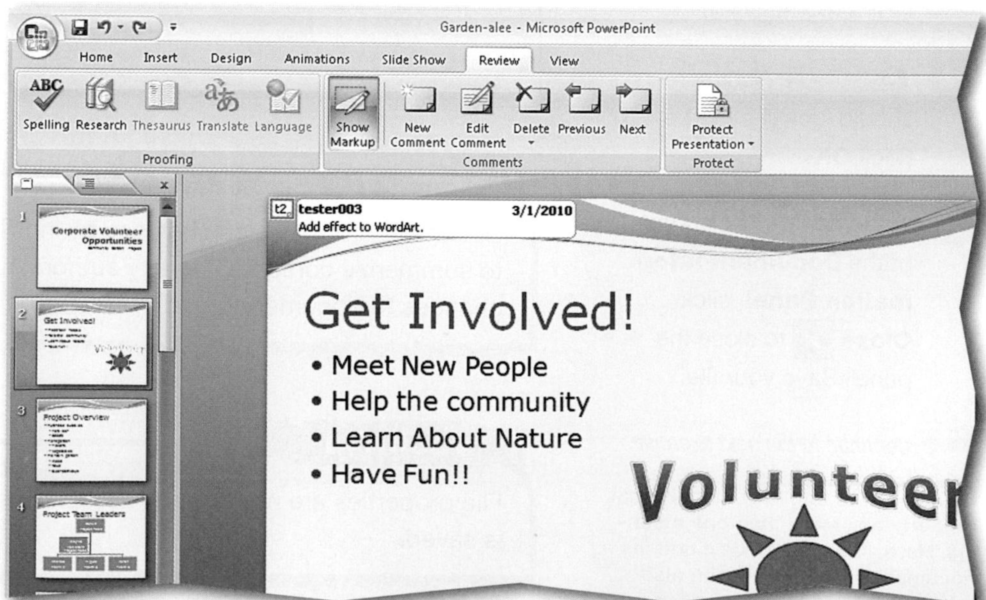

Step-By-Step

1. In your **Business** file, scroll until the top of Page ii is at the top of your screen.
2. Choose **View>Window> Split** . Click near the middle of the document pane.
3. In the bottom pane, click **Select Browse Object** . Click **Browse by Heading** .
4. **CHECK** Your screen should look like Figure 4.38.
5. Choose **Window> Remove Split**.
6. **CHECK** Your screen should look like Figure 4.39. Save your file.

Continue to the next exercise.

Academic Skills

Using a split screen can help you to double-check your work without having to scroll back and torth through a long document.

NCLB/Language Arts (NCTE 12) Many students have anxiety about writing long reports. Explain to students that as they become more skilled at managing large documents their confidence will grow.

Different Strokes Tell students they can split the window by double-clicking the split bar at the top of the vertical scroll bar.

EXERCISE 4-19
Split Windows and Arrange Panes

When you split the window, the Word screen is divided into two panes that you can scroll independently. Splitting the window is useful when you need to compare different parts of a document. For example, you can make sure your table of contents contains all of the formatted headings in your document.

FIGURE 4.38 Split window

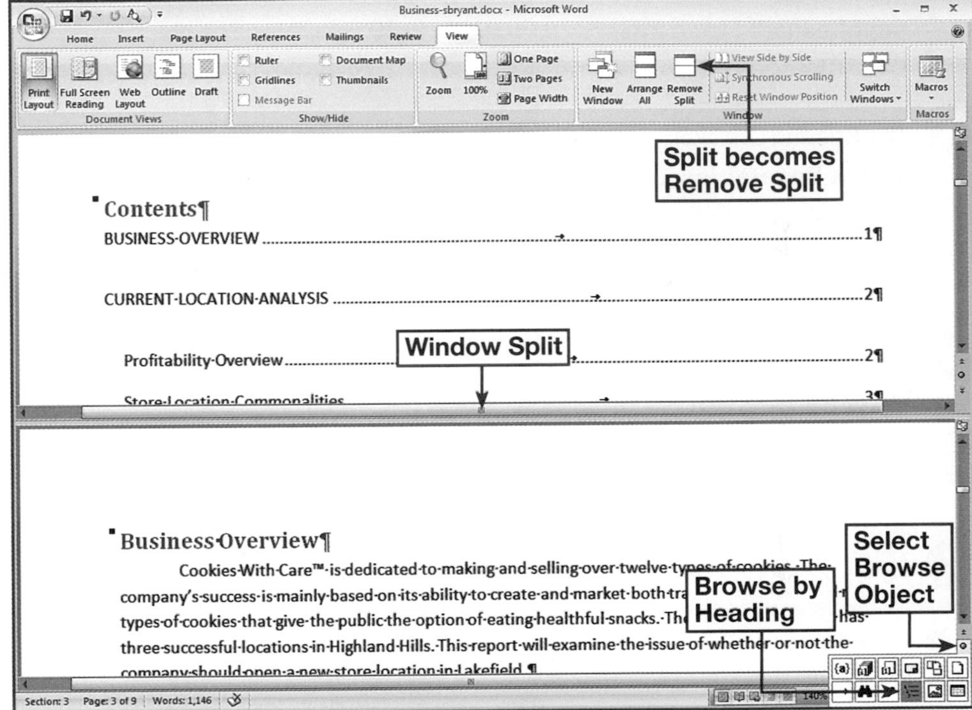

FIGURE 4.39 Single document pane

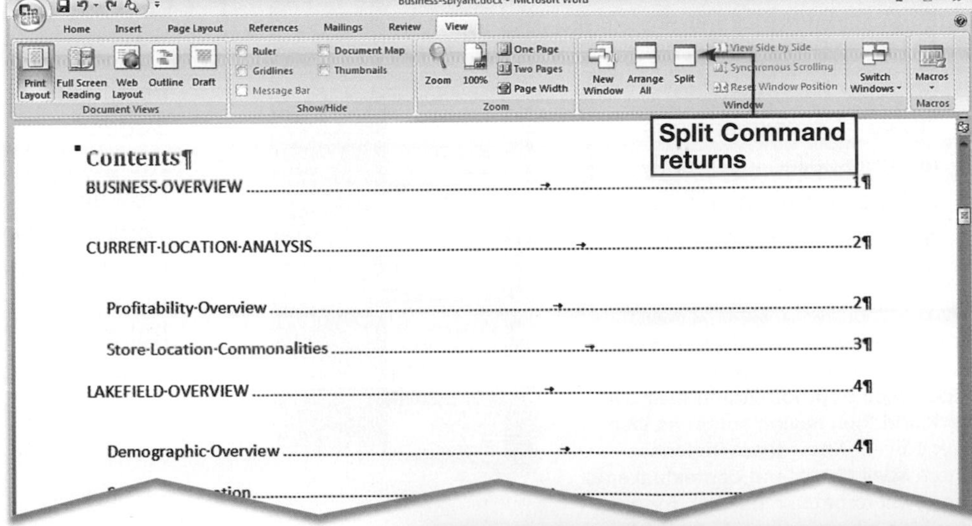

Step-By-Step

1. In your **Garden** file, select **Slide 3**.
2. Choose **Review> Proofing>Spelling** .
3. In the **Spelling** dialog box, under **Suggestions**, click **supplies** (see Figure 2.39). Click **Change**.
4. The Spelling Checker locates **Vegetebles**. Under **Suggestions**, click **Vegetables**. Click **Change**.
5. When the spelling check is complete, click **OK**.
6. **CHECK** Your screen should look like Figure 2.40.
7. Save your file.

Continue to the next exercise.

Microsoft Office 2007

In Microsoft Office 2007 a wavy blue underline indicates a contextual spelling error, such as "their" for "there." Contextual errors are not spelled incorrectly, but they are used incorrectly within the context of the sentence.

NCLB/Language Arts (NCTE 10) Make sure students understand the importance of proofreading their own work and then having someone else look it over. Show them instances where spell check and contextual spell check fail to catch mistakes, for example using "there" instead of "their".

EXERCISE 2-17
Use the Spelling Checker

You might show your PowerPoint presentation to a large audience using a video projector. On a large screen, grammatical errors and misspellings are magnified. You should always use the Spelling Checker to make sure every word in your presentation is spelled correctly. PowerPoint also checks words against its built-in dictionary as you create each slide. A wavy red line appears under any words that the dictionary does not recognize.

Step-By-Step Tip In **Step 3**, let students know that they can click the Ignore All or Change All button to ignore or change all occurrences of a word in presentation.

FIGURE 2.39 Spelling dialog box

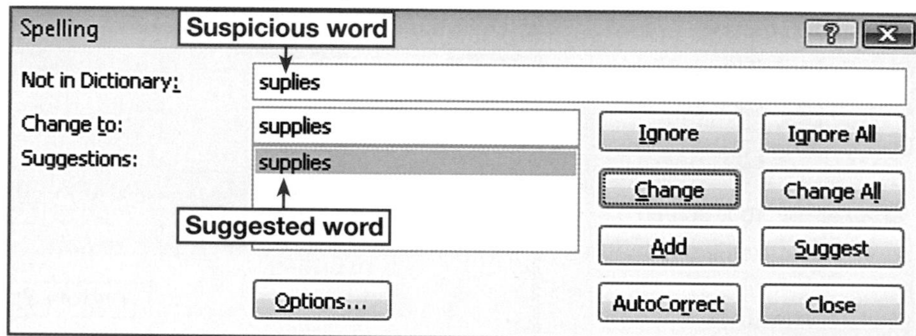

FIGURE 2.40 Spelling check is complete

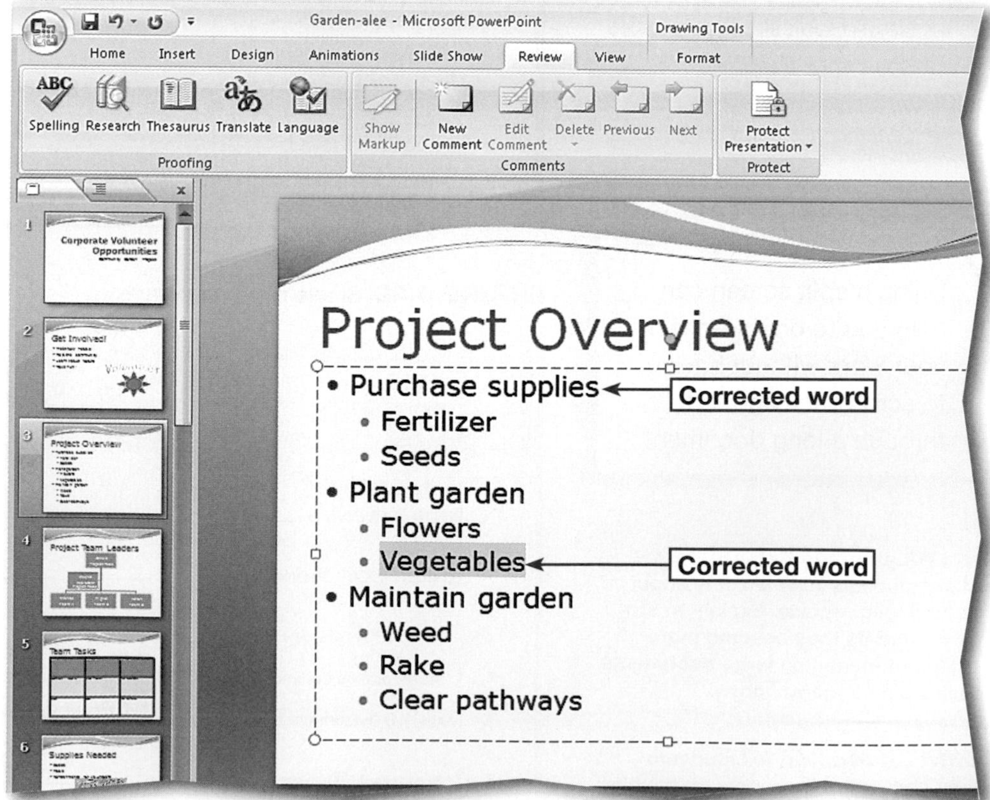

EXERCISE 4-20
Use Outline View

You can use **Outline View** to see the structure of a document. Outline View displays the text in levels—Level 1, then Level 2, and so on. Levels 1, 2, and 3 are equal to the Heading styles 1, 2, and 3. The body text of the document is the lowest level, and is indented furthest to the right in the outline.

FIGURE 4.40 Report in Outline View

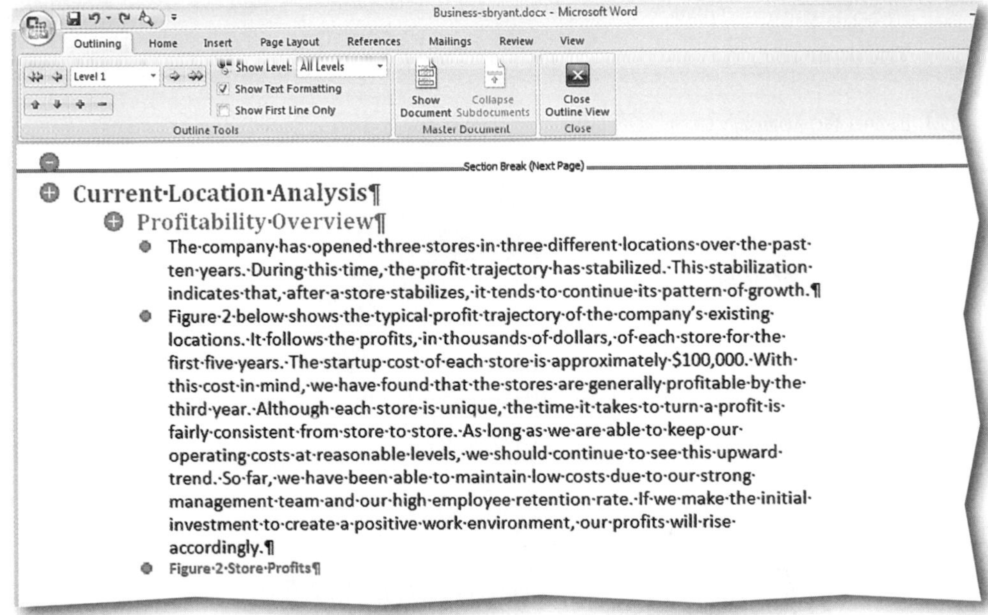

FIGURE 4.41 Promoted and demoted text

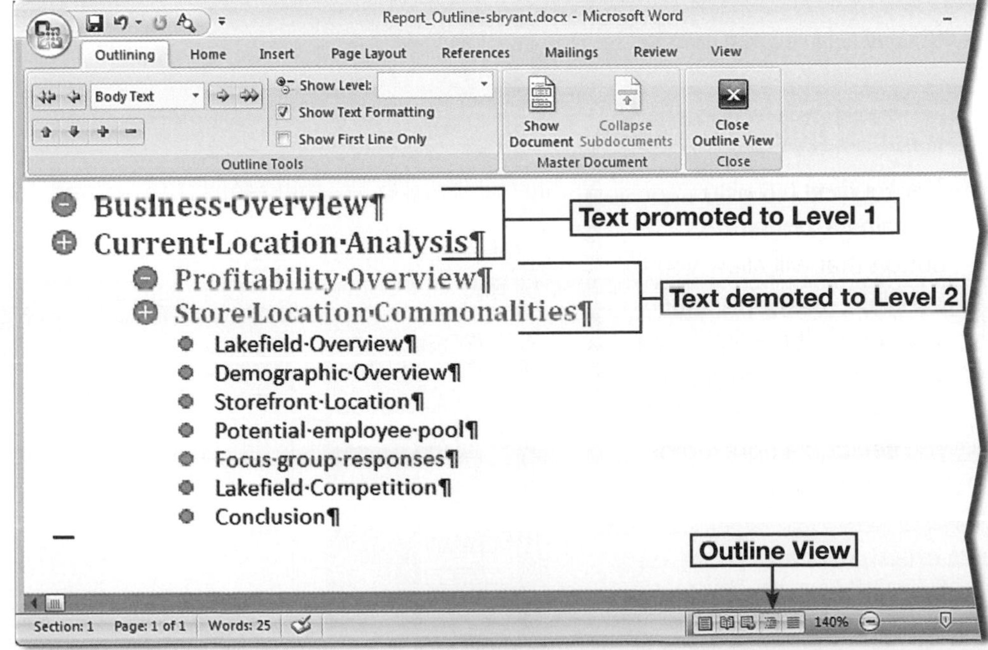

Step-By-Step

1. In your **Business** file, move to Page 4. Choose **View>Document Views>Outline**. Click in the **Current Location Analysis**.
2. **CHECK** Your screen should look like Figure 4.40.
3. Switch to **Print Layout** view. Save and close your **Business** file.
4. Locate and open the data file **Report_Outline.docx**. Save as: Report_Outline-[your first initial and last name].
5. At the bottom of the screen, click **Outline View**.
6. Select the first two lines of text. Choose **Outlining>Outline Tools>Promote to Level 1**.
7. Select the next two lines. Click **Demote**. Deselect the text.
8. **CHECK** Your screen should look like Figure 4.41.

Continued on the next page.

Teaching Tip Reinforce for students the importance of using headings to organize written work. Ask them to discuss how they can use **Outline View** to find and fix organizational errors, to work out the order of their discussion, and to find areas where they need to add more information.

Step-By-Step

1. In your **Garden** file, select **Slide 5**.
2. In the table, select the word **Organize**.
3. On the **Review** tab, in the **Proofing** group, click **Thesaurus**.
4. In the **Research** task pane, move your pointer over **coordinate**. *Coordinate* is a good synonym for *organize*, so click the drop-down arrow (see Figure 2.37).
5. On the drop-down menu, click **Insert**. Close the **Research** task pane.
6. **CHECK** Your screen should look like Figure 2.38.
7. Save your file.

Continue to the next exercise.

Academic Skills

The **Review** tab also contains a **Translate** button that will allow you to translate words into other languages. If English is not your first language, you can use this feature to help you select the right words for your presentation.

NCLB/Language Arts (NCTE 10) Show English Learners how to use the Translate button to help translate their ideas into English.

EXERCISE 2-16
Use the Thesaurus

Slides that contain many words are difficult to read. Your text has to say what you want to say in as few words as possible. The **Thesaurus** contains words with similar meanings, also known as synonyms, allowing you to pick the exact word you need.

Different Strokes Students can also right-click a word and select a synonym from the menu.

FIGURE 2.37 Thesaurus

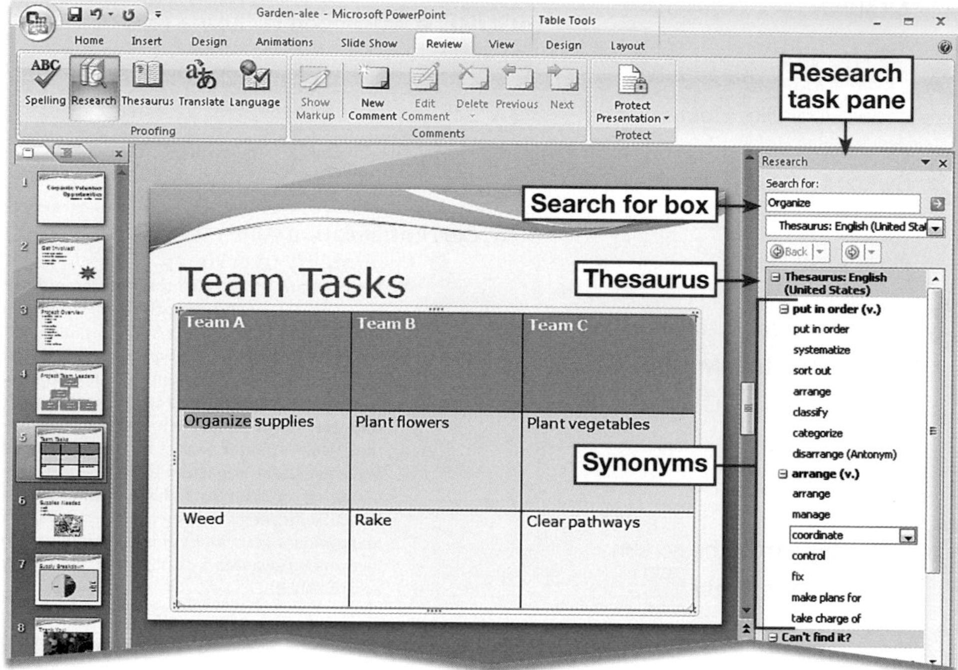

FIGURE 2.38 Replaced word

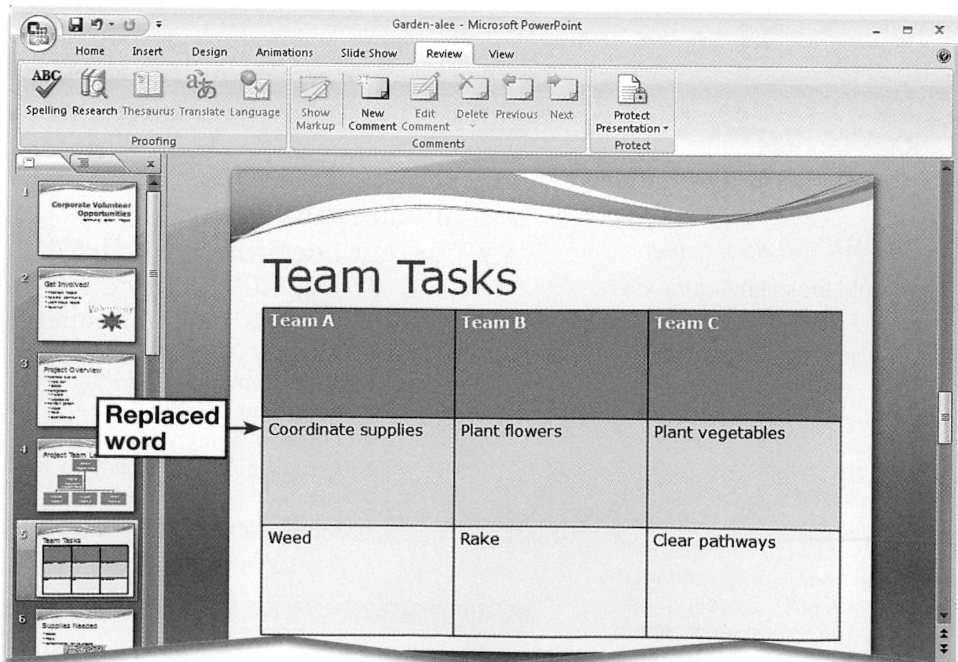

Step-By-Step

EXERCISE 4-20 (Continued)
Use Outline View

9. Promote the text **Lakefield Overview** to **Level 1**.

10. Demote **Demographic Overview** and **Storefront Location** to **Level 2**.

11. Select **Potential employee pool** and **Focus group responses**. Click the **Outline Level** drop-down arrow. Click **Level 3**. Deselect the text.

12. CHECK Your screen should look like Figure 4.42.

13. Promote **Lakefield Competition** to **Level 2**.

14. Promote **Conclusion** to **Level 1**. Deselect the text.

15. CHECK Your screen should look like Figure 4.43.

16. With your teacher's permission, print the outline. Save the file.

Continue to the next exercise.

FIGURE 4.42 Level 3 text

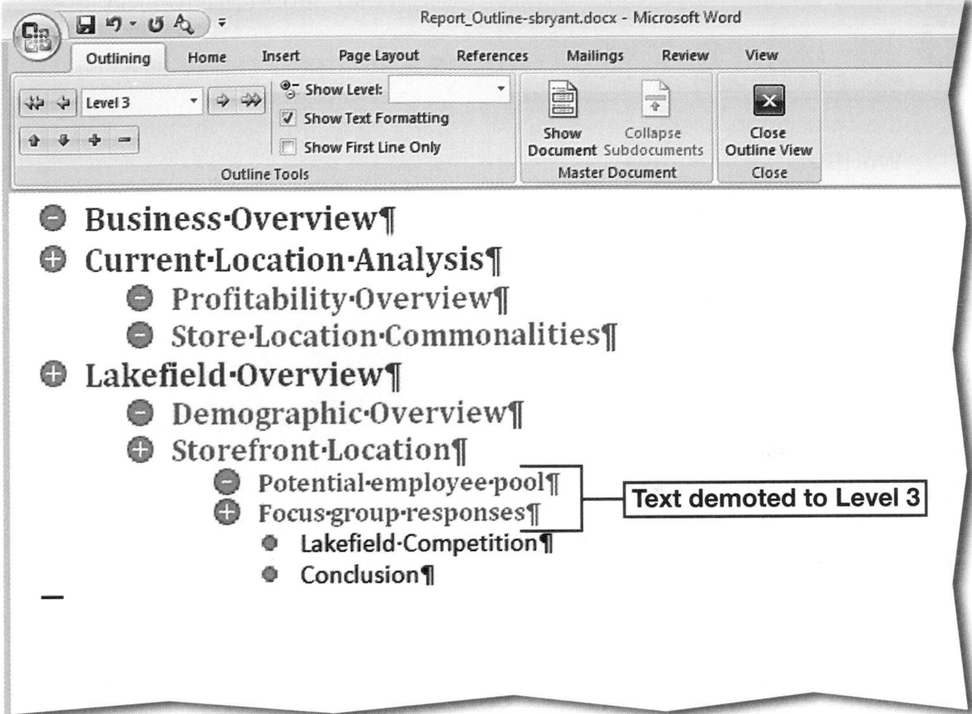

FIGURE 4.43 Final outline

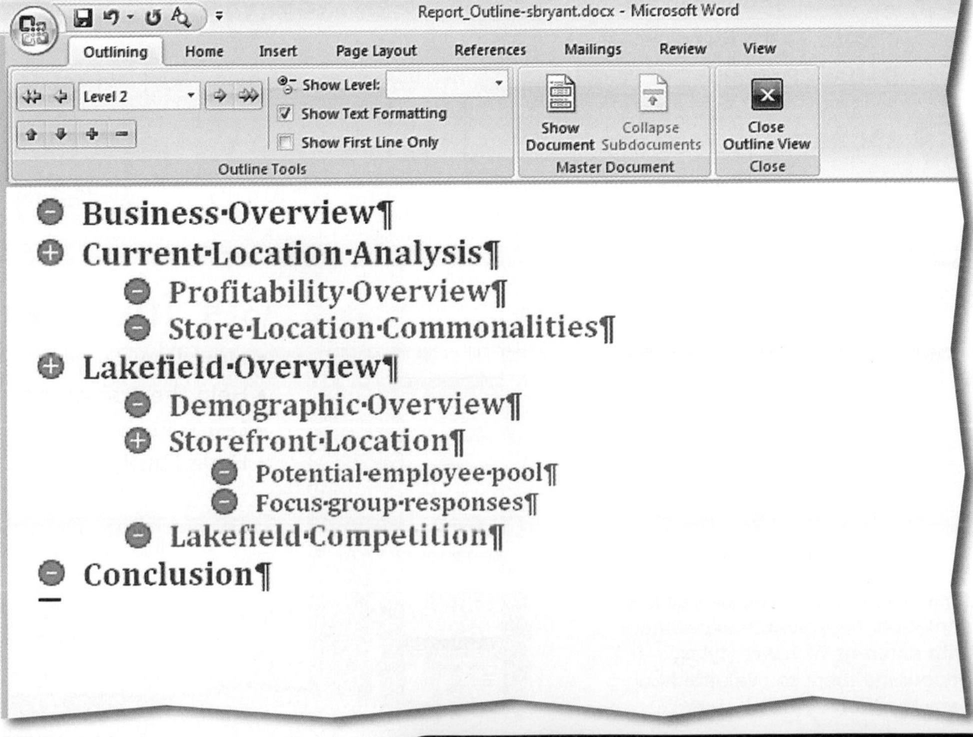

Teaching Tip Have students switch to **Print Layout** view so they can see that the text is not actually indented. Then have them switch back to **Outline View**.

Solution The solution file for this exercise is **Report_Outline-SF.docx**.

Step-By-Step

1. In your **Garden** file, select **Slide 2**.

2. Click in the bulleted list text box. On the **Insert** tab, in the **Text** group, click **WordArt**.

3. In the **WordArt** drop-down list, click the first style in the fourth row (see Figure 2.35).

4. Click inside the **Your Text Here** box. key: Volunteer!

5. Position the WordArt so it is above the sun shape.

6. Under the **Drawing Tools** contextual tab, on the **Format** tab, in the **WordArt Styles** group, choose **Text Effects**.

7. On the drop-down menu choose **Transform**, select **Deflate Bottom**.

8. **CHECK** Your screen should look similar to Figure 2.36.

9. Save your file.

Continue to the next exercise.

Teaching Tip WordArt can sometimes detract from the overall presentation. As students experiment with different WordArt styles, encourage them to evaluate how easy the WordArt is to read.

EXERCISE 2-15
Add and Modify WordArt on a Slide

WordArt allows you to turn text into artwork. As with any graphic, WordArt can make your presentation more effective. Too much WordArt will distract your audience.

FIGURE 2.35 WordArt Gallery dialog box

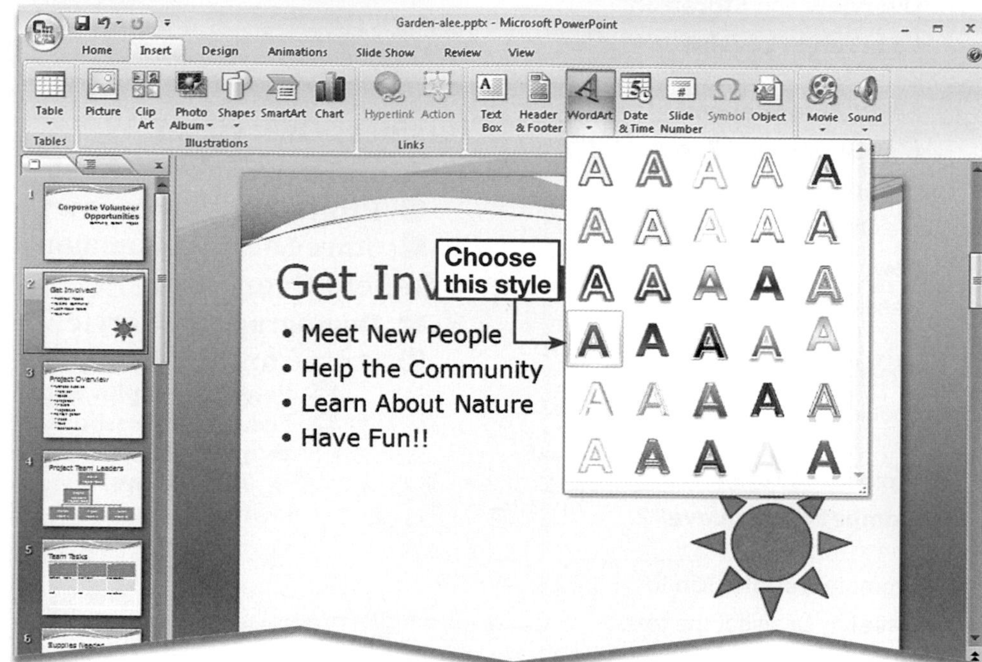

FIGURE 2.36 Inserted WordArt

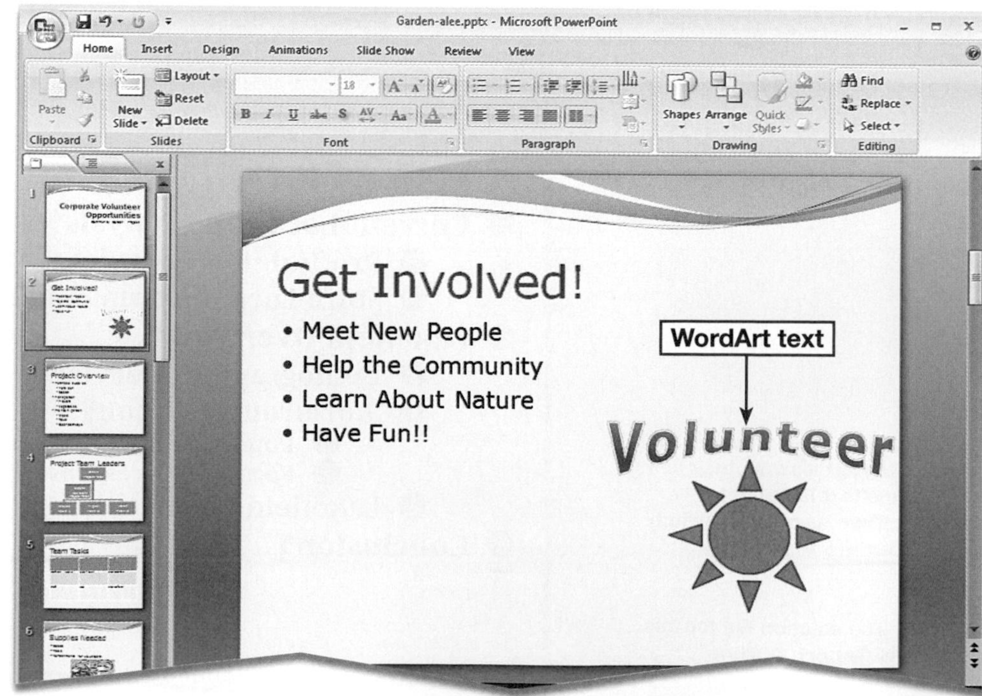

EXERCISE 4-21
Arrange Open Windows

You can open more than one document at a time in order to compare them. Comparing two open documents side by side allows you to scroll through both documents at the same time. (You can also compare documents on two panes split horizontally.)

FIGURE 4.44 Two documents viewed side by side

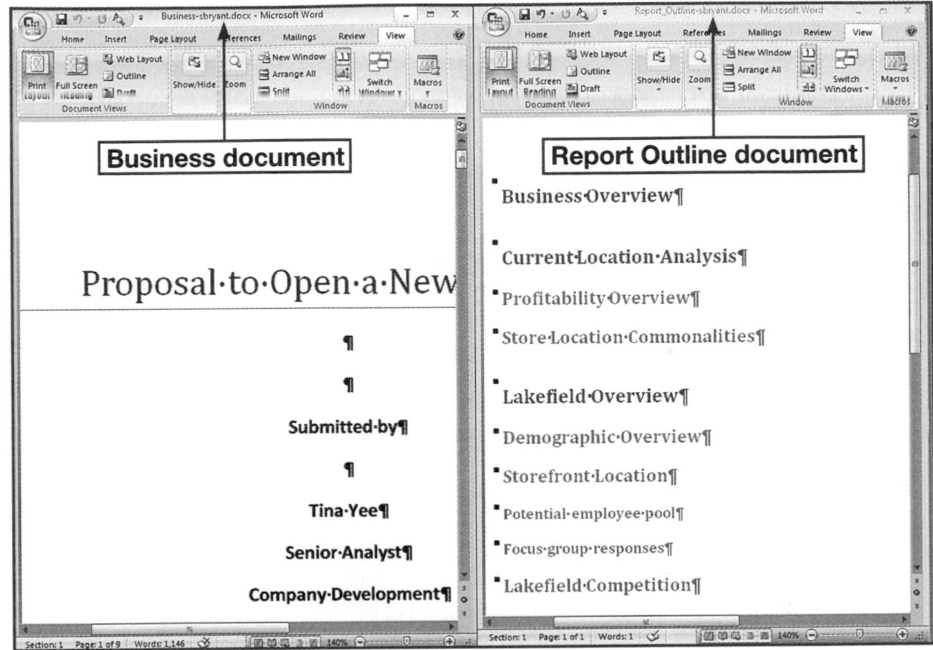

FIGURE 4.45 Window positions reversed

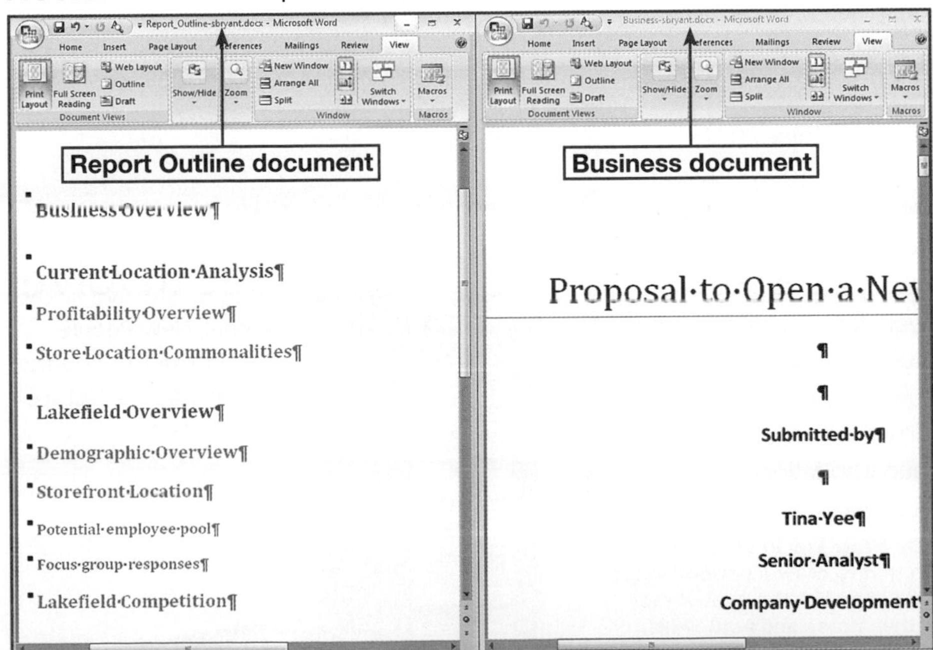

Step-By-Step

1. Make sure your **Report Outline** file is open.
2. Open your **Business** file.
3. In your **Business** file, select **View>Window>View Side by Side**.
4. **CHECK** Your screen should look like Figure 4.44.
5. Scroll down. Notice that the two documents move together.
6. Click anywhere in the **Report Outline** file. Select **View>Window>Reset Window Position**.
7. **CHECK** Your screen should look like Figure 4.45.
8. Click anywhere in the **Report Outline** file. Select **View>Window** and click **View Side by Side** to deselect it. Save and close both files.

Step-By-Step

1. In your **Garden** file, select **Slide 2**.
2. On the **Insert** tab, in the **Illustrations** group, click the **Shapes** button drop-down arrow.
3. Under **Basic Shapes**, click **Sun** (see Figure 2.33).
4. Click in the lower right corner of **Slide 2**.
5. Click and drag the pointer to create a sun. Release your mouse button to finish.
6. **CHECK** Your screen should look similar to Figure 2.34.
7. Save your file.

Continue to the next exercise.

Microsoft Office 2007

Microsoft Office 2007 includes two new categories of shapes to choose from. The **Rectangles** category allows you to choose from seven different shapes. The **Equation Shapes** category allows you to use PowerPoint to illustrate various mathematical equations.

Step-By-Step Tip In Steps 4-5, explain that to draw a perfect shape, students can click the oval or rectangle, then press and hold Shift while dragging the pointer.

EXERCISE 2-14
Add Shapes to Slides

Adding Clip Art and pictures is not the only way you can add interest to your presentation. You can also use PowerPoint's Shapes, which are pre-designed shapes such as rectangles, ovals, and stars.

FIGURE 2.33 Select the Sun shape

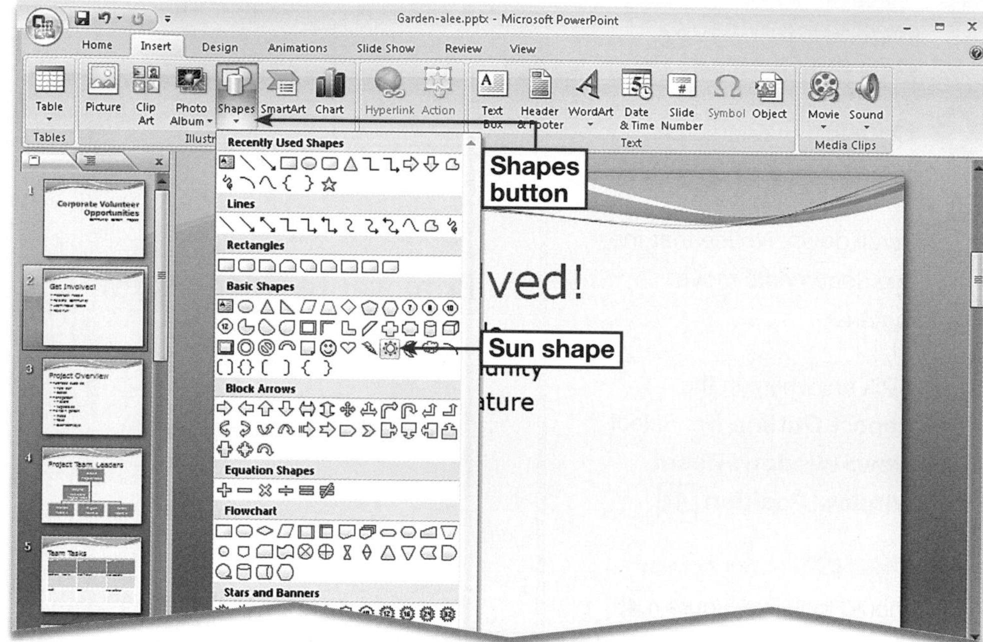

FIGURE 2.34 Sun shape added to slide

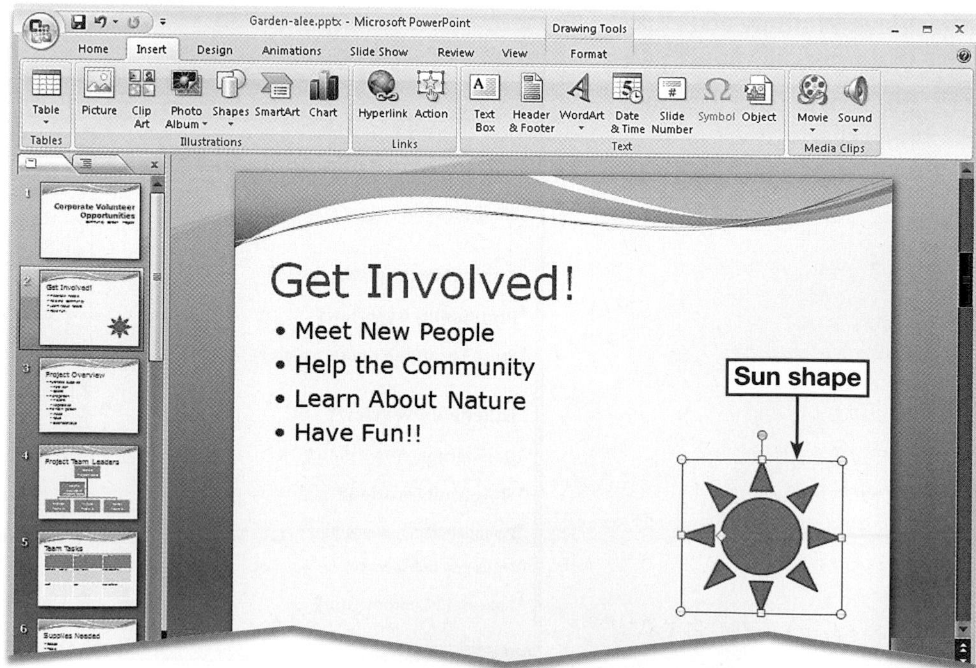

LESSON 4 After You Read

Vocabulary

Key Terms

bibliography
endnote
footer
footnote
header
Outline View
page break
report
section
section break
table of contents
Word Count

Academic Vocabulary

describe
log
navigate

Answer to Vocabulary Activity
Students key a paragraph that contains at least five vocabulary terms from this lesson. In their paragraphs, students explain how they would use each vocabulary term they selected to create and format a lengthy document. Students can exchange paragraphs and review terms they did not understand together.

Review Vocabulary

Complete the following statements on a separate piece of paper. Choose from the Vocabulary list on the left to complete the statements.

1. The Previous Page and Next Page buttons can help you ___navigate___ through, a multiple-page document such as a report. (p. 102)

2. A(n) ___header___ is text that appears at the top of every page. (p. 101)

3. A citation that appears at the end of a document is a(n) ___endnote___ (p. 107)

4. A(n) ___section___ can have different formatting from the rest of a document. (p. 112)

5. Use ___Word Count___ to count the number of paragraphs in a document. (p. 104)

Vocabulary Activity

6. Key a paragraph that includes at least five of the vocabulary terms from this lesson. In your paragraph, identify which Word tools can help you create and format lengthy documents such as reports.
   A. Identify the five vocabulary terms you will use in your paragraph.
   B. Key the paragraph. Explain how you would use each vocabulary term you identified to create and format a lengthy document.
   C. With your teacher's permission, exchange your paragraph with a peer. Review any terms you or your classmate did not understand.

Review Key Concepts

Answer the following questions on a separate piece of paper.

7. What does the Word Count command count in a document? (p. 104)
   A. Number of words.
   B. Number of paragraphs.
   C. Number of characters.
   D. All of the above.

8. What commands do you choose to insert a section break? (p. 110)
   A. Home>Section Break
   B. View>Break
   C. Insert>Section Break
   D. Page Layout>Page Setup> Breaks

9. What is Reveal Formatting used to view? (p. 98)
   A. A document close up.
   B. A document's formatting.
   C. A document's white space.
   D. A document as an outline.

10. Which of following items is used to cite information at the bottom of a page? (p. 108)
   A. Endnote
   B. References
   C. Footnote
   D. Table of contents

Step-By-Step

1. In your **Garden** file, select **Slide 7**.
2. Choose **Home>Slides> New Slide**.
3. In the title box, key: Thank You!
4. Choose **Insert> Illustrations>Picture** .
5. In the **Insert Picture** dialog box, select the data file **Flowers.jpg** (see Figure 2.31). Click **Insert**.
6. In the slide, use the sizing handles to enlarge the photo.
7. **CHECK** Your screen should look similar to Figure 2.32.
8. Save your file.

Continue to the next exercise.

Academic Skills

Never use a picture from the Internet without getting permission from the copyright owner. All original compositions, like photos and music, are copyright protected, even if there is no copyright notice © next to the artwork.

NCLB/Language Arts (NCTE 8) Remind students that they need to receive permission and properly credit all outside resources that they use.

EXERCISE 2-13
Add a Picture to a Slide

Pictures are images that are made up of small dots. A typical picture would be a photograph or artwork created in a software program like Microsoft Paint. You can insert pictures from your own scanned images, digital camera, or picture CD-ROM.

Step-By-Step Tip In **Step 6**, if students insert the wrong picture by mistake, have them press Delete to delete the picture and try again.

FIGURE 2.31 Insert Picture dialog box

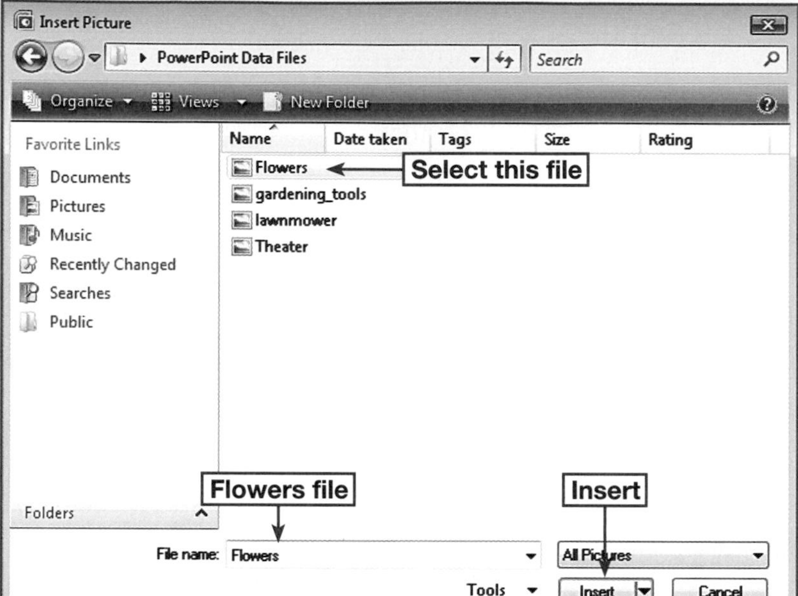

FIGURE 2.32 Inserted picture

LESSON 4 Practice It Activities

Step-By-Step

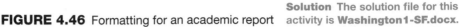

1. Open a new document. Click **Reveal Formatting** [icon]. Change the **Font** to **Times New Roman**, **12 pt**. Click **Default**. Click **No**.
2. Click **Alignment**. Choose **Alignment>Left**. Under **Indentation**, confirm **Right** is **0″**. Change **Line Spacing** to **Double** and **Spacing After** to **0 pt**. Click **Default**. Click **No**.
3. Click the **plus sign** [⊞] next to **Section**. Confirm all four **Margins** are **1″**.
4. **CHECK** Your screen should look like Figure 4.46.
5. Close the **Reveal Formatting** pane. Key the report heading shown in Figure 4.47. Press ENTER.
6. Choose **Insert>Text>Object>Text from File**. Insert the data file **Washington.docx**. Scroll to the top of the page.
7. **CHECK** Your screen should look like Figure 4.47. Save as Washington-[your first initial and last name]1. Close the file.

1. Format an Academic Report

Data File

Follow the steps to complete the activity.

Solution The solution file for this activity is **Washington1-SF.docx**.

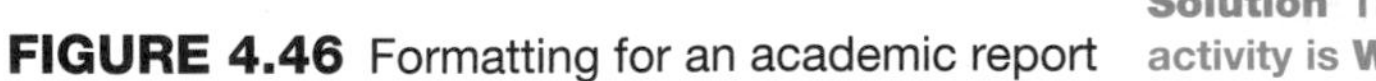

FIGURE 4.46 Formatting for an academic report

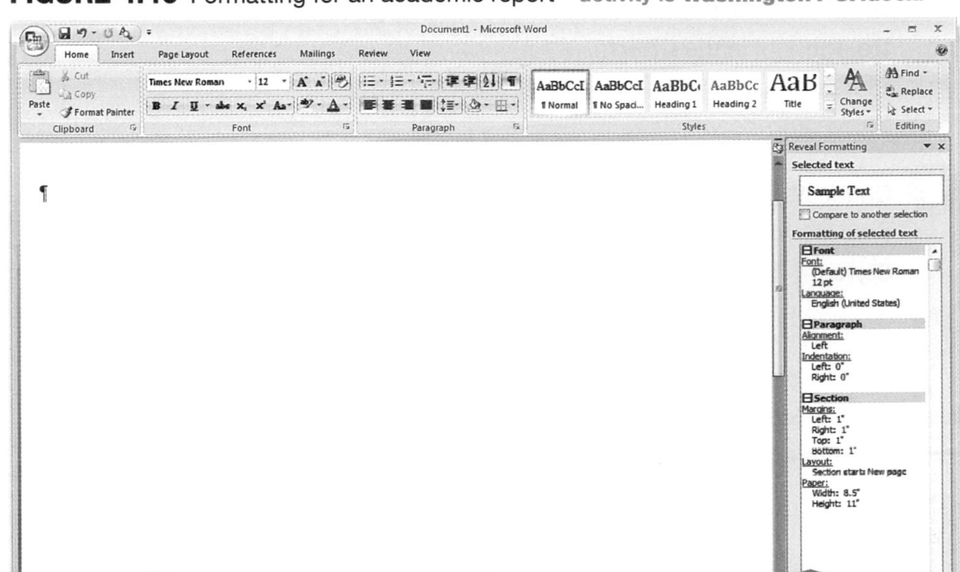

FIGURE 4.47 Academic report with heading and text inserted

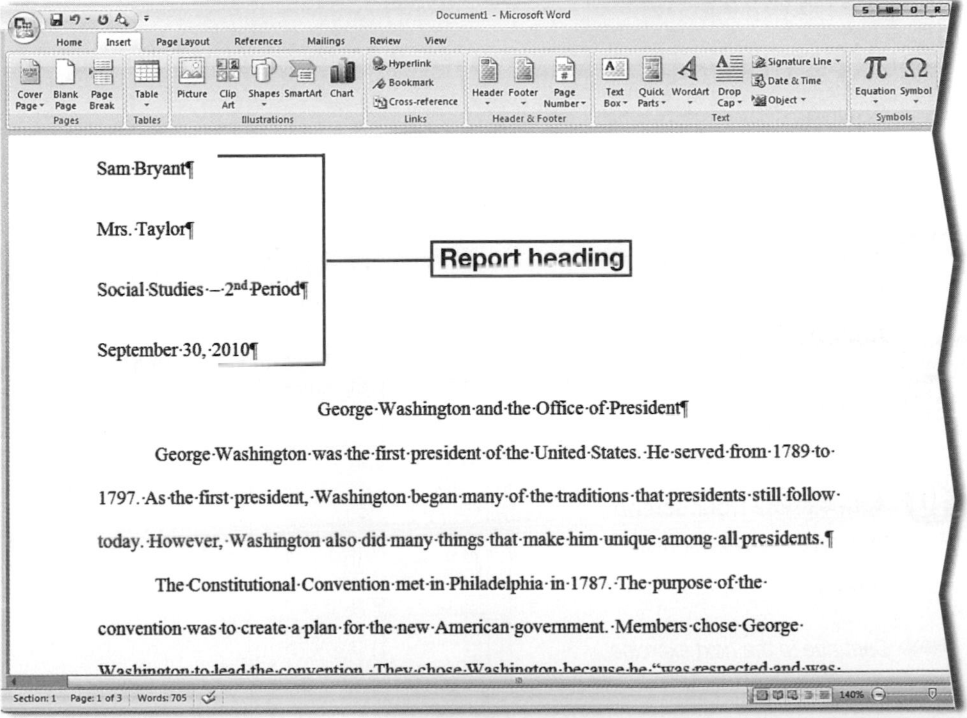

Step-By-Step

1. In your **Garden** file, on **Slide 7**, select the chart, if necessary.
2. Under the **Chart Tools** contextual tab, on the **Design** tab, in the **Chart Styles** group, click the **More** drop-down arrow.
3. On the **More Chart Styles** drop-down menu, click **Style 34** (see Figure 2.29).
4. Click on the Chart. Choose **Chart Tools>Format>Shape Styles>Shape Effects**.
5. Click on **Preset** in the **Preset** group and choose **Preset 5**.
6. Click in the **Chart Area** (see Figure 2.30).
7. Choose **Chart Tools>Format>Shape Styles>Shape Fill**.
8. In the **Shape Fill** drop-down menu, under **Theme Colors**, select **Blue, Accent 2, Lighter, 60%**.
9. Click outside the chart area.
10. CHECK Your screen should look like Figure 2.30. Save your file.

Continue to the next exercise.

EXERCISE 2-12
Apply Quick Styles to a Chart

As with SmartArt diagrams and tables, you can apply Quick Styles to charts as well. With a few simple steps, you can change the chart's colors, effects, and background. The ability to change such styles allows your charts to be clearer to understand and more visually appealing to your audience.

FIGURE 2.29 Chart Styles drop-down menu

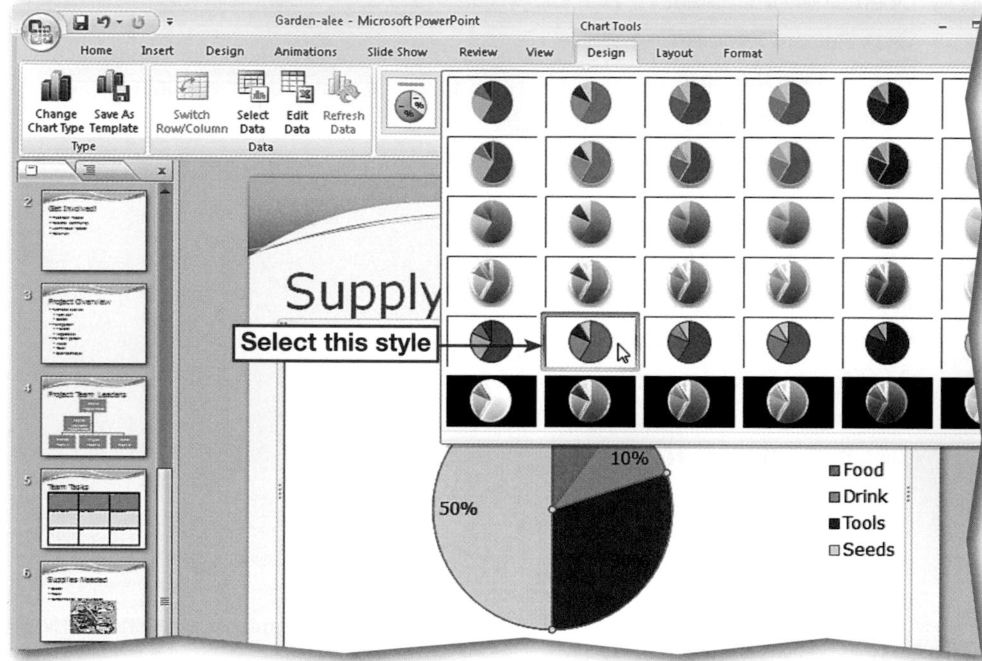

FIGURE 2.30 Pie chart with styles applied

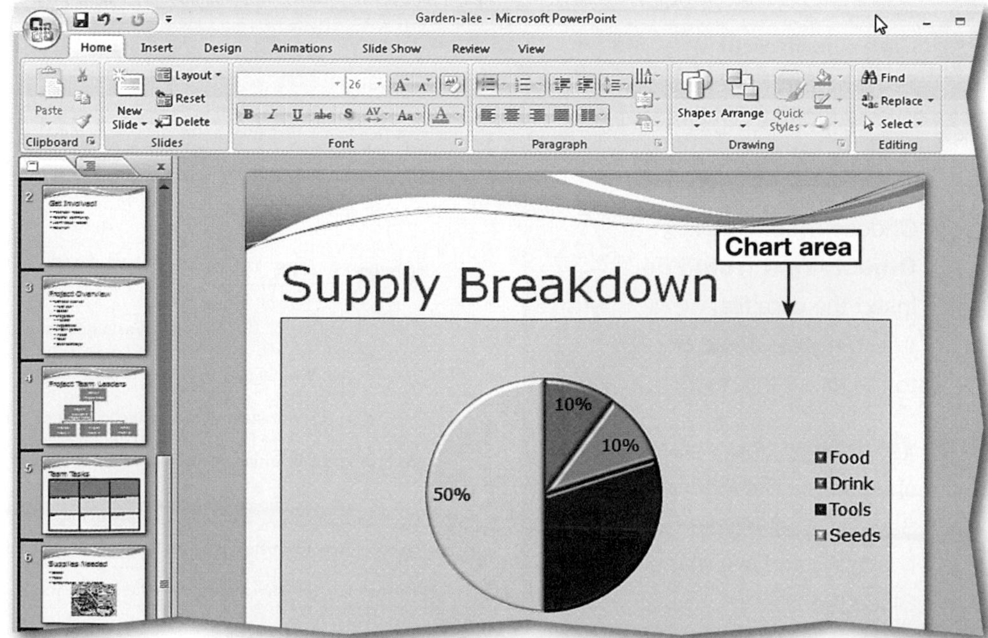

Step-By-Step

1. Open your **Washington-1** file. Save as: Washington-[your first initial and last name]2.
2. Choose **Insert>Header & Footer>Header>Edit Header**.
3. Click in the **Header** box. Key: Bryant. Press the spacebar once.
4. Click **Insert>Header & Footer>Page Number> Current Position>Plain Number**.
5. Select the name and page number. Click **Home> Paragraph>Align Right**. Deselect the text.
6. **CHECK** Your screen should look like Figure 4.48.
7. Press CTRL + HOME. Click **Browse by Page** .
8. Click **Next Page**. Click **Previous Page**.
9. **CHECK** Your screen should look like Figure 4.49. Save and close your file.

Solution The solution file for this activity is **Washington2-SF.docx**.

2. Add a Header and Navigate a Report

Follow the steps to complete the activity. You must complete Practice It Activity 1 before doing this activity.

New Student Strategy If a student did not complete Practice It Activity 1, the solution file for that activity can be used as a data file for this activity.

FIGURE 4.48 Header added to report

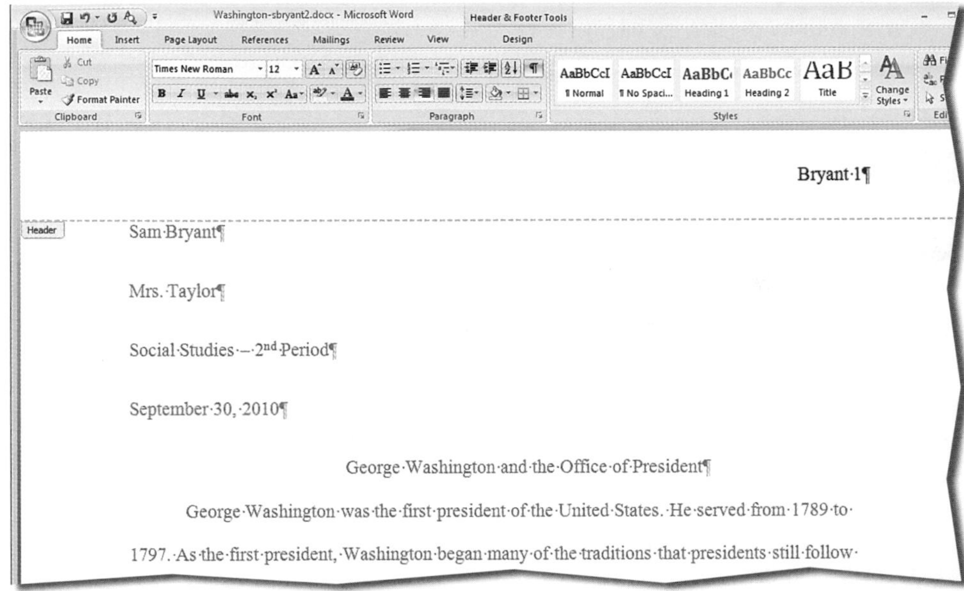

FIGURE 4.49 Use Browse by Page to move to Page 2

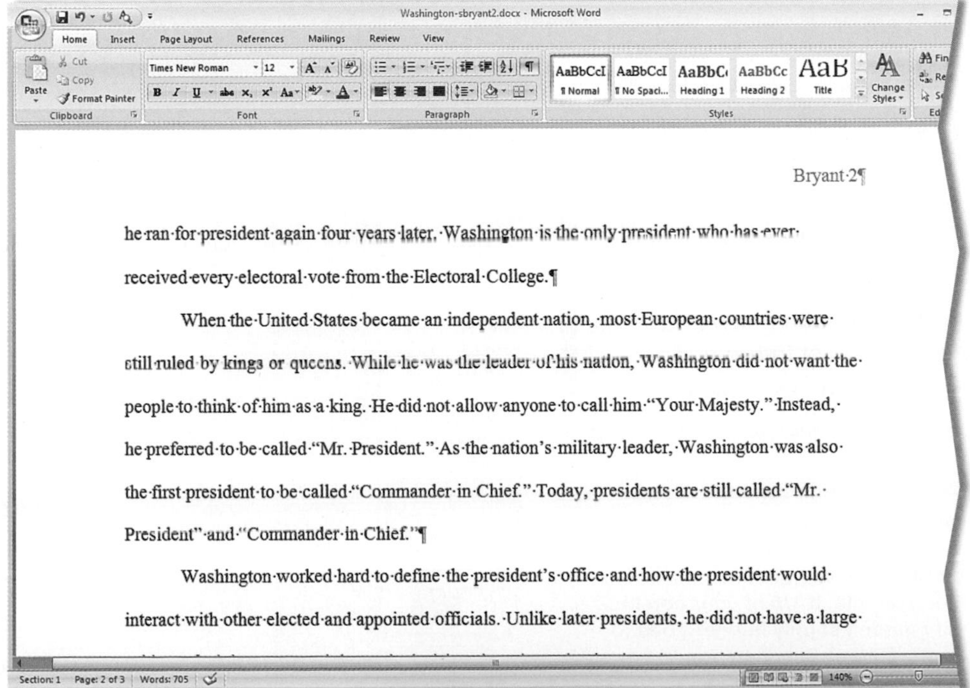

Step-By-Step

9. In the Excel worksheet, right-click **Select All** (see Figure 2.27).
10. Click **Clear Contents**.
11. Enter budget data for the community garden by filling in the datasheet as shown in Figure 2.27.
12. Exit Excel.
13. On the **Chart Tools** contextual tab, on the **Design** tab, click the **Chart Layouts** drop-down arrow. Choose **Layout 6**.
14. CHECK Your screen should look like Figure 2.28.
15. Save your file.

Continue to the next exercise.

Academic Skills

A bar chart or a line chart is not appropriate for displaying percentages and fractions. When deciding which chart to use, students should consider what information they need to convey.

NCLB/Math (Number and Operations) Pie charts represent proportions or fractions of a whole. For example, if 1/5 of your community garden supply budget goes to tools, 20% of the chart would be taken up by this category.

EXERCISE 2-11 (Continued)
Create a Chart

FIGURE 2.27 Information entered into Excel Datasheet window

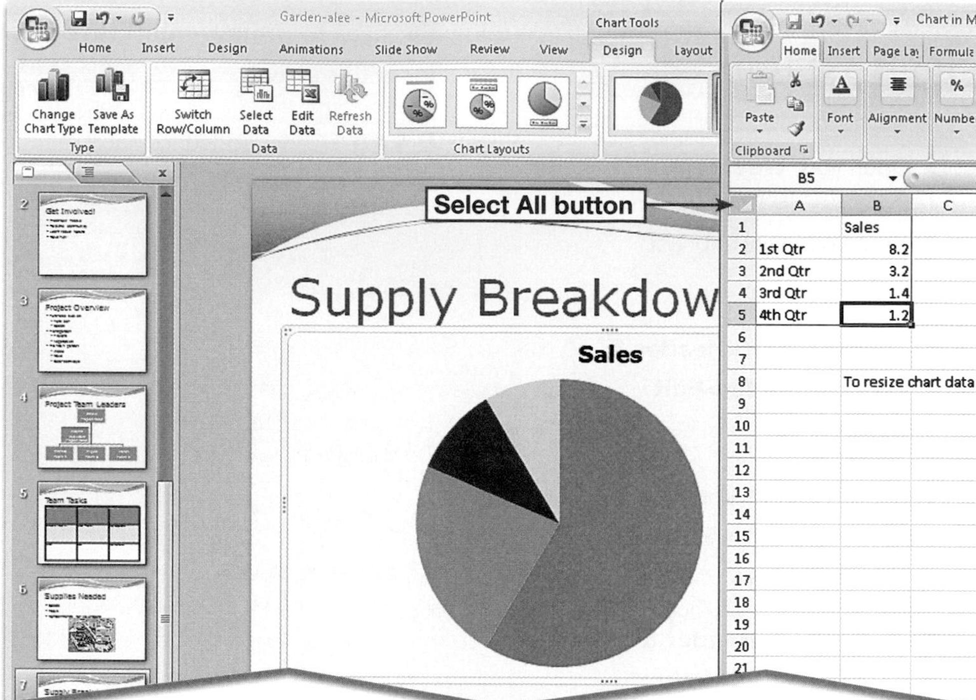

FIGURE 2.28 Completed pie chart

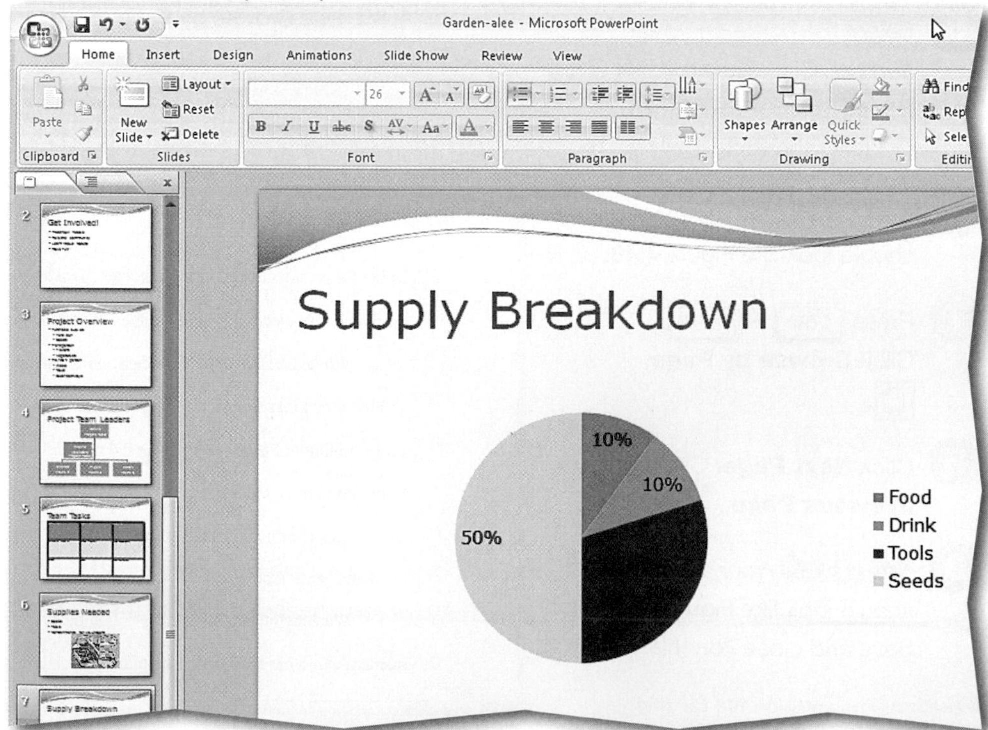

LESSON 4 Practice It Activities

Step-By-Step

1. Open your **Washington-2** file. Save as: Washington-[your first initial and last name]3.
2. On Page 1, click after **disagreed** at the end of the second paragraph. Place the cursor before the period. Press the spacebar once. Key: (Lee 50).
3. CHECK Your screen should look like Figure 4.50.
4. On Page 3, click before **Works Cited**. Choose **Insert>Pages>Page Break**.
5. Click after the last citation on Page 4. Press ENTER.
6. Key: Lee, Jane. "George Washington." The First Presidents. Ed. Marcus Taylor. New York: Presidential Press, 2009. 45-66.
7. Select **The First Presidents**. Click **Underline**.
8. CHECK Your screen should look like Figure 4.51. Save and close the file.

Solution The solution file for this activity is **Washington3-SF.docx**.

3. Modify a Works Cited List

Follow the steps to complete the activity. You must complete Practice It Activity 2 before doing this activity.

New Student Strategy If a student did not complete Practice It Activity 2, then the solution file for that activity can be used as a data file for this activity.

FIGURE 4.50 Parenthetical citation added to report

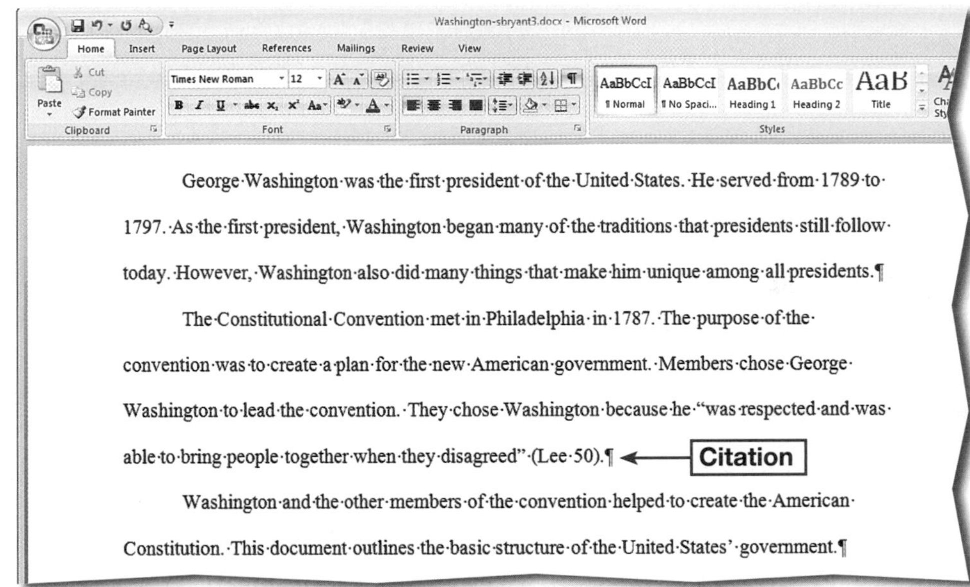

FIGURE 4.51 Works Cited page with citation added

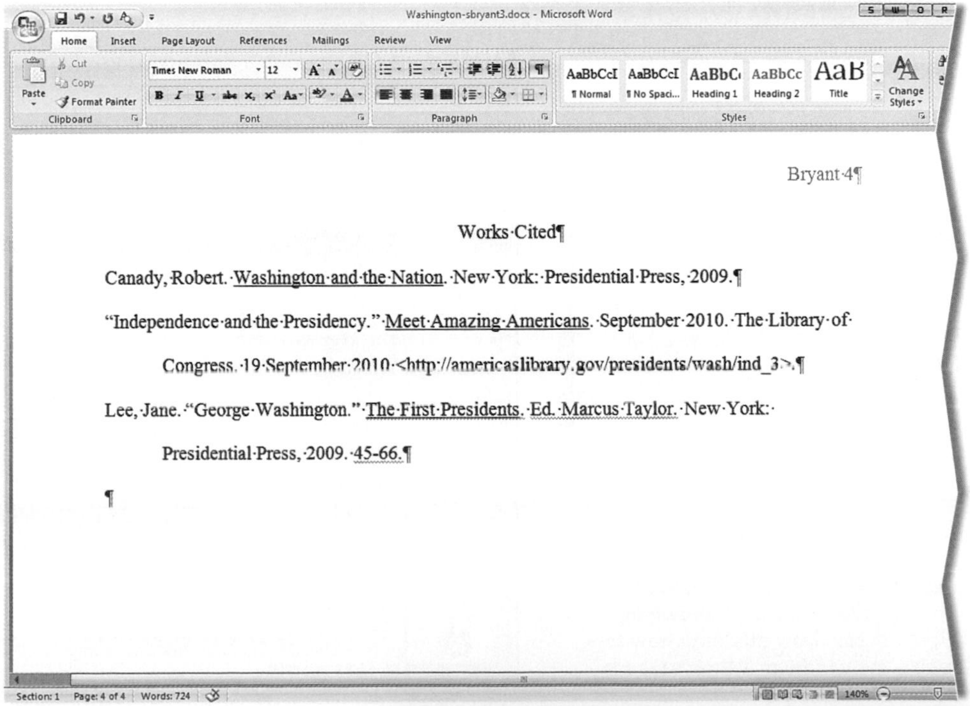

Step-By-Step

1. In your **Garden** file, select **Slide 6**.
2. Choose **Home>Slides> New Slide** drop-down arrow. Click **Title and Content**.
3. In the title box, key: Supply Breakdown.
4. On the **Insert** tab, in the **Illustrations** group, choose **Chart**.
5. In the **Insert Chart** dialog box, click **Pie**.
6. **CHECK** Your dialog box should look like Figure 2.25.
7. Select the chart shown in Figure 2.25. Click **OK**.
8. **CHECK** Your screen should look like Figure 2.26.

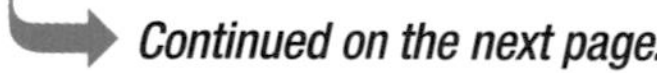

Continued on the next page.

You Should Know

When you select a pie chart, numbers are already included. Replace these numbers with your own project's data.

Step By Step Tip After **Step 5**, the Excel worksheet should automatically open in a window beside the PowerPoint window as shown in Figure 2.26. Show students how to resize the windows if their screens do not match Figure 2.26.

EXERCISE 2-11
Create a Chart

Like a diagram, a **chart** displays information in a visual way. Charts are useful for comparing changes over time. For example, you might use a line chart to show the fluctuation in population of manatees over the last ten years. When you insert a chart into PowerPoint, an Excel worksheet containing default data automatically opens. Once you replace the data with your own data it is shown in the form of a chart.

FIGURE 2.25 Insert Chart dialog box

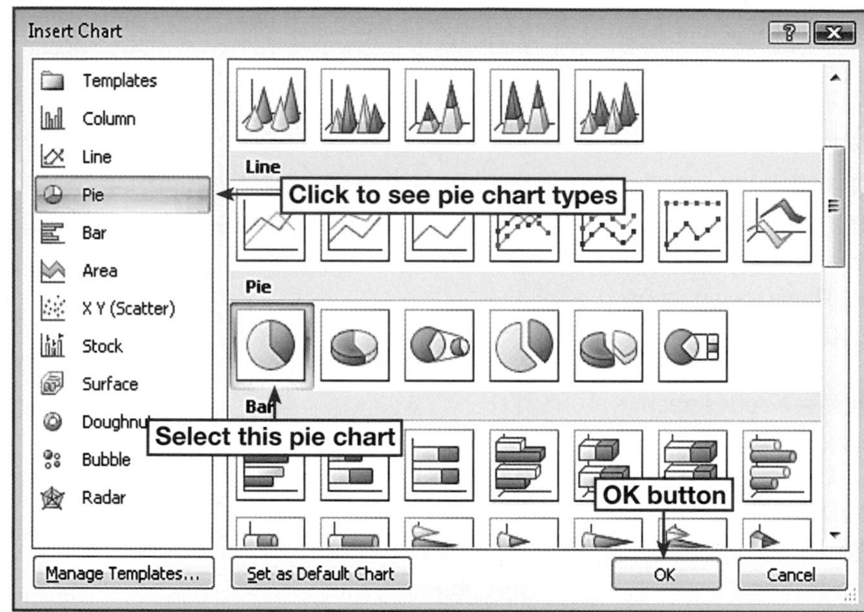

FIGURE 2.26 Sample chart inserted

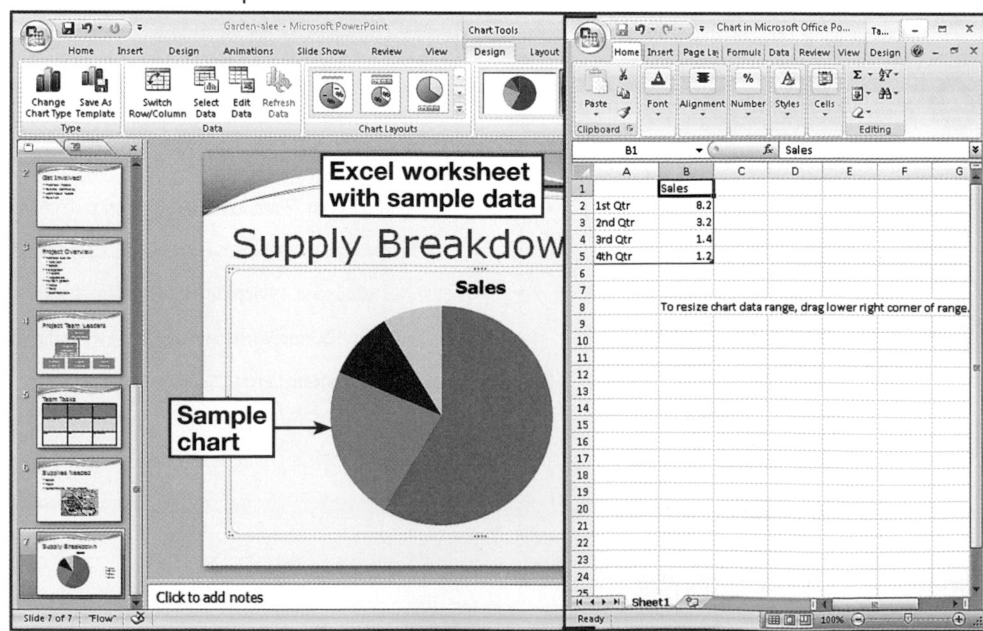

LESSON 4 You Try It Activities

4. Insert Headers and Page Breaks

You have written a report about the country of New Zealand. Before you submit the report to your teacher, you need to change the report's margins, add a header, and add a title. You also need to finish formatting your Works Cited page.

Solution The solution file for this activity is **New Zealand4-SF.docx.**

Step-By-Step

1. Open the data file **New Zealand.docx**. Save as: New Zealand-[your first initial and last name]4.
2. Choose **Reveal Formatting**. Change all the margins to **1″**. Change the default font to **Times New Roman 12 pt**. Close the task pane.
3. Choose **Insert>Header & Footer>Header>Edit Header**. In the **Header** box, key: Bryant. Add a space.
4. Insert a page number. Right-align the name and page number.
5. Just below the date, on a new line, key: New Zealand's Riches. Center the title.
6. **CHECK** Your screen should look like Figure 4.52.
7. On Page 2, insert a page break so the Works Cited list starts on Page 3.
8. **CHECK** Your screen should look like Figure 4.53. Save and close the file.

FIGURE 4.52 Report with header, title, and correct margins

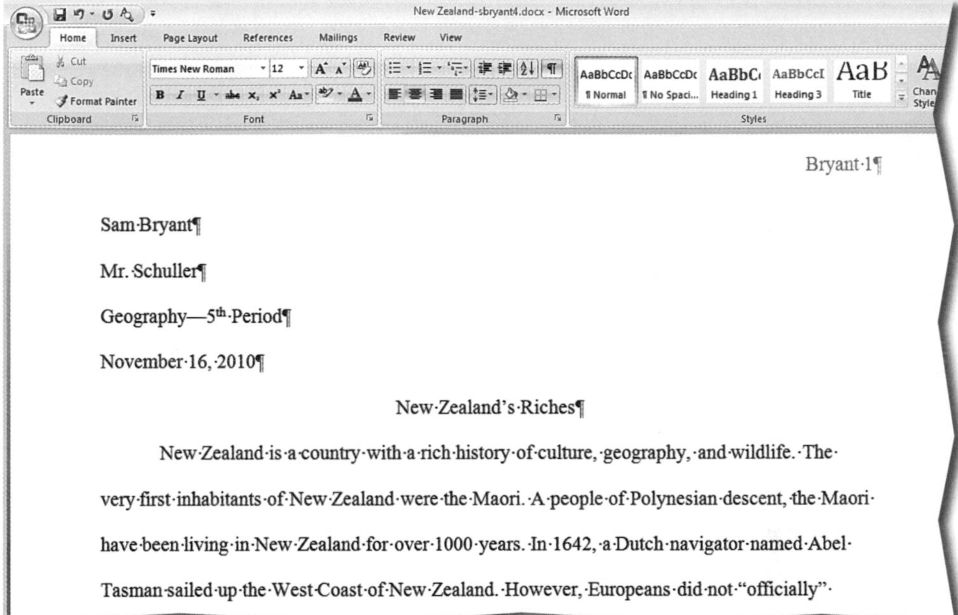

FIGURE 4.53 Page break inserted before Works Cited

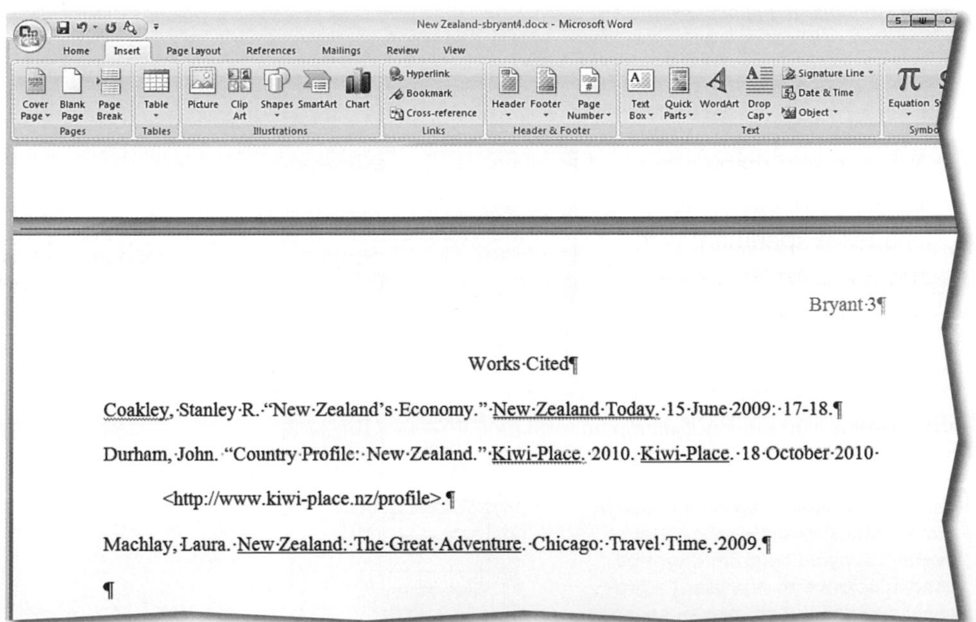

EXERCISE 2-10
Apply Quick Styles to a SmartArt Diagram

You can change the color and style of a SmartArt diagram using Quick Styles. An inserted diagram will automatically appear in the Accent 1 color of the Theme Color. By applying Quick Styles, you can change the color and effects of the diagram.

FIGURE 2.23 Change Colors menu

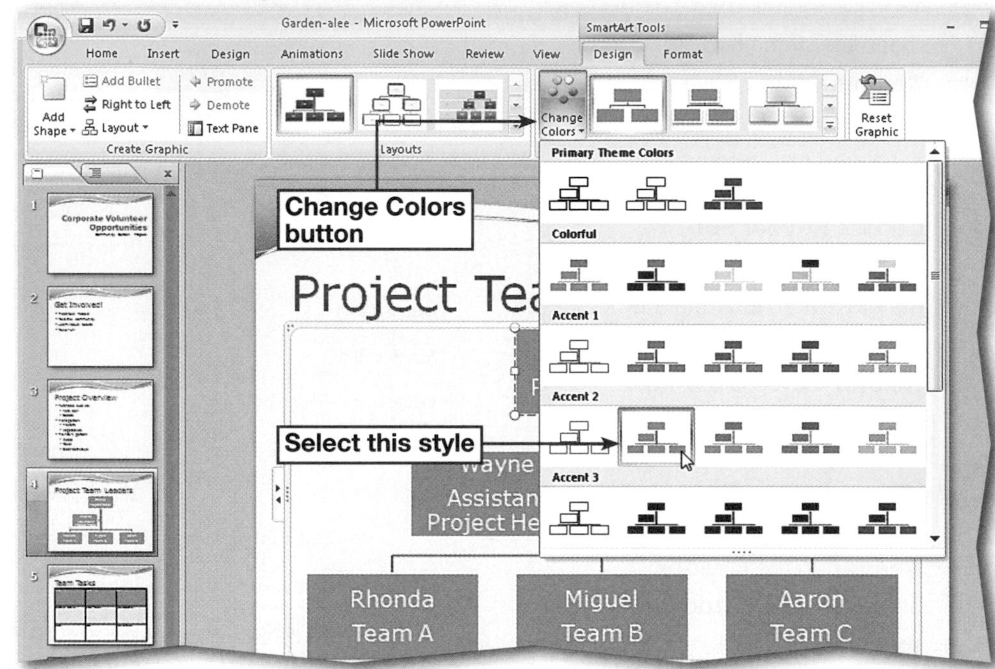

FIGURE 2.24 Diagram with Quick Styles applied

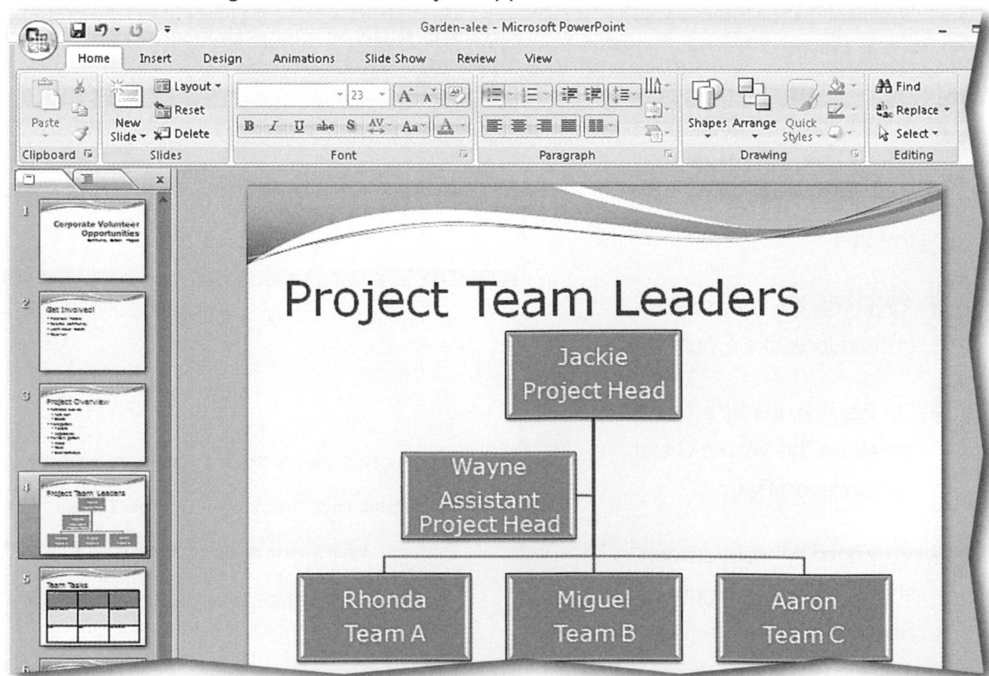

Step-By-Step

1. Select your SmartArt diagram. Choose **SmartArt Tools>Design>SmartArt Styles>Change Colors** .
2. On the **Change Colors** drop-down menu, choose the color shown in Figure 2.23.
3. Choose **SmartArt Tools>Design>SmartArt Styles>More** drop-down arrow.
4. In the **More** drop-down menu, under **3-D**, click **Cartoon**.
5. Click anywhere outside of the text box.
6. **CHECK** Your screen should look like Figure 2.24.
7. Save your file.

Continue to the next exercise.

Shortcuts

You can add many different kinds of effects to shapes. Experiment with the SmartArt Styles menu to see live previews of the style options.

NCLB/Math (Geometry) Explore the different kinds of diagrams and how they are used to explain important concepts. A venn diagram is used in mathematics to show areas that overlap. A cycle diagram might be used in science to represent a process, such as the change of seasons.

LESSON 4 You Try It Activities

5. Review a Report

Your teacher has requested that your geography report be no longer than 600 words. You decide to use the Word tools to make sure your report meets your teacher's requirement. You also decide to modify your report's Document Properties. You must complete You Try It Activity 4 before doing this activity.

Solution The solution file for this activity is New Zealand5-SF.docx.

Step-By-Step

1. Open your **New Zealand-4** file. Save as: New Zealand-[your first initial and last name]5.
2. Open the **Word Count** dialog box. Review the word count and close the dialog box.
3. On Page 2, in the third paragraph, delete the text **a bird with nostrils at the end of its beak,**. Recount the report's word count.
4. **CHECK** Your screen should look like Figure 4.54.
5. Open the **Document Properties** dialog box. On the **Summary** tab, add the report's **Title** and **Author**. Delete extra information contained on the tab. Click **OK**.
6. Go to Page 1. View the report in **Outline** view.
7. **CHECK** Your screen should look similar to Figure 4.55. Save and close the file.

New Student Strategy If a student did not complete You Try It Activity 4, then the solution file for that activity can be used as a data file for this activity.

FIGURE 4.54 Recounted Word Count

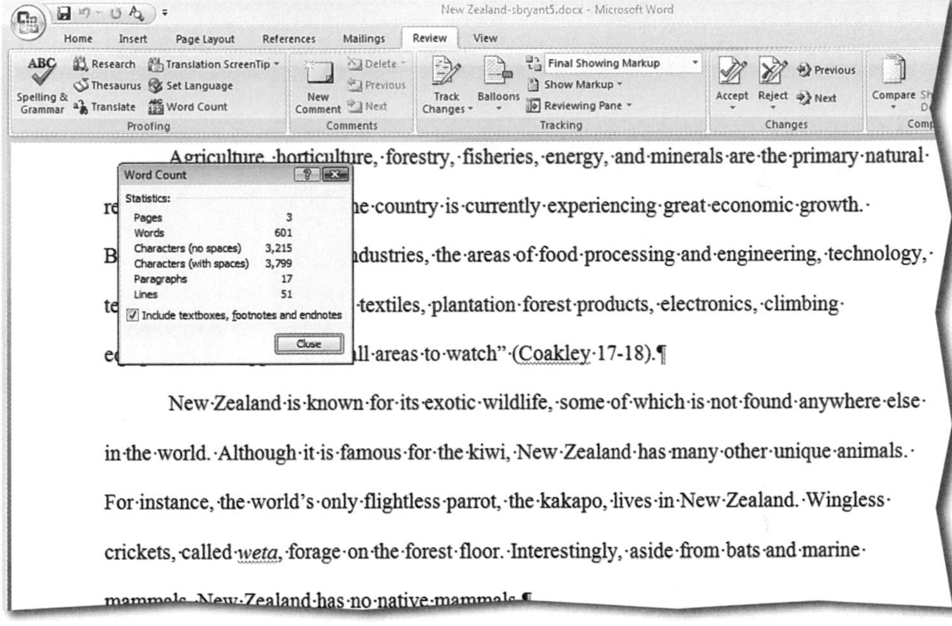

FIGURE 4.55 Report in Outline view

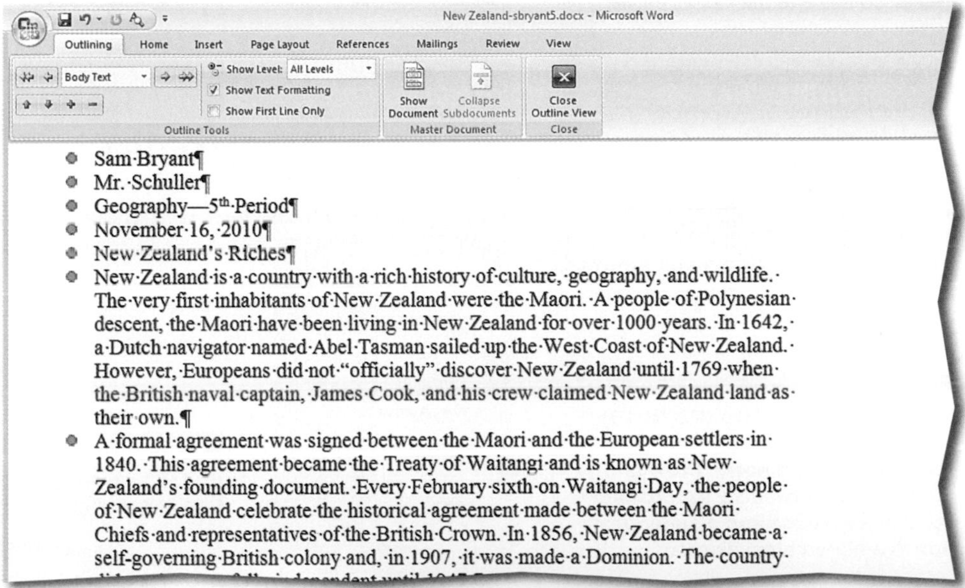

Step-By-Step

EXERCISE 2-9 (Continued)
Create a SmartArt Diagram

10. Click in the Assistant shape (see Figure 2.21). Key: Wayne. Press ENTER. Key: Assistant Project Head.

11. Click in the left subordinate box. Key: Rhonda. Press ENTER. Key: Team A.

12. CHECK Your screen should look like Figure 2.21.

13. Click in the middle subordinate box. Key: Miguel. Press ENTER. Key: Team B.

14. Click in the right subordinate box. Key: Aaron. Press ENTER. Key: Team C.

15. Click anywhere outside the diagram box.

16. CHECK Your screen should look like Figure 2.22.

17. Save your file.

Continue to the next exercise.

Troubleshooter

If you delete something by mistake, press CTRL + Z to undo the deletion.

NCLB/Language Arts (NCTE 10) Remind students of the meaning of the word "subordinate." Draw a comparison between a subordinate point in an outline and a subordinate box in a hierarchical diagram.

FIGURE 2.21 Text keyed into subordinate box

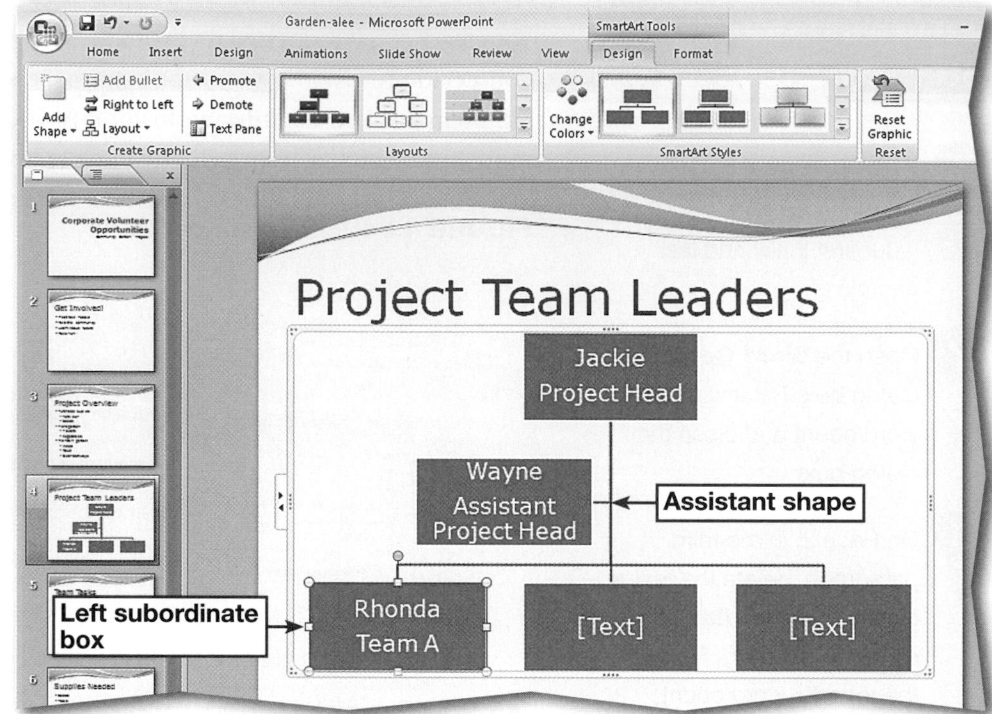

FIGURE 2.22 Final diagram

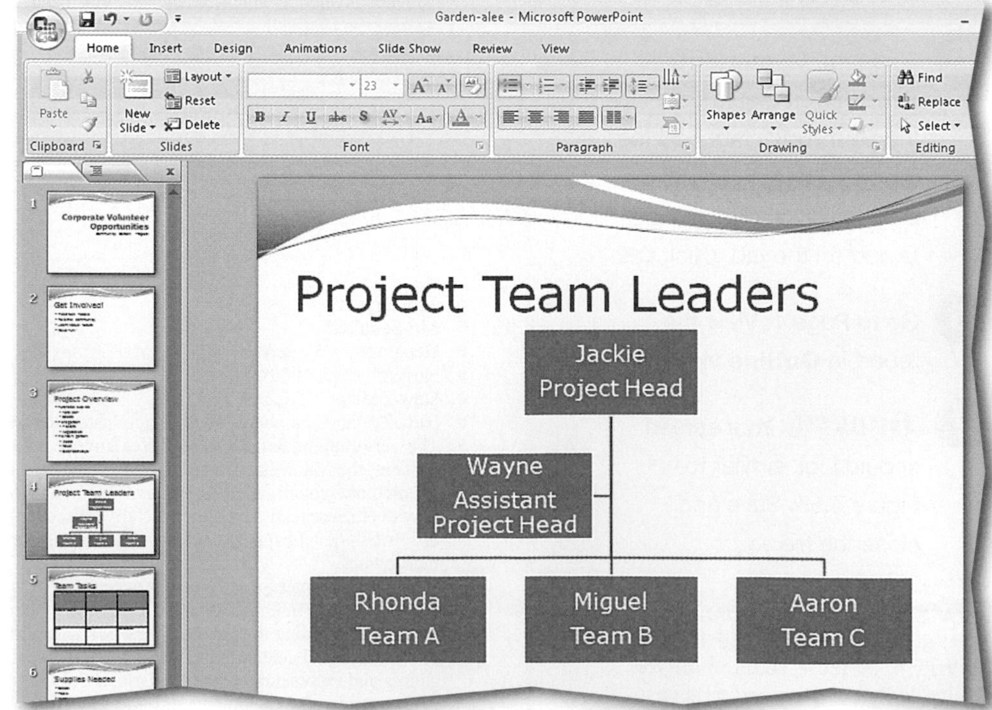

LESSON 4 Critical Thinking Activities

Beyond the Classroom Activity Student outlines will vary, but should include a list of at least four formatting skills learned in this lesson, and a list of at least two viewing skills learned in this lesson. A sample solution file is **w4rev6-SF.docx**.

Standards at Work Activity The solution file for this activity is **Conflict7-SF.docx**.

21st Century Skills Activity Student paragraphs will vary, but should describe a decision that the student made and the process that led up to the decision.

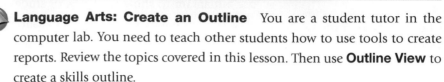

6. Beyond the Classroom Activity

Language Arts: Create an Outline You are a student tutor in the computer lab. You need to teach other students how to use tools to create reports. Review the topics covered in this lesson. Then use **Outline View** to create a skills outline.

- Divide the outline into two main heads: **Formatting Documents** and **Viewing Documents**.
- Under **Formatting Documents**, list at least four lesson skills you would use to format a report.
- Under **Viewing Documents**, list at least four lesson skills you would use to view a report.

Save your outline as: w4rev-[your first initial and last name]6.

7. Standards at Work Activity

Microsoft Certified Application Specialist Correlation
Word 1.2 *Lay Out Documents*

Create Headers and Footers Your supervisor has completed a report on how to resolve conflict in the workplace. Before he submits the report, he wants you to insert a header and footer into the document.

Open the data file **Conflict.docx**. Save as: Conflict-[your first initial and last name]7. Insert a header that contains the name of the report and the page number. Insert a footer that contains today's date. Format the header and footer content so they align right. Use **Page Setup** to make sure the report's title page contains no header or footer information.

8. 21st Century Skills Activity

Analyze Your Decision-Making Skills To make a good decision, you have to gather information, evaluate your choices, and predict what the outcome of your decision will be. Think about an important decision that you recently made. Then, key one or two paragraphs. In your paragraphs:

- State what decision you had to make.
- Describe the process you took to make that decision.
- Evaluate the outcome of your decision. Did you make a good decision? Why or why not? How might you change your decision-making process to make better decisions in the future?

Save your file as: w4rev-[your first initial and last name]8.

Go Online e-REVIEW
glencoe.com

Go to the **Online Learning Center** to complete the following review activities.

Online Self Check
To test your knowledge of the material, click **Unit 1> Lesson 4** and choose **Self Checks**.

Interactive Review
To review the main points of this lesson, click **Unit 1> Lesson 4** and choose **Interactive Review**.

Step-By-Step

1. In your **Garden** file, select **Slide 3**.
2. Choose **Home>Slides> New Slide**.
3. In the **Slides** group, click **Layout**. In the drop-down menu, click **Title and Content**.
4. In the title box, key: Project Team Leaders.
5. Click in the content text box. Choose **Insert> Illustrations>SmartArt**.
6. In the **Choose SmartArt Graphic** dialog box, click **Hierarchy**. Select **Organization Chart**. Click **OK**. Close the window.
7. **CHECK** Your screen should look like Figure 2.19.
8. Click in the diagram's top box. Key: Jackie. Press ENTER. Key: Project Head.
9. **CHECK** Your screen should look like Figure 2.20.

Continued on the next page.

Tech Tip

The text will automatically resize itself as you type. As you type more text, the font size becomes smaller to fit all the text in the box.

EXERCISE 2-9
Create a SmartArt Diagram

A **diagram** is a graphic that organizes information visually. For example, you might use a diagram to show the levels of student government at your school. The senior class vice-president, secretary, and treasurer all report to the senior class president, so the senior class president would be at the top of the diagram. PowerPoint provides many different types of diagrams that can be easily inserted into a presentation.

Step-By-Step Tip In **Step 6** tell students to use the **ScreenTip** to identify the correct chart.

FIGURE 2.19 Diagram inserted into slide

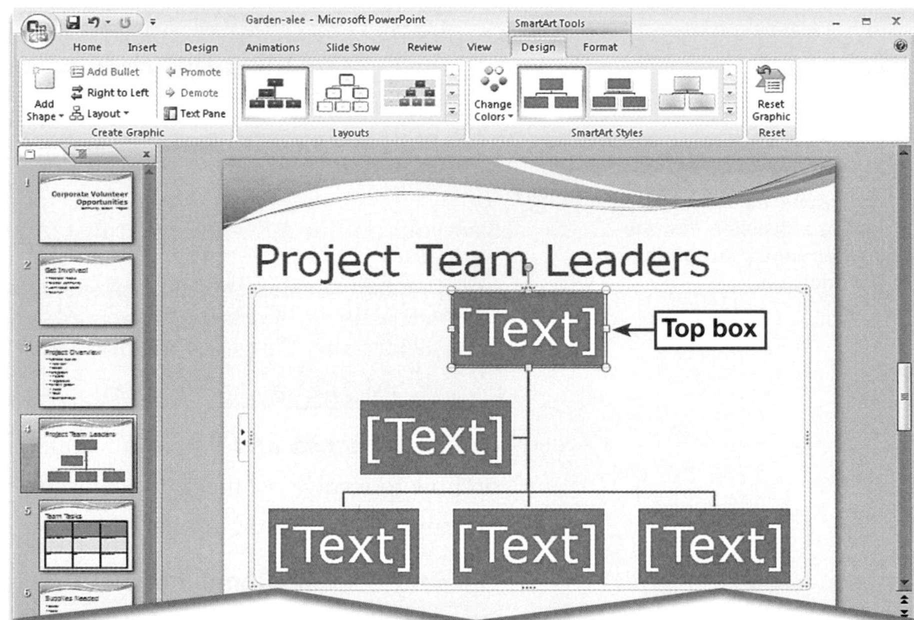

FIGURE 2.20 Text keyed into top box

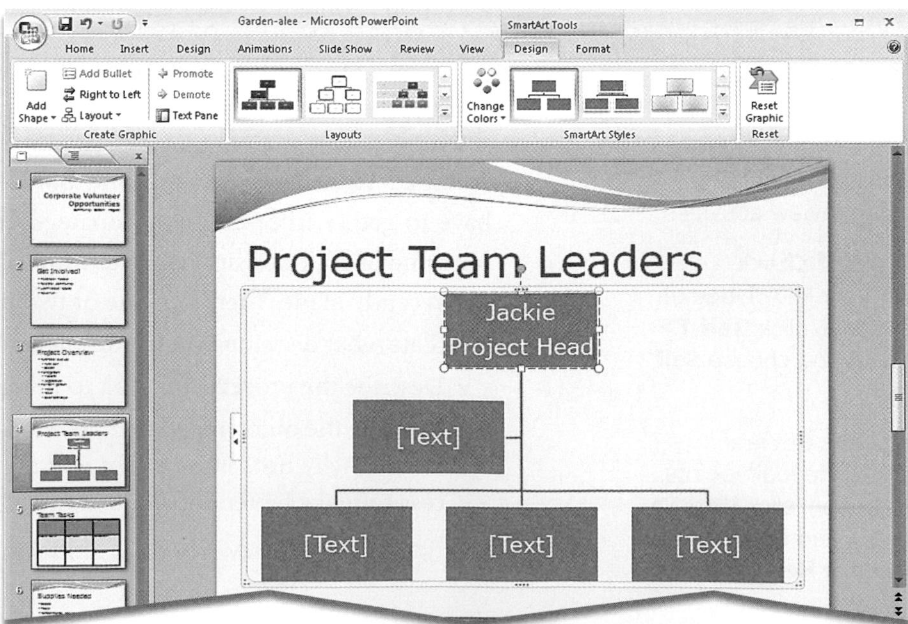

LESSON 4 Challenge Yourself Projects

Before You Begin

Take a Point of View You will often be asked to write reports that provide facts and recommendations based on your research and analysis. These projects show you the skills you need to present a superior report.

Reflect Once you complete the projects, open a Word document and answer the following:

1. Why is it important to use proper formatting when citing sources?
2. What are the benefits of using headers, footers, and a table of contents?
3. How can creating an outline help you organize your ideas at the start and end of a research project?

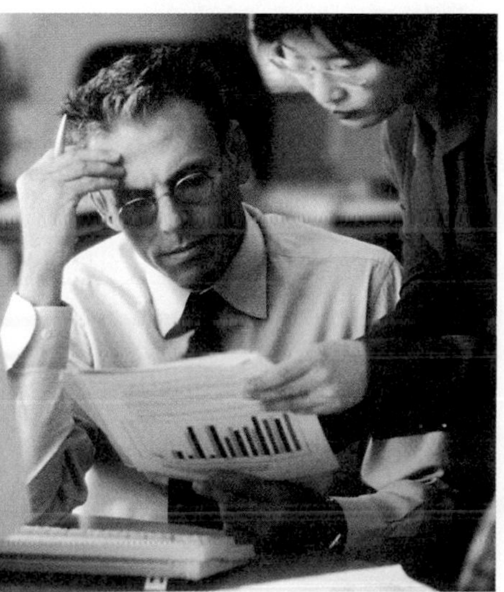

Answers Rubrics for each Challenge Yourself Project are available at **glencoe.com**. You may want to download the rubrics and make them available to students as they complete each project.

9. Cite Sources

Rubric

LEVEL This is an intermediate level project.

Language Arts: Insert Footnotes and References You are writing a report on the importance of marketing research. Open the data file **Marketing_Report.docx**. Save as: Marketing_Report-[your first initial and last name]9. Then:

Solution A sample solution file is **Marketing_Report9-SF.docx**.

- Use the **Footnotes** group on the **References** tab to insert two footnotes to the report. Create appropriate sources and make sure that the sources are formatted in Chicago style.
- Use a page break to create a **Bibliography** page. Using the **Citations & Bibliography** group on the **References** tab, insert the two sources you created.
- Add your name and the current date to the report's title page.

10. Format a Report

Rubric

LEVEL This is an intermediate level project.

Language Arts: Insert Headers, Footers, and a Table of Contents You need to finish formatting your marketing report. Open your **Marketing_Report-9** file. Save as: Marketing_Report-[your first initial and last name]10. Then:

Solution A sample solution file is **Marketing_Report10-SF.docx**.

- Use a section break to add a table of contents page. Add the head **CONTENTS**, but do not insert the table of contents yet.
- Add headers and footers to the report. The title page should contain no header or footer information.
- The Table of Contents page should have **ii** centered in the footer. The report body should have **Marketing Report [Page Number]** right aligned in the header. Use the **Link to Previous** button to format each section differently.
- Insert the table of contents. Format the table to reflect the report formatting.

11. Use Outline View

Rubric

LEVEL This is an advanced level project.

Language Arts: Outline a Report Outlining a report that you have already written can help you identify organizational problems. Open your **Marketing_Report-10** file. Save as: Marketing_Report-[your first initial and last name]11.

Solution A sample solution file is **Marketing_Report11-SF.docx**.

View the report in **Outline View**. Delete all the text that is not a **Heading 1** or **Heading 2**. The remaining text is your "skeleton" outline. Review the outline to identify any organizational problems. Make your final corrections.

Step-By-Step

10 Close the **Clip Art** task pane.

11 Click the image and drag it under the bulleted text.

12 Press SHIFT and drag the sizing handle in the lower right corner down to enlarge the image (see Figure 2.17).

13 Release the mouse button. Click anywhere in the slide.

14 CHECK Your screen should look similar to Figure 2.18.

15 Save your file.

Continue to the next exercise.

Shortcuts

Another way to insert Clip Art is to drag an image from the **Clip Art** task pane to your slide.

Academic Skills

In **Step 12**, you press the **Shift** key so that the image will maintain the same proportion as you drag the handle. Proportion means that the ratio of the height to the width remains the same.

NCLB/Math (Geometry) Explain to students that maintaining the same proportions will keep an image from becoming distorted when it is resized. Show them what happens if the proportions are changed.

EXERCISE 2-8 (Continued)
Add Clip Art to a Slide

FIGURE 2.17 Enlarging the image

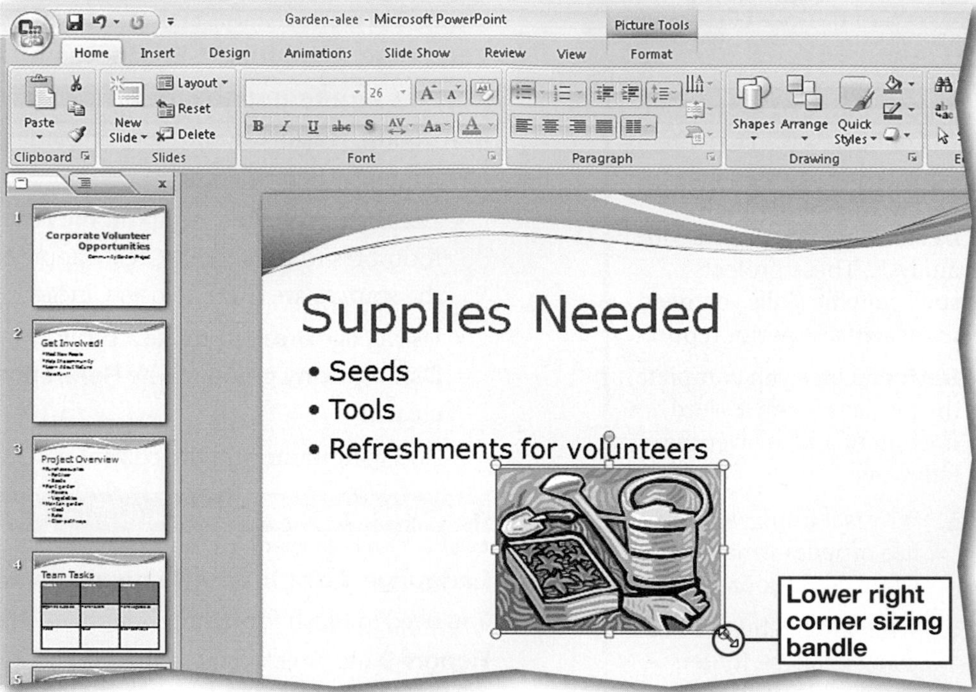

Differentiated Instruction/Advanced Students Students can use Clip Art as a background to their text. To place Clip Art behind text, right-click the Clip Art in the slide and choose **Send to Back>Send to Back.**

FIGURE 2.18 Slide with Clip Art inserted

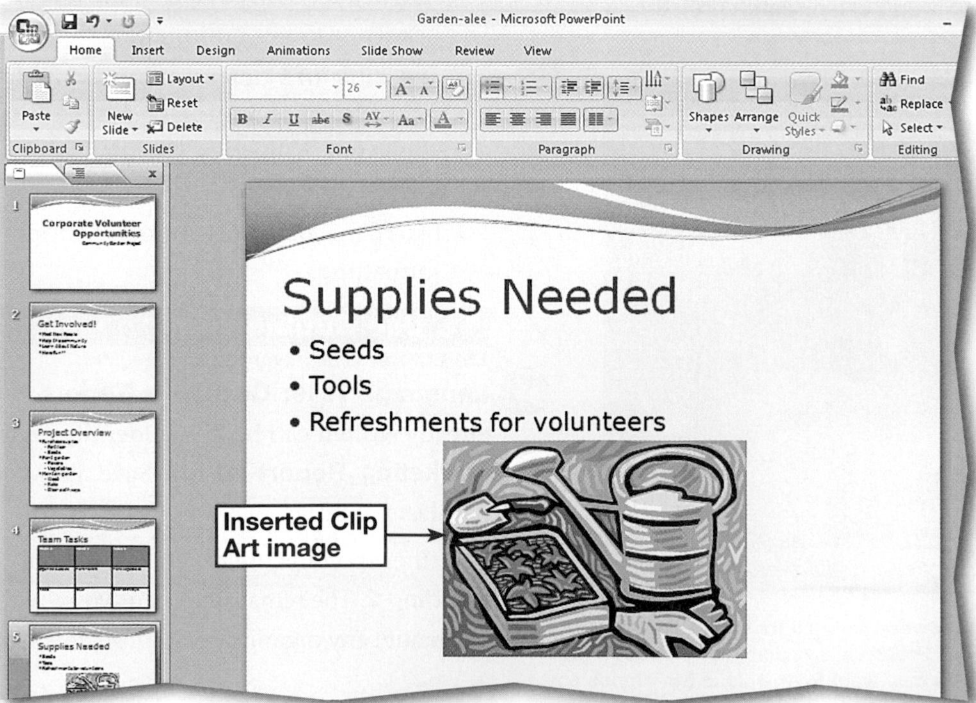

LESSON 5

Columns, Tables, and Graphics

Key Concepts

- Create and format columns
- Insert and modify a table and a chart
- Insert and manipulate Clip Art, SmartArt, and WordArt
- Work with a text box
- Insert, position, and modify a shape

Standard

The following standards are covered in this lesson. Refer to pages xxv and 715 for a description of the standards listed here.

ISTE Standards Correlation

NETS•S

1a, 1b, 1c, 2b, 3d, 6a, 6b

Microsoft Certified Application Specialist

Word

1.2, 3.1, 3.2, 3.3, 3.4, 4.2, 4.3

When creating a document, you do not always need to present your information using plain text. Using Microsoft Word, you have many options from which to choose when deciding how to present your work. In this lesson, you will learn how to use columns, tables, and graphics to organize and display information visually in a Word document. Choose your graphic elements carefully, and your work will really stand out!

21st CENTURY SKILLS

See page TM63 for answer to 21st Century Skills.

Take Responsibility Think about your strengths and weaknesses associated with your school and work performances. Assessing what you are good at—and areas that need improvement—can help you take responsibility for your own learning and improve on your weaknesses. Take the initiative to study hard for tests, get involved in your community, and participate in extracurricular activities. *What is one thing you can do to become a more responsible student or employee?*

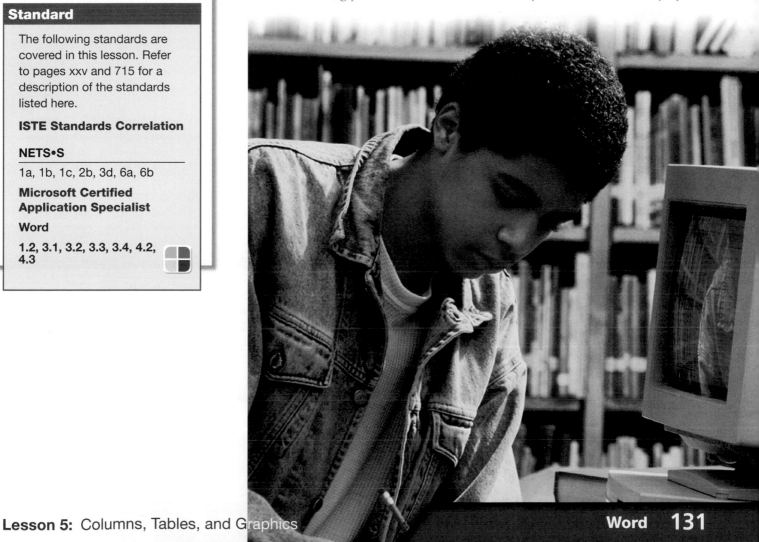

Step-By-Step

1. In your **Garden** file, select **Slide 4**. Choose **Home>Slides>New Slide**.
2. In the title box, key: Supplies Needed.
3. In the text box, key the three bullet points shown in Figure 2.15.
4. On the **Insert** tab, in the **Illustrations** group, click **Clip Art**.
5. In the **Clip Art** task pane, under **Search for**, key: garden.
6. Under **Search in**, make sure **All collections** is selected.
7. Click the **Results should be** drop-down arrow. Make sure only **Clip Art** is selected. Click **Go**.
8. **CHECK** Your screen should look similar to Figure 2.16.
9. Click the image (or a similar image) shown in Figure 2.16.

Continued on the next page.

Step-By-Step Tip In **Step 8**, be aware that students may be sent online to search Clip Art on Office Online. If students are unable to go online, you can provide them with the data file **Garden.jpg**.

EXERCISE 2-8
Add Clip Art to a Slide

Images help make your presentation visually interesting. You can use PowerPoint to locate premade graphics known as **Clip Art**. The Clip Art task pane helps you search for the image that best fits your presentation.

FIGURE 2.15 Slide 6 text

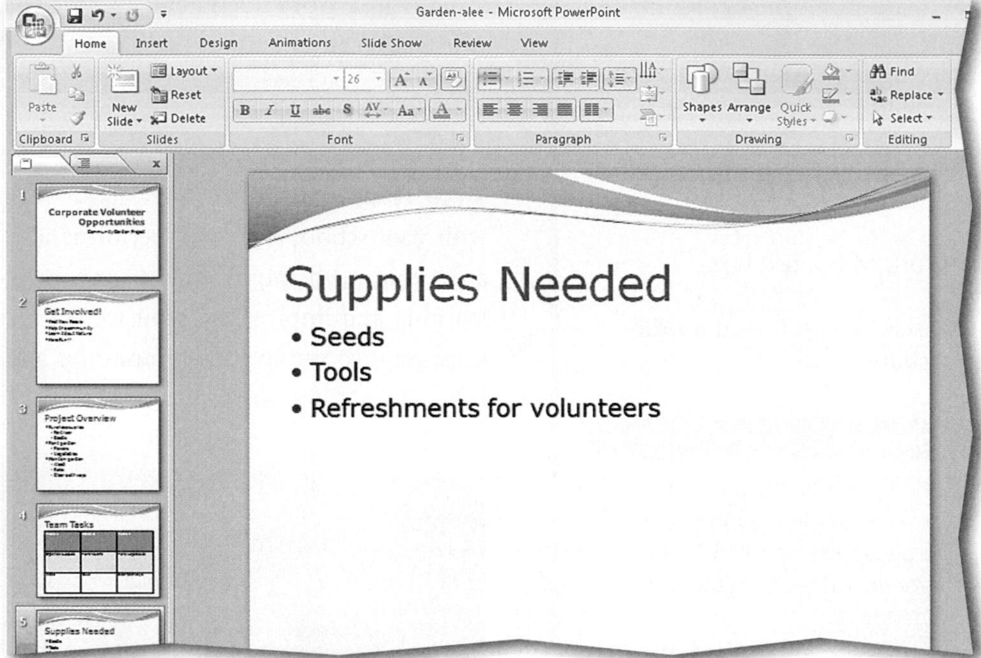

FIGURE 2.16 Clip Art task pane

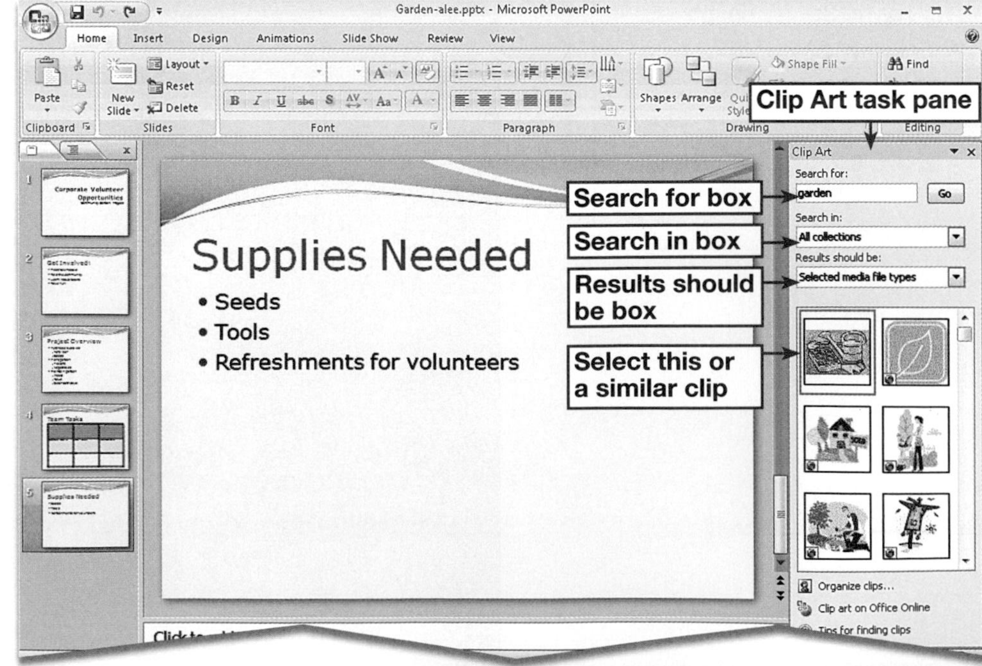

LESSON 5 Reading Guide

Before You Read

See page TM42 for English Learner activity suggestions.

Helpful Memory Tools Successful readers use tricks to help them remember. For example, the acronym *HOMES* is a memory aid where each letter stands for one of the five Great Lakes. Some students may try to create a song using the information. As you read the lesson, look for opportunities to make up your own memory aids.

Read To Learn

- Consider how columns affect the readability and flow of your document.
- Explore ways in which data and information can be conveyed visually.
- Determine how graphics can effectively add visual interest to your document.

Main Idea

Word provides several features to enhance the appearance and readability of your documents.

Vocabulary

Key Terms

cell	diagram	SmartArt
chart	graphic	style
Clip Art	newsletter	table
column	shape	text box
column break	sizing handle	WordArt

Academic Vocabulary

These words appear in your reading and on your tests. Make sure you know their meanings.

restore
survey
visual

Quick Write Activity

Describe On a separate sheet of paper, describe how a popular magazine, newspaper, or Web site combines text and graphics to grab attention and to convey important information. How might you use this example as a model for adding graphics to your own memo, letter, or flyer?

Study Skills

Motivate Yourself When you work on a project, do not wait until the last minute to start your tasks. Deadline anxiety can slow you down and cause you to lose your motivation. Remember, past success is the greatest motivator for your next project!

Academic Standards

English Language Arts

NCTE 4 Use written language to communicate effectively.

NCTE 5 Use different writing process elements to communicate effectively.

Math

NCTM (Number and Operations) Compute fluently and make reasonable estimates.

NCTM (Geometry) Analyze characteristics and properties of two- and three-dimensional geometric shapes and develop mathematical arguments about geometric relationships.

Step-By-Step

1. In your **Garden** file, click the **Slides** pane. On **Slide 4** move your pointer to the bottom border of the table (see Figure 2.13). The pointer will become a double-headed arrow.
2. Click and drag the sizing handle down as shown in Figure 2.13.
3. **CHECK** Your screen should look like Figure 2.13.
4. On the **Table Tools** contextual tab, on the **Design** tab, in the **Table Styles** group, click the **More Styles** drop-down arrow (see Figure 2.13).
5. On the drop-down menu, under **Medium**, choose **Medium Style 2, Accent 2**.
6. Select the whole table. Select **Table Tools>Design>Table Styles>Border** drop-down arrow. Select **All Borders**.
7. **CHECK** Your screen should look like Figure 2.14.
8. Save your file.

Continue to the next exercise.

Step-By-Step Tip After **Step 6**, have students compare how the black borders enhance the table by improving the contrast between the table rows and columns.

EXERCISE 2-7
Apply Quick Styles to Tables

Tables placed on a slide that already has a theme applied to it will automatically appear in a style that complements the theme. However, you can always change the appearance of your tables if you find them difficult to read or prefer another color. You can use Quick Styles to change the overall look of a table. The Quick Styles gallery in the Table Styles drop-down arrow contains a variety of choices that are based on the color scheme of the slide's theme.

Troubleshooting Note that there are two Design tabs on the Ribbon when the table is selected. Be sure students select the **Design** tab on the **Table Tools** contextual tab.

FIGURE 2.13 Resized table

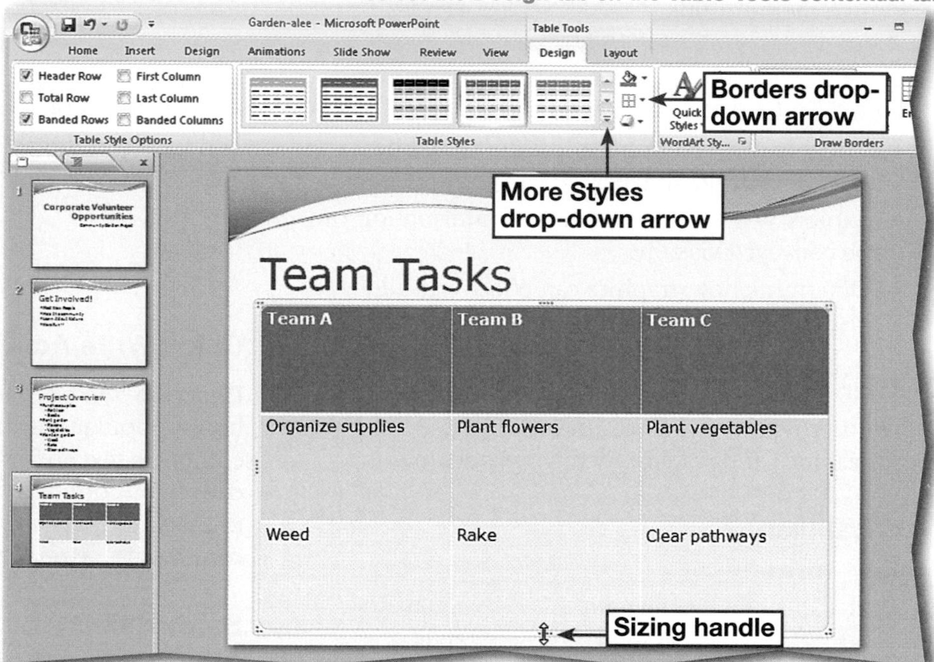

FIGURE 2.14 Table with Quick Style applied

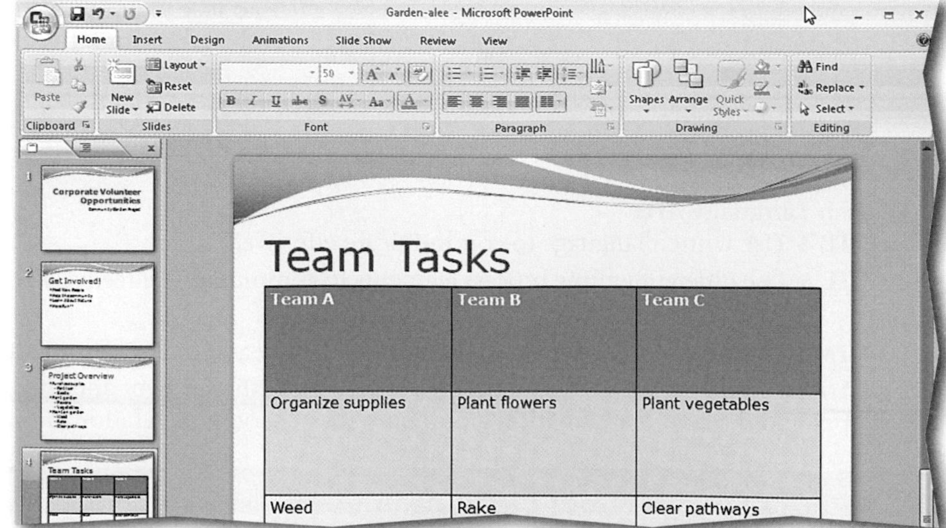

EXERCISE 5-1
Create Columns

Step-By-Step

1. Start **Word**. Open the data file **Newsletter.docx**.
2. Save as: Newsletter-[your first initial and last name] (for example, *Newsletter-sbryant)*.
3. Turn on **Show/Hide** ¶ [¶].
4. Click before the heading **BIKE SALES RISING**.
5. Choose **Page Layout> Page Setup>Columns> More Columns** [▥].
6. In the **Columns** dialog box, under **Presets**, click **Three** (see Figure 5.1).
7. Make sure the **Equal column width** box is selected.
8. In the **Apply to** box, make sure **This section** is selected.
9. Click **OK**.
10. **CHECK** Your screen should look like Figure 5.2.
11. Save your file.

Continue to the next exercise.

Troubleshooting If students see boxes or lines on their screens, have them choose **Office>Word Options>Advanced**. Then, under **Show Document Content**, uncheck the **Text boundaries** box.

Many companies use a printed report called a **newsletter** to keep their employees informed about important events. A **column** groups text vertically and makes it easier to read many stories on a single page. Newsletter text is usually displayed in two or three columns.

FIGURE 5.1 Columns dialog box

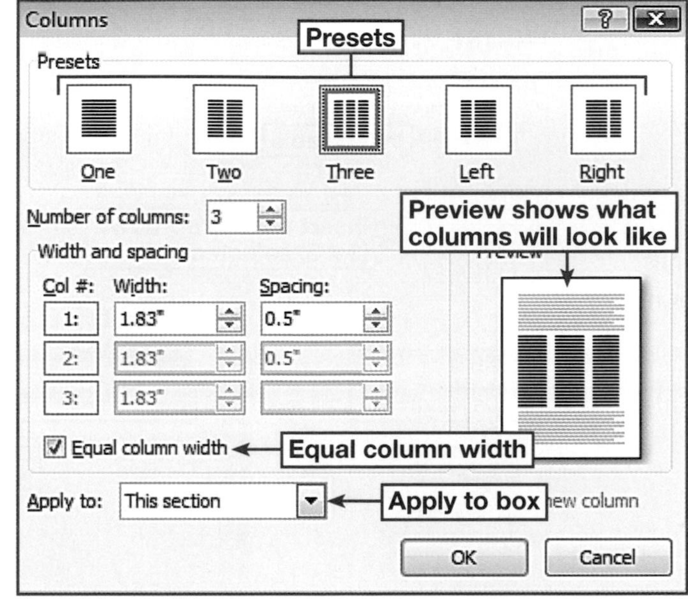

FIGURE 5.2 Created three columns of equal width

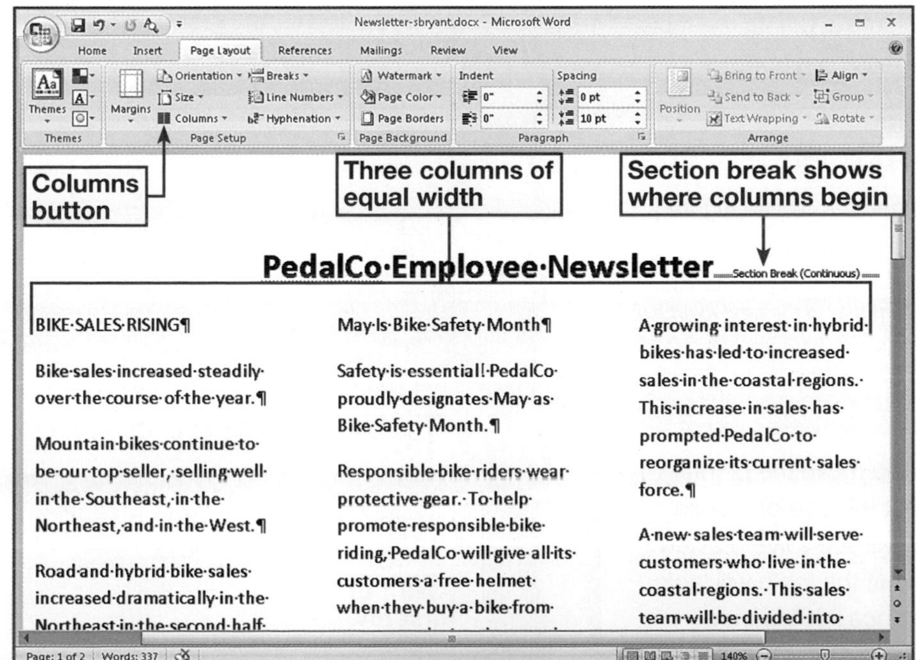

Step-By-Step

1. In your **Garden** file, select **Slide 3**.
2. Choose the **New Slide** drop-down arrow. Select **Title and Content**.
3. In the title box, key: Team Tasks.
4. Click in the content text box. Choose **Insert> Tables>Table** .
5. Drag to select 3 columns across and 3 rows down (see Figure 2.11).
6. Release the mouse button to insert the table.
7. In the first cell of the first row, key: Team A. Press TAB.
8. Key the text shown in Figure 2.12 into the table. Press TAB to move between cells.
9. **CHECK** Your screen should look like Figure 2.12. Save your file.

Continue to the next exercise.

Microsoft Office 2007

As you move the pointer to select the size of a table, you will see a live preview of what the table will look like once it is inserted.

EXERCISE 2-6
Create a Table

A **table** organizes your information into rows and columns. PowerPoint tables work like Word tables. Including tables in your presentations is a great way to organize information. You might use tables when you want to compare information side by side, as when comparing team responsibilities on a large project. The area where a row and a column intersect is called a cell. Enter text into cells like you do into a text box. Press the Tab key to move from cell to cell.

FIGURE 2.11 Select columns and rows

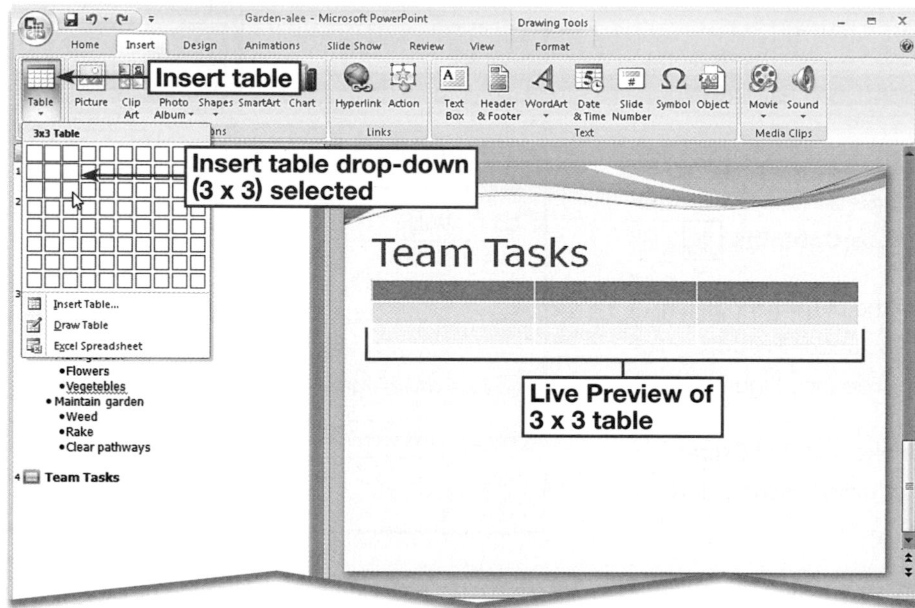

FIGURE 2.12 Finished table

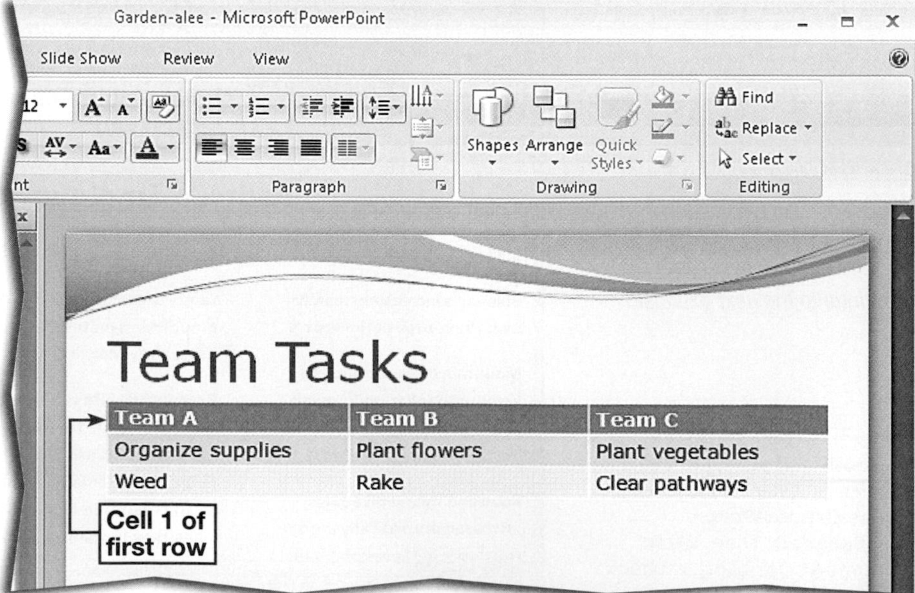

EXERCISE 5-2
Insert Column Breaks

When text reaches the end of a column, it automatically wraps, or moves, to the top of the next column. You can insert a **column break** to force text to begin at the top of the next column.

Step-By-Step

1. In your **Newsletter** file, scroll down and click before the text **USE YOUR HEAD!** in the bottom of the first column.
2. Choose **Page Layout> Page Setup>Breaks**. Under **Page Breaks**, select **Column** (see Figure 5.3).
3. Click before the text **NEW MARKET PROMPTS REORGANIZATION** in the second column.
4. Repeat Step 2.
5. **CHECK** Your screen should look like Figure 5.4.
6. Save your file.

Continue to the next exercise.

FIGURE 5.3 Breaks menu

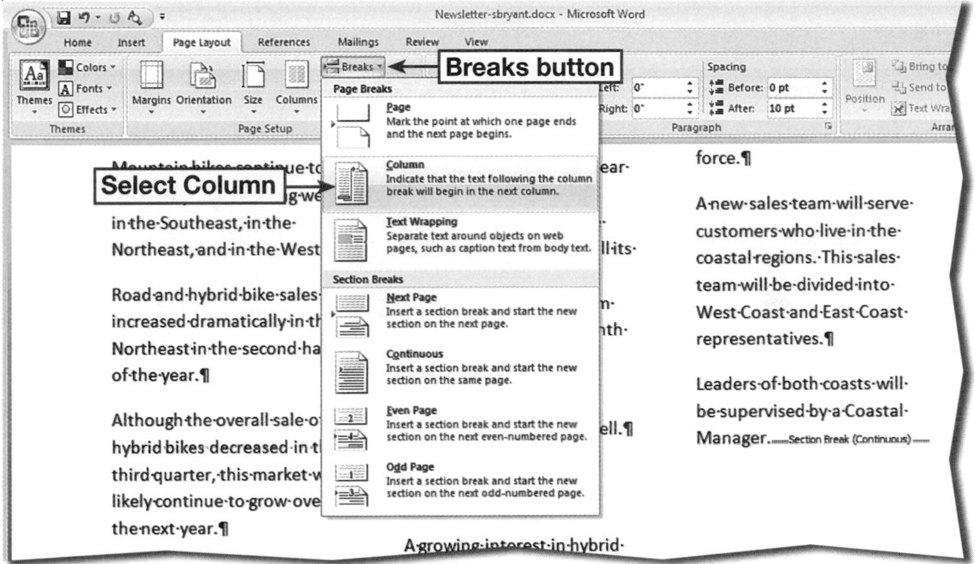

FIGURE 5.4 Text with column breaks

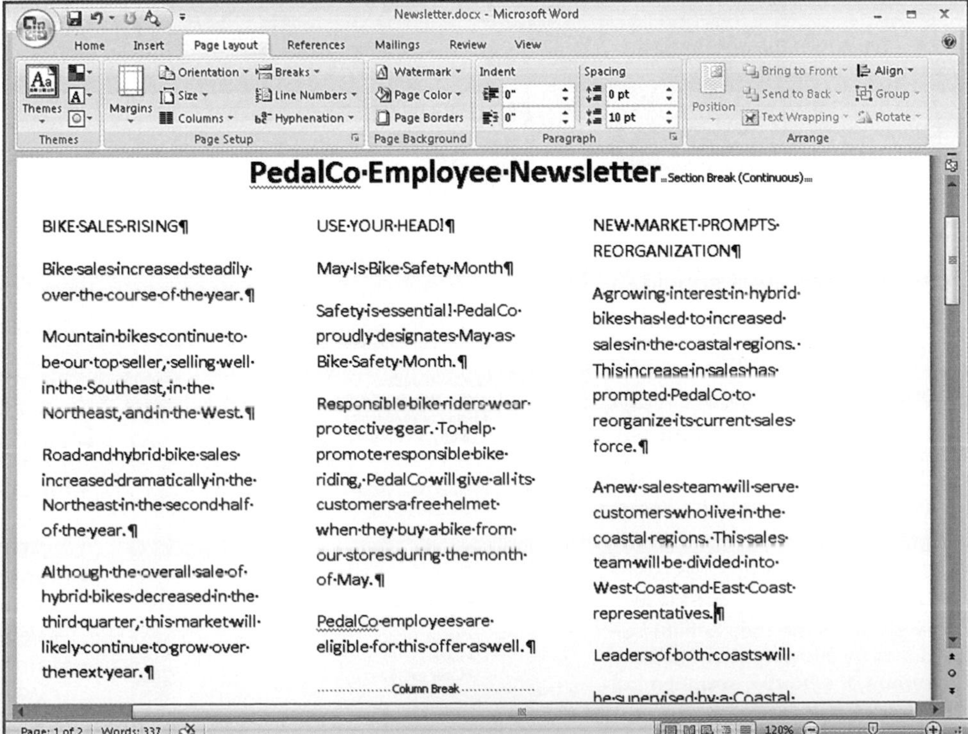

Academic Skills

It is important to make your documents look attractive. Controlling the way columns are formatted in your document leads to a more consistent appearance and ensures effective communication.

NCLB/Language Arts (NCTE 4)
Explain that an easy-to-read appearance is important for effective communication. If a document is messy and hard to read, a student may not be able to effectively communicate a point, as the messiness could be distracting.

Step-By-Step

1. In your **Garden** file, click the **Outline** tab.
2. On the **Outline** pane, select the text **Plant garden**.
3. Choose **Home>Paragraph>Decrease List Level**.
4. CHECK Your screen should look like Figure 2.9.
5. On the **Slide**, select the word **Weed**.
6. Click **Increase List Level**.
7. CHECK Your screen should look like Figure 2.10.
8. Save your file.

Continue to the next exercise.

Academic Skills

In this outline, the text "Plant garden" is promoted because it should be a main point. The text "Weed" is demoted because it is a supporting point for the main point "Maintain garden."

NCLB/Language Arts (NCTE 8) Show students the idea behind bulleted text by allowing them to list the rooms of a house, and then bullet out appliances and furniture found in each room.

EXERCISE 2-5
Promote and Demote Text

On the Outline pane, text for each slide is organized in levels. The slide title appears on the first level, subtitles or main bullet points appear on the second level, and supporting points are on the third level. These levels help you to organize your presentation. If you want to emphasize the importance of an item, you can **promote** it and make it a main point. If you decide an item should be **subordinate**, or below, another main point, you can **demote** it to make it a supporting point.

FIGURE 2.9 Promoted text

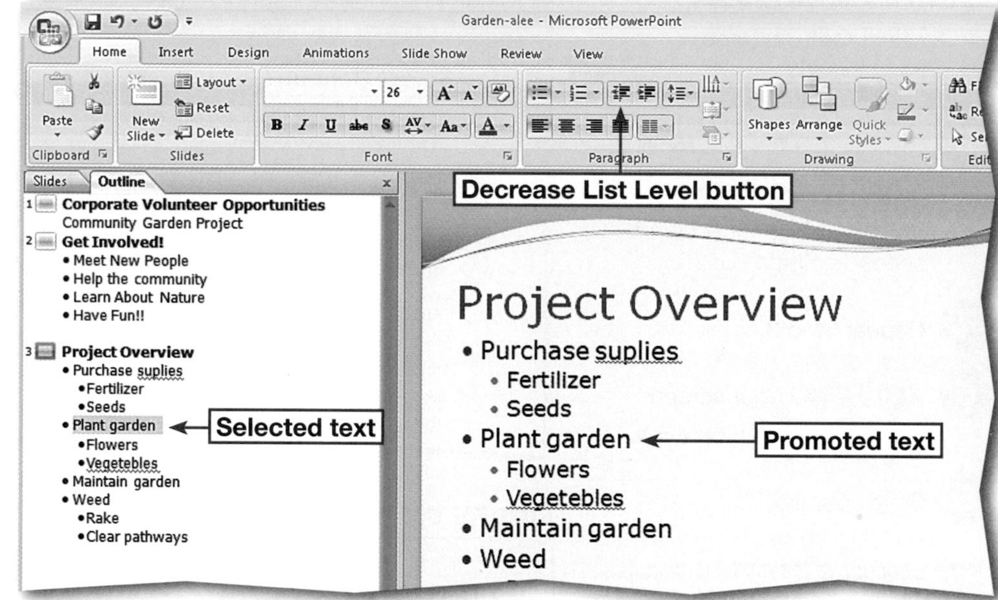

FIGURE 2.10 Demoted text

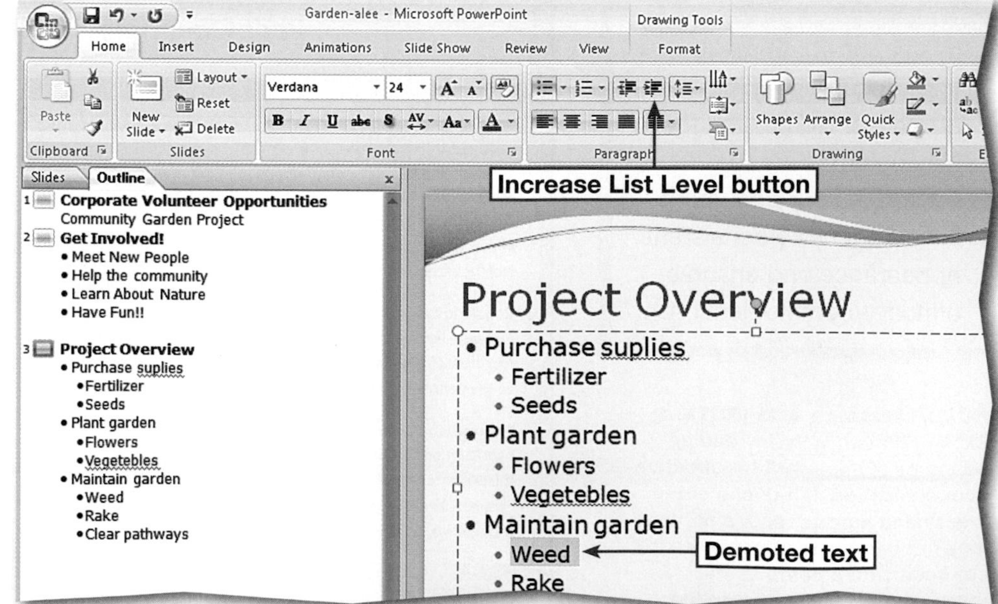

Step-By-Step

1. In your **Newsletter** file, click before **BIKE SALES RISING**.
2. Choose **Page Layout>Page Setup>Columns>More Columns**.
3. In the **Columns** dialog box, uncheck **Equal column width**. Select the **Line between** box. Change the **Width** of column 3 to **2.35″** (see Figure 5.5). Press TAB. Click **OK**.
4. Select the text **BIKE SALES RISING**. Choose **Home>Styles>More>Heading 3**. Click **Center**.
5. Apply **Heading 3** to the text **USE YOUR HEAD! May is Bike Safety Month**. Click **Center**.
6. With the heading selected, choose **Page Layout>Paragraph**. Click the **Spacing Before** drop-down arrow. Choose **0 pt**.
7. Apply **Heading 3** and **Center** to the text **NEW MARKET PROMPTS REORGANIZATION**.
8. **CHECK** Your screen should look like Figure 5.6. Save your file.

Continue to the next exercise.

EXERCISE 5-3
Format Columns and Column Text

You can format columns by adjusting column width, or by changing the number of columns you use. Format column text the same way you would format other text in a document.

Step-By-Step Tip In **Step 3**, ask students to look at the [Preview] in the **Columns** dialog box when they change the column width.

FIGURE 5.5 Revised Columns dialog box

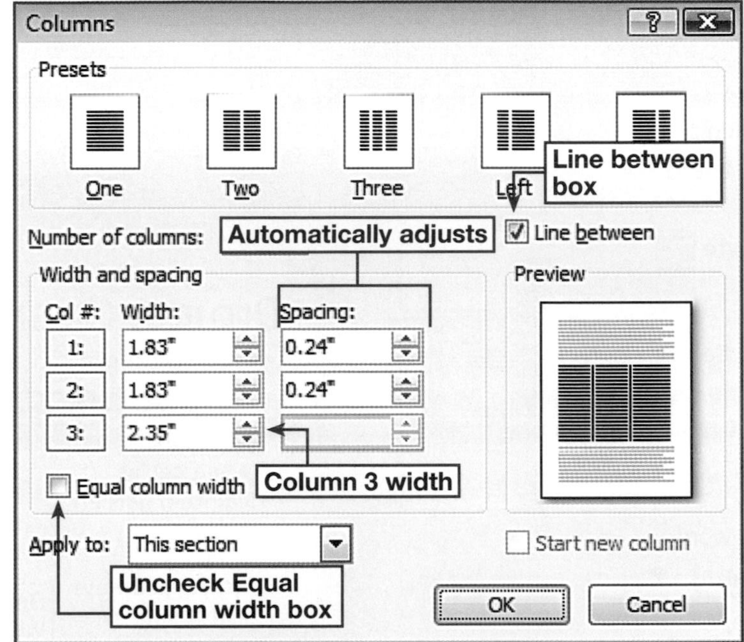

FIGURE 5.6 Formatted columns and text

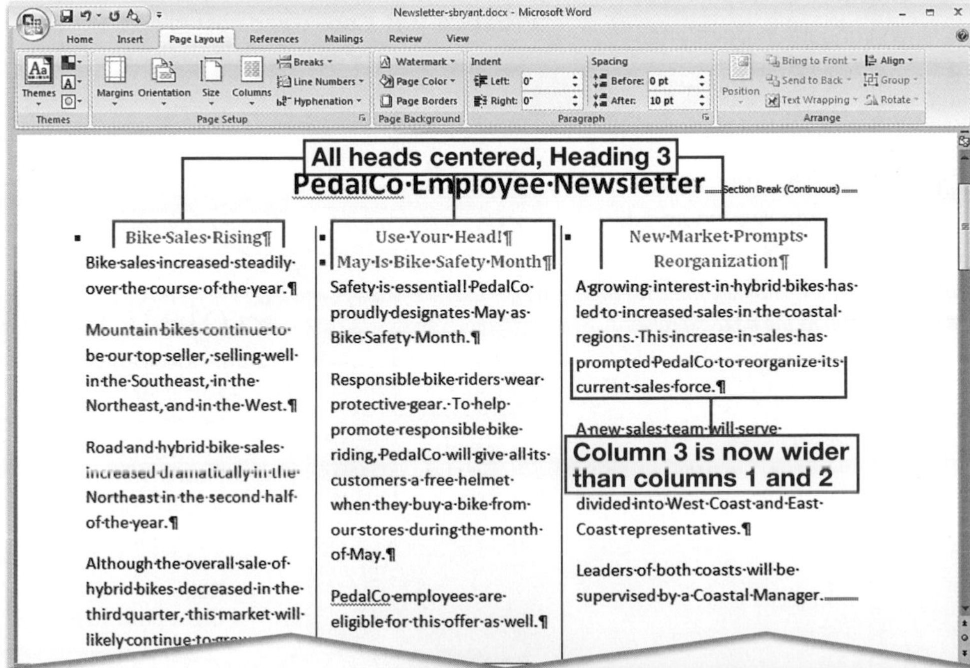

Step-By-Step

1. In your **Garden** file, double-click the word **Fertilizer**.
2. Choose **Home>Clipboard>Cut** . After the word **Fertilizer** is removed, delete the open space, if necessary.
3. Move the insertion point before the word **Plant**. Choose **Home>Clipboard>Paste** . Press ENTER.
4. Select the word **Seeds**. Click and drag the insertion point under the word **Fertilizer** (see Figure 2.7).
5. Click before the word **Plant**. Press ENTER.
6. Double-click the word **garden**. Choose **Home>Clipboard>Copy**. Place your insertion point after the word **Plant**. Click **Paste**.
7. **CHECK** Your screen should look like Figure 2.8. Save your file.

Continue to the next exercise.

EXERCISE 2-4
Cut, Copy, and Paste Text

If text is not in the proper order, you can easily move it into the correct position. If you **cut** a word or words, you can remove it from one place and move, or **paste**, it into the correct position. If you want to use the same text in more than one place, you can **copy** the text and paste it into the new location.

Step-By-Step Tip In **Step 7**, note that the **AutoFit** button will appear automatically after students create this slide.

FIGURE 2.7 Drag-and-Drop arrow

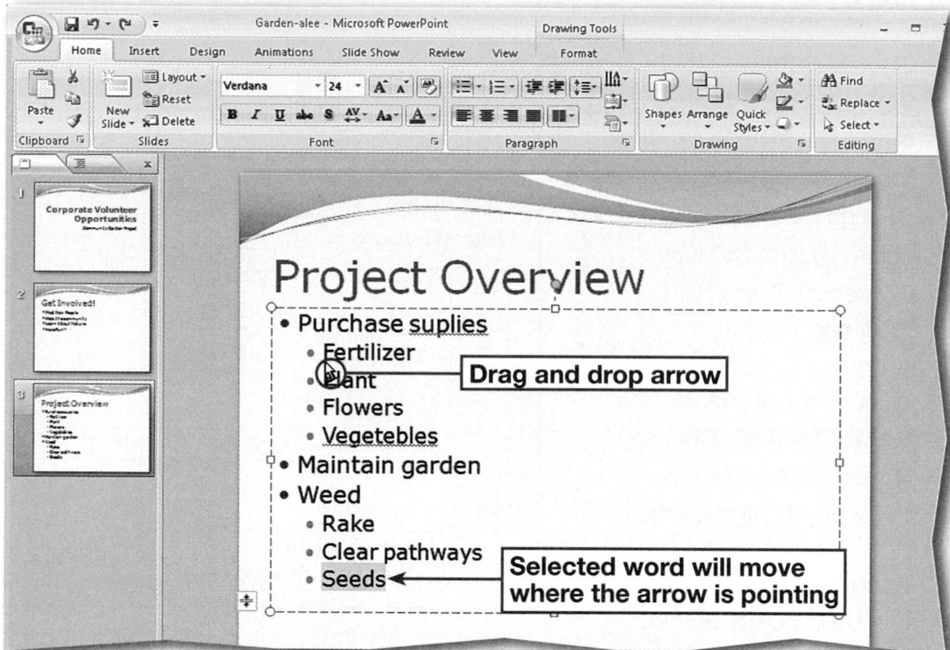

FIGURE 2.8 Copied and pasted text

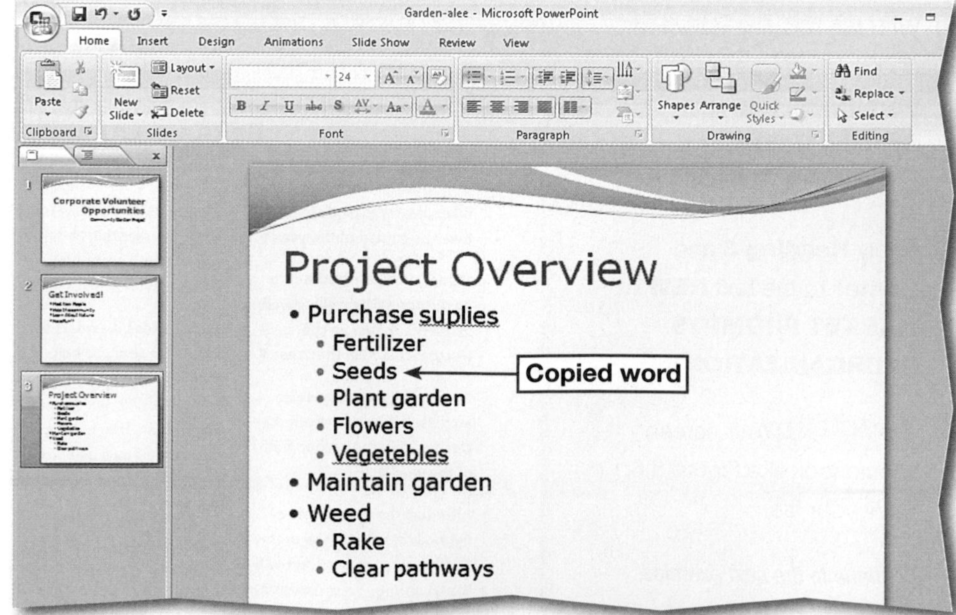

Step-By-Step

1. In your **Newsletter** file, scroll to the second page.
2. At the bottom of the third column, click after the text **Congratulations to all!**
3. Choose **Page Layout> Page Setup>Columns> More Columns** .
4. In the **Columns** dialog box, under **Presets**, click **One**. In the **Apply to** box, click the drop-down arrow and select **This point forward**. Click **OK**.
5. Click before the ¶ mark after the section break. Choose **Insert>Tables> Table>Insert Table** .
6. In the **Insert Table** dialog box, in the **Number of columns**, key: 4.
7. In the **Number of rows** box, key: 6 (see Figure 5.7). Click **OK**.
8. CHECK Your screen should look like Figure 5.8. Save your file.

Continue to the next exercise.

Microsoft Office 2007

You can use the **Live Preview** feature to see how your table will look on the page.

EXERCISE 5-4
Insert a Table

A **table** consists of vertical columns and horizontal rows. Tables can help you to organize information or to line up items next to each other. Tables are excellent for presenting complicated information. You might use a table to present the results of a survey, or detailed analysis of information collected.

FIGURE 5.7 Insert Table dialog box

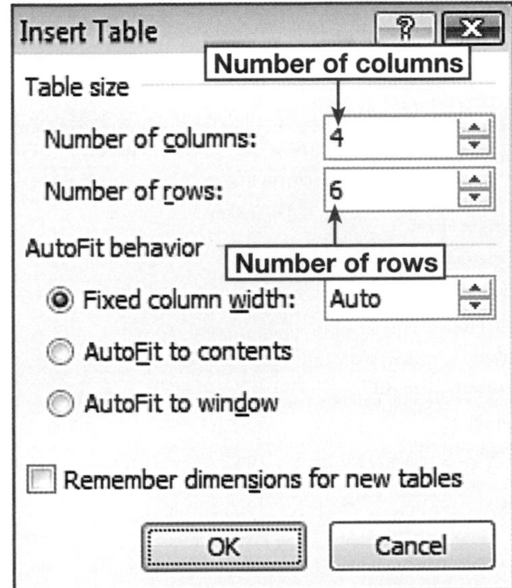

FIGURE 5.8 Inserted table

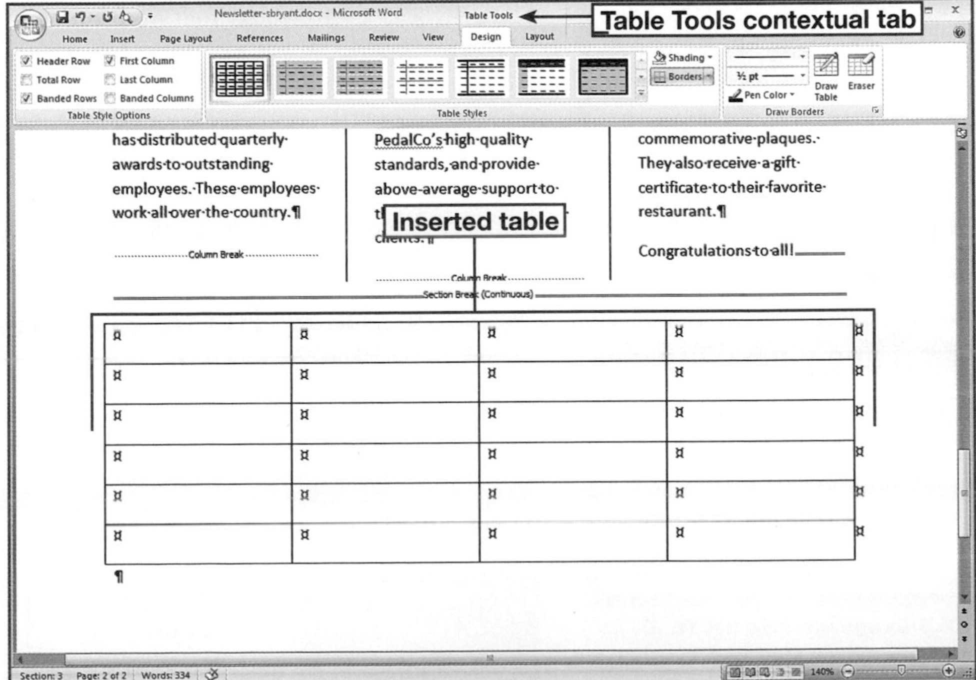

Step-By-Step

1. In your **Garden** file, choose the **Home>Slides>New Slide** drop-down arrow.
2. Select **Slides from Outline.** In the **Insert Outline** dialog box, browse to the data file **Outline.docx** (see Figure 2.5).
3. Select **Outline.docx**.
4. Click **Insert**.
5. **CHECK** Your screen should look like Figure 2.6. Notice the outline is inserted on Slide 3.
6. Save your file.

Continue to the next exercise.

You Should Know

Using heading styles to create an outline in Word allows you to import the structure of your outline, not just the content, into PowerPoint.

Academic Skills

Outlines are effective for organizing ideas and generating statements to present the main purpose of a presentation or essay.

NCLB/Language Arts (NCTE 8) Emphasize the importance of using an outline across disciplines.

EXERCISE 2-3
Import Text from Other Sources

PowerPoint allows you to **import**, or bring in, text from different sources into your presentation. For example, you might write an outline for your presentation in Word and then import that outline into your presentation. When you insert the outline, PowerPoint automatically creates slide titles, subtitles, and bulleted lists.

Differentiated Instruction/Advanced Students Let advanced students know that they can double-click to open a file.

FIGURE 2.5 Insert Outline dialog box

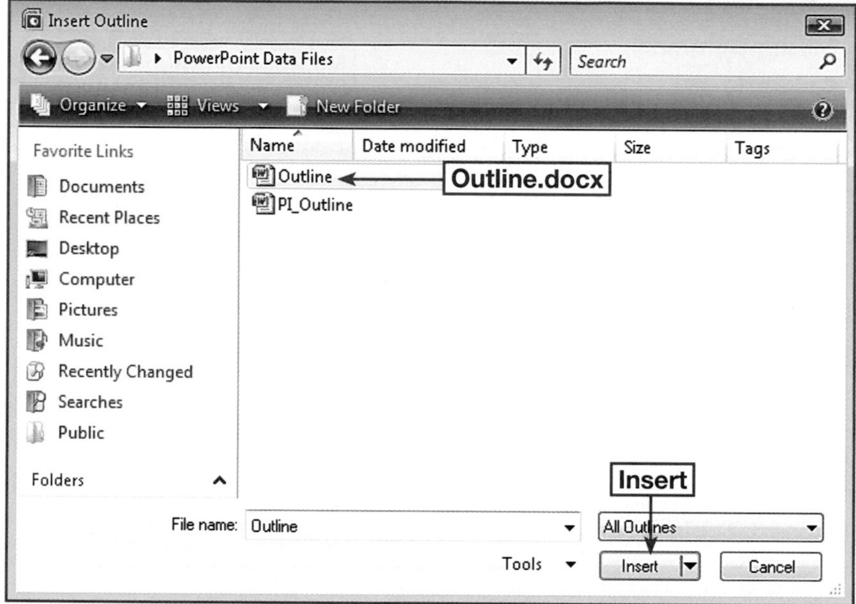

FIGURE 2.6 Slide created from Word outline

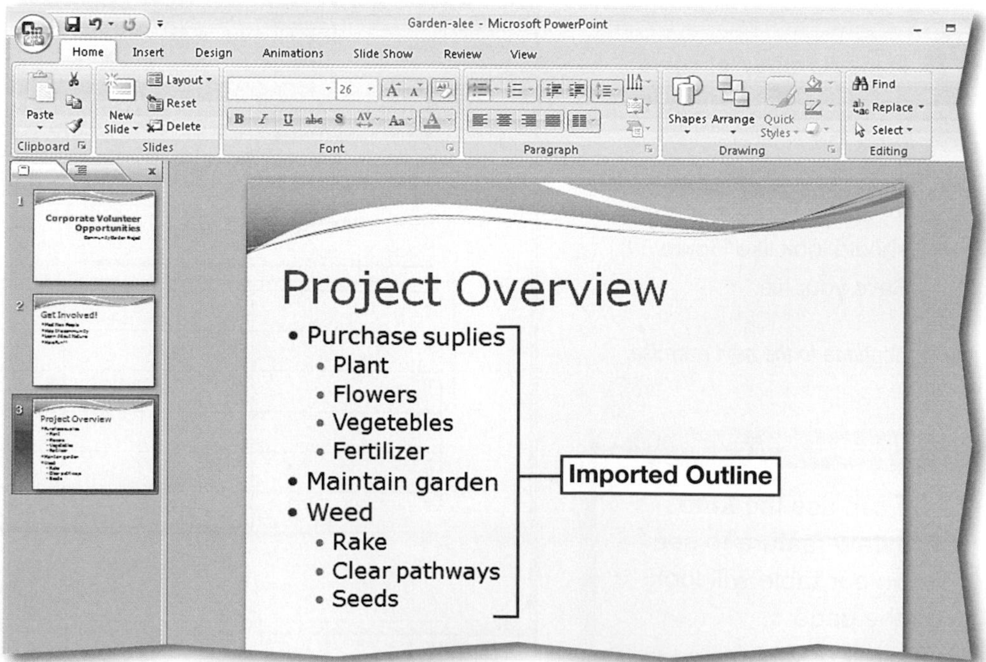

Step-By-Step

1. In your **Newsletter** file, click in the table's first cell.
2. Key: Award.
3. Press TAB.
4. Key the remaining text shown in Figure 5.9 into the table.
5. Use the keyboard shortcuts listed in Table 5.1 to move through the cells.
6. CHECK Your screen should look like Figure 5.9.
7. Save your file.

Continue to the next exercise.

You Should Know

Pressing ENTER in a cell creates a new paragraph within the cell.

Shortcuts

When the insertion point is in the last cell of the last row, press TAB to insert a new row below the current last row.

Differentiated Instruction/Visually Impaired Students with visual impairments can enlarge a table in a document by using the Zoom tool at the bottom of the screen.

EXERCISE 5-5
Key Text in a Table

When columns and rows cross in a table, they form a **cell**. Cells are where text is keyed into a table. To enter text in a cell, position the insertion point in the cell and then start keying text. Table 5.1 describes how to move among cells in a table.

TABLE 5.1 Ways to Move Within a Table

Move To:	Keyboard Shortcut
Next cell	TAB
Previous cell	SHIFT + TAB
Next row	↓
Previous row	↑
First cell in row	ALT + HOME
Last cell in row	ALT + END
First cell in column	ALT + PAGE DOWN
Last cell in column	ALT + PAGE UP

FIGURE 5.9 Table with text

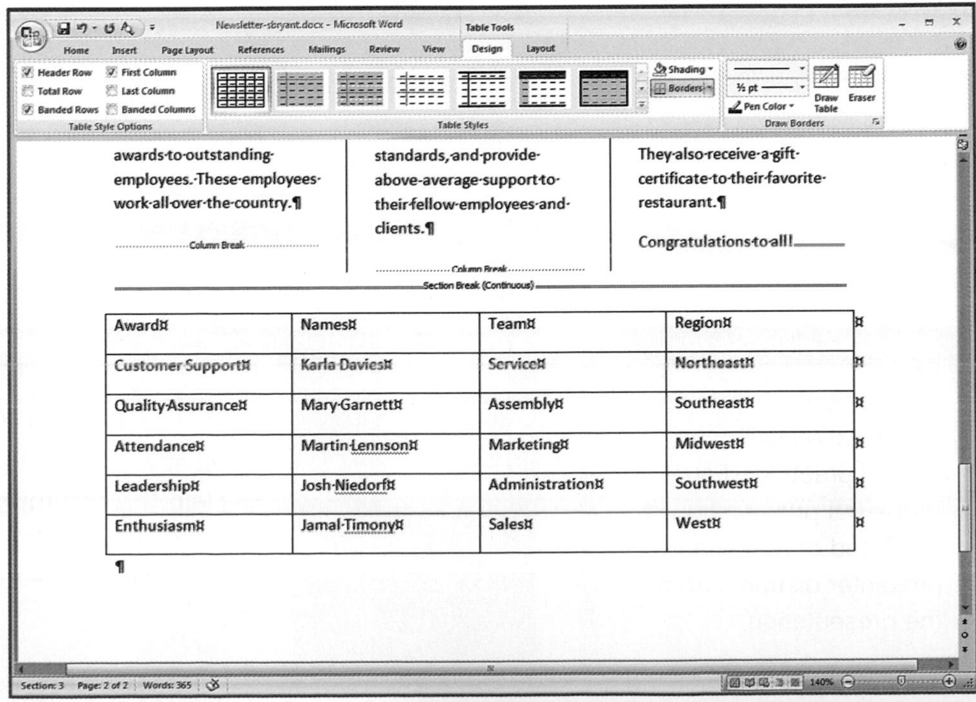

awards to outstanding employees. These employees work all over the country.

standards, and provide above-average support to their fellow employees and clients.

They also receive a gift certificate to their favorite restaurant.

Congratulations to all!

Award	Names	Team	Region
Customer Support	Karla Davies	Service	Northeast
Quality Assurance	Mary Garnett	Assembly	Southeast
Attendance	Martin Lennson	Marketing	Midwest
Leadership	Josh Niedorf	Administration	Southwest
Enthusiasm	Jamal Timony	Sales	West

Step-By-Step

1. In your **Garden** file, choose **Home>Slides> New Slide** .
2. In the title box, key: Get Involved Now!
3. Click in the bulleted text box and key: Meet New People. Press ENTER.
4. Key the remaining four bulleted points shown in Figure 2.3.
5. CHECK Your screen should look like Figure 2.3.
6. Double-click the word **Now** to select it. Press ←BACKSPACE.
7. Select the fourth bulleted item.
8. Press ←BACKSPACE.
9. CHECK Your screen should look like Figure 2.4.
10. Save your file.

Continue to the next exercise.

Academic Skills

Think about the different presentation skills you should practice when you prepare a presentation. A confused or unprepared presenter distracts from the presentation.

NCLB/Language Arts (NCTE 10)

EXERCISE 2-2
Add and Delete Text on Slides

PowerPoint provides text boxes (also called placeholders) to make it easy for you to enter text. Use the title text box for the slide titles. The first slide of a presentation also has a subtitle text box. When a text box or other object is selected, one or more contextual tabs will appear on the Ribbon. A **contextual tab** contains commands that can be used only with the selected object. For example, selecting a text box will make the Drawing Tools contextual tab appear.

Differentiated Instruction/Advanced Student Have students click on the contextual tab. Let them explore the available options.

FIGURE 2.3 New Slide with bulleted text

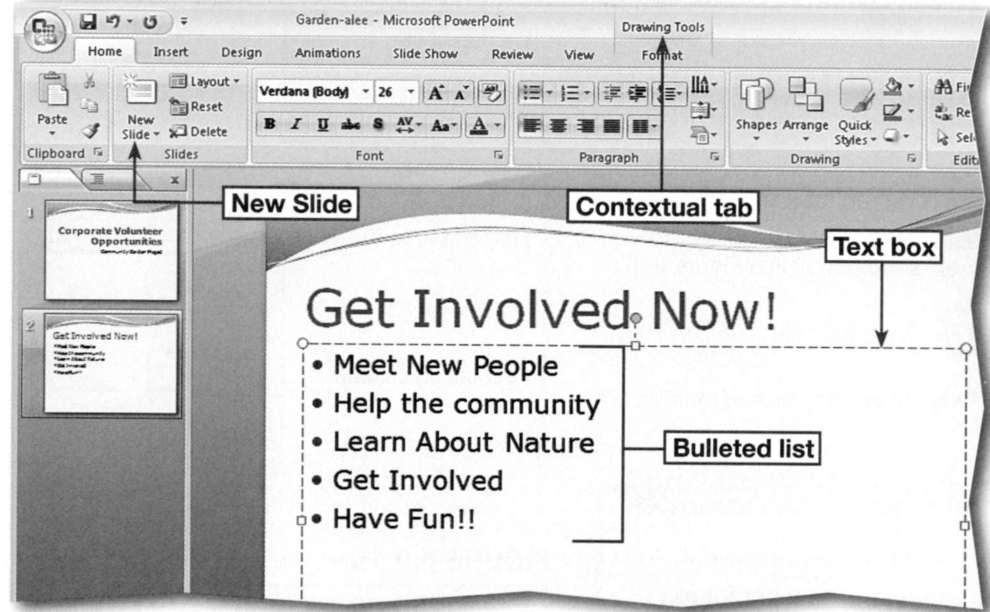

EL Consider partnering an English Learner with a classmate to help with entering text.

FIGURE 2.4 Edited text

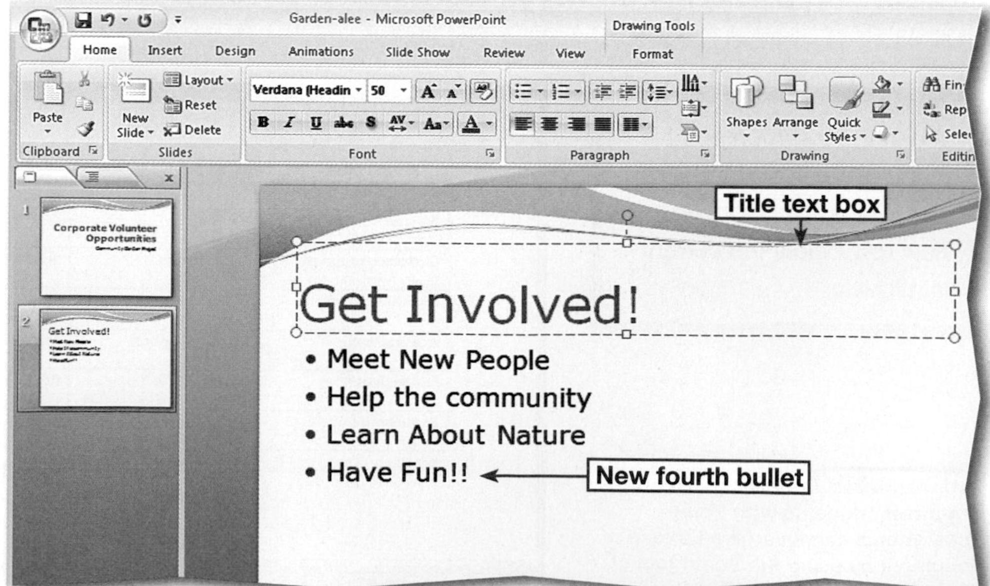

Step-By-Step

EXERCISE 5-6
Insert Columns and Rows in a Table

Sometimes you may need to add another column or row to a table to insert more information. Word makes it easy to add rows and columns to a table.

1. In your **Newsletter** file, click anywhere in the table's bottom row.
2. In the **Table Tools** contextual tab, choose **Layout>Rows & Columns>Insert Below**.
3. In the first column of the new row, key: Motivation.
4. CHECK Your screen should look like Figure 5.10.
5. Press TAB twice.
6. Select **Layout>Rows & Columns>Insert Right**.
7. In the first row of the new column, key: Title.
8. CHECK Your screen should look like Figure 5.11.
9. Save your file.

Continue to the next exercise.

FIGURE 5.10 Inserting a row

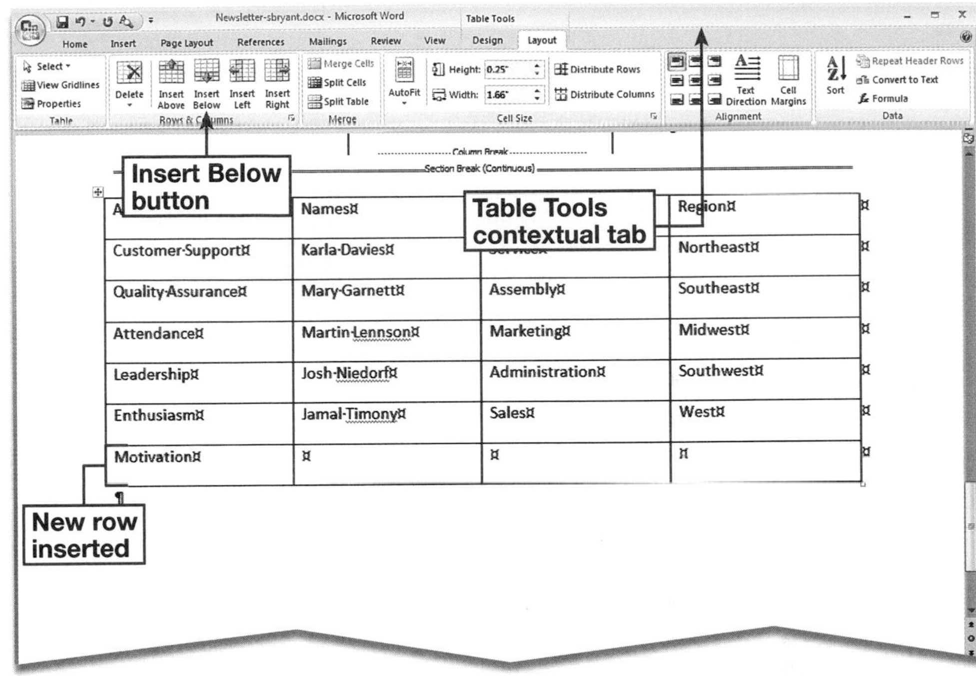

FIGURE 5.11 Inserting a column

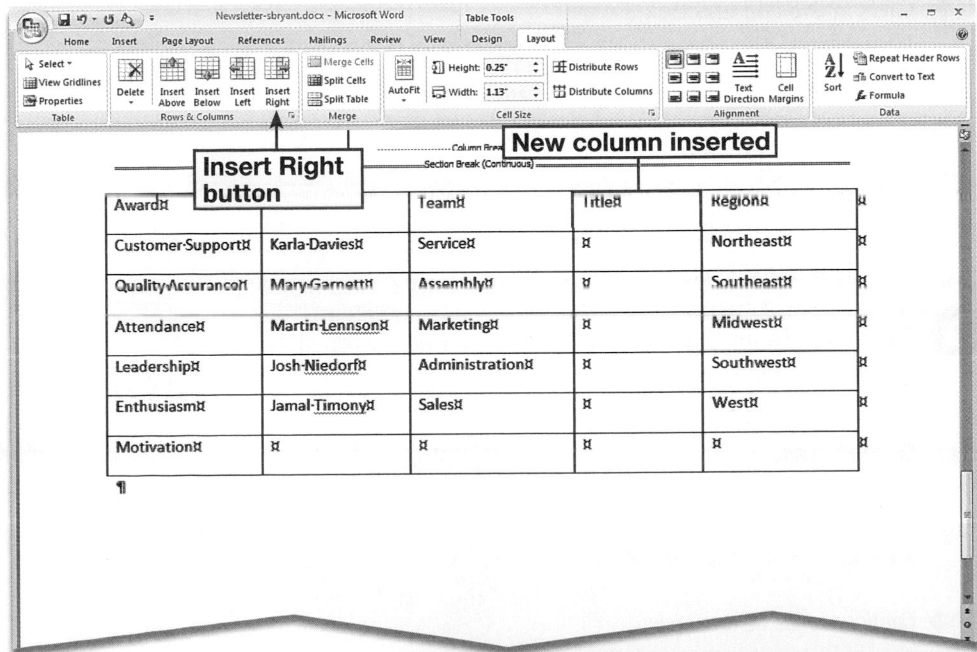

Step-By-Step Tip In **Step 2**, point out that if the insertion point is in the wrong row, the row will be inserted in the wrong place. If students make this error, have them click **Undo** and try again.

Teaching Tip Have students discuss scenarios in other classes in which they might need to add columns or rows to tables.

Step-By-Step

1. Start PowerPoint. Choose **Office>New**. Under **Templates**, click **Blank and Recent** (see Figure 2.1).
2. Select **Blank Presentation**. Click **Create**.
3. On the **Design** tab, in the **Themes** group, click the **More** drop-down arrow (see Figure 2.2) Select **Flow**.
4. Click the **Colors** drop-down arrow. Select **Oriel**.
5. Click the **Fonts** drop-down arrow. Select **Aspect**.
6. On the **Design** tab, in the **Background** group, click **Background Styles**. Choose **Style 10**.
7. Click in the title text box. Key: Corporate Volunteer Opportunities.
8. Click in the subtitle text box and key: Community Garden Project. Click outside the text box.
9. Save your file as: Garden-[your first initial and last name]. (For example, *Garden-alee*).
10. CHECK Your screen should look like Figure 2.2.

Continue to the next exercise.

EXERCISE 2-1
Create a Presentation with a Blank Template

Themes make it easy to create professional-looking presentations. A **theme** includes colors, fonts, and graphics designed to work together throughout a presentation. Text boxes indicate where to place **content** (the text and graphics included on a slide).

Teaching Tip Explain to students that the text on-screen may look smaller or bigger depending on their screen's resolution.

FIGURE 2.1 New Presentation dialog box

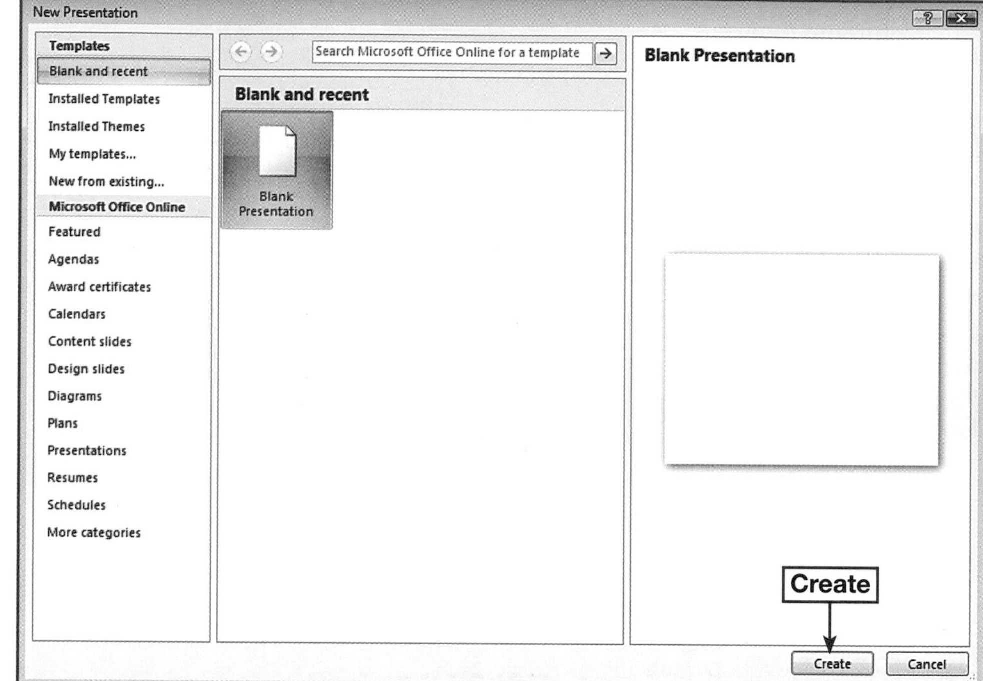

FIGURE 2.2 Modified Flow design theme

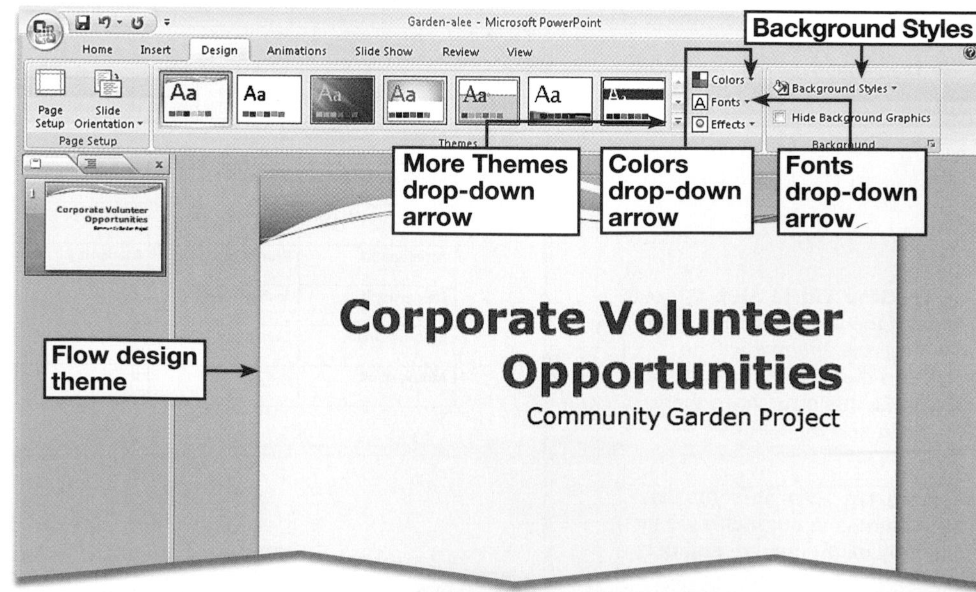

Step-By-Step

1. In your **Newsletter** file, move the pointer next to the left side of the table's bottom row until it becomes a small black arrow.
2. Double-click to select the entire row (see Figure 5.12). Press DELETE. The text is deleted.
3. Click anywhere in the bottom row. In the **Table Tools** contextual tab, choose **Layout>Rows & Columns>Delete> Delete Rows**.
4. Click anywhere in the **Title** column.
5. Choose **Layout>Rows & Columns>Delete> Delete Columns**.
6. **CHECK** Your screen should look like Figure 5.13. Save your file.

Continue to the next exercise.

Academic Skills

You can remember the difference between *row* and *column* by thinking of horizontal rows at a theater or stadium and vertical columns in front of a building.

NCLB/Math (NCTM Geometry 4) Have students discuss other ways to remember the difference between rows and columns.

EXERCISE 5-7
Delete Columns and Rows in a Table

To delete the text from an entire column or row, select the column or row and press Delete. When you perform this action, the text is deleted, but a blank column or row remains in the table. To delete an entire column or row from a table, use the Delete menu command.

Troubleshooting It is easy for students to delete the wrong row by mistake. Remind them to click **Undo** right away if they make a mistake.

FIGURE 5.12 Selecting a row

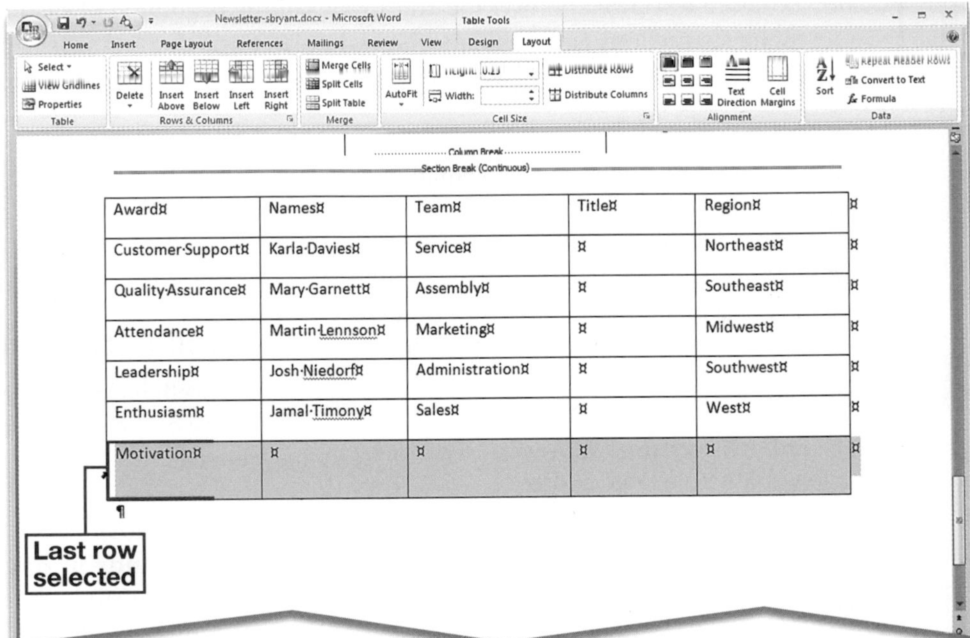

FIGURE 5.13 Column and row deleted

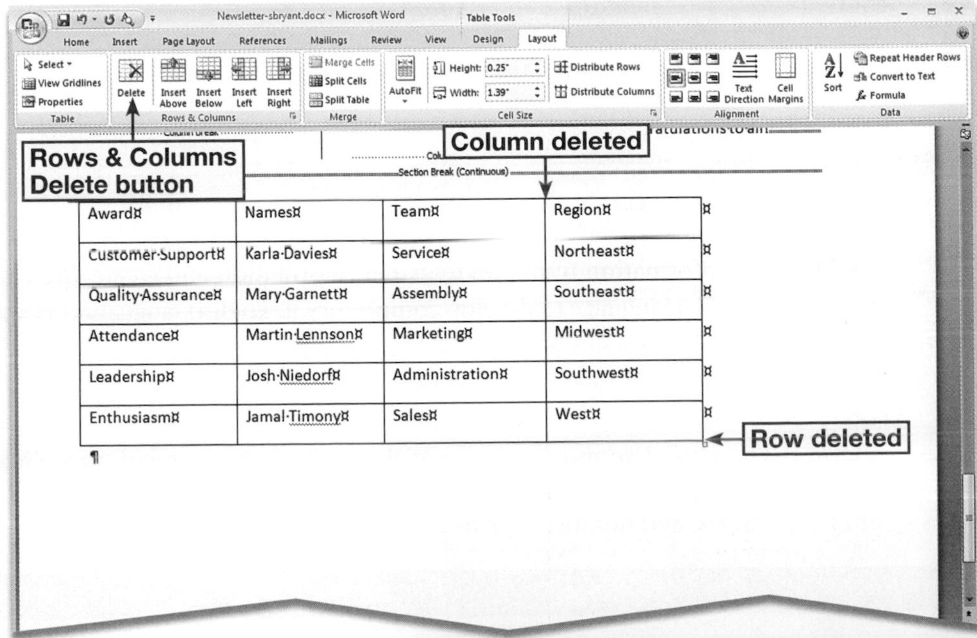

LESSON 2 Reading Guide

Before You Read

See page TM42 for English Learner activity instructions.

Find Your Study Method Think about recurring challenges you have faced when you have tried to study or take a test. Then go over the Study Skills at the beginning of each lesson in the book. Pick the most useful suggestions and try them when you read through a lesson.

Read To Learn

- Consider how the design of a presentation can influence the audience's response.
- Understand how using graphs, charts, and diagrams can show your expertise on a topic.
- Explore techniques for working with others to organize and enhance your presentations.

Main Idea

PowerPoint presentations allow you to convey your message visually to a large audience.

Vocabulary

Key Terms

chart
Clip Art
comment
content
contextual tab
copy
cut
demote
diagram
markup
paste
promote
table
theme
thesaurus
WordArt

Academic Vocabulary

These words appear in your reading and on your tests. Make sure you know their meanings.

import
subordinate

Quick Write Activity

Describe On a separate sheet of paper, describe some of the qualities that make verbal presentations interesting.

Study Skills

Find a Study Buddy Studying with a friend can make your study time more productive and enjoyable. Together you can compare classroom notes and quiz each other.

Academic Standards

English Language Arts

NCTE 8 Use information resources to gather information and create and communicate knowledge.

NCTE 10 Use first language to develop competency in English language arts and develop an understanding of content across the curriculum.

NCTE 11 Participate as members of literacy communities.

Math

NCTM (Geometry) Use visualization, spatial reasoning, and geometric modeling to solve problems.

NCTM (Numbers and Operations) Understand numbers, ways of representing numbers, relationships among numbers, and number systems.

Step-By-Step

1. In your **Newsletter** file, select the table's first row.
2. In the **Table Tools** contextual tab, choose **Design>Table Styles> Shading** . In the drop-down menu, select **Light Green**. Deselect the row.
3. Point just outside the table's upper-left corner. Click the **Move Handle** (see Figure 5.15) to select the table.
4. Choose **Design>Draw Borders>Dialog Box Launcher** . In the **Borders and Shading** dialog box, select the **Borders** tab.
5. Under **Setting**, select **All**. Under **Style**, select the line style in Figure 5.14. Press **OK**.
6. With the table still selected, choose **Layout>Cell Size>AutoFit>AutoFit Contents** . Deselect the table.
7. **CHECK** Your screen should look like Figure 5.15. Save your file.

Continue to the next exercise.

Teaching Tip Point out to the students that as they move the cursor over the colors in the Shading tab, the name of the colors will be displayed.

EXERCISE 5-8
Format a Table

Add shading and borders to help emphasize specific content and make a table look more interesting. To make the text fit better, you can change column widths.

FIGURE 5.14 Borders and Shading dialog box

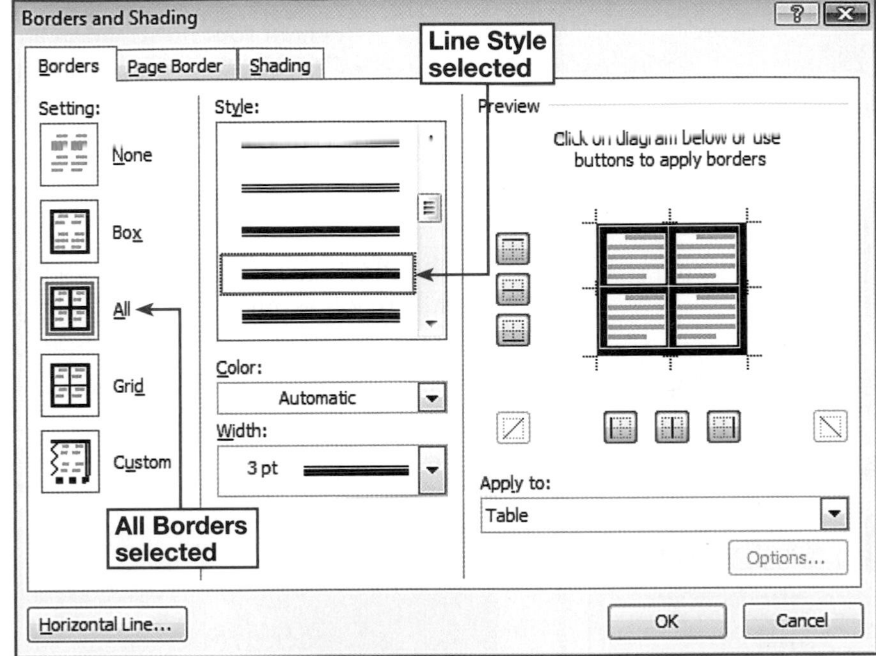

FIGURE 5.15 Formatted table

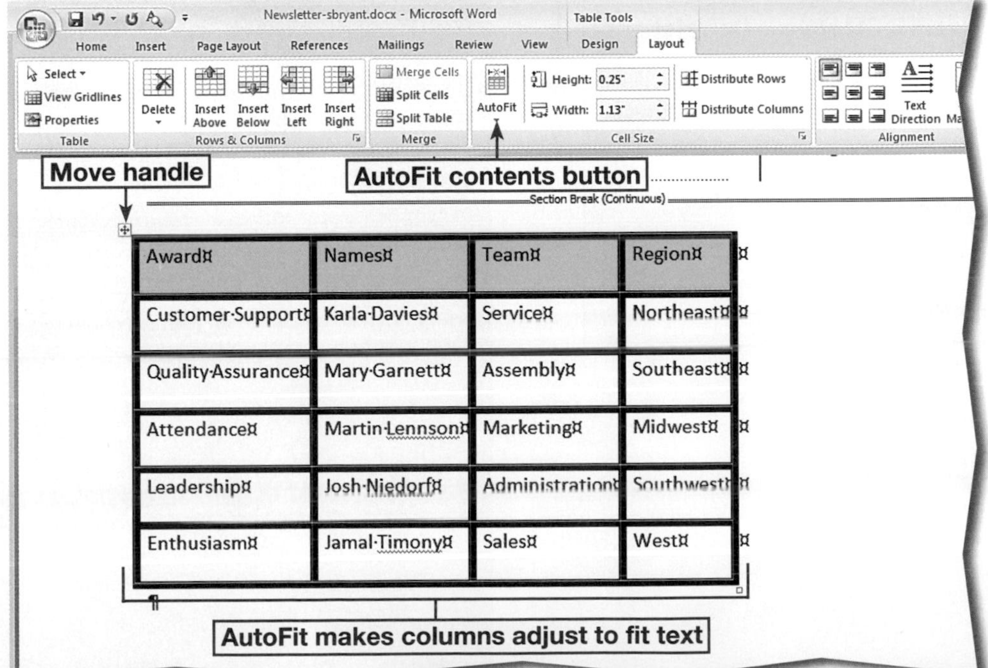

LESSON 2 Create Content and Collaborate

In this lesson, you will learn techniques for making sure that your PowerPoint presentations impress your audience and convey your message. You have already learned how to insert and edit text in PowerPoint slides. In this lesson, you will use ready-made design themes and create visuals such as tables and shapes to make the content in your presentation attractive. You will also learn how to add comments to a presentation and view them, which is very helpful if you are working with a group.

Key Concepts

- Use themes
- Promote and demote text
- Create diagrams, tables, and charts
- Insert Clip Art, pictures, shapes, and WordArt
- Use Spelling Checker and Thesaurus
- Track changes

Standards

The following standards are covered in this lesson. Refer to pages xxv and 715 for a description of the standards listed here.

ISTE Standards Correlation

NETS•S

1a, 1b, 2b, 2d, 4b, 6a, 6b, 6c, 6d

Microsoft Certified Application Specialist

PowerPoint

1.1, 2.2, 3.1, 3.2, 3.3, 3.6, 3.7, 4.1

21st CENTURY SKILLS

See page TM92 for answers to 21st Century Skills.

Get Involved Think of someone you know who spends time helping people in need. This person might promote local charities, visit with senior citizens, or help organize pledge drives. When you volunteer, either on your own or through an organization, you are helping people and helping to build a stronger community. People who volunteer often say that they receive as much or more from their efforts as the people they are helping. *What are a few ways you can get involved?*

Step-By-Step

1. In your **Newsletter** file, click in the table's top row.

2. In the **Table Tools** contextual tab, choose **Layout>Rows & Columns>Insert Above** .

3. With all the cells in the top row selected, choose **Layout>Merge>Merge Cells** .

4. Click in the merged top row. Key: Third Quarter Employee Awards.

5. CHECK Your screen should look like Figure 5.16.

6. Select the entire table. Choose **Table Layout> Table>Properties** . Choose **Layout> Alignment>Align Center** .

7. With the whole table still selected, choose **Home>Paragraph**. Open the **Paragraph** dialog box. Under **Spacing**, set **After** to **0**. Click **OK**.

8. Choose **Table Tools> Layout>Align Center** . Deselect the table.

9. CHECK Your screen should look like Figure 5.17. Save your file.

Continue to the next exercise.

EXERCISE 5-9
Modify Cell Formats

You can change the format of an individual cell or a group of cells. For example, you can merge cells together to create one long row. You can also center the text in a row.

FIGURE 5.16 Merged cells with text added

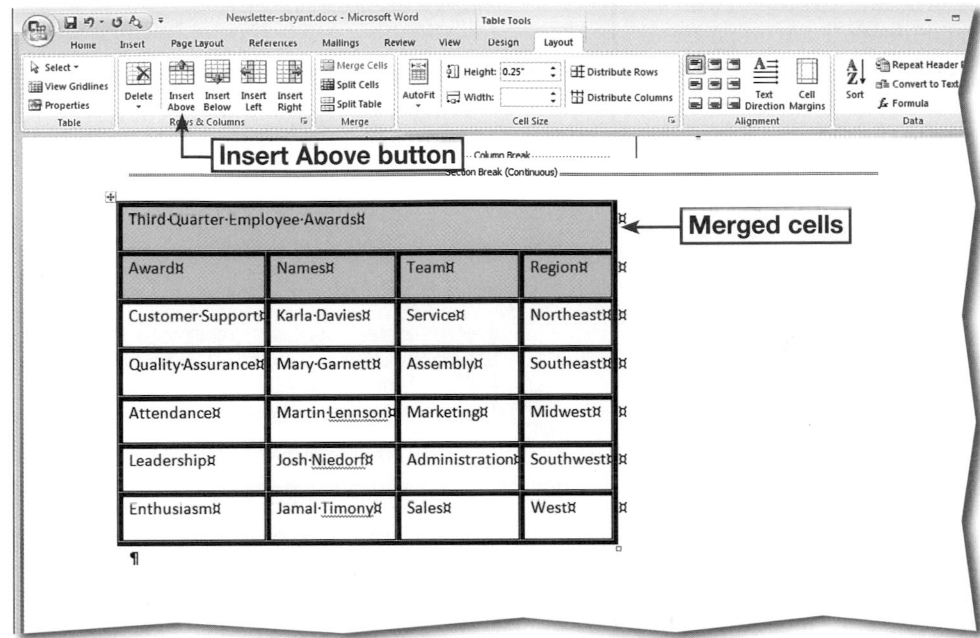

FIGURE 5.17 Table with modified cells

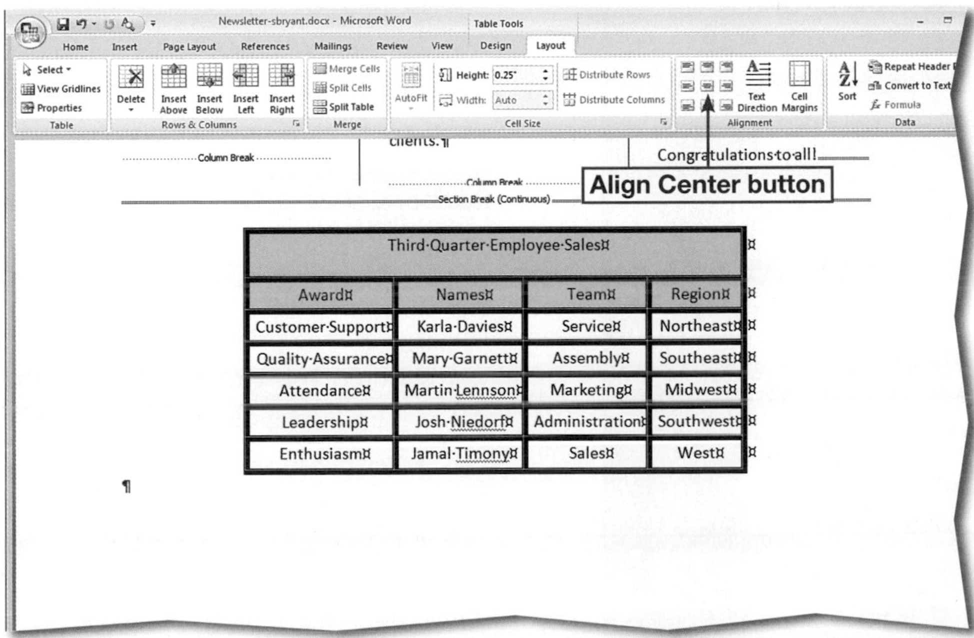

Troubleshooting In **Step 7**, if students notice that the text in their tables is still close to the top of the cells, make sure that there is no spacing before or after text in the **Paragraph** dialog box.

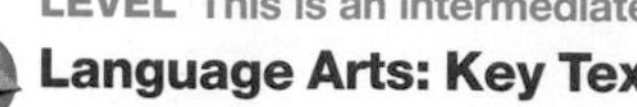

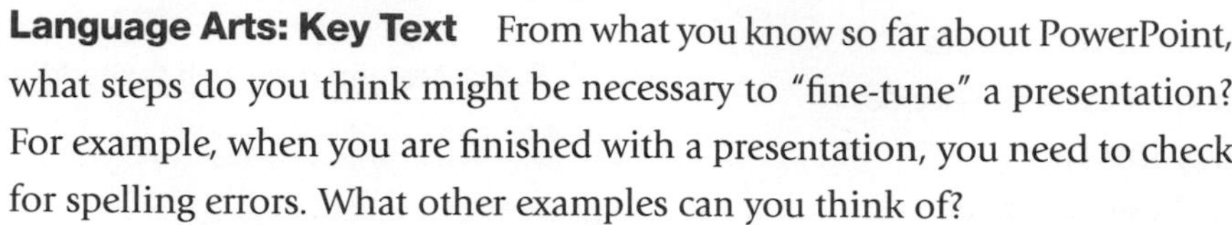

LESSON 1 Challenge Yourself Projects

Before You Begin

Prepare to Present You will be able to present with confidence if you prepare and review your presentation with care. These projects teach you how to further develop your presentation skills so you can create and deliver successful presentations.

Reflect Once you complete the projects, open a document and answer the following:

1. Which presentation tips are most useful and why?
2. How can you use the presentation skills you have learned in a classroom setting?
3. What is the hardest part for you in writing to an audience?

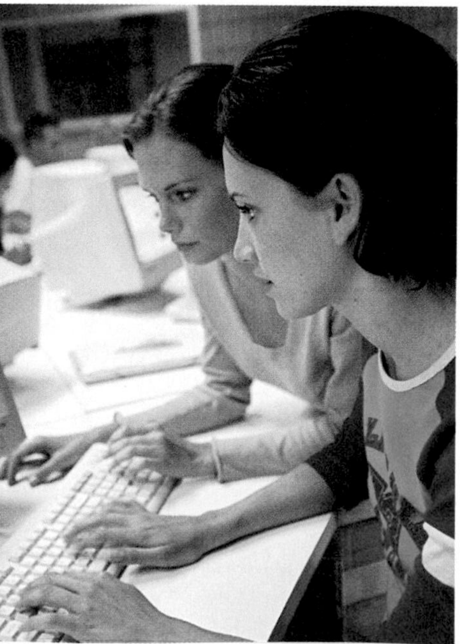

9. Polish Your Presentation

Rubric R

LEVEL This is an intermediate level project.

Language Arts: Key Text From what you know so far about PowerPoint, what steps do you think might be necessary to "fine-tune" a presentation? For example, when you are finished with a presentation, you need to check for spelling errors. What other examples can you think of?

- Key a paragraph that lists at least three steps.
- Explain why you think your three steps are important for creating a good presentation.

Save as: Tips-p1rev-[your first initial and last name]9. Then share your steps with your class.

10. Research a Topic

Rubric R

LEVEL This is an intermediate level project.

Language Arts: Use Research Methods Use the Internet or another method of research (such as your school library) to find information about creating a presentation. What suggestions can you find that are not covered in your **Tips** presentation? What suggestions for creating presentations do you think you might add?

- Open your saved **Tips-7** presentation.
- Save as: Tips-[your first initial and last name]10.
- Use your research to create your own text for the sixth slide.
- Add a title and three bullet points to the slide.
- When finished, print out all six slides as a handout.
- Print the entire presentation and save your work.

11. Rewrite for an Audience

Rubric R

LEVEL This is an advanced level project.

Language Arts: Edit a Presentation Revise the **Tips-7** file for an audience of elementary school students. Rewrite the slides so that the language is appropriate for a younger audience. Simplify the text. Which words would you change? How are the needs of a younger audience different from an audience of your peers?

- Rewrite all six slides.
- Save as: Tips-[your first initial and last name]11.
- Review your work as a slide show.
- Print the entire presentation and save your work.

When completed, modify your project for an older audience. What elements would you change to reach that older audience? What would you still do the same?

Answers Rubrics for each Challenge Yourself Project are available at glencoe.com. You may want to download the rubrics and make them available to students as they complete each project.

Step-By-Step

1. In your **Newsletter** file, select the table's first row.
2. Choose **Home>Styles>Heading 1**. Deselect the text.
3. CHECK Your screen should look like Figure 5.18.
4. Reselect the table's first row. Choose **Home>Styles>More**. From the menu, choose **Clear Formatting**.
5. With the first row still selected, choose **Home>Styles>More**. From the menu, select **Heading 1**. Deselect the text.
6. Select the second row. Select **Heading 2**. Deselect the text.
7. Select the first two rows. Choose **Table Tools>Layout>Align Center**. Deselect the table.
8. CHECK Your screen should look like Figure 5.19. Save your file.

Continue to the next exercise.

Troubleshooting Your students' default **Heading** styles may be different from the ones shown in Figure 5.18. Have students choose **Home>Styles>More** to see the full **Styles** menu.

EXERCISE 5-10
Apply and Clear Styles from Tables

You can apply a **style** (a set of formatting changes) to a table in one step. As with text, you apply styles to tables by using either the Styles group on the Home tab or the Styles task pane.

FIGURE 5.18 Heading 1 style applied to table

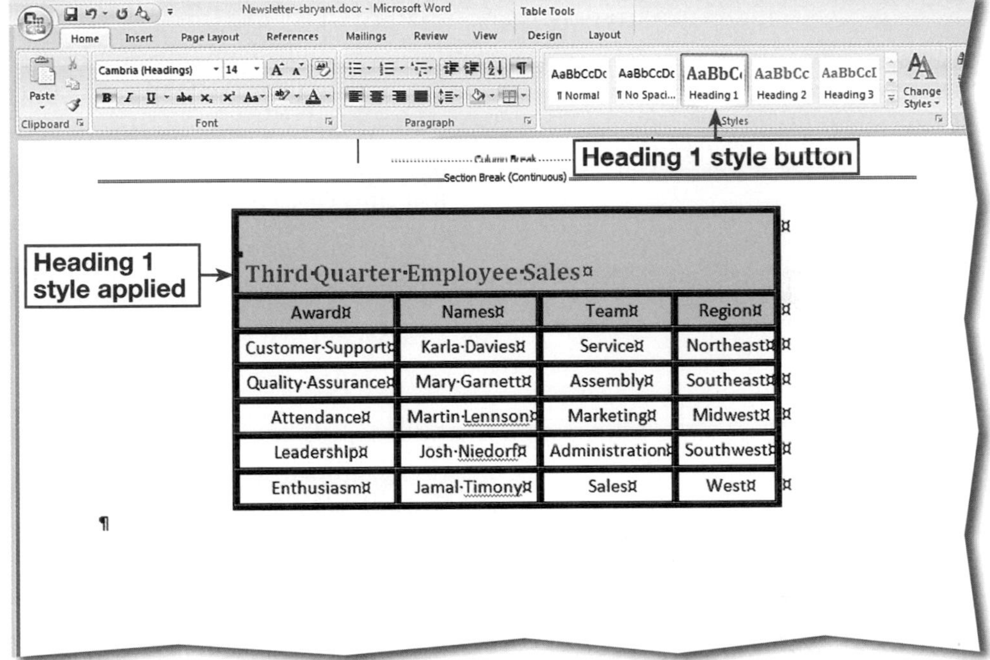

FIGURE 5.19 Heading 2 style applied to table

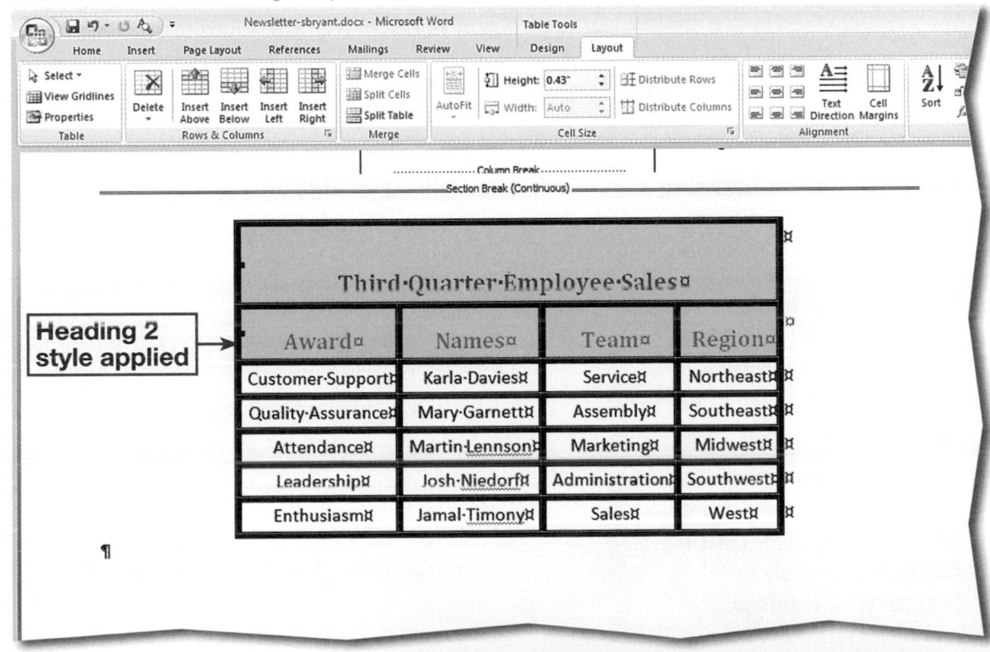

LESSON 1 Critical Thinking Activities

Beyond the Classroom Activity
Paragraphs should include which skills from this lesson will help students prepare a revised presentation for next year's sales.

Standards at Work Activity
Students should add to Slide 5 in their Tips presentation a title and a list of three good presentation skills. Use **Tips7-SF.pptx** as a sample solution file.

21st Century Skills Activity
Students should key a paragraph that describes their experience as an audience member for a presentation.

6. Beyond the Classroom Activity

Language Arts: Revise a Slide Presentation You are the director of sales in a large company. It is your responsibility to forecast next year's sales. You need to update the presentation that you gave last year. The forecast for each quarter was written as a separate report. Each report is contained in a separate slide. To prepare your new presentation, you need to:

- Switch your forecasts for the first and third quarters. This means that the first slide in last year's presentation (Report 1) will become the third slide (Report 3), and the third slide (Report 3) will become the first slide (Report 1).
- Edit the sales numbers for Reports 2 and 4.
- Print a new presentation handout.

Key a paragraph that explains how the skills you learned in this lesson will help you prepare the revised presentation. Save your work as: p2rev-[your first initial and last name]6.

7. Standards at Work Activity

Microsoft Certified Application Specialist Correlation
PP.1.5 *Arrange slides*

Identify Presentation Skills PowerPoint presentations are often used as part of an oral presentation. Evaluate an oral presentation that you gave for school or some other occasion. Then, open your saved **Tips-5** presentation and perform the following tasks:

- Select Slide 5. Key a bulleted list of three skills that an individual should develop to give a great presentation (for example, speak clearly).
- Give the slide an appropriate title.
- Move slide 5 before slide 2 using the slide sorter.

Save your work as: Tips-[your first initial and last name]7.

8. 21st Century Skills Activity

Evaluate a Presentation Think about a time when you were listening to a classmate's report. Then, key a paragraph about your experience. Did the presentation keep your attention? Why or why not? How can evaluating your classmate's presentation make you a better presenter? Save your work as: p2rev-[your first initial and last name]8.

Go Online e-REVIEW
glencoe.com

Go to the **Online Learning Center** to complete the following review activities.

Online Self Check
To test your knowledge of the material, click **Unit 4> Lesson 1** and choose **Self Checks**.

Interactive Review
To review the main points of the lesson, click **Unit 4> Lesson 1** and choose **Interactive Review**.

Step-By-Step

1. In your **Newsletter** file, scroll to the first page.
2. Click at the end of the third paragraph in the first column, after **year**. Press ENTER once.
3. Choose **Insert> Illustrations>Clip Art**.
4. In the **Clip Art** task pane, in the **Search for** box, key: bike.
5. Click the **Search in** drop-down arrow. Make sure **Everywhere** is selected.
6. Click the **Results should be** drop-down arrow. Uncheck everything except **Clip Art**. Click **Go**.
7. Select a clip similar to the one shown in Figure 5.20. Click the clip to insert it. Close the task pane.
8. CHECK Your screen should look similar to Figure 5.21. Save your file.

Continue to the next exercise.

Troubleshooter

In Step 2, be sure to press ENTER after the second-to-last paragraph. The Clip Art should appear before the last paragraph in the first column.

EXERCISE 5-11
Insert Clip Art

The Clip Art gallery contains pictures that you can insert into a document. **Clip Art** can enhance the look of a document and break up long blocks of text.

Step-By-Step Tip In **Step 6**, if the computers are connected to the Internet, students will be sent online to see clips from Web Collections.

FIGURE 5.20 Clip Art task pane

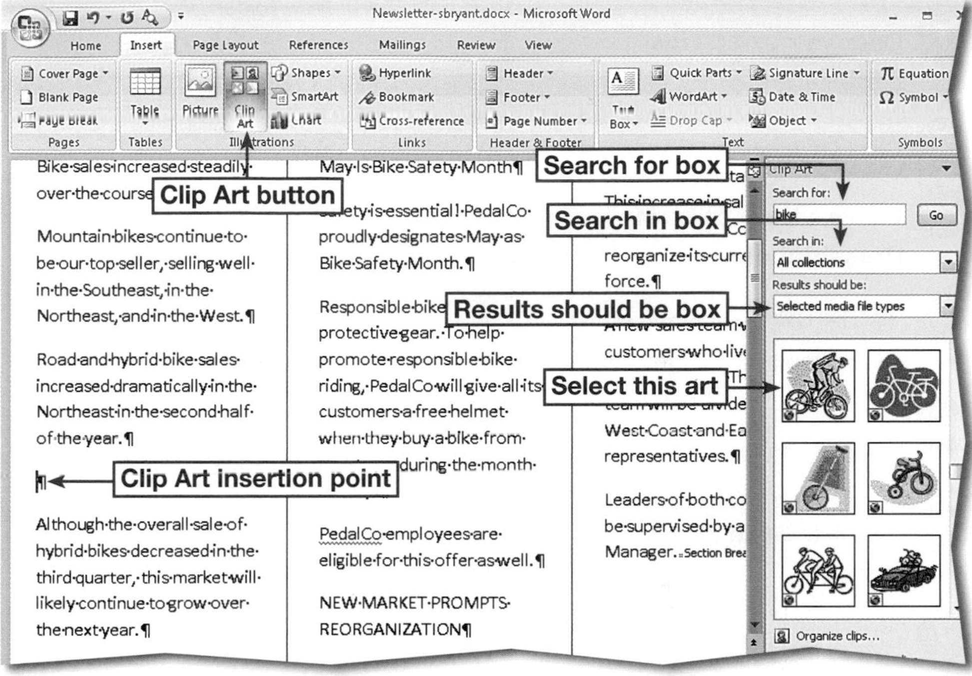

FIGURE 5.21 Clip Art inserted

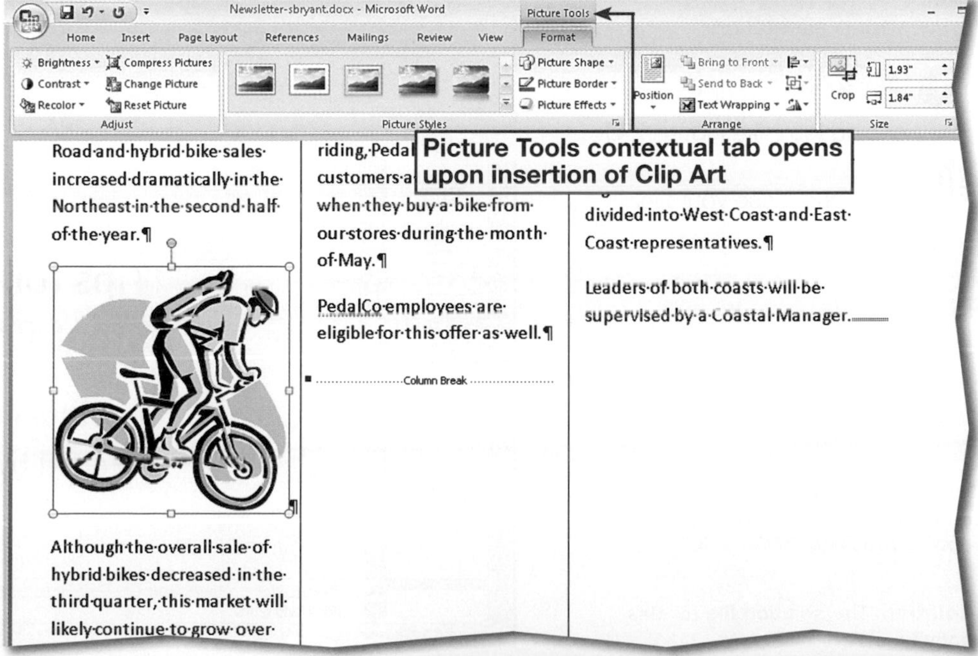

LESSON 1 You Try It Activities

5. Create Folders and Save PowerPoint Presentations

Your classmate is ready to save her PowerPoint presentation. Show her how to create a new folder and save the presentation.

Step-By-Step

1. Open your saved **Tips4** presentation.
2. Click **Office>Save As**.
3. Create a folder called **My Presentations**.
4. **CHECK** Your screen should look like Figure 1.40.
5. Save the file as: Tips-[your first initial and last name]5.
6. Switch to **Slide Show** view.
7. Click through all of the slides in the presentation.
8. Return to the first page of your presentation.
9. **CHECK** Your screen should look like Figure 1.41.
10. Save and close your file.

FIGURE 1.40 New folder

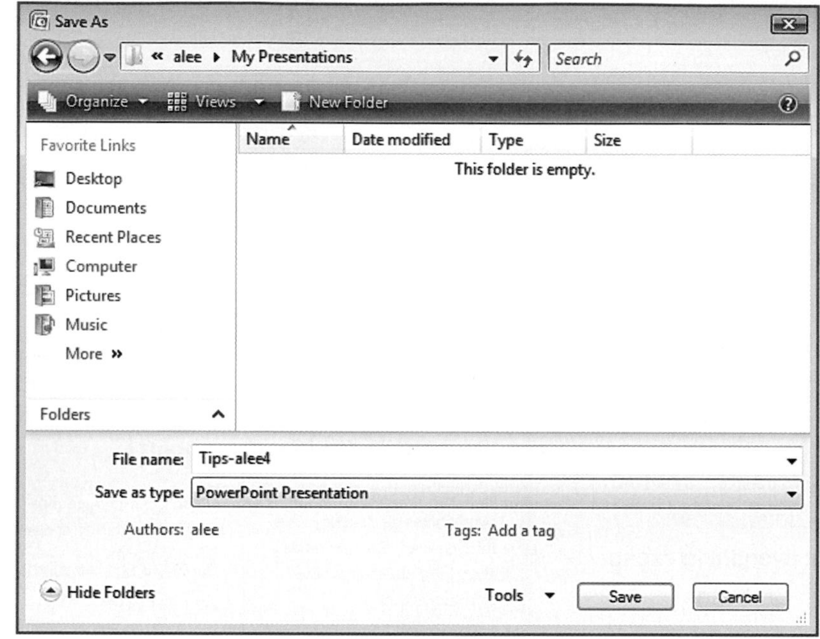

FIGURE 1.41 Saved presentation

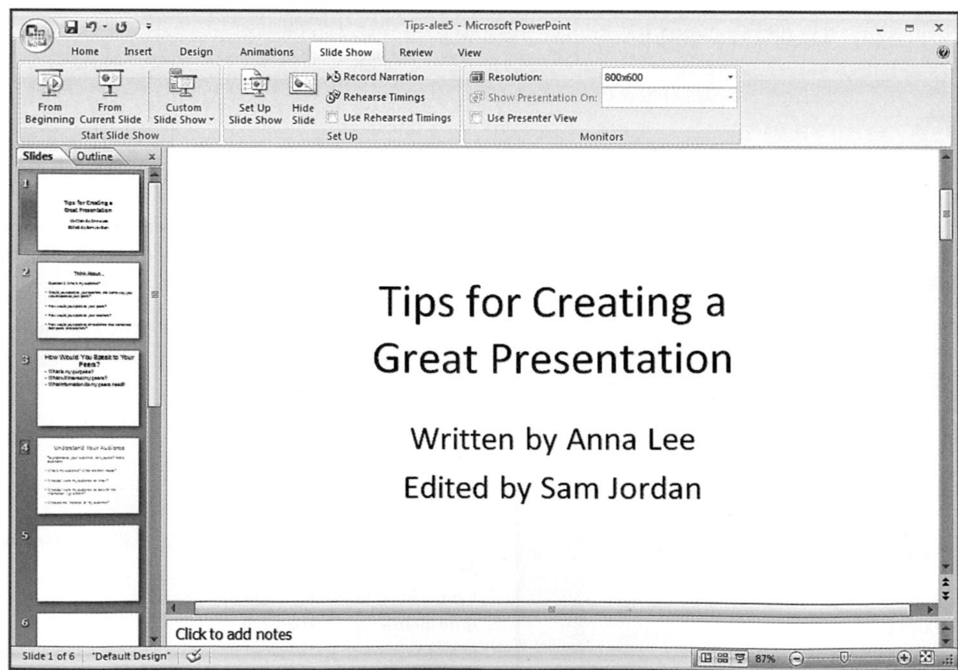

Different Strokes Let students know that they can save a presentation by pressing **CTRL + S**.

Solution The solution file for this activity is **Tips5-SF.pptx**.

Step-By-Step

1. In your **Newsletter** file, click the clip to select it.
2. In the **Picture Tools** contextual tab, choose **Format>Size**.
3. Change the **Shape Height** to **1.4"**. Width changes automatically.
4. Choose **Format> Arrange>Text Wrapping>More Layout Options**.
5. In the **Advanced Layout** dialog box, click the **Text Wrapping** tab. Under **Wrapping Style**, select **Tight**.
6. On the **Picture Position** tab, under **Horizontal**, click **Alignment**. Use the drop-down arrows to select **Centered** relative to **Column** (see Figure 5.22). Click **OK**.
7. Move your pointer over the green rotation handle (see Figure 5.23). Click and rotate slightly clockwise.
8. **CHECK** Your screen should look like Figure 5.23. Save your file.

Continue to the next exercise.

EL Make sure English Learner students understand the word *clockwise*. You may need to clarify the correct rotation direction.

EXERCISE 5-12
Modify Clip Art

You can resize and format Clip Art to fit your document's design. To move Clip Art, point to it and drag it to where you want to place it on the page.

FIGURE 5.22 Advanced Layout dialog box

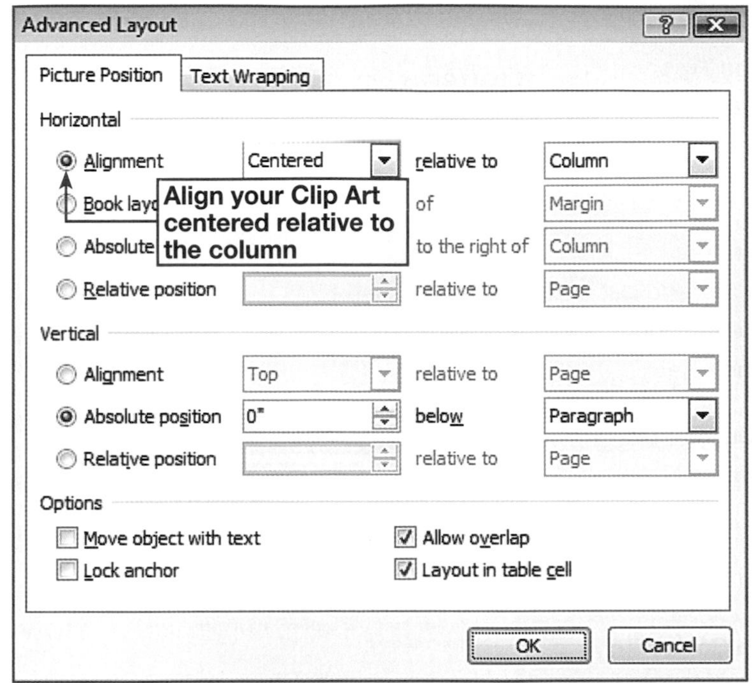

FIGURE 5.23 Clip Art positioned in column

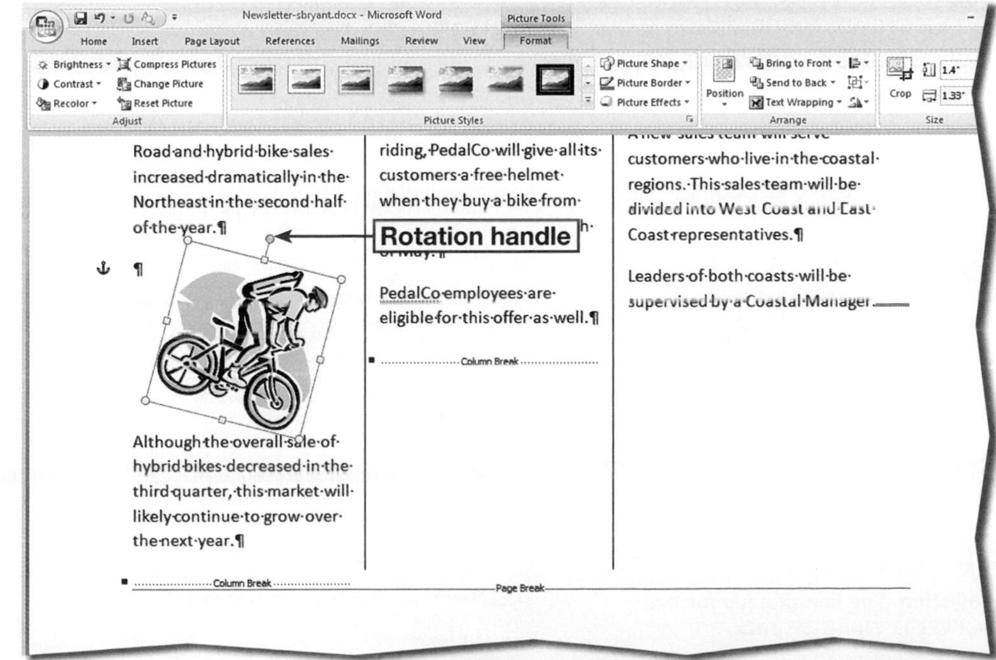

LESSON 1 You Try It Activities

4. Peer Teaching

Your classmate missed the first lesson of your PowerPoint class, so your teacher has asked you to use an existing PowerPoint presentation to teach her some basic skills.

Step-By-Step

1. Open your saved **Tips** presentation. Save as: Tips-[your first initial and last name]4.
2. On the first slide, key: Edited by [your first and last name] under the words **Written by Anna Lee**.
3. Switch to the **Outline** tab. Move to **Slide 2**.
4. **CHECK** Your screen should look like Figure 1.38.
5. Switch to **Slide Sorter View**.
6. Change the order of the third and fourth slides.
7. Double-click the third slide.
8. **CHECK** Your screen should look like Figure 1.39.
9. With your teacher's permission, print the third slide in the presentation.
10. Save and close your file.

Solution The solution file for this activity is **Tips4-SF.pptx**.

FIGURE 1.38 Outline tab

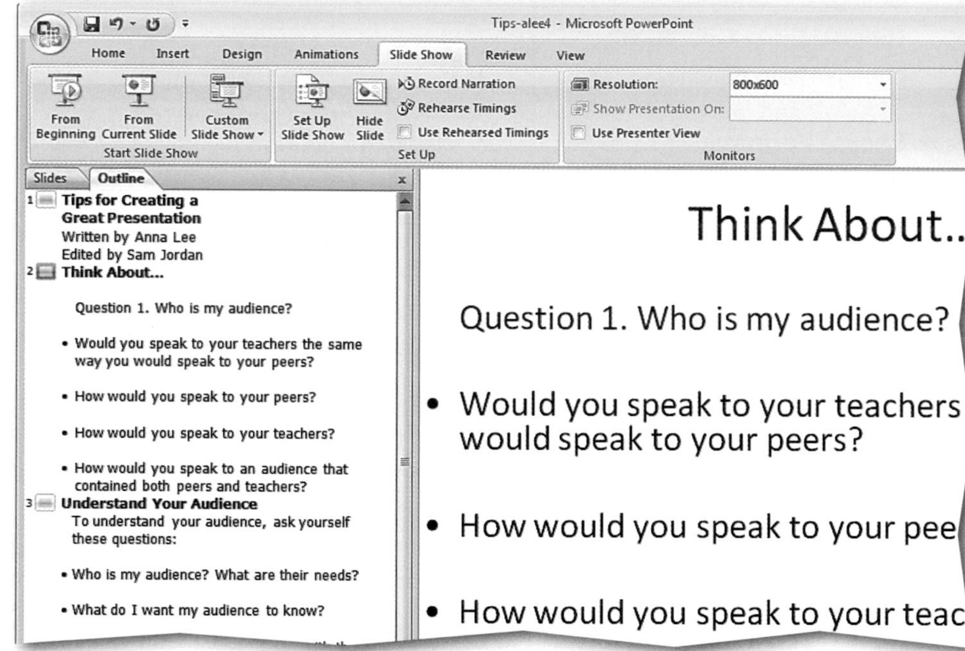

FIGURE 1.39 The third slide

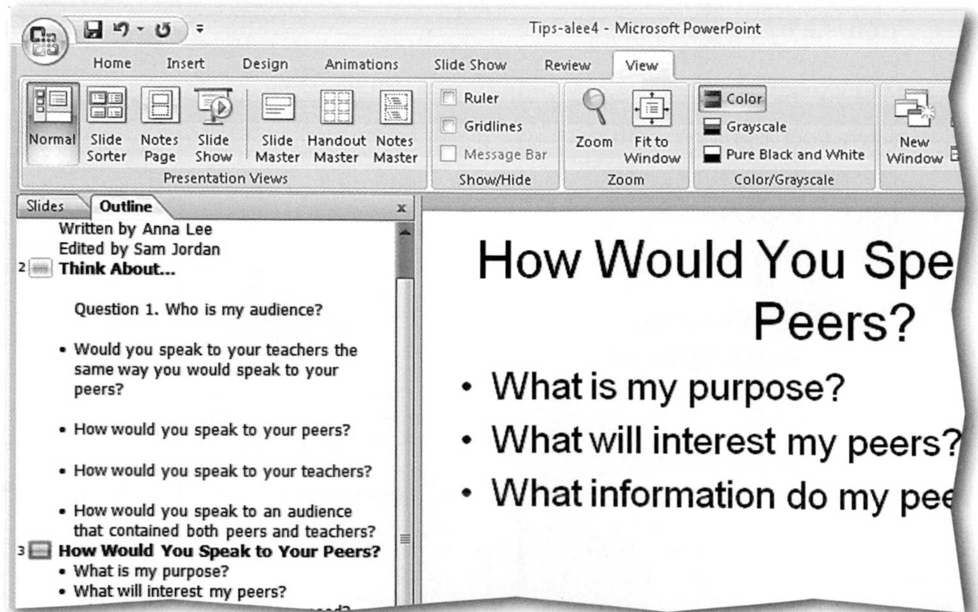

Step-By-Step

1. In your **Newsletter** file, click after **well** at the end of the final paragraph in the second column. Press ENTER.

2. Choose **Insert>Text>Text Box**. In the drop-down menu, select **Simple Text Box**.

3. CHECK Your screen should look like Figure 5.24. Notice the **Text Box Tools** contextual tab appears when you insert a text box.

4. Click the sizing handle on the left side of the text box.

5. Drag the sizing handle inward to reduce the text box size until it fits within the column.

6. CHECK Your screen should look similar to Figure 5.25.

7. Click in the text box. Key: Expand Your Knowledge! Press ENTER.

8. Key: Visit the PedalCo Web site to learn more about helmet safety.

9. Format **Expand Your Knowledge!**: **Bold**, **Centered**, **Font Size 14 pt**. If necessary, resize the box to fit the text.

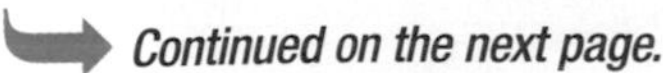

Continued on the next page.

EXERCISE 5-13
Insert, Position, and Size a Text Box

A **text box** is a movable, resizable box that contains text. You can use text boxes to arrange individual blocks of text on a page. Use a **sizing handle** to resize a text box. Sizing handles can also be used to resize objects, such as Clip Art and pictures.

FIGURE 5.24 Text box created

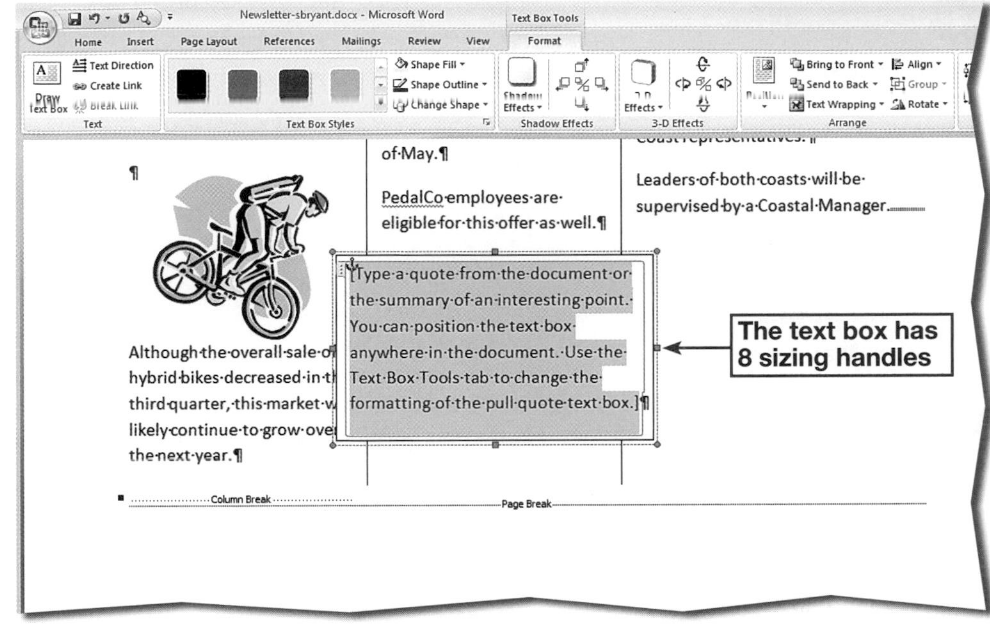

FIGURE 5.25 Text box enlarged

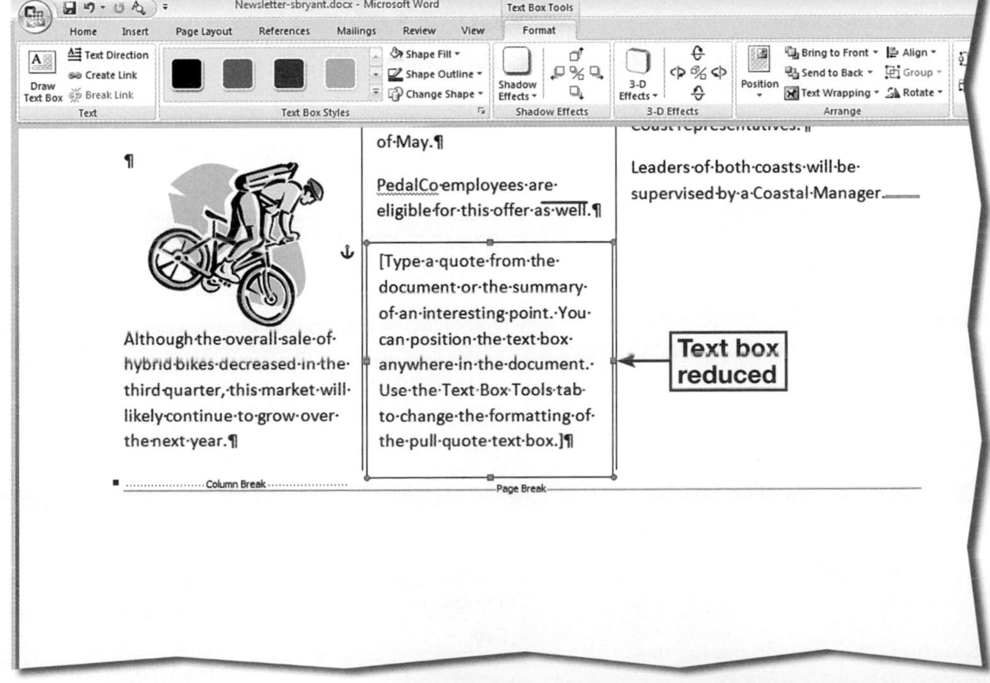

LESSON 1 Practice It Activities

3. Run a Slide Show and Print

Follow the steps to complete the activity. You must complete Practice It Activity 2 before doing this activity.

New Student Strategy If a student did not complete Practice It Activity 2, then the solution file for that activity can be used as a data file for this activity.

Step-By-Step

1. Open your **Pizza-2** file. Save as: Pizza-[your first initial and last name]3.
2. Choose **Slide Show>Set Up>Set Up Slide Show** .
3. Under **Advance slides**, click **Manually**.
4. **CHECK** Your dialog box should look like Figure 1.36. Click **OK**.
5. Choose **Office>Print**. In the **Name** box, click the drop-down arrow. Ask your teacher which printer you should use.
6. In the **Print what** box, click the drop-down arrow. Click **Handouts**. In the **Slides per page** box, select **6**.
7. **CHECK** Your dialog box should look similar to Figure 1.37.
8. With your teacher's permission, click **OK** to print the slides. Save and close your file.

Solution The solution file for this activity is **Pizza3-SF.pptx**.

FIGURE 1.36 Set Up Show dialog box

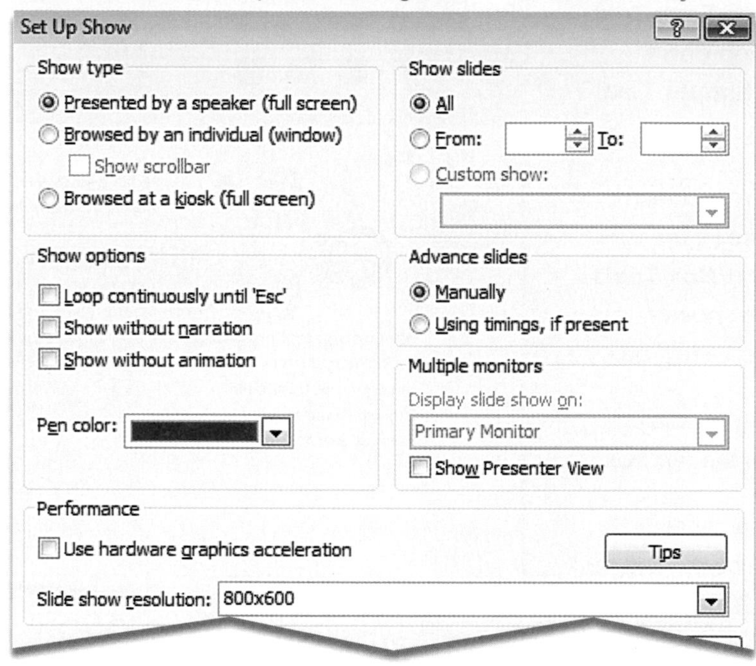

FIGURE 1.37 Print dialog box

Print
Printer
Name: Microsoft XPS Document Writer
Properties
Status: Idle
Find Printer...
Type: Microsoft XPS Document Writer
Where: XPSPort:
Comment:
Print to file
Print range
All
Current slide
Selection
Custom Show:
Slides:
Enter slide numbers and/or slide ranges. For example, 1,3,5-12
Copies
Number of copies:
1
Collate
Print what:
Handouts
Color/grayscale:
Color
Handouts
Slides per page: 6
Order: Horizontal Vertical

Step-By-Step

EXERCISE 5-13 (Continued)
Insert, Position, and Size a Text Box

10 CHECK Your screen should look like Figure 5.26. Click the text box's border. In the **Text Box Tools** contextual tab, choose **Format>Text Box Styles>Dialog Box Launcher** . In the **Format Text Box** dialog box, click the **Text Box** tab. Make sure **Resize AutoShape to fit text** is selected.

11 Click the **Colors and Lines** tab. Under **Fill**, click the **Color** box drop-down arrow. Click **Yellow**. Click the **Layout** tab. Under **Wrapping style**, click **In front of text**. Under **Horizontal alignment**, click **Center**. Click **OK**.

12 Select **Insert>Text>Text Box>Draw Text Box**. Draw a new text box under the first text box. Click the first text box. In the **Text Box Tools** contextual tab, choose **Format>Text>Create Link**. Click in the new text box to link it to the first text box. Click **Undo** twice. Deselect the first text box.

13 CHECK Your screen should look like Figure 5.27. Save your file.

Continue to the next exercise.

FIGURE 5.26 Formatted text in text box

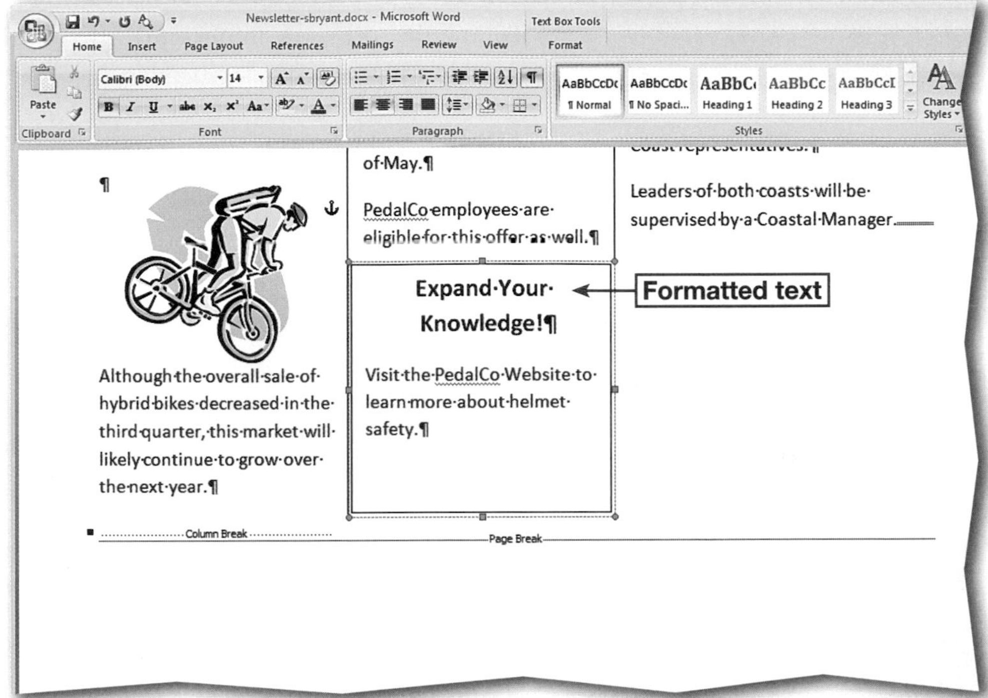

FIGURE 5.27 Finished text box

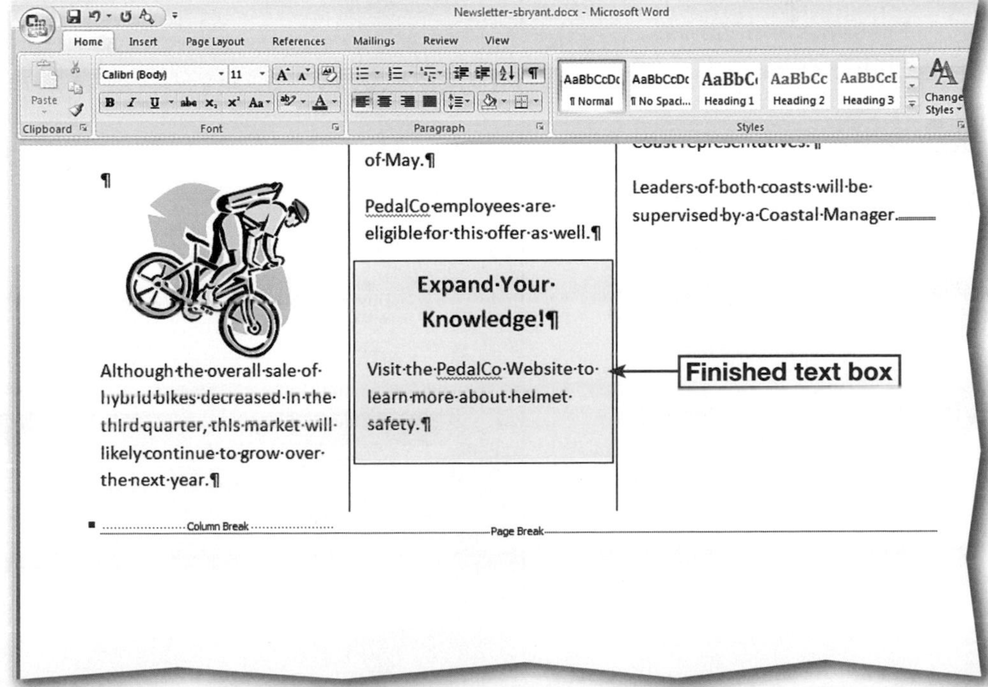

Teaching Tip Tell students to make sure their text boxes are still easy to read after they add color. Dark background colors can make text difficult to read.

LESSON 1 Practice It Activities

Step-By-Step

1. Open your **Pizza-1** file. Save as: Pizza-[your first initial and last name]2.
2. On the **Slides** tab, select **Slide 3**.
3. In the **Slide** pane, click before the word **vegetables**.
4. Key: any. Press the **spacebar** once.
5. **CHECK** Your screen should look like Figure 1.34.
6. Choose **View> Presentation Views> Slide Sorter**.
7. Drag **Slide 2** after **Slide 3**.
8. **CHECK** Your screen should look like Figure 1.35.
9. In the **Presentation Views** group, click **Normal**.
10. Save and close your file.

Solution The solution file for this activity is **Pizza2-SF.pptx.**

2. Edit Text and Use Slide Sorter View

Follow the steps to complete the activity. You must complete Practice It Activity 1 before doing this activity.

New Student Strategy If a student did not complete Practice It Activity 1, then the solution file for that activity can be used as a data file for this activity.

FIGURE 1.34 Editing text

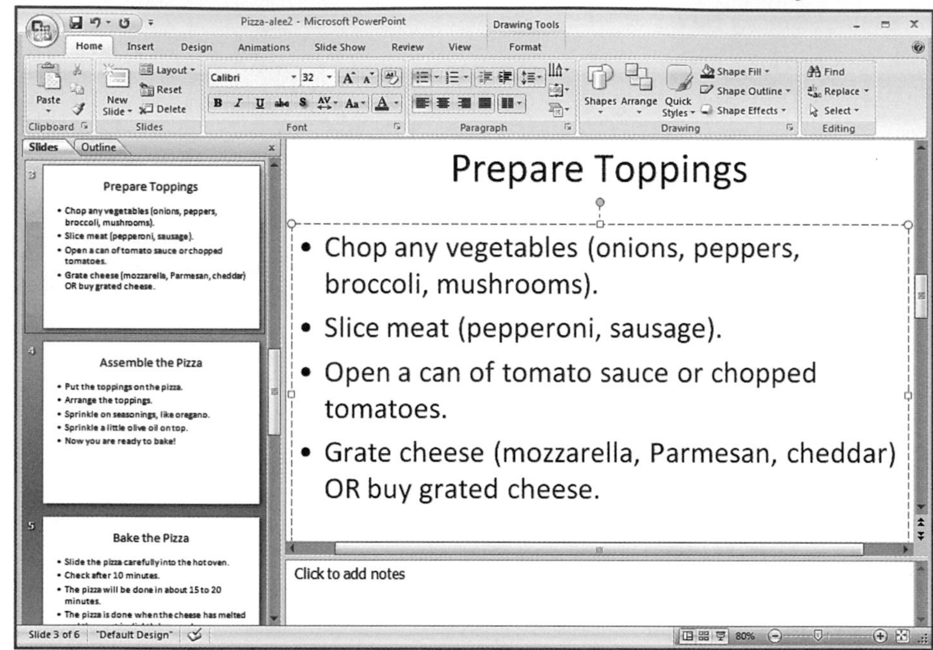

FIGURE 1.35 Rearranged slides

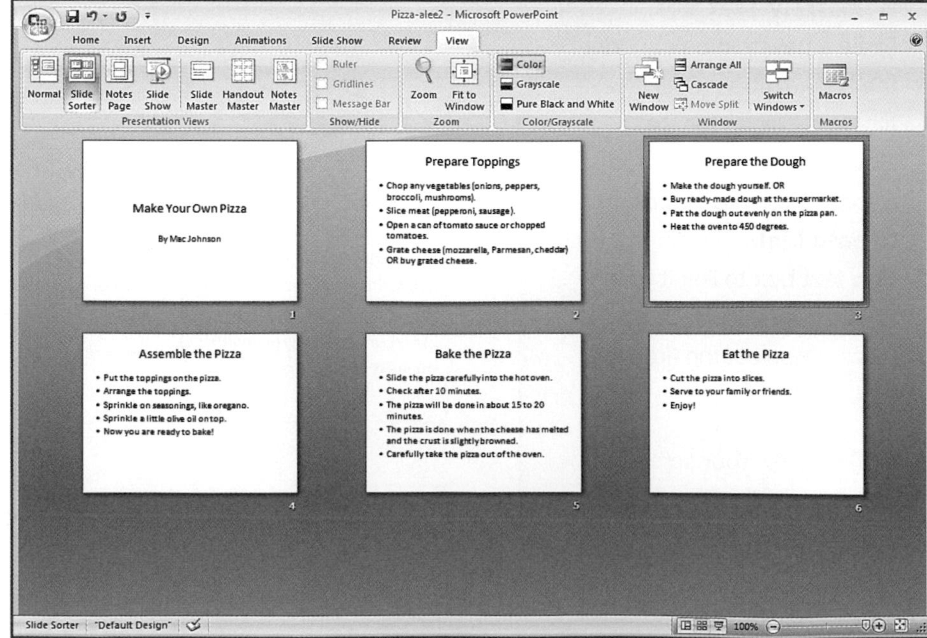

Step-By-Step

1. In your **Newsletter** file, click after **Manager** in the last paragraph in the third column. Press ENTER.

2. Choose **Insert>Illustrations>SmartArt**.

3. In the **Choose a SmartArt Graphic** dialog box, under **Hierarchy**, select the **Organization Chart**. Click **OK**.

4. Right-click the box in the second row of the diagram. Click **Cut**. Right-click one box in the diagram's last row. Click **Cut**.

5. Use the sizing handles to resize the diagram similar to Figure 5.28.

6. Click in each of the diagram's three boxes and key the text shown in Figure 5.29.

7. Format the diagram text: **Bold** and **12 pt**. Resize the text boxes similar to Figure 5.29. Deselect the diagram.

8. **CHECK** Your screen should look like Figure 5.29. Save your file.

Continue to the next exercise.

Troubleshooting In Step 3, if students are using Windows XP, refer them to page xlix to learn about any differences that they may see on the screen.

EXERCISE 5-14
Create and Modify SmartArt

A **diagram** can help you explain an idea or process by displaying it graphically. The **SmartArt** Gallery contains six types of diagrams: List, Process, Cycle, Hierarchy, Relationship, Matrix, and Pyramid.

NCLB/Math (NCTM Geometry) Explain to students that SmartArt diagrams should be chosen depending on the information being conveyed.

FIGURE 5.28 Modified and resized diagram

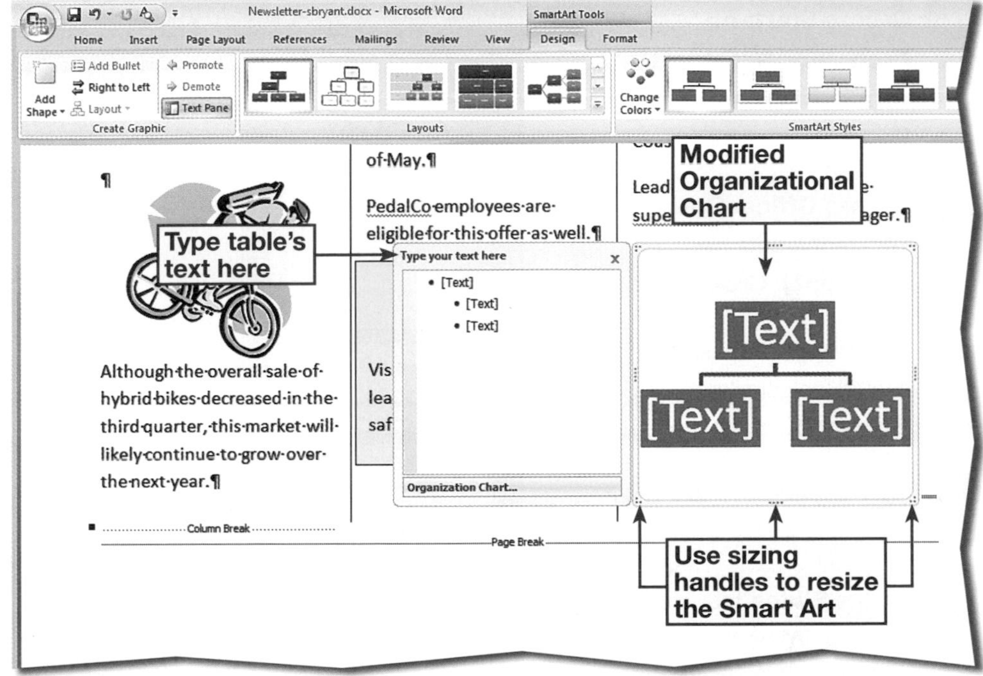

FIGURE 5.29 Finished diagram

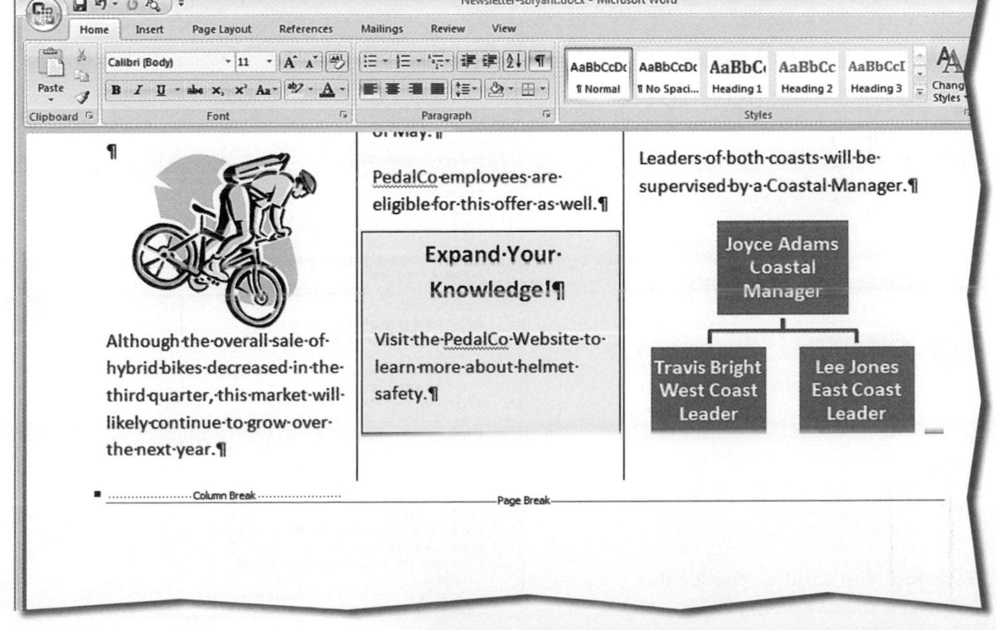

LESSON 1 Practice It Activities

1. Explore the PowerPoint Screen

Follow the steps to complete the activity.

NCLB/Language Arts (NCTE 5) PowerPoint is an ideal tool for students to develop their abilities to logically organize ideas or items using ordered steps.

Step-By-Step

1. Choose **Start>All Programs>Microsoft Office>Microsoft Office PowerPoint 2007**.
2. Choose **Office>Open**. Locate the data file **Pizza.pptx**. Click **Open**.
3. **CHECK** Your screen should look similar to Figure 1.32.
4. Save the file as: Pizza-[your first initial and last name]1.
5. On the **Slides** tab, click **Slide 2**. In the third bullet, double-click **baking**. Key: pizza. Press the **spacebar** once.
6. Click the **Outline** tab. Click the slide icon next to **Slide 1**.
7. **CHECK** Your screen should look like Figure 1.33. Click the **Slides** tab.
8. **CHECK** Your screen should again look like Figure 1.32.
9. Save and close your file.

Solution The solution file for this activity is **Pizza1-SF.pptx**.

FIGURE 1.32 Pizza presentation

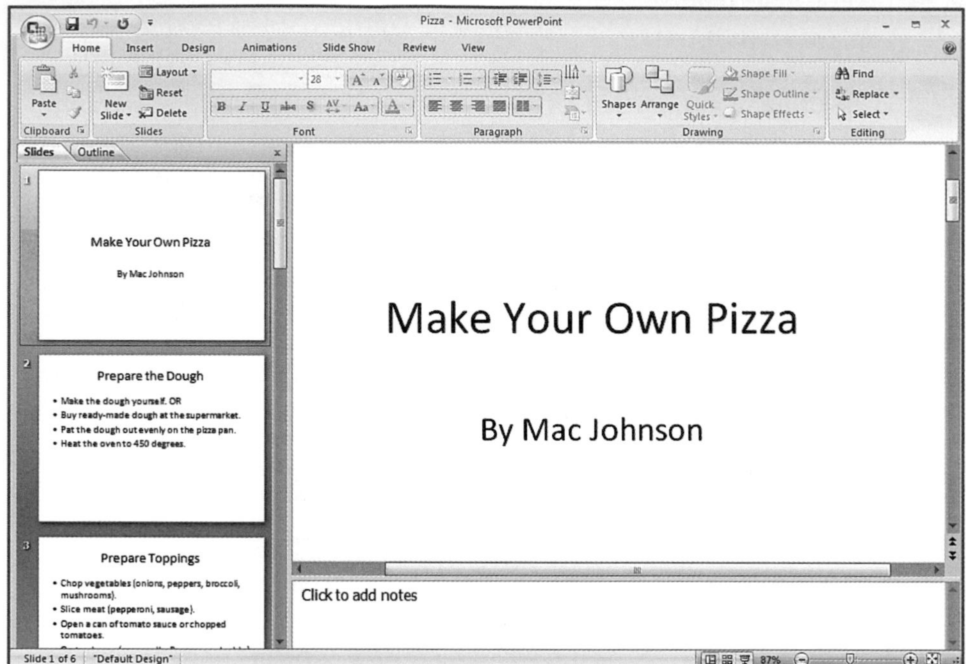

FIGURE 1.33 Using the Outline tab

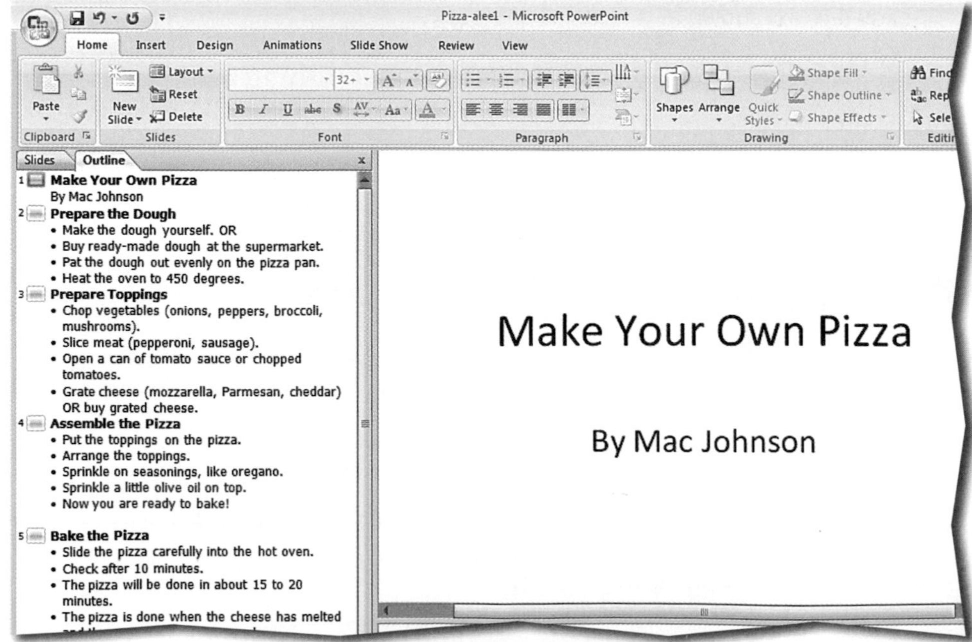

Step-By-Step

1. In your **Newsletter** file, scroll to the table at the bottom of page 2.

2. Choose **Insert>Illustrations>Shapes**. From the drop-down menu, under **Stars and Banners**, select the **5-Point Star** (see Figure 5.30).

3. The cursor turns into a four-pointed arrow. Drag the star to the left side of the table.

4. **CHECK** Your screen should look like Figure 5.31. Right-click the shape. Select **Format AutoShape**.

5. In the **Format AutoShape** dialog box, on the **Colors and Lines** tab, under **Fill**, click the **Color** drop-down arrow. Click **Yellow**.

6. Under **Line**, click the **Style** drop-down arrow. Click **1 pt**.

7. On the **Size** tab, under **Height**, select **Absolute** and key: .75″.

Continued on the next page.

Tech Tip

In Step 4, you can access the **Format AutoShape** dialog box by clicking **Drawing Tools>Format** and clicking the **Shapes** Dialog Box Launcher.

EXERCISE 5-15
Insert, Position, and Size a Shape

A **graphic** is an element that is used to display information and to add visual interest to a document. Word has tools that allow you to create an easy-to-see graphic **shape** such as a circle, square, star, or arrow. Use the Shapes menu to select the type of shape you want to create and use.

FIGURE 5.30 Selecting a Shape

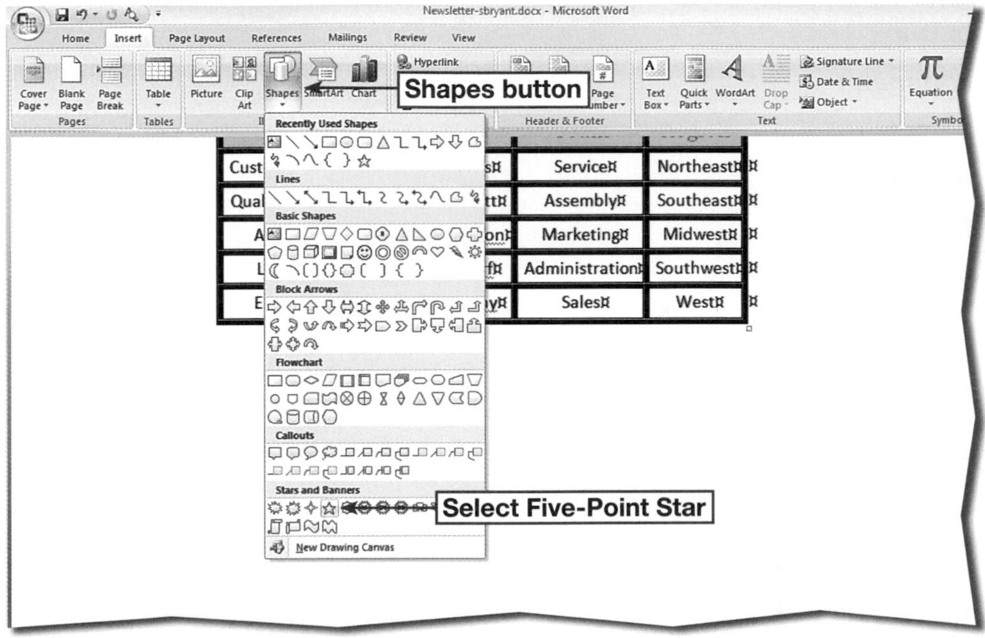

FIGURE 5.31 Shape created

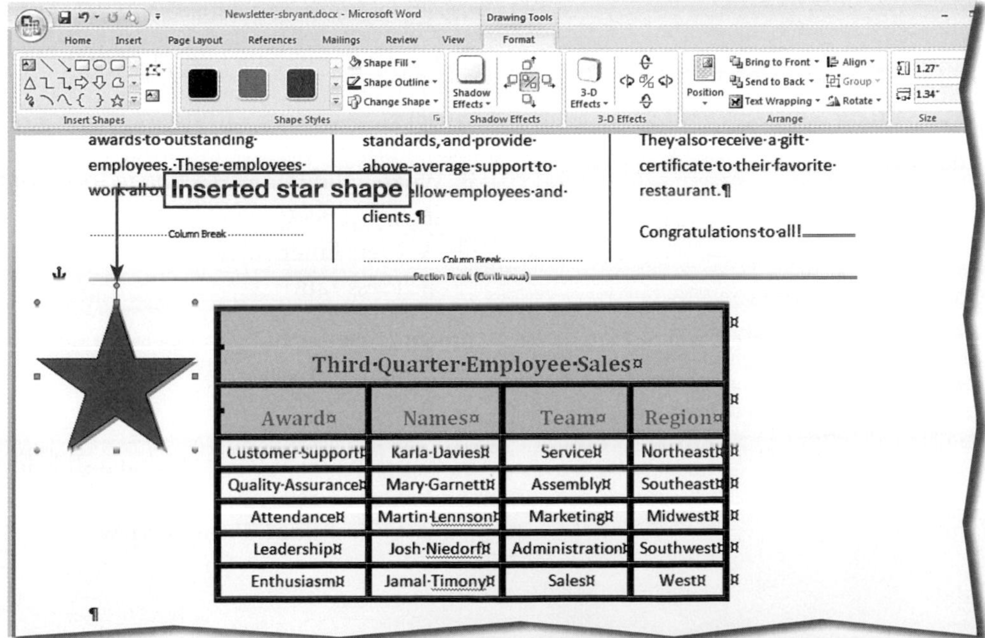

LESSON 1  After You Read 

Vocabulary

Key Terms

button

command

cursor

dialog box

folder

group

placeholder

presentation

Quick Access Toolbar (QAT)

Ribbon

ScreenTip

scroll bar

slide

status bar

tab

title bar

Academic Vocabulary

display

monitor

Answer to Vocabulary Activity
Students write a paragraph about one skill from the lesson. Paragraphs should include at least five vocabulary terms.

Review Vocabulary

Complete the following statements on a separate piece of paper. Choose from the Vocabulary list on the left to complete the statements.

1. A(n) ___slide___ is an individual page within a presentation. (p. 546)

2. The ___title bar___ at the top of the screen displays the name of the current presentation. (p. 544)

3. A(n) ___folder___ is an item that helps the user organize files by grouping related files together. (p. 547)

4. A preset text box on a new slide is called a(n) ___placeholder___. (p. 552)

5. A(n) ___ScreenTip___ is a description of an object that appears when you point to the object. (p. 544)

Vocabulary Activity

6. Key a paragraph that describes one skill you learned in this lesson. (For example, explain how to run a slide show manually.)
A. Decide what topic you are going to write about.
B. List five Key Terms that relate to the topic.
C. Key a paragraph that explains your topic. Include at least five Vocabulary terms in your paragraph.
D. Exchange your paragraph with a classmate. Use your classmate's feedback to revise your paragraph.

Review Key Concepts

Answer the following questions on a separate piece of paper.

7. Which of the following is a tab on the Ribbon? (p. 545)
A. Draw
B. Format
(C.) Insert
D. Help

8. When a slide show is set up to loop continuously, how would you exit the slide show? (p. 555)
A. Press Enter
B. Press Tab
C. Press Backspace
(D.) Press Escape

9. Which tab would you use to set up a slide show? (p. 554)
(A.) Slide Show
B. Review
C. Insert
D. Animations

10. Which path lets you see what a slide looks like before you print it? (p. 557)
A. Office>Save As
(B.) Office>Print>Print Preview
C. View>Slide
D. Office>Open

EXERCISE 5-15 (Continued)
Insert, Position, and Size a Shape

8. On the **Size** tab, under **Scale**, click **Lock aspect ratio**.

9. On the **Layout** tab, under **Wrapping** style, click **In front of text**. Under **Horizontal** alignment, click **Left**. Click **OK**.

10. **CHECK** Your screen should look like Figure 5.32.

11. Use the rotation handle to slightly rotate the shape in either direction.

12. Click the shape and drag it to the table's top-left corner. Deselect the shape. Scroll up to see the table.

13. **CHECK** Your screen should look similar to Figure 5.33. Save your file.

Continue to the next exercise.

FIGURE 5.32 Shape formatted

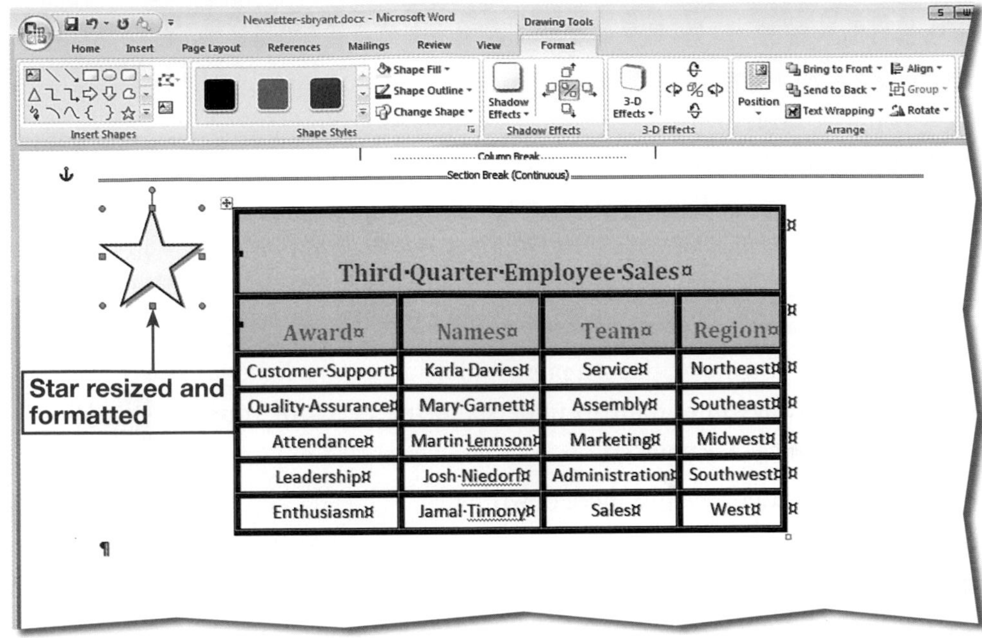

Third·Quarter·Employee·Sales			
Award	Names	Team	Region
Customer·Support	Karla·Davies	Service	Northeast
Quality·Assurance	Mary·Garnett	Assembly	Southeast
Attendance	Martin·Lennson	Marketing	Midwest
Leadership	Josh·Niedorf	Administration	Southwest
Enthusiasm	Jamal·Timony	Sales	West

FIGURE 5.33 Rotated shape positioned on table

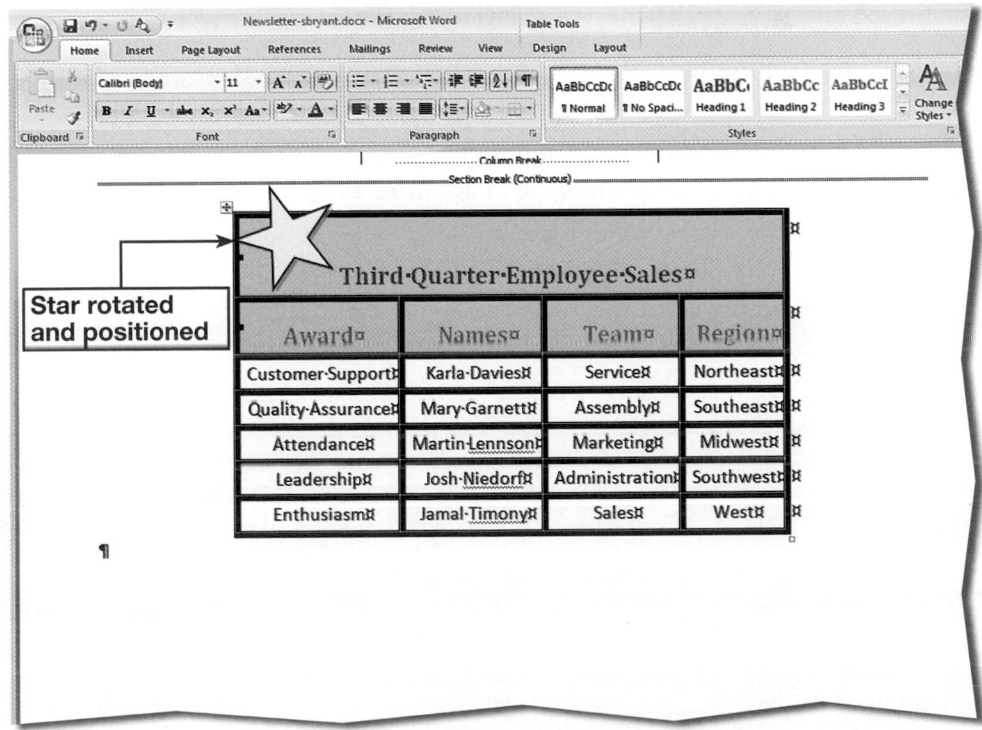

Third·Quarter·Employee·Sales			
Award	Names	Team	Region
Customer·Support	Karla·Davies	Service	Northeast
Quality·Assurance	Mary·Garnett	Assembly	Southeast
Attendance	Martin·Lennson	Marketing	Midwest
Leadership	Josh·Niedorf	Administration	Southwest
Enthusiasm	Jamal·Timony	Sales	West

Academic Skills

Using tables in documents allows you to simplify information and clarify your main points. For example, if you are writing a paper for your science class, you might list research results in a table.

NCLB/Language Arts (NCTE 5) Reinforce to students that tables are essential to effective written communication because they allow students to organize information.

Teaching Tip Tell students to delete any extra paragraph marks in the document. This will make the formatting go more smoothly.

Writing MATTERS

Know Your Audience

You have been invited to give a presentation about your prized comic book collection to an art class at the local community college. You are excited to share your love of comics, but you are not sure how to do it.

Evaluate Your Audience's Needs

No matter what you are writing—a presentation, a report, a letter, a memo—it is always important to understand the needs of your particular audience. Ask yourself:

1. Who will read or see this piece of writing?
2. What do I want them to know?
3. What background do they bring?
4. What do I want this piece of writing or presentation to accomplish?

Focus on the Audience

You call the community college and learn that the class is a beginning art class on creating comics. Most of the students have little experience in art, and may know nothing about comic books. The class is made up of adults, ranging in age from 19 to 25. You decide to bring several examples of good comic books. You make sure to leave time for plenty of questions. You even try to predict a few of the questions audience members may ask, so that you can be prepared with good answers.

PowerPoint is an excellent tool for customizing presentations, such as the comic book presentation described here.

NCLB/Language Arts (NCTE 4) Reinforce to students that an effective presentation will contain spoken, written, and visual language that is appropriate for the audience.

SKILLBUILDER

1. **List** What are three questions to ask yourself about your audience?
2. **Explain** Why is it a good idea to understand your audience?
3. **Apply** You are invited to give your presentation again. This time, however, your audience is fifth and sixth graders. Key a paragraph that introduces your comic book collection. Make sure your paragraph is appropriate for your new, younger audience.

SkillBuilder answers can be found on page TM90.

Step-By-Step

EXERCISE 5-16
Use WordArt

Use **WordArt** to create text that is stretched, shadowed, or shaped. You can use WordArt to create an exciting title for your document or to create a logo.

Solution Use the file **Newsletter-SF.docx** as a solution file for Exercises 5-1 through 5-16.

1. In your **Newsletter** file, go to page one. Click after the text **PedalCo Employee Newsletter**. Press ENTER.
2. Select the text **PedalCo Employee Newsletter** (*do not* include the paragraph mark). Click **Insert>Text>WordArt**. In the drop-down menu, select **WordArt style 7** (see Figure 5.34).
3. In the **Edit WordArt Text** box, with **PedalCo Employee Newsletter** selected, click the **Size** drop-down arrow. Click **20**. Click **Bold**. Click **OK**.
4. Right-click the WordArt. Select **Format WordArt**. On the **Colors and Lines** tab, under **Fill**, click the **Color** drop-down arrow. Click **Light Blue**.
5. Under **Line**, change **Weight** to **1.5 pt**. Click **OK**. Deselect the WordArt.
6. **CHECK** Your screen should look like Figure 5.35.
7. Select the headline and click **Copy**. Scroll to the top of page two. Delete the headline there and click **Paste**. Save and close your file.

Continue to the next exercise.

FIGURE 5.34 WordArt Gallery

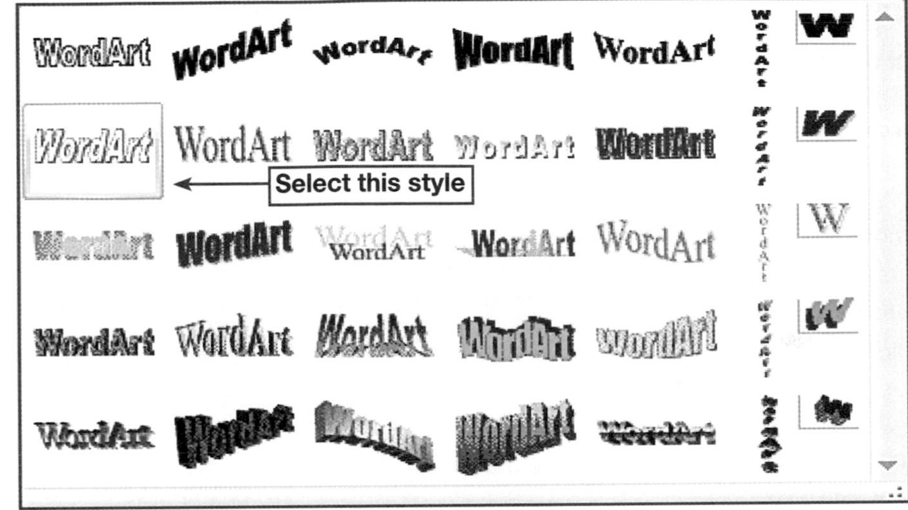

FIGURE 5.35 Finished WordArt

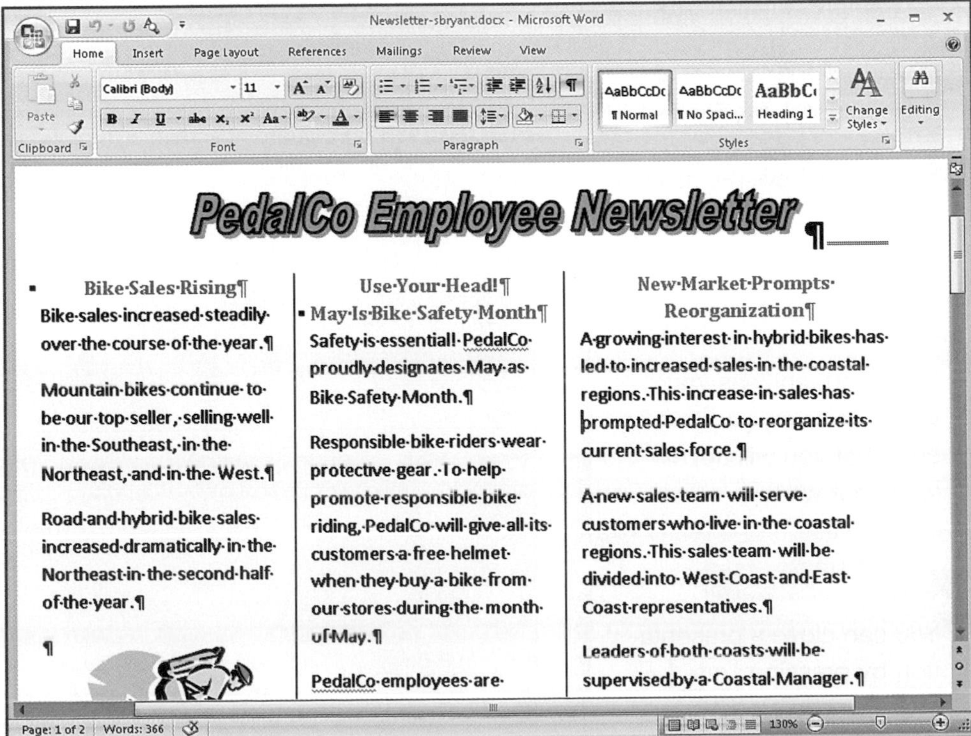

Step-By-Step

1. In your **Tips** file, choose **Office>Print**.
2. In the **Print** dialog box, under **Print what**, click the drop-down arrow to see the list of options.
3. Click **Handouts** (see Figure 1.30).
4. Under **Handouts**, click the drop-down arrow in the **Slides per page** box. Click **6**.
5. With your teacher's permission, click **OK** to print. Save your file.
6. Choose **Office>Close**. Your presentation closes.
7. CHECK Your screen should look like Figure 1.31.
8. To close PowerPoint, click **Close** [X] on the title bar.

You Should Know

Save frequently as you work. This way you can be sure that you will never lose your work.

Shortcuts

You can close a presentation by pressing CTRL + F4. You can close PowerPoint by pressing ALT + F4.

EXERCISE 1-16
Print a Presentation Handout

Instead of printing slides, you can print handouts, which have one or more slides on each page and space to take notes. Handouts allow your audience to follow your presentation, and they provide a record of the items discussed.

Solution Use the file **Tips-SF.pptx** as a solution file for Exercises 1-3 through 1-16.

FIGURE 1.30 Printing handouts

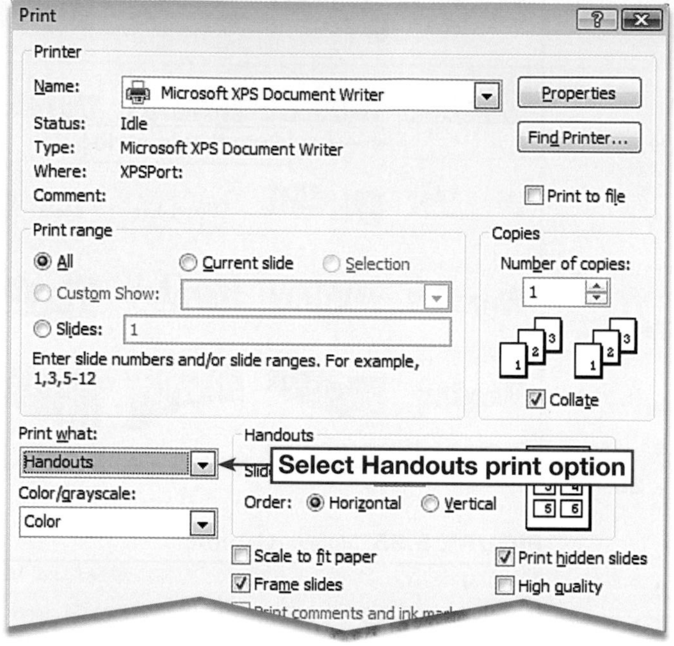

FIGURE 1.31 PowerPoint screen with presentation closed

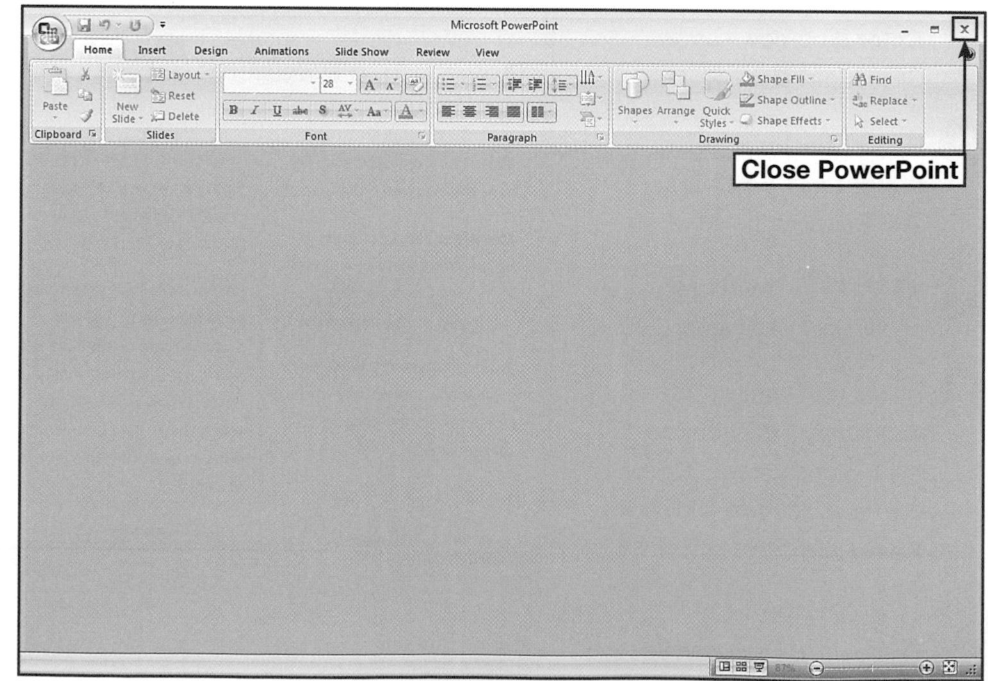

Step-By-Step

1. Open the data file **Sales .docx**. Save as: Sales-[your first initial and last name].

2. Click at the end of the paragraph under **Sales by Quarter**. Press ENTER.

3. Choose **Insert> Illustrations>Chart**. In the **Insert Chart** dialog box, under **Column**, use the ScreenTips to select **3-D Clustered Column**. Click **OK**.

4. A Microsoft Excel worksheet opens. Click the upper-left button to select the entire worksheet. Press DELETE.

5. Key the data shown in Figure 5.36. Close the worksheet.

6. In your **Sales** document, select the chart. In the **Chart Tools** contextual tab, choose **Layout> Labels>Axis Titles> Primary Vertical Axis Title>Horizontal Title**.

7. Click the **Axis Title** text box. Key: Percent of Market. Click outside the text box.

8. CHECK Your screen should look like Figure 5.37. Save your file.

Continue to the next exercise.

EXERCISE 5-17
Create and Modify a Chart

A **chart** makes it easy to compare and contrast numerical information. You enter data for the chart in an Excel worksheet. You can choose from several chart types, including column, bar, line, and pie.

Step-By-Step Tip In **Step 5**, show students how to resize the rows in the worksheet to see all the data.

FIGURE 5.36 New data for an Excel worksheet

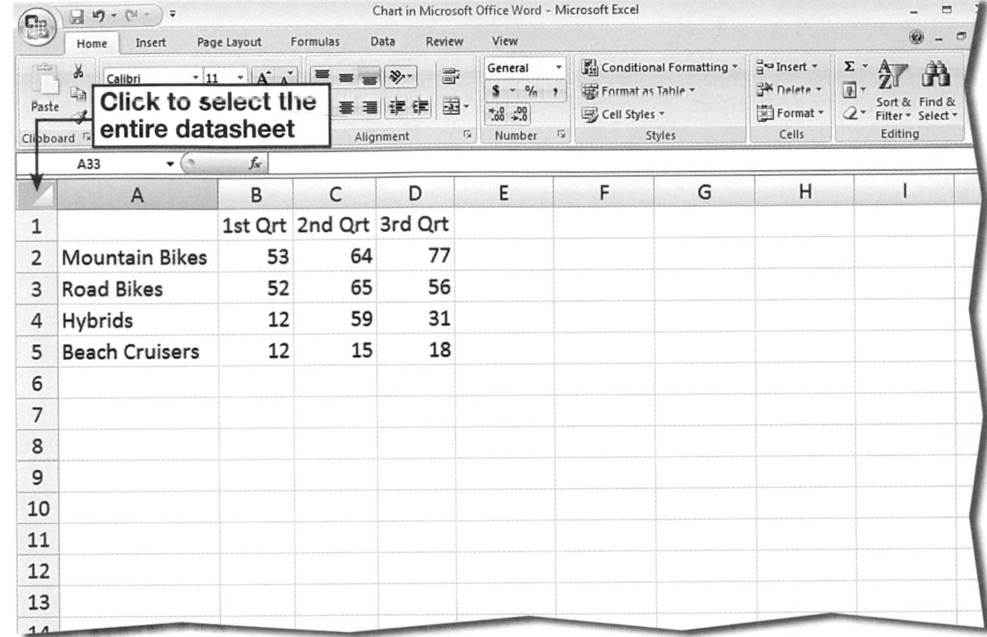

FIGURE 5.37 Modified chart

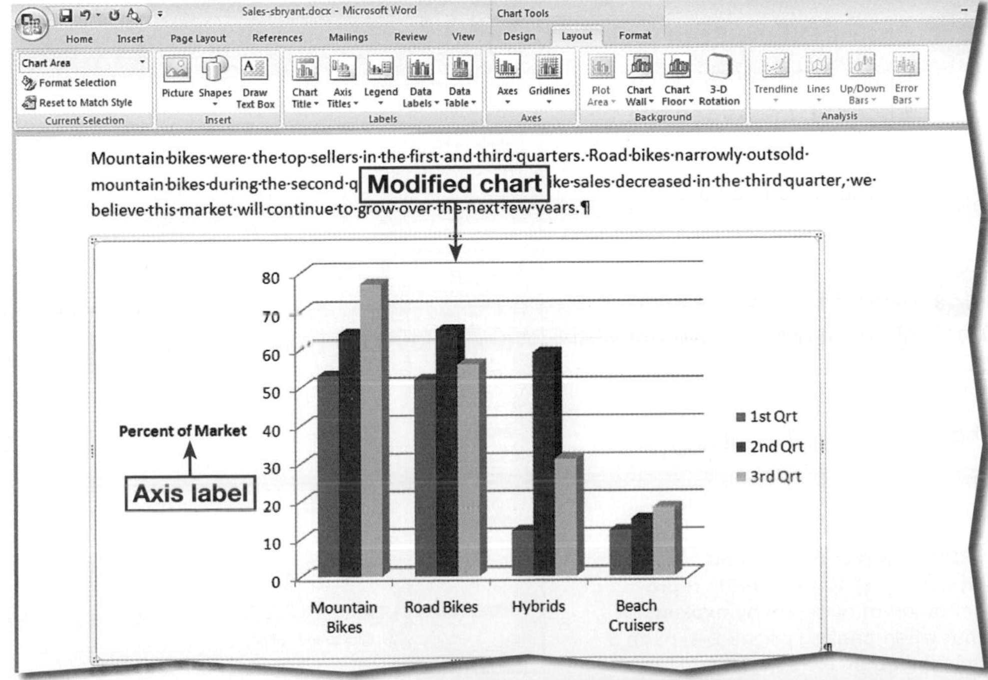

Step-By-Step

1. In your **Tips** file, choose **Office>Print**.
2. In the **Print** dialog box, in the **Name** box, click the drop-down arrow to select a printer. Ask your teacher which printer you should use.
3. Check that there is a **1** in the **Number of copies** box.
4. Under **Print range,** click **Slides**. In the **Slides** box, key: 1.
5. **CHECK** Your dialog box should look similar to Figure 1.28. With your teacher's permission, click **OK**.
6. **CHECK** Your screen should look like Figure 1.29.
7. Choose **Office>Print**. Under **Print range**, click **Slides**. In the **Slides** box, key: 2-4. With your teacher's permission, click **OK**.
8. **CHECK** Your screen should again look like Figure 1.29. Save your file.

Continue to the next exercise.

NCLB/Math (Number and Operations) Reinforce the representation of numbers by explaining that when printing pages 2-4, page 3 is included by the symbol "-".

EXERCISE 1-15
Print Slides

You can choose to print any number of slides—from a single slide to the entire presentation. Indicate which slides you want to print in the Print dialog box.

Step-By-Step Tip In **Step 2**, to save time, write the name of the printer on the board where students can see it.

FIGURE 1.28 Print dialog box

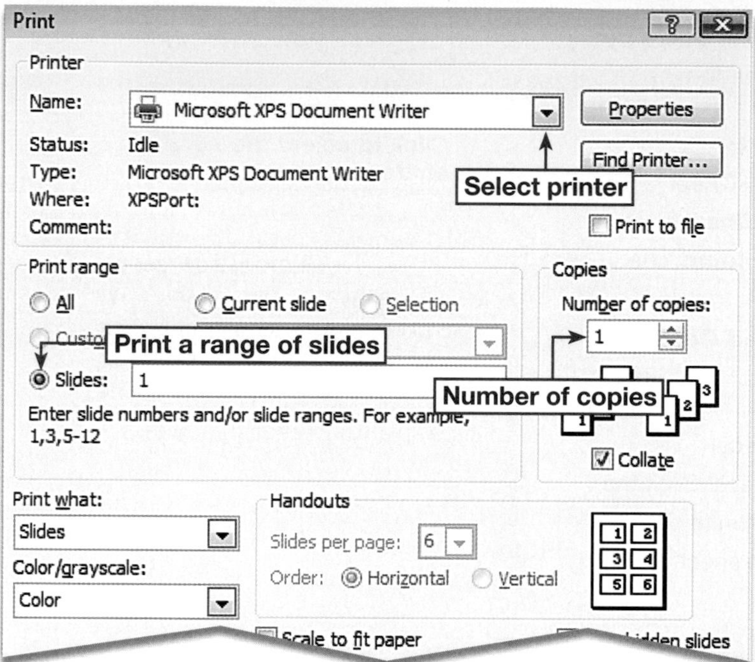

FIGURE 1.29 PowerPoint screen after printing

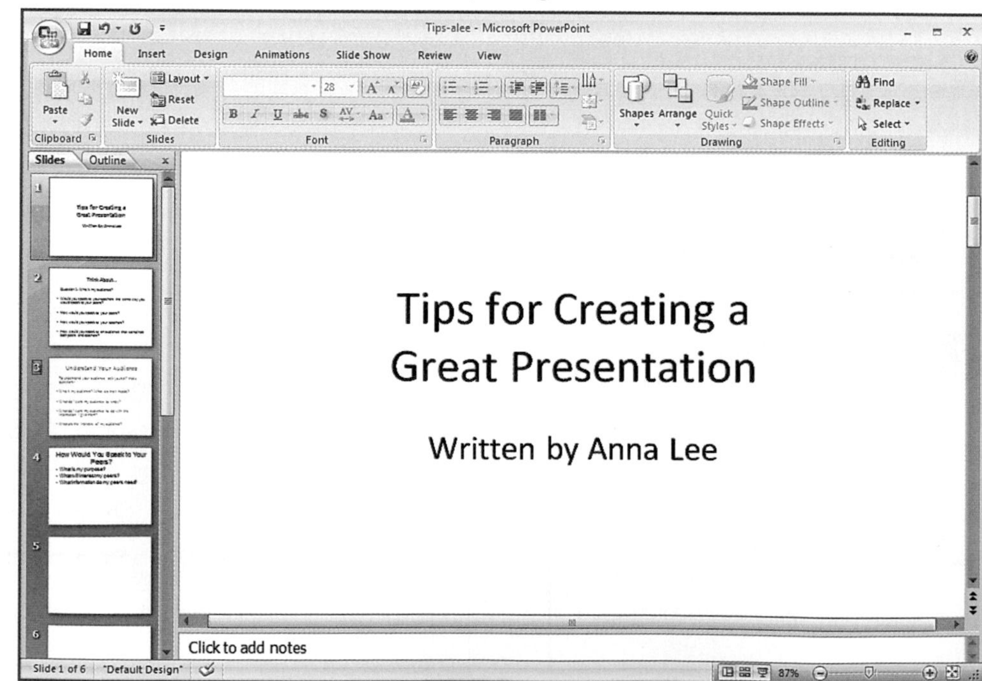

Step-By-Step

1. In your **Sales** file, select the last six lines at the bottom of the page.
2. Choose **Insert>Tables>Table>Convert Text to Table**.
3. In the **Convert Text to Table** dialog box, make sure the **Number of columns** is **4**.
4. Under **Separate text at**, click **Commas**. Click **OK**. Click outside the table to deselect the text.
5. **CHECK** Your screen should look like Figure 5.38.
6. Select the table under **Quarterly Breakdown**. Choose **Table Tools>Layout>Convert to Text**.
7. In the **Convert Table to Text** dialog box, make sure **Tabs** is selected. Click **OK**.
8. **CHECK** Your screen should look like Figure 5.39. Save and close your file.

You Should Know

The **Convert Table to Text** option will convert a table to text even if the table has formatting applied.

Solution Use the file **Sales-SF.docx** as a solution file for Exercises 5-17 and 5-18.

EXERCISE 5-18

Convert Text to Tables and Convert Tables to Text

Before you can organize text into a table, you must first separate the original text with commas, tabs, paragraphs, or other characters so that the Convert Text to Table feature can determine where each new column begins. In addition to converting text to a table, you can also change a table to text. You might convert text to a table to see what it looks like and then **restore** it, or return it to its original state, if you like it better as text.

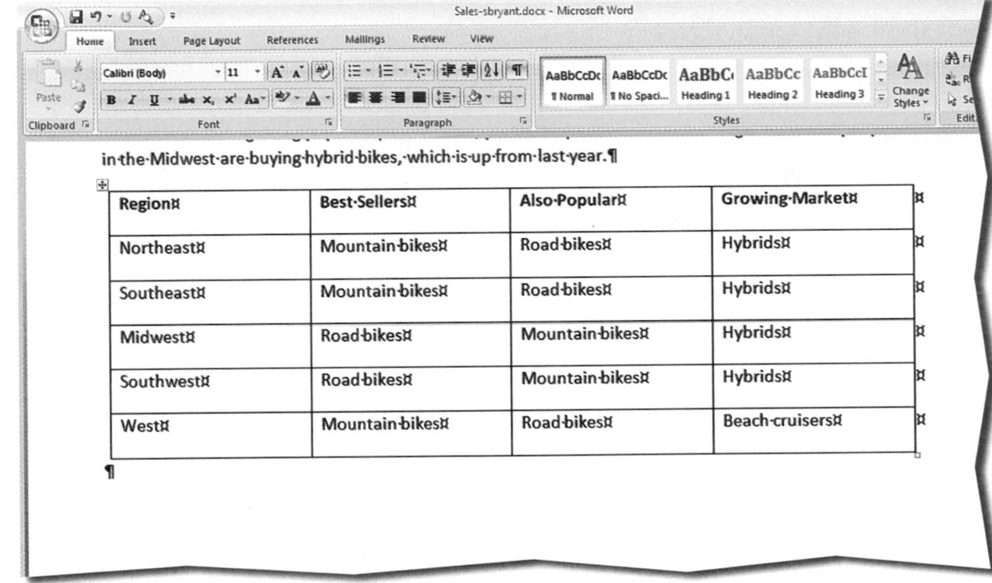

in the Midwest are buying hybrid bikes, which is up from last year.

Region	Best Sellers	Also Popular	Growing Market
Northeast	Mountain bikes	Road bikes	Hybrids
Southeast	Mountain bikes	Road bikes	Hybrids
Midwest	Road bikes	Mountain bikes	Hybrids
Southwest	Road bikes	Mountain bikes	Hybrids
West	Mountain bikes	Road bikes	Beach cruisers

FIGURE 5.38 Text converted into a table

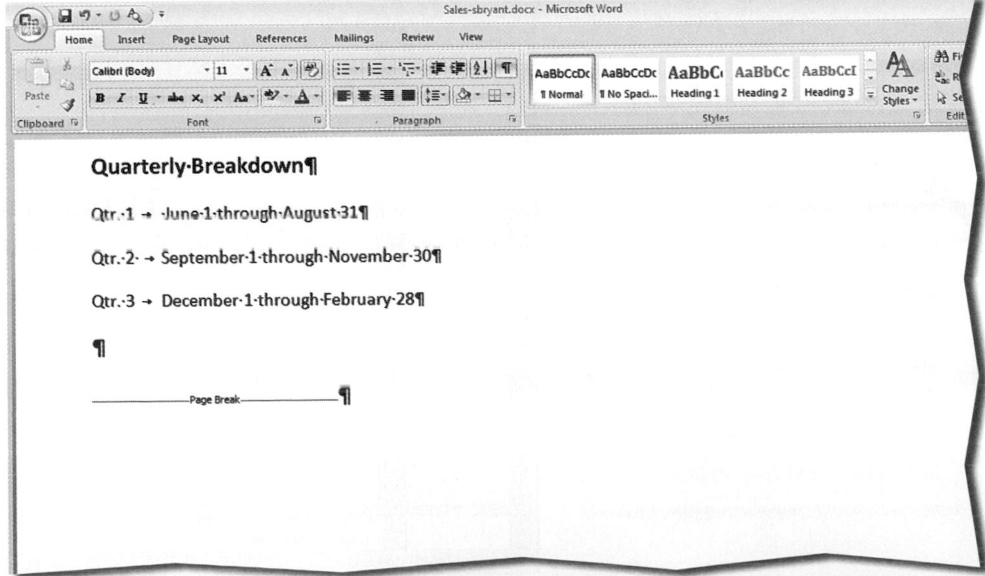

Quarterly Breakdown

Qtr. 1 → June 1 through August 31

Qtr. 2 → September 1 through November 30

Qtr. 3 → December 1 through February 28

Page Break

FIGURE 5.39 Table converted to text

Step-By-Step

1. In your **Tips** file, go to **Slide 1**.

2. Choose **Office>Print>Print Preview**.

3. **CHECK** Your screen should look like Figure 1.26.

4. Click the slide to zoom in. Notice the text in the slide gets larger.

5. Click again on the slide to zoom out.

6. Press PAGE DOWN. You are now previewing Slide 2.

7. Press PAGE UP. You are again previewing Slide 1.

8. In the **Preview** group, click **Close Print Preview** to close Print Preview (see Figure 1.26).

9. **CHECK** Your screen should look like Figure 1.27. Save your file.

Continue to the next exercise.

Tech Tip

It is always important to preview your work before you print, regardless of the application you are using. In Print Preview, PowerPoint allows you to zoom in to be sure your text is correct.

EXERCISE 1-14
Use Print Preview

Print Preview shows you what a slide will look like when you print it. Using Print Preview before you print can help you to catch and fix mistakes in your presentation.

FIGURE 1.26 Print Preview

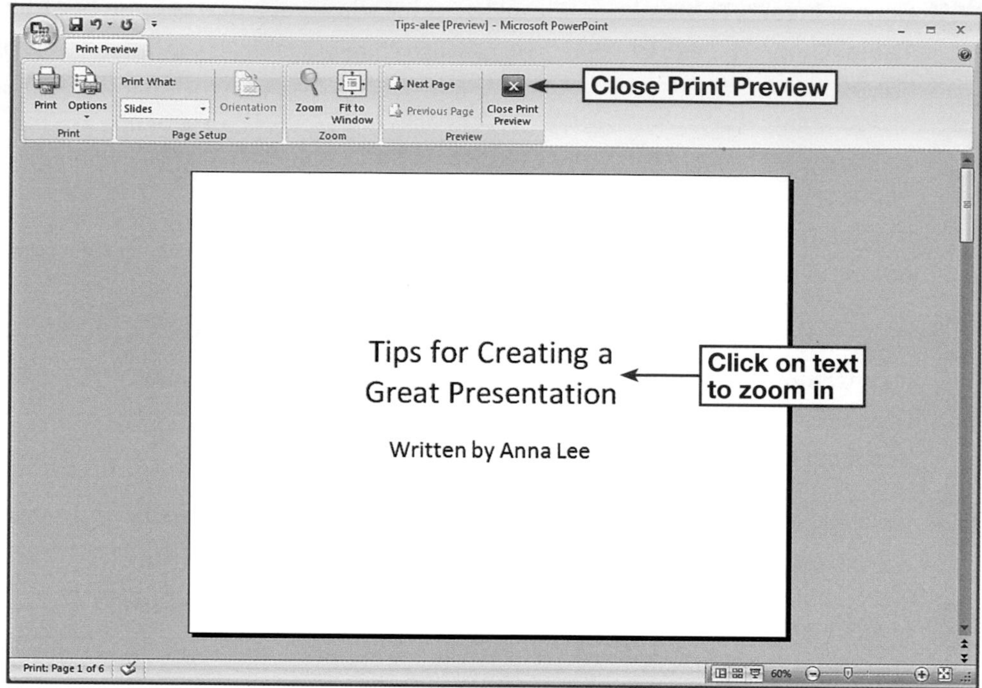

FIGURE 1.27 PowerPoint screen after closing Print Preview

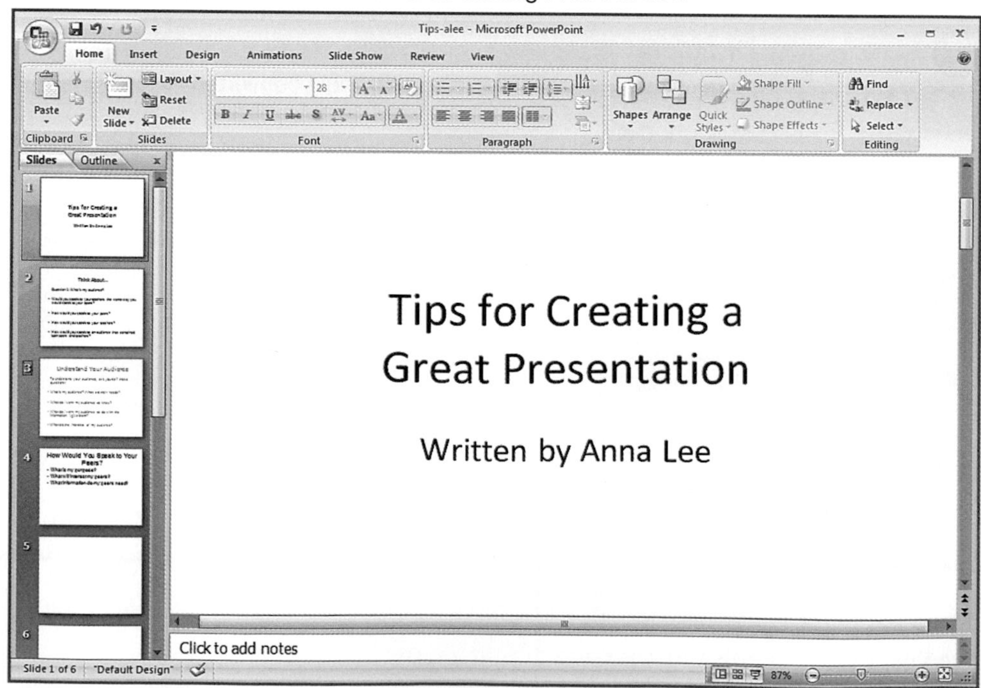

MATH MATTERS

Read Charts, Graphs, and Diagrams

You are in charge of marketing two new video games to teens: The Battle of Zorq and Lar's Quest. You have done your research and must make a presentation to your boss and the other staff. What would be the best way to present the data?

Reading a Graph

Often, statistical information is best understood visually. Charts, graphs, and diagrams organize information so that you can compare numbers easily. Below is the data collected for the two video games:

- 74 teens ages 13–15 preferred playing Battle of Zorq
- 59 teens ages 13–15 preferred playing Lar's Quest
- 102 teens ages 16–19 preferred playing Lar's Quest
- 21 teens ages 16–19 preferred playing Battle of Zorq

Now look at the chart shown to the right. Which is easier to understand, the text data above or the chart shown at the right?

The chart actually shows you the comparison in video game preferences. You can see that the teens were divided by age first. You can then analyze the data as follows: the red-and-yellow bars show the data for Battle of Zorq, and the blue bars show the data for Lar's Quest. Creating a chart or other visual representation of data is an effective communication tool.

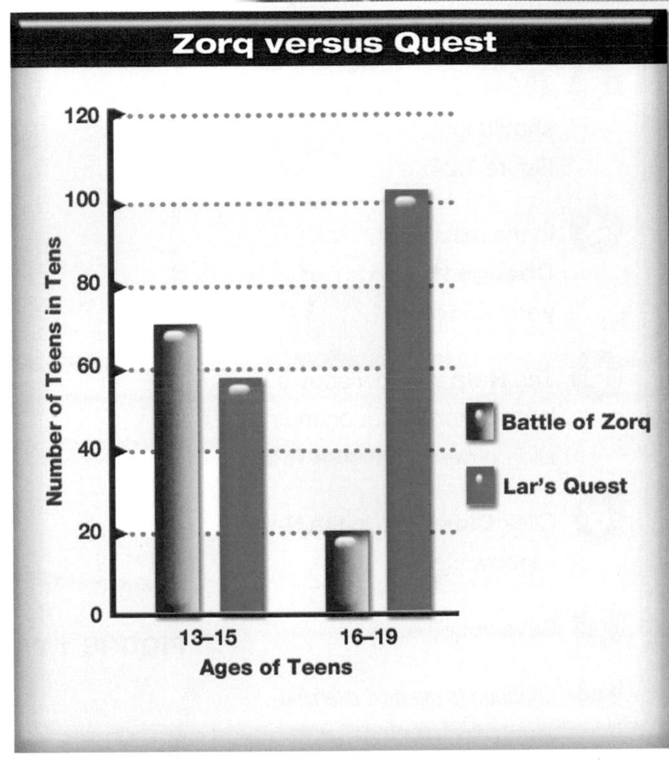

A chart can help you convey information at a glance.

NCLB/Math (NCTM Number and Operations) Students should understand how to read the graph and explain that the information on the horizontal, or *x* axis, represents the age breakdowns of the teens who were surveyed. The information on the vertical, or *y* axis, represents the number of teens surveyed, broken into segments of 20.

SKILLBUILDER

1. **Identify** What is the main purpose of a chart, graph, or diagram?
2. **Evaluate** Why do you think a manager would value an employee who can accurately read charts and graphs?
3. **Apply** Study the chart shown above. Which game would you be more likely to market to 16- to 19-year-old teens? Explain your reasoning.

Skillbuilder answers can be found on page TM63.

Step-By-Step

1. In your **Tips** file, click **Help** [Help icon] in the upper right-hand corner. The PowerPoint **Help** window opens.
2. In the **Search** box, key: move slide order. Press ENTER.
3. CHECK Your screen should look similar to Figure 1.24.
4. In the results list, click **Change the order of your slides**.
5. The **Help** window shows information about changing slide order (see Figure 1.25).
6. Click **Close** [X] in the **Help** window.
7. Save your file.

Continue to the next exercise.

Academic Skills

You can use Help to learn how to use the Spelling function. Why is it important to both proofread your presentation and use the Spelling function before giving your presentation to the class? What might an audience think of a presentation with misspelled words?

EXERCISE 1-13
Use the Help Feature

NCLB/Language Arts (NCTE 6) Reinforce for students how important it is to create presentations that are free of spelling and punctuation errors.

Use the **Help** feature to answer questions as you work. Enter the topic you want to find in the Help window, and PowerPoint will produce a list of search results.

Troubleshooting Note that Steps 1 and 4 may send students online.

FIGURE 1.24 PowerPoint Help window

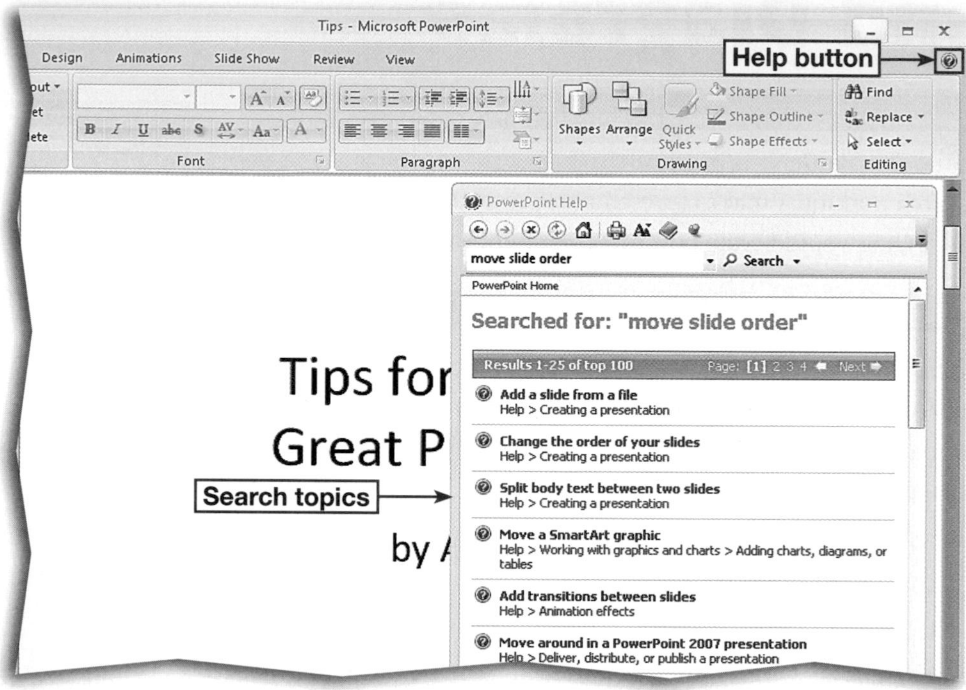

FIGURE 1.25 Help window

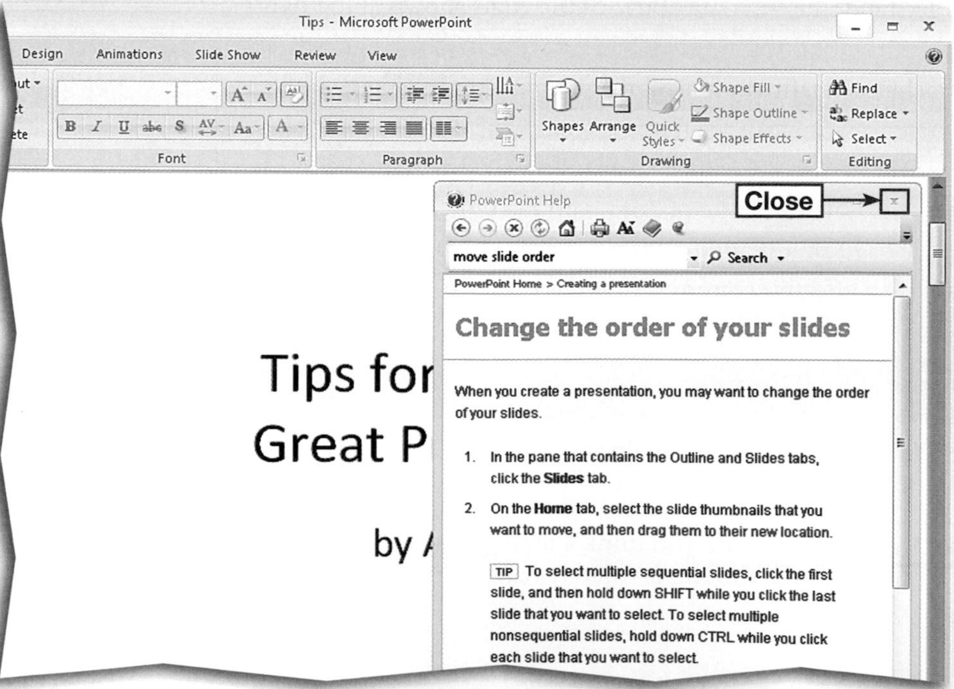

LESSON 5 After You Read

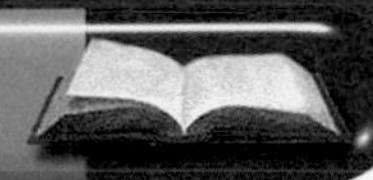

Vocabulary

Key Terms

cell
chart
Clip Art
column
column break
diagram
graphic
newsletter
shape
sizing handle
SmartArt
style
table
text box
WordArt

Academic Vocabulary

restore
survey
visual

Answer to Vocabulary Activity
The pieces of paper should contain vocabulary terms on half of the papers and definitions on the rest.

Review Vocabulary

Complete the following statements on a separate piece of paper. Choose from the Vocabulary list on the left to complete the statements.

1. SmartArt is an example of a(n) ___visual___ tool used to convey information. (p. 148)

2. A(n) ___text box___ is a movable, resizable rectangle that contains text. (p. 145)

3. You can use a ___sizing handle___ to change the size of a graphic. (p. 145)

4. A(n) ___table___ is a set of rows and columns used to organize information. (p. 136)

5. When creating a newsletter, you must decide how many ___column___s to include. (p. 133)

Vocabulary Activity

6. Create a memory game using the vocabulary terms from this lesson.
   A. Select seven vocabulary terms. Write each term on a separate piece of paper. Write the definition for each term on seven more pieces of paper.
   B. Turn the papers face down, keeping the definitions in one group and the terms in another group. Mix the papers in each group.
   C. With your teacher's permission, pair up with a classmate and take turns turning over terms and their definitions. If you pick up the wrong definition, turn the paper face down. If you pick up the right definition, keep both pieces of paper.

Review Key Concepts

Answer the following questions on a separate piece of paper.

7. What keys can you use to move between cells in a table? (p. 137)
   A. Enter and Tab
   B. Tab and Arrows
   C. Spacebar and Page Down
   D. Page Down and Arrows

8. What can you use to resize an object? (p. 145)
   A. sizing handles
   B. text box
   C. Clip Art
   D. AutoFormat

9. What tab can you use to apply a style to a table? (p. 142)
   A. Insert
   B. View
   C. Home
   D. Page Layout

10. Which command path do you choose to create a chart? (p. 151)
   A. Insert>Diagram
   B. Insert>Illustrations>Chart
   C. Format>Picture
   D. Chart>Chart Type

Step-By-Step

1. In your **Tips** file, choose **Slide Show>Set Up>Set Up Slide Show** .
2. Under **Show slides**, click **From**. The numbers **1** and **6** appear in the **From** and **To** boxes.
3. In the **From** box, key: 2. Press TAB. Key: 4.
4. Under **Show Options**, select **Loop continuously until 'Esc'**.
5. CHECK Your screen should look like Figure 1.22.
6. Click **OK**.
7. In the **Slides** tab, select **Slide 3**. In the **Set Up** group, click **Hide Slide** .
8. In the **Start Slide Show** group, click **From Beginning** .
9. CHECK Your screen should look like Figure 1.23. Notice that the slide show now begins on Slide 2.
10. Click to advance to the next slide. **Slide 4** appears. Click again. The presentation loops back to Slide 2.
11. Press ESC to exit the slide show. Save your file.

Continue to the next exercise.

EXERCISE 1-12
Select Slides for a Show

If necessary, you can choose to show only selected slides instead of an entire presentation. You use the Set Up Show dialog box to identify the slide numbers you want to include in your customized presentation. This feature also allows you to hide specific slides in a presentation and to let your presentation loop from the last slide back to the first. Be careful not to let a presentation loop more times than is necessary to make your point.

Different Strokes Tell students that they can also run a slide show by clicking the Slide Show button in the lower right on the status bar.

FIGURE 1.22 Set Up Show dialog box

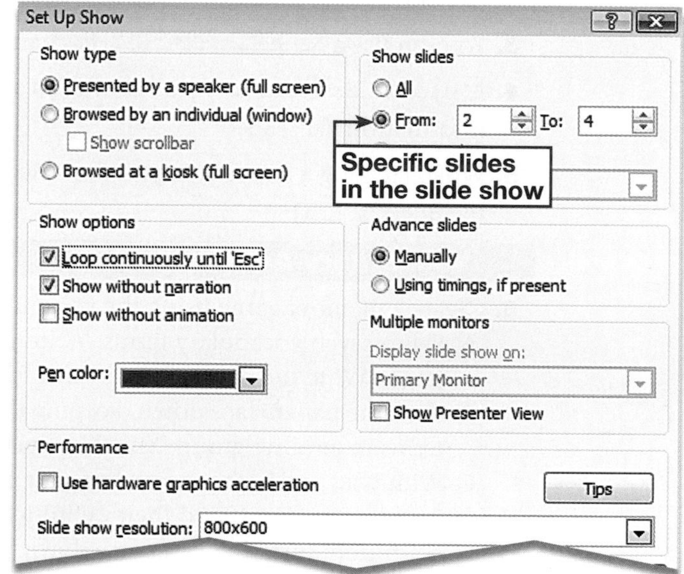

FIGURE 1.23 Slide show beginning with Slide 2

Think About...

Question 1. Who is my audience?

- Would you speak to your teachers the same way you would speak to your peers?
- How would you speak to your peers?
- How would you speak to your teachers?
- How would you speak to an audience that contained both peers and teachers?

LESSON 5 Practice It Activities

Step-By-Step

1. Open the data file **Hillside .docx**. Save as: Hillside-[your first initial and last name]1.
2. Click before **Band Tryouts on Tuesday**. Select **Page Layout>Page Setup> Columns>Two**.
3. Click before **Bike Week Continues** at the bottom of the left column. Select **Page Layout>Page Setup>Breaks>Page Breaks>Column**.
4. **CHECK** Your screen should look like Figure 5.40.
5. Select the text **The Hillside High Gazette**. Choose **Insert>Text> WordArt**. Select **WordArt Style 9**.
6. Select the heading **Band Tryouts on Tuesday**. Choose **Home>Styles** and select **Heading 1**.
7. Repeat **Step 6** for the other two headings.
8. **CHECK** Your screen should look like Figure 5.41. Save and close your file.

1. Insert Columns and WordArt

Data File

Follow the steps to complete the activity.

Solution The solution file for this activity is **Hillside1-SF.docx.**

FIGURE 5.40 Text in two columns

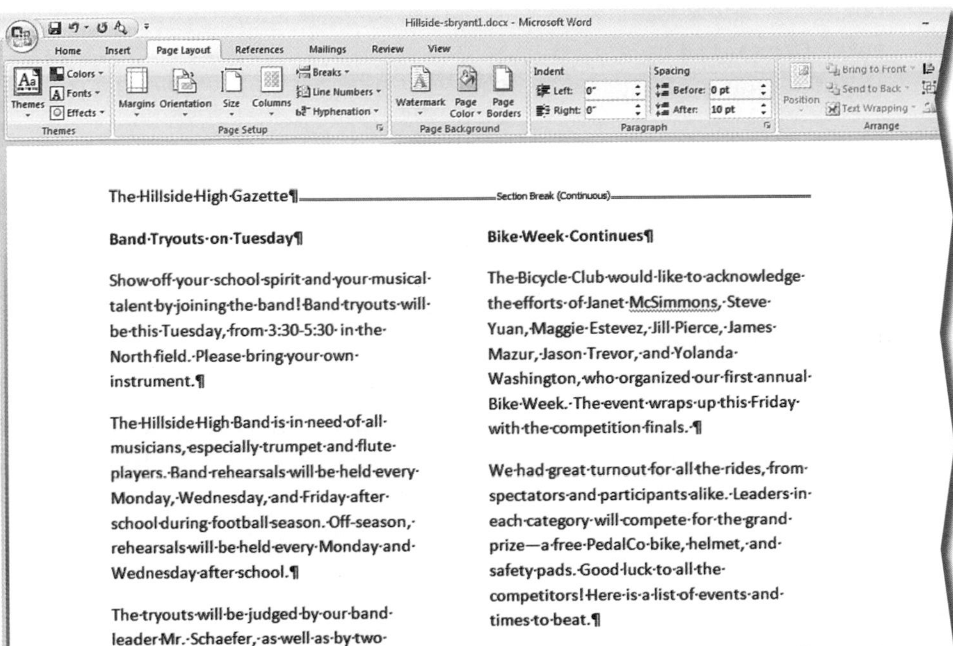

FIGURE 5.41 WordArt added to page

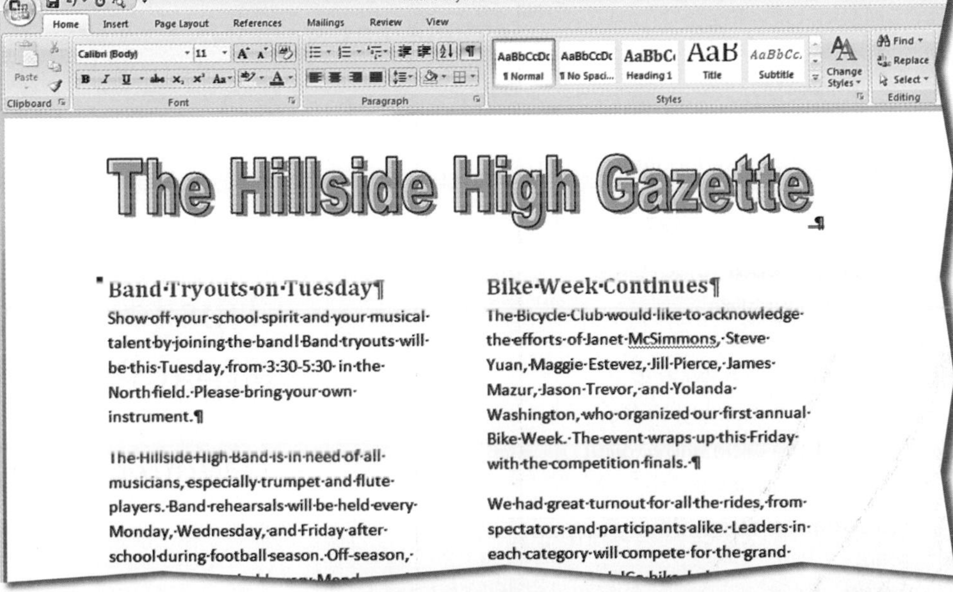

Step-By-Step Tip In **Step 5**, remind students to select only the text, not the paragraph mark next to it.

Step-By-Step

1 In your **Tips** file, choose **Slide Show>Set Up>Set Up Slide Show**.

2 In the **Set Up Show** dialog box, under **Show type**, select **Presented by a speaker (full screen)**.

3 Under **Show slides**, select **All**. Under **Advance slides**, click **Manually**.

4 Under **Show Options**, select **Show without Narration**. Under **Performance**, click the **Slide Show Resolution** drop-down arrow. Select **800x600**.

5 **CHECK** Your dialog box should look like Figure 1.20. Click **OK**.

6 In the **Start Slide Show** group, click **From Beginning**.

7 **CHECK** Your screen should look like Figure 1.21.

8 Click the mouse OR press the **spacebar** to advance to the next slide.

9 Repeat Step 8 twice to view the remaining slides. To exit the slide show, click twice OR press the **spacebar** twice. Save your file.

Continue to the next exercise.

EXERCISE 1-11
Set Up and Run a Slide Show

You can set up a slide show to run automatically, or you can manually move from slide to slide. In this exercise, you will use the Set Up Show dialog box to run a show manually. You can also change other settings, such as the presentation's resolution and narration. When setting up the show, you will use some of PowerPoint's preset, or default, settings.

Step-By-Step Tip In **Step 10**, after pressing the spacebar twice, a black screen will appear that reads "End of Slide Show. Click to Exit." Have students click anywhere on that screen to return to PowerPoint.

FIGURE 1.20 Set Up Show dialog box

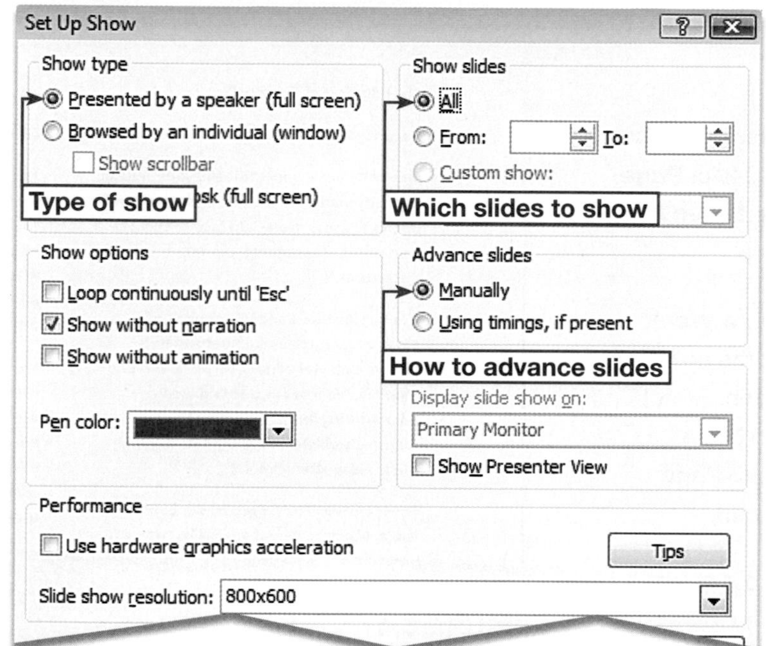

FIGURE 1.21 Slide show

Tips for Creating a Great Presentation

Written by Anna Lee

LESSON 5 Practice It Activities

Step-By-Step

1. Open your **Hillside-1** file. Save as: Hillside-[your first initial and last name]2.
2. Select the text shown in Figure 5.42.
3. Choose **Insert>Tables> Table>Convert Text to Table** .
4. Under **Number of columns**, key: 3. Under **AutoFit behavior**, click **AutoFit to contents**. Click **OK**.
5. In the **Table Tools** contextual tab, choose **Design>Table Styles>More** .
6. In the **Table Styles** drop-down menu, choose **Table Contemporary** (second column, third row).
7. In the first row of the table, change the font size to **14**. In the body of the table, change the font size to **12**.
8. **CHECK** Your screen should look like Figure 5.43.
9. Save and close your file.

Solution The solution file for this activity is **Hillside2-SF.docx**.

2. Create a Table

Follow the steps to complete the activity. You must complete Practice It Activity 1 before doing this activity.

New Student Strategy If a student did not complete Practice It Activity 1, then the solution file for that activity can be used as a data file for this activity.

FIGURE 5.42 Text to select

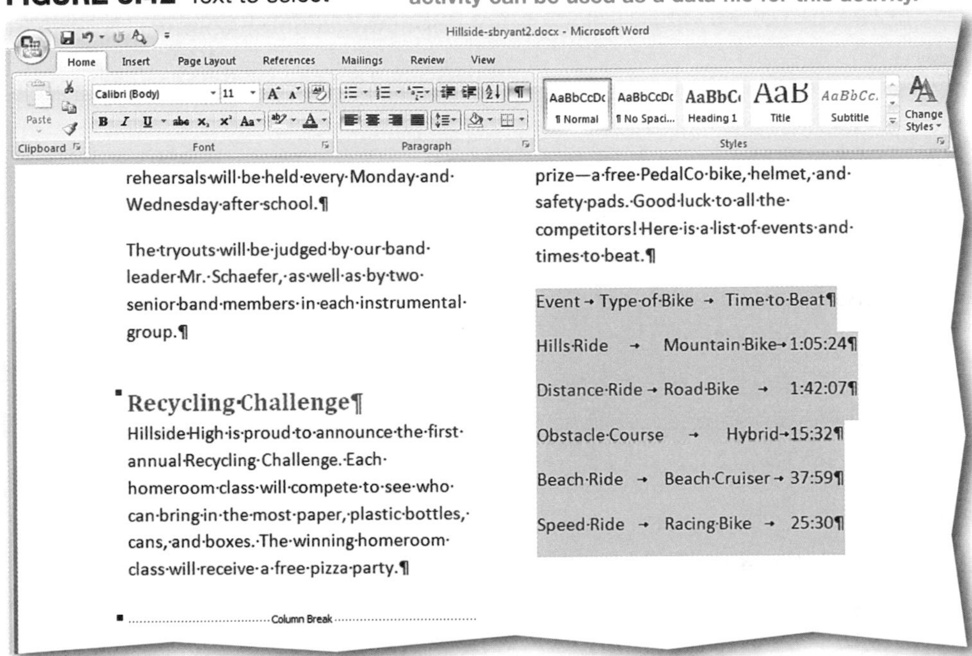

Troubleshooting If students are not able to find the **Table Contemporary** style, have them choose a different style.

FIGURE 5.43 Finished table

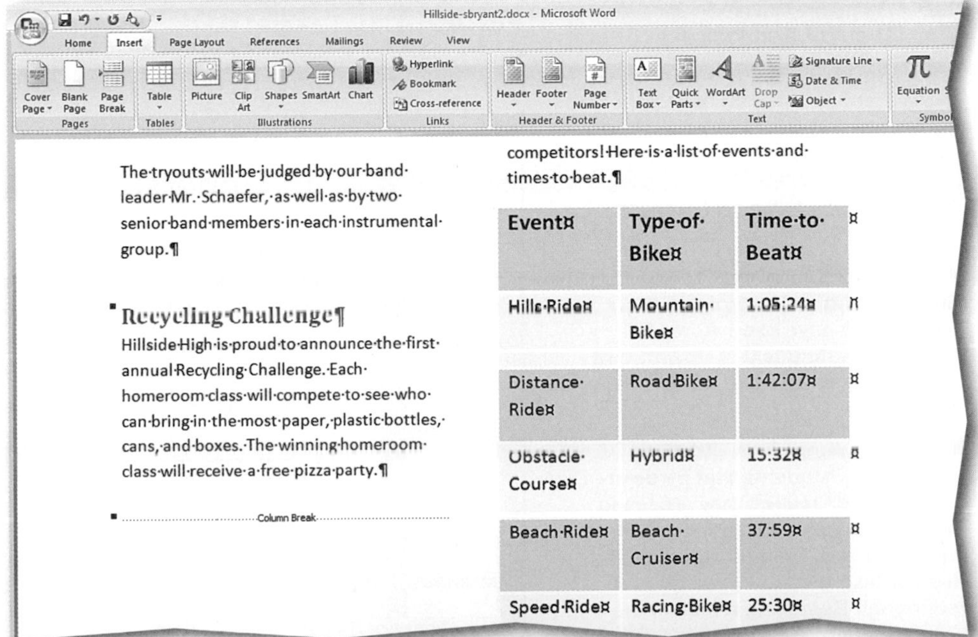

Step-By-Step

1. In your **Tips** file, move to **Slide 1**. Click to the left of the word **by**.
2. Key: Written. Press the **spacebar** once. Click in a blank part of the slide.
3. CHECK Your screen should look like Figure 1.18.
4. On the keyboard, press PAGE DOWN twice.
5. Double-click the word **really**. The word is selected and the mini toolbar appears (see Figure 1.19).
6. On the keyboard, press DELETE. The word is deleted.
7. Press PAGE UP twice.
8. CHECK Your screen should again look like Figure 1.18.
9. Save your file.

Continue to the next exercise.

New Student Strategy Ask students who are just joining the class if they have used Word. Tell them that editing text in PowerPoint is similar to editing text in Word.

NCLB/Language Arts (NCTE 4) Reinforce to students that by deleting the word "really," they are using their vocabulary skills to communicate effectively with an audience. In this context, the word "really" is redundant. Removing it makes the point more concise.

EXERCISE 1-10
Edit Text on a Slide

You might want to add or delete text, or make other edits to a presentation. To edit or add text to a slide, use the I-pointer to place the insertion point (also called a **cursor**) where you want new text to go. **Monitor**, or watch and confirm, that your cursor is in the correct place. Then click and key, or type, the new text into the slide pane. When a word is double-clicked in a slide, the Mini toolbar will appear. The Mini toolbar contains many common commands available in different groups on the Home tab.

FIGURE 1.18 Edited text

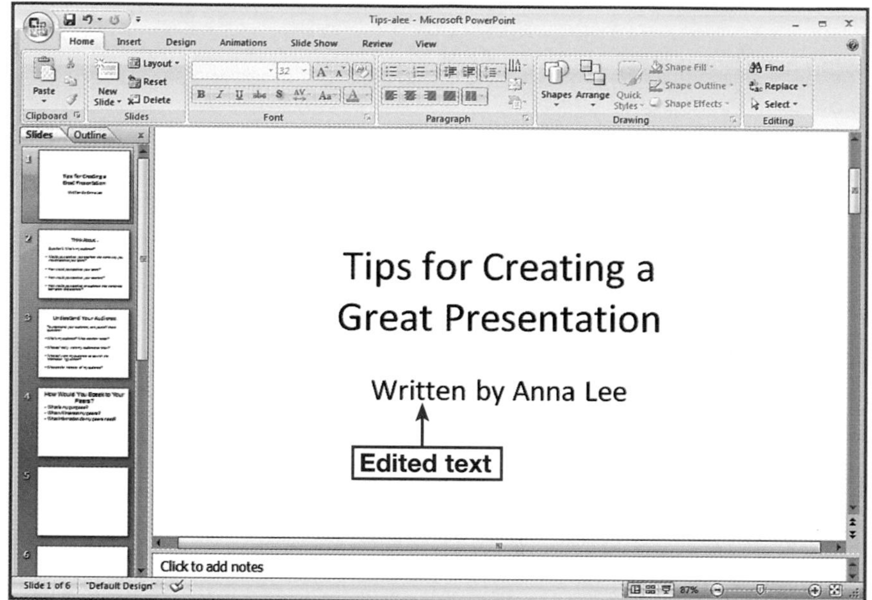

FIGURE 1.19 Selected word

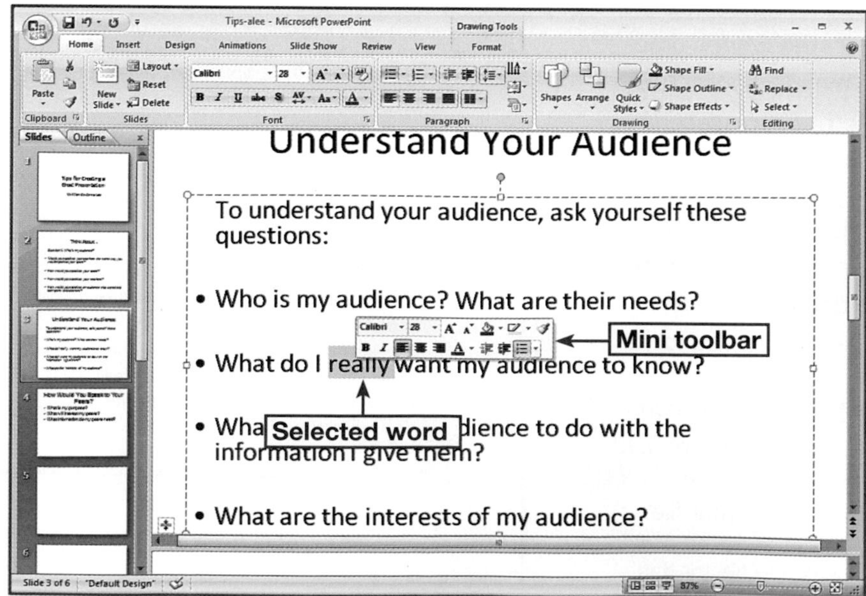

Step-By-Step

1. Open your **Hillside-2** file. Save as: Hillside-[your first initial and last name]3.
2. Click before the text **The tryouts** (see Figure 5.44).
3. Choose **Insert>Illustrations>Clip Art**.
4. In the **Clip Art** task pane, in the **Search for** box, key: band. Click **Go**.
5. Select a clip like the one shown in Figure 5.44. Close the task pane.
6. Select the clip. Under the **Picture Tools** contextual tab, choose **Format>Arrange>Text Wrapping>Tight**.
7. Click the graphic and drag it to the left side of the second column. Use the sizing handles to resize the graphic as needed.
8. **CHECK** Your screen should look similar to Figure 5.45. Save and close your file.

Solution The solution file for this activity is **Hillside3-SF.docx**.

3. Insert Clip Art

Follow the steps to complete the activity. You must complete Practice It Activity 2 before doing this activity.

New Student Strategy If a student did not complete Practice It Activity 2, then the solution file for that activity can be used as a data file for this activity.

FIGURE 5.44 Clip Art task pane

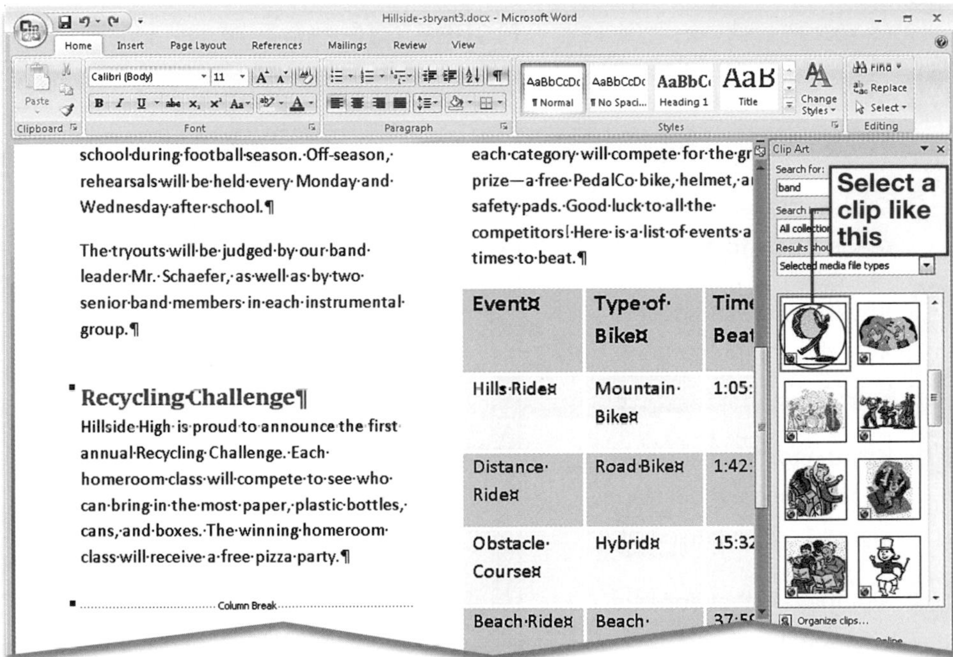

FIGURE 5.45 Clip art inserted into column

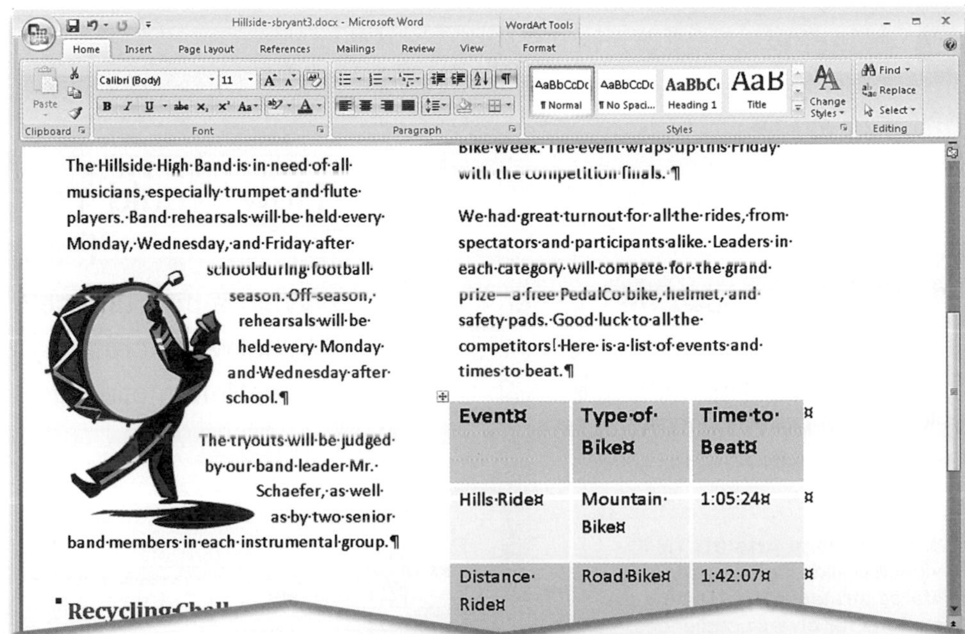

Step-By-Step

1. In your **Tips** file, in the **Slides** tab, click **Slide 4**.
2. Click in the text box that reads **Click to add title**.
3. Key: How Would You Speak to Your Peers?
4. CHECK Your screen should look like Figure 1.16.
5. Click in the text box that reads **Click to add text**.
6. Key the text that appears after the first bullet in Figure 1.17. Press ENTER.
7. Key the text that appears after the second bullet in Figure 1.17. Press ENTER.
8. Key the text that appears after the third bullet in Figure 1.17. Click in a blank space in the slide.
9. CHECK Your screen should look like Figure 1.17. Save your file.

Continue to the next exercise.

Academic Skills

When writing a bulleted list, use parallel structure and keep your points concise.

NCLB/Language Arts (NCTE 5) Review the slides with students to reinforce strategies for creating presentations for diverse audiences.

EXERCISE 1-9
Add Text to Blank Slides

Presentations usually begin with a title slide that displays the title. When you create a new title slide, it contains a preset text box called a **placeholder** for the title and subtitle. When you create a new content slide, it contains text boxes for the title and text. Each text box contains instructions such as "Click to add title." To add text, click in one of these boxes and begin keying text.

Step-By-Step Tip In **Step 8**, tell students that they do not need to press **Enter** after they type the last line in a text box. They can simply click on another part of the slide.

FIGURE 1.16 Slide 4 with title added

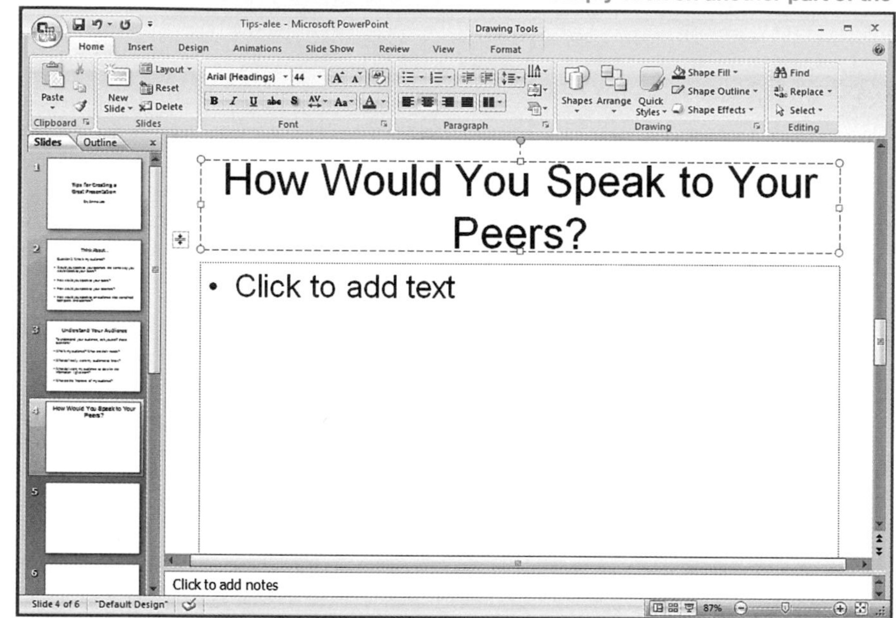

FIGURE 1.17 Text added to a slide

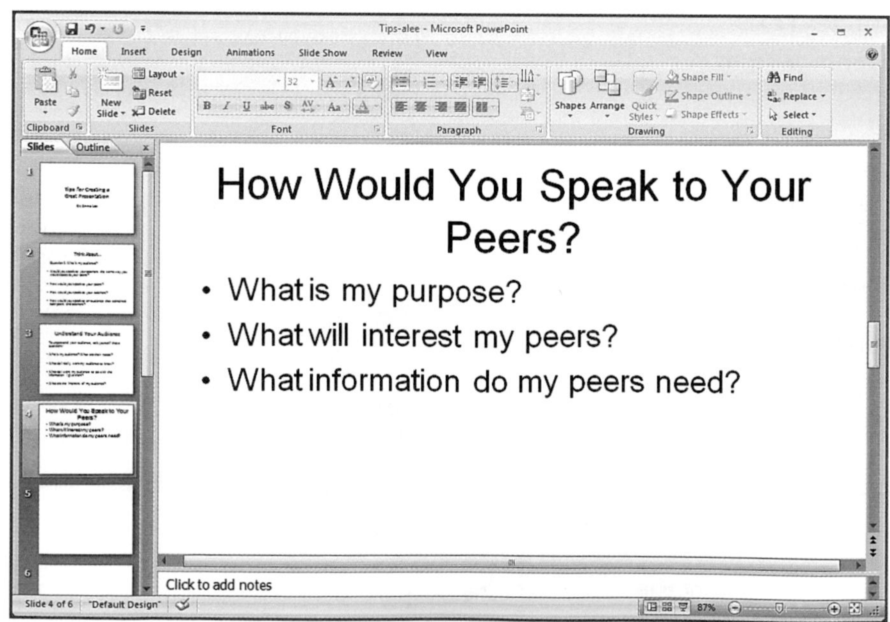

4. Create a Sales Table

You are the sales manager at a car dealership and are responsible for presenting information to your boss on car sales for the year. You need to let her know the sales from each quarter for the three salespeople that you manage. You decide to display the information in a table.

Step-By-Step

1. Create a new document. Save as: w4rev-[your first initial and last name]4.
2. Create a table with five columns and four rows.
3. Key the text as it is shown in Figure 5.46.
4. Insert a new row above the first row.
5. Merge the cells in the new row. Key the text: Yearly Car Sales (in $) into the row.
6. Apply the style **Heading 1** to the first row.
7. Apply the style **Heading 2** to the second row. Center the text in both the first and second rows.
8. Use **Table Tools** to **Align Center Left** text in the remaining three rows.
9. **AutoFit** the table text to contents.
10. **CHECK** Your screen should look like Figure 5.47. Save and close your file.

Solution The solution file for this activity is **w4rev-4-SF.docx.**

FIGURE 5.46 Sales table

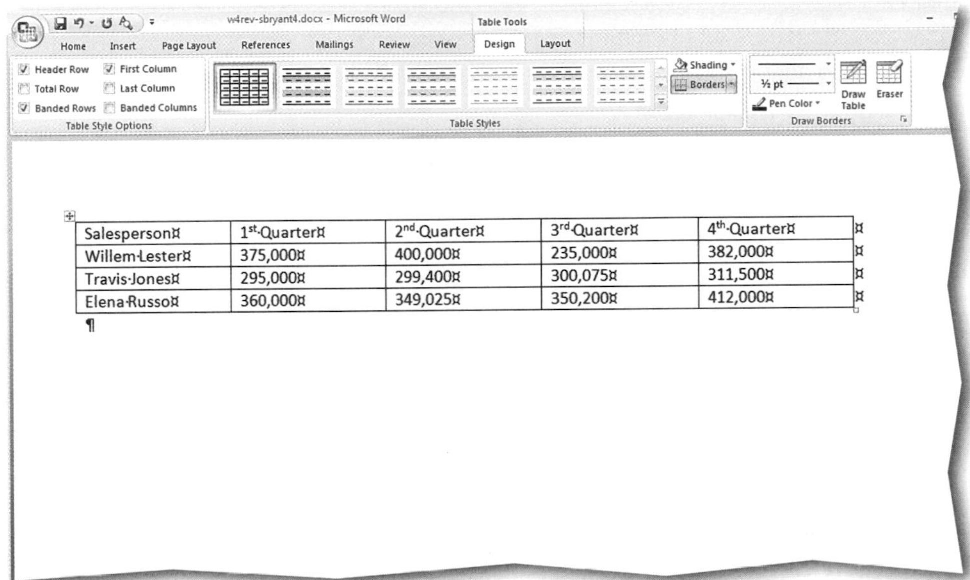

Salesperson	1st Quarter	2nd Quarter	3rd Quarter	4th Quarter
Willem Lester	375,000	400,000	235,000	382,000
Travis Jones	295,000	299,400	300,075	311,500
Elena Russo	360,000	349,025	350,200	412,000

FIGURE 5.47 Formatted table

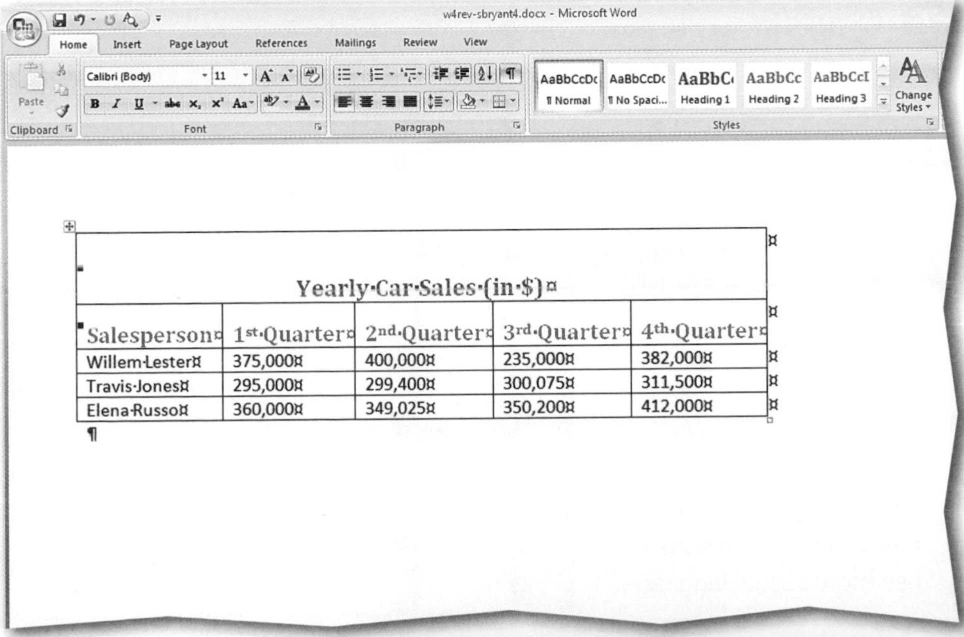

Yearly Car Sales (in $)				
Salesperson	1st Quarter	2nd Quarter	3rd Quarter	4th Quarter
Willem Lester	375,000	400,000	235,000	382,000
Travis Jones	295,000	299,400	300,075	311,500
Elena Russo	360,000	349,025	350,200	412,000

Step-By-Step

1. In your **Tips** file, click the **down arrow** on the scroll bar once (see Figure 1.14).
2. CHECK Your screen should look like Figure 1.15. On the scroll bar, click the **up arrow**.
3. CHECK Your screen should again look like Figure 1.14. Click **Next Slide**. Your screen should again look like Figure 1.15.
4. Click **Previous Slide**. Your screen should again look like Figure 1.14.
5. On the keyboard, press PAGE DOWN. You move to **Slide 2**.
6. On the keyboard, press PAGE UP. You move back to **Slide 1**.
7. CHECK Your screen should again look like Figure 1.14. Save your file.

Continue to the next exercise.

Academic Skills

Review the text in Figure 1.15. Tailor a presentation's words to fit your audience. A school or business presentation requires more formal language, while a presentation for friends can use more casual language.

EXERCISE 1-8
Move Among Slides

To move from slide to slide, use the **scroll bar** on the right edge of the screen. The Next Slide and Previous Slide buttons will also help you move among slides. Use the navigation keys on the keyboard to move through a presentation quickly.

NCLB/Language Arts (NCTE 4) Reinforce with students how they need to adjust their language to communicate effectively with diverse audiences.

FIGURE 1.14 The scroll bar

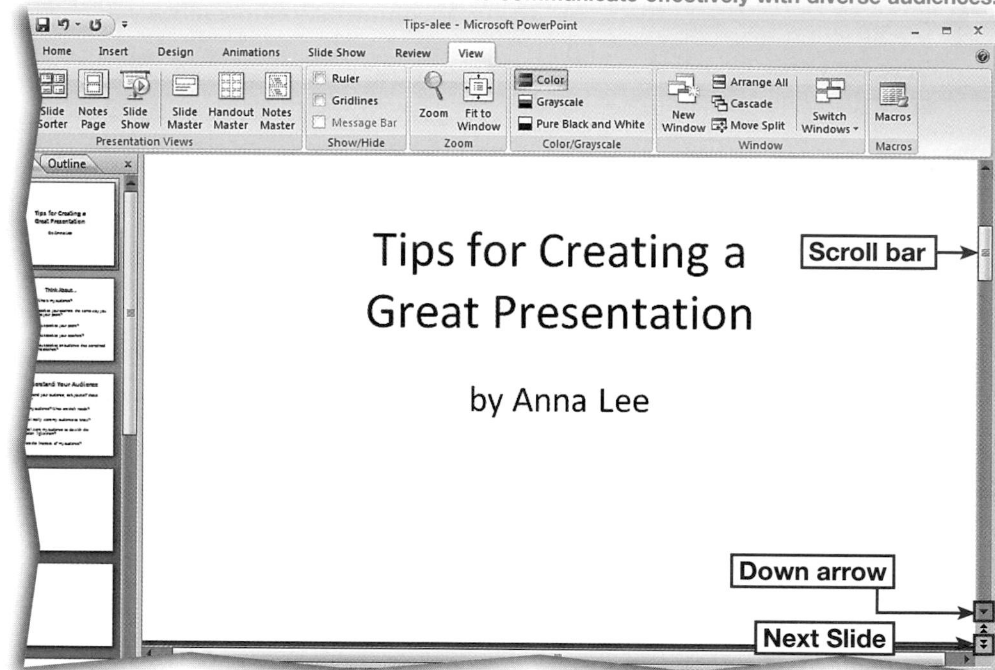

FIGURE 1.15 Slide 2

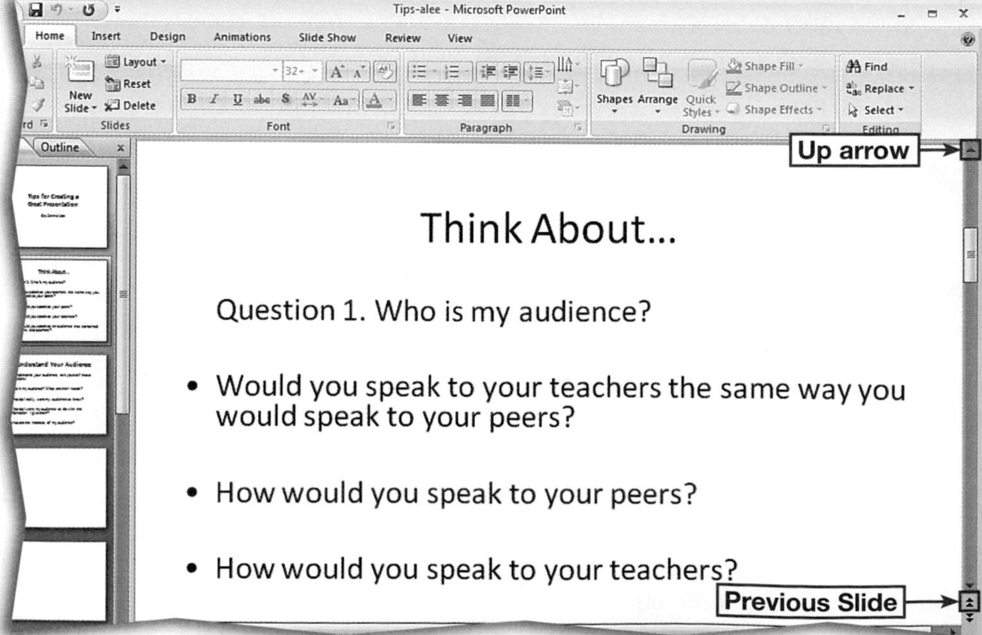

Step-By-Step

1. Open your **Hillside-3** file. Save as: Hillside-[your first initial and last name]5
2. Click after **party.** at the bottom of the first column. Press ENTER.
3. Insert a **Text Cycle** SmartArt graphic.
4. Delete two text boxes. Three arrows will remain.
5. Key the text shown in Figure 5.48 into the diagram.
6. On the **SmartArt Tools** contextual tab, choose **Design>SmartArt Styles**. Select **Intense Effect**.
7. Resize and reposition the diagram so that it fits at the bottom of column 1.
8. **CHECK** Your screen should look like Figure 5.49. Save and close your file.

Solution The solution file for this activity is **Hillside5-SF.docx**.

5. Insert SmartArt

The Hillside High Gazette advisor likes your newsletter's design, but he thinks you should add another graphic. You decide to add a diagram to the Recycling Challenge story. You must complete Practice It Activity 3 before doing this activity.

New Student Strategy If a student did not complete Practice It Activity 3, then the solution file for that activity can be used as a data file for this activity.

FIGURE 5.48 SmartArt diagram

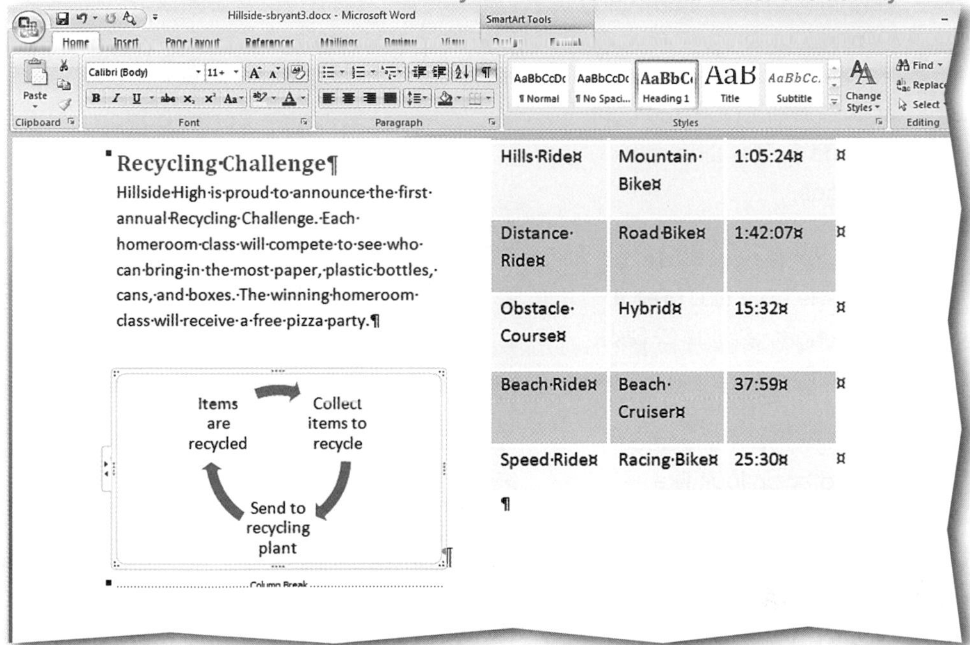

FIGURE 5.49 Finished diagram

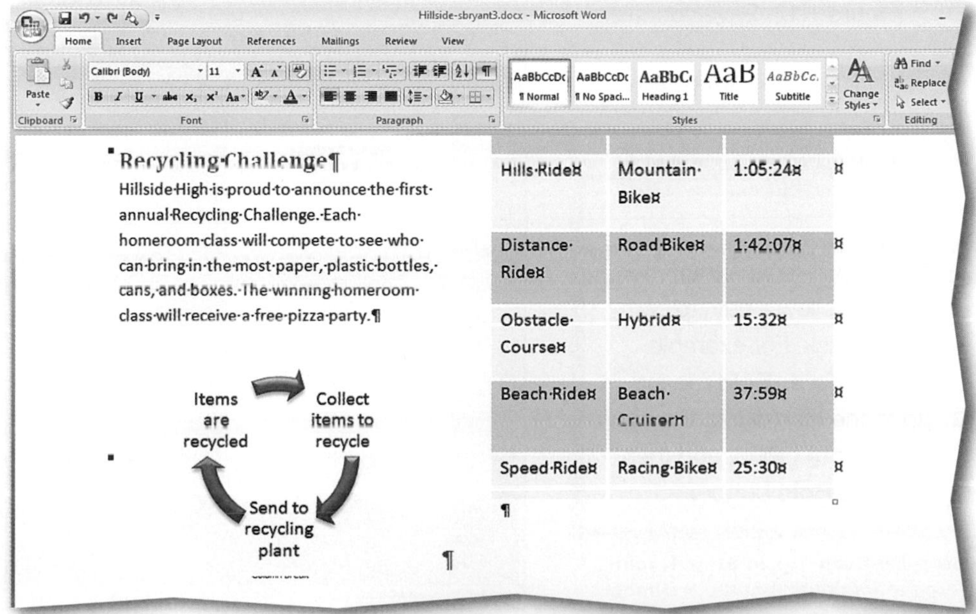

Step-By-Step

1. In your **Tips** file, choose **View** tab**>Presentation Views** group**>Slide Sorter** button (see Figure 1.12).
2. **CHECK** Your screen should look like Figure 1.13.
3. Point to **Slide 1**. Click the slide and drag it to the right of Slide 2. The slide order changes.
4. Point to the new **Slide 1**. Click the slide and drag it to the right of Slide 2. Click **Slide 1**.
5. **CHECK** Your screen should again look like Figure 1.13.
6. Double-click **Slide 1**.
7. **CHECK** Your screen should again look like Figure 1.12. Save your file.

Continue to the next exercise.

Microsoft Office 2007

When the > symbol appears in a step, it means that you need to follow a path to complete a task. For example, **Home>Font>Bold** means go to the **Home** tab, then go to the **Font** group, and then click the **Bold** button.

Step-By-Step Tip In **Step 1**, reinforce to students that the > symbol is navigating them through the path **tabs>groups>buttons.**

EXERCISE 1-7
Use Slide Sorter View

Slide Sorter View shows you small images of all the slides in your presentation in the slides pane. You can use Slide Sorter View to add more slides and to change the order of slides in a presentation.

Teaching Tip If students accidentally switch back to Normal View, have them click the **Slide Sorter View** button again.

FIGURE 1.12 Presentation in Normal View

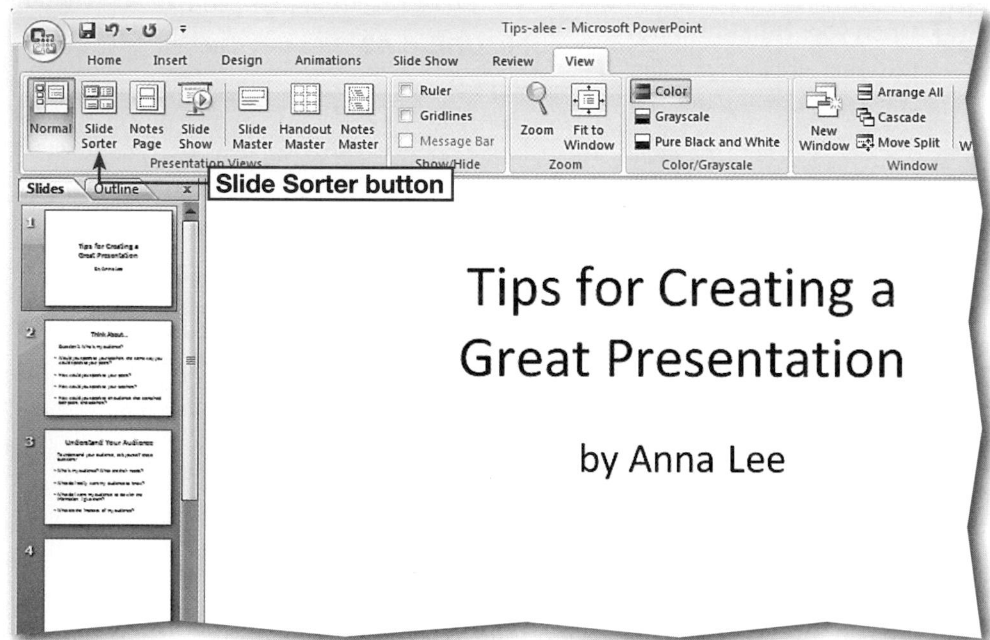

FIGURE 1.13 Presentation in Slide Sorter View

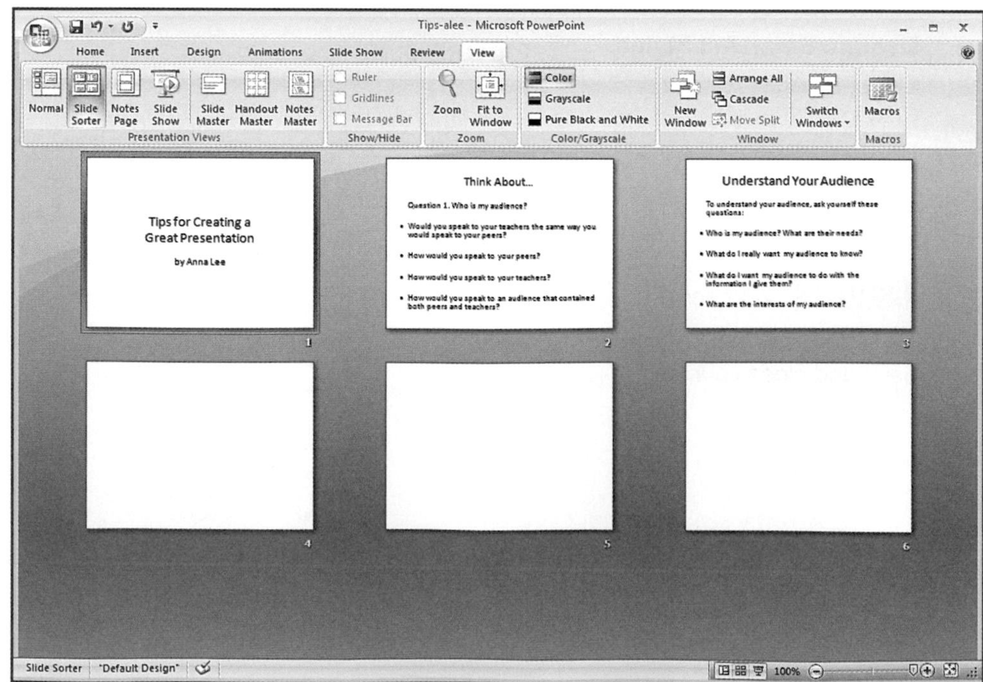

LESSON 5 Critical Thinking Activities

Beyond the Classroom Activity
Student sales overviews will vary but should include a WordArt title, a chart, and a table.

Standards at Work Activity
Students create a one-page newsletter. The newsletter should have a title and three columns. Students key text about three different cities into the newsletter and add a heading to each column.

21st Century Skills Activity
Student paragraphs will vary but should discuss an example of responsible behavior as well as predict an alternate outcome.

NCLB/Math (Number and Operations) In this activity, students should demonstrate their ability to determine what percentage each type of CD takes of the total market.

Go Online e-REVIEW
glencoe.com

Go to the **Online Learning Center** to complete the following review activities.

Online Self Check
To test your knowledge of the material, click **Unit 1> Lesson 5** and choose **Self Checks**.

Interactive Review
To review the main points of the lesson, click **Unit 1> Lesson 5** and choose **Interactive Review**.

6. Beyond the Classroom Activity

Math: Create a Sales Overview You are a business analyst for a company that sells CDs. Your boss has asked you to create a sales overview showing how many different types of CDs have been sold in various regions over the last quarter. Create a sales overview that includes the following:

- A WordArt title
- A chart that shows how the following four types of CDs have sold over the last quarter: classical, country, rock, alternative
- A table that shows which types of CDs were most popular in which region

Use the PedalCo Sales Overview created in the lesson as a model for your sales overview. Save your file as: w4rev-[your first initial and last name]6.

7. Standards at Work Activity

Microsoft Certified Application Specialist Correlation
Word 1.2 *Lay Out Documents*

Create Columns The company you work for is opening three new offices in three different cities. Your boss has asked you to create a one-page newsletter that will provide information about the three cities where these offices are located.

- First, create a title for your newsletter.
- Then, create three columns below the heading (remember to use the **Apply to** box in the **Columns** dialog box).
- In each column, key three or four sentences about three different cities.
- Add a heading to each column.

Save your file as: w4rev-[your first initial and last name]7.

8. 21st Century Skills Activity

Take Responsibility You decide to write an editorial for your local paper explaining why you think it is important for people to take more responsibility for their actions. Key two or three short paragraphs. Describe a time when you tried to act responsibly. Predict what would have been the result if you had not acted responsibly. Format your text as two columns and add a piece of Clip Art that illustrates what you are describing in your editorial. Save your file as: w4rev-[your first initial and last name]8.

Step-By-Step

1. In your **Tips** file, in the **Slides** tab, click on **Slide 2**.
2. On the **Home** tab, in the **Clipboard** group, click **Cut**.
3. Move the pointer between **Slide 2** and **Slide 3** and click to place a blinking line in the space (see Figure 1.10).
4. On the **Home** tab, in the **Clipboard** group, click **Paste**. **Slide 2** is now **Slide 3**.
5. In the **Slides** tab, click and hold **Slide 3**.
6. Move the pointer above **Slide 2**. Release the mouse button. **Slide 3** is now **Slide 2**.
7. **CHECK** Your screen should look like Figure 1.11.
8. Save your file.

Continue to the next exercise.

You Should Know

The **Cut** button does not delete a slide completely. Objects that are cut are automatically placed on the **Clipboard**. Anything on the Clipboard can be pasted into a new location.

EXERCISE 1-6
Use Normal View to Arrange Slides

The Slides tab allows you to organize the slides in your presentation. You can cut a slide from one location and paste it into another. You can also drag a slide from one position and drop it in another.

FIGURE 1.10 The pointer in between slides

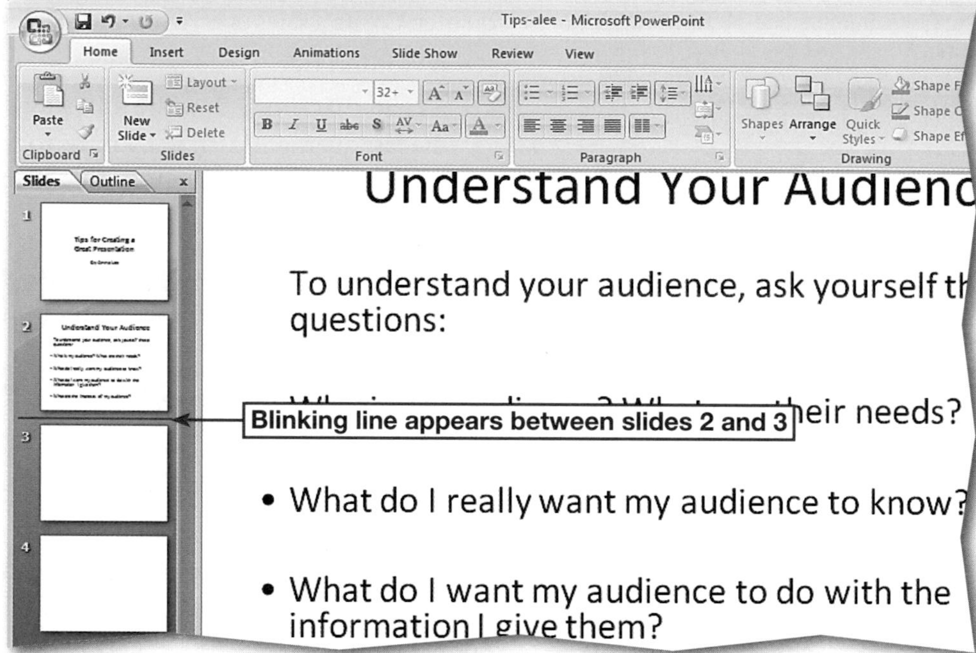

FIGURE 1.11 After dragging slides

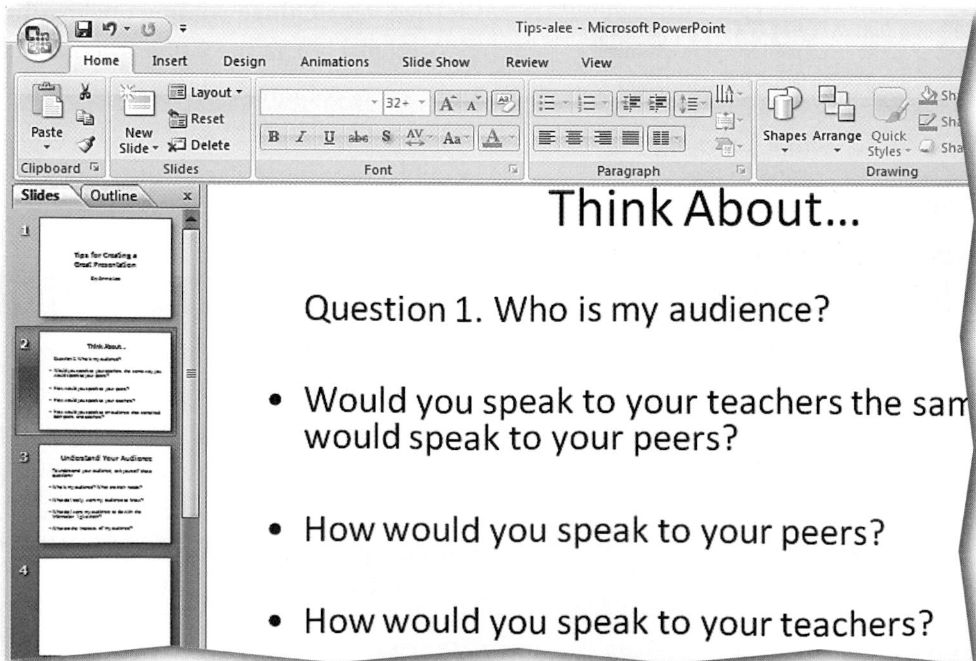

LESSON 5 Challenge Yourself Projects

Before You Begin

Elements of Good Design Graphical elements, such as art and tables, can improve your written communications. A good design works well and is memorable without being distracting.

Reflect After you complete the projects, open a Word document and answer the following questions:

1. How important were the graphics to the purpose of the document?
2. Which of your graphics do you think is most memorable? Why?

Answers Rubrics for each Challenge Yourself Project are available at **glencoe.com**. You may want to download the rubrics and make them available to students as they complete each project.

9. Create an Advertisement

LEVEL This is an intermediate level project.

Language Arts: Create Content for an Ad You work as a graphic designer. A client has hired you to design an advertisement for her. The product that she is advertising is a new state-of-the-art toaster. Create an advertisement that, at the minimum, includes the following:

- At least one graphic, such as Clip Art, WordArt, or a shape
- A text box with several sentences promoting the product
- A title that will attract the viewer's attention

Limit the advertisement to one page. Save your file as: w4rev-[your first initial and last name]9. Remember, your responsibility as the graphic designer for this job is to provide the client with a well-designed advertisement that will help her to sell her product!

10. Produce a Newsletter

LEVEL This is an intermediate level project.

Language Arts: Create a Newsletter The local community theater you work for has asked you to create a newsletter. This newsletter will include information about upcoming auditions and plays being performed. Use the information in the data file **Theater_Newsletter.docx** to create a one-page newsletter.

- Create a newsletter that has two columns.
- Include at least two graphics in the newsletter.
- Use WordArt to format the newsletter title. Place the title above the columns.

Solution Use the file **Theater_Newsletter10-SF.docx** as a sample solution file.

Save your newsletter as: Theater_Newsletter-[your first initial and last name]10.

11. Organize Information

LEVEL This is an advanced level project.

Math: Organize Data in a Table Your principal has asked you to submit grades for the ten students you teach. To organize your grades:

- Create a table that has 5 columns and 11 rows. Label the columns: Student, Quiz 1, Quiz 2, Test, and Homework.
- Enter the information from the data file **Grades.docx** into the table.
- Add a column labeled Average to the right side of the table. Add together the four grades each student has and divide that number by four to determine each student's average.

Solution Use the file **Grades-SF.docx** as a solution file for this project.

Format the table so it is clear and easy to read. Save your file as: Grades-[your first initial and last name]11.

Step-By-Step

1. In your **Tips** file, locate the **Outline** tab and the **Slides** tab (see Figure 1.8).
2. In the **Slides** tab, click **Slide 2**. This moves the presentation to Slide 2.
3. Click **Slide 1**. Your screen should again look like Figure 1.8.
4. Click the **Outline** tab.
5. **CHECK** Your screen should look like Figure 1.9.
6. In the **Outline** tab, click the slide icon next to **2**.
7. Click the slide icon next to **1**.
8. **CHECK** Your screen should again look like Figure 1.9.
9. Click the **Slides** tab.
10. Click **Save** to save your work.

Continue to the next exercise.

Step-By-Step Tip In **Step 1**, tell students that their **Slides** and **Outline** tabs may show either images or the words **Slides** or **Outline**, depending on their screen settings.

Differentiated Instruction/Visually Impaired If students have trouble reading the presentation's outline, tell them they can use the **Zoom** feature to enlarge the text.

EXERCISE 1-5
Use the Slides and Outline Tabs

The Slides and Outline tabs show you different ways to view your presentation. The Slides tab shows you a miniature of each slide in your presentation. The Outline tab displays the content of your presentation in outline form. You can use both panes to move around in your presentation. In the Outline tab, click the slide icon next to each slide to move among slides.

FIGURE 1.8 Slides tab

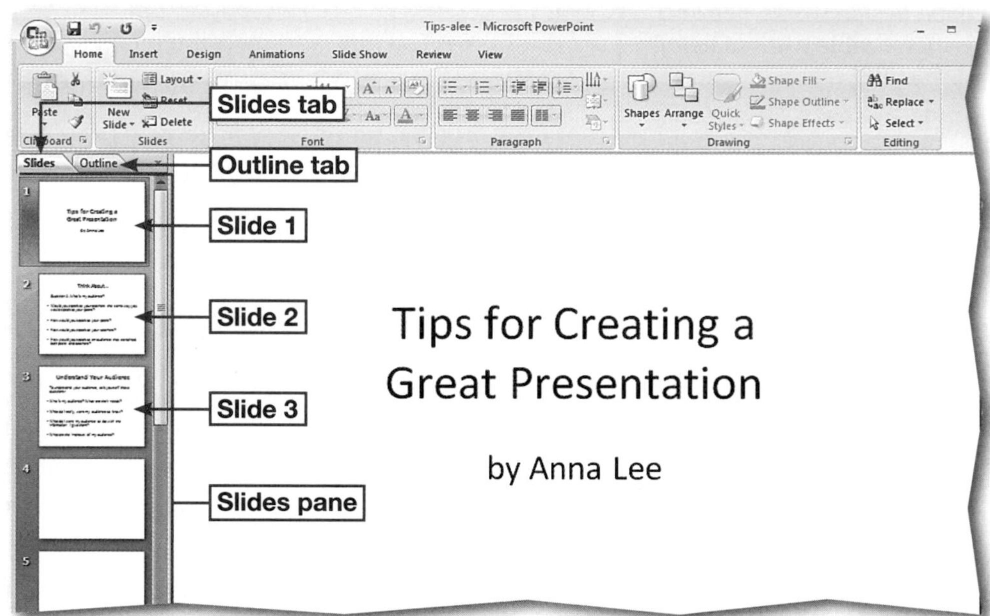

FIGURE 1.9 Outline tab

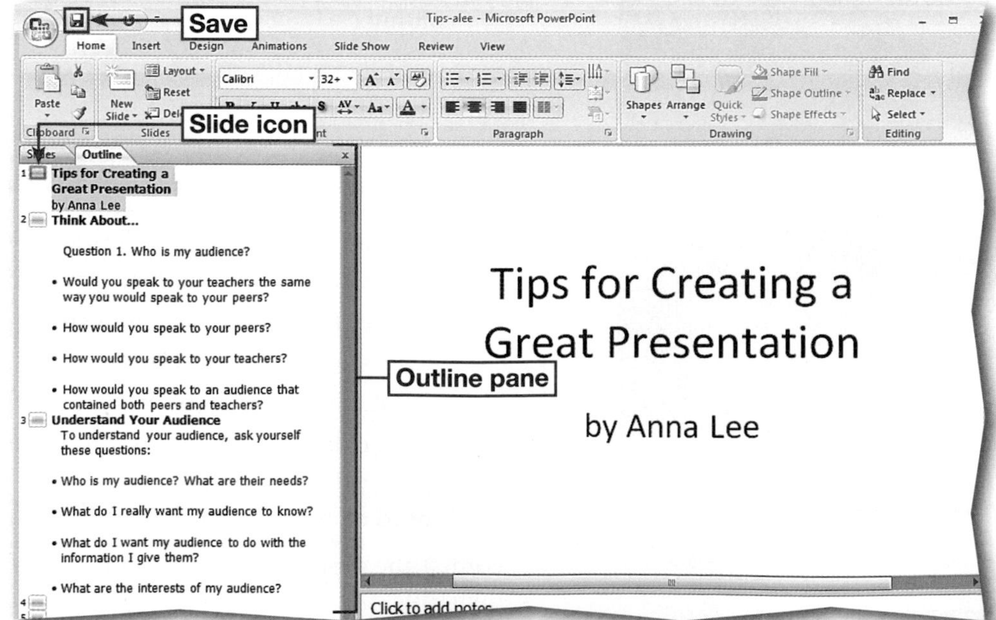

LESSON 6 Collaborate with Others

Key Concepts

- Insert and edit hyperlinks
- Send documents for review
- Use Track Changes
- Compare and merge documents
- Create and preview a Web page
- Perform a mail merge
- Select printing options
- Create and print labels
- Convert documents into different formats
- Create a letterhead

Standards

The following standards are covered in this lesson. Refer to pages xxv and 715 for a description of the standards listed here.

ISTE Standards Correlation

NETS•S

1b, 2a, 2b, 2d, 5a, 5b, 6b

Microsoft Certified Application Specialist

Word

1.1, 1.2, 1.3, 4.5, 5.2, 5.3, 5.4, 6.1

At school and at work, it is important that people collaborate, or work together, to get projects done. In this lesson, you will learn how to use Track Changes and other Word tools that will help you work collaboratively. You will also learn how to create a Web page using Word and how to perform a mail merge so you can share your work with others either online or in print.

21st CENTURY SKILLS

See page TM65 for answer to 21st Century Skills.

Work It Out Today, businesses rely more and more on teams to get work done. While most teams have a leader, all team members work together to meet team goals. There are some situations, however, where team members may not get along with others. This conflict can keep teams from working productively. Learning how to resolve conflicts can help keep a project on track. Discussing differences, listening to others, and seeing issues from different points of view are important steps in conflict resolution. *How did you handle a recent conflict you had with someone?*

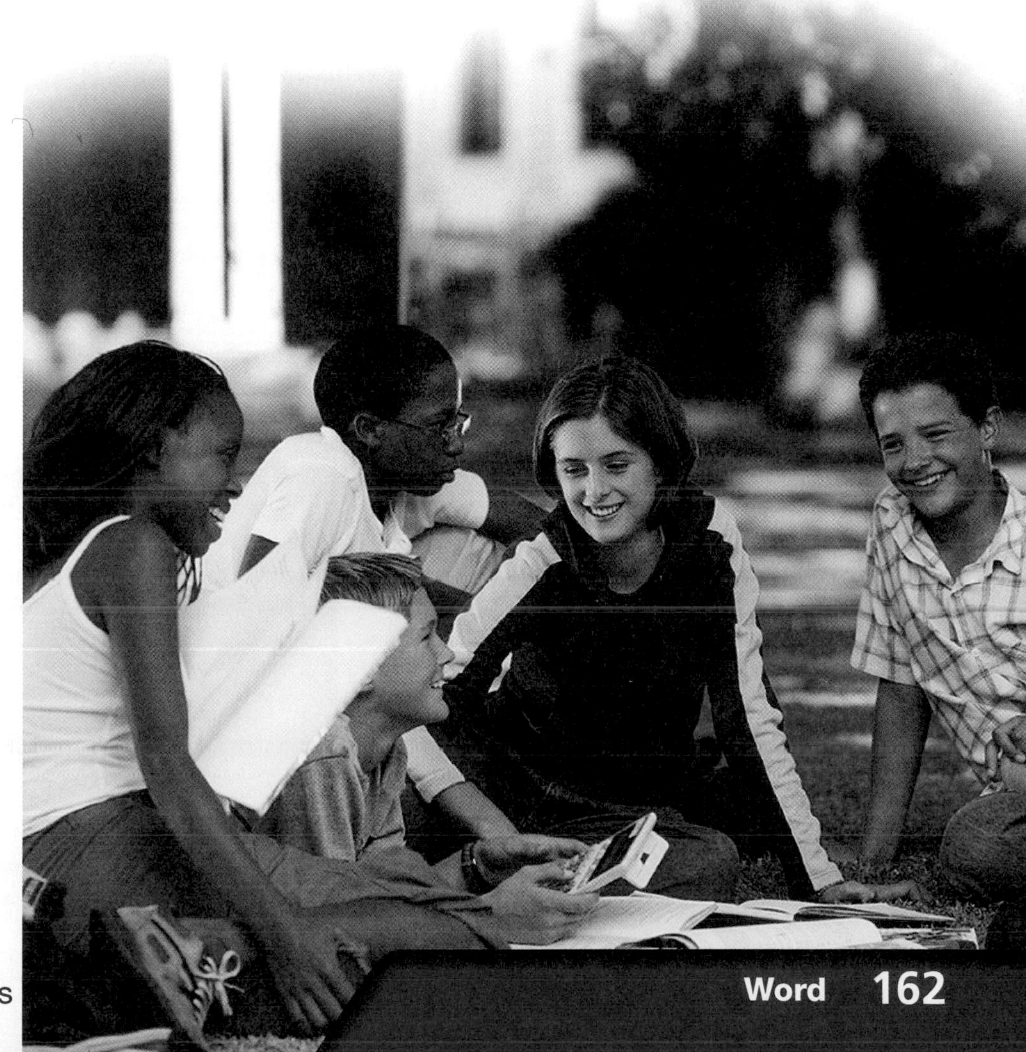

Step-By-Step

1. In your **Tips** file, click **Office** . In the **Office** drop-down menu, click **Save As**. The **Save As** dialog box opens.

2. With your teacher's permission, click the **New Folder** button (see Figure 1.6).

3. In the **New Folder** text box that appears, key: [your first initial and last name] as the new folder name (for example, *alee*).

4. Click outside the text box. The new folder opens automatically.

5. In the **File name** box, in the **Save As** dialog box, key: Tips-. Then key your first initial and your last name (for example, *Tips-alee*).

6. **CHECK** Your dialog box should look similar to Figure 1.6.

7. Click **Save** in the **Save As** dialog box.

8. **CHECK** Your screen should look similar to Figure 1.7. The document's name appears on the title bar.

Continue to the next exercise.

EXERCISE 1-4
Name and Save a Presentation in a New Folder

Instead of storing all of your presentations in one place, you can store them in folders. A **folder** helps you organize your presentations by grouping related presentations together. One way to create a new folder is to use the Save As dialog box. A **dialog box** is used to enter specific information to perform a task, such as naming and saving a document.

Teaching Tip Explain to students that they will save a data file as [file name]-[student's first initial and last name]. Students will sometimes work in the same file throughout multiple exercises. Check that students know where to locate their saved file.

FIGURE 1.6 Save As dialog box

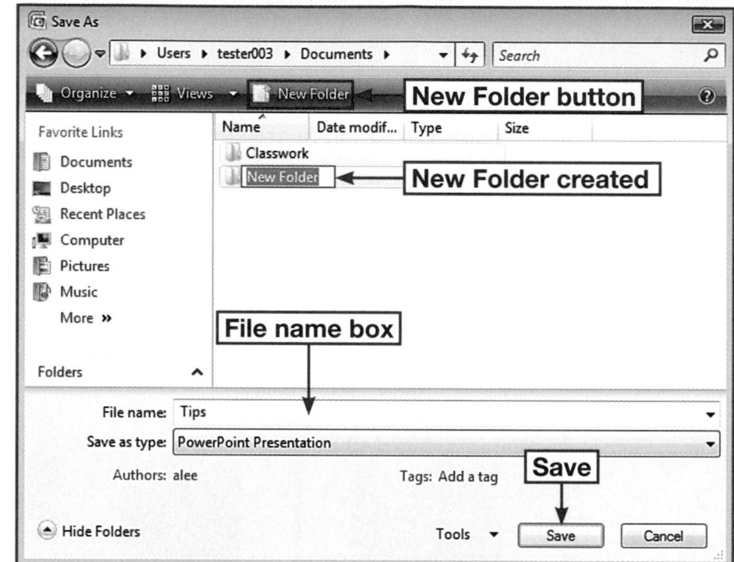

FIGURE 1.7 Saved presentation

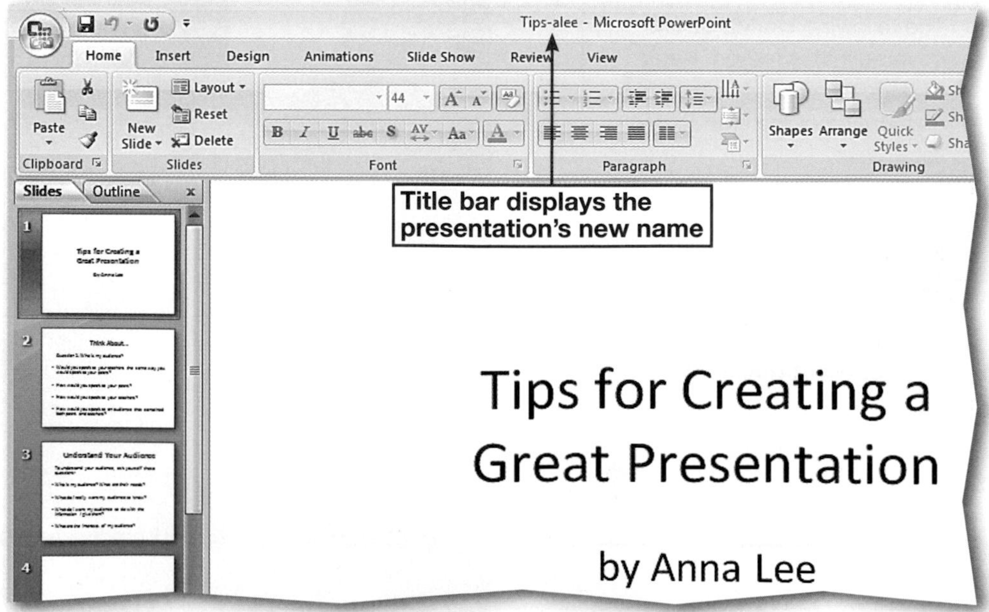

Differentiated Instruction/Advanced Students Have advanced students practice saving files from other applications in the new folder.

Before You Read

See page TM42 for English Learner activity suggestions.

Stay Engaged One way to stay engaged when reading is to turn each of the exercise titles into a question, then read the section to find the answers. For example, Exercise 6-1 might be "How do I insert a hyperlink into a document?"

Read To Learn

- Explore using hyperlinks and HTML to navigate between documents electronically.
- Consider how tracking changes electronically can improve your writing skills.
- Discover how you can use mail merge to send professional, personalized letters.

Main Idea

Word offers several tools that help you exchange, review, and present your documents.

Vocabulary

Key Terms

attachment
background
combine
comment
data source
hyperlink
Hypertext Markup Language (HTML)
mail merge
main document
merge field
page orientation
Track Changes
Web browser
Web Layout View
Web page

Academic Vocabulary

These words appear in your reading and on your tests. Make sure you know their meanings.

contribute
enable
vary

Quick Write Activity

Describe In previous lessons you learned how to create several kinds of documents, including business letters, reports, and newsletters. On a separate sheet of paper, describe how a Web page might be different from these types of documents. How does a Web page use color and graphics to communicate a message? In what ways is a Web page like a flyer?

Study Skills

Listen with a Purpose Listening is one of the most important skills you can develop to do better in school and on the job. When learning new skills, ask questions and take notes. Remember that listening is an active—not a passive—activity!

Academic Standards

English Language Arts

NCTE 4 Adjust use of language to communicate effectively with a variety of audiences.

NCTE 5 Employ a wide range of strategies while writing to communicate effectively with different audiences.

NCTE 12 Use language to accomplish individual purposes.

Math

NCTM (Measurement) Apply appropriate techniques, tools, and formulas to determine measurements.

Step-By-Step

1. Click **Office** . Click **Open**.
2. In the **Open** dialog box, click the **Look in** box drop-down arrow.
3. Select the location of your data files. Ask your teacher for the correct location.
4. Click **Tips.pptx** (see Figure 1.4).
5. Click **Open**.
6. The **Tips** presentation opens in **Normal View**.
7. CHECK Your screen should look like Figure 1.5.

Continue to the next exercise.

EXERCISE 1-3
View a Presentation in Normal View

A **slide** is an individual page within a presentation. A **presentation** is a group of slides that can be printed or presented as a slide show. PowerPoint automatically opens presentations in Normal View. In this view, the PowerPoint screen is divided into two sections. The Slides and Outline tab is on the left. The slide pane is on the right.

Troubleshooting Let students know that they may or may not see a gray band in their Save As dialog box, depending on their computer's settings.

FIGURE 1.4 Open dialog box

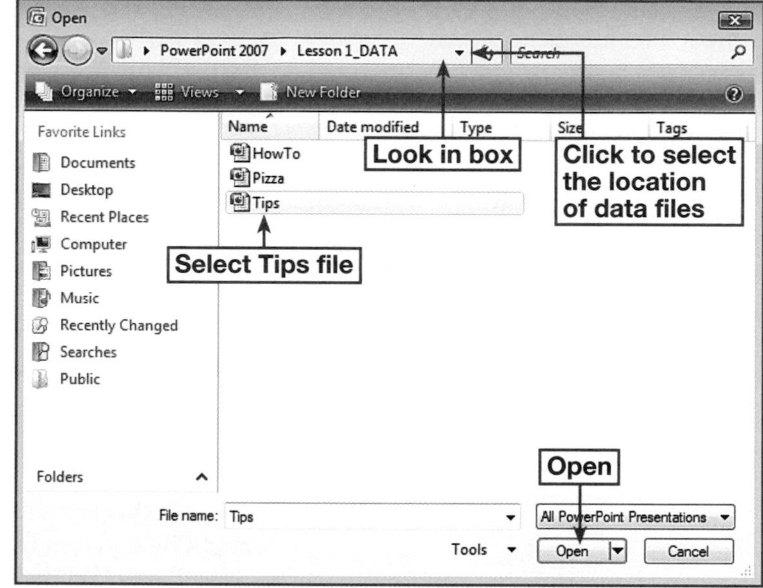

FIGURE 1.5 Tips presentation open in Normal View

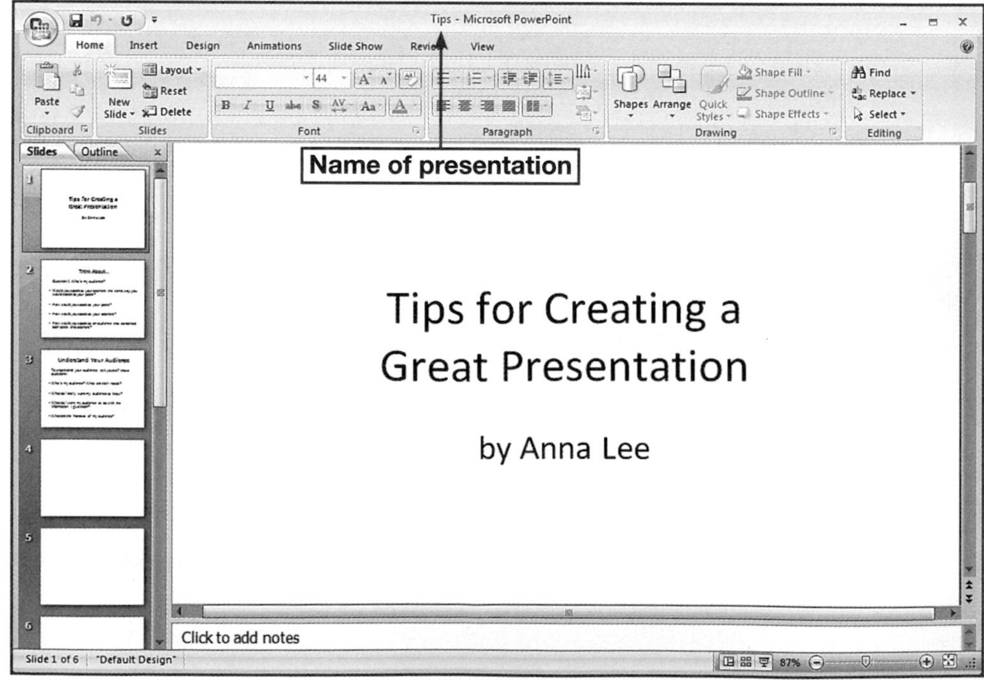

Microsoft Office 2007

PowerPoint presentations created in Office 2007 save by default in the .pptx file format. Files saved in this format will not open in earlier versions of Office.

Troubleshooter

If you are using Windows XP, go to page li to learn how to complete the steps in this exercise and in Exercise 1-4.

Troubleshooting Make it easier for students to navigate to the data files by setting the default file location for the students before class. Click **Office**. Click **PowerPoint Options**. Click **Save**.

Step-By-Step

1. Start **Word**. Open the data file **Flyer_Memo.docx**. Save as: Flyer_Memo-[your first initial and last name] (for example, *Flyer_Memo-sbryant*).

2. Position your cursor after the colon at the end of the memo's body text. Press ENTER once.

3. Choose **Insert>Links>Hyperlink**.

4. In the **Insert Hyperlink** dialog box, under **Link to**, click **Existing File** or **Web Page** (see Figure 6.1).

5. In the **Text to display** box, key: Link to flyer.

6. Under **Look in**, click **Current Folder**.

7. Click the **Look in** drop-down arrow. Locate and select the data file **Flyer.docx**. Click **OK**.

8. **CHECK** Your screen should look like Figure 6.2. Save your file.

Continue to the next exercise.

Tech Tip

Hyperlinks can be used to link to Web pages, e-mail addresses, and even to other portions of longer documents.

EXERCISE 6-1
Insert a Hyperlink to a Word Document

A **hyperlink** is a word, phrase, or graphic that a user can click to move from one online location to another. Hyperlinks make it possible for, or enable, users to move from one Word document to another. Words in a hyperlink usually appear with an underline and in a different color.

FIGURE 6.1 Insert Hyperlink dialog box

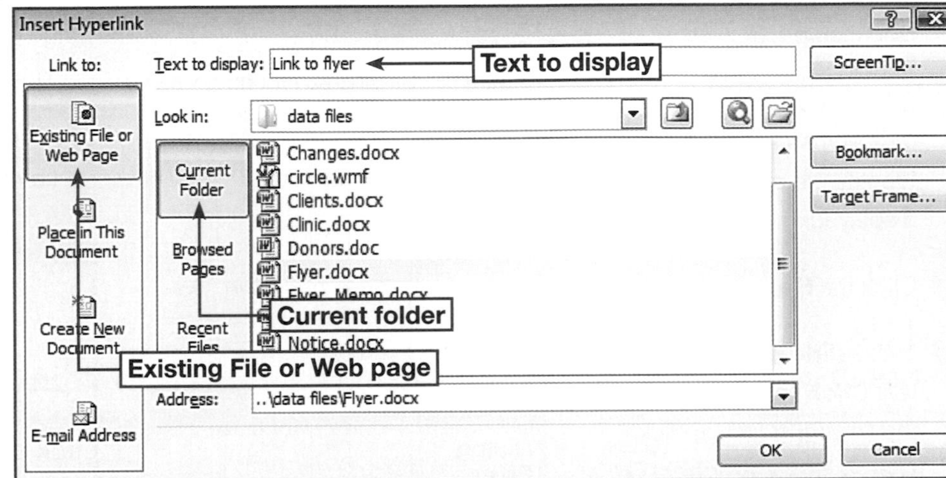

FIGURE 6.2 Hyperlink to a document

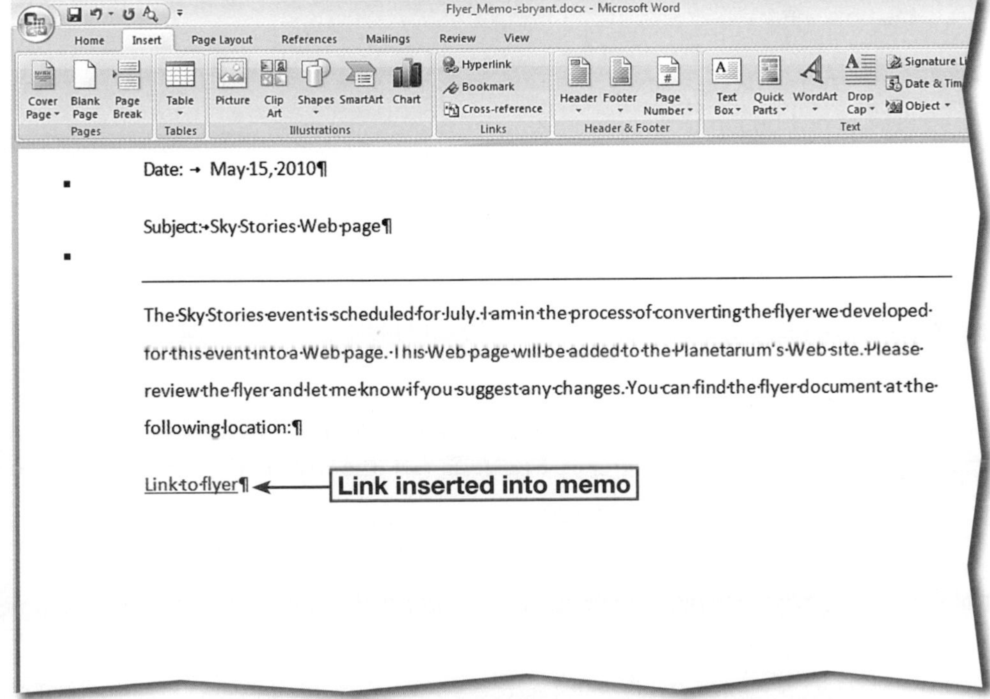

Step-By-Step

1. In PowerPoint, on the **Ribbon**, click the **Home** tab (see Figure 1.2).
2. Roll your pointer arrow over the six different groups in the **Home** tab (see Figure 1.3).
3. Click the seven different tabs across the **Ribbon**. Identify the groups displayed in each tab.
4. Click the **Home** tab.
5. In the **slide pane**, click the text **Click to add title**. In the **Drawing** group, click **Dialog Box Launcher**. At the bottom of the dialog box, click **Close** to close the box.
6. In the **Slides** group, click the **Layout** button. The **Layout** menu opens.
7. **CHECK** Your screen should look like Figure 1.2.
8. Click in a blank area on the screen to close the **Layout** menu.

Continue to the next exercise.

EXERCISE 1-2
Use the Ribbon, Tabs, and Groups

The **Ribbon** is designed to help you quickly find **buttons** (or **commands**), which are organized under tabs and **groups**. Each **tab** contains several related groups, and groups contain closely related buttons. Consider the common text commands grouped under the Home tab. Each group is organized according to the functions of the commands. For instance, all commands that affect the appearance of text are contained in the Font group.

FIGURE 1.2 The Layout menu

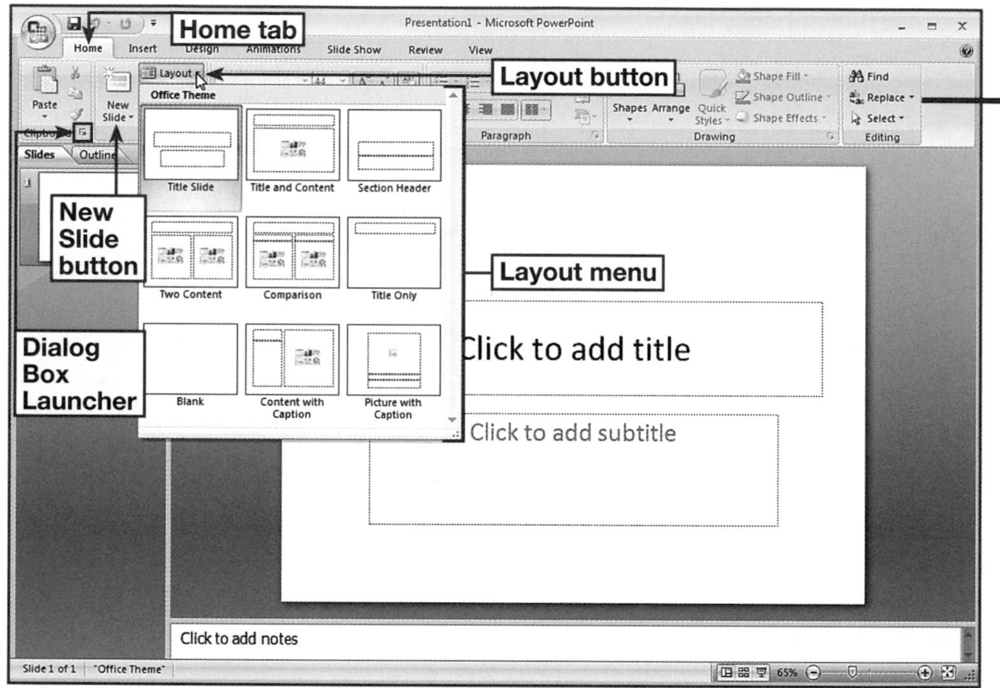

FIGURE 1.3 The Ribbon

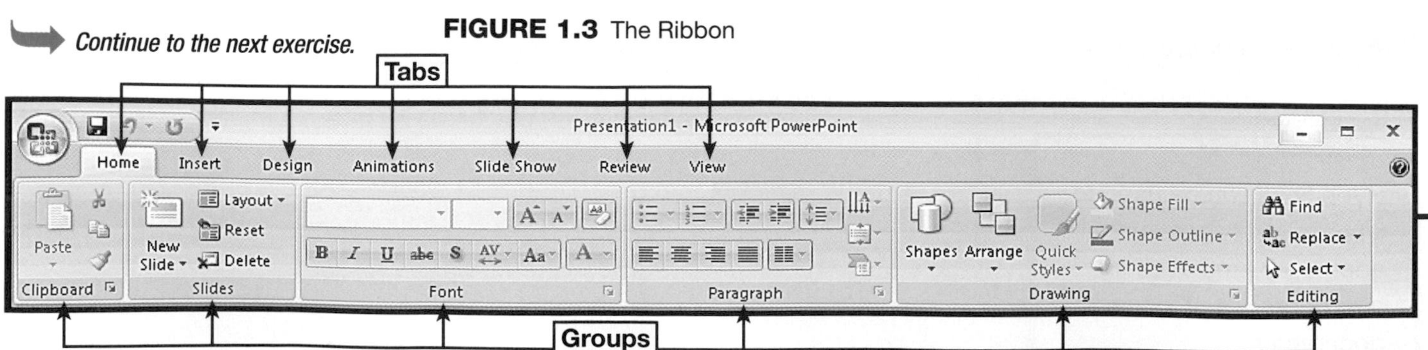

Step-By-Step

1. In your **Flyer Memo** file, choose **Office>Word Options>Customize>All Commands>Send for Review>Add**. Click **OK**.
2. On the **Quick Access Toolbar**, click **Send for Review** (see Figure 6.3).
3. **CHECK** Your screen should look like Figure 6.4. Notice the information that is automatically inserted into the e-mail message.
4. In the **To** box, key your teacher's e-mail address.
5. With your teacher's permission, click **Send**.
6. **CHECK** Your screen should again look like Figure 6.3. Save and close your file.

Continue to the next exercise.

You Should Know

A file can be sent to more than one person for review. Key a comma before each additional e-mail address.

Troubleshooting Note that students may not be able to send e-mails depending on the configuration in the classroom. If e-mail is configured, these steps will automatically open the default e-mail application on each computer. If Outlook is not the default, Figure 6.4 may not match, and students may be asked for a user name and password after **Step 2**.

EXERCISE 6-2
Send a Document for Review via E-mail

When two or more people work together, they all contribute to, or play a significant part in, producing a final result. Sending documents for review via e-mail can speed this process. When you use Send for Review, text automatically appears in the e-mail message asking the person to review the document. The document for review is also automatically sent as an **attachment** to the recipient. When opened, the document is displayed in Reading Layout View.

Solution Use the file **Flyer_Memo-SF.docx** as a solution file for Exercises 6-1 through 6-2.

FIGURE 6.3 Word window before e-mail sent

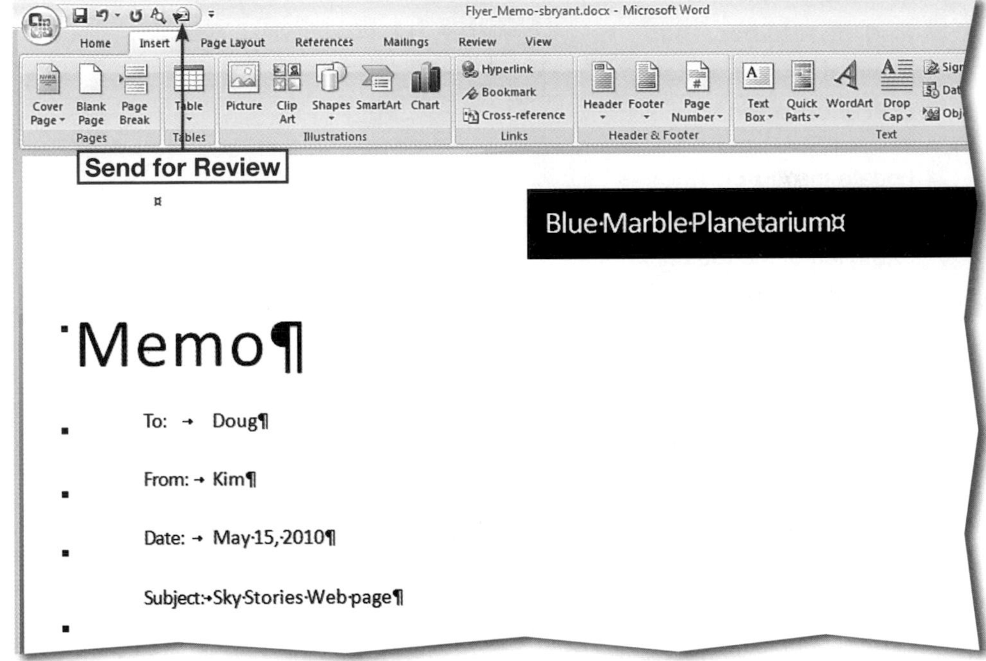

Teaching Tip Point out the different parts of a message to help students who are not familiar with e-mail.

FIGURE 6.4 Sending a document by e-mail

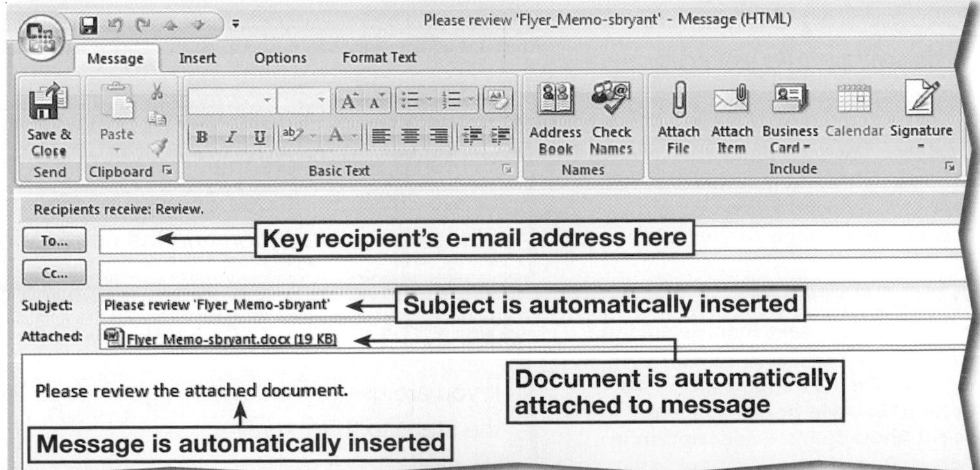

Step-By-Step

1. To start PowerPoint, click the **Start** button (see Figure 1.1). Choose **Programs>Microsoft Office®>Microsoft Office PowerPoint 2007**.
2. iCHECK Your screen should look like Figure 1.1.
3. Find the **title bar**. The name of your presentation is **Presentation1**.
4. Locate the **Quick Access Toolbar (QAT)**. The button to the left of the toolbar is the **Office Button**.
5. Move your pointer over the **Office Button**. A **ScreenTip** appears.
6. In the **slide pane**, click inside the first text box.
7. Click the **Office** button. Read the list of menu options. Click in a blank area on the screen to close the menu.

Continue to the next exercise.

EL Review Key Terms with English Learners. As needed, show them how the terms apply to the lesson.

Teaching Tip If students do not see any ScreenTips, have them select the **Office** button and click **PowerPoint Options**. On the **Popular** tab, in the **ScreenTip style** box, have them select **Show feature description in ScreenTips**.

EXERCISE 1-1
Identify Parts of the PowerPoint Screen

You need to know your way around the PowerPoint screen before you can create a presentation. The **title bar** displays, or shows, the name of the current presentation. The **Quick Access Toolbar (QAT)** is a customizable toolbar for easy access to your most commonly used functions. The **status bar** displays information, such as the number of the slide you are viewing. You use the pointer to select tools on the screen. When you point to an object, a **ScreenTip** appears that tells you what the object does. When you move your pointer, the ScreenTip disappears.

Teaching Tip Review with students the purpose of the iCheck icon in Step 2. The iCheck icon lets the student know that their screen should look like the figure at that step. Students can use the iCheck icon to check their own work.

FIGURE 1.1 PowerPoint screen

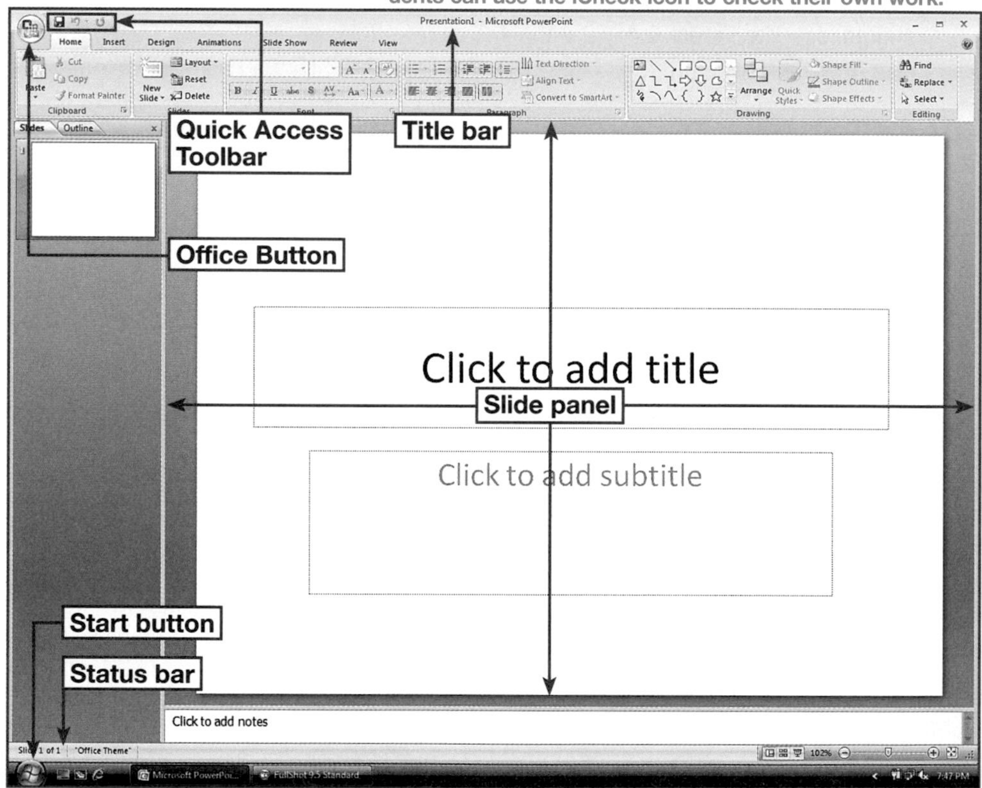

Microsoft Office 2007

ScreenTips do more than just show you the names of buttons. In Office 2007, Enhanced ScreenTips also provide a brief description of the button's function and the corresponding keyboard shortcut.

Troubleshooter

If you are using Windows XP, go to page I to learn how to complete the steps in this exercise.

Step-By-Step

1. Open the data file **Flyer**. Save as: Flyer-[your first initial and last name].
2. Choose **Review>Tracking>Track Changes**. Make sure the **Track Changes** button is active (see Figure 6.5).
3. Click before the first **Friday** in the flyer. Key: every. Press the **spacebar** once.
4. In the **Where** line in your flyer, select the text **Main**. Press DELETE.
5. **CHECK** Your screen should look like Figure 6.5.
6. Choose **View>Document Views>Draft**.
7. **CHECK** Your screen should look like Figure 6.6. Save your file.
8. Switch to **Print Layout View**.

Continue to the next exercise.

Academic Skills

The audience for this flyer would be interested in learning about mythology and astronomy, which is the study of stars and constellations. Many constellations, such as Andromeda, Orion, and Cassiopeia, draw their names from Greek mythology.

EXERCISE 6-3
Use Track Changes

When reviewing a document, you can use **Track Changes** to help you mark changes as you make them. Text that you add to the document is displayed in a different color and underlined. Text that you delete from the document is marked with a strikethrough effect when you are in Draft View. In Print Layout View, deletions are displayed in balloons.

EL Two words in this exercise that might need explanation are *constellation* and *planetarium*. The exercise can be completed without knowing the meanings, but students may not grasp the purpose of the flyers.

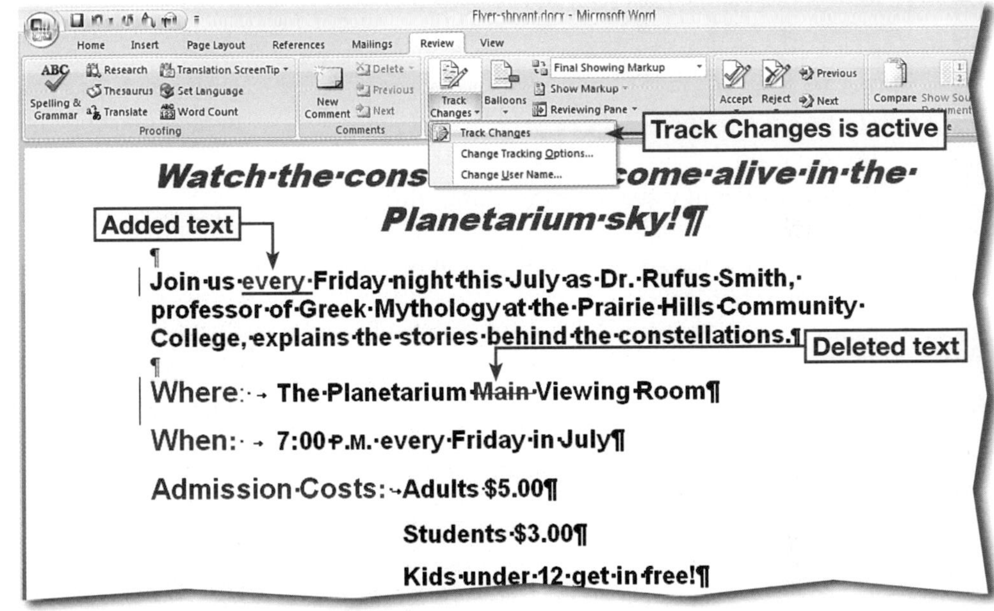

FIGURE 6.5 Text added using Track Changes

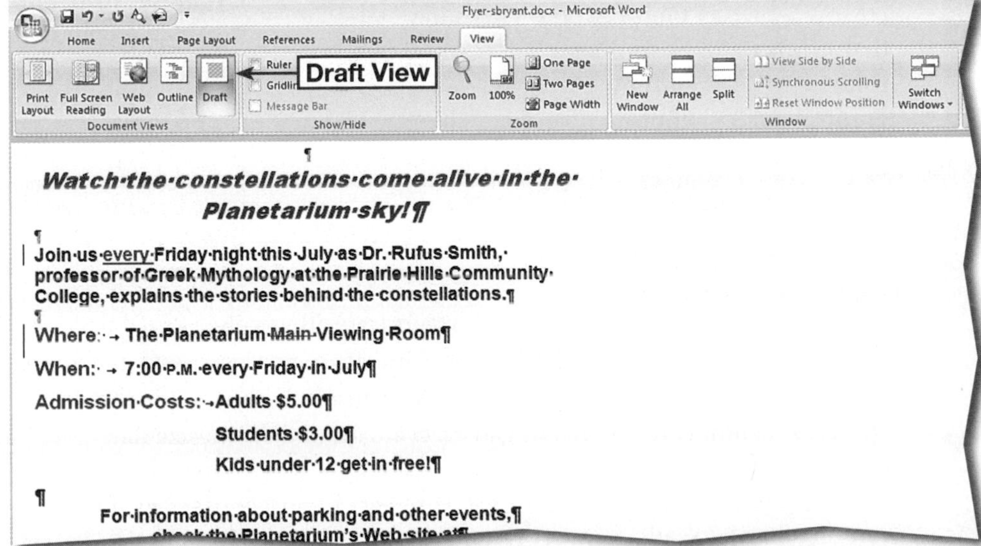

FIGURE 6.6 Text deleted using Track Changes

NCLB/Language Arts (NCTE 5) Ask students to define the audience of the flyer. Students should notice that the flyer appeals to those interested in astronomy and mythology. Also note that the way the admission costs are broken down indicates that this is a family-oriented event.

LESSON 1 Reading Guide

Before You Read

See page TM42 for English Learner activity suggestions.

How Can You Improve? Before starting the lesson, think about the last exam you took on material you had to read. What reading strategies helped you on the test? Make a list of ways to improve your strategies in order to succeed on your next exam.

Read to Learn

- Understand basic principles of creating a good presentation.
- Explore different views when working with slides.
- Consider how to organize information on a slide using placeholders.
- Learn how to set up an organized presentation.

Main Idea

Presentation software can be used to explain and present information to many different audiences.

Vocabulary

Key Terms

button	placeholder	ScreenTip
command	presentation	scroll bar
cursor	Quick Access Toolbar (QAT)	slide
dialog box		status bar
folder		tab
group	Ribbon	title bar

Academic Vocabulary

These words appear in your reading and on your tests. Make sure you know their meanings.

display
monitor

Quick Write Activity

Describe On a separate piece of paper, describe a presentation that you have seen. Consider the following questions. What was the subject? Who was in the audience? Was the presentation interesting? What made it interesting? What part of the presentation helped you to learn about its subject matter? Include any other details that you remember about the presentation.

Study Skills

Organize Your Thoughts If you have trouble organizing your ideas, try creating a list, outline, or diagram. These tools will help you organize your thoughts so you can create presentations that are easy to follow.

Academic Standards

English Language Arts

NCTE 4 Use written language to communicate effectively.

NCTE 5 Use different writing process elements to communicate effectively.

NCTE 6 Apply knowledge of language structure and conventions to discuss texts.

NCTE 7 Conduct research and gather, evaluate, and synthesize data to communicate discoveries.

Math

NCTM (Number and Operations) Understand numbers, ways of representing numbers, relationships among numbers, and number systems.

Step-By-Step

EXERCISE 6-4
Insert, View, and Edit Comments

You can make a note in a document by inserting a **comment**. When you insert a comment, it is automatically labeled with your user initials and the comment's number. In Print Layout View, comments are shown in balloons on the screen. In Draft View, comments are identified only by the user's initials.

Teaching Tip Ask students for examples of situations when they might insert comments—in their own documents and in others' documents.

FIGURE 6.7 Comment inserted into document

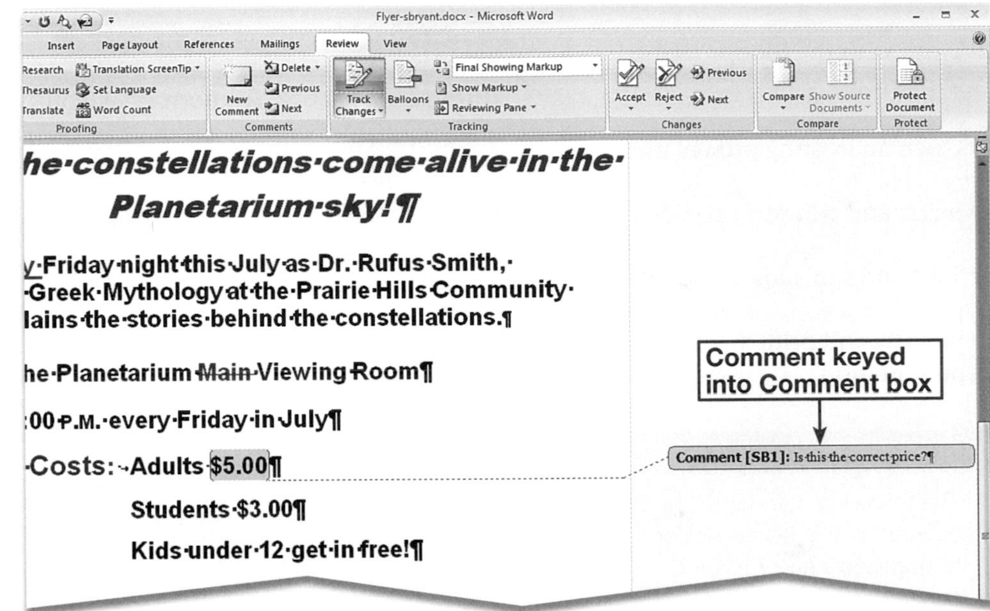

1. In your **Flyer** file, in the **Admission Costs** line, select **$5.00**.
2. Choose **Review>Comments>New Comment**.
3. In the **Comment** box, key: Is this the correct price?
4. **CHECK** Your screen should look similar to Figure 6.7.
5. Choose **Review>Tracking** and click the **Show Markup** drop-down arrow. Click **Comments** to deselect it.
6. **CHECK** Your screen should look like Figure 6.8.
7. Click the **Show Markup** drop-down arrow again. Click **Comments**. The comments are visible again.

Continued on the next page.

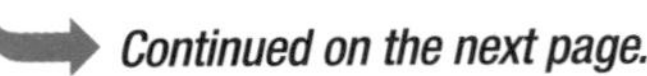

FIGURE 6.8 Comment hidden

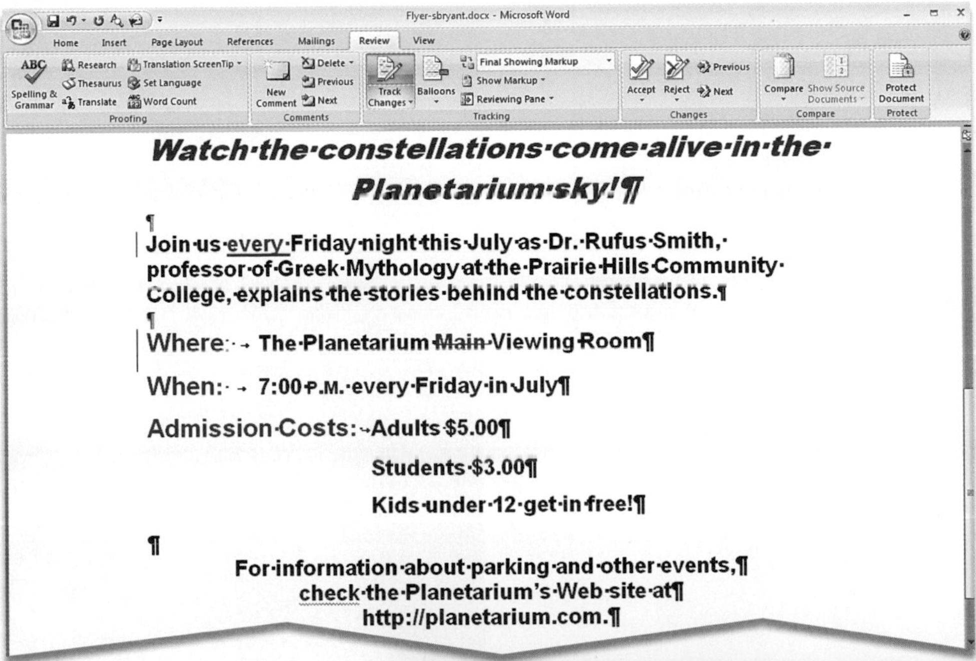

Shortcuts

You can also add a new comment by pressing ALT + R + C on your keyboard.

Troubleshooting If students do not see all changes in balloons, have them choose **Review>Tracking>Balloons>Show Revisions in Balloons.**

LESSON 1 PowerPoint Basics

Key Concepts

- Identify parts of the PowerPoint screen
- Work with the Ribbon, tabs, and groups
- Open an existing presentation
- Insert and edit text on slides
- Start and run slide shows
- Preview and print a presentation

Standards

The following standards are covered in this lesson. Refer to pages xxv and 715 for a description of the standards listed here.

ISTE Standards Correlation

NETS•S

1a, 1b, 2a, 2b, 2d, 3a, 3b, 3c, 3d, 4b, 4c, 5a, 5b, 6a, 6b, 6c

Microsoft Certified Application Specialist

PowerPoint

1.5, 4.4, 4.5

From the classroom to the boardroom, people love to use PowerPoint when giving presentations. PowerPoint gives you an easy way to display information in an interesting and visual way. In this lesson, you will become familiar with PowerPoint by learning how to open, run, modify, and print an existing presentation.

21st CENTURY SKILLS

See page TM90 for answers to 21st Century Learning Skills.

Understand Your Audience As you plan a presentation, ask yourself some questions. How can I make my presentation interesting to my audience? Who is my audience? What will keep their attention? What do they already know, and what do they need to know? These questions will help you understand your audience. This understanding will help you make a presentation that gives your audience the information they need in a way that is interesting to them. *Why is it important to catch your audience's interest when you are giving a presentation?*

Step-By-Step

EXERCISE 6-4 (Continued)
Insert, View, and Edit Comments

8 Choose **View>Document View>Draft**.

9 Move your pointer over your initials to make the comment appear.

10 CHECK Your screen should look like Figure 6.9.

11 Choose **Review>Tracking> Reviewing Pane**.

12 Choose **View>Document Views>Print Layout**.

13 In the **Reviewing** pane, under **Comment**, click after the word **price** and before the question mark. Press the **spacebar** once.

14 Key: for adults.

15 CHECK Your screen should look like Figure 6.10.

16 In the **Reviewing** pane, click **Close**.

17 Save your file.

Continue to the next exercise.

FIGURE 6.9 Comment in Normal View

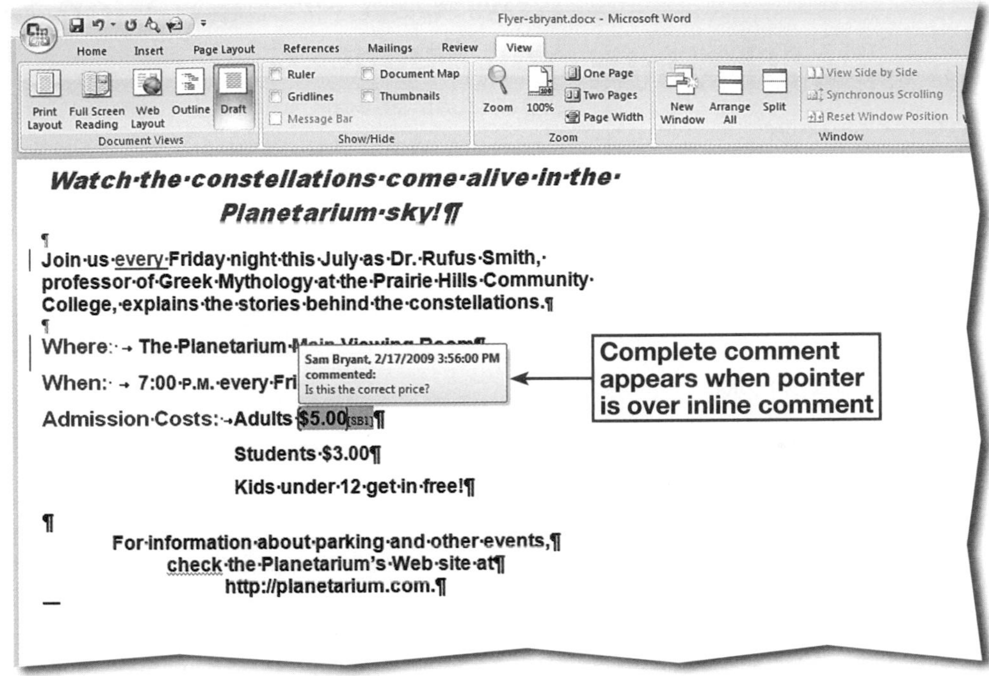

FIGURE 6.10 Edited comment

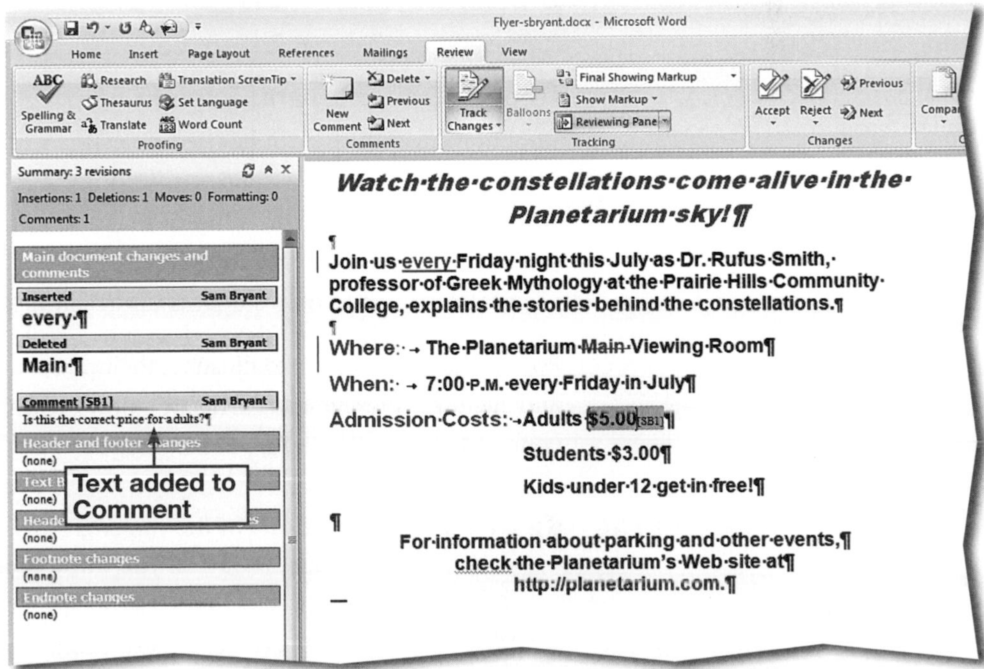

You Should Know

If you rest the insertion point over a comment balloon, the name of the reviewer and the date and time the comment was made will be displayed.

UNIT 4 Careers and Technology

How Can Presentation Skills Help You Succeed?

Career Checklist

To use presentations as an effective communication tool in the workplace, remember to:

- ✓ Identify your audience.
- ✓ Keep text brief and to the point.
- ✓ Use attractive color schemes.
- ✓ Use animation sparingly.
- ✓ Rehearse your presentation.
- ✓ Revise your presentation.
- ✓ Speak clearly.
- ✓ Speak to your audience. Do not just read the slides.

Differentiated Instruction/ Advanced Students Have students write a paragraph describing how professionals in various careers would use PowerPoint.

NCLB/Math (Representation) Have students go to the book Web site at **glencoe.com** to learn more about math theory. Students should click the Math Handbook link.

Presentation software such as PowerPoint can be used to present information in a classroom setting. Businesses also use PowerPoint to provide information to a variety of audiences. PowerPoint can help you give professional-looking presentations that are well-organized, focused, and engaging. A well-designed presentation will help you make a good impression on your co-workers, as well as your superiors.

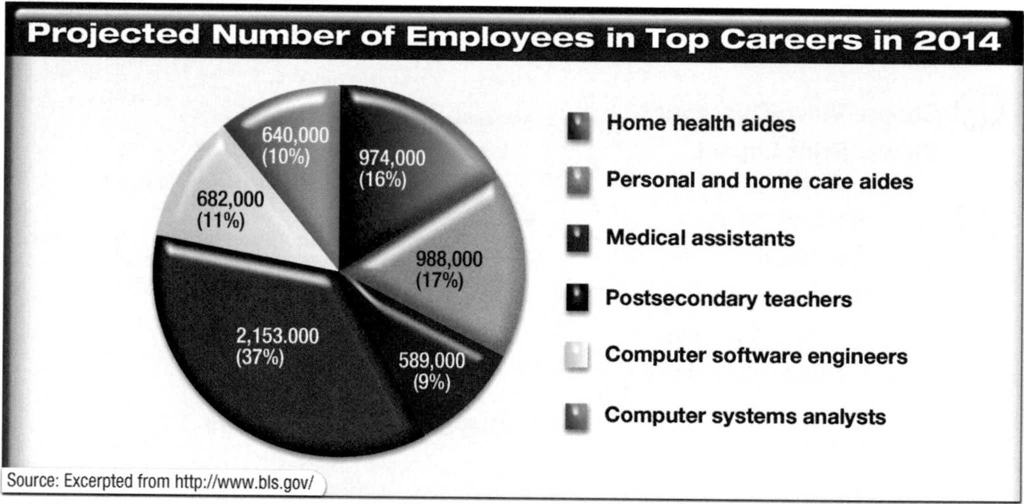

Report, Educate, and Explain

Presentation software can be used in a wide variety of career paths. Professionals in all industries often report activities or findings. Presentation software is the tool of choice when companies need to educate or train their employees. In the medical industry, presentations are often given to demonstrate new techniques and procedures. Teachers use presentations to help students understand topics.

PowerPoint allows users to illustrate their presentations with charts, tables, text, diagrams, and pictures. Presentation software allows you to display information visually so that your audience understands your message.

READING CHECK

1. **Evaluate** Choose one of the career groups in the chart above that interests you. List down three ways that you think presentation skills might be useful in that occupation.
2. **Math** Of the top six careers in the chart, which occupation will have the greatest number of members in 2014?

See page TM88 for answers to the Reading Check.

EXERCISE 6-5
Compare and Merge Documents

1. In your **Flyer** file, choose **Review>Compare**. Select **Combine**.
2. In the **Combine Documents** dialog box, click the **Original document** drop-down arrow.
3. Browse to and select your **Flyer** file (see Figure 6.11).
4. Click the **Revised document** drop-down arrow. Select the data file **Changes.docx**.
5. **CHECK** Your screen should look like Figure 6.11. Click **OK**.
6. Choose **Review>Compare**. Click the **Show Source Documents** drop-down arrow and choose **Hide Source Documents**.
7. **CHECK** Your screen should look like Figure 6.12.
8. Save the new file as Combined-[your first initial and last name]. Close your **Flyer** file.

Continue to the next exercise.

Solution Use the file **Flyer-SF.docx** as a solution file for Exercise 6-3 through 6-5.

When two or more people have made changes to two different copies of the same document, you can **combine** the documents. When you Compare and Merge a document, Word creates one final document that contains all of the comments and suggestions. Changes and comments are color coded to help you identify each reviewer.

Intervention Strategy Help students understand how to read the combined document by reading aloud through the changes and descriptions with them.

FIGURE 6.11 Combine Documents dialog box

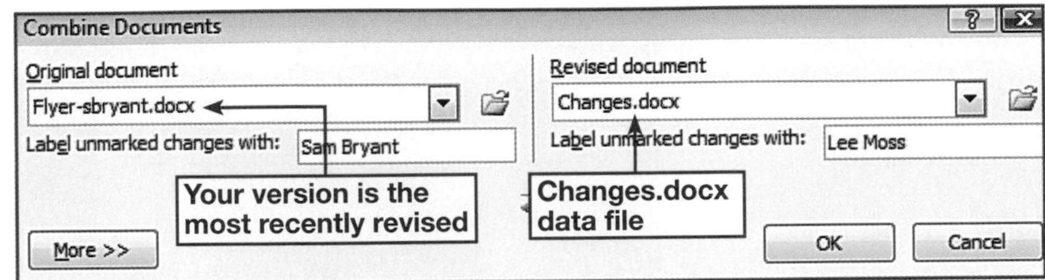

FIGURE 6.12 Merged document

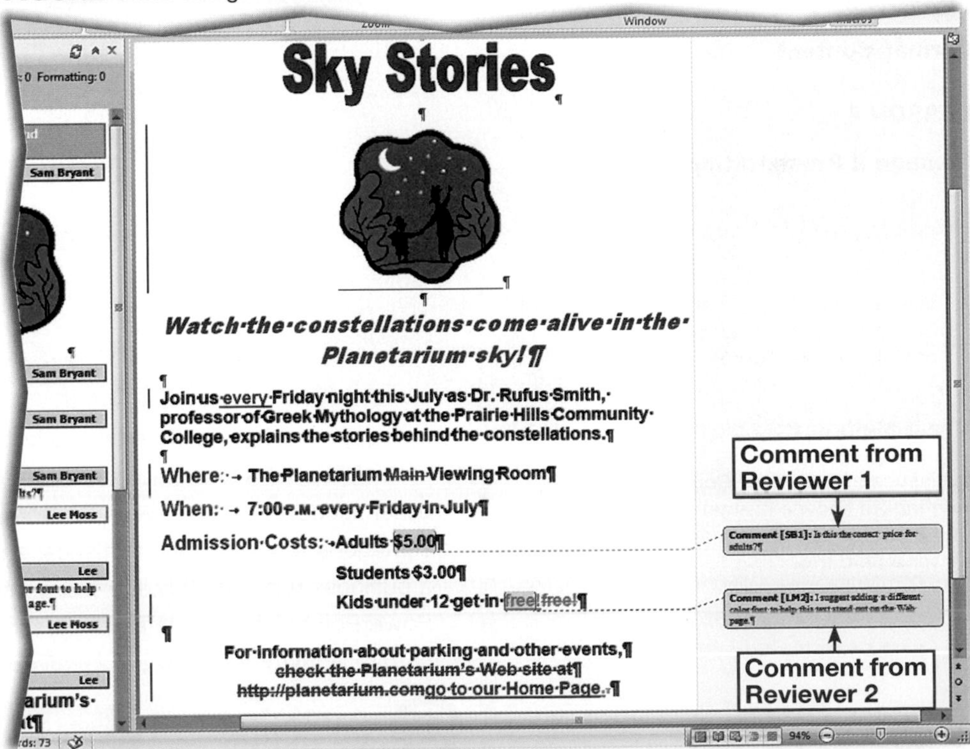

You Should Know

If you want to keep a record of the edits made by reviewers, you can print the document with the changes.

PowerPoint 2007: The Power of Presentations

Unit Objectives:

After completing this Unit, you will be able to:

LESSON 1

PowerPoint Basics

LESSON 2

Create Content and Collaborate

LESSON 3

Format Content

LESSON 4

Manage a Presentation

See page TM88 for an overview of Unit level resources.

Why It Matters Possible answers include using PowerPoint to present issues at a Student Council meeting, to show a budget at a club meeting, or to share an itinerary for a field trip.

Why It Matters

In today's world, it is important to know how to share information. At school, teachers and students share the information needed to master essential concepts and skills. At work, employees use documents and presentations to share data, statistics, and other types of information that help a business run smoothly. For many schools and businesses, Microsoft PowerPoint has become essential for sharing information. ***How might a club or activity that you are involved with use PowerPoint?***

Go Online — REAL WORLD CONNECTION

glencoe.com

Go to the **Online Learning Center** and select your book. Choose **Unit 4** to learn more about how different organizations use PowerPoint presentations.

Step-By-Step

1. In your **Combined** file, scroll up and click before the word **Presents**.
2. On the **Review** tab, in the **Changes** group, click **Next** .
3. **CHECK** Your screen should look like Figure 6.13. The Clip Art is selected as the first change in the document.
4. Click **Next** again. The next change is highlighted.
5. In the **Changes** group, click **Previous** once to go back to the first change.
6. In the **Changes** group, click **Next** four times.
7. **CHECK** Your screen should look like Figure 6.14. Save your file.

Continue to the next exercise.

You Should Know

You can print a list of changes made to a document by selecting **Office>Print**. In the **Print what** box, click **List of markup**.

EXERCISE 6-6
Locate and Review Combined Changes in a Document

You can use the Changes group in the Review tab to review changes in a document. Clicking Next Change will take you to the next change in your document. Clicking Previous Change will take you to the change before the one you are currently viewing. You can also click Next Comment and Previous Comment to review comments. Word will highlight one change at a time so you can see which changes you want to keep.

FIGURE 6.13 First change highlighted

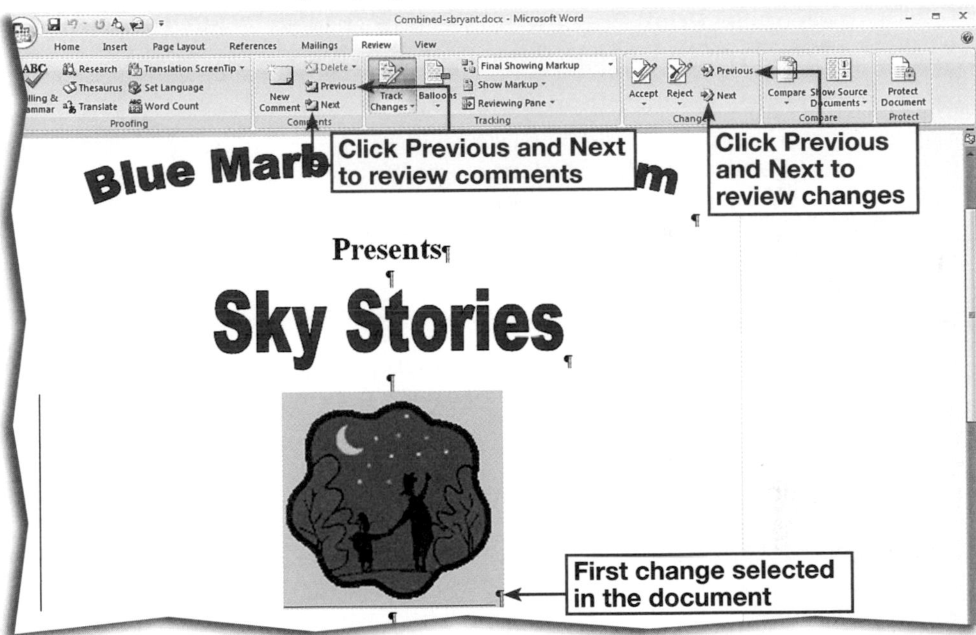

FIGURE 6.14 Last change highlighted

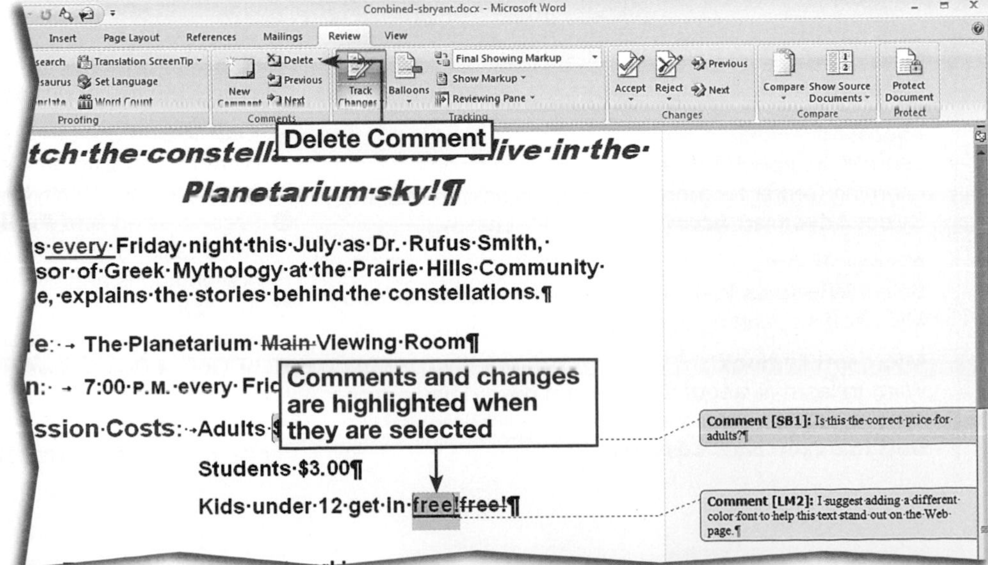

Portfolio Project

Part 4: Create a Report

LEVEL This is an advanced level project.

Goal The student council needs to identify which grade has raised the most money. You need to create a report that shows the numbers in descending order. Then you need to view the report in **Print Preview** to see how it looks before you present it to the student council.

Create Use the **Report Wizard** to create a report.

- The report should be based on your **Fundraiser Per Student** query. Include all of the fields in your report.
- Keep the title **Fundraiser Per Student** for your report.
- Open your finished report in **Design View**. Click **Group & Sort** [icon]. Sort the **Per Student** field in descending order.
- View your report in **Print Preview**. Use **Page** Setup to change the top and bottom margins to 0.5″.
- With your teacher's permission, print the report.

Self Assess Use the Have You ...? checklist to review your report. Make sure you have completed all of the items noted in the checklist. Check it carefully. The student council will use this report to decide which grades receive prizes.

	Have You...?
✔	Used the **Report Wizard** to create a report
✔	Based the report on your **Fundraiser Per Student** query
✔	Sorted in descending order the **Per Student** field in your report
✔	Viewed your report in **Print Preview**
✔	Changed the top and bottom margin of the report

Solution The solution file for this project is the **Fundraiser Per Student** report in the **BakeSale-SF .accdb** database file.

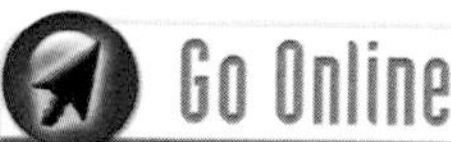

BEYOND THE BOOK

glencoe.com

Go to the Online Learning Center to learn additional skills, review what you have already learned.

Microsoft Access
Learn more about Access by visiting the Online Learning Center for more MCAS-based exercises. Select **Advanced Access Exercises> Lessons**.

Microsoft Vista
Select **Windows Vista Exercises>Lessons** to explore Microsoft's operating system fully.

Microsoft Outlook
Want to learn all about Outlook and how to use e-mail communication and scheduling? Select **Microsoft Outlook Exercises>Lessons**.

Additional Projects
Complete additional projects in the following areas:

- **Real-World Business Projects** reinforce Microsoft Word by focusing on real-world business applications.
- **Presentation and Publishing Projects** Use your Word skills to create exciting PowerPoint presentations and desktop publishing activities.
- **Academic Projects** Integrate academic skills while enriching your understanding of Microsoft Word.

More Online Resources
Access additional Web sites and online information relating to key topics covered in Glencoe's *iCheck Series*. Select **Additional Resources>Links**.

Step-By-Step

1. In your **Combined** file, click **Track Changes** to turn off Track Changes.
2. Select the first change, the Clip Art. On the **Review** tab, click **Changes> Accept**.
3. The next change is automatically highlighted. Click **Reject**. Press the spacebar to insert a space between **us** and **Friday**.
4. **CHECK** Your screen should look like Figure 6.15.
5. Select the word **free** and choose **Home>Font**. Click the **Font Color** drop-down menu and choose **Red**.
6. On the **Review** tab, click the **Accept** drop-down arrow. Click **Accept All Changes in Document**.
7. Choose **Review> Comments**. Click the **Delete** drop-down menu. Choose **Delete All Comments in Document**.
8. **CHECK** Your screen should look like Figure 6.16.
9. Save your file.

Continue to the next exercise.

EXERCISE 6-7
Accept and Reject Changes

After a document is reviewed, you can decide to either accept or reject the suggested changes. You can also delete comments that you have read and no longer need. You can accept and reject/delete changes and comments one at a time. There are also options to accept or reject all of the changes in a document or to delete every comment at one time.

Different Strokes Tell students that they can press **Ctrl** + **Shift** + **E** to turn Track Changes on and off.

FIGURE 6.15 Accepted and rejected changes

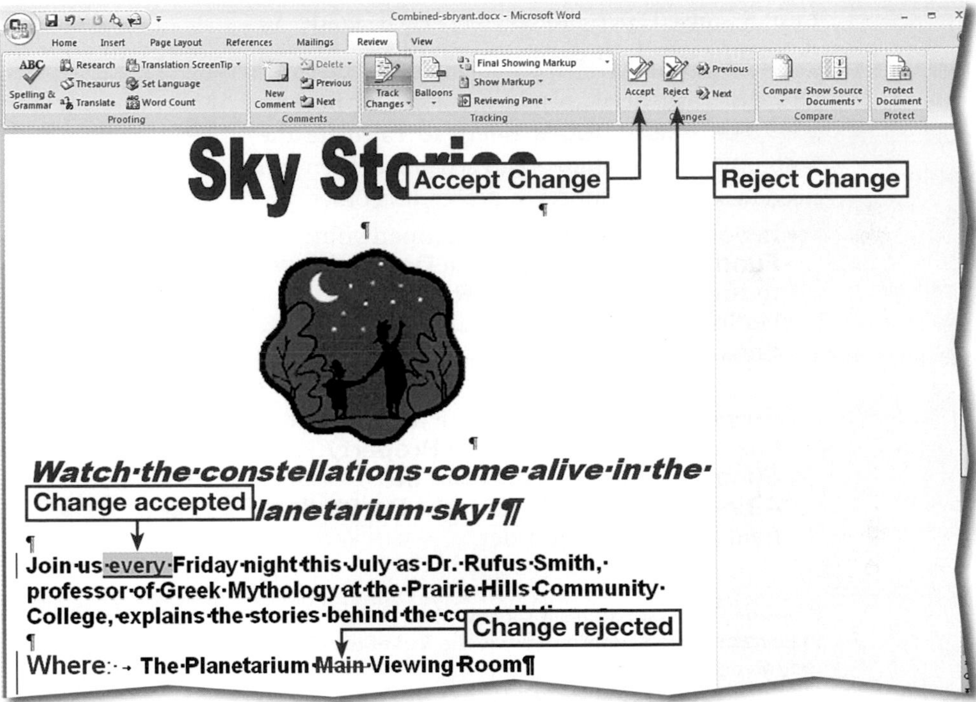

FIGURE 6.16 All comments deleted and all changes accepted

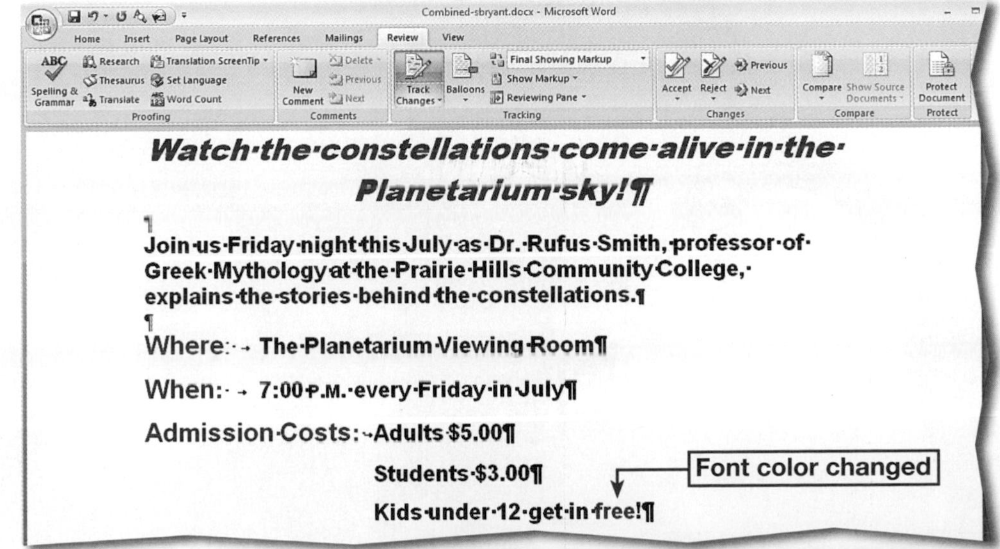

Portfolio Project

Part 3: Add a Calculated Field to a Query

LEVEL This is an advanced level project.

Goal The student council discussed whether grades with more students had an unfair advantage in the fundraiser. You decided to calculate the money raised per student by each grade to determine which three classes win prizes.

Create You need to add a calculated field to your **Fundraiser Totals** query to calculate the amount raised per student by each grade. Then you need to sort the numbers in descending order.

- In your **BakeSale** database, open your **Fundraiser Totals** query in **Design View**. In the field after **AmountRaised**, key: PerStudent: AmountRaised/TotalStudents. Press ENTER.
- Click in the **PerStudent** field. Click **Property Sheet**. Change the **Format** box to **Currency**. Close the **Property Sheet**. Remove the sort from the **AmountRaised** field. Sort the **PerStudent** field in descending order.

Solution The solution file for this project is the **Fundraiser Per Student** query in the **BakeSale-SF .accdb** database file.

- Save the query as: Fundraiser Per Student. View your query in **Datasheet View**. The grades with the highest fundraising amount per student should be at the top.
- With your teacher's permission, print your query.

Self Assess Use the Have You...? checklist to review your query. Make sure you have completed all of the items noted in the checklist.

When finished, proceed to Part 4.

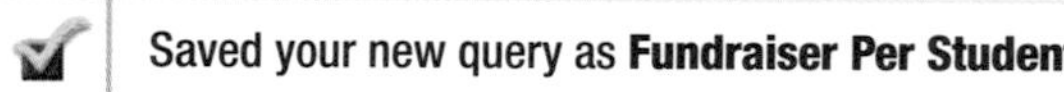

Have You...?

- ✓ Added a new field to your **Fundraiser Totals** query
- ✓ Keyed the correct formula in the field
- ✓ Changed the format of the new field to **Currency**
- ✓ Sorted the numbers in descending order
- ✓ Saved your new query as **Fundraiser Per Student**

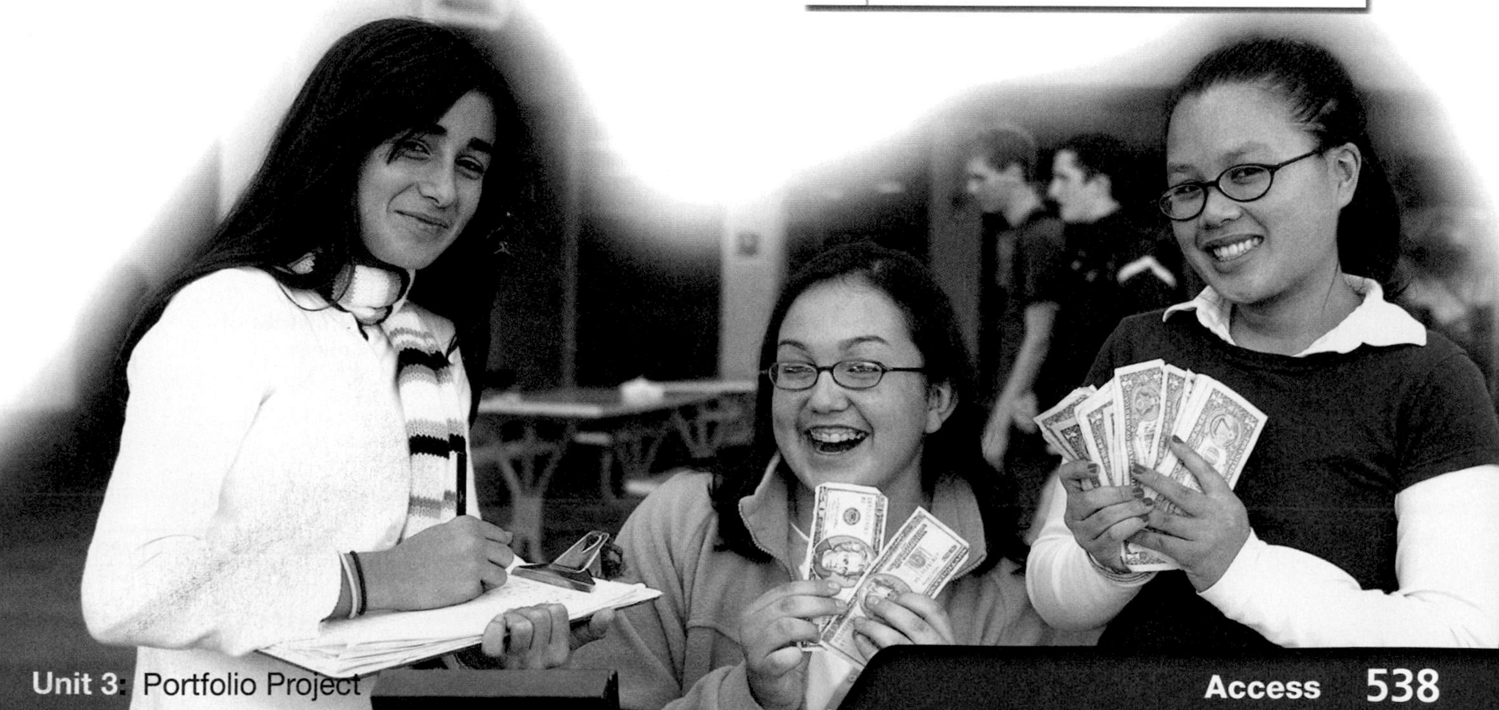

Step-By-Step

1. In your **Combined** file, select the text **Home Page** at the bottom of the page.
2. Choose **Insert> Hyperlink** .
3. In the **Insert Hyperlink** dialog box, under **Link to**, select **Existing File or Web Page**.
4. In the **Address** box, key: www.planetarium.html.
5. CHECK Your dialog box should look like Figure 6.17. Click **OK**.
6. In the flyer, reselect the text **Home Page**.
7. Click **Insert Hyperlink** . Notice the dialog box is now named **Edit Hyperlink**.
8. Select the the text in the **Address** box. Key: www.homepage.html. Click **OK**.
9. CHECK Your screen should look like Figure 6.18. Save your **Combined** file.

Continue to the next exercise.

Troubleshooting Explain to students that Word automatically inserts the **http://** when they key a Web address. Have students double-check their Web addresses before clicking **OK** in the **Insert Hyperlink** dialog box to make sure parts of it have not been duplicated by **Auto Complete**.

EXERCISE 6-8
Insert and Edit a Hyperlink to a Web Page

You can use hyperlinks to link a document to one or more Web pages. Hyperlinks help your readers get more information. Remember to check your hyperlinks regularly, because Web page addresses change frequently.

Teaching Tip Explain to students that display text can be more descriptive than a Web address.

FIGURE 6.17 Insert Hyperlink dialog box

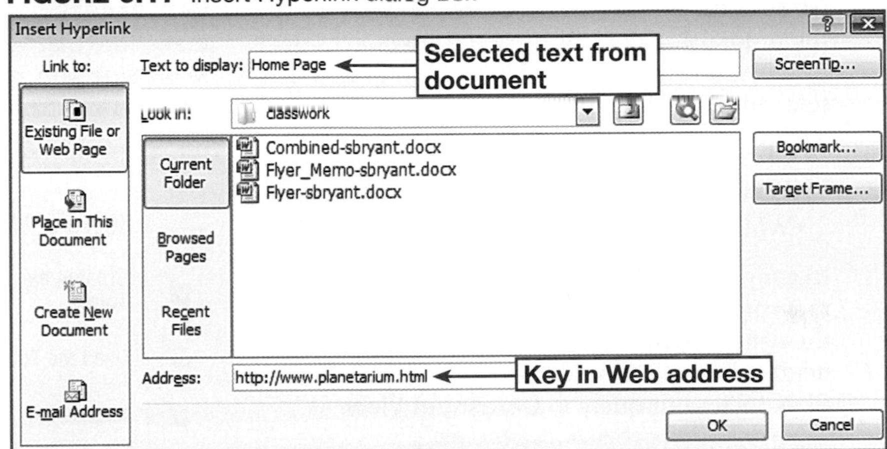

FIGURE 6.18 Edited hyperlink to a Web page

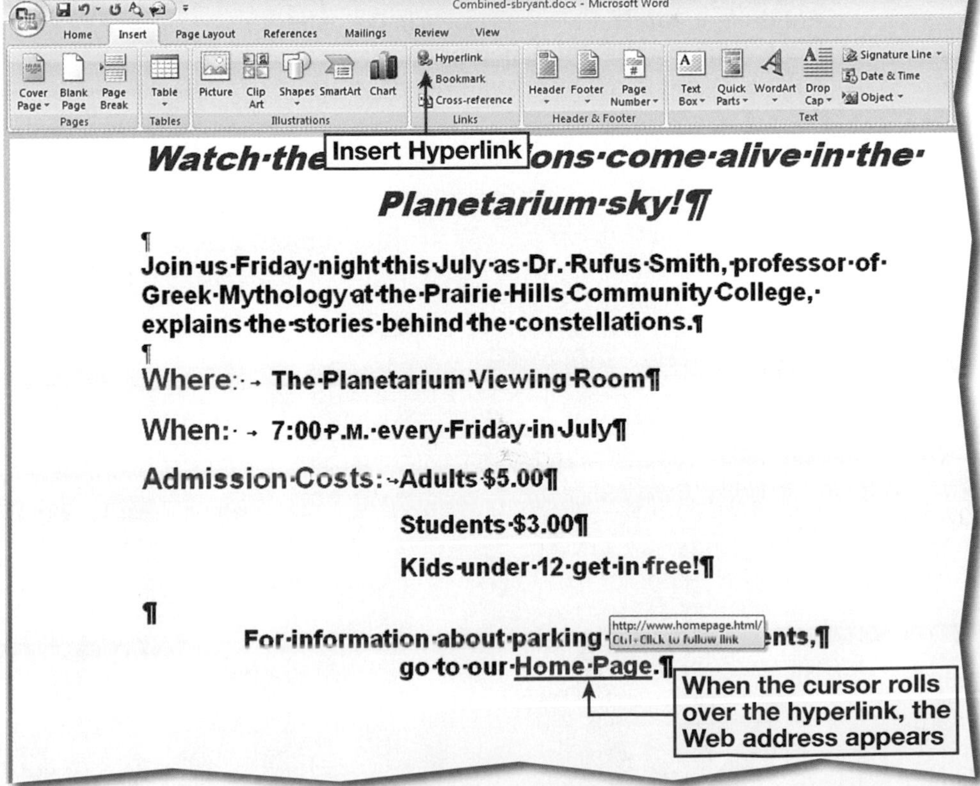

Portfolio Project

Part 2: Create Queries

LEVEL This is an intermediate level project.

Goal The student council has collected all of the fundraising data. You need to organize your data by the number of students per grade and the total amount raised per grade.

Create Create queries to find the following:

- Which grades have the most students.
- Which grades raised the most money.

In your **BakeSale** database, use the **Totals** table to create a query in **Design View**. Include all of the fields in your query. Sort the **TotalStudents** field in descending order. Save the query as: **Class Size**. View your query in **Datasheet View**.

Create a second query in **Design View**. Use the **Totals** table to create the query. Include all of the fields in your query. Sort the **AmountRaised** field in descending order. Save the query as: **Fundraiser Totals**. View your query in **Datasheet View**. With your teacher's permission, print your Class Size and Fundraiser Totals queries.

Self Assess Use the Have You...? checklist to make sure that you created the queries correctly. Make sure you have completed all of the items noted in the Checklist.

When finished, proceed to Part 3.

	Have You...?
✓	Created two queries: **Class Size** and **Fundraiser Totals**
✓	Used the **Totals** table to create both queries
✓	Included all of the fields in your queries
✓	Sorted in descending order the **TotalStudents** field in the **Class Size** query
✓	Sorted in descending order the **AmountRaised** field in the **Fundraiser Totals** query

Solution The solution file for this project is the **Fundraiser Totals** query in the **BakeSale-SF.accdb** database file.

Step-By-Step

1. In your **Combined** file, choose **Page Layout> Page Background**. Click the **Page Color** drop-down menu and choose **Fill Effects**.
2. In the **Fill Effects** dialog box, click the **Gradient** tab. Choose **Two Colors**. Choose **White** for **Color 1**. Choose **Aqua, Accent 5, Lighter 60%** for **Color 2**.
3. **CHECK** Your dialog box should look like Figure 6.19. Click **OK**.
4. Choose **View>Document Views>Web Layout View**.
5. **CHECK** Your screen should look similar to Figure 6.20.
6. Save your **Flyer** file.

Continue to the next exercise.

You Should Know

When applying a background to a document, you should be aware of readability. Avoid choosing a textured or patterned background that will make the words on your page difficult to read.

Solution Use the file **Combined-SF.docx** as a solution file for Exercises 6-5 through 6-9.

EXERCISE 6-9
Preview a Web Page for Publication

You can use Word to create a **Web page**. Word's **Web Layout View** lets you see how your document will look as a Web page. Applying a **background** to your document will help add visual interest to your Web page.

FIGURE 6.19 Fill Effects dialog box

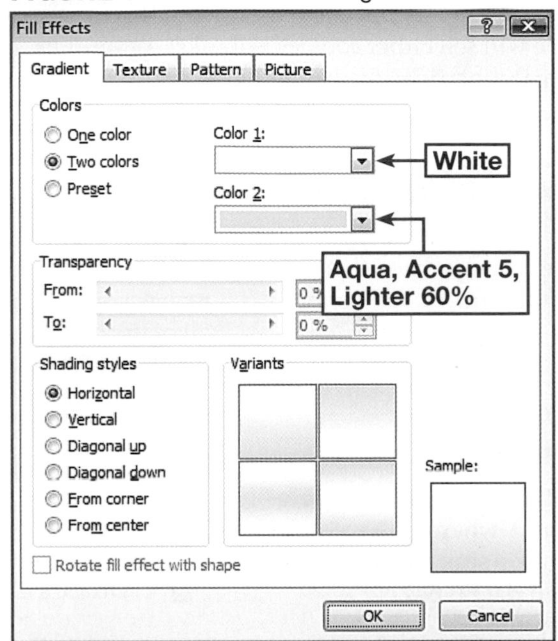

FIGURE 6.20 File as it would appear in a Web browser

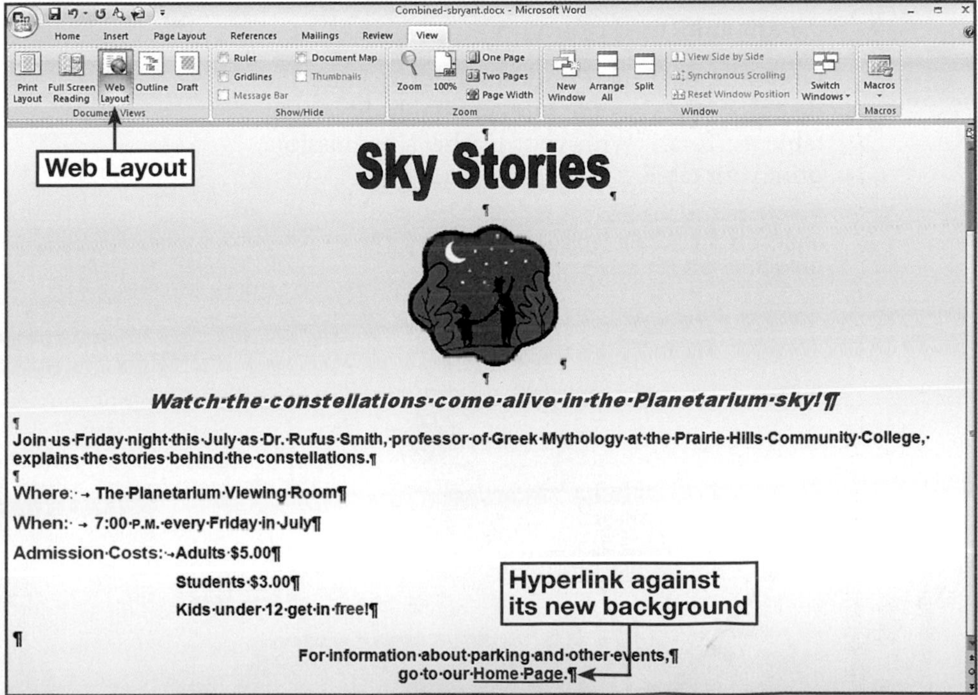

UNIT 3 Portfolio Project

School Fundraiser

Your school needs to raise money to buy new books for the school library. You and the other members of the student council decide to hold a school-wide bake sale. Each grade will sell either cookies, cupcakes, or muffins. In order to motivate students to participate, you will give first, second, and third place prizes to the three grades that raise the most money.

Answers Rubrics for each part of the Portfolio Project are available at **glencoe.com.** You may want to download the rubrics and make them available to students as they complete each project.

Part 1: Create a Table

LEVEL This is a beginning level project.

Goal You need to create a database that will store the following information:

- Grade level
- Which product this grade sold
- Number of students in each grade
- Total amount raised per grade

Create Create a database named **BakeSale.** Ask your teacher how and where to save your database. Create a table in **Design View**. Add the following field names and data types:

- Grade (AutoNumber)
- Product (Text)
- TotalStudents (Number)
- AmountRaised (Currency)

Open the data file **Fundraiser.docx**. Enter the data from the data file into your table. Save your table as: Totals. With your teacher's permission, print your table.

Solution The solution file for this project is the **Totals** table in the **BakeSale-SF.accdb** database.

Self Assess Use the Have You...? checklist to review your table. Make sure you have completed all of the items noted in the checklist. Use **Design View** and **Datasheet View** to check your work.

When finished, proceed to Part 2.

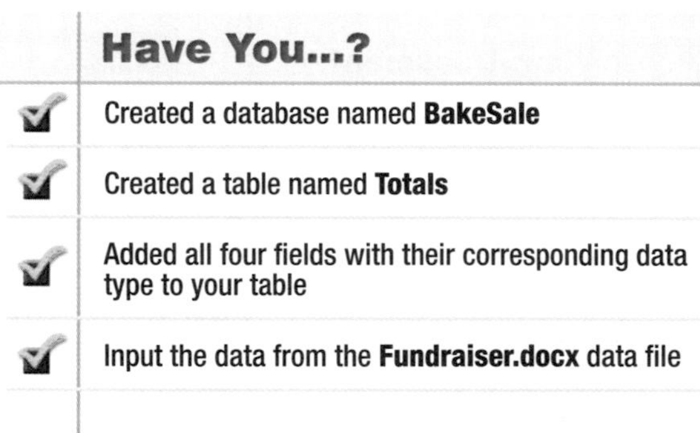

	Have You...?
✓	Created a database named **BakeSale**
✓	Created a table named **Totals**
✓	Added all four fields with their corresponding data type to your table
✓	Input the data from the **Fundraiser.docx** data file

Step-By-Step

1 In your **Combined** file, choose **Office>Save As**.

2 In the **Save As** dialog box, click **New Folder**.

3 In the **Name** box, key: New. Click outside the box.

4 Click **Back to**. Select the **New** folder.

5 Click the **Organize** drop-down arrow. Select **Rename** (see Figure 6.21).

6 Key: Lesson 6-[your first initial and last name]. Deselect the folder.

7 **CHECK** Your screen should look like Figure 6.22.

8 Click **Cancel**. Save your **Combined** file.

Continue to the next exercise.

Tech Tip

You can delete selected files and folders in the **Save As** dialog box by selecting the file or folder and clicking the **Organize** drop-down arrow. Choose **Delete**.

Different Strokes Tell students that they can also rename a folder by right-clicking the folder name and selecting **Rename**.

Troubleshooting Students using Windows XP may refer to pages li-liii about any differences they see in the **Save As** dialog box.

EXERCISE 6-10
Rename a Folder

If a folder name does not reflect the information in the folder, you may decide to rename it. You can rename a folder so that it describes its contents more accurately and makes it easier for you to locate information.

Step-By-Step Tip In **Step 4**, the **Back to Documents** button may have a different name depending on the file structure your students are using. The ScreenTip inserts the name of the previous folder after the words Back to.

FIGURE 6.21 Rename option in Save As dialog box

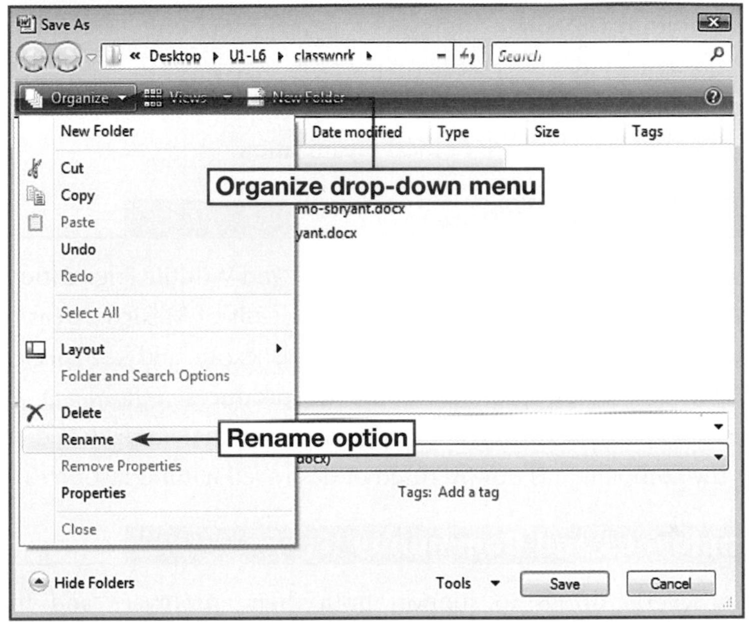

FIGURE 6.22 Renamed folder

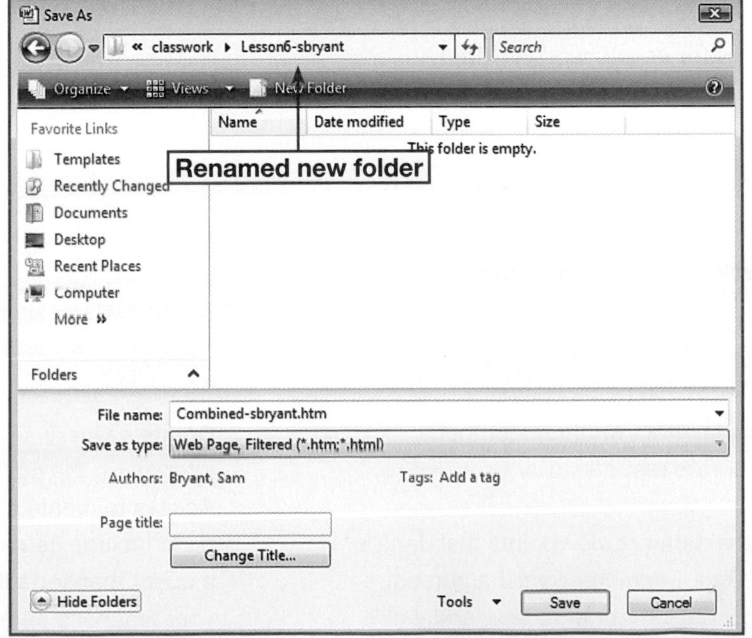

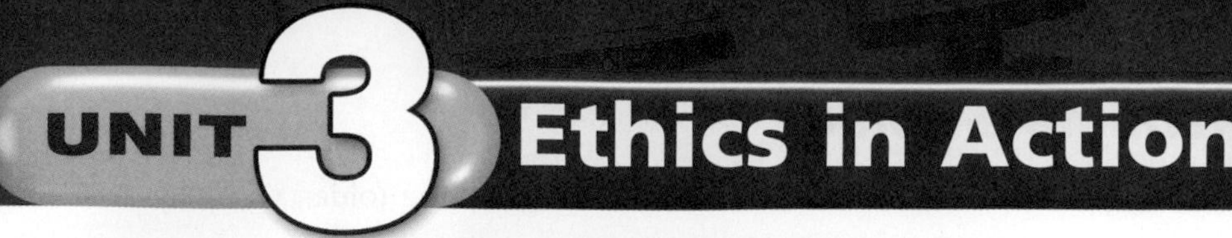

Corporate Responsibility

The ethical climate of a company is a reflection of the ethics of its owners and managers. Just as people have a responsibility to treat others in an ethical manner, companies have a responsibility to deal ethically with their employees and their community. The ethical policy of many corporations includes the practice of giving back to those in need. These companies may spend large amounts of money on socially responsible programs, such as those that help support the environment or local organization.

Support the Environment

A major oil company, in cooperation with the National Fish and Wildlife Foundation, has created a marine habitat conservation program for the Gulf of Mexico. Areas of focus are barrier island protection, coral reefs, marine debris, exotic and key species, and wetlands. A paper and forest products company produces a *Roadmap for Sustainability* report, which assesses the company's environmental impact and its efforts to ensure that the company has not overused or destroyed natural resources.

Support the Employees and Community

Many companies do several things to support both their employees and the community, such as the following:

- Allow employees to donate their vacation time to other employees with serious illnesses.
- Offer scholarships for employees' children.
- Give time off to employees to volunteer after a natural disaster.
- Match employee contributions to charitable organizations.
- Provide services to community projects.

These and other actions help demonstrate to the general public that companies care about their employees and their communities.

CASE STUDY

Janelle and Mark are shopping for furniture for their new home. They are on a tight budget and want to get the most value for their dollar. Mark wants to buy a living room suite for $1,500 from a discount furniture company. Janelle wants to buy a similar suite from a different furniture company. While this suite costs $2,250, Janelle likes the fact that the company has been recognized as a "best company" for how it treats employees and for its forestry replanting program. Mark also likes the company, but is not sure he wants to spend the extra money to buy its furniture.

See page TM77 for answers to You Decide and Application Activity.

YOU DECIDE

1. **Recall** How does Janelle's furniture company demonstrate corporate responsibility?

2. **Decide** Explain the different viewpoints that Janelle and Mark have taken. Each has a valid argument. Which argument seems stronger to you, and why?

APPLICATION ACTIVITY

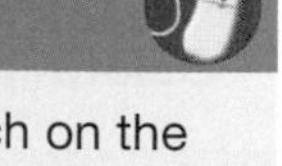

3. **Create a Query** Do some preliminary research on the Internet on the costs for public landscaping. Then, use Access to create a table of expenses for building a park. Include items such as labor and materials. Create a query that sorts the costs in ascending order. With your teacher's permission, print your query.

EXERCISE 6-11
Save a Document as a Web Page

Hypertext Markup Language (HTML) is the code used to create Web pages. If you want to post a document to a Web site, you must save it with the extension .htm or .html so that it can be opened with a **Web browser**.

FIGURE 6.23 Save As dialog box

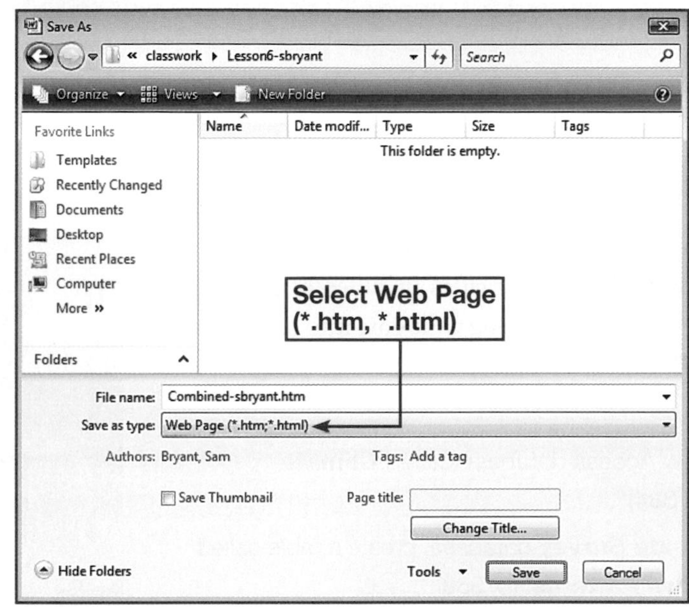

FIGURE 6.24 Flyer with new extension

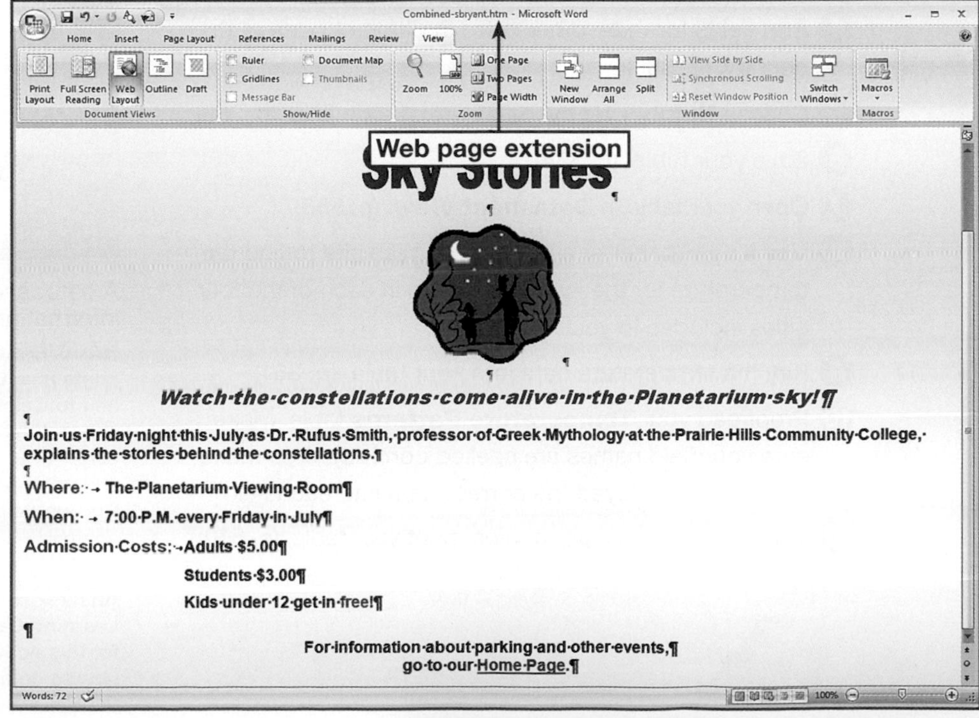

Step-By-Step

1. In your **Combined** file, choose **Office>Save As**.
2. In the **Save As** dialog box, in the **Save in** box, browse to your new **Lesson 6** folder.
3. Click the folder. Click **Open**.
4. Click the **Save as type** drop-down arrow. Choose **Web Page (*.htm; *.html)**.
5. **CHECK** Your dialog box should look like Figure 6.23. Click **Save**.
6. If a warning box opens, click **Continue**.
7. **CHECK** Your screen should look like Figure 6.24.
8. Save and close your file.

Continue to the next exercise.

Academic Skills

The audience for a Web page is different than the audience for an academic report. Online content should be short and to the point, with clickable graphical elements.

NCLB/Language Arts (NCTE 12) Students should customize the content in their Web pages to meet the expectations of an online audience.

Solution Use the file **Combined-SF.html** and its associated files in the folder **Combined-sbryant_files** as a solution file for Exercises 6-10 and 6-11.

Academic Connections

SCIENCE | SOCIAL STUDIES | LANGUAGE ARTS | MATH

In this activity, you will use your Access knowledge to record weather data.

Rubric R

Keep Track of the Temperature

You are part of a team of scientists that is comparing temperature patterns in your city with three other cities in different parts of the country. You decide to start inputting your data into an Access table so that you will be able to create reports and queries quickly and easily.

1. Create a new Access database called **Climate Survey**. (p. 384)
2. In your **Climate Survey** database, create a table called **Temperature Patterns**. (p. 386)
3. In your **Temperature Patterns** table, add a field for your city. (p. 386)
4. Add fields for three other cities in different parts of the country. (p. 386)
5. Choose **Number** for the data type of each field. (p. 386)
6. Save your table. (p. 364)
7. Open your table in **Datasheet View**. (p. 356)
8. Use a newspaper or a newspaper Web site to find the temperature for the last seven days in each of the four cities included in your table.
9. Key the temperature data into your table. (p. 361)
10. Proofread your **Temperature Patterns** table. Make sure your field names are spelled correctly. Also make sure you have keyed the correct data into each field.
11. With your teacher's permission, print your table. (p. 510)

A database can help you keep track of information, such as weather patterns.

NCLB/Math (Number and Operations) Show students how to convert the temperature from Fahrenheit to Celsius. For example, if it is 75 degrees Fahrenheit, the conversion looks like this: $75 - 32 = 43$. $43/9 = 4.8$. $4.8 \times 5 = 24$ degrees Celsius. Students should enter the converted temperatures into a new Celsius field in their tables.

Answer to Academic Connections Go to the Online Learning Center at **glencoe.com** to access the rubric for this activity. If students need help remembering how to complete specific skills, have them turn to the page number listed after selected steps.

Step-By-Step

1. Open the data file **Notice. docx**. Save as: Notice-[your first initial and last name].
2. Choose **Page Layout> Page Setup>Dialog Box Launcher** . On the **Margins tab**, under **Orientation**, click **Landscape**.
3. On the **Paper** tab, under **Paper size**, key the **Width** as 8″ and the **Height** as 6″.
4. **CHECK** Your dialog box should look like Figure 6.25.
5. On the **Layout** tab, under **Page**, click **Vertical alignment**. Select **Center**. Click **OK**. Click **Office> Print>Print Preview**.
6. **CHECK** Your screen should look like Figure 6.26. Close **Print Preview**. Save your file.

Academic Skills

Measure the dimensions used in this exercise on a sheet of standard notebook paper.

EXERCISE 6-12
Change Page Orientation and Paper Size

Page orientation refers to whether a page is laid out vertically or horizontally. Portrait orientation is the default layout in Word. The page is taller than it is wide. To make a page wider than it is tall, you can use Page Layout to change the orientation to Landscape. You can also change the size of the paper on which a page will be printed.

NCLB/Math (Measurement) Students' marked pages should be 8″ wide and 6″ tall.

FIGURE 6.25 Page Setup dialog box

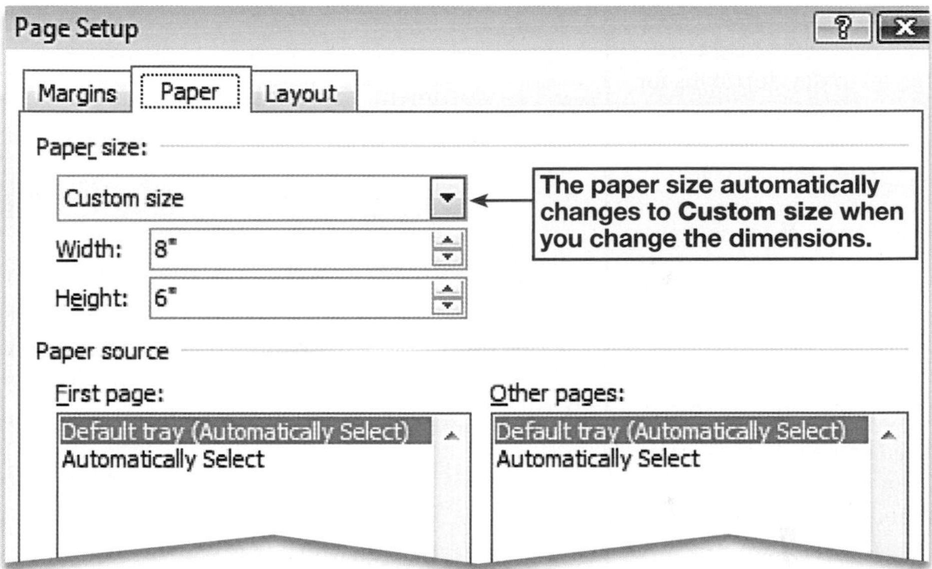

FIGURE 6.26 Document with paper size and page orientation changed

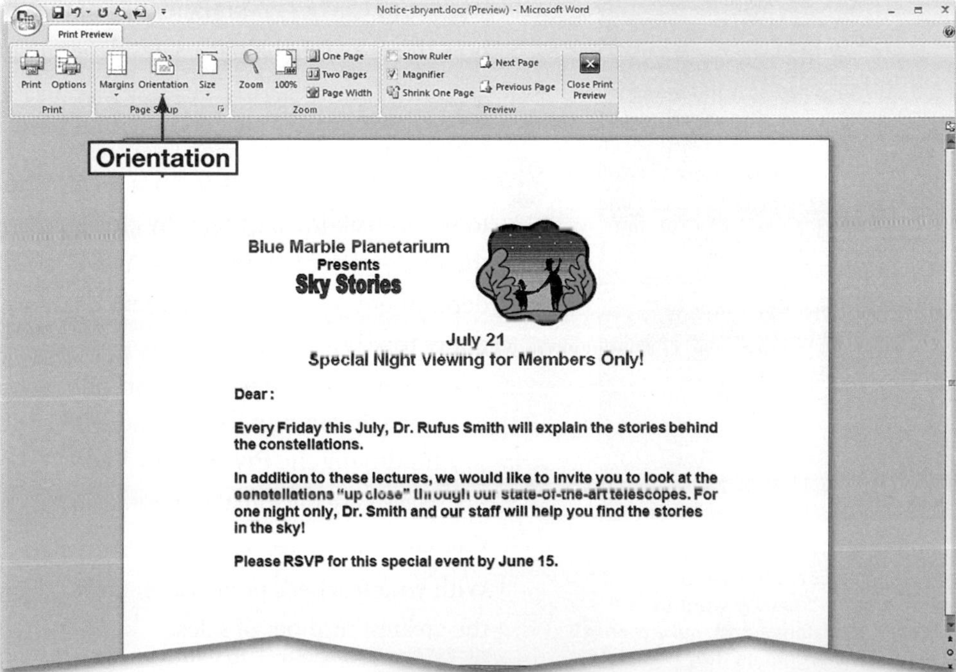

LESSON 5 Challenge Yourself Projects

Before You Begin

Documentation When you work on a project, document every step so that you have a record of what was done. That way, you or others can refer to that record later. These exercises help you to develop skills for documenting changes you make to a database.

Reflect

1. Give three reasons you might want to document your work.
2. How can documenting work help you manage your time and database?
3. List some other ways you can use Access to document the changes you make to a database.

Answers Rubrics for each Challenge Yourself Project are available at **glencoe.com**. You may want to download the rubrics and make them available to students as they complete each project.

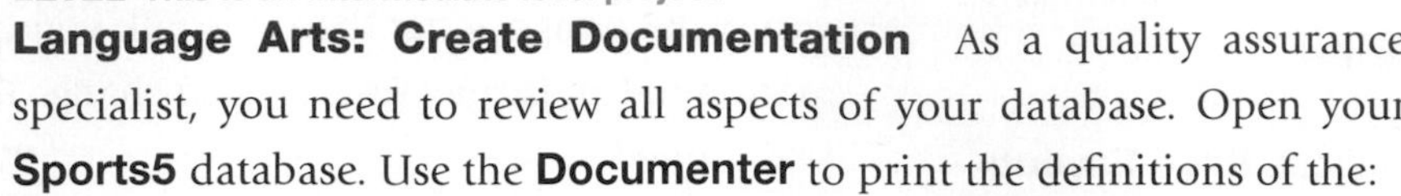

9. Document Table and Query Properties

Rubric R

LEVEL This is an intermediate level project.

Language Arts: Create Documentation As a quality assurance specialist, you need to review all aspects of your database. Open your **Sports5** database. Use the **Documenter** to print the definitions of the:

- Customer table
- Product table
- CustOrderDet query

Solution Use the printed reports as solution files for Project 9.

Write your name on each of the printed definitions. In a separate Word document, explain why you may want to preview the properties of your database objects, and how such documentation is useful to a business.

10. Track Sales by Quantity

Rubric 

LEVEL This is an intermediate level project.

Math: Modify a PivotChart The sales department would like to track sales trends with a chart that plots the quantity ordered for each product in the **Sports5** database. Open your **Sports5** database. Modify the **Order_PivotChart** query to match the sales department's request. In your PivotChart, make sure that:

Solution The solution file for Project 10 is the query **Order_PivotChart10-SF** in the database **Sports5-SF.accdb.**

- The vertical axis uses only **Sum of Quantity**.
- The horizontal axis uses only **Product Name**.
- The z-axis remains **Year**.

Save your new query as: Order_PivotChart-[your first initial and last name]10. With your teacher's permission, print the chart. In a Word document, explain how the chart will help the sales department track sales trends.

11. Track Sales by City

Rubric 

LEVEL This is an intermediate level project.

Math: Add Information to a PivotChart The sales department wants to see a breakdown of sales by city. However, **City** is not one of the fields in the **Order_PivotChart** query. You need to modify the query for the sales department. Open your **Sports5** database. Modify the **Order-PivotChart** query to:

- Add a **City** field to the PivotChart. (Hint: Open the **Order_PivotChart** query in **Design View** to add **City** to the query result before modifying the **PivotChart View**.)
- Make **City** the initial horizontal axis.

Solution The solution file for Project 11 is the query **Order_PivotChart11-SF** in the database **Sports5-SF.accdb.**

Save your new query as: Order_PivotChart-[your first initial and last name]11. With your teacher's permission, print the PivotChart. Identify which city had the greatest number of sales.

NCTM/Math (Algebra) To reinforce the importance of using charts, ask students to create their own chart in Project 11. Ask students to discuss the factors they considered when creating their chart.

Step-By-Step

1. In your **Notice** file, choose **Mailings>Start Mail Merge** .
2. Click **Step by Step Mail Merge Wizard** .
3. In the **Mail Merge** task pane, under **Select document type**, make sure **Letters** is selected. Click **Next: Starting document** (see Figure 6.27).
4. Under **Select starting document**, make sure **Use the current document** is selected. Click **Next: Select recipients**.
5. Under **Select recipients**, select **Use an existing list**. Click **Browse**.
6. In the **Select Data Source** dialog box, navigate to and open the data file **List.docx**.
7. **CHECK** Your screen should look like Figure 6.28. Click **OK**. Save your file.

Continue to the next exercise.

EL You might consider pairing English Learners with native speakers for this exercise. Working one-on-one, native speakers can help English Learners understand the material.

EXERCISE 6-13
Prepare a Mail Merge

Perform a **mail merge** to create a large mailing, such as personalized form letters. Information, such as names and addressess, may vary, or be different, from letter to letter. If the information varies, it is stored in the **data source**. The data source for a mail merge can be a Word table, an Excel spreadsheet, or an Access database. You can either use existing data or create your own data source while preparing the merge.

FIGURE 6.27 Mail Merge task pane

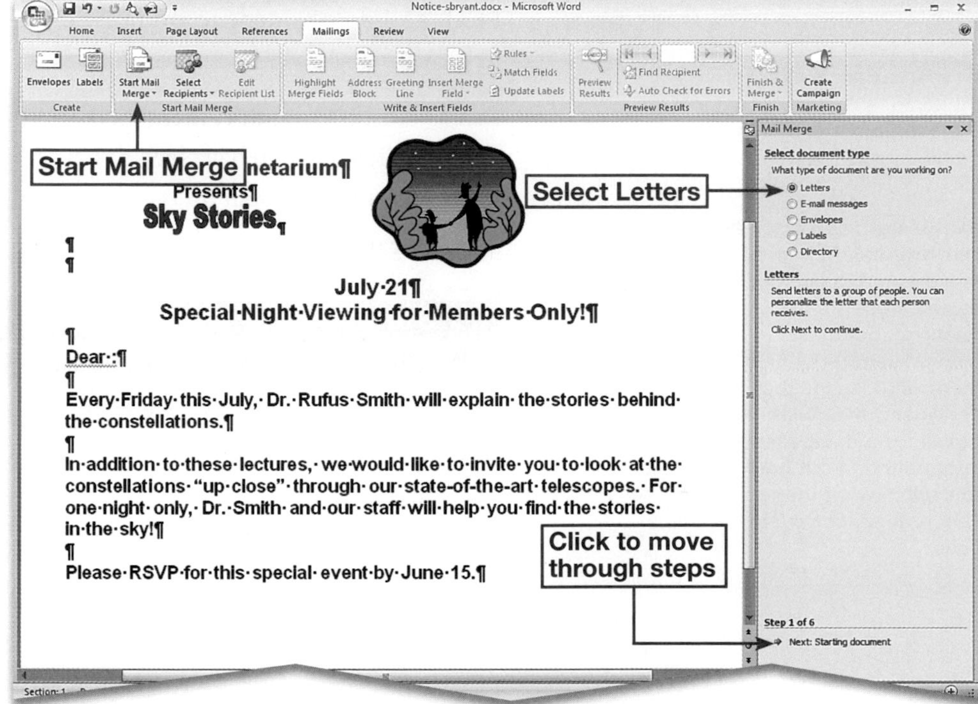

FIGURE 6.28 Mail Merge Recipients dialog box

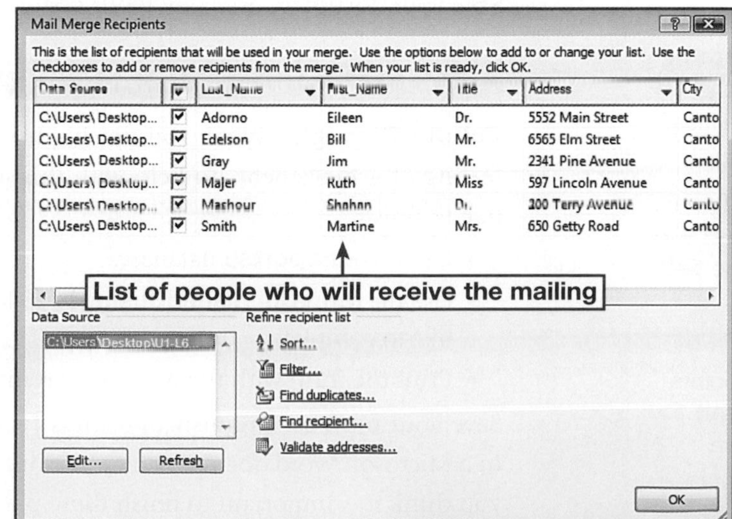

Data Source		Last_Name	First_Name	Title	Address	City
C:\Users\ Desktop...	☑	Adorno	Eileen	Dr.	5552 Main Street	Canto
C:\Users\ Desktop...	☑	Edelson	Bill	Mr.	6565 Elm Street	Canto
C:\Users\ Desktop...	☑	Gray	Jim	Mr.	2341 Pine Avenue	Canto
C:\Users\ Desktop...	☑	Majer	Ruth	Miss	597 Lincoln Avenue	Canto
C:\Users\ Desktop...	☑	Mashour	Shahan	Dr.	300 Terry Avenue	Canto
C:\Users\ Desktop...	☑	Smith	Martine	Mrs.	650 Getty Road	Canto

LESSON 5 Critical Thinking Activities

Beyond the Classroom Activity Students' lists should include six to ten dependent relationships. Answers should be similar to the examples in the text at right.

Standards at Work Activity Students' answers will vary but should conform to strong password standards.

21st Century Skills Activity Students' answers should include projects to complete and reasons to do so.

NCLB/Math (Number and Operations) Reinforce the importance of database relationships by asking students to explain how, in a relational database, relationships help prevent redundant data. Ask them what issues they would have to consider if they were designing tables for a database that will track information about books. Ask them to explain what they can do to prevent redundant data in their database.

Go Online e-REVIEW
glencoe.com

Go to the **Online Learning Center** to complete the following review activities.

Online Self Check
To test your knowledge of the material, click **Unit 3> Lesson 5** and choose **Self Checks**.

Interactive Review
To review the main points of the lesson, click **Unit 3> Lesson 5** and choose **Interactive Review**.

6. Beyond the Classroom Activity

Language Arts: Identify Dependencies In Exercise 5-9, you looked at how tables, queries, forms, and reports depend on each other. These dependencies are positive. You see dependencies around you every day. People depend on buses to get them to work and school, and bus drivers would not have a job if no one rode the bus. Bees depend on flowers for food, and flowers depend on bees to carry their pollen to other flowers to grow.

In a Microsoft Word document, make a list of six to ten positive dependent relationships that you have seen or have heard about. Explain why and how the items are dependent on each other.

Save your document as: a5rev-[your first initial and last name]6.

7. Standards at Work Activity

Microsoft Certified Application Specialist Correlation
Access 6.2 *Manage Databases*

Protect Data Keeping important information safe is a good idea for more than just Access databases. More and more passwords are required for different information transactions every day. Strong passwords are one way to ensure that your personal information stays secure.

In a Microsoft Word document, write down six examples of strong passwords. Make sure they conform to the rules of a strong password: at least eight characters combining letters, numbers, and symbols.

Save your document as: a5rev-[your first initial and last name]7.

8. 21st Century Skills Activity

Follow Through When you finish what you start, you get to enjoy the feeling of achievement. To help with this, make a list of what you would like to finish.

- Open your **Sports5** database.
- Use the form **UnfinishedBusiness** to key in some projects you would like to complete.
- Print the form with the most important projects first.

Save your form as: UnfinishedBusiness-[your first initial and last name]8. In a Microsoft Word document, key one or two paragraphs that explain why you think it is important to finish these particular projects.

Step-By-Step

1. In your **Notice** file, be sure the **Mail Merge** task pane is open.

2. In the **Mail Merge** task pane, click **Next: Write your letter**.

3. In the **Notice**, click after **Dear**, right before the colon (see Figure 6.29).

4. In the **Mail Merge** task pane, under **Write your letter**, click **More items**.

5. In the **Insert Merge Field** dialog box, under **Fields**, select **Title**. Click **Insert**. Click **Close**.

6. In the **Mail Merge** task pane, under **Write your letter**, click **More items**.

7. In the **Insert Merge Field** dialog box, under **Fields**, click **Last_Name**. Click **Insert**. Click **Close**.

8. **CHECK** Your screen should look like Figure 6.30.

Continued on the next page.

Troubleshooting Have students make sure the spacing between merge codes is correct. There should be a space between **Dear** and *Title*, and a space between the *Title* and *Last Name* fields.

EXERCISE 6-14
Perform a Mail Merge

Insert a code called a **merge field** in the **main document** to show where the unique information should go. For example, you might insert the merge field First Name to show where the first name should go in a letter.

FIGURE 6.29 Field in main document

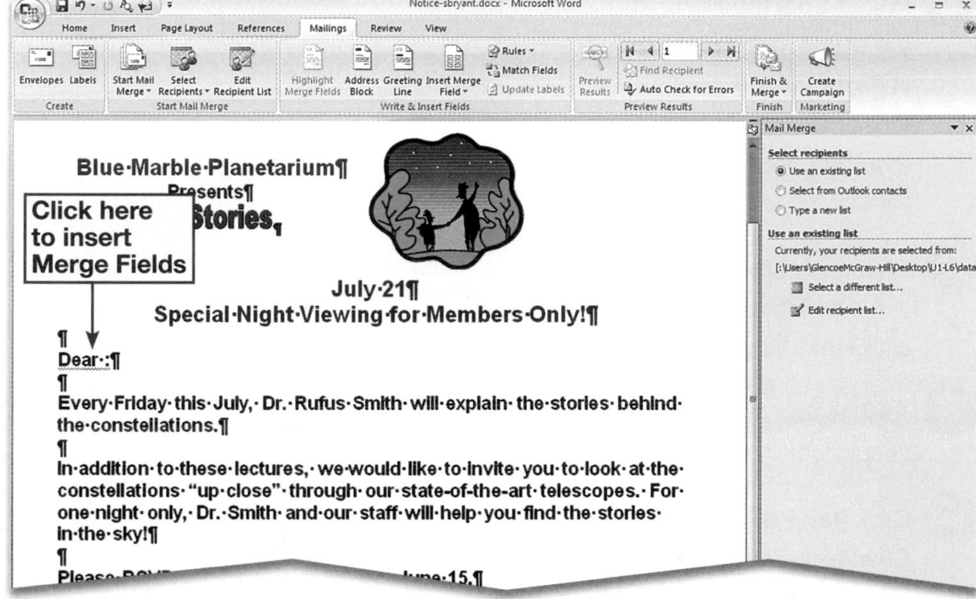

FIGURE 6.30 Notice with Title field inserted

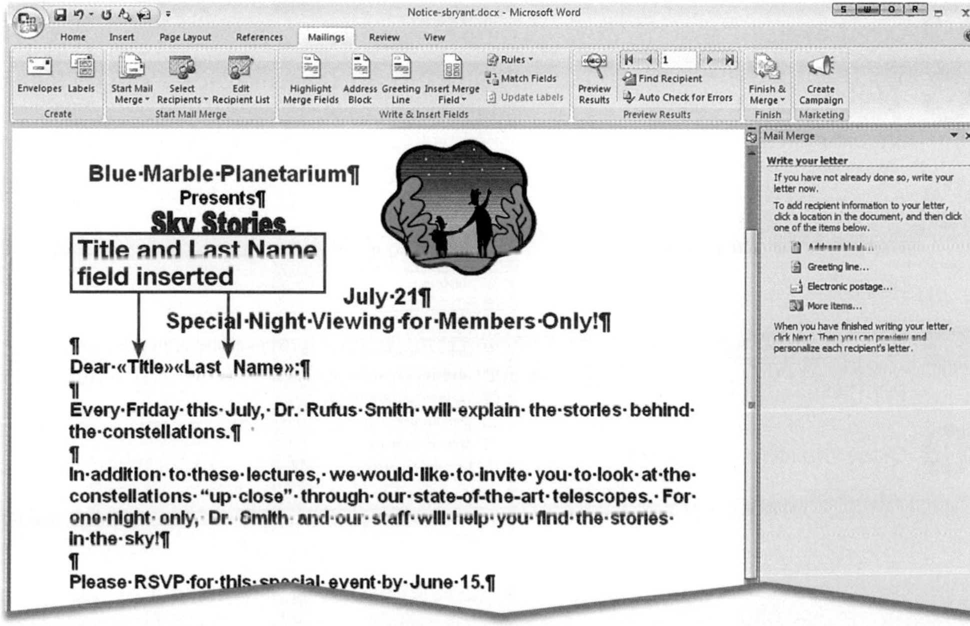

5. Print Full Forms on a Page

Step-By-Step

1. In your **Sports5** file, open the **CustomerOrders** form in **Form View**. Choose **Office>Print>Print Preview**. Maximize the window.
2. Change the **Zoom** to **75%**. In the **Navigation Pane**, click **Next Page**.
3. CHECK Your screen should look like Figure 5.39.
4. Click **Page Setup**. Change the **Top Margin** to: 2.2. Change the **Bottom Margin** to: 2.2. Click **OK**.
5. Click **Save**.
6. CHECK Your screen should look like Figure 5.40.
7. Click **Print**. Under **Print range**, enter page 1 to page 2.
8. With your teacher's permission, click **OK**.
9. Close the form. Close the database.

Solution The solution file for this activity is the **CustomerOrders** form in the **Sports5-SF.accdb** database.

You need to print forms from the Customer Order form. Since the size of a sheet of paper does not always match the form height, only part of a form may print at the bottom of a page. You decide to adjust the margins of your form in Print Preview so that each form fits on a printed page.

FIGURE 5.39 CustomerOrders with partial form at top

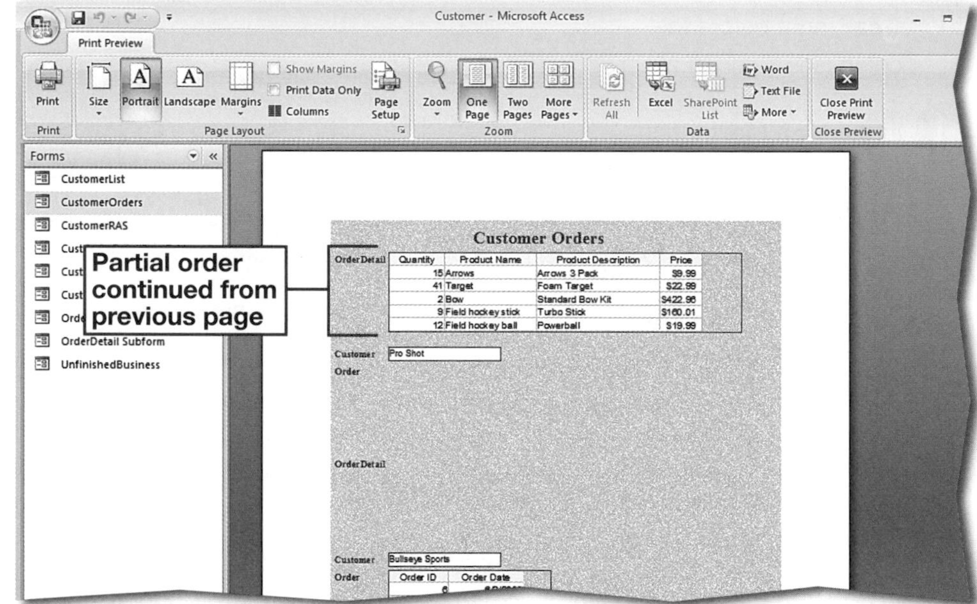

FIGURE 5.40 CustomerOrders with full form displayed

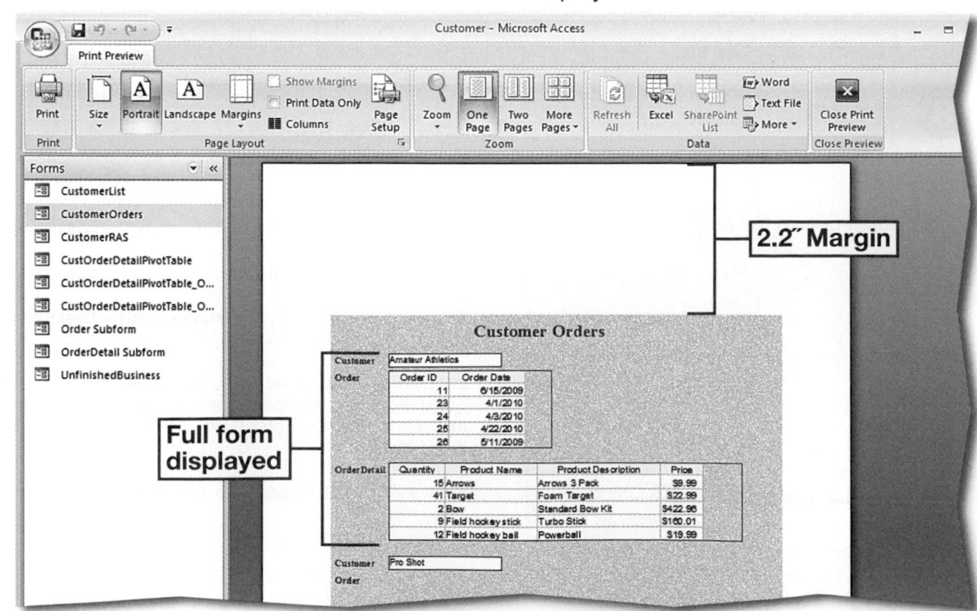

Step-By-Step

EXERCISE 6-14 (Continued)
Perform a Mail Merge

9. In the **Mail Merge** task pane, click **Next: Preview your letters**. Then click **Next: Complete the merge**.

10. CHECK Your screen should look like Figure 6.31.

11. In the task pane, under **Merge**, click **Edit individual letters**. In the **Merge to New Document** dialog box, choose **All**. Click **OK**.

12. CHECK Your screen should look like Figure 6.32. Scroll through the letters to see all of the different names in place.

13. Keep the **Letters1** file open but do not save it.

Continue immediately to the next exercise.

Academic Skills

Remember to proofread and edit your document before you complete the mail merge. If you wait until after you have completed the mail merge, you will have to make any edits to each letter.

NCLB/Language Arts (NCTE 4) Explain to students that editing the letter before they complete the merge will ensure that everyone receiving the mailing will get exactly the same information.

Solution Use the file **Notice-Landscape-SF.docx** as a solution file for Exercises 6-13 through 6-14.

FIGURE 6.31 Notice with Last_Name field inserted

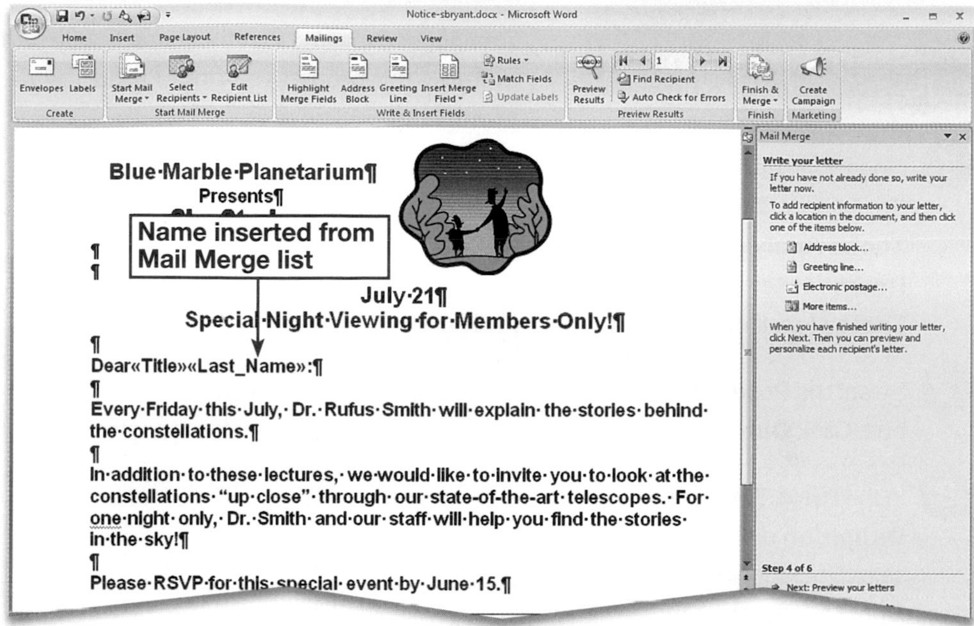

FIGURE 6.32 List of names merged with main document

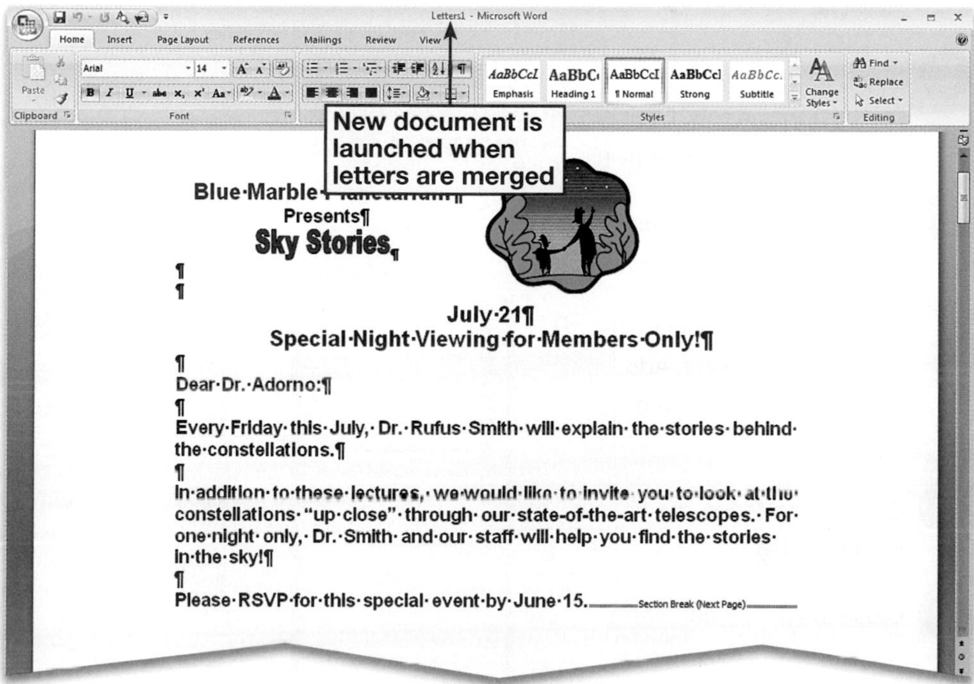

Teaching Tip You may or may not want to have students save the personalized letters. This file is large and can be recreated by merging the main document and the data source.

LESSON 5 You Try It Activities

4. Print Database Object Definitions

Step-By-Step

1. Open your **Sports5.accdb** file. Choose **Database Tools>Analyze>Database Documenter**. Click the **Tables** tab, if necessary.
2. Select the **Product** check box. Click **Options**.
3. In the **Print Table Definition** dialog box, select the options (see Figure 5.37). Click **OK**.
4. In the **Documenter** box, click **OK**.
5. Maximize the **Object Definition** window. Click in the window once to zoom in.
6. **CHECK** Your screen should look like Figure 5.38.
7. With your teacher's permission, print the report. Add your name to the printed report.
8. Click **Close Print Preview**.
9. Close the database.

Solution The solution file for this activity is **Sports5.accdb**.

Your supervisor says that the marketing department is upgrading software and needs to know the properties of the Product table. You decide to send them a printout through interoffice mail.

FIGURE 5.37 Print Table Definition dialog box

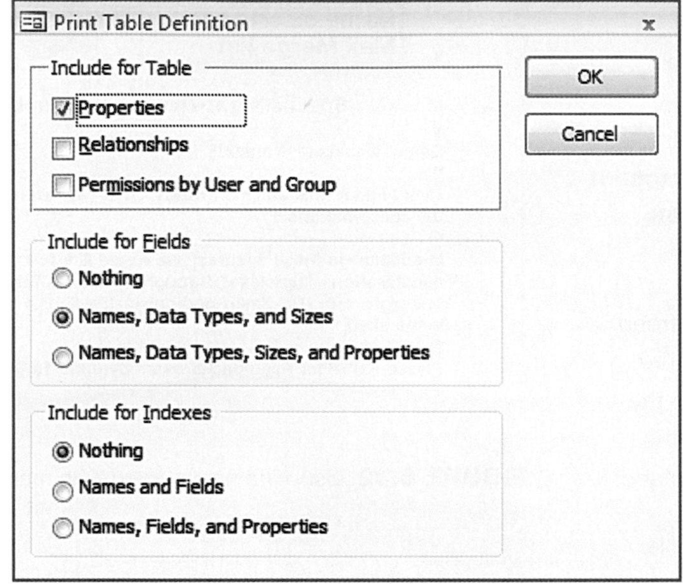

FIGURE 5.38 Object Definition window

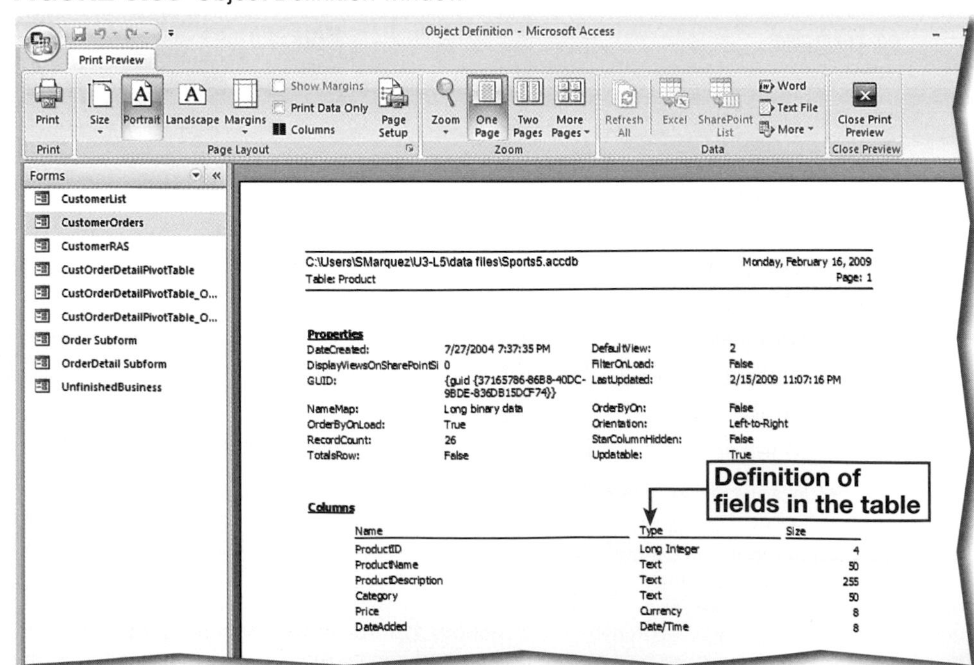

Step-By-Step

1. In your **Letters1** file, choose **Office>Print**.
2. In the **Print** dialog box, under **Page range**, click **Pages**. In the **Pages** box, key: 1-6.
3. Under **Copies**, make sure the **Number of copies** is **1**.
4. **CHECK** Your dialog box should look like Figure 6.33.
5. Click **Options**. Click **Display**. Under **Printing options**, select **Print drawings created in Word** and **Print background colors and images**.
6. Click **Advanced**. Under **Print**, make sure that **Use draft quality** and **Print in background** are selected (see Figure 6.34). Click **OK**.
7. With your teacher's permission, click **OK** to print the notices.
8. Close the **Letters1** file without saving your changes.
9. Close the **Mail Merge** task pane. Save your **Notice** file.

Continue to the next exercise.

Step-By-Step Tip In **Step 5**, explain that **Use draft quality** prints the document faster and saves toner or ink.

EXERCISE 6-15
Choose Printing Options

Printing options are changes that affect the printout of a document. Options include the print quality, order of the pages, and other items. When printing a large document such as a mail merge, you may want to use the Draft output option to save time and ink. You may also decide to print just a range of pages instead of the entire document.

FIGURE 6.33 Print dialog box

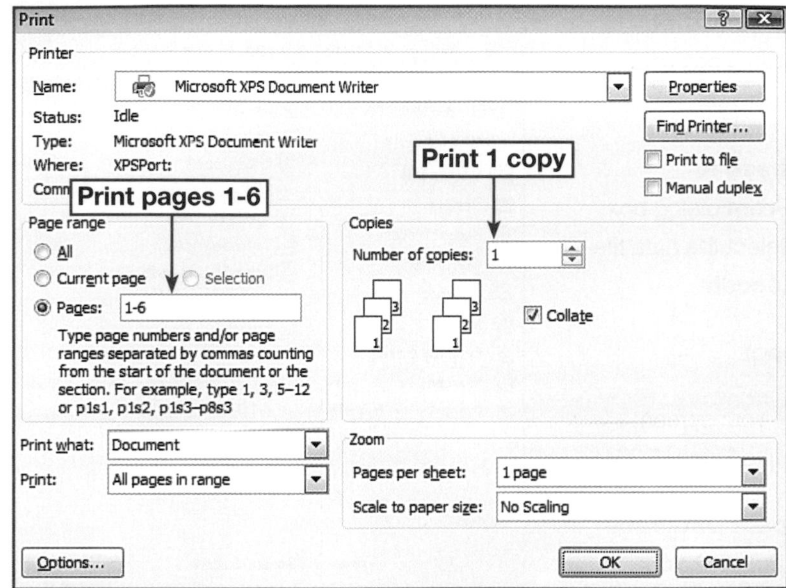

FIGURE 6.34 Print options

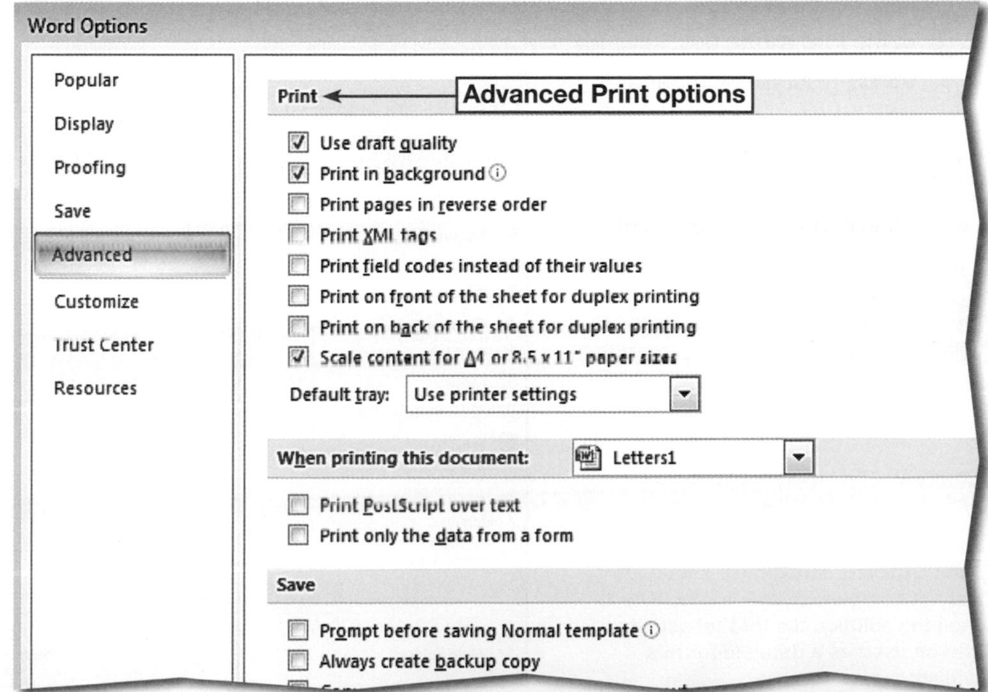

LESSON 5 Practice It Activities

3. Repair a Database

Data File

Follow the steps to complete the activity. You must complete Practice It Activity 2 before doing this activity.

Step-By-Step

1. Open your **Sports5b** database. Select **Office> Manage>Compact and Repair Database**.
2. In the **Database to Compact From** dialog box, locate and select the data file **BrokenDB.accdb**.
3. Click **Compact**.
4. CHECK Your screen should look like Figure 5.35.
5. In the **Compact Database Into** dialog box, ask your teacher where to save the file.
6. In the **File name** box, key: a5-p3-[your first initial and last name].
7. CHECK Your screen should look like Figure 5.36.
8. Click **Save**.

Solution The solution file for this activity is **a5-p3-SF.accdb**.

New Student Strategy If a student did not complete Practice It Activity 2, then the solution file for that activity can be used as a data file for this activity.

FIGURE 5.35 Database to Compact From dialog box

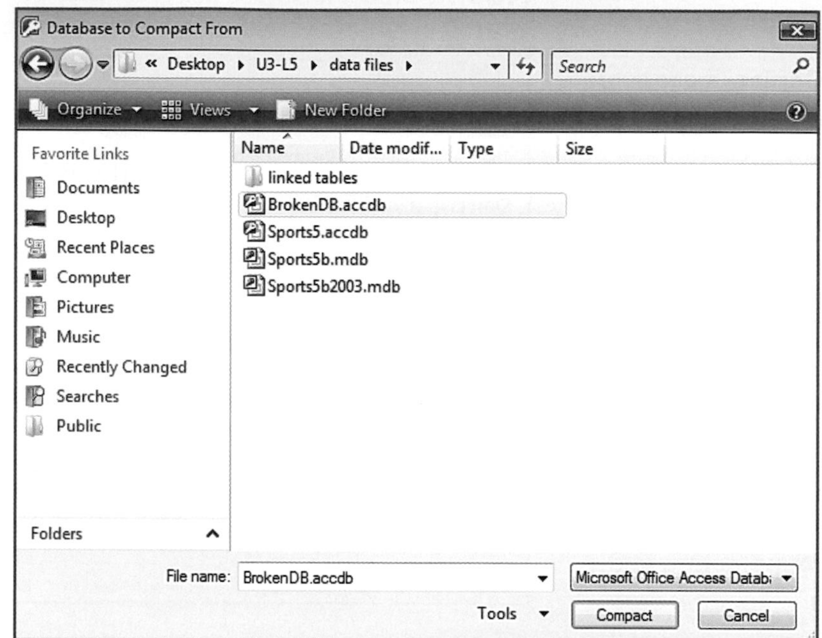

FIGURE 5.36 Compact Database Into dialog box

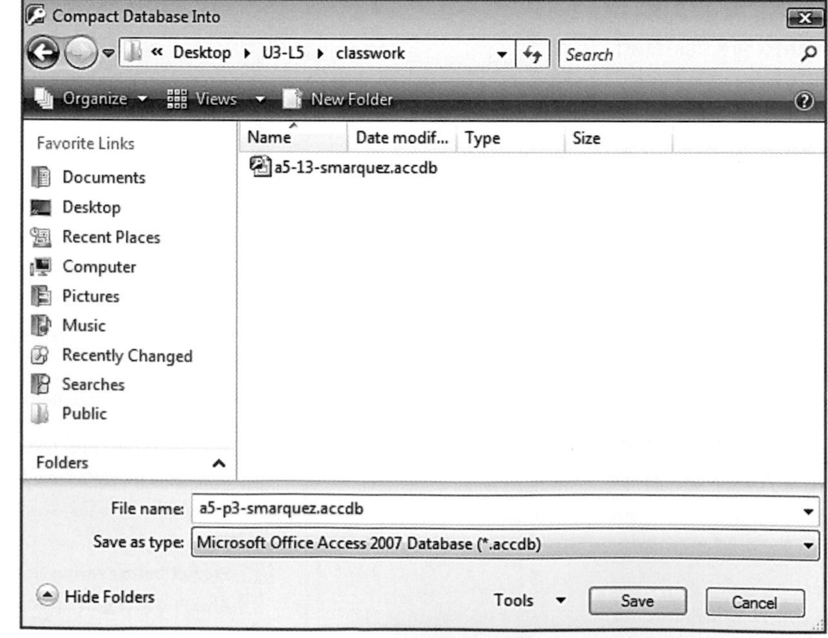

Step-By-Step

1. In your **Notice** file, choose **Mailings>Create> Labels**.
2. On the **Labels** tab, under **Address**, key the return address shown in Figure 6.35.
3. Click **Options**. In the **Label Options** dialog box, under **Label vendors**, choose **Avery US Letter**.
4. Under **Product number**, scroll to and choose **5960**.
5. Click **OK**. Click **New Document**.
6. With your teacher's permission, click **Office> Print>Print**. The **Printer** dialog box will prompt you to put a sheet of labels in the manual feeder.
7. Save the new file as: Labels-[your first initial and last name].
8. **CHECK** Your screen should look like Figure 6.36.
9. Close the **Labels** file.

Continue to the next exercise.

Teaching Tip To save labels, you might want to have the students print on plain paper for this exercise.

Step-By-Step Tip In **Step 4**, you may want to have students choose a different style of label. Students will have to scroll down a long list to get to style 5960.

EXERCISE 6-16
Create and Print Labels

When performing a mail merge, you will often have to create labels. You can create individual labels for every recipient on your mailing list. You can also create a sheet of the same mailing label to make, for example, return address labels.

Solution Use the file **Labels-SF.docx** as a solution file for this exercise.

FIGURE 6.35 Label address

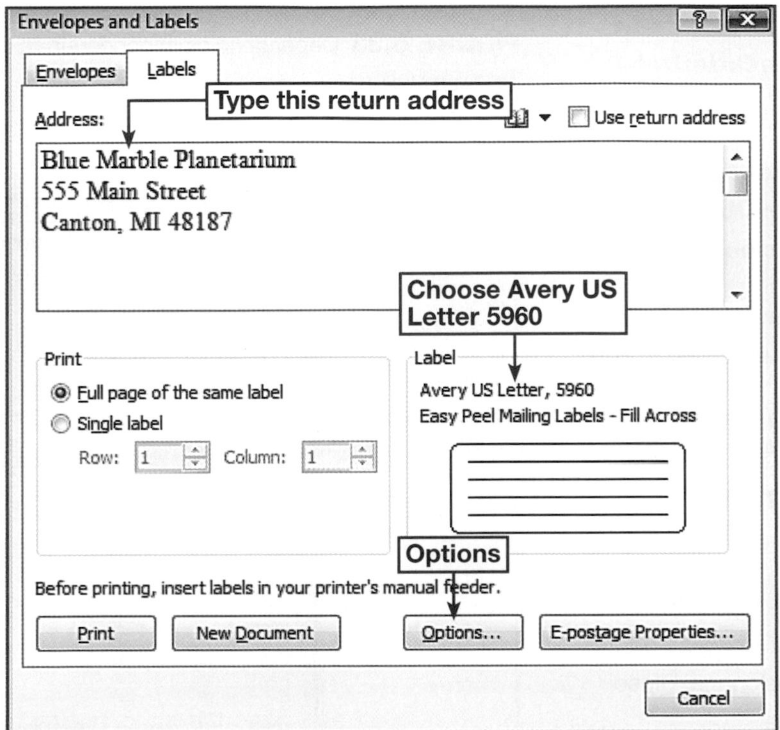

FIGURE 6.36 Print Preview of a sheet of labels

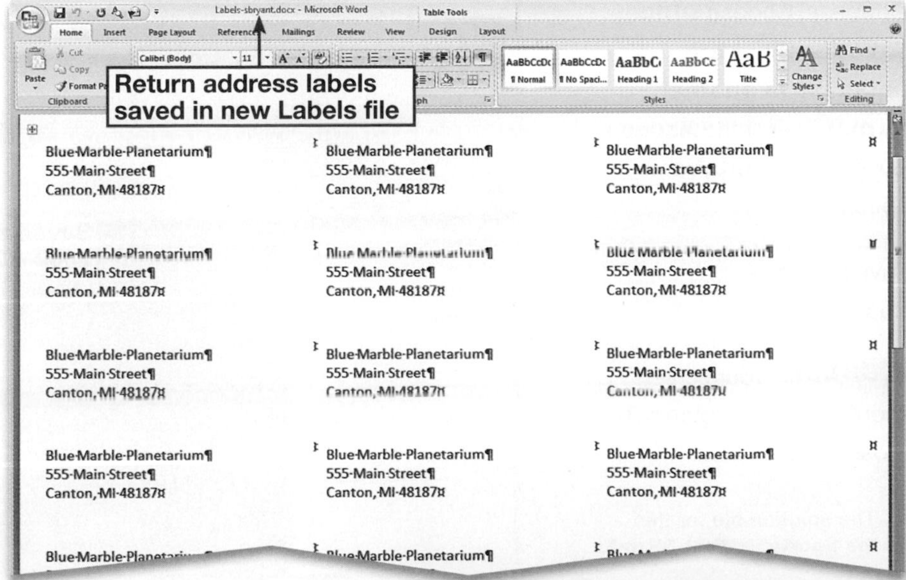

LESSON 5 Practice It Activities

2. Show Dependencies for a Table and Save Database as Previous Version

Step-By-Step

1. Open the **Sports5.accdb** file. Open the **OrderDetail** table.
2. Choose **Database Tools> Show/Hide>Object Dependencies**.
3. Click the **plus sign** next to the **Product** table.
4. Click the **plus sign** next to the **CustOrderDet** query and next to **Table: Category**.
5. **CHECK** Your screen should look like Figure 5.33. Close the task pane. Close the database.
6. Open your **Sports5b** database. Choose **Office> Save As>Save the database in another format**. Select the **Access 2002–2003 Database** option.
7. Save the file as Sports5b2003.
8. **CHECK** Your screen should look like Figure 5.34. Close the database.

Solution The solution file for this activity is the **Sports5b2003-SF.mdb** database.

Follow the steps to complete the activity. You must complete Practice It Activity 1 before doing this activity.

New Student Strategy If a student did not complete **Practice It Activity 1**, then the solution file for that activity can be used as a data file for this activity.

FIGURE 5.33 Dependencies expanded in task pane

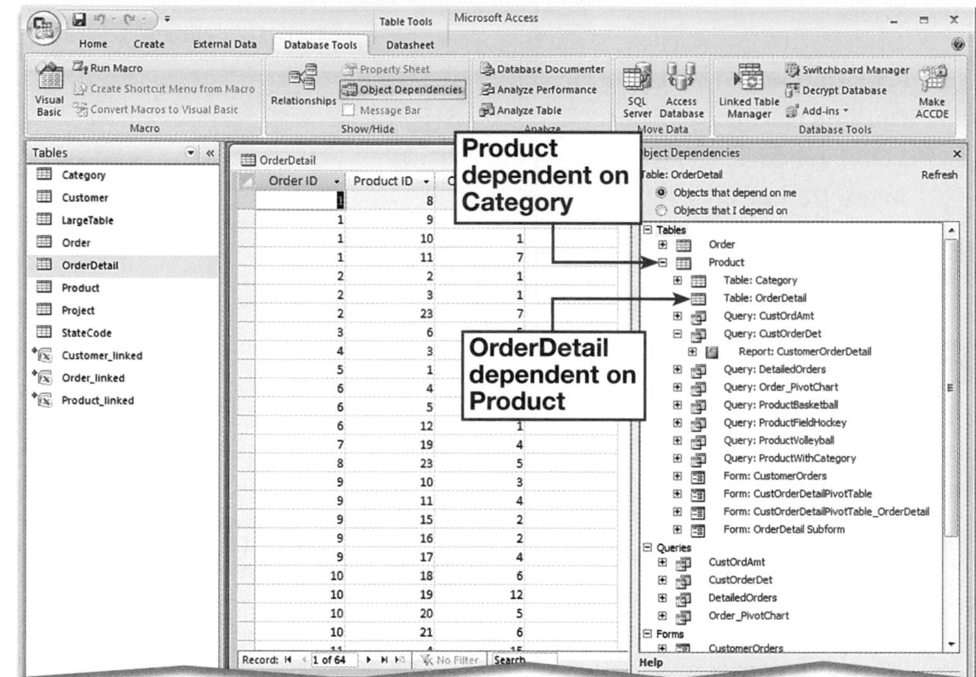

FIGURE 5.34 Database saved in Access 2002–2003 file format

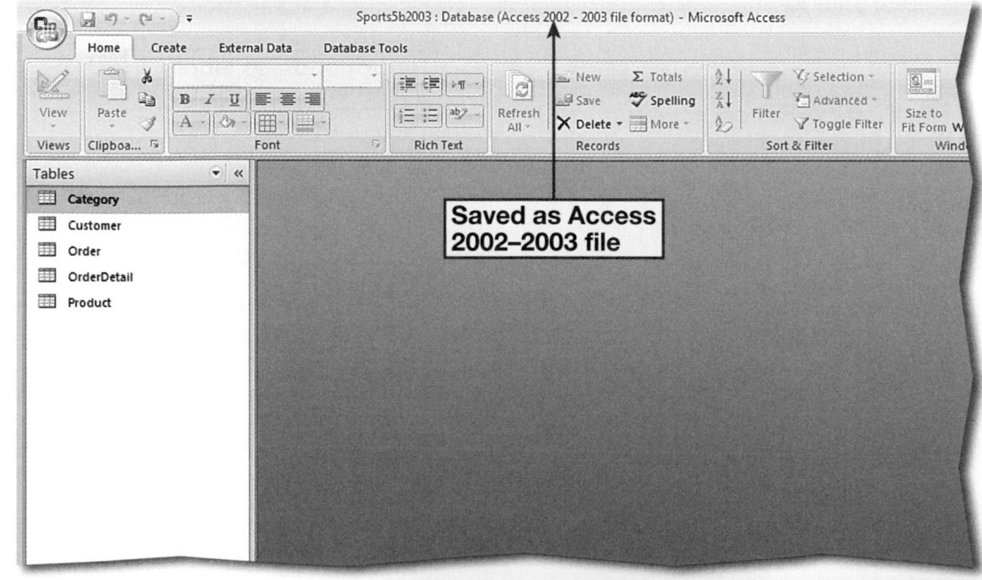

Step-By-Step

1. In your **Notice** file, choose **Office>Save As**.
2. Under **Save in**, locate your lesson folder.
3. In the **Save as type** drop-down list, choose **Word 97-2003 (*.doc)** (see Figure 6.37). Click **Save**.
4. **CHECK** Your screen should look like Figure 6.38.
5. Choose **Office>Save As**.
6. In the **Save as type** drop-down list, choose **Rich Text Format (*.rtf)**. Click **Save**. Click **Continue**.
7. Save and close your .docx, .doc, and .rtf files.

Continue to the next exercise.

Microsoft Office 2007

When you save a file as a Word 97-2003 document (.doc), the words Compatibility Mode appear on the title bar. Such files are compatible with earlier versions of the software, but are not capable of supporting some new Office 2007 features.

Differentiated Instruction/ Advanced Students Ask students if they can identify any other file extensions that they know.

Teaching Tip Point out to students that .rtf appears after the document's name in the **Title** bar.

EXERCISE 6-17
Convert Documents to Different Formats

When you save a Word document, it has the file extension .docx. Sometimes, you might need to save a document in a different format so it can be used by an earlier version of Word. Other times, you might want to save a file as an RTF, or Rich Text Format, file. You might do this if you do not know what word processing program the person receiving the file uses.

Solution Use the file **Notice-SF.doc** and **Notice-SF.rtf** as solution files for this exercise.

FIGURE 6.07 Save As dialog box

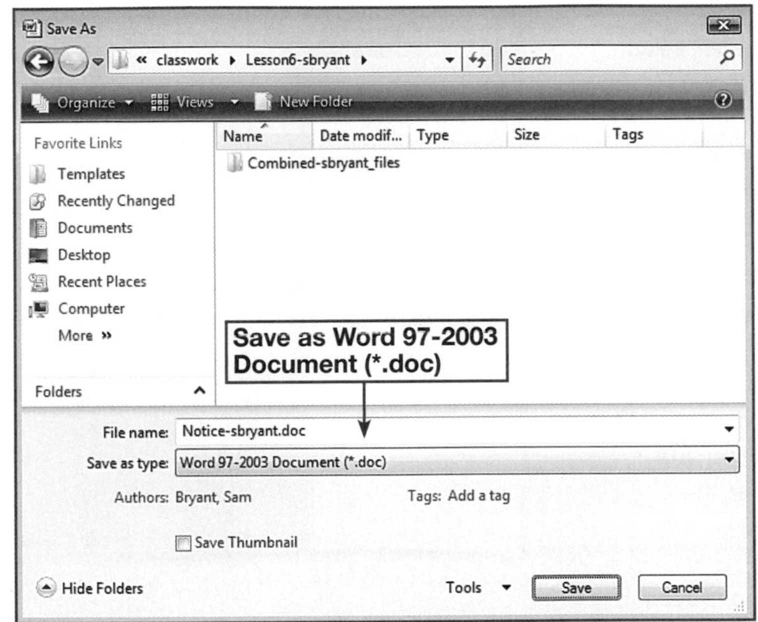

FIGURE 6.38 Document saved in Word 97-2003 format

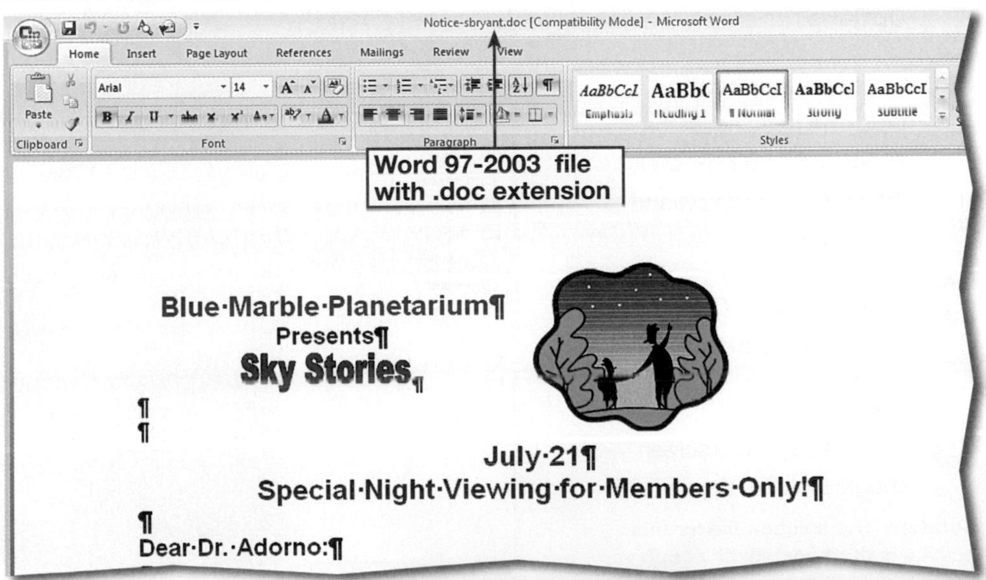

LESSON 5 Practice It Activities

1. Configure Database Options

Follow the steps to complete the activity.

Step-By-Step Tip In **Steps 1**, **4**, and **7**, students will be prompted to enter their password. Remind them that the password is case-sensitive.

Step-By-Step

1. Open your **Sports5.accdb** database. Choose **Office> Access Options**.
2. In the categories list, select **Current Database**.
3. Under the **Application Options** heading, in the **Display Form** box, click the drop-down arrow and select **CustomerRAS**.
4. Click **OK** in the **Access Options** window. Click **OK** in the confirmation box. Close and reopen the **Sports5** database.
5. **CHECK** Your screen should look like Figure 5.31. Choose **Office>Access Options**.
6. Under the **Application Options** heading, in the **Display Form** box, click the drop-down arrow and select **(none)**.
7. Click **OK** twice. Close and reopen the **Sports5** database.
8. **CHECK** Your screen should look like Figure 5.32.

Solution The solution file for this activity is the **Sports5-SF.accdb** database.

FIGURE 5.31 Database with CustomerRAS form initialized

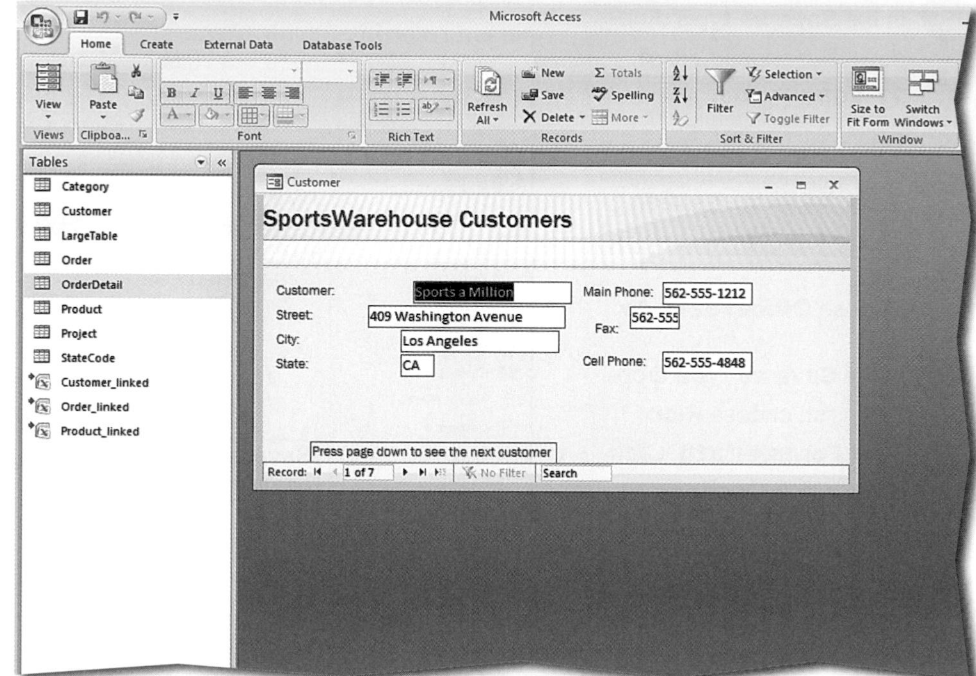

FIGURE 5.32 Database with no form initialized

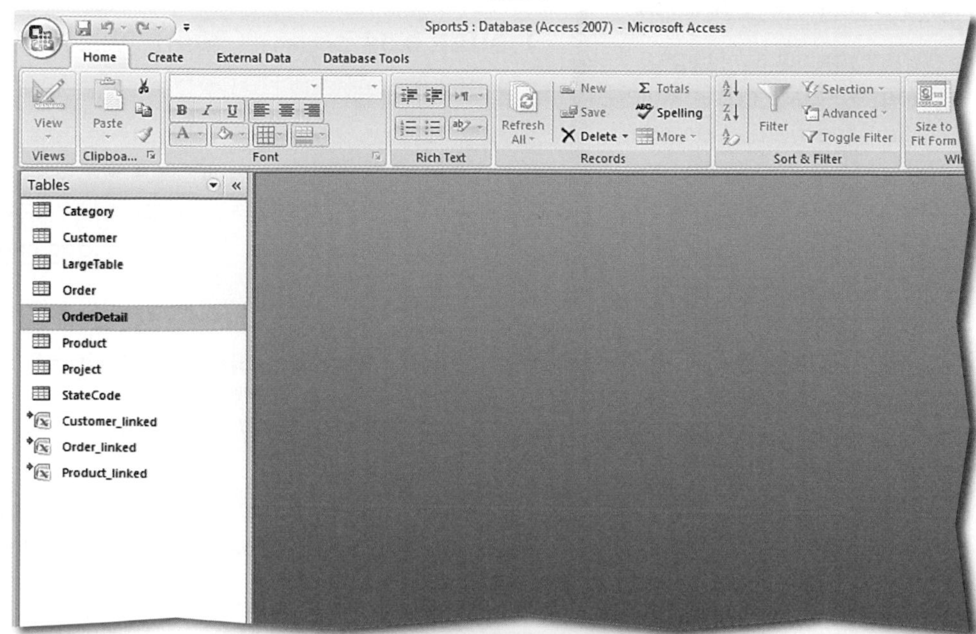

Step-By-Step

1 Choose **Office>New>Blank Document**. Click **Create**. Save the document as: Letterhead-[your first initial and last name].

2 Choose **Page Layout>Page Setup>Dialog Box Launcher**. On the **Margin** tab, change the top margin to **.5″**. Click **OK**.

3 Choose **Insert>Picture**. In the **Insert Picture** dialog box, locate the data file **circle.wmf**. Click **Insert**.

4 Select the shape. Choose **Home>Paragraph>Center** .

5 CHECK Your screen should look like Figure 6.39.

6 On the **Picture Tools** contextual tab, select **Format>Size>Dialog Box Launcher**.

7 Change the **Height** and **Width** to **.6″**. Press ENTER.

8 Click to the right of the shape. Press ENTER. Key the name and address as shown in Figure 6.40. Format the text as shown in Figure 6.40.

9 CHECK Your screen should look like Figure 6.40.

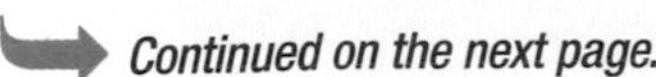
Continued on the next page.

EXERCISE 6-18
Create Personal Letterhead

One easy way to personalize your correspondence is to create your own letterhead. Letterhead typically contains the sender's name, address, and phone number. The letterhead can also contain an e-mail address and the address of a Web site. Letterhead should take up the top two inches of the page. Use a different font, and increase the size. The font size of the name should be larger than the rest of the text in the address.

FIGURE 6.39 The Circle shape

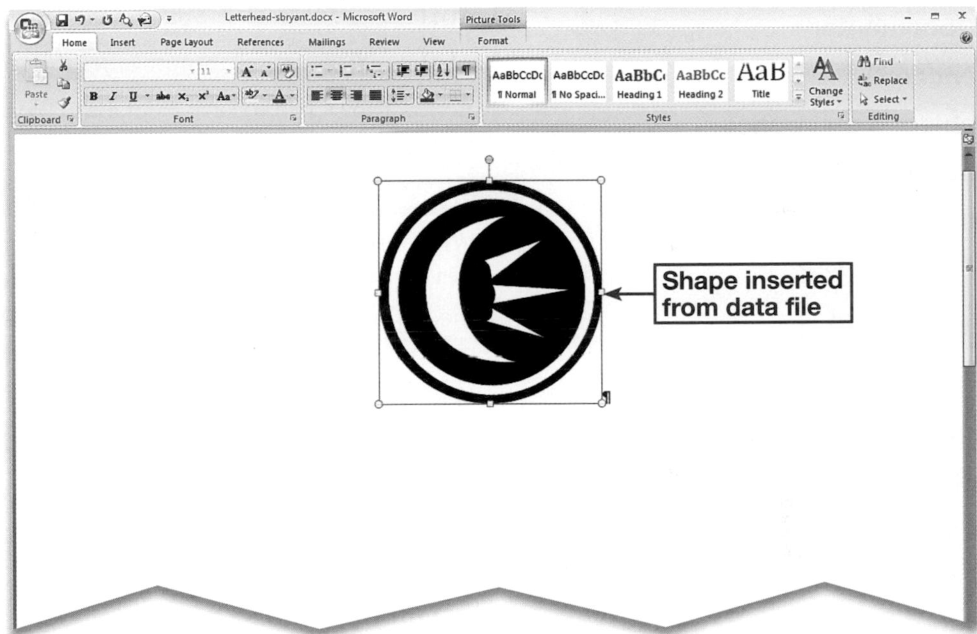

FIGURE 6.40 Return address

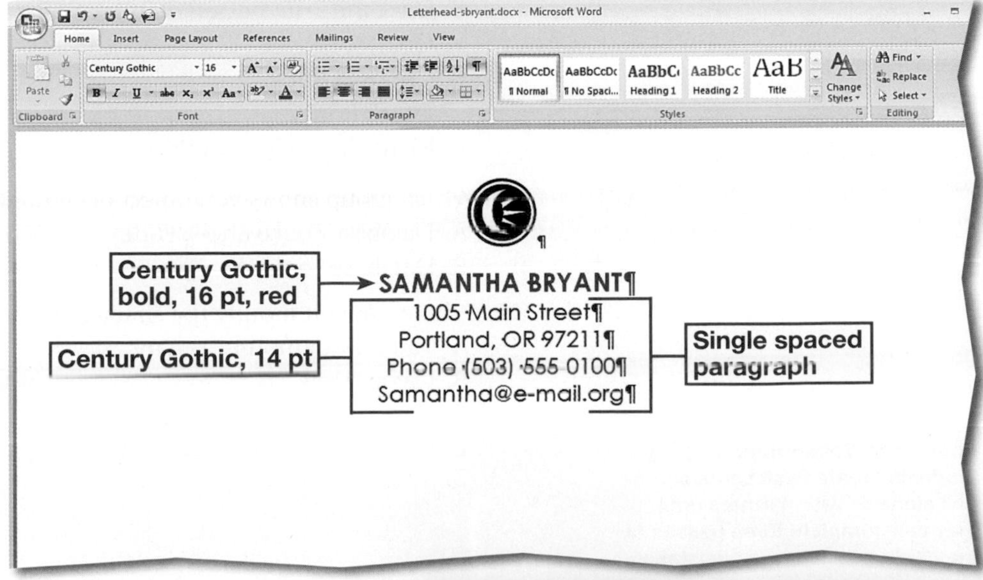

LESSON 5 After You Read

Vocabulary

Key Terms

chart
Documenter
encrypt
object dependency
password
preview
Print Preview
Quick Print
union query

Academic Vocabulary

display
ensure
source
version

Answer to Vocabulary Activity
Students create flash cards and drill alone or with partners until they can complete three passes of the cards with few or no mistakes.

Review Vocabulary

Complete the following statements on a separate piece of paper. Choose from the Vocabulary list on the left to complete the statements.

1. To make your database more secure, you could ___encrypt___ it with a password. (p. 518)

2. Use the ___Documenter___ to preview database object properties. (p. 514)

3. A(n) ___chart___ displays data visually. (p. 511)

4. A(n) ___union query___ combines the results of several queries. (p. 515)

5. Access allows you to save a database file as a previous ___version___. (p. 523)

Vocabulary Activity

6. Write a short definition for each vocabulary word on one side of separate 3x5 cards. On the back of each card, write the vocabulary word that matches the definition. With this set of flash cards, work either alone or with a partner until you can read the terms or the definitions and correctly match the appropriate answers to the back of the cards three times with no mistakes.

Review Key Concepts

Answer the following questions on a separate piece of paper.

7. Where would you configure database options? (p. 519)
A. Database Tools>Database Tools
B. Office>Manage
C. Office>Access Options
D. All of the above

8. What is the quickest way to print a report? (p. 516)
A. Click Print.
B. Click the Print button on the QAT.
C. Choose Office>Print>Quick Print.
D. Right-click, and click Print.

9. Which group shows you object dependencies? (p. 521)
A. Database Tools>Show/Hide
B. Database Tools>Analyze
C. Create>Objects
D. None of the above

10. Where can you modify the characteristics of a chart? (p. 511)
A. You cannot modify a chart.
B. Layout View
C. Design View
D. the Microsoft Graph window

Step-By-Step

EXERCISE 6-18 (Continued)
Create Personal Letterhead

Data File

10 Select the shape. Right-click the image. Choose **Edit Picture**.

11 Choose **Drawing Tools> Format>Shape Styles**. Click the **Shape Styles** dialog box launcher.

12 In the **Format Drawing Canvas** dialog box, select the **Colors and Lines** tab. Under **Fill**, click **Fill Effects**.

13 On the **Gradient** tab, under **Colors**, select **Preset**. In the **Preset colors** drop-down menu, choose **Early Sunset**.

14 Under **Shading styles**, select **From center**. Under **Variants**, click the second **Variant**.

15 CHECK Your dialog box should look like Figure 6.41. Click **OK**. Click **OK** again.

16 CHECK Your letterhead should look like Figure 6.42. Save your file. Exit Word.

Teaching Tip Ask students to experiment with their letterhead. Address information can be separated from the name and put along either the left or right margin, and graphical images can be placed in a corner instead of the center.

Solution Use the file **Letterhead-SF.docx** as the solution file for **Exercise 6-18**.

FIGURE 6.41 Fill Effects dialog box

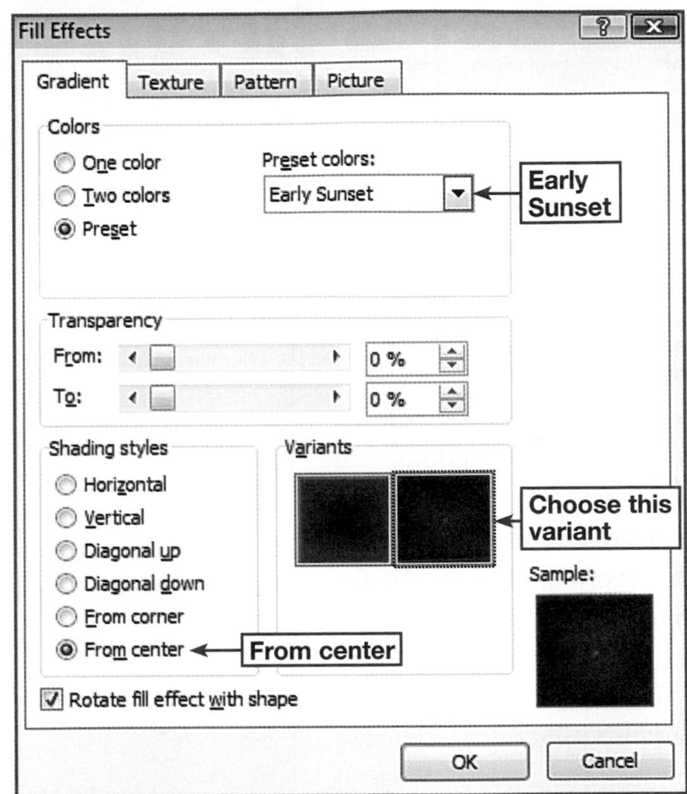

FIGURE 6.42 Finished letterhead

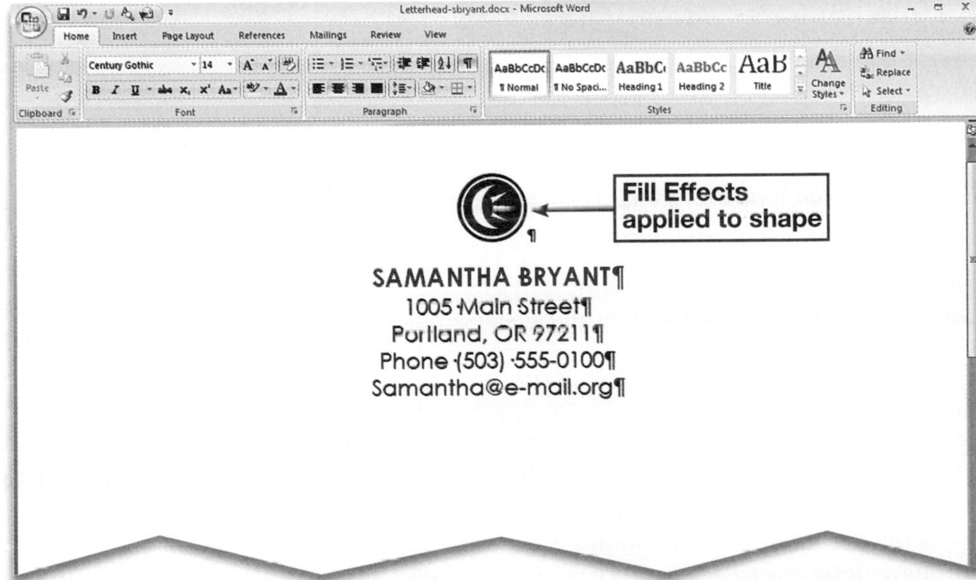

Troubleshooting Students must click in the center of the image to edit the image. The blue sizing handles should appear inside the outer border. If they appear outside, the student has selected the background of the image.

MATH MATTERS

Reading a Sales Invoice

Justine Bennett has her own business, Justine Time. She provides custom-designed items such as plaques, posters, lawn signs, and banners. Justine has customers all over the United States and Canada. How does she get paid for her work? She sends out sales invoices.

Using Sales Invoices

An invoice is an itemized list of goods that indicates price, quantity, total amounts, payment options, and other information. Although many goods and services are paid for immediately, many businesses obtain the money from their sales by invoicing their clients. For example, Bill Jackson wants signs for his mother's 80th birthday party. He contacts Justine and places an order. Then Justine sends Bill a sales invoice. Bill receives the invoice in the mail and checks it against the merchandise he received. Then he sends Justine a check for the total stated on the invoice.

Sales Invoice Information

Most sales invoices contain similar information, such as the company's and client's names, addresses, and telephone numbers. The invoice then describes or itemizes the services or products rendered, and states the amount due. Invoices usually contain a reference number that a company can use to keep track of bills that have been paid and accounts that are still outstanding.

Justine Time
123 Main Street
Brooklyn, NY 11212
718-555-SIGN

Invoice
INVOICE #172
DATE: 5/19/10

Bill To:
Bill Jackson
34 Overbrook Lane
Sioux Falls, SD 57109
(605) 555-6789

Reference #: 3272

Item #	Price	Quantity	Description	AMOUNT
4702	$10.00	5	Happy Birthday Banners	$50.00
4687	$15.00	3	Lawn Signs	$45.00
			SUBTOTAL	$95.00
			TAX	$6.00
			TOTAL DUE	**$101.00**

Make all checks payable to **Justine Time**. Please include the invoice number on your check and mail all payments to the above address.

THANK YOU FOR YOUR BUSINESS!

Businesses use invoices to let customers know how much they owe for items or services they have purchased.

NCLB/Math (Representation) Step students through the invoice above. Explain that the Item column includes the items being invoiced and that the Price and Quantity columns refer to each item being invoiced. Finally, explain that the Description column describes each item. Allow students to work out how the amounts in the AMOUNT column were determined (Price × Quantity). Have them reflect on other types of businesses that might use invoices.

SKILLBUILDER

1. **Identify** What is the purpose of a sales invoice?
2. **Connect** Have you ever received or seen an invoice for a purchase? What information was on the invoice? If you have never received an invoice, describe a situation in which you might receive one.
3. **Decide** If you had your own business, would you choose to have customers pay immediately, or would you use an invoicing system instead? What are the advantages and disadvantages of each choice? Explain your answer.

SkillBuilder answers can be found on page TM87.

21st Century WORKPLACE

Learn to Collaborate

Collaboration means working with other people. It means sharing ideas and tasks to make a project run well. Since most jobs involve the efforts of many people, knowing how to collaborate is a critical skill in today's workplace.

People bring different backgrounds and skills to each project. For projects to run smoothly, it is important that team members treat each other with respect. Being a good team member often involves looking at ideas and tasks from someone else's point of view. Ultimately, all team members benefit by being open to each other's ideas and suggestions.

NCLB/Language Arts (NCTE 7) Collaborating is useful in group projects. For example, if more than one person is conducting research, everyone will have to work together to synthesize conflicting information.

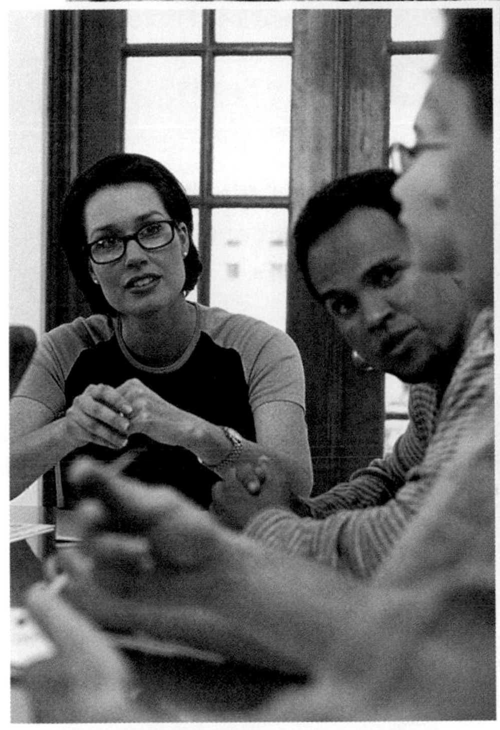

Working well with others is a critical skill to learn in today's workplace.

NCLB/Language Arts (NCTE 4) An important aspect of effective communication is understanding other people's differences. By relating with others, students can adjust their messages so that they have greater impact.

MEET THE MANAGER

Sweet Potato Kids in Baltimore, Maryland, is a hands-on museum for children ages 1–10. Working collaboratively allows Michelle Hall-Davis, the museum's manager and owner, and her staff to provide the best possible activities and programs to their community. "Sweet Potato Kids is in a diverse neighborhood," notes Michelle. "Our employees need to be sensitive to the cultural, religious, economic, and racial backgrounds of our customers. They are also sensitive to these differences among themselves. Because we all work together, Sweet Potato Kids has become a 'melting pot' for the children in our community."

SKILLBUILDER

1. **Describe** Tell about a time when you had to collaborate with others to meet a goal. What were the challenges and benefits of the collaboration?

2. **Analyze** Suppose you are an employer, and you have to choose between two applicants for a job. One person has excellent collaboration skills and poor technical skills. The other has poor collaboration skills and excellent technical skills. Which one would you choose? Explain your choice.

3. **Create** Use Word to design a flyer in which you provide pointers for being a good collaborator. Include examples of how collaboration can help a business grow. Illustrate your flyer with Clip Art or other graphics.

Skillbuilder answers can be found on page TM65.

Step-By-Step

1. Open your copy of the **Sports5** file.
2. Choose **Office>Manage> Compact and Repair Database** (see Figure 5.29).
3. Close the **Sports5** database.
4. Choose **Office>Manage> Compact and Repair Database**.
5. In the **Database to Compact From** dialog box, locate and select the data file **BrokenDB.accdb**. Click **Compact**.
6. In the **Compact Database Into** dialog box, ask your teacher where to navigate to save the file.
7. In the **File name** box, key: a5-13-[your first initial and last name].
8. **CHECK** Your screen should look like Figure 5.30.
9. Click **Save**. Exit Access.

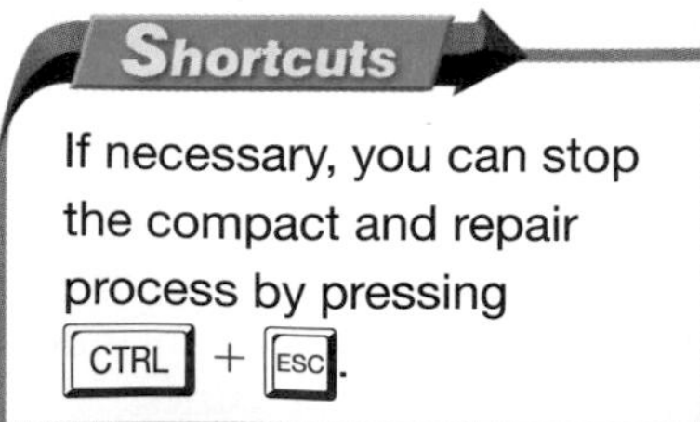

Shortcuts

If necessary, you can stop the compact and repair process by pressing CTRL + ESC.

EXERCISE 5-12
Repair a Database

Sometimes Access databases can get damaged. If the damage is not too serious, Access may be able to fix the problem. If a database opens in Access but displays error messages, use the Compact and Repair tool to repair the open database. If Access cannot open the database because of the damage, you can tell the Compact and Repair tool which database to repair. In this exercise, you will repair an open database. Then you will repair a database you choose from a list.

Solution The solution file for this exercise is **a5-12-SF.accdb**.

FIGURE 5.29 Repairing an open database

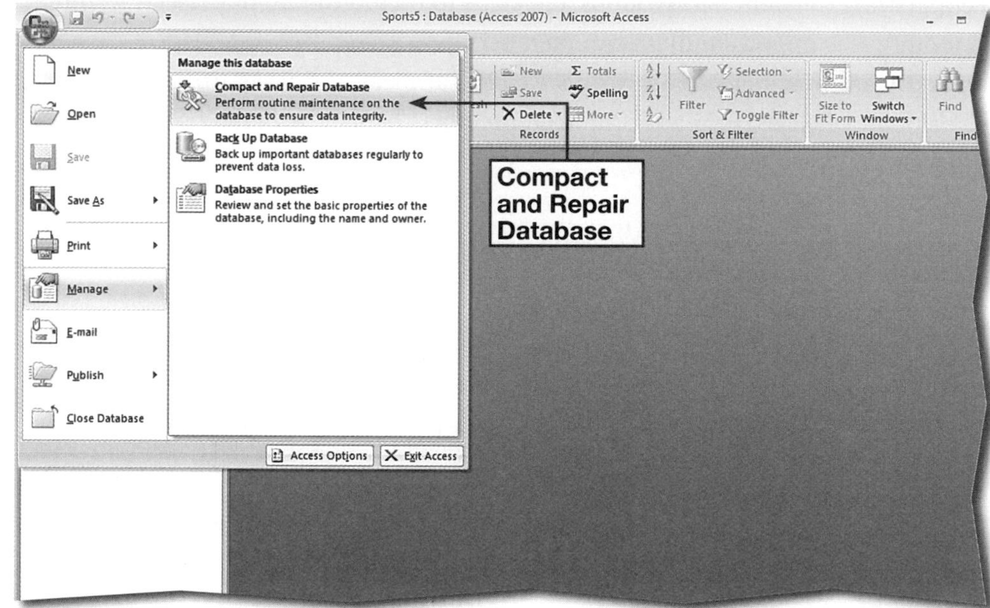

Step-By-Step Tip In **Step 5**, students may need help navigating to the **BrokenDB.accdb** file.

FIGURE 5.30 Repairing a database from a list

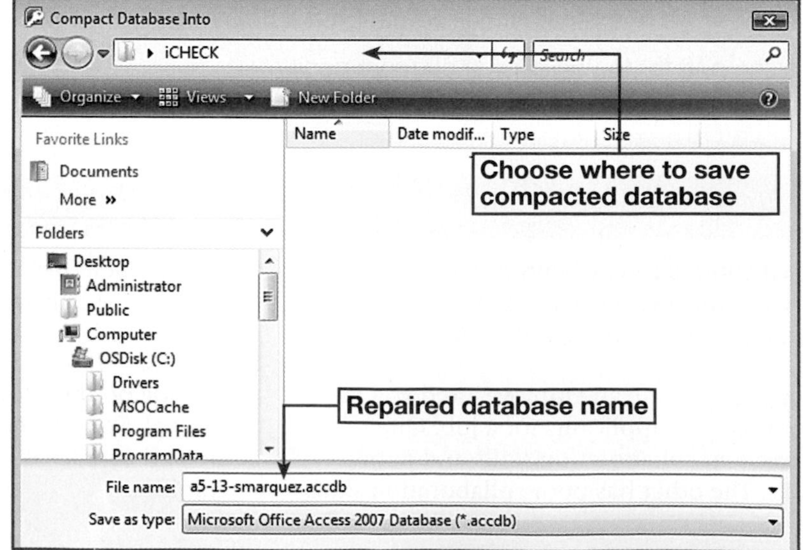

LESSON  After You Read 

Vocabulary

Key Terms

attachment
background
combine
comment
data source
hyperlink
Hypertext Markup Language (HTML)
mail merge
main document
merge field
page orientation
Track Changes
Web browser
Web Layout View
Web page

Academic Vocabulary

contribute
enable
vary

Answer to Vocabulary Activity
Students create a dictionary that contains every vocabulary term in the lesson. Students use the glossary to create the dictionary, and then they use each term in a sentence to make sure they understand the term's meaning.

Review Vocabulary

Complete the following statements on a separate piece of paper. Choose from the Vocabulary list on the left to complete the statements.

1. A(n) ___hyperlink___ is a word, phrase, or graphic that you click to move from one location to another (p. 164).
2. ___Page orientation___ refers to whether a page is laid out vertically or horizontally. (p. 176)
3. A(n) ___comment___ is a note that you can insert in a document. (p. 167)
4. You can ___contribute___ to a document by collaborating with a classmate. (p. 165)
5. You can use ___Track Changes___ to record changes to a document. (p. 166)

Vocabulary Activity

6. Write a Word "dictionary" that will help other students understand all of the vocabulary terms in this lesson.
   A. Write all of the vocabulary terms, in alphabetical order, on a piece of paper.
   B. Use a dictionary and the glossary to see how terms are defined.
   C. Define each term. Then, use each term in a sentence that relates to something that you learned in the lesson.

Review Key Concepts

Answer the following questions on a separate piece of paper.

7. What application displays Web pages? (p. 175)
   (A.) a Web browser
   B. an e-mail application
   C. the Internet
   D. the World Wide Web

8. Which group allows you to accept and reject changes in a document? (p. 171)
   A. Home>Reviewing
   B. View>Show/Hide
   (C.) Review>Changes
   D. Insert>Changes

9. What document is combined with the main document in the mail merge process? (p. 177)
   A. Worksheet
   B. Mail Merge
   C. Landscape
   (D.) Data Source

10. Which dialog box is used to change paper size and page orientation? (p. 176)
   (A.) Page Setup
   B. Options
   C. Print Preview
   D. Paragraph

Step-By-Step

1. Locate the data file **Sports5b.accdb**. Ask your teacher where to copy the file.
2. Open your copy of the file. Click **Office** and hold the pointer over the **Save As** option (see Figure 5.27).
3. Under the **Save the database in another format** header, note the different versions available.
4. Select the **Access 2000 Database** option.
5. In the **Save As** dialog box, navigate to the folder with the **Sports5b.accdb** database file and click **Save**.
6. 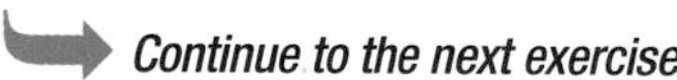 Your screen should look like Figure 5.28. Note the **Access 2000 file format** label in the Access title bar.
7. Close the database.

Continue to the next exercise.

Troubleshooter

Access does not allow you to convert a database that is encrypted with a password. You must first remove the password and then reapply it after the conversion.

Solution Use the file **Sports5b-SF.mdb** as a solution file for Exercise 5-11.

EXERCISE 5-11
Save Databases as Previous Versions

Office Access 2007 works with all previous **versions**, or types, of Access. However, you cannot make design changes in some older forms of databases without some conversion. Once you have worked on the database, you might have to change it back to a previous version so that others not using Access 2007 can work on it. Some features of Access 2007 are not supported by earlier versions of Access and will not be converted.

Teaching Tip Although students can open files created in Access 95 and 97, they cannot save these file types.

FIGURE 5.27 Office Save As option

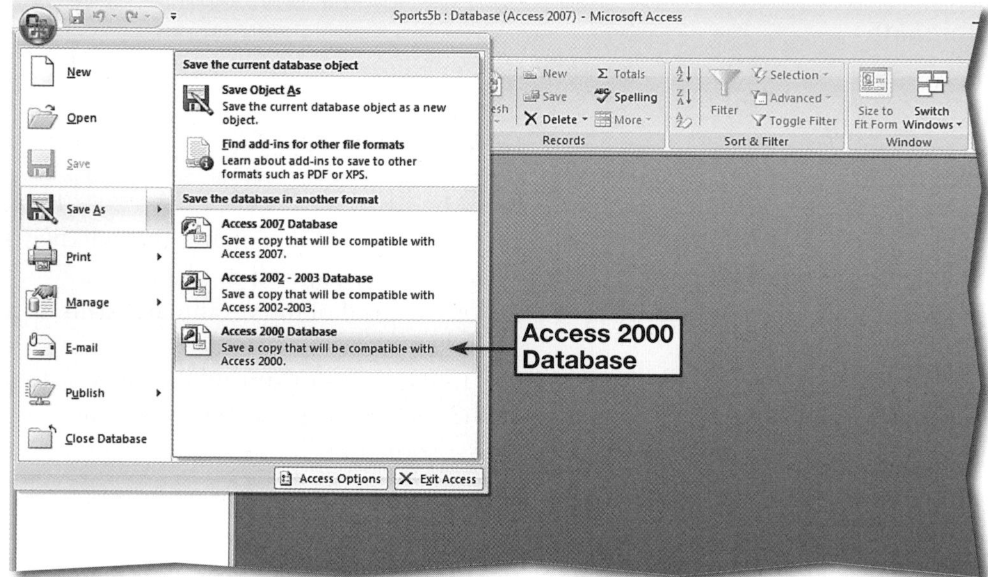

FIGURE 5.28 Access 2000 format

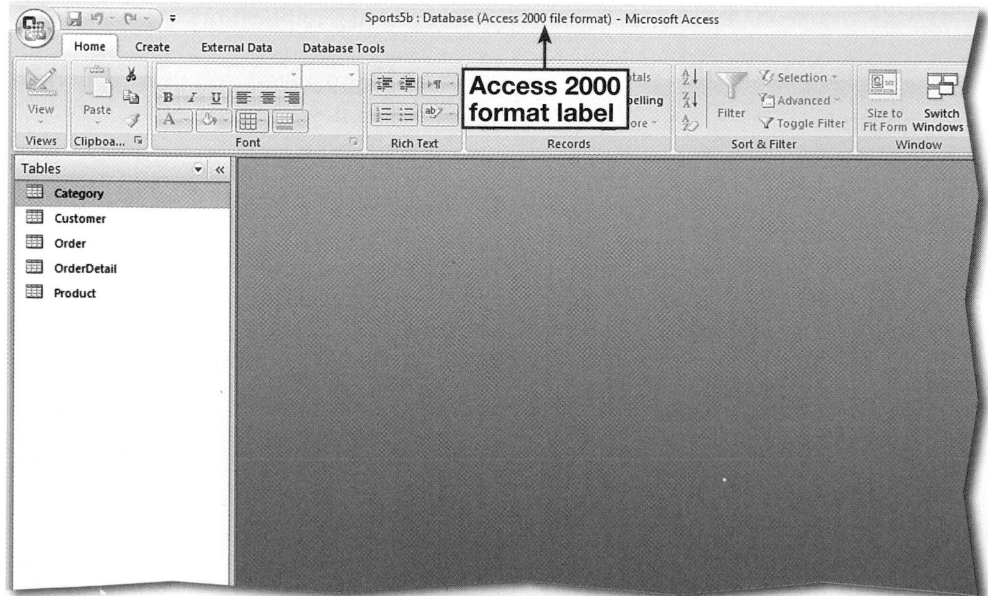

LESSON 6 Practice It Activities

1. Use Track Changes and Send E-mail

Follow the steps to complete the activity.

Step-By-Step

1. Open the data file **Book Sale.docx**. Save as: Book Sale-[your first initial and last name]1.
2. Click **Review>Tracking**. Click **Track Changes**.
3. Select **April 4th**. Click **New Comment**.
4. Key: Is this the correct date?
5. Select **Main**. Key: 2nd.
6. In the **Why? line**, click before **Library**. Key: the. Press the **spacebar** once.
7. CHECK Your screen should look like Figure 6.43.
8. On the **Quick Access Toolbar**, click **Send for Review**.
9. In the **To** box, key your teacher's e-mail address.
10. Your screen should look similar to Figure 6.44. Click **Send**.
11. Save and close the file.

Solution The solution file for this activity is **Book Sale1-SF.docx**.

FIGURE 6.43 Changes made to document

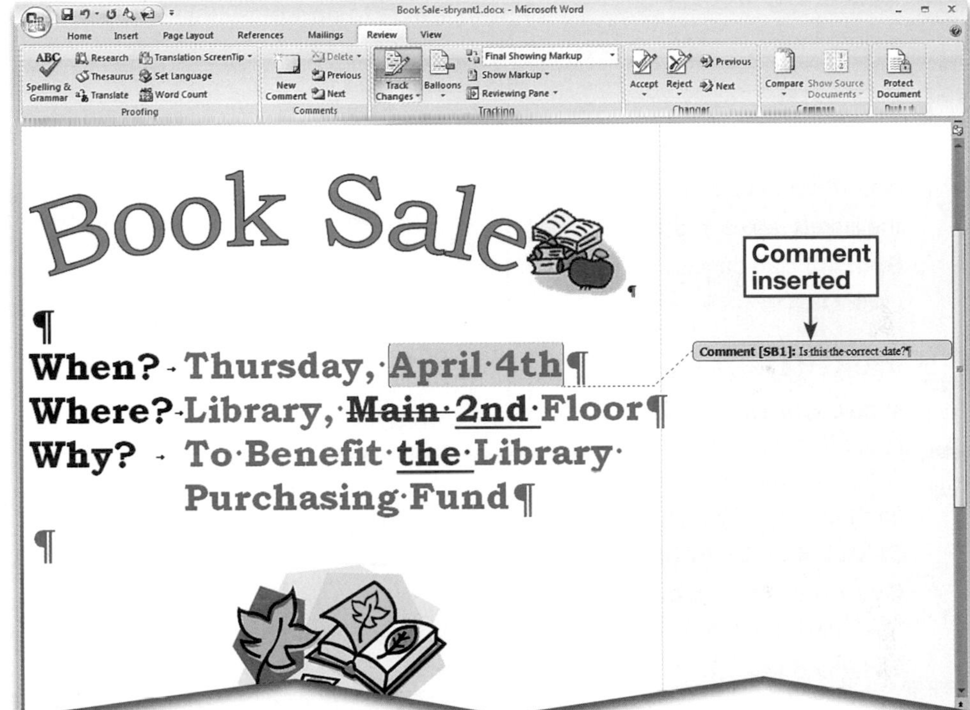

FIGURE 6.44 Document sent for review

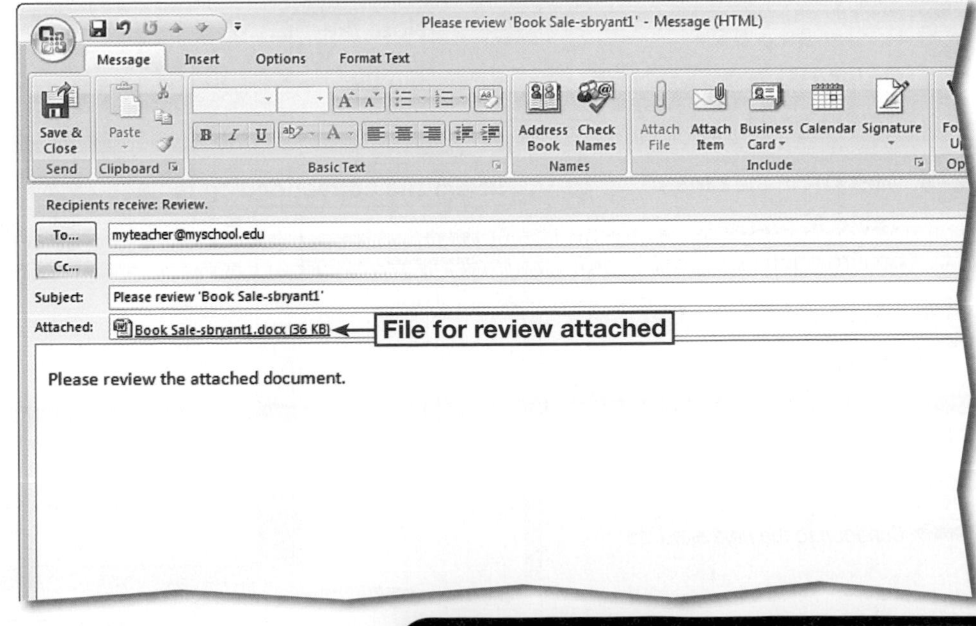

Step-By-Step

1. In your **Sports5** file, choose **Database Tools> Database Tools>Linked Table Manager**.
2. **CHECK** Your screen should look like Figure 5.25.
3. In the **Linked Table Manager**, click the **Select All** button to update all of the linked tables in the **Sports5** database. Click **OK**.
4. **CHECK** Your screen should look like Figure 5.26.
5. Ask your teacher where to find the linked files. In the **Select New Location of Customer_linked** dialog box, navigate to the correct folder and select **Customer.xlsx**.
6. Click **Open**.
7. Repeat **Step 5** for **Order.xlsx** and **Product.xlsx**.
8. Click **OK** in the **Linked Table Manager** confirmation box.
9. Close the **Linked Table Manager**.
10. Close the **Sports5** database.

Continue to the next exercise.

EXERCISE 5-10
Manage Table Links Using the Linked Table Manager

Your database might contain one or more tables that are linked to data sources outside the database. If the data sources are moved, or if the database is moved, Access cannot maintain the link. In order to ensure, or make certain, that Access knows where to find moved data, use the Linked Table Manager to update the links.

Solution Use the file **Sports5-SF.accdb** as a solution file for **Exercises 5-1** through **5-10**.

FIGURE 5.25 Linked Table Manager

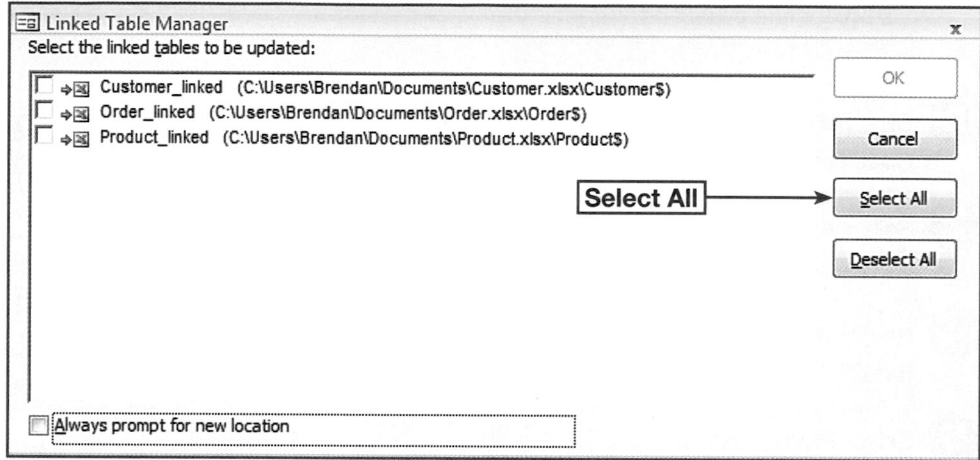

FIGURE 5.26 Select New Location of Customer_linked dialog box

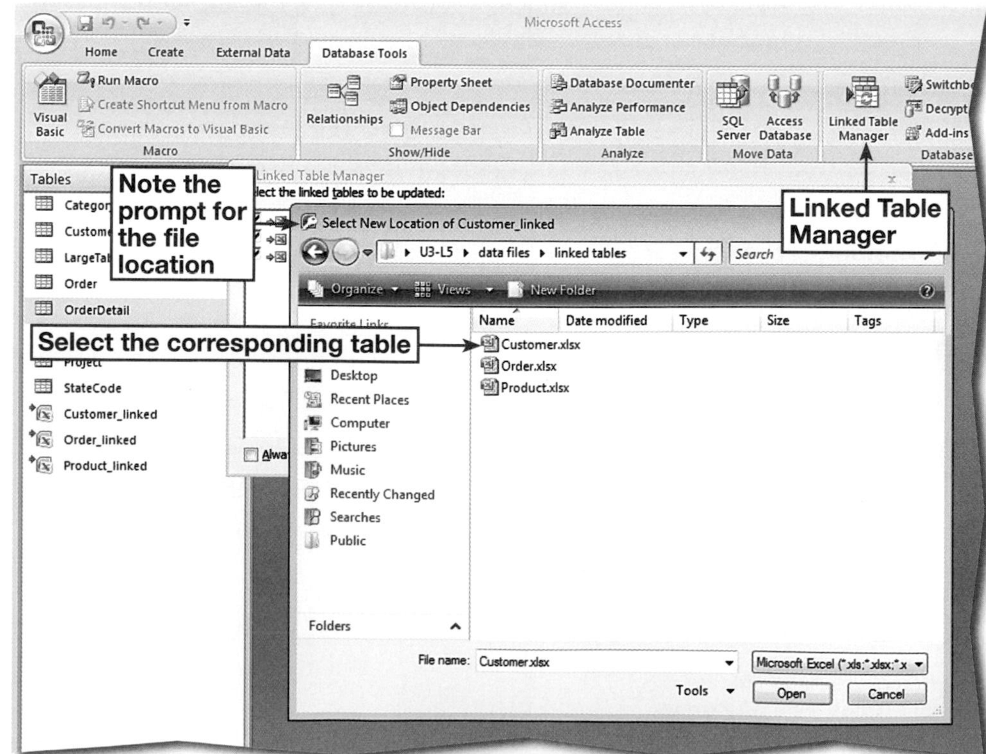

2. Track Successive Changes

Follow the steps to complete the activity. You must complete Practice It Activity 1 before doing this activity.

Step-By-Step

1. Open your **Book Sale-1** file. Save as: Book Sale-[your first initial and last name]2. Make sure **Track Changes** is activated.
2. Click before **When?** Choose **Comments> Next** .
3. Click **Delete Comment** .
4. Click **Review Changes> Next** .
5. Click the **Accept** drop-down menu. Choose **Accept All Changes in Document**.
6. **CHECK** Your screen should look like Figure 6.45. Deactivate **Track Changes**.
7. Save the file as a **Word 97-2003** document.
8. **CHECK** Your screen should look similar to Figure 6.46. Close the document.

New Student Strategy If a student did not complete Practice It Activity 1, then the solution file for that activity can be used as a data file for this activity.

Solution The solution file for this activity is **Book Sale2-SF.doc.**

FIGURE 6.45 Document with changes accepted

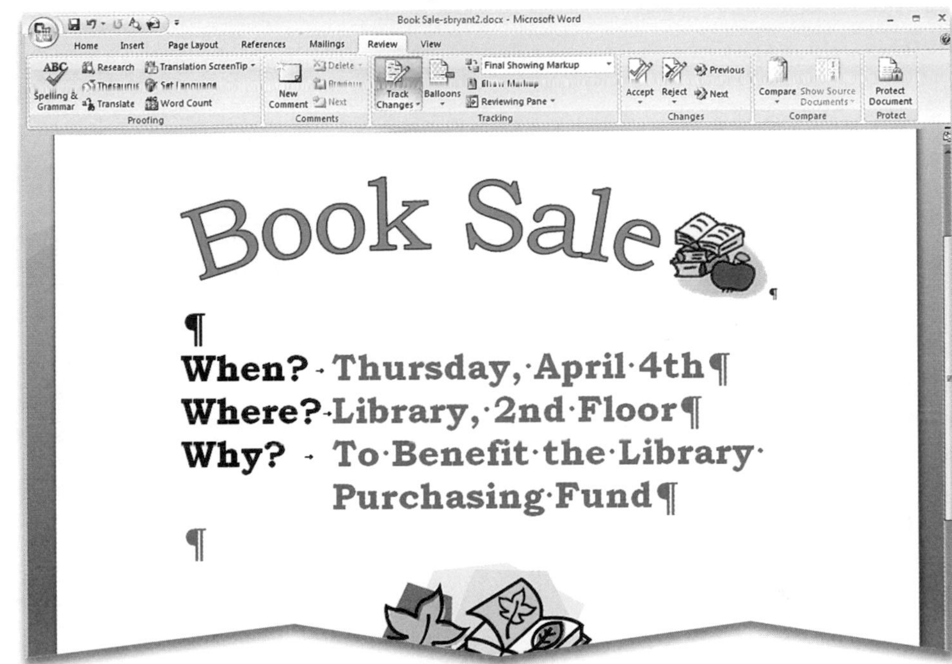

FIGURE 6.46 Document sent as attachment

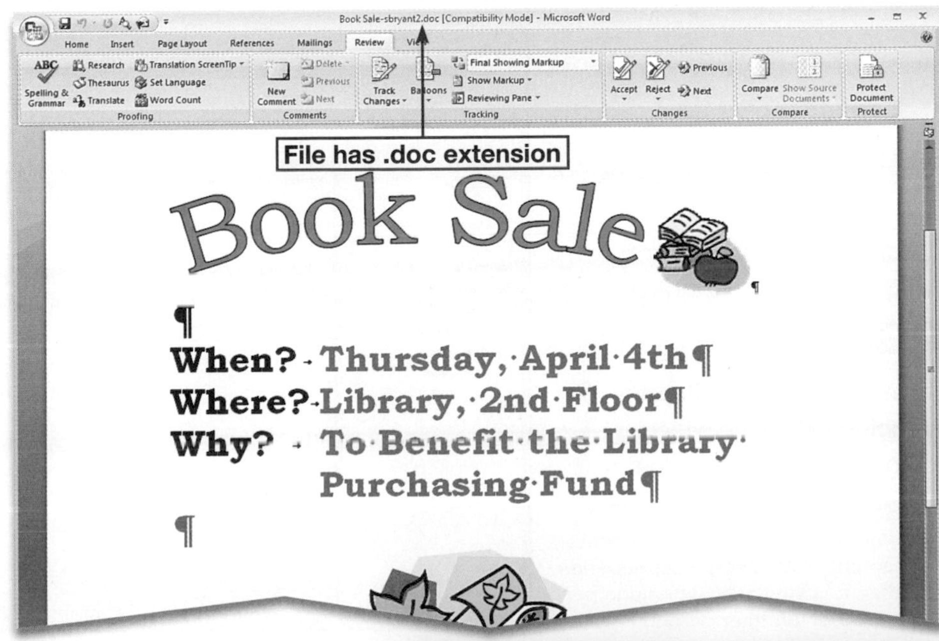

Step-By-Step

1. In your **Sports5** file, open the **CustOrderDet** query. Choose **Database Tools> Show/Hide>Object Dependencies**.

2. **CHECK** Your screen should look like Figure 5.23.

3. Click **Object Dependencies** to close the task pane.

4. Navigate to and open the **OrderDetail** table. Choose **Database Tools> Show/Hide>Object Dependencies**.

5. In the **Object Dependencies** task pane, click the **plus sign** next to the query **CustOrderDet**.

6. **CHECK** Your screen should look like Figure 5.24.

7. Close the **Object Dependencies** pane.

8. Close the database objects.

Continue to the next exercise.

Tech Tip

To make the **Object Dependencies** task pane wider, drag the left window edge.

EL Explain to English Learner students that when one database object *depends* on another, it is similar to when one person *depends* on another person in order to complete a task.

EXERCISE 5-9
Identify Object Dependencies

When a database object **displays**, or shows, records from another database object, their relationship is called an **object dependency**. For example, if a form cannot work without a table, then the form is dependent on the table. Access can help you keep track of dependencies.

FIGURE 5.23 Dependencies for CustOrderDet query

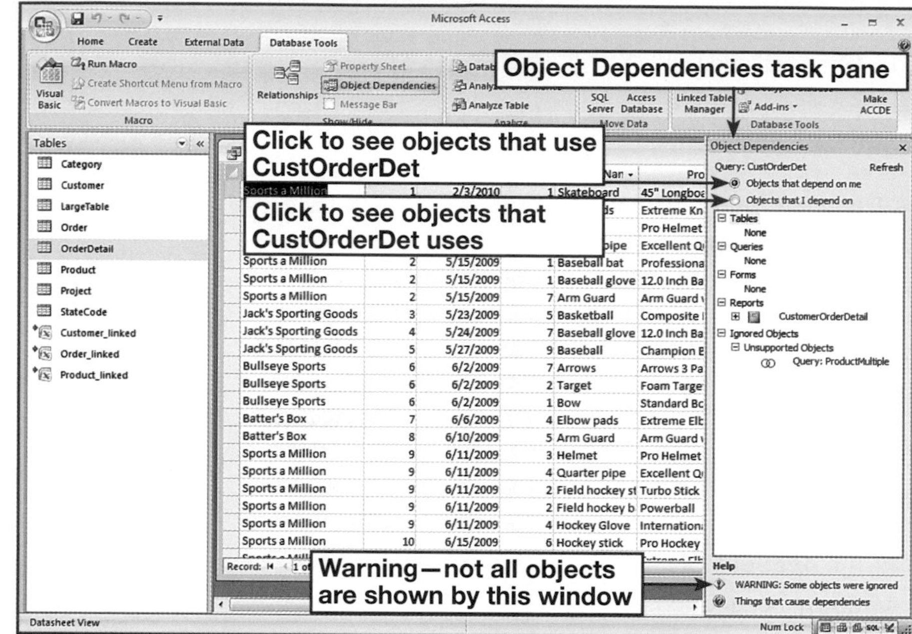

FIGURE 5.24 Dependencies for OrderDetail table

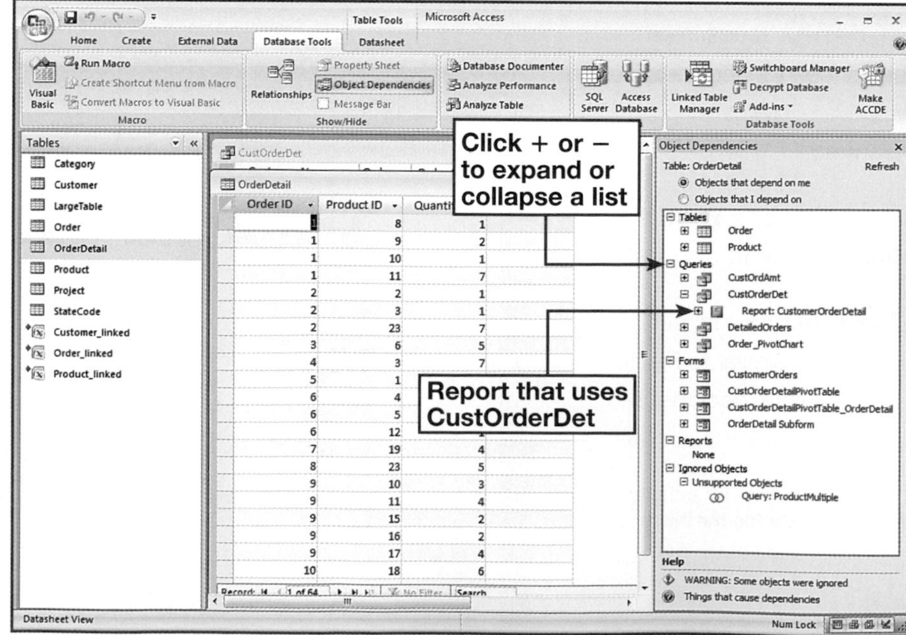

LESSON 6 Practice It Activities

Step-By-Step

1. Open your **Book Sale-1.docx** file. Save as: Book Sale-[your first initial and last name]3.
2. Select **Central High School**. Click **Insert>Links>Hyperlink** .
3. In the **Address** box, key: www.homepage.com. Click **OK**.
4. **CHECK** Your screen should look like Figure 6.47.
5. Choose **Page Layout>Page Background**. Click the **Page Color>Fill Effects**. Click **Texture** and select **Papyrus**. Click **OK**.
6. Choose **Office>Save As**. Under **Save in**, browse to your **Lesson Folder**. Create a new folder named: Book Sale-[your first initial and last name]3. Open the folder.
7. Click the **Save as type** drop-down arrow. Click **Web Page (*.htm; *.html)**. Click **Save**.
8. **CHECK** Your screen should look like Figure 6.48. Save and close the file.

3. Create and Save a Web Page

Follow the steps to complete the activity. You must complete Practice It Activity 2 before doing this activity.

New Student Strategy If a student did not complete You Try It Activity 2, then the solution file for that activity can be used as a data file for this activity.

FIGURE 6.47 Hyperlink inserted into page

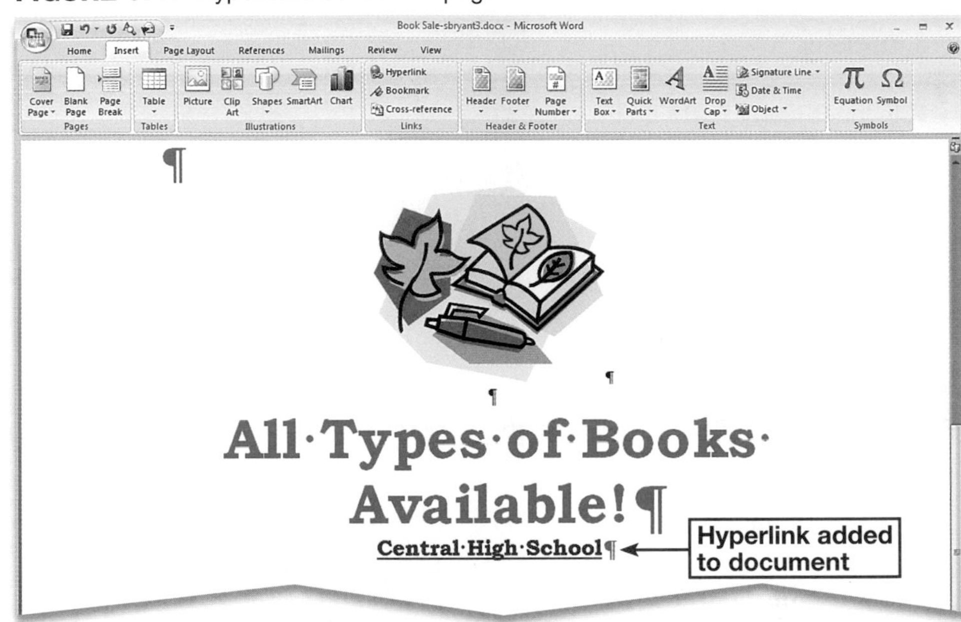

FIGURE 6.48 Document saved as a Web page

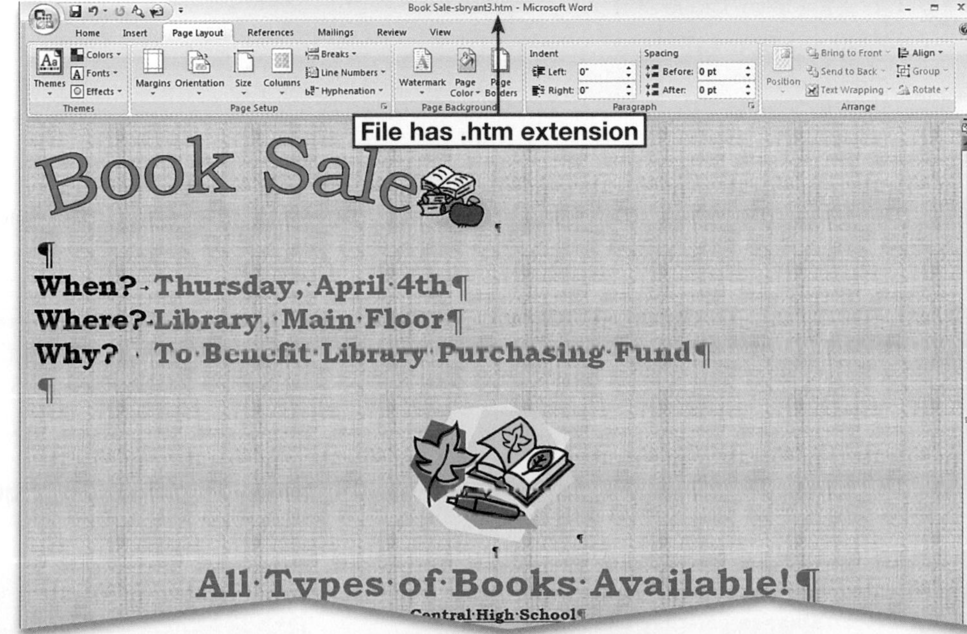

Solution The solution file for this activity is **Book Sale3-SF.htm**. This file is located in the **Book Sale 3-SF** folder.

Step-By-Step

EXERCISE 5-8 (Continued)
Configure Database Options

Step-By-Step Tip In **Steps 1**, **11**, and **17**, students will be prompted to enter the database password in the **Password Required** dialog box.

11 Open the **Sports5** database.

12 CHECK Your screen should look like Figure 5.21.

13 Choose **Office>Access Options**.

14 In the **Display Form** box, locate the **Current Database** category under the **Application Options** heading. Click the drop-down arrow, and select **(none)**.

15 Under the **Navigation** heading, click the **Display Navigation Pane** check box. Click **OK**.

16 In the **Confirmation** box, click **OK**.

17 Close the form. Close and reopen the **Sports5** database.

18 CHECK Your screen should look like Figure 5.22.

Continue to the next exercise.

FIGURE 5.21 New Sports5 options

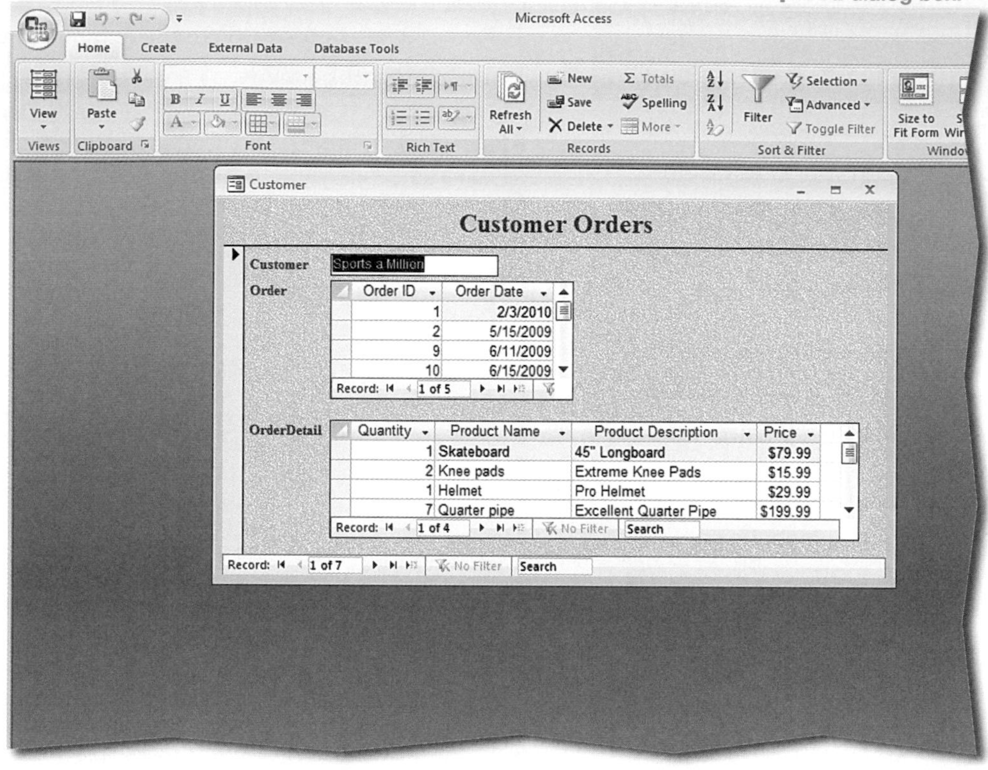

FIGURE 5.22 Access Options reset

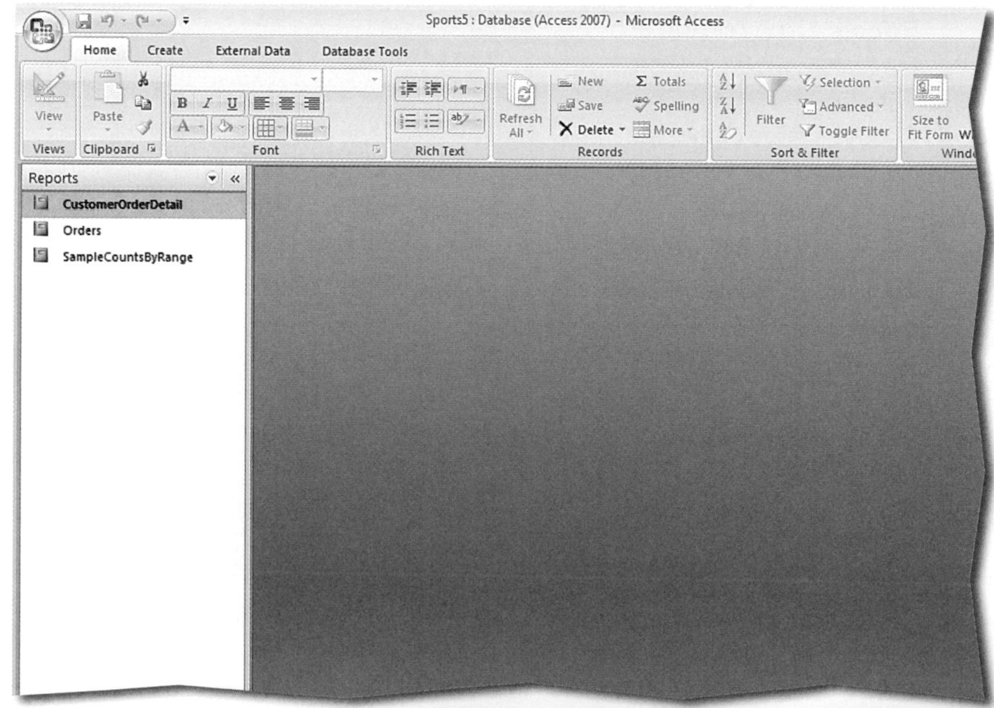

You Should Know

Access Options allow you to set preferences for specific view, display, and editing settings.

Teaching Tip Explain to students that the **Current Database** category of options is useful when you want users to have access to a form but not to the other objects in the database.

4. Change Page Setup

After school, you work for an animal clinic. You have been asked to prepare a reminder notice that will be sent to clients whose pets have their yearly exam and shots due this month.

Step-By-Step

1. Open the data file **Clinic.docx**. Save as: Clinic-[your first initial and last name]4. Choose **Page Layout> Page Setup Dialog Box Launcher**.
2. Change the **Page orientation** to **Landscape**.
3. On the **Margins** tab, make the **Top** and **Bottom** margins **1″**. Make the **Left** and **Right** margins **1.25″**.
4. On the **Paper** tab, under **Paper size**, select **Custom size**. Change the **Width** to **8″**. Change the **Height** to **6″** (see Figure 6.49).
5. On the **Layout** tab, change the page's **Vertical Alignment** to **Center**. Click **OK**.
6. Switch to **Print Preview**.
7. **CHECK** Your screen should look like Figure 6.50. Close **Print Preview**.
8. With your teacher's permission, choose **Use Draft quality** to print your notice. Save and close the file.

Solution The solution file for this activity is **Clinic4-SF.docx**.

FIGURE 6.49 Paper tab

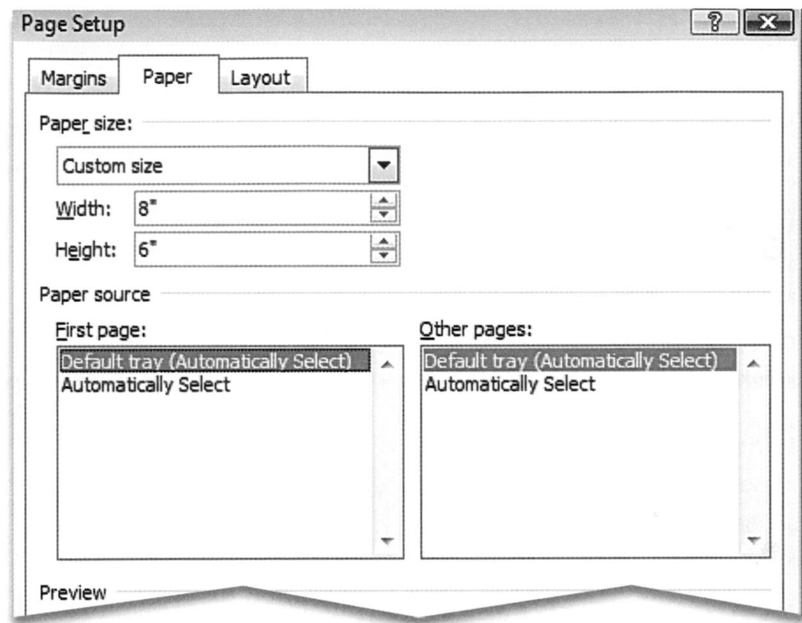

FIGURE 6.50 Notice with new page setup

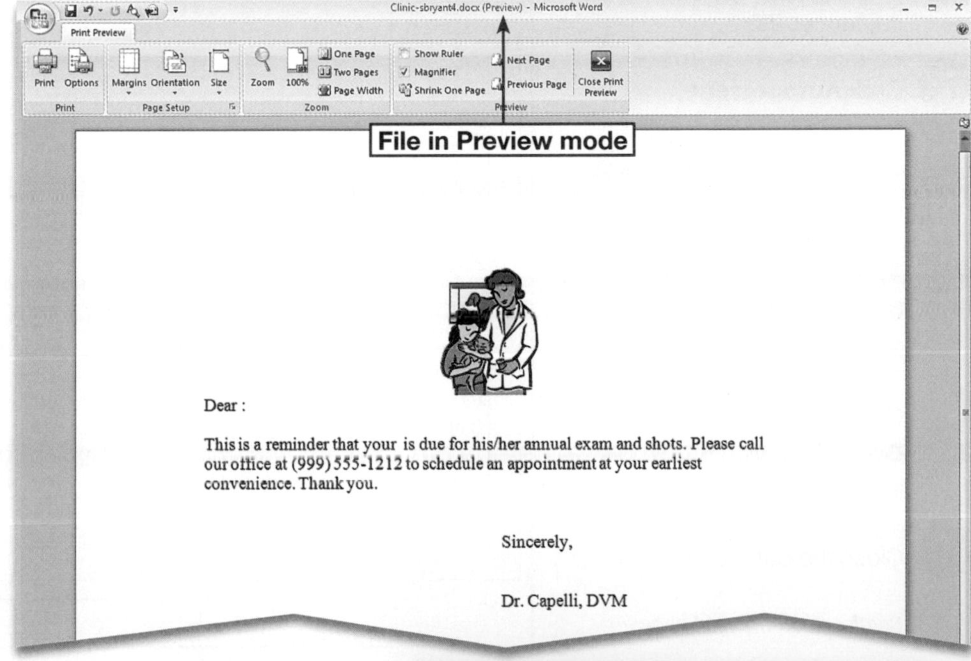

Step-By-Step

1. Open your **Sports5** database. Choose **Office> Access Options**.
2. **CHECK** Your screen should look similar to Figure 5.19.
3. In the categories listed on the left side of the **Access Options** dialog box, click **Current Database**.
4. Under the **Application Options** heading in the **Display Form** box, click the drop-down arrow and select **CustomerOrders**.
5. Under the **Navigation** heading, remove the check from the box in front of **Display Navigation Pane**.
6. Click **Proofing** in the categories list.
7. Click **Autocorrect Options**. Make sure all the options in the **AutoCorrect** dialog box are checked.
8. **CHECK** Your dialog box should look like Figure 5.20. Click **OK**.
9. Click **OK** in the **Access Options** window. Click **OK** in the confirmation box.
10. Close the database.

Continued on the next page.

EXERCISE 5-8
Configure Database Options

Access lets you customize the database you have open and gives you options for customizing how Access itself controls various settings. These include your preferences for the way datasheets look, how the Spelling function works, and how files are saved. These options are reached through the Office menu.

FIGURE 5.19 Access Options screen

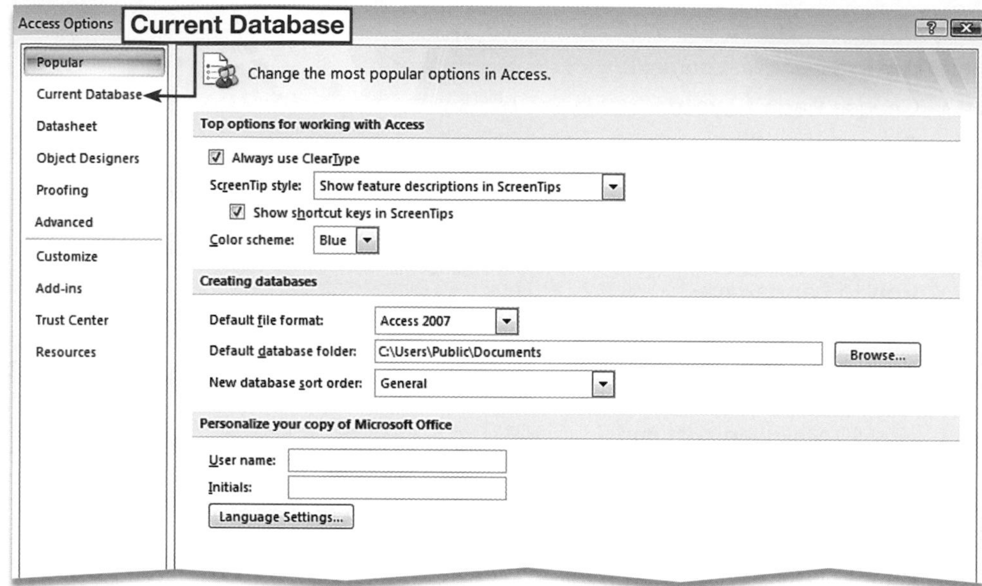

FIGURE 5.20 AutoCorrect dialog box

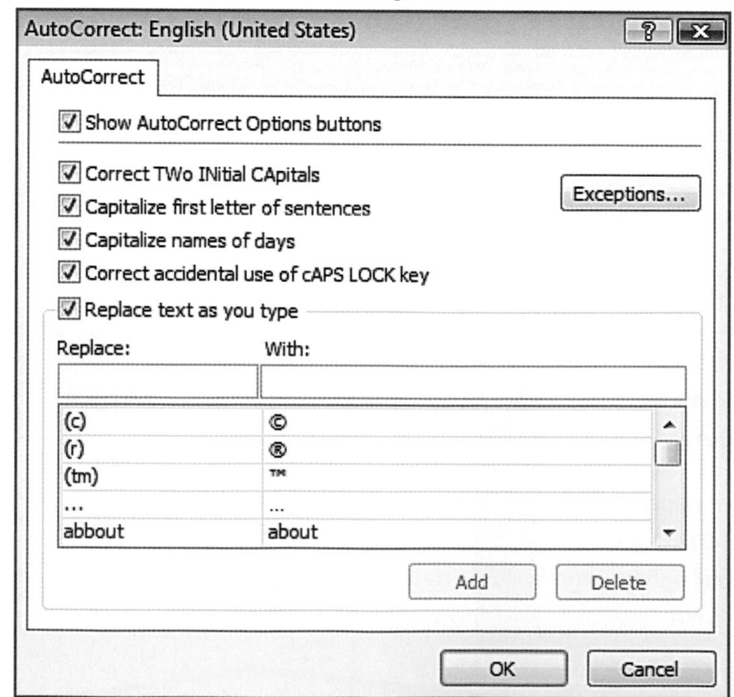

5. Perform a Mail Merge

Now that the notice is ready, it must be mailed to clients by using a mail merge. You must complete You Try It Activity 4 before doing this activity.

Step-By-Step

1. Open your **Clinic-4** file. Save as: Clinic-[your first initial and last name]5.
2. Open the **Mail Merge** task pane.
3. Step 1, select **Letters**. Click **Next: Starting document**.
4. Step 2, select **Use the current document**. Click **Next: Select recipients**.
5. Step 3, select **Use an existing list**. Click **Next: Write your letter**. Locate and open the data file **Clients.docx**. In the **Mail Merge Recipients** dialog box, click **OK**. Click **Next: Write your letter**.
6. Use **More Items** to add fields for **Title**, **Last Name**, and **Animal Type** (see Figure 6.51). Complete the mail merge process.
7. **CHECK** Your screen should look like Figure 6.52.
8. Close the **Mail Merge** task pane. Save and close your **Clinic** file.

Solution The solution file for this activity is **Clinic5-SF.docx**.

FIGURE 6.51 Fields added to document

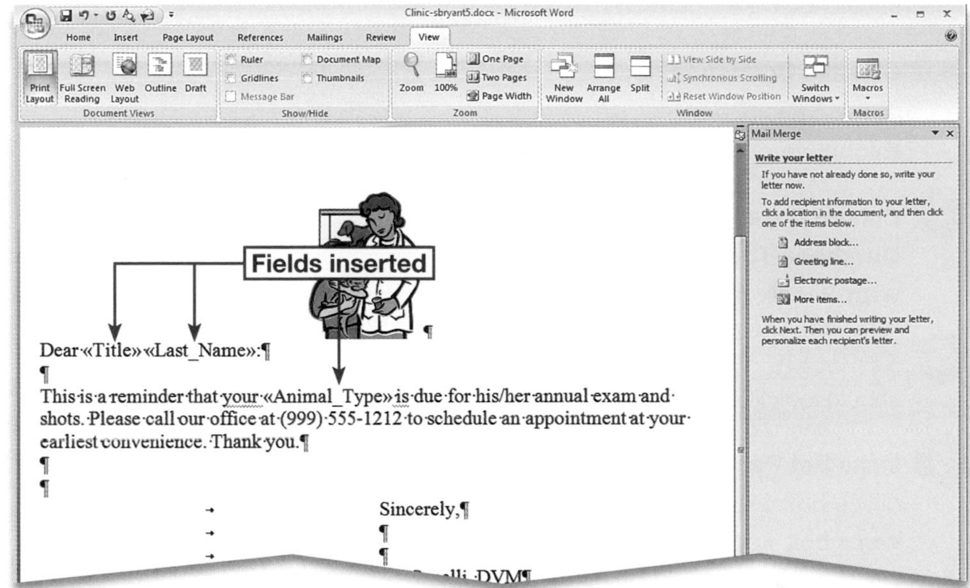

FIGURE 6.52 Merged letter

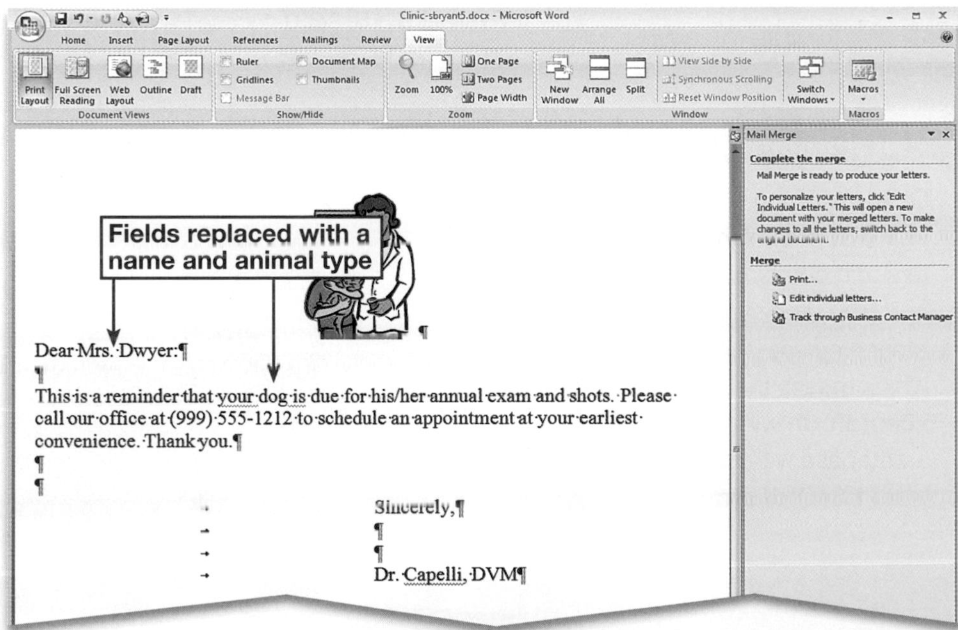

New Student Strategy If a student did not complete You Try It Activity 4, then the solution file for that activity can be used as a data file for this activity.

Step-By-Step

1. Choose **Office>Open**. In the **Open** dialog box, navigate to your **Sports5** database and select it.
2. **CHECK** Your screen should look like Figure 5.17.
3. Click the **Open** drop-down arrow. Select **Open Exclusive**.
4. Choose **Database Tools>Database Tools>Encrypt with Password**.
5. **CHECK** Your screen should look like Figure 5.18.
6. In the **Set Password** dialog box, in the **Password** box, key: Password.
7. In the **Verify** box, key: Password. Click **OK**.

Continue to the next exercise.

Academic Skills

Create a strong password that is at least eight characters and combines letters, numbers, and symbols. Most are case-sensitive, which means that keying **k8sordform** will not open a database with the password **K8sOrdForm**.

EXERCISE 5-7
Encrypt Databases Using Passwords

A **password** is a short sequence of characters that protects data. A password will **encrypt** a database, keeping your data safe and secure, because only users who know the password can use the database. Remember your password, because without it there is no way to retrieve your data.

Teaching Tip Students can remove a password at any time by opening it, clicking **Database Tools>Database Tools>Decrypt Database**, and entering the password in the **Unset Database Password** dialog box.

FIGURE 5.17 Open dialog box

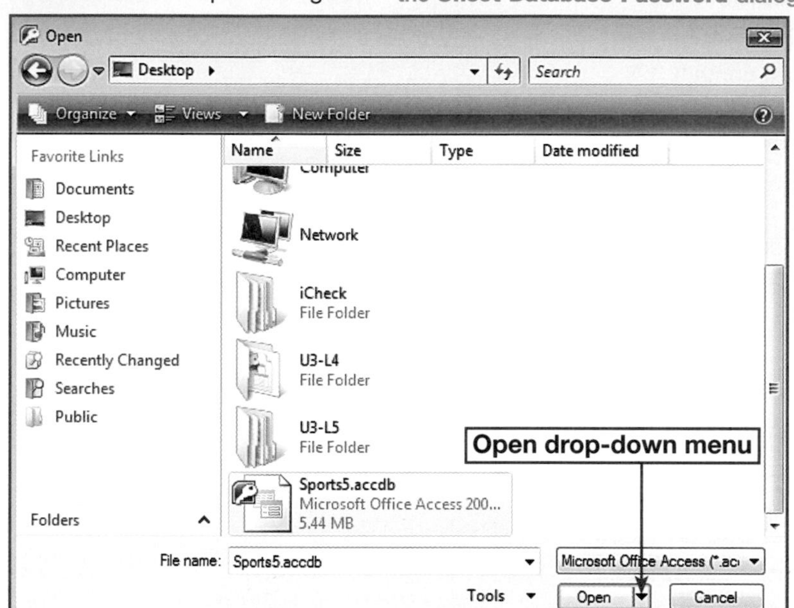

FIGURE 5.18 Set Database Password dialog box

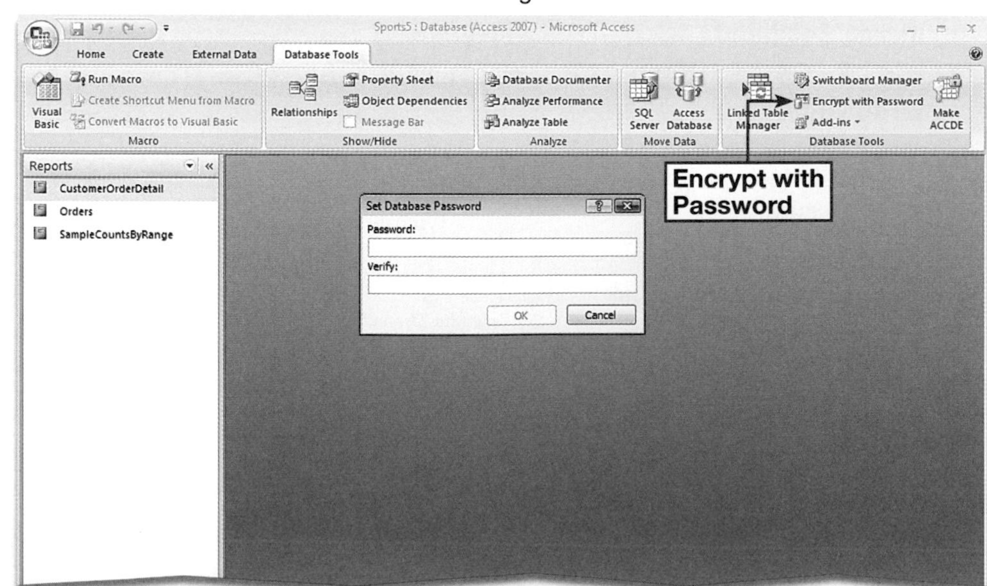

NCLB/Math (Number and Operations) Explain to students that passwords are codes. A code that follows a simple pattern, such as *abcd1234*, is easy to guess. A password with a random combination of letters and numbers, like *f20N1c68*, is much more difficult to guess because there is no pattern. Ask students to create their own passwords and test their strength.

Beyond the Classroom Activity
Students can create a one-page ad promoting their participation in the next local art fair. Students should save the final ad in Word 2007 format.

Standards at Work Activity
Students create a one-page document about an upcoming open house. Students should use Word tools to illustrate the page, view the page in Web Layout View, and save the document as a Web page.

21st Century Skills Activity
Student paragraphs will vary but should include a description of a conflict and how the situation was resolved. If students are comfortable with the idea, have them exchange their paragraphs with other classmates and use Track Changes to add suggestions and comments about the conflict's resolution.

6. Beyond the Classroom Activity

Language Arts: Create an Advertisement You plan to sell your crafts at the next local art fair. You decide to create an advertisement that can be sent as a postcard to past buyers and be posted as a flyer in local stores.

Create a one-page advertisement that notes the date and time of the art fair. Describe who you are, what you are selling, and include any other information that you think is necessary. Use Word tools to illustrate your advertisement. Design the document so that it has a Landscape orientation. Finally, save your advertisement in a Word 2007 format.

Save as: w6rev-[your first initial and last name]6.

7. Standards at Work Activity

Microsoft Certified Application Specialist Correlation
Word 1.3 *Insert Hyperlinks*

Create a Web Page You work for a real estate agency. One of the agents has asked you to create a Web page that announces an upcoming open house. Create a one-page document. In your document:

- State the date, time, and address of the open house. Include any other information that you think is necessary (a description of the house, its price, and so on).
- Use Clip Art, WordArt, backgrounds, and other Word tools to illustrate the page.
- Include a hyperlink to the real estate agency's home page.
- Preview your document in Web Layout View. Save your document as a Web page.

Save the file as: w6rev-[your first initial and last name]7.

8. 21st Century Skills Activity

Handle Conflict Learning how to handle conflict is an important life skill. Think about a recent conflict you experienced. Perhaps you jumped to a conclusion, assumed something, or listened to a rumor that was not true. Then, key a paragraph that describes the situation. Explain how the conflict was or was not finally resolved. Evaluate the resolution—could the situation have been handled differently? Why or why not?

Save your file as: w6rev-[your first initial and last name] 8.

Go Online **e-REVIEW**
glencoe.com

Go to the **Online Learning Center** to complete the following review activities.

Online Self Check
To test your knowledge of the material, click **Unit 1> Lesson 6** and choose **Self Checks**.

Interactive Review
To review the main points of the lesson, click **Unit 1> Lesson 6** and choose **Interactive Review**.

EXERCISE 5-6 (Continued)
Preview and Print a Form or Report

11 Close the form. In your **Sports5** file, open the **CustomerOrder Detail** report.

12 With your teacher's permission, choose **Office> Print>Quick Print** to print the report right away. Add your name to the printed report.

13 Click **Print** . Under **Number of Copies**, click the **up arrow** to **5**. Deselect the **Collate** box (see Figure 5.15).

14 CHECK Your dialog box should look like Figure 5.16.

15 Click **Collate**. The box is checked again.

16 In the **Number of Copies** box, click the **down arrow** and select **1**.

17 With your teacher's permission, click **OK** to print the page. Close the report. Close the **Sports5** database.

EL Tell English Learners that the Collate option controls the order of printed pages. If you print three copies of a two-page document without the Collate option selected, all copies of page 1 will print, and then all copies of page 2 will print. With the Collate option, Access prints page 1, followed by page 2. This sequence is repeated two more times.

FIGURE 5.15 Print dialog box with Collate selected

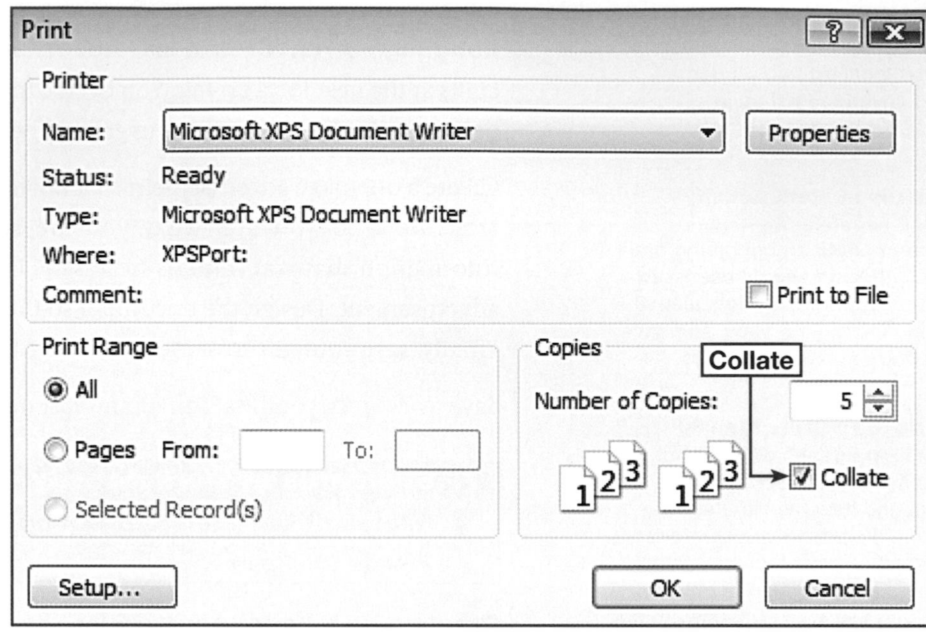

FIGURE 5.16 Print dialog box without Collate selected

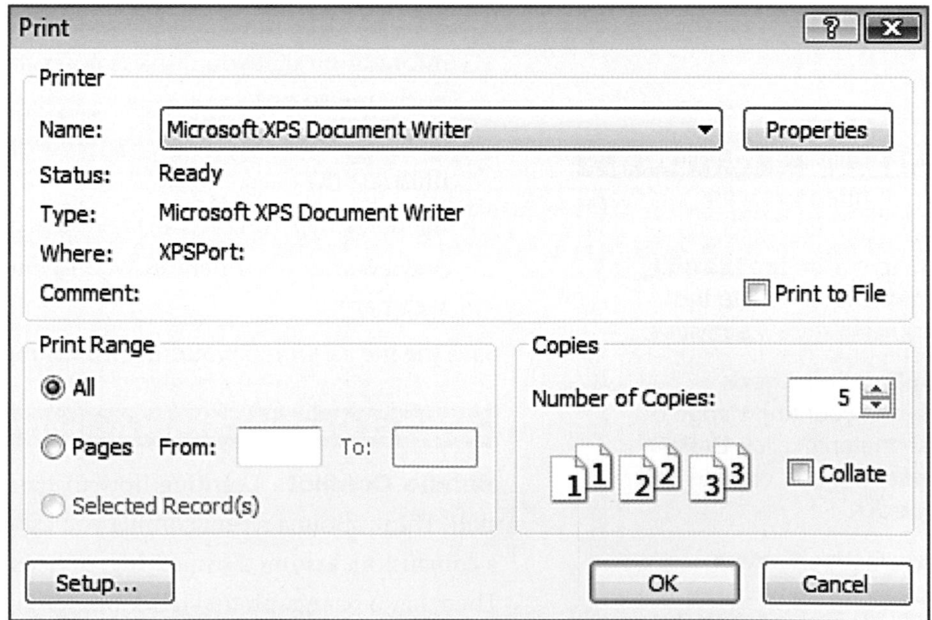

LESSON 6 Challenge Yourself Projects

Before You Begin

Work Together Collaboration is an everyday part of working in the business world. These projects show you how to use Word to share your documents with others, whether they are coworkers, classmates, or clients.

Reflect Once you complete the projects, open a Word document and answer the following:

1. How might you use mail merge for your next event or party?
2. How might you use Comments and Track Changes for your next group project?

Answers Rubrics for Challenge Yourself Projects are available at **glencoe.com**. You may want to download the rubrics and make them available to students as they complete each project.

9. Create a Company Summary

Rubric R

LEVEL This is an intermediate level project.

Language Arts: Review and Edit a Document You and a friend are going to start a small Internet company that sells comic books. Write a brief summary of the company. In your summary, state:

- What the company will do
- Who the company will appeal to

Use e-mail to exchange summaries with a classmate. Make comments and suggest changes for your classmate's summary. When you receive your classmate's review of your work, accept or reject the changes that were suggested. Save your summary as: w6rev-[your first initial and last name]9. Save the summary document as a Web page, and preview your work in a Web browser. Save your Web page in a new **Summary** folder.

10. Prepare a Mail Merge

LEVEL This is an advanced level project.

Language Arts: Write a Business Letter You work for a nonprofit agency that is having its annual fund-raiser for children with special needs. You have been put in charge of sending a letter to last year's donors. Write a generic fund-raising letter that:

- Tells the recipient about the upcoming fund-raiser.
- Notes how much the recipient gave last year.
- Asks if he or she will support the organization again this year.

Add a letterhead to your letter and format the letter correctly. Use Anytown, NY 01245 for the recipient's address. For now, leave spaces for each recipient's individual name, street address, and previous donation amount. Save your letter as: w6rev-[your first initial and last name]10. Exchange your letter with another classmate. Review your classmate's work, and accept or reject your classmate's suggestions for your letter.

11. Perform a Mail Merge

LEVEL This is an advanced level project.

Language Arts: Merge Letters and Create Labels Perform a mail merge using the letter you created in Challenge Yourself Project 10. Use the data file **Donors.docx** as your source. Insert fields for Title, First Name, Last Name, Address, and Previous Donation Amount into your main document. Check the spacing between fields carefully, and perform the merge. Choose **Use Draft quality** to print a copy of each letter. Do not save your merged letters. Create return address labels with the fund-raising organization's address. Save your labels as: w6rev-[your first initial and last name]11.

Step-By-Step

1. In your **Sports5** file, open the **CustomerOrders** form.

2. Choose **Office>Print> Print Preview**. Maximize the window.

3. CHECK Your screen should look like Figure 5.13.

4. Click the window once to zoom in. Click **Next Page** ▶.

5. Click **Print**. In the **Print** dialog box, under **Print Range**, in the **From** box, key: 1. In the **To** box, key: 2.

6. With your teacher's permission, click **OK** to print the forms. Add your name to the printed forms.

7. Click **Close Print Preview** ✕.

8. Click the **Record Selector** (see Figure 5.14).

9. Choose **Office>Print> Print**. Under **Print Range**, click **Selected Record(s)**.

10. With your teacher's permission, click **OK**. Only one form prints. Add your name to the printed form.

Continued on the next page.

EXERCISE 5-6
Preview and Print a Form or Report

Although forms are designed to be used on the screen, they are also printable. There are several ways to print a report. In this exercise, you will print a page of a form, print a single form by selecting it with the record selector, and use **Quick Print** to print a report immediately.

Teaching Tip Tell students they can print one form per page by changing the **Force New Page** property in the form header or footer in **Design View.**

FIGURE 5.13 Form in Print Preview

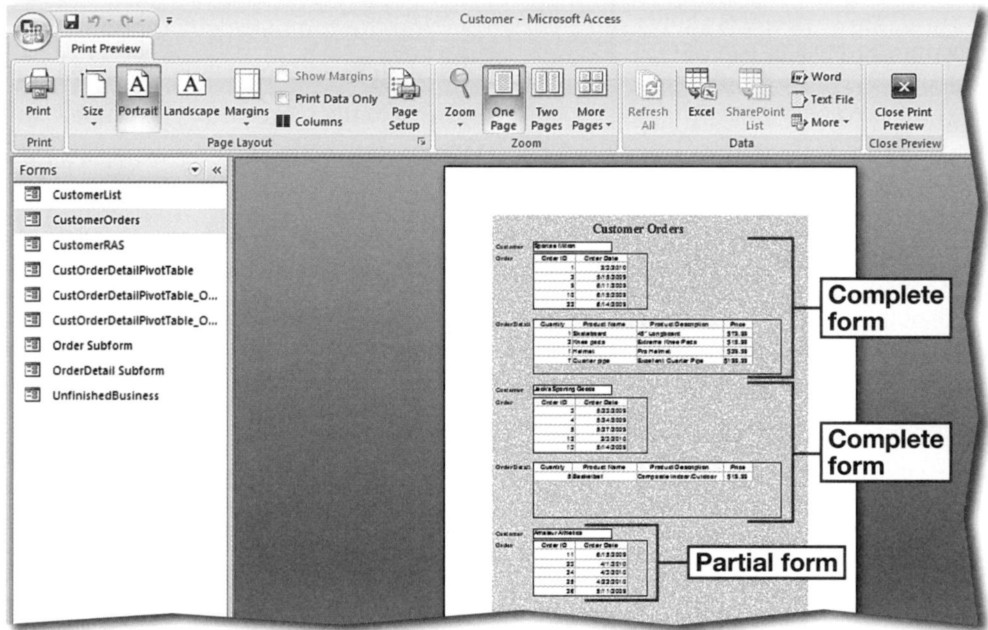

FIGURE 5.14 Print dialog box with Selected Record(s) selected

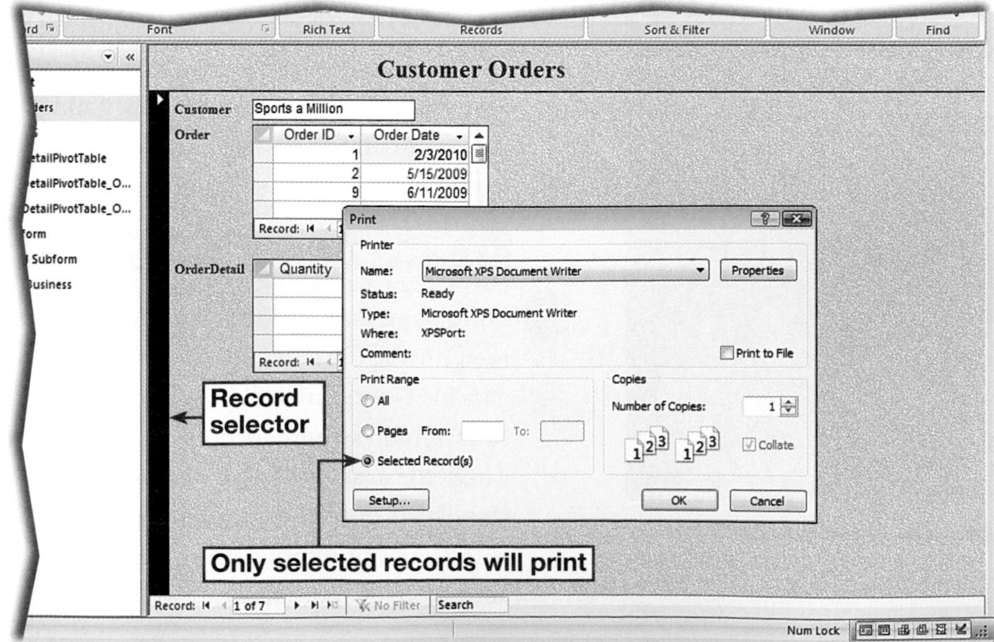

In this activity, you will use your writing skills to create a business letter.

Rubric

Writing a Business Letter

The company you work for is planning its annual event to raise money for Food Share, an organization that collects and purchases food for people in need. As a member of the Planning Committee, you have been asked to write a business letter to send to your coworkers. In the letter you must explain what Food Share does and convince people to come to the event to support this wonderful cause.

1. Open a Word 2007 document. (p. 17)
2. Change the top margin to 2″. (p. 35)
3. Create a letterhead for your letter. Key your company's name and address at the top of the letter. Your company is Brownville Clothing, Inc., 2275 Riverside Road, Brownville, NH 00023.
4. Change the font of the letterhead to 14 point Arial and make it bold. Center the name and address. (p. 38)
5. Set the font for the rest of the letter at 11 point Calibri. (p. 38)
6. Insert the date. Address the letter to your coworkers.
7. Key the body of the letter. In the letter, describe your event (it may be a food drive, a carnival, a charity auction, a dinner, and so on). Be sure to explain the purpose of the event. Explain what Food Share does and how it uses the money it collects.
8. In the letter encourage people to attend the event. Explain how supporting Food Share through the event will benefit the community.
9. Add a closing. (p. 68)
10. Proofread the letter.

NCLB/Language Arts (NCTE 8) Have students research statistics regarding hunger in your local area. Have them use the information they find to support the Food Share cause in their letters.

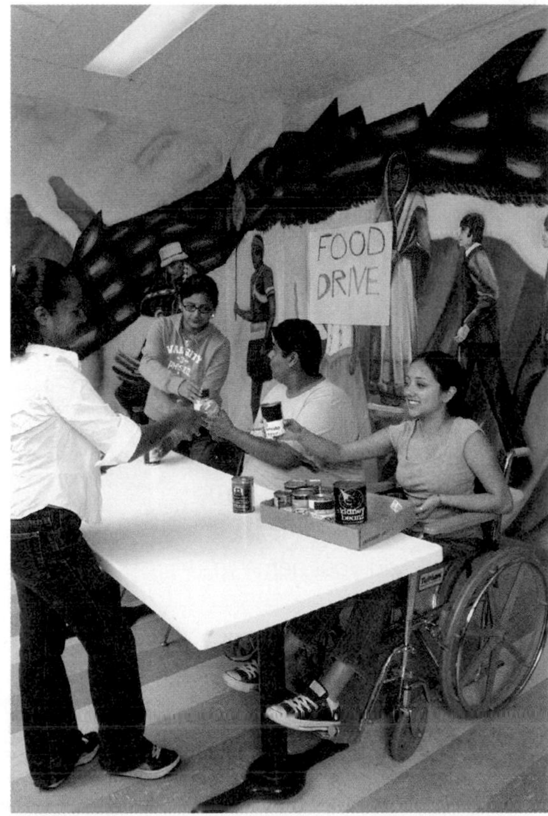

An effective business letter can help you realize your goals.

Step-By-Step Tip In **Step 4**, direct students to page 39 for help with applying bold to text. Refer students to page 44 for help with centering the text.

Answer to Academic Connections Go to the Online Learning Center at **glencoe.com** to access the rubric for this activity. If students need help remembering how to complete specific skills, have them turn to the page number listed after selected steps.

Step-By-Step

1. In your **Sports5** file, open the **ProductBasketball** query in **Datasheet View**. Only the basketball products are displayed. Close the query.

2. Open the **ProductMultiple** query in **Design View**. Click in the query window.

3. **CHECK** Your screen should look like Figure 5.11.

4. Read the query definition. Find the three **SELECT** statements that obtain the fields from the three queries.

5. Click **Datasheet View** .

6. **CHECK** Your screen should look like Figure 5.12.

7. With your teacher's permission, print the merged query. Add your name to the printed query.

8. Close the datasheet.

Continue to the next exercise.

Academic Skills

Finding the **SELECT** statements in the union query requires proofreading skills. In a Word document, key three types of errors you might catch while proofreading.

EXERCISE 5-5
Print Results of Multiple Queries

Sometimes you will need to use data from several sources of information as if the data were one large table or query. This is done using a **union query**, or merged query. Queries that are merged together for a union query must have exactly the same number and type of fields. In this exercise, you will merge the data from three queries into one query. Each of the three queries lists products from different categories.

NCLB/Language Arts (NCTE 4) Reinforce the importance of proofreading. Ask students to discuss what might happen to data in the database if it is not proofread and corrected.

FIGURE 5.11 ProductMultiple query in Design View

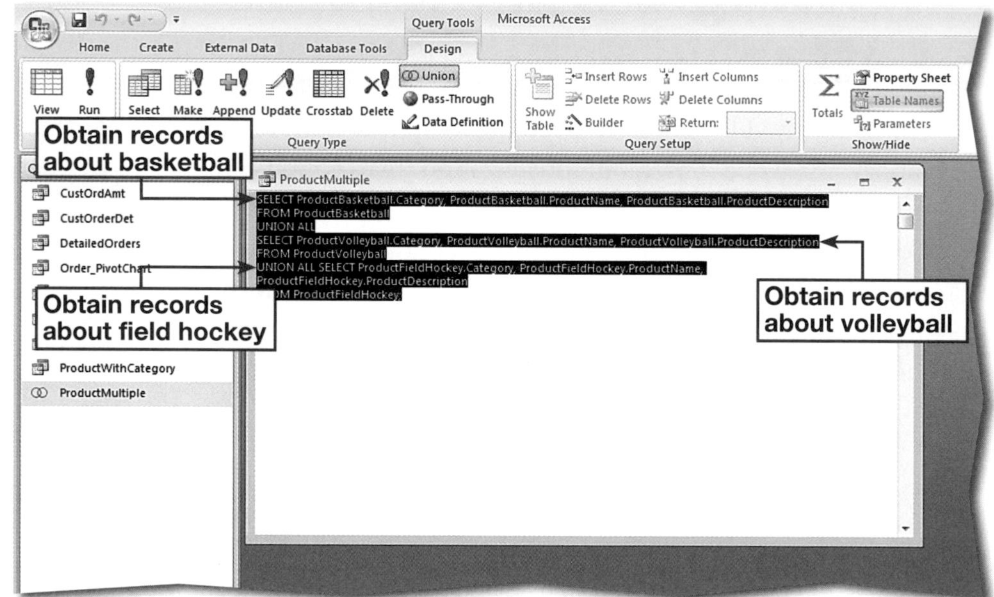

FIGURE 5.12 ProductMultiple query in Datasheet View

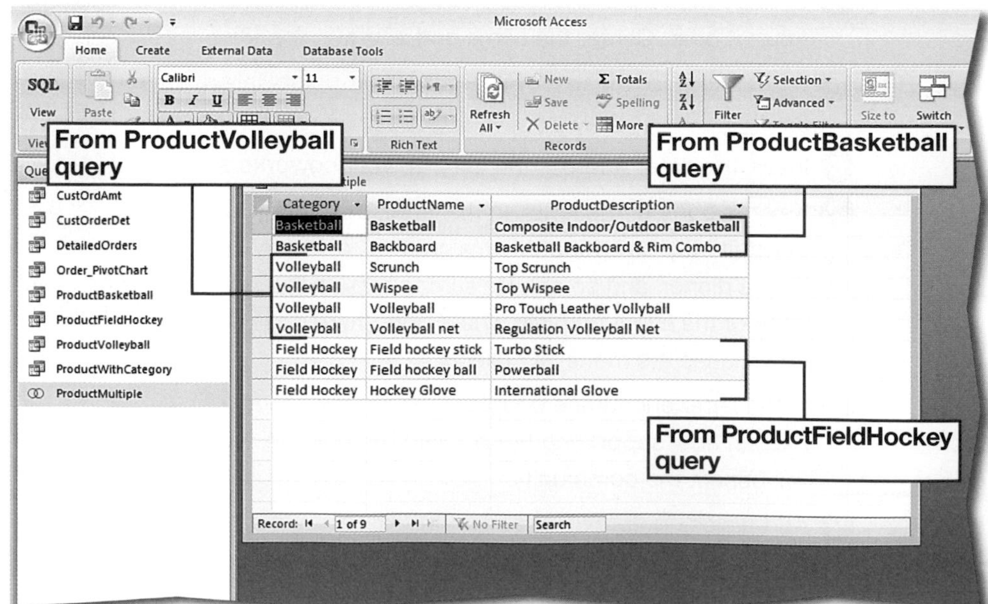

What Are Ethics?

Ethics are the moral rules that people live by, or the principles of conduct that govern a group or society. The rules are based on ideas of right and wrong behaviors. For example, most people believe that cheating on a test or telling a lie to avoid being punished are unethical behaviors.

Businesses also have codes of ethics. Many corporations and large companies require their employees to sign a document agreeing to follow the standards of behavior set by the organization. Revealing confidential information or using company resources for personal use are examples of unethical business practices.

Making Ethical Decisions

How does a business decide what it will or will not do? When considering whether an action is ethical or unethical, there are some questions that both businesses—and individuals—must answer.

- Is the action against the law?
- Does it violate company or professional policies?
- What if everyone did this? How would I feel if someone did this to me?
- Am I sacrificing long-term benefits for short-term gains?

When you make ethical decisions, people are more likely to trust you and to feel that they can depend on you. When businesses make ethical decisions, there is more trust between buyer and seller, employer and employee, business and government, and business and society. Business works best when it is based on a firm foundation of ethics.

CASE STUDY

Jim and Bob are making plans to start a landscaping business together. While sharing these plans with friends, Bob is told that in high school Jim was caught cheating on tests several times. Jim's attitude was that if it did not hurt anyone, it was alright to do it. This makes Bob wonder about Jim's ethics. Bob has very strong ethics and wants customers to know that their company does business honestly. Bob is not sure what he should do.

YOU DECIDE

1. **Recall** List four questions that should be asked when determining whether an action is right or wrong.
2. **Evaluate** Key a paragraph explaining how you think Bob should handle his dilemma.

APPLICATION ACTIVITY

3. **Create a Memo** Key a memo from Bob to Jim stating what Bob thinks the landscaping business's code of ethics should be. Carefully proofread the memo and make any necessary corrections.

See page TM53 for answers to You Decide and Application Activity.

EXERCISE 5-4
Print Database Object Definitions

The database **Documenter** report enables you to preview and print the properties of your database objects. For form objects and report objects, the Documenter also shows the properties of all the controls you have used.

FIGURE 5.9 Print Table Definition dialog box

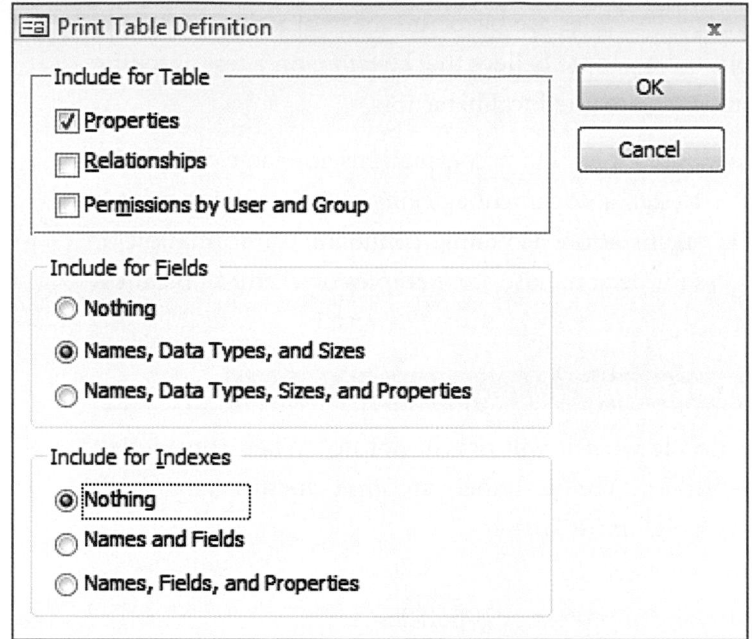

FIGURE 5.10 Object Definition window in Print Preview

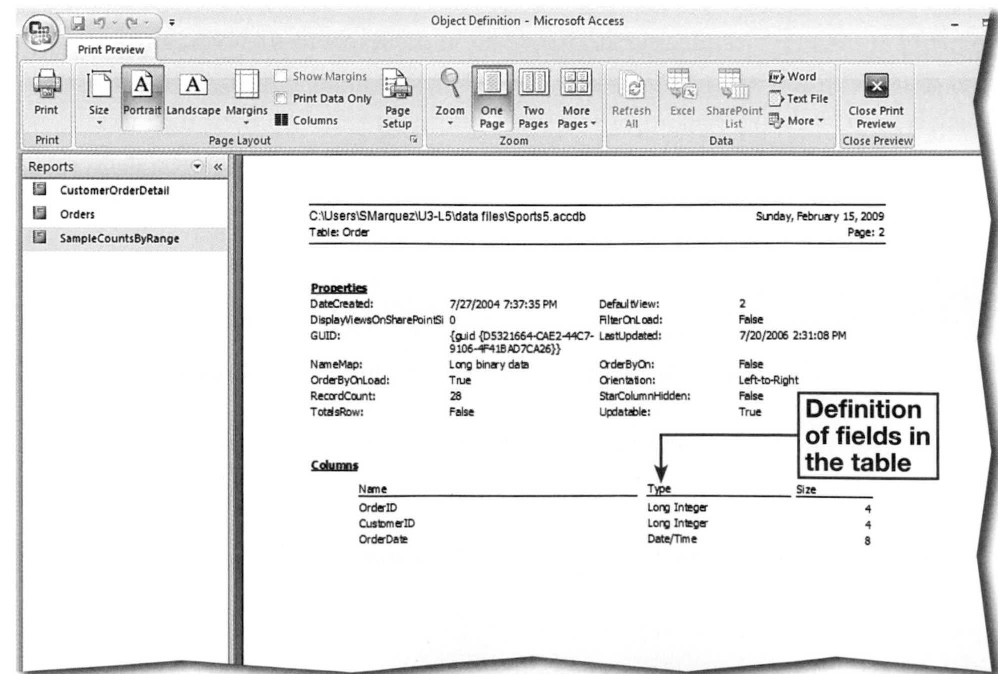

Step-By-Step

1. In your **Sports5** file, choose **Database Tools> Analyze>Database Documenter**. Click on each tab to see the objects that can be described. Click the **Tables** tab.
2. Select the **Customer**, **Order**, and **OrderDetail** check boxes. Click **Options**.
3. In the **Print Table Definition** dialog box, select only those options shown in Figure 5.9. Click **OK**.
4. In the **Documenter** box, click **OK**.
5. Maximize the **Object Definition** window. Click on the window once to zoom in. Click **Next Page** ▶.
6. **CHECK** Your screen should look like Figure 5.10.
7. With your teacher's permission, print the report. Add your name to the printed report.
8. Click **Close Print Preview** ✕.

Continue to the next exercise.

Step-By-Step Tip In **Step 7**, make sure the page range for the report is correct. Otherwise, students may print too many pages.

UNIT 1 Portfolio Project

Summer Day Camp Fun

The day camp you work for is putting together its schedule for the coming summer. Your supervisor has asked you to arrange six fun and exciting classes for seven- and eight-year-olds. The classes will be held at the local community center. You do not have a large budget, so you will have to be creative to meet your goal.

Answers Rubrics for each part of the Portfolio Project are available at **glencoe.com**. You may want to download the rubrics and make them available to students as they complete each project.

Part 1: Write a Letter

LEVEL This is a beginning level project.

Rubric

Goal Your task is to find individuals who can teach activities at your camp. For example:

- The owner of the local gardening center might agree to teach gardening skills.
- Someone in your community might have a craft or hobby they would like to share.

Create Key a general letter that you can send to people. Use the standard business letter format when creating your letter (see page 710). Your letter should have at least three paragraphs. In the first paragraph:

- State why you are sending the letter.
- Ask whether the person has any skills or talents that they would like to share with children.

In the second paragraph:

- Ask the person to describe the skill or talent they would like to teach.
- Ask the person what days and times they might be available to teach.

Self Assess Use the Have You...? checklist to review your letter. Then, print your letter and proofread it carefully. Make necessary corrections. Follow your teacher's instructions for naming the document and saving it to your Portfolio Folder.

When finished, proceed to Part 2.

	Have You...?
✓	Included standard margins for a business letter
✓	Included a letterhead
✓	Included today's date
✓	Included a greeting
✓	Included three or more paragraphs in the letter's body
✓	Included a closing

Step-By-Step

1. In your **Sports5** file, open the **SampleCountsBy Range** report.
2. Maximize the window. Click **Two Pages** .
3. Choose **Print Preview> Page Layout> Landscape** .
4. Click **One Page** .
5. **Choose Print Preview> Page Layout> Columns** .
6. CHECK Your screen should look like Figure 5.7.
7. In the **Page Setup** dialog box, key: 3 in the **Number of Columns** box.
8. Under **Column Layout**, select **Down, then Across**. Click **OK**.
9. CHECK Your screen should look like Figure 5.8.
10. With your teacher's permission, click **Print** .
11. Click **OK**. Click **Close Print Preview** .

Continue to the next exercise.

Microsoft Office 2007

Access has a built-in Help reference. To search or browse for Help, click **Help** on the **Ribbon**.

EXERCISE 5-3
Use Print Preview to Prepare Reports for Printing

Print Preview helps you make sure that text and fields are in the correct place with the correct formatting. By contrast, Layout View allows you to manipulate fields and groups, but it does not show page breaks or certain other elements.

Differentiated Instruction/Advanced Students Have advanced students open the report in **Design View** and place the **Range** and **Count** headers over each column.

FIGURE 5.7 SampleCountsByRange Page Setup dialog box

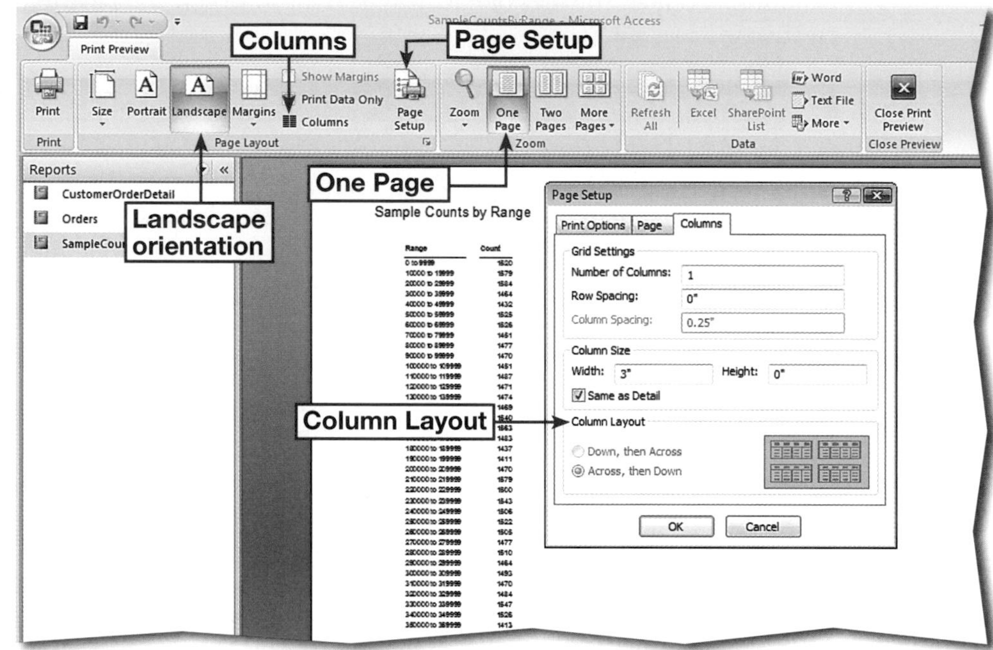

FIGURE 5.8 SampleCountsByRange in Print Preview

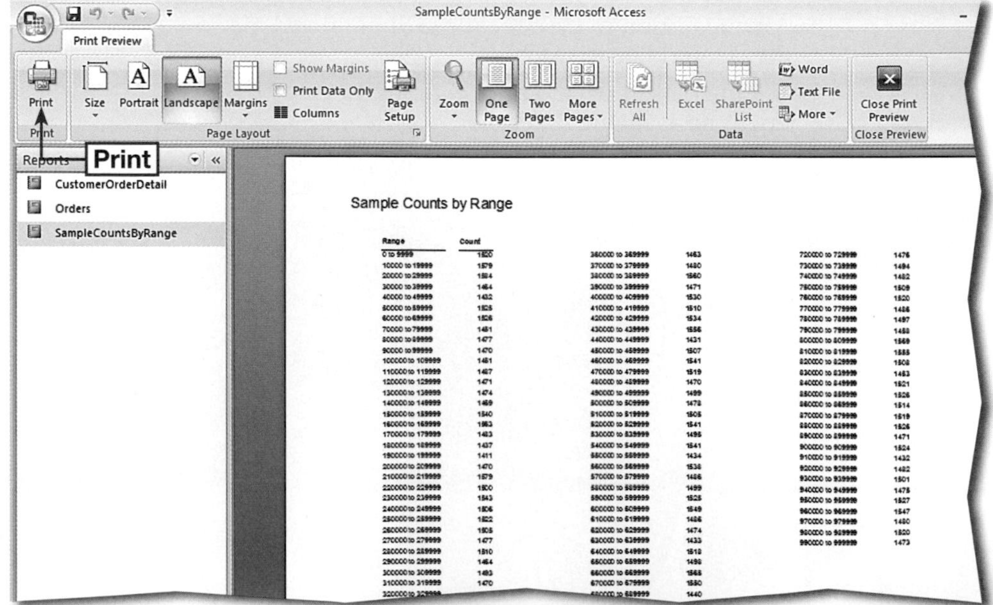

UNIT 1 Portfolio Project

Part 2: Develop a Schedule

LEVEL This is an intermediate level project.

Goal You sent out your letter and received a great response! Many people have agreed to teach classes this summer. Your task now is to *compile* (put together) the information so you can develop a schedule of classes.

Create Use the information from the data file **Schedule.docx** to create a Word table of the Class Schedule. The table should include the following heads:

- Class
- Day
- Time
- Room
- Teacher

Insert the information from the data file into your table. Make sure you place information under the correct head. Then, format your table with bold lines around the outside border. Bold the heads. Remember to create a title for your table.

Self Assess Use the Have You...? checklist to review your table. Make sure your table reflects all of the items noted in the checklist.

Carefully proofread your table and make the necessary corrections. (Tip: It is often a good idea to have another person proofread your documents. Pair up with a friend to proofread each other's table.) Follow your teacher's instructions for naming the document and saving it to your Portfolio Folder.

When finished, proceed to Part 3.

	Have You...?
✓	Adjusted the column width as needed
✓	Included heads in each column
✓	Bolded the heads
✓	Applied styles to the heads
✓	Added a title for the table
✓	Added a border to the table

Step-By-Step

11 Return to **Design View** and double-click the chart. The **Microsoft Graph** window opens.

12 **CHECK** Your screen should look like Figure 5.5. With the chart selected, click the **Chart Objects** drop-down menu. Select **Value Axis**. In the toolbar at the top of the screen, choose **Format>Number**.

13 In the **Format Axis** dialog box, under **Category**, select **Currency**. In the **Decimal places** box, key: 0. Click **OK**.

14 Choose **Chart>Chart Type**. Under **Chart Type**, select **Bar**. Click **OK**.

15 Click in an open area of the design grid to return to **Design View**. Click **Report View**.

16 **CHECK** Your screen should look like Figure 5.6. Close the report. Click **Yes** to save changes, and in the **Save As** dialog box, key: Orders. Click **OK**.

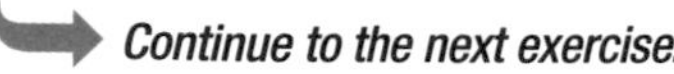

Continue to the next exercise.

Tech Tip

In **Design View**, you can edit a report's text box control sources without using the **Property Sheet**.

EXERCISE 5-2 (Continued) Create and Modify Charts

Step-By-Step Teaching Tip In **Step 13**, explain to students that the graph they see in **Design View** is only a sample chart. The actual chart can be seen only in **Layout** or **Report View**.

FIGURE 5.5 Microsoft Graph window

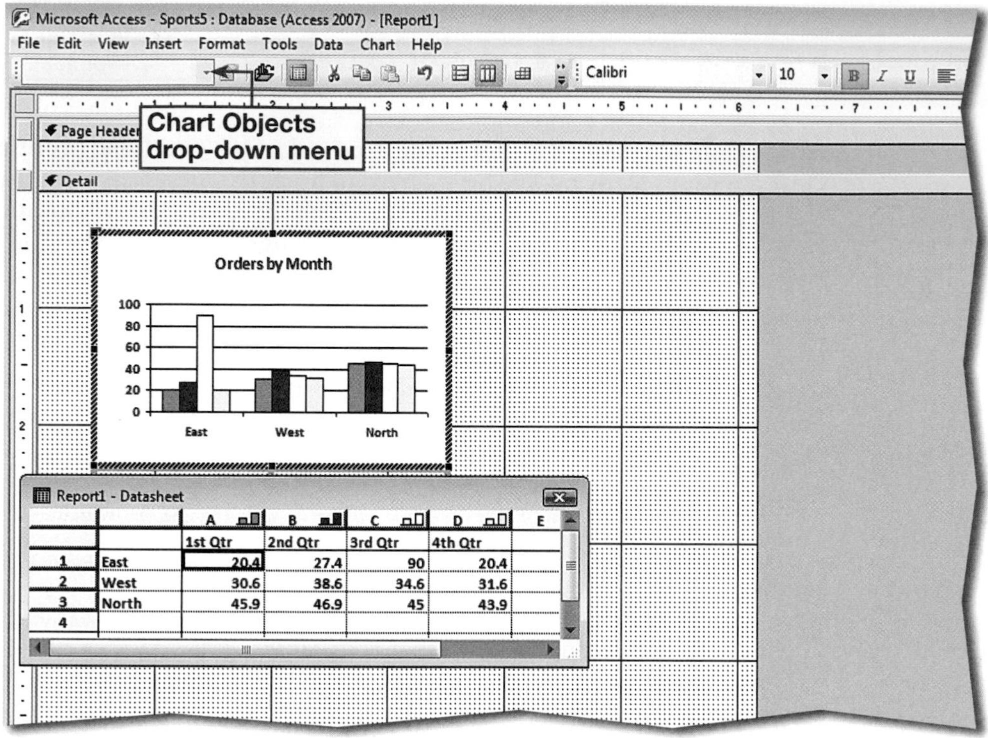

FIGURE 5.6 Orders bar chart in Report View

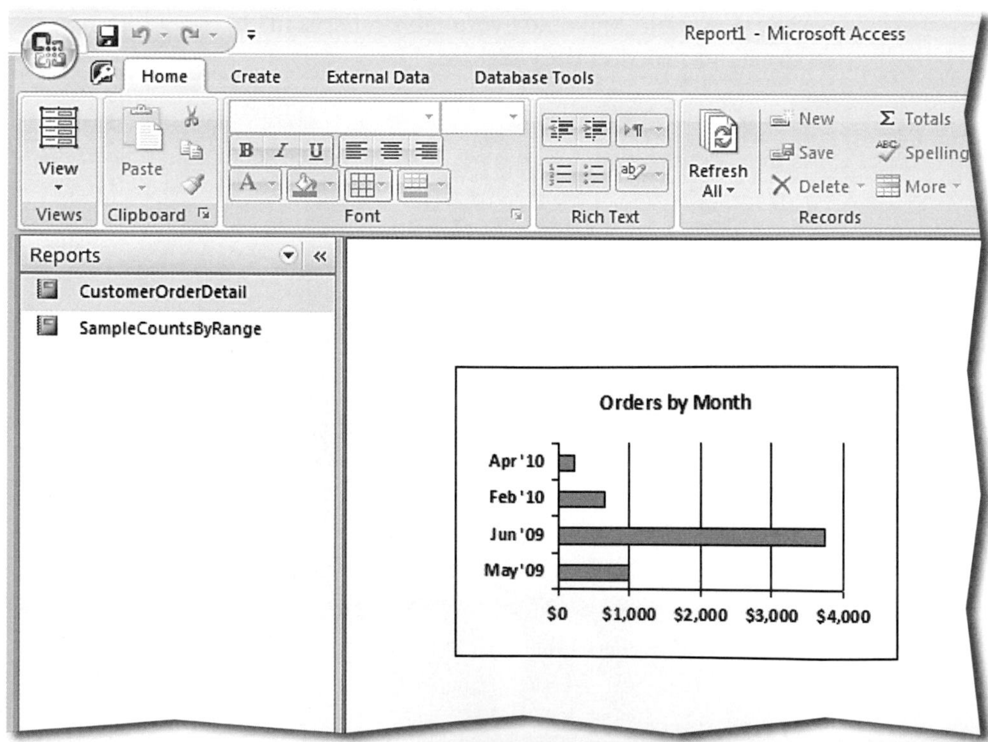

UNIT 1 Portfolio Project

Part 3: Make a Flyer

LEVEL This is an intermediate level project.

Rubric R

Goal It is your responsibility to publicize the camp's summer classes. To do this, you decide to create an eye-catching notice, or flyer, which students will want to read and take home to their families.

Create Use Word to create a simple flyer. Your flyer should contain the following information:

- The name of the summer day camp
- The location of the camp
- When the camp is taking place
- A list of the classes being taught
- Contact information for people who want to learn more about the camp

Use Clip Art, WordArt, and other graphics to make your flyer visually interesting.

Self Assess Use the Have You...? checklist to review your flyer. Make sure your flyer follows the design rules noted in the checklist.

Carefully proofread your flyer and make corrections. Follow your teacher's instructions for naming the document and saving it to your Portfolio Folder.

When finished, proceed to Part 4.

	Have You...?
✓	Used no more than three different fonts
✓	Used no more than three different colors
✓	Varied font size (the most important information should be the largest size)
✓	Used WordArt
✓	Inserted Clip Art
✓	Provided the camp's name, location, and dates
✓	Provided a list of classes being taught
✓	Provided contact information

Step-By-Step

1. In your **Sports5** file, choose **Create>Reports> Blank Report** .
2. Choose **Report Layout Tools>Format>View**. Select **Design View**. Maximize the window.
3. Choose **Design>Controls> Insert Chart** .
4. Click under **Detail**. The **Chart Wizard** opens.
5. **CHECK** Your screen should look like Figure 5.3.
6. Under **View**, select **Queries**. Select **Query: Order_PivotChart**. Click **Next**.
7. In the **Available Fields** box, double-click **OrderDate**. Double-click **Price**. The fields are moved to the **Fields for Chart** box. Click **Next**.
8. Click **Next** twice. In the chart title box, key: Orders by Month. Select **No, don't display a legend**. Click **Finish**.
9. Click **Report View** in the lower right corner of the screen.
10. **CHECK** Your screen should look like Figure 5.4.

Continued on the next page.

EXERCISE 5-2
Create and Modify Charts

A **chart** is useful for presenting database information visually. You can insert a chart into an existing form or report, or you can create a new chart by creating a blank form or report into which you can insert the chart. Once a chart is created, you can format it and even change its type in the Microsoft Graph window.

Step-By-Step Tip In **Step 3**, students can close the Field List by choosing **Design Tools>Add Existing Fields.**

FIGURE 5.3 Orders chart in Design View

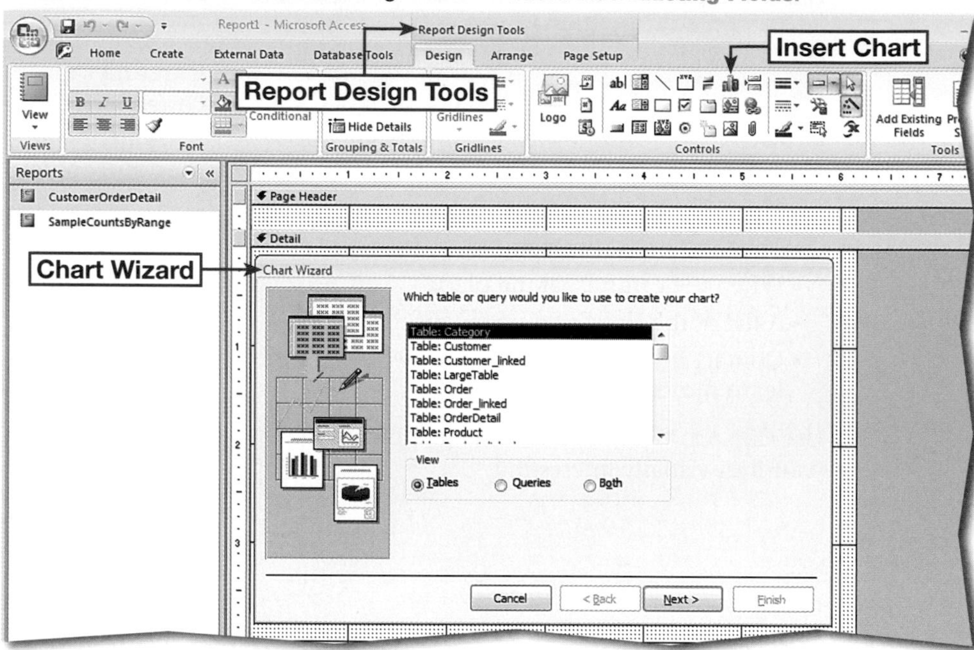

FIGURE 5.4 Orders column chart in Report View

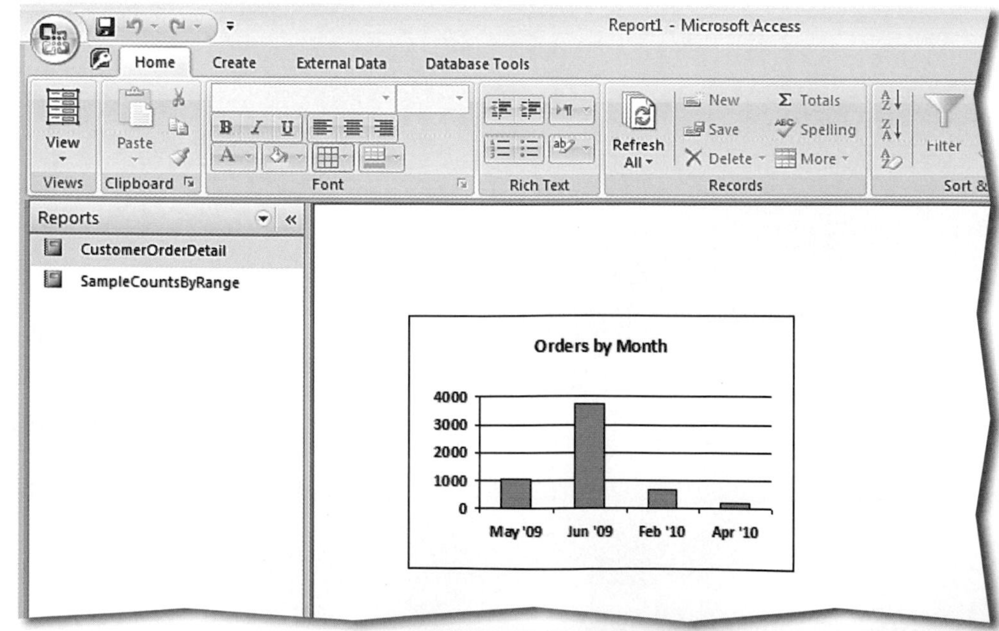

UNIT 1 Portfolio Project

Part 4: Create a Newsletter

LEVEL This is an advanced level project.

Goal The summer day camp was a big success! You have now been asked to develop a newsletter to report what happened at the camp. The newsletter will also advertise the next camp session.

Create Use Word to create a newsletter. In your newsletter:

- Include photos, Clip Art, and other graphics of the camp's activities.
- Include two or three brief stories about the camp's activities, events, and highlights.
- Provide the camp's name, location, and dates for the next session.
- State why kids love to participate in the camp.

For your newsletter, use either a two-column or a three-column design as needed to fit your content.

Self Assess Use the Have You...? checklist to review your newsletter. Make sure your newsletter follows the design rules noted in the checklist. Carefully proofread your newsletter and make corrections. Follow your teacher's instructions for naming the document and saving it to your Portfolio Folder.

	Have You...?
✓	Used no more than three different fonts
✓	Used no more than three different colors
✓	Varied font size (the most important information should be the largest size)
✓	Used WordArt and Clip Art as needed
✓	Inserted photos
✓	Used either a two- or three-column design
✓	Provided two or three brief stories about the camp
✓	Provided the camp's contact information
✓	Provided dates for the next session

Go Online — BEYOND THE BOOK

glencoe.com

Go to the Online Learning Center to learn additional skills and review what you have already learned.

Microsoft Word
Extend your knowledge of Word by visiting the Online Learning Center for more MCAS-based exercises. Select **Advanced Word Exercises>Lessons**

Windows Vista
Select **Windows Vista Exercises>Lessons** to explore Microsoft's operating system fully.

Microsoft Outlook
Want to learn all about Outlook and how to use e-mail communication and scheduling? Select **Microsoft Outlook Exercises>Lessons** for all you need to know.

Additional Projects
Complete additional projects in the following areas:

- **Real-World Business Projects** reinforce Microsoft Word by focusing on real-world business applications.
- **Presentation and Publishing Projects** Use your Word skills to create exciting PowerPoint presentations and desktop publishing activities.
- **Academic Projects** Integrate academic skills while enriching your understanding of Microsoft Word.

More Online Resources
Access additional Web sites and online information relating to key topics covered in Glencoe's *iCheck Series*. Select **Additional Resources>Links**.

Step-By-Step

1. Start **Access**. Ask your teacher where to copy the **Sports5.accdb** database, and open your copy of the **Sports5** database.
2. In the **Navigation Pane**, display **Reports**.
3. Open the report **CustomerOrderDetail**.
4. Maximize the **Print Preview** window.
5. Choose **Print Preview>Zoom**, and click the **Zoom** drop-down arrow. Select **200%**.
6. **CHECK** Your screen should look like Figure 5.1.
7. Click the middle of the screen. Choose **Print Preview>Zoom>Two Pages**.
8. Click **Zoom**.
9. Choose **Print Preview>Zoom>More Pages** and select **Four Pages**.
10. **CHECK** Your screen should look like Figure 5.2. Click **Close Print Preview**.

Continue to the next exercise.

Teaching Tip Remind students that they can view a report by right-clicking the report in the **Navigation Pane** and selecting **Design** or **Layout View**.

EXERCISE 5-1
Preview for Print

A report **preview** shows you what a report will look like when it is printed. **Print Preview** lets you review each page before sending the whole report to the printer. Print Preview gives you an accurate picture of all of the data and calculations in a report. When you open a report in Access, it automatically opens in Print Preview.

Troubleshooting Make sure students understand that using the **Zoom** drop-down arrow will provide them with more zoom choices than using the **Zoom** button.

FIGURE 5.1 Print Preview at 200%

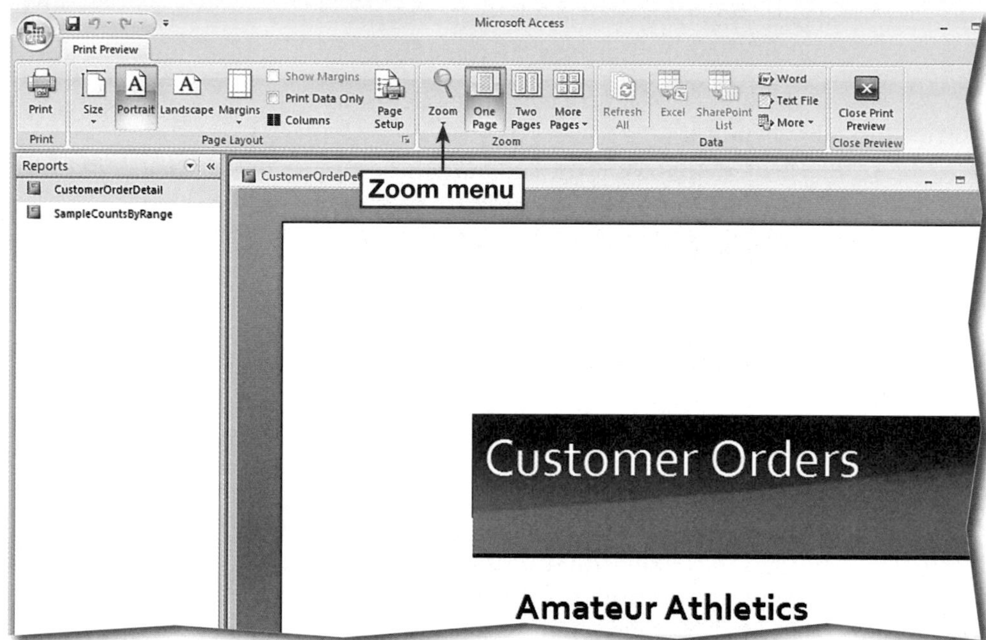

FIGURE 5.2 Print Preview with four pages

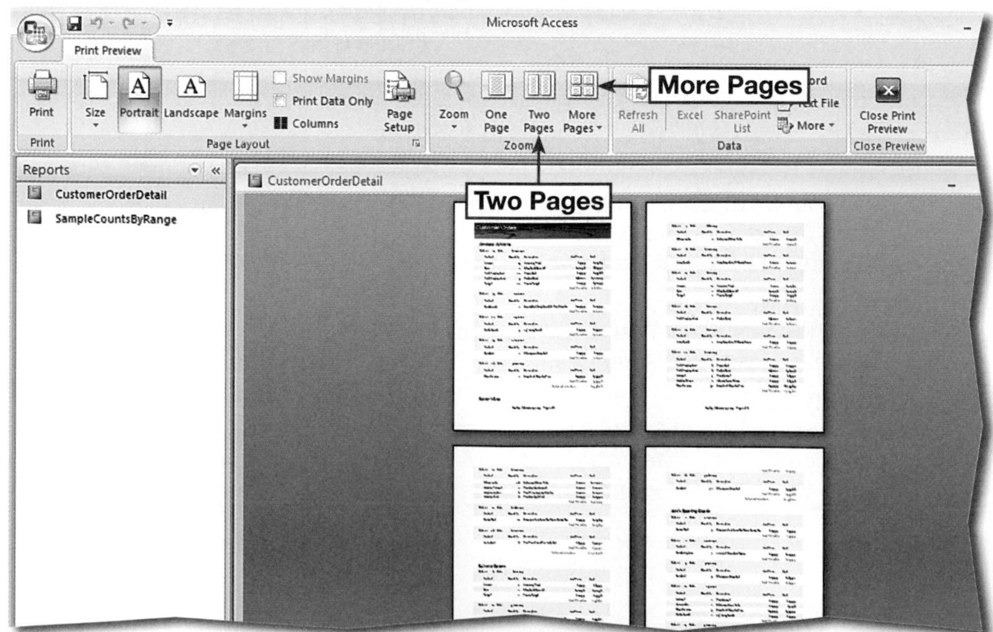

UNIT 2 Excel 2007: Business and Personal Finances

Unit Objectives:

After completing this Unit, you will be able to:

LESSON 1

Excel Basics

LESSON 2

Create Data and Content

LESSON 3

Format Data and Content

LESSON 4

Analyze Data

LESSON 5

Manage Workbooks

See page TM66 for an overview of Unit level resources.

Why It Matters Have students identify examples of how they might use Excel to help with their schoolwork. For example, students could use Excel to organize their grades, assignments, and due dates.

Why It Matters

Microsoft Excel is a powerful business tool. Using Excel, you can organize lists of data, calculate expenses for a project, create charts, and much more. A skilled Excel user is a good candidate for a variety of jobs. ***What is one way that Excel might help you with your schoolwork?***

Go Online — **REAL WORLD CONNECTION**

glencoe.com

Go to the **Online Learning Center** and select your book. Choose **Unit 2** to learn how businesses use spreadsheet applications in the real world.

LESSON 5 Reading Guide

Before You Read

See page TM42 for English Learner activity suggestions.

Take a Nap The more well rested and alert you are when you sit down to study, the more likely you will be to remember the information later. Studying in the same state of mind as when you are likely to take a test—fully rested and mentally sharp—will help to ensure your best performance.

Read To Learn

- Prepare data for formal reports.
- Make data easier to interpret by creating charts.
- Troubleshoot problems by documenting the properties of all objects in a database.
- Protect a database by encrypting it with a password.

Main Idea

Access is an excellent tool for managing, maintaining, and safeguarding valuable information in a database.

Vocabulary

Key Terms

chart
Documenter
encrypt
object dependency
password
preview
Print Preview
Quick Print
union query

Academic Vocabulary

These words appear in your reading and on your tests. Make sure you know their meanings:

display
ensure
source
version

Quick Write Activity

Describe On a separate sheet of paper, explain why users might want to protect and save their databases. Why might a business want to ensure that its data is protected? What type of data would you want to protect in a database?

Study Skills

Use Your Tools All Microsoft Office programs provide a certain level of error-checking. Use the error-correcting tools that are available to you, and pay attention to the errors they correct. Proofread your own work, and take the opportunity to make sure that you have produced the most accurate and presentable work possible.

Academic Standards

English Language Arts

NCTE 4 Use written language to communicate effectively.

Math

NCTM (Number and Operations) Understand numbers, ways of representing numbers, relationships among numbers, and number systems.

NCTM (Representation) Create and use representations to organize, record, and communicate mathematical ideas.

NCTM (Algebra) Use mathematical models to represent and understand quantitative relationships.

Careers and Technology

How Can Spreadsheet Skills Advance Your Career?

Career Checklist

To use spreadsheets effectively in the workplace, remember to:

- ✓ Use standard formats and fonts.
- ✓ Group related worksheets into a single file.
- ✓ Hide distracting rows, columns, or worksheets to focus on essential information.
- ✓ Use color to group and classify information.
- ✓ Format your spreadsheet for easy printing.

Spreadsheets are complex tools that are used to measure performance, plan a budget, and make other calculations. If you have spreadsheet skills you can also learn to manage and manipulate information in the workplace. Spreadsheets are used to maintain schedules, track expenses, and manage large-scale projects in a variety of careers.

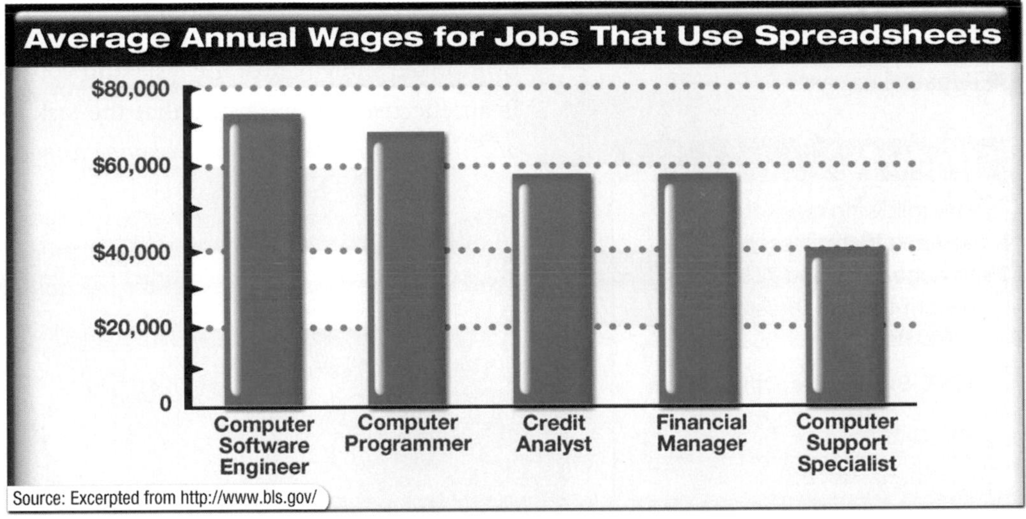

Differentiated Instruction/Advanced Students Have students write a paragraph describing how they might use Excel in the career of their choice.

NCLB/Math (Representation) Have students go visit the book Web site at **glencoe.com** to learn more about math theory. Students should click the Math Handbook link.

Business

Spreadsheet software is valuable in the world of business. Credit analysts and financial managers use a wide range of spreadsheet functions to input and assess credit histories, financial portfolios, and budgets.

Computer Occupations

There are a wide variety of high-salary jobs in the computer industry that use spreadsheets for their non-mathematical capabilities. Computer software engineers and computer programmers use spreadsheets to classify and manipulate the huge amount of complex information needed to analyze programming problems, write programs, and create software. A computer support specialist might use spreadsheets to log and track data from their support calls.

1. **Evaluate** How could spreadsheet skills improve your chances of obtaining a higher salary?
2. **Math** Which of the careers listed in the chart has the highest annual wage potential?

See page TM66 for answers to the Reading Check.

LESSON 5 Manage Databases

In this lesson, you will learn how to manage your databases. You will preview reports, print various objects, and repair databases. Knowing these skills will help you to make the most of your databases.

Key Concepts

- Preview reports
- Print documentation on database objects
- Identify object dependencies
- Repair databases

Standards

The following standards are covered in this lesson. Refer to pages xxiv and 715 for descriptions of the standards listed here.

ISTE Standards Correlation

NETS•S

2a, 3d, 6a, 6b, 6c

Microsoft Certified Application Specialist Standards

Access

2.6, 5.3, 5.6, 6.1, 6.2

21st CENTURY SKILLS

See page TM87 for answers to 21st Century Skills.

Follow Up Even when you think you are finished with a task or project, there is always one last thing you can do: ask if there is anything else left. Whether you are performing work for someone else or for yourself, always return to a project after you have finished and ask, "What else can I do?" You may discover that you overlooked some part of the task, and you will be glad you asked. Following up is an effective way to ensure that the task has been completed. *What are some additional things you could have done as part of a recently completed task?*

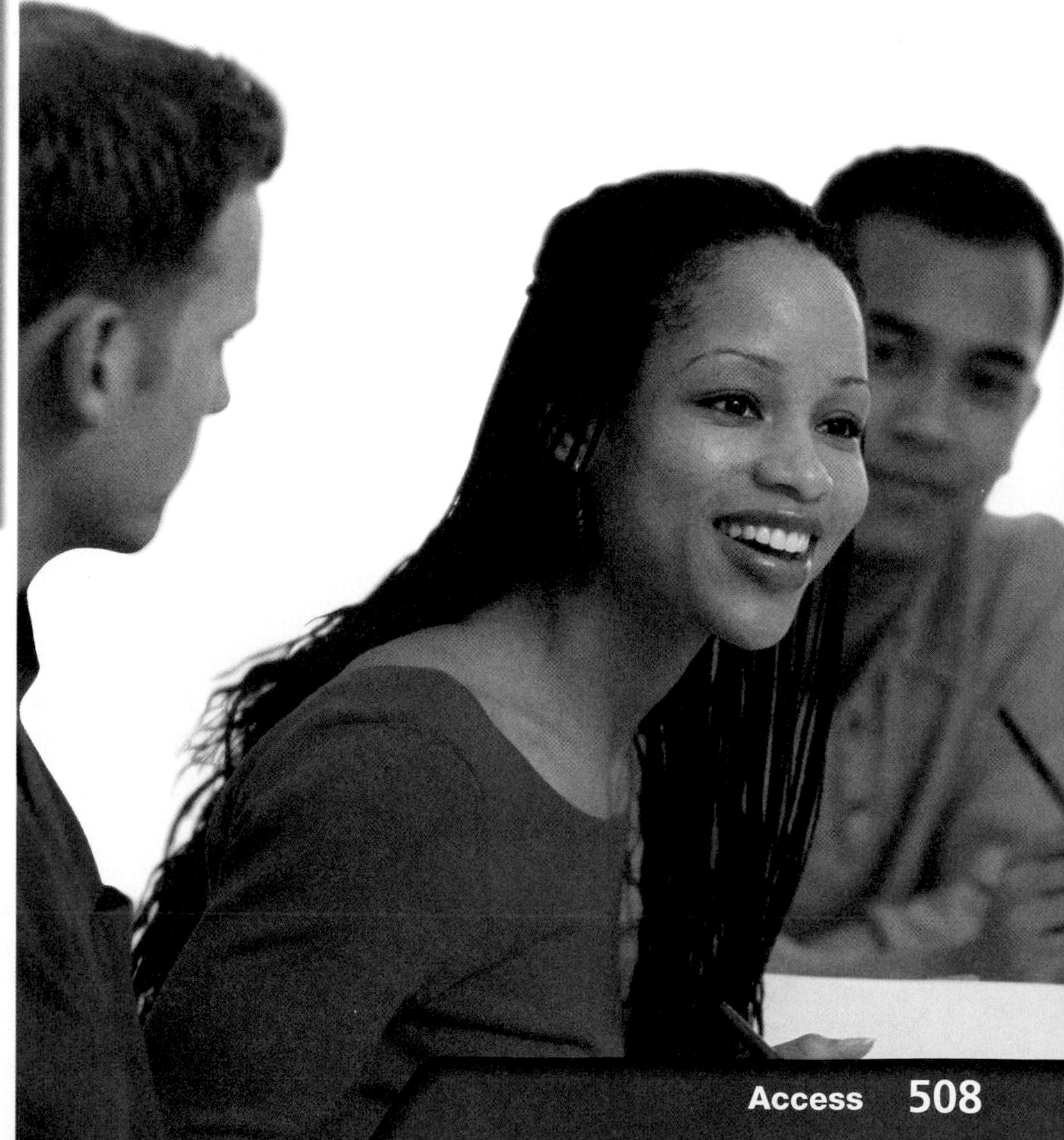

LESSON 1 Excel Basics

In this lesson, you will learn basic Excel skills such as opening and closing a workbook, inserting and editing cell contents, and naming and saving a workbook. These basic skills will give you the foundation you need to learn more complex Excel skills.

Key Concepts

- Identify parts of the Excel screen
- Open and close workbooks
- Name and save a workbook
- Insert and edit cell contents
- Calculate a sum
- Print a worksheet

Standards

The following standards are covered in this lesson. Refer to pages xxv and 715 for a description of the standards listed here.

ISTE Standards Correlation

NETS•S

2b, 3b, 3d, 4c, 6a, 6b,

Microsoft Certified Applications Specialist

Excel

1.4, 3.2

21st CENTURY SKILLS

See page TM68 for answer to 21st Century Skills.

Be Productive Productivity is a measure of how well you use resources, such as time or money. If you think the results you are getting are worth the time and effort you put into a project, then you are probably being productive. Two people may spend the same amount of time on a project, but one person may be more productive if he or she has better tools or is more organized. Excel is a tool that can help you organize your work more productively. *What tools do you use to organize your work?*

LESSON 4 Challenge Yourself Projects

Before You Begin

Manage Data A database is an important tool for sharing, updating, and protecting information. These projects give you the skills you need to gather and present data normally found in an Access database.

Reflect Once you complete the projects, open a Word document and answer the following:

1. How might filtering data help manage queries?
2. How else might you use Access to manage data?
3. How else might you have completed the project? Are there other methods that you could use to gather this information?

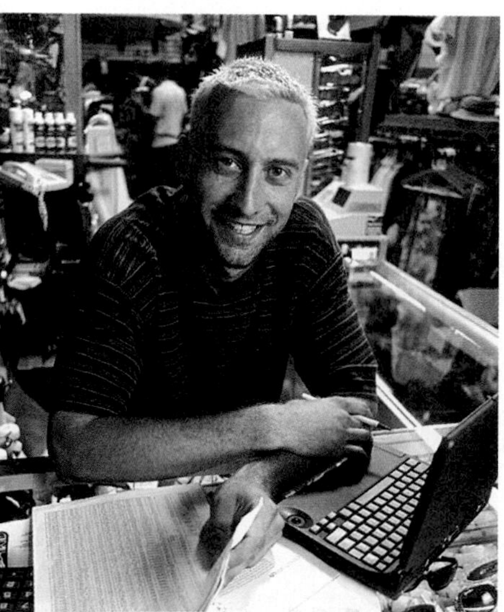

Answers Rubrics for each Challenge Yourself Project are available at **glencoe.com**. You may want to download the rubrics and make them available to students as they complete each project.

9. Filter Data within Queries

LEVEL This is an intermediate level project.

Math: Verify Data The sales department has identified a discrepancy in their sales reports during the last six-month period. To try and find the error, it needs to look at your detailed order information for that period of time. Open your **Sports4** database and create a filter in the **DetailedOrders** query that will return the order information from June 2009 to June 2010. Double-check that the information falls within the correct parameters.

Solution The solution file for Project 9 is the query **DetailedOrders-9SF** in the **Sports4-SF.accdb** database.

Save your new query as: DetailedOrders-[your first initial and last name]9.

10. Export Data From Queries

LEVEL This is an intermediate level project.

Export Data to Excel The sales department needs to receive the June 2009 to June 2010 order information as an Excel spreadsheet. Using the **DetailedOrders** query you created in Exercise 9:

- Run the proper filter on the data.
- Export the data from Access to an Excel worksheet.

Save your file as: DetailedOrders-[your first initial and last name]10. Ask your teacher where to save the file.

Solution The solution file for Project 10 is the Excel file **DetailedOrders-10SF.xlsx**.

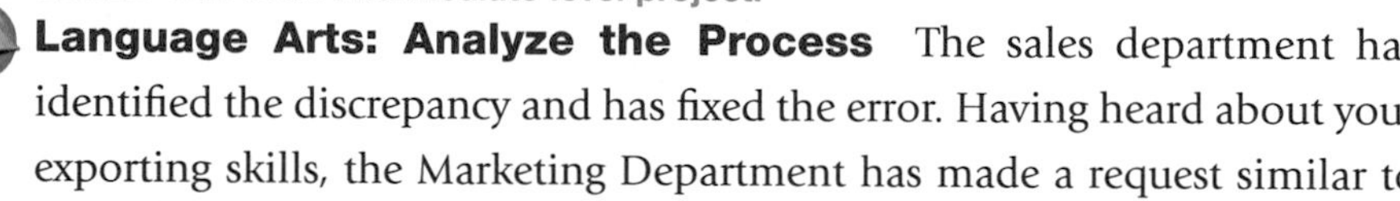

11. Sort Data

LEVEL This is an intermediate level project.

Language Arts: Analyze the Process The sales department has identified the discrepancy and has fixed the error. Having heard about your exporting skills, the Marketing Department has made a request similar to the one made by the sales department. You must:

- Create a filter for items sold during the months of November 2009 to February 2010
- Sort the records by area.
- When completed, double-check that the information falls within the correct parameters.

Solution The solution file for Project 11 is the Excel file **From Sales.xlsx**.

Save your new query as: DetailedOrders-[your first initial and last name]11.

In a Word document, make a list of five types of data that a business might want to gather from a database. For example, a business might want information to track how many of one item was sold during a specific period of time. Why might this information be helpful to the business?

LESSON 1 Reading Guide

Before You Read

See page TM42 for English Learner activity suggestions.

Prior Knowledge Look over the Key Concepts at the beginning of the lesson. Write down what you already know about each concept and what you want to find out by reading the lesson. As you read, find examples for both categories.

Read to Learn

- Explore the Excel application and how it works.
- Understand how to enter values and formulas into worksheet cells.
- Consider how Excel can help you organize important data, such as an inventory.

Main Idea

Excel is an important tool that allows you to create and edit spreadsheets.

Vocabulary

Key Terms

button	Quick Access Toolbar (QAT)
cell	Ribbon
cell reference	ScreenTip
command	spreadsheet
dialog box	sheet tab
folder	tab
formula	title bar
formula bar	workbook
group	worksheet

Academic Vocabulary

These words appear in your reading and on your tests. Make sure you know their meanings.

illustrate
learn

Quick Write Activity

Create a List Chances are that everyday you do simple calculations such as adding or substracting numbers. Think about the tools you use on a daily basis to work with numbers (e.g., calculator, pencil and paper, etc.). On a separate piece of paper, make a list of these tools. In your list, describe how these tools help you make sense of numbers. How could these tools be improved to help you work better?

Study Skill

Avoid Distractions Is it sometimes hard for you to finish your homework? Talk to your family about establishing a set time every day for homework. Make sure both family and friends know that you are not available during this time.

Academic Standards

English Language Arts

NCTE 3 Apply strategies to interpret texts.

NCTE 4 Use written language to communicate effectively.

Math

NCTM (Number and Operations) Understand numbers, ways of representing numbers, relationships among numbers, and number systems.

NCTM (Number and Operations) Compute fluently and make reasonable estimates.

LESSON 4 Critical Thinking Activities

Beyond the Classroom Activity Students' answers may include customer name, date of purchase, product, style, or price. Students may notice how often customers make purchases, how much they are spending, and what styles they prefer.

Standards at Work Activity Students' answers should include three math-related instances during their day, including school-related assignments.

21st Century Skills Activity Students' answers will vary but should identify at least two projects and give concrete reasons for finishing.

6. Beyond the Classroom Activity

Language Arts: Analyze Data In Exercise 4-11, you learned how to sort records in forms and reports. Being able to check related information at a glance is important because it can help you recognize patterns in the data. In a Microsoft Word document, list five ways you might sort information in a sales report. Explain how these sorting criteria can reveal patterns in the data. Save your document as: a4rev-[your first initial and last name]6.

7. Standards at Work Activity

Microsoft Certified Application Specialist Correlation
Access 4.2 *Modify Queries*

Perform Calculations We all perform mathematical calculations every day. When you total the cost of items bought at the supermarket or determine how much it would cost to ride the bus a certain distance, you are performing a calculation. You can perform calculations in a database.

In a Microsoft Word document, identify three times when you might calculate a total, average, percentage, or other mathematical calculations during a typical day. Explain how you could use Access to perform these calculations. Save your document as: a4rev-[your first initial and last name]7.

8. 21st Century Skills Activity

Outline Important Tasks Finishing what you start gives you a feeling of achievement. To help with this, make a list of the tasks you would like to finish. Do you have to review for a test? Complete a science project? Organize a fundraiser for the local community theater?

- Open your **Sports4** database.
- Use the form **UnfinishedBusiness** to key in some projects you would like to complete.
- Print the form with the most important projects first.

Save your form as: UnfinishedBusiness-[your first initial and last name]8. In Microsoft Word, key one or two paragraphs explaining why it is important for you to finish these projects.

glencoe.com

Go to the **Online Learning Center** to complete the following review activities.

Online Self Check
Test your knowledge of the material by clicking **Unit 3> Lesson 4** and then choosing **Self Checks**.

Interactive Review
To review the main points of this lesson, click **Unit 3> Lesson 4** and then choose **Interactive Review**.

MATH MATTERS

Introduction to Excel

Excel is a type of spreadsheet software. Spreadsheet software allows users to organize and manipulate numbers and other data.

How Can I Use Excel?

Although Excel can be used to organize text, it is more commonly used to organize and process numbers in rows and columns. Businesses use Excel for many kinds of data, including budgets, sales figures, expense statements, and time cards.

You could use Excel to organize and process information about a variety of things, including:

- Your class schedule
- Your grades
- Your friends' addresses and phone numbers
- Your personal budget

When Should I Use Excel?

It is best to use Excel whenever you need to store and process data, especially numbers. There are many advantages to entering data in an Excel spreadsheet instead of a table in Word, including:

- A spreadsheet has ready-made columns and rows.
- Excel has built-in formulas that can automatically calculate sums, averages, maximum values, and minimum values.
- The formulas in Excel can be copied to other columns and rows to make quick and accurate calculations.

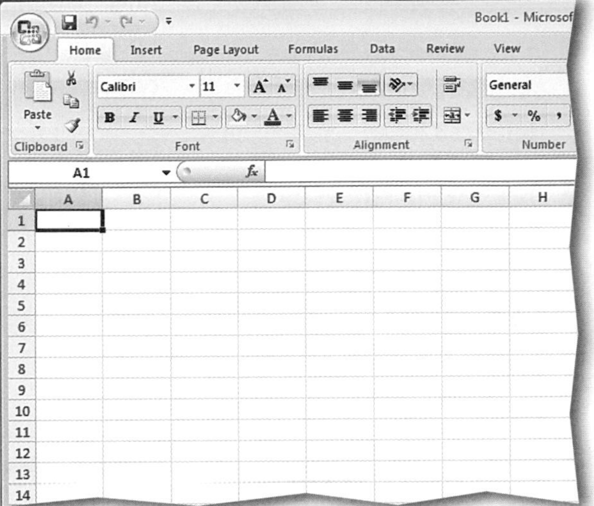

Excel is an excellent tool for tracking financial information.

NCLB/Language Arts (NCTE 3) Reinforce comprehension and evaluation of text by having students use Excel to alphabetize a list of words in the same column.

NCLB/Math (Number and Operations) Reinforce the representation of numbers by having students use Excel to key in phone numbers, budget amounts, and work hours.

SkillBuilder answers can be found on page TM68.

SKILLBUILDER

1. **Identify** What are some additional ways that businesses might use Excel?
2. **Evaluate** Why do you think many people prefer using Excel's built-in formulas instead of calculators to process data?
3. **Analyze** Explain how Excel is different from Word.
4. **Describe** Use the Internet to find out more about Excel. Describe one new use for Excel that you learned.

LESSON 4 You Try It Activities

5. Export Data from Tables

Step-By-Step

1. In your **Sports4** file, open the **Sport Record Holders3** table.
2. Click **Toggle Filter** .
3. Choose **External Data>Export>Word** .
4. **CHECK** Your screen should look like Figure 4.63.
5. In the **Export-RTF File** dialog box, click **Browse**. Ask your teacher where you should save the file and navigate there in the **File Save** dialog box. Click **Save**.
6. Click the check box labeled **Open the destination file after the export operation is complete**.
7. Click **OK**.
8. **CHECK** Your screen should look like Figure 4.64.
9. Close the exported file.
10. Close the **Export-RTF File** dialog box. Exit **Access**.

Solution The solution file for this activity is **Sport Record Holders3.rtf**.

Your supervisor says the marketing department is not familiar with Microsoft Access. She asks you to export the data you gathered from the Sport Records Holders information to another file format. You decide to export the filtered data from the Sport Record Holders table to a Word document so that the marketing department can access the information it needs for its campaign.

FIGURE 4.63 Export-RTF File dialog box

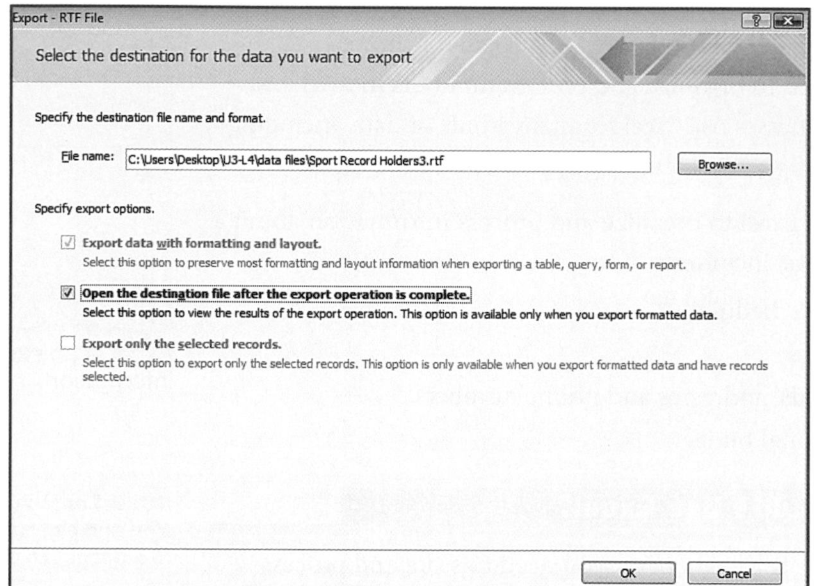

FIGURE 4.64 Exported Sport Record Holders3 filtered data

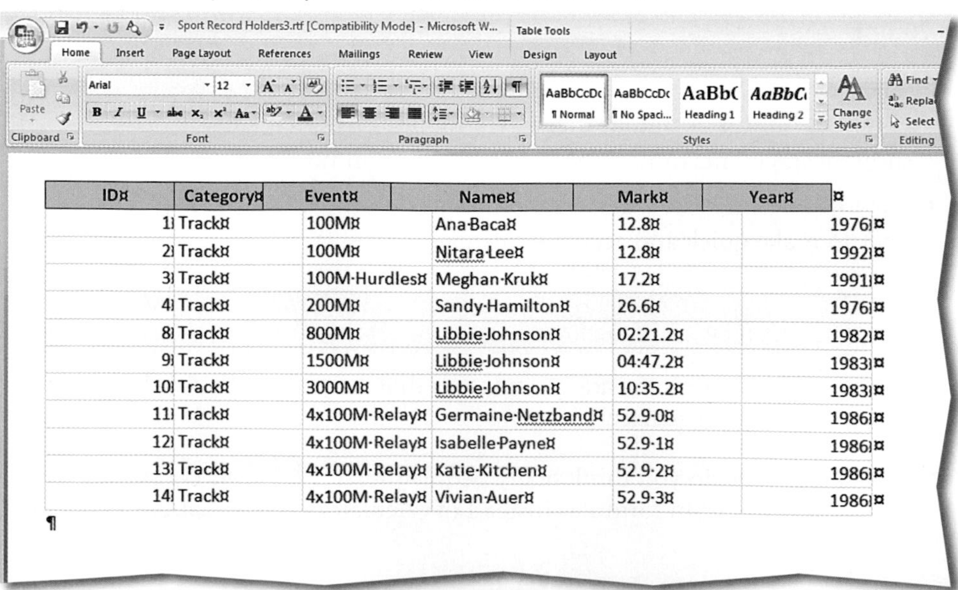

ID	Category	Event	Name	Mark	Year
1	Track	100M	Ana Baca	12.8	1976
2	Track	100M	Nitara Lee	12.8	1992
3	Track	100M Hurdles	Meghan Kruk	17.2	1991
4	Track	200M	Sandy Hamilton	26.6	1976
8	Track	800M	Libbie Johnson	02:21.2	1982
9	Track	1500M	Libbie Johnson	04:47.2	1983
10	Track	3000M	Libbie Johnson	10:35.2	1983
11	Track	4x100M Relay	Germaine Netzband	52.9-0	1986
12	Track	4x100M Relay	Isabelle Payne	52.9-1	1986
13	Track	4x100M Relay	Katie Kitchen	52.9-2	1986
14	Track	4x100M Relay	Vivian Auer	52.9-3	1986

Step-By-Step

1. To start **Excel**, click the **Start** button (see Figure 1.1). Choose **Programs>Microsoft Office®>Microsoft Office Excel 2007**.
2. **CHECK** Your screen should look like Figure 1.1.
3. Find the **title bar** (see Figure 1.1). The name of your file should be **Book1**.
4. Find the **Quick Access Toolbar (QAT)**. Click the **drop-down arrow** for the **QAT**. Read the items listed in the menu.
5. Click the **Office Button**. Read the items listed in the menu. Click in a blank area to close the menu.
6. Locate the **scroll bars** at the right side and bottom of the screen. Scroll bars allow you to move up and down and left and right in a worksheet.
7. Locate the **status bar** at the bottom of the screen.

Continue to the next exercise.

Step-By-Step Tip If the name of the workbook in **Step 2** is **Book2**, have the student close and reopen Excel.

EXERCISE 1-1
Identify Parts of the Excel Screen

In this exercise, you will **learn**, or become familiar with, the different parts of the Excel window. You must know the parts of the Excel screen to use Excel productively. The **title bar** displays the Excel file name. The **Quick Access Toolbar** (or **QAT**) allows users to quickly find commands. You use scroll bars to scroll, or move up and down or left and right in the document. Use the pointer to select tabs and other tools.

FIGURE 1.1 The Excel screen

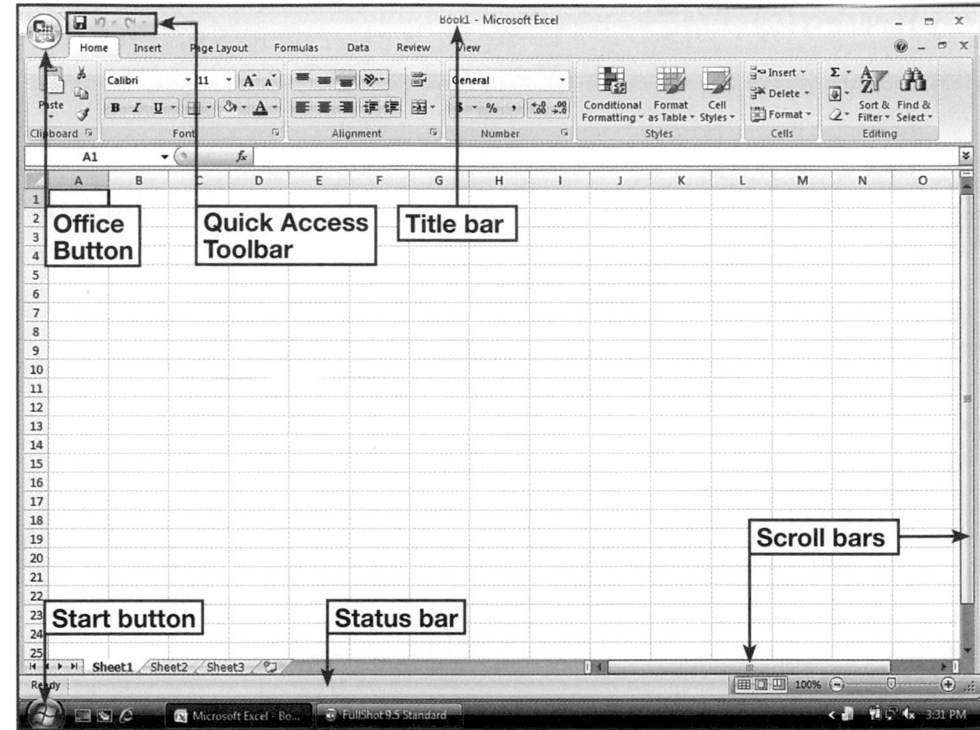

You Should Know

The location of Excel's functions may shift depending on the size of your viewing window.

Microsoft Office 2007

The Office Button is a new 2007 feature. You can use this button to perform important tasks such as creating, saving, and printing a document.

LESSON 4 You Try It Activities

4. Filter Data within Tables

Your supervisor says the marketing department needs a specific segment of the Sport Record Holders information for a marketing campaign and asks you to gather the data. You decide to filter the data within the Sport Record Holders table. This method leaves only the information that the marketing department needs for its campaign.

Solution The solution file for this activity is the **Sport Record Holders3** table in the **Sports4-SF.accdb** database.

Step-By-Step

1. In your **Sports4** file, open the **Sport Record Holders3** table.
2. Click the **Category** heading. Choose **Home>Sort & Filter>Filter**.
3. Clear all the selections except **Track**. Click **OK**.
4. CHECK Your screen should look like Figure 4.61.
5. Under the **Event** heading, click **400M**. Click **Selection**. Select **Does Not Contain "400M"**.
6. Click the **Filtered** button on the **Navigation** bar at the bottom of the **Sport Record Holders3** table.
7. Click **Advanced** and select **Advanced Filter/Sort**.
8. In the **Criteria** box, key: Not Like "*RELAY*". Press ⌄.
9. Click **Toggle Filter**.
10. CHECK Your screen should look like Figure 4.62. Close and save the table.

FIGURE 4.61 Table filtered for Track

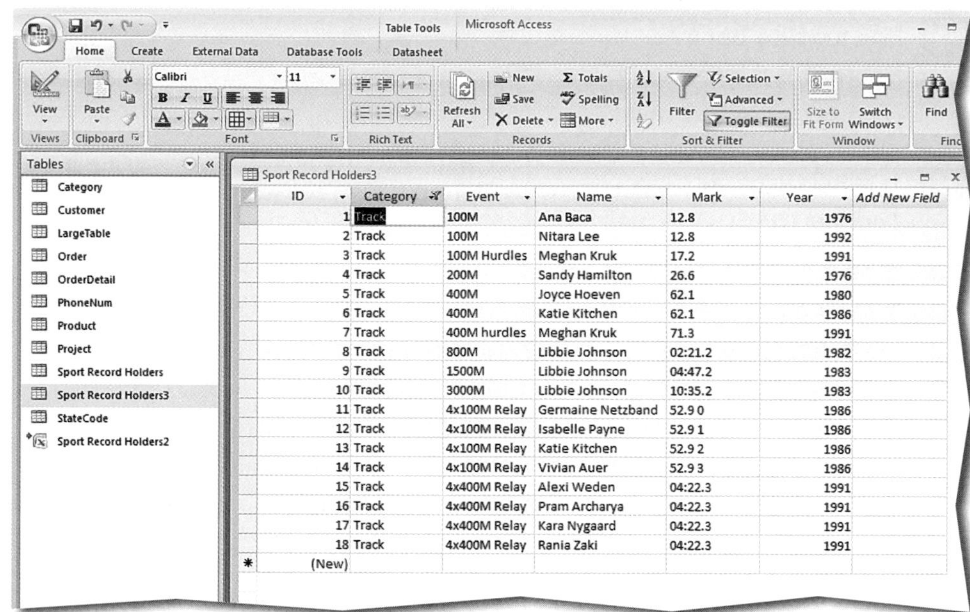

FIGURE 4.62 Table filtered for no relays

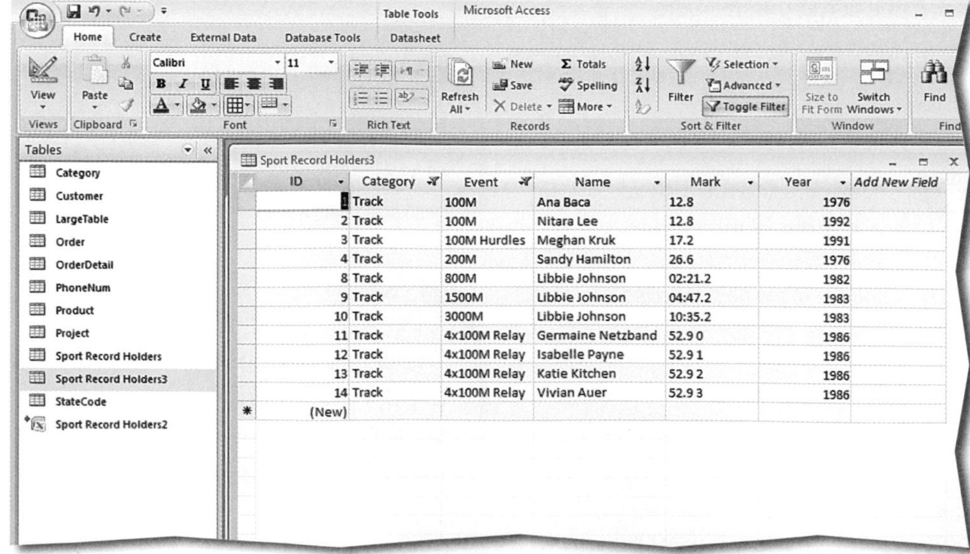

Step-By-Step

1. In Excel, on the **Ribbon**, click the **Home** tab (see Figure 1.2).
2. Roll your pointer arrow over the seven groups in the **Home** tab (see Figure 1.3).
3. Click the seven tabs across the Ribbon. Identify the groups displayed in the tab.
4. Click the **Home** tab. Read the **ScreenTip** for each button in the **Font** group.
5. In the **Font** group, click the arrow next to the **Font Color** button to display the drop-down menu. Click outside the menu to close it.
6. In the **Font** group, click the **Dialog Box Launcher**.
7. CHECK Your screen should look like Figure 1.2. Click the **Close** button on the dialog box.

Continue to the next exercise.

EXERCISE 1-2
Use Tabs, Groups, and Buttons

The **Ribbon** contains all of the buttons that you can use in Excel. Across the top of the Ribbon are **tabs**. The tabs display **buttons** (or **commands**) organized in logical **groups** that relate to a specific activity, such as keying text. When you point to a button, a **ScreenTip** appears to show you the button's name. More commands are available in **dialog boxes** that are located within the groups. Use the Dialog Box Launcher to open a group's dialog box. Not every group wil have a Dialog Box Launcher.

FIGURE 1.2 The Excel Screen

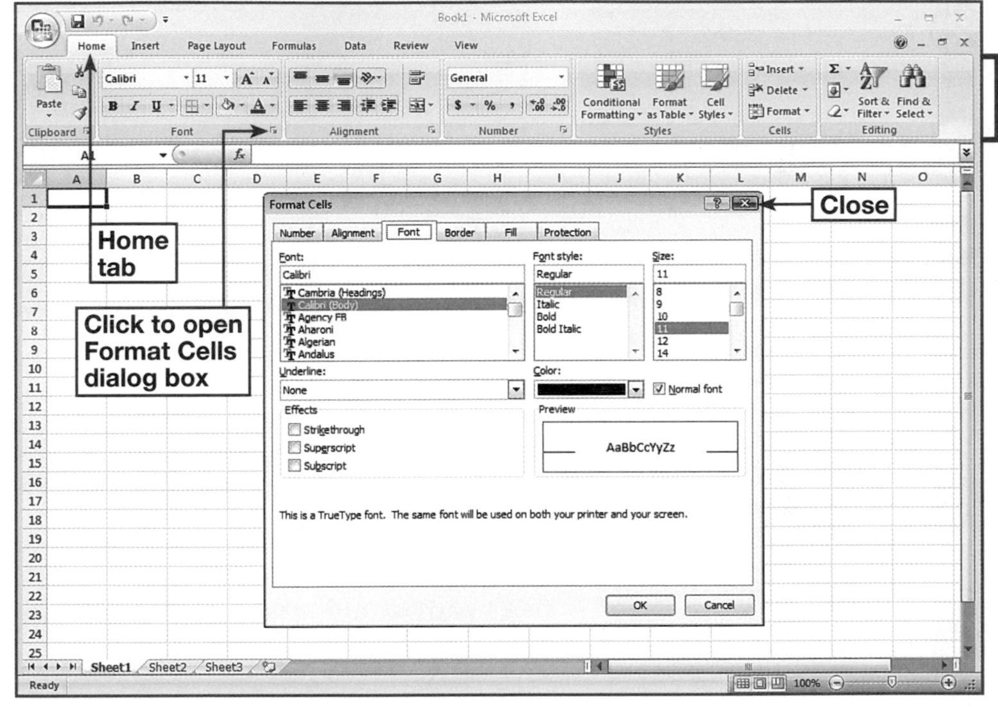

FIGURE 1.3 The Ribbon

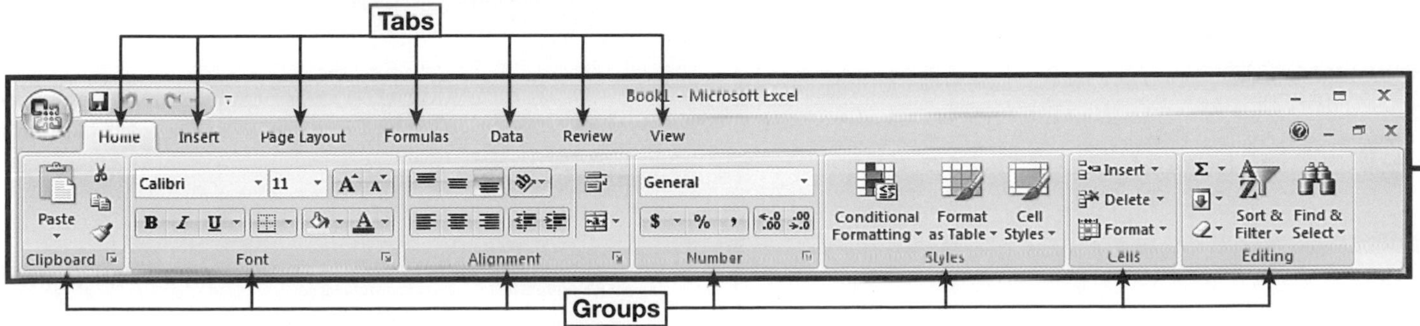

Teaching Tip Point out to students that the **Dialog Box Launcher** is the same button in all groups where it appears.

3. Sort Records in a Form

Follow the steps to complete the activity. You must complete Practice It Activity before doing this activity.

Step-By-Step

1. In your **Sports4 file**, open the **CustomerOrders** form.
2. Choose **Home>Sort & Filter>Ascending**.
3. CHECK Your screen should look like Figure 4.59.
4. Press PAGE DOWN three times. Notice the records are sorted in alphabetical order. Press PAGE UP three times to return to the first customer.
5. On the form, under **OrderDetail**, click the **Quantity** header.
6. Click **Descending**.
7. CHECK Your screen should look like Figure 4.60.
8. Press PAGE DOWN to note the order of the quantity column.
9. Close the form.

Solution The solution file for this activity is the **CustomerOrders** form in the **Sports4-SF.accdb** database.

FIGURE 4.59 CustomerOrders form sorted alphabetically by customer

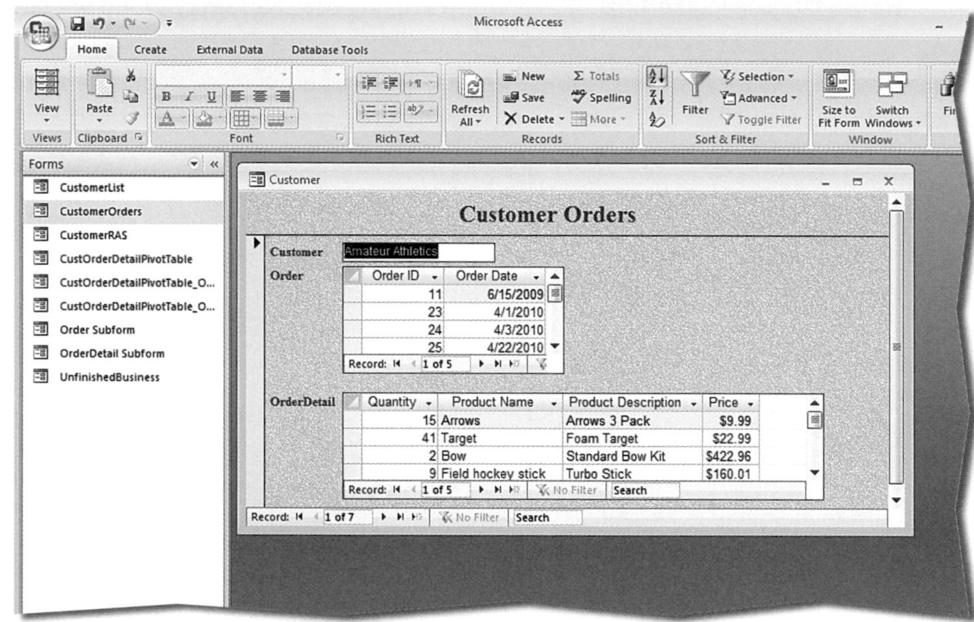

FIGURE 4.60 CustomerRAS form sorted by quantity ordered

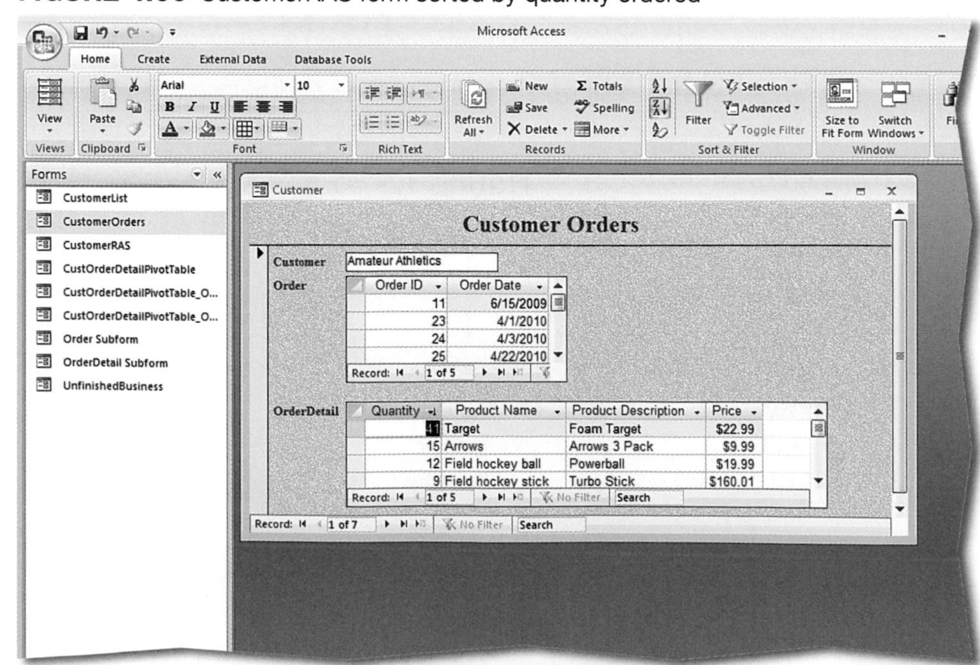

Step-By-Step

1. In your **Book1** file, click **Close Window** [X] (see Figure 1.4).

2. If prompted to save, click **No**. The current workbook closes.

3. Click the **Office Button** and select **New**.

4. In the **New Workbook** dialog box, under **Templates**, select **Blank and recent**.

5. In the middle pane, select **Blank Workbook**. Click **Create**.

6. **CHECK** Your screen should look like Figure 1.5. Notice that the name of the workbook is now **Book2**.

Continue to the next exercise.

Troubleshooter

When closing a workbook, be careful not to click the **Close** button on the title bar. The two **Close** buttons look the same. The **Close** button on the title bar will exit Excel and not just your workbook!

Different Strokes Let students know they can create a new workbook by pressing **Ctrl + N**. Students can also close a workbook by choosing **Office>Close**.

EXERCISE 1-3
Close and Create a Workbook

An Excel file is called a **workbook**. A workbook contains one or more sheets called **worksheets**, also known as **spreadsheets**. A worksheet contains data such as numbers and formulas. When you launch Excel, a new workbook appears automatically. In this exercise, you will learn how to close a workbook and how to create a new one.

FIGURE 1.4 Closing a workbook

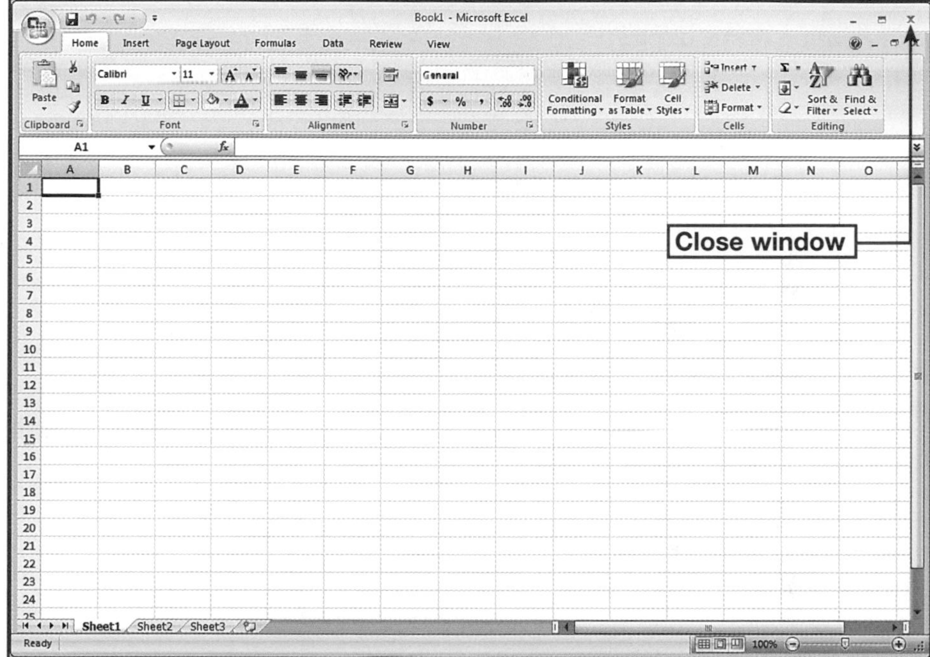

FIGURE 1.5 New workbook

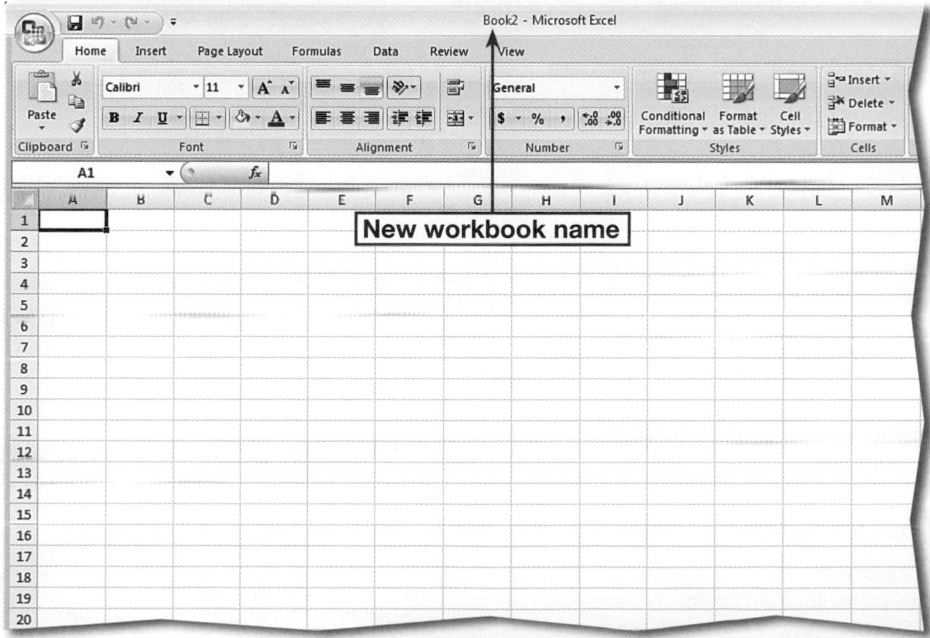

2. Sort Records in a Query

Follow the steps to complete the activity. You must complete Practice It Activity 1 before doing this activity.

Step-By-Step

1. In your **Sports4** file, in the **Navigation Pane**, display **Queries**.
2. Right-click the **CustomerOrdAmt** query and select **Copy**. Click **Paste**.
3. In the **Paste As** dialog box, key: CustOrdAmt By Order Date. Click **OK**.
4. Open the copied query in **Design View**. In the design grid, under **OrderDate**, click in the **Sort** box.
5. Click the drop-down arrow and select **Ascending**.
6. **CHECK** Your screen should look like Figure 4.57.
7. Click **Datasheet View**.
8. **CHECK** Your screen should look like Figure 4.58.
9. In the **OrderDate** heading, click the drop-down arrow and select **Sort Newest to Oldest**.
10. Click **Save**. Close the query.

Solution The solution file for this activity is the **CustOrdAmt By Order Date** query in the **Sports4-SF.accdb** database.

FIGURE 4.57 Sort CustOrdAmt by ascending dates Design View

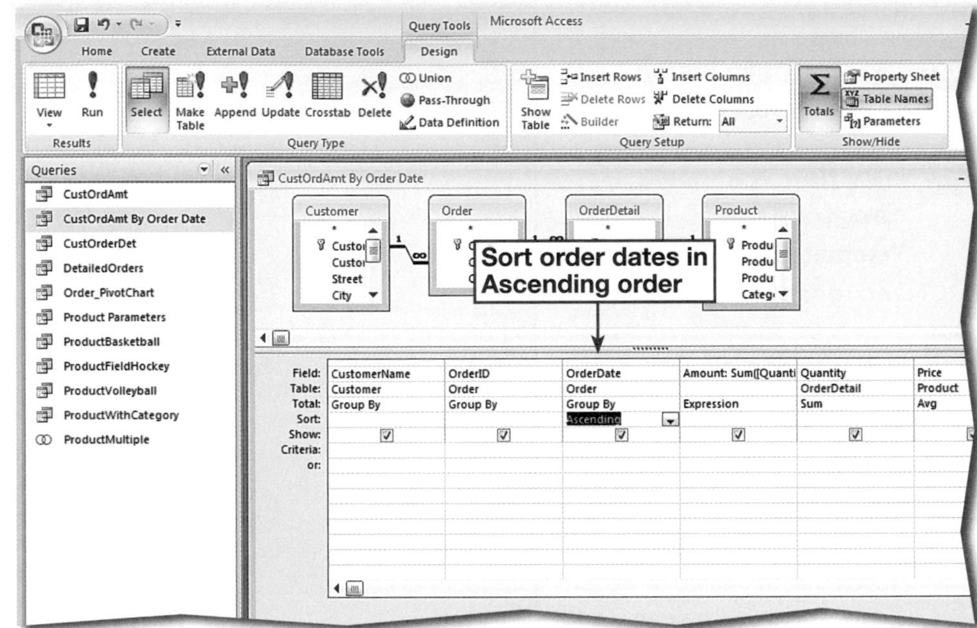

FIGURE 4.58 Sort CustOrdAmt by ascending dates

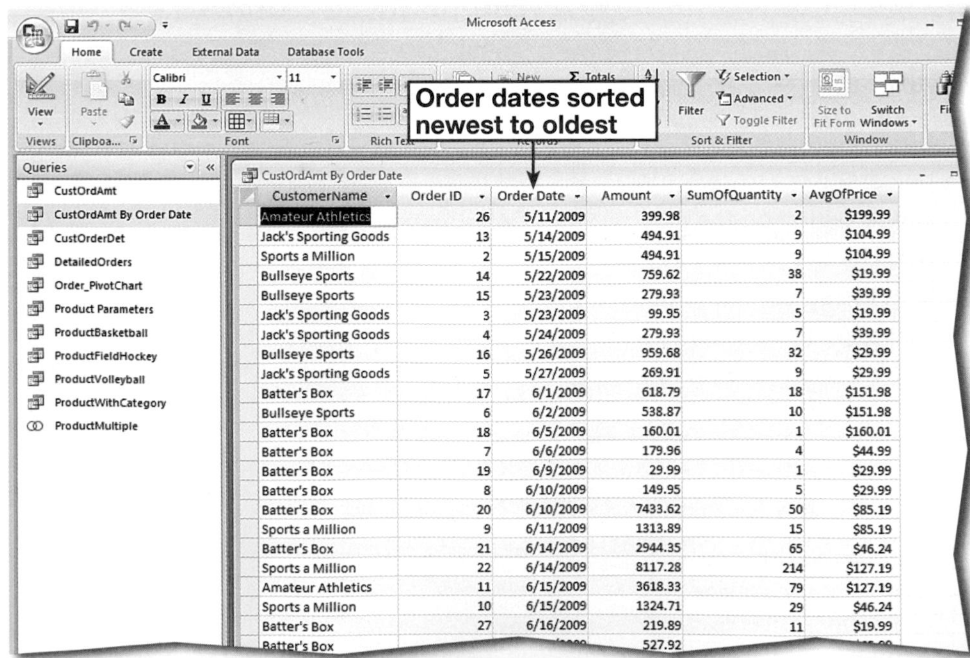

Step-By-Step

1. In your **Book2** file, click the **down arrow** on the vertical scroll bar (see Figure 1.6). The numbers along the worksheet's left edge increase as you scroll down.
2. Click the **up arrow** to return to the top of the worksheet.
3. Click the **right arrow** on the horizontal scroll bar. The letters along the top change as you scroll right.
4. Click the **left arrow**.
5. **CHECK** Your screen should look like Figure 1.6.
6. Locate the **sheet tabs**. Click the **Sheet2** tab.
7. **CHECK** Your screen should look like Figure 1.7. The **Sheet2** tab turns white to show that you are currently using Sheet 2.
8. Click the **Sheet3** tab. Click the **Sheet1** tab to return to Sheet 1.
9. **CHECK** Your screen should look like Figure 1.6.

Continue to the next exercise.

Shortcuts

You can drag the scroll bar to scroll through a worksheet faster.

EXERCISE 1-4
Scroll and Move Through Worksheets

Use the scroll bars to move left, right, up, or down through a worksheet. By default, when you create a new workbook, it always contains three worksheets. The **sheet tabs** allow you to move from one worksheet to another.

FIGURE 1.6 Scroll bars

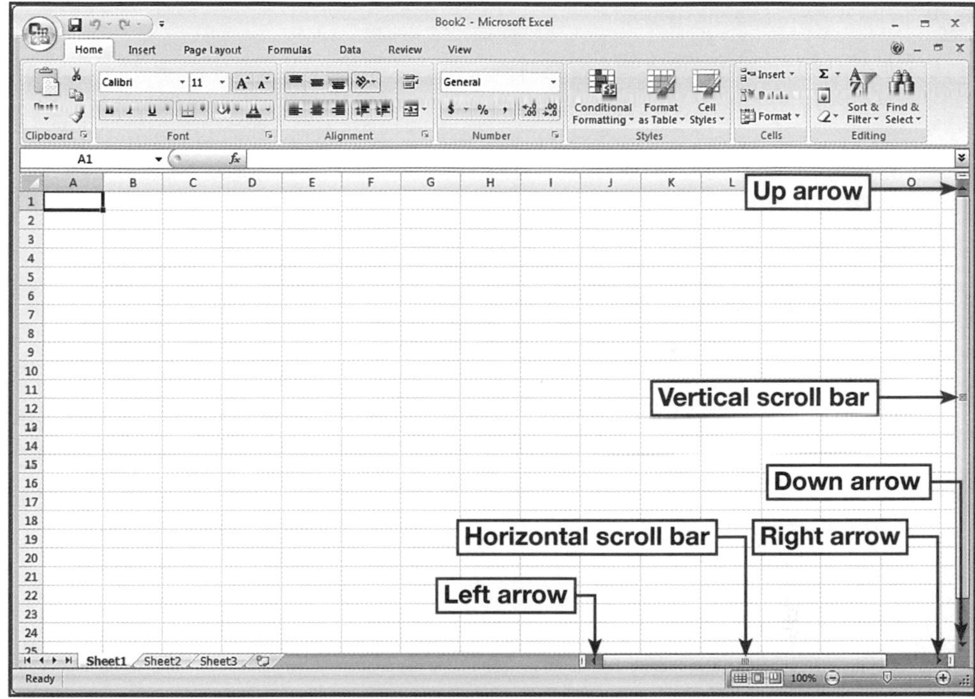

FIGURE 1.7 Identifying the sheet you are using

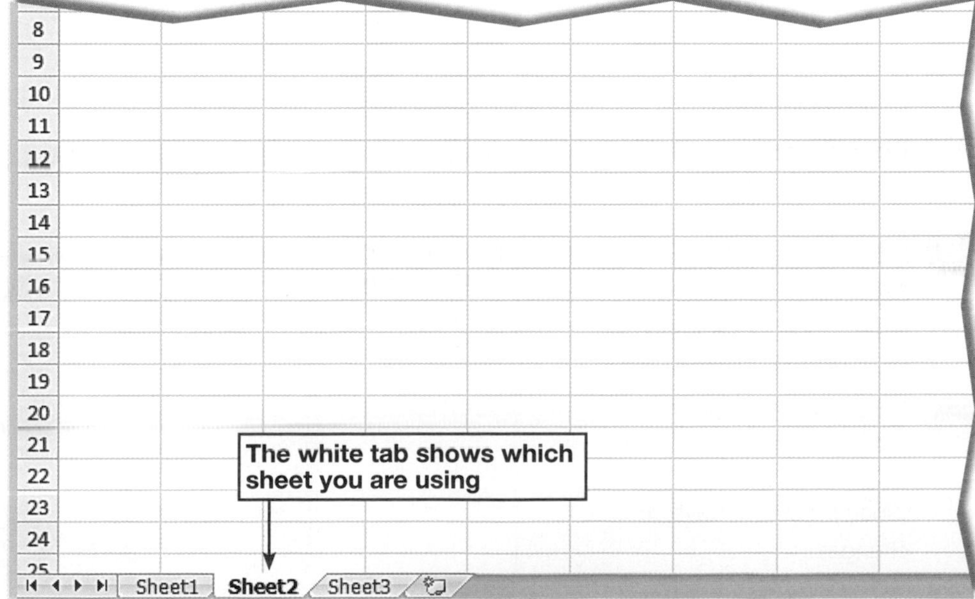

LESSON 4 Practice It Activities

1. Add and Remove Tables from Queries

Follow the steps to complete the activity.

Solution The solution file for this activity is the **DetailedOrders** query in the **Sports4-SF.accdb** database.

Step-By-Step

1. In your **Sports4** file, open the **Detailed Orders** query in **Design View**.
2. In query design, right-click the **Product** table and select **Remove Table**.
3. Click **Datasheet View**.
4. CHECK Your screen should look like Figure 4.55.
5. Click **Design View**. Choose **Design>Query Setup>Show Table**.
6. Select the **Product** table and the **StateCode** table. Add them to the query design window. Close the **Show Table** box.
7. Double-click the **StateName** field in the **PhoneNum** table to add it to the field list.
8. In the field list, click the **StateName** drop-down arrow and select the **State**. Click **Datasheet View**.
9. CHECK Your screen should look like Figure 4.56. Close the query. Save your changes.

FIGURE 4.55 DetailedOrders query with Product Table removed

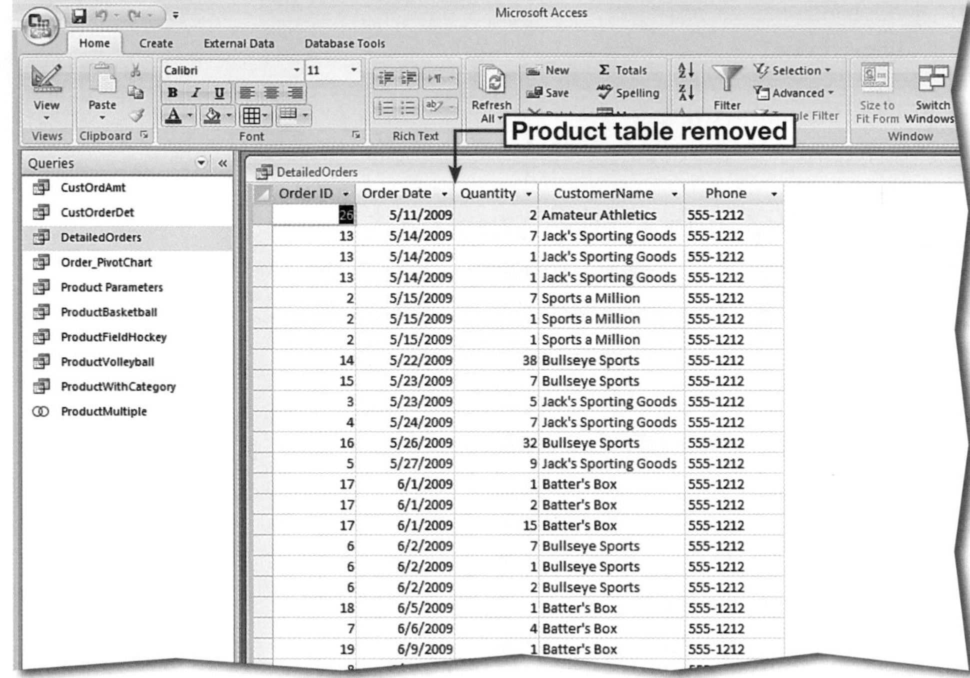

FIGURE 4.56 DetailedOrders query with StateCode table added

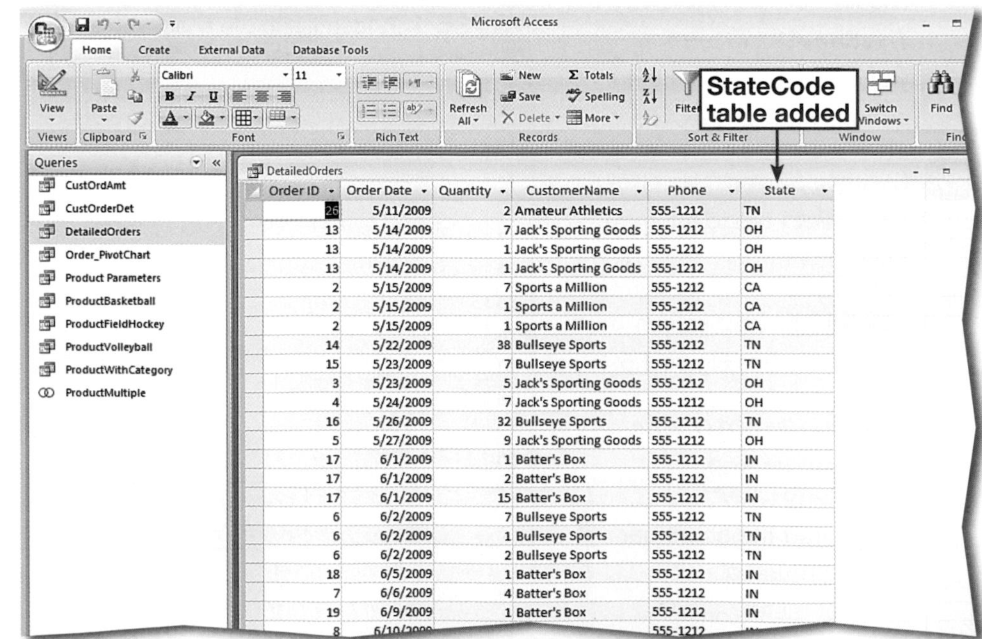

Step-By-Step

1. In your **Book2** file, choose **Office>Save As**. The **Save As** dialog box opens.
2. With your teacher's permission, click **New Folder** (see Figure 1.8).
3. In the **New Folder** text box, key: [your first initial and last name] (for example, *jking*). Press ENTER.
4. Click outside the text box. The new folder opens automatically.
5. Click **Back to Document** (see Figure 1.9).
6. CHECK Your dialog box should look like Figure 1.9. Notice the folder's name has changed.
7. Click **Close** X to close the dialog box.

Continue to the next exercise.

Microsoft Office 2007

When the **>** symbol appears in a step, it means that you need to follow a path to complete a task. For example, **Home>Font>Bold** means go to the **Home** tab, then go to the **Font** group, then click the **Bold** button.

Step-By-Step Tip In Step 1, the direction to the **Save As** dialog box is in path form. Explain that this means click the **Office Button** and then choose **Save As**.

EXERCISE 1-5
Create a New Folder

You can store documents in folders. A **folder** helps you organize your files so you can find them quickly. One way to create a new folder is to use the Save As dialog box. The dialog box can be used to enter specific information to perform a task, such as naming and saving a workbook.

Troubleshooting Students using Windows XP should go to page I to complete Exercises 1-5 and 1-6.

FIGURE 1.8 Save As dialog box

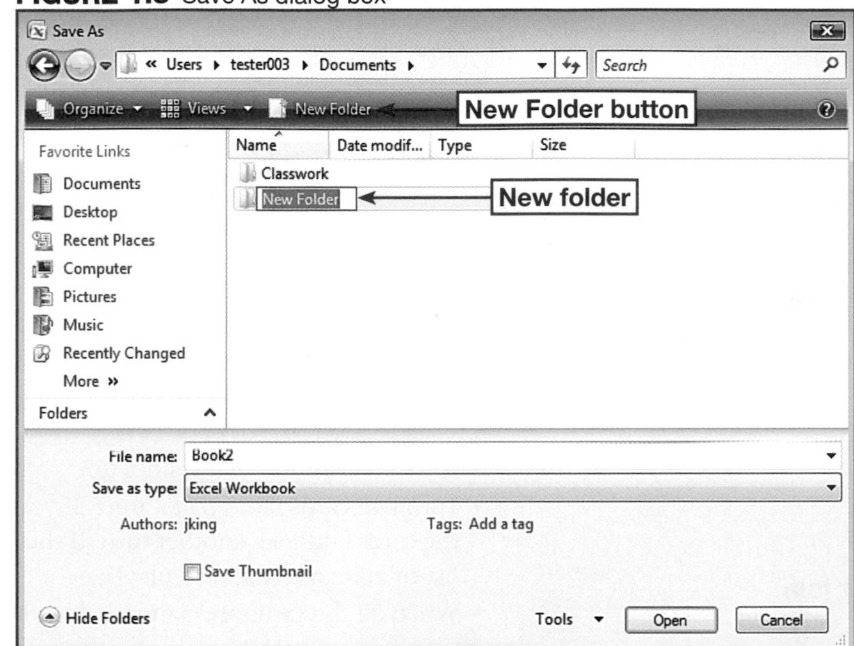

FIGURE 1.9 Naming a new folder

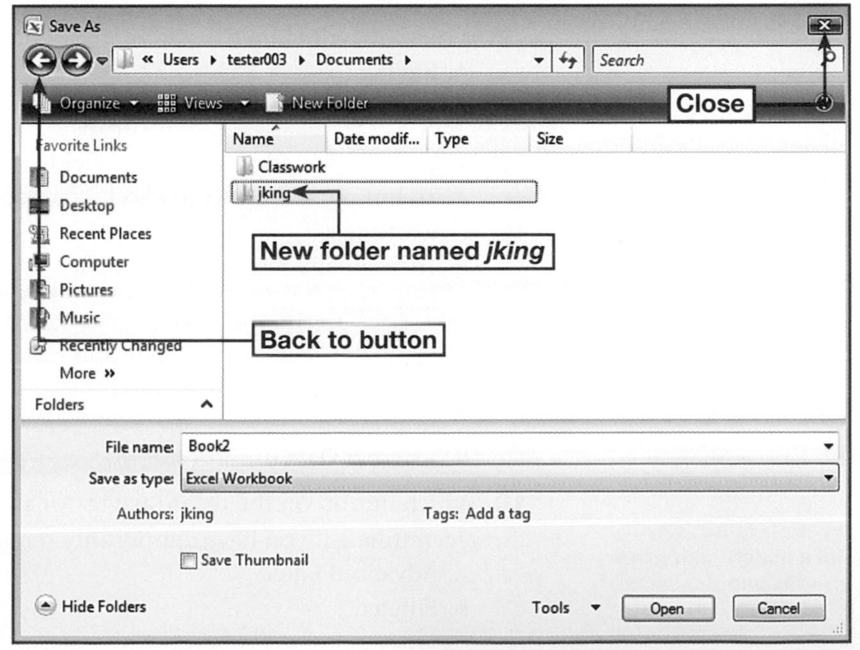

LESSON 4 After You Read

Vocabulary

Key Terms

aggregate
alias
database object
document
export specifications
import specifications
inner join
left-outer join
link
normalize
parameter
right-outer join

Academic Vocabulary

common
criteria
design
element
refine

Answer to Vocabulary Activity
Students create a match-card game using the Key Terms and Academic Vocabulary.

Review Vocabulary

Complete the following statements on a separate piece of paper. Choose from the Vocabulary on the left to complete the statements.

1. To __normalize__ a table is to make sure it has no repeating groups of data. (p. 472)

2. __Import specifications__ allow you to save the steps you use to import data from external sources so that you use them again. (p. 475)

3. A join that displays all the records of the first table and related records in the second is a __left-outer join__. (p. 480)

4. You can attach different types of __criteria__ to a database. (p. 478)

5. A(n) __linked__ table is a table connected to data outside the database. (p. 472)

Vocabulary Activity

6. Write each vocabulary term on a separate piece of paper. Write each definition on a separate piece of paper. Then:
- Lay the cards out, blank sides up.
- Turn two cards face up at a time. If you match a term to a definition, claim the cards and take another turn. If the cards do not match, lay them back down and go to the next player.
- When all the cards are claimed, the winner has the most cards.

Review Key Concepts

Answer the following questions on a separate piece of paper.

7. Which term describes an alternative name given to a table or field? (p. 483)
A. Element
(B.) Alias
C. Report
D. All of the above

8. Why might you add a calculated field to a query? (p. 482)
A. To link a database to an Excel worksheet
B. To manually recalculate the data in a query
(C.) To automatically recalculate the data every time it changes
D. To ensure that equations in a database are accurate

9. Which path allows you to view and run saved import operations? (p. 476)
(A.) External Data>Import>Saved Imports
B. External Data>Import>More
C. External Data>Export>Saved Exports
D. None of the above

10. Which button on the record navigator should you use to reapply the most recent filters if you have temporarily removed them from view? (p. 495)
A. Advanced Filter
B. Filtered
C. Sort & Filter
(D.) Unfiltered

Step-By-Step

1. In your **Book2** file, choose **Office>Save As**. The **Save As** dialog box opens (see Figure 1.10).

2. In the **File name** box, key: e1-6-. Then key your first initial and your last name (for example, *e1-6-jking*).

3. Locate the folder you created in Exercise 1-5 or ask your teacher for the location you should select in the **Save in** box.

4. Click the folder twice to select that location.

5. Click **Save** in the **Save As** dialog box.

6.  Your screen should look like Figure 1.11. Notice that the workbook's new name appears on the title bar.

Continue to the next exercise.

Troubleshooter

If you are using Windows XP, go to page li to learn how to complete the steps in this exercise and in Exercise 1-5.

EXERCISE 1-6
Name and Save a Workbook

You must save a workbook if you want to use it again. Save your work every few minutes to keep it from being lost.

Troubleshooting Remind students where you want them to save their work.

FIGURE 1.10 Save As dialog box with new file name

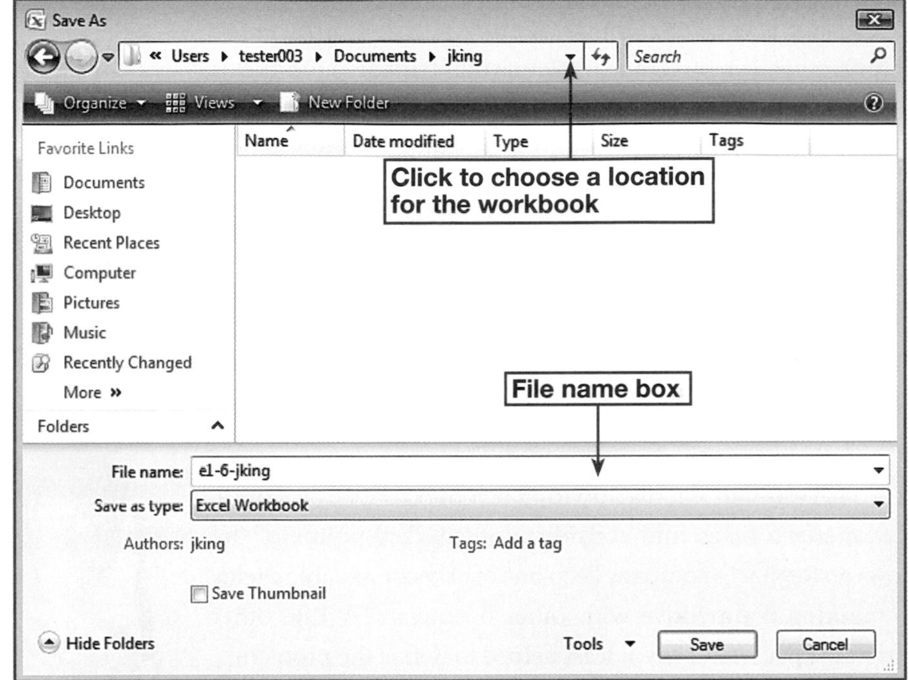

FIGURE 1.11 New file name in title bar

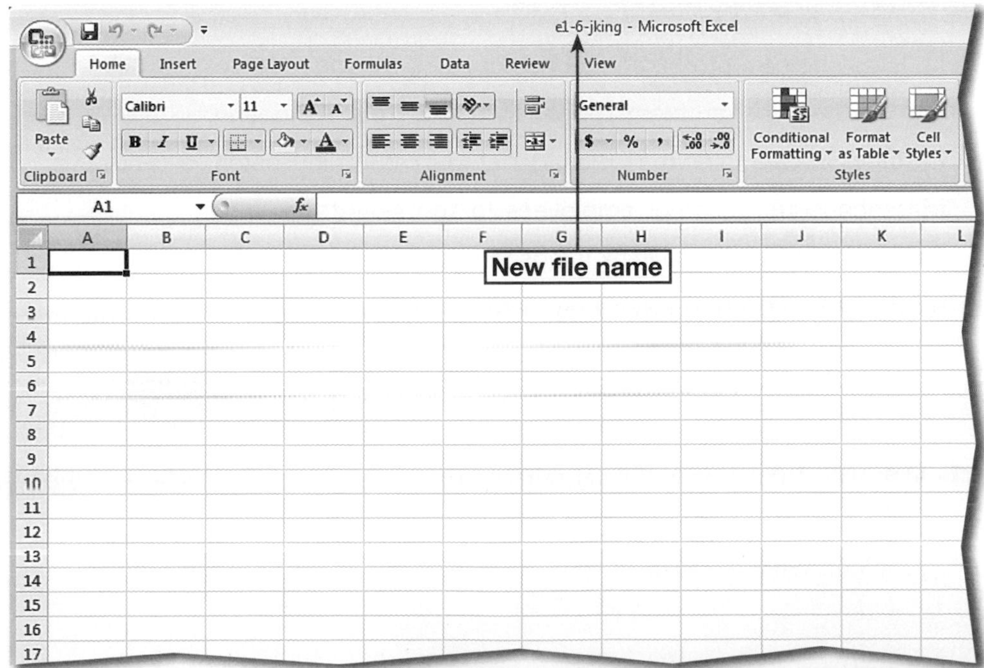

21st Century WORKPLACE

Problem Solving

Raphael's major client, Douglas Contractors, just switched to another vendor. Mr. Douglas claims that Raphael's product is more expensive than his competitor's product. Raphael immediately tells his staff that they will have to find new clients.

Evaluate the Problem

In today's workplace, employers value employees who have the ability to solve problems. Being able to recognize problems and understand their causes is the first step to finding solutions that will work.

Maria knows that Raphael's company needs Douglas Contractors as a client. She suggests that Raphael try to match the competitor's price. Maria's suggestion takes into consideration the key points of the issue: how can Raphael's company keep one of its most valuable clients while remaining competitive with other businesses? While other solutions may exist, Maria has at least helped to define the problem.

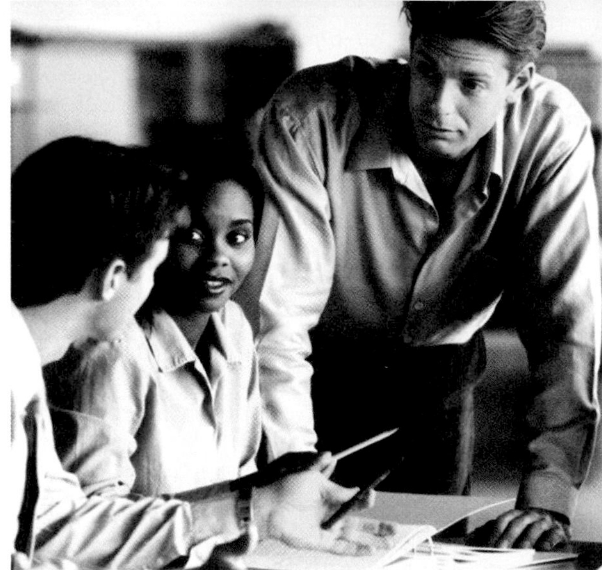

Communication is an important part of solving problems in the workplace.

In fields such as information technology (IT), the main part of the job involves problem recognition and troubleshooting. Brittney St. Germain, an IT manager at MarketSoft in Boston, Massachusetts, tells her employees to "go slow to go fast" because "taking time to think things through is ultimately more efficient than trying to solve a problem in a panic."

NCTE/Language Arts (NCTE 12) Reinforce the role that communication plays in solving problems by asking students to list three problems that they have solved and how communication helped them evaluate and find a solution for each problem. Ask them to share an experience with the class.

SkillBuilder answers can be found on page TM84.

SKILLBUILDER

1. **Discuss** How does Maria use effective problem solving?
2. **Plan** Recommend an alternate solution to Raphael's problem. What issues must you consider?
3. **Predict** Think of a problem that you might encounter in the near future. Write a short paragraph predicting how you can use the "go slow to go fast" strategy to solve the problem.

Step-By-Step

1. In your **e1-6** file, click cell **A1** (see Figure 1.12).
2. Key: First Quarter Sales. Press ENTER.
3. Click cell **A1**. Look in the formula bar to read the cell's content (see Figure 1.12).
4. Click cell **B1**. Notice the formula bar is empty. **B1** appears to contain text, but it does not.
5. Click cell **A1**.
6. In the column head row, move the pointer to the line between **A** and **B** until the pointer becomes a two-headed arrow (see Figure 1.13).
7. Click and drag to the right to make the column wider until *First Quarter Sales* fits in cell **A1**.
8. CHECK Your screen should look like Figure 1.13.
9. Click **Save** on the **QAT** to save your work.

Continue to the next exercise.

Teaching Tip Point out to students how the row and column heads change color when a cell is selected.

EXERCISE 1-7
Insert and View Cell Contents

Worksheets are made up of boxes called **cells**. Cells are organized into horizontal rows and vertical columns. Rows are labeled with numbers, and columns are labeled with letters.

A cell is named by its **cell reference**, or its column letter and row number. For example, cell E14 is in column E, row 14. The **formula bar** shows a cell's contents. Sometimes cells must be resized to view all of the contents.

FIGURE 1.12 Cell content shown in formula bar

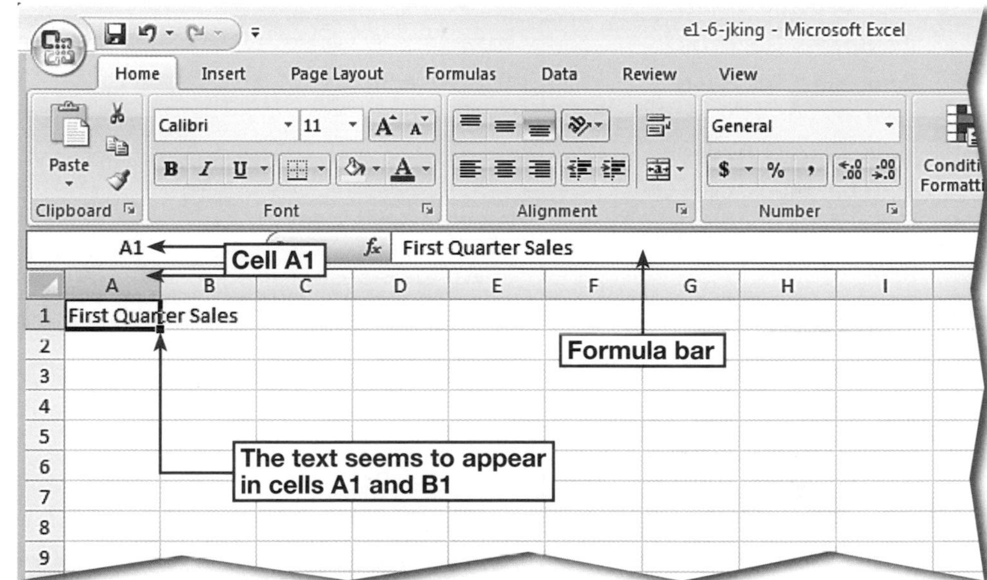

FIGURE 1.13 Making a column wider

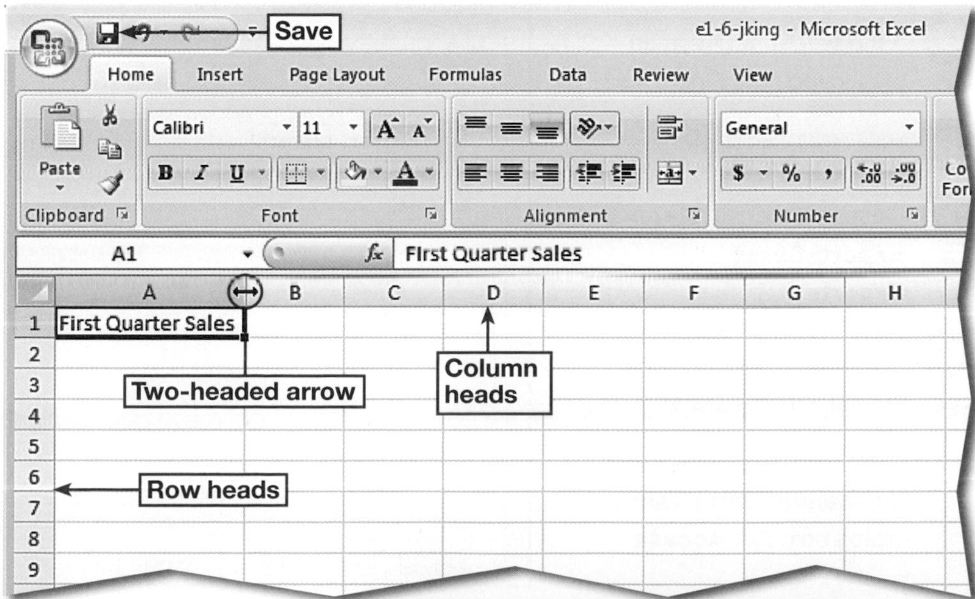

Step-By-Step

1. In your **Sports4** file, in the **Navigation Pane**, display **Tables**. Select **Sport Record Holders3**.
2. Choose **External Data>Export>More** and select **Access Database**.
3. Click **Browse**. Select the **Sports Records** database. Click **Save**.
4. In the **Export-Access Database** box, click **OK**. In the **Export** dialog box, click **OK**.
5. In the **Export-Access Database** dialog box, click the **Save export steps** check box.
6. In the **Description** box, key: Export Sports Record Holders table to Sports Records database.
7. CHECK Your screen should look like Figure 4.53.
8. Click **Save Export**.
9. Choose **External Data>Export>Saved Exports**.
10. CHECK Your screen should look like Figure 4.54.
11. Click **Run**. Click **OK**. Close the **Manage Data Tasks** dialog box. Exit **Access**.

EXERCISE 4-19
Save and Run Export Specifications

Access allows you to set up and save **export specifications** so that you can run them later. If you plan to repeat the export process more than a few times, export specifications can be very useful.

Solution The solution file for **Exercise 4-1** through **Exercise 4-19** is **Sports4-SF.accdb**.

FIGURE 4.53 Export-Access Database save steps dialog box

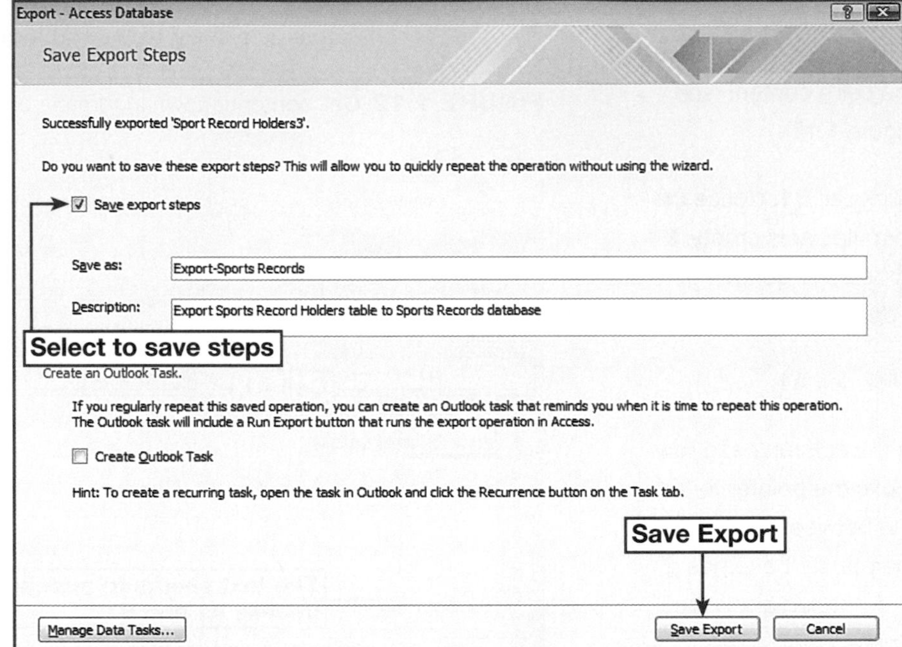

FIGURE 4.54 Manage Data Tasks dialog box

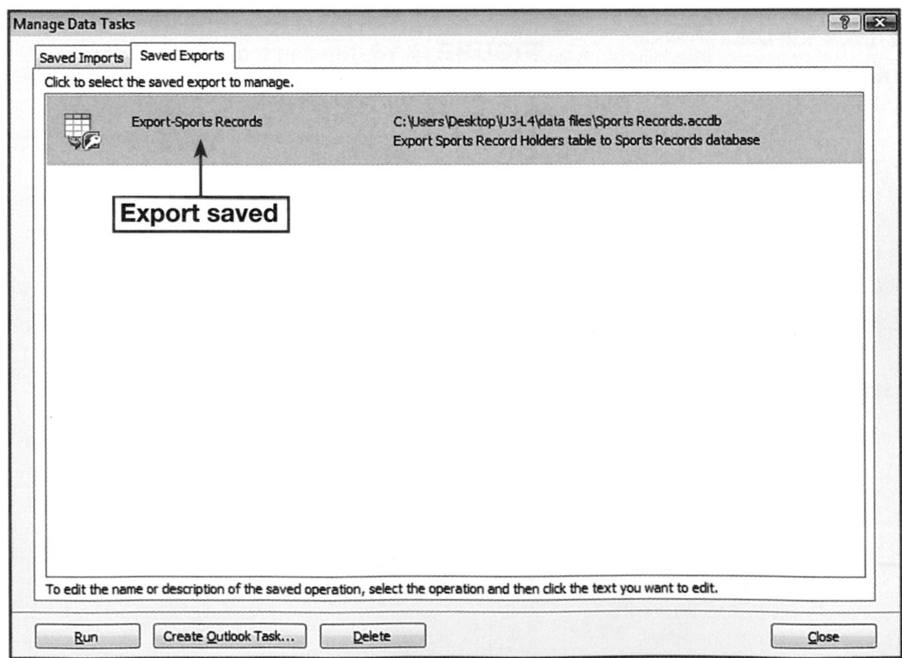

Step-By-Step

1. In your **e1-6** file, Choose **View>Zoom>Zoom** . The **Zoom** dialog box opens. Click **75%**. Click **OK**.
2. Click **Zoom** . Click **Custom** and key: 200. Cliolc **OK**.
3. **CHECK** Your screen should look like Figure 1.14.
4. Locate the **Zoom In** and **Zoom Out** buttons in the lower right corner of your screen. Click the **Zoom Out** button until the **Zoom** level is **100%**.
5. Click the **Customize Quick Access Toolbar** button on the **QAT** and choose **Minimize the Ribbon**. The Ribbon is now minimized.
6. Repeat **Step 5**. Save your file.
7. Choose **View>Workbook Views>Full Screen** .
8. **CHECK** Your screen should look like Figure 1.15.
9. Right-click the **Select All** button. Choose **Close Full Screen**. Your screen returns to **Normal View**.

Continue to the next exercise.

EXERCISE 1-8
Change the View of a Screen

There are several ways to change the appearance of the Excel screen. One way is to use the zoom option. Increasing the zoom percentage makes everything appear larger, so it is easier to see a cell's content. Decreasing the zoom percentage makes everything appear smaller, which allows you to see more of the worksheet at once. Although items may appear larger or smaller on screen, depending on the zoom, the item itself will appear normal size when it prints. Another way is to minimize the Ribbon in order to see more of the screen.

FIGURE 1.14 Screen at 200% zoom

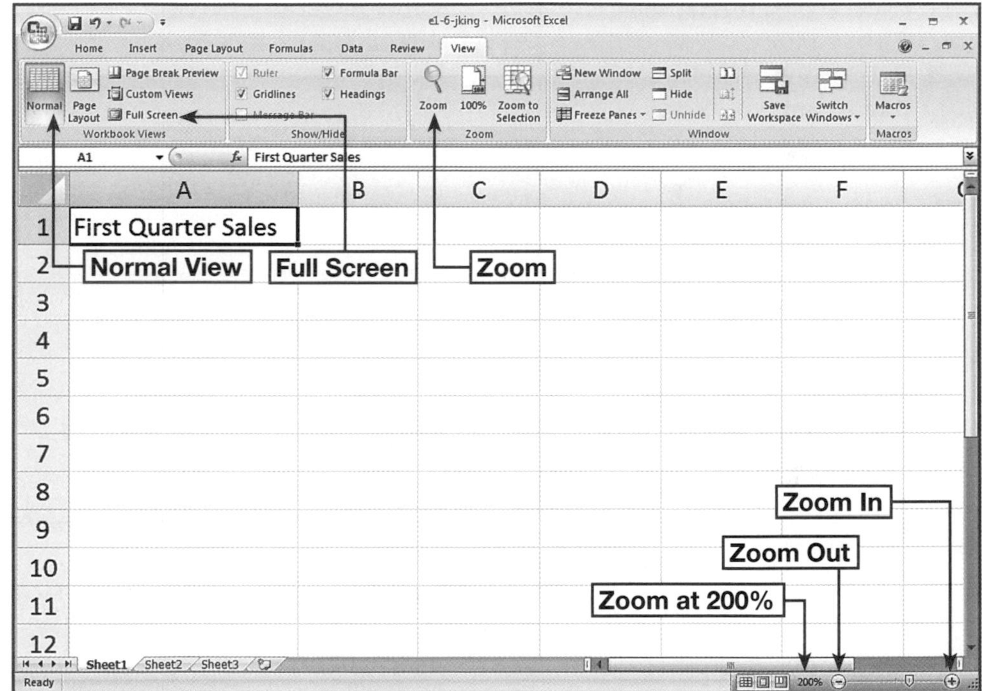

FIGURE 1.15 Full Screen Toggle View

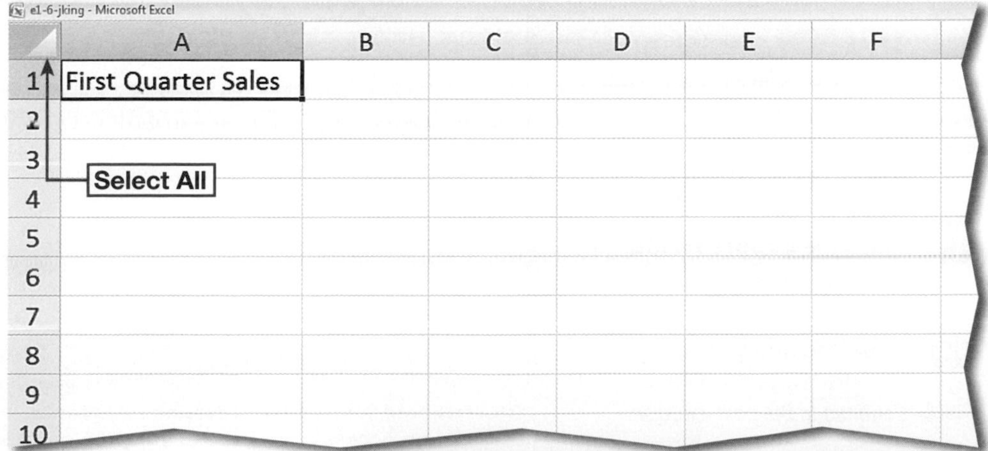

Step-By-Step

1. In your **Sports4** file, in the **Navigation Pane**, display **Queries**.
2. Click the **ProductFieldHockey** query to select it.
3. Choose **External Data> Export>More** and select **HTML Document**.
4. In the **Export-HTML Document** box, click **Browse**. Save the file.
5. Click the **Export data with formatting and layout** check box.
6. Click the check box labeled **Open the destination file after the export operation is complete**.
7. CHECK Your screen should look like Figure 4.51.
8. Click **OK**. In the **HTML Output Options** dialog box, leave the defaults and click **OK**.
9. CHECK Your screen should look like Figure 4.52.
10. Close the exported **ProductFieldHockey** file.
11. Close the **Export-HTML Document** dialog box.
12. Close the query.

Continue to the next exercise.

EXERCISE 4-18
Export Data from Queries

Like tables, Access allows you to export data from queries in the current database file to many different files, programs, or databases. You can only export one query at a time, and you must also export the underlying record sources for the query. Otherwise, the query will not work in the database or program to which it has been exported. to.

FIGURE 4.51 Export-HTML Document dialog box

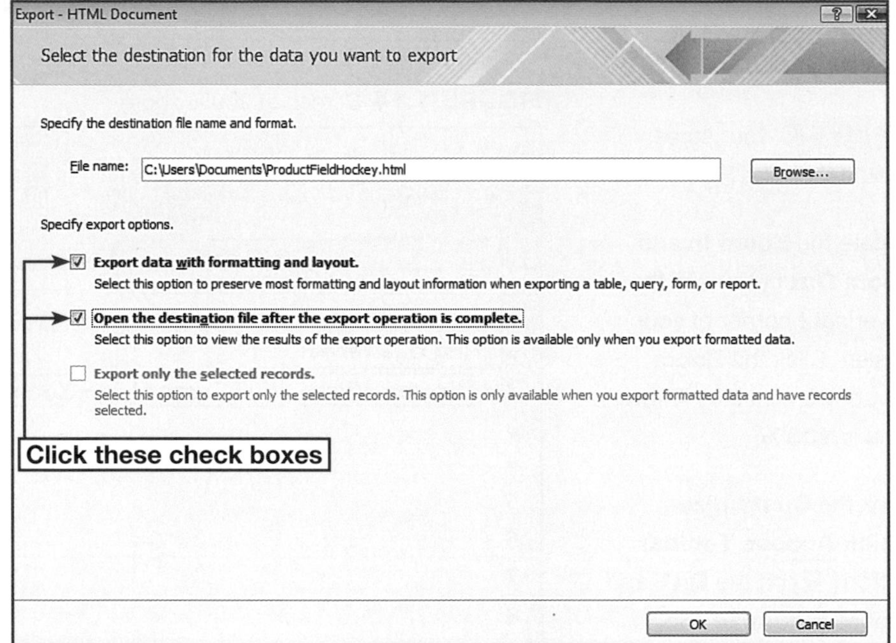

FIGURE 4.52 Exported ProductFieldHockey data

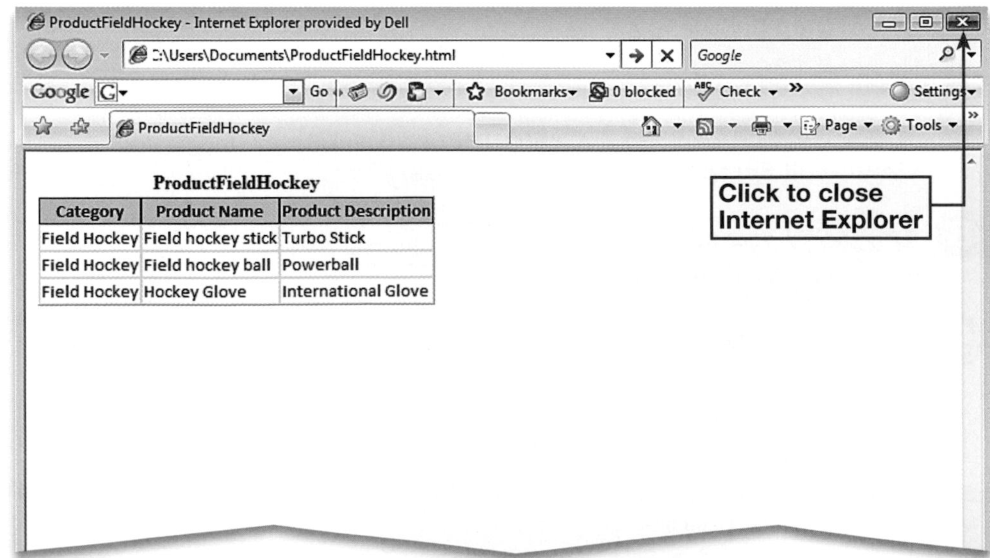

ProductFieldHockey

Category	Product Name	Product Description
Field Hockey	Field hockey stick	Turbo Stick
Field Hockey	Field hockey ball	Powerball
Field Hockey	Hockey Glove	International Glove

Differentiated Instruction/Advanced Students Ask advanced students to export another query into an Access database exporting the query's data sources.

Step-By-Step

1. In your **e1-6** file, click cell **A1**.
2. Key: Surplus Inventory. Press ENTER.
3. CHECK Your screen should look like Figure 1.16.
4. On the **QAT**, click **Undo**. *First Quarter Sales* reappears.
5. CHECK Your screen should look like Figure 1.17.
6. Click **Redo**. *Surplus Inventory* reappears.
7. Click **Undo**. *First Quarter Sales* reappears.
8. Click **Save**.
9. Choose **Office>Close** to close the workbook.

Continue to the next exercise.

You Should Know

After you close and reopen a file, the **Undo** and **Redo** buttons will no longer be available.

Intervention Strategy Let students know that the zoom on their computer may not match the zoom shown in the figures. The zoom level in the figures has been increased to improve readability.

EXERCISE 1-9
Use Undo and Redo

If you ever make a mistake or change your mind while working with Excel, choose Undo. Undo reverses your last action. You can choose Undo multiple times to undo multiple actions. If you choose Undo by accident, you can choose Redo.

FIGURE 1.16 Replacing text in a cell

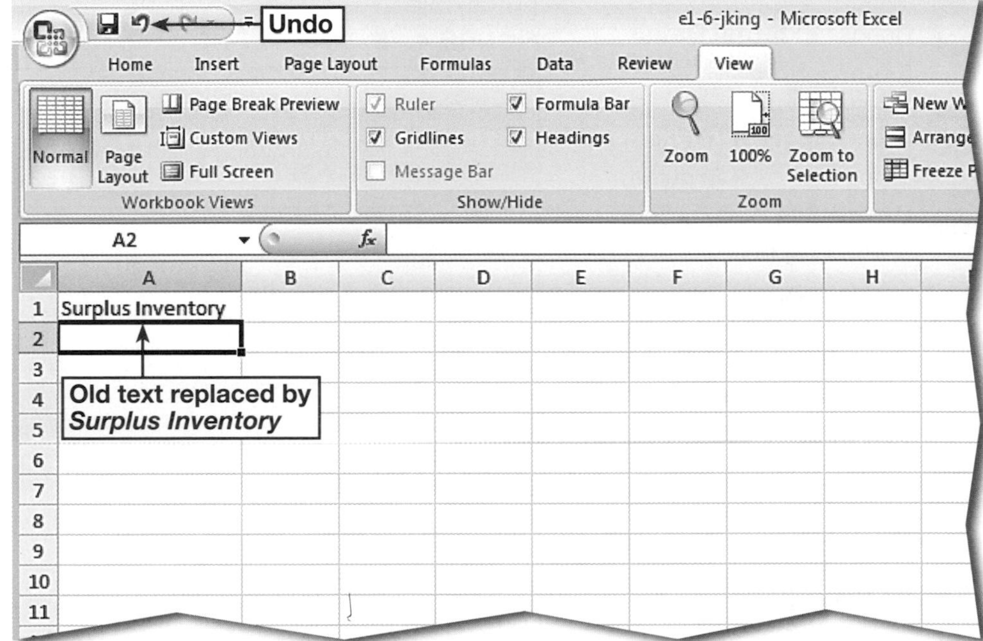

FIGURE 1.17 Using Undo

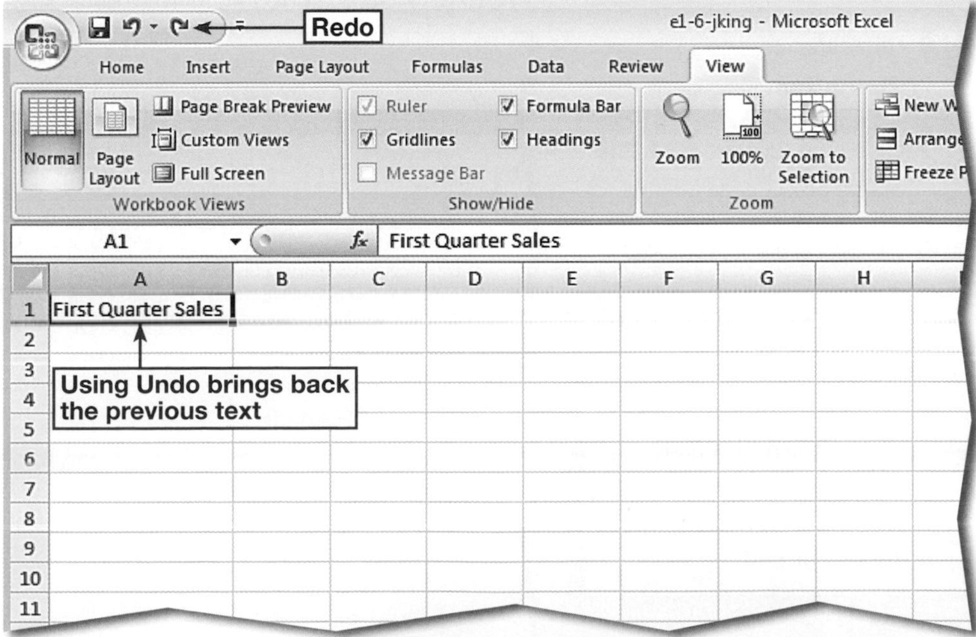

Step-By-Step

1. In your **Sports4** file, in the **Navigation Pane**, display **Tables**.
2. Select the **PhoneNum** table by clicking it once.
3. Choose **External Data> Export>Word** .
4. In the **Export-RTF File** dialog box, click **Browse**. Use the **File Save** dialog box to save the file.
5. Click the check box labeled **Open the destination file after the export operation is complete**.
6. CHECK Your screen should look like Figure 4.49.
7. Click **OK**.
8. CHECK Your screen should look like Figure 4.50.
9. Close the exported **PhoneNum** file.
10. Close the **Export-RTF File** dialog box.

Continue to the next exercise.

Tech Tip

When you export a table, query, or form, the field names are placed in the first row of the table in the Word document.

EXERCISE 4-17
Export Data from Tables

Access allows you to export the data in tables from the table's current database file to many different files, programs, or databases. You can export the table with the data in it, or export only the structure of the table itself. You can import all your data at once, but you can export only one table at a time, and you must export the whole table or table structure, not individual records.

Teaching Tip Explain to students that the **PhoneNum** file is exported as an RTF, or rich-text format word processing file.

FIGURE 4.49 Export-RTF File dialog box

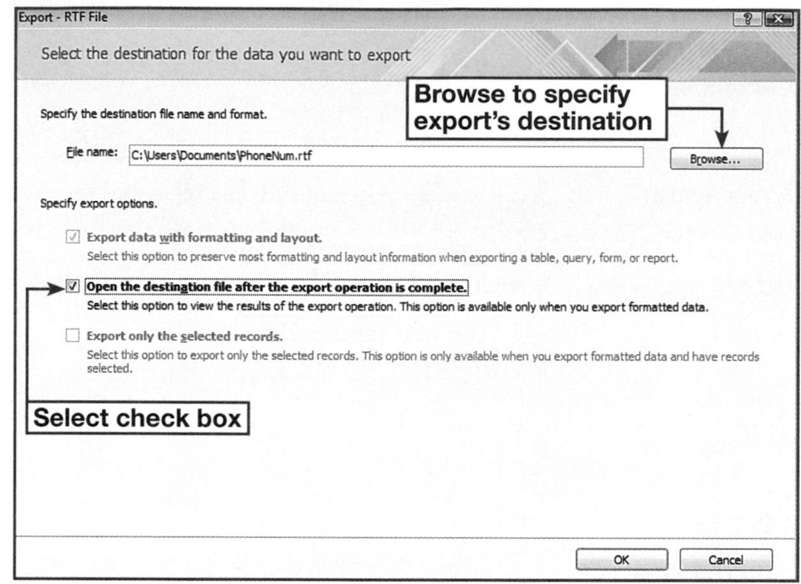

FIGURE 4.50 Exported PhoneNum data

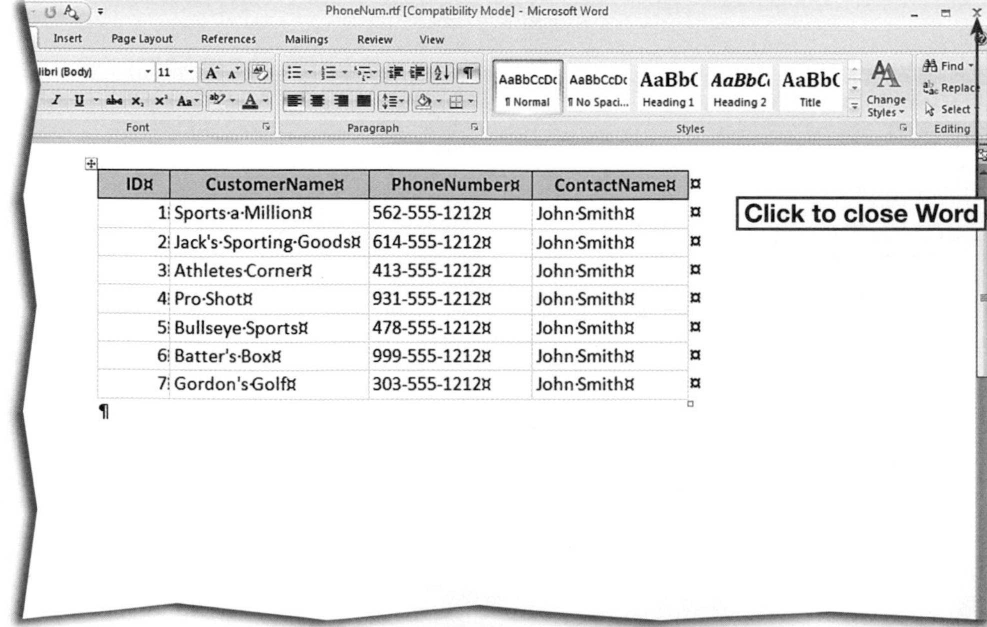

ID	CustomerName	PhoneNumber	ContactName
1	Sports a Million	562-555-1212	John Smith
2	Jack's Sporting Goods	614-555-1212	John Smith
3	Athletes Corner	413-555-1212	John Smith
4	Pro-Shot	931-555-1212	John Smith
5	Bullseye Sports	478-555-1212	John Smith
6	Batter's Box	999-555-1212	John Smith
7	Gordon's Golf	303-555-1212	John Smith

Step-By-Step

1. Click **Office>Open**. The **Open** dialog box opens.
2. Click the up arrow on the **Folders** box.
3. Locate the folder where you save your work.
4. Select the name of the workbook that you saved and closed in Exercise 1-9 (the workbook named **e1-6**).
5. **CHECK** Your dialog box should look similar to Figure 1.18.
6. Click **Open**. The workbook that you saved in Exercise 1-9 will open.
7. **CHECK** Your screen should look like Figure 1.19.
8. Save your file.

Continue to the next exercise.

Academic Skills

When working with others, it is especially important to give your files memorable names. Your file names and folder structures should be logical to everyone who needs to access the files.

NCLB/Language Arts (NCTE 4) Show students examples of poorly organized files. Discuss how properly named files can save students time and relieve their anxiety about losing their work.

EXERCISE 1-10
Open an Existing Workbook

To open an existing workbook, you need to know where (on what drive, in which folder, and so on) the workbook was saved and what the file was named.

FIGURE 1.18 Open dialog box

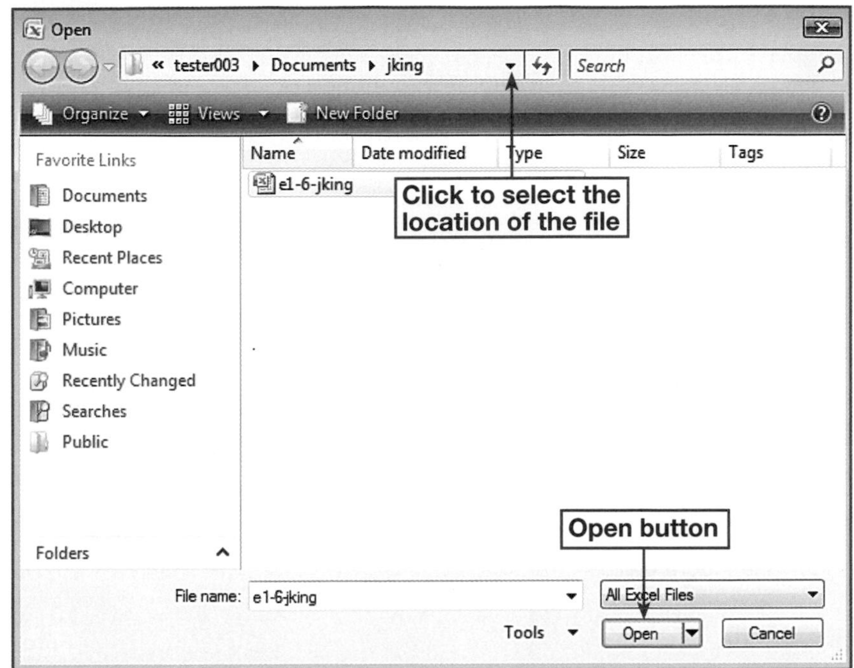

FIGURE 1.19 Open Excel workbook

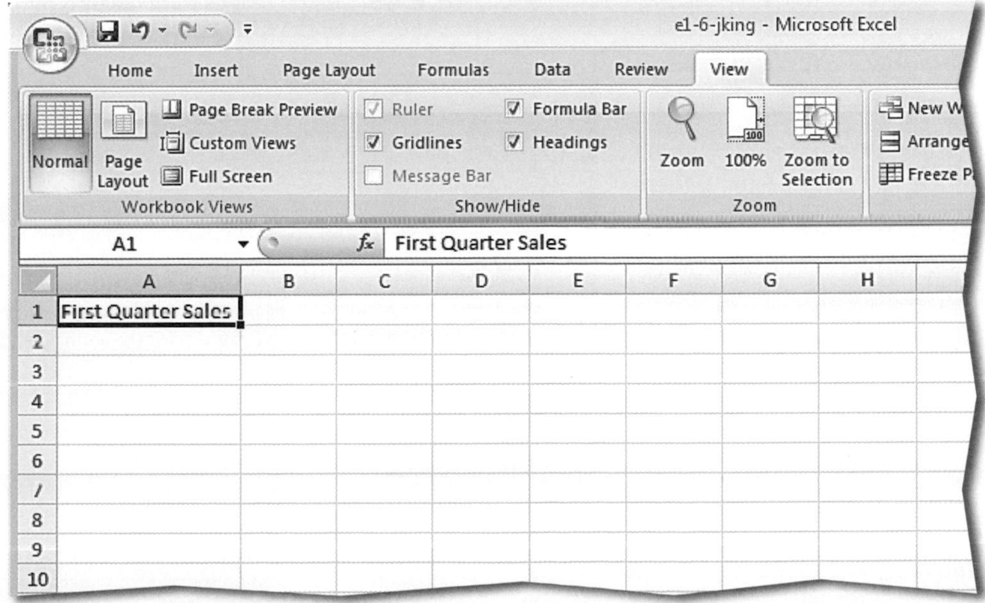

Troubleshooting Direct students who are using Windows XP to page I for more information on completing these steps.

Step-By-Step

1. In your **Sports4** file, open the **CustomerRAS** form.
2. **CHECK** Your screen should look like Figure 4.47.
3. Click **Toggle Filter**. Notice that the filter settings are reapplied.
4. On the **Navigation** bar at the bottom of the **CustomerRAS** form window, click the **Filtered** button to turn off the filter.
5. Click **Advanced** and select **Clear All Filters**.
6. **CHECK** Your screen should look like Figure 4.48.
7. Close the form.

Continue to the next exercise.

You Should Know

Click **Unfiltered** in the **Navigation** bar to reapply the last saved filter. If there are no saved filters, this box will appear grayed out.

Teaching Tip Explain to students that the procedure for clearing filters from other database objects is the same.

EXERCISE 4-16
Remove Filters

When you create filters in most database objects, the filter remains until you turn it off or remove it permanently. Reports do not save filters, but tables, queries, and reports do. You must clear these filters in order to remove them completely.

FIGURE 4.47 CustomerRAS form with filters

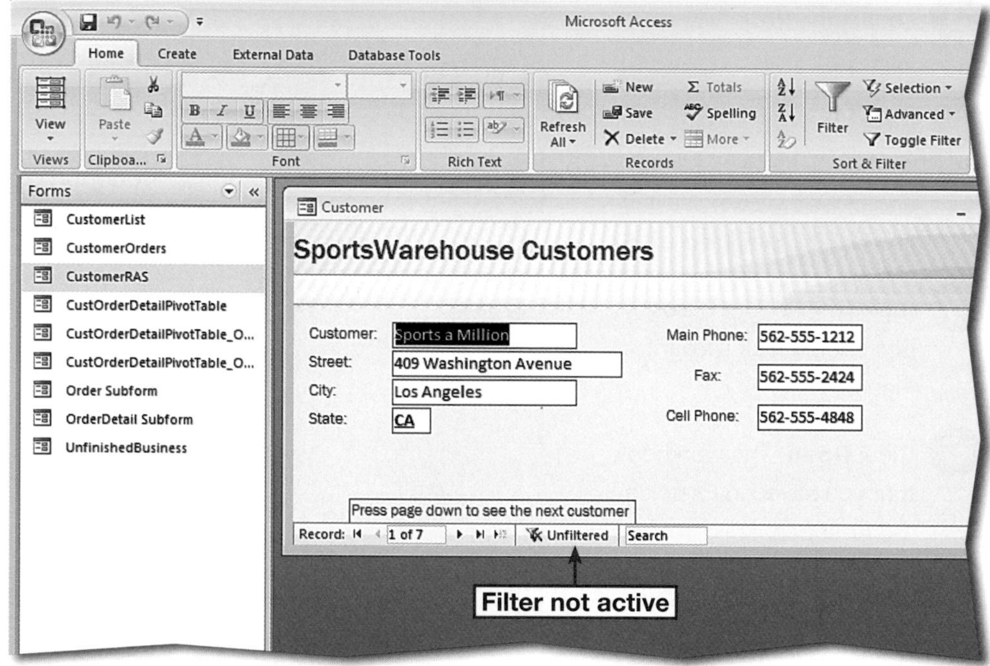

FIGURE 4.48 CustomerRAS form cleared of filters

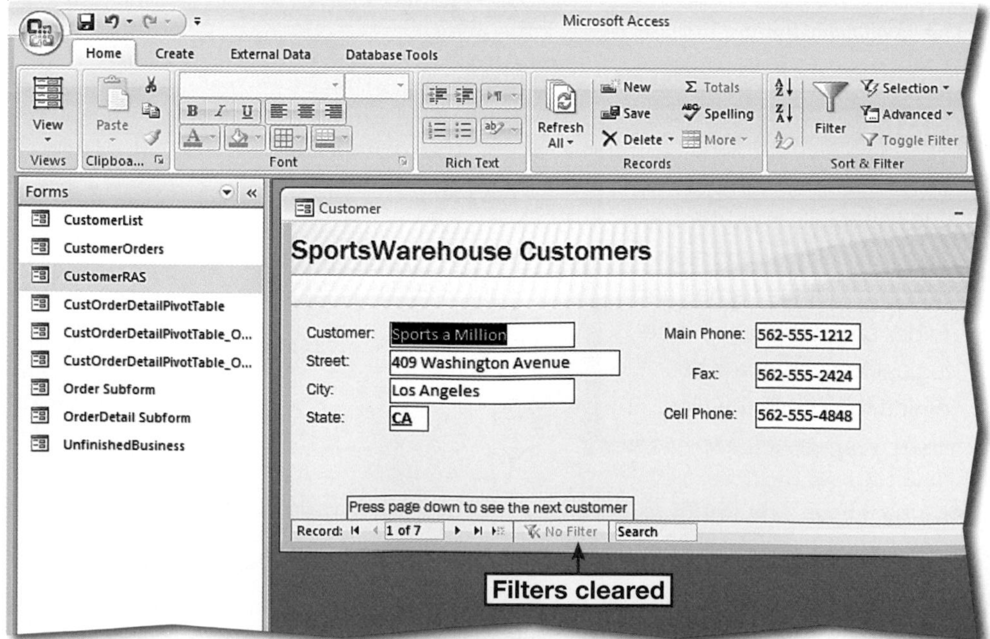

EXERCISE 1-11
Calculate a Sum

Excel has preprogrammed formulas that allow you to quickly add columns or rows of numbers. A **formula** is an equation that begins with an equal sign (=) and includes values or cell references. The **formula bar** displays the formulas and contents of selected cells. Different formulas allow you to perform different actions. For example, the formula used in this exercise allows you to add a column of numbers.

FIGURE 1.20 Sum button clicked once

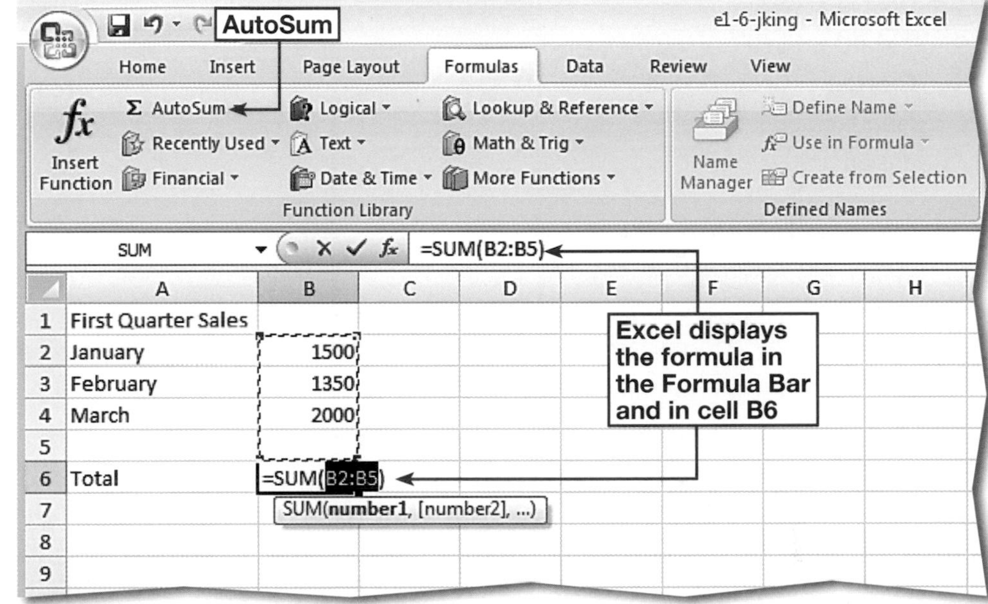

FIGURE 1.21 Sum of cells B2:B5

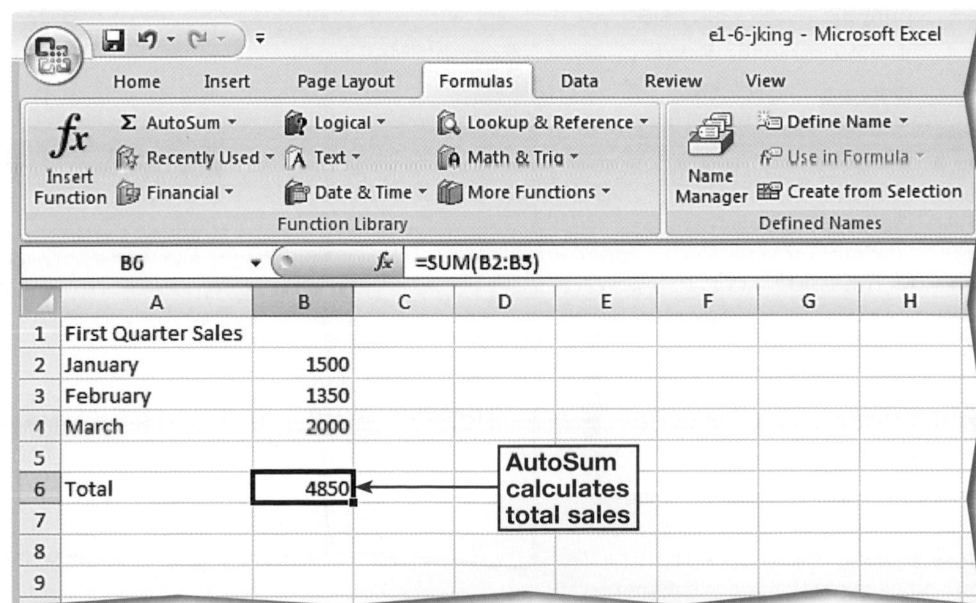

Step-By-Step

1. In your **e1-6** file, click cell **A2** and key: January. Press TAB. In cell **B2** key: 1500.
2. Click cell **A3** and key: February. Press TAB. In cell **B3** key: 1350.
3. Click cell **A4** and key: March. Press TAB. In cell **B4** key: 2000.
4. Click cell **A6** and key: Total.
5. Click cell **B6** and then choose **Formulas> Function Library> AutoSum** Σ.
6. **CHECK** Your screen should look like Figure 1.20. In cell B6 Excel displays **=SUM(B2:B5)**. This is also displayed in the formula bar. This indicates that Excel will add (sum) the numbers in cells B2, B3, B4, and B5 and display the answer in cell B6.
7. Click **AutoSum** Σ again.
8. **CHECK** Your screen should look like Figure 1.21. Excel enters the sum of the First Quarter Sales in cell **B6**. Save your file.

Continue to the next exercise.

NCTM/Math (Number and Operations) Reinforce the idea of "sum" by having students use a calculator to add up the numbers and then compare them to the sum on the worksheet.

Step-By-Step

EXERCISE 4-15 (Continued)
Filter Data within Reports

9. Choose **Home>Sort & Filter>Advanced** and select **Advanced Filter/ Sort**.

10. **CHECK** Your screen should look like Figure 4.45.

11. Double-click the **TotalCost** in the **CustomerOrderDetail** report to add it to the design grid.

12. Under the **TotalCost** field, click in the **Criteria** box and key: >200.

13. Click **Toggle Filter**.

14. **CHECK** Your screen should look like Figure 4.46.

15. Click **Print Preview**. Click **Print**.

16. Ask your teacher where to print the report, and select that printer in the **Print** dialog box. Click **OK**.

17. Close the report.

Continue to the next exercise.

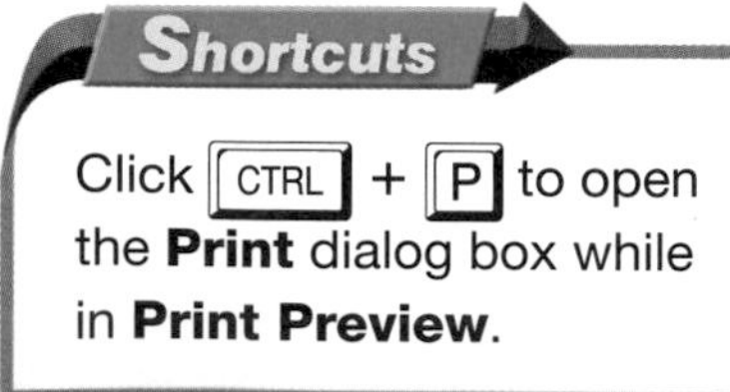

Shortcuts

Click CTRL + P to open the **Print** dialog box while in **Print Preview**.

Step-By-Step Tip In **Step 17**, remind students that reports do not save the filtering changes, so there will be no confirmation box.

FIGURE 4.45 Advanced filter/sort for report

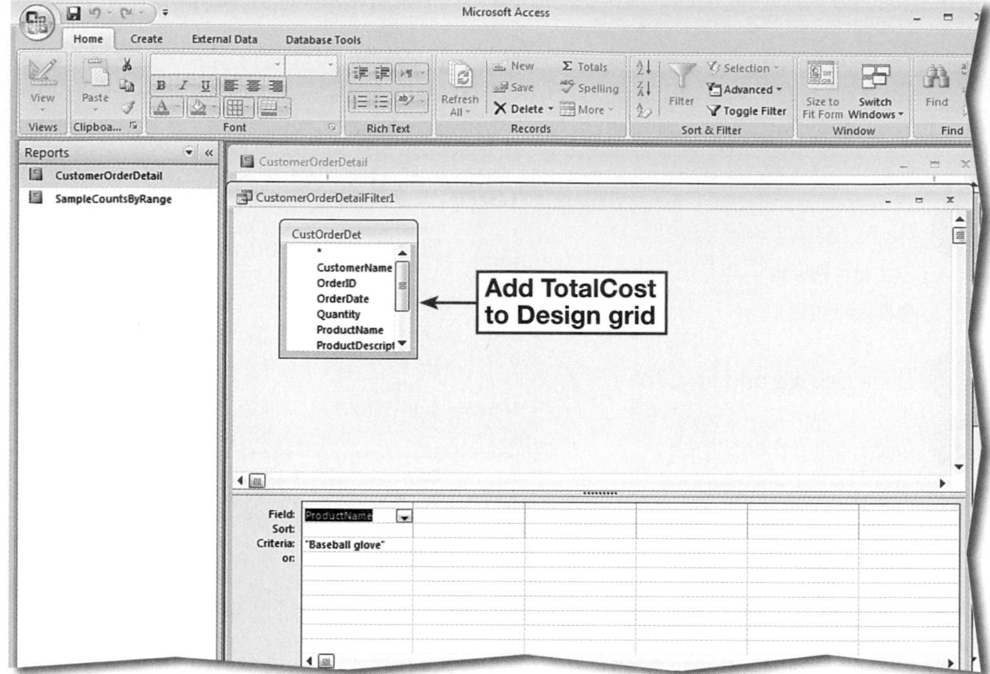

FIGURE 4.46 Report filtered for more than $200

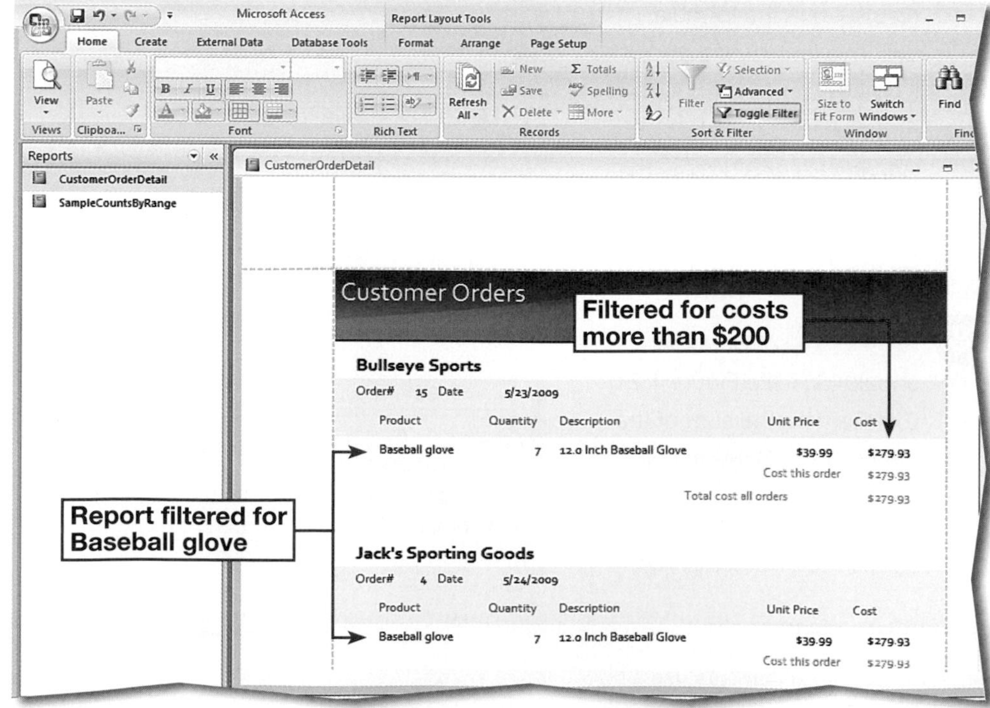

Step-By-Step

1. In your **e1-6** file, choose **Office>Print>Print Preview**.
2. **CHECK** Your screen should look like Figure 1.22. Your worksheet is open in **Print Preview** view.
3. Click **Close Print Preview** to return to your file (see Figure 1.22).
4. Choose **Office>Print**. The **Print** dialog box opens.
5. Check with your teacher to make sure that the correct printer name is in the **Name** box.
6. Check that there is a **1** in the **Number of copies** box.
7. **CHECK** Your dialog box should look similar to Figure 1.23. With your teacher's permission, print the worksheet.
8. Save your file.

Continue to the next exercise.

Shortcuts

You can zoom in on the worksheet by clicking the **Zoom** button in **Print Preview** view.

EXERCISE 1-12
Preview and Print a Worksheet

Print Preview view illustrates, or shows, what your worksheet will look like when you print it. The Print dialog box allows you to make choices such as the number of copies that will print, or where the document will print.

FIGURE 1.22 Worksheet in Print Preview view

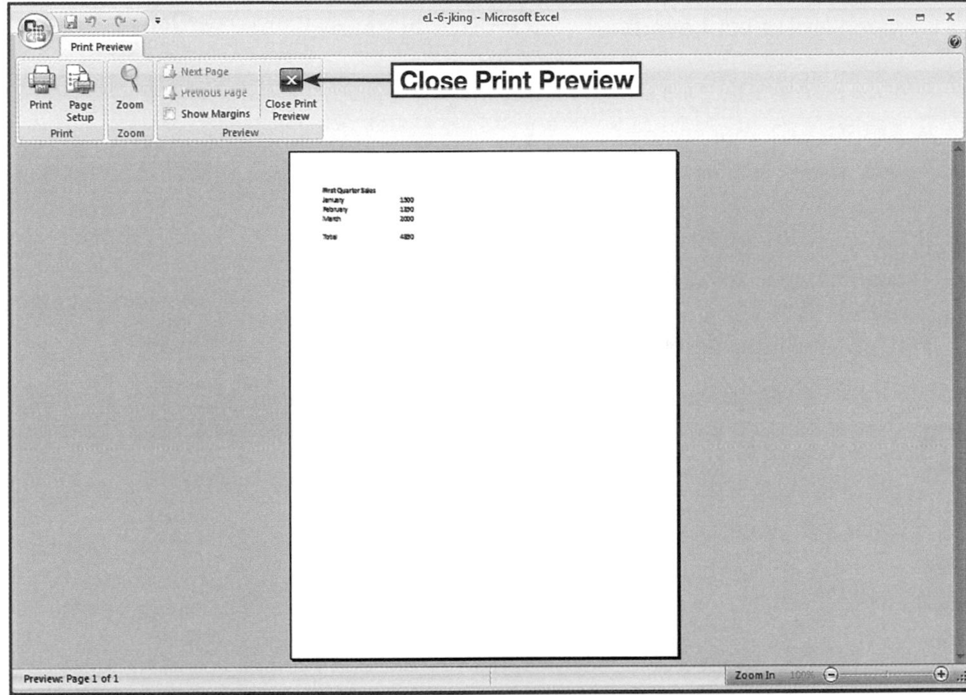

FIGURE 1.23 Print dialog box

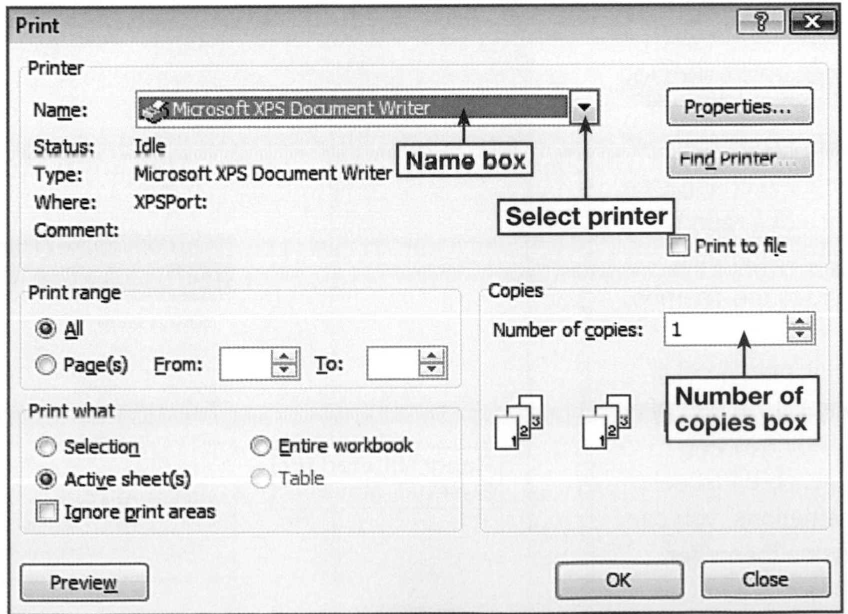

Step-By-Step

1. In your **Sports4** file, in the **Navigation Pane**, display **Reports**.
2. Right-click the **CustomerOrderDetail** report and select **Layout View**.
3. **CHECK** Your screen should look like Figure 4.43.
4. Under the **Product** heading, click **Arrows**.
5. Choose **Home>Sort & Filter>Filter** .
6. Click **Select All** to clear the selections. Click the **Baseball glove** check box.
7. Click **OK**.
8. **CHECK** Your screen should look like Figure 4.44.

Continued on the next page.

> **Microsoft Office 2007**
>
> You can apply different AutoFormats to change the appearance of a report. Many of these formats correspond to the Themes available in Word, PowerPoint, and Excel. If your report will be part of a larger project involving documents, spreadsheets, and presentations, you can use the same theme for each element.

EXERCISE 4-15
Filter Data within Reports

When compared with a table or a query, a report is a complete file, or **document**, that contains information. You can edit results in these documents. As in a table or query, report filters show only the data that fit the criteria. You can design advanced filters or use common filter tools. However, the filters won't be saved after you close the report.

FIGURE 4.43 CustomerOrderDetail layout view

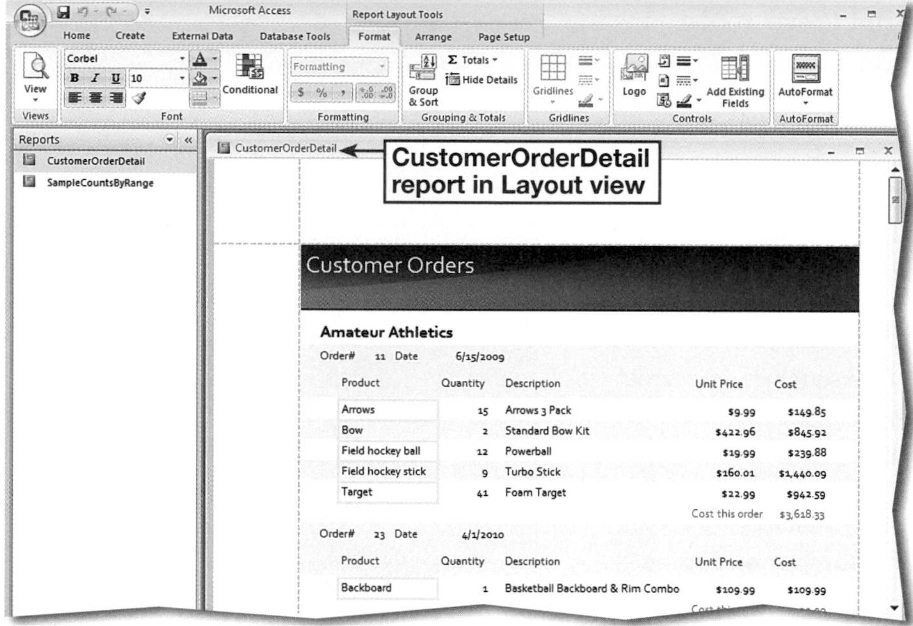

FIGURE 4.44 Report filtered for Baseball glove

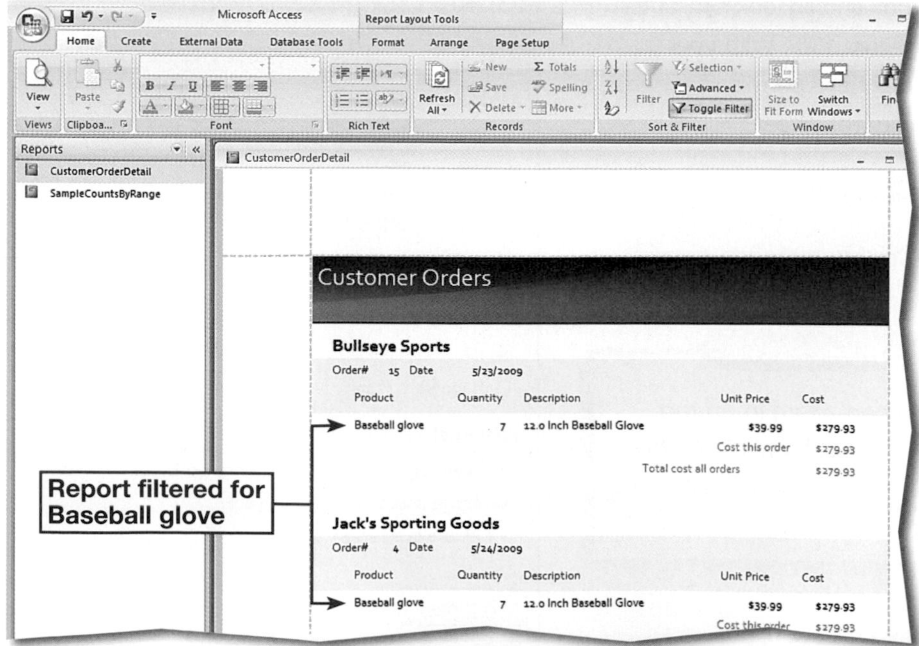

Step-By-Step

1. In your **e1-6** file, in the upper right corner, click **Microsoft Office Excel Help** [icon]. The Excel Help window opens.

2. In the **Search** box, key: cell contents.

3. Click **Search**.

4. CHECK Your screen should look similar to Figure 1.24.

5. Scroll down the **Results** list and click **Edit cell contents**. A **Help** window appears with information about editing cell contents.

6. CHECK Your screen should look like Figure 1.25.

7. Click **Close** [X] in the **Excel Help** window.

8. Choose **Office>Close**. The workbook closes. If a warning box appears, click **Yes** to save your file.

9. To exit the **Excel** program, choose **Office>Exit Excel**.

Troubleshooting Be aware that Step 2 may send students online.

Step-By-Step Tip In Step 6, let students know that their **Help** window may be a different size than the one shown in Figure 1.24.

Solution Use the file e1-6-SF.xlsx as a solution file for Exercises 1-6 through 1-13.

EXERCISE 1-13
Use the Help Feature

You can work more productively if you know how to find help quickly. Use Microsoft Excel Help to find answers to questions about using Excel. Choosing Help brings up the Help window, allowing you to search for Help by keying the name of a topic.

FIGURE 1.24 Search Results in Excel Help window

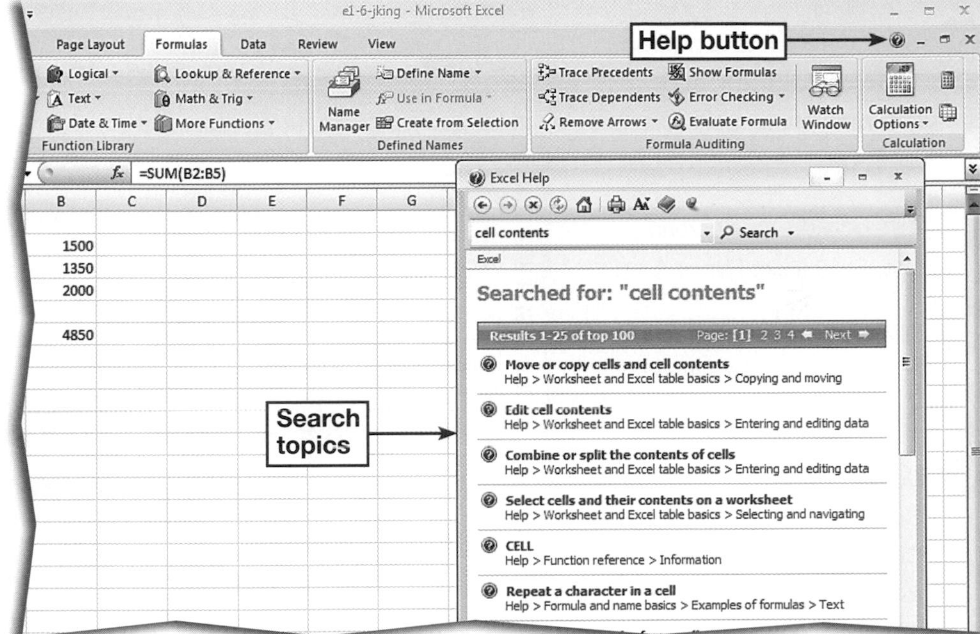

FIGURE 1.25 Help window

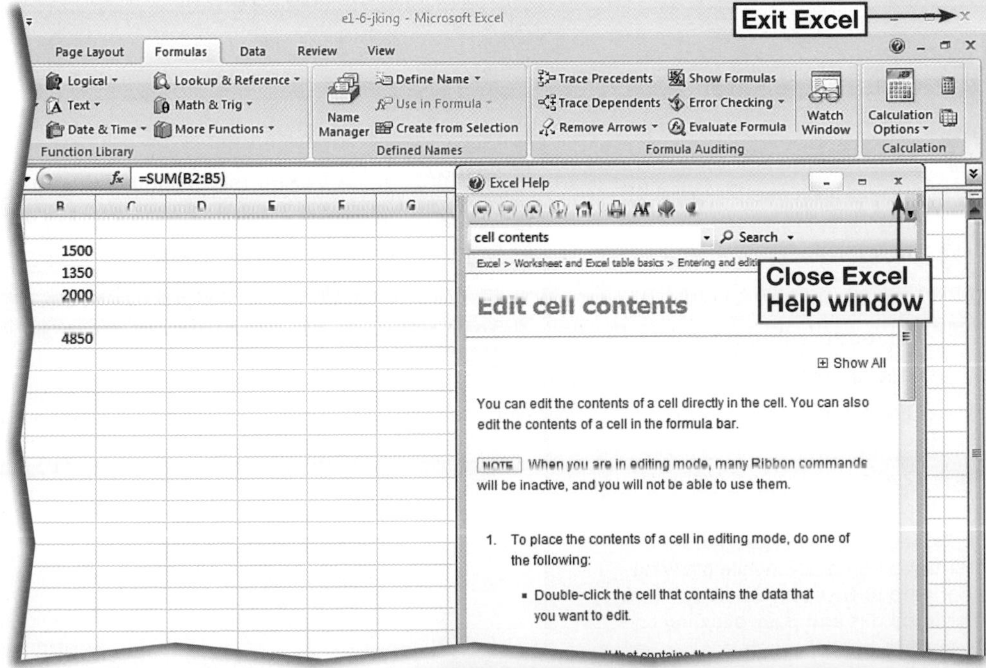

Step-By-Step

1. In your **Sports4** file, open the **CustomerRAS** form.
2. In the form, click in the **Customer** field. Click **Filter**.
3. Clear the **Sports a Million**, **Sven's Ski Shop**, and **(Blanks)** check boxes. Click **OK**.
4. CHECK Your screen should look like Figure 4.41.
5. Click **Advanced** and select **Advanced Filter/Sort**.
6. Double-click the **CustomerID** field in the **Customer** table to add it to the design grid.
7. Under the **CustomerID** field, click in the **Criteria** box and key: >3.
8. Click **Toggle Filter**.
9. CHECK Your screen should look like Figure 4.42.
10. Press PAGE DOWN twice. The form should show only the records that have a CustomerID greater than 3. Close the form.

Continue to the next exercise.

EL Explain to English Learners that a filter traps some data while allowing other data to be seen. Similarly, an air filter traps dirt and dust, allowing clean air to pass through.

EXERCISE 4-14
Filter Data within Forms

Sometimes you may need to filter the data within a form as you would in a table or query. A filter in a form shows only the data that fits the criteria. You can design advanced filters or use the common filter tools available on the Ribbon.

FIGURE 4.41 CustomerRAS filtered

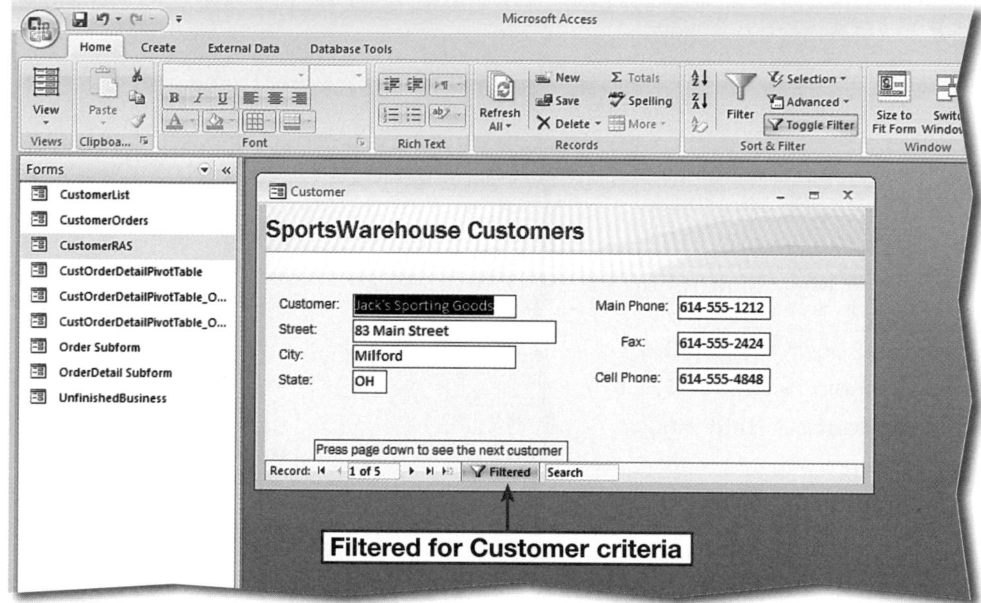

FIGURE 4.42 CustomerRAS advanced filter

LESSON **After You Read** 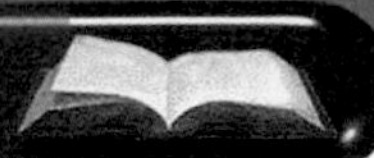

Vocabulary

Key Terms

button

cell

cell reference

command

dialog box

folder

formula

formula bar

group

Quick Access Toolbar (QAT)

Ribbon

ScreenTip

spreadsheet

sheet tab

tab

title bar

workbook

worksheet

Academic Vocabulary

illustrate

learn

Answer to Vocabulary Activity
Students make flash cards for every vocabulary word used in the lesson. Students should use the glossary to make sure their definitions are accurate.

Review Vocabulary

Complete the following statements on a separate piece of paper. Choose from the Vocabulary list on the left to complete the statements.

1. To ___learn___ is to become familiar with a new concept or idea. (p. 205)

2. Tabs on the ___Ribbon___ display commands and buttons organized in logical groups that relate to a specific activity. (p. 206)

3. The name of the workbook is shown in the ___title bar___ at the top of the screen. (p. 205)

4. You can view the contents of a cell in the ___formula bar___. (p. 211)

5. You can click a(n) ___button___ to perform a specific task. (p. 206)

Vocabulary Activity

6. Make flash cards for each vocabulary word used in Lesson 1.
- A. On the front of the card, write the word.
- B. On the back of the card, write the definition.
- C. Team up with a classmate and take turns using the flash cards to quiz each other.
- D. When you know the definitions for all the terms, save the flash cards to review for the year-end or term-end assessment.

Review Key Concepts

Answer the following questions on a separate piece of paper.

7. Where can you find the Print and Print Preview commands? (p. 216)
- A. Home tab
- B. Quick Access Toolbar (QAT)
- C. Insert tab
- (D.) Office button

8. Which button allows you to quickly add columns or rows of numbers? (p. 215)
- (A.) AutoSum
- B. Equation
- C. Format
- D. Insert

9. Which feature makes everything in a workbook appear larger or smaller? (p. 212)
- A. Redo
- (B.) Zoom
- C. New
- D. Undo

10. Which button do you use to reverse your last action? (p. 213)
- A. Zoom
- B. Save
- (C.) Undo
- D. Close

11. Which bar displays the contents of a cell? (p. 211)
- A. Title bar
- B. Quick Access Toolbar (QAT)
- C. Scroll bar
- (D.) Formula bar

EXERCISE 4-13 (Continued)
Filter Data within Queries

10 Choose **Home>Sort & Filter>Advanced** and select **Advanced Filter/ Sort**.

11 **CHECK** Your screen should look like Figure 4.39.

12 Double-click the **Quantity** field in the **CustOrderDet** query to add it to the design grid.

13 Under the **Quantity** field, click in the **Criteria** box and key: >2.

14 Click the **Toggle Filter**.

15 **CHECK** Your screen should look like Figure 4.40.

16 Close the query. Click **Yes** to save the changes.

Continue to the next exercise.

Troubleshooter

In order to apply a filter within a query, open the query in **Datasheet**, **Form**, **Report**, or **Layout View**. If you do not see any filter commands in these views, the designer of the data-base might have disabled the filtering function.

NCLB/Math (Number and Operations) Remind students that the >2 symbol means greater than 2.

FIGURE 4.39 Advanced filter/sort for query

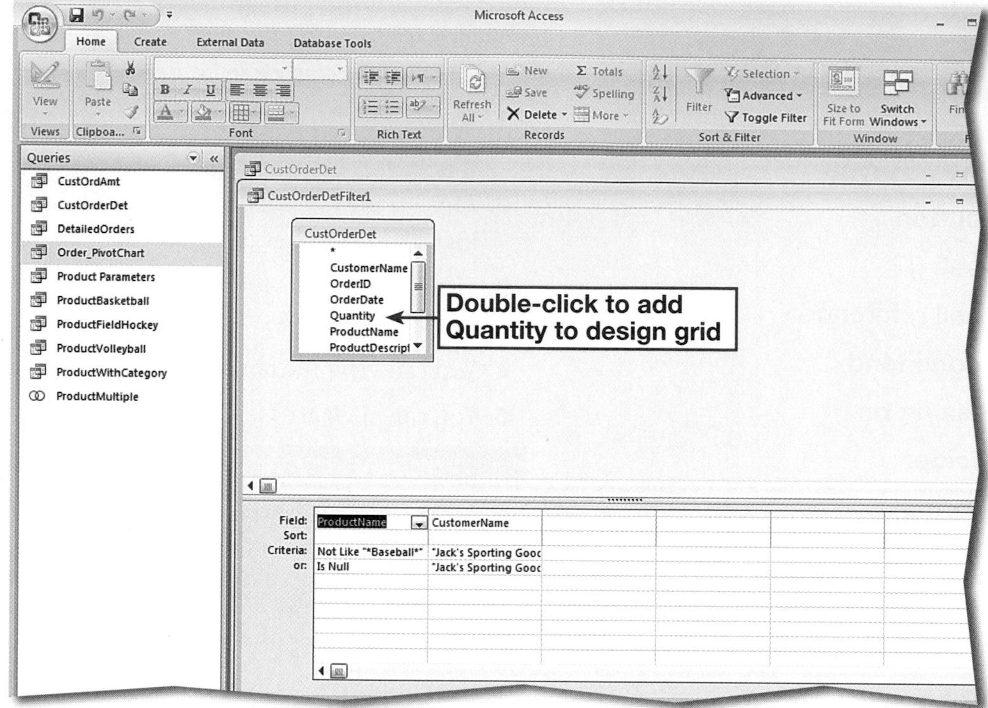

FIGURE 4.40 Query filtered for more than 2

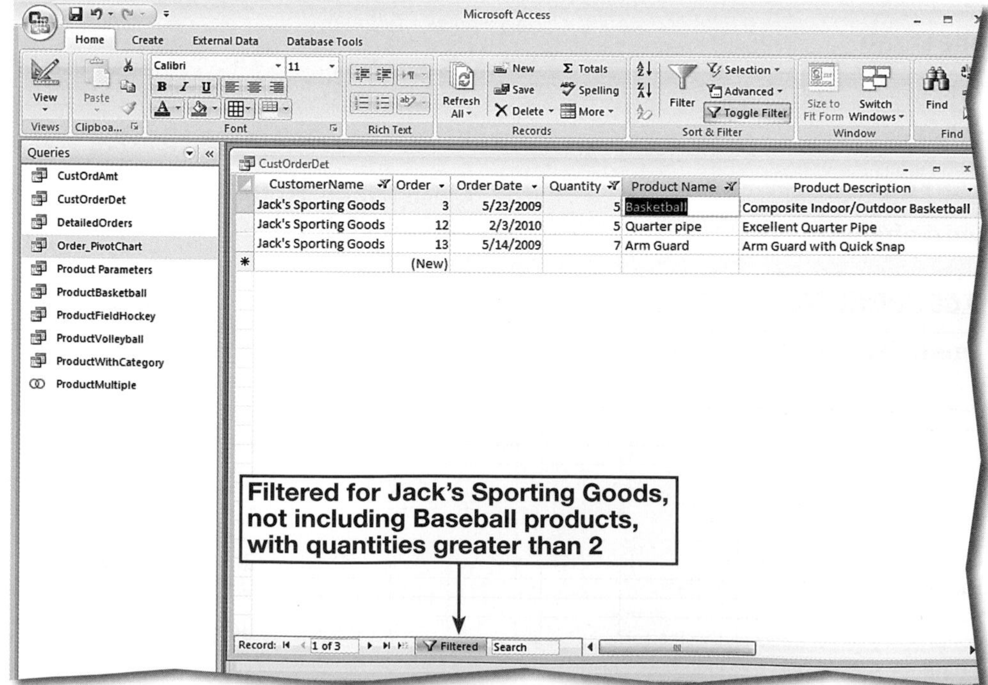

LESSON 1 Practice It Activities

1. Insert Cell Contents and Change Zoom View

Follow the steps to complete the activity.

Step-By-Step

1. Open your **e1-6** file.
2. Choose **Office>Save As**. In the File name box, key: e1rev-[your first initial and last name]1.
3. Ask your teacher for the location you should select in the **Save in** box. Select that location. Click **Save**.
4. In cells **D1** through **E4**, key the new data shown in Figure 1.26.
5. Point to the line between the letters **D** and **E**. Drag the double arrow until all of the contents fit in column **D**.
6. Choose **View>Zoom**.
7. Click **Custom**. Key: 125. Click **OK**.
8. **CHECK** Your screen should look like Figure 1.27.
9. Choose **View>100%**.
10. Save and close your file.

Solution The solution file for this activity is **e1rev1-SF.xlsx**.

FIGURE 1.26 New data added to worksheet

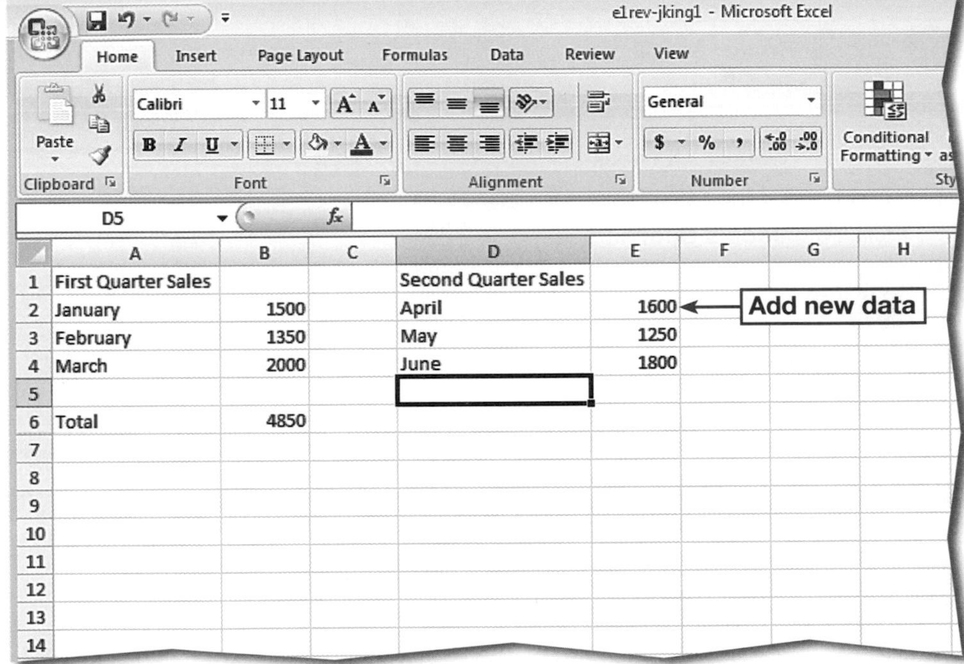

FIGURE 1.27 Screen at 125% zoom

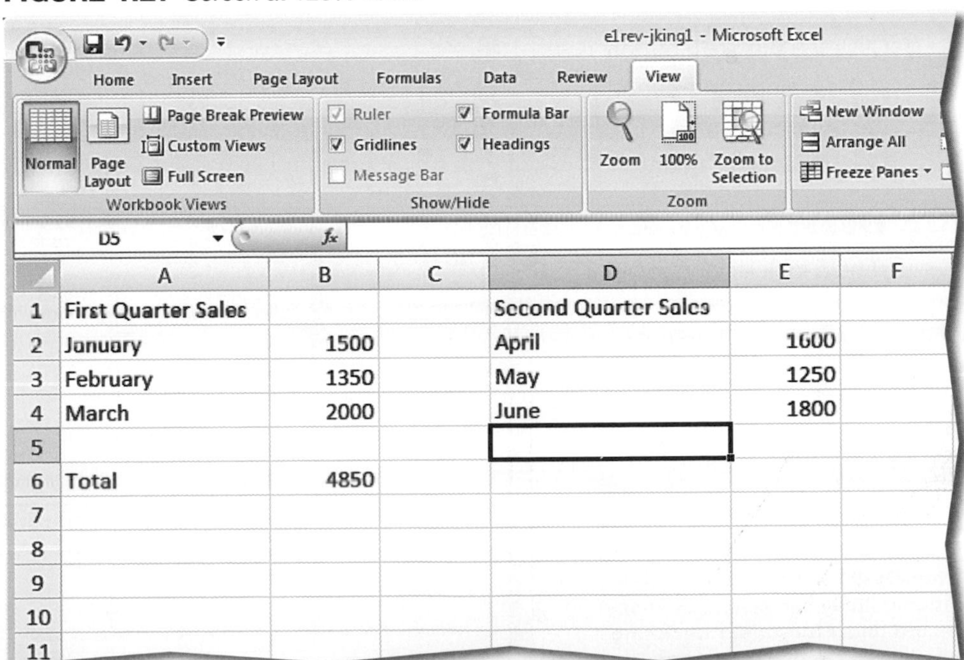

Step-By-Step

EXERCISE 4-13
Filter Data within Queries

1. In your **Sports4** file, open the **CustOrderDet** query.
2. In the query, click the **CustomerName** heading.
3. Choose **Home>Sort & Filter>Filter**.
4. Click the **Select All** check box to clear the selections. Click the **Jack's Sporting Goods** check box. Click **OK**.
5. CHECK Your screen should look like Figure 4.37.
6. Under the **Product Name** heading click **Baseball**.
7. Choose **Home>Sort & Filter>Selection** and select **Does Not Contain "Baseball"**.
8. Click the **Filtered** button in the **Navigation** bar at the bottom of the **CustOrderDet** query.
9. CHECK Your screen should look like Figure 4.38.

Continued on the next page.

Differentiated Instructions/ Advanced Students Have advanced students experiment with the other available filters.

Step-By-Step Tip In **Step 2**, tell students they can also click in any record under the **CustomerName** heading to set the same filter.

Just as in tables, you can also filter the data within a query. These filters show only the data that fit the criteria, hiding the information you do not want to see. Access has tools for creating common query filters, as well as ways to design advanced filters.

FIGURE 4.37 Table filtered for Jack's Sporting Goods

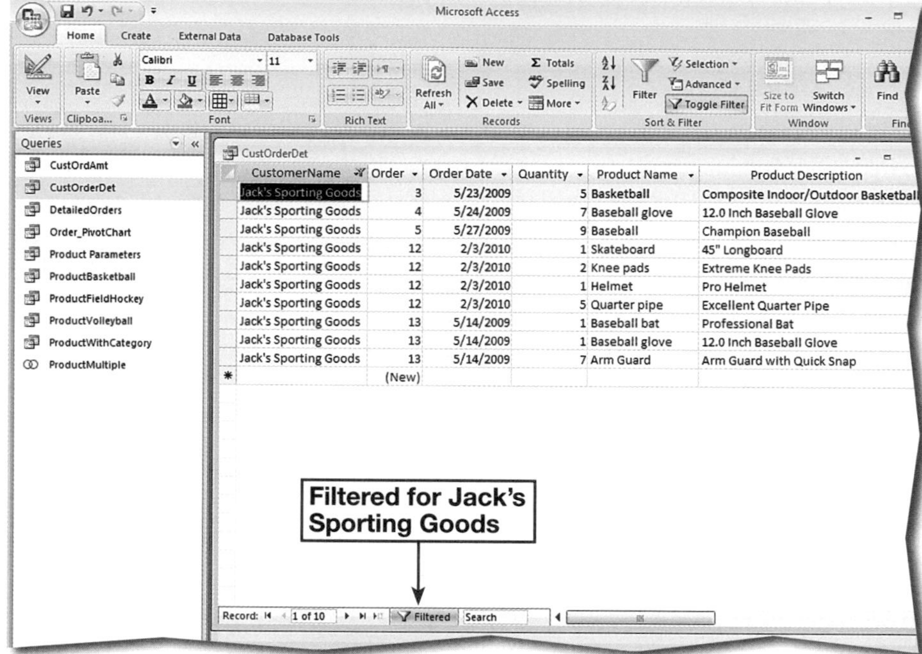

FIGURE 4.38 Table filtered for "Not Baseball"

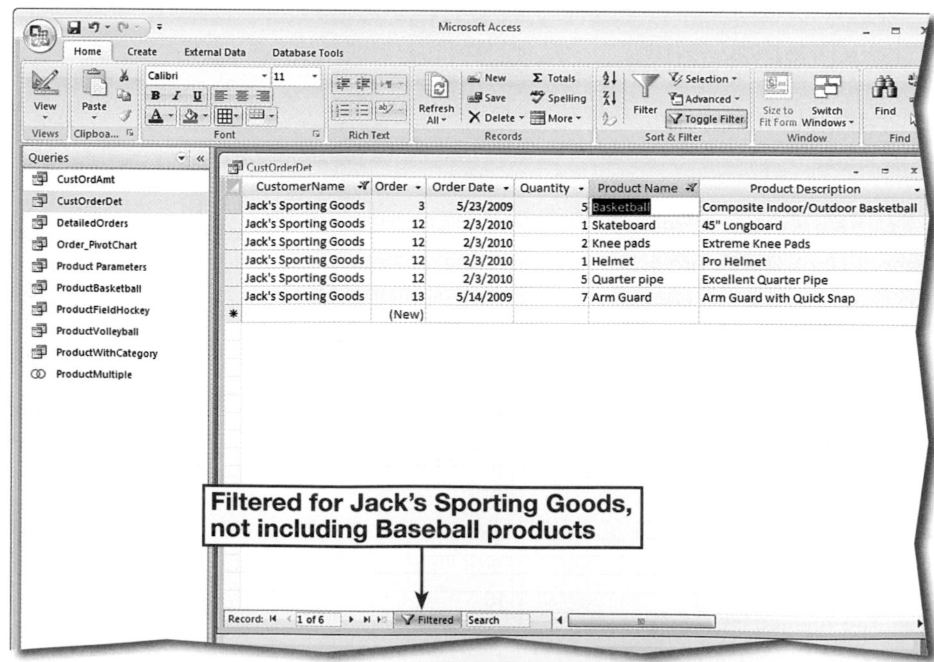

LESSON 1 Practice It Activities

Step-By-Step

1. Open your **e1rev-1** file. Save as: e1rev-[your first initial and last name]2.
2. Click cell **B2**.
3. Key: 1550.
4. Press ENTER.
5. CHECK Your screen should look like Figure 1.28.
6. Click **Undo**.
7. CHECK Your screen should look like Figure 1.29.
8. Click **Redo**. The changes you made to cell B2 reappear, the total is recalculated.
9. CHECK Your screen should look like Figure 1.28.
10. Save and close your file.

Solution The solution file for this activity is **e1rev2-SF.xlsx**.

2. Edit Cell Contents

Follow the steps to complete the activity. You must complete Practice It Activity 1 before doing this activity.

New Student Strategy If a student did not complete Practice It Activity 1, then the solution file for that activity can be used as a data file for this activity.

FIGURE 1.28 Edited cell

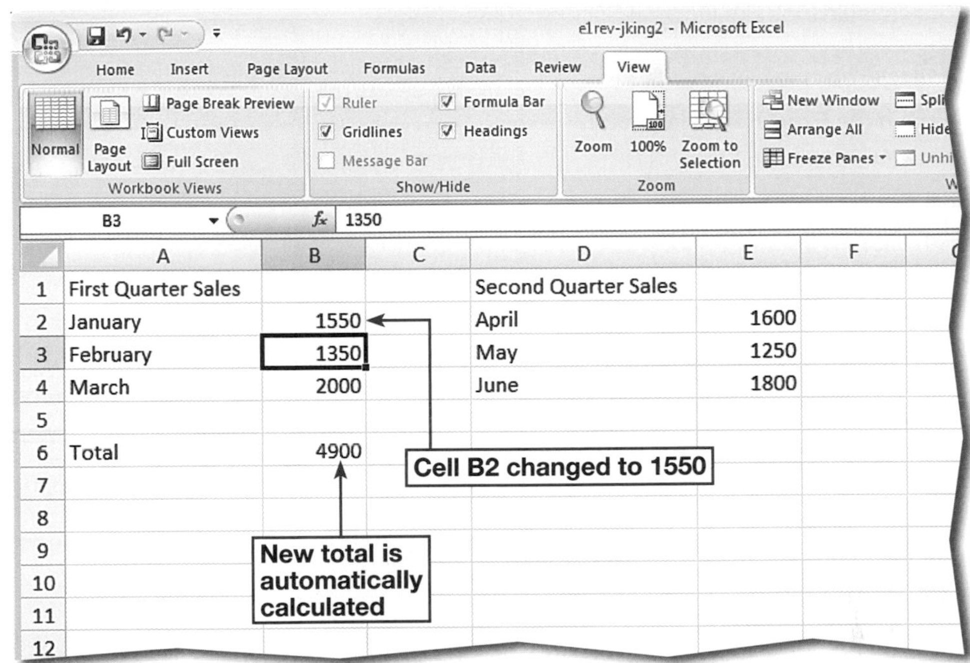

FIGURE 1.29 Undo

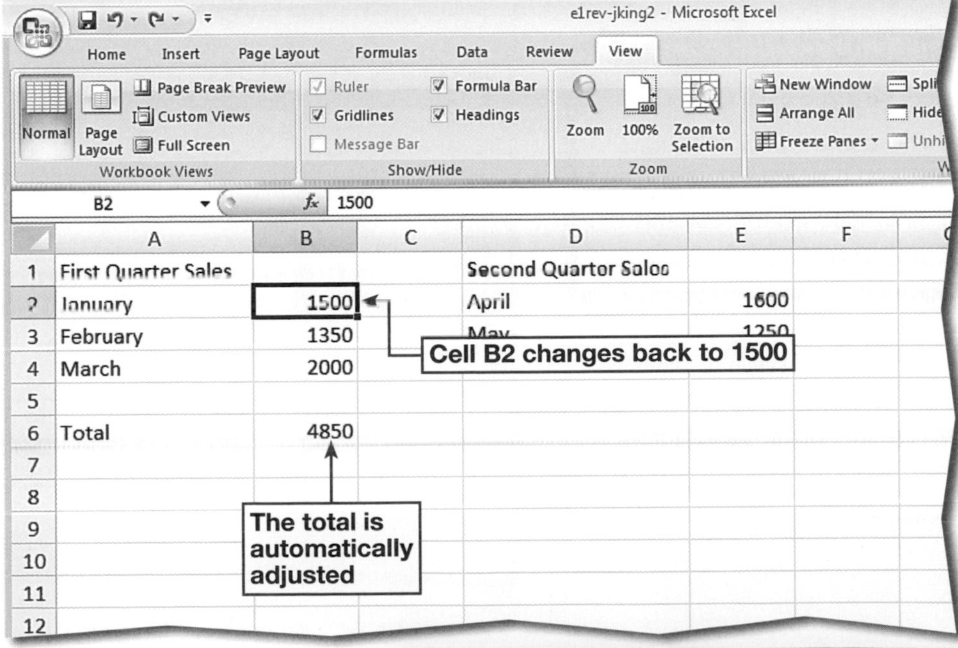

EXERCISE 4-12 (Continued)
Filter Data within Tables

Step-By-Step

10. Choose **Home>Sort & Filter>Advanced** and select **Advanced Filter/Sort**.
11. CHECK Your screen should look like Figure 4.35.
12. Double-click the **Price** field in the **Product** table to add it to the design grid.
13. Under the **Price** field, click in the **Criteria** box and key: >20.
14. Click the **Toggle Filter** button.
15. CHECK Your screen should look like Figure 4.36.
16. Close the table. Click **Yes** to save the changes.

Continue to the next exercise.

You Should Know

To display a tip showing the current filter criterion, rest the pointer over the filter icon on the column heading.

Teaching Tip Explain to students that in addition to using the **Sort & Filter** tools group to add filters, they can also use the **Advanced Filter/Sort** design grid. The advanced grid will allow further and more specific sorting capabilities.

FIGURE 4.35 Advanced filter/sort

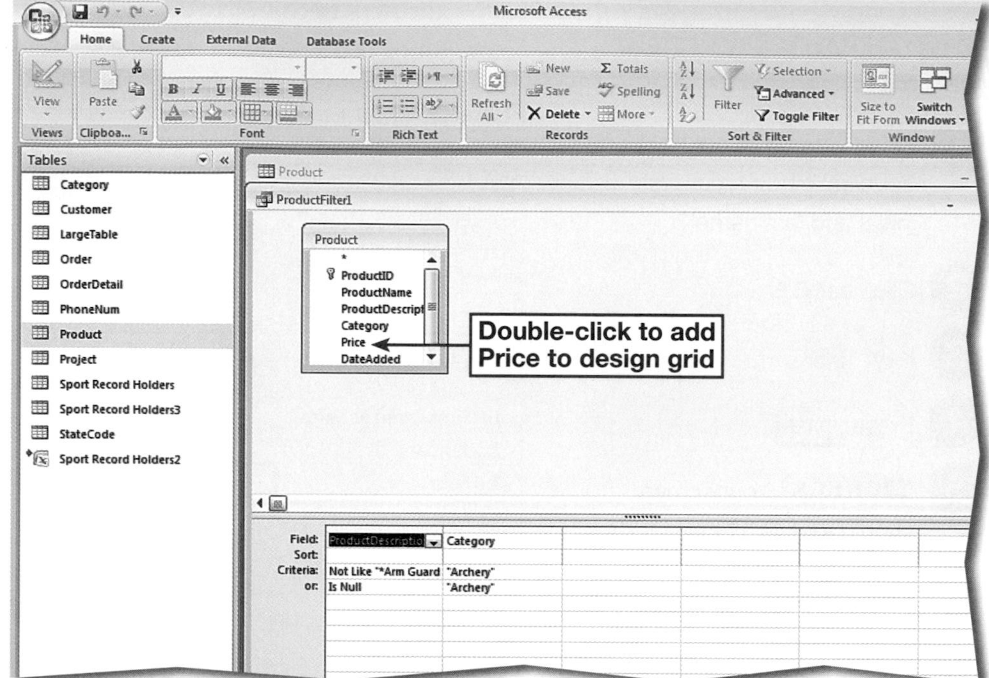

FIGURE 4.36 Table filtered for more than $20

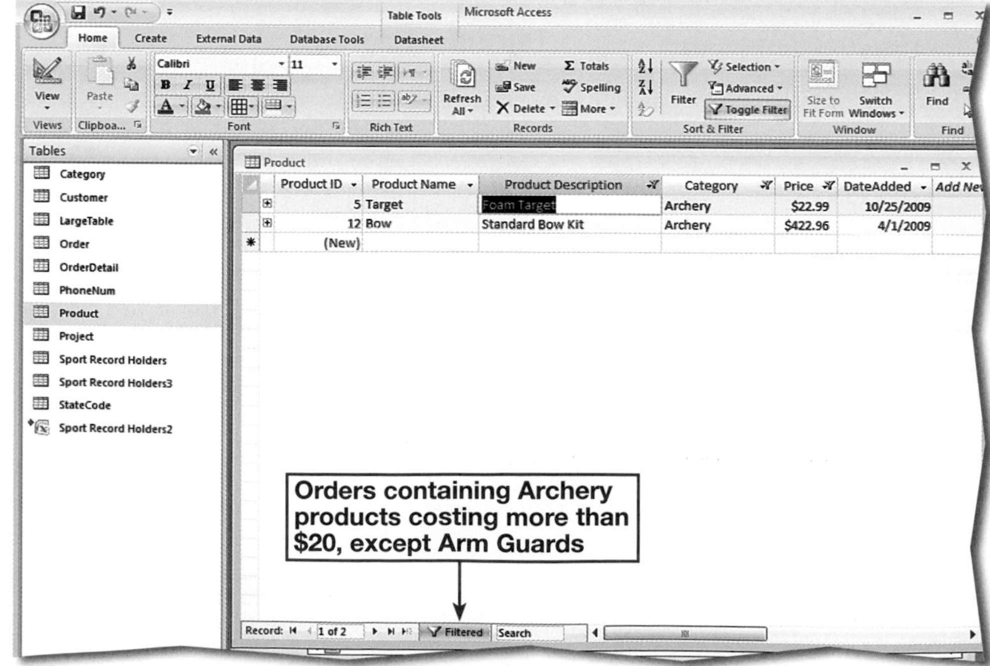

LESSON 1 Practice It Activities

Step-By-Step

1. Open your **e1rev-2** file. Save as: e1rev-[your first initial and last name]3.
2. Click cell **E6**.
3. Choose **Formulas>Function Library>AutoSum** Σ.
4. Select cells **E2** to **E4**. Press ENTER.
5. CHECK Your screen should look like Figure 1.30.
6. Choose **Office>Print>Print Preview**.
7. CHECK Your screen should look like Figure 1.31.
8. Click **Close Print Preview** to close Print Preview.
9. Choose **Office>Print**. With your teacher's permission, click **OK** to print the document.
10. Save and close your file.

Solution The solution file for this activity is **e1rev3-SF.xlsx**.

3. Calculate a Sum and Print a Worksheet

Follow the steps to complete the activity. You must complete Practice It Activity 2 before doing this activity.

New Student Strategy If a student did not complete Practice It Activity 2, then the solution file for that activity can be used as a data file for this activity.

FIGURE 1.30 AutoSum results

e1rev-jking3 - Microsoft Excel

E6 =SUM(E2:E5)

	A	B	C	D	E	F	G
1	First Quarter Sales			Second Quarter Sales			
2	January	1500		April	1600		
3	February	1350		May	1250		
4	March	2000		June	1800		
5							
6	Total	4850			4650		
7							
8							
9							
10							
11							
12							

Sum of second quarter sales

FIGURE 1.31 Print Preview

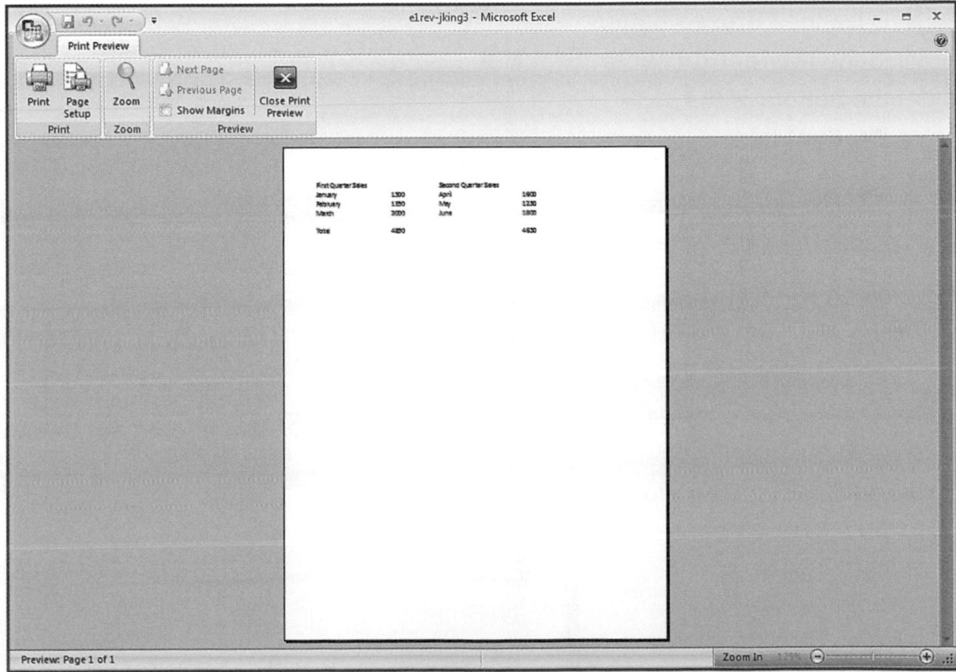

Step-By-Step

1 In your **Sports4** file, open the **Product** table.

2 Click the **Product** table **Category** heading.

3 Choose **Home>Sort & Filter>Filter**.

4 Click the **Select All** check box to clear the selections. Check **Archery**. Click **OK**.

5 CHECK Your screen should look like Figure 4.33.

6 Under the **Product Description** heading click **Arm Guard with Quick Snap**.

7 Choose **Home>Sort & Filter>Selection** and select **Does Not Contain "Arm Guard with Quick Snap"**.

8 Click the **Filtered** button in the **Navigation** bar at the bottom of the **Product** table.

9 CHECK Your screen should look like Figure 4.34.

Continued on the next page.

EXERCISE 4-12
Filter Data within Tables

Rather than take the time to build a query to return data from a single table, you can instead filter the data within the table itself. The filters will show only the data that fit the criteria, leaving out the information that you do not want to see. Access offers several tools for creating common filters, as well as the ability to design, or create, advanced filters in a filter Design View.

FIGURE 4.33 Table filtered for "Archery"

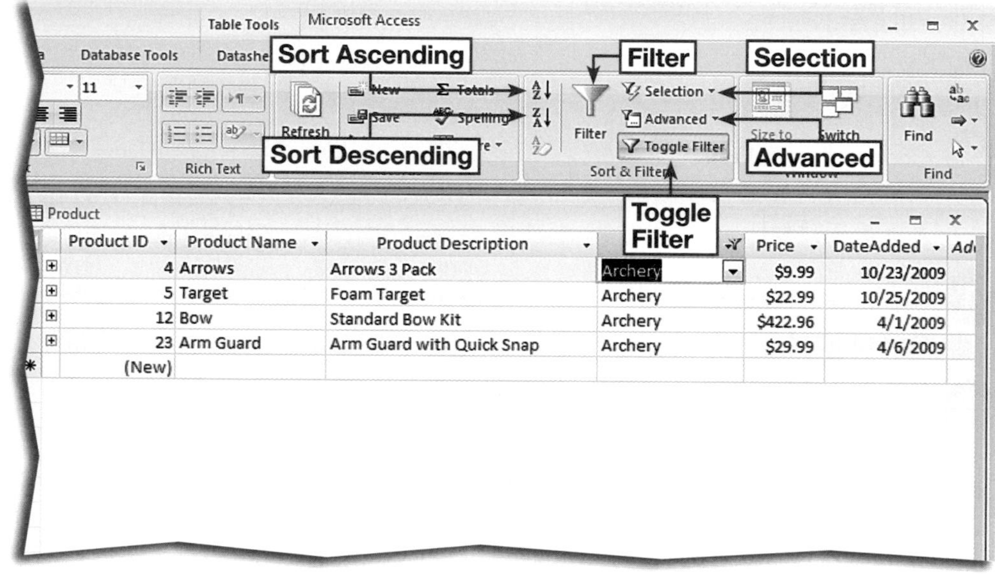

FIGURE 4.34 Table filtered for "Not Arm Guard"

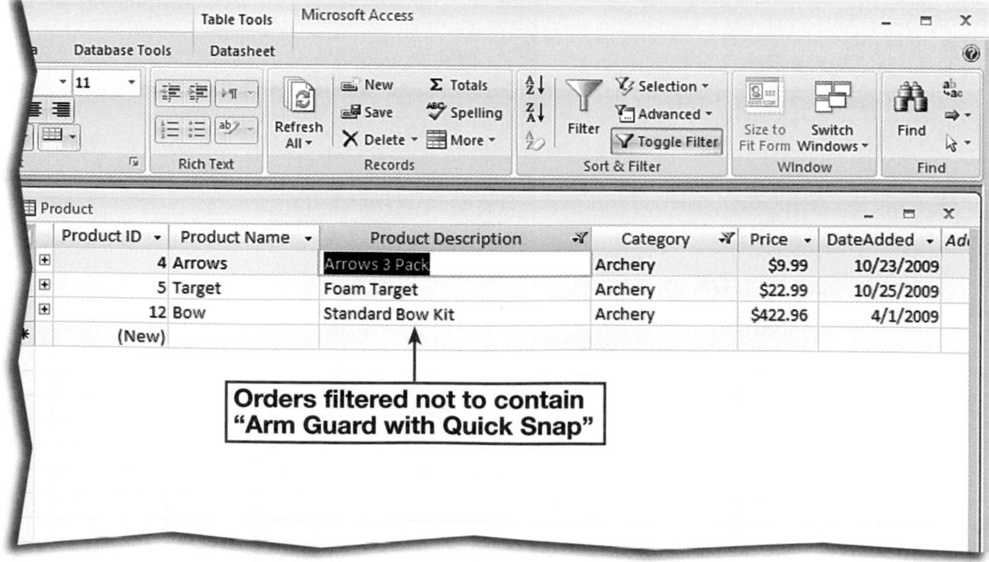

Academic Skills

You can use similar filters, called Boolean Operators, to limit your searches on search engines and in other large databases, such as library catalogs.

NCLB/Language Arts (NCTE 12)

LESSON 1 You Try It Activities

4. Make a Schedule

You have just started a new job. You have new responsibilities and a busy schedule. You decide to use Excel to create a schedule for each day of the work week.

Step-By-Step

1. Create a new workbook.
2. Save as: e1rev-[your first initial and last name]4.
3. In cell **A2**, key: Monday. In cell **A3**, key: Tuesday. Continue until Wednesday, Thursday, Friday, Saturday, and Sunday are keyed down the first column of the workbook.
4. Adjust the line between **A** and **B** until *Wednesday* fits in cell **A4**.
5. In cell **B1**, key: Week 1.
6. In cells **B2** to **B8**, key the number of hours shown in Figure 1.32.
7. Zoom in to **200%**.
8. **CHECK** Your screen should look like Figure 1.33.
9. Change the zoom back to **100%**.
10. Save and close your file.

Solution The solution file for this activity is e1rev4-SF.xlsx.

FIGURE 1.32 Work schedule

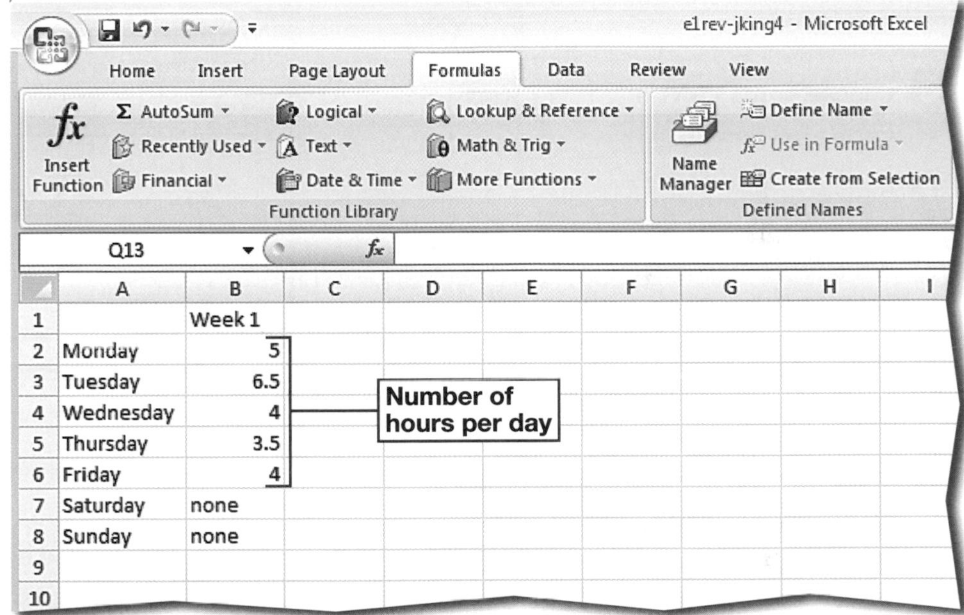

FIGURE 1.33 200% zoom

	A	B	C	D	E	F
1		Week 1				
2	Monday	5				
3	Tuesday	6.5				
4	Wednesday	4				
5	Thursday	3.5				
6	Friday	4				
7	Saturday	none				
8	Sunday	none				
9						

Step-By-Step

13 Click **Close Print Preview** .

14 CHECK Your screen should look like Figure 4.31.

15 Under the **OrderID** header, select the **OrderDate** control.

16 Choose **Home>Sort & Filter>Ascending** .

17 Click **Print Preview** .

18 CHECK Your screen should look like Figure 4.32.

19 Click **Close Print Preview** .

20 Close the report. Click **No** to close without saving changes.

Continue to the next exercise.

Academic Skills

Consider how you might incorporate data from a form or a report into a PowerPoint presentation or a business report written in Word. Being able to explain data results to others is an important part of managing a database.

NCLB/Language Arts (NCTE 12) Tell students that they can incorporate data from Access reports and forms into the reports and presentations they create with Word, PowerPoint, and Excel.

EXERCISE 4-11 (Continued)
Sort Records in Forms and Reports

FIGURE 4.31 CustomerOrderDetail Design View

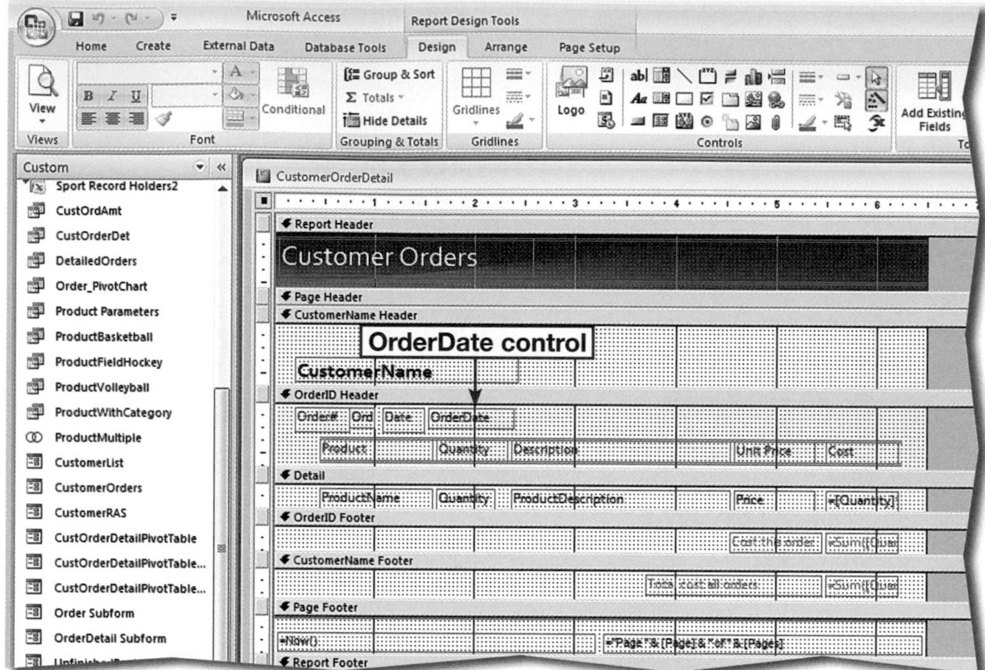

FIGURE 4.32 CustomerOrderDetail sorted by ascending date

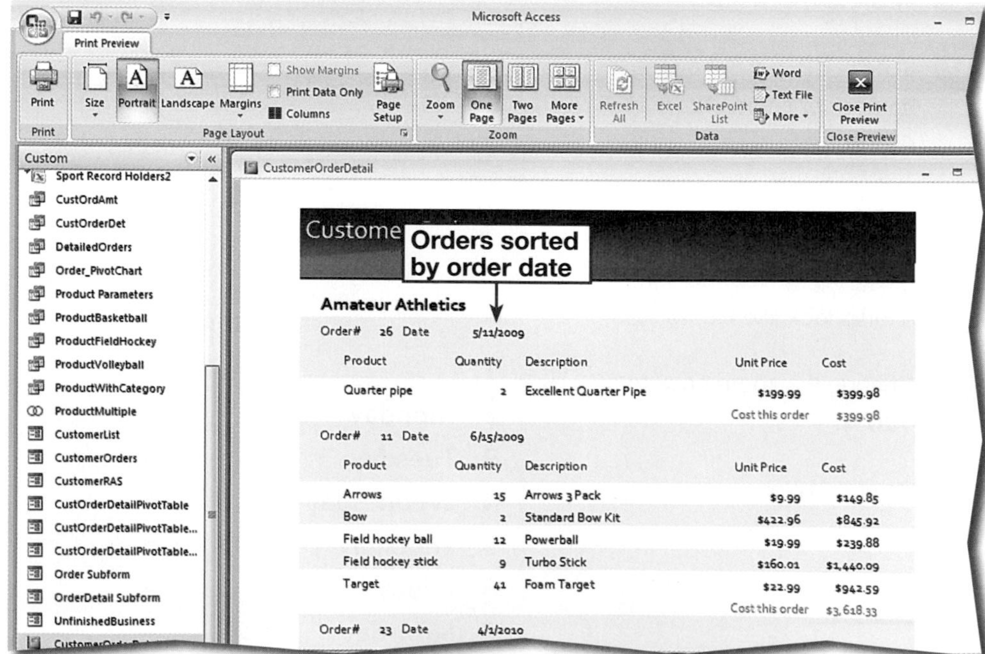

Troubleshooting Explain to students the difference between *sorting* and *grouping* in a report. Sorting take items and puts them in order, alphabetical for example. Grouping takes items that are similar in some way and groups them together.

LESSON 1 You Try It Activities

Step-By-Step

1. Open your **e1rev-4** file.
2. Save as: e1rev-[your first initial and last name]5.
3. In cell **C1**, key: Week 2.
4. In cells **C2** to **C8**, key the number of hours shown in Figure 1.34.
5. In cell **C3**, change **5** to **6**.
6. In cell **A10**, key: Total Hours.
7. Click cell **B10**. Use **AutoSum** to calculate the total hours for Week 1.
8. Click cell **C10**. Use **AutoSum** to calculate the total hours for Week 2.
9. **CHECK** Your screen should look like Figure 1.35.
10. Save and close your file.

Solution The solution file for this activity is **e1rev5-SF.xlsx**.

5. Calculate Weekly Hours

You decide to use AutoSum to compare how many hours you are working each week at your new job. You must complete You Try It Activity 4 before doing this activity. **New Student Strategy** If a student did not complete You Try It Activity 4, then the solution file for that activity can be used as a data file for this activity.

FIGURE 1.34 Week 2 schedule

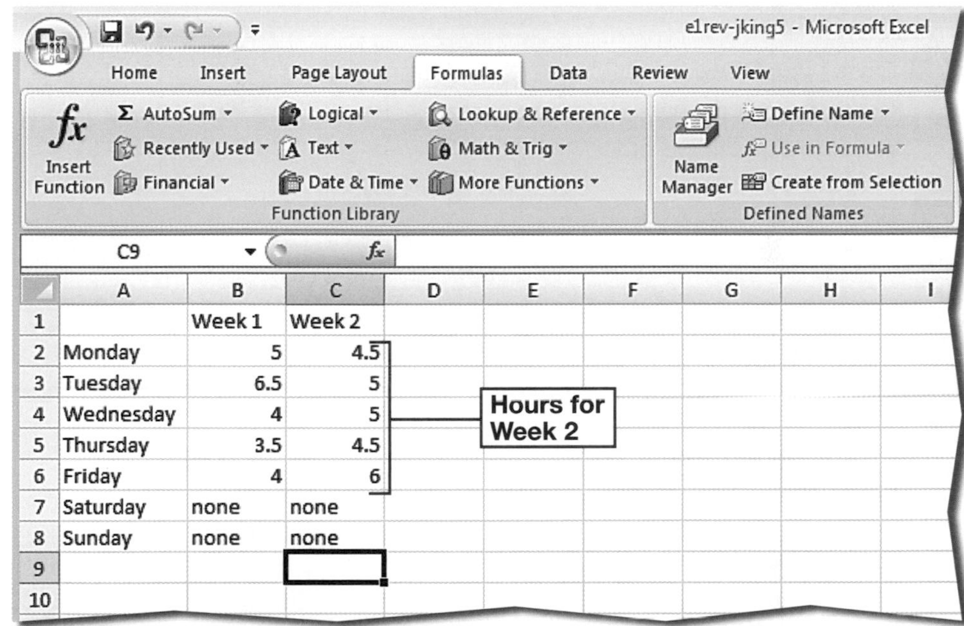

FIGURE 1.35 AutoSum results

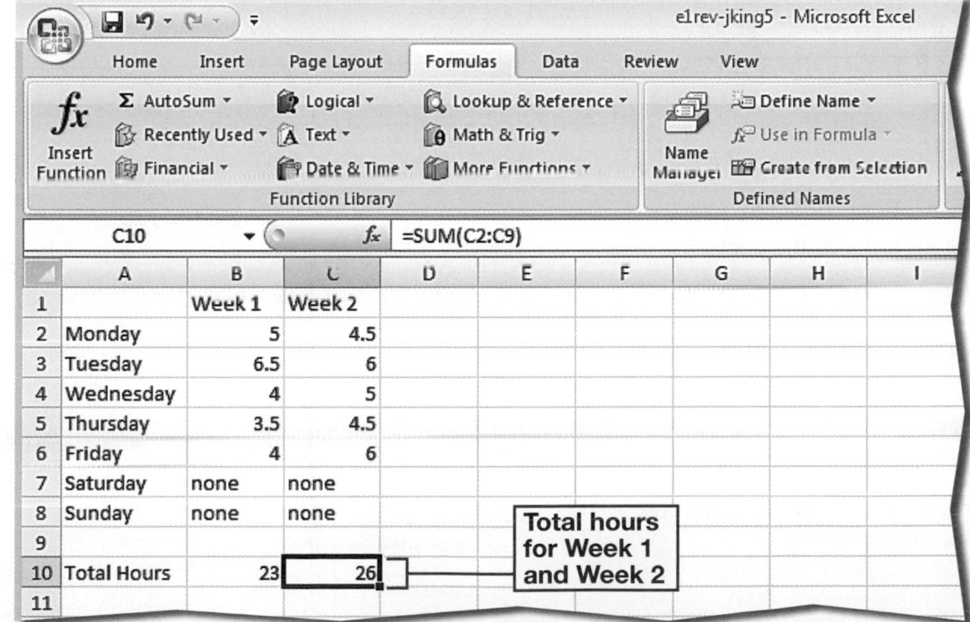

Step-By-Step

1. In your **Sports4** file, open the **CustomerRAS** form.
2. Choose **Home>Sort & Filter>Ascending** .
3. CHECK Your screen should look like Figure 4.29.
4. Press PAGE DOWN three times. Notice the records are sorted in alphabetical order.
5. On the form, click in the **City** box.
6. Click **Ascending** .
7. Press PAGE DOWN three times.
8. Choose **Home>Sort & Filter>Clear All Sorts** .
9. Close the form.
10. Right-click to open the **CustomerOrderDetail** report in **Design View**.
11. Click **Print Preview** .
12. CHECK Your screen should look like Figure 4.30. Scroll down to note the order of the customer order dates.

Continued on the next page.

Differentiated Instruction/ Advanced Students Have advanced students open the **CustomerOrders** form and sort by **subform** fields.

EXERCISE 4-11
Sort Records in Forms and Reports

Information in forms is sortable in much the same way you sort the information in a table or other **database object**. To sort records, determine the sorting order for each field and then use the Sort & Filter tools to set the order. Reports are set up to present data for printing, so you should avoid changing the order of the records after you have finished designing the report. However, you can sort records in a report in Design View by selecting the specific element you want to sort and applying the Sort & Filter tools.

Step-By-Step Tip In **Step 7**, point out to students that the records are now sorted in alphabetical order by state.

FIGURE 4.29 CustomerRAS form sorted alphabetically by customer

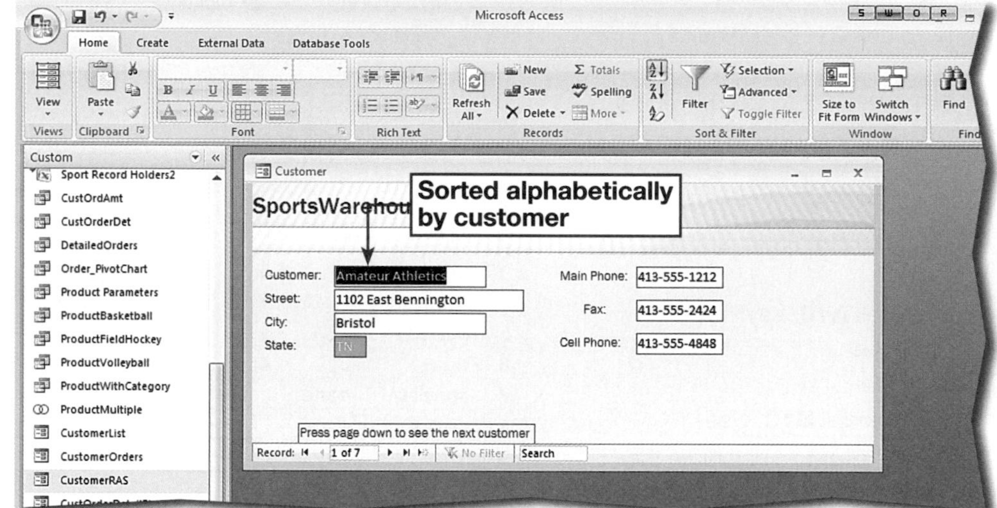

FIGURE 4.30 CustomerOrderDetail Print Preview

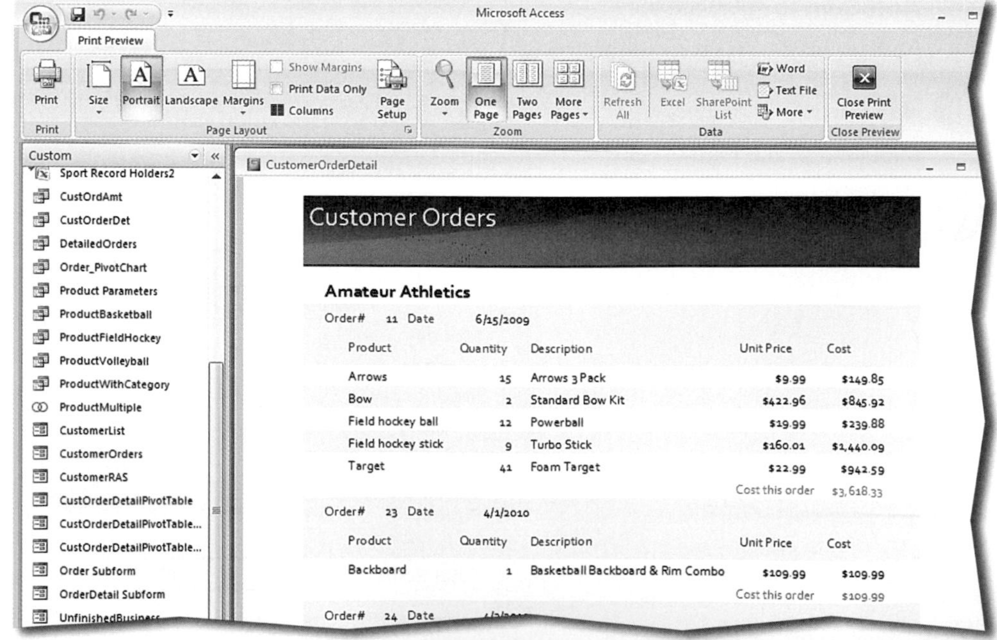

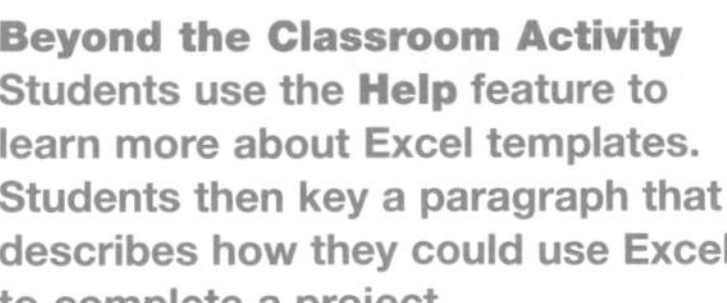

LESSON 1 Critical Thinking Activities

Beyond the Classroom Activity Students use the **Help** feature to learn more about Excel templates. Students then key a paragraph that describes how they could use Excel to complete a project.

Standards at Work Activity Students' worksheets should look similar to the solution file **e1rev7-SF.xlsx.**

21st Century Skills Activity Students' worksheets should look similar to the solution file called **e1rev8-SF.xlsx.**

NCLB/Math (Number and Operations) Reinforce number recognition by allowing students to add a new column to their 21st Century Skills Activity and entering in birthdates as well as zip codes.

NCLB/Language Arts (NCTE 4) Reinforce language arts skills by allowing students to read their paragraphs to the class.

Go Online e-REVIEW

glencoe.com

Go to the **Online Learning Center** to complete the following review activities.

Online Self Check
To test your knowledge of the material, click **Unit 2> Lesson 1** and choose **Self Checks.**

Interactive Review
To review the main points of the lesson, click **Unit 2> Lesson 1** and choose **Interactive Review.**

6. Beyond the Classroom Activity

Language Arts: Describe Excel Excel can help you accomplish many tasks in your daily life. To learn more about how to use Excel, open the Excel Help feature. In the Excel Help window, search for Excel templates. Review the results of your search. You will see that Excel can be used to track anything from home repairs to sports results. Read any items that interest you. Then, key a paragraph in Word that describes how Excel could help you to track or complete a specific project you are currently working on.

Save your document as: e1rev-[your first initial and last name]6.

7. Standards at Work Activity

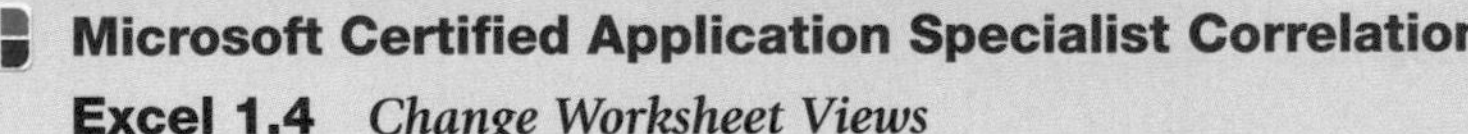

Microsoft Certified Application Specialist Correlation

Excel 1.4 *Change Worksheet Views*

Organize Contact Information Your boss has asked you to create an Excel worksheet that will be used to store employees' contact information.

Create a new Excel worksheet. List the following titles in the first row: Name, Street Address, City, State, Zip Code. In the second row, fill in your contact data. Then add the contact information of three friends. Adjust column width so that all of the categories fit. Zoom in to 125%. Review your document and edit any cells with incorrect data. With your teacher's permission, print your worksheet. Key a paragraph explaining why you would want to change the zoom of a document.

Save your document as: e1rev-[your first initial and last name]7.

8. 21st Century Skills Activity

Increase Productivity One way to increase your productivity for a particular task is to practice. Practice will help you enter, edit, and calculate data quickly and efficiently. Another way to increase productivity is to ask others how they complete certain tasks efficiently.

Open your **e1rev-7** file. Add three more friends to your worksheet. Remember to adjust column width so that all of the categories fit. Share with your classmates any tips that help you enter and edit data more quickly in Excel. Add two relatives to your worksheet, using your classmates' productivity tips.

Save your document as: e1rev-[your first initial and last name]8.

Step-By-Step

1. In your **Sports4** file, open the **DetailedOrders** query in **Design View**.
2. In the design grid under **OrderDate**, click in the **Sort** box.
3. Click the drop-down arrow and select **Ascending**.
4. **CHECK** Your screen should look like Figure 4.27.
5. Click **Datasheet View**.
6. **CHECK** Your screen should look like Figure 4.28.
7. In the **OrderDate** heading, click the drop-down arrow and select **Sort Newest to Oldest**.
8. Click **Save**.
9. Close the query.

Continue to the next exercise.

You Should Know

Ascending sort will display the record with the smallest value at the top and the record with the largest value at the bottom. *Descending* sort will do the opposite.

Teaching Tip Explain to students that all fields can be arranged in ascending/descending order, alphabetically, numerically, or in other ways.

EXERCISE 4-10
Sort Records in Tables and Queries

To organize and find records in Datasheet View, it helps to sort the records in a table or query. In a query that lists customer orders, you should list all of a customer's orders together, not scattered throughout the listing. In other cases, you may want to view the largest orders first.

FIGURE 4.27 Sort DetailedOrders by ascending dates Design View

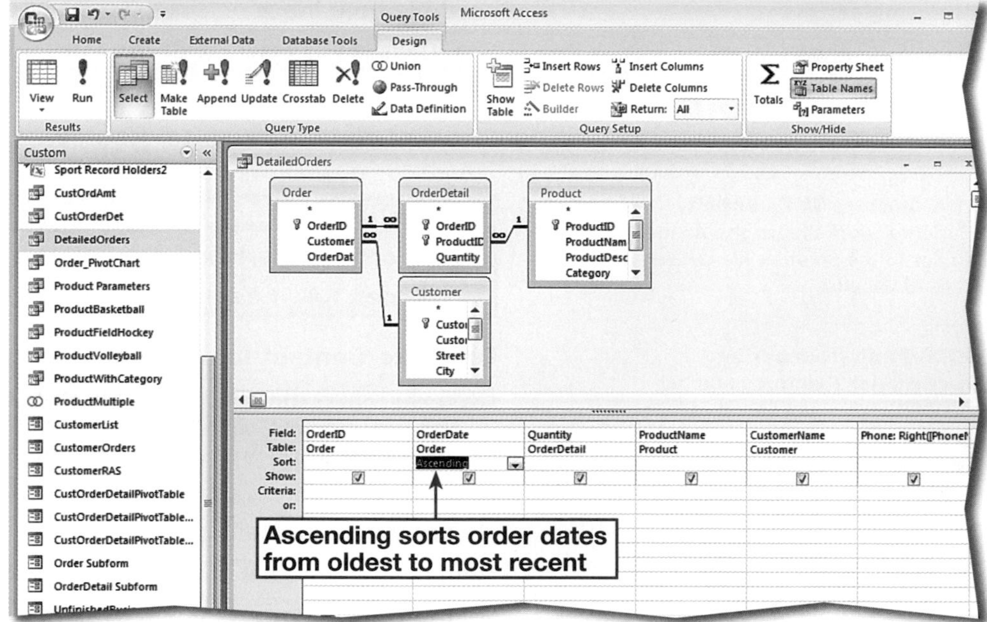
Ascending sorts order dates from oldest to most recent

FIGURE 4.28 Sort DetailedOrders by ascending dates

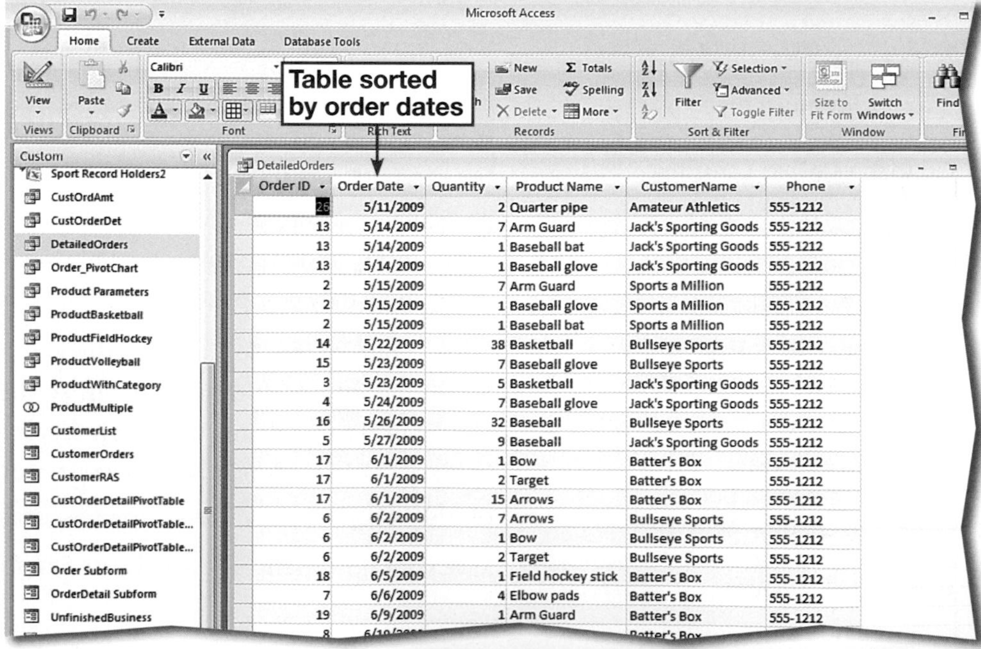
Table sorted by order dates

LESSON 1 Challenge Yourself Projects

Before You Begin

Budget Expenses Whether you need to plan a party or buy school supplies, creating a budget can help you track costs and monitor your spending. These projects teach you how to use a spreadsheet to create a budget.

Reflect Once you complete the projects, open a Word document and answer the following questions:

1. What are some of the benefits of using Excel to create a budget?
2. How did Excel help you determine whether or not you were within your budget?
3. How might you use Excel to budget your time?

Answers Rubrics for each Challenge Yourself Project and Before You Begin are available at **glencoe.com**. You may want to download the rubrics and make them available to students as they complete each project.

9. Create a Budget

Rubric R

LEVEL This is an intermediate level project.

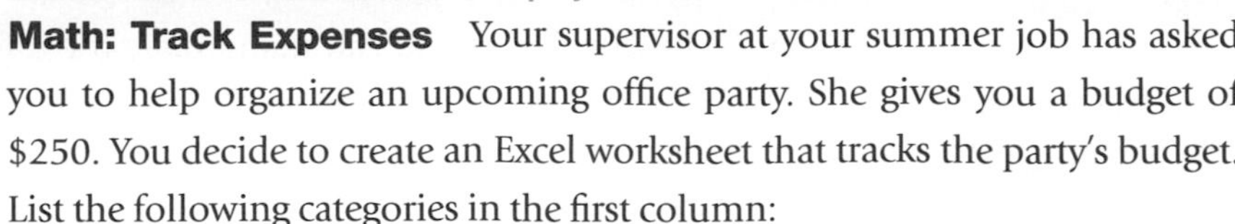

Math: Track Expenses Your supervisor at your summer job has asked you to help organize an upcoming office party. She gives you a budget of $250. You decide to create an Excel worksheet that tracks the party's budget. List the following categories in the first column:

- Food
- Music
- Decorations
- Gift

Adjust column width so that all of the categories fit.

Save your worksheet as: e1rev-[your first initial and last name]9.

Solution Students' worksheets should look like solution file **e1rev9-SF.xlsx**.

10. Calculate Total Costs

Rubric R

LEVEL This is an intermediate level project.

Math: Calculate Costs After looking into prices for your office party, you come up with estimates for each category. Enter the following costs in your party budget worksheet:

- Food = $85
- Music = $150
- Decorations = $25
- Gifts = $40

Use **AutoSum** to calculate the total cost of the party. Are the costs within your budget? Save your worksheet as: e1rev-[your first initial and last name]10.

Solution Students' worksheets should look like solution file **e1rev10-SF.xlsx**.

11. Create an Alternative Budget

Rubric R

LEVEL This is an advanced level project.

Math: Analyze Data Your supervisor looks at your budget and asks you to create a new budget that costs no more than $200.

- Create a new worksheet.
- In the third column of your worksheet, enter a different cost for each category.
- Use **AutoSum** to find the total cost of the alternative budget.
- If the budget is still over $200, reduce some of the costs and recalculate the total price of the party.

Save your workbook as: e1rev-[your first initial and last name]11.

Solution Students' worksheets should look like solution file **e1rev11-SF.xlsx**.

Step-By-Step

1. In your **Sports4** file, open the **CustOrdAmt** query in **Design View**.
2. Confirm **Design>Show/Hide>Totals** Σ is selected.
3. In the design grid, click in the first open **Field** box to the right of **Amount**. Key: Quantity.
4. Click in the **Total** box under **Quantity**. Click the drop-down arrow and select **Sum**.
5. Fill in the four fields to the right of the Quantity field as shown in Figure 4.25.
6. Click **Datasheet View**.
7. **CHECK** Your screen should look like Figure 4.26.
8. Close the query. Click **Yes** to save the changes.

Continue to the next exercise.

Academic Skills

The **Sum** function adds the numbers in a column to give you a total quantity. The **Count** function tells you how many separate numbers are in the column. For example, if you add 5 + 10 + 6 + 9 + 25, your sum is 55. However, the count is 5.

EXERCISE 4-9
Use Aggregate Functions in Queries

Normally, calculated fields only use fields from one record. You can use an aggregate function to gather together, or **aggregate**, data from different records and display it in the query. You also can manipulate the information in the field to display the result of expressions in the query.

FIGURE 4.25 CustOrdAmt Design View

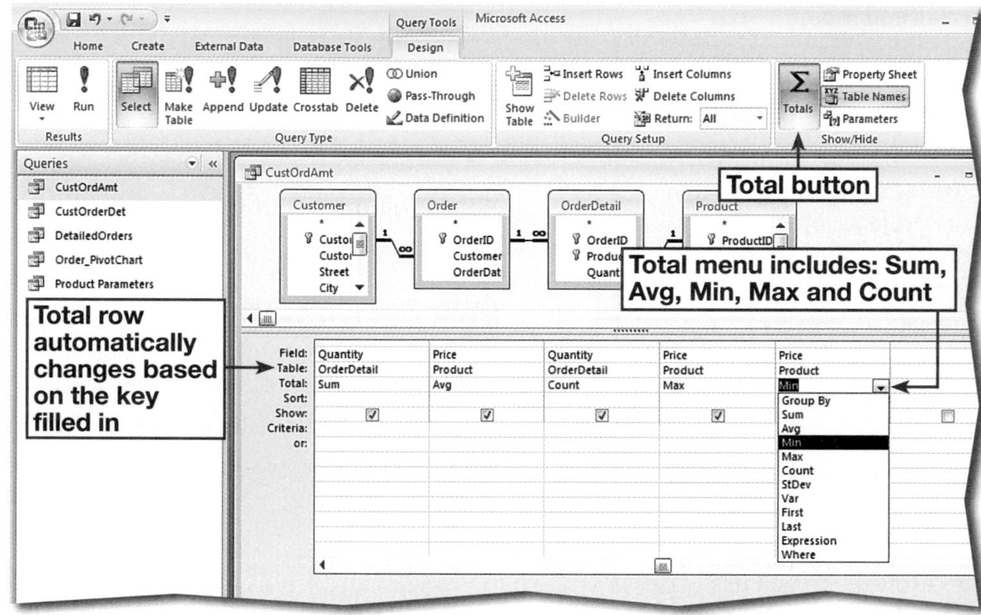

FIGURE 4.26 CustOrdAmt with aggregate functions

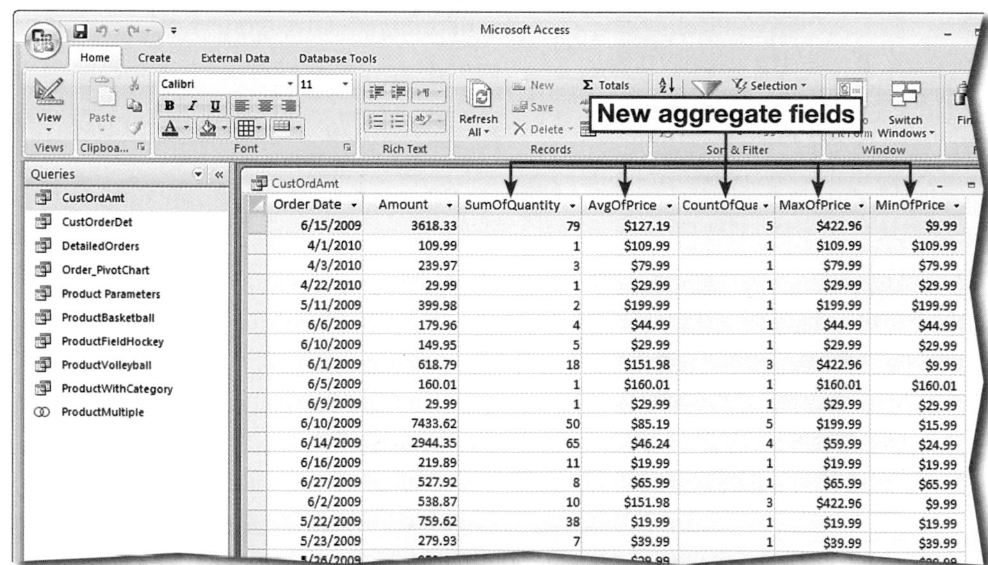

NCLB/Math (NCTM Number and Operations) Show students how a company could use the Count function to see how many separate orders are being placed by customers. The Sum function can help a company maintain their inventory, but the Count function can help them keep track of how often customers are ordering.

LESSON 2 Create Data and Content

In this lesson, you will learn many new skills, including how AutoSum can add numerals and how to use Cut, Copy, and Paste commands. These skills will help you to use Excel to track budgets and inventory.

Key Concepts

- Enter, edit, clear, find, and replace cell contents
- Use AutoSum, AVERAGE, MIN, and MAX functions
- Use Cut, Copy, and Paste
- Use the Fill handle tool
- Insert, modify, and remove hyperlinks

Standards

The following standards are covered in this lesson. Refer to pages xxv and 715 for a description of the standards listed here.

ISTE Standards Correlation

NETS•S

1a, 1d, 2b, 2d, 4a, 4c, 5c, 6a, 6b

Microsoft Certified Application Specialist

Excel

1.1, 2.2, 2.3, 3.2

NCLB/Math (Problem Solving)
Reinforce to students that it is important to always create weekly or monthly budgets to prevent spending funds they do not have.

See page TM70 for answer to 21st Century Skills.

21st CENTURY SKILLS

Manage Money Responsibly Have you ever bought two CDs on a Saturday afternoon and then found yourself without money the next week? Nearly everybody can improve their money management skills. The first step to managing your money is to create a budget, which is an estimate of income and expenses over a stated time. To create a monthly budget, write down the amount of money you have to spend each month. Then make a list of essential items that you buy each month, such as clothes or school supplies. Also list how much these items will cost over a month's time. Subtract this number from the amount you have to spend to find how much you have for things you would like but do not need.

Microsoft Excel is an excellent budgeting tool. In this lesson, you will learn the skills you need to create a budget. *Do you believe that a budget would help you better manage your money?*

Step-By-Step

1. In your **Sports4** file, open the **DetailedOrders** query in **Design View**.
2. Click in the **Field** box to the right of **CustomerName**.
3. Key: Phone: Right(PhoneNumber,8).
4. Press ENTER.
5. CHECK Your screen should look like Figure 4.23.
6. Click **Datasheet View**.
7. CHECK Your screen should look like Figure 4.24.
8. Close table. Save the changes.

Continue to the next exercise.

Troubleshooter

Notice that Access always puts the field names in brackets like this: **[PhoneNumber]**. The brackets tell Access that this is a field name. When writing an expression, put field names in brackets so that Access will read its function correctly.

Teaching Tip Explain that the expression keyed into the field box includes the field alias **(Phone)** and the expression that tells the query to display the first eight characters from the right in the **PhoneNumber** field.

EXERCISE 4-8
Add Aliases

An **alias** is an alternative name given to a table or field in an expression. In the previous exercise, the names of the two new fields you created are actually aliases that give a better descriptive name to the calculated fields in the query. You can identify aliases by the fact they have a colon following the field name in Design View.

FIGURE 4.23 Detailed Orders Design View

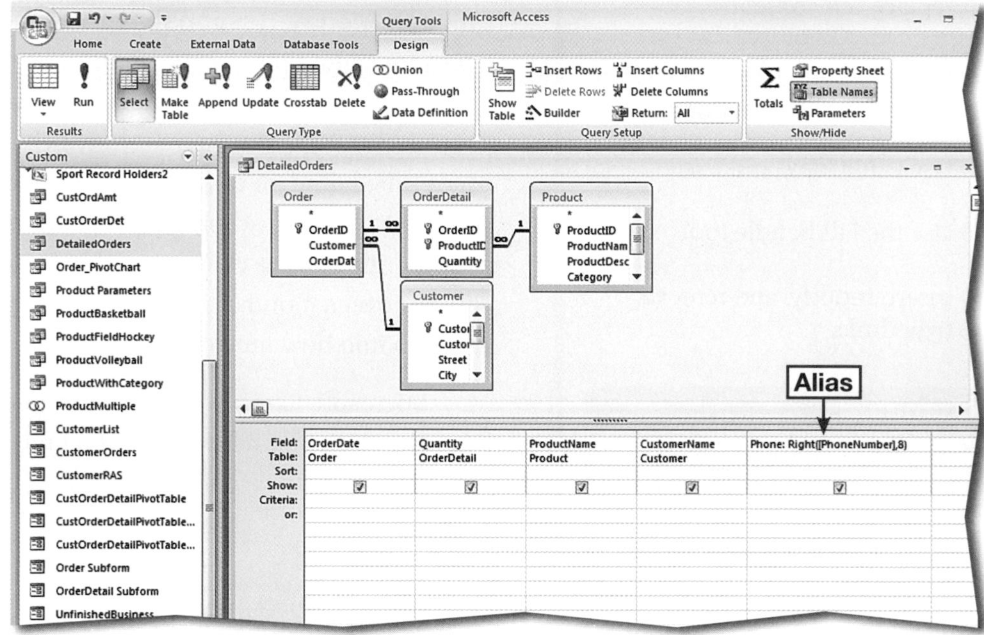

FIGURE 4.24 Detailed Orders with phone number

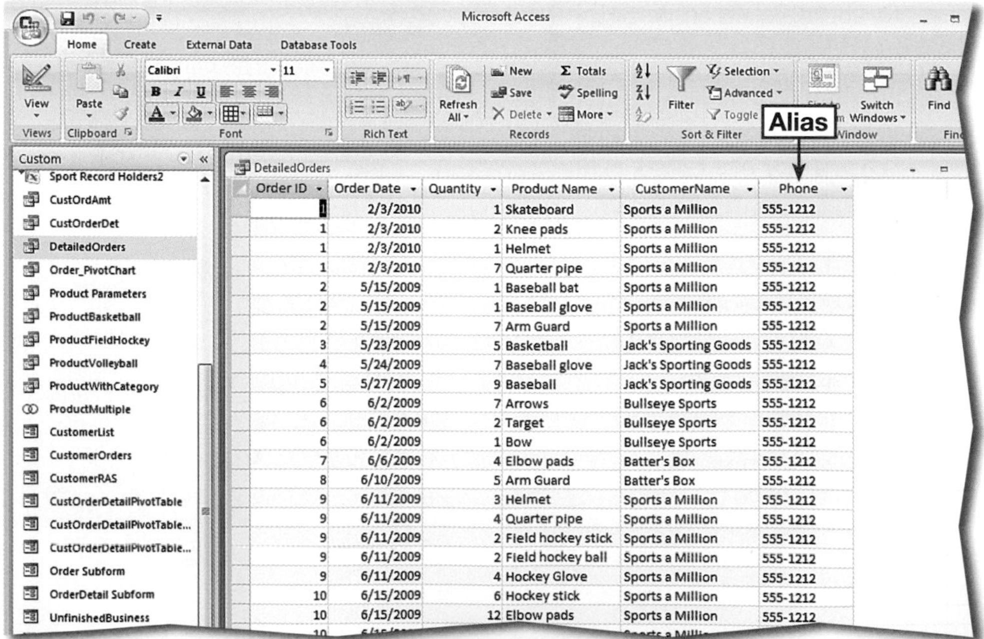

LESSON 2 Reading Guide

Before You Read

See page TM42 for English Learner activity suggestions.

Prepare with a Partner Before you read, work with a partner. Read the exercise titles and ask each other questions about the topics that will be discussed. Write down the questions you both have about each section. As you read, answer the questions you have identified.

Read To Learn

- Perform tasks quickly and easily with Excel's automated tools and commands.
- Create and modify a budget to track expenses.
- Explore worksheet and workbook editing tools.
- Create and work with formulas and functions.

Main Idea

Excel has many functions that can help users create data and content for a spreadsheet.

Vocabulary

Key Terms

AutoSum	Clipboard	function
AVERAGE	copy	hyperlink
budget	cut	MAX
cell content	edit	MIN
clear	Fill handle	paste

Academic Vocabulary

These words appear in your reading and on your tests. Make sure you know their meanings.

determine
insert

Quick Write Activity

Explain On a separate sheet of paper, explore how you currently track how much you spend and how much money you save. Why is it important to track expenses? How might you use Excel to help you save money for an important purchase?

Study Skill

Make an Outline An outline is a good tool for organizing information. When you understand how information fits together, you will be more likely to remember what you have learned. On a separate sheet of paper, list the most important information from each exercise in the lesson.

Academic Standards

Math

NCTM (Number and Operations) Understand numbers, ways of representing numbers, relationships among numbers, and number systems.

NCTM (Number and Operations) Understand meanings of operations and how they relate to one another.

NCTM (Number and Operations) Compute fluently and make reasonable estimates.

NCTM (Algebra) Represent and analyze mathematical situations and structures using algebraic symbols.

Step-By-Step

1. In your **Sports4** file, open the **CustOrderDet** query in **Design View**.
2. In the **design grid**, scroll to the right and click in the **Field** box to the right of the **Price** column.
3. Key: TotalCost: [Price]*[Quantity]. Press ENTER.
4. Key: AreaCode: Left([PhoneNumber],3). Press ENTER.
5. **CHECK** Your screen should look like Figure 4.21.
6. Click **Datasheet View**.
7. Scroll to the right to see the new calculated fields.
8. **CHECK** Your screen should look like Figure 4.22.
9. Click **Save**. Close the query.

Continue to the next exercise.

Academic Skills

In Step 3, the phrase **Total Cost:[Price]*[Quantity]** means that the **Total Cost** is equal to the **Price** multiplied by the **Quantity**.

Step-By-Step Tip In **Steps 3 and 4**, make sure students key the names without using spaces. Remind students that they can **AutoFit** the calculated fields if they cannot see all the text that they keyed in the new calculated fields.

EXERCISE 4-7
Add Calculated Fields to Queries

Access allows you to set up a calculated field in a query to perform a calculation. The calculated data is not stored in your tables. Instead, when you change the data in the query, Access recalculates the field.

NCLB/Math (NCTM Number and Operations) Have students multiply the numbers themselves.

FIGURE 4.21 CustOrderDet Design View

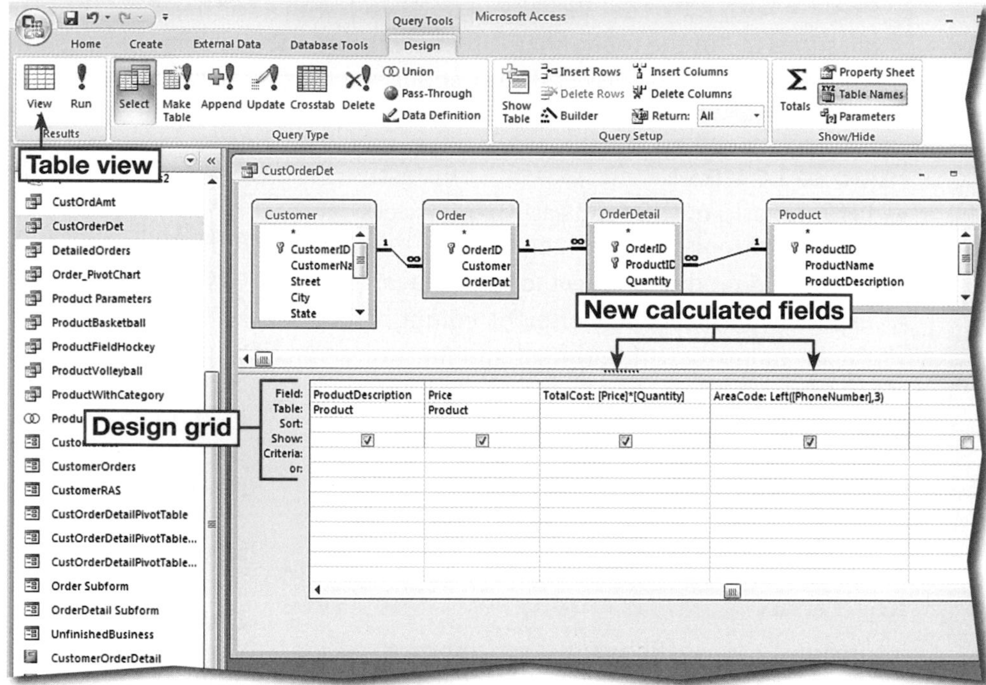

FIGURE 4.22 CustOrderDet query with calculated fields

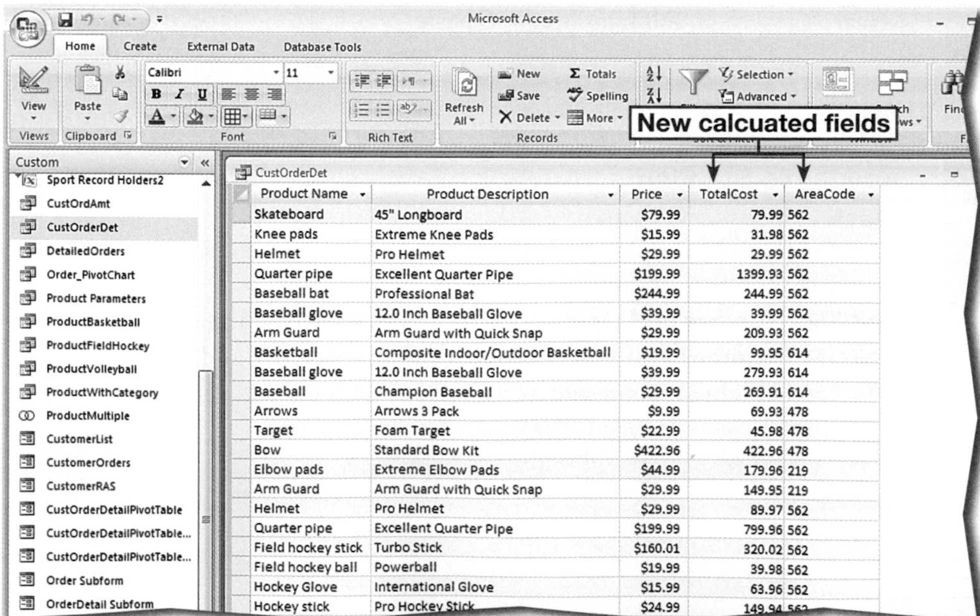

Product Name	Product Description	Price	TotalCost	AreaCode
Skateboard	45" Longboard	$79.99	79.99	562
Knee pads	Extreme Knee Pads	$15.99	31.98	562
Helmet	Pro Helmet	$29.99	29.99	562
Quarter pipe	Excellent Quarter Pipe	$199.99	1399.93	562
Baseball bat	Professional Bat	$244.99	244.99	562
Baseball glove	12.0 Inch Baseball Glove	$39.99	39.99	562
Arm Guard	Arm Guard with Quick Snap	$29.99	209.93	562
Basketball	Composite Indoor/Outdoor Basketball	$19.99	99.95	614
Baseball glove	12.0 Inch Baseball Glove	$39.99	279.93	614
Baseball	Champion Baseball	$29.99	269.91	614
Arrows	Arrows 3 Pack	$9.99	69.93	478
Target	Foam Target	$22.99	45.98	478
Bow	Standard Bow Kit	$422.96	422.96	478
Elbow pads	Extreme Elbow Pads	$44.99	179.96	219
Arm Guard	Arm Guard with Quick Snap	$29.99	149.95	219
Helmet	Pro Helmet	$29.99	89.97	562
Quarter pipe	Excellent Quarter Pipe	$199.99	799.96	562
Field hockey stick	Turbo Stick	$160.01	320.02	562
Field hockey ball	Powerball	$19.99	39.98	562
Hockey Glove	International Glove	$15.99	63.96	562
Hockey stick	Pro Hockey Stick	$24.99	149.94	562

Step-By-Step

1. Start **Excel**. Choose **Office>Open**. The **Open** dialog box opens.

2. Click the **Look in** box drop-down arrow and select the location of your data files. Ask your teacher for the correct location.

3. Click the file **Budget.xlsx**. Click **Open**.

4. Choose **Office>Save As**. In the **File name** box, key: Budget-[your first initial and last name] (for example, *Budget-jking*). Ask your teacher which location to select in the **Save in** box. Click **Save**.

5. Click cell **F2**. Key: 300. Press ENTER.

6. **CHECK** Your screen should look like Figure 2.1.

7. Key: 650 in cell **F3**. Press ENTER.

8. Key: 250 in cell **F4**. Press ENTER.

9. **CHECK** Your screen should look like Figure 2.2. Save your file.

Continue to the next exercise.

Different Strokes Let students know that after entering the contents of a cell, they can move to the cell to the right by pressing Tab.

EXERCISE 2-1
Enter Cell Contents

Each cell in a worksheet can contain words, numbers, or both. The **cell contents** will depend on the type of worksheet you are making. In this case, you are creating a budget for a business. A **budget** is an estimate of income and expenses over time. After you have entered what you want in a cell, press Enter to move to the cell below.

EL If students have trouble understanding instructions, pair them with native speakers to follow the steps.

FIGURE 2.1 Content entered into cell F2

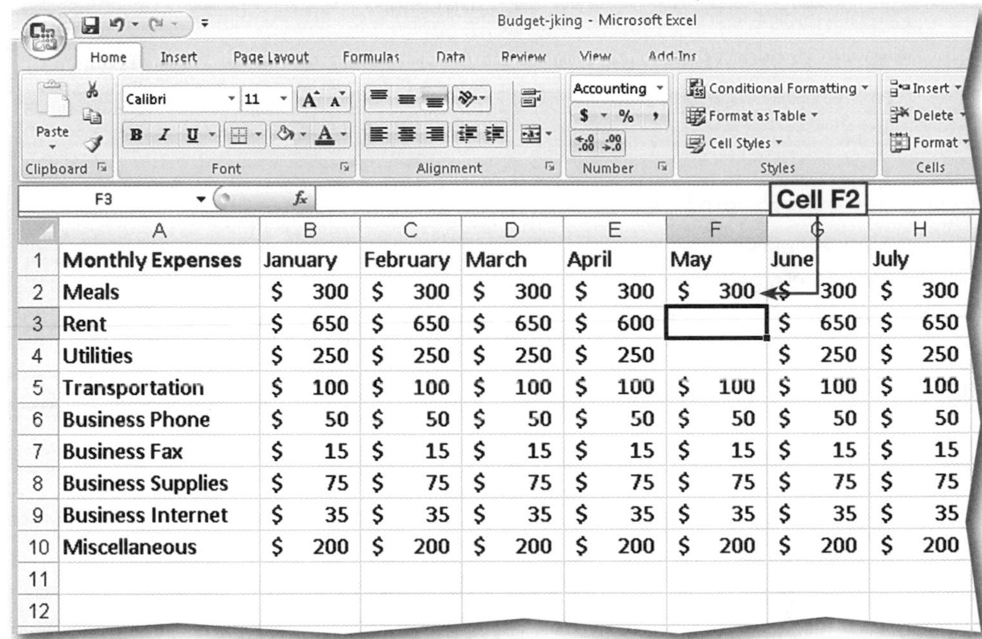

	A	B	C	D	E	F	G	H
1	Monthly Expenses	January	February	March	April	May	June	July
2	Meals	$ 300	$ 300	$ 300	$ 300	$ 300	$ 300	$ 300
3	Rent	$ 650	$ 650	$ 650	$ 600		$ 650	$ 650
4	Utilities	$ 250	$ 250	$ 250	$ 250		$ 250	$ 250
5	Transportation	$ 100	$ 100	$ 100	$ 100	$ 100	$ 100	$ 100
6	Business Phone	$ 50	$ 50	$ 50	$ 50	$ 50	$ 50	$ 50
7	Business Fax	$ 15	$ 15	$ 15	$ 15	$ 15	$ 15	$ 15
8	Business Supplies	$ 75	$ 75	$ 75	$ 75	$ 75	$ 75	$ 75
9	Business Internet	$ 35	$ 35	$ 35	$ 35	$ 35	$ 35	$ 35
10	Miscellaneous	$ 200	$ 200	$ 200	$ 200	$ 200	$ 200	$ 200
11								
12								

FIGURE 2.2 Cells F2, F3, and F4 with content

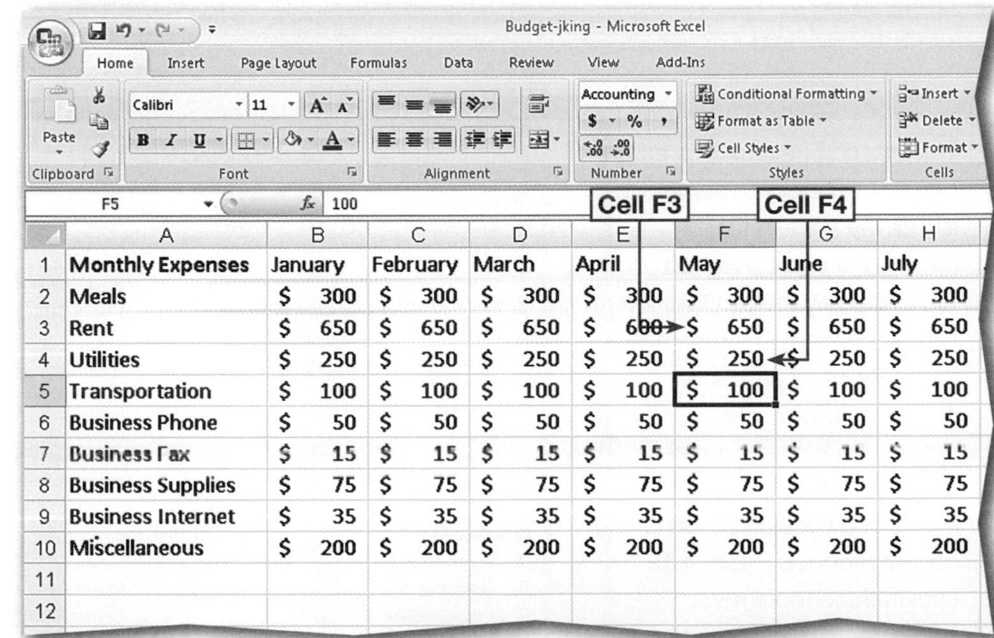

	A	B	C	D	E	F	G	H
1	Monthly Expenses	January	February	March	April	May	June	July
2	Meals	$ 300	$ 300	$ 300	$ 300	$ 300	$ 300	$ 300
3	Rent	$ 650	$ 650	$ 650	$ 600	$ 650	$ 650	$ 650
4	Utilities	$ 250	$ 250	$ 250	$ 250	$ 250	$ 250	$ 250
5	Transportation	$ 100	$ 100	$ 100	$ 100	$ 100	$ 100	$ 100
6	Business Phone	$ 50	$ 50	$ 50	$ 50	$ 50	$ 50	$ 50
7	Business Fax	$ 15	$ 15	$ 15	$ 15	$ 15	$ 15	$ 15
8	Business Supplies	$ 75	$ 75	$ 75	$ 75	$ 75	$ 75	$ 75
9	Business Internet	$ 35	$ 35	$ 35	$ 35	$ 35	$ 35	$ 35
10	Miscellaneous	$ 200	$ 200	$ 200	$ 200	$ 200	$ 200	$ 200
11								
12								

Step-By-Step

7. Click **OK**. Click **Datasheet View**.

8. **CHECK** Your screen should look like Figure 4.19.

9. Click **Design View**. Double-click the relationship line between the **Product** and **Category** tables.

10. In the **Join Properties** dialog box, click the third option to create a right-outer join.

11. Click **OK.** Click **Datasheet View**.

12. **CHECK** Your screen should look like Figure 4.20.

13. Close the query. Click **Yes** to save the changes.

Continue to the next exercise.

You Should Know

The reason Figure 4.17 and Figure 4.20 look the same is that the right-outer join returns the entire **Product** table and any rows in the **Category** table that match them. Since all products have a category, this returns the same information as the inner join. However, since not all categories have a product, Figure 4.19 shows three more rows.

EXERCISE 4-6 (Continued)

Create Joins

Teaching Tip Let students know that if they create a join by mistake, they can either click the join they want to remove and press the **Delete** key or right-click the join and select **Delete**.

FIGURE 4.19 ProductWithCategory left-outer join

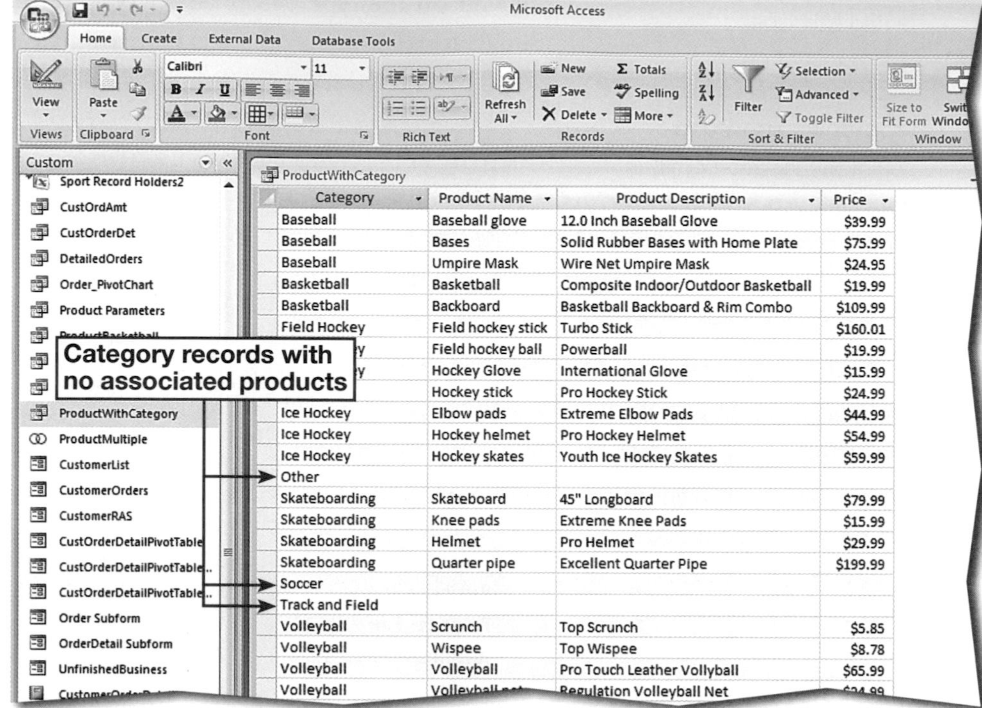

FIGURE 4.20 ProductWithCategory right-outer join

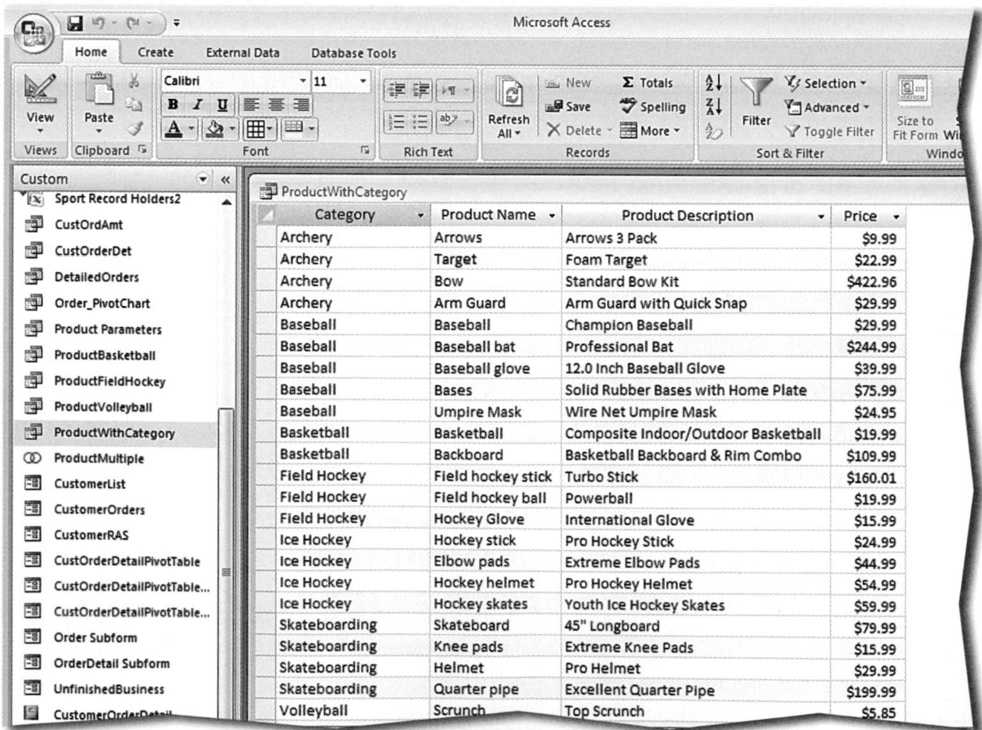

EXERCISE 2-2
Use AutoSum, AVERAGE, MIN, and MAX

Excel provides built-in formulas called **functions**. The **AutoSum** function is used to add values in rows or columns. The **AVERAGE** function is used to find the numeric average of a list of cells. Use the **MAX** function to **determine**, or identify, the largest number in a group of selected cells. Use the **MIN** function to identify the smallest number.

Teaching Tip Discuss with students how identifying the largest and smallest cost in a budget can help track how money is being spent.

Step-By-Step

1. In your **Budget** file, key the new row labels for cells **A12** through **A15** (see Figure 2.3).
2. Click cell **B12**. Choose **Formulas** and click **AutoSum** [Σ] (see Figure 2.4). Press [ENTER].
3. With cell **B13** selected, click the **AutoSum** drop-down arrow. From the drop-down list, choose **Average**.
4. Click cell **B2** and drag the pointer down to cell **B10**. Press [ENTER].
5. With cell **B14** selected, click the **AutoSum** drop-down arrow and click **Min**.
6. Click cell **B2** and drag the pointer down to cell **B10**. Press [ENTER].
7. With cell **B15** selected, click the **AutoSum** drop-down arrow and click **Max**.
8. Click cell **B2** and drag the pointer down to cell **B10**. Press [ENTER].
9. **CHECK** Your screen should look like Figure 2.4. Save your file.

Continue to the next exercise.

FIGURE 2.3 Row labels added to worksheet

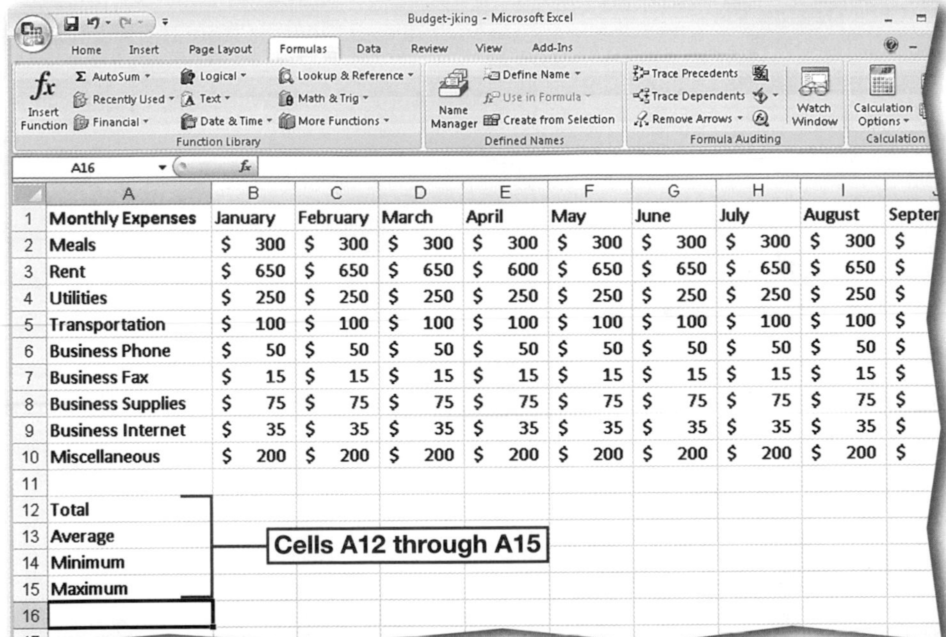

	A	B	C	D	E	F	G	H	I
1	Monthly Expenses	January	February	March	April	May	June	July	August
2	Meals	$ 300	$ 300	$ 300	$ 300	$ 300	$ 300	$ 300	$ 300
3	Rent	$ 650	$ 650	$ 650	$ 600	$ 650	$ 650	$ 650	$ 650
4	Utilities	$ 250	$ 250	$ 250	$ 250	$ 250	$ 250	$ 250	$ 250
5	Transportation	$ 100	$ 100	$ 100	$ 100	$ 100	$ 100	$ 100	$ 100
6	Business Phone	$ 50	$ 50	$ 50	$ 50	$ 50	$ 50	$ 50	$ 50
7	Business Fax	$ 15	$ 15	$ 15	$ 15	$ 15	$ 15	$ 15	$ 15
8	Business Supplies	$ 75	$ 75	$ 75	$ 75	$ 75	$ 75	$ 75	$ 75
9	Business Internet	$ 35	$ 35	$ 35	$ 35	$ 35	$ 35	$ 35	$ 35
10	Miscellaneous	$ 200	$ 200	$ 200	$ 200	$ 200	$ 200	$ 200	$ 200
11									
12	Total								
13	Average								
14	Minimum								
15	Maximum								
16									

FIGURE 2.4 Function results

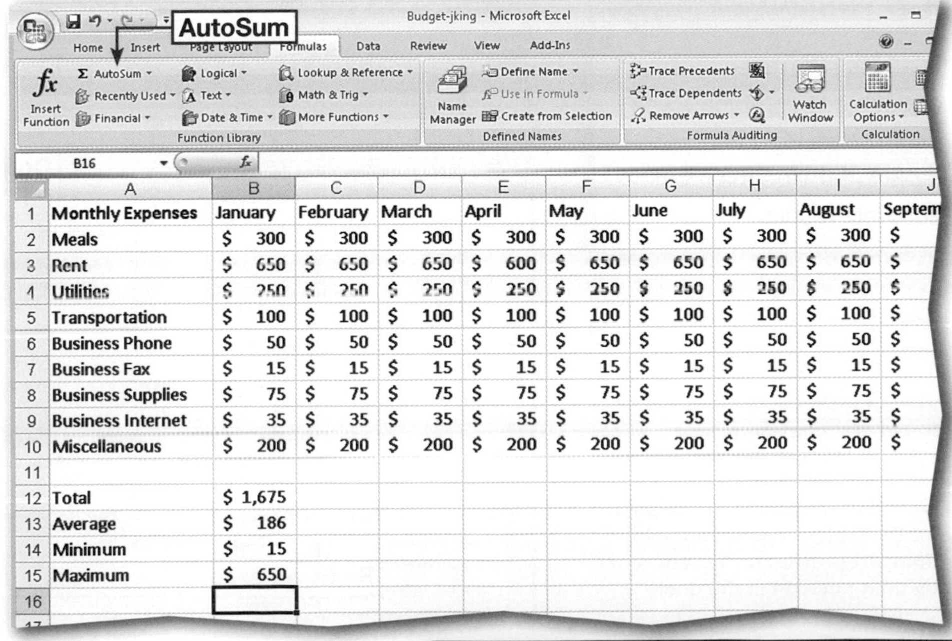

	A	B	C	D	E	F	G	H	I
1	Monthly Expenses	January	February	March	April	May	June	July	August
2	Meals	$ 300	$ 300	$ 300	$ 300	$ 300	$ 300	$ 300	$ 300
3	Rent	$ 650	$ 650	$ 650	$ 600	$ 650	$ 650	$ 650	$ 650
4	Utilities	$ 250	$ 250	$ 250	$ 250	$ 250	$ 250	$ 250	$ 250
5	Transportation	$ 100	$ 100	$ 100	$ 100	$ 100	$ 100	$ 100	$ 100
6	Business Phone	$ 50	$ 50	$ 50	$ 50	$ 50	$ 50	$ 50	$ 50
7	Business Fax	$ 15	$ 15	$ 15	$ 15	$ 15	$ 15	$ 15	$ 15
8	Business Supplies	$ 75	$ 75	$ 75	$ 75	$ 75	$ 75	$ 75	$ 75
9	Business Internet	$ 35	$ 35	$ 35	$ 35	$ 35	$ 35	$ 35	$ 35
10	Miscellaneous	$ 200	$ 200	$ 200	$ 200	$ 200	$ 200	$ 200	$ 200
11									
12	Total	$ 1,675							
13	Average	$ 186							
14	Minimum	$ 15							
15	Maximum	$ 650							
16									

Step-By-Step

1. In your **Sports4** file, open the **ProductWithCategory** query.
2. **CHECK** Your screen should look like Figure 4.17.
3. Click **Design View**.
4. Double-click the relationship line between the **Product** and **Category** tables.
5. **CHECK** Your screen should look like Figure 4.18.
6. In the **Join Properties** dialog box, click the second option, **Include ALL records from 'Category'...**, to create a left-outer join.

Continued on the next page.

You Should Know

In a *join*, information from one table is combined with information from another table to provide the most accurate results.

Troubleshooting The terms *left-outer join* and *right-outer join* come from the position of the tables when referenced in the query. Explain to students that the left and right position of the tables is determined in the **Join Properties** dialog box and not by their position in the query design window.

EXERCISE 4-6
Create Joins

When you add a table to a query, Access creates a join based on the relationships between the tables. Joins help you refine the way a query presents the table's information. The default join that Access creates is an **inner join**, which tells the query to return only those rows that share a common value. There also are outer joins, which return all the rows from one table and only the rows from the other table that match. A **left-outer join** includes all the rows from the first table, and a **right-outer join** includes all the rows from the second table.

FIGURE 4.17 ProductWithCategory query inner join

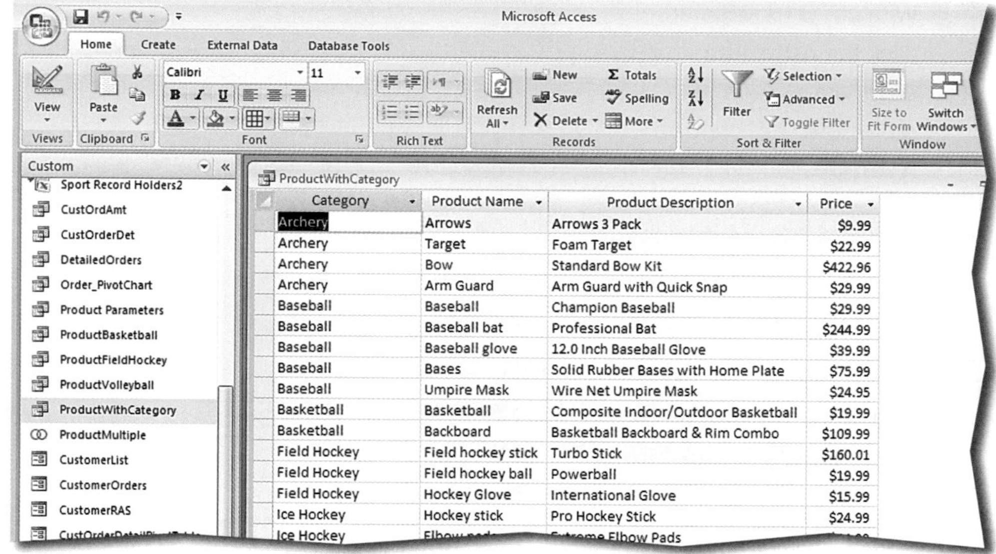

FIGURE 4.18 Join Properties dialog box

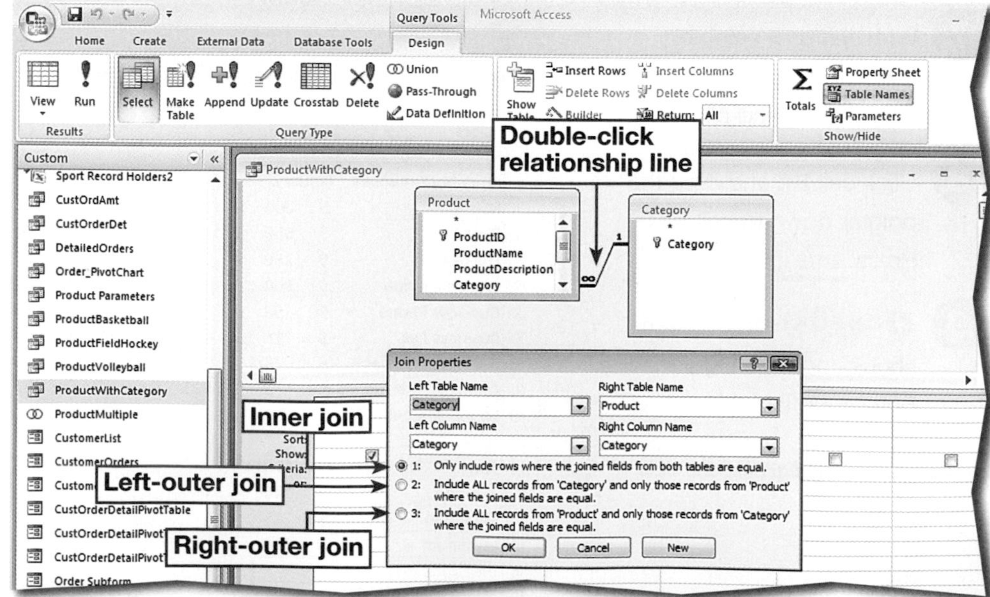

Step-By-Step

1. In your **Budget** file, double-click cell **E3**.
2. Click to the right of **600**.
3. Press BACKSPACE twice
4. CHECK Your screen should look like Figure 2.5.
5. Key: 50.
6. Press ENTER.
7. CHECK Your screen should look like Figure 2.6.
8. Save your file.

Continue to the next exercise.

EXERCISE 2-3
Edit Cell Contents

Step-By-Step Tip In **Step 2**, reinforce to students that in Excel formulas are calculations that you type in yourself. Functions are built-in formulas such as a sum or an average.

Sometimes you will find a cell that contains incorrect information. Other times, you may need to enter new or updated data in a cell that already contains information. In either case, you can change, or **edit**, the contents of a cell by double-clicking in that cell.

Intervention Strategy Students can double-click by accident. Show them that double-clicking causes an insertion point to appear so they can edit the cell.

FIGURE 2.5 Deleted zeroes

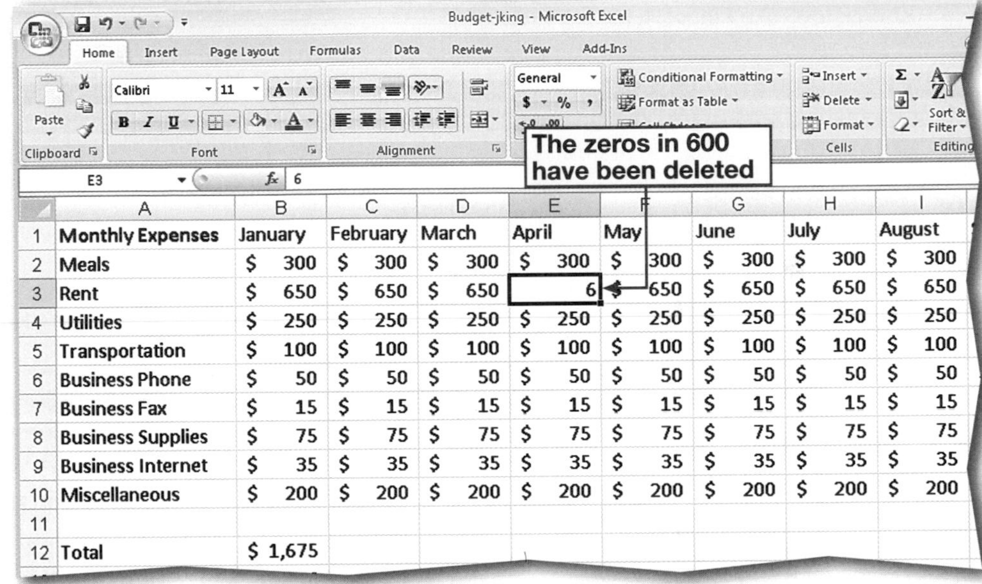

	A	B	C	D	E	F	G	H	I
1	Monthly Expenses	January	February	March	April	May	June	July	August
2	Meals	$ 300	$ 300	$ 300	$ 300	$ 300	$ 300	$ 300	$ 300
3	Rent	$ 650	$ 650	$ 650	6	$ 650	$ 650	$ 650	$ 650
4	Utilities	$ 250	$ 250	$ 250	$ 250	$ 250	$ 250	$ 250	$ 250
5	Transportation	$ 100	$ 100	$ 100	$ 100	$ 100	$ 100	$ 100	$ 100
6	Business Phone	$ 50	$ 50	$ 50	$ 50	$ 50	$ 50	$ 50	$ 50
7	Business Fax	$ 15	$ 15	$ 15	$ 15	$ 15	$ 15	$ 15	$ 15
8	Business Supplies	$ 75	$ 75	$ 75	$ 75	$ 75	$ 75	$ 75	$ 75
9	Business Internet	$ 35	$ 35	$ 35	$ 35	$ 35	$ 35	$ 35	$ 35
10	Miscellaneous	$ 200	$ 200	$ 200	$ 200	$ 200	$ 200	$ 200	$ 200
11									
12	Total	$ 1,675							

FIGURE 2.6 Edited cell

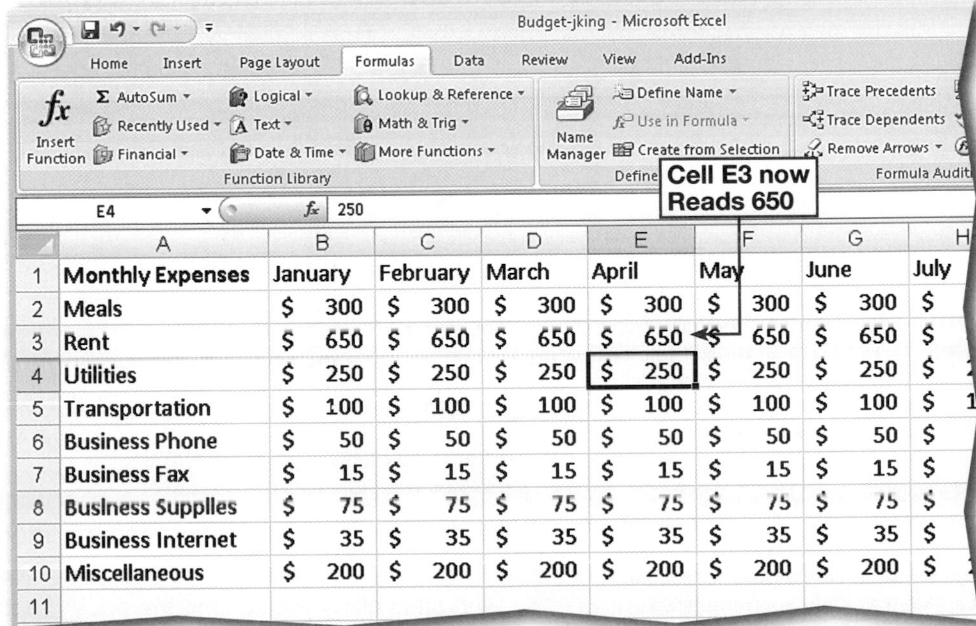

	A	B	C	D	E	F	G	H
1	Monthly Expenses	January	February	March	April	May	June	July
2	Meals	$ 300	$ 300	$ 300	$ 300	$ 300	$ 300	$
3	Rent	$ 650	$ 650	$ 650	$ 650	$ 650	$ 650	$
4	Utilities	$ 250	$ 250	$ 250	$ 250	$ 250	$ 250	$
5	Transportation	$ 100	$ 100	$ 100	$ 100	$ 100	$ 100	$
6	Business Phone	$ 50	$ 50	$ 50	$ 50	$ 50	$ 50	$
7	Business Fax	$ 15	$ 15	$ 15	$ 15	$ 15	$ 15	$
8	Business Supplies	$ 75	$ 75	$ 75	$ 75	$ 75	$ 75	$
9	Business Internet	$ 35	$ 35	$ 35	$ 35	$ 35	$ 35	$
10	Miscellaneous	$ 200	$ 200	$ 200	$ 200	$ 200	$ 200	$
11								

You Should Know

You can also edit the contents of a cell in the formula bar. Click in the cell you wish to edit. The cell contents will appear in the formula bar, where you can edit them.

Academic Skills

Using a budget can help ensure you are not spending more money than you have. Review the file used in this exercise and identify the costs being tracked. What other costs might a business need to track on a monthly basis?

NCLB/Math (Number and Operations) Ask students to identify three monthly expenses that they have. Let them consider if those expenses can be reduced. Have students calculate how much they might be able to save in a year.

Step-By-Step

10 Click **Run** [!].

11 In the **Enter Parameter Value** dialog box, key: Archery. Click **OK**.

12 CHECK Your screen should look like Figure 4.15.

13 Close the query. Click **Yes** to save the query.

14 Open the **Product Parameters** query.

15 In the **Enter Parameter Value** box, key: Basketball. Click **OK**.

16 CHECK Your screen should look like Figure 4.16.

17 Close the query.

Continue to the next exercise.

Shortcuts

To add **Criteria** to a query, the query must be in **Design View**.

Step-By-Step Tip In **Step 11**, explain to students that the query presents all the products in the **Archery** category that are priced less than $10.

NCLB/Math (Number and Operations) Ask students to name the types of criteria they might use when purchasing a product online. Explain that by limiting the price range of items shown, they will be less tempted to buy items they cannot afford.

EXERCISE 4-5 (Continued)
Add Criteria to Queries

FIGURE 4.15 Product Parameters query with Archery

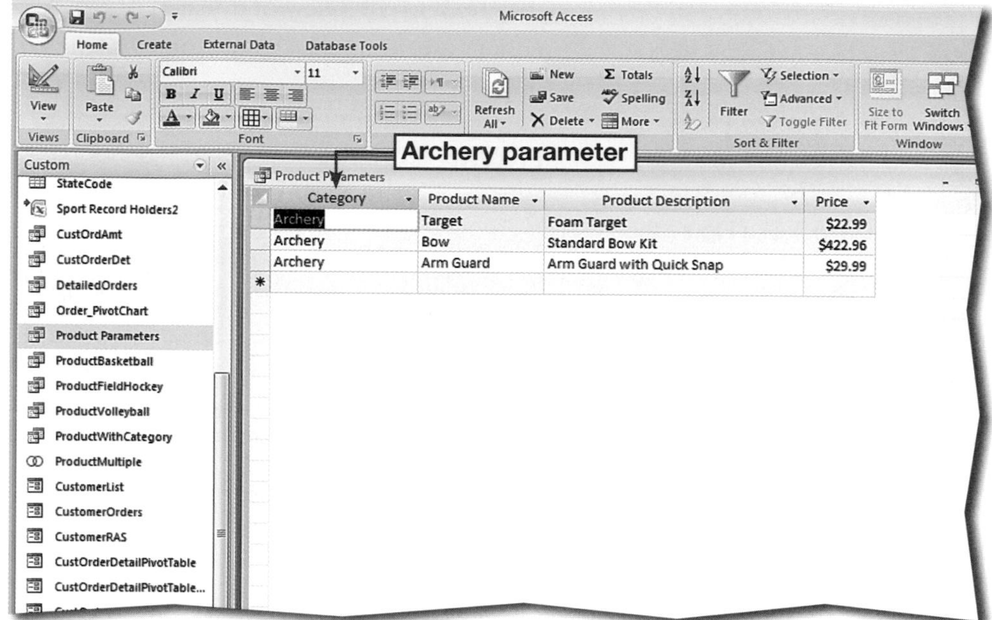

FIGURE 4.16 Product Parameters query with Basketball

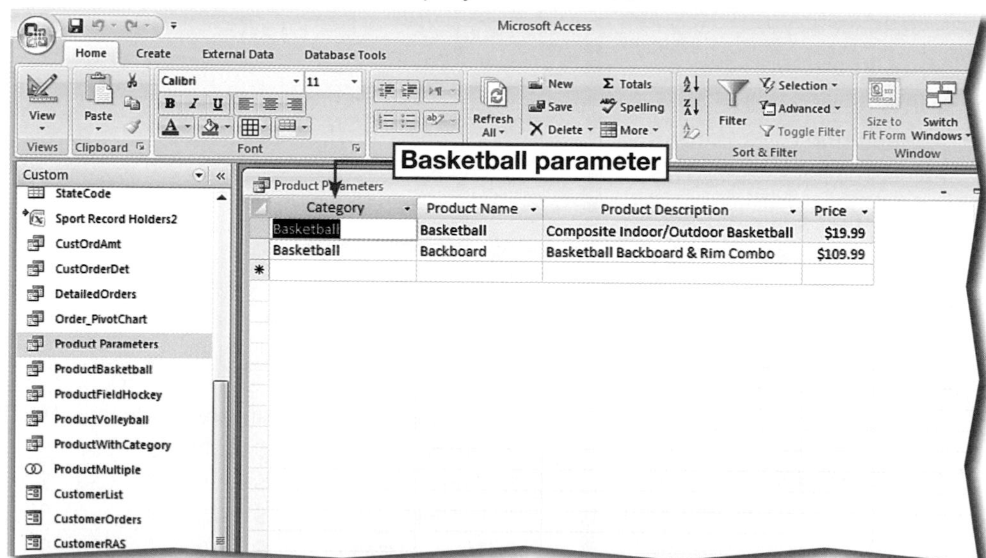

Academic Skills

When you search for products on the internet, you are actually running a query on the company's database of products. Often, Web sites allow you to limit the price range of a type of item so that you see only products that fit in your budget.

Step-By-Step

1. In your **Budget** file, click cell **C5**.
2. Press DELETE.
3. CHECK Your screen should look like Figure 2.7.
4. Click cell **D5**.
5. Press DELETE.
6. Click cell **E5**.
7. Press DELETE.
8. CHECK Your screen should look like Figure 2.8.
9. Save your file.

Continue to the next exercise.

Microsoft Office 2007

Pressing DELETE is the same as using the **Clear Contents** button.

Step-By-Step Tip In **Step 3**, show students that the cell does not go away when they press **Delete**; the contents are simply cleared.

EXERCISE 2-4
Clear Cell Contents

When you need to make changes to the contents of a cell, you can edit the cell contents. There will be other times when you will just want to **clear**, or empty, the contents of a cell.

FIGURE 2.7 Clearing cell content

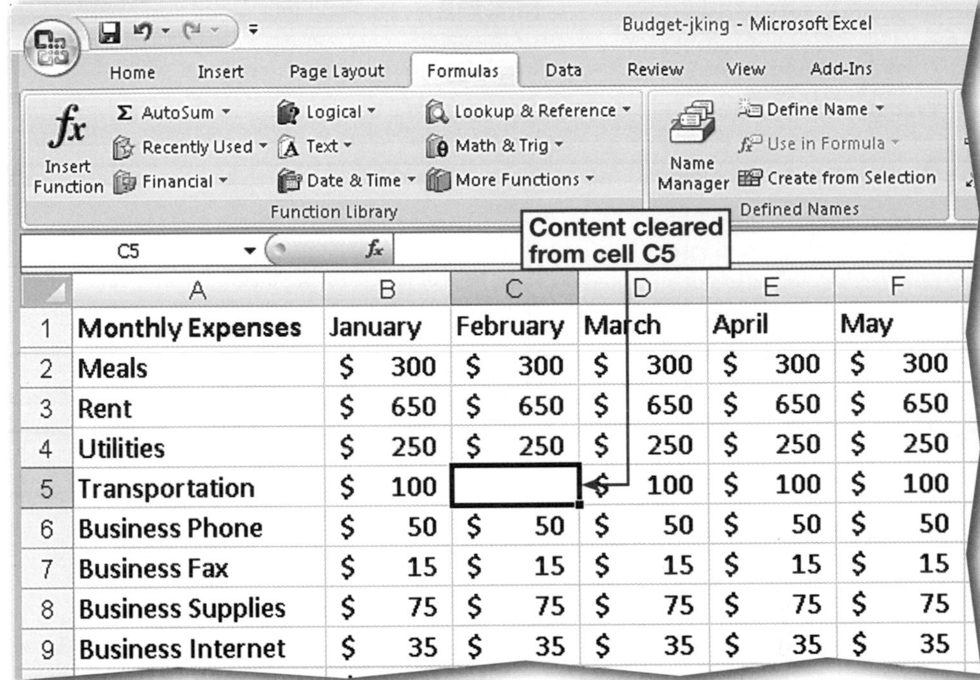

	A	B	C	D	E	F
1	Monthly Expenses	January	February	March	April	May
2	Meals	$ 300	$ 300	$ 300	$ 300	$ 300
3	Rent	$ 650	$ 650	$ 650	$ 650	$ 650
4	Utilities	$ 250	$ 250	$ 250	$ 250	$ 250
5	Transportation	$ 100		$ 100	$ 100	$ 100
6	Business Phone	$ 50	$ 50	$ 50	$ 50	$ 50
7	Business Fax	$ 15	$ 15	$ 15	$ 15	$ 15
8	Business Supplies	$ 75	$ 75	$ 75	$ 75	$ 75
9	Business Internet	$ 35	$ 35	$ 35	$ 35	$ 35

FIGURE 2.8 More cell content deleted

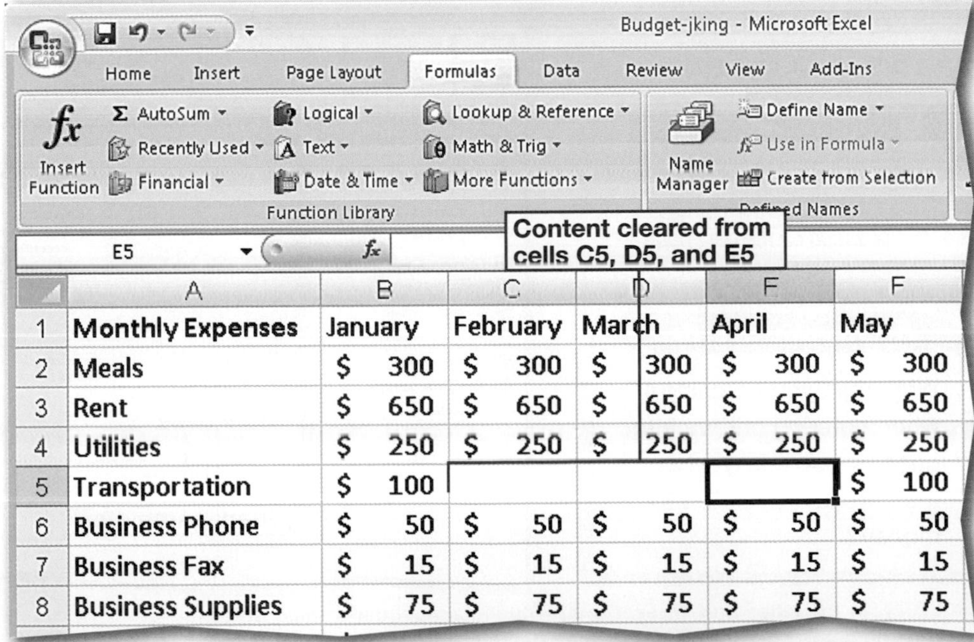

	A	B	C	D	E	F
1	Monthly Expenses	January	February	March	April	May
2	Meals	$ 300	$ 300	$ 300	$ 300	$ 300
3	Rent	$ 650	$ 650	$ 650	$ 650	$ 650
4	Utilities	$ 250	$ 250	$ 250	$ 250	$ 250
5	Transportation	$ 100				$ 100
6	Business Phone	$ 50	$ 50	$ 50	$ 50	$ 50
7	Business Fax	$ 15	$ 15	$ 15	$ 15	$ 15
8	Business Supplies	$ 75	$ 75	$ 75	$ 75	$ 75

EXERCISE 4-5
Add Criteria to Queries

To further refine, or narrow down, the information that Access queries present, you can update or edit queries. Add criteria, or conditions, to an existing query using the criteria fields to change the query, or set a **parameter**, or value, for the query, which will then prompt you for the proper criteria each time you run the query.

FIGURE 4.13 Product Parameters query

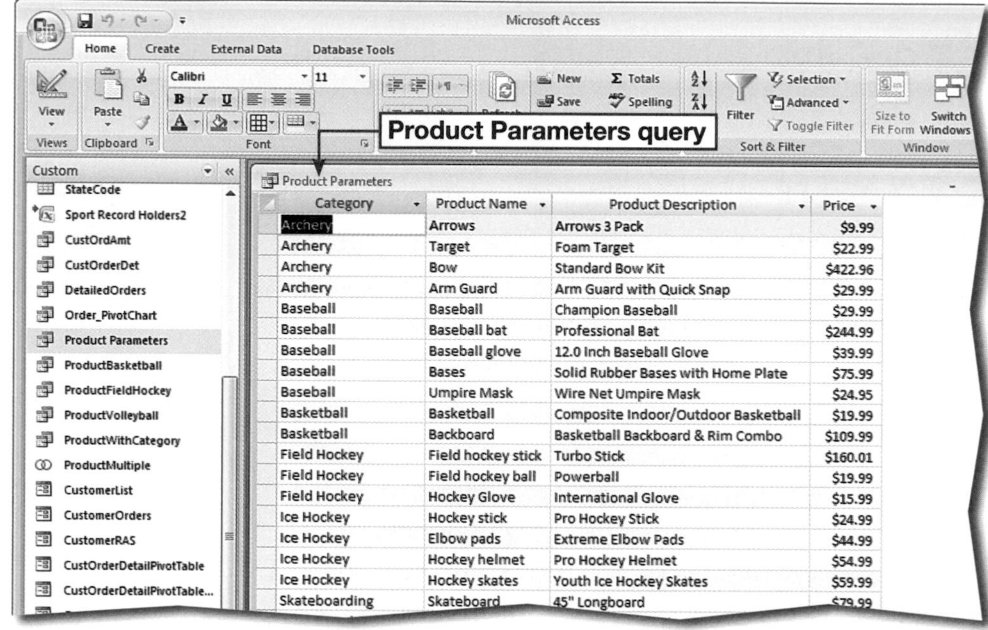

FIGURE 4.14 Product Parameters query Design View

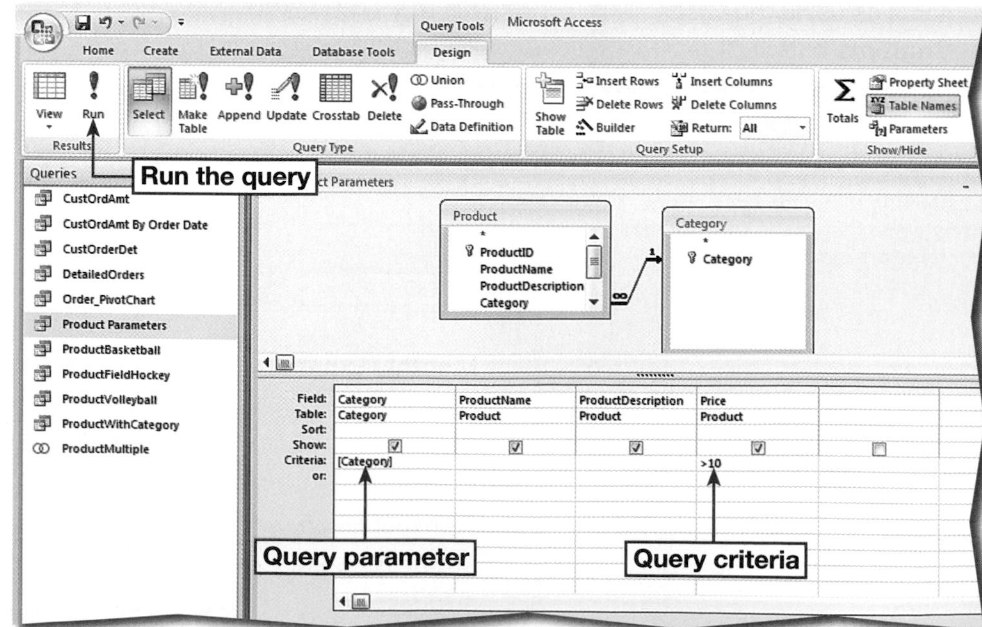

Step-By-Step

1. In your **Sports4** file, in the **Navigation Pane**, right-click the **ProductWithCategory** query and select **Copy**.
2. Right-click in a blank area of the **Navigation Pane** and select **Paste**.
3. In the **Paste As** dialog box, key: Product Parameters. Click **OK**.
4. Open the **Product Parameters** query.
5. **CHECK** Your screen should look like Figure 4.13.
6. Click **Design View**.
7. Under the **Price** field, click in the **Criteria** box and key: >10.
8. Under the **Category** field, click in the **Criteria** box and key: [Category:].
9. **CHECK** Your screen should look like Figure 4.14.

Continued on the next page.

Academic Skills

Why must you be careful when entering criteria into queries, especially when the criteria are related to money?

NCLB/Math (Number and Operations) Students must understand that the way the numbers are represented in their database are important. An error could lead to inaccurate daily sales counts, for example.

Step-By-Step

1. In your **Budget** file, choose **Home>Editing>Find & Select**. Click **Replace**.
2. In the **Find and Replace** dialog box, in the **Find what** box, key: Miscellaneous (see Figure 2.9). Press TAB.
3. In the **Replace with** box, key: Insurance.
4. Click **Replace All**.
5. Click **OK** in the message box.
6. In the **Find and Replace** dialog box, click **Close**.
7. CHECK Your screen should look like Figure 2.10.
8. Save your file.

Continue to the next exercise.

You Should Know

Use the **Options** button in the **Find and Replace** dialog box to select whether you want to search within a worksheet or within an entire workbook.

Step-By-Step Tip Before students replace the text in **Step 4**, point out where the word *Miscellaneous* appears in the worksheet.

EXERCISE 2-5
Find and Replace Cell Contents

You may sometimes want to find all the cells that contain particular contents and replace the contents with another phrase or number. Although you could do this cell by cell, there is an easier way. The Find and Replace dialog box will automatically find all the cells with particular content and replace it. For instance, you might want to find the word *business* and replace it everywhere with the word *company*.

FIGURE 2.9 Find and Replace dialog box

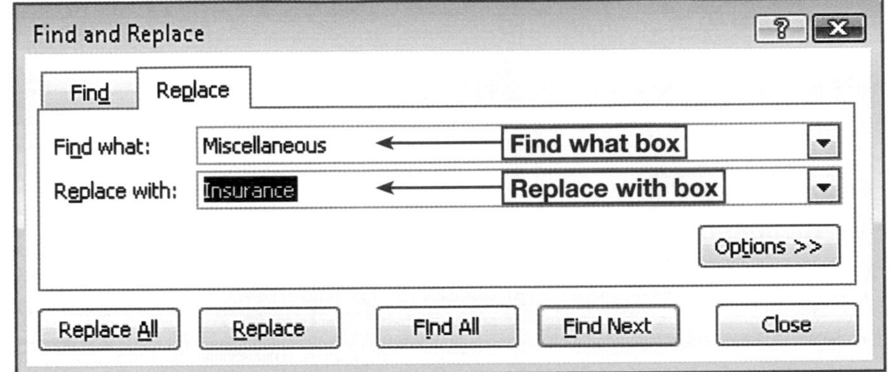

FIGURE 2.10 The replaced text

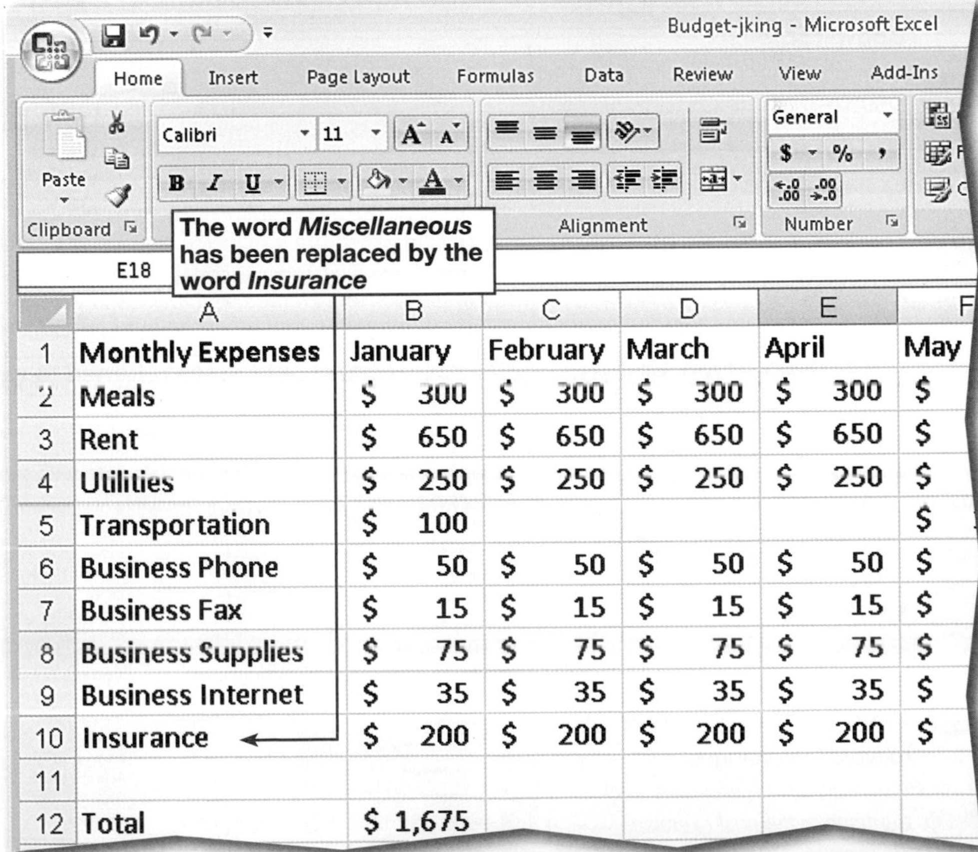

	A	B	C	D	E	F
1	Monthly Expenses	January	February	March	April	May
2	Meals	$ 300	$ 300	$ 300	$ 300	$
3	Rent	$ 650	$ 650	$ 650	$ 650	$
4	Utilities	$ 250	$ 250	$ 250	$ 250	$
5	Transportation	$ 100				$
6	Business Phone	$ 50	$ 50	$ 50	$ 50	$
7	Business Fax	$ 15	$ 15	$ 15	$ 15	$
8	Business Supplies	$ 75	$ 75	$ 75	$ 75	$
9	Business Internet	$ 35	$ 35	$ 35	$ 35	$
10	Insurance	$ 200	$ 200	$ 200	$ 200	$
11						
12	Total	$ 1,675				

Step-By-Step

1. In your **Sports4** file, open the **ProductWithCategory** query in **Design View**.

2. In the query design window, right-click the **Category** table and select **Remove Table**. Click **Datasheet View**.

3. CHECK Your screen should look like Figure 4.11.

4. Click **Design View**. Choose **Design>Query Setup>Show Table**.

5. In the **Show Table** box, select the **Category** table and add it to the query design window. Close the **Show Table** box.

6. Double-click the **Category** field in the **Category** table to add it to the field list.

7. In the field list, move the pointer above the **Category** field until it becomes a small arrow pointing down. Click to select the **Category** field, and drag it to the left of the **ProductName** field.

8. Click **Datasheet View**.

9. CHECK Your screen should look like Figure 4.12.

10. Close the query. Click **Yes** to save the changes.

Continue to the next exercise.

EXERCISE 4-4
Add and Remove Tables from Queries

You can update or edit queries in Access by adding or removing tables from the existing queries. You might want to add new tables that you have imported or remove tables from the query so that it only shows information that is up-to-date or that has been changed.

FIGURE 4.11 Product without Category query

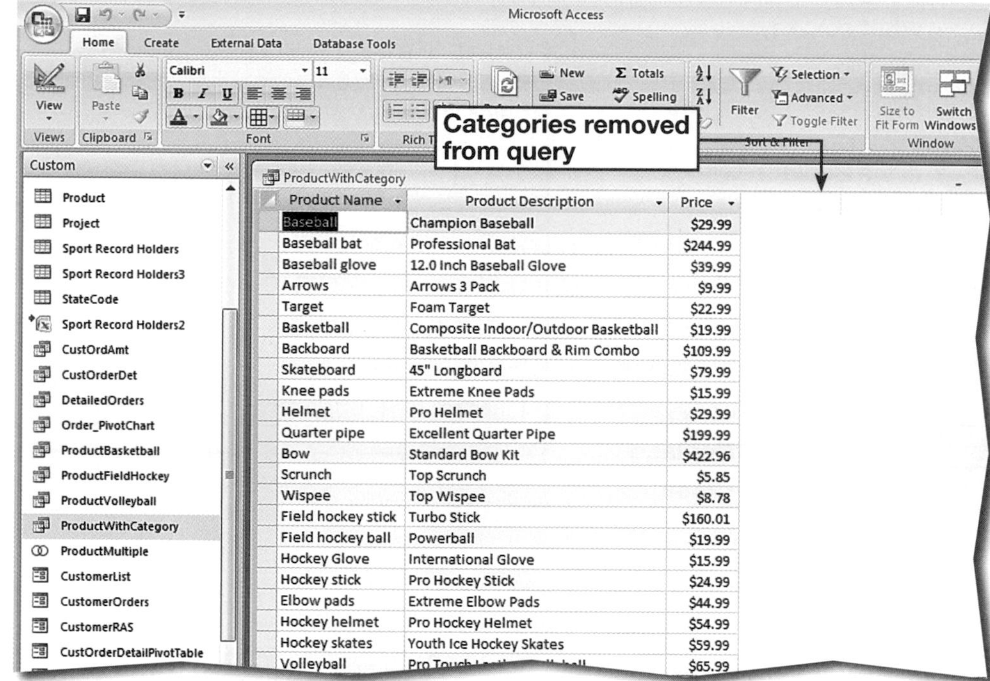

FIGURE 4.12 Product with Category query

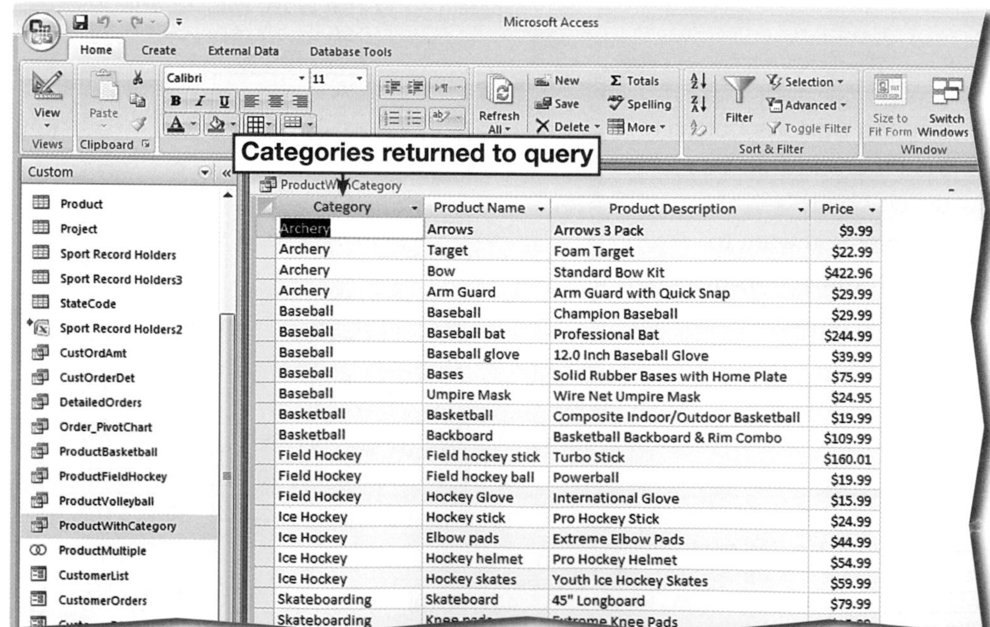

EXERCISE 2-6
Move Selected Cells

Sometimes a cell or cells are originally keyed in the wrong place. Instead of deleting the contents of the cells and rekeying them in the correct place, you can simply move the cell or cells to the correct place.

1. In your **Budget** file, click cell **A10**.
2. Place the pointer over the edge of cell **A10** so that the four-headed arrow pointer [four-headed arrow icon] appears (see Figure 2.11).
3. Click on the edge of cell **A10** and hold the mouse button down.
4. Drag the pointer over cell **A11** and release the mouse button.
5. **CHECK** Your screen should look like Figure 2.12. The content of cell A10 has been moved to A11.
6. Save your file.

Continue to the next exercise.

FIGURE 2.11 Pointer turned into the four-headed arrow pointer

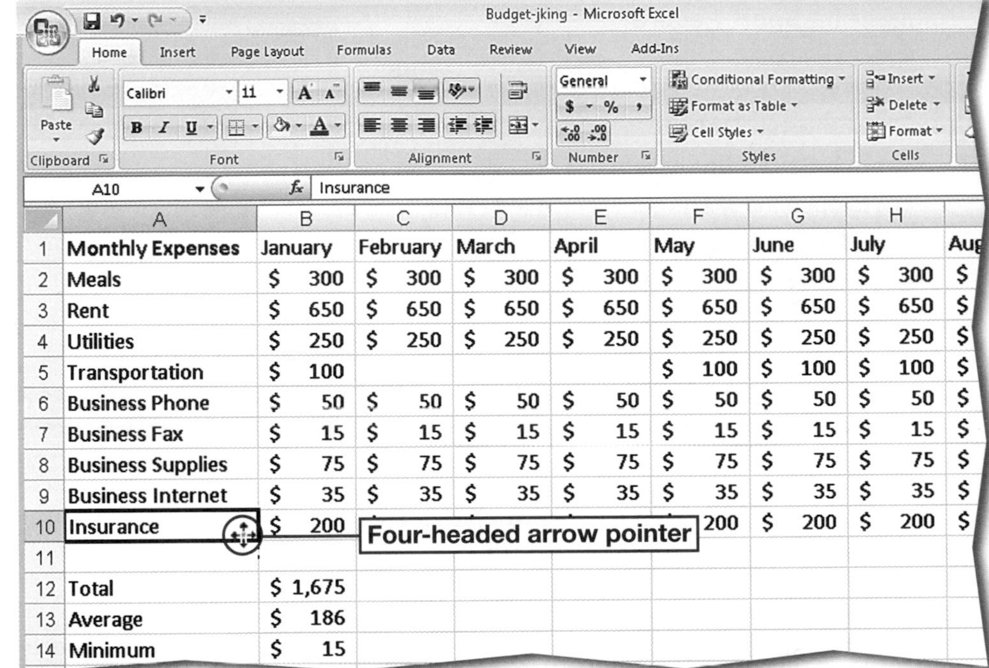

FIGURE 2.12 New cell placement

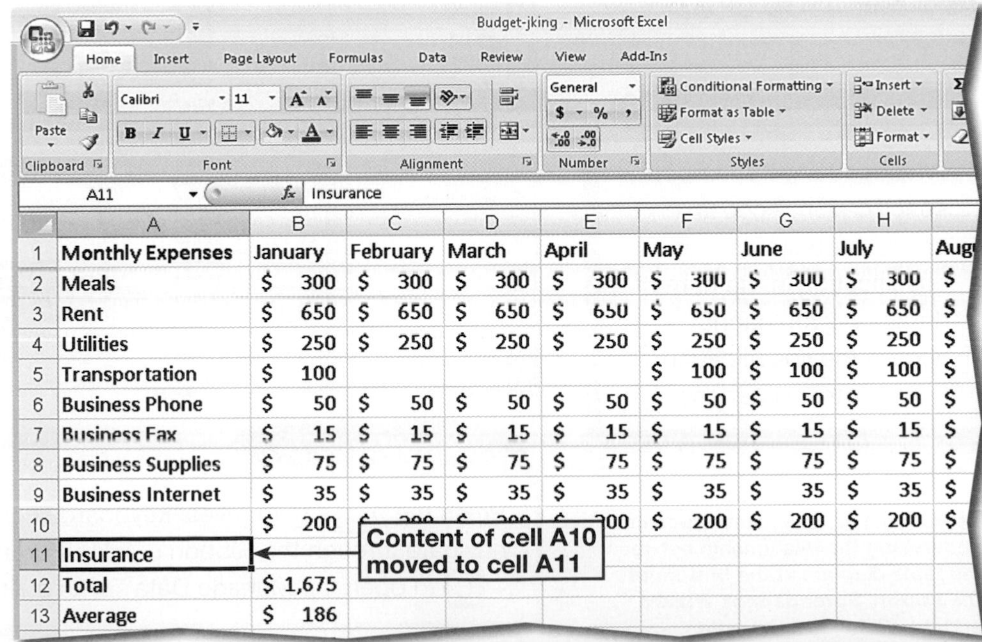

Shortcuts

You can move more than one cell at a time. Select all of the cells you want to move. Then grab the edge of the selection and drag the cells to their new location.

Differentiated Instruction/ Physically Impaired If students are having difficulty locating the four-headed arrow pointer, suggest that they rest the whole weight of their hand on the mouse to allow them to steady it.

Step-By-Step

EXERCISE 4-3 (Continued)
Save and Run Import Specifications

9 Open the **Sport Record Holders3** table. Note the field names at the top of the table. Close the table.

10 In the **Navigation Pane**, delete the **Sport Record Holders3** table.

11 Click **External Data> Import>Saved Imports** to open the **Manage Data Tasks** dialog box (see Figure 4.9).

12 Click **Run** to run the import specification **Import-GRecord**. Click **OK**. Click **Close**. Open the **Sport Record Holders3** table.

13 **CHECK** Your screen should look like Figure 4.10. Close the table. Save your work.

Continue to the next exercise.

You Should Know

When you save an import specification, Access creates and stores that specification in the current database. You cannot access the specification from another database.

Teaching Tip Make sure students understand the relationship between the table diagram at the bottom of the **Import Spreadsheet Wizard** and the **Field Options** area.

Step-By-Step Tip In **Step 12**, make sure students key the **3** without using a space after **Holders**.

FIGURE 4.9 Manage Data Tasks dialog box

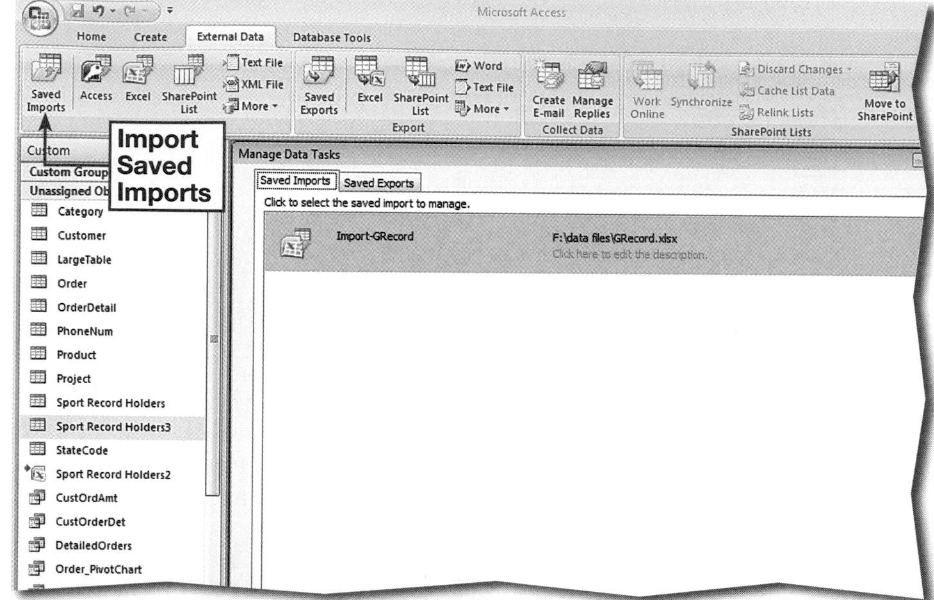

FIGURE 4.10 Sport Record Holders3 table

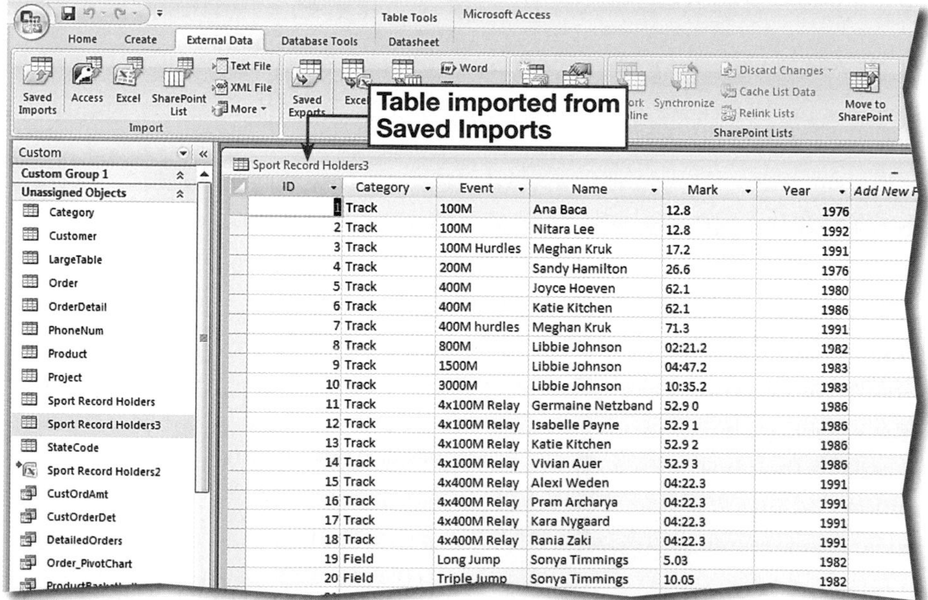

ID	Category	Event	Name	Mark	Year
1	Track	100M	Ana Baca	12.8	1976
2	Track	100M	Nitara Lee	12.8	1992
3	Track	100M Hurdles	Meghan Kruk	17.2	1991
4	Track	200M	Sandy Hamilton	26.6	1976
5	Track	400M	Joyce Hoeven	62.1	1980
6	Track	400M	Katie Kitchen	62.1	1986
7	Track	400M hurdles	Meghan Kruk	71.3	1991
8	Track	800M	Libbie Johnson	02:21.2	1982
9	Track	1500M	Libbie Johnson	04:47.2	1983
10	Track	3000M	Libbie Johnson	10:35.2	1983
11	Track	4x100M Relay	Germaine Netzband	52.9 0	1986
12	Track	4x100M Relay	Isabelle Payne	52.9 1	1986
13	Track	4x100M Relay	Katie Kitchen	52.9 2	1986
14	Track	4x100M Relay	Vivian Auer	52.9 3	1986
15	Track	4x400M Relay	Alexi Weden	04:22.3	1991
16	Track	4x400M Relay	Pram Archarya	04:22.3	1991
17	Track	4x400M Relay	Kara Nygaard	04:22.3	1991
18	Track	4x400M Relay	Rania Zaki	04:22.3	1991
19	Field	Long Jump	Sonya Timmings	5.03	1982
20	Field	Triple Jump	Sonya Timmings	10.05	1982

Shortcuts

Press the ALT key to reveal keyboard shortcuts that can help you navigate through the Ribbon quickly. For example, click ALT + X + C to open the Manage Data Tasks dialog box.

Step-By-Step

1. In your **Budget** file, click cell **B10**. Click and hold the mouse button down. Drag the pointer to cell **G10**. The range **B10:G10** is now selected.
2. Choose **Home> Clipboard>Cut** .
3. Click cell **B11**.
4. Choose **Home>Clipboard.** Click **Paste** .
5. **CHECK** Your screen should look like Figure 2.13.
6. Select cells **H10** through **M10**.
7. Choose **Home> Clipboard>Copy** .
8. Click cell **H11**.
9. Click **Paste** . Press ESC to make the moving line disappear.
10. **CHECK** Your screen should look like Figure 2.14.
11. Save your file.

Continue to the next exercise.

Teaching Tip Review with students why they would find it useful to be able to copy and paste cells in a budget. Tell them that if they are dealing with costs that remain constant, like rent, they can copy cells from month to month instead of keying those costs in one at a time.

EL Make sure English Learners understand all key terms.

EXERCISE 2-7
Cut, Copy, and Paste Cells

One way to move and copy cells is to use the **Cut**, **Copy**, and **Paste** commands. When you use the Cut command, the cells are removed from their original location and placed on the **Clipboard**. When you use the Copy command, the selected cells are copied, and the copy is placed on the Clipboard. The Paste command then allows you to move cut or copied cells from the Clipboard into your worksheet. Cutting, copying, and pasting cells can help you ensure that your budget is accurate while also saving time.

FIGURE 2.13 Using Cut and Paste

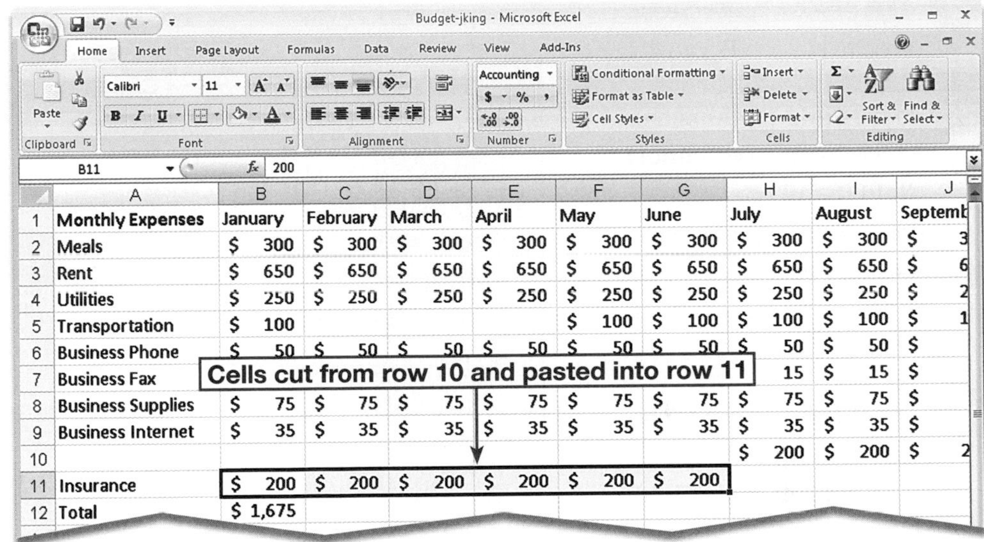

	A	B	C	D	E	F	G	H	I	J
1	Monthly Expenses	January	February	March	April	May	June	July	August	Septemb
2	Meals	$ 300	$ 300	$ 300	$ 300	$ 300	$ 300	$ 300	$ 300	$ 3
3	Rent	$ 650	$ 650	$ 650	$ 650	$ 650	$ 650	$ 650	$ 650	$ 6
4	Utilities	$ 250	$ 250	$ 250	$ 250	$ 250	$ 250	$ 250	$ 250	$ 2
5	Transportation	$ 100				$ 100	$ 100	$ 100	$ 100	$ 1
6	Business Phone	$ 50	$ 50	$ 50	$ 50	$ 50	$ 50	$ 50	$ 50	$
7	Business Fax							$ 15	$ 15	$
8	Business Supplies	$ 75	$ 75	$ 75	$ 75	$ 75	$ 75	$ 75	$ 75	$
9	Business Internet	$ 35	$ 35	$ 35	$ 35	$ 35	$ 35	$ 35	$ 35	$
10								$ 200	$ 200	$ 2
11	Insurance	$ 200	$ 200	$ 200	$ 200	$ 200	$ 200			
12	Total	$ 1,675								

FIGURE 2.14 Using Copy and Paste

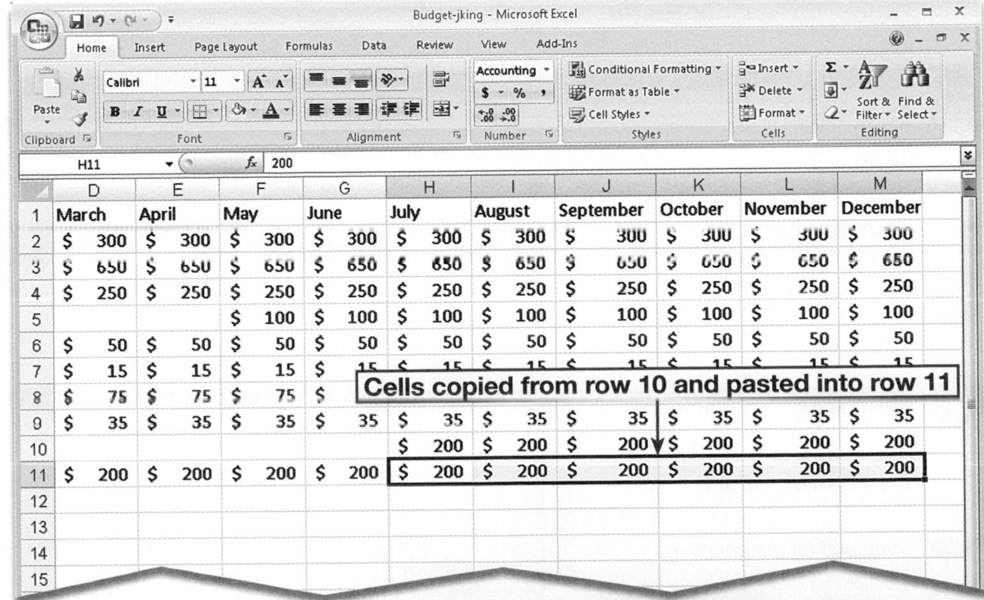

	D	E	F	G	H	I	J	K	L	M
1	March	April	May	June	July	August	September	October	November	December
2	$ 300	$ 300	$ 300	$ 300	$ 300	$ 300	$ 300	$ 300	$ 300	$ 300
3	$ 650	$ 650	$ 650	$ 650	$ 650	$ 650	$ 650	$ 650	$ 650	$ 650
4	$ 250	$ 250	$ 250	$ 250	$ 250	$ 250	$ 250	$ 250	$ 250	$ 250
5			$ 100	$ 100	$ 100	$ 100	$ 100	$ 100	$ 100	$ 100
6	$ 50	$ 50	$ 50	$ 50	$ 50	$ 50	$ 50	$ 50	$ 50	$ 50
7	$ 15	$ 15	$ 15	$ 15	$ 15	$ 15	$ 15	$ 15	$ 15	$ 15
8	$ 75	$ 75	$ 75	$						
9	$ 35	$ 35	$ 35	$ 35	$ 35	$ 35	$ 35	$ 35	$ 35	$ 35
10					$ 200	$ 200	$ 200	$ 200	$ 200	$ 200
11	$ 200	$ 200	$ 200	$ 200	$ 200	$ 200	$ 200	$ 200	$ 200	$ 200
12										
13										
14										
15										

EXERCISE 4-3
Save and Run Import Specifications

Access can save the steps you use to import data from external sources so that you do not have to perform the same operations over and over again. When you want to import more data, simply run the **import specifications** that you saved the last time you imported data. The new data will be entered with the same specifications.

FIGURE 4.7 Import Spreadsheet Wizard

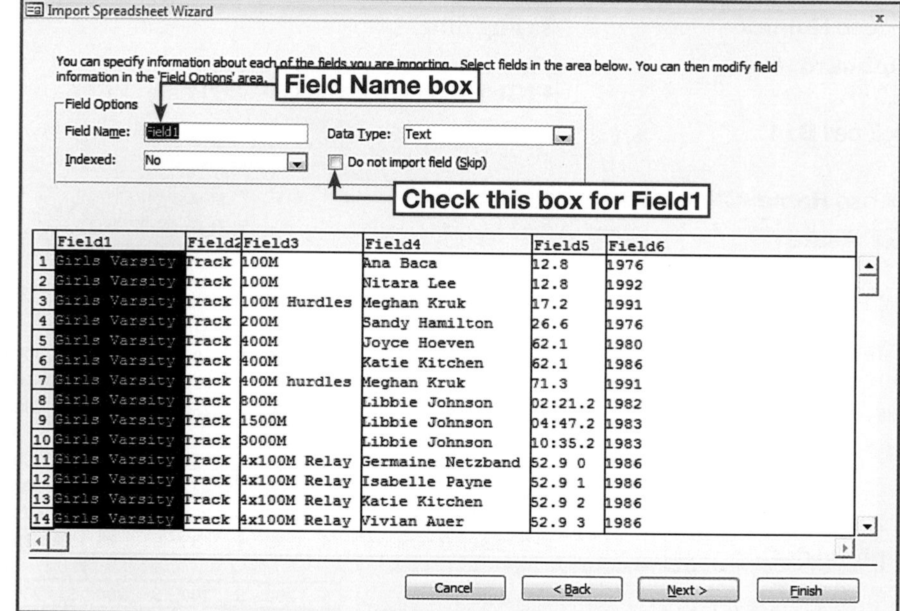

FIGURE 4.8 Save Import Steps page

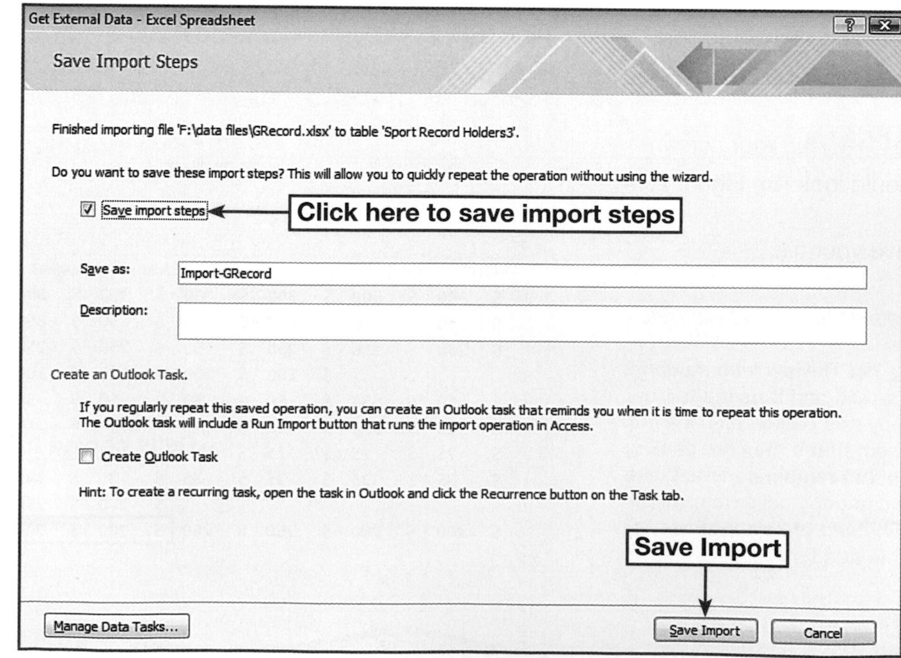

Step-By-Step

1. In your **Sports4** file, choose **External Data> Import>Excel** . Select **Import the source data**. Click **Browse**.
2. Locate the **GRecord** data file and click **Open**. Click **OK**. Click **Next**.
3. **CHECK** Your screen should look like Figure 4.7.
4. In the **Field Options** area, check the **Do not import field (Skip)** box. In the table diagram, click the **Field2** header. In the **Field Options** area of the **Field Name** box, key: Category.
5. Click **Field3**. In the **Field Name** box, key: Event. Click **Field4**. In the **Field Name** box, key: Name. Click **Field5**. In the **Field Name** box, key: Mark. Click **Field6**. In the **Field Name** box, key: Year.
6. Click **Next** twice. In the **Import to table** box, at the end of the text, key: 3. Click **Finish**.
7. Check the **Save import steps** box.
8. **CHECK** Your screen should look like Figure 4.8. Click **Save Import**.

Continued on the next page.

Step-By-Step

1. In your **Budget** file, scroll left until you can see column A.
2. Click row heading **10** to select row 10.
3. CHECK Your screen should look like Figure 2.15.
4. Right-click and select **Delete**. Row 10 is deleted, and row 11 becomes row 10.
5. Click column-heading **C** to select column C (see Figure 2.15).
6. Choose **Home>Cells> Delete>Delete Cells** Column C is deleted.
7. CHECK Your screen should look like Figure 2.16. Notice that column D has become column C.
8. Save your file.

Continue to the next exercise.

You Should Know

You can delete all of the contents in a row or column. Select the row or column and press DELETE.

New Student Strategy Ask a student who is comfortable with the material to partner with a new student to help them get started.

EXERCISE 2-8
Delete Rows and Columns

As you update files, you may often find it necessary to delete an entire row or column. When you delete a row or column, both the contents of the cells and the cells themselves are removed from the worksheet.

FIGURE 2.15 Selecting a row or a column

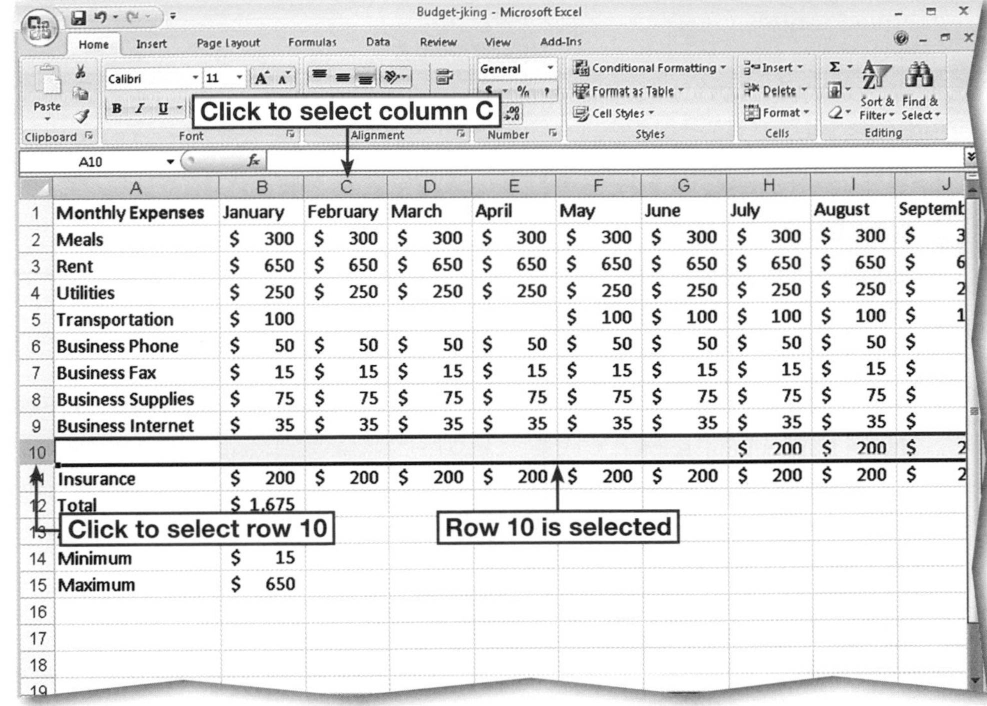

FIGURE 2.16 Deleting rows and columns

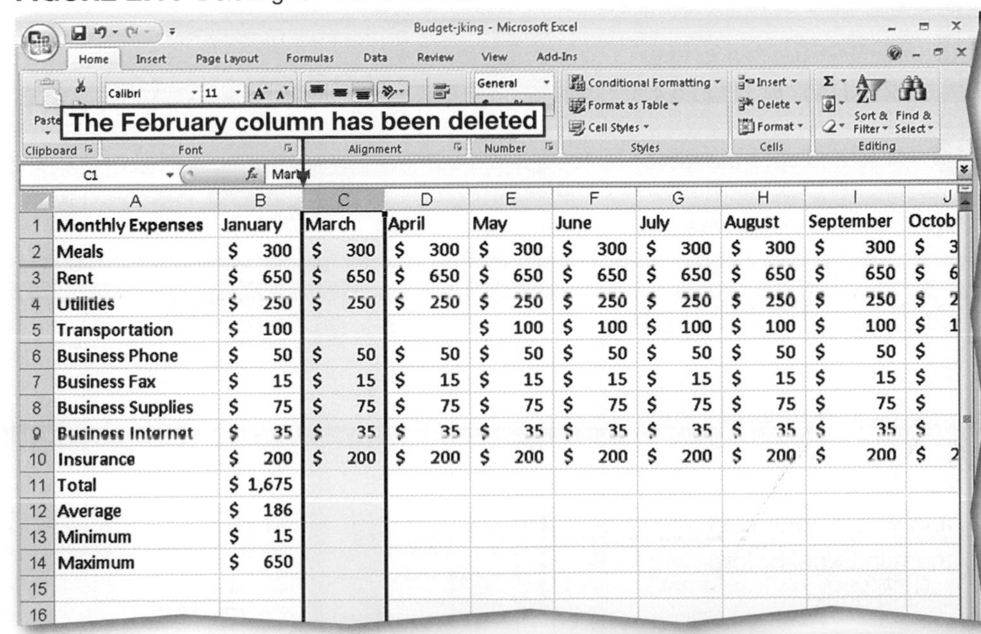

Step-By-Step

1. In your **Sports4** file, choose **External Data> Import>Excel**.
2. Select **Link to the data source by creating a linked table**.
3. Click **Browse**. Locate the **GRecord** data file and select it. Click **Open**.
4. **CHECK** Your screen should look like Figure 4.5.
5. Click **OK**. Click **Next**.
6. In the **Linked Table Name** box, put the pointer at the end of the default table name and key: 2. Click **Finish**. Click **OK**.
7. In the **Navigation Pane**, double-click the **Sport Record Holders2** table. AutoFit column **F5**.
8. **CHECK** Your screen should look like Figure 4.6.
9. Close and save the table.

Continue to the next exercise.

Troubleshooter

After you link the table, open it in **Datasheet View** to check that the information is correct. If you find errors, you must edit them in Excel before linking again.

EXERCISE 4-2
Link to External Data Sources

Sometimes you might not want to import data. Perhaps another department in the company does not use Access and wants to keep the information in Excel spreadsheets. Instead of importing the data, you can create a **link** to it from within Access. A linked table in Access will show the data, but you must work in Excel to edit or add information.

Step-By-Step Tip In **Step 6**, make sure students key the **2** without adding a space after the default table name.

FIGURE 4.5 Link to External Data wizard

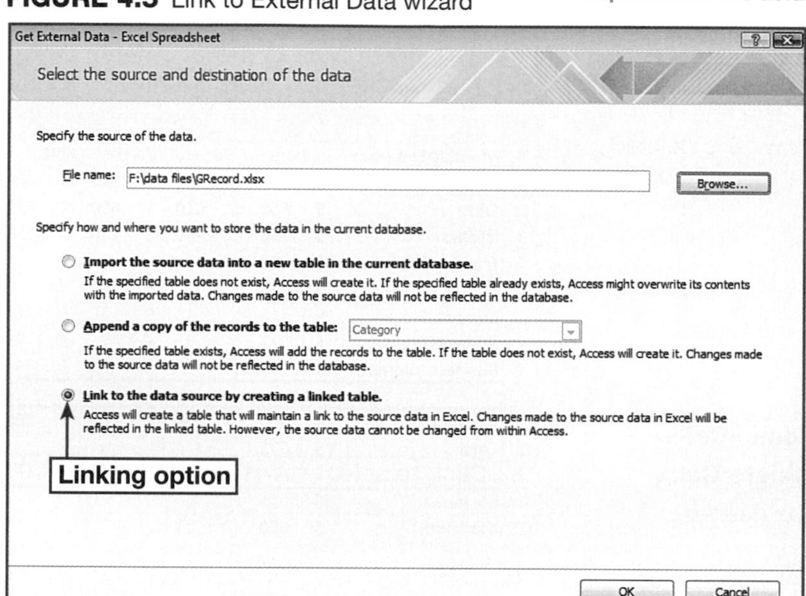

FIGURE 4.6 Sport Record Holders2 table

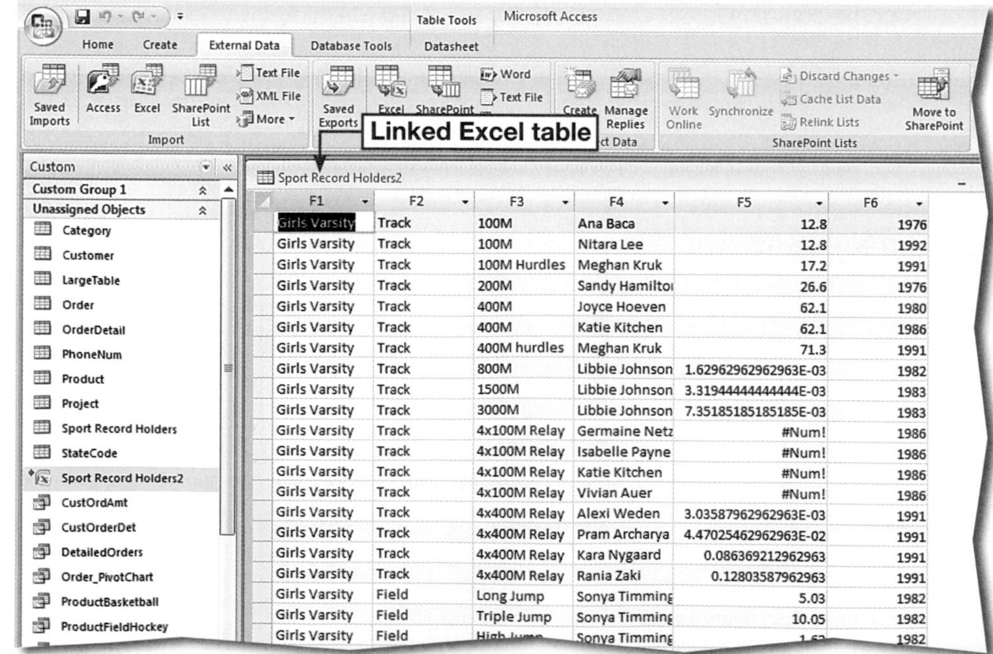

Step-By-Step

1. In your **Budget** file, click column heading **C** to select column C, if necessary.
2. Choose **Home>Cells> Insert** and click the **Insert Cells** drop-down arrow. Click **Insert Sheet Columns**.
3. Select cells **B1 through B10**. Drag the selected cells one column to the right. The word *February* appears in cell C1. The rest of the contents are copied.
4. **CHECK** Your screen should look like Figure 2.17.
5. Click row heading **11** to select row 11. Click the **Insert Cells** drop-down arrow and select **Insert Sheet Rows**.
6. Select row heading **10** and click **Insert**. A new row is added.
7. **CHECK** Your screen should look like Figure 2.18. Save your file.

Continue to the next exercise.

Troubleshooting Tell students that to insert multiple rows or columns, select the number of rows or columns to be inserted at the location and choose **Insert Cells**.

Teaching Tip Review with students why they would need to add or remove rows in a budget. Tell them they may need to add a row for another expense or delete a row if they cut back on expenses.

EXERCISE 2-9
Insert Rows and Columns

You can also **insert**, or add, new rows and columns between existing rows and columns. The new row or column will be empty when you add it.

FIGURE 2.17 Inserting columns

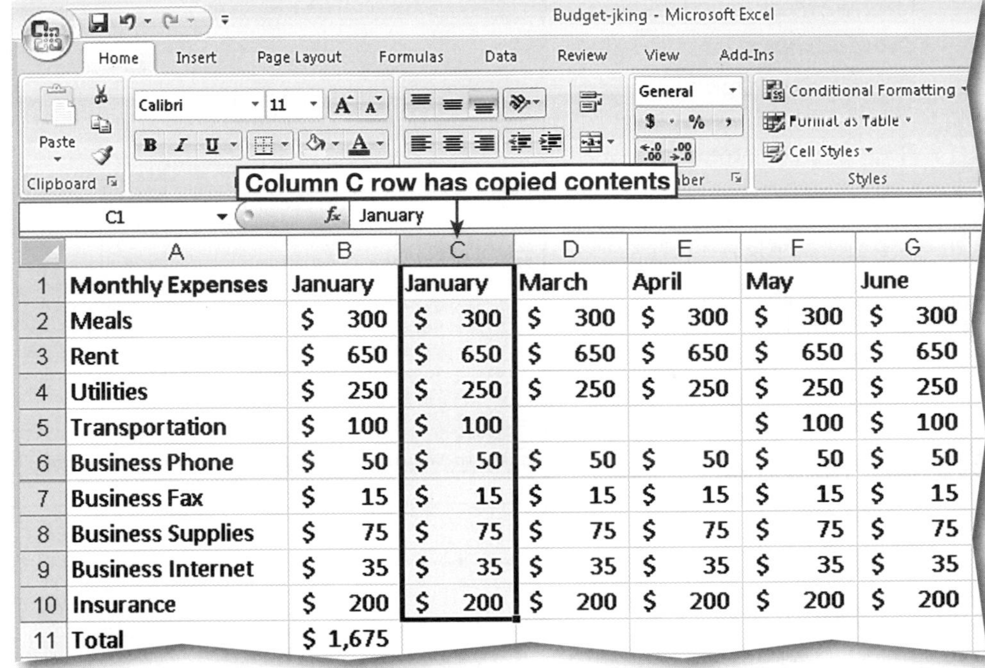

	A	B	C	D	E	F	G
1	Monthly Expenses	January	January	March	April	May	June
2	Meals	$ 300	$ 300	$ 300	$ 300	$ 300	$ 300
3	Rent	$ 650	$ 650	$ 650	$ 650	$ 650	$ 650
4	Utilities	$ 250	$ 250	$ 250	$ 250	$ 250	$ 250
5	Transportation	$ 100	$ 100			$ 100	$ 100
6	Business Phone	$ 50	$ 50	$ 50	$ 50	$ 50	$ 50
7	Business Fax	$ 15	$ 15	$ 15	$ 15	$ 15	$ 15
8	Business Supplies	$ 75	$ 75	$ 75	$ 75	$ 75	$ 75
9	Business Internet	$ 35	$ 35	$ 35	$ 35	$ 35	$ 35
10	Insurance	$ 200	$ 200	$ 200	$ 200	$ 200	$ 200
11	Total	$ 1,675					

FIGURE 2.18 Inserting rows

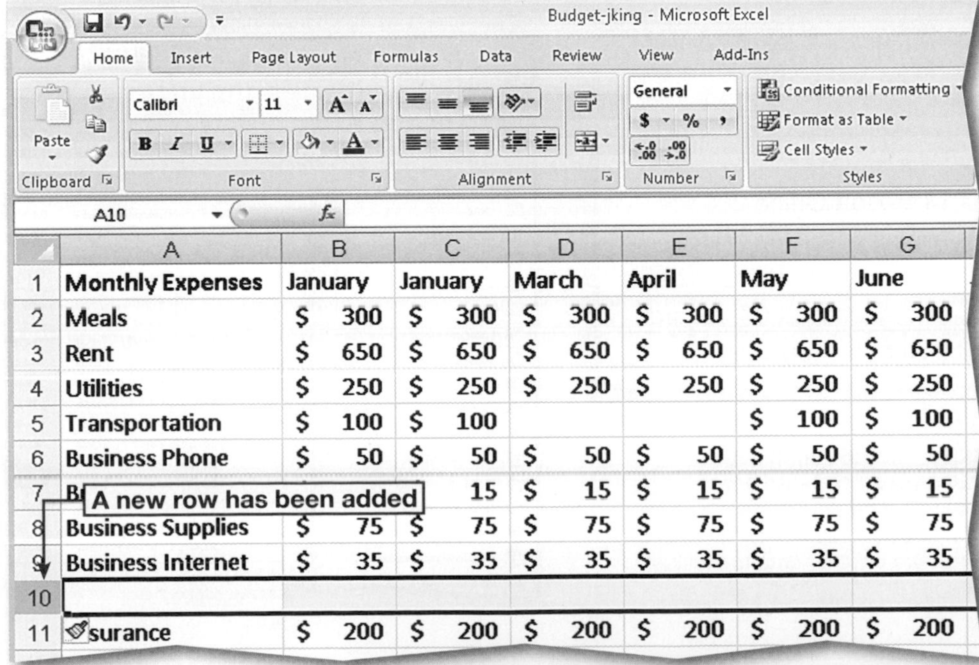

	A	B	C	D	E	F	G
1	Monthly Expenses	January	January	March	April	May	June
2	Meals	$ 300	$ 300	$ 300	$ 300	$ 300	$ 300
3	Rent	$ 650	$ 650	$ 650	$ 650	$ 650	$ 650
4	Utilities	$ 250	$ 250	$ 250	$ 250	$ 250	$ 250
5	Transportation	$ 100	$ 100			$ 100	$ 100
6	Business Phone	$ 50	$ 50	$ 50	$ 50	$ 50	$ 50
7	B		15	$ 15	$ 15	$ 15	$ 15
8	Business Supplies	$ 75	$ 75	$ 75	$ 75	$ 75	$ 75
9	Business Internet	$ 35	$ 35	$ 35	$ 35	$ 35	$ 35
10							
11	surance	$ 200	$ 200	$ 200	$ 200	$ 200	$ 200

Step-By-Step

EXERCISE 4-1 (Continued) Import Structured Data into Tables

12 Close the table. Choose **External Data>Import>Excel** .

13 Click **Browse**. Ask your teacher where to find the **GRecord.xlsx** data file and select it. Click **Open**.

14 Click **OK**. Click **Next**.

15 **CHECK** Your screen should look like Figure 4.3.

16 Click **Next** twice. Click **Finish** and then click **Close**.

17 In the **Navigation Pane**, open the **Sport Record Holders** table.

18 **CHECK** Your screen should look like Figure 4.4.

19 Close the table.

Continue to the next exercise.

FIGURE 4.3 Get External Data – Excel Spreadsheet

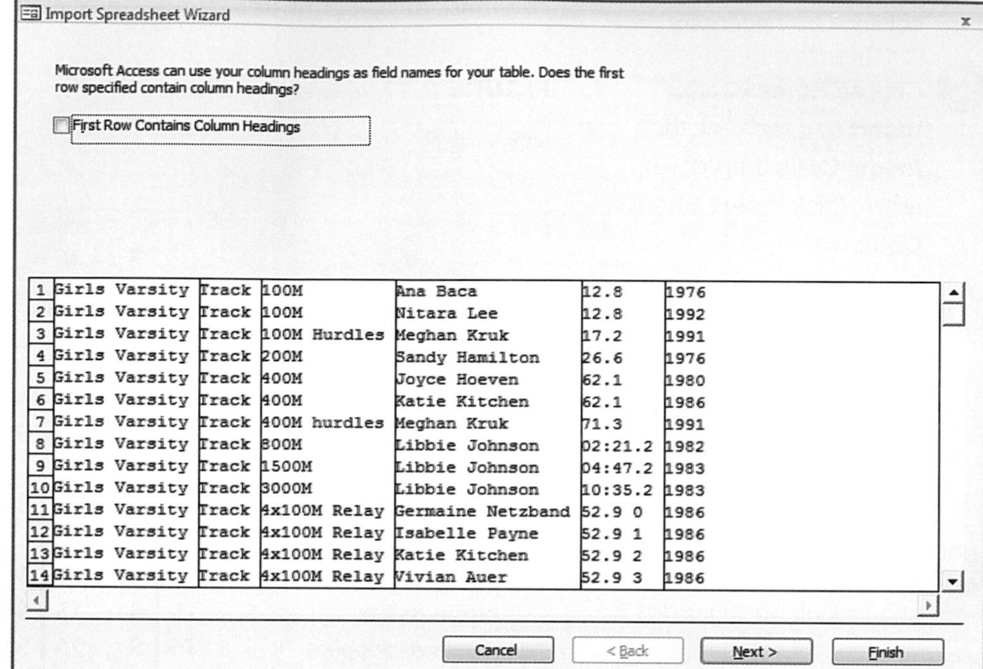

1	Girls Varsity	Track	100M	Ana Baca	12.8	1976
2	Girls Varsity	Track	100M	Nitara Lee	12.8	1992
3	Girls Varsity	Track	100M Hurdles	Meghan Kruk	17.2	1991
4	Girls Varsity	Track	200M	Sandy Hamilton	26.6	1976
5	Girls Varsity	Track	400M	Joyce Hoeven	62.1	1980
6	Girls Varsity	Track	400M	Katie Kitchen	62.1	1986
7	Girls Varsity	Track	400M hurdles	Meghan Kruk	71.3	1991
8	Girls Varsity	Track	800M	Libbie Johnson	02:21.2	1982
9	Girls Varsity	Track	1500M	Libbie Johnson	04:47.2	1983
10	Girls Varsity	Track	3000M	Libbie Johnson	10:35.2	1983
11	Girls Varsity	Track	4x100M Relay	Germaine Netzband	52.9 0	1986
12	Girls Varsity	Track	4x100M Relay	Isabelle Payne	52.9 1	1986
13	Girls Varsity	Track	4x100M Relay	Katie Kitchen	52.9 2	1986
14	Girls Varsity	Track	4x100M Relay	Vivian Auer	52.9 3	1986

FIGURE 4.4 Sport Record Holders table

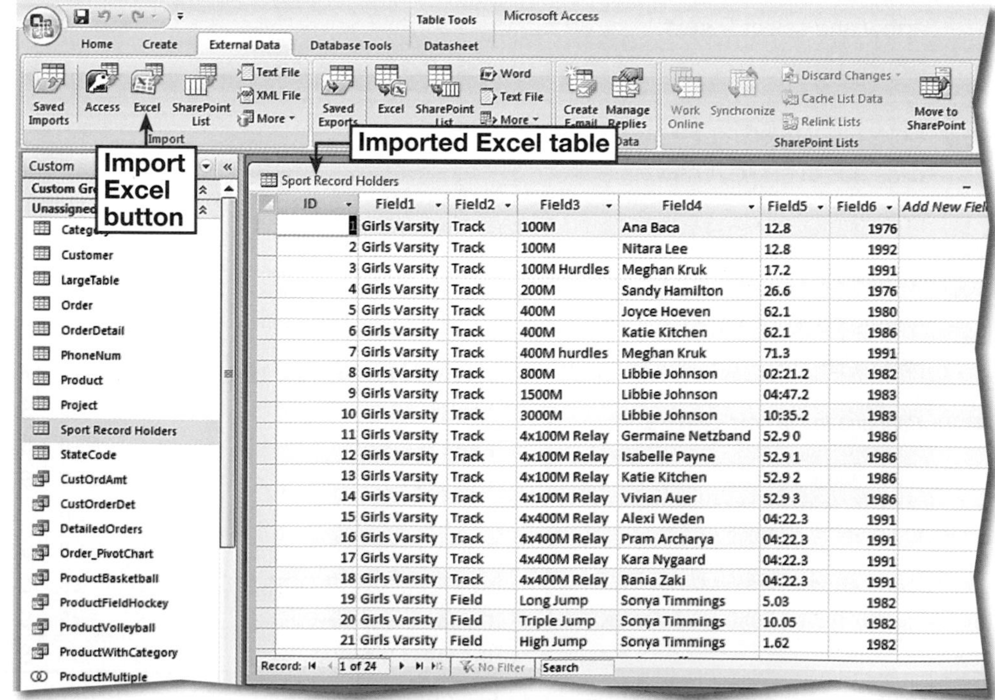

ID	Field1	Field2	Field3	Field4	Field5	Field6	Add New Field
1	Girls Varsity	Track	100M	Ana Baca	12.8	1976	
2	Girls Varsity	Track	100M	Nitara Lee	12.8	1992	
3	Girls Varsity	Track	100M Hurdles	Meghan Kruk	17.2	1991	
4	Girls Varsity	Track	200M	Sandy Hamilton	26.6	1976	
5	Girls Varsity	Track	400M	Joyce Hoeven	62.1	1980	
6	Girls Varsity	Track	400M	Katie Kitchen	62.1	1986	
7	Girls Varsity	Track	400M hurdles	Meghan Kruk	71.3	1991	
8	Girls Varsity	Track	800M	Libbie Johnson	02:21.2	1982	
9	Girls Varsity	Track	1500M	Libbie Johnson	04:47.2	1983	
10	Girls Varsity	Track	3000M	Libbie Johnson	10:35.2	1983	
11	Girls Varsity	Track	4x100M Relay	Germaine Netzband	52.9 0	1986	
12	Girls Varsity	Track	4x100M Relay	Isabelle Payne	52.9 1	1986	
13	Girls Varsity	Track	4x100M Relay	Katie Kitchen	52.9 2	1986	
14	Girls Varsity	Track	4x100M Relay	Vivian Auer	52.9 3	1986	
15	Girls Varsity	Track	4x400M Relay	Alexi Weden	04:22.3	1991	
16	Girls Varsity	Track	4x400M Relay	Pram Archarya	04:22.3	1991	
17	Girls Varsity	Track	4x400M Relay	Kara Nygaard	04:22.3	1991	
18	Girls Varsity	Track	4x400M Relay	Rania Zaki	04:22.3	1991	
19	Girls Varsity	Field	Long Jump	Sonya Timmings	5.03	1982	
20	Girls Varsity	Field	Triple Jump	Sonya Timmings	10.05	1982	
21	Girls Varsity	Field	High Jump	Sonya Timmings	1.62	1982	

Microsoft Office 2007

Microsoft Office 2007 allows you to link tables from any Access database into Access 2007, regardless of file format.

Differentiated Instruction/ Advanced Students Have advanced students open the data file **GRecord.xlsx** in Excel to see what the original data looks like.

EXERCISE 2-10
Insert and Delete Cells

You can insert or delete a single cell. Be careful—when you insert or delete a cell, the cells around the inserted cell shift, and data may no longer line up with the column or row headings. Usually, you will insert or delete an entire row or column.

FIGURE 2.19 Cell B11 shifted down

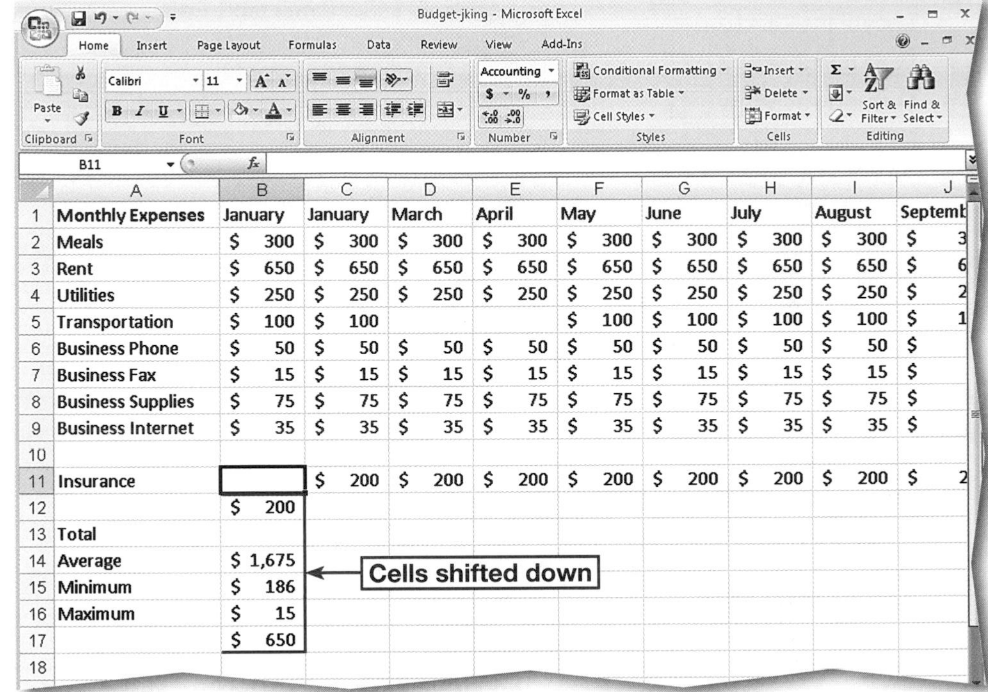

	A	B	C	D	E	F	G	H	I	J
1	Monthly Expenses	January	January	March	April	May	June	July	August	Septemb
2	Meals	$ 300	$ 300	$ 300	$ 300	$ 300	$ 300	$ 300	$ 300	$ 3
3	Rent	$ 650	$ 650	$ 650	$ 650	$ 650	$ 650	$ 650	$ 650	$ 6
4	Utilities	$ 250	$ 250	$ 250	$ 250	$ 250	$ 250	$ 250	$ 250	$ 2
5	Transportation	$ 100	$ 100			$ 100	$ 100	$ 100	$ 100	$ 1
6	Business Phone	$ 50	$ 50	$ 50	$ 50	$ 50	$ 50	$ 50	$ 50	$
7	Business Fax	$ 15	$ 15	$ 15	$ 15	$ 15	$ 15	$ 15	$ 15	$
8	Business Supplies	$ 75	$ 75	$ 75	$ 75	$ 75	$ 75	$ 75	$ 75	$
9	Business Internet	$ 35	$ 35	$ 35	$ 35	$ 35	$ 35	$ 35	$ 35	$
10										
11	Insurance		$ 200	$ 200	$ 200	$ 200	$ 200	$ 200	$ 200	$ 2
12		$ 200								
13	Total									
14	Average	$ 1,675								
15	Minimum	$ 186								
16	Maximum	$ 15								
17		$ 650								
18										

FIGURE 2.20 Row 10 deleted and row 11 taking its place

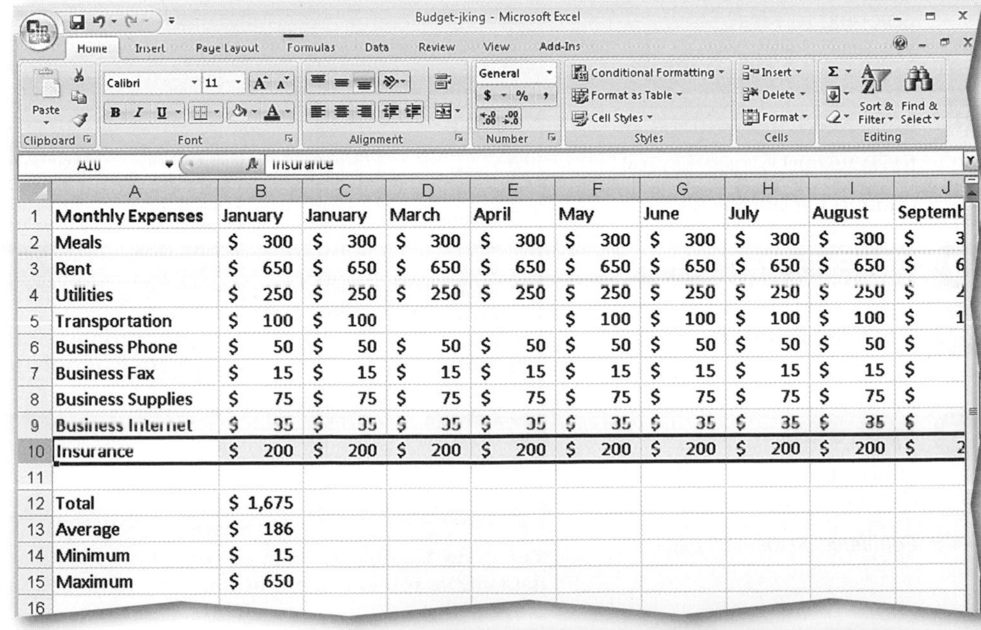

	A	B	C	D	E	F	G	H	I	J
1	Monthly Expenses	January	January	March	April	May	June	July	August	Septemb
2	Meals	$ 300	$ 300	$ 300	$ 300	$ 300	$ 300	$ 300	$ 300	$ 3
3	Rent	$ 650	$ 650	$ 650	$ 650	$ 650	$ 650	$ 650	$ 650	$ 6
4	Utilities	$ 250	$ 250	$ 250	$ 250	$ 250	$ 250	$ 250	$ 250	$ 2
5	Transportation	$ 100	$ 100			$ 100	$ 100	$ 100	$ 100	$ 1
6	Business Phone	$ 50	$ 50	$ 50	$ 50	$ 50	$ 50	$ 50	$ 50	$
7	Business Fax	$ 15	$ 15	$ 15	$ 15	$ 15	$ 15	$ 15	$ 15	$
8	Business Supplies	$ 75	$ 75	$ 75	$ 75	$ 75	$ 75	$ 75	$ 75	$
9	Business Internet	$ 35	$ 35	$ 35	$ 35	$ 35	$ 35	$ 35	$ 35	$
10	Insurance	$ 200	$ 200	$ 200	$ 200	$ 200	$ 200	$ 200	$ 200	$ 2
11										
12	Total	$ 1,675								
13	Average	$ 186								
14	Minimum	$ 15								
15	Maximum	$ 650								
16										

Step-By-Step

1. In your **Budget** file, click cell **B11**.
2. Choose **Home>Cells**. Click the **Insert Cells** drop-down arrow. Select **Insert Cells**.
3. In the **Insert** dialog box, select **Shift cells down**. Click **OK**.
4. **CHECK** Your screen should look like Figure 2.19.
5. With **B11** still selected, right-click and select **Delete**.
6. In the **Delete** dialog box, select **Shift cells up**.
7. Click **OK**.
8. Click row heading **10** to select row 10.
9. Right-click and choose **Delete**. Row 10 is deleted and row 11 moves up to replace it.
10. **CHECK** Your screen should look like Figure 2.20.
11. Save your file.

Continue to the next exercise.

Teaching Tip Let students know that they may need to insert or delete cells if they forget to include an entry in a worksheet.

Differentiated Instruction/ Hearing Impaired Be sure to face the class whenever you speak so that students may pick up facial or speech reading cues.

EXERCISE 4-1
Import Structured Data into Tables

You can import data into the database to create a table from outside sources, such as CSV files, Excel files, and other Access databases. A wizard will guide you through the process. To make your table efficient, you must **normalize** it, or make sure it is structured correctly and that there are no repeated groups of information.

Step-By-Step

1. Locate the **Sports4.accdb** data file. Copy the database before opening it. Open the **Customer** table.
2. Click **Design View**. Locate the **Customer** table's **Primary Key**. Click **Datasheet View**.
3. **CHECK** Your screen should look like Figure 4.1.
4. Close the table. Choose **External Data>Import> Text File**.
5. In the **Get External Data Text File** wizard, make sure the first option is selected. Click **Browse**.
6. Find the **PhoneNum.csv** data file. Click **Open**. Click **OK**.
7. Click **Next**. Click the check box next to **First Row Contains Field Names**.
8. Click **Next** and read the three wizard pages. Do not change the default settings.
9. Click **Finish**. Click **Close**.
10. Open the **PhoneNum** table.
11. **CHECK** Your screen should look like Figure 4.2.

Continued on the next page.

FIGURE 4.1 Customer table Datasheet View

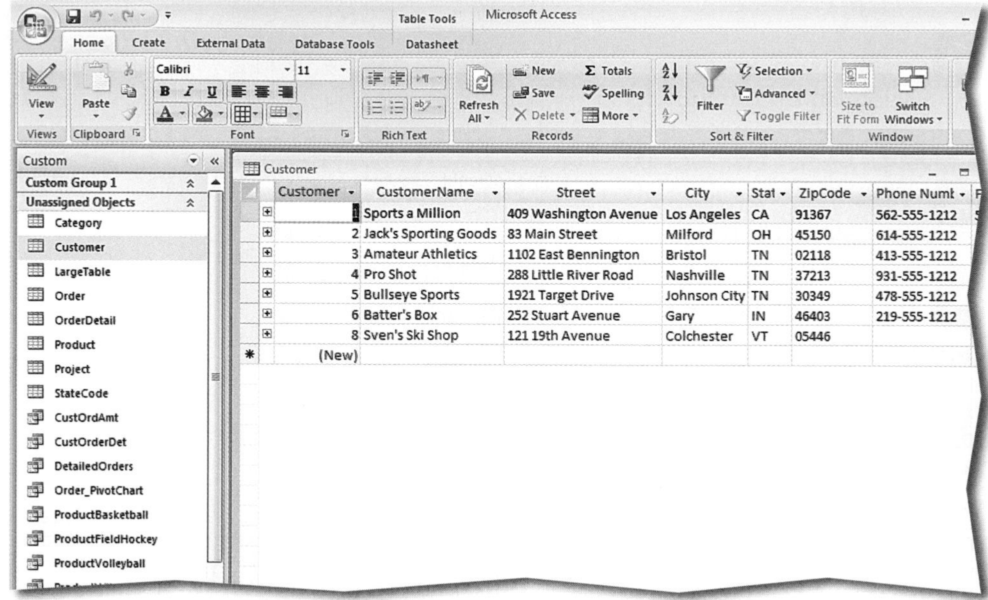

FIGURE 4.2 PhoneNum table datasheet

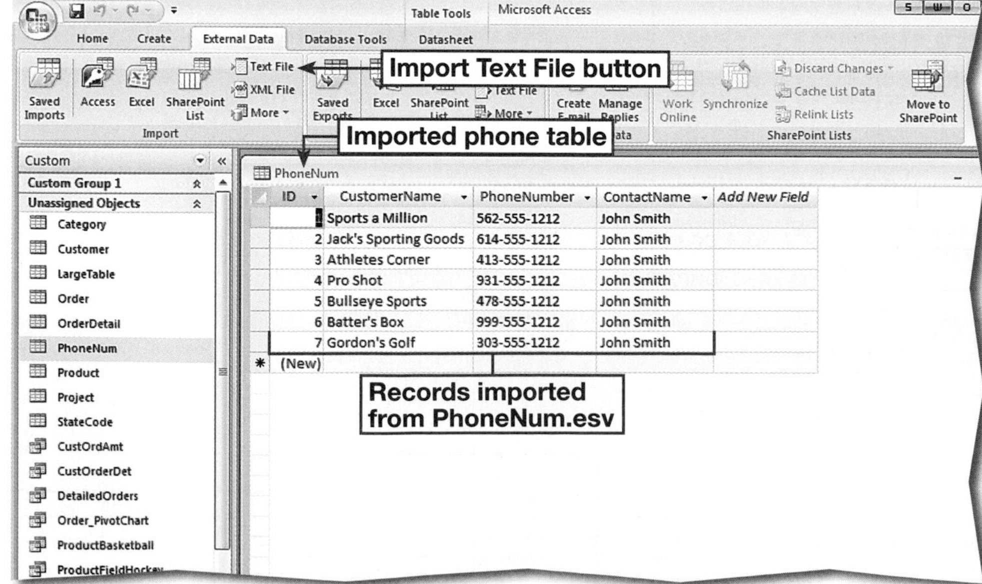

Teaching Tip Discuss with students the benefits of having linked data in a database. Linked data allows you to find corresponding information faster than having to search through multiple tables.

Step-By-Step

1. In your **Budget** file, click cell **B1**. Point to the small square that appears on the lower right corner of the cell (see Figure 2.21). The pointer takes the shape of a plus sign [+].

2. Click and hold the mouse button. Drag the pointer to the right until it is on cell **C1**. Release the mouse button.

3. Click cell **B12**. Drag the Fill handle to the right until it is in cell **G12**.

4. Click cell **G12**. Drag the Fill handle to the right until it is in cell **M12**.

5. **CHECK** Your screen should look like Figure 2.22.

6. Save your file.

Continue to the next exercise.

Differentiated Instruction/ Advanced Students Tell students that when they key **January, Monday**, or any date and then use the Fill handle, Excel automatically fills in the rest of the months or days. Have students create a new file and practice this task.

EXERCISE 2-11
Use the Fill Handle

Sometimes you may want to insert the same contents into many different cells. For example, a bill may cost the same amount of money every month. You can use the **Fill handle** to insert repeated content into several cells at once.

FIGURE 2.21 The Fill handle

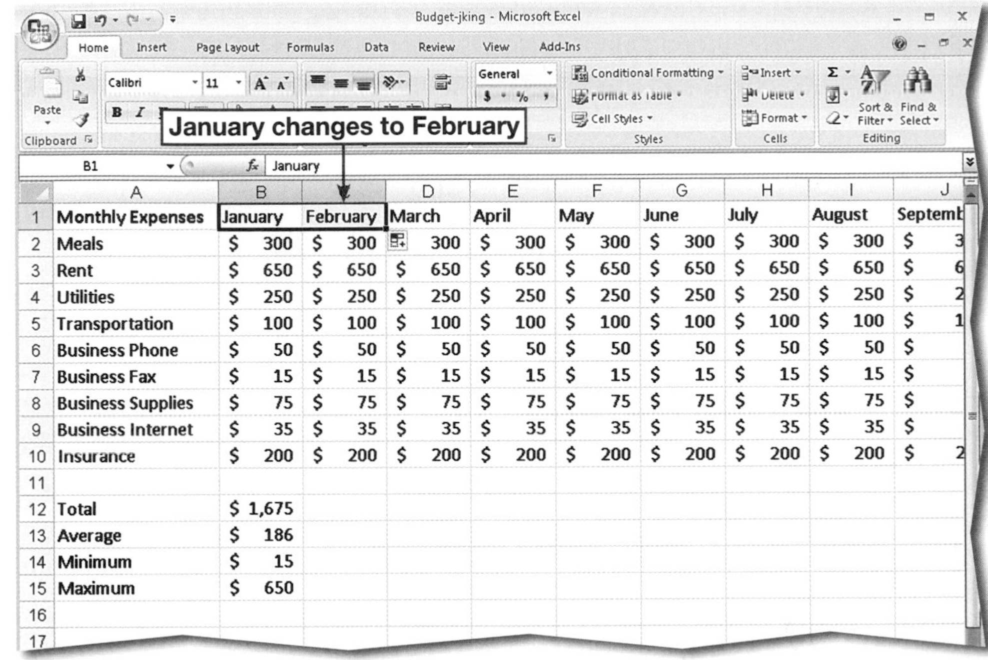

	A	B		D	E	F	G	H	I	J
1	Monthly Expenses	January	February	March	April	May	June	July	August	Septemb
2	Meals	$ 300	$ 300	300	$ 300	$ 300	$ 300	$ 300	$ 300	$ 3
3	Rent	$ 650	$ 650	$ 650	$ 650	$ 650	$ 650	$ 650	$ 650	$ 6
4	Utilities	$ 250	$ 250	$ 250	$ 250	$ 250	$ 250	$ 250	$ 250	$ 2
5	Transportation	$ 100	$ 100	$ 100	$ 100	$ 100	$ 100	$ 100	$ 100	$ 1
6	Business Phone	$ 50	$ 50	$ 50	$ 50	$ 50	$ 50	$ 50	$ 50	$
7	Business Fax	$ 15	$ 15	$ 15	$ 15	$ 15	$ 15	$ 15	$ 15	$
8	Business Supplies	$ 75	$ 75	$ 75	$ 75	$ 75	$ 75	$ 75	$ 75	$
9	Business Internet	$ 35	$ 35	$ 35	$ 35	$ 35	$ 35	$ 35	$ 35	$
10	Insurance	$ 200	$ 200	$ 200	$ 200	$ 200	$ 200	$ 200	$ 200	$ 2
11										
12	Total	$ 1,675								
13	Average	$ 186								
14	Minimum	$ 15								
15	Maximum	$ 650								

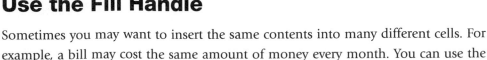

FIGURE 2.22 After using the Fill handle

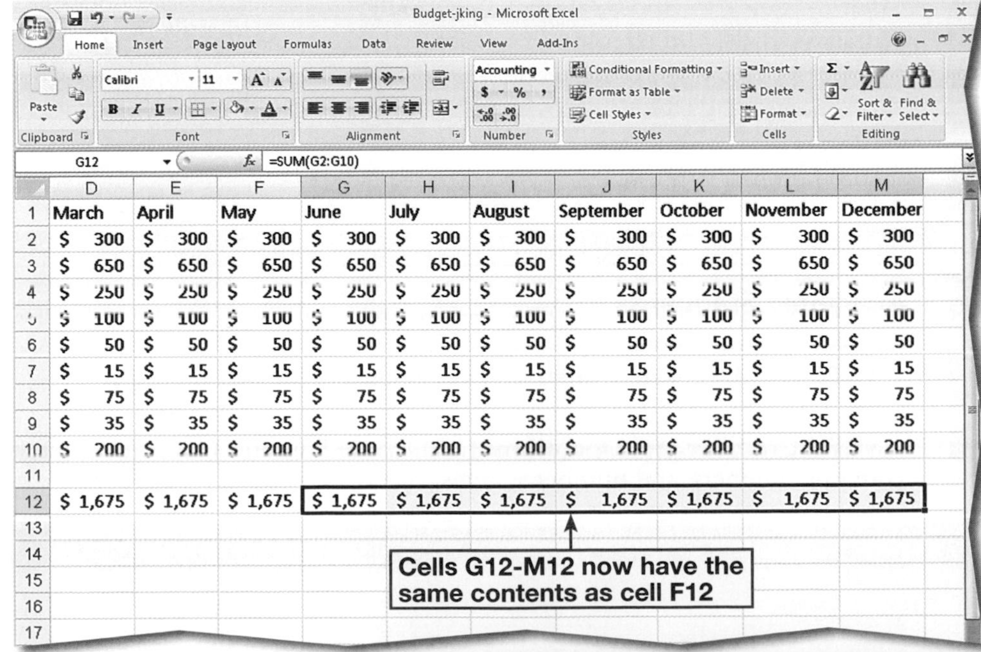

	D	E	F	G	H	I	J	K	L	M
1	March	April	May	June	July	August	September	October	November	December
2	$ 300	$ 300	$ 300	$ 300	$ 300	$ 300	$ 300	$ 300	$ 300	$ 300
3	$ 650	$ 650	$ 650	$ 650	$ 650	$ 650	$ 650	$ 650	$ 650	$ 650
4	$ 250	$ 250	$ 250	$ 250	$ 250	$ 250	$ 250	$ 250	$ 250	$ 250
5	$ 100	$ 100	$ 100	$ 100	$ 100	$ 100	$ 100	$ 100	$ 100	$ 100
6	$ 50	$ 50	$ 50	$ 50	$ 50	$ 50	$ 50	$ 50	$ 50	$ 50
7	$ 15	$ 15	$ 15	$ 15	$ 15	$ 15	$ 15	$ 15	$ 15	$ 15
8	$ 75	$ 75	$ 75	$ 75	$ 75	$ 75	$ 75	$ 75	$ 75	$ 75
9	$ 35	$ 35	$ 35	$ 35	$ 35	$ 35	$ 35	$ 35	$ 35	$ 35
10	$ 200	$ 200	$ 200	$ 200	$ 200	$ 200	$ 200	$ 200	$ 200	$ 200
11										
12	$ 1,675	$ 1,675	$ 1,675	$ 1,675	$ 1,675	$ 1,675	$ 1,675	$ 1,675	$ 1,675	$ 1,675

LESSON 4 Reading Guide

Before You Read

See page TM42 for English Learner activity suggestions.

Buddy Up for Success One advantage to sharing your notes with a buddy is that you can fill in gaps in each other's information. You can also compare notes before you start quizzing each other.

Read To Learn

- Add criteria and calculated fields to queries and sort records in tables and queries.
- Maintain inventory and research data by sorting and filtering data.
- Export and import data, attach and detach documents from records, and link to external data sources.

Main Idea

A better understanding of the tools available in Access will enable you to gather and present database information in a useful format.

Vocabulary

Key Terms

aggregate
alias
database object
document
export specifications
import specifications
inner join
left-outer join
link
normalize
parameter
right-outer join

Academic Vocabulary

These words appear in your reading and on your tests. Make sure you know their meanings.

common
criteria
design
element
refine

Quick Write Activity

Describe On a separate sheet of paper list five different documents you might find attached to a database for a sports equipment manufacturing company.

Study Skills

Divide and Conquer At first glance, an assignment may look too big to handle. Break it down. Identify the steps you need to take to finish the task. Then, plan a timeline. Each step brings you closer to your goal.

Academic Standards

English Language Arts

NCTE 12 Use spoken, written, and visual language to accomplish your own purposes.

Math

NCTM (Number and Operations) Understand numbers, ways of representing numbers, relationships among numbers, and number systems.

Step-By-Step

1. In your **Budget** file, click cell **C1**. Click **Insert> Links>Insert Hyperlink** .

2. In the **Insert Hyperlink** dialog box, use the **Look in** box to locate and select the data file **Months.xlsx** (see Figure 2.23).

3. Click **OK**. The text in cell C1 turns blue to indicate the presence of a hyperlink.

4. Click cell **C1**, hold, and then release to follow the link. The workbook **Months** opens.

5. Click **Close** to close Months.

6. Right-click cell **C1**. Choose **Edit Hyperlink**. Click **Remove Link**.

7. **CHECK** Your screen should look like Figure 2.24. Save and close your file.

Academic Skills

Money management involves both tracking past costs and anticipating future costs. How can identifying these fixed costs help you estimate how much you might spend over a year?

NCLB/Math (Number and Operations)

EXERCISE 2-12
Insert and Edit Hyperlinks

A **hyperlink** is a shortcut that connects to a file in another location. If parts of your worksheet are associated with other files, you can insert a hyperlink that will open these files when you click a link in your worksheet. For example, perhaps you track monthly expenses in a separate worksheet and you want to be able to access these expenses from your overall budget file. Adding a hyperlink helps you link related files so that you can easily access them.

Solution Use the file **Budget-SF** as a solution file for Exercises 2-1 through 2-12.

FIGURE 2.23 Insert Hyperlink dialog box

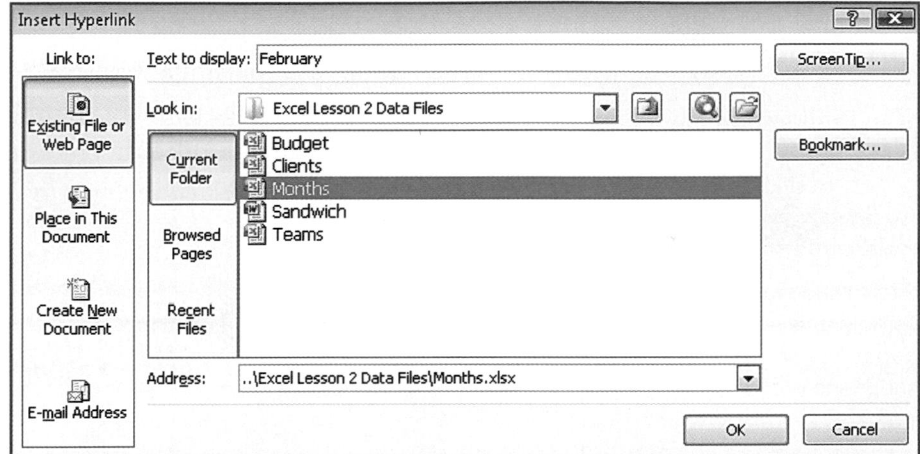

FIGURE 2.24 Workbook with hyperlink removed

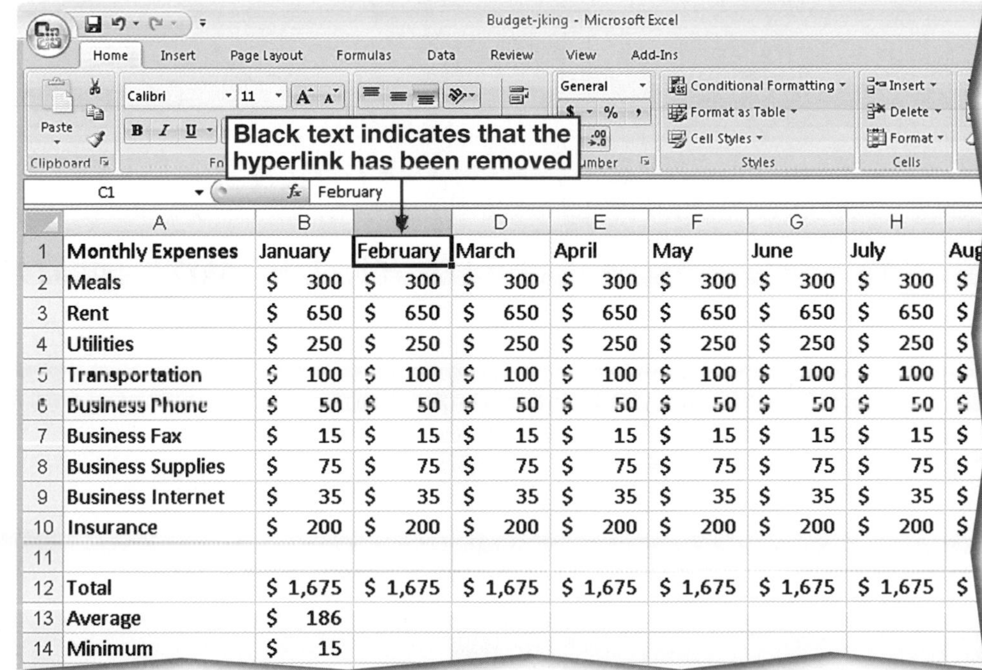

	A	B	C	D	E	F	G	H	
1	Monthly Expenses	January	February	March	April	May	June	July	Aug
2	Meals	$ 300	$ 300	$ 300	$ 300	$ 300	$ 300	$ 300	$
3	Rent	$ 650	$ 650	$ 650	$ 650	$ 650	$ 650	$ 650	$
4	Utilities	$ 250	$ 250	$ 250	$ 250	$ 250	$ 250	$ 250	$
5	Transportation	$ 100	$ 100	$ 100	$ 100	$ 100	$ 100	$ 100	$
6	Business Phone	$ 50	$ 50	$ 50	$ 50	$ 50	$ 50	$ 50	$
7	Business Fax	$ 15	$ 15	$ 15	$ 15	$ 15	$ 15	$ 15	$
8	Business Supplies	$ 75	$ 75	$ 75	$ 75	$ 75	$ 75	$ 75	$
9	Business Internet	$ 35	$ 35	$ 35	$ 35	$ 35	$ 35	$ 35	$
10	Insurance	$ 200	$ 200	$ 200	$ 200	$ 200	$ 200	$ 200	$
11									
12	Total	$ 1,675	$ 1,675	$ 1,675	$ 1,675	$ 1,675	$ 1,675	$ 1,675	$
13	Average	$ 186							
14	Minimum	$ 15							

Troubleshooting In **Step 4**, be aware that the font and font size change to Arial 10 pt. in cell C1. Tell students to change the font and size back to Calibri 11 pt.

LESSON 4 Maximize Database Functions

Key Concepts

- Link to external data sources
- Import and export data
- Sort and filter data within different database objects
- Save and run import and export specifications

Standards

The following standards are covered in this lesson. Refer to pages xxv and 715 for descriptions of the standards listed here.

ISTE Standards Correlation

NETS•S

4a, 6a, 6b, 6c, 6d

Microsoft Certified Application Specialist

Access

3.5, 4.2, 5.1, 5.2, 5.4

In this lesson, you will learn how to format the data in your database to improve search results. You also will also learn how to import data and structures from inside and outside the database, and to filter data within database objects.

21st CENTURY SKILLS

See page TM84 for answer to 21st Century Skills.

Complete a Task Believe it or not, finishing is a skill that can be learned. Incomplete projects slow you down, drain your energy, and weaken your self-confidence. Look around for things you have left undone. What needs to be done? Do it. Is it something you like? Finish it. If the time has passed for an incomplete project to be useful or enjoyable, get rid of it. This frees up your time and energy for current work or hobbies and builds your confidence in your own abilities. *What is a task that you recently completed?*

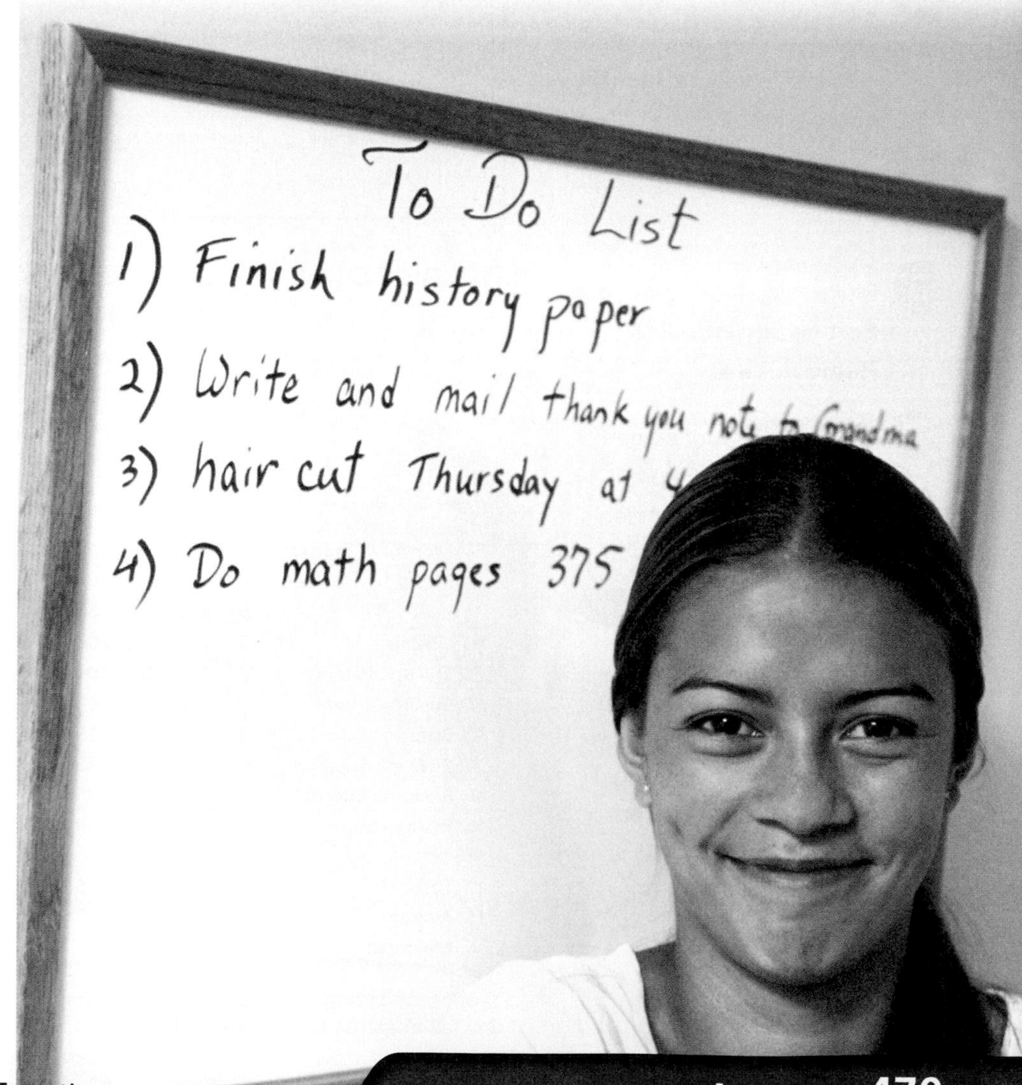

MATH MATTERS

Using Math Formulas

You use math formulas every day without even realizing it. You might calculate how much money it will cost for a movie and snacks. Or, you might use a formula to figure out how much you will earn taking care of your neighbor's house.

The Problem

Your neighbors hire you to take care of their house for three days while they are on a trip. They will pay you $5 to check the mail, $2 each day to get the newspaper, and $7 to water the lawn and plants. You want to figure out how much you will earn.

How Excel Calculates

Excel uses formulas to do calculations like the one described above. Excel can also help you balance your checkbook or figure out how much it will cost to give a party.

Excel calculates formulas the same way you do calculations in your math class. Math follows certain rules to find the correct answer. The *order of precedence* states which part of the formula you calculate first. Some math operations, such as multiplication, take precedence over others. In other words, some operations are done before others. If you key a formula that has an addition symbol (+), a subtraction sign (−), a multiplication symbol (*), and a division (/) symbol, Excel will compute the multiplication first, then division, then addition, and then subtraction.

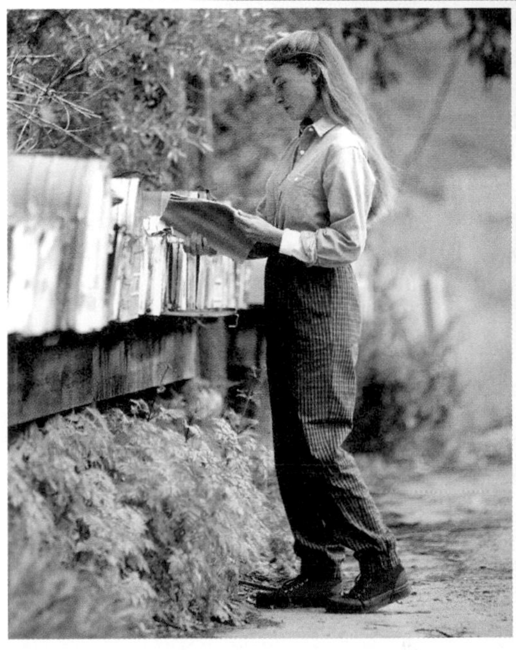

You can use Excel to calculate your earnings in a small business, such as taking care of people's houses while they are on vacation.

NCLB/Math (Algebra) Ask students to calculate the cost for a movie, snacks, and bus fare. Then ask students to recalculate the cost using a coupon for $3 off the purchase of a movie ticket, and a round trip bus fare to the theater. Reinforce to students that Excel calculates formulas using the same algebraic symbols and equations that they used in their calculations.

SKILLBUILDER

1. **State** If you key a formula that includes addition, subtraction, multiplication, and division, in what order will Excel do the calculations?

2. **Discuss** Explain why the order of precedence is important.

3. **Apply** Solve this problem using the order of precedence. You checked the mail and got the paper each day, but you paid your little sister $4 to water the lawn. How much money will you get to keep? The formula is: 5 + 2 * 3 + 7 − 4. Multiply 2 times 3 first, then do the other operations from left to right.

SkillBuilder answers can be found on page TM70.

LESSON 3 Challenge Yourself Projects

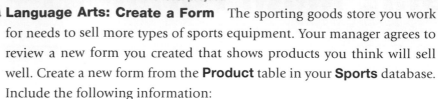

Before You Begin

Organize Data An important aspect of managing information is presenting it in an easy-to-read format. Access provides the tools you need to sort, group, and view selected information in a database. These projects teach you how to create a form, how to format a report, and how to create labels based on the data in your database.

Reflect Once you complete the projects, open a Word document and answer the following:

1. Describe the methods you used to create a readable form.
2. In what ways do you think labels can help you better organize and quickly manage data?

Rubric

9. Create a New Sports Product Form

LEVEL This is an intermediate level project.

Language Arts: Create a Form The sporting goods store you work for needs to sell more types of sports equipment. Your manager agrees to review a new form you created that shows products you think will sell well. Create a new form from the **Product** table in your **Sports** database. Include the following information:

- ProductCategory (such as baseball or basketball)
- ProductName
- ProductPrice

Solution The solution file for Project 9 is the **Product9-SF** form in the **Sports-SF.accdb.**

Save the form as: Product-[your first initial and last name]9.

In Word, key a paragraph summarizing why the new form is more readable. In your paragraph, provide examples to support your ideas.

Rubric

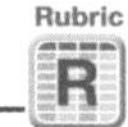

10. Create Reports

LEVEL This is an intermediate level project.

Language Arts: Create a Report You want to generate and print a report for your supervisor to review. Open your **Sports** database. Create a report based on the form in your **Product-9** file. Add group headers to the report to make it easier to read.

Save the report as: ProdReport-[your first initial and last name]10. With your teacher's permission, print the report.

Solution The solution file for Project 10 is the **ProdReport10-SF** report in the **Sports-SF.accdb** database.

In Word, make a list of five types of data that are often easier to read when divided into groups. For example, grouping sales information by state or zip code makes it much easier to track data trends over a period of time.

Rubric

R

11. Track Product Orders

LEVEL This is an advanced level project.

Create Labels Your supervisor has asked you to create a set of inventory labels.

Solution The solution file for Project 11 is the **ProdLabels11-SF** table in the **Sports-SF.accdb** database.

- Open your **Sports** database.
- Create inventory labels for the **Product** table.
- Save your file as: ProdLabels-[your first initial and last name]11.

In a separate Word document key a paragraph explaining how you would use inventory labels. For example, you might use them to help track inventory or to track the overall status of your business's finances.

Answers Rubrics for each Challenge Yourself Project are available at **glencoe.com.** You may want to download the rubrics and make them available to students as they complete each project.

LESSON 2 After You Read

Vocabulary

Key Terms

AutoSum
AVERAGE
budget
cell content
clear
Clipboard
copy
cut
edit
Fill handle
function
hyperlink
MAX
MIN
paste

Academic Vocabulary

determine
insert

Answer to Vocabulary Activity
Students create a matching game using six of the lesson's vocabulary words. Students should use the vocabulary chart to make sure their definitions are accurate.

EL The Vocabulary Activity may be especially helpful for English Learners.

Review Vocabulary

Complete the following statements on a separate piece of paper. Choose from the Vocabulary list on the left to complete the statements.

1. The letters and numbers in a cell are called ___cell content___. (p. 228)
2. You can ___insert___ new rows between existing rows. (p. 236)
3. A(n) ___hyperlink___ is a shortcut to other files. (p. 239)
4. The ___AutoSum___ function allows you to add values in rows and columns. (p. 229)
5. A(n) ___function___ is a preset formula. (p. 229)

Vocabulary Activity

6. Create a matching game.
A. Write six of this lesson's vocabulary words on index cards or squares of paper. Write the definitions for the six terms you selected on a different set of index cards or squares of paper.
B. Place all of the cards face down on your desk and mix them up. Arrange the cards four across and three down.
C. With your teacher's permission, pair up with a classmate. Take turns turning over two cards at a time. If the two cards are a vocabulary word and its correct definition, keep the cards. If not, put the cards back.
D. Continue until you have reviewed all of your cards. The person who collects the most pairs at the end of the game wins.

Review Key Concepts

Answer the following questions on a separate piece of paper.

7. Which key should you press to move down one cell in a worksheet? (p. 228)
A. Backspace
B. Delete
C. Insert
(D.) Enter

8. Which group would you use to insert and delete rows and columns? (p. 235)
A. Page Layout
(B.) Cells
C. Add-Ins
D. Editing

9. Which of the following is a function? (p. 229)
A. MIN
B. AVERAGE
C. AutoSum
(D.) All of the above

10. How do you select a cell that you want to edit? (p. 230)
A. Choose Home>Cells>Format.
B. Click Copy
C. Click the cell
(D.) Double-click the cell.

NCLB/Language Arts (NCTE 12)
Reinforce the importance of prioritizing by asking students to discuss why they sorted the demands on their time the way they did. Ask them to compare and contrast the highest and lowest priority activities.

Beyond the Classroom Activity
Students' answers will vary. Possible answers include test scores (percentage), tax and/or change on a purchase, miles per gallon for fuel economy, and travel time.

Standards at Work Activity
Students' answers may include simple entry labels and extra space added between items in the form.

21st Century Skills Activity
Students' answers might include homework, chores, volunteer work, movies to see, friends to call, job searches, and sports or music practices. Tables should be sorted by importance and should be filtered to show only unfinished activities.

Go Online **e-REVIEW**
glencoe.com

Go to the **Online Learning Center** to complete the following review activities.

Online Self Check
To test your knowledge of the material, click **Unit 3> Lesson 3** and choose **Self Checks**.

Interactive Review
To review the main points of the lesson, click **Unit 3> Lesson 3** and choose **Interactive Review**.

6. Beyond the Classroom Activity

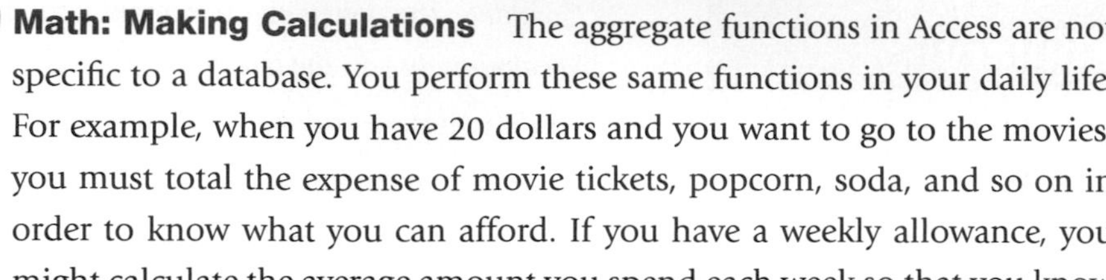
Math: Making Calculations The aggregate functions in Access are not specific to a database. You perform these same functions in your daily life. For example, when you have 20 dollars and you want to go to the movies, you must total the expense of movie tickets, popcorn, soda, and so on in order to know what you can afford. If you have a weekly allowance, you might calculate the average amount you spend each week so that you know how much to save for something special.

Think about the kinds of calculations you make in daily life. In Word, key a list of ten calculations you make. Save your document as: a3rev-[your first initial and last name]6.

7. Standards at Work Activity

Microsoft Certified Application Specialist Correlation
Access 2.5 *Create Forms*

Organize Information Forms are useful in Access because they present information in an easy-to-read format.

In Word, make a list of at least three forms you have encountered. For example, you might have filled out a survey that used a form. Or, you might have filled out a product registration card for something you bought. Think about what made these forms readable. Key a paragraph that describes how a form's formatting makes data easier to read. Save your document as: a3rev-[your first initial and last name]7.

8. 21st Century Skills Activity

Prioritize Tasks One of the best ways to make sure that you get important work done on time is to keep a to-do list. Make a list of the tasks you have to complete today, this week, and in the weeks ahead. Organize your list by marking each task with a number to show its importance.

- Open your **Sports** file.
- Enter your own to-do activities in the **To-do List** table in the database.
- In your table, include both tasks that you have not finished and tasks that you have already finished.

Then, do the following:

- Sort your table by importance.
- Use a filter to show only those activities not yet finished.

Save your table as: a3rev-[your first initial and last name]8.

LESSON 

Practice It Activities

1. Enter, Edit, and Clear Cell Contents

Follow the steps to complete the activity.

Step-By-Step

1. Open the data file **Clients.xlsx**. Close the task pane, if necessary.
2. Save the file as: Clients-[your first initial and last name]1.
3. Click cell **A6**. Key: Chris. Press ENTER.
4. Key: Sam. Press ENTER.
5. CHECK Your screen should look like Figure 2.25.
6. Double-click cell **B1**. Click between the *k* and *1*. Press the spacebar.
7. Click cell **D5**. Press ←BACKSPACE.
8. CHECK Your screen should look like Figure 2.26.
9. Save and close your file.

Solution Use the file **Clients1-SF** as a solution file for this activity.

FIGURE 2.25 List of months

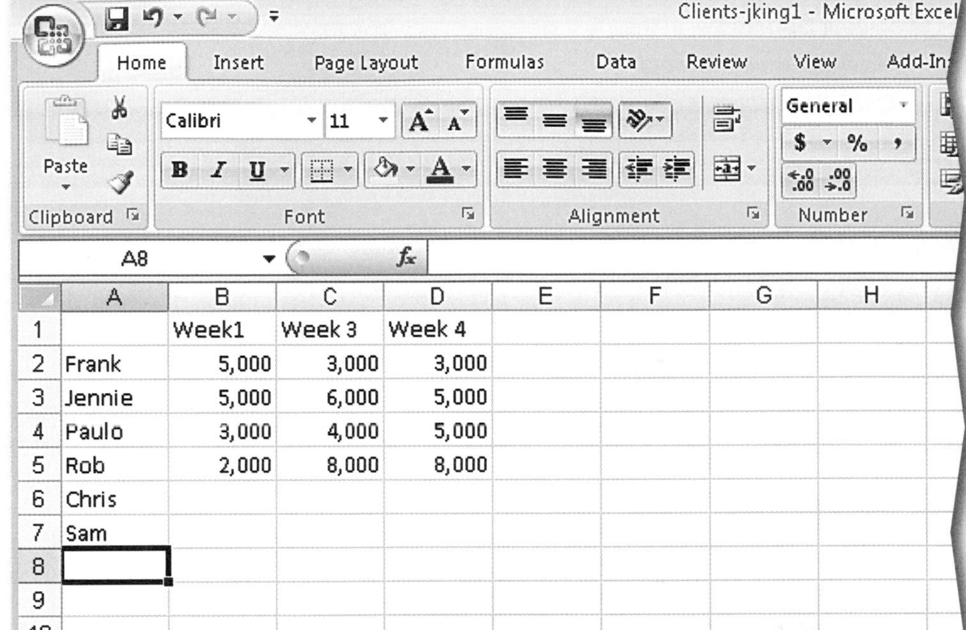

FIGURE 2.26 Editing and clearing contents

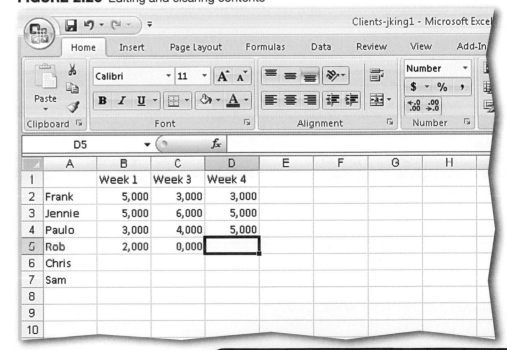

Clients-jking1 - Microsoft Excel

D5

	A	B	C	D	E	F	G	H
1		Week 1	Week 3	Week 4				
2	Frank	5,000	3,000	3,000				
3	Jennie	5,000	6,000	5,000				
4	Paulo	3,000	4,000	5,000				
5	Rob	2,000	0,000					
6	Chris							
7	Sam							
8								
9								
10								

LESSON 3 You Try It Activities

5. Add Group Headers to a Report

You need to create a more reader-friendly version of the customer order details in the Sports database. You must add group headers to the details query and present the report to your boss.

Step-By-Step

1. In your **Sports** file, in the **Navigation** pane, open the **OrderWithDetail** query.
2. Create a report.
3. In the **Grouping & Totals** group, choose **Group & Sort**.
4. Click **Add a group**.
5. Select **CustomerName**.
6. **CHECK** Your screen should look like Figure 3.76.
7. Click **Add a group** and select **OrderID**.
8. Close the **Group, Sort, and Total** pane. Select the **Order ID** column and move the column to the left of **CustomerName**. Click **Report View**.
9. **CHECK** Your screen should look like Figure 3.77. **Save** the report as: Orders With Groups.
10. Close the report and query. Close the database. Exit **Access**.

Solution The solution file for this activity is the **Orders With Groups** report in the **Sports-SF.accdb** database.

FIGURE 3.76 CustomerName added

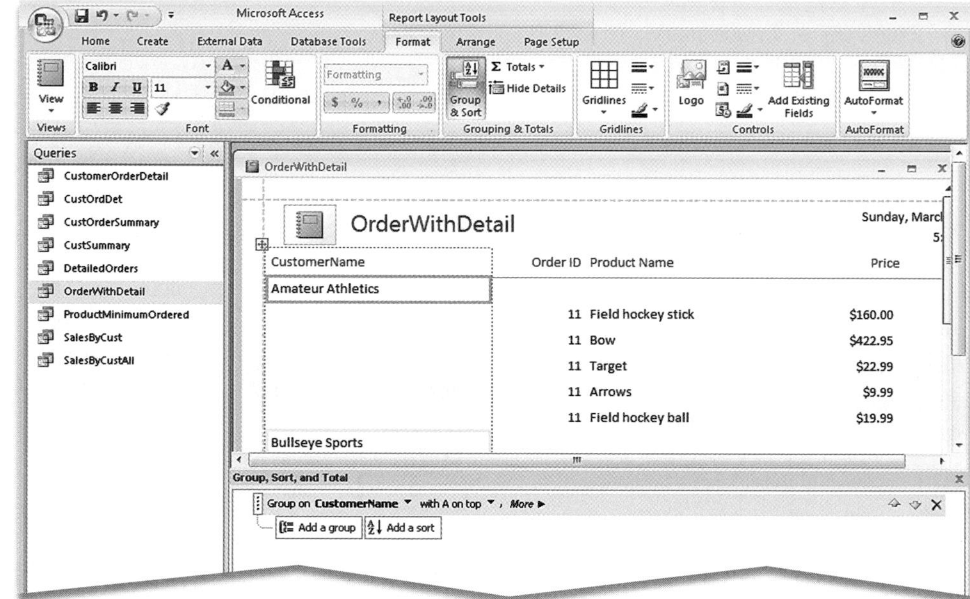

FIGURE 3.77 Orders With Groups report

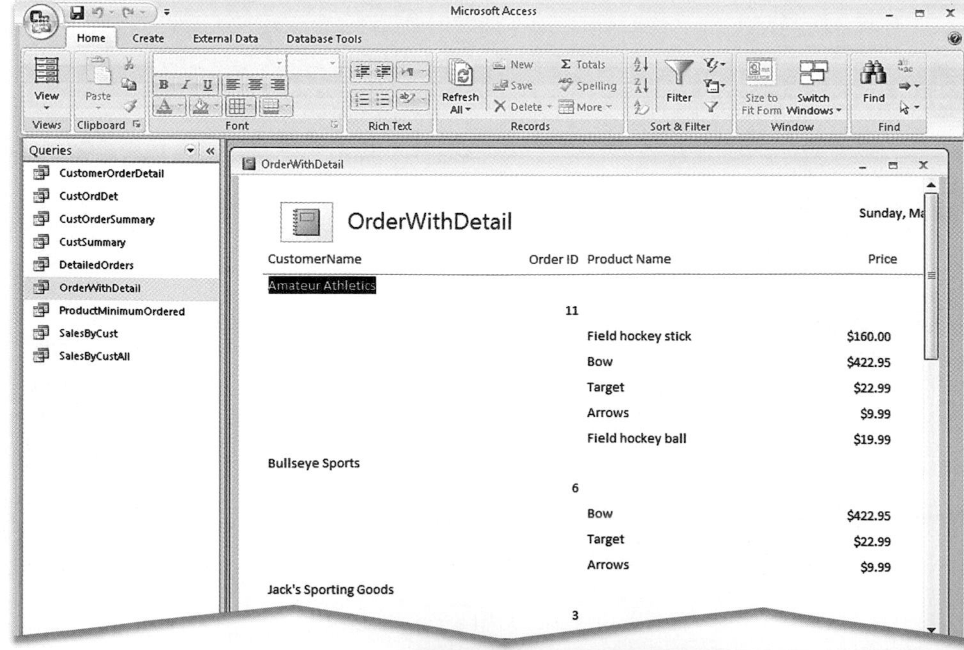

2. Insert and Delete Rows, Columns, and Cells

Follow the steps to complete the activity.

Solution Use the file **Clients2-SF** as a solution file for this activity.

Step-By-Step

1. Open your **Clients-1** file.
2. Save the file as: Clients-[your first initial and last name]2.
3. Click column heading **C**. Choose **Home>Cells**. Click the **Insert Cells** drop-down arrow. Select **Insert Sheet Columns**.
4. **CHECK** Your screen should look like Figure 2.27.
5. Click cell **C1**. Key: Week 2. Click row heading **5**. Click the **Insert Cells** drop-down arrow. Select **Insert Sheet Rows**. Click cell **A5**. Key: Quentin. Click cell **B5**. Key: 4,000.
6. Point to the lower right corner of cell **B5**. Drag the box to cover cells **B5** through **E5**.
7. Click cell **C5**. Click the **Insert Cells** drop-down arrow. Select **Insert Cells**. Select **Shift cells down**. Click **OK**.
8. **CHECK** Your screen should look like Figure 2.28.

FIGURE 2.27 Inserting columns

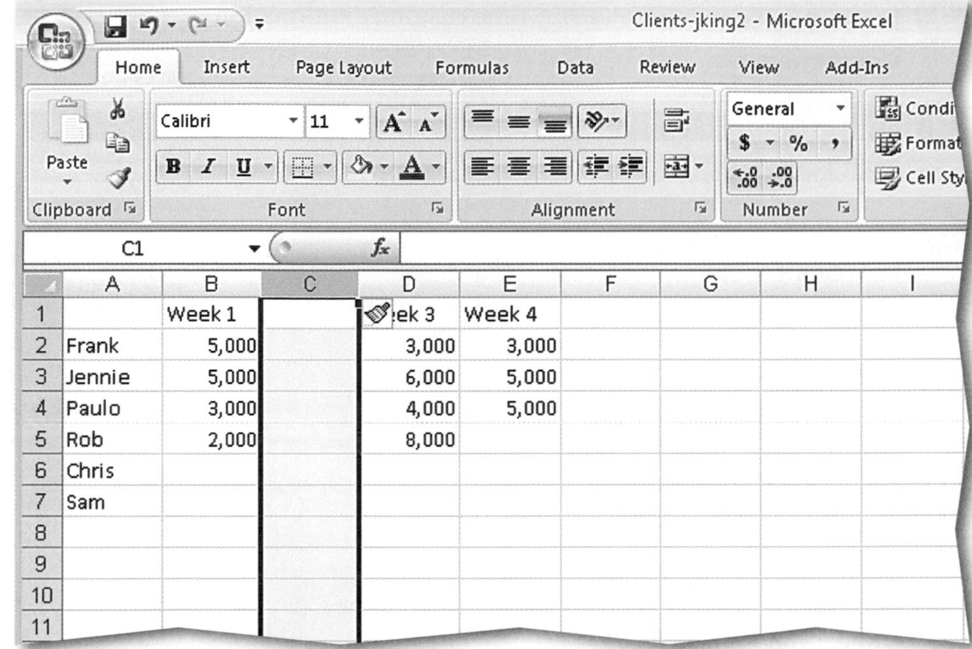

FIGURE 2.28 Inserting rows and cells

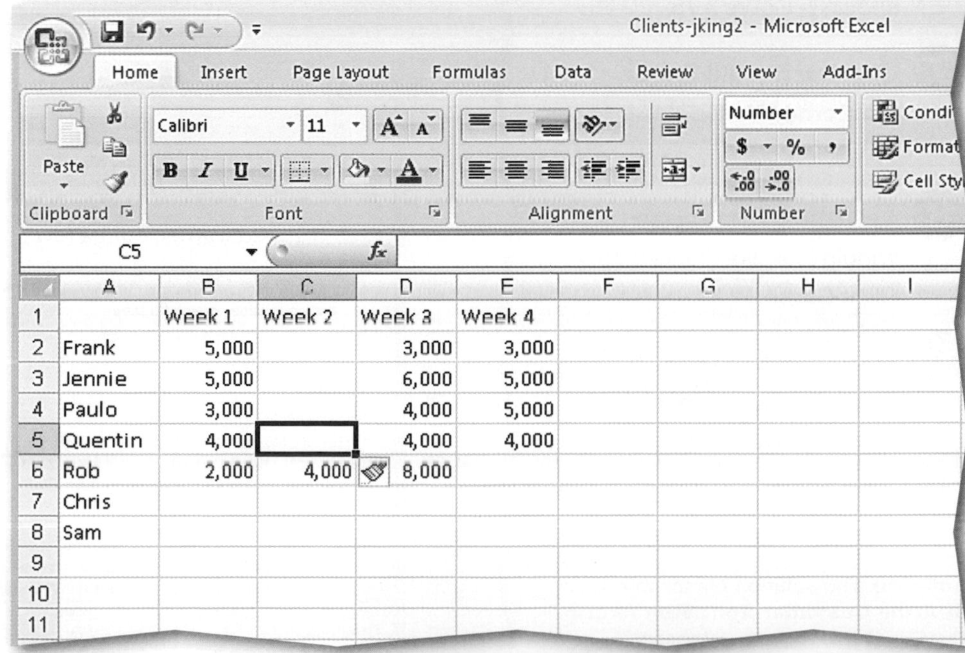

LESSON 3 You Try It Activities

Step-By-Step

1. In your **Sports** file, open the **Customer** table.
2. Choose **Create>Forms> Split Form** .
3. Change the name of the form from **Customer** to **Customer Split View**.
4. **CHECK** Your screen should look like Figure 3.74.
5. Locate the **Sven's Ski Shop** record in the split form. Note that the split form does not contain phone numbers for the ski shop.
6. Enter the phone numbers as shown in Figure 3.75.
7. Click **Sven's Ski Shop Customer Name** in the datasheet.
8. **CHECK** Your screen should look like Figure 3.75. Click **Close** [x].
9. Save your changes. In the **Save As** dialog box, key: Customer Split View.
10. Close the **Customer** table.

Solution The solution file for this activity is the **Customer Split View** form in the **Sports-SF.accdb** database.

4. Create a Split Form

Your boss wants to revise the Customer table in the Sports database. She says that the table needs to be easier to read, but the original table should still be viewable. She asks you to create a split form from the Customer table and to revise some of the customer information in the datasheet.

FIGURE 3.74 Customer Split View Form

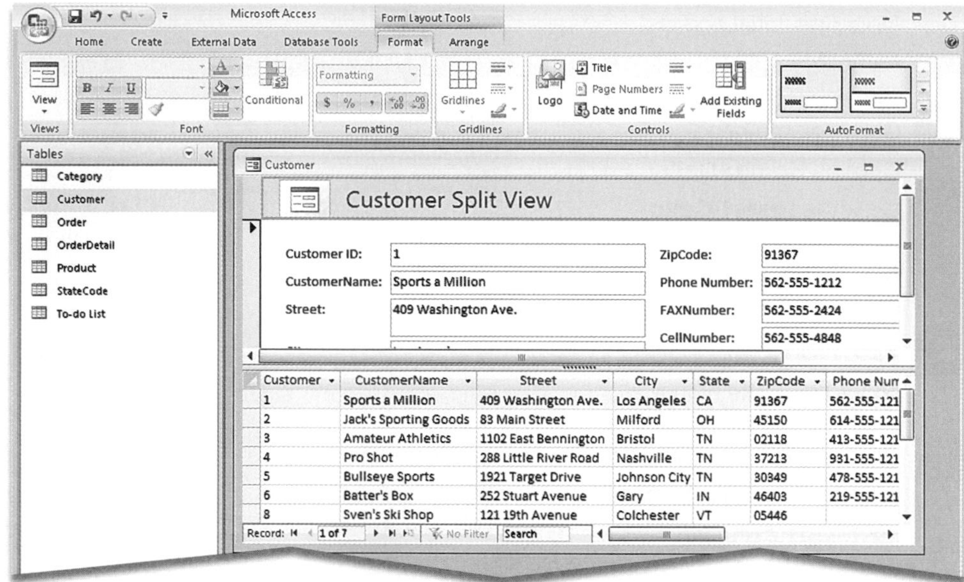

FIGURE 3.75 Changes made to Sven's Ski Shop in Split View form

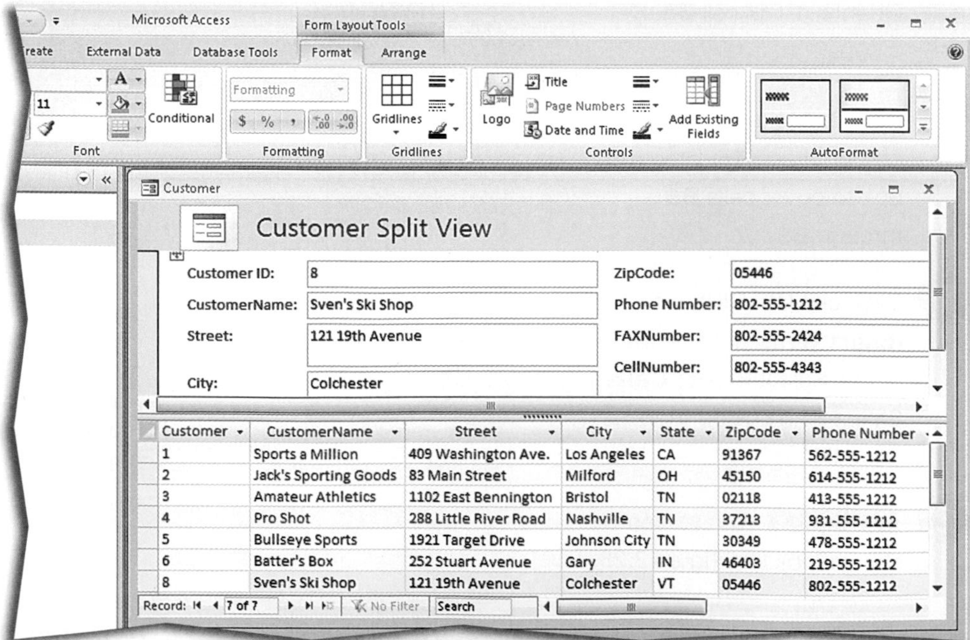

LESSON 2 Practice It Activities

3. Use AutoSum, AVERAGE, MIN, and MAX

Follow the steps to complete the activity. You must complete Practice It Activity 2 before doing this activity.

New Student Strategy If a student did not complete Practice It Activity 2, then the solution file for that activity can be used as a data file for this activity.

Step-By-Step

1. Open your **Clients-2** file. Save the file as: Clients-[your first initial and last name]3.
2. Select cells **B2** to **B5**. Point to the lower right corner of cell **B5**. Drag to cells **C2** through **C5** (see Figure 2.29).
3. Delete cells **A7** and **A8**. In cell **E6**, key: 5,000. In **A8** through **A11**, key the four cells shown in Figure 2.29.
4. Click cell **B8**. Choose **Formulas>Function Library>AutoSum**. Press ENTER.
5. Click the **AutoSum** drop-down arrow. Choose **Average**. Select cells **B2** to **B6**. Press ENTER.
6. Repeat step 5 but choose **Min**. Select cells **B2** to **B6**. Press ENTER.
7. Repeat step 6 but choose **Max**. Select cells **B2** to **B6**. Press ENTER.
8. **CHECK** Your screen should look like Figure 2.30. Save and close your file.

FIGURE 2.29 Copy cells

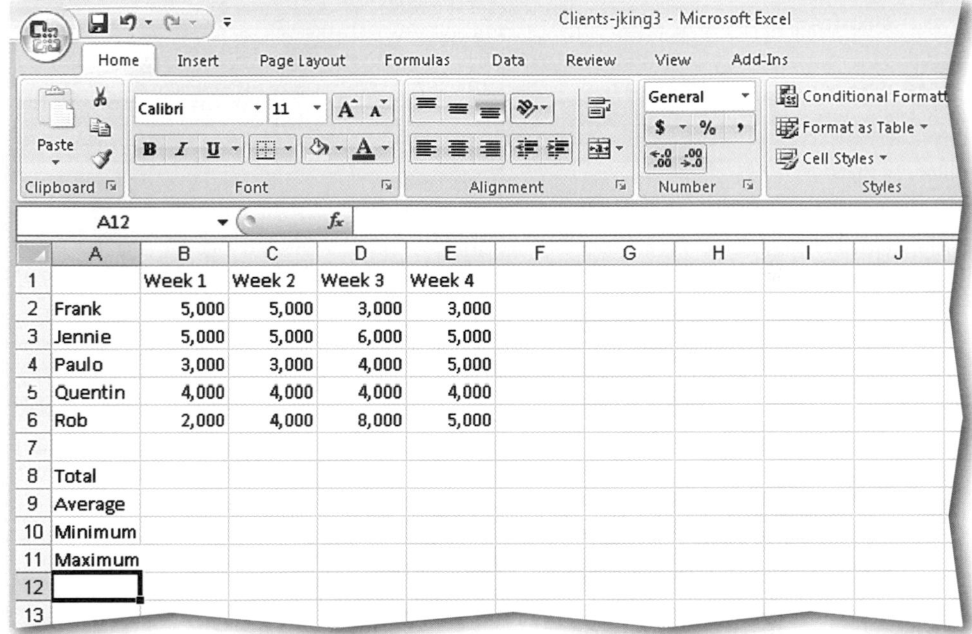

	A	B	C	D	E
1		Week 1	Week 2	Week 3	Week 4
2	Frank	5,000	5,000	3,000	3,000
3	Jennie	5,000	5,000	6,000	5,000
4	Paulo	3,000	3,000	4,000	5,000
5	Quentin	4,000	4,000	4,000	4,000
6	Rob	2,000	4,000	8,000	5,000
7					
8	Total				
9	Average				
10	Minimum				
11	Maximum				
12					
13					

Solution Use the file **Clients3-SF** as a solution file for this activity.

FIGURE 2.30 Function results

	A	B	C	D	E
1		Week 1	Week 2	Week 3	Week 4
2	Frank	5,000	5,000	3,000	3,000
3	Jennie	5,000	5,000	6,000	5,000
4	Paulo	3,000	3,000	4,000	5,000
5	Quentin	4,000	4,000	4,000	4,000
6	Rob	2,000	4,000	8,000	5,000
7					
8	Total	19,000			
9	Average	3,800			
10	Minimum	2,000			
11	Maximum	5,000			
12					
13					

LESSON 3 Practice It Activities

3. Create Labels

Follow the steps to complete the activity. You must complete Practice It Activity 2 before doing this activity.

New Student Strategy If a student did not complete Practice It Activity 2, then the solution file for that activity can be used as a data file for this

Step-By-Step

1. In your **Sports** file, open the **Product** table.
2. Choose **Create>Reports> Labels** to open the **Label Wizard**. Select **Mailing Labels**. Click **Next** twice.
3. In the **Available Fields** box, double-click **Category** to move it to the **Prototype label** box.
4. Press ENTER. Double-click **ProductName** to move it to the label. Add the **Price** field to the same line.
5. In the label, click between **ProductName** and **Price**. Add a space and a dollar sign ($).
6. **CHECK** Your screen should look like Figure 3.72.
7. Click **Next**. Double-click **Category** to move it to the **Sort by** box. Click **Next**.
8. For the name, key: Inventory Labels. Click **Finish**.
9. **CHECK** Your screen should look like Figure 3.73. Close the labels and the **Product** table.

FIGURE 3.72 Label fields

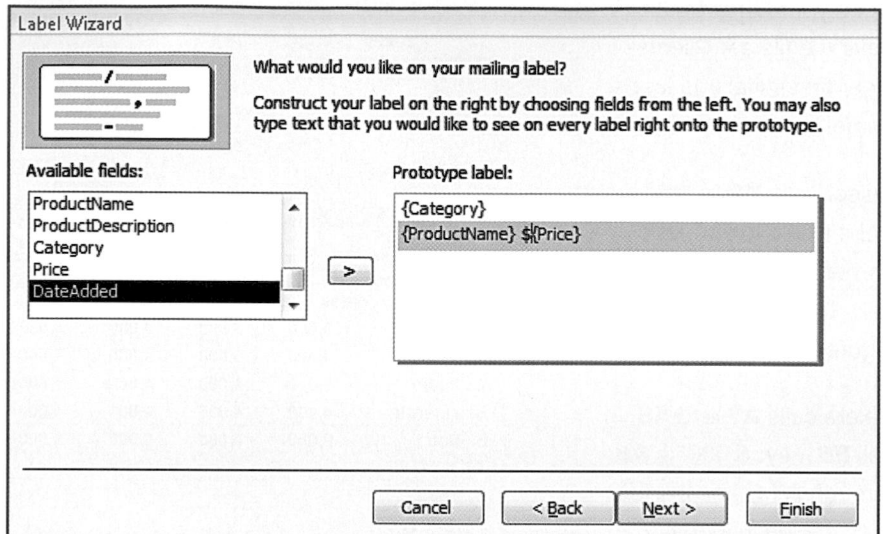

Solution The solution file for this activity is the **Inventory Labels** report in the **Sports-SF.accdb** database.

FIGURE 3.73 Completed labels

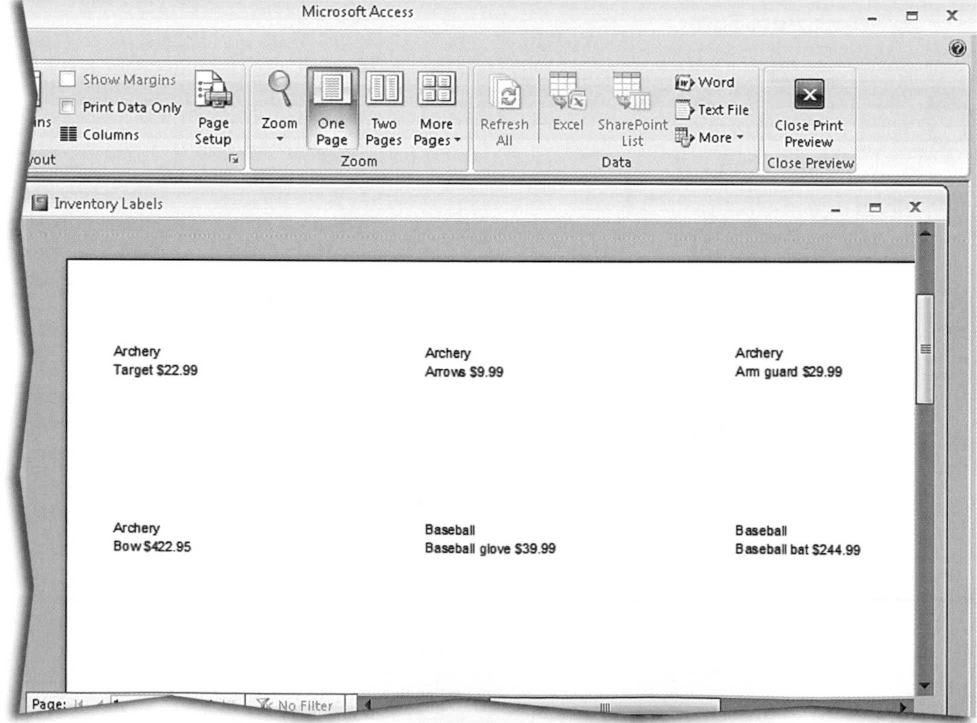

LESSON 2 You Try It Activities

4. Edit a Worksheet

You are creating a chart that shows your classmates' favorite sports teams. While proofreading your chart, you notice that there are some errors you need to correct.

Step-By-Step

1. Open the data file **Teams.xlsx**. Close the task pane if necessary.
2. CHECK Your screen should look like Figure 2.31. Save the file as: Teams-[your first initial and last name]4.
3. In cell **A10**, change **Jessic** to **Jessica**.
4. Clear the contents of cell **A11**.
5. Use **Replace** to change every **Jagwars** to **Jaguars**.
6. In cell **D3**, change **RED** to **Red**.
7. Click cell **D2**. Shift the cells in the column down so **D2** becomes cell **D3**.
8. Move the contents of cell **C11** to cell **D2**.
9. Press CTRL + HOME.
10. CHECK Your screen should look like Figure 2.32. Save and close your file.

Solution Use the file **Teams4-SF** as a solution file for this activity.

FIGURE 2.31 Favorite teams chart

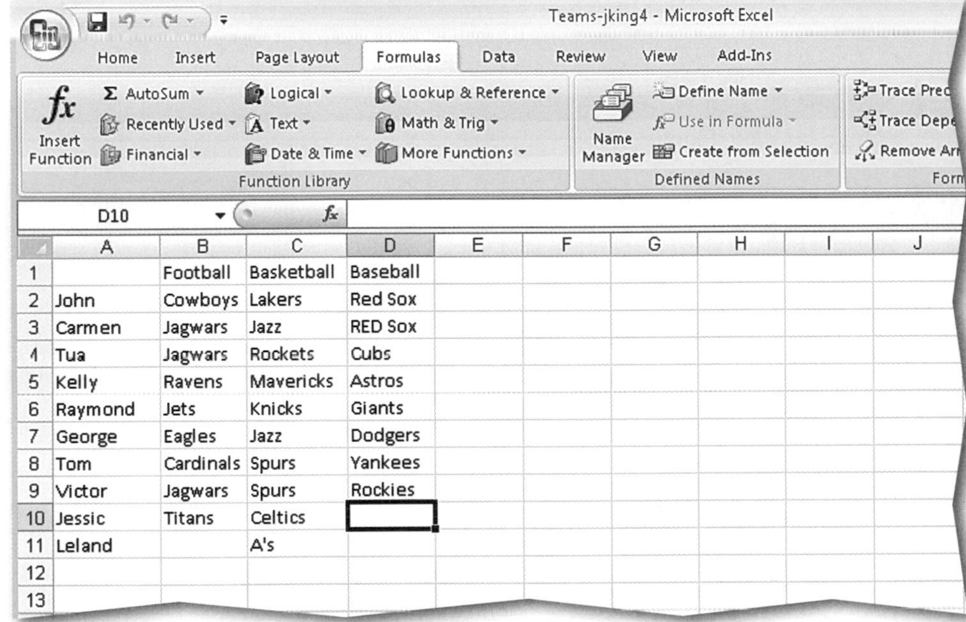

FIGURE 2.32 Favorite teams chart after editing

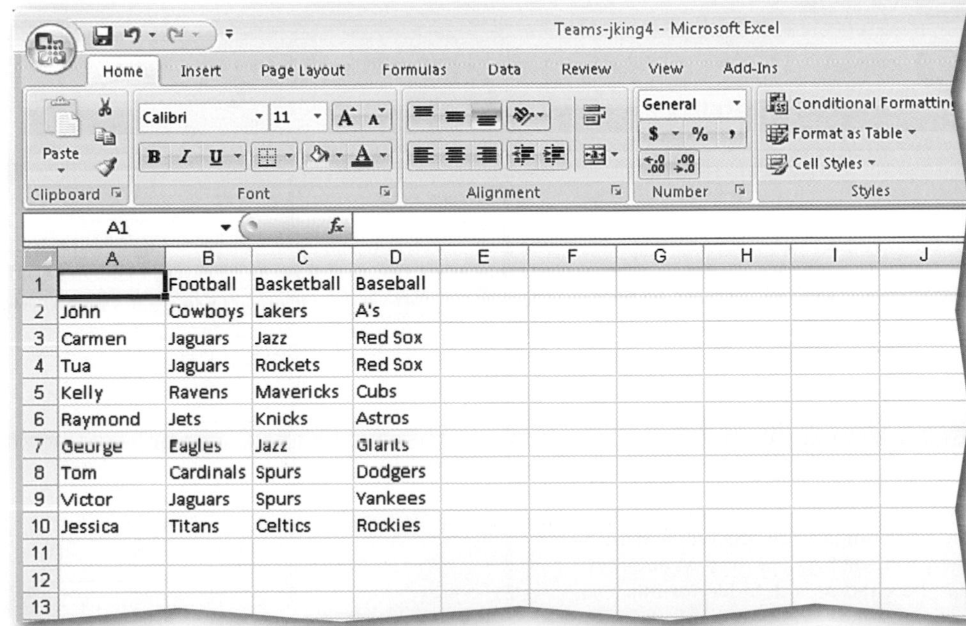

Step-By-Step

1. In your **Sports** file, open the **OrderWithDetail** query.
2. **CHECK** Your screen should look like Figure 3.70.
3. Choose **Create>Reports> Report**.
4. **CHECK** Your screen should look like Figure 3.71.
5. Click **Close**.
6. Click **Yes** to close the report and save changes.
7. In the **Save As** dialog box, key: Order Detail.
8. Click **OK**.
9. Close the **OrderWithDetail** query.

Solution The solution for this exercise is the **Order Detail** report in the **Sports-SF.accdb** data file.

New Student Strategy If a student did not complete Practice It Activity 1, then the solution file for that activity can be used as a data file for this activity.

2. Create Simple Reports

Follow the steps to complete the activity. You must complete Practice It Activity 1 before doing this activity.

FIGURE 3.70 OrderWithDetail query

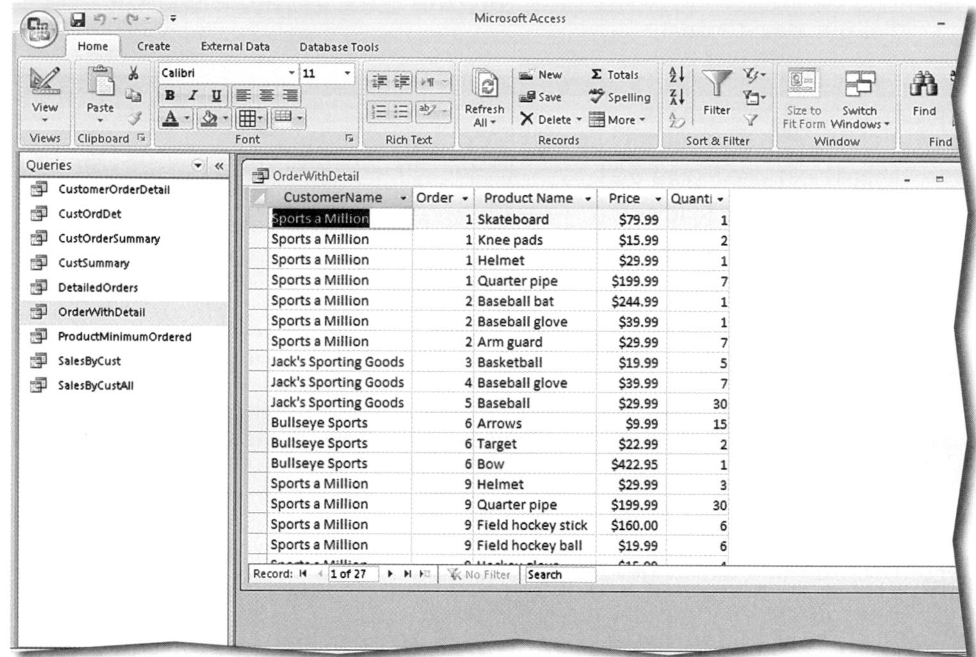

FIGURE 3.71 Order Detail Report

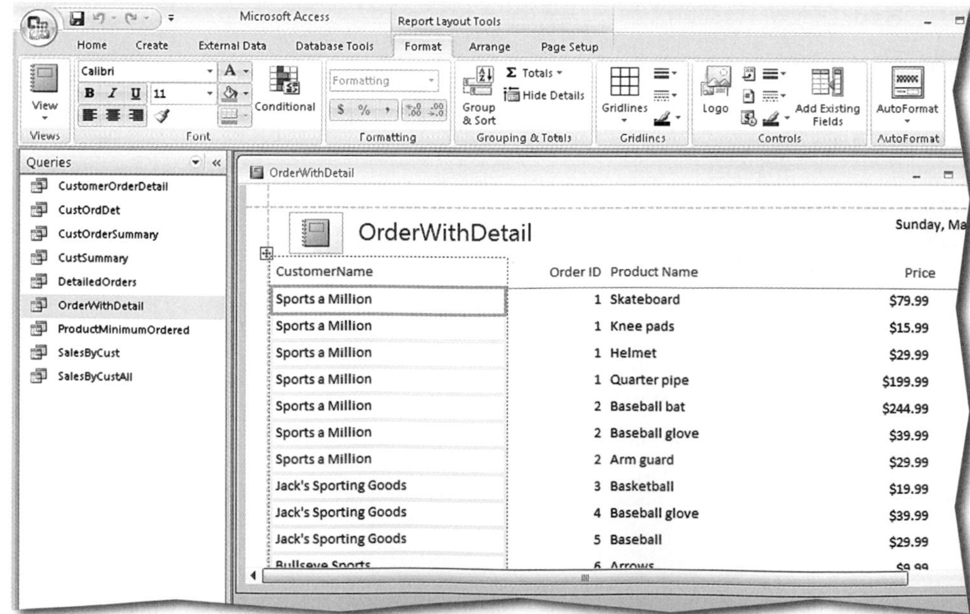

LESSON 2 You Try It Activities

Step-By-Step

1. Create a new workbook. Save the blank workbook as: Sporting-[your first initial and last name]5.
2. In cells **A2** through **A5**, key the four items shown in Figure 2.33.
3. In cells **A7** through **A10**, key the labels shown in Figure 2.33.
4. In cells **B1** through **G1**, key the months **January**, **February**, **March**, **April**, **May**, and **June**.
5. Enter the numbers as shown in Figure 2.33.
6. **CHECK** Your screen should look like Figure 2.33.
7. Use the **AutoSum** functions on the **Formula** tab to determine the **total**, **average**, **minimum**, and **maximum** for each month's sales.
8. **CHECK** Your screen should look like Figure 2.34.
9. Save and close your file.

NCLB/Math (Number and Operations) Have students determine which item sold the most and least in each month. Ask them to describe why they think some items sold better during different months.

5. Compute Sales

You are a salesperson at a sporting goods store. Your supervisor has given you the amount of units sold for four items during the months of January through June. The items are baseballs, skis, sleds, and tents. He wants you to create a workbook to analyze the sales.

Solution Use the file Sporting5-SF as a solution file for this activity.

FIGURE 2.33 Sporting goods sales

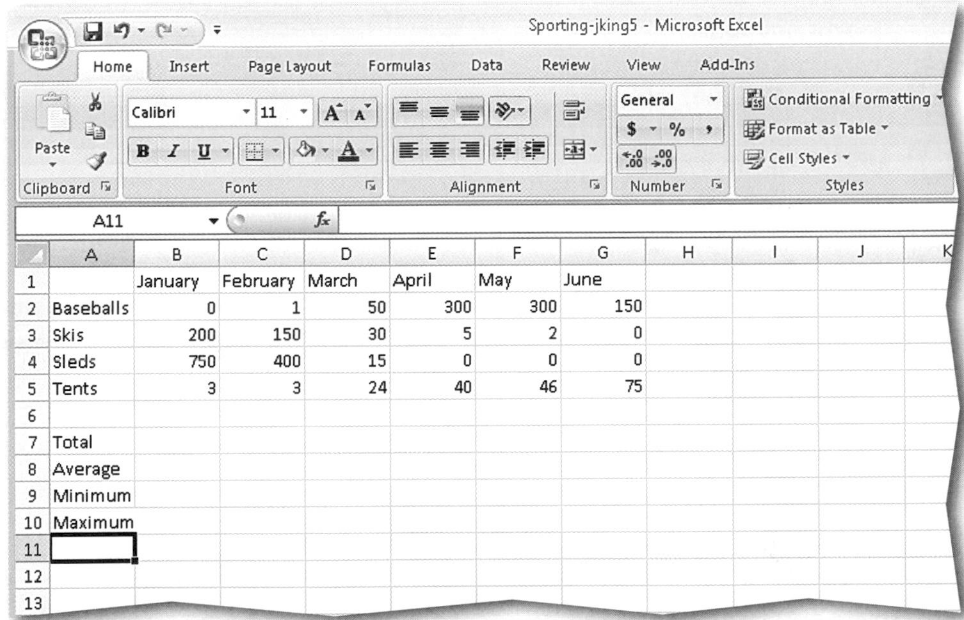

	A	B	C	D	E	F	G
1		January	February	March	April	May	June
2	Baseballs	0	1	50	300	300	150
3	Skis	200	150	30	5	2	0
4	Sleds	750	400	15	0	0	0
5	Tents	3	3	24	40	46	75
6							
7	Total						
8	Average						
9	Minimum						
10	Maximum						

FIGURE 2.34 Function results

	A	B	C	D	E	F	G
1		January	February	March	April	May	June
2	Baseballs	0	1	50	300	300	150
3	Skis	200	150	30	5	2	0
4	Sleds	750	400	15	0	0	0
5	Tents	3	3	24	40	46	75
6							
7	Total	953	554	119	345	348	225
8	Average	238.25	138.5	29.75	86.25	87	56.25
9	Minimum	0	1	15	0	0	0
10	Maximum	750	400	50	300	300	150

1. Create Simple Forms

Step-By-Step

1. Start **Access**.
2. Locate and open your **Sports.accdb** file.
3. Open the **Product** table.
4. CHECK Your screen should look like Figure 3.68.
5. Choose **Create>Forms>Form** .
6. CHECK Your screen should look like Figure 3.69.
7. Click **Close** x.
8. Click **Yes** to save changes.
9. In the **Save As** dialog box, key: Product Form.
10. Click **OK**.
11. Close the **Product** table.

Solution The solution for this exercise is the **Product Form** of the **Sports-SF.accdb** file.

Follow the steps to complete the activity.

FIGURE 3.68 Sports database Product table

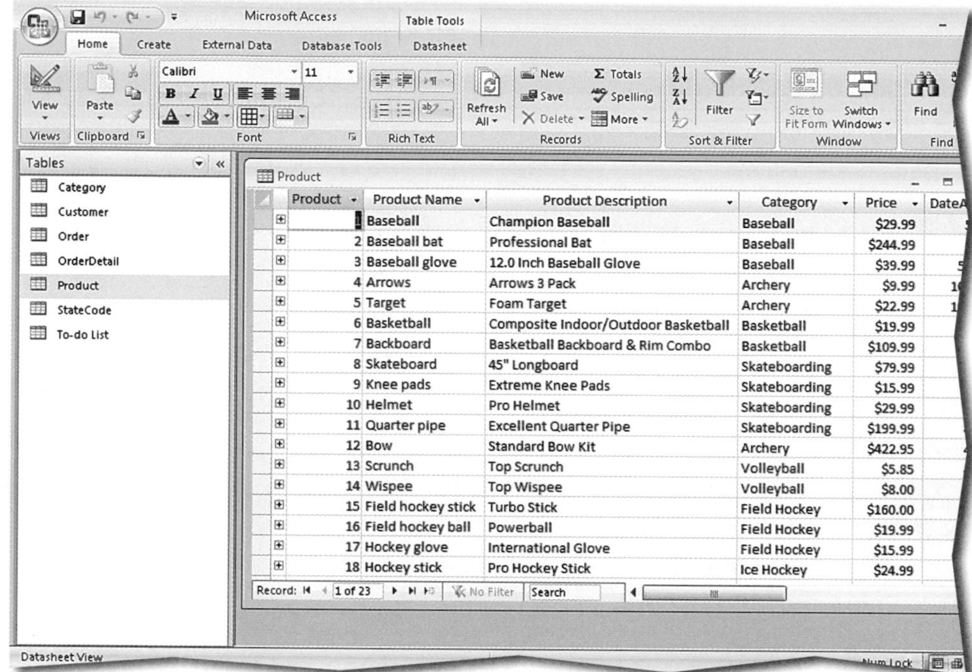

FIGURE 3.69 Product Form

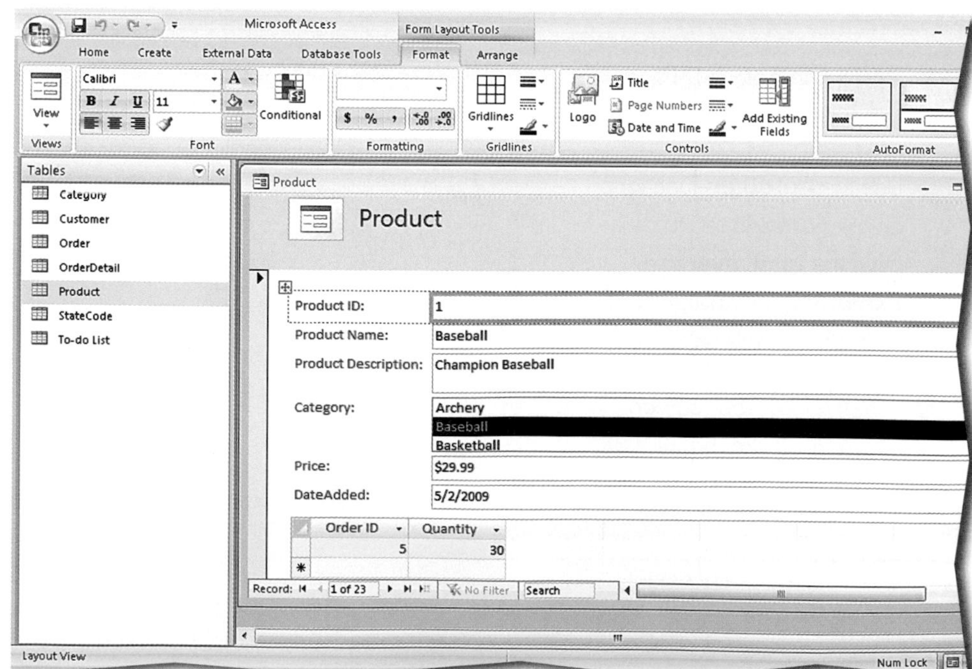

Beyond the Classroom Activity Student workbooks should show two labeled columns: "Sources of Income," listing at least five items for sales, and "Expenses," listing at least five expense items, such as rent, salaries, and advertising.

Standards at Work Activity Students' workbooks should show the company name keyed in cell A1. A hyperlink from the company name should open the workbook students created in the Beyond the Classroom Activity.

21st Century Skills Activity Student workbooks should include one column with at least six items and one column with amounts spent. Have students review their workbooks to see how they might budget more responsibly.

NCLB/Math (Number and Operations) Students should understand that the MIN and MAX functions are effective tools when looking for ways to cut back on expenses.

glencoe.com

Go to the **Online Learning Center** to complete the following review activities.

Online Self Check
To test your knowledge of the material, click **Unit 2> Lesson 2** and choose **Self Checks**.

Interactive Review
To review the main points of this lesson, click **Unit 2> Lesson 2** and choose **Interactive Review**.

6. Beyond the Classroom Activity

Math: Identify Income and Expenses You are applying for a job working in the accounting department of a furniture store. The owner wants to check your spreadsheet skills. Create a new workbook. Then perform the following tasks:

- Label the first column "Sources of Income". In this column, list at least five products sold by the store (such as sofas, chairs, and tables).
- Label the second column "Expenses". In this column, list at least five things that the store must spend money on each month (such as rent, salaries, and gas for the delivery truck).

Save your workbook as: e2rev-[your first initial and last name]6.

7. Standards at Work Activity

Microsoft Certified Application Specialist Correlation
Excel 2.3 *Format Cells and Cell Content*

Use a Hyperlink Create a new workbook and insert a hyperlink to the workbook you created for the owner of the furniture store. To do this:

- Label the first column "Prospective Employers".
- Give the furniture store a name and key the name into cell A2.
- Create a hyperlink to the workbook you saved above in cell A2.
- Key another employer that has a job opening that you are thinking of applying for into cell A3.
- Create a hyperlink to a new workbook that contains at least five things you will need to provide on a personal data form (such as the position you are applying for, education, and employment history).

Save your workbook as: e2rev-[your first initial and last name]7.

8. 21st Century Skills Activity

Create a Budget Identify at least six things that you spend money on each month. You might include food, clothes, movies, and music. Make sure to include all of your major expenses. Then, in a new workbook:

- Key the items you identified into column A. Enter one item per row.
- Enter the amount that you spend on each item into column B.
- Use AutoSum to calculate your total expenses.

Use MAX and MIN to identify items you spend the most and least amount of money on. Include these at the bottom of your worksheet. Save your workbook as: e2rev-[your first initial and last name]8.

LESSON 3 After You Read

Vocabulary

Key Terms

aggregate function
AutoFormat
control
criteria
datasheet
find
form
group header
Layout View
multiple item form
PivotTable
replace
sort
split form
subform
wildcard

Academic Vocabulary

document
revise

Answer to Vocabulary Activity
Answers will vary. Students should note that the dictionary definition may differ slightly or greatly from the way the application term is defined.

Review Vocabulary

Complete the following statements on a separate piece of paper. Choose from the Vocabulary list on the left to complete the statements.

1. Layout View allows you to make changes to a database object while viewing the data. (p. 440)
2. You can use a(n) aggregate function to gather together data from different records. (p. 455)
3. A(n) subform is inserted inside another form. (p. 435)
4. You can apply AutoFormat to both forms and reports. (p. 457)
5. The Access Report Wizard allows you to revise, or make changes to, a simple report. (p. 449)

Vocabulary Activity

6. Each industry or area of study will sometimes give a slightly different meaning to a familiar word.
   A. Use a dictionary to look up the meaning of the words in the vocabulary list.
   B. For compound words that do not have a definition, such as PivotTable, look up the individual words that make up the compound word. Write down the dictionary definition that is closest to the definition of the term. If necessary, explain why you think the two definitions are different.

Review Key Concepts

Answer the following questions on a separate piece of paper.

7. Which button is used to give you a total of a column of figures? (p. 455)
   A. Sum (circled)
   B. Totals
   C. Group & Sort
   D. Apply Filter
8. What feature can make it easier for you to sort information into groups in a Report? (p. 453)
   A. Control
   B. PivotTable
   C. Group Header (circled)
   D. Form Header
9. What tool allows you to format controls in a form or report? (p. 442)
   A. Property Sheet (circled)
   B. Add Existing Fields tool
   C. Bound Objects frame
   D. Report Header
10. Which wizard would help you in setting up a mailing list? (p. 459)
    A. Import Table Wizard
    B. AutoReport Wizard
    C. Label Wizard (circled)
    D. Export Text Wizard
11. Which type of form includes both a datasheet and a form together? (p. 433)
    A. AutoForm
    B. subform
    C. multiple item form
    D. split form (circled)

LESSON 2 Challenge Yourself Projects

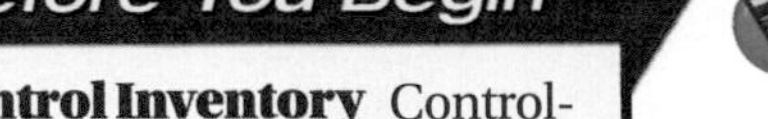

Before You Begin

Control Inventory Controlling inventory is an essential part of managing a budget. These projects teach you how to use a spreadsheet to create, track, and update an inventory to meet customer business needs.

Reflect Once you complete the projects, open a Word document and key a paragraph that answers the following:

1. What are the benefits of using AVG, MIN, MAX when creating an inventory in Excel?
2. Which sandwich requires the most inventory, which the least?
3. Which is the most and least expensive sandwich to produce?

Answers Rubrics for each Challenge Yourself Project are available at **glencoe.com**. You may want to download the rubrics and make them available to students as they complete each project.

9. Track Inventory

LEVEL This is an intermediate level project.

Math: Create a Worksheet and Convert Quantities The Tastee Sandwich Shop has hired you to do inventory. Their sandwiches include:

- Roast beef
- Ham
- Chicken
- Turkey
- Veggies

Create a new Excel workbook. Use information in the data file **Sandwich .docx**. In one column, list the types of sandwiches. In a second column, enter the number of ounces of filling in each sandwich. In a third column, show how much of each filling is available. Convert the amount of meat from pounds to ounces (one pound is 16 ounces) and enter the number of ounces in column four. Name each column.

Save as: e2rev-[your first initial and last name]9.

Solution Use the file **e2rev9-SF** as a solution file for Project 9.

10. Look Ahead

LEVEL This is an intermediate level project.

Math: Add Columns and Analyze Data Your boss wants you to track how quickly the items are being sold. Open your **e2rev-9** workbook. Add a column to the workbook named **Number of sandwiches sold per day**. Then, add another column named **Filling needed per week**. Using the information in the data file **Sandwich.docx**, enter into the columns the number or sandwiches sold per day and how much of each type of filling the shop needs for one week.

Save as: e2rev-[your first initial and last name]10.

Solution Use the file **e2rev10-SF** as a solution file for Project 10.

11. Add Products

LEVEL This is an advanced level project.

Math: Calculate and Analyze Data Two new sandwiches have been added. You need to add these items to your inventory. Open your **e2rev-10** workbook. Then, using the information in the data file **Sandwich.docx**, insert two rows between "Chicken" and "Veggies" on your chart.

- Name the rows for the two new sandwiches. Fill in all the cells in each row. Use the other rows as models.
- Use AutoSum to calculate the total **Number of sandwiches sold per day** and **Filling needed per week** for those columns. Find the AVG, MIN, and MAX in each column.

Solution Use the file **e2rev11-SF** as a solution file for Project 11.

Identify the type of sandwiches you sell the most and least of in a day. Then identify the filling you use the most and least of per week. Save as: e2rev-[your first initial and last name]11.

MATH MATTERS

Showing a Profit or Loss

Your summer lawn-care business keeps you busy. Every day, you record the cash and checks you receive, and you keep all expense receipts. However, the overall status of your finances is a mystery. Are you making more than you spend? A profit and loss statement will show you how your business is doing.

What Is a Profit and Loss Statement?

A profit and loss statement follows this basic formula:

Revenue − Expenses = Net Profit (or Net Loss)

If your revenues are higher than your expenses, your business has earned money. If your expenses are higher than your revenue, your business has lost money. To calculate the revenue of your lawn-care business, add the money customers have paid you. To calculate your expenses, add the costs of running your business (such as flyers, new rakes, and lawn mower fuel). Finally, subtract your expenses from your revenue. The result is your net profit or loss.

Large businesses issue profit and loss statements, also called income statements. Their reports are much more complex, but they follow the same basic pattern.

Using a Profit and Loss Statement

If you know you are making a profit, you might buy a new lawn mower or hire someone to work with you. If you are losing money, you can decide how to reduce expenses or expand your business to increase your income.

You can use a profit and loss statement to keep track of your business's income and expenses.

NCLB/Math (Algebra) Reinforce the importance of the basic formula for a profit and loss statement by asking students to create a profit and loss statement for a summer lawn care business. Ask students to calculate revenue and expenses. Then, ask them to explain whether they had a net profit or loss and what they plan to do with the profit or how they plan to increase income.

Skillbuilder answers can be found on page TM83.

SKILLBUILDER

1. **Identify** What is the basic formula for a profit and loss statement?
2. **Prepare** Invent a business, and write a profit and loss statement for it. Include details of income and business expenses. Be creative!
3. **Discuss** Why is it important to know the status of your business's finances?
4. **Evaluate** Do an Internet search for profit and loss statement software. Key a short paragraph about which software you think would be best for a small company.

LESSON 3 Format Data and Content

In this lesson you will learn to format, or adjust the appearance of, Excel worksheets. You will change the way the font looks and adjust the size of rows and columns. You will also learn to adjust alignment and to insert and size SmartArt graphics.

Key Concepts

- Change font, font size, font style, and font color
- Convert text to columns
- Apply cell and table styles
- Modify the size of rows and columns
- Hide and unhide rows, columns, and worksheets
- Change horizontal and vertical alignment
- Insert, move, and modify SmartArt graphics

Standards

The following standards are covered in this lesson. Refer to pages xxv and 715 for a description of the standards listed here.

ISTE Standards Correlation

NETS•S

1a, 1c, 2b, 3d, 4c, 5c, 6a, 6b

Microsoft Certified Application Specialist

Excel

1.1, 1.3, 1.5, 2.1, 2.2, 2.3, 2.4, 4.4

21st CENTURY SKILLS

See page TM72 for answer to 21st Century Skills.

Even when you are organized and have a set plan, the unexpected can happen. In order to meet unexpected challenges successfully, you must be flexible. One of the best ways to prepare for the unexpected is to have a backup plan. First, make plans for how you expect things to turn out. Then, come up with an alternate plan in case your original plan does not work out. Your backup plan will help you to be flexible if you need to change plans. For example, if you are taking a car trip, you might want to plan an alternate route to reach your destination. That way, if a road is blocked, you will still get where you need to go. *Can you think of a time when you had to be flexible in order to meet your goals?*

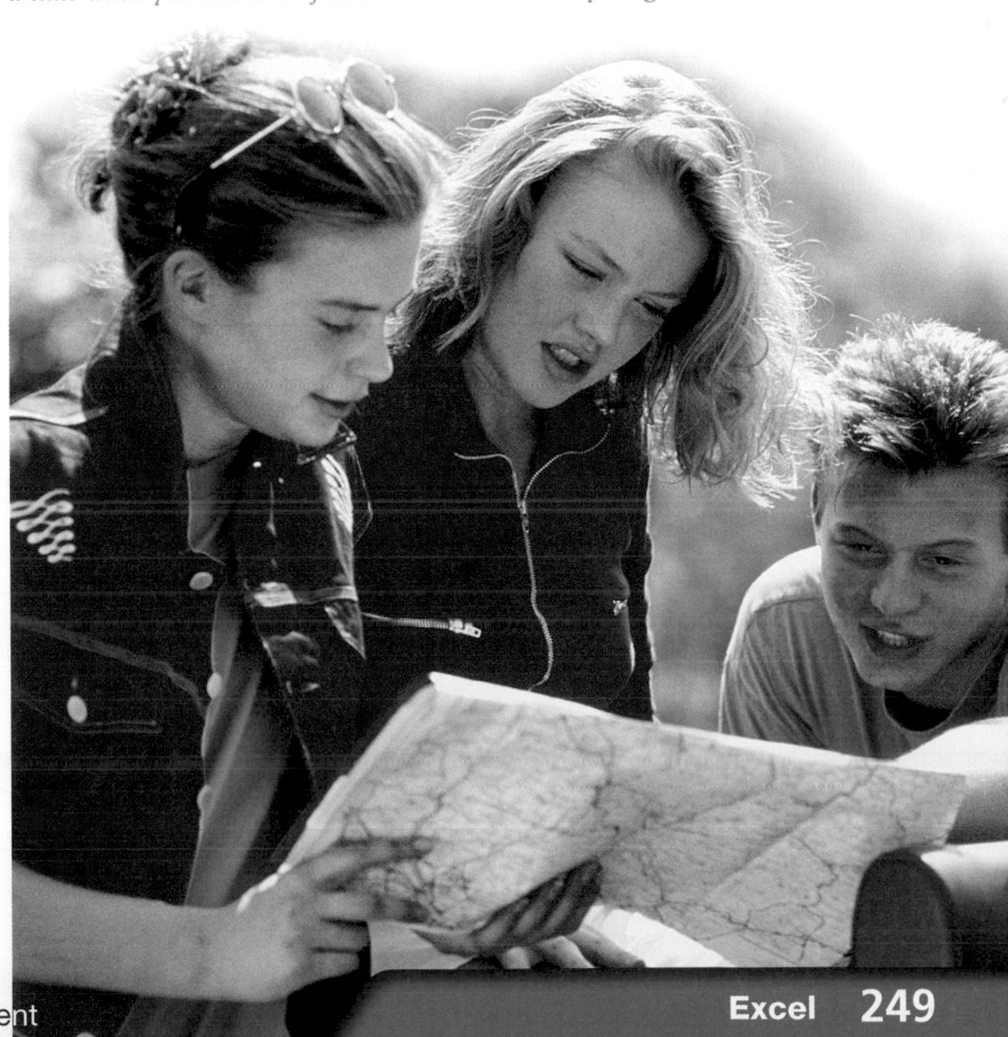

Step-By-Step

EXERCISE 3-21 (Continued)
Create Labels Using the Label Wizard

10 Click between **City** and **State** in the label, and add a comma and a space. Add a space between **State** and **ZipCode**.

11 CHECK Your screen should look like Figure 3.66.

12 Click **Next**.

13 Double-click **State** to move it to the **Sort by** box. Click **Next**.

14 For the name of the label report, key: Customer Labels. Click **Finish**.

15 CHECK Your screen should look like Figure 3.67. Notice that Access displays the labels in **Print Preview**.

16 Click **Close** to close the labels. Close the table.

17 Exit **Access**.

Troubleshooter

When using the Label Wizard, you can only add fields with the data types **Text**, **Number**, **Date/Time**, **Currency**, **Yes/No**, or **Attachment**.

Differentiated Instruction/ Advanced Students Have students change the formatting of the labels in **Design View** and print them.

Solution Use the file **Sports-SF .accdb** as a solution file for Exercises 3-1 through Exercise 3-21.

FIGURE 3.66 Filling out label in Label Wizard

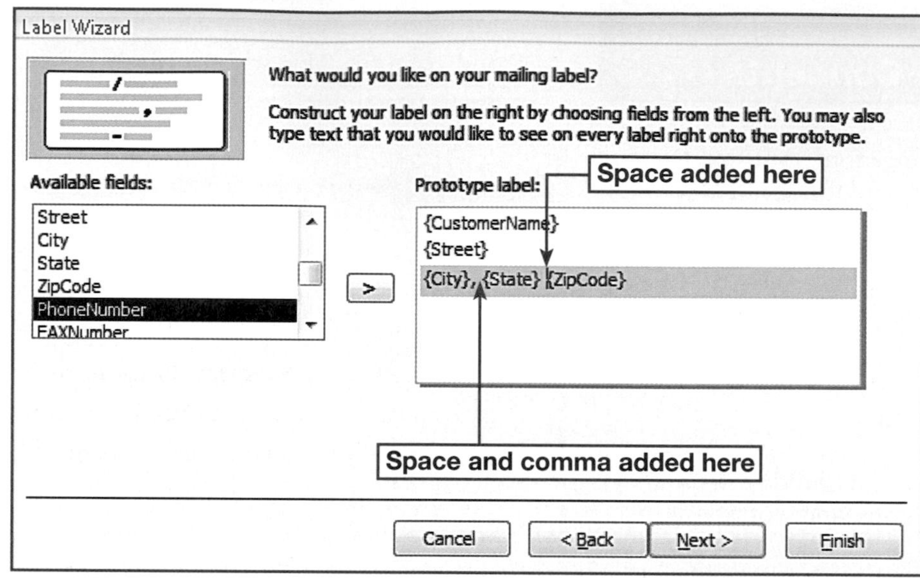

FIGURE 3.67 Completed Customer Labels

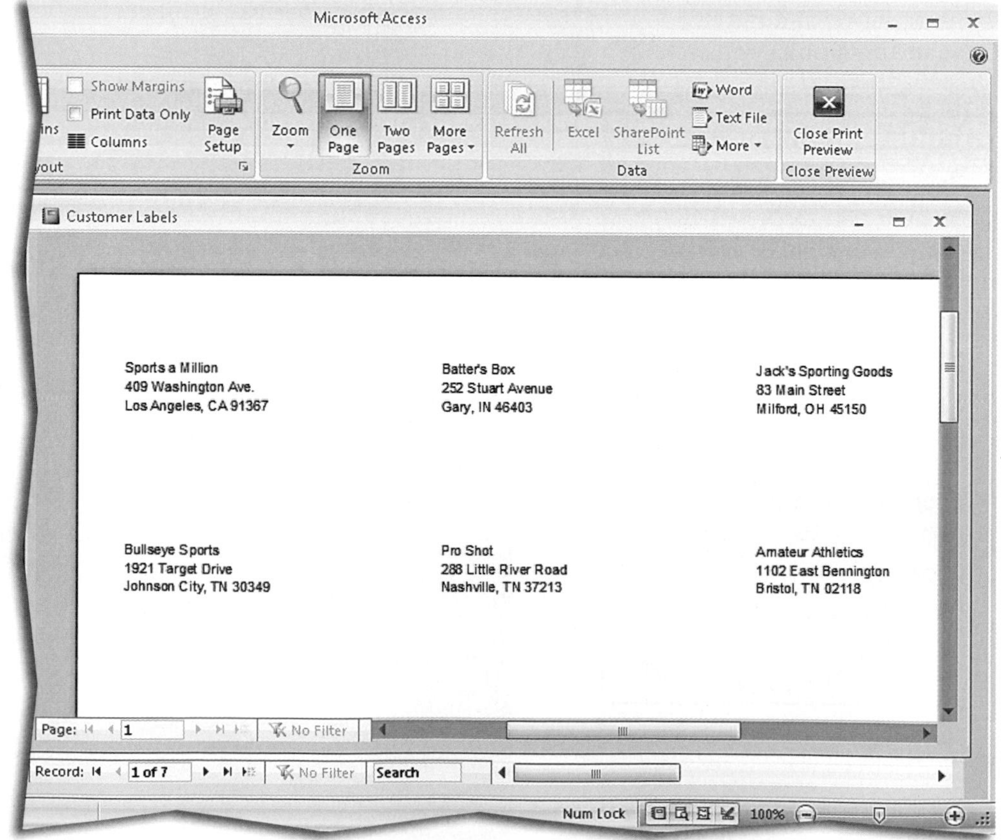

LESSON 3 Reading Guide

Before You Read

See page TM42 for English Learner activity suggestions.

Use Notes When you are reading, keep a notepad handy. Whenever you come upon a section or term you are unfamiliar with, write the word or a question on the paper. After you have finished the lesson, look up the terms or try to answer your questions based on what you have read.

Read To Learn

- Create and modify tables to showcase data.
- Explore ways to format content in order to have an easily understandable worksheet.
- Place and modify graphics in an Excel spreadsheet.

Main Idea

Excel has many ways to format the data and overall look of a spreadsheet.

Vocabulary

Key Terms

background
border
cell style
delimiter
font
font style
graphical list
horizontal alignment
SmartArt
table style
theme
vertical alignment

Academic Vocabulary

These words appear in your reading and on your tests. Make sure you know their meanings.

convey
distinct

Quick Write Activity

Explain On a separate sheet of paper, write a paragraph that explains the kind of formatting you use in your Word documents to organize and present information. How might you use formatting such as **boldface**, *italics*, underlining, fonts, borders, colors, and more in a workbook that contains financial data for an entire year? Try to come up with several different examples.

Study Skills

Take Good Notes Taking good notes and reviewing them frequently reinforces what you learned and helps you prepare for tests.

Academic Standards

English Language Arts

NCTE 5 Employ a wide range of strategies while writing to communicate effectively with different audiences.

Math

NCTM (Number and Operations) Understand numbers, ways of representing numbers, relationships among numbers, and number systems.

NCTM (Number and Operations) Understand meanings and operations and how they relate to one another.

NCTM (Algebra) Represent and analyze mathematical situations and structures using algebraic symbols.

Step-By-Step

1. In your **Sports** file, open the **Customer** table.
2. Choose **Create>Reports>Labels** to open the **Label Wizard** (see Figure 3.64).
3. Select the first label size in the list. Click **Next**.
4. Read the text on the next Wizard page. When you are finished, click **Next**.
5. In the **Available Fields** box, double-click **CustomerName** to move it to the **Prototype label** box.
6. Press ENTER to move the cursor to the next line.
7. Double-click **Street**. Press ENTER.
8. Double-click the **City**, **State**, and **ZipCode** fields to move them over on the same line.
9. **CHECK** Your screen should look like Figure 3.65.

Continued on the next page.

You Should Know

You can customize a label by clicking **Customize** on the first page of the **Label Wizard** and then clicking **New**. The **New Label** dialog box will display.

EXERCISE 3-21
Create Labels Using the Label Wizard

The Label Wizard allows you to quickly create labels based on information stored in your database tables. You can easily create address labels for a customer mailing list or to send orders to customers.

Step-By-Step Tip In **Step 3**, have students select a different label type, if necessary.

FIGURE 3.64 Label Wizard

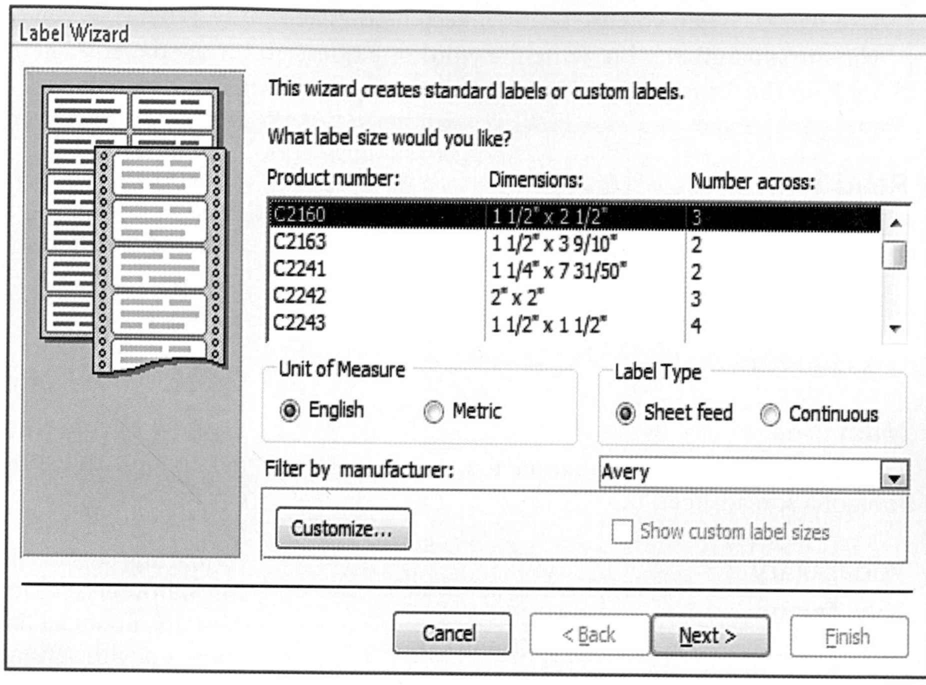

FIGURE 3.65 Adding fields to Prototype label.

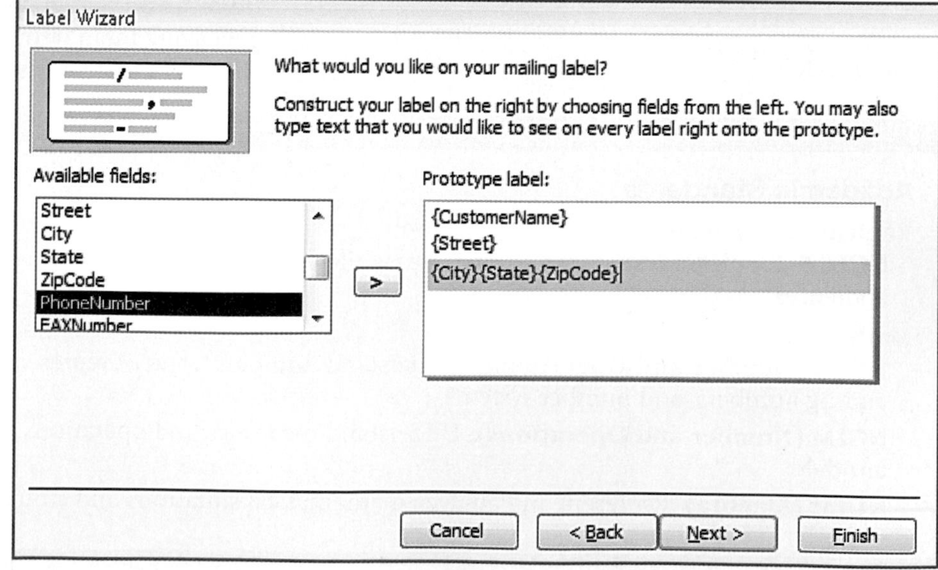

EXERCISE 3-1
Change Font, Font Size, and Style

The **font** is the "look" of the characters. A **font style** is a trait such as **bold**, *italic*, or <u>underline</u> that is applied to a font. Choosing the right fonts helps to make your worksheet more readable. You can either use the Format group or launch the Format Cells dialog box to change a font.

Troubleshooting Make sure students know where to save their files each time they use a data file.

FIGURE 3.1 Font group

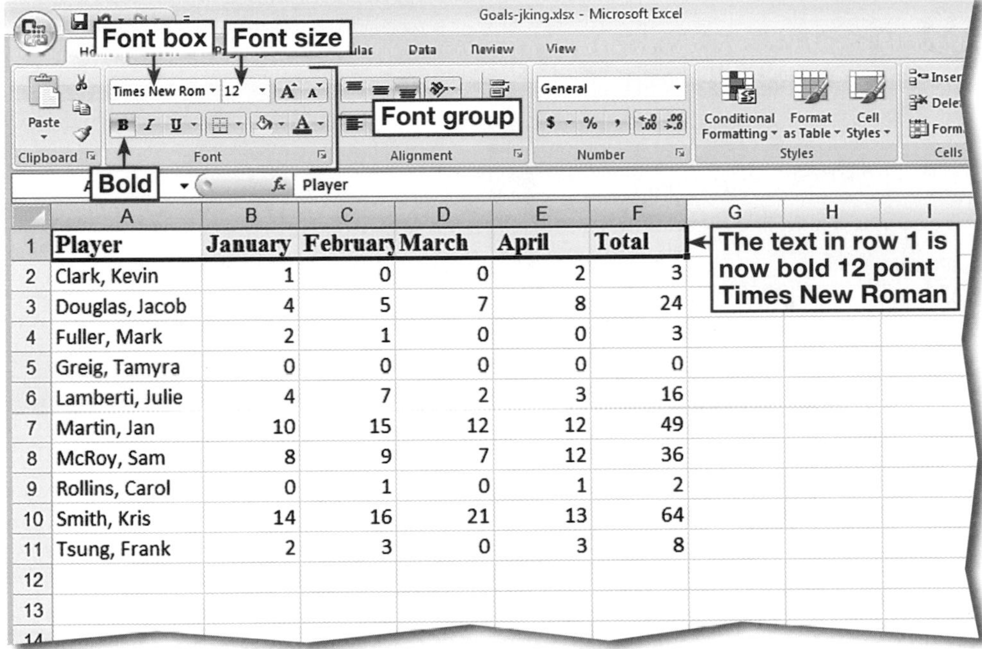

	A	B	C	D	E	F
1	**Player**	**January**	**February**	**March**	**April**	**Total**
2	Clark, Kevin	1	0	0	2	3
3	Douglas, Jacob	4	5	7	8	24
4	Fuller, Mark	2	1	0	0	3
5	Greig, Tamyra	0	0	0	0	0
6	Lamberti, Julie	4	7	2	3	16
7	Martin, Jan	10	15	12	12	49
8	McRoy, Sam	8	9	7	12	36
9	Rollins, Carol	0	1	0	1	2
10	Smith, Kris	14	16	21	13	64
11	Tsung, Frank	2	3	0	3	8

FIGURE 3.2 Font, font size, and font style changed for selected cells

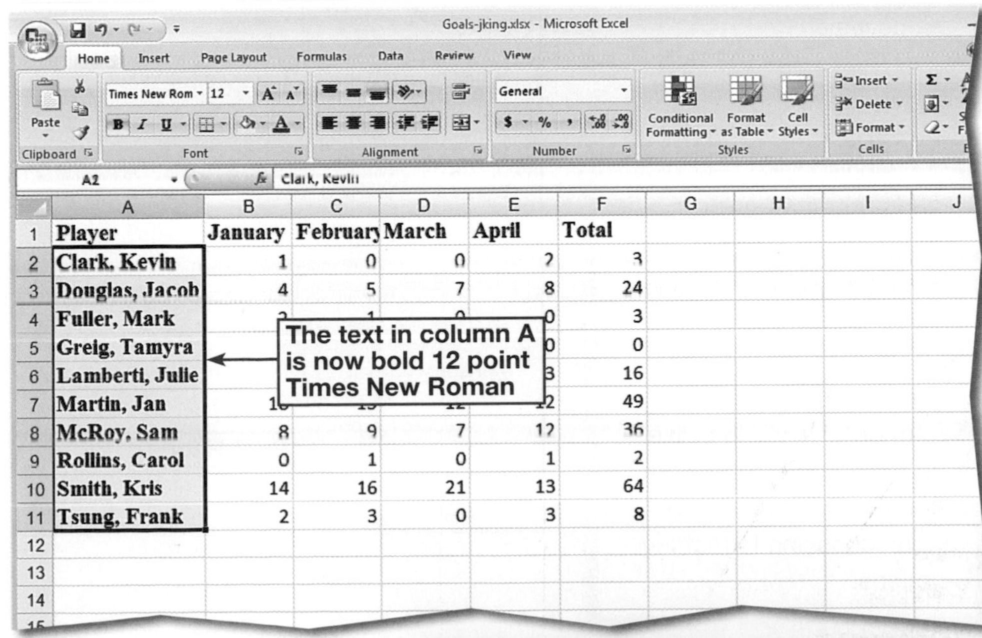

	A	B	C	D	E	F
1	Player	January	February	March	April	Total
2	**Clark, Kevin**	1	0	0	2	3
3	**Douglas, Jacob**	4	5	7	8	24
4	**Fuller, Mark**					3
5	**Greig, Tamyra**					0
6	**Lamberti, Julie**					16
7	**Martin, Jan**					49
8	**McRoy, Sam**	8	9	7	12	36
9	**Rollins, Carol**	0	1	0	1	2
10	**Smith, Kris**	14	16	21	13	64
11	**Tsung, Frank**	2	3	0	3	8

Step-By-Step

1. Start **Excel**.
2. Open the data file **Goals.xlsx**. Save as: Goals-[your first initial and last name] (for example, *Goals-jking*). Ask your teacher where to save your file.
3. Select **A1:F1**.
4. Choose **Home>Font** and click the **Font** drop-down arrow. Select **Times New Roman**.
5. In the **Font** group, click **Bold** **B**. In the **Font Size** box, click **12**.
6. **CHECK** Your screen should look like Figure 3.1.
7. Select **A2:A11**. Click the **Font** drop-down arrow and choose **Times New Roman** (see Figure 3.2).
8. Click the **Font Size** drop-down arrow. Choose **12**. Click **Bold** **B**.
9. **CHECK** Your screen should look like Figure 3.2. Save your file.

Continue to the next exercise.

Step-By-Step Tip In **Step 3**, remind students that selecting A1:F1 means selecting the contents in cells A1 through F1.

Step-By-Step Tip In **Step 7**, make sure that students know that they can scroll down to find more fonts.

Step-By-Step

10. Click **OK**. Choose **Design> View>Print Preview**.
11. **CHECK** Your screen should look like Figure 3.62.
12. Click **Print** .
13. In the **Print range** section, select **Pages** and enter **1 to 1**.
14. **CHECK** Your screen should look like Figure 3.63.
15. With your teacher's permission, click **OK** to print. Close the report and click **No** to close without saving changes.

Continue to the next exercise.

You Should Know

AutoFormats are applied to forms and reports the same way.

Tech Tip

Some AutoFormats will work better than others when printed in grayscale (black and white). *Print Preview* will give you a good idea of what your form or table will look like. You also need to consider the quality of your printer when choosing formatting options.

EXERCISE 3-20 (Continued)
Apply AutoFormat to Forms and Reports

FIGURE 3.62 Customer Orders report with new format

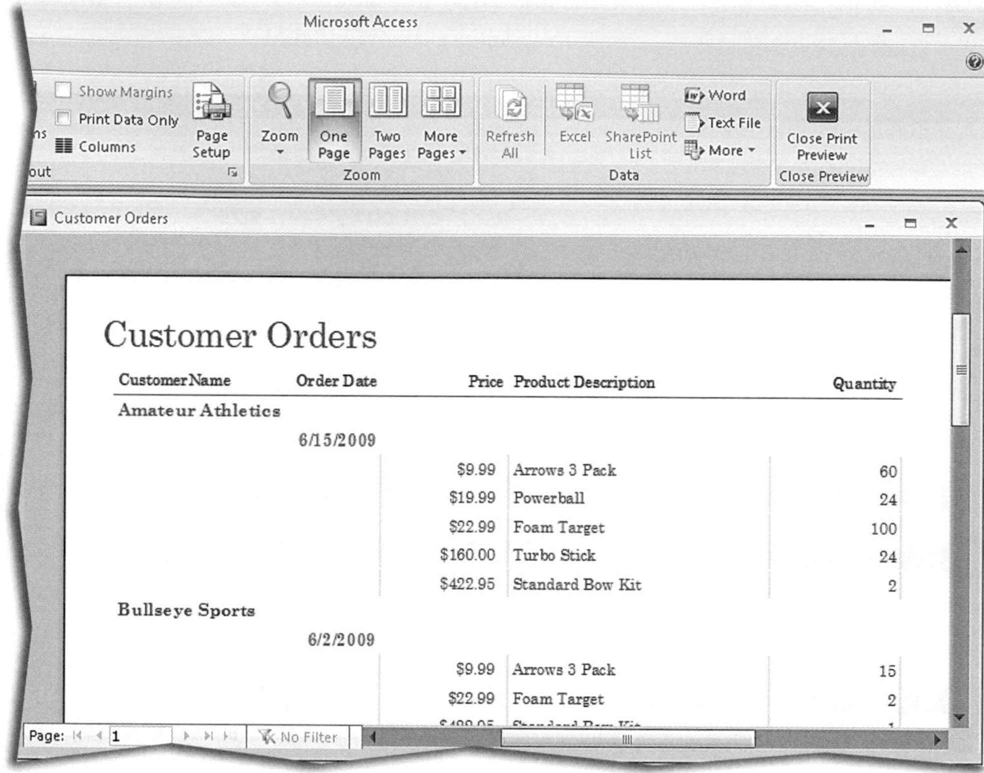

FIGURE 3.63 Page range in Print dialog box

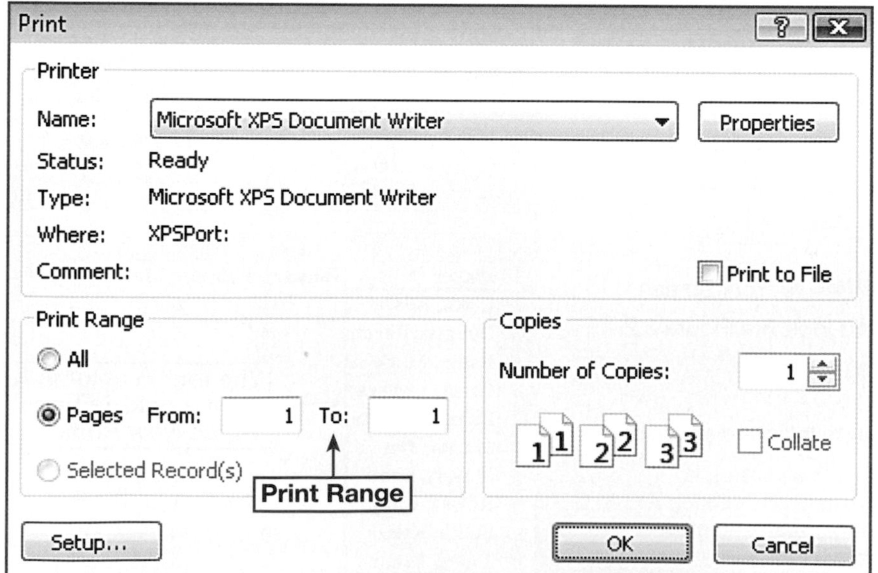

Step-By-Step

1. In your **Goals** file, select **A1:F1**.
2. Choose **Home>Font**. Click the **Borders** drop-down arrow.
3. Click **Bottom Border** (see Figure 3.3).
4. Select **A2:A11**.
5. Click the **Borders** drop-down arrow.
6. In the drop-down menu, click **Right Border**.
7. Select cell **A11**. Click **Bottom Border**. A bottom border is added to the cell.
8. Click **No Border**. The borders are removed from A11.
9. Click **Right Border**. Now the right border is added back to the cell.
10. **CHECK** Your screen should look like Figure 3.4.

Continued on the next page.

Shortcuts

Font, alignment, and other formatting changes only affect the cells that are selected. Remember to select a range, or group of cells, first, and then make the formatting change.

EXERCISE 3-2
Apply Borders and Copy Cell Contents

A **border** is a line along one or more edges of a cell. Borders make worksheet labels easier to find. By applying a border to a cell or groups of cells, you can make information easier and quicker to find. Sometimes you want a border around certain cells and not around others. Excel allows you to copy text without copying the border. You should use the Paste Special dialog box to control which information is pasted into a new cell.

FIGURE 3.3 Bottom border

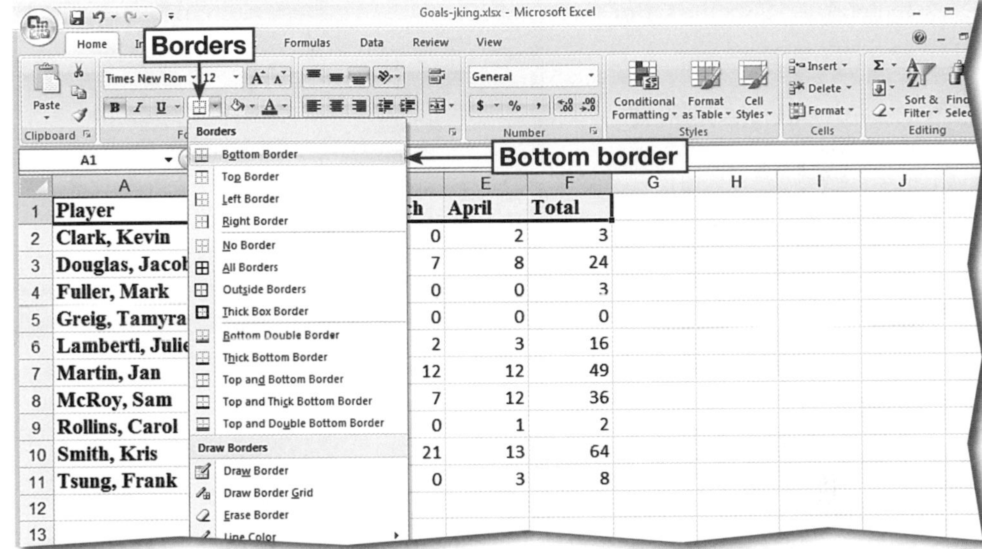

FIGURE 3.4 Cell Borders

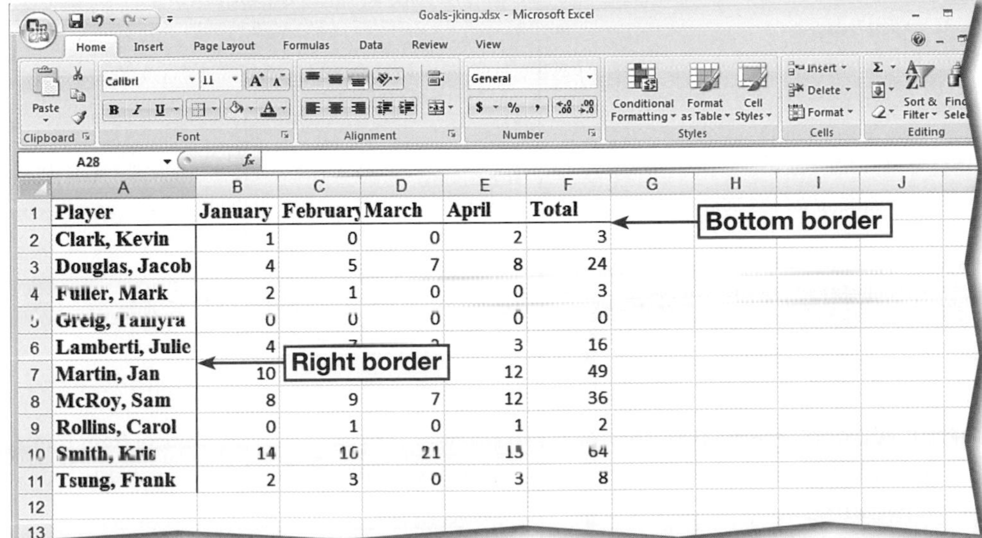

Troubleshooting In Step 8, make sure students do not drag the contents of cell A12 into A13 and then choose **Fill without Formatting** from the **AutoFill Options** box. The name will be pasted in Calibri 11 point font instead of Times New Roman 12 point. Only the Paste Special dialog box gives you the option of retaining all formatting except the border.

Step-By-Step

1. In your **Sports** file, open the **Customer Orders** report in **Design View**.
2. Choose **Arrange> AutoFormat> AutoFormat**.
3. Move your pointer over the thumbnails. Click the **Oriel** format thumbnail.
4. Choose **Design>Report View**.
5. **CHECK** Your screen should look like Figure 3.60.
6. Click **Design View** in the lower-right corner of the screen.
7. Choose **Arrange> AutoFormat** and select the **AutoFormat Wizard**.
8. In the wizard, click **Options**.
9. **CHECK** Your screen should look like Figure 3.61.

Continued on the next page.

Microsoft Office 2007

You cannot customize any of the built-in AutoFormats, but you can create and customize your own AutoFormats.

EXERCISE 3-20
Apply AutoFormat to Forms and Reports

Instead of designing every element for a form or report from scratch, you can choose an **AutoFormat** already available in Access to apply to your existing database object. You select the formats while viewing the form or report in Design View or Layout View.

FIGURE 3.60 Oriel format on Customer Orders report

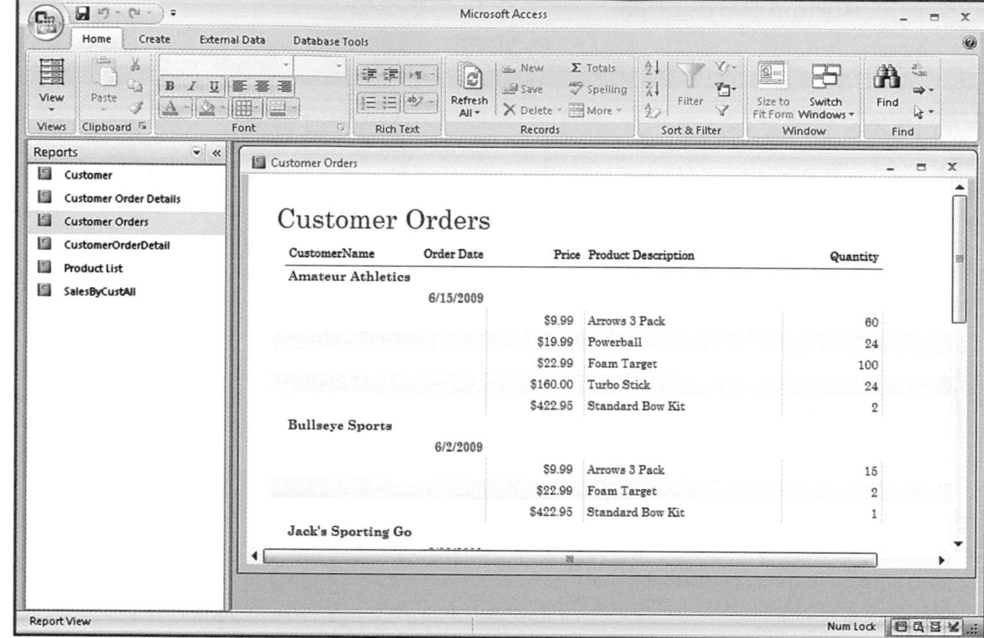

FIGURE 3.61 AutoFormat Wizard

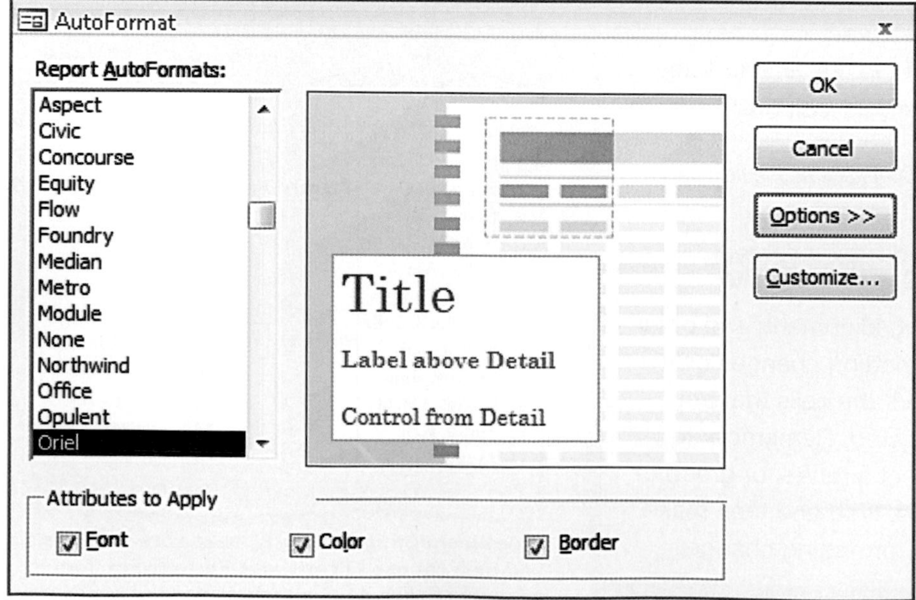

Step-By-Step

11 With **A11** selected, choose **Home>Clipboard>Copy**.

12 Click cell **A12**. Then click the **Paste** drop-down menu. Choose **Paste Special**.

13 In the **Paste Special** dialog box, click the **All except borders** button (see Figure 3.5). Click **OK**.

14 CHECK Your screen should look like Figure 3.6. Notice that the name **Tsung**, **Frank**, with the correct font, is copied, but the border is not.

15 Click **Undo**. Click ESC.

16 Save your file.

Continue to the next exercise.

You Should Know

Borders are used to keep different types of information separate. Just as a border separates two countries, a border in an Excel worksheet tells viewers that the information in one column or row is distinct from the information in another column or row.

EXERCISE 3-2 (Continued)
Apply Borders and Copy Cell Contents

FIGURE 3.5 Paste Special dialog box.

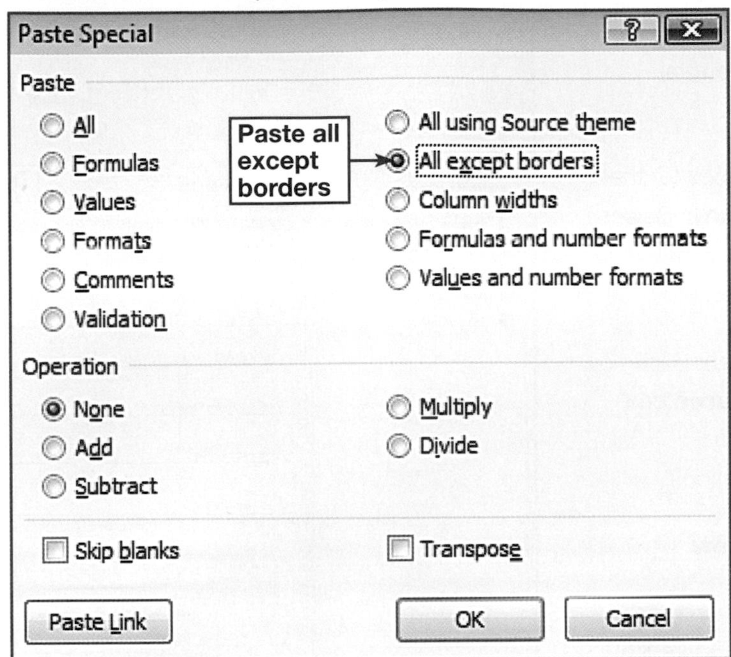

FIGURE 3.6 Cell borders

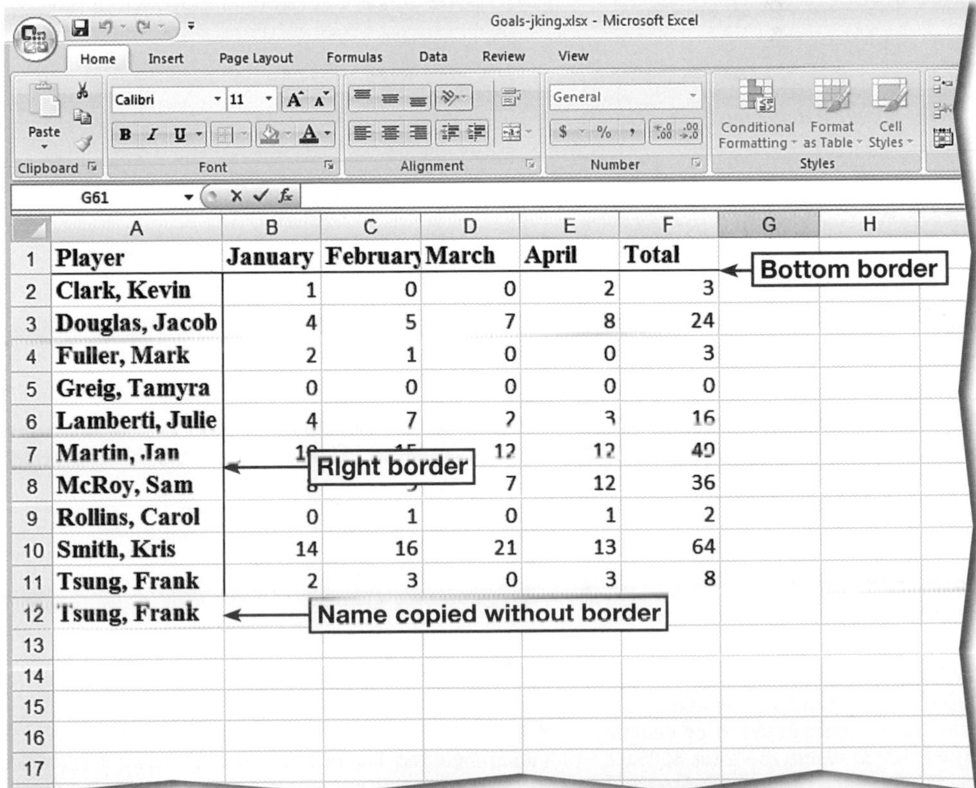

	A	B	C	D	E	F
1	Player	January	February	March	April	Total
2	Clark, Kevin	1	0	0	2	3
3	Douglas, Jacob	4	5	7	8	24
4	Fuller, Mark	2	1	0	0	3
5	Greig, Tamyra	0	0	0	0	0
6	Lamberti, Julie	4	7	2	3	16
7	Martin, Jan	1[illegible]	[illegible]	12	12	40
8	McRoy, Sam	[illegible]	[illegible]	7	12	36
9	Rollins, Carol	0	1	0	1	2
10	Smith, Kris	14	16	21	13	64
11	Tsung, Frank	2	3	0	3	8
12	Tsung, Frank					

EXERCISE 3-19 (Continued)
Create Aggregate Fields in Reports

12. Click the **Text Box** [ab] control. Click in the **Report Footer** to the right of the **Price** total (see Figure 3.58).

13. Select the label box for the control and delete it. Select the text box and click **Property Sheet**.

14. Click the **Data** tab. Click the **Control Source** box and key: =Count ([ProductDescription]).

15. Click **Report View**.

16. **CHECK** Your screen should look like Figure 3.59.

17. Close the report. Click **No** to close without saving changes.

Continue to the next exercise.

Academic Skills

Access can display minimums, maximums, averages, and counts of fields within a report. On a separate sheet of paper, figure out the average price of the Amateur Athletics products in the **Customer Orders** report.

NCLB/Math (Number and Operations) Students should add the five numbers in the Price column. They should divide the total, $635.92, by five to reach the answer $127.18.

FIGURE 3.58 Customer Orders report in Design View

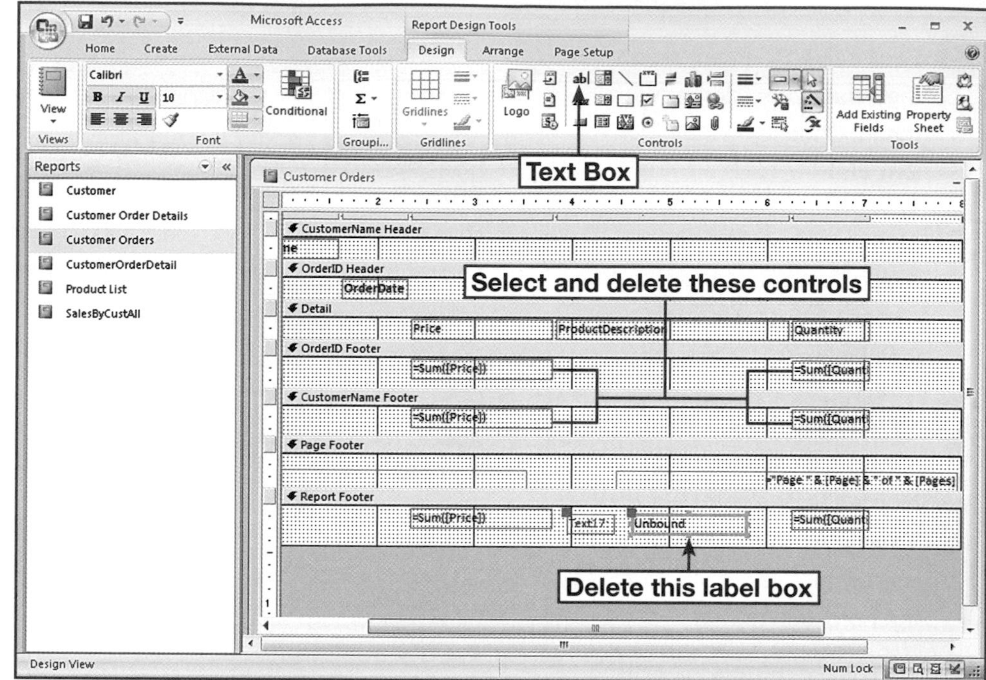

FIGURE 3.59 Customer Orders report in Report View

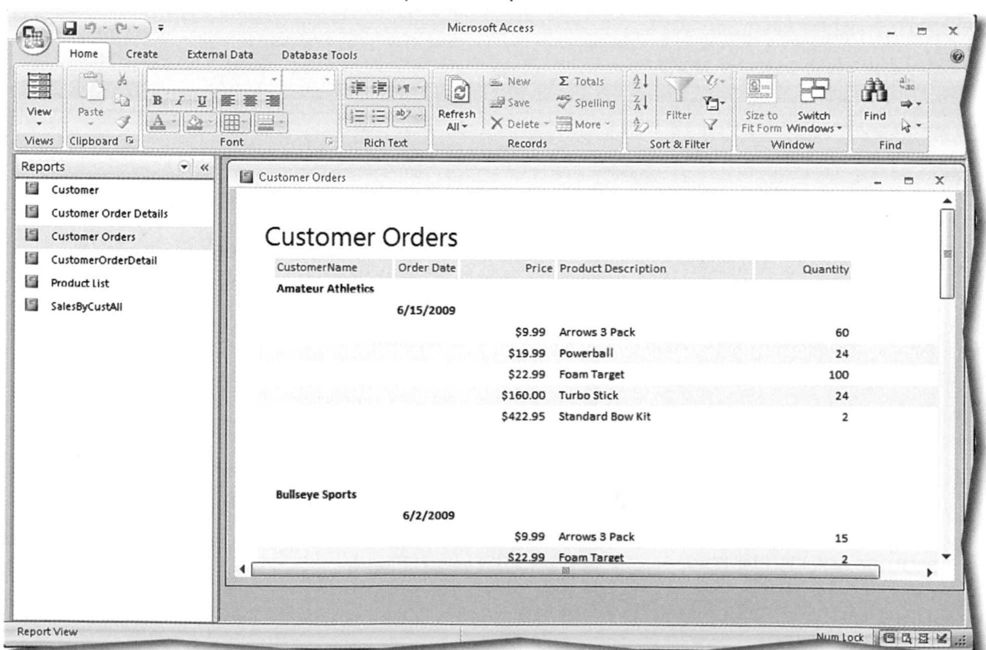

Step-By-Step Tip In **Step 11**, make sure that students type in the expression correctly. Explain to them that this aggregate function counts the number of product descriptions in the report.

EXERCISE 3-3
Convert Text to Columns

Use the Convert Text to Columns Wizard to separate the content of a cell, such as a list of first names and last names, into different columns. Excel makes use of a **delimiter**, or divider, to separate the text. The Convert Text to Columns function saves time by making many changes to a group of data in one step.

FIGURE 3.7 Convert Text to Columns Wizard

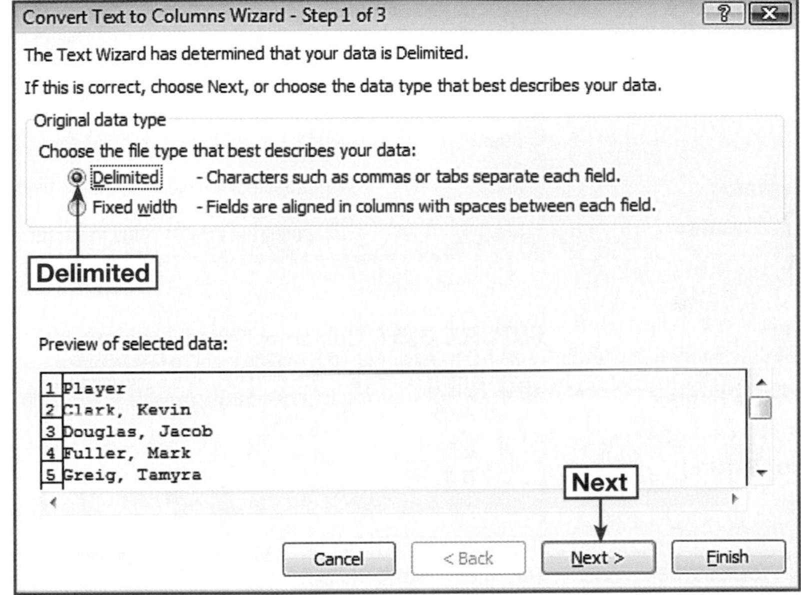

FIGURE 3.8 Players' last names in column A

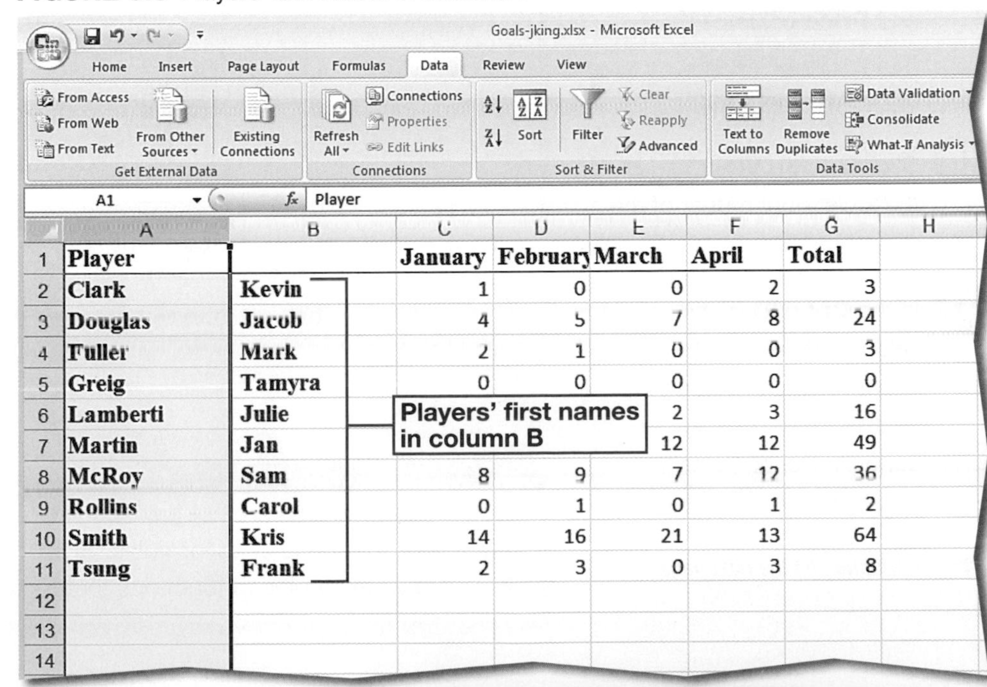

	A	B	C	D	E	F	G	H
1	Player		January	February	March	April	Total	
2	Clark	Kevin	1	0	0	2	3	
3	Douglas	Jacob	4	5	7	8	24	
4	Fuller	Mark	2	1	0	0	3	
5	Greig	Tamyra	0	0	0	0	0	
6	Lamberti	Julie			2	3	16	
7	Martin	Jan			12	12	49	
8	McRoy	Sam	8	9	7	12	36	
9	Rollins	Carol	0	1	0	1	2	
10	Smith	Kris	14	16	21	13	64	
11	Tsung	Frank	2	3	0	3	8	
12								
13								
14								

Step-By-Step

1. In your **Goals** file, click column heading **B**.
2. Right-click and select **Insert**. A new column is inserted. Notice that column B has become column C.
3. Select **A2:A11**. Choose **Data>Data Tools>Text to Columns**. The Convert Text to Columns Wizard opens (see Figure 3.7).
4. Make sure **Delimited** is selected. Click **Next**.
5. In the **Convert Text to Columns Wizard** dialog box, under **Delimiters**, click **Comma**. Unclick **Tabs**.
6. Click **Next**. Click **Finish**. The contents of column A have been separated out into two columns.
7. **CHECK** Your screen should look like Figure 3.8.
8. Click column heading **B** to select column B. Right-click and select **Delete**.
9. Save your file.

Continue to the next exercise.

Teaching Tip Explain to students that the Convert Text to Columns Wizard can select a cell, range, or entire column of data to distribute across other cells.

Step-By-Step

1. In your **Sports** file, in the **Navigation Pane**, select **Reports**.
2. Open the **Customer Orders** report.
3. Click **Layout View** .
4. Select the **Quantity** header.
5. Choose **Format> Grouping & Totals> Totals** Σ.
6. Select **Sum**.
7. Select the **Price** header.
8. Click **Totals** Σ and select **Sum**.
9. **CHECK** Your screen should look like Figure 3.57. All groups of the **Quantity** and **Price** columns have totals. The totals also appear at the bottom.
10. Click **Design View** in the lower-right corner of the screen.
11. In the **OrderID** footer, select and delete the **=Sum ([Price])** and the **=Sum ([Quantity])** controls. Do the same in the **CustomerName** footer.

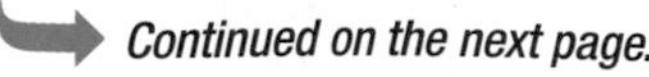

Continued on the next page.

EXERCISE 3-19
Create Aggregate Fields in Reports

Aggregate information is information that has been gathered together. To gather together data from different records, use the aggregate fields in Design View and Layout View. Common **aggregate functions** are shown in Table 3.1.

TABLE 3.1 Common aggregate functions

Function	Purpose
Sum	Adds the field values
Avg	Computes the average value of a field
Count	Counts the number of field values
Min	Computes the smallest value in a field
Max	Computes the largest value in a field

FIGURE 3.57 Customer Orders report with totals

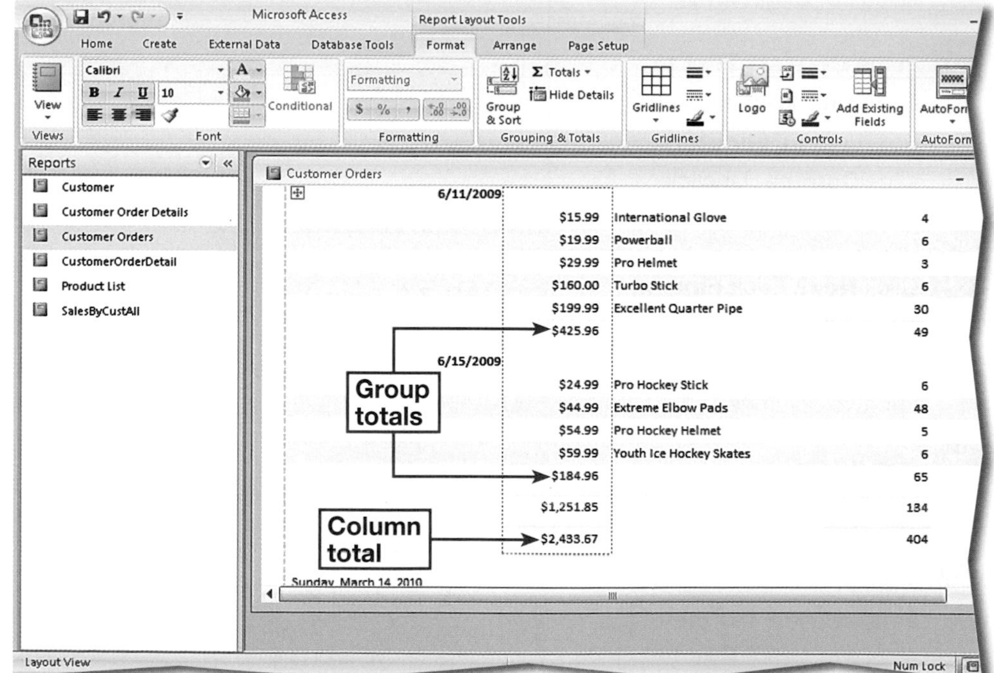

You Should Know

Aggregate functions are not just specific to Access. Excel also uses aggregate functions in its formulas. SUM, AVERAGE, MIN, and MAX are all examples of functions that Excel and Access share.

Step-By-Step

1 In your **Goals** file, select **A1:F11**.

2 Choose **Home>Styles> Format as Table**. Under Light, click **Table Style Light 17**. Click **OK**. Notice that the contextual tab **Table Tools** and **Design** tab are now displayed on the Ribbon.

3 **CHECK** Your screen should look like Figure 3.9.

4 With your table still selected, click the **Table Styles** group drop-down arrow in the upper-right corner of your screen (see Figure 3.9).

5 Rest your pointer on each of the Quick Style thumbnails in the Table Styles menu. Note how each style affects your table with the Live Preview (see Figure 3.10).

Continued on the next page.

Microsoft Office 2007

When you format a table in Microsoft Office 2007, table headers are added by default. You can change the default names, or you can turn them on or off by choosing **Design> Table Style Options.**

Step-By-Step Tip In **Step 2**, explain to students that the header data displayed in the table because the table specified to view the Header Row in the Table Style Options.

EXERCISE 3-4
Apply Table Styles

A **theme** is a predefined set of colors, fonts, and effects that you can apply to an entire workbook to ensure that the cells have consistent formatting. Microsoft Office Excel 2007 has 16 built-in themes that you can apply or modify to create your own. You can also use the Format as Table command to apply a **table style**, or predefined set of formats, to a range of data. Themes and table styles save time by making formatting changes, such as adding borders and changing font colors, in one step.

Teaching Tip Explain to students that table styles are based on the theme that is applied to the workbook and that when they choose another theme, the styles are updated to match the new theme.

FIGURE 3.9 Table Style Light 17 applied to cells

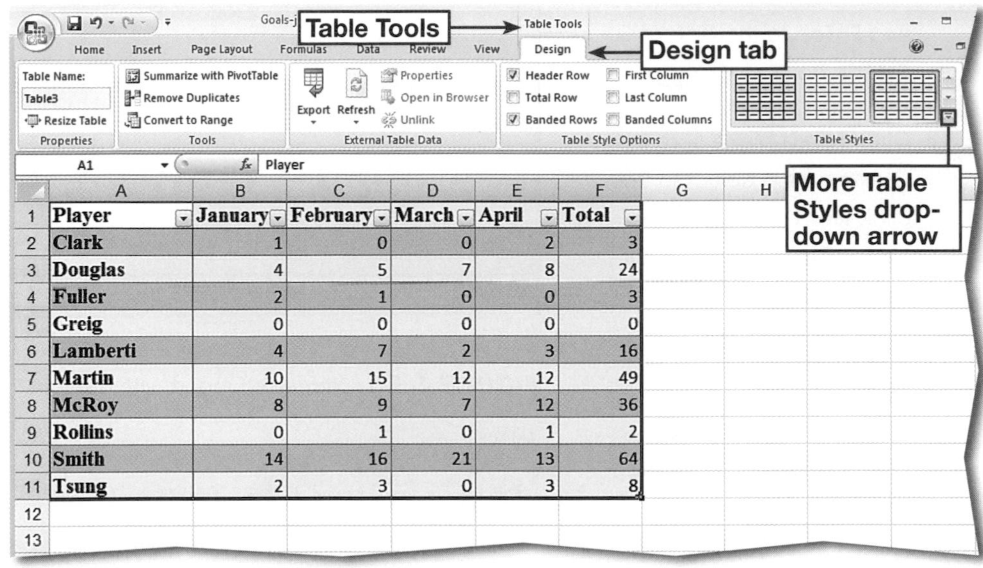

FIGURE 3.10 Table Styles drop-down menu

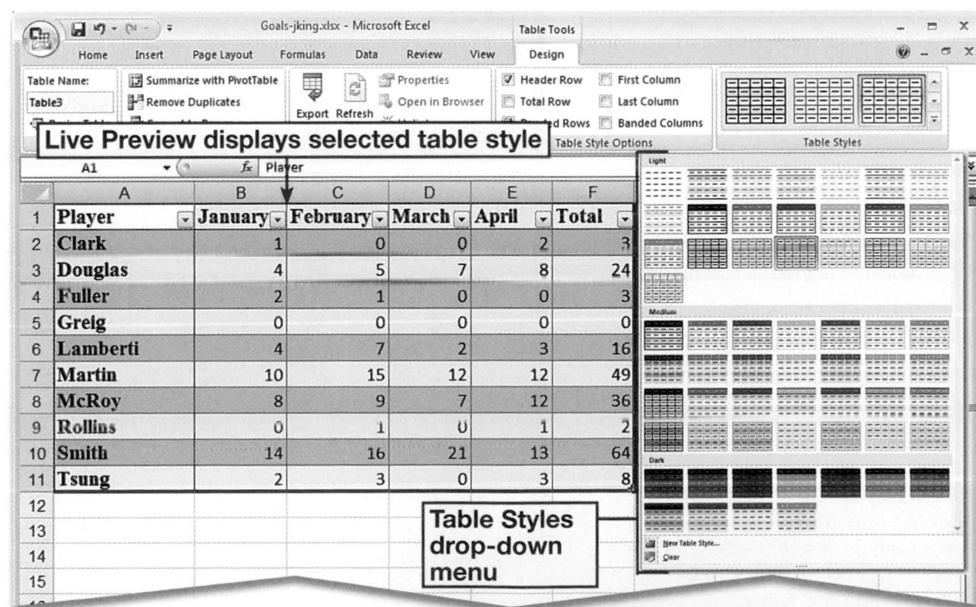

Step-By-Step

EXERCISE 3-18 (Continued)
Define Group Headers in Reports

12 Choose **Create>Reports> Report Wizard** .

13 In the **Tables/Queries** menu, select **Query: CustOrdDet**.

14 Move **CustomerName**, **OrderID**, **OrderDate**, **Quantity**, **ProductName**, and **Price** to the **Selected Fields** box.

15 Click **Next**. Make sure **by Customer** is selected and click **Next**. Double-click **OrderDate**. Double-click **ProductName**.

16 CHECK Your screen should look like Figure 3.55.

17 Click **Finish**. Click **Close Print Preview**.

18 Click the **View** drop-down arrow and select **Layout View**. Select the column headers for columns displaying ##### and adjust them for fit.

19 CHECK Your screen should look like Figure 3.56. Close the report. Click **Yes** to save changes.

Continue to the next exercise.

Step-By-Step Tip In **Step 14**, students may move each field over individually or move them all at once by clicking and holding the **CTRL** key while clicking the fields.

FIGURE 3.55 Grouping in Report Wizard

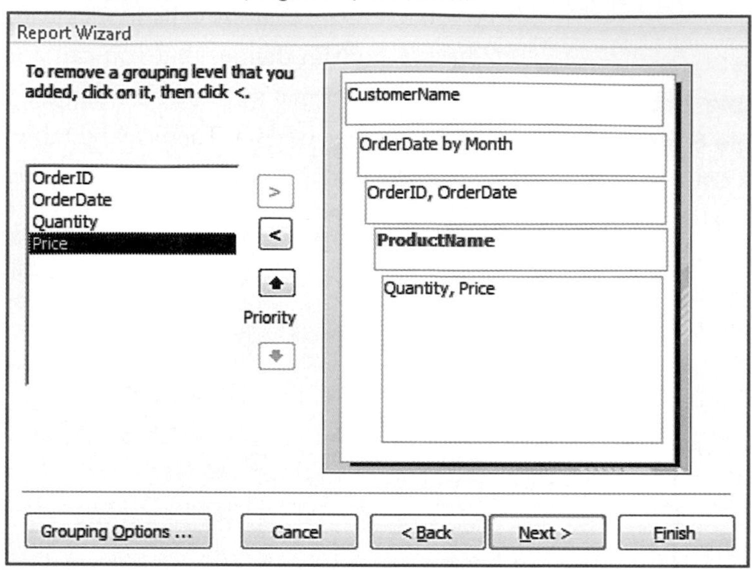

FIGURE 3.56 Completed report with groups

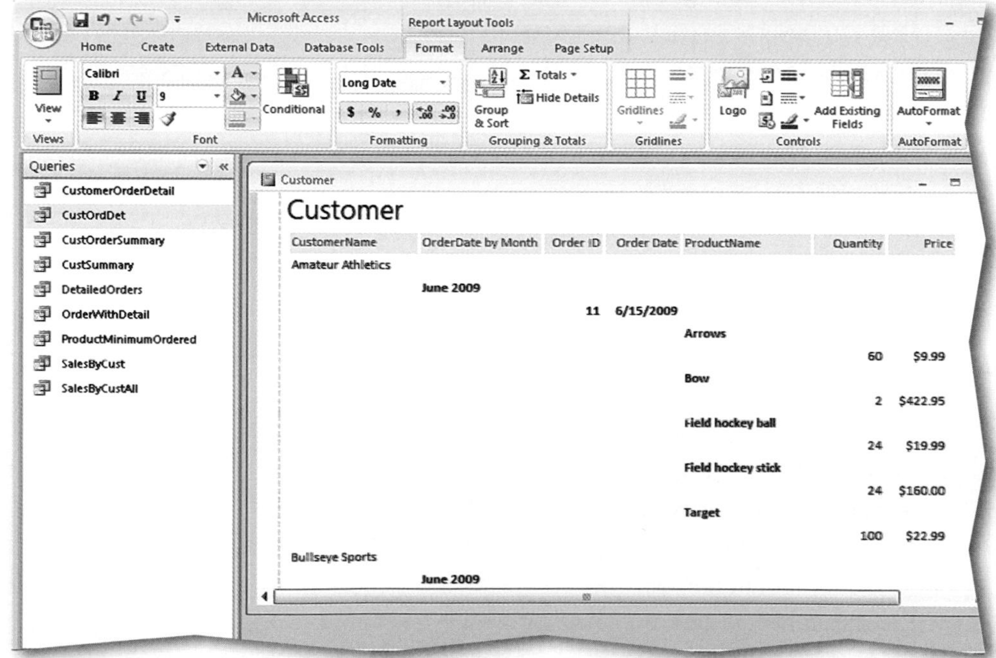

Step-By-Step

6 Click **Table Style Light 19**.

7 With your table still selected, choose **Page Layout>Themes> Themes** (see Figure 3.11). Move your pointer over the built-in themes.

8 Click **Verve**. Notice how the style is updated. Click **Undo** . Click cell **F11**.

9 Under **Table Tools**, click the **Design** tab. In the **Table Styles Options** group, click to add a checkmark next to **Banded Columns**. Note the difference on-screen. Uncheck **Banded Columns**.

10 Uncheck **Header Row**. Note row 1 is now empty. Check **Header Row**.

11 Click to add checkmarks next to **Total Row and Last Column**.

12 **CHECK** Your screen should look like Figure 3.12. Note that the numbers in the last column are bold and that a Total has been added to Row 12.

13 Save your file.

Continue to the next exercise.

EXERCISE 3-4 (Continued)
Apply Table Styles

FIGURE 3.11 Page Layout Themes

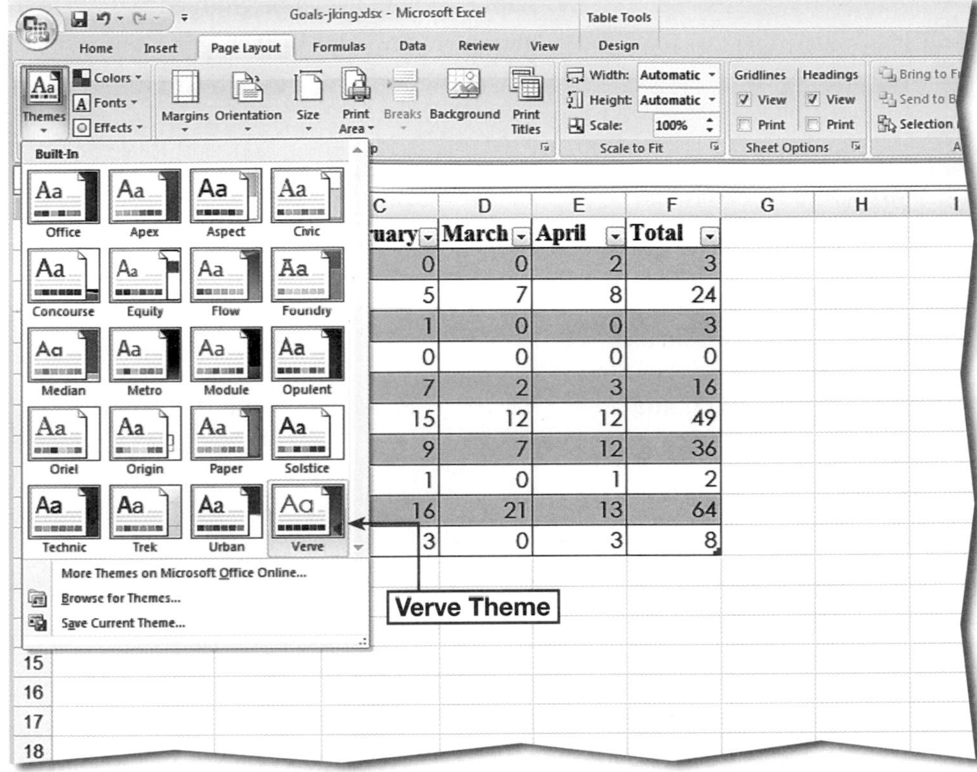

FIGURE 3.12 Format applied to cells

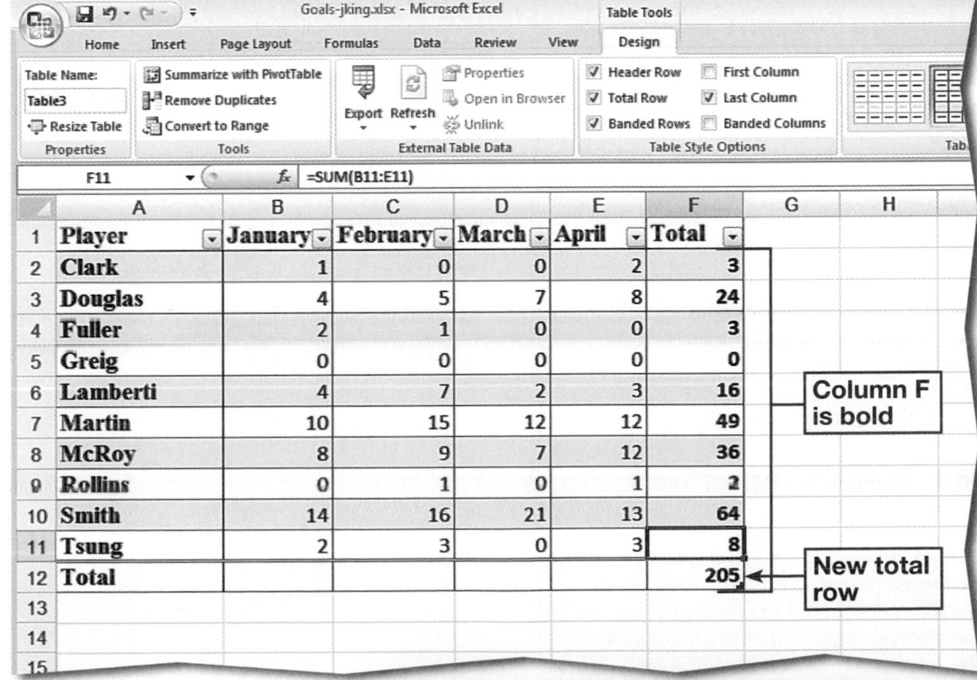

Step-By-Step

1 In your **Sports** file, open the **CustOrdDet** query.

2 Choose **Create>Reports> Report**.

3 Choose **Format> Grouping & Totals> Group & Sort**.

4 CHECK Your screen should look like Figure 3.53.

5 In the **Group, Sort, and Total** pane, click **Add a group**.

6 Select **CustomerName**. The report groups by customer name and alphabetizes the list.

7 Click **Add a group**. Select **OrderID**.

8 Click **Group & Sort** to close the pane. Click **Report View**.

9 CHECK Your screen should look like Figure 3.54.

10 Click **Save**. Name the report: Customer Order Details. Click **OK**.

11 Close the report. Close the **CustOrdDet** query.

Continued on the next page.

Differentiated Instruction/Advanced Students Have advanced students format the report so it fits on two pages in Landscape view, and have them print the report.

EXERCISE 3-18
Define Group Headers in Reports

Information is often easier to read when it is divided into groups. For example, group sales information can be grouped by state to track trends over time and by location. A **group header** helps further refine reports by sorting information into helpful groups. Use the Group & Sort tool to **sort** information into groups and group headers.

FIGURE 3.53 Group, Sort, and Total pane

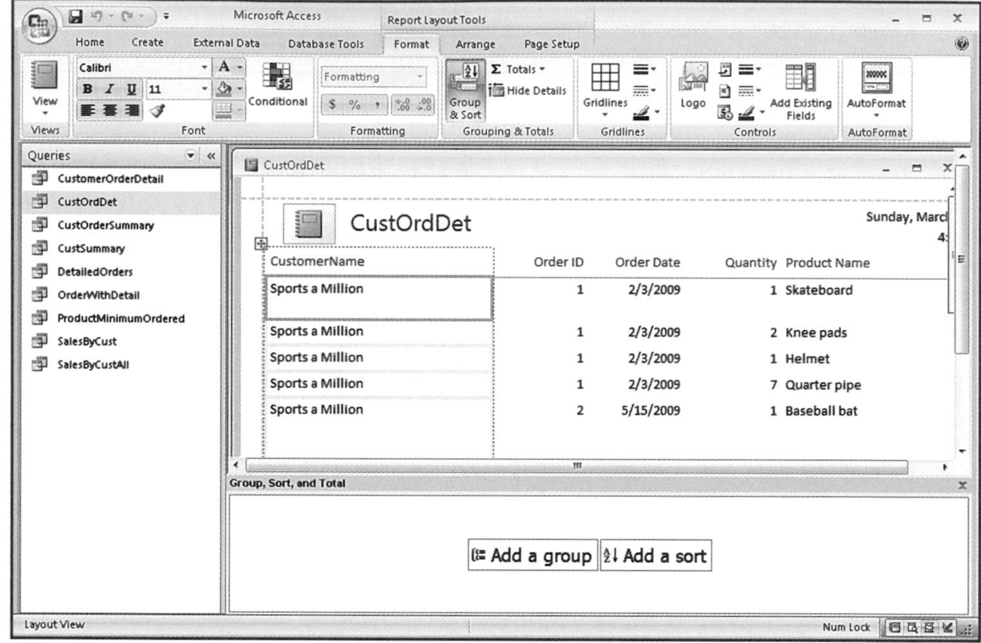

FIGURE 3.54 Completed report in Report View

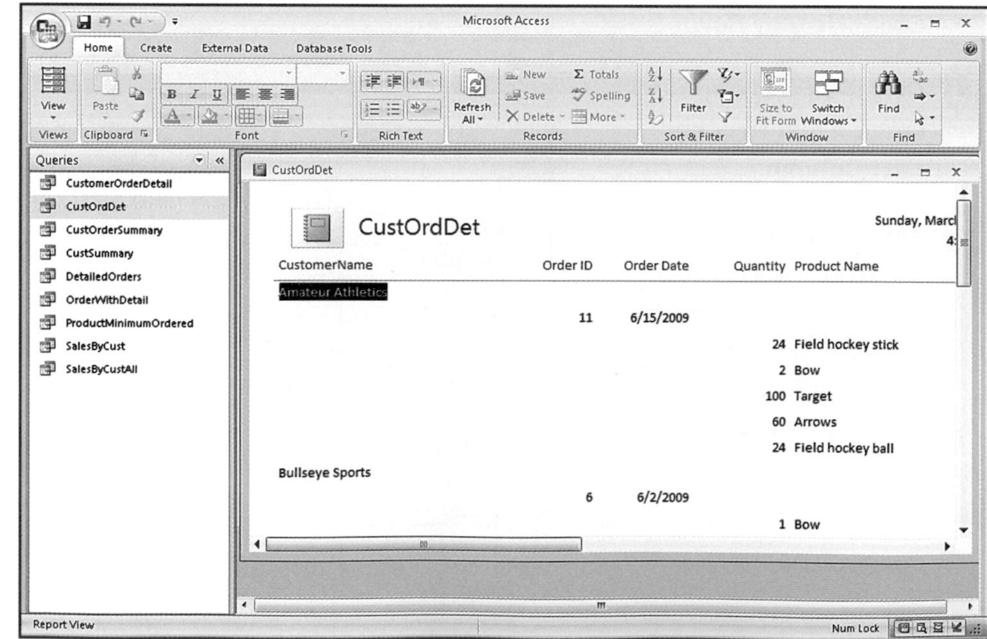

EXERCISE 3-5
Modify Tables to Show New Data

As you create your table, you may decide that you would like Excel to show data in a different way. For example, maybe you would like to see the average number of goals kicked by your team, but later you want to see the total number of goals. you may also discover that you need to include more data in a table. You can either key a value or text in a cell that is directly below or adjacent to the right of the table, or drag the resize handle at the lower-right corner of the table to select rows and columns.

Step By Step Tip In **Step 4**, point out that the default header for column G is Column1. Remind students that they can change the table header.

Step-By-Step

1. In your **Goals** file, select **F12**. Click the **AutoSum** drop-down menu. Choose **More Functions**. In the **Insert Function** dialog box, select **Average** and click **OK**.
2. In the **Function Arguments** dialog box, make sure the range of cells is F2:F11. Click **OK**. The number 20.5 appears as a total.
3. Repeat Step 1 but choose **SUM** from the list. Click **OK**.
4. Repeat Step 2. Click **OK**. The number 205 appears.
5. **CHECK** Your screen should look like Figure 3.13.
6. Position the pointer over the lower right corner of cell **F12** so that the resize handle appears (see Figure 3.14).

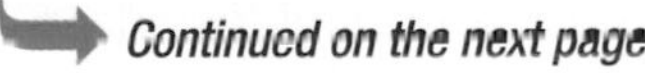
Continued on the next page.

You Should Know

If you need to add a row or column between existing rows and columns in a table, select the row or column where you want the contents to appear, right-click, and choose **Insert**.

FIGURE 3.13 SUM function

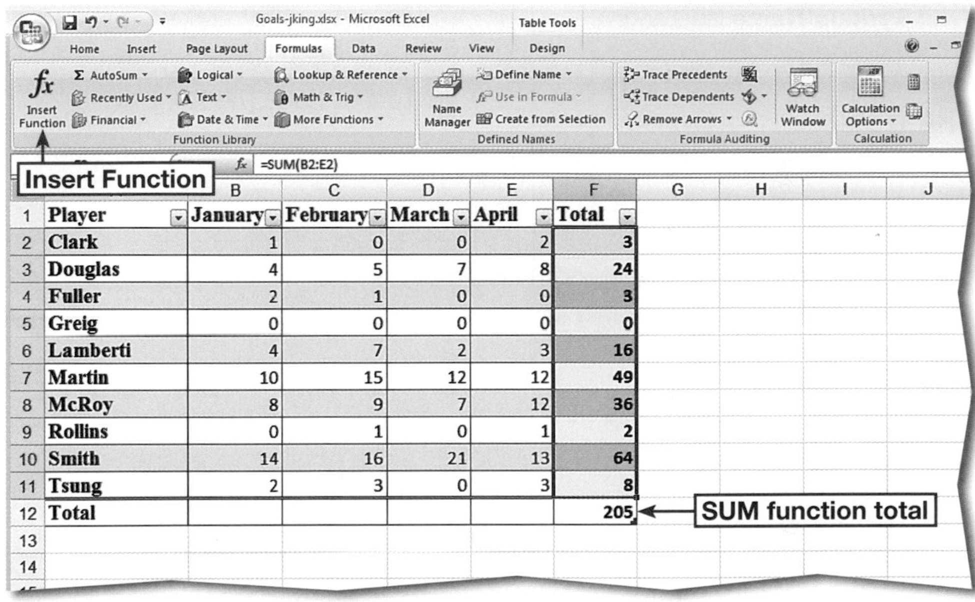

FIGURE 3.14 Resize handle in F12

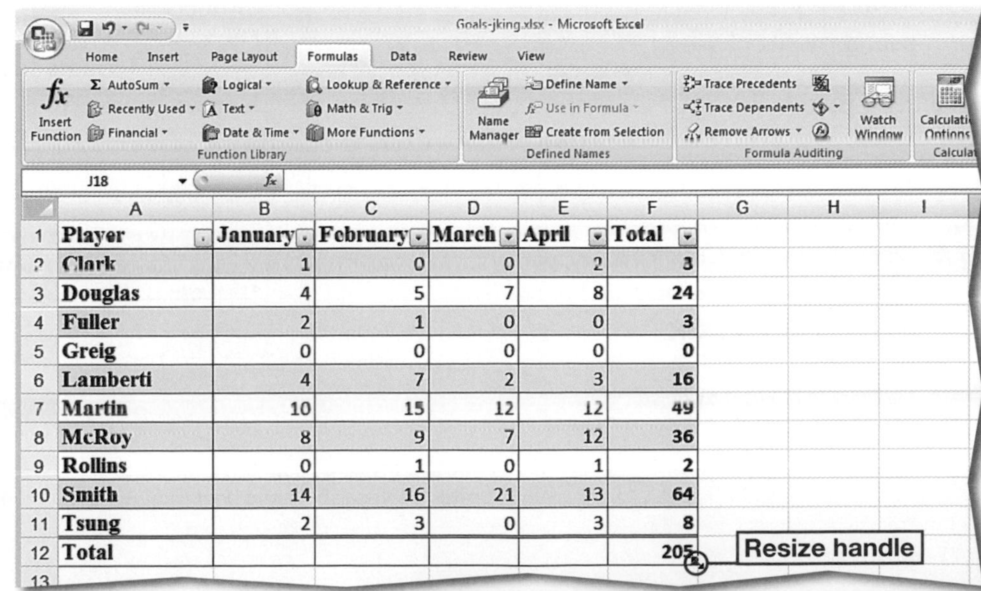

Step-By-Step

EXERCISE 3-17 (Continued)
Create a Report in Design View

10 CHECK Your dialog box should look like Figure 3.51. Click **OK**. Close the **Field List**.

11 Drag the **Page Footer** bar up until it is just under the **Product Description**. Right-click the **ProductName** label and select **Cut**.

12 Right-click in the window beneath the page header bar and select **Paste**. Move the label so that it is over the **ProductName** text box.

13 Cut and paste the **Price** label the same way you did the **ProductName** label.

14 CHECK Your screen should look like Figure 3.52.

15 Choose **Office>Print> Print Preview**. Look through all the pages.

16 Click **Print**. With your teacher's permission, click **OK**.

17 Close the report. Click **Yes**. In the **Save As** box, key: Product List. Click **OK**.

Continue to the next exercise.

FIGURE 3.51 Page Numbers dialog box

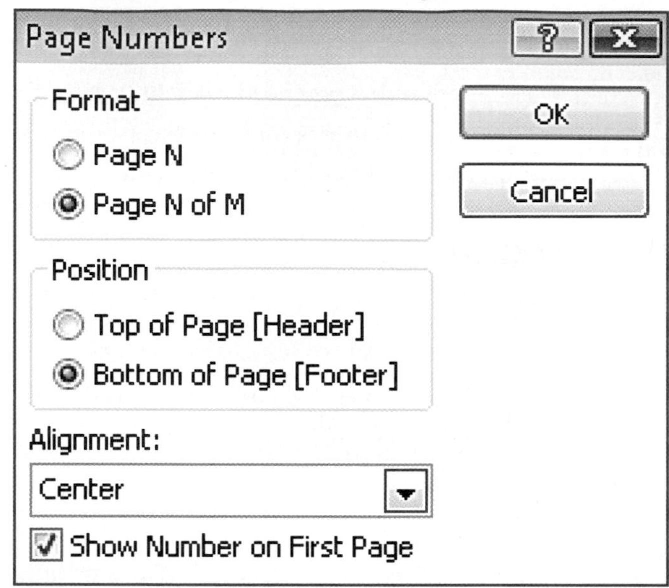

Step-By-Step Tip In **Step 12**, let students know that they will have to scroll down to see the **Page Footer**.

FIGURE 3.52 Finished Report in Design View

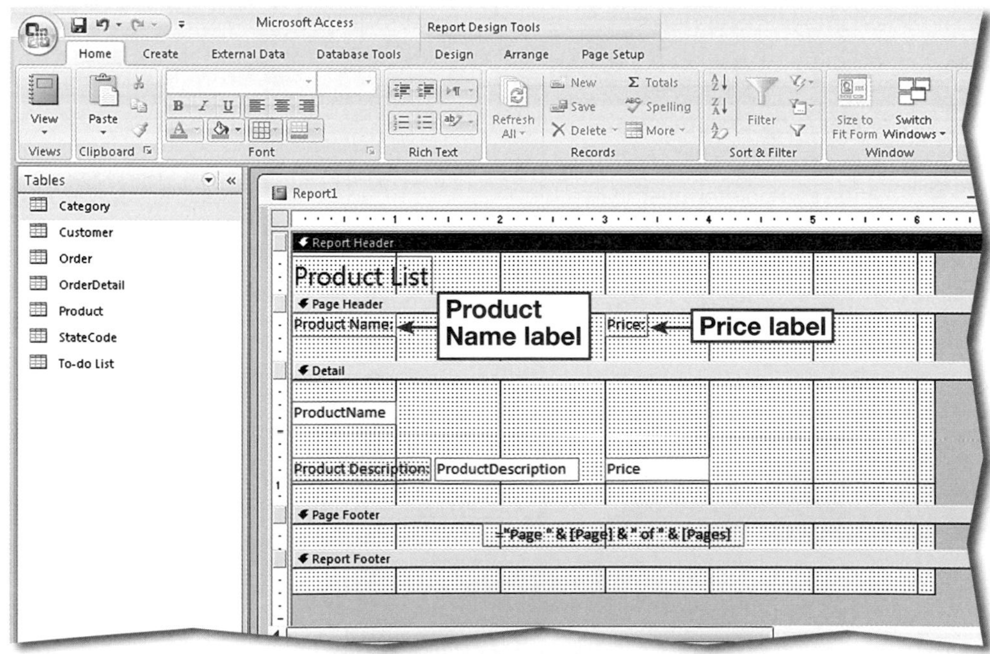

Differentiated Instruction/Advanced Students Have advanced students format the **Price** and **ProductName** labels and background color using the **Font** group.

Step-By-Step

7. Drag the pointer over cell **G12** and release the mouse button. A new column is added to the table.
8. **CHECK** Your screen should look like Figure 3.15
9. Click **Undo** [Undo button].
10. Click cell **B12**. Choose **Formulas>Function Library>AutoSum** to calculate the total goals for January. Continue until you have the total goals for totals for February, March, and April.
11. Click cell **F13**.
12. **CHECK** Your screen should look like Figure 3.16.
13. Save your file.

Continue to the next exercise.

You Should Know

To delete a table row or column, select the row or column and press DELETE.

Troubleshooting In Step 9, if the number 0 still appears in cell G12, have students delete it.

NCLB/Math (Algebra) Walk students through the example given. Explain in detail the process and show all work to the class.

EXERCISE 3-5 (Continued)
Modify Tables to Show New Data

FIGURE 3.15 New column added to table

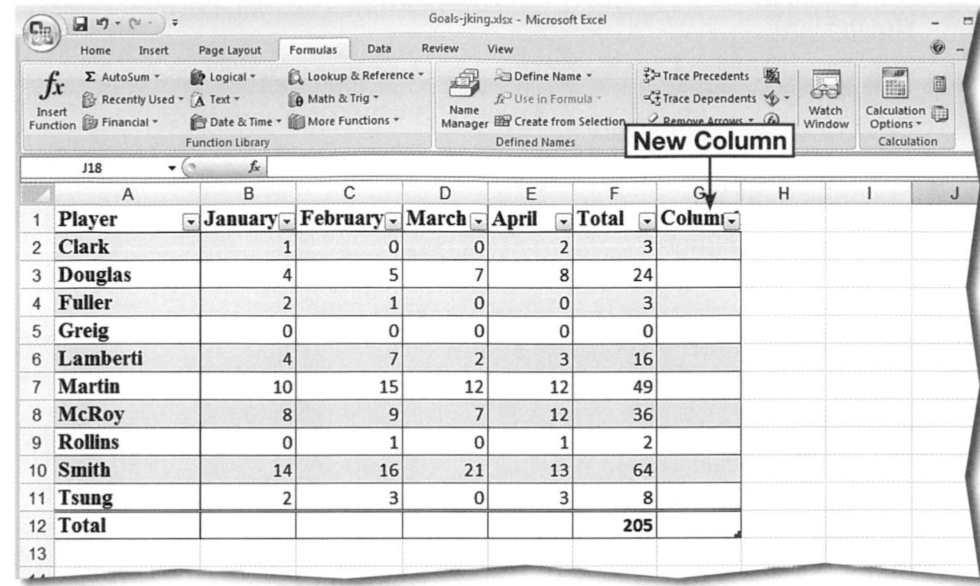

	Player	January	February	March	April	Total	Column
2	Clark	1	0	0	2	3	
3	Douglas	4	5	7	8	24	
4	Fuller	2	1	0	0	3	
5	Greig	0	0	0	0	0	
6	Lamberti	4	7	2	3	16	
7	Martin	10	15	12	12	49	
8	McRoy	8	9	7	12	36	
9	Rollins	0	1	0	1	2	
10	Smith	14	16	21	13	64	
11	Tsung	2	3	0	3	8	
12	Total					205	

FIGURE 3.16 Total row added

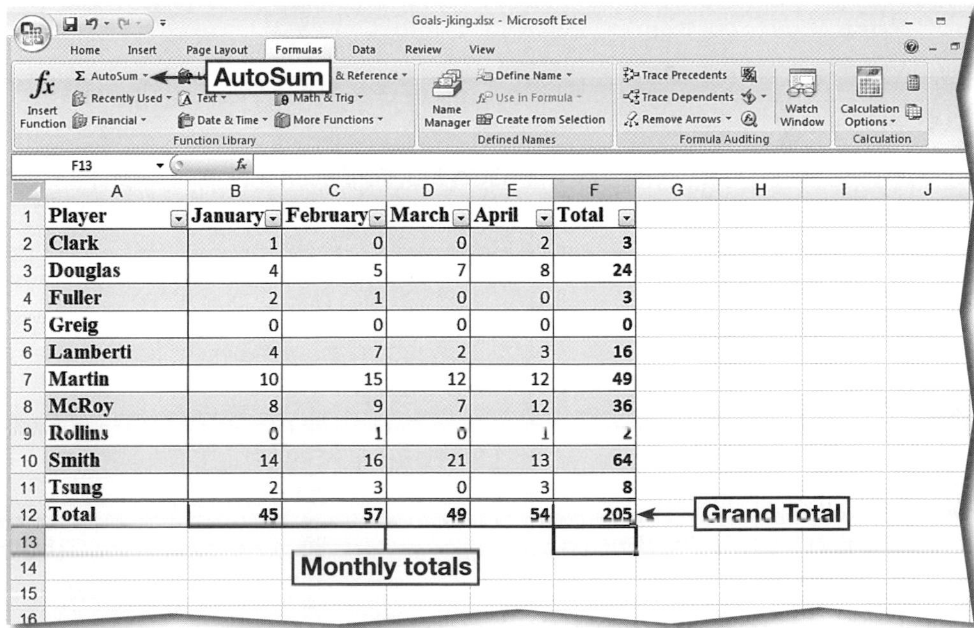

	Player	January	February	March	April	Total
2	Clark	1	0	0	2	3
3	Douglas	4	5	7	8	24
4	Fuller	2	1	0	0	3
5	Greig	0	0	0	0	0
6	Lamberti	4	7	2	3	16
7	Martin	10	15	12	12	49
8	McRoy	8	9	7	12	36
9	Rollins	0	1	0	1	2
10	Smith	14	16	21	13	64
11	Tsung	2	3	0	3	8
12	Total	45	57	49	54	205

Academic Skills

Investigate how the number 20.5 was arrived at in **Step 3**. The AVERAGE function added (+) all the goals together (205). Then they were divided (/) by the total number of players (10).

Step-By-Step

1. In your **Sports** file, choose **Create>Reports>Report Design**.
2. **CHECK** Your screen should look like Figure 3.49.
3. Click **Add Existing Fields**. Click **Show all tables**.
4. Click the **plus sign** + to expand the **Product** table fields. Drag the **ProductName** field onto the design window under the **Detail** header.
5. Double-click the **ProductDescription** and **Price** fields to put them in the design window.
6. Click **Title** and key: Product List. Drag the **Price** field and label to the right of the **ProductDescription** boxes.
7. **CHECK** Your screen should look like Figure 3.50.
8. Click **Insert Page Number** to open the **Page Numbers** dialog box.
9. Under **Format** select **Page N of M**. Under **Position** select **Bottom of Page [Footer]**.

Continued on the next page.

EXERCISE 3-17
Create a Report in Design View

You can also build or change a report in Design View. Using the Report Design tool to start your form gives you the most control over how the form looks, since Design View gives you the most control over the form.

FIGURE 3.49 Blank Report Design View

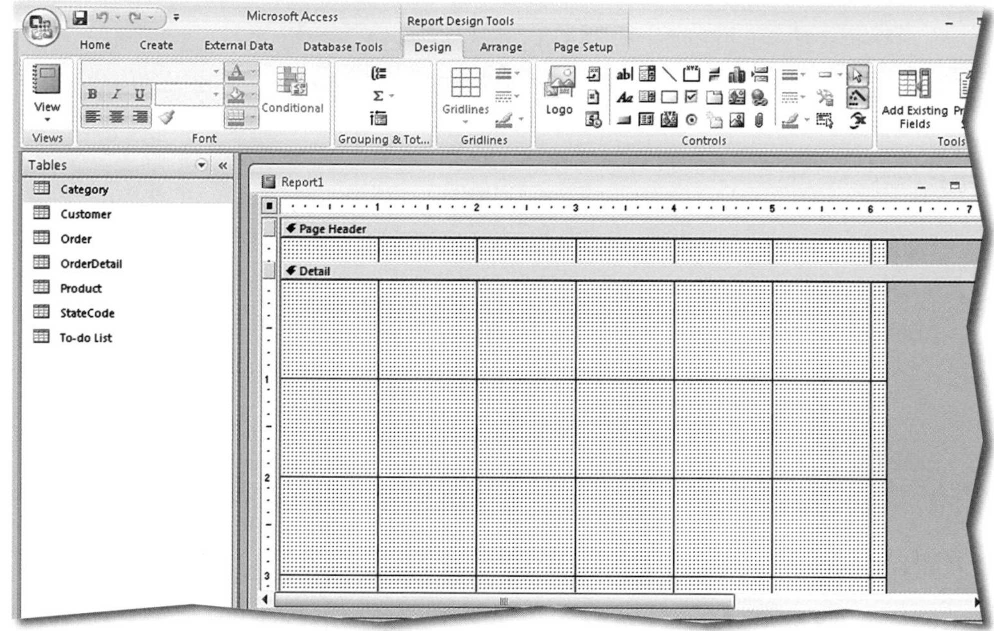

FIGURE 3.50 Report with fields added

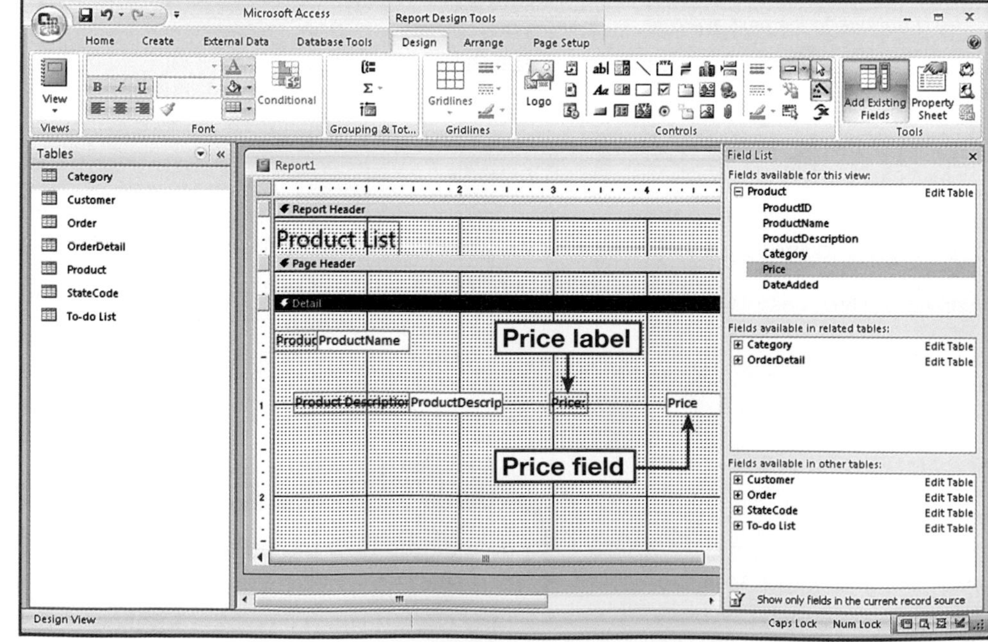

EXERCISE 3-6
Change Font Color

You can change the font color of text and numbers. You might use different font colors for headings and totals to make them distinct, or separate, from the rest of the worksheet. You can use the Format menu or the Formatting toolbar to change font color. You can also copy a font color from one cell to another without changing any of the data in the cell.

FIGURE 3.17 Font color selected in dialog box

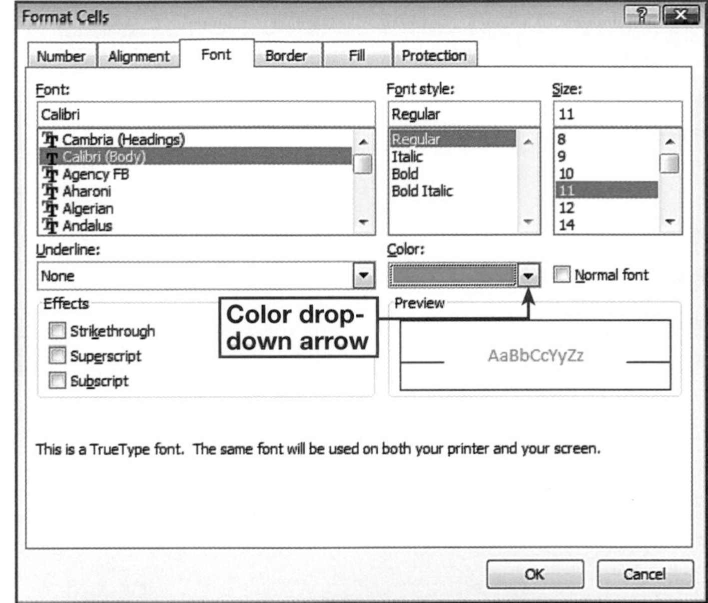

FIGURE 3.18 Font color changed for selected cells

	A	B	C	D	E	F
1	Player	January	February	March	April	Total
2	Clark	1	0	0	2	3
3	Douglas	4	5	7	8	24
4	Fuller	2	1	0	0	3
5	Greig	0	0	0	0	0
6	Lamberti	4	7	2	3	16
7	Martin	10	15	12	12	49
8	McRoy	8	9	7	12	36
9	Rollins	0	1	0	1	2
10	Smith	14	16	21	13	64
11	Tsung	2	3	0	3	8
12	Total	45	57	49	54	205

Grand total is red

Monthly totals are green

Step-By-Step

1. In your **Goals** file, select **B12:E12**.
2. Choose **Home>Font**. Click the **Font** group dialog box launcher.
3. In the **Format Cells** dialog box, click the **Font** tab.
4. Click the **Color** drop-down arrow. Under **Standard Colors**, choose **Green** (see Figure 3.17). Click **OK**.
5. Click on the lower right corner of cell **E12** and drag it to the right to cell **F12**. In the **Auto Fill Options** drop-down menu, choose **Fill Formatting Only**.
6. Click **F12**. Choose **Home>Font** and click the **Font Color** drop-down arrow. Under **Standard Colors**, choose **Red**.
7. **CHECK** Your screen should look like Figure 3.18.
8. Save and close your file.

Continue to the next exercise.

Differentiated Instruction/Visually Impaired If students cannot distinguish color, point out that the name of each color appears when you place the pointer over the color tile in the Font Color drop-down menu.

Solution Use the file **Goals-SF.xlsx** as a solution file for Exercises 3-1 through 3-6.

Step-By-Step

EXERCISE 3-16 (Continued)
Create a Report Using the Report Wizard

12 Select **Access 2007**. Click **Next** to accept the style. Name the report **Customer Orders**. Select **Modify the report's design**. Click **Finish**.

13 CHECK Your screen should look like Figure 3.47.

14 Click the **View** drop-down arrow and select **Layout View**.

15 Click the **Quantity** header to select the quantity column and drag it to the right of **Product Description**. Narrow the quantity column so the form fits in the window.

16 Select the **Price** column header and narrow it to fit.

17 Select the **Customer Name** header. Resize the column until all the customer names fit.

18 CHECK Your screen should look like Figure 3.48.

19 Choose **Office>Print> Print Preview**. Click **Print**. Ask your teacher where to print the form and click **OK** to print. Close the form and click **Yes** to save changes.

Continue to the next exercise.

FIGURE 3.47 Customer Orders form in Design View

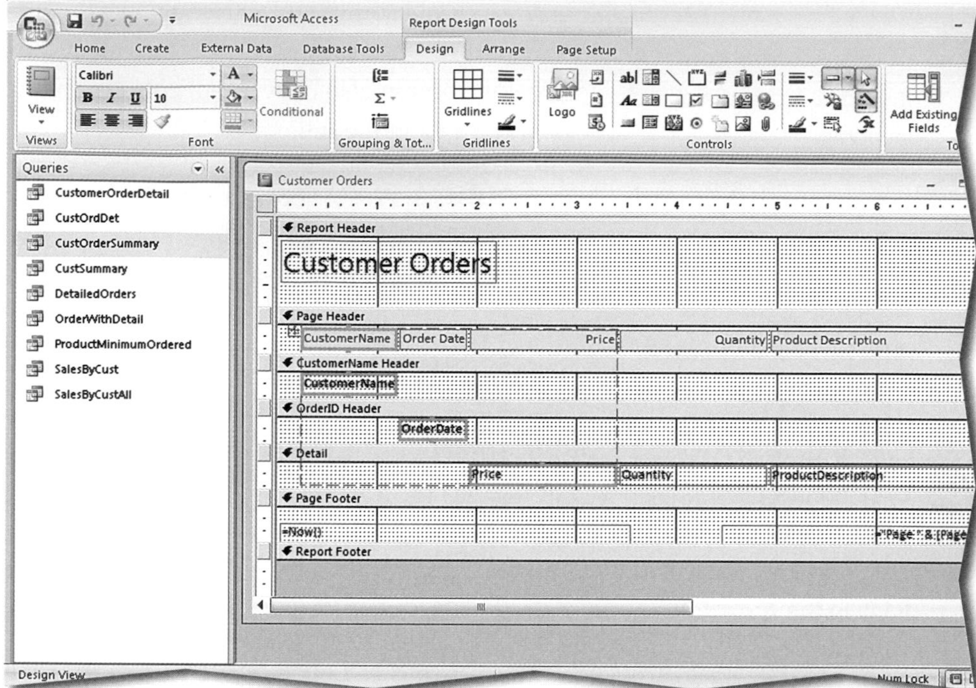

FIGURE 3.48 Customer Orders form in Layout View

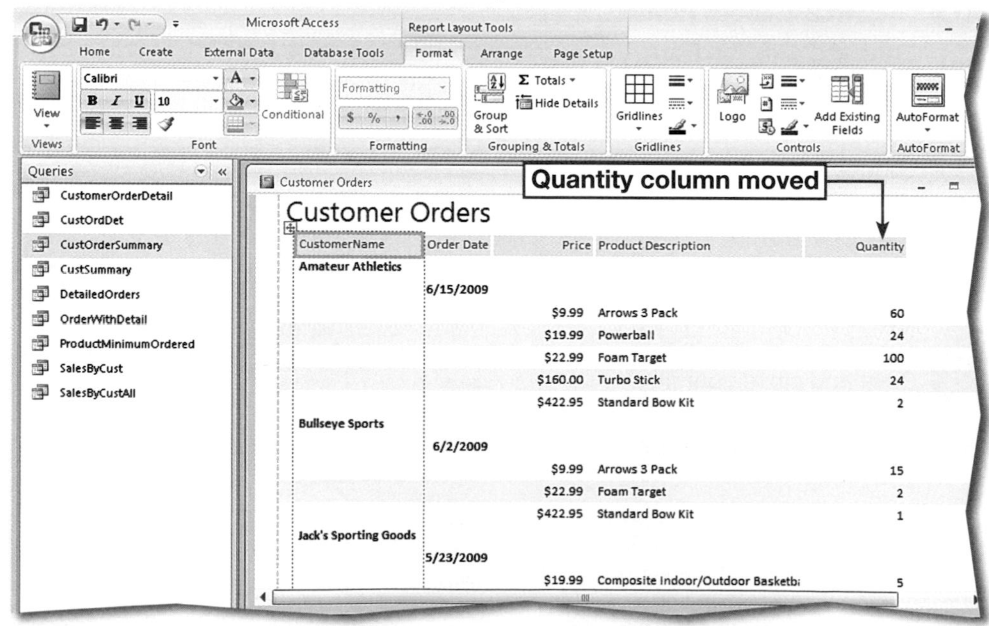

Step-By-Step Tip In **Steps 16 and 17**, let students know that if they try to **AutoFit** the columns, they will not be able to view all the text in other columns and all the entries in the **Price** column will change to ####.

Step-By-Step

1. Open the data file **Supplies.xlsx**. Save as: Supplies-[your first initial and last name].
2. Select **B2:B9**.
3. Choose **Home>Styles>Cell Styles**.
4. In the Cell Styles list, under Number Format, choose **Currency** (see Figure 3.19).
5. Select **C2:C8**.
6. Choose **Home>Styles>Cell Styles**.
7. In the Cell Styles list under Number Format, click **Percent**.
8. Click **C9**.
9. **CHECK** Your screen should look like Figure 3.20.
10. Save your file.

Continue to the next exercise.

Microsoft Office 2007

When you rest your pointer on a cell style thumbnail without clicking, the Microsoft Office 2007 Quick Styles feature allows you to see how the style affects your data.

EXERCISE 3-7
Apply Cell Styles

A **cell style** is a set of formatting traits that has been given a name. When you apply a cell style, you apply all of the formatting traits of that style. Microsoft Office 2007 has several built-in cell styles, called Quick Styles, which allow you to change the look of a group of data (such as currency or percentages) in one quick step.

Teaching Tip Explain to students that Excel cell styles can be modified to customize data. For example, one currency style may not always be appropriate for a column of monetary data.

FIGURE 3.19 Cell Styles

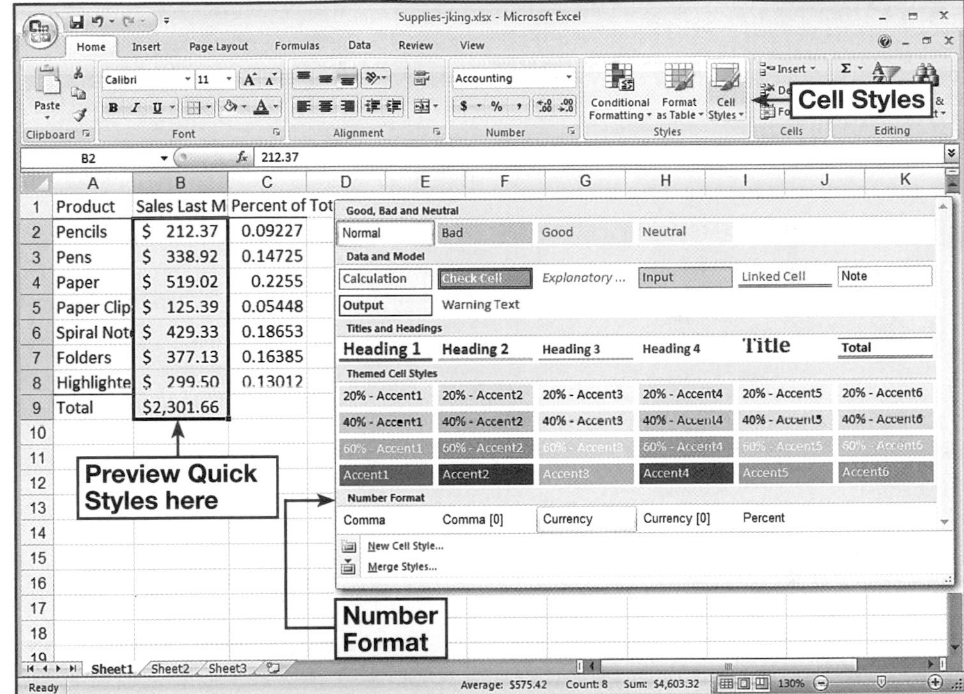

FIGURE 3.20 Percent style applied to selected cells

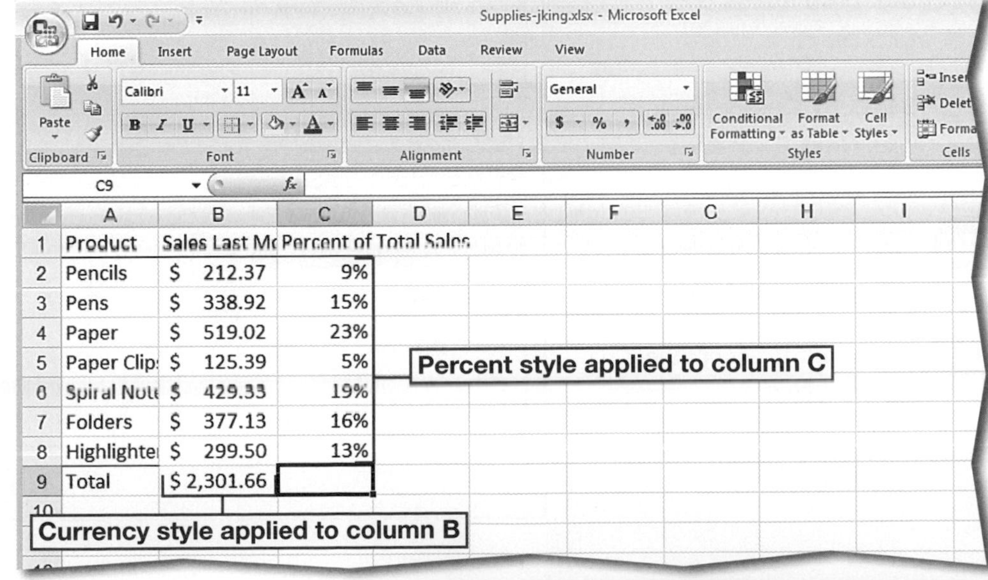

EXERCISE 3-16

Create a Report Using the Report Wizard

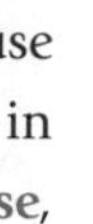

A report is a document that presents findings. In business, inventory reports may indicate that more parts need to be ordered, while financial reports help a company **document**, or track, how money is used. The simplest way to create a report is to use the Report Tool, which creates a report from the table or query you have selected in the Navigation Pane. The Access Report Wizard also makes it easy to create and **revise**, or make changes to, a simple report.

FIGURE 3.45 CustOrderSummary Simple Form

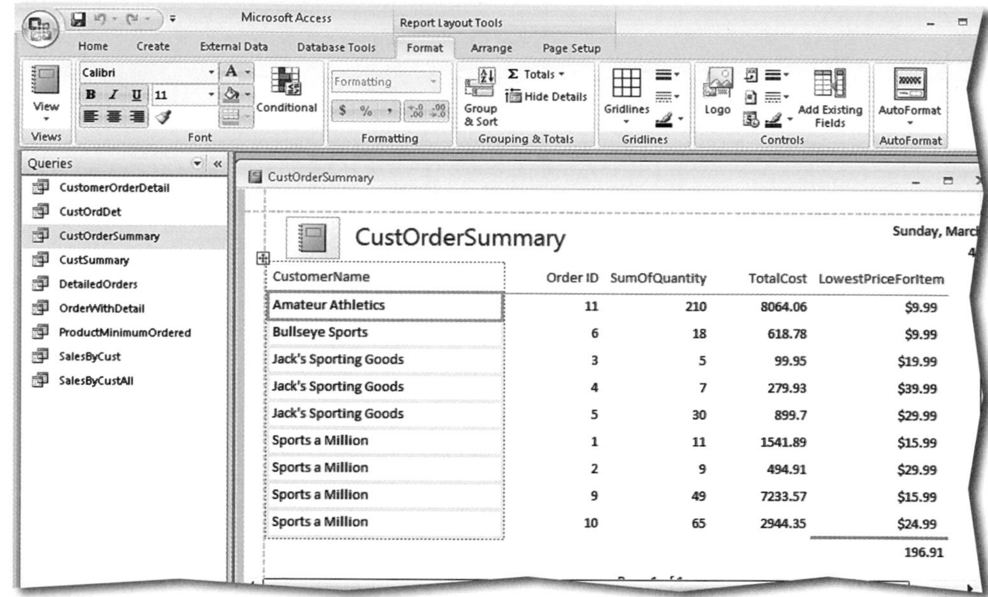

FIGURE 3.46 Report Wizard

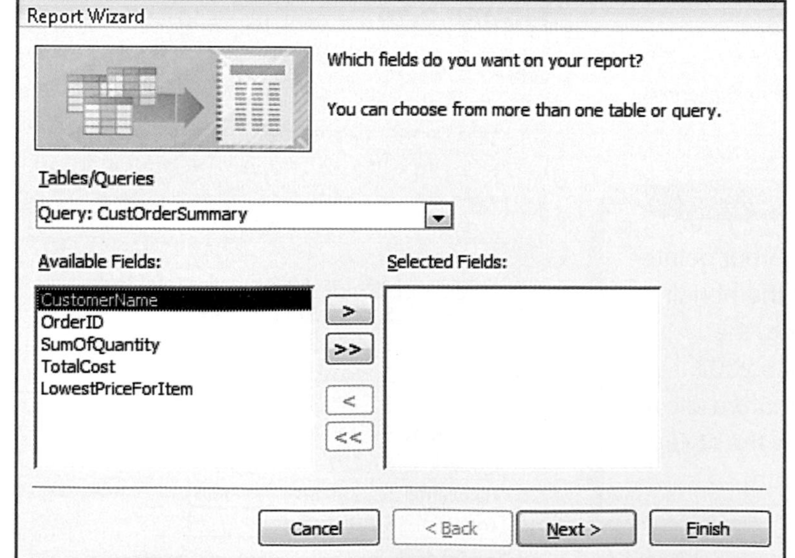

Step-By-Step

1. In your **Sports** file, open the **CustOrderSummary** query.
2. Choose **Create>Reports> Report** .
3. **CHECK** Your screen should look like Figure 3.45.
4. Click **Close** . Click **No**. Close the query.
5. Choose **Create>Reports> Report Wizard** .
6. **CHECK** Your screen should look like Figure 3.46.
7. In the **Tables/Queries** box, select **Query: CustomerOrderDetail**.
8. Move **CustomerName, OrderDate, Quantity, ProductDescription**, and **Price** from the **Available Fields** box to the **Selected Fields** box. Click **Next**.
9. Select **by Customer** and click **Next**. Click **Next** again.
10. Select **Price** in the first sort order box. Click **Next**.
11. Click **Next** to accept the current layout.

Continued on the next page.

Step-By-Step

1. In your **Supplies** file, click **A1**.
2. In the column heading row, move the pointer to the line between column headings A and B until the pointer becomes a double arrow (see Figure 3.21).
3. Click and drag to the right to make the column wider until you can see all of the text in the cells.
4. Double-click the line between column headings B and C (see Figure 3.21).
5. Click **C1**.
6. Choose **Home>Cells>Format**. Click **Column Width**.
7. In the **Column Width** box, key: 19.
8. Click **OK**.
9. **CHECK** Your screen should look like Figure 3.22.
10. Save your file.

Continue to the next exercise.

Teaching Tip Remind students that they can see the entire contents of a cell in the formula bar.

EXERCISE 3-8
Change Column Width

Often, the contents of a cell do not fit in the cell. Excel has several methods to change column width. You can drag the line between the column headings, double-click the line between the column headings to AutoFit them, or use the Format menu to adjust column width using a specified value.

FIGURE 3.21 Adjusting column width by dragging

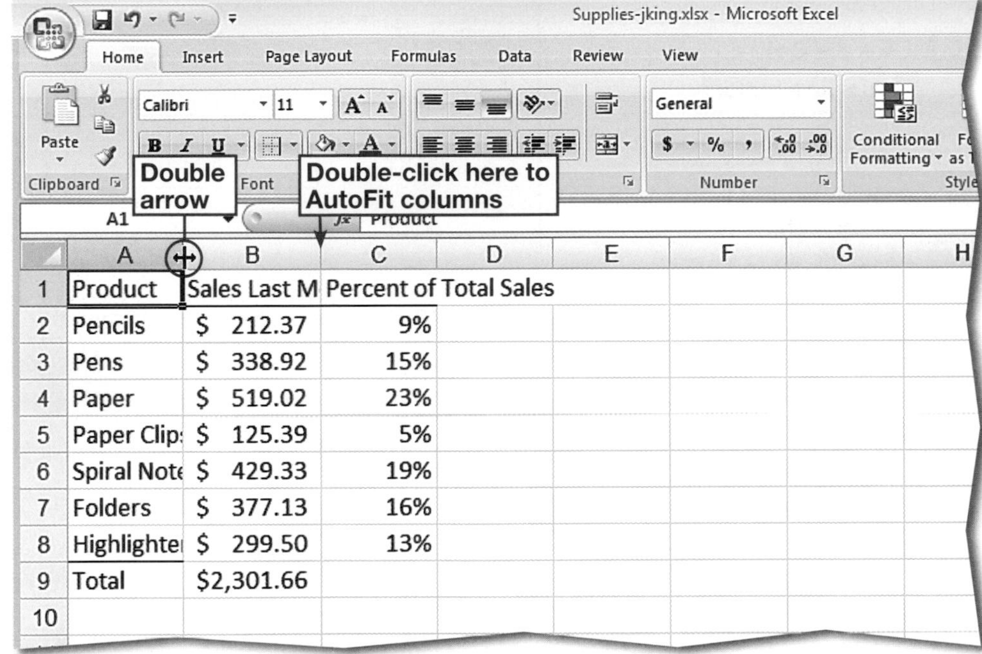

FIGURE 3.22 Resized columns

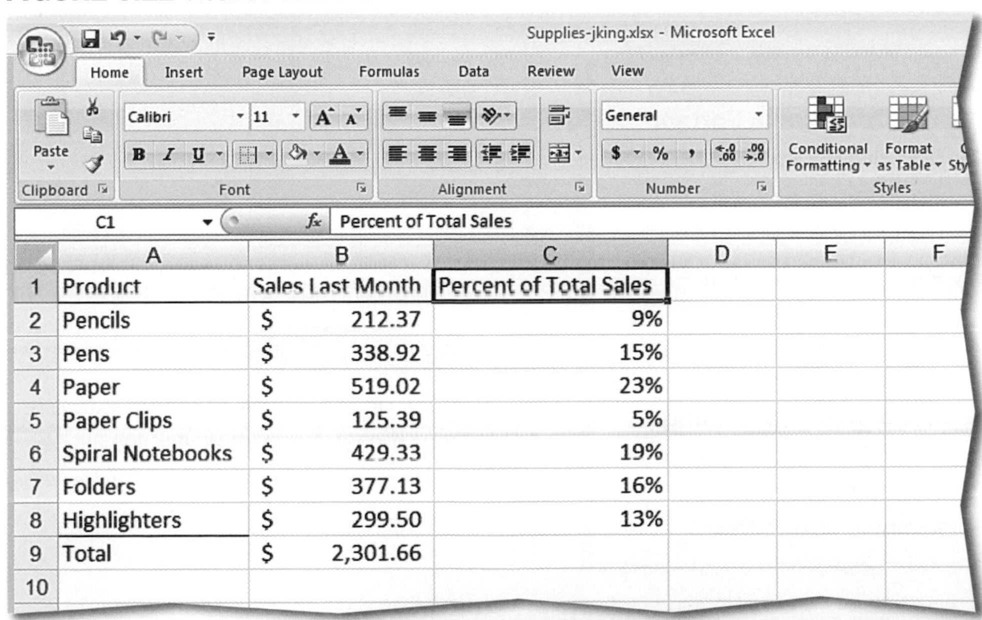

Step-By-Step

EXERCISE 3-15 (Continued)
Apply and Change Conditional Formatting on Controls

11. Under Condition 2, click the drop-down arrow in the second box and select **equal to**.

12. Click in the third box and key: CA.

13. Click the **Bold** and **Underline** buttons.

14. CHECK Your screen should look like Figure 3.43.

15. Click **OK**. Click **Form View**.

16. Press PAGE DOWN twice.

17. CHECK Your screen should look like Figure 3.44.

18. Close the form. Click **Yes** to save the changes.

Continue to the next exercise.

FIGURE 3.43 Condition 2 in dialog box

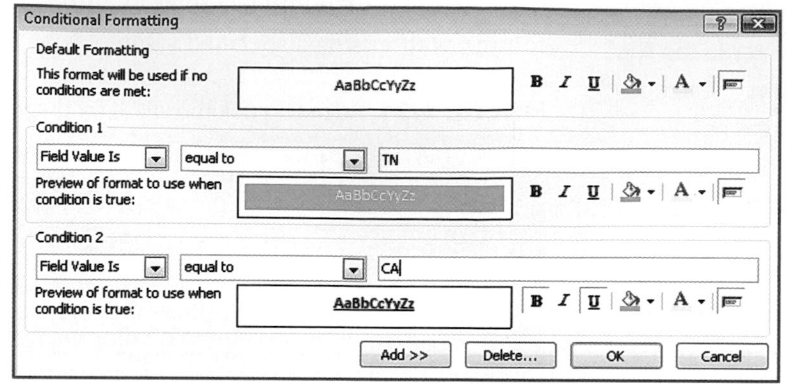

FIGURE 3.44 Form with conditional formats

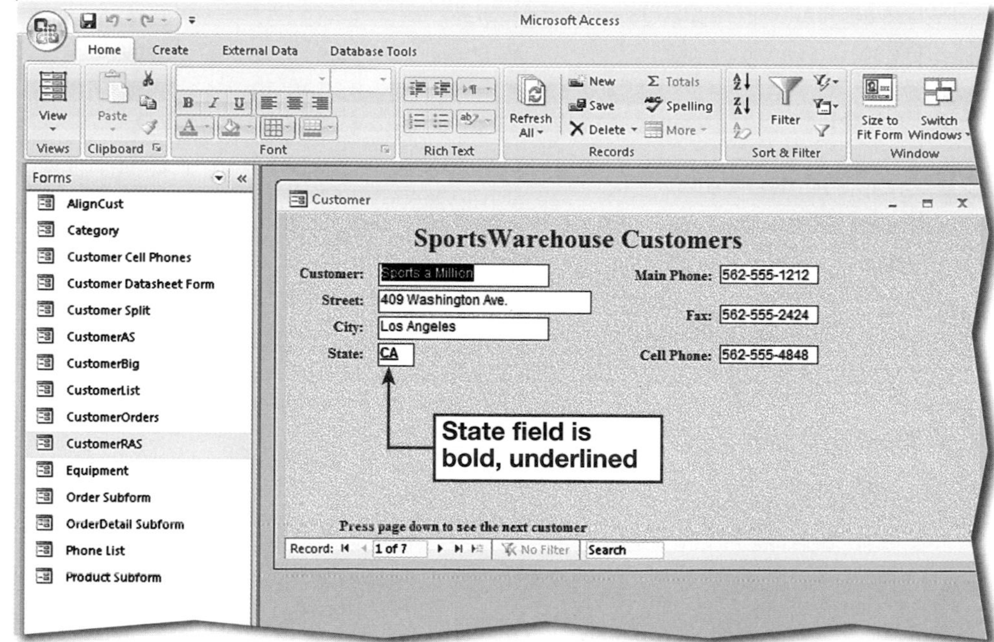

Academic Skills

The **Conditional Formatting** dialog box depends on expressions that are mathematical operators. On a separate sheet of paper, write down the expressions from the second box of the first condition in the **Conditional Formatting** dialog box. Also write the expressions' mathematical symbols next to them.

Tech Tip

Click on the edges of the form to expand the window border so that the whole form is visible.

NCLB/Math (Number and Operations) Ask students to identify what mathematical symbols correspond with the **equal to** condition.

EXERCISE 3-9
Change Row Height

You can change row height to fit the contents of a cell or to call attention to labels or totals. You can change row height by dragging the line between row headings or using the Format menu.

FIGURE 3.23 Adjusting row height by dragging

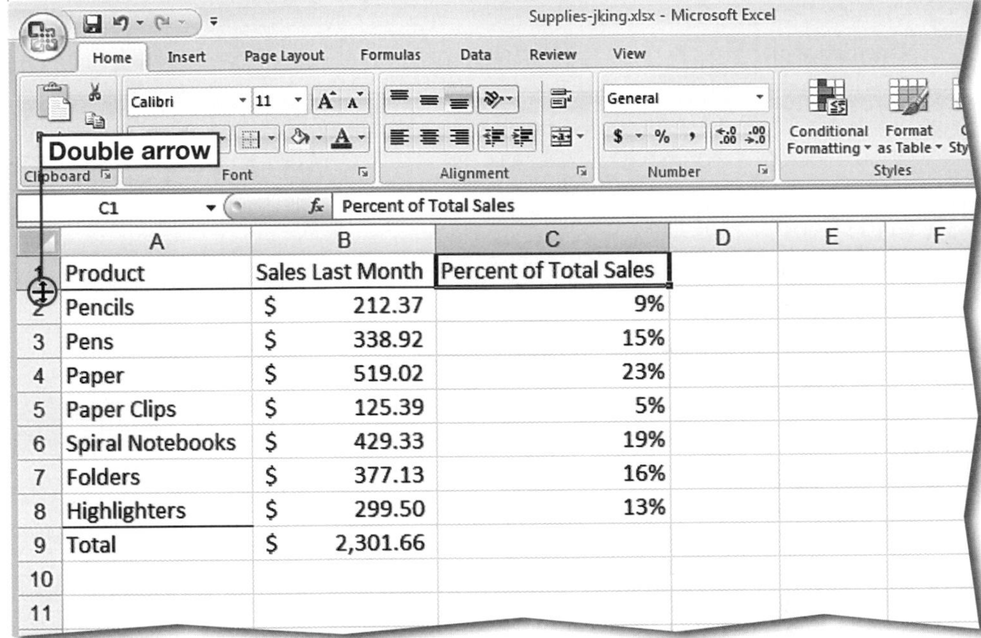

FIGURE 3.24 Row height resized

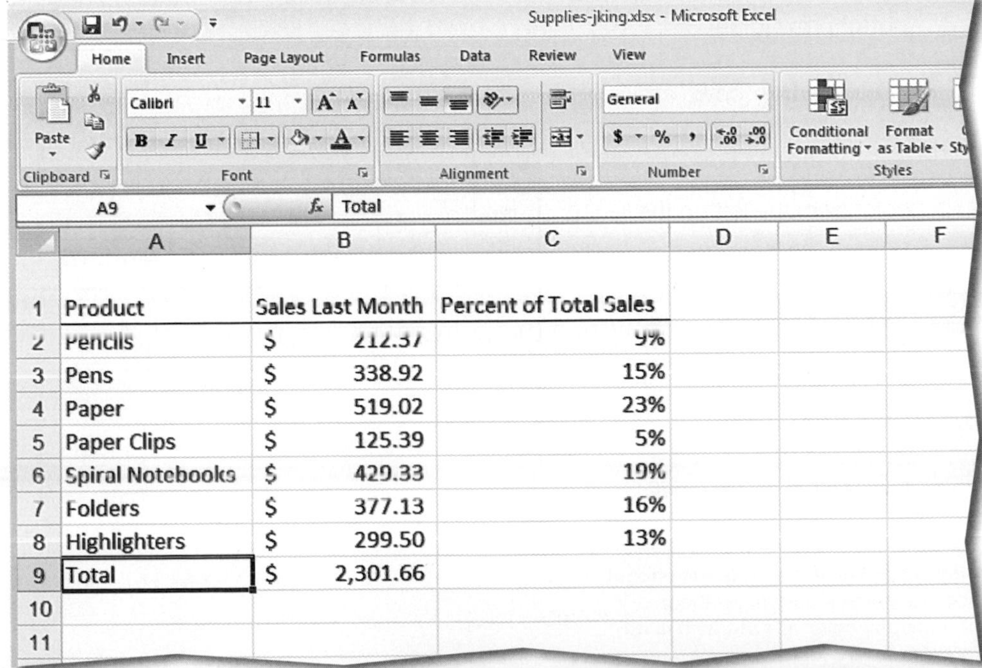

Step-By-Step

1. In your **Supplies** file, move the pointer to the line between row headings 1 and 2 (see Figure 3.23).
2. Click and drag down until the line is even with the bottom of row 2.
3. Click **A9**.
4. Choose **Home>Cells> Format**. Click **Row Height**.
5. In the Row Height box, key: 25. Click **OK**.
6. Click cell **A9**. Choose **Home>Cells>Format** and then click **AutoFit Row Height**. Now row 9 is just tall enough for the contents in the row.
7. **CHECK** Your screen should look like Figure 3.24.
8. Save your file.

Continue to the next exercise.

Different Strokes In **Step 6**, you can also double-click on the line between rows to AutoFit.

Differentiated Instruction/ Advanced Students Show students that they can drag to change the height of several rows at once. Select the rows and then drag the line between any of the highlighted row headings to change the height of all.

Step-By-Step

1. In your **Sports** file, open the **CustomerRAS** form in **Design View**.
2. Click the **State** control.
3. Choose **Design>Font>Conditional** .
4. CHECK Your screen should look like Figure 3.41.
5. In the **Conditional Formatting** dialog box under **Condition 1**, click the drop-down arrow in the second box and select **equal to**.
6. Click in the third box and key: TN.
7. Click the drop-down arrow next to **Fill/Back Color** and select the fourth color from the right on the bottom row (blue).
8. Click the drop-down arrow next to the **Font/Fore Color** and select the fourth color from the left on the bottom row (yellow).
9. CHECK Your screen should look like Figure 3.42.
10. Click **Add**.

Continued on the next page.

Teaching Tip If the students cannot find the correct colors, let them choose any color as long as it is different from the default.

EXERCISE 3-15
Apply and Change Conditional Formatting on Controls

Conditional formatting means that a control can be set to appear one way for most data displayed in the control, and another way when certain conditions are met. You can set several conditional formats for one control. You can also set the control to display the different conditions differently.

FIGURE 3.41 Conditional Formatting dialog box

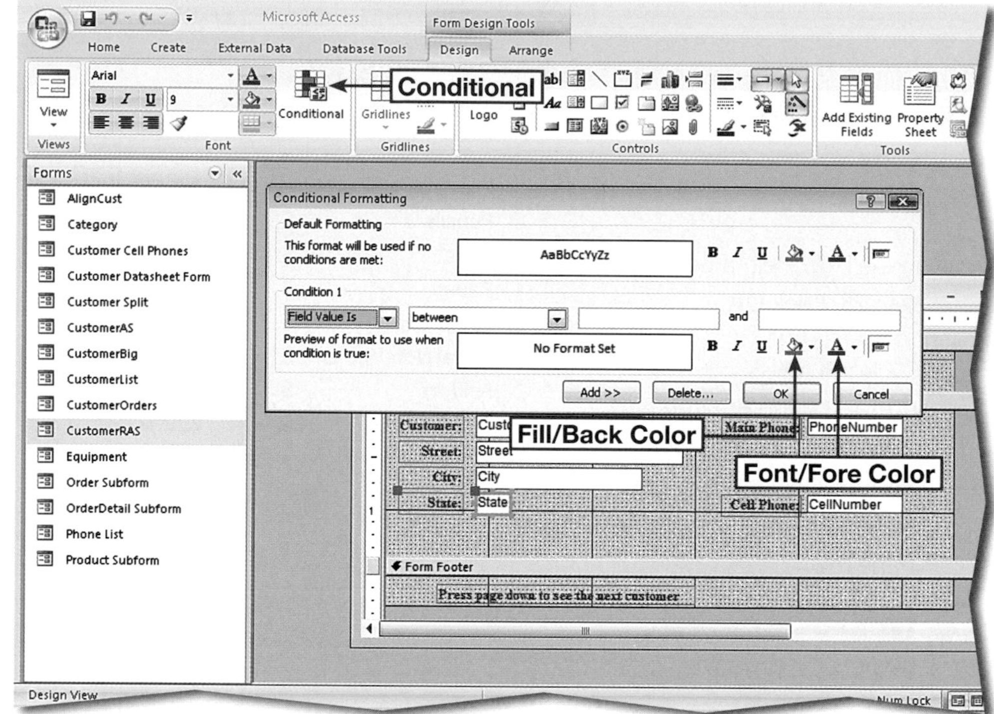

FIGURE 3.42 Condition 1 in dialog box

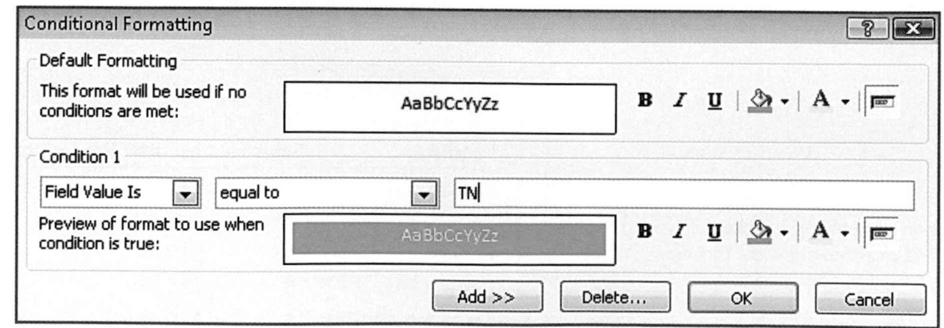

Step-By-Step

1. In your **Supplies** file, key the data shown in column D of Figure 3.25.
2. Use the **Cell Styles** drop-down menu to apply the Currency Number Format to cells D2:D9. AutoFit column D.
3. Click column heading **C** to select column C.
4. Choose **Home>Cells> Format**. Under Visibility, choose **Hide & Unhide> Hide Columns**.
5. Click row heading **9** to select the row.
6. Choose **Home>Cells> Format**. Under **Visibility**, choose **Hide & Unhide> Hide Rows**.
7. **CHECK** Your screen should look like Figure 3.26.
8. Select column heading **B** through column heading **D**. Choose **Home>Cells> Format>Hide & Unhide**. Click **Unhide Columns**.
9. Select row heading **8** through row heading **10**. Choose **Home>Cells> Format>Hide & Unhide**. Click **Unhide Rows**. Save your file.

Continue to the next exercise.

EXERCISE 3-10
Hide and Unhide Columns and Rows

To make your worksheet easier to read, you can hide columns or rows. Hiding a column can make it easier to compare data side by side, and hiding a row can help you to focus only on certain data. Unhide columns and rows when you want to see them again.

Teaching Tip Explain to students that Hide can be used to simplify a worksheet. In this worksheet, hiding row 9 and column C allows students to quickly compare last month's sales with this month's sales.

FIGURE 3.25 Data added to worksheet

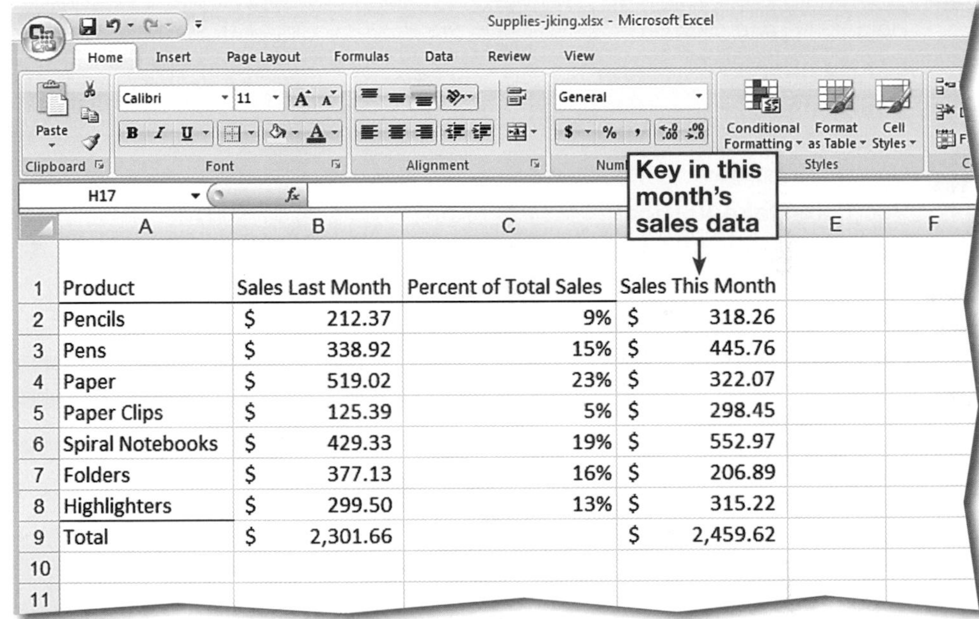

	A	B	C	D
1	Product	Sales Last Month	Percent of Total Sales	Sales This Month
2	Pencils	$ 212.37	9%	$ 318.26
3	Pens	$ 338.92	15%	$ 445.76
4	Paper	$ 519.02	23%	$ 322.07
5	Paper Clips	$ 125.39	5%	$ 298.45
6	Spiral Notebooks	$ 429.33	19%	$ 552.97
7	Folders	$ 377.13	16%	$ 206.89
8	Highlighters	$ 299.50	13%	$ 315.22
9	Total	$ 2,301.66		$ 2,459.62

FIGURE 3.26 Column and row hidden

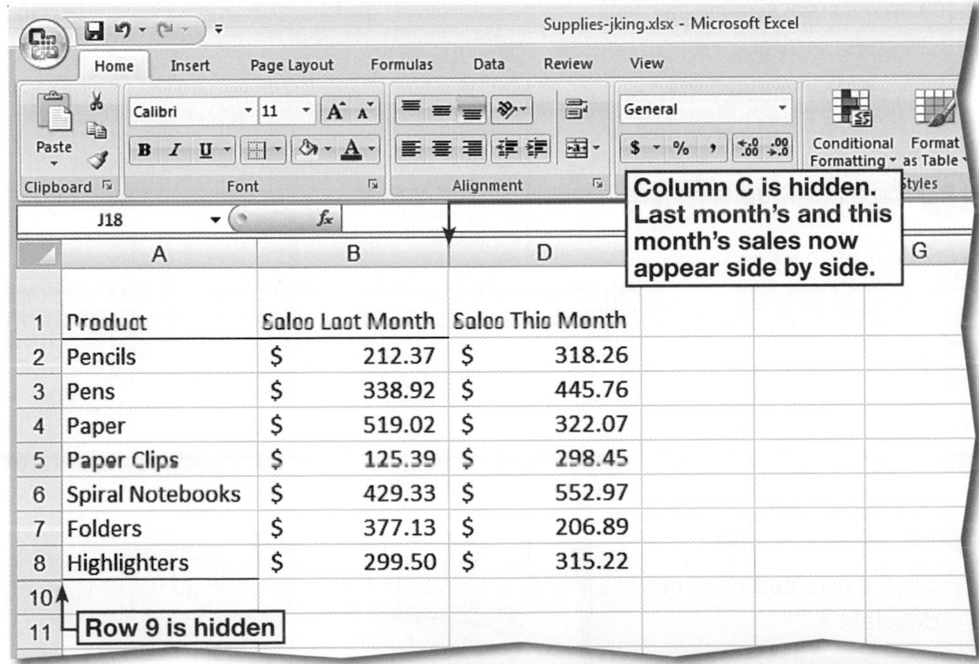

	A	B	D
1	Product	Sales Last Month	Sales This Month
2	Pencils	$ 212.37	$ 318.26
3	Pens	$ 338.92	$ 445.76
4	Paper	$ 519.02	$ 322.07
5	Paper Clips	$ 125.39	$ 298.45
6	Spiral Notebooks	$ 429.33	$ 552.97
7	Folders	$ 377.13	$ 206.89
8	Highlighters	$ 299.50	$ 315.22

Step-By-Step

10 Click the **FAXNumber** control. Hold SHIFT and click the **Fax** label box. Choose **Arrange>Control Alignment>Align Top**.

11 Click **PhoneNumber**. Hold SHIFT and click **FAXNumber** and **CellNumber**.

12 Choose **Arrange> Position>Make Vertical Spacing Equal**.

13 CHECK Your screen should look like Figure 3.39.

14 Click **CustomerName**. Hold SHIFT and click the **Street**, **City**, and **State** controls.

15 Choose **Design>Tools> Property Sheet**.

16 In the **Property Sheet** click the **Format** tab. Click in the **Left** box and key: 0.875. Close the **Property Sheet**.

17 Click **Form View**.

18 CHECK Your screen should look like Figure 3.40.

19 Close the form. Click **Yes**.

Continue to the next exercise.

Shortcuts

Click a selected control to deselect it.

EXERCISE 3-14 (Continued)
Resize, Align, and Space Controls

FIGURE 3.39 Controls aligned vertically

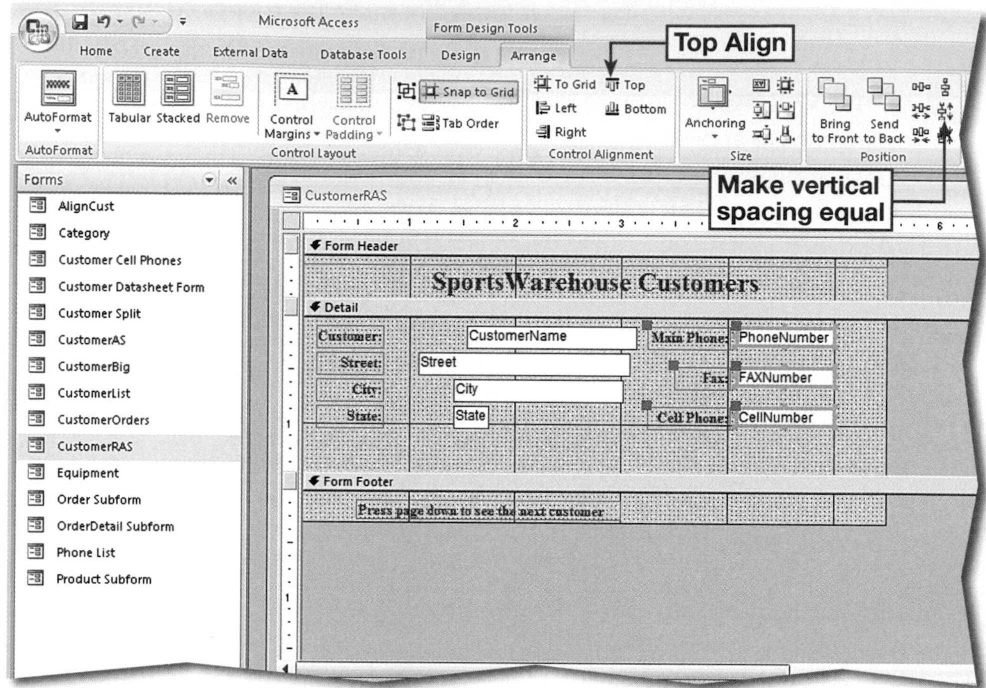

FIGURE 3.40 Properly spaced form

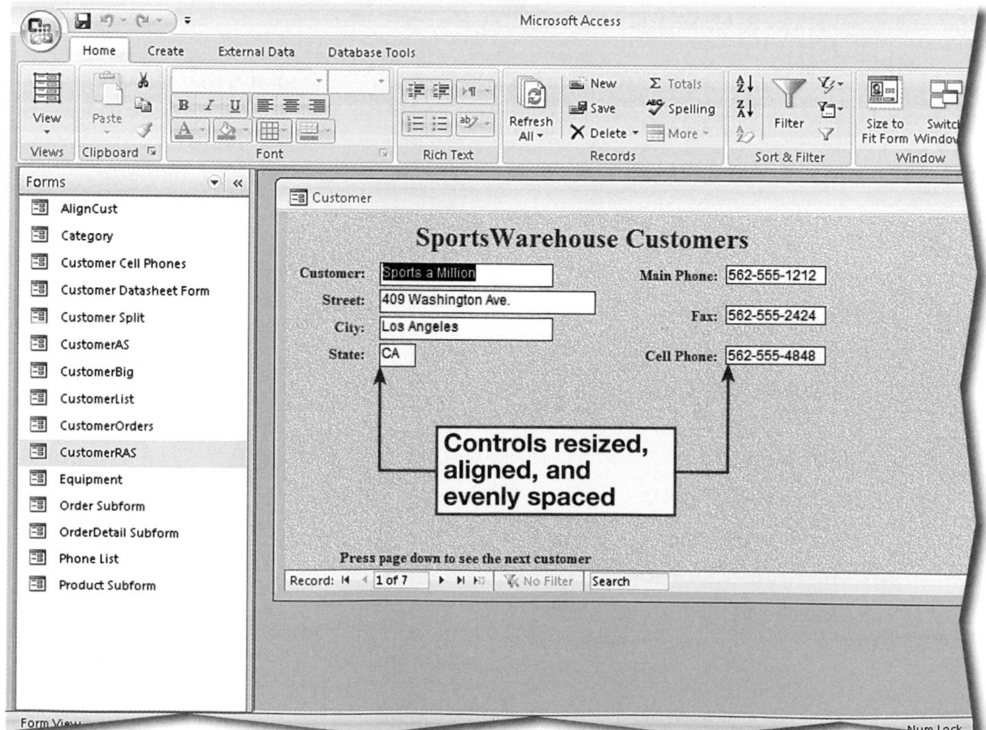

Step-By-Step

1. In your **Supplies** file, select **C2:C8**.
2. On the **Home** tab, click the **Alignment** group dialog box launcher (see Figure 3.27).
3. In the **Format Cells** dialog box, click the **Alignment** tab.
4. Click the **Horizontal** drop-down arrow. Select **Center**. Click **OK**.
5. CHECK Your screen should look like Figure 3.28.
6. Save and close your file.

Continue to the next exercise.

Microsoft Office 2007

When you select text, use the Left, Center, and Right buttons on the Mini toolbar to change alignment more quickly.

EL Explain to English learners that horizontal refers to formatting that spans from left to right and that vertical refers to formatting that spans from top to bottom.

Differentiated Instruction/ Advanced Students Encourage advanced students to experiment with the Orientation options in the Alignment group.

Solution Use the file **Supplies-SF** as a solution file for Exercises 3-7 through 3-11.

EXERCISE 3-11
Change Horizontal Alignment

Change the **horizontal alignment** to align the contents of a cell to the left, center, or right. You can use the Format Cells dialog box or the buttons in the Alignment group on the Home tab to change the alignment of a cell's contents.

FIGURE 3.27 Alignment tab in Format Cells dialog box

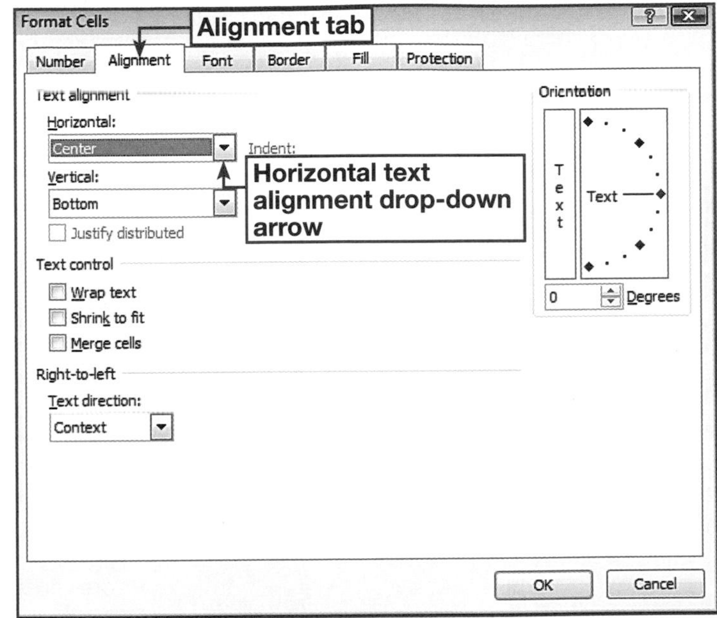

FIGURE 3.28 Cells with center alignment

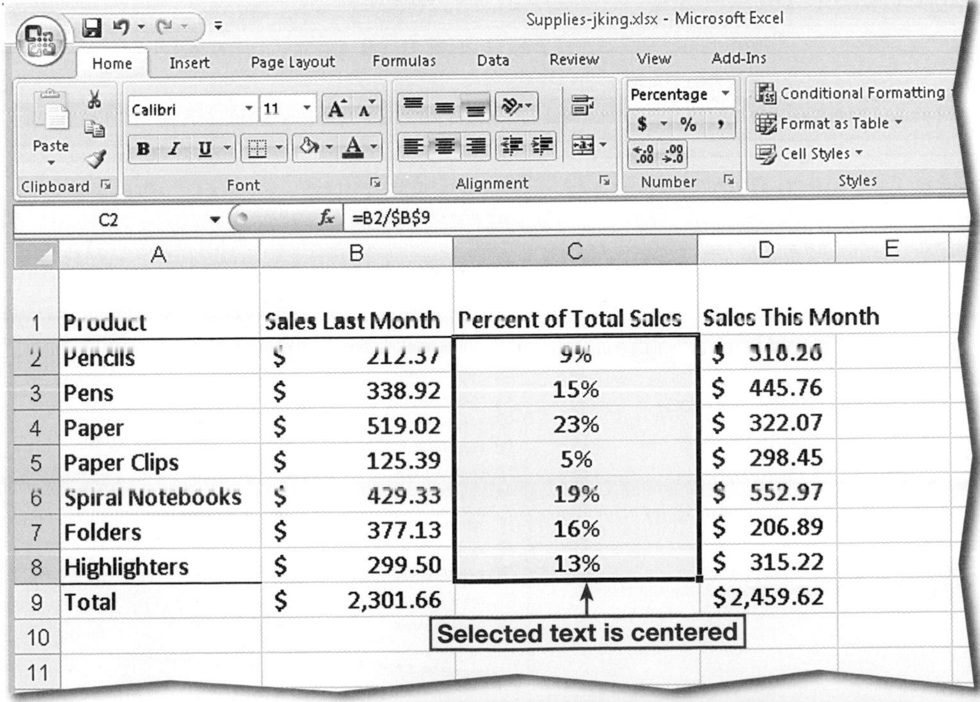

	A	B	C	D	E
1	Product	Sales Last Month	Percent of Total Sales	Sales This Month	
2	Pencils	$ 212.37	9%	$ 318.26	
3	Pens	$ 338.92	15%	$ 445.76	
4	Paper	$ 519.02	23%	$ 322.07	
5	Paper Clips	$ 125.39	5%	$ 298.45	
6	Spiral Notebooks	$ 429.33	19%	$ 552.97	
7	Folders	$ 377.13	16%	$ 206.89	
8	Highlighters	$ 299.50	13%	$ 315.22	
9	Total	$ 2,301.66		$2,459.62	
10					
11					

EXERCISE 3-14
Resize, Align, and Space Controls

In professional forms and reports, controls are equally sized, neatly aligned, and evenly spaced. Fields that are too big or too small can be resized. Access also provides tools to align and space controls correctly so that you do not have to make more than minor adjustments.

Step-By-Step Tip In **Step 5**, remind students to hold down the **Shift** key when selecting multiple controls.

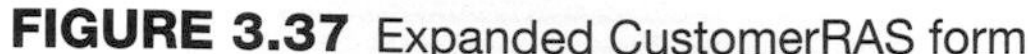

FIGURE 3.37 Expanded CustomerRAS form

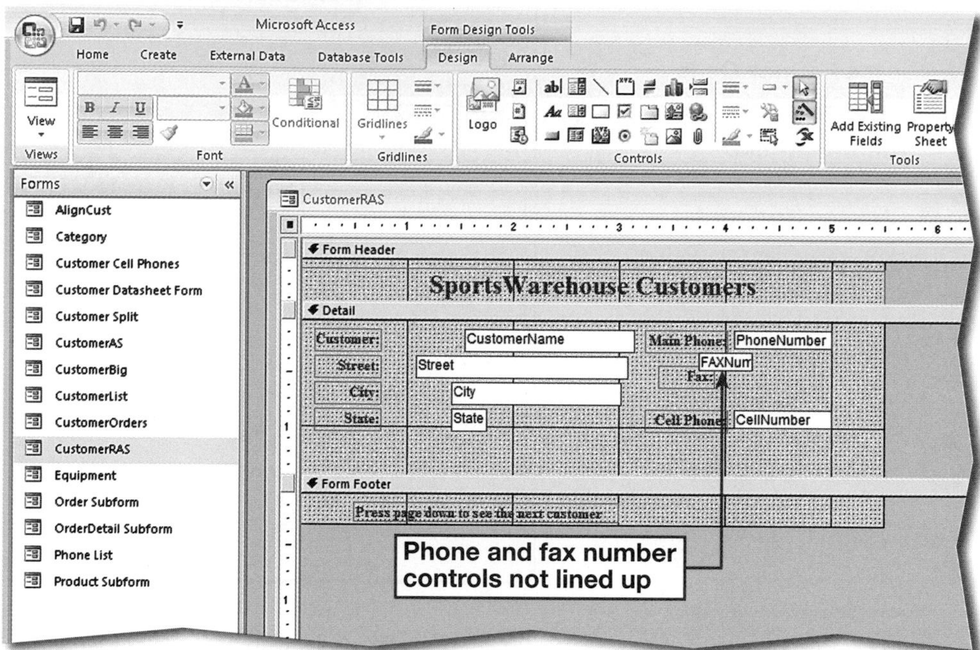

FIGURE 3.38 Controls aligned right

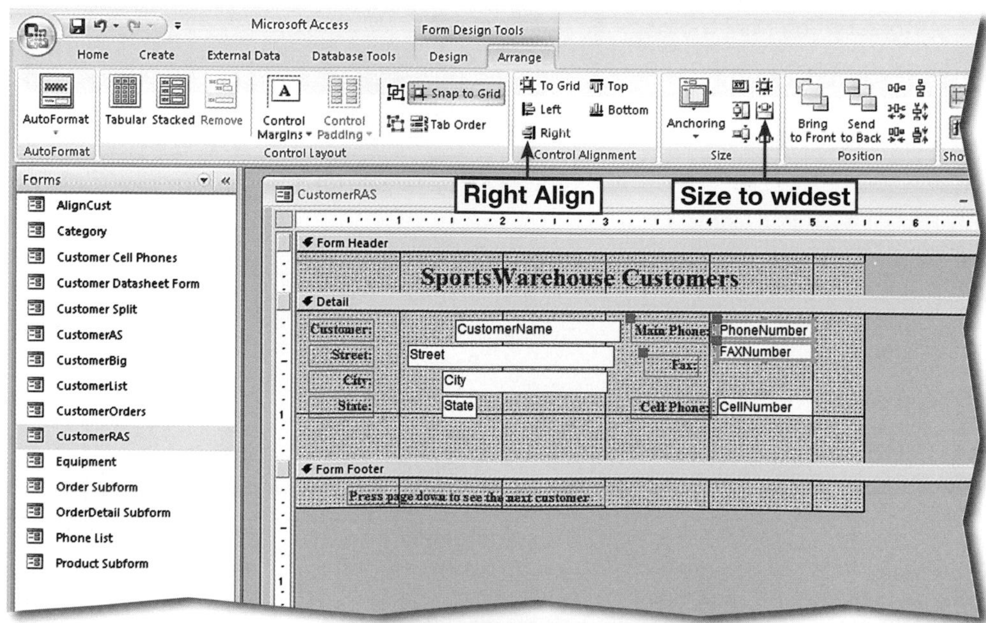

Step-By-Step

1. In your **Sports** file, open the **CustomerRAS** form in **Design View**.
2. Expand the window border so that the whole form is visible.
3. **CHECK** Your screen should look like Figure 3.37.
4. Press and hold SHIFT and click the **PhoneNumber** and **FAXNum** controls.
5. Choose **Arrange>Size>Size to Widest**.
6. Choose **Arrange>Control Alignment>Align Right**.
7. **CHECK** Your screen should look like Figure 3.38.
8. Click the **Main Phone** label box. Press and hold SHIFT and click the **FAX** label box.
9. Click **Align Right**.

Continued on the next page.

Troubleshooter

Many of the tools used to format controls are accessible only when your form is displayed in **Design View**.

Step-By-Step

1. Open the data file **Computers.xlsx**. Save as: Computers-[your first initial and last name].
2. Click **B1**.
3. Key: Monthly Sales.
4. Press ENTER.
5. Select **B1:D1**.
6. On the **Home** tab, click the **Alignment** dialog box launcher.
7. In the **Format Cells** dialog box, click the **Alignment** tab.
8. Click the **Horizontal** drop-down arrow. Select **Center Across Selection** (see Figure 3.29). Click **OK**.
9. **CHECK** Your screen should look like Figure 3.30.
10. Save your file.

Continue to the next exercise.

Shortcuts

In Microsoft Office 2007, you can merge and center cell contents by choosing **Home>Alignment> Merge & Center.**

Teaching Tip Show students that the contents of cell B1 are in B1 even though they look to be in C1. Have them click B1 and C1 and look in the formula bar.

EXERCISE 3-12
Center Across Selection

If you want to center text across a range of cells, use the Center Across Selection feature. For example, you can center a title over a range of cells for extra emphasis. You can also use this feature to emphasize headings.

FIGURE 3.29 Center Across Selection selected on Alignment tab

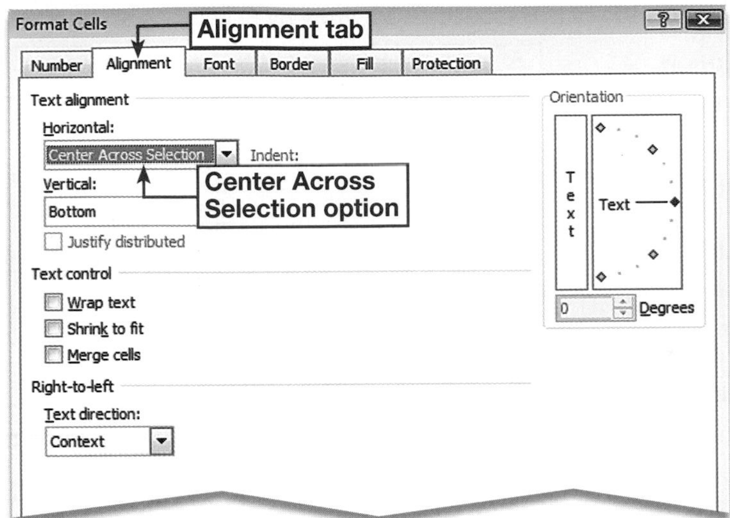

FIGURE 3.30 Center Across Selection applied to selected text

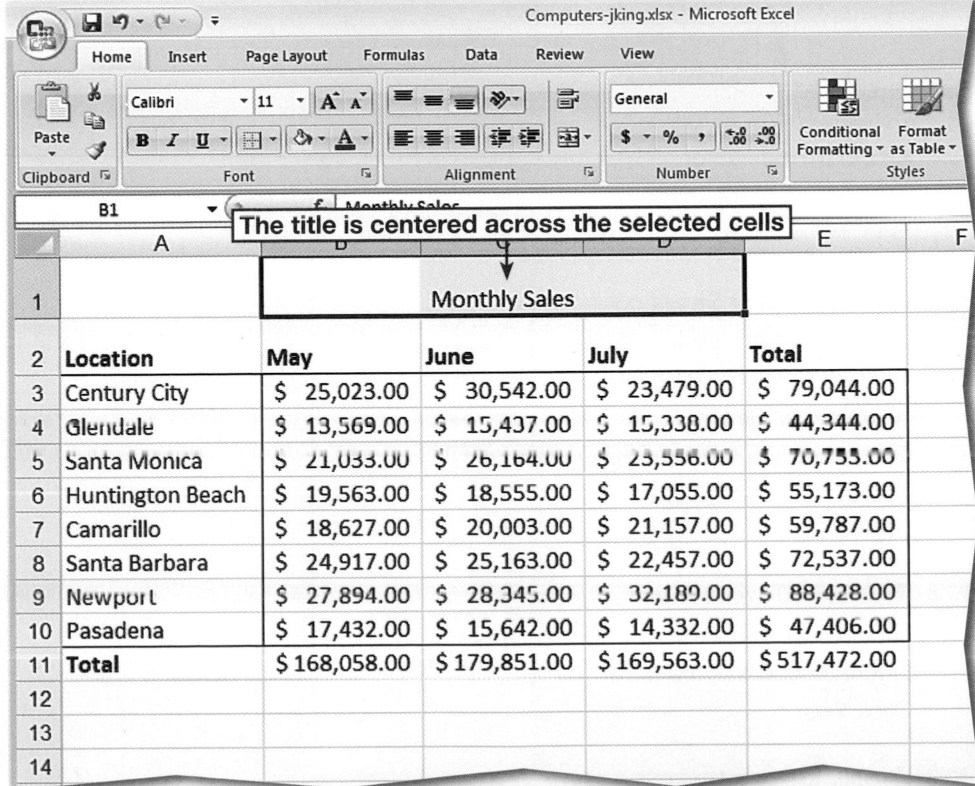

	A	B	C	D	E
1			Monthly Sales		
2	Location	May	June	July	Total
3	Century City	$ 25,023.00	$ 30,542.00	$ 23,479.00	$ 79,044.00
4	Glendale	$ 13,569.00	$ 15,437.00	$ 15,338.00	$ 44,344.00
5	Santa Monica	$ 21,033.00	$ 26,164.00	$ 23,556.00	$ 70,753.00
6	Huntington Beach	$ 19,563.00	$ 18,555.00	$ 17,055.00	$ 55,173.00
7	Camarillo	$ 18,627.00	$ 20,003.00	$ 21,157.00	$ 59,787.00
8	Santa Barbara	$ 24,917.00	$ 25,163.00	$ 22,457.00	$ 72,537.00
9	Newport	$ 27,894.00	$ 28,345.00	$ 32,189.00	$ 88,428.00
10	Pasadena	$ 17,432.00	$ 15,642.00	$ 14,332.00	$ 47,406.00
11	Total	$ 168,058.00	$ 179,851.00	$ 169,563.00	$ 517,472.00
12					
13					
14					

Step-By-Step

1. Open the **Customer-Orders** form in **Design View**. Click on the **CustomerOrders** title in the **Form Header**. Click **Property Sheet**.

2. In the **Property Sheet**, click the **Format** tab. Click the **Fore Color** box. Click **Builder**. Select **Purple**.

3. In the **Form** window in the **Detail** section, select the **CustomerName** control.

4. In the **Property Sheet**, click **Back Color**. Click **Builder**. Select **Yellow**.

5. CHECK Your screen should look similar to Figure 3.35.

6. In the **CustomerOrders** design window in the **OrderDetail** subform, scroll down to the **Price** field and select it.

7. In the **Property Sheet** on the **Format** tab, click **Format**. Click the drop-down arrow. Select **Standard**. Click **Property Sheet**. Click **Form View**.

8. CHECK Your screen should look similar to Figure 3.36. Close the form. Click **Yes**.

Continue to the next exercise.

EXERCISE 3-13
Format Controls

The format controls in Access help you make forms more presentable and the information more readable. You can change font sizes, colors, the background color and even the font of controls. You also can format the information that each control presents, such as the unit of currency, the current date and time, and more.

Differentiated Instruction/Advanced Students Have advanced students format additional controls in the form.

FIGURE 3.35 Property Sheet

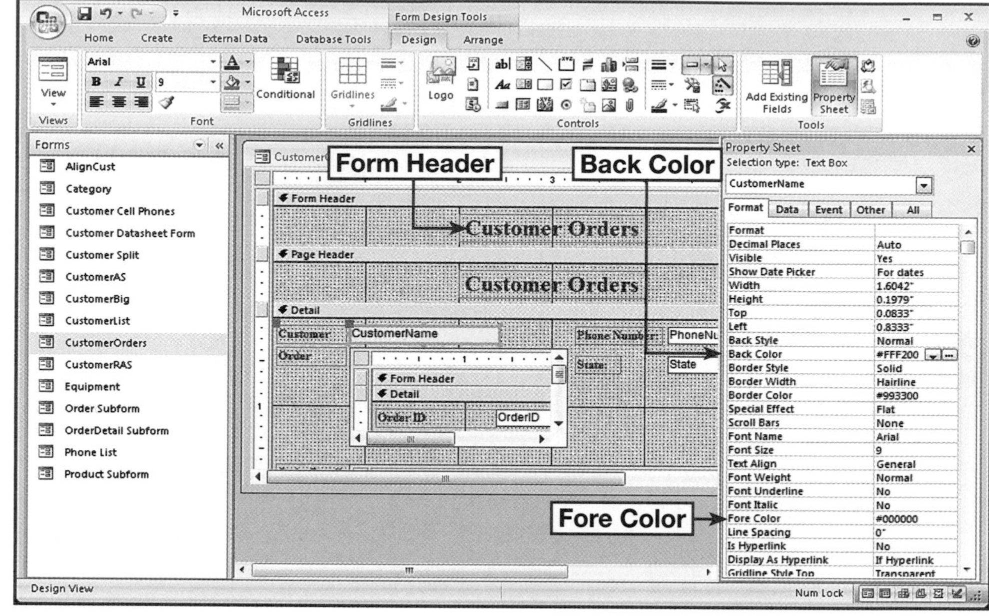

FIGURE 3.36 Revised CustomerOrders form

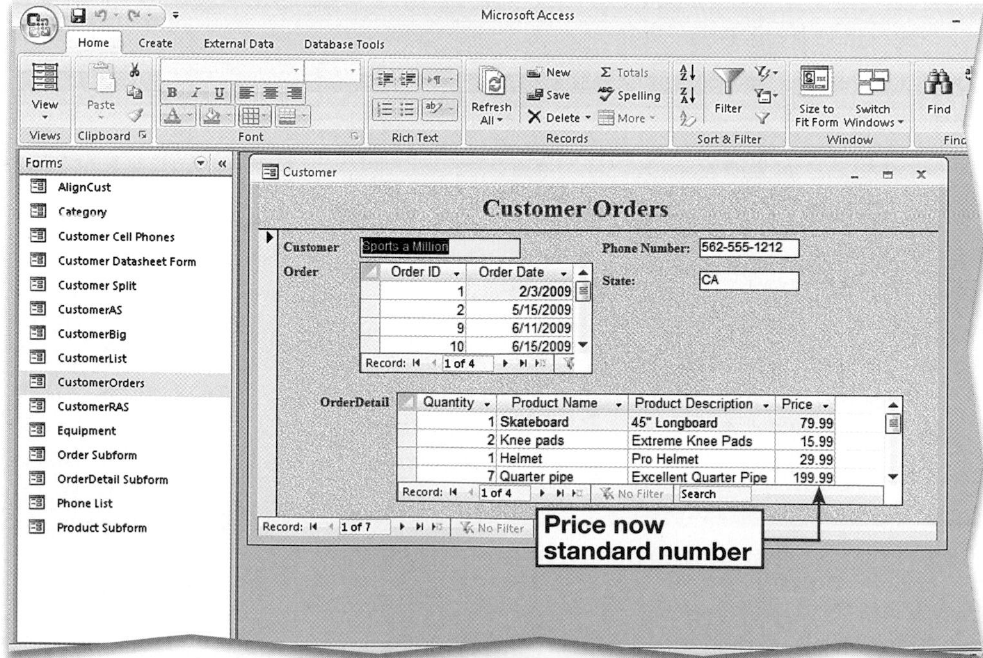

Step-By-Step

1. In your **Computers** file, select **A2:E2**.
2. On the **Home** tab, click the **Alignment** group dialog box launcher.
3. In the **Format Cells** dialog box, click the **Alignment** tab.
4. Click the **Vertical** drop-down arrow. Select **Top** (see Figure 3.31).
5. Click **OK**.
6. **CHECK** Your screen should look like Figure 3.32.
7. Save your file.

Continue to the next exercise.

You Should Know

Use the **Top Align**, **Middle Align**, and **Bottom Align** buttons on the **Home** tab to change vertical alignment more quickly.

Shortcuts

You can open the **Format Cells** dialog box by right-clicking a cell or range of cells and choosing **Format Cells** in the shortcut menu.

Step-By-Step Tip In **Step 4**, tell students that they may have to scroll up in the Vertical drop-down list to see the Top option.

EXERCISE 3-13
Change Vertical Alignment

You can use the Format Cells dialog box to change the vertical alignment of a cell's contents. **Vertical alignment** refers to how the content is positioned in relation to the top and bottom of the cell. For example, content that is top aligned is placed near the top of a cell.

FIGURE 3.31 Vertical alignment selected

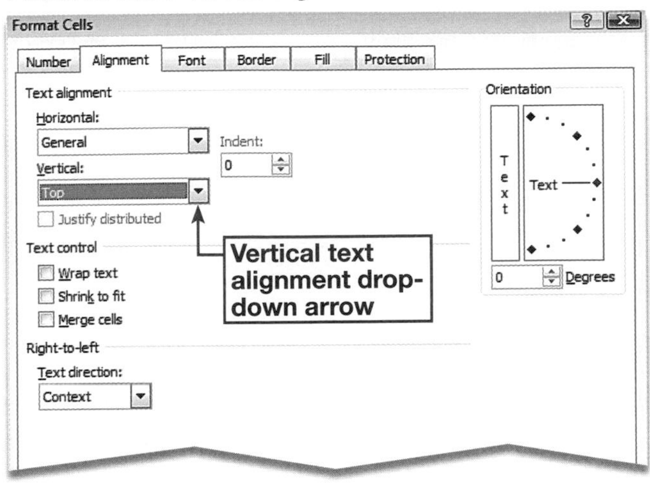

FIGURE 3.32 Cells with top alignment applied

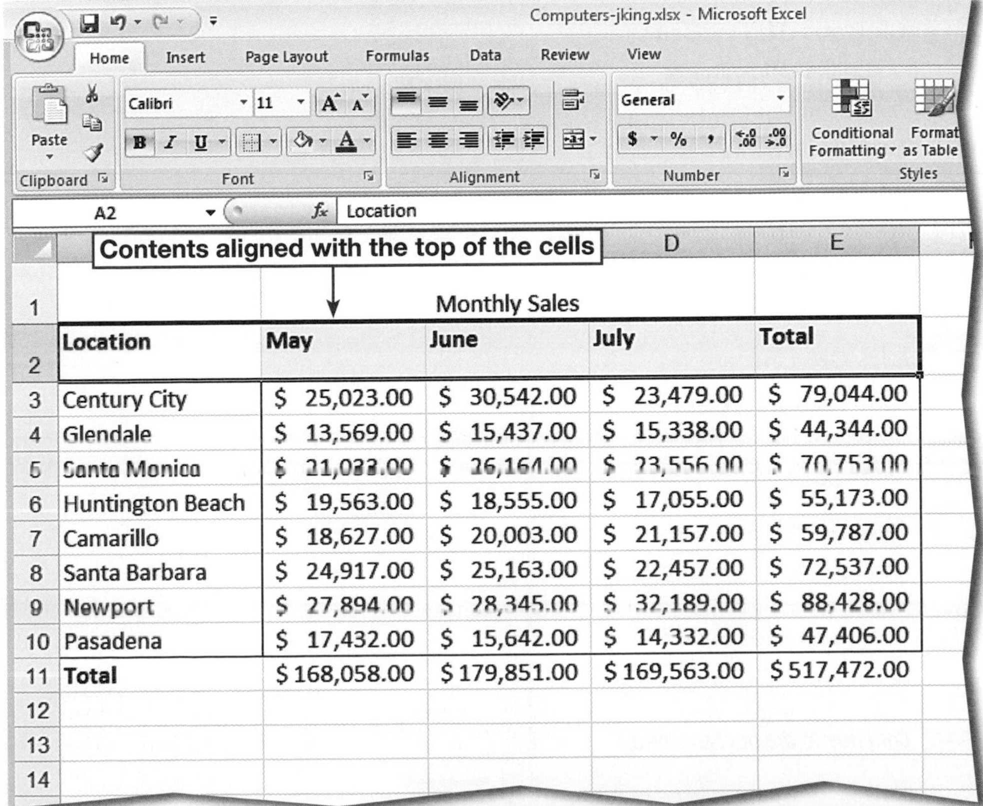

	A	B	C	D	E
1			Monthly Sales		
2	Location	May	June	July	Total
3	Century City	$ 25,023.00	$ 30,542.00	$ 23,479.00	$ 79,044.00
4	Glendale	$ 13,569.00	$ 15,437.00	$ 15,338.00	$ 44,344.00
5	Santa Monica	$ 21,033.00	$ 26,164.00	$ 23,556.00	$ 70,753.00
6	Huntington Beach	$ 19,563.00	$ 18,555.00	$ 17,055.00	$ 55,173.00
7	Camarillo	$ 18,627.00	$ 20,003.00	$ 21,157.00	$ 59,787.00
8	Santa Barbara	$ 24,917.00	$ 25,163.00	$ 22,457.00	$ 72,537.00
9	Newport	$ 27,894.00	$ 28,345.00	$ 32,189.00	$ 88,428.00
10	Pasadena	$ 17,432.00	$ 15,642.00	$ 14,332.00	$ 47,406.00
11	Total	$ 168,058.00	$ 179,851.00	$ 169,563.00	$ 517,472.00
12					
13					
14					

Step-By-Step

1. Open the **Customer Orders** form in **Design View**.

2. Choose **Arrange>Control Layout>Tab Order**.

3. In the **Tab Order** dialog box in the **Section** pane, make sure **Detail** is selected.

4. In the **Custom Order** pane, move the pointer over the grey box to the left of **PhoneNumber** until it becomes a right-facing arrow. Click and drag the pointer down so that **PhoneNumber** and **State** are selected.

5. Click and drag the selection up until a black line is displayed under **CustomerName**. Release the mouse.

6. **CHECK** Your screen should look like Figure 3.33.

7. Click **OK**. Choose **Home>Form View**.

8. Press TAB twice.

9. **CHECK** Your screen should look like Figure 3.34.

10. Click **Close** x. Click **Yes** to save the changes.

Continue to the next exercise.

EXERCISE 3-12
Define Tab Order

A form is the public face of your database. An effective form speeds the use of the database, allowing people to view information in it more easily. To move through a form more efficiently, you can press Tab to move from one control or field to the next. With the Tab Order tool, you can define the order in which the Tab key moves from control to control through a form. Changing the tab order of controls on a form makes the form more efficient because users will not have to search the database for what they need.

Differentiated Instruction/Advanced Students Have advanced students determine and implement a different tab order in another form in the database.

FIGURE 3.33 Tab Order dialog box

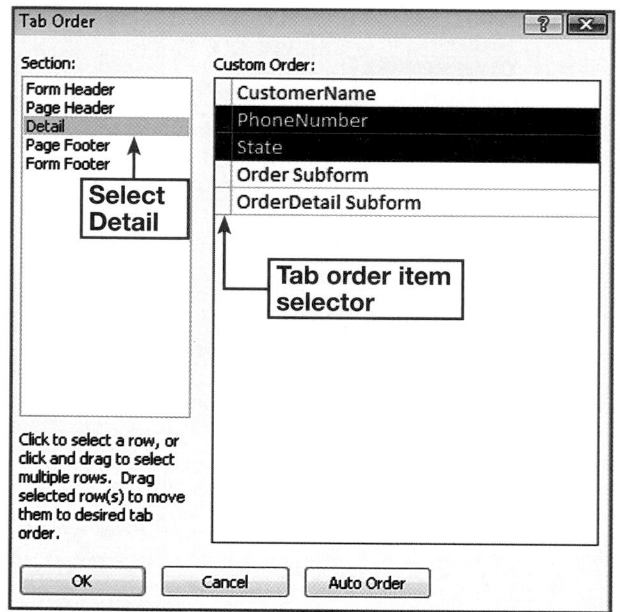

Step-By-Step Tip In **Step 9**, explain to students that the second tab skipped the **Order** field and moved to the **State** field.

FIGURE 3.34 Tab Order rearranged

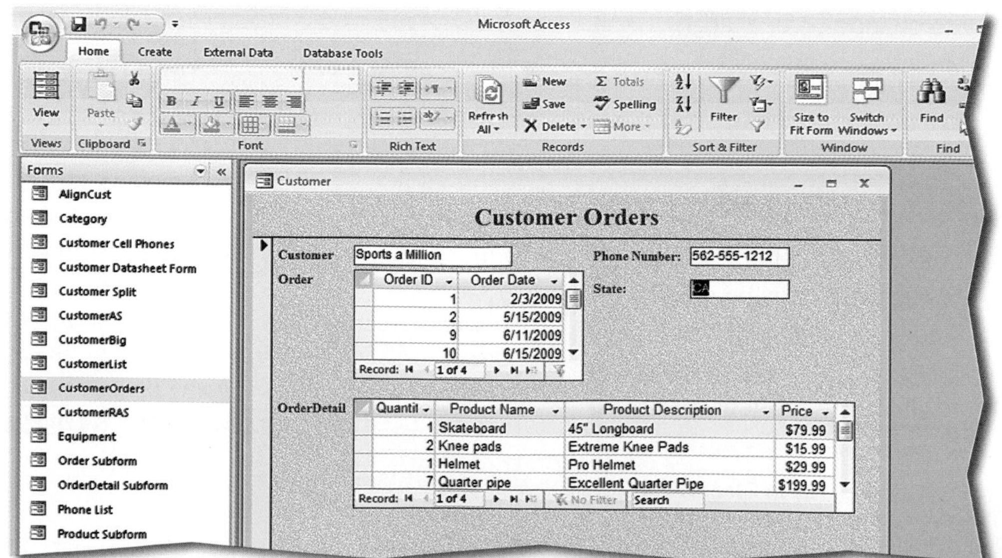

EXERCISE 3-14
Show and Hide Gridlines and Headings

Just as you can hide and unhide rows and columns, you can hide and unhide a worksheet or an entire workbook's gridlines and headings. Viewing a worksheet without gridlines and headings allows you to see what a chart or table will look like when you print it.

FIGURE 3.33 Hidden gridlines

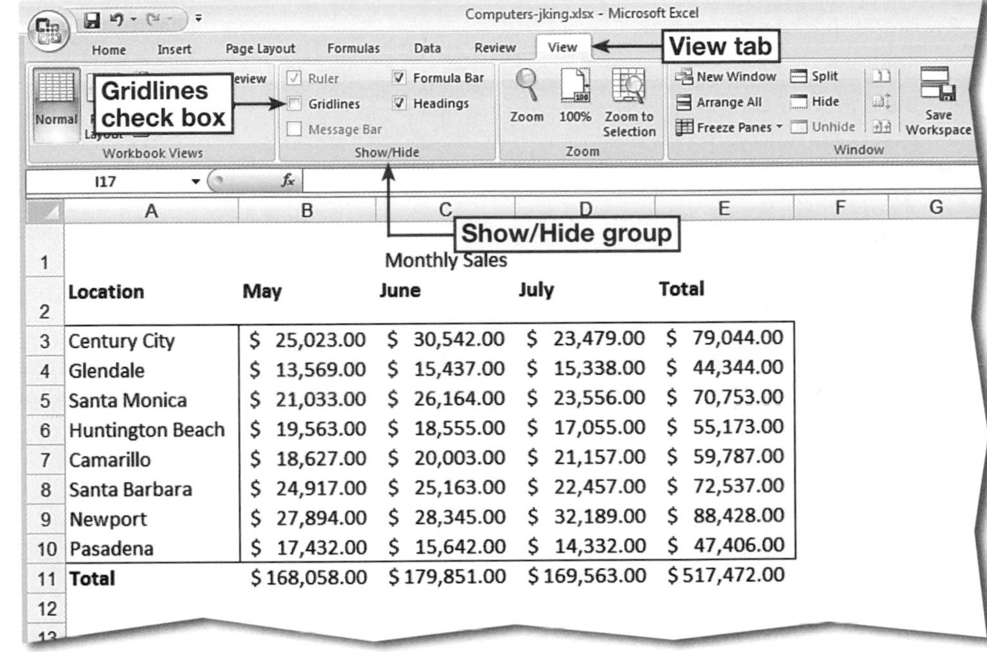

	A	B	C	D	E
1			Monthly Sales		
2	**Location**	**May**	**June**	**July**	**Total**
3	Century City	$ 25,023.00	$ 30,542.00	$ 23,479.00	$ 79,044.00
4	Glendale	$ 13,569.00	$ 15,437.00	$ 15,338.00	$ 44,344.00
5	Santa Monica	$ 21,033.00	$ 26,164.00	$ 23,556.00	$ 70,753.00
6	Huntington Beach	$ 19,563.00	$ 18,555.00	$ 17,055.00	$ 55,173.00
7	Camarillo	$ 18,627.00	$ 20,003.00	$ 21,157.00	$ 59,787.00
8	Santa Barbara	$ 24,917.00	$ 25,163.00	$ 22,457.00	$ 72,537.00
9	Newport	$ 27,894.00	$ 28,345.00	$ 32,189.00	$ 88,428.00
10	Pasadena	$ 17,432.00	$ 15,642.00	$ 14,332.00	$ 47,406.00
11	**Total**	$ 168,058.00	$ 179,851.00	$ 169,563.00	$ 517,472.00

FIGURE 3.34 The gridlines and headings are visible

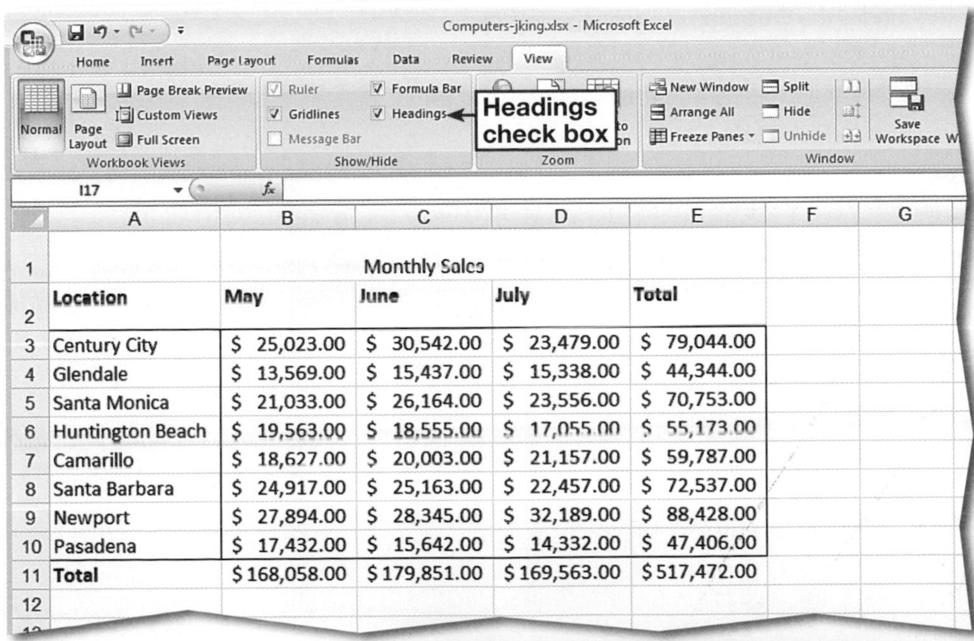

	A	B	C	D	E
1			Monthly Sales		
2	**Location**	**May**	**June**	**July**	**Total**
3	Century City	$ 25,023.00	$ 30,542.00	$ 23,479.00	$ 79,044.00
4	Glendale	$ 13,569.00	$ 15,437.00	$ 15,338.00	$ 44,344.00
5	Santa Monica	$ 21,033.00	$ 26,164.00	$ 23,556.00	$ 70,753.00
6	Huntington Beach	$ 19,563.00	$ 18,555.00	$ 17,055.00	$ 55,173.00
7	Camarillo	$ 18,627.00	$ 20,003.00	$ 21,157.00	$ 59,787.00
8	Santa Barbara	$ 24,917.00	$ 25,163.00	$ 22,457.00	$ 72,537.00
9	Newport	$ 27,894.00	$ 28,345.00	$ 32,189.00	$ 88,428.00
10	Pasadena	$ 17,432.00	$ 15,642.00	$ 14,332.00	$ 47,406.00
11	**Total**	$ 168,058.00	$ 179,851.00	$ 169,563.00	$ 517,472.00

Step-By-Step

1. In your **Computers** file, click cell **A1**.
2. Choose **View>Show/Hide** and remove the checkmark from the **Gridlines** check-box. Notice that the gridlines are hidden.
3. **CHECK** Your screen should look like Figure 3.33.
4. Choose **View>Show/Hide** and check **Gridlines**. The gridlines reappear.
5. Choose **View>Show/Hide** and remove the checkmark from the **Headings** box. Notice that the row and column headings are hidden.
6. Choose **View>Show/Hide**. Click the **Headings** box. The headings reappear.
7. **CHECK** Your screen should look like Figure 3.34.
8. Save your file.

Continue to the next exercise.

Tech Tip

You can print without gridlines by choosing **Page Layout>Sheet Options** and deselecting, or clearing, the **Gridlines** check box.

Step-By-Step

1 Open the **CustomerOrders** form in **Design View**. Choose **Design>Tools>Add Existing Fields**.

2 In the **Field List** pane, drag the **PhoneNumber** field onto the form to the right of the **CustomerName** box.

3 CHECK Your screen should look like Figure 3.31.

4 Choose **Design> Controls>Text Box** ab. Click under the **Phone Number** control on the form to place the **Text Box**. Select the text in the **Text Box** label and key: State:. Double-click the **Text Box** control.

5 In the **Property Sheet** under the **Data** tab, click in the **Control Source** box. Click the drop-down arrow and select **State**.

6 Click the **Other** tab and select the text in the **Name** box and key: State. Click **Form View**.

7 CHECK Your screen should look like Figure 3.32. Click Close x.

Continue to the next exercise.

EXERCISE 3-11
Add and Bind Controls

In previous exercises, you created simple forms for entering and editing data. You can add a new **control** to those forms by adding new fields as controls. Controls can be added without pulling them from fields. You can bind the new controls to other data sources once they are on the form.

Step-By-Step Tip In **Step 8**, explain to students that double-clicking the form control is the same as clicking the Property Sheet button.

FIGURE 3.31 CustomerOrders with Phone Number

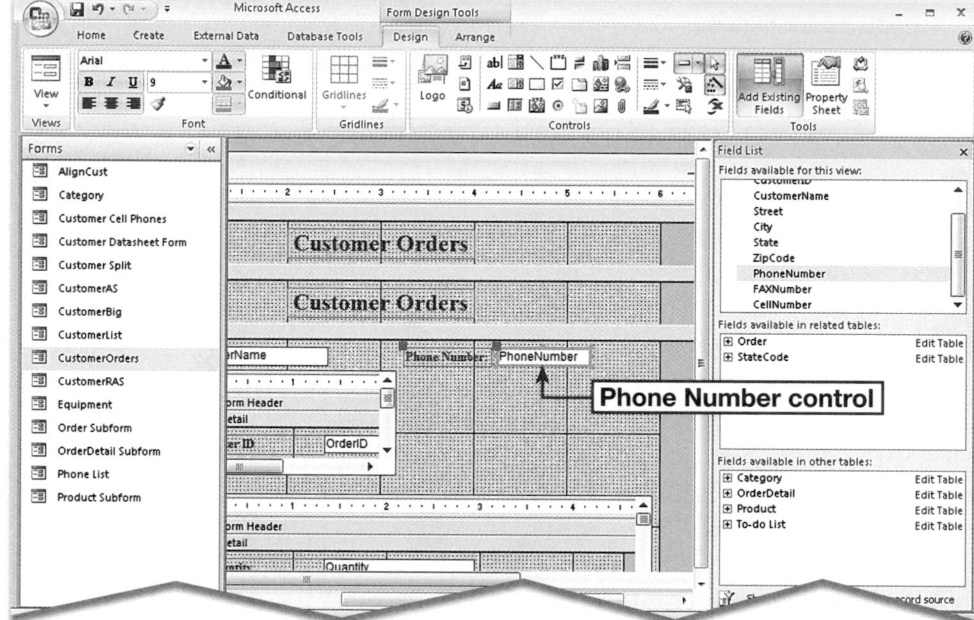

FIGURE 3.32 Form with Phone Number, State controls

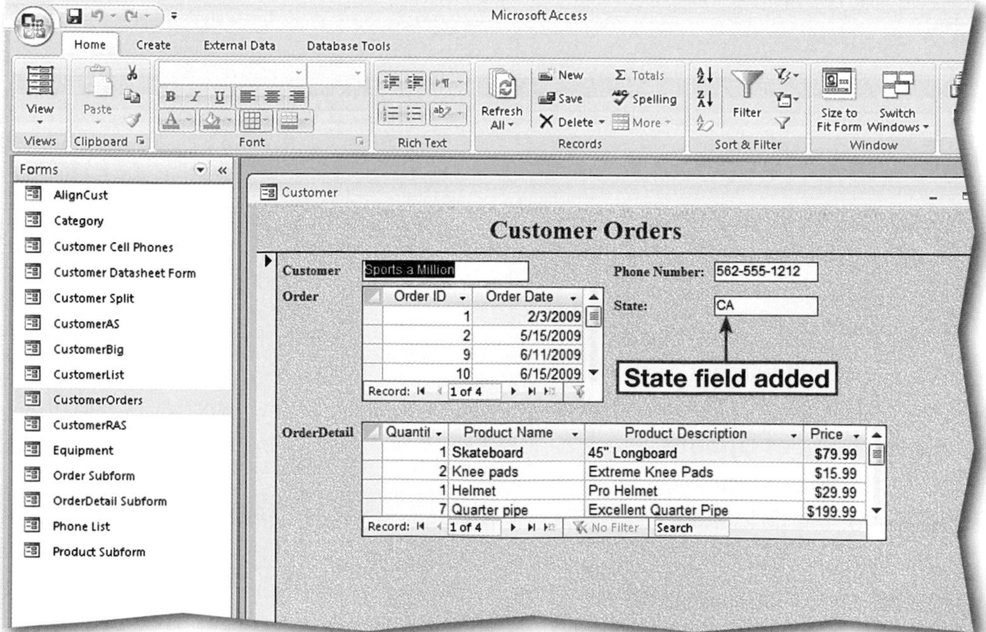

EXERCISE 3-15
Rename a Worksheet and Change the Tab Color

You can organize your work by storing information on multiple sheets. For example, if you are compiling quarterly sales reports for your company, you might create four worksheets, one for each quarter. Each worksheet should have a name that is easy to understand. Change the tab color so you can find each sheet quickly.

New Student Strategy Show students just joining the class how to switch from sheet to sheet.

FIGURE 3.35 Renaming a worksheet

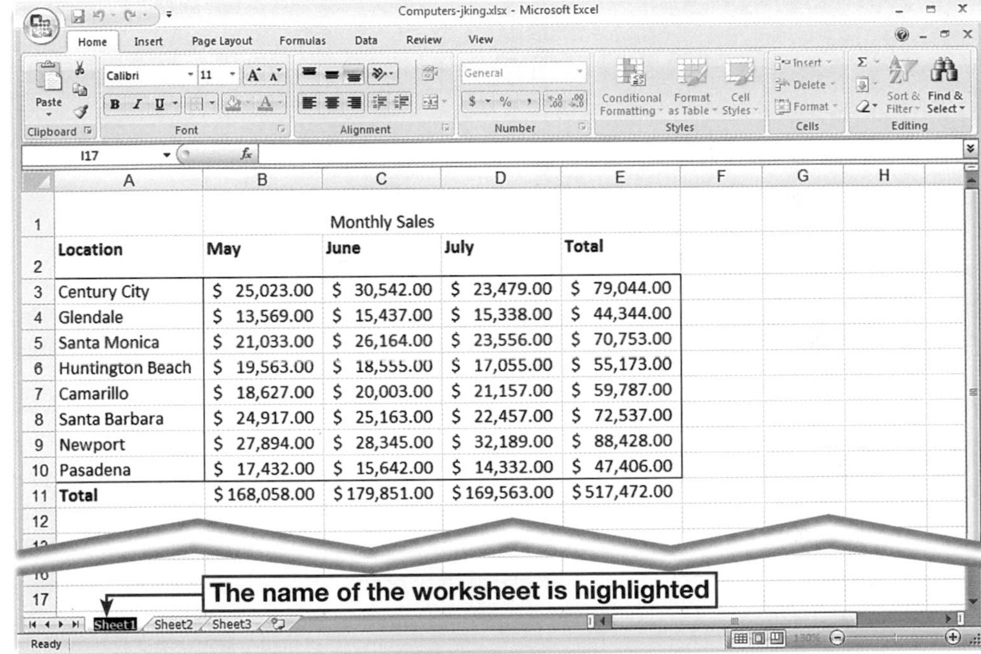

	Location	May	June	July	Total
1			Monthly Sales		
2	Location	May	June	July	Total
3	Century City	$ 25,023.00	$ 30,542.00	$ 23,479.00	$ 79,044.00
4	Glendale	$ 13,569.00	$ 15,437.00	$ 15,338.00	$ 44,344.00
5	Santa Monica	$ 21,033.00	$ 26,164.00	$ 23,556.00	$ 70,753.00
6	Huntington Beach	$ 19,563.00	$ 18,555.00	$ 17,055.00	$ 55,173.00
7	Camarillo	$ 18,627.00	$ 20,003.00	$ 21,157.00	$ 59,787.00
8	Santa Barbara	$ 24,917.00	$ 25,163.00	$ 22,457.00	$ 72,537.00
9	Newport	$ 27,894.00	$ 28,345.00	$ 32,189.00	$ 88,428.00
10	Pasadena	$ 17,432.00	$ 15,642.00	$ 14,332.00	$ 47,406.00
11	Total	$ 168,058.00	$ 179,851.00	$ 169,563.00	$ 517,472.00

FIGURE 3.36 Change tab color

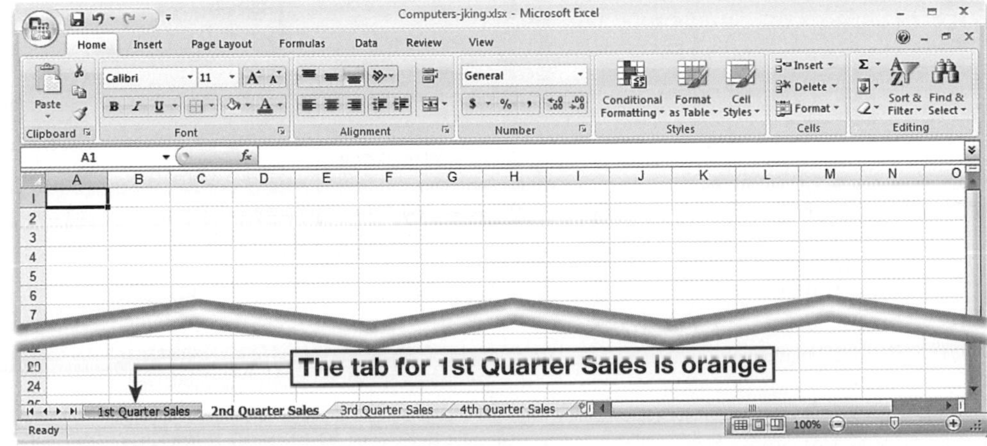

Teaching Tip Financial reports are divided into quarters just like the school year is divided into semesters and quarters.

Step-By-Step

1. In your **Computers** file, choose **Home>Cells>Format**. Under **Organize Sheets**, click **Rename Sheet**. **Sheet1** is highlighted (see Figure 3.35).
2. Key: 1st Quarter Sales.
3. Press ENTER.
4. Repeat Step 1 choosing **Sheet 2**. Key: 2nd Quarter Sales.
5. Click **Insert Worksheet** twice. Rename the two worksheets: 3rd Quarter Sales and 4th Quarter Sales.
6. Click **1st Quarter Sales** tab. Choose **Home>Cells>Format**. Under **Organize Sheets**, select **Tab Color**.
7. Under **Standard Colors**, select **Orange, Accent 6**.
8. Click the tab for **2nd Quarter Sales**.
9. **CHECK** Your screen should look like Figure 3.36.
10. Save your file.

Continue to the next exercise.

Step-By-Step

11 Double-click on the **State** label and select the text. Key: Home State:.

12 Double-click on **CustomerName** and delete **Name** from the text.

13 CHECK Your screen should look like Figure 3.29.

14 Double-click on **CellNumber** and add a space between the two words.

15 To remove the white space, drag the bottom of the form up under the information. Click **Form View**.

16 CHECK Your screen should look like Figure 3.30.

17 Click **Save**. In the **Save As** dialog box, key: Customer Cell Phones. Click **OK**.

18 Close the form.

Continue to the next exercise.

Shortcuts

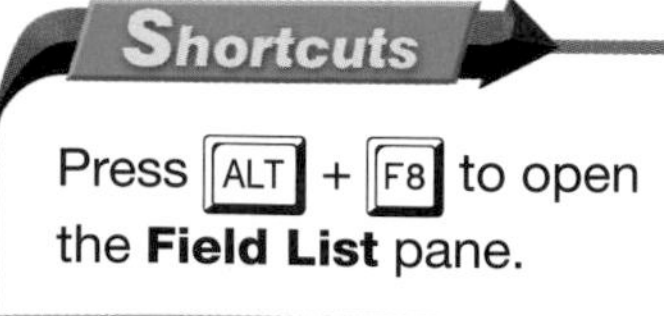

Press ALT + F8 to open the **Field List** pane.

NCLB/Language Arts (NCTE 8)
Ask students how being able to see the data while they are modifying the form helps improve the form's overall appearance and organization.

EXERCISE 3-10 (Continued)
Create Forms Using Layout View

FIGURE 3.29 Modified Form in Layout View

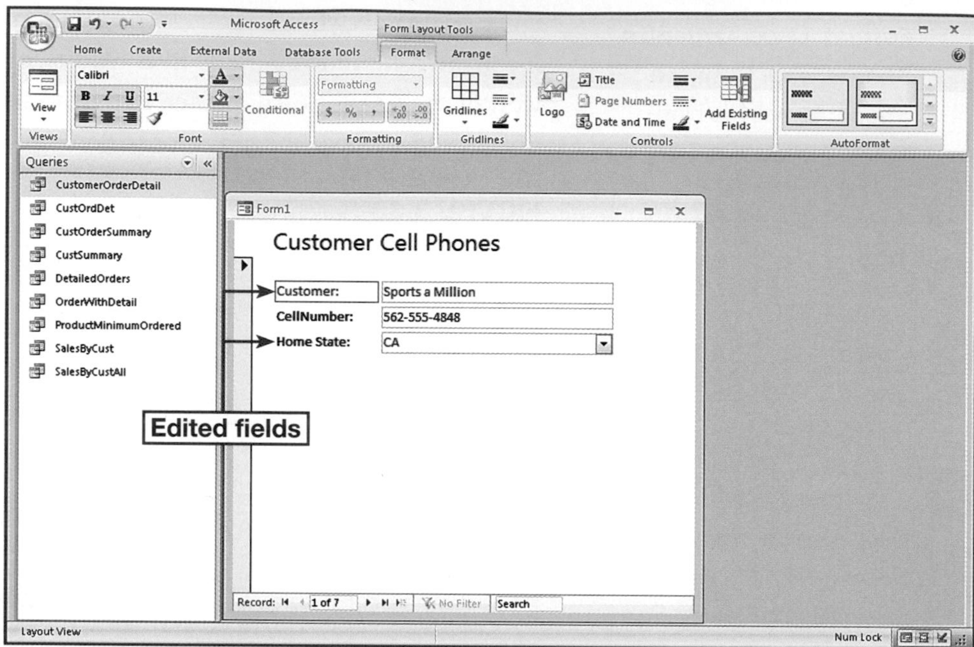

FIGURE 3.30 Customer Cell Phones form in Form View

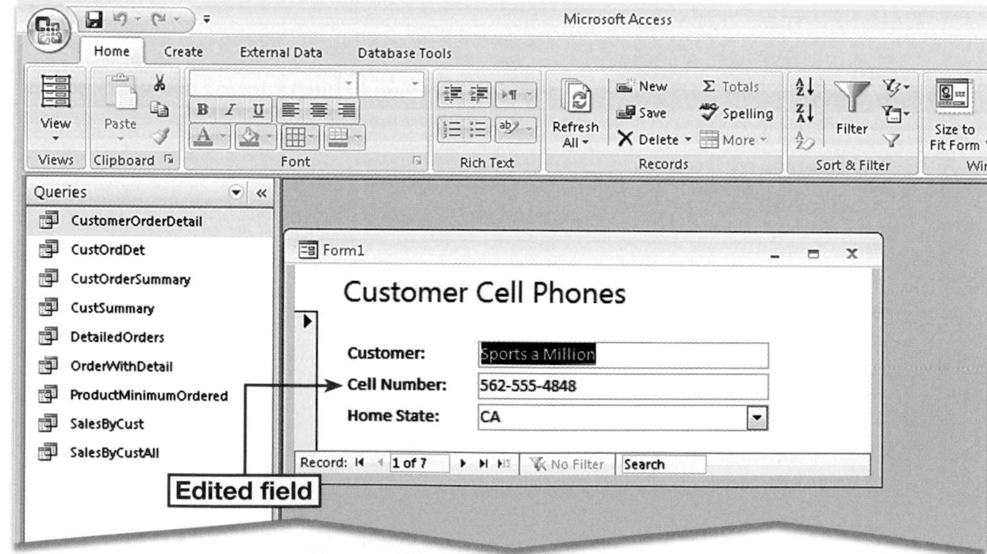

Microsoft Office 2007

In addition to closing a window by using **Close**, you can also click on the window's icon on the left edge of the window title bar and select **Close** from the drop-down menu.

Step-By-Step

1. In your **Computers** file, click the **2nd Quarter Sales** tab.
2. Click the **Select All** button in the top left corner of the worksheet, just to the left of column A and just above row 1.
3. Choose **Home>Styles> Cell Styles**. Select **Neutral**.
4. **CHECK** Your screen should look like Figure 3.37.
5. Select the **1st Quarter Sales** tab. Choose **Page Layout> Page Setup>Background**.
6. In the **Sheet Background** dialog box, browse to and select your data file folder.
7. In the **Files of type** box, make sure **All Pictures** is selected. In the data file list, select the file **CompuBold.JPG**.
8. **CHECK** Your screen should look like Figure 3.38.
9. Save your file.

Continue to the next exercise.

Teaching Tip Explain to students that watermarks will not appear on a colored background. In Step 2 they are learning how to add a colored background to a worksheet.

EXERCISE 3-16
Choose a Background

A **background** is a graphic or color that appears behind the information in your worksheet. Sometimes backgrounds act as watermarks. Logos often appear as watermarks. They are usually translucent, which means you can see through them. A background will only show on the computer screen, it will not appear if you print the document out.

FIGURE 3.37 Worksheet with a background color

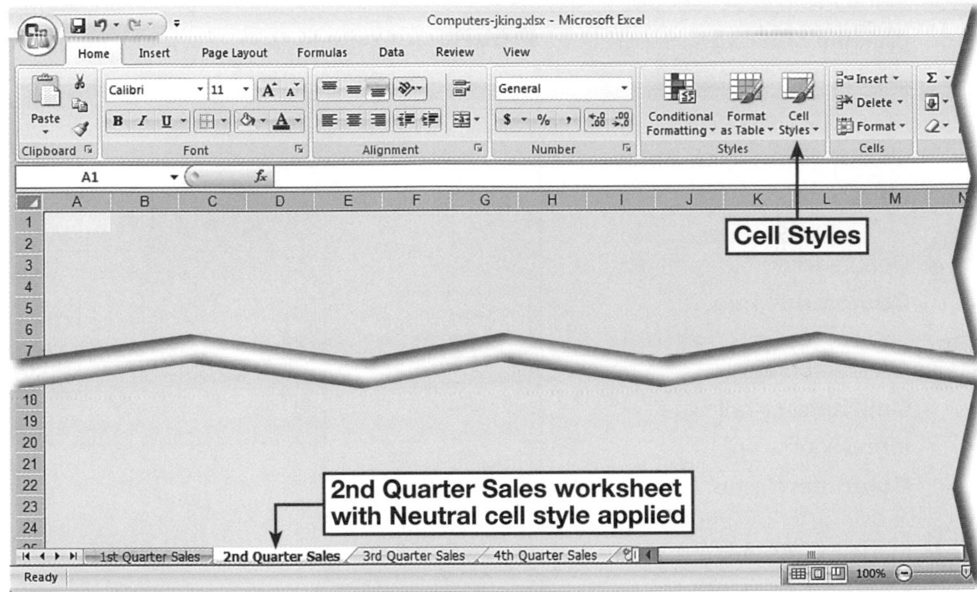

FIGURE 3.38 Background logo inserted in sheet

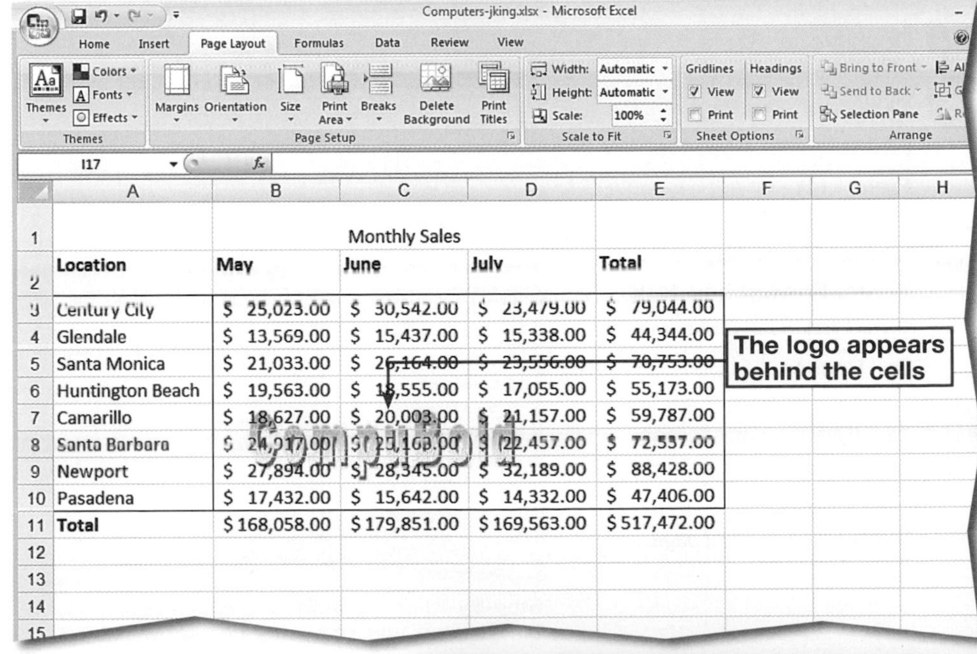

Location	May	June	July	Total
	Monthly Sales			
Century City	$ 25,023.00	$ 30,542.00	$ 23,479.00	$ 79,044.00
Glendale	$ 13,569.00	$ 15,437.00	$ 15,338.00	$ 44,344.00
Santa Monica	$ 21,033.00	$ 26,164.00	$ 23,556.00	$ 70,753.00
Huntington Beach	$ 19,563.00	$ 18,555.00	$ 17,055.00	$ 55,173.00
Camarillo	$ 18,627.00	$ 20,003.00	$ 21,157.00	$ 59,787.00
Santa Barbara	$ 24,917.00	$ 25,163.00	$ 22,457.00	$ 72,537.00
Newport	$ 27,894.00	$ 28,345.00	$ 32,189.00	$ 88,428.00
Pasadena	$ 17,432.00	$ 15,642.00	$ 14,332.00	$ 47,406.00
Total	$ 168,058.00	$ 179,851.00	$ 169,563.00	$ 517,472.00

Step-By-Step

1. In your **Sports** file, choose **Create>Forms>Blank Form** .
2. **CHECK** Your screen should look like Figure 3.27.
3. In the **Field List** window, click the **plus sign** + to expand the **Customer** table. If tables are not already visible, click **Show all tables**.
4. Double-click **CustomerName**.
5. Click and drag **CellNumber** onto the form window under **CustomerName**.
6. In the **Fields available in related tables** window, click the **plus sign** + to expand **StateCode**.
7. Double-click **State**.
8. Click **Add Existing Fields** to close the **Field List**.
9. Choose **Form Layout Tools>Format** and click **Title** . Key: Customer Cell Phones.
10. **CHECK** Your screen should look like Figure 3.28.

Continued on the next page.

EXERCISE 3-10
Create Forms Using Layout View

In a database that contains thousands of records, it can take a long time to create a report with totals because the report needs to process all the records. In addition to using the different form tools and Design View to create forms, you can also use **Layout View** which to see how your data will look when printed. The Layout View also allows you to make design changes and helps you ensure that the data is in the right place with the correct formatting.

FIGURE 3.27 Blank form in Layout View started

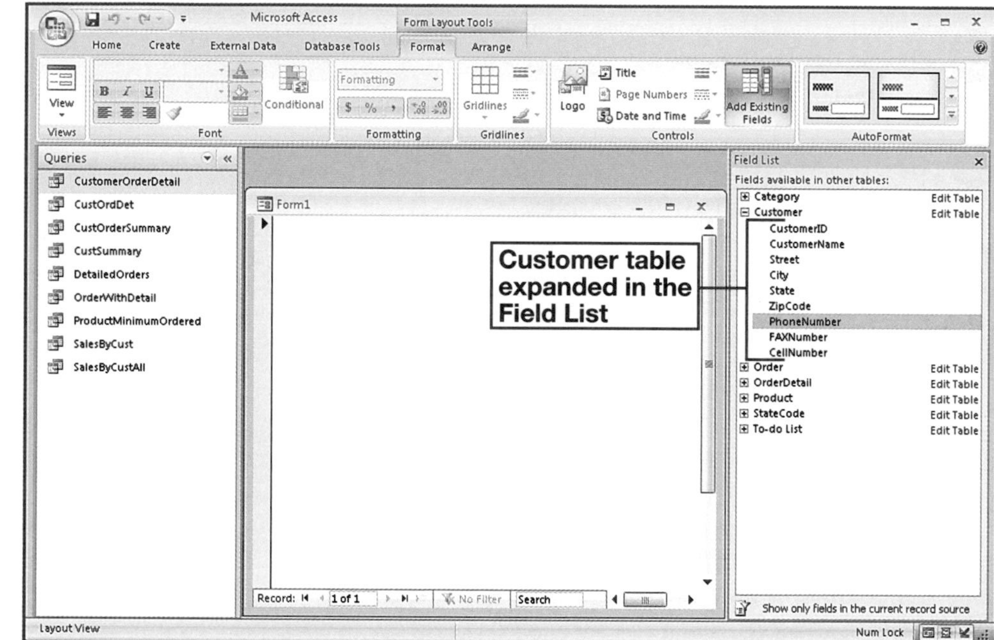

FIGURE 3.28 Customer Cell Phones form in Layout View

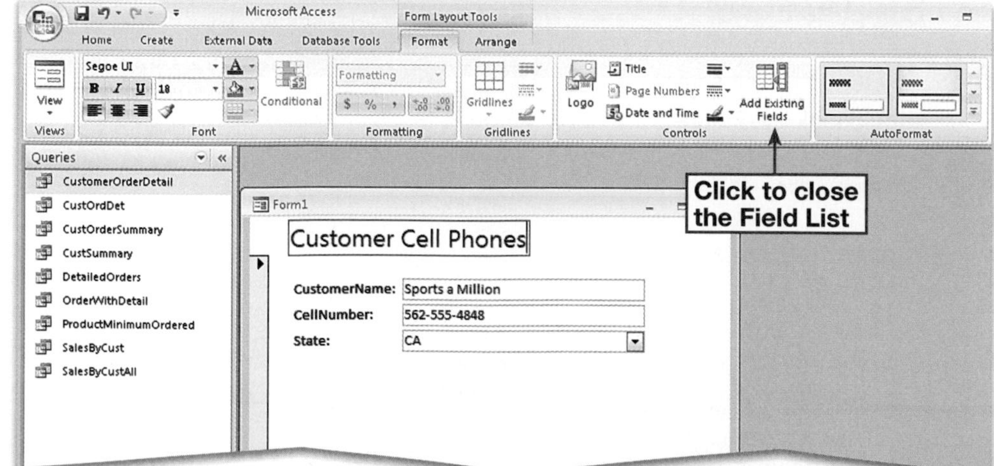

Step-By-Step Tip In **Step 9**, reinforce to students the difference between the *text* box and the *label* box and make sure they know which they should select.

Step-By-Step

1. In your **Computers** file, click the **2nd Quarter Sales** tab. Choose **Home>Cells>Format**. Under **Visibility**, click **Hide & Unhide** and select **Hide Sheet**.

2. Click the **3rd Quarter Sales** tab if it does not automatically become selected.

3. Choose **Home>Cells> Format**. Click **Hide & Unhide** and select **Hide Sheet**. Repeat steps 3 and 4 with the **4th Quarter Sales** tab. The only visible worksheet is **1st Quarter Sales** (see Figure 3.39).

4. Choose **Home>Cells> Format**. Click **Hide & Unhide** and select **Unhide Sheet**.

5. In the **Unhide** dialog box, click **2nd Quarter Sales** (see Figure 3.40). Click **OK**.

6. Repeat Step 5 and click **3rd Quarter Sales**. Click **OK**. Repeat using the **4th Quarter Sales** tab.

7. **CHECK** Your screen should look like Figure 3.40.

8. Save your file.

Continue to the next exercise.

EXERCISE 3-17
Hide and Unhide Worksheets

Just as you can hide and unhide rows and columns, you can hide and unhide entire worksheets. When a worksheet is hidden, it is still available. It is just not visible. Hide worksheets to focus on just one part of your workbook.

FIGURE 3.39 Hidden sheets

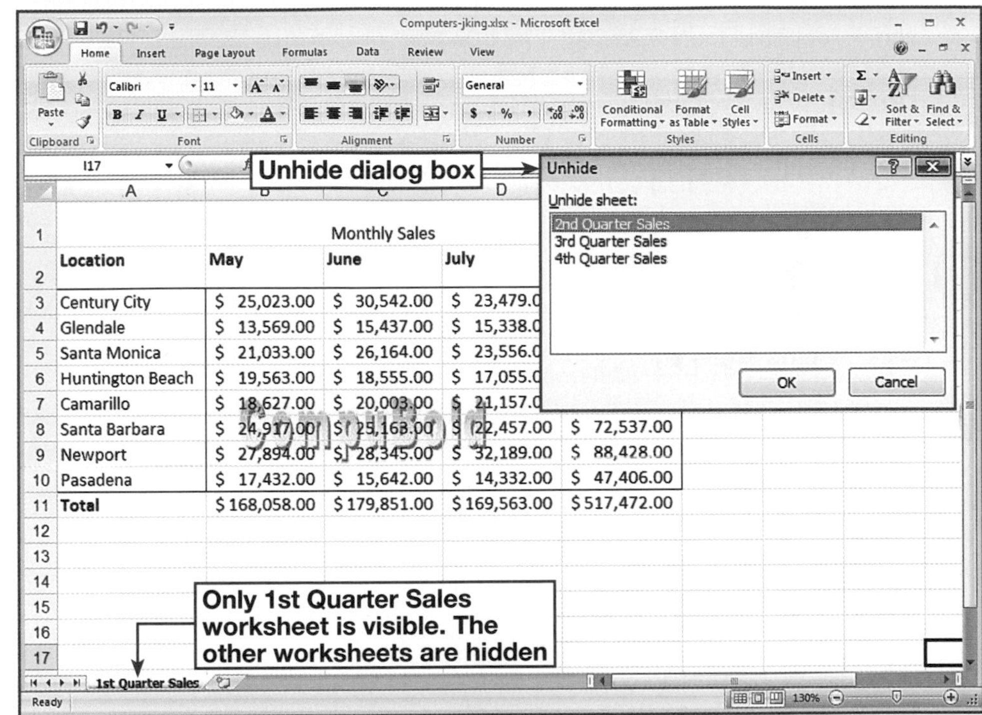

FIGURE 3.40 Unhiding worksheets

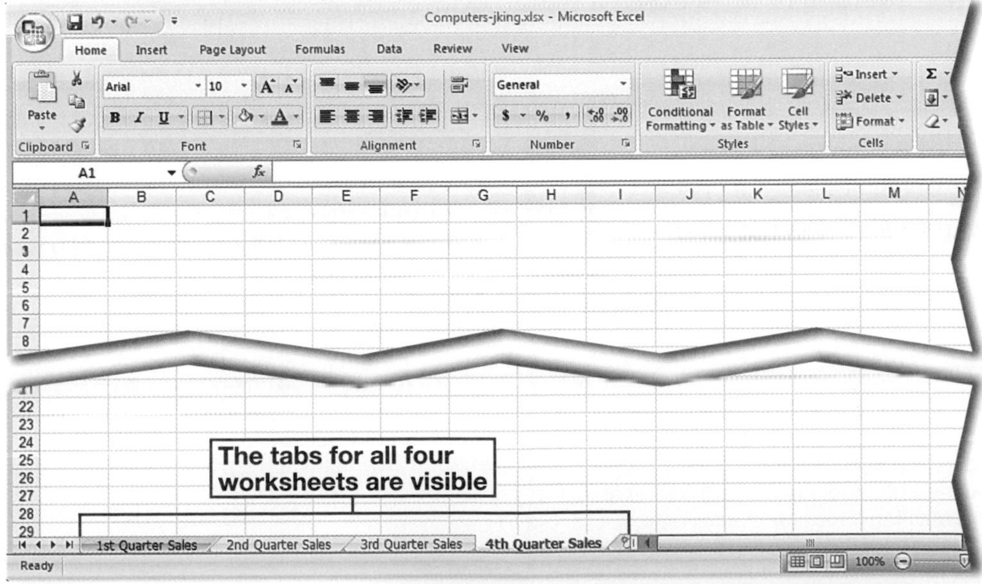

Step-By-Step

11 Click the drop-down arrow next to **CustomerName** and clear the **Sports a Million** check box.

12 **CHECK** Your screen should look like Figure 3.25.

13 Click **OK**.

14 Click the **plus sign** + next to **June**.

15 Under the **June** heading, under the **Total** heading, click the **plus sign** +.

16 **CHECK** Your screen should look like Figure 3.26.

17 Close the form. Click **No** to close without saving changes.

18 Close the **CustomerOrderDetail** query.

Continue to the next exercise.

Troubleshooter

Press the **Spacebar** to select or clear the check box for the current item in a field's drop-down list.

Teaching Tip Explain to students that PivotTable forms display the data that you decide is most relevant. Discuss with students how a PivotTable containing information about the timing of customer orders and prices and their totals can be used.

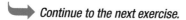

EXERCISE 3-9 (Continued)
Create PivotTable Forms

Teaching Tip Review with students that a crosstab query displays summary data for data that has been grouped into two fields.

FIGURE 3.25 Removing Sports a Million from form

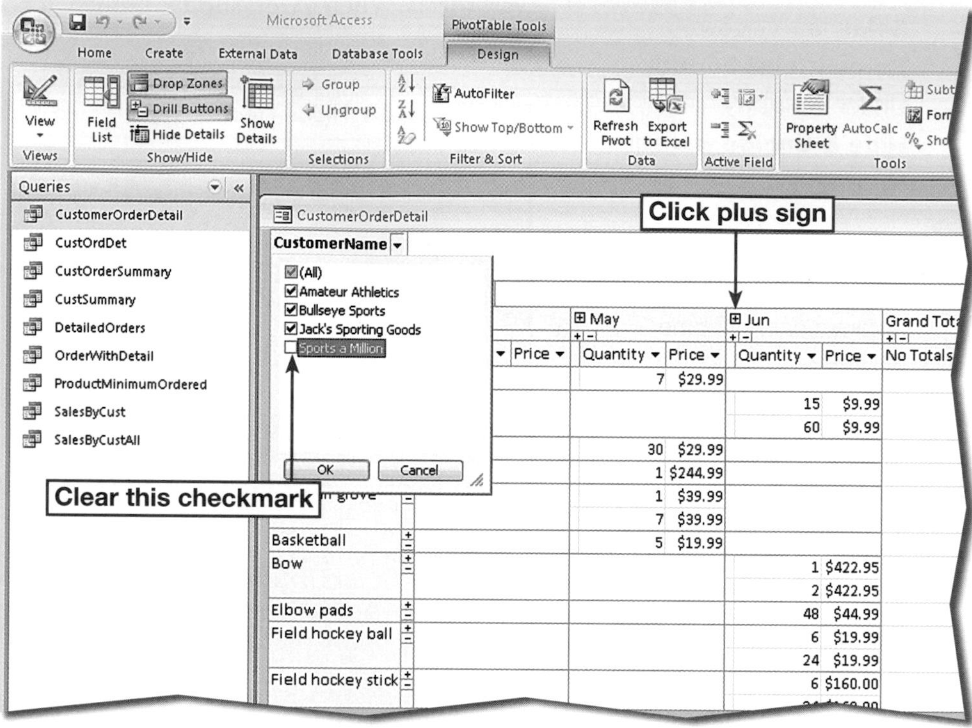

FIGURE 3.26 Expanded PivotTable form

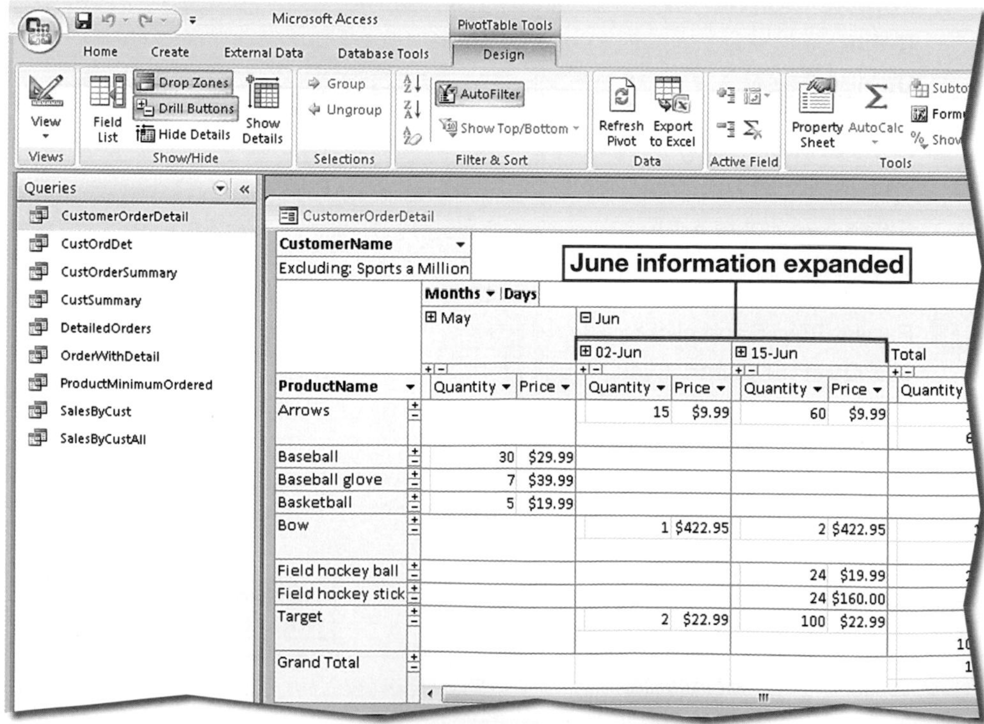

Step-By-Step

1. In your **Computers** file, click the **1st Quarter Sales** tab.
2. Choose **Insert>SmartArt**.
3. In the **Choose a SmartArt Graphic** dialog box, under **Process**, scroll down and click **Upward Arrow** (see Figure 3.41). Click **OK**.
4. Right-click anywhere on the blue SmartArt arrow. Choose **Add a Shape> Add a Shape After**. A new blue dot is added to the graphic.
5. Click the word **Text** at the bottom of the arrow. Key: May. Press ENTER. Key: $27,894. Press ENTER.
6. Enter the remainder of the sales data into the **Text** pane as shown in Figure 3.42: June $28,345, July $32,189, Newport's Total Sales $88,428. Press ENTER between entries.
7. CHECK Your screen should look like Figure 3.42.
8. Click the **SmartArt Tools** tab. Then click **Format**.

Continued on the next page.

EXERCISE 3-18
Insert, Move, and Size SmartArt Graphics

In this exercise you will create a SmartArt graphic for a monthly sales report. Excel provides a variety of **SmartArt** shapes, such as a **graphical list** (like a bulleted or numbered list), a process diagram (which shows how information changes in a process), and an organizational chart (which demonstrates an organized arrangement), to visually communicate, or convey, information. Graphics are often used to summarize information and demonstrate the data's significance.

FIGURE 3.41 Choose a SmartArt Graphic dialog box

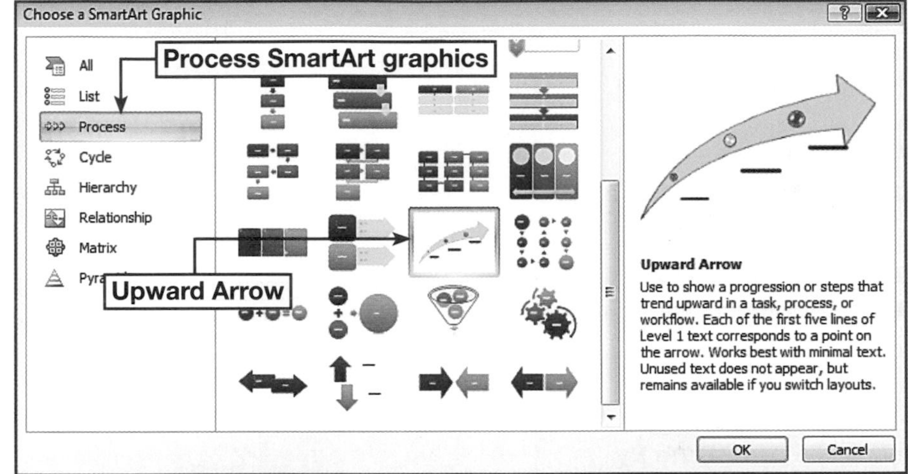

FIGURE 3.42 Newport Sales data added to

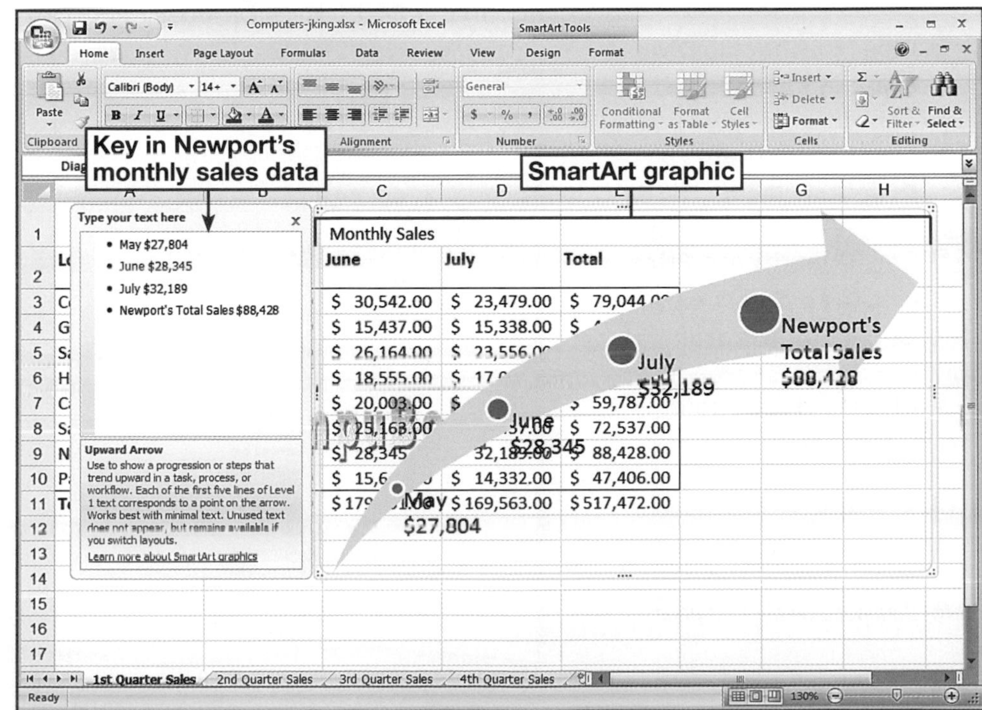

Step-By-Step

1. In your **Sports** file, in the **Navigation Pane**, select **Queries** and open the **CustomerOrderDetail** query.
2. Choose **Create>Forms> More Forms** and select **PivotTable** from the list.
3. **CHECK** Your screen should look like Figure 3.23.
4. In the **PivotTable Field List**, click **CustomerName** and drag and drop it into the form window where **Drop Filter Fields Here** appears.
5. Click the **plus sign** [+] in front of the **OrderDate By Month** field and select **Months**.
6. Drag **Months** onto **Drop Column Fields Here**.
7. Drag **ProductName** onto **Drop Row Fields Here**.
8. Drag **Quantity** and **Price** onto **Drop Totals or Detail Fields Here**.
9. Close the **PivotTable Field List**.
10. **CHECK** Your screen should look like Figure 3.24.

Continued on the next page.

EXERCISE 3-9
Create PivotTable Forms

A **PivotTable** is similar to a crosstab query. However, a PivotTable can display much more data and present it in several different ways, depending on how you want to use that data. You create a PivotTable form from existing database objects.

FIGURE 3.23 PivotTable form window

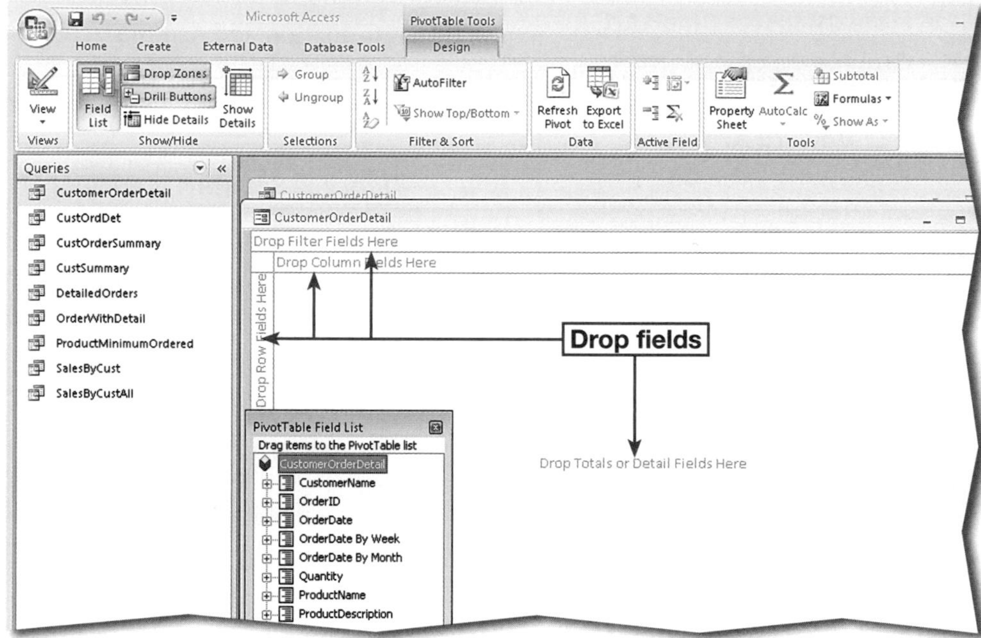

FIGURE 3.24 CustomerOrderDetail PivotTable form

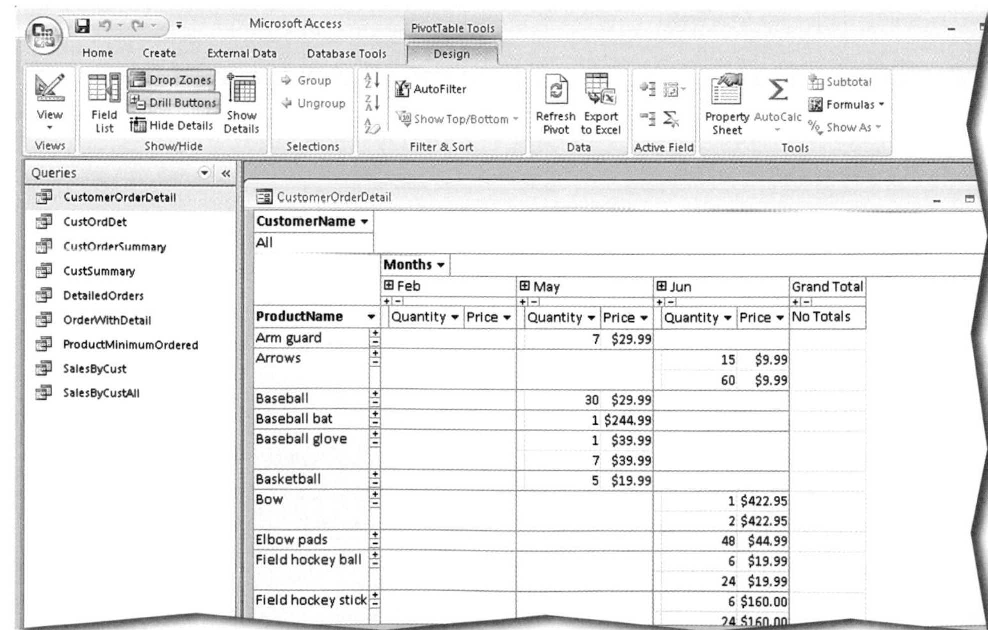

Step-By-Step

9. Click the **Shape Effects** button and select **Preset 9** (see Figure 3.43).
10. Click the arrow to select the SmartArt graphic.
11. Position your pointer over the left corner of the graphic until it takes the shape of the four-headed arrow.
12. Click and drag the four-headed arrow down and to the left so it is directly under the Monthly Sales figures in the worksheet.
13. Choose **SmartArt Tools> Design**. Then click **Change Colors** and select **Colored Fill**, **Accent 3**.
14. **CHECK** Your screen should look like Figure 3.44.
15. Click the arrow to select the SmartArt graphic.
16. Position your pointer over the arrow's lower-right dot (see Figure 3.44) until it becomes a two-headed arrow. Click and drag the dot down and to the right.
17. Resize the arrow until you are satisfied with how it looks. Save your workbook. Close the workbook and exit Excel.

Solution Use the file **Computers-SF.xlsx** as a solution file for Exercises 3-12 through 3-18.

EXERCISE 3-18 (Continued)
Insert, Move, and Size SmartArt Graphics

FIGURE 3.43 Shape Effects

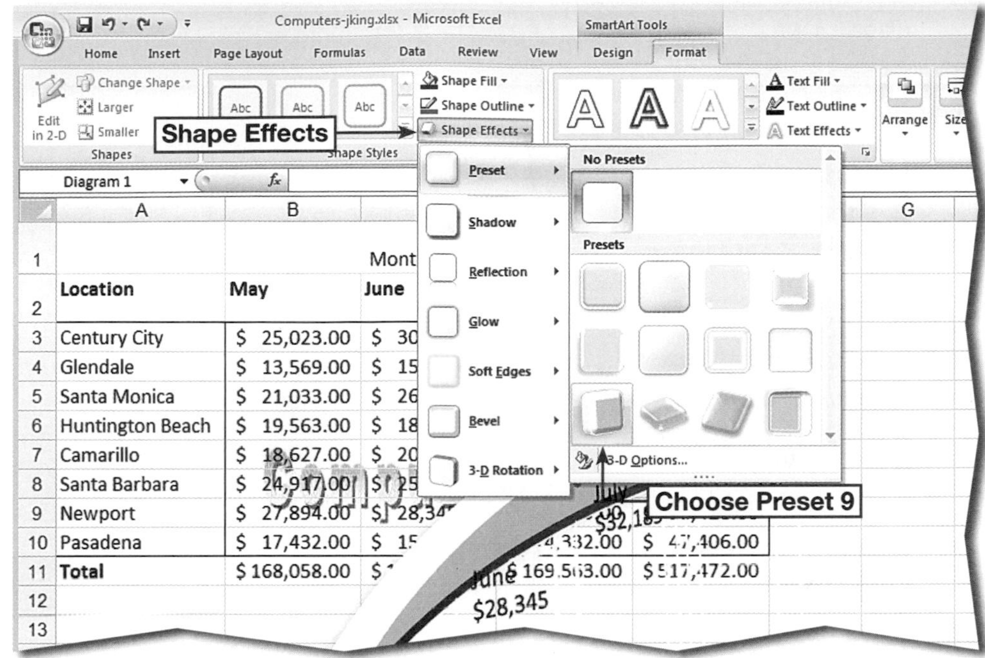

FIGURE 3.44 SmartArt displays Newport's sales figures

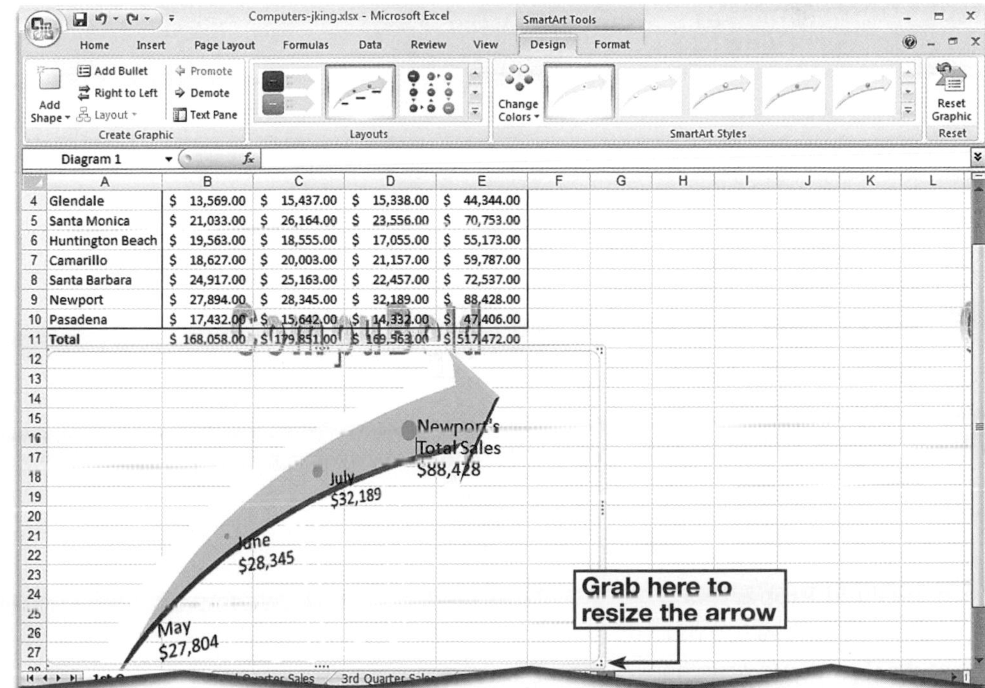

Troubleshooter Check to make sure each student is comfortable with SmartArt. If not, ask students who have mastered the skill to tutor students who need extra help.

Step-By-Step

9 In the **Property Sheet** drop-down menu select **Phone List**.

10 Click the **Data** tab and then click the **Link Master Fields** box. Click the **Builder** [...] button. The **Subform Field Linker** box opens.

11 In the box under **Master Fields**, pull down the menu and select **PhoneNumber**.

12 In the **Child Fields** pull-down menu, select **PhoneNumber**.

13 CHECK Your screen should look like Figure 3.21.

14 Click **OK**. Press F4. Click **Form View**.

15 CHECK Your screen should look like Figure 3.22. Press PAGE DOWN to move through the records.

16 Close the forms. Click **No to all** to close the forms without saving changes.

Continue to the next exercise.

Troubleshooter

If the **Field Properties** dialog box hides too much of **Design View**, drag its borders to change its size.

EXERCISE 3-8 (Continued)
Create Subforms by Dragging and Dropping

FIGURE 3.21 Subform Field Linker

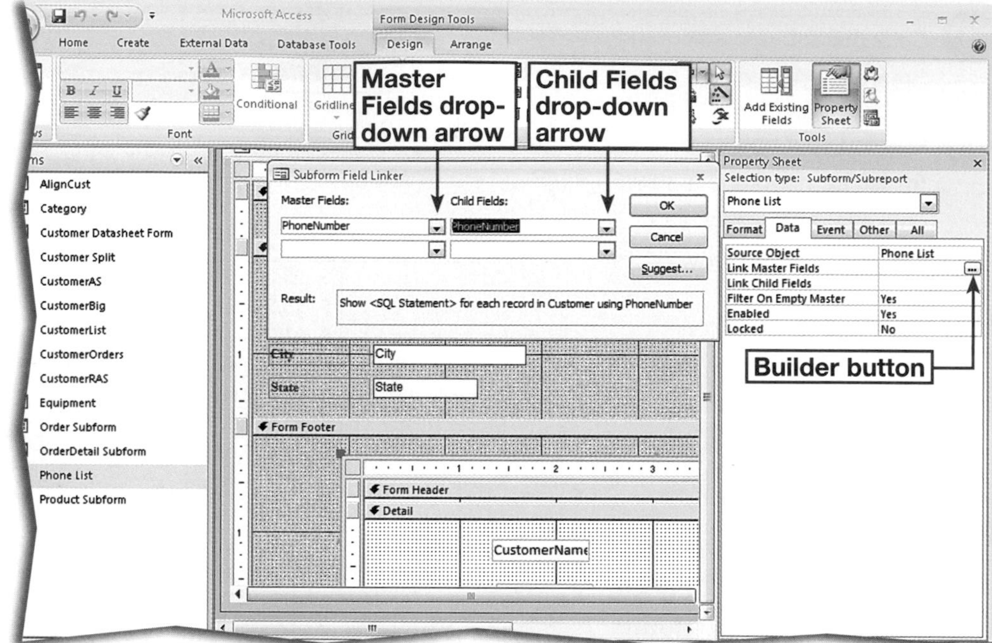

FIGURE 3.22 Completed Subform

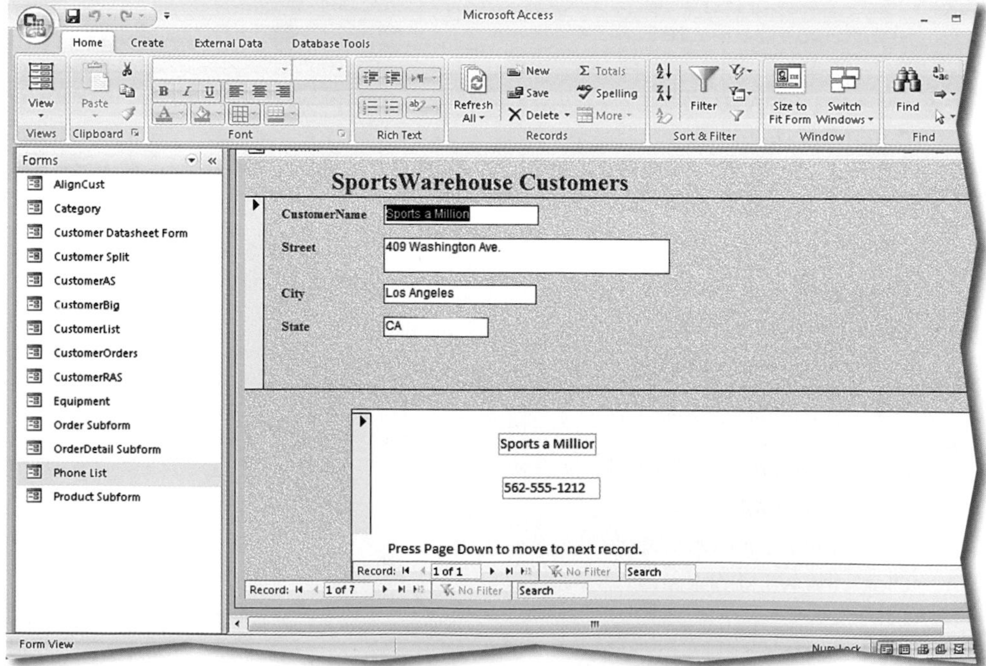

21st Century WORKPLACE

Develop Interview Skills

Rosa sits up straight and calmly describes her past work experience. She wears a brown suit and little makeup. Her hair is tied back in a neat ponytail. She asks about training on the job at the company.

Shayn fidgets and looks at the floor. His shirt is partially untucked. He gives one-word answers to the questions, and he does not have any questions for the interviewer.

Imagine you are the interviewer. Which candidate would probably interest you more? Who would make the better impression?

When you interview for a job, dress in a way that is appropriate. Speaking clearly, making eye contact with the interviewer, and showing that you can think quickly by responding to questions will also help you make a good impression.

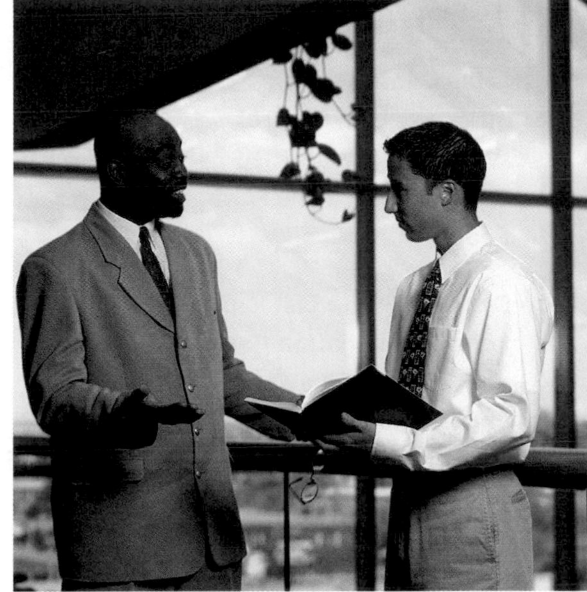

Making the right impression at an interview includes dressing appropriately and making eye contact.

MEET THE MANAGER

Rachel Orzoff, a career counselor in Minneapolis, Minnesota, teaches students how to prepare for interviews. She says, "Every interviewer is looking for the answers to three questions: Can you do the job? Will you do the job? And do I want to do the job with you?" Job candidates need to be able to perform the tasks of the position, she says. They also need to be likable, professional, and ready to be part of a team.

NCLB/Language Arts (NCTE 5) Have students discuss how they might act in front of a possible employer during an interview. Would they talk differently then if they were in front of their friends or family? Why would they change the way they speak in front of that audience as opposed to other audiences?

SKILLBUILDER

1. **List** Create a list of pointers for a person getting ready for an interview.
2. **Write** Imagine you are interested in a job in the data-entry department of a jewelry manufacturing business. Write three questions you might ask the interviewer about the company, the job, or the work environment.
3. **Prioritize** Write a sentence explaining which of the following you think is most important for a successful interview. Then rank the other four.
   - **a.** wearing conservative clothing
   - **b.** having good manners
   - **c.** asking intelligent questions
   - **d.** making eye contact and smiling
   - **e.** appearing calm and confident

SkillBuilder answers can be found on page TM72.

EXERCISE 3-8
Create Subforms by Dragging and Dropping

Subforms also can be created using a drag-and-drop technique. This technique works well when you want to modify forms that already exist.

Step-By-Step Tip Students may need to enlarge the Form window in **Step 1**.

FIGURE 3.19 Phone List subform

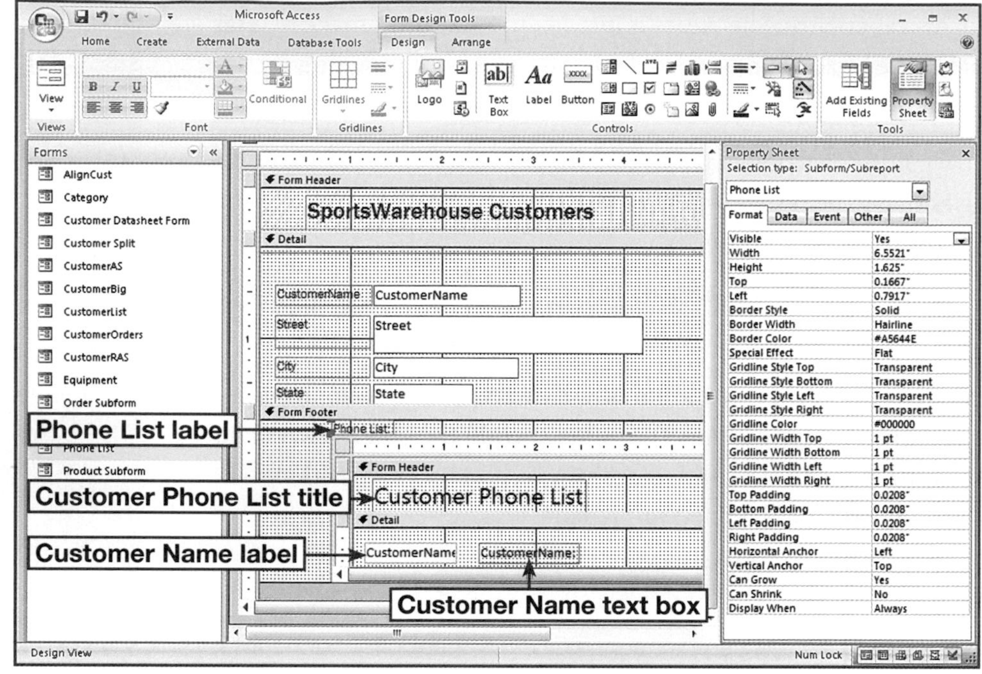

FIGURE 3.20 Subform property sheet

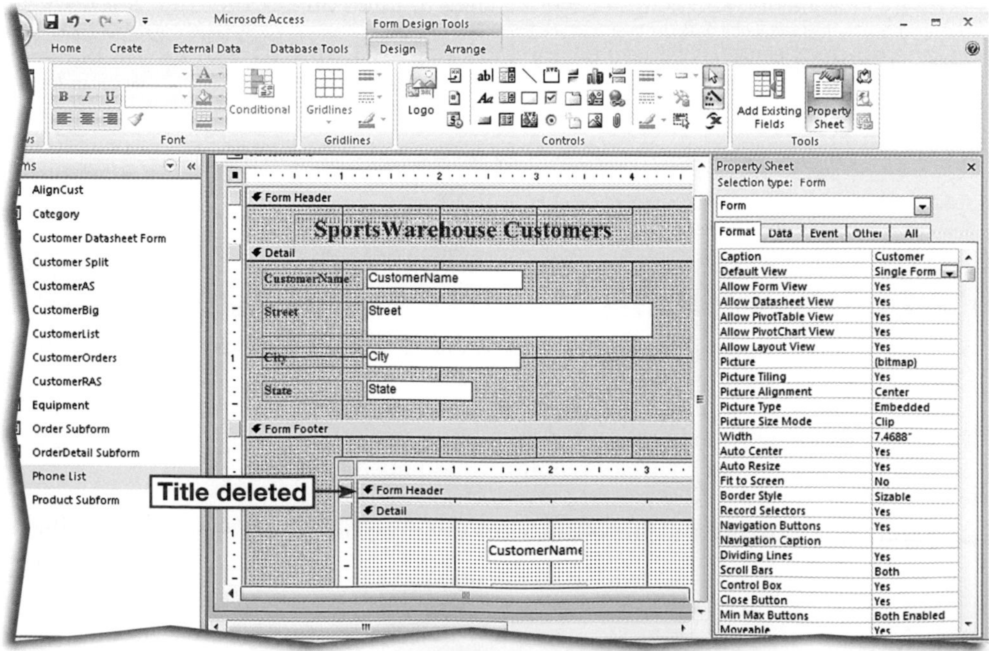

Step-By-Step

1. In your **Sports** file, in the **Navigation Pane**, right-click the **CustomerAS** form and open it in **Design View**. Press F4 to close the **Property Sheet**.
2. In the **Controls** group, make sure **Use Control Wizards** is selected. Select the text in the **Form Footer**. Press DELETE.
3. Drag the **Phone List** form from the **Navigation Pane** and drop it into the **Form Footer** of the **CustomerAS** form.
4. **CHECK** Your screen should look like Figure 3.19.
5. Select the **Customer Phone List** title and press DELETE. Drag the **Detail** bar up to the **Form Header** bar.
6. Select the **Customer Name** label and press DELETE. Select the **Phone Number** label and press DELETE.
7. Select the **Phone List** label at the top of the **Phone List** form and delete it. Press F4 to display the **Property Sheet**.
8. **CHECK** Your screen should look like Figure 3.20.

Continued on the next page.

LESSON 3 After You Read

Vocabulary

Key Terms

background

border

cell style

delimiter

font

font style

graphical list

horizontal alignment

SmartArt

table style

theme

vertical alignment

Academic Vocabulary

convey

distinct

Answer to Vocabulary Activity
Students create a matching quiz using six vocabulary words from the lesson. Students write vocabulary words on the left side, and definitions on the right side. Students then exchange quizzes with a classmate and take each other's quiz.

Review Vocabulary

Complete the following statements on a separate piece of paper. Choose from the Vocabulary list on the left to complete the statements.

1. A(n) __background__ is a graphic or color that appears behind the information in a worksheet. (p. 269)

2. The side-to-side placement of a cell's contents is called the __horizontal alignment__. (p. 264)

3. A(n) __SmartArt graphic__ is a movable, resizable graphic used to visually communicate information. (p. 271)

4. Font colors help to make certain cells __distinct__ from the rest of the worksheet (p. 259)

5. A(n) __border__ is a line along one or more sides of a cell. (p. 252)

Vocabulary Activity

6. Create a matching quiz based on this lesson's vocabulary words.

A. Choose six terms from the vocabulary list. On the left side of a piece of paper, write the terms. On the right side, write the definitions—but not in the same order as the terms.

B. After you have created your quiz, with your teacher's permission, team up with a classmate and exchange quizzes.

C. Match the vocabulary word to its correct definition with a line. Note any definitions that you did not know and find the correct answer.

Reviewing Key Concepts

Answer the following questions on a separate piece of paper.

7. Which tab would you use to change a workbook's theme? (p. 255)

A. Data
B. Home
(C.) Page Layout
D. View

8. What group on the Home tab do you use to change the horizontal alignment of a cell's contents? (p. 264)

A. Clipboard
B. Cells
(C.) Alignment
D. Editing

9. Which tab would you use to create a SmartArt graphic? (p. 271)

A. Review
B. Add-Ins
C. Formulas
(D.) Insert

10. Which would you use to center your table's heading across columns A, B, and C? (p. 265)

(A.) Center Across Selection
B. Center
C. Align Right
D. General

Step-By-Step

1. In your **Sports** data file, choose **Create>Forms> More Forms** and select **Form Wizard**.

2. In the **Form Wizard**, in the **Tables/Queries** pull-down menu, select **Table: Category**. In the **Available Fields** box, double-click **Category**.

3. In the **Tables/Queries** pull-down menu, select **Table: Product**. Select **ProductName** and **Price** and move them to the **Selected Fields** box.

4. **CHECK** Your screen should look like Figure 3.17. Click **Next**.

5. Select **by Category** and make sure **Form with subform(s)** at the bottom of the wizard is selected. Click **Next**.

6. Select **Tabular**. Click **Next**. Select the **Access 2007** style and click **Next**. Click **Finish**.

7. **CHECK** Your screen should look like Figure 3.18. Press PAGE DOWN to move through the records. Click **Close** x to close the form.

Continue to the next exercise.

EXERCISE 3-7
Create Subforms Using Form Wizard

A **subform** is a form that is inserted into another form. They are most effective if the forms are based on tables or queries with one-to-many relationships so that the main form can show one piece of information and the subform can show the many related fields or records. For example, you can use a form to view the shipping date on a customer's order, and then use a subform to see the customer's mailing address. The Subform Wizard is the easiest way to create a form with subforms.

FIGURE 3.17 Form Wizard

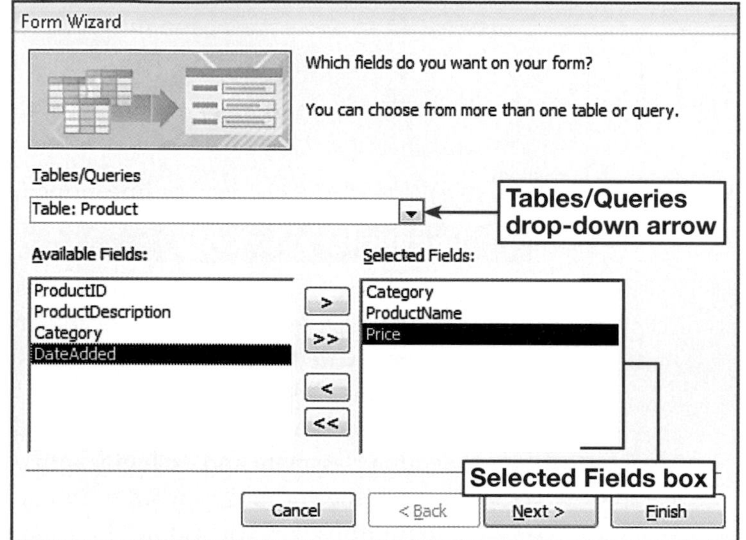

FIGURE 3.18 Category form with Product subform

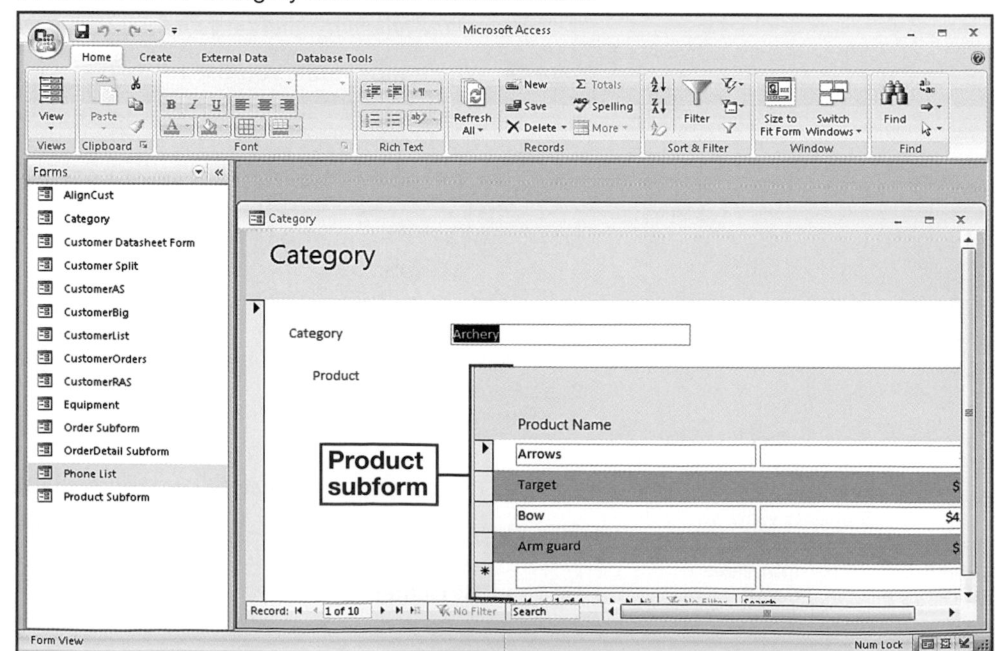

LESSON 3 Practice It Activities

Step-By-Step

1. Open the data file **Office.xlsx**. Save as: Office-[your first initial and last name]1.

2. Select **A1:E7**. On the **Home** tab, in the **Font** group, choose the font **Bookman Old Style** (see Figure 3.45).

3. Select **A2:A7**. Change the **Font Size** to **12**. Click **Bold** **B**.

4. From the **Border** drop-down list, choose **Right Border**.

5. Select **B1:E1**. Click **Bold** **B**.

6. Change the **Font Size** to **12**.

7. On the **Border** drop-down list, choose **Bottom Border**.

8. Double-click the lines between the column heads to increase the width of columns A, B, C, D, and E.

9. **CHECK** Your screen should look like Figure 3.46. Save and close your file.

Solution The solution file for this activity is **Office1-SF.xlsx**.

1. Format a Worksheet

Data File

Follow the steps to complete the activity.

FIGURE 3.45 Font box in Font group

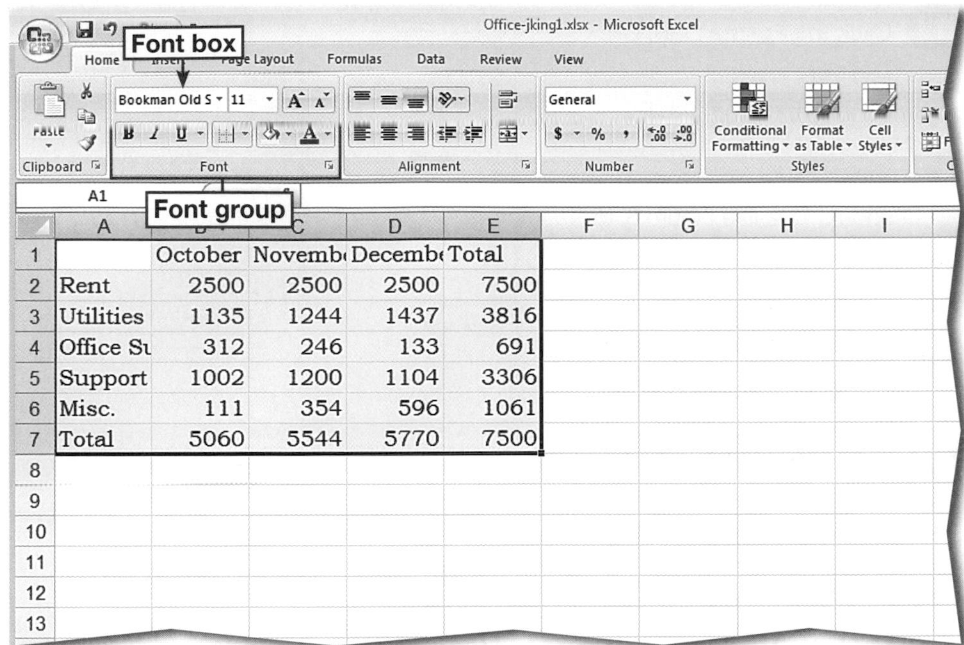

FIGURE 3.46 Modify column width

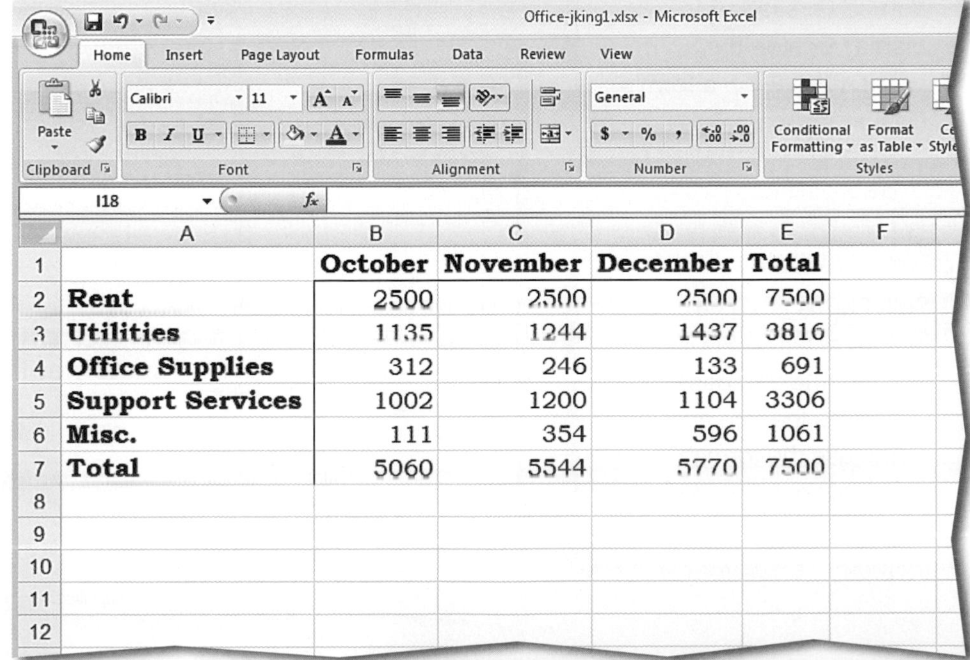

Step-By-Step

EXERCISE 3-6 (Continued)
Create Split Forms

9. Click **Property Sheet**.
10. In the drop-down menu at the top of the property sheet, select **Form**.
11. Click the **Format** tab. Click **Default View** and select **Split Form** from the list.
12. **CHECK** Your screen should look like Figure 3.15.
13. Click **Form View**.
14. **CHECK** Your screen should look like Figure 3.16.
15. Click **Close** [x]. Click **No** to close the form without saving changes.

Continue to the next exercise.

Tech Tip

You can press [F4] to display or hide the property sheet in a form's Design View.

Microsoft Office 2007

Split Forms are a new feature of Office 2007. Many of the database templates that are available online use the form portion as a functional header for the datasheet portion.

FIGURE 3.15 Phone list split form in Design View

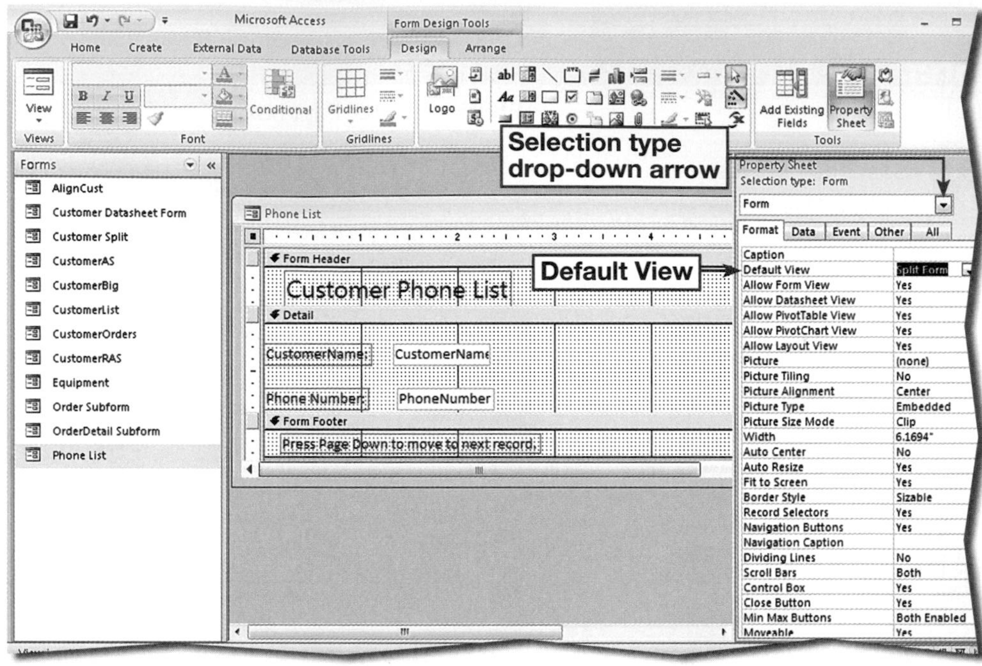

FIGURE 3.16 Phone list split form in Form View

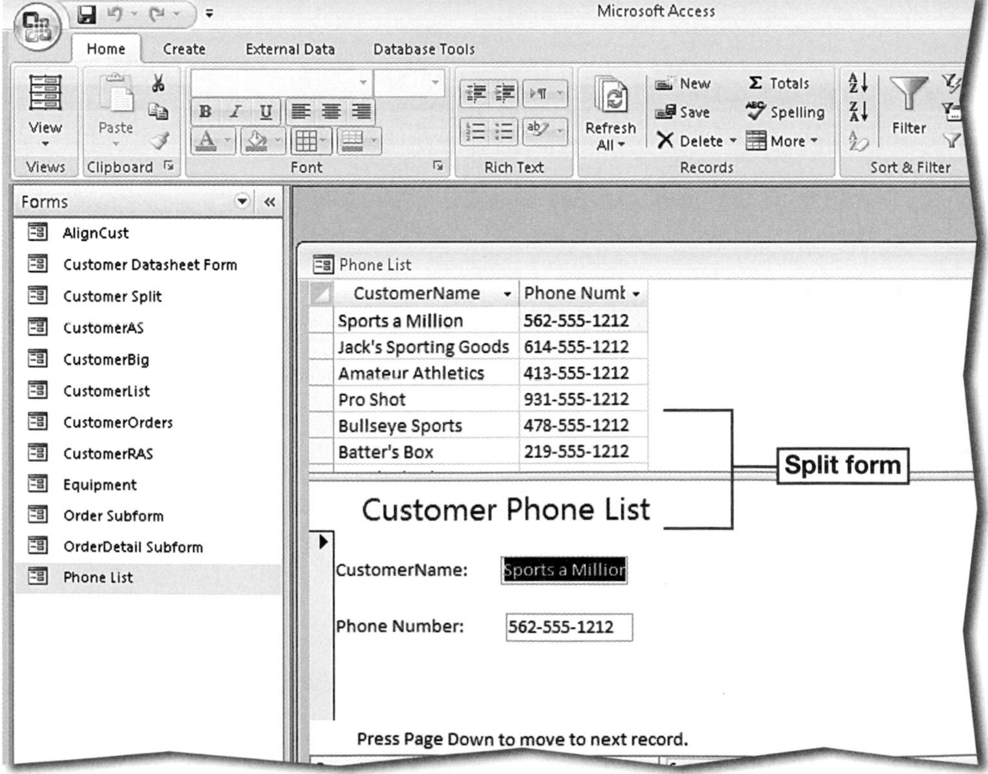

LESSON 3 Practice It Activities

Step-By-Step

1. Open your **Office-1** file. Save as: Office-[your first initial and last name]2.

2. Select **A1:E7**. Choose **Home> Styles>Format as a Table**. Select **Table Style Light 9**. Click **OK**.

3. Select **B2:E7**. Choose **Home>Cell Styles> Currency** (see Figure 3.47). If necessary, double-click the lines between column headings to increase the width of columns B, C, D, and E.

4. In cell **A1**, change the column heading to **Monthly Expenses**.

5. Change the **Font Size** to **12**. Adjust the column width, if necessary.

6. **CHECK** Your screen should look like Figure 3.48.

7. Save and close your file.

Solution The solution file for this activity is **Office2-SF**.

2. Format As a Table and Use Cell Styles

Follow the steps to complete the activity. You must complete Practice It Activity 1 before doing this activity.

New Student Strategy If a student did not complete Practice It Activity 1, then the solution file for that activity can be used as a data file for this activity.

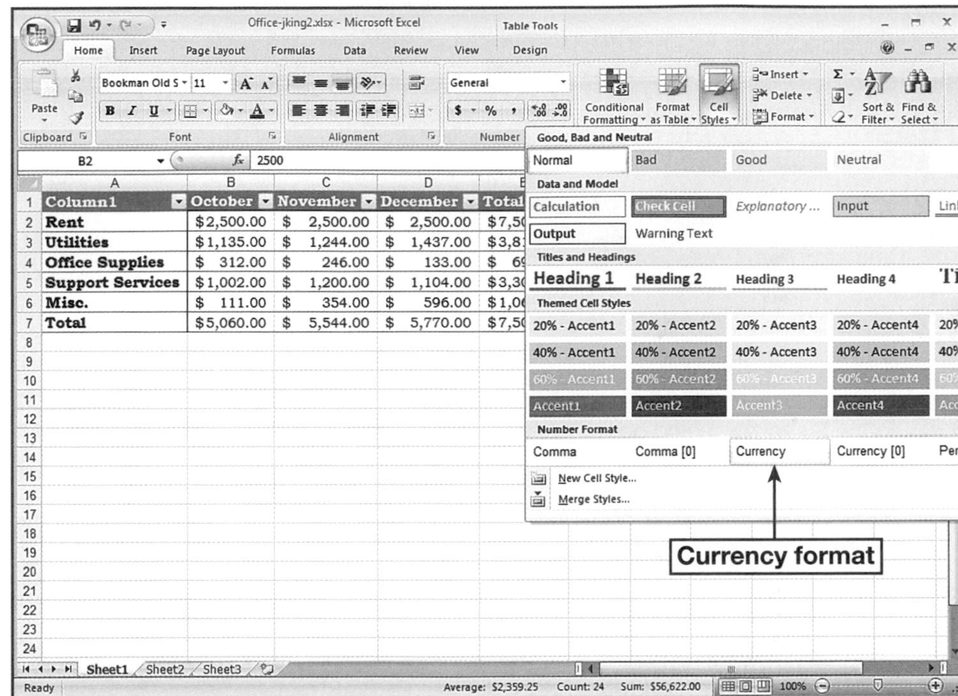

FIGURE 3.47 Currency style selected in Cell Style menu

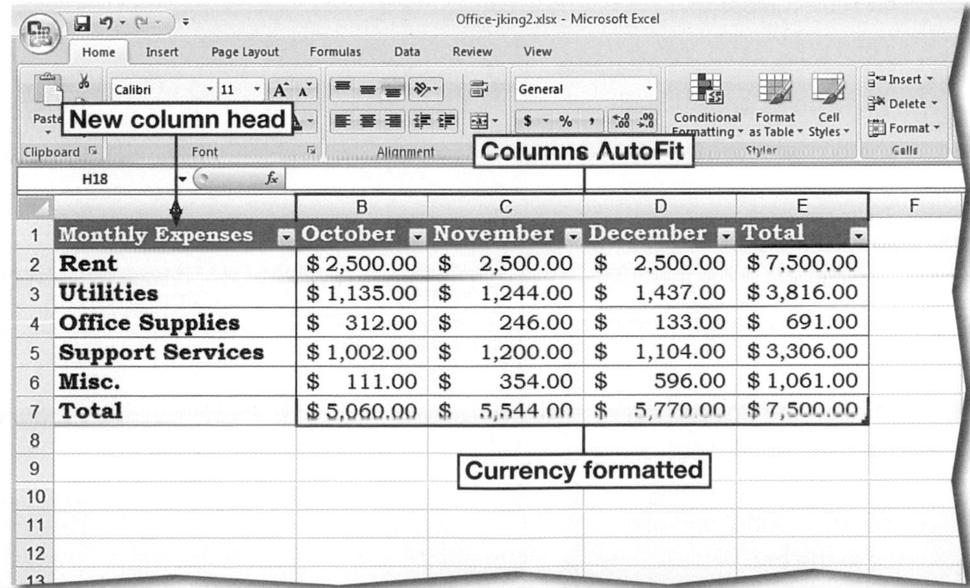

FIGURE 3.48 Column header added to cell A1

Step-By-Step

1. In your **Sports** file, open the **Customer** table, if necessary. Choose **Create>Forms>Split Form** .
2. **CHECK** Your screen should look like Figure 3.13.
3. Click **Form View** . Press TAB twice.
4. Delete the word **Avenue** and key: Ave. Press ENTER.
5. Click **Close** x and click **Yes** to save changes.
6. In the **Save As** dialog box, key: Customer Split. Click **OK**. Close the **Customer** table.
7. In the **Navigation Pane**, select **Forms** and open the **Phone List** form. Click the **View** drop-down arrow, and select **Design View** .
8. **CHECK** Your screen should look like Figure 3.14.

Continued on the next page.

Shortcuts

You can draw out a form control on the design grid to the size and shape you want, or you can simply select the control and click once in the grid.

EXERCISE 3-6
Create Split Forms

A **split form** contains a datasheet in one half and a form in the other. Split forms allow you to select data from a record in the datasheet on the bottom of the screen and edit that data in the form at the top of the screen. You can create a split form from a table using the Split Form Tool button, or you can split an existing form.

Teaching Tip Tell students that pressing the **Page Down** key will take them through records.

FIGURE 3.13 Customer table split

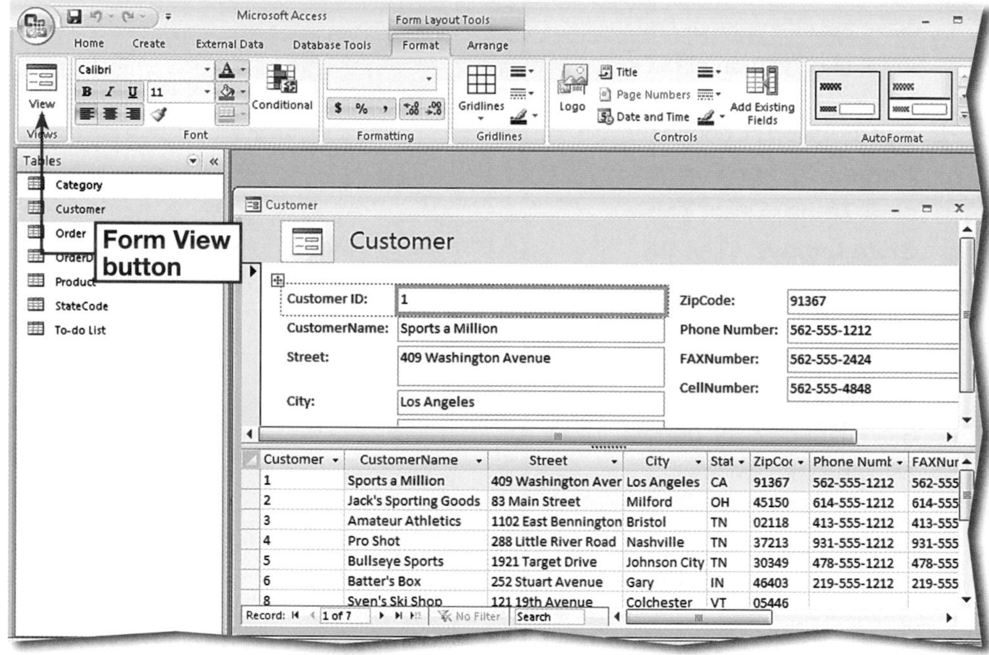

FIGURE 3.14 Phone list Design View

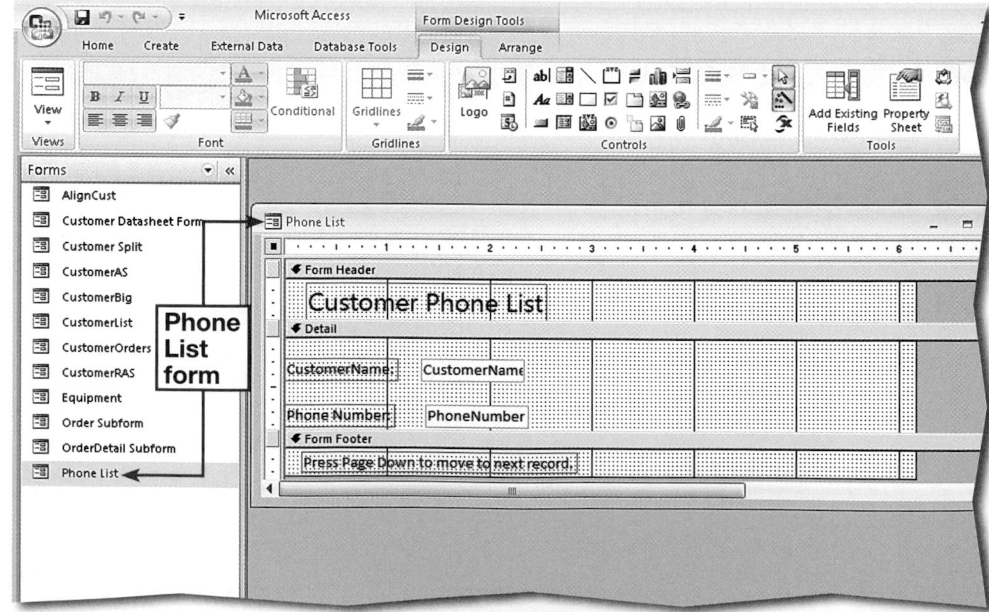

LESSON 3 Practice It Activities

Step-By-Step

1. Open your **Office-2** file. Save as: Office-[your first initial and last name]3.
2. Choose **Home>Cells> Format**. Under **Organize Sheets**, click **Rename Sheet**.
3. Key: Monthly Expenses. Press ENTER.
4. Choose **Home>Cells> Format**. Under **Organize Sheets**, click **Tab Color**.
5. Select **Red**.
6. CHECK Your screen should look like Figure 3.49.
7. Choose **Page Layout> Page Setup> Background**.
8. Navigate to the folder containing the data file **OfficeInc.JPG**. Select the file. Click **Insert**.
9. CHECK Your screen should look like Figure 3.50.
10. Save and close your file.

Solution The solution file for this activity is **Office3-SF.xlsx**.

3. Add a Background and Rename a Worksheet

Data File

Follow the steps to complete the activity. You must complete Practice It Activity 2 before doing this activity.

New Student Strategy If a student did not complete Practice It Activity 2, then the solution file for that activity can be used as a data file for this activity.

FIGURE 3.49 Tab color added to worksheet

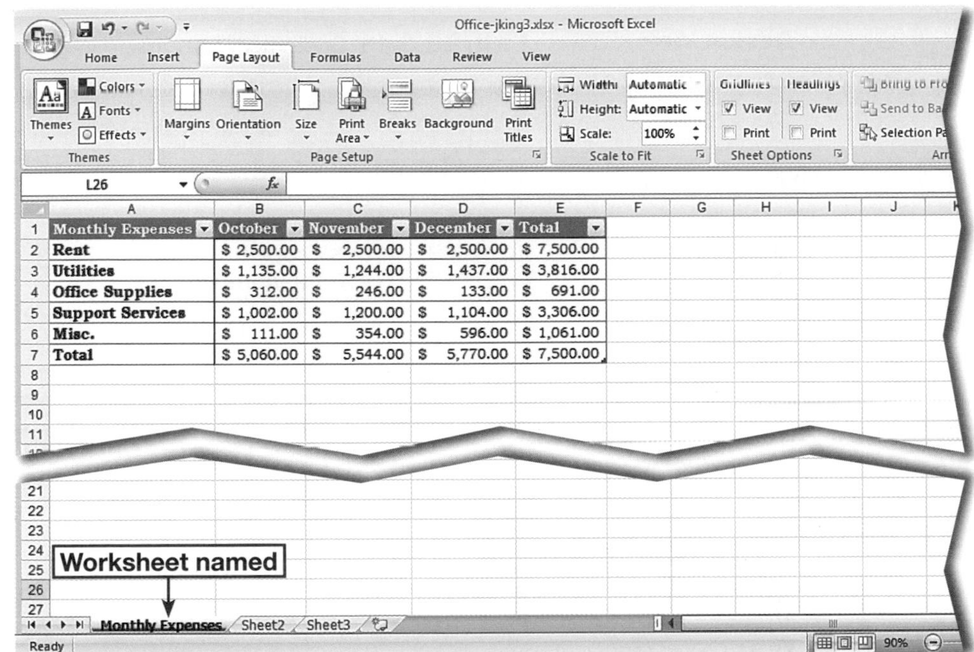

FIGURE 3.50 Office Inc. background added to worksheet

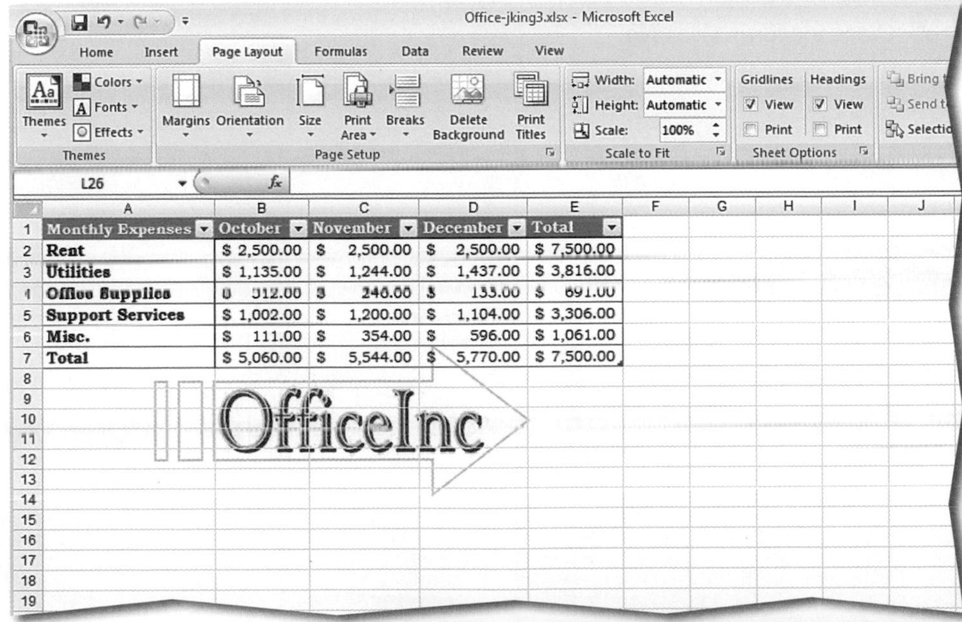

Step-By-Step

1. In your **Sports** file, open the **Customer** table.

2. Choose **Create>Forms> More Forms** and select **Datasheet**.

3. Click the **Design View** icon in the lower-right corner of the screen.

4. CHECK Your screen should look like Figure 3.11.

5. Click **Save**. In the **Save As** dialog box, key: Customer Datasheet Form. Click **OK**.

6. Choose **Create>Forms> Multiple Items**.

7. CHECK Your screen should look like Figure 3.12.

8. Click the **View** drop-down arrow and select **Design View**.

9. Close the form. Click **No** when asked to save changes.

Continue to the next exercise.

Tech Tip

The **Form View** button is not available in a datasheet form.

EXERCISE 3-5
Create Datasheet and Multiple Item Forms

Access provides several tools that help you avoid having to create every form from scratch. Use the **datasheet** form tool to create a simple form that presents the information from a specific table in Datasheet View. To display multiple records, use the multiple items tool. A **multiple item form** shows multiple items in a datasheet, with each record from the datasheet making up one row in the form.

FIGURE 3.11 Customer form Design View

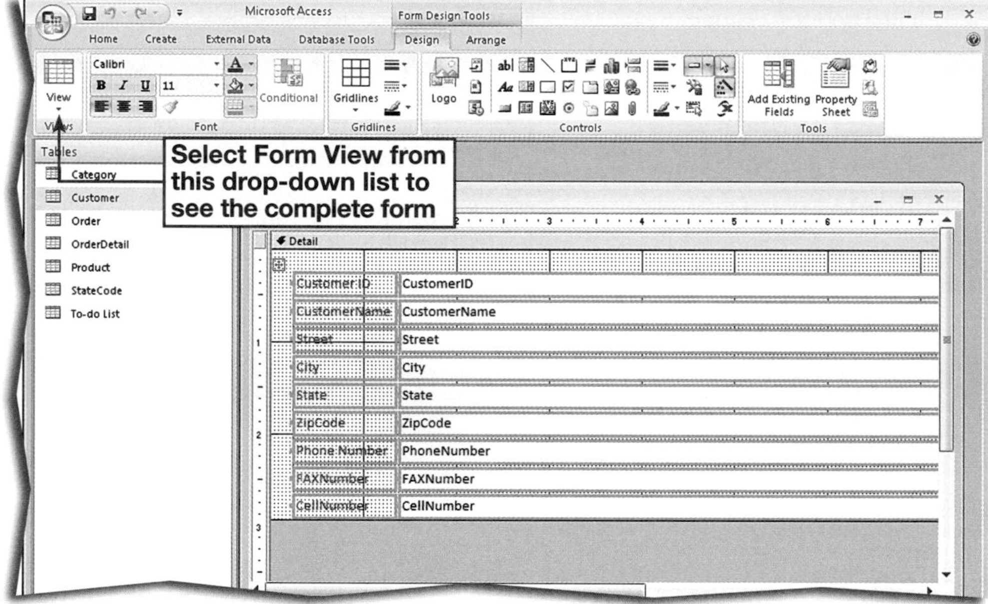

FIGURE 3.12 Customer Multiple Item form

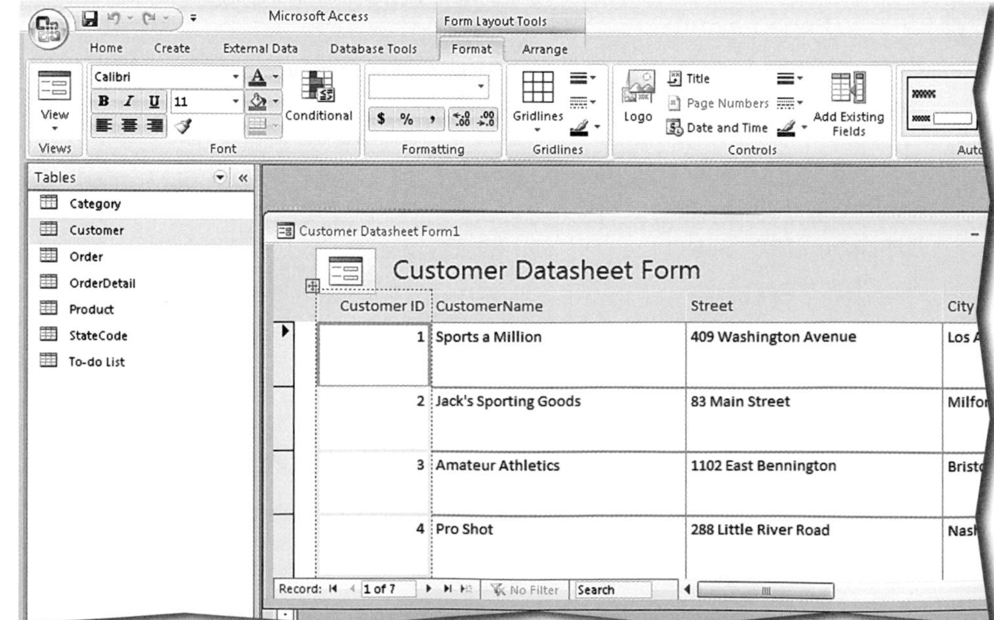

LESSON 3 You Try It Activities

Step-By-Step

1. Open the data file **Planner.xlsx**. Save as: Planner-[your first initial and last name]4.
2. Change the **Font Size** of **A2:C2** to **12**.
3. Bold the text in **A2:C2**. Change the font of **A1** to font size **14** and **Bold**.
4. Adjust the width of column **A**.
5. Change the **Font Color** of row 2 and column A to **blue**. Center the title in **A1** across **A1:C1**.
6. CHECK Your screen should look like Figure 3.51.
7. In column **B**, list how you spend your after-school hours. In column **C**, list how you could spend your time more efficiently.
8. Adjust the width of columns **B** and **C**.
9. CHECK Your screen should look similar to Figure 3.52.
10. Save and close your file.

Solution The solution file for this activity is **Planner-SF.xlsx**.

4. Schedule Change

One characteristic of being flexible is the willingness to change the way you do things. Create a schedule that lists the way you typically spend your after-school and evening time. Consider the things you normally do such as chores. Next to that list, key in how you think you might be more efficient during those hours. Remember to proofread for mistakes.

FIGURE 3.51 Planner with formatting applied

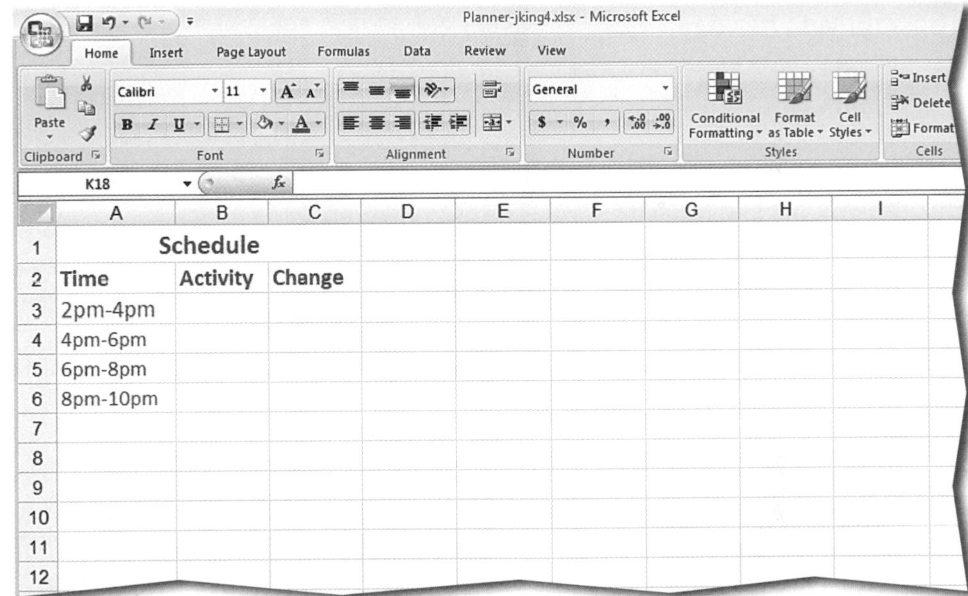

FIGURE 3.52 Completed planner

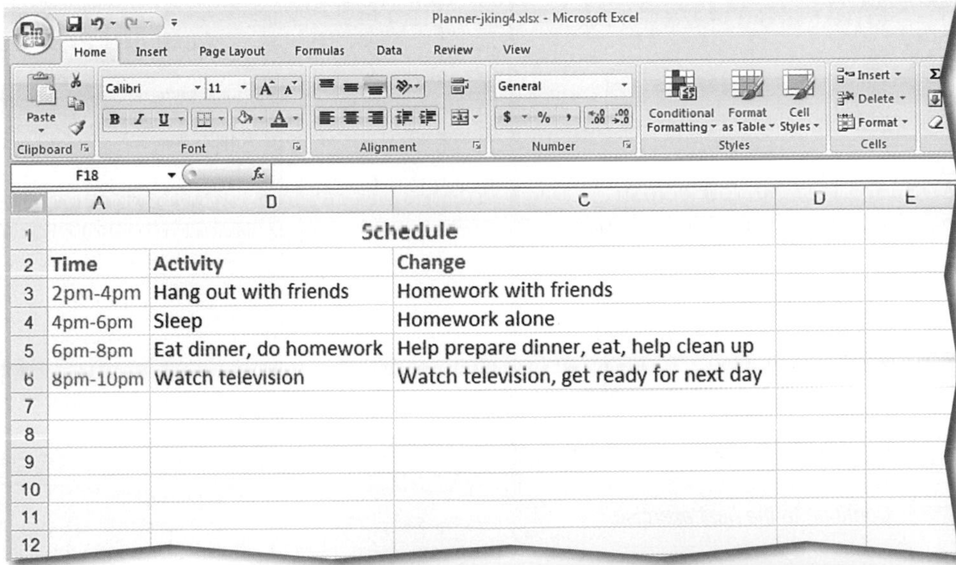

Step-By-Step

EXERCISE 3-4 (Continued)
Create Simple Forms

12 Click the **CustomerName** field and drag and drop it into the form under the **Detail** bar. Do the same with the **PhoneNumber** field.

13 CHECK Your screen should look like Figure 3.9.

14 Click **Add Existing Fields** to close the **Field List**.

15 Scroll to the bottom of the **Form1** window. Move the pointer over the bar labeled **Form Footer** until the two-headed arrow appears. Click and drag the bar up until it is just under **Phone Number**.

16 Choose **Design> Controls>Label**. Draw a box under the **Form Footer** bar and key: Press Page Down to move to next record. Press ENTER.

17 Click the **Form View** button.

18 CHECK Your screen should look like Figure 3.10.

19 Click **Save** and name the form **Phone List**. Click **OK** and then press PAGE DOWN to move through the phone list. Close the form.

Continue to the next exercise.

FIGURE 3.9 Phone List form

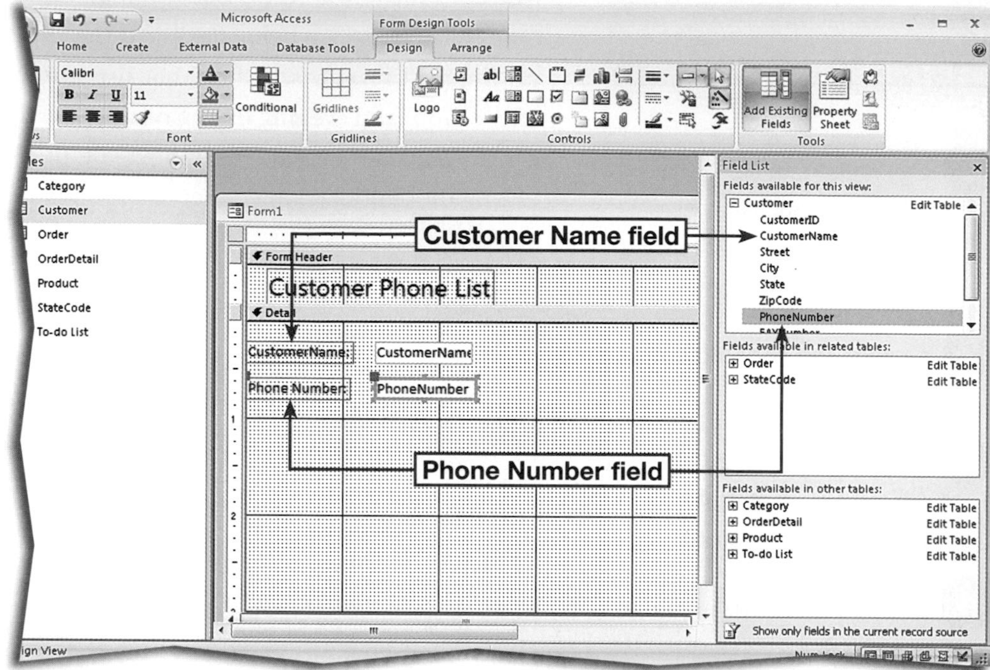

FIGURE 3.10 Phone List form running

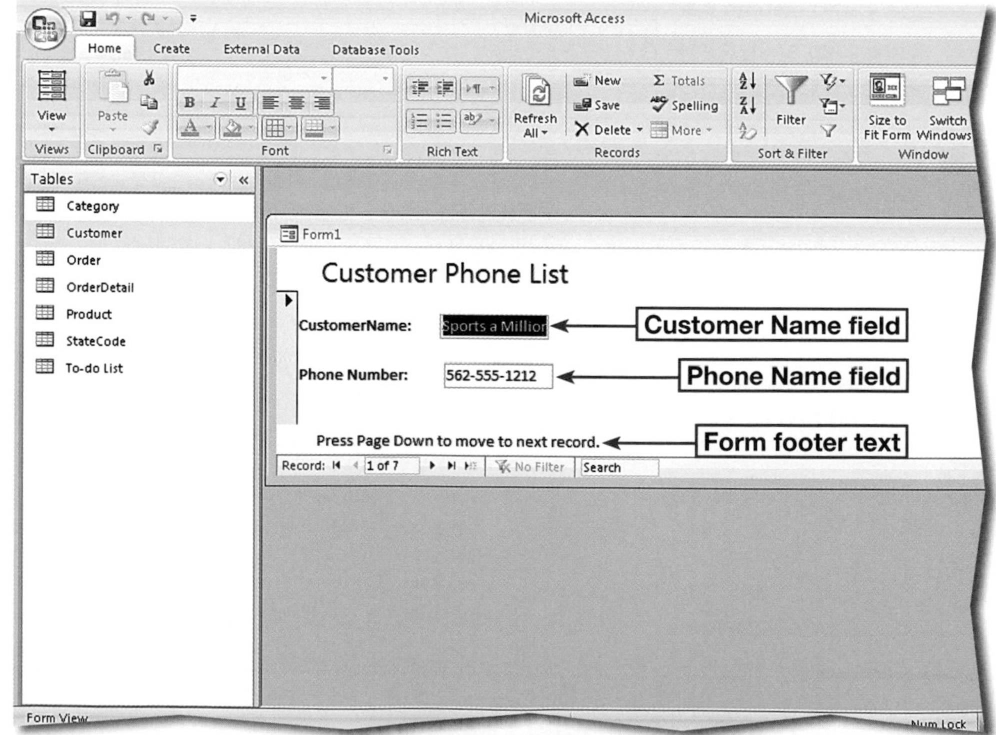

Step-By-Step Tip In **Step 12**, if students are not sure where to drop the **CustomerName** field in the form, have them line their pointer up with the **C** in the **Customer Phone List** header.

LESSON 3 You Try It Activities

5. Being Prepared

Data File

As part of a contest, you and a group of friends must spend a week in the wilderness living out of a backpack. Create a worksheet to list what you should take on your trip.

Solution The solution file for this activity is **Backpacking-SF.xlsx**.

Step-By-Step

1. Open the data file **Backpacking.xlsx**. Save the file as: Backpacking-[your first initial and last name]5.
2. Add a bottom border for cells **A1:C1**.
3. Select **A1:C1**. Bold and center the cell contents.
4. In each column, list three items you would need for that category. Adjust the width of each column.
5. CHECK Your screen should look similar to Figure 3.53.
6. Rename the worksheet tab Packing and change the tab color to **Green**.
7. Choose Page **Layout>Page Setup> Background**. Locate the data file **Pack.JPG** and insert it.
8. Hide **Sheet2** and **Sheet3**.
9. CHECK Your screen should look similar to Figure 3.54.
10. Save and close your file.

FIGURE 3.53 Backpacking list

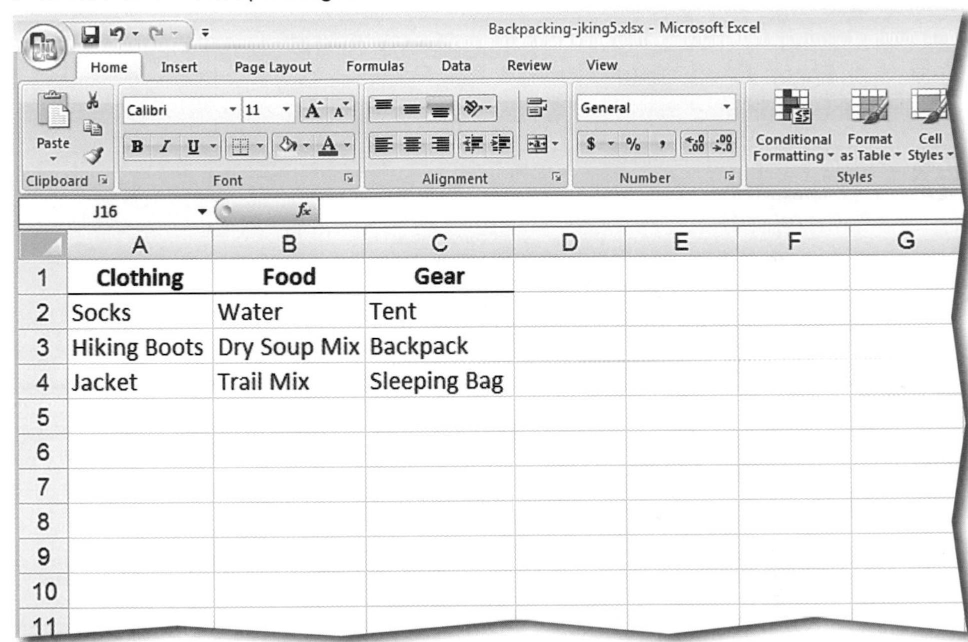

	A	B	C
1	Clothing	Food	Gear
2	Socks	Water	Tent
3	Hiking Boots	Dry Soup Mix	Backpack
4	Jacket	Trail Mix	Sleeping Bag

FIGURE 3.54 Formatted backpacking list

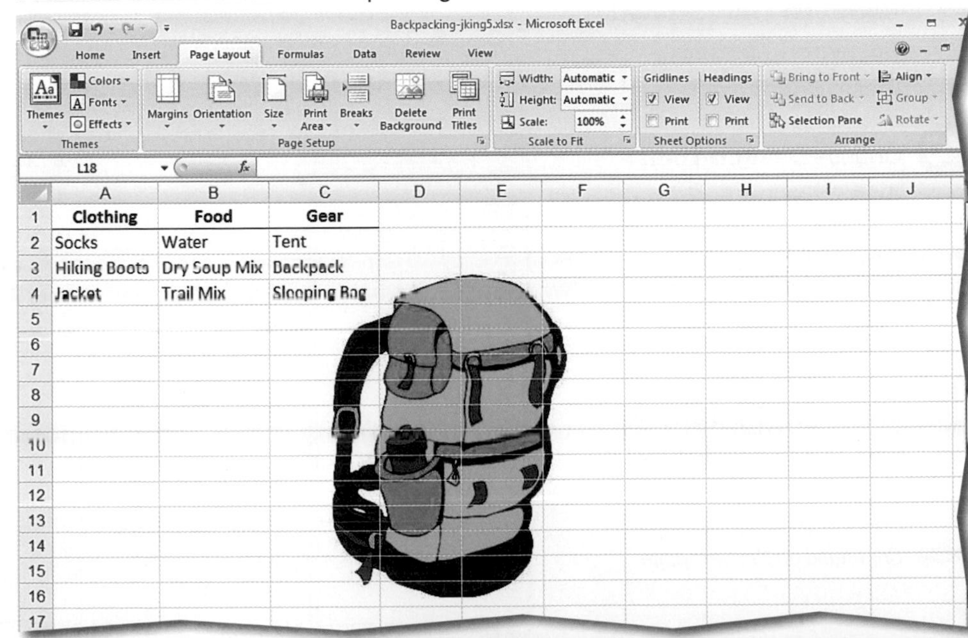

	A	B	C
1	Clothing	Food	Gear
2	Socks	Water	Tent
3	Hiking Boots	Dry Soup Mix	Backpack
4	Jacket	Trail Mix	Sleeping Bag

EXERCISE 3-4
Create Simple Forms

When you enter your billing information into a **form** at your favorite online store, chances are the information will be saved into a database. In Access, forms provide a way to enter, edit, or display data from a table or query. They can be used to limit access to the data, for example, by not showing fields that should not be changed, and make it easier for users to enter or change information. The easiest way to create a form is to use the Form tool.

Teaching Tip Let students know that a *simple form* displays a single record at a time.

FIGURE 3.7 Simple Customer form

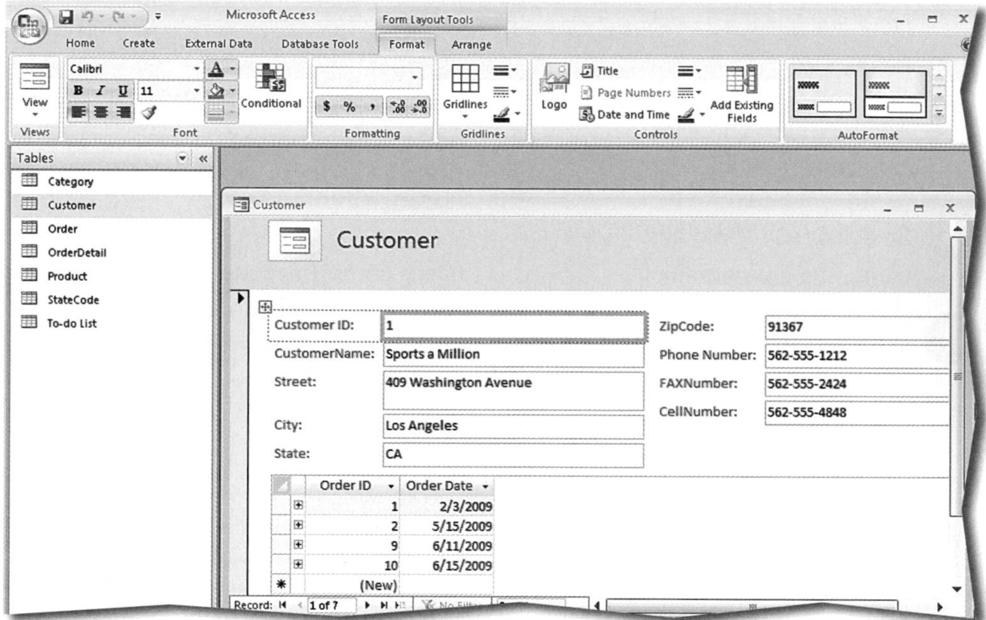

FIGURE 3.8 Form Design View

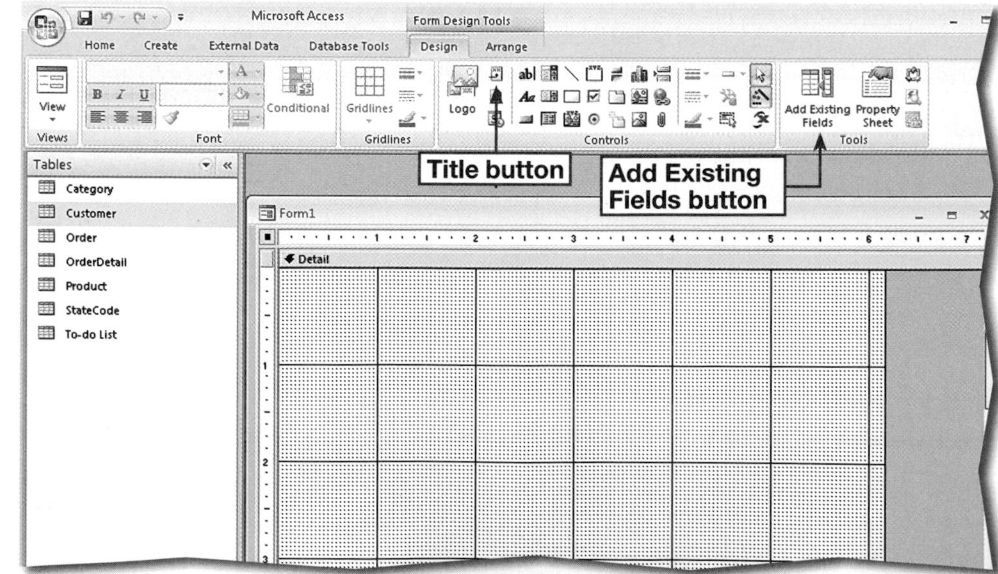

Step-By-Step

1. In your **Sports** file, open the **Customer** table.
2. Choose **Create>Forms>Form**.
3. **CHECK** Your screen should look like Figure 3.7.
4. Click **Form View** to see the completed form.
5. Press PAGE DOWN to view different records.
6. Close the form. Click **No** to close the form without saving changes. Close the table.
7. Choose **Create>Forms>Form Design**.
8. **CHECK** Your screen should look like Figure 3.8.
9. Choose **Design>Controls>Title**. Key: Customer Phone List. Press ENTER.
10. Choose **Design>Tools>Add Existing Fields**. Click **Show all tables** if tables are not already visible.
11. In the **Field List**, click the **plus sign** + to the left of the Customer table to show the fields in that table.

Continued on the next page.

LESSON 3 Critical Thinking Activities

Beyond the Classroom Activity Student workbooks will vary but should include entries for ten people. Column labels should be easy to read, and the worksheet should include a column for additional information about people.

Standards at Work Activity Student workbooks will vary but should show the data formatted and a reason for selecting the styles. For example, "This table or cell style makes totals at the bottom of the worksheet easy to read."

21st Century Skills Activity Student workbooks will vary but should include two jobs and a list of qualifications for both jobs. They should be formatted with color, bold, and italics, and the column should be large enough to fit the content.

6. Beyond the Classroom Activity

Language Arts: Create a Directory Use Excel to create a directory that includes information about ten of your friends and family members. Use one row for each person. Include a column for each of the following:

- address
- home phone number
- cellular phone number
- e-mail address
- birthday

Use a large font and bold for column labels. AutoFit rows and columns as necessary. Add a new column to include additional information about the people, such as how many children they have, what you bought them for their last birthday, the best time to reach them, and so on.

Save your workbook as: e3rev-[your first initial and last name]6.

7. Standards at Work Activity

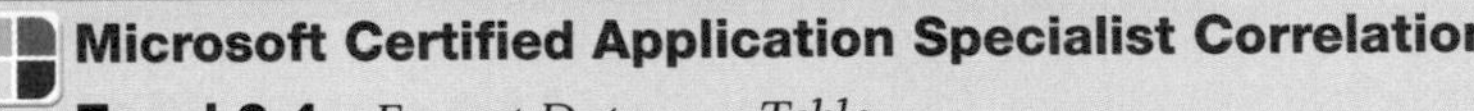

Microsoft Certified Application Specialist Correlation

Excel 2.4 *Format Data as a Table*

Format a Table You work for a small company that makes pottery. Your supervisor has asked you to format a worksheet that contains information about specific pottery items that the company makes and has sold in recent months. Your boss wants you to format the worksheet so the information stands out. Open the data file **Pottery.xlsx**. Save as: e3rev-[your first initial and last name]7. Decide which table and cell styles are the most appropriate for the data. Apply the styles. Key a paragraph in cell H6 that identifies why you chose the styles. In your paragraph, list the styles that you selected to format your data.

8. 21st Century Skills Activity

Create a Backup Plan Having a backup plan is a great step towards being flexible. Think of your first choice for a summer job. Open a new workbook. List the job at the top of a column in a worksheet. Underneath the job, list the reasons that you are qualified for the job. In case you do not get this job, list a second job choice in the second column. Include the reasons that you are qualified for your second job choice. The second column is now your backup plan. Modify the format so that your first job choice is in red and bold, and your backup job is in blue and italics. Adjust the column size to fit the content.

Save your workbook as: e3rev-[your first initial and last name]8.

glencoe.com

Go to the **Online Learning Center** to complete the following review activities.

Online Self Check
To test your knowledge of the material, click **Unit 2> Lesson 3** and choose **Self Checks**.

Interactive Review
To review the main points of the lesson, click **Unit 2> Lesson 3** and choose **Interactive Review**.

Step-By-Step

EXERCISE 3-3
Find and Replace Data

If you feel uncomfortable using queries or filters, or you want to **find** and **replace** a small amount of data in a single table, use the Find and Replace tools. You can find data in an individual field or in the entire table. To refine your search, use specific conditions, or **criteria**, to narrow your results. You can also use **wildcard** characters to search for different forms of the same word.

Step-By-Step Tip In **Step 10**, students' screens may highlight the word *Avenue* in a different record.

1. In your **Sports** file, open the **Customer** table. Choose **Home>Find>Find** . The **Find and Replace** dialog box opens (see Figure 3.5).
2. In the **Find What** box, key: 999.
3. Click the **Look In** drop-down arrow and select **Customer** to search the entire **Customer** table. Click the **Match** drop-down arrow and select **Any Part of Field**.
4. Click the **Replace** tab. In the **Replace With** box, key: 219.
5. **CHECK** Your screen should look like Figure 3.5.
6. Click **Find Next**. Click **Replace** twice. Click the **Find** tab. In the **Find What** box, key: *Avenue. Click the **Match** drop-down arrow and select **Whole Field**. Click **Find Next**.
7. **CHECK** Your screen should look similar to Figure 3.6.
8. Click **Cancel**. Close the table. Save the changes.

Continue to the next exercise.

FIGURE 3.5 Find and Replace dialog box

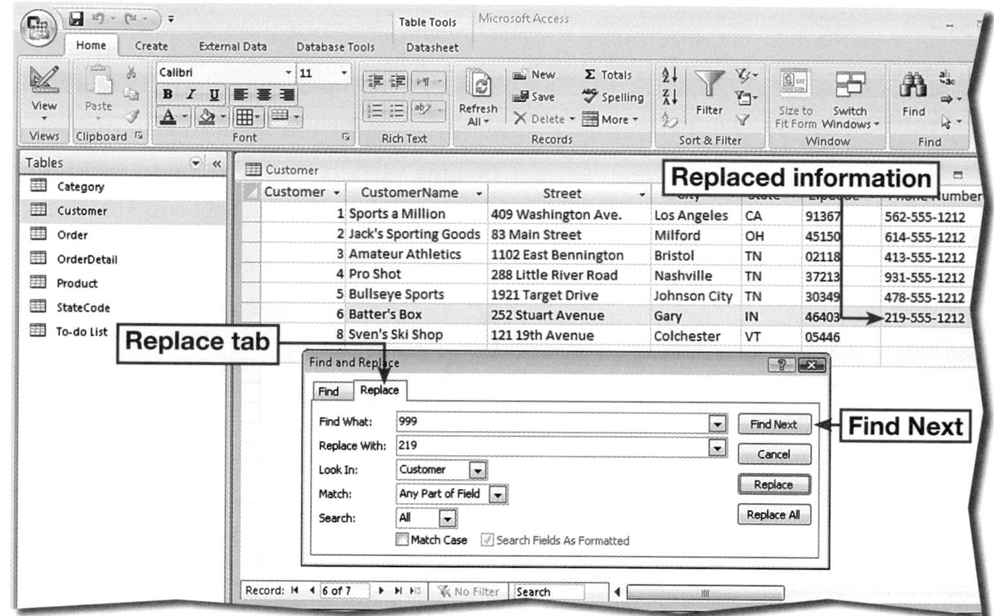

FIGURE 3.6 Find and Replace with wildcard character

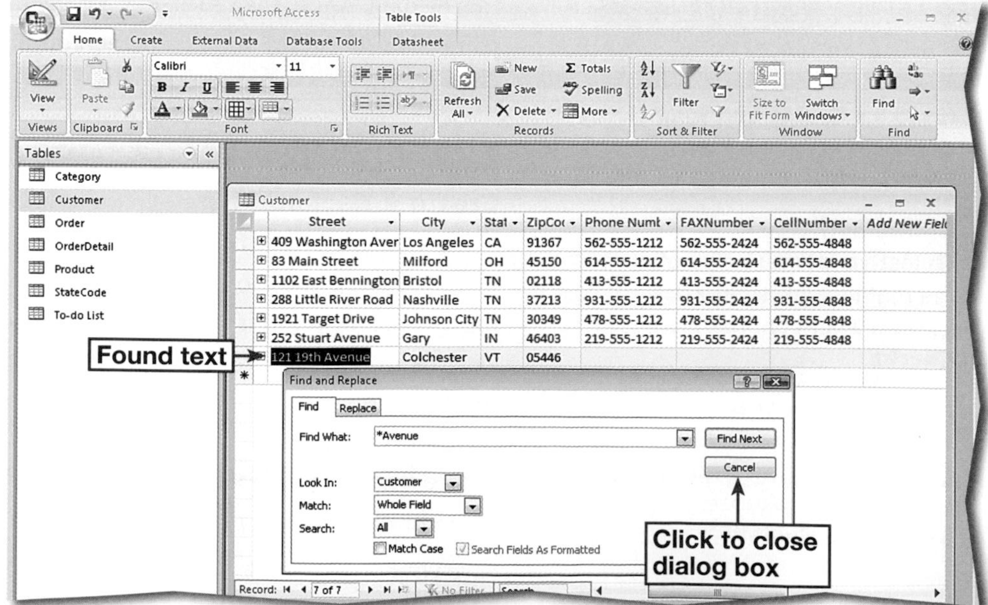

Teaching Tip Explain to students that the asterisk is a wildcard character. By keying **Avenue* and selecting **Whole Field** in the **Match** field they will find every field in the table that ends in the word *Avenue*.

Before You Begin

Format Data Formatting influences how an audience responds to a document. These projects teach you how to format a worksheet so it is easy to read and to understand.

Reflect Once you complete the projects, open a Word document and answer the following:

1. How can formatting be used to draw the reader's attention?
2. How did Excel's Quick Styles feature help you maintain consistency in your worksheets?

Answers Rubrics for each Challenge Yourself Project are available at **glencoe.com**. You may want to download the rubrics and make available to students as they complete each project.

9. Create a Sales Worksheet

Rubric R

LEVEL This is an intermediate level project.

Math: Create a Worksheet You are the owner of a small business that sells frames. Make a worksheet that shows the monthly sales for each size of frame. Include the following:

- three frame sizes: 8″ × 10″, 11″ × 14″, and 16″ × 20″
- prices for each frame size (8″ × 10″ = $11.95; 11″ × 14″ = $12.95; 16″ × 20″ = $13.95)
- sales for three months, assuming that smaller frames sell better
- total, average, minimum, and maximum for each month

Create a row for each size and a column for each month. Use AutoSum functions to calculate the total, average, minimum, and maximum for each month. Save as: e3rev-[your first initial and last name]9.

10. Format a Sales Worksheet

Rubric R

LEVEL This is an intermediate level project.

Language Arts: Change Font and Use Formats You decide to post your frame sales worksheet (created in Project 9 above) for your employees. Make the following format changes to increase the readibility:

- Make the font size for column and row labels larger.
- Use a different color for each month, and add the title **Quarterly Sales**. Center it across three cells, and apply an appropriate format.

Then, key a paragraph below the table that describes how the format changes add to the readability. Save your workbook as: e3rev-[your first initial and last name]10.

11. Design a Work Schedule

Rubric R

LEVEL This is an advanced level project.

Math: Insert and Format SmartArt You need to create a work schedule for the five employees at your frame shop. Design a worksheet that shows a schedule, in hourly increments, from 9:00 a.m. to 6:00 p.m. for Monday through Saturday. Include a column for each day and a row for each hour increment. For each day, assign two employees to the 9 a.m. to 1 p.m. shift and two employees to the 1 p.m. to 6 p.m. shift. Do your best to evenly distribute the hours among the employees, and avoid having any employee work two shifts in a row. Include the following:

- Below the schedules, add a SmartArt graphic that lists each employee's total hours. (Hint: Choose a SmartArt graphic from the **List** category in the **Choose a SmartArt** graphic dialog box).
- Save your workbook as: e3rev-[your first initial and last name]11.

Step-By-Step

1. In your **Sports** file, open the **Customer** table.
2. In the **Street** column, locate the field that contains **252 Linden Avenue**.
3. Select the word **Linden** (see Figure 3.3). Key: Stuart.
4. Select the seventh row.
5. Choose **Home>Records** and click the **Delete** drop-down arrow. Select **Delete Record**. When the warning dialog box opens, click **Yes**. The **Gordon's Golf** customer record is deleted.
6. In the sixth row of the **Phone Number** column, select the text **999**. Key: 219. Press scroll down.
7. CHECK Your screen should look like Figure 3.4.
8. Close the datasheet. Click **Yes**, if necessary.

Continue to the next exercise.

Tech Tip

To resize rows in the **Form** and **Datasheet Views**, place your pointer between two record selectors and drag up or down, or right-click a record selector and select **Row Height** on the menu.

EXERCISE 3-2
Edit and Delete Records in a Datasheet

Datasheets are not just for adding data to a table. You can also change and delete a table's fields and records in Datasheet View. Access has tools to help you edit the data from the Datasheet View without creating a form or using a delete, update, or append query.

Teaching Tip Explain to students that **AutoNumber** fields cannot be changed. For example, if students tried to change the Pro Shot **Customer ID** from 4 to 9, they would not be able to do so.

FIGURE 3.3 Customer table datasheet

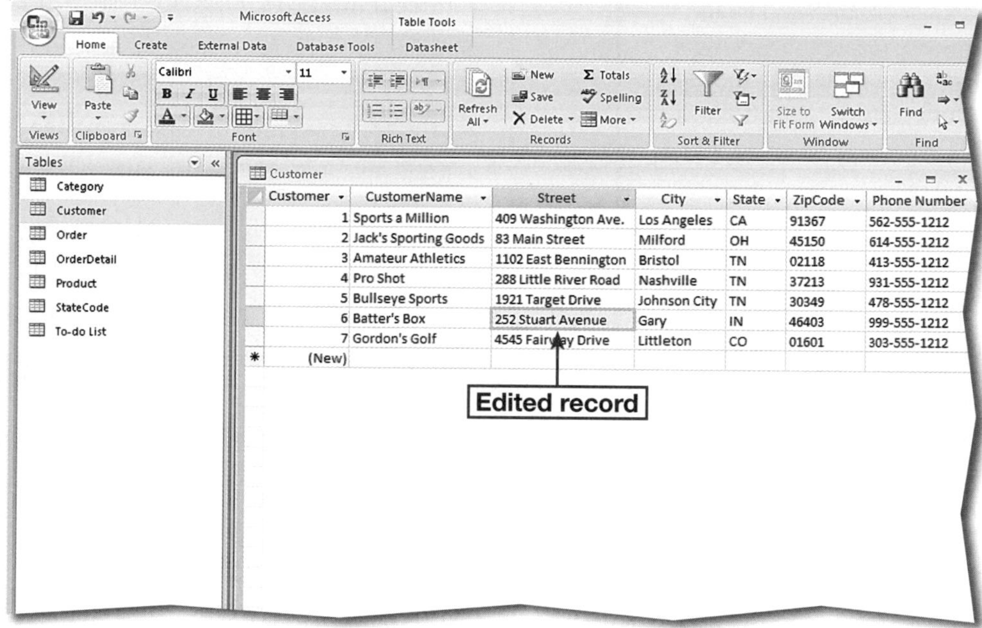

FIGURE 3.4 Customer table datasheet after changes

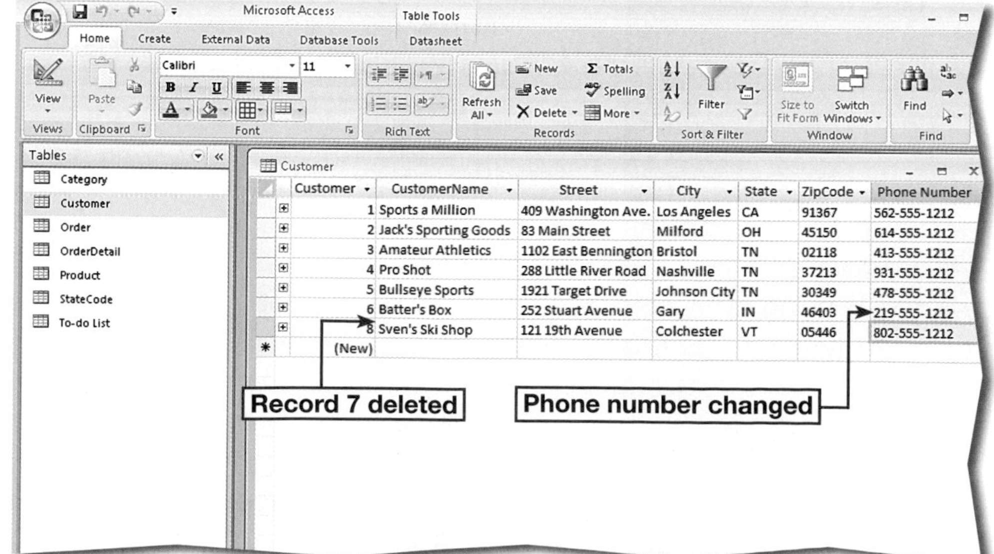

LESSON 4 Analyze Data

Key Concepts

- Filter and sort data
- Write, edit, and use formulas
- Use absolute, relative, and mixed references
- Create, modify, and position diagrams
- Create, modify, and position charts

Standards

The following standards are covered in this lesson. Refer to pages xxv and 715 for a description of the standards listed here.

ISTE Standards Correlation

NETS•S

1a, 3b, 3c, 3d, 4d, 6b

Microsoft Certified Application Specialist

Excel

2.3, 3.1, 3.2, 4.1, 4.2, 4.6 

In this lesson, you will use Excel to help you analyze data. You will sort data in ascending and descending order, as well as filter data to see only the information that you need. You will learn to use absolute and relative references to make different calculations, and create charts to visually represent your data.

See page TM74 for answer to 21st Century Skills.

21st CENTURY SKILLS

Improve Self-Management Successful self-management means setting a goal, figuring out what you need to do to meet that goal, and having the discipline to work steadily toward achieving it. For example, imagine that you want to run in a 10-mile race six months from now. What do you need to do now to prepare yourself? Once you determine your needs, use organizational tools such as calendars and Microsoft Excel to check your progress every week. It is easier to stick to a plan if you chart your progress so that you can see that you are getting closer to your goal. *Which of your goals require successful self-management?*

EXERCISE 3-1
Enter Records in a Datasheet

Forms are a good way to enter data in a large or complex table, but building forms takes time. When you are working with a simple table with a smaller amount of data, it is easier to use the Datasheet View to add data manually rather than create an entire form to enter the information.

Troubleshooting Review with students how to copy and save their database before starting the exercise.

FIGURE 3.1 New customer record entered in datasheet

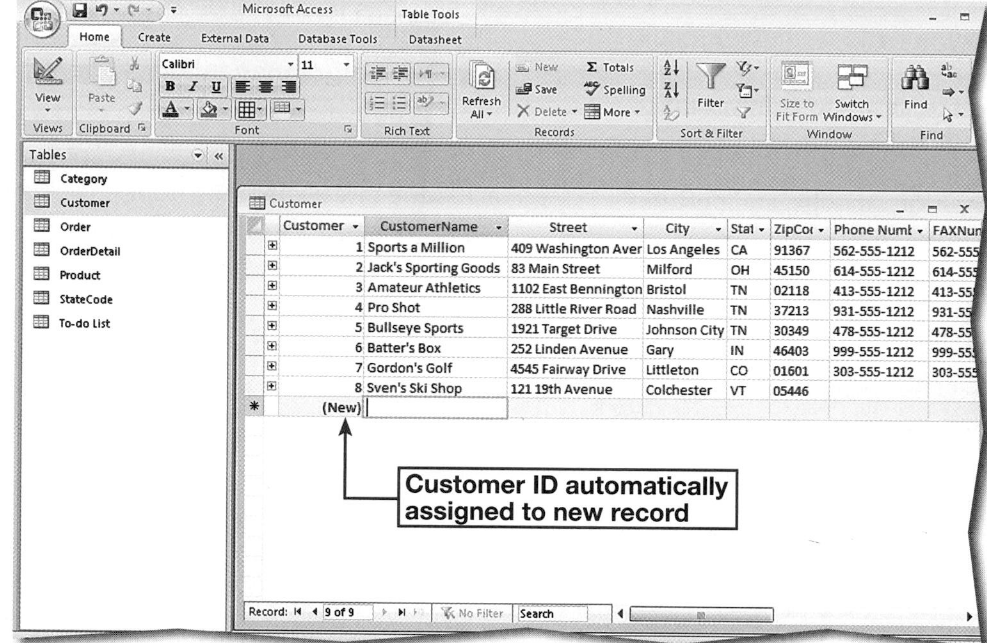

Teaching Tip Encourage students to resize columns in the table so that they can read the text for each column head.

FIGURE 3.2 New record with invalid state data

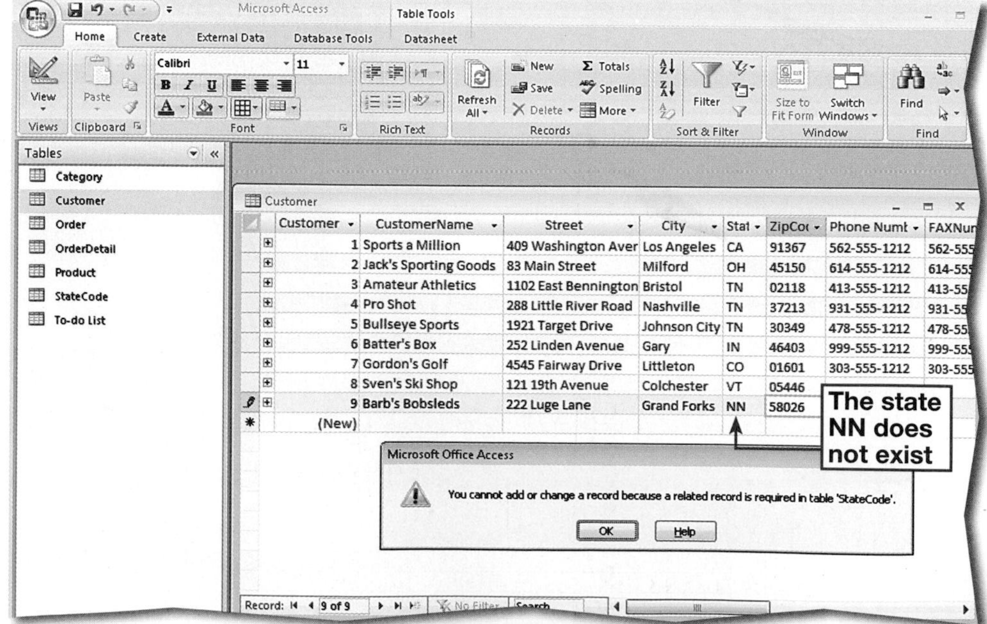

Step-By-Step

1. Start **Access**. With your teacher's help, locate the **Sports.accdb** data file and ask your teacher how to copy the database to your folder before working in it.
2. Open the **Sports** database file. In the **Navigation Pane**, select **Tables**.
3. Open the **Customer** table. Click in the eighth row of the **CustomerName** column.
4. Complete the row as shown in Figure 3.1. Click in the ninth row of the **CustomerName** column.
5. **CHECK** Your screen should look like Figure 3.1.
6. Complete the ninth row according to the data in Figure 3.2.
7. Click in the tenth row of the **CustomerName** column.
8. **CHECK** Your screen should look like Figure 3.2.
9. In the warning box, click **OK**. Click **Undo**. The new record is gone.
10. Close the datasheet. Click **Yes** to save the information you entered into the eighth record, if necessary.

Continue to the next exercise.

LESSON 4 Reading Guide

Before You Read

See page TM42 for English Learner activity suggestions.

Understanding It is normal to have questions when you read. Write down questions while reading—many of them will be answered as you continue. If they are not, you will have a list ready for your teacher when you finish.

Read To Learn

- Sort and filter columns to target the data you need.
- Create worksheets to calculate loan options.
- Customize how data is calculated using relative and absolute references.
- Make numerical data easier to understand by using charts and diagrams.

Main Idea

Excel is an excellent tool for analyzing, developing, and displaying data.

Vocabulary

Key Terms

absolute reference	filter	operator
chart	function	PMT
condition	IF	range
COUNT	mixed reference	relative reference
COUNTA	NOW	sort

Academic Vocabulary

These words appear in your reading and on your tests. Make sure you know their meanings.

adjust
version

Quick Write Activity

Describe When reading a report, seeing pages of words or figures can hinder the learning process. On a separate sheet of paper, describe why a full page of data and text may be difficult for viewers to understand. Explain how you think a chart or diagram can display information more clearly.

Study Skills

Study with a Friend When you explain something to another person, you are likely to remember that conversation at a later date. If you study with a friend, you are more likely to remember that discussion at test time. Verbalizing a concept lets you know if you really understand it. Discuss and compare a lesson's main ideas with a partner.

Academic Standards

NCLB/Math (Algebra) Reinforce the representation of data as a chart, graph, or diagram as an effective tool to visually convey information by having students go online to find examples to share with the class.

Math

NCTM (Data Analysis and Probability) Select and use appropriate statistical methods to analyze data.

NCTM (Number and Operations) Understand meanings and operations and how they relate to one another.

NCTM (Algebra) Understand patterns, relations, and functions.

NCTM (Algebra) Represent and analyze mathematical situations and structures using algebraic symbols.

NCTM (Algebra) Use mathematical models to represent and understand quantitative relationships.

NCTM (Algebra) Analyze change in various contexts.

LESSON 3 Reading Guide

Before You Read

See page TM42 for English Learner activity suggestions.

Study with a Buddy It can be difficult to review your own notes and quiz yourself on what you have just read. According to research, studying with a partner for just twelve minutes can help you study better.

Read To Learn

- Improve data entry and accessibility with forms and subforms.
- Use reports and labels to highlight and present data.
- Sort related data into groups and identify relationships between data with group headers.
- Gather data from various records in one report to offer the most complete information.

Main Idea

Access contains a variety of formatting features to ensure that your data is easy to understand.

Vocabulary

Key Terms

aggregate function	find	PivotTable
AutoFormat	form	replace
control	group header	sort
criteria	Layout View	split form
datasheet	multiple item form	subform
		wildcard

Academic Vocabulary

These words appear in your reading and on your tests. Make sure you know their meanings.

document
revise

Quick Write Activity

Identify Make a list of field names for information that could be included in an order form for an athletic shoe company's catalog. Think of all the information that a shoe manufacturer would want to track.

Study Skills

Why Prioritize? There are many times when we are faced with having to do multiple tasks in the same time frame. Manage you tasks by listing them and putting them in order of what should get completed first. Always try to remember what you need to do today, this week, and in the weeks ahead. Take the necessary time each day to work on tasks from each of these three time frames.

Academic Standards

English Language Arts

NCTE 8 Use information resources to gather information and create and communicate knowledge.

NCTE 12 Use language to accomplish individual purposes.

Math

NCTM (Algebra) Use mathematical models to represent and understand quantitative relationships.

NCTM (Number and Operations) Understand meanings of operations and how they relate to one another.

Step-By-Step

1. Start Excel. Open the data file **February Sales.xlsx**. Save as: February Sales-[your first initial and last name] (for example, *February Sales-jking*). Ask your teacher where to save your file.
2. Click cell **A2**. Choose **Data>Sort & Filter> Filter**. Click the drop-down arrow at the top of column A (see Figure 4.1).
3. Click **(Select All)** to remove the check marks next to every name. Then choose **Carmen Estrella**. Click **OK**. Only the products that Carmen sold are shown.
4. Click the column A drop-down arrow again and choose **(Select All)**. Click **OK**. The screen displays all of the employees.
5. Click the column B drop-down arrow. Choose **(Select All)**. Select **Thunderhead Parka**. Click **OK**.
6. **CHECK** Your screen should look like Figure 4.2.
7. Choose **Data>Sort & Filter>Filter** to turn off the AutoFilter. Save your file.

Continue to the next exercise.

EXERCISE 4-1
Use AutoFilter

Some worksheets contain so much information that it is difficult to understand the data. You can **filter** the worksheet, or show only the parts that you need. To use the AutoFilter command, you must first click on a cell in the **range**, or group of cells, that you wish to filter.

FIGURE 4.1 AutoFilter arrows

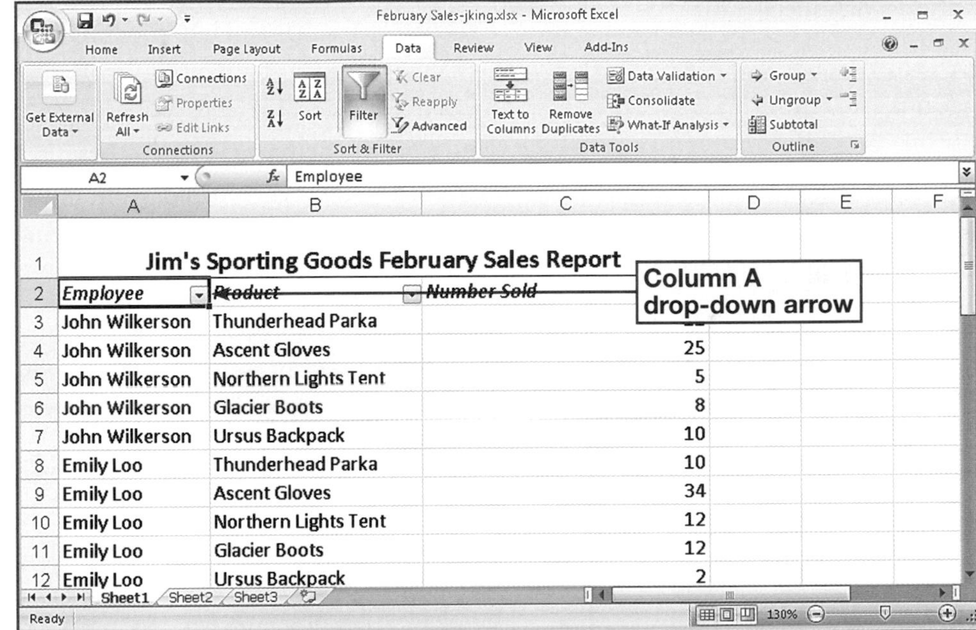

FIGURE 4.2 Thunderhead parkas sold

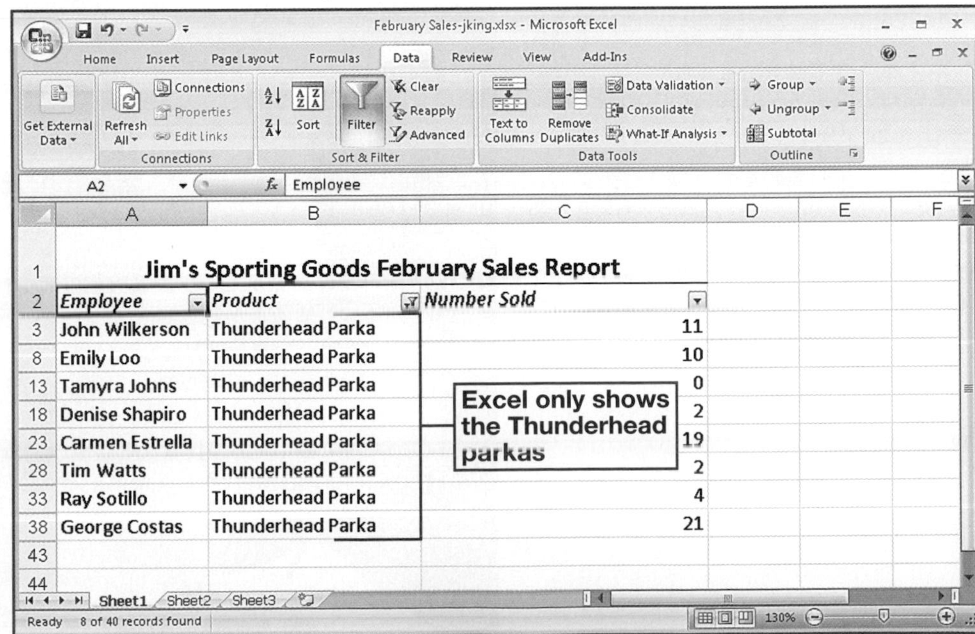

LESSON 3 Enter and Organize Data

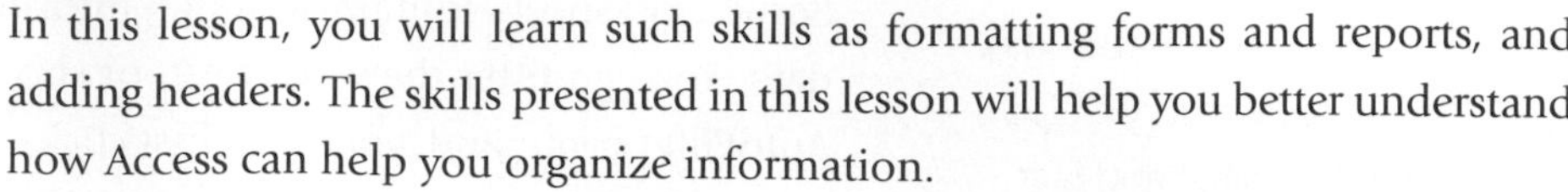

Key Concepts

- Enter, edit, and delete records from a datasheet
- Create, change, and format forms and reports
- Define and format controls
- Create multiple item, split, and subforms, and PivotTables
- Create and print labels

Standards

The following standards are covered in this lesson. Refer to pages xxv and 715 for a description of the standards listed here.

ISTE Standards Correlation

NETS•S

1c, 2b, 3c, 6a, 6b, 6d

Microsoft Certified Application Specialist

Access

2.5, 2.6, 2.7, 3.1, 3.3

In this lesson, you will learn such skills as formatting forms and reports, and adding headers. The skills presented in this lesson will help you better understand how Access can help you organize information.

21st CENTURY SKILLS

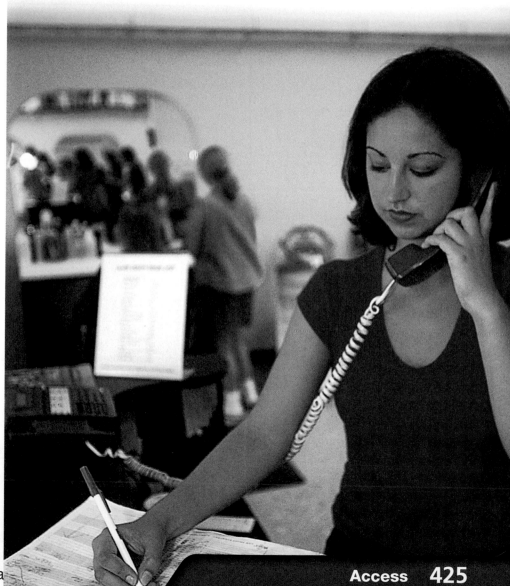

See page TM83 for answer to 21st Century Skills.

Prioritize You have an important test tomorrow that you need to study for. Your best friend calls to tell you the movie you have been waiting to see has finally arrived at the local theater. What do you do? Learning to sort the demands on your time can help you make the best use of your time, energy, money, and other resources. Whether you are working, studying, or planning your weekend, prioritizing will help you fit it all in. *What activities are a priority in your life?*

Step-By-Step

1. In your **February Sales** file, click any cell in column **A**.
2. Choose **Data>Sort & Filter>Sort A to Z** .
3. **CHECK** Your screen should look like Figure 4.3.
4. Click cell **C2**.
5. In the **Sort & Filter** group, click **Sort Z to A** .
6. **CHECK** Your screen should look like Figure 4.4.
7. Save and close your file.

Continue to the next exercise.

You Should Know

You do not have to select the cell at the top of a column to use **Sort**. You can click any cell in that column to sort.

NCLB/Math (Algebra) Reinforce how using the **AutoSort** feature in the data file helped to identify best-selling products. Explain to students that this is an example of how they can use **AutoSort** to identify patterns in a worksheet's data.

Solution Use the file **February Sales-SF.xlsx** as a solution file for Exercises 4-1 and 4-2.

Teaching Tip Tell students that they can sort more than one column by using **Data>Sort & Filter>Sort**. For instance, they can sort by employee name, then by number of items sold, and then by type of product.

EXERCISE 4-2
Sort Data

Excel can automatically **sort**, or organize, information for you. The Sort A to Z button alphabetizes names from A to Z or lists numbers in increasing order. You can choose Sort Z to A to sort from Z to A or in decreasing numerical order. You can also sort by more than one criteria, such as A to Z and in decreasing numerical order.

FIGURE 4.3 Using Sort to alphabetize

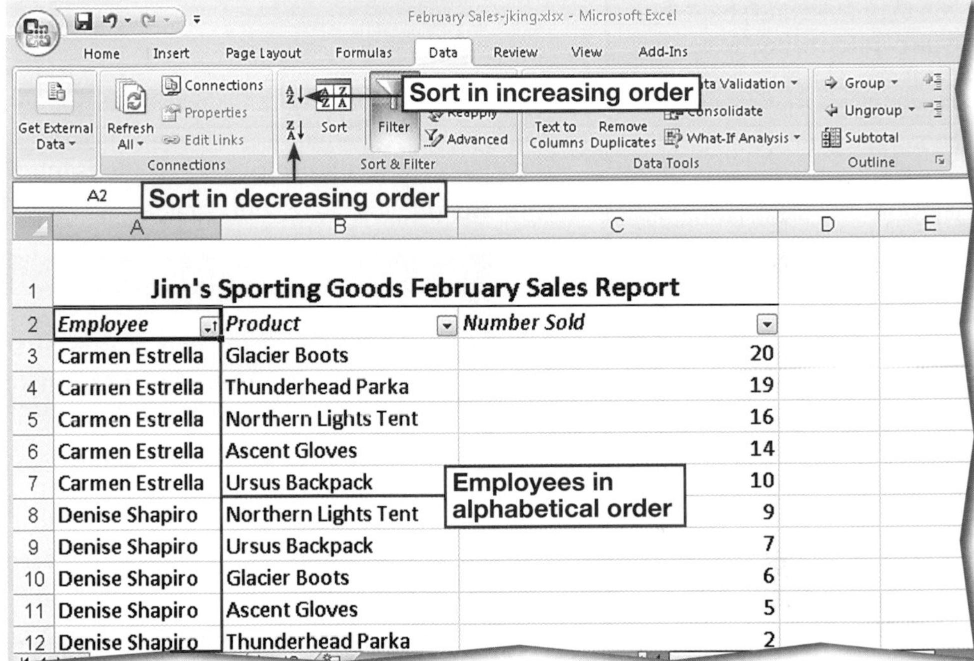

FIGURE 4.4 Using Sort on lists of numbers

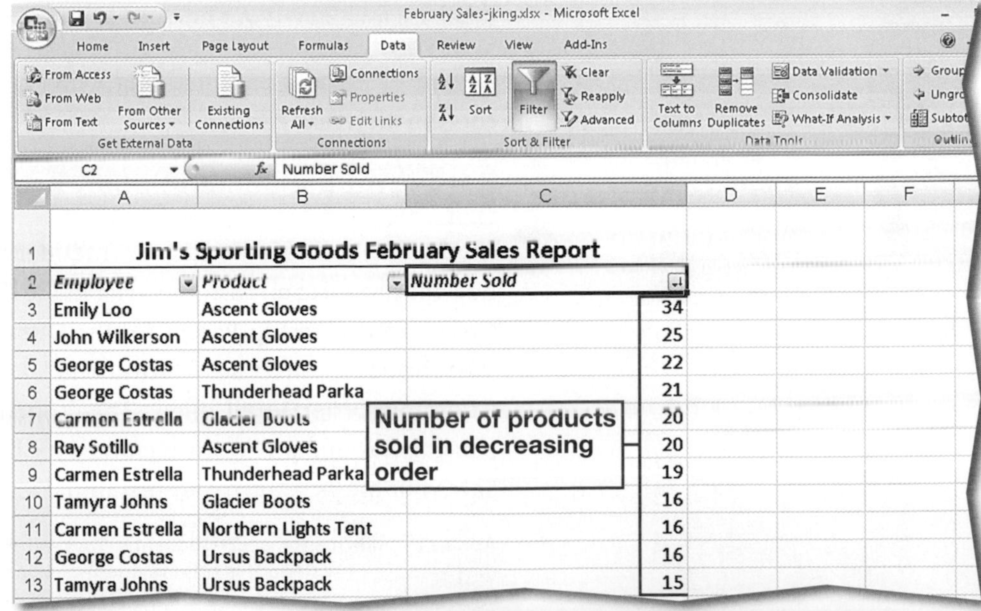

LESSON 2 Challenge Yourself Projects

Before You Begin

Gather Data Gathering data for a business with thousands of orders can be complicated. Access allows you to process and share this type of information in a database. These projects teach you how to record, coordinate, and query data quickly.

Reflect Once you complete the projects, open a Word document and answer the following:

1. In what ways do you think a template can help you better coordinate and quickly manage data?
2. What are some other ways you can use Access to gather and share information in a database easily?

9. Record Research Test Results

Rubric 

LEVEL This is an intermediate level project.

Create Relationships You are helping a scientist with an experiment that will test different drugs on different kinds of bacteria. You will record the results of the experiments in an Access database. Create a database that contains tables named:

- Bacteria
- Drug
- Test Result

Create a relationship between the **Bacteria** and **Drug** tables and the **Test Result** table. Save your database as: a2rev-[your first initial and last name]9.

10. Coordinate a Conference

Rubric 

LEVEL This is an intermediate level project.

Language Arts: Synthesize and Organize Information You have just been assigned the job of coordinating a nationwide conference. Create a database to organize and record information about the event, registration, and payments. Use a database template to create an **Events** database.

Everyone attending the conference will receive a souvenir. There will be many different souvenirs offered, and each attendee can choose which one they want. Create a table called **Souvenir**. This table will track the types of souvenirs available. Create a second table called **Attendee**. Add a field to the **Attendee** table to record which souvenir that person has chosen. Create a relationship between the **Souvenir** and the **Attendee** tables. Save your database as: a2rev-[your first initial and last name]10.

Key a paragraph summarizing why a database template made the coordination task easier.

11. Create a Sales Summary Query

Rubric 

LEVEL This is an advanced level project.

Math: Consolidate Data The president of the company wants to know how the product and customer data in the **Warehouse** database are related. Create a Relationship Report for the **CustomerOrderDetail** query in the **Warehouse** database. Print the Relationship Report for the **CustomerOrderDetail** query. Then, open a Word document and key a paragraph summarizing the relationships between the tables in your report. Save your file as: a2rev-[your first initial and last name]11.

Answers Rubrics for each Challenge Yourself Project are available at **glencoe.com**. You may want to download the rubrics and make them available to students as they complete each project.

EXERCISE 4-3
Key a Basic Formula

In Excel, a formula is an equation that performs a calculation, such as a sum or an average. You can tell Excel which numbers to use and what mathematical operation to perform by creating a formula. Every formula begins with an equal sign (=) and includes values or cell references. Depending on the type of calculation you wish to perform, you will need to use an **operator**, or a symbol for mathematical operations, such as * for multiplication, + for addition, − for subtraction, and / for division. In this exercise, you will calculate the two-percent bonus of an employee.

Step-By-Step

1. Open the data file **Bonus.xlsx**. Save as: Bonus-[your first initial and last name].
2. Click cell **C3**.
3. Key: =B3*.02.
4. **CHECK** Your screen should look like Figure 4.5.
5. Press ENTER. The results of the calculation appear in cell C2.
6. Press ↑.
7. **CHECK** Your screen should look like Figure 4.6.
8. Save your file.

Continue to the next exercise.

Step-By-Step Tip In **Step 3**, remind students that all formulas begin with an equal sign (=).

FIGURE 4.5 Entering a formula

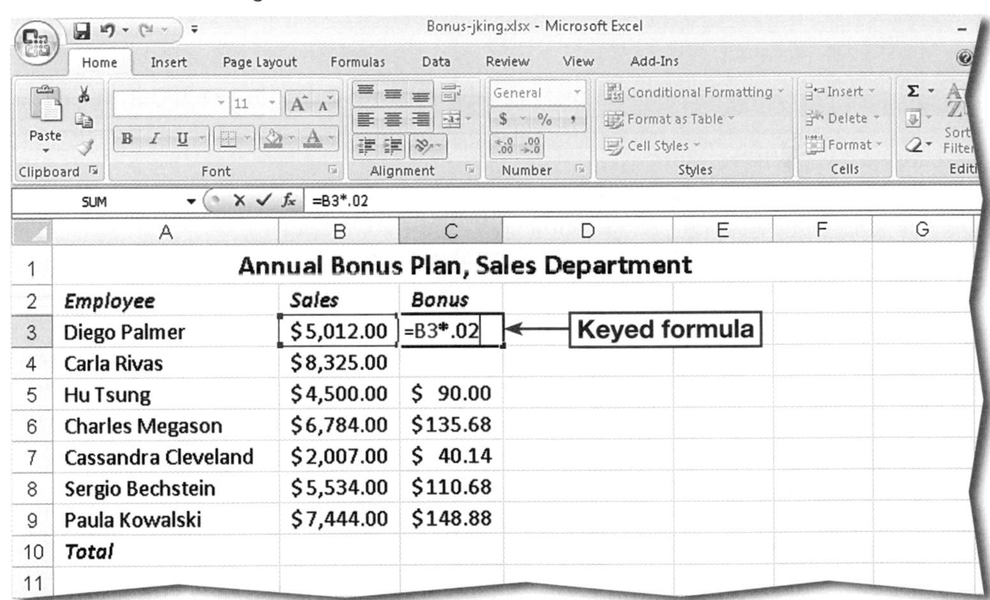

FIGURE 4.6 Formula results

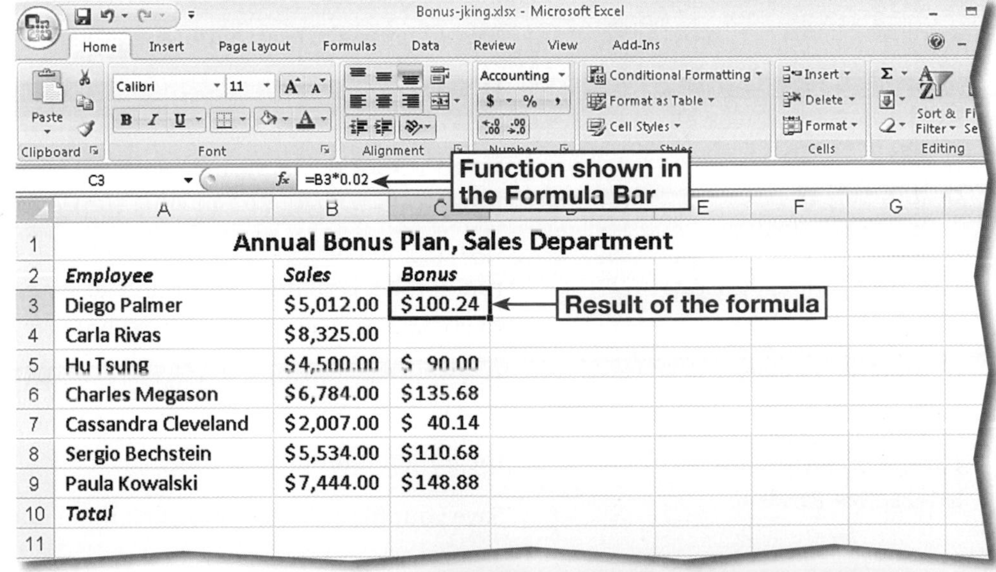

Academic Skills

Try to analyze how Excel formulas work. Then you can practice writing your own formulas in Excel. Test the formulas to make sure they work.

NCLB/Math (Algebra) Explain to students that there may be times when they will need to create a formula on their own. For example, there is no built-in function that creates a percent formula, so they have to key this formula in themselves using an operator.

NCLB/ Math (Number and Operations) Remind students how to move a decimal point. The decimal .02 represents 2 percent, 2 represents 20 percent, and .002 represents two-tenths of a percent.

LESSON 2 Critical Thinking Activities

Beyond the Classroom Activity
Students use database templates to create a database. They arrange the tables in the **Relationships** window so that no relationship lines cross. They then examine how the tables are related and identify which fields are part of each relationship. They pick a one-to-many relationship and describe why the relationship makes sense.

Standards at Work Activity
Students create a well-organized query that pulls information from at least three fields from the different tables in the database. Students run the query, and they format and print the datasheet in Datasheet View.

21st Century Skills Activity
Students key a paragraph that describes a project they rushed to finish and then had to redo. Students describe the steps they could have used to do the project right the first time.

Go Online e-REVIEW
glencoe.com

Go to the **Online Learning Center** to complete the following review activities.

Online Self Check
To test your knowledge of the material, click **Unit 3> Lesson 2** and choose **Self Checks**.

Interactive Review
To review the main points of the lesson, click **Unit 3> Lesson 2** and choose **Interactive Review**.

6. Beyond the Classroom Activity

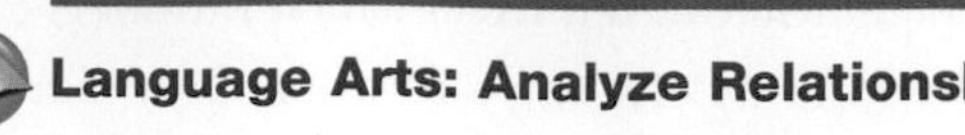

Language Arts: Analyze Relationships You need to understand the structure of the tables and relationships in your database before you can make any changes to them. Use a database template to create a database. Consider the following for types of databases you may want to create:

- Pets
- Types of stores in your neighborhood
- Your CD/DVD collection

Open the **Relationships** window and arrange the tables so that no relationship lines cross each other. Then examine the fields in each table. Look at how the tables are related. In a Word document, answer the following question: Which fields are part of each relationship? Pick a one-to-many relationship and describe in your document why the relationship makes sense.

Save your database as: a2rev-[your first initial and last name]6.

7. Standards at Work Activity

Microsoft Certified Application Specialist Correlation
Access 4.1 *Create Queries*

Create a Query Use the database you created in Activity 6 to design a query that will pull information in at least three fields from the different tables in the database. After you have run the query, format the datasheet so that the information arranged will be easy to read and understand when you print the datasheet view.

Save your database as: a2rev-[your first initial and last name]7.

8. 21st Century Skills Activity

Use Patience In the business world, there is a cautionary saying: "Never time to do it right, always time to do it over." Take time to do a project correctly the first time so you do not have to redo your work. In the long run, it takes less time and trouble to plan, prepare, and do a job well than to go back and repair a poorly completed project.

In a Word document, key a paragraph describing a project that you finished in a hurry and had to redo. Describe the steps you could have used to do the project right the first time.

Save your file as: a2rev-[your first initial and last name]8.

Step-By-Step

1. In your **Bonus** file, click cell **C4**.
2. Key: =B3*.05.
3. Press ENTER. This formula calculates the bonus amount for row 3.
4. CHECK Your screen should look like Figure 4.7. Notice the exclamation point in the yellow diamond next to cell C4. This symbol is an error message.
5. In the **Formula Bar**, change **B3** to **B4** and change **.05** to **.02**.
6. Press ENTER.
7. CHECK Your screen should look like Figure 4.8.
8. Save your file.

Continue to the next exercise.

Microsoft Office 2007

The total number of characters that you can enter into one cell in Excel 2007 is 32,767.

Step-By-Step Tip In Step 4, explain to students that the error message appears because the formula keyed into cell C4 does not match the formula entered into cell C3 in Exercise 4-3. Excel alerts the user to a possible inconsistency that may need to be resolved.

EXERCISE 4-4
Edit Formulas

If a formula has been keyed incorrectly, you can edit the formula in the formula bar. You can also edit a formula by double-clicking the cell that contains the formula. When you edit a formula, make sure that it contains the correct numbers and cell references.

Teaching Tip Point out that editing a formula uses the same skills as editing the contents of a cell. Students can use the **Backspace** key to remove text if they make a mistake.

FIGURE 4.7 Inconsistent formula identified in worksheet

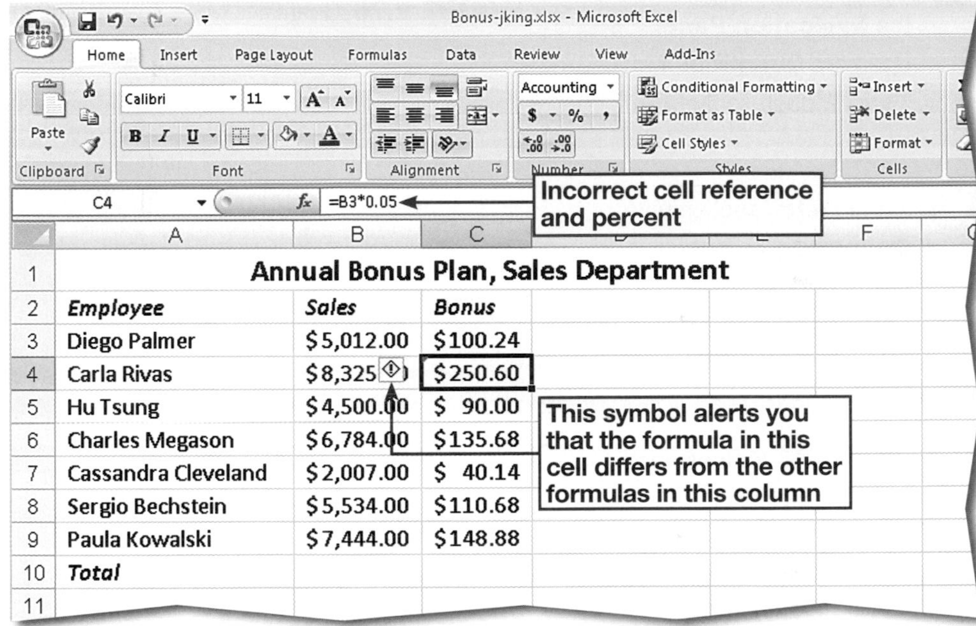

FIGURE 4.8 Edited formula

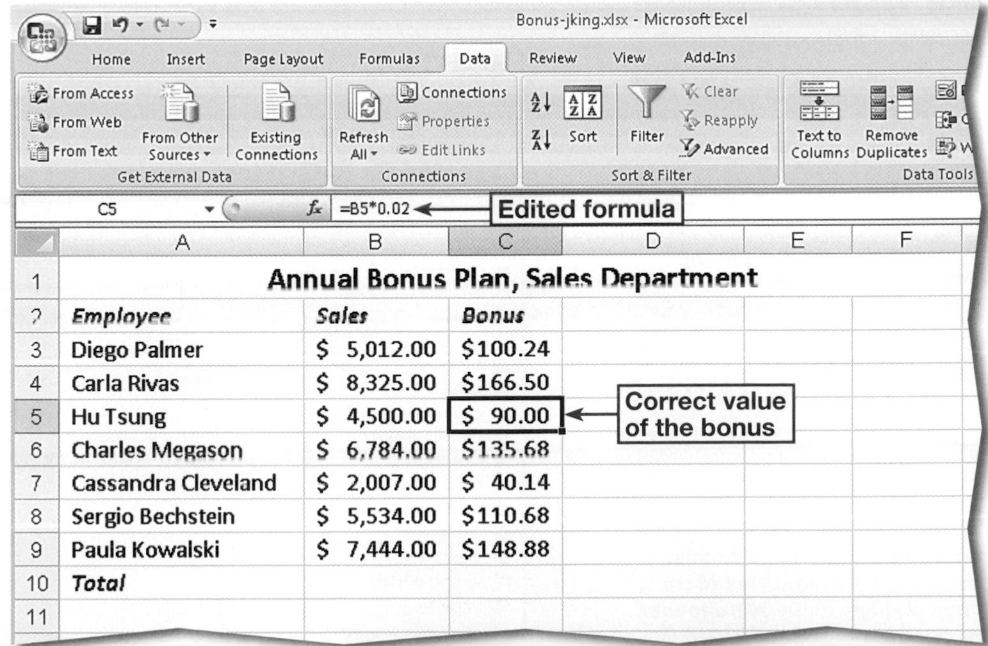

LESSON 2 You Try It Activities

5. Modify a Select Query

Your boss wants to put the Quantities More Than 2 query on the company Web site. Now that you have renamed the query, she asks you to modify the data to reflect the new name. You must complete You Try It Activity 4 before doing this activity.

New Student Strategy If a student did not complete You Try It Activity 4, then the solution file for that activity can be used as a data file for this activity.

Step-By-Step

1. In your **Warehouse** file, in the **Navigation Pane**, open the **Quantities More Than 2** query in **Design View**.
2. In the **Fields** section under **Quantity**, click in the **Criteria** box.
3. Change the **Criteria** to >2.
4. **CHECK** Your screen should look like Figure 2.76.
5. Run the **Quantities More Than 2** query.
6. **CHECK** Your screen should look like Figure 2.77.
7. Close the **Quantities More Than 2** query.
8. Click **Yes** to save the changes.
9. Exit **Access**.

Solution The solution for this activity is the **Quantities More Than 2** query in the **Warehouse-SF.accdb** database.

FIGURE 2.76 Quantities More Than 2 query in Design View

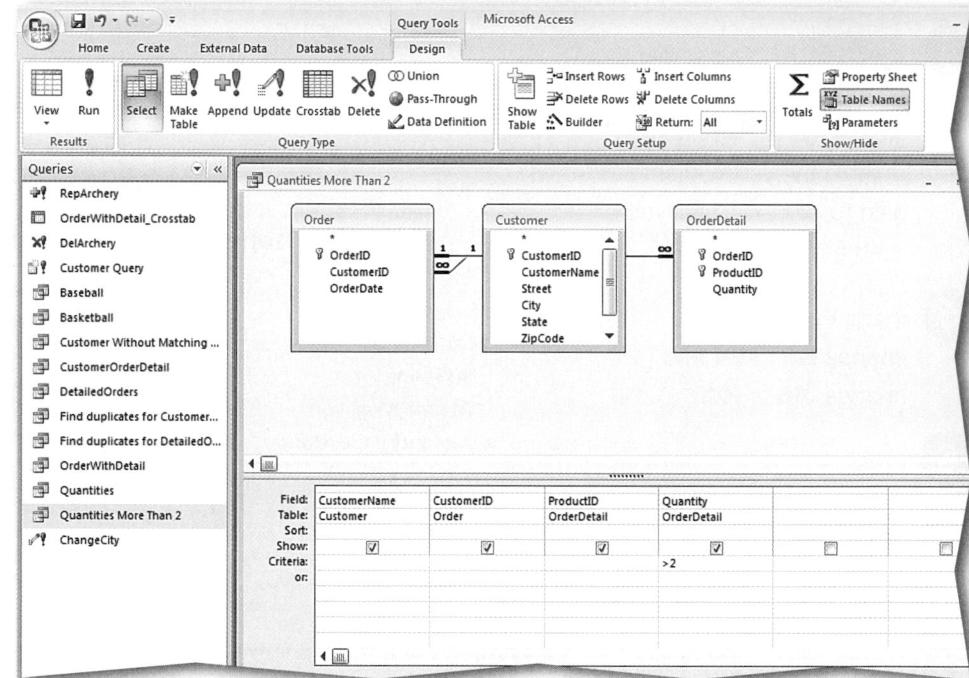

FIGURE 2.77 Results of Quantities More Than 2 query

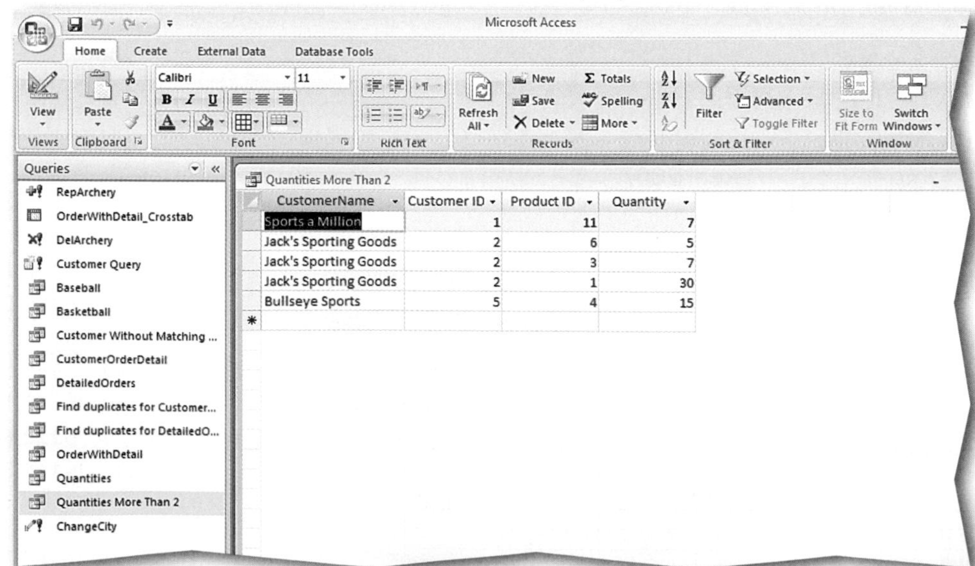

CustomerName	Customer ID	Product ID	Quantity
Sports a Million	1	11	7
Jack's Sporting Goods	2	6	5
Jack's Sporting Goods	2	3	7
Jack's Sporting Goods	2	1	30
Bullseye Sports	5	4	15

Step-By-Step

1. In your **Bonus** file, click cell **B10**.
2. On the formula bar, click **Insert Function** f_x.
3. In the **Insert Function** dialog box, under **Select a function**, click **SUM** (see Figure 4.9).
4. Click **OK**. The **Function Arguments** dialog box opens.
5. In the dialog box, check the line labeled **Number1** to make sure it reads **B3:B9**.
6. Click **OK**.
7. **CHECK** Your screen should look like Figure 4.10.
8. Save your file.

Continue to the next exercise.

Academic Skills

In this exercise, you use the **SUM** function to tell Excel to add the numbers in column B. Math problems use an addition sign (+) to indicate when numbers should be added together.

Step-By-Step Tip In **Step 3**, if students cannot find **SUM** in the **Select a Function** drop-down list, tell them to make sure that **All** is selected in the **Or Select a Category** drop-down list.

EXERCISE 4-5
Use Functions to Create Formulas

In addition to keying in formulas, you can create a formula by choosing a **function**, or preset formula, from a list. All you have to do is choose the function you want to use and fill in the correct numbers or cell references.

FIGURE 4.9 Insert Function dialog box

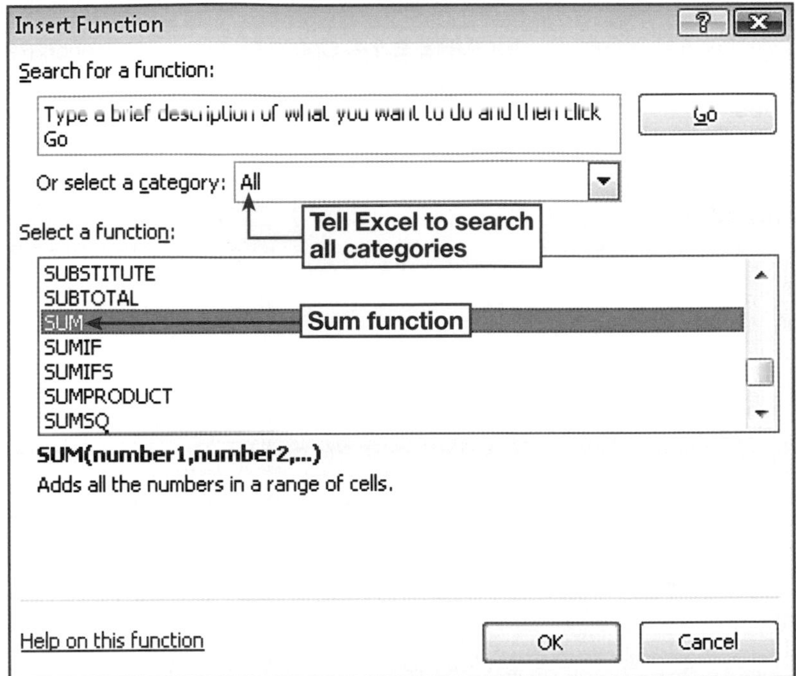

FIGURE 4.10 Numbers added using the SUM function

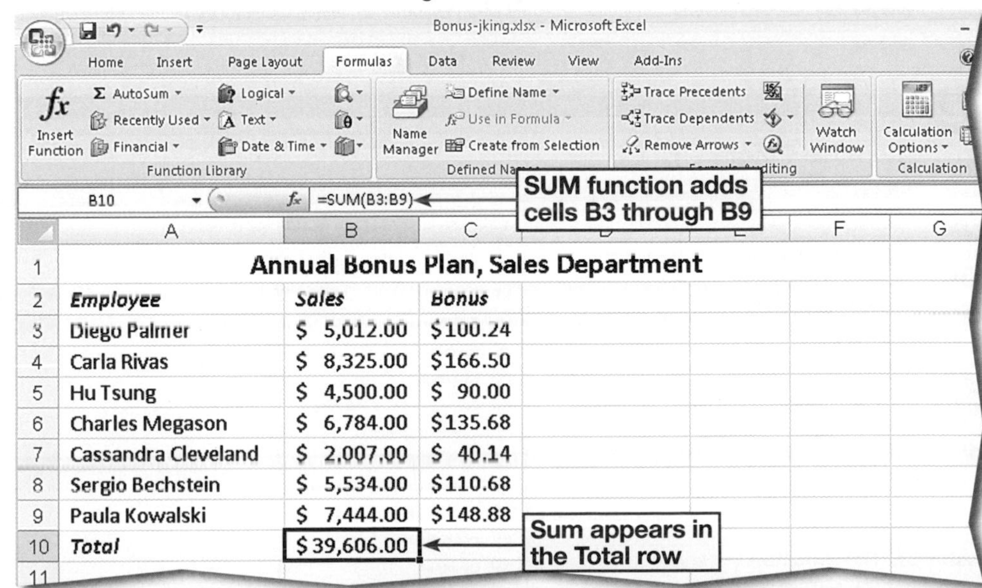

NCLB/Math (Number and Operations) Explain to students that **operators** are used to perform mathematical functions. The division symbol (÷) is also an operator.

4. Copy and Rename a Query

Your boss wants a copy of the Quantities query, but she only wants to know the quantities ordered that are more than two. She also thinks that the name should be more descriptive. She asks you to copy the Quantities query and rename it.

Step-By-Step

1. In your **Warehouse** file, in the **Navigation Pane**, select **Queries**.
2. In the **Navigation Pane**, select the **Quantities** query.
3. Create a copy of the **Quantities** query.
4. Name the new query **Copy Of Quantities**.
5. **CHECK** Your screen should look like Figure 2.74.
6. In the **Navigation Pane**, change the name of the **Copy Of Quantities** query.
7. Rename the query **Quantities More Than 2**.
8. **CHECK** Your screen should look like Figure 2.75.
9. Exit **Access**.

Solution The **solution** for this activity is the **Quantities More Than 2** query in the **Warehouse-SF.accdb** database.

FIGURE 2.74 Copy of query in Navigation Pane

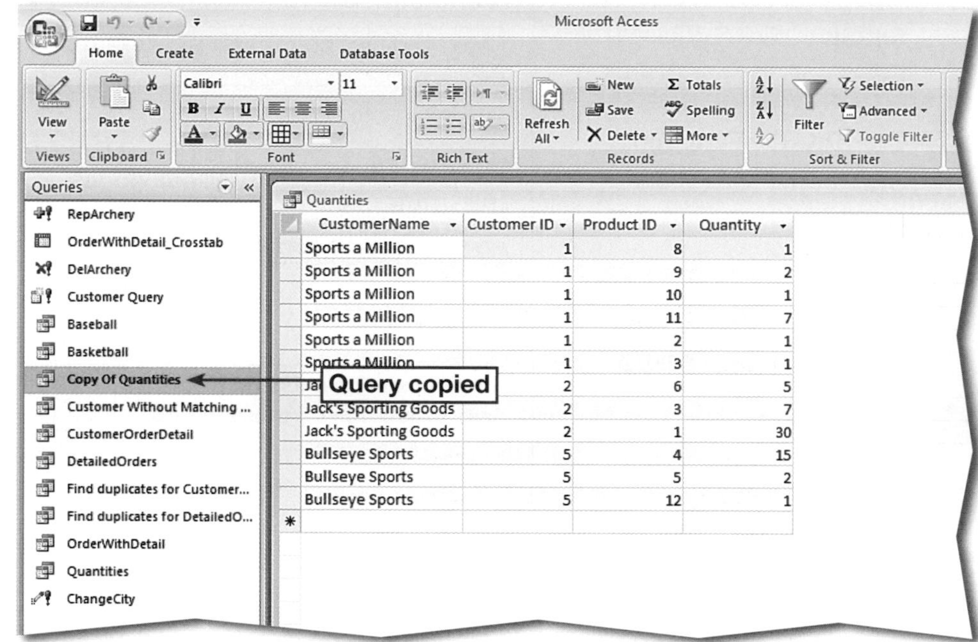

FIGURE 2.75 New query name in Navigation Pane

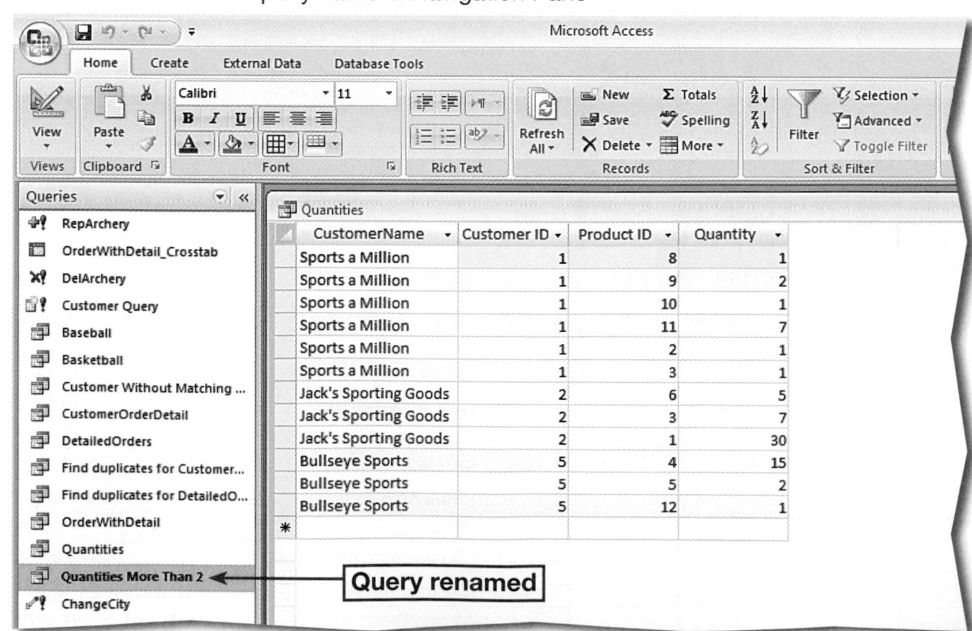

Step-By-Step

1. In your **Bonus** file, click cell **B10**.
2. Choose **Home> Clipboard>Copy** (see Figure 4.11).
3. Click cell **C10**.
4. Choose **Home> Clipboard>Paste**.
5. **CHECK** Your screen should look like Figure 4.12.
6. Save and close your file.

Continue to the next exercise.

Tech Tip

To keep the original row number or column letter when you move or copy a formula, use a dollar sign ($) in the cell address, a technique known as **absolute addressing**. For example, if you use $D$3 in a formula, the cell address *will not* change when the formula is copied.

Inclusion Strategy It may be helpful to do a class demo of copying a formula to show visual learners how the cell references automatically change in the new formula.

Teaching Tip You may wish to tell students that using the Fill handle to insert content is faster than using Copy and Paste buttons.

Solution Use the file **Bonus-SF.xlsx** as a solution file for Exercises 4-3 through 4-6.

EXERCISE 4-6
Copy and Move Formulas

If you want to put the same kind of formula in one cell that you have already created in another cell, you can use the Copy and Paste commands. Instead of creating another formula, you can copy the first formula into the second cell. Excel will automatically **adjust**, or modify, the cell references accordingly in the new formula so it calculates correctly.

FIGURE 4.11 Formula in cell B10 copied

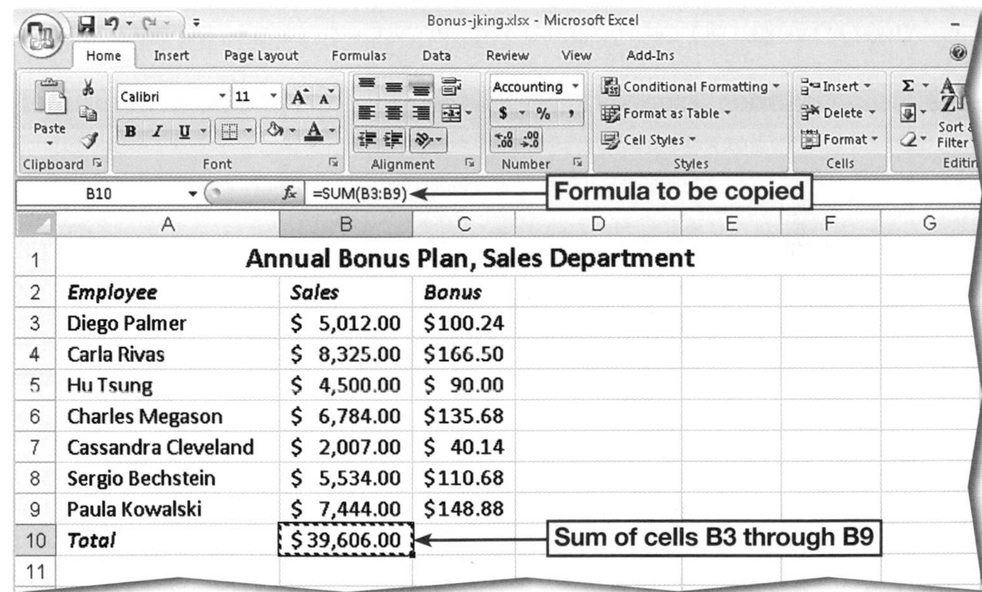

FIGURE 4.12 Formula copied and pasted into cell C10

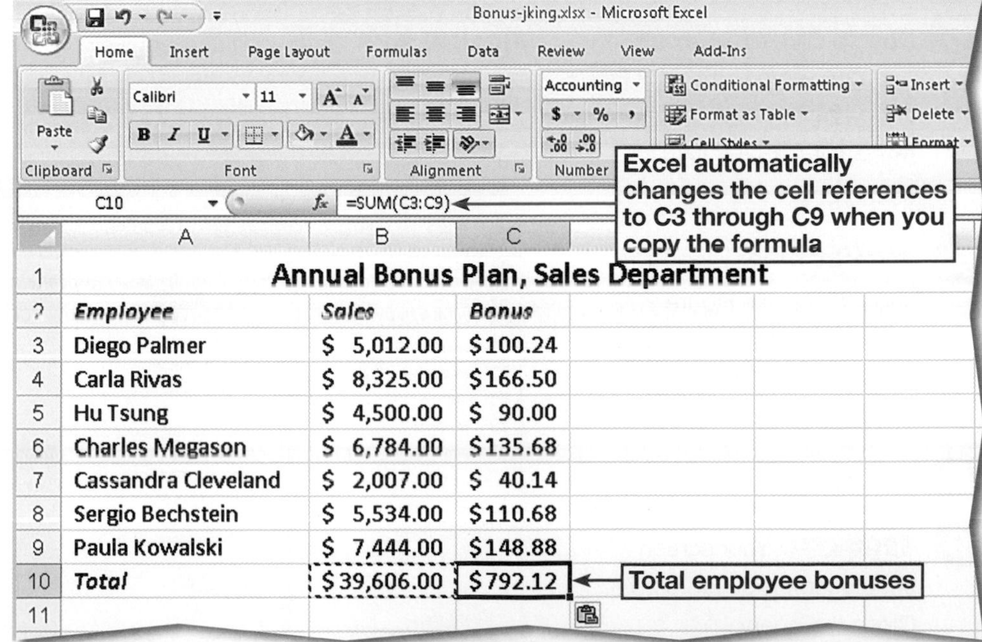

LESSON  Practice It Activities

3. Create a Select Query

Follow the steps to complete the activity. You must complete Practice It Activity 2 before doing this activity.

New Student Strategy If a student did not complete Practice It Activity 2, then the solution file for that activity can be used as a data file for this activity.

Step-By-Step

1. In your **Warehouse** file, select **Create>Other> Query Design** .
2. Select the **Order** table and add it to the design window.
3. Add the **Customer** and **OrderDetail** tables to the design window. Close the **Show Table** dialog box.
4. Double-click **CustomerName** in the **Customer** table to add it to the field section.
5. Double-click **CustomerID** in the **Order** table to add it to the field section.
6. Double-click **ProductID** and **Quantity** in the **OrderDetail** table to add those fields to the field section.
7. **CHECK** Your screen should look like Figure 2.72. Click **Save** . In the **Save As** dialog box, key: Quantities. Click **OK**.
8. Click **Run** .
9. **CHECK** Your screen should look like Figure 2.73. Close the query.

FIGURE 2.72 Query in Design View

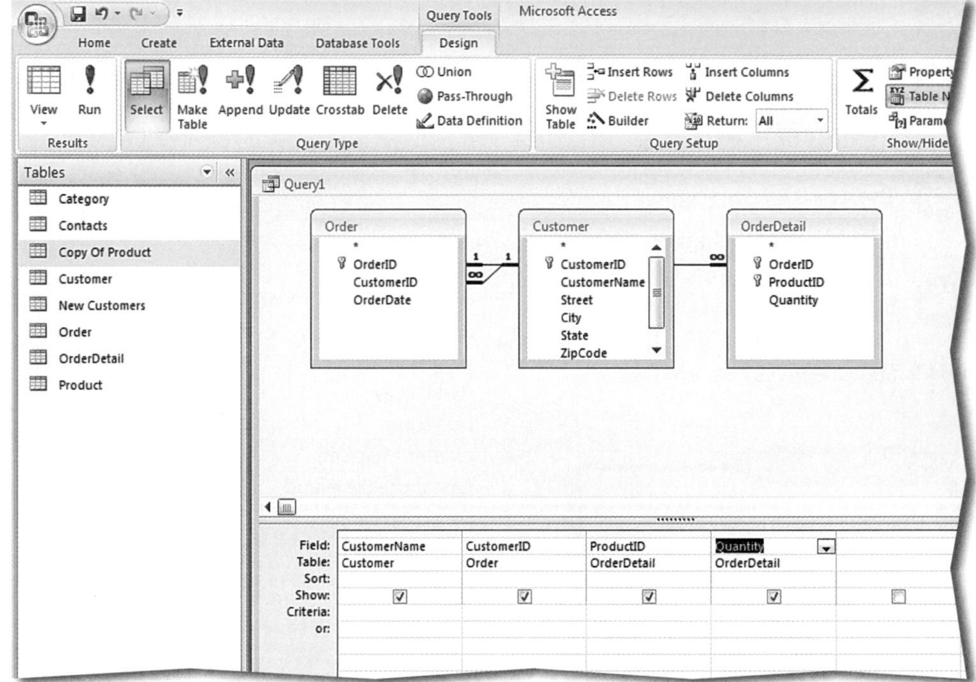

Solution The solution file for this activity is the **Quantities** query in the **Warehouse-SF.accdb** database.

FIGURE 2.73 Query in Datasheet View

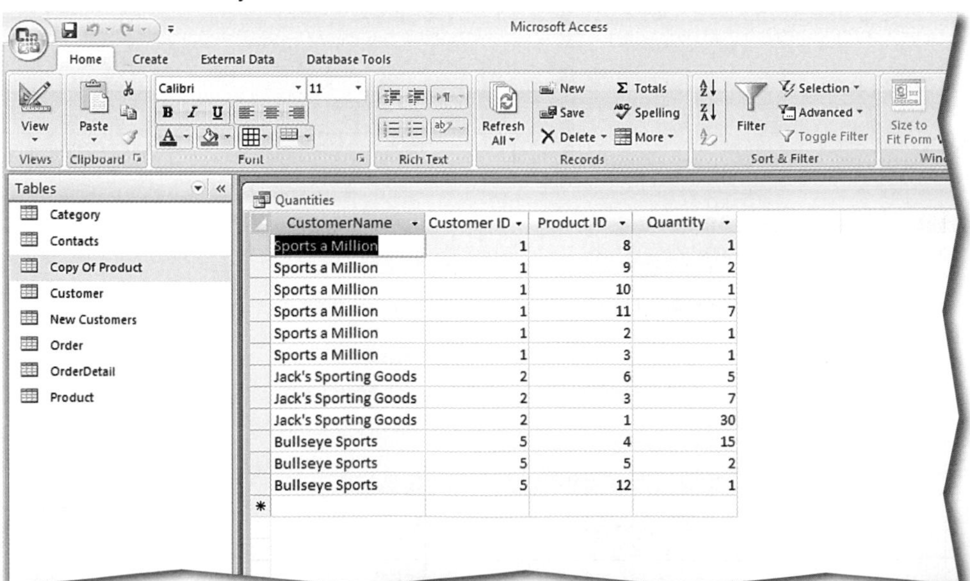

CustomerName	Customer ID	Product ID	Quantity
Sports a Million	1	8	1
Sports a Million	1	9	2
Sports a Million	1	10	1
Sports a Million	1	11	7
Sports a Million	1	2	1
Sports a Million	1	3	1
Jack's Sporting Goods	2	6	5
Jack's Sporting Goods	2	3	7
Jack's Sporting Goods	2	1	30
Bullseye Sports	5	4	15
Bullseye Sports	5	5	2
Bullseye Sports	5	12	1

Step-By-Step

1. Open the data file **Books.xlsx**. Save as: Books-[your first initial and last name].
2. Click cell **C13**.
3. Key: =SUM(. Make sure you do not forget the left parenthesis.
4. In the pop-up box that appears, click **number1**.
5. Click cell **C3**. Hold the mouse button down and drag the pointer down to cell **C11**. Release the mouse button.
6. **CHECK** Your screen should look like Figure 4.13.
7. Press ENTER.
8. **CHECK** Your screen should look like Figure 4.14.
9. Save your file.

Continue to the next exercise.

Shortcuts

Entering a range in a formula by dragging can be more accurate than keying in a range because you see exactly which range you are selecting.

Troubleshooting If students have difficulty getting a sum for February, tell them to key =SUM(C2 before they drag from C2 to C10 in Step 4. Then they should press ENTER.

EXERCISE 4-7
Enter a Range by Dragging

When you are keying a formula, you do not have to key the range for the formula. Instead, you can enter a range by dragging the pointer over the range you wish to enter.

FIGURE 4.13 Range entered in formula by dragging

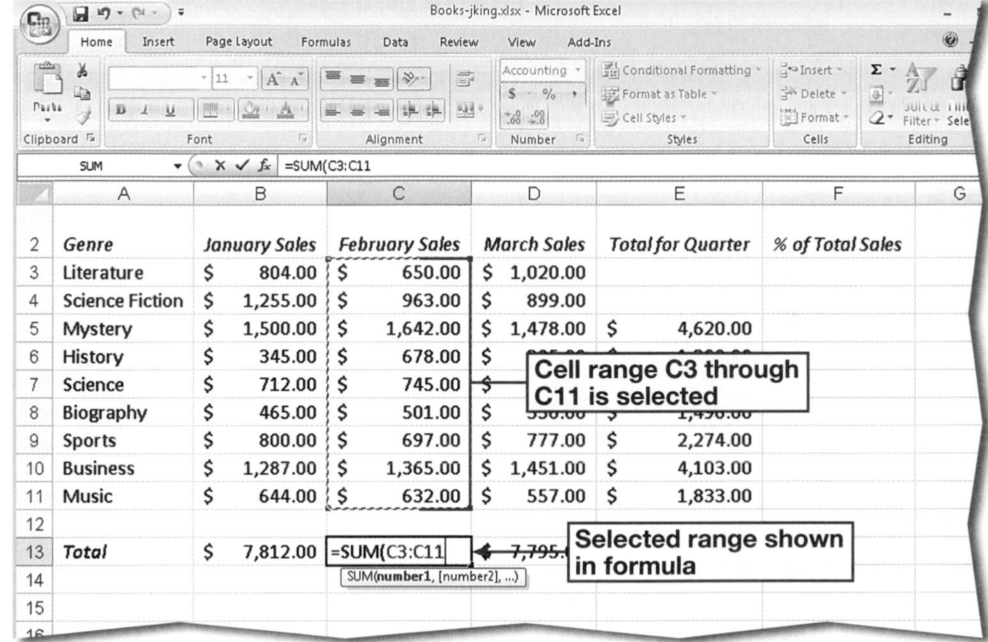

FIGURE 4.14 Total calculated using new formula

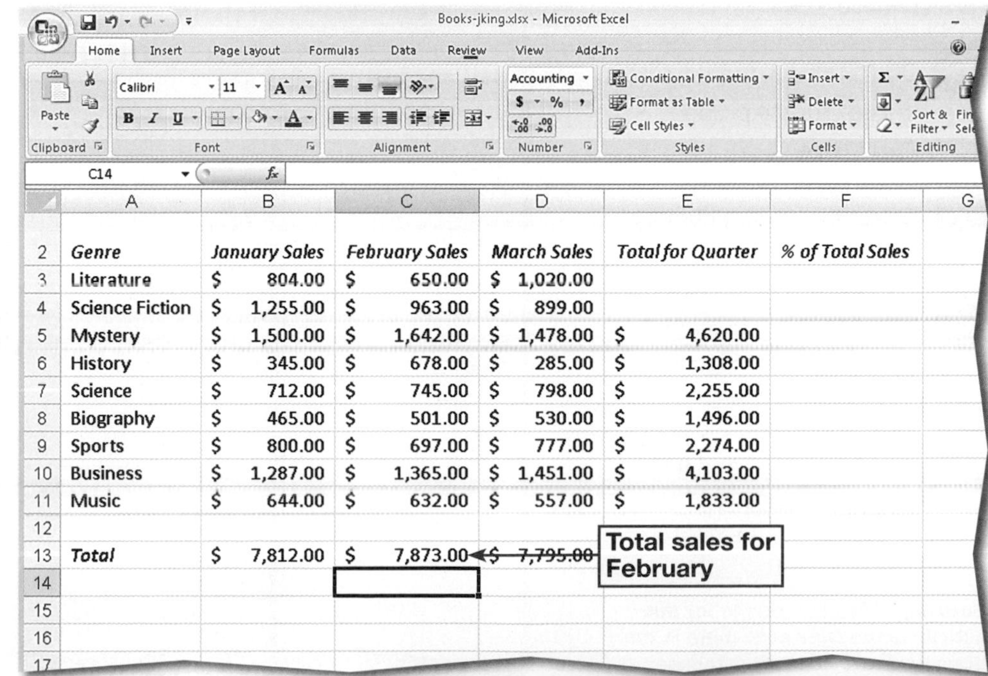

	A	B	C	D	E	F
2	Genre	January Sales	February Sales	March Sales	Total for Quarter	% of Total Sales
3	Literature	$ 804.00	$ 650.00	$ 1,020.00		
4	Science Fiction	$ 1,255.00	$ 963.00	$ 899.00		
5	Mystery	$ 1,500.00	$ 1,642.00	$ 1,478.00	$ 4,620.00	
6	History	$ 345.00	$ 678.00	$ 285.00	$ 1,308.00	
7	Science	$ 712.00	$ 745.00	$ 798.00	$ 2,255.00	
8	Biography	$ 465.00	$ 501.00	$ 530.00	$ 1,496.00	
9	Sports	$ 800.00	$ 697.00	$ 777.00	$ 2,274.00	
10	Business	$ 1,287.00	$ 1,365.00	$ 1,451.00	$ 4,103.00	
11	Music	$ 644.00	$ 632.00	$ 557.00	$ 1,833.00	
12						
13	Total	$ 7,812.00	$ 7,873.00	~~$ 7,795.00~~		

LESSON 2 Practice It Activities

2. Create a Table and Change Its Fields

Step-By-Step

1. In your **Warehouse** file, choose **Create>Tables> Table Templates**. Select **Contacts**.
2. **CHECK** Your screen should look like Figure 2.70.
3. Click the **Datasheet** tab. Click **Design View** . In the **Save As** box, key: Contacts. Click **OK**.
4. Click the **Last Name** field.
5. Under **Field Properties**, click the box for the property **Required**. Click the drop-down arrow and choose **Yes**.
6. Click **Company** field. Click the box for the property **Field Size**.
7. Select the current number and key: 30.
8. **CHECK** Your screen should look like Figure 2.71.
9. Save your table. Close the design window, and then close the datasheet.

Solution The solution file for this activity is the **Contacts** table in the **Warehouse-SF.accdb** database.

Follow the steps to complete the activity. You must complete Practice It Activity 1 before doing this activity.

New Student Strategy If a student did not complete Practice It Activity 1, then the solution file for that activity can be used as a data file for this activity.

FIGURE 2.70 Contacts Table

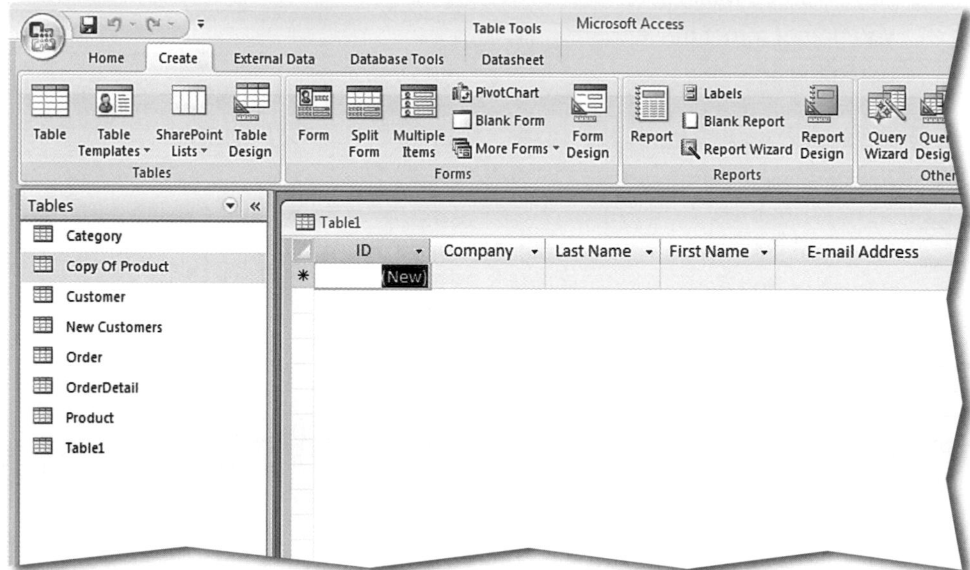

FIGURE 2.71 Table Design View

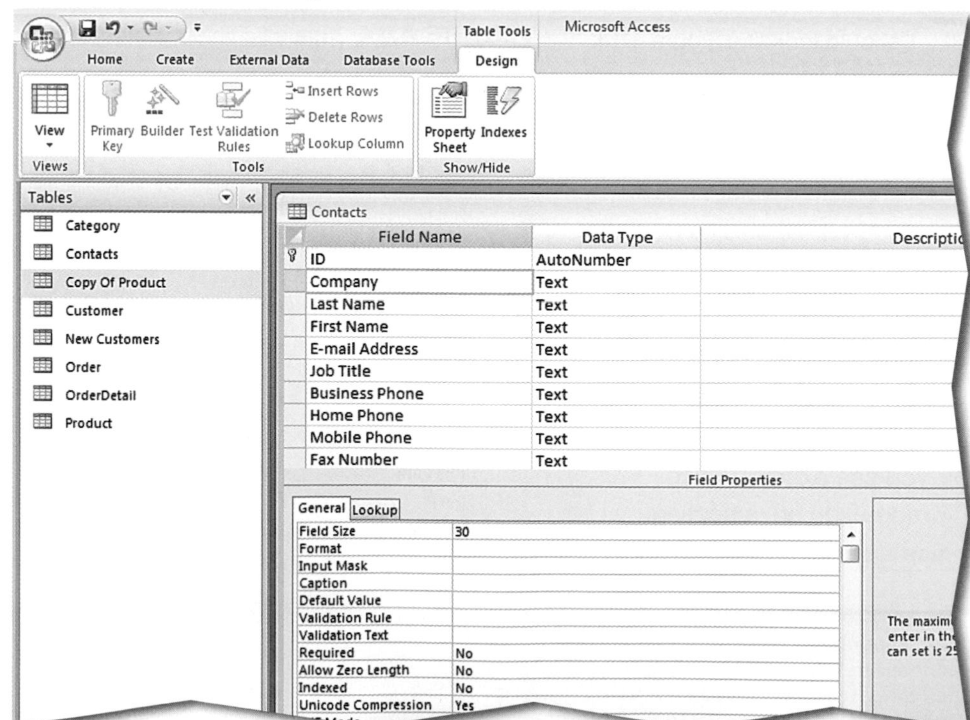

Step-By-Step

1. In your **Books** file, click cell **E3**.
2. Key: =SUM(B3:D3).
3. **CHECK** Your screen should look like Figure 4.15.
4. Press ENTER. The total quarterly sales for Literature appear in cell **E3**.
5. Click cell **E3**. Choose **Home>Clipboard>Copy** .
6. Click cell **E3**. Choose **Home>Clipboard>Paste** .
7. **CHECK** Your screen should look like Figure 4.16. Save your file.

Continue to the next exercise.

Academic Skills

The word *relative* refers to an object that is dependent on something else. In Step 6, when you copy the formula from cell E3 into cell E4, the formula changes to include the numbers in row 4. The total then changes. This shows how the formula is *relative* to the data in row 4. What would happen if you copied the formula from cell E4 to cell E5?

EXERCISE 4-8
Use Relative References

There are two types of cell references for formulas in Excel. The first type, which you have already used, is called a **relative reference**. A relative reference changes when the formula is pasted into a new location. A relative reference is written with the column letter and row number, such as B2.

EL If English Learner students have trouble entering the formulas, pair them with native English speakers to help them complete the exercise.

FIGURE 4.15 Keying a relative reference

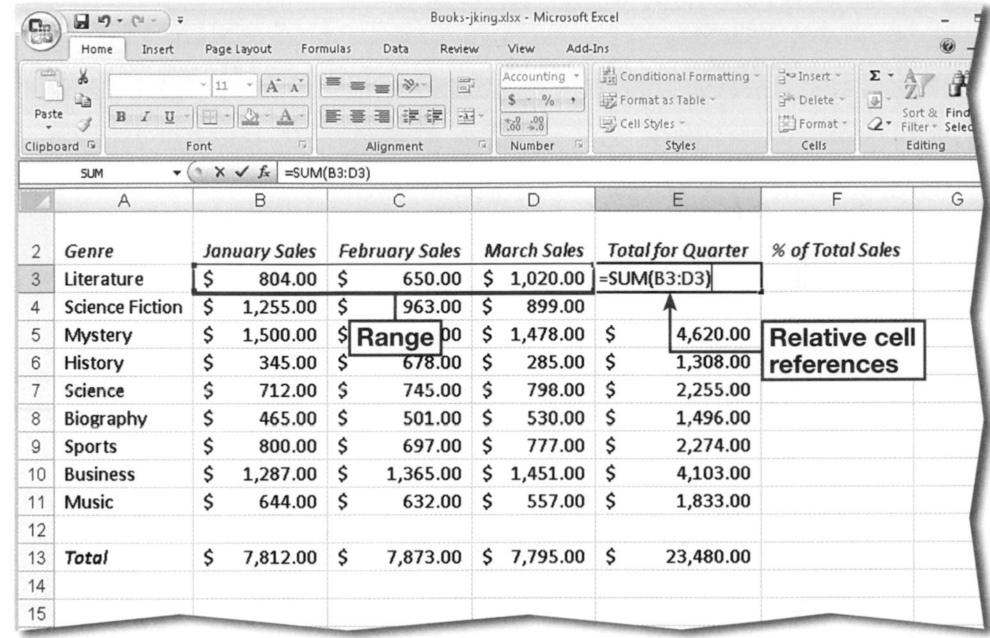

	A	B	C	D	E	F
2	Genre	January Sales	February Sales	March Sales	Total for Quarter	% of Total Sales
3	Literature	$ 804.00	$ 650.00	$ 1,020.00	=SUM(B3:D3)	
4	Science Fiction	$ 1,255.00	$ 963.00	$ 899.00		
5	Mystery	$ 1,500.00	$ [illegible]	$ 1,478.00	$ 4,620.00	
6	History	$ 345.00	$ 678.00	$ 285.00	$ 1,308.00	
7	Science	$ 712.00	$ 745.00	$ 798.00	$ 2,255.00	
8	Biography	$ 465.00	$ 501.00	$ 530.00	$ 1,496.00	
9	Sports	$ 800.00	$ 697.00	$ 777.00	$ 2,274.00	
10	Business	$ 1,287.00	$ 1,365.00	$ 1,451.00	$ 4,103.00	
11	Music	$ 644.00	$ 632.00	$ 557.00	$ 1,833.00	
12						
13	Total	$ 7,812.00	$ 7,873.00	$ 7,795.00	$ 23,480.00	
14						
15						

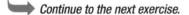

FIGURE 4.16 Pasting a relative reference

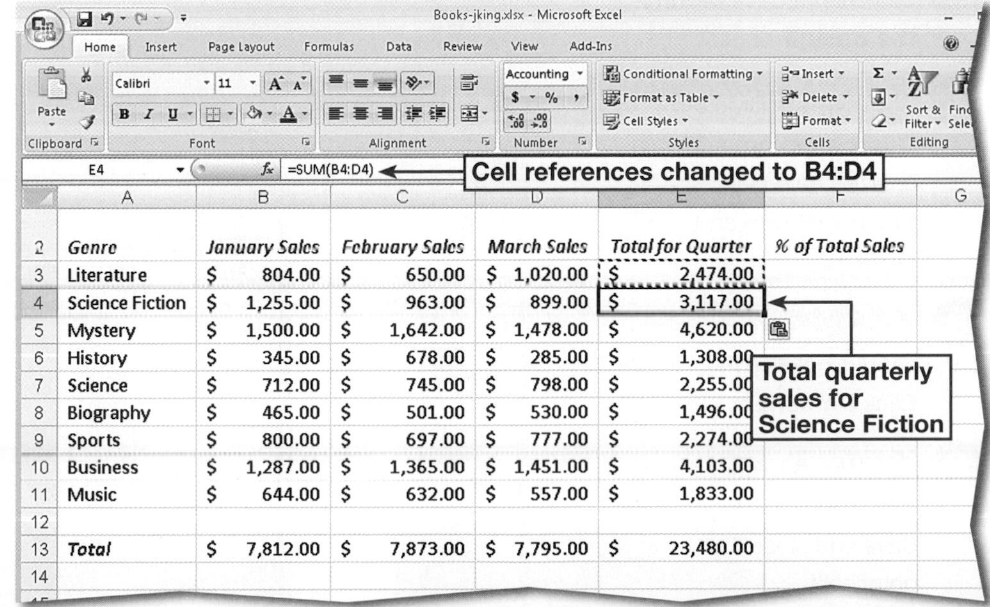

	A	B	C	D	E	F
2	Genre	January Sales	February Sales	March Sales	Total for Quarter	% of Total Sales
3	Literature	$ 804.00	$ 650.00	$ 1,020.00	$ 2,474.00	
4	Science Fiction	$ 1,255.00	$ 963.00	$ 899.00	$ 3,117.00	
5	Mystery	$ 1,500.00	$ 1,642.00	$ 1,478.00	$ 4,620.00	
6	History	$ 345.00	$ 678.00	$ 285.00	$ 1,308.00	
7	Science	$ 712.00	$ 745.00	$ 798.00	$ 2,255.00	
8	Biography	$ 465.00	$ 501.00	$ 530.00	$ 1,496.00	
9	Sports	$ 800.00	$ 697.00	$ 777.00	$ 2,274.00	
10	Business	$ 1,287.00	$ 1,365.00	$ 1,451.00	$ 4,103.00	
11	Music	$ 644.00	$ 632.00	$ 557.00	$ 1,833.00	
12						
13	Total	$ 7,812.00	$ 7,873.00	$ 7,795.00	$ 23,480.00	
14						

NCLB/Math (Number and Operations) Explain to students that the total in E5 would also change depending on the numbers in row 5.

LESSON 2 Practice It Activities

1. Find Records with Duplicate Values

Follow the steps to complete the activity.

Solution The solution file for this activity is the **Find duplicates for DetailedOrders** query in the **Warehouse-SF.accdb** database.

FIGURE 2.68 Find duplicate values in Design View

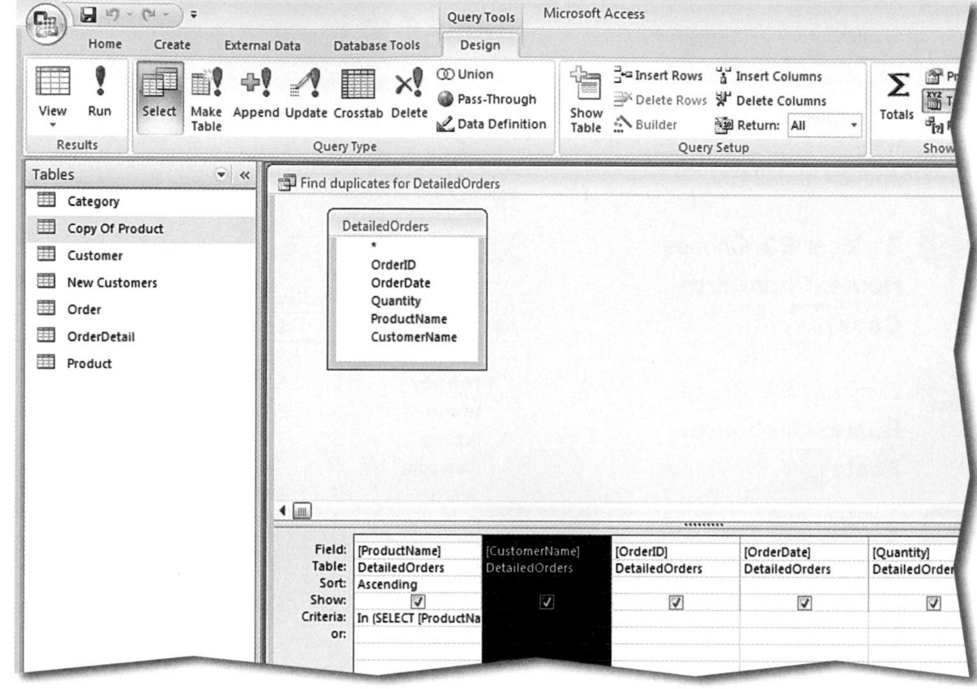

FIGURE 2.69 Find duplicates query in Datasheet View

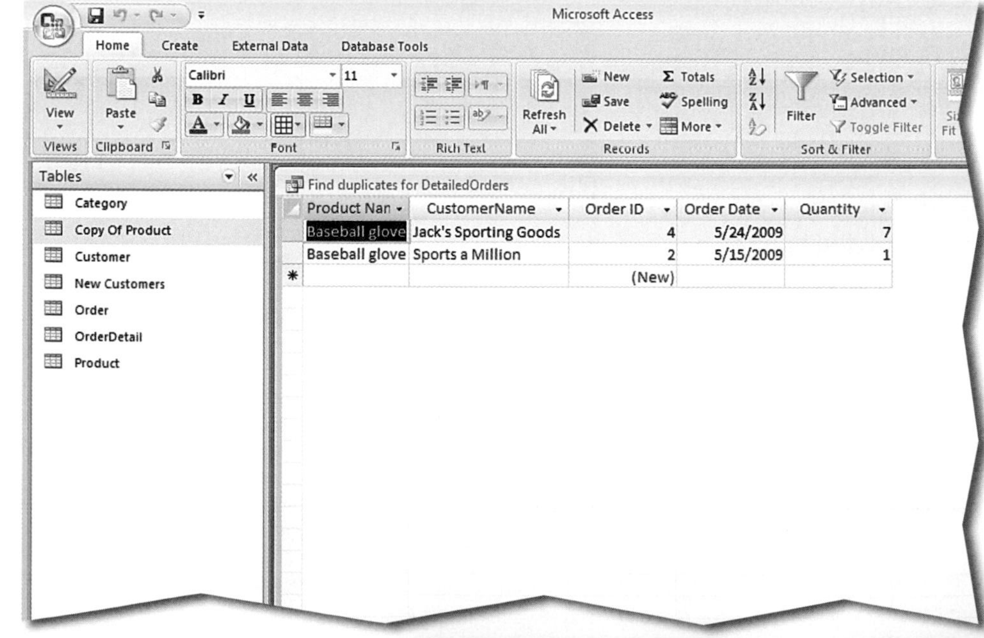

Step-By-Step

1. Start **Access**. Click **Open**. Locate and open your **Warehouse** file.
2. Choose **Create>Query Wizard**. Select **Find Duplicates Query Wizard** and click **OK**.
3. Under **View**, click **Queries**. Double-click **Query: DetailedOrders**.
4. Double-click **ProductName**.
5. Click **Next**. Click the **double-arrow** >> to select all fields.
6. Click **Next**. Click **Modify the design**.
7. Click **Finish**. Drag the **CustomerName** column until it is between **ProductName** and **OrderID**.
8. **CHECK** Your screen should look like Figure 2.68. Click **Datasheet View**.
9. **CHECK** Your screen should look like Figure 2.69. Save and close the datasheet.

Step-By-Step

1. In your **Books** file, click cell **F3**.
2. Key: =E3/$E$13. Press ENTER.
3. CHECK Your screen should look like Figure 4.17.
4. Click cell **F3**.
5. Click **Copy**.
6. Select cells **F4:F11**.
7. Click **Paste**.
8. CHECK Your screen should look like Figure 4.18.
9. Save your file.

Continue to the next exercise.

Academic Skills

The equation =E3/$E$13 means that the contents of cell E3 should be divided by the total in cell E13 to determine the percentage of Literature sales for the quarter. What would the equation be in order to determine the percentage of Sports sales?

NCLB/Math (Number and Operations) Explain to students that the equation =**E9/EE13** would determine the percentage of Sports sales.

Step-By-Step Tip In **Step 8**, have students watch the formula bar when they copy formulas. The relative reference, **E3**, changes, but the absolute reference, **E13**, does not.

EXERCISE 4-9
Use Absolute References

An **absolute reference** is a locked cell that maintains a constant reference when copied to another location. Unlike a relative reference, an absolute reference does not change when you copy the formula to a new location. Use an absolute reference when more than one formula should refer to the same cell. For example, the formulas to calculate the percent of total sales for Literature and Science Fiction will both include the sales total $23,480 in cell E12. To write an absolute reference, place a dollar sign ($) in front of both the column letter and the row number. In this exercise, you will use the absolute reference $E$12.

Troubleshooting If students do not see the numbers as percents, have them select the range **F2:F10**, then choose **Cell Styles>Styles>Percent.**

FIGURE 4.17 Literature sales percentage

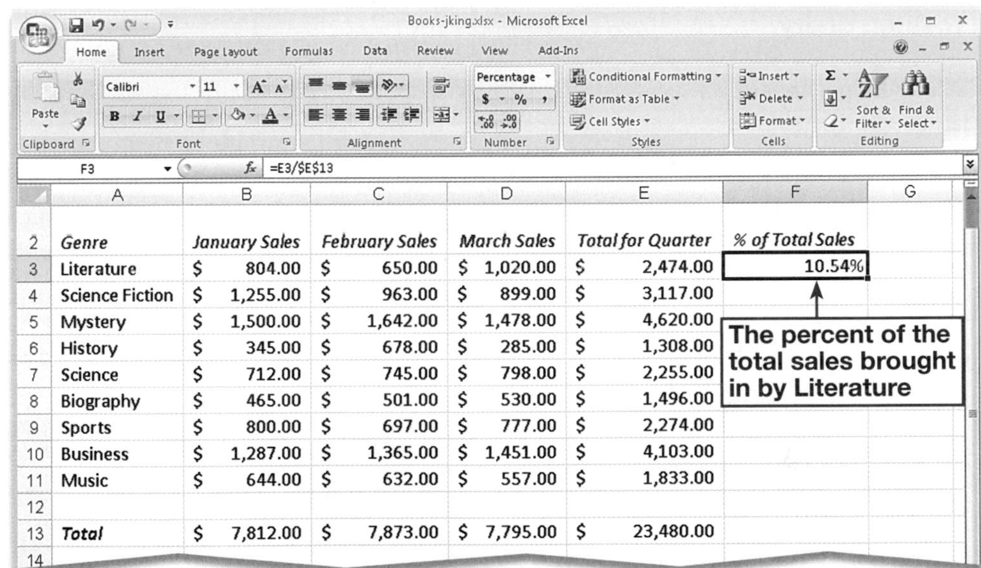

	A	B	C	D	E	F
2	Genre	January Sales	February Sales	March Sales	Total for Quarter	% of Total Sales
3	Literature	$ 804.00	$ 650.00	$ 1,020.00	$ 2,474.00	10.54%
4	Science Fiction	$ 1,255.00	$ 963.00	$ 899.00	$ 3,117.00	
5	Mystery	$ 1,500.00	$ 1,642.00	$ 1,478.00	$ 4,620.00	
6	History	$ 345.00	$ 678.00	$ 285.00	$ 1,308.00	
7	Science	$ 712.00	$ 745.00	$ 798.00	$ 2,255.00	
8	Biography	$ 465.00	$ 501.00	$ 530.00	$ 1,496.00	
9	Sports	$ 800.00	$ 697.00	$ 777.00	$ 2,274.00	
10	Business	$ 1,287.00	$ 1,365.00	$ 1,451.00	$ 4,103.00	
11	Music	$ 644.00	$ 632.00	$ 557.00	$ 1,833.00	
12						
13	Total	$ 7,812.00	$ 7,873.00	$ 7,795.00	$ 23,480.00	

FIGURE 4.18 Absolute reference

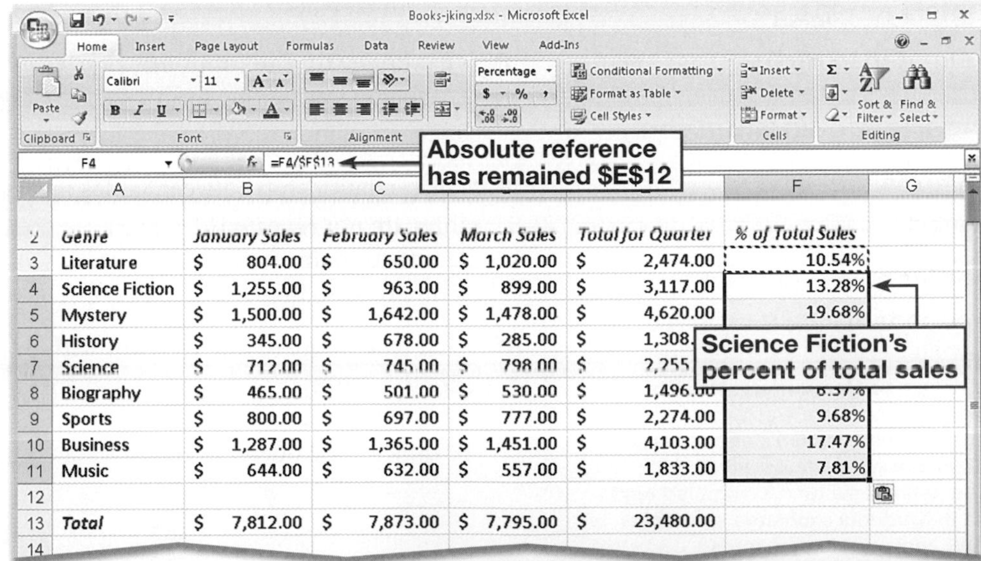

	A	B	C	D	E	F
2	Genre	January Sales	February Sales	March Sales	Total for Quarter	% of Total Sales
3	Literature	$ 804.00	$ 650.00	$ 1,020.00	$ 2,474.00	10.54%
4	Science Fiction	$ 1,255.00	$ 963.00	$ 899.00	$ 3,117.00	13.28%
5	Mystery	$ 1,500.00	$ 1,642.00	$ 1,478.00	$ 4,620.00	19.68%
6	History	$ 345.00	$ 678.00	$ 285.00	$ 1,308.	[illegible]
7	Science	$ 712.00	$ 745.00	$ 798.00	$ 2,255	[illegible]
8	Biography	$ 465.00	$ 501.00	$ 530.00	$ 1,496.00	[illegible]
9	Sports	$ 800.00	$ 697.00	$ 777.00	$ 2,274.00	9.68%
10	Business	$ 1,287.00	$ 1,365.00	$ 1,451.00	$ 4,103.00	17.47%
11	Music	$ 644.00	$ 632.00	$ 557.00	$ 1,833.00	7.81%
12						
13	Total	$ 7,812.00	$ 7,873.00	$ 7,795.00	$ 23,480.00	

LESSON 2

After You Read

Vocabulary

Key Terms

attachment field
caption
control
crosstab query
data type
database template
Design View
duplicate query
input mask
Lookup field
primary key
property
property sheet
referential integrity
relationship
Table Analyzer Wizard
Totals row
unmatched query

Academic Vocabulary

analyze
insert
portion
redundant

Answer to Vocabulary Activity
Students create a word scramble based on the lesson's vocabulary. Students write the definition with the definition's term scrambled next to it. Students exchange scrambles and unscramble the words.

Review Vocabulary

Complete the following statements on a separate sheet of paper. Choose from the Vocabulary list on the left to complete the statements.

1. A(n) ___relationship___ is a link between two tables with a common field. (p. 399)

2. The Totals row function will ___insert___ a new row in a table. (p. 387)

3. The window that lists field properties is a(n) ___property sheet___. (p. 389)

4. You can change the structure of a table in ___Design View___. (p. 386)

5. A(n) ___input mask___ allows you to specify how certain information should be formatted in a database. (p. 398)

Vocabulary Activity

6. Create a word scramble to help you review this lesson's Vocabulary. To create the scramble:
   A. On the right side of a sheet of paper, write each definition.
   B. To the left of each definition, write the vocabulary word, but with the letters scrambled.
   C. With your teacher's permission, in class, exchange scrambles with another classmate. Solve the scramble by unscrambling the words and writing them next to their definition.

Review Key Concepts

Answer the following questions on a separate piece of paper.

7. Where can you see the properties of each field in a database template? (p. 386)
   A. Form View
   B. Print preview
   C. Datasheet View
   (D.) Design View

8. What does using an input mask on a field help to prevent? (p. 398)
   A. Opening the wrong form
   (B.) Entering incorrect data
   C. Accidentally changing data
   D. Using the wrong field type

9. Which relationship between tables means that both fields in their respective tables are not repeated? (p. 399)
   A. one-to-many
   B. many-to-many
   (C.) one-to-one
   D. one-to-none

10. What type of query finds records with duplicate field values in a single tab or query? (p. 408)
   A. crosstab query
   B. unmatched query
   (C.) duplicate query
   D. simple query

Step-By-Step

EXERCISE 4-10
Use Mixed References

A **mixed reference** is a cell reference that is part relative and part absolute. This means it has either an absolute column and a relative row, or a relative column and an absolute row. For example, if you place a dollar sign in front of the reference to column A ($A1), when you drag the formula to the right the column reference will not change, because the column reference is absolute. However, if you drag the formula down, the row reference will automatically adjust incrementally, because it is relative. If you copy a formula across rows or down columns, a relative reference automatically adjusts, and an absolute reference does not change.

1. In your **Books** file, click cell **F3**. This displays the formula that you keyed into the worksheet in the last exercise. Double-click cell **F3** and change the formula to read **=E3/$E13**.
2. Click outside cell **F3**. Notice that the percentage for Literature sales did not change.
3. Click cell **F3**. Click **Copy**.
4. Select cells **F4:F11**. Click **Paste**.
5. **CHECK** Your screen should look like Figure 4.19.
6. Click cell **F4**. The mixed cell reference **$E13** causes the formula to automatically increment to **$E14** when it is copied to the range **F4:F11**. The formula now contains a reference to a blank cell, or zero, which cannot be a divisor.
7. Click **Undo** twice. Repeat Steps 3 and 4.
8. **CHECK** Your screen should look like Figure 4.20. Save and close your file.

Continue to the next exercise.

Solution Use the file **Books-SF.xlsx** as a solution file for Exercises 4-8 through 4-10.

FIGURE 4.19 #DIV/0! errors in column F

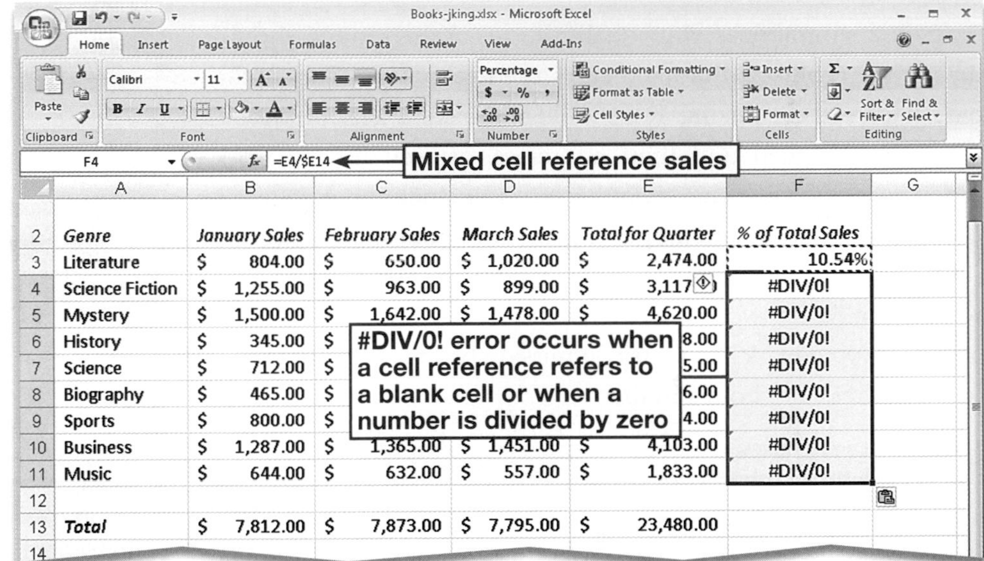

FIGURE 4.20 Literature percent formula

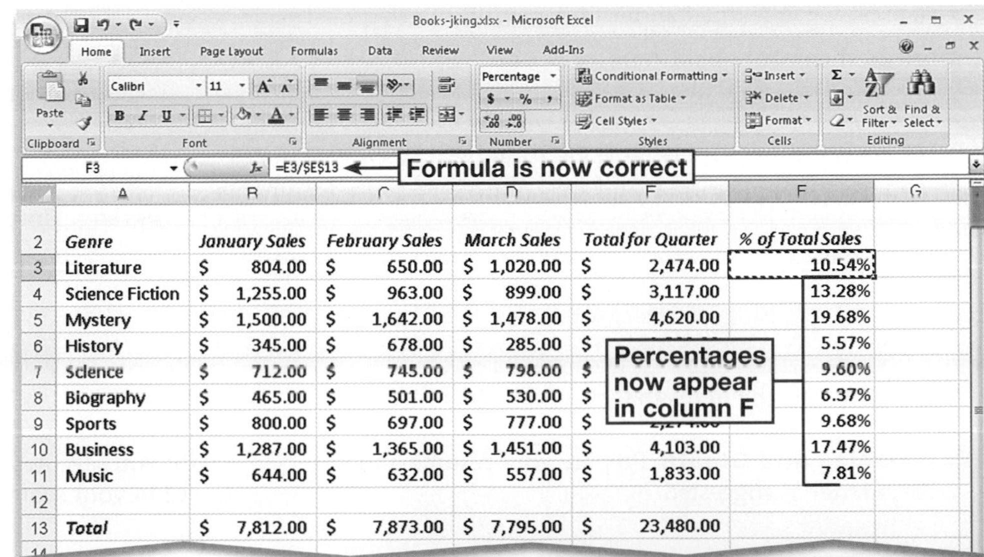

Writing MATTERS

Preparing a Résumé

Summer is coming, and you need a job! A local fruit company needs a person to work in the office. The ad asks you to mail a résumé and cover letter. You want to come across as professional, responsible, and hardworking.

Prepare a Résumé

A résumé summarizes your qualifications. Your résumé should include your contact information and a general statement about the type of job you are seeking. You should also include a list of schools you have attended and their addresses, as well as any work experience you might have. For each job, include the employer's contact information and a brief statement of your duties. List any skills you have acquired through job experience, volunteering, and so on. Finally, list two or three references. These should be people who know your work habits. Ask permission before you list anyone's name, address, or phone number.

Prepare a Cover Letter

A cover letter is a short, formal business letter that expresses your interest in the job and requests an interview. A cover letter should:

- state the specific job or position for which you are applying.
- state how you learned about the position.
- briefly state your qualifications.
- request an interview.

Key the résumé and cover letter separately. Keep them to one page each and use the same format and style. Proofread both documents carefully.

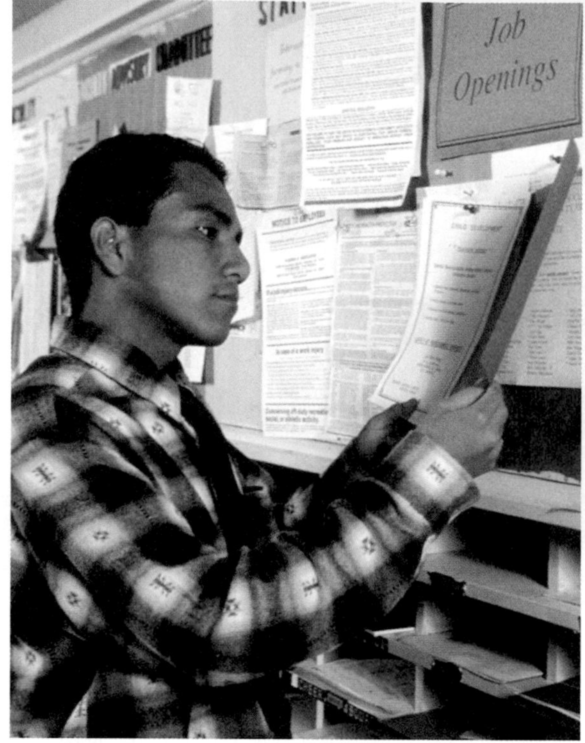

Employment ads often request a résumé and cover letter from applicants before scheduling an interview.

NCLB/Language Arts (NCTE 12) Reinforce the importance of preparing a résumé and cover letter that shows a potential employer that the applicant is professional, responsible, and hardworking. Ask students to explain why it is important to be brief and to the point. Ask them to discuss why a poorly created résumé or cover letter may eliminate them from consideration for a job.

Teaching Tip Have students go online to learn more about résumés and cover letters and why careful preparation of these items is so important in a job search.

SKILLBUILDER

1. **Identify** List the items that should be included on a résumé.
2. **Organize and Create** Prepare your résumé and cover letter as suggested.
3. **Explain** How could an Access database of prospective employers be useful in your job search? What data might you save in your Access database that might be useful in your search?

SkillBuilder answers can be found on page TM81.

EXERCISE 4-11
Create Diagrams and Charts

A **chart** is a graphic that organizes data visually so that you can compare different kinds of data or evaluate how data changes over time. In order to understand the data in a worksheet quickly, you can create bar charts, column charts, line charts, and pie charts. The Charts group allows you to create charts automatically based on the data that you select.

FIGURE 4.21 Column drop-down menu

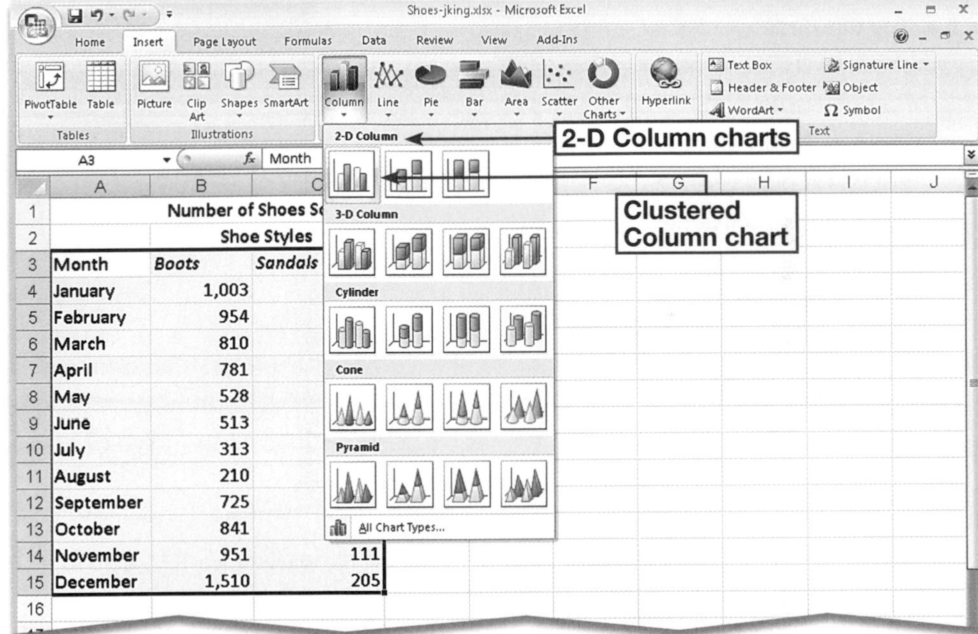

FIGURE 4.22 Completed chart

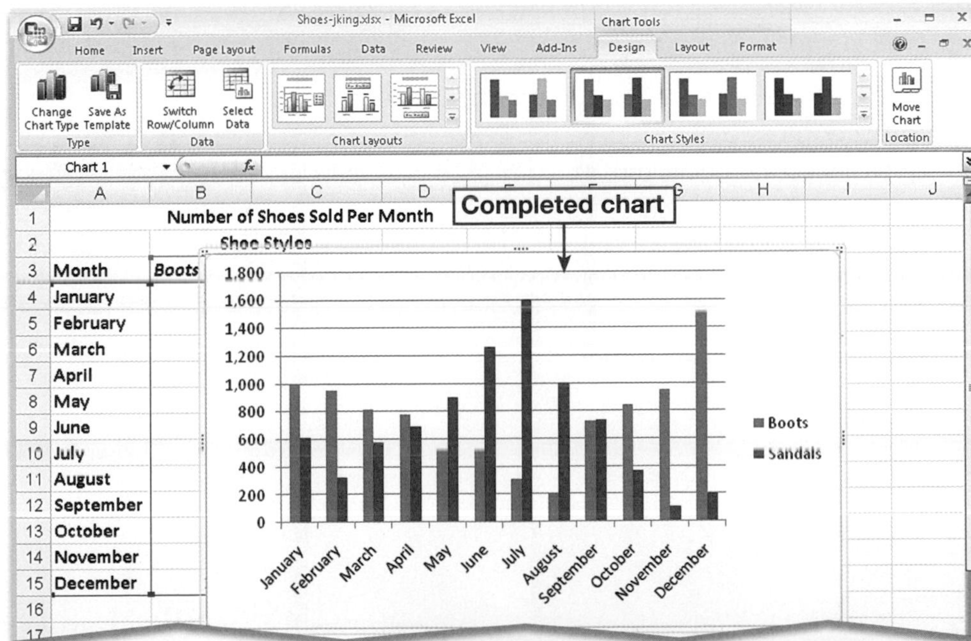

Step-By-Step

1. Open the data file **Shoes.xlsx**. Save as: Shoes-[your first initial and last name].
2. Select cells **A3** through **C15**.
3. Choose **Insert>Charts>Column**.
4. In the drop-down menu, under **2-D Column**, select **Clustered Column** (see Figure 4.21).
5. **CHECK** Your screen should look like Figure 4.22.
6. Save your file.

Continue to the next exercise.

Academic Skills

In this exercise, you created a chart to compare the number of boots and sandals sold within a specific month. Based on this chart, identify which type of shoe sold the most in December. Which shoe sold the most in July? How does the chart help you to identify this information quickly?

NOLD/Math (Data Analysis and Probability) Explain to students that more boots were sold in December and that more sandals were sold in July. A bar chart is good for making sales comparisons. A pie chart, on the other hand, could be used for showing percentages.

Step-By-Step

EXERCISE 2-22 (Continued)
Create Subqueries

10 In the **SQL View** window, at the end of the second line, click to position the cursor after the "**t**" in Product and before the "**;**". Press ENTER.

11 Key this code exactly as shown: WHERE Product.ProductName IN (SELECT Product.ProductName FROM Product WHERE Product.ProductName = "Basketball") (see Figure 2.66).Make sure a semi-colon appears at the end of the line you keyed.

12 Click **Run** !.

13 CHECK Your screen should look like Figure 2.67.

14 Click **Save**. Close the query. Close the database, and close **Access**.

You Should Know

A *subquery* is an SQL expression, or combination of mathematical or logical operators and functions, that is created inside another query.

FIGURE 2.66 New code for Basketball query

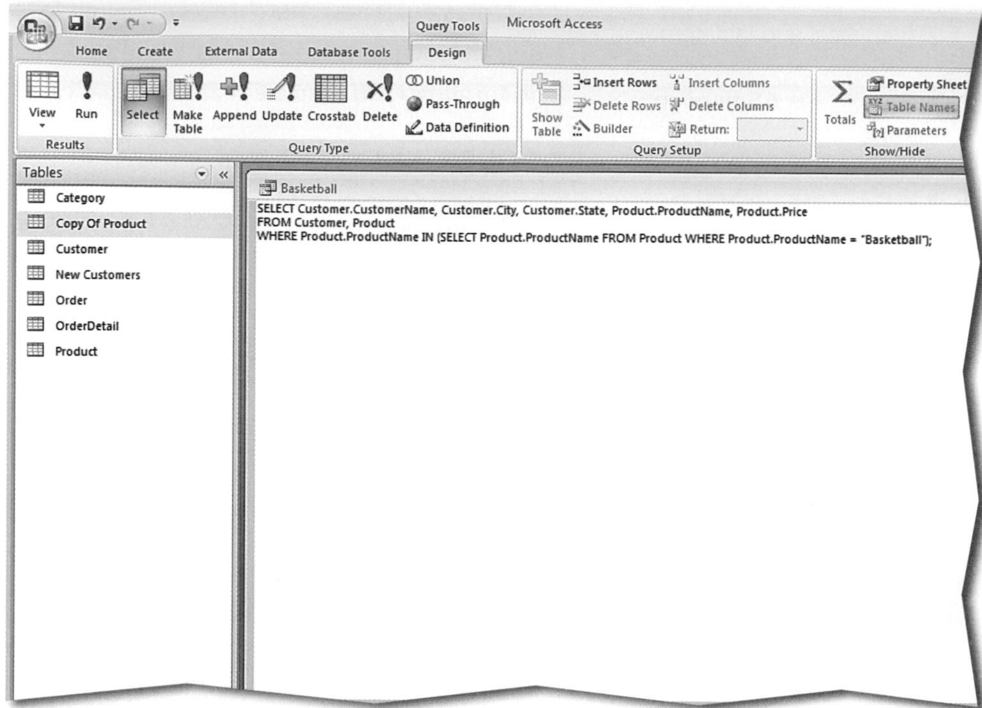

Solution Use the file **Warehouse-SF.accdb** as a solution file for Exercises 2-17 through 2-22.

FIGURE 2.67 Run new Basketball query

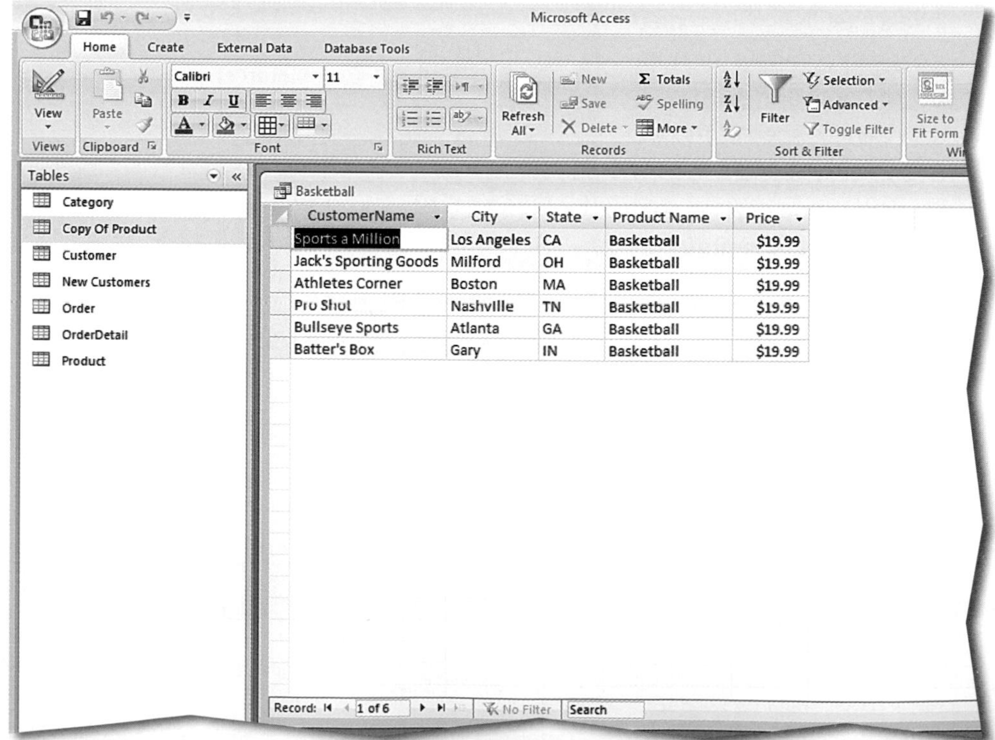

Step-By-Step

1. If necessary, in your **Shoes** file, click the white area of the chart box to display the **Chart Tools**. Choose **Layout>Labels>Axis Titles** (see Figure 4.23).

2. Choose **Primary Horizontal Axis Title> Title Below Axis**. In the **Horizontal (Category) Axis Title** box, key: Month.

3. Choose **Layout>Labels> Axis Titles**. Choose **Primary Vertical Axis Title>Rotated Title**. In the **Vertical Axis (Value) Title** box, key: Monthly Totals. Choose **Layout> Labels>Chart Title> Above Chart**. In the **Chart Title** text box, key: Sales Comparison for Year 2009.

4. Click the white area of the chart once to display the sizing handles. Drag a bottom corner sizing handle to make the chart bigger yet still keep its scale.

5. Choose **Chart Tools> Format**. In the **Size** group, in the first drop-down list, select **3**. In the second drop-down list, choose **5**.

6. **CHECK** Your screen should look like Figure 4.24. Save your file.

Continue to the next exercise.

EXERCISE 4-12
Modify and Position Chart Elements

There are many ways that you can modify charts to make data easier to read. For example, you can change the size of the chart to highlight sales trends, salary increases, or the decrease of a loan balance as payments are made.

NCLB/Math (NCTM Geometry) Reinforce that the horizontal axis is the *x* axis. The vertical axis is the *y* axis.

FIGURE 4.23 Labels group on Layout tab

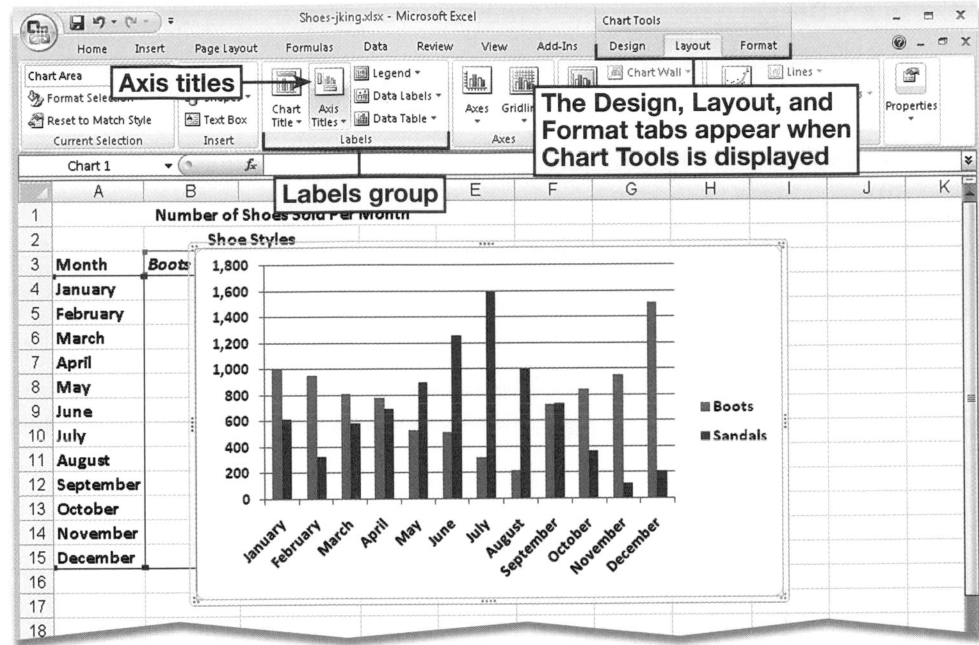

FIGURE 4.24 Sizing and positioning chart

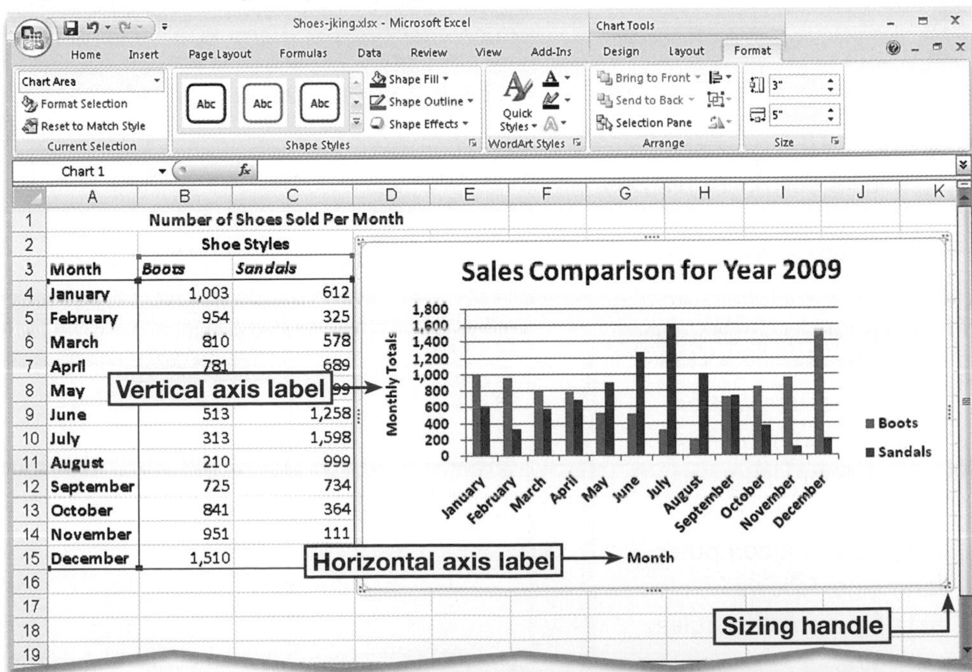

Step-By-Step

1. In your **Warehouse** file, select **Create>Other> Query Design**.
2. Add the **Customer** and **Product** tables to the **Query Design** window and close the **Show Table** dialog box.
3. Add the **CustomerName**, **City**, and **State** fields from the **Customer** table.
4. Add the **ProductName** and **Price** fields from the **Product** table.
5. Click **Save**. In the **Save As** dialog box, key: Basketball. Click **OK**.
6. Click **Run**.
7. **CHECK** Your screen should look like Figure 2.64.
8. Click the **View** drop-down menu and select **SQL View**.
9. **CHECK** Your screen should look like Figure 2.65.

Continued on the next page.

Academic Skills

Subqueries are written in SQL, a computer language. Every language, whether it is a human language or a computer language, follows its own set of grammatical rules.

EXERCISE 2-22
Create Subqueries

Subqueries are queries created within existing select queries using SQL, or Structured Query Language. Creating a subquery is similar to writing a simple computer program that refines the programming of the original Access query. In this exercise, you will create a subquery that selects all customers who have bought basketballs. The expression includes the customer's city and state, as well as the price paid for the product.

FIGURE 2.64 Basketball query

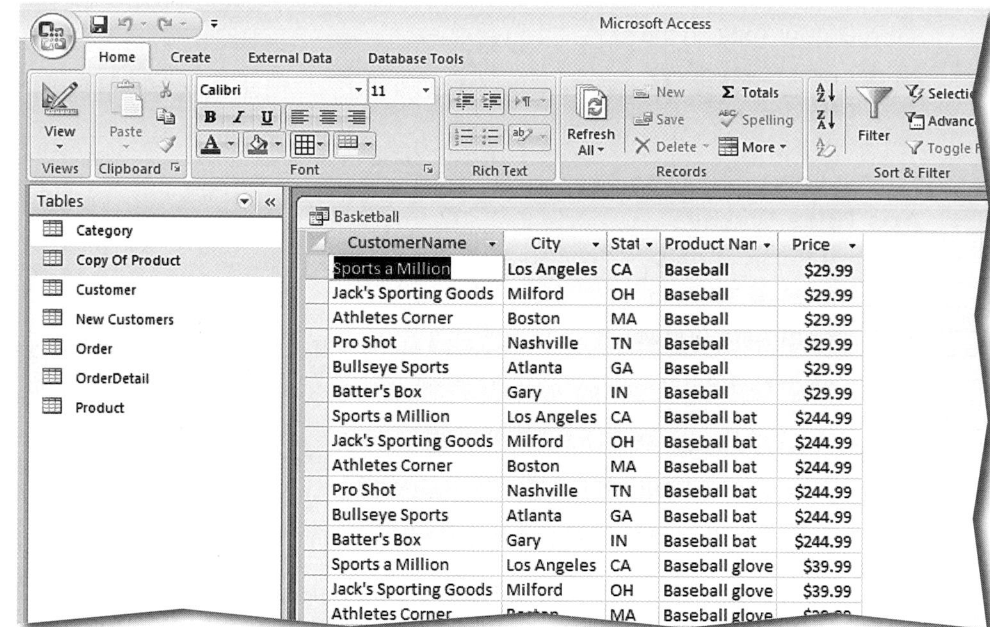

NCLB/Language Arts (NCTE 6) Have students discuss and identify possible grammatical rules in the SQL query shown in Figure 2.65.

FIGURE 2.65 SQL Basketball query

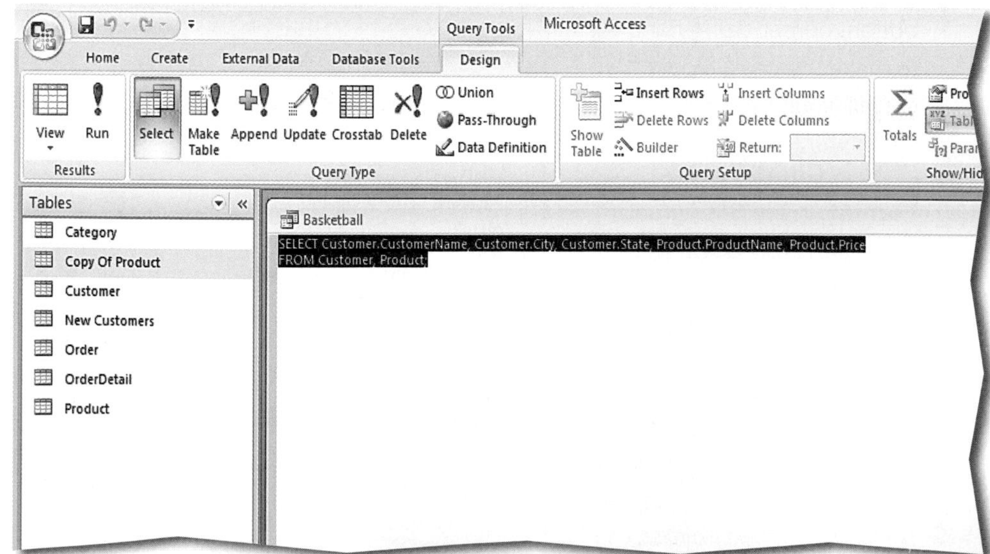

Step-By-Step

1. If necessary, in your **Shoes** file, click in the white area of the chart box to display the **Chart Tools**.

2. Choose **Design>Type>Change Chart Type**. The **Change Chart Type** dialog box opens (see Figure 4.25).

3. In the **Change Chart Type** dialog box, under **Line**, choose **Line with Markers**. Click **OK**.

4. Click cell **A3**.

5. **CHECK** Your screen should look like Figure 4.26. Save your file.

Continue to the next exercise.

Academic Skills

Consider your data when choosing a chart type. For example, use a *bar chart* to compare items to each other. Use a *pie chart* to show how one item is part of a whole. A *line chart* can help you compare sales over time. In this exercise, how did the amount of boots sold compare with the number of sandals sold during summer? Why do you think that is?

NCLB/Math (Data Analysis and Probability) Tell students that in the summer, when sales of boots are low, sales of sandals are high. The opposite is true in the winter, when the weather is colder.

EXERCISE 4-13
Change Chart Type

One way to modify an existing chart is to change the chart type. For example, you can give a clustered column chart a completely different look by changing its chart type to a line, bar, or area chart. Sometimes changing a chart type is the best way to make information easy for viewers to read and understand.

FIGURE 4.25 Change Chart Type dialog box

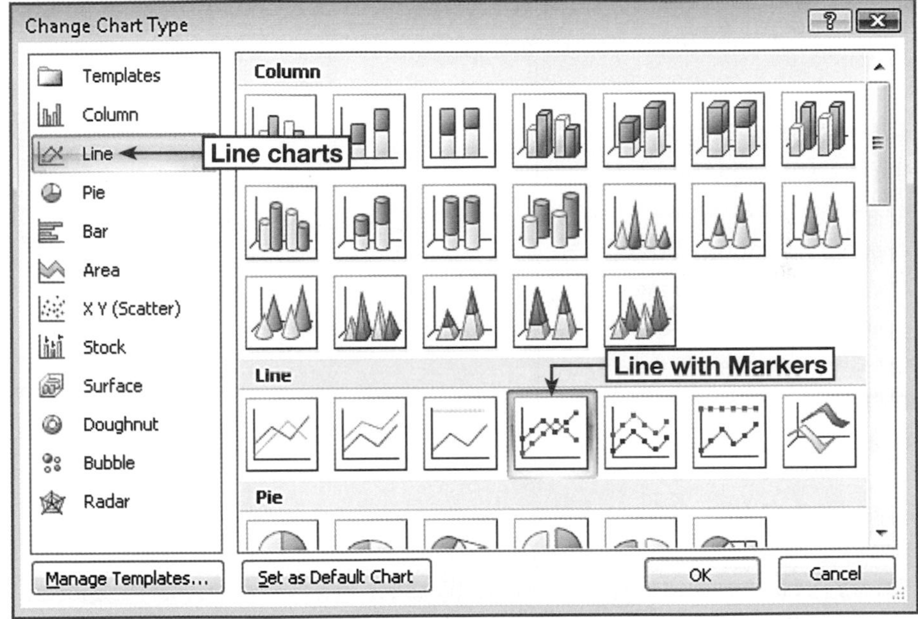

FIGURE 4.26 Chart type changed to Line with Markers

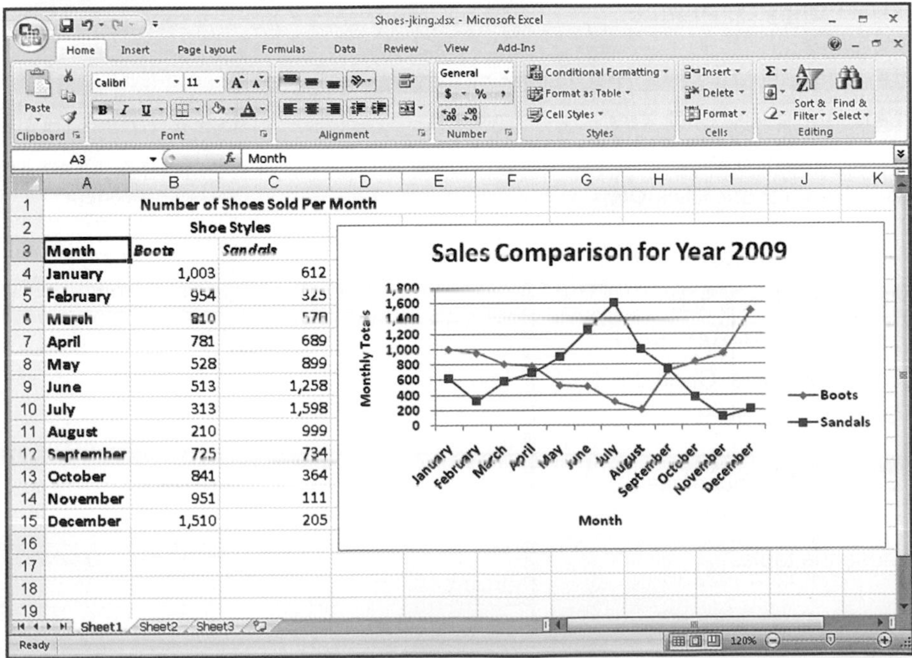

EXERCISE 2-21 (Continued)
Create Action Queries: Append and Delete

Step-By-Step

9 Click **Run** [!]. Click **Yes**. Open the **Copy Of Product** table.

10 CHECK Your screen should look like Figure 2.62. Close the table and the **DelArchery** query.

11 Choose **Create>Other> Query Design** [icon]. Add the **Product** table and close the **Table Show** dialog box. Double-click each field to add it to the query design grid. Under the **Category** field in the **Criteria** box, key: Archery. Click **Run** [!].

12 Click **Design View** [icon]. Choose **Design> QueryType>Append** [icon]. Click the **Table Name** drop-down arrow and select **Copy Of Product**. Click **OK**.

13 Close the query. Click **Yes**. In the **Query Name** box, key: RepArchery. Click **OK**.

14 In the **Navigation Pane**, display **Queries** and double-click **RepArchery**. Click **Yes** twice. Open the **Copy Of Product** table.

15 CHECK Your screen should look like Figure 2.63. Close the table.

Continue to the next exercise.

FIGURE 2.62 Copy Of Product table without Archery

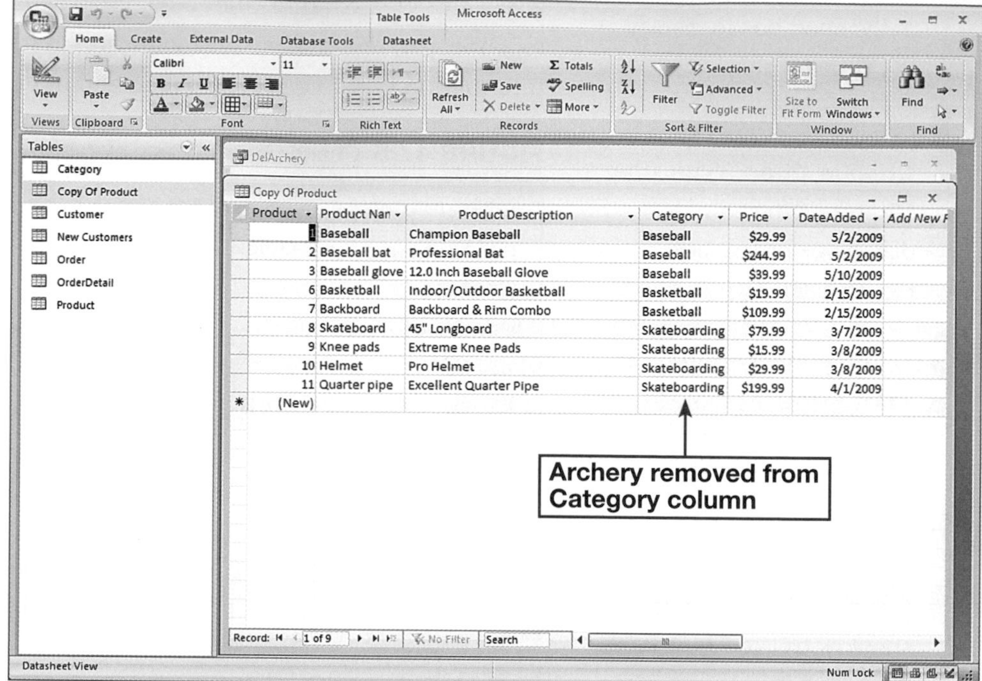

Teaching Tip Explain to students the value of running the query as a select query first and checking the results before returning to the query **Design View** and creating an action query.

FIGURE 2.63 Appended Copy Of Product table

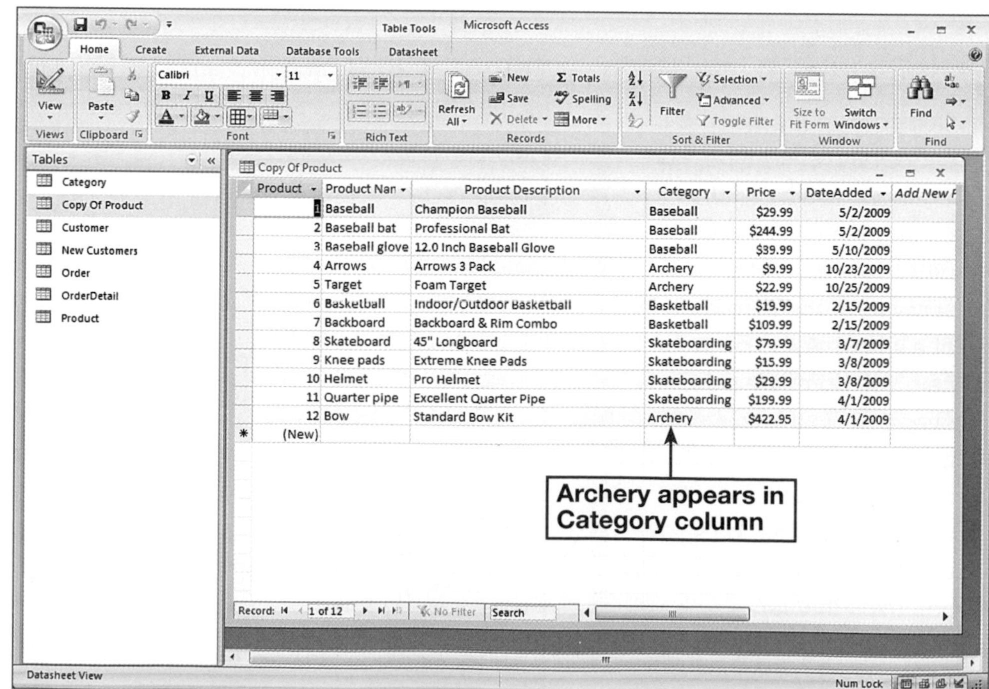

Step-By-Step

1. If necessary, in your **Shoes** file, click the white area of the chart box to display the **Chart Tools**. Click the **Design** tab.
2. Click the **Move Chart Location** button.
3. In the **Move Chart** dialog box, Choose **New Sheet**.
4. In the text box, key: Shoe Sales (see Figure 4.27).
5. Click **OK**.
6. CHECK Your file should look like Figure 4.28. Notice the chart moves from Sheet1 to a new sheet named **Shoe Sales**.
7. In the **Shoe Sales** sheet, right-click the chart and select **Move Chart**.
8. In the **Move Chart** dialog box, choose **Object In**.
9. Make sure **Sheet1** is selected. Click **OK**. The chart is moved back to Sheet1, and the Shoe Sales sheet is deleted.
10. Save and close your file.

Continue to the next exercise.

Solution Use the file **Shoes-SF.xlsx** as a solution file for Exercises 4-14 through 4-16.

EXERCISE 4-14
Add a Chart to a New Sheet

Sometimes crowding a worksheet with numbers and a chart can be overwhelming. A good strategy is to put the data in one sheet and move the accompanying chart to another sheet in the same workbook. You can move a chart from one sheet to another, or you can add it as an object.

FIGURE 4.27 Move Chart dialog box

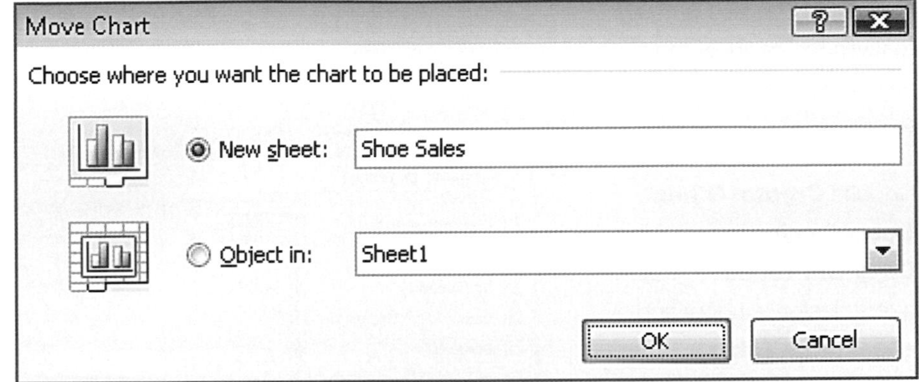

FIGURE 4.28 Chart moved to a new sheet

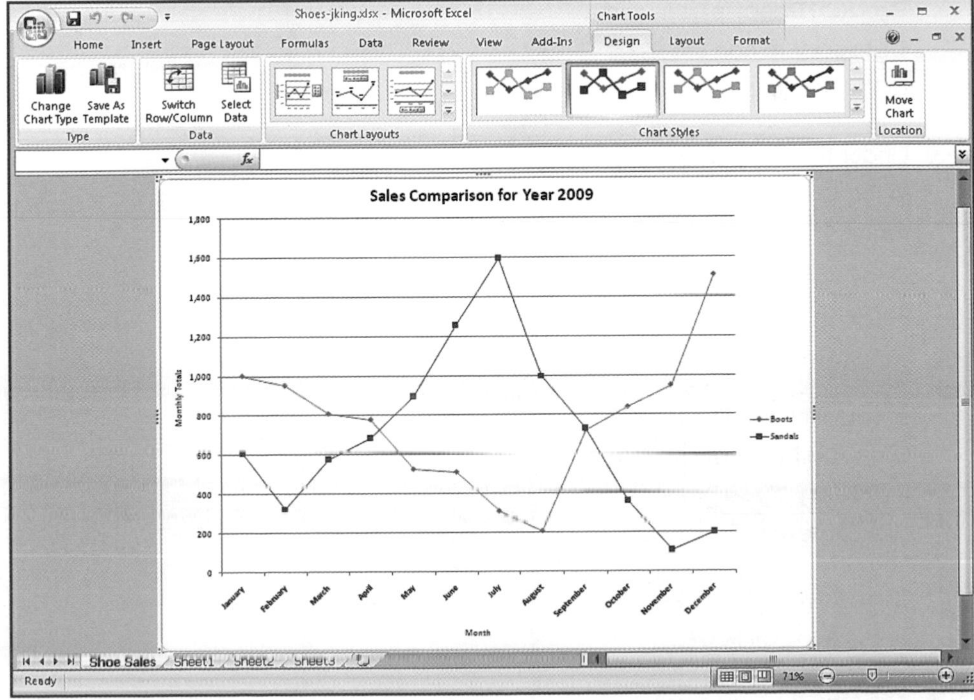

Step-By-Step

1. In your **Warehouse** file, in the **Navigation** pane, right-click the **Product** table and select **Copy**.
2. Right-click in an open area of the **Navigation Pane** and select **Paste**. Click **OK** to keep the name of the new table **Copy Of Product**.
3. Choose **Create>Other>Query Design**. Add **Copy Of Product** to the query design window and close **Show Table**.
4. In the window, double-click **ProductName**, **ProductDescription**, and **Category** to add the fields to the design grid.
5. Under the **Category** field, in the **Criteria** box, key: Archery. Click **Run** to check the results of the query.
6. **CHECK** Your screen should look like Figure 2.60. Click **Design View**. In the **Query Type** group, click **Delete**.
7. Click **Save** and key: DelArchery. Click **OK**.
8. **CHECK** Your screen should look like Figure 2.61.

Continued on the next page.

EXERCISE 2-21
Create Action Queries: Append and Delete

You can use action queries to delete entire records in an existing table, as with a delete query, or insert new records into an existing table, as with an append query.

FIGURE 2.60 Select query for Archery

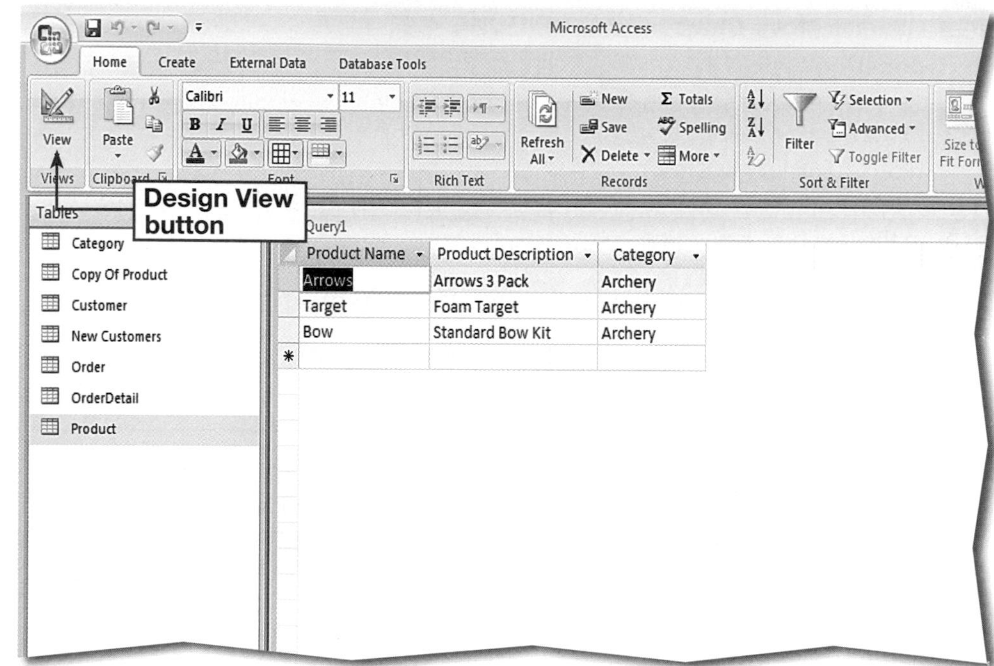

FIGURE 2.61 Delete query for Copy Of Product table

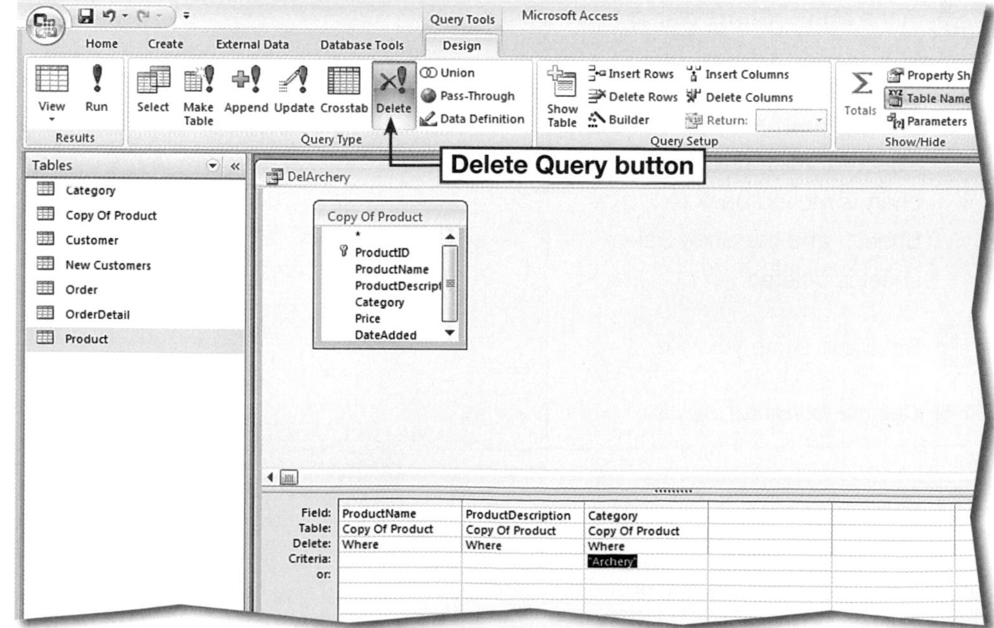

EXERCISE 4-15
Use the COUNT and COUNTA Functions

To find the number of cells in a range that contain numerals, use the **COUNT** function. For example, you can use this function to find the number of expenses, as opposed to the total amount of those expenses. In some places in Excel, such as in the Sum drop-down list, the COUNT function is called Count Numbers. To find the number of cells in a range that contain any kind of data (both numbers and text), use the **COUNTA** function.

Step-By-Step

1. Open the data file **Expenses.xlsx**. Save as: Expenses-[your first initial and last name].
2. Click cell **C29**. Choose **Home>Editing**. Click the **Sum** Σ drop-down arrow. Click **Count Numbers** (see Figure 4.29).
3. Select cells **C3** through **C27**. Press ENTER. The number of expenses (13) appears in cell **C29**. Because this cell is formatted for dollar values, the number displays as a dollar value.
4. Click cell **C24**. Key: 33.36. Press ENTER. The number of expenses increases to 14.
5. **CHECK** Your screen should look like Figure 4.30

Continued on the next page.

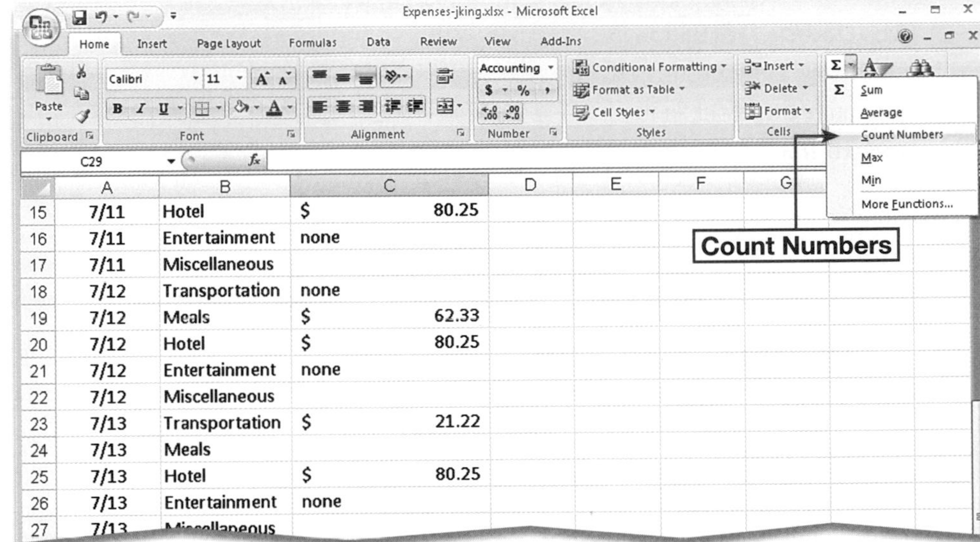

FIGURE 4.29 Count Numbers function in Sum list

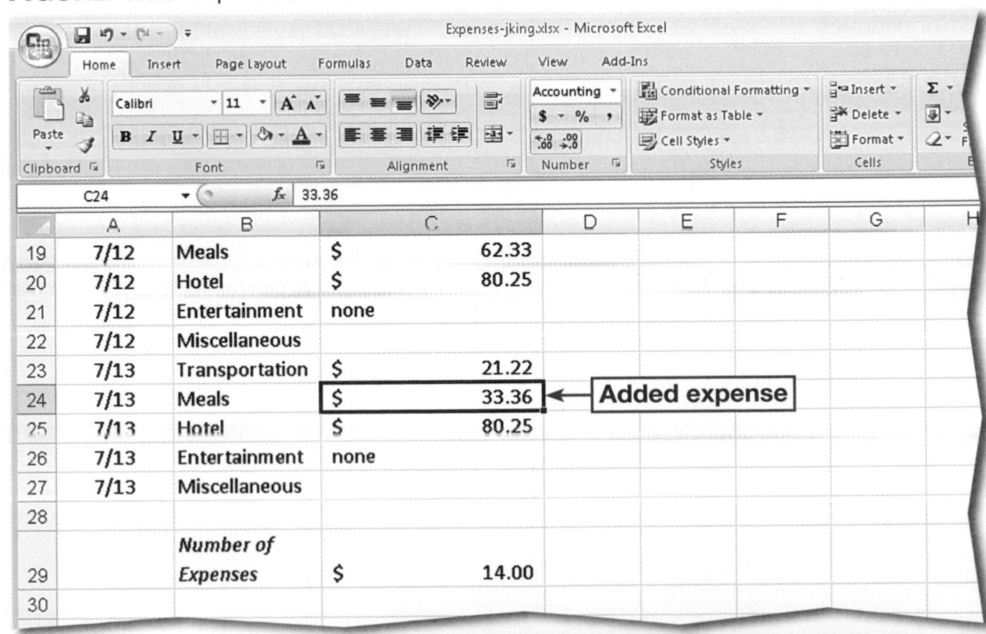

FIGURE 4.30 Expense added to worksheet

Tech Tip

The COUNT (or Count Numbers) function counts all cells in a range that contain numbers, even if the number is 0. If you do not want the COUNT function to count a cell, leave it blank or replace any numbers with text.

Troubleshooting Explain to students that the COUNT function is called the Count Numbers function when you select it from the SUM drop-down list.

EXERCISE 2-20 (Continued)
Create Action Queries: Make-Table and Update

7. Add the **New Customers** table to the query window and close the **Show Table** dialog box.
8. Double-click the **CustomerName**, **Street**, **City**, and **State** fields to add them to the query.
9. Click **Update** button in the **Query Type** group. Under the **City** field, in the **Update to** box, key: "LA".
10. In the same column in the **Criteria** box, key: "Los Angeles" (see Figure 2.58).
11. Click **Run** . Click **Yes** to update the table.
12. Click **Save** and name the query **ChangeCity**.
13. Click **OK**. Close the query. Click **Yes** to save the changes.
14. Locate and open the **New Customers** table, and then set the **Navigation Pane** to display **Queries**.
15. CHECK Your screen should look like Figure 2.59.
16. Close the table.

Continue to the next exercise.

FIGURE 2.58 Update query

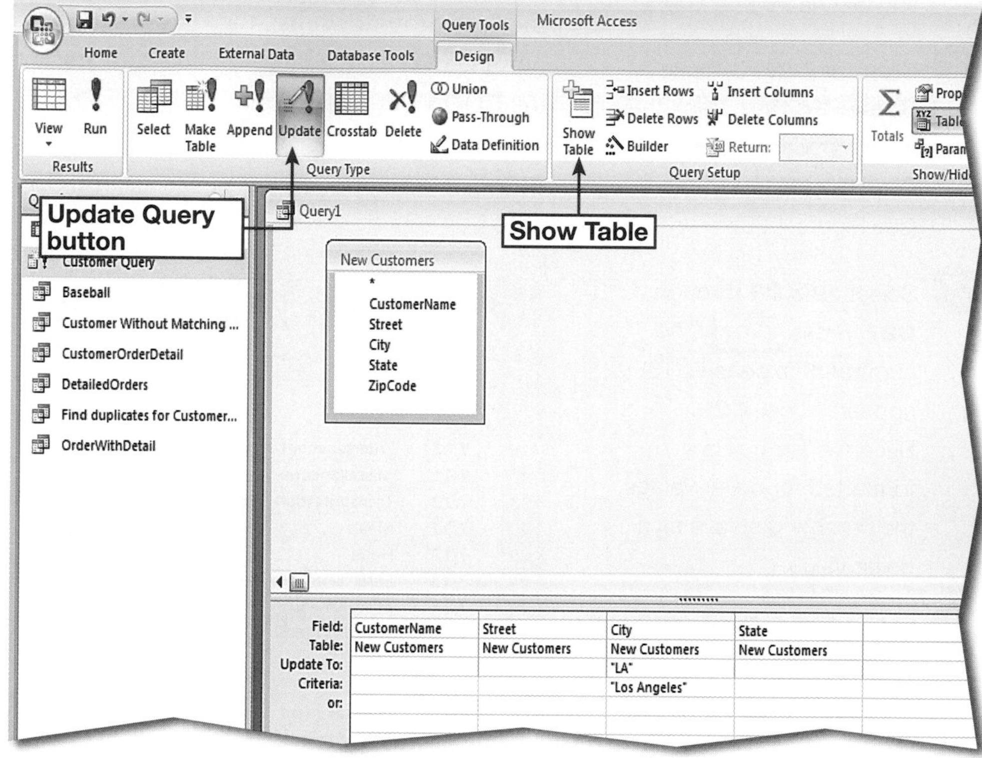

FIGURE 2.59 Update query results

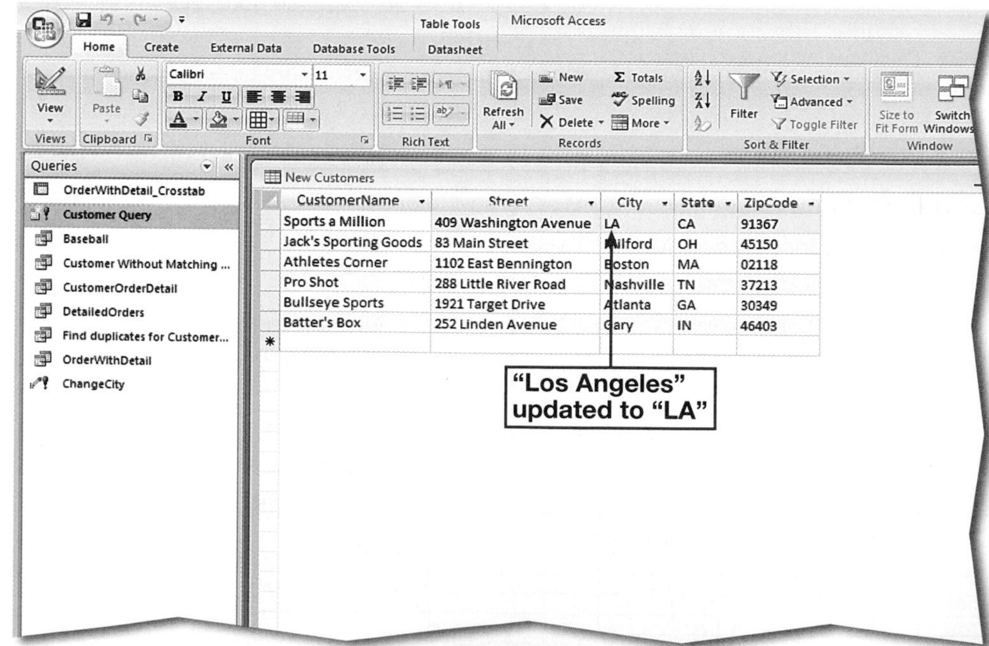

Step-By-Step

EXERCISE 4-15 (Continued)
Use the COUNT and COUNTA Functions

6. Click cell **C30**. Click the **Sum** [Σ] drop-down arrow. Choose **More Functions**.

7. Make sure **Or select a category** is set to **All**. Under **Select a function**, choose **COUNTA**. Click **OK**.

8. In the **Value1** box, key: C3:C27. Only 20 of the expense category amounts have been filled out.

9. Click **OK**. A number appears in cell **C30** (see Figure 4.31).

10. Click **Undo** [↶]. To complete the expense report, in each empty cell in column C, key: none.

11. **CHECK** Your screen should look like Figure 4.32. Save and close your file.

Continue to the next exercise.

FIGURE 4.31 Number appears using COUNTA function

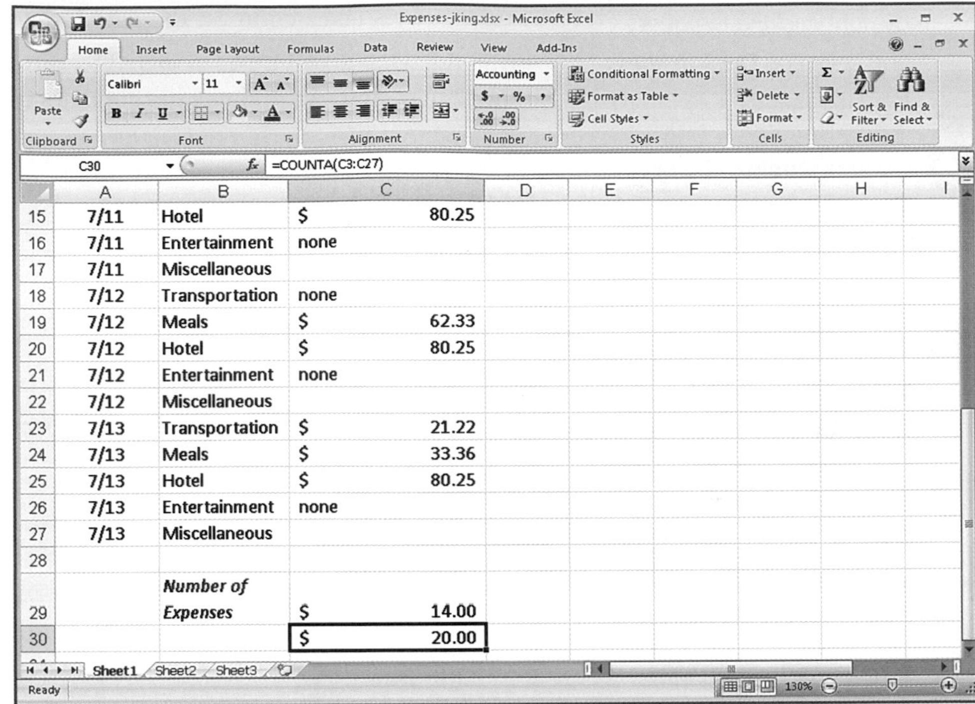

Expenses-jking.xlsx - Microsoft Excel

C30 | =COUNTA(C3:C27)

	A	B	C
15	7/11	Hotel	$ 80.25
16	7/11	Entertainment	none
17	7/11	Miscellaneous	
18	7/12	Transportation	none
19	7/12	Meals	$ 62.33
20	7/12	Hotel	$ 80.25
21	7/12	Entertainment	none
22	7/12	Miscellaneous	
23	7/13	Transportation	$ 21.22
24	7/13	Meals	$ 33.36
25	7/13	Hotel	$ 80.25
26	7/13	Entertainment	none
27	7/13	Miscellaneous	
28			
29		*Number of Expenses*	$ 14.00
30			$ 20.00

FIGURE 4.32 Final spreadsheet

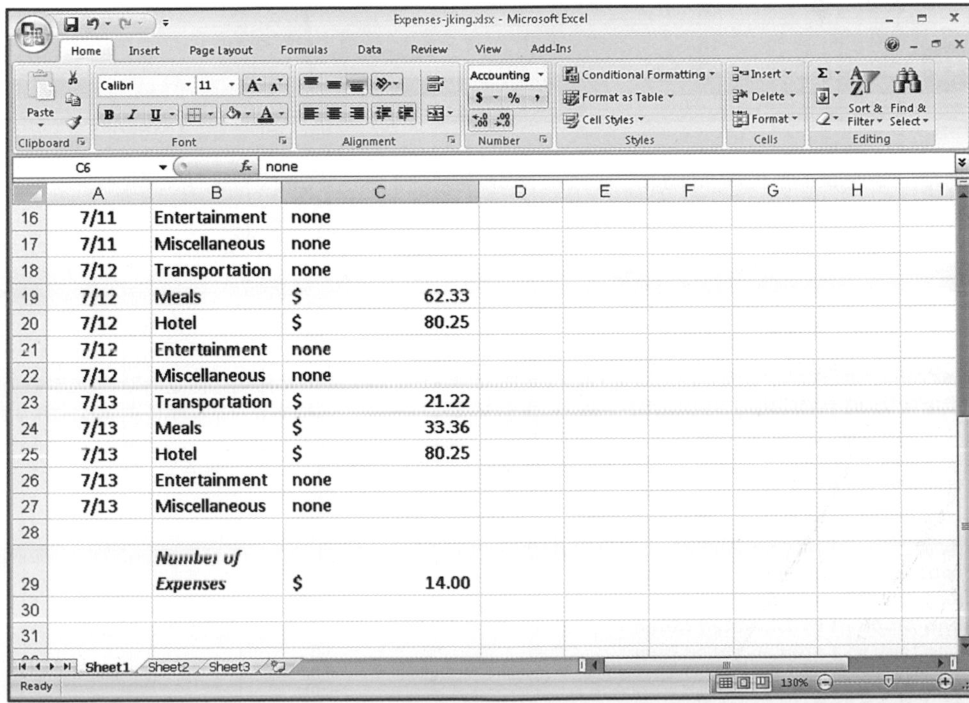

Expenses-jking.xlsx - Microsoft Excel

C6 | none

	A	B	C
16	7/11	Entertainment	none
17	7/11	Miscellaneous	none
18	7/12	Transportation	none
19	7/12	Meals	$ 62.33
20	7/12	Hotel	$ 80.25
21	7/12	Entertainment	none
22	7/12	Miscellaneous	none
23	7/13	Transportation	$ 21.22
24	7/13	Meals	$ 33.36
25	7/13	Hotel	$ 80.25
26	7/13	Entertainment	none
27	7/13	Miscellaneous	none
28			
29		*Number of Expenses*	$ 14.00
30			
31			

Different Strokes Tell students that they can also Insert a COUNT or COUNTA function with the **Insert Function** button on the formula bar.

Solution Use the file **Expenses-SF.xlsx** as a solution file for this exercise.

Step-By-Step

1 In your **Warehouse** file, open the **Customer Query** by right-clicking the query and selecting **Design View** from the menu.

2 Choose **Design>Query Type>Make Table**. The **Make Table** dialog box opens (see Figure 2.56).

3 In the dialog box, in the **Table Name** field, key: New Customers. Click **OK**.

4 Choose **Design>Results> Run** to activate the **Customer Query**. Click **Yes** to create the table.

5 **CHECK** Your screen should look like Figure 2.57. Close the query and save changes.

6 Choose **Create>Query Design**.

Continued on the next page.

You Should Know

Action queries start out as simple select queries that are then modified with the **Query Type** buttons in the **Query Tools** tab.

Troubleshooting If students see the message **This action or event has been blocked by Disabled Mode** when they try to run an action query, show them how to change the **Microsoft Office Access Trust Center Settings** to enable all macros.

EXERCISE 2-20
Create Action Queries: Make-Table and Update

Action queries take action on the data in database objects by adding, changing, or deleting data. For example, a make-table query retrieves information and assembles it into a new table. An update query updates information in existing tables. You must run an action query for it to take effect.

FIGURE 2.56 Make Table dialog box

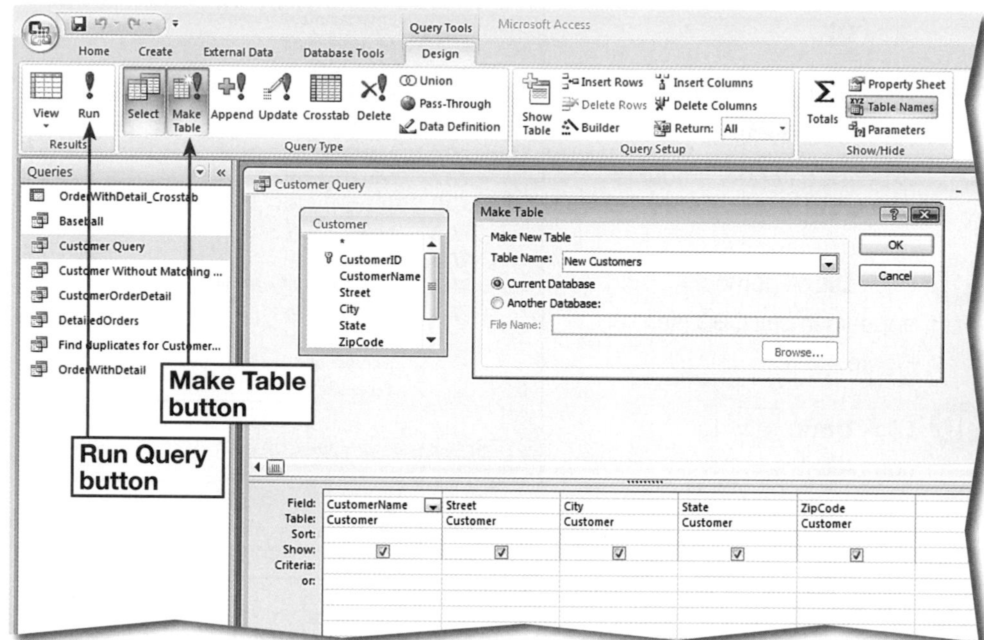

FIGURE 2.57 Make Table query results

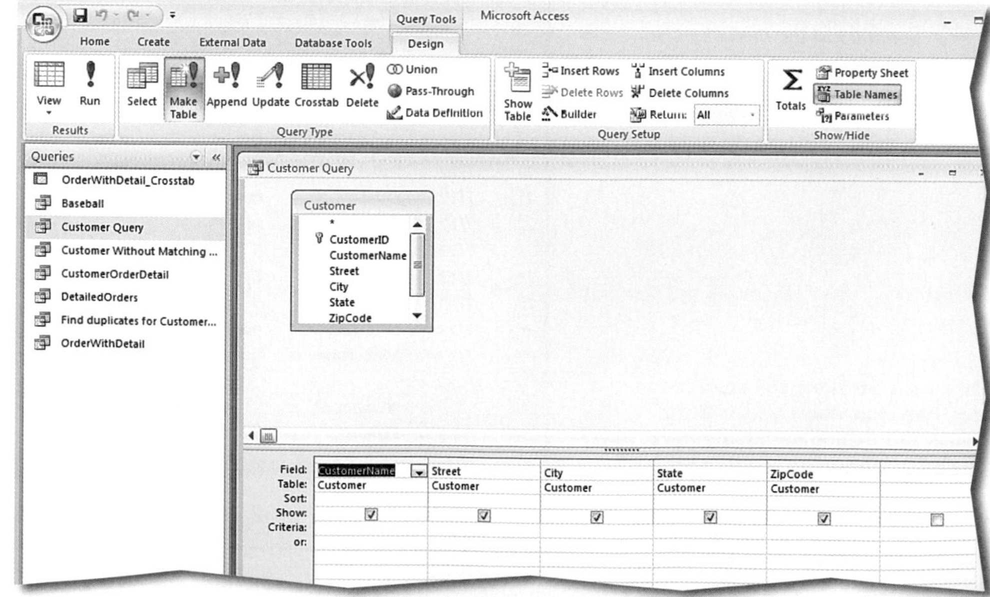

EXERCISE 4-16
Use the NOW and PMT Functions

The **NOW** function displays the date and time that a worksheet is opened or used. This feature can be useful when a worksheet has been changed many times. The date and time shown on a printout of the worksheet will tell you which **version**, or variation of the original, of the file you are using. The **PMT** function calculates the monthly payment for a loan using the amount of the loan, the interest rate, and the number of payments. Both of these functions are very useful if you want to create and update your own personal budget.

NCLB/Math (Number and Operations)

FIGURE 4.33 Date and time added to worksheet

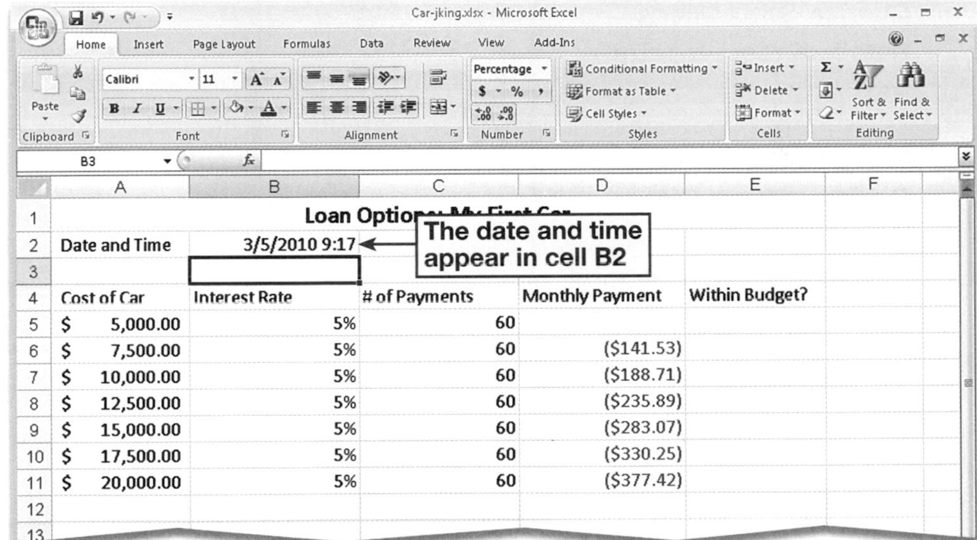

FIGURE 4.34 Insert Function dialog box

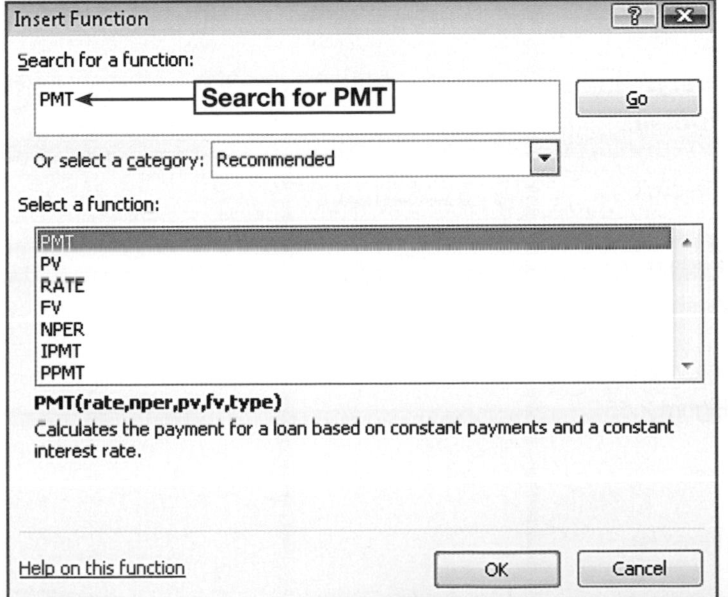

Step-By-Step

1. Open the data file **Car.xlsx**. Save as: Car-[your first initial and last name].
2. Click cell **B2**. Key: =NOW(). Press ENTER.
3. CHECK Your screen should look similar to Figure 4.33. Your current date and time should appear in cell **B2**.
4. Click cell **D5**.
5. On the formula bar, click **Insert Function** *fx*.
6. In the **Insert Function** dialog box, under **Search for a function**, key: PMT (see Figure 4.34). Click **Go**.
7. Click **OK**. The **Function Arguments** dialog box opens.

Continued on the next page.

Academic Skills

You need to know how much you can afford to spend in order to create an effective budget. Be sure to consider taxes, interest rates, and other expenses. Excel can help you to incorporate these items into your budget.

Troubleshooting Let students know that, in the **Insert Function** dialog box, they can click once on a function to display a description of what the function does.

Step-By-Step

EXERCISE 2-19 (Continued)
Create Crosstab, Unmatched, and Duplicate Queries

Different Strokes Explain to students that double-clicking fields in the **Query Wizard** is an acceptable alternative to selecting the fields and moving them into the selected-fields pane with the arrow (<, >) buttons.

7. Close the query. Click **Query Wizard**. Double-click **Find Unmatched Query Wizard**.
8. Select **Table: Customer** and click **Next**.
9. Under **View**, click **Queries**. Select **Query: DetailedOrders** and click **Next**.
10. In both field lists, select **CustomerName**. Click **Next**. Double-click **CustomerName**. Click **Next**. Click **Finish**.
11. **CHECK** Your screen should look like Figure 2.54.
12. Close the datasheet. Click **Query Wizard**. Double-click **Find Duplicates Query Wizard**.
13. Under **View**, click **Queries**. Click **Query: CustomerOrderDetail**.
14. Click **Next**. Double-click **ProductName**. Click **Next**. Click **Next** again, and then click **Finish**.
15. **CHECK** Your screen should look like Figure 2.55.
16. Close the datasheet.

Continue to the next exercise.

FIGURE 2.54 Unmatched query

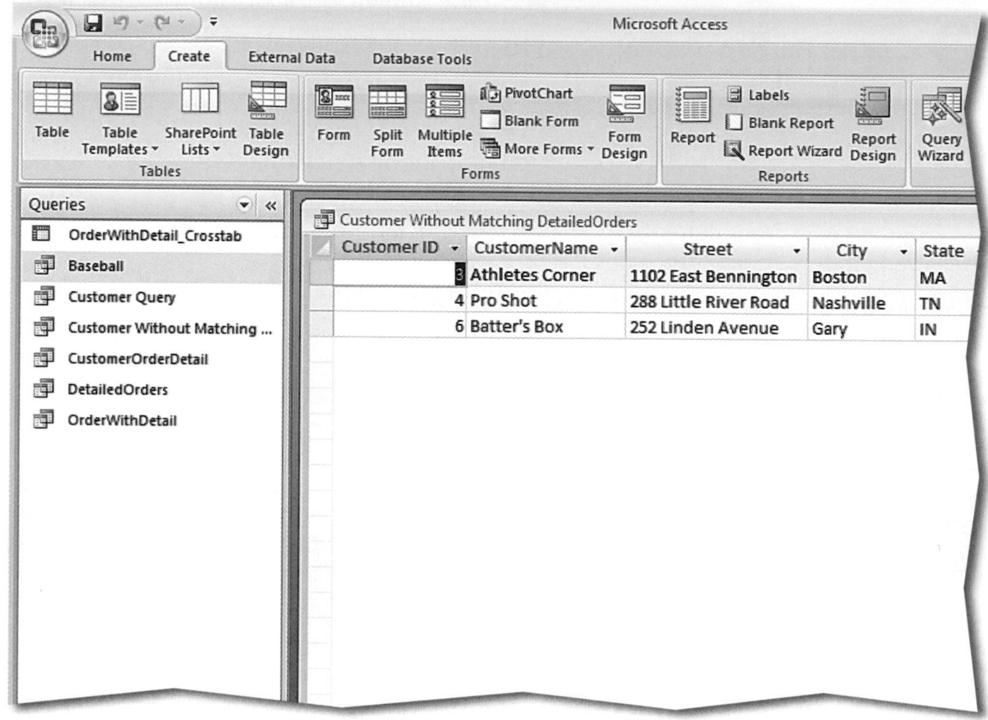

FIGURE 2.55 Duplicate query

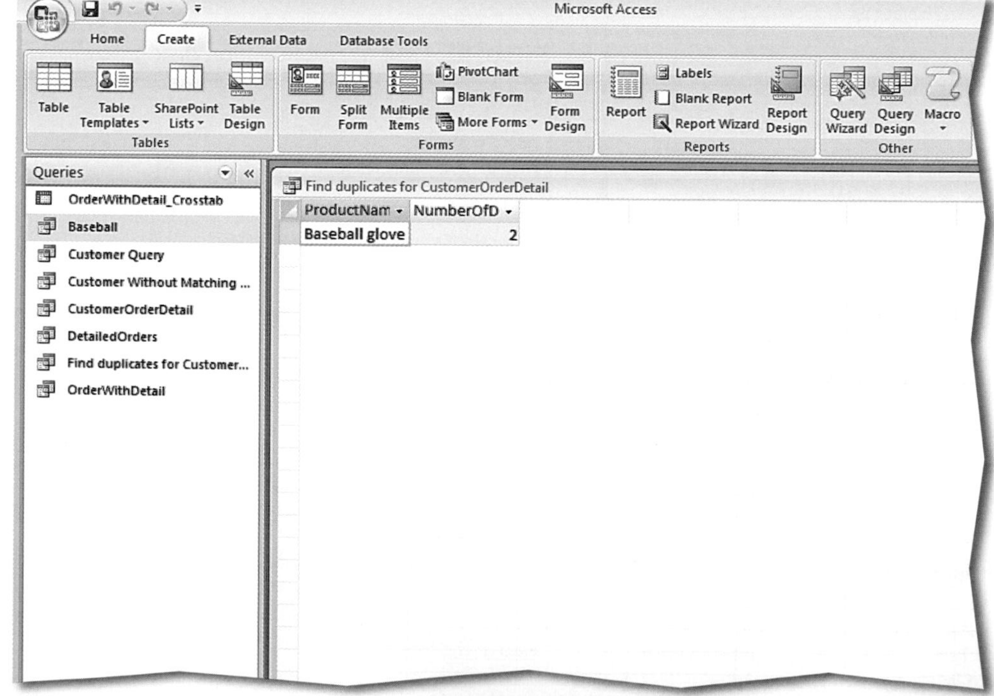

Step-By-Step

8 In the **Rate** line, key: 0.05/12 (see Figure 4.35).

9 In the **Nper** line, key: 60. Nper is the total number of payments to be made.

10 In the **Pv** line, key: A5. Pv is the amount of the loan. Click **OK**.

11 **CHECK** Your screen should look like Figure 4.36. Save your file.

Continue to the next exercise.

You Should Know

The Function Arguments dialog box will help you calculate your monthly payments if you take out a loan. Rate refers to the interest rate for a loan, presented as a percentage. Nper is the total number of payments for the loan (a five-year loan would have 60 monthly payments). Pv is the present value or amount of the loan.

Academic Skills

The results from the PMT function are red and in parentheses because they represent negative amounts. The numbers represent money that you owe for the car. In finance, the amount owed is usually represented like this.

EXERCISE 4-16 (Continued)
Use the NOW and PMT Functions

FIGURE 4.35 Function Arguments dialog box

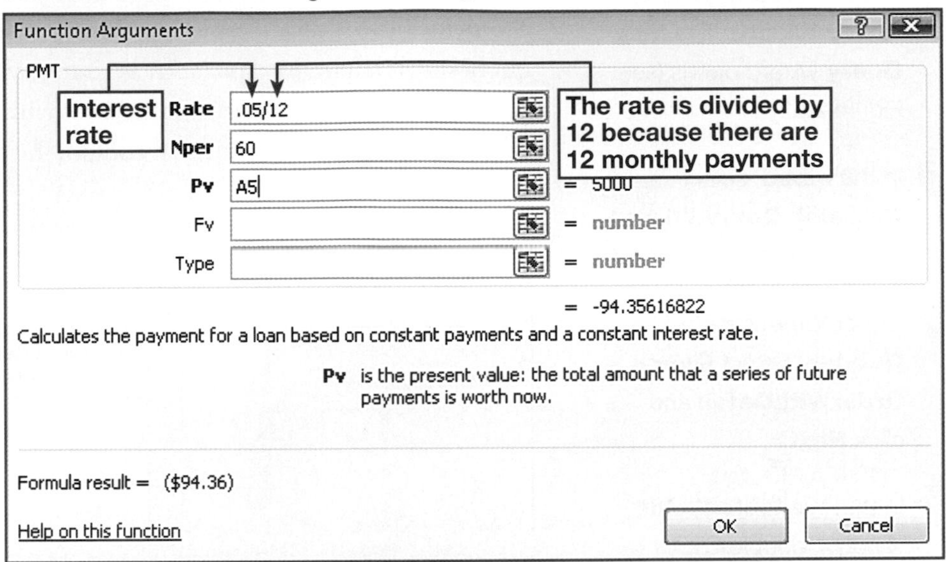

FIGURE 4.36 Payment amounts calculated

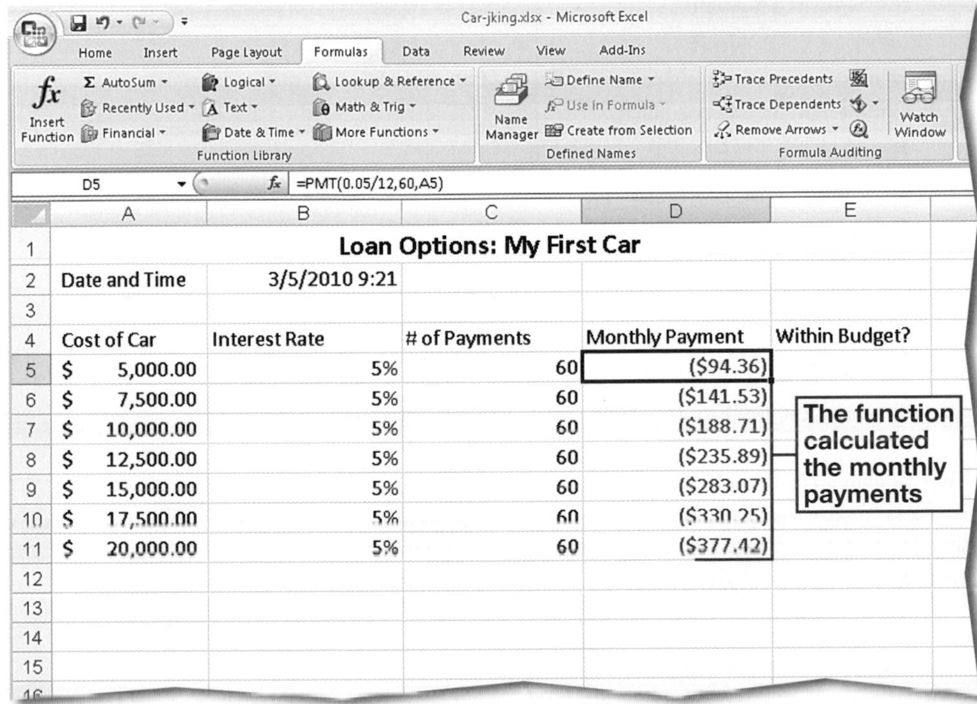

	A	B	C	D	E
1	Loan Options: My First Car				
2	Date and Time	3/5/2010 9:21			
3					
4	Cost of Car	Interest Rate	# of Payments	Monthly Payment	Within Budget?
5	$ 5,000.00	5%	60	($94.36)	
6	$ 7,500.00	5%	60	($141.53)	
7	$ 10,000.00	5%	60	($188.71)	
8	$ 12,500.00	5%	60	($235.89)	
9	$ 15,000.00	5%	60	($283.07)	
10	$ 17,500.00	5%	60	($330.25)	
11	$ 20,000.00	5%	60	($377.42)	

Differentiated Instruction/Advanced Students See if advanced students can explain why the rate is divided by 12 in Step 11. The correct answer would be that the annual loan is based on 12 monthly payments for 60 months, or 5 years.

NCLB/Math (Number and Operations)

EXERCISE 2-19
Create Crosstab, Unmatched, and Duplicate Queries

Access includes several queries to help you analyze and manage your data. A **crosstab query** shows summary data (such as count, average, or sum) for data grouped by two fields. An **unmatched query** finds records without matching related data. A **duplicate query** finds multiple records that contain the same data in a field.

FIGURE 2.52 New Query wizard

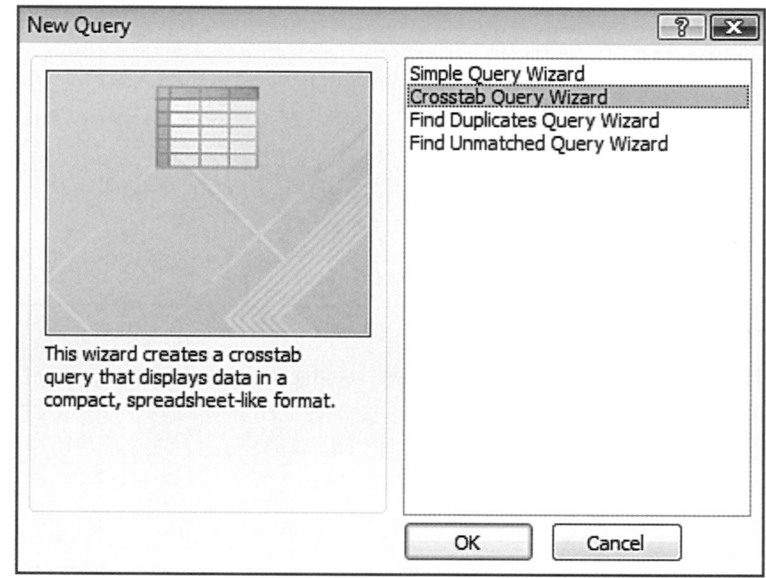

FIGURE 2.53 Crosstab query datasheet

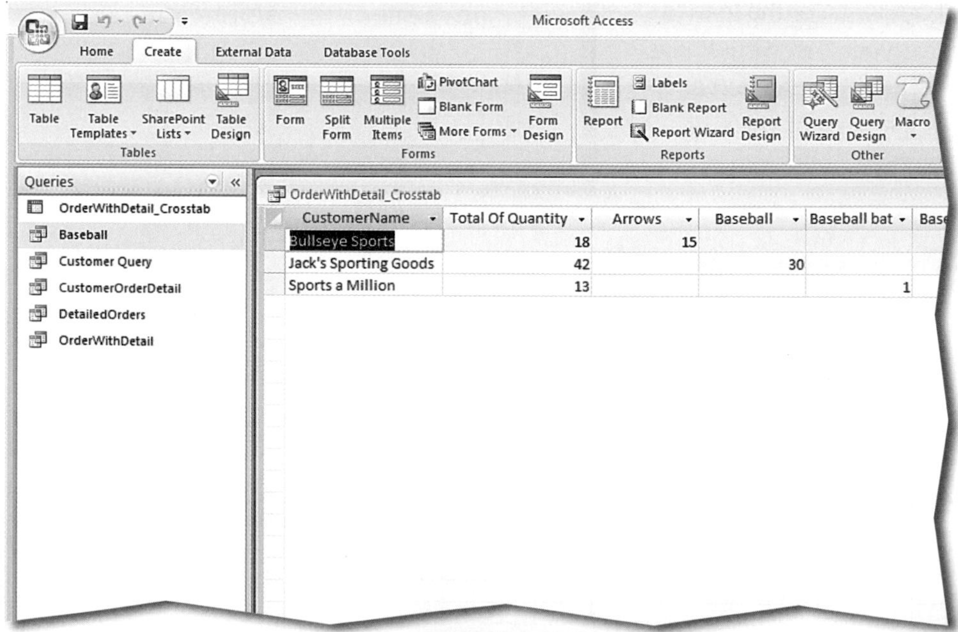

Step-By-Step

1. In your **Warehouse** file, choose **Create>Other> Query Wizard**. The **New Query** wizard opens (see Figure 2.52).
2. In the wizard, select **Crosstab Query Wizard** and click **OK**.
3. Under **View**, click **Queries**. Select **Query: OrderWithDetail** and click **Next**.
4. In the **Available Fields** window, double-click **CustomerName**. **CustomerName** moves to the **Selected Fields** window. Click **Next**.
5. Click **ProductName**. Click **Next**. In the **Fields** list, click **Quantity**. In the **Functions** list, click **Sum**. Click **Next**. Leave the title as is and click **Finish**.
6. **CHECK** Your screen should look like Figure 2.53.

Continued on the next page.

You Should Know

Existing queries can be added to query **Design View**, just like tables.

Step-By-Step Tip In **Step 5**, if students do not see the **Functions** list, have them double-click **Quantity** in the **Fields** list. The **Functions** list will appear.

Step-By-Step

1. In your **Car** file, click **E5**.
2. On the formula bar, click **Insert Function** *fx*.
3. In the **Insert Function** dialog box, under **Search for a function**, key: IF.
4. **CHECK** Your dialog box should look like Figure 4.37.
5. Click **Go**.
6. Click **OK**.

Continued on the next page.

EXERCISE 4-17
Use the IF Function

The **IF** function allows a worksheet to compare numbers. In this exercise, you will use the IF function to determine whether a monthly car payment is within your budget. To do this, the IF function compares numbers to see if a **condition**, or rule, that you create is true.

For example, you might want to buy a car, under one condition—you cannot spend more than $250 a month. If the condition is true, meaning that the payment will be less than $250, the function displays one result, such as *Yes*. If the condition is false, meaning that the payment will be more than $250, the function displays another result, such as *No*. By using the IF function, Excel will tell you whether the car payment will be within your budget.

The IF function can also be used to make other comparisons. It can be used to compare weights, measurements, or almost any kind of data that can be entered as a number.

FIGURE 4.37 Insert Function dialog box

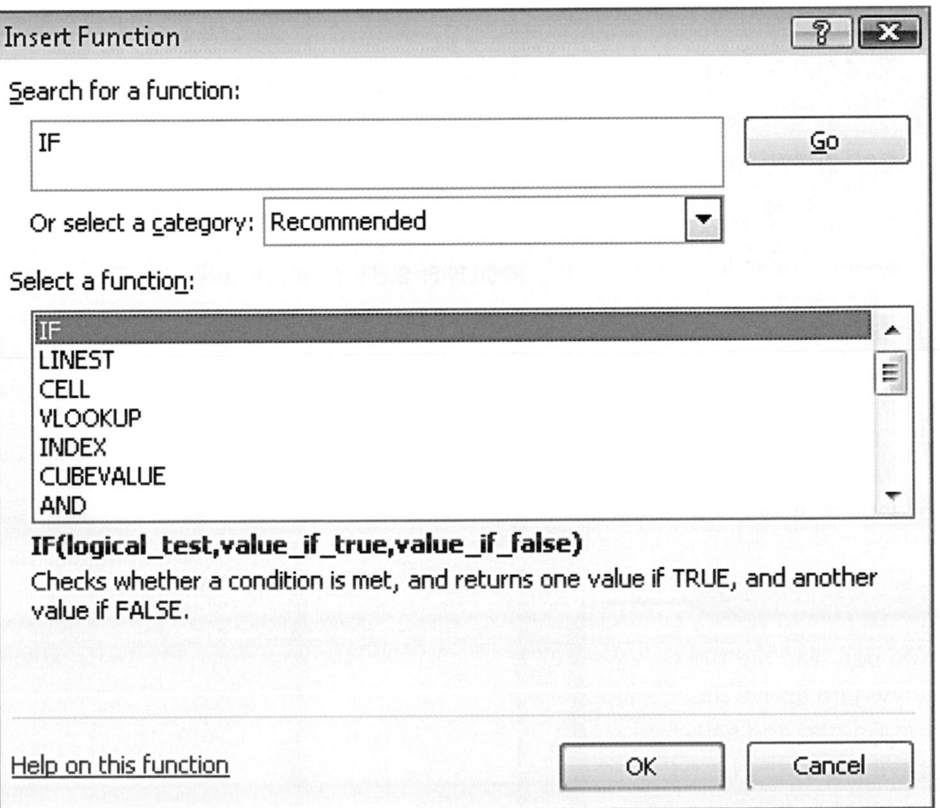

You Should Know

Instead of having the IF function display text, you can have it display numbers. For example, you can test to see if you owe more than $500 for a particular bill. If you do, you can have a standard response, such as *$500*, appear.

Intervention Strategy If students find the **IF** function confusing, give a non-mathematical example: If it rains, I will watch a movie. If it does not rain, I will take a walk.

Differentiated Instruction/Advanced Students Encourage students to discuss other ways to use the IF function. Have students create and explain new worksheets that demonstrate these ways.

Step-By-Step

EXERCISE 2-18 (Continued)
Save Filters as Queries

9 Click **Advanced** and select **Advanced Filter/ Sort**.

10 Click **Advanced** again and select **Save As Query**.

11 The **Save As Query** dialog box opens (see Figure 2.50). Key: Baseball. Click **OK**.

12 Close the **ProductFilter1** window.

13 Close the **Product** table. Click **No** when asked to save changes.

14 Display **Queries** in the **Navigation Pane**.

15 Double-click the **Baseball** query to open it.

16 CHECK Your screen should look like Figure 2.51.

17 Close the **Baseball** query.

Continue to the next exercise.

Shortcuts

You can also right-click anywhere above the design grid and select **Save As Query** from the list to open the **Save As Query** dialog box.

FIGURE 2.50 Save As Query dialog box

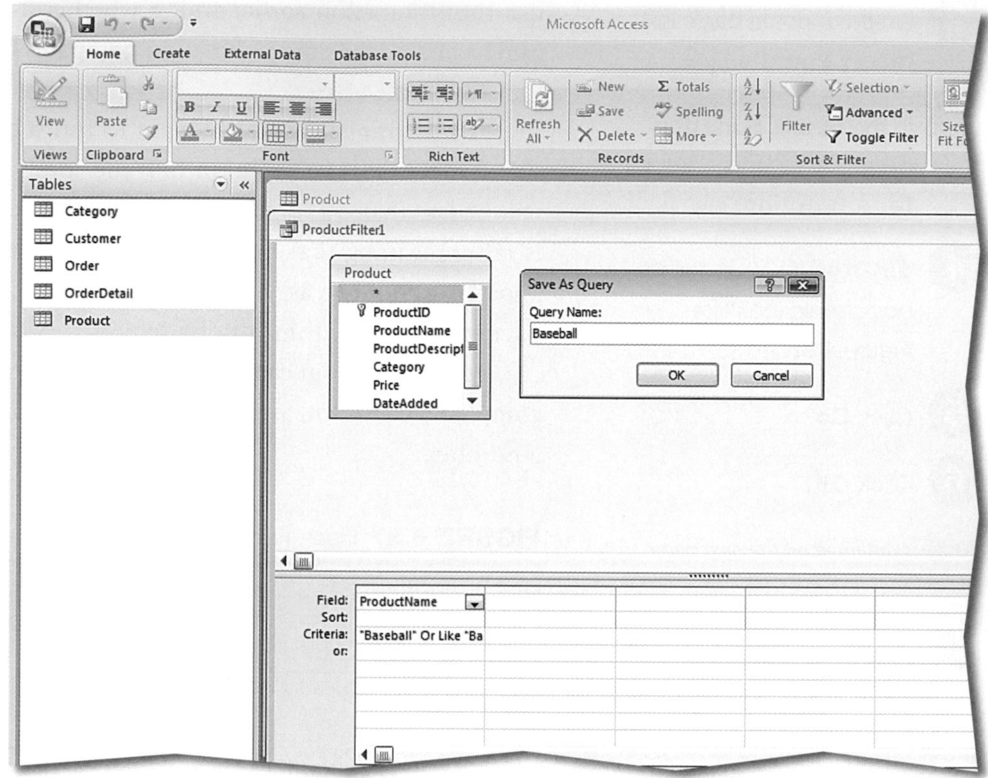

FIGURE 2.51 Baseball query

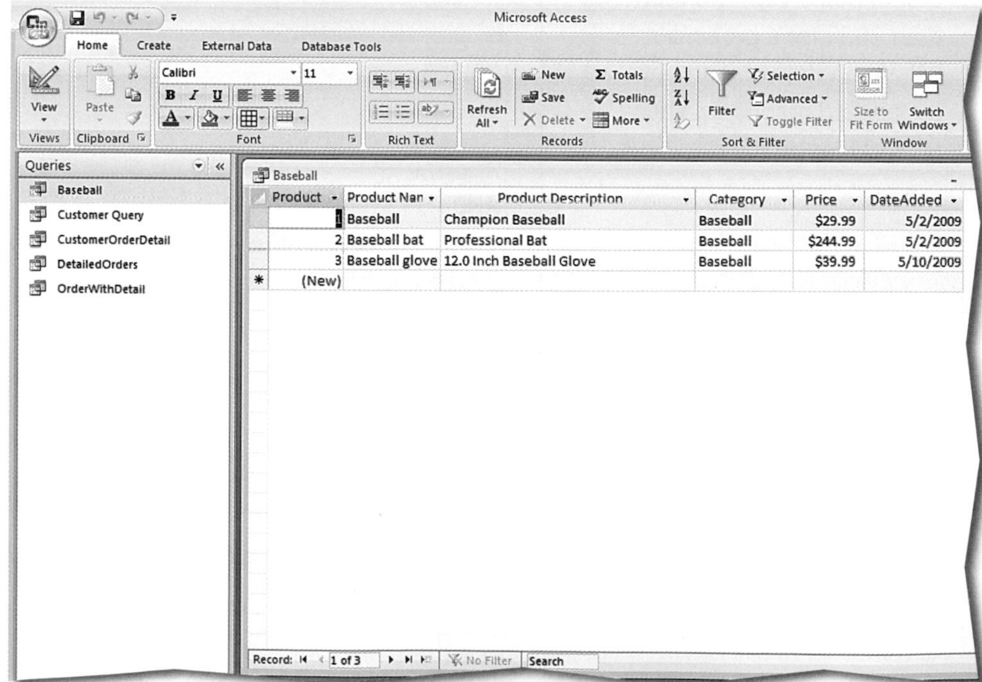

Step-By-Step

7 In the **Function Arguments** dialog box, in the **Logical_test** box, key: D5>=250 (see Figure 4.38).

8 In **Value_if_true** box, key: Yes.

9 In the **Value_if_false** box, key: No. Excel automatically inserts quotation marks in the **Value_if_false** box.

10 CHECK Your dialog box should look like Figure 4.38. Click **OK**.

11 Click the lower right corner of cell **E5** and drag it down to cell **E11**. Release the mouse button.

12 CHECK Your screen should look like Figure 4.39. The most expensive car you can afford is $12,500.

13 Save and close your file.

Continue to the next exercise.

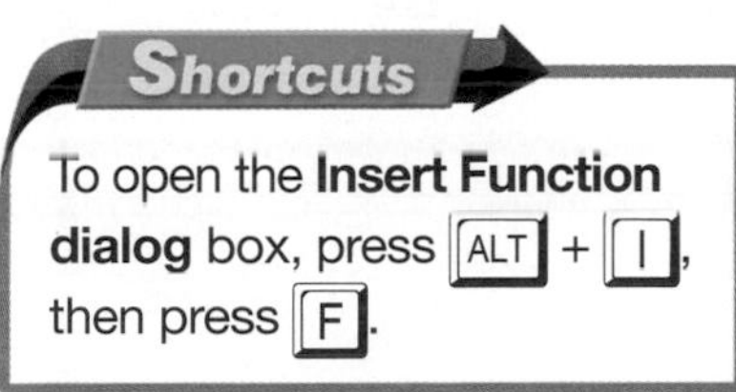

Shortcuts

To open the **Insert Function dialog** box, press ALT + I, then press F.

Step-By-Step Tip In **Step 5**, point out to students that the value of 250 in the IF function is negative because payments are subtracted from the total.

Solution Use the file **Car-SF.xlsx** as a solution file for Exercises 4-16 through 4-17.

EXERCISE 4-17 (Continued)
Use the IF Function

FIGURE 4.38 Function Arguments for IF

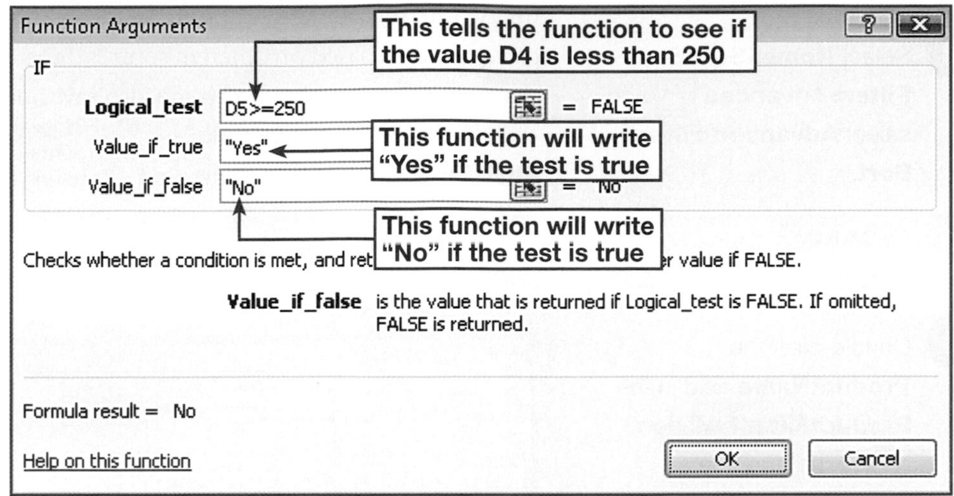

FIGURE 4.39 Budget check

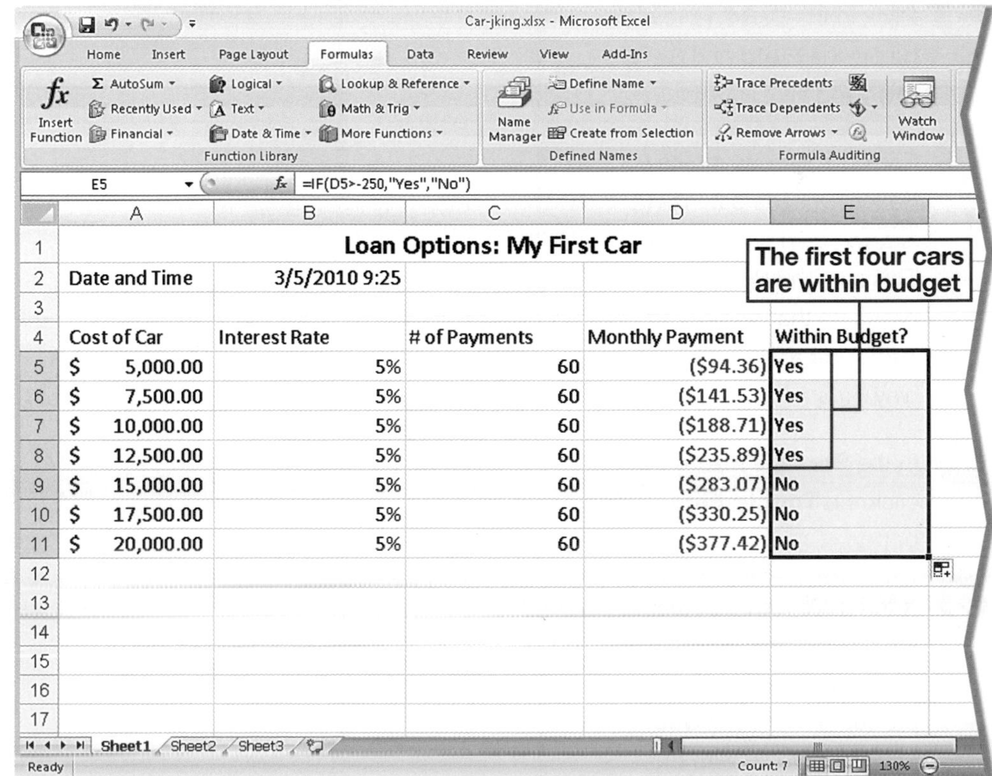

Step-By-Step

1. In your **Warehouse** file, open the **Product** table.

2. Select **Home>Sort & Filter>Advanced** and select **Advanced Filter/ Sort**.

3. **CHECK** Your screen should look like Figure 2.48.

4. Double-click the **ProductName** field in the **ProductFilter1** window. Notice that the name appears below in the **Field** row.

5. Click in the **Criteria** row below the **Field** and **Sort** rows and key: Baseball.

6. Click the **or** row and key: Baseball *. The asterisk (*) is a wildcard search term. This search will find all products that begin with **Baseball** and end in any way.

7. In the **Sort & Filter** group, click the **Toggle Filter** button.

8. **CHECK** Your screen should look like Figure 2.49. The filter shows only the products in the **Product** table that begin with the word **Baseball**.

Continued on the next page.

EXERCISE 2-18
Save Filters as Queries

Filters allow you to view only a portion, or a part, of the data in a given table or query, filtering out information based on criteria you set. While queries create new groups of data based on different sources, most filters only change how you see the data that is already assembled. You can also save and use some advanced filters as queries.

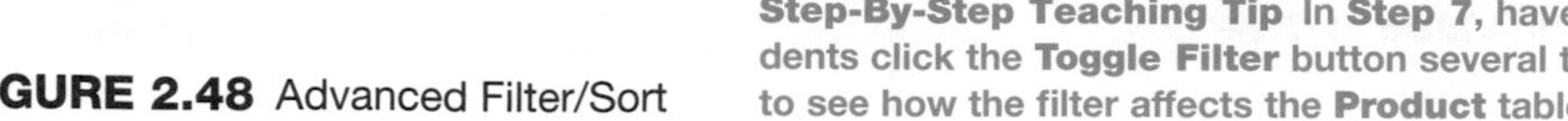

Step-By-Step Teaching Tip In **Step 7**, have students click the **Toggle Filter** button several times to see how the filter affects the **Product** table.

FIGURE 2.48 Advanced Filter/Sort

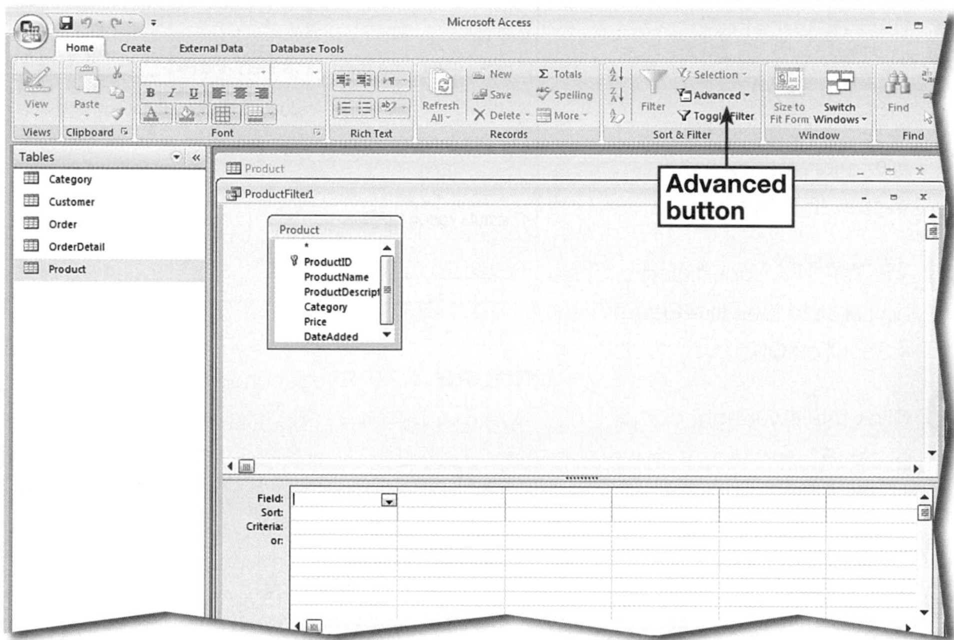

FIGURE 2.49 Filter applied to Product table

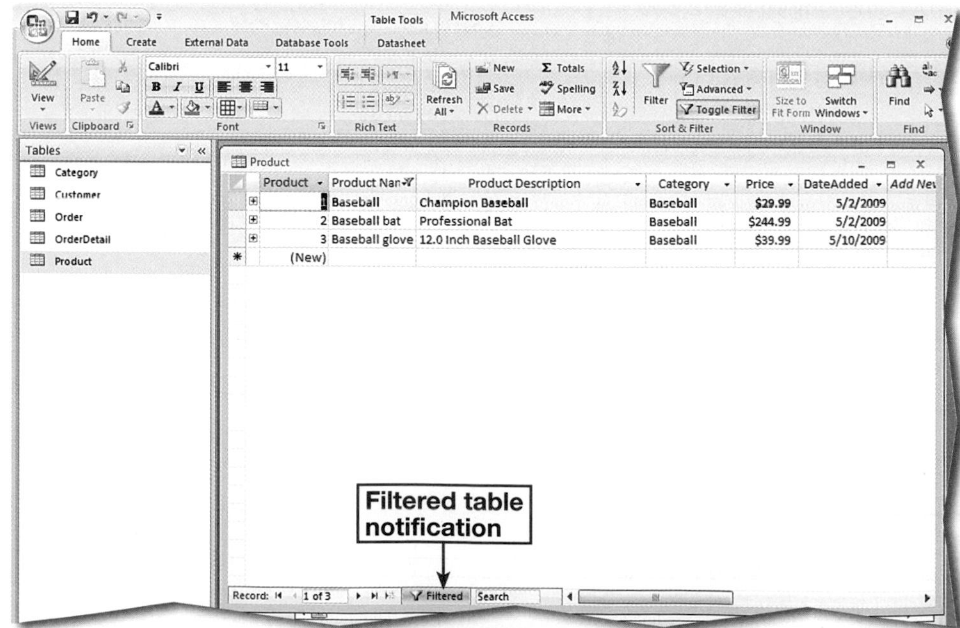

MATH MATTERS

Presenting Information Graphically

Your boss is worried that the restaurant he manages is losing sales. He asks you to prepare a report that analyzes the current sales data. You need to decide how you want to present the data so it is easily understandable.

Using Graphics

When you need information about a business's performance, a good place to look is a business report. A business report can be anything from a one-page summary of sales to a 200-page analysis of an entire industry. It may propose a new product or marketing strategy, describe a current development, or track profits over a period of time.

While business reports are good for analyzing and summarizing large amounts of data, there are times when you want to show your data so it is immediately understandable. Using a graphic such as a chart or graph allows you to organize data so it can be evaluated at a glance. For instance, an upward line on a graph shows that sales are increasing, while a downward line will signal that sales are on the decline.

Seeing the Numbers

You decide to create a graph that shows your boss the amount of burger sales over the last seven months. Your graph (shown above right) illustrates how sales have generally increased over the last few months—which is a relief for your boss!

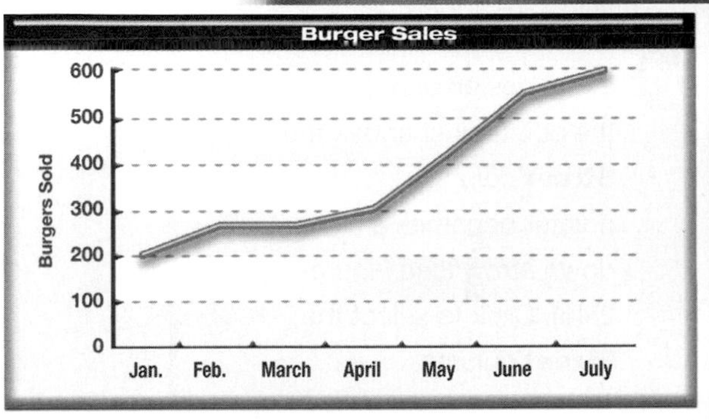

Use graphics to display information visually.

NCLB/Math (Algebra) Reinforce the importance of using graphics to display information visually by asking students to create their own SmartArt graphic or to choose a different chart type to display the data in the figure on this page.

Academic Integration/Math Have students go online to learn more about math theory.

 SkillBuilder answers can be found on page TM74.

SKILLBUILDER

1. **Describe** What are some of the purposes of a business report?
2. **Evaluate** Why is it sometimes better to present data as a graphic than as numbers or words?
3. **Connect** How can math and writing skills help you to read or write a business report? How might your business report be improved with a basic knowledge of Excel? Explain your answer in a brief paragraph.

Step-By-Step

9 The query opens in **Datasheet View**. Click **Design View**.

10 In the **Customer** table, double-click **Street**. Double-click **ZipCode**. The fields are added.

11 In the design grid, position the pointer just above the **Street** column until the pointer becomes a small down arrow (see Figure 2.46). Click to select the **Street** column.

12 With the pointer in the same place, drag and drop the **Street** column between the **CustomerName** and **City** columns.

13 Click **Datasheet View**.

14 **CHECK** Your screen should look like Figure 2.47. Save and close the datasheet.

Continue to the next exercise.

You Should Know

The **Query Wizard** allows you to create a query by choosing fields from other tables. You can even choose fields from other queries to create new queries.

EXERCISE 2-17 (Continued)
Create Queries

Differentiated Instruction/Advanced Students Have students try creating another query from other tables.

FIGURE 2.46 Query design with added fields

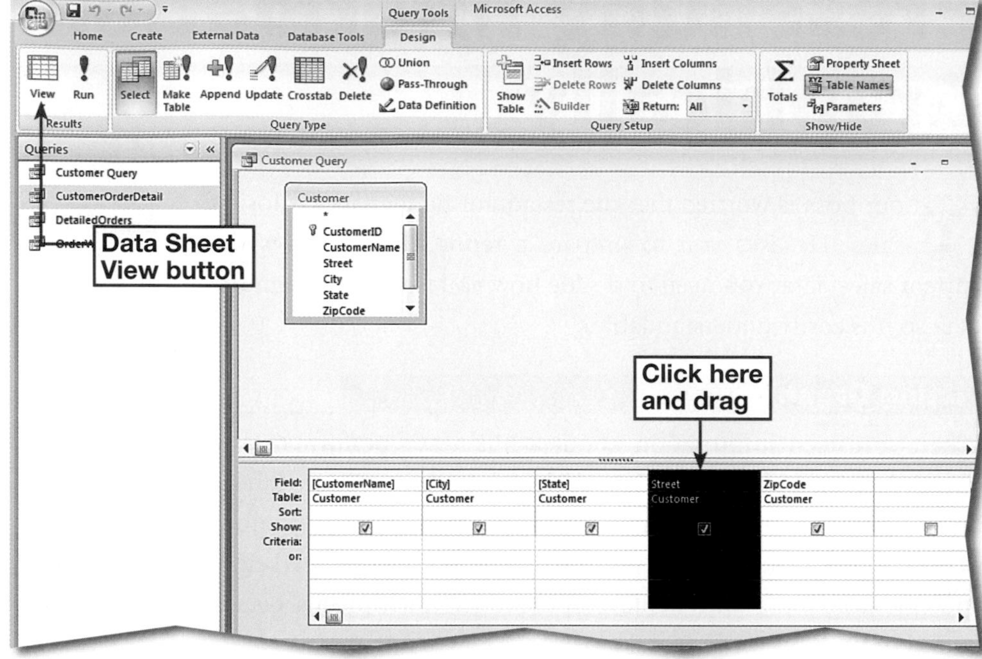

FIGURE 2.47 Datasheet with added fields

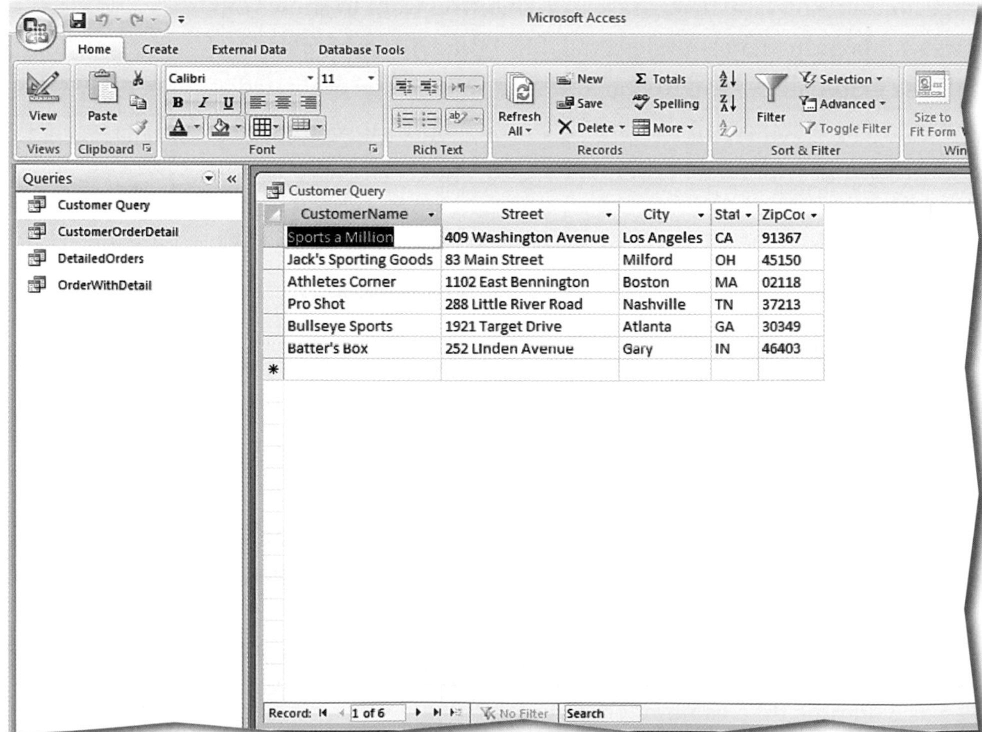

LESSON 4 After You Read

Vocabulary

Key Terms

absolute reference
chart
condition
COUNT
COUNTA
filter
function
IF
mixed reference
NOW
operator
PMT
range
relative reference
sort

Academic Vocabulary

adjust
version

Answer to Vocabulary Activity
Quizzes will vary but should contain definitions of the vocabulary words from this lesson and the correct answers.

Review Vocabulary

Complete the following statements on a separate piece of paper. Choose from the Vocabulary list on the left to complete the statements.

1. A reference that does not change when the formula is copied to a new location is a(n) absolute reference. (p. 292)
2. A group of cells is called a(n) range. (p. 284)
3. You can use the NOW function to add the current date and time to a worksheet. (p. 300)
4. The sort buttons can organize cells in ascending or descending order. (p. 285)
5. You cannot change, or adjust an absolute reference. (p. 289)

Vocabulary Activity

6. Create a quiz to review this lesson's Vocabulary words.
   A. On a separate sheet of paper, write the definitions for this lesson's list of Vocabulary words. Do not write the words themselves.
   B. Exchange quizzes with a partner and then take your partner's quiz. Write the correct Vocabulary word beside each definition.
   C. Note any definitions that you did not know and identify the correct answer.

Review Key Concepts

Answer the following questions on a separate piece of paper.

7. Which of the following tabs contains the Filter command? (p. 284)
   A. File
   B. Edit
   C. Insert
   D. Data
8. Which of these buttons would you use to create a formula? (p. 288)
   A. Copy
   B. Insert Function
   C. Sum
   D. Sort Ascending
9. In which of these references will both the column letter and row number change when the formula is copied to a new location? (p. 291)
   A. A1
   B. $A1
   C. A$1
   D. $A$1
10. Which of these functions calculates the monthly payment on a loan? (p. 300)
    A. SUM
    B. IF
    C. PMT
    D. COUNTA

Step-By-Step

1. In Access, choose **Office> Open**. Locate the data file **Warehouse.accdb**.
2. Ask your teacher how to copy the **Warehouse** database to your folder before working in it.
3. Open your **Warehouse** file. Choose **Create> Other>Query Wizard** (see Figure 2.44).
4. Make sure the **Simple Query Wizard** option is selected. Click **OK**.
5. In the **Simple Query Wizard** dialog box, under **Tables/Queries**, click the drop-down arrow and select **Table: Customer**.
6. Under **Available Fields**, double-click **CustomerName**, **City**, and **State**.
7. **CHECK** Your dialog box should look like Figure 2.45. Note that the fields you double-clicked have moved to the **Selected Fields** list.
8. Click **Next**. Leave **Customer Query** as the title for your query and click **Finish**.

Continued on the next page.

EXERCISE 2-17
Create Queries

Queries, unlike table Datasheet Views, do not always show all fields and all rows. The Query Wizard creates a query that shows the fields you choose in the order you want. The wizard also helps you to create queries that will find records with duplicate fields or records that have no related records in another table. You can also create a query in Design View.

FIGURE 2.44 Queries selected in Objects list

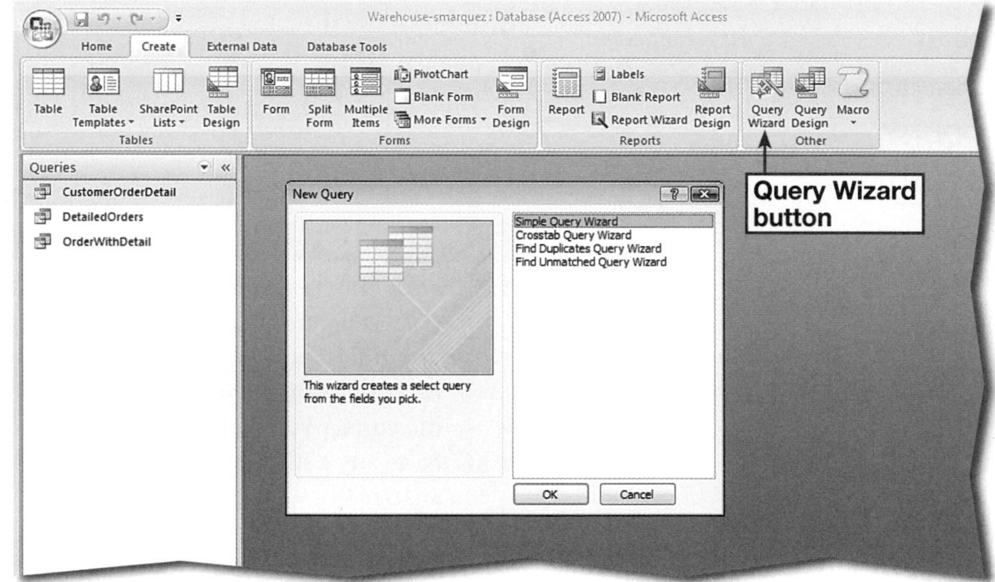

FIGURE 2.45 Simple Query Wizard dialog box

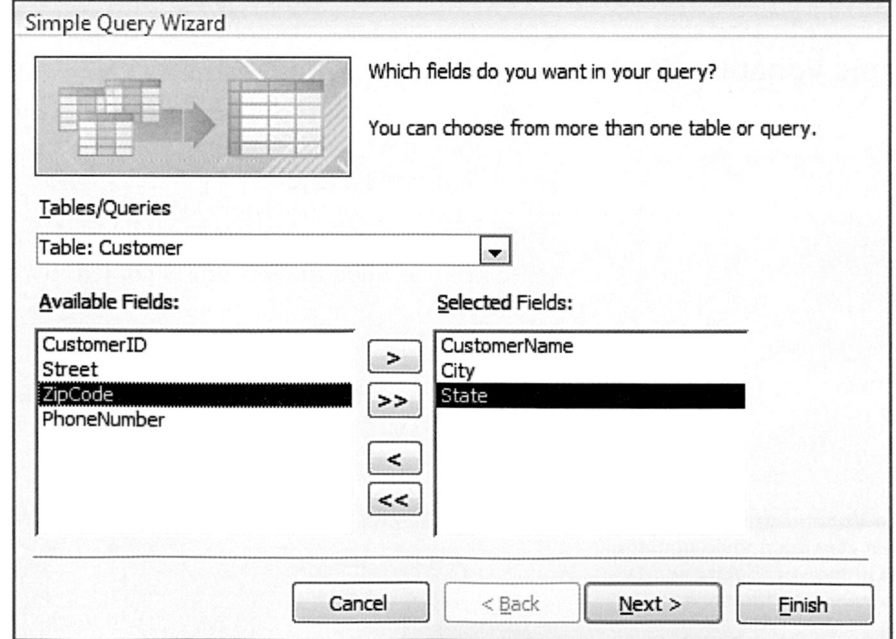

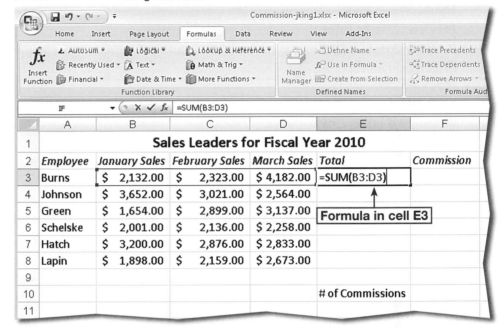

LESSON 4 Practice It Activities

1. Create, Copy, and Paste Formulas

Data File

Follow the steps to complete the activity.

Step-By-Step

1. Open the data file **Commission.xlsx**. Save as: Commission [your first initial and last name]1.
2. Click cell **E3**.
3. Key: =SUM(B3:D3).
4. CHECK Your screen should look like Figure 4.40.
5. Press ENTER. Press the up arrow. Cell **E3** should be selected.
6. Click **Copy**.
7. Select cells **E3** through **E8**.
8. Click **Paste**.
9. CHECK Your screen should look like Figure 4.41.
10. Save and close your file.

Solution The solution file for this activity is **Commission1-6F.xlsx**.

Differentiated Instruction/ Advanced Students Encourage students to think of other spreadsheets in which they could copy and paste formulas.

FIGURE 4.40 Creating a formula

Commission-jking1.xlsx - Microsoft Excel

IF =SUM(B3:D3)

	A	B	C	D	E	F
1	Sales Leaders for Fiscal Year 2010					
2	*Employee*	*January Sales*	*February Sales*	*March Sales*	*Total*	*Commission*
3	Burns	$ 2,132.00	$ 2,323.00	$ 4,182.00	=SUM(B3:D3)	
4	Johnson	$ 3,652.00	$ 3,021.00	$ 2,564.00		
5	Green	$ 1,654.00	$ 2,899.00	$ 3,137.00		
6	Schelske	$ 2,001.00	$ 2,136.00	$ 2,258.00		
7	Hatch	$ 3,200.00	$ 2,876.00	$ 2,833.00		
8	Lapin	$ 1,898.00	$ 2,159.00	$ 2,673.00		
9						
10					# of Commissions	
11						

Formula in cell E3

FIGURE 4.41 Pasted formula

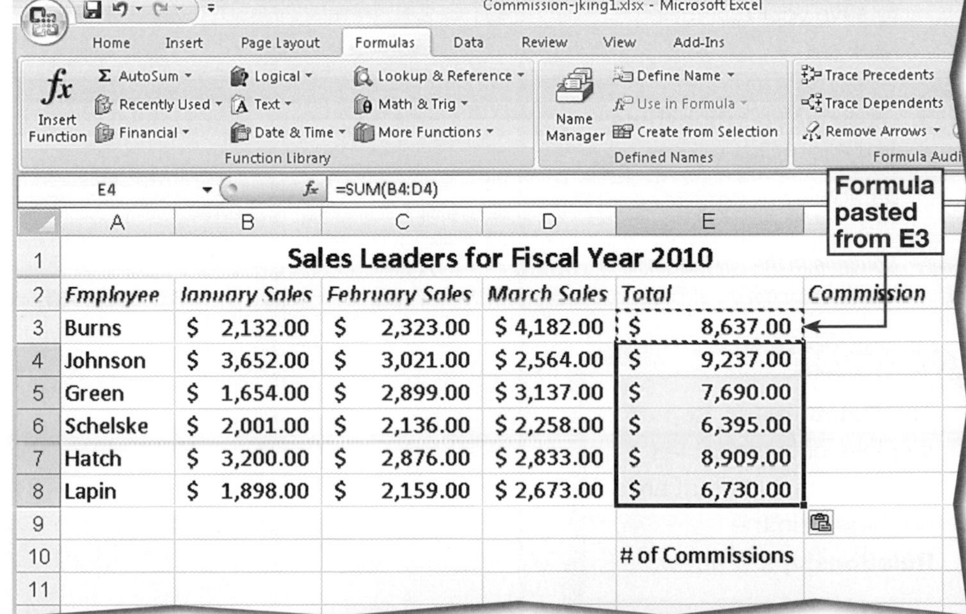

	A	B	C	D	E	F
1	Sales Leaders for Fiscal Year 2010					
2	*Employee*	*January Sales*	*February Sales*	*March Sales*	*Total*	*Commission*
3	Burns	$ 2,132.00	$ 2,323.00	$ 4,182.00	$ 8,637.00	
4	Johnson	$ 3,652.00	$ 3,021.00	$ 2,564.00	$ 9,237.00	
5	Green	$ 1,654.00	$ 2,899.00	$ 3,137.00	$ 7,690.00	
6	Schelske	$ 2,001.00	$ 2,136.00	$ 2,258.00	$ 6,395.00	
7	Hatch	$ 3,200.00	$ 2,876.00	$ 2,833.00	$ 8,909.00	
8	Lapin	$ 1,898.00	$ 2,159.00	$ 2,673.00	$ 6,730.00	
9						
10					# of Commissions	
11						

Step-By-Step

1. In your **Depot** file, choose **Design>Tools> Relationship Report** .

2. **CHECK** Your screen should look like Figure 2.42. The report is in **Print Preview**. Choose **Print Preview>Print** . The **Print** dialog box opens.

3. In the **Name** box, click the **drop-down arrow** to select a printer. Ask your teacher which printer to use. With your teacher's permission, click **OK** to print the report.

4. Click **Close Print Preview** .

5. **CHECK** Your screen should look like Figure 2.43. Click **Close** to close **Report1**. When asked to save your changes, click **No**.

6. Close the **Relationships** window. Close your **Depot** database.

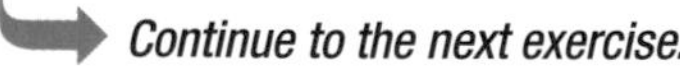
Continue to the next exercise.

Troubleshooter

The **Relationship Report** displays only the tables and relationships that are not hidden in the **Relationships** window.

EXERCISE 2-16
Print Table Relationships

Relationships between database objects can become confusing. Sometimes it can be helpful to have a printed copy of the relationships available. You can print the table relationships from the Relationships window with a Relationship Report.

Solution Use the file **Depot-SF.accdb** as a solution file for Exercises 2-5 through 2-16.

FIGURE 2.42 Relationship Report Print Preview

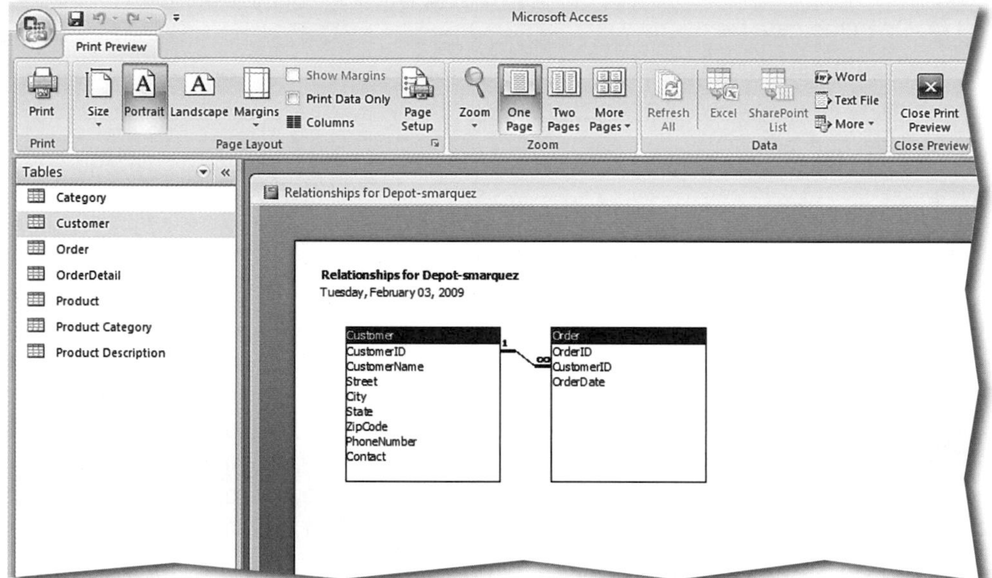

Teaching Tip Have students navigate the report to the **Print Preview** window and print a Landscape version of the relationship report.

FIGURE 2.43 Report1 page

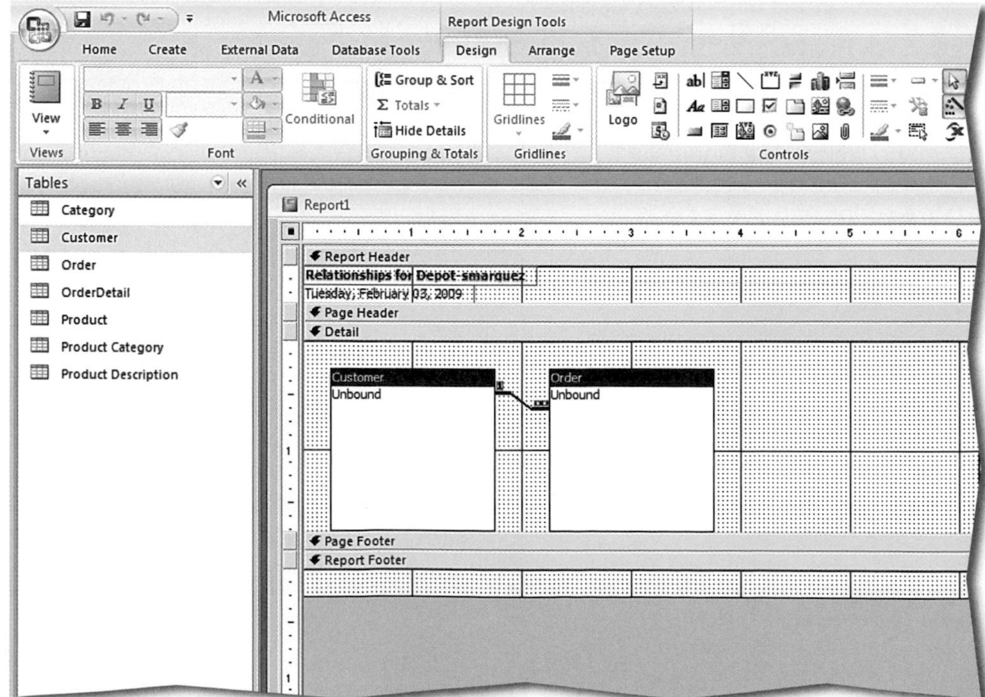

LESSON 4 Practice It Activities

2. Create a Formula and Use the Count Numbers Function

Follow the steps to complete the activity. You must complete Practice It Activity 1 before doing this activity. **New Student Strategy** If a student did not complete Practice It Activity 1, then the solution for that activity can be used as a data file for this activity.

Step-By-Step

1. Open your **Commission-1** file. Save as: Commission-[your first initial and last name]2.
2. In cell **F3**, key: =E3*.06. Press ENTER.
3. Press the up arrow. Click **Copy**.
4. Select cells **F4** through **F8**. Click **Paste**.
5. CHECK Your screen should look like Figure 4.42.
6. Select cell **F10**. Click the **Sum** drop-down arrow. Click **Count Numbers**.
7. Select cells **F3:F8**. Press ENTER. With cell **F10** selected, choose **Home>Accounting**. Click the **$** drop-down arrow and select **More Accounting Formats**.
8. In the **Format Cells** dialog box, choose **General**. Click **OK**.
9. CHECK Your screen should look like Figure 4.43.
10. Save and close your file.

FIGURE 4.42 Calculating 6% commission

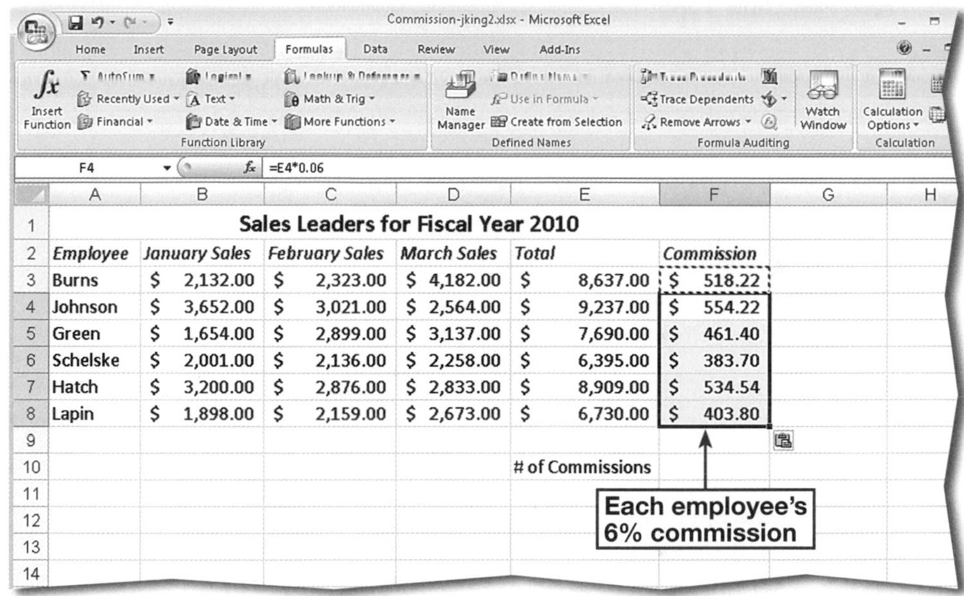

	A	B	C	D	E	F
1			Sales Leaders for Fiscal Year 2010			
2	Employee	January Sales	February Sales	March Sales	Total	Commission
3	Burns	$ 2,132.00	$ 2,323.00	$ 4,182.00	$ 8,637.00	$ 518.22
4	Johnson	$ 3,652.00	$ 3,021.00	$ 2,564.00	$ 9,237.00	$ 554.22
5	Green	$ 1,654.00	$ 2,899.00	$ 3,137.00	$ 7,690.00	$ 461.40
6	Schelske	$ 2,001.00	$ 2,136.00	$ 2,258.00	$ 6,395.00	$ 383.70
7	Hatch	$ 3,200.00	$ 2,876.00	$ 2,833.00	$ 8,909.00	$ 534.54
8	Lapin	$ 1,898.00	$ 2,159.00	$ 2,673.00	$ 6,730.00	$ 403.80
10					# of Commissions	

FIGURE 4.43 Commission count

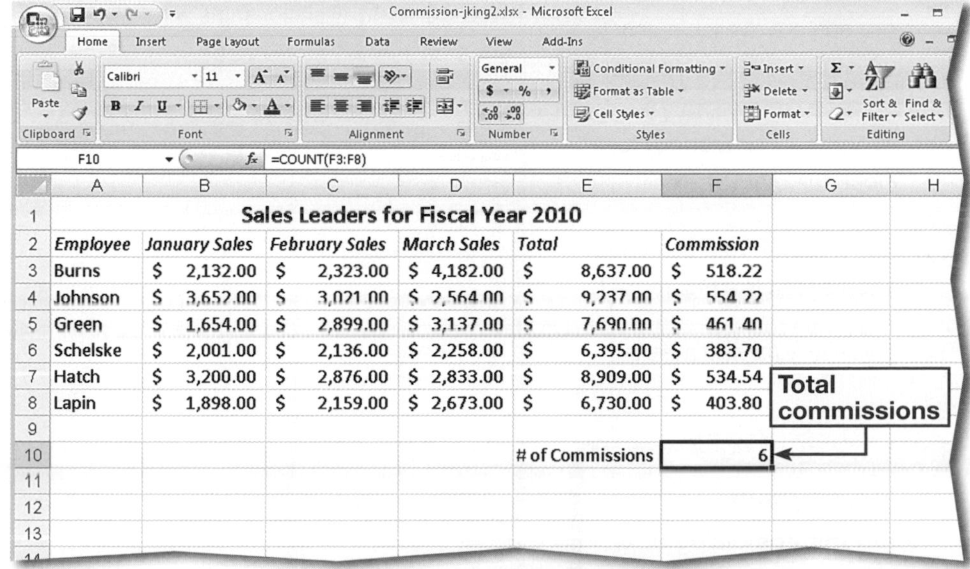

	A	B	C	D	E	F
1			Sales Leaders for Fiscal Year 2010			
2	Employee	January Sales	February Sales	March Sales	Total	Commission
3	Burns	$ 2,132.00	$ 2,323.00	$ 4,182.00	$ 8,637.00	$ 518.22
4	Johnson	$ 3,652.00	$ 3,021.00	$ 2,564.00	$ 9,237.00	$ 554.22
5	Green	$ 1,654.00	$ 2,899.00	$ 3,137.00	$ 7,690.00	$ 461.40
6	Schelske	$ 2,001.00	$ 2,136.00	$ 2,258.00	$ 6,395.00	$ 383.70
7	Hatch	$ 3,200.00	$ 2,876.00	$ 2,833.00	$ 8,909.00	$ 534.54
8	Lapin	$ 1,898.00	$ 2,159.00	$ 2,673.00	$ 6,730.00	$ 403.80
10					# of Commissions	6

Solution The solution file for this activity is **Commission2-SF.xlsx**.

Step-By-Step

1 In your **Depot** file, double-click the relationship line between the **Order** and **Customer** tables to open the **Edit Relationships** dialog box. In the dialog box, click **Join Type**.

2 CHECK Your screen should look like Figure 2.40.

3 The **Join Properties** dialog box lets you control the related information in the tables. Leave the first option selected. Click **OK**.

4 In the **Edit Relationships** box under **Enforce Referential Integrity** are two **Cascade** options. Deselect the **Enforce Referential Integrity** check box.

5 Notice that the **Cascade** options are available only when the relationship has enforced referential integrity. Click **Cancel** to close the dialog box.

6 CHECK Your screen should look like Figure 2.41.

Continue to the next exercise.

Shortcuts

To open the **Edit Relationships** dialog box, choose **Design>Tools> Edit Relationships**.

EXERCISE 2-15
Modify Relationships

There are a few other ways to modify relationships to ensure that data is not lost, duplicated, or garbled. For example, to modify the way the information in tables is linked, use the Join option. To control how data is added or deleted in related fields, use the Cascade Update and Cascade Delete options.

FIGURE 2.40 Join Properties dialog box

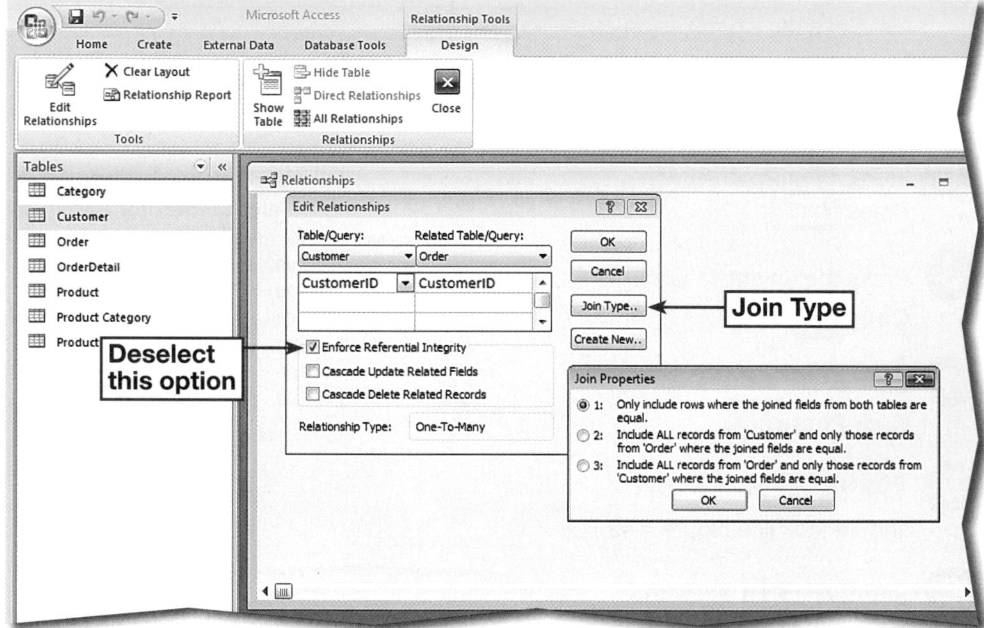

Step-By-Step Tip In **Step 1**, reinforce to students that double-clicking the relationship line in the **Relationships** window is another way to open the **Edit Relationships** dialog box.

FIGURE 2.41 Relationships window

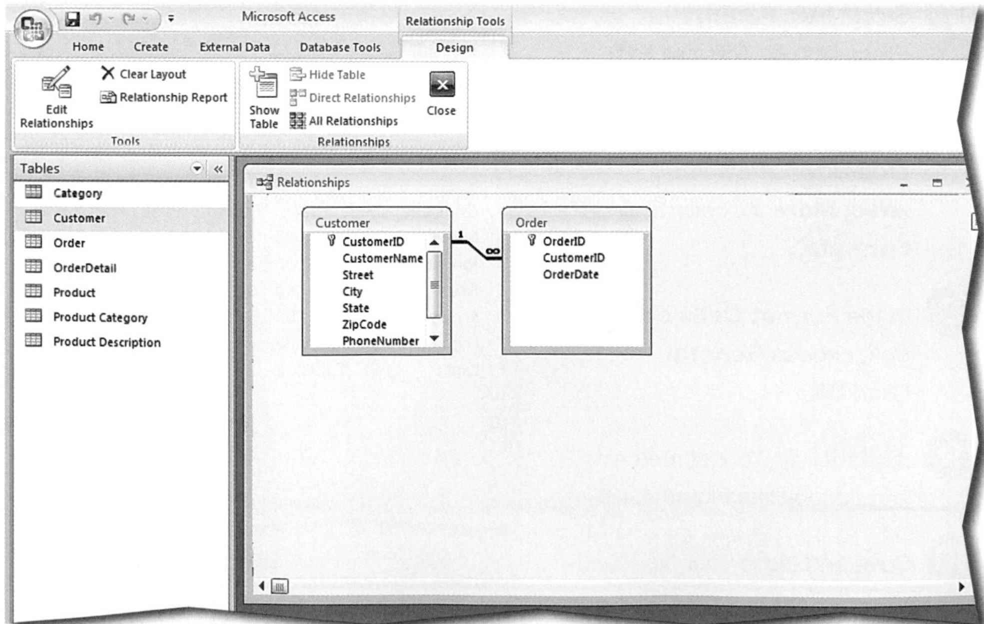

LESSON 4 Practice It Activities

3. Create, Modify, and Position a Chart

Step-By-Step

1 Open your **Commission-2** file. Save as: Commission-[your first initial and last name]3.

2 Select the range **A2:B8**. Choose **Insert>Charts> Column**. Under **2-D Column**, choose **Clustered Column** (see Figure 4.44).

3 With the chart still selected, choose **Layout>Labels> Axis Titles.** Select **Primary Horizontal Axis Title>Title Below Axis**. In the **Horizontal (Category) Axis Title** box, key: Employee. Press ENTER.

4 Choose **Axis Titles> Primary Vertical Axis Title>Rotated Title**. In the **Vertical (Value) Axis Title** box, key: Sales (Dollars). Press ENTER.

5 Use the sizing handles to make the chart bigger. Position the chart below the data in your worksheet.

6 CHECK Your screen should look like Figure 4.45. Save and close your file.

Solution The solution file for this activity is **Commission3-SF.xlsx**.

Follow the steps to complete the activity. You must complete Practice It Activity 2 before doing this activity. **New Student Strategy** If a student did not complete Practice It Activity 2, then the solution for that activity can be used as a data file for this activity.

FIGURE 4.44 Column drop-down menu

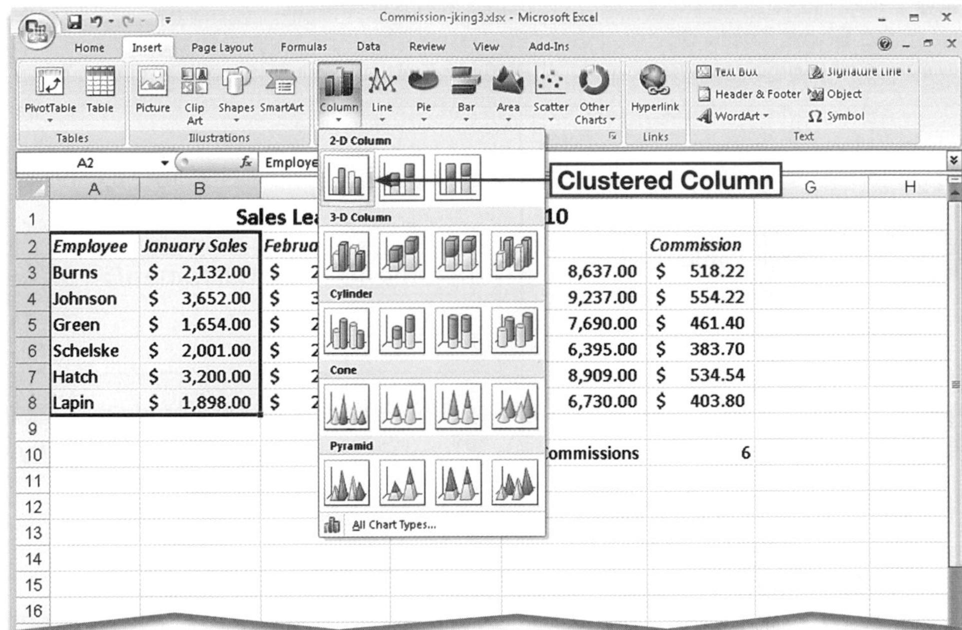

FIGURE 4.45 Completed chart

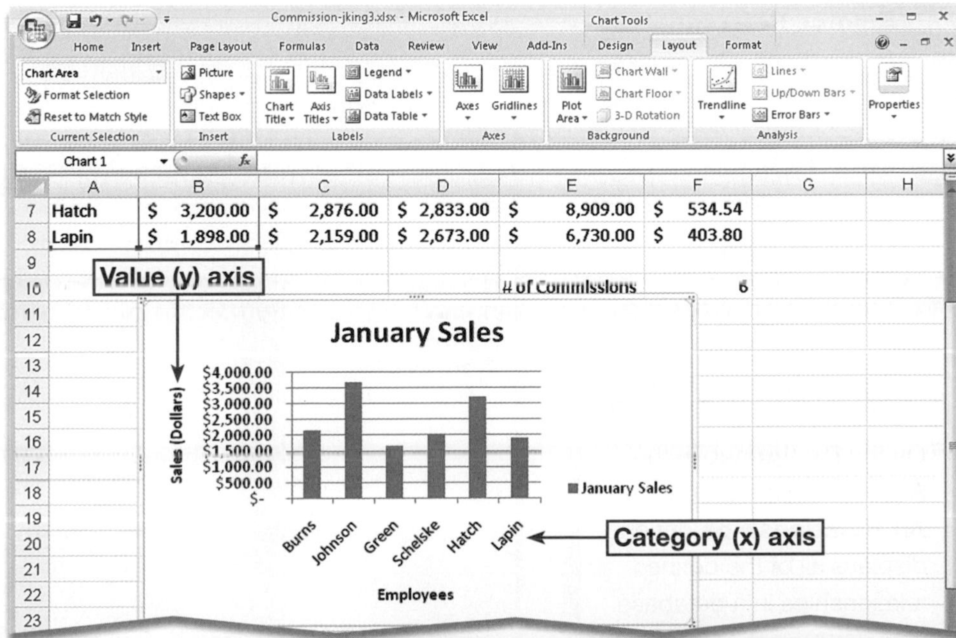

Step-By-Step

1. In your **Depot** file, open the **Relationships** window by choosing **Database Tools>Show/Hide Relationships**.
2. Click **Show Table**. In the **Show Table** dialog box, click **Customer**. Click **Add** to add the **Customer** table to the **Relationships** window.
3. In the **Show Table** dialog box, click **Order**. Click **Add**. Close the **Show Table** dialog box.
4. Drag the **CustomerID** field from the **Customer** table and drop it in the **CustomerID** field in the **Order** table.
5. In the **Edit Relationships** dialog box, click the **Enforce Referential Integrity** check box (see Figure 2.38). Click **Create**.
6. **CHECK** Your screen should look like Figure 2.39. Click **Save**.

Continue to the next exercise.

You Should Know

On the **Design** tab in the **Relationships** group, the **All Relationships** option displays all of the defined relationships in a database.

EXERCISE 2-14
Enforce Referential Integrity in a Relationship

Data must be complete in order for a database to be useful. For example, an order must specify which customer is making a purchase. That customer must exist in the database. The Order table and the Customer table have a relationship based on the customer who made the order. **Referential integrity** makes sure that the related data in two tables always exists and is complete.

Step-By-Step Tip In **Step 4**, show students how to drag a field from one table and drop it onto another. The technique is similar in other Office 2007 software.

FIGURE 2.38 Edit Relationships dialog box

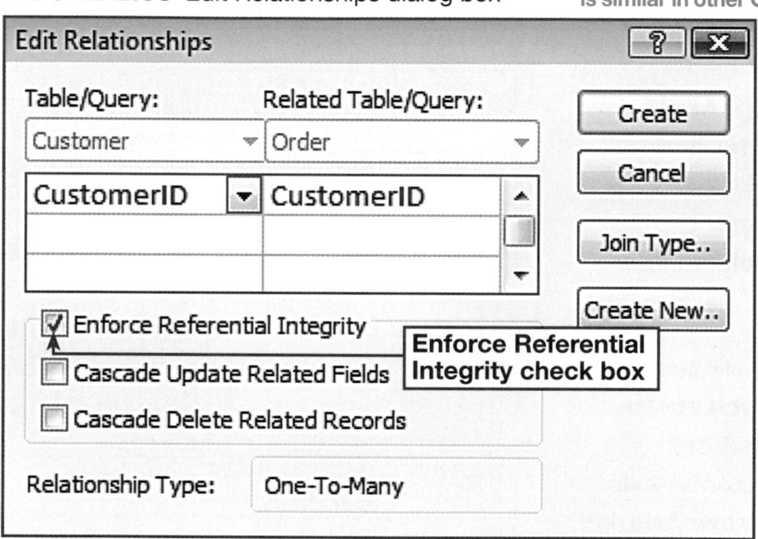

FIGURE 2.39 Relationships window with referential integrity

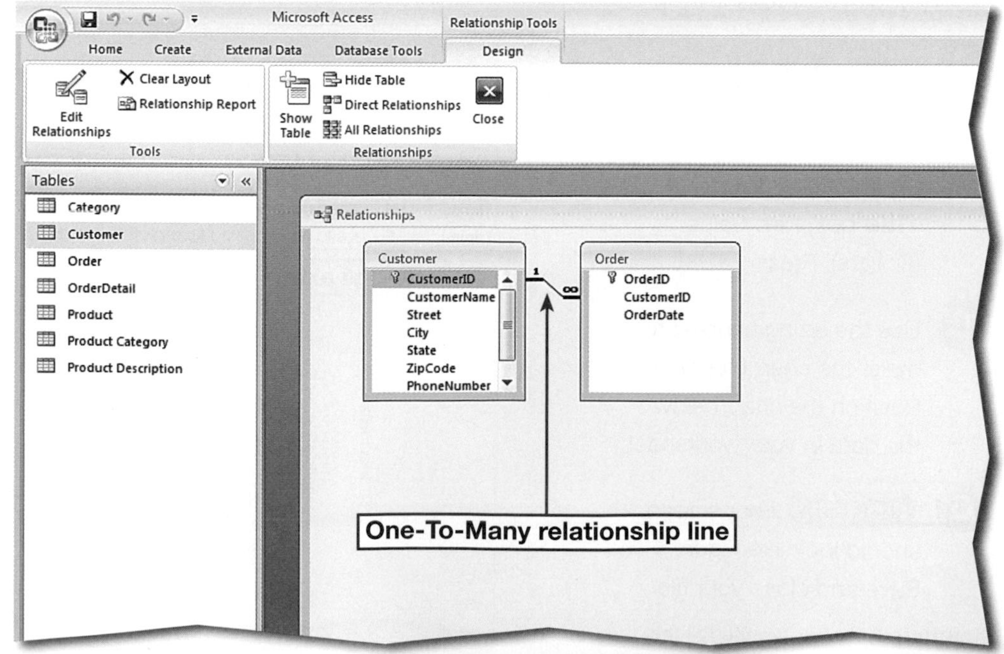

LESSON 4 You Try It Activities

Step-By-Step

1. Open the data file **Homework.xlsx**. Save as: Homework-[your first initial and last name]4.
2. In cells **B2:F2**, enter the amount of time (in hours) you want to study each day for Week 1.
3. In cells **B3:F3**, enter the amount of time (in hours) you want to study each day for Week 2.
4. In cell **G2**, write a formula to find the total study time for Week 1 (see Figure 4.46).
5. Copy the formula from cell **G2** and paste it into cell **G3**.
6. In cell **H1**, key: Average.
7. Use **SUM** to put the average number of hours per day you want to study in Week 1 in cell H2, and the **AVG** for Week 2 in cell H3.
8. **CHECK** Your screen should look similar to Figure 4.47.
9. Save and close your file.

4. Make a Study Schedule

Data File

Think about how much time you have after school each day to study. Be realistic about how much time you schedule for yourself. For instance, you probably need to schedule less study time on days when you have after-school activities. You can use Excel to track your study time.

Solution The solution file for this activity is **Homework4-SF.xlsx**.

FIGURE 4.46 Homework total

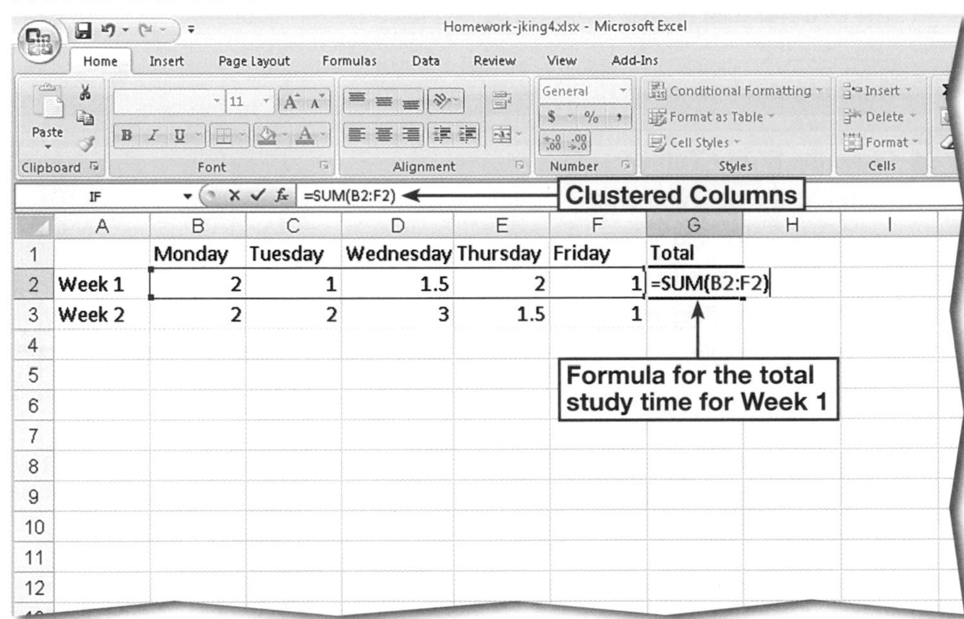

FIGURE 4.47 Average hours per day

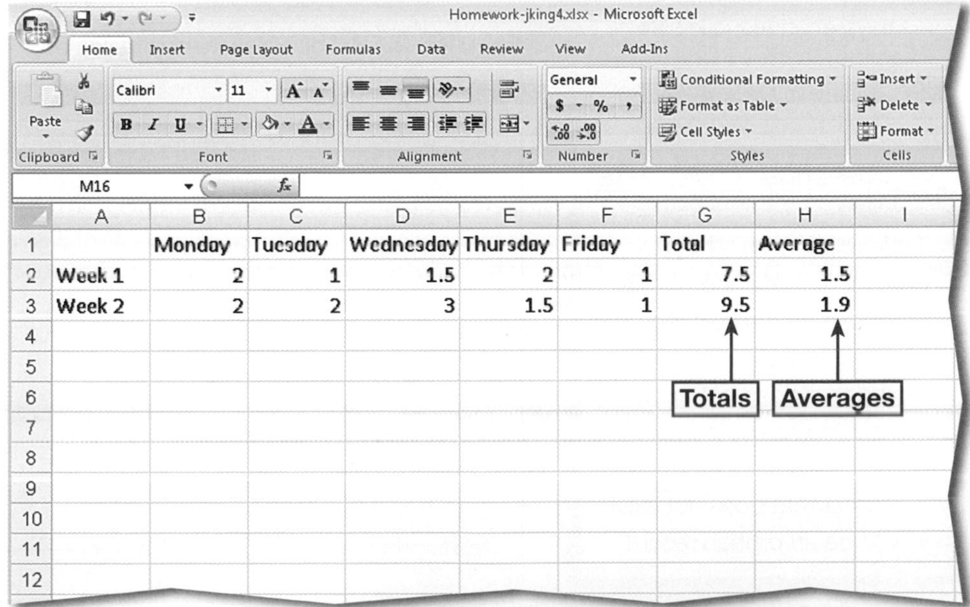

Step-By-Step

1. In your **Depot** file, click **Show Table** . In the **Show Table** dialog box, on the **Tables** tab, select **OrderDetail**. Click **Add**.

2. CHECK Your screen should look like Figure 2.36. The **OrderDetail** table is shown in the **Relationships** window.

3. Close the **Show Table** dialog box. Select and drag the **ProductID** field in the **OrderDetail** table to the **ProductID** field in the **Product** table.

4. Notice that in the **Edit Relationships** dialog box, this relationship is **One-To-Many** (see Figure 2.37). Click **Cancel**.

5. Close the **Relationships** window. When prompted to save changes, click **No**.

Continue to the next exercise.

You Should Know

Table relationships help to prevent orphan records in a database. An *orphan record* has a reference to another record that does not exist. For example, a customer order that references a customer that does not exist would be an orphan record.

EXERCISE 2-13
Create and Modify One-to-Many Relationships

In the Depot file, the Product table contains all the details about the items ordered in the OrderDetail table. The common field that relates the two tables is the ProductID field. Because one record in the Product table describes many items in the OrderDetail table, the tables have a one-to-many relationship.

FIGURE 2.36 OrderDetail table in Relationships window

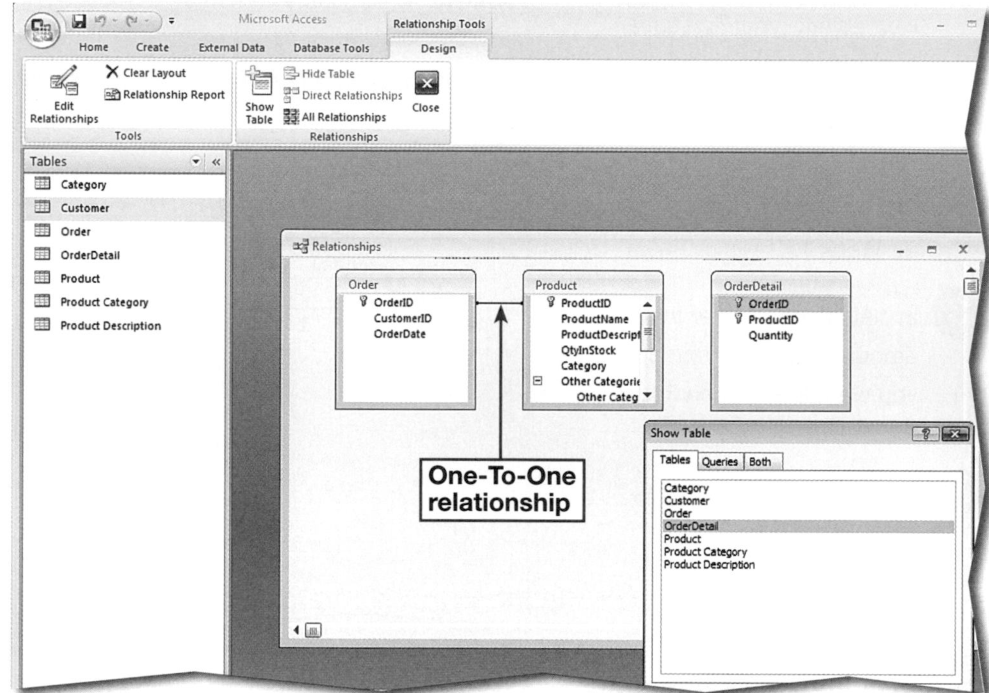

FIGURE 2.37 Edit Relationships dialog box

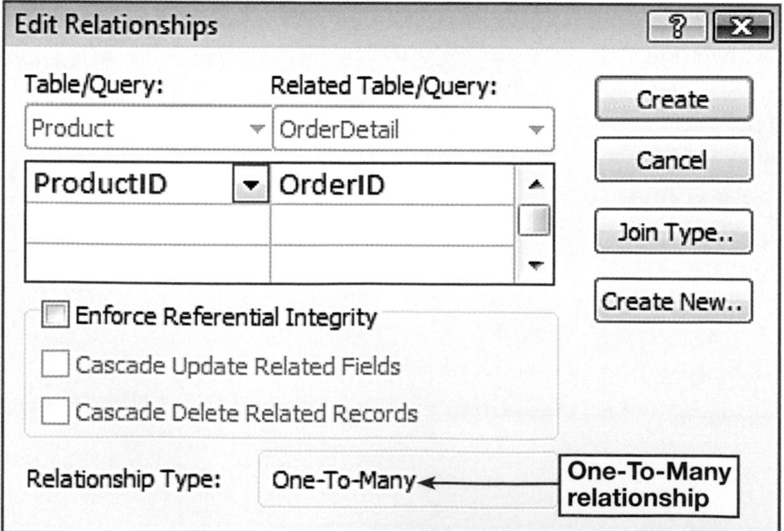

LESSON 4 You Try It Activities

5. Make a Study Chart

You want to compare how many hours you will study each day in Week 1 and in Week 2. The best way to do this is to create a bar graph for each week. You must complete You Try It Activity 4 before starting this activity.

New Student Strategy If a student did not complete You Try It Activity 4, then the solution for that activity can be used as a data file for this activity.

Step-By-Step

1. Open your **Homework-4** file. Save as: Homework-[your first initial and last name]5.
2. Select the range **A1:F3**.
3. Use the **Chart Tools** to create a clustered column graph that shows how many hours you will study each day of Week 1 and Week 2.
4. Title the chart **Homework Schedule**. Name the horizontal axis **Day** and name the vertical axis **Time (Hours)** (see Figure 4.48).
5. Position the chart below the schedule. Adjust the size of the chart so that it is readable.
6. **CHECK** Your screen should look similar to Figure 4.49.
7. Save and close your file.

FIGURE 4.48 Chart with axis information

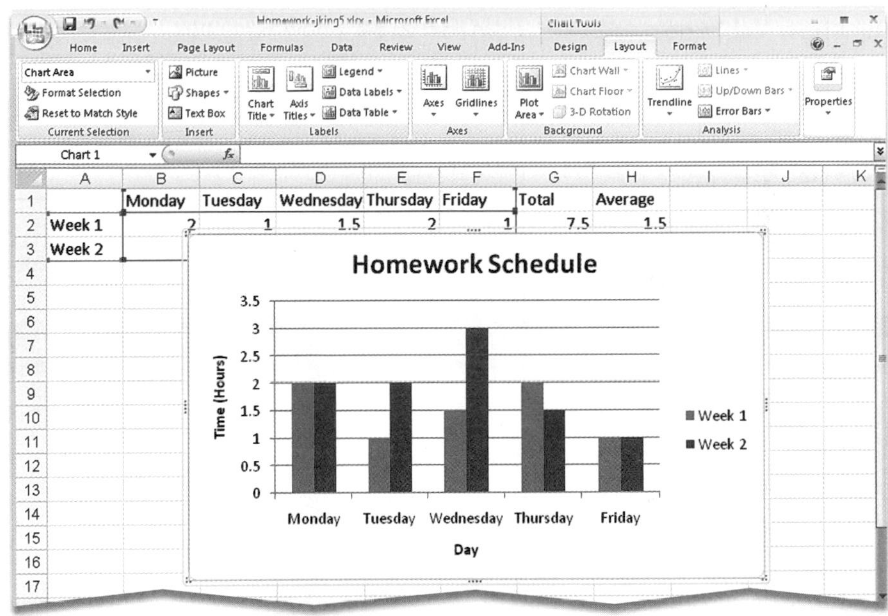

FIGURE 4.49 Completed chart

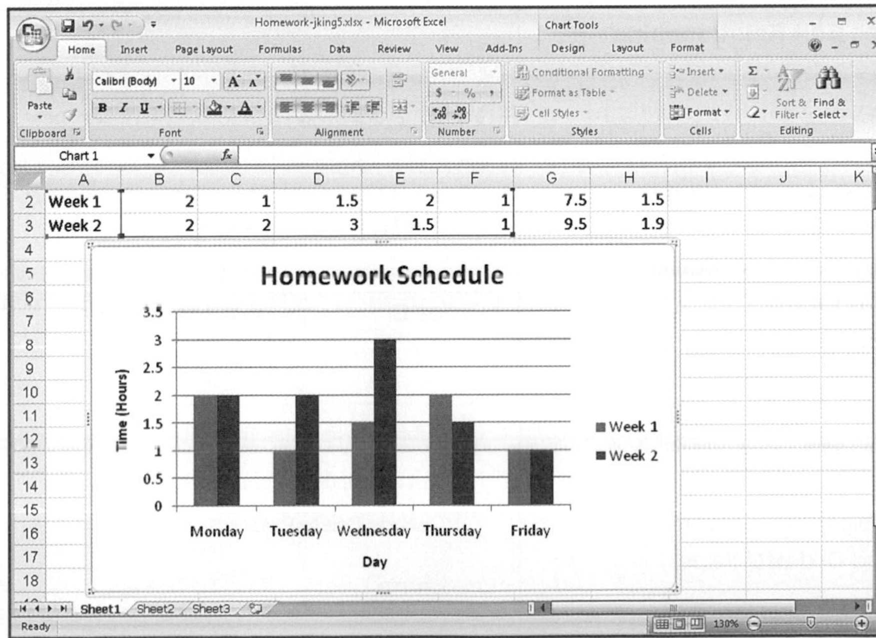

Solution The solution file for this activity is **Homework5-SF.xlsx**.

Step-By-Step

1. In your **Depot** file, choose **Database Tools>Show/Hide>Relationships**. The **Relationships** window opens. Choose **Design>Relationships>Show Table**.

2. The **Show Table** box allows you to add tables to the **Relationships** window to create new relationships. In the **Show Table** box, select **Order**. Click **Add**. Add the **Product** table.

3. **CHECK** Your screen should look like Figure 2.34. Close the **Show Table** dialog box. In the **Order** table in the **Relationships** window, select the **OrderID** field and drag it to the **ProductID** field in the **Product** table.

4. The **Edit Relationships** dialog box opens (see Figure 2.35). At the bottom of the box, note that the **Relationship Type** is **One-To-One**. This is because the **OrderID** and **ProductID** fields are both unique in each table.

5. Click **Create**. The black line denotes a one-to-one relationship between the tables at the **ProductID** and **OrderID** fields.

Continue to the next exercise.

EXERCISE 2-12
Create and Modify One-to-One Relationships

A **relationship** is a link between two tables based on a common field. Access is a relational database because it lets you define these relationships as part of the database structure. A one-to-one relationship means that both fields in their respective tables are not repeated. For example, a one-to-one relationship could be created between a student in one table and his or her guardian in another table.

FIGURE 2.34 Show Table box

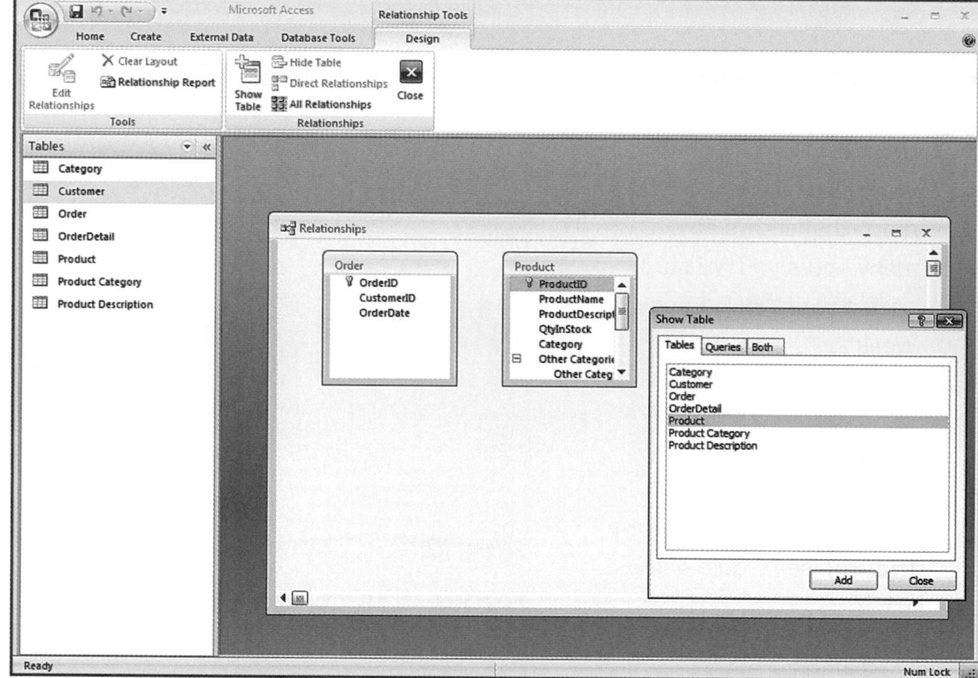

FIGURE 2.35 Edit Relationships dialog box

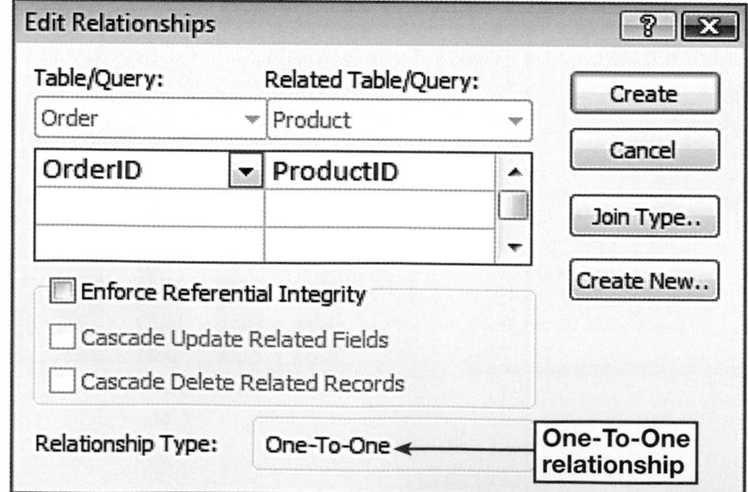

Beyond the Classroom Activity Students' worksheets should look similar to solution file **e4rev6-SF.xlsx**.

Standards at Work Activity Students' final files should look like the solution file **e4rev7-SF.xlsx.**

21st Century Skills Activity Students' worksheets should look similar to solution file **e4rev8-SF.xlsx.**

NCLB/Math (Number and Operations) To reinforce students' understanding of meanings and operations and how they relate to one another, ask students to calculate and include the grand total for all four weeks.

6. Beyond the Classroom Activity

Math: Create an Income Sheet Each week you earn money doing the following chores for your neighbors:

- For sweeping one neighbor's sidewalk and porch, you earn $5.00.
- For mowing another neighbor's lawn, you earn $20.00.
- For cleaning another neighbor's windows, you earn $15.00.

Create a worksheet that has columns for three chores and rows for four weeks. For each week, show the amount you earn for each chore and use the **SUM** function to show how much you earned that week.

Save your worksheet as: e4rev-[your first initial and last name]6.

7. Standards at Work Activity

Microsoft Certified Application Specialist Correlation
Excel 4.1 *Create and Format Charts*

Create a Column Chart Your supervisor has asked you to create a clustered column chart comparing January and February sales in your **Books** file.

Open the latest version of your **Books** file. Save it as: e4rev-[your first initial and last name]7. Select cells **A1:C10**. Use the **Chart Tools** to create a **Clustered Column** chart. Enlarge the chart and position it so that it does not cover the data in your worksheet.

8. 21st Century Skills Activity

Design an Academic Calendar One way to manage your time well is to create a calendar to schedule your schoolwork. Imagine that you have a five-page English paper due in two weeks. Use Excel to create a schedule for working on your English paper. Your schedule should include the following steps:

A. Research
B. Write a draft
C. Edit the draft
D. Write a final draft

Remember that you have five pages to write. Make sure you schedule all ten weekdays in the two weeks you have to finish the paper. Give yourself at least three days to research and at least one day to complete each of the remaining stages of the writing process.

Save your worksheet as: e4rev-[your first initial and last name]8.

Go Online **e-REVIEW**

glencoe.com

Go to the **Online Learning Center** to complete the following review activities.

Online Self Check
To test your knowledge of the material, click **Unit 2> Lesson 4** and choose **Self Checks**.

Interactive Review
To review the main points of the lesson, click **Unit 2> Lesson 4** and choose **Interactive Review.**

Step-By-Step

1. In your **Depot** file, open the **Customer** table in **Design View**.
2. Click the **ZipCode** field.
3. Under **Field Properties**, click in the **Input Mask** box.
4. Click the **Input Mask Builder** [...] button.
5. **CHECK** Your screen should look like Figure 2.32.
6. In the **Input Mask Wizard** dialog box, click **Zip Code**.
7. Click **Finish**.
8. **CHECK** Your screen should look like Figure 2.33.
9. Save and close the datasheet.

Continue to the next exercise.

Tech Tip

To see what each mask character does, search **Access Help** for input mask syntax examples.

Step-By-Step Tip In **Step 4**, point out to students that the **Builder** button for the **Input Mask** box is visible only when the insertion point is in the property field. If students see a dialog box asking them to install this feature, tell them to click **Yes**.

EXERCISE 2-11
Create an Input Mask

You want only accurate data in your database. Applying an **input mask** allows you to specify how you want information such as zip codes and phone numbers to be formatted in your database. For example, you can use an input mask to specify that phone numbers be keyed with the area code first, such as (405) 555-5555 instead of 555-5555. Input masks help to prevent errors by keeping users from entering the wrong types of characters into certain fields.

FIGURE 2.32 Input Mask Wizard dialog box

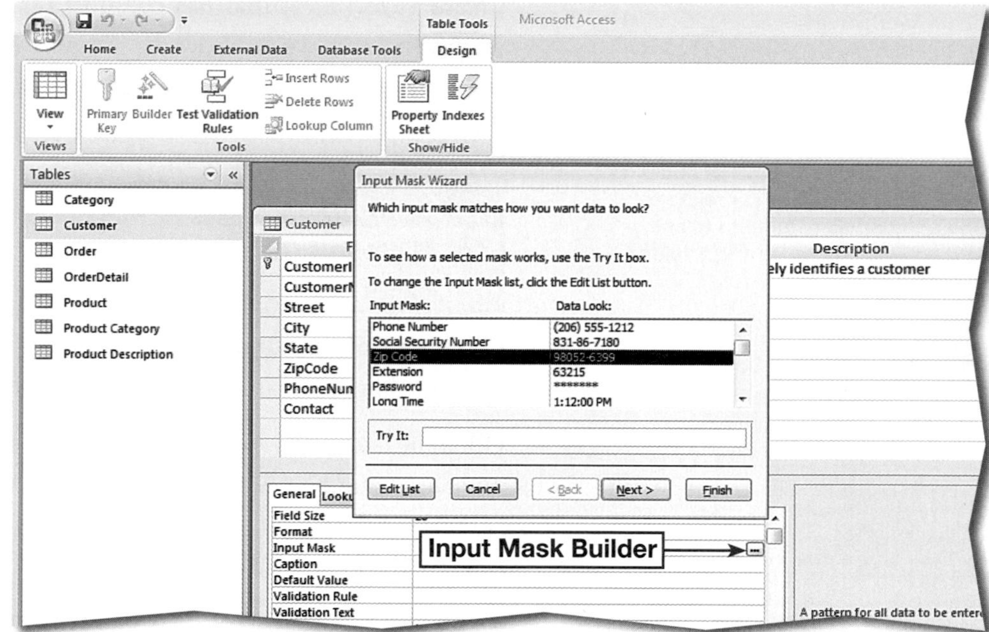

FIGURE 2.33 Input mask for zip code created

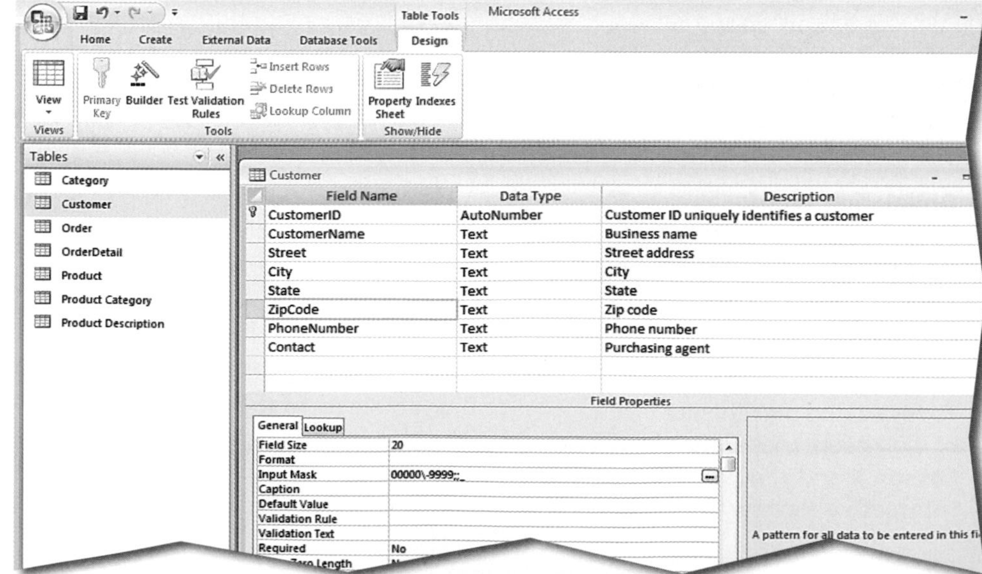

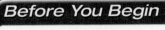

LESSON 4 Challenge Yourself Projects

Before You Begin

Self-Management Use self-management skills to direct your activities and achieve your goals. These projects show you how to use an Excel workbook as an organizational tool to help set and meet your goals.

Reflect Once you complete the projects, open a Word document and answer the following:

1. Describe the factors you considered when designing the schedule.
2. How can you use an Excel schedule to improve your self-management skills?

Answers Rubrics for each Challenge Yourself Project are available at **glencoe.com**. You may want to download the rubrics and make them available to students as they complete each project.

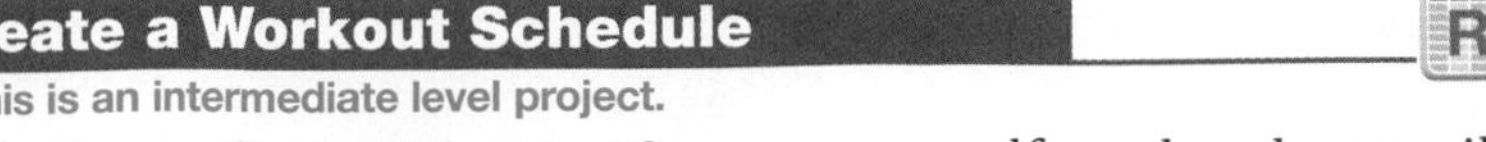

9. Create a Workout Schedule

Rubric R

LEVEL This is an intermediate level project.

Math: Design a Spreadsheet If you are ever self-employed, you will benefit from knowing how to create a workbook. For this project, imagine that you work as a trainer in a gym. Your job is to create a workout schedule for your clients. Each client's schedule must show the following:

- day of the week
- the type of exercise (aerobics, weights, or running)
- the time of day

Solution Students' worksheets should look similar to solution file **e4rev9-SF.xlsx**.

Design a spreadsheet with a column for each day of the week. Include a row for each type of exercise and the time of day. Create a one-week schedule for a client who wants to work out four days a week, three hours each day. Include all three types of exercise.

Save your worksheet as: e4rev-[your first initial and last name]9.

10. Set Hourly Rates

Rubric R

LEVEL This is an intermediate level project.

Math: Create Formulas As a personal trainer, you need to set an hourly rate for each type of exercise. Create a sample training schedule for four days a week, two hours each day. The schedule should include each type of exercise (aerobics, weights, or running).

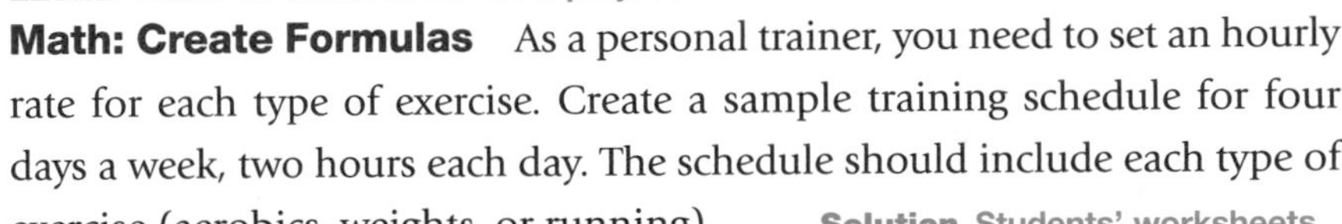

Solution Students' worksheets should look similar to solution file **e4rev10-SF.xlsx**.

Use formulas to calculate:

- cost for each exercise session
- cost for each day
- total cost for the week

Save your worksheet as: e4rev-[your first initial and last name]10.

11. Plan a Discount Program

Rubric R

LEVEL This is an advanced level project.

Math: Use Functions As a personal trainer, you decide to offer a discount program for your clients. Create a sample schedule that includes:

- five days of exercise a week
- each day's workout schedule
- cost for each day

You decide to give clients a 10 percent discount for each day that costs more than $20. Write a formula that will calculate which days receive a discount (Hint: use the **IF** function).

NCLB/Math (Algebra) Have students discuss other uses for the IF function.

Save your worksheet as: e4rev-[your first initial and last name]11.

Solution Students' worksheets should look similar to solution file **e4rev11-SF.xlsx**.

Step-By-Step

EXERCISE 2-10 (Continued)
Create and Modify Attachment Fields

9 CHECK Your screen should look like Figure 2.30.

10 Double-click the **Attachment** field of the **Baseball Glove** record.

11 Click **Add** in the **Attachments** dialog box. Select the first **Baseball Glove** file (with the **.gif** extension) and click **Open**.

12 Click **Add** again and select the second **Baseball Glove** file (with the **.jpeg** extension). Click **Open**.

13 Click **OK** in the **Attachments** dialog box.

14 Double-click the **Baseball Glove Attachment** field. Select the jpeg image **Baseball Glove.jpg** in the **Attachments** dialog box.

15 Click **Remove**. Select the remaining image and click **Save As**.

16 Navigate to the folder containing your **Depot** database file and click **Save**. Click **OK**.

17 CHECK Your screen should look like Figure 2.31. Close the table.

Continue to the next exercise.

FIGURE 2.30 Product table with Baseball attachment

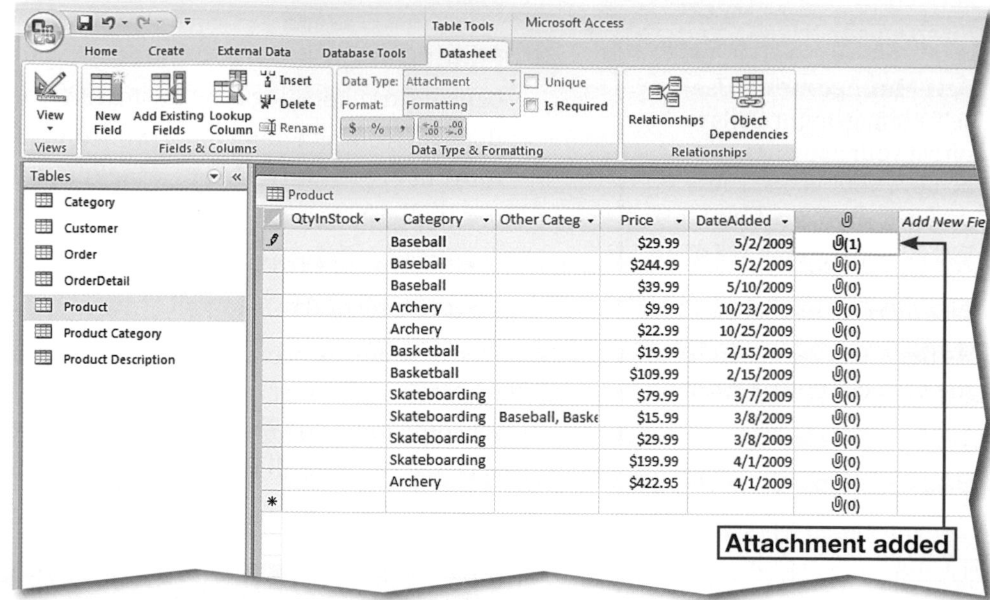

FIGURE 2.31 Product table with Baseball Glove.gif attachment

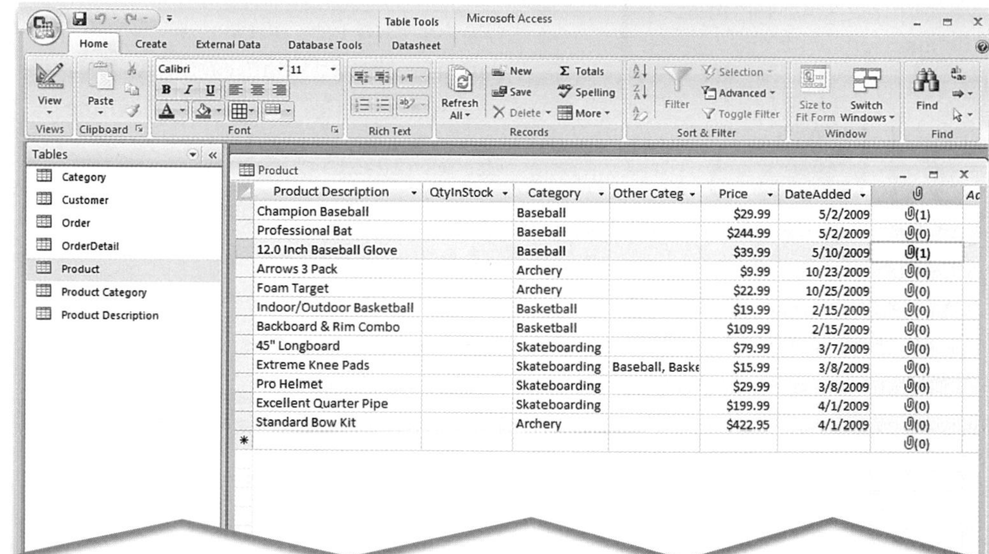

Step-By-Step Tip In **Step 10**, tell students to scroll left if they do not know which attachment field to double-click for the **Baseball Glove** record.

Microsoft Office 2007

You can attach documents only to databases that are created in Office Access 2007. You cannot share attachments between an Office 2007 (.accdb) database and other versions of Access that use the (.mdb) file format.

LESSON 5 Manage Workbooks

Key Concepts

- Use a template
- Organize worksheets
- Split, freeze, hide, and arrange workbooks
- Save and preview worksheets as Web pages
- Set up pages for printing
- Rename folders and convert files to different formats

Standards

The following standards are covered in this lesson. Refer to pages xxv and 715 for a description of the standards listed here.

ISTE Standards Correlation

NETS•S

1a, 1c, 1d, 2b, 2d, 3d, 4a, 4b, 4c, 5a, 5c, 6a, 6b, 6d

Microsoft Certified Application Specialist

Excel

1.4 1.5, 5.4, 5.5

You have learned how to format cells and create formulas. In this lesson, you will learn how to manage workbooks. You will insert, delete, split, and rearrange worksheets. Learning how to split and arrange workbooks will help you manage your work environment. You will also set up a workbook for printing by setting the print area and changing Page Setup options.

21st CENTURY SKILLS

See page TM76 for answer to 21st Century Skills.

Be Honest Honesty is more than just telling the truth. It is also about speaking up in support of your values and opinions. It can also be a trait of a hard-working employee. Honesty is essential for building trust, whether it be with friends or co-workers. If you have a reputation for being an honest person, people will trust you. Trust is an important part of any business or personal relationship. *How has honesty played a role in your week so far?*

Step-By-Step

1. In your **Depot** file, make sure the **Product** table is open. Scroll to the right and select the **Add New Field** column.

2. Choose **Datasheet>Data Type & Formatting**. Click the **Data Type** drop-down arrow and select **Attachment**.

3. **CHECK** Your screen should look like Figure 2.28.

4. To add an attachment to the **Attachment** field of the first record **(Baseball)**, double-click the **Attachment** icon 0(0) in the first row. The **Attachments** dialog box opens (see Figure 2.29).

5. Click **Add** to open the **Choose File** dialog box. Locate the data file **Baseball.gif**. After you find the data file, click **Open**.

6. The **Choose File** dialog box closes, and the **Attachments** dialog box now lists the **Baseball.gif** file.

7. **CHECK** Your screen should look like Figure 2.29.

8. Click **OK**.

Continued on the next page.

EXERCISE 2-10
Create and Modify Attachment Fields

Some forms of information are best presented in their original format, such as images, Word documents, and spreadsheets. An **attachment field** is useful for linking to a database files and other objects that might not fit into one field. For example, multiple illustrations of a company's products would not fit well into the fields of the product table. Access allows you to attach those documents to records in the database so that you can open them by selecting them from their associated records.

Teaching Tip Let students know that to open attachments, they should double-click in the Attachments field, select the attachment in the dialog box, and click Open.

FIGURE 2.28 Product table with Attachment field

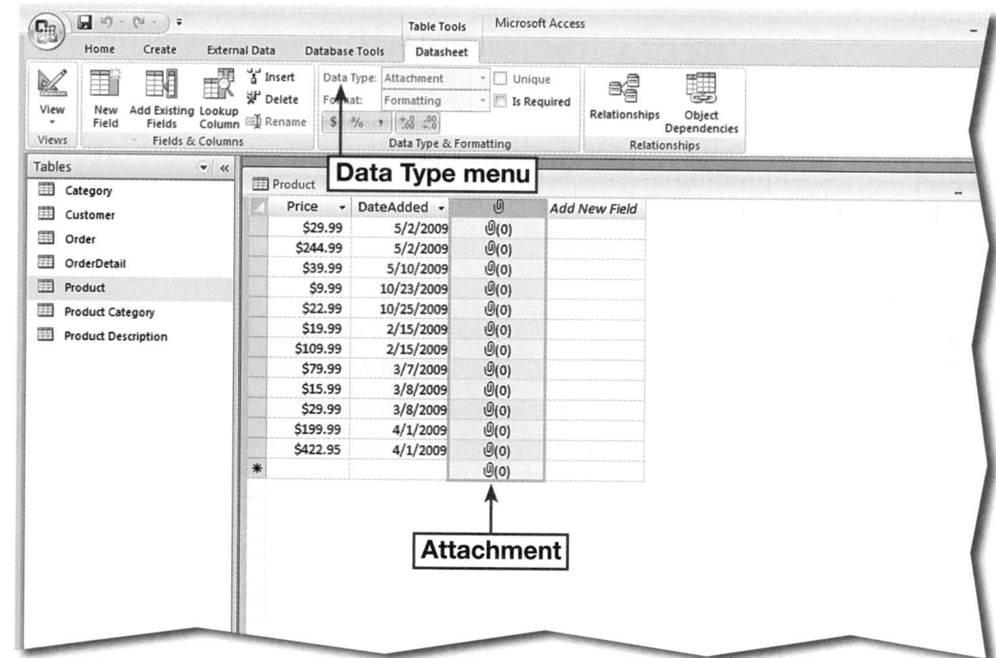

FIGURE 2.29 Attachments dialog box

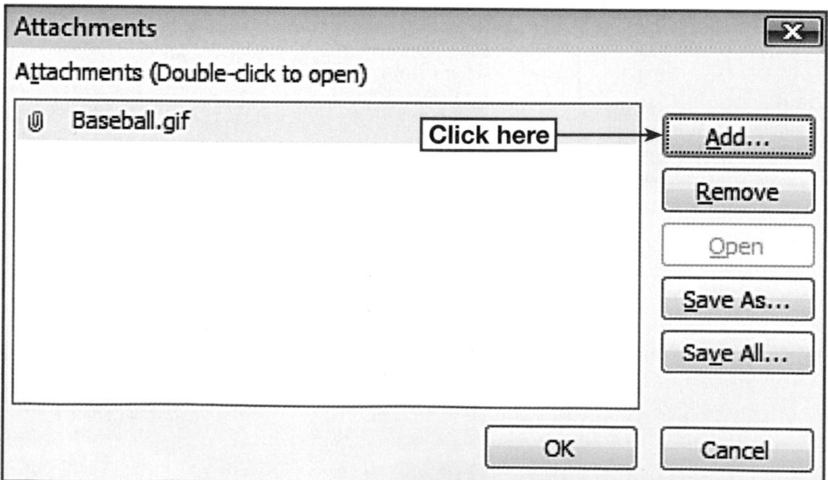

LESSON 5 Reading Guide

Before You Read

See page TM42 for English Learner activity suggestions.

Use Diagrams to Help Understanding As you are reading through this lesson, write down the main idea. Write down any facts, explanations, or examples you find in the exercise. Start at the main idea and draw arrows to the information that directly supports it. Then draw arrows from these examples to any information that supports them.

Read To Learn

- Learn different ways to create and display your Excel files.
- Use templates to improve the usefulness of your worksheets.
- Explore how to use printing options to adjust the margins, create headers and footers, or print specific parts of a page.
- Consider how to convert your Excel files easily into functioning Web pages.
- Insert, delete, and arrange worksheets as needed to keep track of your hours while on the job.

Main Idea

Excel is an excellent tool that provides multiple ways to view data.

Vocabulary

Key Terms

footer
freeze
header
landscape
margin
page break
page orientation
portrait
print area
split
template

Academic Vocabulary

These words appear in your reading and on your tests. Make sure you know their meanings.

arrange
common
convert
locate

Quick Write Activity 

Describe Think about all the individuals in your class. When you turn in completed Excel worksheet assignments, your teacher needs to know whose work belongs to whom. On a separate sheet of paper, list the information you would place on your worksheet so that the teacher can tell your paper apart from your classmates' papers.

Study Skills

Discover How You Learn Some people learn best by seeing diagrams and charts. Others learn best by listening. Know what learning style works best for you and in which situation.

Academic Standards

English Language Arts

NCTE 12 Use language to accomplish individual purposes.

Math

NCTM (Number and Operations) Compute fluently and make reasonable estimates.

NCTM (Algebra) Represent and analyze mathematical situations and structures using algebraic symbols.

NCTM (Representation) Create and use representations to organize, record, and communicate mathematical ideas.

Step-By-Step

EXERCISE 2-9 (Continued)
Create and Modify Multivalued Fields

9 Click **Finish**.

10 **CHECK** Your screen should look like Figure 2.26.

11 Go to the table's **Design View** and click in the **Other Categories** field row selector.

12 While holding the mouse button down, drag the row so that the black line is under the **Category** field.

13 Click **Save** and return to the **Datasheet View**.

14 Click in the **Other Categories** column of the **Knee pads** record, and click the **drop-down arrow**.

15 In the drop-down menu, select **Baseball** and **Basketball**.

16 **CHECK** Your screen should look like Figure 2.27. Click **OK**.

Continue to the next exercise.

Shortcuts

The **View** buttons are toggle buttons. Clicking them switches between **Design View** and **Datasheet View**.

Teaching Tip Discuss with students other uses for multivalued fields in a database.

FIGURE 2.26 Product table with Other Categories

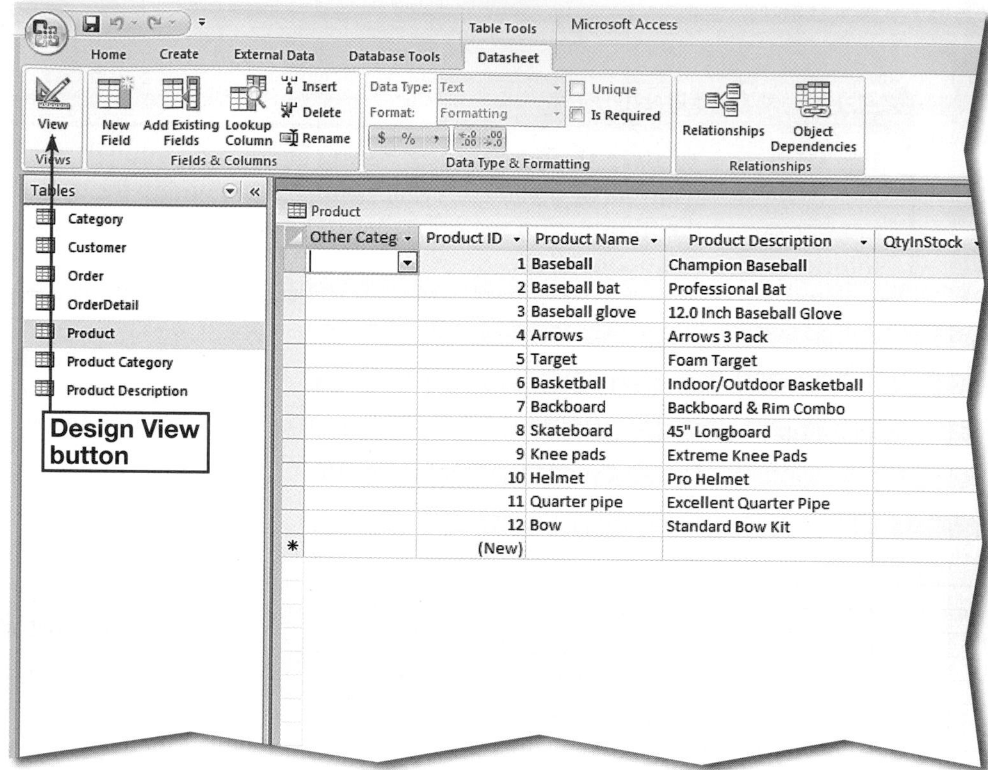

FIGURE 2.27 Product table with edited Other Categories column

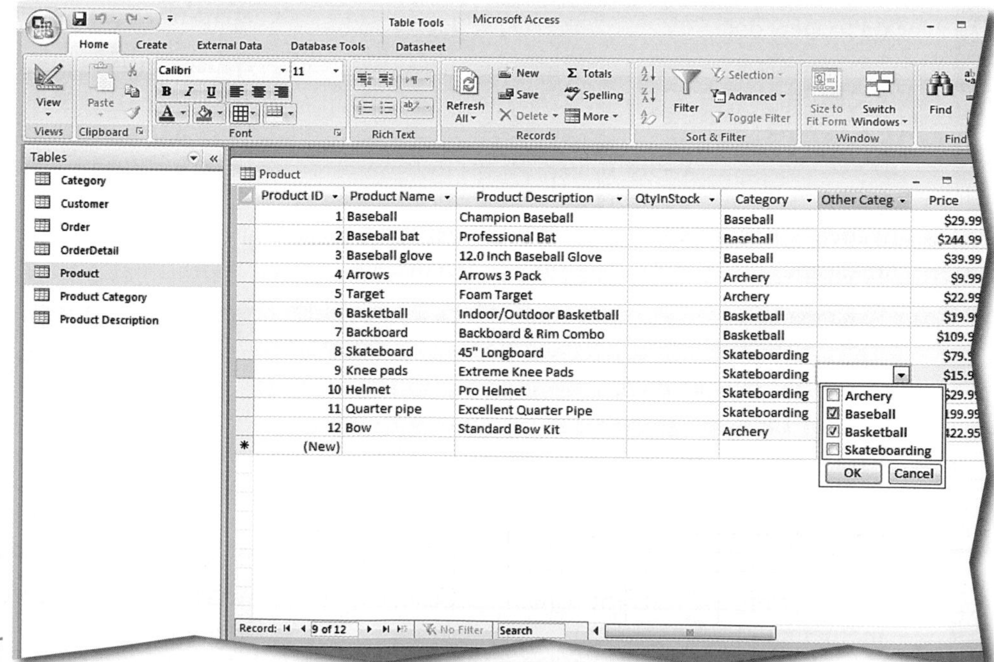

Step-By-Step

1 Start **Excel**.

2 Choose **Office>New**.

3 In the **New Workbook** dialog box, under **Templates**, click **Installed Templates** (see Figurc 5.1).

4 Scroll down and select the **Time Card** template. Click **Create**.

5 Save the file as: TimeCard-[your first initial and last name] (for example, *TimeCard-jking*).

6 CHECK Your screen should look like Figure 5.2.

7 Save your file.

Continue to the next exercise.

EXERCISE 5-1
Create a Workbook from a Template

You can use a **template** to create workbooks that complete specific tasks. Once you choose your template, you can fill in the details. Excel comes with **common**, or most frequently used, templates, such as invoices, time cards, and personal budgets that contain useful formulas and preset formatting.

New Student Strategy If students are just joining the class, review creating a blank workbook before creating a workbook from a template.

FIGURE 5.1 New Workbook dialog box

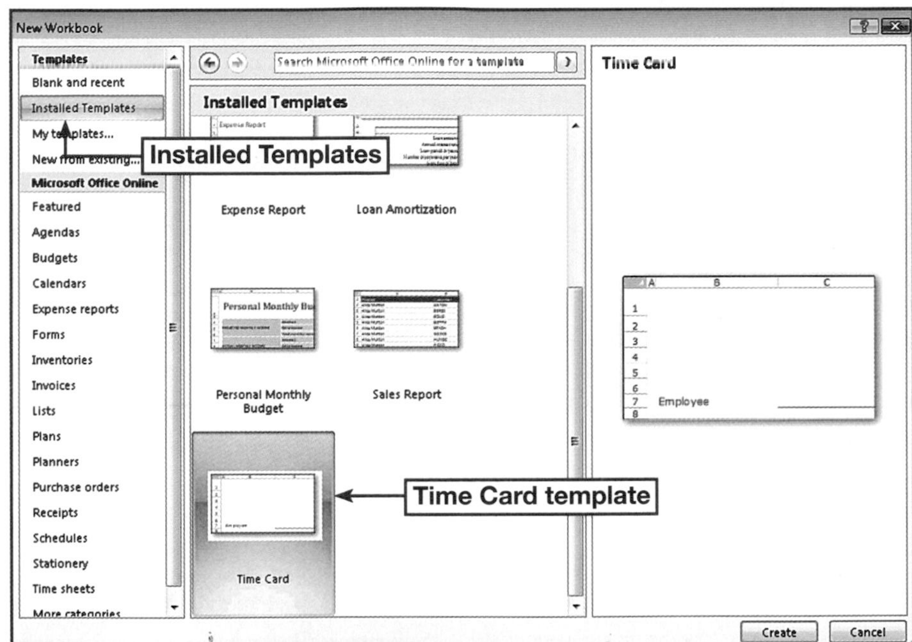

FIGURE 5.2 Time Card template

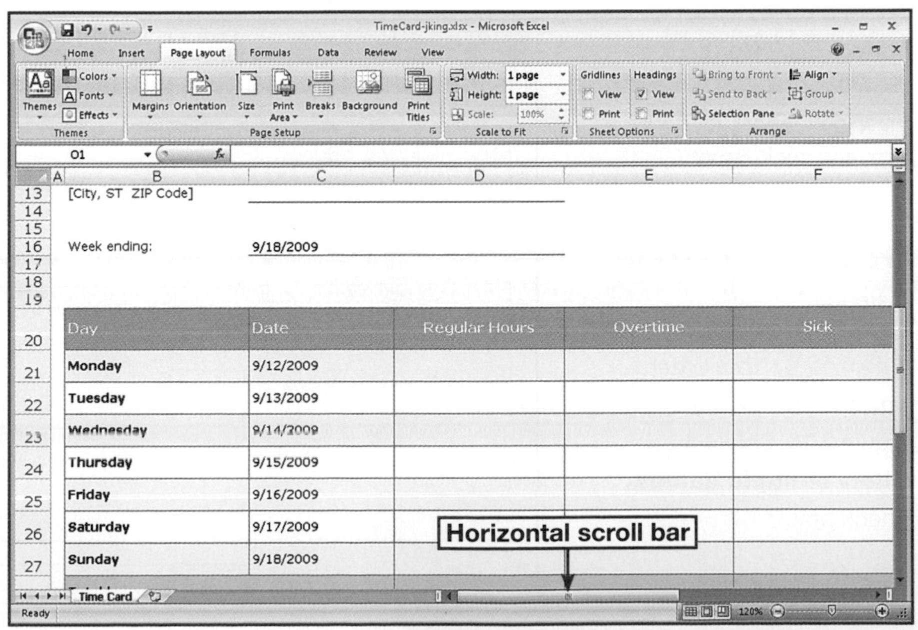

Tech Tip

If you are connected to the Internet, you can find many Excel templates at Microsoft Templates Online. In the **New Workbook** dialog box, under **Microsoft Office Online**, click a specific template category. Choose a template and, with your teacher's permission, click **Download**.

Teaching Tip The Time Card workbook is larger than the screen, so make sure that students use the scroll bars to view the template.

Step-By-Step

1. In your **Depot** file, open the **Product** table. Choose **Datasheet>Fields & Columns>Lookup Column** . The **Lookup Wizard** starts (see Figure 2.24).

2. Read the **Lookup Wizard** box. Make sure the first option in the box (the option to have the lookup column look up the values) is selected. Click **Next**.

3. In the Wizard, select **Table: Category**, and click **Next**.

4. In the **Available Fields** box, double-click **Category** to move it into the **Selected Fields** box. Click **Next**.

5. This box allows you to select how the items in the field's drop-down list will be sorted. Click **Next**.

6. Read the contents of this box and click **Next**.

7. In the label box for the lookup column, key: Other Categories.

8. **CHECK** Your Wizard box should look like Figure 2.25. Select the **Allow Multiple Values** check box.

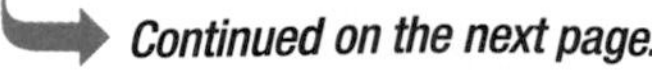
Continued on the next page.

EXERCISE 2-9
Create and Modify Multivalued Fields

Multivalued fields are useful for storing more than one answer in a single field. For example, a sporting goods store might categorize knee pads as items that belong in both the skateboarding and baseball categories. You can create a **Lookup field**, which will contain all the possible data choices for the field. You can edit or change multivalued fields in the table's Design View.

Teaching Tip Explain to students that they can also move fields with the arrows between the **Available Fields** and **Selected Fields** boxes.

FIGURE 2.24 Starting Lookup Wizard

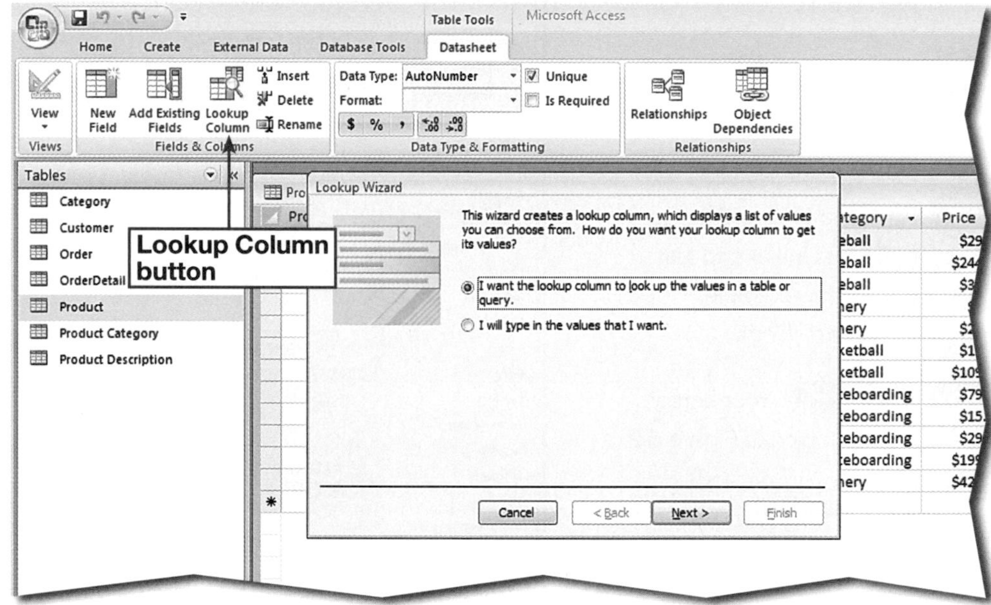

FIGURE 2.25 Finishing Lookup Wizard

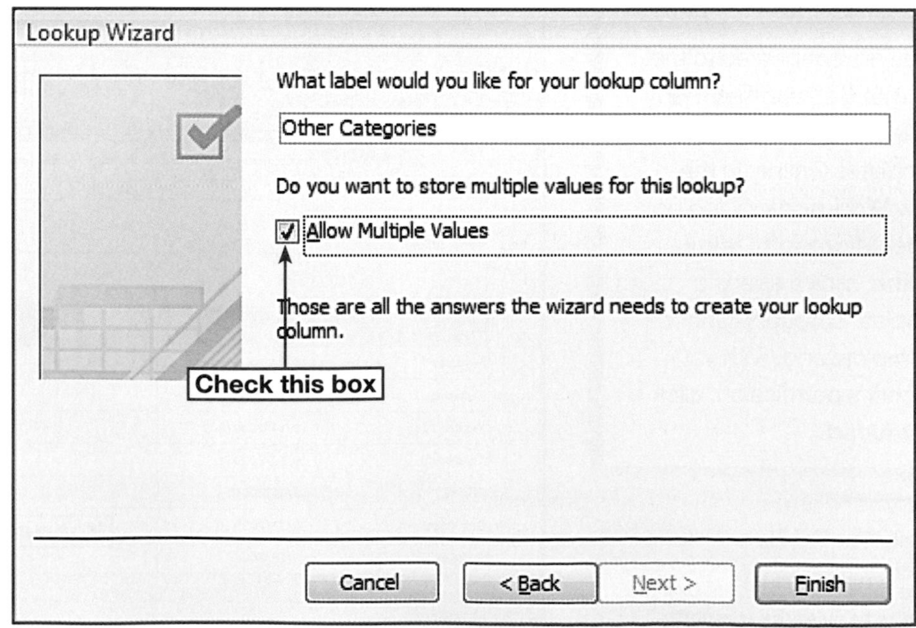

EXERCISE 5-2
Enter Data into a Template

The Time Card template is designed to automatically total your hours for you and calculate your weekly gross, or pretax, pay. All you have to do is enter your hours and the wage per hour.

NCLB/Math (Number and Operations) Tell students that H30 is the total amount of money due to the employee. It multiplies the total number of hours being worked (cells D28 and E28) by the respective pay rates (cells D29 and E29).

FIGURE 5.3 Entering data

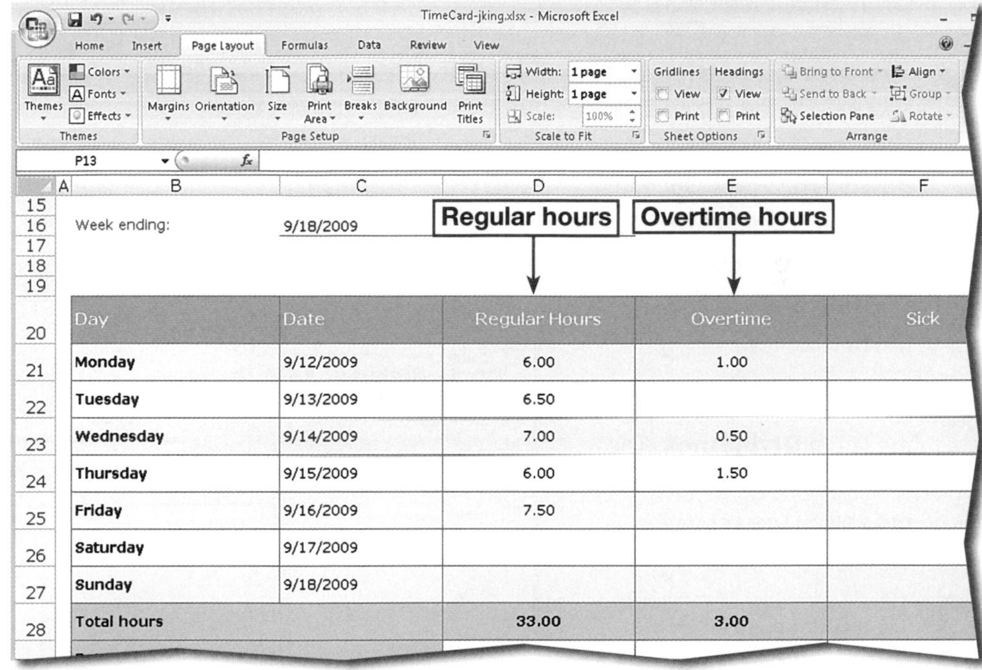

Step-By-Step

1. In your **TimeCard** file, click the cell for **Monday's Regular Hours**.
2. Key: 6. Press ENTER.
3. In the **Tuesday** row, key: 6.5.
4. Fill in the rest of the regular hours and overtime hours according to Figure 5.3.
5. In cell **D29**, key: 8. In cell **E29**, key: 12.
6. Scroll to the bottom right of the spreadsheet.
7. CHECK Your screen should look like Figure 5.4.
8. Save your file.

Continue to the next exercise.

FIGURE 5.4 Totals

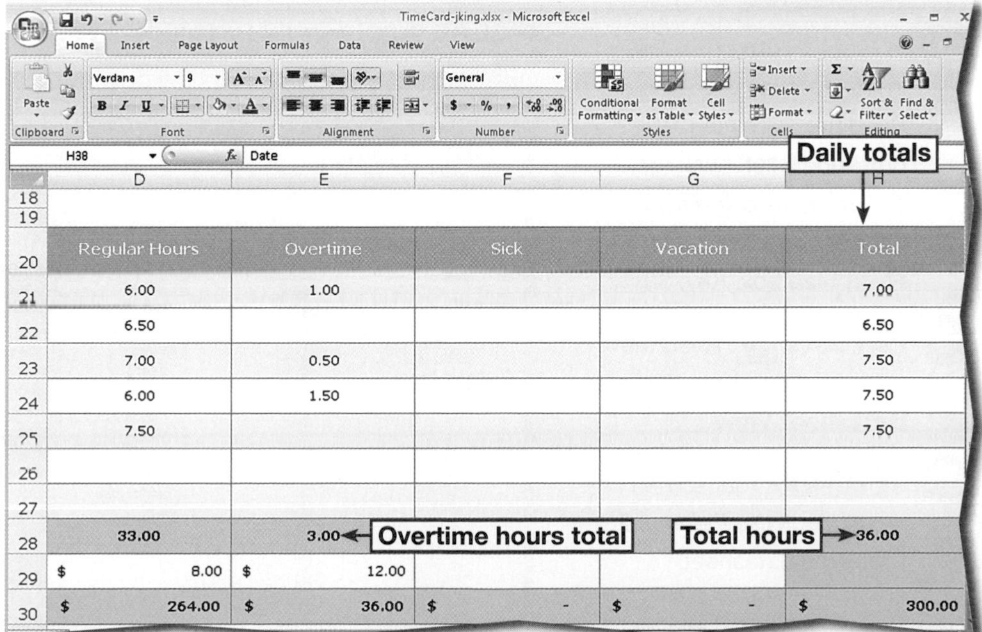

Shortcuts

You can use TAB to move across the spreadsheet. When you finish a row, use the Scroll key or mouse to move down to the next row.

Academic Skills

Click cell **D30** and look at the formula being used. The formula multiplies cell **D28** (hours being worked) by cell **D29** (the pay rate). Now scroll to cell **H30**. How does this formula work?

Step-By-Step

1. In your **Depot** file, open the **Product** table in **Design View**. Click the blank cell under **DateAdded** and key: QtyInStock. Press TAB.

2. CHECK Your screen should look like Figure 2.22. Click the **Data Type drop-down arrow**. Choose **Number**. Under **Field Properties**, click the **Caption** box and key: Stock Quantity.

3. Click the **row selector** to the left of **QtyinStock**. The field is selected. Drag the bold black line above the **Category** field.

4. Click **Save**. Click the **Price** field and press TAB. In the **Data Type** drop-down list, click **Currency**.

5. In **Field Properties**, click in the **Format** box. Choose **Currency** from the drop-down list. Click the **Category** field. In **Field Properties**, click in the **Field Size** box. Key: 30.

6. Click **Save**. Read the warning. Click **Yes**. Click **Datasheet View**.

7. CHECK Your screen should look like Figure 2.23. Close the datasheet.

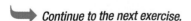

Continue to the next exercise.

EXERCISE 2-8
Modify Table Structure

Although it is easy to create a table with a template or the Table Analyzer Wizard, you may not get exactly what you need. With a little patience, you can change anything in your tables. For example, you can add a new field, change the order of the fields, change the field type, and change the field's **caption**, or column heading.

Step-By-Step Tip In **Step 1**, let students know that spaces are not used in field names.

FIGURE 2.22 New field added in Design View

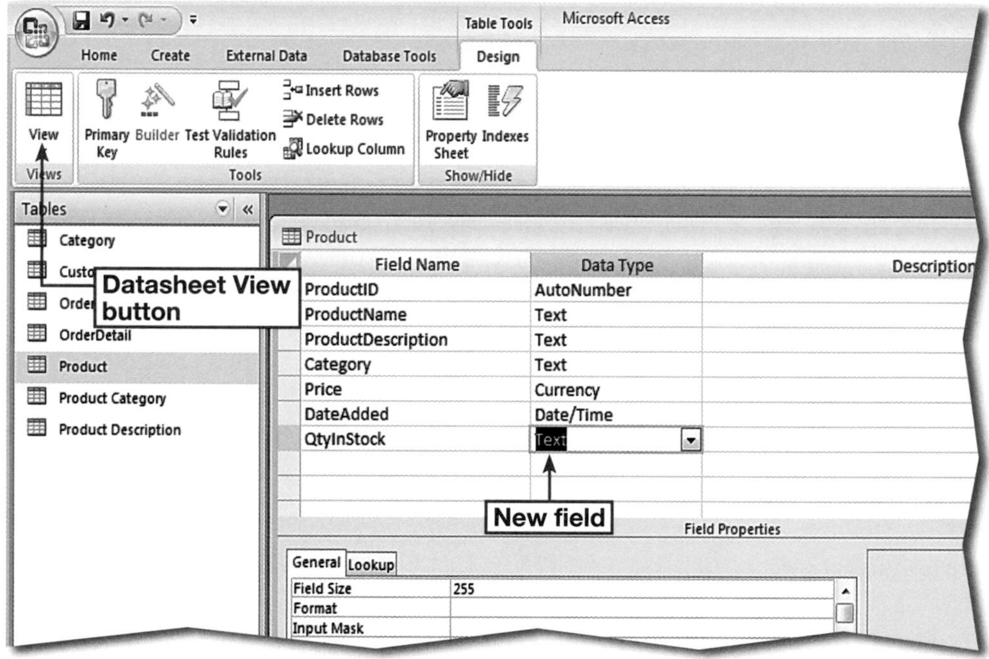

FIGURE 2.23 Price field in Datasheet View

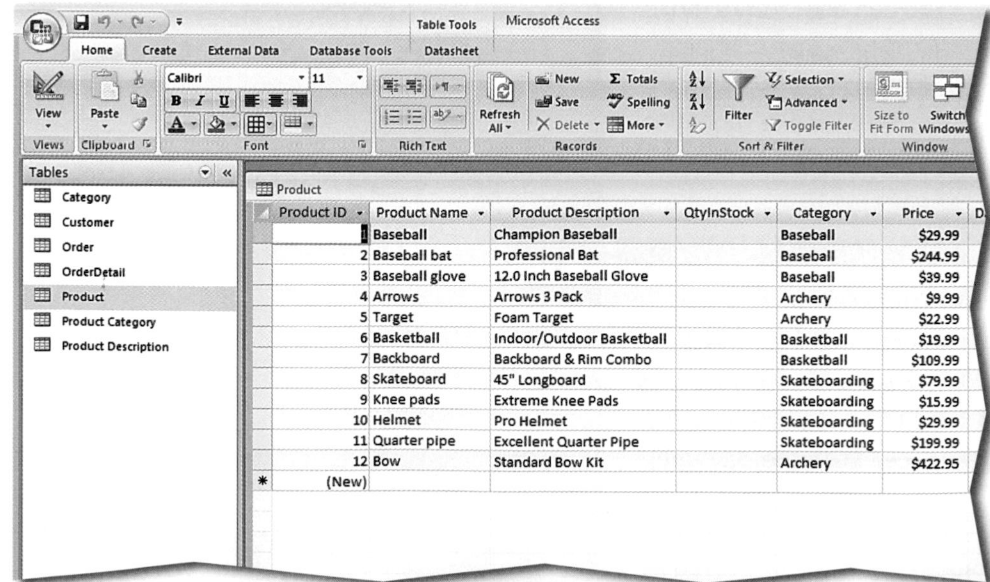

Product ID	Product Name	Product Description	QtyInStock	Category	Price
1	Baseball	Champion Baseball		Baseball	$29.99
2	Baseball bat	Professional Bat		Baseball	$244.99
3	Baseball glove	12.0 Inch Baseball Glove		Baseball	$39.99
4	Arrows	Arrows 3 Pack		Archery	$9.99
5	Target	Foam Target		Archery	$22.99
6	Basketball	Indoor/Outdoor Basketball		Basketball	$19.99
7	Backboard	Backboard & Rim Combo		Basketball	$109.99
8	Skateboard	45" Longboard		Skateboarding	$79.99
9	Knee pads	Extreme Knee Pads		Skateboarding	$15.99
10	Helmet	Pro Helmet		Skateboarding	$29.99
11	Quarter pipe	Excellent Quarter Pipe		Skateboarding	$199.99
12	Bow	Standard Bow Kit		Archery	$422.95
(New)					

Step-By-Step

1. In your **TimeCard** file, click **Insert Worksheet** . A blank worksheet appears after the **Time Card** worksheet (see Figure 5.5).
2. Click **Insert Worksheet** again. There are now three worksheets in the workbook.
3. Click the **Sheet1** tab.
4. Right-click and select **Delete**. Click the **Time Card** tab.
5. **CHECK** Your screen should look like Figure 5.6.
6. Save your file.

Continue to the next exercise.

Tech Tip

To rename a worksheet, right-click the sheet tab and select **Rename** in the shortcut menu or double-click the sheet tab.

Step-By-Step Tip In **Step 2**, let students know that the sheet number (for example, Sheet2) indicates the order in which it was added to the workbook.

Differentiated Instruction/Advanced If students want to insert a second timesheet into an existing workbook, they can right-click the **Time Card** tab at the bottom of the screen. In the **Insert** dialog box, they should click the **Spreadsheet Solutions** tab and select the template they want to include.

EXERCISE 5-3
Insert and Delete Worksheets

If you need more worksheets in a workbook, you can insert a new worksheet. If a workbook has more worksheets than you need, you can delete a worksheet. You might want your workbook to have four worksheets if you want to submit all your weekly time cards for the month of April, for example.

FIGURE 5.5 New worksheet added to workbook

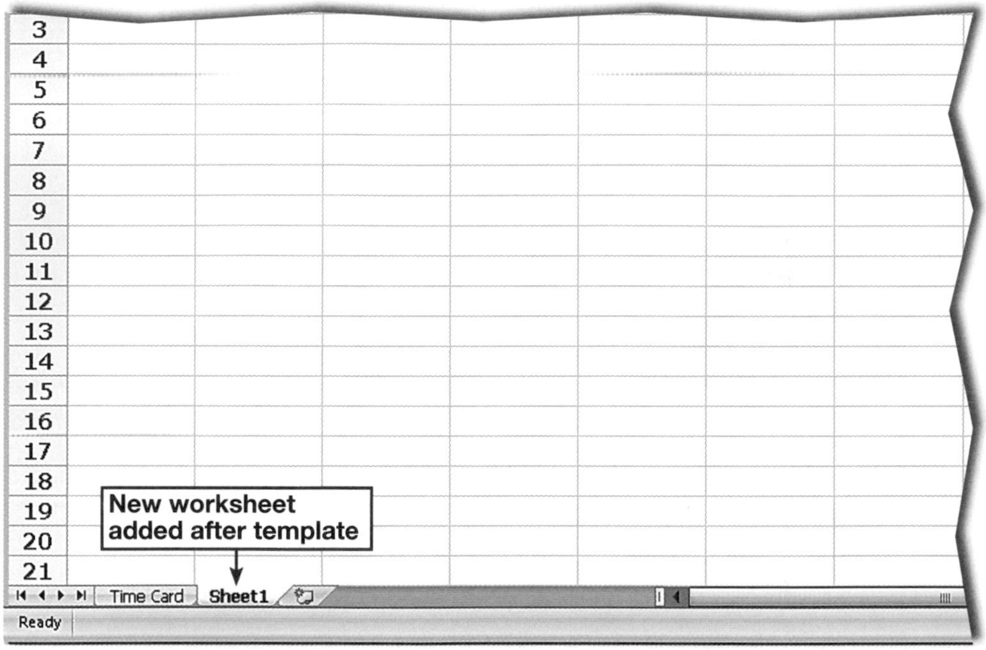

New worksheet added after template

FIGURE 5.6 Worksheet deleted

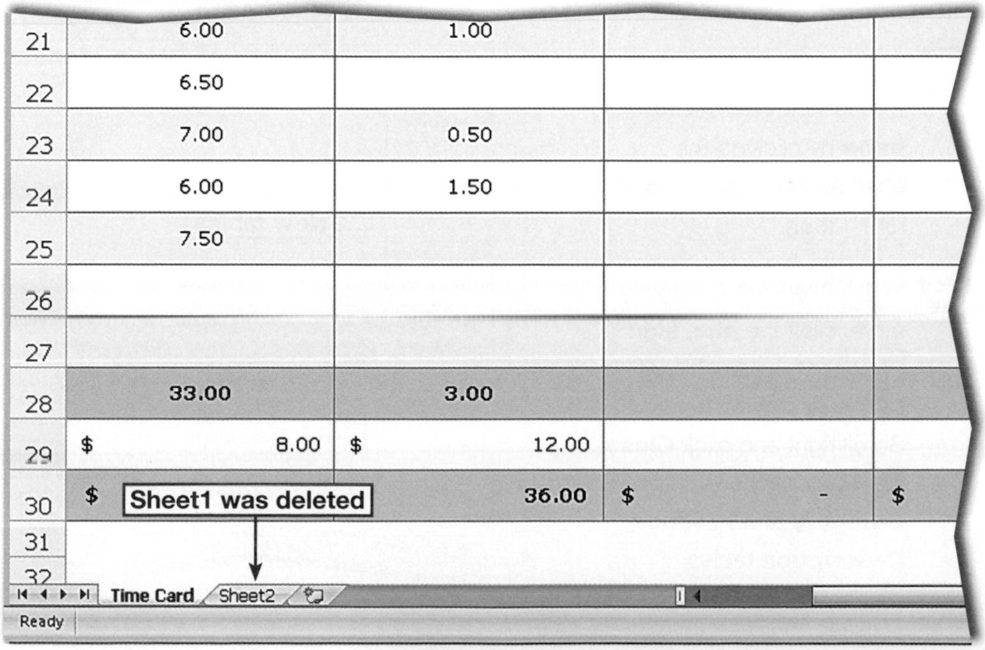

Sheet1 was deleted

Step-By-Step

EXERCISE 2-7 (Continued)
Evaluate Table Design

8. **CHECK** Your screen should look like Figure 2.20. In the Wizard, select **Table1**. Click the **Rename Table** button. Key: Product Description. Click **OK**.

9. Click **Table2**. Click **Rename Table**. Key: Product Category. Click **OK**.

10. Click **Next**. The fields highlighted in the Wizard uniquely identify each record. Click **Next**. Select **No**. Click **Finish**.

11. **CHECK** Your screen should look like Figure 2.21. Access has opened the two new tables, minimized the **Navigation pane**, and opened the **Access Help** window.

12. Close the **Help** window. Expand the **Navigation pane** by clicking the **shutter bar open/close** » button.

13. In the **Product Category** table, click the **plus sign** + left of the **Archery** field to see all archery items. Scroll right and click **Close** × to close the **Product Category** and **Product Description** tables.

Continue to the next exercise.

FIGURE 2.20 Renaming tables in Table Analyzer Wizard

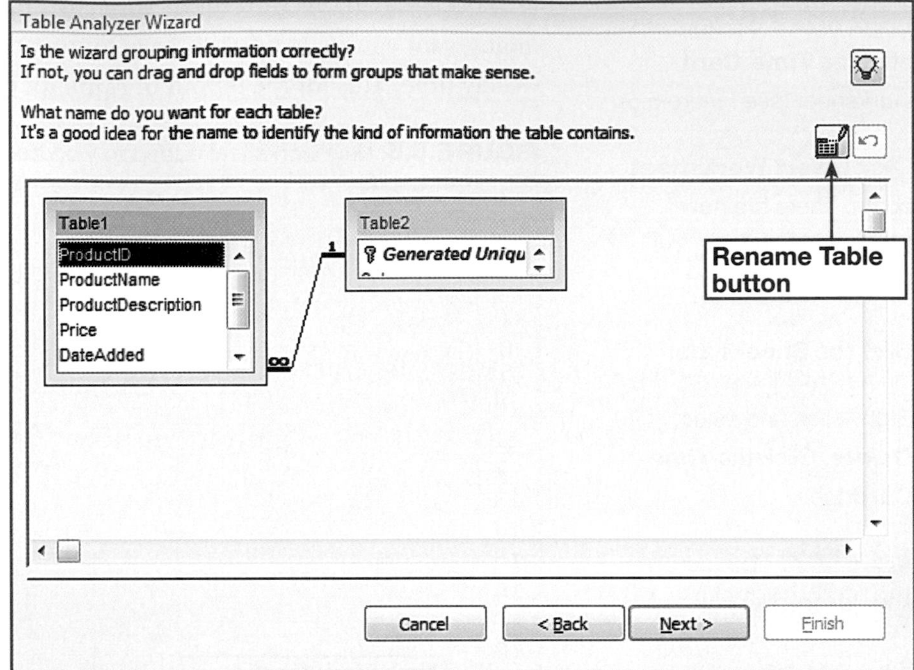

Step-By-Step Tip In **Step 13**, point out to students that all products related to archery are listed in the Archery field.

FIGURE 2.21 New tables created

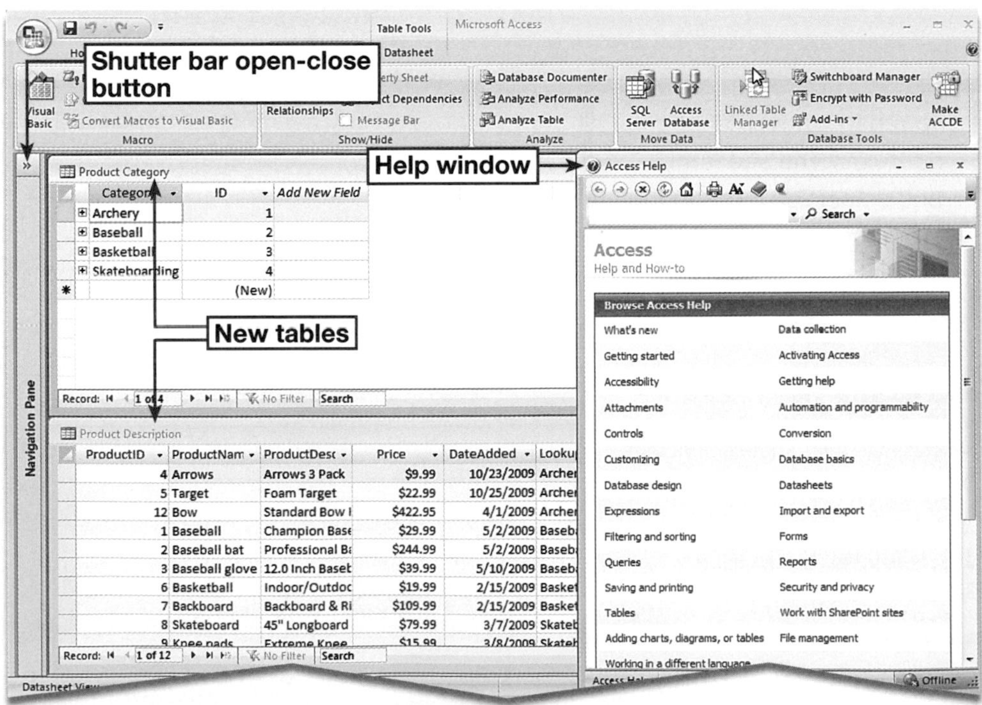

Step-By-Step

1. In your **TimeCard** file, click the **Sheet2** tab.
2. Choose **Home>Cells> Format**.
3. Under **Organize Sheets**, select **Move or Copy Sheet**. The **Move or Copy** dialog box opens (see Figure 5.7).
4. Under **Before sheet**, click **Time Card**.
5. Click **OK**.
6. **CHECK** Your screen should look like Figure 5.8.
7. Save and close your file.

Continue to the next exercise.

Shortcuts

To rearrange worksheets faster, drag a sheet tab left or right to its new position.

Tech Tip

You can also move or copy a worksheet between workbooks by right-clicking the **Sheet** tab, selecting **Move** or **Copy**, and choosing the workbook from the **To book** list.

Solution Use the file **TimeCard-SF.xlsx** as a solution file for **Exercises 5-1** through **5-4**.

EXERCISE 5-4
Rearrange Worksheets

You can change the order of worksheets in a workbook. Excel allows you to arrange, or order, worksheets in the way that is most logical to you.

FIGURE 5.7 Move or Copy dialog box

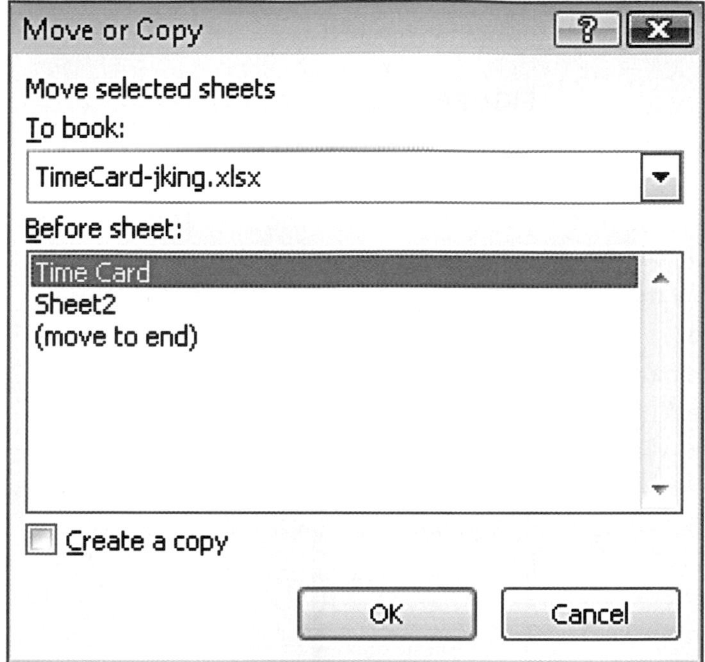

FIGURE 5.8 Repositioned worksheet

Sheet2 moved before Time Card worksheet

Step-By-Step

1. In your **Depot** file, choose **Database Tools> Analyze>Analyze Table**. The **Table Analyzer Wizard** dialog box opens.

2. CHECK Your screen should look like Figure 2.18.

3. Read the text in the Wizard's pane. Click the arrows next to **Show me an example** to see examples of what is being described. Click **Next** when you are done.

4. When you have read and understand the second page of the Wizard, click **Next**.

5. CHECK Your screen should look like Figure 2.19.

6. In the **Table Analyzer Wizard**, under **Tables**, make sure that the **Product** table is selected. Click **Next**.

7. Make sure the button next to **Yes, let the Wizard decide** is selected. Click **Next**.

Continued on the next page.

EL Check to see that English Learner students understand all vocabulary words.

EXERCISE 2-7
Evaluate Table Design

Access has several tools to help you modify your database to run more efficiently. One of those tools is the **Table Analyzer Wizard**. The wizard can **analyze**, or study, the information in a table and then make changes to streamline the data. For example, if a table stores customer address information, the Table Analyzer Wizard ensures that the addresses are listed consistently and gets rid of **redundant**, or repeated, listings.

FIGURE 2.18 Table Analyzer Wizard

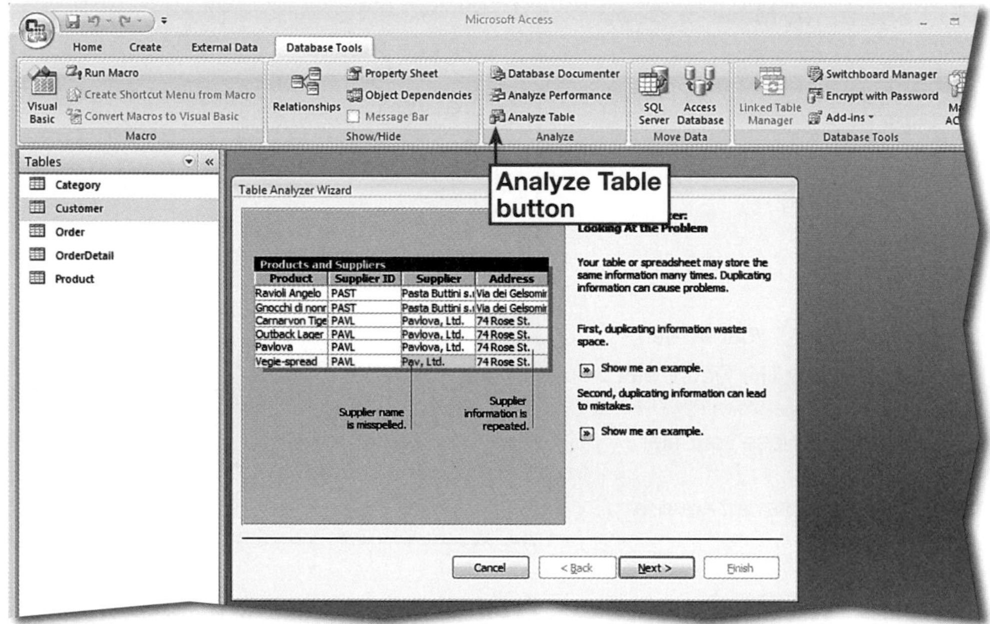

FIGURE 2.19 Select Product table

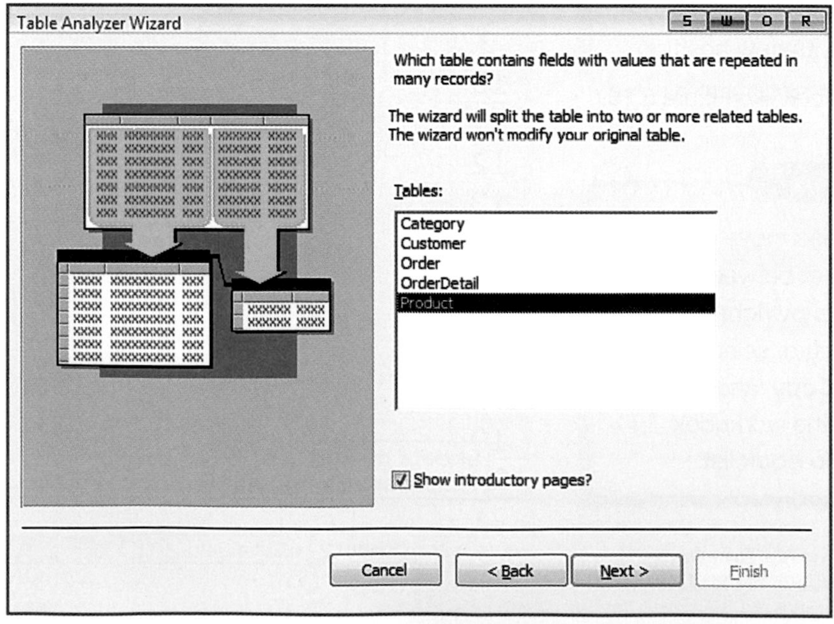

EXERCISE 5-5
Split, Freeze, and Unfreeze Workbooks

Data File

If you move far enough down or to the right in a worksheet, you will no longer see the row and column headings. Excel allows you to **freeze** headings to keep them in place while you move around. If you need to look at two parts of a worksheet that are too far apart to view at the same time, you can **split** the window. Splitting the window divides it into two panes that you can scroll independently.

EL Review with English Learners the difference between *freeze* and *split*.

FIGURE 5.9 Freeze a workbook

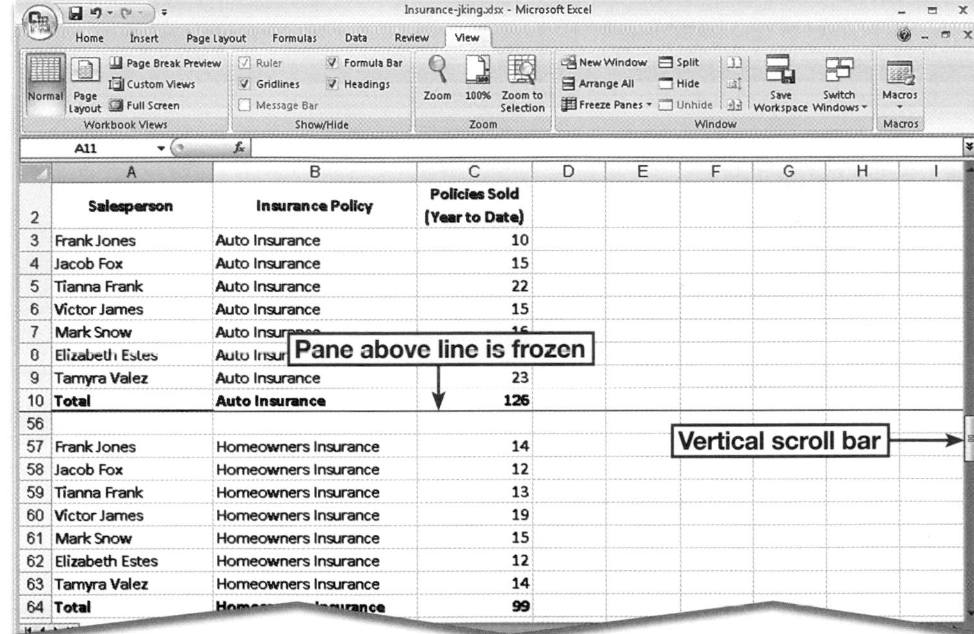

FIGURE 5.10 Split a workbook

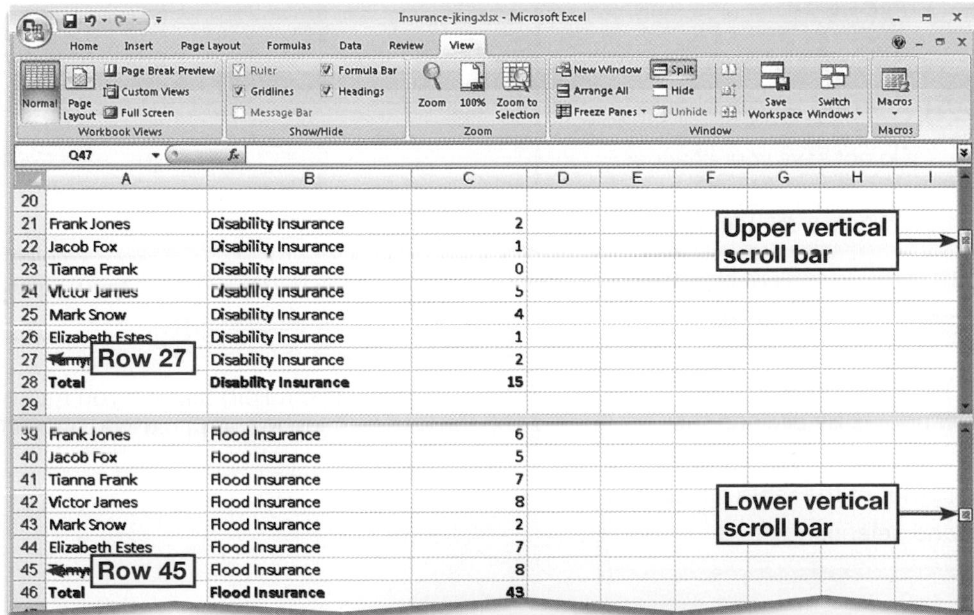

Step-By-Step

1. Open the data file **Insurance.xlsx**. Save as: Insurance-[your first initial and last name].
2. Click the **Year-to-Date Sales** worksheet tab. If necessary, scroll up and click cell **A11**.
3. Choose **View>Windows> Freeze Panes**. Choose **Freeze Panes**. Scroll down to row **64**. Only the bottom window scrolls down (see Figure 5.9).
4. Click **Freeze Panes** and select **Unfreeze Panes**.
5. Choose **Window>Split**.
6. Use the upper vertical scroll bar to scroll down to row **28**. Use the lower vertical scroll bar to scroll down to row **46**.
7. **CHECK** Your screen should look like Figure 5.10.
8. Click **Split**. Save your file.

Continue to the next exercise.

Tech Tip

If your window is split into two panes, double-click any part of the split bar that divides the panes to restore the window.

Step-By-Step

EXERCISE 2-6 (Continued)
Modify Table and Field Properties

13. Open the **Customer** table. Click **Design View**.

14. Click in the **Street** field. In the **Field Properties** section, select the text in the **Field Size** box. Review Table 2.1 to identify the meanings of common field properties, such as **Field Size**.

15. In the **Field Size** box, key: 45.

16. Click in the **Required** box. Click the **drop-down arrow** and select **Yes**.

17. Click in the **State** field. Under **Field Properties**, select the text in the **Field Size** box. Key: 2.

18. Click **Default Value**. Key: TX. Press ENTER.

19. CHECK Your screen should look like Figure 2.17.

20. Close the **Customer** table. Do not save your changes.

Continue to the next exercise.

TABLE 2.1 Common field properties

Property	Meaning
Field Size	How much data you can enter in that field
Format	How the field is displayed
Caption	What heading is displayed in Datasheet View
Default Value	The initial value for a new field
Required	If *Yes*, this field cannot be empty
Indexed	Helps you find records more quickly by field

FIGURE 2.17 Field properties changed

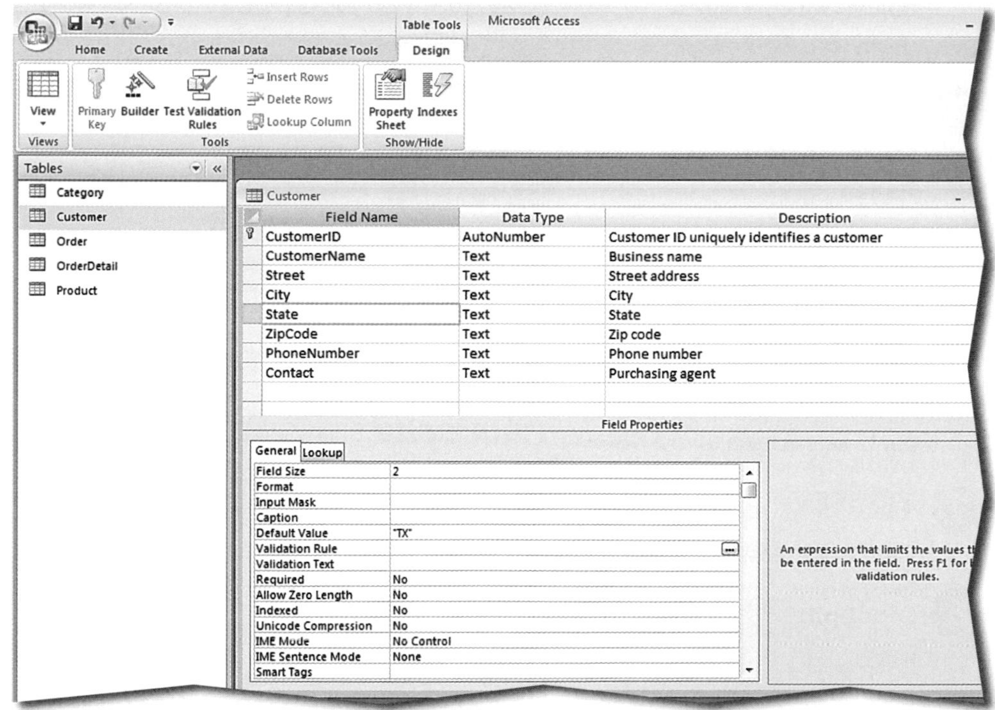

Shortcuts

You can also close table windows by clicking the table icon in the upper-left corner of the table title bar and selecting **Close**.

Troubleshooter

You cannot leave a field blank if you make the field required, even if you do not have the data yet.

Step-By-Step

1. With your **Insurance** file still open, open the data files **Pricing.xlsx** and **Guidelines.xlsx**. Be sure to open the files in order so **Guidelines** is the active file.
2. In the **Guidelines** file, choose **View>Window>Hide** (see Figure 5.11). This will hide **Guidelines**.
3. Choose **View>Window>Arrange All**. In the **Arrange Windows** box, click **Horizontal**. Click **OK**.
4. **CHECK** Your screen should look like Figure 5.12.
5. Choose **View>Window>Unhide**. Select **Guidelines**. Click **OK**.
6. Close **Guidelines** and **Pricing**. Do not save your changes.
7. Click **Maximize** in the **Insurance** window.
8. Save your file.

Continue to the next exercise.

Tech Tip

You can delete a worksheet quickly by right-clicking on the sheet's tab and selecting **Delete**.

EXERCISE 5-6
Hide, Unhide, and Arrange Workbooks

You can arrange several workbooks to organize them on the screen. You can also hide a workbook from view without closing it.

Differentiated Instruction/Advanced Students
Encourage students to try different ways of arranging workbooks (such as vertical and cascade).

FIGURE 5.11 Window group

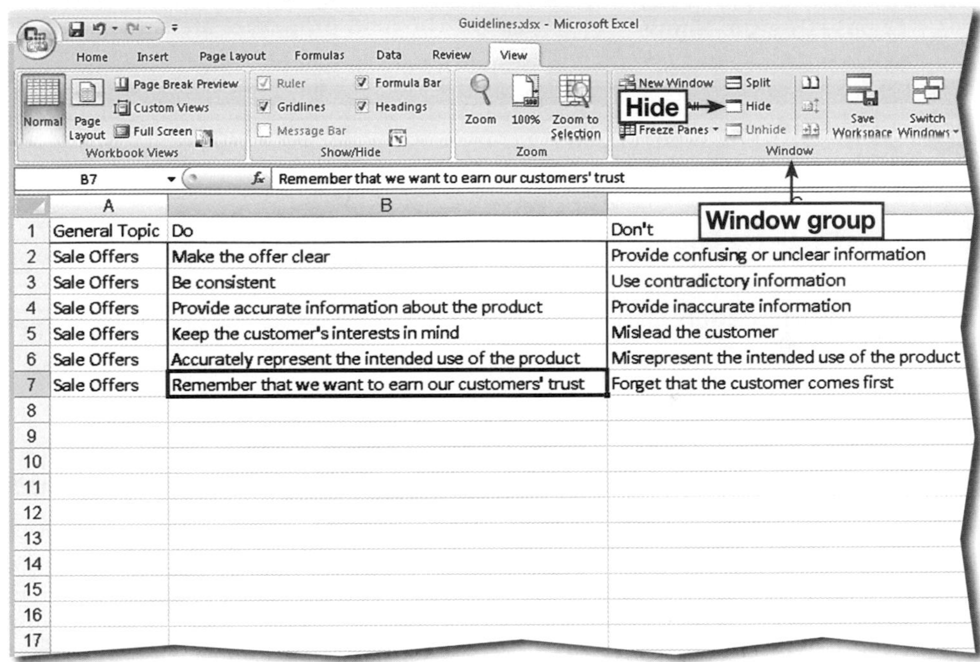

FIGURE 5.12 Windows arranged horizontally

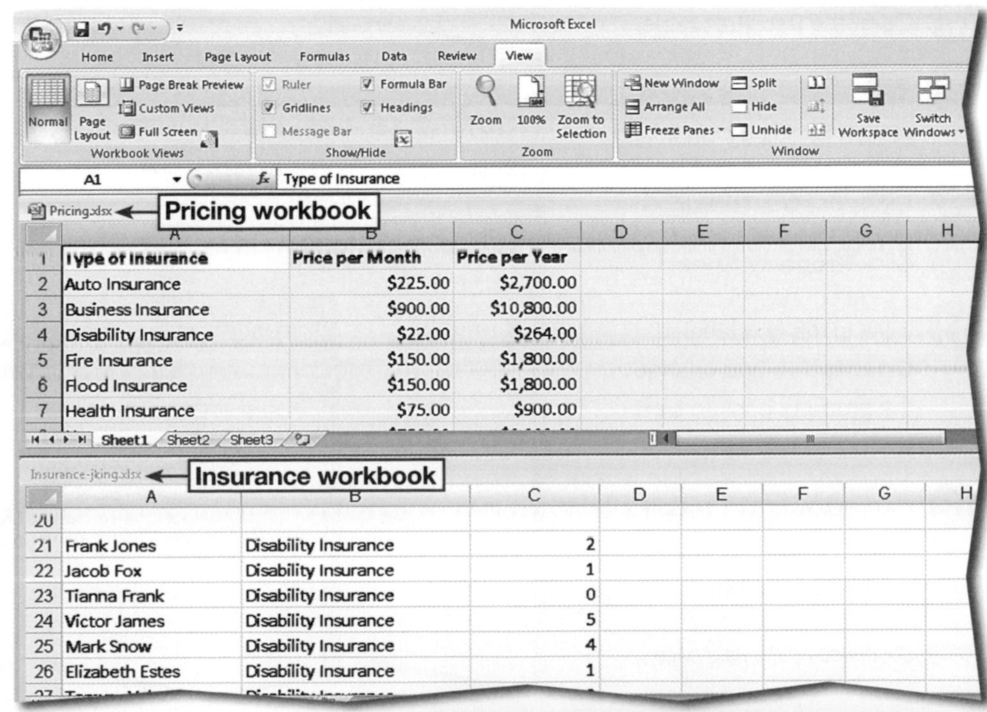

Step-By-Step

1. In Access, locate and open your **Depot** file. Open the **Product** table.
2. Click **Design View**. Choose **Design>Show/Hide>Property Sheet**.
3. **CHECK** Your screen should look like Figure 2.15.
4. In the **Property Sheet**, click in the box that is labeled **Orientation**. Click the **drop-down arrow** that appears and select **Right-to-Left**.
5. Click **Save** on the **Quick Access Toolbar**.
6. Click **Property Sheet** again to close the table's properties. Close the table.
7. Open the **Product** table.
8. **CHECK** Your screen should look like Figure 2.16.
9. Click **Design View**.
10. Click **Property Sheet**.
11. Click in the box labeled **Orientation** and change the property back to **Left-to-Right**.
12. Click **Save**. Close the **Property Sheet**. Close the **Product** table.

Continued on the next page.

EXERCISE 2-6
Modify Table and Field Properties

Access allows you to set properties for entire tables of data and for individual fields. Table properties include the default view, the order in which the table will sort data, and how much of the table will appear on the screen. Field properties can be set for forms, for reports, and for each **control**, or object that displays data or performs an action. The field properties are shown as a list in a **property sheet**. Common field properties are shown in Table 2.1 on the next page (see page 390).

Teaching Tip Emphasize to students the difference between modifying table properties and database properties.

FIGURE 2.15 Table Property Sheet open

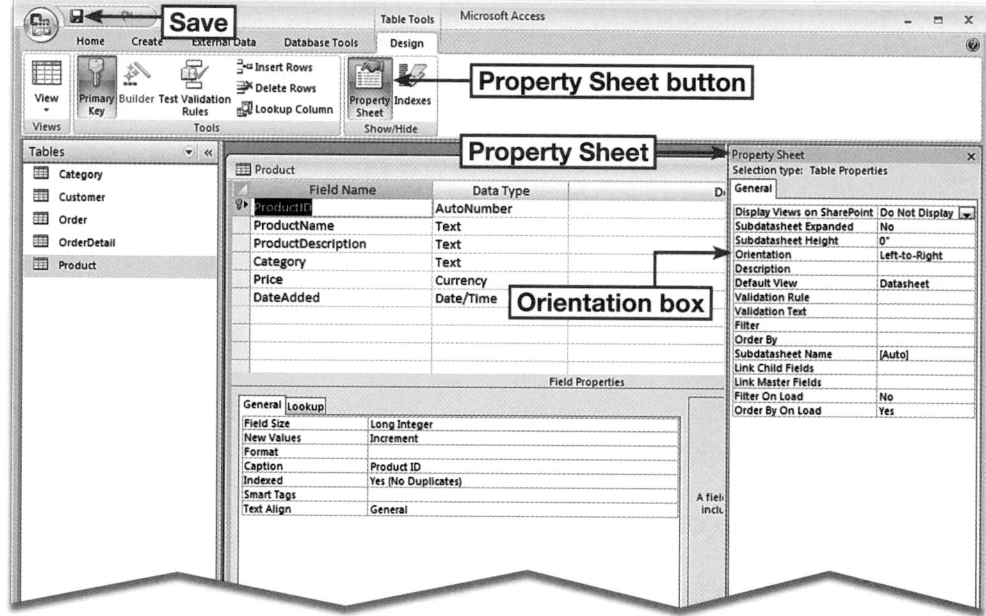

FIGURE 2.16 Product table in right-to-left orientation

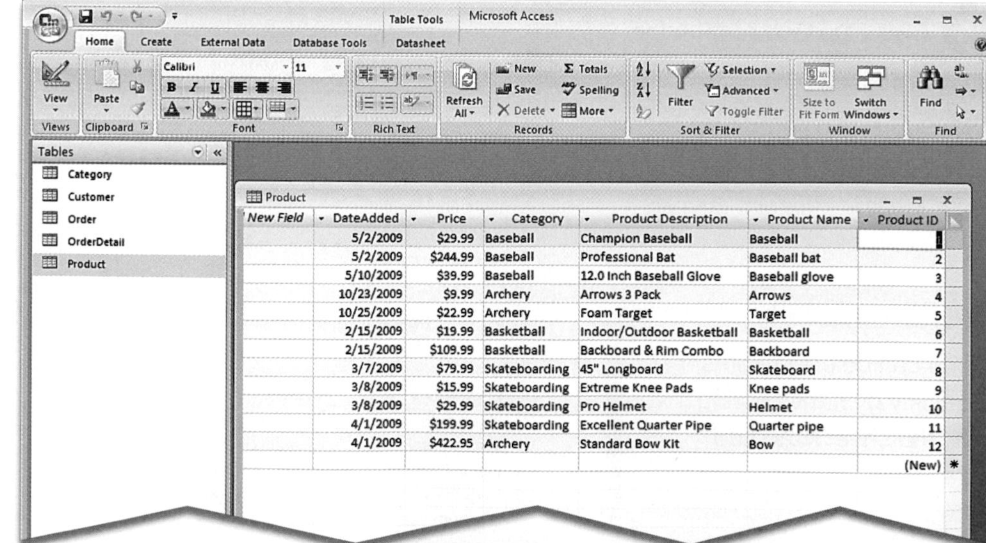

Step-By-Step

1. In your **Insurance** file, choose **Office>Save As**. The **Save As** dialog box opens.
2. In the **Save as type** box, select **Web page**. Next to **Save**, click **Selection: Sheet**.
3. In the **File** name box, change the file name to Sales Numbers.
4. **CHECK** Your dialog box should look like Figure 5.13. Click **Publish**.
5. In the **Publish as Web Page** dialog box, click **Publish**.
6. Choose **Office>Open**. Select **Sales Numbers .html**.
7. **CHECK** Your screen should look like Figure 5.14.
8. Close the Web browser.
9. Save your file.

Continue to the next exercise.

You Should Know

The extension for a Web page is .htm or .html. You do not have to key this extension in the **File** name box as long as **Web Page** is selected in the **Save as type** box.

EXERCISE 5-7
Save and Publish Worksheets as Web Pages

You can save a worksheet, or an entire workbook, as a Web page. This will **convert**, or change, the information into a format that can be viewed on the Web. When you open an Excel file that has been saved as a Web page, the file opens in a Web browser, not in Excel. Saving an Excel document to a Web format means that people can view it even if they do not have Excel. They just need access to a Web browser. You can use Web Page Preview to see what your worksheet will look like on the Web.

Solution Use the file **Sales Numbers.htm** as a solution file for this exercise.

FIGURE 5.13 Save As dialog box

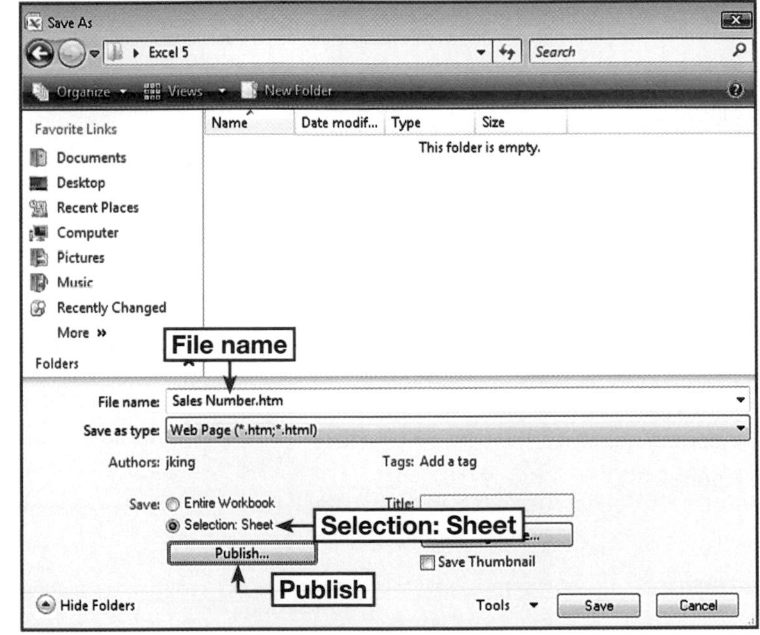

FIGURE 5.14 Sales numbers Web page

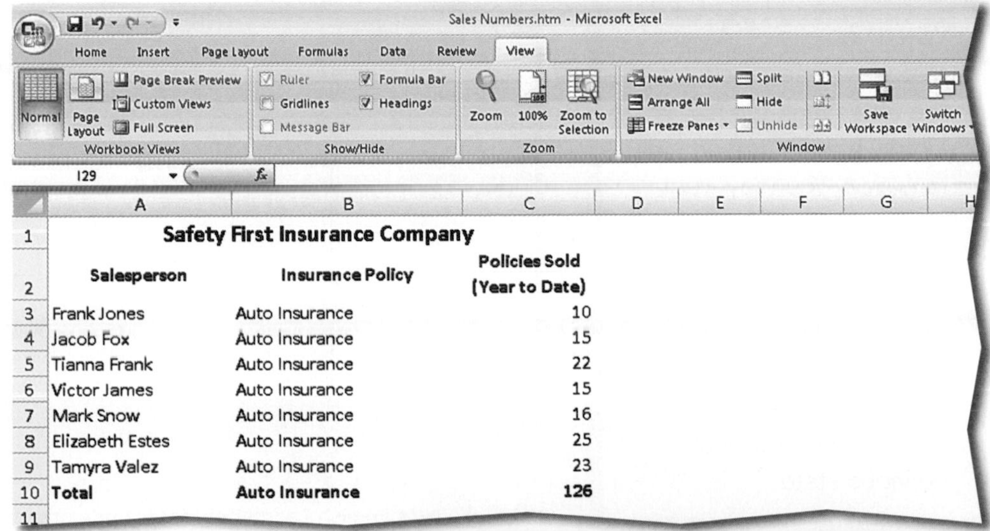

	A	B	C
1	Safety First Insurance Company		
2	Salesperson	Insurance Policy	Policies Sold (Year to Date)
3	Frank Jones	Auto Insurance	10
4	Jacob Fox	Auto Insurance	15
5	Tianna Frank	Auto Insurance	22
6	Victor James	Auto Insurance	15
7	Mark Snow	Auto Insurance	16
8	Elizabeth Estes	Auto Insurance	25
9	Tamyra Valez	Auto Insurance	23
10	**Total**	**Auto Insurance**	**126**
11			

Step-By-Step

7 Click the **drop-down arrow** [▾] again. Select **Minimum**.

8 In the **Total** row, click in the cell under the **Date Added** column. A down arrow appears.

9 Click the **drop-down arrow** [▾]. Select **Maximum**.

10 CHECK Your screen should look like Figure 2.13. The **Total** row now shows what the least expensive product is and when the latest product was added.

11 To remove the **Total** row, click **Totals** [Σ] again.

12 CHECK Your screen should look like Figure 2.14. Save your file.

Continue to the next exercise.

You Should Know

When you click **Totals** to remove the Total row from the datasheet, the row is simply hidden, not actually removed. You may want to hide a row to protect confidential information or to make the table easier to read by minimizing the amount of data. When you display the row again, the row appears in its previous state.

EXERCISE 2-5 (Continued)
Summarize Data with a Totals Row

FIGURE 2.13 Least expensive and latest products in Totals row

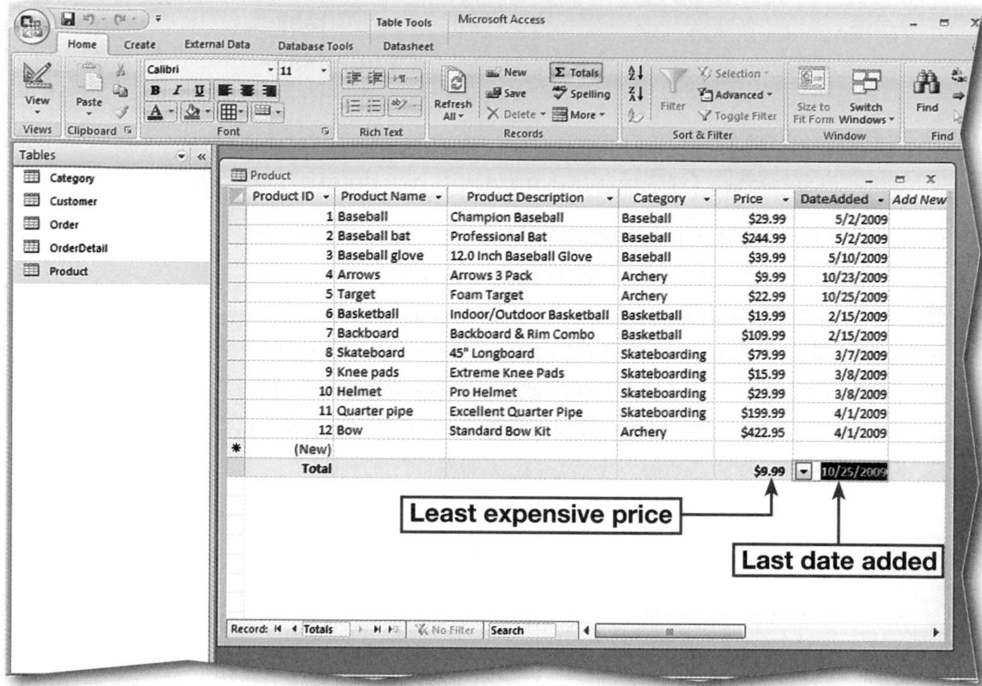

FIGURE 2.14 Return to Products Table

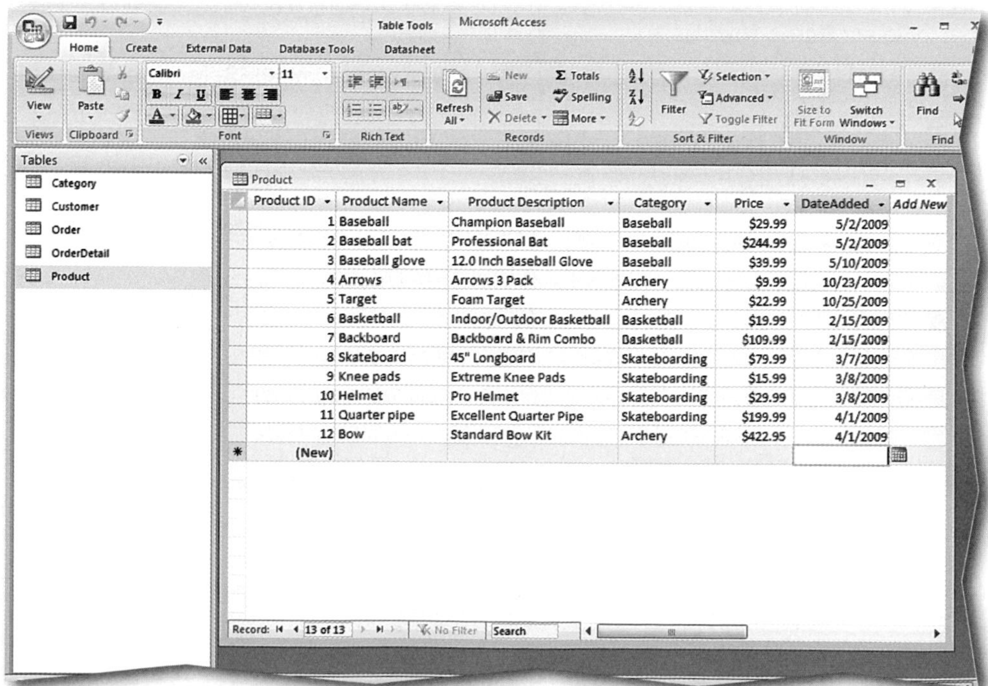

EL Make sure English Learner students understand all directions and can follow the steps.

EXERCISE 5-8
Use Print Preview Features

You can use Print Preview to see what a worksheet will look like before you print it. This preview helps you decide whether your printout will be readable and balanced, and whether all the data will fit on a single page.

Step-By-Step

1. In your **Insurance** file, choose **Office>Print>Print Preview**. The **Print Preview** screen opens (see Figure 5.15).
2. Click **Next Page** to view the second page that will be printed.
3. Click **Previous Page**.
4. Click **Zoom**.
5. CHECK Your screen should look like Figure 5.16.
6. Click **Close Print Preview**.
7. Save your file.

Continue to the next exercise.

FIGURE 5.15 Print Preview screen

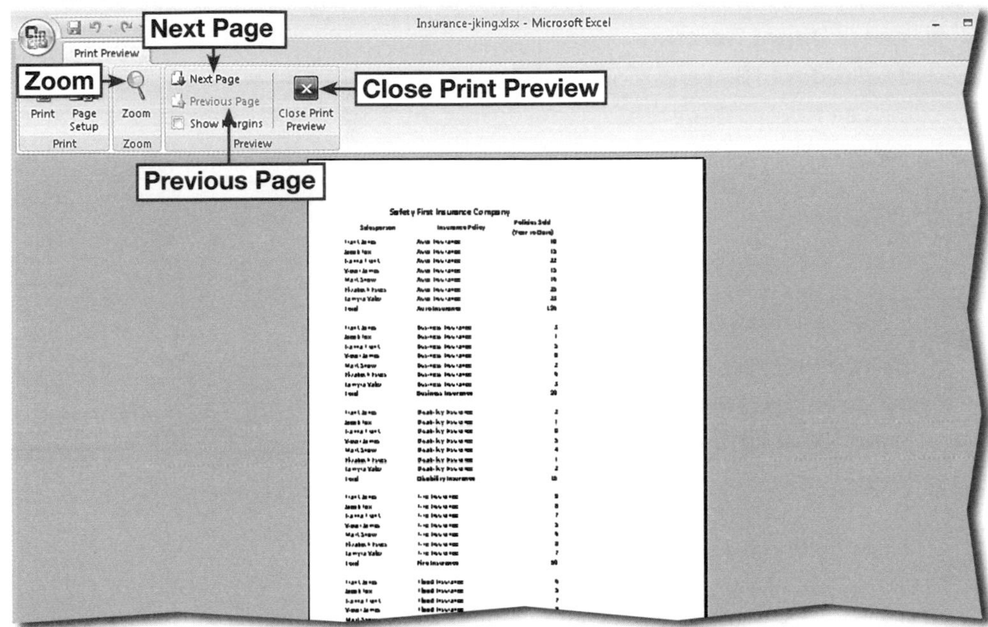

FIGURE 5.16 Zoom used in Print Preview view

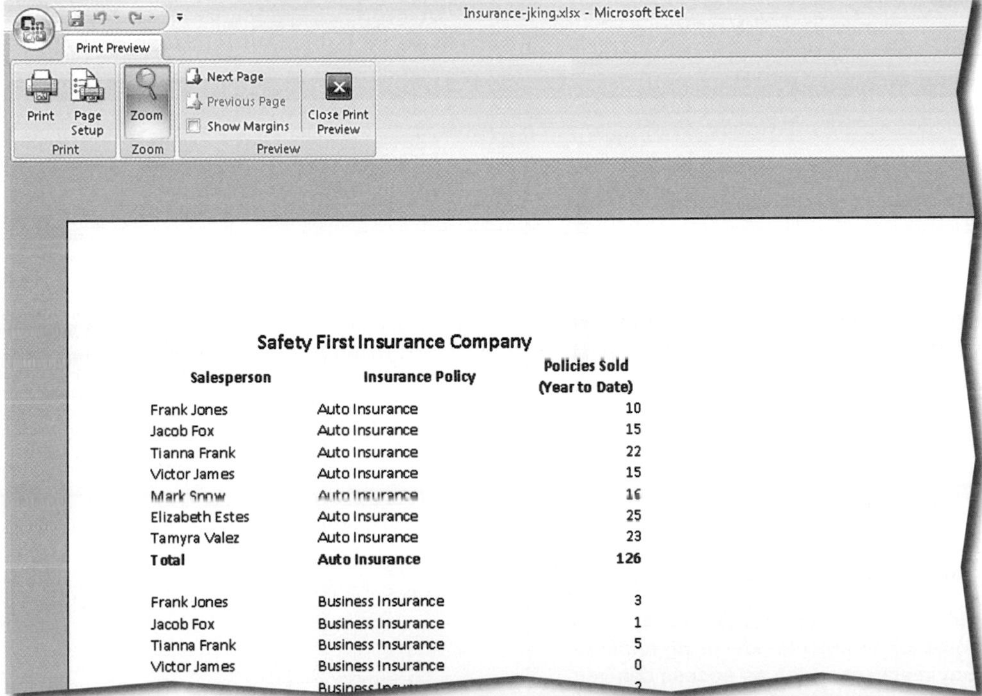

You Should Know

In **Print Preview**, your pointer becomes a magnifying glass. Clicking on the document will automatically zoom.

Microsoft Office 2007

You can customize Excel and place the Print Preview feature onto the Quick Access Toolbar (QAT) in order to quickly preview a worksheet.

Troubleshooting In **Step 7**, if a dialog box appears, tell students to click Yes.

EXERCISE 2-5
Summarize Data with a Totals Row

The **Totals row** function offers and quick and simple way to summarize columns of data in a table to get totals, averages, maximums, minimums, and other calculations. The Totals row also can be used with queries or forms. The Totals row function inserts, or adds, a new row in a table.

Intervention Strategy Before starting this exercise, show students how to find the **Depot** file and where to save their database.

FIGURE 2.11 Table with Totals row added

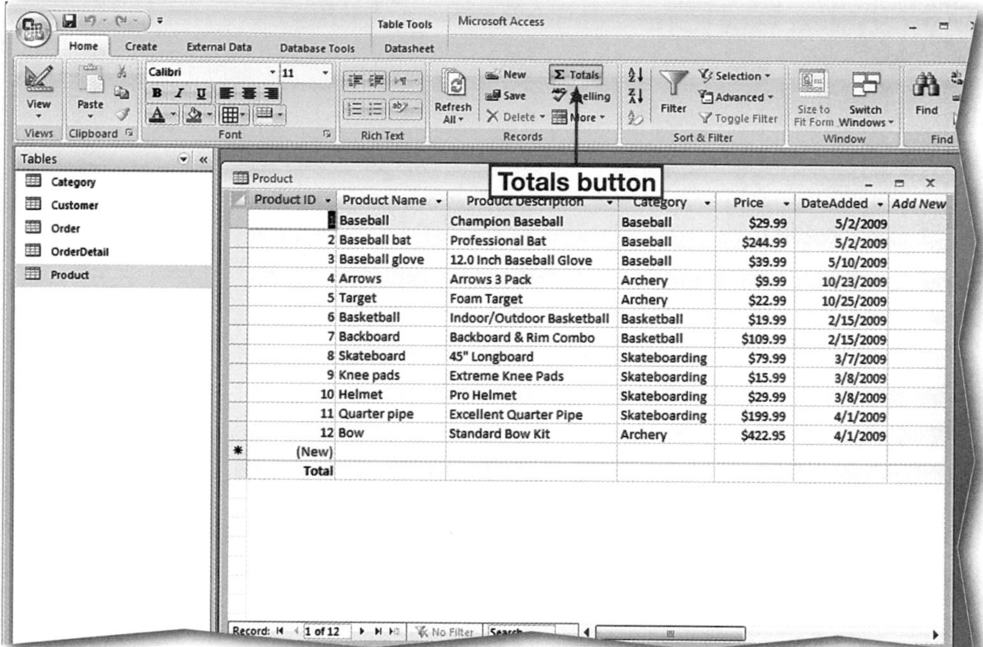

Teaching Tip Let students know that to see a list of all view options, they can click the **View** drop-down arrow.

FIGURE 2.12 Table with Totals row showing Average

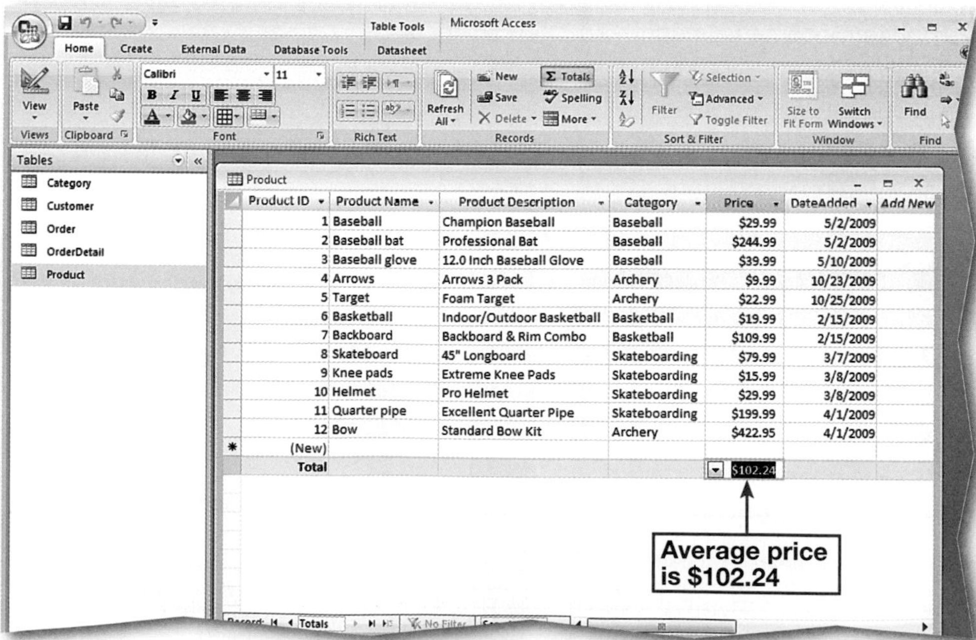

Step-By-Step

1. In Access, locate the data file **Depot.accdb**. Ask your teacher how to copy the database to your folder before working in it.
2. In your **Depot** file, open the **Product** table and choose **Home>Records>Totals** Σ.
3. CHECK Your screen should look like Figure 2.11.
4. Locate the **Total** row near the bottom of the table. In the **Total** row, click in the cell under the **Price** column.
5. Click the **drop-down arrow** ▾. Select **Average**.
6. CHECK Your screen should look like Figure 2.12.

Continued on the next page.

Academic Skills

Organization is crucial to learning, as well as to maintaining an efficient database. It is easier to analyze and synthesize information if it is well organized. By using totals to summarize your data, you are on track to becoming more organized.

NCLB/Language Arts (NCTE 8) Reinforce with students how using technology resources such as Access can help them to organize information.

EXERCISE 5-9
Change Page Orientation

Use Page Setup to change paper size and **page orientation**. The default page orientation is **portrait**, or vertical. For a horizontal layout, change the orientation to **landscape**, or horizontal. Landscape orientation can be very helpful if your worksheets contain a lot of data in columns.

Teaching Tip Help students remember the terms by thinking of a vertical *portrait* of someone and a *horizontal* painting of a landscape.

Step-By-Step

1. In your **Insurance** file, select the **Page Layout** tab. Click the **Page Setup** dialog box launcher.
2. In the **Page Setup** dialog box, click the **Page** tab. Under **Orientation**, click **Landscape** (see Figure 5.17).
3. In the dialog box, click **Print Preview**. If necessary, click **Zoom**.
4. **CHECK** Your screen should look like Figure 5.18.
5. Click **Page Setup**.
6. In the **Page Setup** dialog box, click **Portrait**. Click **OK**. Your preview should now be in **Portrait** view.
7. Click **Close Print Preview**. Your worksheet should now be in **Normal** view.
8. Save your file.

Continue to the next exercise.

FIGURE 5.17 Page Setup dialog box

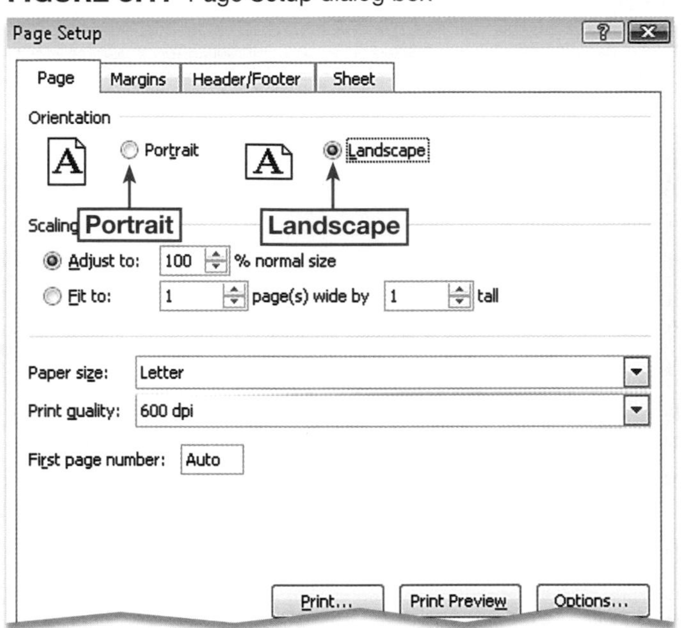

FIGURE 5.18 Worksheet viewed in Landscape orientation

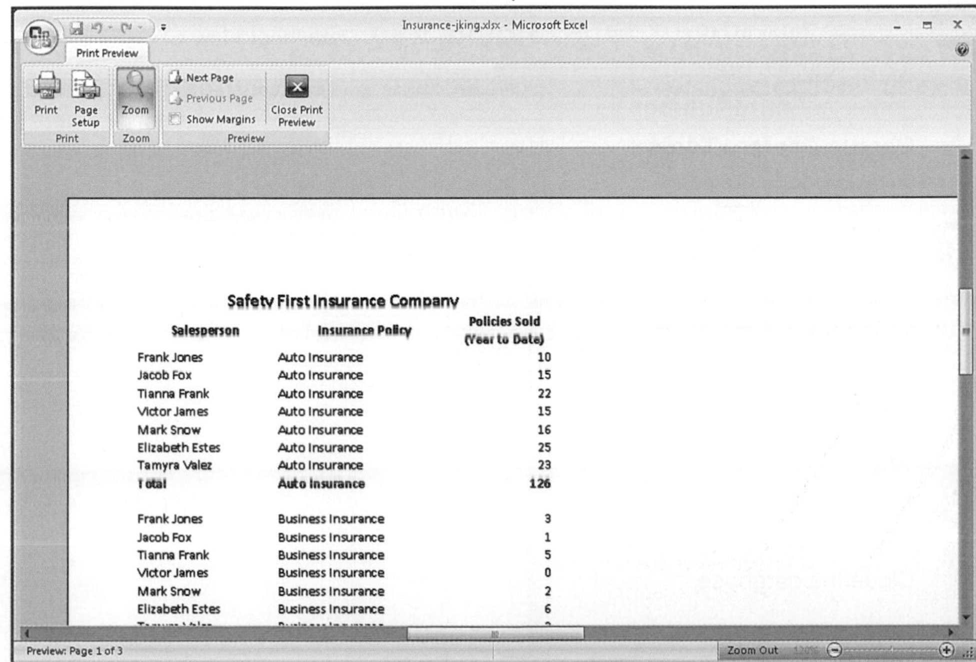

Shortcuts

To confirm that the worksheet is in **Normal** view, click the **View** tab. **Normal View** should be selected in the **Workbook Views** group.

Step-By-Step

1. In your **Database** file, choose **Create>Tables> Table Design** [icon]. Under **Field Name**, key: Company Name. Press [TAB].

2. Click the **Data Type drop-down arrow** [▼]. Select **AutoNumber**.

3. Notice that the **Field Properties** change when you change the data type. Click the **drop-down arrow** [▼]. Select **Text**.

4. Press [TAB] twice. Key: Founded. Press [TAB]. Click the **drop-down arrow** [▼] and select **Date/Time**.

5. Click in the **Company Name** field. Choose **Design>Tools>Primary Key** [icon].

6. Move to the third row of the table. Key: ID. Press [TAB] and select **AutoNumber**. Choose **Design>Tools> Primary Key** [icon].

7. **CHECK** Your screen should look like Figure 2.9. Click **Datasheet View** [icon]. Click **Yes**. In the **Save As** dialog box, key: Companies. Click **OK**.

8. **CHECK** Your screen should look like Figure 2.10. Close the database.

Continue to the next exercise.

EXERCISE 2-4
Create Tables in Design View

Use **Design View** to design tables. In a table, you can change a field's **property**, such as the number of characters, or change a field **data type**, such as whether it represents a date/time. Every table must have a field called a **primary key**, which ensures that each record is unique. Changes to the primary key must be made in Design View.

Intervention Strategy Show students how and where to save their database before starting this exercise.

FIGURE 2.9 Design View finished table

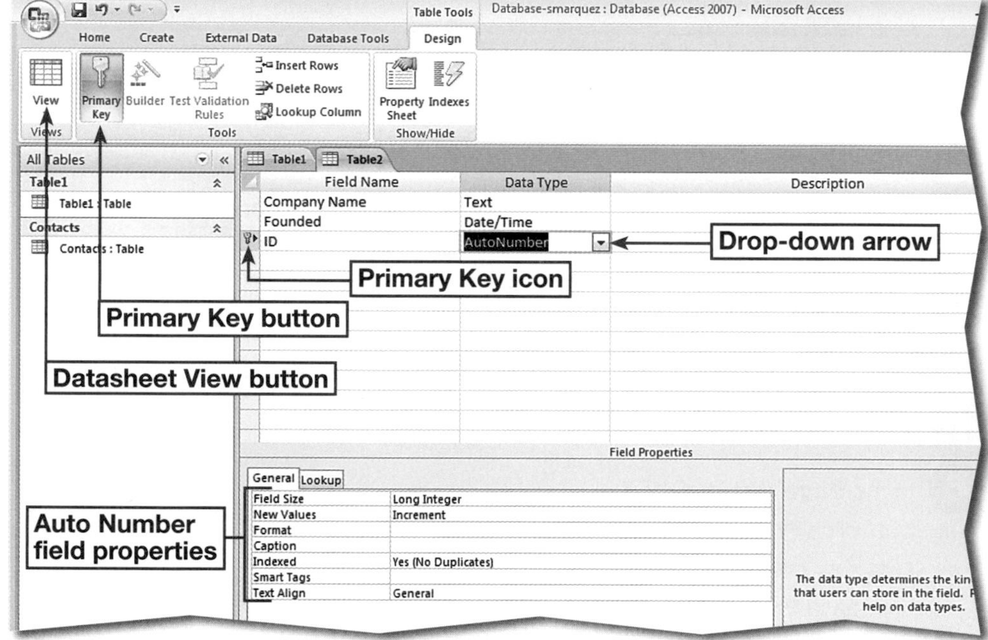

Solution The solution file for this exercise is the **Companies** table in the **Database-SF.accdb** database.

FIGURE 2.10 Datasheet View

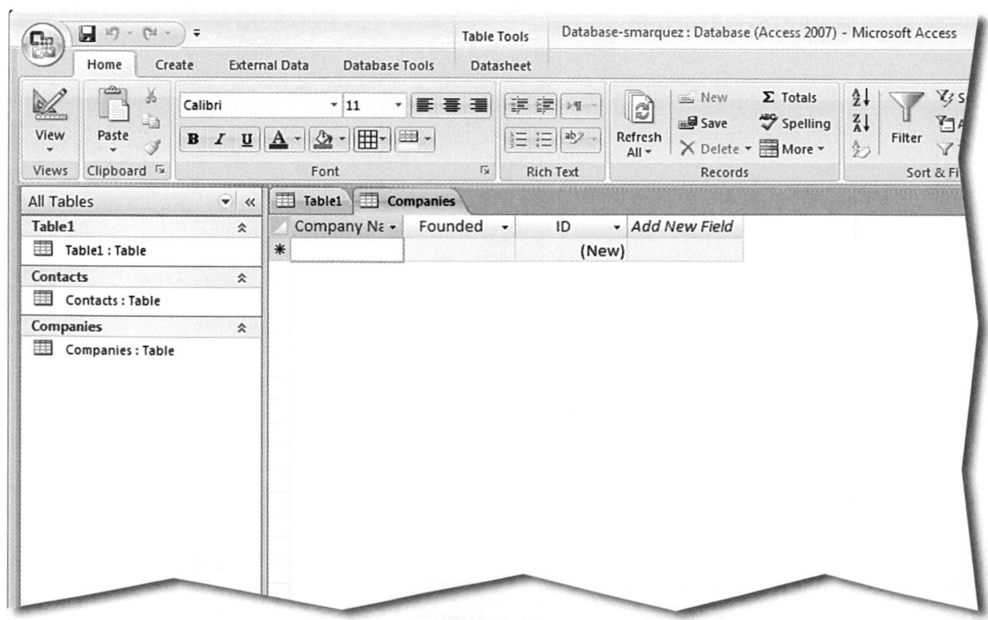

Step-By-Step

1. In your **Insurance** file, select **A1:C9**.
2. Choose **Page Layout> Page Setup>Print Area** and select **Set Print Area**.
3. Choose **Office>Print> Print Preview**. If necessary, click **Zoom**. Notice that only the area that you selected as the print area will print (see Figure 5.19).
4. Click **Close Print Preview**.
5. Click cell **A1**.
6. **CHECK** Your screen should look like Figure 5.20.
7. Choose **Page Layout> Page Setup>Print Area** and select **Clear Print Area**.
8. Save your file.

Continue to the next exercise.

Troubleshooter

Once a print area has been set, it remains the same until you clear or change it, even after you save and close a file.

Differentiated Instruction/ Visually Impaired If students have trouble seeing the cells, have them change the zoom.

EXERCISE 5-10
Set the Print Area

By default, when you choose Print, the entire worksheet prints. If you want to print only a selection of the worksheet, such as a range of cells, set the **print area**. The next time you open the worksheet in Excel, the print area settings you created will be in place. To print the entire worksheet, clear the print area.

FIGURE 5.19 Print Preview of print area

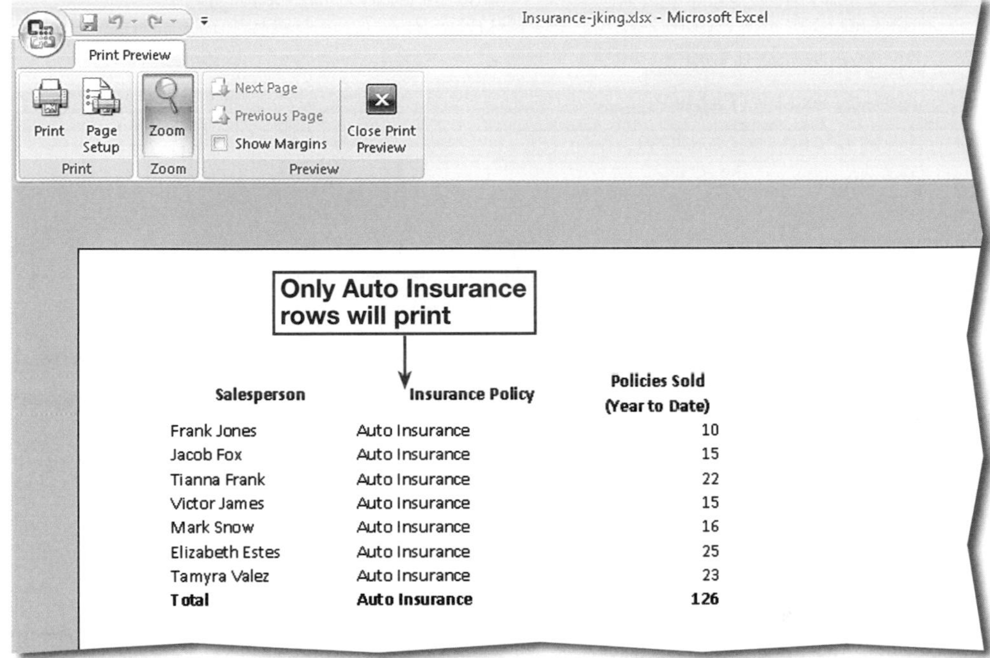

FIGURE 5.20 Print area selected in worksheet

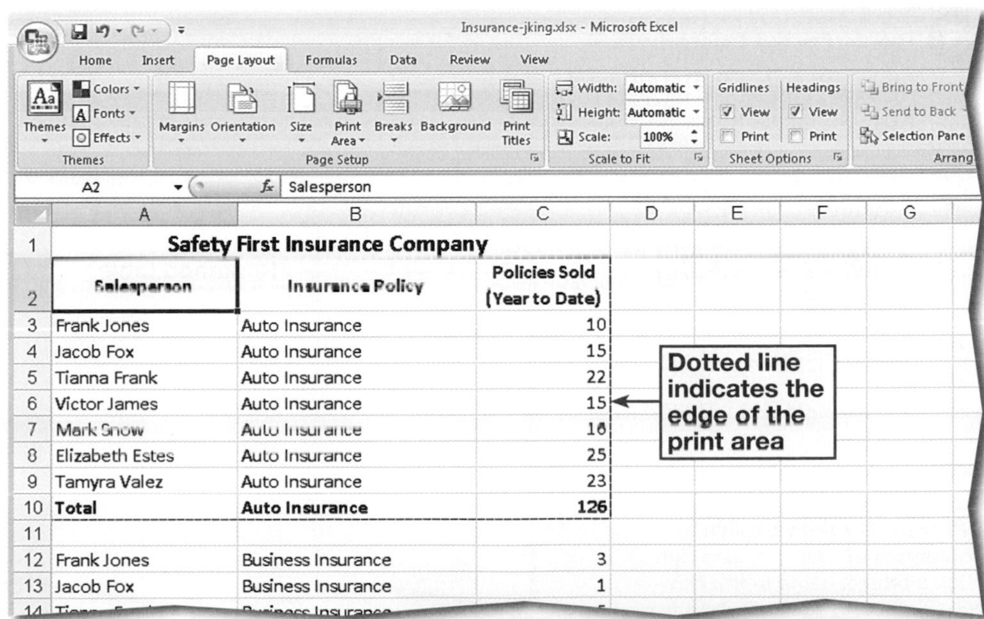

Step-By-Step

1. In your **Database** file, choose **Create>Tables> Table Templates**. In the drop-down menu, select **Contacts**.

2. **CHECK** Your screen should look like Figure 2.7. Notice the fields that already exist in **Table2**. Click **Close** [x] to close the datasheet. Click **Yes** to save the changes.

3. In the table **Save As** dialog box that opens, key: Customers. Click **OK**. Right-click the **Customers** table and select **Copy**.

4. Choose **Home> Clipboard>Paste**. The **Paste Table As** dialog box opens. In the **Table Name** box, key: Vendors. Click **OK**.

5. Right-click the **Customers** table and select **Rename**. Key: Contacts. Press ENTER.

6. Click the **Vendors** table and choose **Home> Records>Delete**. Click **Yes**.

7. **CHECK** Your screen should look like Figure 2.8.

Continue to the next exercise.

Different Strokes Explain to students that they can also right-click a table's name in the **Navigation pane** and select **Delete** from the pop-up menu to delete a table.

EXERCISE 2-3
Add and Remove Tables from Templates

You can add new tables to any database, even those created with templates. Access has dozens of table templates ready for business and personal use. Each table has the most common fields already defined for you and organized for easy use. If you use a template to build your database, you may need to modify it to suit your needs. You can also rename or delete tables as needed.

Solution The solution file for this exercise is the **Contacts** table in the **Database-SF.accdb** database.

FIGURE 2.7 Table created using Table Template

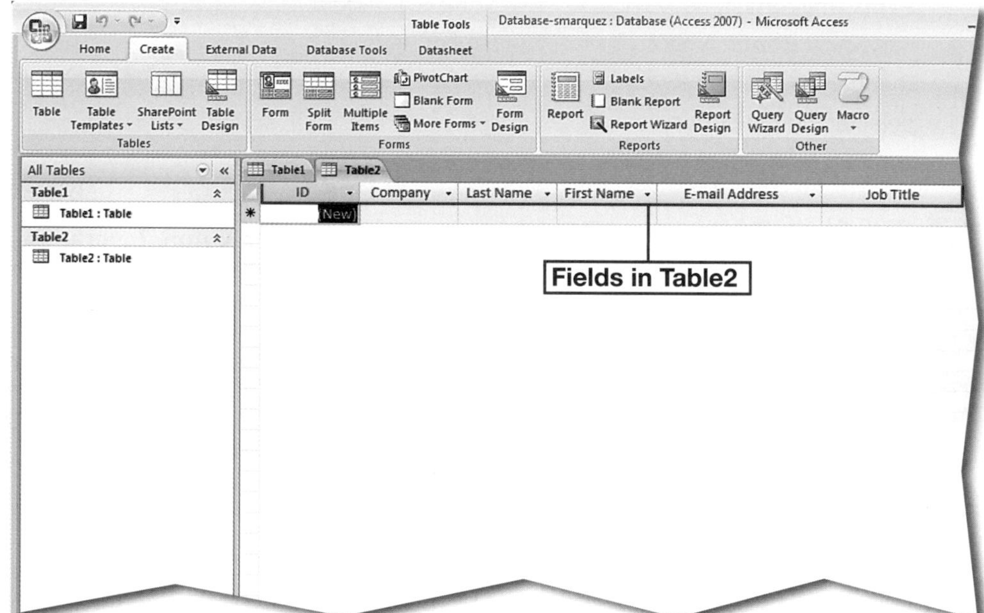

FIGURE 2.8 Vendors table deleted

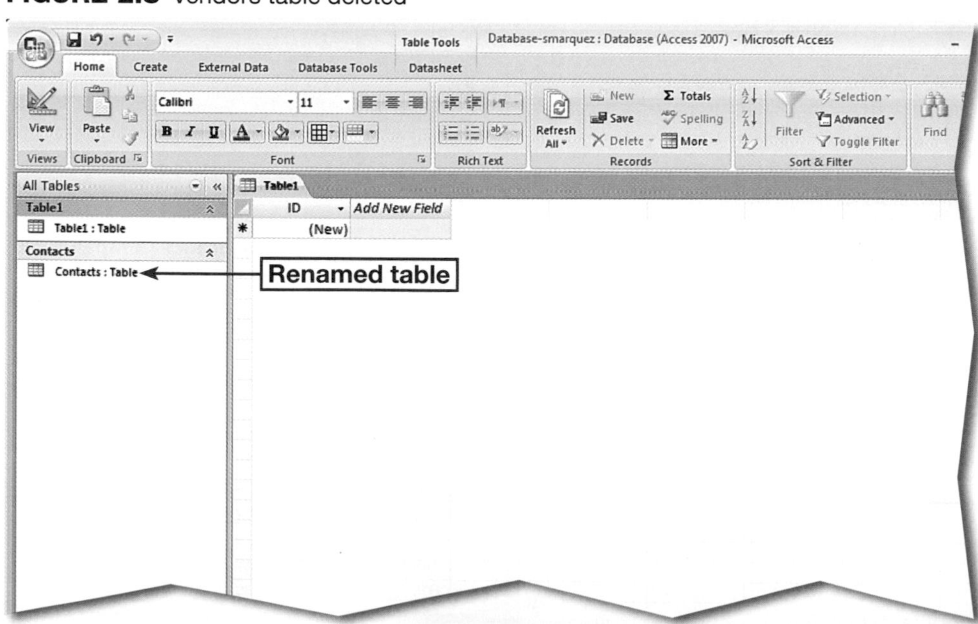

Step-By-Step

1. In your **Insurance** file, click the **Page Setup** dialog box launcher.
2. In the **Page Setup** dialog box, click the **Header/ Footer** tab. Click the **Header** drop-down arrow. Select your **Insurance** file (see Figure 5.21).
3. Click the **Footer** drop-down arrow. Select **Page 1**.
4. **CHECK** Your dialog box should look like Figure 5.21. Click **OK**.
5. Choose **Office>Print> Print Preview**. If necessary, click **Zoom** to zoom out.
6. **CHECK** Your screen should look like Figure 5.22.
7. Click **Close Print Preview**.
8. Save your file.

Continue to the next exercise.

Microsoft Office 2007

Use Excel's **Header & Footer Tools** contextual tab to add built-in header and footer elements, such as the page number, number of pages, current date or time, file name, or file path.

EXERCISE 5-11
Create Headers and Footers

A **header** is text that appears at the top of the printed page. A **footer** is text that appears at the bottom of the printed page. The header and footer often contain the file name, sheet name, page number, current date, or name of the author.

FIGURE 5.21 Page Setup dialog box

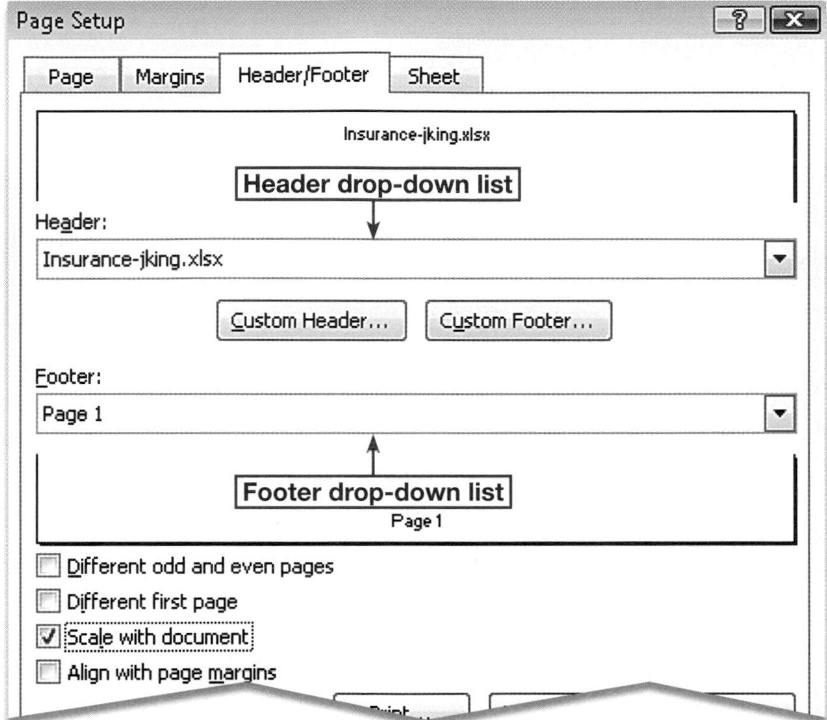

FIGURE 5.22 Header and footer

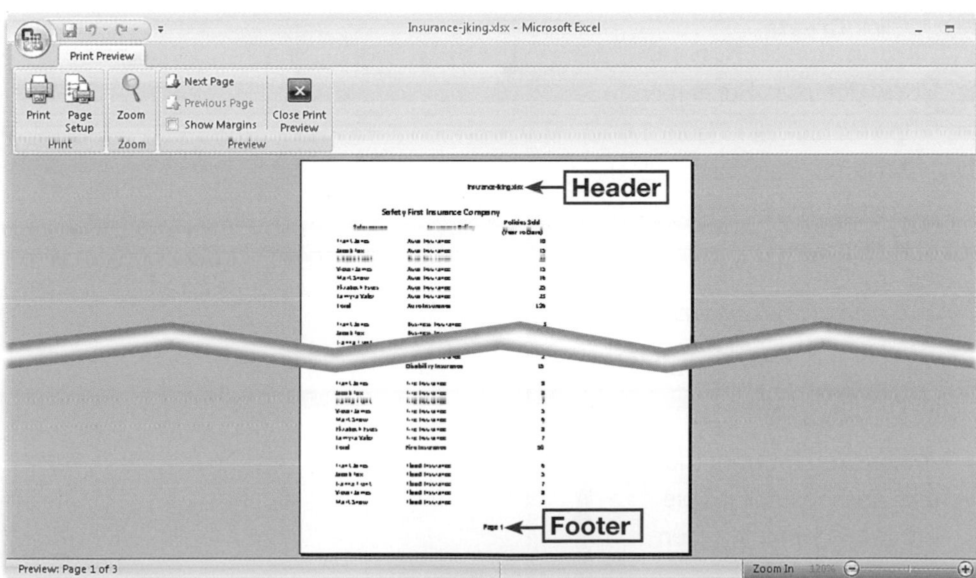

Step-By-Step

1. Start **Access**.
2. On the top of the **Getting Started with Microsoft Access** page, under **New Blank Database**, click **Blank Database**.
3. In the **File Name** box, key: Database-[your first initial and last name] (for example, *Database-smarquez*).
4. **CHECK** Your screen should look like Figure 2.5.
5. Ask your teacher where you should save your database. Click the **Browse folders** icon next to the **File Name** box to open the **File New Database** dialog box, and navigate to the proper location.
6. Click **OK**. The dialog box closes.
7. Click **Create**.
8. **CHECK** Your screen should look like Figure 2.6. An empty database is created and an empty table is displayed.

Continue to the next exercise.

Tech Tip

Access remembers the size and position of the database window when you close it.

EXERCISE 2-2
Create a Blank Database

If you cannot find a template to meet your needs, Access lets you create a completely blank database that does not contain any database objects. You can then design your own tables, forms, and reports and add them to the database.

Different Strokes Let students know that they can also click in the **File name** box and press Home on the keyboard. Then they can press **Delete** until the box is blank.

FIGURE 2.5 The new blank database

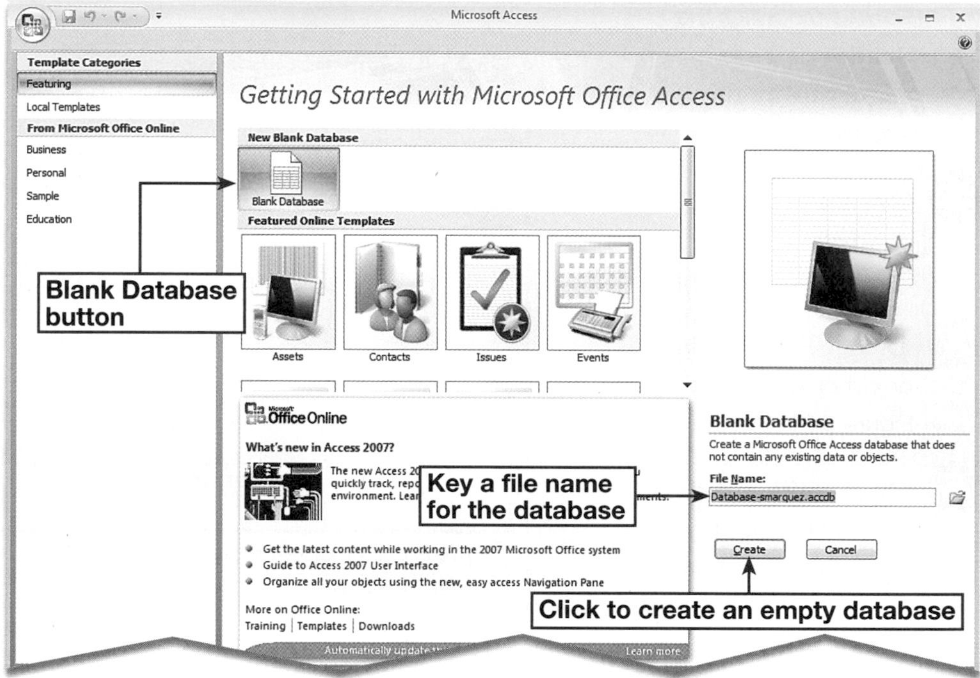

FIGURE 2.6 View of a blank database

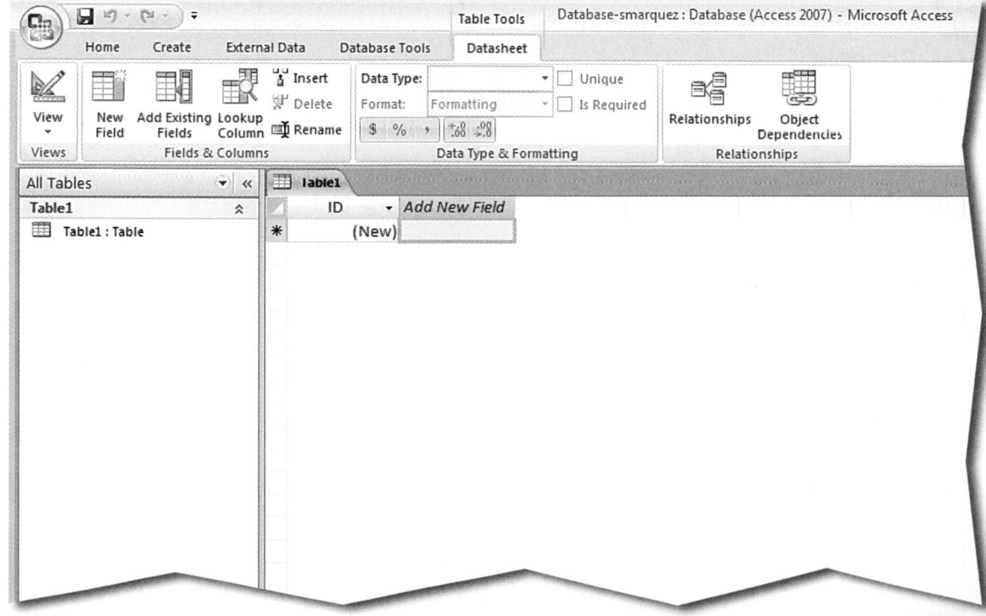

Step-By-Step

1. In your **Insurance** file, choose **View>Workbook Views>Page Break Preview**. Click **OK**.
2. Click on the blue vertical line and drag it between columns **D** and **E**. Click on the blue vertical line and drag it between **F** and **G** (see Figure 5.23).
3. Scroll down until you see the dotted blue horizontal line between rows **43** and **44** (see Figure 5.23).
4. Point to the horizontal page break. Drag it down between rows **46** and **47**.
5. Choose **Workbook Views>Normal**.
6. Choose **Office>Print>Print Preview**. Click **Zoom** .
7. Click **Next Page** .
8. **CHECK** Your screen should look like Figure 5.24.
9. Click **Close Print Preview**.
10. Save your file.

Continue to the next exercise.

Step-By-Step Tip If the **Welcome to Page Break Preview** dialog box opens in **Step 1**, tell students to click **OK**.

EXERCISE 5-12
Preview and Modify Page Breaks

A **page break** is the place where one printed page ends and the next begins. You can move a page break to control which information prints on each page. You can also insert page breaks to force a page to break at a certain point.

Differentiated Instruction/Advanced Students Encourage advanced students to practice switching workbook views using the **View** tab.

FIGURE 5.23 Page Break Preview

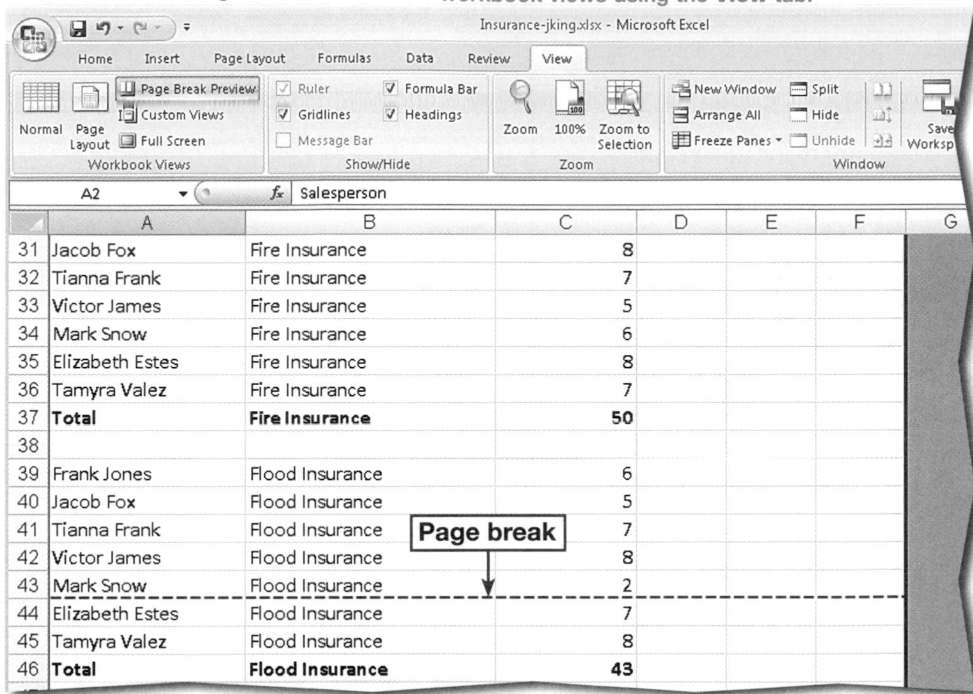

FIGURE 5.24 Modified page break

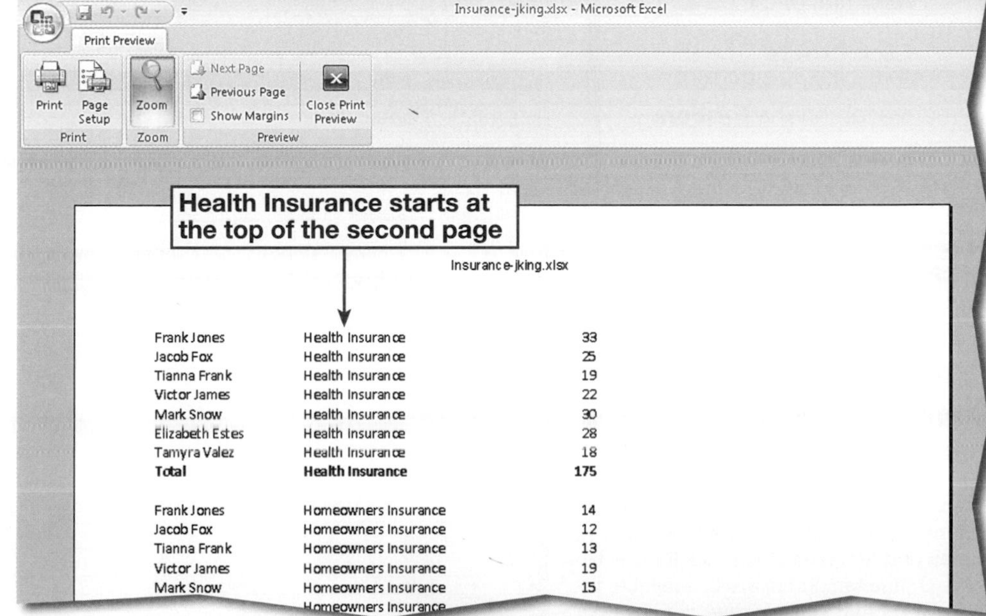

EXERCISE 2-1 (Continued)
Create Databases Using Templates

Step-By-Step

10 **CHECK** Your screen should look like Figure 2.3. The **File New Database** dialog box opens. Ask your teacher where you should store the database.

11 Once you have selected a location, click **OK** at the bottom of the dialog box. The **File New Database** dialog box closes.

12 Click **Create**.

13 **CHECK** Your screen should look similar to Figure 2.4. A new database has been created using the **Contacts** template. Click **Close** [x] to exit **Access**.

Continue to the next exercise.

Troubleshooting A security warning may pop up when creating a new database. Let students know that this is one of Office's new security features.

FIGURE 2.3 File New Database dialog box

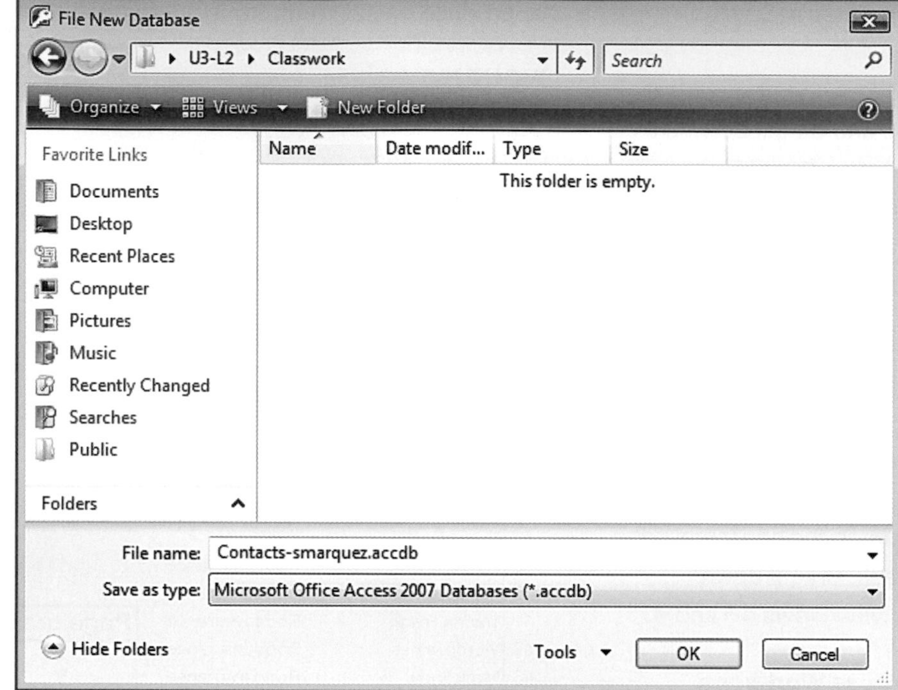

FIGURE 2.4 New database

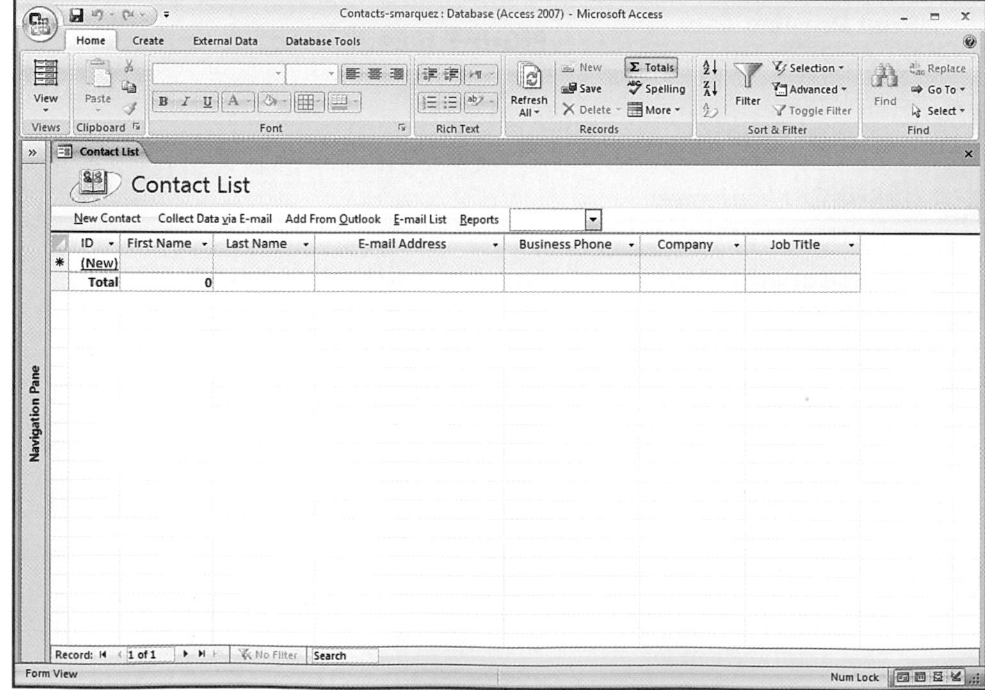

Microsoft Office 2007

To see more of the database object you are working on, double-click the current active tab on the **Ribbon**. This will minimize the Ribbon and allow more screen space for the table, query, or other object you are working on. To return to the Ribbon, double-click a tab header on the minimized Ribbon.

Teaching Tip Explain to students the difference between locally stored templates and templates available for download. Online templates are unavailable to computers that lack Internet access.

Step-By-Step

1. In your **Insurance** file, select **A3:C91**.
2. Change the **Font Size** to **12**.
3. Choose **Office>Print> Print Preview**.
4. Click **Next Page**.
5. **CHECK** Your screen should look like Figure 5.25.
6. Click **Close Print Preview**.
7. Choose **Page Layout** and then click the **Page Setup** dialog box launcher.
8. In the **Page Setup** dialog box, click the **Margins** tab.
9. In the **Top** and **Bottom** boxes, click the down arrow until the boxes read **0.75** (see Figure 5.26).
10. Click **Print Preview**.

Continued on the next page.

Academic Skills

In Step 9, 0.75 represents that the top and bottom margins are 3/4 of an inch from the top and bottom of the page. What does the number 0.5 represent in the Footer box?

EXERCISE 5-13
Setup Options for Printing

If your worksheet does not fit on a single printed page and you would like it to, you can decrease the **margin**, the amount of space between the text and edge of the page. Use the Page Setup group or Page Setup dialog box to change a worksheet's margins. You can also use the Options button in the Page Setup dialog box to select other printing options. For example, you can choose to have certain rows or columns repeat on every page.

FIGURE 5.25 Split data in Print Preview

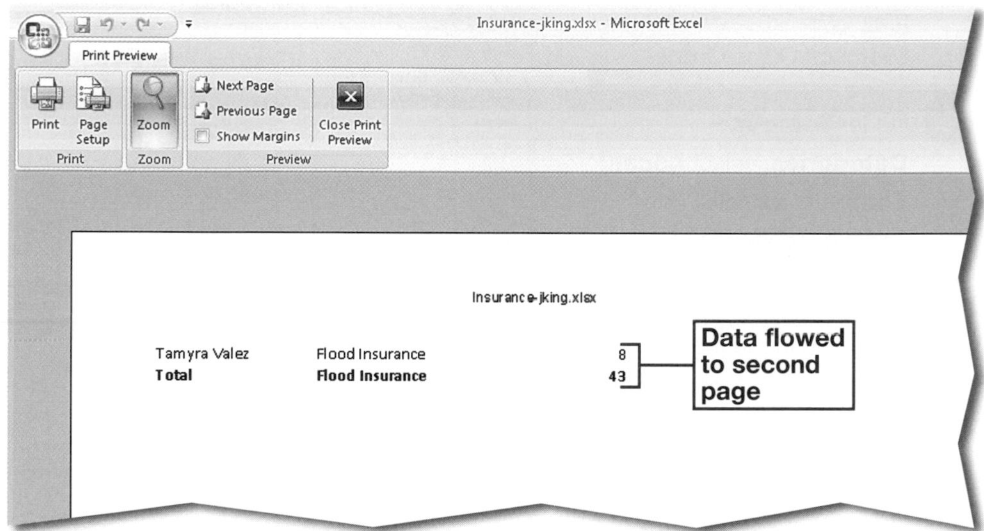

FIGURE 5.26 Page Setup dialog box

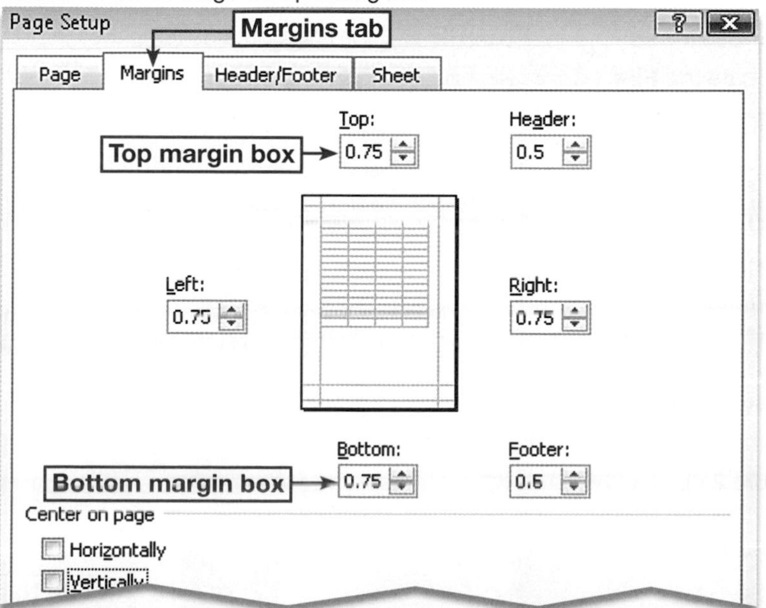

NCLB/Math (Representation) Tell students that the number 0.5 represents that the top of the footer is 1/2 an inch from the bottom of the page.

Step-By-Step

1. Start **Access**.
2. **CHECK** Your screen should look like Figure 2.1.
3. In the **Template Categories** pane, notice that you can use templates from your own computer or download templates from Microsoft Office Online.
4. Under **Template Categories**, select **Local Templates** to pick one from your computer.
5. Local templates are now displayed in the main screen. Select **Contacts** (see Figure 2.1).
6. **CHECK** Your screen should look like Figure 2.2.
7. On the right side of the screen, under **Business Contacts**, locate the **File Name** box (see Figure 2.2).
8. In the **File Name** box, key: Contacts-[your first initial and last name] (for example, *Contacts-smarquez*).
9. Click the **Browse folders** icon next to the **File Name** box (see Figure 2.2).

Continued on the next page.

EXERCISE 2-1
Create Databases Using Templates

To create a database using a **database template**, you can search both Access and online to find the appropriate style. The templates come complete with tables and fields that allow you to organize and track any kind of information, such as inventory, customer orders, personal contact information, and to-do lists. You can use database templates as they are or modify them to suit your needs.

FIGURE 2.1 Access 2007 Getting Started page

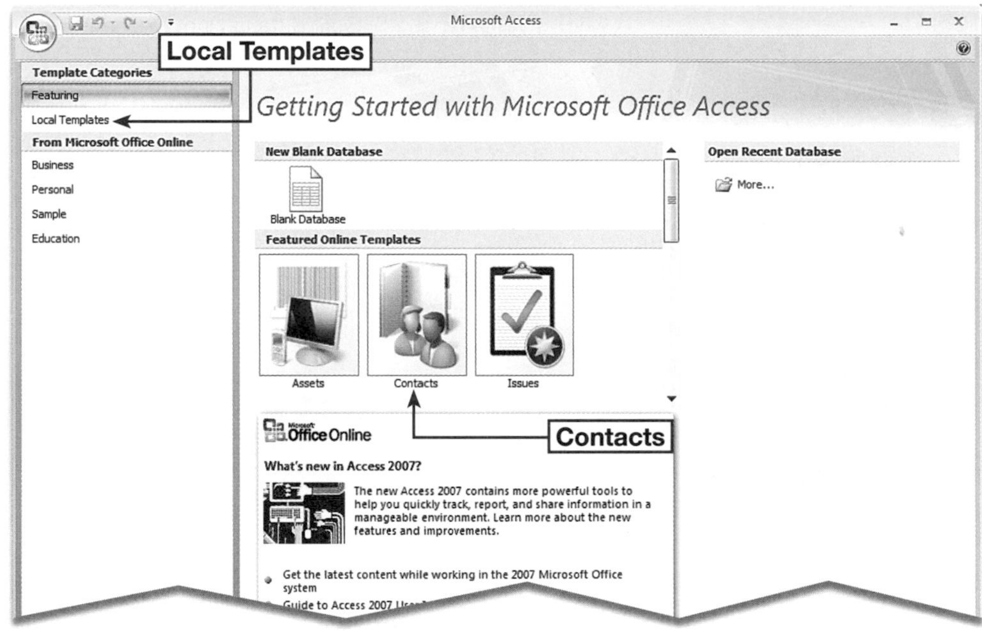

FIGURE 2.2 Saving Contacts template

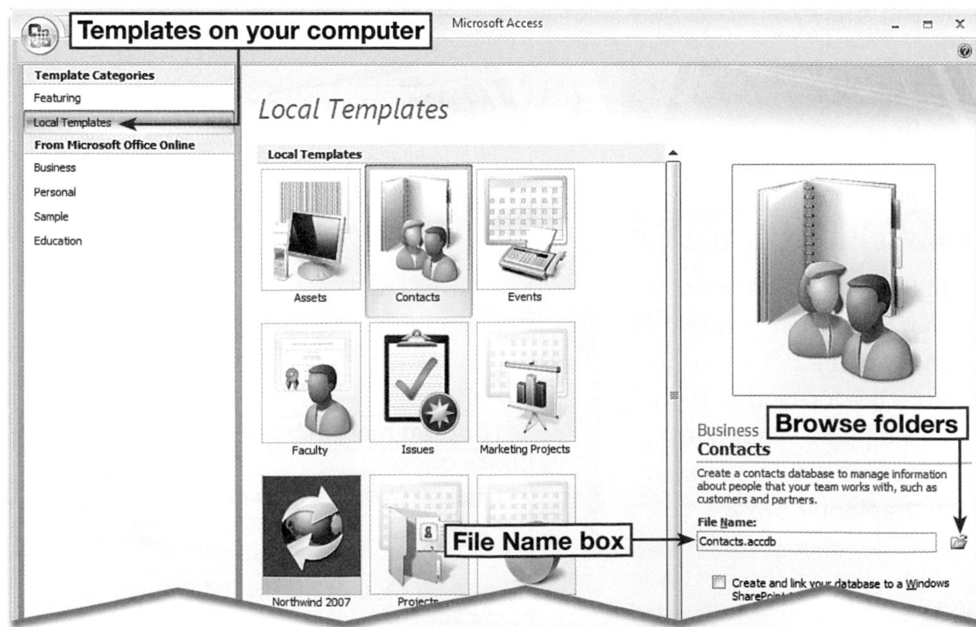

Step-By-Step

11 Use the vertical scroll bar to scroll to the bottom of the first page.

12 CHECK Your screen should look like Figure 5.27.

13 Click **Next Page**. Scroll to the top of the page. The column headings are not on the second page.

14 Click **Close Print Preview**. Click the **Page Setup** dialog box launcher. Click the **Sheet** tab.

15 Under **Print titles**, in the **Rows to repeat at top** pane, key: A1:C1. Click **OK**.

16 Choose **Office>Print> Print Preview**. Click **Next Page**.

17 CHECK Your screen should look similar to Figure 5.28.

18 Click **Close Print Preview**.

19 Save your file.

Continue to the next exercise.

Microsoft Office 2007

You can also specify custom page margins by choosing **Page Layout> Page Setup>Margins** and selecting **Custom Margins**.

EXERCISE 5-13 (Continued)
Setup Options for Printing

FIGURE 5.27 New bottom margin

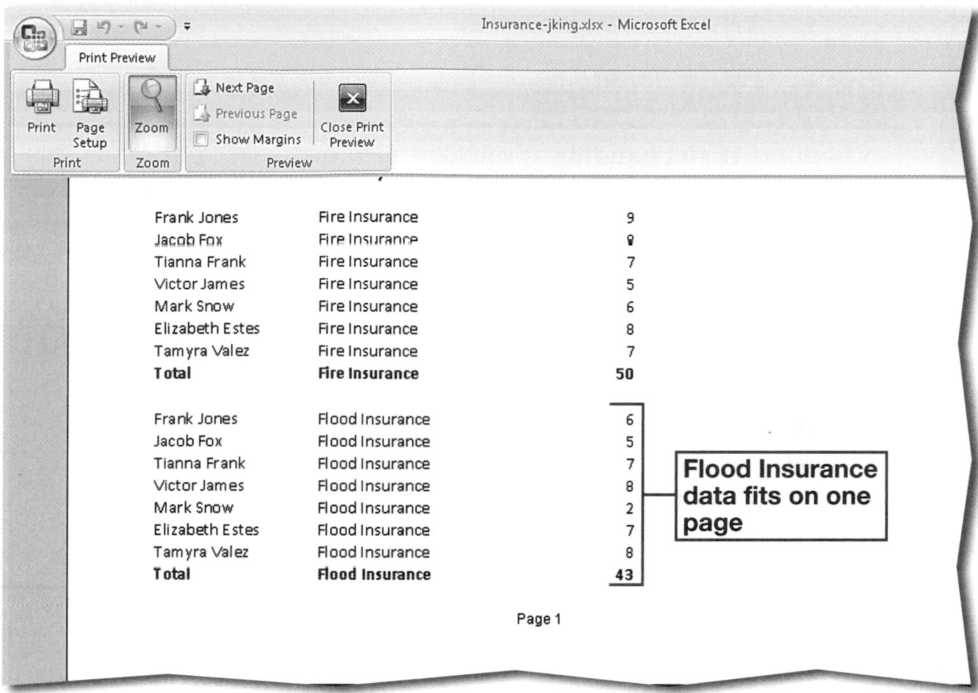

FIGURE 5.28 Repeated row

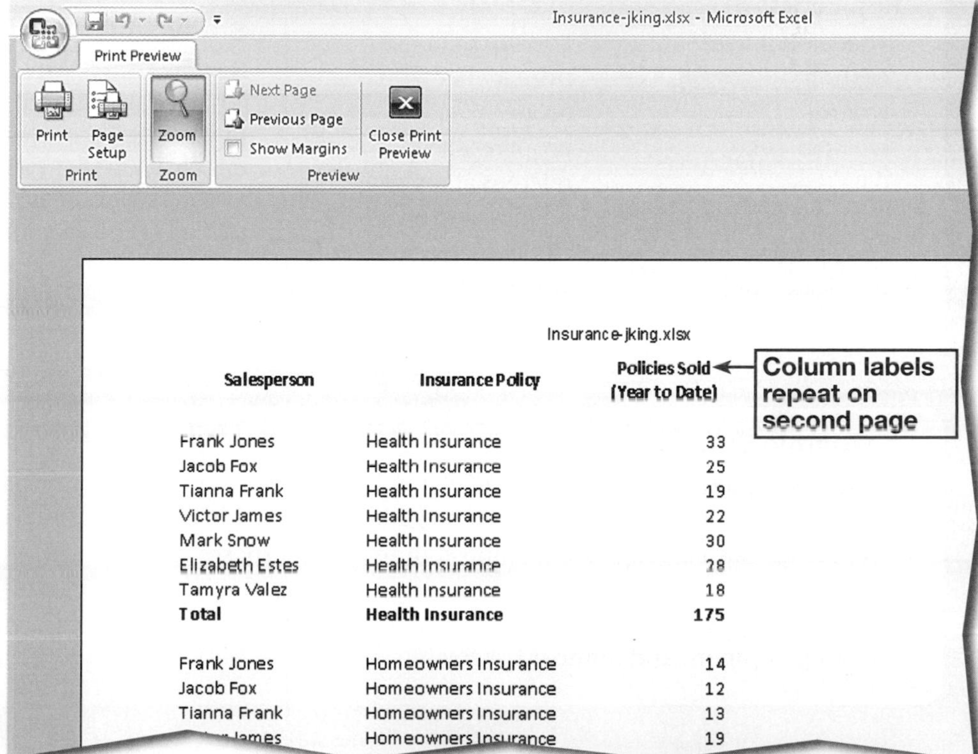

Before You Read

See page TM42 for English Learner activity suggestions.

Check for Understanding If you have questions as you are reading, that means you are checking your understanding of the material. To get the most out of the text, try to answer those questions.

Read To Learn

- Understand how you can compare data such as store sales by creating and modifying tables.
- Discover how specific kinds of queries can extend the way you search, view, change, and analyze data.
- Consider how selecting information to print can focus attention on the most important data.

Main Idea

By understanding various formats and relationships in tables and queries, you will make the information in your database easier to find and interpret.

Vocabulary

Key Terms

attachment field
caption
control
crosstab query
data type
database template
Design View
duplicate query
input mask
Lookup field
primary key
property
property sheet
referential integrity
relationship
Table Analyzer Wizard
Totals row
unmatched query

Academic Vocabulary

These words appear in your reading and on your tests. Make sure you know their meanings.

analyze
insert
portion
redundant

Quick Write Activity

List A catalog company that sells camping gear has a database that contains a table with customer information and a separate table with inventory information. On a separate sheet of paper, write down the type of information that you think might be in each table.

Study Skills

Review Class Notes Review your notes the same day you take them. Add anything you did not have time to write down in class. You may also remember other information that you would like to add to your notes as you review. Reviewing your notes will enable you to study for tests more effectively.

Academic Standards

English Language Arts

NCTE 8 Use information resources to gather information and create and communicate knowledge.

NCTE 12 Use language to accomplish individual purposes.

Math

NCTM (Number and Operations) Understand numbers, ways of representing numbers, relationships among numbers, and number systems.

Step-By-Step

1. In your **Insurance** file, select **A12:C19**.
2. Choose **Office>Print**.
3. In the **Print** dialog box, under **Print what**, click **Selection** (see Figure 5.29).
4. Click **Preview**.
5. **CHECK** Your screen should look like Figure 5.30.
6. With your teacher's permission, click **Print** in the **Print Preview** screen to print the selection.
7. Click **Close Print Preview**.
8. Save your file.

Continue to the next exercise.

Troubleshooter

It is not enough to select a range of cells before you print. Remember to choose **Selection** in the **Print** dialog box.

EXERCISE 5-14
Print a Selection

If you always want to print a certain range, make it the print area. The next time you open the file, you will not have to change the print area, because Excel will remember your settings. If you want to print a range just once, you should print it as a selection.

FIGURE 5.29 Print dialog box

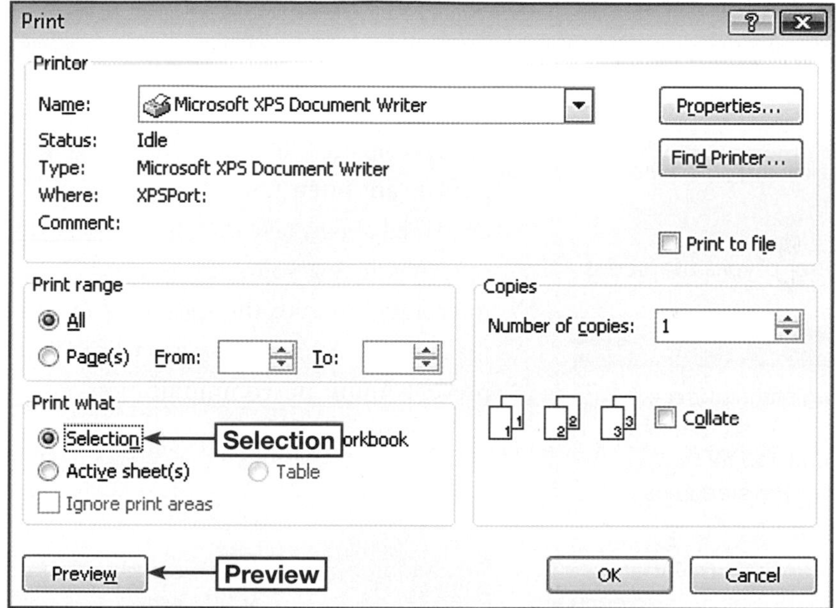

FIGURE 5.30 Print Selection in Print Preview

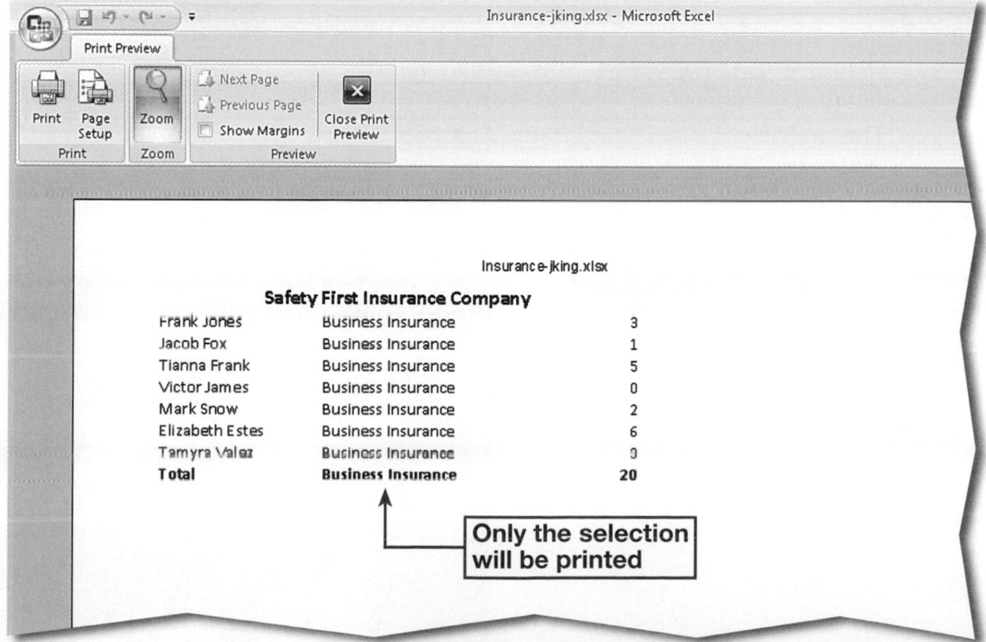

LESSON 2 Structure a Database

Key Concepts

- Use database templates and create blank databases
- Create tables and change their structure
- Create relationships between tables
- Create different types of queries

Standards

The following standards are covered in this lesson. Refer to pages xxv and 715 for a description of the standards listed here.

ISTE Standards Correlation

NETS•S

1a, 1b, 1c, 2a, 2b, 2d, 3a, 3b, 3c, 3d, 4a, 4b, 5a, 5b, 5c, 6a, 6b, 6c, 6d

Microsoft Certified Application Specialist Standards

Access

1.1, 1.2, 1.3, 2.1, 2.2, 2.3, 2.4, 4.1

In this lesson, you will continue learning skills to use Access in your daily life. You will learn to create the following elements in this lesson: databases, tables, simple queries, action queries, and subqueries. Wizards will allow you to quickly implement your knowledge of Access.

21st CENTURY SKILLS

See page TM81 for answer to 21st Century Skills.

Be Patient Your best friend has a problem. Your boss wants things done a certain way. To help each person, you need to be patient. Being patient involves doing your best to understand another person's perspective. People who are patient are often good listeners. To be more patient with the friend or boss described above, take the time to focus on and actively think about what is being said to you. Ask yourself questions about what you are hearing, and check your interpretation with the speaker. You will be rewarded by finding out what you really need to know. The extra time you spend to understand the person may prevent future miscommunication. *How might being patient help make you a better student?*

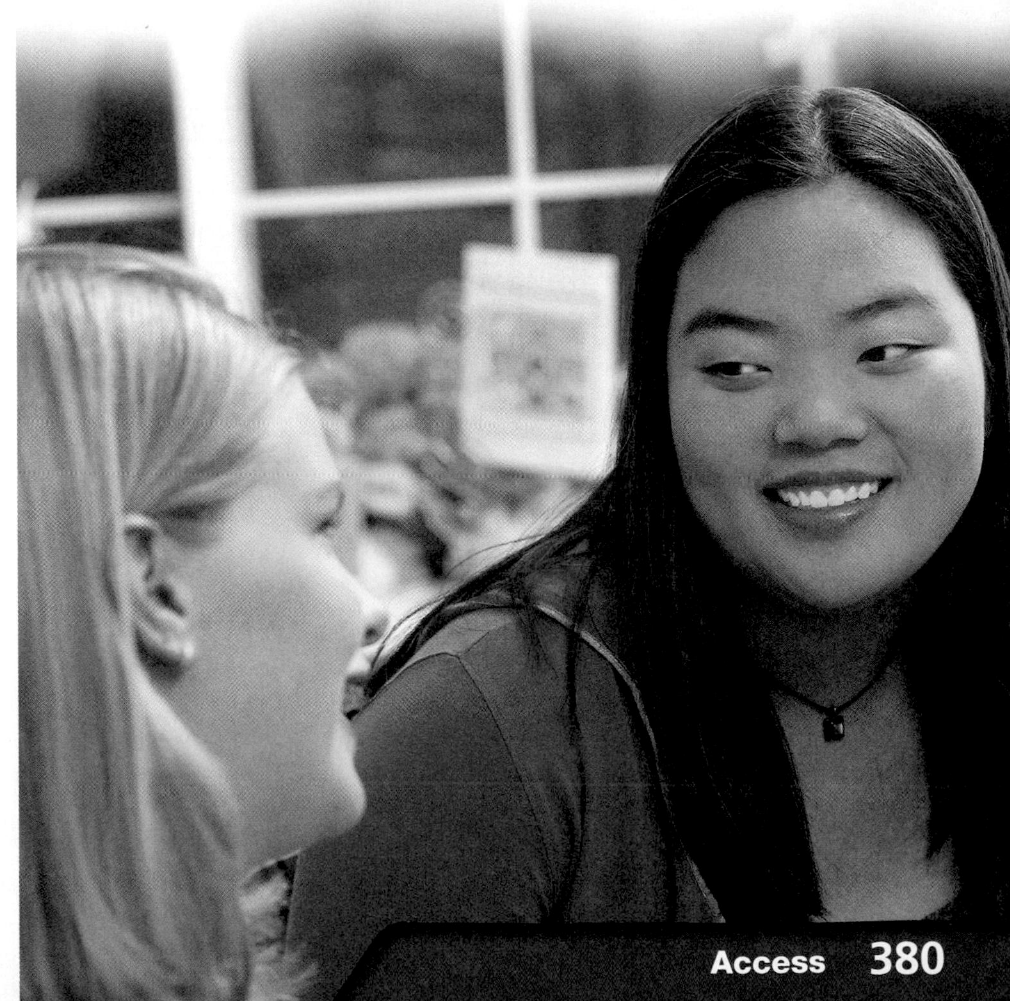

Step-By-Step

1. In your **Insurance** file, scroll up and click cell **A1** so the range is no longer selected.
2. Choose **Office>Print**.
3. In the **Print** dialog box, under **Print what**, click **Active sheet(s)** (see Figure 5.31).
4. With your teacher's permission, click **OK** to print the worksheet.
5. Choose **Office>Print**.
6. In the **Print** dialog box, under **Print what**, click **Entire workbook**.
7. With your teacher's permission, click **OK** to print the workbook.
8. **CHECK** Your screen should look like Figure 5.32.
9. Save your file.

Continue to the next exercise.

Microsoft Office 2007

If a workbook has a defined print area, Excel will only print the area. Check **Ignore print areas** in the **Print** dialog box if you do not want to print a defined print area.

EXERCISE 5-15
Print a Workbook

By default, when you choose Print, the current worksheet prints. You can also choose to print the entire workbook.

Teaching Tip Show students that the changes they made to the header, orientation, and so on, have only been applied to the first worksheet in the workbook.

FIGURE 5.31 Print dialog box

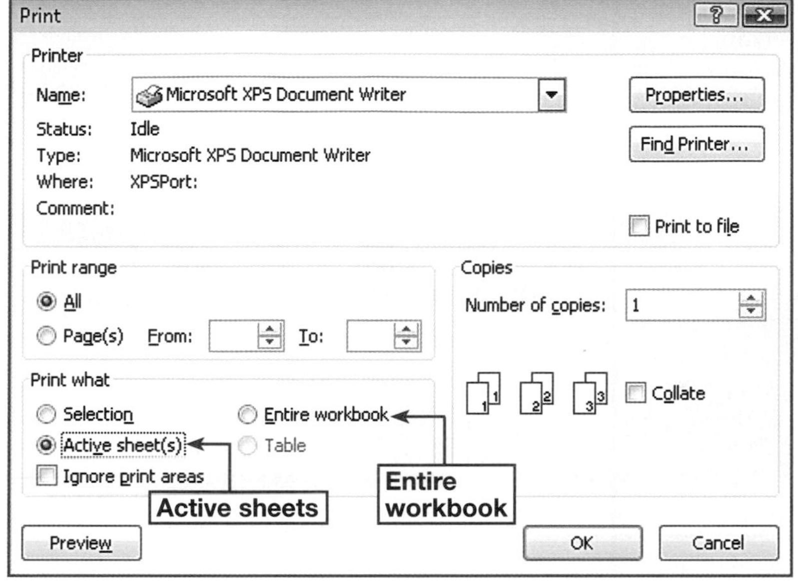

FIGURE 5.32 Workbook

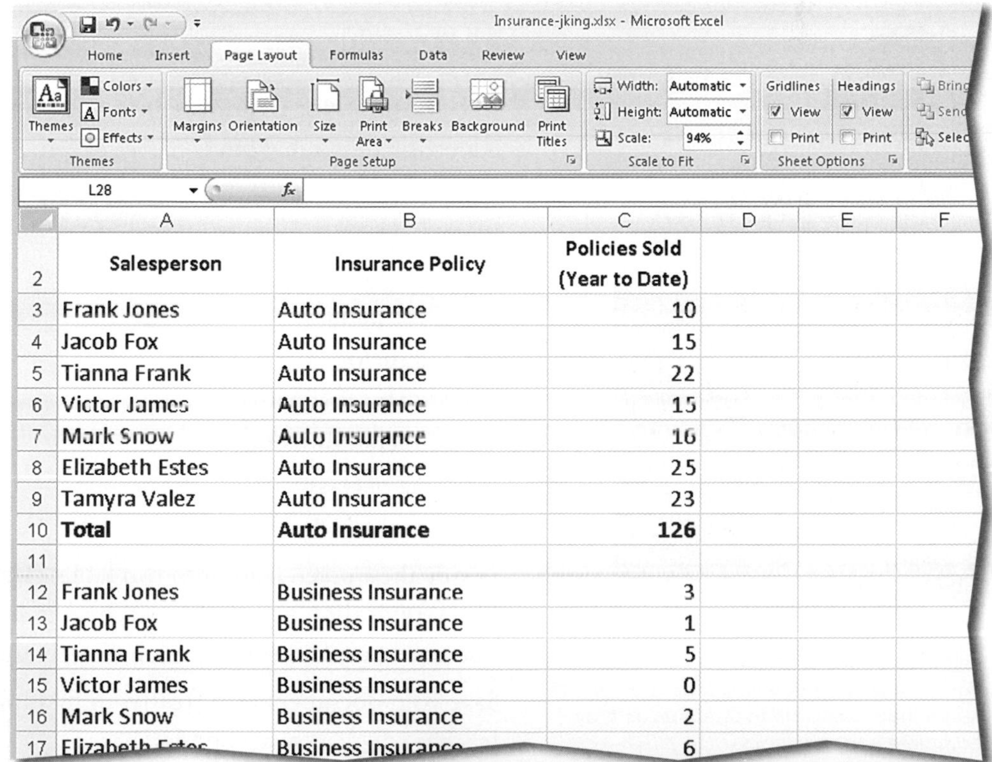

	A	B	C	D	E	F
2	Salesperson	Insurance Policy	Policies Sold (Year to Date)			
3	Frank Jones	Auto Insurance	10			
4	Jacob Fox	Auto Insurance	15			
5	Tianna Frank	Auto Insurance	22			
6	Victor James	Auto Insurance	15			
7	Mark Snow	Auto Insurance	16			
8	Elizabeth Estes	Auto Insurance	25			
9	Tamyra Valez	Auto Insurance	23			
10	**Total**	**Auto Insurance**	**126**			
11						
12	Frank Jones	Business Insurance	3			
13	Jacob Fox	Business Insurance	1			
14	Tianna Frank	Business Insurance	5			
15	Victor James	Business Insurance	0			
16	Mark Snow	Business Insurance	2			
17	Elizabeth Estes	Business Insurance	6			

Before You Begin

Customized Criteria A database allows you to find information based on the criteria that you choose. These projects will help you understand how to work with your data.

Reflect Once you complete the projects, answer the following:

1. What formatting changes did you apply to the **Camp** queries? How did these changes improve its appearance?
2. How does Access help you organize and locate information better than Word?

Answers Rubrics for each Challenge Yourself Project are available at **glencoe.com**. You may want to download the rubrics and make them available to students as they complete each project.

Rubric

9. Format an Unfinished Datasheet

LEVEL This is an intermediate level project.

Format Text Your supervisor wants you to finish formatting the queries in the **Camp** database for a staff meeting. In particular, your supervisor wants you to format the two datasheets so they are easy to read.

In your **Camp** database, open the **Hart Lodge Activities** and **Spring Lake Activities** queries. Apply three formatting changes to each query to make the datasheet more readable. Ask your teacher how to save your work.

10. Plan a Database

LEVEL This is an intermediate level project.

Math: Enter Data Think about objects or information that you need to organize. For example, do you have collections of CDs or books? Do you need to organize information about your friends, such as e-mail addresses and phone numbers?

Use the data file **My Collections.accdb** to create a database to organize your collection. Include at least three to five fields in your database. (For example, if you are creating a database to organize your CD collection, one of your fields could be the CD title.) Fill the fields in with information about your collection. Ask your teacher where and how to save your database.

11. Organize Data

LEVEL This is an advanced level project.

Language Arts: Organize Information You are opening a young adult education center that offers classes in sports, crafts, and foreign languages. To help maintain class registration information, you plan to create a database that will keep track of the following information:

- Student ID number
- Class name
- Instructor
- Student first name
- Student last name
- Cost of class
- Class start date

Divide these seven fields into two tables. Then, enter the fields into the data file **Registration.accdb**. Give each table in the database a name. In a Word document, explain your decisions for dividing the fields as you did.

Save your document as: a1rev-[your first initial and last name]11. Ask your teacher where to save your database.

Step-By-Step

1. In your **Insurance** file, choose **Office>Save As**. Ask your teacher which location to choose in the **Save in** box.
2. Click **New Folder** [New Folder icon]. Key: Insurance. Press ENTER (see Figure 5.33).
3. Click the back arrow to get to the previous screen.
4. Click **Organize**. Click **Rename**.
5. Key: Insurance Sales. Press ENTER. If necessary, click **OK** in the warning box.
6. **CHECK** Your dialog box should look like Figure 5.34.
7. Click **Open**. Click **Save**. Your **Insurance** file is now saved in the **Insurance Sales** folder.

Continue to the next exercise.

Shortcuts

You can also rename a folder by right-clicking the folder and choosing **Rename**.

EXERCISE 5-16
Rename Folders

You can create and rename folders in the Save As dialog box. Make your folder names as descriptive as possible so you can locate, or find, your files quickly and easily.

FIGURE 5.33 Save As dialog box

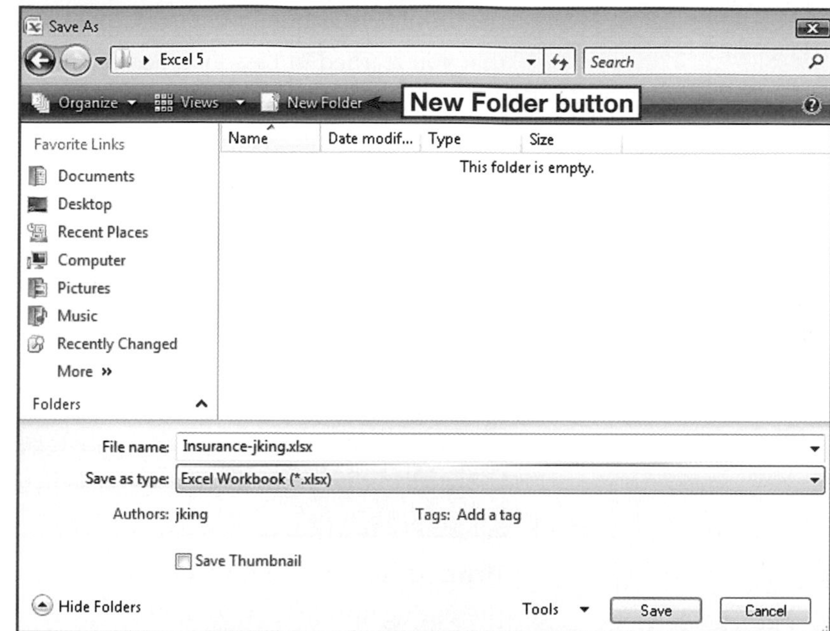

FIGURE 5.34 Insurance Sales folder in Save As dialog box

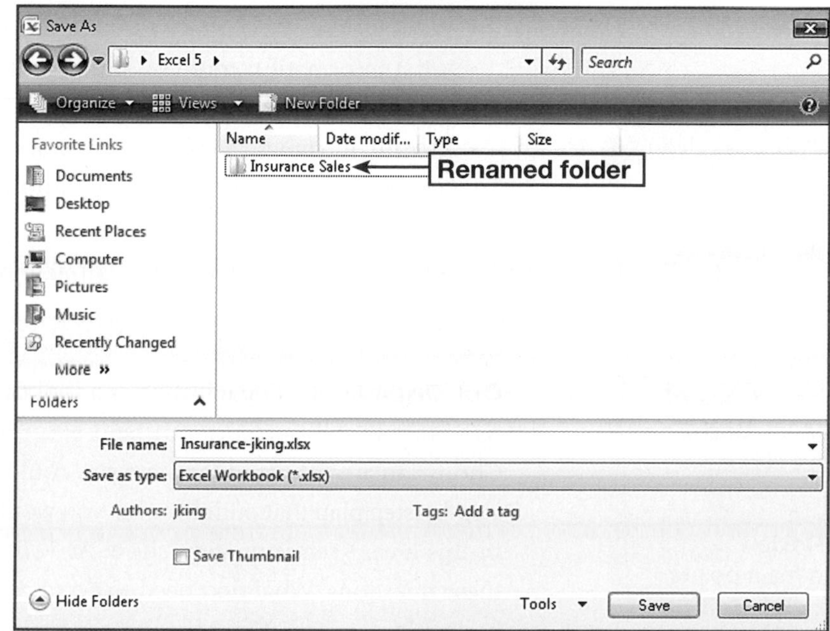

Teaching Tip If you do not want to keep the folder students create in this exercise, have students delete it.

NCLB/Language Arts (NCTE 12) Remind students that when renaming folders they must use clear naming conventions. If a teacher needs to see their report, but they renamed the folder "Old," the folder name does not help them communicate where that report is.

Beyond the Classroom Activity Student paragraphs will vary but should tell how to perform three of the skills learned in Lesson 1 and provide a useful tip for each skill. The paragraph should be clear but concise.

Standards at Work Activity Student paragraphs will vary but should list three characteristics that would make a field the best Primary Key.

21st Century Skills Activity Each student's plan should include a step-by-step list of what he or she would do to become more organized in one area of his or her life. The steps should be short.

6. Beyond the Classroom Activity

Language Arts: Spread the Word Your new job at the local newspaper is to write the Tech Tip column. Your supervisor tells you that your first story will be about helpful Microsoft Access commands. Choose three skills that you learned in Lesson 1. For example, you could choose:

- Open and close a table or query
- View and enter data
- Format a datasheet
- Print a table or query
- Compact a database

Key a paragraph telling readers how to perform each skill. Provide a useful tip for each skill. Remember that newspaper columns have limited space. Write clearly, but be concise.

Save the file as: a1rev-[your first initial and last name]6.

7. Standards at Work Activity

Microsoft Certified Application Specialist Correlation
Access 5.6 *Print Database Objects*

Print Objects Printing data from the database is a primary means of presenting information to others. Open any table in the **Sports Equipment** database and preview it in Print Preview. Key a paragraph that answers the following question:

- What formatting changes would make the table more readable?
- What information could be added to the printout or the table itself that would make the information even more useful?
- Identify the types of information stored in the database. Why would a business need to store this information, and how would they use it to make the business successful?

Save your file as: a1rev-[your first initial and last name]7.

8. 21st Century Skills Activity

Get Organized Organization is a tool that helps you do tasks efficiently. As with any skill, practice can help you improve your ability to organize. Choose an area of your life where you could be more organized. Then, key a step-by-step plan that outlines what you would do to become more organized in this area. Keep your steps short. As you develop your plan, ask yourself these questions: What do I need to do to complete step 1? Step 2? Is there a better place to start? Can I break these steps down into smaller parts?

Save your file as: a1rev-[your first initial and last name]8.

Go Online e-REVIEW
glencoe.com

Go to the **Online Learning Center** to complete the following review activities.

Online Self Check
To test your knowledge of the material, click **Unit 3> Lesson 1** and choose **Self Checks**.

Interactive Review
To review the main points of the lesson, click **Unit 3> Lesson 1** and choose **Interactive Review**.

Step-By-Step

1. In your **Insurance** file, choose **Office>Save As**.
2. In the **Save as type** box, click the **drop-down arrow** (see Figure 5.35).
3. Choose **Formatted Text (Space delimited) (*.prn)**. Click **Save**.
4. A box opens explaining that only the active sheet will be saved. Click **OK**.
5. Another box opens explaining that some features will be lost in the new format. Click **Yes**.
6. **CHECK** Your screen should look like Figure 5.36. Save and close your file. Exit **Excel**.

You Should Know

Whenever you save a file in another file format, some of its formatting may not be supported and may be lost. Microsoft will let you know in a warning that some data and content may not open correctly if saved to a different format.

Teaching Tip Give students an example of a file format. You might explain that the CSV format (comma separated values) saves only the data and commas that separate the data.

Solution Use the file **Insurance-SF.xlsx** as a solution file for **Exercises 5-5** through **5-17**.

EXERCISE 5-17
Convert Files to Different Formats

You might need to save a workbook in a different format so it can be used by another application. For example, you can save a worksheet as formatted text so it is easier to work with in Microsoft Word.

Teaching Tip Explain that a PRN file can be opened in Excel or in any text editor, such as Notepad. The file format is used for printing purposes. It will retain all the information, but not all the formatting.

FIGURE 5.35 Save as type

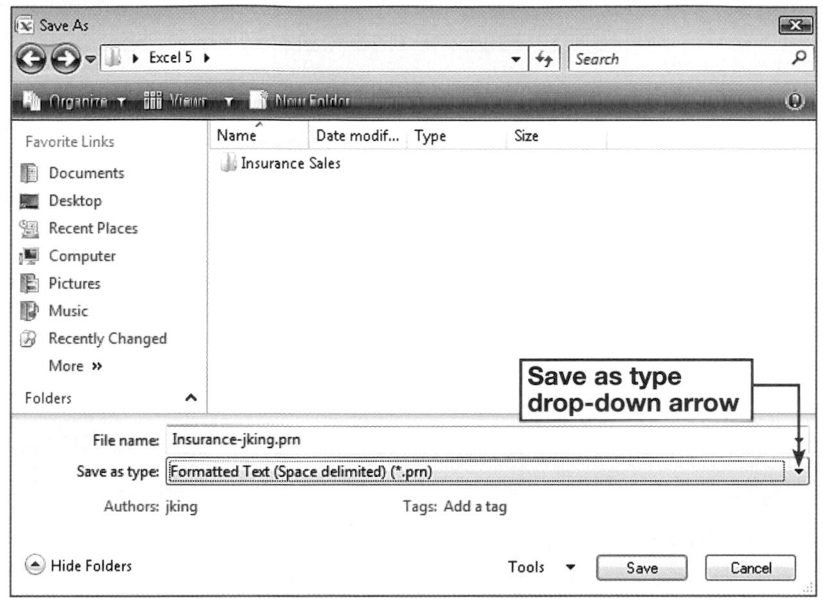

FIGURE 5.36 Workbook saved in .prn format

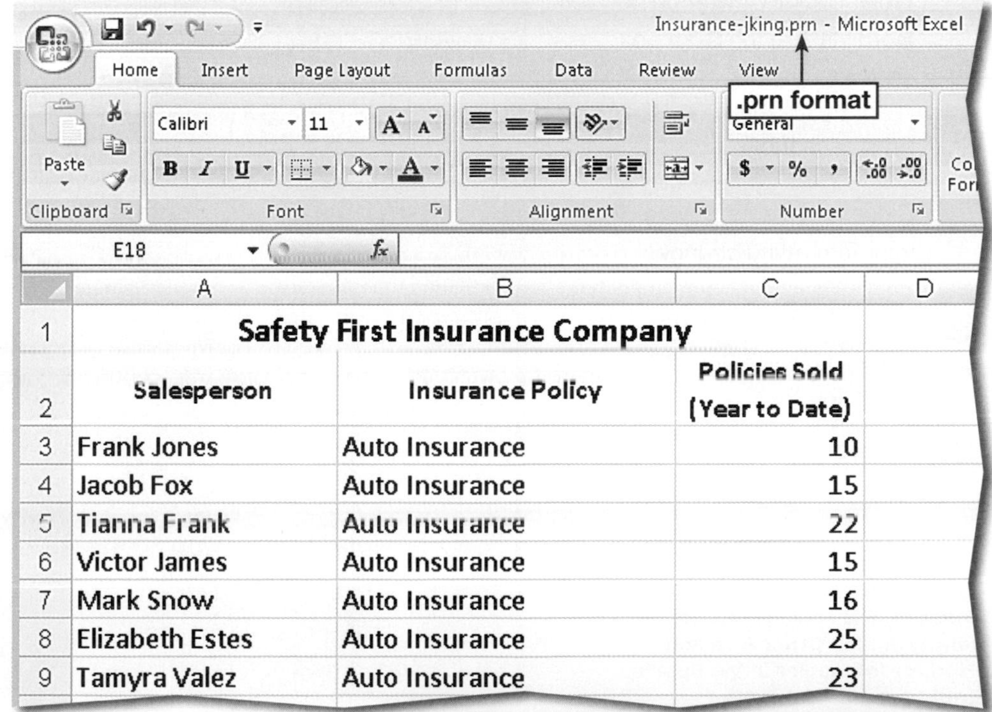

	A	B	C	D
1	Safety First Insurance Company			
2	Salesperson	Insurance Policy	Policies Sold (Year to Date)	
3	Frank Jones	Auto Insurance	10	
4	Jacob Fox	Auto Insurance	15	
5	Tianna Frank	Auto Insurance	22	
6	Victor James	Auto Insurance	15	
7	Mark Snow	Auto Insurance	16	
8	Elizabeth Estes	Auto Insurance	25	
9	Tamyra Valez	Auto Insurance	23	

5. View Multiple Tables and Queries

Your employer needs you to format a table so that it is easier to read. One table has already been formatted according to the new company policy. You want to compare one table to another to make sure you are formatting the data correctly.

Step-By-Step

1. Open your **Sports Equipment** database.
2. Open all three tables. Move them on the screen so you can see part of two different tables at the same time.
3. CHECK Your screen should look similar to Figure 1.46.
4. Switch to the **Order Info** table. Click **Home>Font> Bold** **B**. In the **Size** box, click **12**.
5. Switch to the **Product Info** table. Click **Home>Font> Bold** **B**. In the **Size** box, click **12**.
6. Print each table.
7. Close each table, saving your formatting changes.
8. CHECK Your screen should look like Figure 1.47. Close the file.
9. Exit Access.

Solution The solution files for this activity are the **Order Info** and **Product Info** tables in the **Sports Equipment-SF** database.

FIGURE 1.46 Multiple windows open in Access

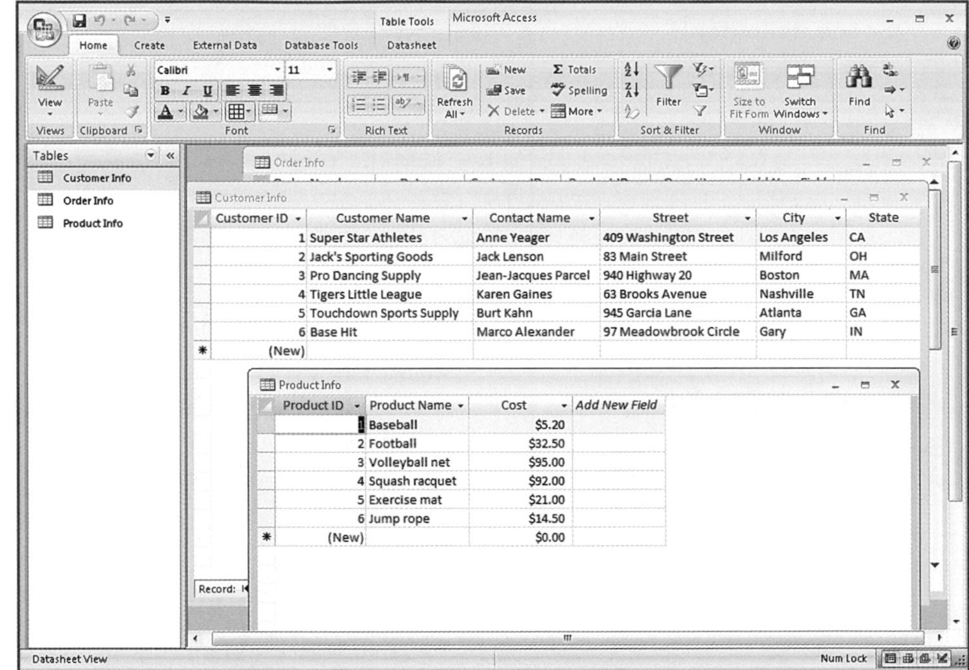

FIGURE 1.47 Database window after closing the tables

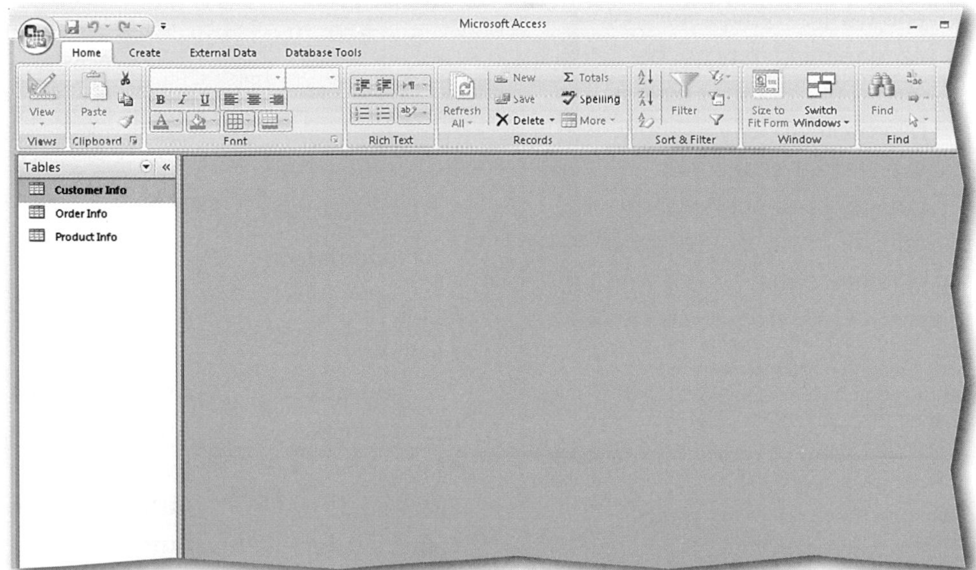

MATH MATTERS

Balance an Account

It is important to keep track of your financial accounts. Always know how much money goes into your account—and how much you spend! If you do not keep track, you may not have enough money in your account to pay for your transactions. You can use Excel to record your money flow, and to calculate how much money you have left in your account.

Using Excel Workbooks

Look at the Excel workbook below. It has columns for the date, check numbers, types of transaction, and amounts added or withdrawn from your account. To get the balance, use this calculation:

= <cell with the beginning balance> − <cell showing withdrawal or payment> + <cell showing deposits>

In the workbook below, you would click F3, and key: "=F2−E3+D3." Then, click on the little black square in the lower right corner of F3, and drag the box down along the F column to calculate the new balance.

Checking.xlsx

	A	B	C	D	E	F	G	H
1	Date	Check	Transaction	Deposit	Payment	Balance		
2	1-Jul					$350.00		
3	2-Jul	301	Phone bill		$ 23.75	$326.25		
4	5-Jul		Gift from Grandma	$ 50.00		$376.25		
5	7-Jul	302	New CD		$ 16.99	$359.26		
6	8-Jul	303	Credit card bill		$ 147.96	$211.30		
7	9-Jul		Paycheck	$175.00		$386.30		
8	11-Jul	304	Donation to the homeless shelter		$ 25.00	$ 36.30		
9	12-Jul	305	Movie tickets		$ 20.00	$341.30		
10								
11								

Sheet1 Sheet2 Sheet3

Use Excel to balance your accounts.

NCLB/Math (Number and Operations)
Reinforce the importance of balancing an account by asking students to explain why it is important to compare the dollar amounts of checks and deposits listed on a bank statement with the amounts listed on a checkbook or savings account register.

NCLB/Math (Number and Operations)
Have students go online to learn more about the skills needed to balance a checkbook, track their expenses, and help them prepare a budget.

SKILLBUILDER

1. **List** List some of the benefits of balancing an account in Excel. Include reasons for both personal and business use.
2. **Predict** What are some of the effects of not balancing an account? What might happen if records are not kept accurately? Give an example.
3. **Math** Imagine you have an account with $200. You wrote a check today for $25. Your credit card bill for $247.98 is due in two weeks. You will receive your paycheck for your part-time job ($150) in one week. When should you pay your bill? How much will you have left in your account after paying the bill?

SkillBuilder answers can be found on page TM76.

4. Look at Data in Three Tables

Your supervisor wants to know which customers are buying volleyball nets. You decide to find the information by comparing three separate tables in the database.

FIGURE 1.44 Order Info table

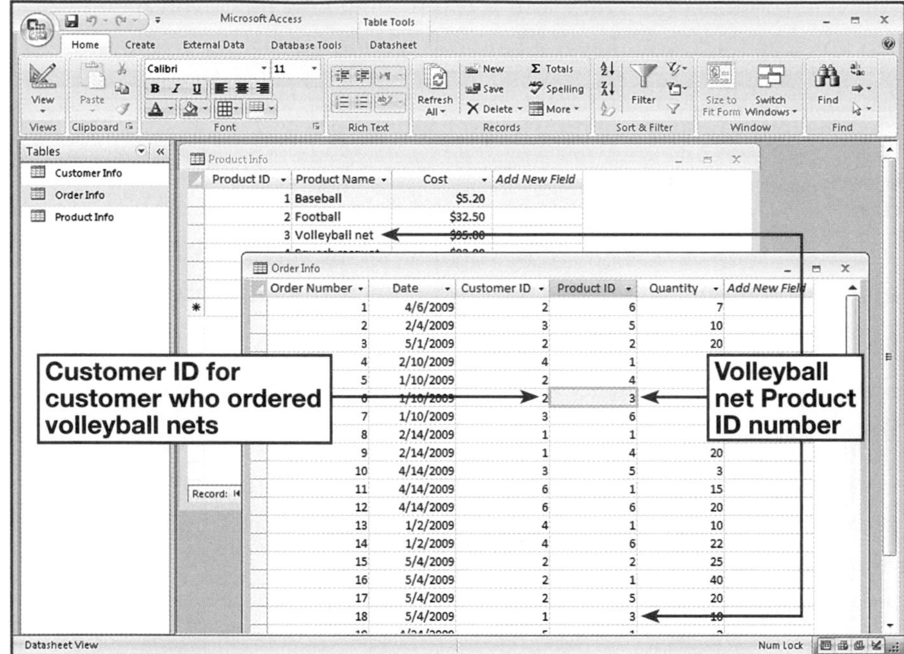

FIGURE 1.45 Customer Info table

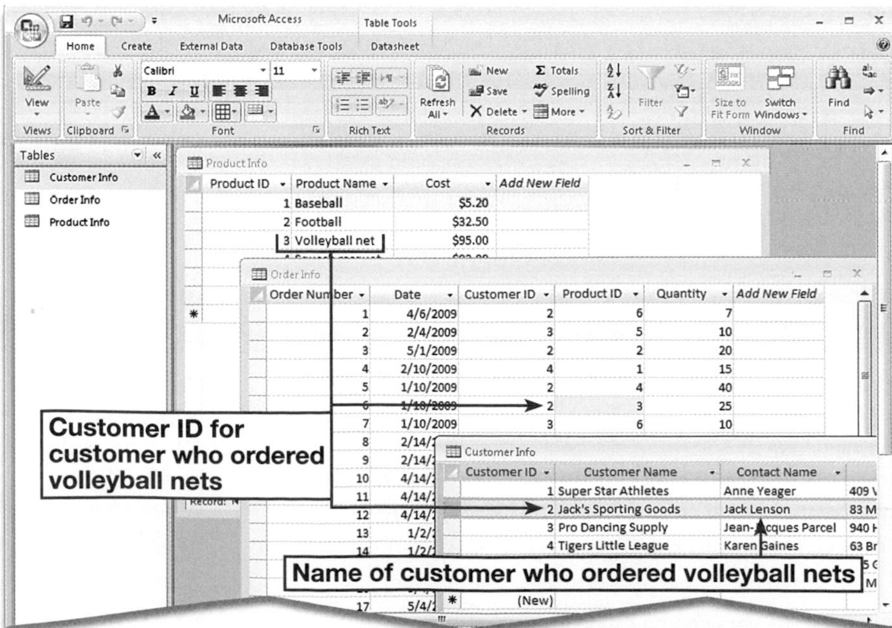

Step-By-Step

1. Open your **Sports Equipment** database.
2. Open the **Product Info** table. Find the **Product ID** field. Note that the volleyball net Product ID number is **3**.
3. Open the **Order Info** table. In the **Product ID** field, find the Product ID number identified in Step 2.
4. **CHECK** Your screen should look like Figure 1.44.
5. Open the **Customer Info** table. In the **Customer ID** field, match the Customer ID numbers identified in Step 3 with the **Customer Name** field.
6. **CHECK** Your screen should look like Figure 1.45.
7. Close the three tables. Close the database.

Solution The answer to **Step 3** is 2, 1. The answer to **Step 5** is **Jack's Sporting Goods** and **Super Star Athletes**.

LESSON 5 After You Read

Vocabulary

Key Terms

footer

freeze

header

landscape

margin

page break

page orientation

portrait

print area

split

template

Academic Vocabulary

arrange

common

convert

locate

Answer to Vocabulary Activity
Students should draw vocabulary words and guess each other's drawings.

Review Vocabulary

Complete the following statements on a separate piece of paper. Choose from the Vocabulary list on the left to complete the statements.

1. Text that appears at the bottom of the printed page is the footer. (p. 325)
2. In landscape orientation, the printed worksheet is wider than it is tall. (p. 323)
3. One printed page ends and the next begins at a(n) page break. (p. 326)
4. When saving a file, you need to locate the properly named file in the correct folder in order to find it again quickly. (p. 331)
5. You can use a(n) template as the basis for other workbooks. (p. 315)

Vocabulary Activity

6. Create a guessing game using five of the vocabulary words.
   A. Pick five vocabulary words, but do not reveal the terms you have chosen.
   B. With your teacher's permission, form groups of five students each.
   C. Each student will take a turn trying to help the other students guess a vocabulary word by drawing a picture on a sheet of paper. Each student will have one minute to draw. If a student guesses correctly, the student who drew the picture wins one point, and the student who guessed correctly draws the next picture.

Review Key Concepts

Answer the following questions on a separate piece of paper.

7. Excel's printing options allow you to ______________. (p. 327)
   A. adjust margins
   B. create headers and footers
   C. print specific parts of a page
   D. all of the above
8. Which of the following allows you to view your worksheet as a Web page? (p. 321)
   A. Web Page Preview
   B. Save As
   C. Publish as a Web Page
   D. Print Preview
9. Which of these commands would you use to display two workbooks on your computer screen at once? (p. 320)
   A. Arrange All
   B. Freeze Panes
   C. Hide
   D. Split
10. Which group on the Home tab allows you to insert and delete a worksheet? (p. 317)
    A. Styles
    B. Cells
    C. Editing
    D. Format

LESSON 1 Practice It Activities

3. Print a Query

Follow the steps to complete the activity.

Solution The solution file for this activity is the **Hart Lodge Activities** query located in the **Camp-SF** database.

Step-By-Step

1. Open your **Camp** database. In the **Navigation Pane** menu, select **Queries**. Double-click **Hart Lodge Activities**.
2. Select **Home>Font>Italic** *I*. In the Font Size drop-down menu, click **14**.
3. In the **Hart Lodge Activities** table, click and drag the line between the fields **Activity Name** and **Meeting Place** until all the text is visible.
4. Click and drag the line between the fields **Meeting Place** and **Cost** until all the text is visible.
5. **CHECK** Your screen should look like Figure 1.42.
6. Select **Office>Print**.
7. Select a printer. Make sure the **Number of Copies** box contains **1**.
8. With your teacher's permission, click **OK** to print.
9. Click **Save**. Close the table. Close the database.

FIGURE 1.42 Formatted query

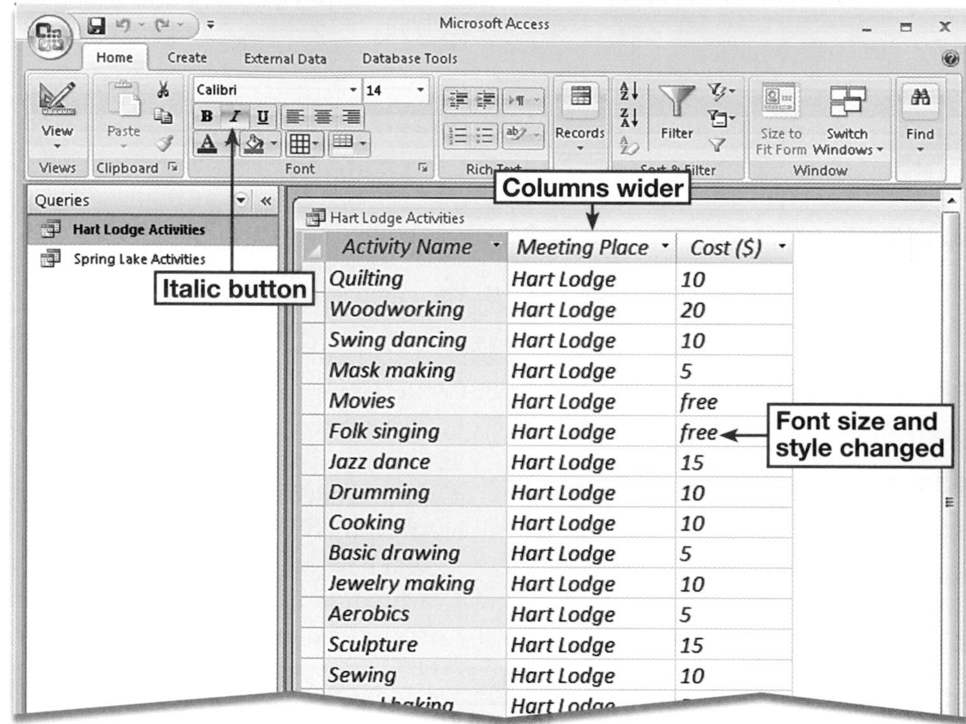

FIGURE 1.43 Print dialog box

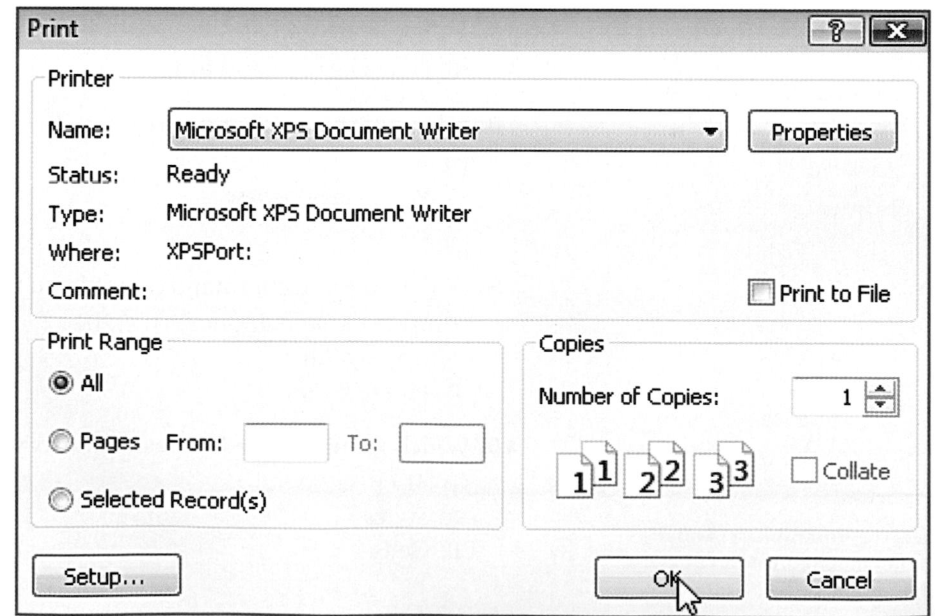

LESSON 5 Practice It Activities

1. Publish a Web Page and Insert and Freeze a Worksheet

Data File

Follow the steps to complete the activity.

Solution The solution file for this activity is **Costs1-SF.xlsx**.

Step-By-Step

1. Open the data file **Costs .xlsx**. Save as: Costs-[your first initial and last name]1.
2. Choose **Office>Save As**. In the **Save as type** dialog box, select **Web Page** and then click **Publish** twice.
3. In the **Excel** version of the file, choose **Insert Worksheet**. Right-click the **Sheet1** tab and select **Move or Copy**.
4. In the **Before sheet** box, click **(2009)**. Click **OK**.
5. **CHECK** Your screen should look like Figure 5.37.
6. Click the **2010** tab.
7. Click cell **E1**. Choose **View>Window>Freeze Panes** and select **Freeze Panes**. Scroll to the right side of the sheet.
8. **CHECK** Your screen should look like Figure 5.38.
9. Choose **View>Window> Freeze Panes** and select **Unfreeze Panes**.
10. Save and close your file.

FIGURE 5.37 Inserted worksheet

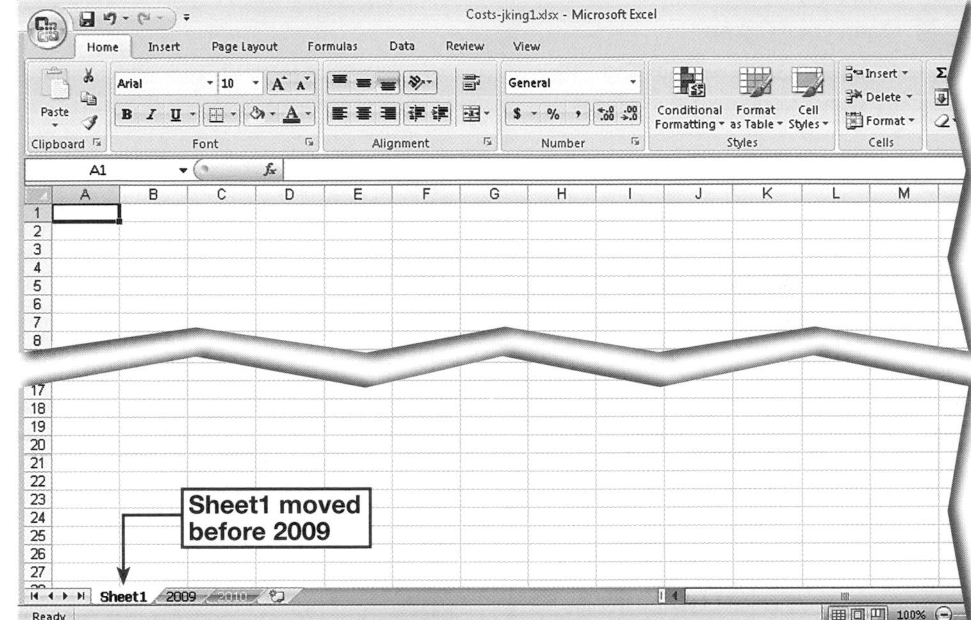

FIGURE 5.38 Worksheet with frozen pane

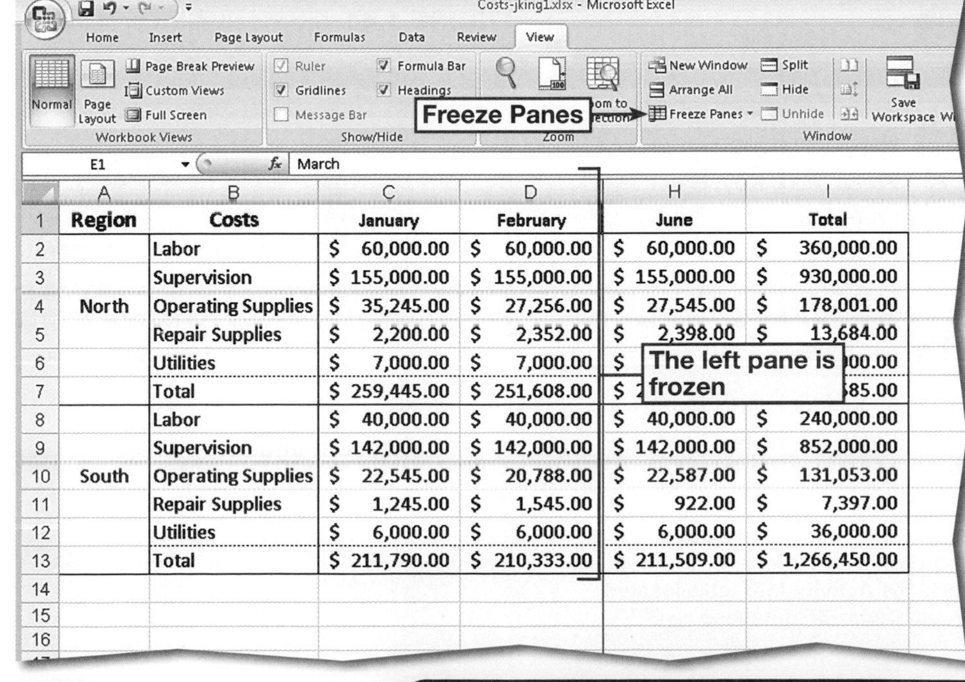

	A	B	C	D	H	I
1	Region	Costs	January	February	June	Total
2		Labor	$ 60,000.00	$ 60,000.00	$ 60,000.00	$ 360,000.00
3		Supervision	$ 155,000.00	$ 155,000.00	$ 155,000.00	$ 930,000.00
4	North	Operating Supplies	$ 35,245.00	$ 27,256.00	$ 27,545.00	$ 178,001.00
5		Repair Supplies	$ 2,200.00	$ 2,352.00	$ 2,398.00	$ 13,684.00
6		Utilities	$ 7,000.00	$ 7,000.00	$	00.00
7		Total	$ 259,445.00	$ 251,608.00	$ 2	85.00
8		Labor	$ 40,000.00	$ 40,000.00	$ 40,000.00	$ 240,000.00
9		Supervision	$ 142,000.00	$ 142,000.00	$ 142,000.00	$ 852,000.00
10	South	Operating Supplies	$ 22,545.00	$ 20,788.00	$ 22,587.00	$ 131,053.00
11		Repair Supplies	$ 1,245.00	$ 1,545.00	$ 922.00	$ 7,397.00
12		Utilities	$ 6,000.00	$ 6,000.00	$ 6,000.00	$ 36,000.00
13		Total	$ 211,790.00	$ 210,333.00	$ 211,509.00	$ 1,266,450.00

LESSON 1 Practice It Activities

2. View Data in a Datasheet

Follow the steps to complete the activity.

Step-By-Step

1. Open your **Camp** database. Double-click the **Activity Info table**.
2. CHECK Your screen should look like Figure 1.40.
3. Click the **down arrow** [▼] repeatedly.
4. Press [PAGE UP].
5. Click **Next Record** [▶] several times.
6. Click **First Record** [|◀].
7. Select the text in the **Current Record** box. Key: 20. Press [ENTER].
8. Click **New Record** [▶*]. Press [TAB].
9. Key: Jazz dance. Press [TAB]. Key: Hart Lodge. Press [TAB]. Key: A. Press [TAB]. Key: 5. Press [TAB].
10. CHECK Your screen should look like Figure 1.41. Close the table. Close the database.

Solution The solution for this activity is the **Activity Info** table located in the **Camp-SF** database.

FIGURE 1.40 Activity Info table

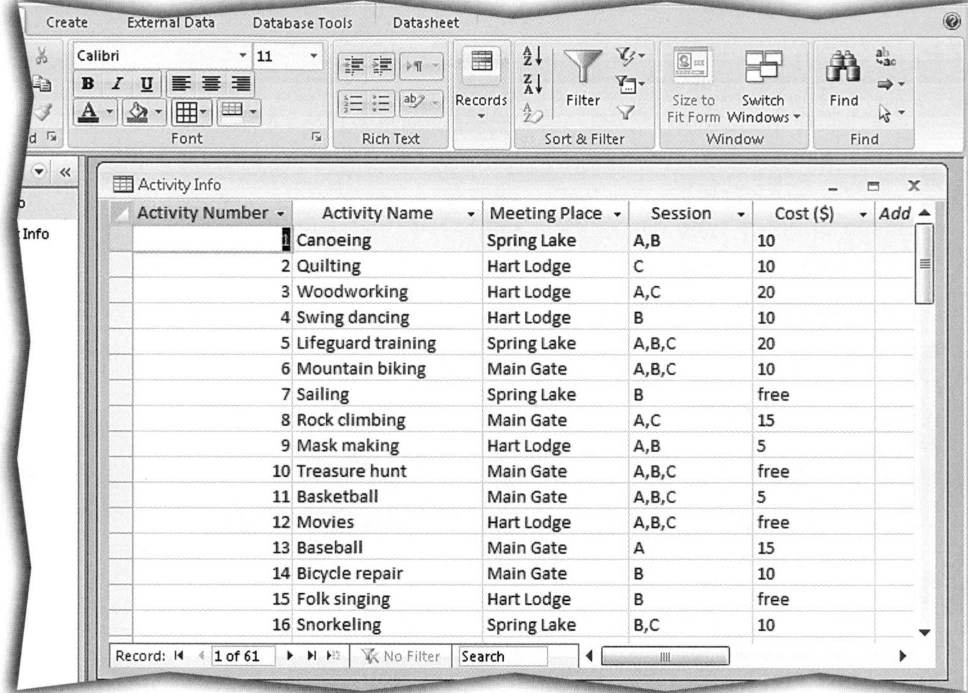

FIGURE 1.41 Access screen with record added

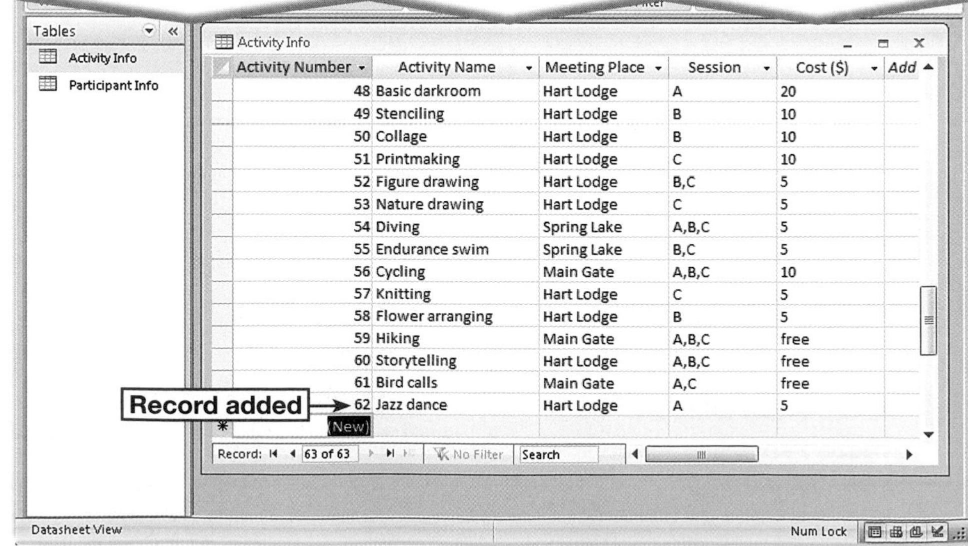

LESSON 5 Practice It Activities

Step-By-Step

1. Open your **Costs-1** file. Save as: Costs-[your first initial and last name]2.
2. On the **Page Layout** tab, click the **Page Setup** dialog box launcher. In the **Page Setup** dialog box, click the **Page** tab.
3. Under **Orientation**, click **Landscape**.
4. In the **Page Setup** dialog box, click the **Header/ Footer** tab.
5. In the **Header** drop-down list, choose **Page 1 of ?** (see Figure 5.39).
6. In the **Footer** drop-down list, choose **Costs-[your first initial and last name]2**.
7. Click **Print Preview**. If necessary, click **Zoom**.
8. **CHECK** Your screen should look like Figure 5.40.
9. Click **Close Print Preview**. Save and close your file.

New Student Strategy If a student did not complete Practice Activity 1, then the solution file for that activity can be used as a data file for this exercise.

2. Change Page Orientation and Add a Header and Footer

Follow the steps to complete the activity. You must complete Practice It Activity 1 before doing this activity. **Solution** The solution file for this activity is **Costs2-SF.xlsx.**

FIGURE 5.39 Page Setup dialog box

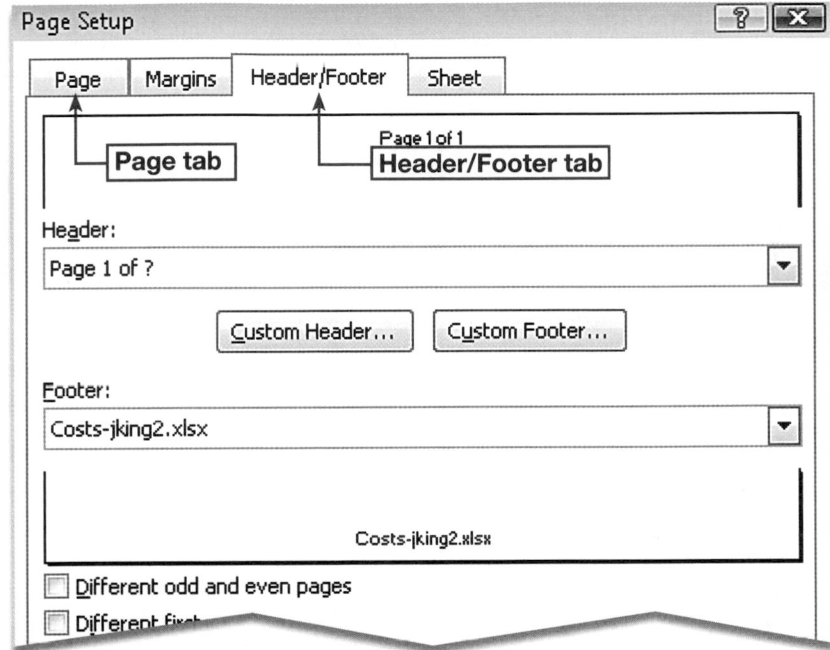

FIGURE 5.40 Header and footer

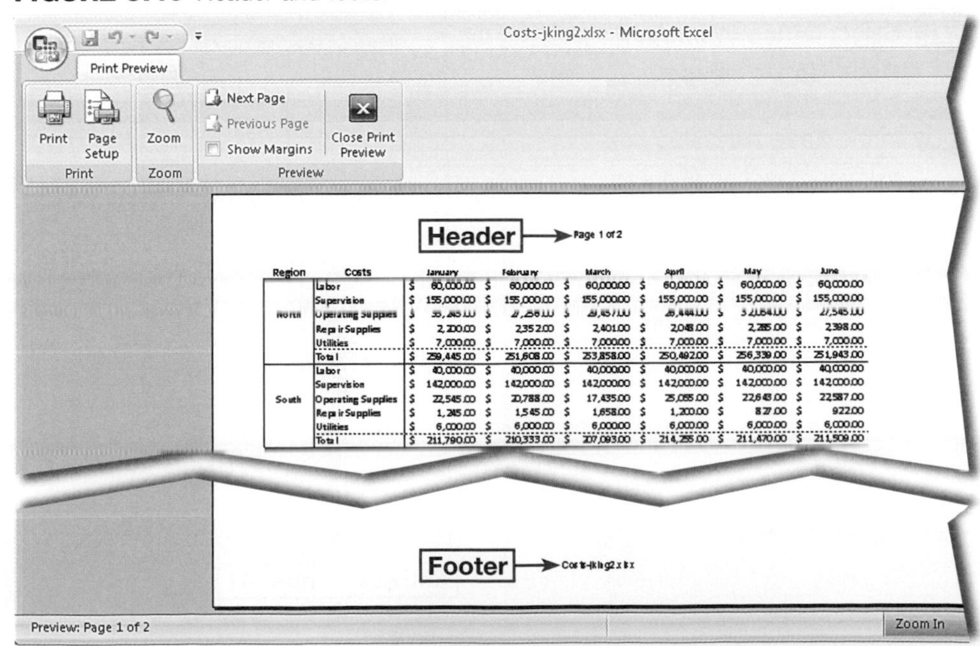

LESSON 1 Practice It Activities

Step-By-Step

1. Start **Access**. Choose **Office>Open**. Locate and copy the data file **Camp.accdb**. Open the database.
2. Open the **Activity Info** table.
3. CHECK Your screen should look like Figure 1.38.
4. Click **New Record**. Press TAB.
5. Key the information for Activity Number 61 as it appears in Figure 1.39.
6. Click **Close** x to close the **Activity Info** table.
7. Select **Office>Manage> Back Up Database**.
8. In the **Save As** dialog box, ask your teacher where to save your backup file.
9. Click **Save** to back up the database. Close the file.

Solution The solution file for this activity is the **Activity Info** table in the **Camp-SF** database.

1. Open and Copy a Database

Follow the steps to complete the activity.

FIGURE 1.38 Activity Info table

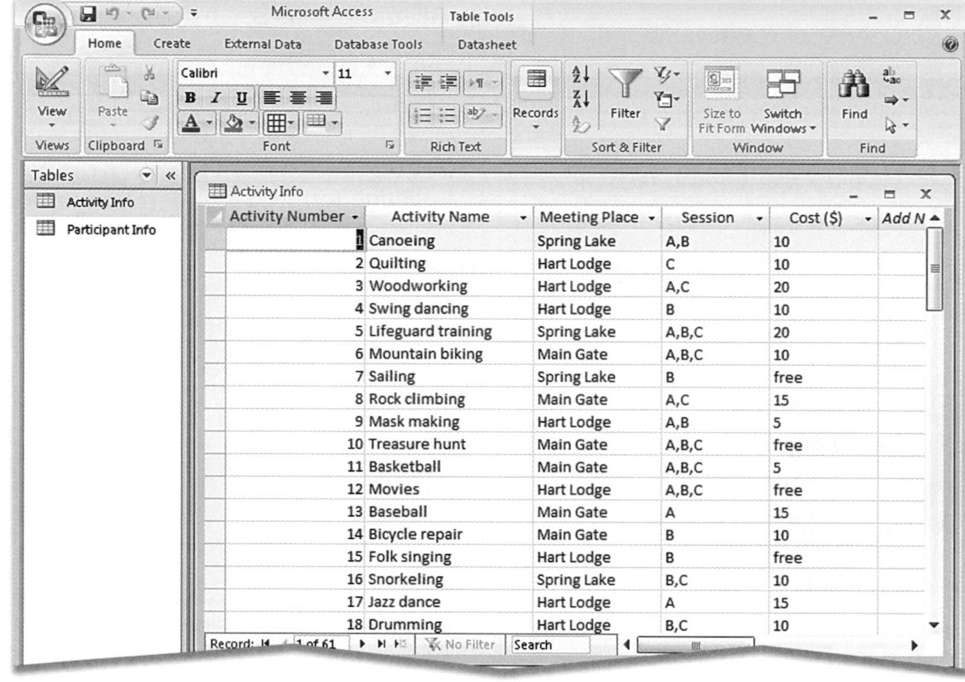

Activity Number	Activity Name	Meeting Place	Session	Cost ($)
1	Canoeing	Spring Lake	A,B	10
2	Quilting	Hart Lodge	C	10
3	Woodworking	Hart Lodge	A,C	20
4	Swing dancing	Hart Lodge	B	10
5	Lifeguard training	Spring Lake	A,B,C	20
6	Mountain biking	Main Gate	A,B,C	10
7	Sailing	Spring Lake	B	free
8	Rock climbing	Main Gate	A,C	15
9	Mask making	Hart Lodge	A,B	5
10	Treasure hunt	Main Gate	A,B,C	free
11	Basketball	Main Gate	A,B,C	5
12	Movies	Hart Lodge	A,B,C	free
13	Baseball	Main Gate	A	15
14	Bicycle repair	Main Gate	B	10
15	Folk singing	Hart Lodge	B	free
16	Snorkeling	Spring Lake	B,C	10
17	Jazz dance	Hart Lodge	A	15
18	Drumming	Hart Lodge	B,C	10

FIGURE 1.39 Record added to table

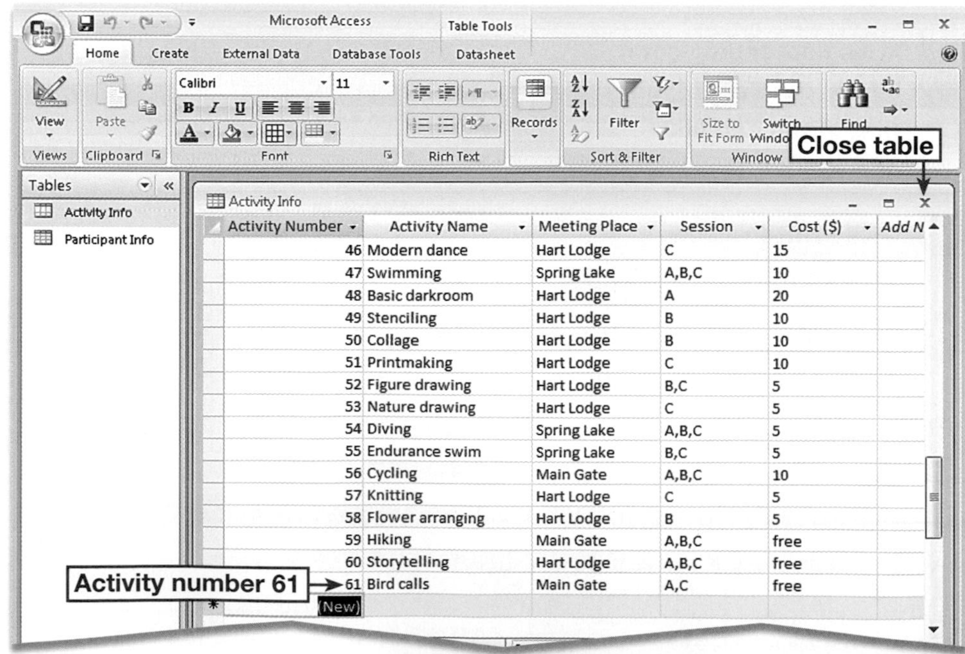

Activity Number	Activity Name	Meeting Place	Session	Cost ($)
46	Modern dance	Hart Lodge	C	15
47	Swimming	Spring Lake	A,B,C	10
48	Basic darkroom	Hart Lodge	A	20
49	Stenciling	Hart Lodge	B	10
50	Collage	Hart Lodge	B	10
51	Printmaking	Hart Lodge	C	10
52	Figure drawing	Hart Lodge	B,C	5
53	Nature drawing	Hart Lodge	C	5
54	Diving	Spring Lake	A,B,C	5
55	Endurance swim	Spring Lake	B,C	5
56	Cycling	Main Gate	A,B,C	10
57	Knitting	Hart Lodge	C	5
58	Flower arranging	Hart Lodge	B	5
59	Hiking	Main Gate	A,B,C	free
60	Storytelling	Hart Lodge	A,B,C	free
61	Bird calls	Main Gate	A,C	free
(New)				

LESSON 5 Practice It Activities

Step-By-Step

1. Open your **Costs-2** file. Save as: Costs-[your first initial and last name]3.
2. Click the **2009** tab. Select **A1:D13**.
3. On the **Page Layout** tab, choose **Page Setup>Print Area>Set Print Area**.
4. Click the **2010** tab. Select **A1:D13**.
5. Choose **Page Setup> Print Area>Set Print Area**.
6. Choose **Office>Print> Print Preview**. Click **Zoom** .
7. **CHECK** Your screen should look like Figure 5.41.
8. Click **Print**. In the **Print what** area, click **Entire Workbook**.
9. With your teacher's permission, click **Print** to print the workbook.
10. **CHECK** Your screen should look like Figure 5.42. Save and close your workbook.

Solution The solution file for this activity is **Costs3-SF.xlsx**.

3. Set Print Area and Print a Workbook

Follow the steps to complete the activity. You must complete Practice It Activity 2 before doing this activity.

New Student Strategy If a student did not complete Practice Activity 2, then the solution file for that activity can be used as a data file for this exercise.

FIGURE 5.41 Print area in Print Preview

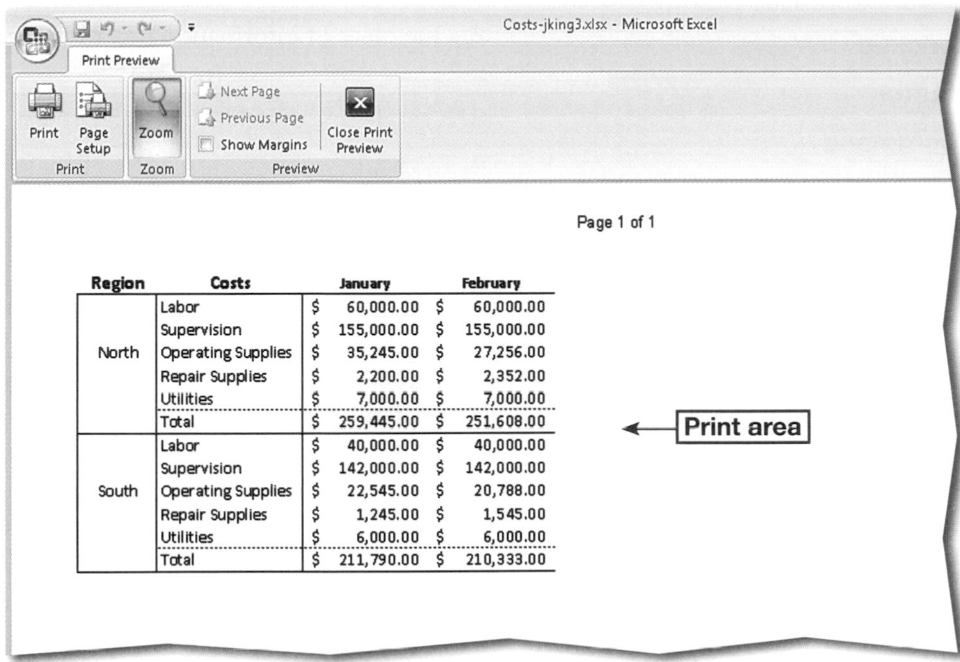

Region	Costs	January	February
North	Labor	$ 60,000.00	$ 60,000.00
	Supervision	$ 155,000.00	$ 155,000.00
	Operating Supplies	$ 35,245.00	$ 27,256.00
	Repair Supplies	$ 2,200.00	$ 2,352.00
	Utilities	$ 7,000.00	$ 7,000.00
	Total	$ 259,445.00	$ 251,608.00
South	Labor	$ 40,000.00	$ 40,000.00
	Supervision	$ 142,000.00	$ 142,000.00
	Operating Supplies	$ 22,545.00	$ 20,788.00
	Repair Supplies	$ 1,245.00	$ 1,545.00
	Utilities	$ 6,000.00	$ 6,000.00
	Total	$ 211,790.00	$ 210,333.00

FIGURE 5.42 Print area selected

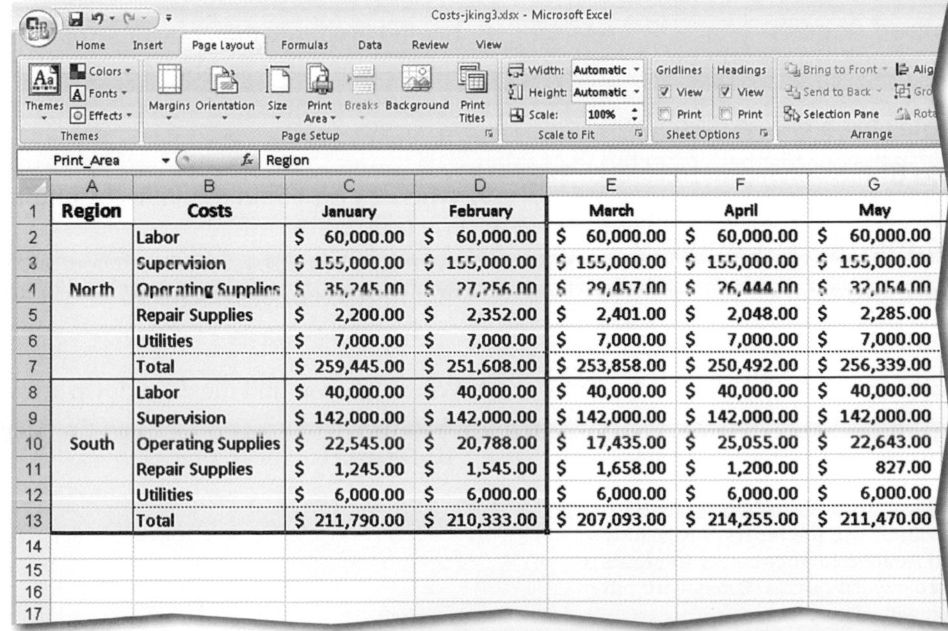

	A	B	C	D	E	F	G
1	Region	Costs	January	February	March	April	May
2	North	Labor	$ 60,000.00	$ 60,000.00	$ 60,000.00	$ 60,000.00	$ 60,000.00
3		Supervision	$ 155,000.00	$ 155,000.00	$ 155,000.00	$ 155,000.00	$ 155,000.00
4		Operating Supplies	$ 35,245.00	$ 27,256.00	$ 29,457.00	$ 26,444.00	$ 32,054.00
5		Repair Supplies	$ 2,200.00	$ 2,352.00	$ 2,401.00	$ 2,048.00	$ 2,285.00
6		Utilities	$ 7,000.00	$ 7,000.00	$ 7,000.00	$ 7,000.00	$ 7,000.00
7		Total	$ 259,445.00	$ 251,608.00	$ 253,858.00	$ 250,492.00	$ 256,339.00
8	South	Labor	$ 40,000.00	$ 40,000.00	$ 40,000.00	$ 40,000.00	$ 40,000.00
9		Supervision	$ 142,000.00	$ 142,000.00	$ 142,000.00	$ 142,000.00	$ 142,000.00
10		Operating Supplies	$ 22,545.00	$ 20,788.00	$ 17,435.00	$ 25,055.00	$ 22,643.00
11		Repair Supplies	$ 1,245.00	$ 1,545.00	$ 1,658.00	$ 1,200.00	$ 827.00
12		Utilities	$ 6,000.00	$ 6,000.00	$ 6,000.00	$ 6,000.00	$ 6,000.00
13		Total	$ 211,790.00	$ 210,333.00	$ 207,093.00	$ 214,255.00	$ 211,470.00

LESSON 1 After You Read

Review Vocabulary

Complete the following statements on a separate piece of paper. Choose from the vocabulary list on the left to complete the statements.

1. A query pulls information from a database based on certain ___criteria___. (p. 357)
2. One piece of information that describes something is called a(n) ___field___. (p. 356)
3. A single row of fields in a database table is a(n) ___record___. (p. 356)
4. To ensure you don't lose valuable data you should always create a(n) ___backup___ of your database. (p. 368)
5. A table contains rows and columns of ___data___. (p. 352)

Vocabulary Activity

6. Use the Key Terms and Academic Vocabulary from this lesson to create a crossword puzzle. Use graph paper to create the puzzle. Make up hints using the definitions of the words. You do not have to use all the Key Terms and Academic Vocabulary. Exchange your puzzle with a classmate.

Review Key Concepts

Answer the following questions on a separate piece of paper.

7. Which of the following can be used to move to the first record in a table? (p. 360)
   A. Page Up key
   B. Scroll bars
   C. Navigation buttons
   (D.) All of the above

8. If you have more than one table open, where can you find the button to switch from table to table? (p. 358)
   A. Office menu
   B. Views button>View menu
   (C.) Home>Window
   D. Create>Other

9. Where can you find the subject, author, and comments about a database? (p. 366)
   A. Datasheet >Views
   (B.) Office>Manage>Database Properties
   C. Office >Print
   D. Save As dialog box

10. Where can you find the drop-down arrow to change a record's font size? (p. 363)
   A. Office
   B. Datasheet tab
   C. Database Tools tab
   (D.) Home tab

Vocabulary

Key Terms

backup
button
command
criteria
database
dialog box
field
folder
group
pointer
query
Quick Access Toolbar (QAT)
record
Ribbon
scroll bar
shared access
tab
table
title bar

Academic Vocabulary

compare
control
data
function

Answer to Vocabulary Activity
Students use the lesson's Key Terms and Academic Vocabulary to create a crossword puzzle. Crossword puzzles will vary.

LESSON 5 You Try It Activities

4. Create an Expense Statement

You are going on a five-day business trip, and your employer has agreed to reimburse you for all of your expenses. You need to keep track of what you spend in order to get paid back, so you decide to use the Expense Statement template in Excel.

Step-By-Step

1. In **Excel**, open the **New Workbook** dialog box (see Figure 5.43). Click **Installed Templates**.
2. Choose **Expense Report**. Click **Create**. Save as: Expenses-[your first initial and last name]4.
3. On the **Expense Report**, after **Name**, key: your first and last name.
4. Scroll to the right. Under **Pay Period**, by **From**, key: 6/10/2009. By **To**, key: 6/14/2009.
5. Scroll to the left. In the first row under **Date**, key: 6/10/2009. Under **Hotel**, key: 75. Click **Scroll Right**.
6. Add four rows to the table. In those rows, fill in the hotel, transportation, fuel, meals, phone, and entertainment expenses as shown in Figure 5.44.
7. **CHECK** Your screen should look like Figure 5.44.
8. Save and close your file.

Solution The solution file for this activity is **Expenses4-SF.xlsx**.

FIGURE 5.43 Templates dialog box

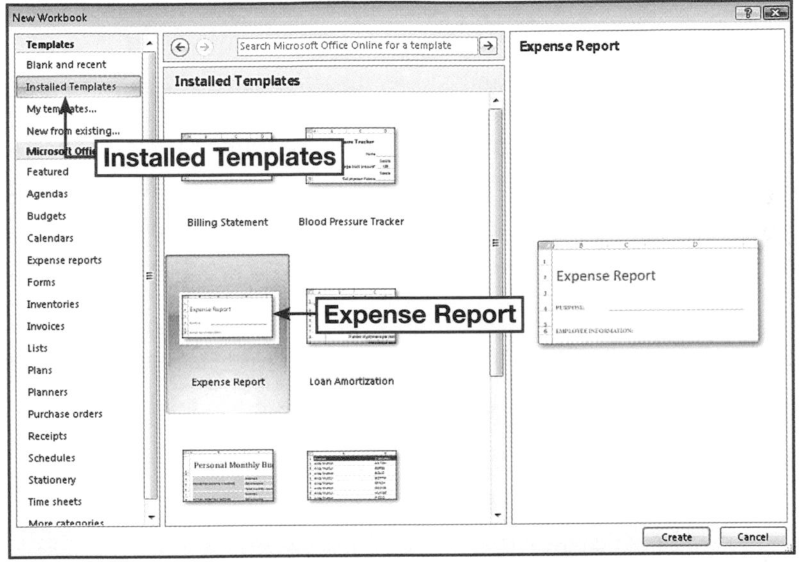

FIGURE 5.44 Expense statement

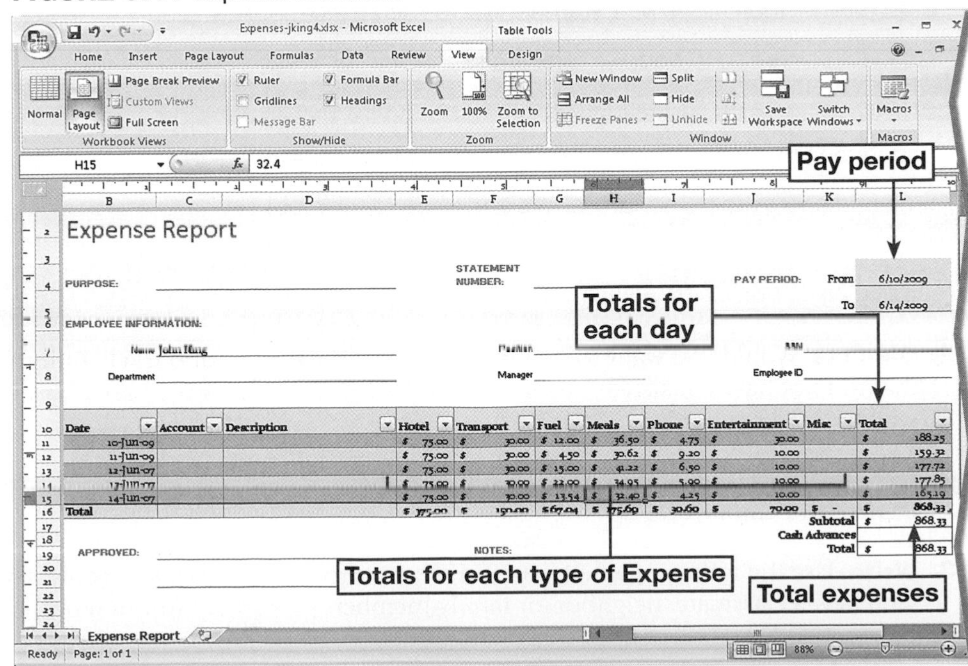

21st Century WORKPLACE

Can You Be Counted On?

Reliability is an idea involving a person who will perform in a way that friends, family, or employers expect. In the workplace, this means that the person completes the tasks he or she is expected to do. In other words, managers need someone they hire to arrive at work on time and to complete a number of tasks in a friendly and cooperative manner.

If an employee fails to report to work, another person must be found to take their place. If an employee has consistently not done the job entrusted to him or her, managers may have to step in and do the job themselves or move people from other positions. This process is time consuming and costly, and could result in poor service for a customer. For these reasons, hiring reliable employees is critical in the 21st century workplace.

MEET THE MANAGER

Connie Kamedulski is the owner of Animal Fair, a pet store in Ridgefield, Connecticut. At Animal Fair some of the young people she hires do not understand that showing up late or not showing up at all can get them fired. Mrs. Kamedulski feels that reliability is a real issue for some young people. "They miss the boat on what reliability means," she says. To succeed on the job, young people need to understand that when they are at work, they must devote less of their time and energy to personal matters and more to their job.

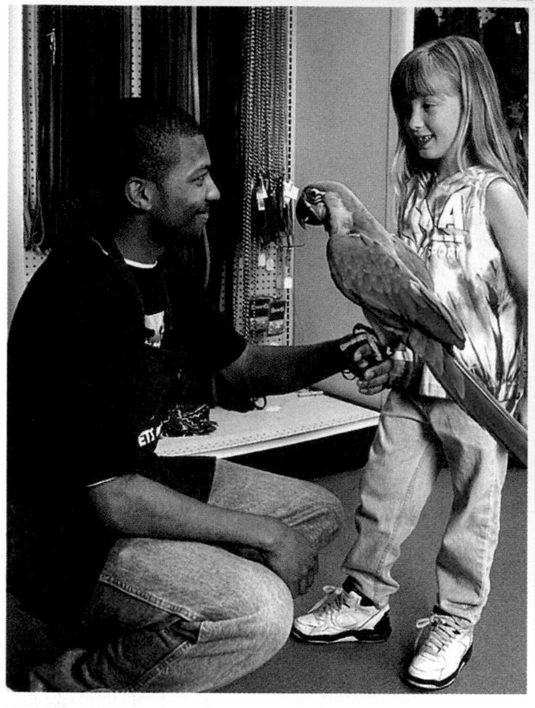

Employers need reliable staff that can be counted on to help satisfy their customer's needs.

NCLB/Language Arts (NCTE 12) Reinforce to students that a person can be seen as reliable through spoken, written, and visual language. A friend who always keeps his word is reliable. An employee not doing her work is labeled by her boss as unreliable. Students demonstrate their reliability by making sure that what they communicate is in line with their actions.

SKILLBUILDER

1. **Discuss** Would you want to do business with a shop that did not have consistent business hours? Why or why not?
2. **Explain** How is reliability important for business owners and employees?
3. **Write** Use the following questions and prompts to interview a classmate, neighbor, or family member about reliability. Use a word processor to write a brief story based on the answers.
   - **a.** Tell me about a time when you relied on someone to help you.
   - **b.** What do you think might have happened if he or she had been unreliable?
   - **c.** If you could say anything to that person now, what would it be?

SkillBuilder answers can be found on page TM79.

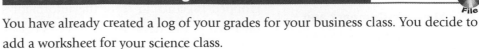

LESSON 5 You Try It Activities

5. Create a Grades Log

You have already created a log of your grades for your business class. You decide to add a worksheet for your science class.

Step-By-Step

1. Open the data file **Subjects.xlsx**. Save as: Subjects-[your first initial and last name]5.
2. Insert one new worksheet. Rename the new worksheet **Science**.
3. Copy the column and row labels in the **Business** worksheet.
4. Click the **Science** tab. Paste the column and row labels into your **Science** worksheet (see Figure 5.45).
5. Fill in your science grades (see Figure 5.46).
6. Change the page orientation to **Landscape**.
7. **CHECK** Your screen should look like Figure 5.46.
8. With your teacher's permission, print the entire workbook.
9. Save and close your file.

Solution The solution file for this activity is **Subjects5-SF.xlsx**.

FIGURE 5.45 Science worksheet

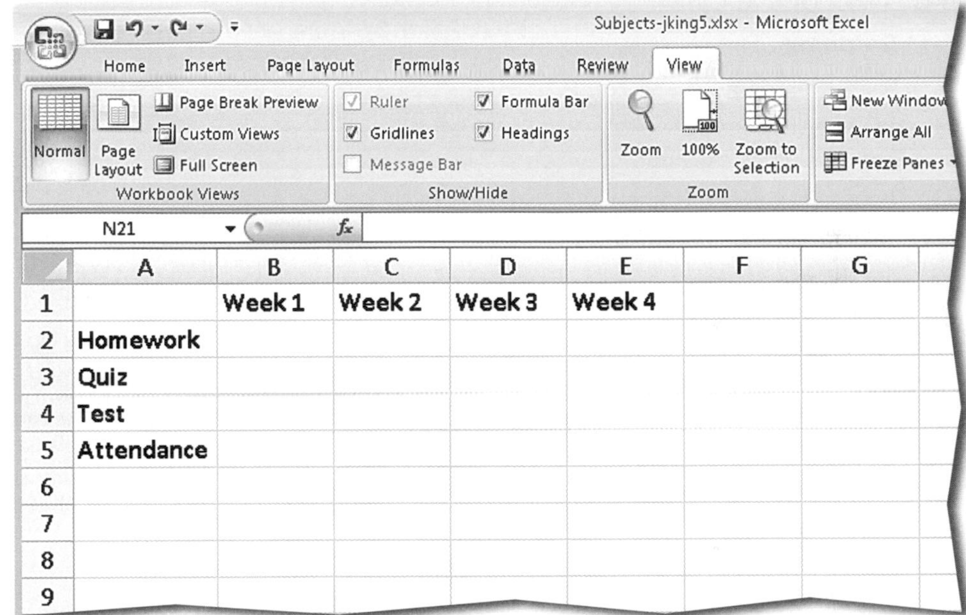

FIGURE 5.46 Science grades

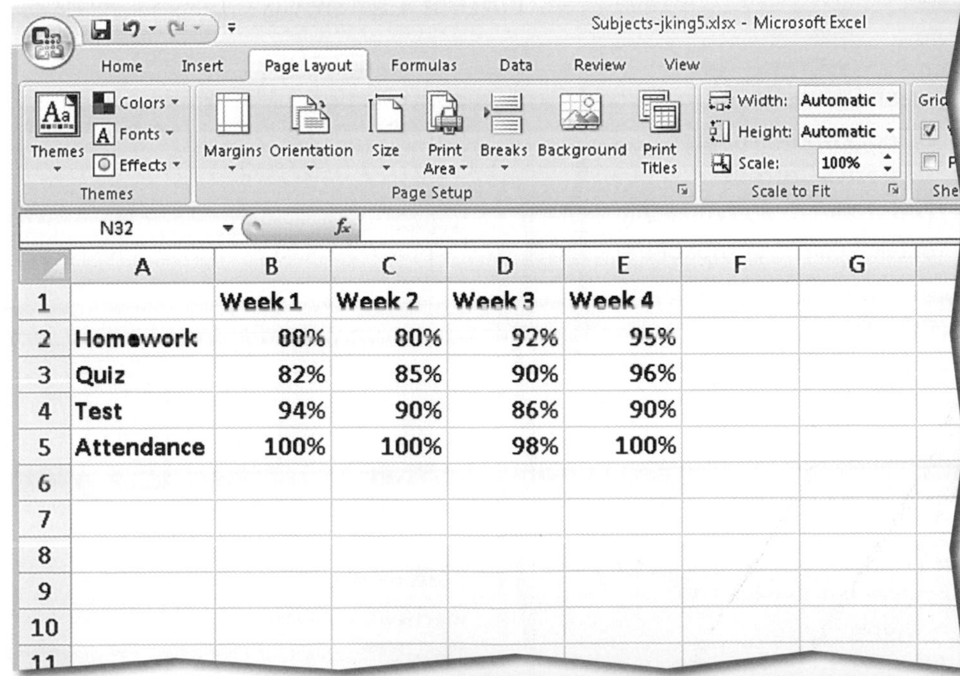

Step-By-Step

1. In the **Sports Equipment** database, select **Office> Manage>Compact and Repair Database** (see Figure 1.36).
2. Select **Office>Close Database**. This will only close the database, not Access. In order to close both the database and Access at the same time, select the Close button on the Access screen.
3. CHECK Your screen should look like Figure 1.37.
4. Click the **Close** [x] button in the upper right corner of the window (see Figure 1.37). You can also exit Access by selecting the **Office Button** and then clicking **Exit Access**.

Shortcuts

Select **Office>Access Options>Current Database** to automatically set Access to compact the database each time it is closed.

Solution Use the files **Sports Equipment-SF_be.accdb** as a solution file for Exercises 1-4 through 1-19. Use the file **Sports Equipment-SF_be.accdb** as a solution file for Exercises 1-16 through 1-19.

EXERCISE 1-19
Compact and Close a Database

When you compact a database, you organize it into a smaller file. Similar data is grouped together to store the information more efficiently. Compacting is like organizing your desk. You put books back on the shelves. You throw away scratch paper, and you move pencils to one side of the desk. Once your desk is organized, everything takes up less space, just like when you split a database in Exercise 1-16.

FIGURE 1.36 Compact database

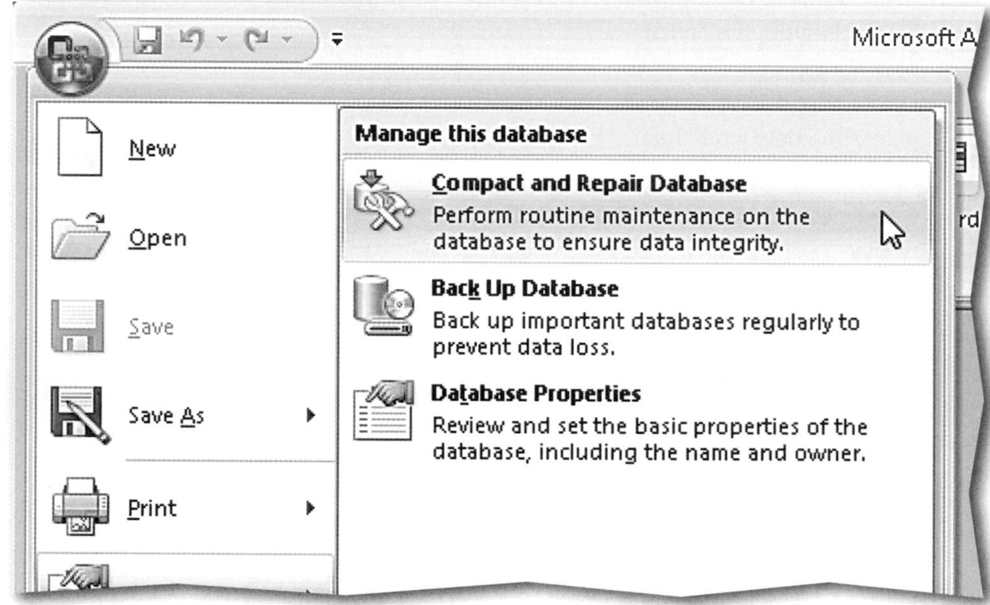

FIGURE 1.37 Closing a database and closing Access

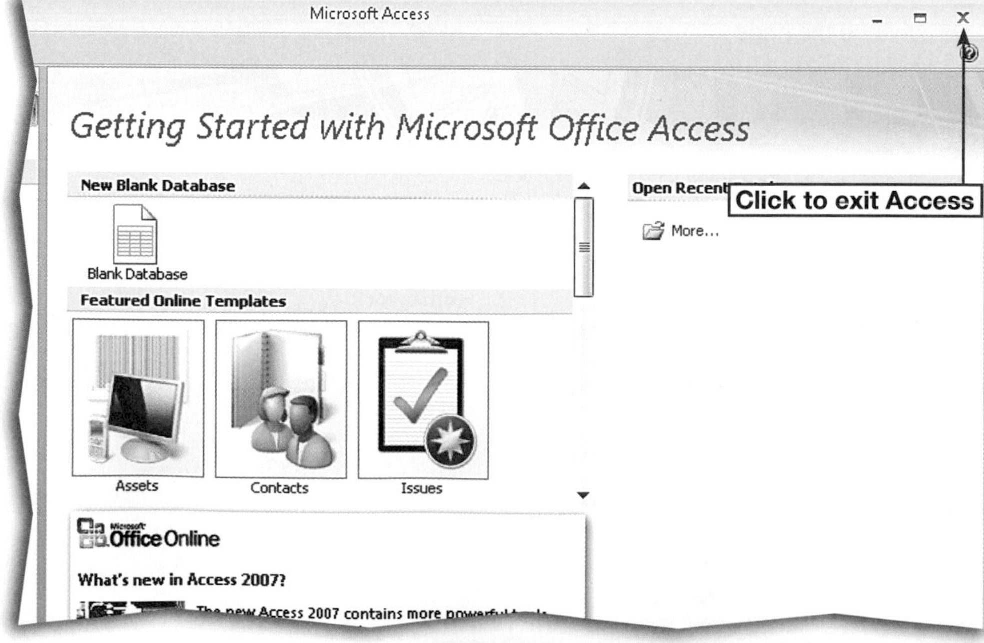

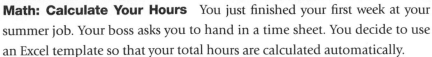

LESSON 5 Critical Thinking Activities

Beyond the Classroom Activity The Solution file for this activity is e5rev6-SF.xlsx.

Standards at Work Activity Students' printouts should be in Web Page Preview.

21st Century Skills Activity Student worksheets should contain information that sales associates should tell customers. Worksheets should have top, bottom, left, and right margins of 1 inch. The page orientation should be landscape.

6. Beyond the Classroom Activity

Math: Calculate Your Hours You just finished your first week at your summer job. Your boss asks you to hand in a time sheet. You decide to use an Excel template so that your total hours are calculated automatically.

Open the Excel **Time Card** template. Enter your first and last name. Key the first *full* week in July for the pay period. Open the data file **Hours.docx**. Enter the hours from the data file into the time card template. With your teacher's permission, print your worksheet.

Save as: e5rev-[your first initial and last name]6.

7. Standards at Work Activity

Microsoft Certified Application Specialist Correlation
Excel 5.4 *Save Workbooks*

Publish a Worksheet as a Web Page Your boss has asked you to put the company's sales figures on the company's Web site. You decide to preview the sales figures as a Web page beforehand to see if you need to make any changes to make the data more readable.

- Open the data file **Web.xlsx**.
- Publish the worksheet as a Web page.

With your teacher's permission, print the worksheet.

Save as: Web-[your first initial and last name]7.

8. 21st Century Skills Activity

Be Honest with Customers You work as a sales associate in a store that sells footwear for hiking and other outdoor activities. Create a workbook that includes everything your sales associates should tell customers before they make a purchase. List information about three of your products.

- Include a column for each product.
- Include a row for sizes available, cost, how long the product should last, recommended use, and the return policy.
- Change the page orientation to landscape.
- Change the top, bottom, left, and right margins to 1 inch.
- With your teacher's permission, print the worksheet.

Save your file as: e5rev-[your first initial and last name]8.

glencoe.com

Go to the **Online Learning Center** to complete the following review activities.

Online Self Check
To test your knowledge of the material, click **Unit 2> Lesson 5** and choose **Self Checks**.

Interactive Review
To review the main points of the lesson, click **Unit 2> Lesson 5** and choose **Interactive Review**.

Step-By-Step

1 In the **Sports Equipment** database, at the right-hand end of the **Ribbon**, click **Help**. The Access **Help** window opens.

2 In the **Search for** box, key: convert database. Press ENTER.

3 CHECK Your screen should look like Figure 1.34. The **Help** window contains a list of topics.

4 Scroll down the list (if necessary) and select **Convert a database to the Access 2007 file format**.

5 The **Help** window shows a list of related topics (see Figure 1.35).

6 Click **Close** x in the **Help** window.

Continue to the next exercise.

Microsoft Office 2007

The information on converting databases will prove useful if you need to use a database that was created in a previous version of Access. Converting the database will change its file type from .mdb to .accdb.

Step-By-Step Tip Be aware that **Step 2** may send students online.

EXERCISE 1-18
Use the Help Feature

You work more productively when you know how to find help quickly. Use Microsoft Office Access Help to find answers to your questions about using Access. Choosing Help brings up the Help task pane, which allows you to search for Help by keying the name of a topic.

FIGURE 1.34 Help window

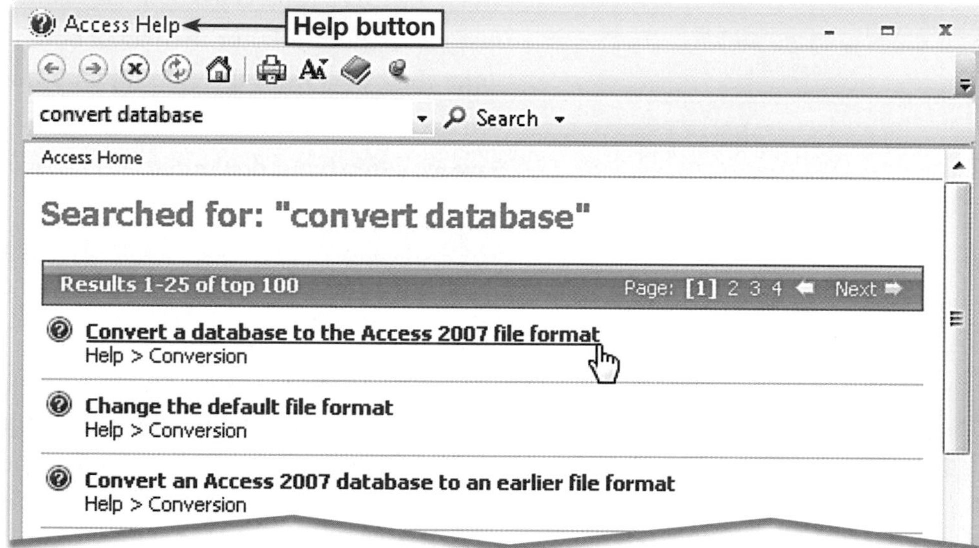

FIGURE 1.35 Search Results

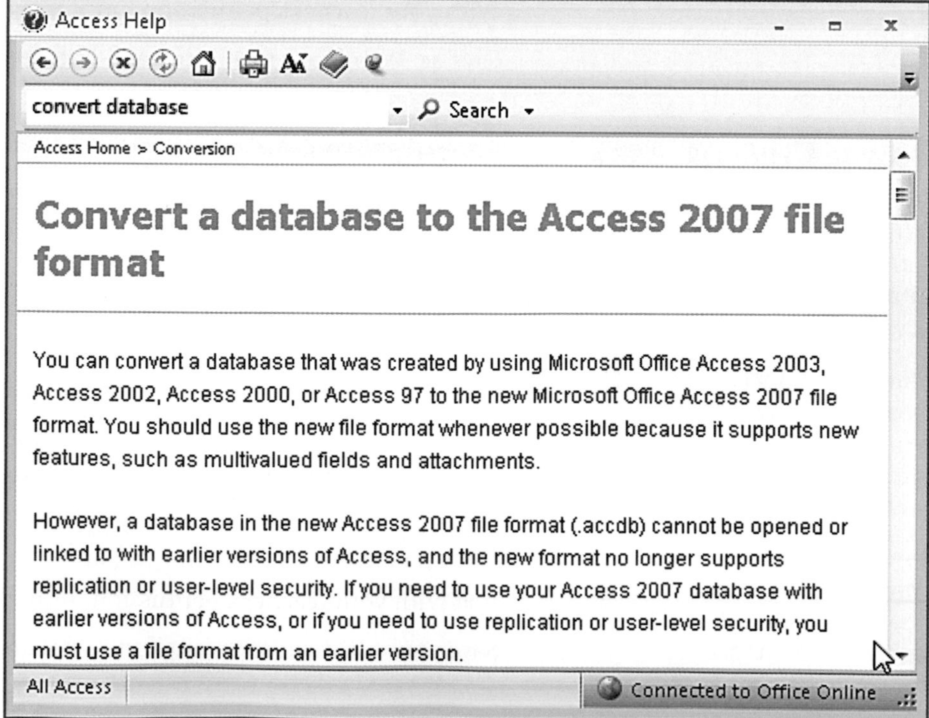

Before You Begin

Taking Inventory Everyone needs to organize and analyze data to decide how to spend time and money effectively. Whether you are analyzing how you spend your time, or cataloging your CD collection, you need to make sure you use your resources properly.

Reflect Once you complete the projects, open a Word document and answer the following:

1. How can Excel help you manage time effectively?
2. How can Excel help you budget effectively?

Answers Rubrics for each Challenge Yourself Project are available at **glencoe.com**. You may want to download the rubrics and make them available to students as they complete each project.

9. Keep Track of Your Time

Rubric R

LEVEL This is an intermediate level project.

Math: Calculate Your Weekly Activities A balance of activities and a mix of work and play are important. Create a worksheet that shows how you spent your time last month. Make a column for each week. Insert the following rows:

- Hours at school
- Hours at extracurricular activities
- Hours with family/friends
- Hours at work

Fill in the hours for each week. Add up the hours for each row. Create a pie chart based on your totals showing the percentages of how much time you spend each week completing the tasks in the bulleted list. Save your file as: e5rev-[your first initial and last name]9.

10. Organize Your Music Collection

Rubric R

LEVEL This is an intermediate level project.

Math: Run a MIN and MAX Formula Create a worksheet to keep track of your music collection. Include a column for each of your five favorite artists. Label the following rows:

- Type of music
- CDs I own
- Favorite song

Fill in the spreadsheet. Highlight the column of the artist that has the highest number of CDs in your collection. Create a MIN and MAX formula to see the minimum and maximum numbers of the types of CDs you own. Select the highlighted column. Set this column as the print area. With your teacher's permission, print this column. Save your file as: e5rev-[your first initial and last name]10.

11. Keep Track of Travel Expenses

Rubric R

LEVEL This is an advanced level project.

Math: Calculate Expenses You won a plane ticket to anywhere in the United States plus $500 spending money. Use the **Expense Report** template to calculate your budget for each day. Include expenses for the following:

- Lodging
- Meals
- Transportation
- Entertainment

Your trip can last from five to seven days, depending on how you budget your money. Make sure your total expenses do not go over $500. When finished, look over your report. How did you have to divide your money to stay within your budget? Which expenses cost the most? Which cost the least? How did you decide to estimate your costs? Save your file as: e5rev-[your first initial and last name]11.

Step-By-Step

1 Open your **Sports Equipment Split** file.

2 In the database, select **Office>Manage>Back Up Database**. The **Save As** dialog box opens.

3 Access provides a new suggested file name (see Figure 1.32).

4 Ask your teacher which location you should use, and navigate to that location so that it appears in the **Save In** box.

5 Click **Save**.

6 CHECK Your screen should look like Figure 1.33.

Continue to the next exercise.

Tech Tip

Backing up data is very important. Just as you know to save your work often, you should remember to back up your data often. You will lose all work done since the last time you backed up your data, if something happens to your database.

Intervention Strategy Be sure students understand that their backup copy will not have any changes students made to the database since it was backed up.

Teaching Tip Make sure students understand that after they back up the database, they are still working with the original and not the backup copy.

EXERCISE 1-17
Back Up a Database

It is important to keep valuables in a safe place. Information in a database is valuable, too. For example, you would not want to lose a customer's name and address if your computer failed.

Be sure to save design changes to your database often. As an added safeguard, make a **backup**, or a copy, of your database in another location. If there is ever a problem with the database or with your computer, you will have a backup copy. Any changes you make to the database after backing it up will not be reflected in the backup copy. You must back up again to see these changes.

FIGURE 1.32 Save Backup As dialog box

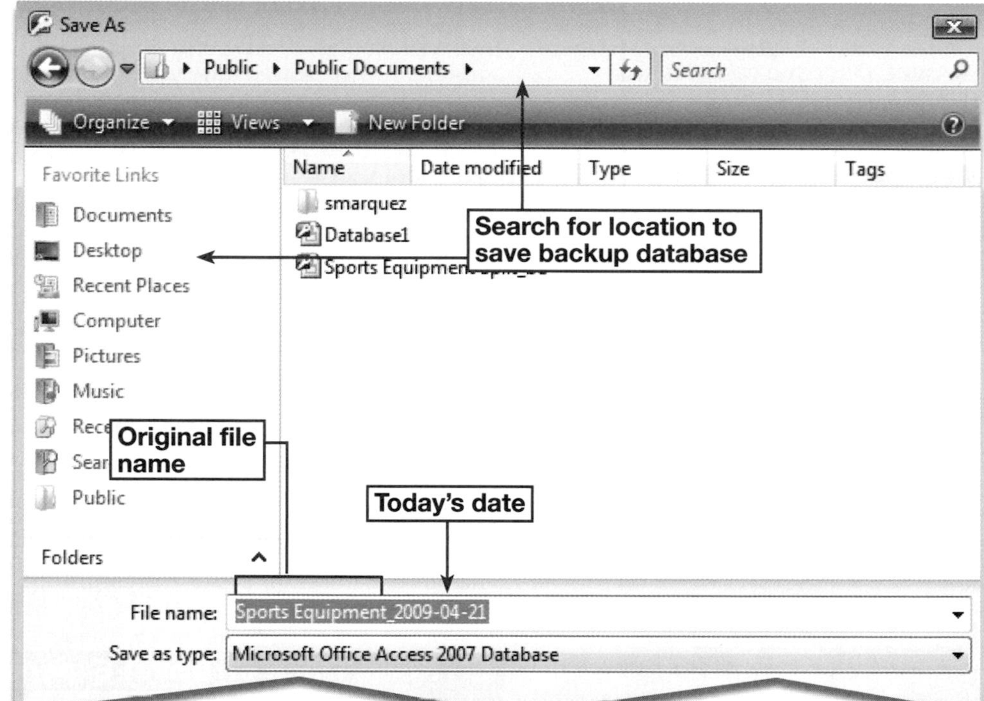

FIGURE 1.33 Access screen after backing up database

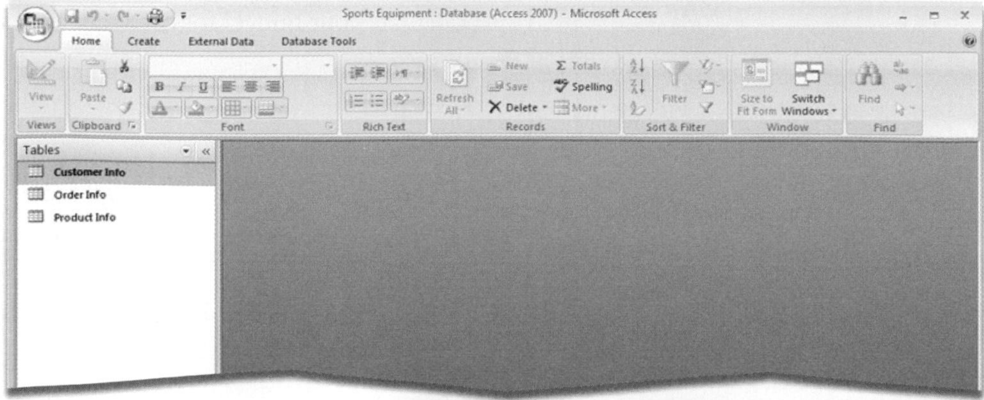

UNIT 2 Academic Connections

MATH | SCIENCE | LANGUAGE ARTS | SOCIAL STUDIES

Rubric R

In this activity, you will use your math skills to create formulas.

Calculate Percentages

The used car lot that you work for is developing a bonus plan for its sales team. Your boss has given you each employee's total sales for last month. He wants you to calculate how much a 5%, 10%, and 15% bonus will be for each employee. Then he will decide what percent to give each salesperson. You decide to create a workbook that calculates the percentages for you.

1. Create a new Excel workbook. (p. 207)
2. In cell **A1**, key: Employee Names. Key 10 names (last name, first initial) in cells **A2** through **A11**.
3. In cells **B1** through **E1**, key the following column labels: **Total Sales, 5% Sales Bonus, 10% Sales Bonus, 15% Sales Bonus**. Adjust the width of each column so that cell contents fit. (p. 261)
4. In cells **B2** through **B11**, key each employee's total sales. Use numbers between 15,000 and 30,000. Apply the **Currency** style to the numbers in column B. (p. 260)
5. Click cell **C2**. Key a formula that calculates 5% of the first employee's total sales. (p. 286)
6. Copy that formula to cells **C3** to **C11**.
7. Click cell **D2**. Key a formula that calculates 10% of the first employee's total sales. (p. 286)
8. Copy that formula to cells **D3** to **D11**.
9. Click cell **E2**. Key a formula that calculates 15% of the first employee's total sales. (p. 286)
10. Copy that formula to cells **E3** to **E11**.

You can use Excel to calculate how much money you may make on a sale or how much money it will cost to buy a new car.

NCLB/Math (Representation) Reinforce that representing data as a chart, graph, or diagram is an effective tool to visually convey information. Ask students to use the percentages to create pie charts that display the bonus plan data.

Answer to Academic Connections Go to the Online Learning Center at **glencoe.com** to access the rubric for this activity. If students need help remembering how to complete specific skills, have them turn to the page number listed after selected steps.

Step-By-Step

1. In Access, select **Office> Open**. Locate and open the data file **Sports Equipment Split.accdb**. Ask your teacher how and where to copy the database before working in it.

2. Select **Database Tools> Move Data> Access Database** .

3. CHECK Your screen should look like Figure 1.30.

4. In the **Database Splitter Wizard**, click the **Split Database** button.

5. Ask your teacher where the file should be saved. In the **Create Back-end Database** dialog box click the **Split** button (see Figure 1.31).

6. When the Splitter Wizard is complete, click **OK**.

7. Select **Office>Close Database**.

8. Select **Office>Open**. Your **Sporting Equipment Split** database is now two different files: A back-end database (labeled **-be**) and a front end.

9. Click **Cancel** Cancel.

Continue to the next exercise.

Troubleshooting In **Step 1**, make sure students open the **Sports Equipment Split** database, not the **Sports Equipment** database.

EXERCISE 1-16
Split a Database

An Access database can be split to include its data in one file and all the queries, forms, and reports in another. You would want to split a database if several different programs are going to be used on the same database. Splitting a database also overcomes any size restrictions because it makes the individual database files smaller. The database file is split into two parts, the front and back-ends. The back end stores main information while the front-end stores objects such as queries and reports

FIGURE 1.30 Database Splitter Wizard

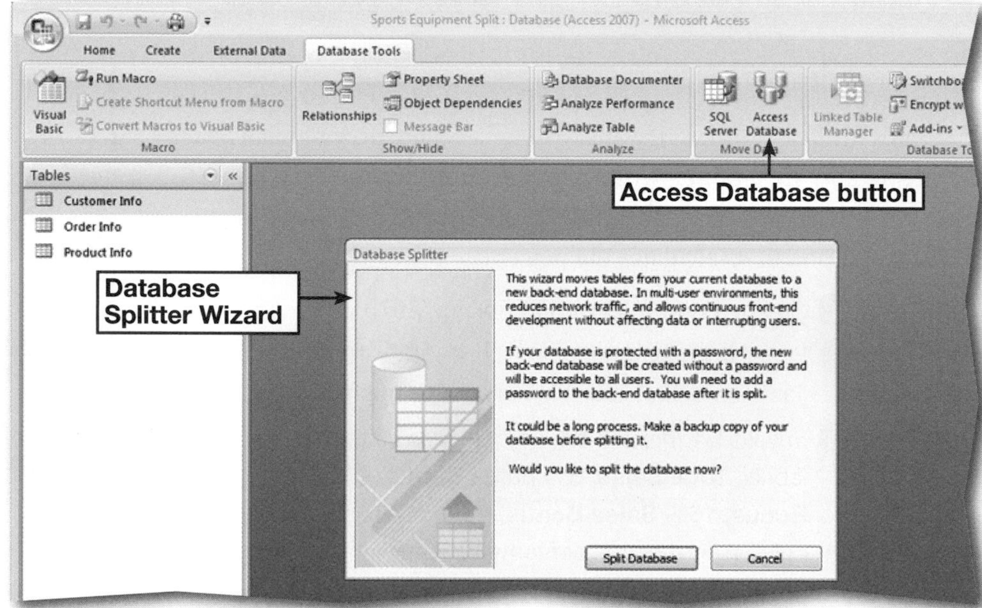

FIGURE 1.31 Create Back-end Database dialog box

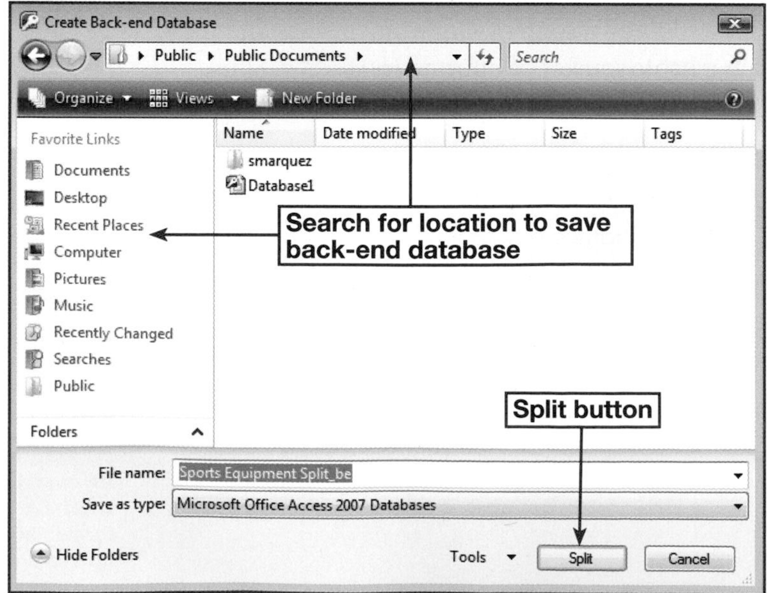

UNIT 2 Ethics in Action

Using Online Resources Responsibly

The Internet provides an enormous amount of free information. You can use the Internet to do research, stay informed about world events, or check the weather. Ethical Internet use involves using the information you obtain responsibly, honestly, and in a way that is not harmful to others.

Avoiding Plagiarism

Sometimes it is tempting to present information that you find on the Internet as your own. Plagiarism is using another person's ideas as your own, and is unethical and dishonest. Always cite, or state, the source of your information. When you use information from the Internet, include the Web address to show where you found it. This also helps the reader evaluate the validity of your sources.

Evaluating Internet Sources

How trustworthy is information on the Internet? Facts presented in reference books and textbooks are checked and double-checked for accuracy. But facts on the Internet may not have been checked. Some information on the Internet may even be intentionally misleading. Here are some things you can do to make sure that you are using reliable information:

1. Use reputable and well-known sources. Government sites and many university sites are reliable sources of information.
2. Make sure that the source you are using has cited other sources. Do the other sources appear trustworthy?
3. Back up the research that you do on the Internet with more than one source—online or print.

CASE STUDY

Samantha and Jay are researching a group project about public transportation. Samantha finds information on the Internet that supports the main idea of the project. The information comes from a source unfamiliar to most people. Because few people are aware of their source, Jay proposes that they use the information without citing the source. Samantha is not sure whether this is a good idea.

See page TM66 for answers to You Decide and Application Activity.

YOU DECIDE

1. **State** Name one thing that Jay and Samantha could do to make sure the information that they found on the Internet is reliable.
2. **Justify** Write a short paragraph that describes what you think Samantha should do.

APPLICATION ACTIVITY

3. **Create Guidelines** Create an Excel worksheet that lists ethical guidelines for using books, periodicals, and online resources. Ask permission to post the list in your classroom, the computer lab, or library.

Step-By-Step

1. In your **Sports Equipment** file, select **Office> Manage>Database Properties**.
2. In the **Sports Equipment Properties** dialog box, click the **Custom** tab (see Figure 1.28).
3. In the **Custom** tab, click **Checked by** in the list under the **Name** box.In the **Value** box, key: [your first initial and last name].
4. Click **Add** to create the custom property.
5. CHECK Your dialog box should look like Figure 1.29.
6. Click the tabs **General**, **Statistics**, and **Contents** to see the other database properties.
7. Click the **Summary** tab. In the **Category** box, key: Sports. Click **OK** (see Figure 1.28).
8. Select **Office>Close Database**.

Continue to the next exercise.

You Should Know

Text under the **Summary** tab can be changed by keying in new text or by deleting existing text.

EXERCISE 1-15
Change and Display Database Properties

Database Properties include information about your database such as the author's name, comments about the database, tables included in the database, and the last date the database was modified. You can use Database Properties to search for a database, or to organize the different databases on your computer. You can also add properties to help you identify a database.

Differentiated Instruction/Advanced Students Tell students who have an interest in computers that they can find more technical information under the **General** tab.

FIGURE 1.28 Sports Equipment Properties dialog box

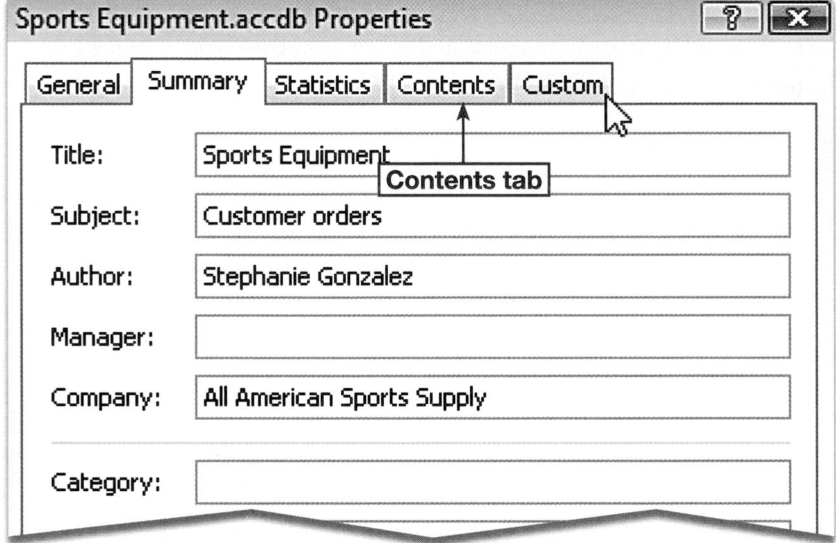

FIGURE 1.29 Summary tab

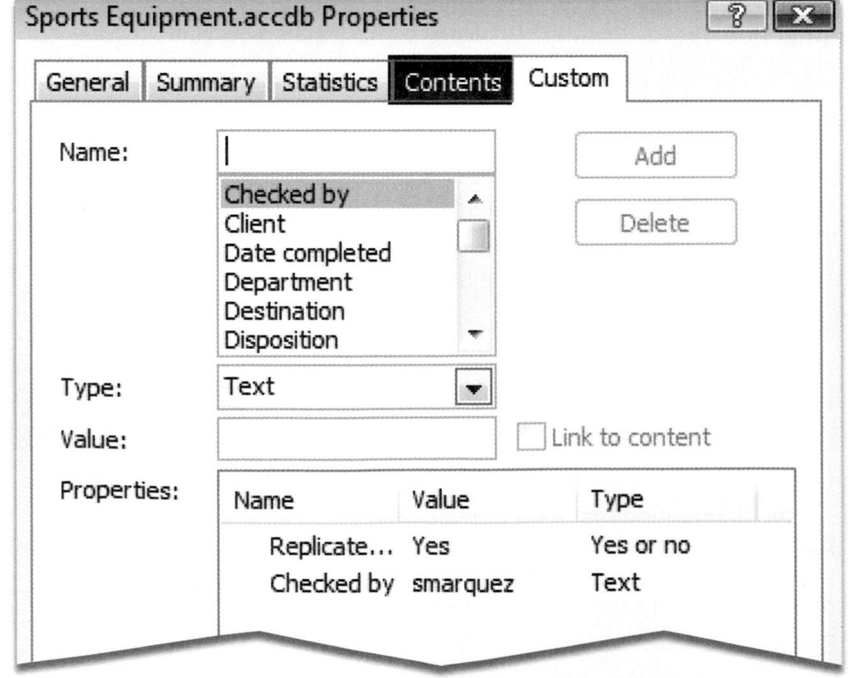

Portfolio Project

Organize Your Landscape Business

You and three friends have decided to start a landscaping business. You want to use Excel to create all of your business records.

Answers Rubrics for each part of the Portfolio Project are available at **glencoe.com**. You may want to download the rubrics and make them available to students as they complete each project.

Part 1: Create a Payroll Record

LEVEL This is a beginning level project.

Goal Your first task is to create a worksheet to track how many hours you work.

Create Create a worksheet.

- In cells **A2** through **A5**, list your name along with the names **Taylor**, **Sharon**, and **Mark** (your business partners).
- Start in cell **B1** and use seven columns to list the days of the week. Label the column to the right of the weekday columns **Total Hours**.
- Label the column next to the **Total Hours** column **Paycheck**.
- Adjust the column width as necessary. Bold the heads of the columns. Place a border on the right edge of cells **A2** through **A5** and a bottom border on cells **B1** through **J1**.
- Use the information from the data file **Hours.docx** to fill in the payroll record.

Self Assess Use the Have You...? checklist to review your worksheet. With your teacher's permission, print your worksheet and proofread it carefully. Make any necessary corrections. Follow your teacher's instructions for naming the file and saving it to your Portfolio Folder.

When finished, proceed to Part 2.

	Have You...?
✓	Correctly labeled the rows
✓	Correctly labeled the columns
✓	Bolded the column heads
✓	Added borders to the row and column heads
✓	Entered the data correctly

NCLB/Math (Number and Operations) Reinforce the importance of tracking expenses by asking students to define money management and the types of activities that are part of money management. Encourage students to discuss the benefits of balancing an account.

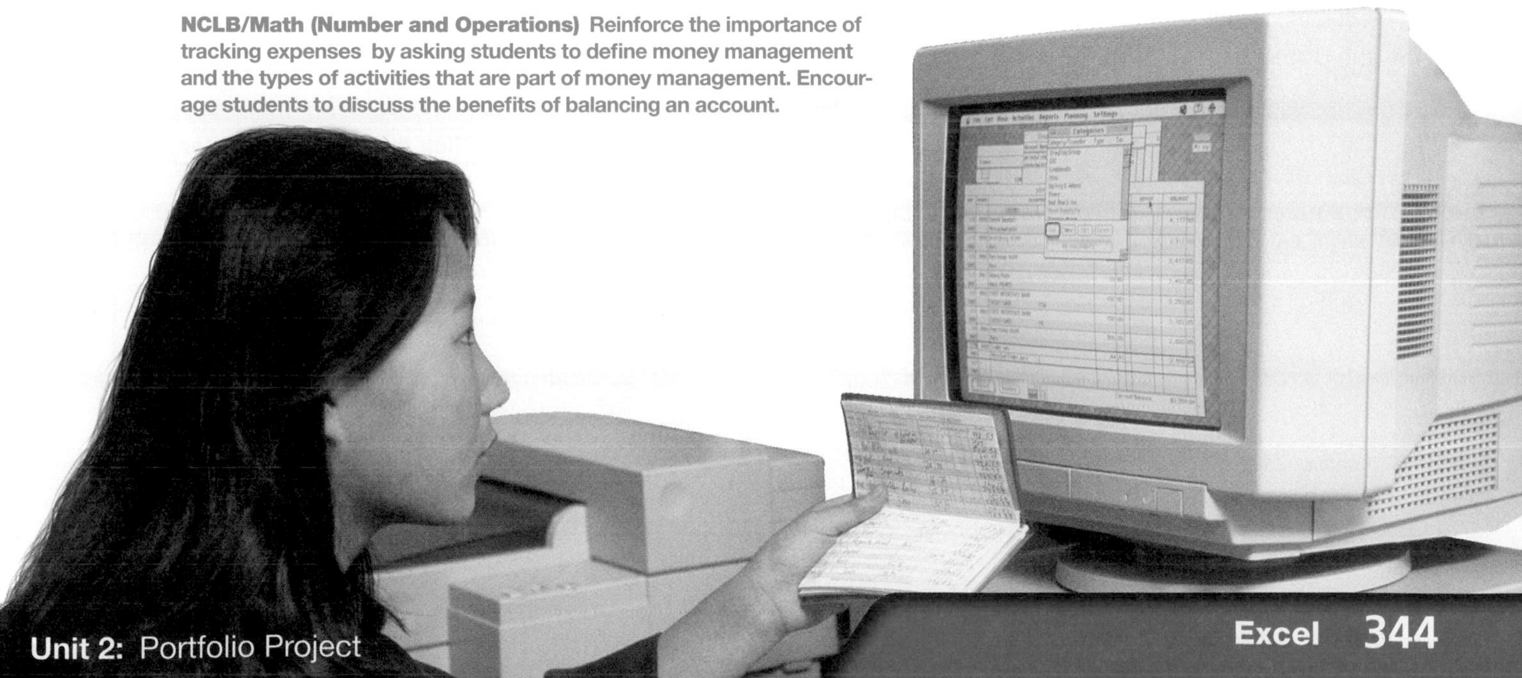

Step-By-Step

1 In your **Sports Equipment** file, select **Office>Print> Print Preview**.

2 Point to a customer name and click to zoom in.

3 CHECK Your screen should look like Figure 1.26.

4 Click anywhere on the page to zoom out.

5 On the **Print Preview** tab click the **Print** button. The **Print** dialog box opens (see Figure 1.27).

6 In the **Name** box, click the **down arrow** to select a printer. Ask your teacher which printer you should use.

7 In the **Number of Copies** box, check that there is a **1**.

8 Under **Print Range,** check that **All** is selected.

9 With your teacher's permission, click **OK**.

10 Click the **Close Print Preview** button to close **Print Preview** (see Figure 1.26).

11 Close the **Customer Info** table.

Continue to the next exercise.

EXERCISE 1-14
Preview and Print a Table or Query

There are two easy ways to print a datasheet:

- Click Office and select one of the print options.
- Press CTRL + P.

Both tables and queries automatically print in Datasheet View.

Step-By-Step Tip In **Step 5**, point out that the **Ribbon** has changed to show the **Close Print Preview** button.

FIGURE 1.26 Print Preview

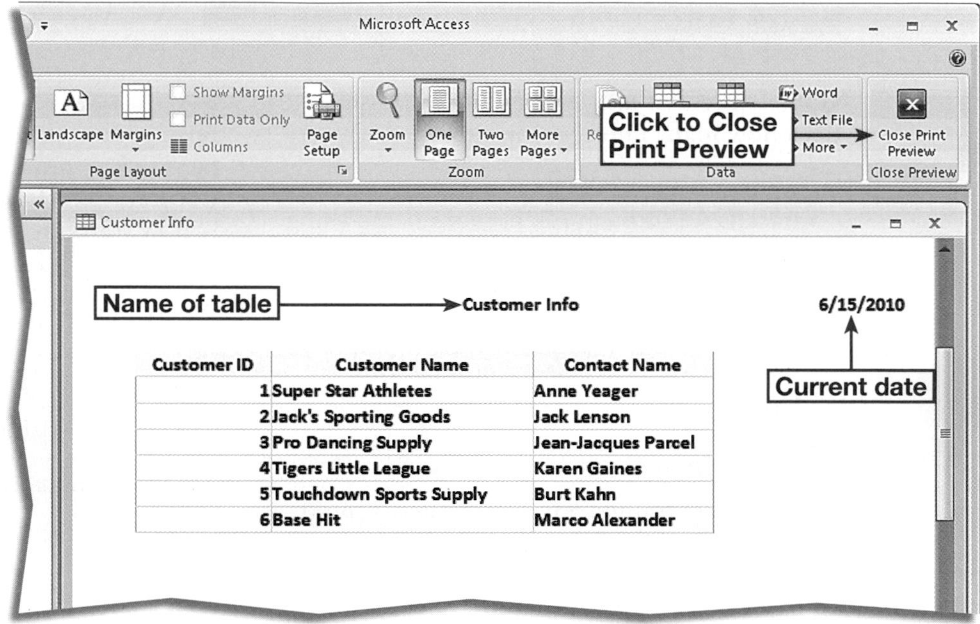

Step-By-Step Tip In **Step 8**, explain to students that you also can print individual pages or a selection, as well.

FIGURE 1.27 Print dialog box

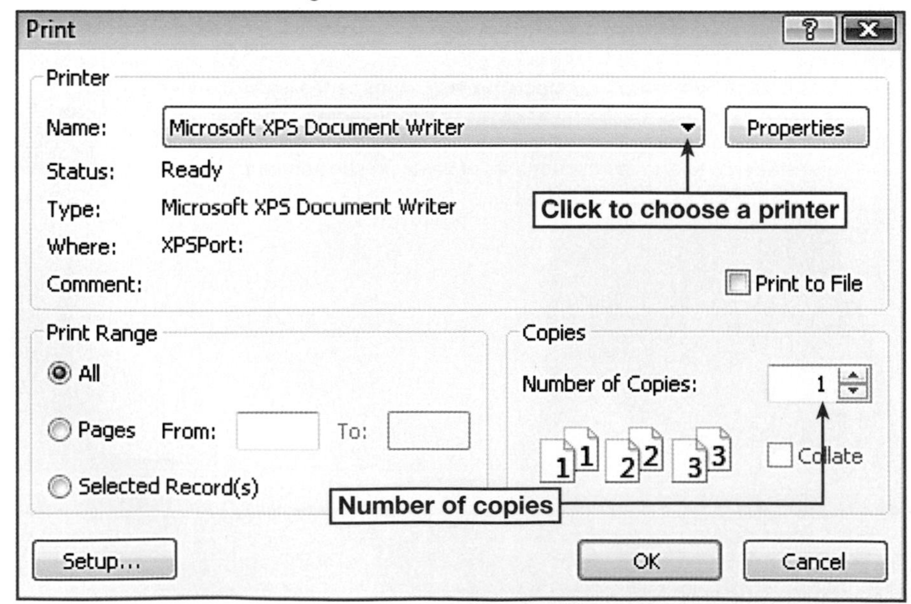

Portfolio Project

Part 2: Calculate Paychecks

LEVEL This is an intermediate level project.

Goal At the end of the first week, your new business is doing well. Now you need to figure out how many total hours you, Taylor, Sharon, and Mark worked and how much each of you earned for the week.

Create Follow the steps below to make the calculations:

- Open the worksheet that you created in **Portfolio Project 1**.
- In this worksheet, calculate the total number of hours that each person worked.
- Place this figure in the **Total Hours** column. Then write a formula to find how much each person made your first week. The hourly rate is $8.50.
- Finally, calculate the total payroll for that week by adding the **Paycheck** column. Apply the **Currency** style to the **Paycheck** column.

Self Assess Use the Have You...? checklist to review your worksheet. Make sure your worksheet reflects all of the items noted in the checklist.

Carefully proofread your worksheet and make the necessary corrections. Follow your teacher's instructions for naming the file and saving it to your Portfolio Folder.

When finished, proceed to Part 3.

	Have You...?
✓	Calculated the total hours each person worked
✓	Created a formula to find how much each person earned
✓	Calculated the total payroll for the week
✓	Placed the formulas in the correct cells
✓	Applied Currency style to the Paycheck column

Step-By-Step

1. In your **Sports Equipment** file, in the **Customer Info** table, move the pointer to the line between **Street** and **City** until the pointer becomes a two-headed arrow (see Figure 1.25).

2. Drag the arrow to the right until you can see all the text in the **Street** column.

3. In the upper left cornor of the screen, click the **Office Button**. Scroll down the list, and select **Save**.

4. CHECK Your screen should look like Figure 1.25.

Continue to the next exercise.

You Should Know

If you own a cellphone, the phone may contain a list of contacts. That list of contacts is a database. When you scroll through your contact list, you are scrolling through a database. Just as your phone has a database, so do most major retail stores. A store might have databases to manage inventory and also customer information.

EXERCISE 1-13
Save a Table or Query

In Access, data is saved automatically. You will need to save design changes. For example, when you change the column width, font, or page setup of a datasheet, you need to save these changes before closing the object. Access will prompt you to save the changes if you try to close the table without saving.

Different Strokes Tell students that they can also use **Ctrl + S** to save changes.

FIGURE 1.25 Formatting changes saved

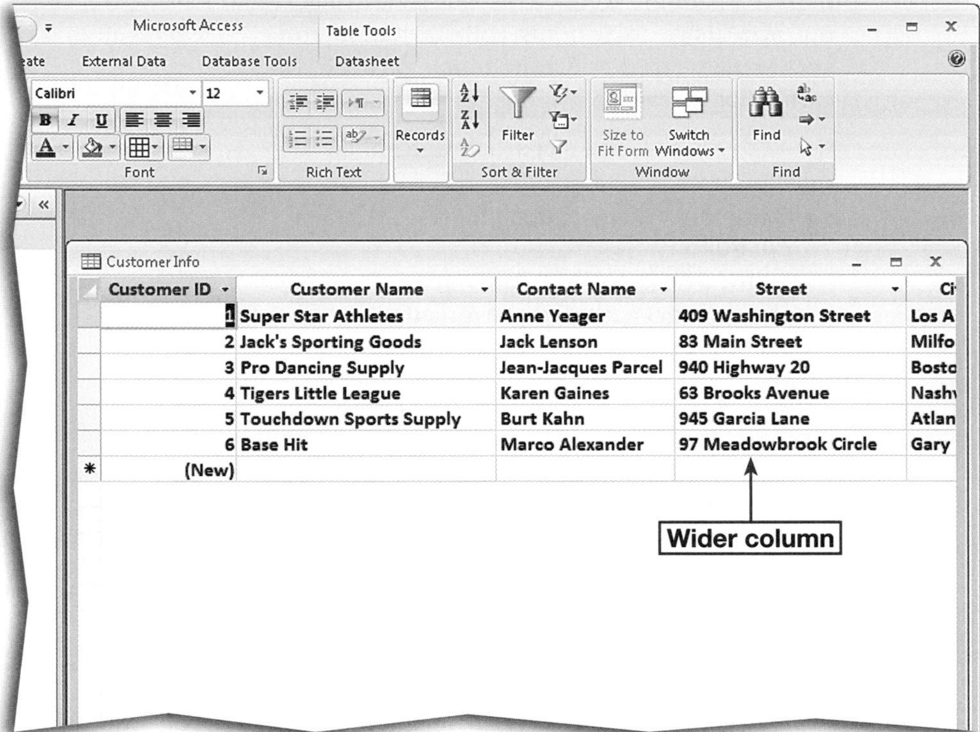

Shortcuts

To rename a table or query, right-click the table or query name in the **Navigation Pane** and click **Rename** in the shortcut menu.

You Should Know

When you change the font in a datasheet, it does not matter which data you have selected. All of the text fonts in the entire datasheet are automatically changed.

Portfolio Project

Part 3: Keep Track of Your Work

LEVEL This is an intermediate level project.

Goal You and your business partners want to keep track of the types of work that you do so that you can see how much money each type of work is bringing in. You decide to use Excel to create a worksheet.

Create In a new worksheet, create a column for each of the following data:

- Customer Name
- Lawn Maintenance
- Leaf Raking
- Planting
- Fertilizing
- Customer Total

Use the data in the **Lawns.docx** data file to fill in your worksheet. Apply **Currency** style to the numbers you enter. In the **Customer Total** column, calculate the total for each customer.

- At the bottom of your worksheet, add a row labeled **Total per Service**. Adjust column width as necessary. Find the sum of the column for lawn maintenance, leaf raking, planting, and fertilizing.
- Use borders, shading, and bolding to make your worksheet clear and readable.

Self Assess Use the Have You...? checklist to review your customer worksheet. Make sure your worksheet follows all of the guidelines set out in the previous section.

Carefully proofread your worksheet and make any necessary corrections. Pay special attention to the formulas as you proofread. Follow your teacher's instructions for naming the file and saving it to your Portfolio Folder.

When finished, proceed to Part 4.

	Have You...?
✓	Labeled each column and row correctly
✓	Entered the data from the **Lawns.docx** data file
✓	Adjusted column width as necessary
✓	Calculated the total per service and the total overall revenue
✓	Used borders, shading, and bolding to make your worksheet more readable

Step-By-Step

1. In your **Sports Equipment** file, in the **Navigation Pane**, open the **Customer Info** table.
2. In the **Home** tab, in the **Font** group, click the **Font Size** drop-down arrow. Select **12**. Click **Home>Font>Bold** **B**.
3. **CHECK** Your screen should look like Figure 1.23.
4. In the row of field names, move the pointer to the line between **Customer Name** and **Contact Name** until the pointer becomes a two-headed arrow (see Figure 1.24).
5. Click and drag to the right to make the column wider until you can see all the text in the **Customer Name** column.

Continue to the next exercise.

Academic Skills

Not all fonts of the same point size are equally readable. Unlike inches and centimeters which are always the same size, point size is a relative measurement. Text in 12 pt. Arial is not quite the same size as text in 12 pt. Calibri.

NCLB/Math (Measurement)

EXERCISE 1-12
Format a Datasheet

You can make data easier to read by changing the look of the datasheet. You might want to change the width of a column, make the text larger, or change the font style. You can apply these formatting changes to both tables and queries.

Differentiated Instruction/Visually Impaired If a student has trouble reading the text, increase the datasheet's font size. There is no equivalent in the Access table to the **Zoom** feature in other applications.

FIGURE 1.23 Formatted datasheet

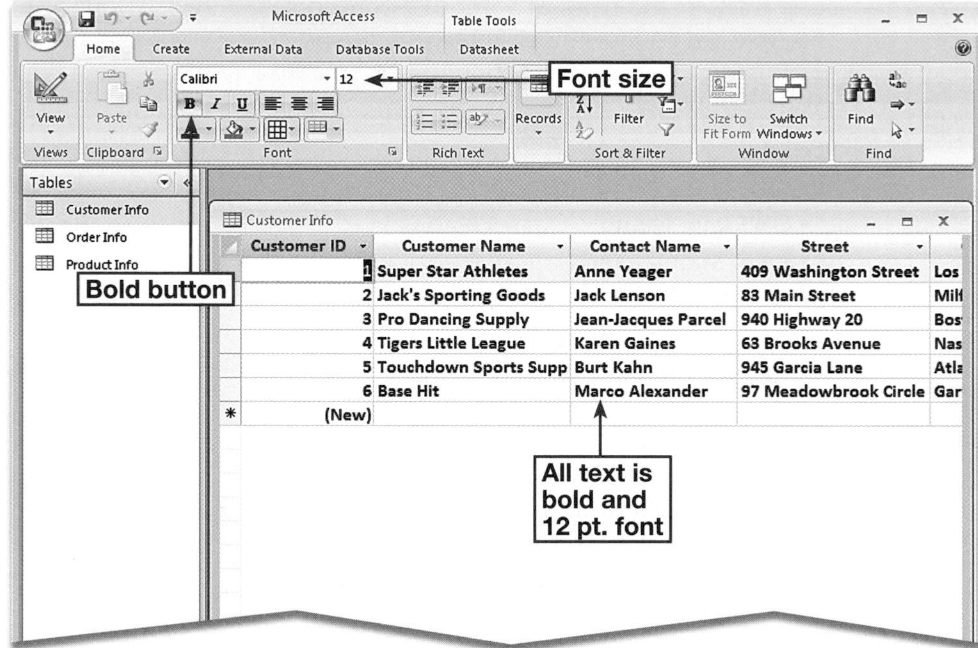

FIGURE 1.24 Changing the width of a column

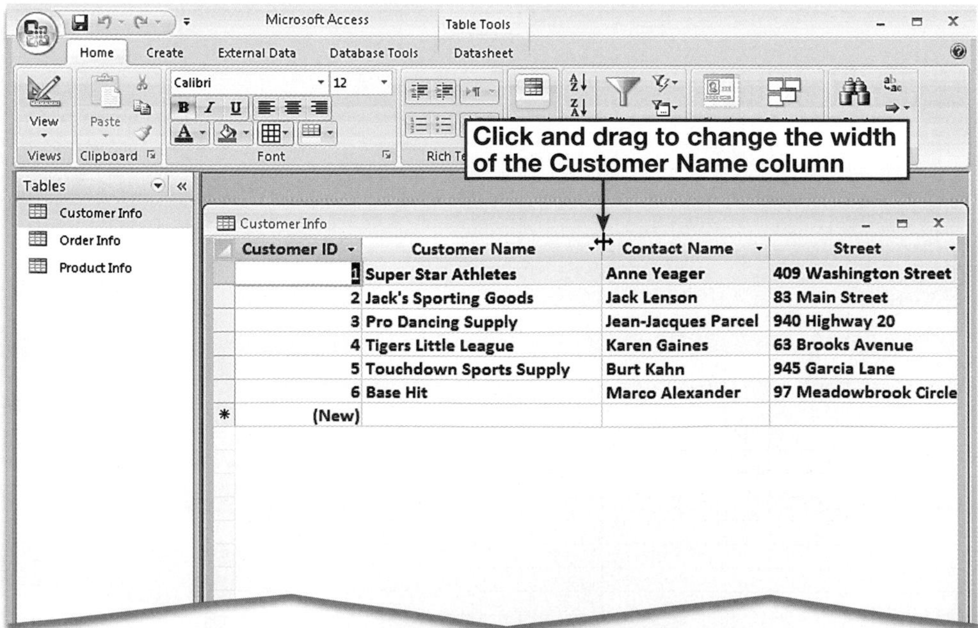

Portfolio Project

Part 4: Create a Chart

LEVEL This is an advanced level project.

Goal You want to be able to see who your best customers are quickly. You decide to sort your worksheet and create a chart.

Create In the worksheet you created in **Portfolio Project 3**, select a cell in the **Customer Total** column.

- Sort the column in descending order so that your best customers are at the top of the worksheet.
- Select cells **A1** to **E11**. Create a column chart that shows how much each customer spent on each service. Include the title **Customer Totals** in the chart.
- Identify the highest amount spent and the lowest amount spent.
- Drag the column chart below your data and adjust the size so that it is readable.

Self Assess Use the Have You...? checklist to review your worksheet. Make sure your worksheet fulfills all the requirements listed in the previous section.

Carefully proofread your worksheet and make corrections. Pay special attention to the chart as you proofread. Follow your teacher's instructions for naming the file and saving it to your Portfolio Folder.

	Have You...?
✓	Sorted the totals for each service
✓	Created a column chart that shows the totals for each service
✓	Added a title to the chart
✓	Added vertical and horizontal axis labels
✓	Positioned the chart below the data
✓	Adjusted the chart's size so that it is readable

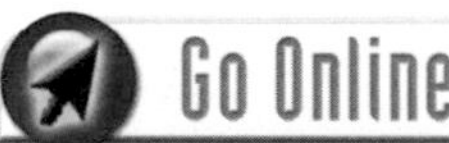

BEYOND THE BOOK

glencoe.com

Go to the Online Learning Center to learn additional skills and review what you have already learned.

Microsoft Excel
Extend your knowledge of Excel by visiting the Online Learning Center for more MCAS-based exercises. Select **Advanced Excel Exercises>Lessons**.

Windows Vista
Select **Windows Vista Exercises>Lessons** to explore Microsoft's operating system fully.

Microsoft Outlook
Want to learn all about Outlook and how to e-mail communication and scheduling? Select **Microsoft Outlook Exercises>Lessons** for all you need to know.

Additional Projects
Complete additional projects in the following areas:

- **Real-World Business Projects** reinforce Microsoft Word by focusing on real-world business applications.
- **Presentation and Publishing Projects** Use your Word skills to create exciting PowerPoint presentations and desktop publishing activities.
- **Academic Projects** Integrate academic skills while enriching your understanding of Microsoft Office.

More Online Resources
Access additional Web sites and online information relating to key topics covered in Glencoe's *iCheck Series*. Select **Additional Resources>Links**.

Step-By-Step

1. In your **Sports Equipment** file, select **Office>Open**.
2. Ask your teacher which location to select in the box at the top of the **Open** dialog box.
3. With your teacher's permission, right-click in the blank area of the **Open** dialog box and click **New**.
4. Click **Folder**.
5. A folder named **New Folder** appears in the **Open** dialog box (see Figure 1.21).
6. Key: [your first initial and last name]. (For example, *smarquez*.) Press ENTER.
7. CHECK Your dialog box should look like Figure 1.22. Note that the folder's name has changed.
8. Click **Cancel** Cancel to close the dialog box.

Continue to the next exercise.

Troubleshooter

Take a moment and proofread the name of the new folder you have just created before pressing ENTER. Mislabeled folders can cause problems when you try to manage your files later.

EXERCISE 1-11
Create a New Folder

Teacher Tip If students are using Windows XP to complete exercises, refer them to page I to read about differences between XP and Windows Vista.

You can store databases in folders. Just as you may keep your math assignments in a separate folder from your English homework, **folders** in Access help you organize various databases so you can find them quickly. One way to create a new folder is to use the Open dialog box. A **dialog box** is used to enter specific information to perform a task, such as naming and saving a document.

Differentiated Instruction/Advanced Students Let advanced students explore **Save As** instead of **Open** to see the difference between the two features.

FIGURE 1.21 Creating a new folder

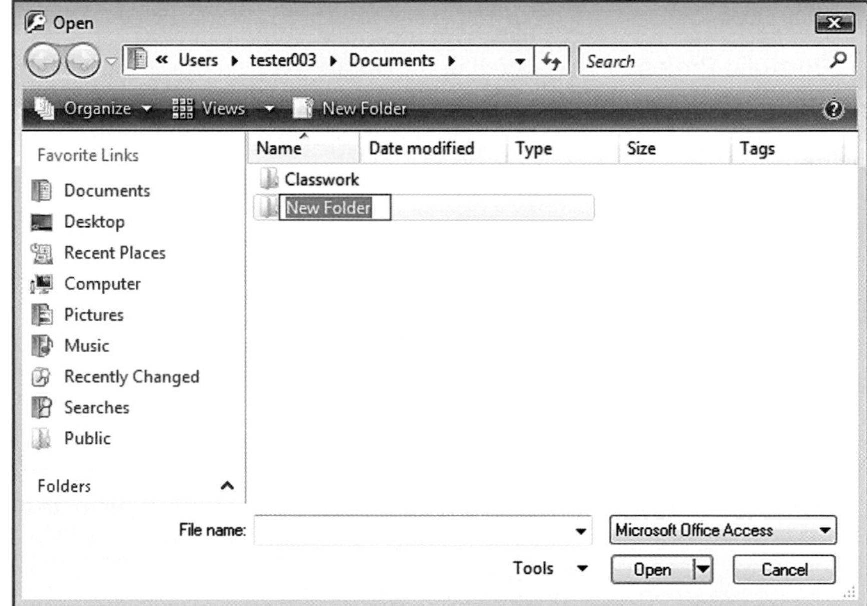

FIGURE 1.22 Naming a new folder

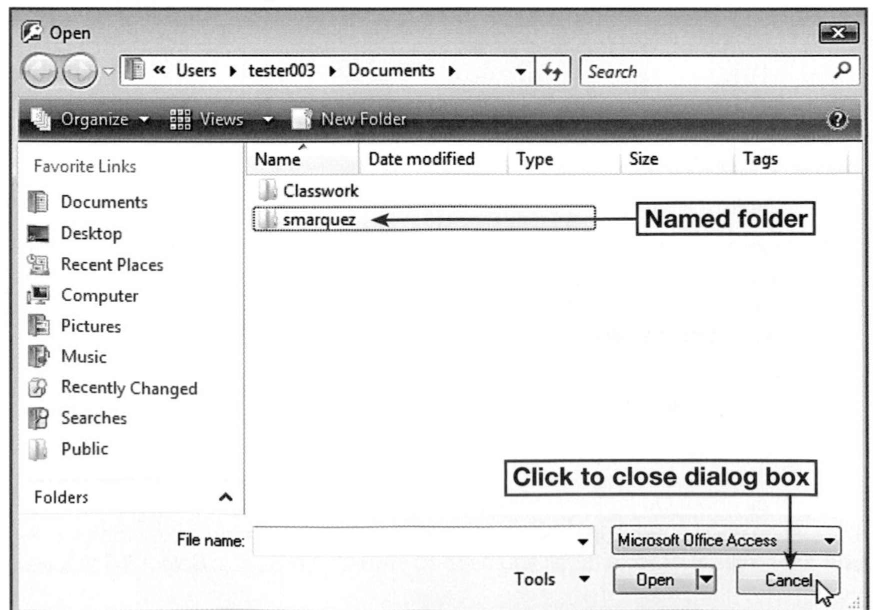

Access 2007: Use Databases

Unit Objectives:

After completing this Unit, you will be able to:

LESSON 1

Access Basics

LESSON 2

Structure a Database

LESSON 3

Enter and Organize Data

LESSON 4

Maximize Database Functions

LESSON 5

Manage Databases

See page TM77 for an overview of Unit level resources.

Why It Matters Students' answers may vary. Students might use library databases and e-mail contacts. They might also encounter databases when searching the Internet or shopping online.

Why It Matters

A database is an organized collection of information. You may be using databases every day without realizing it. For example, personal music players, such as iPods, organize thousands of music, photo, and video files by title, artist, year, and more. The best thing about databases is that they make it easy to search for information using different criteria saving time and effort. ***What other common databases might you use daily?***

Go Online REAL WORLD CONNECTION

glencoe.com

Go to the **Online Learning Center** and select your book. Choose **Unit 3** to learn more about how businesses use database applications in the real world.

EXERCISE 1-10
Enter Data

When you enter data in a table, Access saves it automatically. If you enter data and then close the table, you will not be asked to save the data or any changes you made to existing data. The new data and the changes will be there when you reopen the table. When you enter or modify data in a table, you should always be careful because your changes will be difficult to undo.

Step-By-Step Tip In **Step 6**, explain that the **Cost** field is set up to automatically add a dollar sign and two decimal places to the number.

Step-By-Step

1. Select **Office>Open**. Open the **Sports Equipment** database. Ask your teacher how and where to copy the database before working in it.
2. In the **Navigation Pane**, open the **Product Info** table.
3. On the **Navigation** toolbar, click **New Record** [button] (see Figure 1.19).
4. Press TAB. Your insertion point should be in the last row of the **Product Name** field.
5. Key: Skates. Press TAB.
6. Key: 37.50. Press TAB.
7. **CHECK** Your screen should look like Figure 1.20.
8. In the table window, click **Close** [x].

Continue to the next exercse.

FIGURE 1.19 New Record inserted

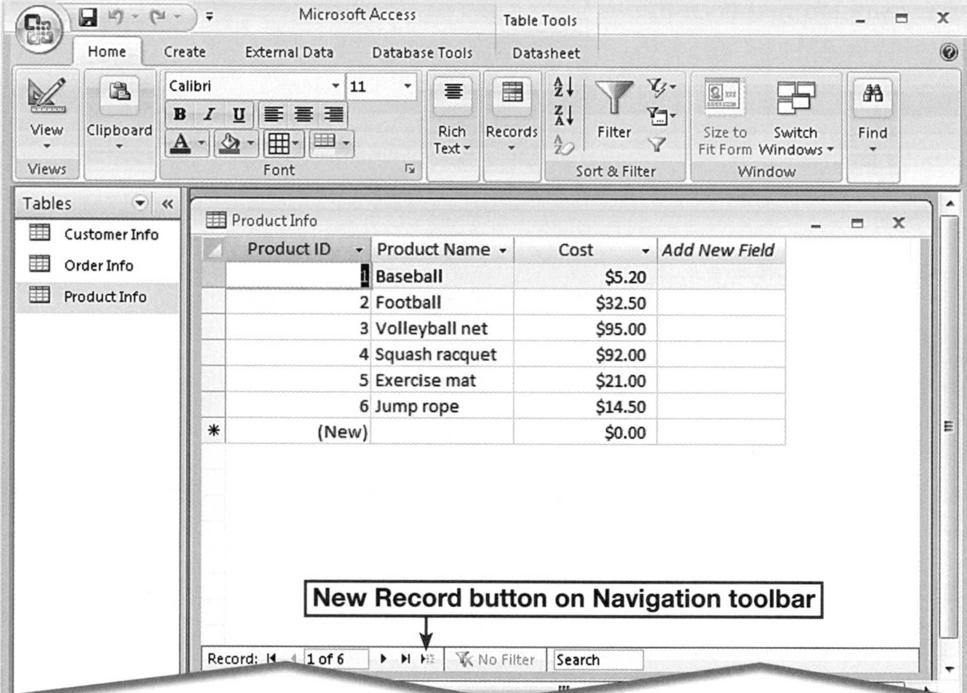

FIGURE 1.20 Data entered in record

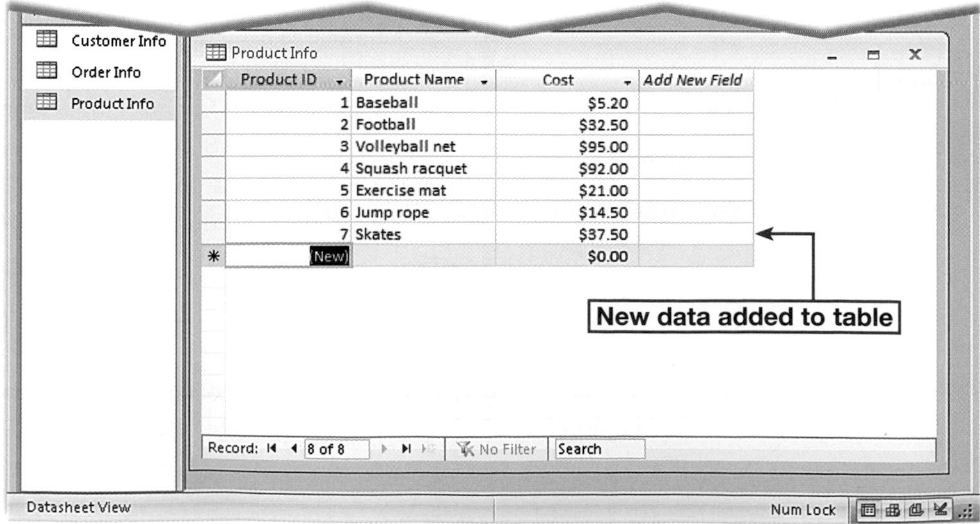

Academic Skills

All data must be entered correctly. If you are looking for the records of a client named John Smith, a query will not find them if his name was originally entered as Jon Smiht.

NCLB/Language Arts (NCTE 8) Explain to students that correct spelling and accuracy is as important in a database as it is when they do their homework.

Career Checklist

To use databases effectively in the workplace, remember that you will need to:

- ✓ Identify what you want to find before you search.
- ✓ Search the database using keywords.
- ✓ Evaluate query results and revise keywords.
- ✓ Create forms and reports to organize and display data.

How Are Databases Used in the Professional World?

Organizing the vast amount of information at our fingertips has become an important part of everyday business. Trends indicate that the number of jobs that involve working with databases will increase. Database administrators organize databases so that information can be accessed, manipulated, added to, and maintained. Computer and information systems managers ensure that information is available to those who need it and blocked for those who should not access it.

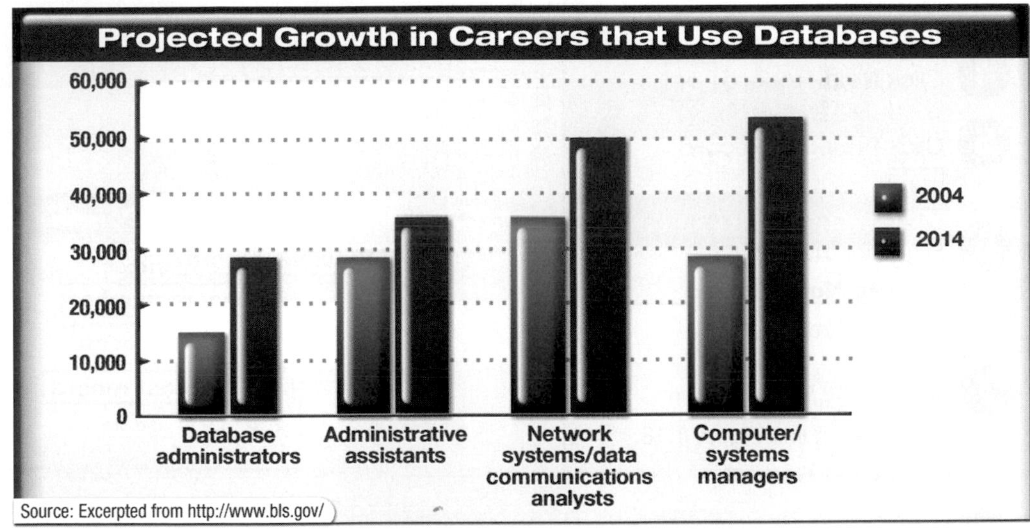

Differentiated Instruction/ Advanced Students Have students write a paragraph describing how the career of their choice would use Access.

NCLB/Math (Representation) Have students go to the book Web site at **glencoe.com** to learn more about math theory. Students should click the Math Handbook link.

Databases and the Internet

The Internet contains millions of databases that organize information and make it available to users. Computer programmers work with database administrators to create databases for business, educational, and personal use. Business databases, such as Apple iTunes, organize music files so that they can be searched, purchased, and downloaded to another kind of database on a personal music player. Reference databases offer factual information of all kinds. Some online reference databases, called "wikis", are created and maintained by the public. Wikipedia is the best-known public database. It contains entries on almost every imaginable topic.

1. **Evaluate** Why is the number of jobs that involve working with databases projected to increase?
2. **Math** How much growth is the database administrator career field expected to experience from 2004 to 2014?

See page TM77 for answers to the Reading Check.

EXERCISE 1-9
Navigate Among Records

Navigation buttons allow you to move quickly from one record in a field to another record in the same field. A highlighted box to the left of the record indicates which record you are currently using. Both tables and queries use the same navigation buttons. For large databases that contain thousands, or even millions of entries, the navigation buttons are extremely useful.

EL Observe EL students often to make sure they understand the directions.

FIGURE 1.17 Navigation buttons

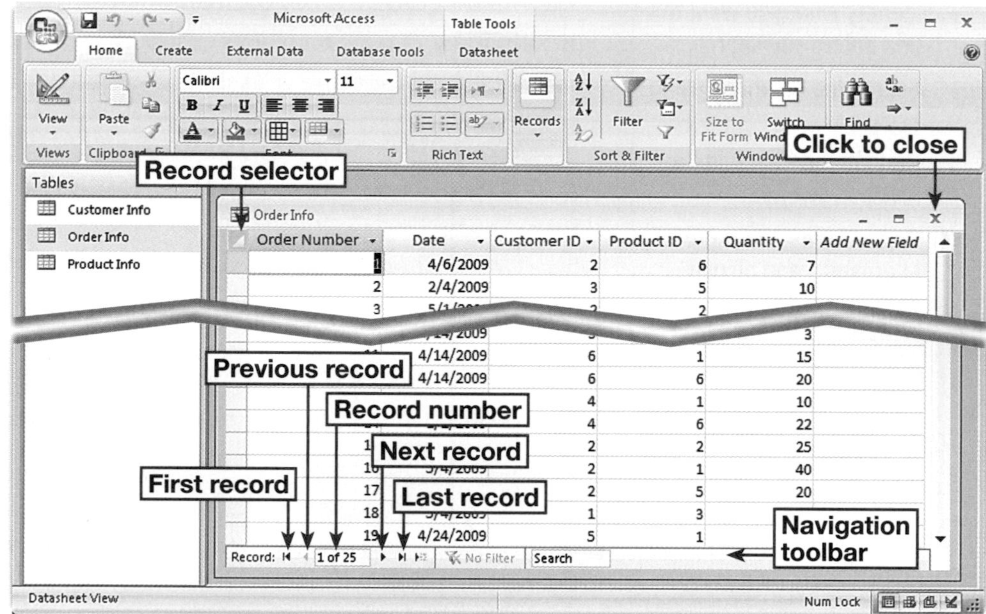

FIGURE 1.18 Record number 23

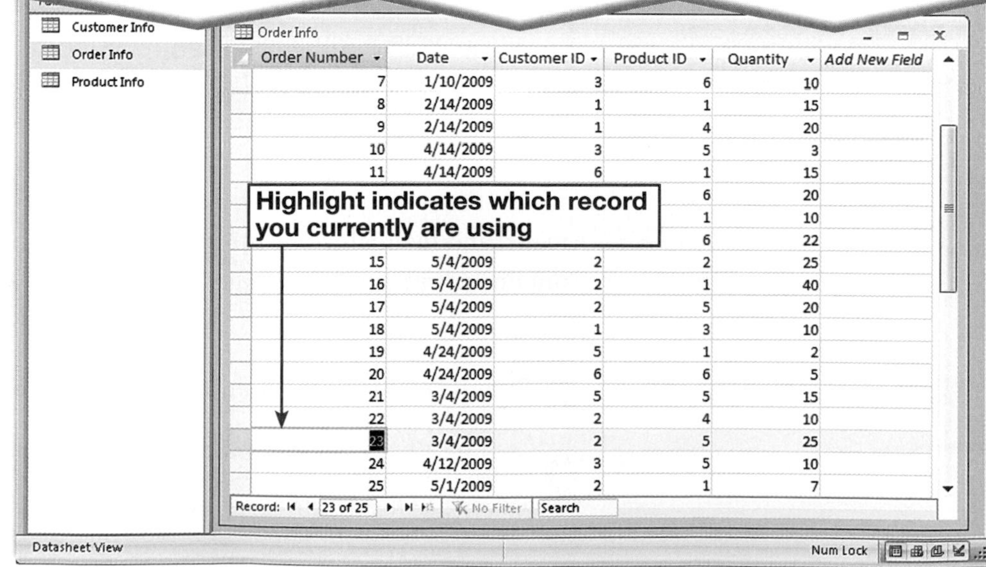

Step-By-Step

1. In your **Sports Equipment** file, in the **Navigation Pane** menu, select **Tables**. Open the **Order Info** table. On the navigation toolbar, click **Last Record** [▶|] (see Figure 1.17).
2. Click **First Record** [|◀].
3. **CHECK** Your screen should look like Figure 1.17.
4. Click **Next Record** [▶].
5. Click **Previous Record** [◀].
6. Highlight the text in the **Record Number** box. Key: 23. Press ENTER.
7. **CHECK** Your screen should look like Figure 1.18. Click **First Record**.
8. **CHECK** Your screen should look like Figure 1.17.
9. In the table window, click **Close** [x].
10. Click **Office** and select **Close Database**.

Continue to the next exercise.

Teaching Tip Ask students to think of large public databases. Some answers might include public libraries, motor vehicle records, and social security records.

Step-By-Step Tip In **Step 3**, point out that if students click the record selector, they will select the entire record.

LESSON 1 Access Basics

In this lesson, you will learn the basics of Access. You will explore tables and queries and learn how to view, insert, and format data. You will also learn how to print and save the data in your database, copy a database, and finally compact and close your database.

Key Concepts

- Identify parts of the Access screen
- Open a database
- Insert and format data
- View and print data from a database
- Copy a database
- Compact and close a database

Standards

The following standards are covered in this lesson. Refer to pages xxv and 715 for a description of the standards listed here.

ISTE Standards Correlation

NETS•S

2b, 3d, 4b, 4c, 5a, 6a, 6b, 6d

Microsoft Certified Application Specialist

Access

1.4, 3.2, 5.6, 6.1, 6.2

21st CENTURY SKILLS

See page TM79 for answer to 21st Century Skills.

Get Organized Tests and project due dates can sneak up on you if you are not well organized. Buy a calendar that is small enough to keep with you yet large enough to show a whole month on one page. Write tests, assignments, and due dates on your calendar as soon as they are assigned. Put an X through each day when it is over so you can see what is due next. Microsoft Access databases give you even more ways to stay organized. You can view and print tasks by start date, due date, importance, or any other category you choose. *What methods do you use to stay organized?*

Step-By-Step

1. In your **Sports Equipment** file, in the **Navigation Pane** menu, click **Queries**. The list of queries in the database opens. Double-click **April Orders** (see Figure 1.15).
2. In the **Navigation Pane**, double-click **May Orders**. Click the **May Orders** title bar. Drag the query down until your screen looks similar to Figure 1.16.
3. Click the **April Orders** title bar. The **April Orders** query is now on top.
4. In the **Window** group, click **Switch Windows** . Select **Tile Horizontally**.
5. Click **Switch Windows** . Select **Tile Vertically**.
6. Click **Switch Windows** . Select **April Orders**.
7. In the **April Orders** query window, click **Close** x.
8. In the **May Orders** query window, click **Close** x.
9. **CHECK** Your screen should look like Figure 1.15.

Continue to the next exercise.

Differentiated Instruction/Advanced Students Have students arrange the two windows on the screen by resizing and moving each window.

EXERCISE 1-8
Open Multiple Queries

Access also allows you to have more than one query open at the same time. This can help you put information located in different queries side by side so that you can compare, or measure similarities and differences. For example, a business might want to compare what customers ordered in April and May. That way, in June, when a mailer is sent to customers, it can be targeted to match customer needs.

FIGURE 1.15 List of queries in Sports Equipment database

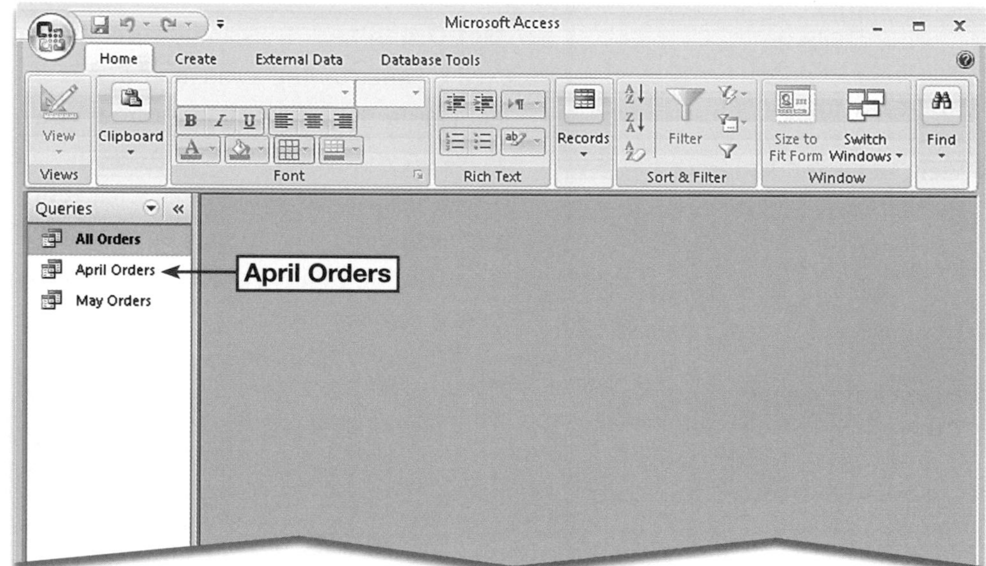

FIGURE 1.16 Access screen with multiple queries open

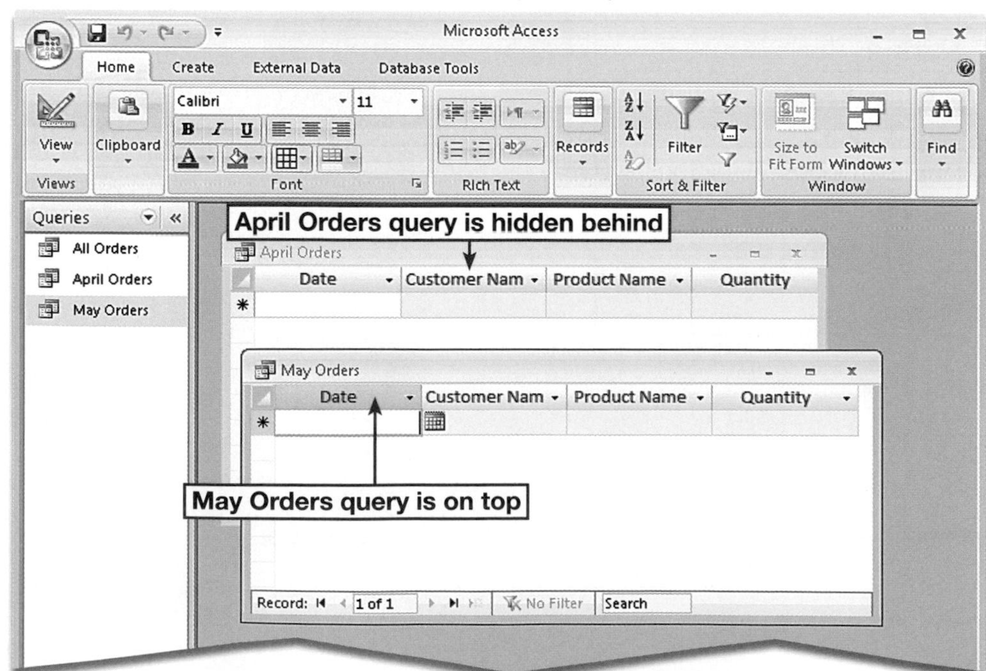

LESSON 1 Reading Guide

Before You Read

See page TM42 for English Learner activity suggestions.

Two-Column Notes Two-column notes are a useful way to study and organize what you have read. Divide a piece of paper into two columns. In the left column, write down main ideas. In the right column, list supporting details.

Read To Learn

- Explore information management by learning some of the basics of Access.
- Learn the basics of creating and using tables and queries.
- Create a database tracking inventory and customer information.

Main Idea

Database management enables you to track, manipulate, and control the presentation of data.

Vocabulary

Key Terms

backup	field	record
button	folder	Ribbon
command	group	scroll bar
criteria	pointer	shared access
database	query	tab
default	Quick Access Toolbar (QAT)	table
dialog box		title bar

Academic Vocabulary

These words appear in your reading and on your tests. Make sure you know their meanings:

compare
control
data
function

Quick Write Activity

Describe On a separate sheet of paper, describe how you would keep track of a music or movie collection. What information would be necessary for your tracking? How might tracking your collection on a computer be easier than by hand?

Study Skills

Be Prepared Preparing to study makes the time you spend on schoolwork more effective. Plan on working on your assignments at the same time and place each day. It can be at home, library, or any other plan that you'll find some quiet time. Make sure you have gathered all of the tools and supplies you will need beforehand.

Academic Standards

English Language Arts

NCTE 8 Use information resources to gather information and create and communicate knowledge.

NCTE 12 Use language to accomplish individual purposes.

Math

NCTM (Measurement) Understand measurable attributes of objects and the units, systems, and processes of measurement.

Step-By-Step

1. In your **Sports Equipment** file, In the **Navigation Pane**, click **Tables**. Double-click **Customer Info** to open the table (see Figure 1.13).

2. In the **Navigation Pane**, double-click **Order Info**.

3. **CHECK** Your screen should look like Figure 1.14.

4. In the **Navigation Pane**, double-click **Customer Info**.

5. Click the title bar on the **Customer Info** table. Drag it down until you see the **Order Info** window.

6. In the **Window** group, click **Switch Windows**. Select **Tile Horizontally**.

7. Click **Switch Windows**. Select **Tile Vertically**.

8. Click **Switch Windows**. Select **Order Info**.

9. In the **Order Info** table window, click **Close** [x].

10. In the **Customer Info** table window, click **Close** [x].

11. **CHECK** Your screen should again look like Figure 1.13.

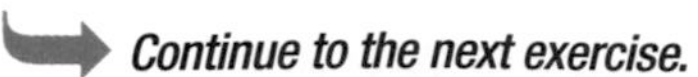
Continue to the next exercise.

Intervention Strategy If a student has trouble understanding or conceptualizing opening multiple windows, show a similar example using three pieces of paper on top of each other on a desk.

EXERCISE 1-7
Open Multiple Tables

Access allows you to have more than one table open at the same time. This can help you compare data located in different tables. For example, you can keep track of your customers in one table, and the items that they order in another.

Troubleshooting If students have trouble locating the bottom table, make sure they moved the top table enough to see the bottom table.

FIGURE 1.13 Navigation Pane with list of tables

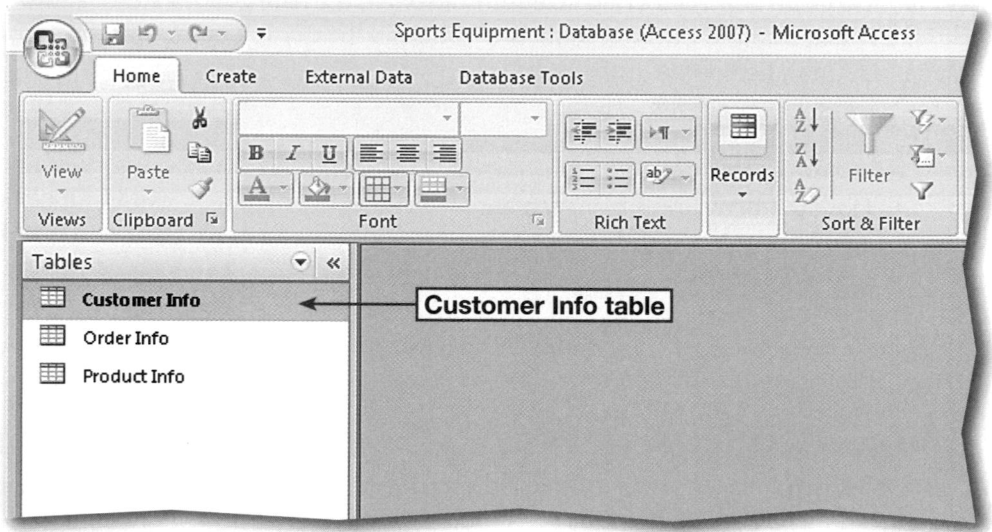

FIGURE 1.14 Access screen with multiple tables open

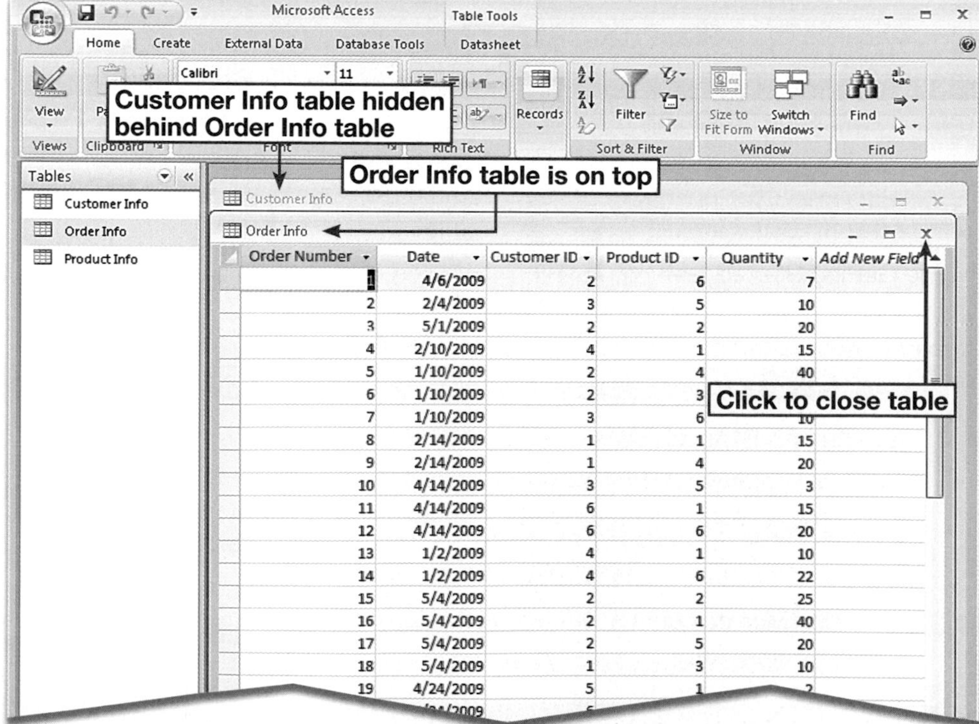

Order Number	Date	Customer ID	Product ID	Quantity	Add New Field
1	4/6/2009	2	6	7	
2	2/4/2009	3	5	10	
3	5/1/2009	2	2	20	
4	2/10/2009	4	1	15	
5	1/10/2009	2	4	40	
6	1/10/2009	2	3		
7	1/10/2009	3	6	10	
8	2/14/2009	1	1	15	
9	2/14/2009	1	4	20	
10	4/14/2009	3	5	3	
11	4/14/2009	6	1	15	
12	4/14/2009	6	6	20	
13	1/2/2009	4	1	10	
14	1/2/2009	4	6	22	
15	5/4/2009	2	2	25	
16	5/4/2009	2	1	40	
17	5/4/2009	2	5	20	
18	5/4/2009	1	3	10	
19	4/24/2009	5	1	2	

Step-By-Step

1. To start Access, choose **Start>All Programs> Microsoft Office®> Microsoft Office Access 2007**.
2. **CHECK** Your screen should look like Figure 1.1.
3. At the top of the page, under the **New Blank Database** heading, click the **Blank Database** icon.
4. Click the **Create** button to create a new blank database labeled **Database1**.
5. **CHECK** Your screen should look like Figure 1.2. Notice the tab that indicates that the file is in Datasheet View.

Continue to the next exercise.

Microsoft Office 2007

The Getting Started task pane in Access has been expanded into the opening page for Access 2007, the Getting Started page. The Getting Started page offers helpful tips and information on what is new in Access 2007.

EL Make sure English Learners understand all vocabulary terms. Suggest that they create flashcards to help them memorize the terms and definitions.

EXERCISE 1-1
Get Started with Access

Access automatically opens to a Getting Started page that offers many options to help you learn how to work with a **database.** A database stores information, or **data**. From this page you can start a blank database file or choose from database templates. When you create a new database, it will automatically open in Datasheet view. This is the **default**, or automatic, setting for Access. You can also open existing database files.

FIGURE 1.1 The Getting Started page

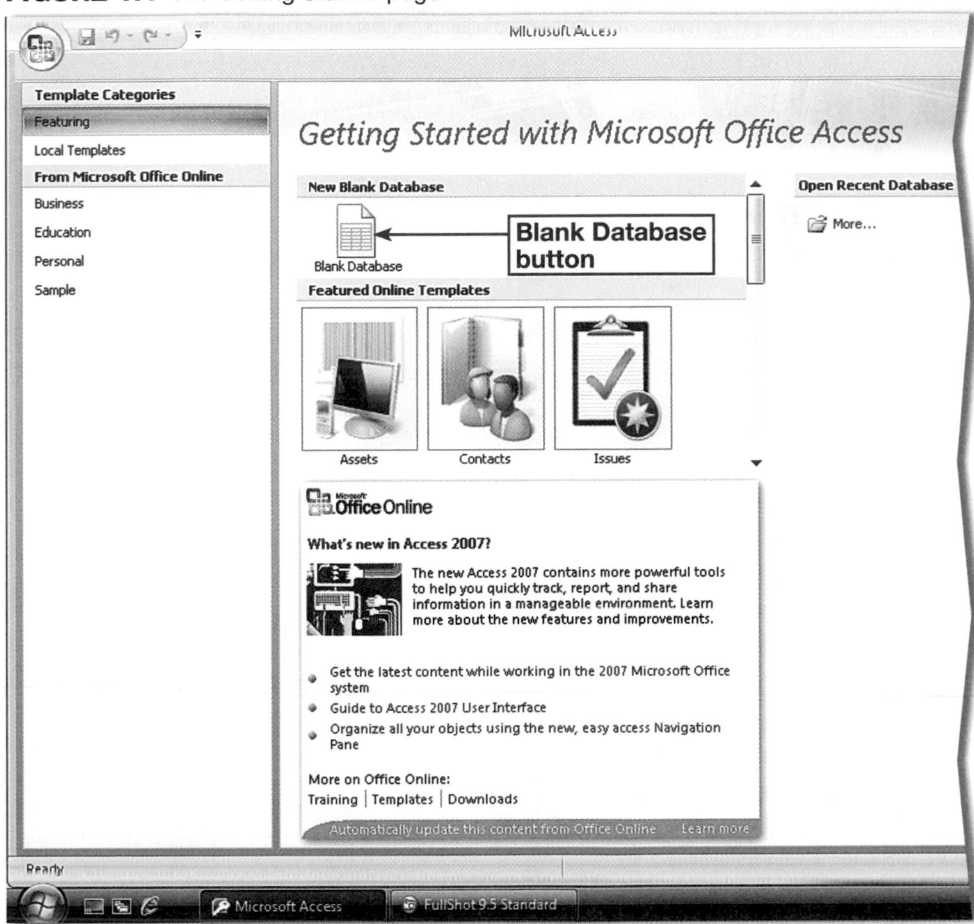

FIGURE 1.2 New database file

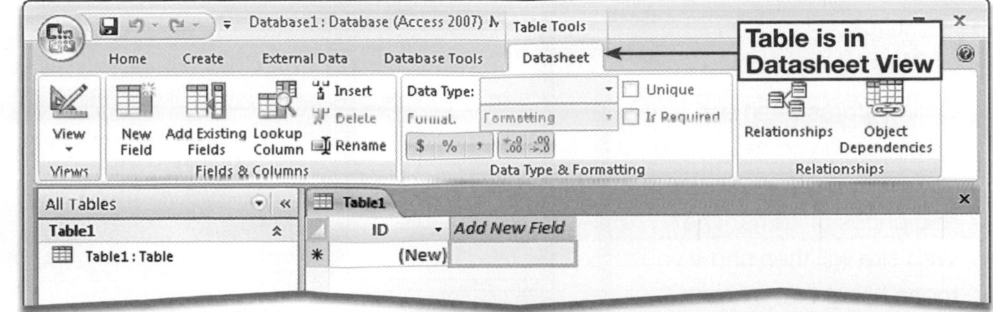

Step-By-Step

1. In your **Sports Equipment** file, click the **Navigation Pane** menu. Select **Queries** (see Figure 1.11).

2. In the list of queries, right-click **All Orders**. In the menu, click **Open**.

3. **CHECK** Your screen should look like Figure 1.12.

4. Click the **down arrow** [▼] until you reach the bottom of the query.

5. Click the **up arrow** [▲] until you reach the top of the query.

6. On the keyboard, press [PAGE DOWN] twice.

7. Press [PAGE UP] twice to move back to the top.

8. Click **Close** [x] in the query window.

9. **CHECK** Your screen should again look like Figure 1.11.

Continue to the next exercise.

You Should Know

Online stores often use a query when you request to find certain colors, styles, and prices of items. The Web site will then show you those items that match.

EXERCISE 1-6
Open a Query

A **query** asks Access to find data from one or more tables that matches specific **criteria**, or conditions. For example, one query might find all the products that cost over $50.00. Another query might find all the customers who live in Detroit. Like a table, a query is made up of columns (fields) and rows (records). To view a query or a table, use the scroll bars or the keyboard.

Teaching Tip Tell students that if a query had more columns than fit in the window, there would also be a horizontal scroll bar.

FIGURE 1.11 Opening a query from the Navigation Pane

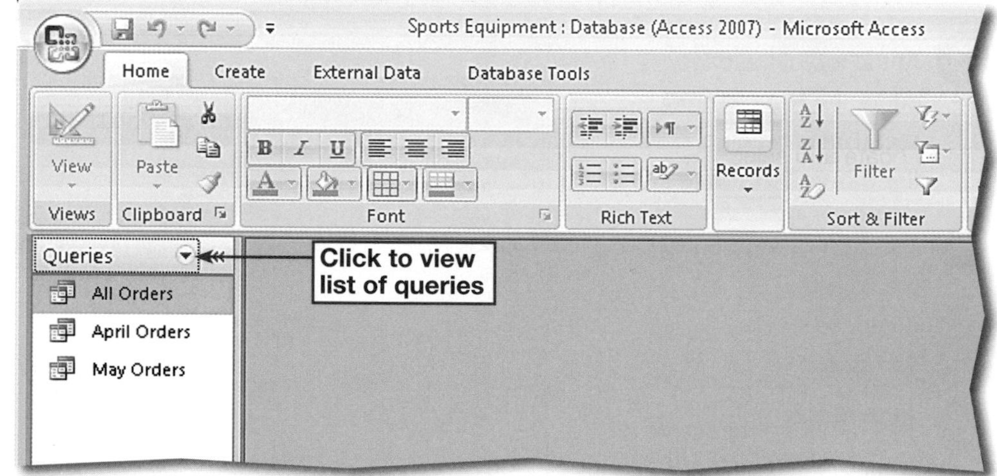

FIGURE 1.12 All Orders query

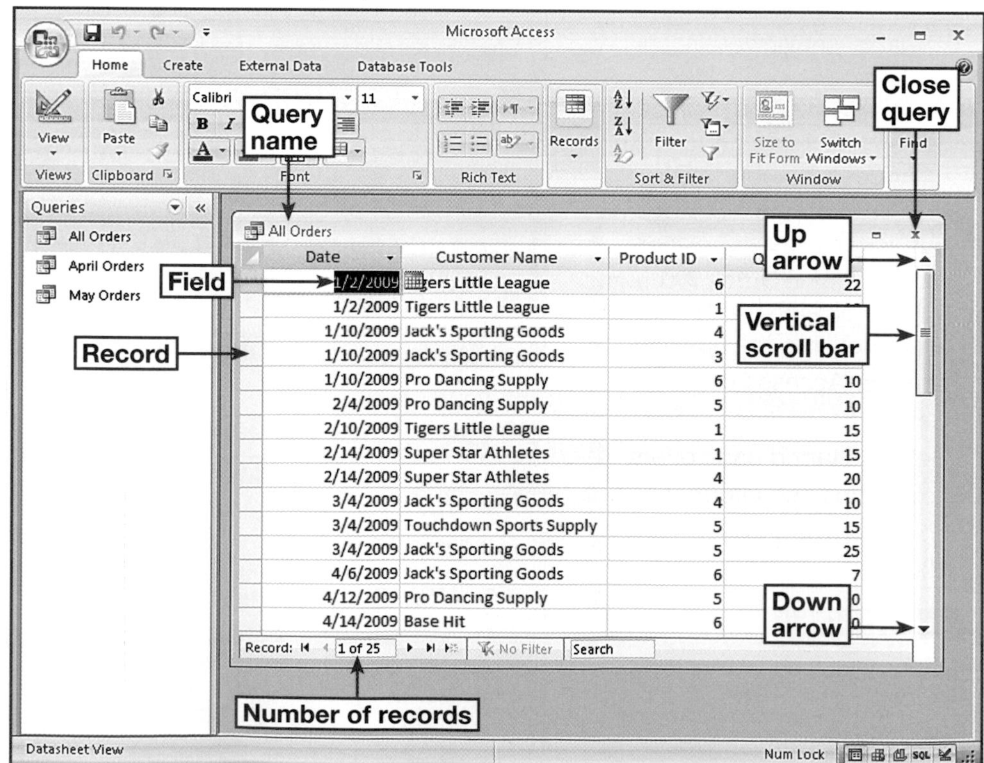

Step-By-Step

1. In the upper-left corner of the screen, click the **Home** tab.
2. CHECK Your screen should look like Figure 1.3.
3. Locate the **Title bar**.
4. Locate the **Navigation Pane**.
5. Locate and select the **Office Button**. Click in a blank area to close the menu.
6. Minimize the **Navigation Pane** by clicking the **Shutter Bar Open/ Close** button « (see Figure 1.4).
7. Locate the **Quick Access Toolbar**. Select the drop-down arrow to display the **Customize Quick Access Toolbar** menu.
8. Click anywhere on-screen to close the **Quick Access Toolbar**.

Continue to the next exercise.

EXERCISE 1-2
Identify Parts of the Access Screen

The Access screen contains several useful tools. The **title bar** displays a database's name. The **Quick Access Toolbar (QAT)** is a customizable toolbar where you can place the functions you use most often. The Navigation Pane allows you to see all of the different tables, reports, queries, or forms associated with the database.

FIGURE 1.3 The Access screen

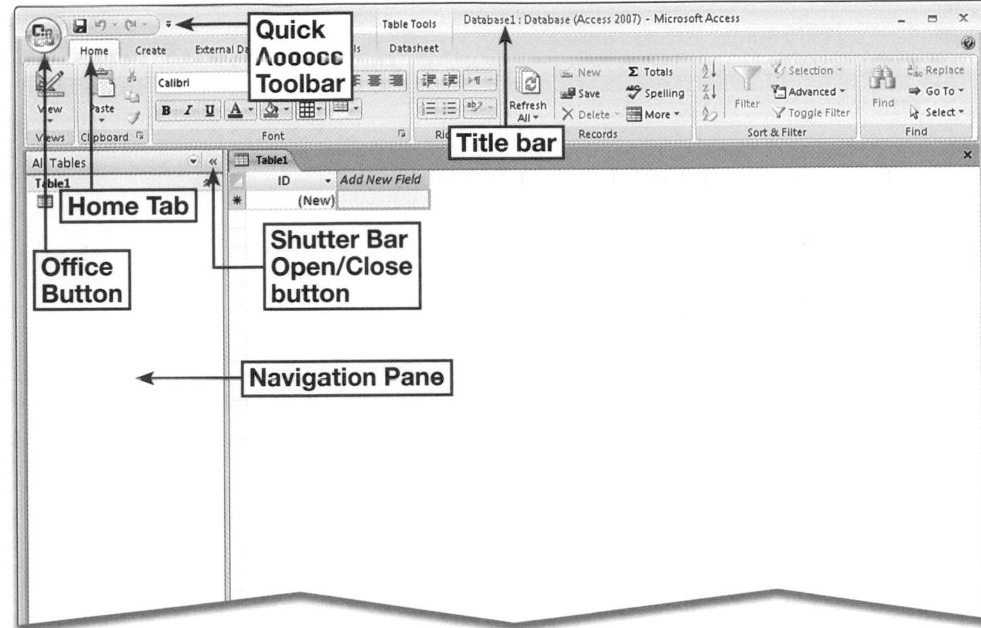

FIGURE 1.4 The Access screen with the Navigation Pane open

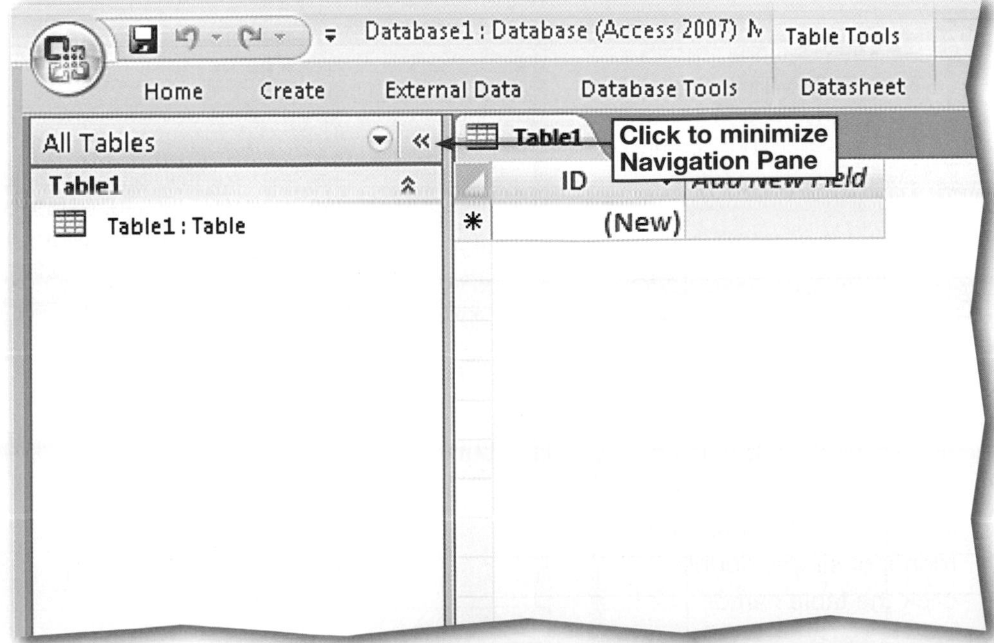

Step-By-Step

1. In your **Sports Equipment** file, in the **Navigation Pane**, in the list of tables, make sure **Customer Info** is selected (see Figure 1.9).

2. In the **pane**, right-click **Customer Info** and select **Open** from the menu.

3. **CHECK** Your screen should look like Figure 1.10. Notice that the table has six records.

4. On the horizontal scroll bar, click the **right arrow** ▶ to view all the table's fields.

5. Click the **left arrow** ◀ to scroll to the left.

6. Click **Close** x in the **Customer Info** table window.

7. **CHECK** Your screen should again look like Figure 1.9.

Continue to the next exercise.

Microsoft Office 2007

There is more than one way to open a table in Access 2007. You can right-click the table name in the **Navigation Pane** and select **Open** from the menu, or simply double-click the table name.

EXERCISE 1-5
Open a Table

By default, Access opens databases in Datasheet View. In this view, a **table** contains columns and rows of data, or information, about one topic such as a business' customers or products. A table's columns contain fields. A **field** is one piece of data, such as a customer's name in a database for contacts or the color of a product in an inventory database. A table's rows contain records. A **record** is made up of all the fields related to one particular item in the table. **Scroll bars** allow you to see all the data in a table.

Teaching Tip Tell students that if the table had more records, the window would also have a vertical scroll bar.

FIGURE 1.9 Opening a table from the Navigation pane

FIGURE 1.10 Customer Info table in Datasheet View

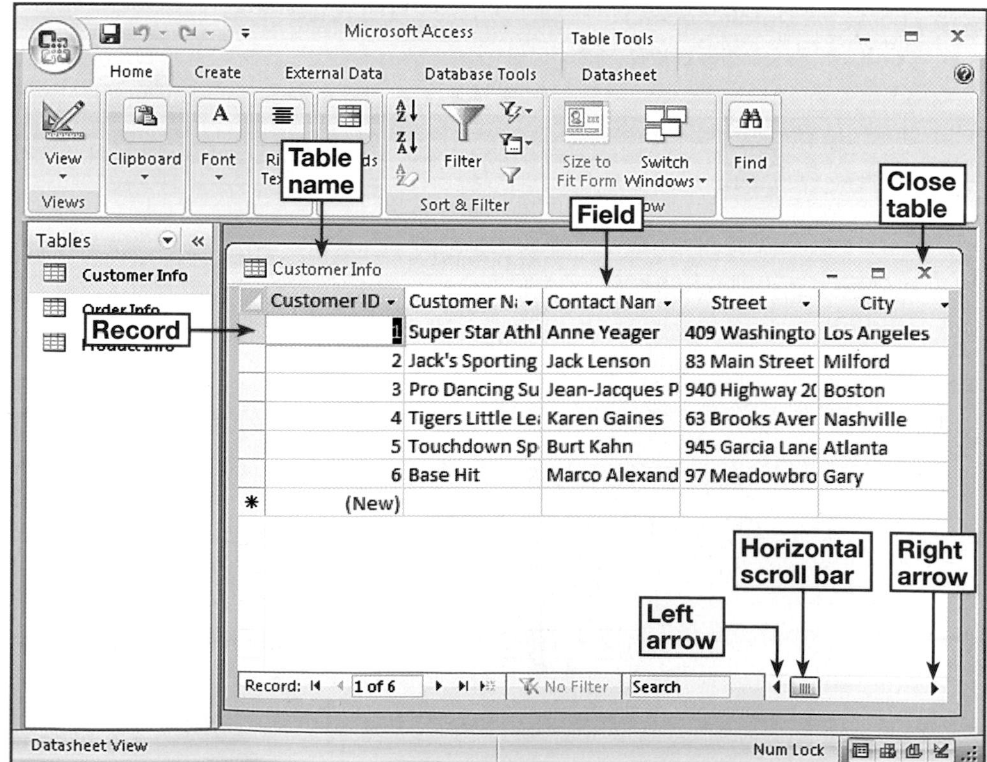

Step-By-Step

1. On the **Ribbon**, click the **Create** tab (see Figure 1.5).
2. Roll your pointer over the four different groups in the Create tab (see Figure 1.6).
3. Click the four tabs across the Ribbon. Identify the groups displayed in each tab. Click the **Create** tab.
4. In the **Tables** group, place the pointer on the **Table Design** button. A **ScreenTip** opens under the button to show the button name and function.
5. Click the **Table Templates** button. Read the available views in the drop-down menu (see Figure 1.5).
6. Click the **Office Button** and click **Close Database**.

Continue to the next exercise.

EXERCISE 1-3
Use the Ribbon, Tabs, and Groups

Across the top of the Access window is the **Ribbon**. The Ribbon has different **tabs** that contain major Access tasks, or functions. The tabs are broken up into **groups** of similar actions. Each group contains **buttons** (or **commands**) that you click to perform specific tasks. Use the **pointer** to select tabs and other tools.

FIGURE 1.5 Table Design screen tip

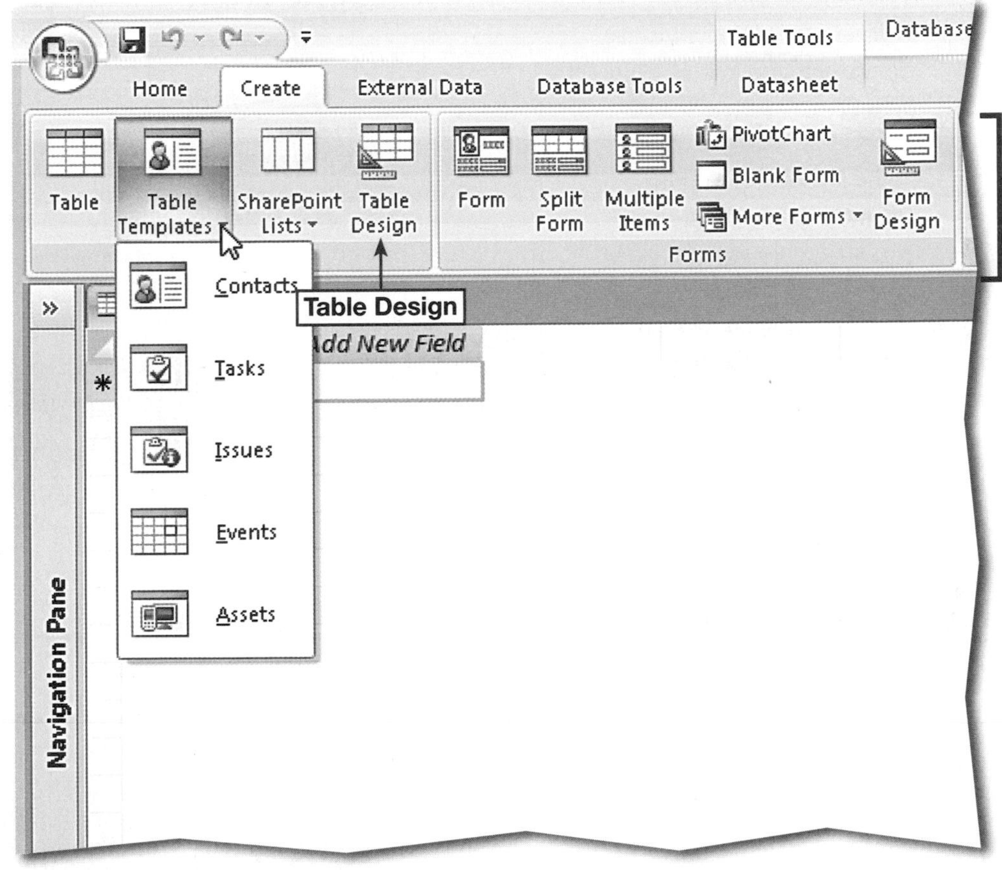

FIGURE 1.6 Table Templates options

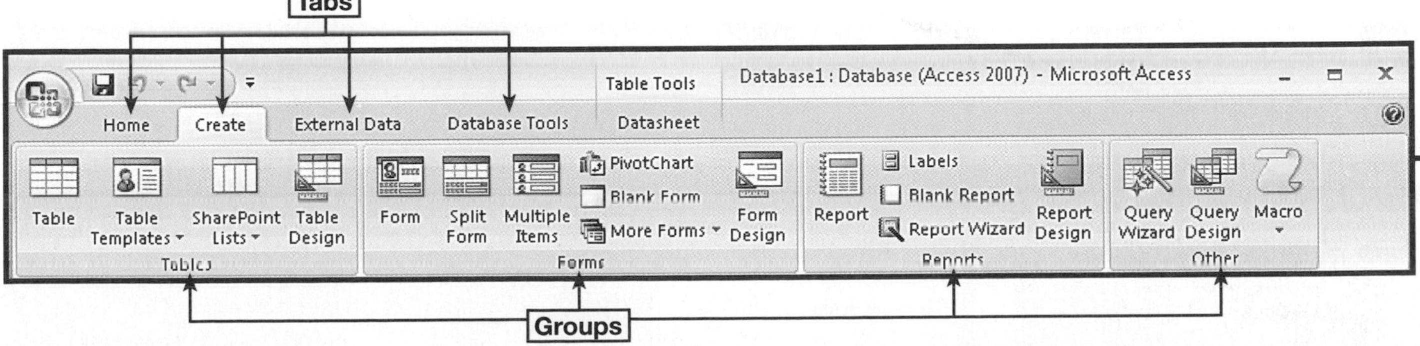

Teaching Tip Explain to students that buttons with downward-pointing arrows below them always have drop-down menus that allow students to select additional options.

Step-By-Step

1. Click the **Office Button**. Click **Open**.
2. With your teacher's help, locate the data file **Sports Equipment.accdb**. Ask your teacher how and where to copy the database before working in it.
3. Select the database shown in the **Open** dialog box. Click the **Open** drop-down arrow (see Figure 1.7).
4. Read the options. Notice the third choice, **Open Exclusive**.
5. Click **Open** to open the database.
6. **CHECK** Your screen should look like Figure 1.8.
7. Click the **Navigation Pane** menu bar and select **Queries**.
8. Click **Forms**. There are no forms in this database. Click **Reports**. There are no reports in the database.
9. Click **Tables.**
10. **CHECK** Your screen should again look like Figure 1.8.

Continue to the next exercise.

EXERCISE 1-4
Open and Explore a Database

A database is used to store information. The database used in this exercise helps a sports equipment company store and organize information about customers, products, and customer orders. When you open a database, it can still be opened and edited by other users. This is called **shared access**. If you need to ensure that you are the only one making changes to the database, you can select Open Exclusive. That means that no one else has control, or power, to open or edit the database.

Step-By-Step Tip In **Step 2**, show students how and where to save their database.

FIGURE 1.7 Open dialog box

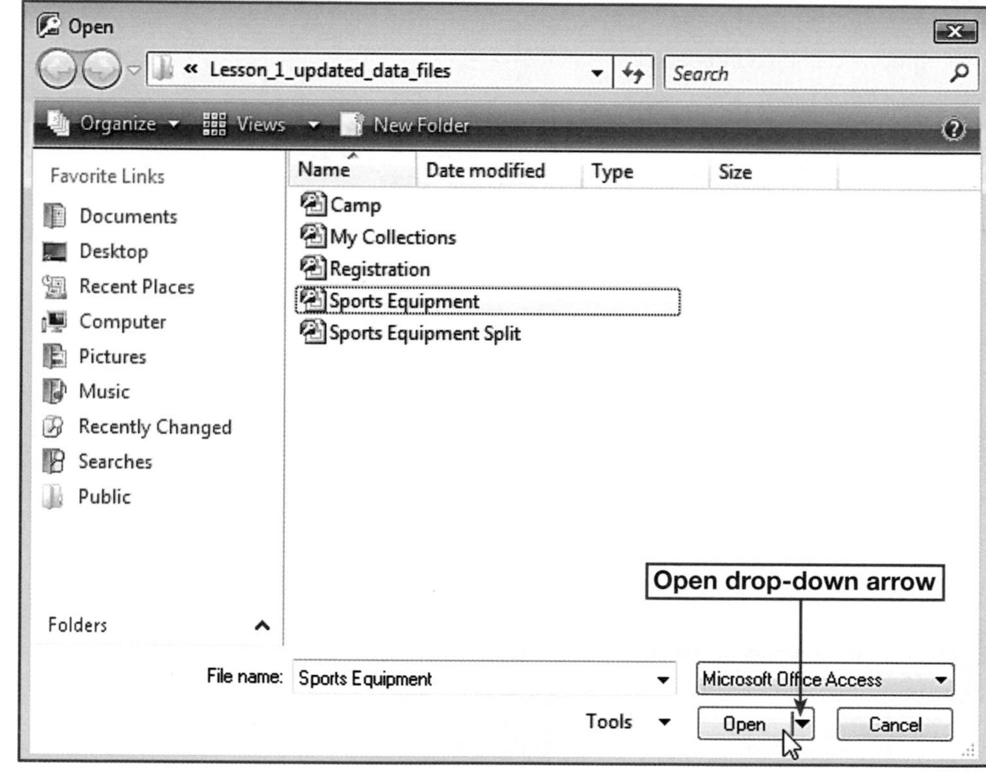

FIGURE 1.8 Sports Equipment Database window

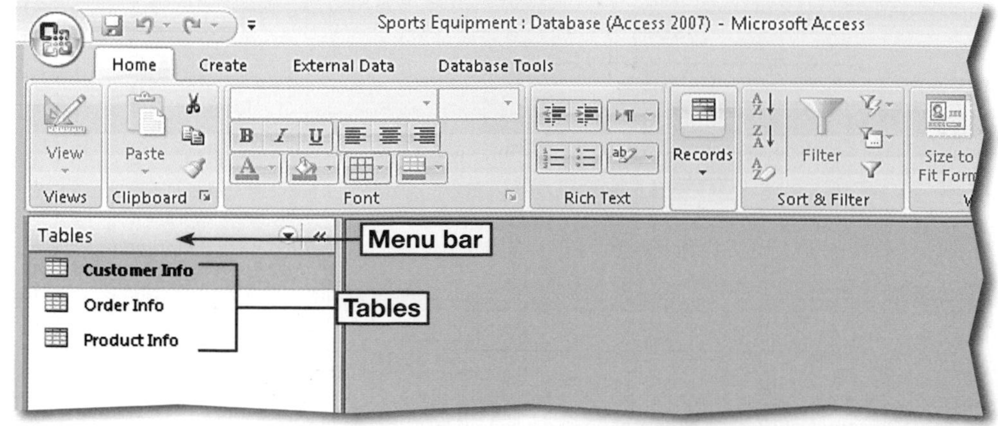